GREAT BOOKS OF THE WESTERN WORLD

GREAT BOOKS
OF THE WESTERN WORLD

ROBERT MAYNARD HUTCHINS, *EDITOR IN CHIEF*

40.

GIBBON: I

GREAT BOOKS
OF THE WESTERN WORLD

40.

GIBBON I

THE DECLINE AND FALL
OF THE
ROMAN EMPIRE

VOLUME I

BY EDWARD GIBBON

WILLIAM BENTON, *Publisher*

ENCYCLOPÆDIA BRITANNICA, INC.

CHICAGO · LONDON · TORONTO · GENEVA

The annotations in this edition are derived from
the edition in Everyman's Library, edited by Oliphant Smeaton,
by permission of J. M. Dent & Sons Ltd., London,
and E. P. Dutton & Co. Inc., New York

THE UNIVERSITY OF CHICAGO

The Great Books
is published with the editorial advice of the faculties
of The University of Chicago

BIOGRAPHICAL NOTE
Edward Gibbon, 1737-1794

Edward Gibbon was the eldest of seven children born to Edward Gibbon and Julia Porten, and their only child to survive infancy. He attributed his survival to the affectionate care of his aunt, Catherine Porten, "the true mother of my mind as well as my health." It was she who encouraged him in his "invincible love of reading," which he pursued widely in his grandfather's library until his "indiscriminate appetite subsided by degrees in the historic line."

Gibbon's early schooling had been irregular and frequently interrupted by illness. Then, suddenly, as he approached his sixteenth year, "his disorders wonderfully vanished." Shortly afterwards his father sent him to Oxford. Here he received neither instruction nor companionship, finding the boys frivolous, the dons indolent, and his fourteen months at the university "the most idle and unprofitable" of his whole life.

In the course of his solitary literary rambles during these fourteen months, Gibbon became converted to Catholicism. He wrote to his father of the step, and the elder Gibbon, with the impetuosity that seems to have characterized his dealings with his son, sent the sixteen-year-old youth to Lausanne. Here under the tutelage of the Calvinist minister, M. Pavilliard, young Gibbon repudiated his Catholicism and followed a carefully supervised program of studies with particular emphasis on the French and Latin classics and on the mastery of these languages.

At the age of twenty, Gibbon fell in love with Suzanne Curchod, who found his unprepossessing appearance "spirituelle et singulière" and reciprocated his affections. His request for his father's permission to marry her met with refusal. He quietly acceded: "Without his consent," he wrote, "I was destitute and helpless. I sighed as a lover, I obeyed as a son."

The Seven Years' War had already been in progress for a year, when, in 1758, Gibbon returned to England, more French than English in his outlook. From 1759 until the war ended in 1763, he served as a captain under his father in the Hampshire Militia. He assessed the value of this experience as making him "an Englishman and a soldier" and as giving him insight into military organization and tactics,

"so that the Captain of the Hampshire Grenadiers has not been useless to the historian of the Roman Empire."

Upon his release from the militia, Gibbon decided to embark on a long-projected tour of Europe. In 1761 he completed, in French, his first work, *Essay on the Study of Literature*, in defense of classical studies. This had given him some status abroad and when, in 1763, he visited Paris, his essay "entitled" him to a "favorable reception." But it was Rome that moved him to an unwonted enthusiasm, that seemed to give a new form and vividness to all he had read and studied. Here, according to a celebrated passage of the *Memoirs:* "On the fifteenth of October 1764, as I sat musing amidst the ruins of the Capitol, while the barefooted friars were singing Vespers in the Temple of Jupiter, the idea of writing the decline and fall of the city first started to my mind."

But it was not until 1772, two years after the death of his father, that Gibbon settled in London and submitted himself to the rigours of his life work. In the interim, he made several sallies into the field of polite letters, dividing his time between the family home at Buriton and the fashionable clubs of London. His membership in Johnson's literary club was an annoyance to Boswell, who described him as "an ugly, affected, disgusting fellow."

Gibbon was elected to the House of Commons in 1774. Although he held his seat during the stormy years of the American Revolution, he did not speak once. Like his stint in the Hampshire militia, his eight sessions in parliament he considered not wasted; they comprised "a school of civic prudence, the first and most essential virtue of a historian."

The first volume of *The Decline and Fall*, published in 1776, was immediately acclaimed as a classic and attacked for its discussion of Christianity. Volumes II and III, which followed shortly afterwards, were more quietly received.

Since 1779 Gibbon had been serving on the Board of Trade, a sinecure which added to his income. The Board existed in a state of "perpetual virtual adjournment" and "unbroken sitting vacation" until it was dissolved as a result of the campaign conducted against it by

Edmund Burke in 1782. Shortly afterwards, the historian also lost his seat in parliament. As it now became impossible for him to maintain himself in London, he arranged to live in Lausanne with his life-long friend, George Deyverdun.

At Lausanne, in the comfort of his well-appointed bachelor quarters, the last three volumes reached rapid completion. In a famous passage of his autobiography, he commemorates his deliverance from his labors: "It was on the night of the 27th of June 1787, between the hours of eleven and twelve, that I wrote the last line of the last page in a summer-house in my garden. After laying down my pen, I took several turns in a *berceau*, or covered walk of acacias . . . I will not dissemble the first emotions of joy on the recovery of my freedom, and, perhaps the establishment of my fame. But my pride was soon humbled, and a sober mel-

ancholy was spread over my mind by the idea that I had taken an everlasting leave of an old and agreeable companion, and that whatsoever might be the future fate of my history, the life of the historian must be short and precarious." For Gibbon it had always been reading and study that "supplied each day, each hour, with a perpetual source of independent and rational pleasure," just as his library had been "the foundation" of his works and the "best comfort" of his life.

In the "autumnal felicity" that followed in the wake of the completion of *The Decline and Fall*, Gibbon began work on his autobiography. But the mood was shattered by the death of Deyverdun in 1789, and in 1793 Gibbon returned to London. He had been suffering for some time from dropsy and the gout and upon his return, underwent a number of operations. Gibbon died January 16, 1794.

CONTENTS: VOLUME ONE

CHAPTERS I—XL

VII. *The Elevation and Tyranny of Maximin. Rebel-
lion in Africa and Italy under the Authority of the
Senate. Civil Wars and Seditions. Violent Deaths of
Maximin and his Son, of Maximus and Balbinus,
and of the Three Gordians. Usurpation and Secular
Games of Philip*

A.D.

VIII. *Of the State of Persia after the Restoration of
the Monarchy by Artaxerxes*

A.D.

IX. *The State of Germany Till the Invasion of the Barbarians in the Time of the Emperor Decius*

A.D.

XV. *The Progress of the Christian Religion, and the Sentiments, Manners, Numbers, and Condition of the Primitive Christians*

Contents

XXXVII. *Origin, Progress, and Effects of the Monastic Life. Conversion of the Barbarians to Christianity and Arianism. Persecution of the Vandals in Africa. Extinction of Arianism among the Barbarians*

A.D.

XXXVIII. *Reign and Conversion of Clovis. His Victories over the Alemanni, Burgundians, and Visigoths. Establishment of the French Monarchy in Gaul. Laws of the Barbarians. State of the Romans. The Visigoths of Spain. Conquest of Britain by the Saxons*

A.D.

Contents

NOTES: Chapters I—XL, p. 673

MAPS, p. 901

I. The Extent of the Roman Empire
at the Death of Trajan
II. Italy
III. Rome under the Emperors
IV. Byzantine Constantinople
V. Asia Minor
VI. The Empire of Attila
VII. Roman Britain

CHAPTER I

The Extent and Military Force of the Empire in the Age of the Antonines.

I N the second century of the Christian era, the Empire of Rome comprehended the fairest part of the earth, and the most civilised portion of mankind. The frontiers of that extensive monarchy were guarded by ancient renown and disciplined valour. The gentle but powerful influence of laws and manners had gradually cemented the union of the provinces. Their peaceful inhabitants enjoyed and abused the advantages of wealth and luxury. The image of a free constitution was preserved with decent reverence: the Roman senate appeared to possess the sovereign authority, and devolved on the emperors all the executive powers of government. During a happy period (A.D. 98–180) of more than fourscore years, the public administration was conducted by the virtue and abilities of Nerva, Trajan, Hadrian, and the two Antonines. It is the design of this, and of the two succeeding chapters, to describe the prosperous condition of their empire; and afterwards, from the death of Marcus Antoninus, to deduce the most important circumstances of its decline and fall; a revolution which will ever be remembered, and is still felt by the nations of the earth.

The principal conquests of the Romans were achieved under the republic; and the emperors, for the most part, were satisfied with preserving those dominions which had been acquired by the policy of the senate, the active emulation of the consuls, and the martial enthusiasm of the people. The seven first centuries were filled with a rapid succession of triumphs; but it was reserved for Augustus to relinquish the ambitious design of subduing the whole earth, and to introduce a spirit of moderation into the public councils. Inclined to peace by his temper and situation, it was easy for him to discover that Rome, in her present exalted situation, had much less to hope than to fear from the chance

of arms; and that, in the prosecution of remote wars, the undertaking became every day more difficult, the event more doubtful, and the possession more precarious, and less beneficial. The experience of Augustus added weight to these salutary reflections, and effectually convinced him that, by the prudent vigour of his counsels, it would be easy to secure every concession which the safety or the dignity of Rome might require from the most formidable Barbarians. Instead of exposing his person and his legions to the arrows of the Parthians, he obtained, by an honourable treaty, the restitution of the standards and prisoners which had been taken in the defeat of Crassus.[1]

His generals, in the early part of his reign, attempted the reduction of Æthiopia and Arabia Felix. They marched near a thousand miles to the south of the tropic; but the heat of the climate soon repelled the invaders, and protected the unwarlike natives of those sequestered regions.[2] The northern countries of Europe scarcely deserved the expense and labour of conquest. The forests and morasses of Germany were filled with a hardy race of barbarians, who despised life when it was separated from freedom; and though, on the first attack, they seemed to yield to the weight of the Roman power, they soon, by a signal act of despair, regained their independence, and reminded Augustus of the vicissitude of fortune.[3] On the death of that emperor, his testament was publicly read in the senate. He bequeathed, as a valuable legacy to his successors, the advice of confining the empire within those limits, which Nature seemed to have placed as its permanent bulwarks and boundaries; on the west the Atlantic ocean; the Rhine and Danube on the north; the Euphrates on the east; and towards the south, the sandy deserts of Arabia and Africa.[4]

Happily for the repose of mankind, the moderate system recommended by the wisdom of Augustus, was adopted by the fears and vices of his immediate successors. Engaged in the pursuit of pleasure, or in the exercise of tyranny, the first Cæsars seldom showed themselves to the armies, or to the provinces; nor were they disposed to suffer, that those triumphs which *their* indolence neglected should be usurped by the conduct and valour of their lieutenants. The military frame of a subject was considered as an insolent invasion of the Imperial prerogative; and it became the duty, as well as interest, of every Roman general, to guard the frontiers intrusted to his care, without aspiring to conquests which might have proved no less fatal to himself than to the vanquished barbarians.[5]

The only accession which the Roman empire received, during the first century of the Christian era, was the province of Britain. In this single instance the successors of Cæsar and Augustus were persuaded to follow the example of the former, rather than the precept of the latter. The proximity of its situation to the coast of Gaul seemed to invite their arms; the pleasing, though doubtful intelligence, of a pearl fishery, attracted their avarice;[6] and as Britain was viewed in the light of a distinct and insulated world, the conquest scarcely formed any exception to the general system of continental measures. After a war of about forty years, undertaken by the most stupid, maintained by the most dissolute, and terminated by the most timid of all the emperors, the far greater part of the island submitted to the Roman yoke.[7] The various tribes of Britons possessed valour without conduct, and the love of freedom without the spirit of union. They took up arms with savage fierceness; they laid them down, or turned them against each other with wild inconstancy; and while they fought singly, they were successively subdued. Neither the fortitude of Caractacus, nor the despair of Boadicea, nor the fanaticism of the Druids, could avert the slavery of their country, or resist the steady progress of the Imperial generals, who maintained the national glory, when the throne was disgraced by the weakest, or the most vicious of mankind. At the very time when Domitian, confined to his palace, felt the terrors which he inspired; his legions, under the command of the virtuous Agricola, defeated the collected force of the Caledonians at the foot of the Grampian hills; and his fleets, venturing to explore an unknown and dangerous navigation, displayed the Roman arms round every part of the island. The conquest of Britain was considered as already achieved;[8] and it was the design of Agricola to complete and ensure his success by the easy reduction of Ireland, for which in his opinion, one legion and a few auxiliaries were sufficient.[9] The western isle might be improved into a valuable possession, and the Britons would wear their chains with the less reluctance, if the prospect and example of freedom were on every side removed from before their eyes.

But the superior merit of Agricola soon occasioned his removal from the government of Britain; and for ever disappointed this rational, though extensive scheme of conquest. Before his departure, the prudent general had provided for security as well as for dominion. He had observed that the island is almost divided into two unequal parts by the opposite gulfs, or, as they are now called, the Firths of Scotland. Across the narrow interval of about forty miles, he had drawn a line of military stations, which was afterwards fortified in the reign of Antoninus Pius, by a turf rampart erected on foundations of stone.[10] This wall of Antoninus, at a small distance beyond the modern cities of Edinburgh and Glasgow, was fixed as the limit of the Roman province. The native Caledonians preserved in the northern extremity of the island their wild independence, for which they were not less indebted to their poverty than to their valour. Their incursions were frequently repelled and chastised; but their country was never subdued.[11] The masters of the fairest and most wealthy climates of the globe turned with contempt from gloomy hills assailed by the winter tempest, from lakes concealed in a blue mist, and from cold and lonely heaths, over which the deer of the forest were chased by a troop of naked barbarians.[12]

Such was the state of the Roman frontiers, and such the maxims of Imperial policy, from the death of Augustus to the accession of Trajan. That virtuous and active prince had received the education of a soldier, and possessed the talents of a general.[13] The peaceful system of his predecessors was interrupted by scenes of war and conquest; and the legions, after a long interval, beheld a military emperor at their head. The first exploits of Trajan were against the Dacians, the most warlike of men, who dwelt beyond the Danube, and who, during the reign of Domitian, had insulted with impunity the Majesty of Rome.[14] To the strength and fierceness of barbarians, they added a contempt for life, which was derived from a warm persuasion of the immortality and transmigration of the soul.[15] Decebalus, the Dacian king, approved himself a rival not unworthy of Trajan; nor did he despair of his own and the public fortune, till, by the confession of his enemies, he had exhausted every resource both of valour and policy.[16] This memorable war, with a very short suspension of hostilities, lasted five years; and as the emperor could exert, without control, the whole force of the state, it was terminated by an absolute submission of the barbarians.[17] The new province of Dacia, which formed a second exception to the precept of Augustus, was about 1300 miles in circumference. Its natural boundaries were the Dniester, the Teyss [Theiss modern form], or Tibiscus, the Lower Danube, and the Euxine Sea. The vestiges of a military road may still be traced from the banks of the Danube to the neighbourhood of Bender, a place famous in modern history, and the actual frontier of the Turkish and Russian empires.[18]

Trajan was ambitious of fame; and as long as mankind shall continue to bestow more liberal applause on their destroyers than on their benefactors, the thirst of military glory will ever be the vice of the most exalted characters. The praises of Alexander, transmitted by a succession of poets and historians, had kindled a dangerous emulation in the mind of Trajan. Like him the Roman emperor undertook an expedition against the nations of the east, but he lamented with a sigh, that his advanced age scarcely left him any hopes of equalling the renown of the son of Philip.[19] Yet the success of Trajan, however transient, was rapid and specious. The degenerate Parthians, broken by intestine discord, fled before his arms. He descended the river Tigris in triumph, from the mountains of Armenia to the Persian gulf. He enjoyed the honour of being the first, as he was the last, of the Roman generals, who ever navigated that remote sea. His fleets ravaged the coasts of Arabia; and Trajan vainly flattered himself that he was approaching towards the confines of India.[20] Every day the astonished senate received the intelligence of new names and new nations, that acknowledged his sway. They were informed that the kings of Bosphorus, Colchos, Iberia, Albania, Osrhoene, and even the Parthian monarch himself, had accepted their diadems from the hands of the emperor; that the independent tribes of the Median and Carduchian hills had implored his protection; and that the rich countries of Armenia, Mesopotamia, and Assyria, were reduced into the state of provinces.[21] But the death of Trajan soon clouded the splendid prospect; and it was justly to be dreaded that so many distant nations would throw off the unaccustomed yoke, when they were no longer restrained by the powerful hand which had imposed it.

It was an ancient tradition, that when the Capitol was founded by one of the Roman kings, the god Terminus (who presided over boundaries, and was represented according to the fashion of that age by a large stone) alone, among all the inferior deities, refused to yield his place to Jupiter himself. A favourable inference was drawn from his obstinacy, which was interpreted by the augurs as a sure presage that the boundaries of the Roman power would never recede.[22] During many ages, the prediction, as it is usual, contributed to its own accomplishment. But though Terminus had resisted the majesty of Jupiter, he submitted to the authority of the emperor Hadrian.[23] The resignation of all the eastern conquests of Trajan was the first measure of his reign. He restored to the Parthians the election of an independent sovereign, withdrew the Roman garrisons from the provinces of Armenia, Mesopotamia, and Assyria, and, in compliance with the precept of Augustus, once more established the Euphrates as the frontier of the empire.[24] Censure, which arraigns the public actions and the private motives of princes, has ascribed to envy, a conduct, which might be attributed to the prudence and moderation of Hadrian. The various character of that emperor, capable, by turns, of the meanest and the most generous sentiments, may afford some colour to the suspicion. It was, however, scarcely in his power to place the superiority of his predecessor in a more conspicuous light, than by thus confessing himself unequal to the task of defending the conquests of Trajan.

The martial and ambitious spirit of Trajan formed a very singular contrast with the moderation of his successor. The restless activity of Hadrian was not less remarkable, when compared with the gentle repose of Antoninus Pius. The life of the former was almost a perpetual journey; and as he possessed the various talents of the soldier, the statesman, and the scholar, he gratified his curiosity in the discharge of his duty. Careless of the difference of seasons and of climates, he marched on foot, and bareheaded, over the snows of Caledonia, and the sultry plains of the Upper Egypt; nor was there a province of the empire which, in the course of his reign, was not honoured with the presence of the monarch.[25] But the tranquil life of Antoninus Pius was spent in the bosom of Italy; and, during the twenty-three years that he directed public administration, the longest journeys of that amiable prince extended no farther than from his palace in Rome to the retirement of his Lanuvian Villa.[26]

Notwithstanding this difference in their personal conduct, the general system of Augustus was equally adopted and uniformly pursued by Hadrian and by the two Antonines. They persisted in the design of maintaining the dignity of the empire, without attempting to enlarge its limits. By every honourable expedient they invited the friendship of the barbarians; and endeavoured to convince mankind that the Roman power, raised above the temptation of conquest, was actuated only by the love of order and justice. During a long period of forty-three years their virtuous labours were crowned with success; and if we except a few slight hostilities that served to exercise the legions of the frontier, the reigns of Hadrian and Antoninus Pius offer the fair prospect of universal peace.[27] The Roman name was revered among the most remote nations of the earth. The fiercest barbarians frequently submitted their differences to the arbitration of the emperor; and we are informed by a contemporary historian, that he had seen ambassadors who were refused the honour which they came to solicit, of being admitted into the rank of subjects.[28]

The terror of the Roman arms added weight and dignity to the moderation of the emperors. They preserved peace by a constant preparation for war; and while justice regulated their conduct, they announced to the nations on their confines that they were as little disposed to endure as to offer an injury. The military strength, which it had been sufficient for Hadrian and the elder Antoninus to display, was exerted against the Parthians and the Germans by the emperor Marcus. The hostilities of the barbarians provoked the resentment of that philosophic monarch, and, in the prosecution of a just defence, Marcus and his generals obtained many signal victories, both on the Euphrates and on the Danube.[29] The military establishment of the Roman empire, which thus assured either its tranquillity or success, will now become the proper and important object of our attention.

In the purer ages of the commonwealth, the use of arms was reserved for those ranks of citizens who had a country to love, a property to defend, and some share in enacting those laws, which it was their interest, as well as duty, to maintain. But in proportion as the public freedom was lost in extent of conquest, war was gradually improved into an art, and degraded into a trade.[30] The legions themselves, even at the time when they were recruited in the most distant provinces, were supposed to consist of Roman citizens. That distinction was generally considered either as a legal qualification or as a proper recompense for the soldier; but a more serious regard was paid to the essential merit of age, strength, and military stature.[31] In all levies, a just preference was given to the climates of the North over those of the South: the race of men born to the exercise of arms was sought for in the country rather than in cities; and it was very reasonably presumed, that the hardy occupations of smiths, carpenters, and huntsmen, would supply more vigour and resolution than the sedentary trades which are employed in the service of luxury.[32] After every qualification of property had been laid aside, the armies of the Roman emperors were still commanded, for the most part, by officers of a liberal birth and education; but the common soldiers, like the mercenary troops of modern Europe, were drawn from the meanest, and very frequently from the most profligate, of mankind.

That public virtue which among the ancients was denominated patriotism, is derived from a strong sense of our own interest in the preservation and prosperity of the free government of which we are members. Such a sentiment, which had rendered the legions of the republic almost invincible, could make but a very feeble impression on the mercenary servants of a despotic prince; and it became necessary to supply that defect by other motives, of a different, but not less forcible nature; honour and religion. The peasant, or mechanic, imbibed the useful prejudice that he was advanced to the more dignified profession of arms, in which his rank and reputation would depend on his own valour; and that, although the prowess of a private soldier must often escape the notice of fame, his own behaviour might sometimes confer glory or disgrace on the company, the legion, or even the army, to whose honours he was associated. On his first entrance into the service, an oath was administered to him, with every circumstance of solemnity. He promised never to desert his standard, to submit his own will to the commands of his leader, and to sacrifice his life for the safety of the emperor and the empire.[33] The attachment of the Roman troops to their standards was inspired by the united influence of religion and of honour. The golden eagle, which glittered in the front of the legion, was the object of their fondest devotion; nor was it esteemed less impious than it was ignominious, to abandon that sacred ensign in the hour of danger.[34] These motives, which derived their strength from the imagination, were enforced by fears and hopes of a more substantial kind. Regular pay, occasional donatives, and a stated recompense, after the appointed time of service, alleviated the hardships of the military life,[35] whilst, on the other hand, it was impossible for cowardice or disobedience to escape the severest punishment. The centurions were authorized to chastise with blows, the generals had a right to punish with death; and it was an inflexible maxim of Roman discipline, that a good soldier should dread his officers far more than the enemy. From such laudable arts did the valour of the Imperial troops receive a degree of firmness and docility, unattainable by the impetuous and irregular passions of barbarians.

And yet so sensible were the Romans of the imperfection of valour without skill and practice, that, in their language, the name of an army was borrowed from the word which signified exercise.[36] Military exercises were the important and unremitted object of their discipline. The recruits and young soldiers were constantly trained both in the morning and in the evening, nor was age or knowledge allowed to excuse the veterans from the daily repetition of what they had completely learnt. Large sheds were erected in the winter-quarters of the troops, that their useful labours might not receive any interruption from the most tempestuous weather; and it was carefully observed, that the arms destined to this imitation of war, should be of double the weight which was required in real action.[37] It is not the purpose of this work to enter into any minute description of the Roman exercises. We shall only remark, that they comprehended whatever could add strength to the body, activity to the limbs, or grace to the motions. The soldiers were diligently instructed to march, to run, to leap, to swim, to carry heavy burdens, to handle every species of arms that was used either for offence or for defence, either in distant engagement or in a closer onset; to form a variety of evolutions; and to move to the sound of flutes, in the Pyrrhic or martial dance.[38] In the midst of peace, the Roman troops familiarised themselves with the practice of war; and it is prettily remarked by

an ancient historian who had fought against them, that the effusion of blood was the only circumstance which distinguished a field of battle from a field of exercise.[39] It was the policy of the ablest generals, and even of the emperors themselves, to encourage these military studies by their presence and example; and we are informed that Hadrian, as well as Trajan, frequently condescended to instruct the unexperienced soldiers, to reward the diligent, and sometimes to dispute with them the prize of superior strength or dexterity.[40] Under the reigns of those princes, the science of tactics was cultivated with success; and as long as the empire retained any vigour, their military instructions were respected as the most perfect model of Roman discipline.

Nine centuries of war had gradually introduced into the service many alterations and improvements. The legions, as they are described by Polybius,[41] in the time of the Punic wars, differed very materially from those which achieved the victories of Cæsar, or defended the monarchy of Hadrian and the Antonines. The constitution of the Imperial legion may be described in a few words.[42] The heavy-armed infantry, which composed its principal strength,[43] was divided into ten cohorts, and fifty-five companies, under the orders of a correspondent number of tribunes and centurions. The first cohort, which always claimed the post of honour and the custody of the eagle, was formed of eleven hundred and five soldiers, the most approved for valour and fidelity. The remaining nine cohorts consisted each of five hundred and fifty-five; and the whole body of legionary infantry amounted to six thousand one hundred men. Their arms were uniform, and admirably adapted to the nature of their service: an open helmet, with a lofty crest; a breast-plate, or coat of mail; greaves on their legs, and an ample buckler on their left arm. The buckler was of an oblong and concave figure, four feet in length, and two and an half in breadth, framed of a light wood, covered with a bull's hide, and strongly guarded with plates of brass. Besides a lighter spear, the legionary soldier grasped in his right hand the formidable *pilum*, a ponderous javelin, whose utmost length was about six feet, and which was terminated by a massy triangular point of steel of eighteen inches.[44] This instrument was indeed much inferior to our modern fire-arms; since it was exhausted by a single discharge, at the distance of only ten or twelve paces. Yet when it was launched by a firm and skilful hand, there was not any cavalry that durst venture within its reach, nor any shield or corslet that could sustain the impetuosity of its weight. As soon as the Roman had darted his *pilum*, he drew his sword, and rushed forwards to close with the enemy. His sword was a short well-tempered Spanish blade, that carried a double edge, and was alike suited to the purpose of striking or of pushing; but the soldier was always instructed to prefer the latter use of his weapon, as his own body remained less exposed, whilst he inflicted a more dangerous wound on his adversary.[45] The legion was usually drawn up eight deep; and the regular distance of three feet was left between the files as well as ranks.[46] A body of troops, habituated to preserve this open order, in a long front and a rapid charge, found themselves prepared to execute every disposition which the circumstances of war, or the skill of their leader, might suggest. The soldier possessed a free space for his arms and motions, and sufficient intervals were allowed, through which seasonable reinforcements might be introduced to the relief of the exhausted combatants.[47] The tactics of the Greeks and Macedonians were formed on very different principles. The strength of the phalanx depended on sixteen ranks of long pikes, wedged together in the closest array.[48] But it was soon discovered by reflection, as well by the event, that the strength of the phalanx was unable to contend with the activity of the legion.[49]

The cavalry, without which the force of the legion would have remained imperfect, was divided into ten troops or squadrons; the first, as the companion of the first cohort, consisted of an hundred and thirty-two men; whilst each of the other nine amounted only to sixty-six. The entire establishment formed a regiment, if we may use the modern expression, of seven hundred and twenty-six horse, naturally connected with its respective legion, but occasionally separated to act in the line, and to compose a part of the wings of the army.[50] The cavalry of the emperors was no longer composed, like that of the ancient republic, of the noblest youths of Rome and Italy, who, by performing their military service on horseback, prepared themselves for the offices of senator and consul; and solicited, by deeds of valour, the future suffrages of their countrymen.[51] Since the alteration of manners and government, the most wealthy of the equestrian order were engaged in the administration of justice, and of the revenue;[52] and whenever they embraced the profession of arms, they were immediately intrusted with a troop of horse, or a cohort of foot.[53]

Trajan and Hadrian formed their cavalry from the same provinces, and the same class of their subjects, which recruited the ranks of the legion. The horses were bred, for the most part, in Spain or Cappadocia. The Roman troopers despised the complete armour with which the cavalry of the East was encumbered. *Their* more useful arms consisted in a helmet, an oblong shield, light boots, and a coat of mail. A javelin, and a long broad-sword, were their principal weapons of offence. The use of lances and of iron maces they seem to have borrowed from the barbarians.[54]

The safety and honour of the empire were principally intrusted to the legions, but the policy of Rome condescended to adopt every useful instrument of war. Considerable levies were regularly made among the provincials, who had not yet deserved the honourable distinction of Romans. Many dependent princes and communities, dispersed round the frontiers, were permitted for a while, to hold their freedom and security by the tenure of military service.[55] Even select troops of hostile barbarians were frequently compelled or persuaded to consume their dangerous valour in remote climates, and for the benefit of the state.[56] All these were included under the general name of auxiliaries; and howsoever they might vary according to the difference of times and circumstances, their numbers were seldom much inferior to those of the legions themselves.[57] Among the auxiliaries, the bravest and most faithful bands were placed under the command of præfects and centurions, and severely trained in the arts of Roman discipline; but the far greater part retained those arms, to which the nature of their country, or their early habits of life, more peculiarly adapted them. By this institution each legion, to whom a certain proportion of auxiliaries was allotted, contained within itself every species of lighter troops, and of missile weapons, and was capable of encountering every nation, with the advantages of its respective arms and discipline.[58] Nor was the legion destitute of what, in modern language, would be styled a train of artillery. It consisted in ten military engines of the largest, and fifty-five of a smaller size; but all of which, either in an oblique or horizontal manner, discharged stones and darts with irresistible violence.[59]

The camp of a Roman legion presented the appearance of a fortified city.[60] As soon as the space was marked out, the pioneers carefully levelled the ground, and removed every impediment that might interrupt its perfect regularity.

Its form was an exact quadrangle; and we may calculate that a square of about seven hundred yards was sufficient for the encampment of twenty thousand Romans; though a similar number of our own troops would expose to the enemy a front of more than treble that extent. In the midst of the camp, the prætorium, or general's quarters, rose above the others; the cavalry, the infantry, and the auxiliaries occupied their respective stations; the streets were broad and perfectly straight, and a vacant space of two hundred feet was left on all sides, between the tents and the rampart. The rampart itself was usually twelve feet high, armed with a line of strong and intricate palisades, and defended by a ditch of twelve feet in depth as well as in breadth. This important labour was performed by the hands of the legionaries themselves, to whom the use of the spade and the pick-axe was no less familiar than that of the sword or *pilum*. Active valour may often be the present of nature; but such patient diligence can be the fruit only of habit and discipline.[61]

Whenever the trumpet gave the signal of departure, the camp was almost instantly broke up, and the troops fell into their ranks without delay or confusion. Besides their arms, which the legionaries scarcely considered as an encumbrance, they were laden with their kitchen urniture, the instruments of fortification, and the provision of many days.[62] Under this weight, which would oppress the delicacy of a modern soldier, they were trained by a regular step to advance, in about six hours, near twenty miles.[63] On the appearance of an enemy, they threw aside their baggage, and by easy and rapid evolutions converted the column of march into an order of battle.[64] The slingers and archers skirmished in the front; the auxiliaries formed the first line, and were seconded or sustained by the strength of the legions: the cavalry covered the flanks, and the military engines were placed in the rear.

Such were the arts of war by which the Roman emperors defended their extensive conquests, and preserved a military spirit, at a time when every other virtue was oppressed by luxury and despotism. If, in the consideration of their armies, we pass from their discipline to their numbers, we shall not find it easy to define them with any tolerable accuracy. We may compute, however, that the legion, which was itself a body of six thousand eight hundred and thirty-one Romans, might, with its attendant auxiliaries, amount to about twelve thousand five hundred men. The peace establishment of Hadrian and his successors was composed of no less than thirty of these formidable brigades; and most probably formed a standing force of three hundred and seventy-five thousand men. Instead of being confined within the walls of fortified cities, which the Romans considered as the refuge of weakness or pusillanimity, the legions were encamped on the banks of the great rivers, and along the frontiers of the barbarians. As their stations, for the most part, remained fixed and permanent, we may venture to describe the distribution of the troops. Three legions were sufficient for Britain. The principal strength lay upon the Rhine and Danube, and consisted of sixteen legions, in the following proportions: two in the Lower and three in the Upper Germany; one in Rhætia, one in Noricum, four in Pannonia, three in Mæsia, and two in Dacia. The defence of the Euphrates was entrusted to eight legions, six of whom were planted in Syria, and the other two in Cappadocia. With regard to Egypt, Africa, and Spain, as they were far removed from any important scene of war, a single legion maintained the domestic tranquillity of each of those great provinces. Even Italy was not left destitute of a military force. Above twenty thousand chosen soldiers, distinguished by the titles of City Cohorts and Prætorian Guards, watched over the safety of the monarch and the capital. As the authors of almost every revolution that distracted the empire, the Prætorians will, very soon, and very loudly, demand our attention; but in their arms and institution, we cannot find any circumstance which discriminated them from the legions, unless it were a more splendid appearance, and a less rigid discipline.[65]

The navy maintained by the emperors might seem inadequate to their greatness; but it was fully sufficient for every useful purpose of government. The ambition of the Romans was confined to the land; nor was that warlike people ever actuated by the enterprising spirit which had prompted the navigators of Tyre, of Carthage, and even of Marseilles, to enlarge the bounds of the world, and to explore the most remote coasts of the ocean. To the Romans the ocean remained an object of terror rather than of curiosity;[66] the whole extent of the Mediterranean, after the destruction of Carthage, and the extirpation of the pirates, was included within their provinces. The policy of the emperors was directed only to preserve the peaceful dominion of that sea, and to protect the commerce of their subjects. With these moderate views, Augustus stationed two permanent fleets in the most convenient ports of Italy, the one at Ravenna, on the Adriatic, the other at Misenum, in the bay of Naples. Experience seems at length to have convinced the ancients, that as soon as their galleys exceeded two, or at the most three ranks of oars, they were suited rather for vain pomp than for real service. Augustus himself, in the victory of Actium, had seen the superiority of his own light frigates (they were called Liburnians) over the lofty but unwieldy castles of his rival.[67] Of these Liburnians he composed the two fleets of Ravenna and Misenum, destined to command, the one the eastern, the other the western division of the Mediterranean; and to each of the squadrons he attached a body of several thousand marines. Besides these two ports, which may be considered as the principal seats of the Roman navy, a very considerable force was stationed at Frejus, on the coast of Provence, and the Euxine was guarded by forty ships, and three thousand soldiers. To all these we add the fleet which preserved the communication between Gaul and Britain, and a great number of vessels constantly maintained on the Rhine and Danube, to harass the country, or to intercept the passage of the barbarians.[68] If we review this general state of the Imperial forces; of the cavalry as well as infantry; of the legions, the auxiliaries, the guards, and the navy; the most liberal computation will not allow us to fix the entire establishment by sea and by land at more than four hundred and fifty thousand men; a military power, which, however, formidable it may seem, was equalled by a monarch of the last century, whose kingdom was confined within a single province of the Roman empire.[69]

We have attempted to explain the spirit which moderated, and the strength which supported, the power of Hadrian and the Antonines. We shall now endeavour, with clearness and precision, to describe the provinces once united under their sway, but, at present, divided into so many independent and hostile states.

Spain, the western extremity of the empire, of Europe, and of the ancient world, has, in every age, invariably preserved the same natural limits; the Pyrenæan mountains, the Mediterranean, and the Atlantic Ocean. That great peninsula, at present so unequally divided between two sovereigns, was distributed by Augustus into three provinces, Lusitania, Bætica, and Tarraconensis. The kingdom of Portugal now fills the place of the warlike country

of the Lusitanians; and the loss sustained by the former, on the side of the East is compensated by an accession of territory towards the North. The confines of Grenada and Andalusia correspond with those of ancient Bætica. The remainder of Spain, Gallicia and the Asturias, Biscay and Navarre, Leon and the two Castilles, Murcia, Valencia, Catalonia, and Arragon, all contributed to form the third and most considerable of the Roman governments, which, from the name of its capital, was styled the province of Tarragona.[70] Of the native barbarians, the Celtiberians were the most powerful, as the Cantabrians and Asturians proved the most obstinate. Confident in the strength of their mountains, they were the last who submitted to the arms of Rome, and the first who threw off the yoke of the Arabs.

Ancient Gaul, as it contained the whole country between the Pyrenees, the Alps, the Rhine, and the Ocean, was of greater extent than modern France. To the dominions of that powerful monarchy, with its recent acquisitions of Alsace and Lorraine, we must add the duchy of Savoy, the cantons of Switzerland, the four electorates of the Rhine, and the territories of Liege, Luxemburg, Hainault, Flanders, and Brabant. When Augustus gave laws to the conquests of his father, he introduced a division of Gaul equally adapted to the progress of the legions, to the course of the rivers, and to the principal national distinctions, which had comprehended above an hundred independent states.[71] The seacoast of the Mediterranean, Languedoc, Provence, and Dauphiné, received their provincial appellation from the colony of Narbonne. The government of Aquitaine was extended from the Pyrenees to the Loire. The country between the Loire and the Seine was styled the Celtic Gaul, and soon borrowed a new denomination from the celebrated colony of Lugdunum, or Lyons. The Belgic lay beyond the Seine, and in more ancient times had been bounded only by the Rhine; but a little before the age of Cæsar the Germans, abusing their superiority of valour, had occupied a considerable portion of the Belgic territory. The Roman conquerors very eagerly embraced so flattering a circumstance, and the Gallic frontier of the Rhine, from Basil to Leyden, received the pompous names of the Upper and the Lower Germany.[72] Such, under the reign of the Antonines, were the six provinces of Gaul; the Narbonnese, Aquitaine, the Celtic, or Lyonnese, the Belgic, and the two Germanies.

We have already had occasion to mention

the conquest of Britain, and to fix the boundary of the Roman province in this island. It comprehended all England, Wales, and the Lowlands of Scotland, as far as Dumbarton and Edinburgh. Before Britain lost her freedom, the country was irregularly divided between thirty tribes of barbarians, of whom the most considerable were the Belgæ in the West, the Brigantes in the North, the Silures in South Wales, and the Iceni in Norfolk and Suffolk.[73] As far as we can either trace or credit the resemblance of manners and language, Spain, Gaul, and Britain were peopled by the same hardy race of savages. Before they yielded to the Roman arms, they often disputed the field, and often renewed the contest. After their submission they constituted the western division of the European provinces, which extended from the columns of Hercules to the wall of Antoninus and from the mouth of the Tagus to the sources of the Rhine and Danube.

Before the Roman conquest, the country which is now called Lombardy was not considered as a part of Italy. It had been occupied by a powerful colony of Gauls, who settling themselves along the banks of the Po, from Piedmont to Romagna, carried their arms and diffused their names from the Alps to the Apennine. The Ligurians dwelt on the rocky coast, which now forms the republic of Genoa. Venice was yet unborn; but the territories of that state, which lie to the east of the Adige, were inhabited by the Venetians.[74] The middle part of the peninsula that now composes the duchy of Tuscany and the ecclesiastical state, was the ancient seat of the Estruscans and Umbrians; to the former of whom Italy was indebted for the first rudiments of civilised life.[75] The Tiber rolled at the foot of the seven hills of Rome, and the country of the Sabines, the Latins, and the Volsci, from that river to the frontiers of Naples, was the theatre of her infant victories. On that celebrated ground the first consuls deserved triumphs; their successors adorned villas, and *their* posterity have erected convents.[76] Capua and Campania possessed the immediate territory of Naples; the rest of the kingdom was inhabited by many warlike nations, the Marsi, the Samnites, the Apulians, and the Lucanians; and the sea coasts had been covered by the flourishing colonies of the Greeks. We may remark, that when Augustus divided Italy into eleven regions, the little province of Istria was annexed to that seat of Roman sovereignty.[77]

The European provinces of Rome were protected by the course of the Rhine and the Danube. The latter of those mighty streams, which rises at the distance of only thirty miles from the former, flows above thirteen hundred miles, for the most part, to the south-east, collects the tribute of sixty navigable rivers, and is, at length, through six mouths, received into the Euxine, which appears scarcely equal to such an accession of waters.[78] The provinces of the Danube soon acquired the general appellation of Illyricum, or the Illyrian frontier,[79] and were esteemed the most warlike of the empire; but they deserve to be more particularly considered under the names of Rhætia, Noricum, Pannonia, Dalmatia, Dacia, Mæsia, Thrace, Macedonia, and Greece.

The province of Rhætia, which soon extinguished the name of the Vindelicians, extended from the summit of the Alps to the banks of the Danube; from its source, as far as its conflux with the Inn. The greatest part of the flat country is subject to the elector of Bavaria; the city of Augsburg is protected by the constitution of the German empire; the Grisons are safe in their mountains, and the country of Tyrol is ranked among the numerous provinces of the house of Austria.

The wide extent of territory, which is included between the Inn, the Danube, and the Save; Austria, Styria, Carinthia, Carniola, the Lower Hungary, and Sclavonia, was known to the ancients under the names of Noricum and Pannonia. In their original state of independence, their fierce inhabitants were intimately connected. Under the Roman government they were frequently united, and they still remain the patrimony of a single family. They now contain the residence of a German prince, who styles himself Emperor of the Romans, and form the centre, as well as strength, of the Austrian power. It may not be improper to observe, that if we except Bohemia, Moravia, the northern skirts of Austria, and a part of Hungary, between the Theiss and the Danube, all the other dominions of the House of Austria were comprised within the limits of the Roman empire.

Dalmatia, to which the name of Illyricum more properly belonged, was a long but narrow tract between the Save and the Adriatic. The best part of the sea-coast, which still retains its ancient appellation, is a province of the Venetian state, and the seat of the little republic of Ragusa. The inland parts have assumed the Sclavonian names of Croatia and Bosnia; the former obeys an Austrian governor, the latter a Turkish pasha; but the whole country is still infested by tribes of barbarians, whose savage independence irregularly marks the doubtful limit of the Christian and Mahometan power.[80]

After the Danube had received the waters of the Theiss and the Save, it acquired, at least among the Greeks, the name of Ister.[81] It formerly divided Mæsia and Dacia, the latter of which, as we have already seen, was a conquest of Trajan, and the only province beyond the river. If we inquire into the present state of those countries, we shall find that, on the left hand of the Danube, Temeswar and Transylvania have been annexed, after many revolutions, to the crown of Hungary; whilst the principalities of Moldavia and Wallachia acknowledge the supremacy of the Ottoman Porte. On the right hand of the Danube, Mæsia, which, during the middle ages, was broken into the barbarian kingdoms of Servia and Bulgaria, is again united in Turkish slavery.

The appellation of Roumelia, which is still bestowed by the Turks on the extensive countries of Thrace, Macedonia, and Greece, preserves the memory of their ancient state under the Roman empire. In the time of the Antonines, the martial regions of Thrace, from the mountains of Hæmus and Rhodope, to the Bosphorus and the Hellespont, had assumed the form of a province. Notwithstanding the change of masters and of religion, the new city of Rome, founded by Constantine on the banks of the Bosphorus, has ever since remained the capital of a great monarchy. The kingdom of Macedonia, which, under the reign of Alexander, gave laws to Asia, derived more solid advantages from the policy of the two Philips; and with its dependencies of Epirus and Thessaly, extended from the Ægean to the Ionian Sea. When we reflect on the fame of Thebes and Argos, of Sparta and Athens, we can scarcely persuade ourselves that so many immortal republics of ancient Greece were lost in a single province of the Roman empire, which, from the superior influence of the Achæan league, was usually denominated the province of Achaia.

Such was the state of Europe under the Roman emperors. The provinces of Asia, without excepting the transient conquests of Trajan, are all comprehended within the limits of the Turkish power. But, instead of following the arbitrary divisions of despotism and ignorance, it will be safer for us, as well as more agreeable, to observe the indelible characters of nature. The name of Asia Minor is attributed with some propriety to the peninsula, which, confined betwixt the Euxine and the Mediterra-

nean, advances from the Euphrates towards Europe. The most extensive and flourishing district, westward of Mount Taurus and the river Halys, was dignified by the Romans with the exclusive title of Asia. The jurisdiction of that province extended over the ancient monarchies of Troy, Lydia, and Phrygia, the maritime countries of the Pamphylians, Lycians, and Carians, and the Grecian colonies of Ionia, which equalled in arts, though not in arms, the glory of their parent. The kingdoms of Bithynia and Pontus possessed the northern side of the peninsula from Constantinople to Trebizond. On the opposite side, the province of Cilicia was terminated by the mountains of Syria: the inland country, separated from the Roman Asia by the river Halys, and from Armenia by the Euphrates, had once formed the independent kingdom of Cappadocia. In this place we may observe that the northern shores of the Euxine, beyond Trebizond in Asia, and beyond the Danube in Europe, acknowledged the sovereignty of the emperors, and received at their hands either tributary princes or Roman garrisons. Budzak, Crim Tartary, Circassia, and Mingrelia, are the modern appellations of those savage countries.[82]

Under the successors of Alexander, Syria was the seat of the Seleucidæ, who reigned over Upper Asia, till the successful revolt of the Parthians confined their dominions between the Euphrates and the Mediterranean. When Syria became subject to the Romans, it formed the eastern frontier of their empire; nor did that province, in its utmost latitude, know any other bounds than the mountains of Cappadocia to the north, and towards the south the confines of Egypt, and the Red Sea. Phœnicia and Palestine were sometimes annexed to, and sometimes separated from, the jurisdiction of Syria. The former of these was a narrow and rocky coast; the latter was a territory scarcely superior to Wales, either in fertility or extent. Yet Phœnicia and Palestine will for ever live in the memory of mankind; since America, as well as Europe, has received letters from the one, and religion from the other.[83] A sandy desert alike destitute of wood and water skirts along the doubtful confine of Syria, from the Euphrates to the Red Sea. The wandering life of the Arabs was inseparably connected with their independence; and wherever, on some spots less barren than the rest, they ventured to form any settled habitation, they soon became subjects to the Roman empire.[84]

The geographers of antiquity have frequently

hesitated to what portion of the globe they should ascribe Egypt.[85] By its situation that celebrated kingdom is included within the immense peninsula of Africa; but it is accessible only on the side of Asia, whose revolutions, in almost every period of history, Egypt has humbly obeyed. A Roman præfect was seated on the splendid throne of the Ptolemies; and the iron sceptre of the Mamalukes is now in the hands of a Turkish pasha. The Nile flows down the country, above five hundred miles from the tropic of Cancer to the Mediterranean, and marks, on either side, the extent of fertility by the measure of its inundations. Cyrene, situate towards the west, and along the sea-coast, was first a Greek colony, afterwards a province of Egypt, and is now lost in the desert of Barca.

From Cyrene to the ocean, the coast of Africa extends above fifteen hundred miles; yet so closely is it pressed between the Mediterranean and the Sahara, or sandy desert, that its breadth seldom exceeds fourscore or an hundred miles. The eastern division was considered by the Romans as the more peculiar and proper province of Africa. Till the arrival of the Phœnician colonies, that fertile country was inhabited by the Libyans, the most savage of mankind. Under the immediate jurisdiction of Carthage, it became the centre of commerce and empire; but the republic of Carthage is now degenerated into the feeble and disorderly states of Tripoli and Tunis. The military government of Algiers oppresses the wide extent of Numidia, as it was once united under Massinissa and Jugurtha: but in the time of Augustus, the limits of Numidia were contracted; and, at least, two-thirds of the country acquiesced in the name of Mauritania, with the epithet of Cæsariensis. The genuine Mauritania, or country of the Moors, which, from the ancient city of Tingi, or Tangier, was distinguished by the appellation of Tingitana, is represented by the modern kingdom of Fez. Sallè, on the Ocean, long infamous for its piratical depredations, was noticed by the Romans, as the extreme object of their power, and almost of their geography. A city of their foundation may still be discovered near Mequinez, the residence of the barbarian whom we condescend to style the Emperor of Morocco; but it does not appear that his more southern dominions, Morocco itself, and Segelmessa, were ever comprehended within the Roman province. The western parts of Africa are intersected by the branches of Mount Atlas, a name so idly celebrated by the fancy of poets;[86] but which is

now diffused over the immense ocean that rolls between the ancient and the new continent.[87]

Having now finished the circuit of the Roman empire, we may observe, that Africa is divided from Spain by a narrow strait of about twelve miles, through which the Atlantic flows into the Mediterranean. The columns of Hercules, so famous among the ancients, were two mountains which seemed to have been torn asunder by some convulsion of the elements; and at the foot of the European mountain the fortress of Gibraltar is now seated. The whole extent of the Mediterranean Sea, its coasts, and its islands, were comprised within the Roman dominion. Of the larger islands, the two Baleares, which derive their name of Majorca and Minorca from their respective size, are subject at present, the former to Spain, the latter to Great Britain. It is easier to deplore the fate, than to describe the actual condition, of Corsica. Two Italian sovereigns assume a regal title from Sardinia and Sicily. Crete, or Candia, with Cyprus, and most of the smaller islands of Greece and Asia, have been subdued by the Turkish arms; whilst the little rock of Malta defies their power, and has emerged, under the government of its military Order, into fame and opulence.

This long enumeration of provinces, whose broken fragments have formed so many powerful kingdoms, might almost induce us to forgive the vanity or ignorance of the ancients. Dazzled with the extensive sway, the irresistible strength, and the real or affected moderation of the emperors, they permitted themselves to despise, and sometimes to forget, the outlying countries which had been left in the enjoyment of a barbarous independence; and they gradually usurped the licence of confounding the Roman monarchy with the globe of the earth.[88] But the temper, as well as knowledge, of a modern historian requires a more sober and accurate language. He may impress a juster image of the greatness of Rome, by observing that the empire was above two thousand miles in breadth, from the wall of Antoninus and the northern limits of Dacia, to mount Atlas and the tropic of Cancer; that it extended, in length, more than three thousand miles from the Western Ocean to the Euphrates; that it was situated in the finest part of the Temperate Zone, between the twenty-fourth and fifty-sixth degrees of northern latitude; and that it was supposed to contain above sixteen hundred thousand square miles, for the most part of fertile and well-cultivated land.[89]

CHAPTER II

*Of the Union and Internal Prosperity of the Roman Empire
in the Age of the Antonines.*

I T is not alone by the rapidity, or extent of conquest, that we should estimate the greatness of Rome. The sovereign of the Russian deserts commands a larger portion of the globe. In the seventh summer after his passage of the Hellespont, Alexander erected the Macedonian trophies on the banks of the Hyphasis.[1] Within less than a century, the irresistible Zingis, and the Mogul princes of his race, spread their cruel devastations and transient empire from the sea of China to the confines of Egypt and Germany.[2] But the firm edifice of Roman power was raised and preserved by the wisdom of ages. The obedient provinces of Trajan and the Antonines were united by laws and adorned by arts. They might occasionally suffer from the partial abuse of delegated authority; but the general principle of government was wise, simple, and beneficent. They enjoyed the religion of their ancestors, whilst in civil honours and advantages they were exalted, by just degrees, to an equality with their conquerors.

I. The policy of the emperors and the senate, as far as it concerned religion, was happily seconded by the reflections of the enlightened, and by the habits of the superstitious, part of their subjects. The various modes of worship, which prevailed in the Roman world, were all considered by the people, as equally true; by the philosopher, as equally false; and by the magistrate, as equally useful. And thus toleration produced not only mutual indulgence, but even religious concord.

The superstition of the people was not embittered by any mixture of theological rancour; nor was it confined by the chains of any speculative system. The devout polytheist, though fondly attached to his national rites, admitted with implicit faith the different religions of the earth.[3] Fear, gratitude, and curiosity, a dream or an omen, a singular disorder, or a distant journey, perpetually disposed him to multiply the articles of his belief, and to enlarge the list of his protectors. The thin texture of the Pagan mythology was interwoven with various but not discordant materials. As soon as it was allowed that sages and heroes, who had lived, or who had died for the benefit of their country, were exalted to a state of power and immortality, it was universally confessed that they deserved, if not the adoration, at least the reverence of all mankind. The deities of a thousand groves and a thousand streams possessed, in peace, their local and respective influence; nor could the Roman who deprecated the wrath of the Tiber, deride the Egyptian who presented his offering to the beneficent genius of the Nile. The visible powers of Nature, the planets, and the elements, were the same throughout the universe. The invisible governors of the moral world were inevitably cast in a similar mould of fiction and allegory. Every virtue, and even vice, acquired its divine representative; every art and profession its patron, whose attributes, in the most distant ages and countries, were uniformly derived from the character of their peculiar votaries. A republic of gods of such opposite tempers and interest required, in every system, the moderating hand of a supreme magistrate, who, by the progress of knowledge and flattery, was gradually invested with the sublime perfections of an Eternal Parent, and an Omnipotent Monarch.[4] Such was the mild spirit of antiquity, that the nations were less attentive to the difference than to the resemblance of their religious worship. The Greek, the Roman, and the Barbarian, as they met before their respective altars, easily persuaded themselves, that under various names, and with various ceremonies, they adored the same deities. The elegant mythology of Homer gave a beautiful, and almost a regular form, to the polytheism of the ancient world.[5]

The philosophers of Greece deduced their morals from the nature of man, rather than from that of God. They meditated, however, on the Divine Nature, as a very curious and important speculation; and in the profound inquiry, they displayed the strength and weakness of the human understanding.[6] Of the four most celebrated schools, the Stoics and the Platonists endeavoured to reconcile the jarring interests of reason and piety. They have left us the most sublime proofs of the existence and perfections of the first cause; but, as it was impossible for them to conceive the creation of matter, the workman in the Stoic philosophy was not sufficiently distinguished from the work; whilst, on the contrary, the spiritual God of Plato and his disciples resembled an idea rather than a substance. The opinions of the Academics and Epicureans were of a less religious cast; but whilst the modest science of the former induced them to doubt, the positive ignorance of the latter urged them to deny, the providence of a Supreme Ruler. The spirit of inquiry, prompted by emulation, and supported by freedom, had divided the public teachers of philosophy into a variety of contending sects; but the ingenuous youth who, from every part, resorted to Athens, and the other seats of learning in the Roman empire, were alike instructed in every school to reject and to despise the religion of the multitude. How, indeed, was it possible, that a philosopher should accept, as divine truths, the idle tales of the poets, and the incoherent traditions of antiquity; or, that he should adore, as gods, those imperfect beings whom he must have despised, as men! Against such unworthy adversaries, Cicero condescended to employ the arms of reason and eloquence; but the satire of Lucian was a much more adequate, as well as more efficacious weapon. We may be well assured, that a writer conversant with the world would never have ventured to expose the gods of his country to public ridicule, had they not already been the objects of secret contempt among the polished and enlightened orders of society.[7]

Notwithstanding the fashionable irreligion which prevailed in the age of the Antonines, both the interests of the priests and the credulity of the people were sufficiently respected. In their writings and conversation, the philosophers of antiquity asserted the independent dignity of reason; but they resigned their actions to the commands of law and of custom. Viewing, with a smile of pity and indulgence, the various errors of the vulgar, they diligently practised the ceremonies of their fathers, devoutly frequented the temples of the gods; and sometimes condescending to act a part on the theatre of superstition, they concealed the sentiments of an Atheist under the sacerdotal robes. Reasoners of such a temper were scarcely inclined to wrangle about their respective modes of faith, or of worship. It was indifferent to them what shape the folly of the multitude might choose to assume; and they approached, with the same inward contempt, and the same external reverence, the altars of the Libyan, the Olympian, or the Capitoline Jupiter.[8]

It is not easy to conceive from what motives a spirit of persecution could introduce itself into the Roman councils. The magistrates could not be actuated by a blind, though honest bigotry, since the magistrates were themselves philosophers; and the schools of Athens had given laws to the senate. They could not be impelled by ambition or avarice, as the temporal and ecclesiastical powers were united in the same hands. The pontiffs were chosen among the most illustrious of the senators; and the office of Supreme Pontiff was constantly exercised by the emperors themselves. They knew and valued the advantages of religion, as it is connected with civil government. They encouraged the public festivals which humanise the manners of the people. They managed the arts of divination, as a convenient instrument of policy: and they respected as the firmest bond of society, the useful persuasion that, either in this or in a future life, the crime of perjury is most assuredly punished by the avenging gods.[9] But whilst they acknowledged the general advantages of religion, they were convinced that the various modes of worship contributed alike to the same salutary purposes; and that, in every country, the form of superstition, which had received the sanction of time and experience, was the best adapted to the climate and to its inhabitants. Avarice and taste very frequently despoiled the vanquished nations of the elegant statues of their gods, and the rich ornaments of their temples;[10] but, in the exercise of the religion which they derived from their ancestors, they uniformly experienced the indulgence, and even protection, of the Roman conquerors. The province of Gaul seems, and indeed only seems, an exception to this universal toleration. Under the specious pretext of abolishing human sacrifices, the emperors Tiberius and Claudius suppressed the dangerous power of the Druids,[11] but the priests themselves, their gods and their altars, subsisted in peaceful obscurity till the final destruction of Paganism.[12]

Rome, the capital of a great monarchy, was incessantly filled with subjects and strangers from every part of the world,[13] who all introduced and enjoyed the favourite superstitions of their native country.[14] Every city in the empire was justified in maintaining the purity of its ancient ceremonies; and the Roman senate, using the common privilege, sometimes interposed, to check this inundation of foreign rites. The Egyptian superstition, of all the most contemptible and abject, was frequently prohibited; the temples of Serapis and Isis demolished and their worshippers banished from Rome and

Italy.[15] But the zeal of fanaticism prevailed over the cold and feeble efforts of policy. The exiles returned, the proselytes multiplied, the temples were restored with increasing splendour, and Isis and Serapis at length assumed their place among the Roman deities.[16] Nor was this indulgence a departure from the old maxims of government. In the purest ages of the commonwealth, Cybele and Æsculapius had been invited by solemn embassies;[17] and it was customary to tempt the protectors of besieged cities, by the promise of more distinguished honours than they possessed in their native country.[18] Rome gradually became the common temple of her subjects; and the freedom of the city was bestowed on all the gods of mankind.[19]

II. The narrow policy of preserving, without any foreign mixture, the pure blood of the ancient citizens, had checked the fortune, and hastened the ruin, of Athens and Sparta. The aspiring genius of Rome sacrificed vanity to ambition, and deemed it more prudent, as well as honourable, to adopt virtue and merit for her own wheresoever they were found, among slaves or strangers, enemies or barbarians.[20] During the most flourishing era of the Athenian commonwealth, the number of citizens gradually decreased from thirty[21] to twenty-one thousand.[22] If, on the contrary, we study the growth of the Roman republic, we may discover, that, notwithstanding the incessant demands of wars and colonies, the citizens, who, in the first census of Servius Tullius, amounted to no more than eighty-three thousand, were multiplied, before the commencement of the social war, to the number of four hundred and sixty-three thousand men, able to bear arms in the service of their country.[23] When the allies of Rome claimed an equal share of honours and privileges, the senate indeed preferred the chance of arms to an ignominious concession. The Samnites and the Lucanians paid the severe penalty of their rashness; but the rest of the Italian states, as they successively returned to their duty, were admitted into the bosom of the republic,[24] and soon contributed to the ruin of public freedom. Under a democratical government, the citizens exercise the powers of sovereignty; and those powers will be first abused, and afterwards lost, if they are committed to an unwieldy multitude. But when the popular assemblies had been suppressed by the administration of the emperors, the conquerors were distinguished from the vanquished nations, only as the first and most honourable

order of subjects; and their increase, however rapid, was no longer exposed to the same dangers. Yet the wisest princes, who adopted the maxims of Augustus, guarded with the strictest care the dignity of the Roman name, and diffused the freedom of the city with a prudent liberality.[25]

Till the privileges of Romans had been progressively extended to all the inhabitants of the empire, an important distinction was preserved between Italy and the provinces. The former was esteemed the centre of public unity, and the firm basis of the constitution. Italy claimed the birth, or at least the residence, of the emperors and the senate.[26] The estates of the Italians were exempt from taxes, their persons from the arbitrary jurisdiction of governors. Their municipal corporations, formed after the perfect model of the capital, were entrusted, under the immediate eye of the supreme power, with the execution of the laws. From the foot of the Alps to the extremity of Calabria, all the natives of Italy were born citizens of Rome. Their partial distinctions were obliterated, and they insensibly coalesced into one great nation, united by language, manners, and civil institutions, and equal to the weight of a powerful empire. The republic gloried in her generous policy, and was frequently rewarded by the merit and services of her adopted sons. Had she always confined the distinction of Romans to the ancient families within the walls of the city, that immortal name would have been deprived of some of its noblest ornaments. Virgil was a native of Mantua; Horace was inclined to doubt whether he should call himself an Apulian or a Lucanian: it was in Padua that an historian was found worthy to record the majestic series of Roman victories. The patriot family of the Catos emerged from Tusculum; and the little town of Arpinum claimed the double honour of producing Marius and Cicero, the former of whom deserved, after Romulus and Camillus, to be styled the Third Founder of Rome; and the latter, after saving his country from the designs of Catiline, enabled her to contend with Athens for the palm of eloquence.[27]

The provinces of the empire (as they have been described in the preceding chapter) were destitute of any public force, or constitutional freedom. In Etruria, in Greece,[28] and in Gaul,[29] it was the first care of the senate to dissolve those dangerous confederacies, which taught mankind, that as the Roman arts prevailed by division, they might be resisted by union. Those princes, whom the ostentation of gratitude or generosity permitted for a while to hold a precarious sceptre, were dismissed from their thrones as soon as they had performed their appointed task of fashioning to the yoke the vanquished nations. The free states and cities which had embraced the cause of Rome, were rewarded with a nominal alliance, and insensibly sunk into real servitude. The public authority was everywhere exercised by the ministers of the senate and of the emperors, and that authority was absolute, and without control. But the same salutary maxims of government, which had secured the peace and obedience of Italy, were extended to the most distant conquests. A nation of Romans was gradually formed in the provinces, by the double expedient of introducing colonies, and of admitting the most faithful and deserving of the provincials to the freedom of Rome.

"Wheresoever the Roman conquers, he inhabits," [30] is a very just observation of Seneca, confirmed by history and experience. The natives of Italy, allured by pleasure or by interest, hastened to enjoy the advantages of victory; and we may remark, that about forty years after the reduction of Asia, eighty thousand Romans were massacred in one day, by the cruel orders of Mithridates. [31] These voluntary exiles were engaged, for the most part, in the occupations of commerce, agriculture, and the farm of the revenue. But after the legions were rendered permanent by the emperors, the provinces were peopled by a race of soldiers; and the veterans, whether they received the reward of their service in land or in money, usually settled with their families in the country where they had honourably spent their youth. Throughout the empire, but more particularly in the western parts, the most fertile districts, and the most convenient situations, were reserved for the establishment of colonies; some of which were of a civil, and others of a military nature. In their manners and internal policy, the colonies formed a perfect representation of their great parent; and as they were soon endeared to the natives by the ties of friendship and alliance, they effectually diffused a reverence for the Roman name, and a desire, which was seldom disappointed, of sharing, in due time, its honours and advantages. [32] The municipal cities insensibly equalled the rank and splendour of the colonies; and in the reign of Hadrian, it was disputed which was the preferable condition, of those societies which had issued from, or those which had been received into the bosom of Rome. [33] The right of Latium, as it was called, conferred on the cities to which it had been granted a more partial favour. The magistrates only, at the expiration of their office, assumed the quality of Roman citizens; but as those offices were annual, in a few years they circulated round the principal families. [34] Those of the provincials who were permitted to bear arms in the legions; [35] those who exercised any civil employment; all, in a word, who performed any public service, or displayed any personal talents, were rewarded with a present, whose value was continually diminished by the increasing liberality of the emperors. Yet even, in the age of the Antonines, when the freedom of the city had been bestowed on the greater number of their subjects, it was still accompanied with very solid advantages. The bulk of the people acquired, with that title, the benefit of the Roman laws, particularly in the interesting articles of marriage, testaments, and inheritances; and the road of fortune was open to those whose pretensions were seconded by favour or merit. The grandsons of the Gauls, who had besieged Julius Caesar in Alesia, commanded legions, governed provinces, and were admitted into the senate of Rome. [36] Their ambition, instead of disturbing the tranquillity of the state, was intimately connected with its safety and greatness.

So sensible were the Romans of the influence of language over national manners, that it was their most serious care to extend, with the progress of their arms, the use of the Latin tongue. [37] The ancient dialects of Italy, the Sabine, the Etruscan, and the Venetian, sunk into oblivion; but in the provinces, the east was less docile than the west, to the voice of its victorious preceptors. This obvious difference marked the two portions of the empire with a distinction of colours, which, though it was in some degree concealed during the meridian splendour of prosperity, became gradually more visible as the shades of night descended upon the Roman world. The western countries were civilised by the same hands which subdued them. As soon as the barbarians were reconciled to obedience, their minds were opened to any new impressions of knowledge and politeness. The language of Virgil and Cicero, though with some inevitable mixture of corruption, was so universally adopted in Africa, Spain, Gaul, Britain, and Pannonia, [38] that the faint traces of the Punic or Celtic idioms were preserved only in the mountains, or among the peasants. [39] Education and study insensibly inspired the natives of those countries with the sentiments of Romans; and Italy gave fashions as well as laws to her Latin provincials. They solicited with more ardour, and obtained with more facility, the freedom and honours of the state; supported the national dignity in letters [40] and in arms; and, at length, in the person of Trajan, produced an emperor whom the Scipios would not have disowned for their countryman. The situation of the Greeks was very different from that of the Barbarians. The former had been long since civilised and corrupted. They had too much taste to relinquish their language, and too much vanity to adopt any foreign institutions. Still preserving the prejudices after they had lost the virtues of their ancestors, they affected to despise the unpolished manners of the Roman conquerors, whilst they were compelled to respect their superior wisdom and power. [41] Nor was the influence of the Grecian language and sentiments confined to the narrow limits of that once celebrated country. Their empire, by the progress of colonies and conquest, had been diffused from the Hadriatic to the Euphrates and the Nile. Asia was covered with Greek cities, and the long reign of the Macedonian kings had introduced a silent revolution into Syria and Egypt. In their pompous courts those princes united the elegance of Athens with the luxury of the East, and the example of the court was imitated, at an humble distance, by the higher ranks of their subjects. Such was the general division of the Roman empire into the Latin and Greek languages. To these we may add a third distinction for the body of the natives in Syria, and especially in Egypt. The use of their ancient dialects, by secluding them from the commerce of mankind, checked the improvements of those barbarians. [42] The slothful effeminacy of the former, exposed them to the contempt; the sullen ferociousness of the latter, excited the aversion of the conquerors. [43] Those nations had submitted to the Roman power, but they seldom desired or deserved the freedom of the city; and it was remarked that more than two hundred and thirty years elapsed after the ruin of the Ptolemies before an Egyptian was admitted into the senate of Rome. [44]

It is a just though trite observation, that victorious Rome was herself subdued by the arts of Greece. Those immortal writers who still command the admiration of modern Europe, soon became the favourite object of study and imitation in Italy and the western provinces. But the elegant amusements of the Romans

were not suffered to interfere with their sound maxims of policy. Whilst they acknowledged the charms of the Greek, they asserted the dignity of the Latin tongue, and the exclusive use of the latter was inflexibly maintained in the administration of civil as well as military government. [45] The two languages exercised at the same time their separate jurisdiction throughout the empire: the former as the natural idiom of science; the latter as the legal dialect of public transactions. Those who united letters with business were equally conversant with both; and it was almost impossible, in any province, to find a Roman subject of a liberal education, who was at once a stranger to the Greek and to the Latin language.

It was by such institutions that the nations of the empire insensibly melted away into the Roman name and people. But there still remained, in the centre of every province and of every family, an unhappy condition of men who endured the weight, without sharing the benefits, of society. In the free states of antiquity the domestic slaves were exposed to the wanton rigour of despotism. The perfect settlement of the Roman empire was preceded by ages of violence and rapine. The slaves consisted, for the most part, of barbarian captives, taken in thousands by the chance of war, purchased at a vile price, [46] accustomed to a life of independence, and impatient to break and to revenge their fetters. Against such internal enemies, whose desperate insurrections had more than once reduced the republic to the brink of destruction, [47] the most severe regulations, [48] and the most cruel treatment, seemed almost justified by the great law of self-preservation. But when the principal nations of Europe, Asia, and Africa, were united under the laws of one sovereign, the source of foreign supplies flowed with much less abundance, and the Romans were reduced to the milder but more tedious method of propagation. In their numerous families, and particularly in their country estates, they encouraged the marriage of their slaves. The sentiments of nature, the habits of education, and the possession of a dependent species of property, contributed to alleviate the hardships of servitude. [49] The existence of a slave became an object of greater value, and though his happiness still depended on the temper and circumstances of the master, the humanity of the latter, instead of being restrained by fear, was encouraged by the sense of his own interest. The progress of manners was accelerated by the virtue or policy of the emperors; and by the edicts of Hadrian and the Antonines, the protection of the laws was extended to the most abject part of mankind. The jurisdiction of life and death over the slaves, a power long exercised and often abused, was taken out of private hands, and reserved to the magistrates alone. The subterraneous prisons were abolished; and, upon a just complaint of intolerable treatment, the injured slave obtained either his deliverance, or a less cruel master.[50]

Hope, the best comfort of our imperfect condition, was not denied to the Roman slave; and if he had any opportunity of rendering himself either useful or agreeable, he might very naturally expect that the diligence and fidelity of a few years would be rewarded with the inestimable gift of freedom. The benevolence of the master was so frequently prompted by the meaner suggestions of vanity and avarice, that the laws found it more necessary to restrain than to encourage a profuse and undistinguishing liberality, which might degenerate into a very dangerous abuse.[51] It was a maxim of ancient jurisprudence, that as a slave had not any country of his own, he acquired with his liberty an admission into the political society of which his patron was a member. The consequences of this maxim would have prostituted the privileges of the Roman city to a mean and promiscuous multitude. Some seasonable exceptions were therefore provided; and the honourable distinction was confined to such slaves only, as for just causes, and with the approbation of the magistrate, should receive a solemn and legal manumission. Even these chosen freed-men obtained no more than the private rights of citizens, and were rigorously excluded from civil or military honours. Whatever might be the merit or fortune of their sons, *they* likewise were esteemed unworthy of a seat in the senate; nor were the traces of a servile origin allowed to be completely obliterated till the third or fourth generation.[52] Without destroying the distinction of ranks, a distant prospect of freedom and honours was presented, even to those whom pride and prejudice almost disdained to number among the human species.

It was once proposed to discriminate the slaves by a peculiar habit; but it was justly apprehended that there might be some danger in acquainting them with their own numbers.[53] Without interpreting, in their utmost strictness, the liberal appellations of legions and myriads,[54] we may venture to pronounce, that the proportion of slaves, who were valued as prop-

erty, was more considerable than that of servants, who can be computed only as an expense.[55] The youths of a promising genius were instructed in the arts and sciences, and their price was ascertained by the degree of their skill and talents.[56] Almost every profession, either liberal[57] or mechanical, might be found in the household of an opulent senator. The ministers of pomp and sensuality were multiplied beyond the conception of modern luxury.[58] It was more for the interest of the merchant or manufacturer to purchase than to hire his workmen; and in the country, slaves were employed as the cheapest and most laborious instruments of agriculture. To confirm the general observation, and to display the multitude of slaves, we might allege a variety of particular instances. It was discovered, on a very melancholy occasion, that four hundred slaves were maintained in a single palace of Rome.[59] The same number of four hundred belonged to an estate which an African widow, of a very private condition, resigned to her son, whilst she reserved for herself a much larger share of her property.[60] A freedman, under the reign of Augustus, though his fortune had suffered great losses in the civil wars, left behind him three thousand six hundred yoke of oxen, two hundred and fifty thousand head of smaller cattle, and, what was almost included in the description of cattle, four thousand and one hundred and sixteen slaves.[61]

The number of subjects who acknowledged the laws of Rome, of citizens, of provincials, and of slaves, cannot now be fixed with such a degree of accuracy, as the importance of the object would deserve. We are informed that when the emperor Claudius exercised the office of censor, he took an account of six millions nine hundred and forty-five thousand Roman citizens, who, with the proportion of women and children, must have amounted to about twenty millions of souls. The multitude of subjects of an inferior rank was uncertain and fluctuating. But, after weighing with attention every circumstance which could influence the balance, it seems probable that there existed, in the time of Claudius, about twice as many provincials as there were citizens, of either sex, and of every age; and that the slaves were at least equal in number to the free inhabitants of the Roman world. The total amount of this imperfect calculation would rise to about one hundred and twenty millions of persons; a degree of population which possibly exceeds that of modern Europe,[62] and forms the most numerous society that has ever been united under the same system of government.

Domestic peace and union were the natural consequences of the moderate and comprehensive policy embraced by the Romans. If we turn our eyes towards the monarchies of Asia, we shall behold despotism in the centre, and weakness in the extremities; the collection of the revenue, or the administration of justice, enforced by the presence of an army; hostile barbarians established in the heart of the country, hereditary satraps usurping the dominion of the provinces, and subjects inclined to rebellion, though incapable of freedom. But the obedience of the Roman world was uniform, voluntary, and permanent. The vanquished nations, blended into one great people, resigned the hope, nay even the wish, of resuming their independence, and scarcely considered their own existence as distinct from the existence of Rome. The established authority of the emperors pervaded without an effort the wide extent of their dominions, and was exercised with the same facility on the banks of the Thames, or of the Nile, as on those of the Tiber. The legions were destined to serve against the public enemy, and the civil magistrate seldom required the aid of a military force.[63] In this state of general security, the leisure as well as opulence both of the prince and people were devoted to improve and to adorn the Roman empire.

Among the innumerable monuments of architecture constructed by the Romans, how many have escaped the notice of history, how few have resisted the ravages of time and barbarism! And yet even the majestic ruins that are still scattered over Italy and the provinces, would be sufficient to prove that those countries were once the seat of a polite and powerful empire. Their greatness alone, or their beauty, might deserve our attention; but they are rendered more interesting by two important circumstances, which connect the agreeable history of the arts with the more useful history of human manners. Many of those works were erected at private expense, and almost all were intended for public benefit.

It is natural to suppose that the greatest number, as well as the most considerable of the Roman edifices, were raised by the emperors, who possessed so unbounded a command both of men and money. Augustus was accustomed to boast that he had found his capital of brick, and that he had left it of marble.[64] The strict economy of Vespasian was the source of his magnificence. The works of Trajan bear the stamp of his genius. The public monuments with which Hadrian adorned every province of the empire, were executed not only by his orders, but under his immediate inspection. He was himself an artist; and he loved the arts, as they conduced to the glory of the monarch. They were encouraged by the Antonines, as they contributed to the happiness of the people. But if the emperors were the first, they were not the only architects of their dominions. Their example was universally imitated by their principal subjects, who were not afraid of declaring to the world that they had spirit to conceive, and wealth to accomplish, the noblest undertakings. Scarcely had the proud structure of the Coliseum been dedicated at Rome, before the edifices of a smaller scale indeed, but of the same design and materials, were erected for the use and at the expense, of the cities of Capua and Verona.[65] The inscription of the stupendous bridge of Alcantara attests that it was thrown over the Tagus by the contribution of a few Lusitanian communities. When Pliny was intrusted with the government of Bithynia and Pontus, provinces by no means the richest or most considerable of the empire, he found the cities within his jurisdiction striving with each other in every useful and ornamental work, that might deserve the curiosity of strangers, or the gratitude of their citizens. It was the duty of the Proconsul to supply their deficiencies, to direct their taste, and sometimes to moderate their emulation.[66] The opulent senators of Rome and the provinces esteemed it an honour, and almost an obligation, to adorn the splendour of their age and country; and the influence of fashion very frequently supplied the want of taste or generosity. Among a crowd of these private benefactors, we may select Herodes Atticus, an Athenian citizen, who lived in the age of the Antonines. Whatever might be the motive of his conduct, his magnificence would have been worthy of the greatest kings.

The family of Herod, at least after it had been favoured by fortune, was lineally descended from Cimon and Miltiades, Theseus and Cecrops, Æacus and Jupiter. But the posterity of so many gods and heroes was fallen into the most abject state. His grandfather had suffered by the hands of justice, and Julius Atticus, his father, must have ended his life in poverty and contempt, had he not discovered an immense treasure buried under an old house, the last remains of his patrimony. According to the rigour of law, the emperor might have asserted his claim, and the prudent Atticus prevented, by a frank confession, the officiousness of informers. But the equitable Nerva, who then filled the throne, refused to accept any part of it, and commanded him to use, without scruple, the present of fortune. The cautious Athenian still insisted that the treasure was too considerable for a subject, and that he knew not how to *use it. Abuse it, then*, replied the monarch, with a good-natured peevishness; for it is your own.[67] Many will be of opinion that Atticus literally obeyed the emperor's last instructions; since he expended the greatest part of his fortune, which was much increased by an advantageous marriage, in the service of the Public. He had obtained for his son Herod the prefecture of the free cities of Asia; and the young magistrate, observing that the town of Troas was indifferently supplied with water, obtained from the munificence of Hadrian three hundred myriads of drachms (about a hundred thousand pounds) for the construction of a new aqueduct. But in the execution of the work the charge amounted to more than double the estimate, and the officers of the revenue began to murmur, till the generous Atticus silenced their complaints, by requesting that he might be permitted to take upon himself the whole additional expense.[68]

The ablest preceptors of Greece and Asia had been invited by liberal rewards to direct the education of young Herod. Their pupil soon became a celebrated orator according to the useless rhetoric of that age, which, confining itself to the schools, disdained to visit either the Forum or the senate. He was honoured with the consulship at Rome; but the greatest part of his life was spent in a philosophic retirement at Athens, and his adjacent villas; perpetually surrounded by sophists, who acknowledged, without reluctance, the superiority of a rich and generous rival.[69] The monuments of his genius have perished; some considerable ruins still preserve the fame of his taste and munificence: modern travellers have measured the remains of the stadium which he constructed at Athens. It was six hundred feet in length, built entirely of white marble, capable of admitting the whole body of the people, and finished in four years, whilst Herod was president of the Athenian games. To the memory of his wife Regilla he dedicated a theatre, scarcely to be paralleled in the empire; no wood except cedar, very curiously carved, was employed in any part of the building. The Odeum, designed by Pericles for musical performances, and the rehearsal of new tragedies, had been a trophy of the victory of the arts over Barbaric greatness, as the timbers employed in the construction consisted chiefly of the masts of the Persian vessels. Notwithstanding the repairs bestowed on that ancient edifice by a king of Cappadocia, it was again fallen to decay. Herod restored its ancient beauty and magnificence. Nor was the liberality of that illustrious citizen confined to the walls of Athens. The most splendid ornaments bestowed on the temple of Neptune in the Isthmus, a theatre at Corinth, a stadium at Delphi, a bath at Thermopylae, and an aqueduct at Canusium in Italy, were insufficient to exhaust his treasures. The people of Epirus, Thessaly, Eubœa, Bœotia, and Peloponnesus, experienced his favours; and many inscriptions of the cities of Greece and Asia gratefully style Herodes Atticus their patron and benefactor.[70]

In the commonwealths of Athens and Rome, the modest simplicity of private houses announced the equal condition of freedom; whilst the sovereignty of the people was represented in the majestic edifices destined to the public use;[71] nor was this republican spirit totally extinguished by the introduction of wealth and monarchy. It was in works of national honour and benefit, that the most virtuous of the emperors affected to display their magnificence. The golden palace of Nero excited a just indignation, but the vast extent of ground which had been usurped by his selfish luxury, was more nobly filled under the succeeding reigns by the Coliseum, the baths of Titus, the Claudian portico, and the temples dedicated to the goddess of Peace, and to the genius of Rome.[72] These monuments of architecture, the property of the Roman people, were adorned with the most beautiful productions of Grecian painting and sculpture; and in the temple of Peace a very curious library was open to the curiosity of the learned. At a small distance from thence was situated the Forum of Trajan. It was surrounded with a lofty portico, in the form of a quadrangle, into which four triumphal arches opened a noble and spacious entrance: in the centre arose a column of marble, whose height, of one hundred and ten feet, denoted the elevation of the hill that had been cut away. This column, which still subsists in its ancient beauty, exhibited an exact representation of the Dacian victories of its founder. The veteran soldier contemplated the story of his own campaigns, and by an easy illusion of national vanity, the peaceful citizen associated himself to the honours of the triumph. All the other quarters of the capital, and all the provinces of the empire, were embellished by the same liberal spirit of public magnificence, and were filled with amphitheatres, theatres, temples, porticos, triumphal arches, baths, and aqueducts, all variously conducive to the health, the devotion, and the pleasures of the meanest citizen. The last mentioned of those edifices deserve our peculiar attention. The boldness of the enterprise, the solidity of the execution, and the uses to which they were subservient, rank the aqueducts among the noblest monuments of Roman genius and power. The aqueducts of the capital claim a just pre-eminence; but the curious traveller, who, without the light of history, should examine those of Spoleto, of Metz, or of Segovia, would very naturally conclude that those provincial towns had formerly been the residence of some potent monarch. The solitudes of Asia and Africa were once covered with flourishing cities, whose populousness, and even whose existence, was derived from such artificial supplies of a perennial stream of fresh water.[73]

We have computed the inhabitants and contemplated the public works of the Roman empire. The observation of the number and greatness of its cities will serve to confirm the former, and to multiply the latter. It may not be unpleasing to collect a few scattered instances relative to that subject, without forgetting, however, that from the vanity of nations and the poverty of language, the vague appellation of city has been indifferently bestowed on Rome and upon Laurentum. *Ancient* Italy is said to have contained eleven hundred and ninety-seven cities; and for whatsoever era of antiquity the expression might be intended,[74] there is not any reason to believe the country less populous in the age of the Antonines than in that of Romulus. The petty states of Latium were contained within the metropolis of the empire, by whose superior influence they had been attracted. Those parts of Italy which have so long languished under the lazy tyranny of priests and viceroys, had been afflicted only by the more tolerable calamities of war; and the first symptoms of decay which *they* experienced were amply compensated by the rapid improvements of the Cisalpine Gaul. The splendour of Verona may be traced in its remains: yet Verona was less celebrated than Aquileia or Padua, Milan or Ravenna. II. The spirit of improvement had passed the Alps, and been felt even in the woods of Britain, which were gradually cleared away to open a free space for convenient and elegant habitations. York was the seat of government; London was already enriched by commerce; and Bath was celebrated for the salutary effects of its medicinal waters. Gaul could boast of her twelve hundred cities;[75] and though, in the northern parts, many of them, without excepting Paris itself, were little more than the rude and imperfect townships of a rising people, the southern provinces imitated the wealth and elegance of Italy.[76] Many were the cities of Gaul, Marseilles, Arles, Nismes, Narbonne, Thoulouse, Bourdeaux, Autun, Vienna, Lyons, Langres, and Treves, whose ancient condition might sustain an equal, and perhaps advantageous comparison with their present state. With regard to Spain, that country flourished as a province, and has declined as a kingdom. Exhausted by the abuse of her strength, by America, and by superstition, her pride might possibly be confounded, if we required such a list of three hundred and sixty cities, as Pliny has exhibited under the reign of Vespasian.[77] III. Three hundred African cities had once acknowledged the authority of Carthage,[78] nor is it likely that their numbers diminished under the administration of the emperors: Carthage itself rose with new splendour from its ashes; and that capital, as well as Capua and Corinth, soon recovered all the advantages which can be separated from independent sovereignty. IV. The provinces of the east present the contrast of Roman magnificence with Turkish barbarism. The ruins of antiquity scattered over uncultivated fields, and ascribed, by ignorance, to the power of magic, scarcely afford a shelter to the oppressed peasant or wandering Arab. Under the reign of the Cæsars, the proper Asia alone contained five hundred populous cities,[79] enriched with all the gifts of nature, and adorned with all the refinements of art. Eleven cities of Asia had once disputed the honour of dedicating a temple to Tiberius, and their respective merits were examined by the senate.[80] Four of them were immediately rejected as unequal to the burden; and among these was Laodicea, whose splendour is still displayed in its ruins.[81] Laodicea collected a very considerable revenue from its flocks of sheep, celebrated for the fineness of their wool, and had received, a little before the contest, a legacy of above four hundred thousand pounds by the testament of a generous citizen.[82] If such was the poverty of Laodicea, what must have been the wealth of those cities, whose claim appeared preferable, and particularly of Pergamus, of Smyrna, and of Ephesus, who so long disputed with each other over the titular primacy of Asia.[83] The capitals of Syria and Egypt held a still superior rank in the empire: Antioch and Alexandria looked down with disdain on a crowd of dependent cities,[84] and yielded, with reluctance, to the majesty of Rome itself.

All these cities were connected with each other, and with the capital, by the public highways, which issuing from the Forum of Rome, traversed Italy, pervaded the provinces, and were terminated only by the frontiers of the empire. If we carefully trace the distance from the wall of Antoninus to Rome, and from thence to Jerusalem, it will be found that the great chain of communication, from the north-west to the south-east point of the empire, was drawn out to the length of four thousand and eighty Roman miles.[85] The public roads were accurately divided by mile-stones, and ran in a direct line from one city to another, with very little respect for the obstacles either of nature or private property. Mountains were perforated, and bold arches thrown over the broadest and most rapid streams.[86] The middle part of the road was raised into a terrace which commanded the adjacent country, consisted of several strata of sand, gravel, and cement, and was paved with large stones, or in some places, near the capital, with granite.[87] Such was the solid construction of the Roman highways, whose firmness has not entirely yielded to the effort of fifteen centuries. They united the subjects of the most distant provinces by an easy and familiar intercourse; but their primary object had been to facilitate the marches of the legions; nor was any country considered as completely subdued, till it had been rendered, in all its parts, pervious to the arms and authority of the conqueror. The advantage of receiving the earliest intelligence, and of conveying their orders with celerity, induced the emperors to establish throughout their extensive dominions, the regular institution of posts.[88] Houses were everywhere erected at the distance only of five or six miles; each of them was constantly provided with forty horses, and by the help of these relays it was easy to travel an hundred miles in a day along the Roman roads.[89] The use of the posts was allowed to those who claimed it by an Imperial mandate; but though originally intended for the public service, it was sometimes indulged to the business or conveniency of private citizens.[90] Nor was the communication of the Roman empire less free and open by sea than it was by land. The provinces surrounded and inclosed the Mediterranean; and Italy, in the shape of an immense promontory, advanced into the midst of that great lake. The coasts of Italy are, in general, destitute of safe harbours; but human industry had corrected the deficiencies of nature; and the artificial port of Ostia, in particular, situate at the mouth of the Tyber, and formed by the emperor Claudius, was a useful monument of Roman greatness.[91] From this port, which was only sixteen miles from the capital, a favourable breeze frequently carried vessels in seven days to the columns of Hercules, and in nine or ten, to Alexandria in Egypt.[92]

Whatever evils either reason or declamation have imputed to extensive empire, the power of Rome was attended with some beneficial consequences to mankind; and the same freedom of intercourse which extended the vices, diffused likewise the improvements of social life. In the more remote ages of antiquity, the world was unequally divided. The east was in the immemorial possession of arts and luxury; whilst the west was inhabited by rude and warlike barbarians, who either disdained agriculture, or to whom it was totally unknown. Under the protection of an established government, the productions of happier climates, and the industry of more civilised nations, were gradually introduced into the western countries of Europe; and the natives were encouraged, by an open and profitable commerce, to multiply the former, as well as to improve the latter. It would be almost impossible to enumerate all the articles, either of the animal or the vegetable reign, which were successively imported into Europe, from Asia and Egypt;[93] but it will not be unworthy of the dignity, and much less of the utility, of an historical work, slightly to touch on a few of the principal heads. 1. Almost all the flowers, the herbs, and the fruits, that grow in our European gardens, are of foreign extraction, which, in many cases, is betrayed even by their names: the apple was a native of Italy, and when the Romans had tasted the richer flavour of the apricot, the peach, the pomegranate, the citron, and the orange, they contented themselves with applying to all these new fruits the common denomination of apple, discriminating them from each other by the additional epithet of their country. 2. In the time of Homer, the vine grew wild in the island of Sicily, and most probably in the adjacent continent; but it was not improved by the skill, nor did it afford a liquor grateful to the taste, of the savage inhabitants.[94]

A thousand years afterwards, Italy could boast, that of the fourscore most generous and celebrated wines, more than two-thirds were produced from her soil.[95] The blessing was soon communicated to the Narbonnese province of Gaul; but so intense was the cold to the north of the Cevennes, that, in the time of Strabo, it was thought impossible to ripen the grapes in those parts of Gaul.[96] This difficulty, however, was gradually vanquished; and there is some reason to believe, that the vineyards of Burgundy are as old as the age of the Antonines.[97] The olive, in the western world, followed the progress of peace, of which it was considered as the symbol. Two centuries after the foundation of Rome, both Italy and Africa were strangers to that useful plant; it was naturalised in those countries; and at length carried into the heart of Spain and Gaul. The timid errors of the ancients, that it required a certain degree of heat, and could only flourish in the neighbourhood of the sea, were insensibly exploded by industry and experience.[98] The cultivation of flax was transported from Egypt to Gaul, and enriched the whole country, however it might impoverish the particular lands on which it was sown.[99] 3. The use of artificial grasses became familiar to the farmers both of Italy and the provinces, particularly the Lucerne, which derived its name and origin from Media.[100] The assured supply of wholesome and plentiful food for the cattle during winter multiplied the number of the flocks and herds, which in their turn contributed to the fertility of the soil. To all these improvements may be added an assiduous attention to mines and fisheries, which, by employing a multitude of laborious hands, serve to increase the pleasures of the rich, and the subsistence of the poor. The elegant treatise of Columella describes the advanced state of the Spanish husbandry, under the reign of Tiberius; and it may be observed, that those famines which so frequently afflicted the infant republic, were seldom or never experienced by the extensive empire of Rome. The accidental scarcity, in any single province, was immediately relieved by the plenty of its more fortunate neighbours.

Agriculture is the foundation of manufactures; since the productions of nature are the materials of art. Under the Roman empire, the labour of an industrious and ingenious people was variously, but incessantly employed, in the service of the rich. In their dress, their table, their houses, and their furniture, the favourites of fortune united every refinement of conveniency, of elegance, and of splendour, whatever could soothe their pride or gratify their sensuality. Such refinements, under the odious name of luxury, have been severely arraigned by the moralists of every age; and it might perhaps be more conducive to the virtue, as well as happiness, of mankind, if all possessed the necessities, and none of the superfluities, of life. But in the present imperfect condition of society, luxury, though it may proceed from vice or folly, seems to be the only means that can correct the unequal distribution of property. The diligent mechanic, and the skilful artist, who have obtained no share in the division of the earth, receive a voluntary tax from the possessors of land; and the latter are prompted, by a sense of interest, to improve those estates, with whose produce they may purchase additional pleasures. This operation, the particular effects of which are felt in every society, acted with much more diffusive energy in the Roman world. The provinces would soon have been exhausted of their wealth, if the manufactures and commerce of luxury had not insensibly restored to the industrious subjects the sums which were exacted from them by the arms and authority of Rome. As long as the circulation was confined within the bounds of the empire, it impressed the political machine with a new degree of activity, and its consequences, sometimes beneficial, could never become pernicious.

But it is no easy task to confine luxury within the limits of an empire. The most remote countries of the ancient world were ransacked to supply the pomp and delicacy of Rome. The forests of Scythia afforded some valuable furs. Amber was brought over land from the shores of the Baltic to the Danube; and the barbarians were astonished at the price which they received in exchange for so useless a commodity.[101] There was a considerable demand for Babylonian carpets and other manufactures of the East; but the most important and unpopular branch of foreign trade was carried on with Arabia and India. Every year, about the time of the summer solstice, a fleet of a hundred and twenty vessels sailed from Myos-hormos, a port of Egypt, on the Red Sea. By the periodical assistance of the Monsoons, they traversed the ocean in about forty days. The coast of Malabar, or the island of Ceylon,[102] was the usual term of their navigation, and it was in those markets that the merchants from the more remote countries of Asia expected their arrival. The return of the fleet of Egypt was fixed to the months of December or January; and as soon as their rich cargo had been transported on the backs of camels, from the Red Sea to the Nile, and had descended that river as far as Alexandria, it was poured, without delay, into the capital of the empire.[103] The objects of oriental traffic were splendid and trifling; silk, a pound of which was esteemed not inferior in value to a pound of gold;[104] precious stones, among which the pearl claimed the first rank after the diamond;[105] and a variety of aromatics, that were consumed in religious worship and the pomp of funerals. The labour and risk of the voyage was rewarded with almost incredible profit; but the profit was made upon Roman subjects, and a few individuals were enriched at the expense of the Public. As the natives of Arabia and India were contented with the productions and manufactures of their own country, silver, on the side of the Romans, was the principal, if not the only instrument of commerce. It was a complaint worthy of the gravity of the senate, that in the purchase of female ornaments, the wealth of the state was irrevocably given away to foreign and hostile nations.[106] The annual loss is computed, by a writer of an inquisitive but censorious temper, at upwards of eight hundred thousand pounds sterling.[107] Such was the style of discontent, brooding over the dark prospect of approaching poverty. And yet, if we compare the proportion between gold and silver, as it stood in the time of Pliny, and as it was fixed in the reign of Constantine, we shall discover within that period a very considerable increase.[108] There is not the least reason to suppose that gold was become more scarce; it is therefore evident that silver was grown more common; that whatever might be the amount of the Indian and Arabian exports, they were far from exhausting the wealth of the Roman world; and that the produce of the mines abundantly supplied the demands of commerce.

Notwithstanding the propensity of mankind to exalt the past, and to depreciate the present, the tranquil and prosperous state of the empire was warmly felt, and honestly confessed, by the provincials as well as Romans. "They acknowledged that the true principles of social life, laws, agriculture, and science, which had been first invented by the wisdom of Athens, were now firmly established by the power of Rome, under whose auspicious influence the fiercest barbarians were united by an equal government and common language. They affirm, that with the improvement of arts, the human species was visibly multiplied. They celebrate the increasing splendour of the cities, the beautiful face of the country, cultivated and adorned like an immense garden; and the long festival of peace, which was enjoyed by so many nations, forgetful of their ancient animosities, and delivered from the apprehension of future danger."[109] Whatever suspicions may be suggested by the air of rhetoric and declamation, which seems to prevail in these passages, the substance of them is perfectly agreeable to historic truth.

It was scarcely possible that the eyes of contemporaries should discover in the public felicity the latent causes of decay and corruption. This long peace, and the uniform government of the Romans, introduced a slow and secret poison into the vitals of the empire. The minds of men were gradually reduced to the same level, the fire of genius was extinguished, and even the military spirit evaporated. The natives of Europe were brave and robust, Spain, Gaul, Britain, and Illyricum supplied the legions with excellent soldiers, and constituted the real strength of the monarchy. Their personal valour remained, but they no longer possessed that public courage which is nourished by the love of independence, the sense of national honour, the presence of danger, and the habit of command. They received laws and governors from the will of their sovereign, and trusted for their defence to a mercenary army. The posterity of their boldest leaders was contented with the rank of citizens and subjects. The most aspiring spirits resorted to the court or standard of the emperors; and the deserted provinces, deprived of political strength or union, insensibly sunk into the languid indifference of private life.

The love of letters, almost inseparable from peace and refinement, was fashionable among the subjects of Hadrian and the Antonines, who were themselves men of learning and curiosity. It was diffused over the whole extent of their empire; the most northern tribes of Britons had acquired a taste for rhetoric; Homer as well as Virgil were transcribed and studied on the banks of the Rhine and Danube; and the most liberal rewards sought out the faintest glimmerings of literary merit.[110] The sciences of physic and astronomy were successfully cultivated by the Greeks; the observations of Ptolemy and the writings of Galen are studied by those who have improved their discoveries and corrected their errors; but if we except the inimitable Lucian, this age of indolence passed away without having produced a single writer of original genius, or who excelled in the arts of elegant composition. The authority of Plato and Aristotle, of

Zeno and Epicurus, still reigned in the schools; and their systems, transmitted with blind deference from one generation of disciples to another, precluded every generous attempt to exercise the powers, or enlarge the limits, of the human mind. The beauties of the poets and orators, instead of kindling a fire like their own, inspired only cold and servile imitations: or if any ventured to deviate from those models, they deviated at the same time from good sense and propriety. On the revival of letters, the youthful vigour of the imagination, after a long repose, national emulation, a new religion, new languages, and a new world, called forth the genius of Europe. But the provincials of Rome, trained by a uniform artificial foreign education, were engaged in a very unequal competition with those bold ancients, who, by expressing their genuine feelings in their native tongue, had already occupied every place of honour. The name of Poet was almost forgotten; that of Orator was usurped by the sophists. A cloud of critics, of compilers, of commentators, darkened the face of learning, and the decline of genius was soon followed by the corruption of taste.

The sublime Longinus, who in somewhat a later period, and in the court of a Syrian queen, preserved the spirit of ancient Athens, observes and laments this degeneracy of his contemporaries, which debased their sentiments, enervated their courage, and depressed their talents. "In the same manner," says he, "as some children always remain pigmies, whose infant limbs have been too closely confined; thus our tender minds, fettered by the prejudices and habits of a just servitude, are unable to expand themselves, or to attain that well-proportioned greatness which we admire in the ancients; who living under a popular government, wrote with the same freedom as they acted."[111] This diminutive stature of mankind, if we pursue the metaphor, was daily sinking below the old standard, and the Roman world was indeed peopled by a race of pygmies; when the fierce giants of the north broke in, and mended the puny breed. They restored a manly spirit of freedom; and after the revolution of ten centuries, freedom became the happy parent of taste and science.

CHAPTER III

Of the Constitution of the Roman Empire, in the Age of the Antonines.

THE obvious definition of a monarchy seems to be that of a state, in which a single person, by whatsoever name he may be distinguished, is entrusted with the execution of the laws, the management of the revenue, and the command of the army. But, unless public liberty is protected by intrepid and vigilant guardians, the authority of so formidable a magistrate will soon degenerate into despotism. The influence of the clergy, in an age of superstition, might be usefully employed to assert the rights of mankind; but so intimate is the connection between the throne and the altar, that the banner of the church has very seldom been seen on the side of the people. A martial nobility and stubborn commons, possessed of arms, tenacious of property, and collected into constitutional assemblies, form the only balance capable of preserving a free constitution against enterprises of an aspiring prince.

Every barrier of the Roman constitution had been levelled by the vast ambition of the dictator; every fence had been extirpated by the cruel hand of the Triumvir. After the victory of Actium, the fate of the Roman world depended on the will of Octavianus, surnamed Cæsar, by his uncle's adoption, and afterwards Augustus, by the flattery of the senate. The conqueror was at the head of forty-four veteran legions,[1] conscious of their own strength, and of the weakness of the constitution, habituated, during twenty years civil war, to every act of blood and violence, and passionately devoted to the house of Cæsar, from whence alone they had received, and expected, the most lavish rewards. The provinces, long oppressed by the ministers of the republic, sighed for the government of a single person, who would be the master, not the accomplice, of those petty tyrants. The people of Rome, viewing, with a secret pleasure, the humiliation of the aristocracy, demanded only bread and public shows; and were supplied with both by the liberal hand of Augustus. The rich and polite Italians, who had almost universally embraced the philosophy of Epicurus, enjoyed the present blessings of ease and tranquillity, and suffered not the pleasing dream to be interrupted by the memory of their old tumultuous freedom. With its power, the senate had lost its dignity; many of the most noble families were extinct. The republicans of spirit and ability had perished in the field of battle, or in the proscription. The door of the assembly had been designedly left open, for a mixed multitude of more than a thousand persons, who reflected disgrace upon their rank, instead of deriving honour from it.[2]

The reformation of the senate was one of the first steps in which Augustus laid aside the tyrant, and professed himself the father of his country. He was elected censor; and, in concert with his faithful Agrippa, he examined the list of the senators, expelled a few members, whose vices or whose obstinacy required a public example, persuaded near two hundred to prevent the shame of an expulsion by a voluntary retreat, raised the qualification of a senator to about ten thousand pounds, created a sufficient number of Patrician families, and accepted for himself the honourable title of Prince of the Senate, which had always been bestowed, by the censors, on the citizen the most eminent for his honours and services.[3] But whilst he thus restored the dignity, he destroyed the independence of the senate. The principles of a free constitution are irrevocably lost, when the legislative power is nominated by the executive.

Before an assembly thus modelled and prepared, Augustus pronounced a studied oration, which displayed his patriotism, and disguised his ambition. "He lamented, yet excused, his past conduct. Filial piety had required at his hands the revenge of his father's murder; the humanity of his own nature had sometimes given way to the stern laws of necessity, and to a forced connection with two unworthy colleagues: as long as Antony lived, the republic forbade him to abandon her to a degenerate Roman, and a barbarian queen. He was now at liberty to satisfy his duty and his inclination. He solemnly restored the senate and people to all their ancient rights; and wished only to mingle with the crowd of his fellow-citizens, and to share the blessings which he had obtained for his country."[4]

It would require the pen of Tacitus (if Tacitus had assisted at this assembly) to describe the various emotions of the senate; those that were suppressed, and those that were affected. It was dangerous to trust the sincerity of Augustus; to seem to distrust it was still more dangerous. The respective advantages of monarchy and a republic have often divided speculative inquirers; the present greatness of the Roman state, the corruption of manners, and the licence of the soldiers, supplied new arguments to the advocates of monarchy; and these general views of government were again warped by the hopes and fears of each individual. Amidst this confusion of sentiments, the answer of the senate was unanimous and decisive. They refused to accept the resignation of Augustus; they conjured him not to desert the republic, which he had saved. After a decent resistance, the crafty tyrant submitted to the orders of the senate; and consented to receive the government of the provinces, and the general command of the Roman armies, under the well-known names of PROCONSUL and IMPERATOR.[5] But he would receive them only for ten years. Even before the expiration of that period, he hoped that the wounds of civil discord would be completely healed, and that the republic, restored to its pristine health and vigour, would no longer require the dangerous interposition of so extraordinary a magistrate. The memory of this comedy, repeated several times during the life of Augustus, was preserved to the last ages of the empire, by the peculiar pomp with which the perpetual monarchs of Rome always solemnised the tenth years of their reign.[6]

Without any violation of the principles of the constitution, the general of the Roman armies might receive and exercise an authority almost despotic over the soldiers, the enemies, and the subjects of the republic. With regard to the soldiers, the jealousy of freedom had, even from the earliest ages of Rome, given way to the hopes of conquest, and a just sense of military discipline. The dictator, or consul, had a right to command the service of the Roman youth; and to punish an obstinate or cowardly disobedience by the most severe and ignominious penalties, by striking the offender out of the list of citizens, by confiscating his property, and by selling his person into slavery.[7] The most sacred rights of freedom, confirmed by the Porcian and Sempronian laws, were suspended by the military engagement. In his camp the general exercised an absolute power of life and death; his jurisdiction was not confined by any forms of trial or rules of proceeding, and the execution of the sentence was immediate and without appeal.[8] The choice of the enemies of Rome was regularly decided by the legislative authority. The most important resolutions of peace and war were seriously debated in the senate, and solemnly ratified by the people. But when the arms of the legions were carried to a great distance from Italy, the generals assumed the liberty of directing them against whatever people, and in whatever manner, they judged most advantageous for the public service. It was from the success, not from the justice, of their enterprises, that they expected the honours of a triumph. In the use of victory, especially after they were no longer controlled by the commissioners of the senate, they exercised the most unbounded despotism. When Pompey commanded in the East, he rewarded his soldiers and allies, dethroned princes, divided kingdoms, founded colonies, and distributed the treasures of Mithridates. On his return to Rome, he obtained, by a single act of the senate and people, the universal ratification of all his proceedings. [9] Such was the power over the soldiers, and over the enemies of Rome, which was either granted to, or assumed by, the generals of the republic. They were, at the same time, the governors, or rather monarchs, of the conquered provinces, united the civil with the military character, administered justice as well as the finances, and exercised both the executive and legislative power of the state.

From what has been already observed in the first chapter of this work, some notion may be formed of the armies and provinces thus intrusted to the ruling hand of Augustus. But as it was impossible that he could personally command the legions of so many distant frontiers, he was indulged by the senate, as Pompey had already been, in the permission of devolving the execution of his great office on a sufficient number of lieutenants. In rank and authority these officers seemed not inferior to the ancient proconsuls; but their station was dependent and precarious. They received and held their commissions at the will of a superior, to whose *auspicious* influence the merit of their action was legally attributed. [10] They were the representatives of the emperor. The emperor alone was the general of the republic, and his jurisdiction, civil as well as military, extended over all the conquests of Rome. It was some satisfaction, however, to the senate, that he always delegated his power to the members of their body. The Imperial lieutenants were of consular or prætorian dignity; the legions were commanded by senators, and the præfecture of Egypt was the only important trust committed to a Roman knight.

Within six days after Augustus had been compelled to accept so very liberal a grant, he resolved to gratify the pride of the senate by an easy sacrifice. He represented to them, that they had enlarged his powers, even beyond that degree which might be required by the melancholy condition of the times. They had not permitted him to refuse the laborious command of the armies and the frontiers; but he must insist on being allowed to restore the more peaceful and secure provinces, to the mild administration of the civil magistrate. In the division of the provinces, Augustus provided for his own power, and for the dignity of the republic. The proconsuls of the senate, particularly those of Asia, Greece, and Africa, enjoyed a more honourable character than the lieutenants of the emperor, who commanded in Gaul or Syria. The former were attended by lictors, the latter by soldiers. A law was passed that wherever the emperor was present, his extraordinary commission should supersede the ordinary jurisdiction of the governor; a custom was introduced, that the new conquest belonged to the Imperial portion; and it was soon discovered that the authority of the *Prince*, the favourite epithet of Augustus, was the same in every part of the empire.

In return for this imaginary concession, Augustus obtained an important privilege, which rendered him master of Rome and Italy. By a dangerous exception to the ancient maxims, he was authorised to preserve his military command, supported by a numerous body of guards, even in time of peace, and in the heart of the capital. His command, indeed, was confined to those citizens who were engaged in the service by the military oath; but such was the propensity of the Romans to servitude, that the oath was voluntarily taken by the magistrates, the senators, and the equestrian order, till the homage of flattery was insensibly converted into an annual and solemn protestation of fidelity.

Although Augustus considered a military force as the firmest foundation, he wisely rejected it, as a very odious instrument of government. It was more agreeable to his temper, as well as to his policy, to reign under the venerable names of ancient magistracy, and artfully to collect, in his own person, all the scattered rays of civil jurisdiction. With this view, he permitted the senate to confer upon him, for his life, the powers of the consular[11] and tribunitian offices,[12] which were, in the same manner, continued to all his successors. The consuls had succeeded to the kings of Rome, and represented the dignity of the state. They superintended the ceremonies of religion, levied and commanded the legions, gave audience to foreign ambassadors, and presided in the assemblies both of the senate and people. The general control of the finances was intrusted to their care; and though they seldom had leisure to administer justice in person, they were considered as the supreme guardians of law, equity, and the public peace. Such was their ordinary jurisdiction; but whenever the senate empowered the first magistrate to consult the safety of the commonwealth, he was raised by that decree above the laws, and exercised, in the defence of liberty, a temporary despotism.[13] The character of the tribunes was, in every respect, different from that of the consuls. The appearance of the former was modest and humble; but their persons were sacred and inviolable. Their force was suited rather for opposition than for action. They were instituted to defend the oppressed, to pardon offences, to arraign the enemies of the people, and, when they judged it necessary, to stop, by a single word, the whole machine of government. As long as the republic subsisted, the dangerous influence, which either the consul or the tribune might derive from their respective jurisdiction, was diminished by several important restrictions. Their authority expired with the year in which they were elected; the former office was divided between two, the latter among ten persons; and, as both in their private and public interest they were averse to each other, their mutual conflicts contributed, for the most part, to strengthen rather than to destroy the balance of the constitution. But when the consular and tribunitian powers were united, when they were vested for life in a single person, when the general of the army was, at the same time, the minister of the senate, and the representative of the Roman people, it was impossible to resist the exercise, nor was it easy to define the limits, of his Imperial prerogative.

To these accumulated honours, the policy of Augustus soon added the splendid as well as important dignities of supreme pontiff, and of censor. By the former he acquired the management of the religion, and by the latter a legal inspection over the manners and fortunes, of the Roman people. If so many distinct and independent powers did not exactly unite with each other, the complaisance of the senate was prepared to supply every deficiency by the most ample and extraordinary concessions. The emperors, as the first ministers of the republic, were exempted from the obligation and penalty of many inconvenient laws: they were authorised to convoke the senate, to make several motions in the same day, to recommend candidates for the honours of the state, to enlarge the bounds of the city, to employ the revenue at their discretion, to declare peace and war, to ratify treaties; and by a most comprehensive clause, they were empowered to execute whatsoever they should judge advantageous to the empire, and agreeable to the majesty of things private or public, human or divine.[14]

When all the various powers of executive government were committed to the *Imperial magistrate*, the ordinary magistrates of the commonwealth languished in obscurity, without vigour, and almost without business. The names and forms of the ancient administration were preserved by Augustus with the most anxious care. The usual number of consuls, prætors, tribunes,[15] were annually invested with their respective ensigns of office, and continued to discharge some of their least important functions. Those honours still attracted the vain ambition of the Romans; and the emperors themselves, though invested for life with the powers of the consulship, frequently aspired to the title of that annual dignity, which they condescended to share with the most illustrious of their fellow-citizens.[16] In the election of these magistrates, the people, during the reign of Augustus, were permitted to expose all the inconveniences of a wild democracy. That artful prince, instead of discovering the least symptom of impatience, humbly solicited their suffrages for himself or his friends, and scrupulously practised all the duties of an ordinary candidate.[17] But we may venture to ascribe to his councils, the first measure of the succeeding reign, by which the elections were transferred to the senate.[18] The assemblies of the people were for ever abolished, and the emperors were delivered from a dangerous multitude, who, without restoring liberty, might have disturbed, and perhaps endangered, the established government.

By declaring themselves the protectors of the people, Marius and Cæsar had subverted the constitution of their country. But as soon as the senate had been humbled and disarmed, such an assembly, consisting of five or six hundred persons, was found a much more tractable and useful instrument of dominion. It was on the dignity of the senate, that Augustus and his successors founded their new empire; and they affected, on every occasion, to adopt the language and principles of Patricians. In the administration of their own powers they frequently consulted the great national council, and *seemed* to refer to its decision the most important concerns of peace and war. Rome, Italy, and the internal provinces, were subject to the immediate jurisdiction of the senate. With regard to civil objects, it was the supreme court of appeal; with regard to criminal matters, a tribunal constituted for the trial of all offences that were committed by men in any public station, or that affected the peace and majesty of the Roman people. The exercise of the judicial power became the most frequent and serious occupation of the senate; and the important causes that were pleaded before them afforded a last refuge to the spirit of ancient eloquence. As a council of state, and as a court of justice, the senate possessed very considerable prerogatives; but in its legislative capacity, in which it was supposed virtually to represent the people, the rights of sovereignty were acknowledged to reside in that assembly. Every power was derived from their authority, every law was ratified by their sanction. Their regular meetings were held on three stated days in every month, the Calends, the Nones, and the Ides. The debates were conducted with decent freedom; and the emperors themselves, who glorified in the name of senators, sat, voted, and divided with their equals.

To resume, in a few words, the system of the Imperial government, as it was instituted by Augustus, and maintained by those princes who understood their own interest and that of the people, it may be defined an absolute monarchy disguised by the forms of a commonwealth. The masters of the Roman world surrounded their throne with darkness, concealed their irresistible strength, and humbly professed themselves the accountable ministers of the senate, whose supreme decrees they dictated and obeyed.[19]

The face of the court corresponded with the forms of the administration. The emperors, if we except those tyrants whose capricious folly violated every law of nature and decency, disdained that pomp and ceremony which might offend their countrymen, but could add nothing to their real power. In all the offices of life they affected to confound themselves with their subjects, and maintained with them an equal intercourse of visits and entertainments. Their habit, their palace, their table, were suited only to the rank of an opulent senator. Their family, however numerous or splendid, was composed entirely of their domestic slaves and freedmen.[20] Augustus or Trajan would have blushed at employing the meanest of the Romans in those menial offices, which, in the household and bedchamber of a limited monarch, are so eagerly solicited by the proudest nobles of Britain.

The deification of the emperors[21] is the only instance in which they departed from their accustomed prudence and modesty. The Asiatic Greeks were the first inventors, the successors of Alexander the first objects, of this servile and impious mode of adulation. It was easily transferred from the kings to the governors of Asia; and the Roman magistrates very frequently were adored as provincial deities, with the pomp of altars and temples, of festivals and sacrifices.[22] It was natural that the emperors should not refuse what the proconsuls had accepted; and the divine honours which both the one and the other received from the provinces, attested rather the despotism than the servitude of Rome. But the conquerors soon imitated the vanquished nations in the arts of flattery; and the imperious spirit of the first Cæsar too easily consented to assume, during his lifetime, a place among the tutelar deities of Rome. The milder temper of his successor declined so dangerous an ambition, which was never afterwards revived, except by the madness of Caligula and Domitian. Augustus permitted indeed some of the provincial cities to erect temples to his honour, on condition that they should associate the worship of Rome with that of the sovereign; he tolerated private superstition, of which he might be the object;[23] but he contented himself with being revered by the senate and people in his human character, and wisely left to his successor the care of his public deification. A regular custom was introduced, that on the decease of every emperor who had neither lived nor died like a tyrant, the senate by a solemn decree should place him in the number of the gods: and the ceremonies of his Apotheosis were blended with those of his funeral. This legal, and, as it should seem, injudicious profanation, so abhorrent to our stricter principles, was received with a faint murmur,[24] by the easy nature of polytheism; but it was received as an institution, not of religion, but of policy. We should disgrace the virtues of the Antonines, by comparing them with the vices of Hercules or Jupiter. Even the character of Cæsar or Augustus were far superior to those of the popular deities. But it was the misfortune of the former to live in an enlightened age, and their actions were too faithfully recorded to admit of such a mixture of fable and mystery, as the devotion of the vulgar requires. As soon as their divinity was established by law, it sunk into oblivion, without contributing either to their own fame, or to the dignity of succeeding princes.

In the consideration of the Imperial government, we have frequently mentioned the artful founder, under his well-known title of Augustus, which was not however conferred upon him till the edifice was almost completed. The obscure name of Octavianus he derived from a mean family in the little town of Aricia. It was stained with the blood of the proscription; and he was desirous, had it been possible, to erase all memory of his former life. The illustrious surname of Cæsar he had assumed as the adopted son of the dictator; but he had too much good sense, either to hope to be confounded, or to wish to be compared, with that extraordinary man. It was proposed in the senate, to dignify their minister with a new appellation: and after a very serious discussion, that of Augustus was chosen, among several others, as being the most expressive of the character of peace and sanctity, which he uniformly affected.[25] *Augustus* was therefore a personal, *Cæsar* a family distinction. The former should naturally have expired with the prince on whom it was bestowed; and however the latter was diffused by adoption and female alliance, Nero was the last prince who could allege any hereditary claim to the honours of the Julian line. But, at the time of his death, the practice of a century had inseparably connected those appellations with the Imperial dignity, and they have been preserved by a long succession of emperors, Romans, Greeks, Franks, and Germans, from the fall of the republic to the present time. A distinction was, however, soon introduced. The sacred title of Augustus was always reserved for the monarch, whilst the name of Cæsar was more freely communicated to his relations; and, from the reign of Hadrian, at least, was appropriated to the second person in the state, who was considered as the presumptive heir of the empire.

The tender respect of Augustus for a free constitution which he had destroyed, can only be explained by an attentive consideration of the character of that subtle tyrant. A cool head, an unfeeling heart, and a cowardly disposition, prompted him, at the age of nineteen, to assume the mask of hypocrisy, which he never afterwards laid aside. With the same hand, and probably with the same temper, he signed the proscription of Cicero, and the pardon of Cinna. His virtues, and even his vices, were artificial; and according to the various dictates of his interest, he was at first the enemy, and at last the father, of the Roman world.[26] When he framed the artful system of the Imperial authority, his moderation was inspired by his

fears. He wished to deceive the people by an image of civil liberty, and the armies by an image of civil government.

I. The death of Cæsar was ever before his eyes. He had lavished wealth and honours on his adherents; but the most favoured friends of his uncle were in the number of the conspirators. The fidelity of the legions might defend his authority against open rebellion; but their vigilance could not secure his person from the dagger of a determined republican; and the Romans, who revered the memory of Brutus,[27] would applaud the imitation of his virtue. Cæsar had provoked his fate, as much by the ostentation of his power as by his power itself. The consul or the tribune might have reigned in peace. The title of king had armed the Romans against his life. Augustus was sensible that mankind is governed by names; nor was he deceived in his expectation, that the senate and people would submit to slavery, provided they were respectfully assured that they still enjoyed their ancient freedom. A feeble senate and enervated people cheerfully acquiesced in the pleasing illusion, as long as it was supported by the virtue, or even by the prudence, of the successors of Augustus. It was a motive of self-preservation, not a principle of liberty, that animated the conspirators against Caligula, Nero, and Domitian. They attacked the person of the tyrant, without aiming their blow at the authority of the emperor.

There appears, indeed, *one* memorable occasion, in which the senate, after seventy years of patience, made an ineffectual attempt to reassume its long-forgotten rights. When the throne was vacant by the murder of Caligula, the consuls convoked that assembly in the Capitol, condemned the memory of the Cæsars, gave the watchword *liberty* to the few cohorts who faintly adhered to their standard, and during eight and forty hours acted as the independent chiefs of a free commonwealth. But while they deliberated, the Prætorian Guards had resolved. The stupid Claudius, brother of Germanicus, was already in their camp, invested with the Imperial purple, and prepared to support his election by arms. The dream of liberty was at an end; and the senate awoke to all the horrors of inevitable servitude. Deserted by the people, and threatened by a military force, that feeble assembly was compelled to ratify the choice of the Prætorians, and to embrace the benefit of an amnesty, which Claudius had the prudence to offer, and the generosity to observe.[28]

II. The insolence of the armies inspired Augustus with fears of a still more alarming nature. The despair of the citizens could only attempt what the power of the soldiers was, at any time, able to execute. How precarious was his own authority over men whom he had taught to violate every social duty! He had heard their seditious clamours; he dreaded their calmer moments of reflection. One revolution had been purchased by immense rewards; but a second revolution might double those rewards. The troops professed the fondest attachment to the house of Cæsar; but the attachments of the multitude are capricious and inconstant. Augustus summoned to his aid whatever remained in those fierce minds of Roman prejudices; enforced the rigour of discipline by the sanction of law; and interposing the majesty of the senate between the emperor and the army, boldly claimed their allegiance, as the first magistrate of the republic.[29]

During a long period of two hundred and twenty years, from the establishment of this artful system to the death of Commodus, the dangers inherent to a military government were, in a great measure, suspended. The soldiers were seldom roused to that fatal sense of their own strength, and of the weakness of the civil authority, which was, before and afterwards, productive of such dreadful calamities. Caligula and Domitian were assassinated in their palace by their own domestics; the convulsions which agitated Rome on the death of the former, were confined to the walls of the city. But Nero involved the whole empire in his ruin. In the space of eighteen months, four princes perished by the sword; and the Roman world was shaken by the fury of the contending armies. Excepting only this short, though violent, eruption of military licence, the two centuries from Augustus to Commodus passed away unstained with civil blood, and undisturbed by revolutions. The emperor was elected by *the authority of the senate*, and *the consent of the soldiers*.[30] The legions respected their oath of fidelity; and it requires a minute inspection of the Roman annals to discover three inconsiderable rebellions, which were all suppressed in a few months, and without even the hazard of a battle.[31]

In elective monarchies, the vacancy of the throne is a moment big with danger and mischief. The Roman emperors, desirous to spare the legions that interval of suspense, and the temptation of an irregular choice, invested their designed successor with so large a share of present power, as should enable him, after their decease, to assume the remainder, without suffering the empire to perceive the change of masters. Thus Augustus, after all his fairer prospects had been snatched from him by untimely deaths rested his last hopes on Tiberius, obtained for his adopted son the censorial and tribunitian powers, and dictated a law by which the future prince was invested with an authority equal to his own, over the provinces and the armies.[32] Thus Vespasian subdued the generous mind of his eldest son. Titus was adored by the eastern legions, which, under his command, had recently achieved the conquest of Judæa. His power was dreaded, and, as his virtues were clouded by the intemperance of youth, his designs were suspected. Instead of listening to such unworthy suspicions, the prudent monarch associated Titus to the full powers of the Imperial dignity; and the grateful son ever approved himself the humble and faithful minister of so indulgent a father.[33]

The good sense of Vespasian engaged him indeed to embrace every measure that might confirm his recent and precarious elevation. The military oath, and the fidelity of the troops, had been consecrated by the habits of an hundred years, to the name and family of the Cæsars; and although that family had been continued only by the fictitious rite of adoption, the Romans still revered, in the person of Nero, the grandson of Germanicus, and the lineal successor of Augustus. It was not without reluctance and remorse that the Prætorian Guards had been persuaded to abandon the cause of the tyrant.[34] The rapid downfall of Galba, Otho, and Vitellius, taught the armies to consider the emperors as the creatures of *their* will, and the instruments of *their* licence. The birth of Vespasian was mean; his grandfather had been a private soldier, his father a petty officer of the revenue;[35] his own merit had raised him, in an advanced age, to the empire; but his merit was rather useful, than shining, and his virtues were disgraced by a strict and even sordid parsimony. Such a prince consulted his true interest by the association of a son, whose more splendid and amiable character might turn the public attention from the obscure origin to the future glories of the Flavian house. Under the mild administration of Titus, the Roman world enjoyed a transient felicity, and his beloved memory served to protect, above fifteen years, the vices of his brother Domitian.

Nerva had scarcely accepted the purple from the assassins of Domitian before he discovered that his feeble age was unable to stem the torrent of public disorders, which had multiplied under the long tyranny of his predecessor. His mild disposition was respected by the good; but the degenerate Romans required a more vigorous character, whose justice should strike terror into the guilty. Though he had several relations, he fixed his choice on a stranger. He adopted Trajan, then about forty years of age, and who commanded a powerful army in the Lower Germany; and immediately, by a decree of the senate, declared him his colleague and successor in the empire.[36] It is sincerely to be lamented, that whilst we are fatigued with the disgustful relation of Nero's crimes and follies, we are reduced to collect the actions of Trajan from the glimmerings of an abridgment, or the doubtful light of a panegyric. There remains, however, one panegyric far removed beyond the suspicion of flattery. Above two hundred and fifty years after the death of Trajan, the senate, in pouring out the customary acclamations on the accession of a new emperor, wished that he might surpass the felicity of Augustus, and the virtue of Trajan.[37]

We may readily believe, that the father of his country hesitated whether he ought to intrust the various and doubtful character of his kinsman Hadrian with sovereign power. In his last moments, the arts of the empress Plotina either fixed the irresolution of Trajan, or boldly supposed a fictitious adoption;[38] the truth of which could not be safely disputed, and Hadrian was peaceably acknowledged as his lawful successor. Under his reign, as has been already mentioned, the empire flourished in peace and prosperity. He encouraged the arts, reformed the laws, asserted military discipline, and visited all his provinces in person. His vast and active genius was equally suited to the most enlarged views, and the minute details of civil policy. But the ruling passions of his soul were curiosity and vanity. As they prevailed, and as they were attracted by different objects, Hadrian was, by turns, an excellent prince, a ridiculous sophist, and a jealous tyrant. The general tenor of his conduct deserved praise for its equity and moderation. Yet in the first days of his reign, he put to death four consular senators, his personal enemies, and men who had been judged worthy of empire; and the tediousness of a painful illness rendered him, at last, peevish and cruel. The senate doubted whether they should pronounce him a god or a tyrant; and the honours decreed to his memory were granted to the prayers of the pious Antoninus.[39]

The caprice of Hadrian influenced his choice of a successor. After revolving in his mind several men of distinguished merit, whom he esteemed and hated, he adopted Ælius Verus, a gay and voluptuous nobleman, recommended by uncommon beauty to the lover of Antinous.[40] But while Hadrian was delighting himself with his own applause, and the acclamations of the soldiers, whose consent had been secured by an immense donative, the new Cæsar[41] was ravished from his embraces by an untimely death. He left only one son. Hadrian commended the boy to the gratitude of the Antonines. He was adopted by Pius; and, on the accession of Marcus, was invested with an equal share of sovereign power. Among the many vices of this younger Verus he possessed one virtue; a dutiful reverence for his wiser colleague, to whom he willingly abandoned the ruder cares of empire. The philosophic emperor dissembled his follies, lamented his early death, and cast a decent veil over his memory.

As soon as Hadrian's passion was either gratified or disappointed, he resolved to deserve the thanks of posterity, by placing the most exalted merit on the Roman throne. His discerning eye easily discovered a senator about fifty years of age, blameless in all the offices of life, and a youth of about seventeen, whose riper years opened the fair prospect of every virtue: the elder of these was declared the son and successor of Hadrian, on condition, however, that he himself should immediately adopt the younger. The two Antonines (for it is of them that we are now speaking) governed the Roman world forty-two years, with the same invariable spirit of wisdom and virtue. Although Pius had two sons,[42] he preferred the welfare of Rome to the interest of his family, gave his daughter Faustina in marriage to young Marcus, obtained from the senate the tribunitian and proconsular powers, and with a noble disdain, or rather ignorance of jealousy, associated him to all the labours of government. Marcus, on the other hand, revered the character of his benefactor, loved him as a parent, obeyed him as his sovereign,[43] and, after he was no more, regulated his own administration by the example and maxims of his predecessor. Their united reigns are possibly the only period of history in which the happiness of a great people was the sole object of government.

Titus Antoninus Pius has been justly denominated a second Numa. The same love of religion, justice, and peace, was the distinguishing characteristic of both princes. But the situation of the latter opened a much larger field for the exercise of those virtues. Numa could only prevent a few neighbouring villages from plundering each other's harvests. Antoninus diffused order and tranquillity over the greatest part of the earth. His reign is marked by the rare advantage of furnishing very few materials for history; which is, indeed, little more than the register of the crimes, follies, and misfortunes of mankind. In private life, he was an amiable as well as a good man. The native simplicity of his virtue was a stranger to vanity or affectation. He enjoyed with moderation the conveniencies of his fortune, and the innocent pleasures of society:[44] and the benevolence of his soul displayed itself in a cheerful serenity of temper.

The virtue of Marcus Aurelius Antoninus was of a severer and more laborious kind.[45] It was the well-earned harvest of many a learned conference, of many a patient lecture, and many a midnight lucubration. At the age of twelve years he embraced the rigid system of the Stoics, which taught him to submit his body to his mind, his passions to his reason; to consider virtue as the only good, vice as the only evil, all things external as things indifferent.[46] His meditations, composed in the tumult of a camp, are still extant; and he even condescended to give lessons of philosophy in a more public manner than was perhaps consistent with the modesty of a sage, or the dignity of an emperor.[47] But his life was the noblest commentary on the precepts of Zeno. He was severe to himself, indulgent to the imperfections of others, just and beneficent to all mankind. He regretted that Avidius Cassius, who excited a rebellion in Syria, had disappointed him, by a voluntary death, of the pleasure of converting an enemy into a friend; and he justified the sincerity of that sentiment, by moderating the zeal of the senate against the adherents of the traitor.[48] War he detested, as the disgrace and calamity of human nature; but when the necessity of a just defence called upon him to take up arms, he readily exposed his person to eight winter campaigns on the frozen banks of the Danube, the severity of which was at last fatal to the weakness of his constitution. His memory was revered by a grateful posterity, and above a century after his death, many persons preserved the image of Marcus Antoninus, among those of their household gods.[49]

If a man were called to fix the period in the history of the world, during which the condition of the human race was most happy and prosperous, he would, without hesitation, name that which elapsed from the death of Domitian to the accession of Commodus. The vast extent of the Roman empire was governed by absolute power, under the guidance of virtue and wisdom. The armies were restrained by the firm but gentle hand of four successive emperors, whose characters and authority commanded involuntary respect. The forms of the civil administration were carefully preserved by Nerva, Trajan, Hadrian, and the Antonines, who delighted in the image of liberty, and were pleased with considering themselves as the accountable ministers of the laws. Such princes deserved the honour of restoring the republic had the Romans of their days been capable of enjoying a rational freedom.

The labours of these monarchs were overpaid by the immense reward that inseparably waited on their success; by the honest pride of virtue, and by the exquisite delight of beholding the general happiness of which they were the authors. A just, but melancholy reflection embittered, however, the noblest of human enjoyments. They must often have recollected the instability of a happiness which depended on the character of a single man. The fatal moment was perhaps approaching, when some licentious youth, or some jealous tyrant, would abuse, to the destruction, that absolute power which they had exerted for the benefit of their people. The ideal restraints of the senate and the laws might serve to display the virtues, but could never correct the vices, of the emperor. The military force was a blind and irresistible instrument of oppression; and the corruption of Roman manners would always supply flatterers eager to applaud, and ministers prepared to serve the fear or the avarice, the lust or the cruelty, of their masters.

These gloomy apprehensions had been already justified by the experience of the Romans. The annals of the emperors exhibit a strong and various picture of human nature, which we should vainly seek among the mixed and doubtful characters of modern history. In the conduct of those monarchs we may trace the utmost lines of vice and virtue; the most exalted perfection, and the meanest degeneracy of our own species. The golden age of Trajan and the Antonines had been preceded by an age of iron. It is almost superfluous to enumerate the unworthy successors of Augustus. Their unparalleled vices, and the splendid theatre on which they were acted, have saved them from oblivion. The dark unrelenting Tiberius, the furious Caligula, the feeble Claudius, the profligate and cruel Nero, the beastly Vitellius,[50] and the timid inhuman Domitian, are condemned to everlasting infamy. During fourscore years (excepting only the short and doubtful respite of Vespasian's reign[51]) Rome groaned beneath an unremitting tyranny, which exterminated the ancient families of the republic, and was fatal to almost every virtue, and every talent, that arose in that unhappy period.

Under the reign of these monsters the slavery of the Romans was accompanied with two peculiar circumstances, the one occasioned by their former liberty, the other by their extensive conquests, which rendered their condition more completely wretched than that of the victims of tyranny in any other age or country. From these causes were derived, 1. The exquisite sensibility of the sufferers; and, 2, the impossibility of escaping from the hand of the oppressor.

I. When Persia was governed by the descendants of Sefi, a race of princes whose wanton cruelty often stained their divan, their table, and their bed, with the blood of their favourites, there is a saying recorded of a young nobleman, that he never departed from the sultan's presence without satisfying himself whether his head was still on his shoulders. The experience of every day might almost justify the scepticism of Rustan.[52] Yet the fatal sword, suspended above him by a single thread, seems not to have disturbed the slumbers, or interrupted the tranquillity, of the Persian. The monarch's frown, he well knew, could level him with the dust; but the stroke of lightning or apoplexy might be equally fatal; and it was the part of a wise man to forget the inevitable calamities of human life in the enjoyment of the fleeting hour. He was dignified with the appellation of the king's slave; had, perhaps, been purchased from obscure parents in a country which he had never known; and was trained up from his infancy in the severe discipline of the seraglio.[53] His name, his wealth, his honours, were the gift of a master, who might, without injustice, resume what he had bestowed. Rustan's knowledge, if he possessed any, could only serve to confirm his habits by prejudices. His language afforded not words for any form of government, except absolute monarchy. The history of the East informed him, that such had ever been the condition of mankind.[54] The Koran, and the interpreters of that divine book, inculcated to him, that the sultan was the descendant of the prophet, and

the vice-regent of heaven; that patience was the first virtue of a Mussulman, and unlimited obedience the great duty of a subject.

The minds of the Romans were very differently prepared for slavery. Oppressed beneath the weight of their own corruption and of military violence, they for a long while preserved the sentiments, or at least the ideas, of their free-born ancestors. The education of Helvidius and Thrasea, of Tacitus and Pliny, was the same as that of Cato and Cicero. From Grecian philosophy they had imbibed the justest and most liberal notions of the dignity of human nature, and the origin of civil society. The history of their own country had taught them to revere a free, a virtuous, and a victorious commonwealth; to abhor the successful crimes of Cæsar and Augustus; and inwardly to despise those tyrants whom they adored with the most abject flattery. As magistrates and senators, they were admitted into the great council which had once dictated laws to the earth, whose name still gave a sanction to the acts of the monarch, and whose authority was so often prostituted to the vilest purposes of tyranny. Tiberius, and those emperors who adopted his maxims, attempted to disguise their murders by the formalities of justice, and perhaps enjoyed a secret pleasure in rendering the senate their accomplice as well as their victim. By this assembly the last of the Romans were condemned for imaginary crimes and real virtues. Their infamous accusers assumed the language of independent patriots, who arraigned a dangerous citizen before the tribunal of his country; and the public service was rewarded by riches and honours.[55] The servile judges professed to assert the majesty of the commonwealth, violated in the person of its first magistrate;[56] whose clemency they most applauded when they trembled the most at his inexorable and impending cruelty.[57] The tyrant beheld their baseness with just contempt, and encountered their secret sentiments of detestation with sincere and avowed hatred for the whole body of the senate.

II. The division of Europe into a number of independent states, connected, however, with each other, by the general resemblance of religion, language, and manners, is productive of the most beneficial consequences to the liberty of mankind. A modern tyrant, who should find no resistance either in his own breast, or in his people, would soon experience a gentle restraint from the example of his equals, the dread of present censure, the advice of his allies, and the apprehension of his enemies. The object of his displeasure, escaping from the narrow limits of his dominions, would easily obtain, in a happier climate, a secure refuge, a new fortune adequate to his merit, the freedom of complaint, and perhaps the means of revenge. But the empire of the Romans filled the world, and when that empire fell into the hands of a single person, the world became a safe and dreary prison for his enemies. The slave of Imperial despotism, whether he was condemned to drag his gilded chain in Rome and the senate, or to wear out a life of exile on the barren rock of Seriphus, or the frozen banks of the Danube, expected his fate in silent despair.[58]

To resist was fatal, and it was impossible to fly. On every side he was encompassed with a vast extent of sea and land, which he could never hope to traverse without being discovered, seized, and restored to his irritated master. Beyond the frontiers, his anxious view could discover nothing, except the ocean, inhospitable deserts, hostile tribes of barbarians, of fierce manners and unknown language, or dependent kings, who would gladly purchase the emperor's protection by the sacrifice of an obnoxious fugitive.[59] "Wherever you are," said Cicero to the exiled Marcellus, "remember that you are equally within the power of the conqueror."[60]

CHAPTER IV

The Cruelty, Follies, and Murder of Commodus. Election of Pertinax. His Attempts to Reform the State. His Assassination by the Prætorian Guards.

THE mildness of Marcus, which the rigid discipline of the Stoics was unable to eradicate, formed, at the same time, the most amiable, and the only defective, part of his character. His excellent understanding was often deceived by the unsuspecting goodness of his heart. Artful men, who study the passions of princes, and conceal their own, approached his person in the disguise of philosophic sanctity, and acquired riches and honours by affecting to despise them.[1] His excessive indulgence to his brother, his wife, and his son, exceeded the bounds of private virtue, and became a public injury, by the example and consequences of their vices.

Faustina, the daughter of Pius and the wife of Marcus, has been as much celebrated for her gallantries as for her beauty. The grave simplicity of the philosopher was ill calculated to engage her wanton levity, or to fix that unbounded passion for variety, which often discovered personal merit in the meanest of mankind. The Cupid of the ancients was, in general, a very sensual deity; and the amours of an empress, as they exact on her side the plainest advances, are seldom susceptible of much sentimental delicacy. Marcus was the only man in the empire who seemed ignorant or insensible of the irregularities of Faustina; which, according to the prejudices of every age, reflected some disgrace on the injured husband. He promoted several of her lovers to posts of honour and profit,[2] and during a connection of

thirty years, invariably gave her proofs of the most tender confidence, and of a respect which ended not with her life. In his Meditations, he thanks the gods, who had bestowed on him a wife, so faithful, so gentle, and of such a wonderful simplicity of manners. The obsequious senate, at his earnest request, declared her a goddess. She was represented in her temples, with the attributes of Juno, Venus, and Ceres; and it was decreed, that on the day of their nuptials, the youth of either sex should pay their vows before the altar of their chaste patroness.[3]

The monstrous vices of the son have cast a shade on the purity of the father's virtues. It has been objected to Marcus, that he sacrificed the happiness of millions to a fond partiality for a worthless boy; and that he chose a successor in his own family, rather than in the republic. Nothing, however, was neglected by the anxious father, and by the men of virtue and learning whom he summoned to his assistance, to expand the narrow mind of young Commodus, to correct his growing vices, and to render him worthy of the throne, for which he was designed. But the power of instruction is seldom of much efficacy, except in those happy dispositions where it is almost superfluous. The distasteful lesson of a grave philosopher was in a moment obliterated by the whisper of a profligate favourite; and Marcus himself blasted the fruits of this laboured education, by admitting his son, at the age of fourteen or fifteen, to a full participation of the Imperial power. He lived but four years afterwards; but he lived long enough to repent a rash measure, which raised the impetuous youth above the restraint of reason and authority.

Most of the crimes which disturb the internal peace of society are produced by the restraints which the necessary, but unequal, laws of property have imposed on the appetites of mankind, by confining to a few the possession of those objects that are coveted by many. Of all our passions and appetites, the love of power is of the most imperious and unsociable nature, since the pride of one man requires the submission of the multitude. In the tumult of civil discord, the laws of society lose their force, and their place is seldom supplied by those of humanity. The ardour of contention, the pride of victory, the despair of success, the memory of past injuries, and the fear of future dangers, all contribute to inflame the mind, and to silence the voice of pity. From such motives almost every page of history has been stained with civil blood; but these motives will not account for the unprovoked cruelties of Commodus, who had nothing to wish and everything to enjoy. The beloved son of Marcus succeeded (A.D. 180) to his father, amidst the acclamations of the senate and armies,[4] and when he ascended the throne the happy youth saw round him neither competitor to remove nor enemies to punish. In this calm elevated station it was surely natural that he should prefer the love of mankind to their detestation, the mild glories of his five predecessors, to the ignominious fate of Nero and Domitian.

Yet Commodus was not, as he has been represented, a tiger born with an insatiate thirst of human blood, and capable, from his infancy, of the most inhuman actions.[5] Nature had formed him of a weak, rather than a wicked, disposition. His simplicity and timidity rendered him the slave of his attendants, who gradually corrupted his mind. His cruelty, which at first obeyed the dictates of others, degenerated into habit, and at length became the ruling passion of his soul.[6]

Upon the death of his father, Commodus found himself embarrassed with the command of a great army, and the conduct of a difficult war against the Quadi and Marcomanni.[7] The servile and profligate youths whom Marcus had banished, soon regained their station and influence about the new emperor. They exaggerated the hardships and dangers of a campaign in the wild countries beyond the Danube;

and they assured the indolent prince, that the terror of his name and the arms of his lieutenants would be sufficient to complete the conquest of the dismayed barbarians; or to impose such conditions as were more advantageous than any conquest. By a dexterous application to his sensual appetites, they compared the tranquillity, the splendour, the refined pleasures of Rome, with the tumult of a Pannonian camp, which afforded neither leisure nor materials for luxury.[8] Commodus listened to the pleasing advice; but whilst he hesitated between his own inclination and the awe which he still retained for his father's counsellors, the summer insensibly elapsed, and his triumphal entry into the capital was deferred till the autumn. His graceful person,[9] popular address, and imagined virtues, attracted the public favour; the honourable peace which he had recently granted to the barbarians diffused an universal joy;[10] his impatience to revisit Rome was fondly ascribed to the love of his country; and his dissolute course of amusements was faintly condemned in a prince of nineteen years of age.

During the three first years of his reign, the forms, and even the spirit, of the old administration were maintained by those faithful counsellors, to whom Marcus had recommended his son, and for whose wisdom and integrity Commodus still entertained a reluctant esteem. The young prince and his profligate favourites revelled in all the licence of sovereign power; but his hands were yet unstained with blood; and he had even displayed a generosity of sentiment, which might perhaps have ripened into solid virtue.[11] A fatal incident decided his fluctuating character.

One evening (A.D. 183), as the emperor was returning to the palace through a dark and narrow portico in the amphitheatre,[12] an assassin, who waited his passage, rushed upon him with a drawn sword, loudly exclaiming, "*The senate sends you this.*" The menace prevented the deed; the assassin was seized by the guards, and immediately revealed the authors of the conspiracy. It had been formed, not in the state, but within the walls of the palace. Lucilla, the emperor's sister, and widow of Lucius Verus, impatient of the second rank, and jealous of the reigning empress, had armed the murderer against her brother's life. She had not ventured to communicate the black design to her second husband Claudius Pompeianus, a senator of distinguished merit and unshaken loyalty; but among the crowd of her lovers (for she imitated the manners of Faustina), she found men of desperate fortunes and wild ambition, who were prepared to serve her more violent as well as her tender passions. The conspirators experienced the rigour of justice, and the abandoned princess was punished, first with exile, and afterwards with death.[13]

But the words of the assassin sunk deep into the mind of Commodus, and left an indelible impression of fear and hatred against the whole body of the senate. Those whom he had dreaded as importunate ministers, he now suspected as secret enemies. The Delators, a race of men discouraged, and almost extinguished, under the former reigns, again became formidable, as soon as they discovered that the emperor was desirous of finding disaffection and treason in the senate. That assembly, whom Marcus had ever considered as the great council of the nation, was composed of the most distinguished of the Romans; and distinction of every kind soon became criminal. The possession of wealth stimulated the diligence of the informers; rigid virtue implied a tacit censure of the irregularities of Commodus; important services implied a dangerous superiority of merit; and the friendship of the father always insured the aversion of the son. Suspicion was equivalent to proof; trial to condemnation. The execution of a considerable senator was attended with the death of all who might lament or revenge his fate; and when Commodus had once tasted human blood, he became incapable of pity or remorse.

Of these innocent victims of tyranny, none died more lamented than the two brothers of the Quintilian family, Maximus and Condianus; whose fraternal love has saved their names from oblivion, and endeared their memory to posterity. Their studies and their occupations, their pursuits and their pleasures, were still the same. In the enjoyment of a great estate, they never admitted the idea of a separate interest; some fragments are now extant of a treatise which they composed in common; and in every action of life it was observed that their two bodies were animated by one soul. The Antonines, who valued their virtues, and delighted in their union, raised them, in the same year, to the consulship; and Marcus afterwards intrusted to their joint care the civil administration of Greece, and a great military command, in which they obtained a signal victory over the Germans. The kind cruelty of Commodus united them in death.[14]

The tyrant's rage, after having shed the noblest blood of the senate, at length recoiled on the principal instrument of his cruelty. Whilst Commodus was immersed in blood and luxury, he devolved the detail of the public business on Perennis; a servile and ambitious minister, who had obtained his post by the murder of his predecessor, but who possessed a considerable share of vigour and ability. By acts of extortion, and the forfeited estates of the nobles sacrificed to his avarice, he had accumulated an immense treasure. The Prætorian guards were under his immediate command; and his son, who already discovered a military genius, was at the head of the Illyrian legions. Perennis aspired to the empire; or what, in the eyes of Commodus, amounted to the same crime, he was capable of aspiring to it, had he not been prevented, surprised, and (A.D. 186) put to death. The fall of a minister is a very trifling incident in the general history of the empire; but it was hastened by an extraordinary circumstance, which proved how much the nerves of discipline were already relaxed. The legions of Britain, discontented with the administration of Perennis, formed a deputation of fifteen hundred select men, with instructions to march to Rome, and lay their complaints before the emperor. These military petitioners, by their own determined behaviour, by inflaming the divisions of the guards, by exaggerating the strength of the British army, and by alarming the fears of Commodus, exacted and obtained the minister's death, as the only redress of their grievances.[15] This presumption of a distant army, and their discovery of the weakness of government, was a sure presage of the most dreadful convulsions.

The negligence of the public administration was betrayed soon afterwards by a new disorder which arose from the smallest beginnings. A spirit of desertion began to prevail among the troops; and the deserters, instead of seeking their flight in safety or concealment, infested the highways. Maternus, a private soldier, of a daring boldness above his station, collected these bands of robbers into a little army, set open the prisons, invited the slaves to assert their freedom, and plundered with impunity the rich and defenceless cities of Gaul and Spain. The governors of the provinces, who had long been the spectators, and perhaps the partners, of his depredations, were, at length, roused from their supine indolence by the threatening commands of the emperor. Maternus found that he was encompassed, and foresaw that he must be overpowered. A great effort of despair was his last resource. He ordered his followers to disperse, to pass the Alps in small parties and various disguises, and to assemble at Rome, during the licentious tumult of the festival of Cybele.[16] To murder Commodus, and to ascend the vacant throne, was the ambition of no vulgar robber. His measures were so ably concerted, that his concealed troops already filled the streets of Rome. The envy of an accomplice discovered and ruined this singular enterprise, in the moment when it was ripe for execution.[17]

Suspicious princes often promote the last of mankind from a vain persuasion that those who have no dependence, except on their favour, will have no attachment, except to the person of their benefactor. Cleander, the successor of Perennis, was a Phrygian by birth; of a nation, over whose stubborn, but servile temper, blows only could prevail.[18] He had been sent from his native country to Rome, in the capacity of a slave. As a slave he entered the Imperial palace, rendered himself useful to his master's passions, and rapidly ascended to the most exalted station which a subject could enjoy. His influence over the mind of Commodus was much greater than that of his predecessor; for Cleander was devoid of any ability or virtue which could inspire the emperor with envy or distrust. Avarice was the reigning passion of his soul, and the great principle of his administration. The rank of Consul, of Patrician, of Senator, was exposed to public sale; and it would have been considered as disaffection if any one had refused to purchase these empty and disgraceful honours with the greatest part of his fortune.[19] In the lucrative provincial employments, the minister shared with the governor the spoils of the people. The execution of the laws was venal and arbitrary. A wealthy criminal might obtain, not only the reversal of the sentence by which he was justly condemned; but might likewise inflict whatever punishment he pleased on the accuser, the witnesses, and the judge.

By these means, Cleander, in the space of three years, had accumulated more wealth than had ever yet been possessed by any freedman.[20] Commodus was perfectly satisfied with the magnificent presents which the artful courtier laid at his feet in the most seasonable moments. To divert the public envy, Cleander, under the emperor's name, erected baths, porticos, and places of exercise, for the use of the people.[21] He flattered himself that the Romans, dazzled and amused by this apparent liberality, would be less affected by the bloody scenes which were

daily exhibited; that they would forget the death of Byrrhus, a senator to whose superior merit the late emperor had granted one of his daughters; and that they would forgive the execution of Arrius Antoninus, the last representative of the name and virtues of the Antonines. The former, with more integrity than prudence, had attempted to disclose, to his brother-in-law, the true character of Cleander. An equitable sentence pronounced by the latter, when Proconsul of Asia, against a worthless creature of the favourite, proved fatal to him.[22] After the fall of Perennis, the terrors of Commodus had, for a short time, assumed the appearance of a return to virtue. He repealed the most odious of his acts, loaded his memory with the public execration, and ascribed to the pernicious counsels of that wicked minister, all the errors of his inexperienced youth. But his repentance lasted only thirty days; and, under Cleander's tyranny, the administration of Perennis was often regretted.

Pestilence and famine contributed to fill up the measure of the calamities of Rome.[23] The first could be only imputed to the just indignation of the gods; but (A.D. 189) a monopoly of corn, supported by the riches and power of the minister, was considered as the immediate cause of the second. The popular discontent, after it had long circulated in whispers, broke out in the assembled circus. The people quitted their favourite amusements for the more delicious pleasure of revenge, rushed in crowds towards a palace in the suburbs, one of the emperor's retirements, and demanded, with angry clamours, the head of the public enemy. Cleander, who commanded the Prætorian guards,[24] ordered a body of cavalry to sally forth, and disperse the seditious multitude. The multitude fled with precipitation towards the city; several were slain, and many more were trampled to death: but when the cavalry entered the streets, their pursuit was checked by a shower of stones and darts from the roofs and windows of the houses. The foot guards[25] who had been long jealous of the prerogatives and insolence of the Prætorian cavalry, embraced the party of the people. The tumult became a regular engagement, and threatened a general massacre. The Prætorians, at length, gave way, oppressed with numbers; and the tide of popular fury returned with redoubled violence against the gates of the palace, where Commodus lay, dissolved in luxury, and alone unconscious of the civil war. It was death to approach his person with the unwelcome news. He would have perished in this supine security, had not two women, his elder sister Fadilla, and Marcia, the most favoured of his concubines, ventured to break into his presence. Bathed in tears, and with dishevelled hair, they threw themselves at his feet; and with all the pressing eloquence of fear, discovered to the affrighted emperor, the crimes of the minister, the rage of the people, and the impending ruin, which, in a few minutes, would burst over his palace and person. Commodus started from his dream of pleasure, and commanded that the head of Cleander should be thrown out to the people. The desired spectacle instantly appeased the tumult; and the son of Marcus might even yet have regained the affection and confidence of his outraged subjects.[26]

But every sentiment of virtue and humanity was extinct in the mind of Commodus. Whilst he thus abandoned the reins of empire to these unworthy favourites, he valued nothing in sovereign power, except the unbounded licence of indulging his sensual appetites. His hours were spent in a seraglio of three hundred beautiful women, and as many boys, of every rank, and of every province; and, wherever the arts of seduction proved ineffectual, the brutal lover had recourse to violence. The ancient historians have expatiated on these abandoned scenes of prostitution, which scorned every restraint of nature or modesty; but it would not be easy to translate their too faithful descriptions into the decency of modern language. The intervals of lust were filled up with the basest amusements. The influence of a polite age, and the labour of an attentive education, had never been able to infuse into his rude and brutish mind the least tincture of learning; and he was the first of the Roman emperors totally devoid of taste for the pleasures of the understanding. Nero himself excelled, or affected to excel, in the elegant arts of music and poetry; nor should we despise his pursuits had he not converted the pleasing relaxation of a leisure hour into the serious business and ambition of his life. But Commodus, from his earliest infancy, discovered an aversion to whatever was rational or liberal, and a fond attachment to the amusements of the populace; the sports of the circus and amphitheatre, the combats of gladiators, and the hunting of wild beasts. The masters in every branch of learning, whom Marcus provided for his son, were heard with inattention and disgust; whilst the Moors and Parthians, who taught him to dart the javelin and to shoot with the bow, found a disciple who delighted in his application, and

soon equalled the most skilful of his instructors, in the steadiness of the eye, and the dexterity of the hand.

The servile crowd, whose fortune depended on their master's vices, applauded these ignoble pursuits. The perfidious voice of flattery reminded him that by exploits of the same nature, by the defeat of the Nemæn lion, and the slaughter of the wild boar of Erymanthus, the Grecian Hercules had acquired a place among the gods, and an immortal memory among men. They only forgot to observe, that, in the first ages of society, when the fiercer animals often dispute with man the possession of an unsettled country, a successful war against those savages is one of the most innocent and beneficial labours of heroism. In the civilised state of the Roman empire, the wild beasts had long since retired from the face of man, and the neighbourhood of populous cities. To surprise them in their solitary haunts, and to transport them to Rome, that they might be slain in pomp by the hand of an emperor, was an enterprise equally ridiculous for the prince, and oppressive for the people.[27] Ignorant of these distinctions, Commodus eagerly embraced the glorious resemblance, and styled himself (as we still read on his medals[28]) the *Roman Hercules*. The club and the lion's hide were placed by the side of the throne, amongst the ensigns of sovereignty; and statues were erected, in which Commodus was represented in the character, and with the attributes, of the god, whose valour and dexterity he endeavoured to emulate in the daily course of his ferocious amusements.[29]

Elated with these praises, which gradually extinguished the innate sense of shame, Commodus resolved to exhibit, before the eyes of the Roman people, those exercises, which till then he had decently confined within the walls of his palace, and to the presence of a few favourites. On the appointed day, the various motives of flattery, fear, and curiosity, attracted to the amphitheatre an innumerable multitude of spectators: and some degree of applause was deservedly bestowed on the uncommon skill of the Imperial performer. Whether he aimed at the head or heart of the animal, the wound was alike certain and mortal. With arrows, whose point was shaped into the form of a crescent, Commodus often intercepted the rapid career, and cut asunder the long bony neck of the ostrich.[30] A panther was let loose; and the archer waited till he had leaped upon a trembling malefactor. In the same instant the shaft flew, the beast dropped dead, and the man remained unhurt. The dens of the amphitheatre disgorged at once a hundred lions; a hundred darts from the unerring hand of Commodus laid them dead as they ran raging around the *Arena*. Neither the huge bulk of the elephant, nor the scaly hide of the rhinoceros, could defend them from his stroke. Ethiopia and India yielded their most extraordinary productions; and several animals were slain in the amphitheatre, which had been seen only in the representations of art, or perhaps of fancy.[31] In all these exhibitions, the securest precautions were used to protect the person of the Roman Hercules from the desperate spring of any savage; who might possibly disregard the dignity of the emperor, and the sanctity of the god.[32]

But the meanest of the populace were affected with shame and indignation when they beheld their sovereign enter the lists as a gladiator, and glory in a profession which the laws and manners of the Romans had branded with the justest note of infamy.[33] He chose the habit and arms of the *Secutor*, whose combat with the *Retiarius* formed one of the most lively scenes in the bloody sports of the amphitheatre. The *Secutor* was armed with an helmet, sword, and buckler; his naked antagonist had only a large net and a trident; with the one he endeavoured to entangle, with the other to dispatch, his enemy. If he missed the first throw, he was obliged to fly from the pursuit of the *Secutor*, till he had prepared his net for a second cast.[34] The emperor fought in this character seven hundred and thirty-five times. These glorious achievements were carefully recorded in the public acts of the empire; and that he might omit no circumstance of infamy, he received from the common fund of gladiators, a stipend so exorbitant, that it became a new and most ignominious tax upon the Roman people.[35] It may be easily supposed that in these engagements the master of the world was always successful: in the amphitheatre his victories were not often sanguinary; but when he exercised his skill in the school of gladiators, or his own palace, his wretched antagonists were frequently honoured with a mortal wound from the hand of Commodus, and obliged to seal their flattery with their blood.[36] He now disdained the appellation of Hercules. The name of Paulus, a celebrated Secutor, was the only one which delighted his ear. It was inscribed on his colossal statues, and repeated in the redoubled acclamations[37] of the mournful and applauding senate.[38] Claudius Pompeianus, the virtuous husband of Lucilla, was the only senator who asserted the honour of his rank. As a father, he permitted his sons to consult their safety by attending the amphitheatre. As a Roman, he declared, that his own life was in the emperor's hands, but that he would never behold the son of Marcus prostituting his person and dignity. Notwithstanding his manly resolution, Pompeianus escaped the resentment of the tyrant, and with his honour had the good fortune to preserve his life.[39]

Commodus had now attained the summit of vice and infamy. Amidst the acclamations of a flattering court, he was unable to disguise, from himself, that he had deserved the contempt and hatred of every man of sense and virtue in his empire. His ferocious spirit was irritated by the consciousness of that hatred, by the envy of every kind of merit, by the just apprehension of danger, and by the habit of slaughter, which he contracted in his daily amusements. History has preserved a long list of consular senators sacrificed to his wanton suspicion, which sought out, with peculiar anxiety, those unfortunate persons connected, however remotely, with the family of the Antonines, without sparing even the ministers of his crimes or pleasures.[40] His cruelty proved at last fatal to himself. He had shed with impunity the noblest blood of Rome: he perished as soon as he was dreaded by his own domestics. Marcia his favourite concubine, Eclectus his chamberlain, and Lætus his Prætorian præfect, alarmed by the fate of their companions and predecessors, resolved to prevent the destruction which every hour hung over their heads, either from the mad caprice of the tyrant, or the sudden indignation of the people. Marcia seized the occasion of presenting a draught of wine to her lover, after he had fatigued himself with hunting some wild beasts. Commodus retired to sleep; but whilst he was labouring with the effects of poison and drunkenness, a robust youth, by profession a wrestler, entered his chamber, and strangled him without resistance. The body was secretly conveyed out of the palace, before the least suspicion was entertained in the city, or even in the court, of the emperor's death. Such was the fate of the son of Marcus, and so easy was it to destroy a hated tyrant, who, by the artificial powers of government, had oppressed, during thirteen years, so many millions of subjects, each of whom was equal to their master in personal strength and personal abilities.[41]

The measures of the conspirators were conducted with the deliberate coolness and celerity which the greatness of the occasion required. They resolved instantly to fill the vacant throne with an emperor whose character would justify and maintain the action that had been committed. They fixed on Pertinax, præfect of the city, an ancient senator of consular rank, whose conspicuous merit had broke through the obscurity of his birth, and raised him to the first honours of the state. He had successively governed most of the provinces of the empire; and in all his great employments, military as well as civil, he had uniformly distinguished himself by the firmness, the prudence, and the integrity of his conduct.[42] He now remained almost alone of the friends and ministers of Marcus; and when, at a late hour of the night, he was awakened with the news, that the chamberlain and the præfect were at his door, he received them with intrepid resignation, and desired they would execute their master's orders. Instead of death, they offered him the throne of the Roman world. During some moments he distrusted their intentions and assurances. Convinced at length of the death of Commodus, he accepted the purple with a sincere reluctance, the natural effect of his knowledge both of the duties and of the dangers of the supreme rank.[43]

Lætus conducted without delay his new emperor to the camp of the Prætorians, diffusing at the same time through the city a seasonable report that Commodus died suddenly of an apoplexy; and that the virtuous Pertinax had *already* succeeded to the throne. The guards were rather surprised than pleased with the suspicious death of a prince whose indulgence and liberality they alone had experienced; but the emergency of the occasion, the authority of their præfect, the reputation of Pertinax, and the clamours of the people, obliged them to stifle their secret discontents, to accept the donative promised of the new emperor, to swear allegiance to him, and with joyful acclamations and laurels in their hands to conduct him to the senate-house, that the military consent might be ratified by the civil authority.

This important night was now far spent; with the dawn of day, and (A.D. 193, 1st January) the commencement of the new year, the senators expected a summons to attend an ignominious ceremony. In spite of all remonstrances, even of those of his creatures, who yet preserved any regard for prudence or decency, Commodus had resolved to pass the night in the gladiators' school, and from thence to take possession of the consulship, in the habit and with the attendance of that infamous crew. On a sudden, before the break of day, the senate was called together in the temple of Concord, to meet the guards, and to ratify the election of a new emperor. For a few minutes they sat in silent suspense, doubtful of their unexpected deliverance, and suspicious of the cruel artifices of Commodus; but when at length they were assured that the tyrant was no more, they resigned themselves to all the transports of joy and indignation. Pertinax, who modestly represented the meanness of his extraction, and pointed out several noble senators more deserving than himself of the empire, was constrained by their dutiful violence to ascend the throne, and received all the titles of Imperial power, confirmed by the most sincere vows of fidelity. The memory of Commodus was branded with eternal infamy. The names of tyrant, of gladiator, of public enemy, resounded in every corner of the house. They decreed in tumultuous votes, that his honours should be reversed, his titles erased from the public monuments, his statues thrown down, his body dragged with a hook into the stripping-room of the gladiators, to satiate the public fury; and they expressed some indignation against those officious servants who had already presumed to screen his remains from the justice of the senate. But Pertinax could not refuse those last rites to the memory of Marcus, and the tears of his first protector Claudius Pompeianus, who lamented the cruel fate of his brother-in-law, and lamented still more that he had deserved it.[44]

These effusions of impotent rage against a dead emperor, whom the senate had flattered when alive with the most abject servility, betrayed a just but ungenerous spirit of revenge. The legality of these decrees was however supported by the principles of the Imperial constitution. To censure, to depose, or to punish with death, the first magistrate of the republic, who had abused his delegated trust, was the ancient and undoubted prerogative of the Roman senate;[45] but that feeble assembly was obliged to content itself with inflicting on a fallen tyrant that public justice, from which, during his life and reign, he had been shielded by the strong arm of military despotism.

Pertinax found a nobler way of condemning his predecessor's memory; by the contrast of his own virtues with the vices of Commodus. On the day of his accession, he resigned over to his wife and son his whole private fortune; that they might have no pretence to solicit favours at the expense of the state. He refused to flatter the vanity of the former with the title of Augusta; or to corrupt the inexperienced youth of the latter by the rank of Cæsar. Accurately distinguishing between the duties of a parent and those of a sovereign, he educated his son with a severe simplicity, which, while it gave him no assured prospect of the throne, might in time have rendered him worthy of it. In public, the behaviour of Pertinax was grave and affable. He lived with the virtuous part of the senate (and in a private station, he had been acquainted with the true character of each individual), without either pride or jealousy; considered them as friends and companions, with whom he had shared the dangers of the tyranny, and with whom he wished to enjoy the security of the present time. He very frequently invited them to familiar entertainments, the frugality of which was ridiculed by those who remembered and regretted the luxurious prodigality of Commodus.[46]

To heal, as far as it was possible, the wounds inflicted by the hand of tyranny, was the pleasing, but melancholy, task of Pertinax. The innocent victims, who yet survived, were recalled from exile, released from prison, and restored to the full possession of their honours and fortunes. The unburied bodies of murdered senators (for the cruelty of Commodus endeavoured to extend itself beyond death) were deposited in the sepulchres of their ancestors; their memory was justified; and every consolation was bestowed on their ruined and afflicted families. Among these consolations, one of the most grateful was the punishment of the Delators; the common enemies of their master, of virtue, and of their country. Yet even in the inquisition of these legal assassins, Pertinax proceeded with a steady temper, which gave everything to justice, and nothing to popular prejudice and resentment.

The finances of the state demanded the most vigilant care of the emperor. Though every measure of injustice and extortion had been adopted, which could collect the property of the subject into the coffers of the prince; the rapaciousness of Commodus had been so very inadequate to his extravagance, that, upon his death, no more than eight thousand pounds were found in the exhausted treasury,[47] to defray the current expenses of government, and to discharge the pressing demand of a liberal donative, which the new emperor had been obliged to promise to the Prætorian guards. Yet under these distressed circumstances, Pertinax had the generous firmness to remit all the oppressive taxes invented by Commodus, and to cancel all the unjust claims of the treasury; declaring, in a decree of the senate, "that he was

better satisfied to administer a poor republic with innocence, than to acquire riches by the ways of tyranny and dishonour." Economy and industry he considered as the pure and genuine sources of wealth; and from them he soon derived a copious supply for the public necessities. The expense of the household was immediately reduced to one half. All the instruments of luxury, Pertinax exposed to public auction,[48] gold and silver plate, chariots of a singular construction, a superfluous wardrobe of silk and embroidery, and a great number of beautiful slaves of both sexes; excepting only, with attentive humanity, those who were born in a state of freedom, and had been ravished from the arms of their weeping parents. At the same time that he obliged the worthless favourites of the tyrant to resign a part of their ill-gotten wealth, he satisfied the just creditors of the state, and unexpectedly discharged the long arrears of honest services. He removed the oppressive restrictions which had been laid upon commerce, and granted all the uncultivated lands in Italy and the provinces to those who would improve them; with an exemption from tribute, during the term of ten years.[49]

Such an uniform conduct had already secured to Pertinax the noblest reward of a sovereign, the love and esteem of his people. Those who remembered the virtues of Marcus were happy to contemplate in their new emperor the features of that bright original; and flattered themselves that they should long enjoy the benign influence of his administration. A hasty zeal to reform the corrupted state, accompanied with less prudence than might have been expected from the years and experience of Pertinax, proved fatal to himself and to his country. His honest indiscretion united against him the servile crowd, who found their private benefit in the public disorders, and who preferred the favour of a tyrant to the inexorable equality of the laws.[50]

Amidst the general joy, the sullen and angry countenance of the Prætorian guards betrayed their inward dissatisfaction. They had reluctantly submitted to Pertinax; they dreaded the strictness of the ancient discipline, which he was preparing to restore; and they regretted the licence of the former reign. Their discontents were secretly fomented by Lætus their præfect, who found, when it was too late, that this new emperor would reward a servant, but would not be ruled by a favourite. On the third day of his reign the soldiers seized on a noble senator, with a design to carry him to the camp, and to invest him with the Imperial purple. Instead of being dazzled by the dangerous honour, the affrighted victim escaped from their violence, and took refuge at the feet of Pertinax. A short time afterwards Sosius Falco, one of the consuls of the year, a rash youth,[51] but of an ancient and opulent family, listened to the voice of ambition; and a conspiracy was formed during a short absence of Pertinax, which was crushed by his sudden return to Rome, and his resolute behaviour. Falco was on the point of being justly condemned to death as a public enemy, had he not been saved by the earnest and sincere entreaties of the injured emperor; who conjured the senate, that the purity of his reign might not be stained by the blood even of a guilty senator.

These disappointments served only to irritate the rage of the Prætorian guards. On the twenty-eighth of March, eighty-six days only after the death of Commodus, a general sedition broke out in the camp, which the officers wanted either power or inclination to suppress. Two or three hundred of the most desperate soldiers marched at noon-day, with arms in their hands and fury in their looks, towards the Imperial palace. The gates were thrown open by their companions upon guard; and by the domestics of the old court, who had already formed a secret conspiracy against the life of the too virtuous emperor. On the news of their approach, Pertinax, disdaining either flight or concealment, advanced to meet his assassins; and recalled to their minds his own innocence, and the sanctity of their recent oath. For a few moments they stood in silent suspense, ashamed of their atrocious design, and awed by the venerable aspect and majestic firmness of their sovereign, till at length the despair of pardon reviving their fury, a barbarian of the country of Tongres[52] levelled the first blow against Pertinax, who was instantly dispatched with a multitude of wounds. His head separated from his body, and placed on a lance, was carried in triumph to the Prætorian camp, in the sight of a mournful and indignant people, who lamented the unworthy fate of that excellent prince, and the transient blessings of a reign, the memory of which could serve only to aggravate their approaching misfortunes.[53]

CHAPTER V

Public Sale of the Empire to Didius Julianus by the Prætorian Guards. Clodius Albinus in Britain, Pescennius Niger in Syria, and Septimius Severus in Pannonia, declare against the Murderers of Pertinax. Civil Wars and Victory of Severus over his three Rivals. Relaxation of Discipline. New Maxims of Government.

THE power of the sword is more sensibly felt in an extensive monarchy than in a small community. It has been calculated by the ablest politicians, that no state, without being soon exhausted, can maintain above the hundredth part of its members in arms and idleness. But although this relative proportion may be uniform, the influence of the army over the rest of the society will vary according to the degree of its positive strength. The advantages of military science and discipline cannot be exerted, unless a proper number of soldiers are united into one body, and actuated by one soul. With a handful of men, such an union would be ineffectual; with an unwieldy host, it would be impracticable; and the powers of the machine would be alike destroyed by the extreme minuteness, or the excessive weight, of its springs. To illustrate this observation we need only reflect, that there is no superiority of natural strength, artificial weapons, or acquired skill, which could enable one man to keep in constant subjection one hundred of his fellow-creatures: the tyrant of a single town, or a small district, would soon discover that an hundred armed followers were a weak defence against ten thousand peasants or citizens; but an hundred thousand well-disciplined soldiers will command, with despotic sway, ten millions of subjects; and a body of ten or fifteen thousand guards will strike terror into the most numerous populace that ever crowded the streets of an immense capital.

The Prætorian bands, whose licentious fury was the first symptom and cause of the decline of the Roman empire, scarcely amounted to the last-mentioned number.[1] They derived their institution from Augustus. That crafty tyrant, sensible that laws might colour, but that arms alone could maintain, his usurped dominion, had gradually formed this powerful body of guards in constant readiness to protect his person, to awe the senate, and either to prevent or to crush the first motions of rebellion. He distinguished these favoured troops by a double pay, and superior privileges; but, as their formidable aspect would at once have alarmed and irritated the Roman people, three cohorts only were stationed in the capital; whilst the remainder was dispersed in the adjacent towns of Italy.[2] But after fifty years of peace and servitude, Tiberius ventured on a decisive measure, which for ever riveted the fetters of his country. Under the fair pretences of relieving Italy from the heavy burthen of military quarters, and of introducing a stricter discipline among the guards, he assembled them at Rome, in a permanent camp,[3] which was fortified with skilful care,[4] and placed on a commanding situation.[5]

Such formidable servants are always necessary, but often fatal to the throne of despotism. By thus introducing the Prætorian guards, as it were, into the palace and the senate, the emperors taught them to perceive their own strength, and the weakness of the civil government; to view the vices of their masters with familiar contempt, and to lay aside that reverential awe, which distance only, and mystery, can preserve towards an imaginary power. In the luxurious idleness of an opulent city, their pride was nourished by the sense of their irresistible weight; nor was it possible to conceal from them, that the person of the sovereign, the authority of the senate, the public treasure, and the seat of empire, were all in their hands. To divert the Prætorian bands from these dangerous reflections, the firmest and best established princes were obliged to mix blandishments with commands, rewards with punishments, to flatter their pride, indulge their pleasures, connive at their irregularities, and to purchase their precarious faith by a liberal donative; which, since the elevation of Claudius, was exacted as a legal claim, on the accession of every new emperor.[6]

The advocates of the guards endeavoured to justify by arguments, the power which they asserted by arms; and to maintain that, according to the purest principles of the constitution, *their* consent was essentially necessary in the appointment of an emperor. The election of consuls, of generals, and of magistrates, however it had been recently usurped by the senate, was the ancient and undoubted right of the Roman people.[7] But where was the Roman people to be found? Not surely amongst the mixed multitude of slaves and strangers that filled the streets of Rome; a servile populace, as devoid of spirit as destitute of property. The defenders of the state, selected from the flower of the Italian youth,[8] and trained in the exercise of arms and virtue, were the genuine representatives of the people, and the best entitled to elect the military chief of the republic. These assertions, however defective in reason, became unanswerable, when the fierce Prætorians increased their weight, by throwing, like the barbarian conqueror of Rome, their swords into the scale.[9]

The Prætorians had violated the sanctity of the throne, by the atrocious murder of Pertinax; they dishonoured the majesty of it, by their subsequent conduct. The camp was without a leader, for even the Præfect Lætus, who had excited the tempest, prudently declined the public indignation. Amidst the wild disorder Sulpicianus, the emperor's father-in-law, and governor of the city, who had been sent to the camp on the first alarm of mutiny, was endeavouring to calm the fury of the multitude, when he was silenced by the clamorous return of the murderers, bearing on a lance the head of Pertinax. Though history has accustomed us to observe every principle and every passion yielding to the imperious dictates of ambition, it is scarcely credible that, in these moments of horror, Sulpicianus should have aspired to ascend a throne polluted with the recent blood of so near a relation, and so excellent a prince. He had already begun to use the only effectual argument, and to treat for the Imperial dignity; but the more prudent of the Prætorians, apprehensive that, in this private contract, they should not obtain a just price for so valuable a commodity, ran out upon the ramparts; and, with a loud voice, proclaimed that the Roman world was to be disposed of to the best bidder by public auction.[10]

This infamous offer, the most insolent excess of military licence, diffused an universal grief, shame, and indignation throughout the city. It reached at length the ears of Didius Julianus, a wealthy senator, who, regardless of the public calamities, was indulging himself in the luxury of the table.[11] His wife and his daughter, his freedmen and his parasites, easily convinced him that he deserved the throne, and earnestly conjured him to embrace so fortunate an opportunity. The vain old man (A.D. 193, March 28th) hastened to the Prætorian camp, where Sulpicianus was still in treaty with the guards; and began to bid against him from the foot of the rampart. The unworthy negotiation was transacted by faithful emissaries, who passed alternately from one candidate to the other, and acquainted each of them with the offers of his rival. Sulpicianus had already promised a donative of five thousand drachms (above one hundred and sixty pounds) to each soldier; when Julian, eager for the prize, rose at once to the sum of six thousand two hundred and fifty drachms, or upwards of two hundred pounds sterling. The gates of the camp were instantly thrown open to the purchaser; he was declared emperor, and received an oath of allegiance from the soldiers, who retained humanity enough to stipulate that he should pardon and forget the competition of Sulpicianus.

It was now incumbent on the Prætorians to fulfil the conditions of the sale. They placed their new sovereign, whom they served and despised, in the centre of their ranks, surrounded him on every side with their shields, and conducted him in close order of battle through the deserted streets of the city. The senate was commanded to assemble; and those who had been the distinguished friends of Pertinax, or the personal enemies of Julian, found it necessary to affect a more than common share of satisfaction at this happy revolution.[12] After Julian had filled the senate-house with armed soldiers, he expatiated on the freedom of his election, his own eminent virtues, and his full assurance of the affections of the senate. The obsequious assembly congratulated their own and the public felicity; engaged their allegiance, and conferred on him all the several branches of the Imperial power.[13] From the senate Julian was conducted, by the same military procession, to take possession of the palace. The first objects that struck his eyes were the abandoned trunk of Pertinax and the frugal entertainment prepared for his supper. The one he viewed with indifference; the other with contempt. A magnificent feast was prepared by his order, and he amused himself till a very late hour with dice, and the performances of Pylades, a celebrated dancer. Yet it was observed, that after the crowd of flatterers dispersed, and left him to darkness, solitude, and terrible reflection, he passed a sleepless night; revolving most probably in his mind his own rash folly, the fate of his virtuous predecessor, and the doubtful and dangerous tenure of an empire, which had not been acquired by merit, but purchased by money.[14]

He had reason to tremble. On the throne of the world he found himself without a friend, and even without an adherent. The guards themselves were ashamed of the prince whom their avarice had persuaded them to accept; nor was there a citizen who did not consider his elevation with horror, as the last insult on the Roman name. The nobility, whose conspicuous station and ample possessions exacted the strict-est caution, dissembled their sentiments, and met the affected civility of the emperor with smiles of complacency and professions of duty. But the people, secure in their numbers and obscurity, gave a free vent to their passions. The streets and public places of Rome resounded with clamours and imprecations. The enraged multitude affronted the person of Julian, rejected his liberality, and conscious of the impotence of their own resentment, they called aloud on the legions of the frontiers to assert the violated majesty of the Roman empire.

The public discontent was soon diffused from the centre to the frontiers of the empire. The armies of Britain, of Syria, and of Illyricum, lamented the death of Pertinax, in whose company, or under whose command, they had so often fought and conquered. They received with surprise, with indignation, and perhaps with envy, the extraordinary intelligence that the Prætorians had disposed of the empire by public auction; and they sternly refused to ratify the ignominious bargain. Their immediate and unanimous revolt was fatal to Julian, but it was fatal at the same time to the public peace; as the generals of the respective armies, Clodius Albinus, Pescennius Niger, and Septimius Severus, were still more anxious to succeed than to revenge the murdered Pertinax. Their forces were exactly balanced. Each of them was at the head of three legions,[15] with a numerous train of auxiliaries; and however different in their characters, they were all soldiers of experience and capacity.

Clodius Albinus, governor of Britain, surpassed both his competitors in the nobility of his extraction, which he derived from some of the most illustrious names of the old republic.[16] But the branch from whence he claimed his descent was sunk into mean circumstances, and transplanted into a remote province. It is difficult to form a just idea of his true character. Under the philosophic cloak of austerity, he stands accused of concealing most of the vices which degrade human nature.[17] But his accusers are those venal writers who adored the fortune of Severus, and trampled on the ashes of an unsuccessful rival. Virtue, or the appearances of virtue, recommended Albinus to the confidence and good opinion of Marcus; and his preserving with the son the same interest which he had acquired with the father, is a proof, at least, that he was possessed of a very flexible disposition. The favour of a tyrant does not always suppose a want of merit in the object of it; he may, without intending it, reward a man of worth and ability, or he may find such a man useful to his own service. It does not appear that Albinus served the son of Marcus, either as the minister of his cruelties, or even as the associate of his pleasures. He was employed in a distant honourable command, when he received a confidential letter from the emperor, acquainting him of the treasonable designs of some discontented generals, and authorising him to declare himself the guardian and successor of the throne, by assuming the title and ensigns of Cæsar.[18] The governor of Britain wisely declined the dangerous honour, which would have marked him for the jealousy, or involved him in the approaching ruin, of Commodus. He courted power by nobler, or, at least, by more specious arts. On a premature report of the death of the emperor, he assembled his troops; and, in an eloquent discourse, deplored the inevitable mischiefs of despotism, described the happiness and glory which their ancestors had enjoyed under the consular government, and declared his firm resolution to reinstate the senate and people in their legal authority. This popular harangue was answered by the loud acclamations of the British legions, and received at Rome with a secret murmur of applause. Safe in the possession of this little world, and in the command of an army less distinguished indeed for discipline than for numbers and valour,[19] Albinus braved the menaces of Commodus, maintained towards Pertinax a stately ambiguous reserve, and instantly declared against the usurpation of Julian. The convulsions of the capital added new weight to his sentiments, or rather to his professions of patriotism. A regard to decency induced him to decline the lofty titles of Augustus and Emperor; and he imitated perhaps the example of Galba, who, on a similar occasion, had styled himself the Lieutenant of the senate and people.[20]

Personal merit alone had raised Pescennius Niger from an obscure birth and station to the government of Syria; a lucrative and important command, which in times of civil confusion gave him a near prospect of the throne. Yet his parts seem to have been better suited to the second than to the first rank; he was an unequal rival, though he might have approved himself an excellent lieutenant, to Severus, who afterwards displayed the greatness of his mind by adopting several useful institutions from a vanquished enemy.[21] In his government, Niger acquired the esteem of the soldiers, and the love of the provincials. His rigid discipline fortified the valour and confirmed the obedience of the former,

whilst the voluptuous Syrians were less delighted with the mild firmness of his administration, than with the affability of his manners, and the apparent pleasure with which he attended their frequent and pompous festivals.[22] As soon as the intelligence of the atrocious murder of Pertinax had reached Antioch, the wishes of Asia invited Niger to assume the Imperial purple and revenge his death. The legions of the eastern frontier embraced his cause; the opulent but unarmed provinces from the frontiers of Æthiopia[23] to the Hadriatic cheerfully submitted to his power; and the kings beyond the Tigris and the Euphrates congratulated his election, and offered him their homage and services. The mind of Niger was not capable of receiving this sudden tide of fortune; he flattered himself that his accession would be undisturbed by competition, and unstained by civil blood; and whilst he enjoyed the vain pomp of triumph, he neglected to secure the means of victory. Instead of entering into an effectual negotiation with the powerful armies of the west, whose resolution might decide, or at least must balance, the mighty contest; instead of advancing without delay towards Rome and Italy, where his presence was impatiently expected,[24] Niger trifled away in the luxury of Antioch those irretrievable moments which were diligently improved by the decisive activity of Severus.[25]

The country of Pannonia and Dalmatia, which occupied the space between the Danube and the Hadriatic, was one of the last and most difficult conquests of the Romans. In the defence of national freedom, two hundred thousand of these barbarians had once appeared in the field, alarmed the declining age of Augustus, and exercised the vigilant prudence of Tiberius at the head of the collected force of the empire.[26] The Pannonians yielded at length to the arms and institutions of Rome. Their recent subjection, however, the neighbourhood, and even the mixture, of the unconquered tribes, and perhaps the climate, adapted, as it has been observed, to the production of great bodies and slow minds,[27] all contributed to preserve some remains of their original ferocity, and under the tame and uniform countenance of Roman provincials, the hardy features of the natives were still to be discerned. Their warlike youth afforded an inexhaustible supply of recruits to the legions stationed on the banks of the Danube, and which, from a perpetual warfare against the Germans and Sarmatians, were deservedly esteemed the best troops in the service.

The Pannonian army was at this time commanded by Septimius Severus, a native of Africa, who, in the gradual ascent of private honours, had concealed his daring ambition, which was never diverted from its steady course by the allurements of pleasure, the apprehension of danger, or the feelings of humanity.[28] On the first news of the murder of Pertinax, he assembled his troops, painted in the most lively colours the crime, the insolence, and the weakness of the Prætorian guards, and animated the legions to arms and to revenge. He concluded (and the peroration was thought extremely eloquent) with promising every soldier about four hundred pounds; an honourable donative, double in value to the infamous bribe with which Julian had purchased the empire.[29] The acclamations of the army immediately saluted Severus with the names of Augustus, Pertinax, and Emperor; and he (A.D. 193, April 13th) thus attained the lofty station to which he was invited, by conscious merit and a long train of dreams and omens, the fruitful offspring either of his superstition or policy.[30]

The new candidate for empire saw and improved the peculiar advantage of his situation. His province extended to the Julian Alps, which gave an easy access into Italy; and he remembered the saying of Augustus, That a Pannonian army might in ten days appear in sight of Rome.[31] By a celerity proportioned to the greatness of the occasion, he might reasonably hope to revenge Pertinax, punish Julian, and receive the homage of the senate and people, as their lawful emperor, before his competitors, separated from Italy by an immense tract of sea and land, were apprised of his success, or even of his election. During the whole expedition he scarcely allowed himself any moments for sleep or food; marching on foot, and in complete armour, at the head of his columns, he insinuated himself into the confidence and affection of his troops, pressed their diligence, revived their spirits, animated their hopes, and was well satisfied to share the hardships of the meanest soldier, whilst he kept in view the infinite superiority of this reward.

The wretched Julian had expected, and thought himself prepared, to dispute the empire with the governor of Syria; but in the invincible and rapid approach of the Pannonian legions, he saw his inevitable ruin. The hasty arrival of every messenger increased his just apprehensions. He was successively informed that Severus had passed the Alps; that the Italian cities, unwilling or unable to oppose his progress, had received him with the warmest professions of joy and duty; that the important place of Ravenna had surrendered without resistance, and that the Hadriatic fleet was in the hands of the conqueror. The enemy was now within two hundred and fifty miles of Rome; and every moment diminished the narrow span of life and empire allotted to Julian.

He attempted, however, to prevent, or at least to protract, his ruin. He implored the venal faith of the Prætorians, filled the city with unavailing preparations for war, drew lines round the suburbs, and even strengthened the fortifications of the palace; as if those last intrenchments could be defended without hope of relief against a victorious invader. Fear and shame prevented the guards from deserting his standard; but they trembled at the name of the Pannonian legions, commanded by an experienced general, and accustomed to vanquish the barbarians on the frozen Danube.[32] They quitted, with a sigh, the pleasures of the baths and theatres, to put on arms, whose use they had almost forgotten, and beneath the weight of which they were oppressed. The unpractised elephants, whose uncouth appearance, it was hoped, would strike terror into the army of the north, threw their unskilful riders; and the awkward evolutions of the marines, drawn from the fleet of Misenum, were an object of ridicule to the populace; whilst the senate enjoyed, with secret pleasure, the distress and weakness of the usurper.[33]

Every motion of Julian betrayed his trembling perplexity. He insisted that Severus should be declared a public enemy by the senate. He intreated that the Pannonian general might be associated to the empire. He sent public ambassadors of consular rank to negotiate with his rival; he dispatched private assassins to take away his life. He designed that the Vestal virgins, and all the colleges of priests, in their sacerdotal habits, and bearing before them the sacred pledges of the Roman religion, should advance, in solemn procession, to meet the Pannonian legions; and, at the same time, he vainly tried to interrogate, or to appease, the fates, by magic ceremonies, and unlawful sacrifices.[34]

Severus, who dreaded neither his arms nor his enchantments, guarded himself from the only danger of secret conspiracy, by the faithful attendance of six hundred chosen men, who never quitted his person or their cuirasses, either by night or by day, during the whole march. Advancing with a steady and rapid course, he passed, without difficulty, the defiles of the Apennine, received into his party the troops and ambassadors sent to retard his progress, and made a short halt at Interamnia, about seventy miles from Rome. His victory was already secure; but the despair of the Prætorians might have rendered it bloody; and Severus had the laudable ambition of ascending the throne without drawing the sword.[35] His emissaries, dispersed in the capital, assured the guards, that provided they would abandon their worthless prince, and the perpetrators of the murder of Pertinax, to the justice of the conqueror, he would no longer consider that melancholy event as the act of the whole body. The faithless Prætorians, whose resistance was supported only by sullen obstinacy, gladly complied with the easy conditions, seized the greatest part of the assassins, and signified to the senate that they no longer defended the cause of Julian. That assembly, convoked by the consul, unanimously acknowledged Severus as lawful emperor, decreed divine honours to Pertinax, and pronounced a sentence of deposition and death against his unfortunate successor. Julian was conducted into a private apartment of the baths of the palace, and (A.D. 193, June 2) beheaded as a common criminal, after having purchased, with an immense treasure, an anxious and precarious reign of only sixty-six days.[36] The almost incredible expedition of Severus, who, in so short a space of time, conducted a numerous army from the banks of the Danube to those of the Tiber, proves at once the plenty of provisions produced by agriculture and commerce, the goodness of the roads, the discipline of the legions, and the indolent subdued temper of the provinces.[37]

The first cares of Severus were bestowed on two measures, the one dictated by policy, the other by decency; the revenge, and the honours, due to the memory of Pertinax. Before the new emperor entered Rome, he issued his commands to the Prætorian guards, directing them to wait his arrival on a large plain near the city, without arms, but in the habits of ceremony, in which they were accustomed to attend their sovereign. He was obeyed by those haughty troops, whose contrition was the effect of their just terrors. A chosen part of the Illyrian army encompassed them with levelled spears. Incapable of flight or resistance, they expected their fate in silent consternation. Severus mounted the tribunal, sternly reproached them with perfidy and cowardice, dismissed them with ignominy from the trust which they had betrayed, despoiled them of their splendid ornaments, and banished them, on pain of death, to the distance of an hundred miles from the capital. During the transaction, another detachment had been sent to seize their arms, occupy their camp, and prevent the hasty consequences of their despair.[38]

The funeral and consecration of Pertinax was next solemnised with every circumstance of sad magnificence.[39] The senate, with a melancholy pleasure, performed the last rites to that excellent prince, whom they had loved, and still regretted. The concern of his successor was probably less sincere. He esteemed the virtues of Pertinax, but those virtues would for ever have confined his ambition to a private station. Severus pronounced his funeral oration with studied eloquence, inward satisfaction, and well-acted sorrow; and by this pious regard to his memory, convinced the credulous multitude that *he alone* was worthy to supply his place. Sensible, however, that arms, not ceremonies, must assert his claim to the empire, he left Rome at the end of thirty days, and, without suffering himself to be elated by this easy victory, prepared to encounter his more formidable rivals.

The uncommon abilities and fortune of Severus have induced an elegant historian to compare him with the first and greatest of the Cæsars.[40] The parallel is, at least, imperfect. Where shall we find, in the character of Severus, the commanding superiority of soul, the generous clemency, and the various genius, which could reconcile and unite the love of pleasure, the thirst of knowledge, and the fire of ambition?[41] In one instance only they may be compared with some degree of propriety, in the celerity of their motions and their civil victories. In less than four years[42] (A.D. 193–197), Severus subdued the riches of the East, and the valour of the West. He vanquished two competitors of reputation and ability, and defeated numerous armies, provided with weapons and discipline equal to his own. In that age, the art of fortification, and the principles of tactics, were well understood by all the Roman generals; and the constant superiority of Severus was that of an artist who uses the same instruments with more skill and industry than his rivals. I shall not, however, enter into a minute narrative of these military operations; but as the two civil wars against Niger and against Albinus were almost the same in their conduct, event, and consequences, I shall collect into one point of view the most striking circumstances, tending to develop the character of the conqueror, and the state of the empire.

Falsehood and insincerity, unsuitable as they seem to the dignity of public transactions, offend us with a less degrading idea of meanness than when they are found in the intercourse of private life. In the latter, they discover a want of courage; in the other, only a defect of power: and, as it is impossible for the most able statesman to subdue millions of followers and enemies by their own personal strength, the world, under the name of policy, seems to have granted them a very liberal indulgence of craft and dissimulation. Yet the arts of Severus cannot be justified by the most ample privileges of state reason. He promised only to betray, he flattered only to ruin; and however he might occasionally bind himself by oaths and treaties, his conscience, obsequious to his interest, always released him from the inconvenient obligation.[43]

If his two competitors, reconciled by their common danger, had advanced upon him without delay, perhaps Severus would have sunk under their united effort. Had they even attacked him, at the same time, with separate views and separate armies, the contest might have been long and doubtful. But they fell, singly and successively, an easy prey to the arts as well as arms of their subtle enemy, lulled into security by the moderation of his professions, and overwhelmed by the rapidity of his action. He first marched against Niger, whose reputation and power he the most dreaded: but he declined any hostile declarations, suppressed the name of his antagonist, and only signified to the senate and people, his intention of regulating the eastern provinces. In private he spoke of Niger, his old friend and intended successor,[44] with the most affectionate regard, and highly applauded his generous design of revenging the murder of Pertinax. To punish the vile usurper of the throne, was the duty of every Roman general. To persevere in arms, and to resist a lawful emperor, acknowledged by the senate, would alone render him criminal.[45] The sons of Niger had fallen into his hands among the children of the provincial governors, detained at Rome as pledges for the loyalty of their parents.[46] As long as the power of Niger inspired terror, or even respect, they were educated with the most tender care, with the children of Severus himself; but they were soon involved in their father's ruin, and removed, first by exile, and afterwards by death, from the eye of public compassion.[47]

Whilst Severus was engaged in his eastern war, he had reason to apprehend that the governor of Britain might pass the sea and the Alps, occupy the vacant seat of empire, and oppose his return with the authority of the senate and the forces of the West. The ambiguous conduct of Albinus, in not assuming the Imperial title, left room for negotiation. Forgetting, at once, his professions of patriotism, and the jealousy of sovereign power, he accepted the precarious rank of Cæsar, as a reward for his fatal neutrality. Till the first contest was decided, Severus treated the man, whom he had doomed to destruction, with every mark of esteem and regard. Even in the letter, in which he announced his victory over Niger, he styles Albinus the brother of his soul and empire, sends him the affectionate salutations of his wife Julia, and his young family, and intreats him to preserve the armies and the republic faithful to their common interest. The messengers charged with this letter were instructed to accost the Cæsar with respect, to desire a private audience, and to plunge their daggers into his heart.[48] The conspiracy was discovered, and the too credulous Albinus, at length, passed over to the continent, and prepared for an unequal contest with his rival, who rushed upon him at the head of a veteran and victorious army.

The military labours of Severus seem inadequate to the importance of his conquests. Two engagements, the one near the Hellespont, the other in the narrow defiles of Cilicia, decided the fate of his Syrian competitor; and the troops of Europe asserted their usual ascendant over the effeminate natives of Asia.[49] The battle of Lyons, where one hundred and fifty thousand[50] Romans were engaged, was equally fatal to Albinus. The valour of the British army maintained, indeed, a sharp and doubtful contest with the hardy discipline of the Illyrian legions. The fame and person of Severus appeared, during a few moments, irrecoverably lost, till that warlike prince rallied his fainting troops, and led them on to a decisive victory.[51] The war was finished by that memorable day.

The civil wars of modern Europe have been distinguished, not only by the fierce animosity, but likewise by the obstinate perseverance, of the contending factions. They have generally been justified by some principle, or, at least, coloured by some pretext, of religion, freedom, or loyalty. The leaders were nobles of independent property and hereditary influence. The troops fought like men interested in a decision of the quarrel; and as military spirit and party zeal were strongly diffused throughout the whole community, a vanquished chief was immediately supplied with new adherents, eager to shed their blood in the same cause. But the Romans, after the fall of the republic, combated only for the choice of masters. Under the standard of a popular candidate for empire, a few enlisted from affection, some from fear, many from interest, none from principle. The legions, uninflamed by party zeal, were allured into civil war by liberal donatives, and still more liberal promises. A defeat, by disabling the chief from the performance of his engagements, dissolved the mercenary allegiance of his followers; and left them to consult their own safety, by a timely desertion of an unsuccessful cause. It was of little moment to the provinces, under whose name they were oppressed or governed; they were driven by the impulsion of the present power, and as soon as that power yielded to a superior force, they hastened to implore the clemency of the conqueror, who, as he had an immense debt to discharge, was obliged to sacrifice the most guilty countries to the avarice of his soldiers. In the vast extent of the Roman empire, there were few fortified cities capable of protecting a routed army; nor was there any person, or family, or order of men, whose natural interest, unsupported by the powers of government, was capable of restoring the cause of a sinking party.[52]

Yet, in the contest between Niger and Severus, a single city deserves an honourable exception. As Byzantium was one of the greatest passages from Europe into Asia, it had been provided with a strong garrison, and a fleet of five hundred vessels was anchored in the harbour.[53] The impetuosity of Severus disappointed this prudent scheme of defence; he left to his generals the siege of Byzantium, forced the less guarded passage of the Hellespont, and, impatient of a meaner enemy, pressed forward to encounter his rival. Byzantium, attacked by a numerous and increasing army, and afterwards by the whole naval power of the empire, sustained a siege of three years, and remained faithful to the name and memory of Niger. The citizens and soldiers (we know not from what cause) were animated with equal fury; several of the principal officers of Niger, who despaired of, or who disdained, a pardon, had thrown themselves into this last refuge: the fortifications were esteemed impregnable, and, in the defence of the place, a celebrated engineer displayed all the mechanical powers known to the ancients.[54] Byzantium, at length, surrendered to famine. The magistrates and soldiers were put to the sword, the walls demolished, the privileges suppressed, and the destined capital of the east subsisted only as an open village, subject to the insulting jurisdiction of Perinthus. The historian Dion, who had admired the flourishing, and lamented the desolate, state of Byzantium, accused the revenge of Severus, for depriving the Roman people of the strongest bulwark against the barbarians of Pontus and Asia.[55] The truth of this observation was but too well justified in the succeeding age, when the Gothic fleets covered the Euxine, and passed through the undefended Bosphorus into the centre of the Mediterranean.

Both Niger and Albinus were discovered and put to death in their flight from the field of battle. Their fate excited neither surprise nor compassion. They had staked their lives against the chance of empire, and suffered what they would have inflicted; nor did Severus claim the arrogant superiority of suffering his rivals to live in a private station. But his unforgiving temper, stimulated by avarice, indulged a spirit of revenge where there was no room for apprehension. The most considerable of the provincials, who, without any dislike to the fortunate candidate, had obeyed the governor under whose authority they were accidentally placed, were punished by death, exile, and especially by the confiscation of their estates. Many cities of the east were stript of their ancient honours, and obliged to pay, into the treasury of Severus, four times the amount of the sums contributed by them for the service of Niger.[56]

Till the final decision of the war, the cruelty of Severus was, in some measure, restrained by the uncertainty of the event, and his pretended reverence for the senate. The head of Albinus, accompanied with a menacing letter, announced to the Romans that he was resolved to spare none of the adherents of his unfortunate competitors. He was irritated by the just suspicion, that he had never possessed the affections of the senate, and he concealed his old malevolence under the recent discovery of some treasonable correspondences. Thirty-five senators, however, accused of having favoured the party of Albinus, he freely pardoned; and, by his subsequent behaviour, endeavoured to convince them that he had forgotten, as well as forgiven, their supposed offences. But, at the same time, he condemned forty-one[57] other senators, whose names history has recorded; their wives, children, and clients, attended them in death, and the noblest provincials of Spain and Gaul were involved in the same ruin. Such rigid justice, for so he termed it, was, in the opinion of Severus, the only conduct capable of ensuring peace to the people, or stability to the prince; and he condescended slightly to lament, that, to be mild, it was necessary that he should first be cruel.[58]

The true interest of an absolute monarch generally coincides with that of his people. Their numbers, their wealth, their order, and their security, are the best and only foundations of his real greatness; and were he totally devoid of virtue, prudence might supply its place, and would dictate the same rule of conduct. Severus considered the Roman empire as his property, and had no sooner secured the possession, than he bestowed his care on the cultivation and improvement of so valuable an acquisition. Salutary laws, executed with inflexible firmness, soon corrected most of the abuses with which, since the death of Marcus, every part of the government had been infected. In the administration of justice, the judgments of the emperor were characterised by attention, discernment, and impartiality; and whenever he deviated from the strict line of equity, it was generally in favour of the poor and oppressed; not so much indeed from any sense of humanity, as from the natural propensity of a despot, to humble the pride of greatness, and to sink all his subjects to the same common level of absolute dependence. His expensive taste for building, magnificent shows, and above all a constant and liberal distribution of corn and provisions, were the surest means of captivating the affection of the Roman people.[59] The misfortunes of civil discord were obliterated. The calm of peace and prosperity was once more experienced in the provinces; and many cities, restored by the munificence of Severus, assumed the title of his colonies, and attested by public monuments their gratitude and felicity.[60] The fame of the Roman arms was revived by that war-like and successful emperor,[61] and he boasted with a just pride, that, having received the empire oppressed with foreign and domestic wars, he left it established in profound, universal, and honourable peace.[62]

Although the wounds of civil war appeared completely healed, its mortal poison still lurked in the vitals of the constitution. Severus possessed a considerable share of vigour and ability; but the daring soul of the first Cæsar, or the deep policy of Augustus, were scarcely equal to the task of curbing the insolence of the victorious legions. By gratitude, by misguided policy, by seeming necessity, Severus was induced to relax the nerves of discipline.[63] The vanity of his soldiers was flattered with the honour of

wearing gold rings; their ease was indulged in the permission of living with their wives in the idleness of quarters. He increased their pay beyond the example of former times, and taught them to expect, and soon to claim, extraordinary donatives on every public occasion of danger or festivity. Elated by success, enervated by luxury, and raised above the level of subjects by their dangerous privileges,[64] they soon became incapable of military fatigue, oppressive to the country, and impatient of a just subordination. Their officers asserted the superiority of rank by a more profuse and elegant luxury. There is still extant a letter of Severus, lamenting the licentious state of the army, and exhorting one of his generals to begin the necessary reformation from the tribunes themselves; since, as he justly observes, the officer who has forfeited the esteem, will never command the obedience, of his soldiers.[65] Had the emperor pursued the train of reflection, he would have discovered that the primary cause of this general corruption might be ascribed, not indeed to the example, but to the pernicious indulgence, however, of the commander in chief.

The Prætorians, who murdered their emperor and sold the empire, had received the just punishment of their treason; but the necessary, though dangerous, institution of guards, was soon restored on a new model by Severus, and increased to four times the ancient number.[66] Formerly these troops had been recruited in Italy; and as the adjacent provinces gradually imbibed the softer manners of Rome, the levies were extended to Macedonia, Noricum, and Spain. In the room of these elegant troops, better adapted to the pomp of courts than to the uses of war, it was established by Severus, that from all the legions of the frontiers, the soldiers most distinguished for strength, valour, and fidelity, should be occasionally draughted; and promoted, as an honour and reward, into the more eligible service of the guards.[67] By this new institution, the Italian youth were diverted from the exercise of arms, and the capital was terrified by the strange aspect and manners of a multitude of barbarians. But Severus flattered himself that the legions would consider these chosen Prætorians as the representatives of the whole military order; and that the present aid of fifty thousand men, superior in arms and appointments to any force that could be brought into the field against them, would for ever crush the hopes of rebellion, and secure the empire to himself and his posterity.

The command of these favoured and formidable troops soon became the first office of the empire. As the government degenerated into military despotism, the Prætorian Præfect, who in his origin had been a simple captain of the guards, was placed, not only at the head of the army, but of the finances, and even of the law. In every department of administration he represented the person and exercised the authority of the emperor. The first Præfect who enjoyed and abused this immense power was Plautianus, the favourite minister of Severus. His reign lasted above ten years, till the marriage of his daughter with the eldest son of the emperor, which seemed to assure his fortune, proved the occasion of his ruin.[68] The animosities of the palace, by irritating the ambition and alarming the fears of Plautianus, threatened to produce a revolution, and obliged the emperor, who still loved him, to consent with reluctance to his death.[69] After the fall of Plautianus an eminent lawyer, the celebrated Papinian, was appointed to execute the motley office of Prætorian Præfect.

Till the reign of Severus, the virtue and even the good sense of the emperors had been distinguished by their real or affected reverence for the senate, and by a tender regard to the nice frame of civil policy instituted by Augustus. But the youth of Severus had been trained in the implicit obedience of camps, and his riper years spent in the despotism of military command. His haughty and inflexible spirit could not discover, or would not acknowledge, the advantage of preserving an intermediate power, however imaginary, between the emperor and the army. He disdained to profess himself the servant of an assembly that detested his person and trembled at his frown; he issued his commands, where his request would have proved as effectual; assumed the conduct and style of a sovereign and a conqueror, and exercised, without disguise, the whole legislative as well as the executive power.

The victory over the senate was easy and inglorious. Every eye and every passion was directed to the supreme magistrate, who possessed the arms and treasure of the state; whilst the senate, neither elected by the people, nor guarded by military force, nor animated by public spirit, rested its declining authority on the frail and crumbling basis of ancient opinion. The fine theory of a republic insensibly vanished, and made way for the more natural and substantial feelings of monarchy. As the freedom and honours of Rome were successively communicated to the provinces, in which the old government had been either unknown, or was remembered with abhorrence, the tradition of republican maxims was gradually obliterated. The Greek historians of the age of the Antonines[70] observe with a malicious pleasure, that although the sovereign of Rome, in compliance with an obsolete prejudice, abstained from the name of king, he possessed the full measure of regal power. In the reign of Severus, the senate was filled with polished and eloquent slaves from the eastern provinces, who justified personal flattery by speculative principles of servitude. These new advocates of prerogative were heard with pleasure by the court, and with patience by the people, when they inculcated the duty of passive obedience, and descanted on the inevitable mischiefs of freedom. The lawyers and the historians concurred in teaching that the Imperial authority was held, not by the delegated commission, but by the irrevocable resignation of the senate; that the emperor was freed from the restraint of civil laws, could command by his arbitrary will the lives and fortunes of his subjects, and might dispose of the empire as of his private patrimony.[71] The most eminent of the civil lawyers, and particularly Papinian, Paulus, and Ulpian, flourished under the house of Severus; and the Roman jurisprudence having closely united itself with the system of monarchy, was supposed to have attained its full maturity and perfection.

The contemporaries of Severus, in the enjoyment of the peace and glory of his reign, forgave the cruelties by which it had been introduced. Posterity, who experienced the fatal effects of his maxims and example, justly considered him as the principal author of the decline of the Roman empire.

CHAPTER VI

The Death of Severus. Tyranny of Caracalla. Usurpation of Macrinus. Follies of Elagabalus. Virtues of Alexander Severus. Licentiousness of the Army. General State of the Roman Finances.

THE ascent to greatness, however steep and dangerous, may entertain an active spirit with the consciousness and exercise of its own powers; but the possession of a throne could never yet afford a lasting satisfaction to an ambitious mind. This melancholy truth was felt and acknowledged by Severus. Fortune and merit had, from an humble station, elevated him to the first place among mankind. "He had been all things," as he said himself, "and all was of little value."[1] Distracted with the care, not of acquiring, but of preserving an empire, oppressed with age and infirmities, careless of fame,[2] and satiated with power, all his prospects of life were closed. The desire of perpetuating the greatness of his family was the only remaining wish of his ambition and paternal tenderness.

Like most of the Africans, Severus was passionately addicted to the vain studies of magic and divination, deeply versed in the interpretation of dreams and omens, and perfectly acquainted with the science of judicial astrology; which, in almost every age, except the present, has maintained its dominion over the mind of man. He had lost his first wife whilst he was governor of the Lyonnese Gaul.[3] In the choice of a second, he sought only to connect himself with some favourite of fortune; and as soon as he had discovered that a young lady of Emesa in Syria had *a royal nativity*, he solicited, and obtained her hand.[4] Julia Domna (for that was her name) deserved all that the stars could promise her. She possessed, even in an advanced age, the attractions of beauty,[5] and united to a lively imagination a firmness of mind, and strength of judgment, seldom bestowed on her sex. Her amiable qualities never made any deep impression on the dark and jealous temper of her husband; but in her son's reign she administered the principal affairs of the empire, with a prudence that supported his authority; and with a moderation that sometimes corrected his wild extravagancies.[6] Julia applied herself to letters and philosophy, with some success, and with the most splendid reputation. She was the patroness of every art, and the friend of every man of genius.[7] The grateful flattery of the learned has celebrated her virtue; but, if we may credit the scandal of ancient history, chastity was very far from being the most conspicuous virtue of the empress Julia.[8]

Two sons, Caracalla[9] and Geta, were the fruit of this marriage, and the destined heirs of the empire. The fond hopes of the father, and of the Roman world, were soon disappointed by these vain youths, who displayed the indolent security of hereditary princes; and a presumption that fortune would supply the place of merit and application. Without any emulation of virtue or talents, they discovered, almost from their infancy, a fixed and implacable antipathy for each other. Their aversion, confirmed by years, and fomented by the arts of their interested favourites, broke out in childish, and gradually in more serious, competitions; and, at length, divided the theatre, the circus, and the court, into two factions; actuated by the hopes and fears of their respective leaders. The prudent emperor endeavoured, by every expedient of advice and authority, to allay this growing animosity. The unhappy discord of his sons clouded all his prospects, and threatened to overturn a throne raised with so much labour, cemented with so much blood, and guarded with every defence of arms and treasure. With an impartial hand he maintained between them an exact balance of favour, conferred on both the rank of Augustus, with the revered name of Antoninus; and for the first time the Roman world beheld three emperors.[10] Yet even this equal conduct served only to inflame the contest, whilst the fierce Caracalla asserted the right of primogeniture, and the milder Geta courted the affections of the people and the soldiers. In the anguish of a disappointed father, Severus foretold that the weaker of his sons would fall a sacrifice to the stronger; who, in his turn, would be ruined by his own vices.[11]

In these circumstances the intelligence of a war in Britain and of an invasion (A.D. 208) of the province by the barbarians of the North, was received with pleasure by Severus. Though the vigilance of his lieutenants might have been sufficient to repel the distant enemy, he resolved to embrace the honourable pretext of withdrawing his sons from the luxury of Rome, which enervated their minds and irritated their passions; and of inuring their youth to the toils of war and government. Notwithstanding his advanced age (for he was above three-score), and his gout, which obliged him to be carried in a litter, he transported himself in person into that remote island, attended by his two sons, his whole court, and a formidable army. He immediately passed the walls of Hadrian and Antoninus, and entered the enemy's country, with a design of completing the long-attempted conquest of Britain. He penetrated to the northern extremity of the island without meeting an enemy. But the concealed ambuscades of the Caledonians, who hung unseen on the rear and flanks of his army, the coldness of the climate, and the severity of a winter march across the hills and morasses of Scotland, are reported to have cost the Romans above fifty thousand men. The Caledonians at length yielded to the powerful and obstinate attack, sued for peace, and surrendered a part of their arms, and a large tract of territory. But their apparent submission lasted no longer than the present terror. As soon as the Roman legions had retired, they resumed their hostile independence. Their restless spirit provoked Severus to send a new army into Caledonia, with the most bloody orders, not to subdue but to extirpate the natives. They were saved by the death of their haughty enemy.[12]

This Caledonian war, neither marked by decisive events, nor attended with any important consequences, would ill deserve our attention; but it is supposed, not without a considerable degree of probability, that the invasion of Severus is connected with the most shining period of the British history or fable. Fingal, whose fame, with that of his heroes and bards, has been revived in our language by a recent publication, is said to have commanded the Caledonians in that memorable juncture, to have eluded the power of Severus, and to have obtained a signal victory on the banks of the Carun, in which the son of the King of the World, Caracul, fled from his arms along the fields of his pride.[13] Something of a doubtful mist still hangs over these Highland traditions; nor can it be entirely dispelled by the most ingenious researches of modern criticism:[14] but if we could, with safety, indulge the pleasing supposition, that Fingal lived, and that Ossian sung, the striking contrast of the situation and manners of the contending nations might amuse a philosophic mind. The parallel would be little to the advantage of the more civilised people, if we compared the unrelenting revenge of Severus with the generous clemency of Fingal; the timid and brutal cruelty of Caracalla, with the bravery, the tenderness, the elegant genius of Ossian; the mercenary chiefs who, from motives of fear or interest, served under the Imperial standard, with the freeborn warriors who started to arms at the voice of the king of Morven; if, in a word, we contemplated the untutored Caledonians, glowing with the warm virtues of nature, and the degenerate Romans, polluted with the mean vices of wealth and slavery.

The declining health and last illness of Severus inflamed the wild ambition and black passions of Caracalla's soul. Impatient of any delay or division of empire, he attempted, more than once, to shorten the small remainder of his father's days, and endeavoured, but without success, to excite a mutiny among the troops.[15] The old emperor had often censured the misguided lenity of Marcus, who, by a single act of justice, might have saved the Romans from the tyranny of his worthless son. Placed in the same situation, he experienced how easily the rigour of a judge dissolves away in the tenderness of a parent. He deliberated, he threatened, but he could not punish; and this last and only instance of mercy was more fatal to the empire than a long series of cruelty.[16] The disorder of his mind irritated the pains of his body; he wished impatiently for death, and hastened the instant of it by his impatience. He expired (A.D. 211, February 4th) at York in the sixty-fifth year of his life, and in the eighteenth of a glorious and successful reign. In his last moments he recommended concord to his sons, and his sons to the army. The salutary advice never reached the heart, or even the understanding, of the impetuous youths; but the more obedient troops, mindful of their oath of allegiance, and of the authority of their deceased master, resisted the solicitations of Caracalla, and proclaimed both brothers emperors of Rome. The new princes soon left the Caledonians in peace, returned to the capital, celebrated their father's funeral with divine honours, and were cheerfully acknowledged as lawful sovereigns, by the senate, the people, and the provinces. Some pre-eminence of rank seems to have been allowed to the elder brother; but they both administered the empire with equal and independent power.[17]

Such a divided form of government would have proved a source of discord between the most affectionate brothers. It was impossible that it could long subsist between two implacable enemies, who neither desired nor could trust a reconciliation. It was visible that one only could reign, and that the other must fall; and each of them judging of his rival's designs by his own, guarded his life with the most jealous vigilance from the repeated attacks of poison or the sword. Their rapid journey through Gaul and Italy, during which they never ate at the same table, or slept in the same house, displayed to the provinces the odious spectacle of fraternal discord. On their arrival at Rome, they immediately divided the vast extent of the Imperial palace.[18] No communication was allowed between their apartments: the doors and passages were diligently fortified, and guards posted and relieved with the same strictness as in a besieged place. The emperors met only in public, in the presence of their afflicted mother; and each surrounded by a numerous train of armed followers. Even on these occasions of ceremony, the dissimulation of courts could ill disguise the rancour of their hearts.[19]

This latent civil war already distracted the whole government, when a scheme was suggested that seemed of mutual benefit to the hostile brothers. It was proposed, that since it was impossible to reconcile their minds, they should separate their interest, and divide the empire between them. The conditions of the treaty were already drawn with some accuracy. It was agreed that Caracalla, as the elder brother, should remain in possession of Europe and the western Africa; and that he should relinquish the sovereignty of Asia and Egypt to Geta, who might fix his residence at Alexandria or Antioch, cities little inferior to Rome itself in wealth and greatness; that numerous armies should be constantly encamped on either side of the Thracian Bosphorus, to guard the frontiers of the rival monarchies; and that the senators of European extraction should acknowledge the sovereign of Rome, whilst the natives of Asia followed the emperor of the East. The tears of the empress Julia interrupted the negotiation, the first idea of which had filled every Roman breast with surprise and indignation. The mighty mass of conquest was so intimately united by the hand of time and policy, that it required the most forcible violence to rend it asunder. The Romans had reason to dread that the disjoined members would soon be reduced by a civil war under the dominion of one master; but if the separation was permanent, the division of the provinces must terminate in the dissolution of an empire whose unity had hitherto remained inviolate.[20]

Had the treaty been carried into execution, the sovereign of Europe might soon have been the conqueror of Asia; but Caracalla obtained an easier though a more guilty victory. He artfully listened to his mother's entreaties, and consented (A.D. 212, 27th February) to meet his brother in her apartment, on terms of peace and reconciliation. In the midst of their conversation, some centurions, who had contrived to conceal themselves, rushed with drawn swords upon the unfortunate Geta. His distracted mother strove to protect him in her arms; but, in the unavailing struggle, she was wounded in the hand, and covered with the blood of her younger son, while she saw the elder animating and assisting[21] the fury of the assassins. As soon as the deed was perpetrated, Caracalla, with hasty steps, and horror in his countenance, ran towards the Prætorian camp as his only refuge, and threw himself on the ground before the statues of the tutelar deities.[22] The soldiers attempted to raise and comfort him. In broken and disordered words he informed them of his imminent danger and fortunate escape; insinuating that he had prevented the designs of his enemy, and declared his resolution to live and die with his faithful troops. Geta had been the favourite of the soldiers; but complaint was useless, revenge was dangerous, and they still reverenced the son of Severus. Their discontent died away in idle murmurs, and Caracalla soon convinced them of the justice of his cause, by distributing in one lavish donative the accumulated treasures of his father's reign.[23] The real *sentiments* of the soldiers alone were of importance to his power or safety. Their declaration in his favour commanded the dutiful *professions* of the senate. The obsequious assembly was always prepared to ratify the decision of fortune; but as Caracalla wished to assuage the first emotions of public indignation, the name of Geta was mentioned with decency, and he received the funeral honours of a Roman emperor.[24] Posterity, in pity to his misfortune, has cast a veil over his vices. We consider that young prince as the innocent victim of his brother's ambition, without recollecting that he himself wanted power, rather than inclination, to consummate the same attempts of revenge and murder.

The crime went not unpunished. Neither business, nor pleasure, nor flattery, could defend Caracalla from the stings of a guilty conscience; and he confessed, in the anguish of a tortured mind, that his disordered fancy often beheld the angry forms of his father and his brother rising into life, to threaten and upbraid him.[25] The consciousness of his crime should have induced him to convince mankind, by the virtues of his reign, that the bloody deed had been the involuntary effect of fatal necessity. But the repentance of Caracalla only prompted him to remove from the world whatever could remind him of his guilt, or recall the memory of his murdered brother. On his return from the senate to the palace, he found his mother in the company of several noble matrons, weeping over the untimely fate of her younger son. The jealous emperor threatened them with instant death; the sentence was executed against Fadilla, the last remaining daughter of the emperor Marcus; and even the afflicted Julia was obliged to silence her lamentations, to suppress her sighs, and to receive the assassin with smiles of joy and approbation. It was computed that, under the vague appellation of the friends of Geta, above twenty thousand persons of both sexes suffered death. His guards and freedmen, the ministers of his serious business, and the companions of his looser hours, those who by his interest had been promoted to any commands in the army or provinces, with the long-connected chain of their dependents, were included in the proscription; which endeavoured to reach every one who had maintained the smallest correspondence with Geta, who lamented his death, or who even mentioned his name.[26] Helvius Pertinax, son to the prince of that name, lost his life by an unseasonable witticism.[27] It was a sufficient crime of Thrasea Priscus, to be descended from a family in which the love of liberty seemed an hereditary quality.[28] The particular causes of calumny and suspicion were at length exhausted; and when a senator was accused of being a secret enemy to the government, the emperor was satisfied with the general proof that he was a man of property and virtue. From this well-grounded principle he frequently drew the most bloody inferences.

The execution of so many innocent citizens was bewailed by the secret tears of their friends and families. The death of Papinian, the Prætorian præfect, was lamented as a public calamity. During the last seven years of Severus, he had exercised the most important office of the state, and, by his salutary influence, guided the emperor's steps in the paths of justice and moderation. In full assurance of his virtues and abilities, Severus, on his death-bed, had conjured him to watch over the prosperity and union of the Imperial family.[29] The honest labours of Papinian served only to inflame the hatred which Caracalla had already conceived against his father's minister. After the murder of Geta, the Præfect was commanded to exert the powers of his skill and eloquence in a studied apology for that atrocious deed. The philosophic Seneca had condescended to compose a similar epistle to the senate, in the name of the son and assassin of Agrippina.[30] That it was easier to commit than to justify a "parricide," was the glorious reply of Papinian,[31] who did not hesitate between the loss of life and that of honour. Such intrepid virtue, which had escaped pure and unsullied from the intrigues of courts, the habits of business, and the arts of his profession, reflects more lustre on the memory of Papinian, than all his great employments, his numerous writings, and the superior reputation as a lawyer, which he has preserved through every age of the Roman jurisprudence.[32]

It had hitherto been the peculiar felicity of the Romans, and in the worst of times their consolation, that the virtue of the emperors was active, and their vice indolent. Augustus, Trajan, Hadrian, and Marcus, visited their extensive dominions in person, and their progress was marked by acts of wisdom and beneficence. The tyranny of Tiberius, Nero, and Domitian, who resided almost constantly at Rome, or in the adjacent villas, was confined to the senatorial and equestrian orders.[33] But Caracalla was the common enemy of mankind. He left (A.D. 213) the capital (and he never returned to it) about a year after the murder of Geta. The rest of his reign was spent in the several provinces of the empire, particularly those of the East, and every province was by turns the scene of his rapine and cruelty. The senators, compelled by fear to attend his capricious motions, were obliged to provide daily entertainments at an immense expense, which he abandoned with contempt to his guards; and to erect, in every city, magnificent palaces and theatres, which he either disdained to visit, or ordered to be immediately thrown down. The most wealthy families were ruined by partial fines and confiscations, and the great body of his subjects oppressed by ingenious and aggravated taxes.[34] In the midst of peace, and upon the slightest provocation, he issued his commands, at Alexandria in Egypt, for a general massacre. From a secure post in the temple of Serapis, he viewed and directed the slaughter of many thousand citizens, as well as strangers, without distinguishing either the number or the crime of the sufferers; since, as he coolly informed the senate, *all* the Alexandrians, those who had perished and those who had escaped, were alike guilty.[35]

The wise instructions of Severus never made any lasting impression on the mind of his son, who, although not destitute of imagination and eloquence, was equally devoid of judgment and humanity.[36] One dangerous maxim, worthy of a tyrant, was remembered and abused by Caracalla, "To secure the affections of the army, and to esteem the rest of his subjects as of little moment."[37] But the liberality of the father had been restrained by prudence, and his indulgence to the troops was tempered by firmness and authority. The careless profusion of the son was the policy of one reign, and the inevitable ruin both of the army and of the empire. The vigour of the soldiers, instead of being confirmed by the severe discipline of camps, melted away in the luxury of cities. The excessive increase of their pay and donatives[38] exhausted the state to enrich the military order, whose modesty in peace, and service in war, is best secured by an honourable poverty. The demeanour of Caracalla was haughty and full of pride; but with the troops he forgot even the proper dignity of his rank, encouraged their insolent familiarity, and, neglecting the essential duties of a general, affected to imitate the dress and manners of a common soldier.

It was impossible that such a character, and such a conduct as that of Caracalla, could inspire either love or esteem; but as long as his vices were beneficial to the armies, he was secure from the danger of rebellion. A secret conspiracy, provoked by his own jealousy, was fatal to the tyrant. The Prætorian præfecture was divided between two ministers. The military department was intrusted to Adventus, an experienced rather than an able soldier; and the civil affairs were transacted by Opilius Macrinus, who, by his dexterity in business, had raised himself, with a fair character, to that high office. But his favour varied with the caprice of the emperor, and his life might depend on the slightest suspicion, or the most casual circumstance. Malice or fanaticism had suggested to an African, deeply skilled in the knowledge of futurity, a very dangerous prediction, that Macrinus and his son were destined to reign over the empire. The report was soon diffused through the province; and when the man was sent in chains to Rome, he still asserted, in the presence of the Præfect of the city, the faith of his prophecy. That magistrate, who had received the most pressing instructions to inform himself of the *successors* of Caracalla, im-

mediately communicated the examination of the African to the Imperial court, which at that time resided in Syria. But, notwithstanding the diligence of the public messengers, a friend of Macrinus found means to apprise him of the approaching danger. The emperor received the letters from Rome; and as he was then engaged in the conduct of a chariot-race, he delivered them unopened to the Prætorian Præfect, directing him to dispatch the ordinary affairs, and to report the more important business that might be contained in them. Macrinus read his fate, and resolved to prevent it. He inflamed the discontents of some inferior officers, and employed the hand of Martialis, a desperate soldier, who had been refused the rank of centurion. The devotion of Caracalla prompted him to make a pilgrimage from Edessa to the celebrated temple of the Moon at Carrhæ.[39] He (A.D. 217, 8th March) was attended by a body of cavalry; but having stopped on the road for some necessary occasion, his guards preserved a respectful distance, and Martialis approaching his person under a pretence of duty, stabbed him with a dagger. The bold assassin was instantly killed by a Scythian archer of the Imperial guard. Such was the end of a monster whose life disgraced human nature, and whose reign accused the patience of the Romans. The grateful soldiers forgot his vices, remembered only his partial liberality, and obliged the senate to prostitute their own dignity and that of religion by granting him a place among the gods. Whilst he was upon earth, Alexander the Great was the only hero whom this god deemed worthy his admiration. He assumed the name and ensigns of Alexander, formed a Macedonian phalanx of guards, persecuted the disciples of Aristotle, and displayed with a puerile enthusiasm the only sentiment by which he discovered any regard for virtue or glory. We can easily conceive, that after the battle of Narva, and the conquest of Poland, Charles the Twelfth (though he still wanted the more elegant accomplishments of the son of Philip) might boast of having rivalled his valour and magnanimity; but in no one action of his life did Caracalla express the faintest resemblance of the Macedonian hero, except in the murder of a great number of his own and of his father's friends.[40]

After the extinction of the house of Severus, the Roman world remained three days without a master. The choice of the army (for the authority of a distant and feeble senate was little regarded) hung in an anxious suspense; as no candidate presented himself whose distinguished birth and merit could engage their attachment and unite their suffrages. The decisive weight of the Prætorian guards elevated the hopes of their præfects, and these powerful ministers began to assert their *legal* claim to fill the vacancy of the Imperial throne. Adventus, however, the senior præfect, conscious of his age and infirmities, of his small reputation, and his smaller abilities, resigned the dangerous honour to the crafty ambition of his colleague Macrinus, whose well-dissembled grief removed all suspicion of his being accessory to his master's death.[41] The troops neither loved nor esteemed his character. They cast their eyes around in search of a competitor, and at last yielded with reluctance to his promises of unbounded liberality and indulgence. A short time after his accession (A.D. 217, March 11) he conferred on his son Diadumenianus, at the age of only ten years, the Imperial title and the popular name of Antoninus. The beautiful figure of the youth, assisted by an additional donative, for which the ceremony furnished a pretext, might attract, it was hoped, the favour of the army, and secure the doubtful throne of Macrinus.

The authority of the new sovereign had been ratified by the cheerful submission of the senate and provinces. They exulted in their unexpected deliverance from a hated tyrant, and it seemed of little consequence to examine into the virtues of the successor of Caracalla. But as soon as the first transports of joy and surprise had subsided, they began to scrutinise the merits of Macrinus with a critical severity, and to arraign the hasty choice of the army. It had hitherto been considered as a fundamental maxim of the constitution, that the emperor must be always chosen in the senate, and the sovereign power, no longer exercised by the whole body, was always delegated to one of its members. But Macrinus was not a senator.[42] The sudden elevation of the Prætorian præfects betrayed the meanness of their origin; and the equestrian order was still in possession of that great office, which commanded with arbitrary sway the lives and fortunes of the senate. A murmur of indignation was heard, that a man whose obscure[43] extraction had never been illustrated by any signal service, should dare to invest himself with the purple, instead of bestowing it on some distinguished senator, equal in birth and dignity to the splendour of the Imperial station.

As soon as the character of Macrinus was surveyed by the sharp eye of discontent, some vices, and many defects, were easily discovered.

The choice of his ministers was in many instances justly censured, and the dissatisfied people, with their usual candour, accused at once his indolent tameness and his excessive severity.[44]

His rash ambition had climbed a height where it was difficult to stand with firmness, and impossible to fall without instant destruction. Trained in the arts of courts, and the forms of civil business, he trembled in the presence of the fierce and undisciplined multitude, over whom he had assumed the command; his military talents were despised, and his personal courage suspected; a whisper that circulated in the camp disclosed the fatal secret of the conspiracy against the late emperor, aggravated the guilt of murder by the baseness of hypocrisy, and heightened contempt by detestation. To alienate the soldiers, and to provoke inevitable ruin, the character of a reformer was only wanting: and such was the peculiar hardship of his fate, that Macrinus was compelled to exercise that invidious office. The prodigality of Caracalla had left behind it a long train of ruin and disorder; and if that worthless tyrant had been capable of reflecting on the sure consequences of his own conduct, he would perhaps have enjoyed the dark prospect of the distress and calamities which he bequeathed to his successors.

In the management of this necessary reformation, Macrinus proceeded with a cautious prudence, which would have restored health and vigour to the Roman army, in an easy and almost imperceptible manner. To the soldiers already engaged in the service, he was constrained to leave the dangerous privileges and extravagant pay given by Caracalla; but the new recruits were received on the more moderate though liberal establishment of Severus, and gradually formed to modesty and obedience.[45] One fatal error destroyed the salutary effects of this judicious plan. The numerous army, assembled in the East by the late emperor, instead of being immediately dispersed by Macrinus through the several provinces, was suffered to remain united in Syria, during the winter that followed his elevation. In the luxurious idleness of their quarters, the troops viewed their strength and numbers, communicated their complaints, and revolved in their minds the advantages of another revolution. The veterans, instead of being flattered by the advantageous distinction, were alarmed by the first steps of the emperor, which they considered as the presage of his future intentions. The recruits, with sullen reluctance, entered on a service, whose labours were increased while its rewards were diminished by a covetous and unwarlike sovereign. The murmurs of the army swelled with impunity into seditious clamours; and the partial mutinies betrayed a spirit of discontent and disaffection, that waited only for the slightest occasion to break out on every side into a general rebellion. To minds thus disposed, the occasion soon presented itself.

The empress Julia had experienced all the vicissitudes of fortune. From an humble station she had been raised to greatness, only to taste the superior bitterness of an exalted rank. She was doomed to weep over the death of one of her sons, and over the life of the other. The cruel fate of Caracalla, though her good sense must have long taught her to expect it, awakened the feelings of a mother and of an empress. Notwithstanding the respectful civility expressed by the usurper towards the widow of Severus, she descended with a painful struggle into the condition of a subject, and soon withdrew herself by a voluntary death from the anxious and humiliating dependence. Julia Mæsa, her sister, was ordered to leave the court and Antioch.[46] She retired to Emesa with an immense fortune, the fruit of twenty years' favour, accompanied by her two daughters, Soæmias and Mamæa, each of whom was a widow, and each had an only son. Bassianus, for that was the name of the son of Soæmias, was consecrated to the honourable ministry of high priest of the Sun; and this holy vocation, embraced either from prudence or superstition, contributed to raise the Syrian youth to the empire of Rome. A numerous body of troops was stationed at Emesa; and, as the severe discipline of Macrinus had constrained them to pass the winter encamped, they were eager to revenge the cruelty of such unaccustomed hardships. The soldiers, who resorted in crowds to the temple of the Sun, beheld with veneration and delight the elegant dress and figure of a young Pontiff: they recognised, or they thought that they recognised, the features of Caracalla, whose memory they now adored. The artful Mæsa saw and cherished their rising partiality, and readily sacrificing her daughter's reputation to the fortune of her grandson, she insinuated that Bassianus was the natural son of their murdered sovereign. The sums distributed by her emissaries with a lavish hand silenced every objection, and the profusion sufficiently proved the affinity, or at least the resemblance, of Bassianus with the great original. The young Antoninus (for he had assumed and polluted that

respectable name) was (A.D. 218, May 16) declared emperor by the troops of Emesa, asserted his hereditary right, and called aloud on the armies to follow the standard of a young and liberal prince, who had taken up arms to revenge his father's death and the oppression of the military order.[47]

Whilst a conspiracy of women and eunuchs was concerted with prudence, and conducted with rapid vigour, Macrinus, who, by a decisive motion, might have crushed his infant enemy, floated between the opposite extremes of terror and security, which alike fixed him inactive at Antioch. A spirit of rebellion diffused itself through all the camps and garrisons of Syria, successive detachments murdered their officers,[48] and joined the party of the rebels; and the tardy restitution of military pay and privileges was imputed to the acknowledged weakness of Macrinus. At length he marched out of Antioch, to meet the increasing and zealous army of the young pretender. His own troops seemed to take the field with faintness and reluctance; but (A.D. 218, June 7), in the heat of the battle,[49] the Prætorian guards, almost by an involuntary impulse, asserted the superiority of their valour and discipline. The rebel ranks were broken; when the mother and grandmother of the Syrian prince, who, according to their eastern custom, had attended the army, threw themselves from their covered chariots, and, by exciting the compassion of the soldiers, endeavoured to animate their drooping courage. Antoninus himself, who, in the rest of his life, never acted like a man, in this important crisis of his fate approved himself a hero, mounted his horse, and, at the head of his rallied troops, charged sword in hand among the thickest of the enemy; whilst the eunuch Gannys, whose occupations had been confined to female cares and the soft luxury of Asia, displayed the talents of an able and experienced general. The battle still raged with doubtful violence, and Macrinus might have obtained the victory, had he not betrayed his own cause by a shameful and precipitate flight. His cowardice served only to protract his life a few days, and to stamp deserved ignominy on his misfortunes. It is scarcely necessary to add, that his son Diadumenianus was involved in the same fate. As soon as the stubborn Prætorians could be convinced that they fought for a prince who had basely deserted them, they surrendered to the conqueror; the contending parties of the Roman army, mingling tears of joy and tenderness, united under the banners of the imagined son of Caracalla, and the East acknowledged with pleasure the first emperor of Asiatic extraction.

The letters of Macrinus had condescended to inform the senate of the slight disturbance occasioned by an impostor in Syria, and a decree immediately passed, declaring the rebel and his family public enemies; with a promise of pardon, however, to such of his deluded adherents as should merit it by an immediate return to their duty. During the twenty days that elapsed from the declaration to the victory of Antoninus (for in so short an interval was the fate of the Roman world decided), the capital and the provinces, more especially those of the East, were distracted with hopes and fears, agitated with tumult, and stained with a useless effusion of civil blood, since whosoever of the rivals prevailed in Syria, must reign over the empire. The specious letters in which the young conqueror announced his victory to the obedient senate, were filled with professions of virtue and moderation; the shining examples of Marcus and Augustus he should ever consider as the great rule of his administration; and he affected to dwell with pride on the striking resemblance of his own age and fortunes with those of Augustus, who in the earliest youth had revenged by a successful war the murder of his father. By adopting the style of Marcus Aurelius Antoninus, son of Antoninus and grandson of Severus, he tacitly asserted his hereditary claim to the empire; but, by assuming the tribunitian and proconsular powers before they had been conferred on him by a decree of the senate, he offended the delicacy of Roman prejudice. This new and injudicious violation of the constitution was probably dictated either by the ignorance of his Syrian courtiers, or the fierce disdain of his military followers.[50]

As the attention of the new emperor was diverted by the most trifling amusements, he (A.D. 219) wasted many months in his luxurious progress from Syria to Italy, passed at Nicomedia his first winter after his victory, and deferred till the ensuing summer his triumphal entry into the capital. A faithful picture, however, which preceded his arrival, and was placed by his immediate order over the altar of Victory in the senate-house, conveyed to the Romans the just but unworthy resemblance of his person and manners. He was drawn in his sacerdotal robes of silk and gold, after the loose flowing fashion of the Medes and Phœnicians; his head was covered with a lofty tiara, his numerous collars and bracelets were adorned with gems of an inestimable value. His eyebrows were tinged with black, and his cheeks painted with an artificial red and white.[51] The grave senators confessed with a sigh, that, after having long experienced the stern tyranny of their own countrymen, Rome was at length humbled beneath the effeminate luxury of Oriental despotism.

The Sun was worshipped at Emesa, under the name of Elagabalus,[52] and under the form of a black conical stone, which, as it was universally believed, had fallen from heaven on that sacred place. To this protecting deity, Antoninus, not without some reason, ascribed his elevation to the throne. The display of superstitious gratitude was the only serious business of his reign. The triumph of the God of Emesa over all the religions of the earth, was the great object of his zeal and vanity: and the appellation of Elagabalus (for he presumed as pontiff and favourite to adopt that sacred name) was dearer to him than all the titles of Imperial greatness. In a solemn procession through the streets of Rome, the way was strewed with gold dust; the black stone, set in precious gems, was placed on a chariot drawn by six milk-white horses richly caparisoned. The pious emperor held the reins, and, supported by his ministers, moved slowly backwards, that he might perpetually enjoy the felicity of the divine presence. In a magnificent temple raised on the Palatine Mount, the sacrifices of the god of Elagabalus were celebrated with every circumstance of cost and solemnity. The richest wines, the most extraordinary victims, and the rarest aromatics, were profusely consumed on his altar. Around the altar a chorus of Syrian damsels performed their lascivious dances to the sound of barbarian music, whilst the gravest personages of the state and army, clothed in long Phœnician tunics, officiated in the meanest functions, with affected zeal and secret indignation.[53]

To this temple, as to the common centre of religious worship, the Imperial fanatic attempted to remove the Ancilia, the Palladium,[54] and all the sacred pledges of the faith of Numa. A crowd of inferior deities attended in various stations the majesty of the god of Emesa; but his court was still imperfect, till a female of distinguished rank was admitted to his bed. Pallas had been first chosen for his comfort; but as it was dreaded lest her warlike terrors might affright the soft delicacy of a Syrian deity, the Moon, adored by the Africans under the name of Astarte, was deemed a more suitable companion for the Sun. Her image, with the rich offerings of her temple as a marriage portion, was transported with solemn pomp from Carthage to Rome, and the day of these mystic nuptials was a general festival in the capital and throughout the empire.[55]

A rational voluptuary adheres with invariable respect to the temperate dictates of nature, and improves the gratifications of sense by social intercourse, endearing connections, and the soft colouring of taste and the imagination. But Elagabalus (I speak of the emperor of that name), corrupted by his youth, his country, and his fortune, abandoned himself to the grossest pleasures with ungoverned fury, and soon found disgust and satiety in the midst of his enjoyments. The inflammatory powers of art were summoned to his aid: the confused multitude of women, of wines, and of dishes, and the studied variety of attitudes and sauces, served to revive his languid appetites. New terms and new inventions in these sciences, the only ones cultivated and patronised by the monarch,[56] signalised his reign, and transmitted his infamy to succeeding times. A capricious prodigality supplied the want of taste and elegance; and whilst Elagabalus lavished away the treasures of his people in the wildest extravagance, his own voice and that of his flatterers applauded a spirit and magnificence unknown to the tameness of his predecessors. To confound the order of seasons and climates,[57] to sport with the passions and prejudices of his subjects, and to subvert every law of nature and decency, were in the number of his most delicious amusements. A long train of concubines, and a rapid succession of wives, among whom was a vestal virgin, ravished by force from her sacred asylum,[58] were insufficient to satisfy the impotence of his passions. The master of the Roman world affected to copy the dress and manners of the female sex, preferred the distaff to the sceptre, and dishonoured the principal dignities of the empire by distributing them among his numerous lovers; one of whom was publicly invested with the title and authority of the emperor's, or, as he more properly styled himself, of the empress's husband.[59]

It may seem probable, the vices and follies of Elagabalus have been adorned by fancy, and blackened by prejudice.[60] Yet confining ourselves to the public scenes displayed before the Roman people, and attested by grave and contemporary historians, their inexpressible infamy surpasses that of any other age or country. The licence of an eastern monarch is secluded from the eye of curiosity by the inaccessible walls of his seraglio. The sentiments of honour and gallantry have introduced a refinement of pleasure, a regard for decency, and a respect for the public opinion, into the modern courts of Europe; but the corrupt and opulent nobles of Rome gratified every vice that could be collected from the mighty conflux of nations and manners. Secure of impunity, careless of censure, they lived without restraint in the patient and humble society of their slaves and parasites. The emperor, in his turn, viewing every rank of his subjects with the same contemptuous indifference, asserted without control his sovereign privilege of lust and luxury.

The most worthless of mankind are not afraid to condemn in others the same disorders which they allow in themselves; and can readily discover some nice difference of age, character, or station, to justify the partial distinction. The licentious soldiers, who had raised to the throne the dissolute son of Caracalla, blushed at their ignominious choice, and turned with disgust from that monster, to contemplate with pleasure the opening virtues of his cousin Alexander the son of Mamæa. The crafty Mæsa, sensible that her grandson Elagabalus must inevitably destroy himself by his own vices, had provided another and surer support of her family. Embracing a favourable moment of fondness and devotion, she had persuaded the young emperor to adopt Alexander, and to invest him (A.D. 221) with the title of Cæsar, that his own divine occupations might be no longer interrupted by the care of the earth. In the second rank that amiable prince soon acquired the affections of the public, and excited the tyrant's jealousy, who resolved to terminate the dangerous competition, either by corrupting the manners, or by taking away the life, of his rival. His arts proved unsuccessful; his vain designs were constantly discovered by his own loquacious folly, and disappointed by those virtuous and faithful servants whom the prudence of Mamæa had placed about the person of her son. In a hasty sally of passion, Elagabalus resolved to execute by force what he had been unable to compass by fraud, and by a despotic sentence degraded his cousin from the rank and honours of Cæsar. The message was received in the senate with silence, and in the camp with fury. The Prætorian guards swore to protect Alexander, and to revenge the dishonoured majesty of the throne. The tears and promises of the trembling Elagabalus, who only begged them to spare his life, and to leave him in the possession of his beloved Hierocles, diverted their just indignation; and they contented themselves with empowering their præfects to watch over the safety of Alexander, and the conduct of the emperor.[61]

It was impossible that such a reconciliation should last, or that even the mean soul of Elagabalus could hold an empire on such humiliating terms of dependence. He soon attempted, by a dangerous experiment, to try the temper of the soldiers. The report of the death of Alexander, and the natural suspicion that he had been murdered, inflamed their passions into fury, and the tempest of the camp could only be appeased by the presence and authority of the popular youth. Provoked at this new instance of their affection for his cousin, and their contempt for his person, the emperor ventured to punish some of the leaders of the mutiny. His unseasonable severity proved instantly fatal to his minions, his mother, and himself. Elagabalus was (A.D. 222, 10th March) massacred by the indignant Prætorians, his mutilated corpse dragged through the streets of the city, and thrown into the Tiber. His memory was branded with eternal infamy by the senate; the justice of whose decree has been ratified by posterity.[62]

In the room of Elagabalus, his cousin Alexander was raised to the throne by the Prætorian guards. His relation to the family of Severus, whose name he assumed, was the same as that of his predecessor; his virtue and his danger had already endeared him to the Romans, and the eager liberality of the senate conferred upon him, in one day, the various titles and powers of the Imperial dignity.[63] But as Alexander was a modest and dutiful youth, of only seventeen years of age, the reins of government were in the hands of two women, of his mother Mamæa, and of Mæsa, his grandmother. After the death of the latter, who survived but a short time the elevation of Alexander, Mamæa remained the sole regent of her son and of the empire.

In every age and country, the wiser, or at least the stronger, of the two sexes, has usurped the powers of the state, and confined the other to the cares and pleasures of domestic life. In hereditary monarchies, however, and especially in those of modern Europe, the gallant spirit of chivalry, and the law of succession, have accustomed us to allow a singular exception; and a woman is often acknowledged the absolute sovereign of a great kingdom, in which she would be deemed incapable of exercising the smallest employment, civil or military. But as the Roman emperors were still considered as the generals and magistrates of the republic, their wives and mothers, although distinguished by the name of Augusta, were never associated to their personal honours; and a female reign would have appeared an inexpiable prodigy in the eyes of those primitive Romans, who married without love, or loved without delicacy and respect.[64] The haughty Agrippina aspired, indeed, to share the honours of the empire, which she had conferred on her son; but her mad ambition, detested by every citizen who felt for the dignity of Rome, was disappointed by the artful firmness of Seneca and Burrhus.[65] The good sense, or the indifference, of succeeding princes, restrained them from offending the prejudices of their subjects; and it was reserved for the profligate Elagabalus to discharge the acts of the senate, with the name of his mother Soæmias, who was placed by the side of the consuls, and subscribed, as a regular member, the decrees of the legislative assembly. Her more prudent sister, Mamæa, declined the useless and odious prerogative, and a solemn law was enacted, excluding women for ever from the senate, and devoting to the infernal gods the head of the wretch by whom this sanction should be violated.[66] The substance, not the pageantry, of power was the object of Mamæa's manly ambition. She maintained an absolute and lasting empire over the mind of her son, and in his affection the mother could not brook a rival. Alexander, with her consent, married the daughter of a Patrician; but his respect for his father-in-law, and love for the empress, were inconsistent with the tenderness or interest of Mamæa. The Patrician was executed on the ready accusation of treason, and the wife of Alexander driven with ignominy from the palace, and banished into Africa.[67]

Notwithstanding this act of jealous cruelty, as well as some instances of avarice, with which Mamæa is charged, the general tenor of her administration was equally for the benefit of her son and of the empire. With the approbation of the senate, she chose sixteen of the wisest and most virtuous senators, as a perpetual council of state, before whom every public business of moment was debated and determined. The celebrated Ulpian, equally distinguished by his knowledge of, and his respect for, the laws of Rome, was at their head; and the prudent firmness of this aristocracy restored order and authority to the government. As soon as they had purged the city from foreign superstition and luxury, the remains of the capricious tyranny of Elagabalus, they applied themselves to remove his worthless creatures from every department of public administration, and to supply their places with men of virtue and ability.

Learning, and the love of justice, became the only recommendations for civil offices; valour, and the love of discipline, the only qualifications for military employments.[68]

But the most important care of Mamæa and her wise counsellors, was to form the character of the young emperor, on whose personal qualities the happiness or misery of the Roman world must ultimately depend. The fortunate soil assisted, and even prevented, the hand of cultivation. An excellent understanding soon convinced Alexander of the advantages of virtue, the pleasure of knowledge, and the necessity of labour. A natural mildness and moderation of temper preserved him from the assaults of passion, and the allurements of vice. His unalterable regard for his mother, and his esteem for the wise Ulpian, guarded his inexperienced youth from the poison of flattery.

The simple journal of his ordinary occupations exhibits a pleasing picture of an accomplished emperor,[69] and with some allowance for the difference of manners, might well deserve the imitation of modern princes. Alexander rose early; the first moments of the day were consecrated to private devotion, and his domestic chapel was filled with the images of those heroes, who, by improving or reforming human life, had deserved the grateful reverence of posterity. But, as he deemed the service of mankind the most acceptable worship of the gods, the greatest part of his morning hours was employed in his council, where he discussed public affairs, and determined private causes, with a patience and discretion above his years. The dryness of business was relieved by the charms of literature; and a portion of time was always set apart for his favourite studies of poetry, history, and philosophy. The works of Virgil and Horace, the Republics of Plato and Cicero, formed his taste, enlarged his understanding, and gave him the noblest ideas of man and government. The exercises of the body succeeded to those of the mind; and Alexander, who was tall, active, and robust, surpassed most of his equals in the gymnastic arts. Refreshed by the use of the bath and a slight dinner, he resumed, with new vigour, the business of the day; and, till the hour of supper, the principal meal of the Romans, he was attended by his secretaries, with whom he read and answered the multitude of letters, memorials, and petitions, that must have been addressed to the master of the greatest part of the world. His table was served with the most frugal simplicity; and whenever he was at liberty to consult his own inclination, the company

consisted of a few select friends, men of learning and virtue, amongst whom Ulpian was constantly invited. Their conversation was familiar and instructive; and the pauses were occasionally enlivened by the recital of some pleasing composition, which supplied the place of the dancers, comedians, and even gladiators, so frequently summoned to the tables of the rich and luxurious Romans.[70] The dress of Alexander was plain and modest, his demeanour courteous and affable: at the proper hours his palace was open to all his subjects, but the voice of a crier was heard, as in the Eleusinian mysteries, pronouncing the same salutary admonition; "Let none enter those holy walls, unless he is conscious of a pure and innocent mind."[71]

Such an uniform tenor of life, which left not a moment for vice or folly, is a better proof of the wisdom and justice of Alexander's government, than all the trifling details preserved in the compilation of Lampridius. Since the accession of Commodus, the Roman world had experienced, during a term of forty years, the successive and various vices of four tyrants. From the death of Elagabalus it enjoyed (A.D. 222-235) an auspicious calm of thirteen years. The provinces, relieved from the oppressive taxes invented by Caracalla and his pretended son, flourished in peace and prosperity, under the administration of magistrates, who were convinced by experience, that to deserve the love of the subjects was their best and only method of obtaining the favour of their sovereign. While some gentle restraints were imposed on the innocent luxury of the Roman people, the price of provisions, and the interest of money, were reduced, by the paternal care of Alexander, whose prudent liberality, without distressing the industrious, supplied the wants and amusements of the populace. The dignity, the freedom, the authority of the senate were restored; and every virtuous senator might approach the person of the emperor, without fear, and without a blush.

The name of Antoninus, ennobled by the virtues of Pius and Marcus, had been communicated by adoption to the dissolute Verus, and by descent to the cruel Commodus. It became the honourable appellation of the sons of Severus, was bestowed on young Diadumenianus, and at length prostituted to the infamy of the high priest of Emesa. Alexander, though pressed by the studied, and perhaps sincere, importunity of the senate, nobly refused the borrowed lustre of a name; whilst in his whole conduct he laboured to restore the glories and felicity of the age of the genuine Antonines.[72]

In the civil administration of Alexander, wisdom was enforced by power, and the people, sensible of the public felicity, repaid their benefactor with their love and gratitude. There still remained a greater, a more necessary, but a more difficult enterprise; the reformation of the military order, whose interest and temper, confirmed by long impunity, rendered them impatient of the restraints of discipline, and careless of the blessings of public tranquillity. In the execution of his design the emperor affected to display his love, and to conceal his fear, of the army. The most rigid economy in every other branch of the administration, supplied a fund of gold and silver for the ordinary pay and the extraordinary rewards of the troops. In their marches he relaxed the severe obligation of carrying seventeen days' provision on their shoulders. Ample magazines were formed along the public roads, and as soon as they entered the enemy's country, a numerous train of mules and camels waited on their haughty laziness. As Alexander despaired of correcting the luxury of his soldiers, he attempted, at least, to direct it to objects of martial pomp and ornament, fine horses, splendid armour, and shield enriched with silver and gold. He shared whatever fatigues he was obliged to impose, visited, in person, the sick and wounded, preserved an exact register of their services and his own gratitude, and expressed, on every occasion, the warmest regard for a body of men, whose welfare, as he affected to declare, was so closely connected with that of the state.[73] By the most gentle arts he laboured to inspire the fierce multitude with a sense of duty, and to restore at least a faint image of that discipline to which the Romans owed their empire over so many other nations, as warlike and more powerful than themselves. But his prudence was vain, his courage fatal, and the attempt towards a reformation served only to inflame the ills it was meant to cure.

The Prætorian guards were attached to the youth of Alexander. They loved him as a tender pupil, whom they had saved from a tyrant's fury, and placed on the Imperial throne. That amiable prince was sensible of the obligation; but as his gratitude was restrained within the limits of reason and justice, they soon were more dissatisfied with the virtues of Alexander, than they had ever been with the vices of Elagabalus. Their præfect, the wise Ulpian, was the friend of the laws and of the people; he was considered as the enemy of the soldiers, and to his pernicious counsels every scheme of reformation was imputed. Some trifling accident blew up their discontent into a furious mutiny; and a civil war raged, during three days, in Rome, whilst the life of that excellent minister was defended by the grateful people. Terrified, at length, by the sight of some houses in flames, and by the threats of a general conflagration, the people yielded with a sigh, and left the virtuous, but unfortunate, Ulpian to his fate. He was pursued into the Imperial palace, and massacred at the feet of his master, who vainly strove to cover him with the purple, and to obtain his pardon from the inexorable soldiers. Such was the deplorable weakness of government, that the emperor was unable to revenge his murdered friend and his insulted dignity, without stooping to the arts of patience and dissimulation. Epagathus, the principal leader of the mutiny, was removed from Rome, by the honourable employment of præfect of Egypt; from that high rank he was gently degraded to the government of Crete; and, when, at length, his popularity among the guards was effaced by time and absence, Alexander ventured to inflict the tardy, but deserved punishment of his crimes.[74] Under the reign of a just and virtuous prince, the tyranny of the army threatened with instant death his most faithful ministers, who were suspected of an intention to correct their intolerable disorders. The historian Dion Cassius had commanded the Pannonian legions with the spirit of ancient discipline. Their brethren of Rome, embracing the common cause of military licence, demanded the head of the reformer. Alexander, however, instead of yielding to their seditious clamours, showed a just sense of his merit and services, by appointing him his colleague in the consulship, and defraying from his own treasury the expense of that vain dignity: but as it was justly apprehended, that if the soldiers beheld him with the ensigns of his office, they would revenge the insult in his blood, the nominal first magistrate of the state retired, by the emperor's advice, from the city, and spent the greatest part of his consulship at his villas in Campania.[75]

The lenity of the emperor confirmed the insolence of the troops; the legions imitated the example of the guards, and defended their prerogative of licentiousness with the same furious obstinacy. The administration of Alexander was an unavailing struggle against the corruption of his age. In Illyricum, in Mauritania, in Armenia, in Mesopotamia, in Germany, fresh mutinies perpetually broke out; his officers were murdered, his authority was insulted, and his life at last sacrificed to the fierce discontents of the army.[76] One particular fact well deserves to be recorded, as it illustrates the manners of the troops, and exhibits a singular instance of their return to a sense of duty and obedience. Whilst the emperor lay at Antioch, in his Persian expedition, the particulars of which we shall hereafter relate, the punishment of some soldiers, who had been discovered in the baths of women, excited a sedition in the legion to which they belonged. Alexander ascended his tribunal, and with a modest firmness represented to the armed multitude the absolute necessity as well as his inflexible resolution of correcting the vices introduced by his impure predecessor, and of maintaining the discipline, which could not be relaxed without the ruin of the Roman name and empire. Their clamours interrupted his mild expostulation. "Reserve your shouts," said the undaunted emperor, "till you take the field against the Persians, the Germans, and the Sarmatians. Be silent in the presence of your sovereign and benefactor, who bestows upon you the corn, the clothing, and the money of the provinces; Be silent, or I shall no longer style you soldiers, but *citizens*,[77] if those indeed who disclaim the laws of Rome deserve to be ranked among the meanest of the people." His menaces inflamed the fury of the legion, and their brandished arms already threatened his person. "Your courage," resumed the intrepid Alexander, "would be more nobly displayed in the field of battle; *me* you may destroy, you cannot intimidate; and the severe justice of the republic would punish your crime, and revenge my death." The legion still persisted in clamorous sedition, when the emperor pronounced, with a loud voice, the decisive sentence, "*Citizens!* lay down your arms, and depart in peace to your respective habitations." The tempest was instantly appeased; the soldiers, filled with grief and shame, silently confessed the justice of their punishment and the power of discipline, yielded up their arms and military ensigns, and retired in confusion, not to their camp, but to the several inns of the city. Alexander enjoyed, during thirty days, the edifying spectacle of their repentance; nor did he restore them to their former rank in the army, till he had punished with death those tribunes whose connivance had occasioned the mutiny. The grateful legion served the emperor, whilst living, and revenged him when dead.[78]

The resolutions of the multitude generally depend on a moment; and the caprice of passion might equally determine the seditious legion to lay down their arms at the emperor's feet, or to plunge them into his breast. Perhaps, if the singular transaction had been investigated by the penetration of a philosopher, we should discover the secret causes which on that occasion authorised the boldness of the prince, and commanded the obedience of the troops; and perhaps, if it had been related by a judicious historian, we should find this action, worthy of Cæsar himself, reduced nearer to the level of probability and the common standard of the character of Alexander Severus. The abilities of that amiable prince seem to have been inadequate to the difficulties of his situation, the firmness of his conduct inferior to the purity of his intentions. His virtues, as well as the vices of Elagabalus, contracted a tincture of weakness and effeminacy from the soft climate of Syria, of which he was a native; though he blushed at his foreign origin, and listened with a vain complacency to the flattering genealogists, who derived his race from the ancient stock of Roman nobility.[79] The pride and avarice of his mother cast a shade on the glories of his reign; and by exacting from his riper years the same dutiful obedience which she had justly claimed from his inexperienced youth, Mamæa exposed to public ridicule, both her son's character and her own.[80] The fatigues of the Persian war irritated the military discontent; the unsuccessful event degraded the reputation of the emperor as a general, and even as a soldier. Every cause prepared, and every circumstance hastened, a revolution, which distracted the Roman empire with a long series of intestine calamities.

The dissolute tyranny of Commodus, the civil wars occasioned by his death, and the new maxims of policy introduced by the house of Severus, had all contributed to increase the dangerous power of the army, and to obliterate the faint image of laws and liberty that was still impressed on the minds of the Romans. This internal change, which undermined the foundations of the empire, we have endeavoured to explain with some degree of order and perspicuity. The personal characters of the emperors, their victories, laws, follies, and fortunes, can interest us no farther than as they are connected with the general history of the Decline and Fall of the monarchy. Our constant attention to that great object will not suffer us to overlook a most important edict of Antoninus Caracalla, which communicated to all the free inhabitants of the empire the name and privileges of Roman citizens. His unbounded liberality flowed not, however, from the sentiments of a generous mind; it was the sordid result of avarice, and will naturally be illustrated by some observations on the finances of that state, from the victorious ages of the commonwealth to the reign of Alexander Severus.

The siege of Veii in Tuscany, the first considerable enterprise of the Romans, was protracted to the tenth year, much less by the strength of the place than by the unskilfulness of the besiegers. The unaccustomed hardships of so many winter campaigns, at the distance of near twenty miles from home,[81] required more than common encouragements; and the senate wisely prevented the clamours of the people, by the institution of a regular pay for the soldiers, which was levied by a general tribute, assessed according to an equitable proportion on the property of the citizens.[82] During more than two hundred years after the conquest of Veii, the victories of the republic added less to the wealth than to the power of Rome. The states of Italy paid their tribute in military service only, and the vast force both by sea and land, which was exerted in the Punic wars, was maintained at the expense of the Romans themselves. That high-spirited people (such is often the generous enthusiasm of freedom) cheerfully submitted to the most excessive but voluntary burdens, in the just confidence that they should speedily enjoy the rich harvest of their labours. Their expectations were not disappointed. In the course of a few years, the riches of Syracuse, of Carthage, of Macedonia, and of Asia, were brought in triumph to Rome. The treasures of Perseus alone amounted to near two millions sterling, and the Roman people, the sovereign of so many nations, was for ever delivered from the weight of taxes.[83] The increasing revenue of the provinces was found sufficient to defray the ordinary establishment of war and government, and the superfluous mass of gold and silver was deposited in the temple of Saturn, and reserved for any unforeseen emergency of the state.[84]

History has never perhaps suffered a greater or more irreparable injury, than in the loss of the curious register bequeathed by Augustus to the senate, in which that experienced prince so accurately balanced the revenues and expenses of the Roman empire.[85] Deprived of this clear and comprehensive estimate, we are reduced to collect a few imperfect hints from such of the ancients as have accidentally turned aside from the splendid to the more useful parts of history. We are informed that, by the conquests of Pompey, the tributes of Asia were raised from fifty to one hundred and thirty-five millions of drachms; or about four millions and a half sterling.[86] Under the last and most indolent of the Ptolemies, the revenue of Egypt is said to have amounted to twelve thousand five hundred talents; a sum equivalent to more than two millions and a half of our money, but which was afterwards considerably improved by the more exact economy of the Romans, and the increase of the trade of Æthiopia and India.[87] Gaul was enriched by rapine, as Egypt was by commerce, and the tributes of those two great provinces have been compared as nearly equal to each other in value.[88] The ten thousand Euboic or Phœnician talents, about four millions sterling,[89] which vanquished Carthage was condemned to pay within the term of fifty years, were a slight acknowledgment of the superiority of Rome,[90] and cannot bear the least proportion with the taxes afterwards raised both on the lands and on the persons of the inhabitants, when the fertile coast of Africa was reduced into a province.[91]

Spain, by a very singular fatality, was the Peru and Mexico of the old world. The discovery of the rich western continent by the Phœnicians, and the oppression of the simple natives, who were compelled to labour in their own mines for the benefit of strangers, form an exact type of the more recent history of Spanish America.[92] The Phœnicians were acquainted only with the sea-coast of Spain; avarice, as well as ambition, carried the arms of Rome and Carthage into the heart of the country, and almost every part of the soil was found pregnant with copper, silver, and gold. Mention is made of a mine near Carthagena which yielded every day twenty-five thousand drachms of silver, or about three hundred thousand pounds a year.[93] Twenty thousand pound weight of gold was annually received from the provinces of Asturia, Gallicia, and Lusitania.[94]

We want both leisure and materials to pursue this curious inquiry through the many potent states that were annihilated in the Roman empire. Some notion, however, may be formed of the revenue of the provinces where considerable wealth had been deposited by nature, or collected by man, if we observe the severe attention that was directed to the abodes of solitude and sterility. Augustus once received a petition from the inhabitants of Gyarus, humbly praying that they might be relieved from one-third of their excessive impositions. Their whole tax amounted indeed to no more than one hundred and fifty drachms, or about five pounds; but Gyarus was a little island, or rather a rock, of the Ægean Sea, destitute of fresh water and every necessary of life, and inhabited only by a few wretched fishermen.[95]

From the faint glimmerings of such doubtful and scattered lights we should be inclined to believe, 1st, That (with every fair allowance for the difference of times and circumstances) the general income of the Roman provinces could seldom amount to less than fifteen or twenty millions of our money;[96] and, 2ndly, That so ample a revenue must have been fully adequate to all the expenses of the moderate government instituted by Augustus, whose court was the modest family of a private senator, and whose military establishment was calculated for the defence of the frontiers, without any aspiring views of conquest, or any serious apprehension of a foreign invasion.

Notwithstanding the seeming probability of both these conclusions, the latter of them at least is positively disowned by the language and conduct of Augustus. It is not easy to determine whether, on this occasion, he acted as the common father of the Roman world, or as the oppressor of liberty; whether he wished to relieve the provinces, or to impoverish the senate and the equestrian order. But no sooner had he assumed the reins of government than he frequently intimated the insufficiency of the tributes, and the necessity of throwing an equitable proportion of the public burden upon Rome and Italy. In the prosecution of this unpopular design, he advanced, however, by cautious and well-weighed steps. The introduction of customs was followed by the establishment of an excise, and the scheme of taxation was completed by an artful assessment on the real and personal property of the Roman citizens, who had been exempted from any kind of contribution above a century and a half.

I. In a great empire like that of Rome, a natural balance of money must have gradually established itself. It has been already observed, that as the wealth of the provinces was attracted to the capital by the strong hand of conquest and power, so a considerable part of it was restored to the industrious provinces by the gentle influence of commerce and arts. In the reign of Augustus and his successors, duties were imposed on every kind of merchandise, which through a thousand channels flowed to the great centre of opulence and luxury; and in whatsoever manner the law was expressed, it was the Roman purchaser, and not the provincial merchant, who paid the tax.[97] The rate of the customs varied from the eighth to the fortieth part of the value of the commodity; and

we have a right to suppose that the variation was directed by the unalterable maxims of policy: that a higher duty was fixed on the articles of luxury than on those of necessity, and that the productions raised or manufactured by the labour of the subjects of the empire were treated with more indulgence than was shown to the pernicious, or at least the unpopular, commerce of Arabia and India.[98] There is still extant a long but imperfect catalogue of eastern commodities, which about the time of Alexander Severus were subject to the payment of duties; cinnamon, myrrh, pepper, ginger, and the whole tribe of aromatics, a great variety of precious stones, among which the diamond was the most remarkable for its price, and the emerald for its beauty,[99] Parthian and Babylonian leather, cottons, silks, both raw and manufactured, ebony, ivory, and eunuchs.[100] We may observe that the use and value of those effeminate slaves gradually rose with the decline of the empire.

II. The excise, introduced by Augustus after the civil wars, was extremely moderate, but it was general. It seldom exceeded one per cent.; but it comprehended whatever was sold in the markets or by public auction, from the most considerable purchases of lands and houses to those minute objects which can only derive a value from their infinite multitude and daily consumption. Such a tax, as it affects the body of the people, has ever been the occasion of clamour and discontent. An emperor well acquainted with the wants and resources of the state, was obliged to declare by a public edict that the support of the army depended in a great measure on the produce of the excise.[101]

III. When Augustus resolved to establish a permanent military force for the defence of his government against foreign and domestic enemies, he instituted a peculiar treasury for the pay of the soldiers, the rewards of the veterans, and the extraordinary expenses of war. The ample revenue of the excise, though peculiarly appropriated to those uses, was found inadequate. To supply the deficiency, the emperor suggested a new tax of five per cent. on all legacies and inheritances. But the nobles of Rome were more tenacious of property than of freedom. Their indignant murmurs were received by Augustus with his usual temper. He candidly referred the whole business to the senate, and exhorted them to provide for the public service by some other expedient of a less odious nature. They were divided and perplexed. He insinuated to them that their obstinacy would oblige him to *propose* a general land-tax and capitation. They acquiesced in silence.[102] The new imposition on legacies and inheritances was however mitigated by some restrictions. It did not take place unless the object was of a certain value, most probably of fifty or an hundred pieces of gold,[103] nor could it be exacted from the nearest of kin on the father's side.[104] When the rights of nature and poverty were thus secured, it seemed reasonable that a stranger, or a distant relation, who acquired an unexpected accession of fortune, should cheerfully resign a twentieth part of it for the benefit of the state.[105]

Such a tax, plentiful as it must prove in every wealthy community, was most happily suited to the situation of the Romans, who could frame their arbitrary wills, according to the dictates of reason or caprice, without any restraint from the modern fetters of entails and settlements. From various causes the partiality of paternal affection often lost its influence over the stern patriots of the commonwealth and the dissolute nobles of the empire; and if the father bequeathed to his son the fourth part of his estate, he removed all ground of legal complaint.[106] But a rich childless old man was a domestic tyrant, and his power increased with his years and infirmities. A servile crowd, in which he frequently reckoned prætors and consuls, courted his smiles, pampered his avarice, applauded his follies, served his passions, and waited with impatience for his death. The arts of attendance and flattery were formed into a most lucrative science; those who professed it acquired a peculiar appellation; and the whole city, according to the lively descriptions of satire, was divided between two parties, the hunters and their game.[107] Yet, while so many unjust and extravagant wills were every day dictated by cunning, and subscribed by folly, a few were the result of rational esteem and virtuous gratitude. Cicero, who had so often defended the lives and fortunes of his fellow-citizens, was rewarded with legacies to the amount of an hundred and seventy thousand pounds;[108] nor do the friends of the younger Pliny seem to have been less generous to that amiable orator.[109] Whatever was the motive of the testator, the treasury claimed, without distinction, the twentieth part of his estate; and in the course of two or three generations, the whole property of the subject must have gradually passed through the coffers of the state.

In the first and golden years of the reign of Nero, that prince, from a desire of popularity, and perhaps from a blind impulse of benevolence, conceived a wish of abolishing the oppression of the customs and excise. The wisest senators applauded his magnanimity; but they diverted him from the execution of a design, which would have dissolved the strength and resources of the republic.[110] Had it indeed been possible to realise this dream of fancy, such princes as Trajan and the Antonines would surely have embraced with ardour the glorious opportunity of conferring so signal an obligation on mankind. Satisfied, however, with alleviating the public burden, they attempted not to remove it. The mildness and precision of their laws ascertained the rule and measure of taxation, and protected the subject of every rank against arbitrary interpretations, antiquated claims, and the insolent vexation of the farmers of the revenue.[111] For it is somewhat singular that, in every age, the best and wisest of the Roman governors persevered in this pernicious method of collecting the principal branches at least of the excise and customs.[112]

The sentiments, and, indeed, the situation of Caracalla, were very different from those of the Antonines. Inattentive, or rather averse, to the welfare of his people, he found himself under the necessity of gratifying the insatiate avarice which he had excited in the army. Of the several impositions introduced by Augustus, the twentieth on inheritances and legacies was the most fruitful, as well as the most comprehensive. As its influence was not confined to Rome or Italy, the produce continually increased with the gradual extension of the ROMAN CITY. The new citizens, though charged, on equal terms,[113] with the payment of new taxes, which had not affected them as subjects, derived an ample compensation from the rank they obtained, the privileges they acquired, and the fair prospect of honours and fortune that was thrown open to their ambition. But the favour which implied a distinction, was lost in the prodigality of Caracalla, and the reluctant provincials were compelled to assume the vain title, and the real obligations, of Roman citizens. Nor was the rapacious son of Severus contented with such a measure of taxation, as had appeared sufficient to his moderate predecessors. Instead of a twentieth, he exacted a tenth of all legacies and inheritances; and during his reign (for the ancient proportion was restored after his death) he crushed alike every part of the empire under the weight of his iron sceptre.[114]

When all the provincials became liable to the peculiar impositions of Roman citizens, they seemed to acquire a legal exemption from the tributes which they had paid in their former condition of subjects. Such were not the maxims of government adopted by Caracalla and his pretended son. The old as well as the new taxes were, at the same time, levied in the provinces. It was reserved for the virtue of Alexander to relieve them in a great measure from this intolerable grievance, by reducing the tributes to a thirtieth part of the sum exacted at the time of his accession.[115] It is impossible to conjecture the motive that engaged him to spare so trifling a remnant of the public evil; but the noxious weed, which had not been totally eradicated, again sprang up with the most luxuriant growth, and in the succeeding age darkened the Roman world with its deadly shade. In the course of this history, we shall be too often summoned to explain the land-tax, the capitation, and the heavy contributions of corn, wine, oil, and meat, which were exacted from the provinces for the use of the court, the army, and the capital.

As long as Rome and Italy were respected as the centre of government, a national spirit was preserved by the ancient, and insensibly imbibed by the adopted, citizens. The principal commands of the army were filled by men who had received a liberal education, were well instructed in the advantages of laws and letters, and who had risen, by equal steps, through the regular succession of civil and military honours.[116] To their influence and example we may partly ascribe the modest obedience of the legions during the two first centuries of the Imperial history.

But when the last enclosure of the Roman constitution was trampled down by Caracalla, the separation of professions gradually succeeded to the distinction of ranks. The more polished citizens of the internal provinces were alone qualified to act as lawyers and magistrates. The rougher trade of arms was abandoned to the peasants and barbarians of the frontiers, who knew no country but their camp, no science but that of war, no civil laws, and scarcely those of military discipline. With bloody hands, savage manners, and desperate resolutions, they sometimes guarded, but much oftener subverted, the throne of the emperors.

CHAPTER VII

The Elevation and Tyranny of Maximin. Rebellion in Africa and Italy under the Authority of the Senate. Civil Wars and Seditions. Violent Deaths of Maximin and his Son, of Maximus and Balbinus, and of the three Gordians. Usurpation and Secular Games of Philip.

OF the various forms of government which have prevailed in the world, an hereditary monarchy seems to present the fairest scope for ridicule. Is it possible to relate, without an indignant smile, that, on the father's decease, the property of a nation, like that of a drove of oxen, descends to his infant son, as yet unknown to mankind and to himself; and that the bravest warriors and the wisest statesmen, relinquishing their natural right to empire, approach the royal cradle with bended knees and protestations of inviolable fidelity? Satire and declamation may paint these obvious topics in the most dazzling colours, but our more serious thoughts will respect a useful prejudice, that establishes a rule of succession, independent of the passions of mankind; and we shall cheerfully acquiesce in any expedient which deprives the multitude of the dangerous, and indeed the ideal, power of giving themselves a master.

In the cool shade of retirement, we may easily devise imaginary forms of government, in which the sceptre shall be constantly bestowed on the most worthy, by the free and incorrupt suffrage of the whole community. Experience overturns these airy fabrics, and teaches us that, in a large society, the election of a monarch can never devolve to the wisest, or to the most numerous, part of the people. The army is the only order of men sufficiently united to concur in the same sentiments, and powerful enough to impose them on the rest of their fellow-citizens: but the temper of soldiers, habituated at once to violence and to slavery, renders them very unfit guardians of a legal, or even a civil, constitution. Justice, humanity, or political wisdom, are qualities they are too little acquainted with in themselves, to appreciate them in others. Valour will acquire their esteem, and liberality will purchase their suffrage; but the first of these merits is often lodged in the most savage breasts; the latter can only exert itself at the expense of the public; and both may be turned against the possessor of the throne, by the ambition of a daring rival.

The superior prerogative of birth, when it has obtained the sanction of time and popular opinion, is the plainest and least invidious of all distinctions among mankind. The acknowledged right extinguishes the hopes of faction, and the conscious security disarms the cruelty of the monarch. To the firm establishment of this idea, we owe the peaceful succession, and mild administration, of European monarchies. To the defect of it, we must attribute the frequent civil wars, through which an Asiatic despot is obliged to cut his way to the throne of his fathers. Yet, even in the East, the sphere of contention is usually limited to the princes of the reigning house, and as soon as the more fortunate competitor has removed his brethren, by the sword and the bow-string, he no longer entertains any jealousy of his meaner subjects. But the Roman empire, after the authority of the senate had sunk into contempt, was a vast scene of confusion. The royal, and even noble, families of the provinces, had long since been led in triumph before the car of the haughty republicans. The ancient families of Rome had successively fallen beneath the tyranny of the Cæsars; and whilst those princes were shackled by the forms of a commonwealth, and disappointed by the repeated failure of their posterity,[1] it was impossible that any idea of hereditary succession should have taken root in the minds of their subjects. The right to the throne, which none could claim from birth, every one assumed from merit. The daring hopes of ambition were set loose from the salutary restraints of law and prejudice; and the meanest of mankind might, without folly, entertain a hope of being raised by valour and fortune to a rank in the army, in which a single crime would enable him to wrest the sceptre of the world from his feeble and unpopular master. After the murder of Alexander Severus, and the elevation of Maximin, no emperor could think himself safe upon the throne, and every barbarian peasant of the frontier might aspire to that august, but dangerous station.

About thirty-two years before that event, the emperor Severus, returning from an eastern expedition, halted in Thrace, to celebrate, with military games, the birthday of his younger son, Geta. The country flocked in crowds to behold their sovereign, and a young barbarian of gigantic stature earnestly solicited, in his rude dialect, that he might be allowed to contend for the prize of wrestling. As the pride of discipline would have been disgraced in the overthrow of a Roman soldier by a Thracian peasant, he was matched with the stoutest followers of the camp, sixteen of whom he successively laid on the ground. His victory was rewarded by some trifling gifts, and a permission to enlist in the troops. The next day, the happy barbarian was distinguished above a crowd of recruits, dancing and exulting after the fashion of his country. As soon as he perceived that he had attracted the emperor's notice, he instantly ran up to his horse, and followed him on foot, without the least appearance of fatigue, in a long and rapid career. "Thracian," said Severus, with astonishment, "art thou disposed to wrestle after thy race?" Most willingly, Sir, replied the unwearied youth, and, almost in a breath, overthrew seven of the strongest soldiers in the army. A gold collar was the prize of his matchless vigour and activity, and he was immediately appointed to serve in the horse-guards who always attended on the person of the sovereign.[2]

Maximin, for that was his name, though born on the territories of the empire, descended from a mixed race of barbarians. His father was a Goth, and his mother of the nation of the Alani. He displayed, on every occasion, a valour equal to his strength; and his native fierceness was soon tempered or disguised by the knowledge of the world. Under the reign of Severus and his son, he obtained the rank of centurion, with the favour and esteem of both those princes, the former of whom was an excellent judge of merit. Gratitude forbade Maximin to serve under the assassin of Caracalla. Honour taught him to decline the effeminate insults of Elagabalus. On the accession of Alexander he returned to court, and was placed by that prince in a station useful to the service and honourable to himself. The fourth legion, to which he was appointed tribune, soon became, under his care, the best disciplined of the whole army. With the general applause of the soldiers, who bestowed on their favourite hero the names of Ajax and Hercules, he was successively promoted to the first military command;[3] and had not he still retained too much of his savage origin, the emperor might perhaps have given his own sister in marriage to the son of Maximin.[4]

Instead of securing his fidelity, these favours served only to inflame the ambition of the Thracian peasant, who deemed his fortune inadequate to his merit, as long as he was constrained to acknowledge a superior. Though a stranger to real wisdom, he was not devoid of a selfish cunning, which showed him that the emperor had lost the affection of the army, and taught him to improve their discontent to his own advantage. It is easy for faction and calumny to shed their poison on the administration of the best of princes, and to accuse even their virtues, by artfully confounding them with those vices to which they bear the nearest affinity. The troops listened with pleasure to the emissaries of Maximin. They blushed at their own ignominious patience, which, during thirteen years, had supported the vexatious discipline imposed by an effeminate Syrian, the timid slave of his mother and of the senate. It was time, they cried, to cast away that useless phantom of the civil power, and to elect for their prince and general a real soldier, educated in camps, exercised in war, who would assert the glory, and distribute among his companions the treasures, of the empire. A great army was at that time assembled on the banks of the Rhine, under the command of the emperor himself, who, almost immediately after his return from the Persian war, had been obliged to march against the barbarians of Germany. The important care of training and reviewing the new levies was intrusted to Maximin. One day (A.D. 235, March 19), as he entered the field of exercise the troops, either from a sudden impulse or a formed conspiracy, saluted him emperor, silenced by their loud acclamations his obstinate refusal, and hastened to consummate their rebellion by the murder of Alexander Severus.

The circumstances of his death are variously related. The writers, who supposed that he died in ignorance of the ingratitude and ambition of Maximin, affirm that, after taking a frugal repast in the sight of the army, he retired to sleep, and that, about the seventh hour of the day, a part of his own guards broke into the imperial tent, and with many wounds assassinated their virtuous and unsuspecting prince.[5] If we credit another, and indeed a more probable account, Maximin was invested with the purple by a numerous detachment, at the distance of several miles from the head-quarters; and he trusted for success rather to the secret wishes than to the public declarations of the great army. Alexander had sufficient time to awaken a faint sense of loyalty among his troops; but their reluctant professions of fidelity quickly vanished on the appearance of Maximin, who declared himself the friend and advocate of the military order, and was unanimously acknowledged emperor of the Romans by the applauding legions. The son of Mamæa, betrayed and deserted, withdrew into his tent, desirous at least to conceal his approaching fate from the insults of the multitude. He was soon followed by a tribune and some centurions, the ministers of death; but, instead of receiving with manly resolution the inevitable stroke, his unavailing cries and entreaties disgraced the last moments of his life, and converted into contempt some portion of the just pity which his innocence and misfortunes must inspire. His mother Mamæa, whose pride and avarice he loudly accused as the cause of his ruin, perished with her son. The most faithful of his friends were sacrificed to the first fury of the soldiers. Others were reserved for the more deliberate cruelty of the usurper; and those who experienced the mildest treatment, were stripped of their employments, and ignominiously driven from the court and army.[6]

The former tyrants, Caligula and Nero, Commodus and Caracalla, were all dissolute and inexperienced youths,[7] educated in the purple, and corrupted by the pride of empire, the luxury of Rome, and the perfidious voice of flattery. The cruelty of Maximin was derived from a different source, the fear of contempt. Though he depended on the attachment of the soldiers, who loved him for virtues like their own, he was conscious that his mean and barbarian origin, his savage appearance, and his total ignorance of the arts and institutions of civil life,[8] formed a very unfavourable contrast with the amiable manners of the unhappy Alexander. He remembered that, in his humbler fortune, he had often waited before the door of the haughty nobles of Rome, and had been denied admittance by the insolence of their slaves. He recollected, too, the friendship of a few who had relieved his poverty, and assisted his rising hopes. But those who had spurned, and those who had protected the Thracian, were guilty of the same crime, the knowledge of his original obscurity. For this crime many were put to death; and by the execution of several of his benefactors, Maximin published, in characters of blood, the indelible history of his baseness and ingratitude.[9]

The dark and sanguinary soul of the tyrant was open to every suspicion against those among his subjects who were the most distinguished by their birth or merit. Whenever he was alarmed with the sound of treason, his cruelty was unbounded and unrelenting. A conspiracy against his life was either discovered or imagined, and Magnus, a consular senator, was named as the principal author of it. Without a witness, without a trial, and without an opportunity of defence, Magnus, with four thousand of his supposed accomplices, was put to death. Italy and the whole empire were infested with innumerable spies and informers. On the slightest accusation, the first of the Roman nobles, who had governed provinces, commanded armies, and been adorned with the consular and triumphal ornaments, were chained on the public carriages, and hurried away to the emperor's presence. Confiscation, exile, or simple death, were esteemed uncommon instances of his lenity. Some of the unfortunate sufferers he ordered to be sewed up in the hides of slaughtered animals, others to be exposed to wild beasts, others again to be beaten to death with clubs. During the three years of his reign, he disdained to visit either Rome or Italy. His camp, occasionally removed from the banks of the Rhine to those of the Danube, was the seat of his stern despotism, which trampled on every principle of law and justice, and was supported by the avowed power of the sword.[10] No man of noble birth, elegant accomplishments, or knowledge of civil business, was suffered near his person; and the court of a Roman emperor revived the idea of those ancient chiefs of slaves and gladiators, whose savage power had left a deep impression of terror and detestation.[11]

As long as the cruelty of Maximin was confined to the illustrious senators, or even to the bold adventurers, who in the court or army expose themselves to the caprice of fortune, the body of the people viewed their sufferings with indifference, or perhaps with pleasure. But the tyrant's avarice, stimulated by the insatiate desires of the soldiers, at length attacked the public property. Every city of the empire was possessed of an independent revenue, destined to purchase corn for the multitude, and to supply the expenses of the games and entertainments. By a single act of authority, the whole mass of wealth was at once confiscated for the use of the Imperial treasury. The temples were stripped of their most valuable offerings of gold and silver, and the statues of gods, heroes, and emperors, were melted down and coined into money. These impious orders could not be executed without tumults and massacres, as in many places the people chose rather to die in the defence of their altars, than to behold in the midst of peace their cities exposed to the rapine and cruelty of war. The soldiers themselves, among whom this sacrilegious plunder was distributed, received it with a blush; and, hardened as they were in acts of violence, they dreaded the just reproaches of their friends and relations. Through-

out the Roman world a general cry of indignation was heard, imploring vengeance on the common enemy of human kind; and at length, by an act of private oppression, a peaceful and unarmed province was driven into rebellion against him.[12]

The procurator of Africa was a servant worthy of such a master, who considered the fines and confiscations of the rich as one of the most fruitful branches of the Imperial revenue. An iniquitous sentence had been (A.D. 237, April) pronounced against some opulent youths of that country, the execution of which would have stripped them of far the greater part of their patrimony. In this extremity, a resolution that must either complete or prevent their ruin, was dictated by despair. A respite of three days, obtained with difficulty from the rapacious treasurer, was employed in collecting from their estates a great number of slaves and peasants, blindly devoted to the commands of their lords, and armed with the rustic weapons of clubs and axes. The leaders of the conspiracy, as they were admitted to the audience of the procurator, stabbed him with the daggers concealed under their garments, and, by the assistance of their tumultuary train, seized on the little town of Thysdrus,[13] and erected the standard of rebellion against the sovereign of the Roman empire. They rested their hopes on the hatred of mankind against Maximin, and they judiciously resolved to oppose to that detested tyrant an emperor whose mild virtues had already acquired the love and esteem of the Romans, and whose authority over the province would give weight and stability to the enterprise. Gordianus, their proconsul, and the object of their choice, refused, with unfeigned reluctance, the dangerous honour, and begged with tears that they would suffer him to terminate in peace a long and innocent life, without staining his feeble age with civil blood. Their menaces compelled him to accept the Imperial purple, his only refuge indeed against the jealous cruelty of Maximin; since, according to the reasoning of tyrants, those who have been esteemed worthy of the throne deserve death, and those who deliberate have already rebelled.[14]

The family of Gordianus was one of the most illustrious of the Roman senate. On the father's side, he was descended from the Gracchi; on his mother's, from the emperor Trajan. A great estate enabled him to support the dignity of this birth, and, in the enjoyment of it, he displayed an elegant taste and beneficent disposition. The palace in Rome, formerly inhabited by the great

Pompey, had been, during several generations, in the possession of Gordian's family.[15] It was distinguished by ancient trophies of naval victories, and decorated with the works of modern painting. His villa on the road to Præneste was celebrated for baths of singular beauty and extent, for three stately rooms of an hundred feet in length, and for a magnificent portico, supported by two hundred columns of the four most curious and costly sorts of marble.[16] The public shows exhibited at his expense, and in which the people were entertained with many hundreds of wild beasts and gladiators,[17] seem to surpass the fortune of a subject; and whilst the liberality of other magistrates was confined to a few solemn festivals in Rome, the magnificence of Gordian was repeated, when he was ædile, every month in the year, and extended, during his consulship, to the principal cities of Italy. He was twice elevated to the last-mentioned dignity, by Caracalla and by Alexander; for he possessed the uncommon talent of acquiring the esteem of virtuous princes, without alarming the jealousy of tyrants. His long life was innocently spent in the study of letters and the peaceful honours of Rome; and, till he was named proconsul of Africa by the voice of the senate and the approbation of Alexander,[18] he appears prudently to have declined the command of armies and the government of provinces. As long as that emperor lived, Africa was happy under the administration of his worthy representative; after the barbarous Maximin had usurped the throne, Gordianus alleviated the miseries which he was unable to prevent. When he reluctantly accepted the purple, he was above fourscore years old; a last and valuable remains of the happy age of the Antonines, whose virtues he revived in his own conduct and celebrated in an elegant poem of thirty books. With the venerable proconsul, his son, who had accompanied him into Africa as his lieutenant, was likewise declared emperor. His manners were less pure, but his character was equally amiable with that of his father. Twenty-two acknowledged concubines, and a library of sixty-two thousand volumes, attested the variety of his inclinations, and from the productions which he left behind him, it appears that the former as well as the latter were designed for use rather than ostentation.[19] The Roman people acknowledged in the features of the younger Gordian the resemblance of Scipio Africanus, recollected with pleasure that his mother was the grand-daughter of Antoninus Pius, and rested the public hope on those latent virtues which had hitherto, as they fondly imagined, lain concealed in the luxurious indolence of a private life.

As soon as the Gordians had appeased the first tumult of a popular election, they removed their court to Carthage. They were received with the acclamations of the Africans, who honoured their virtues, and who, since the visit of Hadrian, had never beheld the majesty of a Roman emperor. But these vain acclamations neither strengthened nor confirmed the title of the Gordians. They were induced by principle, as well as interest, to solicit the approbation of the senate; and a deputation of the noblest provincials was sent, without delay, to Rome, to relate and justify the conduct of their countrymen, who, having long suffered with patience, were at length resolved to act with vigour. The letters of the new princes were modest and respectful, excusing the necessity which had obliged them to accept the Imperial title; but submitting their election and their fate to the supreme judgment of the senate.[20]

The inclinations of the senate were neither doubtful nor divided. The birth and noble alliances of the Gordians had intimately connected them with the most illustrious houses of Rome. Their fortune had created many dependents in that assembly, their merit had acquired many friends. Their mild administration opened the flattering prospect of the restoration not only of the civil but even of the republican government. The terror of military violence, which had first obliged the senate to forget the murder of Alexander, and to ratify the election of a barbarian peasant,[21] now produced a contrary effect, and provoked them to assert the injured rights of freedom and humanity. The hatred of Maximin towards the senate was declared and implacable; the tamest submission had not appeased his fury, the most cautious innocence would not remove his suspicions; and even the care of their own safety urged them to share the fortune of an enterprise, of which (if unsuccessful) they were sure to be the first victims. These considerations, and perhaps others of a more private nature, were debated in a previous conference of the consuls and the magistrates. As soon as their resolution was decided, they convoked in the temple of Castor the whole body of the senate, according to an ancient form of secrecy,[22] calculated to awaken their attention, and to conceal their decrees. "Conscript fathers," said the consul Syllanus, "the two Gordians, both of consular dignity, the one your proconsul, the other your lieutenant, have been declared emperors by the general consent of Africa. Let us return thanks," he boldly continued, "to the youth of Thysdrus; let us return thanks to the faithful people of Carthage, our generous deliverers from an horrid monster—Why do you hear me thus coolly, thus timidly? Why do you cast those anxious looks on each other? Why hesitate? Maximin is a public enemy! May his enmity soon expire with him, and may we long enjoy the prudence and felicity of Gordian the father, the valour and constancy of Gordian the son!"[23] The noble ardour of the consul revived the languid spirit of the senate. By an unanimous decree the election of the Gordians was ratified, Maximin, his son, and his adherents, were pronounced enemies of their country, and liberal rewards were offered to whomsoever had the courage and good fortune to destroy them.

During the emperor's absence, a detachment of the Prætorian guards remained at Rome, to protect, or rather to command, the capital. The Præfect Vitalianus had signalised his fidelity to Maximin, by the alacrity with which he had obeyed, and even prevented, the cruel mandates of the tyrant. His death alone could rescue the authority of the senate, and the lives of the senators, from a state of danger and suspense. Before their resolves had transpired, a quæstor and some tribunes were commissioned to take his devoted life. They executed the order with equal boldness and success; and, with their bloody daggers in their hands, ran through the streets proclaiming to the people and the soldiers the news of the happy revolution. The enthusiasm of liberty was seconded by the promise of a large donative, in lands and money; the statues of Maximin were thrown down; the capital of the empire acknowledged, with transport, the authority of the two Gordians and the senate,[24] and the example of Rome was followed by the rest of Italy.

A new spirit had arisen in that assembly, whose long patience had been insulted by wanton despotism and military licence. The senate assumed the reins of government, and, with a calm intrepidity, prepared to vindicate by arms the cause of freedom. Among the consular senators recommended by their merit and services to the favour of the emperor Alexander, it was easy to select twenty, not unequal to the command of an army, and the conduct of a war. To these was the defence of Italy intrusted. Each was appointed to act in his respective department, authorised to enrol and discipline the Italian youth; and instructed to fortify the ports and highways against the impending invasion of Maximin. A number of deputies, chosen from the most illustrious of the senatorian and equestrian orders, were dispatched at the same time to the governors of the several provinces, earnestly conjuring them to fly to the assistance of their country, and to remind the nations of their ancient ties of friendship with the Roman senate and people. The general respect with which these deputies were received, and the zeal of Italy and the provinces in favour of the senate, sufficiently prove that the subjects of Maximin were reduced to that uncommon distress, in which the body of the people has more to fear from oppression than from resistance. The consciousness of that melancholy truth inspires a degree of persevering fury seldom to be found in those civil wars which are artificially supported for the benefit of a few factious and designing leaders.[25]

For while the cause of the Gordians was embraced with such diffusive ardour, the Gordians themselves (A.D. 237, 3rd July) were no more. The feeble court of Carthage was alarmed with the rapid approach of Capelianus, governor of Mauritania, who, with a small band of veterans, and a fierce host of barbarians, attacked a faithful but unwarlike province. The younger Gordian sallied out to meet the enemy at the head of a few guards, and a numerous undisciplined multitude, educated in the peaceful luxury of Carthage. His useless valour served only to procure him an honourable death, in the field of battle. His aged father, whose reign had not exceeded thirty-six days, put an end to his life on the first news of the defeat. Carthage, destitute of defence, opened her gates to the conqueror, and Africa was exposed to the rapacious cruelty of a slave, obliged to satisfy his unrelenting master with a large account of blood and treasure.[26]

The fate of the Gordians filled Rome with just, but unexpected terror. The senate convoked in the temple of Concord, affected to transact the common business of the day; and seemed to decline, with trembling anxiety, the consideration of their own and the public danger. A silent consternation prevailed on the assembly, till a senator, of the name and family of Trajan, awakened his brethren from their fatal lethargy. He represented to them, that the choice of cautious dilatory measures had been long since out of their power; that Maximin, implacable by nature, and exasperated by injuries, was advancing towards Italy, at the head of the military force of the empire; and that their only remaining alternative was either to meet him bravely in the field, or tamely to expect the tortures and ignominious death reserved for unsuccessful rebellion. "We have lost," continued he, "two excellent princes; but unless we desert ourselves, the hopes of the republic have not perished with the Gordians. Many are the senators whose virtues have deserved, and whose abilities would sustain, the Imperial dignity. Let us elect two emperors, one of whom may conduct the war against the public enemy, whilst his colleague remains at Rome to direct the civil administration. I cheerfully expose myself to the danger and envy of the nomination, and give my vote in favour of Maximus and Balbinus. Ratify my choice, conscript fathers, or appoint, in their place, others more worthy of the empire." The general apprehension silenced the whispers of jealousy; the merit of the candidates was universally acknowledged; and the house resounded with the sincere acclamations, of "long life and victory to the emperors Maximus and Balbinus. You are happy in the judgment of the senate; may the republic be happy under your administration!"[27]

The virtues and the reputation of the new emperors justified the most sanguine hopes of the Romans. The various nature of their talents seemed to appropriate to each his peculiar department of peace and war, without leaving room for jealous emulation. Balbinus was an admired orator, a poet of distinguished fame, and a wise magistrate, who had exercised with innocence and applause the civil jurisdiction in almost all the interior provinces of the empire. His birth was noble,[28] his fortune affluent, his manners liberal and affable. In him the love of pleasure was corrected by a sense of dignity, nor had the habits of ease deprived him of a capacity for business. The mind of Maximus was formed in a rougher mould. By his valour and abilities he had raised himself from the meanest origin to the first employments of the state and army. His victories over the Sarmatians and the Germans, the austerity of his life, and the rigid impartiality of his justice, whilst he was Præfect of the city, commanded the esteem of a people, whose affections were engaged in favour of the more amiable Balbinus. The two colleagues had both been consuls (Balbinus had twice enjoyed that honourable office), both had been named among the twenty lieutenants of the senate; and since the one was sixty and the other seventy-four years old,[29] they had both attained the full maturity of age and experience.

After the senate had conferred on Maximus and Balbinus an equal portion of the consular and tribunitian powers, the title of Fathers of their country, and the joint office of Supreme Pontiff, they ascended to the Capitol, to return thanks to the gods, protectors of Rome.[30] The solemn rites of sacrifice were disturbed by a sedition of the people. The licentious multitude neither loved the rigid Maximus, nor did they sufficiently fear the mild and humane Balbinus. Their increasing numbers surrounded the temple of Jupiter; with obstinate clamours they asserted their inherent right of consenting to the election of their sovereign; and demanded, with an apparent moderation, that, besides the two emperors chosen by the senate, a third should be added of the family of the Gordians, as a just return of gratitude to those princes who had sacrificed their lives for the republic. At the head of the city-guards, and the youth of the equestrian order, Maximus and Balbinus attempted to cut their way through the seditious multitude. The multitude, armed with sticks and stones, drove them back into the Capitol. It is prudent to yield when the contest, whatever may be the issue of it, must be fatal to both parties. A boy, only thirteen years of age, the grandson of the elder, and nephew of the younger, Gordian, was produced to the people, invested with the ornaments and title of Cæsar. The tumult was appeased by this easy condescension; and the two emperors, as soon as they had been peaceably acknowledged in Rome, prepared to defend Italy against the common enemy.

Whilst in Rome and Africa revolutions succeeded each other with such amazing rapidity, the mind of Maximin was agitated by the most furious passions. He is said to have received the news of the rebellion of the Gordians, and of the decree of the senate against him, not with the temper of a man, but the rage of a wild beast; which, as it could not discharge itself on the distant senate, threatened the life of his son, of his friends, and of all who ventured to approach his person. The grateful intelligence of the death of the Gordians was quickly followed by the assurance that the senate, laying aside all hopes of pardon or accommodation, had substituted in their room two emperors, with whose merit he could not be unacquainted. Revenge was the only consolation left to Maximin, and revenge could only be obtained by arms. The strength of the legions had been assembled by Alexander from all parts of the empire. Three successful campaigns against the Germans and the Sarmatians had raised their fame, confirmed their discipline, and even increased their numbers, by filling the ranks with the flower of the barbarian youth. The life of Maximin had been spent in war, and the candid severity of history cannot refuse him the valour of a soldier, or even the abilities of an experienced general.[31] It might naturally be expected that a prince of such a character, instead of suffering the rebellion to gain stability by delay, should immediately have marched from the banks of the Danube to those of the Tiber, and that his victorious army, instigated by contempt for the senate, and eager to gather the spoils of Italy, should have burned with impatience to finish the easy and lucrative conquest. Yet as far as we can trust to the obscure chronology of that period,[32] it appears that the operations of some foreign war deferred the Italian expedition till the ensuing spring. From the prudent conduct of Maximin, we may learn that the savage features of his character have been exaggerated by the pencil of party, that his passions, however impetuous, submitted to the force of reason, and that the barbarian possessed something of the generous spirit of Sylla, who subdued the enemies of Rome before he suffered himself to revenge his private injuries.[33]

When the troops of Maximin, advancing in excellent order, arrived at the foot of the Julian Alps, they were terrified by the silence and desolation that reigned on the frontiers of Italy. The villages and open towns had been abandoned on their approach by the inhabitants, the cattle was driven away, the provisions removed, or destroyed, the bridges broke down, nor was anything left which could afford either shelter or give subsistence to an invader. Such had been the wise orders of the generals of the senate, whose design was to protract the war, to ruin the army of Maximin by the slow operation of famine, and to consume his strength in the sieges of the principal cities of Italy, which they had plentifully stored with men and provisions from the deserted country. Aquileia received and withstood the first shock of the invasion. The streams that issue from the head of the Hadriatic gulf, swelled by the melting of the winter snows,[34] opposed an unexpected obstacle to the arms of Maximin. At length, on a singular bridge, constructed with art and difficulty of large hogsheads, he transported his army to the opposite bank, rooted up the beautiful vineyards in the neighborhood of Aquileia, demolished the suburbs, and employed the timber of the buildings in the engines and towers, with which on every side he attacked the city. The walls, fallen to decay during the security of a long peace, had been hastily repaired on this sudden

emergency; but the firmest defence of Aquileia consisted in the constancy of the citizens; all ranks of whom, instead of being dismayed, were animated by the extreme danger, and their knowledge of the tyrant's unrelenting temper. Their courage was supported and directed by Crispinus and Menophilus, two of the twenty lieutenants of the senate, who, with a small body of regular troops, had thrown themselves into the besieged place. The army of Maximin was repulsed on repeated attacks, his machines destroyed by showers of artificial fire; and the generous enthusiasm of the Aquileians was exalted into a confidence of success, by the opinion that Belenus, their tutelar deity, combated in person in the defence of his distressed worshippers.[35]

The emperor Maximus, who had advanced as far as Ravenna, to secure that important place, and to hasten the military preparations beheld the event of the war in the more faithful mirror of reason and policy. He was too sensible that a single town could not resist the persevering efforts of a great army; and he dreaded lest the enemy, tired with the obstinate resistance of Aquileia, should on a sudden relinquish the fruitless siege, and march directly towards Rome. The fate of the empire and the cause of freedom must then be committed to the chance of a battle; and what arms could he oppose to the veteran legions of the Rhine and the Danube? Some troops newly levied among the generous but enervated youth of Italy; and a body of German auxiliaries, on whose firmness, in the hour of trial, it was dangerous to depend. In the midst of these just alarms, the stroke of domestic conspiracy punished the crimes of Maximin, and delivered Rome and the senate from the calamities that would surely have attended the victory of an enraged barbarian.

The people of Aquileia had scarcely experienced any of the common miseries of a siege, their magazines were plentifully supplied, and several fountains within the walls assured them of an inexhaustible resource of fresh water. The soldiers of Maximin were, on the contrary, exposed to the inclemency of the season, the contagion of disease, and the horrors of famine. The open country was ruined, the rivers filled with the slain, and polluted with blood. A spirit of despair and disaffection began to diffuse itself among the troops; and as they were cut off from all intelligence, they easily believed that the whole empire had embraced the cause of the senate, and that they were left as devoted victims to perish under the impregnable walls of Aquileia. The fierce temper of the tyrant was exasperated by disappointments, which he imputed to the cowardice of his army; and his wanton and ill-timed cruelty, instead of striking terror, inspired hatred and a just desire of revenge. A party of Prætorian guards, who trembled for their wives and children in the camp of Alba, near Rome, executed the sentence of the senate. Maximin, abandoned by his guards, was (A.D. 238, April) slain in his tent, with his son (whom he had associated to the honours of the purple), Anulinus the præfect, and the principal ministers of his tyranny.[36] The sight of their heads, borne on the point of spears, convinced the citizens of Aquileia, that the siege was at an end; the gates of the city were thrown open, a liberal market was provided for the hungry troops of Maximin, and the whole army joined in solemn protestations of fidelity to the senate and the people of Rome, and to their lawful emperors Maximus and Balbinus. Such was the deserved fate of a brutal savage, destitute, as he has generally been represented, of every sentiment that distinguishes a civilised, or even a human being. The body was suited to the soul. The stature of Maximin exceeded the measure of eight feet, and circumstances almost incredible are related of his matchless strength and appetite.[37] Had he lived in a less enlightened age, tradition and poetry might well have described him as one of those monstrous giants, whose supernatural power was constantly exerted for the destruction of mankind.

It is easier to conceive than to describe the universal joy of the Roman world on the fall of the tyrant, the news of which is said to have been carried in four days from Aquileia to Rome. The return of Maximus was a triumphal procession, his colleague and young Gordian went out to meet him, and the three princes made their entry into the capital, attended by the ambassadors of almost all the cities of Italy, saluted with the splendid offerings of gratitude and superstition, and received with the unfeigned acclamations of the senate and people, who persuaded themselves that a golden age would succeed to an age of iron.[38] The conduct of the two emperors correspond with these expectations. They administered justice in person; and the rigour of the one was tempered by the other's clemency. The oppressive taxes with which Maximin had loaded the rights of inheritance and succession were repealed, or at least moderated. Discipline was revived, and with the advice of the senate many wise laws were enacted by their imperial ministers, who endeavoured to restore a civil constitution on the ruins of military tyranny. "What reward may we expect for delivering Rome from a monster?" was the question asked by Maximus, in a moment of freedom and confidence. Balbinus answered it without hesitation. "The love of the senate, of the people, and of all mankind." "Alas!" replied his more penetrating colleague, "Alas! I dread the hatred of the soldiers, and the fatal effects of their resentment."[39] His apprehensions were but too well justified by the event.

Whilst Maximus was preparing to defend Italy against the common foe, Balbinus, who remained at Rome, had been engaged in scenes of blood and intestine discord. Distrust and jealousy reigned in the senate; and even in the temples where they assembled, every senator carried either open or concealed arms. In the midst of their deliberations, two veterans of the guards, actuated either by curiosity or a sinister motive, audaciously thrust themselves into the house, and advanced by degrees beyond the altar of Victory. Gallicanus, a consular, and Mæcenas, a Prætorian senator, viewed with indignation their insolent intrusion: drawing their daggers, they laid the spies, for such they deemed them, dead at the foot of the altar, and then advancing to the door of the senate, imprudently exhorted the multitude to massacre the Prætorians, as the secret adherents of the tyrant. Those who escaped the first fury of the tumult took refuge in the camp, which they defended with superior advantage against the reiterated attacks of the people, assisted by the numerous bands of gladiators, the property of opulent nobles. The civil war lasted many days, with infinite loss and confusion on both sides. When the pipes were broken that supplied the camp with water, the Prætorians were reduced to intolerable distress; but in their turn they made desperate sallies into the city, set fire to a great number of houses, and filled the street with the blood of the inhabitants. The emperor Balbinus attempted, by ineffectual edicts and precarious truces, to reconcile the factions at Rome. But their animosity, though smothered for a while, burnt with redoubled violence. The soldiers, detesting the senate and the people, despised the weakness of a prince who wanted either the spirit or the power to command the obedience of his subjects.[40]

After the tyrant's death, his formidable army had acknowledged, from necessity rather than from choice, the authority of Maximus, who transported himself without delay to the camp before Aquileia. As soon as he had received their oath of fidelity, he addressed them in terms full of mildness and moderation; lamented, rather than arraigned, the wild disorders of the times, and assured the soldiers, that of all their past conduct, the senate would remember only their generous desertion of the tyrant, and their voluntary return to their duty. Maximus enforced his exhortations by a liberal donative, purified the camp by a solemn sacrifice of expiation, and then dismissed the legions to their several provinces, impressed, as he hoped, with a lively sense of gratitude and obedience.[41] But nothing could reconcile the haughty spirit of the Prætorians. They attended the emperors on the memorable day of their public entry into Rome; but amidst the general acclamations, the sullen dejected countenance of the guards sufficiently declared that they considered themselves as the object, rather than the partners, of the triumph. When the whole body was united in their camp, those who had served under Maximin, and those who had remained at Rome, insensibly communicated to each other their complaints and apprehensions. The emperors chosen by the army had perished with ignominy; those elected by the senate were seated on the throne.[42] The long discord between the civil and military powers was decided by a war, in which the former had obtained a complete victory. The soldiers must now learn a new doctrine of submission to the senate; and whatever clemency was affected by that politic assembly, they dreaded a slow revenge, coloured by the name of discipline, and justified by fair pretences of the public good. But their fate was still in their own hands; and if they had courage to despise the vain terrors of an impotent republic, it was easy to convince the world that those who were masters of the arms were masters of the authority, of the state.

When the senate elected two princes, it is probable that, besides the declared reason of providing for the various emergencies of peace and war, they were actuated by the secret desire of weakening by division the despotism of the supreme magistrate. Their policy was effectual, but it proved fatal both to their emperors and to themselves. The jealousy of power was soon exasperated by the difference of character. Maximus despised Balbinus as a luxurious noble, and was in his turn disdained by his colleague as an obscure soldier. Their silent discord was understood rather than seen;[43] but the mutual consciousness prevented them from uniting in any vigorous measures of defence against their common enemies of the Prætorian camp. The whole city was (A.D. 238, July 15) employed in the Capitoline games, and the emperors were left almost alone in the palace. On a sudden they were alarmed by the approach of a troop of desperate assassins. Ignorant of each other's situation or designs, for they already occupied very distant apartments, afraid to give or to receive assistance, they wasted the important moments in idle debates and fruitless recriminations. The arrival of the guards put an end to the vain strife. They seized on these emperors of the senate, for such they called them with malicious contempt, stripped them of their garments, and dragged them in insolent triumph through the streets of Rome, with a design of inflicting a slow and cruel death on those unfortunate princes. The fear of a rescue from the faithful Germans of the Imperial guards, shortened their tortures; and their bodies, mangled with a thousand wounds, were left exposed to the insults or to the pity of the populace.[44]

In the space of a few months, six princes had been cut off by the sword. Gordian, who had already received the title of Cæsar, was the only person that occurred to the soldiers as proper to fill the vacant throne.[45] They carried him to the camp, and unanimously saluted him Augustus and Emperor. His name was dear to the senate and people; his tender age promised a long impunity of military licence; and the submission of Rome and the provinces to the choice of the Prætorian guards, saved the republic, at the expense indeed of its freedom and dignity, from the horrors of a new civil war in the heart of the capital.[46]

As the third Gordian was only nineteen years of age at the time of his death, the history of his life, were it known to us with greater accuracy than it really is, would contain little more than the account of his education, and the conduct of the ministers, who by turns abused or guided the simplicity of his inexperienced youth. Immediately after his accession, he fell into the hands of his mother's eunuchs, that pernicious vermin of the East, who, since the days of Elagabalus, had infested the Roman palace. By the artful conspiracy of these wretches, an impenetrable veil was drawn between an innocent prince and his oppressed subjects, the virtuous disposition of Gordian was deceived, and the honours of the empire sold without his knowledge, though in a very public manner, to the most worthless of mankind. We are ignorant by what fortunate accident the emperor escaped from this ignominious slavery, and devolved his confidence on a minister whose wise counsels had no object except the glory of his sovereign and the happiness of the people. It should seem that (A.D. 240) love and learning introduced Misitheus to the favour of Gordian. The young prince married the daughter of his master of rhetoric, and promoted his father-in-law to the first offices of the empire. Two admirable letters that passed between them are still extant. The minister, with the conscious dignity of virtue, congratulates Gordian that he is delivered from the tyranny of the eunuchs,[47] and still more that he is sensible of his deliverance. The emperor acknowledges, with an amiable confusion, the errors of his past conduct; and laments, with singular propriety, the misfortune of a monarch, from whom a venal tribe of courtiers perpetually labour to conceal the truth.[48]

The life of Misitheus had been spent in the profession of letters, not of arms; yet such was the versatile genius of that great man, that, when (A.D. 242) he was appointed Prætorian Præfect, he discharged the military duties of his place with vigour and ability. The Persians had invaded Mesopotamia, and threatened Antioch. By the persuasion of his father-in-law, the young emperor quitted the luxury of Rome, opened, for the last time recorded in history, the temple of Janus, and marched in person into the East. On his approach with a great army, the Persians withdrew their garrisons from the cities which they had already taken, and retired from the Euphrates to the Tigris. Gordian enjoyed the pleasure of announcing to the senate the first success of his arms, which he ascribed with a becoming modesty and gratitude to the wisdom of his father and Præfect. During the whole expedition, Misitheus watched over the safety and discipline of the army; whilst he prevented their dangerous murmurs by maintaining a regular plenty in the camp, and by establishing ample magazines of vinegar, bacon, straw, barley, and wheat, in all the cities of the frontier.[49] But the prosperity of Gordian expired with Misitheus, who died of a flux, not without very strong suspicions of poison. Philip, his successor (A.D. 243) in the præfecture, was an Arab by birth, and consequently, in the earlier part of his life, a robber by profession. His rise from so obscure a station to the first dignities of the empire, seems to prove that he was a bold and able leader. But his boldness prompted him to aspire to the throne, and his abilities were employed to supplant, not to serve, his indulgent master. The minds of the soldiers were irritated by an artificial scarcity, created by his contrivance in the camp; and the distress of the army was attributed to the youth and incapacity of the prince. It is not in our power to trace the successive steps of the secret conspiracy and open sedition, which were at length fatal to Gordian. A sepulchral monument was erected to his memory on the spot[50] where (A.D. 244, March) he was killed, near the conflux of the Euphrates with the little river Aboras.[51] The fortunate Philip, raised to the empire by the votes of the soldiers, found a ready obedience from the senate and the provinces.[52]

We cannot forbear transcribing the ingenious, though somewhat fanciful description, which a celebrated writer of our own times has traced of the military government of the Roman empire. "What in that age was called the Roman empire, was only an irregular republic, not unlike the Aristocracy[53] of Algiers,[54] where the militia, possessed of the sovereignty, creates and deposes a magistrate, who is styled a Dey. Perhaps, indeed, it may be laid down as a general rule, that a military government is, in some respects, more republican than monarchical. Nor can it be said that the soldiers only partook of the government by their disobedience and rebellions. The speeches made to them by the emperors, were they not at length of the same nature as those formerly pronounced to the people by the consuls and the tribunes? And although the armies had no regular place or forms of assembly; though their debates were short, their action sudden, and their resolves seldom the result of cool reflection, did they not dispose, with absolute sway, of the public fortune? What was the emperor, except the minister of a violent government elected for the private benefit of the soldiers?

"When the army had elected Philip, who was Prætorian præfect to the third Gordian; the latter demanded that he might remain sole emperor; he was unable to obtain it. He requested that the power might be equally divided between them; the army would not listen to his speech. He consented to be degraded to the rank of Cæsar; the favour was refused him. He desired, at least, he might be appointed Prætorian præfect; his prayer was rejected. Finally, he pleaded for his life. The army, in these several judgments, exercised the supreme magistracy." According to the historian, whose doubtful narrative the president De Montesquieu has adopted, Philip, who, during the whole transaction, had preserved a sullen silence, was inclined to spare the innocent life of his benefactor; till, recollecting that his innocence might excite a dangerous compassion in the Roman world; he commanded, without regard to his suppliant cries, that he should be seized, stript, and led away to instant death. After a moment's pause the inhuman sentence was executed.[55]

On his return from the East to Rome, Philip, desirous of obliterating the memory of his crimes, and of captivating the affections of the people, solemnised (A.D. 248, April 21) the secular games with infinite pomp and magnificence. Since their institution or revival by Augustus,[56] they had been celebrated by Claudius, by Domitian, and by Severus, and were now renewed the fifth time, on the accomplishment of the full period of a thousand years from the foundation of Rome. Every circumstance of the secular games was skilfully adapted to inspire the superstitious mind with deep and solemn reverence. The long interval between them[57] exceeded the term of human life; and as none of the spectators had already seen them, none could flatter themselves with the expectation of beholding them a second time. The mystic sacrifices were performed, during three nights, on the banks of the Tiber; and the Campus Martius resounded with music and dances, and was illuminated with innumerable lamps and torches. Slaves and strangers were excluded from any participation in these national ceremonies. A chorus of twenty-seven youths, and as many virgins, of noble families, and whose parents were both alive, implored the propitious gods in favour of the present, and for the hope of the rising generation; requesting, in religious hymns, that, according to the faith of their ancient oracles, they would still maintain the virtue, the felicity, and the empire of the Roman people.[58] The magnificence of Philip's shows and entertainments dazzled the eyes of the multitude. The devout were employed in the rites of superstition, whilst the reflecting few revolved in their anxious minds the past history and the future fate of the empire.

Since Romulus, with a small band of shepherds and outlaws, fortified himself on the hills near the Tiber, ten centuries had already elapsed.[59] During the first four ages, the Romans, in the laborious school of poverty, had acquired the virtues of war and government; by the vigorous exertion of those virtues, and by the assistance of fortune, they had obtained, in the course of the three succeeding centuries, an absolute empire over many countries of Europe, Asia, and Africa. The last three hundred years had been consumed in apparent prosperity and internal decline. The nation of soldiers, magistrates, and legislators, who composed the thirty-five tribes of the Roman people, was dissolved into the common mass of mankind and confounded with the millions of servile provincials, who had received the name without adopting the spirit of Romans. A mercenary army, levied among the subjects and barbarians of the frontier, was the only order of men who preserved and abused their independence. By their tumultuary election, a Syrian, a Goth, or an Arab, was exalted to the throne of Rome, and invested with despotic power over the conquests and over the country of the Scipios.

The limits of the Roman empire still extended from the Western Ocean to the Tigris, and from Mount Atlas to the Rhine and the Danube. To the undiscerning eye of the vulgar, Philip appeared a monarch no less powerful than Hadrian or Augustus had formerly been. The form was still the same, but the animating health and vigour were fled. The industry of the people was discouraged and exhausted by a long series of oppression. The discipline of the legions, which alone, after the extinction of every other virtue, had propped the greatness of the state, was corrupted by the ambition, or relaxed by the weakness, of the emperors. The strength of the frontiers, which had always consisted in arms rather than in fortifications, was insensibly undermined; and the fairest provinces were left exposed to the rapaciousness or ambition of the barbarians, who soon discovered the decline of the Roman empire.

CHAPTER VIII

Of the State of Persia after the Restoration of the Monarchy by Artaxerxes.

WHENEVER Tacitus indulges himself in those beautiful episodes, in which he relates some domestic transaction of the Germans or of the Parthians, his principal object is to relieve the attention of the reader from a uniform scene of vice and misery. From the reign of Augustus to the time of Alexander Severus, the enemies of Rome were in her bosom; the tyrants, and the soldiers; and her prosperity had a very distant and feeble interest in the revolutions that might happen beyond the Rhine and the Euphrates. But when the military order had levelled, in wild anarchy, the power of the prince, the laws of the senate, and even the discipline of the camp, the barbarians of the north and of the east, who had long hovered on the frontier, boldly attacked the provinces of a declining monarchy. Their vexatious inroads were changed into formidable irruptions, and, after a long vicissitude of mutual calamities, many tribes of the victorious invaders established themselves in the provinces of the Roman empire. To obtain a clearer knowledge of these great events, we shall endeavour to form a previous idea of the character, forces, and designs of those nations who avenged the cause of Hannibal and Mithridates.

In the more early ages of the world, whilst the forest that covered Europe afforded a retreat to a few wandering savages, the inhabitants of Asia were already collected into populous cities, and reduced under extensive empires, the seat of the arts, of luxury, and of despotism. The Assyrians reigned over the East,[1] till the sceptre of Ninus and Semiramis dropt from the hands of their enervated successors. The Medes and the Babylonians divided their power, and were themselves swallowed up in the monarchy of the Persians, whose arms could not be confined within the narrow limits of Asia. Followed, as it is said, by two millions of *men*, Xerxes, the descendant of Cyrus, invaded Greece. Thirty thousand *soldiers*, under the command of Alexander, the son of Philip, who was intrusted by the Greeks with their glory and revenge, were sufficient to subdue Persia. The princes of the house of Seleucus usurped and lost the Macedonian command over the East. About the same time that, by an ignominious treaty, they resigned to the Romans the country on this side Mount Taurus, they were driven by the Parthians, an obscure horde of Scythian origin, from all the provinces of Upper Asia. The formidable power of the Parthians, which spread from India to the frontiers of Syria, was in its turn subverted by Ardshir, or Artaxerxes; the founder of a new dynasty, which, under the name of Sassanides, governed Persia till the invasion of the Arabs. This great revolution, whose fatal influence was soon experienced by the Romans, happened in the fourth year of Alexander Severus, two hundred and twenty-six years after the Christian era.[2]

Artaxerxes had served with great reputation in the armies of Artaban, the last king of the Parthians, and it appears that he was driven in-

to exile and rebellion by royal ingratitude, the customary reward for superior merit. His birth was obscure, and the obscurity equally gave room to the aspersions of his enemies, and the flattery of his adherents. If we credit the scandal of the former, Artaxerxes sprang from the illegitimate commerce of a tanner's wife with a common soldier.[3] The latter represent him as descended from a branch of the ancient kings of Persia, though time and misfortune had gradually reduced his ancestors to the humble station of private citizens.[4] As the lineal heir of the monarchy, he asserted his right to the throne, and challenged the noble task of delivering the Persians from the oppression under which they groaned above five centuries since the death of Darius. The Parthians were defeated in three great battles. In the last of these their king Artaban was slain, and the spirit of the nation was for ever broken.[5] The authority of Artaxerxes was solemnly acknowledged in a great assembly held at Balch in Khorasan. Two younger branches of the royal house of Arsaces were confounded among the prostrate satraps. A third, more mindful of ancient grandeur than of present necessity, attempted to retire, with a numerous train of vassals, towards their kinsman, the king of Armenia; but this little army of deserters was intercepted, and cut off, by the vigilance of the conqueror,[6] who boldly assumed the double diadem, and the title of King of Kings, which had been enjoyed by his predecessor. But these pompous titles, instead of gratifying the vanity of the Persian, served only to admonish him of his duty, and to inflame in his soul the ambition of restoring, in their full splendour, the religion and empire of Cyrus.

I. During the long servitude of Persia under the Macedonian and the Parthian yoke, the nations of Europe and Asia had mutually adopted and corrupted each other's superstitions. The Arsacides, indeed, practised the worship of the Magi; but they disgraced and polluted it with a various mixture of foreign idolatry. The memory of Zoroaster, the ancient prophet and philosopher of the Persians,[7] was still revered in the East; but the obsolete and mysterious language in which the Zendavesta was composed,[8] opened a field of dispute to seventy sects, who variously explained the fundamental doctrines of their religion, and were all indifferently derided by a crowd of infidels, who rejected the divine mission and miracles of the Prophet. To suppress the idolaters, reunite the schismatics, and confute the unbelievers, by the infallible decision of a general council, the pious Artaxerxes summoned the Magi from all parts of his dominions. These priests, who had so long sighed in contempt and obscurity, obeyed the welcome summons; and on the appointed day appeared, to the number of about eighty thousand. But as the debates of so tumultuous an assembly could not have been directed by the authority of reason, or influenced by the art of policy, the Persian synod was reduced, by successive operations, to forty thousand, to four thousand, to four hundred, to forty, and at last to seven Magi, the most respected for their learning and piety. One of these, Erdaviraph, a young but holy prelate, received from the hands of his brethren three cups of soporiferous wine. He drank them off, and instantly fell into a long and profound sleep. As soon as he waked, he related to the king and to the believing multitude his journey to Heaven, and his intimate conferences with the Deity. Every doubt was silenced by this supernatural evidence; and the articles of the faith of Zoroaster were fixed with equal authority and precision.[9] A short delineation of that celebrated system will be found useful, not only to display the character of the Persian nation, but to illustrate many of their most important transactions, both in peace and war, with the Roman empire.[10]

The great and fundamental article of the system was the celebrated doctrine of the two principles; a bold and injudicious attempt of Eastern philosophy to reconcile the existence of moral and physical evil with the attributes of a beneficent Creator and Governor of the world. The first and original Being, in whom, or by whom, the universe exists, is denominated in the writings of Zoroaster, *Time without bounds*; but it must be confessed that this infinite substance seems rather a metaphysical abstraction of the mind, than a real object endowed with self-consciousness, or possessed of moral perfections. From either the blind or the intelligent operation of this infinite Time, which bears but too near an affinity with the chaos of the Greeks, the two secondary but active principles of the universe were from all eternity produced, Ormusd and Ahriman, each of them possessed of the powers of creation, but each disposed by his invariable nature, to exercise them with different designs. The principle of good is eternally absorbed in light; the principle of evil eternally buried in darkness. The wise benevolence of Ormusd formed man capable of virtue, and abundantly provided his fair habitation with the materials of happiness. By his vigilant providence, the motion of the planets, the order of

the seasons, and the temperate mixture of the elements, are preserved. But the malice of Ahriman has long since pierced *Ormusd's egg*; or, in other words, has violated the harmony of his works. Since that fatal irruption the most minute articles of good and evil are intimately intermingled and agitated together; the rankest poisons spring up amidst the most salutary plants; deluges, earthquakes, and conflagrations, attest the conflict of Nature, and the little world of man is perpetually shaken by vice and misfortune. Whilst the rest of human kind are led away captives in the chains of their infernal enemy, the faithful Persian alone reserves his religious adoration for his friend and protector Ormusd, and fights under his banner of light, in the full confidence that he shall, in the last day, share the glory of his triumph. At that decisive period, the enlightened wisdom of goodness will render the power of Ormusd superior to the furious malice of his rival. Ahriman and his followers, disarmed and subdued, will sink into their native darkness; and virtue will maintain the eternal peace and harmony of the universe.[11]

The theology of Zoroaster was darkly comprehended by foreigners, and even by the far greater number of his disciples; but the most careless observers were struck with the philosophic simplicity of the Persian worship. "That people," says Herodotus,[12] "rejects the use of temples, of altars, and of statues, and smiles at the folly of those nations who imagine that the gods are sprung from, or bear any affinity with, the human nature. The tops of the highest mountains are the places chosen for sacrifices. Hymns and prayers are the principal worship; the Supreme God who fills the wide circle of Heaven is the object to whom they are addressed." Yet, at the same time, in the true spirit of a polytheist, he accuses them of adoring Earth, Water, Fire, the Winds, and the Sun and Moon. But the Persians of every age have denied the charge, and explained the equivocal conduct, which might appear to give a colour to it. The elements, and more particularly Fire, Light, and the Sun, whom they called Mithra, were the objects of their religious reverence, because they considered them as the purest symbols, the noblest productions, and the most powerful agents of the Divine Power and Nature.[13]

Every mode of religion, to make a deep and lasting impression on the human mind, must exercise our obedience, by enjoining practices of devotion; and must acquire our esteem, by inculcating moral duties analogous to the dictates of our own hearts. The religion of Zoroaster was abundantly provided with the former, and possessed a sufficient portion of the latter. At the age of puberty, the faithful Persian was invested with a mysterious girdle, the badge of the divine protection, and from that moment all the actions of his life, even the most indifferent, or the most necessary, were sanctified by their peculiar prayers, ejaculations, or genuflexions; the omission of which, under any circumstances, was a grievous sin, not inferior in guilt to the violation of the moral duties. The moral duties, however, of justice, mercy, liberality, etc., were in their turn required of the disciple of Zoroaster, who wished to escape the persecution of Ahriman, and to live with Ormusd in a blissful eternity, where the degree of felicity will be exactly proportioned to the degree of virtue and piety.[14]

But there are some remarkable instances, in which Zoroaster lays aside the prophet, assumes the legislator, and discovers a liberal concern for private and public happiness, seldom to be found among the grovelling or visionary schemes of superstition. Fasting and celibacy, the common means of purchasing the Divine favour, he condemns with abhorrence, as a criminal rejection of the best gifts of Providence. The saint, in the Magian religion, is obliged to beget children, to plant useful trees, to destroy noxious animals, to convey water to the dry lands of Persia, and to work out his salvation by pursuing all the labours of agriculture. We may quote from the Zendavesta a wise and benevolent maxim, which compensates for many an absurdity. "He who sows the ground with care and diligence, acquires a greater stock of religious merit, than he could gain by the repetition of ten thousand prayers."[15] In the spring of every year a festival was celebrated, destined to represent the primitive equality, and the present connection, of mankind. The stately kings of Persia, exchanging their vain pomp for more genuine greatness, freely mingled with the humblest but most useful of their subjects. On that day the husbandmen were admitted, without distinction, to the table of the king, and his satraps. The monarch accepted their petitions, inquired into their grievances, and conversed with them on the most equal terms. "From your labours," was he accustomed to say (and to say with truth, if not with sincerity), "from your labours, we receive our subsistence; you derive your tranquillity from our vigilance; since, therefore, we are mutually necessary to each other, let us live together like brothers in con-

cord and love."[16] Such a festival must indeed have degenerated, in a wealthy and despotic empire, into a theatrical representation; but it was at least a comedy well worthy of a royal audience, and which might sometimes imprint a salutary lesson on the mind of a young prince.

Had Zoroaster, in all his institutions, invariably supported this exalted character, his name would deserve a place with those of Numa and Confucius, and his system would be justly entitled to all the applause which it has pleased some of our divines, and even some of our philosophers, to bestow on it. But in that motley composition, dictated by reason and passion, by enthusiasm and by selfish motives, some useful and sublime truths were disgraced by a mixture of the most abject and dangerous superstition. The Magi, or sacerdotal order, were extremely numerous, since, as we have already seen, fourscore thousand of them were convened in a general council. Their forces were multiplied by discipline. A regular hierarchy was diffused through all the provinces of Persia; and the Archimagus, who resided at Balch, was respected as the visible head of the church, and the lawful successor of Zoroaster.[17] The property of the Magi was very considerable. Besides the less invidious possession of a large tract of the most fertile lands of Media,[18] they levied a general tax on the fortunes and the industry of the Persians.[19] "Though your good works," says the interested prophet, "exceed in number the leaves of the trees, the drops of rain, the stars in the heaven, or the sands on the sea-shore, they will all be unprofitable to you, unless they are accepted by the *destour*, or priest. To obtain the acceptation of this guide to salvation, you must faithfully pay him *tithes* of all you possess, of your goods, of your lands, and of your money. If the destour be satisfied, your soul will escape hell tortures; you will secure praise in this world and happiness in the next. For the destours are the teachers of religion; they know all things, and they deliver all men."[20]

These convenient maxims of reverence and implicit faith were doubtless imprinted with care on the tender minds of youth; since the Magi were the masters of education in Persia, and to their hands the children even of the royal family were intrusted.[21] The Persian priests, who were of a speculative genius, preserved and investigated the secrets of Oriental philosophy; and acquired, either by superior knowledge or superior art, the reputation of being well versed in some occult sciences, which have derived their appellation from the Magi.[22] Those of more active dispositions mixed with the world in courts and cities; and it is observed, that the administration of Artaxerxes was in a great measure directed by the counsels of the sacerdotal order, whose dignity, either from policy or devotion, that prince restored to its ancient splendour.[23]

The first counsel of the Magi was agreeable to the unsociable genius of their faith,[24] to the practice of ancient kings,[25] and even to the example of their legislator, who had fallen a victim to a religious war, excited by his own intolerant zeal.[26] By an edict of Artaxerxes, the exercise of every worship, except that of Zoroaster, was severely prohibited. The temples of the Parthians, and the statues of their deified monarchs, were thrown down with ignominy.[27] The sword of Aristotle (such was the name given by the Orientals to the polytheism and philosophy of the Greeks) was easily broken;[28] the flames of persecution soon reached the more stubborn Jews and Christians;[29] nor did they spare the heretics of their own nation and religion. The majesty of Ormusd, who was jealous of a rival, was seconded by the despotism of Artaxerxes, who could not suffer a rebel; and the schismatics within his vast empire were soon reduced to the inconsiderable number of eighty thousand.[30] This spirit of persecution reflects dishonour on the religion of Zoroaster; but as it was not productive of any civil commotion, it served to strengthen the new monarchy, by uniting all the various inhabitants of Persia in the bands of religious zeal.

II. Artaxerxes, by his valour and conduct, had wrested the sceptre of the East from the ancient royal family of Parthia. There still remained the more difficult task of establishing, throughout the vast extent of Persia, a uniform and vigorous administration. The weak indulgence of the Arsacides had resigned to their sons and brothers the principal provinces, and the greatest offices of the kingdom, in the nature of hereditary possessions. The *vitaxæ*, or eighteen most powerful satraps, were permitted to assume the regal title; and the vain pride of the monarch was delighted with a nominal dominion over so many vassal kings. Even tribes of barbarians in their mountains, and the Greek cities of Upper Asia,[31] within their walls, scarcely acknowledged, or seldom obeyed, any superior; and the Parthian empire exhibited, under other names, a lively image of the feudal system[32] which has since prevailed in Europe. But the active victor, at the head of a numerous and disciplined army, visited in person every province of Persia. The defeat of the boldest rebels, and the reduction of the strongest fortifications,[33] diffused the terror of his arms, and prepared the way for the peaceful reception of his authority. An obstinate resistance was fatal to the chiefs; but their followers were treated with lenity.[34] A cheerful submission was rewarded with honours and riches; but the prudent Artaxerxes, suffering no person except himself to assume the title of king, abolished every intermediate power between the throne and the people. His kingdom, nearly equal in extent to modern Persia, was, on every side, bounded by the sea, or by great rivers; by the Euphrates, the Tigris, the Araxes, the Oxus, and the Indus, by the Caspian Sea, and the Gulf of Persia.[35] That country was computed to contain, in the last century, five hundred and fifty-four cities, sixty thousand villages, and about forty millions of souls.[36] If we compare the administration of the house of Sassan with that of the house of Sefi, the political influence of the Magian with that of the Mahometan religion, we shall probably infer, that the kingdom of Artaxerxes contained at least as great a number of cities, villages, and inhabitants. But it must likewise be confessed, that in every age the want of harbours on the sea-coast, and the scarcity of fresh water in the inland provinces, have been very unfavourable to the commerce and agriculture of the Persians; who, in the calculation of their numbers, seem to have indulged one of the meanest, though most common, articles of national vanity.

As soon as the ambitious mind of Artaxerxes had triumphed over the resistance of his vassals, he began to threaten the neighbouring states, who, during the long slumber of his predecessors, had insulted Persia with impunity. He obtained some easy victories over the wild Scythians and the effeminate Indians; but the Romans were an enemy who, by their past injuries and present power, deserved the utmost efforts of his arms. A forty years' tranquillity, the fruit of valour and moderation, had succeeded the victories of Trajan. During the period that elapsed from the accession of Marcus to the reign of Alexander, the Roman and the Parthian empires were twice engaged in war; and although the whole strength of the Arsacides contended with a part only of the forces of Rome, the event was most commonly in favour of the latter. Macrinus, indeed, prompted by his precarious situation and pusillanimous temper, purchased a peace at the expense of near two millions of our money;[37] but the generals of

Marcus, the emperor Severus, and his son, erected many trophies in Armenia, Mesopotamia, and Assyria. Among their exploits, the imperfect relation of which would have unseasonably interrupted the more important series of domestic revolutions, we shall only mention the repeated calamities of the two great cities of Seleucia and Ctesiphon.

Seleucia, on the western bank of the Tigris, about forty-five miles to the north of ancient Babylon, was the capital of the Macedonian conquests in Upper Asia.[38] Many ages after the fall of their empire, Seleucia retained the genuine characters of a Grecian colony, arts, military virtue, and the love of freedom. The independent republic was governed by a senate of three hundred nobles; the people consisted of six hundred thousand citizens; the walls were strong, and as long as concord prevailed among the several orders of the state, they viewed with contempt the power of the Parthian: but the madness of faction was sometimes provoked to implore the dangerous aid of the common enemy, who was posted almost at the gates of the colony.[39] The Parthian monarchs, like the Mogul sovereigns of Hindostan, delighted in the pastoral life of their Scythian ancestor; and the Imperial camp was frequently pitched in the plain of Ctesiphon, on the eastern bank of the Tigris, at the distance of only three miles from Seleucia.[40] The innumerable attendants on luxury and despotism resorted to the court, and the little village of Ctesiphon insensibly swelled into a great city.[41] Under the reign of Marcus, the Roman generals (A.D. 165) penetrated as far as Ctesiphon and Seleucia. They were received as friends by the Greek colony; they attacked as enemies the seat of the Parthian kings; yet both cities experienced the same treatment. The sack and conflagration of Seleucia, with the massacre of three hundred thousand of the inhabitants, tarnished the glory of the Roman triumph.[42] Seleucia, already exhausted by the neighbourhood of a too powerful rival, sunk under the fatal blow; but Ctesiphon (A.D. 198), in about thirty-three years, had sufficiently recovered its strength to maintain an obstinate siege against the emperor Severus. The city was, however, taken by assault; the king, who defended it in person, escaped with precipitation; an hundred thousand captives, and a rich booty, rewarded the fatigues of the Roman soldiers.[43] Notwithstanding these misfortunes, Ctesiphon succeeded to Babylon and to Seleucia, as one of the great capitals of the East. In summer, the monarch of Persia enjoyed at Ecbatana the cool breezes of the mountains of Media; but the mildness of the climate engaged him to prefer Ctesiphon for his winter residence.

From these successful inroads, the Romans derived no real or lasting benefit; nor did they attempt to preserve such distant conquests, separated from the provinces of the empire by a large tract of intermediate desert. The reduction of the kingdom of Osrhoene was an acquisition of less splendour indeed, but of a far more solid advantage. That little state occupied the northern and most fertile part of Mesopotamia, between the Euphrates and the Tigris. Edessa, its capital, was situated about twenty miles beyond the former of those rivers; and the inhabitants, since the time of Alexander, were a mixed race of Greeks, Arabs, Syrians, and Armenians.[44] The feeble sovereigns of Osrhoene, placed on the dangerous verge of two contending empires, were attached from inclination to the Parthian cause; but the superior power of Rome exacted from them a reluctant homage, which is still attested by their medals. After the conclusion of the Parthian war under Marcus, it was judged prudent to secure some substantial pledges of their doubtful fidelity. Forts were constructed in several parts of the country, and a Roman garrison was fixed in the strong town of Nisibis. During the troubles that followed the death of Commodus, the princes of Osrhoene attempted to shake off the yoke; but the stern policy of Severus confirmed their dependence,[45] and the perfidy of Caracalla completed the easy conquest. Abgarus, the last king of Edessa, was (A.D. 216) sent in chains to Rome, his dominions reduced into a province, and his capital dignified with the rank of colony; and thus the Romans, about ten years before the fall of the Parthian monarchy, obtained a firm and permanent establishment beyond the Euphrates.[46]

Prudence as well as glory might have justified a war on the side of Artaxerxes, had his views been confined to the defence or the acquisition of a useful frontier. But the ambitious Persian openly avowed a far more extensive design of conquest; and (A.D. 230) he thought himself able to support his lofty pretensions by the arms of reason as well as by those of power. Cyrus, he alleged, had first subdued, and his successors had for a long time possessed, the whole extent of Asia, as far as the Propontis and the Ægean sea; the provinces of Caria and Ionia, under their empire, had been governed by Persian satraps, and all Egypt, to the confines of Æthiopia, had acknowledged their sovereignty.[47] Their rights had been suspended, but not destroyed, by a long usurpation; and as soon as he received the Persian diadem, which birth and successful valour had placed upon his head, the first great duty of his station called upon him to restore the ancient limits and splendour of the monarchy. The Great King, therefore (such was the haughty style of his embassies to the emperor Alexander), commanded the Romans instantly to depart from all the provinces of his ancestors, and, yielding to the Persians the empire of Asia, to content themselves with the undisturbed possession of Europe. This haughty mandate was delivered by four hundred of the tallest and most beautiful of the Persians; who, by their fine horses, splendid arms, and rich apparel, displayed the pride and greatness of their master.[48] Such an embassy was much less an offer of negotiation than a declaration of war. Both Alexander Severus and Artaxerxes, collecting the military force of the Roman and Persian monarchies, resolved in this important contest to lead their armies in person.

If we credit what should seem the most authentic of all records, an oration, still extant, and delivered by the emperor himself to the senate, we must allow that the victory of Alexander Severus was not inferior to any of those formerly obtained over the Persians by the son of Philip. The army of the Great King consisted of one hundred and twenty thousand horse, clothed in complete armour of steel; of seven hundred elephants, with towers filled with archers on their backs; and of eighteen hundred chariots, armed with scythes. This formidable host, the like of which is not to be found in eastern history, and has scarcely been imagined in eastern romance,[49] was (A.D. 233) discomfited in a great battle, in which the Roman Alexander approved himself an intrepid soldier and a skilful general. The Great King fled before his valour; an immense booty, and the conquest of Mesopotamia, were the immediate fruits of this signal victory. Such are the circumstances of this ostentatious and improbable relation, dictated, as it too plainly appears, by the vanity of the monarch, adorned by the unblushing servility of his flatterers, and received without contradiction by a distant and obsequious senate.[50] Far from being inclined to believe that the arms of Alexander obtained any memorable advantage over the Persians, we are induced to suspect that all this blaze of imaginary glory was designed to conceal some real disgrace.

Our suspicions are confirmed by the authority of a contemporary historian, who mentions

the virtues of Alexander with respect, and his faults with candour. He describes the judicious plan which had been formed for the conduct of the war. Three Roman armies were destined to invade Persia at the same time, and by different roads. But the operations of the campaign, though wisely concerted, were not executed either with ability or success. The first of these armies, as soon as it had entered the marshy plains of Babylon, towards the artificial conflux of the Euphrates and the Tigris,[51] was encompassed by the superior numbers, and destroyed by the arrows, of the enemy. The alliance of Chosroes, king of Armenia,[52] and the long tract of mountainous country, in which the Persian cavalry was of little service, opened a secure entrance into the heart of Media to the second of the Roman armies. These brave troops laid waste the adjacent provinces, and by several successful actions against Artaxerxes, gave a faint colour to the emperor's vanity. But the retreat of this victorious army was imprudent, or at least unfortunate. In repassing the mountains great numbers of soldiers perished by the badness of the roads, and the severity of the winter season. It had been resolved, that whilst these two great detachments penetrated into the opposite extremes of the Persian dominions, the main body, under the command of Alexander himself, should support their attack by invading the centre of the kingdom. But the inexperienced youth, influenced by his mother's counsels, and perhaps by his own fears, deserted the bravest troops and the fairest prospect of victory; and after consuming in Mesopotamia an inactive and inglorious summer, he led back to Antioch an army diminished by sickness, and provoked by disappointment. The behaviour of Artaxerxes had been very different. Flying with rapidity from the hills of Media to the marshes of the Euphrates, he had everywhere opposed the invaders in person; and in either fortune had united with the ablest conduct the most undaunted resolution. But in several obstinate engagements against the veteran legions of Rome, the Persian monarch had lost the flower of his troops. Even his victories had weakened his power. The favourable opportunities of the absence of Alexander, and of the confusions that followed that emperor's death, presented themselves in vain to his ambition. Instead of expelling the Romans, as he pretended, from the continent of Asia, he found himself unable to wrest from their hands the little province of Mesopotamia.[53]

The reign of Artaxerxes, which from the last

defeat of the Parthians (A.D. 240) lasted only fourteen years, forms a memorable era in the history of the East, and even in that of Rome. His character seems to have been marked by those bold and commanding features that generally distinguished the princes who conquer, from those who inherit, an empire. Till the last period of the Persian monarchy his code of laws was respected as the ground-work of their civil and religious policy.[54] Several of his sayings are preserved. One of them in particular discovers a deep insight into the constitution of government. "The authority of the prince," said Artaxerxes, "must be defended by a military force; that force can only be maintained by taxes; all taxes must, at last, fall upon agriculture; and agriculture can never flourish except under the protection of justice and moderation."[55] Artaxerxes bequeathed his new empire, and his ambitious designs against the Romans, to Sapor, a son not unworthy of his great father; but those designs were too extensive for the power of Persia, and served only to involve both nations in a long series of destructive wars and reciprocal calamities.

The Persians, long since civilised and corrupted, were very far from possessing the martial independence and the intrepid hardness, both of mind and body, which have rendered the northern barbarians masters of the world. The science of war, that constituted the more rational force of Greece and Rome, as it now does of Europe, never made any considerable progress in the East. Those disciplined evolutions which harmonise and animate a confused multitude were unknown to the Persians. They were equally unskilled in the arts of constructing, besieging, or defending regular fortifications. They trusted more to their courage than to their discipline. The infantry was a half-armed spiritless crowd of peasants, levied in haste by the allurements of plunder, and as easily dispersed by a victory as by a defeat. The monarch and his nobles transported into the camp the pride and luxury of the seraglio. Their military operations were impeded by a useless train of women, eunuchs, horses, and camels, and in the midst of a successful campaign the Persian host was often separated or destroyed by an unexpected famine.[56]

But the nobles of Persia, in the bosom of luxury and despotism, preserved a strong sense of personal gallantry and national honour. From the age of seven years they were taught to speak truth, to shoot with the bow, and to ride; and it was universally confessed, that in the two last of these arts they had made a more than common proficiency.[57] The most distinguished youth were educated under the monarch's eye, practised their exercises in the gate of his palace, and were severely trained up to the habits of temperance and obedience in their long and laborious parties of hunting. In every province the satrap maintained a like school of military virtue. The Persian nobles (so natural is the idea of feudal tenures) received from the king's bounty lands and houses, on the condition of their service in war. They were ready on the first summons to mount on horseback, with a martial and splendid train of followers, and to join the numerous bodies of guards, who were carefully selected from amongst the most robust slaves, and the bravest adventurers of Asia. These armies, both of light and of heavy cavalry, equally formidable by the impetuosity of their charge, and the rapidity of their motions, threatened, as an impending cloud, the eastern provinces of the declining empire of Rome.[58]

CHAPTER IX

The State of Germany till the Invasion of the Barbarians in the time of the Emperor Decius.

THE government and religion of Persia have deserved some notice from their connection with the decline and fall of the Roman empire. We shall occasionally mention the Scythian or Sarmatian tribes, which, with their arms and horses, their flocks and herbs, their wives and families, wandered over the immense plains which spread themselves from the Caspian Sea to the Vistula, from the confines of Persia to those of Germany. But the warlike Germans, who first resisted, then invaded, and at length overturned, the western monarchy of Rome, will occupy a much more important place in this history, and possess a stronger, and, if we may use the expression, a more domestic, claim to our attention and regard. The most civilised nations of modern Europe issued from the woods of Germany, and in the rude institutions of those barbarians we may still distinguish the original principles of our present laws and manners. In their primitive state of simplicity and independence the Germans were surveyed by the discerning eye, and delineated by the masterly pencil, of Tacitus, the first of historians who applied the science of philosophy to the study of facts. The expressive conciseness of his descriptions has deserved to exercise the diligence of innumerable antiquarians, and to excite the genius and penetration of the philosophic historians of our own times. The subject, however, various and important, has already been so frequently, so ably, and so successfully discussed, that it is now grown familiar to the reader, and difficult to the writer. We shall therefore content ourselves with observing, and indeed with repeating, some of the most important circumstances of climate, of manners, and of institutions, which rendered the wild barbarians of Germany such formidable enemies to the Roman power.

Ancient Germany, excluding from its independent limits the province westward of the Rhine, which had submitted to the Roman yoke, extended itself over a third part of Europe. Almost the whole of modern Germany, Denmark, Norway, Sweden, Finland, Livonia, Prussia, and the greater part of Poland, were peopled by the various tribes of one great nation, whose complexion, manners, and language denoted a common origin and preserved a striking resemblance. On the west, ancient Germany was divided by the Rhine from the Gallic, and on the south by the Danube from the Illyrian, provinces of the empire. A ridge of hills, rising from the Danube, and called the Carpathian mountains, covered Germany on the side of Dacia or Hungary. The eastern frontier was faintly marked by the mutual fears of the Germans and the Sarmatians, and was often confounded by the mixture of warring and confederating tribes of the two nations. In the remote darkness of the north, the ancients imperfectly descried a frozen ocean that lay beyond the Baltic Sea, and beyond the Peninsula, or islands,[1] of Scandinavia.

Some ingenious writers[2] have suspected that Europe was much colder formerly than it is at present; and the most ancient descriptions of the climate of Germany tend exceedingly to confirm their theory. The general complaints of intense frost, and eternal winter, are perhaps little to be regarded, since we have no method of reducing to the accurate standard of the thermometer the feelings or the expressions of an orator, born in the happier regions of Greece or Asia. But I shall select two remarkable circumstances of a less equivocal nature. 1. The great rivers which covered the Roman provinces, the Rhine and the Danube, were frequently frozen over, and capable of supporting the most enormous weights. The barbarians, who often chose that severe season for their inroads, transported, without apprehension or danger, their numerous armies, their cavalry, and their heavy wagons, over a vast and solid bridge of ice.[3] Modern ages have not presented an instance of a like phenomenon. 2. The reindeer, that useful animal, from whom the savage of the North derives the best comforts of his dreary life, is of a constitution that supports, and even requires, the most intense cold. He is found on the rock of Spitzberg, within ten degrees of the Pole; he seems to delight in the snows of Lapland and Siberia; but at present he cannot subsist, much less multiply, in any country to the south of the Baltic.[4] In the time of Cæsar, the reindeer, as well as the elk and the wild bull, was a native of the Hercynian forest, which then overshadowed a great part of Germany and Poland.[5] The modern improvements sufficiently explain the causes of the diminution of the cold. These immense woods have been gradually cleared, which intercepted from the earth the rays of the sun.[6] The morasses have been drained, and, in proportion as the soil has been cultivated, the air has become more temperate. Canada, at this day, is an exact picture of ancient Germany. Although situated in the same parallel with the finest provinces of France and England, that country experiences the most rigorous cold. The reindeer are very numerous, the ground is covered with deep and lasting snow, and the great river of St. Lawrence is regularly frozen, in a season when the waters of the Seine and the Thames are usually free from ice.[7]

It is difficult to ascertain, and easy to exaggerate, the influence of the climate of ancient Germany over the minds and bodies of the natives. Many writers have supposed, and most have allowed, though, as it should seem, without any adequate proof, that the rigorous cold of the North was favourable to long life and generative vigour, that the women were more fruitful, and the human species more prolific, than in warmer or more temperate climates.[8] We may assert, with greater confidence, that the keen air of Germany formed the large and masculine limbs of the natives, who were, in general, of a more lofty stature than the people of the South,[9] gave them a kind of strength better adapted to violent exertions than to patient labour, and inspired them with constitutional bravery, which is the result of nerves and spirits. The severity of a winter campaign, that chilled the courage of the Roman troops, was scarcely felt by these hardy children of the North,[10] who in their turn were unable to resist the summer heats, and dissolved away in languor and sickness under the beams of an Italian sun.[11]

There is not anywhere upon the globe a large tract of country which we have discovered destitute of inhabitants, or whose first population can be fixed with any degree of historical certainty. And yet, as the most philosophic minds can seldom refrain from investigating the infancy of great nations, our curiosity consumes itself in toilsome and disappointed efforts. When Tacitus considered the purity of the German blood, and the forbidding aspect of the country, he was disposed to pronounce those barbarians *Indigenæ*, or natives of the soil. We may allow with safety, and perhaps with truth, that ancient Germany was not originally peopled by any foreign colonies already formed into a political society;[12] but that the name and nation received their existence from the gradual union of some wandering savages of the Hercynian woods. To assert those savages to have been the spontaneous production of the earth which they inhabited would be a rash inference, condemned by religion and unwarranted by reason.

Such rational doubt is but ill-suited with the genius of popular vanity. Among the nations who have adopted the Mosaic history of the world, the ark of Noah has been of the same use as was formerly to the Greeks and Romans the siege of Troy. On a narrow basis of acknowledged truth an immense but rude superstructure of fable has been erected, and the "Wild Irishman," as well as the Wild Tartar, could point out the individual son of Japhet, from whose loins his ancestors were lineally descended. The last century abounded with antiquarians of profound learning and easy faith, who by the dim light of legends and traditions, of conjectures and etymologies, conducted the great-grandchildren of Noah from the tower of Babel to the extremities of the globe. Of these judicious critics, one of the most entertaining was Olaus Rudbeck, professor in the University of Upsal.[13] Whatever is celebrated, either in history or fable, this zealous patriot ascribes to his country. From Sweden (which formed so considerable a part of ancient Germany) the Greeks themselves derived their alphabetical characters, their astronomy, and their religion. Of

that delightful region (for such it appeared to the eyes of a native) the Atlantis of Plato, the country of the Hyperboreans, the gardens of the Hesperides, the Fortunate Islands, and even the Elysian Fields, were all but faint and imperfect transcripts. A clime so profusely favoured by Nature could not long remain desert after the flood. The learned Rudbeck allows the family of Noah a few years to multiply from eight to about twenty thousand persons. He then disperses them into small colonies to replenish the earth and to propagate the human species. The German or Swedish detachment (which marched, if I am not mistaken, under the command of Askenaz, the son of Gomer, the son of Japhet) distinguished itself by a more than common diligence in the prosecution of this great work. The northern hive cast its swarms over the greatest part of Europe, Africa, and Asia; and (to use the author's metaphor) the blood circulated from the extremities to the heart.

But all this well-laboured system of German antiquities is annihilated by a single fact, too well attested to admit of any doubt, and of too decisive a nature to leave room for any reply. The Germans, in the age of Tacitus, were unacquainted with the use of letters;[14] and the use of letters is the principal circumstance that distinguishes a civilized people from a herd of savages incapable of knowledge or reflection. Without that artificial help, the human memory soon dissipates or corrupts the ideas intrusted to her charge; and the nobler faculties of the mind, no longer supplied with models or with materials, gradually forget their powers; the judgment becomes feeble and lethargic, the imagination languid or irregular. Fully to apprehend this important truth, let us attempt, in an improved society, to calculate the immense distance between the man of learning and the *illiterate* peasant. The former, by reading and reflection, multiplies his own experience, and lives in distant ages and remote countries; whilst the latter, rooted to a single spot, and confined to a few years of existence, surpasses, but very little, his fellow-labourer the ox in the exercise of his mental faculties. The same, and even a greater, difference will be found between nations than between individuals; and we may safely pronounce that, without some species of writing, no people has ever preserved the faithful annals of their history, ever made any considerable progress in the abstract sciences, or ever possessed, in any tolerable degree of perfection, the useful and agreeable arts of life.

Of these arts, the ancient Germans were

wretchedly destitute. They passed their lives in a state of ignorance and poverty, which it has pleased some declaimers to dignify with the appellation of virtuous simplicity. Modern Germany is said to contain about two thousand three hundred walled towns.[15] In a much wider extent of country, the geographer Ptolemy could discover no more than ninety places, which he decorates with the name of cities;[16] though according to our ideas, they would but ill deserve that splendid title. We can only suppose them to have been rude fortifications, constructed in the centre of the woods, and designed to secure the women, children, and cattle, whilst the warriors of the tribe marched out to repel a sudden invasion.[17] But Tacitus asserts, as a well-known fact, that the Germans, in his time, had *no* cities;[18] and that they affected to despise the works of Roman industry as places of confinement rather than of security.[19] Their edifices were not even contiguous, or formed into regular villages;[20] each barbarian fixed his independent dwelling on the spot to which a plain, a wood or a stream of fresh water had induced him to give the preference. Neither stone, nor brick, nor tiles, were employed in these slight habitations.[21] They were indeed no more than low huts of a circular figure, built of rough timber, thatched with straw, and pierced at the top to leave a free passage for the smoke. In the most inclement winter, the hardy German was satisfied with a scanty garment made of the skin of some animal . The nations who dwelt towards the North clothed themselves in furs; and the women manufactured for their own use a coarse kind of linen.[22] The game of various sorts, with which the forests of Germany were plentifully stocked, supplied its inhabitants with food and exercise.[23] Their monstrous herds of cattle, less remarkable indeed for their beauty than for their utility,[24] formed the principal object of their wealth. A small quantity of corn was the only produce exacted from the earth: the use of orchards or artificial meadows was unknown to the Germans; nor can we expect any improvements in agriculture from a people whose property every year experienced a general change by a new division of the arable lands, and who, in that strange operation, avoided disputes by suffering a great part of their territory to lie waste and without tillage.[25]

Gold, silver, and iron were extremely scarce in Germany. Its barbarous inhabitants wanted both skill and patience to investigate those rich veins of silver, which have so liberally rewarded the attention of the princes of Brunswick and Saxony. Sweden, which now supplies Europe with iron, was equally ignorant of its own riches; and the appearance of the arms of the Germans furnished a sufficient proof how little iron they were able to bestow on what they must have deemed the noblest use of that metal. The various transactions of peace and war had introduced some Roman coins (chiefly silver) among the borderers of the Rhine and Danube; but the more distant tribes were absolutely unacquainted with the use of money, carried on their confined traffic by the exchange of commodities, and prized their rude earthen vessels as of equal value with the silver vases, the presents of Rome to their princes and ambassadors.[26] To a mind capable of reflection, such leading facts convey more instruction than a tedious detail of subordinate circumstances. The value of money has been settled by general consent to express our wants and our property, as letters were invented to express our ideas; and both these institutions, by giving a more active energy to the powers and passions of human nature, have contributed to multiply the objects they were designed to represent. The use of gold and silver is in a great measure fictitious; but it would be impossible to enumerate the important and various services which agriculture, and all the arts, have received from iron, when tempered and fashioned by the operation of fire and the dexterous hand of man. Money, in a word, is the most universal incitement, iron the most powerful instrument, of human industry; and it is very difficult to conceive by what means a people, neither actuated by the one nor seconded by the other, could emerge from the grossest barbarism.[27]

If we contemplate a savage nation in any part of the globe, a supine indolence and carelessness of futurity will be found to constitute their general character. In a civilised state, every faculty of man is expanded and exercised; and the great chain of mutual dependence connects and embraces the several members of society. The most numerous portion of it is employed in constant and useful labour. The select few, placed by fortune above that necessity, can, however, fill up their time by the pursuits of interest or glory, by the improvement of their estate or of their understanding, by the duties, the pleasures, and even the follies of social life. The Germans were not possessed of their varied resources. The care of the house and family, the management of the land and cattle, were delegated to the old and the infirm, to women and slaves. The lazy warrior, destitute of every art that might employ his leisure hours, consumed his days and nights in the animal gratifications of sleep and food. And yet, by a wonderful diversity of Nature (according to the remark of a writer who had pierced into its darkest recesses), the same barbarians are by turns the most indolent and the most restless of mankind. They delight in sloth, they detest tranquillity.[28] The languid soul, oppressed with its own weight, anxiously required some new and powerful sensation; and war and danger were the only amusements adequate to its fierce temper. The sound that summoned the German to arms was grateful to his ear. It roused him from his uncomfortable lethargy, gave him an active pursuit, and, by strong exercise of the body, and violent emotions of the mind, restored him to a more lively sense of his existence. In the dull intervals of peace, these barbarians were immoderately addicted to deep gaming and excessive drinking; both of which, by different means, the one by inflaming their passions, the other by extinguishing their reason, alike relieved them from the pain of thinking. They gloried in passing whole days and nights at table; and the blood of friends and relations often stained their numerous and drunken assemblies.[29] Their debts of honour (for in that light they have transmitted to us those of play) they discharged with the most romantic fidelity. The desperate gamester, who had staked his person and liberty on a last throw of the dice, patiently submitted to the decision of fortune, and suffered himself to be bound, chastised, and sold into remote slavery, by his weaker but more lucky antagonist.[30]

Strong beer, a liquor extracted with very little art from wheat or barley, and *corrupted* (as it is strongly expressed by Tacitus) into a certain semblance of wine, was sufficient for the gross purposes of German debauchery. But those who had tasted the rich wines of Italy, and afterwards of Gaul, sighed for that more delicious species of intoxication. They attempted not, however (as has since been executed with so much success), to naturalise the vine on the banks of the Rhine and Danube; nor did they endeavour to procure by industry the materials of an advantageous commerce. To solicit by labour what might be ravished by arms was esteemed unworthy of the German spirit.[31] The intemperate thirst of strong liquors often urged the barbarians to invade the provinces on which art or nature had bestowed those much envied presents. The Tuscan who betrayed his country

to the Celtic nations attracted them into Italy by the prospect of the rich fruits and delicious wines, the productions of a happier climate.[32] And in the same manner the German auxiliaries, invited into France during the civil wars of the sixteenth century, were allured by the promise of plenteous quarters in the provinces of Champagne and Burgundy.[33] Drunkenness, the most illiberal, but not the most dangerous, of *our* vices, was sometimes capable, in a less civilised state of mankind, of occasioning a battle, a war, or a revolution.

The climate of ancient Germany had been mollified, and the soil fertilised, by the labour of ten centuries from the time of Charlemagne. The same extent of ground which at present maintains, in ease and plenty, a million of husbandmen and artificers, was unable to supply an hundred thousand lazy warriors with the simple necessaries of life.[34] The Germans abandoned their immense forests to the exercise of hunting, employed in pasturage the most considerable part of their lands, bestowed on the small remainder a rude and careless cultivation, and then accused the scantiness and sterility of a country that refused to maintain the multitude of its inhabitants. When the return of famine severely admonished them of the importance of the arts, the national distress was sometimes alleviated by the emigration of a third, perhaps, or a fourth part of their youth.[35] The possession and the enjoyment of property are the pledges which bind a civilised people to an improved country. But the Germans, who carried with them what they most valued, their arms, their cattle, and their women, cheerfully abandoned the vast silence of their woods for the unbounded hopes of plunder and conquest. The innumerable swarms that issued, or seemed to issue, from the great storehouse of nations, were multiplied by the fears of the vanquished and by the credulity of succeeding ages. And from facts thus exaggerated, an opinion was gradually established, and has been supported by writers of distinguished reputation, that, in the age of Cæsar and Tacitus, the inhabitants of the North were far more numerous than they are in our days.[36] A more serious inquiry into the causes of population seems to have convinced modern philosophers of the falsehood, and indeed the impossibility, of the supposition. To the names of Mariana and of Machiavel,[37] we can oppose the equal names of Robertson and Hume.[38]

A warlike nation like the Germans, without either cities, letters, arts, or money, found some compensation for this savage state in the enjoyment of liberty. Their poverty secured their freedom, since our desires and our possessions are the strongest fetters of despotism. "Among the Suiones (says Tacitus), riches are held in honour. They are *therefore* subject to an absolute monarch, who, instead of intrusting his people with the free use of arms, as is practised in the rest of Germany, commits them to the safe custody not of a citizen, or even of a freedman, but of a slave. The neighbours of the Suiones, the Sitones, are sunk even below servitude; they obey a woman."[39] In the mention of these exceptions, the great historian sufficiently acknowledges the general theory of government. We are only at a loss to conceive by what means riches and despotism could penetrate into a remote corner of the North, and extinguish the generous flame that blazed with such fierceness on the frontier of the Roman provinces: or how the ancestors of those Danes and Norwegians, so distinguished in latter ages by their unconquered spirit, could thus tamely resign the great character of German liberty.[40] Some tribes, however, on the coast of the Baltic, acknowledged the authority of kings, though without relinquishing the rights of men;[41] but in the far greater part of Germany, the form of government was a democracy tempered indeed, and controlled, not so much by general and positive laws, as by the occasional ascendant of birth or valour, of eloquence or superstition.[42]

Civil governments, in their first institutions, are voluntary associations for mutual defence. To obtain the desired end, it is absolutely necessary that each individual should conceive himself obliged to submit his private opinion and actions to the judgment of the greater number of his associates. The German tribes were contented with this rude but liberal outline of political society. As soon as a youth, born of free parents, had attained the age of manhood, he was introduced into the general council of his countrymen, solemnly invested with a shield and spear, and adopted as an equal and worthy member of the military commonwealth. The assembly of the warriors of the tribe was convened at stated seasons or on sudden emergencies. The trial of public offences, the election of magistrates, and the great business of peace and war, were determined by its independent voice. Sometimes, indeed, these important questions were previously considered and prepared in a more select council of the principal chieftains.[43] The magistrates might deliberate and persuade, the people only could resolve and execute; and

the resolutions of the Germans were for the most part hasty and violent. Barbarians accustomed to place their freedom in gratifying the present passion, and their courage in overlooking all future consequences, turned away with indignant contempt from the remonstrance of justice and policy, and it was the practice to signify by a hollow murmur their dislike of such timid counsels. But whenever a more popular orator proposed to vindicate the meanest citizen from either foreign or domestic injury, whenever he called upon his fellow-countrymen to assert the national honour, or to pursue some enterprise full of danger and glory, a loud clashing of shields and spears expressed the eager applause of the assembly. For the Germans always met in arms, and it was constantly to be dreaded lest an irregular multitude, inflamed with faction and strong liquors, should use those arms to enforce, as well as to declare, their furious resolves. We may recollect how often the diets of Poland have been polluted with blood, and the more numerous party has been compelled to yield to the more violent and seditious.[44]

A general of the tribe was elected on occasions of danger; and, if the danger was pressing and extensive, several tribes concurred in the choice of the same general. The bravest warrior was named to lead his countrymen into the field by his example rather than by his commands. But this power, however limited, was still invidious. It expired with the war, and in time of peace the German tribes acknowledged not any supreme chief.[45] *Princes* were, however, appointed in the general assembly, to administer justice, or rather to compose differences,[46] in their respective districts. In the choice of these magistrates as much regard was shown to birth as to merit.[47] To each was assigned, by the public, a guard and a council of an hundred persons; and the first of the princes appears to have enjoyed a pre-eminence of rank and honour which sometimes tempted the Romans to compliment him with the regal title.[48]

The comparative view of the powers of the magistrates, in two remarkable instances, is alone sufficient to represent the whole system of German manners. The disposal of the landed property within their district was absolutely vested in their hands, and they distributed it every year according to a new division.[49] At the same time they were not authorised to punish with death, to imprison, or even to strike, a private citizen.[50] A people thus jealous of their persons, and careless of their possessions, must have been totally destitute of industry and the arts, but animated with a high sense of honour and independence.

The Germans respected only those duties which they imposed on themselves. The most obscure soldier resisted with disdain the authority of the magistrates. "The noblest youths blushed not to be numbered among the faithful companions of some renowned chief, to whom they devoted their arms and service. A noble emulation prevailed among the companions to obtain the first place in the esteem of their chief; amongst the chiefs, to acquire the greatest number of valiant companions. To be ever surrounded by a band of select youths was the pride and strength of the chiefs, their ornament in peace, their defence in war. The glory of such distinguished heroes diffused itself beyond the narrow limits of their own tribe. Presents and embassies solicited their friendship, and the fame of their arms often ensured victory to the party which they espoused. In the hour of danger it was shameful for the chief to be surpassed in valour by his companions; shameful for the companions not to equal the valour of their chief. To survive his fall in battle was indelible infamy. To protect his person and to adorn his glory with the trophies of their own exploits were the most sacred of their duties. The chiefs combated for victory, the companions for the chief. The noblest warriors, whenever their native country was sunk in the laziness of peace, maintained their numerous bands in some distant scene of action, to exercise their restless spirit and to acquire renown by voluntary dangers. Gifts worthy of soldiers, the warlike steed, the bloody and ever victorious lance, were the rewards which the companions claimed from the liberality of their chief. The rude plenty of his hospitable board was the only pay that *he* could bestow or *they* would accept. War, rapine, and the free-will offerings of his friends, supplied the materials of this munificence."[51] This institution, however it might accidentally weaken the several republics, invigorated the general character of the Germans, and even ripened amongst them all the virtues of which barbarians are susceptible; the faith and valour, the hospitality and the courtesy, so conspicuous long afterwards in the ages of chivalry. The honourable gifts, bestowed by the chief on his brave companions, have been supposed, by an ingenious writer, to contain the first rudiments of the fiefs, distributed, after the conquest of the Roman provinces, by the barbarian lords among their vassals, with a similar duty of homage and military service.[52] These conditions are, however, very repugnant to the maxims of the ancient Germans, who delighted in mutual presents; but without either imposing, or accepting, the weight of obligations.[53]

"In the days of chivalry, or more properly of romance, all the men were brave, and all the women were chaste;" and notwithstanding the latter of these virtues is acquired and preserved with much more difficulty than the former, it is ascribed, almost without exception, to the wives of the ancient Germans. Polygamy was not in use, except among the princes, and among them only for the sake of multiplying their alliances. Divorces were prohibited by manners rather than by laws. Adulteries were punished as rare and inexpiable crimes; nor was seduction justified by example and fashion.[54] We may easily discover that Tacitus indulges an honest pleasure in the contrast of barbarian virtue with the dissolute conduct of the Roman ladies; yet there are some striking circumstances that give an air of truth, or at least of probability, to the conjugal faith and chastity of the Germans.

Although the progress of civilisation has undoubtedly contributed to assuage the fiercer passions of human nature, it seems to have been less favourable to the virtue of chastity, whose most dangerous enemy is the softness of the mind. The refinements of life corrupt while they polish the intercourse of the sexes. The gross appetite of love becomes most dangerous when it is elevated, or rather, indeed, disguised by sentimental passion. The elegance of dress, of motion, and of manners gives a lustre to beauty, and inflames the senses through the imagination. Luxurious entertainments, midnight dances, and licentious spectacles, present at once temptations and opportunity to female frailty.[55] From such dangers the unpolished wives of the barbarians were secured by poverty, solitude, and the painful cares of a domestic life. The German huts, open on every side to the eye of indiscretion or jealousy, were a better safeguard of conjugal fidelity than the walls, the bolts, and the eunuchs of a Persian harem. To this reason, another may be added of a more honourable nature. The Germans treated their women with esteem and confidence, consulted them on every occasion of importance, and fondly believed that in their breasts resided a sanctity and wisdom more than human. Some of these interpreters of fate, such as Velleda, in the Batavian war, governed, in the name of the deity, the fiercest nations of Germany.[56] The rest of the sex, without being adored as goddesses, were respected as the free and equal companions of soldiers; associated even by the marriage ceremony to a life of toil, of danger, and of glory.[57] In their great invasions, the camps of the barbarians were filled with a multitude of women, who remained firm and undaunted amidst the sound of arms, the various forms of destruction, and the honourable wounds of their sons and husbands.[58] Fainting armies of Germans have more than once been driven back upon the enemy by the generous despair of the women who dreaded death much less than servitude. If the day was irrecoverably lost, they well knew how to deliver themselves and their children, with their own hands, from an insulting victor.[59] Heroines of such a cast may claim our admiration; but they were most assuredly neither lovely, nor very susceptible of love. Whilst they affected to emulate the stern virtues of *man*, they must have resigned that attractive softness in which principally consists the charm of *woman*. Conscious pride taught the German females to suppress every tender emotion that stood in competition with honour, and the first honour of the sex has ever been that of chastity. The sentiments and conduct of these high-spirited matrons may, at once, be considered as a cause, as an effect, and as a proof of the general character of the nation. Female courage, however it may be raised by fanaticism, or confirmed by habit, can be only a faint and imperfect imitation of the manly valour that distinguishes the age or country in which it may be found.

The religious system of the Germans (if the wild opinions of savages can deserve that name) was dictated by their wants, their fears, and their ignorance.[60] They adored the great visible objects and agents of nature, the Sun and the Moon, the Fire and the Earth; together with those imaginary deities, who were supposed to preside over the most important occupations of human life. They were persuaded that, by some ridiculous arts of divination, they could discover the will of the superior beings, and that human sacrifices were the most precious and acceptable offering to their altars. Some applause has been hastily bestowed on the sublime notion, entertained by that people, of the Deity, whom they neither confined within the walls of a temple, nor represented by any human figure; but when we recollect that the Germans were unskilled in architecture, and totally unacquainted with the art of sculpture, we shall readily assign the true reason of a scruple which arose not so much from a superi-

ority of reason as from a want of ingenuity. The only temples in Germany were dark and ancient groves, consecrated by the reverence of succeeding generations. Their secret gloom, the imagined residence of an invisible power, by presenting no distinct object of fear or worship, impressed the mind with a still deeper sense of religious horror;[61] and the priests, rude and illiterate as they were, had been taught by experience the use of every artifice that could preserve and fortify impressions so well suited to their own interest.

The same ignorance, which renders barbarians incapable of conceiving or embracing the useful restraints of laws, exposes them naked and unarmed to the blind terrors of superstition. The German priests, improving this favourable temper of their countrymen, had assumed a jurisdiction, even in temporal concerns, which the magistrate could not venture to exercise; and the haughty warrior patiently submitted to the lash of correction, when it was inflicted, not by any human power, but by the immediate order of the god of war.[62] The defects of civil policy were sometimes supplied by the interposition of ecclesiastical authority. The latter was constantly exerted to maintain silence and decency in the popular assemblies; and was sometimes extended to a more enlarged concern for the national welfare. A solemn procession was occasionally celebrated in the present countries of Mecklenburgh and Pomerania. The unknown symbol of the *Earth*, covered with a thick veil, was placed on a carriage drawn by cows; and in this manner the goddess, whose common residence was in the isle of Rugen, visited several adjacent tribes of her worshippers. During her progress the sound of war was hushed, quarrels were suspended, arms laid aside, and the restless Germans had an opportunity of tasting the blessings of peace and harmony.[63] The *truce of God*, so often and so ineffectually proclaimed by the clergy of the eleventh century, was an obvious imitation of this ancient custom.[64]

But the influence of religion was far more powerful to inflame than to moderate the fierce passions of the Germans. Interest and fanaticism often prompted its ministers to sanctify the most daring and the most unjust enterprises, by the approbation of Heaven, and full assurances of success. The consecrated standards, long revered in the groves of superstition, were placed in the front of the battle;[65] and the hostile army was devoted with dire execrations to the gods of war and of thunder.[66] In the faith of soldiers (and such were the Germans) cowardice is the most unpardonable of sins. A brave man was the worthy favourite of their martial deities; the wretch, who had lost his shield, was alike banished from the religious and civil assemblies of his countrymen. Some tribes of the north seem to have embraced the doctrine of transmigration,[67] others imagined a gross paradise of immortal drunkenness.[68] All agreed that a life spent in arms, and a glorious death in battle, were the best preparations for a happy futurity either in this or in another world.

The immortality so vainly promised by the priests was in some degree conferred by the bards. That singular order of men has most deservedly attracted the notice of all who have attempted to investigate the antiquities of the Celts, the Scandinavians, and the Germans. Their genius and character, as well as the reverence paid to that important office, have been sufficiently illustrated. But we cannot so easily express, or even conceive, the enthusiasm of arms and glory, which they kindled in the breast of their audience. Among a polished people, a taste for poetry is rather an amusement of the fancy than a passion of the soul. And yet, when in calm retirement we peruse the combats described by Homer or Tasso, we are insensibly seduced by the fiction, and feel a momentary glow of martial ardour. But how faint, how cold is the sensation which a peaceful mind can receive from solitary study! It was in the hour of battle, or in the feast of victory, that the bards celebrated the glory of heroes of ancient days, the ancestors of those warlike chieftains who listened with transport to their artless but animated strains. The view of arms and of danger heightened the effect of the military song; and the passions which it tended to excite, the desire of fame and the contempt of death, were the habitual sentiments of a German mind.[69]

Such was the situation, and such were the manners, of the ancient Germans. Their climate, their want of learning, of arts, and of laws, their notions of honour, of gallantry, and of religion, their sense of freedom, impatience of peace, and thirst of enterprise, all contributed to form a people of military heroes. And yet we find that, during more than two hundred and fifty years that elapsed from the defeat of Varus to the reign of Decius, these formidable barbarians made few considerable attempts, and not any material impression on the luxurious and enslaved provinces of the empire. Their progress was checked by their want of arms and discipline, and their fury was diverted by the intestine divisions of ancient Germany.

I. It has been observed, with ingenuity, and not without truth, that the command of iron soon gives a nation the command of gold. But the rude tribes of Germany, alike destitute of both those valuable metals, were reduced slowly to acquire, by their unassisted strength, the possession of the one as well as the other. The face of a German army displayed their poverty of iron. Swords, and the longer kind of lances, they could seldom use. Their *frameæ* (as they called them in their own language) were long spears headed with a sharp but narrow iron point, and which, as occasion required, they either darted from a distance or pushed in close onset. With this spear, and with a shield, their cavalry was contented. A multitude of darts, scattered[70] with incredible force, were an additional resource of the infantry. Their military dress, when they wore any, was nothing more than a loose mantle. A variety of colours was the only ornament of their wooden or osier shields. Few of the chiefs were distinguished by cuirasses, scarce any by helmets. Though the horses of Germany were neither beautiful, swift, nor practised in the skilful evolutions of the Roman manege, several of the nations obtained renown by their cavalry; but, in general, the principal strength of the Germans consisted in their infantry,[71] which was drawn up in several deep columns, according to the distinction of tribes and families. Impatient of fatigue or delay, these half-armed warriors rushed to battle with dissonant shouts and disordered ranks; and sometimes, by the effort of native valour, prevailed over the constrained and more artificial bravery of the Roman mercenaries. But as the barbarians poured forth their whole souls on the first onset, they knew not how to rally or to retire. A repulse was a sure defeat; and a defeat was most commonly total destruction. When we recollect the complete armour of the Roman soldiers, their discipline, exercises, evolutions, fortified camps, and military engines, it appears a just matter of surprise how the naked and unassisted valour of the barbarians could dare to encounter in the field the strength of the legions, and the various troops of the auxiliaries which seconded their operations. The contest was too unequal, till the introduction of luxury had enervated the vigour, and a spirit of disobedience and sedition had relaxed the discipline, of the Roman armies. The introduction of barbarian auxiliaries into those armies was a measure attended with very obvious dangers, as it might gradually instruct the Germans in the arts of war and of policy. Although they were admitted in small numbers and with the strictest precaution, the example of Civilis was proper to convince the Romans that the danger was not imaginary, and that their precautions were not always sufficient.[72] During the civil wars that followed the death of Nero, that artful and intrepid Batavian, whom his enemies condescended to compare with Hannibal and Sertorius,[73] formed a great design of freedom and ambition. Eight Batavian cohorts, renowned in the wars of Britain and Italy, repaired to his standard. He introduced an army of Germans into Gaul, prevailed on the powerful cities of Treves and Langres to embrace his cause, defeated the legions, destroyed their fortified camps, and employed against the Romans the military knowledge which he had acquired in their service. When at length, after an obstinate struggle, he yielded to the power of the empire, Civilis secured himself and his country by an honourable treaty. The Batavians still continued to occupy the islands of the Rhine,[74] the allies not the servants of the Roman monarchy.

II. The strength of ancient Germany appears formidable when we consider the effects that might have been produced by its united effort. The wide extent of country might very possibly contain a million of warriors, as all who were of age to bear arms were of a temper to use them. But this fierce multitude, incapable of concerting or executing any plan of national greatness, was agitated by various and often hostile intentions. Germany was divided into more than forty independent states; and even in each state the union of the several tribes was extremely loose and precarious. The barbarians were easily provoked; they knew not how to forgive an injury, much less an insult; their resentments were bloody and implacable. The casual disputes that so frequently happened in their tumultuous parties of hunting or drinking were sufficient to inflame the minds of whole nations; the private feud of any considerable chieftains diffused itself among their followers and allies. To chastise the insolent, or to plunder the defenceless, were alike causes of war. The most formidable states of Germany affected to encompass their territories with a wide frontier of solitude and devastation. The awful distance preserved by their neighbours attested the terror of their arms, and in some measure defended them from the danger of unexpected incursions.[75]

"The Bructeri (it is Tacitus who now speaks) were totally exterminated by the neighbouring tribes,[76] provoked by their insolence, allured by the hopes of spoil, and perhaps inspired by the tutelar deities of the empire. Above sixty thousand barbarians were destroyed; not by the Roman arms, but in our sight, and for our entertainment. May the nations, enemies of Rome, ever preserve this enmity to each other! We have now attained the utmost verge of prosperity,[77] and have nothing left to demand of Fortune, except the discord of these barbarians."[78] These sentiments, less worthy of the humanity than of the patriotism of Tacitus, express the invariable maxims of the policy of his countrymen. They deemed it a much safer expedient to divide than to combat the barbarians, from whose defeat they could derive neither honour nor advantage. The money and negotiations of Rome insinuated themselves into the heart of Germany; and every art of seduction was used with dignity to conciliate those nations whom their proximity to the Rhine or Danube might render the most useful friends as well as the most troublesome enemies. Chiefs of renown and power were flattered by the most trifling presents, which they received either as marks of distinction, or as the instruments of luxury. In civil dissensions, the weaker faction endeavoured to strengthen its interest by entering into secret connections with the governors of the frontier provinces. Every quarrel among the Germans was fomented by the intrigues of Rome; and every plan of union and public good was defeated by the stronger bias of private jealousy and interest.[79]

The general conspiracy which terrified the Romans under the reign of Marcus Antoninus comprehended almost all the nations of Germany, and even Sarmatia, from the mouth of the Rhine to that of the Danube.[80] It is impossible for us to determine whether this hasty confederation was formed by necessity, by reason, or by passion; but we may rest assured that the barbarians were neither allured by the indolence, nor provoked by the ambition, of the Roman monarch. This dangerous invasion required all the firmness and vigilance of Marcus. He fixed generals of ability in the several stations of attack, and assumed in person the conduct of the most important province on the Upper Danube. After a long and doubtful conflict, the spirit of the barbarians was subdued. The Quadi and the Marcomanni,[81] who had taken the lead in the war, were the most severely punished in its catastrophe. They were commanded to retire five miles[82] from their own banks of the

Danube, and to deliver up the flower of the youth, who were immediately sent into Britain, a remote island, where they might be secure as hostages, and useful as soldiers.[83] On the frequent rebellions of the Quadi and Marcomanni, the irritated emperor resolved to reduce their country into the form of a province. His designs were disappointed by death. This formidable league, however, the only one that appears in the two first centuries of the Imperial history, was entirely dissipated, without leaving any traces behind in Germany.

In the course of this introductory chapter, we have confined ourselves to the general outlines of the manners of Germany, without attempting to describe or to distinguish the various tribes which filled the great country in the time of Cæsar, of Tacitus, or of Ptolemy. As the ancient, or as new tribes successively present themselves in the series of this history, we shall concisely mention their origin, their situation, and their particular character. Modern nations are fixed and permanent societies, connected among themselves by laws and government, bound to their native soil by arts and agriculture. The German tribes were voluntary and fluctuating associations of soldiers, almost of savages. The same territory often changed its inhabitants in the tide of conquest and emigration. The same communities, uniting in a plan of defence or invasion, bestowed a new title on their new confederacy. The dissolution of an ancient confederacy restored to the independent tribes their peculiar but long-forgotten appellation. A victorious state often communicated its own name to a vanquished people. Sometimes crowds of volunteers flocked from all parts to the standard of a favourite leader; his camp became their country, and some circumstance of the enterprise soon gave a common denomination to the mixed multitude. The distinctions of the ferocious invaders were perpetually varied by themselves, and confounded by the astonished subjects of the Roman empire.[84]

Wars, and the administration of public affairs, are the principal subjects of history; but the number of persons interested in these busy scenes is very different according to the different condition of mankind. In great monarchies, millions of obedient subjects pursue their useful occupations in peace and obscurity. The attention of the writer, as well as of the reader, is solely confined to a court, a capital, a regular army, and the districts which happen to be the occasional scene of military operations. But a state of freedom and barbarism, the season of civil commotions, or the situation of petty republics,[85] raises almost every member of the community into action, and consequently into notice. The irregular divisions, and the restless motions, of the people of Germany dazzle our imagination and seem to multiply their numbers. The profuse enumeration of kings and warriors of armies and nations inclines us to forget that the same objects are continually repeated under a variety of appellations, and that the most splendid appellations have been frequently lavished on the most inconsiderable objects.

CHAPTER X

The Emperors Decius, Gallus, Æmilianus, Valerian, and Gallienus. The general Irruption of the Barbarians. The Thirty Tyrants.

FROM the great secular games celebrated by Philip to the death of the emperor Gallienus there elapsed (A.D. 248–268) twenty years of shame and misfortune. During that calamitous period every instant of time was marked, every province of the Roman world was afflicted by barbarous invaders and military tyrants, and the ruined empire seemed to approach the last and fatal moment of its dissolution. The confusion of the times, and the scarcity of authentic memorials, oppose equal difficulties to the historian, who attempts to preserve a clear and unbroken thread of narration. Surrounded with imperfect fragments, always concise, often obscure, and sometimes contradictory, he is reduced to collect, to compare, and to conjecture: and though he ought never to place his conjectures in the rank of facts, yet the knowledge of human nature, and of the sure operation of its fierce and unrestrained passions, might, on some occasions, supply the want of historical materials.

There is not, for instance, any difficulty in conceiving that the successive murders of so many emperors had loosened all the ties of allegiance between the prince and people; that all the generals of Philip were disposed to imitate the example of their master; and that the caprice of armies, long since habituated to frequent and violent revolutions, might any day raise to the throne the most obscure of their fellow-soldiers. History can only add that the rebellion against the emperor Philip broke out in the summer of the year two hundred and forty-nine, among the legions of Mæsia; and that a subaltern officer,[1] named Marinus, was the object of their seditious choice. Philip was alarmed. He dreaded lest the treason of the Mæsian army should prove the first spark of a general conflagration. Distracted with the consciousness of his guilt and of his danger, he communicated the intelligence to the senate. A gloomy silence prevailed, the effect of fear, and perhaps of disaffection: till at length Decius, one of the assembly, assuming a spirit worthy of his noble extraction, ventured to discover more intrepidity than the emperor seemed to possess. He treated the whole business with contempt, as a hasty and inconsiderate tumult, and Philip's rival as a phantom of royalty, who in a very few days would be destroyed by the same inconstancy that had created him. The speedy completion of the prophecy inspired Philip with a just esteem for so able a counsellor: and Decius appeared to him the only person capable of restoring peace and discipline to an army whose tumultuous spirit did not immediately subside after the murder of Marinus. Decius who long resisted his own nomination, seems to have insinuated the danger of presenting a leader of merit to the angry and apprehensive minds of the soldiers; and his prediction was again confirmed by the event. The legion of Mæsia forced their judge to become (A.D. 249) their accomplice. They left him only the alternative of death or the purple. His subsequent conduct, after that decisive measure, was unavoidable. He conducted or followed his army to the confines of Italy, whither Philip, collecting all his force to repel the formidable competitor whom he had raised up, advanced to meet him. The Imperial troops were superior in number; but the rebels formed an army of veterans, commanded by an able and experienced leader.[2] Philip was either killed in the battle or put to death a few days afterwards at Verona. His son and associate in the empire was massacred at Rome by the Prætorian guards; and the victorious Decius, with more favourable circumstances than the ambition of that age can usually plead, was universally acknowledged by the senate and provinces. It is reported that, immediately after his reluctant acceptance of the title of Augustus, he had assured Philip, by a private message, of his innocence and loyalty, solemnly protesting that, on his arrival in Italy, he would resign the imperial ornaments and return to the condition of an obedient subject. His professions might be sincere. But in the situation where fortune had placed him it was scarcely possible that he could either forgive or be forgiven.[3]

The emperor Decius had employed a few months in the works of peace and the administration of justice, when (A.D. 250) he was summoned to the banks of the Danube by the invasion of the GOTHS. This is the first considerable occasion in which history mentions that great people, who afterwards broke the Roman power, sacked the Capitol, and reigned in Gaul, Spain, and Italy. So memorable was the part which they acted in the subversion of the Western empire that the name of GOTHS is frequently but improperly used as a general appellation of rude and warlike barbarism.

In the beginning of the sixth century, and after the conquest of Italy, the Goths, in possession of present greatness, very naturally indulged themselves in the prospect of past and of future glory. They wished to preserve the memory of their ancestors, and to transmit to posterity their own achievements. The principal minister of the court of Ravenna, the learned Cassiodorus, gratified the inclination of the conquerors in a Gothic history, which consisted of twelve books, now reduced to the imperfect abridgment of Jornandes.[4] These writers passed with the most artful conciseness over the misfortunes of the nation, celebrated its successful valour, and adorned the triumph with many Asiatic trophies that more properly belonged to the people of Scythia. On the faith of ancient songs, the uncertain, but the only, memorials of barbarians, they deduced the first origin of the Goths from the vast island, or peninsula, of Scandinavia.[5] That extreme country of the north was not unknown to the conquerors of Italy: the ties of ancient consanguinity had been strengthened by recent offices of friendship; and a Scandinavian king had cheerfully abdicated his savage greatness that he might pass the remainder of his days in the peaceful and polished court of Ravenna.[6] Many vestiges, which cannot be ascribed to the arts of popular vanity, attest the ancient residence of the Goths in the countries beyond the Baltic. From the time of the geographer Ptolemy, the southern part of Sweden seems to have continued in the possession of the less enterprising remnant of the nation, and a large territory is even at present divided into east and west Gothland. During the middle ages (from the ninth to the twelfth century), whilst Christianity was advancing with a slow progress into the north, the Goths and the Swedes composed two distinct and sometimes hostile members of the same monarchy.[7] The latter of these two names has prevailed without extinguishing the former. The Swedes, who might well be satisfied with their own fame in arms, have in every age claimed the kindred glory of the Goths. In a moment of discontent against the court of Rome, Charles the Twelfth insinuated that his victorious troops were not degenerated from their brave ancestors who had already subdued the mistress of the world.[8]

Till the end of the eleventh century, a celebrated temple subsisted at Upsal, the most considerable town of the Swedes and Goths. It was enriched with the gold which the Scandinavians had acquired in their piratical adventures, and sanctified by the uncouth representations of the three principal deities, the god of war, the goddess of generation, and the god of thunder. In the general festival that was solemnised every ninth year, nine animals of every species (without excepting the human) were sacrificed, and their bleeding bodies suspended in the sacred grove adjacent to the temple.[9] The only traces that now subsist of this barbaric superstition are contained in the Edda, a system of mythology compiled in Iceland about the thirteenth century, and studied by the learned of Denmark and Sweden as the most valuable remains of their ancient traditions.

Notwithstanding the mysterious obscurity of the Edda, we can easily distinguish two persons confounded under the name of Odin, the god of war, and the great legislator of Scandinavia. The latter, the Mahomet of the north, instituted a religion adapted to the climate and to the people. Numerous tribes on either side of the Baltic were subdued by the invincible valour of Odin, by his persuasive eloquence, and by the fame, which he acquired, of a most skilful magician. The faith that he had propagated during a long and prosperous life he confirmed by a voluntary death. Apprehensive of the ignominious approach of disease and infirmity, he resolved to expire as became a warrior. In a solemn assembly of the Swedes and Goths, he wounded himself in nine mortal places, hastening away (as he asserted with his dying voice) to prepare the feast of heroes in the palace of the god of war.[10]

The native and proper habitation of Odin is distinguished by the appellation of As-gard. The happy resemblance of that name with As-burg,

or As-of[11] words of a similar signification, has given rise to an historical system of so pleasing a contexture that we could almost wish to persuade ourselves of its truth. It is supposed that Odin was the chief of a tribe of barbarians which dwelt on the banks of the lake Mætois, till the fall of Mithridates and the arms of Pompey menaced the north with servitude. That Odin, yielding with indignant fury to a power which he was unable to resist, conducted his tribe from the frontiers of the Asiatic Sarmatia into Sweden, with the great design of forming, in that inaccessible retreat of freedom, a religion and a people which, in some remote age, might be subservient to his immortal revenge; when his invincible Goths, armed with martial fanaticism, should issue in numerous swarms from the neighbourhood of the Polar circle, to chastise the oppressors of mankind.[12]

If so many successive generations of Goths were capable of preserving a faint tradition of their Scandinavian origin, we must not expect, from such unlettered barbarians, any distinct account of the time and circumstances of their emigration. To cross the Baltic was an easy and natural attempt. The inhabitants of Sweden were masters of a sufficient number of large vessels, with oars,[13] and the distance is little more than one hundred miles from Carlscrona to the nearest ports of Pomerania and Prussia. Here, at length, we land on firm and historic ground. At least as early as the Christian era,[14] and as late as the age of the Antonines,[15] the Goths were established towards the mouth of the Vistula, and in that fertile province where the commercial cities of Thorn, Elbing, Koningsberg, and Dantzic were long afterwards founded.[16] Westward of the Goths, the numerous tribes of the Vandals were spread along the banks of the Oder, and the sea-coast of Pomerania and Mecklenburg. A striking resemblance of manners, complexion, religion, and language, seemed to indicate that the Vandals and the Goths were originally one great people.[17] The latter appear to have been subdivided into Ostrogoths, Visigoths, and Gepidæ.[18] The distinction among the Vandals was more strongly marked by the independent names of Heruli, Burgundians, Lombards, and a variety of other petty states, many of which, in a future age, expanded themselves into powerful monarchies.

In the age of the Antonines, the Goths were still seated in Prussia. About the reign of Alexander Severus, the Roman province of Dacia had already experienced their proximity by frequent and destructive inroads.[19] In this interval, therefore, of about seventy years, we must place the second migration of the Goths from the Baltic to the Euxine; but the cause that produced it lies concealed among the various motives which actuate the conduct of unsettled barbarians. Either a pestilence or a famine, a victory or a defeat, an oracle of the gods or the eloquence of a daring leader, were sufficient to impel the Gothic arms on the milder climates of the south. Besides the influence of a martial religion, the numbers and spirit of the Goths were equal to the most dangerous adventures. The use of round bucklers and short swords rendered them formidable in a close engagement; the manly obedience which they yielded to hereditary kings gave uncommon union and stability to their councils;[20] and the renowned Amala, the hero of that age, and the tenth ancestor of Theodoric, king of Italy, enforced, by the ascendant of personal merit, the prerogative of his birth, which he derived from the *Anses*, or demigods of the Gothic nation.[21]

The fame of a great enterprise excited the bravest warriors from all the Vandalic states of Germany, many of whom are seen a few years afterwards combating under the common standard of the Goths.[22] The first motions of the emigrants carried them to the banks of the Prypec, a river universally conceived by the ancients to be the southern branch of the Borysthenes.[23] The windings of that great stream through the plains of Poland and Russia gave a direction to their line of march, and a constant supply of fresh water and pasturage to their numerous herds of cattle. They followed the unknown course of the river, confident in their valour, and careless of whatever power might oppose their progress. The Bastarnæ and the Venedi were the first who presented themselves; and the flower of their youth, either from choice or compulsion, increased the Gothic army. The Bastarnæ dwelt on the northern side of the Carpathian mountains; the immense tract of land that separated the Bastarnæ from the savages of Finland was possessed, or rather wasted, by the Venedi;[24] we have some reason to believe that the first of these nations, which distinguished itself in the Macedonian war,[25] and was afterwards divided into the formidable tribes of the Peucini, the Borani, the Carpi, etc., derived its origin from the Germans. With better authority, a Sarmatian extraction may be assigned to the Venedi, who rendered themselves so famous in the middle ages.[26] But the confusion of blood and manners on that doubtful frontier often perplexed the most accurate observers.[27] As the

Goths advanced near the Euxine Sea, they encountered a purer race of Sarmatians, the Jazyges, the Alani, and the Roxolani; and they were probably the first Germans who saw the mouth of the Borysthenes and of the Tanais. If we inquire into the characteristic marks of the people of Germany and of Sarmatia, we shall discover that those two great portions of human kind were principally distinguished by fixed huts or movable tents, by a close dress of flowing garments, by the marriage of one or of several wives, by a military force consisting, for the most part, either of infantry or cavalry; and above all by the use of the Teutonic or of the Sclavonian language the last of which has been diffused by conquest from the confines of Italy to the neighbourhood of Japan.

The Goths were now in possession of the Ukraine, a country of considerable extent and uncommon fertility, intersected with navigable rivers, which, from either side, discharge themselves into the Borysthenes; and interspersed with large and lofty forests of oaks. The plenty of game and fish, the innumerable bee-hives, deposited in the hollows of old trees, and in the cavities of rocks, and forming, even in that rude age, a valuable branch of commerce, the size of the cattle, the temperature of the air, the aptness of the soil for every species of grain, and the luxuriancy of the vegetation, all displayed the liberality of Nature, and tempted the industry of man.[28] But the Goths withstood all these temptations, and still adhered to a life of idleness, of poverty, and of rapine.

The Scythian hordes, which, towards the east, bordered on the new settlements of the Goths, presented nothing to their arms except the doubtful chance of an unprofitable victory. But the prospect of the Roman territories was far more alluring; and the fields of Dacia were covered with rich harvests, sown by the hands of an industrious, and exposed to be gathered by those of a warlike, people. It is probable that the conquests of Trajan maintained by his successors, less for any real advantage than for ideal dignity, had contributed to weaken the empire on that side. The new and unsettled province of Dacia was neither strong enough to resist, nor rich enough to satiate, the rapaciousness of the barbarians. As long as the remote banks of the Dniester were considered as the boundary of the Roman power, the fortifications of the Lower Danube were more carelessly guarded, and the inhabitants of Mæsia lived in supine security, fondly conceiving themselves at an inaccessible distance from any barbarian invaders. The irruptions of the Goths, under the reign of Philip, fatally convinced them of their mistake. The king, or leader, of that fierce nation traversed with contempt the province of Dacia, and passed both the Dniester and the Danube without encountering any opposition capable of retarding his progress. The relaxed discipline of the Roman troops betrayed the most important posts where they were stationed, and the fear of deserved punishment induced great numbers of them to enlist under the Gothic standard. The various multitude of barbarians appeared, at length, under the walls of Marcianopolis, a city built by Trajan in honour of his sister, and at that time the capital of the second Mæsia.[29] The inhabitants consented to ransom their lives and property by the payment of a large sum of money, and the invaders retreated back into their deserts, animated, rather than satisfied, with the first success of their arms against an opulent but feeble country. Intelligence was soon transmitted to the emperor Decius that Cniva, king of the Goths, had passed the Danube a second time, with more considerable forces; that his numerous detachments scattered devastation over the province of Mæsia, whilst the main body of the army, consisting of seventy thousand Germans and Sarmatians, a force equal to the most daring achievements, required the presence of the Roman monarch, and the exertion of his military power.

Decius found (A.D. 250) the Goths engaged before Nicopolis, on the Jatrus, one of the many monuments of Trajan's victories.[30] On his approach they raised the siege, but with a design only of marching away to a conquest of greater importance, the siege of Philippopolis, a city of Thrace, founded by the father of Alexander, near the foot of mount Hæmus.[31] Decius followed them through a difficult country, and by forced marches; but when he imagined himself at a considerable distance from the rear of the Goths, Cniva turned with rapid fury on his pursuers. The camp of the Romans was surprised and pillaged, and, for the first time, their emperor fled in disorder before a troop of half-armed barbarians. After a long resistance, Philippopolis, destitute of succour, was taken by storm. A hundred thousand persons are reported to have been massacred in the sack of that great city.[32] Many prisoners of consequence became a valuable accession to the spoil; and Priscus, a brother of the late emperor Philip, blushed not to assume the purple under the protection of the barbarous enemies of Rome.[33] The time, however, consumed in that tedious siege enabled Decius to revive the courage, restore the discipline, and recruit the numbers of his troops. He intercepted several parties of Carpi, and other Germans, who were hastening to share the victory of their countrymen,[34] intrusted the passes of the mountains to officers of approved valour and fidelity;[35] repaired and strengthened the fortifications of the Danube, and exerted his utmost vigilance to oppose either the progress or the retreat of the Goths. Encouraged by the return of fortune, he anxiously waited for an opportunity to retrieve, by a great and decisive blow, his own glory and that of the Roman arms.[36]

At the same time when Decius was struggling with the violence of the tempest, his mind, calm and deliberate amidst the tumult of war, investigated the more general causes that, since the age of the Antonines, had so impetuously urged the decline of the Roman greatness. He soon discovered that it was impossible to replace that greatness on a permanent basis without restoring public virtue, ancient principles and manners, and the oppressed majesty of the laws. To execute this noble but arduous design, he first resolved to revive the obsolete office of censor; an office which, as long as it had subsisted in its pristine integrity, had so much contributed to the perpetuity of the state,[37] till it was usurped and gradually neglected by the Cæsars.[38] Conscious that the favour of the sovereign may confer power, but that the esteem of the people can alone bestow authority, he submitted the choice of the censor to the unbiassed voice of the senate. By their unanimous votes, or rather acclamations, Valerian, who was afterwards emperor, and who then served with distinction in the army of Decius, was (A.D. 251, 27 Oct.) declared the most worthy of that exalted honour. As soon as the decree of the senate was transmitted to the emperor, he assembled a great council in his camp, and, before the investiture of the censor elect, he apprised him of the difficulty and importance of his great office. "Happy Valerian," said the prince to his distinguished subject, "happy in the general approbation of the senate and of the Roman republic! Accept the censorship of mankind; and judge of our manners. You will select those who deserve to continue members of the senate; you will restore the equestrian order to its ancient splendour; you will improve the revenue, yet moderate the public burdens. You will distinguish into regular classes the various and infinite multitude of citizens, and accurately review the military strength, the wealth, the virtue, and the resources of Rome. Your decisions shall obtain the force of laws. The army, the palace, the ministers of justice, and the great officers of the empire, are all subject to your tribunal. None are exempted, excepting only the ordinary consuls,[39] the prefect of the city, the king of the sacrifices, and (as long as she preserves her chastity inviolate) the eldest of the vestal virgins. Even these few, who may not dread the severity, will anxiously solicit the esteem, of the Roman censor."[40]

A magistrate, invested with such extensive powers, would have appeared not so much the minister as the colleague of his sovereign.[41] Valerian justly dreaded an elevation so full of envy and of suspicion. He modestly urged the alarming greatness of the trust, his own insufficiency, and the incurable corruption of the times. He artfully insinuated that the office of censor was inseparable from the Imperial dignity, and that the feeble hands of a subject were unequal to the support of such an immense weight of cares and of power.[42] The approaching event of war soon put an end to the prosecution of a project so specious but so impracticable; and whilst it preserved Valerian from the danger, saved the emperor Decius from the disappointment which would most probably have attended it. A censor may maintain, he can never restore, the morals of a state. It is impossible for such a magistrate to exert his authority with benefit, or even with effect, unless he is supported by a quick sense of honour and virtue in the minds of the people, by a decent reverence for the public opinion, and by a train of useful prejudices combating on the side of national manners. In a period when these principles are annihilated, the censorial jurisdiction must either sink into empty pageantry, or be converted into a partial instrument of vexatious oppression.[43] It was easier to vanquish the Goths than to eradicate the public vices; yet even in the first of these enterprises Decius lost his army and his life.

The Goths were now, on every side, surrounded and pursued by the Roman arms. The flower of their troops had perished in the long siege of Philippopolis, and the exhausted country could no longer afford subsistence for the remaining multitude of licentious barbarians. Reduced to this extremity, the Goths would gladly have purchased, by the surrender of all their booty and prisoners, the permission of an undisturbed retreat. But the emperor, confident of victory, and resolving, by the chastisement of these invaders, to strike a salutary terror into the nations of the North, refused to listen to any

terms of accommodation. The high-spirited barbarians preferred death to slavery. An obscure town of Mæsia, called Forum Terebronii,[44] was the scene of the battle. The Gothic army was drawn up in three lines, and, either from choice or accident, the front of the third line was covered by a morass. In the beginning of the action, the son of Decius, a youth of the fairest hopes, and already associated to the honours of the purple, was slain by an arrow, in the sight of his afflicted father; who, summoning all his fortitude, admonished the dismayed troops that the loss of a single soldier was of little importance to the republic.[45] The conflict was terrible; it was the combat of despair against grief and rage. The first line of the Goths at length gave way in disorder; the second, advancing to sustain it, shared its fate; and the third only remained entire, prepared to dispute the passage of the morass, which was imprudently attempted by the presumption of the enemy. "Here the fortune of the day turned, and all things became adverse to the Romans: the place deep with ooze, sinking under those who stood, slippery to such as advanced; their armour heavy, the waters deep; nor could they wield, in that uneasy situation, their weighty javelins. The barbarians, on the contrary, were enured to encounters in the bogs, their persons tall, their spears long, such as could wound at a distance."[46] In the morass the Roman army, after an ineffectual struggle, was irrecoverably lost; nor could the body of the emperor ever be found.[47] Such was the fate of Decius, in the fiftieth year of his age; an accomplished prince, active in war, and affable in peace;[48] who, together with his son, has deserved to be compared, both in life and death, with the brightest examples of ancient virtue.[49]

This fatal blow humbled, for a very little time, the insolence of the legions. They appear to have patiently expected, and submissively obeyed, the decree of the senate, which regulated the succession to the throne. From a just regard for the memory of Decius, the Imperial title was (A.D. 251, Dec.) conferred on Hostilianus, his only surviving son; but an equal rank, with more effectual power, was granted to Gallus, whose experience and ability seemed equal to the great trust of guardian to the young prince and the distressed empire.[50] The first care of the new emperor was to deliver the Illyrian provinces from the intolerable weight of the victorious Goths. He (A.D. 252) consented to leave in their hands the rich fruits of their invasion, an immense booty, and, what was still more disgraceful, a great number of prisoners of the highest merit and quality. He plentifully supplied their camp with every conveniency that could assuage their angry spirits, or facilitate their so much wished-for departure; and he even promised to pay them annually a large sum of gold, on condition they should never afterwards infest the Roman territories by their incursions.[51]

In the age of the Scipios, the most opulent kings of the earth, who courted the protection of the victorious commonwealth, were gratified with such trifling presents as could only derive a value from the hand that bestowed them; an ivory chair, a coarse garment of purple, an inconsiderable piece of plate, or a quantity of copper coin.[52] After the wealth of nations had centred in Rome, the emperors displayed their greatness, and even their policy, by the regular exercise of a steady and moderate liberality towards the allies of the state. They relieved the poverty of the barbarians, honoured their merit, and recompensed their fidelity. These voluntary marks of bounty were understood to flow not from the fears, but merely from the generosity or the gratitude of the Romans; and whilst presents and subsidies were liberally distributed among friends and suppliants, they were sternly refused to such as claimed them as a debt.[53] But this stipulation of an annual payment to a victorious enemy appeared without disguise in the light of an ignominious tribute; the minds of the Romans were not yet accustomed to accept such unequal laws from a tribe of barbarians; and the prince who by a necessary concession had probably saved his country, became the object of the general contempt and aversion. The death of Hostilianus, though it happened in the midst of a raging pestilence, was interpreted as the personal crime of Gallus;[54] and even the defeat of the late emperor was ascribed by the voice of suspicion to the perfidious counsels of his hated successor.[55] The tranquillity which the empire enjoyed during the first year of his administration[56] served rather to inflame than to appease the public discontent; and, as soon as the apprehensions of war were removed, the infamy of the peace was more deeply and more sensibly felt.

But the Romans were irritated to a still higher degree when they discovered that they had not even secured their repose, though at the expense of their honour. The dangerous secret of the wealth and weakness of the empire had been revealed to the world. New swarms of barbarians, encouraged (A.D. 253) by the success, and not conceiving themselves bound by the obligation, of their brethren, spread devastation through the Illyrian provinces, and terror as far as the gates of Rome. The defence of the monarchy, which seemed abandoned by the pusillanimous emperor, was assumed by Æmilianus, governor of Pannonia and Mæsia; who rallied the scattered forces, and revived the fainting spirits of the troops. The barbarians were unexpectedly attacked, routed, chased, and pursued beyond the Danube. The victorious leader distributed as a donative the money collected for the tribute, and the acclamations of the soldiers proclaimed him emperor on the field of battle.[57] Gallus, who, careless of the general welfare, indulged himself in the pleasures of Italy, was almost in the same instant informed of the success of the revolt and of the rapid approach of his aspiring lieutenant. He advanced to meet him as far as the plains of Spoleto. When the armies came in sight of each other, the soldiers of Gallus compared the ignominious conduct of their sovereign with the glory of his rival. They admired the valour of Æmilianus; they were attracted by his liberality, for he offered a considerable increase of pay to all deserters.[58] The murder of Gallus, and of his son Volusianus, put an end to the civil war; and the senate (A.D. 253, May) gave a legal sanction to the rights of conquest. The letters of Æmilianus to that assembly displayed a mixture of moderation and vanity. He assured them that he should resign to their wisdom the civil administration; and, contenting himself with the quality of their general, would in a short time assert the glory of Rome, and deliver the empire from all the barbarians both of the North and of the East.[59] His pride was flattered by the applause of the senate; and medals are still extant representing him with the name and attributes of Hercules and Victor and of Mars the Avenger.[60]

If the new monarch possessed the abilities, he wanted the time necessary to fulfil these splendid promises. Less than four months intervened between his victory and his fall.[61] He had vanquished Gallus: he sunk under the weight of a competitor more formidable than Gallus. That unfortunate prince had sent Valerian, already distinguished by the honourable title of censor, to bring the legions of Gaul and Germany to his aid.[62] Valerian executed that commission with zeal and fidelity; and as he arrived too late to save his sovereign, he resolved to revenge him. The troops of Æmilianus, who still lay encamped in the plains of Spoleto, were awed by the sanctity of his character, but much more by the superior strength of his army; and as they were now become as incapable of personal attachment as they had always been of constitutional principle, they (A.D. 253, Aug.) readily imbrued their hands in the blood of a prince who had so lately been the object of their partial choice. The guilt was theirs, but the advantage of it was Valerian's; who obtained the possession of the throne by the means indeed of a civil war, but with a degree of innocence singular in that age of revolutions; since he owned neither gratitude nor allegiance to his predecessor whom he dethroned.

Valerian was about sixty years of age[63] when he was invested with the purple, not by the caprice of the populace, or the clamours of the army, but by the unanimous voice of the Roman world. In his gradual ascent through the honours of the state, he had deserved the favour of virtuous princes, and had declared himself the enemy of tyrants.[64] His noble birth, his mild but unblemished manners, his learning, prudence, and experience, were revered by the senate and people; and if mankind (according to the observation of an ancient writer) had been left at liberty to choose a master, their choice would most assuredly have fallen on Valerian.[65] Perhaps the merit of this emperor was inadequate to his reputation; perhaps his abilities, or at least his spirit, were affected by the languor and coldness of old age. The consciousness of his decline engaged him to share the throne with a younger and more active associate:[66] the emergency of the times demanded a general no less than a prince; and the experience of the Roman censor might have directed him where to bestow the Imperial purple, as the reward of military merit. But instead of making a judicious choice, which would have confirmed his reign and endeared his memory, Valerian, consulting only the dictates of affection or vanity, immediately invested with the supreme honours his son Gallienus, a youth whose effeminate vices had been hitherto concealed by the obscurity of a private station. The joint government of the father and the son subsisted about seven, and the sole administration of Gallienus continued about eight years (A.D. 253–268). But the whole period was one uninterrupted series of confusion and calamity. As the Roman empire was at the same time, and on every side, attacked by the blind fury of foreign invaders, and the wild ambition of domestic usurpers, we shall consult order and perspicuity by pursuing not so much the doubtful arrangement of dates as the more natural distribution of subjects. The most dangerous enemies of Rome, during the reigns of Valerian and Gallienus, were, 1. The Franks; 2. The Alemanni; 3. The Goths; and 4. The Persians. Under these general appellations we may comprehend the adventures of less considerable tribes, whose obscure and uncouth names would only serve to oppress the memory and perplex the attention of the reader.

I. As the posterity of the Franks compose one of the greatest and most enlightened nations of Europe, the powers of learning and ingenuity have been exhausted in the discovery of their unlettered ancestors. To the tales of credulity have succeeded the systems of fancy. Every passage has been sifted, every spot has been surveyed, that might possibly reveal some faint traces of their origin. It has been supposed that Pannonia,[67] that Gaul, that the northern parts of Germany,[68] gave birth to that celebrated colony of warriors. At length the most rational critics, rejecting the fictitious emigrations of ideal conquerors, have acquiesced in a sentiment whose simplicity persuades us of its truth.[69] They suppose that, about the year two hundred and forty,[70] a new confederacy was formed under the name of Franks, by the old inhabitants of the Lower Rhine and the Weser. The present circle of Westphalia, the Landgraviate of Hesse, and the duchies of Brunswick and Luneburg, were the ancient seat of the Chauci, who, in their inaccessible morasses, defied the Roman arms;[71] of the Cherusci, proud of the fame of Arminius; of the Catti, formidable by their firm and intrepid infantry; and of several other tribes of inferior power and renown.[72] The love of liberty was the ruling passion of these Germans; the enjoyment of it their best treasure; the word that expressed that enjoyment the most pleasing to their ear. They deserved, they assumed, they maintained the honourable epithet of Franks or Freemen; which concealed, though it did not extinguish, the peculiar names of the several states of the confederacy.[73] Tacit consent, and mutual advantage, dictated the first laws of the union; it was gradually cemented by habit and experience. The league of the Franks may admit of some comparison with the Helvetic body; in which every canton, retaining its independent sovereignty, consults with its brethren in the common cause, without acknowledging the authority of any supreme head or representative assembly.[74] But the principle of the two confederacies were extremely different. A peace of two hundred years has rewarded the wise and honest policy of the Swiss. An inconstant spirit, the thirst of rapine, and a disregard to the most solemn treaties, disgraced the character of the Franks.

The Romans had long experienced the daring valour of the people of Lower Germany. The union of their strength threatened Gaul with a more formidable invasion, and required the presence of Gallienus, the heir and colleague of imperial power.[75] Whilst that prince, and his infant son Salonius, displayed, in the court of Treves, the majesty of the empire, its armies were ably conducted by their general Posthumus, who, though he afterwards betrayed the family of Valerian, was ever faithful for the great interest of the monarchy. The treacherous language of panegyrics and medals darkly announces a long series of victories. Trophies and titles attest (if such evidence can attest) the fame of Posthumus, who is repeatedly styled The Conqueror of the Germans, and the saviour of Gaul.[76]

But a single fact, the only one indeed of which we have any distinct knowledge, erases, in a great measure, these monuments of vanity and adulation. The Rhine, though dignified with the title of Safeguard of the provinces, was an imperfect barrier against the daring spirit of enterprise with which the Franks were actuated. Their rapid devastations stretched from the river to the foot of the Pyrenees: nor were they stopped by those mountains. Spain, which had never dreaded, was unable to resist, the inroads of the Germans. During twelve years, the greatest part of the reign of Gallienus, that opulent country was the theatre of unequal and destructive hostilities. Tarragona, the flourishing capital of a peaceful province, was sacked and almost destroyed,[77] and so late as the days of Orosius, who wrote in the fifth century, wretched cottages, scattered amidst the ruins of magnificent cities, still recorded the rage of the barbarians.[78] When the exhausted country no longer supplied a variety of plunder, the Franks seized on some vessels in the ports of Spain,[79] and transported themselves into Mauritania. The distant province was astonished with the fury of these barbarians, who seemed to fall from a new world, as their name, manners, and complexion were equally unknown on the coast of Africa.[80]

II. In that part of Upper Saxony beyond the Elbe, which is at present called the Marquisate of Lusace, there existed, in ancient times, a sacred wood, the awful seat of the superstition of the Suevi. None were permitted to enter the holy precincts without confessing, by their servile bonds and suppliant posture, the immediate presence of the sovereign Deity.[81] Patriotism contributed as well as devotion to consecrate the Sonnenwald, or wood of the Semnones.[82] It

was universally believed that the nation had received its first existence on that sacred spot. At stated periods, the numerous tribes who gloried in the Suevic blood resorted thither by their ambassadors; and the memory of their common extraction was perpetuated by barbaric rites and human sacrifices. The wide extended name of Suevi filled the interior countries of Germany from the banks of the Oder to those of the Danube. They were distinguished from the other Germans by their peculiar mode of dressing their long hair, which they gathered into a rude knot on the crown of the head; and they delighted in an ornament that showed their ranks more lofty and terrible in the eyes of the enemy.[83] Jealous as the Germans were of military renown, they all confessed the superior valour of the Suevi; and the tribes of the Usipetes and Tencteri, who, with a vast army, encountered the dictator Cæsar, declared that they esteemed it not a disgrace to have fled before a people to whose arms the immortal gods themselves were unequal.[84]

In the reign of the emperor Caracalla, an innumerable swarm of Suevi appeared on the banks of the Mein, and in the neighbourhood of the Roman provinces, in quest either of food, of plunder, or of glory.[85] The hasty army of volunteers gradually coalesced into a great and permanent nation, and as it was composed from so many different tribes, assumed the name of Alemanni, or *All-men*; to denote at once their various lineage and their common bravery.[86] The latter was soon felt by the Romans in many a hostile inroad. The Alemanni fought chiefly on horseback; but their cavalry was rendered still more formidable by a mixture of light infantry, selected from the bravest and most active of the youth, whom frequent exercise had enured to accompany the horsemen in the longest march, the most rapid charge, or the most precipitate retreat.[87]

This warlike people of Germans had been astonished by the immense preparations of Alexander Severus; they were dismayed by the arms of his successor, a barbarian equal in valour and fierceness to themselves. But still hovering on the frontiers of the empire, they increased the general disorder that ensued after the death of Decius. They inflicted severe wounds on the rich provinces of Gaul; they were the first who removed the veil that covered the feeble majesty of Italy. A numerous body of the Alemanni penetrated across the Danube, and through the Rhætian Alps, into the plains of Lombardy, advanced as far as Ravenna, and displayed the victorious banners of barbarians almost in sight of Rome.[88] The insult and the danger rekindled in the senate some sparks of their ancient virtue. Both the emperors were engaged in far distant wars, Valerian in the East and Gallienus on the Rhine. All the hopes and resources of the Romans were in themselves. In this emergency, the senators resumed the defence of the republic, drew out the Prætorian guards, who had been left to garrison the capital, and filled up their numbers by enlisting into the public service the stoutest and most willing of the Plebeians. The Alemanni, astonished with the sudden appearance of an army more numerous than their own, retired into Germany laden with spoil; and their retreat was esteemed as a victory by the unwarlike Romans.[89]

When Gallienus received the intelligence that his capital was delivered from the barbarians, he was much less delighted than alarmed with the courage of the senate, since it might one day prompt them to rescue the republic from domestic tyranny as well as from foreign invasion. His timid ingratitude was published to his subjects in an edict which prohibited the senators from exercising any military employment, and even from approaching the camps of the legions. But his fears were groundless. The rich and luxurious nobles, sinking into their natural character, accepted, as a favour, this disgraceful exemption from military service; and as long as they were indulged in the enjoyment of their baths, their theatres, and their villas, they cheerfully resigned the more dangerous cares of empire to the rough hands of peasants and soldiers.[90]

Another invasion of the Alemanni, of a more formidable aspect, but more glorious event, is mentioned by a writer of the lower empire. Three hundred thousand of that warlike people are said to have been vanquished, in a battle near Milan, by Gallienus in person at the head of only ten thousand Romans.[91] We may, however, with great probability, ascribe this incredible victory either to the credulity of the historian or to some exaggerated exploits of one of the emperor's lieutenants. It was by arms of a very different nature that Gallienus endeavoured to protect Italy from the fury of the Germans. He espoused Pipa, the daughter of a king of the Marcomanni, a Suevic tribe, which was often confounded with the Alemanni in their wars and conquests.[92] To the father, as the price of his alliance, he granted an ample settlement in Pannonia. The native charms of unpolished beauty seem to have fixed the daughter in the affections of the inconstant emperor, and the bands of policy were more firmly connected by those of love. But the haughty prejudice of Rome still refused the name of marriage to the profane mixture of a citizen and a barbarian; and has stigmatised the German princess with the opprobrious title of concubine of Gallienus.[93]

III. We have already traced the emigration of the Goths from Scandinavia, or at least from Prussia, to the mouth of the Borysthenes, and have followed their victorious arms from the Borysthenes to the Danube. Under the reigns of Valerian and Gallienus, the frontier of the last-mentioned river was perpetually infested by the inroads of Germans and Sarmatians but it was defended by the Romans with more than usual firmness and success. The provinces that were the seat of war recruited the armies of Rome with an inexhaustible supply of hardy soldiers; and more than one of these Illyrian peasants attained the station and displayed the abilities of a general. Though flying parties of the barbarians, who incessantly hovered on the banks of the Danube, penetrated sometimes to the confines of Italy and Macedonia, their progress was commonly checked, or their return intercepted, by the Imperial lieutenants.[94] But the great stream of the Gothic hostilities was diverted into a very different channel. The Goths, in their new settlement of the Ukraine, soon became masters of the northern coast of the Euxine: to the south of that inland sea were situated the soft and wealthy provinces of Asia Minor, which possessed all that could attract, and nothing that could resist, a barbarian conqueror.

The banks of the Borysthenes are only sixty miles distant from the narrow entrance[95] of the peninsula of Crim Tartary, known to the ancients under the name of Chersonesus Taurica.[96] On that inhospitable shore, Euripides, embellishing with exquisite art the tales of antiquity, has placed the scene of one of his most affecting tragedies.[97] The bloody sacrifices of Diana, the arrival of Orestes and Pylades, and the triumph of virtue and religion over savage fierceness, serve to represent an historical truth, that the Tauri, the original inhabitants of the peninsula, were, in some degree, reclaimed from their brutal manners by a gradual intercourse with the Grecian colonies which settled along the maritime coast. The little kingdom of Bosphorus, whose capital was situated on the Straits, through which the Mæotis communicates itself to the Euxine, was composed of degenerate Greeks and half-civilised barbarians. It subsisted, as an independent state, from the time of the Peloponnesian war,[98] was at last swallowed up by the ambition of Mithridates,[99] and, with the rest of his dominions, sunk under the weight of the Roman arms. From the reign of Augustus,[100] the kings of Bosphorus were the humble, but not useless, allies of the empire. By presents, by arms, and by a slight fortification drawn across the Isthmus, they effectually guarded against the roving plunderers of Sarmatia the access of a country which, from its peculiar situation and convenient harbours, commanded the Euxine Sea and Asia Minor.[101] As long as the sceptre was possessed by a lineal succession of kings, they acquitted themselves of their important charge with vigilance and success. Domestic factions, and the fears, or private interest, of obscure usurpers, who seized on the vacant throne, admitted the Goths into the heart of Bosphorus. With the acquisition of a superfluous waste of fertile soil, the conquerors obtained the command of a naval force, sufficient to transport their armies to the coast of Asia.[102] The ships used in the navigation of the Euxine were of a very singular construction. They were slight flat-bottomed barks framed of timber only, without the least mixture of iron, and occasionally covered with a shelving roof on the appearance of a tempest.[103] In these floating houses, the Goths carelessly trusted themselves to the mercy of an unknown sea, under the conduct of sailors pressed into the service, and whose skill and fidelity were equally suspicious. But the hopes of plunder had banished every idea of danger, and a natural fearlessness of temper supplied in their minds the more rational confidence which is the just result of knowledge and experience. Warriors of such a daring spirit must have often murmured against the cowardice of their guides, who required the strongest assurances of a settled calm before they would venture to embark; and would scarcely ever be tempted to lose sight of the land. Such, at least, is the practise of the modern Turks,[104] and they are probably not inferior in the art of navigation to the ancient inhabitants of Bosphorus.

The fleet of the Goths, leaving the coast of Circassia on the left hand, first appeared before Pityus,[105] the utmost limits of the Roman provinces; a city provided with a convenient port and fortified with a strong wall. Here they met with a resistance more obstinate than they had reason to expect from the feeble garrison of a distant fortress. They were repulsed; and their disappointment seemed to diminish the terror of the Gothic name. As long as Successianus, an officer of superior rank and merit, defended that frontier, all their efforts were ineffectual; but as

soon as he was removed by Valerian to a more honourable but less important station, they resumed the attack of Pityus; and, by the destruction of that city, obliterated the memory of their former disgrace.[106]

Circling round the eastern extremity of the Euxine Sea, the navigation from Pityus to Trebizond is about three hundred miles.[107] The course of the Goths carried them in sight of the country of Colchis, so famous by the expedition of the Argonauts, and they even attempted, though without success, to pillage a rich temple at the mouth of the river Phasis. Trebizond, celebrated in the retreat of the Ten Thousand as an ancient colony of Greeks,[108] derived its wealth and splendour from the munificence of the emperor Hadrian, who had constructed an artificial port on a coast left destitute by nature of secure harbours.[109] The city was large and populous; a double enclosure of walls seemed to defy the fury of the Goths, and the usual garrison had been strengthened by a reinforcement of ten thousand men. But there are not any advantages capable of supplying the absence of discipline and vigilance. The numerous garrison of Trebizond, dissolved in riot and luxury, disdained to guard their impregnable fortifications. The Goths soon discovered the supine negligence of the besieged, erected a lofty pile of fascines, ascended the walls in the silence of the night, and entered the defenceless city sword in hand. A general massacre of the people ensued, whilst the affrighted soldiers escaped through the opposite gates of the town. The most holy temples, and the most splendid edifices, were involved in a common destruction. The booty that fell into the hands of the Goths was immense: the wealth of the adjacent countries had been deposited in Trebizond, as in a secure place of refuge. The number of captives was incredible, as the victorious barbarians ranged without opposition through the extensive province of Pontus.[110] The rich spoils of Trebizond filled a great fleet of ships that had been found in the port. The robust youth of the sea-coast were chained to the oar; and the Goths, satisfied with the success of their first naval expedition, returned in triumph to their new establishments in the kingdom of Bosphorus.[111]

The second expedition of the Goths was undertaken with greater powers of men and ships; but they steered a different course, and, disdaining the exhausted provinces of Pontus, followed the western coast of the Euxine, passed before the wide mouths of the Borysthenes, the Dniester, and the Danube, and increasing their fleet by the capture of a great number of fishing barks, they approached the narrow outlet through which the Euxine Sea pours its waters into the Mediterranean, and divides the continents of Europe and Asia. The garrison of Chalcedon was encamped near the temple of Jupiter Urius, on a promontory that commanded the entrance of the Strait; and so dreaded were the invasions of the barbarians, that this body of troops surpassed in number the Gothic army. But it was in numbers alone that they surpassed it. They deserted with precipitation their advantageous post, and abandoned the town of Chalcedon, most plentifully stored with arms and money, to the discretion of the conquerors. Whilst they hesitated whether they should prefer the sea or land, Europe or Asia, for the scene of their hostilities, a perfidious fugitive pointed out Nicomedia, once the capital of the kings of Bithynia, as a rich and easy conquest. He guided the march, which was only sixty miles from the camp of Chalcedon,[112] directed the resistless attack, and partook of the booty; for the Goths had learned sufficient policy to reward the traitor whom they detested. Nice, Prusa, Apamæa, Cius, cities that had sometimes rivalled, or imitated, the splendour of Nicomedia, were involved in the same calamity, which, in a few weeks, raged without control through the whole province of Bithynia. Three hundred years of peace, enjoyed by the soft inhabitants of Asia, had abolished the exercise of arms and removed the apprehension of danger. The ancient walls were suffered to moulder away, and all the revenue of the most opulent cities was reserved for the construction of baths, temples, and theatres.[113]

When the city of Cyzicus withstood the utmost effort of Mithridates,[114] it was distinguished by wise laws, a naval power of two hundred galleys, and three arsenals: of arms, of military engines, and of corn.[115] It was still the seat of wealth and luxury; but of its ancient strength nothing remained except the situation, in a little island of the Propontis, connected with the continent of Asia only by two bridges. From the recent sack of Prusa, the Goths advanced within eighteen miles[116] of the city, which they had devoted to destruction; but the ruin of Cyzicus was delayed by a fortunate accident. The season was rainy, and the lake Apolloniates, the reservoir of all the springs of Mount Olympus, rose to an uncommon height. The little river of Rhyndacus, which issues from the lake, swelled into a broad and rapid stream, and stopped the progress of the Goths. Their retreat to the mari-

time city of Heraclea, where the fleet had probably been stationed, was attended by a long train of waggons, laden with the spoils of Bithynia, and was marked by the flames of Nice and Nicomedia, which they wantonly burnt.[117] Some obscure hints are mentioned of a doubtful combat that secured their retreat.[118] But even a complete victory would have been of little moment, as the approach of the autumnal equinox summoned them to hasten their return. To navigate the Euxine before the month of May, or after that of September, is esteemed by the modern Turks the most unquestionable instance of rashness and folly.[119]

When we are informed that the third fleet, equipped by the Goths in the ports of Bosphorus, consisted of five hundred sail of ships,[120] our ready imagination instantly computes and multiplies the formidable armament; but as we are assured, by the judicious Strabo,[121] that the piratical vessels used by the barbarians of Pontus and the Lesser Scythia were not capable of containing more than twenty-five or thirty men, we may safely affirm that fifteen thousand warriors, at the most, embarked in this great expedition. Impatient of the limits of the Euxine, they steered their destructive course from the Cimmerian to the Thracian Bosphorus. When they had almost gained the middle of the Straits, they were suddenly driven back to the entrance of them, till a favourable wind springing up the next day carried them in a few hours into the placid sea, or rather lake, of the Propontis. Their landing on the little island of Cyzicus was attended with the ruin of that ancient and noble city. From thence issuing again through the narrow passage of the Hellespont, they pursued their winding navigation amidst the numerous islands scattered over the Archipelago, or the Ægean Sea. The assistance of captives and deserters must have been very necessary to pilot their vessels and to direct their various incursions, as well on the coast of Greece as on that of Asia. At length the Gothic fleet anchored in the port of Piræus, five miles distant from Athens,[122] which had attempted to make some preparations for a vigorous defence. Cleodamus, one of the engineers employed by the emperor's orders to fortify the maritime cities against the Goths, had already begun to repair the ancient walls fallen to decay since the time of Sulla. The efforts of his skill were ineffectual, and the barbarians became masters of the native seat of the muses and the arts. But while the conquerors abandoned themselves to the licence of plunder and intemperance, their fleet, that lay with a slender guard in the harbour of Piræus, was un-expectedly attacked by the brave Dexippus, who, flying with the engineer Cleodamus from the sack of Athens, collected a hasty band of volunteers, peasants as well as soldiers, and in some measure avenged the calamities of his country.[123]

But this exploit, whatever lustre it might shed on the declining age of Athens, served rather to irritate than to subdue the undaunted spirit of the northern invaders. A general conflagration blazed out at the same time in every district of Greece. Thebes and Argos, Corinth and Sparta, which had formerly waged such memorable wars against each other, were now unable to bring an army into the field, or even to defend their ruined fortifications. The rage of war, both by land and by sea, spread from the eastern point of Sunium to the western coast of Epirus. The Goths had already advanced within sight of Italy, when the approach of such imminent danger awakened the indolent Gallienus from his dream of pleasure. The emperor appeared in arms; and his presence seems to have checked the ardour, and to have divided the strength, of the enemy. Naulobatus, a chief of the Heruli, accepted an honourable capitulation, entered with a large body of his countrymen into the service of Rome, and was invested with the or-naments of the consular dignity, which had never before been profaned by the hands of a barbarian.[124] Great numbers of the Goths, dis-gusted with the perils and hardships of a tedious voyage, broke into Mæsia, with a design of forc-ing their way over the Danube to their settle-ments in the Ukraine. The wild attempt would have proved inevitable destruction if the dis-cord of the Roman generals had not opened to the barbarians the means of an escape.[125] The small remainder of this destroying host returned on board their vessels; and measuring back their way through the Hellespont and the Bosphorus, ravaged in their passage the shores of Troy, whose fame, immortalised by Homer, will prob-ably survive the memory of the Gothic con-quests. As soon as they found themselves in safety within the basin of the Euxine, they landed at Anchialus in Thrace, near the foot of Mount Hæmus; and, after all their toils, indulged them-selves in the use of those pleasant and salutary hot baths. What remained of the voyage was a short and easy navigation.[126] Such was the vari-ous fate of this third and greatest of their naval enterprises. It may seem difficult to conceive how the original body of fifteen thousand war-riors could sustain the losses and divisions of so

bold an adventure. But as their numbers were gradually wasted by the sword, by shipwrecks, and by the influence of a warm climate, they were perpetually renewed by troops of banditti and deserters, who flocked to the standard of plunder, and by a crowd of fugitive slaves, often of German or Sarmatian extraction, who eagerly seized the glorious opportunity of freedom and revenge. In these expeditions, the Gothic nation claimed a superior share of honour and danger; but the tribes that fought under the Gothic ban-ners are sometimes distinguished and sometimes confounded in the imperfect histories of that age; and as the barbarian fleets seemed to issue from the mouth of the Tanais, the vague but familiar appellation of Scythians was frequently bestowed on the mixed multitude.[127]

In the general calamities of mankind the death of an individual, however exalted, the ruin of an edifice, however famous, are passed over with careless inattention. Yet we cannot forget that the temple of Diana at Ephesus, after having risen with increasing splendour from seven repeated misfortunes,[128] was finally burnt by the Goths in their third naval invasion. The arts of Greece, and the wealth of Asia, had con-spired to erect that sacred and magnificent struc-ture. It was supported by an hundred and twenty-seven marble columns of the Ionic order. They were the gifts of devout monarchs, and each was sixty feet high. The altar was adorned with the masterly sculptures of Praxiteles, who had, perhaps, selected from the favourite leg-ends of the place the birth of the divine children of Latona, the concealment of Apollo after the slaughter of the Cyclops, and the clemency of Bacchus to the vanquished Amazons.[129] Yet the length of the temple of Ephesus was only four hundred and twenty-five feet, about two-thirds of the measure of the church of St. Peter's at Rome.[130] In the other dimensions it was still more inferior to that sublime production of mod-ern architecture. The spreading arms of a Chris-tian cross require a much greater breadth than the oblong temples of the Pagans; and the bold-est artists of antiquity would have been startled at the proposal of raising in the air a dome of the size and proportions of the Pantheon. The temple of Diana was, however, admired as one of the wonders of the world. Successive empires, the Persian, the Macedonian, and the Roman, had revered its sanctity and enriched its splen-dour.[131] But the rude savages of the Baltic were destitute of a taste for the elegant arts, and they despised the ideal terrors of a foreign super-stition.[132]

Another circumstance is related of these invasions, which might deserve our notice, were it not justly to be suspected as the fanciful conceit of a recent sophist. We are told that in the sack of Athens the Goths had collected all the libraries, and were on the point of setting fire to this funeral pile of Grecian learning, had not one of their chiefs, of more refined policy than his brethren, dissuaded them from the design; by the profound observation that as long as the Greeks were addicted to the study of books, they would never apply themselves to the exercise of arms.[133] The sagacious counsellor (should the truth of the fact be admitted) reasoned like an ignorant barbarian. In the most polite and powerful nations, genius of every kind has displayed itself about the same period; and the age of science has generally been the age of military virtue and success.

IV. The new sovereigns of Persia, Artaxerxes and his son Sapor, had triumphed over the house of Arsaces. Of the many princes of that ancient race, Chosroes, king of Armenia, had alone preserved both his life and his independence. He defended himself by the natural strength of his country; by the perpetual resort of fugitives and malcontents; by the alliance of the Romans, and, above all, by his own courage. Invincible in arms, during a thirty years' war, he was at length assassinated by the emissaries of Sapor, king of Persia. The patriotic satraps of Armenia, who asserted the freedom and dignity of the crown, implored the protection of Rome in favour of Tiridates the lawful heir. But the son of Chosroes was an infant, the allies were at a distance, and the Persian monarch advanced towards the frontier at the head of an irresistible force. Young Tiridates, the future hope of his country, was saved by the fidelity of a servant, and Armenia continued above twenty-seven years a reluctant province of the great monarchy of Persia.[134] Elated with this easy conquest, and presuming on the distresses or the degeneracy of the Romans, Sapor obliged the strong garrisons of Carrhæ and Nisibis to surrender, and spread devastation and terror on either side of the Euphrates.

The loss of an important frontier, the ruin of a faithful and natural ally, and the rapid success of Sapor's ambition, affected Rome with a deep sense of the insult as well as of the danger. Valerian flattered himself that the vigilance of his lieutenants would sufficiently provide for the safety of the Rhine and of the Danube; but he resolved, notwithstanding his advanced age, to march in person to the defence of the Euphrates.

During his progress through Asia Minor, the naval enterprises of the Goths were suspended, and the afflicted province enjoyed a transient and fallacious calm. He passed the Euphrates, encountered the Persian monarch near the walls of Edessa, was (A.D. 260) vanquished and taken prisoner by Sapor. The particulars of this great event are darkly and imperfectly represented; yet by the glimmering light which is afforded us, we may discover a long series of imprudence, of error, and of deserved misfortunes on the side of the Roman emperor. He reposed an implicit confidence in Macrinus, his Prætorian præfect.[135] That worthless minister rendered his master formidable only to the oppressed subjects, and contemptible to the enemies of Rome. By his weak or wicked counsels, the Imperial army was betrayed into a situation where valour and military skill were equally unavailing.[136] The vigorous attempt of the Romans to cut their way through the Persian host was repulsed with great slaughter;[137] and Sapor, who encompassed the camp with superior numbers, patiently waited till the increasing rage of famine and pestilence had ensured his victory. The licentious murmurs of the legions soon accused Valerian as the cause of their calamities; their seditious clamours demanded an instant capitulation. An immense sum of gold was offered to purchase the permission of a disgraceful retreat. But the Persian, conscious of his superiority, refused the money with disdain; and detaining the deputies, advanced in order of battle to the foot of the Roman rampart, and insisted on a personal conference with the emperor. Valerian was reduced to the necessity of intrusting his life and dignity to the faith of an enemy. The interview ended as it was natural to expect. The emperor was made a prisoner, and his astonished troops laid down their arms.[138] In such a moment of triumph, the pride and policy of Sapor prompted him to fill the vacant throne with a successor entirely dependent on his pleasure. Cyriades, an obscure fugitive of Antioch, stained with every vice, was chosen to dishonour the Roman purple; and the will of the Persian victor could not fail of being ratified by the acclamations, however reluctant, of the captive army.[139]

The Imperial slave was eager to secure the favour of his master by an act of treason to his native country. He conducted Sapor over the Euphrates, and by the way of Chalcis to the metropolis of the East. So rapid were the motions of the Persian cavalry that, if we may credit a very judicious historian,[140] the city of Antioch was surprised when the idle multitude was fondly gazing on the amusements of the theatre. The splendid buildings of Antioch, private as well as public, were either pillaged or destroyed; and the numerous inhabitants were put to the sword, or led away into captivity.[141] The tide of devastation was stopped for a moment by the resolution of the high priest of Emesa. Arrayed in his sacerdotal robes, he appeared at the head of a great body of fanatic peasants, armed only with slings, and defended his god and his property from the sacrilegious hands of the followers of Zoroaster.[142] But the ruin of Tarsus, and many other cities, furnishes a melancholy proof that, except in this single instance, the conquest of Syria and Cilicia scarcely interrupted the progress of the Persian arms. The advantages of the narrow passes of Mount Taurus were abandoned, in which an invader, whose principal force consisted in his cavalry, would have been engaged in a very unequal combat: and Sapor was permitted to form the siege of Cæsarea, the capital of Cappadocia; a city, though of the recond rank, which was supposed to contain four hundred thousand inhabitants. Demosthenes commanded in the place, not so much by the commission of the emperor, as in the voluntary defence of his country. For a long time he deferred its fate; and, when at last Cæsarea was betrayed by the perfidy of a physician, he cut his way through the Persians, who had been ordered to exert their utmost diligence to take him alive. This heroic chief escaped the power of a foe, who might either have honoured or punished his obstinate valour; but many thousands of his fellow-citizens were involved in a general massacre, and Sapor is accused of treating his prisoners with wanton and unrelenting cruelty.[143] Much should undoubtedly be allowed for national animosity, much for humbled pride and impotent revenge; yet, upon the whole, it is certain that the same prince, who, in Armenia, had displayed the mild aspect of a legislator, showed himself to the Romans under the stern features of a conqueror. He despaired of making any permanent establishment in the empire, and sought only to leave behind him a wasted desert, whilst he transported into Persia the people and the treasures of the provinces.[144]

At the time when the East trembled at the name of Sapor, he received a present not unworthy of the greatest kings; a long train of camels laden with the most rare and valuable merchandises. The rich offering was accompanied with an epistle, respectful but not servile, from Odenathus, one of the noblest and most opulent senators of Palmyra. "Who is this Odenathus" (said the haughty victor, and he commanded that the presents should be cast into the Euphrates), "that he thus insolently presumes to write to his lord? If he entertains a hope of mitigating his punishment let him fall prostrate before the foot of our throne with his hands bound behind his back. Should he hesitate, swift destruction shall be poured on his head, on his whole race, and on his country."[145] The desperate extremity to which the Palmyrenian was reduced called into action all the latent powers of his soul. He met Sapor; but he met him in arms. Infusing his own spirit into a little army collected from the villages of Syria[146] and the tents of the desert,[147] he hovered round the Persian host, harassed their retreat, carried off part of the treasure, and, what was dearer than any treasure, several of the women of the Great King; who was at last obliged to repass the Euphrates with some marks of haste and confusion.[148] By this exploit, Odenathus laid the foundations of his future fame and fortunes. The majesty of Rome, oppressed by a Persian, was protected by a Syrian or Arab of Palmyra.

The voice of history, which is often little more than the organ of hatred or flattery, reproaches Sapor with a proud abuse of the rights of conquest. We are told that Valerian, in chains, but invested with the Imperial purple, was exposed to the multitude, a constant spectacle of fallen greatness; and that whenever the Persian monarch mounted on horseback, he placed his foot on the neck of a Roman emperor. Notwithstanding all the remonstrances of his allies, who repeatedly advised him to remember the vicissitude of fortune, to dread the returning power of Rome, and to make his illustrious captive the pledge of peace, not the object of insult, Sapor still remained inflexible. When Valerian sunk under the weight of shame and grief, his skin, stuffed with straw, and formed into the likeness of a human figure, was preserved for ages in the most celebrated temple of Persia; a more real monument of triumph than the fancied trophies of brass and marble so often erected by Roman vanity.[149] The tale is moral and pathetic, but the truth of it may very fairly be called in question. The letters still extant from the princes of the East to Sapor are manifest forgeries;[150] nor is it natural to suppose that a jealous monarch should, even in the person of a rival, thus publicly degrade the majesty of kings. Whatever treatment the unfortunate Valerian might experience in Persia, it is at least certain that the only emperor of Rome who had ever fallen into the hands of the enemy languished away his life in hopeless captivity.

The emperor Gallienus, who had long supported with impatience the censorial severity of his father and colleague, received the intelligence of his misfortunes with secret pleasure and avowed indifference. "I knew that my father was a mortal," said he, "and since he has acted as becomes a brave man, I am satisfied." Whilst Rome lamented the fate of her sovereign, the savage coldness of his son was extolled by the servile courtiers as the perfect firmness of a hero and a stoic.[151] It is difficult to paint the light, the various, the inconstant character of Gallienus, which he displayed without constraint, as soon as he became sole possessor of the empire. In every art that he attempted his lively genius enabled him to succeed; and as his genius was destitute of judgment, he attempted every art except the important ones of war and government. He was a master of several curious but useless sciences, a ready orator and elegant poet,[152] a skilful gardener, an excellent cook, and most contemptible prince. When the great emergencies of the state required his presence and attention, he was engaged in conversation with the philosopher Plotinus,[153] wasting his time in trifling or licentious pleasures, preparing his initiation to the Grecian mysteries, or soliciting a place in the Areopagus of Athens. His profuse magnificence insulted the general poverty; the solemn ridicule of his triumphs impressed a deeper sense of the public disgrace.[154] The repeated intelligence of invasions, defeats, and rebellions, he received with a careless smile; and singling out, with affected contempt, some particular production of the lost province, he carelessly asked whether Rome must be ruined unless it was supplied with linen from Egypt and Arras cloth from Gaul? There were, however, a few short moments in the life of Gallienus when, exasperated by some recent injury, he suddenly appeared the intrepid soldier and the cruel tyrant; till satiated with blood, or fatigued by resistance, he insensibly sunk into the natural mildness and indolence of his character.[155]

At a time when the reins of government were held with so loose a hand, it is not surprising that a crowd of usurpers should start up in every province of the empire against the son of Valerian. It was probably some ingenious fancy, of comparing the thirty tyrants of Rome with the thirty tyrants of Athens, that induced the writers of the Augustan History to select that celebrated number, which has been gradu-ally received into a popular appellation.[156] But in every light the parallel is idle and defective. What resemblance can we discover between a council of thirty persons, the united oppressors of a single city, and an uncertain list of independent rivals, who rose and fell in irregular succession through the extent of a vast empire? Nor can the number of thirty be completed, unless we include in the account the women and children who were honoured with the Imperial title. The reign of Gallienus, distracted as it was, produced only nineteen pretenders to the throne; Cyriades, Macrianus, Balista, Odenathus, and Zenobia in the East; in Gaul, and the western provinces, Posthumus, Lollianus, Victorinus and his mother Victoria, Marius, and Tetricus. In Illyricum and the confines of the Danube, Ingenuus, Regillianus, and Aureolus; in Pontus,[157] Saturninus; in Isauria, Trebellianus; Piso in Thessaly; Valens in Achaia; Æmilianus in Egypt; and Celsus in Africa. To illustrate the obscure monuments of the life and death of each individual would prove a laborious task, alike barren of instruction and of amusement. We may content ourselves with investigating some general characters that most strongly mark the condition of the times and the manners of the men, their pretensions, their motives, their fate, and the destructive consequences of their usurpation.[158]

It is sufficiently known that the odious appellation of *Tyrant* was often employed by the ancients to express the illegal seizure of supreme power, without any reference to the abuse of it. Several of the pretenders, who raised the standard of rebellion against the emperor Gallienus, were shining models of virtue, and almost all possessed a considerable share of vigour and ability. Their merit had recommended them to the favour of Valerian, and gradually promoted them to the most important commands of the empire. The generals, who assumed the title of Augustus, were either respected by their troops for their able conduct and severe discipline, or admired for valour and success in war, or beloved for frankness and generosity. The field of victory was often the scene of their election; and even the armourer Marius, the most contemptible of all the candidates for the purple, was distinguished however by intrepid courage, matchless strength, and blunt honesty.[159] His mean and recent trade cast indeed an air of ridicule on his elevation; but his birth could not be more obscure than was that of the greater part of his rivals, who were born of peasants and enlisted in the army as private soldiers. In times of confusion, every active genius finds the place assigned him by Nature: in a general state of war, military merit is the road to glory and to greatness. Of the nineteen tyrants, Tetricus only was a senator; Piso alone was a noble. The blood of Numa, through twenty-eight successive generations, ran in the veins of Calphurnius Piso,[160] who, by female alliances, claimed a right of exhibiting, in his house, the images of Crassus and of the great Pompey.[161] His ancestors had been repeatedly dignified with all the honours which the commonwealth could bestow; and of all the ancient families of Rome, the Calphurnian alone had survived the tyranny of the Cæsars. The personal qualities of Piso added new lustre to his race. The usurper Valens, by whose order he was killed, confessed, with deep remorse, that even an enemy ought to have respected the sanctity of Piso; and although he died in arms against Gallienus, the senate, with the emperor's generous permission, decreed the triumphal ornaments to the memory of so virtuous a rebel.[162]

The lieutenants of Valerian were grateful to the father, whom they esteemed. They disdained to serve the luxurious indolence of his unworthy son. The throne of the Roman world was unsupported by any principle of loyalty; and treason against such a prince might easily be considered as patriotism to the state. Yet if we examine with candour the conduct of these usurpers, it will appear that they were much oftener driven into rebellion by their fears than urged to it by their ambition. They dreaded the cruel suspicions of Gallienus; they equally dreaded the capricious violence of their troops. If the dangerous favour of the army had imprudently declared them deserving of the purple, they were marked for sure destruction; and even prudence would counsel them to secure a short enjoyment of empire, and rather to try the fortune of war than to expect the hand of an executioner. When the clamour of the soldiers invested the reluctant victims with the ensigns of sovereign authority, they sometimes mourned in secret their approaching fate. "You have lost," said Saturninus on the day of his elevation, "you have lost a useful commander, and you have made a very wretched emperor."[163]

The apprehensions of Saturninus were justified by the repeated experience of revolutions. Of the nineteen tyrants who started up under the reign of Gallienus, there was not one who enjoyed a life of peace or a natural death. As soon as they were invested with the bloody purple, they inspired their adherents with the same fears and ambition which had occasioned their own revolt. Encompassed with domestic conspiracy, military sedition, and civil war, they trembled on the edge of precipices, in which, after a longer or shorter term of anxiety, they were inevitably lost. The precarious monarchs received, however, such honours as the flattery of their respective armies and provinces could bestow; but their claim, founded on rebellion, could never obtain the sanction of law or history. Italy, Rome, and the senate constantly adhered to the cause of Gallienus, and he alone was considered as the sovereign of the empire. That prince condescended indeed to acknowledge the victorious arms of Odenathus, who deserved the honourable distinction, by the respectful conduct which he always maintained towards the son of Valerian. With the general applause of the Romans, and the consent of Gallienus, the senate conferred the title of Augustus on the brave Palmyrenian and seemed to intrust him with the government of the East, which he already possessed, in so independent a manner, that, like a private succession, he bequeathed it to his illustrious widow Zenobia.[164]

The rapid and perpetual transitions from the cottage to the throne and from the throne to the grave, might have amused an indifferent philosopher; were it possible for a philosopher to remain indifferent amidst the general calamities of human kind. The election of these precarious emperors, their power and their death, were equally destructive to their subjects and adherents. The price of their fatal elevation was instantly discharged to the troops, by an immense donative, drawn from the bowels of the exhausted people. However virtuous was their character, however pure their intentions, they found themselves reduced to the hard necessity of supporting their usurpation by frequent acts of rapine and cruelty. When they fell, they involved armies and provinces in their fall. There is still extant a most savage mandate from Gallienus to one of his ministers, after the suppression of Ingenuus, who had assumed the purple in Illyricum. "It is not enough," says that soft but inhuman prince, "that you exterminate such as have appeared in arms: the chance of battle might have served me as effectually. The male sex of every age must be extirpated; provided that, in the execution of the children and old men, you can contrive means to save our reputation. Let every one die who has dropped an expression, who has entertained a thought against me, against *me*, the son of Valerian, the father and brother of so many princes.[165] Remember that Ingenuus was made emperor: tear, kill, hew in pieces. I write to you with my own hand, and would inspire you with my own feelings."[166] Whilst the public forces of the state were dissipated in private quarrels, the defenceless provinces lay exposed to every invader. The bravest usurpers were compelled, by the perplexity of their situation, to conclude ignominious treaties with the common enemy, to purchase with oppressive tributes the neutrality or services of the barbarians, and to introduce hostile and independent nations into the heart of the Roman monarchy.[167]

Such were the barbarians, and such the tyrants, who, under the reigns of Valerian and Gallienus, dismembered the provinces, and reduced the empire to the lowest pitch of disgrace and ruin, from whence it seemed impossible that it should ever emerge. As far as the barrenness of materials would permit, we have attempted to trace, with order and perspicuity, the general events of that calamitous period. There still remain some particular facts; I. The disorders of Sicily; II. The tumults of Alexandria; and, III. The rebellion of the Isaurians, which may serve to reflect a strong light on the horrid picture.

I. Whenever numerous troops of banditti, multiplied by success and impunity, publicly defy, instead of eluding the justice of their country, we may safely infer that the excessive weakness of the government is felt and abused by the lowest ranks of the community. The situation of Sicily preserved it from the barbarians; nor could the disarmed province have supported an usurper. The sufferings of that once flourishing and still fertile island were inflicted by baser hands. A licentious crown of slaves and peasants reigned for a while over the plundered country, and renewed the memory of the servile wars of more ancient times.[168] Devastations, of which the husbandman was either the victim or the accomplice, must have ruined the agriculture of Sicily; and as the principal estates were the property of the opulent senators of Rome, who often enclosed within a farm the territory of an old republic, it is not improbable that this private injury might affect the capital more deeply than all the conquests of the Goths or the Persians.

II. The foundation of Alexandria was a noble design, at once conceived and executed by the son of Philip. The beautiful and regular form of that great city, second only to Rome itself, comprehended a circumference of fifteen miles;[169] it was peopled by three hundred thousand inhabitants, besides at least an equal number of slaves.[170] The lucrative trade of Arabia and India flowed through the port of Alexandria to the capital and provinces of the empire. Idleness was unknown. Some were employed in blowing of glass, others in weaving of linen, others again manufacturing the papyrus. Either sex, and every age, was engaged in the pursuits of industry, nor did even the blind or the lame want occupations suited to their condition.[171] But the people of Alexandria, a various mixture of nations, united the vanity and inconstancy of the Greeks with the superstition and obstinacy of the Egyptians. The most trifling occasion, a transient scarcity of flesh or lentils, the neglect of an accustomed salutation, a mistake of precedency in the public baths, or a religious dispute,[172] were at any time sufficient to kindle a sedition among that vast multitude, whose resentments were furious and implacable.[173] After the captivity of Valerian and the insolence of his son had relaxed the authority of the laws, the Alexandrians abandoned themselves to the ungoverned rage of their passions, and their unhappy country was the theatre of a civil war, which continued (with a few short and suspicious truces) above twelve years.[174] All intercourse was cut off between the several quarters of the afflicted city, every street was polluted with blood, every building of strength converted into a citadel; nor did the tumults subside, till a considerable part of Alexandria was irretrievably ruined. The spacious and magnificent district of Bruchion, with its palaces and museum, the residence of the kings and philosophers of Egypt, is described above a century afterwards as already reduced to its present state of dreary solitude.[175]

III. The obscure rebellion of Trebellianus, who assumed the purple in Isauria, a petty province of Asia Minor, was attended with strange and memorable consequences. The pageant of royalty was soon destroyed by an officer of Gallienus; but his followers, despairing of mercy, resolved to shake off their allegiance, not only to the emperor, but to the empire, and suddenly returned to the savage manners, from which they had never perfectly been reclaimed. Their craggy rocks, a branch of the wide-extended Taurus, protected their inaccessible retreat. The tillage of some fertile valleys[176] supplied them with necessaries, and a habit of rapine with the luxuries of life. In the heart of the Roman monarchy, the Isaurians long continued a nation of wild barbarians. Succeeding princes, unable to reduce them to obedience either by arms or policy, were compelled to acknowledge their weakness by surrounding the hostile and independent spot with a strong chain of fortifications,[177] which often proved insufficient to restrain the incursions of these domestic foes. The Isaurians, gradually extending their territory to the sea-coast, subdued the western and mountainous part of Cilicia, formerly the nest of those daring pirates, against whom the republic had once been obliged to exert its utmost force, under the conduct of the great Pompey.[178]

Our habits of thinking so fondly connect the order of the universe with the fate of man, that this gloomy period of history has been decorated with inundations, earthquakes, uncommon meteors, preternatural darkness, and a crowd of prodigies fictitious or exaggerated.[179] But a long and general famine was a calamity of a more serious kind. It was the inevitable consequence of rapine and oppression, which extirpated the produce of the present, and the hope of future harvests. Famine is almost always followed by epidemical diseases, the effect of scanty and unwholesome food. Other causes must however have contributed to the furious plague,

which, from the year two hundred and fifty to the year two hundred and sixty-five, raged without interruption in every province, every city, and almost every family, of the Roman empire. During some time five thousand persons died daily in Rome; and many towns, that had escaped the hands of the barbarians, were entirely depopulated.[180]

We have the knowledge of a very curious circumstance, of some use perhaps in the melancholy calculation of human calamities. An exact register was kept at Alexandria, of all the citizens entitled to receive the distribution of corn. It was found that the ancient number of those comprised between the ages of forty and seventy had been equal to the whole sum of claimants, from fourteen to fourscore years of age, who remained alive after the reign of Gallienus.[181] Applying this authentic fact to the most correct tables of mortality, it evidently proves that above half the people of Alexandria had perished; and could we venture to extend the analogy to the other provinces, we might suspect that war, pestilence, and famine had consumed, in a few years, the moiety of the human species.[182]

CHAPTER XI

Reign of Claudius. Defeat of the Goths. Victories, Triumph, and Death of Aurelian.

UNDER the deplorable reigns of Valerian and Gallienus the empire was oppressed and almost destroyed by the soldiers, the tyrants, and the barbarians. It was saved by a series of great princes, who derived their obscure origin from the martial provinces of Illyricum. Within a period of about thirty years, Claudius, Aurelian, Probus, Diocletian and his colleagues, triumphed over the foreign and domestic enemies of the state, re-established, with the military discipline, the strength of the frontiers, and deserved the glorious title of Restorers of the Roman world.

The removal of an effeminate tyrant made way for a succession of heroes. The indignation of the people imputed all their calamities to Gallienus, and the far greater part were, indeed, the consequence of his dissolute manners and careless administration. He was even destitute of a sense of honour, which so frequently supplies the absence of public virtue; and as long as he was permitted to enjoy the possession of

Italy, a victory of the barbarians, the loss of a province, or the rebellion of a general, seldom disturbed the tranquil course of his pleasures. At length a considerable army, stationed on the Upper Danube, invested with the Imperial purple their leader Aureolus, who, disdaining a confined and barren reign over the mountains of Rhætia, passed the Alps, occupied Milan, threatened Rome, and challenged Gallienus to dispute in the field the sovereignty of Italy. The emperor, provoked by the insult, and alarmed by the instant danger, suddenly exerted that latent vigour which sometimes broke through the indolence of his temper. Forcing himself from the luxury of the palace, he appeared in arms at the head of his legions, and advanced beyond the Po to encounter his competitor. The corrupted name of Pontirolo[1] still preserves the memory of a bridge over the Adda, which, during the action, must have proved an object of the utmost importance to both armies. The Rhætian usurper, after receiving a total defeat and a dangerous wound, retired into Milan. The siege of that great city was immediately formed; the walls were battered with every engine in use among the ancients; and Aureolus, doubtful of his internal strength and hopeless of foreign succours, already anticipated the fatal consequences of unsuccessful rebellion.

His last resource was an attempt to seduce the loyalty of the besiegers. He scattered libels through their camp, inviting the troops to desert an unworthy master, who sacrificed the public happiness to his luxury, and the lives of his most valuable subjects to the slightest suspicions. The arts of Aureolus diffused fears and discontent among the principal officers of his rival. A conspiracy was formed by Heraclianus, the Prætorian præfect, by Marcian, a general of rank and reputation, and by Cecrops, who commanded a numerous body of Dalmatian guards. The death of Gallienus was resolved, and, notwithstanding their desire of first terminating the siege of Milan, the extreme danger which accompanied every moment's delay obliged them to hasten the execution of their daring purpose. At a late hour of the night, but while the emperor still protracted the pleasures of the table, an alarm was suddenly given that Aureolus, at the head of all his forces, had made a desperate sally from the town; Gallienus, who was never deficient in personal bravery, started from his silken couch, and, without allowing himself time either to put on his armour or to assemble his guards, he mounted on horseback and rode full speed towards the supposed place of the attack. Encompassed by his declared or concealed enemies, he soon, amidst the nocturnal tumult, received a mortal dart from an uncertain hand. Before he expired, a patriotic sentiment rising in the mind of Gallienus induced him to name a deserving successor, and it was his last request that the Imperial ornaments should be delivered to Claudius, who then commanded a detached army in the neighbourhood of Pavia. The report at least was diligently propagated, and the order cheerfully obeyed by the conspirators, who had already agreed to place Claudius on the throne. On the first news of the emperor's death the troops expressed some suspicion and resentment, till the one was removed and the other assuaged by a donative of twenty pieces of gold to each soldier. They then ratified the election and acknowledged the merit of their new sovereign.[2]

The obscurity which covered the origin of Claudius, though it was afterwards embellished by some flattering fictions,[3] sufficiently betrays the meanness of his birth. We can only discover that he was a native of one of the provinces bordering on the Danube, that his youth was spent in arms, and that his modest valour attracted the favour and confidence of Decius. The senate and people already considered him as an excellent officer, equal to the most important trusts, and censured the inattention of Valerian, who suffered him to remain in the subordinate station of a tribune. But it was not long before that emperor distinguished the merit of Claudius, by declaring him general and chief of the Illyrian frontier, with the command of all the troops in Thrace, Mæsia, Dacia, Pannonia, and Dalmatia, the appointments of the præfect of Egypt, the establishment of the proconsul of Africa, and the sure prospect of the consulship. By his victories over the Goths he deserved from the senate the honour of a statue, and excited the jealous apprehensions of Gallienus. It was impossible that a soldier could esteem so dissolute a sovereign, nor is it easy to conceal a just contempt. Some unguarded expressions which dropped from Claudius were officiously transmitted to the royal ear. The emperor's answer to an officer of confidence describes in very lively colours his own character and that of the times. "There is not anything capable of giving me more serious concern than the intelligence contained in your last despatch,[4] that some malicious suggestions have indisposed towards us the mind of our friend and *parent* Claudius. As you regard your allegiance, use every means to appease his resentment, but conduct your negotiation with secrecy; let it not reach the knowledge of the Dacian troops; they are already provoked, and it might inflame their fury. I myself have sent him some presents: be it your care that he accept them with pleasure. Above all, let him not suspect that I am made acquainted with his impudence. The fear of my anger might urge him to desperate counsels."[5] The presents which accompanied this humble epistle, in which the monarch solicited a reconciliation with his discontented subject, consisted of a considerable sum of money, a splendid wardrobe, and a valuable service of silver and gold plate. By such arts Gallienus softened the indignation and dispelled the fears of his Illyrian general, and during the remainder of that reign the formidable sword of Claudius was always drawn in the cause of a master whom he despised. At last, indeed, he received from the conspirators the bloody purple of Gallienus; but he had been absent from their camp and counsels; and however he might applaud the deed, we may candidly presume that he was innocent of the knowledge of it.[6] When Claudius ascended the throne he was about fifty-four years of age.

The siege of Milan was still continued, and Aureolus soon discovered that the success of his artifices had only raised up a more determined adversary. He attempted to negotiate with Claudius a treaty of alliance and partition. "Tell him," replied the intrepid emperor, "that such proposals should have been made to Gallienus; *he*, perhaps, might have listened to them with patience, and accepted a colleague as despicable as himself."[7] This stern refusal, and a last unsuccessful effort, obliged Aureolus to yield the city and himself to the discretion of the conqueror. The judgment of the army pronounced him worthy of death, and Claudius, after a feeble resistance, consented to the execution of the sentence. Nor was the zeal of the senate less ardent in the cause of their new sovereign. They ratified, perhaps with a sincere transport of zeal, the election of Claudius; and as his predecessor had shown himself the personal enemy of their order, they exercised, under the name of justice, a severe revenge against his friends and family. The senate was permitted to discharge the ungrateful office of punishment, and the emperor reserved for himself the pleasure and merit of obtaining by his intercession a general act of indemnity.[8]

Such ostentatious clemency discovers less of the real character of Claudius than a trifling circumstance in which he seems to have consulted only the dictates of his heart. The frequent rebellions of the provinces had involved almost every person in the guilt of treason, almost every estate in the case of confiscation; and Gallienus often displayed his liberality by distributing among his officers the property of his subjects. On the accession of Claudius, an old woman threw herself at his feet and complained that a general of the late emperor had obtained an arbitrary grant of her patrimony. This general was Claudius himself, who had not entirely escaped the contagion of the times. The emperor blushed at the reproach, but deserved the confidence which she had reposed in his equity. The confession of his fault was accompanied with immediate and ample restitution.[9]

In the arduous task which Claudius had undertaken of restoring the empire to its ancient splendour, it was first necessary to revive among his troops a sense of order and obedience. With the authority of a veteran commander, he represented to them that the relaxation of discipline had introduced a long train of disorders, the effects of which were at length experienced by the soldiers themselves; that a people ruined by oppression, and indolent from despair, could no longer supply a numerous army with the means of luxury, or even of subsistence; that the danger of each individual had increased with the despotism of the military order, since princes who tremble on the throne will guard their safety by the instant sacrifice of every obnoxious subject. The emperor expatiated on the mischiefs of a lawless caprice, which the soldiers could only gratify at the expense of their own blood, as their seditious elections had so frequently been followed by civil wars, which consumed the flower of the legions either in the field of battle or in the cruel abuse of victory. He painted in the most lively colours the exhausted state of the treasury, the desolation of the provinces, the disgrace of the Roman name, and the insolent triumph of rapacious barbarians. It was against those barbarians, he declared, that he intended to point the first effort of their arms. Tetricus might reign for a while over the West, and even Zenobia might preserve the dominion of the East.[10] These usurpers were his personal adversaries, nor could he think of indulging any private resentment till he had saved an empire whose impending ruin would, unless it was timely prevented, crush both the army and the people.

The various nations of Germany and Sarmatia who fought under the Gothic standard had already collected an armament more formidable than any which had yet issued from the Euxine. On the banks of the Dniester, one of the great rivers that discharge themselves into that sea, they constructed a fleet of two thousand, or even of six thousand vessels;[11] numbers, which, however incredible they may seem, would have been insufficient to transport their pretended army of three hundred and twenty thousand barbarians. Whatever might be the real strength of the Goths, the vigour and success of the expedition were not adequate to the greatness of the preparations. In their passage through the Bosphorus the unskilful pilots were overpowered by the violence of the current; and while the multitude of their ships were crowded in a narrow channel, many were dashed against each other or against the shore. The barbarians made several descents on the coasts both of Europe and Asia; but the open country was already plundered, and they were repulsed with shame and loss from the fortified cities which they assaulted. A spirit of discouragement and division arose in the fleet, and some of their chiefs sailed away towards the islands of Crete and Cyprus; but the main body, pursuing a more steady course, anchored at length near the foot of Mount Athos, and assaulted the city of Thessalonica, the wealthy capital of all the Macedonian provinces. Their attacks, in which they displayed a fierce but artless bravery, were soon interrupted by the rapid approach of Claudius, hastening to a scene of action that deserved the presence of a warlike prince at the head of the remaining powers of the empire. Impatient for battle, the Goths immediately broke up their camp, relinquished the siege of Thessalonica, left their navy at the foot of Mount Athos, traversed the hills of Macedonia, and pressed forwards to engage the last defence of Italy.

We still possess an original letter addressed by Claudius to the senate and people on this memorable occasion. "Conscript fathers," says the emperor, "know that three hundred and twenty thousand Goths have invaded the Roman territory. If I vanquish them, your gratitude will reward my services. Should I fall, remember that I am the successor of Gallienus. The whole republic is fatigued and exhausted. We shall fight after Valerian, after Ingenuus, Regillianus, Lollianus, Posthumus, Celsus, and a thousand others, whom a just contempt for Gallienus provoked into rebellion. We are in want of darts, of spears, and of shields. The strength of the empire, Gaul, and Spain, are usurped by Tetricus; and we blush to acknowledge that the archers of the East serve under the banners of Zenobia. Whatever we shall perform will be sufficiently great."[12] The melancholy firmness of this epistle announces a hero careless of his fate, conscious of his danger, but still deriving a well-grounded hope from the resources of his own mind.

The event surpassed his own expectations and those of the world. By the most signal victories he delivered the empire from this host of barbarians, and was distinguished by posterity under the glorious appellation of the Gothic Claudius. The imperfect historians of an irregular war[13] do not enable us to describe the order and circumstances of his exploits; but, if we could be indulged in the allusion, we might distribute into three acts this memorable tragedy. I. The decisive battle was fought near Naissus, a city of Dardania. The legions at first gave way, oppressed by numbers and dismayed by misfortunes. Their ruin was inevitable, had not the abilities of their emperor prepared a seasonable

relief. A large detachment, rising out of the secret and difficult passes of the mountains, which by his order they had occupied, suddenly assailed the rear of the victorious Goths. The favourable instant was improved by the activity of Claudius. He revived the courage of his troops, restored their ranks, and pressed the barbarians on every side. Fifty thousand men are reported to have been slain in the battle of Naissus. Several large bodies of barbarians, covering their retreat with a movable fortification of waggons, retired, or rather escaped, from the field of slaughter. II. We may presume that some insurmountable difficulty—the fatigue, perhaps, or the disobedience of the conquerors—prevented Claudius from completing in one day the destruction of the Goths. The war was diffused over the provinces of Mæsia, Thrace, and Macedonia, and its operations drawn out into a variety of marches, surprises, and tumultuary engagements, as well by sea as by land. When the Romans suffered any loss, it was commonly occasioned by their own cowardice or rashness; but the superior talents of the emperor, his perfect knowledge of the country, and his judicious choice of measures as well as officers, assured on most occasions the success of his arms. The immense booty, the fruit of so many victories, consisted for the greater part of cattle and slaves. A select body of the Gothic youth was received among the Imperial troops; the remainder was sold into servitude; and so considerable was the number of female captives that every soldier obtained as his share two or three women. A circumstance from which we may conclude that the invaders entertained some designs of settlement as well as of plunder; since even in a naval expedition they were accompanied by their families. III. The loss of their fleet, which was either taken or sunk, had intercepted the retreat of the Goths. A vast circle of Roman posts, distributed with skill, supported with firmness, and gradually closing towards a common centre, forced the barbarians into the most inaccessible parts of Mount Hæmus, where they found a safe refuge, but a very scanty subsistence. During the course of a rigorous winter, in which they were besieged by the emperor's troops, famine and pestilence, desertion and the sword, continually diminished the imprisoned multitude. On the return of spring nothing appeared in arms except a hardy and desperate band, the remnant of that mighty host which had embarked at the mouth of the Dniester.

The pestilence which swept away such numbers of the barbarians at length proved fatal to their conqueror. After a short but glorious reign of two years, Claudius expired at Sirmium, amidst the tears and acclamations of his subjects. In his last illness he convened the principal officers of the state and army, and in their presence recommended Aurelian,[14] one of his generals, as the most deserving of the throne, and the best qualified to execute the great design which he himself had been permitted only to undertake. The virtues of Claudius, his valour, affability, justice, and temperance, his love of fame and of his country, place him in that short list of emperors who added lustre to the Roman purple. Those virtues, however, were celebrated with peculiar zeal and complacency by the courtly writers of the age of Constantine, who was the great-grandson of Crispus, the elder brother of Claudius. The voice of flattery was soon taught to repeat that the gods, who so hastily had snatched Claudius from the earth, rewarded his merit and piety by the perpetual establishment of the empire in his family.[15]

Notwithstanding these oracles, the greatness of the Flavian family (a name which it had pleased them to assume) was deferred above twenty years, and the elevation of Claudius occasioned the immediate ruin of his brother Quintilius, who possessed not sufficient moderation or courage to descend into the private station to which the patriotism of the late emperor had condemned him. Without delay or reflection he assumed the purple at Aquileia, where he commanded a considerable force; and though his reign lasted only seventeen days, he had time to obtain the sanction of the senate and to experience a mutiny of the troops. As soon as he was informed that the great army of the Danube had invested the well-known valour of Aurelian with Imperial power, he sunk under the fame and merit of his rival; and, ordering his veins to be opened, prudently withdrew himself from the unequal contest.[16]

The general design of this work will not permit us minutely to relate the actions of every emperor after he ascended the throne, much less to deduce the various fortunes of his private life. We shall only observe that the father of Aurelian was a peasant of the territory of Sirmium, who occupied a small farm, the property of Aurelius, a rich senator. His warlike son enlisted in the troops as a common soldier, successively rose to the rank of a centurion, a tribune, the præfect of a legion, the inspector of the camp, the general, or, as it was then called, the duke of a frontier; and at length, during the Gothic war, exercised the important office of commander-in-chief of the cavalry. In every station he distinguished himself by matchless valour,[17] rigid discipline, and successful conduct. He was invested with the consulship by the emperor Valerian, who styles him, in the pompous language of that age, the deliverer of Illyricum, the restorer of Gaul, and the rival of the Scipios. At the recommendation of Valerian, a senator of the highest rank and merit, Ulpius Crinitus, whose blood was derived from the same source as that of Trajan, adopted the Pannonian peasant, gave him his daughter in marriage, and relieved with his ample fortune the honourable poverty which Aurelian had preserved inviolate.[18]

The reign of Aurelian lasted only four years and about nine months; but every instant of that short period was filled by some memorable achievement. He put an end to the Gothic war, chastised the Germans who invaded Italy, recovered Gaul, Spain, and Britain out of the hands of Tetricus, and destroyed the proud monarchy which Zenobia had erected in the East on the ruins of the afflicted empire.

It was the rigid attention of Aurelian even to the minutest articles of discipline which bestowed such uninterrupted success on his arms. His military regulations are contained in a very concise epistle to one of his inferior officers, who is commanded to enforce them, as he wishes to become a tribune, or as he is desirous to live. Gaming, drinking, and the arts of divination were severely prohibited. Aurelian expected that his soldiers should be modest, frugal, and laborious; that their armour should be constantly kept bright, their weapons sharp, their clothing and horses ready for immediate service; that they should live in their quarters with chastity and sobriety, without damaging the corn-fields, without stealing even a sheep, a fowl, or a bunch of grapes, without exacting from their landlords either salt, or oil, or wood. "The public allowance," continues the emperor, "is sufficient for their support; their wealth should be collected from the spoil of the enemy, not from the tears of the provincials."[19] A single instance will serve to display the rigour, and even cruelty, of Aurelian. One of the soldiers had seduced the wife of his host. The guilty wretch was fastened to two trees forcibly drawn towards each other, and his limbs were torn asunder by their sudden separation. A few such examples impressed a salutary consternation. The punishments of Aurelian were terrible; but he had seldom occasion to punish more than once the same offence. His own conduct gave a sanction to his laws, and the seditious legions dreaded a chief who had learned to obey, and who was worthy to command.

The death of Claudius had revived the fainting spirit of the Goths. The troops which guarded the passes of Mount Hæmus and the banks of the Danube had been drawn away by the apprehension of a civil war; and it seems probable that the remaining body of the Gothic and Vandalic tribes embraced the favourable opportunity, abandoned their settlements of the Ukraine, traversed the rivers, and swelled with new multitudes the destroying host of their countrymen. Their united numbers were at length encountered by Aurelian, and the bloody and doubtful conflict ended only with the approach of night.[20] Exhausted by so many calamities, which they had mutually endured and inflicted during a twenty years' war, the Goths and the Romans consented to a lasting and beneficial treaty. It was earnestly solicited by the barbarians, and cheerfully ratified by the legions, to whose suffrage the prudence of Aurelian referred the decision of that important question. The Gothic nation engaged to supply the armies of Rome with a body of two thousand auxiliaries, consisting entirely of cavalry, and stipulated in return an undisturbed retreat, with a regular market as far as the Danube, provided by the emperor's care, but at their own expense. The treaty was observed with such religious fidelity that, when a party of five hundred men straggled from the camp in quest of plunder, the king or general of the barbarians commanded that the guilty leader should be apprehended and shot to death with darts, as a victim devoted to the sanctity of their engagements. It is, however, not unlikely that the precaution of Aurelian, who had exacted as hostages the sons and daughters of the Gothic chiefs, contributed something to this pacific temper. The youths he trained in the exercise of arms, and near his own person; to the damsels he gave a liberal and Roman education, and, by bestowing them in marriage on some of his principal officers, gradually introduced between the two nations the closest and most endearing connections.[21]

But the most important condition of peace was understood rather than expressed in the treaty. Aurelian withdrew the Roman forces from Dacia, and tacitly relinquished that great province to the Goths and Vandals.[22] His manly judgment convinced him of the solid advantages, and taught him to despise the seeming disgrace, of thus contracting the frontiers of the monarchy. The Dacian subjects, removed from those distant possessions which they were unable to cultivate or defend, added strength and populousness to the southern side of the Danube. A fertile territory, which the repetition of barbarous inroads had changed into a desert, was yielded to their industry, and a new province of Dacia still preserved the memory of Trajan's conquests. The old country of that name detained, however, a considerable number of its inhabitants, who dreaded exile more than a Gothic master.[23] These degenerate Romans continued to serve the empire, whose allegiance they had renounced, by introducing among their conquerors the first notions of agriculture, the useful arts, and the conveniences of civilised life. An intercourse of commerce and language was gradually established between the opposite banks of the Danube; and, after Dacia became an independent state, it often proved the firmest barrier of the empire against the invasions of the savages of the North. A sense of interest attached these more settled barbarians to the alliance of Rome, and a permanent interest very frequently ripens into sincere and useful friendship. This various colony, which filled the ancient province, and was insensibly blended into one great people, still acknowledged the superior renown and authority of the Gothic tribe, and claimed the fancied honour of a Scandinavian origin. At the same time the lucky, though accidental, resemblance of the name of Getæ infused among the credulous Goths a vain persuasion that, in a remote age, their own ancestors, already seated in the Dacian provinces, had received the instructions of Zamolxis, and checked the victorious arms of Sesostris and Darius.[24]

While the vigorous and moderate conduct of Aurelian restored the Illyrian frontier, the nation of the Alemanni[25] violated the conditions of peace which either Gallienus had purchased, or Claudius had imposed, and, inflamed by their impatient youth, suddenly flew to arms. Forty thousand horses appeared in the field,[26] and the numbers of the infantry doubled those of the cavalry.[27] The first objects of their avarice were a few cities of the Rhætian frontier; but their hopes soon rising with success, the rapid march of the Alemanni traced a line of devastation from the Danube to the Po.[28]

The emperor was almost at the same time informed of the irruption, and of the retreat, of the barbarians. Collecting an active body of troops, he marched with silence and celerity along the skirts of the Hercynian forest; and the Alemanni, laden with the spoils of Italy, arrived at the Danube, without suspecting that on the opposite bank, and in an advantageous post, a Roman army lay concealed and prepared to intercept their return. Aurelian indulged the fatal security of the barbarians, and permitted about half their forces to pass the river without disturbance and without precaution. Their situation and astonishment gave him an easy victory; his skilful conduct improved the advantage. Disposing the legions in a semicircular form, he advanced the two horns of the crescent across the Danube, and, wheeling them on a sudden towards the centre, enclosed the rear of the German host. The dismayed barbarians, on whatsoever side they cast their eyes, beheld with despair a wasted country, a deep and rapid stream, a victorious and implacable enemy.

Reduced to this distressed condition, the Alemanni no longer disdained to sue for peace. Aurelian received their ambassadors at the head of his camp, and with every circumstance of martial pomp that could display the greatness and discipline of Rome. The legions stood to their arms in well-ordered ranks and awful silence. The principal commanders, distinguished by the ensigns of their rank, appeared on horseback on either side of the Imperial throne. Behind the throne the consecrated images of the emperor and his predecessors,[29] the golden eagles, and the various titles of the legions, engraved in letters of gold, were exalted in the air on lofty pikes covered with silver. When Aurelian assumed his seat, his manly grace and majestic figure[30] taught the barbarians to revere the person as well as the purple of their conqueror. The ambassadors fell prostrate on the ground in silence. They were commanded to rise, and permitted to speak. By the assistance of interpreters they extenuated their perfidy, magnified their exploits, expatiated on the vicissitudes of fortune and the advantages of peace, and, with an ill-timed confidence, demanded a large subsidy as the price of the alliance which they offered to the Romans. The answer of the emperor was stern and imperious. He treated their offer with contempt, and their demand with indignation; reproached the barbarians that they were as ignorant of the arts of war as of the laws of peace; and finally dismissed them with the choice only of submitting to his unconditioned mercy, or awaiting the utmost severity of his resentment.[31] Aurelian had resigned a distant province to the Goths; but it was dangerous to trust or to pardon these perfidious barbarians, whose formidable power kept Italy itself in perpetual alarms.

Immediately after this conference it should seem that some unexpected emergency required the emperor's presence in Pannonia. He devolved on his lieutenants the care of finishing the destruction of the Alemanni, either by the sword, or by the surer operation of famine. But an active despair has often triumphed over the indolent assurance of success. The barbarians, finding it impossible to traverse the Danube and the Roman camp, broke through the posts in their rear, which were more feebly or less carefully guarded; and with incredible diligence, but by a different road, returned towards the mountains of Italy.[32] Aurelian, who considered the war as totally extinguished, received the mortifying intelligence of the escape of the Alemanni, and of the ravage which they already committed in the territory of Milan. The legions were commanded to follow, with as much expedition as those heavy bodies were capable of exerting, the rapid flight of an enemy, whose infantry and cavalry moved with almost equal swiftness. A few days afterwards the emperor himself marched to the relief of Italy, at the head of a chosen body of auxiliaries (among whom were the hostages and cavalry of the Vandals), and of all the Prætorian guards who had served in the wars on the Danube.[33]

As the light troops of the Alemanni had spread themselves from the Alps to the Apennine, the incessant vigilance of Aurelian and his officers was exercised in the discovery, the attack, and the pursuit of the numerous detachments. Notwithstanding this desultory war, three considerable battles are mentioned, in which the principal force of both armies was obstinately engaged.[34] The success was various. In the first, fought near Placentia, the Romans received so severe a blow that, according to the expression of a writer extremely partial to Aurelian, the immediate dissolution of the empire was apprehended.[35] The crafty barbarians, who had lined the woods, suddenly attacked the legions in the dusk of the evening, and, it is most probable, after the fatigue and disorder of a long march. The fury of their charge was irresistible; but at length, after a dreadful slaughter, the patient firmness of the emperor rallied his troops, and restored, in some degree, the honour of his arms. The second battle was fought near Fano in Umbria; on the spot which, five hundred years before, had been fatal to the brother of Hannibal.[36] Thus far the successful Germans had advanced along the Æmilian and Flaminian way, with a design of sacking the defenceless mistress of the world. But Aurelian, who, watchful for the safety of Rome, still hung on their rear, found in this place the decisive moment of giving them a total and irretrievable defeat.[37] The flying remnant of their host was exterminated in a third and last battle near Pavia; and Italy was delivered from the inroads of the Alemanni.

Fear has been the original parent of superstition, and every new calamity urges trembling mortals to deprecate the wrath of their invisible enemies. Though the best hope of the republic was in the valour and conduct of Aurelian, yet such was the public consternation, when the barbarians were hourly expected at the gates of Rome, that, by a decree of the senate, the Sibylline books were consulted. Even the emperor himself, from a motive either of religion or of policy, recommended this salutary measure, chided the tardiness of the senate,[38] and offered to supply whatever expense, whatever animals, whatever captives of any nation, the gods should require. Notwithstanding this liberal offer, it does not appear that any human victims expiated with their blood the sins of the Roman people. The Sibylline books enjoined ceremonies of a more harmless nature—processions of priests in white robes, attended by a chorus of youths and virgins; lustrations of the city and adjacent country; and sacrifices, whose powerful influence disabled the barbarians from passing the mystic ground on which they had been celebrated. However puerile in themselves, these superstitious arts were subservient to the success of the war; and if, in the decisive battle of Fano, the Alemanni fancied they saw an army of spectres combating on the side of Aurelian, he received a real and effectual aid from this imaginary reinforcement.[39]

But whatever confidence might be placed in ideal ramparts, the experience of the past, and the dread of the future, induced the Romans to construct fortifications of a grosser and more substantial kind. The seven hills of Rome had been surrounded, by the successors of Romulus, with an ancient wall of more than thirteen miles.[40] The vast enclosure may seem disproportioned to the strength and numbers of the infant state. But it was necessary to secure an ample extent of pasture and arable land against the frequent and sudden incursions of the tribes of Latium, the perpetual enemies of the republic. With the progress of Roman greatness, the city and its inhabitants gradually increased, filled up the vacant space, pierced through the useless walls, covered the field of Mars, and, on every side, followed the public highways in long

and beautiful suburbs.[41] The extent of the new walls, erected by Aurelian, and finished in the reign of Probus, was magnified by popular estimation to near fifty,[42] but is reduced by accurate measurement to about twenty-one miles.[43] It was a great but a melancholy labour, since the defence of the capital betrayed the decline of the monarchy. The Romans of a more prosperous age, who trusted to the arms of the legions the safety of the frontier camps,[44] were very far from entertaining a suspicion that it would ever become necessary to fortify the seat of empire against the inroads of the barbarians.[45]

The victory of Claudius over the Goths, and the success of Aurelian against the Alemanni, had already restored to the arms of Rome their ancient superiority over the barbarous nations of the North. To chastise domestic tyrants, and to reunite the dismembered parts of the empire, was a task reserved for the second of those warlike emperors. Though he was acknowledged by the senate and people, the frontiers of Italy, Africa, Illyricum, and Thrace, confined the limits of his reign. Gaul, Spain, and Britain, Egypt, Syria, and Asia Minor, were still possessed by two rebels, who alone, out of so numerous a list, had hitherto escaped the dangers of their situation; and to complete the ignominy of Rome, these rival thrones had been usurped by women.

A rapid succession of monarchs had arisen and fallen in the provinces of Gaul. The rigid virtues of Posthumus served only to hasten his destruction. After suppressing a competitor who had assumed the purple at Mentz, he refused to gratify his troops with the plunder of the rebellious city; and, in the seventh year of his reign, became the victim of their disappointed avarice.[46] The death of Victorinus, his friend and associate, was occasioned by a less worthy cause. The shining accomplishments[47] of that prince were stained by a licentious passion, which he indulged in acts of violence, with too little regard to the laws of society, or even to those of love.[48] He was slain at Cologne, by a conspiracy of jealous husbands, whose revenge would have appeared more justifiable had they spared the innocence of his son. After the murder of so many valiant princes, it is somewhat remarkable that a female for a long time controlled the fierce legions of Gaul, and still more singular that she was the mother of the unfortunate Victorinus. The arts and treasures of Victoria enabled her successively to place Marius and Tetricus on the throne, and to reign with a manly vigour under the name of those dependent emperors. Money of copper, of silver, and of gold, was coined in her name; she assumed the titles of Augusta and Mother of the Camps: her power ended only with her life; but her life was perhaps shortened by the ingratitude of Tetricus.[49]

When, at the instigation of his ambitious patroness, Tetricus assumed the ensigns of royalty, he was governor of the peaceful province of Aquitaine, an employment suited to his character and education. He reigned four or five years over Gaul, Spain, and Britain, the slave and sovereign of a licentious army, whom he dreaded, and by whom he was despised. The valour and fortune of Aurelian at length opened the prospect of a deliverance. He ventured to disclose his melancholy situation, and conjured the emperor to hasten to the relief of his unhappy rival. Had this secret correspondence reached the ears of the soldiers, it would most probably have cost Tetricus his life; nor could he resign the sceptre of the West without committing an act of treason against himself. He affected the appearances of a civil war, led his forces into the field against Aurelian, posted them in the most disadvantageous manner, betrayed his own counsels to the enemy, and with a few chosen friends deserted in the beginning of the action. The rebel legions, though disordered and dismayed by the unexpected treachery of their chief, defended themselves with desperate valour, till they were cut in pieces almost to a man, in this bloody and memorable battle, which was fought near Châlons in Champagne.[50] The retreat of the irregular auxiliaries, Franks and Batavians,[51] whom the conqueror soon compelled or persuaded to repass the Rhine, restored the general tranquillity, and the power of Aurelian was acknowledged from the wall of Antoninus to the Columns of Hercules.

As early as the reign of Claudius, the city of Autun, alone and unassisted, had ventured to declare against the legions of Gaul. After a siege of seven months they stormed and plundered that unfortunate city, already wasted by famine.[52] Lyons, on the contrary, had resisted with obstinate disaffection the arms of Aurelian. We read of the punishment of Lyons,[53] but there is not any mention of the rewards of Autun. Such, indeed, is the policy of civil war: severely to remember injuries, and to forget the most important services. Revenge is profitable, gratitude is expensive.

Aurelian had no sooner secured the person and provinces of Tetricus than he turned his arms against Zenobia, the celebrated queen of Palmyra and the East. Modern Europe has produced several illustrious women who have sustained with glory the weight of empire; nor is our own age destitute of such distinguished characters. But if we except the doubtful achievements of Semiramis, Zenobia is perhaps the only female whose superior genius broke through the servile indolence imposed on her sex by the climate and manners of Asia.[54] She claimed her descent from the Macedonian kings of Egypt, equalled in beauty her ancestor Cleopatra, and far surpassed that princess in chastity[55] and valour. Zenobia was esteemed the most lovely as well as the most heroic of her sex. She was of a dark complexion (for in speaking of a lady these trifles become important). Her teeth were of a pearly whiteness, and her large black eyes sparkled with uncommon fire, tempered by the most attractive sweetness. Her voice was strong and harmonious. Her manly understanding was strengthened and adorned by study. She was not ignorant of the Latin tongue, but possessed in equal perfection the Greek, the Syriac, and the Egyptian languages. She had drawn up for her own use an epitome of oriental history, and familiarly compared the beauties of Homer and Plato under the tuition of the sublime Longinus.

This accomplished woman gave her hand to Odenathus, who, from a private station, raised himself to the dominion of the East. She soon became the friend and companion of a hero. In the intervals of war Odenathus passionately delighted in the exercise of hunting; he pursued with ardour the wild beasts of the desert, lions, panthers, and bears; and the ardour of Zenobia in that dangerous amusement was not inferior to his own. She had inured her constitution to fatigue, disdained the use of a covered carriage, generally appeared on horseback in a military habit, and sometimes marched several miles on foot at the head of the troops. The success of Odenathus was in a great measure ascribed to her incomparable prudence and fortitude. Their splendid victories over the Great King, whom they twice pursued as far as the gates of Ctesiphon, laid the foundations of their united fame and power. The armies which they commanded, and the provinces which they had saved, acknowledged not any other sovereigns than their invincible chiefs. The senate and people of Rome revered a stranger who had avenged their captive emperor, and even the insensible son of Valerian accepted Odenathus for his legitimate colleague.

After a successful expedition against the

Gothic plunderers of Asia, the Palmyrenian prince returned to the city of Emesian Syria. Invincible in war, he was there cut off by domestic treason, and his favourite amusement of hunting was the cause, or at least the occasion, of his death.[56] His nephew, Mæonius, presumed to dart his javelin before that of his uncle; and, though admonished of his error, repeated the same insolence. As a monarch, and as a sportsman, Odenathus was provoked, took away his horse, a mark of ignominy among the barbarians, and chastised the rash youth by a short confinement. The offence was soon forgot, but the punishment was remembered; and Mæonius, with a few daring associates, assassinated his uncle in the midst of a great entertainment. Herod, the son of Odenathus, though not of Zenobia, a young man of a soft and effeminate temper,[57] was killed with his father. But Mæonius obtained only the pleasure of revenge by this bloody deed. He had scarcely time to assume the title of Augustus before he was sacrificed by Zenobia to the memory of her husband.[58]

With the assistance of his most faithful friends, she immediately filled the vacant throne, and governed with manly counsels Palmyra, Syria, and the East, above five years. By the death of Odenathus, that authority was at an end which the senate had granted him only as a personal distinction; but his martial widow, disdaining both the senate and Gallienus, obliged one of the Roman generals who was sent against her to retreat into Europe, with the loss of his army and his reputation.[59] Instead of the little passions which so frequently perplex a female reign, the steady administration of Zenobia was guided by the most judicious maxims of policy. If it was expedient to pardon, she could calm her resentment; if it was necessary to punish, she could impose silence on the voice of pity. Her strict economy was accused of avarice; yet on every proper occasion she appeared magnificent and liberal. The neighbouring states of Arabia, Armenia, and Persia, dreaded her enmity, and solicited her alliance. To the dominions of Odenathus, which extended from the Euphrates to the frontiers of Bithynia, his widow added the inheritance of her ancestors, the populous and fertile kingdom of Egypt.[60] The emperor Claudius acknowledged her merit, and was content that, while *he* pursued the Gothic war, *she* should assert the dignity of the empire in the East. The conduct, however, of Zenobia was attended with some ambiguity; nor is it unlikely that she had conceived the design of erecting an independent and hostile monarchy. She blended with the popular manners of Roman princes the stately pomp of the courts of Asia, and exacted from her subjects the same adoration that was paid to the successors of Cyrus. She bestowed on her three sons[61] a Latin education, and often showed them to the troops adorned with the Imperial purple. For herself she reserved the diadem, with the splendid but doubtful title of Queen of the East.

When Aurelian passed over into Asia, against an adversary whose sex alone could render her an object of contempt, his presence restored obedience to the province of Bithynia, already shaken by the arms and intrigues of Zenobia.[62] Advancing at the head of his legions, he accepted the submission of Ancyra, and was admitted into Tyana, after an obstinate siege, by the help of a perfidious citizen. The generous though fierce temper of Aurelian abandoned the traitor to the rage of the soldiers: a superstitious reverence induced him to treat with lenity the countrymen of Apollonius the philosopher.[63] Antioch was deserted on his approach, till the emperor, by his salutary edicts, recalled the fugitives, and granted a general pardon to all who, from necessity rather than choice, had been engaged in the service of the Palmyrenian queen. The unexpected mildness of such a conduct reconciled the minds of the Syrians, and, as far as the gates of Emesa, the wishes of the people seconded the terror of his arms.[64]

Zenobia would have ill deserved her reputation had she indolently permitted the emperor of the West to approach within an hundred miles of her capital. The fate of the East was decided in two great battles; so similar in almost every circumstance, that we can scarcely distinguish them from each other, except by observing that the first was fought near Antioch,[65] and the second near Emesa.[66] In both the queen of Palmyra animated the armies by her presence, and devolved the execution of her orders on Zabdas, who had already signalised his military talents by the conquest of Egypt. The numerous forces of Zenobia consisted for the most part of light archers, and of heavy cavalry clothed in complete steel. The Moorish and Illyrian horse of Aurelian were unable to sustain the ponderous charge of their antagonists. They fled in real or affected disorder, engaged the Palmyrenians in a laborious pursuit, harassed them by a desultory combat, and at length discomfited this impenetrable but unwieldy body of cavalry. The light infantry, in the meantime, when they had exhausted their quivers, remaining without protection against a closer onset, exposed their naked sides to the swords of the legions. Aurelian had chosen these veteran troops who were usually stationed on the Upper Danube, and whose valour had been severely tried in the Alemannic war.[67] After the defeat of Emesa, Zenobia found it impossible to collect a third army. As far as the frontier of Egypt, the nations subject to her empire had joined the standard of the conqueror, who detached Probus, the bravest of his generals, to possess himself of the Egyptian provinces. Palmyra was the last resource of the widow of Odenathus. She retired within the walls of her capital, made every preparation for a vigorous resistance, and declared, with the intrepidity of a heroine, that the last moment of her reign and of her life should be the same.

Amid the barren deserts of Arabia a few cultivated spots rise like islands out of the sandy ocean. Even the name of Tadmor, or Palmyra, by its signification in the Syriac as well as in the Latin language, denoted the multitude of palm-trees which afforded shade and verdure to that temperate region. The air was pure, and the soil, watered by some invaluable springs, was capable of producing fruits as well as corn. A place possessed of such singular advantages, and situated at a convenient distance[68] between the Gulf of Persia and the Mediterranean, was soon frequented by the caravans which conveyed to the nations of Europe a considerable part of the rich commodities of India. Palmyra insensibly increased into an opulent and independent city, and, connecting the Roman and the Parthian monarchies by the mutual benefits of commerce, was suffered to observe an humble neutrality, till at length, after the victories of Trajan, the little republic sunk into the bosom of Rome, and flourished more than one hundred and fifty years in the subordinate though honourable rank of a colony. It was during that peaceful period, if we may judge from a few remaining inscriptions, that the wealthy Palmyrenians constructed those temples, palaces, and porticos of Grecian architecture, whose ruins, scattered over an extent of several miles, have deserved the curiosity of our travellers. The elevation of Odenathus and Zenobia appeared to reflect new splendour on their country, and Palmyra, for a while, stood forth the rival of Rome; but the competition was fatal, and ages of prosperity were sacrificed to a moment of glory.[69]

In his march over the sandy desert between Emesa and Palmyra, the emperor Aurelian was perpetually harassed by the Arabs; nor could he always defend his army, and especially his baggage, from those flying troops of active and daring robbers, who watched the moment of surprise, and eluded the slow pursuit of the legions. The siege of Palmyra was an object far more difficult and important, and the emperor, who, with incessant vigour, pressed the attacks in person, was himself wounded with a dart. "The Roman people," says Aurelian, in an original letter, "speak with contempt of the war which I am waging against a woman. They are ignorant both of the character and of the power of Zenobia. It is impossible to enumerate her warlike preparations, of stones, of arrows, and of every species of missile weapons. Every part of the walls is provided with two or three *balistæ*, and artificial fires are thrown from her military engines. The fear of punishment has armed her with a desperate courage. Yet still I trust in the protecting deities of Rome, who have hitherto been favourable to all my undertakings."[70] Doubtful, however, of the protection of the gods, and of the event of the siege, Aurelian judged it more prudent to offer terms of an advantageous capitulation; to the queen, a splendid retreat; to the citizens, their ancient privileges. His proposals were obstinately rejected, and the refusal was accompanied with insult.

The firmness of Zenobia was supported by the hope that in a very short time famine would compel the Roman army to repass the desert; and by the reasonable expectation that the kings of the East, and particularly the Persian monarch, would arm in the defence of their most natural ally. But fortune and the perseverance of Aurelian overcame every obstacle. The death of Sapor, which happened about this time,[71] distracted the councils of Persia, and the inconsiderable succours that attempted to relieve Palmyra were easily intercepted either by the arms or the liberality of the emperor. From every part of Syria a regular succession of convoys safely arrived in the camp, which was increased by the return of Probus with his victorious troops from the conquest of Egypt. It was then that Zenobia resolved to fly. She mounted the fleetest of her dromedaries,[72] and had already reached the banks of the Euphrates, about sixty miles from Palmyra, when she was overtaken by the pursuit of Aurelian's light horse, seized and brought back a captive to the feet of the emperor. Her capital soon afterwards surrendered, and was treated with unexpected lenity. The arms, horses, and camels, with an immense treasure of gold, silver, silk, and precious stones, were all delivered to the conqueror, who, leaving only a garrison of six hundred archers, returned to Emesa, and employed some time in the distribution of rewards and punishments at the end of so memorable a war, which restored to the obedience of Rome those provinces that had renounced their allegiance since the captivity of Valerian.

When the Syrian queen was brought into the presence of Aurelian, he sternly asked her, How she had presumed to rise in arms against the emperors of Rome? The answer of Zenobia was a prudent mixture of respect and firmness. "Because I disdained to consider as Roman emperors an Aureolus or a Gallienus. You alone I acknowledge as my conqueror and my sovereign."[73] But as female fortitude is commonly artificial, so it is seldom steady or consistent. The courage of Zenobia deserted her in the hour of trial; she trembled at the angry clamours of the soldiers, who called aloud for her immediate execution, forgot the generous despair of Cleopatra, which she had proposed as her model, and ignominiously purchased life by the sacrifice of her fame and her friends. It was to their counsels, which governed the weakness of her sex, that she imputed the guilt of her obstinate resistance; it was on their heads that she directed the vengeance of the cruel Aurelian. The fame of Longinus, who was included among the numerous and perhaps innocent victims of her fear, will survive that of the queen who betrayed, or the tyrant who condemned him. Genius and learning were incapable of moving a fierce unlettered soldier, but they had served to elevate and harmonise the soul of Longinus. Without uttering a complaint, he calmly followed the executioner, pitying his unhappy mistress, and bestowing comfort on his afflicted friends.[74]

Returning from the conquest of the East, Aurelian had already crossed the Straits which divide Europe from Asia, when he was provoked by the intelligence that the Palmyrenians had massacred the governor and garrison which he had left among them, and again erected the standard of revolt. Without a moment's deliberation, he once more turned his face towards Syria. Antioch was alarmed by his rapid approach, and the helpless city of Palmyra felt the irresistible weight of his resentment. We have a letter of Aurelian himself, in which he acknowledges[75] that old men, women, children, and peasants, had been involved in that dreadful execution, which should have been confined to armed rebellion; and although his principal concern seems directed to the re-establishment of a temple of the Sun, he discovers some pity for the remnant of the Palmyrenians, to whom he grants the permission of rebuilding and inhabiting their city. But it is easier to destroy than to restore. The seat of commerce, of arts, and of Zenobia, gradually sunk into an obscure town, a trifling fortress, and at length a miserable village. The present citizens of Palmyra, consisting of thirty or forty families, have erected their mud-cottages within the spacious court of a magnificent temple.

Another and a last labour still awaited the indefatigable Aurelian; to suppress a dangerous though obscure rebel, who, during the revolt of Palmyra, had arisen on the banks of the Nile. Firmus, the friend and ally, as he proudly styled himself, of Odenathus and Zenobia, was no more than a wealthy merchant of Egypt. In the course of his trade to India he had formed very intimate connections with the Saracens and the Blemmyes, whose situation, on either coast of the Red Sea, gave them an easy introduction into the Upper Egypt. The Egyptians he inflamed with the hope of freedom, and, at the head of their furious multitude, broken into the city of Alexandria, where he assumed the Imperial purple, coined money, published edicts, and raised an army, which, as he vainly boasted, he was capable of maintaining from the sole profits of his paper trade. Such troops were a feeble defence against the approach of Aurelian; and it seems almost unnecessary to relate that Firmus was routed, taken, tortured, and put to death.[76] Aurelian might now congratulate the senate, the people, and himself, that, in little more than three years, he had restored universal peace and order to the Roman world.

Since the foundation of Rome no general had more nobly deserved a triumph than Aurelian; nor was a triumph ever celebrated with superior pride and magnificence.[77] The pomp was opened by twenty elephants, four royal tigers, and above two hundred of the most curious animals from every climate of the North, the East, and the South. They were followed by sixteen hundred gladiators, devoted to the cruel amusement of the amphitheatre. The wealth of Asia, the arms and ensigns of so many conquered nations, and the magnificent plate and wardrobe of the Syrian queen, were disposed in exact symmetry or artful disorder. The ambassadors of the most remote parts of the earth, of Æthiopia, Arabia, Persia, Bactriana, India, and China, all remarkable by their rich or singular dresses, displayed the fame and power of the

Roman emperor, who exposed likewise to the public view the presents that he had received, and particularly a great number of crowns of gold, the offerings of grateful cities. The victories of Aurelian were attested by the long train of captives who reluctantly attended his triumph—Goths, Vandals, Sarmatians, Alemanni, Franks, Gauls, Syrians, and Egyptians. Each people was distinguished by its peculiar inscription, and the title of Amazons was bestowed on ten martial heroines of the Gothic nation who had been taken in arms.[78] But every eye, disregarding the crowd of captives, was fixed on the emperor Tetricus and the queen of the East. The former, as well as his son, whom he had created Augustus, was dressed in Gallic trousers,[79] a saffron tunic, and a robe of purple. The beauteous figure of Zenobia was confined by fetters of gold; a slave supported the gold chain which encircled her neck, and she almost fainted under the intolerable weight of jewels. She preceded on foot the magnificent chariot in which she once hoped to enter the gates of Rome. It was followed by two other chariots, still more sumptuous, of Odenathus and of the Persian monarch. The triumphal car of Aurelian (it had formerly been used by a Gothic king) was drawn, on this memorable occasion, either by four stags or by four elephants.[80] The most illustrious of the senate, the people, and the army closed the solemn procession. Unfeigned joy, wonder, and gratitude swelled the acclamations of the multitude; but the satisfaction of the senate was clouded by the appearance of Tetricus; nor could they suppress a rising murmur that the haughty emperor should thus expose to public ignominy the person of a Roman and a magistrate.[81]

But, however in the treatment of his unfortunate rivals Aurelian might indulge his pride, he behaved towards them with a generous clemency which was seldom exercised by the ancient conquerors. Princes who, without success, had defended their throne or freedom, were frequently strangled in prison as soon as the triumphal pomp ascended the Capitol. These usurpers, whom their defeat had convicted of the crime of treason, were permitted to spend their lives in affluence and honourable repose. The emperor presented Zenobia with an elegant villa at Tibur or Tivoli, about twenty miles from the capital; the Syrian queen insensibly sunk into a Roman matron, her daughters married into noble families, and her race was not yet extinct in the fifth century.[82] Tetricus and his son were reinstated in their rank and fortunes. They erected on the Cælian hill a magnificent palace, and, as soon as it was finished, invited Aurelian to supper. On his entrance he was agreeably surprised with a picture which represented their singular history. They were delineated offering to the emperor a civic crown and the sceptre of Gaul, and again receiving at his hands the ornaments of the senatorial dignity. The father was afterwards invested with the government of Lucania,[83] and Aurelian, who soon admitted the abdicated monarch to his friendship and conversation, familiarly asked him, Whether it were not more desirable to administer a province of Italy than to reign beyond the Alps? The son long continued a respectable member of the senate; nor was there any one of the Roman nobility more esteemed by Aurelian, as well as by his successors.[84]

So long and so various was the pomp of Aurelian's triumph, that, although it opened with the dawn of day, the slow majesty of the procession ascended not the Capitol before the ninth hour; and it was already dark when the emperor returned to the palace. The festival was protracted by theatrical representations, the games of the circus, the hunting of wild beasts, combats of gladiators, and naval engagements. Liberal donatives were distributed to the army and people, and several institutions, agreeable or beneficial to the city, contributed to perpetuate the glory of Aurelian. A considerable portion of his oriental spoils was consecrated to the gods of Rome; the Capitol, and every other temple, glittered with the offerings of his ostentatious piety; and the temple of the Sun alone received above fifteen thousand pounds of gold.[85] This last was a magnificent structure, erected by the emperor on the side of the Quirinal hill, and dedicated, soon after the triumph, to that deity whom Aurelian adored as the parent of his life and fortunes. His mother had been an inferior priestess in a chapel of the Sun; a peculiar devotion to the god of Light was a sentiment which the fortunate peasant imbibed in his infancy; and every step of his elevation, every victory of his reign, fortified superstition by gratitude.[86]

The arms of Aurelian had vanquished the foreign and domestic foes of the republic. We are assured that, by his salutary rigour, crimes and factions, mischievous arts and pernicious connivance, the luxuriant growth of a feeble and oppressive government, were eradicated throughout the Roman world.[87] But if we attentively reflect how much swifter is the progress of corruption than its cure, and if we remember that the years abandoned to public disorders exceeded the months allotted to the martial reign of Aurelian, we must confess that a few short intervals of peace were insufficient for the arduous work of reformation. Even his attempt to restore the integrity of the coin was opposed by a formidable insurrection. The emperor's vexation breaks out in one of his private letters: "Surely," says he, "the gods have decreed that my life should be a perpetual warfare. A sedition within the walls has just now given birth to a very serious civil war. The workmen of the mint, at the instigation of Felicissimus, a slave to whom I had intrusted an employment in the finances, have risen in rebellion. They are at length suppressed; but seven thousand of my soldiers have been slain in the contest, of those troops whose ordinary station is in Dacia and the camps along the Danube."[88] Other writers, who confirm the same fact, add likewise, that it happened soon after Aurelian's triumph; that the decisive engagement was fought on the Cælian hill; that the workmen of the mint had adulterated the coin; and that the emperor restored the public credit, by delivering out good money in exchange for the bad, which the people were commanded to bring into the treasury.[89]

We might content ourselves with relating this extraordinary transaction, but we cannot dissemble how much, in its present form, it appears to us inconsistent and incredible. The debasement of the coin is indeed well suited to the administration of Gallienus; nor is it unlikely that the instruments of the corruption might dread the inflexible justice of Aurelian. But the guilt, as well as the profit, must have been confined to a few; nor is it easy to conceive by what arts they could arm a people whom they had injured against a monarch whom they had betrayed. We might naturally expect that such miscreants should have shared the public detestation with the informers and the other ministers of oppression; and that the reformation of the coin should have been an action equally popular with the destruction of those obsolete accounts which, by the emperor's order, were burnt in the forum of Trajan.[90] In an age when the principles of commerce were so imperfectly understood, the most desirable end might perhaps be effected by harsh and injudicious means; but a temporary grievance of such a nature can scarcely excite and support a serious civil war. The repetition of intolerable taxes, imposed either on the land or on the necessaries of life, may at last provoke those who will not, or who cannot, relinquish their country. But the case is far otherwise in every operation which, by whatsoever expedients, restores the just value of money. The transient evil is soon obliterated by the permanent benefit, the loss is divided among multitudes; and if a few wealthy individuals experience a sensible diminution of treasure, with their riches they at the same time lose the degree of weight and importance which they derived from the possession of them. However Aurelian might choose to disguise the real cause of the insurrection, his reformation of the coin could furnish only a faint pretence to a party already powerful and discontented. Rome, though deprived of freedom, was distracted by faction. The people, towards whom the emperor, himself a plebeian, always expressed a peculiar fondness, lived in perpetual dissension with the senate, the equestrian order, and the Prætorian guards.[91] Nothing less than the firm though secret conspiracy of those orders, of the authority of the first, the wealth of the second, and the arms of the third, could have displayed a strength capable of contending in battle with the veteran legions of the Danube, which, under the conduct of a martial sovereign, had achieved the conquest of the West and of the East.

Whatever was the cause or the object of this rebellion, imputed with so little probability to the workmen of the mint, Aurelian used his victory with unrelenting rigour.[92] He was naturally of a severe disposition. A peasant and a soldier, his nerves yielded not easily to the impressions of sympathy, and he could sustain without emotion the sight of tortures and death. Trained from his earliest youth in the exercise of arms, he set too small a value on the life of a citizen, chastised by military execution the slightest offences, and transferred the stern discipline of the camp into the civil administration of the laws. His love of justice often became a blind and furious passion; and, whenever he deemed his own or the public safety endangered, he disregarded the rules of evidence and the proportion of punishments. The unprovoked rebellion with which the Romans rewarded his services exasperated his haughty spirit. The noblest families of the capital were involved in the guilt or suspicion of this dark conspiracy. A hasty spirit of revenge urged the bloody prosecution, and it proved fatal to one of the nephews of the emperor. The executioners (if we may use the expression of a contemporary poet) were fatigued, the prisons were crowded, and the unhappy senate lamented the death or absence of its most illustrious members.[93] Nor was the pride of Aurelian less offensive to that assembly than his cruelty. Ignorant or impatient of the restraints of civil institutions, he disdained to hold his power by any other title than that of the sword, and governed by right of conquest an empire which he had saved and subdued.[94]

It was observed by one of the most sagacious of the Roman princes, that the talents of his predecessor Aurelian were better suited to the command of an army than to the government of an empire.[95] Conscious of the character in which nature and experience had enabled him to excel, he again took the field a few months after his triumph. It was expedient to exercise the restless temper of the legions in some foreign war, and the Persian monarch, exulting in the shame of Valerian, still braved with impunity the offended majesty of Rome. At the head of an army, less formidable by its numbers than by its discipline and valour, the emperor advanced as far as the Straits which divide Europe from Asia. He there experienced that the most

absolute power is a weak defence against the effects of despair. He had threatened one of his secretaries who was accused of extortion, and it was known that he seldom threatened in vain. The last hope which remained for the criminal was to involve some of the principal officers of the army in his danger, or at least in his fears. Artfully counterfeiting his master's hand, he showed them, in a long and bloody list, their own names devoted to death. Without suspecting or examining the fraud, they resolved to secure their lives by the murder of the emperor. On his march, between Byzantium and Heraclea, Aurelian was suddenly attacked by the conspirators, whose stations gave them a right to surround his person, and, after a short resistance, fell by the hand of Mucapor, a general whom he had always loved and trusted. He died regretted by the army, detested by the senate, but universally acknowledged as a warlike and fortunate prince, the useful though severe reformer of a degenerate state.[96]

CHAPTER XII

Conduct of the Army and Senate after the Death of Aurelian. Reigns of Tacitus, Probus, Carus and his Sons

SUCH was the unhappy condition of the Roman emperors, that, whatever might be their conduct, their fate was commonly the same. A life of pleasure or virtue, of severity or mildness, of indolence or glory, alike led to an untimely grave; and almost every reign is closed by the same disgusting repetition of treason and murder. The death of Aurelian, however, is remarkable by its extraordinary consequences. The legions admired, lamented, and revenged their victorious chief. The artifice of his perfidious secretary was discovered and punished. The deluded conspirators attended the funeral of their injured sovereign with sincere or well-feigned contrition, and submitted to the unanimous resolution of the military order, which was signified by the following epistle: "The brave and fortunate armies to the senate and people of Rome.—The crime of one man, and the error of many, have deprived us of the late emperor Aurelian. May it please you, venerable lords and fathers! to place him in the number of the gods, and to appoint a successor whom your judgment shall declare worthy of the Imperial purple! None of those whose guilt or misfortune have contributed to our loss shall

ever reign over us."[1] The Roman senators heard, without surprise, that another emperor had been assassinated in his camp; they secretly rejoiced in the fall of Aurelian; but the modest and dutiful address of the legions, when it was communicated in full assembly by the consul, diffused the most pleasing astonishment. Such honours as fear and perhaps esteem could extort they liberally poured forth on the memory of their deceased sovereign. Such acknowledgments as gratitude could inspire they returned to the faithful armies of the republic, who entertained so just a sense of the legal authority of the senate in the choice of an emperor. Yet, notwithstanding this flattering appeal, the most prudent of the assembly declined exposing their safety and dignity to the caprice of an armed multitude. The strength of the legions was, indeed, a pledge of their sincerity, since those who may command are seldom reduced to the necessity of dissembling; but could it naturally be expected that a hasty repentance would correct the inveterate habits of fourscore years? Should the soldiers relapse into their accustomed seditions, their insolence might disgrace the majesty of the senate and prove fatal to the object of its choice. Motives like these dictated a decree by which the election of a new emperor was referred to the suffrage of the military order.

The contention that ensued is one of the best attested but most improbable events in the history of mankind.[2] The troops, as if satiated with the exercise of power, again conjured the senate to invest one of its own body with the Imperial purple. The senate still persisted in its refusal; the army in its request. The reciprocal offer was pressed and rejected at least three times, and, whilst the obstinate modesty of either party was resolved to receive a master from the hands of the other, eight months insensibly elapsed; an amazing period of tranquil anarchy, during which the Roman world remained without a sovereign, without an usurper, and without a sedition. The generals and magistrates appointed by Aurelian continued to execute their ordinary functions; and it is observed that a proconsul of Asia was the only considerable person removed from his office in the whole course of the interregnum.

An event somewhat similar but much less authentic is supposed to have happened after the death of Romulus, who, in his life and character, bore some affinity with Aurelian. The throne was vacant during twelve months till the election of a Sabine philosopher, and the public peace was guarded in the same manner by the union of the several orders of the state. But, in the time of Numa and Romulus, the arms of the people were controlled by the authority of the Patricians; and the balance of freedom was easily preserved in a small and virtuous community.[3] The decline of the Roman state, far different from its infancy, was attended with every circumstance that could banish from an interregnum the prospect of obedience and harmony: an immense and tumultuous capital, a wide extent of empire, the servile equality of despotism, an army of four hundred thousand mercenaries, and the experience of frequent revolutions. Yet, notwithstanding all these temptations, the discipline and memory of Aurelian still restrained the seditious temper of the troops, as well as the fatal ambition of their leaders. The flower of the legions maintained their stations on the banks of the Bosphorus, and the Imperial standard awed the less powerful camps of Rome and of the provinces. A generous though transient enthusiasm seemed to animate the military order; and we may hope that a few real patriots cultivated the returning friendship of the army and the senate as the only expedient

capable of restoring the republic to its ancient beauty and vigour.

On the twenty-fifth of September, near eight months after the murder of Aurelian, the consul convoked an assembly of the senate, and reported the doubtful and dangerous situation of the empire. He slightly insinuated that the precarious loyalty of the soldiers depended on the chance of every hour and of every accident; but he represented, with the most convincing eloquence, the various dangers that might attend any farther delay in the choice of an emperor. Intelligence, he said, was already received that the Germans had passed the Rhine and occupied some of the strongest and most opulent cities of Gaul. The ambition of the Persian king kept the East in perpetual alarms; Egypt, Africa, and Illyricum were exposed to foreign and domestic arms; and the levity of Syria would prefer even a female sceptre to the sanctity of the Roman laws. The consul then, addressing himself to Tacitus, the first of the senators,[4] required his opinion on the important subject of a proper candidate for the vacant throne.

If we can prefer personal merit to accidental greatness, we shall esteem the birth of Tacitus more truly noble than that of kings. He claimed his descent from the philosophic historian whose writings will instruct the last generations of mankind.[5] The senator Tacitus was then seventy-five years of age.[6] The long period of his innocent life was adorned with wealth and honours. He had twice been invested with the consular dignity,[7] and enjoyed with elegance and sobriety his ample patrimony of between two and three millions sterling.[8] The experience of so many princes, whom he had esteemed or endured, from the vain follies of Elagabalus to the useful rigour of Aurelian, taught him to form a just estimate of the duties, the dangers, and the temptations of their sublime station. From the assiduous study of his immortal ancestor he derived the knowledge of the Roman constitution and of human nature.[9] The voice of the people had already named Tacitus as the citizen the most worthy of empire. The ungrateful rumour reached his ears, and induced him to seek the retirement of one of his villas in Campania. He had passed two months in the delightful privacy of Baiæ, when he reluctantly obeyed the summons of the consul to resume his honourable place in the senate, and to assist the republic with his counsels on this important occasion.

He arose to speak, when, from every quarter of the house, he was saluted with the names of Augustus and Emperor. "Tacitus Augustus, the gods preserve thee, we choose thee for our sovereign, to thy care we intrust the republic and the world. Accept the empire from the authority of the senate. It is due to thy rank, to thy conduct, to thy manners." As soon as the tumult of acclamations subsided, Tacitus attempted to decline the dangerous honour, and to express his wonder that they should elect his age and infirmities to succeed the martial vigour of Aurelian. "Are these limbs, conscript fathers! fitted to sustain the weight of armour, or to practise the exercises of the camp? The variety of climates, and the hardships of a military life, would soon oppress a feeble constitution, which subsists only by the most tender management. My exhausted strength scarcely enables me to discharge the duty of a senator; how insufficient would it prove to the arduous labours of war and government! Can you hope that the legions will respect a weak old man, whose days have been spent in the shade of peace and retirement? Can you desire that I should ever find reason to regret the favourable opinion of the senate?"[10]

The reluctance of Tacitus, and it might possibly be sincere, was encountered by the affectionate obstinacy of the senate. Five hundred voices repeated at once, in eloquent confusion, that the greatest of the Roman princes, Numa, Trajan, Hadrian, and the Antonines, had ascended the throne in a very advanced season of life; that the mind, not the body, a sovereign, not a soldier, was the object of their choice; and that they expected from him no more than to guide by his wisdom the valour of the legions. These pressing though tumultuary instances were seconded by a more regular oration of Metius Falconius, the next on the consular bench to Tacitus himself. He reminded the assembly of the evils which Rome had endured from the vices of headstrong and capricious youths, congratulated them on the election of a virtuous and experienced senator, and with a manly, though perhaps a selfish, freedom, exhorted Tacitus to remember the reasons of his elevation, and to seek a successor, not in his own family, but in the republic. The speech of Falconius was enforced by a general acclamation. The emperor elect submitted to the authority of his country, and received the voluntary homage of his equals. The judgment of the senate was confirmed by the consent of the Roman people and of the Prætorian guards.[11]

The administration of Tacitus was not unworthy of his life and principles. A grateful servant of the senate, he considered that national

council as the author, and himself as the subject, of the laws.[12] He studied to heal the wounds which Imperial pride, civil discord, and military violence had inflicted on the constitution, and to restore, at least, the image of the ancient republic as it had been preserved by the policy of Augustus and the virtues of Trajan and the Antonines. It may not be useless to recapitulate some of the most important prerogatives which the senate appeared to have regained by the election of Tacitus.[13] 1. To invest one of their body, under the title of emperor, with the general command of the armies and the government of the frontier provinces. 2. To determine the list, or, as it was then styled, the College of Consuls. They were twelve in number, who, in successive pairs, each during the space of two months, filled the year, and represented the dignity of that ancient office. The authority of the senate, in the nomination of the consuls, was exercised with such independent freedom, that no regard was paid to an irregular request of the emperor in favour of his brother Florianus. "The senate," exclaimed Tacitus, with the honest transport of a patriot, "understand the character of a prince whom they have chosen." 3. To appoint the proconsuls and presidents of the provinces, and to confer on all the magistrates their civil jurisdiction. 4. To receive appeals through the intermediate office of the præfect of the city from all the tribunals of the empire. 5. To give force and validity, by their decrees, to such as they should approve of the emperor's edicts. 6. To these several branches of authority we may add some inspection over the finances, since, even in the stern reign of Aurelian, it was in their power to divert a part of the revenue from the public service.[14]

Circular epistles were sent, without delay, to all the principal cities of the empire—Treves, Milan, Aquileia, Thessalonica, Corinth, Athens, Antioch, Alexandria, and Carthage—to claim their obedience, and to inform them of the happy revolution which had restored the Roman senate to its ancient dignity. Two of these epistles are still extant. We likewise possess two very singular fragments of the private correspondence of the senators on this occasion. They discover the most excessive joy and the most unbounded hopes. "Cast away your indolence," it is thus that one of the senators addresses his friend, "emerge from your retirements of Baiæ and Puteoli. Give yourself to the city, to the senate. Rome flourishes, the whole republic flourishes. Thanks to the Roman army, to an army truly Roman, at length we have recovered our just authority, the end of all our de-sires. We hear appeals, we appoint proconsuls, we create emperors; perhaps, too, we may re-strain them—to the wise a word is sufficient."[15] These lofty expectations were, however, soon disappointed; nor, indeed, was it possible that the armies and the provinces should long obey the luxurious and unwarlike nobles of Rome. On the slightest touch the unsupported fabric of their pride and power fell to the ground. The expiring senate displayed a sudden lustre, blazed for a moment, and was extinguished for ever.

All that had yet passed at Rome was no more than a theatrical representation, unless it was ratified by the more substantial power of the legions. Leaving the senators to enjoy their dream of freedom and ambition, Tacitus pro-ceeded to the Thracian camp, and was there, by the Prætorian præfect, presented to the as-sembled troops as the prince whom they them-selves had demanded, and whom the senate had bestowed. As soon as the præfect was silent the emperor addressed himself to the soldiers with eloquence and propriety. He gratified their av-arice by a liberal distribution of treasure under the names of pay and donative. He engaged their esteem by a spirited declaration that, although his age might disable him from the performance of military exploits, his counsels should never be unworthy of a Roman general, the successor of the brave Aurelian.[16]

Whilst the deceased emperor was making preparations for a second expedition into the East, he had negotiated with the Alani, a Scyth-ian people, who pitched their tents in the neigh-borhood of the lake Mætis. Those barbarians, allured by presents and subsidies, had promised to invade Persia with a numerous body of light cavalry. They were faithful to their engage-ments; but when they arrived on the Roman frontier Aurelian was already dead, the design of the Persian war was at least suspended, and the generals who, during the interregnum, ex-ercised a doubtful authority, were unprepared either to receive or to oppose them. Provoked by such treatment, which they considered as trifling and perfidious, the Alani had recourse to their own valour for their payment and re-venge; and as they moved with the usual swift-ness of Tartars, they had soon spread themselves over the provinces of Pontus, Cappadocia, Cili-cia, and Galatia. The legions who, from the opposite shores of the Bosphorus, could almost distinguish the flames of the cities and villages, impatiently urged their general to lead them against the invaders. The conduct of Tacitus

was suitable to his age and station. He convinced the barbarians of the faith, as well as of the power, of the empire. Great numbers of the Alani, appeased by the punctual discharge of the engagements which Aurelian had contracted with them, relinquished their booty and cap-tives, and quietly retreated to their own deserts beyond the Phasis. Against the remainder, who refused peace, the Roman emperor waged, in person, a successful war. Seconded by an army of brave and experienced veterans, in a few weeks he delivered the provinces of Asia from the terror of the Scythian invasion.[17]

But the glory and life of Tacitus were of short duration. Transported in the depth of winter from the soft retirement of Campania to the foot of Mount Caucasus, he sunk under the un-accustomed hardships of a military life. The fa-tigues of the body were aggravated by the cares of the mind. For a while the angry and selfish passions of the soldiers had been suspended by the enthusiasm of public virtue. They soon broke out with redoubled violence, and raged in the camp, and even in the tent of the aged emperor. His mild and amiable character served only to inspire contempt, and he was incessantly tor-mented with factions which he could not as-suage, and by demands which it was impossible to satisfy. Whatever flattering expectations he had conceived of reconciling the public disor-ders, Tacitus soon was convinced that the licen-tiousness of the army disdained the feeble re-straint of laws, and his last hour was hastened by anguish and disappointment. It may be doubtful whether the soldiers imbrued their hands in the blood of this innocent prince.[18] It is certain that their insolence was the cause of his death. He expired at Tyana in Cappadocia, after a reign of only six months and about twenty days.[19]

The eyes of Tacitus were scarcely closed be-fore his brother Florianus showed himself un-worthy to reign by the hasty usurpation of the purple, without expecting the approbation of the senate. The reverence for the Roman con-stitution, which yet influenced the camp and the provinces, was sufficiently strong to dispose them to censure, but not to provoke them to oppose, the precipitate ambition of Florianus. The discontent would have evaporated in idle murmurs, had not the general of the East, the heroic Probus, boldly declared himself the aveng-er of the senate. The contest, however, was still unequal; nor could the most able leader, at the head of the effeminate troops of Egypt and Syr-ia, encounter, with any hopes of victory, the legions of Europe, whose irresistible strength appeared to support the brother of Tacitus. But the fortune and activity of Probus triumphed over every obstacle. The hardy veterans of his rival, accustomed to cold climates, sickened and consumed away in the sultry heats of Cilicia, where the summer proved remarkably unwholesome. Their numbers were diminished by frequent desertion, the passes of the mountains were feebly defended; Tarsus opened its gates; and the soldiers of Florianus, when they had permitted him to enjoy the Imperial title about three months, delivered the empire from civil war by the easy sacrifice of a prince whom they despised.[20]

The perpetual revolutions of the throne had so perfectly erased every notion of hereditary right, that the family of an unfortunate emperor was incapable of exciting the jealousy of his successors. The children of Tacitus and Florianus were permitted to descend into a private station, and to mingle with the general mass of the people. Their poverty indeed became an additional safeguard to their innocence. When Tacitus was elected by the senate he resigned his ample patrimony to the public service,[21] an act of generosity specious in appearance, but which evidently disclosed his intention of transmitting the empire to his descendants. The only consolation of their fallen state was the remembrance of transient greatness, and a distant hope, the child of a flattering prophecy, that, at the end of a thousand years, a monarch of the race of Tacitus should arise, the protector of the senate, the restorer of Rome, and the conqueror of the whole earth.[22]

The peasants of Illyricum, who had already given Claudius and Aurelian to the sinking empire, had an equal right to glory in the elevation of Probus.[23] Above twenty years before, the emperor Valerian, with his usual penetration, had discovered the rising merit of the young soldier, on whom he conferred the rank of tribune long before the age prescribed by the military regulations. The tribune soon justified his choice by a victory over a great body of Sarmatians, in which he saved the life of a near relation of Valerian; and deserved to receive from the emperor's hand the collars, bracelets, spears, and banners, the mural and the civic crown, and all the honourable rewards reserved by ancient Rome for successful valour. The third, and afterwards the tenth, legion were intrusted to the command of Probus, who, in every step of his promotion, showed himself superior to the station which he filled. Africa and Pontus, the Rhine, the Danube, the Euphrates, and the Nile, by turns afforded him the most splendid occasions of displaying his personal prowess and his conduct in war. Aurelian was indebted to him for the conquest of Egypt, and still more indebted for the honest courage with which he often checked the cruelty of his master. Tacitus, who desired by the abilities of his generals to supply his own deficiency of military talents, named him commander-in-chief of all the eastern provinces, with five times the usual salary, the promise of the consulship, and the hope of a triumph. When Probus ascended the Imperial throne he was about forty-four years of age;[24] in the full possession of his fame, of the love of the army, and of a mature vigour of mind and body.

His acknowledged merit, and the success of his arms against Florianus, left him without an enemy or a competitor. Yet, if we may credit his own professions, very far from being desirous of the empire, he had accepted it with the most sincere reluctance. "But it is no longer in my power," says Probus in a private letter, "to lay down a title so full of envy and of danger. I must continue to personate the character which the soldiers have imposed upon me."[25] His dutiful address to the senate displayed the sentiments, or at least the language, of a Roman patriot: "When you elected one of your order, conscript fathers! to succeed the emperor Aurelian, you acted in a manner suitable to your justice and wisdom. For you are the legal sovereigns of the world, and the power which you derive from your ancestors will descend to your posterity. Happy would it have been if Florianus, instead of usurping the purple of his brother, like a private inheritance, had expected what your majesty might determine, either in his favour, or in that of any other person. The prudent soldiers have punished his rashness. To me they have offered the title of Augustus; but I submit to your clemency my pretensions and my merits."[26] When this respectful epistle was read by the consul, the senators were unable to disguise their satisfaction that Probus should condescend thus humbly to solicit a sceptre which he already possessed. They celebrated with the warmest gratitude his virtues, his exploits, and above all his moderation. A decree immediately passed, without a dissenting voice, to ratify the election of the eastern armies, and to confer on their chief all the several branches of the Imperial dignity; the names of Cæsar and Augustus, the title of Father of his country, the right of making in the same day three motions in the senate,[27] the office of Pontifex Maximus, the tribunitian power, and the proconsular command; a mode of investiture which, though it seemed to multiply the authority of the emperor, expressed the constitution of the ancient republic. The reign of Probus corresponded with this fair beginning. The senate was permitted to direct the civil administration of the empire. Their faithful general asserted the honour of the Roman arms, and often laid at their feet crowns of gold and barbaric trophies, the fruits of his numerous victories.[28] Yet, whilst he gratified their vanity, he must secretly have despised their indolence and weakness. Though it was every moment in their power to repeal the disgraceful edict of Gallienus, the proud successors of the Scipios patiently acquiesced in their exclusion from all military employments. They soon experienced that those who refuse the sword must renounce the sceptre.

The strength of Aurelian had crushed on every side the enemies of Rome. After his death they seemed to revive with an increase of fury and of numbers. They were again vanquished by the active vigour of Probus, who, in a short reign of about six years,[29] equalled the fame of ancient heroes, and restored peace and order to every province of the Roman world. The dangerous frontier of Rhætia he so firmly secured that he left it without the suspicion of an enemy. He broke the wandering power of the Sarmatian tribes, and by the terror of his arms compelled those barbarians to relinquish their spoil. The Gothic nation courted the alliance of so warlike an emperor.[30] He attacked the Isaurians in their mountains, besieged and took several of their strongest castles,[31] and flattered himself that he had for ever suppressed a domestic foe whose independence so deeply wounded the majesty of the empire. The troubles excited by the usurper Firmus in the Upper Egypt had never been perfectly appeased, and the cities of Ptolemais and Coptos, fortified by the alliance of the Blemmyes, still maintained an obscure rebellion. The chastisement of those cities, and of their auxiliaries the savages of the South, is said to have alarmed the court of Persia,[32] and the Great King sued in vain for the friendship of Probus. Most of the exploits which distinguished his reign were achieved by the personal valour and conduct of the emperor, insomuch that the writer of his Life expresses some amazement how, in so short a time, a single man could be present in so many distant wars. The remaining actions he intrusted to the care of his lieutenants, the judicious choice of whom forms no inconsiderable part of his glory. Carus, Diocle-

tian, Maximian, Constantius, Galerius, Asclepiodatus, Annibalianus, and a crowd of other chiefs, who afterwards ascended or supported the throne, were trained to arms in the severe school of Aurelian and Probus.[33]

But the most important service which Probus rendered to the republic was the deliverance of Gaul, and the recovery of seventy flourishing cities oppressed by the barbarians of Germany, who, since the death of Aurelian, had ravaged that great province with impunity.[34] Among the various multitude of those fierce invaders, we may distinguish, with some degree of clearness, three great armies, or rather nations, successively vanquished by the valour of Probus. He drove back the Franks into their morasses; a descriptive circumstance from whence we may infer that the confederacy known by the manly appellation of *Free* already occupied the flat maritime country, intersected and almost overflown by the stagnating waters of the Rhine, and that several tribes of the Frisians and Batavians had acceded to their alliance. He vanquished the Burgundians, a considerable people of the Vandalic race. They had wandered in quest of booty from the banks of the Oder to those of the Seine. They esteemed themselves sufficiently fortunate to purchase, by the restitution of all their booty, the permission of an undisturbed retreat. They attempted to elude that article of the treaty. Their punishment was immediate and terrible.[35] But of all the invaders of Gaul, the most formidable were the Lygians, a distant people who reigned over a wide domain on the frontiers of Poland and Silesia.[36] In the Lygian nation the Arii held the first rank by their numbers and fierceness. "The Arii" (it is thus that they are described by the energy of Tacitus) "study to improve by art and circumstances the innate terrors of their barbarism. Their shields are black, their bodies are painted black. They choose for the combat the darkest hour of the night. Their host advances, covered as it were with a funeral shade;[37] nor do they often find an enemy capable of sustaining so strange and infernal an aspect. Of all our senses, the eyes are the first vanquished in battle."[38] Yet the arms and discipline of the Romans easily discomfited these horrid phantoms. The Lygii were defeated in a general engagement, and Semno, the most renowned of their chiefs, fell alive into the hands of Probus. That prudent emperor, unwilling to reduce a brave people to despair, granted them an honourable capitulation, and permitted them to return in safety to their native country. But the losses which they suffered in the march, the battle, and the retreat, broke the power of the nation: nor is the Lygian name ever repeated in the history either of Germany or of the empire. The deliverance of Gaul is reported to have cost the lives of four hundred thousand of the invaders; a work of labour to the Romans, and of expense to the emperor, who gave a piece of gold for the head of every barbarian.[39] But as the fame of warriors is built on the destruction of human kind, we may naturally suspect that the sanguinary account was multiplied by the avarice of the soldiers, and accepted without any very severe examination by the liberal vanity of Probus.

Since the expedition of Maximin, the Roman generals had confined their ambition to a defensive war against the nations of Germany, who perpetually pressed on the frontiers of the empire. The more daring Probus pursued his Gallic victories, passed the Rhine, and displayed his invincible eagles on the banks of the Elbe and the Neckar. He was fully convinced that nothing could reconcile the minds of the barbarians to peace, unless they experienced in their own country the calamities of war. Germany, exhausted by the ill success of the last emigration, was astonished by his presence. Nine of the most considerable princes repaired to his camp, and fell prostrate at his feet. Such a treaty was humbly received by the Germans as it pleased the conqueror to dictate. He exacted a strict restitution of the effects and captives which they had carried away from the provinces; and obliged their own magistrates to punish the more obstinate robbers who presumed to detain any part of the spoil. A considerable tribute of corn, cattle, and horses, the only wealth of barbarians, was reserved for the use of the garrisons which Probus established on the limits of their territory. He even entertained some thoughts of compelling the Germans to relinquish the exercise of arms, and to trust their differences to the justice, their safety to the power, of Rome. To accomplish these salutary ends, the constant residence of an Imperial governor, supported by a numerous army, was indispensably requisite. Probus therefore judged it more expedient to defer the execution of so great a design; which was indeed rather of specious than solid utility.[40] Had Germany been reduced into the state of a province, the Romans, with immense labour and expense, would have acquired only a more extensive boundary to defend against the fiercer and more active barbarians of Scythia.

Instead of reducing the warlike natives of Germany to the condition of subjects, Probus contented himself with the humble expedient of raising a bulwark against their inroads. The country which now forms the circle of Swabia had been left desert in the age of Augustus by the emigration of its ancient inhabitants.[41] The fertility of the soil soon attracted a new colony from the adjacent provinces of Gaul. Crowds of adventurers, of a roving temper and of desperate fortunes, occupied the doubtful possession, and acknowledged, by the payment of tithes, the majesty of the empire.[42] To protect these new subjects, a line of frontier garrisons was gradually extended from the Rhine to the Danube. About the reign of Hadrian, when that mode of defence began to be practised, these garrisons were connected and covered by a strong entrenchment of trees and palisades. In the place of so rude a bulwark, the emperor Probus constructed a stone wall of a considerable height and strengthened it by towers at convenient distances. From the neighbourhood of Neustadt and Ratisbon on the Danube, it stretched across hills, valleys, rivers, and morasses, as far as Wimpfen on the Neckar, and at length terminated on the banks of the Rhine, after a winding course of near two hundred miles.[43] This important barrier, uniting the two mighty streams that protected the provinces of Europe, seemed to fill up the vacant space through which the barbarians, and particularly the Alemanni, could penetrate with the greatest facility into the heart of the empire. But the experience of the world, from China to Britain, has exposed the vain attempt of fortifying any extensive tract of country.[44] An active enemy, who can select and vary his points of attack, must in the end discover some feeble spot, or some unguarded moment. The strength, as well as the attention, of the defenders is divided; and such are the blind effects of terror on the firmest troops that a line broken in a single place is almost instantly deserted. The fate of the wall which Probus erected may confirm the general observation. Within a few years after his death it was overthrown by the Alemanni. Its scattered ruins, universally ascribed to the power of the Dæmon, now serve only to excite the wonder of the Swabian peasant.

Among the useful conditions of peace imposed by Probus on the vanquished nations of Germany was the obligation of supplying the Roman army with sixteen thousand recruits, the bravest and most robust of their youth. The emperor dispersed them through all the provinces, and distributed this dangerous reinforcement, in small bands of fifty or sixty each, among the national troops; judiciously observing that the aid which the republic derived from the barbarians should be felt but not seen.[45] Their aid was now become necessary. The feeble elegance of Italy and the internal provinces could no longer support the weight of arms. The hardy frontier of the Rhine and Danube still produced minds and bodies equal to the labours of the camp; but a perpetual series of wars had gradually diminished their numbers. The infrequency of marriage, and the ruin of agriculture, affected the principles of population, and not only destroyed the strength of the present, but intercepted the hope of future generations. The wisdom of Probus embraced a great and beneficial plan of replenishing the exhausted frontiers by new colonies of captive or fugitive barbarians, on whom he bestowed lands, cattle, instruments of husbandry, and every encouragement that might engage them to educate a race of soldiers for the service of the republic. Into Britain, and most probably into Cambridgeshire,[46] he transported a considerable body of Vandals. The impossibility of an escape reconciled them to their situation, and in the subsequent troubles of that island they approved themselves the most faithful servants of the state.[47] Great numbers of Franks and Gepidæ were settled on the banks of the Danube and the Rhine. An hundred thousand Bastarnæ, expelled from their own country, cheerfully accepted an establishment in Thrace, and soon imbibed the manners and sentiments of Roman subjects.[48] But the expectations of Probus were too often disappointed. The impatience and idleness of the barbarians could ill brook the slow labours of agriculture. Their unconquerable love of freedom, rising against despotism, provoked them into hasty rebellions, alike fatal to themselves and to the provinces,[49] nor could these artificial supplies, however repeated by succeeding emperors, restore the important limit of Gaul and Illyricum to its ancient and native vigour.

Of all the barbarians who abandoned their new settlements, and disturbed the public tranquillity, a very small number returned to their own country. For a short season they might wander in arms through the empire, but in the end they were surely destroyed by the power of a warlike emperor. The successful rashness of a party of Franks was attended, however, with such memorable consequences that it ought not to be passed unnoticed. They had been established by Probus on the sea-coast of Pontus, with a view of strengthening the frontier against the inroads of the Alani. A fleet stationed in one of the harbours of the Euxine fell into the hands of the Franks; and they resolved, through unknown seas, to explore their way from the mouth of the Phasis to that of the Rhine. They easily escaped through the Bosphorus and the Hellespont, and, cruising along the Mediterranean, indulged their appetite for revenge and plunder by frequent descents on the unsuspecting shores of Asia, Greece, and Africa. The opulent city of Syracuse, in whose port the navies of Athens and Carthage had formerly been sunk, was sacked by a handful of barbarians, who massacred the greatest part of the trembling inhabitants. From the island of Sicily the Franks proceeded to the Columns of Hercules, trusted themselves to the ocean, coasted round Spain and Gaul, and, steering their triumphant course through the British Channel, at length finished their surprising voyage by landing in safety on the Batavian or Frisian shores.[50] The example of their success, instructing their countrymen to conceive the advantages and to despise the dangers of the sea, pointed out to their enterprising spirit a new road to wealth and glory.

Notwithstanding the vigilance and activity of Probus, it was almost impossible that he could at once contain in obedience every part of his wide-extended dominions. The barbarians who broke their chains had seized the favourable opportunity of a domestic war. When the emperor marched to the relief of Gaul, he devolved the command of the East on Saturninus. That general, a man of merit and experience, was driven into rebellion by the absence of his sovereign, the levity of the Alexandrian people, the pressing instances of his friends, and his own fears; but from the moment of his elevation he never entertained a hope of empire or even of life. "Alas!" he said, "the republic has lost a useful servant, and the rashness of an hour has destroyed the services of many years. You know not," continued he, "the misery of sovereign power: a sword is perpetually suspended over our head. We dread our very guards, we distrust our companions. The choice of action or of repose is no longer in our disposition, nor is there any age, or character, or conduct, that can protect us from the censure of envy. In thus exalting me to the throne, you have doomed me to a life of cares, and to an untimely fate. The only consolation which remains is the assurance that I shall not fall alone."[51] But as the former part of his prediction was verified by the victory, so the latter was disappointed by the clemency, of Probus. That amiable prince attempted even to save the unhappy Saturninus from the fury of the soldiers. He had more than once solicited the usurper himself to place some confidence in the mercy of a sovereign who so highly esteemed his character that he had punished as a malicious informer the first who related the improbable news of his defection.[52] Saturninus might perhaps have embraced the generous offer had he not been restrained by the obstinate distrust of his adherents. Their guilt was deeper, and their hopes more sanguine, than those of their experienced leader.

The revolt of Saturninus was scarcely extinguished in the East before new troubles were excited in the West by the rebellion of Bonosus and Proculus in Gaul. The most distinguished merit of those two officers was their respective prowess, of the one in the combats of Bacchus, of the other in those of Venus,[53] yet neither of them were destitute of courage and capacity, and both sustained with honour the august character which the fear of punishment had engaged them to assume, till they sunk at length beneath the superior genius of Probus. He used the victory with his accustomed moderation, and spared the fortunes as well as the lives of their innocent families.[54]

The arms of Probus had now suppressed all the foreign and domestic enemies of the state. His mild but steady administration confirmed the re-establishment of the public tranquillity; nor was there left in the provinces a hostile barbarian, a tyrant, or even a robber, to revive the memory of past disorders. It was time that the emperor should revisit Rome, and celebrate his own glory and the general happiness. The triumph due to the valour of Probus was conducted with a magnificence suitable to his fortune; and the people, who had so lately admired the trophies of Aurelian, gazed with equal pleasure on those of his heroic successor.[55] We cannot on this occasion forget the desperate courage of about fourscore gladiators, reserved, with near six hundred others, for the inhuman sports of the amphitheatre. Disdaining to shed their blood for the amusement of the populace, they killed their keepers, broke from the place of their confinement, and filled the streets of Rome with blood and confusion. After an obstinate resistance, they were overpowered and cut in pieces by the regular forces; but they obtained at least an honourable death, and the satisfaction of a just revenge.[56]

The military discipline which reigned in the camps of Probus was less cruel than that of Aurelian, but it was equally rigid and exact. The latter had punished the irregularities of the

soldiers with unrelenting severity, the former prevented them by employing the legions in constant and useful labours. When Probus commanded in Egypt, he executed many considerable works for the splendour and benefit of that rich country. The navigation of the Nile, so important to Rome itself, was improved; and temples, bridges, porticoes, and palaces, were constructed by the hands of the soldiers, who acted by turns as architects, as engineers, and as husbandmen.[57] It was reported of Hannibal that, in order to preserve his troops from the dangerous temptations of idleness, he had obliged them to form large plantations of olive-trees along the coast of Africa.[58] From a similar principle, Probus exercised his legions in covering with rich vineyards the hills of Gaul and Pannonia, and two considerable spots are described which were entirely dug and planted by military labour.[59] One of these, known under the name of Mount Alma, was situated near Sirmium, the country where Probus was born, for which he ever retained a partial affection, and whose gratitude he endeavoured to secure, by converting into tillage a large and unhealthy tract of marshy ground. An army thus employed constituted perhaps the most useful as well as the bravest portion of Roman subjects.

But, in the prosecution of a favourite scheme, the best of men, satisfied with the rectitude of their intentions, are subject to forget the bounds of moderation; nor did Probus himself sufficiently consult the patience and disposition of his fierce legionaries.[60] The dangers of the military profession seem only to be compensated by a life of pleasure and idleness; but if the duties of the soldier are incessantly aggravated by the labours of the peasant, he will at last sink under the intolerable burden or shake it off with indignation. The imprudence of Probus is said to have inflamed the discontent of his troops. More attentive to the interests of mankind than to those of the army, he expressed the vain hope that, by the establishment of universal peace, he should soon abolish the necessity of a standing and mercenary force.[61] The unguarded expression proved fatal to him. In one of the hottest days of summer, as he severely urged the unwholesome labour of draining the marshes of Sirmium, the soldiers, impatient of fatigue, on a sudden threw down their tools, grasped their arms, and broke out into a furious mutiny. The emperor, conscious of his danger, took refuge in a lofty tower constructed for the purpose of surveying the progress of the work.[62] The tower was instantly forced, and a thousand swords were plunged at once into the bosom of the unfortunate Probus. The rage of the troops subsided as soon as it had been gratified. They then lamented their fatal rashness, forgot the severity of the emperor whom they had massacred, and hastened to perpetuate, by an honourable monument, the memory of his virtues and victories.[63]

When the legions had indulged their grief and repentance for the death of Probus, their unanimous consent declared Carus, his Prætorian præfect, the most deserving of the Imperial throne. Every circumstance that relates to this prince appears of a mixed and doubtful nature. He gloried in the title of Roman Citizen; and affected to compare the purity of *his* blood with the foreign, and even barbarous, origin of the preceding emperors; yet the most inquisitive of his contemporaries, very far from admitting his claim, have variously deduced his own birth, or that of his parents, from Illyricum, from Gaul, or from Africa.[64] Though a soldier, he had received a learned education; though a senator, he was invested with the first dignity of the army; and in an age when the civil and military professions began to be irrecoverably separated from each other, they were united in the person of Carus. Notwithstanding the severe justice which he exercised against the assassins of Probus, to whose favour and esteem he was highly indebted, he could not escape the suspicion of being accessory to a deed from whence he derived the principal advantage. He enjoyed, at least before his elevation, an acknowledged character of virtue and abilities;[65] but his austere temper insensibly degenerated into moroseness and cruelty; and the imperfect writers of his life almost hesitate whether they shall not rank him in the number of Roman tyrants.[66] When Carus assumed the purple he was about sixty years of age, and his two sons, Carinus and Numerian, had already attained the season of manhood.[67]

The authority of the senate expired with Probus; nor was the repentance of the soldiers displayed by the same dutiful regard for the civil power which they had testified after the unfortunate death of Aurelian. The election of Carus was decided without expecting the approbation of the senate, and the new emperor contented himself with announcing, in a cold and stately epistle, that he had ascended the vacant throne.[68] A behaviour so very opposite to that of his amiable predecessor afforded no favourable presage of the new reign: and the Romans, deprived of power and freedom, asserted their privilege of licentious murmurs.[69] The voice of congratulation and flattery was not however silent; and we may still peruse, with pleasure and contempt, an eclogue which was composed on the accession of the emperor Carus. Two shepherds, avoiding the noontide heat, retire into the cave of Faunus. On a spreading beech they discover some recent characters. The rural deity had described, in prophetic verses, the felicity promised to the empire under the reign of so great a prince. Faunus hails the approach of that hero, who, receiving on his shoulders the sinking weight of the Roman world, shall extinguish war and faction, and once again restore the innocence and security of the golden age.[70]

It is more than probable that these elegant trifles never reached the ears of a veteran general who, with the consent of the legions, was preparing to execute the long-suspended design of the Persian war. Before his departure for this distant expedition, Carus conferred on his two sons, Carinus and Numerian, the title of Cæsar, and, investing the former with almost an equal share of the Imperial power, directed the young prince first to suppress some troubles which had arisen in Gaul, and afterwards to fix the seat of his residence at Rome, and to assume the government of the Western provinces.[71] The safety of Illyricum was confirmed by a memorable defeat of the Sarmatians; sixteen thousand of those barbarians remained on the field of battle, and the number of captives amounted to twenty thousand. The old emperor, animated with the fame and prospect of victory, pursued his march, in the midst of winter, through the countries of Thrace and Asia Minor, and at length, with his younger son Numerian, arrived on the confines of the Persian monarchy. There, encamping on the summit of a lofty mountain, he pointed out to his troops the opulence and luxury of the enemy whom they were about to invade.

The successor of Artaxerxes, Varanes, or Bahram, though he had subdued the Segestans, one of the most warlike nations of Upper Asia,[72] was alarmed at the approach of the Romans, and endeavoured to retard their progress by a negotiation of peace. His ambassadors entered the camp about sunset, at the time when the troops were satisfying their hunger with a frugal repast. The Persians expressed their desire of being introduced to the presence of the Roman emperor. They were at length conducted to a soldier who was seated on the grass. A piece of stale bacon and a few hard peas composed his supper. A coarse woollen garment of purple was the only circumstance that announced his dignity. The conference was conducted with the same disregard of courtly elegance. Carus, taking off a cap which he wore to conceal his baldness, assured the ambassadors that, unless their master acknowledged the superiority of Rome, he would speedily render Persia as naked of trees as his own head was destitute of hair.[73] Notwithstanding some traces of art and preparation, we may discover in this scene the manners of Carus, and the severe simplicity which the martial princes who succeeded Gallienus had already restored in the Roman camps. The ministers of the Great King trembled and retired.

The threats of Carus were not without effect. He ravaged Mesopotamia, cut in pieces whatever opposed his passage, made himself master of the great cities of Seleucia and Ctesiphon (which seem to have surrendered without resistance), and carried his victorious arms beyond the Tigris.[74] He had seized the favourable moment for an invasion. The Persian councils were distracted by domestic factions, and the greater part of their forces were detained on the frontiers of India. Rome and the East received with transport the news of such important advantages. Flattery and hope painted in the most lively colours the fall of Persia, the conquest of Arabia, the submission of Egypt, and a lasting deliverance from the inroads of the Scythian nations.[75] But the reign of Carus was destined to expose the vanity of predictions. They were scarcely uttered before they were contradicted by his death; an event attended with such ambiguous circumstances that it may be related in a letter from his own secretary to the præfect of the city. "Carus," says he, "our dearest emperor, was confined by sickness to his bed, when a furious tempest arose in the camp. The darkness which overspread the sky was so thick that we could no longer distinguish each other; and the incessant flashes of lightning took from us the knowledge of all that passed in the general confusion. Immediately after the most violent clap of thunder we heard a sudden cry that the emperor was dead; and it soon appeared that his chamberlains, in a rage of grief, had set fire to the royal pavilion, a circumstance which gave rise to the report that Carus was killed by lightning. But, as far as we have been able to investigate the truth, his death was the natural effect of his disorder."[76]

The vacancy of the throne was not productive of any disturbance. The ambition of the aspiring generals was checked by their mutual fears; and young Numerian, with his absent brother Carinus, were unanimously acknowledged as Roman emperors. The public expected that the successor of Carus would pursue his father's footsteps, and, without allowing the Persians to recover from their consternation, would advance sword in hand to the palaces of Susa and Ecbatana.[77] But the legions, however strong in numbers and discipline, were dismayed by the most abject superstition. Notwithstanding all the arts that were practised to disguise the manner of the late emperor's death, it was found impossible to remove the opinion of the multitude, and the power of opinion is irresistible. Places or persons struck with lightning were considered by the ancients with pious horror, as singularly devoted to the wrath of Heaven.[78] An oracle was remembered which marked the river Tigris as the fatal boundary of the Roman arms. The troops, terrified with the fate of Carus and with their own danger, called aloud on young Numerian to obey the will of the gods, and to lead them away from this inauspicious scene of war. The feeble emperor was unable to subdue their obstinate prejudice, and the Persians wondered at the unexpected retreat of a victorious enemy.[79]

The intelligence of the mysterious fate of the late emperor was soon carried from the frontiers of Persia to Rome; and the senate, as well as the provinces, congratulated the accession of the sons of Carus. These fortunate youths were strangers, however, to that conscious superiority, either of birth or of merit, which can alone render the possession of a throne easy, and as it were natural. Born and educated in a private station, the election of their father raised them at once to the rank of princes; and his death, which happened about sixteen months afterwards, left them the unexpected legacy of a vast empire. To sustain with temper this rapid elevation, an uncommon share of virtue and prudence was requisite; and Carinus, the elder of the brothers, was more than commonly deficient in those qualities. In the Gallic war he discovered some degree of personal courage;[80] but from the moment of his arrival at Rome he abandoned himself to the luxury of the capital, and to the abuse of his fortune. He was soft, yet cruel; devoted to pleasure, but destitute of taste; and, though exquisitely susceptible of vanity, indifferent to the public esteem. In the course of a few months he successively married and divorced nine wives, most of whom he left pregnant; and, notwithstanding this legal inconstancy, found time to indulge such a variety of irregular appetites as brought dishonour on himself and on the noblest houses of Rome. He beheld with inveterate hatred all those who might remember his former obscurity, or censure his present conduct. He banished or put to death the friends and counsellors whom his father had placed about him to guide his inexperienced youth; and he persecuted with the meanest revenge his schoolfellows and companions who had not sufficiently respected the latent majesty of the emperor. With the senators Carinus affected a lofty and regal demeanour, frequently declaring that he designed to distribute their estates among the populace of Rome. From the dregs of that populace he selected his favourites, and even his ministers. The palace, and even the Imperial table, was filled with singers, dancers, prostitutes, and all the various retinue of vice and folly. One of his doorkeepers[81] he intrusted with the government of the city. In the room of the Prætorian præfect, whom he put to death, Carinus substituted one of the ministers of his looser pleasures. Another, who possessed the same or even a more infamous title to favour, was invested with the consulship. A confidential secretary, who had acquired uncommon skill in the art of forgery, delivered the indolent emperor, with his own consent, from the irksome duty of signing his name.

When the emperor Carus undertook the Persian war, he was induced, by motives of affection as well as policy, to secure the fortunes of his family by leaving in the hands of his eldest son the armies and provinces of the West. The intelligence which he soon received of the conduct of Carinus filled him with shame and regret; nor had he concealed his resolution of satisfying the republic by a severe act of justice, and of adopting, in the place of an unworthy son, the brave and virtuous Constantius, who at that time was governor of Dalmatia. But the elevation of Constantius was for a while deferred; and as soon as the father's death had released Carinus from the control of fear or decency, he displayed to the Romans the extravagancies of Elagabalus, aggravated by the cruelty of Domitian.[82]

The only merit of the administration of Carinus that history could record, or poetry celebrate, was the uncommon splendour with which, in his own and his brother's name, he exhibited the Roman games of the theatre, the circus, and the amphitheatre. More than twenty years afterwards, when the courtiers of Diocletian represented to their frugal sovereign the fame and popularity of his munificent predecessor, he acknowledged that the reign of Carinus had indeed been a reign of pleasure.[83] But this vain prodigality, which the prudence of Diocletian might justly despise, was enjoyed with surprise and transport by the Roman people. The oldest of the citizens, recollecting the spectacles of former days, the triumphal pomp of Probus or Aurelian, and the secular games of the emperor Philip, acknowledged that they were all surpassed by the superior magnificence of Carinus.[84]

The spectacles of Carinus may therefore be best illustrated by the observation of some particulars which history has condescended to relate concerning those of his predecessors. If we confine ourselves solely to the hunting of wild beasts, however we may censure the vanity of the design or the cruelty of the execution, we are obliged to confess that neither before nor since the time of the Romans so much art and expense have ever been lavished for the amusement of the people.[85] By the order of Probus, a great quantity of large trees, torn up by the roots, were transplanted into the midst of the circus. The spacious and shady forest was immediately filled with a thousand ostriches, a thousand stags, a thousand fallow-deer, and a thousand wild boars; and all this variety of game was abandoned to the riotous impetuosity of the multitude. The tragedy of the succeeding day consisted in the massacre of an hundred lions, an equal number of lionesses, two hundred leopards, and three hundred bears.[86] The collection prepared by the younger Gordian for his triumph, and which his successor exhibited in the secular games, was less remarkable by the number than by the singularity of the animals. Twenty zebras displayed their elegant forms and variegated beauty to the eyes of the Roman people.[87] Ten elks, and as many camelopards, the loftiest and most harmless creatures that wander over the plain of Sarmatia and Æthiopia, were contrasted with thirty African hyænas and ten Indian tigers, the most implacable savages of the torrid zone. The unoffending strength with which Nature has endowed the greater quadrupeds was admired in the rhinoceros, the hippopotamus of the Nile,[88] and a majestic troop of twenty-two elephants.[89] While the populace gazed with stupid wonder on the splendid show, the naturalist might indeed observe the figure and properties of so many different species, transported from every part of the ancient world into the amphitheatre of Rome. But this accidental benefit which science might derive from folly is surely insufficient to justify such a wanton abuse of the public riches. There occurs, however, a single instance in the first Punic war in which the senate wisely connected this amusement of the multitude with the interest of the state. A considerable number of elephants, taken in the defeat of the Carthaginian army, were driven through the circus by a few slaves, armed only with blunt javelins.[90] The useful spectacle served to impress the Roman soldier with a just contempt for those unwieldy animals; and he no longer dreaded to encounter them in the ranks of war.

The hunting or exhibition of wild beasts was conducted with a magnificence suitable to a people who styled themselves the masters of the world; nor was the edifice appropriated to that entertainment less expensive of Roman greatness. Posterity admires, and will long admire, the awful remains of the amphitheatre of Titus, who so well deserved the epithet of Colossal.[91] It was a building of an elliptic figure, five hundred and sixty-four feet in length, and four hundred and sixty-seven in breadth, founded on fourscore arches, and rising, with four successive orders of architecture, to the height of one hundred and forty feet.[92] The outside of the edifice was encrusted with marble and decorated with statues. The slopes of the vast concave, which formed the inside, were filled and surrounded with sixty or eighty rows of seats, of marble likewise, covered with cushions, and capable of receiving with ease above four-score thousand spectators.[93] Sixty-four *vomitories* (for by that name the doors were very aptly distinguished) poured forth the immense multitude; and the entrances, passages, and staircases were contrived with such exquisite skill, that each person, whether of the senatorial, the equestrian, or the plebeian order, arrived at his destined place without trouble or confusion.[94] Nothing was omitted which, in any respect, could be subservient to the convenience and pleasure of the spectators. They were protected from the sun and rain by an ample canopy, occasionally drawn over their heads. The air was continually refreshed by the playing of fountains, and profusely impregnated by the grateful scent of aromatics. In the centre of the edifice, the *arena*, or stage, was strewed with the finest sand, and successively assumed the most different forms. At one moment it seemed to rise out of the earth, like the garden of the Hesperides, and was afterwards broken into the rocks and caverns of Thrace. The subterraneous pipes conveyed an inexhaustible supply of water; and what had just before appeared a level plain might be suddenly converted into a wide lake, covered with armed vessels, and replenished with the monsters of the deep.[95] In the decoration of these scenes the Roman emperors displayed their wealth and liberality; and we read on various occasions that the whole furniture of the amphitheatre consisted either of silver, or of gold, or of amber.[96] The poet who describes the games of Carinus, in the character of a shepherd attracted to the capital by the fame of their magnificence, affirms that the nets designed as a defence against the wild beasts were of gold wire; that the porticoes were gilded; and that the *belt* or circle which divided the several ranks of spectators from each other was studded with a precious mosaic of beautiful stones.[97]

In the midst of this glittering pageantry, the emperor Carinus, secure of his fortune, enjoyed the acclamations of the people, the flattery of his courtiers, and the songs of the poets, who, for want of a more essential merit, were reduced to celebrate the divine graces of his person.[98] In the same hour, but at the distance of nine hundred miles from Rome, his brother expired; and a sudden revolution transferred into the hands of a stranger the sceptre of the house of Carus.[99]

The sons of Carus never saw each other after their father's death. The arrangements which their new situation required were probably deferred till the return of the younger brother to Rome, where a triumph was decreed to the young emperors for the glorious success of the Persian war.[100] It is uncertain whether they intended to divide between them the administration or the provinces of the empire; but it is very unlikely that their union would have proved of any long duration. The jealousy of power must have been inflamed by the opposition of characters. In the most corrupt of times Carinus was unworthy to live: Numerian deserved to reign in a happier period. His affable manners and gentle virtues secured him, as soon as they became known, the regard and affections of the public. He possessed the elegant accomplishments of a poet and orator, which dignify as well as adorn the humblest and the most exalted station. His eloquence, however it was applauded by the senate, was formed not so much on the model of Cicero as on that of the modern declaimers; but in an age very far from being destitute of poetical merit, he contended for the prize with the most celebrated of his contemporaries, and still remained the friend of his rivals; a circumstance which evinces either the goodness of his heart, or the superiority of his genius.[101] But the talents of Numerian were rather of the contemplative than of the active kind. When his father's elevation reluctantly forced him from the shade of retirement, neither his temper nor his pursuits had qualified him for the command of armies. His constitution was destroyed by the hardships of the Persian war; and he had contracted, from the heat of the climate,[102] such a weakness in his eyes, as obliged him, in the course of a long retreat, to confine himself to the solitude and darkness of a tent or litter. The administration of all affairs, civil as well as military, was devolved on Arrius Aper, the Prætorian præfect, who, to the power of his important office, added the honour of being father-in-law to Numerian. The Imperial pavilion was strictly guarded by his most trusty adherents; and during many days Aper delivered to the army the supposed mandates of their invisible sovereign.[103]

It was not till eight months after the death of Carus that the Roman army, returning by slow marches from the banks of the Tigris, arrived on those of the Thracian Bosphorus. The legions halted at Chalcedon in Asia, while the court passed over to Heraclea, on the European side of the Propontis.[104] But a report soon circulated through the camp, at first in secret whispers, and at length in loud clamours, of the emperor's death, and of the presumption of his ambitious minister, who still exercised the sovereign power in the name of a prince who was no more. The impatience of the soldiers could not long support a state of suspense. With rude curiosity they broke into the imperial tent, and discovered only the corpse of Numerian.[105] The gradual decline of his health might have induced them to believe that his death was natural; but the concealment was interpreted as an evidence of guilt, and the measures which Aper had taken to secure his election became the immediate occasion of his ruin. Yet, even in the transport of their rage and grief, the troops observed a regular proceeding, which proves how firmly discipline had been re-established by the martial successors of Gallienus. A general assembly of the army was appointed to be held at Chalcedon, whither Aper was transported in chains, as a prisoner and a criminal. A vacant tribunal was erected in the midst of the camp, and the generals and tribunes formed a great military council. They soon announced to the multitude that their choice had fallen on Diocletian, commander of the domestics or bodyguards, as the person the most capable of revenging and succeeding their beloved emperor. The future fortunes of the candidate depended on the chance or conduct of the present hour. Conscious that the station which he had filled exposed him to some suspicions, Diocletian ascended the tribunal, and, raising his eyes towards the Sun, made a solemn profession of his own innocence, in the presence of that all-seeing Deity.[106] Then, assuming the tone of a sovereign and a judge, he commanded that Aper should be brought in chains to the foot of the tribunal. "This man," said he, "is the murderer of Numerian;" and without giving him time to enter on a dangerous justification, drew his sword, and buried it in the breast of the unfortunate præfect. A charge supported by such decisive proof was admitted without contradiction, and the legions, with repeated acclamations, acknowledged the justice and authority of the emperor Diocletian.[107]

Before we enter upon the memorable reign of that prince, it will be proper to punish and dismiss the unworthy brother of Numerian. Carinus possessed arms and treasures sufficient to support his legal title to the empire. But his personal vices overbalanced every advantage of birth and situation. The most faithful servants of the father despised the incapacity, and dreaded the cruel arrogance of the son. The hearts of the people were engaged in favour of his rival, and even the senate was inclined to prefer an usurper to a tyrant. The arts of Diocletian inflamed the general discontent; and the winter was employed in secret intrigues and open preparations for a civil war. In the spring the forces of the East and of the West encountered each other in the plains of Margus, a small city of Mæsia, in the neighbourhood of the Danube.[108] The troops, so lately returned from the Persian war, had acquired their glory at the expense of health and numbers, nor were they in a condition to contend with the unexhausted strength of the legions of Europe. Their ranks were broken, and, for a moment, Diocletian despaired of the purple and of life. But the advantage which Carinus had obtained by the valour of his soldiers he quickly lost by the infidelity of his officers. A tribune, whose wife he had seduced, seized the opportunity of revenge, and by a single blow extinguished civil discord in the blood of the adulterer.[109]

CHAPTER XIII

The Reign of Diocletian and his Three Associates, Maximian, Galerius, and Constantius. General Re-establishment of Order and Tranquillity. The Persian War, Victory, and Triumph. The new Form of Administration. Abdication and Retirement of Diocletian and Maximian.

As the reign of Diocletian was more illustrious than that of any of his predecessors, so was his birth more abject and obscure. The strong claims of merit and of violence had frequently superseded the ideal prerogatives of nobility; but a distinct line of separation was hitherto preserved between the free and the servile part of mankind. The parents of Diocletian had been slaves in the house of Anulinus, a Roman senator; nor was he himself distinguished by any other name than that which he derived from a small town in Dalmatia, from whence his mother deduced her origin.[1] It is, however, probable that his father obtained the freedom of the family, and that he soon acquired an office of scribe, which was commonly exercised by persons of his condition.[2] Favourable oracles, or rather the consciousness of superior merit, prompted his aspiring son to pursue the profession of arms and the hopes of fortune; and it would be extremely curious to observe the graduation of arts and accidents which enabled him in the end to fulfil those oracles, and to display that merit to the world. Diocletian was successively promoted to the government of Mæsia, the honours of the consulship, and the important command of the guards of the palace. He distinguished his abilities in the Persian war; and after the death of Numerian, the slave, by the confession and judgment of his rivals, was declared the most worthy of the Imperial throne. The malice of religious zeal, whilst it arraigns the savage fierceness of his colleague Maximian, has affected to cast suspicion on the personal courage of the emperor Diocletian.[3] It would not be easy to persuade us of the cowardice of a soldier of fortune who acquired and preserved the esteem of the legions, as well as the favour of so many warlike princes. Yet even calumny is sagacious enough to discover and to attack the most vulnerable part. The valour of Diocletian was never found inadequate to his duty, or to the occasion; but he appears not to have possessed the daring and generous spirit of a hero, who courts danger and fame, disdains artifice, and boldly challenges the allegiance of his equals. His abilities were useful rather than splendid—a vigorous mind improved by the experience and study of mankind; dexterity and application in business; a judicious mixture of liberality and economy, of mildness and rigour; profound dissimulation under the disguise of military frankness; steadiness to pursue his ends; flexibility to vary his means; and, above all, the great art of submitting his own passions, as well as those of others, to the interest of his ambition, and of colouring his ambition with the most specious pretences of justice and public utility. Like Augustus, Diocletian may be considered as the founder of a new empire. Like the adopted son of Cæsar, he was distinguished as a statesman rather than as a warrior; nor did either of those princes employ force, whenever their purpose could be effected by policy.

The victory of Diocletian was remarkable for its singular mildness. A people accustomed to applaud the clemency of the conqueror, if the usual punishments of death, exile, and confiscation were inflicted with any degree of temper and equity, beheld, with the most pleasing astonishment, a civil war, the flames of which were extinguished in the field of battle. Diocletian received into his confidence Aristobulus, the principal minister of the house of Carus, respected the lives, the fortunes, and the dignity of his adversaries, and even continued in their respective stations the greater number of the servants of Carinus.[4] It is not improbable that motives of prudence might assist the humanity of the artful Dalmatian: of these servants, many had purchased his favour by secret treachery; in others, he esteemed their grateful fidelity to an unfortunate master. The discerning judgment of Aurelian, of Probus, and of Carus, had filled the several departments of the state and army with officers of approved merit, whose removal would have injured the public service, without promoting the interest of the successor. Such a conduct, however, displayed to the Roman world the fairest prospect of the new reign, and the emperor affected to confirm this favourable prepossession by declaring that, among all the virtues of his predecessors, he was the most ambitious of imitating the humane philosophy of Marcus Antoninus.[5]

The first considerable action of his reign seemed to evince his sincerity as well as his moderation. After the example of Marcus, he gave himself a colleague in the person of Maximian, on whom he bestowed at first the title of Cæsar, and afterwards that of Augustus.[6] But the motives of his conduct, as well as the object of his choice, were of a very different nature from those of his admired predecessor. By investing a luxurious youth with the honours of the purple, Marcus had discharged a debt of private gratitude, at the expense, indeed, of the happiness of the state. By associating a friend and a fellow-soldier to the favours of government, Diocletian, in a time of public danger, provided for the defence both of the East and of the West. Maximian was born a peasant, and, like Aurelian, in the territory of Sirmium. Ignorant of letters,[7] careless of laws, the rusticity of his appearance and manners still betrayed in the most elevated fortune the meanness of his extraction. War was the only art which he professed. In a long course of service he had distinguished himself on every frontier of the empire; and though his military talents were formed to obey rather than to command, though, perhaps, he never attained the skill of a consummate general, he was capable, by his valour, constancy, and experience, of executing the most arduous undertakings. Nor were the vices of Maximian less useful to his benefactor. Insensible to pity, and fearless of consequences, he was the ready instrument of every act of cruelty which the policy of that artful prince might at once suggest and disclaim. As soon as a bloody sacrifice had been offered to prudence or to revenge, Diocletian, by his seasonable intercession, saved the remaining few whom he had never designed to punish, gently censured the severity of his stern colleague, and enjoyed the comparison of a golden and an iron age, which was universally applied to their opposite maxims of government. Notwithstanding the difference of their characters, the two emperors maintained, on the throne, that friendship which they had contracted in a private station. The haughty, turbulent spirit of Maximian, so fatal afterwards to himself and to the public peace, was accustomed to respect the genius of Diocletian, and confessed the ascendant of reason over brutal violence.[8] From a motive either of pride or superstition, the two emperors assumed the titles, the one of Jovius, the other of Herculius.

Whilst the motion of the world (such was the language of their venal orators) was maintained by the all-seeing wisdom of Jupiter, the invincible arm of Hercules purged the earth from monsters and tyrants.[9]

But even the omnipotence of Jovius and Herculius was insufficient to sustain the weight of the public administration. The prudence of Diocletian discovered that the empire, assailed on every side by the barbarians, required on every side the presence of a great army and of an emperor. With this view, he resolved once more to divide his unwieldy power, and, with the inferior title of Cæsar, to confer on two generals of approved merit an equal share of the sovereign authority.[10] Galerius, surnamed Armentarius, from his original profession of a herdsman, and Constantius, who from his pale complexion had acquired the denomination of Chlorus,[11] were the two persons invested with the second honours of the Imperial purple. In describing the country, extraction, and manners of Herculius, we have already delineated those of Galerius, who was often, and not improperly, styled the younger Maximian, though, in many instances both of virtue and ability, he appears to have possessed a manifest superiority over the elder. The birth of Constantius was less obscure than that of his colleagues. Eutropius, his father, was one of the most considerable nobles of Dardania, and his mother was the niece of the emperor Claudius.[12] Although the youth of Constantius had been spent in arms, he was endowed with a mild and amiable disposition, and the popular voice had long since acknowledged him worthy of the rank which he at last attained. To strengthen the bonds of political, by those of domestic, union, each of the emperors assumed the character of a father to one of the Cæsars, Diocletian to Galerius, and Maximian to Constantius; and each, obliging them to repudiate their former wives, bestowed his daughter in marriage on his adopted son.[13] These four princes distributed among themselves the wide extent of the Roman empire. The defence of Gaul, Spain,[14] and Britain was intrusted to Constantius: Galerius was stationed on the banks of the Danube, as the safeguard of the Illyrian provinces. Italy and Africa were considered as the department of Maximian; and for his peculiar portion Diocletian reserved Thrace, Egypt, and the rich countries of Asia. Every one was sovereign within his own jurisdiction; but their united authority extended over the whole monarchy, and each of them was prepared to assist his colleagues with his counsels or presence. The Cæsars, in their exalted rank, revered the majesty of the emperors, and the three younger princes invariably acknowledged, by their gratitude and obedience, the common parent of their fortunes. The suspicious jealousy of power found not any place among them; and the singular happiness of their union has been compared to a chorus of music, whose harmony was regulated and maintained by the skilful hand of the first artist.[15]

This important measure was not carried into execution till about six years after the association of Maximian, and that interval of time had not been destitute of memorable incidents. But we have preferred for the sake of perspicuity, first to describe the more perfect form of Diocletian's government, and afterwards to relate the actions of his reign, following rather the natural order of the events than the dates of a very doubtful chronology.

The first exploit of Maximian, though it is mentioned in a few words by our imperfect writers, deserves, from its singularity, to be recorded in a history of human manners. He suppressed the peasants of Gaul, who, under the appellation of Bagaudæ,[16] had risen in a general insurrection; very similar to those which in the fourteenth century successively afflicted both France and England.[17] It should seem that very many of those institutions, referred by an easy solution to the feudal system, are derived from the Celtic barbarians. When Cæsar subdued the Gauls, that great nation was already divided into three orders of men; the clergy, the nobility, and the common people. The first governed by superstition, the second by arms, but the third and last was not of any weight or account in their public councils. It was very natural for the plebeians, oppressed by debt or apprehensive of injuries, to implore the protection of some powerful chief, who acquired over their persons and property the same absolute rights as, among the Greeks and Romans, a master exercised over his slaves.[18] The greatest part of the nation was gradually reduced in a state of servitude; compelled to perpetual labour on the estates of the Gallic nobles, and confined to the soil, either by the real weight of fetters, or by the no less cruel and forcible restraints of the laws. During the long series of troubles which agitated Gaul, from the reign of Gallienus to that of Diocletian, the condition of those servile peasants was peculiarly miserable; and they experienced at once the complicated tyranny of their masters, of the barbarians, of the soldiers, and of the officers of the revenue.[19]

Their patience was at last provoked into despair. On every side they rose in multitudes, armed with rustic weapons, and with irresistible fury. The ploughman became a foot soldier, the shepherd mounted on horseback, the deserted villages and open towns were abandoned to the flames, and the ravages of the peasants equalled those of the fiercest barbarians.[20] They asserted the natural rights of men, but they asserted those rights with the most savage cruelty. The Gallic nobles, justly dreading their revenge, either took refuge in the fortified cities, or fled from the wild scene of anarchy. The peasants reigned without control; and two of their most daring leaders had the folly and rashness to assume the Imperial ornaments.[21] Their power soon expired at the approach of the legions. The strength of union and discipline obtained an easy victory over a licentious and divided multitude.[22] A severe retaliation was inflicted on the peasants who were found in arms: the affrighted remnant returned to their respective habitations, and their unsuccessful effort for freedom served only to confirm their slavery. So strong and uniform is the current of popular passions, that we might almost venture, from very scanty materials, to relate the particulars of this war; but we are not disposed to believe that the principal leaders, Ælianus and Amandus, were Christians,[23] or to insinuate that the rebellion, as it happened in the time of Luther, was occasioned by the abuse of those benevolent principles of Christianity which inculcate the natural freedom of mankind.

Maximian had no sooner recovered Gaul from the hands of the peasants, than he lost Britain by the usurpation of Carausius. Ever since the rash but successful enterprise of the Franks under the reign of Probus, their daring countrymen had constructed squadrons of light brigantines, in which they incessantly ravaged the provinces adjacent to the ocean.[24] To repel their desultory incursions, it was found necessary to create a naval power; and the judicious measure was prosecuted with prudence and vigour. Gessoriacum, or Boulogne, in the straits of the British Channel, was chosen by the emperor for the station of the Roman fleet; and the command of it was intrusted to Carausius, a Menapian of the meanest origin,[25] but who had long signalised his skill as a pilot and his valour as a soldier. The integrity of the new admiral corresponded not with his abilities. When the German pirates sailed from their own harbours he connived at their passage, but he diligently intercepted their return, and appropriated to his own use an ample share of the spoil which they had acquired. The wealth of Carausius was, on this occasion, very justly considered as an evidence of his guilt; and Maximian had already given orders for his death. But the crafty Menapian foresaw and prevented the severity of the emperor. By his liberality he had attached to his fortunes the fleet which he commanded, and secured the barbarians in his interest. From the port of Boulogne he sailed over to Britain, persuaded the legions and the auxiliaries which guarded that island to embrace his party, and boldly assuming, with the Imperial purple, the title of Augustus, defied the justice and the arms of his injured sovereign.[26]

When Britain was thus dismembered from the empire its importance was sensibly felt and its loss sincerely lamented. The Romans celebrated, and perhaps magnified, the extent of that noble island, provided on every side with convenient harbours; the temperature of the climate, and the fertility of the soil, alike adapted for the production of corn or of vines; the valuable minerals with which it abounded; its rich pastures covered with innumerable flocks, and its woods free from wild beasts or venomous serpents. Above all, they regretted the large amount of the revenue of Britain, whilst they confessed that such a province well deserved to become the seat of an independent monarchy.[27] During the space of seven years it was possessed by Carausius; and fortune continued propitious to a rebellion supported with courage and ability. The British emperor defended the frontiers of his dominions against the Caledonians of the North, invited from the continent a great number of skilful artists, and displayed, on a variety of coins that are still extant, his taste and opulence. Born on the confines of the Franks, he courted the friendship of that formidable people by the flattering imitation of their dress and manners. The bravest of their youths he enlisted among his land or sea forces; and, in return for their useful alliance, he communicated to the barbarians the dangerous knowledge of military and naval arts. Carausius still preserved the possession of Boulogne and the adjacent country. His fleets rode triumphant in the channel, commanded the mouths of the Seine and of the Rhine, ravaged the coasts of the ocean, and diffused beyond the Columns of Hercules the terror of his name. Under his command, Britain, destined in a future age to obtain the empire of the sea, already assumed its natural and respectable station of a maritime power.[28]

By seizing the fleet of Boulogne, Carausius had deprived his master of the means of pursuit and revenge. And when, after a vast expense of time and labour, a new armament was launched into the water,[29] the Imperial troops, unaccustomed to that element, were easily baffled and defeated by the veteran sailors of the usurper. This disappointed effort was soon productive of a treaty of peace. Diocletian and his colleague, who justly dreaded the enterprising spirit of Carausius, resigned to him the sovereignty of Britain, and reluctantly admitted their perfidious servant to a participation of the Imperial honours.[30] But the adoption of the two Cæsars restored new vigour to the Roman arms; and while the Rhine was guarded by the presence of Maximian, his brave associate Constantius assumed the conduct of the British war. His first enterprise was against the important place of Boulogne. A stupendous mole, raised across the entrance of the harbour, intercepted all hopes of relief. The town surrendered after an obstinate defence; and a considerable part of the naval strength of Carausius fell into the hands of the besiegers. During the three years which Constantius employed in preparing a fleet adequate to the conquest of Britain, he secured the coast of Gaul, invaded the country of the Franks, and deprived the usurper of the assistance of those powerful allies.

Before the preparations were finished, Constantius received the intelligence of the tyrant's death, and it was considered as a sure presage of the approaching victory. The servants of Carausius imitated the example of treason which he had given. He was murdered by his first minister Allectus, and the assassin succeeded to his power and to his danger. But he possessed not equal abilities either to exercise the one or to repel the other. He beheld with anxious terror the opposite shores of the continent, already filled with arms, with troops, and with vessels; for Constantius had very prudently divided his forces, that he might likewise divide the attention and resistance of the enemy. The attack was at length made by the principal squadron, which, under the command of the præfect Asclepiodotus, an officer of distinguished merit, had been assembled in the mouth of the Seine. So imperfect in those times was the art of navigation, that orators have celebrated the daring courage of the Romans, who ventured to set sail with a side-wind, and on a stormy day. The weather proved favourable to their enterprise. Under the cover of a thick fog they escaped the fleet of Allectus, which had been stationed off the Isle of Wight to receive them, landed in safety on some part of the western coast, and convinced the Britons that a superiority of naval strength will not always protect their country from a foreign invasion. Asclepiodotus had no sooner disembarked the imperial troops than he set fire to his ships; and, as the expedition proved fortunate, his heroic conduct was universally admired. The usurper had posted himself near London, to expect the formidable attack of Constantius, who commanded in person the fleet of Boulogne; but the descent of a new enemy required his immediate presence in the West. He performed this long march in so precipitate a manner that he encountered the whole force of the præfect with a small body of harassed and disheartened troops. The engagement was soon terminated by the total defeat and death of Allectus; a single battle, as it has often happened, decided the fate of this great island; and when Constantius landed on the shores of Kent, he found them covered with obedient subjects. Their acclamations were loud and unanimous; and the virtues of the conqueror may induce us to believe that they sincerely rejoiced in a revolution which, after a separation of ten years, restored Britain to the body of the Roman empire.[31]

Britain had none but domestic enemies to dread; and as long as the governors preserved their fidelity, and the troops their discipline, the incursions of the naked savages of Scotland or Ireland could never materially affect the safety of the province. The peace of the continent, and the defence of the principal rivers which bounded the empire, were objects of far greater difficulty and importance. The policy of Diocletian, which inspired the councils of his associates, provided for the public tranquillity, by encouraging a spirit of dissension among the barbarians, and by strengthening the fortifications of the Roman limit. In the East he fixed a line of camps from Egypt to the Persian dominions, and, for every camp, he instituted an adequate number of stationary troops, commanded by their respective officers, and supplied with every kind of arms, from the new arsenals which he had formed at Antioch, Emesa, and Damascus.[32] Nor was the precaution of the emperor less watchful against the well-known valour of the barbarians of Europe. From the mouth of the Rhine to that of the Danube, the ancient camps, towns, and citadels were diligently reestablished, and, in the most exposed places, new ones were skilfully constructed; the strictest vigilance was introduced among the garrisons

of the frontier, and every expedient was practised that could render the long chain of fortifications firm and impenetrable.[33] A barrier so respectable was seldom violated, and the barbarians often turned against each other their disappointed rage. The Goths, the Vandals, the Gepidæ, the Burgundians, the Alemanni, wasted each other's strength by destructive hostilities: and whosoever vanquished, they vanquished the enemies of Rome. The subjects of Diocletian enjoyed the bloody spectacle, and congratulated each other that the mischiefs of civil war were now experienced only by the barbarians.[34]

Notwithstanding the policy of Diocletian, it was impossible to maintain an equal and undisturbed tranquillity during a reign of twenty years, and along a frontier of many hundred miles. Sometimes the barbarians suspended their domestic animosities, and the relaxed vigilance of the garrisons sometimes gave a passage to their strength or dexterity. Whenever the provinces were invaded, Diocletian conducted himself with that calm dignity which he always affected or possessed; reserved his presence for such occasions as were worthy of his interposition, never exposed his person or reputation to any unnecessary danger, ensured his success by every means that prudence could suggest, and displayed, with ostentation, the consequences of his victory. In wars of a more difficult nature, and more doubtful event, he employed the rough valour of Maximian; and that faithful soldier was content to ascribe his own victories to the wise counsels and auspicious influence of his benefactor. But after the adoption of the two Cæsars, the emperors, themselves retiring to a less laborious scene of action, devolved on their adopted sons the defence of the Danube and of the Rhine. The vigilant Galerius was never reduced to the necessity of vanquishing an army of barbarians on the Roman territory.[35] The brave and active Constantius delivered Gaul from a very furious inroad of the Alemanni; and his victories of Langres and Vindonissa appear to have been actions of considerable danger and merit. As he traversed the open country with a feeble guard, he was encompassed on a sudden by the superior multitude of the enemy. He retreated with difficulty towards Langres; but, in the general consternation, the citizens refused to open their gates, and the wounded prince was drawn up the wall by the means of a rope. But, on the news of his distress, the Roman troops hastened from all sides to his relief, and before the evening he had satisfied his honour and revenge by the slaughter of six thousand Alemanni.[36] From the monuments of those times the obscure traces of several other victories over the barbarians of Sarmatia and Germany might possibly be collected; but the tedious search would not be rewarded either with amusement or with instruction. The conduct which the emperor Probus had adopted in the disposal of the vanquished was imitated by Diocletian and his associates. The captive barbarians, exchanging death for slavery, were distributed among the provincials, and assigned to those districts (in Gaul, the territories of Amiens, Beauvais, Cambray, Treves, Langres, and Troyes, are particularly specified)[37] which had been depopulated by the calamities of war. They were usefully employed as shepherds and husbandmen, but were denied the exercise of arms, except when it was found expedient to enrol them in the military service. Nor did the emperors refuse the property of lands, with a less servile tenure, to such of the barbarians as solicited the protection of Rome. They granted a settlement to several colonies of the Carpi, the Bastarnæ, and the Sarmatians; and, by a dangerous indulgence, permitted them in some measure to retain their national manners and independence.[38] Among the provincials it was a subject of flattering exultation that the barbarian, so lately an object of terror, now cultivated their lands, drove their cattle to the neighbouring fair, and contributed by his labour to the public plenty. They congratulated their masters on the powerful accession of subjects and soldiers; but they forgot to observe that multitudes of secret enemies, insolent from favour, or desperate from oppression, were introduced into the heart of the empire.[39]

While the Cæsars exercised their valour on the banks of the Rhine and Danube, the presence of the emperors was required on the southern confines of the Roman world. From the Nile to Mount Atlas Africa was in arms. A confederacy of five Moorish nations issued from their deserts to invade the peaceful provinces.[40] Julian had assumed the purple at Carthage.[41] Achilleus at Alexandria, and even the Blemmyes, renewed, or rather continued, their incursions into the Upper Egypt. Scarcely any circumstances have been preserved of the exploits of Maximian in the western parts of Africa; but it appears, by the event, that the progress of his arms was rapid and decisive, that he vanquished the fiercest barbarians of Mauritania, and that he removed them from the mountains, whose inaccessible strength had inspired their

inhabitants with a lawless confidence, and habituated them to a life of rapine and violence.[42] Diocletian, of his side, opened the campaign in Egypt by the siege of Alexandria, cut off the aqueducts which conveyed the waters of the Nile into every quarter of that immense city,[43] and, rendering his camp impregnable to the sallies of the besieged multitude, he pushed his reiterated attacks with caution and vigour. After a siege of eight months, Alexandria, wasted by the sword and by fire, implored the clemency of the conqueror, but it experienced the full extent of his severity. Many thousands of the citizens perished in a promiscuous slaughter, and there were few obnoxious persons in Egypt who escaped a sentence either of death or at least of exile.[44] The fate of Busiris and of Coptos was still more melancholy than that of Alexandria; those proud cities, the former distinguished by its antiquity, the latter enriched by the passage of the Indian trade, were utterly destroyed by the arms and by the severe order of Diocletian.[45] The character of the Egyptian nation, insensible to kindness, but extremely susceptible of fear, could alone justify this excessive rigour. The seditions of Alexandria had often affected the tranquillity and subsistence of Rome itself. Since the usurpation of Firmus, the province of Upper Egypt, incessantly relapsing into rebellion, had embraced the alliance of the savages of Æthiopia. The number of the Blemmyes, scattered between the island of Meroe and the Red Sea, was very inconsiderable, their disposition was unwarlike, their weapons rude and inoffensive.[46] Yet in the public disorders these barbarians, whom antiquity, shocked with the deformity of their figure, had almost excluded from the human species, presumed to rank themselves among the enemies of Rome.[47] Such had been the unworthy allies of the Egyptians; and while the attention of the state was engaged in more serious wars, their vexatious inroads might again harass the repose of the province. With a view of opposing to the Blemmyes a suitable adversary, Diocletian persuaded the Nobatæ, or people of Nubia, to remove from their ancient habitations in the deserts of Libya, and resigned to them an extensive but unprofitable territory above Syene and the cataracts of the Nile, with the stipulation that they should ever respect and guard the frontier of the empire. The treaty long subsisted; and till the establishment of Christianity introduced stricter notions of religious worship, it was annually ratified by a solemn sacrifice in the isle of Elephantine, in which the Romans, as well as the barbarians, adored the same visible or invisible powers of the universe.[48]

At the same time that Diocletian chastised the past crimes of the Egyptians, he provided for their future safety and happiness by many wise regulations, which were confirmed and enforced under the succeeding reigns.[49] One very remarkable edict which he published, instead of being condemned as the effect of jealous tyranny, deserves to be applauded as an act of prudence and humanity. He caused a diligent inquiry to be made "for all the ancient books which treated of the admirable art of making gold and silver, and without pity committed them to the flames; apprehensive, as we are assured, lest the opulence of the Egyptians should inspire them with confidence to rebel against the empire."[50] But if Diocletian had been convinced of the reality of that valuable art, far from extinguishing the memory, he would have converted the operation of it to the benefit of the public revenue. It is much more likely that his good sense discovered to him the folly of such magnificent pretensions, and that he was desirous of preserving the reason and fortunes of his subjects from the mischievous pursuit. It may be remarked that these ancient books, so liberally ascribed to Pythagoras, to Solomon, or to Hermes, were the pious frauds of more recent adepts. The Greeks were inattentive either to the use or to the abuse of chemistry. In that immense register, where Pliny has deposited the discoveries, the arts, and the errors of mankind, there is not the least mention of the transmutation of metals; and the persecution of Diocletian is the first authentic event in the history of alchymy. The conquest of Egypt by the Arabs diffused that vain science over the globe. Congenial to the avarice of the human heart, it was studied in China as in Europe, with equal eagerness and with equal success. The darkness of the middle ages ensured a favourable reception to every tale of wonder, and the revival of learning gave new vigour to hope, and suggested more specious arts of deception. Philosophy, with the aid of experience, has at length banished the study of alchymy; and the present age, however desirous of riches, is content to seek them by the humbler means of commerce and industry.[51]

The reduction of Egypt was immediately followed by the Persian war. It was reserved for the reign of Diocletian to vanquish that powerful nation, and to extort a confession from the successors of Artaxerxes of the superior majesty of the Roman empire.

We have observed, under the reign of Valerian, that Armenia was subdued by the perfidy and the arms of the Persians, and that, after the assassination of Chosroes, his son Tiridates, the infant heir of the monarchy, was saved by the fidelity of his friends, and educated under the protection of the emperors. Tiridates derived from his exile such advantages as he could never have obtained on the throne of Armenia; the early knowledge of adversity, of mankind, and of the Roman discipline. He signalised his youth by deeds of valour, and displayed a matchless dexterity, as well as strength, in every martial exercise, and even in the less honourable contests of the Olympian games.[52] Those qualities were more nobly exerted in the defence of his benefactor Licinius.[53] That officer, in the sedition which occasioned the death of Probus, was exposed to the most imminent danger, and the enraged soldiers were forcing their way into his tent when they were checked by the single arm of the Armenian prince. The gratitude of Tiridates contributed soon afterwards to his restoration. Licinius was in every station the friend and companion of Galerius, and the merit of Galerius, long before he was raised to the dignity of Cæsar, had been known and esteemed by Diocletain. In the third year of that emperor's reign, Tiridates was invested with the kingdom of Armenia. The justice of the measure was not less evident than its expediency. It was time to rescue from the usurpation of the Persian monarch an important territory, which, since the reign of Nero, had been always granted under the protection of the empire to a younger branch of the house of Arsaces.[54]

When Tiridates appeared on the frontiers of Armenia, he was received with an unfeigned transport of joy and loyalty. During twenty-six years the country had experienced the real and imaginary hardships of a foreign yoke. The Persian monarchs adorned their new conquest with magnificent buildings; but those monuments had been erected at the expense of the people, and were abhorred as badges of slavery. The apprehension of a revolt had inspired the most rigorous precautions: oppression had been aggravated by insult, and the consciousness of the public hatred had been productive of every measure that could render it still more implacable. We have already remarked the intolerant spirit of the Magian religion. The statues of the deified kings of Armenia, and the sacred images of the sun and moon, were broke in pieces by the zeal of the conqueror and the perpetual fire of Ormuzd was kindled and preserved upon an altar erected on the summit of Mount Bagavan.[55] It was natural that a people exasperated by so many injuries should arm with zeal in the cause of their independence, their religion, and their hereditary sovereign. The torrent bore down every obstacle, and the Persian garrisons retreated before its fury. The nobles of Armenia flew to the standard of Tiridates, all alleging their past merit, offering their future service, and soliciting from the new king those honours and rewards from which they had been excluded with disdain under the foreign government.[56] The command of the army was bestowed on Artavasdes, whose father had saved the infancy of Tiridates, and whose family had been massacred for that generous action. The brother of Artavasdes obtained the government of a province. One of the first military dignities was conferred on the satrap Otas, a man of singular temperance and fortitude, who presented to the king his sister,[57] and a considerable treasure, both of which, in a sequestered fortress, Otas had preserved from violation. Among the Armenian nobles appeared an ally whose fortunes are too remarkable to pass unnoticed. His name was Mamgo, his origin was Scythian, and the horde which acknowledged his authority had encamped a very few years before on the skirts of the Chinese empire,[58] which at that time extended as far as the neighbourhood of Sogdiana.[59] Having incurred the displeasure of his master, Mamgo, with his followers, retired to the banks of the Oxus, and implored the protection of Sapor. The emperor of China claimed the fugitive, and alleged the rights of sovereignty. The Persian monarch pleaded the laws of hospitality, and with some difficulty avoided a war by the promise that he would banish Mamgo to the uttermost parts of the West, a punishment, as he described it, not less dreadful than death itself. Armenia was chosen for the place of exile, and a large district was assigned to the Scythian horde, on which they might feed their flocks and herds, and remove their encampment from one place to another, according to the different seasons of the year. They were employed to repel the invasion of Tiridates; but their leader, after weighing the obligations and injuries which he had received from the Persian monarch, resolved to abandon his party. The Armenian prince, who was well acquainted with the merit as well as power of Mamgo, treated him with distinguished respect; and, by admitting him into his confidence, acquired a brave and faithful servant, who contributed very effectually to his restoration.[60]

For a while fortune appeared to favour the enterprising valour of Tiridates. He not only expelled the enemies of his family and country from the whole extent of Armenia, but in the prosecution of his revenge he carried his arms, or at least his incursions, into the heart of Assyria. The historian who has preserved the name of Tiridates from oblivion, celebrates, with a degree of national enthusiasm, his personal prowess; and, in the true spirit of eastern romance, describes the giants and the elephants that fell beneath his invincible arm. It is from other information that we discover the distracted state of the Persian monarchy, to which the king of Armenia was indebted for some part of his advantages. The throne was disputed by the ambition of contending brothers; and Hormuz, after exerting without success the strength of his own party, had recourse to the dangerous assistance of the barbarians who inhabited the banks of the Caspian Sea.[61] The civil war was, however, soon terminated, either by a victory or by a reconciliation; and Narses, who was universally acknowledged as king of Persia, directed his whole force against the foreign enemy. The contest then became too unequal: nor was the valour of the hero able to withstand the power of the monarch. Tiridates, a second time expelled from the throne of Armenia, once more took refuge in the court of the emperors. Narses soon re-established his authority over the revolted province; and, loudly complaining of the protection afforded by the Romans to rebels and fugitives, aspired to the conquest of the East.[62]

Neither prudence nor honour could permit the emperors to forsake the cause of the Armenian king, and it was resolved to exert the force of the empire in the Persian war. Diocletian, with the calm dignity which he constantly assumed, fixed his own station in the city of Antioch, from whence he prepared and directed the military operations.[63] The conduct of the legions was intrusted to the intrepid valour of Galerius, who, for that important purpose, was removed from the banks of the Danube to those of the Euphrates. The armies soon encountered each other in the plains of Mesopotamia, and two battles were fought with various and doubtful success; but the third engagement was of a more decisive nature; and the Roman army received a total overthrow, which is attributed to the rashness of Galerius, who, with an inconsiderable body of troops, attacked the innumerable host of the Persians.[64] But the consideration of the country that was the scene of action may suggest another reason for his defeat. The same ground on which Galerius was vanquished had been rendered memorable by the death of Crassus and the slaughter of ten legions. It was a plain of more than sixty miles, which extended from the hills of Carrhæ to the Euphrates; a smooth and barren surface of sandy desert, without a hillock, without a tree, and without a spring of fresh water.[65] The steady infantry of the Romans, fainting with heat and thirst, could neither hope for victory if they preserved their ranks, nor break their ranks without exposing themselves to the most imminent danger. In this situation they were gradually encompassed by the superior numbers, harassed by the rapid evolutions and destroyed by the arrows of the barbarian cavalry. The king of Armenia had signalised his valour in the battle, and acquired personal glory by the public misfortune. He was pursued as far as the Euphrates; his horse was wounded, and it appeared impossible for him to escape the victorious enemy. In this extremity Tiridates embraced the only refuge which he saw before him: he dismounted and plunged into the stream. His armour was heavy, the river very deep, and at those parts at least half a mile in breadth;[66] yet such was his strength and dexterity, that he reached in safety the opposite bank.[67] With regard to the Roman general, we are ignorant of the circumstances of his escape; but when he returned to Antioch, Diocletian received him, not with the tenderness of a friend and colleague, but with the indignation of an offended sovereign. The haughtiest of men, clothed in his purple, but humbled by the sense of his fault and misfortune, was obliged to follow the emperor's chariot above a mile on foot, and to exhibit, before the whole court, the spectacle of his disgrace.[68]

As soon as Diocletian had indulged his private resentment, and asserted the majesty of supreme power, he yielded to the submissive entreaties of the Cæsar, and permitted him to retrieve his own honour, as well as that of the Roman arms. In the room of the unwarlike troops of Asia, which had most probably served in the first expedition, a second army was drawn from the veterans and new levies of the Illyrian frontier, and a considerable body of Gothic auxiliaries were taken into the Imperial pay.[69] At the head of a chosen army of twenty-five thousand men Galerius again passed the Euphrates; but, instead of exposing his legions in the open plains of Mesopotamia, he advanced through the mountains of Armenia, where he found the inhabitants devoted to his cause, and the country as favourable to the operations of infantry as it was inconvenient for the motions of cavalry.[70] Adversity had confirmed the Roman discipline, while the barbarians, elated by success, were become so negligent and remiss that, in the moment when they least expected it, they were surprised by the active conduct of Galerius, who, attended only by two horsemen, had with his own eyes secretly examined the state and position of their camp. A surprise, especially in the night-time, was for the most part fatal to a Persian army. "Their horses were tied, and generally shackled, to prevent their running away; and if an alarm happened, a Persian had his housing to fix, his horse to bridle, and his corselet to put on, before he could mount."[71] On this occasion the impetuous attack of Galerius spread disorder and dismay over the camp of the barbarians. A slight resistance was followed by a dreadful carnage, and in the general confusion the wounded monarch (for Narses commanded his armies in person) fled towards the deserts of Media. His sumptuous tents, and those of his satraps, afforded an immense booty to the conqueror; and an incident is mentioned which proves the rustic but martial ignorance of the legions in the elegant superfluities of life. A bag of shining leather, filled with pearls, fell into the hands of a private soldier; he carefully preserved the bag, but he threw away its contents, judging that whatever was of no use could not possibly be of any value.[72] The principal loss of Narses was of a much more affecting nature. Several of his wives, his sisters, and children, who had attended the army, were made captives in the defeat. But though the character of Galerius had in general very little affinity with that of Alexander, he imitated, after his victory, the amiable behaviour of the Macedonian towards the family of Darius. The wives and children of Narses were protected from violence and rapine, conveyed to a place of safety, and treated with every mark of respect and tenderness that was due from a generous enemy to their age, their sex, and their royal dignity.[73]

While the East anxiously expected the decision of this great contest, the emperor Diocletian, having assembled in Syria a strong army of observation, displayed from a distance the resources of the Roman power, and reserved himself for any future emergency of the war. On the intelligence of the victory he condescended to advance towards the frontier, with a view of moderating, by his presence and counsels, the pride of Galerius. The interview of the Roman princes at Nisibis was accompanied with every expression of respect on one side, and of esteem on the other. It was in that city that they soon afterwards gave audience to the ambassador of the Great King.[74] The power, or at least the spirit, of Narses had been broken by his last defeat; and he considered an immediate peace as the only means that could stop the progress of the Roman arms. He despatched Apharban, a servant who possessed his favour and confidence, with a commission to negotiate a treaty, or rather to receive whatever conditions the conqueror should impose. Apharban opened the conference by expressing his master's gratitude for the generous treatment of his family, and by soliciting the liberty of those illustrious captives. He celebrated the valour of Galerius, without degrading the reputation of Narses, and thought it no dishonor to confess the superiority of the victorious Cæsar over a monarch who had surpassed in glory all the princes of his race. Notwithstanding the justice of the Persian cause, he was empowered to submit the present differences to the decision of the emperors themselves; convinced as he was that, in the midst of prosperity, they would not be unmindful of the vicissitudes of fortune. Apharban concluded his discourse in the style of Eastern allegory, by observing that the Roman and Persian monarchies were the two eyes of the world, which would remain imperfect and mutilated if either of them should be put out.

"It well becomes the Persians," replied Galerius, with a transport of fury which seemed to convulse his whole frame, "it well becomes the Persians to expatiate on the vicissitudes of fortune, and calmly to read us lectures on the virtues of moderation. Let them remember their own *moderation* towards the unhappy Valerian. They vanquished him by fraud, they treated him with indignity. They detained him till the last moment of his life in shameful captivity, and after his death they exposed his body to perpetual ignominy." Softening, however, his tone, Galerius insinuated to the ambassador that it had never been the practice of the Romans to trample on a prostrate enemy; and that, on this occasion, they should consult their own dignity rather than the Persian merit. He dismissed Apharban with a hope that Narses would soon be informed on what conditions he might obtain, from the clemency of the emperors, a lasting peace and the restoration of his wives and children. In this conference we may discover the fierce passions of Galerius, as well as his deference to the superior wisdom and authority of Diocletian. The ambition of the former grasped at the conquest of the East, and had proposed to reduce Persia into the state of a province. The prudence of the latter, who adhered to the moderate policy of Augustus and the Antonines, embraced the favourable opportunity of terminating a successful war by an honourable and advantageous peace.[75]

In pursuance of their promise, the emperors soon afterwards appointed Sicorius Probus, one of their secretaries, to acquaint the Persian court with their final resolution. As the minister of peace, he was received with every mark of politeness and friendship; but, under the pretence of allowing him the necessary repose after so long a journey, the audience of Probus was deferred from day to day, and he attended the slow motions of the king, till at length he was admitted to his presence, near the river Asprudus, in Media. The secret motive of Narses in this delay had been to collect such a military force as might enable him, though sincerely desirous of peace, to negotiate with the greater weight and dignity. Three persons only assisted at this important conference, the minister Apharban, the præfect of the guards, and an officer who had commanded on the Armenian frontier.[76] The first condition proposed by the ambassador is not at present of a very intelligible nature; that the city of Nisibis might be established for the place of mutual exchange, or, as we should formerly have termed it, for the staple of trade, between the two empires. There is no difficulty in conceiving the intention of the Roman princes to improve their revenue by some restraints upon commerce; but as Nisibis was situated within their own dominions, and as they were masters both of the imports and exports, it should seem that such restraints were the objects of an internal law, rather than of a foreign treaty. To render them more effectual, some stipulations were probably required on the side of the king of Persia, which appeared so very repugnant either to his interest or to his dignity that Narses could not be persuaded to subscribe them. As this was the only article to which he refused his consent, it was no longer insisted on; and the emperors either suffered the trade to flow in its natural channels, or contented themselves with such restrictions as it depended on their own authority to establish.

As soon as this difficulty was removed, a solemn peace was concluded and ratified between the two nations. The conditions of a treaty so glorious to the empire, and so necessary to Persia, may deserve a more peculiar attention, as the history of Rome presents very few transactions of a similar nature; most of her wars having either been terminated by absolute conquest, or waged against barbarians ignorant of the use of letters. I. The Aboras, or, as it is called by Xenophon, the Araxes, was fixed as the boundary between the two monarchies.[77] That river, which rose near the Tigris, was increased, a few miles below Nisibis, by the little stream of the Mygdonius, passed under the walls of Singara, and fell into the Euphrates at Circesium, a frontier town which, by the care of Diocletian, was very strongly fortified.[78] Mesopotamia, the object of so many wars, was ceded to the empire; and the Persians, by this treaty, renounced all pretensions to that great province. II. They relinquished to the Romans five provinces beyond the Tigris.[79] Their situation formed a very useful barrier, and their natural strength was soon improved by art and military skill. Four of these, to the north of the river, were districts of obscure fame and inconsiderable extent—Intiline, Zabdicene, Arzanene, and Moxoene; but on the east of the Tigris the empire acquired the large and mountainous territory of Carduene, the ancient seat of the Carduchians, who preserved for many ages their manly freedom in the heart of the despotic monarchies of Asia. The ten thousand Greeks traversed their country after a painful march, or rather engagement, of seven days; and it is confessed by their leader, in his incomparable relation of the retreat, that they suffered more from the arrows of the Carduchians than from the power of the Great King.[80] Their posterity, the Curds, with very little alteration either of name or manners, acknowledged the nominal sovereignty of the Turkish sultan. III. It is almost needless to observe that Tiridates, the faithful ally of Rome, was restored to the throne of his fathers, and that the rights of the Imperial supremacy were fully asserted and secured. The limits of Armenia were extended as far as the forests of Sintha in Media, and this increase of dominion was not so much an act of liberality as of justice. Of the provinces already mentioned beyond the Tigris, the four first had been dismembered by the Parthians from the crown of Armenia;[81] and when the Romans acquired the possession of them, they stipulated, at the expense of the usurpers, an ample compensation, which invested their ally with the extensive and fertile country of Atropatene. Its principal city, in the same situation perhaps as the modern Tauris, was frequently honoured with the residence of Tiridates; and as it sometimes bore the name of Ecbatana, he imitated, in the buildings and fortifications, the splendid capital of the Medes.[82] IV. The country of Iberia was barren, its inhabitants rude and savage. But they were accustomed to the use of arms, and they separated from the empire barbarians much fiercer and more formidable than themselves. The narrow defiles of Mount Caucasus were in their hands, and it was in their choice either to admit or to exclude the wandering tribes of Sarmatia, whenever a rapacious spirit urged them to penetrate into the richer climates of the South.[83] The nomination of the kings of Iberia, which was resigned by the Persian monarch to the emperors, contributed to the strength and security of the Roman power in Asia.[84] The East enjoyed a profound tranquillity during forty years; and the treaty between the rival monarchies was strictly observed till the death of Tiridates; when a new generation, animated with different views and different passions, succeeded to the government of the world; and the grandson of Narses undertook a long and memorable war against the princes of the house of Constantine.

The arduous work of rescuing the distressed empire from tyrants and barbarians had now been completely achieved by a succession of Illyrian peasants. As soon as Diocletian entered into the twentieth year of his reign, he celebrated that memorable era, as well as the success of his arms, by the pomp of a Roman triumph.[85] Maximian, the equal partner of his power, was his only companion in the glory of that day. The two Cæsars had fought and conquered, but the merit of their exploits was ascribed, according to the rigour of ancient maxims, to the auspicious influence of their fathers and emperors.[86] The triumph of Diocletian and Maximian was less magnificent, perhaps, than those of Aurelian and Probus, but it was dignified by several circumstances of superior fame and good fortune. Africa and Britain, the Rhine, the Danube, and the Nile, furnished their respective trophies; but the most distinguished ornament was of a more singular nature, a Persian victory followed by an important conquest. The representations of rivers, mountains, and provinces were carried before the Imperial car. The images of the captive wives, the sisters, and the children of the Great King afforded a new and grateful spectacle to the vanity of the people.[87] In the eyes of posterity this triumph is remarkable by a distinction of a less honourable kind. It was the last that Rome ever beheld. Soon after this period the emperors ceased to vanquish, and Rome ceased to be the capital of the empire.

The spot on which Rome was founded had been consecrated by ancient ceremonies and imaginary miracles. The presence of some god, or the memory of some hero, seemed to animate every part of the city, and the empire of the world had been promised to the Capitol.[88] The native Romans felt and confessed the power of this agreeable illusion. It was derived from their ancestors, had grown up with their earliest habits of life, and was protected, in some measure, by the opinion of political utility. The form and the seat of government were intimately blended together, nor was it esteemed possible to transport the one without destroying the other.[89] But the sovereignty of the capital was gradually annihilated in the extent of conquest; the provinces rose to the same level, and the vanquished nations acquired the name and privileges, without imbibing the partial affections, of Romans. During a long period, however, the remains of the ancient constitution and the influence of custom preserved the dignity of Rome. The emperors, though perhaps of African or Illyrian extraction, respected their adopted country as the seat of their power and the centre of their extensive dominions. The emergencies of war very frequently required their presence on the frontiers; but Diocletian and Maximian were the first Roman princes who fixed, in time of peace, their ordinary residence in the provinces; and their conduct, however it might be suggested by private motives, was justified by very specious considerations of policy. The court of the emperor of the West was, for the most part, established at Milan, whose situation, at the foot of the Alps, appeared far more convenient than that of Rome, for the important purpose of watching the motions of the barbarians of Germany. Milan soon assumed the splendour of an Imperial city. The houses are described as numerous and well built; the manners of the people as polished and liberal. A circus, a theatre, a mint, a palace, baths, which bore the name of their founder Maximian; porticoes adorned with statues, and a double circumference of walls, contributed to the beauty of the new capital; nor did it seem oppressed even by the proximity of Rome.[90] To rival the majesty of Rome was the ambition likewise of Diocletian, who employed his leisure and the wealth of the East in the embellishment of Nicomedia, a city placed on the verge of Europe and Asia, almost at an equal distance between the Danube and the Euphrates. By the taste of the monarch, and at the expense of the people, Nicomedia acquired, in the space of a few years, a degree of magnifi-cence which might appear to have required the labour of ages, and became inferior only to Rome, Alexandria, and Antioch in extent or populousness.[91] The life of Diocletian and Maximian was a life of action, and a considerable portion of it was spent in camps, or in their long and frequent marches; but whenever the public business allowed them any relaxation, they seemed to have retired with pleasure to their favourite residences of Nicomedia and Milan. Till Diocletian, in the twentieth year of his reign, celebrated his Roman triumph, it is extremely doubtful whether he ever visited the ancient capital of the empire. Even on that memorable occasion his stay did not exceed two months. Disgusted with the licentious familiarity of the people, he quitted Rome with precipitation thirteen days before it was expected that he should have appeared in the senate invested with the ensigns of the consular dignity.[92]

The dislike expressed by Diocletian towards Rome and Roman freedom was not the effect of momentary caprice, but the result of the most artful policy. The crafty prince had framed a new system of Imperial government, which was afterwards completed by the family of Constantine; and as the image of the old constitution was religiously preserved in the senate, he resolved to deprive that order of its small remains of power and consideration. We may recollect, about eight years before the elevation of Diocletian, the transient greatness and the ambitious hopes of the Roman senate. As long as that enthusiasm prevailed, many of the nobles imprudently displayed their zeal in the cause of freedom; and after the successors of Probus had withdrawn their countenance from the republican party, the senators were unable to disguise their impotent resentment. As the sovereign of Italy, Maximian was intrusted with the care of extinguishing this troublesome rather than dangerous spirit, and the task was perfectly suited to his cruel temper. The most illustrious members of the senate, whom Diocletian always affected to esteem, were involved, by his colleague, in the accusation of imaginary plots; and the possession of an elegant villa, or a well-cultivated estate, was interpreted as a convincing evidence of guilt.[93] The camp of the Prætorians, which had so long oppressed, began to protect, the majesty of Rome; and as those haughty troops were conscious of the decline of their power, they were naturally disposed to unite their strength with the authority of the senate. By the prudent measures of Diocletian, the numbers of the Prætorians were insensibly reduced, their privileges abolished,[94] and their place supplied by two faithful legions of Illyricum, who, under the new titles of Jovians and Herculians, were appointed to perform the service of the Imperial guards.[95] But the most fatal though secret wound which the senate received from the hands of Diocletian and Maximian was inflicted by the inevitable operation of their absence. As long as the emperors resided at Rome, that assembly might be oppressed, but it could scarcely be neglected. The successors of Augustus exercised the power of dictating whatever laws their wisdom or caprice might suggest; but those laws were ratified by the sanction of the senate. The model of ancient freedom was preserved in its deliberations and decrees; and wise princes, who respected the prejudices of the Roman people, were in some measure obliged to assume the language and behaviour suitable to the general and first magistrate of the republic. In the armies and in the provinces they displayed the dignity of monarchs; and when they fixed their residence at a distance from the capital, they forever laid aside the dissimulation which Augustus had recommended to his successors. In the exercise of the legislative as well as the executive power, the sovereign advised with his ministers, instead of consulting the great council of the nation. The name of the senate was mentioned with honour till the last period of the empire; the vanity of its members was still flattered with honorary distinctions;[96] but the assembly which had so long been the source, and so long the instrument of power, was respectfully suffered to sink into oblivion. The senate of Rome, losing all connection with the Imperial court and the actual constitution, was left a venerable but useless monument of antiquity on the Capitoline hill.

When the Roman princes had lost sight of the senate and of their ancient capital, they easily forgot the origin and nature of their legal power. The civil offices of consul, of proconsul, of censor, and of tribune, by the union of which it had been formed, betrayed to the people its republican extraction. Those modest titles were laid aside;[97] and if they still distinguished their high station by the appellation of Emperor, or IMPERATOR, that word was understood in a new and more dignified sense, and no longer denoted the general of the Roman armies, but the sovereign of the Roman world. The name of Emperor, which was at first of a military nature, was associated with another of a more servile kind. The epithet of DOMINUS, or Lord, in its primitive signification, was expressive not of the authority of a prince over his subjects, or of a commander over his soldiers, but of the despotic power of a master over his domestic slaves.[98] Viewing it in that odious light, it had been rejected with abhorrence by the first Cæsars. Their resistance insensibly became more feeble, and the name less odious; till at length the style of *our Lord and Emperor* was not only bestowed by flattery, but was regularly admitted into the laws and public monuments. Such lofty epithets were sufficient to elate and satisfy the most excessive vanity; and if the successors of Diocletian still declined the title of King, it seems to have been the effect not so much of their moderation as of their delicacy. Wherever the Latin tongue was in use (and it was the language of government throughout the empire), the Imperial title, as it was peculiar to themselves, conveyed a more respectable idea than the name of king, which they must have shared with an hundred barbarian chieftains; or which, at the best, they could derive only from Romulus, or from Tarquin. But the sentiments of the East were very different from those of the West. From the earliest period of history, the sovereigns of Asia had been celebrated in the Greek language by the title of BASILEUS, or King; and since it was considered as the first distinction among men, it was soon employed by the servile provincials of the East in their humble addresses to the Roman throne.[99] Even the attributes, or at least the titles, of the DIVINITY were usurped by Diocletian and Maximian, who transmitted them to a succession of Christian emperors.[100] Such extravagant compliments, however, soon lose their impiety by losing their meaning; and when the ear is once accustomed to the sound, they are heard with indifference as vague though excessive professions of respect.

From the time of Augustus to that of Diocletian, the Roman princes, conversing in a familiar manner among their fellow-citizens, were saluted only with the same respect that was usually paid to senators and magistrates. Their principal distinction was the Imperial or military robe of purple; whilst the senatorial garment was marked by a broad, and the equestrian by a narrow, band or stripe of the same honourable colour. The pride, or rather the policy, of Diocletian, engaged that artful prince to introduce the stately magnificence of the court of Persia.[101] He ventured to assume the diadem, an ornament detested by the Romans as the odious ensign of royalty, and the use of which had been considered as the most desperate act of the madness of Caligula. It was no more than a broad white fillet set with pearls, which encircled the emperor's head. The sumptuous robes of Diocletian and his successors were of silk and gold; and it is remarked with indignation that even their shoes were studded with the most precious gems. The access to their sacred person was every day rendered more difficult by the institution of new forms and ceremonies. The avenues of the palace were strictly guarded by the various *schools*, as they began to be called, of domestic officers. The interior apartments were intrusted to the jealous vigilance of the eunuchs; the increase of whose numbers and influence was the most infallible symptom of the progress of despotism. When a subject was at length admitted to the Imperial presence, he was obliged, whatever might be his rank, to fall prostrate on the ground, and to adore, according to the eastern fashion, the divinity of his lord and master.[102] Diocletian was a man of sense, who, in the course of private as well as public life, had formed a just estimate both of himself and of mankind: nor is it easy to conceive that in substituting the manners of Persia to those of Rome he was seriously actuated by so mean a principle as that of vanity. He flattered himself that an ostentation of splendour and luxury would subdue the imagination of the multitude; that the monarch would be less exposed to the rude licence of the people and the soldiers, as his person was secluded from the public view; and that habits of submission would insensibly be productive of sentiments of veneration. Like the modesty affected by Augustus, the state maintained by Diocletian was a theatrical representation; but it must be confessed that, of the two comedies, the former was of a much more liberal and manly character than the latter. It was the aim of the one to disguise, and the object of the other to display, the unbounded power which the emperors possessed over the Roman world.

Ostentation was the first principle of the new system instituted by Diocletian. The second was division. He divided the empire, the provinces, and every branch of the civil as well as military administration. He multiplied the wheels of the machine of government, and rendered its operations less rapid but more secure. Whatever advantages and whatever defects might attend these innovations, they must be ascribed in a very great degree to the first inventor; but as the new frame of policy was gradually improved and completed by succeeding princes, it will be more satisfactory to delay the consideration of it till the season of its full maturity and perfection.[103] Reserving, therefore, for the reign of

Constantine a more exact picture of the new empire, we shall content ourselves with describing the principal and decisive outline, as it was traced by the hand of Diocletian. He had associated three colleagues in the exercise of the supreme power; and as he was convinced that the abilities of a single man were inadequate to the public defence, he considered the joint administration of four princes not as a temporary expedient, but as a fundamental law of the constitution. It was his intention that the two elder princes should be distinguished by the use of the diadem and the title of *Augusti;* that, as affection or esteem might direct their choice, they should regularly call to their assistance two subordinate colleagues; and that the *Cæsars*, rising in their turn to the first rank, should supply an uninterrupted succession of emperors. The empire was divided into four parts. The East and Italy were the most honourable, the Danube and the Rhine the most laborious stations. The former claimed the presence of the *Augusti*, the latter were intrusted to the administration of the *Cæsars*. The strength of the legions was in the hands of the four partners of sovereignty, and the despair of successively vanquishing four formidable rivals might intimidate the ambition of an aspiring general. In their civil government the emperors were supposed to exercise the undivided power of the monarch, and their edicts, inscribed with their joint names, were received in all the provinces as promulgated by their mutual councils and authority. Notwithstanding these precautions, the political union of the Roman world was gradually dissolved, and a principle of division was introduced, which, in the course of a few years, occasioned the perpetual separation of the eastern and western empires.

The system of Diocletian was accompanied with another very material disadvantage, which cannot even at present be totally overlooked; a more expensive establishment, and consequently an increase of taxes, and the oppression of the people. Instead of a modest family of slaves and freedmen, such as had contented the simple greatness of Augustus and Trajan, three or four magnificent courts were established in the various parts of the empire, and as many Roman *kings* contended with each other and with the Persian monarch for the vain superiority of pomp and luxury. The number of ministers, of magistrates, of officers, and of servants, who filled the different departments of the state, was multiplied beyond the example of former times; and (if we may borrow the warm expression of a contemporary), "when the proportion of those who received exceeded the proportion of those who contributed, the provinces were oppressed by the weight of tributes."[104] From this period to the extinction of the empire, it would be easy to deduce an uninterrupted series of clamours and complaints. According to his religion and situation, each writer chooses either Diocletian, or Constantine, or Valens, or Theodosius, for the object of his invectives; but they unanimously agree in representing the burden of the public impositions, and particularly the land-tax and capitation, as the intolerable and increasing grievance of their own times. From such a concurrence, an impartial historian, who is obliged to extract truth from satire, as well as from panegyric, will be inclined to divide the blame among the princes whom they accuse, and to ascribe their exactions much less to their personal vices than to the uniform system of their administration. The emperor Diocletian was indeed the author of that system; but during his reign the growing evil was confined within the bounds of modesty and discretion, and he deserves the reproach of establishing pernicious precedents, rather than of exercising actual oppression.[105] It may be added, that his revenues were managed with prudent economy; and that, after all the current expenses were discharged, there still remained in the Imperial treasury an ample provision either for judicious liberality or for any emergency of the state.

It was in the twenty first year of his reign that Diocletian executed his memorable resolution of abdicating the empire; an action more naturally to have been expected from the elder or the younger Antoninus than from a prince who had never practised the lessons of philosophy either in the attainment or in the use of supreme power. Diocletian acquired the glory of giving to the world the first example of a resignation[106] which has not been very frequently imitated by succeeding monarchs. The parallel of Charles the Fifth, however, will naturally offer itself to our mind, not only since the eloquence of a modern historian has rendered that name so familiar to an English reader, but from the very striking resemblance between the characters of the two emperors, whose political abilities were superior to their military genius, and whose specious virtues were much less the effect of nature than of art. The abdication of Charles appears to have been hastened by the vicissitude of fortune; and the disappointment of his favourite schemes urged him to relinquish a power which he found inadequate to his ambition. But the reign of Diocletian had flowed with a

tide of uninterrupted success; nor was it till after he had vanquished all his enemies, and accomplished all his designs, that he seems to have entertained any serious thoughts of resigning the empire. Neither Charles nor Diocletian were arrived at a very advanced period of life; since the one was only fifty-five, and the other was no more than fifty-nine years of age; but the active life of those princes, their wars and journeys, the cares of royalty, and their application to business, had already impaired their constitution, and brought on the infirmities of a premature old age.[107]

Notwithstanding the severity of a very cold and rainy winter, Diocletian left Italy soon after the ceremony of his triumph, and began his progress towards the East round the circuit of the Illyrian provinces. From the inclemency of the weather and the fatigue of the journey, he soon contracted a slow illness; and though he made easy marches, and was generally carried in a close litter, his disorder, before he arrived at Nicomedia, about the end of the summer, was become very serious and alarming. During the whole winter he was confined to his palace; his danger inspired a general and unaffected concern; but the people could only judge of the various alterations of his health from the joy or consternation which they discovered in the countenances and behaviour of his attendants. The rumour of his death was for some time universally believed, and it was supposed to be concealed with a view to prevent the troubles that might have happened during the absence of the Cæsar Galerius. At length, however, on the first of March, Diocletian once more appeared in public, but so pale and emaciated that he could scarcely have been recognised by those to whom his person was the most familiar. It was time to put an end to the painful struggle, which he had sustained during more than a year, between the care of his health and that of his dignity. The former required indulgence and relaxation, the latter compelled him to direct, from the bed of sickness, the administration of a great empire. He resolved to pass the remainder of his days in honourable repose, to place his glory beyond the reach of fortune, and to relinquish the theatre of the world to his younger and more active associates.[108]

The ceremony of his abdication was performed in a spacious plain, about three miles from Nicomedia. The emperor ascended a lofty throne, and, in a speech full of reason and dignity, declared his intention, both to the people and to the soldiers who were assembled on this extraordinary occasion. As soon as he had divested himself of the purple, he withdrew from the gazing multitude, and, traversing the city in a covered chariot, proceeded without delay to the favourite retirement which he had chosen in his native country of Dalmatia. On the same day, which was the first of May,[109] Maximian, as it had been previously concerted, made his resignation of the Imperial dignity at Milan. Even in the splendour of the Roman triumph, Diocletian had meditated his design of abdicating the government. As he wished to secure the obedience of Maximian, he exacted from him either a general assurance that he would submit his actions to the authority of his benefactor, or a particular promise that he would descend from the throne whenever he should receive the advice and the example. This engagement, though it was confirmed by the solemnity of an oath before the altar of the Capitoline Jupiter,[110] would have proved a feeble restraint on the fierce temper of Maximian, whose passion was the love of power, and who neither desired present tranquillity nor future reputation. But he yielded, however reluctantly, to the ascendant which his wiser colleague had acquired over him, and retired immediately after his abdication to a villa in Lucania, where it was almost impossible that such an impatient spirit could find any lasting tranquillity.

Diocletian, who, from a servile origin, had raised himself to the throne, passed the nine last years of his life in a private condition. Reason had dictated, and content seems to have accompanied, his retreat, in which he enjoyed for a long time the respect of those princes to whom he had resigned the possession of the world.[111] It is seldom that minds long exercised in business have formed any habits of conversing with themselves, and in the loss of power they principally regret the want of occupation. The amusements of letters and of devotion, which afford so many resources in solitude, were incapable of fixing the attention of Diocletian; but he had preserved, or at least he soon recovered, a taste for the most innocent as well as natural pleasures, and his leisure hours were sufficiently employed in building, planting, and gardening. His answer to Maximian is deservedly celebrated. He was solicited by that restless old man to reassume the reins of government and the Imperial purple. He rejected the temptation with a smile of pity, calmly observing that, if he could show Maximian the cabbages which he had planted with his own hands at Salona, he should no longer be urged to relinquish the enjoyment of

happiness for the pursuit of power.[112] In his conversations with his friends he frequently acknowledged that of all arts the most difficult was the art of reigning; and he expressed himself on that favourite topic with a degree of warmth which could be the result only of experience. "How often," was he accustomed to say, "is it the interest of four or five ministers to combine together to deceive their sovereign! Secluded from mankind by his exalted dignity, the truth is concealed from his knowledge; he can see only with their eyes, he hears nothing but their misrepresentations. He confers the most important offices upon vice and weakness, and disgraces the most virtuous and deserving among his subjects. By such infamous arts," added Diocletian, "the best and wisest princes are sold to the venal corruption of their courtiers."[113] A just estimate of greatness, and the assurance of immortal fame, improve our relish for the pleasures of retirement; but the Roman emperor had filled too important a character in the world to enjoy without alloy the comforts and security of a private condition. It was impossible that he could remain ignorant of the troubles which afflicted the empire after his abdication. It was impossible that he could be indifferent to their consequences. Fear, sorrow, and discontent sometimes pursued him into the solitude of Salona. His tenderness, or at least his pride, was deeply wounded by the misfortunes of his wife and daughter; and the last moments of Diocletian were embittered by some affronts, which Licinius and Constantine might have spared the father of so many emperors, and the first author of their own fortune. A report, though of a very doubtful nature, has reached our times that he prudently withdrew himself from their power by a voluntary death.[114]

Before we dismiss the consideration of the life and character of Diocletian, we may for a moment direct our view to the place of his retirement. Salona, a principal city of his native province of Dalmatia, was near two hundred Roman miles (according to the measurement of the public highways) from Aquileia and the confines of Italy, and about two hundred and seventy from Sirmium, the usual residence of the emperors whenever they visited the Illyrian frontier.[115] A miserable village still preserves the name of Salona; but so late as the sixteenth century the remains of a theatre, and a confused prospect of broken arches and marble columns, continued to attest its ancient splendour.[116] About six or seven miles from the city Diocletian constructed a magnificent palace, and we may infer, from the greatness of the work, how long he had med-itated his design of abdicating the empire. The choice of a spot which united all that could con-tribute either to health or to luxury did not re-quire the partiality of a native. "The soil was dry and fertile, the air is pure and wholesome, and, though extremely hot during the summer months, this country seldom feels those sultry and noxious winds to which the coasts of Istria and some parts of Italy are exposed. The views from the palace are no less beautiful than the soil and climate were inviting. Towards the west lies the fertile shore that stretches along the Adriatic, in which a number of small islands are scattered in such a manner as to give this part of the sea the appearance of a great lake. On the north side lies the bay, which led to the ancient city of Salona; and the country beyond it, ap-pearing in sight, forms a proper contrast to that more extensive prospect of water which the Adriatic presents both to the south and to the east. Towards the north the view is terminated by high and irregular mountains, situated at a proper distance, and in many places covered with villages, woods, and vineyards."[117]

Though Constantine, from a very obvious prejudice, affects to mention the palace of Dio-cletian with contempt,[118] yet one of their succes-sors, who could only see it in a neglected and mutilated state, celebrates its magnificence in terms of the highest admiration.[119] It covered an extent of ground consisting of between nine and ten English acres. The form was quadrangular, flanked with sixteen towers. Two of the sides were near six hundred, and the other two near seven hundred, feet in length. The whole was constructed of a beautiful free-stone, extracted from the neighbouring quarries of Trau, or Tra-gutium, and very little inferior to marble itself. Four streets, intersecting each other at right an-gles, divided the several parts of this great edi-fice, and the approach to the principal apart-ment was from a very stately entrance, which is still denominated the Golden Gate. The ap-proach was terminated by a *peristylium* of gran-ite columns, on one side of which we discover the square temple of Æsculapius, on the other the octagon temple of Jupiter. The latter of those deities Diocletian revered as the patron of his fortunes, the former as the protector of his health. By comparing the present remains with the precepts of Vitruvius, the several parts of the building, the baths, bedchamber, the *atrium*, the *basilica*, and the Cyzicene, Corinthian, and Egyptian halls have been described with some degree of precision, or at least of probability.

Their forms were various, their proportions just, but they were all attended with two imperfec-tions, very repugnant to our modern notions of taste and conveniency. These stately rooms had neither windows nor chimneys. They were light-ed from the top (for the building seems to have consisted of no more than one story), and they received their heat by the help of pipes that were conveyed along the walls. The range of principal apartments was protected towards the south-west by a portico five hundred and seven-teen feet long, which must have formed a very noble and delightful walk, when the beauties of painting and sculpture were added to those of the prospect.

Had this magnificent edifice remained in a solitary country, it would have been exposed to the ravages of time; but it might, perhaps, have escaped the rapacious industry of man. The vil-lage of Aspalathus,[120] and, long afterwards, the provincial town of Spalatro, have grown out of its ruins. The Golden Gate now opens into the market-place. St. John the Baptist has usurped the honours of Æsculapius; and the temple of Ju-piter, under the protection of the Virgin, is con-verted into the cathedral church. For this ac-count of Diocletian's palace we are principally indebted to an ingenious artist of our own time and country, whom a very liberal curiosity car-ried into the heart of Dalmatia.[121] But there is room to suspect that the elegance of his designs and engraving has somewhat flattered the ob-jects which it was their purpose to represent. We are informed by a more recent and very judi-cious traveller that the awful ruins of Spalatro are not less expressive of the decline of the arts than of the greatness of the Roman empire in the time of Diocletian.[122] If such was indeed the state of architecture, we must naturally believe that painting and sculpture had experienced a still more sensible decay. The practice of archi-tecture is directed by a few general and even mechanical rules. But sculpture, and, above all, painting, propose to themselves the imitation not only of the forms of nature, but of the char-acters and passions of the human soul. In those sublime arts the dexterity of the hand is of little avail unless it is animated by fancy and guided by the most correct taste and observation.

It is almost unnecessary to remark that the civil distractions of the empire, the licence of the soldiers, the inroads of the barbarians, and the progress of despotism, had proved very unfa-vourable to genius, and even to learning. The succession of Illyrian princes restored the em-pire without restoring the sciences. Their military education was not calculated to inspire them with the love of letters; and even the mind of Diocletian, however active and capacious in business, was totally uninformed by study or speculation. The professions of law and physic are of such common use and certain profit that they will always secure a sufficient number of practitioners endowed with a reasonable degree of abilities and knowledge; but it does not appear that the students in those two faculties appeal to any celebrated masters who have flourished within that period. The voice of poetry was silent. History was reduced to dry and confused abridgments, alike destitute of amusement and instruction. A languid and affected eloquence was still retained in the pay and service of the emperors, who encouraged not any arts except those which contributed to the gratification of their pride or the defence of their power.[123]

The declining age of learning and of mankind is marked, however, by the rise and rapid progress of the new Platonists. The school of Alexandria silenced those of Athens; and the ancient sects enrolled themselves under the banners of the more fashionable teachers, who recommended their system by the novelty of their method and the austerity of their manners. Several of these masters—Ammonius, Plotinus, Amelius, and Porphyry[124]—were men of profound thought and intense application; but, by mistaking the true object of philosophy, their labours contributed much less to improve than to corrupt the human understanding. The knowledge that is suited to our situation and powers, the whole compass of moral, natural, and mathematical science, was neglected by the new Platonists; whilst they exhausted their strength in the verbal disputes of metaphysics, attempted to explore the secrets of the invisible world, and studied to reconcile Aristotle with Plato, on subjects of which both these philosophers were as ignorant as the rest of mankind. Consuming their reason in these deep but unsubstantial meditations, their minds were exposed to illusions of fancy. They flattered themselves that they possessed the secret of disengaging the soul from its corporeal prison; claimed a familiar intercourse with dæmons and spirits; and, by a very singular revolution, converted the study of philosophy into that of magic. The ancient sages had derided the popular superstition; after disguising its extravagance by the thin pretence of allegory, the disciples of Plotinus and Porphyry became its most zealous defenders. As they agreed with the Christians in a few mysterious points of faith, they attacked the remainder of their theological system with all the fury of civil war. The new Platonists would scarcely deserve a place in the history of science, but in that of the church the mention of them will very frequently occur.

CHAPTER XIV

Troubles after the Abdication of Diocletian. Death of Constantius. Elevation of Constantine and Maxentius. Six Emperors at the same Time. Death of Maximian and Galerius. Victories of Constantine over Maxentius and Licinius. Reunion of the Empire under the Authority of Constantine.

THE balance of power established by Diocletian subsisted no longer than while it was sustained by the firm and dexterous hand of the founder. It required such a fortunate mixture of different tempers and abilities as could scarcely be found, or even expected, a second time; two emperors without jealousy, two Cæsars without ambition and the same general interest invariably pursued by four independent princes. The abdication of Diocletian and Maximian was succeeded by eighteen years of discord and confusion. The empire was afflicted by five civil wars; and the remainder of the time was not so much a state of tranquillity as a suspension of arms between several hostile monarchs, who, viewing each other with an eye of fear and hatred, strove to increase their respective forces at the expense of their subjects.

As soon as Diocletian and Maximian had resigned the purple, their station, according to the rules of the new constitution, was filled by the two Cæsars, Constantius and Galerius, who immediately assumed the title of Augustus.[1] The honours of seniority and precedence were allowed to the former of those princes, and he continued under a new appellation to administer his ancient department of Gaul, Spain, and Britain. The government of those ample provinces was sufficient to exercise his talents and to satisfy his ambition. Clemency, temperance, and moderation distinguished the amiable character of Constantius, and his fortunate subjects had frequently occasion to compare the virtues of their sovereign with the passions of Maximian, and even with the arts of Diocletian.[2] Instead of imitating their eastern pride and magnificence, Constantius preserved the modesty of a Roman prince. He declared, with unaffected sincerity, that his most valued treasure was in the hearts of his people; and that, whenever the dignity of the throne or the danger of the state required any extraordinary supply, he could depend with confidence on their gratitude and liberality.[3] The provincials of Gaul, Spain, and Britain, sensible of his worth, and of their own happiness, reflected with anxiety on the declining health of the emperor Constantius, and the tender age of his numerous family, the issue of his second marriage with the daughter of Maximian.

The stern temper of Galerius was cast in a very different mould; and while he commanded the esteem of his subjects, he seldom condescended to solicit their affections. His fame in arms, and, above all, the success of the Persian war, had elated his haughty mind, which was naturally impatient of a superior, or even of an equal. If it were possible to rely on the partial testimony of an injudicious writer, we might ascribe the abdication of Diocletian to the menaces of Galerius, and relate the particulars of a *private* conversation between the two princes, in which the former discovered as much pusillanimity as the latter displayed ingratitude and arrogance.[4] But these obscure anecdotes are sufficiently refuted by an impartial view of the character and conduct of Diocletian. Whatever might otherwise have been his intentions, if he had apprehended any danger from the violence of Galerius, his good sense would have instructed him to prevent the ignominious contest; and as he had held the sceptre with glory, he would have resigned it without disgrace.

After the elevation of Constantius and Galerius to the rank of *Augusti*, two new *Cæsars* were required to supply their place, and to complete the system of the Imperial government. Diocletian was sincerely desirous of withdrawing himself from the world; he considered Galerius, who had married his daughter, as the firmest support of his family and of the empire; and he consented, without reluctance, that his successor should assume the merit as well as the envy of the important nomination. It was fixed without consulting the interest or inclination of the princes of the West. Each of them had a son who was arrived at the age of manhood, and who might have been deemed the most natural candidates for the vacant honour. But the impotent resentment of Maximian was no longer to be dreaded; and the moderate Constantius, though he might despise the dangers, was humanely apprehensive of the calamities, of civil war. The two persons whom Galerius promoted to the rank of Cæsar were much better suited to serve the views of his ambition; and their principal recommendation seems to have consisted in the want of merit or personal consequence. The first of these was Daza, or, as he was afterwards called, Maximin, whose mother was the sister of Galerius. The inexperienced youth still betrayed by his manners and language his rustic education, when, to his own astonishment, as well as that of the world, he was invested by Diocletian with the purple, exalted to the dignity of Cæsar, and intrusted with the sovereign command of Egypt and Syria.[5] At the same time Severus, a faithful servant, addicted to pleasure but not incapable of business, was sent to Milan to receive from the reluctant hands of Maximian the Cæsarian ornaments and the possession of Italy and Africa.[6] According to the forms of the constitution, Severus acknowledged the supremacy of the western emperor; but he was absolutely devoted to the commands of his benefactor Galerius, who, reserving to himself the intermediate countries from the confines of Italy to those of Syria, firmly established his power over three-fourths of the monarchy. In the full confidence that the approaching death of Constantius would leave him sole master of the Roman world, we are assured that he had arranged in his mind a long succession of future princes, and that he meditated his own retreat from public life after he should have accomplished a glorious reign of about twenty years.[7]

But, within less than eighteen months, two unexpected revolutions overturned the ambitious schemes of Galerius. The hopes of uniting the western provinces to his empire were disappointed by the elevation of Constantine; whilst Italy and Africa were lost by the successful revolt of Maxentius.

I. The fame of Constantine has rendered posterity attentive to the most minute circumstances of his life and actions. The place of his birth, as well as the condition of his mother Helena, have been the subject not only of literary but of national disputes. Notwithstanding the recent tradition which assigns for her father a British king,[8] we are obliged to confess that Helena was the daughter of an innkeeper; but at the same time we may defend the legality of her marriage against those who have represented her as the concubine of Constantius.[9] The great Constantine was most probably born at Naissus, in Dacia;[10] and it is not surprising that, in a family and province distinguished only by the profession of arms, the youth should discover very little inclination to improve his mind by the acquisition of knowledge.[11] He was about eighteen years of age when his father was promoted to the rank of Cæsar; but that fortunate event was attended with his mother's divorce; and the splendour of an Imperial alliance reduced the son of Helena to a state of disgrace and humiliation. Instead of following Constantius in the West, he remained in the service of Diocletian, signalising his valour in the wars of Egypt and Persia, and gradually rose to the honourable station of a tribune of the first order. The figure of Constantine was tall and majestic; he was dexterous in all his exercises, intrepid in war, affable in peace; in his whole conduct the active spirit of youth was tempered by habitual prudence; and while his mind was engrossed by ambition, he appeared cold and insensible to the allurements of pleasure. The favour of the people and soldiers, who had named him as a worthy candidate for the rank of Cæsar, served only to exasperate the jealousy of Galerius; and though prudence might restrain him from exercising any open violence, an absolute monarch is seldom at a loss how to execute a sure and secret revenge.[12] Every hour increased the danger of Constantine and the anxiety of his father, who, by repeated letters, expressed the warmest desire of embracing his son. For some time the policy of Galerius supplied him with delays and excuses, but it was impossible long to refuse so natural a request of his associate without maintaining his refusal by arms. The permission of the journey was reluctantly granted, and, whatever precautions the emperor might have taken to intercept a return, the consequences of which he with so much reason apprehended, they were effectually disappointed by the incredible diligence of Constantine.[13] Leaving the palace of Nicomedia in the night, he travelled post through Bithynia, Thrace, Dacia, Pannonia, Italy, and, amidst the joyful acclamations of the people, reached the port of Boulogne in the very moment when his father was preparing to embark for Britain.[14]

The British expedition, and an easy victory over the barbarians of Caledonia, were the last exploits of the reign of Constantius. He ended his life in the Imperial palace of York, fifteen months after he had received the title of Augustus, and almost fourteen years and a half after he had been promoted to the rank of Cæsar. His death was immediately succeeded by the elevation of Constantine. The ideas of inheritance and succession are so very familiar that the generality of mankind consider them as founded not only in reason but in nature itself. Our imagination readily transfers the same principles from private property to public dominion: and whenever a virtuous father leaves behind him a son whose merit seems to justify the esteem, or even the hopes, of the people, the joint influence of prejudice and of affection operates with irresistible weight. The flower of the western armies had followed Constantius into Britain, and the national troops were reinforced by a numerous body of Alemanni, who obeyed the orders of Crocus, one of their hereditary chieftains.[15] The opinion of their own importance, and the assurance that Britain, Gaul, and Spain would acquiesce in their nomination, were diligently inculcated to the legions by the adherents of Constantine. The soldiers were asked whether they could hesitate a moment between the honour of placing at their head the worthy son of their beloved emperor and the ignominy of tamely expecting the arrival of some obscure stranger, on whom it might please the sovereign of Asia to bestow the armies and provinces of the West? It was insinuated to them that gratitude and liberality held a distinguished place among the virtues of Constantine; nor did that artful prince show himself to the troops till they were prepared to salute him with the names of Augustus and Emperor. The throne was the object of his desires; and had he been less actuated by ambition, it was his only means of safety. He was well acquainted with the character and sentiments of Galerius, and sufficiently apprised that, if he wished to live, he must determine to reign. The decent, and even obstinate, resistance which he chose to affect[16] was contrived to justify his usurpation; nor did he yield to the acclamations of the army till he had provided the proper materials for a letter, which he immediately despatched to the emperor of the East. Constantine informed him of the melancholy event of his father's death, modestly asserted his natural claim to the succession, and respectfully lamented that the affectionate violence of his troops had not permitted him to solicit the Imperial purple in the regular and constitutional manner. The first emotions of Galerius were those of surprise, disappointment, and rage; and, as he could seldom restrain his passions, he loudly threatened that he would commit to the flames both the letter and the messenger. But his resentment insensibly subsided; and when he recollected the doubtful chance of war, when he had weighed the character and strength of his adversary, he consented to embrace the honourable accommodation which the prudence of Constantine had left open to him. Without either condemning or ratifying the choice of the British army, Galerius accepted the son of his deceased colleague as the sovereign of the provinces beyond the Alps; but he gave him only the title of Cæsar, and the fourth rank among the Roman princes, whilst he conferred the vacant place of Augustus on his favourite Severus. The apparent harmony of the empire was still preserved, and Constantine, who already possessed the substance, expected, without impatience, an opportunity of obtaining the honours of supreme power.[17]

The children of Constantius by his second marriage were six in number, three of either sex, and whose Imperial descent might have solicited a preference over the meaner extraction of the son of Helena. But Constantine was in the thirty-second year of his age, in the full vigour both of mind and body, at the time when the eldest of his brothers could not possibly be more than thirteen years old. His claim of superior merit had been allowed and ratified by the dying emperor.[18] In his last moments Constantius bequeathed to his eldest son the care of the safety, as well as greatness, of the family; conjuring him to assume both the authority and the sentiments of a father with regard to the children of Theodora. Their liberal education, advantageous marriages, the secure dignity of their lives, and the first honours of the state with which they were invested, attest the fraternal affection of Constantine; and, as those princes possessed a mild and grateful disposition, they submitted without reluctance to the superiority of his genius and fortune.[19]

II. The ambitious spirit of Galerius was scarcely reconciled to the disappointment of his views upon the Gallic provinces before the unexpected loss of Italy wounded his pride as well as power in a still more sensible part. The long absence of the emperors had filled Rome with discontent and indignation; and the people gradually discovered that the preference given to Nicomedia and Milan was not to be ascribed to the particular inclination of Diocletian, but to the permanent form of government which he had instituted. It was in vain that, a few months after his abdication, his successors dedicated, under his name, those magnificent baths whose ruins still supply the ground as well as the materials for so many churches and convents.[20] The tranquillity of those elegant recesses of ease and luxury was disturbed by the impatient murmurs of the Romans, and a report was insensibly circulated that the sums expended in erecting those buildings would soon be required at their hands. About that time the avarice of Galerius, or perhaps the exigencies of the state, had induced him to make a very strict and rigorous inquisition into the property of his subjects for the purpose of a general taxation, both on their lands and on their persons. A very minute survey appears to have been taken of their real estates; and, wherever there was the slightest suspicion of concealment, torture was very freely employed to obtain a sincere declaration of their personal wealth.[21] The privileges which had exalted Italy above the rank of the provinces were no longer regarded: and the officers of the revenue already began to number the Roman people, and to settle the proportion of the new taxes. Even when the spirit of freedom had been utterly extinguished, the tamest subjects have sometimes ventured to resist an unprecedented invasion of their property; but on this occasion the injury was aggravated by the insult, and the sense of private interest was quickened by that of national honour. The conquest of Macedonia, as we have already observed, had delivered the Roman people from the weight of personal taxes. Though they had experienced every form of despotism, they had now enjoyed that exemption near five hundred years; nor could they patiently brook the insolence of an Illyrian peasant, who, from his distant residence in Asia, presumed to number Rome among the tributary cities of his empire. The rising fury of the people was encouraged by the authority, or at least the connivance, of the senate; and the feeble remains of the Prætorian guards, who had reason to apprehend their own dissolution, embraced so honourable a pretence, and declared their readiness to draw their swords in the service of their oppressed country. It was the wish, and it soon became the hope, of every citizen that, after expelling from Italy their foreign tyrants, they should elect a prince who, by the place of his residence, and by his maxims of government, might once more deserve the title of Roman emperor. The name, as well as the situation of Maxentius, determined in his favour the popular enthusiasm.

Maxentius was the son of the emperor Maximian, and he had married the daughter of Galerius. His birth and alliance seemed to offer him the fairest promise of succeeding to the empire; but his vices and incapacity procured him the same exclusion from the dignity of Cæsar which Constantine had deserved by a dangerous superiority of merit. The policy of Galerius preferred such associates as would never disgrace the choice, nor dispute the commands, of their benefactor. An obscure stranger was therefore raised to the throne of Italy, and the son of the late emperor of the West was left to enjoy the luxury of a private fortune in a villa a few miles distant from the capital. The gloomy passions of his soul, shame, vexation, and rage, were inflamed by envy on the news of Constantine's success; but the hopes of Maxentius revived with the public discontent, and he was easily persuaded to unite his personal injury and pretensions with the cause of the Roman people. Two Prætorian tribunes and a commissary of provisions undertook the management of the conspiracy; and, as every order of men was actuated by the same spirit, the immediate event was neither doubtful nor difficult. The præfect of the city and a few magistrates, who maintained their fidelity to Severus, were massacred by the guards; and Maxentius, invested with the Imperial ornaments, was acknowledged, by the applauding senate and people, as the protector of the Roman freedom and dignity. It is uncertain whether Maximian was previously acquainted with the conspiracy; but as soon as the standard of rebellion was erected at Rome, the old emperor broke from the retirement where the authority of Diocletian had condemned him to pass a life of melancholy solitude, and concealed his returning ambition under the disguise of paternal tenderness. At the request of his son and of the senate he condescended to reassume the purple. His ancient dignity, his experience, and his fame in arms added strength as well as reputation to the party of Maxentius.[22]

According to the advice, or rather the orders, of his colleague, the emperor Severus immediately hastened to Rome, in the full confidence that, by his unexpected celerity, he should easily suppress the tumult of an unwarlike populace, commanded by a licentious youth. But he found on his arrival the gates of the city shut against him, the walls filled with men and arms, an experienced general at the head of the rebels, and his own troops without spirit or affection. A large body of Moors deserted to the enemy, allured by the promise of a large donative; and, if it be true that they had been levied by Maximian in his African war, preferring the natural feelings of gratitude to the artificial ties of allegiance. Anulinus, the Prætorian præfect, declared himself in favour of Maxentius, and drew after him the most considerable part of the troops accustomed to obey his commands. Rome, according to the expression of an orator, recalled her armies; and the unfortunate Severus, destitute of force and of counsel, retired, or rather fled, with precipitation to Ravenna. Here he might for some time have been safe. The fortifications of Ravenna were able to resist the attempts, and the morasses that surrounded the town were sufficient to prevent the approach, of the Italian army. Thesea, which Severus commanded with a powerful fleet, secured him an inexhaustible supply of provisions, and gave a free entrance to the legions which, on the return of spring, would advance to his assistance from Illyricum and the East. Maximian, who conducted the siege in person, was soon convinced that he might waste his time and his army in the fruitless enterprise, and that he had nothing to hope either from force or famine. With an art more suitable to the character of Diocletian than to his own, he directed his attack not so much against the walls of Ravenna as against the mind of Severus. The treachery which he had experienced disposed that unhappy prince to distrust the most sincere of his friends and adherents. The emissaries of Maximian easily persuaded his credulity that a conspiracy was formed to betray the town, and prevailed upon his fears not to expose himself to the discretion of an irritated conqueror, but to accept the faith of an honourable capitulation. He was at first received with humanity and treated with respect. Maximian conducted the captive emperor to Rome, and gave him the most solemn assurances that he had secured his life by the resignation of the purple. But Severus could obtain only an easy death and an Imperial funeral. When the sentence was signified to him, the manner of executing it was left to his own choice; he preferred the favourite mode of the ancients, that of opening his veins; and, as soon as he expired, his body was carried to the sepulchre which had been constructed for the family of Gallienus.[23]

Though the characters of Constantine and Maxentius had very little affinity with each other, their situation and interest were the same, and prudence seemed to require that they should unite their forces against the common enemy. Notwithstanding the superiority of his age and dignity, the indefatigable Maximian passed the Alps, and, courting a personal interview with the sovereign of Gaul, carried with him his daughter Fausta as the pledge of the new alliance. The marriage was celebrated at Arles with every circumstance of magnificence; and the ancient colleague of Diocletian, who again asserted his claim to the Western empire, conferred on his son-in-law and ally the title of Augustus. By consenting to receive that honour from Maximian, Constantine seemed to embrace the cause of Rome and of the senate; but his professions were ambiguous, and his assistance slow and ineffectual. He considered with attention the approaching contest between the masters of Italy and the emperor of the East, and was prepared to consult his own safety or ambition in the event of the war.[24]

The importance of the occasion called for the presence and abilities of Galerius. At the head of a powerful army collected from Illyricum and the East, he entered Italy, resolved to revenge the death of Severus and to chastise the rebellious Romans; or, as he expressed his intentions, in the furious language of a barbarian, to extirpate the senate, and to destroy the people by the sword. But the skill of Maximian had concerted a prudent system of defence. The invader found every place hostile, fortified, and inaccessible; and though he forced his way as far as Narni, within sixty miles of Rome, his dominion in Italy was confined to the narrow limits of his camp. Sensible of the increasing difficulties of his enterprise, the haughty Galerius made the first advances towards a reconciliation, and despatched two of his most considerable officers to tempt the Roman princes by the offer of a conference, and the declaration of his paternal regard for Maxentius, who might obtain much more from his liberality than he could hope from the doubtful chance of war.[25] The offers of Galerius were rejected with firmness, his perfidious friendship refused with contempt, and it was not long before he discovered that unless he provided for his safety by a timely retreat, he had some reason to apprehend the fate of Severus. The wealth which the Romans defended against his rapacious tyranny they freely contributed for his destruction. The name of Maximian, the popular arts of his son, the secret distribution of large sums, and the promise of still more liberal rewards, checked the ardour and corrupted the fidelity of the Illyrian legions; and when Galerius at length gave the signal of the retreat, it was with some difficulty that he could prevail on his veterans not to desert a banner which had so often conducted them to victory and honour. A contemporary writer assigns two other causes for the failure of the expedition; but they are both of such a nature that a cautious historian will scarcely venture to adopt them. We are told that Galerius, who had formed a very imperfect notion of the greatness of Rome by the cities of the East with which he was acquainted, found his forces inadequate to the siege of that immense capital. But the extent of a city serves only to render it more accessible to the enemy: Rome had long since been accustomed to submit on the approach of a conqueror; nor could the temporary enthusiasm of the people have long contended against the discipline and valour of the legions. We are likewise informed that the legions themselves were struck with horror and remorse, and that those pious sons of the republic refused to violate the sanctity of their venerable parent.[26] But when we recollect with how much ease, in the more ancient civil wars, the zeal of party and the habits of military obedience had converted the native citizens of Rome into her most implacable enemies, we shall be inclined to distrust this extreme delicacy of strangers and barbarians who had never beheld Italy till they entered it in a hostile manner. Had they not been restrained by motives of a more interested nature, they would probably have answered Galerius in the words of Cæsar's veterans: "If our general wishes to lead us to the banks of the Tiber, we are prepared to trace out his camp. Whatsoever walls he has determined to level with the ground, our hands are ready to work the engines: nor shall we hesitate, should the name of the devoted city be Rome itself." These are indeed the expressions of a poet; but of a poet who has been distinguished, and even censured, for his strict adherence to the truth of history.[27]

The legions of Galerius exhibited a very melancholy proof of their disposition by the ravages which they committed in their retreat. They murdered, they ravished, they plundered, they drove away the flocks and herds of the Italians; they burnt the villages through which they passed, and they endeavoured to destroy the country which it had not been in their power to subdue. During the whole march Maxentius hung on their rear, but he very prudently declined a general engagement with those brave and desperate veterans. His father had undertaken a second journey into Gaul, with the hope of persuading Constantine, who had assembled an army on the frontier, to join the pursuit, and to complete the victory. But the actions of Constantine were guided by reason, and not by resentment. He persisted in the wise resolution of maintaining a balance of power in the divided empire, and he no longer hated Galerius when that aspiring prince had ceased to be an object of terror.[28]

The mind of Galerius was the most susceptible of the sterner passions, but it was not, however, incapable of a sincere and lasting friendship. Licinius, whose manners as well as character were not unlike his own, seems to have engaged both his affection and esteem. Their intimacy had commenced in the happier period, perhaps, of their youth and obscurity. It had been cemented by the freedom and dangers of a military life; they had advanced almost by equal steps through the successive honours of the service; and as soon as Galerius was invested with the Imperial dignity, he seems to have conceived the design of raising his companion to the same rank with himself. During the short period of his prosperity, he considered the rank of Cæsar as unworthy of the age and merit of Licinius, and rather chose to reserve for him the place of Constantius, and the empire of the West. While the emperor was employed in the Italian war, he intrusted his friend with the defence of the Danube; and immediately after his return from that unfortunate expedition he invested Licinius with the vacant purple of Severus, resigning to his immediate command the provinces of Illyricum.[29] The news of his promotion was no sooner carried into the East, than Maximin, who governed, or rather oppressed, the countries of Egypt and Syria, betrayed his envy and discontent, disdained the inferior name of Cæsar, and, notwithstanding the prayers as well as arguments of Galerius, exacted, almost by violence, the equal title of Augustus.[30] For the first, and indeed for the last time, the Roman world was administered by six emperors. In the West, Constantine and Maxentius affected to reverence their father Maximian. In the East, Licinius and Maximin honoured with more real consideration their benefactor Galerius. The opposition of interest, and the memory of a recent war, divided the empire into two great hostile powers; but their mutual fears produced an apparent tranquillity, and even a feigned reconciliation, till the death of the elder princes, of Maximian, and more particularly of Galerius, gave a new direction to the views and passions of their surviving associates.

When Maximian had reluctantly abdicated the empire, the venal orators of the times applauded his philosophic moderation. When his ambition excited, or at least encouraged, a civil war, they returned thanks to his generous patriotism, and gently censured that love of ease and retirement which had withdrawn him from the public service.[31] But it was impossible that minds like those of Maximian and his son could long possess in harmony an undivided power. Maxentius considered himself as the legal sovereign of Italy, elected by the Roman senate and people; nor would he endure the control of his father, who arrogantly declared that by *his* name and abilities the rash youth had been established on the throne. The cause was solemnly pleaded before the Prætorian guards; and those troops, who dreaded the severity of the old emperor, espoused the party of Maxentius.[32] The life and freedom of Maximian were, however, respected, and he retired from Italy into Illyricum, affecting to lament his past conduct, and secretly contriving new mischiefs. But Galerius, who was well acquainted with his character, soon obliged him to leave his dominions, and the last refuge of the disappointed Maximian was the court of his son-in-law Constantine.[33] He was received with respect by that artful prince, and with the appearance of filial tenderness by the empress Fausta. That he might remove every suspicion, he resigned the Imperial purple a second time,[34] professing himself at length convinced of the vanity of greatness and ambition. Had he persevered in this resolution, he might have ended his life with less dignity, indeed, than in his first retirement, yet, however, with comfort and reputation. But the near prospect of a throne brought back to his remembrance the state from whence he was fallen, and he resolved, by a desperate effort, either to reign or to perish. An incursion of the Franks had summoned Constantine, with a part of his army, to the banks of the Rhine; the remainder of the troops were stationed in the southern provinces of Gaul, which lay exposed to the enterprises of the Italian emperor, and a considerable treasure was deposited in the city of Arles. Maximian either craftily invented, or hastily credited, a vain report of the death of Constantine. Without hesitation he ascended the throne, seized the treasure, and, scattering it with his accustomed profusion among the soldiers, endeavoured to awake in their minds the memory of his ancient dignity and exploits. Before he could establish his authority, or finish the negotiation which he appears to have entered into with his son Maxentius, the celerity of Constantine defeated all his hopes. On the first news of his perfidy and ingratitude, that prince returned by rapid marches from the Rhine to the Saone, embarked on the last-mentioned river at Châlons, and, at Lyons trusting himself to the rapidity of the Rhone, arrived at the gates of Arles with a military force which it was impossible for Maximian to resist, and which scarcely permitted him to take refuge in the neighbouring city of Marseilles. The narrow neck of land which joined that place to the continent was fortified against the besiegers, whilst the sea was open, either for the escape of Maximian, or for the succours of Maxentius, if the latter should choose to disguise his invasion of Gaul under the honourable pretence of defending a distressed, or, as he might allege, an injured father. Apprehensive of the fatal consequences of delay, Constantine gave orders for an immediate assault; but the scaling-ladders were found too short for the height of the walls, and Marseilles might have sustained as long a siege as it formerly did against the arms of Cæsar, if the garrison, conscious either of their fault or of their danger, had not purchased their pardon by delivering up the city and the person of Maximian. A secret but irrevocable sentence of death was pronounced against the usurper; he obtained only the same favour which he had indulged to Severus, and it was published to the world that, oppressed by the remorse of his repeated crimes, he strangled himself with his own hands. After he had lost the assistance, and disdained the moderate counsels, of Diocletian, the second period of his active life was a series of public calamities and personal mortifications, which were terminated, in about three years, by an ignominious death. He deserved his fate; but we should find more reason to applaud the humanity of Constantine if he had spared an old man, the benefactor of his father and the father of his wife. During the whole of this melancholy transaction, it appears that Fausta sacrificed the sentiments of nature to her conjugal duties.[35]

The last years of Galerius were less shameful and unfortunate; and though he had filled with more glory the subordinate station of Cæsar than the superior rank of Augustus, he preserved, till the moment of his death, the first place among the princes of the Roman world. He survived his retreat from Italy about four years; and, wisely relinquishing his views of universal empire, he devoted the remainder of his life to the enjoyment of pleasure and to the execution of some works of public utility, among which we may distinguish the discharging into the Danube the superfluous waters of the lake Pelso, and the cutting down the immense forests that encompassed it: an operation worthy of a monarch, since it gave an extensive country to the agriculture of his Pannonian subjects.[36] His death was occasioned by a very painful and lingering disorder. His body, swelled by an intemperate course of life to an unwieldy corpulence, was covered with ulcers, and devoured by innumerable swarms of those insects who have given their name to a most loathsome disease;[37] but as Galerius had offended a very zealous and powerful party among his subjects, his sufferings, instead of exciting their compassion, have been celebrated as the visible effects of divine justice.[38] He had no sooner expired in his palace of Nicomedia than the two emperors, who were indebted for their purple to his favour, began to collect their forces, with the intention either of disputing or of dividing the dominions which he had left without a master. They were persuaded, however, to desist from the former design, and to agree in the latter. The provinces of Asia fell to the share of Maximin, and those of Europe augmented the portion of Licinius. The Hellespont and the Thracian Bosphorus formed their mutual boundary, and the banks of those narrow seas, which flowed in the midst of the Roman world, were covered with soldiers, with arms and with fortifications. The deaths of Maximian and of Galerius reduced the number of emperors to four. The sense of their true interest soon connected Licinius and Constantine; a secret alliance was concluded between Maximin and Maxentius, and their unhappy subjects expected with terror the bloody consequences of their inevitable dissensions, which were no longer restrained by the fear or the respect which they had entertained for Galerius.[39]

Among so many crimes and misfortunes, occasioned by the passions of the Roman princes, there is some pleasure in discovering a single action which may be ascribed to their virtue. In the sixth year of his reign Constantine visited the city of Autun, and generously remitted the arrears of tribute, reducing at the same time the proportion of their assessment from twenty-five to eighteen thousand heads, subject to the real and personal capitation.[40] Yet even this indulgence affords the most unquestionable proof of the public misery. This tax was so extremely oppressive, either in itself or in the mode of collecting it, that, whilst the revenue was increased by extortion, it was diminished by despair: a considerable part of the territory of Autun was left uncultivated; and great numbers of the provincials rather chose to live as exiles and outlaws than to support the weight of civil society. It is but too probable that the bountiful emperor relieved, by a partial act of liberality, one among the many evils which he had caused by his general maxims of administration. But even those maxims were less the effect of choice than of necessity. And if we except the death of Maximian, the reign of Constantine in Gaul seems to have been the most innocent and even virtuous period of his life. The provinces were protected by his presence from the inroads of the barbarians, who either dreaded or experienced his active valour. After a signal victory over the Franks and Alemanni, several of their princes were exposed by his order to the wild beasts in the amphitheatre of Treves, and the people seem to have enjoyed the spectacle, without discovering, in such a treatment of royal captives, anything that was repugnant to the laws of nations or of humanity.[41]

The virtues of Constantine were rendered more illustrious by the vices of Maxentius. Whilst the Gallic provinces enjoyed as much happiness as the condition of the times was capable of receiving, Italy and Africa groaned under the dominion of a tyrant as contemptible as he was odious. The zeal of flattery and faction has indeed too frequently sacrificed the reputation of the vanquished to the glory of their successful rivals; but even those writers who have revealed, with the most freedom and pleasure, the faults of Constantine, unanimously confess that Maxentius was cruel, rapacious, and profligate.[42] He had the good fortune to suppress a slight rebellion in Africa. The governor and a few adherents had been guilty; the province suffered for their crime. The flourishing cities of Cirtha and Carthage, and the whole extent of that fertile country, were wasted by fire and sword. The abuse of victory was followed by the abuse of law and justice. A formidable army of sycophants and delators invaded Africa; the rich and the noble were easily convicted of a connection with the rebels; and those among them who experienced the emperor's clemency were only punished by the confiscation of their estates.[43] So signal a victory was celebrated by a magnificent triumph, and Maxentius exposed to the eyes of the people the spoils and captives of a Roman province. The state of the capital was no less deserving of compassion than that of Africa. The wealth of Rome supplied an inexhaustible fund for his vain and prodigal expenses, and the ministers

of his revenue were skilled in the arts of rapine. It was under his reign that the method of exacting a *free gift* from the senators was first invented; and as the sum was insensibly increased, the pretences of levying it, a victory, a birth, a marriage, or an Imperial consulship, were proportionately multiplied.[44] Maxentius had imbibed the same implacable aversion to the senate which had characterised most of the former tyrants of Rome; nor was it possible for his ungrateful temper to forgive the generous fidelity which had raised him to the throne and supported him against all his enemies. The lives of the senators were exposed to his jealous suspicions, the dishonour of their wives and daughters heightened the gratification of his sensual passions.[45] It may be presumed that an Imperial lover was seldom reduced to sigh in vain; but whenever persuasion proved ineffectual, he had recourse to violence; and there remains *one* memorable example of a noble matron who preserved her chastity by a voluntary death. The soldiers were the only order of men whom he appeared to respect, or studied to please. He filled Rome and Italy with armed troops, connived at their tumults, suffered them with impunity to plunder, and even to massacre, the defenceless people;[46] and indulging them in the same licentiousness which their emperor enjoyed, Maxentius often bestowed on his military favourites the splendid villa, or the beautiful wife, of a senator. A prince, of such a character, alike incapable of governing either in peace or in war, might purchase the support, but he could never obtain the esteem, of the army. Yet his pride was equal to his other vices. Whilst he passed his indolent life, either within the walls of his palace or in the neighboring gardens of Sallust, he was repeatedly heard to declare that *he alone* was emperor, and that the other princes were no more than his lieutenants, on whom he had devolved the defence of the frontier provinces, that he might enjoy without interruption the elegant luxury of the capital. Rome, which had so long regretted the absence, lamented, during the six years of his reign, the presence of her sovereign.[47]

Though Constantine might view the conduct of Maxentius with abhorrence, and the situation of the Romans with compassion, we have no reason to presume that he would have taken up arms to punish the one or to relieve the other. But the tyrant of Italy rashly ventured to provoke a formidable enemy whose ambition had been hitherto restrained by considerations of prudence rather than by principles of justice.[48] After the death of Maximian, his titles, according to the established custom, had been erased, and his statues thrown down with ignominy. His son, who had persecuted and deserted him when alive, affected to display the most pious regard for his memory, and gave orders that a similar treatment should be immediately inflicted on all the statues that had been erected in Italy and Africa to the honour of Constantine. That wise prince, who sincerely wished to decline a war, with the difficulty and importance of which he was sufficiently acquainted, at first dissembled the insult, and sought for redress by the milder expedients of negotiation, till he was convinced that the hostile and ambitious designs of the Italian emperor made it necessary for him to arm in his own defence. Maxentius, who openly avowed his pretensions to the whole monarchy of the West, had already prepared a very considerable force to invade the Gallic provinces on the side of Rhætia; and though he could not expect any assistance from Licinius, he was flattered with the hope that the legions of Illyricum, allured by his presents and promises, would desert the standard of that prince, and unanimously declare themselves his soldiers and subjects.[49] Constantine no longer hesitated. He had deliberated with caution, he acted with vigour. He gave a private audience to the ambassadors who, in the name of the senate and people, conjured him to deliver Rome from a detested tyrant; and, without regarding the timid remonstrances of his council, he resolved to prevent the enemy, and to carry the war into the heart of Italy.[50]

The enterprise was as full of danger as of glory; and the unsuccessful event of two former invasions was sufficient to inspire the most serious apprehensions. The veteran troops, who revered the name of Maximian, had embraced in both those wars the party of his son, and were now restrained by a sense of honour, as well as of interest, from entertaining an idea of a second desertion. Maxentius, who considered the Prætorian guards as the firmest defence of his throne, had increased them to their ancient establishment; and they composed, including the rest of the Italians who were enlisted into his service, a formidable body of fourscore thousand men. Forty thousand Moors and Carthaginians had been raised since the reduction of Africa. Even Sicily furnished its proportion of troops; and the armies of Maxentius amounted to one hundred and seventy thousand foot and eighteen thousand horse. The wealth of Italy supplied the expenses of the war; and the adjacent provinces were exhausted to form immense magazines of corn and every other kind of provisions.

The whole force of Constantine consisted of ninety thousand foot and eight thousand horse;[51] and as the defence of the Rhine required an extraordinary attention during the absence of the emperor, it was not in his power to employ above half his troops in the Italian expedition, unless he sacrificed the public safety to his private quarrel.[52] At the head of about forty thousand soldiers, he marched to encounter an enemy whose numbers were at least four times superior to his own. But the armies of Rome, placed at a secure distance from danger, were enervated by indulgence and luxury. Habituated to the baths and theatres of Rome, they took the field with reluctance, and were chiefly composed of veterans who had almost forgotten, or of new levies who had never acquired, the use of arms and the practice of war. The hardy legions of Gaul had long defended the frontiers of the empire against the barbarians of the North; and in the performance of that laborious service their valour was exercised and their discipline confirmed. There appeared the same difference between the leaders as between the armies. Caprice or flattery had tempted Maxentius with the hopes of conquest; but these aspiring hopes soon gave way to the habits of pleasure and the consciousness of his inexperience. The intrepid mind of Constantine had been trained from his earliest youth to war, to action, and to military command.

When Hannibal marched from Gaul into Italy, he was obliged first to discover and then to open a way over mountains, and through savage nations that had never yielded a passage to a regular army.[53] The Alps were then guarded by nature, they are now fortified by art. Citadels, constructed with no less skill than labour and expense, command every avenue into the plain, and on that side render Italy almost inaccessible to the enemies of the king of Sardinia.[54] But in the course of the intermediate period, the generals who have attempted the passage have seldom experienced any difficulty or resistance. In the age of Constantine the peasants of the mountains were civilised and obedient subjects; the country was plentifully stocked with provisions, and the stupendous highways which the Romans had carried over the Alps opened several communications between Gaul and Italy.[55] Constantine preferred the road of the Cottian Alps, or, as it is now called, of Mount Cenis, and led his troops with such active diligence, that he descended into the plain of Piedmont before the court of Maxentius had received any certain intelligence of his departure from the banks of the Rhine. The city of Susa, however, which is situated at the foot of Mount Cenis, was surrounded with walls, and provided with a garrison sufficiently numerous to check the progress of an invader; but the impatience of Constantine's troops disdained the tedious forms of a siege. The same day that they appeared before Susa they applied fire to the gates and ladders to the walls; and mounting to the assault amidst a shower of stones and arrows, they entered the place sword in hand, and cut in pieces the greatest part of the garrison. The flames were extinguished by the care of Constantine, and the remains of Susa preserved from total destruction. About forty miles from thence a more severe contest awaited him. A numerous army of Italians was assembled, under the lieutenants of Maxentius, in the plains of Turin. Its principal strength consisted in a species of heavy cavalry, which the Romans, since the decline of their discipline, had borrowed from the nations of the East. The horses, as well as the men, were clothed in complete armour, the joints of which were artfully adapted to the motions of their bodies. The aspect of this cavalry was formidable, their weight almost irresistible; and as, on this occasion, their generals had drawn them up in a compact column or wedge, with a sharp point, and with spreading flanks, they flattered themselves that they should easily break and trample down the army of Constantine. They might, perhaps, have succeeded in their design, had not their experienced adversary embraced the same method of defence which in similar circumstances had been practised by Aurelian. The skilful evolutions of Constantine divided and baffled this massy column of cavalry. The troops of Maxentius fled in confusion towards Turin; and as the gates of the city were shut against them, very few escaped the sword of the victorious pursuers. By this important service Turin deserved to experience the clemency and even favour of the conqueror. He made his entry into the Imperial palace of Milan, and almost all the cities of Italy between the Alps and the Po not only acknowledged the power, but embraced with zeal the party of Constantine.[56]

From Milan to Rome, the Æmilian and Flaminian highways offered an easy march of about four hundred miles; but though Constantine was impatient to encounter the tyrant, he prudently directed his operations against another army of Italians, who, by their strength and position, might either oppose his progress, or, in case of a misfortune, might intercept his retreat. Ruricius Pompeianus, a general distinguished by his valour and ability, had under his command the city of Verona, and all the troops that were stationed in the province of Venetia. As soon as he was informed that Constantine was advancing towards him, he detached a large body of cavalry, which was defeated in an engagement near Brescia, and pursued by the Gallic legions as far as the gates of Verona. The necessity, the importance, and the difficulties of the siege of Verona, immediately presented themselves to the sagacious mind of Constantine.[57] The city was accessible only by a narrow peninsula towards the west, as the other three sides were surrounded by the Adige, a rapid river, which covered the province of Venetia, from whence the besieged derived an inexhaustible supply of men and provisions. It was not without great difficulty, and after several fruitless attempts, that Constantine found means to pass the river at some distance above the city, and in a place where the torrent was less violent. He then encompassed Verona with strong lines, pushed his attacks with prudent vigour, and repelled a desperate sally of Pompeianus. That intrepid general, when he had used every means of defence that the strength of the place or that of the garrison could afford, secretly escaped from Verona, anxious not for his own but for the public safety. With indefatigable diligence he soon collected an army sufficient either to meet Constantine in the field, or to attack him if he obstinately remained within his lines. The emperor, attentive to the motions, and informed of the approach of so formidable an enemy, left a part of his legions to continue the operations of the siege, whilst, at the head of those troops on whose valour and fidelity he more particularly depended, he advanced in person to engage the general of Maxentius. The army of Gaul was drawn up in two lines, according to the usual practice of war; but their experienced leader, perceiving that the numbers of the Italians far exceeded his own, suddenly changed his disposition, and, reducing the second, extended the front of his first line to a just proportion with that of the enemy. Such evolutions, which only veteran troops can execute without confusion in a moment of danger, commonly prove decisive; but as this engagement began towards the close of the day, and was contested with great obstinacy during the whole night, there was less room for the conduct of the generals than for the courage of the soldiers. The return of light displayed the victory of Constantine, and a field of carnage covered with many thousands of the vanquished Italians. Their general, Pompeianus, was found among the slain; Verona immediately surrendered at discretion, and the garrison was made prisoners of war.[58] When the officers of the victorious army congratulated their master on this important success, they ventured to add some respectful complaints, of such a nature, however, as the most jealous monarchs will listen to without displeasure. They represented to Constantine that, not contented with performing all the duties of a commander, he had exposed his own person with an excess of valour which almost degenerated into rashness; and they conjured him for the future to pay more regard to the preservation of a life in which the safety of Rome and of the empire was involved.[59]

While Constantine signalised his conduct and valour in the field, the sovereign of Italy appeared insensible of the calamities and danger of a civil war which raged in the heart of his dominions. Pleasure was still the only business of Maxentius. Concealing, or at least attempting to conceal, from the public knowledge the misfortunes of his arms,[60] he indulged himself in a vain confidence, which deferred the remedies of the approaching evil without deferring the evil itself.[61] The rapid progress of Constantine[62] was scarcely sufficient to awaken him from this fatal security; he flattered himself that his well-known liberality and the majesty of the Roman name, which had already delivered him from two invasions, would dissipate with the same facility the rebellious army of Gaul. The officers of experience and ability who had served under the banners of Maximian were at length compelled to inform his effeminate son of the imminent danger to which he was reduced; and, with a freedom that at once surprised and convinced him, to urge the necessity of preventing his ruin by a vigorous exertion of his remaining power. The resources of Maxentius, both of men and money, were still considerable. The Prætorian guards felt how strongly their own interest and safety were connected with his cause; and a third army was soon collected, more numerous than those which had been lost in the battles of Turin and Verona. It was far from the intention of the emperor to lead his troops in person. A stranger to the exercises of war, he trembled at the apprehension of so dangerous a contest; and, as fear is commonly superstitious, he listened with melancholy attention to the rumours of omens and presages which seemed to menace his life and empire. Shame at length supplied the place of courage, and forced him to take the field. He was unable to sustain the contempt of the Roman people. The circus resounded with their indignant clamours, and they tumultuously besieged the gates of the palace, reproaching the pusillanimity of their indolent sovereign, and celebrating the heroic spirit of Constantine.[63] Before Maxentius left Rome he consulted the Sibylline books. The guardians of these ancient oracles were as well versed in the arts of this world as they were ignorant of the secrets of fate; and they returned him a very prudent answer, which might adapt itself to the event, and secure their reputation, whatever should be the chance of arms.[64]

The celerity of Constantine's march has been compared to the rapid conquest of Italy by the first of the Cæsars; nor is the flattering parallel repugnant to the truth of history, since no more than fifty-eight days elapsed between the surrender of Verona and the final decision of the war. Constantine had always apprehended that the tyrant would consult the dictates of fear, and perhaps of prudence; and that, instead of risking his last hopes in a general engagement, he would shut himself up within the walls of Rome. His ample magazines secured him against the danger of famine; and as the situation of Constantine admitted not of delay, he might have been reduced to the sad necessity of destroying with fire and sword the Imperial city, the noblest reward of his victory, and the deliverance of which had been the motive, or rather indeed the pretence, of the civil war.[65] It was with equal surprise and pleasure that, on his arrival at a place called Saxa Rubra, about nine miles from Rome,[66] he discovered the army of Maxentius prepared to give him battle.[67] Their long front filled a very spacious plain, and their deep array reached to the banks of the Tiber, which covered their rear, and forbade their retreat. We are informed, and we may believe, that Constantine disposed his troops with consummate skill, and that he chose for himself the post of honour and danger. Distinguished by the splendour of his arms, he charged in person the cavalry of his rival; and his irresistible attack determined the fortune of the day. The cavalry of Maxentius was principally composed either of unwieldy cuirassiers or of light Moors and Numidians. They yielded to the vigour of the Gallic horse, which possessed more activity than the one, more firmness than the other. The defeat of the two wings left the infantry without any protection on its flanks, and the undisciplined Italians fled without reluctance from the standard of a tyrant whom they had always hated, and whom they no longer feared. The Prætorians, conscious that their offences were beyond the reach of mercy, were animated by revenge and despair. Notwithstanding their repeated efforts, those brave veterans were unable to recover the victory; they obtained, however, an honourable death; and it was observed that their bodies covered the same ground which had been occupied by their ranks.[68] The confusion then became general, and the dismayed troops of Maxentius, pursued by an implacable enemy, rushed by thousands into the deep and rapid stream of the Tiber. The emperor himself attempted to escape back into the city over the Milvian bridge, but the crowds which pressed together through that narrow passage forced him into the river, where he was immediately drowned by the weight of his armour.[69] His body, which had sunk very deep into the mud, was found with some difficulty the next day. The sight of his head, when it was exposed to the eyes of the people, convinced them of their deliverance, and admonished them to receive with acclamations of loyalty and gratitude the fortunate Constantine, who thus achieved by his valour and ability the most splendid enterprise of his life.[70]

In the use of victory Constantine neither deserved the praise of clemency nor incurred the censure of immoderate rigour.[71] He inflicted the same treatment to which a defeat would have exposed his own person and family, put to death the two sons of the tyrant, and carefully extirpated his whole race. The most distinguished adherents of Maxentius must have expected to share his fate, as they had shared his prosperity and his crimes; but when the Roman people loudly demanded a greater number of victims, the conqueror resisted, with firmness and humanity, those servile clamours, which were dictated by flattery as well as by resentment. Informers were punished and discouraged; the innocent who had suffered under the late tyranny were recalled from exile, and restored to their estates. A general act of oblivion quieted the minds and settled the property of the people both in Italy and in Africa.[72] The first time that Constantine honoured the senate with his presence he recapitulated his own services and exploits in a modest oration, assured that illustrious order of his sincere regard, and promised to re-establish its ancient dignity and privileges.

The grateful senate repaid these unmeaning professions by the empty titles of honour which it was yet in their power to bestow; and, without presuming to ratify the authority of Constantine, they passed a decree to assign him the first rank among the three *Augusti* who governed the Roman world.[73] Games and festivals were instituted to preserve the fame of his victory, and several edifices, raised at the expense of Maxentius, were dedicated to the honour of his successful rival. The triumphal arch of Constantine still remains a melancholy proof of the decline of the arts, and a singular testimony of the meanest vanity. As it was not possible to find in the capital of the empire a sculptor who was capable of adorning that public monument, the arch of Trajan, without any respect either for his memory or for the rules of propriety, was stripped of its most elegant figures. The difference of times and persons, of actions and characters, was totally disregarded. The Parthian captives appear prostrate at the feet of a prince who never carried his arms beyond the Euphrates; and curious antiquarians can still discover the head of Trajan on the trophies of Constantine. The new ornaments which it was necessary to introduce between the vacancies of ancient sculpture are executed in the rudest and most unskilful manner.[74]

The final abolition of the Prætorian guards was a measure of prudence as well as of revenge. Those haughty troops, whose numbers and privileges had been restored, and even augmented, by Maxentius, were forever suppressed by Constantine. Their fortified camp was destroyed, and the few Prætorians who had escaped the fury of the sword were dispersed among the legions and banished to the frontiers of the empire, where they might be serviceable without again becoming dangerous.[75] By suppressing the troops which were usually stationed in Rome, Constantine gave the fatal blow to the dignity of the senate and people, and the disarmed capital was exposed, without protection, to the insults or neglect of its distant master. We may observe that, in this last effort to preserve their expiring freedom, the Romans, from the apprehension of a tribute, had raised Maxentius to the throne. He exacted that tribute from the senate under the name of a free gift. They implored the assistance of Constantine. He vanquished the tyrant, and converted the free gift into a perpetual tax. The senators, according to the declaration which was required of their property, were divided into several classes. The most opulent paid annually eight pounds of gold, the next class paid four, the last two, and those whose poverty might have claimed an exemption were assessed, however, at seven pieces of gold. Besides the regular members of the senate, their sons, their descendants, and even their relations, enjoyed the vain privileges and supported the heavy burdens of the senatorial order; nor will it any longer excite our surprise that Constantine should be attentive to increase the number of persons who were included under so useful a description.[76] After the defeat of Maxentius the victorious emperor passed no more than two or three months in Rome, which he visited twice during the remainder of his life to celebrate the solemn festivals of the tenth and of the twentieth years of his reign. Constantine was almost perpetually in motion, to exercise the legions or to inspect the state of the provinces. Treves, Milan, Aquileia, Sirmium, Naissus, and Thessalonica were the occasional places of his residence till he founded a NEW ROME on the confines of Europe and Asia.[77]

Before Constantine marched into Italy he had secured the friendship, or at least the neutrality, of Licinius, the Illyrian emperor. He had promised his sister Constantia in marriage to that prince; but the celebration of the nuptials was deferred till after the conclusion of the war, and the interview of the two emperors at Milan, which was appointed for that purpose, appeared to cement the union of their families and interests.[78] In the midst of the public festivity they were suddenly obliged to take leave of each other. An inroad of the Franks summoned Constantine to the Rhine, and the hostile approach of the sovereign of Asia demanded the immediate presence of Licinius. Maximin had been the secret ally of Maxentius, and, without being discouraged by his fate, he resolved to try the fortune of a civil war. He moved out of Syria, towards the frontiers of Bithynia, in the depth of winter. The season was severe and tempestuous; great numbers of men as well as horses perished in the snow; and as the roads were broken up by incessant rains, he was obliged to leave behind him a considerable part of the heavy baggage, which was unable to follow the rapidity of his forced marches. By this extraordinary effort of diligence, he arrived, with a harassed but formidable army, on the banks of the Thracian Bosphorus before the lieutenants of Licinius were apprised of his hostile intentions. Byzantium surrendered to the power of Maximin after a siege of eleven days. He was detained some days under the walls of Heraclea; and he had no sooner taken posses-

sion of that city than he was alarmed by the intelligence that Licinius had pitched his camp at the distance of only eighteen miles. After a fruitless negotiation, in which the two princes attempted to seduce the fidelity of each other's adherents, they had recourse to arms. The emperor of the East commanded a disciplined and veteran army of above seventy thousand men; and Licinius, who had collected about thirty thousand Illyrians, was at first oppressed by the superiority of numbers. His military skill and the firmness of his troops restored the day and obtained a decisive victory. The incredible speed which Maximin exerted in his flight is much more celebrated than his prowess in the battle. Twenty-four hours afterwards he was seen pale, trembling, and without his Imperial ornaments, at Nicomedia, one hundred and sixty miles from the place of his defeat. The wealth of Asia was yet unexhausted; and though the flower of his veterans had fallen in the late action, he had still power, if he could obtain time, to draw very numerous levies from Syria and Egypt. But he survived his misfortune only three or four months. His death, which happened at Tarsus, was variously ascribed to despair, to poison, and to the divine justice. As Maximin was alike destitute of abilities and of virtue, he was lamented neither by the people nor by the soldiers. The provinces of the East, delivered from the terrors of civil war, cheerfully acknowledged the authority of Licinius.[79]

The vanquished emperor left behind him two children, a boy of about eight, and a girl of about seven, years old. Their inoffensive age might have excited compassion; but the compassion of Licinius was a very feeble resource, nor did it restrain him from *extinguishing* the name and memory of his adversary. The death of Severianus will admit of less excuse, as it was dictated neither by revenge nor by policy. The conqueror had never received any injury from the father of that unhappy youth, and the short and obscure reign of Severus, in a distant part of the empire, was already forgotten. But the execution of Candidianus was an act of the blackest cruelty and ingratitude. He was the natural son of Galerius, the friend and benefactor of Licinius. The prudent father had judged him too young to sustain the weight of a diadem; but he hoped that, under the protection of princes who were indebted to his favour for the Imperial purple, Candidianus might pass a secure and honourable life. He was now advancing towards the twentieth year of his age, and the royalty of his birth, though unsupported either by merit or ambition, was sufficient to exasperate the jealous mind of Licinius.[80] To these innocent and illustrious victims of his tyranny we must add the wife and daughter of the emperor Diocletian. When that prince conferred on Galerius the title of Cæsar, he had given him in marriage his daughter Valeria, whose melancholy adventures might furnish a very singular subject for tragedy. She had fulfilled and even surpassed the duties of a wife. As she had not any children herself, she condescended to adopt the illegitimate son of her husband, and invariably displayed towards the unhappy Candidianus the tenderness and anxiety of a real mother. After the death of Galerius, her ample possessions provoked the avarice, and her personal attractions excited the desires, of his successor, Maximin.[81] He had a wife still alive; but divorce was permitted by the Roman law, and the fierce passions of the tyrant demanded an immediate gratification. The answer of Valeria was such as became the daughter and widow of emperors; but it was tempered by the prudence which her defenceless condition compelled her to observe. She represented to the persons whom Maximin had employed on this occasion, "that, even if honour could permit a woman of her character and dignity to entertain a thought of second nuptials, decency at least must forbid her to listen to his addresses at a time when the ashes of her husband and his benefactor were still warm, and while the sorrows of her mind were still expressed by her mourning garments. She ventured to declare that she could place very little confidence in the professions of a man whose cruel inconstancy was capable of repudiating a faithful and affectionate wife."[82] On this repulse, the love of Maximin was converted into fury; and as witnesses and judges were always at his disposal, it was easy for him to cover his fury with an appearance of legal proceedings, and to assault the reputation as well as the happiness of Valeria. Her estates were confiscated, her eunuchs and domestics devoted to the most inhuman tortures; and several innocent and respectable matrons, who were honoured with her friendship, suffered death, on a false accusation of adultery. The empress herself, together with her mother Prisca, was condemned to exile; and as they were ignominiously hurried from place to place before they were confined to a sequestered village in the deserts of Syria, they exposed their shame and distress to the provinces of the East, which, during thirty years, had respected their august dignity. Diocletian made

several ineffectual efforts to alleviate the misfortunes of his daughter; and, as the last return that he expected for the Imperial purple, which he had conferred upon Maximin, he entreated that Valeria might be permitted to share his retirement of Salona, and to close the eyes of her afflicted father.[83] He entreated; but as he could no longer threaten, his prayers were received with coldness and disdain; and the pride of Maximin was gratified in treating Diocletian as a suppliant, and his daughter as a criminal. The death of Maximin seemed to assure the empresses of a favourable alteration in their fortune. The public disorders relaxed the vigilance of their guard, and they easily found means to escape from the place of their exile, and to repair, though with some precaution, and in disguise, to the court of Licinius. His behaviour, in the first days of his reign, and the honourable reception which he gave to young Candidianus, inspired Valeria with a secret satisfaction, both on her own account, and on that of her adopted son. But these grateful prospects were soon succeeded by horror and astonishment; and the bloody executions which stained the palace of Nicomedia sufficiently convinced her that the throne of Maximin was filled by a tyrant more inhuman than himself. Valeria consulted her safety by a hasty flight, and, still accompanied by her mother Prisca, they wandered above fifteen months[84] through the provinces, concealed in the disguise of plebeian habits. They were at length discovered at Thessalonica; and as the sentence of their death was already pronounced, they were immediately beheaded, and their bodies thrown into the sea. The people gazed on the melancholy spectacle; but their grief and indignation were suppressed by the terrors of a military guard. Such was the unworthy fate of the wife and daughter of Diocletian. We lament their misfortunes, we cannot discover their crimes; and whatever idea we may justly entertain of the cruelty of Licinius, it remains a matter of surprise that he was not contented with some more secret and decent method of revenge.[85]

The Roman world was now divided between Constantine and Licinius, the former of whom was master of the West, and the latter of the East. It might perhaps have been expected that the conquerors, fatigued with civil war, and connected by a private as well as public alliance, would have renounced, or at least would have suspended, any farther designs of ambition. And yet a year had scarcely elapsed after the death of Maximin, before the victorious emperors turned their arms against each other. The genius, the success, and the aspiring temper of Constantine, may seem to mark him out as the aggressor; but the perfidious character of Licinius justifies the most unfavourable suspicions, and by the faint light which history reflects on this transaction[86] we may discover a conspiracy fomented by his arts against the authority of his colleague. Constantine had lately given his sister Anastasia in marriage to Bassianus, a man of a considerable family and fortune, and had elevated his new kinsman to the rank of Cæsar. According to the system of government instituted by Diocletian, Italy, and perhaps Africa, were designed for his department in the empire. But the performance of the promised favour was either attended with so much delay, or accompanied with so many unequal conditions, that the fidelity of Bassianus was alienated rather than secured by the honourable distinction which he had obtained. His nomination had been ratified by the consent of Licinius; and that artful prince, by the means of his emissaries, soon contrived to enter into a secret and dangerous correspondence with the new Cæsar, to irritate his discontents, and to urge him to the rash enterprise of extorting by violence what he might in vain solicit from the justice of Constantine. But the vigilant emperor discovered the conspiracy before it was ripe for execution; and, after solemnly renouncing the alliance of Bassianus, despoiled him of the purple, and inflicted the deserved punishment on his treason and ingratitude. The haughty refusal of Licinius, when he was required to deliver up the criminals who had taken refuge in his dominions, confirmed the suspicions already entertained of his perfidy; and the indignities offered at Æmona, on the frontiers of Italy, to the statues of Constantine, became the signal of discord between the two princes.[87]

The first battle was fought near Cibalis, a city of Pannonia, situated on the river Save, about fifty miles above Sirmium.[88] From the inconsiderable forces which in this important contest two such powerful monarchs brought into the field, it may be inferred that the one was suddenly provoked, and that the other was unexpectedly surprised. The emperor of the West had only twenty thousand, and the sovereign of the East no more than five-and-thirty thousand, men. The inferiority of number was, however, compensated by the advantage of the ground. Constantine had taken post in a defile about half a mile in breadth, between a steep hill and a deep morass, and in that situation he steadily expected and repulsed the first attack of the enemy. He pursued his success and advanced into the plain. But the veteran legions of Illyricum rallied under the standard of a leader who had been trained to arms in the school of Probus and Diocletian. The missile weapons on both sides were soon exhausted; the two armies, with equal valour, rushed to a closer engagement of swords and spears, and the doubtful contest had already lasted from the dawn of the day to a late hour of the evening, when the right wing, which Constantine led in person, made a vigorous and decisive charge. The judicious retreat of Licinius saved the remainder of his troops from a total defeat; but when he computed his loss, which amounted to more than twenty thousand men, he thought it unsafe to pass the night in the presence of an active and victorious enemy. Abandoning his camp and magazines, he marched away with secrecy and diligence at the head of the greatest part of his cavalry, and was soon removed beyond the danger of a pursuit. His diligence preserved his wife, his son, and his treasures, which he had deposited at Sirmium. Licinius passed through that city, and, breaking down the bridge on the Save, hastened to collect a new army in Dacia and Thrace. In his flight he bestowed the precarious title of Cæsar on Valens, his general of the Illyrian frontier.[89]

The plain of Mardia in Thrace was the theatre of a second battle no less obstinate and bloody than the former. The troops on both sides displayed the same valour and discipline; and the victory was once more decided by the superior abilities of Constantine, who directed a body of five thousand men to gain an advantageous height, from whence, during the heat of the action, they attacked the rear of the enemy, and made a very considerable slaughter. The troops of Licinius, however, presenting a double front, still maintained their ground till the approach of night put an end to the combat, and secured their retreat towards the mountains of Macedonia.[90] The loss of two battles, and of his bravest veterans, reduced the fierce spirit of Licinius to sue for peace. His ambassador, Mistrianus, was admitted to the audience of Constantine: he expatiated on the common topics of moderation and humanity, which are so familiar to the eloquence of the vanquished; represented in the most insinuating language that the event of the war was still doubtful, whilst its inevitable calamities were alike pernicious to both the contending parties; and declared that he was authorised to propose a lasting and honourable peace in the name of the *two* emperors his masters. Constantine received the mention of Valens with indignation and contempt. "It was not for such a purpose," he sternly replied, "that we have advanced from the shores of the western ocean in an uninterrupted course of combats and victories, that, after rejecting an ungrateful kinsman, we should accept for our colleague a contemptible slave. The abdication of Valens is the first article of the treaty."[91] It was necessary to accept this humiliating condition; and the unhappy Valens, after a reign of a few days, was deprived of the purple and of his life. As soon as this obstacle was removed, the tranquillity of the Roman world was easily restored. The successive defeats of Licinius had ruined his forces, but they had displayed his courage and abilities. His situation was almost desperate, but the efforts of despair are sometimes formidable, and the good sense of Constantine preferred a great and certain advantage to a third trial of the chance of arms. He consented to leave his rival, or, as he again styled Licinius, his friend and brother, in the possession of Thrace, Asia Minor, Syria, and Egypt; but the provinces of Pannonia, Dalmatia, Dacia, Macedonia, and Greece were yielded to the Western empire, and the dominions of Constantine now extended from the confines of Caledonia to the extremity of Peloponnesus. It was stipulated by the same treaty that three royal youths, the sons of the emperors, should be called to the hopes of the succession. Crispus and the young Constantine were soon afterwards declared Cæsars in the West, while the younger Licinius was invested with the same dignity in the East. In this double proportion of honours, the conqueror asserted the superiority of his arms and power.[92]

The reconciliation of Constantine and Licinius, though it was embittered by resentment and jealousy, by the remembrance of recent injuries, and by the apprehension of future dangers, maintained, however, above eight years, the tranquillity of the Roman world. As a very regular series of the Imperial laws commences about this period, it would not be difficult to transcribe the civil regulations which employed the leisure of Constantine. But the most important of his institutions are intimately connected with the new system of policy and religion, which was not perfectly established till the last and peaceful years of his reign. There are many of his laws which, as far as they concern the rights of property of individuals, and the practice of the bar, are more properly referred to the private than to the public jurisprudence of the empire; and he published many edicts of so local and temporary a nature that they would ill deserve the notice of a general history. Two laws, however, may be selected from the crowd; the one for its importance, the other for its singularity; the former for its remarkable benevolence, the latter for its excessive severity. 1. The horrid practice, so familiar to the ancients, of exposing or murdering their new-born infants, was becoming every day more frequent in the provinces, and especially in Italy. It was the effect of distress; and the distress was principally occasioned by the intolerable burden of taxes, and by the vexatious as well as cruel prosecutions of the officers of the revenue against their insolvent debtors. The less opulent or less industrious part of mankind, instead of rejoicing in an increase of family, deemed it an act of paternal tenderness to release their children from the impending miseries of a life which they themselves were unable to support. The humanity of Constantine, moved, perhaps, by some recent and extraordinary instances of despair, engaged him to address an edict to all the cities of Italy, and afterwards of Africa, directing immediate and sufficient relief to be given to those parents who should produce before the magistrates the children whom their own poverty would not allow them to educate. But the promise was too liberal, and the provision too vague, to effect any general or permanent benefit.[93] The law, though it may merit some praise, served rather to display than to alleviate the public distress. It still remains an authentic monument to contradict and confound those venal orators who were too well satisfied with their own situation to discover either vice or misery under the government of a generous sovereign.[94] 2. The laws of Constantine against rapes were dictated with very little indulgence for the most amiable weaknesses of human nature; since the description of that crime was applied not only to the brutal violence which compelled, but even to the gentle seduction which might persuade, an unmarried woman, under the age of twenty-five, to leave the house of her parents. "The successful ravisher was punished with death; and as if simple death was inadequate to the enormity of his guilt, he was either burnt alive, or torn in pieces by wild beasts in the amphitheatre. The virgin's declaration that she had been carried away with her own consent, instead of saving her lover, exposed her to share his fate. The duty of a public prosecution was intrusted to the parents of the guilty or unfortunate maid; and if the sentiments of nature prevailed on them to dissemble the injury, and to repair by a subsequent marriage the honour of their family, they were themselves punished by exile and confiscation. The slaves, whether male or female, who were convicted of having been accessary to the rape or seduction, were burnt alive, or put to death by the ingenious torture of pouring down their throats a quantity of melted lead. As the crime was of a public kind, the accusation was permitted even to strangers. The commencement of the action was not limited to any term of years, and the consequences of the sentence were extended to the innocent offspring of such an irregular union."[95] But whenever the offence inspires less horror than the punishment, the rigour of penal law is obliged to give way to the common feelings of mankind. The most odious parts of this edict were softened or repealed in the subsequent reigns;[96] and even Constantine himself very frequently alleviated, by partial acts of mercy, the stern temper of his general institutions. Such, indeed, was the singular humour of that emperor, who showed himself as indulgent, and even remiss, in the execution of his laws, as he was severe, and even cruel, in the enacting of them. It is scarcely possible to observe a more decisive symptom of weakness, either in the character of the prince, or in the constitution of the government.[97]

The civil administration was sometimes interrupted by the military defence of the empire. Crispus, a youth of the most amiable character, who had received with the title of Cæsar the command of the Rhine, distinguished his conduct as well as valour in several victories over the Franks and Alemanni, and taught the barbarians of that frontier to dread the eldest son of Constantine, and the grandson of Constantius.[98] The emperor himself had assumed the more difficult and important province of the Danube. The Goths, who in the time of Claudius and Aurelian had felt the weight of the Roman arms, respected the power of the empire, even in the midst of its intestine divisions. But the strength of that warlike nation was now restored by a peace of near fifty years; a new generation had arisen, who no longer remembered the misfortunes of ancient days: the Sarmatians of the lake Mæotis followed the Gothic standard either as subjects or as allies, and their united force was poured upon the countries of Illyricum. Campona, Margus, and Bononia, appear to have been the scenes of several memorable sieges and battles;[99] and though Constantine

encountered a very obstinate resistance, he prevailed at length in the contest, and the Goths were compelled to purchase an ignominious retreat by restoring the booty and prisoners which they had taken. Nor was this advantage sufficient to satisfy the indignation of the emperor. He resolved to chastise as well as to repulse the insolent barbarians who had dared to invade the territories of Rome. At the head of his legions he passed the Danube, after repairing the bridge which had been constructed by Trajan, penetrated into the strongest recesses of Dacia,[100] and, when he had inflicted a severe revenge, condescended to give peace to the suppliant Goths, on condition that, as often as they were required, they should supply his armies with a body of forty thousand soldiers.[101] Exploits like these were no doubt honourable to Constantine and beneficial to the state; but it may surely be questioned whether they can justify the exaggerated assertion of Eusebius, that ALL SCYTHIA, as far as the extremity of the North, divided as it was into so many names and nations of the most various and savage manners, had been added by his victorious arms to the Roman empire.[102]

In this exalted state of glory it was impossible that Constantine should any longer endure a partner in the empire. Confiding in the superiority of his genius and military power, he determined, without any previous injury, to exert them for the destruction of Licinius, whose advanced age and unpopular vices seemed to offer a very easy conquest.[103] But the old emperor, awakened by the approaching danger, deceived the expectations of his friends as well as of his enemies. Calling forth that spirit and those abilities by which he had deserved the friendship of Galerius and the Imperial purple, he prepared himself for the contest, collected the forces of the East, and soon filled the plains of Hadrianople with his troops, and the Straits of the Hellespont with his fleet. The army consisted of one hundred and fifty thousand foot and fifteen thousand horse; and as the cavalry was drawn, for the most part, from Phrygia and Cappadocia, we may conceive a more favourable opinion of the beauty of the horses than of the courage and dexterity of their riders. The fleet was composed of three hundred and fifty galleys of three ranks of oars. An hundred and thirty of these were furnished by Egypt and the adjacent coast of Africa. An hundred and ten sailed from the ports of Phœnicia and the isle of Cyprus; and the maritime countries of Bithynia, Ionia, and Caria were likewise obliged to provide an hundred and ten galleys. The troops of Constantine were ordered to rendezvous at Thessalonica; they amounted to above an hundred and twenty thousand horse and foot.[104] Their emperor was satisfied with their martial appearance, and his army contained more soldiers, though fewer men, than that of his eastern competitor. The legions of Constantine were levied in the warlike provinces of Europe; action had confirmed their discipline, victory had elevated their hopes, and there were among them a great number of veterans, who, after seventeen glorious campaigns under the same leader, prepared themselves to deserve an honourable dismission by a last effort of their valour.[105] But the naval preparations of Constantine were in every respect much inferior to those of Licinius. The maritime cities of Greece sent their respective quotas of men and ships to the celebrated harbour of Piræus and their united forces consisted of no more than two hundred small vessels; a very feeble armament, if it is compared with those formidable fleets which were equipped and maintained by the republic of Athens during the Peloponnesian war.[106] Since Italy was no longer the seat of government, the naval establishments of Misenum and Ravenna had been gradually neglected; and as the shipping and mariners of the empire were supported by commerce rather than by war, it was natural that they should the most abound in the industrious provinces of Egypt and Asia. It is only surprising that the eastern emperor, who possessed so great a superiority at sea, should have neglected the opportunity of carrying an offensive war into the centre of his rival's dominions.

Instead of embracing such an active resolution, which might have changed the whole face of the war, the prudent Licinius expected the approach of his rival in a camp near Hadrianople, which he had fortified with an anxious care that betrayed his apprehension of the event. Constantine directed his march from Thessalonica towards that part of Thrace, till he found himself stopped by the broad and rapid stream of the Hebrus, and discovered the numerous army of Licinius, which filled the steep ascent of the hill, from the river to the city of Hadrianople. Many days were spent in doubtful and distant skirmishes; but at length the obstacles of the passage and of the attack were removed by the intrepid conduct of Constantine. In this place we might relate a wonderful exploit of Constantine, which, though it can scarcely be paralleled either in poetry or romance, is cele-

brated, not by a venal orator devoted to his fortune, but by an historian, the partial enemy of his fame. We are assured that the valiant emperor threw himself into the river Hebrus accompanied only by *twelve* horsemen, and that by the effort or terror of his invincible arm, he broke, slaughtered, and put to flight a host of an hundred and fifty thousand men. The credulity of Zosimus prevailed so strongly over his passion that, among the events of the memorable battle of Hadrianople, he seems to have selected and embellished, not the most important, but the most marvellous. The valour and danger of Constantine are attested by a slight wound which he received in the thigh; but it may be discovered, even from an imperfect narration, and perhaps a corrupted text, that the victory was obtained no less by the conduct of the general than by the courage of the hero; that a body of five thousand archers marched round to occupy a thick wood in the rear of the enemy, whose attention was diverted by the construction of a bridge; and that Licinius, perplexed by so many artful evolutions, was reluctantly drawn from his advantageous post to combat on equal ground in the plain. The contest was no longer equal. His confused multitude of new levies was easily vanquished by the experienced veterans of the West. Thirty-four thousand men are reported to have been slain. The fortified camp of Licinius was taken by assault the evening of the battle; the greater part of the fugitives, who had retired to the mountains, surrendered themselves the next day to the discretion of the conqueror; and his rival, who could no longer keep the field, confined himself within the walls of Byzantium.[107]

The siege of Byzantium, which was immediately undertaken by Constantine, was attended with great labour and uncertainty. In the late civil wars, the fortifications of that place, so justly considered as the key of Europe and Asia, had been repaired and strengthened; and as long as Licinius remained master of the sea, the garrison was much less exposed to the danger of famine than the army of the besiegers. The naval commanders of Constantine were summoned to his camp, and received his positive orders to force the passage of the Hellespont, as the fleet of Licinius, instead of seeking and destroying their feeble enemy, continued inactive in those narrow straits, where its superiority of numbers was of little use or advantage. Crispus, the emperor's eldest son, was intrusted with the execution of this daring enterprise, which he performed with so much courage and success, that he deserved the esteem, and most probably excited the jealousy, of his father. The engagement lasted two days; and in the evening of the first, the contending fleets, after a considerable and mutual loss, retired into their respective harbours of Europe and Asia. The second day about noon a strong south wind[108] sprang up, which carried the vessels of Crispus against the enemy; and as the casual advantage was improved by his skilful intrepidity, he soon obtained a complete victory. An hundred and thirty vessels were destroyed, five thousand men were slain, and Amandus, the admiral of the Asiatic fleet, escaped with the utmost difficulty to the shores of Chalcedon. As soon as the Hellespont was open, a plentiful convoy of provisions flowed into the camp of Constantine, who had already advanced the operations of the siege. He constructed artificial mounds of earth of an equal height with the ramparts of Byzantium. The lofty towers which were erected on that foundation galled the besieged with large stones and darts from the military engines, and the battering rams had shaken the walls in several places. If Licinius persisted much longer in the defence, he exposed himself to be involved in the ruin of the place. Before he was surrounded, he prudently removed his person and treasures to Chalcedon in Asia; and as he was always desirous of associating companions to the hopes and dangers of his fortune, he now bestowed the title of Cæsar on Martinianus, who exercised one of the most important offices of the empire.[109]

Such were still the resources, and such the abilities, of Licinius that, after so many successive defeats, he collected in Bithynia a new army of fifty or sixty thousand men, while the activity of Constantine was employed in the siege of Byzantium. The vigilant emperor did not, however, neglect the last struggles of his antagonist. A considerable part of his victorious army was transported over the Bosphorus in small vessels, and the decisive engagement was fought soon after their landing on the heights of Chrysopolis, or, as it is now called, of Scutari. The troops of Licinius, though they were lately raised, ill armed, and worse disciplined, made head against their conquerors with fruitless but desperate valour, till a total defeat, and the slaughter of five-and-twenty thousand men, irretrievably determined the fate of their leader.[110] He retired to Nicomedia, rather with the view of gaining some time for negotiation than with the hope of any effectual defence. Constantia, his wife, and the sister of Constantine, interceded

with her brother in favour of her husband, and obtained from his policy, rather than from his compassion, a solemn promise, confirmed by an oath, that after the sacrifice of Martinianus, and the resignation of the purple, Licinius himself should be permitted to pass the remainder of his life in peace and affluence. The behaviour of Constantia, and her relation to the contending parties, naturally recalls the remembrance of that virtuous matron who was the sister of Augustus and the wife of Antony. But the temper of mankind was altered, and it was no longer esteemed infamous for a Roman to survive his honour and independence. Licinius solicited and accepted the pardon of his offences, laid himself and his purple at the feet of his *lord* and *master*, was raised from the ground with insulting pity, was admitted the same day to the imperial banquet, and soon afterwards was sent away to Thessalonica, which had been chosen for the place of his confinement.[111] His confinement was soon terminated by death, and it is doubtful whether a tumult of the soldiers, or a decree of the senate, was suggested as the motive for his execution. According to the rules of tyranny, he was accused of forming a conspiracy, and of holding a treasonable correspondence with the barbarians; but as he was never convicted, either by his own conduct or by any legal evidence, we may perhaps be allowed, from his weakness, to presume his innocence.[112] The memory of Licinius was branded with infamy, his statues were thrown down, and by a hasty edict, of such mischievous tendency that it was almost immediately corrected, all his laws and all the judicial proceedings of his reign were at once abolished.[113] By this victory of Constantine the Roman world was again united under the authority of one emperor, thirty-seven years after Diocletian had divided his power and provinces with his associate Maximian.

The successive steps of the elevation of Constantine, from his first assuming the purple at York, to the resignation of Licinius at Nicomedia, have been related with some minuteness and precision, not only as the events are in themselves both interesting and important, but still more as they contributed to the decline of the empire by the expense of blood and treasure, and by the perpetual increase, as well of the taxes as of the military establishment. The foundation of Constantinople, and the establishment of the Christian religion, were the immediate and memorable consequences of this revolution.

CHAPTER XV

The Progress of the Christian Religion, and the Sentiments, Manners, Numbers, and Condition of the Primitive Christians.

A CANDID but rational inquiry into the progress and establishment of Christianity may be considered as a very essential part of the history of the Roman empire. While that great body was invaded by open violence, or undermined by slow decay, a pure and humble religion gently insinuated itself into the minds of men, grew up in silence and obscurity, derived new vigour from opposition, and finally erected the triumphant banner of the Cross on the ruins of the Capitol. Nor was the influence of Christianity confined to the period or to the limits of the Roman empire. After a revolution of thirteen or fourteen centuries, that religion is still professed by the nations of Europe, the most distinguished portion of human kind in arts and learning as well as in arms. By the industry and zeal of the Europeans it has been widely diffused to the most distant shores of Asia and Africa; and by the means of their colonies has been firmly established from Canada to Chili, in a world unknown to the ancients.

But this inquiry, however useful or entertaining, is attended with two peculiar difficulties. The scanty and suspicious materials of ecclesiastical history seldom enable us to dispel the dark cloud that hangs over the first age of the church. The great law of impartiality too often obliges us to reveal the imperfections of the uninspired teachers and believers of the Gospel; and, to a careless observer, *their* faults may seem to cast a shade on the faith which they professed. But the scandal of the pious Christian, and the fallacious triumph of the Infidel, should cease as soon as they recollect not only *by whom*, but likewise *to whom*, the Divine Revelation was given. The theologian may indulge the pleasing task of describing Religion as she descended from Heaven, arrayed in her native purity. A more melancholy duty is imposed on the historian. He must discover the inevitable mixture of error and corruption which she contracted in a long residence upon earth, among a weak and degenerate race of beings.

Our curiosity is naturally prompted to inquire by what means the Christian faith obtained so remarkable a victory over the established religions of the earth. To this inquiry an obvious but unsatisfactory answer may be returned; that it was owing to the convincing evidence of the doctrine itself, and to the ruling providence of its great Author. But as truth and reason seldom find so favourable a reception in the world, and as the wisdom of Providence frequently condescends to use the passions of the human heart, and the general circumstances of mankind, as instruments to execute its purpose, we may still be permitted, though with becoming submission, to ask, not indeed what were the first, but what were the secondary causes of the rapid growth of the Christian church? It will, perhaps, appear that it was most effectually favoured and assisted by the five following causes: —I. The inflexible, and, if we may use the expression, the intolerant zeal of the Christians, derived, it is true, from the Jewish religion, but purified from the narrow and unsocial spirit which, instead of inviting, had deterred the Gentiles from embracing the law of Moses. II. The doctrine of a future life, improved by every additional circumstance which could give weight and efficacy to that important truth. III. The miraculous powers ascribed to the primitive church. IV. The pure and austere morals of the Christians. V. The union and discipline of the Christian republic, which gradually formed an independent and increasing state in the heart of the Roman empire.

I. We have already described the religious harmony of the ancient world, and the facility with which the most different and even hostile nations embraced, or at least respected, each other's superstitions. A single people refused to join in the common intercourse of mankind. The Jews, who, under the Assyrian and Persian monarchies, had languished for many ages the most despised portion of their slaves,[1] emerged from obscurity under the successors of Alexander; and as they multiplied to a surprising degree in the East, and afterwards in the West, they soon excited the curiosity and wonder of other nations.[2] The sullen obstinacy with which they maintained their peculiar rites and unsocial manners seemed to mark them out a distinct species of men, who boldly professed, or who faintly disguised, their implacable hatred to the rest of human-kind.[3] Neither the violence of Antiochus, nor the arts of Herod, nor the example of the circumjacent nations, could ever persuade the Jews to associate with the institutions of Moses the elegant mythology of the Greeks.[4] According to the maxims of universal toleration, the Romans protected a superstition which they despised.[5] The polite Augustus condescended to give orders that sacrifices should be offered for his prosperity in the temple of Jerusalem;[6] while the meanest of the posterity of Abraham, who should have paid the same homage to the Jupiter of the Capitol, would have been an object of abhorrence to himself and to his brethren. But the moderation of the conquerors was insufficient to appease the jealous prejudices of their subjects, who were alarmed and scandalised at the ensigns of paganism, which necessarily introduced themselves into a Roman province.[7] The mad attempt of Caligula to place his own statue in the temple of Jerusalem was defeated by the unanimous resolution of a people who dreaded death much less than such an idolatrous profanation.[8] Their attachment to the law of Moses was equal to their detestation of foreign religions. The current of zeal and devotion, as it was contracted into a narrow channel, ran with the strength, and sometimes with the fury, of a torrent.

This inflexible perseverance, which appeared so odious or so ridiculous to the ancient world, assumes a more awful character, since Providence has deigned to reveal to us the mysterious history of the chosen people. But the devout and even scrupulous attachment to the Mosaic religion, so conspicuous among the Jews who lived under the second temple, becomes still more surprising if it is compared with the stubborn incredulity of their forefathers. When the law was given in thunder from Mount Sinai; when the tides of the ocean and the course of the planets were suspended for the convenience of the Israelites; and when temporal rewards and punishments were the immediate consequences of their piety or disobedience, they perpetually relapsed into rebellion against the visible majesty of their Divine King, placed the idols of the nations in the sanctuary of Jehovah, and imitated every fantastic ceremony that was practised in the tents of the Arabs, or in the cities of Phœnicia.[9] As the protection of Heaven was deservedly withdrawn from the ungrateful race, their faith acquired a proportionable degree of vigour and purity. The contemporaries of Moses and Joshua had beheld with careless indifference the most amazing miracles. Under the pressure of every calamity, the belief of those miracles has preserved the Jews of a later period

from the universal contagion of idolatry; and in contradiction to every known principle of the human mind, that singular people seems to have yielded a stronger and more ready assent to the traditions of their remote ancestors than to the evidence of their own senses.[10]

The Jewish religion was admirably fitted for defence, but it was never designed for conquest; and it seems probable that the number of proselytes was never much superior to that of apostates. The divine promises were originally made, and the distinguishing rite of circumcision was enjoined, to a single family. When the posterity of Abraham had multiplied like the sands of the sea, the Deity, from whose mouth they received a system of laws and ceremonies, declared himself the proper and as it were the national God of Israel; and with the most jealous care separated his favourite people from the rest of mankind. The conquest of the land of Canaan was accompanied with so many wonderful and with so many bloody circumstances, that the victorious Jews were left in a state of irreconcilable hostility with all their neighbours. They had been commanded to extirpate some of the most idolatrous tribes, and the execution of the Divine will had seldom been retarded by the weakness of humanity. With the other nations they were forbidden to contract any marriages or alliances; and the prohibition of receiving them into the congregation, which in some cases was perpetual, almost always extended to the third, to the seventh, or even to the tenth generation. The obligation of preaching to the Gentiles the faith of Moses had never been inculcated as a precept of the law, nor were the Jews inclined to impose it on themselves as a voluntary duty.

In the admission of new citizens that unsocial people was actuated by the selfish vanity of the Greeks rather than by the generous policy of Rome. The descendants of Abraham were flattered by the opinion that they alone were the heirs of the covenant, and they were apprehensive of diminishing the value of their inheritance by sharing it too easily with the strangers of the earth. A larger acquaintance with mankind extended their knowledge without correcting their prejudices; and whenever the God of Israel acquired any new votaries, he was much more indebted to the inconstant humour of polytheism than to the active zeal of his own missionaries.[11] The religion of Moses seems to be instituted for a particular country as well as for a single nation; and if a strict obedience had been paid to the order that every male, three times in the year, should present himself before the Lord Jehovah, it would have been impossible that the Jews could ever have spread themselves beyond the narrow limits of the promised land.[12] That obstacle was indeed removed by the destruction of the temple of Jerusalem; but the most considerable part of the Jewish religion was involved in its destruction; and the Pagans, who had long wondered at the strange report of an empty sanctuary,[13] were at a loss to discover what could be the object, or what could be the instruments, of a worship which was destitute of temples and of altars, of priests and of sacrifices. Yet even in their fallen state, the Jews, still asserting their lofty and exclusive privileges, shunned, instead of courting, the society of strangers. They still insisted with inflexible rigour on those parts of the law which it was in their power to practise. Their peculiar distinctions of days, of meats, and a variety of trivial though burdensome observances, were so many objects of disgust and aversion for the other nations, to whose habits and prejudices they were diametrically opposite. The painful and even dangerous rite of circumcision was alone capable of repelling a willing proselyte from the door of the synagogue.[14]

Under these circumstances, Christianity offered itself to the world, armed with the strength of the Mosaic law, and delivered from the weight of its fetters. An exclusive zeal for the truth of religion and the unity of God was as carefully inculcated in the new as in the ancient system: and whatever was now revealed to mankind concerning the nature and designs of the Supreme Being was fitted to increase their reverence for that mysterious doctrine. The divine authority of Moses and the prophets was admitted, and even established, as the firmest basis of Christianity. From the beginning of the world an uninterrupted series of predictions had announced and prepared the long-expected coming of the Messiah, who, in compliance with the gross apprehensions of the Jews, had been more frequently represented under the character of a King and Conqueror, than under that of a Prophet, a Martyr, and the Son of God. By his expiatory sacrifice the imperfect sacrifices of the temple were at once consummated and abolished. The ceremonial law, which consisted only of types and figures, was succeeded by a pure and spiritual worship, equally adapted to all climates, as well as to every condition of mankind; and to the initiation of blood, was substituted a more harmless initiation of water. The promise of divine favour, instead of being partially confined to the posterity of Abraham, was universally proposed to the freeman and the slave, to the Greek and to the barbarian, to the Jew and to the Gentile. Every privilege that could raise the proselyte from earth to heaven, that could exalt his devotion, secure his happiness, or even gratify that secret pride which, under the semblance of devotion, insinuates itself into the human heart, was still reserved for the members of the Christian church; but at the same time all mankind was permitted, and even solicited, to accept the glorious distinction, which was not only proffered as a favour, but imposed as an obligation. It became the most sacred duty of a new convert to diffuse among his friends and relations the inestimable blessing which he had received, and to warn them against a refusal that would be severely punished as a criminal disobedience to the will of a benevolent but all-powerful Deity.

The enfranchisement of the church from the bonds of the synagogue was a work, however, of some time and of some difficulty. The Jewish converts, who acknowledged Jesus in the character of the Messiah foretold by their ancient oracles, respected him as a prophetic teacher of virtue and religion; but they obstinately adhered to the ceremonies of their ancestors, and were desirous of imposing them on the Gentiles, who continually augmented the number of believers. These Judaising Christians seem to have argued with some degree of plausibility from the Divine origin of the Mosaic law, and from the immutable perfections of its great Author. They affirmed, that, if the Being who is the same through all eternity had designed to abolish those sacred rites which had served to distinguish his chosen people, the repeal of them would have been no less clear and solemn than their first promulgation: that, instead of those frequent declarations which either suppose or assert the perpetuity of the Mosaic religion, it would have been represented as a provisionary scheme intended to last only till the coming of the Messiah, who should instruct mankind in a more perfect mode of faith and of worship:[15] that the Messiah himself, and his disciples who conversed with him on earth, instead of authorising by their example the most minute observances of the Mosaic law,[16] would have published to the world the abolition of those useless and obsolete ceremonies, without suffering Christianity to remain during so many years obscurely confounded among the sects of the Jewish church. Arguments like these appear to have been used in the defence of the expiring cause of the Mosaic law; but the industry of our learned divines has abundantly explained the ambiguous language of the Old Testament, and the ambiguous conduct of the apostolic teachers. It was proper gradually to unfold the system of the Gospel, and to pronounce with the utmost caution and tenderness a sentence of condemnation so repugnant to the inclination and prejudices of the believing Jews.

The history of the church of Jerusalem affords a lively proof of the necessity of those precautions, and of the deep impression which the Jewish religion had made on the minds of its sectaries. The first fifteen bishops of Jerusalem were all circumcised Jews; and the congregation over which they presided united the law of Moses with the doctrine of Christ.[17] It was natural that the primitive tradition of a church which was founded only forty days after the death of Christ, and was governed almost as many years under the immediate inspection of his apostle, should be received as the standard of orthodoxy.[18] The distant churches very frequently appealed to the authority of their venerable Parent, and relieved her distresses by a liberal contribution of alms. But when numerous and opulent societies were established in the great cities of the empire, in Antioch, Alexandria, Ephesus, Corinth, and Rome, the reverence which Jerusalem had inspired to all the Christian colonies insensibly diminished. The Jewish converts, or, as they were afterwards called, the Nazarenes, who had laid the foundations of the church, soon found themselves overwhelmed by the increasing multitudes that from all the various religions of polytheism enlisted under the banner of Christ: and the Gentiles, who, with the approbation of their peculiar apostle, had rejected the intolerable weight of Mosaic ceremonies, at length refused to their more scrupulous brethren the same toleration which at first they had humbly solicited for their own practice. The ruin of the temple, of the city, and of the public religion of the Jews, was severely felt by the Nazarenes; as in their manners, though not in their faith, they maintained so intimate a connection with their impious countrymen, whose misfortunes were attributed by the Pagans to the contempt, and more justly ascribed by the Christians to the wrath, of the Supreme Deity. The Nazarenes retired from the ruins of Jerusalem to the little town of Pella beyond the Jordan, where that ancient church languished above sixty years in solitude and obscurity.[19] They still enjoyed the comfort of making frequent and devout visits to the *Holy City*, and the hope of being one day restored to those seats which both nature and religion taught them to love as well as to revere. But at length, under the reign of Hadrian, the desperate fanaticism of the Jews filled up the measure of their calamities; and the Romans, exasperated by their repeated rebellions, exercised the rights of victory with unusual rigour. The emperor founded, under the name of Ælia Capitolina, a new city on Mount Sion,[20] to which he gave the privileges of a colony; and denouncing the severest penalties against any of the Jewish people who should dare to approach its precincts, he fixed a vigilant garrison of a Roman cohort to enforce the execution of his orders. The Nazarenes had only one way left to escape the common proscription, and the force of truth was on this occasion assisted by the influence of temporal advantages. They elected Marcus for their bishop, a prelate of the race of the Gentiles, and most probably a native either of Italy or of some of the Latin provinces. At his persuasion the most considerable part of the congregation renounced the Mosaic law, in the practice of which they had persevered above a century. By this sacrifice of their habits and prejudices they purchased a free admission into the colony of Hadrian, and more firmly cemented their union with the Catholic church.[21]

When the name and honours of the church of Jerusalem had been restored to Mount Sion, the crimes of heresy and schism were imputed to the obscure remnant of the Nazarenes which refused to accompany their Latin bishop. They still preserved their former habitation of Pella, spread themselves into the villages adjacent to Damascus, and formed an inconsiderable church in the city of Berœa, or, as it is now called, of Aleppo, in Syria.[22] The name of Nazarenes was deemed too honourable for those Christian Jews, and they soon received, from the supposed poverty of their understanding, as well as of their condition, the contemptuous epithet of Ebionites.[23] In a few years after the return of the church of Jerusalem, it became a matter of doubt and controversy whether a man who sincerely acknowledged Jesus as the Messiah, but who still continued to observe the law of Moses, could possibly hope for salvation. The humane temper of Justin Martyr inclined him to answer this question in the affirmative; and though he expressed himself with the most guarded diffidence, he ventured to determine in favour of such an imperfect Christian, if he were content to practise the Mosaic ceremonies without pretending to assert their general use or necessity. But when Justin was pressed to declare the sentiment of the church, he confessed that there were very many among the orthodox Christians who not only excluded their Judaising brethren from the hope of salvation, but who declined any intercourse with them in the common offices of friendship, hospitality, and social life.[24] The more rigorous opinion prevailed, as it was natural to expect, over the milder; and an eternal bar of separation was fixed between the disciples of Moses and those of Christ. The unfortunate Ebionites, rejected from one religion as apostates, and from the other as heretics, found themselves compelled to assume a more decided character; and although some traces of that obsolete sect may be discovered as late as the fourth century, they insensibly melted away either into the church or the synagogue.[25]

While the orthodox church preserved a just medium between excessive veneration and improper contempt for the law of Moses, the various heretics deviated into equal but opposite extremes of error and extravagance. From the acknowledged truth of the Jewish religion, the Ebionites had concluded that it could never be abolished. From its supposed imperfections, the Gnostics as hastily inferred that it never was instituted by the wisdom of the Deity. There are some objections against the authority of Moses and the prophets which too readily present themselves to the sceptical mind; though they can only be derived from our ignorance of remote antiquity, and from our incapacity to form an adequate judgment of the Divine economy. These objections were eagerly embraced and as petulantly urged by the vain science of the Gnostics.[26] As those heretics were, for the most part, averse to the pleasures of sense, they morosely arraigned the polygamy of the patriarchs, the gallantries of David, and the seraglio of Solomon. The conquest of the land of Canaan, and the extirpation of the unsuspecting natives, they were at a loss how to reconcile with the common notions of humanity and justice. But when they recollected the sanguinary list of murders, of executions, and of massacres, which stain almost every page of the Jewish annals, they acknowledged that the barbarians of Palestine had exercised as much compassion towards their idolatrous enemies as they had ever shown to their friends or countrymen.[27] Passing from the sectaries of the law itself, they asserted that it was impossible that a religion which consisted only of bloody sacrifices and trifling ceremonies, and whose rewards as well as punishments were all of a carnal and temporal nature, could inspire the love of virtue, or restrain the impetuosity of passion. The Mosaic account of the creation and fall of man was treated with profane derision by the Gnostics, who would not listen with patience to the repose of the Deity after six days' labour, to the rib of Adam, the garden of Eden, the trees of life and of knowledge, the speaking serpent, the forbidden fruit, and the condemnation pronounced against human kind for the venial offence of their first progenitors.[28] The God of Israel was impiously represented by the Gnostics as a being liable to passion and to error, capricious in his favour, implacable in his resentment, meanly jealous of his superstitious worship, and confining his partial providence to a single people, and to this transitory life. In such a character they could discover none of the features of the wise and omnipotent Father of the universe.[29] They allowed that the religion of the Jews was somewhat less criminal than the idolatry of the Gentiles: but it was their fundamental doctrine that the Christ whom they adored as the first and brightest emanation of the Deity appeared upon earth to rescue mankind from their various errors, and to reveal a *new* system of truth and perfection. The most learned of the fathers, by a very singular condescension, have imprudently admitted the sophistry of the Gnostics. Acknowledging that the literal sense is repugnant to every principle of faith as well as reason, they deem themselves secure and invulnerable behind the ample veil of allegory, which they carefully spread over every tender part of the Mosaic dispensation.[30]

It has been remarked with more ingenuity than truth that the virgin purity of the church was never violated by schism or heresy before the reign of Trajan or Hadrian, about one hundred years after the death of Christ.[31] We may observe with much more propriety that, during that period, the disciples of the Messiah were indulged in a freer latitude both of faith and practice than has ever been allowed in succeeding ages. As the terms of communion were insensibly narrowed, and the spiritual authority of the prevailing party was exercised with increasing severity, many of its most respectable adherents, who were called upon to renounce, were provoked to assert their private opinions, to pursue the consequences of their mistaken principles, and openly to erect the standard of rebellion against the unity of the church. The Gnostics were distinguished as the most polite, the most learned, and the most wealthy of the Christian name; and that general appellation, which expressed a superiority of knowledge, was either assumed by their own pride, or ironically bestowed by the envy of their adversaries. They were almost without exception of the race of the Gentiles, and their principal founders seem to have been natives of Syria or Egypt, where the warmth of the climate disposes both the mind and the body to indolent and contemplative devotion. The Gnostics blended with the faith of Christ many sublime but obscure tenets, which they derived from oriental philosophy, and even from the religion of Zoroaster, concerning the eternity of matter, the existence of two principles, and the mysterious hierarchy of the invisible world.[32] As soon as they launched out into that vast abyss, they delivered themselves to the guidance of a disordered imagination; and as the paths of error are various and infinite, the Gnostics were imperceptibly divided into more than fifty particular sects,[33] of whom the most celebrated appear to have been the Basilidians, the Valentinians, the Marcionites, and, in a still later period, the Manichæans. Each of these sects could boast of its bishops and congregations, of its doctors and martyrs;[34] and, instead of the Four Gospels adopted by the church, the heretics produced a multitude of histories, in which the actions and discourses of Christ and of his apostles were adapted to their respective tenets.[35] The success of the Gnostics was rapid and extensive.[36] They covered Asia and Egypt, established themselves in Rome, and sometimes penetrated into the provinces of the West. For the most part they arose in the second century, flourished during the third, and were suppressed in the fourth or fifth, by the prevalence of more fashionable controversies, and by the superior ascendant of the reigning power. Though they constantly disturbed the peace, and frequently disgraced the name of religion, they contributed to assist rather than to retard the progress of Christianity. The Gentile converts, whose strongest objections and prejudices were directed against the law of Moses, could find admission into many Christian societies, which required not from their untutored mind any belief of an antecedent revelation. Their faith was insensibly fortified and enlarged, and the church was ultimately benefited by the conquests of its most inveterate enemies.[37]

But whatever difference of opinion might subsist between the Orthodox, the Ebionites, and the Gnostics, concerning the divinity or the obligation of the Mosaic law, they were all equally animated by the same exclusive zeal, and by the same abhorrence for idolatry, which had distinguished the Jews from the other nations of the ancient world. The philosopher, who considered the system of polytheism as a composi-

tion of human fraud and error, could disguise a smile of contempt under the mask of devotion, without apprehending that either the mockery or the compliance would expose him to the resentment of any invisible, or, as he conceived them, imaginary powers. But the established religions of Paganism were seen by the primitive Christians in a much more odious and formidable light. It was the universal sentiment both of the church and of heretics, that the dæmons were the authors, the patrons, and the objects of idolatry.[38] Those rebellious spirits who had been degraded from the rank of angels, and cast down into the infernal pit, were still permitted to roam upon earth, to torment the bodies and to seduce the minds of sinful men. The dæmons soon discovered and abused the natural propensity of the human heart towards devotion, and, artfully withdrawing the adoration of mankind from their Creator, they usurped the place and honours of the Supreme Deity. By the success of their malicious contrivances, they at once gratified their own vanity and revenge, and obtained the only comfort of which they were yet susceptible, the hope of involving the human species in the participation of their guilt and misery. It was confessed, or at least it was imagined, that they had distributed among themselves the most important characters of polytheism, one dæmon assuming the name and attributes of Jupiter, another of Æsculapius, a third of Venus, and a fourth perhaps of Apollo;[39] and that, by the advantage of their long experience and aërial nature, they were enabled to execute, with sufficient skill and dignity, the parts which they had undertaken. They lurked in the temples, instituted festivals and sacrifices, invented fables, pronounced oracles, and were frequently allowed to perform miracles. The Christians, who, by the interposition of evil spirits, could so readily explain every præternatural appearance, were disposed and even desirous to admit the most extravagant fictions of the Pagan mythology. But the belief of the Christian was accompanied with horror. The most trifling mark of respect to the national worship he considered as a direct homage yielded to the dæmon, and as an act of rebellion against the majesty of God.

In consequence of this opinion, it was the first but arduous duty of a Christian to preserve himself pure and undefiled by the practice of idolatry. The religion of the nations was not merely a speculative doctrine professed in the schools or preached in the temples. The innumerable deities and rites of polytheism were closely interwoven with every circumstance of business or pleasure, of public or of private life; and it seemed impossible to escape the observance of them, without, at the same time, renouncing the commerce of mankind, and all the offices and amusements of society.[40] The important transactions of peace and war were prepared or concluded by solemn sacrifices, in which the magistrate, the senator, and the soldier were obliged to preside or to participate.[41] The public spectacles were an essential part of the cheerful devotion of the Pagans, and the gods were supposed to accept, as the most grateful offering, the games that the prince and people celebrated in honour of their peculiar festivals.[42] The Christian, who with pious horror avoided the abomination of the circus or the theatre, found himself encompassed with infernal snares in every convivial entertainment, as often as his friends, invoking the hospitable deities, poured out libations to each other's happiness.[43] When the bride, struggling with well-affected reluctance, was forced in hymenæal pomp over the threshold of her new habitation,[44] or when the sad procession of the dead slowly moved towards the funeral pile,[45] the Christian, on these interesting occasions, was compelled to desert the persons who were the dearest to him, rather than contract the guilt inherent to those impious ceremonies. Every art and every trade that was in the least concerned in the framing or adorning of idols was polluted by the stain of idolatry;[46] a severe sentence, since it devoted to eternal misery the far greater part of the community which is employed in the exercise of liberal or mechanic professions. If we cast our eyes over the numerous remains of antiquity, we shall perceive that, besides the immediate representations of the gods and the holy instruments of their worship, the elegant forms and agreeable fictions consecrated by the imagination of the Greeks were introduced as the richest ornaments of the houses, the dress, and the furniture of the Pagans.[47] Even the arts of music and painting, of eloquence and poetry, flowed from the same impure origin. In the style of the fathers, Apollo and the Muses were the organs of the infernal spirit; Homer and Virgil were the most eminent of his servants; and the beautiful mythology which pervades and animates the compositions of their genius is destined to celebrate the glory of the dæmons. Even the common language of Greece and Rome abounded with familiar but impious expressions, which the imprudent Christian might too carelessly utter, or too patiently hear.[48]

The dangerous temptations which on every side lurked in ambush to surprise the unguarded believer assailed him with redoubled violence on the days of solemn festivals. So artfully were they framed and disposed throughout the year, that superstition always wore the appearance of pleasure, and often of virtue.[49] Some of the most sacred festivals in the Roman ritual were destined to salute the new calends of January with vows of public and private felicity; to indulge the pious remembrance of the dead and living; to ascertain the inviolable bounds of property; to hail, on the return of spring, the genial powers of fecundity; to perpetuate the two memorable eras of Rome, the foundation of the city, and that of the republic; and to restore, during the humane licence of the Saturnalia, the primitive equality of mankind. Some idea may be conceived of the abhorrence of the Christians for such impious ceremonies, by the scrupulous delicacy which they displayed on a much less alarming occasion. On days of general festivity it was the custom of the ancients to adorn their doors with lamps and with branches of laurel, and to crown their heads with a garland of flowers. This innocent and elegant practice might perhaps have been tolerated as a mere civil institution. But it most unluckily happened that the doors were under the protection of the household gods, that the laurel was sacred to the lover of Daphne, and that garlands of flowers, though frequently worn as a symbol either of joy or mourning, had been dedicated in their first origin to the service of superstition. The trembling Christians, who were persuaded in this instance to comply with the fashion of their country and the commands of the magistrate, laboured under the most gloomy apprehensions, from the reproaches of their own conscience, the censures of the church, and the denunciations of divine vengeance.[50]

Such was the anxious diligence which was required to guard the chastity of the Gospel from the infectious breath of idolatry. The superstitious observances of public or private rites were carelessly practised, from education and habit, by the followers of the established religion. But as often as they occurred, they afforded the Christians an opportunity of declaring and confirming their zealous opposition. By these frequent protestations their attachment to the faith was continually fortified; and in proportion to the increase of zeal, they combated with the more ardour and success in the holy war which they had undertaken against the empire of the dæmons.

II. The writings of Cicero[51] represent in the most lively colours the ignorance, the errors, and the uncertainty of the ancient philosophers with regard to the immortality of the soul. When they are desirous of arming their disciples against the fear of death, they inculcate, as an obvious though melancholy position, that the fatal stroke of our dissolution releases us from the calamities of life; and that those can no longer suffer who no longer exist. Yet there were a few sages of Greece and Rome who had conceived a more exalted, and, in some respects, a juster idea of human nature, though it must be confessed that, in the sublime inquiry, their reason had been often guided by their imagination, and that their imagination had been prompted by their vanity. When they viewed with complacency the extent of their own mental powers, when they exercised the various faculties of memory, of fancy, and of judgment, in the most profound speculations or the most important labours, and when they reflected on the desire of fame, which transported them into future ages, far beyond the bounds of death and of the grave, they were unwilling to confound themselves with the beasts of the field, or to suppose that a being, for whose dignity they entertained the most sincere admiration, could be limited to a spot of earth, and to a few years of duration. With this favourable prepossession they summoned to their aid the science, or rather the language, of Metaphysics. They soon discovered that, as none of the properties of matter will apply to the operations of the mind, the human soul must consequently be a substance distinct from the body, pure, simple, and spiritual, incapable of dissolution, and susceptible of a much higher degree of virtue and happiness after the release from its corporeal prison. From these specious and noble principles the philosophers who trod in the footsteps of Plato deduced a very unjustifiable conclusion, since they asserted, not only the future immortality, but the past eternity of the human soul, which they were too apt to consider as a portion of the infinite and self-existing spirit which pervades and sustains the universe.[52] A doctrine thus removed beyond the senses and the experience of mankind might serve to amuse the leisure of a philosophic mind; or, in the silence of solitude, it might sometimes impart a ray of comfort to desponding virtue; but the faint impression which had been received in the schools was soon obliterated by the commerce and business of active life. We are sufficiently acquainted with the eminent persons who flourished in the age of Cicero and of the first Cæsars, with their actions, their characters, and their motives, to be assured that their conduct in this life was never regulated by any serious conviction of the rewards or punishments of a future state. At the bar and in the senate of Rome the ablest orators were not apprehensive of giving offence to their hearers by exposing that doctrine as an idle and extravagant opinion, which was rejected with contempt by every man of a liberal education and understanding.[53]

Since therefore the most sublime efforts of philosophy can extend no farther than feebly to point out the desire, the hope, or, at most, the probability of a future state, there is nothing, except a divine revelation that can ascertain the existence and describe the condition of the invisible country which is destined to receive the souls of men after their separation from the body. But we may perceive several defects inherent to the popular religions of Greece and Rome which rendered them very unequal to so arduous a task. 1. The general system of their mythology was unsupported by any solid proofs; and the wisest among the Pagans had already disclaimed its usurped authority. 2. The description of the infernal regions had been abandoned to the fancy of painters and of poets, who peopled them with so many phantoms and monsters who dispensed their rewards and punishments with so little equity, that a solemn truth, the most congenial to the human heart, was oppressed and disgraced by the absurd mixture of the wildest fictions.[54] 3. The doctrine of a future state was scarcely considered among the devout polytheists of Greece and Rome as a fundamental article of faith. The providence of the gods, as it related to public communities rather than to private individuals, was principally displayed on the visible theatre of the present world. The petitions which were offered on the altars of Jupiter or Apollo expressed the anxiety of their worshippers for temporal happiness, and their ignorance or indifference concerning a future life.[55] The important truth of the immortality of the soul was inculcated with more diligence as well as success in India, in Assyria, in Egypt, and in Gaul; and since we cannot attribute such a difference to the superior knowledge of the barbarians, we must ascribe it to the influence of an established priesthood, which employed the motives of virtue as the instrument of ambition.[56]

We might naturally expect that a principle so essential to religion would have been revealed in the clearest terms to the chosen people of Palestine, and that it might safely have been intrusted to the hereditary priesthood of Aaron. It is incumbent on us to adore the mysterious dispensations of Providence,[57] when we discover that the doctrine of the immortality of the soul is omitted in the law of Moses; it is darkly insinuated by the prophets; and during the long period which elapsed between the Egyptian and the Babylonian servitudes, the hopes as well as fears of the Jews appear to have been confined within the narrow compass of the present life.[58] After Cyrus had permitted the exiled nation to return into the promised land, and after Ezra had restored the ancient records of their religion, two celebrated sects, the Sadducees and the Pharisees, insensibly arose at Jerusalem.[59] The former, selected from the more opulent and distinguished ranks of society, were strictly attached to the literal sense of the Mosaic law, and they piously rejected the immortality of the soul as an opinion that received no countenance from the divine book, which they revered as the only rule of their faith. To the authority of Scripture the Pharisees added that of tradition, and they accepted, under the name of traditions, several speculative tenets from the philosophy or religion of the eastern nations. The doctrines of fate or predestination, of angels and spirits, and of a future state of rewards and punishments, were in the number of these new articles of belief; and as the Pharisees, by the austerity of their manners, had drawn into their party the body of the Jewish people, the immortality of the soul became the prevailing sentiment of the synagogue under the reign of the Asmonæan princes and pontiffs. The temper of the Jews was incapable of contenting itself with such a cold and languid assent as might satisfy the mind of a Polytheist; and as soon as they admitted the idea of a future state, they embraced it with the zeal which has always formed the characteristic of the nation. Their zeal, however, added nothing to its evidence, or even probability; and it was still necessary that the doctrine of life and immortality, which had been dictated by nature, approved by reason, and received by superstition, should obtain the sanction of divine truth from the authority and example of Christ.

When the promise of eternal happiness was proposed to mankind on condition of adopting the faith, and of observing the precepts, of the Gospel, it is no wonder that so advantageous an offer should have been accepted by great numbers of every religion, of every rank, and of every province in the Roman empire. The ancient Christians were animated by a contempt for their present existence, and by a just confidence of immortality, of which the doubtful and imperfect faith of modern ages cannot give us any adequate notion. In the primitive church the influence of truth was very powerfully strengthened by an opinion which, however it may deserve respect for its usefulness and antiquity, has not been found agreeable to experience. It was universally believed that the end of the world, and the kingdom of heaven, were at hand. The near approach of this wonderful event had been predicted by the apostles; the tradition of it was preserved by their earliest disciples, and those who understood in their literal sense the discourses of Christ himself were obliged to expect the second and glorious coming of the Son of Man in the clouds, before that generation was totally extinguished which had beheld his humble condition upon earth, and which might still be witness of the calamities of the Jews under Vespasian or Hadrian. The revolution of seventeen centuries has instructed us not to press too closely the mysterious language of prophecy and revelation; but as long as, for wise purposes, this error was permitted to subsist in the church, it was productive of the most salutary effects on the faith and practice of Christians, who lived in the awful expectation of that moment when the globe itself, and all the various race of mankind, should tremble at the appearance of their divine Judge.[60]

The ancient and popular doctrine of the Millennium was intimately connected with the second coming of Christ. As the works of the creation had been finished in six days, their duration in their present state, according to a tradition which was attributed to the prophet Elijah, was fixed to six thousand years.[61] By the same analogy it was inferred that this long period of labour and contention, which was now almost elapsed,[62] would be succeeded by a joyful Sabbath of a thousand years; and that Christ, with the triumphant band of the saints and the elect who had escaped death, or who had been miraculously revived, would reign upon earth till the time appointed for the last and general resurrection. So pleasing was this hope to the mind of believers, that the *New Jerusalem*, the seat of this blissful kingdom, was quickly adorned with all the gayest colours of the imagination. A felicity consisting only of pure and spiritual pleasure would have appeared too refined for its inhabitants, who were still supposed to possess their human nature and senses. A garden of Eden, with the amusements of the pastoral life, was no longer suited to the advanced state of society which prevailed under the Roman empire. A city was therefore erected of gold and precious stones, and a supernatural plenty of corn and wine was bestowed on the adjacent territory; in the free enjoyment of whose spontaneous productions the happy and benevolent people was never to be restrained by any jealous laws of exclusive property.[63] The assurance of such a Millennium was carefully inculcated by a succession of fathers from Justin Martyr[64] and Irenæus, who conversed with the immediate disciples of the apostles, down to Lactantius, who was preceptor to the son of Constantine.[65] Though it might not be universally received, it appears to have been the reigning sentiment of the orthodox believers; and it seems so well adapted to the desires and apprehensions of mankind, that it must have contributed in a very considerable degree to the progress of the Christian faith. But when the edifice of the church was almost completed, the temporary support was laid aside. The doctrine of Christ's reign upon earth was at first treated as a profound allegory, was considered by degrees as a doubtful and useless opinion, and was at length rejected as the absurd invention of heresy and fanaticism.[66] A mysterious prophecy, which still forms a part of the sacred canon, but which was thought to favour the exploded sentiment, has very narrowly escaped the proscription of the church.[67]

Whilst the happiness and glory of a temporal reign were promised to the disciples of Christ, the most dreadful calamities were denounced against an unbelieving world. The edification of the new Jerusalem was to advance by equal steps with the destruction of the mystic Babylon; and as long as the emperors who reigned before Constantine persisted in the profession of idolatry, the epithet of Babylon was applied to the city and to the empire of Rome. A regular series was prepared of all the moral and physical evils which can afflict a flourishing nation; intestine discord, and the invasion of the fiercest barbarians from the unknown regions of the North; pestilence and famine, comets and eclipses, earthquakes and inundations.[68] All these were only so many preparatory and alarming signs of the great catastrophe of Rome, when the country of the Scipios and Cæsars should be consumed by a flame from Heaven, and the city of the seven hills, with her palaces, her temples, and her triumphal arches, should be buried in a vast lake of fire and brimstone. It might, however, afford some consolation to Roman vanity, that the period of their empire would be that of

the world itself; which, as it had once perished by the element of water, was destined to experience a second and a speedy destruction from the element of fire. In the opinion of a general conflagration the faith of the Christian very happily coincided with the tradition of the East, the philosophy of the Stoics, and the analogy of Nature; and even the country which, from religious motives, had been chosen for the origin and principal scene of the conflagration, was the best adapted for that purpose by natural and physical causes—by its deep caverns, beds of sulphur, and numerous volcanoes, of which those of Ætna, of Vesuvius, and of Lipari exhibit a very imperfect representation. The calmest and most intrepid sceptic could not refuse to acknowledge that the destruction of the present system of the world by fire was in itself extremely probable. The Christian, who founded his belief much less on the fallacious arguments of reason than on the authority of tradition and the interpretation of Scripture, expected it with terror and confidence as a certain and approaching event; and as his mind was perpetually filled with the solemn idea, he considered every disaster that happened to the empire as an infallible symptom of an expiring world.[69]

The condemnation of the wisest and most virtuous of the Pagans, on account of their ignorance or disbelief of the divine truth, seems to offend the reason and the humanity of the present age.[70] But the primitive church, whose faith was of a much firmer consistence, delivered over, without hesitation, to eternal torture the far greater part of the human species. A charitable hope might perhaps be indulged in favour of Socrates, or some other sages of antiquity, who had consulted the light of reason before that of the Gospel had arisen.[71] But it was unanimously affirmed that those who, since the birth or the death of Christ, had obstinately persisted in the worship of the dæmons, neither deserved nor could expect a pardon from the irritated justice of the Deity. These rigid sentiments, which had been unknown to the ancient world, appear to have infused a spirit of bitterness into a system of love and harmony. The ties of blood and friendship were frequently torn asunder by the difference of religious faith; and the Christians, who, in this world, found themselves oppressed by the power of the Pagans, were sometimes seduced by resentment and spiritual pride to delight in the prospect of their future triumph. "You are fond of spectacles," exclaims the stern Tertullian, "expect the greatest of all spectacles, the last and eternal judgment of the universe. How shall I admire, how laugh, how rejoice, how exult, when I behold so many proud monarchs, and fancied gods, groaning in the lowest abyss of darkness; so many magistrates, who persecuted the name of the Lord, liquefying in fiercer fires than they ever kindled against the Christians; so many sage philosophers blushing in red-hot flames with their deluded scholars; so many celebrated poets trembling before the tribunal, not of Minos, but of Christ; so many tragedians, more tuneful in the expression of their own sufferings; so many dancers—" But the humanity of the reader will permit me to draw a veil over the rest of this infernal description, which the zealous African pursues in a long variety of affected and unfeeling witticisms.[72]

Doubtless there were many among the primitive Christians of a temper more suitable to the meekness and charity of their profession. There were many who felt a sincere compassion for the danger of their friends and countrymen, and who exerted the most benevolent zeal to save them from the impending destruction. The careless Polytheist, assailed by new and unexpected terrors, against which neither his priests nor his philosophers could afford him any certain protection, was very frequently terrified and subdued by the menace of eternal tortures. His fears might assist the progress of his faith and reason; and if he could once persuade himself to suspect that the Christian religion might possibly be true, it became an easy task to convince him that it was the safest and most prudent party that he could possibly embrace.

III. The supernatural gifts, which even in this life were ascribed to the Christians above the rest of mankind, must have conduced to their own comfort, and very frequently to the conviction of infidels. Besides the occasional prodigies, which might sometimes be effected by the immediate interposition of the Deity when he suspended the laws of Nature for the service of religion, the Christian church, from the time of the apostles and their first disciples,[73] has claimed an uninterrupted succession of miraculous powers, the gift of tongues, of vision, and of prophecy, the power of expelling dæmons, of healing the sick, and of raising the dead. The knowledge of foreign languages was frequently communicated to the contemporaries of Irenæus, though Irenæus himself was left to struggle with the difficulties of a barbarous dialect whilst he preached the Gospel to the natives of Gaul.[74] The divine inspiration, whether it was conveyed in the form of a waking or of a sleeping vision, is described as a favour very liberally bestowed on all ranks of the faithful, on women as on elders, on boys as well as upon bishops. When their devout minds were sufficiently prepared by a course of prayer, of fasting, and of vigils, to receive the extraordinary impulse, they were transported out of their senses, and delivered in ecstasy that was inspired, being mere organs of the Holy Spirit, just as a pipe or flute is of him who blows into it.[75] We may add that the design of these visions was, for the most part, either to disclose the future history, or to guide the present administration, of the church. The expulsion of the dæmons from the bodies of those unhappy persons whom they had been permitted to torment was considered as a signal though ordinary triumph of religion, and is repeatedly alleged by the ancient apologists as the most convincing evidence of the truth of Christianity. The awful ceremony was usually performed in a public manner, and in the presence of a great number of spectators; the patient was relieved by the power or skill of the exorcist, and the vanquished dæmon was heard to confess that he was one of the fabled gods of antiquity, who had impiously usurped the adoration of mankind.[76] But the miraculous cure of diseases of the most inveterate or even preternatural kind can no longer occasion any surprise, when we recollect that in the days of Irenæus, about the end of the second century, the resurrection of the dead was very far from being esteemed an uncommon event; that the miracle was frequently performed on necessary occasions, by great fasting and the joint supplication of the church of the place, and that the persons thus restored to their prayers had lived afterwards among them many years.[77] At such a period, when faith could boast of so many wonderful victories over death, it seems difficult to account for the scepticism of those philosophers who still rejected and derided the doctrine of the resurrection. A noble Grecian had rested on this important ground the whole controversy, and promised Theophilus, bishop of Antioch, that, if he could be gratified with the sight of a single person who had been actually raised from the dead, he would immediately embrace the Christian religion. It is somewhat remarkable that the prelate of the first eastern church, however anxious for the conversion of his friend, thought proper to decline this fair and reasonable challenge.[78]

The miracles of the primitive church, after obtaining the sanction of ages, have been lately attacked in a very free and ingenious inquiry;[79]

which, though it has met with the most favour-able reception from the public, appears to have excited a general scandal among the divines of our own as well as of the other Protestant churches of Europe.[80] Our different sentiments on this subject will be much less influenced by any particular arguments than by our habits of study and reflection, and, above all, by the de-gree of the evidence which we have accustomed ourselves to require for the proof of a miracu-lous event. The duty of an historian does not call upon him to interpose his private judgment in this nice and important controversy; but he ought not to dissemble the difficulty of adopting such a theory as may reconcile the interest of religion with that of reason, of making a proper application of that theory, and of defining with precision the limits of that happy period, ex-empt from error and from deceit, to which we might be disposed to extend the gift of super-natural powers. From the first of the fathers to the last of the popes, a succession of bishops, of saints, of martyrs, and of miracles, is continued without interruption; and the progress of super-stition was so gradual and almost impercep-tible, that we know not in what particular link we should break the chain of tradition. Every age bears testimony to the wonderful events by which it was distinguished, and its testimony appears no less weighty and respectable than that of the preceding generation, till we are in-sensibly led on to accuse our own inconsistency if, in the eighth or in the twelfth century, we deny to the venerable Bede, or to the holy Ber-nard, the same degree of confidence which, in the second century, we had so liberally granted to Justin or to Irenæus.[81] If the truth of any of those miracles is appreciated by their apparent use and propriety, every age had unbelievers to convince, heretics to confute, and idolatrous na-tions to convert; and sufficient motives might always be produced to justify the interposition of Heaven. And yet, since every friend to reve-lation is persuaded of the reality, and every reasonable man is convinced of the cessation, of miraculous powers, it is evident that there must have been *some period* in which they were either suddenly or gradually withdrawn from the Christian church. Whatever era is chosen for that purpose, the death of the apostles, the con-version of the Roman empire, or the extinction of the Arian heresy,[82] the insensibility of the Christians who lived at that time will equally afford a just matter of surprise. They still sup-ported their pretensions after they had lost their power. Credulity performed the office of faith;

fanaticism was permitted to assume the lan-guage of inspiration, and the effects of accident or contrivance were ascribed to supernatural causes. The recent experience of genuine mir-acles should have instructed the Christian world in the ways of Providence, and habituated their eye (if we may use a very inadequate expres-sion) to the style of the Divine artist. Should the most skilful painter of modern Italy presume to decorate his feeble imitations with the name of Raphael or of Correggio, the insolent fraud would be soon discovered and indignantly re-jected.

Whatever opinion may be entertained of the miracles of the primitive church since the time of the apostles, this unresisting softness of tem-per, so conspicuous among the believers of the second and third centuries, proved of some acci-dental benefit to the cause of truth and religion. In modern times, a latent and even involuntary scepticism adheres to the most pious disposi-tions. Their admission of supernatural truths is much less an active consent than a cold and passive acquiescence. Accustomed long since to observe and to respect the invariable order of Nature, our reason, or at least our imagination, is not sufficiently prepared to sustain the visible action of the Deity. But in the first ages of Christianity the situation of mankind was ex-tremely different. The most curious, or the most credulous, among the Pagans were often per-suaded to enter into a society which asserted an actual claim of miraculous powers. The primi-tive Christians perpetually trod on mystic ground, and their minds were exercised by the habits of believing the most extraordinary events. They felt, or they fancied, that on every side they were incessantly assaulted by dæ-mons, comforted by visions, instructed by prophecy, and surprisingly delivered from dan-ger, sickness, and from death itself, by the sup-plications of the church. The real or imaginary prodigies, of which they so frequently conceived themselves to be the objects, the instruments, or the spectators, very happily disposed them to adopt with the same ease, but with far greater justice, the authentic wonders of the evangelic history; and thus miracles that exceeded not the measure of their own experience inspired them with the most lively assurance of mysteries which were acknowledged to surpass the limits of their understanding. It is this deep impres-sion of supernatural truths which has been so much celebrated under the name of faith; a state of mind described as the surest pledge of the Divine favour and of future felicity, and recommended as the first or perhaps the only merit of a Christian. According to the more rigid doctors, the moral virtues, which may be equally practised by infidels, are destitute of any value or efficacy in the work of our justification.

IV. But the primitive Christian demonstrated his faith by his virtues; and it was very justly supposed that the Divine persuasion, which enlightened or subdued the understanding, must at the same time purify the heart and direct the actions of the believer. The first apologists of Christianity who justify the innocence of their brethren, and the writers of a later period who celebrate the sanctity of their ancestors, display, in the most lively colours, the reformation of manners which was introduced into the world by the preaching of the Gospel. As it is my intention to remark only such human causes as were permitted to second the influence of revelation, I shall slightly mention two motives which might naturally render the lives of the primitive Christians much purer and more austere than those of their Pagan contemporaries or their degenerate successors—repentance for their past sins, and the laudable desire of supporting the reputation of the society in which they were engaged.

It is a very ancient reproach, suggested by the ignorance or the malice of infidelity, that the Christians allured into their party the most atrocious criminals, who, as soon as they were touched by a sense of remorse, were easily persuaded to wash away, in the water of baptism, the guilt of their past conduct, for which the temples of the gods refused to grant them any expiation. But this reproach, when it is cleared from misrepresentation, contributes as much to the honour as it did to the increase of the church.[83] The friends of Christianity may acknowledge without a blush that many of the most eminent saints had been before their baptism the most abandoned sinners. Those persons who in the world had followed, though in an imperfect manner, the dictates of benevolence and propriety, derived such a calm satisfaction from the opinion of their own rectitude as rendered them much less susceptible of the sudden emotions of shame, of grief, and of terror, which have given birth to so many wonderful conversions. After the example of their Divine Master, the missionaries of the Gospel disdained not the society of men, and especially of women, oppressed by the consciousness, and very often by the effects, of their vices. As they emerged from sin and superstition to the glorious hope of immortality, they resolved to devote themselves to a life, not only of virtue, but of penitence. The desire of perfection became the ruling passion of their soul; and it is well known that, while reason embraces a cold mediocrity, our passions hurry us with rapid violence over the space which lies between the most opposite extremes.

When the new converts had been enrolled in the number of the faithful, and were admitted to the sacraments of the church, they found themselves restrained from relapsing into their past disorders by another consideration of a less spiritual but of a very innocent and respectable nature. Any particular society that has departed from the great body of the nation, or the religion to which it belonged, immediately becomes the object of universal as well as invidious observation. In proportion to the smallness of its numbers, the character of the society may be affected by the virtue and vices of the persons who compose it; and every member is engaged to watch with the most vigilant attention over his own behaviour, and over that of his brethren, since, as he must expect to incur a part of the common disgrace, he may hope to enjoy a share of the common reputation. When the Christians of Bithynia were brought before the tribunal of the younger Pliny, they assured the proconsul that, far from being engaged in any unlawful conspiracy, they were bound by a solemn obligation to abstain from the commission of those crimes which disturb the private or public peace of society, from theft, robbery, adultery, perjury, and fraud.[84] Near a century afterwards, Tertullian with an honest pride could boast that very few Christians had suffered by the hand of the executioner, except on account of their religion.[85] Their serious and sequestered life, averse to the gay luxury of the age, inured them to chastity, temperance, economy, and all the sober and domestic virtues. As the greater number were of some trade or profession, it was incumbent on them, by the strictest integrity and the fairest dealing, to remove the suspicions which the profane are too apt to conceive against the appearances of sanctity. The contempt of the world exercised them in the habits of humility, meekness, and patience. The more they were persecuted, the more closely they adhered to each other. Their mutual charity and unsuspecting confidence has been remarked by infidels, and was too often abused by perfidious friends.[86]

It is a very honourable circumstance for the morals of the primitive Christians, that even their faults, or rather errors, were derived from an excess of virtue. The bishops and doctors of the church, whose evidence attests, and whose authority might influence, the professions, the principles, and even the practice of their contemporaries, had studied the Scriptures with less skill than devotion; and they often received in the most literal sense those rigid precepts of Christ and the apostles to which the prudence of succeeding commentators has applied a looser and more figurative mode of interpretation. Ambitious to exalt the perfection of the Gospel above the wisdom of philosophy, the zealous fathers have carried the duties of self-mortification, of purity, and of patience, to a height which it is scarcely possible to attain, and much less to preserve, in our present state of weakness and corruption. A doctrine so extraordinary and so sublime must inevitably command the veneration of the people; but it was ill calculated to obtain the suffrage of those worldly philosophers who, in the conduct of this transitory life, consult only the feelings of nature and the interest of society.[87]

There are two very natural propensities which we may distinguish in the most virtuous and liberal dispositions, the love of pleasure and the love of action. If the former is refined by art and learning, improved by the charms of social intercourse, and corrected by a just regard to economy, to health, and to reputation, it is productive of the greatest part of the happiness of private life. The love of action is a principle of a much stronger and more doubtful nature. It often leads to anger, to ambition, and to revenge; but when it is guided by the sense of propriety and benevolence, it becomes the parent of every virtue, and, if those virtues are accompanied with equal abilities, a family, a state, or an empire may be indebted for their safety and prosperity to the undaunted courage of a single man. To the love of pleasure we may therefore ascribe most of the agreeable, to the love of action we may attribute most of the useful and respectable, qualifications. The character in which both the one and the other should be united and harmonised would seem to constitute the most perfect idea of human nature. The insensible and inactive disposition, which should be supposed alike destitute of both, would be rejected, by the common consent of mankind, as utterly incapable of procuring any happiness to the individual, or any public benefit to the world. But it was not in *this* world that the primitive Christians were desirous of making themselves either agreeable or useful.

The acquisition of knowledge, the exercise of our reason or fancy, and the cheerful flow of unguarded conversation, may employ the leisure of a liberal mind. Such amusements, however, were rejected with abhorrence, or admitted with the utmost caution, by the severity of the fathers, who despised all knowledge that was not useful to salvation, and who considered all levity of discourse as a criminal abuse of the gift of speech. In our present state of existence the body is so inseparably connected with the soul, that it seems to be our interest to taste, with innocence and moderation, the enjoyments of which that faithful companion is susceptible. Very different was the reasoning of our devout predecessors; vainly aspiring to imitate the perfection of angels, they disdained, or they affected to disdain, every earthly and corporeal delight.[88] Some of our senses indeed are necessary for our preservation, others for our subsistence, and others again for our information; and thus far it was impossible to reject the use of them. The first sensation of pleasure was marked as the first moment of their abuse. The unfeeling candidate for heaven was instructed, not only to resist the grosser allurements of the taste or smell, but even to shut his ears against the profane harmony of sounds, and to view with indifference the most finished productions of human art. Gay apparel, magnificent houses, and elegant furniture were supposed to unite the double guilt of pride and of sensuality: a simple and mortified appearance was more suitable to the Christian who was certain of his sins and doubtful of his salvation. In their censures of luxury the fathers are extremely minute and circumstantial;[89] and among the various articles which excite their pious indignation, we may enumerate false hair, garments of any colour except white, instruments of music, vases of gold or silver, downy pillows (as Jacob reposed his head on a stone), white bread, foreign wines, public salutations, the use of warm baths, and the practice of shaving the beard, which, according to the expression of Tertullian, is a lie against our own faces, and an impious attempt to improve the works of the Creator.[90] When Christianity was introduced among the rich and the polite, the observation of these singular laws was left, as it would be at present, to the few who were ambitious of superior sanctity. But it is always easy, as well as agreeable, for the inferior ranks of mankind to claim a merit from the contempt of that pomp and pleasure which fortune has placed beyond their reach. The virtue of the primitive Christians, like that of the first Romans, was very frequently guarded by poverty and ignorance.

The chaste severity of the fathers in whatever related to the commerce of the two sexes flowed from the same principle—their abhorrence of every enjoyment which might gratify the sensual and degrade the spiritual nature of man. It was their favourite opinion, that if Adam had preserved his obedience to the Creator, he would have lived for ever in a state of virgin purity, and that some harmless mode of vegetation might have peopled paradise with a race of innocent and immortal beings.[91] The use of marriage was permitted only to his fallen posterity, as a necessary expedient to continue the human species, and as a restraint, however imperfect, on the natural licentiousness of desire. The hesitation of the orthodox casuists on this interesting subject betrays the perplexity of men unwilling to approve an institution which they were compelled to tolerate.[92] The enumeration of the very whimsical laws which they most circumstantially imposed on the marriage-bed would force a smile from the young and a blush from the fair. It was their unanimous sentiment that a first marriage was adequate to all the purposes of nature and of society. The sensual connection was refined into a resemblance of the mystic union of Christ with his church, and was pronounced to be indissoluble either by divorce or by death. The practice of second nuptials was branded with the name of a legal adultery; and the persons who were guilty of so scandalous an offence against Christian purity were soon excluded from the honours, and even from the arms, of the church.[93] Since desire was imputed as a crime, and marriage was tolerated as a defect, it was consistent with the same principles to consider a state of celibacy as the nearest approach to the Divine perfection. It was with the utmost difficulty that ancient Rome could support the institution of six vestals;[94] but the primitive church was filled with a great number of persons of either sex who had devoted themselves to the profession of perpetual chastity.[95] A few of these, among whom we may reckon the learned Origen, judged it the most prudent to disarm the tempter.[96] Some were insensible and some were invincible against the assaults of the flesh. Disdaining an ignominious flight, the virgins of the warm climate of Africa encountered the enemy in the closest engagement; they permitted priests and deacons to share their bed, and gloried amidst the flames in their unsullied purity. But insulted Nature sometimes vindicated her rights, and this new species of martyrdom served only to introduce a new scandal into the church.[97] Among the Christian ascetics, however (a name which they soon acquired from their painful exercise), many, as they were less presumptuous, were probably more successful. The loss of sensual pleasure was supplied and compensated by spiritual pride. Even the multitude of Pagans were inclined to estimate the merit of the sacrifice by its apparent difficulty; and it was in the praise of these chaste spouses of Christ that the fathers have poured forth the troubled stream of their eloquence.[98] Such are the early traces of monastic principles and institutions, which, in a subsequent age, have counterbalanced all the temporal advantages of Christianity.[99]

The Christians were not less adverse to the business than to the pleasures of this world. The defence of our persons and property they knew not how to reconcile with the patient doctrine which enjoined an unlimited forgiveness of past injuries, and commanded them to invite the repetition of fresh insults. Their simplicity was offended by the use of oaths, by the pomp of magistracy, and by the active contention of public life; nor could their humane ignorance be convinced that it was lawful on any occasion to shed the blood of our fellow-creatures, either by the sword of justice or by that of war, even though their criminal or hostile attempts should threaten the peace and safety of the whole community.[100] It was acknowledged that, under a less perfect law, the powers of the Jewish constitution had been exercised, with the approbation of Heaven, by inspired prophets and by anointed kings. The Christians felt and confessed that such institutions might be necessary for the present system of the world, and they cheerfully submitted to the authority of their Pagan governors. But while they inculcated the maxims of passive obedience, they refused to take any active part in the civil administration or the military defence of the empire. Some indulgence might perhaps be allowed to those persons who, before their conversion, were already engaged in such violent and sanguinary occupations;[101] but it was impossible that the Christians, without renouncing a more sacred duty, could assume the character of soldiers, of magistrates, or of princes.[102] This indolent, or even criminal disregard to the public welfare, exposed them to the contempt and reproaches of the Pagans, who very frequently asked, what must be the fate of the empire, attacked on every side by the barbarians, if all mankind should adopt the pusillanimous sentiments of the new sect?[103] To this insulting question the Christian apologists returned obscure and ambiguous answers, as they were unwilling to reveal the secret cause of their security; the expectation that, before the conversion of mankind was accomplished, war, government, the Roman empire, and the world itself, would be no more. It may be observed that, in this instance likewise, the situation of the first Christians coincided very happily with their religious scruples, and that their aversion to an active life contributed rather to excuse them from the service than to exclude them from the honours of the state and army.

V. But the human character, however it may be exalted or depressed by a temporary enthusiasm, will return by degrees to its proper and natural level, and will resume those passions that seem the most adapted to its present condition. The primitive Christians were dead to the business and pleasures of the world; but their love of action, which could never be entirely extinguished, soon revived, and found a new occupation in the government of the church. A separate society, which attacked the established religion of the empire, was obliged to adopt some form of internal policy, and to appoint a sufficient number of ministers, intrusted not only with the spiritual functions, but even with the temporal direction of the Christian commonwealth. The safety of the society, its honour, its aggrandisement, were productive, even in the most pious minds, of a spirit of patriotism, such as the first of the Romans had felt for the republic, and sometimes of a similar indifference in the use of whatever means might probably conduce to so desirable an end. The ambition of raising themselves or their friends to the honours and offices of the church was disguised by the laudable intention of devoting to the public benefit the power and consideration which, for that purpose only, it became their duty to solicit. In the exercise of their functions they were frequently called upon to detect the errors of heresy or the arts of faction, to oppose the designs of perfidious brethren, to stigmatise their characters with deserved infamy, and to expel them from the bosom of a society whose peace and happiness they had attempted to disturb. The ecclesiastical governors of the Christians were taught to unite the wisdom of the serpent with the innocence of the dove; but as the former was refined, so the latter was insensibly corrupted, by the habits of government. In the church as well as in the world, the persons who were placed in any public station rendered themselves considerable by their eloquence and firmness, by their knowledge of mankind, and by their dexterity in business; and while they concealed from others, and perhaps from themselves, the secret motives of their conduct, they too frequently relapsed into all the turbulent passions of active life, which were tinctured with an additional degree of bitterness and obstinacy from the infusion of spiritual zeal.

The government of the church has often been the subject, as well as the prize, of religious contention. The hostile disputants of Rome, of Paris, of Oxford, and of Geneva, have alike struggled to reduce the primitive and apostolic model[104] to the respective standards of their own policy. The few who have pursued this inquiry with more candour and impartiality are of opinion[105] that the apostles declined the office of legislation, and rather chose to endure some partial scandals and divisions, than to exclude the Christians of a future age from the liberty of varying their forms of ecclesiastical government according to the changes of times and circumstances. The scheme of policy which, under their approbation, was adopted for the use of the first century, may be discovered from the practice of Jerusalem, of Ephesus, or of Corinth. The societies which were instituted in the cities of the Roman empire were united only by the ties of faith and charity. Independence and equality formed the basis of their internal constitution. The want of discipline and human learning was supplied by the occasional assistance of the *prophets*,[106] who were called to that function without distinction of age, of sex, or of natural abilities, and who, as often as they felt the divine impulse, poured forth the effusions of the Spirit in the assembly of the faithful. But these extraordinary gifts were frequently abused or misapplied by the prophetic teachers. They displayed them at an improper season, presumptuously disturbed the service of the assembly, and by their pride or mistaken zeal they introduced, particularly into the apostolic church of Corinth, a long and melancholy train of disorders.[107] As the institution of prophets became useless, and even pernicious, their powers were withdrawn, and their office abolished.

The public functions of religion were solely intrusted to the established ministers of the church, the *bishops* and the *presbyters*; two appellations which, in their first origin, appear to have distinguished the same office and the same order of persons. The name of Presbyter was expressive of their age, or rather of their gravity and wisdom. The title of Bishop denoted their inspection over the faith and manners of the Christians who were committed to their pastoral care. In proportion to the respective numbers of the faithful, a larger or smaller number of these *episcopal presbyters* guided each infant congregation with equal authority and with united counsels.[108]

But the most perfect equality of freedom requires the directing hand of a superior magistrate: and the order of public deliberations soon introduces the office of a president, invested at least with the authority of collecting the sentiments, and of executing the resolutions, of the assembly. A regard for the public tranquillity, which would so frequently have been interrupted by annual or by occasional elections, induced the primitive Christians to constitute an honourable and perpetual magistracy, and to choose one of the wisest and most holy among their presbyters to execute, during his life, the duties of their ecclesiastical governor. It was under these circumstances that the lofty title of Bishop began to raise itself above the humble appellation of Presbyter; and while the latter remained the most natural distinction for the members of every Christian senate, the former was appropriated to the dignity of its new president.[109] The advantages of this espiscopal form of government, which appears to have been introduced before the end of the first century,[110] were so obvious, and so important for the future greatness, as well as the present peace, of Christianity, that it was adopted without delay by all the societies which were already scattered over the empire, had acquired in a very early period the sanction of antiquity,[111] and is still revered by the most powerful churches, both of the East and of the West, as a primitive and even as a divine establishment.[112] It is needless to observe that the pious and humble presbyters who were first dignified with the episcopal title could not possess, and would probably have rejected, the power and pomp which now encircles the tiara of the Roman pontiff, or the mitre of a German prelate. But we may define in a few words the narrow limits of their original jurisdiction, which was chiefly of a spiritual, though in some instances of a temporal nature.[113] It consisted in the administration of the sacraments and discipline of the church, the superintendency of religious ceremonies, which imperceptibly increased in number and variety, the consecration of ecclesiastical ministers, to whom the bishop assigned their respective functions, the management of the public fund, and the determination of all such differences as the faithful

were unwilling to expose before the tribunal of an idolatrous judge. These powers, during a short period, were exercised according to the advice of the presbyteral college, and with the consent and approbation of the assembly of Christians. The primitive bishops were considered only as the first of their equals, and the honourable servants of a free people. Whenever the episcopal chair became vacant by death, a new president was chosen among the presbyters by the suffrage of the whole congregation, every member of which supposed himself invested with a sacred and sacerdotal character.[114]

Such was the mild and equal constitution by which the Christians were governed more than an hundred years after the death of the apostles. Every society formed within itself a separate and independent republic; and although the most distant of these little states maintained a mutual as well as friendly intercourse of letters and deputations, the Christian world was not yet connected by any supreme authority or legislative assembly. As the numbers of the faithful were gradually multiplied, they discovered the advantages that might result from a closer union of their interest and designs. Towards the end of the second century, the churches of Greece and Asia adopted the useful institutions of provincial synods, and they may justly be supposed to have borrowed the model of a representative council from the celebrated examples of their own country, the Amphictyons, the Achæan league, or the assemblies of the Ionian cities. It was soon established as a custom and as a law, that the bishops of the independent churches should meet in the capital of the province at the stated periods of spring and autumn. Their deliberations were assisted by the advice of a few distinguished presbyters, and moderated by the presence of a listening multitude.[115] Their decrees, which were styled Canons, regulated every important controversy of faith and discipline; and it was natural to believe that a liberal effusion of the Holy Spirit would be poured on the united assembly of the delegates of the Christian people. The institution of synods was so well suited to private ambition and to public interest, that in the space of a few years it was received throughout the whole empire. A regular correspondence was established between the provincial councils, which mutually communicated and approved their respective proceedings; and the catholic church soon assumed the form, and acquired the strength, of a great fœderative republic.[116]

As the legislative authority of the particular

churches was insensibly superseded by the use of councils, the bishops obtained by their alliance a much larger share of executive and arbitrary power; and as soon as they were connected by a sense of their common interest, they were enabled to attack, with united vigour, the original rights of their clergy and people. The prelates of the third century imperceptibly changed the language of exhortation into that of command, scattered the seeds of future usurpations, and supplied, by scripture allegories and declamatory rhetoric, their deficiency of force and of reason. They exalted the unity and power of the church, as it was represented in the EPISCOPAL OFFICE, of which every bishop enjoyed an equal and undivided portion.[117] Princes and magistrates, it was often repeated, might boast an earthly claim to a transitory dominion: it was the episcopal authority alone which was derived from the Deity, and extended itself over this and over another world. The bishops were the vicegerents of Christ, the successors of the apostles, and the mystic substitutes of the high priest of the Mosaic law. Their exclusive privilege of conferring the sacerdotal character invaded the freedom both of clerical and of popular elections: and if, in the administration of the church, they still consulted the judgment of the presbyters or the inclination of the people, they most carefully inculcated the merit of such a voluntary condescension. The bishops acknowledged the supreme authority which resided in the assembly of their brethren; but in the government of his peculiar diocese each of them exacted from his *flock* the same implicit obedience as if that favourite metaphor had been literally just, and as if the shepherd had been of a more exalted nature than that of his sheep.[118] This obedience, however, was not imposed without some efforts on the one side, and some resistance on the other. The democratical part of the constitution was, in many places, very warmly supported by the zealous or interested opposition of the inferior clergy. But their patriotism received the ignominious epithets of faction and schism, and the episcopal cause was indebted for its rapid progress to the labours of many active prelates, who like Cyprian of Carthage, could reconcile the arts of the most ambitious statesman with the Christian virtues which seem adapted to the character of a saint and martyr.[119]

The same causes which at first had destroyed the equality of the presbyters introduced among the bishops a pre-eminence of rank, and from thence a superiority of jurisdiction. As often as in the spring and autumn they met in provincial synod, the difference of personal merit and reputation was very sensibly felt among the members of the assembly, and the multitude was governed by the wisdom and eloquence of the few. But the order of public proceedings required a more regular and less invidious distinction; the office of perpetual presidents in the councils of each province was conferred on the bishops of the principal city; and these aspiring prelates, who acquired the lofty titles of Metropolitans and Primates, secretly prepared themselves to usurp over their episcopal brethren the same authority which the bishops had so lately assumed above the college of presbyters.[120] Nor was it long before an emulation of pre-eminence and power prevailed among the Metropolitans themselves, each of them affecting to display, in the most pompous terms, the temporal honours and advantages of the city over which he presided; the numbers and opulence of the Christians who were subject to their pastoral care; the saints and martyrs who had arisen among them; and the purity with which they preserved the tradition of the faith as it had been transmitted through a series of orthodox bishops from the apostle or the apostolic disciple to whom the foundation of their church was ascribed.[121] From every cause, either of a civil or of an ecclesiastical nature, it was easy to foresee that Rome must enjoy the respect, and would soon claim the obedience, of the provinces. The society of the faithful bore a just proportion to the capital of the empire; and the Roman church was the greatest, the most numerous, and, in regard to the West, the most ancient of all the Christian establishments, many of which had received their religion from the pious labours of her missionaries. Instead of *one* apostolic founder, the utmost boast of Antioch, of Ephesus, or of Corinth, the banks of the Tiber were supposed to have been honoured with the preaching and martyrdom of the *two* most eminent among the apostles;[122] and the bishops of Rome very prudently claimed the inheritance of whatsoever prerogatives were attributed either to the person or to the office of St. Peter.[123] The bishops of Italy and of the provinces were disposed to allow them a primacy of order and association (such was their very accurate expression) in the Christian aristocracy.[124] But the power of a monarch was rejected with abhorrence, and the aspiring genius of Rome experienced from the nations of Asia and Africa a more vigorous resistance to her spiritual than she had formerly done to her temporal dominion.

The patriotic Cyprian, who ruled with the most absolute sway the church of Carthage and the provincial synods, opposed with resolution and success the ambition of the Roman pontiff, artfully connected his own cause with that of the eastern bishops, and, like Hannibal, sought out new allies in the heart of Asia.[125] If this Punic war was carried on without any effusion of blood, it was owing much less to the moderation than to the weakness of the contending prelates. Invectives and excommunications were *their* only weapons; and these, during the progress of the whole controversy, they hurled against each other with equal fury and devotion. The hard necessity of censuring either a pope or a saint and martyr distresses the modern Catholics whenever they are obliged to relate the particulars of a dispute in which the champions of religion indulged such passions as seem much more adapted to the senate or to the camp.[126]

The progress of the ecclesiastical authority gave birth to the memorable distinction of the laity and of the clergy, which had been unknown to the Greeks and Romans.[127] The former of these appellations comprehended the body of the Christian people; the latter, according to the signification of the word, was appropriated to the chosen portion that had been set apart for the service of religion; a celebrated order of men which has furnished the most important, though not always the most edifying, subjects for modern history. Their mutual hostilities sometimes disturbed the peace of the infant church, but their zeal and activity were united in the common cause, and the love of power, which (under the most artful disguises) could insinuate itself into the breasts of bishops and martyrs, animated them to increase the number of their subjects, and to enlarge the limits of the Christian empire. They were destitute of any temporal force, and they were for a long time discouraged and oppressed, rather than assisted, by the civil magistrate; but they had acquired, and they employed within their own society, the two most efficacious instruments of government, rewards and punishments; the former derived from the pious liberality, the latter from the devout apprehensions, of the faithful.

I. The community of goods, which had so agreeably amused the imagination of Plato,[128] and which subsisted in some degree among the austere sect of the Essenians,[129] was adopted for a short time in the primitive church. The fervour of the first proselytes prompted them to sell those worldly possessions which they despised, to lay the price of them at the feet of the apostles, and to content themselves with receiving an equal share out of the general distribution.[130] The progress of the Christian religion relaxed, and gradually abolished, this generous institution, which, in hands less pure than those of the apostles, would too soon have been corrupted and abused by the returning selfishness of human nature; and the converts who embraced the new religion were permitted to retain the possession of their patrimony, to receive legacies and inheritances, and to increase their separate property by all the lawful means of trade and industry. Instead of an absolute sacrifice, a moderate proportion was accepted by the ministers of the Gospel; and in their weekly or monthly assemblies every believer, according to the exigency of the occasion, and the measure of his wealth and piety, presented his voluntary offering for the use of the common fund.[131] Nothing, however inconsiderable, was refused; but it was diligently inculcated that, in the article of tithes, the Mosaic law was still of divine obligation; and that, since the Jews, under a less perfect discipline, had been commanded to pay a tenth part of all that they possessed, it would become the disciples of Christ to distinguish themselves by a superior degree of liberality,[132] and to acquire some merit by resigning a superfluous treasure, which must so soon be annihilated with the world itself.[133] It is almost unnecessary to observe that the revenue of each particular church, which was of so uncertain and fluctuating a nature, must have varied with the poverty or the opulence of the faithful, as they were dispersed in obscure villages, or collected in the great cities of the empire. In the time of the emperor Decius it was the opinion of the magistrates that the Christians of Rome were possessed of very considerable wealth, that vessels of gold and silver were used in their religious worship, and that many among their proselytes had sold their lands and houses to increase the public riches of the sect, at the expense, indeed, of their unfortunate children, who found themselves beggars because their parents had been saints.[134] We should listen with distrust to the suspicions of strangers and enemies; on this occasion, however, they receive a very specious and probable colour from the two following circumstances, the only ones that have reached our knowledge which define any precise sums or convey any distinct idea. Almost at the same period the bishop of Carthage, from a society less opulent than that of Rome, collected an hundred thousand sesterces (above eight hundred and fifty pounds sterling), on a sudden call of charity to redeem the brethren of Numidia, who had been carried away captives by the barbarians of the desert.[135] About an hundred years before the reign of Decius the Roman church had received, in a single donation, the sum of two hundred thousand sesterces from a stranger of Pontus, who proposed to fix his residence in the capital.[136] These oblations, for the most part, were made in money; nor was the society of Christians either desirous or capable of acquiring, to any considerable degree, the incumbrance of landed property. It had been provided by several laws, which were enacted with the same design as our statutes of mortmain, that no real estates should be given or bequeathed to any corporate body without either a special privilege or a particular dispensation from the emperor or from the senate;[137] who were seldom disposed to grant them in favour of a sect, at first the object of their contempt, and at last of their fears and jealousy. A transaction, however, is related under the reign of Alexander Severus, which discovers that the restraint was sometimes eluded or suspended, and that the Christians were permitted to claim and to possess lands within the limits of Rome itself.[138] The progress of Christianity, and the civil confusion of the empire, contributed to relax the severity of the laws; and, before the close of the third century, many considerable estates were bestowed on the opulent churches of Rome, Milan, Carthage, Antioch, Alexandria, and the other great cities of Italy and the provinces.

The bishop was the natural steward of the church; the public stock was intrusted to his care without account or control; the presbyters were confined to their spiritual functions, and the more dependent order of deacons was solely employed in the management and distribution of the ecclesiastical revenue.[139] If we may give credit to the vehement declamations of Cyprian, there were too many among his African brethren who, in the execution of their charge, violated every precept, not only of evangelic perfection, but even of moral virtue. By some of these unfaithful stewards the riches of the church were lavished in sensual pleasures; by others they were perverted to the purposes of private gain, of fraudulent purchases, and of rapacious usury.[140] But as long as the contributions of the Christian people were free and unconstrained, the abuse of their confidence could not be very frequent, and the general uses to which their liberality was applied reflected honour on the religious society. A decent portion was reserved for the maintenance of the bishop and his clergy; a sufficient sum was allotted for the expenses of the public worship, of which the feasts of love, the *agapæ*, as they were called, constituted a very pleasing part. The whole remainder was the sacred patrimony of the poor. According to the discretion of the bishop, it was distributed to support widows and orphans, the lame, the sick, and the aged of the community; to comfort strangers and pilgrims, and to alleviate the misfortunes of prisoners and captives, more especially when their sufferings had been occasioned by their firm attachment to the cause of religion.[141] A generous intercourse of charity united the most distant provinces, and the smaller congregations were cheerfully assisted by the alms of their more opulent brethren.[142] Such an institution, which paid less regard to the merit than to the distress of the object, very materially conduced to the progress of Christianity. The pagans, who were actuated by a sense of humanity, while they derided the doctrines, acknowledged the benevolence, of the new sect.[143] The prospect of immediate relief and of future protection allured into its hospitable bosom many of those unhappy persons whom the neglect of the world would have abandoned to the miseries of want, of sickness, and of old age. There is some reason likewise to believe that great numbers of infants who, according to the inhuman practice of the times, had been exposed by their parents, were frequently rescued from death, baptised, educated, and maintained by the piety of the Christians, and at the expense of the public treasure.[144]

II. It is the undoubted right of every society to exclude from its communion and benefits such among its members as reject or violate those regulations which have been established by general consent. In the exercise of this power the censures of the Christian church were chiefly directed against scandalous sinners, and particularly those who were guilty of murder, of fraud, or of incontinence; against the authors, or the followers, of any heretical opinions which had been condemned by the judgment of the episcopal order; and against those unhappy persons who, whether from choice or from compulsion, had polluted themselves after their baptism by any act of idolatrous worship. The consequences of excommunication were of a temporal as well as a spiritual nature. The Christian against whom it was pronounced was deprived of any part in the oblations of the faithful. The ties both of religious and of private friendship were dissolved: he found himself a profane object of abhorrence to the persons whom he the most esteemed, or by whom he had been the most tenderly beloved; and as far as an expulsion from a respectable society could imprint on his character a mark of disgrace, he was shunned or suspected by the generality of mankind. The situation of these unfortunate exiles was in itself very painful and melancholy; but, as it usually happens, their apprehensions far exceeded their sufferings. The benefits of the Christian communion were those of eternal life; nor could they erase from their minds the awful opinion that to those ecclesiastical governors by whom they were condemned the Deity had committed the keys of Hell and of Paradise. The heretics, indeed, who might be supported by the consciousness of their intentions, and by the flattering hope that they alone had discovered the true path of salvation, endeavoured to regain in their separate assemblies those comforts, temporal as well as spiritual, which they no longer derived from the great society of Christians. But almost all those who had reluctantly yielded to the power of vice or idolatry were sensible of their fallen condition, and anxiously desirous of being restored to the benefits of the Christian communion.

With regard to the treatment of these penitents, two opposite opinions, the one of justice, the other of mercy, divided the primitive church. The more rigid and inflexible casuists refused them for ever, and without exception, the meanest place in the holy community which they had disgraced or deserted; and leaving them to the remorse of a guilty conscience, indulged them only with a faint ray of hope that the contrition of their life and death might possibly be accepted by the Supreme Being.[145] A milder sentiment was embraced, in practice as well as in theory, by the purest and most respectable of the Christian churches.[146] The gates of reconciliation and of heaven were seldom shut against the returning penitent; but a severe and solemn form of discipline was instituted, which, while it served to expiate his crime, might powerfully deter the spectators from the imitation of his example. Humbled by a public confession, emaciated by fasting, and clothed in sackcloth, the penitent lay prostrate at the door of the assembly, imploring with tears the pardon of his offences, and soliciting the prayers of the faithful.[147] If the fault was of a very heinous nature, whole years of penance were esteemed an inadequate satisfaction to the Divine justice; and it was always

by slow and painful gradations that the sinner, the heretic, or the apostate was readmitted into the bosom of the church. A sentence of perpetual excommunication was, however, reserved for some crimes of an extraordinary magnitude, and particularly for the inexcusable relapses of those penitents who had already experienced and abused the clemency of their ecclesiastical superiors. According to the circumstances or the number of the guilty, the exercise of the Christian discipline was varied by the discretion of the bishops. The councils of Ancyra and Illiberis were held about the same time, the one in Galatia, the other in Spain; but their respective canons, which are still extant, seem to breathe a very different spirit. The Galatian, who after his baptism had repeatedly sacrificed to idols, might obtain his pardon by a penance of seven years; and if he had seduced others to imitate his example, only three years more were added to the term of his exile. But the unhappy Spaniard who had committed the same offence was deprived of the hope of reconciliation even in the article of death; and his idolatry was placed at the head of a list of seventeen other crimes, against which a sentence no less terrible was pronounced. Among these we may distinguish the inexpiable guilt of calumniating a bishop, a presbyter, or even a deacon.[148]

The well-tempered mixture of liberality and rigour, the judicious dispensation of rewards and punishments, according to the maxims of policy as well as justice, constituted the *human* strength of the church. The bishops, whose paternal care extended itself to the government of both worlds, were sensible of the importance of these prerogatives; and, covering their ambition with the fair pretence of the love of order, they were jealous of any rival in the exercise of a discipline so necessary to prevent the desertion of those troops which had enlisted themselves under the banner of the Cross, and whose numbers every day became more considerable. From the imperious declamations of Cyprian we should naturally conclude that the doctrines of excommunication and penance formed the most essential part of religion; and that it was much less dangerous for the disciples of Christ to neglect the observance of the moral duties than to despise the censures and authority of their bishops. Sometimes we might imagine that we were listening to the voice of Moses, when he commanded the earth to open, and to swallow up, in consuming flames, the rebellious race which refused obedience to the priesthood of Aaron; and we should sometimes suppose that we heard a Roman consul asserting the majesty of the republic, and declaring his inflexible resolution to enforce the rigour of the laws. "If such irregularities are suffered with impunity," (it is thus that the bishop of Carthage chides the lenity of his colleague), "if such irregularities are suffered, there is an end of EPISCOPAL VIGOUR;[149] an end of the sublime and divine power of governing the Church; an end of Christianity itself." Cyprian had renounced those temporal honours which it is probable he would never have obtained; but the acquisition of such absolute command over the consciences and understanding of a congregation, however obscure or despised by the world, is more truly grateful to the pride of the human heart than the possession of the most despotic power imposed by arms and conquest on a reluctant people.

In the course of this important, though perhaps tedious, inquiry, I have attempted to display the secondary causes which so efficaciously assisted the truth of the Christian religion. If among these causes we have discovered any artificial ornaments, any accidental circumstances, or any mixture of error and passion, it cannot appear surprising that mankind should be the most sensibly affected by such motives as were suited to their imperfect nature. It was by the aid of these causes—exclusive zeal, the immediate expectation of another world, the claim of miracles, the practice of rigid virtue, and the constitution of the primitive church—that Christianity spread itself with so much success in the Roman empire. To the first of these the Christians were indebted for their invincible valour, which disdained to capitulate with the enemy whom they were resolved to vanquish. The three succeeding causes supplied their valour with the most formidable arms. The last of these causes united their courage, directed their arms, and gave their efforts that irresistible weight which even a small band of well-trained and intrepid volunteers has so often possessed over an undisciplined multitude, ignorant of the subject and careless of the event of the war. In the various religions of Polytheism, some wandering fanatics of Egypt and Syria, who addressed themselves to the credulous superstition of the populace, were perhaps the only order of priests[150] that derived their whole support and credit from their sacerdotal profession, and were very deeply affected by a personal concern for the safety or prosperity of their tutelar deities. The ministers of Polytheism, both in Rome and in the provinces, were, for the most part, men of a noble birth and of an affluent fortune, who received, as an honourable distinction, the care of a celebrated temple or of a public sacrifice, exhibited, very frequently at their own expense, the sacred games,[151] and with cold indifference performed the ancient rites, according to the laws and fashion of their country. As they were engaged in the ordinary occupations of life, their zeal and devotion were seldom animated by a sense of interest, or by the habits of an ecclesiastical character. Confined to their respective temples and cities, they remained without any connection of discipline or government; and whilst they acknowledged the supreme jurisdiction of the senate, of the college of pontiffs, and of the emperor, those civil magistrates contented themselves with the easy task of maintaining in peace and dignity the general worship of mankind. We have already seen how various, how loose, and how uncertain were the religious sentiments of Polytheists. They were abandoned, almost without control, to the natural workings of a superstitious fancy. The accidental circumstances of their life and situation determined the object as well as the degree of their devotion; and as long as their adoration was successively prostituted to a thousand deities, it was scarcely possible that their hearts could be susceptible of a very sincere or lively passion for any of them.

When Christianity appeared in the world, even these faint and imperfect impressions had lost much of their original power. Human reason, which by its unassisted strength is incapable of perceiving the mysteries of faith, had already obtained an easy triumph over the folly of Paganism; and when Tertullian or Lactantius employ their labours in exposing its falsehood and extravagance, they are obliged to transcribe the eloquence of Cicero or the wit of Lucian. The contagion of these sceptical writings had been diffused far beyond the number of their readers. The fashion of incredulity was communicated from the philosopher to the man of pleasure or business, from the noble to the plebeian, and from the master to the menial slave who waited at his table, and who eagerly listened to the freedom of his conversation. On public occasions the philosophic part of mankind affected to treat with respect and decency the religious institutions of their country, but their secret contempt penetrated through the thin and awkward disguise; and even the people, when they discovered that their deities were rejected and derided by those whose rank or understanding they were accustomed to reverence, were filled with doubts and apprehensions concerning the truth of those doctrines to which they had yielded the most implicit belief. The decline of ancient prejudice exposed a very numerous portion of human kind to the danger of a painful and comfortless situation. A state of scepticism and suspense may amuse a few inquisitive minds. But the practice of superstition is so congenial to the multitude that, if they are forcibly awakened, they still regret the loss of their pleasing vision. Their love of the marvellous and supernatural, their curiosity with regard to future events, and their strong propensity to extend their hopes and fears beyond the limits of the visible world, were the principal causes which favoured the establishment of Polytheism. So urgent on the vulgar is the necessity of believing, that the fall of any system of mythology will most probably be succeeded by the introduction of some other mode of superstition. Some deities of a more recent and fashionable cast might soon have occupied the deserted temples of Jupiter and Apollo, if, in the decisive moment, the wisdom of Providence had not interposed a genuine revelation fitted to inspire the most rational esteem and conviction, whilst, at the same time, it was adorned with all that could attract the curiosity, the wonder, and the veneration of the people. In their actual disposition, as many were almost disengaged from their artificial prejudices, but equally susceptible and desirous of a devout attachment, an object much less deserving would have been sufficient to fill the vacant place in their hearts, and to gratify the uncertain eagerness of their passions. Those who are inclined to pursue this reflection, instead of viewing with astonishment the rapid progress of Christianity, will perhaps be surprised that its success was not still more rapid and still more universal.

It has been observed, with truth as well as propriety, that the conquests of Rome prepared and facilitated those of Christianity. In the second chapter of this work we have attempted to explain in what manner the most civilised provinces of Europe, Asia, and Africa were united under the dominion of one sovereign, and gradually connected by the most intimate ties of laws, of manners, and of language. The Jews of Palestine, who had fondly expected a temporal deliverer, gave so cold a reception to the miracles of the divine prophet, that it was found unnecessary to publish, or at least to preserve, any Hebrew gospel.[152] The authentic histories of the actions of Christ were composed in the Greek language, at a considerable distance from Jerusalem, and after the Gentile converts were grown extremely numerous.[153] As soon as those histories were translated into the Latin tongue they were perfectly intelligible to all the subjects of Rome, excepting only to the peasants of Syria and Egypt, for whose benefit particular versions were afterwards made. The public highways, which had been constructed for the use of the legions, opened an easy passage for the Christian missionaries from Damascus to Corinth, and from Italy to the extremity of Spain or Britain; nor did those spiritual conquerors encounter any of the obstacles which usually retard or prevent the introduction of a foreign religion into a distant country. There is the strongest reason to believe that before the reigns of Diocletian and Constantine the faith of Christ had been preached in every province, and in all the great cities of the empire; but the foundation of the several congregations, the numbers of the faithful who composed them, and their proportion to the unbelieving multitude, are now buried in obscurity or disguised by fiction and declamation. Such imperfect circumstances, however, as have reached our knowledge concerning the increase of the Christian name in Asia and Greece, in Egypt, in Italy, and in the West, we shall now proceed to relate, without neglecting the real or imaginary acquisitions which lay beyond the frontiers of the Roman empire.

The rich provinces that extend from the Euphrates to the Ionian sea were the principal theatre on which the apostle of the Gentiles displayed his zeal and piety. The seeds of the Gospel, which he had scattered in a fertile soil, were diligently cultivated by his disciples; and it should seem that, during the two first centuries, the most considerable body of Christians was contained within those limits. Among the societies which were instituted in Syria, none were more ancient or more illustrious than those of Damascus, of Berœa or Aleppo, and of Antioch. The prophetic introduction of the Apocalypse had described and immortalised the seven churches of Asia—Ephesus, Smyrna, Pergamus, Thyatira,[154] Sardes, Laodicea, and Philadelphia; and their colonies were soon diffused over that populous country. In a very early period, the islands of Cyprus and Crete, the provinces of Thrace and Macedonia, gave a favourable reception to the new religion; and Christian republics were soon founded in the cities of Corinth, of Sparta, and of Athens.[155] The antiquity of the Greek and Asiatic churches allowed a sufficient space of time for their increase and multiplication; and even the swarms of Gnostics and other heretics serve to display the flourishing condition of the orthodox church, since the appellation of heretics has always been applied to the less numerous party. To these domestic testimonies we may add the confession, the complaints, and the apprehensions of the Gentiles themselves. From the writings of Lucian, a philosopher who had studied mankind, and who describes their manners in the most lively colours, we may learn that, under the reign of Commodus, his native country of Pontus was filled with Epicureans and *Christians*.[156] Within fourscore years after the death of Christ,[157] the humane Pliny laments the magnitude of the evil which he vainly attempted to eradicate. In his very curious epistle to the emperor Trajan he affirms that the temples were almost deserted, that the sacred victims scarcely found any purchasers, and that the superstition had not only infected the cities, but had even spread itself into the villages and the open country of Pontus and Bithynia.[158]

Without descending into a minute scrutiny of the expressions or of the motives of those writers who either celebrate or lament the progress of Christianity in the East, it may in general be observed that none of them have left us any grounds from whence a just estimate might be formed of the real numbers of the faithful in those provinces. One circumstance, however, has been fortunately preserved, which seems to cast a more distinct light on this obscure but interesting subject. Under the reign of Theodosius, after Christianity had enjoyed, during more than sixty years, the sunshine of Imperial favour, the ancient and illustrious church of Antioch consisted of one hundred thousand persons, three thousand of whom were supported out of the public oblations.[159] The splendour and dignity of the queen of the East, the acknowledged populousness of Cæsarea, Seleucia, and Alexandria, and the destruction of two hundred and fifty thousand souls in the earthquake which afflicted Antioch under the elder Justin,[160] are so many convincing proofs that the whole number of its inhabitants was not less than half a million, and that the Christians, however multiplied by zeal and power, did not exceed a fifth part of that great city. How different a proportion must we adopt when we compare the persecuted with the triumphant church, the West with the East, remote villages with populous towns, and countries recently converted to the faith with the place where the believers first received the appellation of Christians! It must not, however, be dissembled that, in another passage, Chrysostom, to whom we are indebted for this useful information, computes the multitude of the faithful as even superior to that of the Jews and Pagans.[161] But the solution of this apparent difficulty is easy and obvious. The eloquent preacher draws a parallel between the civil and the ecclesiastical constitution of Antioch; between the list of Christians who had acquired heaven by baptism, and the list of citizens who had a right to share the public liberality. Slaves, strangers, and infants were comprised in the former; they were excluded from the latter.

The extensive commerce of Alexandria, and its proximity to Palestine, gave an easy entrance to the new religion. It was at first embraced by great numbers of the Therapeutæ, or Essenians, of the lake Mareotis, a Jewish sect which had abated much of its reverence for the Mosaic ceremonies. The austere life of the Essenians, their fasts and excommunications, the community of goods, the love of celibacy, their zeal for martyrdom, and the warmth though not the purity of their faith, already offered a very lively image of the primitive discipline.[162] It was in the school of Alexandria that the Christian theology appears to have assumed a regular and scientifical form; and when Hadrian visited Egypt, he found a church composed of Jews and of Greeks, sufficiently important to attract the notice of that inquisitive prince.[163] But the progress of Christianity was for a long time confined within the limits of a single city, which was itself a foreign colony, and till the close of the second century the predecessors of Demetrius were the only prelates of the Egyptian church. Three bishops were consecrated by the hands of Demetrius, and the number was increased to twenty by his successor Heraclas.[164] The body of the natives, a people distinguished by a sullen inflexibility of temper,[165] entertained the new doctrine with coldness and reluctance; and even in the time of Origen it was rare to meet with an Egyptian who had surmounted his early prejudices in favour of the sacred animals of his country.[166] As soon, indeed, as Christianity ascended the throne, the zeal of those barbarians obeyed the prevailing impulsion; the cities of Egypt were filled with bishops, and the deserts of Thebais swarmed with hermits.

A perpetual stream of strangers and provincials flowed into the capacious bosom of Rome. Whatever was strange or odious, whoever was guilty or suspected, might hope, in the obscurity of that immense capital, to elude the vigilance of the law. In such a various conflux of nations, every teacher, either of truth or of falsehood, every founder, whether of a virtuous or a criminal association, might easily multiply his disciples or accomplices. The Christians of Rome, at the time of the accidental persecution of Nero, are represented by Tacitus as already amounting to a very great multitude,[167] and the language of that great historian is almost similar to the style employed by Livy, when he relates the introduction and the suppression of the rites of Bacchus. After the Bacchanals had awakened the severity of the senate, it was likewise apprehended that a very great multitude, as it were *another people*, had been initiated into those abhorred mysteries.

A more careful inquiry soon demonstrated that the offenders did not exceed seven thousand; a number indeed sufficiently alarming when considered as the object of public justice.[168] It is with the same candid allowance that we should interpret the vague expressions of Tacitus, and in a former instance of Pliny, when they exaggerate the crowds of deluded fanatics who had forsaken the established worship of the gods. The church of Rome was undoubtedly the first and most populous of the empire; and we are possessed of an authentic record which attests the state of religion in that city about the middle of the third century, and after a peace of thirty-eight years. The clergy, at that time, consisted of a bishop, forty-six presbyters, seven deacons, as many sub-deacons, forty-two acolythes, and fifty readers, exorcists, and porters. The number of widows, of the infirm, and of the poor, who were maintained by the oblations of the faithful, amounted to fifteen hundred.[169] From reason, as well as from the analogy of Antioch, we may venture to estimate the Christians of Rome at about fifty thousand. The populousness of that great capital cannot perhaps be exactly ascertained; but the most modest calculation will not surely reduce it lower than a million of inhabitants, of whom the Christians might constitute at the most a twentieth part.[170]

The western provincials appeared to have derived the knowledge of Christianity from the same source which had diffused among them the language, the sentiments, and the manners of Rome. In this more important circumstance, Africa, as well as Gaul, was gradually fashioned to the imitation of the capital. Yet notwithstanding the many favourable occasions which might invite the Roman missionaries to visit their Latin provinces, it was late before they passed either the sea or the Alps;[171] nor can we discover in those great countries any assured traces either of faith or of persecution that ascend higher than the reign of the Antonines.[172] The slow progress of the Gospel in the cold climate of Gaul was extremely different from the eagerness with which it seems to have been received on the burning sands of Africa. The African Christians soon formed one of the principal members of the primitive church. The practice introduced into that province of appointing bishops to the most inconsiderable towns, and very frequently to the most obscure villages, contributed to multiply the splendour and importance of their religious societies, which during the course of the third century were animated by the zeal of Tertullian, directed by the abilities of Cyprian, and adorned by the eloquence of Lactantius. But if, on the contrary, we turn our eyes towards Gaul, we must content ourselves with discovering, in the time of Marcus Antoninus, the feeble and united congregations of Lyons and Vienne; and even as late as the reign of Decius we are assured that in a few cities only—Arles, Narbonne, Toulouse, Limoges, Clermont, Tours, and Paris—some scattered churches were supported by the devotion of a small number of Christians.[173] Silence is indeed very consistent with devotion; but as it is seldom compatible with zeal we may perceive and lament the languid state of Christianity in those provinces which had exchanged the Celtic for the Latin tongue, since they did not, during the three first centuries, give birth to a single ecclesiastical writer. From Gaul, which claimed a just pre-eminence of learning and authority over all the countries on this side of the Alps, the light of the Gospel was more faintly reflected on the remote provinces of Spain and Britain; and if we may credit the vehement assertions of Tertullian, they had already received the first rays of the faith when he addressed his Apology to the magistrates of the emperor Severus.[174] But the obscure and imperfect origin of the western churches of Europe had been so negligently recorded, that, if we would relate the time and manner of their foundation, we must supply the silence of antiquity by those legends which avarice or superstition long afterwards dictated to the monks in the lazy gloom of their convents.[175] Of these holy romances, that of the apostle St. James can alone, by its singular extravagance, deserve to be mentioned. From a peaceful fisherman of the lake of Gennesareth, he was transformed into a valorous knight, who charged at the head of the Spanish chivalry in their battles against the Moors. The gravest historians have celebrated his exploits; the miraculous shrine of Compostella displayed his power; and the sword of a military order, assisted by the terrors of the Inquisition, was sufficient to remove every objection of profane criticism.[176]

The progress of Christianity was not confined to the Roman empire; and, according to the primitive fathers, who interpret facts by prophecy, the new religion, within a century after the death of its Divine Author, had already visited every part of the globe. "There exists not," says Justin Martyr, "a people, whether Greek or barbarian, or any other race of men, by whatsoever appellation or manners they may be distinguished, however ignorant of arts or agriculture, whether they dwell under tents, or wander about in covered waggons, among whom prayers are not offered up in the name of a crucified Jesus to the Father and Creator of all things."[177] But this splendid exaggeration, which even at present it would be extremely difficult to reconcile with the real state of mankind, can be considered only as the rash sally of a devout but careless writer, the measure of whose belief was regulated by that of his wishes. But neither the belief nor the wishes of the fathers can alter the truth of history. It will still remain an undoubted fact that the barbarians of Scythia and Germany, who afterwards subverted the Roman monarchy, were involved in the darkness of paganism; and that even the conversion of Iberia, of Armenia, or of Æthiopia, was not attempted with any degree of success till the sceptre was in the hands of an orthodox emperor.[178] Before that time the various accidents of war and commerce might indeed diffuse an imperfect knowledge of the Gospel among the tribes of Caledonia,[179] and among the borderers of the Rhine, the Danube, and the Euphrates.[180] Beyond the last-mentioned river, Edessa was distinguished by a firm and early adherence to the faith.[181] From Edessa the principles of Christianity were easily introduced into the Greek and Syrian cities which obeyed the successors of Artaxerxes; but they do not appear to have made any deep impression on the minds of the Persians, whose religious system, by the labours of a well-disciplined order of priests, had been constructed with much more art and solidity than the uncertain mythology of Greece and Rome.[182]

From this impartial though imperfect survey of the progress of Christianity, it may perhaps seem probable that the number of its proselytes has been excessively magnified by fear on the one side, and by devotion on the other. According to the irreproachable testimony of Origen,[183] the proportion of the faithful was very inconsiderable, when compared with the multitude of an unbelieving world; but, as we are left without any distinct information, it is impossible to determine, and it is difficult even to conjecture, the real numbers of the primitive Christians. The most favourable calculation, however, that can be deduced from the examples of Antioch and of Rome will not permit us to imagine that more than a twentieth part of the subjects of the empire had enlisted themselves under the banner of the Cross before the important conversion of Constantine. But their habits of faith, of zeal, and of union, seemed to multiply their numbers; and the same causes which contributed to their future increase served to render their actual strength more apparent and more formidable.

Such is the constitution of civil society, that, whilst a few persons are distinguished by riches, by honours, and by knowledge, the body of the people is condemned to obscurity, ignorance, and poverty. The Christian religion, which addressed itself to the whole human race, must consequently collect a far greater number of proselytes from the lower than from the superior ranks of life. This innocent and natural circumstance has been improved into a very odious imputation, which seems to be less strenuously denied by the apologists than it is urged by the adversaries of the faith; that the new sect of Christians was almost entirely composed of the dregs of the populace, of peasants and mechanics, of boys and women, of beggars and slaves, the last of whom might sometimes introduce the missionaries into the rich and noble families to which they belonged. These obscure teachers (such was the charge of malice and infidelity) are as mute in public as they are loquacious and dogmatical in private. Whilst they cautiously avoid the dangerous encounter of philosophers, they mingle with the rude and illiterate crowd, and insinuate themselves into those minds whom their age, their sex, or their education has the best disposed to receive the impression of superstitious terrors.[184]

This unfavourable picture, though not devoid of a faint resemblance, betrays, by its dark colouring and distorted features, the pencil of an enemy. As the humble faith of Christ diffused itself through the world, it was embraced by several persons who derived some consequence from the advantages of nature or fortune. Aristides, who presented an eloquent apology to the emperor Hadrian, was an Athenian philosopher.[185] Justin Martyr had sought divine knowledge in the schools of Zeno, of Aristotle, of Pythagoras, and of Plato, before he fortunately was accosted by the old man, or rather the angel, who turned his attention to the study of the Jewish prophets.[186] Clemens of Alexandria had acquired much various reading in the Greek, and Tertullian in the Latin, language. Julius Africanus and Origen possessed a very considerable share of the learning of their times; and although the style of Cyprian is very different from that of Lactantius, we might almost discover that both those writers had been public teachers of rhetoric. Even the study of philosophy was at length introduced among the Christians, but it was not always productive of the most salutary effects; knowledge was as often the parent of heresy as of devotion, and the description which was designed for the followers of Artemon may, with equal propriety, be applied to the various sects that resisted the successors of the apostles. "They presume to alter the holy Scriptures, to abandon the ancient rule of faith, and to form their opinions according to the subtile precepts of logic. The science of the church is neglected for the study of geometry, and they lose sight of heaven while they are employed in measuring the earth. Euclid is perpetually in their hands. Aristotle and Theophrastus are the objects of their admiration; and they express an uncommon reverence for the works of Galen. Their errors are derived from the abuse of the arts and sciences of the infidels, and they corrupt the simplicity of the Gospel by the refinements of human reason."[187] Nor can it be affirmed with truth that the advantages of birth and fortune were always separated from the profession of Christianity. Several Roman citizens were brought before the tribunal of Pliny, and he soon discovered that a great number of persons of *every order* of men in Bithynia had deserted the religion of their ancestors.[188] His unsuspected testimony may, in this instance, obtain more credit than the bold challenge of Tertullian, when he addresses himself to the fears as well as to the humanity of the proconsul of Africa, by assuring him that if he persists in his cruel intentions he must decimate Carthage, and that he will find among the guilty many persons of his own rank, senators and matrons of noblest extraction, and the friends or relations of his most intimate friends.[189] It appears, however, that about forty years afterwards the emperor Valerian was persuaded of the truth of this assertion, since in one of his rescripts he evidently supposes that senators, Roman knights, and ladies of quality, were engaged in the Christian sect.[190] The church still continued to increase its outward splendour as it lost its internal purity; and, in the reign of Diocletian, the palace, the courts of justice, and even the army, concealed a multitude of Christians, who endeavoured to reconcile the interests of the present with those of a future life.

And yet these exceptions are either too few in number, or too recent in time, entirely to remove the imputation of ignorance and obscurity which has been so arrogantly cast on the first proselytes of Christianity. Instead of employing in our defence the fictions of later ages, it will be more prudent to convert the occasion of scandal into a subject of edification. Our serious thoughts will suggest to us that the apostles themselves were chosen by Providence among the fishermen of Galilee, and that, the lower we depress the temporal condition of the first Christians, the more reason we shall find to admire their merit and success. It is incumbent on us diligently to remember that the kingdom of heaven was promised to the poor in spirit, and that minds afflicted by calamity and the contempt of mankind cheerfully listen to the divine promise of future happiness; while, on the contrary, the fortunate are satisfied with the possession of this world; and the wise abuse in doubt and dispute their vain superiority of reason and knowledge.

We stand in need of such reflections to comfort us for the loss of some illustrious characters, which in our eyes might have seemed the most worthy of the heavenly present. The names of Seneca, of the elder and the younger Pliny, of Tacitus, of Plutarch, of Galen, of the slave Epictetus, and of the emperor Marcus Antoninus, adorn the age in which they flourished, and exalt the dignity of human nature. They filled with glory their respective stations, either in active or contemplative life; their excellent understandings were improved by study; philosophy had purified their minds from the prejudices of the popular superstition; and their days were spent in the pursuit of truth and the practice of virtue. Yet all these sages (it is no less an object of surprise than of concern) overlooked or rejected the perfection of the Christian system. Their language or their silence equally discover their contempt for the growing sect which in their time had diffused itself over the Roman empire. Those among them who condescend to mention the Christians consider them only as obstinate and perverse enthusiasts, who exacted an implicit submission to their mysterious doctrines, without being able to produce a single argument that could engage the attention of men of sense and learning.[191]

It is at least doubtful whether any of these philosophers perused the apologies which the primitive Christians repeatedly published in behalf of themselves and of their religion; but it is much to be lamented that such a cause was not defended by abler advocates. They expose with superfluous wit and eloquence the extravagance of Polytheism. They interest our compassion by displaying the innocence and sufferings of their injured brethren. But when they would demonstrate the divine origin of Christianity, they insist much more strongly on the predictions which announced, than on the miracles which accompanied, the appearance of the Messiah. Their favourite argument might serve to edify a Christian or to convert a Jew, since both the one and the other acknowledge the authority of those prophecies, and both are obliged, with devout reverence, to search for their sense and their accomplishment. But this mode of persuasion loses much of its weight and influence when it is addressed to those who neither understand nor respect the Mosaic dispensation and the prophetic style.[192] In the unskilful hands of Justin and of the succeeding apologists, the sublime meaning of the Hebrew oracles evaporates in distant types, affected conceits, and cold allegories; and even their authenticity was rendered suspicious to an unenlightened Gentile, by the mixture of pious forgeries which, under the names of Orpheus, Hermes, and the Sibyls,[193] were obtruded on him as of equal value with the genuine inspirations of Heaven. The adoption of fraud and sophistry in the defence of revelation too often reminds us of the injudicious conduct of those poets who load their *invulnerable* heroes with a useless weight of cumbersome and brittle armour.

But how shall we excuse the supine inattention of the Pagan and philosophic world to those evidences which were presented by the hand of Omnipotence, not to their reason, but to their senses? During the age of Christ, of his apostles, and of their first disciples, the doctrine which they preached was confirmed by innumerable prodigies. The lame walked, the blind saw, the sick were healed, the dead were raised, dæmons were expelled, and the laws of Nature were frequently suspended for the benefit of the church. But the sages of Greece and Rome turned aside from the awful spectacle, and, pursuing the ordinary occupations of life and study, appeared unconscious of any alterations in the moral or physical government of the world. Under the reign of Tiberius, the whole earth,[194] or at least a celebrated province of the Roman empire,[195] was involved in a preternatural darkness of three hours. Even this miraculous event, which ought to have excited the wonder, the curiosity, and the devotion of mankind, passed without notice in an age of science and history.[196] It happened during the lifetime of Seneca and the elder Pliny, who must have experienced the immediate effects, or received the earliest intelligence, of the prodigy. Each of these philosophers, in a laborious work, has recorded all the great phenomena of Nature, earthquakes, meteors, comets, and eclipses, which his indefatigable curiosity could collect.[197] Both the one and the other have omitted to mention the greatest phenomenon to which the mortal eye has been witness since the creation of the globe. A distinct chapter of Pliny[198] is designed for eclipses of an extraordinary nature and unusual duration; but he contents himself with describing the singular defect of light which followed the murder of Cæsar, when, during the greatest part of a year, the orb of the sun appeared pale and without splendour. This season of obscurity, which cannot surely be compared with the preternatural darkness of the Passion, had been already celebrated by most of the poets[199] and historians of that memorable age.[200]

CHAPTER XVI

The Conduct of the Roman Government towards the Christians, from the Reign of Nero to that of Constantine.

IF we seriously consider the purity of the Christian religion, the sanctity of its moral precepts, and the innocent as well as austere lives of the greater number of those who during the first ages embraced the faith of the Gospel, we should naturally suppose that so benevolent a doctrine would have been received with due reverence even by the unbelieving world; that the learned and the polite, however they might deride the miracles, would have esteemed the virtues of the new sect; and that the magistrates, instead of persecuting, would have protected an order of men who yielded the most passive obedience to the laws, though they declined the active cares of war and government. If, on the other hand, we recollect the universal toleration of Polytheism, as it was invariably maintained by the faith of the people, the incredulity of philosophers, and the policy of the Roman senate and emperors, we are at a loss to discover what new offence the Christians had committed, what new provocation could exasperate the mild indifference of antiquity, and what new motives could urge the Roman princes, who beheld without concern a thousand forms of religion subsisting in peace under their gentle sway, to inflict a severe punishment on any part of their subjects who had chosen for themselves a singular but an inoffensive mode of faith and worship.

The religious policy of the ancient world seems to have assumed a more stern and intolerant character to oppose the progress of Christianity. About fourscore years after the death of Christ, his innocent disciples were punished with death by the sentence of a proconsul of the most amiable and philosophic character, and according to the laws of an emperor distinguished by the wisdom and justice of his general administration. The apologies which were repeatedly addressed to the successors of Trajan are filled with the most pathetic complaints that the Christians, who obeyed the dictates and solicited the liberty of conscience, were alone, among all the subjects of the Roman empire, excluded from the common benefits of their auspicious government. The deaths of a few eminent martyrs have been recorded with care; and from the time that Christianity was invested with the supreme power, the governors of the church have been no less diligently employed in displaying the cruelty, than in imitating the conduct, of their Pagan adversaries. To separate (if it be possible) a few authentic as well as interesting facts from an undigested mass of fiction and error, and to relate, in a clear and rational manner, the causes, the extent, the duration, and the most important circumstances of the persecutions to which the first Christians were exposed, is the design of the present chapter.

The sectaries of a persecuted religion, depressed by fear, animated with resentment, and perhaps heated by enthusiasm, are seldom in a proper temper of mind calmly to investigate, or candidly to appreciate the motives of their enemies, which often escape the impartial and discerning view even of those who are placed at a secure distance from the flames of persecution.

A reason has been assigned for the conduct of the emperors towards the primitive Christians, which may appear the more specious and probable as it is drawn from the acknowledged genius of Polytheism. It has already been observed that the religious concord of the world was principally supported by the implicit assent and reverence which the nations of antiquity expressed for their respective traditions and ceremonies. It might therefore be expected that they would unite with indignation against any sect of people which should separate itself from the communion of mankind, and claiming the exclusive possession of divine knowledge, should disdain every form of worship except its own as impious and idolatrous. The rights of toleration were held by mutual indulgence: they were justly forfeited by a refusal of the accustomed tribute. As the payment of this tribute was inflexibly refused by the Jews, and by them alone, the consideration of the treatment which they experienced from the Roman magistrates will serve to explain how far these speculations are justified by facts, and will lead us to discover the true causes of the persecution of Christianity.

Without repeating what has been already mentioned of the reverence of the Roman princes and governors for the temple of Jerusalem, we shall only observe that the destruction of the temple and city was accompanied and followed by every circumstance that could exasperate the minds of the conquerors, and authorise religious persecutions by the most specious arguments of political justice and the public safety. From the reign of Nero to that of Antoninus Pius, the Jews discovered a fierce impatience of the dominion of Rome, which repeatedly broke out in the most furious massacres and insurrections. Humanity is shocked at the recital of the horrid cruelties which they committed in the cities of Egypt, of Cyprus, and of Cyrene, where they dwelt in treacherous friendship with the unsuspecting natives;[1] and we are tempted to applaud the severe retaliation which was exercised by the arms of the legions against a race of fanatics whose dire and credulous superstition seemed to render them the implacable enemies not only of the Roman government, but of human kind.[2] The enthusiasm of the Jews was supported by the opinion that it was unlawful for them to pay taxes to an idolatrous master, and by the flattering promise which they derived from their ancient oracles, that a conquering Messiah would soon arise, destined to break their fetters, and to invest the favourites of heaven with the empire of the earth. It was by announcing himself as their long-expected deliverer, and by calling on all the descendants of Abraham to assert the hope of Israel, that the famous Barchochebas collected a formidable army, with which he resisted during two years the power of the emperor Hadrian.[3]

Notwithstanding these repeated provocations, the resentment of the Roman princes expired after the victory, nor were their apprehensions continued beyond the period of war and danger. By the general indulgence of Polytheism, and by the mild temper of Antoninus Pius, the Jews were restored to their ancient privileges, and once more obtained the permission of circumcising their children, with the easy restraint that they should never confer on any foreign proselyte that distinguishing mark of the Hebrew race.[4] The numerous remains of that people, though they were still excluded from the precincts of Jerusalem, were permitted to form and to maintain considerable establishments both in Italy and in the provinces, to acquire the freedom of Rome, to enjoy municipal honours, and to obtain at the same time an exemption from the burdensome and expensive offices of society. The moderation or the contempt of the Romans gave a legal sanction to the form of ecclesiastical policy which was instituted by the vanquished sect. The patriarch, who had fixed his residence at Tiberias, was empowered to appoint his subordinate ministers and apostles, to exercise a domestic jurisdiction, and to receive from his dispersed brethren an annual contribution.[5] New synagogues were frequently erected in the principal cities of the empire; and the sabbaths, the fasts, and the festivals, which were either commanded by the Mosaic law or enjoined by the traditions of the Rabbis, were celebrated in the most solemn and public manner.[6] Such gentle treatment insensibly assuaged the stern temper of the Jews. Awakened from their dream of prophecy and conquest, they assumed the behaviour of peaceable and industrious subjects. Their irreconcilable hatred of mankind, instead of flaming out in acts of blood and violence, evaporated in less dangerous gratifications. They embraced every opportunity of overreaching the idolaters in trade, and they pronounced secret and ambiguous imprecations against the haughty kingdom of Edom.[7]

Since the Jews, who rejected with abhorrence the deities adored by their sovereign and by their fellow-subjects, enjoyed, however, the free exercise of their unsocial religion, there must have existed some other cause which exposed the disciples of Christ to those severities from which the posterity of Abraham was exempt. The difference between them is simple and obvious, but, according to the sentiments of antiquity, it was of the highest importance. The Jews were a *nation*, the Christians were a *sect*: and if it was natural for every community to respect the sacred institutions of their neighbours, it was incumbent on them to persevere in those of their ancestors. The voice of oracles, the precepts of philosophers, and the authority of the laws, unanimously enforced this national obligation. By their lofty claim of superior sanctity the Jews might provoke the Polytheists to consider them as an odious and impure race. By disdaining the intercourse of other nations they might deserve their contempt. The laws of Moses might be for the most part frivolous or absurd; yet, since they had been received during many ages by a large society, his followers were justified by the example of mankind, and it was universally acknowledged that they had a right to practise what it would have been criminal in them to neglect. But this principle, which protected the Jewish synagogue, afforded not any favour or security to the primitive church. By embracing the faith of the Gospel the Christians incurred the supposed guilt of an unnatural and unpardonable offence. They dissolved the sacred ties of custom and education, violated the religious institutions of their country, and presumptuously despised whatever their fathers had believed as true or had reverenced as sacred. Nor was this apostasy (if we may use the expression) merely of a partial or local kind; since the pious deserter who withdrew himself from the temples of Egypt or Syria would equally disdain to seek an asylum in those of Athens or Carthage. Every Christian rejected with contempt the superstitions of his family, his city, and his province. The whole body of Christians unanimously refused to hold any communion with the gods of Rome, of the empire, and of mankind. It was in vain that the oppressed believer asserted the inalienable rights of conscience and private judgment. Though his situation might excite the pity, his arguments could never reach the understanding, either of the philosophic or of the believing part of the Pagan world. To their apprehensions it was no less a matter of surprise that any individuals should entertain scruples against complying with the established mode of worship than if they had conceived a sudden abhorrence to the manners, the dress, or the language of their native country.[8]

The surprise of the Pagans was soon succeeded by resentment, and the most pious of men were exposed to the unjust but dangerous imputation of impiety. Malice and prejudice concurred in representing the Christians as a society of atheists, who, by the most daring attack on the religious constitution of the empire, had merited the severest animadversion of the civil magistrate. They had separated themselves (they gloried in the confession) from every mode of superstition which was received in any part of the globe by the various temper of Polytheism: but it was not altogether so evident what deity, or what form of worship, they had substituted to the gods and temples of antiquity. The pure and sublime idea which they entertained of the Supreme Being escaped the gross conception of the Pagan multitude, who were at a loss to discover a spiritual and solitary God, that was neither represented under any corporeal figure or visible symbol, nor was adored with the accustomed pomp of libations and festivals, of altars and sacrifices.[9] The sages of Greece and Rome, who had elevated their minds to the contemplation of the existence and attributes of the First Cause, were induced by reason or by vanity to reserve for themselves and their chosen disciples the privilege of this philosophical devotion.[10] They were far from admitting the prejudices of mankind as the standard of truth, but they considered them as flowing from the original disposition of human nature; and they supposed that any popular mode of faith and worship which presumed to disclaim the assistance of the senses would, in proportion as it receded from superstition, find itself incapable of restraining the wonderings of the fancy and the visions of fanaticism. The careless glance which men of wit and learning condescended to cast on the Christian revelation served only to confirm their hasty opinion, and to persuade them that the principle, which they might have revered, of the Divine Unity, was defaced by the wild enthusiasm, and annihilated by the airy speculations, of the new sectaries. The author of a celebrated dialogue, which has been attributed to Lucian, whilst he affects to treat the mysterious subject of the Trinity in a style of ridicule and contempt, betrays his own ignorance of the weakness of human reason, and of the inscrutable nature of the Divine perfections.[11]

It might appear less surprising that the founder of Christianity should not only be revered by his disciples as a sage and a prophet, but that he should be adored as a God. The Polytheists were disposed to adopt every article of faith which seemed to offer any resemblance, however distant or imperfect, with the popular mythology; and the legends of Bacchus, of Hercules, and of Æsculapius had, in some measure, prepared their imagination for the appearance of the Son of God under a human form.[12] But they were astonished that the Christians should abandon the temples of those ancient heroes who, in the infancy of the world, had invented arts, instituted laws, and vanquished the tyrants or monsters who infested the earth; in order to choose for the exclusive object of their religious worship an obscure teacher, who, in a recent age, and among a barbarous people, had fallen a sacrifice either to the malice of his own countrymen, or to the jealousy of the Roman government. The Pagan multitude, reserving their gratitude for temporal benefits alone, rejected the inestimable present of life and immortality which was offered to mankind by Jesus of Nazareth. His mild constancy in the midst of cruel and voluntary sufferings, his universal benevolence, and the sublime simplicity of his actions and character, were insufficient in the opinion of those carnal men, to compensate for the want of fame, of empire, and of success; and whilst they refused to acknowledge his stupendous triumph over the powers of darkness and of the grave, they misrepresented, or they insulted, the equivocal birth, wandering life, and ignominious death, of the divine Author of Christianity.[13]

The personal guilt which every Christian had contracted, in thus preferring his private sentiment to the national religion, was aggravated in a very high degree by the number and union of the criminals. It is well known, and has been already observed, that Roman policy viewed with the utmost jealousy and distrust any association among its subjects; and that the privileges of private corporations, though formed for the most harmless or beneficial purposes, were bestowed with a very sparing hand.[14] The religious assemblies of the Christians, who had separated themselves from the public worship, appeared of a much less innocent nature: they were illegal in their principle, and in their consequences might become dangerous; nor were the emperors conscious that they violated the laws of justice, when, for the peace of society, they prohibited those secret and sometimes nocturnal meetings.[15] The pious disobedience of the Christians made their conduct, or perhaps their designs, appear in a much more serious and criminal light; and the Roman princes, who might perhaps have suffered themselves to be disarmed by a ready submission, deeming their honour concerned in the execution of their commands, sometimes attempted, by rigorous punishments, to subdue this independent spirit, which boldly acknowledged an authority superior to that of the magistrate. The extent and duration of this spiritual conspiracy seemed to render it every day more deserving of his animadversion. We have already seen that the active and successful zeal of the Christians had insensibly diffused them through every province and almost every city of the empire. The new converts seemed to renounce their family and country, that they might connect themselves in an indissoluble band of union with a peculiar society, which everywhere assumed a different character from the rest of mankind. Their gloomy and austere aspect, their abhorrence of the common business and pleasures of life, and their frequent predictions of impending calamities,[16] inspired the Pagans with the apprehension of some danger which would arise from the new sect, the more alarming as it was the more obscure. "Whatever," says Pliny, "may be the principle of their conduct, their inflexible obstinacy appeared deserving of punishment."[17]

The precautions with which the disciples of Christ performed the offices of religion were at first dictated by fear and necessity; but they were continued from choice. By imitating the awful secrecy which reigned in the Eleusinian mysteries, the Christians had flattered themselves that they should render their sacred institutions more respectable in the eyes of the Pagan World.[18] But the event, as it often happens to the operations of subtile policy, deceived their wishes and their expectations. It was concluded that they only concealed what they would have blushed to disclose. Their mistaken prudence afforded an opportunity for malice to invent, and for suspicious credulity to believe, the horrid tales which described the Christians as the most wicked of human kind, who practised in their dark recesses every abomination that a depraved fancy could suggest, and who solicited the favour of their unknown God by the sacrifice of every moral virtue. There were many who pretended to confess or to relate the ceremonies of this abhorred society. It was asserted, "that a new-born infant, entirely covered over with flour, was presented, like some mystic symbol of initiation, to the knife of the proselyte, who unknowingly inflicted many a secret and mortal wound on the innocent victim of his error; that as soon as the cruel deed was perpetrated, the sectaries drank up the blood, greedily tore asunder the quivering members, and pledged themselves to eternal secrecy, by a mutual consciousness of guilt. It was as confidently affirmed that this inhuman sacrifice was succeeded by a suitable entertainment, in which intemperance served as a provocative to brutal lust; till, at the appointed moment, the lights were suddenly extinguished, shame was banished, nature was forgotten; and, as accident might direct, the darkness of the night was polluted by the incestuous commerce of sisters and brothers, of sons and of mothers."[19]

But the perusal of the ancient apologies was sufficient to remove even the slightest suspicion from the mind of a candid adversary. The Christians, with the intrepid security of innocence, appeal from the voice of rumour to the equity of the magistrates. They acknowledge that, if any proof can be produced of the crimes which calumny has imputed to them, they are worthy of the most severe punishment. They provoke the punishment, and they challenge the proof. At the same time they urge, with equal truth and propriety, that the charge is not less devoid of probability than it is destitute of evidence; they ask whether any one can seriously believe that the pure and holy precepts of the Gospel, which so frequently restrain the use of the most lawful enjoyments, should inculcate the practice of the most abominable crimes; that a large society should resolve to dishonour itself in the eyes of its own members; and that a great number of persons, of either sex, and every age and character, insensible to the fear of death or infamy, should consent to violate those principles which nature and education had imprinted most deeply in their minds.[20] Nothing, it should seem, could weaken the force or destroy the effect of so unanswerable a justification, unless it were the injudicious conduct of the apologists themselves, who betrayed the common cause of religion, to gratify their devout hatred to the domestic enemies of the church. It was sometimes faintly insinuated, and sometimes boldly asserted, that the same bloody sacrifices, and the same incestuous festivals, which were so falsely ascribed to the orthodox believers, were in reality celebrated by the Marcionites, by the Carpocratians, and by several other sects of the Gnostics, who, notwithstanding they might deviate into the paths of heresy, were still actuated by the sentiments of men, and still governed by the precepts of Christianity.[21] Accusations of a similar kind were retorted upon the church by the schismatics who had departed from its communion,[22] and it was confessed on all sides that the most scandalous licentiousness of manners prevailed among great numbers of those who affected the name of Christians. A Pagan magistrate, who possessed neither leisure nor abilities to discern the almost imperceptible line which divides the orthodox faith from heretical pravity, might easily have imagined that their mutual animosity had extorted the discovery of their common guilt. It was fortunate for the repose, or at least for the reputation, of the first Christians, that the magistrates sometimes proceeded with more temper and moderation than is usually consistent with religious zeal, and that they reported, as the impartial result of their judicial inquiry, that the sectaries who had deserted the established worship appeared to them sincere in their professions and blameless in their manners, however they might incur, by their absurd and excessive superstition, the censure of the laws.[23]

History, which undertakes to record the transactions of the past, for the instruction of future ages, would ill deserve that honourable office if she condescended to plead the cause of tyrants, or to justify the maxims of persecution. It must, however, be acknowledged that the conduct of the emperors who appeared the least favourable to the primitive church is by no means so criminal as that of modern sovereigns who have employed the arm of violence and terror against the religious opinions of any part of their subjects. From their reflections, or even from their own feelings, a Charles V. or a Louis XIV. might have acquired a just knowledge of the rights of conscience, of the obligation of faith, and of the innocence of error. But the princes and magistrates of ancient Rome were strangers to those principles which inspired and authorised the inflexible obstinacy of the Christians in the cause of truth, nor could they themselves discover in their own breasts any motives which would have prompted them to refuse a legal, and as it were a natural, submission to the sacred institutions of their country. The same reason which contributes to alleviate the guilt, must have tended to abate the rigour, of their persecutions. As they were actuated, not by the furious zeal of bigots, but by the temperate policy of legislators, contempt must often have relaxed, and humanity must frequently have suspended, the execution of those laws which they enacted against the humble and obscure followers of Christ. From the general view of their character and motives we might naturally conclude: I. That a considerable time elapsed before they considered the new sectaries as an object deserving of the attention of government. II. That in the conviction of any of their subjects who were accused of so very singular a crime, they proceeded with caution and reluc-

tance. III. That they were moderate in the use of punishments; and IV. That the afflicted church enjoyed many intervals of peace and tranquillity. Notwithstanding the careless indifference which the most copious and the most minute of the Pagan writers have shown to the affairs of the Christians,[24] it may still be in our power to confirm each of these probable suppositions by the evidence of authentic facts.

I. By the wise dispensation of Providence a mysterious veil was cast over the infancy of the church, which, till the faith of the Christians was matured, and their numbers were multiplied, served to protect them not only from the malice but even from the knowledge of the Pagan world. The slow and gradual abolition of the Mosaic ceremonies afforded a safe and innocent disguise to the more early proselytes of the Gospel. As they were for the greater part of the race of Abraham, they were distinguished by the peculiar mark of circumcision, offered up their devotions in the Temple of Jerusalem till its final destruction, and received both the Law and the Prophets as the genuine inspirations of the Deity. The Gentile converts who by a spiritual adoption had been associated to the hope of Israel, were likewise confounded under the garb and appearance of Jews;[25] and as the Polytheists paid less regard to articles of faith than to the external worship, the new sect, which carefully concealed, or faintly announced, its future greatness and ambition, was permitted to shelter itself under the general toleration which was granted to an ancient and celebrated people in the Roman empire. It was not long, perhaps, before the Jews themselves, animated with a fiercer zeal and a more jealous faith, perceived the gradual separation of their Nazarene brethren from the doctrine of the synagogue: and they would gladly have extinguished the dangerous heresy in the blood of its adherents. But the decrees of Heaven had already disarmed their malice; and though they might sometimes exert the licentious privilege of sedition, they no longer possessed the administration of criminal justice; nor did they find it easy to infuse into the calm breast of a Roman magistrate the rancour of their own zeal and prejudice. The provincial governors declared themselves ready to listen to any accusation that might affect the public safety; but as soon as they were informed that it was a question not of facts but of words, a dispute relating only to the interpretation of the Jewish laws and prophecies, they deemed it unworthy of the majesty of Rome seriously to discuss the obscure differences which might arise among a barbarous and superstitious people. The innocence of the first Christians was protected by ignorance and contempt; and the tribunal of the Pagan magistrate often proved their most assured refuge against the fury of the synagogue.[26] If, indeed, we were disposed to adopt the traditions of a too credulous antiquity, we might relate the distant peregrinations, the wonderful achievements, and the various deaths of the twelve apostles: but a more accurate inquiry will induce us to doubt whether any of those persons who had been witnesses to the miracles of Christ were permitted, beyond the limits of Palestine, to seal with their blood the truth of their testimony.[27] From the ordinary term of human life, it may very naturally be presumed that most of them were deceased before the discontent of the Jews broke out into that furious war which was terminated only by the ruin of Jerusalem. During a long period, from the death of Christ to that memorable rebellion, we cannot discover any traces of Roman intolerance, unless they are to be found in the sudden, the transient, but the cruel persecution, which was exercised by Nero against the Christians of the capital, thirty-five years after the former, and only two years before the latter, of those great events. The character of the philosophic historian, to whom we are principally indebted for the knowledge of this singular transaction, would alone be sufficient to recommend it to our most attentive consideration.

In the tenth year of the reign of Nero the capital of the empire was afflicted by a fire which raged beyond the memory or example of former ages.[28] The monuments of Grecian art and of Roman virtue, the trophies of the Punic and Gallic wars, the most holy temples, and the most splendid palaces were involved in one common destruction. Of the fourteen regions or quarters into which Rome was divided, four only subsisted entire, three were levelled with the ground, and the remaining seven, which had experienced the fury of the flames, displayed a melancholy prospect of ruin and desolation. The vigilance of government appears not to have neglected any of the precautions which might alleviate the sense of so dreadful a calamity. The Imperial gardens were thrown open to the distressed multitude, temporary buildings were erected for their accommodation, and a plentiful supply of corn and provisions was distributed at a very moderate price.[29] The most generous policy seemed to have dictated the edicts which regulated the disposition of the streets and the construction of private houses;

and, as it usually happens in an age of prosperity, the conflagration of Rome, in the course of a few years, produced a new city, more regular and more beautiful than the former. But all the prudence and humanity affected by Nero on this occasion were insufficient to preserve him from the popular suspicion. Every crime might be imputed to the assassin of his wife and mother; nor could the prince who prostituted his person and dignity on the theatre be deemed incapable of the most extravagant folly. The voice of rumour accused the emperor as the incendiary of his own capital; and, as the most incredible stories are the best adapted to the genius of an enraged people, it was gravely reported, and firmly believed, that Nero, enjoying the calamity which he had occasioned, amused himself with singing to his lyre the destruction of ancient Troy.[30] To divert a suspicion which the power of despotism was unable to suppress, the emperor resolved to substitute in his own place some fictitious criminals. "With this view (continues Tacitus) he inflicted the most exquisite tortures on those men who, under the vulgar appellation of Christians, were already branded with deserved infamy. They derived their name and origin from Christ, who, in the reign of Tiberius, had suffered death by the sentence of the procurator Pontius Pilate.[31] For a while this dire superstition was checked, but it again burst forth; and not only spread itself over Judaea, the first seat of this mischievous sect, but was even introduced into Rome, the common asylum which receives and protects whatever is impure, whatever is atrocious. The confessions of those who were seized discovered a great multitude of their accomplices, and they were all convicted, not so much for the crime of setting fire to the city as for their hatred of human kind.[32] They died in torments, and their torments were embittered by insult and derision. Some were nailed on crosses; others sewn up in the skins of wild beasts, and exposed to the fury of dogs; others again, smeared over with combustible materials, were used as torches to illuminate the darkness of the night. The gardens of Nero were destined for the melancholy spectacle, which was accompanied with a horse-race, and honoured with the presence of the emperor, who mingled with the populace in the dress and attitude of a charioteer. The guilt of the Christians deserved indeed the most exemplary punishment, but the public abhorrence was changed into commiseration, from the opinion that those unhappy wretches were sacrificed, not so much to the public welfare as to the cruelty of a jealous tyrant."[33] Those who survey with a curious eye the revolutions of mankind may observe that the gardens and circus of Nero on the Vatican, which were polluted with the blood of the first Christians, have been rendered still more famous by the triumph and by the abuse of the persecuted religion. On the same spot[34] a temple, which far surpasses the ancient glories of the Capitol, has been since erected by the Christian Pontiffs, who, deriving their claim of universal dominion from an humble fisherman of Galilee, have succeeded to the throne of the Cæsars, given laws to the barbarian conquerors of Rome, and extended their spiritual jurisdiction from the coast of the Baltic to the shores of the Pacific Ocean.

But it would be improper to dismiss this account of Nero's persecution till we have made some observations that may serve to remove the difficulties with which it is perplexed, and to throw some light on the subsequent history of the church.

1. The most sceptical criticism is obliged to respect the truth of this extraordinary fact, and the integrity of this celebrated passage of Tacitus. The former is confirmed by the diligent and accurate Suetonius, who mentions the punishment which Nero inflicted on the Christians, a sect of men who had embraced a new and criminal superstition.[35] The latter may be proved by the consent of the most ancient manuscripts; by the inimitable character of the style of Tacitus; by his reputation, which guarded his text from the interpolations of pious fraud; and by the purport of his narration, which accused the first Christians of the most atrocious crimes, without insinuating that they possessed any miraculous or even magical powers above the rest of mankind.[36] 2. Notwithstanding it is probable that Tacitus was born some years before the fire of Rome,[37] he could derive only from reading and conversation the knowledge of an event which happened during his infancy. Before he gave himself to the public he calmly waited till his genius had attained its full maturity, and he was more than forty years of age when a grateful regard for the memory of the virtuous Agricola extorted from him the most early of those historical compositions which will delight and instruct the most distant posterity. After making a trial of his strength in the life of Agricola, and the description of Germany, he conceived, and at length executed, a more arduous work, the history of Rome, in thirty books, from the fall of Nero to the accession of Nerva. The administration of Nerva introduced an age of justice and prosperity, which Tacitus had destined for the occupation of his old age;[38] but when he took a nearer view of his subject, judging, perhaps, that it was a more honourable or a less invidious office to record the vices of past tyrants than to celebrate the virtues of a reigning monarch, he chose rather to relate, under the form of annals, the actions of the four immediate successors of Augustus. To collect, to dispose, and to adorn a series of fourscore years in an immortal work, every sentence of which is pregnant with the deepest observations and the most lively images, was an undertaking sufficient to exercise the genius of Tacitus himself during the greatest part of his life. In the last years of the reign of Trajan, whilst the victorious monarch extended the power of Rome beyond its ancient limits, the historian was describing, in the second and fourth books of his Annals, the tyranny of Tiberius;[39] and the emperor Hadrian must have succeeded to the throne before Tacitus, in the regular prosecution of his work, could relate the fire of the capital and the cruelty of Nero towards the unfortunate Christians. At the distance of sixty years it was the duty of the annalist to adopt the narratives of contemporaries; but it was natural for the philosopher to indulge himself in the description of the origin, the progress, and the character of the new sect, not so much according to the knowledge or prejudices of the age of Nero, as according to those of the time of Hadrian. 3. Tacitus very frequently trusts to the curiosity or reflection of his readers to supply those intermediate circumstances and ideas which, in his extreme conciseness, he has thought proper to suppress. We may therefore presume to imagine some probable cause which could direct the cruelty of Nero against the Christians of Rome, whose obscurity, as well as innocence, should have shielded them from his indignation, and even from his notice. The Jews, who were numerous in the capital and oppressed in their own country, were a much fitter object for the suspicions of the emperor and of the people: nor did it seem unlikely that a vanquished nation, who already discovered their abhorrence of the Roman yoke, might have recourse to the most atrocious means of gratifying their implacable revenge. But the Jews possessed very powerful advocates in the palace, and even in the heart of the tyrant; his wife and mistress, the beautiful Poppæa, and a favourite player of the race of Abraham, who had already employed their intercession on behalf of the obnoxious people.[40] In their room it was necessary to offer some other victims, and

it might easily be suggested that, although the genuine followers of Moses were innocent of the fire of Rome, there had arisen among them a new and pernicious sect of GALILÆANS, which was capable of the most horrid crimes. Under the appellation of GALILÆANS two distinctions of men were confounded, the most opposite to each other in their manners and principles; the disciples who had embraced the faith of Jesus of Nazareth,[41] and the zealots who had followed the standard of Judas the Gaulonite.[42] The former were the friends, the latter were the enemies, of human kind; and the only resemblance between them consisted in the same inflexible constancy which, in the defence of their cause, rendered them insensible of death and tortures. The followers of Judas, who impelled their countrymen into rebellion, were soon buried under the ruins of Jerusalem; whilst those of Jesus, known by the more celebrated name of Christians, diffused themselves over the Roman empire. How natural was it for Tacitus, in the time of Hadrian, to appropriate to the Christians the guilt and the sufferings which he might, with far greater truth and justice, have attributed to a sect whose odious memory was almost extinguished! 4. Whatever opinion may be entertained of this conjecture (for it is no more than a conjecture), it is evident that the effect, as well as the cause, of Nero's persecution, were confined to the walls of Rome;[43] that the religious tenets of the Galilæans, or Christians, were never made a subject of punishment, or even of inquiry; and that, as the idea of their sufferings was, for a long time, connected with the idea of cruelty and injustice, the moderation of succeeding princes inclined them to spare a sect oppressed by a tyrant whose rage had been usually directed against virtue and innocence.

It is somewhat remarkable that the flames of war consumed almost at the same time the Temple of Jerusalem and the Capitol of Rome;[44] and it appears no less singular that the tribute which devotion had destined to the former should have been converted by the power of an assaulting victor to restore and adorn the splendour of the latter.[45] The emperors levied a general capitation tax on the Jewish people; and although the sum assessed on the head of each individual was inconsiderable, the use for which it was designed, and the severity with which it was exacted, were considered as an intolerable grievance.[46] Since the officers of the revenue extended their unjust claim to many persons who were strangers to the blood or religion of the Jews, it was impossible that the Christians, who had so often sheltered themselves under the shade of the synagogue, should now escape this rapacious persecution. Anxious as they were to avoid the slightest infection of idolatry, their conscience forbade them to contribute to the honour of that dæmon who had assumed the character of the Capitoline Jupiter. As a very numerous though declining party among the Christians still adhered to the law of Moses, their efforts to dissemble their Jewish origin were detected by the decisive test of circumcision;[47] nor were the Roman magistrates at leisure to inquire into the difference of their religious tenets. Among the Christians who were brought before the tribunal of the emperor, or, as it seems more probable, before that of the procurator of Judæa, two persons are said to have appeared, distinguished by their extraction, which was more truly noble than that of the greatest monarchs. These were the grandsons of St. Jude the apostle, who himself was the brother of Jesus Christ.[48] Their natural pretensions to the throne of David might perhaps attract the respect of the people, and excite the jealousy of the governor; but the meanness of their garb and the simplicity of their answers soon convinced him that they were neither desirous nor capable of disturbing the peace of the Roman empire. They frankly confessed their royal origin, and their near relation to the Messiah, but they disclaimed any temporal views, and professed that his kingdom, which they devoutly expected, was purely of a spiritual and angelic nature. When they were examined concerning their fortune and occupation, they showed their hands hardened with daily labour, and declared that they derived their whole subsistence from the cultivation of a farm near the village of Cocaba, of the extent of about twenty-four English acres,[49] and of the value of nine thousand drachms, or three hundred pounds sterling. The grandsons of St. Jude were dismissed with compassion and contempt.[50]

But although the obscurity of the house of David might protect them from the suspicions of a tyrant, the present greatness of his own family alarmed the pusillanimous temper of Domitian, which could only be appeased by the blood of those Romans whom he either feared, or hated, or esteemed. Of the two sons of his uncle Flavius Sabinus,[51] the elder was soon convicted of treasonable intentions, and the younger, who bore the name of Flavius Clemens, was indebted for his safety to his want of courage and ability.[52] The emperor for a long time distinguished so harmless a kinsman by his favour and protection, bestowed on him his own niece Domitilla, adopted the children of that marriage to the hope of the succession, and invested their father with the honours of the consulship. But he had scarcely finished the term of his annual magistracy, when on a slight pretence he was condemned and executed; Domitilla was banished to a desolate island on the coast of Campania;[53] and sentences either of death or of confiscation were pronounced against a great number of persons who were involved in the same accusation. The guilt imputed to their charge was that of *Atheism and Jewish manners*;[54] a singular association of ideas, which cannot with any propriety be applied except to the Christians, as they were obscurely and imperfectly viewed by the magistrates and by the writers of that period. On the strength of so probable an interpretation, and too eagerly admitting the suspicions of a tyrant as an evidence of their honourable crime, the church has placed both Clemens and Domitilla among its first martyrs, and has branded the cruelty of Domitian with the name of the second persecution. But this persecution (if it deserves that epithet) was of no long duration. A few months after the death of Clemens and the banishment of Domitilla, Stephen, a freedman belonging to the latter, who had enjoyed the favour, but who had not surely embraced the faith, of his mistress, assassinated the emperor in his palace.[55] The memory of Domitian was condemned by the senate; his acts were rescinded; his exiles recalled; and under the gentle administration of Nerva, while the innocent were restored to their rank and fortunes, even the most guilty either obtained pardon or escaped punishment.[56]

II. About ten years afterwards, under the reign of Trajan, the younger Pliny was intrusted by his friend and master with the government of Bithynia and Pontus. He soon found himself at a loss to determine by what rule of justice or of law he should direct his conduct in the execution of an office the most repugnant to his humanity. Pliny had never assisted at any judicial proceedings against the Christians, with whose name alone he seems to be acquainted; and he was totally uninformed with regard to the nature of their guilt, the method of their conviction, and the degree of their punishment. In this perplexity he had recourse to his usual expedient, of submitting to the wisdom of Trajan an impartial, and, in some respects, a favourable account of the new superstition, requesting the emperor that he would condescend to resolve his doubts and to instruct his ignorance.[57]

The life of Pliny had been employed in the acquisition of learning, and in the business of the world. Since the age of nineteen he had pleaded with distinction in the tribunals of Rome,[58] filled a place in the senate, had been invested with the honours of the consulship, and had formed very numerous connections with every order of men, both in Italy and in the provinces. From *his* ignorance therefore we may derive some useful information. We may assure ourselves that when he accepted the government of Bithynia there were no general laws or decrees of the senate in force against the Christians; that neither Trajan nor any of his virtuous predecessors, whose edicts were received into the civil and criminal jurisprudence, had publicly declared their intentions concerning the new sect; and that, whatever proceedings had been carried on against the Christians, there were none of sufficient weight and authority to establish a precedent for the conduct of a Roman magistrate.

The answer of Trajan, to which the Christians of the succeeding age have frequently appealed, discovers as much regard for justice and humanity as could be reconciled with his mistaken notions of religious policy.[59] Instead of displaying the implacable zeal of an Inquisitor, anxious to discover the most minute particles of heresy, and exulting in the number of his victims, the emperor expresses much more solicitude to protect the security of the innocent than to prevent the escape of the guilty. He acknowledges the difficulty of fixing any general plan; but he lays down two salutary rules, which often afforded relief and support to the distressed Christians. Though he directs the magistrates to punish such persons as are legally convicted, he prohibits them, with a very humane inconsistency, from making any inquiries concerning the supposed criminals. Nor was the magistrate allowed to proceed on every kind of information. Anonymous charges the emperor rejects, as too repugnant to the equity of his government; and he strictly requires, for the conviction of those to whom the guilt of Christianity is imputed, the positive evidence of a fair and open accuser. It is likewise probable that the persons who assumed so invidious an office were obliged to declare the grounds of their suspicions, to specify (both in respect to time and place) the secret assemblies which their Christian adversary had frequented, and to disclose a great number of circumstances which were concealed with the most vigilant jealousy from the eye of the profane. If they succeeded in their prosecution, they were exposed to the resentment of a considerable and active party, to the censure of the more liberal portion of mankind, and to the ignominy which, in every age and country, has attended the character of an informer. If, on the contrary, they failed in their proofs, they incurred the severe and perhaps capital penalty, which, according to a law published by the emperor Hadrian, was inflicted on those who falsely attributed to their fellow-citizens the crime of Christianity. The violence of personal or superstitious animosity might sometimes prevail over the most natural apprehensions of disgrace and danger; but it cannot surely be imagined that accusations of so unpromising an appearance were either lightly or frequently undertaken by the Pagan subjects of the Roman empire.[60]

The expedient which was employed to elude the prudence of the laws affords a sufficient proof how effectually they disappointed the mischievous designs of private malice or superstitious zeal. In a large and tumultuous assembly the restraints of fear and shame, so forcible on the minds of individuals, are deprived of the greatest part of their influence. The pious Christian, as he was desirous to obtain, or to escape, the glory of martyrdom, expected, either with impatience or with terror, the stated returns of the public games and festivals. On those occasions the inhabitants of the great cities of the empire were collected in the circus or the theatre, where every circumstance of the place, as well as of the ceremony, contributed to kindle their devotion and to extinguish their humanity. Whilst the numerous spectators, crowned with garlands, perfumed with incense, purified with the blood of victims, and surrounded with the altars and statues of their tutelar deities, resigned themselves to the enjoyment of pleasures which they considered as an essential part of their religious worship, they recollected that the Christians alone abhorred the gods of mankind, and, by their absence and melancholy on these solemn festivals, seemed to insult or to lament the public felicity. If the empire had been afflicted by any recent calamity, by a plague, a famine, or an unsuccessful war; if the Tiber had, or if the Nile had not, risen beyond its banks; if the earth had shaken, or if the temperate order of the seasons had been interrupted, the superstitious Pagans were convinced that the crimes and the impiety of the Christians, who were spared by the excessive lenity of the government, had at length provoked the Divine justice. It was not among a licentious

and exasperated populace that the forms of legal proceedings could be observed; it was not in an amphitheatre, stained with the blood of wild beasts and gladiators, that the voice of compassion could be heard. The impatient clamours of the multitude denounced the Christians as the enemies of gods and men, doomed them to the severest tortures, and, venturing to accuse by names some of the most distinguished of the new sectaries, required with irresistible vehemence that they should be instantly apprehended and cast to the lions.[61] The provincial governors and magistrates who presided in the public spectacles were usually inclined to gratify the inclinations, and to appease the rage of the people, by the sacrifice of a few obnoxious victims. But the wisdom of the emperors protected the church from the danger of these tumultuous clamours and irregular accusations, which they justly censured as repugnant both to the firmness and to the equity of their administration. The edicts of Hadrian and of Antoninus Pius expressly declared that the voice of the multitude should never be admitted as legal evidence to convict or to punish those unfortunate persons who had embraced the enthusiasm of the Christians.[62]

III. Punishment was not the inevitable consequence of conviction, and the Christians whose guilt was the most clearly proved by the testimony of witnesses, or even by their voluntary confession, still retained in their own power the alternative of life or death. It was not so much the past offence, as the actual resistance, which excited the indignation of the magistrate. He was persuaded that he offered them an easy pardon, since, if they consented to cast a few grains of incense upon the altar, they were dismissed from the tribunal in safety and with applause. It was esteemed the duty of a humane judge to endeavour to reclaim, rather than to punish, those deluded enthusiasts. Varying his tone according to the age, the sex, or the situation of the prisoners, he frequently condescended to set before their eyes every circumstance which could render life more pleasing, or death more terrible; and to solicit, nay to intreat them, that they would show some compassion to themselves, to their families, and to their friends.[63] If threats and persuasions proved ineffectual, he had often recourse to violence; the scourge and the rack were called in to supply the deficiency of argument, and every art of cruelty was employed to subdue such inflexible, and, as it appeared to the Pagans, such criminal obstinacy. The ancient apologists of Christianity have censured, with equal truth and severity, the irregular conduct of their persecutors, who, contrary to every principle of judicial proceeding, admitted the use of torture, in order to obtain, not a confession, but a denial, of the crime which was the object of their inquiry.[64] The monks of succeeding ages, who, in their peaceful solitudes, entertained themselves with diversifying the deaths and sufferings of the primitive martyrs, have frequently invented torments of a much more refined and ingenious nature. In particular, it has pleased them to suppose that the zeal of the Roman magistrates, disdaining every consideration of moral virtue or public decency, endeavoured to seduce those whom they were unable to vanquish, and that by their orders the most brutal violence was offered to those whom they found it impossible to seduce. It is related that pious females, who were prepared to despise death, were sometimes condemned to a more severe trial, and called upon to determine whether they set a higher value on their religion or on their chastity. The youths to whose licentious embraces they were abandoned received a solemn exhortation from the judge to exert their most strenuous efforts to maintain the honour of Venus against the impious virgin who refused to burn incense on her altars. Their violence, however, was commonly disappointed, and the seasonable interposition of some miraculous power preserved the chaste spouses of Christ from the dishonour even of an involuntary defeat. We should not indeed neglect to remark that the more ancient as well as authentic memorials of the church are seldom polluted with these extravagant and indecent fictions.[65]

The total disregard of truth and probability in the representation of these primitive martyrdoms was occasioned by a very natural mistake. The ecclesiastical writers of the fourth or fifth centuries ascribed to the magistrates of Rome the same degree of implacable and unrelenting zeal which filled their own breasts against the heretics or the idolaters of their own times. It is not improbable that some of those persons who were raised to the dignities of the empire might have imbibed the prejudices of the populace, and that the cruel disposition of others might occasionally be stimulated by motives of avarice or of personal resentment.[66] But it is certain, and we may appeal to the grateful confessions of the first Christians, that the greatest part of those magistrates who exercised in the provinces the authority of the emperor or of the senate, and to whose hands alone the jurisdiction of life

and death was intrusted, behaved like men of polished manners and liberal education, who respected the rules of justice, and who were conversant with the precepts of philosophy. They frequently declined the odious task of persecution, dismissed the charge with contempt, or suggested to the accused Christian some legal evasion by which he might elude the severity of the laws.[67] Whenever they were invested with a discretionary power,[68] they used it much less for the oppression than for the relief and benefit of the afflicted church. They were far from condemning all the Christians who were accused before their tribunal, and very far from punishing with death all those who were convicted of an obstinate adherence to the new superstition. Contenting themselves, for the most part, with the milder chastisements of imprisonment, exile, or slavery in the mines,[69] they left the unhappy victims of their justice some reason to hope that a prosperous event, the accession, the marriage, or the triumph of an emperor, might speedily restore them by a general pardon to their former state. The martyrs, devoted to immediate execution by the Roman magistrates, appear to have been selected from the most opposite extremes. They were either bishops and presbyters, the persons the most distinguished among the Christians by their rank and influence, and whose example might strike terror into the whole sect;[70] or else they were the meanest and most abject among them, particularly those of the servile condition, whose lives were esteemed of little value, and whose sufferings were viewed by the ancients with too careless an indifference.[71] The learned Origen, who, from his experience as well as readings, was intimately acquainted with the history of the Christians, declares, in the most express terms, that the number of martyrs was very inconsiderable.[72] His authority would alone be sufficient to annihilate that formidable army of martyrs, whose relics, drawn for the most part from the catacombs of Rome, have replenished so many churches,[73] and whose marvellous achievements have been the subject of so many volumes of holy romance.[74] But the general assertion of Origen may be explained and confirmed by the particular testimony of his friend Dionysius, who, in the immense city of Alexandria, and under the rigorous persecution of Decius, reckons only ten men and seven women who suffered for the profession of the Christian name.[75]

During the same period of persecution, the zealous, the eloquent, the ambitious Cyprian governed the church, not only of Carthage, but even of Africa. He possessed every quality which could engage the reverence of the faithful, or provoke the suspicions and resentment of the Pagan magistrates. His character as well as his station seemed to mark out that holy prelate as the most distinguished object of envy and of danger.[76] The experience, however, of the life of Cyprian is sufficient to prove that our fancy has exaggerated the perilous situation of a Christian bishop; and that the dangers to which he was exposed were less imminent than those which temporal ambition is always prepared to encounter in the pursuit of honours. Four Roman emperors, with their families, their favourites, and their adherents, perished by the sword in the space of ten years, during which the bishop of Carthage guided by his authority and eloquence the councils of the African church. It was only in the third year of his administration that he had reason, during a few months, to apprehend the severe edicts of Decius, the vigilance of the magistrate, and the clamours of the multitude, who loudly demanded that Cyprian, the leader of the Christians, should be thrown to the lions. Prudence suggested the necessity of a temporary retreat, and the voice of prudence was obeyed. He withdrew himself into an obscure solitude, from whence he could maintain a constant correspondence with the clergy and people of Carthage; and, concealing himself till the tempest was past, he preserved his life, without relinquishing either his power or his reputation. His extreme caution did not however escape the censure of the more rigid Christians, who lamented, or the reproaches of his personal enemies, who insulted, a conduct which they considered as a pusillanimous and criminal desertion of the most sacred duty.[77] The propriety of reserving himself for the future exigencies of the church, the example of several holy bishops,[78] and the divine admonitions which, as he declares himself, he frequently received in visions and ecstacies, were the reasons alleged in his justification.[79] But his best apology may be found in the cheerful resolution with which, about eight years afterwards, he suffered death in the cause of religion. The authentic history of his martyrdom has been recorded with unusual candour and impartiality. A short abstract therefore of its most important circumstances will convey the clearest information of the spirit and of the forms of the Roman persecutions.[80]

When Valerian was consul for the third, and Gallienus for the fourth time, Paternus, proconsul of Africa, summoned Cyprian to appear in his private council-chamber. He there acquainted him with the imperial mandate which he had just received,[81] that those who had abandoned the Roman religion should immediately return to the practice of the ceremonies of their ancestors. Cyprian replied without hesitation that he was a Christian and a bishop, devoted to the worship of the true and only Deity, to whom he offered up his daily supplications for the safety and prosperity of the two emperors, his lawful sovereigns. With modest confidence he pleaded the privilege of a citizen in refusing to give any answer to some invidious and indeed illegal questions which the proconsul had proposed. A sentence of banishment was pronounced as the penalty of Cyprian's disobedience; and he was conducted without delay to Curubis, a free and maritime city of Zeugitana, in a pleasant situation, a fertile territory, and at the distance of about forty miles from Carthage.[82] The exiled bishop enjoyed the conveniences of life and the consciousness of virtue. His reputation was diffused over Africa and Italy; an account of his behaviour was published for the edification of the Christian world;[83] and his solitude was frequently interrupted by the letters, the visits, and the congratulations of the faithful. On the arrival of a new proconsul in the province the fortune of Cyprian appeared for some time to wear a still more favourable aspect. He was recalled from banishment, and, though not yet permitted to return to Carthage, his own gardens in the neighbourhood of the capital were assigned for the place of his residence.[84]

At length, exactly one year[85] after Cyprian was first apprehended, Galerius Maximus, proconsul of Africa, received the imperial warrant for the execution of the Christian teachers. The bishop of Carthage was sensible that he should be singled out for one of the first victims, and the fraility of nature tempted him to withdraw himself, by a secret flight, from the danger and the honour of martyrdom; but, soon recovering that fortitude which his character required, he returned to his gardens, and patiently expected the ministers of death. Two officers of rank, who were intrusted with that commission, placed Cyprian between them in a chariot, and, as the proconsul was not then at leisure, they conducted him, not to a prison, but to a private house in Carthage, which belonged to one of them. An elegant supper was provided for the entertainment of the bishop, and his Christian friends were permitted for the last time to enjoy his society, whilst the streets were filled with a multitude of the faithful, anxious and alarmed at the approaching fate of their spiritual father.[86] In the morning he appeared before the tribunal of the proconsul, who, after informing himself of the name and situation of Cyprian, commanded him to offer sacrifice, and pressed him to reflect on the consequences of his disobedience. The refusal of Cyprian was firm and decisive, and the magistrate, when he had taken the opinion of his council, pronounced, with some reluctance, the sentence of death. It was conceived in the following terms: "That Thascius Cyprianus should be immediately beheaded, as the enemy of the gods of Rome, and as the chief and ringleader of a criminal association, which he had seduced into an impious resistance against the laws of the most holy emperors Valerian and Gallienus."[87] The manner of his execution was the mildest and least painful that could be inflicted on a person convicted of any capital offence: nor was the use of torture admitted to obtain from the bishop of Carthage either the recantation of his principles or the discovery of his accomplices.

As soon as the sentence was proclaimed, a general cry of "We will die with him" arose at once among the listening multitude of Christians who waited before the palace gates. The generous effusions of their zeal and affection were neither serviceable to Cyprian nor dangerous to themselves. He was led away under a guard of tribunes and centurions, without resistance and without insult, to the place of his execution, a spacious and level plain near the city, which was already filled with great numbers of spectators. His faithful presbyters and deacons were permitted to accompany their holy bishop. They assisted him in laying aside his upper garment, spread linen on the ground to catch the precious relics of his blood, and received his orders to bestow five-and-twenty pieces of gold on the executioner. The martyr then covered his face with his hands, and at one blow his head was separated from his body. His corpse remained during some hours exposed to the curiosity of the Gentiles, but in the night it was removed, and transported, in a triumphal procession and with a splendid illumination, to the burial-place of the Christians. The funeral of Cyprian was publicly celebrated without receiving any interruption from the Roman magistrates; and those among the faithful who had performed the last offices to his person and his memory were secure from the danger of inquiry or of punishment. It is remarkable that, of so great a multitude of bishops in the province of Africa, Cyprian was the first who was esteemed worthy to obtain the crown of martyrdom.[88]

It was in the choice of Cyprian either to die a martyr or to live an apostate, but on that choice depended the alternative of honour or infamy. Could we suppose that the bishop of Carthage had employed the profession of the Christian faith only as the instrument of his avarice or ambition, it was still incumbent on him to support the character which he had assumed,[89] and, if he possessed the smallest degree of manly fortitude, rather to expose himself to the most cruel tortures than by a single act to exchange the reputation of a whole life for the abhorrence of his Christian brethren and the contempt of the Gentile world. But if the zeal of Cyprian was supported by the sincere conviction of the truth of those doctrines which he preached, the crown of martyrdom must have appeared to him as an object of desire rather than of terror. It is not easy to extract any distinct ideas from the vague though eloquent declamations of the Fathers, or to ascertain the degree of immortal glory and happiness which they confidently promised to those who were so fortunate as to shed their blood in the cause of religion.[90] They inculcated with becoming diligence that the fire of martyrdom supplied every defect and expiated every sin; that, while the souls of ordinary Christians were obliged to pass through a slow and painful purification, the triumphant sufferers entered into the immediate fruition of eternal bliss, where, in the society of the patriarchs, the apostles, and the prophets, they reigned with Christ, and acted as his assessors in the universal judgment of mankind. The assurance of a lasting reputation upon earth, a motive so congenial to the vanity of human nature, often served to animate the courage of the martyrs. The honours which Rome or Athens bestowed on those citizens who had fallen in the cause of their country were cold and unmeaning demonstrations of respect, when compared with the ardent gratitude and devotion which the primitive church expressed towards the victorious champions of the faith. The annual commemoration of their virtues and sufferings was observed as a sacred ceremony, and at length terminated in religious worship. Among the Christians who had publicly confessed their religious principles, those who (as it very frequently happened) had been dismissed from the tribunal or the prisons of the Pagan magistrates obtained such honours as were justly due to their imperfect martyrdom and their generous resolution. The most pious females courted the permission of imprinting kisses on the fetters which they had worn, and on the wounds which they had received. Their persons were esteemed holy, their decisions were admitted with deference, and they too often abused, by their spiritual pride and licentious manners, the pre-eminence which their zeal and intrepidity had acquired.[91] Distinctions like these, whilst they display the exalted merit, betray the inconsiderable number, of those who suffered and of those who died for the profession of Christianity.

The sober discretion of the present age will more readily censure than admire, but can more easily admire than imitate, the fervour of the first Christians, who, according to the lively expression of Sulpicius Severus, desired martyrdom with more eagerness than his own contemporaries solicited a bishopric.[92] The epistles which Ignatius composed as he was carried in chains through the cities of Asia breathe sentiments the most repugnant to the ordinary feelings of human nature. He earnestly beseeches the Romans that, when he should be exposed in the amphitheatre, they would not, by their kind but unseasonable intercession, deprive him of the crown of glory; and he declares his resolution to provoke and irritate the wild beasts which might be employed as the instruments of his death.[93] Some stories are related of the courage of martyrs who actually performed what Ignatius had intended, who exasperated the fury of the lions, pressed the executioner to hasten his office, cheerfully leaped into the fires which were kindled to consume them, and discovered a sensation of joy and pleasure in the midst of the most exquisite tortures. Several examples have been preserved of a zeal impatient of those restraints which the emperors had provided for the security of the church. The Christians sometimes supplied by their voluntary declaration the want of an accuser, rudely disturbed the public service of paganism,[94] and, rushing in crowds round the tribunal of the magistrates, called upon them to pronounce and to inflict the sentence of the law. The behaviour of the Christians was too remarkable to escape the notice of the ancient philosophers, but they seem to have considered it with much less admiration than astonishment. Incapable of conceiving the motives which sometimes transported the fortitude of believers beyond the bounds of prudence or reason, they treated such an eagerness to die as the strange result of obstinate despair, of stupid insensibility, or of superstitious frenzy.[95] "Unhappy men!" exclaimed the proconsul Antoninus to the Chris-

tians of Asia, "unhappy men! if you are thus weary of your lives, is it so difficult for you to find ropes and precipices?"[96] He was extremely cautious (as it is observed by a learned and pious historian) of punishing men who had found no accusers but themselves, the imperial laws not having made any provisions for so unexpected a case; condemning therefore a few as a warning to their brethren, he dismissed the multitude with indignation and contempt.[97] Notwithstanding this real or affected disdain, the intrepid constancy of the faithful was productive of more salutary effects on those which nature or grace had disposed for the easy reception of religious truth. On these melancholy occasions there were many among the Gentiles who pitied, who admired, and who were converted. The generous enthusiasm was communicated from the sufferer to the spectators, and the blood of martyrs, according to a well-known observation, became the seed of the church.

But although devotion had raised, and eloquence continued to inflame, this fever of the mind, it insensibly gave way to the more natural hopes and fears of the human heart, to the love of life, the apprehension of pain, and the horror of dissolution. The more prudent rulers of the church found themselves obliged to restrain the indiscreet ardour of their followers, and to distrust a constancy which too often abandoned them in the hour of trial.[98] As the lives of the faithful became less mortified and austere, they were every day less ambitious of the honours of martyrdom; and the soldiers of Christ, instead of distinguishing themselves by voluntary deeds of heroism, frequently deserted their post, and fled in confusion before the enemy whom it was their duty to resist. There were three methods, however, of escaping the flames of persecution, which were not attended with an equal degree of guilt: the first indeed was generally allowed to be innocent; the second was of a doubtful, or at least of a venial, nature; but the third implied a direct and criminal apostasy from the Christian faith.

1. A modern Inquisitor would hear with surprise, that, whenever an information was given to a Roman magistrate of any person within his jurisdiction who had embraced the sect of the Christians, the charge was communicated to the party accused, and that a convenient time was allowed him to settle his domestic concerns, and to prepare an answer to the crime which was imputed to him.[99] If he entertained any doubt of his own constancy, such a delay afforded him the opportunity of preserving his life and hon-

our by flight, of withdrawing himself into some obscure retirement or some distant province, and of patiently expecting the return of peace and security. A measure so consonant to reason was soon authorised by the advice and example of the most holy prelates; and seems to have been censured by few, except by the Montanists, who deviated into heresy by their strict and obstinate adherence to the rigour of ancient discipline.[100] 11. The provincial governors, whose zeal was less prevalent than their avarice, had countenanced the practice of selling certificates (or libels as they were called), which attested that the persons therein mentioned had complied with the laws, and sacrificed to the Roman deities. By producing these false declarations, the opulent and timid Christians were enabled to silence the malice of an informer, and to reconcile in some measure their safety with their religion. A slight penance atoned for this profane dissimulation.[101] 111. In every persecution there were great numbers of unworthy Christians who publicly disowned or renounced the faith which they had professed; and who confirmed the sincerity of their abjuration by the legal acts of burning incense or of offering sacrifices. Some of these apostates had yielded on the first menace or exhortation of the magistrate; whilst the patience of others had been subdued by the length and repetition of tortures. The affrighted countenances of some betrayed their inward remorse, while others advanced with confidence and alacrity to the altars of the gods.[102] But the disguise which fear had imposed subsisted no longer than the present danger. As soon as the severity of the persecution was abated, the doors of the churches were assailed by the returning multitude of penitents, who detested their idolatrous submission, and who solicited with equal ardour, but with various success, their readmission into the society of Christians.[103]

iv. Notwithstanding the general rules established for the conviction and punishment of the Christians, the fate of those sectaries, in an extensive and arbitrary government, must still, in a great measure, have depended on their own behaviour, the circumstances of the times, and the temper of their supreme as well as subordinate rulers. Zeal might sometimes provoke, and prudence might sometimes avert or assuage, the superstitious fury of the Pagans. A variety of motives might dispose the provincial governors either to enforce or to relax the execution of the laws; and of these motives the most forcible was their regard not only for the public edicts, but

for the secret intentions of the emperor, a glance from whose eye was sufficient to kindle or to extinguish the flames of persecution. As often as any occasional severities were exercised in the different parts of the empire, the primitive Christians lamented and perhaps magnified their own sufferings; but the celebrated number of *ten* persecutions has been determined by the ecclesiastical writers of the fifth century, who possessed a more distinct view of the prosperous or adverse fortunes of the church from the age of Nero to that of Diocletian. The ingenious parallels of the *ten* plagues of Egypt, and of the *ten* horns of the Apocalypse, first suggested this calculation to their minds; and in their application of the faith of prophecy to the truth of history they were careful to select those reigns which were indeed the most hostile to the Christian cause.[104] But these transient persecutions served only to revive the zeal and to restore the discipline of the faithful; and the moments of extraordinary rigour were compensated by much longer intervals of peace and security. The indifference of some princes and the indulgence of others permitted the Christians to enjoy, though not perhaps a legal, yet an actual and public toleration of their religion.

The Apology of Tertullian contains two very ancient, very singular, but at the same time very suspicious instances of Imperial clemency; the edicts published by Tiberius and by Marcus Antoninus, and designed not only to protect the innocence of the Christians, but even to proclaim those stupendous miracles which had attested the truth of their doctrine. The first of these examples is attended with some difficulties which might perplex a sceptical mind.[105] We are required to believe *that* Pontius Pilate informed the emperor of the unjust sentence of death which he had pronounced against an innocent, and, as it appeared, a divine person; and that, without acquiring the merit, he exposed himself to the danger, of martyrdom; *that* Tiberius, who avowed his contempt for all religion, immediately conceived the design of placing the Jewish Messiah among the gods of Rome; *that* his servile senate ventured to disobey the commands of their master; *that* Tiberius, instead of resenting their refusal, contented himself with protecting the Christians from the severity of the laws, many years before such laws were enacted or before the church had assumed any distinct name or existence; and lastly, *that* the memory of this extraordinary transaction was preserved in the most public and authentic records, which escaped the knowledge of the historians of Greece and Rome, and were only visible to the eyes of an African Christian, who composed his Apology one hundred and sixty years after the death of Tiberius. The edict of Marcus Antoninus is supposed to have been the effect of his devotion and gratitude for the miraculous deliverance which he had obtained in the Marcomannic war. The distress of the legions, the seasonable tempest of rain and hail, of thunder and lightning, and the dismay and defeat of the barbarians, have been celebrated by the eloquence of several Pagan writers. If there were any Christians in that army, it was natural that they should ascribe some merit to the fervent prayers which, in the moment of danger, they had offered up for their own and the public safety. But we are still assured by monuments of brass and marble, by the Imperial medals, and by the Antonine column, that neither the prince nor the people entertained any sense of this signal obligation, since they unanimously attribute their deliverance to the providence of Jupiter, and to the interposition of Mercury. During the whole course of his reign Marcus despised the Christians as a philosopher, and punished them as a sovereign.[106]

By a singular fatality, the hardships which they had endured under the government of a virtuous prince immediately ceased on the accession of a tyrant; and as none except themselves had experienced the injustice of Marcus, so they alone were protected by the lenity of Commodus. The celebrated Marcia, the most favoured of his concubines, and who at length contrived the murder of her Imperial lover, entertained a singular affection for the oppressed church; and though it was impossible that she could reconcile the practice of vice with the precepts of the Gospel, she might hope to atone for the frailties of her sex and profession by declaring herself the patroness of the Christians.[107] Under the gracious protection of Marcia they passed in safety the thirteen years of a cruel tyranny; and when the empire was established in the house of Severus, they formed a domestic but more honourable connection with the new court. The emperor was persuaded that, in a dangerous sickness, he had derived some benefit, either spiritual or physical, from the holy oil with which one of his slaves had anointed him. He always treated with peculiar distinction several persons of both sexes who had embraced the new religion. The nurse as well as the preceptor of Caracalla were Christians; and if that young prince ever betrayed a sentiment of humanity, it was occasioned by an incident which,

however trifling, bore some relation to the cause of Christianity.[108] Under the reign of Severus the fury of the populace was checked; the rigour of ancient laws was for some time suspended; and the provincial governors were satisfied with receiving an annual present from the churches within their jurisdiction, as the price, or as the reward, of their moderation.[109] The controversy concerning the precise time of the celebration of Easter armed the bishops of Asia and Italy against each other, and was considered as the most important business of this period of leisure and tranquillity.[110] Nor was the peace of the church interrupted till the increasing numbers of proselytes seem at length to have attracted the attention, and to have alienated the mind, of Severus. With the design of restraining the progress of Christianity, he published an edict, which, though it was designed to affect only the new converts, could not be carried into strict execution without exposing to danger and punishment the most zealous of their teachers and missionaries. In this mitigated persecution we may still discover the indulgent spirit of Rome and of the Polytheism, which so readily admitted every excuse in favour of those who practised the religious ceremonies of their fathers.[111]

But the laws which Severus had enacted soon expired with the authority of that emperor; and the Christians, after this accidental tempest, enjoyed a calm of thirty-eight years.[112] Till this period they had usually held their assemblies in private houses and sequestered places. They were now permitted to erect and consecrate convenient edifices for the purpose of religious worship;[113] to purchase lands, even at Rome itself, for the use of the community; and to conduct the elections of their ecclesiastical ministers in so public, but at the same time in so exemplary a manner, as to deserve the respectful attention of the Gentiles.[114] This long repose of the church was accompanied with dignity. The reigns of those princes who derived their extraction from the Asiatic provinces proved the most favourable to the Christians; the eminent persons of the sect, instead of being reduced to implore the protection of a slave or concubine, were admitted into the palace in the honourable characters of priests and philosophers; and their mysterious doctrines, which were already diffused among the people, insensibly attracted the curiosity of their sovereign. When the empress Mamæa passed through Antioch, she expressed a desire of conversing with the celebrated Origen, the fame of whose piety and learning was spread over the East. Origen obeyed so flattering an invitation, and, though he could not expect to succeed in the conversion of an artful and ambitious woman, she listened with pleasure to his eloquent exhortations, and honourably dismissed him to his retirement in Palestine.[115] The sentiments of Mamæa were adopted by her son Alexander, and the philosophic devotion of that emperor was marked by a singular but injudicious regard for the Christian religion. In his domestic chapel he placed the statues of Abraham, of Orpheus, of Apollonius, and of Christ, as an honour justly due to those respectable sages who had instructed mankind in the various modes of addressing their homage to the supreme and universal Deity.[116] A purer faith, as well as worship, was openly professed and practised among his household. Bishops, perhaps for the first time, were seen at court; and, after the death of Alexander, when the inhuman Maximin discharged his fury on the favourites and servants of his unfortunate benefactor, a great number of Christians, of every rank, and of both sexes, were involved in the promiscuous massacre, which, on their account, has improperly received the name of Persecution.[117]

Notwithstanding the cruel disposition of Maximin, the effects of his resentment against the Christians were of a very local and temporary nature, and the pious Origen, who had been proscribed as a devoted victim, was still reserved to convey the truths of the Gospel to the ear of monarchs.[118] He addressed several edifying letters to the emperor Philip, to his wife, and to his mother, and as soon as that prince, who was born in the neighbourhood of Palestine, had usurped the Imperial sceptre, the Christians acquired a friend and a protector. The public and even partial favour of Philip towards the sectaries of the new religion, and his constant reverence for the ministers of the church, gave some colour to the suspicion, which prevailed in his own times, that the emperor himself was become a convert to the faith;[119] and afforded some grounds for a fable which was afterwards invented, that he had been purified by confession and penance from the guilt contracted by the murder of his innocent predecessor.[120] The fall of Philip introduced, with the change of masters, a new system of government, so oppressive to the Christians, that their former condition, ever since the time of Domitian, was represented as a state of perfect freedom and security, if compared with the rigorous treatment which they experienced under the short reign of Decius.[121] The virtues

of that prince will scarcely allow us to suspect that he was actuated by a mean resentment against the favourites of his predecessor; and it is more reasonable to believe that, in the prosecution of his general design to restore the purity of Roman manners, he was desirous of delivering the empire from what he condemned as a recent and criminal superstition. The bishops of the most considerable cities were removed by exile or death: the vigilance of the magistrates prevented the clergy of Rome during sixteen months from proceeding to a new election; and it was the opinion of the Christians that the emperor would more patiently endure a competitor for the purple than a bishop in the capital.[122] Were it possible to suppose that the penetration of Decius had discovered pride under the disguise of humility, or that he could foresee the temporal dominion which might insensibly arise from the claims of spiritual authority, we might be less surprised that he should consider the successors of St. Peter as the most formidable rivals to those of Augustus.

The administration of Valerian was distinguished by a levity and inconstancy ill suited to the gravity of the *Roman Censor*. In the first part of his reign he surpassed in clemency those princes who had been suspected of an attachment to the Christian faith. In the last three years and a half, listening to the insinuations of a minister addicted to the superstitions of Egypt, he adopted the maxims, and imitated the severity, of his predecessor Decius.[123] The accession of Gallienus, which increased the calamities of the empire, restored peace to the church; and the Christians obtained the free exercise of their religion by an edict addressed to the bishops, and conceived in such terms as seemed to acknowledge their office and public character.[124] The ancient laws, without being formally repealed, were suffered to sink into oblivion; and (excepting only some hostile intentions which are attributed to the emperor Aurelian[125]) the disciples of Christ passed above forty years in a state of prosperity, far more dangerous to their virtue than the severest trials of persecution.

The story of Paul of Samosata, who filled the metropolitan see of Antioch while the East was in the hands of Odenathus and Zenobia, may serve to illustrate the condition and character of the times. The wealth of that prelate was a sufficient evidence of his guilt, since it was neither derived from the inheritance of his fathers, nor acquired by the arts of honest industry. But Paul considered the service of the church as a very lucrative profession.[126] His ecclesiastical jurisdiction was venal and rapacious; he extorted frequent contributions from the most opulent of the faithful, and converted to his own use a considerable part of the public revenue. By his pride and luxury the Christian religion was rendered odious in the eyes of the Gentiles. His council chamber and his throne, the splendour with which he appeared in public, the suppliant crowd who solicited his attention, the multitude of letters and petitions to which he dictated his answers, and the perpetual hurry of business in which he was involved, were circumstances much better suited to the state of a civil magistrate[127] than to the humility of a primitive bishop. When he harangued his people from the pulpit, Paul affected the figurative style and the theatrical gestures of an Asiatic sophist, while the cathedral resounded with the loudest and most extravagant acclamations in the praise of his divine eloquence. Against those who resisted his power, or refused to flatter his vanity, the prelate of Antioch was arrogant, rigid, and inexorable; but he relaxed the discipline, and lavished the treasures of the church on his dependent clergy, who were permitted to imitate their master in the gratification of every sensual appetite. For Paul indulged himself very freely in the pleasures of the table, and he had received into the episcopal palace two young and beautiful women, as the constant companions of his leisure moments.[128]

Notwithstanding these scandalous vices, if Paul of Samosata had preserved the purity of the orthodox faith, his reign over the capital of Syria would have ended only with his life; and had a reasonable persecution intervened, an effort of court might perhaps have placed him in the rank of saints and martyrs. Some nice and subtle errors, which he imprudently adopted and obstinately maintained, concerning the doctrine of the Trinity, excited the zeal and indignation of the Eastern churches.[129] From Egypt to the Euxine Sea, the bishops were in arms and in motion. Several councils were held, confutations were published, excommunications were pronounced, ambiguous explanations were by turns accepted and refused, treaties were concluded and violated, and at length Paul of Samosata was degraded from his episcopal character by the sentence of seventy or eighty bishops who assembled for that purpose at Antioch, and who, without consulting the rights of the clergy or people, appointed a successor by their own authority. The manifest irregularity of this proceeding increased the numbers of the discontented faction; and as Paul,

who was no stranger to the arts of courts, had insinuated himself into the favour of Zenobia, he maintained above four years the possession of the episcopal house and office. The victory of Aurelian changed the face of the East, and the two contending parties, who applied to each other the epithets of schism and heresy, were either commanded or permitted to plead their cause before the tribunal of the conqueror. This public and very singular trial affords a convincing proof that the existence, the property, the privileges, and the internal policy of the Christians, were acknowledged, if not by the laws, at least by the magistrates of the empire. As a Pagan and as a soldier, it could scarcely be expected that Aurelian should enter into the discussion, whether the sentiments of Paul or those of his adversaries were most agreeable to the true standard of the orthodox faith. His determination, however, was founded on the general principles of equity and reason. He considered the bishops of Italy as the most impartial and respectable judges among the Christians, and, as soon as he was informed that they had unanimously approved the sentence of the council, he acquiesced in their opinion, and immediately gave orders that Paul should be compelled to relinquish the temporal possessions belonging to an office, of which, in the judgment of his brethren, he had been regularly deprived. But while we applaud the justice, we should not overlook the policy of Aurelian, who was desirous of restoring and cementing the dependence of the provinces of the capital, by every means which could bind the interest or prejudices of any part of his subjects.[130]

Amidst the frequent revolutions of the empire the Christians still flourished in peace and prosperity; and notwithstanding a celebrated era of martyrs has been deduced from the accession of Diocletian,[131] the new system of policy, introduced and maintained by the wisdom of that prince, continued, during more than eighteen years, to breathe the mildest and most liberal spirit of religious toleration. The mind of Diocletian himself was less adapted indeed to speculative inquiries than to the active labours of war and government. His prudence rendered him averse to any great innovation, and, though his temper was not very susceptible of zeal or enthusiasm, he always maintained an habitual regard for the ancient deities of the empire. But the leisure of the two empresses, of his wife Prisca, and of Valeria his daughter, permitted them to listen with more attention and respect to the truths of Christianity, which in every age has acknowledged its important obligations to female devotion.[132] The principal eunuchs, Lucian[133] and Dorotheus, Gorgonius and Andrew, who attended the person, possessed the favour, and governed the household of Diocletian, protected by their powerful influence the faith which they had embraced. Their example was imitated by many of the most considerable officers of the palace, who, in their respective stations, had the care of the Imperial ornaments, of the robes, of the furniture, of the jewels, and even of the private treasury; and, though it might sometimes be incumbent on them to accompany the emperor when he sacrificed in the temple,[134] they enjoyed, with their wives, their children, and their slaves, the free exercise of the Christian religion. Diocletian and his colleagues frequently conferred the most important offices on those persons who avowed their abhorrence for the worship of the gods, but who had displayed abilities proper for the service of the state.

The bishops held an honourable rank in their respective provinces, and were treated with distinction and respect, not only by the people, but by the magistrates themselves. Almost in every city the ancient churches were found insufficient to contain the increasing multitude of proselytes; and in their place more stately and capacious edifices were erected for the public worship of the faithful. The corruption of manners and principles, so forcibly lamented by Eusebius,[135] may be considered, not only as a consequence, but as a proof, of the liberty which the Christians enjoyed and abused under the reign of Diocletian. Prosperity had relaxed the nerves of discipline. Fraud, envy, and malice prevailed in every congregation. The presbyters aspired to the episcopal office, which every day became an object more worthy of their ambition. The bishops, who contended with each other for ecclesiastical pre-eminence, appeared by their conduct to claim a secular and tyrannical power in the church; and the lively faith which still distinguished the Christians from the Gentiles was shown much less in their lives than in their controversial writings.

Notwithstanding this seeming security, an attentive observer might discern some symptoms that threatened the church with a more violent persecution than any which she had yet endured. The zeal and rapid progress of the Christians awakened the Polytheists from their supine indifference in the cause of those deities whom custom and education had taught them to revere. The mutual provocations of a religious war, which had already continued above two hundred years, exasperated the animosity of the contending parties. The Pagans were incensed at the rashness of a recent and obscure sect, which presumed to accuse their countrymen of error, and to devote their ancestors to eternal misery. The habits of justifying the popular mythology against the invectives of an implacable enemy, produced in their minds some sentiments of faith and reverence for a system which they had been accustomed to consider with the most careless levity. The supernatural powers assumed by the church inspired at the same time terror and emulation. The followers of the established religion intrenched themselves behind a similar fortification of prodigies; invented new modes of sacrifice, of expiation, and of initiation;[136] attempted to revive the credit of their expiring oracles;[137] and listened with eager credulity to every imposter who flattered their prejudices by a tale of wonders.[138] Both parties seemed to acknowledge the truth of those miracles which were claimed by their adversaries; and while they were contented with ascribing them to the arts of magic, and to the power of dæmons, they mutually concurred in restoring and establishing the reign of superstition.[139] Philosophy, her most dangerous enemy, was now converted into her most useful ally. The groves of the Academy, the gardens of Epicurus, and even the portico of the Stoics, were almost deserted, as so many different schools of scepticism or impiety;[140] and many among the Romans were desirous that the writings of Cicero should be condemned and suppressed by the authority of the senate.[141] The prevailing sect of the new Platonicians judged it prudent to connect themselves with the priests, whom perhaps they despised, against the Christians, whom they had reason to fear. These fashionable philosophers prosecuted the design of extracting allegorical wisdom from the fictions of the Greek poets; instituted mysterious rites of devotion for the use of their chosen disciples; recommended the worship of the ancient gods as the emblems or ministers of the Supreme Deity, and composed against the faith of the Gospel many elaborate treatises,[142] which have since been committed to the flames by the prudence of orthodox emperors.[143]

Although the policy of Diocletian and humanity of Constantius inclined them to preserve inviolate the maxims of toleration, it was soon discovered that their two associates, Maximian and Galerius, entertained the most implacable aversion for the name and religion of the Christians. The minds of those princes had never been enlightened by science; education had never softened their temper. They owed their greatness to their swords, and in their most elevated fortune they still retained their superstitious prejudices of soldiers and peasants. In the general administration of the provinces they obeyed the laws which their benefactor had established; but they frequently found occasions of exercising within their camp and palaces a secret persecution,[144] for which the imprudent zeal of the Christians sometimes offered the most specious pretences. A sentence of death was executed upon Maximilianus, an African youth, who had been produced by his own father before the magistrate as a sufficient and legal recruit, but who obstinately persisted in declaring that his conscience would not permit him to embrace the profession of a soldier.[145] It could scarcely be expected that any government should suffer the action of Marcellus the centurion to pass with impunity. On the day of a public festival, that officer threw away his belt, his arms, and the ensigns of his office, and exclaimed with a loud voice that he would obey none but Jesus Christ the eternal King, and that he renounced for ever the use of carnal weapons, and the service of an idolatrous master. The soldiers, as soon as they recovered from their astonishment, secured the person of Marcellus. He was examined in the city of Tingi by the president of that part of Mauritania; and as he was convicted by his own confession, he was condemned and beheaded for the crime of desertion.[146] Examples of such a nature savour much less of religious persecution than of martial or even civil law: but they served to alienate the mind of the emperors, to justify the severity of Galerius, who dismissed a great number of Christian officers from their employments; and to authorise the opinion that a sect of enthusiasts, which avowed principles so repugnant to the public safety, must either remain useless, or would soon become dangerous subjects of the empire.

After the success of the Persian war had raised the hopes and the reputation of Galerius, he passed a winter with Diocletian in the palace of Nicomedia; and the fate of Christianity became the object of their secret consultations.[147] The experienced emperor was still inclined to pursue measures of lenity; and though he readily consented to exclude the Christians from holding any employments in the household or the army, he urged in the strongest terms the danger as well as cruelty of shedding the blood of those deluded fanatics. Galerius at length extorted from him the permission of summoning a council, composed of a few persons the most distinguished in the civil and military departments of the state. The important question was agitated in their presence, and those ambitious courtiers easily discerned that it was incumbent on them to second, by their own eloquence, the importunate violence of the Cæsar. It may be presumed that they insisted on every topic which might interest the pride, the piety, or the fears, of their sovereign in the destruction of Christianity. Perhaps they represented that the glorious work of the deliverance of the empire was left imperfect, as long as an independent people was permitted to subsist and multiply in the heart of the provinces. The Christians (it might speciously be alleged), renouncing the gods and the institutions of Rome, had constituted a distinct republic, which might yet be suppressed before it had acquired any military force; but which was already governed by its own laws and magistrates, was possessed of a public treasure, and was intimately connected in all its parts by the frequent assemblies of the bishops, to whose decrees their numerous and opulent congregations yielded an implicit obedience. Arguments like these may seem to have determined the reluctant mind of Diocletian to embrace a new system of persecution: but though we may suspect, it is not in our power to relate, the secret intrigues of the palace, the private views and resentments, the jealousy of women or eunuchs, and all those trifling but decisive causes which so often influence the fate of empires and the councils of the wisest monarchs.[148]

The pleasure of the emperors was at length signified to the Christians, who, during the course of this melancholy winter, had expected, with anxiety, the result of so many secret consultations. The twenty-third of February, which coincided with the Roman festival of the Terminalia,[149] was appointed (whether from accident or design) to set bounds to the progress of Christianity. At the earliest dawn of day the Prætorian præfect,[150] accompanied by several generals, tribunes, and officers of the revenue, repaired to the principal church of Nicomedia, which was situated on an eminence in the most populous and beautiful part of the city. The doors were instantly broken open; they rushed into the sanctuary; and as they searched in vain for some visible object of worship, they were obliged to content themselves with committing to the flames the volumes of Holy Scripture. The ministers of Diocletian were followed by a numerous body of guards and pioneers, who marched in order of battle, and were provided with all the instruments used in the destruction of fortified cities. By their incessant labour, a sacred edifice, which towered above the Imperial palace, and had long excited the indignation and envy of the Gentiles, was in a few hours levelled with the ground.[151]

The next day the general edict of persecution was published;[152] and though Diocletian, still averse to the effusion of blood, had moderated the fury of Galerius, who proposed that every one refusing to offer sacrifice should immediately be burnt alive, the penalties inflicted on the obstinacy of the Christians might be deemed sufficiently rigorous and effectual. It was enacted that their churches, in all the provinces of the empire, should be demolished to their foundations; and the punishment of death was denounced against all who should presume to hold any secret assemblies for the purpose of religious worship. The philosophers, who now assumed the unworthy office of directing the blind zeal of persecution, had diligently studied the nature and genius of the Christian religion; and as they were not ignorant that the speculative doctrines of the faith were supposed to be contained in the writings of the prophets, of the evangelists, and of the apostles, they most probably suggested the order that the bishops and presbyters should deliver all their sacred books into the hands of the magistrates; who were commanded, under the severest penalties, to burn them in a public and solemn manner. By the same edict, the property of the church was at once confiscated; and the several parts of which it might consist were either sold to the highest bidder, united to the Imperial domain, bestowed on the cities and corporations, or granted to the solicitations of rapacious courtiers. After taking such effectual measures to abolish the worship and to dissolve the government of the Christians, it was thought necessary to subject to the most intolerable hardships the condition of those perverse individuals who should still reject the religion of nature, of Rome, and of their ancestors. Persons of a liberal birth were declared incapable of holding any honours or employments; slaves were for ever deprived of the hopes of freedom; and the whole body of the people were put out of the protection of the law. The judges were authorised to hear and to determine every action that was brought against a Christian. But the Christians were not permitted to complain of any injury which they themselves had suffered; and thus those unfortunate

sectaries were exposed to the severity, while they were excluded from the benefits, of public justice. This new species of martyrdom, so painful and lingering, so obscure and ignominious, was, perhaps, the most proper to weary the constancy of the faithful: nor can it be doubted that the passions and interest of mankind were disposed on this occasion to second the designs of the emperors. But the policy of a well-ordered government must sometimes have interposed in behalf of the oppressed Christians; nor was it possible for the Roman princes entirely to remove the apprehension of punishment, or to connive at every act of fraud and violence, without exposing their own authority and the rest of their subjects to the most alarming dangers.[153]

This edict was scarcely exhibited to the public view, in the most conspicuous place of Nicomedia, before it was torn down by the hands of a Christian, who expressed at the same time, by the bitterest invectives, his contempt as well as abhorrence for such impious and tyrannical governors. His offense, according to the mildest laws, amounted to treason, and deserved death. And if it be true that he was a person of rank and education, those circumstances could serve only to aggravate his guilt. He was burnt, or rather roasted, by a slow fire; and his executioners, zealous to revenge the personal insult which had been offered to the emperors, exhausted every refinement of cruelty, without being able to subdue his patience, or to alter the steady and insulting smile which, in his dying agonies, he still preserved in his countenance. The Christians, though they confessed that his conduct had not been strictly conformable to the laws of prudence, admired the divine fervour of his zeal; and the excessive commendations which they lavished on the memory of their hero and martyr contributed to fix a deep impression of terror and hatred in the mind of Diocletian.[154]

His fears were soon alarmed by the view of a danger from which he very narrowly escaped. Within fifteen days the palace of Nicomedia, and even the bedchamber of Diocletian, were twice in flames; and though both times they were extinguished without any material damage, the singular repetition of the fire was justly considered as an evident proof that it had not been the effect of chance or negligence. The suspicion naturally fell on the Christians; and it was suggested, with some degree of probability, that those desperate fanatics, provoked by their present sufferings, and apprehensive of impending calamities, had entered into a conspiracy with their faithful brethren, the eunuchs of the palace, against the lives of two emperors whom they detested as the irreconcilable enemies of the church of God. Jealousy and resentment prevailed in every breast, but especially in that of Diocletian. A great number of persons, distinguished either by the offices which they had filled or by the favour which they had enjoyed, were thrown into prison. Every mode of torture was put in practice, and the court, as well as city, was polluted with many bloody executions.[155] But as it was found impossible to extort any discovery of this mysterious transaction, it seems incumbent on us either to presume the innocence, or to admire the resolution, of the sufferers. A few days afterwards Galerius hastily withdrew himself from Nicomedia, declaring that, if he delayed his departure from that devoted palace, he should fall a sacrifice to the rage of the Christians. The ecclesiastical historians, from whom alone we derive a partial and imperfect knowledge of this persecution, are at a loss how to account for the fears and danger of the emperors. Two of these writers, a prince and a rhetorician, were eye-witnesses of the fire of Nicomedia. The one ascribes it to lightning and the divine wrath, the other affirms that it was kindled by the malice of Galerius himself.[156]

As the edict against the Christians was designed for a general law of the whole empire, and as Diocletian and Galerius, though they might not wait for the consent, were assured of the concurrence, of the Western princes, it would appear more consonant to our ideas of policy that the governors of all the provinces should have received secret instructions to publish, on one and the same day, this declaration of war within their respective departments. It was at least to be expected that the convenience of the public highways and established posts would have enabled the emperors to transmit their orders with the utmost despatch from the palace of Nicomedia to the extremities of the Roman world; and that they would not have suffered fifty days to elapse before the edict was published in Syria, and near four months before it was signified to the cities of Africa.[157] This delay may perhaps be imputed to the cautious temper of Diocletian, who had yielded a reluctant consent to the measures of persecution, and who was desirous of trying the experiment under his more immediate eye before he gave way to the disorders and discontent which it must inevitably occasion in the distant provinces. At first, indeed, the magistrates were re-

strained from the effusion of blood; but the use of every other severity was permitted, and even recommended to their zeal; nor could the Christians, though they cheerfully resigned the ornaments of their churches, resolve to interrupt their religious assemblies, or to deliver their sacred books to the flames. The pious obstinacy of Felix, an African bishop, appears to have embarrassed the subordinate ministers of the government. The curator of his city sent him in chains to the proconsul. The proconsul transmitted him to the Prætorian præfect of Italy; and Felix, who disdained even to give an evasive answer, was at length beheaded at Venusia, in Lucania, a place on which the birth of Horace has conferred fame.[158] This precedent, and perhaps some Imperial rescript, which was issued in consequence of it, appeared to authorise the governors of provinces in punishing with death the refusal of the Christians to deliver up their sacred books. There were undoubtedly many persons who embraced this opportunity of obtaining the crown of martyrdom; but there were likewise too many who purchased an ignominious life by discovering and betraying the Holy Scripture into the hands of infidels. A great number even of bishops and presbyters acquired, by this criminal compliance, the opprobrious epithet of *Traditors*; and their offence was productive of much present scandal and of much future discord in the African church.[159]

The copies as well as the versions of Scripture were already so multiplied in the empire, that the most severe inquisition could no longer be attended with any fatal consequences; and even the sacrifice of those volumes which, in every congregation, were preserved for public use, required the consent of some treacherous and unworthy Christians. But the ruin of the churches was easily effected by the authority of the government and by the labour of the Pagans. In some provinces, however, the magistrates contented themselves with shutting up the places of religious worship. In others they more literally complied with the terms of the edict; and, after taking away the doors, the benches, and the pulpit, which they burnt as it were in a funeral pile, they completely demolished the remainder of the edifice.[160] It is perhaps to this melancholy occasion that we should apply a very remarkable story, which is related with so many circumstances of variety and improbability that it serves rather to excite than to satisfy our curiosity. In a small town in Phrygia, of whose name as well as situation we are left ignorant, it should seem that the magistrates and the body of the people had embraced the Christian faith; and as some resistance might be apprehended to the execution of the edict, the governor of the province was supported by a numerous detachment of legionaries. On their approach the citizens threw themselves into the church, with the resolution either of defending by arms that sacred edifice or of perishing in its ruins. They indignantly rejected the notice and permission which was given them to retire, till the soldiers, provoked by their obstinate refusal, set fire to the building on all sides, and consumed, by this extraordinary kind of martyrdom, a great number of Phrygians, with their wives and children.[161]

Some slight disturbances, though they were suppressed almost as soon as excited in Syria and the frontiers of Armenia, afforded the enemies of the church a very plausible occasion to insinuate that those troubles had been secretly fomented by the intrigues of the bishops, who had already forgotten their ostentatious professions of passive and unlimited obedience.[162] The resentment, or the fears, of Diocletian at length transported him beyond the bounds of moderation which he had hitherto preserved, and he declared, in a series of cruel edicts, his intention of abolishing the Christian name. By the first of these edicts the governors of the provinces were directed to apprehend all persons of the ecclesiastical order; and the prisons destined for the vilest criminals were soon filled with a multitude of bishops, presbyters, deacons, readers, and exorcists. By a second edict the magistrates were commanded to employ every method of severity which might reclaim them from their odious superstition, and oblige them to return to the established worship of the gods. This rigorous order was extended, by a subsequent edict, to the whole body of Christians, who were exposed to a violent and general persecution.[163] Instead of those salutary restraints which had required the direct and solemn testimony of an accuser, it became the duty as well as the interest of the Imperial officers to discover, to pursue, and to torment the most obnoxious among the faithful. Heavy penalties were denounced against all who should presume to save a proscribed sectary from the just indignation of the gods and of the emperors. Yet, notwithstanding the severity of this law, the virtuous courage of many of the Pagans, in concealing their friends or relations, affords an honourable proof that the rage of superstition had not extinguished in their minds the sentiments of nature and humanity.[164]

Diocletian had no sooner published his edicts against the Christians than, as if he had been desirous of committing to other hands the work of persecution, he divested himself of the Imperial purple. The character and situation of his colleagues and successors sometimes urged them to enforce, and sometimes inclined them to suspend, the execution of these rigorous laws; nor can we acquire a just and distinct idea of this important period of ecclesiastical history unless we separately consider the state of Christianity, in the different parts of the empire, during the space of ten years which elapsed between the first edicts of Diocletian and the final peace of the church.

The mild and humane temper of Constantius was averse to the oppression of any part of his subjects. The principal offices of his palace were exercised by Christians. He loved their persons, esteemed their fidelity, and entertained not any dislike to their religious principles. But as long as Constantius remained in the subordinate station of Cæsar, it was not in his power openly to reject the edicts of Diocletian, or to disobey the commands of Maximian. His authority contributed, however, to alleviate the sufferings which he pitied and abhorred. He consented with reluctance to the ruin of the churches, but he ventured to protect the Christians themselves from the fury of the populace and from the rigour of the laws. The provinces of Gaul (under which we may probably include those of Britain) were indebted for the singular tranquillity which they enjoyed to the gentle interposition of their sovereign.[165] But Datianus, the president or governor of Spain, actuated either by zeal or policy, chose rather to execute the public edicts of the emperors than to understand the secret intentions of Constantius; and it can scarcely be doubted that his provincial administration was stained with the blood of a few martyrs.[166] The elevation of Constantius to the supreme and independent dignity of Augustus gave a free scope to the exercise of his virtues, and the shortness of his reign did not prevent him from establishing a system of toleration of which he left the precept and the example to his son Constantine. His fortunate son, from the first moment of his accession declaring himself the protector of the church, at length deserved the appellation of the first emperor who publicly professed and established the Christian religion. The motives of his conversion, as they may variously be deduced from benevolence, from policy, from conviction, or from remorse, and the progress of the revolution, which, under his powerful influence and that of his sons, rendered Christianity the reigning religion of the Roman empire, will form a very interesting and important chapter in the second volume of this history. At present it may be sufficient to observe that every victory of Constantine was productive of some relief or benefit to the church.

The provinces of Italy and Africa experienced a short but violent persecution. The rigorous edicts of Diocletian were strictly and cheerfully executed by his associate Maximian, who had long hated the Christians, and who delighted in acts of blood and violence. In the autumn of the first year of the persecution the two emperors met at Rome to celebrate their triumph; several oppressive laws appear to have issued from their secret consultations, and the diligence of the magistrates was animated by the presence of their sovereigns. After Diocletian had divested himself of the purple, Italy and Africa were administered under the name of Severus, and were exposed, without defence, to the implacable resentment of his master Galerius. Among the martyrs of Rome, Adauctus deserves the notice of posterity. He was of a noble family in Italy, and had raised himself, through the successive honours of the palace, to the important office of treasurer of the private demesnes. Adauctus is the more remarkable for being the only person of rank and distinction who appears to have suffered death during the whole course of this general persecution.[167]

The revolt of Maxentius immediately restored peace to the churches of Italy and Africa, and the same tyrant who oppressed every other class of his subjects showed himself just, humane, and even partial, towards the afflicted Christians. He depended on their gratitude and affection, and very naturally presumed that the injuries which they had suffered, and the dangers which they still apprehended, from his most inveterate enemy, would secure the fidelity of a party already considerable by their numbers and opulence.[168] Even the conduct of Maxentius towards the bishops of Rome and Carthage may be considered as the proof of his toleration, since it is probable that the most orthodox princes would adopt the same measures with regard to their established clergy. Marcellus, the former of those prelates, had thrown the capital into confusion by the severe penance which he imposed on a great number of Christians who, during the late persecution, had renounced or dissembled their religion. The rage

of faction broke out in frequent and violent seditions; the blood of the faithful was shed by each other's hands; and the exile of Marcellus, whose prudence seems to have been less eminent than his zeal, was found to be the only measure capable of restoring peace to the distracted church of Rome.[169] The behaviour of Mensurius, bishop of Carthage, appears to have been still more reprehensible. A deacon of that city had published a libel against the emperor. The offender took refuge in the episcopal palace, and, though it was somewhat early to advance any claims of ecclesiastical immunities, the bishop refused to deliver him up to the officers of justice. For this treasonable resistance Mensurius was summoned to court, and, instead of receiving a legal sentence of death or banishment, he was permitted, after a short examination, to return to his diocese.[170] Such was the happy condition of the Christian subjects of Maxentius, that, whenever they were desirous of procuring for their own use any bodies of martyrs, they were obliged to purchase them from the most distant provinces of the East. A story is related of Aglae, a Roman lady, descended from a consular family, and possessed of so ample an estate that it required the management of seventy-three stewards. Among these Boniface was the favourite of his mistress, and, as Aglae mixed love with devotion, it is reported that he was admitted to share her bed. Her fortune enabled her to gratify the pious desire of obtaining some sacred relics from the East. She intrusted Boniface with a considerable sum of gold and a large quantity of aromatics, and her lover, attended by twelve horsemen and three covered chariots, undertook a remote pilgrimage as far as Tarsus in Cilicia.[171]

The sanguinary temper of Galerius, the first and principal author of the persecution, was formidable to those Christians whom their misfortunes had placed within the limits of his dominions; and it may fairly be presumed that many persons of a middle rank, who were not confined by the chains either of wealth or of poverty, very frequently deserted their native country, and sought a refuge in the milder climate of the West. As long as he commanded only the armies and provinces of Illyricum, he could with difficulty either find or make a considerable number of martyrs in a warlike country which had entertained the missionaries of the Gospel with more coldness and reluctance than any other part of the empire.[172] But when Galerius had obtained the supreme power and the government of the East, he indulged in their fullest extent his zeal and cruelty, not only in the provinces of Thrace and Asia, which acknowledged his immediate jurisdiction, but in those of Syria, Palestine, and Egypt, where Maximin gratified his own inclination by yielding a rigorous obedience to the stern commands of his benefactor.[173]

The frequent disappointments of his ambitious views, the experience of six years of persecution, and the salutary reflections which a lingering and painful distemper suggested to the mind of Galerius, at length convinced him that the most violent efforts of despotism are insufficient to extirpate a whole people, or to subdue their religious prejudices. Desirous of repairing the mischief that he had occasioned, he published in his own name, and in those of Licinius and Constantine, a general edict, which, after a pompous recital of the Imperial titles, proceeded in the following manner:

"Among the important cares which have occupied our mind for the utility and preservation of the empire, it was our intention to correct and re-establish all things according to the ancient laws and public discipline of the Romans. We were particularly desirous of reclaiming into the way of reason and nature the deluded Christians who had renounced the religion and ceremonies instituted by their fathers, and, presumptuously despising the practice of antiquity, had invented extravagant laws and opinions according to the dictates of their fancy, and had collected a various society from the different provinces of our empire. The edicts which we have published to enforce the worship of the gods having exposed many of the Christians to danger and distress, many having suffered death, and many more, who still persist in their impious folly, being left destitute of *any* public exercise of religion, we are disposed to extend to those unhappy men the effects of our wonted clemency. We permit them, therefore, freely to profess their private opinions, and to assemble in their conventicles without fear or molestation, provided always that they preserve a due respect to the established laws and government. By another rescript we shall signify our intentions to the judges and magistrates, and we hope that our indulgence will engage the Christians to offer up their prayers to the Deity whom they adore for our safety and prosperity, for their own, and for that of the republic."[174] It is not usually in the language of edicts and manifestos that we should search for the real character or the secret motives of princes; but as these were the words of a dying emperor, his situation,

perhaps, may be admitted as a pledge of his sincerity.

When Galerius subscribed this edict of toleration, he was well assured that Licinius would readily comply with the inclinations of his friend and benefactor, and that any measures in favour of the Christians would obtain the approbation of Constantine. But the emperor would not venture to insert in the preamble the name of Maximin, whose consent was of the greatest importance, and who succeeded a few days afterwards to the provinces of Asia. In the first six months, however, of his new reign, Maximin affected to adopt the prudent counsels of his predecessor; and though he never condescended to secure the tranquillity of the church by a public edict, Sabinus, his Prætorian præfect, addressed a circular letter to all the governors and magistrates of the provinces, expatiating on the Imperial clemency, acknowledging the invincible obstinacy of the Christians, and directing the officers of justice to cease their ineffectual prosecutions, and to connive at the secret assemblies of those enthusiasts. In consequence of these orders, great numbers of Christians were released from prison, or delivered from the mines. The confessors, singing hymns of triumph, returned into their own countries, and those who had yielded to the violence of the tempest, solicited with tears of repentance their re-admission into the bosom of the church.[175]

But this treacherous calm was of short duration; nor could the Christians of the East place any confidence in the character of their sovereign. Cruelty and superstition were the ruling passions of the soul of Maximin. The former suggested the means, the latter pointed out the objects, of persecution. The emperor was devoted to the worship of the gods, to the study of magic, and to the belief of oracles. The prophets or philosophers, whom he revered as the favourites of Heaven, were frequently raised to the government of provinces, and admitted into his most secret councils. They easily convinced him that the Christians had been indebted for their victories to their regular discipline, and that the weakness of polytheism had principally flowed from a want of union and subordination among the ministers of religion. A system of government was therefore instituted, which was evidently copied from the policy of the church. In all the great cities of the empire, the temples were repaired and beautified by the order of Maximin, and the officiating priests of the various deities were subjected to the authority of a superior pontiff destined to oppose the bishop, and to promote the cause of paganism. These pontiffs acknowledged, in their turn, the supreme jurisdiction of the metropolitans or high priests of the province, who acted as the immediate vicegerents of the emperor himself. A white robe was the ensign of their dignity; and these new prelates were carefully selected from the most noble and opulent families. By the influence of the magistrates, and of the sacerdotal order, a great number of dutiful addresses were obtained, particularly from the cities of Nicomedia, Antioch, and Tyre, which artfully represented the well-known intentions of the court as the general sense of the people; solicited the emperor to consult the laws of justice rather than the dictates of his clemency; expressed their abhorrence of the Christians, and humbly prayed that those impious sectaries might at least be excluded from the limits of their respective territories. The answer of Maximin to the address which he obtained from the citizens of Tyre is still extant. He praises their zeal and devotion in terms of the highest satisfaction, descants on the obstinate impiety of the Christians, and betrays, by the readiness with which he consents to their banishment, that he considered himself as receiving, rather than as conferring, an obligation. The priests as well as the magistrates were empowered to enforce the execution of his edicts, which were engraved on tables of brass; and though it was recommended to them to avoid the effusion of blood, the most cruel and ignominious punishments were inflicted on the refractory Christians.[176]

The Asiatic Christians had everything to dread from the severity of a bigoted monarch who prepared his measures of violence with such deliberate policy. But a few months had scarcely elapsed before the edicts published by the two Western emperors obliged Maximim to suspend the prosecution of his designs: the civil war which he so rashly undertook against Licinius employed all his attention; and the defeat and death of Maximin soon delivered the church from the last and most implacable of her enemies.[177]

In this general view of the persecution which was first authorised by the edicts of Diocletian, I have purposely refrained from describing the particular sufferings and deaths of the Christian martyrs. It would have been an easy task, from the history of Eusebius, from the declamations of Lactantius, and from the most ancient acts, to collect a long series of horrid and disgusting pictures, and to fill many pages with racks and scourges, with iron hooks and red-hot beds, and with all the variety of tortures which fire and steel, savage beasts, and more savage executioners, could inflict on the human body. These melancholy scenes might be enlivened by a crowd of visions and miracles destined either to delay the death, to celebrate the triumph, or to discover the relics of those canonised saints who suffered for the name of Christ. But I cannot determine what I ought to transcribe, till I am satisfied how much I ought to believe. The gravest of the ecclesiastical historians, Eusebius himself, indirectly confesses that he has related whatever might redound to the glory, and that he has suppressed all that could tend to the disgrace, of religion.[178] Such an acknowledgment will naturally excite a suspicion that a writer who has so openly violated one of the fundamental laws of history has not paid a very strict regard to the observance of the other; and the suspicion will derive additional credit from the character of Eusebius, which was less tinctured with credulity, and more practised in the arts of courts, than that of almost any of his contemporaries. Of some particular occasions, when the magistrates were exasperated by some personal motives of interest or resentment, when the zeal of the martyrs urged them to forget the rules of prudence, and perhaps of decency, to overturn the altars, to pour out imprecations against the emperors, or to strike the judge as he sat on his tribunal, it may be presumed that every mode of torture which cruelty could invent, or constancy could endure, was exhausted on those devoted victims.[179] Two circumstances, however, have been unwarily mentioned, which insinuate that the general treatment of the Christians who had been apprehended by the officers of justice was less intolerable than it is usually imagined to have been. 1. The confessors who were condemned to work in the mines were permitted by the humanity or the negligence of their keepers to build chapels, and freely to profess their religion in the midst of those dreary habitations.[180] 2. The bishops were obliged to check and to censure the forward zeal of the Christians, who voluntarily threw themselves into the hands of the magistrates. Some of these were persons oppressed by poverty and debts, who blindly sought to terminate a miserable existence by a glorious death. Others were allured by the hope that a short confinement would expiate the sins of a whole life; and others again were actuated by the less honourable motive of deriving a plentiful subsistence, and perhaps a considerable profit, from the alms which the charity of the faithful bestowed on the prisoners.[181] After the church had triumphed over all her enemies, the interest as well as vanity of the captives prompted them to magnify the merit of their respective suffering. A convenient distance of time or place gave an ample scope to the progress of fiction; and the frequent instances which might be alleged of holy martyrs whose wounds had been instantly healed, whose strength had been renewed, and whose lost members had miraculously been restored, were extremely convenient for the purpose of removing every difficulty, and of silencing every objection. The most extravagant legends, as they conduced to the honour of the church, were applauded by the credulous multitude, countenanced by the power of the clergy, and attested by the suspicious evidence of ecclesiastical history.

The vague descriptions of exile and imprisonment, of pain and torture, are so easily exaggerated or softened by the pencil of an artful orator, that we are naturally induced to inquire into a fact of a more distinct and stubborn kind; the number of persons who suffered death in consequence of the edicts published by Diocletian, his associates, and his successors. The recent legendaries record whole armies and cities which were at once swept away by the undistinguishing rage of persecution. The more ancient writers content themselves with pouring out a liberal effusion of loose and tragical invectives, without condescending to ascertain the precise number of those persons who were permitted to seal with their blood their belief of the Gospel. From the history of Eusebius it may however be collected that only nine bishops were punished with death; and we are assured, by his particular enumeration of the martyrs of Palestine, that no more than ninety-two Christians were entitled to that honourable appellation.[182] As we are unacquainted with the degree of episcopal zeal and courage which prevailed at that time, it is not in our power to draw any useful inferences from the former of these facts: but the latter may serve to justify a very important and probable conclusion. According to the distribution of Roman provinces, Palestine may be considered as the sixteenth part of the Eastern empire:[183] and since there were some governors who, from a real or affected clemency, had preserved their hands unstained with the blood of the faithful,[184] it is reasonable to believe that the country which had given birth to Christianity produced at least the sixteenth part of the martyrs who suffered death within the dominions of Galerius and Maximin; the whole might consequently amount to about fifteen hundred, a number which, if it is equally divided between the ten years of the persecution, will allow an annual consumption of one hundred and fifty martyrs. Allotting the same proportion to the provinces of Italy, Africa, and perhaps Spain, where, at the end of two or three years, the rigour of the penal laws was either suspended or abolished, the multitude of Christians in the Roman empire, on whom a capital punishment was inflicted by a judicial sentence, will be reduced to somewhat less than two thousand persons. Since it cannot be doubted that the Christians were more numerous, and their enemies more exasperated, in the time of Diocletian than they had ever been in any former persecution, this probable and moderate computation may teach us to estimate the number of primitive saints and martyrs who sacrificed their lives for the important purpose of introducing Christianity into the world.

We shall conclude this chapter by a melancholy truth which obtrudes itself on the reluctant mind; that, even admitting, without hesitation or inquiry, all that history has recorded, or devotion has feigned, on the subject of martyrdoms, it must still be acknowledged that the Christians, in the course of their intestine dissensions, have inflicted far greater severities on each other than they had experienced from the zeal of infidels. During the ages of ignorance which followed the subversion of the Roman empire in the West, the bishops of the Imperial city extended their dominion over the laity as well as clergy of the Latin church. The fabric of superstition which they had erected, and which might long have defied the feeble efforts of reason, was at length assaulted by a crowd of daring fanatics, who, from the twelfth to the sixteenth century, assumed the popular character of reformers. The church of Rome defended by violence the empire which she had acquired by fraud; a system of peace and benevolence was soon disgraced by the proscriptions, wars, massacres, and the institution of the holy office. And as the reformers were animated by the love of civil as well as of religious freedom, the Catholic princes connected their own interest with that of the clergy, and enforced by fire and the sword the terrors of spiritual censures. In the Netherlands alone more than one hundred thousand of the subjects of Charles V. are said to have suffered by the hand of the executioner; and this extraordinary number is attested by Grotius,[185] a man of genius and learning, who preserved his moderation amidst the fury of contending sects, and who composed the annals of his own age and country at a time when the invention of printing had facilitated the means of intelligence and increased the danger of detection. If we are obliged to submit our belief to the authority of Grotius, it must be allowed that the number of Protestants who were executed in a single province and a single reign far exceeded that of the primitive martyrs in the space of three centuries and of the Roman empire. But if the improbability of the fact itself should prevail over the weight of evidence; if Grotius should be convicted of exaggerating the merit and sufferings of the reformers;[186] we shall be naturally led to inquire what confidence can be placed in the doubtful and imperfect monuments of ancient credulity; what degree of credit can be assigned to a courtly bishop and a passionate declaimer, who, under the protection of Constantine, enjoyed the exclusive privilege of recording the persecutions inflicted on the Christians by the vanquished rivals or disregarded predecessors of their gracious sovereign.

CHAPTER XVII

Foundation of Constantinople. Political System of Constantine and his Successors. Military Discipline. The Palace. The Finances.

THE unfortunate Licinius was the last rival who opposed the greatness, and the last captive who adorned the triumph, of Constantine. After a tranquil and prosperous reign the conqueror bequeathed to his family the inheritance of the Roman empire; a new capital, a new policy, and a new religion; and the innovations which he established have been embraced and consecrated by succeeding generations. The age of the great Constantine and his sons is filled with important events; but the historian must be oppressed by their number and variety, unless he diligently separates from each other the scenes which are connected only by the order of time. He will describe the political institutions that gave strength and stability to the empire before he proceeds to relate the wars and revolutions which hastened its decline. He will adopt the division unknown to the ancients of civil and ecclesiastical affairs: the victory of the Christians, and their intestine discord, will supply copious and distinct materials both for edification and for scandal.

After the defeat and abdication of Licinius his victorious rival proceeded to lay the foundations of a city destined to reign in future times the mistress of the East, and to survive the empire and religion of Constantine. The motives, whether of pride or of policy, which first induced Diocletian to withdraw himself from the ancient seat of government, had acquired additional weight by the example of his successors and the habits of forty years. Rome was insensibly confounded with the dependent kingdoms which had once acknowledged her supremacy; and the country of the Cæsars was viewed with cold indifference by a martial prince, born in the neighbourhood of the Danube, educated in the courts and armies of Asia, and invested with the purple by the legions of Britain. The Italians, who had received Constantine as their deliverer, submissively obeyed the edicts which he sometimes condescended to address to the senate and people of Rome; but they were seldom honoured with the presence of their new sovereign. During the vigour of his age Constantine, according to the various exigencies of peace and war, moved with slow dignity or with active diligence along the frontiers of his extensive dominions; and was always prepared to take the field either against a foreign or a domestic enemy. But as he gradually reached the summit of prosperity and the decline of life, he began to meditate the design of fixing in a more permanent station the strength as well as majesty of the throne. In the choice of an advantageous situation he preferred the confines of Europe and Asia; to curb with a powerful arm the barbarians who dwelt between the Danube and the Tanais; to watch with an eye of jealousy the conduct of the Persian monarch, who indignantly supported the yoke of an ignominious treaty. With these views Diocletian had selected and embellished the residence of Nicomedia: but the memory of Diocletian was justly abhorred by the protector of the church; and Constantine was not insensible to the ambition of founding a city which might perpetuate the glory of his own name. During the late operations of the war against Licinius he had sufficient opportunity to contemplate, both as a soldier and as a statesman, the incomparable position of Byzantium; and to observe how strongly it was guarded by nature against an hostile attack, whilst it was accessible on every side to the benefits of commercial intercourse. Many ages before Constantine, one of the most judicious historians of antiquity[1] had described the advantages of a situation from whence a feeble colony of Greeks derived the command of the sea, and the honours of a flourishing and independent republic.[2]

If we survey Byzantium in the extent which it acquired with the august name of Constantinople, the figure of the Imperial city may be represented under that of an unequal triangle. The obtuse point, which advances towards the east and the shores of Asia, meets and repels the waves of the Thracian Bosphorus. The northern side of the city is bounded by the harbour, and the southern is washed by the Propontis or Sea of Marmora. The basis of the triangle is opposed to the west, and terminates the continent of Europe. But the admirable form and division of the circumjacent land and water cannot, without a more ample explanation, be clearly or sufficiently understood.

The winding channel through which the waters of the Euxine flow with a rapid and incessant course towards the Mediterranean received the appellation of Bosphorus, a name not less celebrated in the history than in the fables of antiquity.[3] A crowd of temples and of votive altars, profusely scattered along its steep and woody banks, attested the unskilfulness, the terrors, and the devotion of the Grecian navigators who, after the example of the Argonauts, explored the dangers of the inhospitable Euxine. On these banks tradition long preserved the memory of the palace of Phineus, infested by the obscene harpies;[4] and of the sylvan reign of Amycus, who defied the son of Leda to the combat of the Cestus.[5] The straits of the Bosphorus are terminated by the Cyanean rocks, which, according to the description of the poets, had once floated on the face of the waters, and were destined by the gods to protect the entrance of the Euxine against the eye of profane curiosity.[6] From the Cyanean rocks to the point and harbour of Byzantium the winding length of the Bosphorus extends about sixteen miles,[7] and its most ordinary breadth may be computed at about one mile and a half. The *new* castles of Europe and Asia are constructed, on either continent, upon the foundations of two celebrated temples, of Serapis and of Jupiter Urius. The *old* castles, a work of the Greek emperors, command the narrowest part of the channel, in a place where the opposite banks advance within five hundred paces of each other. These fortresses were restored and strengthened by Mahomet the Second when he meditated the siege of Constantinople:[8] but the Turkish conqueror was most probably ignorant that, near two thousand years before his reign, Darius had chosen the same situation to connect the two continents by a bridge of boats.[9] At a small distance from the old castles we discover the little town of Chrysopolis, or Scutari, which may almost be considered as the Asiatic suburb of Constantinople. The Bosphorus, as it begins to open into the Propontis, passes between Byzantium and Chalcedon. The latter of those cities was built by the Greeks a few years before the former; and the blindness of its founders, who overlooked the superior advantages of the opposite coast, has been stigmatised by a proverbial expression of contempt.[10]

The harbour of Constantinople, which may be considered as an arm of the Bosphorus, obtained, in a very remote period, the denomination of the *Golden Horn*. The curve which it describes might be compared to the horn of a stag, or as it should seem, with more propriety, to that of an ox.[11] The epithet of *golden* was expressive of the riches which every wind wafted from the most distant countries into the secure and capacious port of Constantinople. The river Lycus, formed by the conflux of two little streams, pours into the harbour a perpetual supply of fresh water, which serves to cleanse the bottom and to invite the periodical shoals of fish to seek their retreat in that convenient recess. As the vicissitudes of tides are scarcely felt in those seas, the constant depth of the harbour allows goods to be landed on the quays without the assistance of boats; and it has been observed that, in many places, the largest vessels may rest their prows against the houses while their sterns are floating in the water.[12] From the mouth of the Lycus to that of the harbour this arm of the Bosphorus is more than seven miles in length. The entrance is about five hundred yards broad, and a strong chain could be occasionally drawn across it to guard the port and city from the attack of an hostile navy.[13]

Between the Bosphorus and the Hellespont, the shores of Europe and Asia receding on either side inclose the Sea of Marmora, which was known to the ancients by the denomination of Propontis. The navigation from the issue of the Bosphorus to the entrance of the Hellespont is about one hundred and twenty miles. Those who steer their westward course through the middle of the Propontis may at once descry the high lands of Thrace and Bithynia, and never lose sight of the lofty summit of Mount Olympus, covered with eternal snows.[14] They leave on the left a deep gulf, at the bottom of which Nicomedia was seated, the Imperial residence of Diocletian; and they pass the small islands of Cyzicus and Proconnesus before they cast anchor at Gallipoli, where the sea, which separates Asia from Europe, is again contracted into a narrow channel.

The geographers who, with the most skilful accuracy, have surveyed the form and extent of the Hellespont, assign about sixty miles for the winding course, and about three miles for the ordinary breadth, of those celebrated straits.[15] But the narrowest part of the channel is found to the northward of the old Turkish castles, between the cities of Sestus and Abydus. It was here that the adventurous Leander braved the passage of the flood for the possession of his mistress.[16] It was here likewise, in a place where the distance between the opposite banks cannot exceed five hundred paces, that Xerxes imposed a stupendous bridge of boats, for the purpose of transporting into Europe a hundred and seventy myriads of barbarians.[17] A sea contracted within such narrow limits may seem but ill to deserve the singular epithet of *broad*, which Homer, as well as Orpheus, has frequently bestowed on the Hellespont. But our ideas of greatness are of a relative nature: the traveller, and especially the poet, who sailed along the Hellespont, who pursued the windings of the stream, and contemplated the rural scenery, which appeared on every side to terminate the prospect, insensibly lost the remembrance of the sea; and his fancy painted those celebrated straits with all the attributes of a mighty river, flowing with a swift current, in the midst of a woody and inland country, and at length, through a wide mouth, discharging itself into the Ægean or Archipelago.[18] Ancient Troy,[19] seated on an eminence at the foot of Mount Ida, overlooked the mouth of the Hellespont, which scarcely received an accession of waters from the tribute of those immortal rivulets the Simois and Scamander. The Grecian camp had stretched twelve miles along the shore, from the Sigean to the Rhœtean promontory; and the flanks of the army were guarded by the bravest chiefs who fought under the banners of Agamemnon. The first of those promontories was occupied by Achilles with his invincible myrmidons, and the dauntless Ajax pitched his tents on the other. After Ajax had fallen a sacrifice to his disappointed pride and to the ingratitude of the Greeks, his sepulchre was created on the ground where he had defended the navy against the rage of Jove and Hector; and the citizens of the rising town of Rhœteum celebrated his memory with divine honours.[20] Before Constantine gave a just preference to the situation of Byzantium, he had conceived the design of erecting the seat of empire on this celebrated spot, from whence the Romans derived their fabulous origin. The extensive plain which lies below ancient Troy, towards the Rhœtean promontory and the tomb of Ajax, was first chosen for his new capital; and, though the undertaking was soon relinquished, the stately remains of unfinished walls and towers attracted the notice of all who sailed through the straits of the Hellespont.[21]

We are at present qualified to view the advantageous position of Constantinople, which appears to have been formed by nature for the centre and capital of a great monarchy. Situated in the forty-first degree of latitude, the Imperial city commanded, from her seven hills,[22] the opposite shores of Europe and Asia; the climate was healthy and temperate, the soil fertile, the harbour secure and capacious, and the approach on the side of the continent was of small extent and easy defence. The Bosphorus and the Hellespont may be considered as the two gates of Constantinople, and the prince who possessed those important passages could always shut them against a naval enemy and open them to the fleets of commerce. The preservation of the eastern provinces may, in some degree, be ascribed to the policy of Constantine, as the barbarians of the Euxine, who in the preceding age had poured their armaments into the heart of the Mediterranean, soon desisted from the exercise of piracy, and despaired of forcing this insurmountable barrier. When the gates of the Hellespont and Bosphorus were shut, the capital still enjoyed within their spacious enclosure every production which could supply the wants or gratify the luxury of its numerous inhabitants. The seacoasts of Thrace and Bithynia, which languish under the weight of Turkish oppression, still exhibit a rich prospect of vineyards, of gardens, and of plentiful harvests; and the Propontis has ever been renowned for an inexhaustible store of the most exquisite fish, that are taken in their stated seasons, without skill, and almost without labour.[23] But when the passages of the straits were thrown open for trade, they alternately admitted the natural and artificial riches of the north and south, of the Euxine and of the Mediterranean. Whatever rude commodities were collected in the forests of Germany and Scythia, as far as the sources of the Tanais and the Borysthenes; whatsoever was manufactured by the skill of Europe or Asia; the corn of Egypt, and the gems and spices of the farthest India, were brought by the varying winds into the port of Constantinople, which, for many ages, attracted the commerce of the ancient world.[24]

The prospect of beauty, of safety, and of wealth, united in a single spot, was sufficient to justify the choice of Constantine. But as some decent mixture of prodigy and fable has, in every age, been supposed to reflect a becoming majesty on the origin of great cities,[25] the emperor was desirous of ascribing his resolution not so much to the uncertain counsels of human policy as to the infallible and eternal decrees of divine wisdom. In one of his laws he has been careful to instruct posterity that, in obedience to the commands of God, he laid the everlasting foundations of Constantinople;[26] and though he has not condescended to relate in what manner the celestial inspiration was communicated to his mind, the defect of his modest silence has been liberally supplied by the ingenuity of succeeding writers, who describe the nocturnal vision which appeared to the fancy of Constantine as he slept within the walls of Byzantium. The tutelar genius of the city, a venerable matron sinking under the weight of years and infirmities, was suddenly transformed into a blooming maid, whom his own hands adorned with all the symbols of Imperial greatness.[27] The monarch awoke, interpreted the auspicious omen, and obeyed, without hesitation, the will of Heaven. The day which gave birth to a city or colony was celebrated by the Romans with such ceremonies as had been ordained by a generous superstition;[28] and though Constantine might omit some rites which savoured too strongly of their Pagan origin, yet he was anxious to leave a deep impression of hope and respect on the minds of the spectators. On foot, with a lance in his hand, the emperor himself led the solemn procession, and directed the line which was traced as the boundary of the destined capital, till the growing circumference was observed with astonishment by the assistants, who, at length, ventured to observe that he had already exceeded the most ample measure of a great city. "I shall still advance," replied Constantine, "till HE, the invisible guide who marches before me, thinks proper to stop."[29] Without presuming to investigate the nature or motives of this extraordinary conductor, we shall content ourselves with the more humble task of describing the extent and limits of Constantinople.[30]

In the actual state of the city, the palace and gardens of the Seraglio occupy the eastern promontory, the first of the seven hills, and cover about one hundred and fifty acres of our own measure. The seat of Turkish jealousy and despotism is erected on the foundations of a Grecian republic; but it may be supposed that the Byzantines were tempted by the conveniency of the harbour to extend their habitations on that side beyond the modern limits of the Seraglio. The new walls of Constantine stretched from the port to the Propontis across the enlarged breadth of the triangle, at the distance of fifteen stadia from the ancient fortification, and with the city of Byzantium they enclosed five of the seven hills which, to the eyes of those who approach Constantinople, appear to rise above each other in beautiful order.[31] About a century after the death of the founder, the new buildings, extending on one side up the harbour, and on the other along the Propontis, already covered the narrow ridge of the sixth and the broad summit of the seventh hill. The necessity of protecting those suburbs from the incessant inroads of the barbarians engaged the younger Theodosius to surround his capital with an adequate and permanent enclosure of walls.[32] From the eastern promontory to the golden gate, the extreme length of Constantinople was about three Roman miles,[33] the circumference measured between ten and eleven, and the surface might be computed as equal to about two thousand English acres. It is impossible to justify the vain and credulous exaggerations of modern travellers, who have sometimes stretched the limits of Constantinople over the adjacent villages of the European and even of the Asiatic coast.[34] But the suburbs of Pera and Galata, though situate beyond the harbour, may deserve to be considered as a part of the city;[35] and this addition may perhaps authorise the measure of a Byzantine historian, who assigns sixteen Greek (about fourteen Roman) miles for the circumference of his native city.[36] Such an extent may seem not unworthy of an Imperial residence. Yet Constantinople must yield to Babylon and Thebes,[37] to ancient Rome, to London, and even to Paris.[38]

The master of the Roman world, who aspired to erect an eternal monument of the glories of his reign, could employ in the prosecution of that great work the wealth, the labour, and all that yet remained of the genius, of obedient millions. Some estimate may be formed of the expense bestowed with Imperial liberality on the foundation of Constantinople by the allowance of about two millions five hundred thousand pounds for the construction of the walls, the porticoes, and the aqueducts.[39] The forests that overshadowed the shores of the Euxine, and the celebrated quarries of white marble in the little island of Proconnesus, supplied an inexhaustible stock of materials, ready to be conveyed, by the convenience of a short water-carriage, to the harbour of Byzantium.[40] A multitude of labourers and artificers urged the conclusion of the work with incessant toil; but the impatience of Constantine soon discovered that, in the decline of the arts, the skill as well as numbers of his architects bore a very unequal proportion to the greatness of his designs. The magistrates of the most distant provinces were therefore directed to institute schools, to appoint professors, and, by the hopes of rewards and privileges, to engage in the study and practice of architecture a sufficient number of ingenious youths who had received a liberal education.[41] The buildings of the new city were executed by such artificers as the reign of Constantine could afford; but they were decorated by the hands of the most celebrated masters of the age of Pericles and Alexander. To revive the genius of Phidias and Lysippus surpassed indeed the power of a Roman emperor; but the immortal productions which they had bequeathed to posterity were exposed without defence to the rapacious vanity of a despot. By his commands the cities of Greece and Asia were despoiled of their most valuable ornaments.[42] The trophies of memorable wars, the objects of religious veneration, the most finished statues of the gods and heroes, of the sages and poets of ancient times, contributed to the splendid triumph of Constantinople; and gave occasion to the remark of the historian Cedrenus,[43] who observes, with some enthusiasm, that nothing seemed wanting except the souls of the illustrious men whom these admirable monuments were intended to represent. But it is not in the city of Constantine, nor in the declining period of an empire, when the human mind was depressed by civil and religious slavery, that we should seek for the souls of Homer and of Demosthenes.

During the siege of Byzantium the conqueror had pitched his tent on the commanding eminence of the second hill. To perpetuate the memory of his success, he chose the same advantageous position for the principal Forum,[44] which

appears to have been of a circular or rather elliptical form. The two opposite entrances formed triumphal arches; the porticoes, which enclosed it on every side, were filled with statues, and the centre of the Forum was occupied by a lofty column, of which a mutilated fragment is now degraded by the appellation of the *burnt pillar*. This column was erected on a pedestal of white marble twenty feet high, and was composed of ten pieces of porphyry, each of which measured about ten feet in height, and about thirty-three in circumference.[45] On the summit of the pillar, above one hundred and twenty feet from the ground, stood the colossal statue of Apollo. It was of bronze, had been transported either from Athens or from a town of Phrygia, and was supposed to be the work of Phidias. The artist had represented the god of day, or, as it was afterwards interpreted, the emperor Constantine himself, with a sceptre in his right hand, the globe of the world in his left, and a crown of rays glittering on his head.[46] The Circus, or Hippodrome, was a stately building about four hundred paces in length, and one hundred in breadth.[47] The space between the two *metae* or goals was filled with statues and obelisks; and we may still remark a very singular fragment of antiquity, the bodies of three serpents twisted into one pillar of brass. Their triple heads had once supported the golden tripod which, after the defeat of Xerxes, was consecrated in the temple of Delphi by the victorious Greeks.[48] The beauty of the Hippodrome has been long since defaced by the rude hands of the Turkish conquerors, but, under the similar appellation of Atmeidan, it still serves as a place of exercise for their horses. From the throne, whence the emperor viewed the Circensian games a winding staircase[49] descended to the palace, a magnificent edifice, which scarcely yielded to the residence of Rome itself, and which, together with the dependent courts, gardens, and porticoes, covered a considerable extent of ground upon the banks of the Propontis, between the Hippodrome and the church of St. Sophia.[50] We might likewise celebrate the baths, which still retained the name of Zeuxippus, after they had been enriched by the munificence of Constantine, with lofty columns, various marbles, and above threescore statues of bronze.[51] But we should deviate from the design of this history if we attempted minutely to decribe the different buildings or quarters of the city. It may be sufficient to observe that whatever could adorn the dignity of a great capital, or contribute to the benefit or pleasure of its numerous inhabitants, was contained within the walls of Constantinople. A particular description, composed about a century after its foundation, enumerates a capitol or school of learning, a circus, two theatres, eight public and one hundred and fifty-three private baths, fifty-two porticoes, five granaries, eight aqueducts or reservoirs of water, four spacious halls for the meetings of the senate or courts of justice, fourteen churches, fourteen palaces, and four thousand three hundred and eighty-eight houses which, for their size or beauty, deserved to be distinguished from the multitude of plebeian habitations.[52]

The populousness of his favoured city was the next and most serious object of the attention of its founder. In the dark ages which succeeded the translation of the empire, the remote and the immediate consequences of that memorable event were strangely confounded by the vanity of the Greeks and the credulity of the Latins.[53] It was asserted and believed that all the noble families of Rome, the senate, and the equestrian order, with their innumerable attendants, had followed their emperor to the banks of the Propontis; that a spurious race of strangers and plebeians was left to possess the solitude of the ancient capital; and that the lands of Italy, long since converted into gardens, were at once deprived of cultivation and inhabitants.[54] In the course of this history such exaggerations will be reduced to their just value; yet since the growth of Constantinople cannot be ascribed to the general increase of mankind and of industry, it must be admitted that this artificial colony was raised at the expense of the ancient cities of the empire. Many opulent senators of Rome and of the eastern provinces were probably invited by Constantine to adopt for their country the fortunate spot which he had chosen for his own residence. The invitations of a master are scarcely to be distinguished from commands, and the liberality of the emperor obtained a ready and cheerful obedience. He bestowed on his favourites the palaces which he had built in the several quarters of the city, assigned them lands and pensions for the support of their dignity,[55] and alienated the demesnes of Pontus and Asia to grant hereditary estates by the easy tenure of maintaining a house in the capital.[56] But these encouragements and obligations soon became superfluous, and were gradually abolished. Wherever the seat of government is fixed, a considerable part of the public revenue will be expended by the prince himself, by his ministers, by the officers of justice, and by the domes-

tics of the palace. The most wealthy of the provincials will be attracted by the powerful motives of interest and duty, of amusement and curiosity. A third and more numerous class of inhabitants will insensibly be formed, of servants, of artificers, and of merchants, who derive their subsistence from their own labour, and from the wants or luxury of the superior ranks. In less than a century Constantinople disputed with Rome itself the pre-eminence of riches and numbers. New piles of buildings, crowded together with too little regard to health or convenience, scarcely allowed the intervals of narrow streets for the perpetual throng of men, of horses, and of carriages. The allotted space of ground was insufficient to contain the increasing people, and the additional foundations, which on either side were advanced into the sea, might alone have composed a very considerable city.[57]

The frequent and regular distributions of wine and oil, of corn or bread, of money or provisions, had almost exempted the poorer citizens of Rome from the necessity of labour. The magnificence of the first Cæsars was in some measure imitated by the founder of Constantinople:[58] but his liberality, however it might excite the applause of the people, has incurred the censure of posterity. A nation of legislators and conquerors might assert their claim to the harvests of Africa, which had been purchased with their blood; and it was artfully contrived by Augustus, that, in the enjoyment of plenty, the Romans should lose the memory of freedom. But the prodigality of Constantine could not be excused by any consideration either of public or private interest; and the annual tribute of corn imposed upon Egypt for the benefit of his new capital was applied to feed a lazy and insolent populace, at the expense of the husbandmen of an industrious province.[59] Some other regulations of this emperor are less liable to blame, but they are less deserving of notice. He divided Constantinople into fourteen regions or quarters,[60] dignified the public council with the appellation of senate,[61] communicated to the citizens the privileges of Italy,[62] and bestowed on the rising city the title of Colony, the first and most favoured daughter of ancient Rome. The venerable parent still maintained the legal and acknowledged supremacy, which was due to her age, to her dignity, and to the remembrance of her former greatness.[63]

As Constantine urged the progress of the work with the impatience of a lover, the walls, the porticoes, and the principal edifices were completed in a few years, or, according to another account, in a few months:[64] but this extraordinary diligence should excite the less admiration, since many of the buildings were finished in so hasty and imperfect a manner, that, under the succeeding reign, they were preserved with difficulty from impending ruin.[65] But while they displayed the vigour and freshness of youth, the founder prepared to celebrate the dedication of his city.[66] The games and largesses which crowned the pomp of this memorable festival may easily be supposed; but there is one circumstance of a more singular and permanent nature, which ought not entirely to be overlooked. As often as the birthday of the city returned, the statue of Constantine, framed by his order, of gilt wood, and bearing in its right hand a small image of the genius of the place, was erected on a triumphal car. The guards, carrying white tapers, and clothed in their richest apparel, accompanied the solemn procession as it moved through the Hippodrome. When it was opposite to the throne of the reigning emperor, he rose from his seat, and with grateful reverence adored the memory of his predecessor.[67] At the festival of the dedication, an edict, engraved on a column of marble, bestowed the title of SECOND or NEW ROME on the city of Constantine.[68] But the name of Constantinople[69] has prevailed over that honourable epithet, and after the revolution of fourteen centuries still perpetuates the fame of its author.[70]

The foundation of a new capital is naturally connected with the establishment of a new form of civil and military administration. The distinct view of the complicated system of policy introduced by Diocletian, improved by Constantine, and completed by his immediate successors, may not only amuse the fancy by the singular picture of a great empire, but will tend to illustrate the secret and internal causes of its rapid decay. In the pursuit of any remarkable institution, we may be frequently led into the more early or the more recent times of the Roman history; but the proper limits of this inquiry will be included within a period of about one hundred and thirty years, from the accession of Constantine to the publication of the Theodosian code;[71] from which, as well as from the *Notitia* of the East and West,[72] we derive the most copious and authentic information of the state of the empire. This variety of objects will suspend, for some time, the course of the narrative; but the interruption will be censured only by those readers who are insensible to the importance of laws and manners, while they pe-

ruse, with eager curiosity, the transient intrigues of a court, or the accidental event of a battle.

The manly pride of the Romans, content with substantial power, had left to the vanity of the East the forms and ceremonies of ostentatious greatness.[73] But when they lost even the semblance of those virtues which were derived from their ancient freedom, the simplicity of Roman manners was insensibly corrupted by the stately affectation of the courts of Asia. The distinctions of personal merit and influence, so conspicuous in a republic, so feeble and obscure under a monarchy, were abolished by the despotism of the emperors; who substituted in their room a severe subordination of rank and office, from the titled slaves who were seated on the steps of the throne, to the meanest instruments of arbitrary power. This multitude of abject dependents was interested in the support of the actual government, from the dread of a revolution which might at once confound their hopes and intercept the reward of their services. In this divine hierarchy (for such it is frequently styled) every rank was marked with the most scrupulous exactness, and its dignity was displayed in a variety of trifling and solemn ceremonies, which it was a study to learn, and a sacrilege to neglect.[74] The purity of the Latin language was debased, by adopting, in the intercourse of pride and flattery, a profusion of epithets which Tully would scarcely have understood, and which Augustus would have rejected with indignation. The principal officers of the empire were saluted, even by the sovereign himself, with the deceitful titles of your *Sincerity*, your *Gravity*, your *Excellency*, your *Eminence*, your *sublime and wonderful Magnitude*, your *illustrious and magnificent Highness*.[75] The codicils or patents of their office were curiously emblazoned with such emblems as were best adapted to explain their nature and high dignity— the image or portrait of the reigning emperors; a triumphal car; the book of mandates placed on a table, covered with a rich carpet, and illuminated by four tapers; the allegorical figures of the provinces which they governed; or the appellations and standards of the troops whom they commanded. Some of these official ensigns were really exhibited in their hall of audience; others preceded their pompous march whenever they appeared in public; and every circumstance of their demeanour, their dress, their ornaments, and their train, was calculated to inspire a deep reverence for the representatives of supreme majesty. By a philosophic observer the system of the Roman government might have been mistaken for a splendid theatre, filled with players of every character and degree, who repeated the language, and imitated the passions, of their original model.[76]

All the magistrates of sufficient importance to find a place in the general state of the empire were accurately divided into three classes—1, The *Illustrious;* 2, The *Spectabiles,* or *Respectable*; and, 3, The *Clarissimi,* whom we may translate by the word *Honourable.* In the times of Roman simplicity, the last-mentioned epithet was used only as a vague expression of deference, till it became at length the peculiar and appropriated title of all who were members of the senate,[77] and consequently of all who, from that venerable body, were selected to govern the provinces. The vanity of those who, from their rank and office, might claim a superior distinction above the rest of the senatorial order, was long afterwards indulged with the new appellation of *Respectable:* but the title of *Illustrious* was always reserved to some eminent personages who were obeyed or reverenced by the two subordinate classes. It was communicated only, I. To the consuls and patricians; II. To the Prætorian præfects, with the præfects of Rome and Constantinople; III. To the masters general of the cavalry and the infantry; and, IV. To the seven ministers of the palace, who exercised their *sacred* functions about the person of the emperor.[78] Among those illustrious magistrates who were esteemed co-ordinate with each other, the seniority of appointment gave place to the union of dignities.[79] By the expedient of honorary codicils, the emperors, who were fond of multiplying their favours, might sometimes gratify the vanity, though not the ambition, of impatient courtiers.[80]

I. As long as the Roman consuls were the first magistrates of a free state, they derived their right to power from the choice of the people. As long as the emperors condescended to disguise the servitude which they imposed, the consuls were still elected by the real or apparent suffrage of the senate. From the reign of Diocletian even these vestiges of liberty were abolished, and the successful candidates, who were invested with the annual honours of the consulship, affected to deplore the humiliating condition of their predecessors. The Scipios and the Catos had been reduced to solicit the votes of plebeians, to pass through the tedious and expensive forms of a popular election, and to expose their dignity to the shame of a public refusal; while their own happier fate had reserved them for an age and government in which the rewards of virtue were assigned by the unerring wisdom of a gracious sovereign.[81] In the epistles which the emperor addressed to the two consuls elect, it was declared that they were *created* by his sole authority.[82] Their names and portraits, engraved on gilt tablets of ivory, were dispersed over the empire as presents to the provinces, the cities, the magistrates, the senate, and the people.[83] Their solemn inauguration was performed at the place of the Imperial residence; and during a period of one hundred and twenty years Rome was constantly deprived of the presence of her ancient magistrates.[84] On the morning of the first of January the consuls assumed the ensigns of their dignity. Their dress was a robe of purple, embroidered in silk and gold, and sometimes ornamented with costly gems.[85] On this solemn occasion they were attended by the most eminent officers of the state and army in the habit of senators; and the useless fasces, armed with the once formidable axes, were borne before them by the lictors.[86] The procession moved from the palace[87] to the Forum or principal square of the city; where the consuls ascended their tribunal, and seated themselves in the curule chairs, which were framed after the fashion of ancient times. They immediately exercised an act of jurisdiction, by the manumission of a slave who was brought before them for that purpose; and the ceremony was intended to represent the celebrated action of the elder Brutus, the author of liberty and of the consulship, when he admitted among his fellow-citizens the faithful Vindex, who had revealed the conspiracy of the Tarquins.[88] The public festival was continued during several days in all the principal cities; in Rome, from custom; in Constantinople, from imitation; in Carthage, Antioch, and Alexandria, from the love of pleasure and the superfluity of wealth.[89] In the two capitals of the empire the annual games of the theatre, the circus, and the amphitheatre[90] cost four thousand pounds of gold, (about) one hundred and sixty thousand pounds sterling; and if so heavy an expense surpassed the faculties or the inclination of the magistrates themselves, the sum was supplied from the Imperial treasury.[91] As soon as the consuls had discharged these customary duties, they were at liberty to retire into the shade of private life, and to enjoy during the remainder of the year the undisturbed contemplation of their own greatness. They no longer presided in the national councils; they no longer executed the resolutions of peace or war. Their abilities (unless they were employed in more effective offices) were of little moment; and their names served only as the legal date of the year in which they had filled the chair of Marius and of Cicero. Yet it was still felt and acknowledged, in the last period of Roman servitude, that this empty name might be compared, and even preferred, to the possession of substantial power. The title of consul was still the most splendid object of ambition, the noblest reward of virtue and loyalty. The emperors themselves, who disdained the faint shadow of the republic, were conscious that they acquired an additional splendour and majesty as often as they assumed the annual honours of the consular dignity.[92]

The proudest and most perfect separation which can be found in any age or country between the nobles and the people is perhaps that of the Patricians and the Plebeians, as it was established in the first age of the Roman republic. Wealth and honours, the offices of the state, and the ceremonies of religion, were almost exclusively possessed by the former; who, preserving the purity of their blood with the most insulting jealousy,[93] held their clients in a condition of specious vassalage. But these distinctions, so incompatible with the spirit of a free people, were removed, after a long struggle, by the persevering efforts of the Tribunes. The most active and successful of the Plebeians accumulated wealth, aspired to honours, deserved triumphs, contracted alliances, and, after some generations, assumed the pride of ancient nobility.[94] The Patrician families, on the other hand, whose original number was never recruited till the end of the commonwealth, either failed in the ordinary course of nature, or were extinguished in so many foreign and domestic wars, or, through a want of merit or fortune, insensibly mingled with the mass of the people.[95] Very few remained who could derive their pure and genuine origin from the infancy of the city, or even from that of the republic, when Cæsar and Augustus, Claudius and Vespasian, created from the body of the senate a competent number of new Patrician families, in the hope of perpetuating an order which was still considered as honourable and sacred.[96] But these artificial supplies (in which the reigning house was always included) were rapidly swept away by the rage of tyrants, by frequent revolutions, by the change of manners, and by the intermixture of nations.[97] Little more was left when Constantine ascended the throne than a vague and imperfect tradition that the Patricians had once been the first of the Romans. To form a body of nobles, whose influence may restrain while it secures the authority of the monarch, would

have been very inconsistent with the character and policy of Constantine; but, had he seriously entertained such a design, it might have exceeded the measure of his power to ratify by an arbitrary edict an institution which must expect the sanction of time and of opinion. He revived, indeed, the title of Patricians, but he revived it as a personal, not as an hereditary distinction. They yielded only to the transient superiority of the annual consuls; but they enjoyed the preeminence over all the great officers of state, with the most familiar access to the person of the prince. This honourable rank was bestowed on them for life; and, as they were usually favourites and ministers who had grown old in the Imperial court, the true etymology of the word was perverted by ignorance and flattery; and the Patricians of Constantine were reverenced as the adopted *Fathers* of the emperor and the republic.[98]

II. The fortunes of the Prætorian præfects were essentially different from those of the consuls and Patricians. The latter saw their ancient greatness evaporate in a vain title. The former, rising by degrees from the most humble condition, were invested with the civil and military administration of the Roman world. From the reign of Severus to that of Diocletian, the guards and the palace, the laws and the finances, the armies and the provinces, were intrusted to their superintending care; and, like the vizirs of the East, they held with one hand the seal, and with the other the standard, of the empire. The ambition of the præfects, always formidable, and sometimes fatal to the masters whom they served, was supported by the strength of the Prætorian bands; but, after those haughty troops had been weakened by Diocletian and finally suppressed by Constantine, the præfects, who survived their fall, were reduced without difficulty to the station of useful and obedient ministers. When they were no longer responsible for the safety of the emperor's person, they resigned the jurisdiction which they had hitherto claimed and exercised over all the departments of the palace. They were deprived by Constantine of all military command as soon as they had ceased to lead into the field, under their immediate orders, the flower of the Roman troops; and, at length, by a singular revolution, the captains of the guards were transformed into the civil magistrates of the provinces. According to the plan of government instituted by Diocletian, the four princes had each their Prætorian præfect; and after the monarchy was once more united in the person of Constantine, he still continued to create the same number of FOUR PRÆFECTS, and intrusted to their care the same provinces which they already administered. 1. The præfect of the East stretched his ample jurisdiction into the three parts of the globe which were subject to the Romans, from the cataracts of the Nile to the banks of the Phasis, and from the mountains of Thrace to the frontiers of Persia. 2. The important provinces of Pannonia, Dacia, Macedonia, and Greece once acknowledged the authority of the præfect of Illyricum. 3. The power of the præfect of Italy was not confined to the country from whence he derived his title; it extended over the additional territory of Rhætia as far as the banks of the Danube, over the dependent islands of the Mediterranean, and over that part of the continent of Africa which lies between the confines of Cyrene and those of Tingitania. 4. The præfect of the Gauls comprehended under that plural denomination the kindred provinces of Britain and Spain, and his authority was obeyed from the wall of Antoninus to the foot of Mount Atlas.[99]

After the Prætorian præfects had been dismissed from all military command, the civil functions which they were ordained to exercise over so many subject nations were adequate to the ambition and abilities of the most consummate ministers. To their wisdom was committed the supreme administration of justice and of the finances, the two objects which, in a state of peace, comprehend almost all the respective duties of the sovereign and of the people; of the former, to protect the citizens who are obedient to the laws; of the latter, to contribute the share of their property which is required for the expenses of the state. The coin, the highways, the posts, the granaries, the manufactures, whatever could interest the public prosperity, was moderated by the authority of the Prætorian præfects. As the immediate representatives of the Imperial majesty, they were empowered to explain, to enforce, and on some occasions to modify, the general edicts by their discretionary proclamations. They watched over the conduct of the provincial governors, removed the negligent, and inflicted punishments on the guilty. From all the inferior jurisdictions an appeal in every matter of importance, either civil or criminal, might be brought before the tribunal of the præfect: but *his* sentence was final and absolute; and the emperors themselves refused to admit any complaints against the judgment or the integrity of a magistrate whom they honoured with such unbounded confidence.[100] His

appointments were suitable to his dignity;[101] and, if avarice was his ruling passion, he enjoyed frequent opportunities of collecting a rich harvest of fees, of presents, and of perquisites. Though the emperors no longer dreaded the ambition of their præfects, they were attentive to counterbalance the power of this great office by the uncertainty and shortness of its duration.[102]

From their superior importance and dignity, Rome and Constantinople were alone excepted from the jurisdiction of the Prætorian præfects. The immense size of the city, and the experience of the tardy, ineffectual operation of the laws, had furnished the policy of Augustus with a specious pretence for introducing a new magistrate, who alone could restrain a servile and turbulent populace by the strong arm of arbitrary power.[103] Valerius Messalla was appointed the first præfect of Rome, that his reputation might countenance so invidious a measure; but at the end of a few days that accomplished citizen[104] resigned his office, declaring, with a spirit worthy of the friend of Brutus, that he found himself incapable of exercising a power incompatible with public freedom.[105] As the sense of liberty became less exquisite, the advantages of order were more clearly understood; and the præfect, who seemed to have been designed as a terror only to slaves and vagrants, was permitted to extend his civil and criminal jurisdiction over the equestrian and noble families of Rome. The prætors, annually created as the judges of law and equity, could not long dispute the possession of the Forum with a vigorous and permanent magistrate who was usually admitted into the confidence of the prince. Their courts were deserted; their number, which had once fluctuated between twelve and eighteen,[106] was gradually reduced to two or three; and their important functions were confined to the expensive obligation[107] of exhibiting games for the amusement of the people. After the office of Roman consuls had been changed into a vain pageant, which was rarely displayed in the capital, the præfects assumed their vacant place in the senate, and were soon acknowledged as the ordinary presidents of that venerable assembly. They received appeals from the distance of one hundred miles; and it was allowed as a principle of jurisprudence that all municipal authority was derived from them alone.[108] In the discharge of his laborious employment the governor of Rome was assisted by fifteen officers, some of whom had been originally his equals, or even his superiors. The principal departments were relative to the command of a numerous watch, established as a safeguard against fires, robberies, and nocturnal disorders; the custody and distribution of the public allowance of corn and provisions; the care of the port, of the aqueducts, of the common sewers, and of the navigation and bed of the Tiber; the inspection of the markets, the theatres, and of the private as well as public works. Their vigilance ensured the three principal objects of a regular police—safety, plenty, and cleanliness; and, as a proof of the attention of government to preserve the splendour and ornaments of the capital, a particular inspector was appointed for the statues; the guardian, as it were, of that inanimate people, which, according to the extravagant computation of an old writer, was scarcely inferior in number to the living inhabitants of Rome. About thirty years after the foundation of Constantinople a similar magistrate was created in that rising metropolis, for the same uses and with the same powers. A perfect equality was established between the dignity of the *two* municipal and that of the *four* Prætorian præfects.[109]

Those who in the Imperial hierarchy were distinguished by the title of *Respectable* formed an intermediate class between the *illustrious* præfects and the *honourable* magistrates of the provinces. In this class the proconsuls of Asia, Achaia, and Africa claimed a pre-eminence, which was yielded to the remembrance of their ancient dignity; and the appeal from their tribunal to that of the præfects was almost the only mark of their dependence.[110] But the civil government of the empire was distributed into thirteen great DIOCESES, each of which equalled the just measure of a powerful kingdom. The first of these dioceses was subject to the jurisdiction of the *count* of the East; and we may convey some idea of the importance and variety of his functions by observing that six hundred apparitors, who would be styled at present either secretaries, or clerks, or ushers, or messengers, were employed in his immediate office.[111] The place of *Augustal præfect* of Egypt was no longer filled by a Roman knight, but the name was retained; and the extraordinary powers which the situation of the country and the temper of the inhabitants had once made indispensable were still continued to the governor. The eleven remaining dioceses—of Asiana, Pontica, and Thrace; of Macedonia, Dacia, and Pannonia, or Western Illyricum; of Italy and Africa; of Gaul, Spain, and Britain—were governed by twelve *vicars* or *vice-præfects*,[112] whose name sufficiently explains the nature and dependence of their office. It

may be added that the lieutenant-generals of the Roman armies, the military counts and dukes, who will be hereafter mentioned, were allowed the rank and title of *Respectable*.

As the spirit of jealousy and ostentation prevailed in the councils of the emperors, they proceeded with anxious diligence to divide the substance and to multiply the titles of power. The vast countries which the Roman conquerors had united under the same simple form of administration were imperceptibly crumbled into minute fragments, till at length the whole empire was distributed into one hundred and sixteen provinces, each of which supported an expensive and splendid establishment. Of these, three were governed by *proconsuls*, thirty-seven by *consulars*, five by *correctors*, and seventy-one by *presidents*.[113] The appellations of these magistrates were different; they ranked in successive order, the ensigns of their dignity were curiously varied, and their situation, from accidental circumstances, might be more or less agreeable or advantageous. But they were all (excepting only the proconsuls) alike included in the class of *honourable* persons; and they were alike intrusted, during the pleasure of the prince, and under the authority of the præfects or their deputies, with the administration of justice and the finances in their respective districts. The ponderous volumes of the Codes and Pandects[114] would furnish ample materials for a minute inquiry into the system of provincial government, as in the space of six centuries it was improved by the wisdom of the Roman statesmen and lawyers. It may be sufficient for the historian to select two singular and salutary provisions, intended to restrain the abuse of authority. I. For the preservation of peace and order, the governors of the provinces were armed with the sword of justice. They inflicted corporal punishments, and they exercised, in capital offences, the power of life and death. But they were not authorized to indulge the condemned criminal with the choice of his own execution or to pronounce a sentence of the mildest and most honourable kind of exile. These prerogatives were reserved to the præfects, who alone could impose the heavy fine of fifty pounds of gold: their vicegerents were confined to the trifling weight of a few ounces.[115] This distinction, which seems to grant the larger while it denies the smaller degree of authority, was founded on a very rational motive. The smaller degree was infinitely more liable to abuse. The passions of a provincial magistrate might frequently provoke him into acts of oppression, which affected only the freedom or the fortunes of the subject; though, from a principle of prudence, perhaps of humanity, he might still be terrified by the guilt of innocent blood. It may likewise be considered that exile, considerable fines, or the choice of an easy death, relate more particularly to the rich and the noble; and the persons the most exposed to the avarice or resentment of a provincial magistrate were thus removed from his obscure persecution to the more august and impartial tribunal of the Prætorian præfect. 2. As it was reasonably apprehended that the integrity of the judge might be biassed, if his interest was concerned or his affections were engaged, the strictest regulations were established to exclude any person, without the special dispensation of the emperor, from the government of the province where he was born,[116] and to prohibit the governor or his son from contracting marriage with a native or an inhabitant;[117] or from purchasing slaves, lands, or houses within the extent of his jurisdiction.[118] Notwithstanding these rigorous precautions, the emperor Constantine, after a reign of twenty-five years, still deplores the venal and oppressive administration of justice, and expresses the warmest indignation that the audience of the judge, his despatch of business, his seasonable delays, and his final sentence, were publicly sold, either by himself or by the officers of his court. The continuance, and perhaps the impunity, of these crimes is attested by the repetition of impotent laws and ineffectual menaces.[119]

All the civil magistrates were drawn from the profession of the law. The celebrated Institutes of Justinian are addressed to the youth of his dominions who had devoted themselves to the study of Roman jurisprudence; and the sovereign condescends to animate their diligence by the assurance that their skill and ability would in time be rewarded by an adequate share in the government of the republic.[120] The rudiments of this lucrative science were taught in all the considerable cities of the East and West; but the most famous school was that of Berytus,[121] on the coast of Phœnicia, which flourished above three centuries from the time of Alexander Severus, the author perhaps of an institution so advantageous to his native country. After a regular course of education, which lasted five years, the students dispersed themselves through the provinces in search of fortune and honours; nor could they want an inexhaustible supply of business in a great empire already corrupted by the multiplicity of laws, of arts, and of vices. The court of the Prætorian

præfect of the East could alone furnish employment for one hundred and fifty advocates, sixty-four of whom were distinguished by peculiar privileges, and two were annually chosen with a salary of sixty pounds of gold to defend the causes of the treasury. The first experiment was made of their judicial talents by appointing them to act occasionally as assessors to the magistrates; from thence they were often raised to preside in the tribunals before which they had pleaded. They obtained the government of a province; and, by the aid of merit, of reputation, or of favour, they ascended, by successive steps, to the *illustrious* dignities of the state.[122] In the practice of the bar these men had considered reason as the instrument of dispute; they interpreted the laws according to the dictates of private interest; and the same pernicious habits might still adhere to their characters in the public administration of the state. The honour of a liberal profession has indeed been vindicated by ancient and modern advocates, who have filled the most important stations with pure integrity and consummate wisdom; but in the decline of Roman jurisprudence the ordinary promotion of lawyers was pregnant with mischief and disgrace. The noble art, which had once been preserved as the sacred inheritance of the patricians, was fallen into the hands of freedmen and plebeians,[123] who, with cunning rather than with skill, exercised a sordid and pernicious trade. Some of them procured admittance into families for the purpose of fomenting differences, of encouraging suits, and of preparing a harvest of gain for themselves or their brethren. Others, recluse in their chambers, maintained the gravity of legal professors, by furnishing a rich client with subtleties to confound the plainest truth, and with arguments to colour the most unjustifiable pretensions. The splendid and popular class was composed of the advocates, who filled the Forum with the sound of their turgid and loquacious rhetoric. Careless of fame and of justice, they are described for the most part as ignorant and rapacious guides, who conducted their clients through a maze of expense, of delay, and of disappointment; from whence, after a tedious series of years, they were at length dismissed, when their patience and fortune were almost exhausted.[124]

III. In the system of policy introduced by Augustus, the governors, those at least of the Imperial provinces, were invested with the full powers of the sovereign himself. Ministers of peace and war, the distribution of rewards and punishments depended on them alone, and they successively appeared on their tribunal in the robes of civil magistracy, and in complete armour at the head of the Roman legions.[125] The influence of the revenue, the authority of law, and the command of a military force, concurred to render their power supreme and absolute; and whenever they were tempted to violate their allegiance, the loyal province which they involved in their rebellion was scarcely sensible of any change in its political state. From the time of Commodus to the reign of Constantine near one hundred governors might be enumerated, who, with various success, erected the standard of revolt; and though the innocent were too often sacrificed, the guilty might be sometimes prevented, by the suspicious cruelty of their master.[126] To secure his throne and the public tranquillity from these formidable servants, Constantine resolved to divide the military from the civil administration, and to establish, as a permanent and professional distinction, a practice which had been adopted only as an occasional expedient. The supreme jurisdiction exercised by the Prætorian præfects over the armies of the empire was transferred to the two *masters general* whom he instituted, the one for the *cavalry*, the other for the *infantry*; and though each of these *illustrious* officers was more peculiarly responsible for the discipline of those troops which were under his immediate inspection, they both indifferently commanded in the field the several bodies, whether of horse or foot, which were united in the same army.[127] Their number was soon doubled by the division of the East and West; and as separate generals of the same rank and title were appointed on the four important frontiers of the Rhine, of the Upper and the Lower Danube, and of the Euphrates, the defence of the Roman empire was at length committed to eight masters general of the cavalry and infantry. Under their orders, thirty-five military commanders were stationed in the provinces: three in Britain, six in Gaul, one in Spain, one in Italy, five on the Upper and four on the Lower Danube, in Asia eight, three in Egypt, and four in Africa. The titles of *counts* and *dukes*,[128] by which they were properly distinguished, have obtained in modern languages so very different a sense that the use of them may occasion some surprise. But it should be recollected that the second of those appellations is only a corruption of the Latin word which was indiscriminately applied to any military chief. All these provincial generals were therefore *dukes*; but no more than ten among them were

dignified with the rank of *counts* or companions, a title of honour, or rather of favour, which had been recently invented in the court of Constantine. A gold belt was the ensign which distinguished the office of the counts and dukes; and, besides their pay, they received a liberal allowance sufficient to maintain one hundred and ninety servants and one hundred and fifty-eight horses. They were strictly prohibited from interfering in any matter which related to the administration of justice or the revenue; but the command which they exercised over the troops of their department was independent of the authority of the magistrates. About the same time that Constantine gave a legal sanction to the ecclesiastical order, he instituted in the Roman empire the nice balance of the civil and the military powers. The emulation, and sometimes the discord, which reigned between two professions of opposite interests and incompatible manners, was productive of beneficial and of pernicious consequences. It was seldom to be expected that the general and the civil governor of a province should either conspire for the disturbance, or should unite for the service, of their country. While the one delayed to offer the assistance which the other disdained to solicit, the troops very frequently remained without orders or without supplies, the public safety was betrayed, and the defenceless subjects were left exposed to the fury of the barbarians. The divided administration, which had been formed by Constantine, relaxed the vigour of the state, while it secured the tranquillity of the monarch.

The memory of Constantine has been deservedly censured for another innovation which corrupted military discipline, and prepared the ruin of the empire. The nineteen years which preceded his final victory over Licinius had been a period of licence and intestine war. The rivals who contended for the possession of the Roman world had withdrawn the greatest part of their forces from the guard of the general frontier; and the principal cities which formed the boundary of their respective dominions were filled with soldiers, who considered their countrymen as their most implacable enemies. After the use of these internal garrisons had ceased with the civil war, the conqueror wanted either wisdom or firmness to revive the severe discipline of Diocletian, and to suppress a fatal indulgence which habit had endeared and almost confirmed to the military order. From the reign of Constantine a popular and even legal distinction was admitted between the *Palatines*[129] and the *Borderers*; the troops of the court, as they were improperly styled, and the troops of the frontier. The former, elevated by the superiority of their pay and privileges, were permitted, except in the extraordinary emergencies of war, to occupy their tranquil stations in the heart of the provinces. The most flourishing cities were oppressed by the intolerable weight of quarters.

The soldiers insensibly forgot the virtues of their profession, and contracted only the vices of civil life. They were either degraded by the industry of mechanic trades, or enervated by the luxury of baths and theatres. They soon became careless of their martial exercises, curious in their diet and apparel, and, while they inspired terror to the subjects of the empire, they trembled at the hostile approach of the barbarians.[130] The chain of fortifications which Diocletian and his colleagues had extended along the banks of the great rivers was no longer maintained with the same care, or defended with the same vigilance. The numbers which still remained under the name of the troops of the frontier might be sufficient for the ordinary defence. But their spirit was degraded by the humiliating reflection that *they*, who were exposed to the hardships and dangers of a perpetual warfare, were rewarded only with about two-thirds of the pay and emoluments which were lavished on the troops of the court. Even the bands or legions that were raised the nearest to the level of those unworthy favourites were in some measure disgraced by the title of honour which they were allowed to assume. It was in vain that Constantine repeated the most dreadful menaces of fire and sword against the Borderers who should dare to desert their colours, to connive at the inroads of the barbarians, or to participate in the spoil.[131] The mischiefs which flow from injudicious counsels are seldom removed by the application of partial severities; and though succeeding princes laboured to restore the strength and numbers of the frontier garrisons, the empire, till the last moment of its dissolution, continued to languish under the mortal wound which had been so rashly or so weakly inflicted by the hand of Constantine.

The same timid policy, of dividing whatever is united, of reducing whatever is eminent, of dreading every active power, and of expecting that the most feeble will prove the most obedient, seems to pervade the institutions of several princes, and particularly those of Constantine. The martial pride of the legions, whose victorious camps had so often been the scene of rebellion, was nourished by the memory of their past exploits, and the consciousness of their actual strength. As long as they maintained their ancient establishment of six thousand men, they subsisted, under the reign of Diocletian, each of them singly, a visible and important object in the military history of the Roman empire. A few years afterwards these gigantic bodies were shrunk to a very diminutive size; and when *seven* legions, with some auxiliaries, defended the city of Amida against the Persians, the total garrison, with the inhabitants of both sexes, and the peasants of the deserted country, did not exceed the number of twenty thousand persons.[132] From this fact, and from similar examples, there is reason to believe that the constitution of the legionary troops, to which they partly owed their valour and discipline, was dissolved by Constantine; and that the bands of Roman infantry, which still assumed the same names and the same honours, consisted only of one thousand or fifteen hundred men.[133] The conspiracy of so many separate detachments, each of which was awed by the sense of its own weakness, could easily be checked; and the successors of Constantine might indulge their love of ostentation, by issuing their orders to one hundred and thirty-two legions, inscribed on the muster-roll of their numerous armies. The remainder of their troops was distributed into several hundred cohorts of infantry, and squadrons of cavalry. Their arms, and titles, and ensigns were calculated to inspire terror, and to display the variety of nations who marched under the Imperial standard. And not a vestige was left of that severe simplicity which, in the ages of freedom and victory, had distinguished the line of battle of a Roman army from the confused host of an Asiatic monarch.[134] A more particular enumeration, drawn from the *Notitia*, might exercise the diligence of an antiquary; but the historian will content himself with observing that the number of permanent stations or garrisons established on the frontiers of the empire amounted to five hundred and eighty-three; and that, under the successors of Constantine, the complete force of military establishment was computed at six hundred and forty-five thousand soldiers.[135] An effort so prodigious surpassed the wants of a more ancient and the faculties of a later period.

In the various states of society armies are recruited from very different motives. Barbarians are urged by their love of war; the citizens of a free republic may be prompted by a principle of duty; the subjects, or at least the nobles, of a monarchy are animated by a sentiment of honour; but the timid and luxurious inhabitants of a declining empire must be allured into the service by the hopes of profit, or compelled by the dread of punishment. The resources of the Roman treasury were exhausted by the increase of pay, by the repetition of donatives, and by the invention of new emoluments and indulgences, which, in the opinion of the provincial youth, might compensate the hardships and dangers of a military life. Yet, although the stature was lowered,[136] although slaves, at least by a tacit connivance, were indiscriminately received into the ranks, the insurmountable difficulty of procuring a regular and adequate supply of volunteers obliged the emperors to adopt more effectual and coercive methods. The lands bestowed on the veterans, as the free reward of their valour, were henceforward granted under a condition which contains the first rudiments of the feudal tenures—that their sons, who succeeded to the inheritance, should devote themselves to the profession of arms as soon as they attained the age of manhood; and their cowardly refusal was punished by the loss of honour, of fortune, or even of life.[137] But as the annual growth of the sons of the veterans bore a very small proportion to the demands of the service, levies of men were frequently required from the provinces, and every proprietor was obliged either to take up arms, or to procure a substitute, or to purchase his exemption by the payment of a heavy fine. The sum of forty-two pieces of gold, to which it was *reduced*, ascertains the exhorbitant price of volunteers, and the reluctance with which the government admitted of this alternative.[138] Such was the horror for the profession of a soldier which had affected the minds of the degenerate Romans that many of the youth of Italy and the provinces chose to cut off the fingers of their right hand to escape from being pressed into the service; and this strange expedient was so commonly practised as to deserve the severe animadversion of the laws,[139] and a peculiar name in the Latin language.[140]

The introduction of barbarians into the Roman armies became every day more universal, more necessary, and more fatal. The most daring of the Scythians, of the Goths, and of the Germans, who delighted in war, and who found it more profitable to defend than to ravage the provinces, were enrolled not only in the auxiliaries of their respective nations, but in the legions themselves, and among the most distinguished of the Palatine troops. As they freely mingled with the subjects of the empire, they gradually learned to despise their manners and to imitate their arts. They abjured the implicit reverence which the pride of Rome had exacted from their ignorance, while they acquired the knowledge and possession of those advantages by which alone she supported her declining greatness. The barbarian soldiers who displayed any military talents were advanced, without exception, to the most important commands; and the names of the tribunes, of the counts and dukes, and of the generals themselves, betray a foreign origin, which they no longer condescended to disguise. They were often intrusted with the conduct of a war against their countrymen; and though most of them preferred the ties of allegiance to those of blood, they did not always avoid the guilt, or at least the suspicion, of holding a treasonable correspondence with the enemy, of inviting his invasion, or of sparing his retreat. The camps and the palace of the son of Constantine were governed by the powerful faction of the Franks, who preserved the strictest connection with each other and with their country, and who resented every personal affront as a national indignity.[141] When the tyrant Caligula was suspected of an intention to invest a very extraordinary candidate with the consular robes, the sacrilegious profanation would have scarcely excited less astonishment if, instead of a horse, the noblest chieftain of Germany or Britain had been the object of his choice. The revolution of three centuries had produced so remarkable a change in the prejudices of the people, that, with the public approbation, Constantine showed his successors the example of bestowing the honours of the consulship on the barbarians who, by their merit and services, had deserved to be ranked among the first of the Romans.[142] But as these hardy veterans, who had been educated in the ignorance or contempt of the laws were incapable of exercising any civil offices, the powers of the human mind were contracted by the irreconcilable separation of talents as well as of professions. The accomplished citizens of the Greek and Roman republics, whose characters could adapt themselves to the bar, the senate, the camp, or the schools, had learned to write, to speak, and to act with the same spirit, and with equal abilities.

IV. Besides the magistrates and generals, who at a distance from the court diffused their delegated authority over the provinces and armies, the emperor conferred the rank of *Illustrious* on seven of his more immediate servants, to whose fidelity he intrusted his safety, or his counsels, or his treasures. 1. The private apartments of the palace were governed by a favourite eunuch, who, in the language of that age, was styled the *præpositus*, or præfect of the sacred bedchamber. His duty was to attend the emperor in his hours of state or in those of amusement, and to perform about his person all those menial services which can only derive their splendour from the influence of royalty. Under a prince who deserved to reign, the great chamberlain (for such we may call him) was an useful and humble domestic; but an artful domestic, who improves every occasion of unguarded confidence, will insensibly acquire over a feeble mind that ascendant which harsh wisdom and uncomplying virtue can seldom obtain. The degenerate grandsons of Theodosius, who were invisible to their subjects, and contemptible to their enemies, exalted the præfects of their bedchamber above the heads of all the ministers of the palace;[143] and even his deputy, the first of the splendid train of slaves who waited in the presence, was thought worthy to rank before the *respectable* proconsuls of Greece or Asia. The jurisdiction of the chamberlain was acknowledged by the *counts*, or superintendents, who regulated the two important provinces of the magnificence of the wardrobe, and of the luxury of the Imperial table.[144] 2. The principal administration of public affairs was committed to the diligence and abilities of the *master of the offices*.[145] He was the supreme magistrate of the palace, inspected the discipline of the civil and military *schools*, and received appeals from all parts of the empire, in the causes which related to that numerous army of privileged persons who, as the servants of the court, had obtained for themselves and families a right to decline the authority of the ordinary judges. The correspondence between the prince and his subjects was managed by the four *scrinia*, or offices of this minister of state. The first was appropriated to memorials, the second to epistles, the third to petitions, and the fourth to papers and orders of a miscellaneous kind. Each of these was directed by an inferior *master of respectable* dignity, and the whole business was despatched by an hundred and forty-eight secretaries, chosen for the most part from the profession of the law, on account of the variety of abstracts of reports and references which frequently occurred in the exercise of their several functions. From a condescension which in former ages would have been esteemed unworthy of the Roman majesty, a particular secretary was allowed for the Greek language; and interpreters were appointed to receive the ambassadors of the barbarians; but

the department of foreign affairs, which constitutes so essential a part of modern policy, seldom diverted the attention of the master of the offices. His mind was more seriously engaged by the general direction of the posts and arsenals of the empire. There were thirty-four cities, fifteen in the East and nineteen in the West, in which regular companies of workmen were perpetually employed in fabricating defensive armour, offensive weapons of all sorts, and military engines, which were deposited in the arsenals, and occasionally delivered for the service of the troops. 3. In the course of nine centuries the office of *quæstor* had experienced a very singular revolution. In the infancy of Rome, two inferior magistrates were annually elected by the people, to relieve the consuls from the invidious management of the public treasure;[146] a similar assistant was granted to every proconsul and to every prætor who exercised a military or provincial command; with the extent of conquest, the two quæstors were gradually multiplied to the number of four, of eight, of twenty, and for a short time, perhaps, of forty;[147] and the noblest citizens ambitiously solicited an office which gave them a seat in the senate, and a just hope of obtaining the honours of the republic. Whilst Augustus affected to maintain the freedom of election, he consented to accept the annual privilege of recommending, or rather indeed of nominating, a certain proportion of candidates; and it was his custom to select one of these distinguished youths to read his orations or epistles in the assemblies of the senate.[148] The practice of Augustus was imitated by succeeding princes; the occasional commission was established as a permanent office; and the favoured quæstor, assuming a new and more illustrious character, alone survived the suppression of his ancient and useless colleagues.[149] As the orations which he composed in the name of the emperor[150] acquired the force, and at length the form, of absolute edicts, he was considered as the representative of the legislative power, the oracle of the council, and the original source of the civil jurisprudence. He was sometimes invited to take his seat in the supreme judicature of the Imperial consistory, with the Prætorian præfects and the master of the offices; and he was frequently requested to resolve the doubts of inferior judges: but as he was not oppressed with a variety of subordinate business, his leisure and talents were employed to cultivate that dignified style of eloquence which, in the corruption of taste and language, still preserves the majesty of the Roman laws.[151] In some respects the office of the Imperial quæstor may be compared with that of a modern chancellor; but the use of a great seal, which seems to have been adopted by the illiterate barbarians, was never introduced to attest the public acts of the emperors. 4. The extraordinary title of *count of the sacred largesses* was bestowed on the treasurer-general of the revenue, with the intention perhaps of inculcating that every payment flowed from the voluntary bounty of the monarch. To conceive the almost infinite detail of the annual and daily expense of the civil and military administration in every part of a great empire would exceed the powers of the most vigorous imagination. The actual account employed several hundred persons, distributed into eleven different offices, which were artfully contrived to examine and control their respective operations. The multitude of these agents had a natural tendency to increase; and it was more than once thought expedient to dismiss to their native homes the useless supernumeraries, who, deserting their honest labours, had pressed with too much eagerness into the lucrative profession of the finances.[152] Twenty-nine provincial receivers, of whom eighteen were honoured with the title of count, corresponded with the treasurer, and he extended his jurisdiction over the mines from whence the precious metals were extracted, over the mints in which they were converted into the current coin, and over the public treasuries of the most important cities, where they were deposited for the service of the state. The foreign trade of the empire was regulated by this minister, who directed likewise all the linen and woollen manufactures, in which the successive operations of spinning, weaving, and dyeing were executed, chiefly by women of a servile condition, for the use of the palace and army. Twenty-six of these institutions are enumerated in the West, where the arts had been more recently introduced, and a still larger proportion may be allowed for the industrious provinces of the East.[153] 5. Besides the public revenue, which an absolute monarch might levy and expend according to his pleasure, the emperors, in the capacity of opulent citizens, possessed a very extensive property, which was administered by the *count* or treasurer of *the private estate*. Some part had perhaps been the ancient demesnes of kings and republics; some accessions might be derived from the families which were successively invested with the purple; but the most considerable portion flowed from the impure source of confiscations and forfeitures. The Imperial estates were scattered through the provinces from Mauritania to Britain; but the rich and fertile soil of Cappadocia tempted the monarch to acquire in that country his fairest possessions,[154] and either Constantine or his successors embraced the occasion of justifying avarice by religious zeal. They suppressed the rich temple of Comana, where the high-priest of the goddess of war supported the dignity of a sovereign prince; and they applied to their private use the consecrated lands, which were inhabited by six thousand subjects or slaves of the deity and her ministers.[155] But these were not the valuable inhabitants: the plains that stretch from the foot of Mount Argæus to the banks of the Sarus bred a generous race of horses, renowned above all others in the ancient world for their majestic shape and incomparable swiftness. These *sacred* animals, destined for the service of the palace and the Imperial games, were protected by the laws from the profanation of a vulgar master.[156] The demesnes of Cappadocia were important enough to require the inspection of a *count*,[157] officers of an inferior rank were stationed in the other parts of the empire; and the deputies of the private, as well as those of the public treasurer, were maintained in the exercise of their independent functions, and encouraged to control the authority of the provincial magistrates.[158] 6, 7. The chosen bands of cavalry and infantry, which guarded the person of the emperor, were under the immediate command of the *two counts of the domestics*. The whole number consisted of three thousand and five hundred men, divided into seven *schools*, or troops, of five hundred each; and in the East this honourable service was almost entirely appropriated to the Armenians. Whenever, on public ceremonies, they were drawn up in the courts and porticos of the palace, their lofty stature, silent order, and splendid arms of silver and gold, displayed a martial pomp not unworthy of the Roman majesty.[159] From the seven schools two companies of horse and foot were selected, of the *protectors*, whose advantageous station was the hope and reward of the most deserving soldiers. They mounted guard in the interior apartments, and were occasionally despatched into the provinces, to execute with celerity and vigour the orders of their master.[160] The counts of the domestics had succeeded to the office of the Prætorian præfects; like the præfects, they aspired from the service of the palace to the command of armies.

The perpetual intercourse between the court and the provinces was facilitated by the construction of roads and the institution of posts.

But these beneficial establishments were accidentally connected with a pernicious and intolerable abuse. Two or three hundred *agents* or messengers were employed, under the jurisdiction of the master of the offices, to announce the names of the annual consuls, and the edicts or victories of the emperors. They insensibly assumed the licence of reporting whatever they could observe of the conduct either of magistrates or of private citizens; and were soon considered as the eyes of the monarch[161] and the scourge of the people. Under the warm influence of a feeble reign they multiplied to the incredible number of ten thousand, disdained the mild though frequent admonitions of the laws, and exercised in the profitable management of the posts a rapacious and insolent oppression. These official spies, who regularly corresponded with the palace, were encouraged, by favour and reward, anxiously to watch the progress of every treasonable design, from the faint and latent symptoms of disaffection, to the actual preparation of an open revolt. Their careless or criminal violation of truth and justice was covered by the consecrated mask of zeal; and they might securely aim their poisoned arrows at the breast either of the guilty or the innocent, who had provoked their resentment, or refused to purchase their silence. A faithful subject, of Syria perhaps, or of Britain, was exposed to the danger, or at least to the dread, of being dragged in chains to the court of Milan or Constantinople, to defend his life and fortune against the malicious charge of these privileged informers. The ordinary administration was conducted by those methods which extreme necessity can alone palliate; and the defects of evidence were diligently supplied by the use of torture.[162]

The deceitful and dangerous experiment of the criminal *quæstion*, as it is emphatically styled, was admitted, rather than approved, in the jurisprudence of the Romans. They applied this sanguinary mode of examination only to servile bodies, whose sufferings were seldom weighed by those haughty republicans in the scale of justice or humanity; but they would never consent to violate the sacred person of a citizen till they possessed the clearest evidence of his guilt.[163] The annals of tyranny, from the reign of Tiberius to that of Domitian, circumstantially relate the executions of many innocent victims; but, as long as the faintest remembrance was kept alive of the national freedom and honour, the last hours of a Roman were secure from the danger of ignominious torture.[164] The conduct of the provincial magistrates was not, however, regulated by the practice of the city, or the strict maxims of the civilians. They found the use of torture established not only among the slaves of oriental despotism, but among the Macedonians, who obeyed a limited monarch; among the Rhodians, who flourished by the liberty of commerce; and even among the sage Athenians, who had asserted and adorned the dignity of human kind.[165] The acquiescence of the provincials encouraged their governors to acquire, or perhaps to usurp, a discretionary power of employing the rack, to extort from vagrants or plebeian criminals the confession of their guilt, till they insensibly proceeded to confound the distinctions of rank, and to disregard the privileges of Roman citizens. The apprehensions of the subjects urged them to solicit, and the interest of the sovereign engaged him to grant, a variety of special exemptions, which tacitly allowed, and even authorised, the general use of torture. They protected all persons of illustrious or honourable rank, bishops and their presbyters, professors of the liberal arts, soldiers and their families, municipal officers, and their posterity to the third generation, and all children under the age of puberty.[166] But a fatal maxim was introduced into the new jurisprudence of the empire, that in the case of treason, which included every offence that the subtlety of lawyers could derive from an *hostile intention* towards the prince or republic,[167] all privileges were suspended, and all conditions were reduced to the same ignominious level. As the safety of the emperor was avowedly preferred to every consideration of justice or humanity, the dignity of age and the tenderness of youth were alike exposed to the most cruel tortures; and the terrors of a malicious information, which might select them as the accomplices, or even as the witnesses, perhaps, of an imaginary crime, perpetually hung over the heads of the principal citizens of the Roman world.[168]

These evils, however terrible they may appear, were confined to the smaller number of Roman subjects whose dangerous situation was in some degree compensated by the enjoyment of those advantages, either of nature or of fortune, which exposed them to the jealousy of the monarch. The obscure millions of a great empire have much less to dread from the cruelty than from the avarice of their masters; and *their* humble happiness is principally affected by the grievance of excessive taxes, which, gently pressing on the wealthy, descend with accelerated weight on the meaner and more indigent classes of society. An ingenious philosopher[169] has calculated the universal measure of the public impositions by the degrees of freedom and servitude; and ventures to assert that, according to an invariable law of nature, it must always increase with the former, and diminish in a just proportion to the latter. But this reflection, which would tend to alleviate the miseries of despotism, is contradicted at least by the history of the Roman empire; which accuses the same princes of despoiling the senate of its authority, and the provinces of their wealth. Without abolishing all the various customs and duties on merchandises, which are imperceptibly discharged by the apparent choice of the purchaser, the policy of Constantine and his successors preferred a simple and direct mode of taxation, more congenial to the spirit of an arbitrary government.[170]

The name and use of the *indictions*,[171] which serve to ascertain the chronology of the middle ages, was derived from the regular practice of the Roman tributes.[172] The emperor subscribed with his own hand, and in purple ink, the solemn edict, or indiction, which was fixed up in the principal city of each diocese during two months previous to the first day of September. And, by a very easy connection of ideas, the word *indiction* was transferred to the measure of tribute which it prescribed, and to the annual term which it allowed for the payment. This general estimate of the supplies was proportioned to the real and imaginary wants of the state; but as often as the expense exceeded the revenue, or the revenue fell short of the computation, an additional tax, under the name of *superindiction*, was imposed on the people, and the most valuable attribute of sovereignty was communicated to the Prætorian præfects, who, on some occasions, were permitted to provide for the unforeseen and extraordinary exigencies of the public service. The execution of these laws (which it would be tedious to pursue in their minute and intricate detail) consisted of two distinct operations: the resolving the general imposition into its constituent parts, which were assessed on the provinces, the cities, and the individuals of the Roman world; and the collecting the separate contributions of the individuals, the cities, and the provinces, till the accumulated sums were poured into the Imperial treasuries. But as the account between the monarch and the subject was perpetually open, and as the renewal of the demand anticipated the perfect discharge of the preceding obligation, the weighty machine of the finances was moved

by the same hands round the circle of its yearly revolution. Whatever was honourable or important in the administration of the revenue was committed to the wisdom of the præfects and their provincial representatives; the lucrative functions were claimed by a crowd of subordinate officers, some of whom depended on the treasurer, others on the governor of the province; and who, in the inevitable conflicts of a perplexed jurisdiction, had frequent opportunities of disputing with each other the spoils of the people. The laborious offices, which could be productive only of envy and reproach, of expense and danger, were imposed on the *Decurions*, who formed the corporations of the cities, and whom the severity of the Imperial laws had condemned to sustain the burthens of civil society.[173] The whole landed property of the empire (without excepting the patrimonial estates of the monarch) was the object of ordinary taxation; and every new purchaser contracted the obligations of the former proprietor. An accurate *census*,[174] or survey, was the only equitable mode of ascertaining the proportion which every citizen should be obliged to contribute for the public service; and from the well-known period of the indictions, there is reason to believe that this difficult and expensive operation was repeated at the regular distance of fifteen years. The lands were measured by surveyors, who were sent into the provinces; their nature, whether arable or pasture, or vineyards or woods, was distinctly reported; and an estimate was made of their common value from the average produce of five years. The numbers of slaves and cattle constituted an essential part of the report; an oath was administered to the proprietors which bound them to disclose the true state of their affairs; and their attempts to prevaricate, or elude the intention of the legislator, were severely watched, and punished as a capital crime, which included the double guilt of treason and sacrilege.[175] A large portion of the tribute was paid in money; and of the current coin of the empire, gold alone could be legally accepted.[176] The remainder of the taxes, according to the proportions determined by the annual indiction, was furnished in a manner still more direct, and still more oppressive. According to the different nature of lands, their real produce in the various articles of wine or oil, corn or barley, wood or iron, was transported by the labour or at the expense of the provincials to the Imperial magazines, from whence they were occasionally distributed, for the use of the court, of the army, and of the two capitals, Rome and Constantinople. The commissioners of the revenue were so frequently obliged to make considerable purchases, that they were strictly prohibited from allowing any compensation, or from receiving in money the value of those supplies which were exacted in kind. In the primitive simplicity of small communities this method may be well adapted to collect the almost voluntary offerings of the people; but it is at once susceptible of the utmost latitude and of the utmost strictness, which in a corrupt and absolute monarchy must introduce a perpetual contest between the power of oppression and the arts of fraud.[177] The agriculture of the Roman provinces was insensibly ruined, and, in the progress of despotism, which tends to disappoint its own purpose, the emperors were obliged to derive some merit from the forgiveness of debts, or the remission of tributes, which their subjects were utterly incapable of paying. According to the new division of Italy, the fertile and happy province of Campania, the scene of the early victories and of the delicious retirements of the citizens of Rome, extended between the sea and the Apennine from the Tiber to the Silarus. Within sixty years after the death of Constantine, and on the evidence of an actual survey, an exemption was granted in favour of three hundred and thirty thousand English acres of desert and uncultivated land, which amounted to one-eighth of the whole surface of the province. As the footsteps of the barbarians had not yet been seen in Italy, the cause of this amazing desolation, which is recorded in the laws, can be ascribed only to the administration of the Roman emperors.[178]

Either from design or from accident, the mode of assessment seemed to unite the substance of a land-tax with the forms of a capitation.[179] The returns which were sent of every province or district expressed the number of tributary subjects, and the amount of the public impositions. The latter of these sums was divided by the former; and the estimate, that such a province contained so many *capita*, or heads of tribute, and that each *head* was rated at such a price, was universally received, not only in the popular, but even in the legal computation. The value of a tributary head must have varied, according to many accidental, or at least fluctuating circumstances: but some knowledge has been preserved of a very curious fact, the more important since it relates to one of the richest provinces of the Roman empire, and which now flourishes as the most splendid of the European kingdoms. The rapacious ministers of Constan-

tius had exhausted the wealth of Gaul, by exacting twenty-five pieces of gold for the annual tribute of every head. The humane policy of his successor reduced the capitation to seven pieces.[180] A moderate proportion between these opposite extremes of extraordinary oppression and of transient indulgence may therefore be fixed at sixteen pieces of gold, or about nine pounds sterling, the common standard, perhaps, of the impositions of Gaul.[181] But this calculation, or rather indeed the facts from whence it is deduced, cannot fail of suggesting two difficulties to a thinking mind, who will be at once surprised by the *equality* and by the *enormity* of the capitation. An attempt to explain them may perhaps reflect some light on the interesting subject of the finances of the declining empire.

I. It is obvious that, as long as the immutable constitution of human nature produces and maintains so unequal a division of property, the most numerous part of the community would be deprived of their subsistence by the equal assessment of a tax from which the sovereign would derive a very trifling revenue. Such, indeed, might be the theory of the Roman capitation; but, in the practice, this unjust equality was no longer felt, as the tribute was collected on the principle of a *real*, not of a *personal* imposition. Several indigent citizens contributed to compose a single *head*, or share of taxation; while the wealthy provincial, in proportion to his fortune, alone represented several of those imaginary beings. In a poetical request, addressed to one of the last and most deserving of the Roman princes who reigned in Gaul, Sidonius Apollinaris personifies his tribute under the figure of a triple monster, the Geryon of the Grecian fables, and entreats the new Hercules that he would most graciously be pleased to save his life by cutting off three of his heads.[182] The fortune of Sidonius far exceeded the customary wealth of a poet; but if he had pursued the allusion, he must have painted many of the Gallic nobles with the hundred heads of the deadly Hydra, spreading over the face of the country, and devouring the substance of an hundred families. II. The difficulty of allowing an annual sum of about nine pounds sterling, even for the average of the capitation of Gaul, may be rendered more evident by the comparison of the present state of the same country, as it is now governed by the absolute monarch of an industrious, wealthy, and affectionate people. The taxes of France cannot be magnified, either by fear or by flattery, beyond the annual amount of eighteen millions sterling, which ought, perhaps to be shared among four-and-twenty millions of inhabitants.[183] Seven millions of these, in the capacity of fathers, or brothers, or husbands, may discharge the obligations of the remaining multitude of women and children; yet the equal proportion of each tributary subject will scarcely rise above fifty shillings of our money, instead of a proportion almost four times as considerable, which was regularly imposed on their Gallic ancestors. The reason of this difference may be found, not so much in the relative scarcity or plenty of gold and silver, as in the different state of society in ancient Gaul and in modern France. In a country where personal freedom is the privilege of every subject, the whole mass of taxes, whether they are levied on property or on consumption, may be fairly divided among the whole body of the nation. But the far greater part of the lands of ancient Gaul, as well as of the other provinces of the Roman world, were cultivated by slaves, or by peasants, whose dependent condition was a less rigid servitude.[184] In such a state the poor were maintained at the expense of the masters who enjoyed the fruits of their labour; and as the rolls of tribute were filled only with the names of those citizens who possessed the means of an honourable, or at least of a decent subsistence, the comparative smallness of their numbers explains and justifies the high rate of their capitation. The truth of this assertion may be illustrated by the following example:—The Ædui, one of the most powerful and civilised tribes or *cities* of Gaul, occupied an extent of territory which now contains above five hundred thousand inhabitants, in the two ecclesiastical dioceses of Autun and Nevers;[185] and with the probable accession of those of Châlons and Maçon,[186] the population would amount to eight hundred thousand souls. In the time of Constantine the territory of the Ædui afforded no more than twenty-five thousand *heads* of capitation, of whom seven thousand were discharged by that prince from the intolerable weight of tribute.[187] A just analogy would seem to countenance the opinion of an ingenious historian,[188] that the free and tributary citizens did not surpass the number of half a million; and if, in the ordinary administration of government, their annual payments may be computed at about four millions and a half of our money, it would appear that, although the share of each individual was four times as considerable, a fourth part only of the modern taxes of France was levied on the Imperial province of Gaul. The exactions of Constantius may be calculated at seven millions sterling, which were reduced to two millions by the humanity or the wisdom of Julian.

But this tax or capitation on the proprietors of land would have suffered a rich and numerous class of free citizens to escape. With the view of sharing that species of wealth which is derived from art or labour, and which exists in money or in merchandise, the emperors imposed a distinct and personal tribute on the trading part of their subjects.[189] Some exemptions, very strictly confined both in time and place, were allowed to the proprietors who disposed of the produce of their own estates. Some indulgence was granted to the profession of the liberal arts; but every other branch of commercial industry was affected by the severity of the law. The honourable merchant of Alexandria, who imported the gems and spices of India for the use of the western world; the usurer, who derived from the interest of money a silent and ignominious profit; the ingenious manufacturer, the diligent mechanic, and even the most obscure retailer of a sequestered village, were obliged to admit the officers of the revenue into the partnership of their gain; and the sovereign of the Roman empire, who tolerated the profession, consented to share the infamous salary of public prostitutes. As this general tax upon industry was collected every fourth year, it was styled the *Lustral Contribution*: and the historian Zosimus[190] laments that the approach of the fatal period was announced by the tears and terrors of the citizens, who were often compelled by the impending scourge to embrace the most abhorred and unnatural methods of procuring the sum at which their poverty had been assessed. The testimony of Zosimus cannot indeed be justified from the charge of passion and prejudice; but, from the nature of this tribute, it seems reasonable to conclude that it was arbitrary in the distribution, and extremely rigorous in the mode of collecting. The secret wealth of commerce, and the precarious profits of art or labour, are susceptible only of a discretionary valuation, which is seldom disadvantageous to the interest of the treasury; and as the person of the trader supplies the want of a visible and permanent security, the payment of the imposition, which, in the case of a land-tax, may be obtained by the seizure of property, can rarely be extorted by any other means than those of corporal punishments. The cruel treatment of the insolvent debtors of the state is attested, and was perhaps mitigated, by a very humane edict of Constantine, who, disclaiming the use of racks and of scourges, allots a spacious and airy prison for the place of their confinement.[191]

These general taxes were imposed and levied by the absolute authority of the monarch; but the occasional offerings of the *coronary gold* still retained the name and semblance of popular consent. It was an ancient custom that the allies of the republic, who ascribed their safety or deliverance to the success of the Roman arms, and even the cities of Italy, who admired the virtues of their victorious general, adorned the pomp of his triumph by their voluntary gifts of crowns of gold, which, after the ceremony, were consecrated in the temple of Jupiter, to remain a lasting monument of his glory to future ages. The progress of zeal and flattery soon multiplied the number, and increased the size, of these popular donations; and the triumph of Cæsar was enriched with two thousand eight hundred and twenty-two massy crowns, whose weight amounted to twenty thousand four hundred and fourteen pounds of gold. This treasure was immediately melted down by the prudent dictator, who was satisfied that it would be more serviceable to his soldiers than to the gods: his example was imitated by his successors; and the custom was introduced of exchanging these splendid ornaments for the more acceptable present of the current gold coin of the empire.[192] The spontaneous offering was at length exacted as the debt of duty; and, instead of being confined to the occasion of a triumph, it was supposed to be granted by the several cities and provinces of the monarchy as often as the emperor condescended to announce his accession, his consulship, the birth of a son, the creation of a Cæsar, a victory over the barbarians, or any other real or imaginary event which graced the annals of his reign. The peculiar free gift of the senate of Rome was fixed by custom at sixteen hundred pounds of gold, or about sixty-four thousand pounds sterling. The oppressed subjects celebrated their own felicity that their sovereign should graciously consent to accept this feeble but voluntary testimony of their loyalty and gratitude.[193]

A people elated by pride, or soured by discontent, is seldom qualified to form a just estimate of their actual situation. The subjects of Constantine were incapable of discerning the decline of genius and manly virtue, which so far degraded them below the dignity of their ancestors; but they could feel and lament the rage of tyranny, the relaxation of discipline, and the increase of taxes. The impartial historian, who acknowledges the justice of their complaints, will observe some favourable circumstances which tended to alleviate the misery of their condition. The threatening tempest of barbarians, which so soon subverted the foundations of Roman greatness, was still repelled, or suspended, on the frontiers. The arts of luxury and literature were cultivated, and the elegant pleasures of society were enjoyed, by the inhabitants of a considerable portion of the globe. The forms, the pomp, and the expense of the civil administration contributed to restrain the irregular licence of the soldiers; and although the laws were violated by power, or perverted by subtlety, the sage principles of the Roman jurisprudence preserved a sense of order and equity unknown to the despotic governments of the East. The rights of mankind might derive some protection from religion and philosophy; and the name of freedom, which could no longer alarm, might sometimes admonish, the successors of Augustus, that they did not reign over a nation of Slaves or Barbarians.[194]

CHAPTER XVIII

Character of Constantine. Gothic War. Death of Constantine. Division of the Empire among his three sons. Persian War. Tragic Deaths of Constantine the Younger and Constans. Usurpation of Magnentius. Civil War. Victory of Constantius.

THE character of the prince who removed the seat of empire, and introduced such important changes into the civil and religious constitution of his country, has fixed the attention, and divided the opinions, of mankind. By the grateful zeal of the Christians the deliverer of the church has been decorated with every attribute of a hero, and even of a saint; while the discontent of the vanquished party has compared Constantine to the most abhorred of those tyrants who, by their vice and weakness, dishonoured the Imperial purple. The same passions have, in some degree, been perpetuated to succeeding generations, and the character of Constantine is considered, even in the present age, as an object either of satire or of panegyric. By the impartial union of those defects which are confessed by his warmest admirers, and of those virtues which are acknowledged by his most implacable enemies, we might hope to delineate a just portrait of that extraordinary man, which the truth and candour of history should adopt without a blush.[1] But it would soon appear that the vain attempt to blend such discordant colours, and to reconcile such inconsistent qualities, must produce a figure monstrous rather than human, unless it is viewed in its proper and distinct lights by a careful separation of the different periods of the reign of Constantine.

The person, as well as the mind, of Constantine had been enriched by nature with her choicest endowments. His stature was lofty, his countenance majestic, his deportment graceful; his strength and activity were displayed in every manly exercise, and, from his earliest youth to a very advanced season of life, he preserved the vigour of his constitution by a strict adherence to the domestic virtues of chastity and temperance. He delighted in the social intercourse of familiar conversation; and though he might sometimes indulge his disposition to raillery with less reserve than was required by the severe dignity of his station, the courtesy and liberality of his manners gained the hearts of all who approached him. The sincerity of his friendship has been suspected; yet he showed, on some occasions, that he was not incapable of a warm and lasting attachment. The disadvantage of an illiterate education had not prevented him from forming a just estimate of the value of learning; and the arts and sciences derived some encouragement from the munificent protection of Constantine. In the despatch of business his diligence was indefatigable; and the active powers of his mind were almost continually exercised in reading, writing, or meditating, in giving audience to ambassadors, and in examining the complaints of his subjects. Even those who censured the propriety of his measures were compelled to acknowledge that he possessed magnanimity to conceive, and patience to execute, the most arduous designs, without being checked either by the prejudices of education or by the clamours of the multitude. In the field he infused his own intrepid spirit into the troops, whom he conducted with the talents of a consummate general; and to his abilities, rather than to his fortune, we may ascribe the signal victories which he obtained over the foreign and domestic foes of the republic. He loved glory as the reward, perhaps as the motive, of his labours. The boundless ambition which, from the moment of his accepting the purple at York, appears as the ruling passion of his soul, may be justified by the dangers of his own situation, by the character of his rivals, by the consciousness of superior merit, and by the prospect that his success would enable him to restore peace and order to the distracted empire. In his civil wars against Maxentius and Licinius he had engaged on his side the inclinations of the people, who compared the undissembled vices of those tyrants with the spirit of wisdom and justice which seemed to direct the general tenor of the administration of Constantine.[2]

Had Constantine fallen on the banks of the Tiber, or even in the plains of Hadrianople, such is the character which, with a few exceptions, he might have transmitted to posterity. But the conclusion of his reign (according to the moderate and indeed tender sentence of a writer of the same age) degraded him from the rank which he had acquired among the most deserving of the Roman princes.[3] In the life of Augustus we behold the tyrant of the republic converted almost by imperceptible degrees into the father of his country and of human kind. In that of Constantine we may contemplate a hero, who had so long inspired his subjects with love and his enemies with terror, degenerating into a cruel and dissolute monarch, corrupted by his fortune, or raised by conquest above the necessity of dissimulation. The general peace which he maintained during the last fourteen years of his reign was a period of apparent splendour rather than of real prosperity; and the old age of Constantine was disgraced by the opposite yet reconcilable vices of rapaciousness and prodigality. The accumulated treasures found in the palaces of Maxentius and Licinius were lavishly consumed; the various innovations introduced by the conqueror were attended with an increasing expense; the cost of his buildings, his court, and his festivals required an immediate and plentiful supply; and the oppression of the people was the only fund which could support the magnificence of the sovereign.[4] His unworthy favourites, enriched by the boundless liberality of their master, usurped with impunity the privilege of rapine and corruption.[5] A secret but universal decay was felt in every part of the public administration, and the emperor himself, though he still retained the obedience, gradually lost the esteem, of his subjects. The dress and manners which, towards the decline of life, he chose to effect, served only to degrade him in the eyes of mankind. The Asiatic pomp which had been adopted by the pride of Diocletian assumed an air of softness and effeminacy in the person of Constantine. He is represented with false hair of various colours, laboriously arranged by the skilful artists of the times; a diadem of a new and more expensive fashion; a profusion of gems and pearls, of collars and bracelets; and a variegated flowing robe of silk, most curiously embroidered with flowers of gold. In such apparel, scarcely to be excused by the youth and folly of Elagabalus, we are at a loss to discover the wisdom of an aged monarch and the simplicity of a Roman veteran.[6] A mind thus relaxed by prosperity and indulgence was incapable of rising to that magnanimity which disdains suspicion and dares to forgive. The deaths of Maximian and Licinius may perhaps be justified by the maxims of policy as they are taught in the schools of tyrants; but an impartial narrative of the executions, or rather murders, which sullied the declining age of Constantine, will suggest to our most candid thoughts the idea of a prince who could sacrifice, without reluctance, the laws of justice and the feelings of nature to the dictates either of his passions or of his interest.

The same fortune which so invariably followed the standard of Constantine seemed to secure the hopes and comforts of his domestic life. Those among his predecessors who had enjoyed the longest and most prosperous reigns, Augustus, Trajan, and Diocletian, had been disappointed of posterity; and the frequent revolutions had never allowed sufficient time for any Imperial family to grow up and multiply under the shade of the purple. But the royalty of the Flavian line, which had been first ennobled by the Gothic Claudius, descended through several generations; and Constantine himself derived from his royal father the hereditary honours which he transmitted to his children. The emperor had been twice married. Minervina, the obscure but lawful object of his youthful attachment,[7] had left him only one son, who was called Crispus. By Fausta, the daughter of Maximian, he had three daughters, and three sons known by the kindred names of Constantine, Constantius, and Constans. The unambitious brothers of the Great Constantine, Julius Constantius, Dalmatius, and Hannibalianus,[8] were permitted to enjoy the most honourable rank and the most affluent fortune that could be consistent with a private station. The youngest of the three lived without a name and died without posterity. His two elder brothers obtained in marriage the daughters of wealthy senators, and propagated new branches of the Imperial race. Gallus and Julian afterwards became the most illustrious of the children of Julius Constantius, the *Patrician*. The two sons of Dalmatius, who had been decorated with the vain title of *Censor*, were named Dalmatius and Hannibalianus. The two sisters of the great Constantine, Anastasia and Eutropia, were bestowed on Optatus and Nepotianus, two senators of noble birth and of consular dignity. His third sister, Constantia, was distinguished by her pre-eminence of greatness and of misery. She remained the widow of the vanquished Licinius; and it was by her entreaties that an innocent boy, the offspring of their marriage, preserved, for some time, his life, the title of Cæsar, and a precarious hope of the succession. Besides the females and the allies of the Flavian house, ten or twelve males, to whom the language of modern courts would apply the title of princes of the blood, seemed, according to the order of their birth, to be destined either to inherit or to support the throne of Constantine. But in less than thirty years this numerous and increasing family was reduced to the persons of Constantius and Julian, who alone had survived a series of crimes and calamities such as the tragic poets have deplored in the devoted lines of Pelops and of Cadmus.

Crispus, the eldest son of Constantine, and the presumptive heir of the empire, is represented by impartial historians as an amiable and accomplished youth. The care of his education, or at least of his studies, was intrusted to Lactantius, the most eloquent of the Christians; a preceptor admirably qualified to form the taste and to excite the virtues of his illustrious disciple.[9] At the age of seventeen Crispus was invested with the title of Cæsar, and the administration of the Gallic provinces, where the inroads of the Germans gave him an early occasion of signalising his military prowess. In the civil war which broke out soon afterwards, the father and son divided their powers; and this history has already celebrated the valour as well as conduct displayed by the latter in forcing the straits of the Hellespont, so obstinately defended by the superior fleet of Licinius. This naval victory contributed to determine the event of the war, and the names of Constantine and of Crispus were united in the joyful acclamations of their eastern subjects, who loudly proclaimed that the world had been subdued, and was now governed, by an emperor endowed with every virtue, and by his illustrious son, a prince beloved of Heaven, and the lively image of his father's perfections. The public favour, which seldom accompanies old age, diffused its lustre over the youth of Crispus. He deserved the esteem and he engaged the affections of the court, the army, and the people. The experienced merit of a reigning monarch is acknowledged by his subjects with reluctance, and frequently denied with partial and discontented murmurs; while, from the opening virtues of his successor, they fondly conceive the most unbounded hopes of private as well as public felicity.[10]

This dangerous popularity soon excited the attention of Constantine, who, both as a father and as a king, was impatient of an equal. Instead of attempting to secure the allegiance of his son by the generous ties of confidence and gratitude, he resolved to prevent the mischiefs which might be apprehended from dissatisfied ambition. Crispus soon had reason to complain that, while his infant brother Constantius was sent with the title of Cæsar to reign over his peculiar department of the Gallic provinces,[11] he, a prince of mature years, who had performed such recent and signal services, instead of being raised to the superior rank of Augustus, was confined almost a prisoner to his father's court, and exposed, without power or defence, to every calumny which the malice of his enemies could suggest. Under such painful circumstances the royal youth might not always be able to compose his behaviour or suppress his discontent; and we may be assured that he was encompassed by a train of indiscreet or perfidious followers, who assiduously studied to inflame, and who were perhaps instructed to betray, the unguarded warmth of his resentment. An edict of Constantine, published about this time, manifestly indicates his real or affected suspicions that a secret conspiracy had been formed against his person and government. By all the allurements of honours and rewards he invites informers of every degree to accuse, without exception, his magistrates or ministers, his friends or his most intimate favourites, protesting, with a solemn asseveration, that he himself will listen to the charge, that he himself will revenge his injuries; and concluding with a prayer, which discovers some apprehension of danger, that the providence of the Supreme Being may still continue to protect the safety of the emperor and of the empire.[12]

The informers who complied with so liberal an invitation were sufficiently versed in the arts of courts to select the friends and adherents of Crispus as the guilty persons; nor is there any reason to distrust the veracity of the emperor, who had promised an ample measure of revenge and punishment. The policy of Constantine maintained, however, the same appearances of regard and confidence towards a son whom he began to consider as his most irreconcilable enemy. Medals were struck with the customary vows for the long and auspicious reign of the young Cæsar;[13] and as the people, who was not admitted into the secrets of the palace, still loved his virtues and respected his dignity, a poet, who solicits his recall from exile, adores with equal devotion the majesty of the father and that of the son.[14] The time was now arrived for celebrating the august ceremony of the twentieth year of the reign of Constantine, and the emperor, for that purpose, removed his court from Nicomedia to Rome, where the most splendid preparations had been made for his reception. Every eye and every tongue affected to express their sense of the general happiness, and the veil of ceremony and dissimulation was drawn for a while over the darkest designs of revenge and murder.[15] In the midst of the festival the unfortunate Crispus was apprehended by order of the emperor, who laid aside the tenderness of a father without assuming the equity of a judge. The examination was short and private;[16] and as it was thought decent to conceal the fate of the young prince from the eyes of the Roman people, he was sent under a strong guard to Pola, in Istria, where, soon afterwards, he was put to death, either by the hand of the executioner or by the more gentle operation of poison.[17] The Cæsar Licinius, a youth of amiable manners, was involved in the ruin of Crispus,[18] and the stern jealousy of Constantine was unmoved by the prayers and tears of his favourite sister, pleading for the life of a son whose rank was his only crime, and whose loss she did not long survive. The story of these unhappy princes, the nature and evidence of their guilt, the forms of their trial, and the circumstances of their death, were buried in mysterious obscurity, and the courtly bishop, who has celebrated in an elaborate work the virtues and piety of his hero, observes a prudent silence on the subject of these tragic events.[19] Such haughty contempt for the opinion of mankind, whilst it imprints an indelible stain on the memory of Constantine, must remind us of the very different behaviour of one of the greatest monarchs of the present age. The Czar Peter, in the full possession of despotic power, submitted to the judgment of Russia, of Europe, and of posterity,

the reasons which had compelled him to subscribe the condemnation of a criminal, or at
least of a degenerate, son.[20]

The innocence of Crispus was so universally
acknowledged that the modern Greeks, who
adore the memory of their founder, are reduced
to palliate the guilt of a parricide which the
common feelings of human nature forbade
them to justify. They pretend that, as soon as
the afflicted father discovered the falsehood of
the accusation by which his credulity had been
so fatally misled, he published to the world his
repentance and remorse; that he mourned forty
days, during which he abstained from the use of
the bath and all the ordinary comforts of life;
and that, for the lasting instruction of posterity,
he erected a golden statue of Crispus, with this
memorable inscription,—To MY SON, WHOM I
UNJUSTLY CONDEMNED.[21] A tale so moral and so
interesting would deserve to be supported by
less exceptionable authority; but if we consult
the more ancient and authentic writers, they
will inform us that the repentance of Constantine was manifested only in acts of blood and
revenge, and that he atoned for the murder of
an innocent son by the execution, perhaps, of a
guilty wife. They ascribe the misfortunes of
Crispus to the arts of his stepmother, Fausta,
whose implacable hatred or whose disappointed
love renewed in the palace of Constantine the
ancient tragedy of Hippolytus and of Phædra.[22]
Like the daughter of Minos, the daughter of
Maximian accused her son-in-law of an incestuous attempt on the chastity of his father's wife,
and easily obtained, from the jealousy of the
emperor, a sentence of death against a young
prince whom she considered with reason as the
most formidable rival of her own children. But
Helena, the aged mother of Constantine, lamented and revenged the untimely fate of her
grandson Crispus; nor was it long before a real
or pretended discovery was made that Fausta
herself entertained a criminal connection with a
slave belonging to the Imperial stables.[23] Her
condemnation and punishment were the instant consequences of the charge, and the
adulteress was suffocated by the steam of a
bath, which, for that purpose, had been heated
to an extraordinary degree.[24] By some it will
perhaps be thought that the remembrance of a
conjugal union of twenty years, and the honour
of their common offspring, the destined heirs of
the throne, might have softened the obdurate
heart of Constantine, and persuaded him to
suffer his wife, however guilty she might appear,
to expiate her offences in a solitary prison. But

it seems a superfluous labour to weight the propriety, unless we could ascertain the truth, of
this singular event, which is attended with some
circumstances of doubt and perplexity. Those
who have attacked, and those who have defended, the character of Constantine, have alike
disregarded two very remarkable passages of
two orations pronounced under the succeeding
reign. The former celebrates the virtues, the
beauty, and the fortune of the empress Fausta,
the daughter, wife, sister, and mother of so
many princes.[25] The latter asserts, in explicit
terms, that the mother of the younger Constantine, who was slain three years after his father's
death, survived to weep over the fate of her
son.[26] Notwithstanding the positive testimony of
several writers of the Pagan as well as of the
Christian religion, there may still remain some
reason to believe, or at least to suspect, that
Fausta escaped the blind and suspicious cruelty
of her husband. The deaths of a son and of a
nephew, with the execution of a great number
of respectable and perhaps innocent friends,[27]
who were involved in their fall, may be sufficient,
however, to justify the discontent of the Roman
people, and to explain the satirical verses affixed to the palace gate, comparing the splendid
and bloody reigns of Constantine and Nero.[28]

By the death of Crispus the inheritance of the
empire seemed to devolve on the three sons of
Fausta, who have been already mentioned under the names of Constantine, Constantius, and
of Constans. These young princes were successively invested with the title of Cæsar, and the
dates of their promotion may be referred to the
tenth, the twentieth, and the thirtieth years of
the reign of their father.[29] This conduct, though
it tended to multiply the future masters of the
Roman world, might be excused by the partiality of paternal affection; but it is not so easy to
understand the motives of the emperor, when
he endangered the safety both of his family and
of his people by the unnecessary elevation of his
two nephews, Dalmatius and Hannibalianus.
The former was raised, by the title of Cæsar, to
an equality with his cousins. In favour of the
latter, Constantine invented the new and singular appellation of *Nobilissimus*,[30] to which he
annexed the flattering distinction of a robe of
purple and gold. But of the whole series of Roman princes in any age of the empire Hannibalianus alone was distinguished by the title of
KING, a name which the subjects of Tiberius
would have detested as the profane and cruel
insult of capricious tyranny. The use of such a
title, even as it appears under the reign of Con-

stantine, is a strange and unconnected fact, which can scarcely be admitted on the joint authority of Imperial medals and contemporary writers.[31]

The whole empire was deeply interested in the education of these five youths, the acknowledged successors of Constantine. The exercises of the body prepared them for the fatigues of war and the duties of active life. Those who occasionally mention the education or talents of Constantius allow that he excelled in the gymnastic arts of leaping and running; that he was a dexterous archer, a skilful horseman, and a master of all the different weapons used in the service either of the cavalry or of the infantry.[32] The same assiduous cultivation was bestowed, though not perhaps with equal success, to improve the minds of the sons and nephews of Constantine.[33] The most celebrated professors of the Christian faith, of the Grecian philosophy, and of the Roman jurisprudence, were invited by the liberality of the emperor, who reserved for himself the important task of instructing the royal youths in the science of government and the knowledge of mankind. But the genius of Constantine himself had been formed by adversity and experience. In the free intercourse of private life, and amidst the dangers of the court of Galerius, he had learned to command his own passions, to encounter those of his equals, and to depend for his present safety and future greatness on the prudence and firmness of his personal conduct. His destined successors had the misfortune of being born and educated in the Imperial purple. Incessantly surrounded with a train of flatterers, they passed their youth in the enjoyment of luxury and the expectation of a throne; nor would the dignity of their rank permit them to descend from that elevated station from whence the various characters of human nature appear to wear a smooth and uniform aspect. The indulgence of Constantine admitted them, at a very tender age, to share the administration of the empire; and they studied the art of reigning, at the expense of the people intrusted to their care. The younger Constantine was appointed to hold his court in Gaul; and his brother Constantius exchanged that department, the ancient patrimony of their father, for the more opulent, but less martial, countries of the East. Italy, the Western Illyricum, and Africa, were accustomed to revere Constans, the third of his sons, as the representative of the great Constantine. He fixed Dalmatius on the Gothic frontier, to which he annexed the government of Thrace, Mace-

donia, and Greece. The city of Cæsarea was chosen for the residence of Hannibalianus; and the provinces of Pontus, Cappadocia, and the Lesser Armenia, were designed to form the extent of his new kingdom. For each of these princes a suitable establishment was provided. A just proportion of guards, of legions, and of auxiliaries, was allotted for their respective dignity and defence. The ministers and generals who were placed about their persons were such as Constantine could trust to assist, and even to control, these youthful sovereigns in the exercise of their delegated power. As they advanced in years and experience, the limits of their authority were insensibly enlarged: but the emperor always reserved for himself the title of Augustus; and while he showed the *Cæsars* to the armies and provinces, he maintained every part of the empire in equal obedience to its supreme head.[34] The tranquillity of the last fourteen years of his reign was scarcely interrupted by the contemptible insurrection of a camel-driver in the island of Cyprus,[35] or by the active part which the policy of Constantine engaged him to assume in the wars of the Goths and Sarmatians.

Among the different branches of the human race, the Sarmatians form a very remarkable shade; as they seem to unite the manners of the Asiatic barbarians with the figure and complexion of the ancient inhabitants of Europe. According to the various accidents of peace and war, of alliance or conquest, the Sarmatians were sometimes confined to the banks of the Tanais, and they sometimes spread themselves over the immense plains which lie between the Vistula and the Volga.[36] The care of their numerous flocks and herds, the pursuit of game, and the exercise of war, or rather of rapine, directed the vagrant motions of the Sarmatians. The movable camps or cities, the ordinary residence of their wives and children, consisted only of large waggons drawn by oxen, and covered in the form of tents. The military strength of the nation was composed of cavalry; and the custom of their warriors to lead in their hand one or two spare horses enabled them to advance and to retreat with a rapid diligence, which surprised the security, and eluded the pursuit, of a distant enemy.[37] Their poverty of iron prompted their rude industry to invent a sort of cuirass, which was capable of resisting a sword or javelin, though it was formed only of horses' hoofs, cut into thin and polished slices, carefully laid over each other in the manner of scales or feathers, and strongly sewed upon an under garment of coarse linen.[38] The offensive arms of the Sarmatians were short daggers, long lances, and a weighty bow with a quiver of arrows. They were reduced to the necessity of employing fish-bones for the points of their weapons; but the custom of dipping them in a venomous liquor, that poisoned the wounds which they inflicted, is alone sufficient to prove the most savage manners; since a people impressed with a sense of humanity would have abhorred so cruel a practice, and a nation skilled in the arts of war would have disdained so impotent a resource.[39] Whenever these barbarians issued from their deserts in quest of prey, their shaggy beards, uncombed locks, the furs with which they were covered from head to foot, and their fierce countenances, which seemed to express the innate cruelty of their minds, inspired the more civilised provincials of Rome with horror and dismay.

The tender Ovid, after a youth spent in the enjoyment of fame and luxury, was condemned to an hopeless exile on the frozen banks of the Danube, where he was exposed, almost without defence, to the fury of these monsters of the desert, with whose stern spirits he feared that his gentle shade might hereafter be confounded. In his pathetic, but sometimes unmanly lamentations,[40] he describes in the most lively colours the dress and manners, the arms and inroads, of the Getæ and Sarmatians, who were associated for the purposes of destruction; and from the accounts of history there is some reason to believe that these Sarmatians were the Jazygæ, one of the most numerous and warlike tribes of the nation. The allurements of plenty engaged them to seek a permanent establishment on the frontiers of the empire. Soon after the reign of Augustus they obliged the Dacians, who subsisted by fishing on the banks of the river Theiss or Tibiscus, to retire into the hilly country, and to abandon to the victorious Sarmatians the fertile plains of the Upper Hungary, which are bounded by the course of the Danube and the semicircular enclosure of the Carpathian mountains.[41] In this advantageous position they watched or suspended the moment of attack, as they were provoked by injuries or appeased by presents; they gradually acquired the skill of using more dangerous weapons; and although the Sarmatians did not illustrate their name by any memorable exploits, they occasionally assisted their eastern and western neighbours, the Goths and the Germans, with a formidable body of cavalry. They lived under the irregular aristocracy of their chieftains;[42] but after they had received into their bosom the fugitive Vandals, who yielded to the pressure of the Gothic power, they seem to have chosen a king from that nation, and from the illustrious race of the Astingi, who had formerly dwelt on the shores of the northern ocean.[43]

This motive of enmity must have inflamed the subjects of contention which perpetually arise on the confines of warlike and independent nations. The Vandal princes were stimulated by fear and revenge; the Gothic kings aspired to extend their dominion from the Euxine to the frontiers of Germany; and the waters of the Maros, a small river which falls into the Theiss, were stained with the blood of the contending barbarians. After some experience of the superior strength and numbers of their adversaries, the Sarmatians implored the protection of the Roman monarch, who beheld with pleasure the discord of the nations, but who was justly alarmed by the progress of the Gothic arms. As soon as Constantine had declared himself in favour of the weaker party, the haughty Araric, king of the Goths, instead of expecting the attack of the legions, boldly passed the Danube, and spread terror and devastation through the province of Mæsia. To oppose the inroad of this destroying host the aged emperor took the field in person; but on this occasion either his conduct or his fortune betrayed the glory which he had acquired in so many foreign and domestic wars. He had the mortification of seeing his troops fly before an inconsiderable detachment of the barbarians, who pursued them to the edge of their fortified camp, and obliged him to consult his safety by a precipitate and ignominious retreat.[44] The event of a second and more successful action retrieved the honour of the Roman name; and the powers of art and discipline prevailed, after an obstinate contest, over the efforts of irregular valour. The broken army of the Goths abandoned the field of battle, the wasted province, and the passage of the Danube: and although the eldest of the sons of Constantine was permitted to supply the place of his father, the merit of the victory, which diffused universal joy, was ascribed to the auspicious counsels of the emperor himself.

He contributed at least to improve this advantage by his negotiations with the free and warlike people of Chersonesus,[45] whose capital, situate on the western coast of the Tauric or Crimæan peninsula, still retained some vestiges of a Grecian colony, and was governed by a perpetual magistrate, assisted by a council of senators, emphatically styled the Fathers of the City. The Chersonites were animated against the Goths by the memory of the wars which, in the preceding century, they had maintained with unequal forces against the invaders of their country. They were connected with the Romans by the mutual benefits of commerce; as they were supplied from the provinces of Asia with corn and manufactures, which they purchased with their only productions, salt, wax, and hides. Obedient to the requisition of Constantine, they prepared under the conduct of their magistrate Diogenes, a considerable army, of which the principal strength consisted in crossbows and military chariots. The speedy march and intrepid attack of the Chersonites, by diverting the attention of the Goths, assisted the operations of the Imperial generals. The Goths, vanquished on every side, were driven into the mountains, where, in the course of a severe campaign, above an hundred thousand were computed to have perished by cold and hunger. Peace was at length granted to their humble supplications; the eldest son of Araric was accepted as the most valuable hostage; and Constantine endeavoured to convince their chiefs, by a liberal distribution of honours and rewards, how far the friendship of the Romans was preferable to their enmity. In the expressions of his gratitude towards the faithful Chersonites, the emperor was still more magnificent. The pride of the nation was gratified by the splendid and almost royal decorations bestowed on their magistrate and his successors. A perpetual exemption from all duties was stipulated for their vessels which traded to the ports of the Black Sea. A regular subsidy was promised, of iron, corn, oil, and of every supply which could be useful either in peace or war. But it was thought that the Sarmatians were sufficiently rewarded by their deliverance from impending ruin; and the emperor, perhaps with too strict an economy, deducted some part of the expenses of the war from the customary gratifications which were allowed to that turbulent nation.

Exasperated by this apparent neglect, the Sarmatians soon forgot, with the levity of barbarians, the services which they had so lately received, and the dangers which still threatened their safety. Their inroads on the territory of the empire provoked the indignation of Constantine to leave them to their fate; and he no longer opposed the ambition of Geberic, a renowned warrior, who had recently ascended the Gothic throne. Wisumar, the Vandal king, whilst, alone and unassisted, he defended his dominions with undaunted courage, was vanquished and slain in a decisive battle which swept away the flower of the Sarmatian youth. The remainder of the nation embraced the desperate expedient of arming their slaves, a hardy race of hunters and herdsmen, by whose tumultuary aid they revenged their defeat, and expelled the invader from their confines. But they soon discovered that they had exchanged a foreign for a domestic enemy, more dangerous and more implacable. Enraged by their former servitude, elated by their present glory, the slaves, under the name of Limigantes, claimed and usurped the possession of the country which they had saved. Their masters, unable to withstand the ungoverned fury of the populace, preferred the hardships of exile to the tyranny of their servants. Some of the fugitive Sarmatians solicited a less ignominious dependence under the hostile standard of the Goths. A more numerous band retired beyond the Carpathian mountains, among the Quadi, their German allies, and were easily admitted to share a superfluous waste of uncultivated land. But the far greater part of the distressed nation turned their eyes towards the fruitful provinces of Rome. Imploring the protection and forgiveness of the emperor, they solemnly promised, as subjects in peace, and as soldiers in war, the most inviolable fidelity to the empire which should graciously receive them into its bosom. According to the maxims adopted by Probus and his successors, the offers of this barbarian colony were eagerly accepted; and a competent portion of lands in the provinces of Pannonia, Thrace, Macedonia, and Italy, were immediately assigned for the habitation and subsistence of three hundred thousand Sarmatians.[46]

By chastising the pride of the Goths, and by accepting the homage of a suppliant nation, Constantine asserted the majesty of the Roman empire; and the ambassadors of Æthiopia, Persia, and the most remote countries of India, congratulated the peace and prosperity of his government.[47] If he reckoned among the favours of fortune the death of his eldest son, of his nephew, and perhaps of his wife, he enjoyed an uninterrupted flow of private as well as public felicity till the thirtieth year of his reign; a period which none of his predecessors, since Augustus, had been permitted to celebrate. Constantine survived that solemn festival about ten months; and, at the mature age of sixty-four, after a short illness, he ended his memorable life at the palace of Aquyrion, in the suburbs of Nicomedia, whither he had retired for the benefit of the air, and with the hope of recruiting his exhausted strength by the use of the warm baths. The excessive demonstrations of grief, or at least of mourning, surpassed whatever had been practised on any former occasion. Notwithstanding the claims of the senate and people of ancient Rome, the corpse of the deceased emperor, according to his last request, was transported to the city which was destined to preserve the name and memory of its founder. The body of Constantine, adorned with the vain symbols of greatness, the purple and diadem, was deposited on a golden bed in one of the apartments of the palace, which for that purpose had been splendidly furnished and illuminated. The forms of the court were strictly maintained. Every day, at the appointed hours, the principal officers of the state, the army, and the household, approaching the person of their sovereign with bended knees and a composed countenance, offered their respectful homage as seriously as if he had been still alive. From motives of policy, this theatrical representation was for some time continued; nor could flattery neglect the opportunity of remarking that Constantine alone, by the peculiar indulgence of Heaven, had reigned after his death.[48]

But this reign could subsist only in empty pageantry; and it was soon discovered that the will of the most absolute monarch is seldom obeyed when his subjects have no longer anything to hope from his favour, or to dread from his resentment. The same ministers and generals who bowed with such reverential awe before the inanimate corpse of their deceased sovereign were engaged in secret consultations to exclude his two nephews, Dalmatius and Hannibalianus, from the share which he had assigned them in the succession of the empire. We are too imperfectly acquainted with the court of Constantine to form any judgment of the real motives which influenced the leaders of the conspiracy; unless we should suppose that they were actuated by a spirit of jealousy and revenge against the præfect Ablavius, a proud favourite, who had long directed the counsels and abused the confidence of the late emperor. The arguments by which they solicited the concurrence of the soldiers and people are of a more obvious nature: and they might with decency, as well as truth, insist on the superior rank of the children of Constantine, the danger of multiplying the number of sovereigns, and the impending mischiefs which threatened the republic, from the discord of so many rival princes who were not connected by the tender sympathy of fraternal affection. The intrigue was conducted with zeal and secrecy, till a loud and unanimous declaration was procured from the troops that they would suffer none except the sons of their lamented monarch to reign over the Roman empire.[49] The younger Dalmatius, who was united with his collateral relations by the ties of friendship and interest, is allowed to have inherited a considerable share of the abilities of the great Constantine; but, on this occasion, he does not appear to have concerted any measures for supporting by arms the just claims which himself and his royal brother derived from the liberality of their uncle. Astonished and overwhelmed by the tide of popular fury, they seem to have remained, without the power of flight or of resistance, in the hands of their implacable enemies. Their fate was suspended till the arrival of Constantius, the second,[50] and perhaps the most favoured, of the sons of Constantine.

The voice of the dying emperor had recommended the care of his funeral to the piety of Constantius; and that prince, by the vicinity of his eastern station, could easily prevent the diligence of his brothers, who resided in their distant governments of Italy and Gaul. As soon as he had taken possession of the palace of Constantinople, his first care was to remove the apprehensions of his kinsmen, by a solemn oath which he pledged for their security. His next employment was to find some specious pretence which might release his conscience from the obligation of an imprudent promise. The arts of fraud were made subservient to the designs of cruelty; and a manifest forgery was attested by a person of the most sacred character. From the hands of the bishop of Nicomedia, Constantius received a fatal scroll, affirmed to be the genuine testament of his father; in which the emperor expressed his suspicions that he had been poisoned by his brothers; and conjured his sons to revenge his death, and to consult their own safety, by the punishment of the guilty.[51] Whatever reasons might have been alleged by these unfortunate princes to defend their life and honour against so incredible an accusation, they were silenced by the furious clamours of the soldiers, who declared themselves, at once, their enemies, their judges, and their executioners. The spirit, and even the forms, of legal proceedings were repeatedly violated in a promiscuous massacre; which involved the two uncles of Constantius, seven of his cousins, of whom Dalmatius and Hannibalianus were the most illustrious, the Patrician Optatus, who had married a sister of the late emperor, and the præfect Ablavius, whose power and riches had inspired him with some hopes of obtaining the purple. If it were necessary to aggravate the horrors of this bloody scene, we might add that Constantius himself had espoused the daughter of his uncle Julius, and that he had bestowed his sister in marriage on his cousin Hannibalianus. These alliances, which the policy of Constantine, regardless of the public prejudice,[52] had formed between the several branches of the Imperial house, served only to convince mankind that these princes were as cold to the endearments of conjugal affection, as they were insensible to the ties of consanguinity and the moving entreaties of youth and innocence. Of so numerous a family, Gallus and Julian alone, the two youngest children of Julius Constantius, were saved from the hands of the assassins, till their rage, satiated with slaughter, had in some measure subsided. The emperor Constantius, who, in the absence of his brothers, was the most obnoxious to guilt and reproach, discovered, on some future occasions, a faint and transient remorse for those cruelties which the perfidious counsels of his ministers and the irresistible violence of the troops, had extorted from his inexperienced youth.[53]

The massacre of the Flavian race was succeeded by a new division of the provinces, which was ratified in a personal interview of the three brothers. Constantine, the eldest of the Cæsars, obtained, with a certain pre-eminence of rank, the possession of the new capital, which bore his own name and that of his father. Thrace and the countries of the East were allotted for the patrimony of Constantius; and Constans was acknowledged as the lawful sovereign of Italy, Africa, and the western Illyricum. The armies submitted to their hereditary right, and they condescended, after some delay, to accept from the Roman senate the title of *Augustus*. When they first assumed the reins of government, the eldest of these princes was twenty-one, the second twenty, and the third only seventeen, years of age.[54]

While the martial nations of Europe followed the standards of his brothers, Constantius, at the head of the effeminate troops of Asia, was left to sustain the weight of the Persian war. At the decease of Constantine, the throne of the East was filled by Sapor, son of Hormouz, or Hormisdas, and grandson of Narses, who, after the victory of Galerius, had humbly confessed the superiority of the Roman power. Although Sapor was in the thirtieth year of his long reign, he was still in the vigour of youth, as the date of his accession, by a very strange fatality, had

preceded that of his birth. The wife of Hormouz remained pregnant at the time of her husband's death, and the uncertainty of the sex, as well as of the event, excited the ambitious hopes of the princes of the house of Sassan. The apprehensions of civil war were at length removed by the positive assurance of the Magi that the widow of Hormouz had conceived, and would safely produce a son. Obedient to the voice of superstition, the Persians prepared, without delay, the ceremony of his coronation. A royal bed, on which the queen lay in state, was exhibited in the midst of the palace; the diadem was placed on the spot which might be supposed to conceal the future heir of Artaxerxes, and the prostrate satraps adored the majesty of their invisible and insensible sovereign.[55] If any credit can be given to this marvellous tale, which seems, however, to be countenanced by the manners of the people and by the extraordinary duration of his reign, we must admire not only the fortune but the genius of Sapor. In the soft sequestered education of a Persian harem the royal youth could discover the importance of exercising the vigour of his mind and body, and by his personal merit deserved a throne on which he had been seated while he was yet unconscious of the duties and temptations of absolute power. His minority was exposed to the almost inevitable calamities of domestic discord; his capital was surprised and plundered by Thair, a powerful king of Yemen or Arabia, and the majesty of the royal family was degraded by the captivity of a princess, the sister of the deceased king. But as soon as Sapor attained the age of manhood the presumptuous Thair, his nation, and his country, fell beneath the first effort of the young warrior, who used his victory with so judicious a mixture of rigour and clemency that he obtained from the fears and gratitude of the Arabs the title of *Dhoulacnaf*, or protector of the nation.[56]

The ambition of the Persian, to whom his enemies ascribe the virtues of a soldier and a statesman, was animated by the desire of revenging the disgrace of his fathers, and of wresting from the hands of the Romans the five provinces beyond the Tigris. The military fame of Constantine, and the real or apparent strength of his government, suspended the attack, and, while the hostile conduct of Sapor provoked the resentment, his artful negotiations amused the patience of the Imperial court. The death of Constantine was the signal of war,[57] and the actual condition of the Syrian and Armenian frontier seemed to encourage the Persians by the prospect of a rich spoil and an easy conquest. The example of the massacres of the palace diffused a spirit of licentiousness and sedition among the troops of the East, who were no longer restrained by their habits of obedience to a veteran commander. By the prudence of Constantius, who, from the interview with his brothers in Pannonia, immediately hastened to the banks of the Euphrates, the legions were gradually restored to a sense of duty and discipline; but the season of anarchy had permitted Sapor to form the siege of Nisibis, and to occupy several of the most important fortresses of Mesopotamia.[58] In Armenia the renowned Tiridates had long enjoyed the peace and glory which he deserved by his valour and fidelity to the cause of Rome. The firm alliance which he maintained with Constantine was productive of spiritual as well as of temporal benefits; by the conversion of Tiridates the character of a saint was applied to that of a hero, the Christian faith was preached and established from the Euphrates to the shores of the Caspian, and Armenia was attached to the empire by the double ties of policy and of religion. But as many of the Armenian nobles still refused to abandon the plurality of their gods and of their wives, the public tranquillity was disturbed by a discontented faction, which insulted the feeble age of their sovereign, and impatiently expected the hour of his death. He died at length, after a reign of fifty-six years, and the fortune of the Armenian monarchy expired with Tiridates. His lawful heir was driven into exile, the Christian priests were either murdered or expelled from their churches, the barbarous tribes of Albania were solicited to descend from their mountains, and two of the most powerful governors, usurping the ensigns or the powers of royalty, implored the assistance of Sapor, and opened the gates of their cities to the Persian garrisons. The Christian party, under the guidance of the archbishop of Artaxata, the immediate successor of St. Gregory the Illuminator, had recourse to the piety of Constantius. After the troubles had continued about three years, Antiochus, one of the officers of the household, executed with success the Imperial commission of restoring Chosroes, the son of Tiridates, to the throne of his fathers, of distributing honours and rewards among the faithful servants of the house of Arsaces, and of proclaiming a general amnesty, which was accepted by the greater part of the rebellious satraps. But the Romans derived more honour than advantage from this revolution. Chosroes was a prince of a puny stature and a pusillanimous spirit. Unequal to the fatigues of war, averse to the society of mankind, he withdrew from his capital to a retired palace which he built on the banks of the river Eleutherus, and in the centre of a shady grove, where he consumed his vacant hours in the rural sports of hunting and hawking. To secure this inglorious ease, he submitted to the conditions of peace which Sapor condescended to impose: the payment of an annual tribute, and the restitution of the fertile province of Atropatene, which the courage of Tiridates and the victorious arms of Galerius had annexed to the Armenian monarchy.[59]

During the long period of the reign of Constantius the provinces of the East were afflicted by the calamities of the Persian war. The irregular incursions of the light troops alternately spread terror and devastation beyond the Tigris and beyond the Euphrates, from the gates of Ctesiphon to those of Antioch; and this active service was performed by the Arabs of the desert, who were divided in their interest and affections, some of their independent chiefs being enlisted in the party of Sapor, whilst others had engaged their doubtful fidelity to the emperor.[60] The more grave and important operations of the war were conducted with equal vigour; and the armies of Rome and Persia encountered each other in nine bloody fields, in two of which Constantius himself commanded in person.[61] The event of the day was most commonly adverse to the Romans, but in the battle of Singara their imprudent valour had almost achieved a signal and decisive victory. The stationary troops of Singara retired on the approach of Sapor, who passed the Tigris over three bridges, and occupied near the village of Hilleh an advantageous camp, which, by the labour of his numerous pioneers, he surrounded in one day with a deep ditch and a lofty rampart. His formidable host, when it was drawn out in order of battle, covered the banks of the river, the adjacent heights, and the whole extent of a plain of above twelve miles which separated the two armies. Both were alike impatient to engage, but the barbarians, after a slight resistance, fled in disorder, unable to resist, or desirous to weary, the strength of the heavy legions, who, fainting with heat and thirst, pursued them across the plain, and cut in pieces a line of cavalry clothed in complete armour, which had been posted before the gates of the camp to protect their retreat. Constantius, who was hurried along in the pursuit, attempted, without effect, to restrain the ardour of his troops, by representing to them the dangers of the approaching night, and the certainty of completing their success with the return of day. As they depended much more on their own valour than on the experience or the abilities of their chief, they silenced by their clamours his timid remonstrances, and, rushing with fury to the charge, filled up the ditch, broke down the rampart, and dispersed themselves through the tents to recruit their exhausted strength, and to enjoy the rich harvest of their labours. But the prudent Sapor had watched the moment of victory. His army, of which the greater part, securely posted on the heights, had been spectators of the action, advanced in silence and under the shadow of the night, and his Persian archers, guided by the illumination of the camp, poured a shower of arrows on a disarmed and licentious crowd. The sincerity of history[62] declares that the Romans were vanquished with a dreadful slaughter, and that the flying remnant of the legions was exposed to the most intolerable hardships. Even the tenderness of panegyric, confessing that the glory of the emperor was sullied by the disobedience of his soldiers, chooses to draw a veil over the circumstances of this melancholy retreat. Yet one of those venal orators, so jealous of the fame of Constantius, relates, with amazing coolness, an act of such incredible cruelty, as, in the judgment of posterity, must imprint a far deeper stain on the honour of the Imperial name. The son of Sapor, the heir of his crown, had been made a captive in the Persian camp. The unhappy youth, who might have excited the compassion of the most savage enemy, was scourged, tortured, and publicly executed by the inhuman Romans.[63]

Whatever advantages might attend the arms of Sapor in the field, though nine repeated victories diffused among the nations the fame of his valour and conduct, he could not hope to succeed in the execution of his designs while the fortified towns of Mesopotamia, and, above all, the strong and ancient city of Nisibis, remained in the possession of the Romans. In the space of twelve years Nisibis, which, since the time of Lucullus, had been deservedly esteemed the bulwark of the East, sustained three memorable sieges against the power of Sapor; and the disappointed monarch, after urging his attacks above sixty, eighty, and an hundred days, was thrice repulsed with loss and ignominy.[64] This large and populous city was situate about two days' journey from the Tigris, in the midst of a pleasant and fertile plain at the foot of Mount Masius. A treble enclosure of brick walls was defended by a deep ditch;[65] and the intrepid resistance of Count Lucilianus and his garrison was seconded by the desperate courage of the people. The citizens of Nisibis were animated by the exhortations of their bishop,[66] inured to arms by the presence of danger, and convinced of the intentions of Sapor to plant a Persian colony in their room, and to lead them away into distant and barbarous captivity. The event of the two former sieges elated their confidence and exasperated the haughty spirit of the Great King, who advanced a third time towards Nisibis, at the head of the united forces of Persia and India. The ordinary machines, invented to batter or undermine the walls, were rendered ineffectual by the superior skill of the Romans, and many days had vainly elapsed when Sapor embraced a resolution worthy of an eastern monarch who believed that the elements themselves were subject to his power. At the stated season of the melting of the snows in Armenia, the river Mygdonius, which divides the plain and the city of Nisibis, forms, like the Nile,[67] an inundation over the adjacent country. By the labour of the Persians the course of the river was stopped below the town, and the waters were confined on every side by solid mounds of earth. On this artificial lake a fleet of armed vessels, filled with soldiers, and with engines which discharged stones of five hundred pounds weight, advanced in order of battle, and engaged, almost upon a level, the troops which defended the ramparts. The irresistible force of the waters was alternately fatal to the contending parties, till at length a portion of the walls, unable to sustain the accumulated pressure, gave way at once, and exposed an ample breach of one hundred and fifty feet. The Persians were instantly driven to the assault, and the fate of Nisibis depended on the event of the day. The heavy-armed cavalry, who led the van of a deep column, were embarrassed in the mud, and great numbers were drowned in the unseen holes which had been filled by the rushing waters. The elephants, made furious by their wounds, increased the disorder, and trampled down thousands of the Persian archers. The Great King, who, from an exalted throne, beheld the misfortunes of his arms, sounded, with reluctant indignation, the signal of the retreat, and suspended for some hours the prosecution of the attack. But the vigilant citizens improved the opportunity of the night, and the return of day discovered a new wall of six feet in height rising every moment to fill up the interval of the breach. Notwithstanding the disappointment of his hopes and the loss of more than twenty thousand men, Sapor still pressed the reduction of Nisibis with an obstinate firmness which could have yielded only to the necessity of defending the eastern provinces of Persia against a formidable invasion of the Massagetæ.[68] Alarmed by this intelligence, he hastily relinquished the siege, and marched with rapid diligence from the banks of the Tigris to those of the Oxus. The danger and difficulties of the Scythian war engaged him soon afterwards to conclude, or at least to observe, a truce with the Roman emperor, which was equally grateful to both princes, as Constantius himself, after the deaths of his two brothers, was involved, by the revolutions of the West, in a civil contest which required and seemed to exceed the most vigorous exertion of his undivided strength.

After the partition of the empire three years had scarcely elapsed before the sons of Constantine seemed impatient to convince mankind that they were incapable of contenting themselves with the dominions which they were unqualified to govern. The eldest of those princes soon complained that he was defrauded of his just proportion of the spoils of their murdered kinsmen; and though he might yield to the superior guilt and merit of Constantius, he exacted from Constans the cession of the African provinces, as an equivalent for the rich countries of Macedonia and Greece which his brother had acquired by the death of Dalmatius. The want of sincerity which Constantine experienced in a tedious and fruitless negotiation exasperated the fierceness of his temper, and he eagerly listened to those favourites who suggested to him that his honour, as well as his interest, was concerned in the prosecution of the quarrel. At the head of a tumultuary band, suited for rapine rather than for conquest, he suddenly broke into the dominions of Constans. by the way of the Julian Alps, and the country round Aquileia felt the first effects of his resentment. The measures of Constans, who then resided in Dacia, were directed with more prudence and ability. On the news of his brother's invasion he detached a select and disciplined body of his Illyrian troops, proposing to follow them in person with the remainder of his forces. But the conduct of his lieutenants soon terminated the unnatural contest. By the artful appearances of flight, Constantine was betrayed into an ambuscade, which had been concealed in a wood, where the rash youth, with a few attendants, was surprised, surrounded, and slain. His body, after it had been found in the obscure stream of the Alsa, obtained the honours of an Imperial sepulchre, but his provinces transferred their allegiance to the conqueror, who, refusing to admit his elder brother Constantius to any share in these new acquisitions, maintained the undisputed possession of more than two-thirds of the Roman empire.[69]

The fate of Constans himself was delayed about ten years longer, and the revenge of his brother's death was reserved for the more ignoble hand of a domestic traitor. The pernicious tendency of the system introduced by Constantine was displayed in the feeble administration of his sons, who, by their vices and weakness, soon lost the esteem and affections of their people. The pride assumed by Constans from the unmerited success of his arms was rendered more contemptible by his want of abilities and application. His fond partiality towards some German captives, distinguished only by the charms of youth, was an object of scandal to the people; [70] and Magnentius, an ambitious soldier, who was himself of barbarian extraction, was encouraged by the public discontent to assert the honour of the Roman name.[71] The chosen bands of Jovians and Herculians, who acknowledged Magnentius as their leader, maintained the most respectable and important station in the Imperial camp. The friendship of Marcellinus, count of the sacred largesses, supplied with a liberal hand the means of seduction. The soldiers were convinced, by the most specious arguments, that the republic summoned them to break the bonds of hereditary servitude, and, by the choice of an active and vigilant prince, to reward the same virtues which had raised the ancestors of the degenerate Constans from a private condition to the throne of the world. As soon as the conspiracy was ripe for execution. Marcellinus, under the pretence of celebrating his son's birthday, gave a splendid entertainment to the *illustrious* and *honourable* persons of the court of Gaul, which then resided in the city of Autun. The intemperance of the feast was artfully protracted till a very late hour of the night, and the unsuspecting guests were tempted to indulge themselves in a dangerous and guilty freedom of conversation. On a sudden the doors were thrown open, and Magnentius, who had retired for a few moments, returned into the apartment, invested with the diadem and purple. The conspirators instantly saluted him with the titles of Augustus and Emperor. The surprise, the terror, the intoxication, the ambitious hopes, and the mutual ignorance of the rest of the assembly prompted them to join their voices to the general acclamation. The guards hastened to take the oath of fidelity, the gates of the town were shut, and before the dawn of day Magnentius became master of the troops and treasure of the palace and city of Autun. By his secrecy and diligence he entertained some hopes of surprising the person of Constans, who was pursuing in the adjacent forest his favourite amusement of hunting, or perhaps some pleasures of a more private and criminal nature. The rapid progress of fame allowed him, however, an instant for flight, though the desertion of his soldiers and subjects deprived him of the power of resistance. Before he could reach a seaport in Spain, where he intended to embark, he was overtaken near Helena,[72] at the foot of the Pyrenees, by a party of light cavalry, whose chief, regardless of the sanctity of a temple, executed his commission by the murder of the son of Constantine.[73]

As soon as the death of Constans had decided this easy but important revolution, the example of the court of Autun was imitated by the provinces of the West. The authority of Magnentius was acknowledged through the whole extent of the two great præfectures of Gaul and Italy; and the usurper prepared, by every act of oppression, to collect a treasure which might discharge the obligation of an immense donative and supply the expenses of a civil war. The martial countries of Illyricum, from the Danube to the extremity of Greece, had long obeyed the government of Vetranio, an aged general, beloved for the simplicity of his manners, and who had acquired some reputation by his experience and services in war.[74] Attached by habit, by duty, and by gratitude to the house of Constantine, he immediately gave the strongest assurances to the only surviving son of his late master that he would expose, with unshaken fidelity, his person and his troops to inflict a just revenge on the traitors of Gaul. But the legions of Vetranio were seduced, rather than provoked, by the example of rebellion; their leader soon betrayed a want of firmness or a want of sincerity, and his ambition derived a specious pretence from the approbation of the princess Constantina. That cruel and aspiring woman, who had obtained from the great Constantine, her father, the rank of *Augusta*, placed the diadem with her own hands on the head of the Illyrian general, and seemed to expect from his victory the accomplishment of those unbounded hopes of which she had been disappointed by the death of her husband Hannibalianus. Perhaps it was without the consent of Constantina that the new emperor formed a necessary, though dishonourable, alliance with the usurper of the West,

whose purple was so recently stained with her brother's blood.[75]

The intelligence of these important events, which so deeply affected the honour and safety of the Imperial house, recalled the arms of Constantius from the inglorious prosecution of the Persian war. He recommended the care of the East to his lieutenants, and afterwards to his cousin Gallus, whom he raised from a prison to a throne, and marched towards Europe, with a mind agitated by the conflict of hope and fear, of grief and indignation. On his arrival at Heraclea in Thrace, the emperor gave audience to the ambassadors of Magnentius and Vetranio. The first author of the conspiracy, Marcellinus, who in some measure had bestowed the purple on his new master, boldly accepted this dangerous commission; and his three colleagues were selected from the illustrious personages of the state and army. These deputies were instructed to soothe the resentment, and to alarm the fears, of Constantius. They were empowered to offer him the friendship and alliance of the western princes, to cement their union by a double marriage,—of Constantius with the daughter of Magnentius, and of Magnentius himself with the ambitious Constantina,—and to acknowledge in the treaty the pre-eminence of rank which might justly be claimed by the emperor of the East. Should pride and mistaken piety urge him to refuse these equitable conditions, the ambassadors were ordered to expatiate on the inevitable ruin which must attend his rashness, if he ventured to provoke the sovereigns of the West to exert their superior strength, and to employ against him that valour, those abilities, and those legions, to which the house of Constantine had been indebted for so many triumphs. Such propositions and such arguments appeared to deserve the most serious attention; the answer of Constantius was deferred till the next day; and as he had reflected on the importance of justifying a civil war in the opinion of the people, he thus addressed his council, who listened with real or affected credulity: "Last night," said he, "after I retired to rest, the shade of the great Constantine, embracing the corpse of my murdered brother, rose before my eyes; his well-known voice awakened me to revenge, forbade me to despair of the republic, and assured me of the success and immortal glory which would crown the justice of my arms." The authority of such a vision, or rather of the prince who alleged it, silenced every doubt, and excluded all negotiation. The ignominious terms of peace were rejected with disdain. One of the ambassadors of the tyrant was dismissed with the haughty answer of Constantius; his colleagues, as unworthy of the privileges of the law of nations, were put in irons; and the contending powers prepared to wage an implacable war.[76]

Such was the conduct, and such perhaps was the duty, of the brother of Constans towards the perfidious usurper of Gaul. The situation and character of Vetranio admitted of milder measures; and the policy of the Eastern emperor was directed to disunite his antagonists, and to separate the forces of Illyricum from the cause of rebellion. It was an easy task to deceive the frankness and simplicity of Vetranio, who, fluctuating some time between the opposite views of honour and interest, displayed to the world the insincerity of his temper, and was insensibly engaged in the snares of an artful negotiation. Constantius acknowledged him as a legitimate and equal colleague in the empire, on condition that he would renounce his disgraceful alliance with Magnentius, and appoint a place of interview on the frontiers of their respective provinces, where they might pledge their friendship by mutual vows of fidelity, and regulate by common consent the future operations of the civil war. In consequence of this agreement, Vetranio advanced to the city of Sardica,[77] at the head of twenty thousand horse, and of a more numerous body of infantry; a power so far superior to the forces of Constantius, that the Illyrian emperor appeared to command the life and fortunes of his rival, who, depending on the success of his private negotiations, had seduced the troops and undermined the throne of Vetranio. The chiefs, who had secretly embraced the party of Constantius, prepared in his favour a public spectacle, calculated to discover and inflame the passions of the multitude.[78] The united armies were commanded to assemble in a large plain near the city. In the centre, according to the rules of ancient discipline, a military tribunal, or rather scaffold, was erected, from whence the emperors were accustomed, on solemn and important occasions, to harangue the troops. The well-ordered ranks of Romans and barbarians, with drawn swords, or with erected spears, the squadrons of cavalry, and the cohorts of infantry, distinguished by the variety of their arms and ensigns, formed an immense circle around the tribunal; and the attentive silence which they preserved was sometimes interrupted by loud bursts of clamour or of applause. In the presence of this formidable assembly the two emperors were called upon to explain the situation of public affairs: the precedency of rank was yielded to the royal birth of Constantius; and though he was indifferently skilled in the arts of rhetoric, he acquitted himself, under these difficult circumstances, with firmness, dexterity, and eloquence. The first part of his oration seemed to be pointed only against the tyrant of Gaul; but while he tragically lamented the cruel murder of Constans, he insinuated that none, except a brother, could claim a right to the succession of his brother. He displayed, with some complacency, the glories of his Imperial race; and recalled to the memory of the troops the valour, the triumphs, the liberality of the great Constantine, to whose sons they had engaged their allegiance by an oath of fidelity, which the ingratitude of his most favoured servants had tempted them to violate. The officers, who surrounded the tribunal, and were instructed to act their parts in this extraordinary scene, confessed the irresistible power of reason and eloquence, by saluting the emperor Constantius as their lawful sovereign. The contagion of loyalty and repentance was communicated from rank to rank, till the plain of Sardica resounded with the universal acclamation of "Away with these upstart usurpers! Long life and victory to the son of Constantine! Under his banners alone we will fight and conquer." The shout of thousands, their menacing gestures, the fierce clashing of their arms, astonished and subdued the courage of Vetranio, who stood, amidst the defection of his followers, in anxious and silent suspense. Instead of embracing the last refuge of generous despair, he tamely submitted to his fate, and, taking the diadem from his head, in the view of both armies fell prostrate at the feet of his conqueror. Constantius used his victory with prudence and moderation; and raising from the ground the aged suppliant, whom he affected to style by the endearing name of Father, he gave him his hand to descend from the throne. The city of Prusa was assigned for the exile or retirement of the abdicated monarch, who lived six years in the enjoyment of ease and affluence. He often expressed his grateful sense of the goodness of Constantius, and, with a very amiable simplicity, advised his benefactor to resign the sceptre of the world, and to seek for content (where alone it could be found) in the peaceful obscurity of a private condition.[79]

The behaviour of Constantius on this memorable occasion was celebrated with some appearance of justice; and his courtiers compared the studied orations which a Pericles or a Demosthenes addressed to the populace of Athens with the victorious eloquence which had persuaded an armed multitude to desert and depose the object of their partial choice.[80] The approaching contest with Magnentius was of a more serious and bloody kind. The tyrant advanced by rapid marches to encounter Constantius, at the head of a numerous army, composed of Gauls and Spaniards, of Franks and Saxons; of those provincials who supplied the strength of the legions, and of those barbarians who were dreaded as the most formidable enemies of the republic. The fertile plains[81] of the Lower Pannonia, between the Drave, the Save, and the Danube, presented a spacious theatre; and the operations of the civil war were protracted during the summer months by the skill or timidity of the combatants.[82] Constantius had declared his intention of deciding the quarrel in the fields of Cibalis, a name that would animate his troops by the remembrance of the victory which, on the same auspicious ground, had been obtained by the arms of his father Constantine. Yet, by the impregnable fortifications with which the emperor encompassed his camp, he appeared to decline rather than to invite a general engagement. It was the object of Magnentius to tempt or to compel his adversary to relinquish this advantageous position; and he employed with that view the various marches, evolutions, and stratagems which the knowledge of the art of war could suggest to an experienced officer. He carried by assault the important town of Siscia; made an attack on the city of Sirmium, which lay in the rear of the Imperial camp; attempted to force a passage over the Save into the eastern provinces of Illyricum; and cut in pieces a numerous detachment which he had allured into the narrow passes of Adarne. During the greater part of the summer the tyrant of Gaul showed himself master of the field. The troops of Constantius were harassed and dispirited; his reputation declined in the eye of the world; and his pride condescended to solicit a treaty of peace, which would have resigned to the assassin of Constans the sovereignty of the provinces beyond the Alps. These offers were enforced by the eloquence of Philip the Imperial ambassador; and the council as well as the army of Magnentius were disposed to accept them. But the haughty usurper, careless of the remonstrances of his friends, gave orders that Philip should be detained as a captive, or at least as an hostage; while he despatched an officer to reproach Constantius with the weakness of his reign, and to insult him by the prom-

ise of a pardon if he would instantly abdicate the purple. "That he should confide in the justice of his cause, and the protection of an avenging Deity," was the only answer which honour permitted the emperor to return. But he was so sensible of the difficulties of his situation, that he no longer dared to retaliate the indignity which had been offered to his representative. The negotiation of Philip was not, however, ineffectual, since he determined Sylvanus the Frank, a general of merit and reputation, to desert with a considerable body of cavalry a few days before the battle of Mursa.

The city of Mursa, or Essek, celebrated in modern times for a bridge of boats, five miles in length, over the river Drave, and the adjacent morasses,[83] has been always considered as a place of importance in the wars of Hungary. Magnentius, directing his march towards Mursa, set fire to the gates, and, by a sudden assault, had almost scaled the walls of the town. The vigilance of the garrison extinguished the flames; the approach of Constantius left him no time to continue the operations of the siege; and the emperor soon removed the only obstacle that could embarrass his motions, by forcing a body of troops which had taken post in an adjoining amphitheatre. The field of battle round Mursa was a naked and level plain: on this ground the army of Constantius formed, with the Drave on their right; while their left, either from the nature of their disposition, or from the superiority of their cavalry, extended far beyond the right flank of Magnentius.[84] The troops on both sides remained under arms in anxious expectation during the greatest part of the morning; and the son of Constantine, after animating his soldiers by an eloquent speech, retired into a church at some distance from the field of battle, and committed to his generals the conduct of this decisive day.[85] They deserved his confidence by the valour and military skill which they exerted. They wisely began the action upon the left; and advancing their whole wing of cavalry in an oblique line, they suddenly wheeled it on the right flank of the enemy, which was unprepared to resist the impetuosity of their charge. But the Romans of the West soon rallied by the habits of discipline; and the barbarians of Germany supported the renown of their national bravery. The engagement soon became general; was maintained with various and singular turns of fortune; and scarcely ended with the darkness of the night. The signal victory which Constantius obtained is attributed to the arms of his cavalry. His cuirassiers are described as so many massy statues of steel, glittering with their scaly armour, and breaking with their ponderous lances the firm array of the Gallic legions. As soon as the legions gave way, the lighter and more active squadrons of the second line rode sword in hand into the intervals and completed the disorder. In the meanwhile, the huge bodies of the Germans were exposed almost naked to the dexterity of the Oriental archers; and whole troops of those barbarians were urged by anguish and despair to precipitate themselves into the broad and rapid stream of the Drave.[86] The number of the slain was computed at fifty-four thousand men, and the slaughter of the conquerors was more considerable than that of the vanquished;[87] a circumstance which proves the obstinacy of the contest, and justifies the observation of an ancient writer, that the forces of the empire were consumed in the fatal battle of Mursa, by the loss of a veteran army, sufficient to defend the frontiers, or to add new triumphs to the glory of Rome.[88] Notwithstanding the invectives of a servile orator, there is not the least reason to believe that the tyrant deserted his own standard in the beginning of the engagement. He seems to have displayed the virtues of a general and of a soldier till the day was irrecoverably lost, and his camp in the possession of the enemy. Magnentius then consulted his safety, and, throwing away the Imperial ornaments, escaped with some difficulty from the pursuit of the light horse, who incessantly followed his rapid flight from the banks of the Drave to the foot of the Julian Alps.[89]

The approach of winter supplied the indolence of Constantius with specious reasons for deferring the prosecution of the war till the ensuing spring. Magnentius had fixed his residence in the city of Aquileia, and showed a seeming resolution to dispute the passage of the mountains and morasses which fortified the confines of the Venetian province. The surprisal of a castle in the Alps by the secret march of the Imperialists could scarcely have determined him to relinquish the possession of Italy, if the inclinations of the people had supported the cause of their tyrant.[90] But the memory of the cruelties exercised by his ministers, after the unsuccessful revolt of Nepotian, had left a deep impression of horror and resentment on the minds of the Romans. That rash youth, the son of the princess Eutropia, and the nephew of Constantine, had seen with indignation the sceptre of the West usurped by a perfidious barbarian. Arming a desperate troop of slaves and gladiators, he overpowered the feeble guard of the domestic tranquillity of Rome, received the homage of the senate, and, assuming the title of Augustus, precariously reigned during a tumult of twenty-eight days. The march of some regular forces put an end to his ambitious hopes: the rebellion was extinguished in the blood of Nepotian, of his mother Eutropia, and of his adherents; and the proscription was extended to all who had contracted a fatal alliance with the name and family of Constantine.[91] But as soon as Constantius, after the battle of Mursa, became master of the sea-coast of Dalmatia, a band of noble exiles, who had ventured to equip a fleet in some harbour of the Adriatic, sought protection and revenge in his victorious camp. By their secret intelligence with their countrymen, Rome and the Italian cities were persuaded to display the banners of Constantius on their walls. The grateful veterans, enriched by the liberality of the father, signalised their gratitude and loyalty to the son. The cavalry, the legions, and the auxiliaries of Italy, renewed their oath of allegiance to Constantius; and the usurper, alarmed by the general desertion, was compelled, with the remains of his faithful troops, to retire beyond the Alps into the provinces of Gaul. The detachments, however, which were ordered either to press or to intercept the flight of Magnentius, conducted themselves with the usual imprudence of success; and allowed him, in the plains of Pavia, an opportunity of turning on his pursuers, and gratifying his despair by the carnage of a useless victory.[92]

The pride of Magnentius was reduced, by repeated misfortunes, to sue, and to sue in vain, for peace. He first despatched a senator, in whose abilities he confided, and afterwards several bishops, whose holy character might obtain a more favourable audience, with the offer of resigning the purple, and the promise of devoting the remainder of his life to the services of the emperor. But Constantius, though he granted fair terms of pardon and reconciliation to all who abandoned the standard of rebellion,[93] avowed his inflexible resolution to inflict a just punishment on the crimes of an assassin whom he prepared to overwhelm on every side by the effort of his victorious arms. An Imperial fleet acquired the easy possession of Africa and Spain, confirmed the wavering faith of the Moorish nations, and landed a considerable force, which passed the Pyrenees, and advanced towards Lyons, the last and fatal station of Magnentius.[94] The temper of the tyrant, which was never inclined to clemency, was urged by distress to exercise every act of oppression which could extort an immediate supply from the cities of Gaul.[95] Their patience was at length exhausted; and Treves, the seat of Prætorian government, gave the signal of revolt, by shutting her gates against Decentius, who had been raised by his brother to the rank of either Cæsar or of Augustus.[96] From Treves, Decentius was obliged to retire to Sens, where he was soon surrounded by an army of Germans, whom the pernicious arts of Constantius had introduced into the civil dissensions of Rome.[97] In the meantime the Imperial troops forced the passages of the Cottian Alps, and in the bloody combat of Mount Seleucus irrevocably fixed the title of rebels on the party of Magnentius.[98] He was unable to bring another army into the field; the fidelity of his guards was corrupted; and when he appeared in public to animate them by his exhortations, he was saluted with an unanimous shout of "Long live the emperor Constantius!" The tyrant, who perceived that they were preparing to deserve pardon and rewards by the sacrifice of the most obnoxious criminal, prevented their design by falling on his sword;[99] a death more easy and more honourable than he could hope to obtain from the hands of an enemy whose revenge would have been coloured with the specious pretence of justice and fraternal piety. The example of suicide was imitated by Decentius, who strangled himself on the news of his brother's death. The author of the conspiracy, Marcellinus, had long since disappeared in the battle of Mursa,[100] and the public tranquillity was confirmed by the execution of the surviving leaders of a guilty and unsuccessful faction. A severe inquisition was extended over all who, either from choice or from compulsion, had been involved in the cause of rebellion. Paul, surnamed Catena from his superior skill in the judicial exercise of tyranny, was sent to explore the latent remains of the conspiracy in the remote province of Britain. The honest indignation expressed by Martin, vice-præfect of the island, was interpreted as an evidence of his own guilt; and the governor was urged to the necessity of turning against his breast the sword with which he had been provoked to wound the Imperial minister. The most innocent subjects of the West were exposed to exile and confiscation, to death and torture; and as the timid are always cruel, the mind of Constantius was inaccessible to mercy.[101]

CHAPTER XIX

Constantius sole Emperor. Elevation and Death of Gallus. Danger and Elevation of Julian. Sarmatian and Persian Wars. Victories of Julian in Gaul.

THE divided provinces of the empire were again united by the victory of Constantius; but as that feeble prince was destitute of personal merit either in peace or war; as he feared his generals, and distrusted his ministers; the triumph of his arms served only to establish the reign of the *eunuchs* over the Roman world. Those unhappy beings, the ancient production of Oriental jealousy and despotism,[1] were introduced into Greece and Rome by the contagion of Asiatic luxury.[2] Their progress was rapid; and the eunuchs, who, in the time of Augustus, had been abhorred, as the monstrous retinue of an Egyptian queen,[3] were gradually admitted into the families of matrons, of senators, and of the emperors themselves.[4] Restrained by the severe edicts of Domitian and Nerva,[5] cherished by the pride of Diocletian, reduced to an humble station by the prudence of Constantine,[6] they multiplied in the palaces of his degenerate sons, and insensibly acquired the knowledge, and at length the direction, of the secret councils of Constantius. The aversion and contempt which mankind has so uniformly entertained for that imperfect species appears to have degraded their character, and to have rendered them almost as incapable as they were supposed to be of conceiving any generous sentiment, or of performing any worthy action.[7] But the eunuchs were skilled in the arts of flattery and intrigue; and they alternately governed the mind of Constantius by his fears, his indolence, and his vanity.[8] Whilst he viewed in a deceitful mirror the fair appearance of public prosperity, he supinely permitted them to intercept the complaints of the injured provinces; to accumulate immense treasures by the sale of justice and of honours; to disgrace the most important dignities by the promotion of those who had purchased at their hands the powers of oppression;[9] and to gratify their resentment against the few independent spirits who arrogantly refused to solicit the protection of slaves. Of these slaves the most distinguished was the chamberlain

Eusebius, who ruled the monarch and the palace with such absolute sway, that Constantius, according to the sarcasm of an impartial historian, possessed some credit with this haughty favourite.[10] By his artful suggestions, the emperor was persuaded to subscribe the condemnation of the unfortunate Gallus, and to add a new crime to the long list of unnatural murders which pollute the honour of the house of Constantine.

When the two nephews of Constantine, Gallus and Julian, were saved from the fury of the soldiers, the former was about twelve, and the latter about six, years of age; and, as the eldest was thought to be of a sickly constitution, they obtained with the less difficulty a precarious and dependent life from the affected pity of Constantius, who was sensible that the execution of these helpless orphans would have been esteemed, by all mankind, an act of the most deliberate cruelty.[11] Different cities of Ionia and Bithynia were assigned for the places of their exile and education; but as soon as their growing years excited the jealousy of the emperor, he judged it more prudent to secure those unhappy youths in the strong castle of Macellum, near Cæsarea. The treatment which they experienced during a six years' confinement was partly such as they could hope from a careful guardian, and partly such as they might dread from a suspicious tyrant.[12] Their prison was an ancient palace, the residence of the kings of Cappadocia; the situation was pleasant, the building stately, the enclosure spacious. They pursued their studies, and practised their exercises, under the tuition of the most skilful masters; and the numerous household appointed to attend, or rather to guard, the nephews of Constantine, was not unworthy of the dignity of their birth. But they could not disguise to themselves that they were deprived of fortune, of freedom, and of safety; secluded from the society of all whom they could trust or esteem, and condemned to pass their melancholy hours in the company of slaves devoted to the commands of a tyrant who had already injured them beyond the hope of reconciliation. At length, however, the emergencies of the state compelled the emperor, or rather his eunuchs, to invest Gallus, in the twenty-fifty year of his age, with the title of Cæsar, and to cement this political connection by his marriage with the princess Constantina. After a formal interview, in which the two princes mutually engaged their faith never to undertake anything to the prejudice of each other, they repaired without delay to their respec-

tive stations. Constantius continued his march towards the West, and Gallus fixed his residence at Antioch; from whence, with a delegated authority, he administered the five great dioceses of the eastern præfecture.[13] In this fortunate change, the new Cæsar was not unmindful of his brother Julian, who obtained the honours of his rank, the appearances of liberty, and the restitution of an ample patrimony.[14]

The writers the most indulgent to the memory of Gallus, and even Julian himself, though he wished to cast a veil over the frailties of his brother, are obliged to confess that the Cæsar was incapable of reigning. Transported from a prison to a throne, he possessed neither genius nor application, nor docility to compensate for the want of knowledge and experience. A temper naturally morose and violent, instead of being corrected, was soured by solitude and adversity; the remembrance of what he had endured disposed him to retaliation rather than to sympathy; and the ungoverned sallies of his rage were often fatal to those who approached his person, or were subject to his power.[15] Constantina, his wife, is described, not as a woman, but as one of the infernal furies tormented with an insatiate thirst of human blood.[16] Instead of employing her influence to insinuate the mild counsels of prudence and humanity, she exasperated the fierce passions of her husband; and as she retained the vanity, though she had renounced the gentleness of her sex, a pearl necklace was esteemed an equivalent price for the murder of an innocent and virtuous nobleman.[17] The cruelty of Gallus was sometimes displayed in the undissembled violence of popular or military executions: and was sometimes disguised by the abuse of law and the forms of judicial proceedings. The private houses of Antioch, and the palaces of public resort, were besieged by spies and informers; and the Cæsar himself, concealed in a plebeian habit, very frequently condescended to assume that odious character. Every apartment of the palace was adorned with the instruments of death and torture, and a general consternation was diffused through the capital of Syria. The prince of the East, as if he had been conscious how much he had to fear, and how little he deserved to reign, selected for the objects of his resentment the provincials accused of some imaginary treason, and his own courtiers, whom with more reason he suspected of incensing, by their secret correspondence, the timid and suspicious mind of Constantius. But he forgot that he was depriving himself of his only support, the affection of the people; whilst he furnished the malice of his enemies with the arms of truth, and afforded the emperor the fairest pretence of exacting the forfeit of his purple and of his life.[18]

As long as the civil war suspended the fate of the Roman world, Constantius dissembled his knowledge of the weak and cruel administration to which his choice had subjected the East; and the discovery of some assassins, secretly despatched to Antioch by the tyrant of Gaul, was employed to convince the public that the emperor and the Cæsar were united by the same interest, and pursued by the same enemies.[19] But when the victory was decided in favour of Constantius, his dependent colleague became less useful and less formidable. Every circumstance of his conduct was severely and suspiciously examined, and it was privately resolved either to deprive Gallus of the purple, or at least to remove him from the indolent luxury of Asia to the hardships and dangers of a German war. The death of Theophilus, consular of the provinces of Syria, who in a time of scarcity had been massacred by the people of Antioch, with the connivance and almost at the instigation of Gallus, was justly resented, not only as an act of wanton cruelty, but as a dangerous insult on the supreme majesty of Constantius. Two ministers of illustrious rank, Domitian the Oriental præfect, and Montius, quæstor of the palace, were empowered by a special commission to visit and reform the state of the East. They were instructed to behave towards Gallus with moderation and respect, and, by the gentlest arts of persuasion, to engage him to comply with the invitation of his brother and colleague. The rashness of the præfect disappointed these prudent measures, and hastened his own ruin as well as that of his enemy. On his arrival at Antioch, Domitian passed disdainfully before the gates of the palace; and, alleging a slight pretence of indisposition, continued several days in sullen retirement, to prepare an inflammatory memorial, which he transmitted to the Imperial court. Yielding at length to the pressing solicitations of Gallus, the præfect condescended to take his seat in council; but his first step was to signify a concise and haughty mandate, importing that the Cæsar should immediately repair to Italy, and threatening that he himself would punish his delay or hesitation by suspending the usual allowance of his household. The nephew and daughter of Constantine, who could ill brook the insolence of a subject, expressed their resentment by instantly delivering Domitian to the custody of a guard. The quarrel still admitted of some terms of accommodation. They were rendered impracticable by the imprudent behaviour of Montius, a statesman whose art and experience were frequently betrayed by the levity of his disposition.[20] The quæstor reproached Gallus, in haughty language, that a prince who was scarcely authorised to remove a municipal magistrate should presume to imprison a Prætorian præfect; convoked a meeting of the civil and military officers, and required them, in the name of their sovereign, to defend the person and dignity of his representatives. By this rash declaration of war the impatient temper of Gallus was provoked to embrace the most desperate counsels. He ordered his guards to stand to their arms, assembled the populace of Antioch, and recommended to their zeal the care of his safety and revenge. His commands were too fatally obeyed. They rudely seized the præfect and the quæstor, and, tying their legs together with ropes, they dragged them through the streets of the city, inflicted a thousand insults and a thousand wounds on these unhappy victims, and at last precipitated their mangled and lifeless bodies into the stream of the Orontes.[21]

After such a deed, whatever might have been the designs of Gallus, it was only in a field of battle that he could assert his innocence with any hope of success. But the mind of that prince was formed of an equal mixture of violence and weakness. Instead of assuming the title of Augustus, instead of employing in his defence the troops and treasures of the East, he suffered himself to be deceived by the affected tranquillity of Constantius, who, leaving him the vain pageantry of a court, imperceptibly recalled the veteran legions from the provinces of Asia. But as it still appeared dangerous to arrest Gallus in his capital, the slow and safer arts of dissimulation were practised with success. The frequent and pressing epistles of Constantius were filled with professions of confidence and friendship, exhorting the Cæsar to discharge the duties of his high station, to relive his colleague from a part of the public cares, and to assist the West by his presence, his counsels, and his arms. After so many reciprocal injuries, Gallus had reason to fear and to distrust. But he had neglected the opportunities of flight and of resistance; he was seduced by the flattering assurances of the tribune Scudilo, who, under the semblance of a rough soldier, disguised the most artful insinuation; and he depended on the credit of his wife Constantina till the unseasonable death of that princess completed the ruin in which he had been involved by her impetuous passions.[22]

After a long delay the reluctant Cæsar set forwards on his journey to the Imperial court. From Antioch to Hadrianople he traversed the wide extent of his dominions with a numerous and stately train; and, as he laboured to conceal his apprehensions from the world, and perhaps from himself, he entertained the people of Constantinople with an exhibition of the games of the circus. The progress of the journey might, however, have warned him of the impending danger. In all the principal cities he was met by ministers of confidence, commissioned to seize the offices of government, to observe his motions, and to prevent the hasty sallies of his despair. The persons despatched to secure the provinces which he left behind passed him with cold salutations or affected disdain; and the troops whose station lay along the public road were studiously removed on his approach, lest they might be tempted to offer their swords for the service of a civil war.[23] After Gallus had been permitted to repose himself a few days at Hadrianople he received a mandate, expressed in the most haughty and absolute style, that his splendid retinue should halt in that city, while the Cæsar himself, with only ten post-carriages, should hasten to the Imperial residence at Milan. In this rapid journey the profound respect which was due to the brother and colleague of Constantius was insensibly changed into rude familiarity; and Gallus, who discovered in the countenances of the attendants that they already considered themselves as his guards, and might soon be employed as his executioners, began to accuse his fatal rashness, and to recollect with terror and remorse the conduct by which he had provoked his fate. The dissimulation which had hitherto been preserved was laid aside at Petovio in Pannonia. He was conducted to a palace in the suburbs, where the general Barbatio, with a select band of soldiers, who could neither be moved by pity nor corrupted by rewards, expected the arrival of his illustrious victim. In the close of the evening he was arrested, ignominiously stripped of the ensigns of Cæsar, and hurried away to Pola, in Istria, a sequestered prison, which had been so recently polluted with royal blood. The horror which he felt was soon increased by the appearance of his implacable enemy the eunuch Eusebius, who, with the assistance of a notary and a tribune, proceeded to interrogate him concerning the administration of the East. The Cæsar sunk under the weight of shame and guilt, confessed all the criminal actions and all the treasonable designs with which he was charged; and, by imputing them to the advice of his wife, exasperated the indignation of Constantius, who reviewed with partial prejudice the minutes of the examination. The emperor was easily convinced that his own safety was incompatible with the life of his cousin: the sentence of death was signed, despatched, and executed; and the nephew of Constantine, with his hands tied behind his back, was beheaded in prison, like the vilest malefactor.[24] Those who are inclined to palliate the cruelties of Constantius assert that he soon relented, and endeavoured to recall the bloody mandate; but that the second messenger, intrusted with the reprieve, was detained by the eunuchs, who dreaded the unforgiving temper of Gallus, and were desirous of reuniting to *their* empire the wealthy provinces of the East.[25]

Besides the reigning emperor, Julian alone survived of all the numerous posterity of Constantius Chlorus. The misfortune of his royal birth involved him in the disgrace of Gallus. From his retirement in the happy country of Ionia he was conveyed, under a strong guard, to the court of Milan, where he languished above seven months in the continual apprehension of suffering the same ignominious death which was daily inflicted, almost before his eyes, on the friends and adherents of his persecuted family. His looks, his gestures, his silence, were scrutinised with malignant curiosity, and he was perpetually assaulted by enemies whom he had never offended, and by arts to which he was a stranger.[26] But in the school of adversity Julian insensibly acquired the virtues of firmness and discretion. He defended his honour, as well as his life, against the ensnaring subtleties of the eunuchs, who endeavoured to extort some declaration of his sentiments; and whilst he cautiously suppressed his grief and resentment, he nobly disdained to flatter the tyrant by any seeming approbation of his brother's murder. Julian most devoutly ascribes his miraculous deliverance to the protection of the gods, who had exempted his innocence from the sentence of destruction pronounced by their justice against the impious house of Constantine.[27] As the most effectual instrument of their providence, he gratefully acknowledges the steady and generous friendship of the empress Eusebia,[28] a woman of beauty and merit, who, by the ascendant which she had gained over the mind of her husband, counterbalanced in some measure the powerful conspiracy of the eunuchs. By the intercession of his patroness Julian was admitted into the Imperial presence: he pleaded his cause with a decent freedom; he was heard with favour; and, notwithstanding the efforts of his enemies, who urged the danger of sparing an avenger of the blood of Gallus, the milder sentiment of Eusebia prevailed in the council. But the effects of a second interview were dreaded by the eunuchs; and Julian was advised to withdraw for a while into the neighbourhood of Milan, till the emperor thought proper to assign the city of Athens for the place of his honourable exile. As he had discovered from his earliest youth a propensity, or rather passion, for the language, the manners, the learning, and the religion of the Greeks, he obeyed with pleasure an order so agreeable to his wishes. Far from the tumult of arms and the treachery of courts, he spent six months amidst the groves of the Academy, in a free intercourse with the philosophers of the age, who studied to cultivate the genius, to encourage the vanity, and to inflame the devotion of their royal pupil. Their labours were not unsuccessful; and Julian inviolably preserved for Athens that tender regard which seldom fails to arise in a liberal mind from the recollection of the place where it has discovered and exercised its growing powers. The gentleness and affability of manners which his temper suggested and his situation imposed, insensibly engaged the affections of the strangers, as well as citizens, with whom he conversed. Some of his fellow-students might perhaps examine his behaviour with an eye of prejudice and aversion; but Julian established in the schools of Athens a general prepossession in favour of his virtues and talents, which was soon diffused over the Roman world.[29]

Whilst his hours were passed in studious retirement, the empress, resolute to achieve the generous design which she had undertaken, was not unmindful of the care of his fortune. The death of the late Cæsar had left Constantius invested with the sole command, and oppressed by the accumulated weight, of a mighty empire. Before the wounds of civil discord could be healed, the provinces of Gaul were overwhelmed by a deluge of barbarians. The Sarmatians no longer respected the barrier of the Danube. The impunity of rapine had increased the boldness and numbers of the wild Isaurians; those robbers descended from their craggy mountains to ravage the adjacent country, and had even presumed, though without success, to besiege the important city of Seleucia, which was defended by a garrison of three Roman legions. Above all,

the Persian monarch, elated by victory, again threatened the peace of Asia; and the presence of the emperor was indispensably required both in the West and in the East. For the first time Constantius sincerely acknowledged that his single strength was unequal to such an extent of care and dominion.[30] Insensible to the voice of flattery, which assured him that his all-powerful virtue and celestial fortune would still continue to triumph over every obstacle, he listened with complacency to the advice of Eusebia, which gratified his indolence, without offending his supicious pride. As she perceived that the remembrance of Gallus dwelt on the emperor's mind, she artfully turned his attention to the opposite characters of the two brothers, which from their infancy had been compared to those of Domitian and of Titus.[31] She accustomed her husband to consider Julian as a youth of a mild, unambitious disposition, whose allegiance and gratitude might be secured by the gift of the purple, and who was qualified to fill with honour a subordinate station, without aspiring to dispute the commands or to shade the glories of his sovereign and benefactor. After an obstinate though secret struggle, the opposition of the favourite eunuchs submitted to the ascendancy of the empress; and it was resolved that Julian, after celebrating his nuptials with Helena, sister of Constantius, should be appointed, with the title of Cæsar, to reign over the countries beyond the Alps.[32]

Although the order which recalled him to court was probably accompanied by some intimation of his approaching greatness he appeals to the people of Athens to witness his tears of undissembled sorrow, when he was reluctantly torn away from his beloved retirement.[33] He trembled for his life, for his fame, and even for his virtue; and his sole confidence was derived from the persuasion that Minerva inspired all his actions, and that he was protected by an invisible guard of angels, whom for that purpose she had borrowed from the Sun and Moon. He approached with horror the palace of Milan; nor could the ingenuous youth conceal his indignation when he found himself accosted with false and servile respect by the assassins of his family. Eusebia, rejoicing in the success of her benevolent schemes, embraced him with the tenderness of a sister, and endeavoured, by the most soothing caresses, to dispel his terrors and reconcile him to his fortune. But the ceremony of shaving his beard, and his awkward demeanor when he first exchanged the cloak of a Greek philosopher for the military habit of a

Roman prince, amused during a few days the levity of the Imperial court.[34]

The emperors of the age of Constantine no longer deigned to consult with the senate in the choice of a colleague; but they were anxious that their nomination should be ratified by the consent of the army. On this solemn occasion the guards, with the other troops whose stations were in the neighborhood of Milan, appeared under arms; and Constantius ascended his lofty tribunal, holding by the hand his cousin Julian, who entered the same day into the twenty-fifth year of his age.[35] In a studied speech, conceived and delivered with dignity, the emperor represented the various dangers which threatened the prosperity of the republic, the necessity of naming a Cæsar for the administration of the West, and his own intention, if it was agreeable to their wishes, of rewarding with the honours of the purple the promising virtues of the nephew of Constantine. The approbation of the soldiers was testified by a respectful murmur: they gazed on the manly countenance of Julian, and observed with pleasure that the fire which sparkled in his eyes was tempered by a modest blush on being thus exposed for the first time to the public view of mankind. As soon as the ceremony of his investiture had been performed, Constantius addressed him with the tone of authority which his superior age and station permitted him to assume; and, exhorting the new Cæsar to deserve, by heroic deeds, that sacred and immortal name, the emperor gave his colleague the strongest assurances of a friendship which should never be impaired by time, nor interrupted by their separation into the most distant climates. As soon as the speech was ended, the troops, as a token of applause, clashed their shields against their knees;[36] while the officers who surrounded the tribunal expressed, with decent reserve, their sense of the merits of the representative of Constantius.

The two princes returned to the palace in the same chariot; and, during the slow procession, Julian repeated to himself a verse of his favourite Homer, which he might equally apply to his fortune and to his fears.[37] The four-and-twenty days which the Cæsar spent at Milan after his investiture, and the first months of his Gallic reign, were devoted to a splendid but severe captivity; nor could the acquisition of honour compensate for the loss of freedom.[38] His steps were watched, his correspondence was intercepted; and he was obliged, by prudence, to decline the visits of his most intimate friends. Of his former domestics four only were permitted to attend him—two pages, his physician, and his librarian; the last of whom was employed in the care of a valuable collection of books, the gifts of the empress, who studied the inclinations as well as the interest of her friend. In the room of these faithful servants an household was formed, such, indeed, as became the dignity of a Cæsar; but it was filled with a crowd of slaves, destitute, and perhaps incapable, of any attachment for their new master, to whom, for the most part, they were either unknown or suspected. His want of experience might require the assistance of a wise council; but the minute instructions which regulated the service of his table, and the distribution of his hours, were adapted to a youth still under the discipline of his preceptors rather than to the situation of a prince intrusted with the conduct of an important war. If he aspired to deserve the esteem of his subjects, he was checked by the fear of displeasing his sovereign; and even the fruits of his marriagebed were blasted by the jealous artifices of Eusebia[39] herself, who, on this occasion alone, seems to have been unmindful of the tenderness of her sex and the generosity of her character. The memory of his father and of his brothers reminded Julian of his own danger, and his apprehensions were increased by the recent and unworthy fate of Sylvanus. In the summer which preceded his own elevation that general had been chosen to deliver Gaul from the tyranny of the barbarians; but Sylvanus soon discovered that he had left his most dangerous enemies in the Imperial court. A dexterous informer, countenanced by several of the principal ministers, procured from him some recommendatory letters; and, erasing the whole of the contents, except the signature, filled up the vacant parchment with matters of high and treasonable import. By the industry and courage of his friends the fraud was, however, detected, and in a great council of the civil and military officers, held in the presence of the emperor himself, the innocence of Sylvanus was publicly acknowledged. But the discovery came too late; the report of the calumny, and the hasty seizure of his estate, had already provoked the indignant chief to the rebellion of which he was so unjustly accused. He assumed the purple at his headquarters of Cologne, and his active powers appeared to menace Italy with an invasion and Milan with a siege. In this emergency Ursicinus, a general of equal rank, regained, by an act of treachery, the favour which he had lost by his eminent services in the East. Exasperated, as he might speciously allege, by injuries of a similar nature, he hastened with a few followers to join the standard, and to betray the confidence, of his too credulous friend. After a reign of only twenty-eight days Sylvanus was assassinated: the soldiers who, without any criminal intention, had blindly followed the example of their leader, immediately returned to their allegiance; and the flatterers of Constantius celebrated the wisdom and felicity of the monarch who had extinguished a civil war without the hazard of a battle.[40]

The protection of the Rhætian frontier, and the persecution of the Catholic church, detained Constantius in Italy above eighteen months after the departure of Julian. Before the emperor returned into the East he indulged his pride and curiosity in a visit to the ancient capital.[41] He proceeded from Milan to Rome along the Æmilian and Flaminian ways; and as soon as he approached within forty miles of the city, the march of a prince who had never vanquished a foreign enemy assumed the appearance of a triumphal procession. His splendid train was composed of all the ministers of luxury; but in a time of profound peace he was encompassed by the glittering arms of the numerous squadrons of his guards and cuirassiers. Their streaming banners of silk, embossed with gold, and shaped in the form of dragons, waved round the person of the emperor. Constantius sat alone in a lofty car resplendent with gold and precious gems; and, except when he bowed his head to pass under the gates of the cities, he affected a stately demeanour of inflexible, and, as it might seem, of insensible gravity. The severe discipline of the Persian youth had been introduced by the eunuchs into the Imperial palace; and such were the habits of patience which they had inculcated, that, during a slow and sultry march, he was never seen to move his hand towards his face, or to turn his eyes either to the right or to the left. He was received by the magistrates and senate of Rome; and the emperor surveyed, with attention, the civil honours of the republic and the consular images of the noble families. The streets were lined with an innumerable multitude. Their repeated acclamations expressed their joy at beholding, after an absence of thirty-two years, the sacred person of their sovereign; and Constantius himself expressed, with some pleasantry, his affected surprise that the human race should thus suddenly be collected on the same spot. The son of Constantine was lodged in the ancient palace of Augustus: he presided in the senate, harangued the people from the tribunal which Cicero had so often as-

cended, assisted with unusual courtesy at the games of the circus, and accepted the crowns of gold, as well as the panegyrics, which had been prepared for this ceremony by the deputies of the principal cities. His short visit of thirty days was employed in viewing the monuments of art and power which were scattered over the seven hills and the interjacent valleys. He admired the awful majesty of the Capitol, the vast extent of the baths of Caracalla and Diocletian, the severe simplicity of the Pantheon, the massy greatness of the amphitheatre of Titus, the elegant architecture of the theatre of Pompey and the Temple of Peace, and, above all, the stately structure of the Forum and column of Trajan; acknowledging that the voice of fame, so prone to invent and to magnify, had made an inadequate report of the metropolis of the world. The traveller who has contemplated the ruins of ancient Rome may conceive some imperfect idea of the sentiments which they must have inspired when they reared their heads in the splendour of unsullied beauty.

The satisfaction which Constantius had received from this journey excited him to the generous emulation of bestowing on the Romans some memorial of his own gratitude and munificence. His first idea was to imitate the equestrian and colossal statue which he had seen in the Forum of Trajan; but, when he had maturely weighed the difficulties of the execution,[42] he chose rather to embellish the capital by the gift of an Egyptian obelisk. In a remote but polished age, which seems to have preceded the invention of alphabetical writing, a great number of these obelisks had been erected, in the cities of Thebes and Heliopolis, by the ancient sovereigns of Egypt, in a just confidence that the simplicity of their form, and the hardness of their substance, would resist the injuries of time and violence.[43] Several of these extraordinary columns had been transported to Rome by Augustus and his successors as the most durable monuments of their power and victory;[44] but there remained one obelisk which, from its size or sanctity, escaped for a long time the rapacious vanity of the conquerors. It was designed by Constantine to adorn his new city;[45] and, after being removed by his order from the pedestal where it stood before the Temple of the Sun at Heliopolis, was floated down the Nile to Alexandria. The death of Constantine suspended the execution of his purpose, and this obelisk was destined by his son to the ancient capital of the empire. A vessel of uncommon strength and capaciousness was provided to convey this enormous weight of granite, at least an hundred and fifteen feet in length, from the banks of the Nile to those of the Tiber. The obelisk of Constantius was landed about three miles from the city, and elevated, by the efforts of art and labour, in the great circus of Rome.[46]

The departure of Constantius from Rome was hastened by the alarming intelligence of the distress and danger of the Illyrian provinces. The distractions of civil war, and the irreparable loss which the Roman legions had sustained in the battle of Mursa, exposed those countries, almost without defence, to the light cavalry of the barbarians; and particularly to the inroads of the Quadi, a fierce and powerful nation, who seem to have exchanged the institutions of Germany for the arms and military arts of their Sarmatian allies.[47] The garrisons of the frontier were insufficient to check their progress; and the indolent monarch was at length compelled to assemble, from the extremities of his dominions, the flower of the Palatine troops, to take the field in person, and to employ a whole campaign, with the preceding autumn and the ensuing spring, in the serious prosecution of the war. The emperor passed the Danube on a bridge of boats, cut in pieces all that encountered his march, penetrated into the heart of the country of the Quadi, and severely retaliated the calamities which they had inflicted on the Roman province. The dismayed barbarians were soon reduced to sue for peace: they offered the restitution of his captive subjects as an atonement for the past, and the noblest hostages as a pledge of their future conduct. The generous courtesy which was shown to the first among their chieftains who implored the clemency of Constantius encouraged the more timid, or the more obstinate, to imitate their example; and the Imperial camp was crowded with the princes and ambassadors of the most distant tribes, who occupied the plains of the Lesser Poland, and who might have deemed themselves secure behind the lofty ridge of the Carpathian mountains. While Constantius gave laws to the barbarians beyond the Danube, he distinguished, with specious compassion, the Sarmatian exiles, who had been expelled from their native country by the rebellion of their slaves, and who formed a very considerable accession to the power of the Quadi. The emperor, embracing a generous but artful system of policy, released the Sarmatians from the bands of this humiliating dependence, and restored them, by a separate treaty, to the dignity of a nation united under the government of a king, the friend and ally of the republic. He declared his resolution of asserting the justice of their cause, and of securing the peace of the provinces by the extirpation, or at least the banishment, of the Limigantes, whose manners were still infected with the vices of their servile origin. The execution of this design was attended with more difficulty than glory. The territory of the Limigantes was protected against the Romans by the Danube, against the hostile barbarians by the Theiss. The marshy lands which lay between those rivers, and were often covered by their inundations, formed an intricate wilderness, pervious only to the inhabitants, who were acquainted with its secret paths and inaccessible fortresses. On the approach of Constantius the Limigantes tried the efficacy of prayers, of fraud, and of arms; but he sternly rejected their supplications, defeated their rude stratagems, and repelled with skill and firmness the efforts of their irregular valour. One of their most warlike tribes, established in a small island towards the conflux of the Theiss and the Danube, consented to pass the river with the intention of surprising the emperor during the security of an amicable conference. They soon became the victims of the perfidy which they meditated. Encompassed on every side, trampled down by the cavalry, slaughtered by the swords of the legions, they disdained to ask for mercy; and, with an undaunted countenance, still grasped their weapons in the agonies of death. After this victory a considerable body of Romans was landed on the opposite banks of the Danube; the Taifalæ, a Gothic tribe engaged in the service of the empire, invaded the Limigantes on the side of the Theiss; and their former masters, the free Sarmatians, animated by hope and revenge, penetrated through the hilly country into the heart of their ancient possessions. A general conflagration revealed the huts of the barbarians, which were seated in the depth of the wilderness; and the soldier fought with confidence on marshy ground, which it was dangerous for him to tread. In this extremity the bravest of the Limigantes were resolved to die in arms rather than to yield: but the milder sentiment, enforced by the authority of their elders, at length prevailed; and the suppliant crowd, followed by their wives and children, repaired to the Imperial camp to learn their fate from the mouth of the conqueror. After celebrating his own clemency, which was still inclined to pardon their repeated crimes, and to spare the remnant of a guilty nation, Constantius assigned for the place of their exile a remote country, where they might enjoy a safe and honourable repose. The Limigantes obeyed with reluctance; but before they could reach, at least before they could occupy, their destined habitations, they returned to the banks of the Danube, exaggerating the hardships of their situation, and requesting, with fervent professions of fidelity, that the emperor would grant them an undisturbed settlement within the limits of the Roman provinces. Instead of consulting his own experience of their incurable perfidy, Constantius listened to his flatterers, who were ready to represent the honour and advantage of accepting a colony of soldiers, at a time when it was much easier to obtain the pecuniary contributions than the military service of the subjects of the empire. The Limigantes were permitted to pass the Danube; and the emperor gave audience to the multitude in a large plain near the modern city of Buda. They surrounded the tribunal, and seemed to hear with respect an oration full of mildness and dignity; when one of the barbarians, casting his shoe into the air, exclaimed with a loud voice, *Marha! Marha!* a word of defiance, which was received as the signal of the tumult. They rushed with fury to seize the person of the emperor; his royal throne and golden couch were pillaged by these rude hands; but the faithful defence of his guards, who died at his feet, allowed him a moment to mount a fleet horse, and to escape from the confusion. The disgrace which had been incurred by a treacherous surprise was soon retrieved by the numbers and discipline of the Romans; and the combat was only terminated by the extinction of the name and nation of the Limigantes. The free Sarmatians were reinstated in the possession of their ancient seats; and although Constantius distrusted the levity of their character, he entertained some hopes that a sense of gratitude might influence their future conduct. He had remarked the lofty stature and obsequious demeanour of Zizais, one of the noblest of their chiefs. He conferred on him the title of King; and Zizais proved that he was not unworthy to reign, by a sincere and lasting attachment to the interest of his benefactor, who, after this splendid success, received the name of *Sarmaticus* from the acclamations of his victorious army.[48]

While the Roman emperor and the Persian monarch, at the distance of three thousand miles, defended their extreme limits against the barbarians of the Danube and of the Oxus, their intermediate frontier experienced the vicissitudes of a languid war and a precarious truce. Two of the eastern ministers of Constantius, the Prætorian præfect Musonian, whose abilities were disgraced by the want of truth and integrity, and Cassian duke of Mesopotamia, a hardy and veteran soldier, opened a secret negotiation with the satrap Tamsapor.[49] These overtures of peace, translated into the servile and flattering language of Asia, were transmitted to the camp of the Great King, who resolved to signify, by an ambassador, the terms which he was inclined to grant to the suppliant Romans. Narses, whom he invested with that character, was honourably received in his passage through Antioch and Constantinople: he reached Sirmium after a long journey, and, at his first audience, respectfully unfolded the silken veil which covered the haughty epistle of his sovereign. Sapor, King of Kings, and Brother of the Sun and Moon (such were the lofty titles affected by oriental vanity), expressed his satisfaction that his brother, Constantius Cæsar, had been taught wisdom by adversity. As the lawful successor of Darius Hystaspes, Sapor asserted that the river Strymon, in Macedonia, was the true and ancient boundary of his empire; declaring, however, that, as an evidence of his moderation, he would content himself with the provinces of Armenia and Mesopotamia, which had been fraudulently extorted from his ancestors. He alleged that, without the restitution of these disputed countries, it was impossible to establish any treaty on a solid and permanent basis; and he arrogantly threatened that, if his ambassador returned in vain, he was prepared to take the field in the spring, and to support the justice of his cause by the strength of his invincible arms. Narses, who was endowed with the most polite and amiable manners, endeavoured, as far as was consistent with his duty, to soften the harshness of the message.[50] Both the style and substance were maturely weighed in the Imperial council, and he was dismissed with the following answer: "Constantius had a right to disclaim the officiousness of his ministers, who had acted without any specific orders from the throne: he was not, however, averse to an equal and honourable treaty; but it was highly indecent, as well as absurd, to propose to the sole and victorious emperor of the Roman world the same conditions of peace which he had indignantly rejected at the time when his power was contracted within the narrow limits of the East: the chance of arms was uncertain; and Sapor should recollect that, if the Romans had sometimes been vanquished in battle, they had almost always been successful in the event of the war." A few days after the departure of

Narses, three ambassadors were sent to the court of Sapor, who was already returned from the Scythian expedition to his ordinary residence of Ctesiphon. A count, a notary, and a sophist, had been selected for this important commission; and Constantius, who was secretly anxious for the conclusion of the peace, entertained some hopes that the dignity of the first of these ministers, the dexterity of the second, and the rhetoric of the third,[51] would persuade the Persian monarch to abate the rigour of his demands. But the progress of their negotiation was opposed and defeated by the hostile arts of Antoninus,[52] a Roman subject of Syria, who had fled from oppression, and was admitted into the councils of Sapor, and even to the royal table, where, according to the custom of the Persians, the most important business was frequently discussed.[53] The dexterous fugitive promoted his interest by the same conduct which gratified his revenge. He incessantly urged the ambition of his new master to embrace the favourable opportunity when the bravest of the Palatine troops were employed with the emperor in a distant war on the Danube. He pressed Sapor to invade the exhausted and defenceless provinces of the East, with the numerous armies of Persia, now fortified by the alliance and accession of the fiercest barbarians. The ambassadors of Rome retired without success, and a second embassy, of a still more honourable rank, was detained in strict confinement, and threatened either with death or exile.

The military historian,[54] who was himself despatched to observe the army of the Persians, as they were preparing to construct a bridge of boats over the Tigris, beheld from an eminence the plain of Assyria, as far as the edge of the horizon, covered with men, with horses, and with arms. Sapor appeared in the front, conspicuous by the splendour of his purple. On his left hand, the place of honour among the Orientals, Grumbates, king of the Chionites, displayed the stern countenance of an aged and renowned warrior. The monarch had reserved a similar place on his right hand for the king of the Albanians, who led his independent tribes from the shores of the Caspian. The satraps and generals were distributed according to their several ranks, and the whole army, besides the numerous train of oriental luxury, consisted of more than one hundred thousand effective men, inured to fatigue, and selected from the bravest nations of Asia. The Roman deserter, who in some measure guided the councils of Sapor, had prudently advised, that, instead of wasting the

summer in tedious and difficult sieges, he should march directly to the Euphrates, and press forwards without delay to seize the feeble and wealthy metropolis of Syria. But the Persians were no sooner advanced into the plains of Mesopotamia than they discovered that every precaution had been used which could retard their progress or defeat their design. The inhabitants with their cattle were secured in places of strength, the green forage throughout the country was set on fire, the fords of the river were fortified by sharp stakes, military engines were planted on the opposite banks, and a seasonable swell of the waters of the Euphrates deterred the barbarians from attempting the ordinary passage of the bridge of Thapsacus. Their skilful guide, changing his plan of operations, then conducted the army by a longer circuit, but through a fertile territory, towards the head of the Euphrates, where the infant river is reduced to a shallow and accessible stream. Sapor overlooked, with prudent disdain, the strength of Nisibis; but as he passed under the walls of Amida, he resolved to try whether the majesty of his presence would not awe the garrison into immediate submission. The sacrilegious insult of a random dart, which glanced against the royal tiara, convinced him of his error; and the indignant monarch listened with impatience to the advice of his ministers, who conjured him not to sacrifice the success of his ambition to the gratification of his resentment. The following day Grumbates advanced towards the gates with a select body of troops, and required the instant surrender of the city, as the only atonement which could be accepted for such an act of rashness and insolence. His proposals were answered by a general discharge, and his only son, a beautiful and valiant youth, was pierced through the heart by a javelin, shot from one of the balistæ. The funeral of the prince of the Chionites was celebrated according to the rites of his country; and the grief of his aged father was alleviated by the solemn promise of Sapor, that the guilty city of Amida should serve as a funeral pile to expiate the death, and to perpetuate the memory, of his son.

The ancient city of Amid or Amida,[55] which sometimes assumes the provincial appellation of Diarbekir,[56] is advantageously situate in a fertile plain, watered by the natural and artificial channels of the Tigris, of which the least inconsiderable stream bends in a semicircular form round the eastern part of the city. The emperor Constantius had recently conferred on Amida the honour of his own name, and the additional fortifications of strong walls and lofty towers. It was provided with an arsenal of military engines, and the ordinary garrison had been reinforced to the amount of seven legions, when the place was invested by the arms of Sapor.[57] His first and most sanguine hopes depended on the success of a general assault. To the several nations which followed his standard their respective posts were assigned; the south to the Vertæ; the north to the Albanians; the east to the Chionites, inflamed with grief and indignation; the west to the Segestans, the bravest of his warriors, who covered their front with a formidable line of Indian elephants.[58] The Persians, on every side, supported their efforts, and animated their courage; and the monarch himself, careless of his rank and safety, displayed, in the prosecution of the siege, the ardour of a youthful soldier. After an obstinate combat the barbarians were repulsed; they incessantly returned to the charge; they were again driven back with a dreadful slaughter, and two rebel legions of Gauls, who had been banished into the East, signalised their undisciplined courage by a nocturnal sally into the heart of the Persian camp. In one of the fiercest of these repeated assaults, Amida was betrayed by the treachery of a deserter, who indicated to the barbarians a secret and neglected staircase, scooped out of the rock that hangs over the stream of the Tigris. Seventy chosen archers of the royal guard ascended in silence to the third story of a lofty tower, which commanded the precipice; they elevated on high the Persian banner, the signal of confidence to the assailants, and of dismay to the besieged; and if this devoted band could have maintained their post a few minutes longer, the reduction of the place might have been purchased by the sacrifice of their lives. After Sapor had tried, without success, the efficacy of force and of stratagem, he had recourse to the slower but more certain operations of a regular siege, in the conduct of which he was instructed by the skill of the Roman deserters. The trenches were opened at a convenient distance, and the troops destined for that service advanced, under the portable cover of strong hurdles, to fill up the ditch, and undermine the foundations of the walls. Wooden towers were at the same time constructed, and moved forwards on wheels, till the soldiers, who were provided with every species of missile weapons, could engage almost on level ground with the troops who defended the rampart. Every mode of resistance which art could suggest, or courage could execute, was employed in the defence of Amida,

and the works of Sapor were more than once destroyed by the fire of the Romans. But the resources of a besieged city may be exhausted. The Persians repaired their losses and pushed their approaches; a large breach was made by the battering-ram, and the strength of the garrison, wasted by the sword and by disease, yielded to the fury of the assault. The soldiers, the citizens, their wives, their children, all who had not time to escape through the opposite gate, were involved by the conquerors in a promiscuous massacre.

But the ruin of Amida was the safety of the Roman provinces. As soon as the first transports of victory had subsided, Sapor was at leisure to reflect that to chastise a disobedient city he had lost the flower of his troops and the most favourable season for conquest.[59] Thirty thousand of his veterans had fallen under the walls of Amida during the continuance of a siege which lasted seventy-three days; and the disappointed monarch returned to his capital with affected triumph and secret mortification. It is more than probable that the inconstancy of his barbarian allies was tempted to relinquish a war in which they had encountered such unexpected difficulties; and that the aged king of the Chionites, satiated with revenge, turned away with horror from a scene of action where he had been deprived of the hope of his family and nation. The strength as well as spirit of the army with which Sapor took the field in the ensuing spring was no longer equal to the unbounded views of his ambition. Instead of aspiring to the conquest of the East, he was obliged to content himself with the reduction of two fortified cities of Mesopotamia, Singara and Bezabde;[60] the one situate in the midst of a sandy desert, the other in a small peninsula, surrounded almost on every side by the deep and rapid stream of the Tigris. Five Roman legions, of the diminutive size to which they had been reduced in the age of Constantine, were made prisoners, and sent into remote captivity on the extreme confines of Persia. After dismantling the walls of Singara, the conqueror abandoned that solitary and sequestered place; but he carefully restored the fortifications of Bezabde, and fixed in that important post a garrison or colony of veterans, amply supplied with every means of defence, and animated by high sentiments of honour and fidelity. Towards the close of the campaign the arms of Sapor incurred some disgrace by an unsuccessful enterprise against Virtha, or Tecrit, a strong, or, as it was universally esteemed till the age of Tamerlane, an impregnable fortress of the independent Arabs.[61]

The defence of the East against the arms of Sapor required, and would have exercised, the abilities of the most consummate general; and it seemed fortunate for the state that it was the actual province of the brave Ursicinus, who alone deserved the confidence of the soldiers and people. In the hour of danger Ursicinus[62] was removed from his station by the intrigues of the eunuchs; and the military command of the East was bestowed, by the same influence, on Sabinian, a wealthy and subtle veteran, who had attained the infirmities, without acquiring the experience, of age. By a second order, which issued from the same jealous and inconstant counsels, Ursicinus was again despatched to the frontier of Mesopotamia, and condemned to sustain the labours of a war, the honours of which had been transferred to his unworthy rival. Sabinian fixed his indolent station under the walls of Edessa; and while he amused himself with the idle parade of military exercise, and moved to the sound of flutes in the Pyrrhic dance, the public defence was abandoned to the boldness and diligence of the former general of the East. But whenever Ursicinus recommended any vigorous plan of operations; when he proposed, at the head of a light and active army, to wheel round the foot of the mountains, to intercept the convoys of the enemy, to harass the wide extent of the Persian lines, and to relieve the distress of Amida; the timid and envious commander alleged that he was restrained by his positive orders from endangering the safety of the troops. Amida was at length taken; its bravest defenders, who had escaped the sword of the barbarians, died in the Roman camp by the hand of the executioner; and Ursicinus himself, after supporting the disgrace of a partial inquiry, was punished for the misconduct of Sabinian by the loss of his military rank. But Constantius soon experienced the truth of the prediction which honest indignation had extorted from his injured lieutenant, that, as long as such maxims of government were suffered to prevail, the emperor himself would find it no easy task to defend his eastern dominions from the invasion of a foreign enemy. When he had subdued or pacified the barbarians of the Danube, Constantius proceeded by slow marches into the East; and after he had wept over the smoking ruins of Amida, he formed, with a powerful army, the siege of Bezabde. The walls were shaken by the reiterated efforts of the most enormous of the battering-rams; the town was reduced to the last extremity; but it was still defended by the patient and intrepid valour of the garrison, till the approach of the rainy season obliged the emperor to raise the siege, and ingloriously to retreat into his winter-quarters at Antioch.[63] The pride of Constantius, and the ingenuity of his courtiers, were at a loss to discover any materials for panegyric in the events of the Persian war; while the glory of his cousin Julian, to whose military command he had intrusted the provinces of Gaul, was proclaimed to the world in the simple and concise narrative of his exploits.

In the blind fury of civil discord, Constantius had abandoned to the barbarians of Germany the countries of Gaul, which still acknowledged the authority of his rival. A numerous swarm of Franks and Alemanni were invited to cross the Rhine by presents and promises, by the hopes of spoil, and by a perpetual grant of all the territories which they should be able to subdue.[64] But the emperor, who for a temporary service had thus imprudently provoked the rapacious spirit of the barbarians, soon discovered and lamented the difficulty of dismissing these formidable allies, after they had tasted the richness of the Roman soil. Regardless of the nice distinction of loyalty and rebellion, these undisciplined robbers treated as their natural enemies all the subjects of the empire who possessed any property which they were desirous of acquiring. Forty-five flourishing cities, Tongres, Cologne, Treves, Worms, Spires, Strasburg, etc., besides a far greater number of towns and villages, were pillaged, and for the most part reduced to ashes. The barbarians of Germany, still faithful to the maxims of their ancestors, abhorred the confinement of walls, to which they applied the odious names of prisons and sepulchres; and, fixing their independent habitations on the banks of rivers, the Rhine, the Moselle, and the Meuse, they secured themselves against the danger of a surprise, by a rude and hasty fortification of large trees, which were felled and thrown across the roads. The Alemanni were established in the modern countries of Alsace and Lorraine; the Franks occupied the island of the Batavians, together with an extensive district of Brabant, which was then known by the appellation of Toxandria,[65] and may deserve to be considered as the original seat of their Gallic monarchy.[66] From the sources to the mouth of the Rhine, the conquests of the Germans extended above forty miles to the west of that river, over a country peopled by colonies of their own name and nation; and the scene of their devastations was three times more extensive than that of their conquests. At a still greater distance the open towns of Gaul were deserted, and the inhabitants of the fortified cities, who trusted to their strength and vigilance, were obliged to content themselves with such supplies of corn as they could raise on the vacant land within the enclosure of their walls. The diminished legions, destitute of pay and provisions, of arms and discipline, trembled at the approach, and even at the name, of the barbarians.

Under these melancholy circumstances, an inexperienced youth was appointed to save and to govern the provinces of Gaul, or rather, as he expresses it himself, to exhibit the vain image of Imperial greatness. The retired scholastic education of Julian, in which he had been more conversant with books than with arms, with the dead than with the living, left him in profound ignorance of the practical arts of war and government; and when he awkwardly repeated some military exercise which it was necessary for him to learn, he exclaimed with a sigh, "O Plato, Plato, what a task for a philosopher!" Yet even this speculative philosophy, which men of business are too apt to despise, had filled the mind of Julian with the noblest precepts and the most shining examples; had animated him with the love of virtue, the desire of fame, and the contempt of death. The habits of temperance recommended in the schools are still more essential in the severe discipline of a camp. The simple wants of nature regulated the measure of his food and sleep. Rejecting with disdain the delicacies provided for his table, he satisfied his appetite with the coarse and common fare which was allotted to the meanest soldiers. During the rigour of a Gallic winter he never suffered a fire in his bedchamber; and after a short and interrupted slumber, he frequently rose in the middle of the night from a carpet spread on the floor, to despatch any urgent business, to visit his rounds, or to steal a few moments for the prosecution of his favourite studies.[67] The precepts of eloquence, which he had hitherto practised on fancied topics of declamation, were more usefully applied to excite or to assuage the passions of an armed multitude: and although Julian, from his early habits of conversation and literature, was more familiarly acquainted with the beauties of the Greek language, he had attained a competent knowledge of the Latin tongue.[68] Since Julian was not originally designed for the character of a legislator or a judge, it is probable that the civil jurisprudence of the Romans had not engaged any con-

siderable share of his attention: but he derived from his philosophic studies an inflexible regard for justice, tempered by a disposition to clemency, the knowledge of the general principles of equity and evidence, and the faculty of patiently investigating the most intricate and tedious questions which could be proposed for his discussion. The measures of policy, and the operations of war, must submit to the various accidents of circumstance and character, and the unpractised student will often be perplexed in the application of the most perfect theory. But in the acquisition of this important science Julian was assisted by the active vigour of his own genius, as well as by the wisdom and experience of Sallust, an officer of rank, who soon conceived a sincere attachment for a prince so worthy of his friendship; and whose incorruptible integrity was adorned by the talent of insinuating the harshest truths without wounding the delicacy of a royal ear.[69]

Immediately after Julian had received the purple at Milan he was sent into Gaul with a feeble retinue of three hundred and sixty soldiers. At Vienna, where he passed a painful and anxious winter, in the hands of those ministers to whom Constantius had intrusted the direction of his conduct, the Cæsar was informed of the siege and deliverance of Autun. That large and ancient city, protected only by a ruined wall and pusillanimous garrison, was saved by the generous resolution of a few veterans, who resumed their arms for the defence of their country. In his march from Autun, through the heart of the Gallic provinces, Julian embraced with ardour the earliest opportunity of signalising his courage. At the head of a small body of archers and heavy cavalry, he preferred the shorter but the more dangerous of two roads; and sometimes eluding and sometimes resisting the attacks of the barbarians, who were masters of the field, he arrived with honour and safety at the camp near Rheims, where the Roman troops had been ordered to assemble. The aspect of their young prince revived the drooping spirit of the soldiers, and they marched from Rheims in search of the enemy with a confidence which had almost proved fatal to them. The Alemanni, familiarised to the knowledge of the country, secretly collected their scattered forces, and, seizing the opportunity of a dark and rainy day, poured with unexpected fury on the rear-guard of the Romans. Before the inevitable disorder could be remedied, two legions were destroyed; and Julian was taught by experience that caution and vigilance are the most important lessons of the art of war. In a second and more successful action he recovered and established his military fame; but as the agility of the barbarians saved them from the pursuit, his victory was neither bloody nor decisive. He advanced, however, to the banks of the Rhine, surveyed the ruins of Cologne, convinced himself of the difficulties of the war, and retreated on the approach of winter, discontented with the court, with his army, and with his own success.[70] The power of the enemy was yet unbroken; and the Cæsar had no sooner separated his troops, and fixed his own quarters at Sens, in the centre of Gaul, than he was surrounded and besieged by a numerous host of Germans. Reduced in this extremity to the resources of his own mind, he displayed a prudent intrepidity which compensated for all the deficiencies of the place and garrison; and the barbarians, at the end of thirty days, were obliged to retire with disappointed rage.

The conscious pride of Julian, who was indebted only to his sword for this signal deliverance, was embittered by the reflection that he was abandoned, betrayed, and perhaps devoted to destruction, by those who were bound to assist him by every tie of honour and fidelity. Marcellus, master-general of the cavalry in Gaul, interpreting too strictly the jealous orders of the court, beheld with supine indifference the distress of Julian, and had restrained the troops under his command from marching to the relief of Sens. If the Cæsar had dissembled in silence so dangerous an insult, his person and authority would have been exposed to the contempt of the world; and if an action so criminal had been suffered to pass with impunity, the emperor would have confirmed the suspicions which received a very specious colour from this conduct towards the princes of the Flavian family. Marcellus was recalled, and gently dismissed from his office.[71] In his room Severus was appointed general of the cavalry; an experienced soldier, of approved courage and fidelity, who could advise with respect, and execute with zeal; and who submitted, without reluctance, to the supreme command which Julian, by the interest of his patroness Eusebia, at length obtained over the armies of Gaul.[72] A very judicious plan of operations was adopted for the approaching campaign. Julian himself, at the head of the remains of the veteran bands, and of some new levies which he had been permitted to form, boldly penetrated into the centre of the German cantonments, and carefully reestablished the fortifications of Saverne, in an advantageous

post which would either check the incursions or intercept the retreat of the enemy. At the same time Barbatio, general of the infantry, advanced from Milan with an army of thirty thousand men, and, passing the mountains, prepared to throw a bridge over the Rhine, in the neighbourhood of Basil. It was reasonable to expect that the Alemanni, pressed on either side by the Roman arms, would soon be forced to evacuate the provinces of Gaul, and to hasten to the defence of their native country. But the hopes of the campaign were defeated by the incapacity, or the envy, or the secret instructions of Barbatio, who acted as if he had been the enemy of the Cæsar, and the secret ally of the barbarians. The negligence with which he permitted a troop of pillagers freely to pass, and to return, almost before the gates of his camp, may be imputed to his want of abilities; but the treasonable act of burning a number of boats, and a superfluous stock of provisions, which would have been of the most essential service to the army of Gaul, was an evidence of his hostile and criminal intentions. The Germans despised an enemy who appeared destitute either of power or of inclination to offend them; and the ignominious retreat of Barbatio deprived Julian of the expected support, and left him to extricate himself from a hazardous situation, where he could neither remain with safety, nor retire with honour.[73]

As soon as they were delivered from the fears of invasion, the Alemanni prepared to chastise the Roman youth who presumed to dispute the possession of that country which they claimed as their own by the right of conquest and of treaties. They employed three days, and as many nights, in transporting over the Rhine their military powers. The fierce Chnodomar, shaking the ponderous javelin which he had victoriously wielded against the brother of Magnentius, led the van of the barbarians, and moderated by his experience the martial ardour which his example inspired.[74] He was followed by six other kings, by ten princes of regal extraction, by a long train of high-spirited nobles, and by thirty-five thousand of the bravest warriors of the tribes of Germany. The confidence derived from the view of their own strength was increased by the intelligence which they received from a deserter, that the Cæsar, with a feeble army of thirteen thousand men, occupied a post about one-and-twenty miles from their camp of Strasburg. With this inadequate force Julian resolved to seek and to encounter the barbarian host; and the chance of a general action was preferred to the tedious and uncertain operation of separately engaging the dispersed parties of the Alemanni. The Romans marched in close order, and in two columns; the cavalry on the right, the infantry on the left; and the day was so far spent when they appeared in sight of the enemy, that Julian was desirous of deferring the battle till the next morning, and of allowing his troops to recruit their exhausted strength by the necessary refreshments of sleep and food. Yielding, however, with some reluctance, to the clamours of the soldiers, and even to the opinion of his council, he exhorted them to justify by their valour the eager impatience which, in case of a defeat, would be universally branded with the epithets of rashness and presumption. The trumpets sounded, the military shout was heard through the field, and the two armies rushed with equal fury to the charge. The Cæsar, who conducted in person his right wing, depended on the dexterity of his archers and the weight of his cuirassiers. But his ranks were instantly broken by an irregular mixture of light-horse and of light-infantry, and he had the mortification of beholding the flight of six hundred of his most renowned cuirassiers.[75] The fugitives were stopped and rallied by the presence and authority of Julian, who, careless of his own safety, threw himself before them, and, urging every motive of shame and honour, led them back against the victorious enemy. The conflict between the two lines of infantry was obstinate and bloody. The Germans possessed the superiority of strength and stature, the Romans that of discipline and temper; and as the barbarians who served under the standard of the empire united the respective advantages of both parties, their strenuous efforts, guided by a skilful leader, at length determined the event of the day. The Romans lost four tribunes, and two hundred and forty-three soldiers, in this memorable battle of Strasburg, so glorious to the Cæsar,[76] and so salutary to the afflicted provinces of Gaul. Six thousand of the Alemanni were slain in the field, without including those who were drowned in the Rhine, or transfixed with darts whilst they attempted to swim across the river.[77] Chnodomar himself was surrounded and taken prisoner, with three of his brave companions, who had devoted themselves to follow in life or death the fate of their chieftain. Julian received him with military pomp in the council of his officers; and expressing a generous pity for the fallen state, dissembled his inward contempt for the abject humiliation of his captive. Instead of exhibiting the vanquished king of the Alemanni as a grateful spectacle to the cities of Gaul, he respectfully laid at the feet of the emperor this splendid trophy of his victory. Chnodomar experienced an honourable treatment: but the impatient barbarian could not long survive his defeat, his confinement, and his exile.[78]

After Julian had repulsed the Alemanni from the provinces of the Upper Rhine, he turned his arms against the Franks, who were seated nearer to the ocean, on the confines of Gaul and Germany; and who, from their numbers, and still more from their intrepid valour, had ever been esteemed the most formidable of the barbarians.[79] Although they were strongly actuated by the allurements of rapine, they professed a disinterested love of war, which they considered as the supreme honour and felicity of human nature; and their minds and bodies were so completely hardened by perpetual action, that, according to the lively expression of an orator, the snows of winter were as pleasant to them as the flowers of spring. In the month of December which followed the battle of Strasburg, Julian attacked a body of six hundred Franks who had thrown themselves into two castles on the Meuse.[80] In the midst of that severe season they sustained, with inflexible constancy, a siege of fifty-four days, till at length, exhausted by hunger, and satisfied that the vigilance of the enemy in breaking the ice of the river left them no hopes of escape, the Franks consented, for the first time, to dispense with the ancient law which commanded them to conquer or to die. The Cæsar immediately sent his captives to the court of Constantius, who, accepting them as a valuable present,[81] rejoiced in the opportunity of adding so many heroes to the choicest troops of his domestic guards. The obstinate resistance of this handful of Franks apprised Julian of the difficulties of the expedition which he meditated for the ensuing spring against the whole body of the nation. His rapid diligence surprised and astonished the active barbarians. Ordering his soldiers to provide themselves with biscuit for twenty days, he suddenly pitched his camp near Tongres, while the enemy still supposed him in his winter-quarters of Paris, expecting the slow arrival of his convoys from Aquitain. Without allowing the Franks to unite or to deliberate, he skilfully spread his legions from Cologne to the ocean; and by the terror, as well as by the success of his arms, soon reduced the suppliant tribes to implore the clemency and to obey the commands of their conqueror. The Chamavians submissively retired to their former habitations beyond the Rhine; but the Salians were permitted to possess their new establishment of Toxandria, as the subjects and auxiliaries of the Roman empire.[82] The treaty was ratified by solemn oaths; and perpetual inspectors were appointed to reside among the Franks, with the authority of enforcing the strict observance of the conditions. An incident is related, interesting enough in itself, and by no means repugnant to the character of Julian, who ingeniously contrived both the plot and the catastrophe of the tragedy. When the Chamavians sued for peace, he required the son of their king, as the only hostage on whom he could rely. A mournful silence, interrupted by tears and groans, declared the sad perplexity of the barbarians; and their aged chief lamented, in pathetic language, that his private loss was now embittered by a sense of the public calamity. While the Chamavians lay prostrate at the foot of his throne, the royal captive, whom they believed to have been slain, unexpectedly appeared before their eyes; and as soon as the tumult of joy was hushed into attention, the Cæsar addressed the assembly in the following terms:—"Behold the son, the prince, whom you wept. You had lost him by your fault. God and the Romans have restored him to you. I shall still preserve and educate the youth, rather as a monument of my own virtue than as a pledge of your sincerity. Should you presume to violate the faith which you have sworn, the arms of the republic will avenge the perfidy, not on the innocent, but on the guilty." The barbarians withdrew from his presence, impressed with the warmest sentiments of gratitude and admiration.[83]

It was not enough for Julian to have delivered the provinces of Gaul from the barbarians of Germany. He aspired to emulate the glory of the first and most illustrious of the emperors; after whose example he composed his own commentaries of the Gallic war.[84] Cæsar has related, with conscious pride, the manner in which *twice* passed the Rhine. Julian could boast that, before he assumed the title of Augustus, he had carried the Roman eagles beyond that great river in *three* successful expeditions.[85] The consternation of the Germans after the battle of Strasburg encouraged him to the first attempt; and the reluctance of the troops soon yielded to the persuasive eloquence of a leader who shared the fatigues and dangers which he imposed on the meanest of the soldiers. The villages on either side of the Main, which were plentifully stored with corn and cattle, felt the ravages of an invading army. The principal houses, constructed with some imita-

tion of Roman elegance, were consumed by the flames; and the Cæsar boldly advanced about ten miles, till his progress was stopped by a dark and impenetrable forest, undermined by subterraneous passages, which threatened with secret snares and ambush every step of the assailant. The ground was already covered with snow; and Julian, after repairing an ancient castle which had been erected by Trajan, granted a truce of ten months to the submissive barbarians. At the expiration of the truce Julian undertook a second expedition beyond the Rhine, to humble the pride of Surmar and Hortaire, two of the kings of the Alemanni, who had been present at the battle of Strasburg. They promised to restore all the Roman captives who yet remained alive; and as the Cæsar had procured an exact account from the cities and villages of Gaul of the inhabitants whom they had lost, he detected every attempt to deceive him with a degree of readiness and accuracy which almost established the belief of his supernatural knowledge. His third expedition was still more splendid and important than the two former. The Germans had collected their military powers, and moved along the opposite banks of the river, with a design of destroying the bridge, and of preventing the passage of the Romans. But this judicious plan of defence was disconcerted by a skilful diversion. Three hundred light-armed and active soldiers were detached in forty small boats, to fall down the stream in silence, and to land at some distance from the posts of the enemy. They executed their orders with so much boldness and celerity, that they had almost surprised the barbarian chiefs, who returned in the fearless confidence of intoxication from one of their nocturnal festivals. Without repeating the uniform and disgusting tale of slaughter and devastation, it is sufficient to observe that Julian dictated his own conditions of peace to six of the haughtiest kings of the Alemanni, three of whom were permitted to view the severe discipline and martial pomp of a Roman camp. Followed by twenty thousand captives, whom he had rescued from the chains of the barbarians, the Cæsar repassed the Rhine, after terminating a war the success of which has been compared to the ancient glories of the Punic and Cimbric victories.

As soon as the valour and conduct of Julian had secured an interval of peace, he applied himself to a work more congenial to his humane and philosophic temper. The cities of Gaul, which had suffered from the inroads of the barbarians, he diligently repaired; and seven important posts, between Mentz and the mouth of the Rhine, are particularly mentioned as having been rebuilt and fortified by the order of Julian.[86] The vanquished Germans had submitted to the just but humiliating condition of preparing and conveying the necessary materials. The active zeal of Julian urged the prosecution of the work; and such was the spirit which he had diffused among the troops, that the auxiliaries themselves, waiving their exemption from any duties of fatigue, contended in the most servile labours with the diligence of the Roman soldiers. It was incumbent on the Cæsar to provide for the subsistence as well as for the safety of the inhabitants and of the garrisons. The desertion of the former, and the mutiny of the latter, must have been the fatal and inevitable consequences of famine. The tillage of the provinces of Gaul had been interrupted by the calamities of war; but the scanty harvests of the continent were supplied, by his paternal care, from the plenty of the adjacent island. Six hundred large barques, framed in the forest of the Ardennes, made several voyages to the coast of Britain; and returning from thence, laden with corn, sailed up the Rhine, and distributed their cargoes to the several towns and fortresses along the banks of the river.[87] The arms of Julian had restored a free and secure navigation, which Constantius had offered to purchase at the expense of his dignity, and of a tributary present of two thousand pounds of silver. The emperor parsimoniously refused to his soldiers the sums which he granted with a lavish and trembling hand to the barbarians. The dexterity, as well as the firmness of Julian, was put to a severe trial, when he took the field with a discontented army, which had already served two campaigns without receiving any regular pay or any extraordinary donative.[88]

A tender regard for the peace and happiness of his subjects was the ruling principle which directed, or seemed to direct, the administration of Julian.[89] He devoted the leisure of his winter-quarters to the offices of civil government; and affected to assume with more pleasure the character of a magistrate than that of a general. Before he took the field he devolved on the provincial governors most of the public and private causes which had been referred to his tribunal; but, on his return, he carefully revised their proceedings, mitigated the rigour of the law, and pronounced a second judgment on the judges themselves. Superior to the last temptation of virtuous minds, an indiscreet and intemperate zeal for justice, he restrained, with calmness and dignity, the warmth of an advocate who prosecuted, for extortion, the president of the Narbonnese province. "Who will ever be found guilty," exclaimed the vehement Delphidius, "if it be enough to deny?" "And who," replied Julian, 'will ever be innocent, if it is sufficient to affirm?" In the general administration of peace and war, the interest of the sovereign is commonly the same as that of his people; but Constantius would have thought himself deeply injured, if the virtues of Julian had defrauded him of any part of the tribute which he extorted from an oppressed and exhausted country. The prince who was invested with the ensigns of royalty might sometimes presume to correct the rapacious insolence of the inferior agents, to expose their corrupt arts, and to introduce an equal and easier mode of collection. But the management of the finances was more safely intrusted to Florentius, Prætorian præfect of Gaul, an effeminate tyrant, incapable of pity or remorse: and the haughty minister complained of the most decent and gentle opposition, while Julian himself was rather inclined to censure the weakness of his own behaviour. The Cæsar had rejected with abhorrence a mandate for the levy of an extraordinary tax; a new superindiction, which the præfect had offered for his signature; and the faithful picture of the public misery, by which he had been obliged to justify his refusal, offended the court of Constantius. We may enjoy the pleasure of reading the sentiments of Julian, as he expresses them with warmth and freedom in a letter to one of his most intimate friends. After stating his own conduct, he proceeds in the following terms:— "Was it possible for the disciple of Plato and Aristotle to act otherwise than I have done? Could I abandon the unhappy subjects intrusted to my care? Was I not called upon to defend them from the repeated injuries of these unfeeling robbers? A tribune who deserts his post is punished with death, and deprived of the honours of burial. With what justice could I pronounce *his* sentence, if, in the hour of danger, I myself neglected a duty far more sacred and far more important? God has placed me in this elevated post; his providence will guard and support me. Should I be condemned to suffer, I shall derive comfort from the testimony of a pure and upright conscience. Would to Heaven that I still possessed a counsellor like Sallust! If they think proper to send me a successor, I shall submit without reluctance; and had much rather improve the short opportunity of doing good, than enjoy a long and lasting impunity of evil."[90] The precarious and dependent situation of Julian displayed his virtues and concealed his defects. The young hero who supported, in Gaul, the throne of Constantius, was not permitted to reform the vices of the government; but he had courage to alleviate or to pity the distress of the people. Unless he had been able to revive the martial spirit of the Romans, or to introduce the arts of industry and refinement among their savage enemies, he could not entertain any rational hopes of securing the public tranquillity, either by the peace or conquest of Germany. Yet the victories of Julian suspended for a short time the inroads of the barbarians, and delayed the ruin of the Western Empire.

His salutary influence restored the cities of Gaul, which had been so long exposed to the evils of civil discord, barbarian war, and domestic tyranny; and the spirit of industry was revived with the hopes of enjoyment. Agriculture, manufactures, and commerce again flourished under the protection of the laws; and the *curiæ*, or civil corporations, were again filled with useful and respectable members: the youth were no longer apprehensive of marriage; and married persons were no longer apprehensive of posterity: the public and private festivals were celebrated with customary pomp; and the frequent and secure intercourse of the provinces displayed the image of national prosperity.[91] A mind like that of Julian must have felt the general happiness of which he was the author; but he viewed with peculiar satisfaction and complacency the city of Paris, the seat of his winter residence, and the object even of his partial affection.[92] That splendid capital, which now embraces an ample territory on either side of the Seine, was originally confined to the small

island in the midst of the river, from whence the inhabitants derived a supply of pure and salubrious water. The river bathed the foot of the walls; and the town was accessible only by two wooden bridges. A forest overspread the northern side of the Seine, but on the south, the ground which now bears the name of the University was insensibly covered with houses, and adorned with a palace and amphitheatre, baths, an aqueduct, and a field of Mars for the exercise of the Roman troops. The severity of the climate was tempered by the neighbourhood of the ocean; and with some precautions, which experience had taught, the vine and figtree were successfully cultivated. But in remarkable winters the Seine was deeply frozen; and the huge pieces of ice that floated down the stream might be compared, by an Asiatic, to the blocks of white marble which were extracted from the quarries of Phrygia. The licentiousness and corruption of Antioch recalled to the memory of Julian the severe and simple manners of his beloved Lutetia,[93] where the amusements of the theatre were unknown or despised. He indignantly contrasted the effeminate Syrians with the brave and honest simplicity of the Gauls, and almost forgave the intemperance which was the only stain of the Celtic character.[94] If Julian could now revisit the capital of France, he might converse with men of science and genius, capable of understanding and of instructing a disciple of the Greeks; he might excuse the lively and graceful follies of a nation whose martial spirit has never been enervated by the indulgence of luxury; and he must applaud the perfection of that inestimable art which softens and refines and embellishes the intercourse of social life.

CHAPTER XX

The Motives, Progress, and Effects of the Conversion of Constantine. Legal Establishment and Constitution of the Christian or Catholic Church.

THE public establishment of Christianity may be considered as one of the most important and domestic revolutions which excite the most lively curiosity, and afford the most valuable instruction. The victories and the civil policy of Constantine no longer influence the state of Europe; but a considerable portion of the globe still retains the impression which it received from the conversion of that monarch; and the ecclesiastical institutions of

his reign are still connected, by an indissoluble chain, with the opinions, the passions, and the interests of the present generation.

In the consideration of a subject which may be examined with impartiality, but cannot be viewed with indifference, a difficulty immediately arises of a very unexpected nature—that of ascertaining the real and precise date of the conversion of Constantine. The eloquent Lactantius, in the midst of his court, seems impatient[1] to proclaim to the world the glorious example of the sovereign of Gaul; who, in the first moments of his reign, acknowledged and adored the majesty of the true and only God.[2] The learned Eusebius has ascribed the faith of Constantine to the miraculous sign which was displayed in the heavens whilst he meditated and prepared the Italian expedition.[3] The historian Zosimus maliciously asserts that the emperor had imbrued his hands in the blood of his eldest son before he publicly renounced the gods of Rome and of his ancestors.[4] The perplexity produced by these discordant authorities is derived from the behaviour of Constantine himself. According to the strictness of ecclesiastical language, the first of the *Christian* emperors was unworthy of that name till the moment of his death; since it was only during his last illness that he received, as a catechumen, the imposition of hands,[5] and was afterwards admitted, by the initiatory rites of baptism, into the number of the faithful.[6] The Christianity of Constantine must be allowed in a much more vague and qualified sense; and the nicest accuracy is required in tracing the slow and almost imperceptible gradations by which the monarch declared himself the protector, and at length the proselyte, of the church. It was an arduous task to eradicate the habits and prejudices of his education, to acknowledge the divine power of Christ and to understand that the truth of *his* revelation was incompatible with the worship of the gods. The obstacles which he had probably experienced in his own mind instructed him to proceed with caution in the momentous change of a national religion; and he insensibly discovered his new opinions, as far as he could enforce them with safety and with effect. During the whole course of his reign, the stream of Christianity flowed with a gentle, though accelerated, motion: but its general direction was sometimes checked, and sometimes diverted, by the accidental circumstances of the times, and by the prudence, or possibly by the caprice, of the monarch. His ministers were permitted to signify the intentions of their master in the various language which was best adapted to their respective principles;[7] and he artfully balanced the hopes and fears of his subjects, by publishing in the same year two edicts; the first of which enjoined the solemn observance of Sunday,[8] and the second directed the regular consultation of the Aruspices.[9] While this important revolution yet remained in suspense, the Christians and the Pagans watched the conduct of their sovereign with the same anxiety, but with very opposite sentiments. The former were prompted by every motive of zeal, as well as vanity, to exaggerate the marks of his favour and the evidences of his faith. The latter, till their just apprehensions were changed into despair and resentment, attempted to conceal from the world, and from themselves, that the gods of Rome could no longer reckon the emperor in the number of their votaries. The same passions and prejudices have engaged the partial writers of the times to connect the public profession of Christianity with the most glorious or the most ignominious era of the reign of Constantine.

Whatever symptoms of Christian piety might transpire in the discourses or actions of Constantine, he persevered till he was near forty years of age in the practice of the established religion;[10] and the same conduct which in the court of Nicomedia might be imputed to his fear, could be ascribed only to the inclination or policy of the sovereign of Gaul. His liberality restored and enriched the temples of the gods; the medals which issued from his Imperial mint are impressed with the figures and attributes of Jupiter and Apollo, of Mars and Hercules; and his filial piety increased the council of Olympus by the solemn apotheosis of his father Constantius.[11] But the devotion of Constantine was more peculiarly directed to the genius of the Sun, the Apollo of Greek and Roman mythology; and he was pleased to be represented with the symbols of the God of Light and Poetry. The unerring shafts of that deity, the brightness of his eyes, his laurel wreath, immortal beauty, and elegant accomplishments, seem to point him out as the patron of a young hero. The altars of Apollo were crowned with the votive offerings of Constantine; and the credulous multitude were taught to believe that the emperor was permitted to behold with mortal eyes the visible majesty of their tutelar deity; and that, either waking or in a vision, he was blessed with the auspicious omens of a long and victorious reign. The Sun was universally celebrated as the invincible guide and protector of Constantine; and the Pagans might reasonably expect that the insulted god would pursue with unrelenting vengeance the impiety of his ungrateful favourite.[12]

As long as Constantine exercised a limited sovereignty over the provinces of Gaul, his Christian subjects were protected by the authority, and perhaps by the laws, of a prince who wisely left to the gods the care of vindicating their own honour. If we may credit the assertion of Constantine himself, he had been an indignant spectator of the savage cruelties which were inflicted, by the hands of Roman soldiers, on those citizens whose religion was their only crime.[13] In the East and in the West he had seen the different effects of severity and indulgence; and as the former was rendered still more odious by the example of Galerius, his implacable enemy, the latter was recommended to his imitation by the authority and advice of a dying father. The son of Constantius immediately suspended or repealed the edicts of persecution, and granted the free exercise of their religious ceremonies to all those who had already professed themselves members of the church. They were soon encouraged to depend on the favour as well as on the justice of their sovereign, who had imbibed a secret and sincere reverence for the name of Christ, and for the God of the Christians.[14]

About five months after the conquest of Italy, the emperor made a solemn and authentic declaration of his sentiments by the celebrated edict of Milan, which restored peace to the catholic church. In the personal interview of the two western princes, Constantine, by the ascendant of genius and power, obtained the ready concurrence of his colleague, Licinius; the union of their names and authority disarmed the fury of Maximin; and, after the death of the tyrant of the East, the edict of Milan was received as a general and fundamental law of the Roman world.[15]

The wisdom of the emperors provided for the restitution of all the civil and religious rights of which the Christians had been so unjustly deprived. It was enacted that the places of worship, and public lands, which had been confiscated, should be restored to the church, without dispute, without delay, and without expense: and this severe injunction was accompanied with a gracious promise, that, if any of the purchasers had paid a fair and adequate price, they should be indemnified from the Imperial treasury. The salutary regulations which guard the future tranquillity of the faithful are framed on the principles of enlarged and equal toleration; and such an equality must have been interpreted by a recent sect as an advantageous and honourable distinction. The two emperors proclaim to the world that they have granted a free and absolute power to the Christians, and to all others, of following the religion which each individual thinks proper to prefer, to which he has addicted his mind, and which he may deem the best adapted to his own use. They

carefully explain every ambiguous word, remove every exception, and exact from the governors of the provinces a strict obedience to the true and simple meaning of an edict which was designed to establish and secure, without any limitation, the claims of religious liberty. They condescend to assign two weighty reasons which have induced them to allow this universal toleration: the humane intention of consulting the peace and happiness of their people; and the pious hope that by such a conduct they shall appease and propitiate *the Deity*, whose seat is in heaven. They gratefully acknowledge the many signal proofs which they have received of the divine favour; and they trust that the same Providence will for ever continue to protect the prosperity of the prince and people. From these vague and indefinite expressions of piety three suppositions may be deduced, of a different, but not of an incompatible nature. The mind of Constantine might fluctuate between the Pagan and the Christian religions. According to the loose and complying notions of Polytheism, he might acknowledge the God of the Christians as *one* of the *many* deities who compose the hierarchy of heaven. Or perhaps he might embrace the philosophic and pleasing idea that, notwithstanding the variety of names, of rites, and of opinions, all the sects and all the nations of mankind are united in the worship of the common Father and Creator of the universe.[16]

But the counsels of princes are more frequently influenced by views of temporal advantage than by considerations of abstract and speculative truth. The partial and increasing favour of Constantine may naturally be referred to the esteem which he entertained for the moral character of the Christians, and to a persuasion that the propagation of the Gospel would inculcate the practice of private and public virtue. Whatever latitude an absolute monarch may assume in his own conduct, whatever indulgence he may claim for his own passions, it is undoubtedly his interest that all his subjects should respect the natural and civil obligations of society. But the operation of the wisest laws is imperfect and precarious. They seldom inspire virtue, they cannot always restrain vice. Their power is insufficient to prohibit all that they condemn, nor can they always punish the actions which they prohibit. The legislators of antiquity had summoned to their aid the powers of education and of opinion. But every principle which had once maintained the vigour and purity of Rome and Sparta was long since extinguished in a declining and despotic empire. Philosophy still exercised her temperate sway over the human mind, but the cause of virtue derived very feeble support from the influence of the Pagan superstition. Under these discouraging circumstances a prudent magistrate might observe with pleasure the progress of a religion which diffused among the people a pure, benevolent, and universal system of ethics, adapted to every duty and every condition of life, recommended as the will and reason of the supreme Deity, and enforced by the sanction of eternal rewards or punishments. The experience of Greek and Roman history could not inform the world how far the system of national manners might be reformed and improved by the precepts of a divine revelation; and Constantine might listen with some confidence to the flattering, and indeed reasonable, assurances of Lactantius. The eloquent apologist seemed firmly to expect, and almost ventured to promise, *that* the establishment of Christianity would restore the innocence and felicity of the primitive age; *that* the worship of the true God would extinguish war and dissension among those who mutually considered themselves as the children of a common parent; *that* every impure desire, every angry or selfish passion, would be restrained by the knowledge of the Gospel; and *that* the magistrates might sheath the sword of justice among a people who would be universally actuated by the sentiments of truth and piety, of equity and moderation, of harmony and universal love.[17]

The passive and unresisting obedience which bows under the yoke of authority, or even of oppression, must have appeared in the eyes of an absolute monarch the most conspicuous and useful of the evangelic virtues.[18] The primitive Christians derived the institution of civil government, not from the consent of the people, but from the decrees of Heaven. The reigning emperor, though he had usurped the sceptre by treason and murder, immediately assumed the sacred character of vicegerent of the Deity. To the Deity alone he was accountable for the abuse of his power; and his subjects were indissolubly bound by their oath of fidelity to a tyrant who had violated every law of nature and society. The humble Christians were sent into the world as sheep among wolves; and since they were not permitted to employ force even in the defence of their religion, they should be still more criminal if they were tempted to shed the blood of their fellow-creatures in disputing the vain privileges or the sordid possessions of this transitory life. Faithful to the doctrine of the apostle, who in the reign of Nero had preach-

ed the duty of unconditional submission, the Christians of the three first centuries preserved their conscience pure and innocent of the guilt of secret conspiracy or open rebellion. While they experienced the rigour of persecution, they were never provoked either to meet their tyrants in the field, or indignantly to withdraw themselves into some remote and sequestered corner of the globe.[19] The protestants of France, of Germany, and of Britain, who asserted with such intrepid courage their civil and religious freedom, have been insulted by the invidious comparison between the conduct of the primitive and of the reformed Christians.[20] Perhaps, instead of censure, some applause may be due to the superior sense and spirit of our ancestors, who had convinced themselves that religion cannot abolish the unalienable rights of human nature.[21] Perhaps the patience of the primitive church may be ascribed to its weakness as well as to its virtue. A sect of unwarlike plebeians, without leaders, without arms, without fortifications, must have encountered inevitable destruction in a rash and fruitless resistance to the master of the Roman legions. But the Christians, when they deprecated the wrath of Diocletian, or solicited the favour of Constantine, could allege, with truth and confidence, that they held the principle of passive obedience, and that, in the space of three centuries, their conduct had always been conformable to their principles. They might add that the throne of the emperors would be established on a fixed and permanent basis if all their subjects, embracing the Christian doctrine, should learn to suffer and to obey.

In the general order of Providence princes and tyrants are considered as the ministers of Heaven, appointed to rule or to chastise the nations of the earth. But sacred history affords many illustrious examples of the more immediate interposition of the Deity in the government of his chosen people. The sceptre and the sword were committed to the hands of Moses, of Joshua, of Gideon, of David, of the Maccabees; the virtues of those heroes were the motive or the effect of the divine favour, the success of their arms was destined to achieve the deliverance or the triumph of the church. If the judges of Israel were occasional and temporary magistrates, the kings of Judah derived from the royal unction of their great ancestor an hereditary and indefeasible right, which could not be forfeited by their own vices, nor recalled by the caprice of their subjects. The same extraordinary providence, which was no longer confined to the Jewish people, might elect Constantine and his family as the protectors of the Christian world; and the devout Lactantius announces, in a prophetic tone, the future glories of his long and universal reign.[22] Galerius and Maximin, Maxentius and Licinius, were the rivals who shared with the favourite of Heaven the provinces of the empire. The tragic deaths of Galerius and Maximin soon gratified the resentment, and fulfilled the sanguine expectations, of the Christians. The success of Constantine against Maxentius and Licinius removed the two formidable competitors who still opposed the triumph of the second David, and his cause might seem to claim the peculiar interposition of Providence. The character of the Roman tyrant disgraced the purple and human nature; and though the Christians might enjoy his precarious favour, they were exposed, with the rest of his subjects, to the effects of his wanton and capricious cruelty. The conduct of Licenius soon betrayed the reluctance with which he had consented to the wise and humane regulations of the edict of Milan. The convocation of provincial synods was prohibited in his dominions; his Christian officers were ignominiously dismissed; and if he avoided the guilt, or rather danger, of a general persecution, his partial oppressions were rendered still more odious by the violation of a solemn and voluntary engagement.[23] While the East, according to the lively expression of Eusebius, was involved in the shades of infernal darkness, the auspicious rays of celestial light warmed and illuminated the provinces of the West. The piety of Constantine was admitted as an unexceptionable proof of the justice of his arms; and his use of victory confirmed the opinion of the Christians, that their hero was inspired and conducted by the Lord of Hosts. The conquest of Italy produced a general edict of toleration; and as soon as the defeat of Licinius had invested Constantine with the sole dominion of the Roman world, he immediately, by circular letters, exhorted all his subjects to imitate, without delay, the example of their sovereign, and to embrace the divine truth of Christianity.[24]

The assurance that the elevation of Constantine was intimately connected with the designs of Providence instilled into the minds of the Christians two opinions, which, by very different means, assisted the accomplishment of the prophecy. Their warm and active loyalty exhausted in his favour every resource of human industry; and they confidently expected that their strenuous efforts would be seconded by some divine and miraculous aid. The enemies of Constantine have imputed to interested motives the alliance which he insensibly contracted with the Catholic church, and which apparently contributed to the success of his ambition. In the beginning of the fourth century the Christians still bore a very inadequate proportion to the inhabitants of the empire; but among a degenerate people, who viewed the change of masters with the indifference of slaves, the spirit and union of a religious party might assist the popular leader, to whose service, from a principle of conscience, they had devoted their lives and fortunes.[25] The example of his father instructed Constantine to esteem and to reward the merit of the Christians; and in the distribution of public offices he had the advantage of strengthening his government by the choice of ministers or generals in whose fidelity he could repose a just and unreserved confidence. By the influence of these dignified missionaries the proselytes of the new faith must have multiplied in the court and army; the barbarians of Germany, who filled the ranks of the legions, were of a careless temper, which acquiesced without resistance in the religion of their commander; and when they passed the Alps it may fairly be presumed that a great number of the soldiers had already consecrated their swords to the service of Christ and of Constantine.[26] The habits of mankind and the interest of religion gradually abated the horror of war and bloodshed which had so long prevailed among the Christians; and in the councils which were assembled under the gracious protection of Constantine the authority of the bishops was seasonably employed to ratify the obligation of the military oath, and to inflict the penalty of excommunication on those soldiers who threw away their arms during the peace of the church.[27] While Constantine in his own dominions increased the number and zeal of his faithful adherents, he could depend on the support of a powerful faction in those provinces which were still possessed or usurped by his rivals. A secret disaffection was diffused among the Christian subjects of Maxentius and Licinius; and the resentment which the latter did not attempt to conceal served only to engage them still more deeply in the interest of his competitor. The regular correspondence which connected the bishops of the most distant provinces enabled them freely to communicate their wishes and their designs, and to transmit without danger any useful intelligence, or any pious contributions, which might promote the service of Constantine, who publicly declared that he had taken up arms for the deliverance of the church.[28]

The enthusiasm which inspired the troops, and perhaps the emperor himself, had sharpened their swords while it satisfied their conscience. They marched to battle with the full assurance that the same God who had formerly opened a passage to the Israelites through the waters of Jordan, and had thrown down the walls of Jericho at the sound of the trumpets of Joshua, would display his visible majesty and power in the victory of Constantine. The evidence of ecclesiastical history is prepared to affirm that their expectations were justified by the conspicuous miracle to which the conversion of the first Christian emperor has been almost unanimously ascribed. The real or imaginary cause of so important an event deserves and demands the attention of posterity; and I shall endeavour to form a just estimate of the famous vision of Constantine, by a distinct consideration of the *standard*, the *dream*, and the *celestial sign*; by separating the historical, the natural, and the marvellous parts of this extraordinary story, which, in the composition of a specious argument, have been artfully confounded in one splendid and brittle mass.

I. An instrument of the tortures which were inflicted only on slaves and strangers became an object of horror in the eyes of a Roman citizen; and the ideas of guilt, of pain, and of ignominy, were closely united with the idea of the cross.[29] The piety, rather than the humanity, of Constantine soon abolished in his dominions the punishment which the Saviour of mankind had condescended to suffer;[30] but the emperor had already learned to despise the prejudices of his education and of his people, before he could erect in the midst of Rome his own statue, bearing a cross in its right hand, with an inscription which referred the victory of his arms, and the deliverance of Rome, to the virtue of that salutary sign, the true symbol of force and courage.[31] The same symbol sanctified the arms of the soldiers of Constantine; the cross glittered on their helmet, was engraved on their shields, was interwoven into their banners; and the consecrated emblems which adorned the person of the emperor himself were distinguished only by richer materials and more exquisite workmanship.[32] But the principal standard which displayed the triumph of the cross was styled the *Labarum*,[33] an obscure, though celebrated, name, which has been vainly derived from almost all the languages of the world. It is described[34] as a long pike intersected by a transversal beam. The silken veil which hung down from the beam was curiously inwrought with the images of the reigning monarch and his children. The summit of the pike supported a crown of gold, which enclosed the mysterious monogram, at once expressive of the figure of the cross and the initial letters of the name of Christ.[35] The safety of the labarum was intrusted to fifty guards of approved valour and fidelity; their station was marked by honours and emoluments; and some fortunate accidents soon introduced an opinion that as long as the guards of the labarum were engaged in the execution of their office they were secure and invulnerable amidst the darts of the enemy. In the second civil war Licinius felt and dreaded the power of this consecrated banner, the sight of which in the distress of battle animated the soldiers of Constantine with an invincible enthusiasm, and scattered terror and dismay through the ranks of the adverse legions.[36] The Christian emperors, who respected the example of Constantine, displayed in all their military expeditions the standard of the cross; but when the degenerate successors of Theodosius had ceased to appear in person at the head of their armies, the labarum was deposited as a venerable but useless relic in the palace of Constantinople.[37] Its honours are still preserved on the medals of the Flavian family. Their grateful devotion has placed the monogram of Christ in the midst of the ensigns of Rome. The solemn epithets of safety of the republic, glory of the army, restoration of public happiness, are equally applied to the religious and military trophies; and there is still extant a medal of the emperor Constantius, where the standard of the labarum is accompanied with these memorable words, BY THIS SIGN THOU SHALT CONQUER.[38]

II. In all occasions of danger or distress it was the practice of the primitive Christians to fortify their minds and bodies by the sign of the cross, which they used in all their ecclesiastical rites, in all the daily occurrences of life, as an infallible preservative against every species of spiritual or temporal evil.[39] The authority of the church might alone have had sufficient weight to justify the devotion of Constantine, who, in the same prudent and gradual progress, acknowledged the truth and assumed the symbol of Christianity. But the testimony of a contemporary writer, who in a formal treatise has avenged the cause of religion, bestows on the piety of the emperor a more awful and sublime character. He affirms, with the most perfect confidence, that, in the night which preceded the last battle against Maxentius, Constantine was admonished in a dream to inscribe the shields of his soldiers with the *celestial sign of God*, the sacred monogram of the name of Christ; that he executed the commands of Heaven, and that his valour and obedience were rewarded by the decisive victory of the Milvian Bridge. Some considerations might perhaps incline a sceptical mind to suspect the judgment or the veracity of the rhetorician, whose pen, either from zeal or interest, was devoted to the cause of the prevailing faction.[40] He appears to have published his Deaths of the Persecutors at Nicomedia about three years after the Roman victory; but the interval of a thousand miles, and a thousand days, will allow an ample latitude for the invention of declaimers, the credulity of party, and the tacit approbation of the emperor himself; who might listen without indignation to a marvellous tale which exalted his fame and promoted his designs. In favour of Licinius, who still dissembled his animosity to the Christians, the same author has provided a similar vision, of a form of prayer, which was communicated by an angel, and repeated by the whole army before they engaged the legions of the tyrant Maximin.[41] The frequent repetition of miracles serves to provoke, where it does not subdue, the reason of mankind; but if the dream of Constantine is separately considered, it may be naturally explained either by the policy or the enthusiasm of the emperor. Whilst his anxiety for the approaching day, which must decide the fate of the empire, was suspended by a short and interrupted slumber, the venerable form of Christ, and the well-known symbol of his religion, might forcibly offer themselves to the active fancy of a prince who reverenced the name, and had perhaps secretly implored the power, of the God of the Christians. As readily might a consummate statesman indulge himself in the use of one of those military stratagems, one of those pious frauds, which Philip and Sertorius had employed with such art and effect.[42] The præternatural origin of dreams was universally admitted by the nations of antiquity, and a considerable part of the Gallic army was already prepared to place their confidence in the salutary sign of the Christian religion. The secret vision of Constantine could be disproved only by the event; and the intrepid hero who had passed the Alps and the Apennine might view with careless despair the consequences of a defeat under the walls of Rome. The senate and people, exulting in their own deliverance from an odious tyrant, acknowledged that the victory of Constantine surpassed the powers of man,

without daring to insinuate that it had been obtained by the protection of the *gods*. The triumphal arch, which was erected about three years after the event, proclaims, in ambiguous language, that, by the greatness of his own mind, and by an *instinct* or impulse of the Divinity, he had saved and avenged the Roman republic.[43] The Pagan orator, who had seized an earlier opportunity of celebrating the virtues of the conqueror, supposes that he alone enjoyed a secret and intimate commerce with the Supreme Being, who delegated the care of mortals to his subordinate deities; and thus assigns a very plausible reason why the subjects of Constantine should not presume to embrace the new religion of their sovereign.[44]

III. The philosopher, who with calm suspicion examines the dreams and omens, the miracles and prodigies, of profane or even of ecclesiastical history, will probably conclude that, if the eyes of the spectators have sometimes been deceived by fraud, the understanding of the readers has much more frequently been insulted by fiction. Every event, or appearance, or accident, which seems to deviate from the ordinary course of nature, has been rashly ascribed to the immediate action of the Deity; and the astonished fancy of the multitude has sometimes given shape and colour, language and motion, to the fleeting but uncommon meteors of the air.[45] Nazarius and Eusebius are the two most celebrated orators who, in studied panegyrics, have laboured to exalt the glory of Constantine. Nine years after the Roman victory Nazarius[46] describes an army of divine warriors, who seemed to fall from the sky; he marks their beauty, their spirit, their gigantic forms, the stream of light which beamed from their celestial armour, their patience in suffering themselves to be heard, as well as seen, by mortals; and their declaration that they were sent, that they flew, to the assistance of the great Constantine. For the truth of this prodigy the Pagan orator appeals to the whole Gallic nation, in whose presence he was then speaking; and seems to hope that the ancient apparitions[47] would now obtain credit from this recent and public event. The Christian fable of Eusebius, which, in the space of twenty-six years, might arise from the original dream, is cast in a much more correct and elegant mould. In one of the marches of Constantine he is reported to have seen with his own eyes the luminous trophy of the cross, placed above the meridian sun, and inscribed with the following words: By this conquer. This amazing object in the sky astonished the whole army, as well as the emperor himself, who was yet undetermined in the choice of a religion: but his astonishment was converted into faith by the vision of the ensuing night. Christ appeared before his eyes; and displaying the same celestial sign of the cross, he directed Constantine to frame a similar standard, and to march, with an assurance of victory, against Maxentius and all his enemies.[48] The learned bishop of Cæsarea appears to be sensible that the recent discovery of this marvellous anecdote would excite some surprise and distrust among the most pious of his readers. Yet, instead of ascertaining the precise circumstances of time and place, which always serve to detect falsehood or establish truth;[49] instead of collecting and recording the evidence of so many living witnesses, who must have been spectators of this stupendous miracle,[50] Eusebius contents himself with alleging a very singular testimony, that of the deceased Constantine, who, many years after the event, in the freedom of conversation, had related to him this extraordinary incident of his own life, and had attested the truth of it by a solemn oath. The prudence and gratitude of the learned prelate forbade him to suspect the veracity of his victorious master; but he plainly intimates that, in a fact of such a nature, he should have refused his assent to any meaner authority. This motive of credibility could not survive the power of the Flavian family; and the celestial sign, which the Infidels might afterwards deride,[51] was disregarded by the Christians of the age which immediately followed the conversion of Constantine.[52] But the Catholic church, both of the East and of the West, has adopted a prodigy which favours, or seems to favour, the popular worship of the cross. The vision of Constantine maintained an honourable place in the legend of superstition till the bold and sagacious spirit of criticism presumed to depreciate the triumph, and to arraign the truth, of the first Christian emperor.[53]

The protestant and philosophic readers of the present age will incline to believe that, in the account of his own conversion, Constantine attested a wilful falsehood by a solemn and deliberate perjury. They may not hesitate to pronounce that, in the choice of a religion, his mind was determined only by a sense of interest; and that (according to the expression of a profane poet[54]) he used the altars of the church as a convenient footstool to the throne of the empire. A conclusion so harsh and so absolute is not, however, warranted by our knowledge of human nature, of Constantine, or of Christianity. In an age of religious fervour the most artful statesmen are observed to feel some part of the enthusiasm which they inspire; and the most orthodox saints assume the dangerous privilege of defending the cause of truth by the arms of deceit and falsehood. Personal interest is often the standard of our belief, as well as of our practice; and the same motives of temporal advantage which might influence the public conduct and professions of Constantine would insensibly dispose his mind to embrace a religion so propitious to his fame and fortunes. His vanity was gratified by the flattering assurance that *he* had been chosen by Heaven to reign over the earth: success had justified his divine title to the throne, and that title was founded on the truth of the Christian revelation. As real virtue is sometimes excited by undeserved applause, the specious piety of Constantine, if at first it was only specious, might gradually, by the influence of praise, of habit, and of example, be matured into serious faith and fervent devotion. The bishops and teachers of the new sect, whose dress and manners had not qualified them for the residence of a court, were admitted to the Imperial table; they accompanied the monarch in his expeditions; and the ascendant which one of them, an Egyptian or a Spaniard,[55] acquired over his mind was imputed by the Pagans to the effect of magic.[56] Lactantius, who has adorned the precepts of the Gospel with the eloquence of Cicero,[57] and Eusebius, who has consecrated the learning and philosophy of the Greeks to the service of religion,[58] were both received into the friendship and familiarity of their sovereign; and those able masters of controversy could patiently watch the soft and yielding moments of persuasion, and dexterously apply the arguments which were the best adapted to his character and understanding. Whatever advantages might be derived from the acquisition of an Imperial proselyte, he was distinguished by the splendour of his purple, rather than by the superiority of wisdom or virtue, from the many thousands of his subjects who had embraced the doctrines of Christianity. Nor can it be deemed incredible that the mind of an unlettered soldier should have yielded to the weight of evidence which, in a more enlightened age, has satisfied or subdued the reason of a Grotius, a Pascal, or a Locke. In the midst of the incessant labours of his great office this soldier employed, or affected to employ, the hours of the night in the diligent study of the Scriptures, and the composition of theological discourses, which he afterwards pronounced in the presence of a numerous and applauding audience. In a very long discourse, which is still extant, the royal preacher expatiates on the various proofs of religion; but he dwells with peculiar complacency on the Sibylline verses,[59] and the fourth eclogue of Virgil.[60] Forty years before the birth of Christ, the Mantuan bard, as if inspired by the celestial muse of Isaiah, had celebrated, with all the pomp of oriental metaphor, the return of the Virgin, the fall of the serpent, the approaching birth of a godlike child, the offspring of the great Jupiter, who should expiate the guilt of human kind and govern the peaceful universe with the virtues of his father; the rise and appearance of an heavenly race, a primitive nation throughout the world; and the gradual restoration of the innocence and felicity of the golden age. The poet was perhaps unconscious of the secret sense and object of these sublime predictions, which have been so unworthily applied to the infant son of a consul, or a triumvir:[61] but if a more splendid, and indeed specious, interpretation of the fourth eclogue contributed to the conversion of the first Christian emperor, Virgil may deserve to be ranked among the most successful missionaries of the Gospel.[62]

The awful mysteries of the Christian faith and worship were concealed from the eyes of strangers, and even of catechumens, with an affected secrecy, which served to excite their wonder and curiosity.[63] But the severe rules of discipline which the prudence of the bishops had instituted were relaxed by the same prudence in favour of an Imperial proselyte, whom it was so important to allure, by every gentle condescension, into the pale of the church; and Constantine was permitted, at least by a tacit dispensation, to enjoy *most* of the privileges, before he had contracted *any* of the obligations, of a Christian. Instead of retiring from the congregation when the voice of the deacon dismissed the profane multitude, he prayed with the faithful, disputed with the bishops, preached on the most sublime and intricate subjects of theology, celebrated with sacred rites the vigil of Easter, and publicly declared himself, not only a partaker, but, in some measure, a priest and hierophant of the Christian mysteries.[64] The pride of Constantine might assume, and his services had deserved, some extraordinary distinction; an ill-timed rigour might have blasted the unripened fruits of his conversion; and if the doors of the church had been strictly closed against a prince who had deserted the altars of the gods, the master of the empire would have been left destitute of any form of religious worship. In his last visit to Rome he piously disclaimed and insulted the superstition of his ancestors, by refusing to lead the military procession of the equestrian order, and to offer the public vows to the Jupiter of the Capitoline Hill.[65] Many years before his baptism and death Constantine had proclaimed to the world that neither his person nor his image should evermore be seen within the walls of an idolatrous temple; while he distributed through the provinces a variety of medals and pictures which represented the emperor in an humble and suppliant posture of Christian devotion.[66]

The pride of Constantine, who refused the privileges of a catechumen, cannot easily be explained or excused; but the delay of his baptism may be justified by the maxims and the practice of ecclesiastical antiquity. The sacrament of baptism[67] was regularly administered by the bishop himself, with his assistant clergy, in the cathedral church of the diocese, during the fifty days between the solemn festivals of Easter and Pentecost; and this holy term admitted a numerous band of infants and adult persons into the bosom of the church. The discretion of parents often suspended the baptism of their children till they could understand the obligations which they contracted: the severity of ancient bishops exacted from the new converts a novitiate of two or three years; and the catechumens themselves, from different motives of a temporal or a spiritual nature, were seldom impatient to assume the character of perfect and initiated Christians. The sacrament of baptism was supposed to contain a full and absolute expiation of sin; and the soul was instantly restored to its original purity, and entitled to the promise of eternal salvation. Among the proselytes of Christianity there were many who judged it imprudent to precipitate a salutary rite which could not be repeated; to throw away an inestimable privilege which could never be recovered. By the delay of their baptism they could venture freely to indulge their passions in the enjoyment of this world, while they still retained in their own hands the means of a sure and easy absolution.[68] The sublime theory of the Gospel had made a much fainter impression on the heart than on the understanding of Constantine himself. He pursued the great object of his ambition through the dark and bloody paths of war and policy; and, after the victory, he abandoned himself, without moderation, to the abuse of his fortune. Instead of asserting his just superiority above the imperfect heroism and profane philosophy of Trajan and the Antonines, the mature age of Constantine forfeited the reputation which he had acquired in his youth. As he gradually advanced in the knowledge of truth, he proportionably declined in the practice of virtue; and the same year of his reign in which he convened the council of Nice was polluted by the execution, or rather murder, of his eldest son. This date is alone sufficient to refute the ignorant and malicious suggestions of Zosimus[69] who affirms that, after the death of Crispus, the remorse of his father accepted from the ministers of Christianity the expiation which he had vainly solicited from the Pagan pontiffs. At the time of the death of Crispus the emperor could no longer hesitate in the choice of a religion; he could no longer be ignorant that the church was possessed of an infallible remedy, though he chose to defer the application of it till the approach of death had removed the temptation and danger of a relapse. The bishops whom he summoned in his last illness to the palace of Nicomedia were edified by the fervour with which he requested and received the sacrament of baptism, by the solemn protestation that the remainder of his life should be worthy of a disciple of Christ, and by his humble refusal to wear the Imperial purple after he had been clothed in the white garment of a Neophyte. The example and reputation of Constantine seemed to countenance the delay of baptism.[70] Future tyrants were encouraged to believe that the innocent blood which they might shed in a long reign would instantly be washed away in the waters of regeneration; and the abuse of religion dangerously undermined the foundations of moral virtue.

The gratitude of the church has exalted the virtues and excused the failings of a generous patron, who seated Christianity on the throne of the Roman world; and the Greeks, who celebrate the festival of the Imperial saint, seldom mention the name of Constantine without adding the title of *equal to the Apostles*.[71] Such a comparison, if it alludes to the character of those divine missionaries, must be imputed to the extravagance of impious flattery. But if the parallel is confined to the extent and number of their evangelic victories, the success of Constantine might perhaps equal that of the Apostles themselves. By the edicts of toleration he removed the temporal disadvantages which had hitherto retarded the progress of Christianity; and its active and numerous ministers received a free permission, a liberal encouragement, to recommend the salutary truths of revelation by every argument which could affect the reason or piety of mankind. The exact balance of the two religions continued but a moment; and the piercing eye of ambition and avarice soon discovered that the profession of Christianity might contribute to the interest of the present, as well as of a future life.[72] The hopes of wealth and honours, the example of an emperor, his exhortations, his irresistible smiles, diffused conviction among the venal and obsequious crowds which usually fill the apartments of a palace. The cities which signalised a forward zeal by the voluntary destruction of their temples were distinguished by municipal privileges and rewarded with popular donatives; and the new capital of the East gloried in the singular advantage that Constantinople was never profaned by the worship of idols.[73] As the lower ranks of society are governed by imitation, the conversion of those who possessed any eminence of birth, of power, or of riches, was soon followed by dependent multitudes.[74] The salvation of the common people was purchased at an easy rate, if it be true that, in one year, twelve thousand men were baptised at Rome, besides a proportionable number of women and children, and that a white garment, with twenty pieces of gold, had been promised by the emperor to every convert.[75] The powerful influence of Constantine was not circumscribed by the narrow limits of his life or of his dominions. The education which he bestowed on his sons and nephews secured to the empire a race of princes whose faith was still more lively and sincere, as they imbibed, in their earliest infancy, the spirit, or at least the doctrine, of Christianity. War and commerce had spread the knowledge of the Gospel beyond the confines of the Roman provinces; and the barbarians, who had disdained an humble and proscribed sect, soon learned to esteem a religion which had been so lately embraced by the greatest monarch and the most civilised nation of the globe.[76] The Goths and Germans, who enlisted under the standard of Rome, revered the cross which glittered at the head of the legions, and their fierce countrymen received at the same time the lessons of faith and of humanity. The kings of Iberia and Armenia worshipped the God of their protector; and their subjects, who have invariably preserved the name of Christians, soon formed a sacred and perpetual connection with their Roman brethren. The Christians of Persia were suspected, in time of war, of preferring their religion to their country; but as long as peace subsisted between the two empires, the persecuting spirit of the Magi was effectually restrained by the interposition of Constantine.[77] The rays of the Gospel illuminated the coast of India. The colonies of Jews who had penetrated into Arabia and Æthiopia[78] opposed the progress of Christianity; but the labour of the missionaries was in some measure facilitated by a previous knowledge of the Mosaic revelation; and Abyssinia still reveres the memory of Frumentius, who, in the time of Constantine, devoted his life to the conversion of those sequestered regions. Under the reign of his son Constantius, Theophilus,[79] who was himself of Indian extraction, was invested with the double character of ambassador and bishop. He embarked on the Red Sea with two hundred horses of the purest breed of Cappadocia, which were sent by the emperor of the prince of the Sabæans, or Homerites. Theophilus was intrusted with many other useful or curious presents, which might raise the admiration and conciliate the friendship of the barbarians; and he successfully employed several years in a pastoral visit to the churches of the torrid zone.[80]

The irresistable power of the Roman emperors was displayed in the important and dangerous change of the national religion. The terrors of a military force silenced the faint and unsupported murmurs of the Pagans, and there was reason to expect that the cheerful submission of the Christian clergy, as well as the people, would be the result of conscience and gratitude. It was long since established as a fundamental maxim of the Roman constitution, that every rank of citizens was alike subject to the laws, and that the care of religion was the right as well as duty of the civil magistrate. Constantine and his successors could not easily persuade themselves that they had forfeited, by their conversion, any branch of the Imperial prerogatives, or that they were incapable of giving laws to a religion which they had protected and embraced. The emperors still continued to exercise a supreme jurisdiction over the ecclesiastical order; and the sixteenth book of the Theodosian code represents, under a variety of titles, the authority which they assumed in the government of the Catholic church.

But the distinction of the spiritual and temporal powers,[81] which had never been imposed on the free spirit of Greece and Rome, was introduced and confirmed by the legal establishment of Christianity. The office of supreme pontiff, which, from the time of Numa to that of Augustus, had always been exercised by one of the most eminent of the senators, was at length united to the Imperial dignity. The first magistrate of the state, as often as he was prompted by superstition or policy, performed with his own hands the sacerdotal functions;[82] nor was there any order of priests, either at Rome or in the provinces, who claimed a more sacred character among men, or a more intimate communication with the gods. But in the Christian church, which intrusts the service of the altar to a perpetual succession of consecrated ministers, the monarch, whose spiritual rank is less honourable than that of the meanest deacon, was seated below the rails of the sanctuary, and confounded with the rest of the faithful multitude.[83] The emperor might be saluted as the father of his people, but he owed a filial duty and reverence to the fathers of the church; and the same marks of respect which Constantine had paid to the persons of saints and confessors were soon exacted by the pride of the episcopal order.[84] A secret conflict between the civil and ecclesiastical jurisdictions embarrassed the operations of the Roman government; and a pious emperor was alarmed by the guilt and danger of touching with a profane hand the ark of the covenant. The separation of men into the two orders of the clergy and of the laity was, indeed, familiar to many nations of antiquity; and the priests of India, of Persia, of Assyria, of Judea, of Æthiopia, of Egypt, and of Gaul, derived from a celestial origin the temporal power and possessions which they had acquired. These venerable institutions had gradually assimilated themselves to the manners and government of their respective countries;[85] but the opposition or contempt of the civil power served to cement the discipline of the primitive church. The Christians had been obliged to elect their own magistrates, to raise and distribute a peculiar revenue, and to regulate the internal policy of their republic by a code of laws, which were ratified by the consent of the people and the practice of three hundred years. When Constantine embraced the faith of the Christians, he seemed to contract a perpetual alliance with a distinct and independent society; and the privileges granted or confirmed by that emperor, or by his successors, were accepted, not as the precarious favours of the court, but as the just and inalienable rights of the ecclesiastical order.

The Catholic church was administered by the spiritual and legal jurisdiction of eighteen hundred bishops;[86] of whom one thousand were seated in the Greek, and eight hundred in the Latin, provinces of the empire. The extent and boundaries of their respective dioceses had been variously and accidentally decided by the zeal and success of the first missionaries, by the wishes of the people, and by the propagation of the Gospel. Episcopal churches were closely planted along the banks of the Nile, on the seacoast of Africa, in the proconsular Asia, and through the southern provinces of Italy. The bishops of Gaul and Spain, of Thrace and Pontus, reigned over an ample territory, and delegated their rural suffragans to execute the subordinate duties of the pastoral office.[87] A Christian diocese might be spread over a province, or reduced to a village; but all the bishops possessed an equal and indelible character; they all derived the same powers and privileges from the apostles, from the people, and from the laws. While the *civil* and *military* professions were separated by the policy of Constantine, a new and perpetual order of *ecclesiastical* ministers, always respectable, sometimes dangerous, was established in the church and state. The important review of their station and attributes may be distributed under the following heads: I. Popular election. II. Ordination of the clergy. III. Property. IV. Civil jurisdiction. V. Spiritual censures. VI. Exercise of public oratory. VII. Privilege of legislative assemblies.

I. The freedom of elections subsisted long after the legal establishment of Christianity,[88] and the subjects of Rome enjoyed in the church the privilege which they had lost in the republic, of choosing the magistrates whom they were bound to obey. As soon as a bishop had closed his eyes, the metropolitan issued a commission to one of his suffragans to administer the vacant see, and prepare, within a limited time, the future election. The right of voting was vested in the inferior clergy, who were best qualified to judge of the merit of the candidates; in the senators or nobles of the city, all those who were distinguished by their rank or property; and finally in the whole body of the people, who on the appointed day flocked in multitudes from the most remote parts of the diocese,[89] and sometimes silenced, by their tumultuous acclamations, the voice of reason and the laws of discipline. These acclamations might accidentally fix on the head of the most deserving competitor, of some ancient presbyter, some holy monk, or some layman conspicuous for his zeal and piety. But the episcopal chair was solicited, especially in the great and opulent cities of the empire, as a temporal rather than as a spiritual dignity. The interested views, the selfish and angry passions, the arts of perfidy and dissimulation, the secret corruption, the open and even bloody violence which had formerly disgraced the freedom of election in the commonwealths of Greece and Rome, too often influenced the choice of the successors of the apostles. While one of the candidates boasted the honours of his family, a second allured his judges by the delicacies of a plentiful table, and a third, more guilty than his rivals, offered to share the plunder of the church among the accomplices of his sacrilegious hopes.[90] The civil as well as ecclesiastical laws attempted to exclude the populace from this solemn and important transaction. The canons of ancient discipline, by requiring several episcopal qualifications of age, station, etc., restrained in some measure the indiscriminate caprice of the electors. The authority of the provincial bishops, who were assembled in the vacant church to consecrate the choice of the people, was interposed to moderate their passions and to correct their mistakes. The bishops could refuse to ordain an unworthy candidate, and the rage of contending factions sometimes accepted their impartial mediation. The submission or the resistance of the clergy and people, on various occasions, afforded different precedents, which were insensibly converted into positive laws and provincial customs:[91] but it was everywhere admitted, as a fundamental maxim of religious policy, that no bishop could be imposed on an orthodox church without the consent of its members. The emperors, as the guardians of the public peace, and as the first citizens of Rome and Constantinople, might effectually declare their wishes in the choice of a primate; but those absolute monarchs respected the freedom of ecclesiastical elections, and, while they distributed and resumed the honours of the state and army, they allowed eighteen hundred perpetual magistrates to receive their important offices from the free suffrages of the people.[92] It was agreeable to the dictates of justice that these magistrates should not desert an honourable station from which they could not be removed; but the wisdom of councils endeavoured, without much success, to enforce the residence, and to prevent the translation, of bishops. The discipline of the West was indeed less relaxed than that of the East; but the same passions which made those regulations necessary rendered them ineffectual. The reproaches which angry prelates have so vehemently urged against each other serve only to expose their common guilt and their mutual indiscretion.

II. The bishops alone possessed the faculty of *spiritual* generation, and this extraordinary privilege might compensate, in some degree, for the painful celibacy[93] which was imposed as a virtue, as a duty, and at length as a positive obligation. The religions of antiquity, which established a separate order of priests, dedicated a holy race, a tribe or family, to the perpetual service of the gods.[94] Such institutions were founded for possession rather than conquest. The children of the priests enjoyed, with proud and indolent security, their sacred inheritance; and the fiery spirit of enthusiasm was abated by the cares, the pleasures, and the endearments of domestic life. But the Christian sanctuary was open to every ambitious candidate who aspired to its heavenly promises or temporal possessions. The office of priests, like that of soldiers or magistrates, was strenuously exercised by those men whose temper and abilities had prompted them to embrace the ecclesiastical profession, or who had been selected by a discerning bishop as the best qualified to promote the glory and interest of the church. The bishops[95] (till the abuse was restrained by the prudence of the laws) might constrain the reluctant and protect the distressed, and the imposition of hands for ever bestowed some of the most valuable privileges of civil society. The whole body of the catholic clergy, more numerous, perhaps, than the legions, was exempted by the emperors from all service, private or public, all municipal offices, and all personal taxes and contributions, which pressed on their fellow-citizens with intolerable weight; and the duties of their holy profession were accepted as a full discharge of their obligations to the republic.[96] Each bishop acquired an absolute and indefeasible right to the perpetual obedience of the clerk whom he ordained; the clergy of each episcopal church, with its dependent parishes, formed a regular and permanent society; and the cathedrals of Constantinople[97] and Carthage[98] maintained their peculiar establishment of five hundred ecclesiastical ministers. Their ranks[99] and numbers were insensibly multiplied by the superstition of the times, which introduced into the church the splendid ceremonies of a Jewish or Pagan temple; and a long train of priests, deacons, sub-deacons, acolytes, exorcists, readers, singers, and doorkeepers contributed, in their respective stations, to swell the pomp and harmony of religious worship. The clerical name and privilege were extended to many pious fraternities, who devoutly supported the ecclesiastical throne.[100] Six hundred *parabolani*, or adventurers, visited the sick at Alexandria; eleven hundred *copiatæ*, or gravediggers

buried the dead at Constantinople; and the swarms of monks, who arose from the Nile, overspread and darkened the face of the Christian world.

III. The edict of Milan secured the revenue as well as the peace of the church.[101] The Christians not only recovered the lands and houses of which they had been stripped by the persecuting laws of Diocletian, but they acquired a perfect title to all the possessions which they had hitherto enjoyed by the connivance of the magistrate. As soon as Christianity became the religion of the emperor and the empire, the national clergy might claim a decent and honourable maintenance: and the payment of an annual tax might have delivered the people from the more oppressive tribute which superstition imposes on her votaries. But as the wants and expenses of the church increased with her prosperity, the ecclesiastical order was still supported and enriched by the voluntary oblations of the faithful. Eight years after the edict of Milan, Constantine granted to all his subjects the free and universal permission of bequeathing their fortunes to the holy Catholic church;[102] and their devout liberality, which during their lives was checked by luxury or avarice, flowed with a profuse stream at the hour of their death. The wealthy Christians were encouraged by the example of their sovereign. An absolute monarch, who is rich without patrimony, may be charitable without merit; and Constantine too easily believed that he should purchase the favour of Heaven if he maintained the idle at the expense of the industrious, and distributed among the saints the wealth of the republic. The same messenger who carried over to Africa the head of Maxentius might be intrusted with an epistle to Cæcilian, bishop of Carthage. The emperor acquaints him that the treasurers of the province are directed to pay into his hands the sum of three thousand *folles*, or eighteen thousand pounds sterling, and to obey his farther requisitions for the relief of the churches of Africa, Numidia and Mauritania.[103] The liberality of Constantine increased in a just proportion to his faith and to his vices. He assigned in each city a regular allowance of corn to supply the fund of ecclesiastical charity, and the persons of both sexes who embraced the monastic life became the peculiar favourites of their sovereign. The Christian temples of Antioch, Alexandria, Jerusalem, Constantinople, etc., displayed the ostentatious piety of a prince ambitious in a declining age to equal the perfect labours of antiquity.[104] The form of these religious edifices was simple and oblong, though they might sometimes swell into the shape of a dome, and sometimes branch into the figure of a cross. The timbers were framed for the most part of cedars of Libanus; the roof was covered with tiles, perhaps of gilt brass; and the walls, the columns, the pavement, were incrusted with variegated marbles. The most precious ornaments of gold and silver, of silk and gems, were profusely dedicated to the service of the altar, and this specious magnificence was supported on the solid and perpetual basis of landed property. In the space of two centuries, from the reign of Constantine to that of Justinian, the eighteen hundred churches of the empire were enriched by the frequent and unalienable gifts of the prince and people. An annual income of six hundred pounds sterling may be reasonably assigned to the bishops, who were placed at an equal distance between riches and poverty,[105] but the standard of their wealth insensibly rose with the dignity and opulence of the cities which they governed. An authentic but imperfect[106] rent-roll specifies some houses, shops, gardens, and farms, which belonged to the three *Basilicæ* of Rome—St. Peter, St. Paul, and St. John Lateran—in the provinces of Italy, Africa, and the East. They produce, besides a reserved rent of oil, linen, paper, aromatics, etc., a clear annual revenue of twenty-two thousand pieces of gold, or twelve thousand pounds sterling. In the age of Constantine and Justinian the bishops no longer possessed, perhaps they no longer deserved, the unsuspecting confidence of their clergy and people. The ecclesiastical revenues of each diocese were divided into four parts, for the respective uses of the bishop himself, of his inferior clergy, of the poor, and of the public worship; and the abuse of this sacred trust was strictly and repeatedly checked.[107] The patrimony of the church was still subject to all the public impositions of the state.[108] The clergy of Rome, Alexandria, Thessalonica, etc., might solicit and obtain some partial exemptions; but the premature attempt of the great council of Rimini, which aspired to universal freedom, was successfully resisted by the son of Constantine.[109]

IV. The Latin clergy, who erected their tribunal on the ruins of the civil and common law, have modestly accepted, as the gift of Constantine,[110] the independent jurisdiction which was the fruit of time, of accident, and of their own industry. But the liberality of the Christian emperors had actually endowed them with some legal prerogatives which secured and dignified

the sacerdotal character.[111] 1. Under a despotic government, the bishops alone enjoyed and asserted the inestimable privilege of being tried only by their *peers*; and even in a capital accusation, a synod of their brethren were the sole judges of their guilt or innocence. Such a tribunal, unless it was inflamed by personal resentment or religious discord, might be favourable, or even partial, to the sacerdotal order: but Constantine was satisfied[112] that secret impunity would be less pernicious than public scandal, and the Nicene council was edified by his public declaration, that, if he surprised a bishop in the act of adultery, he should cast his Imperial mantle over the episcopal sinner. 2. The domestic jurisdiction of the bishops was at once a privilege and a restraint of the ecclesiastical order, whose civil causes were decently withdrawn from the cognisance of a secular judge. Their venial offences were not exposed to the shame of a public trial or punishment; and the gentle correction which the tenderness of youth may endure from its parents or instructors was inflicted by the temperate severity of the bishops. But if the clergy were guilty of any crime which could not be sufficiently expiated by their degradation from an honourable and beneficial profession, the Roman magistrate drew the sword of justice, without any regard to ecclesiastical immunities. 3. The arbitration of the bishops was ratified by a positive law; and the judges were instructed to execute, without appeal or delay, the episcopal decrees, whose validity had hitherto depended on the consent of the parties. The conversion of the magistrates themselves, and of the whole empire, might gradually remove the fears and scruples of the Christians. But they still resorted to the tribunal of the bishops, whose abilities and integrity they esteemed; and the venerable Austin enjoyed the satisfaction of complaining that his spiritual functions were perpetually interrupted by the invidious labour of deciding the claim or the possession of silver and gold, of lands and cattle. 4. The ancient privilege of sanctuary was transferred to the Christian temples, and extended, by the liberal piety of the younger Theodosius, to the precincts of consecrated ground.[113] The fugitive, and even guilty, suppliants were permitted to implore either the justice or the mercy of the Deity and his ministers. The rash violence of despotism was suspended by the mild interposition of the church, and the lives or fortunes of the most eminent subjects might be protected by the mediation of the bishop.

V. The bishop was the perpetual censor of

the morals of his people. The discipline of penance was digested into a system of canonical jurisprudence,[114] which accurately defined the duty of private or public confession, the rules of evidence, the degrees of guilt, and the measure of punishment. It was impossible to execute this spiritual censure, if the Christian pontiff who punished the obscure sins of the multitude, respected the conspicuous vices and destructive crimes of the magistrate: but it was impossible to arraign the conduct of the magistrate without controlling the administration of civil government. Some considerations of religion, or loyalty, or fear, protected the sacred persons of the emperors from the zeal or resentment of the bishops; but they boldly censured and excommunicated the subordinate tyrants who were not invested with the majesty of the purple. St. Athanasius excommunicated one of the ministers of Egypt, and the interdict which he pronounced of fire and water was solemnly transmitted to the churches of Cappodocia.[115] Under the reign of the younger Theodosius, the polite and eloquent Synesius, one of the descendants of Hercules,[116] filled the episcopal seat of Ptolemais, near the ruins of ancient Cyrene,[117] and the philosophic bishop supported with dignity the character which he had assumed with reluctance.[118] He vanquished the monster of Libya, the president Andronicus, who abused the authority of a venal office, invented new modes of rapine and torture, and aggravated the guilt of oppression by that of sacrilege.[119] After a fruitless attempt to reclaim the haughty magistrate by mild and religious admonition, Synesius proceeds to inflict the last sentence of ecclesiastical justice,[120] which devotes Andronicus, with his associates and their *families*, to the abhorrence of earth and heaven. The impenitent sinners, more cruel than Phalaris or Sennacherib, more destructive than war, pestilence, or a cloud of locusts, are deprived of the name and privileges of Christians, of the participation of the sacraments, and of the hope of Paradise. The bishop exhorts the clergy, the magistrates, and the people to renounce all society with the enemies of Christ, to exclude them from their houses and tables, and to refuse them the common offices of life, and the decent rites of burial. The church of Ptolemais, obscure and contemptible as she may appear, addresses this declaration to all her sister churches of the world; and the profane who reject her decrees will be involved in the guilt and punishment of Andronicus and his impious followers. These spiritual terrors were enforced by a dexterous application to the Byzantine court; the trembling president implored the mercy of the church, and the descendant of Hercules enjoyed the satisfaction of raising a prostrate tyrant from the ground.[121] Such principles and such examples insensibly prepared the triumph of the Roman pontiffs, who have trampled on the necks of kings.

VI. Every popular government has experienced the effects of rude or artificial eloquence. The coldest nature is animated, the firmest reason is moved, by the rapid communication of the prevailing impulse; and each hearer is affected by his own passions and by those of the surrounding multitude. The ruin of civil liberty had silenced the demagogues of Athens and the tribunes of Rome; the custom of preaching, which seems to constitute a considerable part of Christian devotion, had not been introduced into the temples of antiquity; and the ears of monarchs were never invaded by the harsh sound of popular eloquence till the pulpits of the empire were filled with sacred orators, who possessed some advantages unknown to their profane predecessors.[122] The arguments and rhetoric of the tribune were instantly opposed, with equal arms, by skilful and resolute antagonists; and the cause of truth and reason might derive an accidental support from the conflict of hostile passions. The bishop, or some distinguished presbyter to whom he cautiously delegated the powers of preaching, harangued, without the danger of interruption or reply, a submissive multitude, whose minds had been prepared and subdued by the awful ceremonies of religion. Such was the strict subordination of the Catholic church, that the same concerted sounds might issue at once from an hundred pulpits of Italy or Egypt, if they were *tuned*[123] by the master-hand of the Roman or Alexandrian primate. The design of this institution was laudable, but the fruits were not always salutary. The preachers recommended the practice of the social duties; but they exalted the perfection of monastic virtue, which is painful to the individual, and useless to mankind. Their charitable exhortations betrayed a secret wish that the clergy might be permitted to manage the wealth of the faithful for the benefit of the poor. The most sublime representations of the attributes and laws of the Deity were sullied by an idle mixture of metaphysical subtleties, puerile rites, and fictitious miracles: and they expatiated, with the most fervent zeal, on the religious merit of hating the adversaries and obeying the ministers of the church. When the public peace was distracted by heresy and schism, the sacred orators sounded the trumpet of discord, and perhaps of sedition. The understandings of their congregations were perplexed by mystery, their passions were inflamed by invectives; and they rushed from the Christian temples of Antioch or Alexandria, prepared either to suffer or to inflict martyrdom. The corruption of taste and language is strongly marked in the vehement declamations of the Latin bishops; but the compositions of Gregory and Chrysostom have been compared with the most splendid models of Attic, or at least of Asiatic, eloquence.[124]

VII. The representatives of the Christian republic were regularly assembled in the spring and autumn of each year; and these synods diffused the spirit of ecclesiastical discipline and legislation through the hundred and twenty provinces of the Roman world.[125] The archbishop or metropolitan was empowered by the laws to summon the suffragan bishops of his province; to revise their conduct, to vindicate their rights, to declare their faith, and to examine the merit of the candidates who were elected by the clergy and people to supply the vacancies of the episcopal college. The primates of Rome, Alexandria, Antioch, Carthage, and afterwards Constantinople, who exercised a more ample jurisdiction, convened the numerous assembly of their dependent bishops. But the convocation of great and extraordinary synods was the prerogative of the emperor alone. Whenever the emergencies of the church required this decisive measure, he despatched a peremptory summons to the bishops or the deputies of each province, with an order for the use of post-horses and a competent allowance for the expenses of their journey. At an early period, when Constantine was the protector rather than the proselyte of Christianity, he referred the African controversy to the council of Arles; in which the bishops of York, of Treves, of Milan, and of Carthage, met as friends and brethren, to debate in their native tongue on the common interest of the Latin or Western

church.[126] Eleven years afterwards, a more numerous and celebrated assembly was convened at Nice in Bithynia, to extinguish, by their final sentence, the subtle disputes which had arisen in Egypt on the subject of the Trinity. Three hundred and eighteen bishops obeyed the summons of their indulgent master; the ecclesiastics of every rank and sect and denomination have been computed at two thousand and forty-eight persons;[127] the Greeks appeared in person; and the consent of the Latins was expressed by the legates of the Roman pontiff. The session, which lasted about two months, was frequently honoured by the presence of the emperor. Leaving his guards at the door, he seated himself (with the permission of the council) on a low stool in the midst of the hall. Constantine listened with patience and spoke with modesty; and while he influenced the debates, he humbly professed that he was the minister, not the judge, of the successors of the apostles, who had been established as priests and as gods upon earth.[128] Such profound reverence of an absolute monarch towards a feeble and unarmed assembly of his own subjects can only be compared to the respect with which the senate had been treated by the Roman princes who adopted the policy of Augustus. Within the space of fifty years, a philosophic spectator of the vicissitudes of human affairs might have contemplated Tacitus in the senate of Rome, and Constantine in the council of Nice. The fathers of the Capitol and those of the church had alike degenerated from the virtues of their founders; but as the bishops were more deeply rooted in the public opinion, they sustained their dignity with more decent pride, and sometimes opposed with a manly spirit the wishes of their sovereign. The progress of time and superstition erased the memory of the weakness, the passion, the ignorance, which disgraced these ecclesiastical synods; and the catholic world has unanimously submitted[129] to the *infallible* decrees of the general councils.[130]

CHAPTER XXI

Persecution of Heresy. The Schism of the Donatists. The Arian Controversy. Athanasius. Distracted State of the Church and Empire under Constantine and his Sons. Toleration of Paganism.

THE grateful applause of the clergy has consecrated the memory of a prince, who indulged their passions and promoted their interest. Constantine gave them security, wealth, honours, and revenge; and the support of the orthodox faith was considered as the most sacred and important duty of the civil magistrate. The edict of Milan, the great charter of toleration, had confirmed to each individual of the Roman world the privilege of choosing and professing his own religion. But this inestimable privilege was soon violated: with the knowledge of truth the emperor imbibed the maxims of persecution; and the sects which dissented from the Catholic church were afflicted and oppressed by the triumph of Christianity. Constantine easily believed that the heretics, who presumed to dispute *his* opinions or to oppose *his* commands, were guilty of the most absurd and criminal obstinacy; and that a seasonable application of moderate severities might save those unhappy men from the danger of an everlasting condemnation. Not a moment was lost in excluding the ministers and teachers of the separated congregations from any share of the rewards and immunities which the emperor had so liberally bestowed on the orthodox clergy. But as the sectaries might still exist under the cloud of royal disgrace, the conquest of the East was immediately followed by an edict which announced their total destruction.[1] After a preamble filled with passion and reproach, Constantine absolutely prohibits the assemblies of the heretics, and confiscates their public property to the use either of the revenue or of the Catholic church. The sects against whom the Imperial severity was directed appear to have been the adherents of Paul of Samosata; the Montanists of Phrygia, who maintained an enthusiastic succession of prophecy; the Novatians, who sternly rejected the temporal efficacy of repentance; the Marcionites and Valentinians, under whose leading banners the various Gnostics of Asia and Egypt had insensibly rallied; and perhaps the Manichæans, who had recently imported from Persia a more artful composition of Oriental and Christian theology.[2] The design of extirpating the

name, or at least of restraining the progress, of these odious heretics, was prosecuted with vigour and effect. Some of the penal regulations were copied from the edicts of Diocletian; and this method of conversion was applauded by the same bishops who had felt the hand of oppression, and had pleaded for the rights of humanity. Two immaterial circumstances may serve, however, to prove that the mind of Constantine was not entirely corrupted by the spirit of zeal and bigotry. Before he condemned the Manichæans and their kindred sects, he resolved to make an accurate inquiry into the nature of their religious principles. As if he distrusted the impartiality of his ecclesiastical counsellors, this delicate commission was intrusted to a civil magistrate, whose learning and moderation he justly esteemed, and of whose venal character he was probably ignorant.[3] The emperor was soon convinced that he had too hastily proscribed the orthodox faith and the exemplary morals of the Novatians, who had dissented from the church in some articles of discipline which were not perhaps essential to salvation. By a particular edict he exempted them from the general penalties of the law;[4] allowed them to build a church at Constantinople; respected the miracles of their saints; invited their bishop, Acesius, to the council of Nice; and gently ridiculed the narrow tenets of his sect by a familiar jest, which from the mouth of a sovereign must have been received with applause and gratitude.[5]

The complaints and mutual accusations which assailed the throne of Constantine, as soon as the death of Maxentius had submitted Africa to his victorious arms, were ill adapted to edify an imperfect proselyte. He learned with surprise that the provinces of that great country, from the confines of Cyrene to the Columns of Hercules, were distracted with religious discord.[6] The source of the division was derived from a double election in the church of Carthage, the second in rank and opulence of the ecclesiastical thrones of the West. Cæcilian and Majourinus were the two rival primates of Africa; and the death of the latter soon made room for Donatus, who, by his superior abilities and apparent virtues, was the firmest support of his party. The advantage which Cæcilian might claim from the priority of his ordination was destroyed by the illegal, or at least indecent, haste with which it had been performed, without expecting the arrival of the bishops of Numidia. The authority of these bishops, who, to the number of seventy, condemned Cæcilian, and consecrated Majorinus, is again weakened by the infamy of some of their personal characters; and by the female intrigues, sacrilegious bargains, and tumultuous proceedings, which are imputed to this Numidian council.[7] The bishops of the contending factions maintained, with equal ardour and obstinacy, that their adversaries were degraded, or at least dishonoured, by the odious crime of delivering the Holy Scriptures to the officers of Diocletian. From their mutual reproaches, as well as from the story of this dark transaction, it may justly be inferred that the late persecution had embittered the zeal, without reforming the manners, of the African Christians. That divided church was incapable of affording an impartial judicature; the controversy was solemnly tried in five successive tribunals, which were appointed by the emperor; and the whole proceeding, from the first appeal to the final sentence, lasted above three years. A severe inquisition, which was taken by the prætorian vicar and the proconsul of Africa, the report of two episcopal visitors who had been sent to Carthage, the decrees of the councils of Rome and of Arles, and the supreme judgment of Constantine himself in his sacred consistory, were all favourable to the cause of Cæcilian; and he was unanimously acknowledged by the civil and ecclesiastical powers as the true and lawful primate of Africa. The honours and estates of the church were attributed to *his* suffragan bishops, and it was not without difficulty that Constantine was satisfied with inflicting the punishment of exile on the principal leaders of the Donatist faction. As their cause was examined with attention, perhaps it was determined with justice. Perhaps their complaint was not without foundation, that the credulity of the emperor had been abused by the insidious arts of his favourite Osius. The influence of falsehood and corruption might procure the condemnation of the innocent, or aggravate the sentence of the guilty. Such an act, however, of injustice, if it concluded an importunate dispute, might be numbered among the transient evils of a despotic administration, which are neither felt nor remembered by posterity.

But this incident, so inconsiderable that it scarcely deserves a place in history, was productive of a memorable schism, which afflicted the provinces of Africa above three hundred years, and was extinguished only with Christianity itself. The inflexible zeal of freedom and fanaticism animated the Donatists to refuse obedience to the usurpers, whose election they disputed, and whose spiritual powers they denied. Excluded from the civil and religious communion of mankind, they boldly excommunicated the rest of mankind who had embraced the impious party of Cæcilian, and of the Traditors, from whom he derived his pretended ordination. They asserted with confidence, and almost with exultation, that the Apostolical succession was interrupted; that *all* the bishops of Europe and Asia were infected by the contagion of guilt and schism; and that the prerogatives of the catholic church were confined to the chosen portion of the African believers, who alone had preserved inviolate the integrity of their faith and discipline. This rigid theory was supported by the most uncharitable conduct. Whenever they acquired a proselyte, even from the distant provinces of the East, they carefully repeated the sacred rites of baptism[8] and ordination; as they rejected the validity of those which he had already received from the hands of heretics or schismatics. Bishops, virgins, and even spotless infants, were subjected to the disgrace of a public penance before they could be admitted to the communion of the Donatists. If they obtained possession of a church which had been used by their Catholic adversaries, they purified the unhallowed building with the same jealous care which a temple of idols might have required. They washed the pavement, scraped the walls, burnt the altar (which was commonly of wood), melted the consecrated plate, and cast the Holy Eucharist to the dogs, with every circumstance of ignominy which could provoke and perpetuate the animosity of religious factions.[9] Notwithstanding this irreconcilable aversion, the two parties, who were mixed and separated in all the cities of Africa, had the same language and manners, the same zeal and learning, the same faith and worship. Proscribed by the civil and ecclesiastical powers of the empire, the Donatists still maintained in some provinces, particularly in Numidia, their superior numbers; and four hundred bishops acknowledged the jurisdiction of their primate. But the invincible spirit of the sect sometimes preyed on its own vitals: and the bosom of their schismatical church was torn by intestine divisions. A fourth part of the Donatist bishops followed the independent standard of the Maximianists. The narrow and solitary path which their first leaders had marked out continued to deviate from the great society of mankind. Even the imperceptible sect of the Rogatians could affirm, without a blush, that when Christ should descend to judge the earth, he would find his true religion preserved only in a few nameless villages of the Cæsarean Mauritania.[10]

The schism of the Donatists was confined to Africa; the more diffusive mischief of the Trinitarian controversy successively penetrated into every part of the Christian world. The former was an accidental quarrel, occasioned by the abuse of freedom; the latter was a high and mysterious argument, derived from the abuse of philosophy. From the age of Constantine to that of Clovis and Theodoric, the temporal interests both of the Romans and barbarians were deeply involved in the theological disputes of Arianism. The historian may therefore be permitted respectfully to withdraw the veil of the sanctuary, and to deduce the progress of reason and faith, of error and passion, from the school of Plato to the decline and fall of the empire.

The genius of Plato, informed by his own meditation or by the traditional knowledge of the priests of Egypt,[11] had ventured to explore the mysterious nature of the Deity. When he had elevated his mind to the sublime contemplation of the first self-existent, necessary cause of the universe, the Athenian sage was incapable of conceiving *how* the simple unity of his essence could admit the infinite variety of distinct and successive ideas which compose the model of the intellectual world; *how* a Being purely incorporeal could execute that perfect model, and mould with a plastic hand the rude and independent chaos. The vain hope of extricating himself from these difficulties, which must ever oppress the feeble powers of the human mind, might induce Plato to consider the divine nature under the threefold modification—of the first cause, the reason, or *Logos*, and the soul or spirit of the universe. His poetical imagination sometimes fixed and animated these metaphysical abstractions; the three *archical* or original principles were represented in the Platonic system as three Gods, united with each other by a mysterious and ineffable generation; and the Logos was particularly considered under the more accessible character of the Son of an Eternal Father, and the Creator and Governor of the world. Such appear to have been the secret doctrines which were cautiously whispered in the gardens of the Academy; and which, according to the more recent disciples of Plato, could not be perfectly understood till after an assiduous study of thirty years.[12]

The arms of the Macedonians diffused over Asia and Egypt the language and learning of Greece; and the theological system of Plato was taught, with less reserve, and perhaps with some improvements, in the celebrated school of Alexandria.[13] A numerous colony of Jews had been invited, by the favour of the Ptolemies, to settle in their new capital.[14] While the bulk of the nation practised the legal ceremonies, and pursued the lucrative occupations of commerce, a few Hebrews of a more liberal spirit devoted their lives to religious and philosophical contemplation.[15] They cultivated with diligence, and embraced with ardour, the theological system of the Athenian sage. But their national pride would have been mortified by a fair confession of their former poverty: and they boldly marked, as the sacred inheritance of their ancestors, the gold and jewels which they had so lately stolen from their Egyptian masters. One hundred years before the birth of Christ, a philosophical treatise, which manifestly betrays the style and sentiments of the school of Plato, was produced by the Alexandrian Jews, and unanimously received as a genuine and valuable relic of the inspired Wisdom of Solomon.[16] A similar union of the Mosaic faith and the Grecian philosophy distinguishes the works of Philo, which were composed, for the most part, under the reign of Augustus.[17] The material soul of the universe[18] might offend the piety of the Hebrews; but they applied the character of the Logos to the Jehovah of Moses and the Patriarchs; and the Son of God was introduced upon earth, under a visible and even human appearance, to perform those familiar offices which seem incompatible with the nature and attributes of the Universal Cause.[19]

The eloquence of Plato, the name of Solomon, the authority of the school of Alexandria, and the consent of the Jews and Greeks, were insufficient to establish the truth of a mysterious doctrine, which might please, but could not satisfy, a rational mind. A prophet, or apostle, inspired by the Deity, can alone exercise a lawful dominion over the faith of mankind: and the theology of Plato might have been for ever confounded with the philosophical visions of the Academy, the Porch, and the Lyceum, if the name and divine attributes of the *Logos* had not been confirmed by the celestial pen of the last and most sublime of the Evangelists.[20] The

Christian Revelation, which was consummated under the reign of Nerva, disclosed to the world the amazing secret, that the LOGOS, who was with God from the beginning, and was God, who had made all things, and for whom all things had been made, was incarnate in the person of Jesus of Nazareth; who had been born of a virgin, and suffered death on the cross. Besides the general design of fixing on a perpetual basis the divine honours of Christ, the most ancient and respectable of the ecclesiastical writers have ascribed to the evangelic theologian a particular intention to confute two opposite heresies, which disturbed the peace of the primitive church.[21] I. The faith of the Ebionites,[22] perhaps of the Nazarenes,[23] was gross and imperfect. They revered Jesus as the greatest of the prophets, endowed with supernatural virtue and power. They ascribed to his person and to his future reign all the predictions of the Hebrew oracles which relate to the spiritual and everlasting kingdom of the promised Messiah.[24] Some of them might confess that he was born of a virgin; but they obstinately rejected the preceding existence and divine perfections of the Logos, or Son of God, which are so clearly defined in the Gospel of St. John. About fifty years afterwards, the Ebionites, whose errors are mentioned by Justin Martyr, with less severity than they seem to deserve,[25] formed a very inconsiderable portion of the Christian name. II. The Gnostics, who were distinguished by the epithet of *Docetes*, deviated into the contrary extreme; and betrayed the human, while they asserted the divine nature of Christ. Educated in the school of Plato, accustomed to the sublime idea of the *Logos*, they readily conceived that the brightest *Æon*, or *Emanation* of the Deity, might assume the outward shape and visible appearances of a mortal;[26] but they vainly pretended that the imperfections of matter are incompatible with the purity of a celestial substance. While the blood of Christ yet smoked on Mount Calvary, the Docetes invented the impious and extravagant hypothesis, that, instead of issuing from the womb of the Virgin,[27] he had descended on the banks of the Jordan in the form of perfect manhood; that he had imposed on the senses of his enemies and of his disciples; and that the ministers of Pilate had wasted their impotent rage on an airy phantom, who *seemed* to expire on the cross, and, after three days, to rise from the dead.[28]

The divine sanction which the Apostle had bestowed on the fundamental principle of the theology of Plato encouraged the learned prose-lytes of the second and third centuries to admire and study the writings of the Athenian sage, who had thus marvellously anticipated one of the most surprising discoveries of the Christian revelation. The respectable name of Plato was used by the orthodox,[29] and abused by the heretics,[30] as the common support of truth and error: the authority of his skilful commentators and the science of dialectics were employed to justify the remote consequences of his opinions, and to supply the discreet silence of the inspired writers. The same subtle and profound questions concerning the nature, the generation, the distinction, and the equality of the three divine persons of the mysterious *Triad*, or *Trinity*,[31] were agitated in the philosophical and in the Christian schools of Alexandria. An eager spirit of curiosity urged them to explore the secrets of the abyss; and the pride of the professors and of their disciples was satisfied with the science of words. But the most sagacious of the Christian theologians, the great Athanasius himself, has candidly confessed[32] that, whenever he forced his understanding to meditate on the divinity of the *Logos*, his toilsome and unavailing efforts recoiled on themselves; that the more he thought, the less he comprehended; and the more he wrote, the less capable was he of expressing his thoughts. In every step of the inquiry we are compelled to feel and acknowledge the immeasurable disproportion between the size of the object and the capacity of the human mind. We may strive to abstract the notions of time, of space, and of matter, which so closely adhere to all the perceptions of our experimental knowledge. But as soon as we presume to reason of infinite substance, of spiritual generation, as often as we deduce any positive conclusions from a negative idea, we are involved in darkness, perplexity, and inevitable contradiction. As these difficulties arise from the nature of the subject, they oppress, with the same insuperable weight, the philosophic and the theological disputant; but we may observe two essential and peculiar circumstances which discriminated the doctrines of the catholic church from the opinions of the Platonic school.

I. A chosen society of philosophers, men of a liberal education and curious disposition, might silently meditate, and temperately discuss in the gardens of Athens or the library of Alexandria, the abstruse questions of metaphysical science. The lofty speculations, which neither convinced the understanding nor agitated the passions of the Platonists themselves, were carelessly overlooked by the idle, the busy, and even the studious part of mankind.[33] But after the *Logos* had been revealed as the sacred object of the faith, the hope, and the religious worship of the Christians, the mysterious system was embraced by a numerous and increasing multitude in every province of the Roman world. Those persons who, from their age, or sex, or occupations, were the least qualified to judge, who were the least exercised in the habits of abstract reasoning, aspired to contemplate the economy of the Divine Nature: and it is the boast of Tertullian[34] that a Christian mechanic could readily answer such questions as had perplexed the wisest of the Grecian sages. Where the subject lies so far beyond our reach, the difference between the highest and the lowest of human understandings may indeed be calculated as infinitely small; yet the degree of weakness may perhaps be measured by the degree of obstinacy and dogmatic confidence. These speculations, instead of being treated as the amusement of a vacant hour, became the most serious business of the present, and the most useful preparation for a future life. A theology which it was incumbent to believe, which it was impious to doubt, and which it might be dangerous, and even fatal, to mistake, became the familiar topic of private meditation and popular discourse. The cold indifference of philosophy was inflamed by the fervent spirit of devotion; and even the metaphors of common language suggested the fallacious prejudices of sense and experience. The Christians, who abhorred the gross and impure generation of the Greek mythology,[35] were tempted to argue from the familiar analogy of the filial and paternal relations. The character of *Son* seemed to imply a perpetual subordination to the voluntary author of his existence;[36] but as the act of generation, in the most spiritual and abstracted sense, must be supposed to transmit the properties of a common nature,[37] they durst not presume to circumscribe the powers or the duration of the Son of an eternal and omnipotent Father. Fourscore years after the death of Christ, the Christians of Bithynia declared before the tribunal of Pliny that they invoked him as a god: and his divine honours have been perpetuated in every age and country, by the various sects who assume the name of his disciples.[38] Their tender reverence for the memory of Christ, and their horror for the profane worship of any created being, would have engaged them to assert the equal and absolute divinity of the *Logos*, if their rapid ascent towards the throne of heaven had not been imperceptibly checked by the apprehension of violating the

unity and sole supremacy of the great Father of Christ, and of the Universe. The suspense and fluctuation produced in the minds of the Christians by these opposite tendencies may be observed in the writings of the theologians who flourished after the end of the apostolic age and before the origin of the Arian controversy. Their suffrage is claimed, with equal confidence, by the orthodox and by the heretical parties; and the most inquisitive critics have fairly allowed that, if they had the good fortune of possessing the catholic verity, they have delivered their conceptions in loose, inaccurate, and sometimes contradictory language.[39]

II. The devotion of individuals was the first circumstance which distinguished the Christians from the Platonists: the second was the authority of the church. The disciples of philosophy asserted the rights of intellectual freedom, and their respect for the sentiments of their teachers was a liberal and voluntary tribute which they offered to superior reason. But the Christians formed a numerous and disciplined society; and the jurisdiction of their laws and magistrates was strictly exercised over the minds of the faithful. The loose wanderings of the imagination were gradually confined by creeds and confessions;[40] the freedom of private judgment submitted to the public wisdom of synods; the authority of a theologian was determined by his ecclesiastical rank; and the episcopal successors of the apostles inflicted the censures of the church on those who deviated from the orthodox belief. But in an age of religious controversy every act of oppression adds new force to the elastic vigour of the mind; and the zeal or obstinacy of a spiritual rebel was sometimes stimulated by secret motives of ambition or avarice. A metaphysical argument became the cause or pretence of political contests; the subtleties of the Platonic school were used as the badges of popular factions, and the distance which separated their respective tenets was enlarged or magnified by the acrimony of dispute. As long as the dark heresies of Praxeas and Sabellius laboured to confound the *Father* with the *Son*,[41] the orthodox party might be excused if they adhered more strictly and more earnestly to the *distinction* than to the *equality* of the divine persons. But as soon as the heat of controversy had subsided and the progress of the Sabellians was no longer an object of terror to the churches of Rome, of Africa, or of Egypt, the tide of theological opinion began to flow with a gentle but steady motion toward the contrary extreme; and the most orthodox doctors allowed them-

selves the use of the terms and definitions which
had been censured in the mouth of the sectaries.[42] After the edict of toleration had restored
peace and leisure to the Christians, the Trinitarian controversy was revived in the ancient
seat of Platonism, the learned, the opulent, the
tumultuous city of Alexandria; and the flame
of religious discord was rapidly communicated
from the schools to the clergy, the people, the
provinces, and the East. The abstruse question
of the eternity of the *Logos* was agitated in ecclesiastic conferences and popular sermons; and
the heterodox opinions of Arius[43] were soon
made public by his own zeal and by that of his
adversaries. His most implacable adversaries
have acknowledged the learning and blameless
life of the eminent presbyter, who, in a former
election, had declined, and perhaps generously
declined, his pretensions to the episcopal throne.[44]
His competitor Alexander assumed the office of
his judge. The important cause was argued before him; and if at first he seemed to hesitate, he
at length pronounced his final sentence as an
absolute rule of faith.[45] The undaunted presbyter, who presumed to resist the authority of
his angry bishop, was separated from the communion of the church. But the pride of Arius
was supported by the applause of a numerous
party. He reckoned among his immediate followers two bishops of Egypt, seven presbyters,
twelve deacons, and (what may appear almost
incredible) seven hundred virgins. A large majority of the bishops of Asia appeared to support
or favour his cause; and their measures were
conducted by Eusebius of Cæsarea, the most
learned of the Christian prelates; and by Eusebius of Nicomedia, who had acquired the reputation of a statesman without forfeiting that of a
saint. Synods in Palestine and Bithynia were
opposed to the synods of Egypt. The attention
of the prince and people was attracted by this
theological dispute; and the decision, at the end
of six years,[46] was referred to the supreme authority of the general council of Nice.

When the mysteries of the Christian faith
were dangerously exposed to public debate, it
might be observed that the human understanding was capable of forming three distinct, though
imperfect, systems concerning the nature of the
Divine Trinity, and it was pronounced that
none of these systems, in a pure and absolute
sense, were exempt from heresy and error.[47]
I. According to the first hypothesis, which was
maintained by Arius and his disciples, the *Logos*
was a dependent and spontaneous production,
created from nothing by the will of the Father.

The Son, by whom all things were made,[48] had
been begotten before all worlds, and the longest
of the astronomical periods could be compared
only as a fleeting moment to the extent of his
duration; yet this duration was not infinite,[49]
and there *had* been a time which preceded the
ineffable generation of the *Logos*. On this only-
begotten Son the Almighty Father had trans-
fused his ample spirit, and impressed the efful-
gence of his glory. Visible image of invisible perfection, he saw, at an immeasurable distance
beneath his feet, the thrones of the brightest
archangels; yet he shone only with a reflected
light, and, like the sons of the Roman emperors,
who were invested with the titles of Cæsar or
Augustus,[50] he governed the universe in obedience to the will of his Father and Monarch.
II. In the second hypothesis, the *Logos* possessed
all the inherent, incommunicable perfections
which religion and philosophy appropriate to
the Supreme God. Three distinct and infinite
minds or substances, three co-equal and co-
eternal beings, composed the Divine Essence;[51]
and it would have implied contradiction that
any of them should not have existed, or that
they should ever cease to exist.[52] The advocates
of a system which seemed to establish three independent Deities attempted to preserve the
unity of the First Cause, so conspicuous in the
design and order of the world, by the perpetual
concord of their administration and the essential agreement of their will. A faint resemblance
of this unity of action may be discovered in the
societies of men, and even of animals. The causes
which disturb their harmony proceed only from
the imperfection and inequality of their faculties; but the omnipotence which is guided by infinite wisdom and goodness cannot fail of choosing the same means for the accomplishment of
the same ends. III. Three beings, who, by the
self-derived necessity of their existence, possess
all the divine attributes in the most perfect
degree, who are eternal in duration, infinite in
space, and intimately present to each other and
to the whole universe, irresistibly force themselves on the astonished mind as one and the
same Being,[53] who, in the economy of grace, as
well as in that of nature, may manifest himself
under different forms, and be considered under
different aspects. By this hypothesis a real substantial trinity is refined into a trinity of names
and abstract modifications that subsist only in
the mind which conceives them. The *Logos* is no
longer a person, but an attribute; and it is only
in a figurative sense that the epithet of Son can
be applied to the eternal reason which was with

God from the beginning, and by *which*, not by *whom*, all things were made. The incarnation of the *Logos* is reduced to a mere inspiration of the Divine Wisdom, which filled the soul and directed all the actions of the man Jesus. Thus, after revolving round the theological circle, we are surprised to find that the Sabellian ends where the Ebionite had begun, and that the incomprehensible mystery which excites our adoration eludes our inquiry.[54]

If the bishops of the council of Nice[55] had been permitted to follow the unbiassed dictates of their conscience, Arius and his associates could scarcely have flattered themselves with the hopes of obtaining a majority of votes in favour of an hypothesis so directly adverse to the two most popular opinions of the catholic world. The Arians soon perceived the danger of their situation, and prudently assumed those modest virtues which, in the fury of civil and religious dissensions, are seldom practised, or even praised, except by the weaker party. They recommended the exercise of Christian charity and moderation, urged the incomprehensible nature of the controversy, disclaimed the use of any terms or definitions which could not be found in the Scriptures, and offered, by very liberal concessions, to satisfy their adversaries without renouncing the integrity of their own principles. The victorious faction received all their proposals with haughty suspicion, and anxiously sought for some irreconcilable mark of distinction, the rejection of which might involve the Arians in the guilt and consequences of heresy. A letter was publicly read and ignominiously torn, in which their patron, Eusebius of Nicomedia, ingenuously confessed that the admission of the Homoousion, or Consubstantial, a word already familiar to the Platonists, was incompatible with the principles of their theological system. The fortunate opportunity was eagerly embraced by the bishops, who governed the resolutions of the synod, and, according to the lively expressions of Ambrose,[56] they used the sword, which heresy itself had drawn from the scabbard, to cut off the head of the hated monster. The consubstantiality of the Father and the Son was established by the council of Nice, and has been unanimously received as a fundamental article of the Christian faith by the consent of the Greek, the Latin, the Oriental, and the Protestant churches. But if the same word had not served to stigmatise the heretics and to unite the catholics, it would have been inadequate to the purpose of the majority by whom it was introduced into the or-

thodox creed. This majority was divided into two parties, distinguished by a contrary tendency to the sentiments of the Tritheists and of the Sabellians. But as those opposite extremes seemed to overthrow the foundations either of natural or revealed religion, they mutually agreed to qualify the rigour of their principles, and to disavow the just, but invidious, consequences which might be urged by their antagonists. The interest of the common cause inclined them to join their numbers and to conceal their differences; their animosity was softened by the healing counsels of toleration, and their disputes were suspended by the use of the mysterious *Homoousion*, which either party was free to interpret according to their peculiar tenets. The Sabellian sense, which, about fifty years before, had obliged the council of Antioch[57] to prohibit this celebrated term, had endeared it to those theologians who entertained a secret but partial affection for a nominal Trinity. But the more fashionable saints of the Arian times, the intrepid Athanasius, the learned Gregory Nazianzen, and the other pillars of the church, who supported with ability and success the Nicene doctrine, appeared to consider the expression of *substance* as if it had been synonymous with that of *nature*; and they ventured to illustrate their meaning by affirming that three men, as they belong to the same common species, are consubstantial or homoousian to each other.[58] This pure and distinct equality was tempered, on the one hand, by the internal connection and spiritual penetration which indissolubly unites the divine persons;[59] and, on the other, by the pre-eminence of the Father, which was acknowledged as far as it is compatible with the independence of the Son.[60] Within these limits the almost invisible and tremulous ball of orthodoxy was allowed securely to vibrate. On either side, beyond this consecrated ground, the heretics and the dæmons lurked in ambush to surprise and devour the unhappy wanderer. But as the degrees of theological hatred depend on the spirit of the war rather than on the importance of the controversy, the heretics who degraded were treated with more severity than those who annihilated the person of the Son. The life of Athanasius was consumed in irreconcilable opposition to the impious *madness* of the Arians,[61] but he defended above twenty years the Sabellianism of Marcellus of Ancyra; and when at last he was compelled to withdraw himself from his communion, he continued to mention with an ambiguous smile the venial errors of his respectable friend.[62]

The authority of a general council, to which the Arians themselves had been compelled to submit, inscribed on the banners of the orthodox party the mysterious characters of the word Homoousion, which essentially contributed, notwithstanding some obscure disputes, some nocturnal combats, to maintain and perpetuate the uniformity of faith, or at least of language. The Consubstantialists, who by their success have deserved and obtained the title of Catholics, gloried in the simplicity and steadiness of their own creed, and insulted the repeated variations of their adversaries, who were destitute of any certain rule of faith. The sincerity or the cunning of the Arian chiefs, the fear of the laws or of the people, their reverence for Christ, their hatred of Athanasius, all the causes, human and divine, that influence and disturb the counsels of a theological faction, introduced among the sectaries a spirit of discord and inconstancy, which in the course of a few years erected eighteen different models of religion,[63] and avenged the violated dignity of the church. The zealous Hilary,[64] who, from the peculiar hardships of his situation, was inclined to extenuate rather than to aggravate the errors of the Oriental clergy, declares that, in the wide extent of the ten provinces of Asia to which he had been banished, there could be found very few prelates who had preserved the knowledge of the true God.[65] The oppression which he had felt, the disorders of which he was the spectator and the victim, appeased, during a short interval, the angry passions of his soul; and in the following passage, of which I shall transcribe a few lines, the bishop of Poitiers unwarily deviates into the style of a Christian philosopher. "It is a thing," says Hilary, "equally deplorable and dangerous, that there are as many creeds as opinions among men, as many doctrines as inclinations, and as many sources of blasphemy as there are faults among us; because we make creeds arbitrarily, and explain them as arbitrarily. The Homoousion is rejected, and received, and explained away by successive synods. The partial or total resemblance of the Father and of the Son is a subject of dispute for these unhappy times. Every year, nay, every moon, we make new creeds to describe invisible mysteries. We repent of what we have done, we defend those who repent, we anathematise those whom we defended. We condemn either the doctrine of others in ourselves, or our own in that of others; and, reciprocally tearing one another to pieces, we have been the cause of each other's ruin."[66]

It will not be expected, it would not perhaps be endured, that I should swell this theological digression by a minute examination of the eighteen creeds, the authors of which, for the most part, disclaimed the odious name of their parent Arius. It is amusing enough to delineate the form, and to trace the vegetation, of a singular plant; but the tedious detail of leaves without flowers, and of branches without fruit, would soon exhaust the patience and disappoint the curiosity of the laborious student. One question, which gradually arose from the Arian controversy, may, however, be noticed, as it served to produce and discriminate the three sects who were united only by their common aversion to the Homoousion of the Nicene synod. 1. If they were asked whether the Son was *like* unto the Father, the question was resolutely answered in the negative by the heretics who adhered to the principles of Arius, or indeed to those of philosophy, which seem to establish an infinite difference between the Creator and the most excellent of his creatures. This obvious consequence was maintained by Aëtius,[67] on whom the zeal of his adversaries bestowed the surname of the Atheist. His restless and aspiring spirit urged him to try almost every profession of human life. He was successively a slave, or at least a husbandman, a travelling tinker, a goldsmith, a physician, a schoolmaster, a theologian, and at last the apostle of a new church, which was propagated by the abilities of his disciple Eunomius.[68] Armed with texts of Scripture, and with captious syllogisms from the logic of Aristotle, the subtle Aëtius had acquired the fame of an invincible disputant, whom it was impossible either to silence or to convince. Such talents engaged the friendship of the Arian bishops, till they were forced to renounce and even to persecute a dangerous ally, who, by the accuracy of his reasoning, had prejudiced their cause in the popular opinion, and offended the piety of their most devoted followers. 2. The omnipotence of the Creator suggested a specious and respectful solution of the *likeness* of the Father and the Son; and faith might humbly receive what reason could not presume to deny, that the Supreme God might communicate his infinite perfections, and create a being similar only to himself.[69] These Arians were powerfully supported by the weight and abilities of their leaders, who had succeeded to the management of the Eusebian interest, and who occupied the principal thrones of the East. They detested, perhaps with some affectation, the impiety of Aëtius; they professed to believe, either without reserve or according to the Scriptures, that the Son was different from all *other* creatures, and similar only to the Father. But they denied that he was either of the same or of a similar substance; sometimes boldly justifying their dissent, and sometimes objecting to the use of the word substance, which seems to imply an adequate, or at least a distinct, notion of the nature of the Diety. 3. The sect which asserted the doctrine of a similar substance was the most numerous, at least in the provinces of Asia; and when the leaders of both parties were assembled in the council of Seleucia,[70] *their* opinion would have prevailed by a majority of one hundred and five to forty-three bishops. The Greek word which was chosen to express this mysterious resemblance bears so close an affinity to the orthodox symbol, that the profane of every age have derided the furious contests which the difference of a single diphthong excited between the Homoousians and the Homoiousians. As it frequently happens that the sounds and characters which approach the nearest to each other accidentally represent the most opposite ideas, the observation would be itself ridiculous, if it were possible to mark any real and sensible distinction between the doctrine of the Semi-Arians, as they were improperly styled, and that of the Catholics themselves. The bishop of Poitiers, who in his Phrygian exile very wisely aimed at a coalition of parties, endeavours to prove that, by a pious and faithful interpretation,[71] the *Homoiousion* may be reduced to a consubstantial sense. Yet he confesses that the word has a dark and suspicious aspect; and, as if darkness were congenial to theological disputes, the Semi-Arians, who advanced to the doors of the church, assailed them with the most unrelenting fury.

The provinces of Egypt and Asia, which cultivated the language and manners of the Greeks, had deeply imbibed the venom of the Arian controversy. The familiar study of the Platonic system, a vain and argumentative disposition, a copious and flexible idiom, supplied the clergy and people of the East with an inexhaustible flow of words and distinctions; and, in the midst of their fierce contentions, they easily forgot the doubt which is recommended by philosophy, and the submission which is enjoined by religion. The inhabitants of the West were of a less inquisitive spirit; their passions were not so forcibly moved by invisible objects, their minds were less frequently exercised by the habits of dispute; and such was the happy ignorance of the Gallican church, that Hilary himself, above thirty years after the first general council, was still a stranger to the Nicene creed.[72] The Latins

had received the rays of divine knowledge through the dark and doubtful medium of a translation. The poverty and stubbornness of their native tongue was not always capable of affording just equivalents for the Greek terms, for the technical words of the Platonic philosophy,[73] which had been consecrated, by the Gospel or by the church, to express the mysteries of the Christian faith, and a verbal defect might introduce into the Latin theology a long train of error or perplexity.[74] But as the western provincials had the good fortune of deriving their religion from an orthodox source, they preserved with steadiness the doctrine which they had accepted with docility; and when the Arian pestilence approached their frontiers, they were supplied with the seasonable preservative of the Homoousion by the paternal care of the Roman pontiff. Their sentiments and their temper were displayed in the memorable synod of Rimini, which surpassed in numbers the council of Nice, since it was composed of above four hundred bishops of Italy, Africa, Spain, Gaul, Britain, and Illyricum. From the first debates it appeared that only four score prelates adhered to the party, though *they* affected to anathematise the name and memory of Arius. But this inferiority was compensated by the advantages of skill, of experience, and of discipline; and the minority was conducted by Valens and Ursacius, two bishops of Illyricum, who had spent their lives in the intrigues of courts and councils, and who had been trained under the Eusebian banner in the religious wars of the East. By their arguments and negotiations they embarrassed, they confounded, they at last deceived the honest simplicity of the Latin bishops, who suffered the palladium of the faith to be extorted from their hands by fraud and importunity, rather than by open violence. The council of Rimini was not allowed to separate till the members had imprudently subscribed a captious creed, in which some expressions, susceptible of an heretical sense, were inserted in the room of the Homoousion. It was on this occasion that, according to Jerom, the world was surprised to find itself Arian.[75] But the bishops of the Latin provinces had no sooner reached their respective dioceses than they discovered their mistake, and repented of their weakness. The ignominious capitulation was rejected with disdain and abhorrence, and the Homoousian standard, which had been shaken but not overthrown, was more firmly replanted in all the churches of the West.[76]

Such was the rise and progress, and such were

the natural revolutions, of those theological disputes which disturbed the peace of Christianity under the reigns of Constantine and of his sons. But as those princes presumed to extend their despotism over the faith, as well as over the lives and fortunes of their subjects, the weight of their suffrage sometimes inclined the ecclesiastical balance: and the prerogatives of the King of Heaven were settled, or changed, or modified, in the cabinet of an earthly monarch.

The unhappy spirit of discord which pervaded the provinces of the East interrupted the triumph of Constantine; but the emperor continued for some time to view with cool and careless indifference the object of the dispute. As he was yet ignorant of the difficulty of appeasing the quarrels of theologians, he addressed to the contending parties, to Alexander and to Arius, a moderating epistle;[77] which may be ascribed with far greater reason to the untutored sense of a soldier and statesman than to the dictates of any of his episcopal counsellors. He attributes the origin of the whole controversy to a trifling and subtle question concerning an incomprehensible point of the law, which was foolishly asked by the bishop, and imprudently resolved by the presbyter. He laments that the Christian people, who had the same God, the same religion, and the same worship, should be divided by such inconsiderable distinctions; and he seriously recommends to the clergy of Alexandria the example of the Greek philosophers, who could maintain their arguments without losing their temper and assert their freedom without violating their friendship. The indifference and contempt of the sovereign would have been, perhaps, the most effectual method of silencing the dispute, if the popular current had been less rapid and impetuous, and if Constantine himself, in the midst of faction and fanaticism, could have preserved the calm possession of his own mind. But his ecclesiastical ministers soon contrived to seduce the impartiality of the magistrate, and to awaken the zeal of the proselyte. He was provoked by the insults which had been offered to his statues; he was alarmed by the real as well as the imaginary magnitude of the spreading mischief; and he extinguished the hope of peace and toleration, from the moment that he assembled three hundred bishops within the walls of the same palace. The presence of the monarch swelled the importance of the debate; his attention multiplied the arguments; and he exposed his person with a patient intrepidity which animated the valour of the combatants. Notwithstanding the applause which has been bestowed on the eloquence and sagacity of Constantine,[78] a Roman general, whose religion might be still a subject of doubt, and whose mind had not been enlightened either by study or by inspiration, was indifferently qualified to discuss, in the Greek language, a metaphysical question, or an article of faith. But the credit of his favourite Osius, who appears to have presided in the council of Nice, might dispose the emperor in favour of the orthodox party; and a well-timed insinuation, that the same Eusebius of Nicomedia, who now protected the heretic, had lately assisted the tyrant,[79] might exasperate him against their adversaries. The Nicene creed was ratified by Constantine; and his firm declaration, that those who resisted the divine judgment of the synod must prepare themselves for an immediate exile, annihilated the murmurs of a feeble opposition; which, from seventeen, was almost instantly reduced to two, protesting bishops. Eusebius of Cæsarea yielded a reluctant and ambiguous consent to the homoousion;[80] and the wavering conduct of the Nicomedian Eusebius served only to delay about three months his disgrace and exile.[81] The impious Arius was banished into one of the remote provinces of Illyricum; his person and disciples were branded, by law, with the odious name of Porphyrians; his writings were condemned to the flames, and a capital punishment was denounced against those in whose possession they should be found. The emperor had now imbibed the spirit of controversy, and the angry sarcastic style of his edicts was designed to inspire his subjects with the hatred which he had conceived against the enemies of Christ.[82]

But, as if the conduct of the emperor had been guided by passion instead of principle, three years from the council of Nice were scarcely elapsed before he discovered some symptoms of mercy, and even of indulgence, towards the proscribed sect, which was secretly protected by his favourite sister. The exiles were recalled; and Eusebius, who gradually resumed his influence over the mind of Constantine, was restored to the episcopal throne, from which he had been ignominiously degraded. Arius himself was treated by the whole court with the respect which would have been due to an innocent and oppressed man. His faith was approved by the synod of Jerusalem; and the emperor seemed impatient to repair his injustice, by issuing an absolute command that he should be solemnly admitted to the communion in the cathedral of Constantinople. On the same day which had been fixed for the triumph of Arius, he expired;

and the strange and horrid circumstances of his death might excite a suspicion that the orthodox saints had contributed more efficaciously than by their prayers to deliver the church from the most formidable of her enemies.[83] The three principal leaders of the catholics, Athanasius of Alexandria, Eustathius of Antioch, and Paul of Constantinople, were deposed on various accusations, by the sentence of numerous councils; and were afterwards banished into distant provinces by the first of the Christian emperors, who, in the last moments of his life received the rites of baptism from the Arian bishop of Nicomedia. The ecclesiastical government of Constantine cannot be justified from the reproach of levity and weakness. But the credulous monarch, unskilled in the stratagems of theological warfare, might be deceived by the modest and specious professions of the heretics, whose sentiments he never perfectly understood; and while he protected Arius, and persecuted Athanasius, he still considered the council of Nice as the bulwark of the Christian faith, and the peculiar glory of his own reign.[84]

The sons of Constantine must have been admitted from their childhood into the rank of catechumens, but they imitated, in the delay of their baptism, the example of their father. Like him, they presumed to pronounce their judgment on mysteries into which they had never been regularly initiated:[85] and the fate of the Trinitarian controversy depended, in a great measure, on the sentiments of Constantius, who inherited the provinces of the East, and acquired the possession of the whole empire. The Arian presbyter or bishop, who had secreted for his use the testament of the deceased emperor, improved the fortunate occasion which had introduced him to the familiarity of a prince whose public counsels were always swayed by his domestic favourites. The eunuchs and slaves diffused the spiritual poison through the palace, and the dangerous infection was communicated by the female attendants to the guards, and by the empress to her unsuspicious husband.[86] The partiality which Constantius always expressed towards the Eusebian faction was insensibly fortified by the dexterous management of their leaders; and his victory over the tyrant Magnentius increased his inclination, as well as ability, to employ the arms of power in the cause of Arianism. While the two armies were engaged in the plains of Mursa, and the fate of the two rivals depended on the chance of war, the son of Constantine passed the anxious moments in a church of the martyrs, under the walls of the city. His spiritual comforter, Valens, the Arian bishop of the diocese, employed the most artful precautions to obtain such early intelligence as might secure either his favour or his escape. A secret chain of swift and trusty messengers informed him of the vicissitudes of the battle; and while the courtiers stood trembling round their affrighted master, Valens assured him that the Gallic legions gave way; and insinuated, with some presence of mind, that the glorious event had been revealed to him by an angel. The grateful emperor ascribed his success to the merits and intercession of the bishop of Mursa, whose faith had deserved the public and miraculous approbation of Heaven.[87] The Arians, who considered as their own the victory of Constantius, preferred his glory to that of his father.[88] Cyril, bishop of Jerusalem, immediately composed the description of a celestial cross, encircled with a splendid rainbow, which, during the festival of Pentecost, about the third hour of the day, had appeared over the Mount of Olives, to the edification of the devout pilgrims and the people of the holy city.[89] The size of the meteor was gradually magnified; and the Arian historian has ventured to affirm that it was conspicuous to the two armies in the plains of Pannonia; and that the tyrant, who is purposely represented as an idolater, fled before the auspicious sign of orthodox Christianity.[90]

The sentiments of a judicious stranger, who has impartially considered the progress of civil or ecclesiastical discord, are always entitled to our notice: and a short passage of Ammianus, who served in the armies, and studied the character, of Constantius, is perhaps of more value than many pages of theological invectives. "The Christian religion, which, in itself," says that moderate historian, "is plain and simple, *he* confounded by the dotage of superstition. Instead of reconciling the parties by the weight of his authority, he cherished and propagated, by verbal disputes, the differences which his vain curiosity had excited. The highways were covered with troops of bishops galloping from every side to the assemblies, which they call synods; and while they laboured to reduce the whole sect to their own particular opinions, the public establishment of the posts was almost ruined by their hasty and repeated journey."[91] Our more intimate knowledge of the ecclesiastical transactions of the reign of Constantius would furnish an ample commentary on this remarkable passage; which justifies the rational apprehensions of Athanasius, that the restless activity of the clergy, who wandered round the empire in search of the true faith, would excite the contempt and laughter of the unbelieving world.[92] As soon as the emperor was relieved from the terrors of the civil war, he devoted the leisure of his winter quarters at Arles, Milan, Sirmium, and Constantinople, to the amusement or toils of controversy: the sword of the magistrate, and even of the tyrant, was unsheathed, to enforce the reasons of the theologian; and as he opposed the orthodox faith of Nice, it is readily confessed that his incapacity and ignorance were equal to his presumption.[93] The eunuchs, the women, and the bishops, who governed the vain and feeble mind of the emperor, had inspired him with an insuperable dislike to the Homoousion; but his timid conscience was alarmed by the impiety of Aëtius. The guilt of that atheist was aggravated by the suspicious favour of the unfortunate Gallus; and even the deaths of the Imperial ministers who had been massacred at Antioch were imputed to the suggestions of that dangerous sophist. The mind of Constantius, which could neither be moderated by reason nor fixed by faith, was blindly impelled to either side of the dark and empty abyss by his horror of the opposite extreme; he alternately embraced and condemned the sentiments, he successively banished and recalled the leaders, of the Arian and Semi-Arian factions.[94] During the season of public business or festivity, he employed whole days, and even nights, in selecting the words, and weighing the syllables, which composed his fluctuating creeds. The subject of his meditations still pursued and occupied his slumbers: the incoherent dreams of the emperor were received as celestial visions, and he accepted with complacency the lofty title of bishop of bishops, from those ecclesiastics who forgot the interest of their order for the gratification of their passions. The design of establishing an uniformity of doctrine, which had engaged him to convene so many synods in Gaul, Italy, Illyricum, and Asia, was repeatedly baffled by his own levity, by the divisions of the Arians, and by the resistance of the catholics; and he resolved, as the last and decisive effort, imperiously to dictate the decrees of a general council. The destructive earthquake of Nicomedia, the difficulty of finding a convenient place, and perhaps some secret motives of policy, produced an alteration in the summons. The bishops of the East were directed to meet at Seleucia, in Isauria; while those of the West held their deliberations at Rimini, on the coast of the Hadriatic; and instead of two or three deputies from each province, the whole episcopal body was ordered to march. The Eastern council, after consuming four days in fierce and unavailing debate, separated without any definite conclusion. The council of the West was protracted till the seventh month. Taurus, the Prætorian præfect, was instructed not to dismiss the prelates till they should all be united in the same opinion; and his efforts were supported by a power of banishing fifteen of the most refractory, and a promise of the consulship if he achieved so difficult an adventure. His prayers and threats, the authority of the sovereign, the sophistry of Valens and Ursacius, the distress of cold and hunger, and the tedious melancholy of a hopeless exile, at length extorted the reluctant consent of the bishops of Rimini. The deputies of the East and of the West attended the emperor in the palace of Constantinople, and he enjoyed the satisfaction of imposing on the world a profession of faith which established the *likeness*, without expressing the *consubstantiality*, of the Son of God.[95] But the triumph of Arianism had been preceded by the removal of the orthodox clergy, whom it was impossible either to intimidate or to corrupt; and the reign of Constantius was disgraced by the unjust and ineffectual persecution of the great Athanasius.

We have seldom an opportunity of observing, either in active or speculative life, what effect may be produced, or what obstacles may be surmounted, by the force of a single mind, when it is inflexibly applied to the pursuit of a single object. The immortal name of Athanasius[96] will never be separated from the catholic doctrine of the Trinity, to whose defence he consecrated every moment and every faculty of his being. Educated in the family of Alexander, he had vigorously opposed the early progress of the Arian heresy: he exercised the important functions of secretary under the aged prelate; and the fathers of the Nicene council beheld with surprise and respect the rising virtues of the young deacon. In a time of public danger the dull claims of age and of rank are sometimes superseded; and within five months after his return from Nice the deacon Athanasius was seated on the archiepiscopal throne of Egypt. He filled that eminent station above forty-six years, and his long administration was spent in a perpetual combat against the powers of Arianism. Five times was Athanasius expelled from his throne; twenty years he passed as an exile or a fugitive; and almost every province of the Roman empire was successively witness to his merit, and his sufferings in the cause of the Homoousion, which he considered as the sole pleasure and business, as the duty and as the glory of his life. Amidst the storms of persecution, the archbishop of Alexandria was patient of labour, jealous of fame, careless of safety; and although his mind was tainted by the contagion of fanaticism, Athanasius displayed a superiority of character and abilities which would have qualified him, far better than the degenerate sons of Constantine, for the government of a great monarchy. His learning was much less profound and extensive than that of Eusebius of Cæsarea, and his rude eloquence could not be compared with the polished oratory of Gregory or Basil; but whenever the primate of Egypt was called upon to justify his sentiments or his conduct, his unpremeditated style, either of speaking or writing, was clear, forcible, and persuasive. He has always been revered in the orthodox school as one of the most accurate masters of the Christian theology; and he was supposed to possess two profane sciences, less adapted to the episcopal character—the knowledge of jurisprudence,[97] and that of divination.[98] Some fortunate conjectures of future events, which impartial reasoners might ascribe to the experience and judgment of Athanasius, were attributed by his friends to heavenly inspiration, and imputed by his enemies to infernal magic.

But as Athanasius was continually engaged with the prejudices and passions of every order of men, from the monk to the emperor, the knowledge of human nature was his first and most important science. He preserved a distinct and unbroken view of a scene which was incessantly shifting; and never failed to improve those decisive moments which are irrecoverably past before they are perceived by a common eye. The archbishop of Alexandria was capable of distinguishing how far he might boldly command, and where he must dexterously insinuate; how long he might contend with power, and when he must withdraw from persecution; and while he directed the thunders of the church against heresy and rebellion, he could assume, in the bosom of his own party, the flexible and indulgent temper of a prudent leader. The election of Athanasius has not escaped the reproach of irregularity and precipitation;[99] but the propriety of his behaviour conciliated the affections both of the clergy and of the people. The Alexandrians were impatient to rise in arms for the defence of an eloquent and liberal pastor. In his distress he always derived support, or at least consolation, from the faithful attachment of his parochial clergy; and the hundred bishops of Egypt adhered, with unshaken zeal, to the cause of Athanasius. In the modest equipage which pride and policy would affect, he frequently performed the episcopal visitation of his provinces, from the mouth of the Nile to the confines of Æthiopia; familiarly conversing with the meanest of the populace, and humbly saluting the saints and hermits of the desert.[100] Nor was it only in ecclesiastical assemblies, among men whose education and manners were similar to his own, that Athanasius displayed the ascendancy of his genius. He appeared with easy and respectful firmness in the courts of princes; and in the various turns of his prosperous and adverse fortune he never lost the confidence of his friends, or the esteem of his enemies.

In his youth the primate of Egypt resisted the great Constantine, who had repeatedly signified his will that Arius should be restored to the catholic communion.[101] The emperor respected, and might forgive, this inflexible resolution; and the faction who considered Athanasius as their most formidable enemy were constrained to dissemble their hatred, and silently to prepare an indirect and distant assault. They scattered rumours and suspicions, represented the archbishop as a proud and oppressive tyrant, and boldly accused him of violating the treaty which had been ratified in the Nicene council with the schismatic followers of Meletius.[102] Athanasius had openly disapproved that ignominious peace, and the emperor was disposed to believe that he had abused his ecclesiastical and civil power to persecute those odious sectaries; that he had sacrilegiously broken a chalice in one of their churches of Maræotis; that he had whipped or imprisoned six of their bishops; and that Arsenius, a seventh bishop of the same party, had been murdered, or at least mutilated, by the cruel hand of the primate.[103] These charges, which affected his honour and his life, were referred by Constantine to his brother Dalmatius, the censor, who resided at Antioch; the synods of Cæsarea and Tyre were successively convened; and the bishops of the East were instructed to judge the cause of Athanasius before they proceeded to consecrate the new church of the Resurrection at Jerusalem. The primate might be conscious of his innocence; but he was sensible that the same implacable spirit which had dictated the accusation would direct the proceeding and pronounce the sentence. He prudently declined the tribunal of his enemies, despised the summons of the synod of Cæsarea; and, after a long and artful delay, submitted to the peremptory commands of the emperor, who threatened to punish his criminal disobedience if he refused to appear in the council of Tyre.[104] Before Athanasius, at the head of fifty Egyptian prelates, sailed from Alexandria, he had wisely secured the alliance of the Meletians; and Arsenius himself, his imaginary victim, and his secret friend, was privately concealed in his train. The synod of Tyre was conducted by Eusebius of Cæsarea, with more passion, and with less art, than his learning and experience might promise; his numerous faction repeated the names of homicide and tyrant; and their clamours were encouraged by the seeming patience of Athanasius, who expected the decisive moment to produce Arsenius alive and unhurt in the midst of the assembly. The nature of the other charges did not admit of such clear and satisfactory replies; yet, the archbishop was able to prove that, in the village where he was accused of breaking a consecrated chalice, neither church nor altar nor chalice could really exist. The Arians, who had secretly determined the guilt and condemnation of their enemy, attempted, however, to disguise their injustice by the imitation of judicial forms; the synod appointed an episcopal commission of six delegates to collect evidence on the spot; and this measure, which was vigorously opposed by the Egyptian bishops, opened new scenes of violence and perjury.[105] After the return of the deputies from Alexandria, the majority of the council pronounced the final sentence of degradation and exile against the primate of Egypt. The decree, expressed in the fiercest language of malice and revenge, was communicated to the emperor and the Catholic church; and the bishops immediately resumed a mild and devout aspect, such as became their holy pilgrimage to the Sepulchre of Christ.[106]

But the injustice of these ecclesiastical judges had not been countenanced by the submission, or even by the presence, of Athanasius. He resolved to make a bold and dangerous experiment, whether the throne was inaccessible to the voice of truth; and before the final sentence could be pronounced at Tyre, the intrepid primate threw himself into a bark which was ready to hoist sale for the Imperial city. The request of a formal audience might have been opposed or eluded; but Athanasius concealed his arrival, watched the moment of Constantine's return from an adjacent villa, and boldly encountered his angry sovereign as he passed on horseback through the principal street of Constantinople. So strange an apparition excited his surprise and indignation; and the guards were ordered to remove the importunate suitor; but his resentment was subdued by involuntary respect; and the haughty spirit of the emperor was awed by the courage and eloquence of a bishop who implored his justice and awakened his conscience.[107] Constantine listened to the complaints of Athanasius with impartial and even gracious attention; the members of the synod of Tyre were summoned to justify their proceedings; and the arts of the Eusebian faction would have been confounded if they had not aggravated the guilt of the primate by the dexterous supposition of an unpardonable offence—a criminal design to intercept and detain the corn-fleet of Alexandria, which supplied the subsistence of the new capital.[108] The emperor was satisfied that the peace of Egypt would be secured by the absence of a popular leader; but he refused to fill the vacancy of the archiepiscopal throne; and the sentence which, after long hesitation, he pronounced, was that of a jealous ostracism rather than of an ignominious exile. In the remote province of Gaul, but in the hospitable court of Treves, Athanasius passed about twenty-eight months. The death of the emperor changed the face of public affairs; and, amidst the general indulgence of a young reign, the primate was restored to his country by an honourable edict of the younger Constantine, who expressed a deep sense of the innocence and merit of his venerable guest.[109]

The death of that prince exposed Athanasius to a second persecution; and the feeble Constantius, the sovereign of the East, soon became the secret accomplice of the Eusebians. Ninety bishops of that sect or faction assembled at Antioch under the specious pretence of dedicating the cathedral. They composed an ambiguous creed, which is faintly tinged with the colours of Semi-Arianism, and twenty-five canons, which still regulate the discipline of the orthodox Greeks.[110] It was decided, with some appearance of equity, that a bishop, deprived by a synod, should not resume his episcopal functions till he had been absolved by the judgment of an equal synod; the law was immediately applied to the case of Athanasius; the council of Antioch pronounced, or rather confirmed, his degradation: a stranger, named Gregory, was seated on his throne; and Philagrius,[111] the præfect of Egypt, was instructed to support the new primate with the civil and military powers of the province. Oppressed by the conspiracy of the Asiatic prelates, Athanasius withdrew from Alexandria and passed three years[112] as an exile and a suppliant on the holy threshold of the

Vatican.[113] By the assiduous study of the Latin language he soon qualified himself to negotiate with the western clergy; his decent flattery swayed and directed the haughty Julius: the Roman pontiff was persuaded to consider his appeal as the peculiar interest of the Apostolic see; and his innocence was unanimously declared in a council of fifty bishops of Italy. At the end of three years the primate was summoned to the court of Milan by the emperor Constans, who, in the indulgence of unlawful pleasures, still professed a lively regard for the orthodox faith. The cause of truth and justice was promoted by the influence of gold,[114] and the ministers of Constans advised their sovereign to require the convocation of an ecclesiastical assembly, which might act as the representatives of the Catholic church. Ninety-four bishops of the West, seventy-six bishops of the East, encountered each other at Sardica, on the verge of the two empires, but in the dominions of the protector of Athanasius. Their debates soon degenerated into hostile altercations; the Asiatics, apprehensive for their personal safety, retired to Philippopolis in Thrace; and the rival synods reciprocally hurled their spiritual thunders against their enemies, whom they piously condemned as the enemies of the true God. Their decrees were published and ratified in their respective provinces: and Athanasius, who in the West was revered as a saint, was exposed as a criminal to the abhorrence of the East.[115] The council of Sardica reveals the first symptoms of discord and schism between the Greek and Latin churches, which were separated by the accidental difference of faith and the permanent distinction of language.

During his second exile in the West, Athanasius was frequently admitted to the Imperial presence—at Capua, Lodi, Milan, Verona, Padua, Aquileia, and Treves. The bishop of the diocese usually assisted at these interviews; the master of the offices stood before the veil or curtain of the sacred apartment; and the uniform moderation of the primate might be attested by these respectable witnesses, to whose evidence he solemnly appeals.[116] Prudence would undoubtedly suggest the mild and respectful tone that became a subject and a bishop. In these familiar conferences with the sovereign of the West, Athanasius might lament the error of Constantius, but he boldly arraigned the guilt of his eunuchs and his Arian prelates; deplored the distress and danger of the Catholic church; and excited Constans to emulate the zeal and glory of his father. The emperor declared his

resolution of employing the troops and treasures of Europe in the orthodox cause; and signified, by a concise and peremptory epistle to his brother Constantius, that, unless he consented to the immediate restoration of Athanasius, he himself, with a fleet and army, would seat the archbishop on the throne of Alexandria.[117] But this religious war, so horrible to nature, was prevented by the timely compliance of Constantius; and the emperor of the East condescended to solicit a reconciliation with a subject whom he had injured. Athanasius waited with decent pride till he had received three successive epistles full of the strongest assurances of the protection, the favour, and the esteem of his sovereign; who invited him to resume his episcopal seat, and who added the humiliating precaution of engaging his principal ministers to attest the sincerity of his intentions. They were manifested in a still more public manner by the strict orders which were despatched into Egypt to recall the adherents of Athanasius, to restore their privileges, to proclaim their innocence, and to erase from the public registers the illegal proceedings which had been obtained during the prevalence of the Eusebian faction. After every satisfaction and security had been given which justice or even delicacy could require, the primate proceeded, by slow journeys, through the provinces of Thrace, Asia, and Syria; and his progress was marked by the abject homage of the Oriental bishops, who excited his contempt without deceiving his penetration.[118] At Antioch he saw the emperor Constantius; sustained, with modest firmness, the embraces and protestations of his master; and eluded the proposal of allowing the Arians a single church at Alexandria by claiming, in the other cities of the empire, a similar toleration for his own party; a reply which might have appeared just and moderate in the mouth of an independent prince. The entrance of the archbishop into his capital was a triumphal procession; absence and persecution had endeared him to the Alexandrians; his authority, which he exercised with rigour, was more firmly established; and his fame was diffused from Æthiopia to Britain, over the whole extent of the Christian world.[119]

But the subject who has reduced his prince to the necessity of dissembling can never expect a sincere and lasting forgiveness; and the tragic fate of Constans soon deprived Athanasius of a powerful and generous protector. The civil war between the assassin and the only surviving brother of Constans, which afflicted the empire above three years, secured an interval of repose to the Catholic church; and the two contending parties were desirous to conciliate the friendship of a bishop who, by the weight of his personal authority, might determine the fluctuating resolutions of an important province. He gave audience to the ambassadors of the tyrant, with whom he was afterwards accused of holding a secret correspondence;[120] and the emperor Constantius repeatedly assured his dearest father, the most reverend Athanasius, that, notwithstanding the malicious rumours which were circulated by their common enemies, he had inherited the sentiments, as well as the throne, of his deceased brother.[121] Gratitude and humanity would have disposed the primate of Egypt to deplore the untimely fate of Constans, and to abhor the guilt of Magnentius; but as he clearly understood that the apprehensions of Constantius were his only safeguard, the fervour of his prayers for the success of the righteous cause might perhaps be somewhat abated. The ruin of Athanasius was no longer contrived by the obscure malice of a few bigoted or angry bishops, who abused the authority of a credulous monarch. The monarch himself avowed the resolution, which he had so long suppressed, of avenging his private injuries;[122] and the first winter after his victory, which he passed at Arles, was employed against an enemy more odious to him than the vanquished tyrant of Gaul.

If the emperor had capriciously decreed the death of the most eminent and virtuous citizen of the republic, the cruel order would have been executed without hesitation by the ministers of open violence or of specious injustice. The caution, the delay, the difficulty with which he proceeded in the condemnation and punishment of a popular bishop, discovered to the world that the privileges of the church had already revived a sense of order and freedom in the Roman government. The sentence which was pronounced in the synod of Tyre, and subscribed by a large majority of the Eastern bishops, had never been expressly repealed; and as Athanasius had been once degraded from his episcopal dignity by the judgment of his brethren, every subsequent act might be considered as irregular, and even criminal. But the memory of the firm and effectual support which the primate of Egypt had derived from the attachment of the Western church engaged Constantius to suspend the execution of the sentence till he had obtained the concurrence of the Latin bishops. Two years were consumed in ecclesiastical negotiations; and the important cause between the emperor and one of his subjects was solemnly debated,

first in the synod of Arles, and afterwards in the great council of Milan,[123] which consisted of above three hundred bishops. Their integrity was gradually undermined by the arguments of the Arians, the dexterity of the eunuchs, and the pressing solicitations of a prince who gratified his revenge at the expense of his dignity, and exposed his own passions whilst he influenced those of the clergy. Corruption, the most infallible symptom of constitutional liberty, was successfully practised; honours, gifts, and immunities were offered and accepted as the price of an episcopal vote;[124] and the condemnation of the Alexandrian primate was artfully represented as the only measure which could restore the peace and union of the Catholic church. The friends of Athanasius were not, however, wanting to their leader, or to their cause. With a manly spirit, which the sanctity of their character rendered less dangerous, they maintained, in public debate, and in private conference with the emperor, the eternal obligation of religion and justice. They declared that neither the hope of his favour, nor the fear of his displeasure, should prevail on them to join in the condemnation of an absent, an innocent, a respectable brother.[125] They affirmed, with apparent reason, that the illegal and obsolete decrees of the council of Tyre had long since been tacitly abolished by the Imperial edicts, the honourable re-establishment of the Archbishop of Alexandria, and the silence or recantation of his most clamourous adversaries. They alleged that his innocence had been attested by the unanimous bishops of Egypt, and had been acknowledged in the councils of Rome and Sardica[126] by the impartial judgment of the Latin church. They deplored the hard condition of Athanasius, who, after enjoying so many years his seat, his reputation, and the seeming confidence of his sovereign, was again called upon to confute the most groundless and extravagant accusations. Their language was specious; their conduct was honourable: but in this long and obstinate contest, which fixed the eyes of the whole empire on a single bishop, the ecclesiastical factions were prepared to sacrifice truth and justice to the more interesting object of defending or removing the intrepid champion of the Nicene faith. The Arians still thought it prudent to disguise, in ambiguous language, their real sentiments and designs; but the orthodox bishops, armed with the favour of the people and the decrees of a general council, insisted on every occasion, and particularly at Milan, that their adversaries should purge themselves from the suspicion of heresy, before they presumed to arraign the conduct of the great Athanasius.[127]

But the voice of reason (if reason was indeed on the side of Athanasius) was silenced by the clamours of a factious or venal majority; and the councils of Arles and Milan were not dissolved till the archbishop of Alexandria had been solemnly condemned and deposed by the judgment of the Western, as well as of the Eastern, church. The bishops who had opposed were required to subscribe the sentence; and to unite in religious communion with the suspected leaders of the adverse party. A formulary of consent was transmitted by the messengers of state to the absent bishops: and all those who refused to submit their private opinion to the public and inspired wisdom of the councils of Arles and Milan were immediately banished by the emperor, who affected to execute the decrees of the catholic church. Among those prelates who led the honourable band of confessors and exiles, Liberius of Rome, Osius of Cordova, Paulinus of Treves, Dionysius of Milan, Eusebius of Vercellæ, Lucifer of Cagliari, and Hilary of Poitiers, may deserve to be particularly distinguished. The eminent station of Liberius, who governed the capital of the empire; the personal merit and long experience of the venerable Osius, who was revered as the favourite of the great Constantine, and the father of the Nicene faith, placed those prelates at the head of the Latin church: and their example, either of submission or resistance, would probably be imitated by the episcopal crowds. But the repeated attempts of the emperor to seduce or to intimidate the bishops of Rome and Cordova were for some time ineffectual. The Spaniard declared himself ready to suffer under Constantius, as he had suffered threescore years before under his grandfather Maximian. The Roman, in the presence of his sovereign, asserted the innocence of Athanasius, and his own freedom. When he was banished to Beræa in Thrace, he sent back a large sum which had been offered for the accommodation of his journey; and insulted the court of Milan by the haughty remark, that the emperor and his eunuchs might want that gold to pay their soldiers and their bishops.[128] The resolution of Liberius and Osius was at length subdued by the hardships of exile and confinement. The Roman pontiff purchased his return by some criminal compliances; and afterwards expiated his guilt by a seasonable repentance. Persuasion and violence were employed to extort the reluctant signature of the decrepit bishop of Cordova, whose strength was broken, and

whose faculties were perhaps impaired, by the weight of an hundred years; and the insolent triumph of the Arians provoked some of the orthodox party to treat with inhuman severity the character, or rather the memory, of an unfortunate old man, to whose former services Christianity itself was so deeply indebted.[129]

The fall of Liberius and Osius reflected a brighter lustre on the firmness of those bishops who still adhered, with unshaken fidelity, to the cause of Athanasius and religious truth. The ingenious malice of their enemies had deprived them of the benefit of mutual comfort and advice, separated those illustrious exiles into distant provinces, and carefully selected the most inhospitable spots of a great empire.[130] Yet they soon experienced that the deserts of Libya, and the most barbarous tracts of Cappadocia, were less inhospitable than the residence of those cities in which an Arian bishop could satiate, without restraint, the exquisite rancour of theological hatred.[131] Their consolation was derived from the consciousness of rectitude and independence, from the applause, the visits, the letters, and the liberal alms of their adherents;[132] and from the satisfaction which they soon enjoyed of observing the intestine divisions of the adversaries of the Nicene faith. Such was the nice and capricious taste of the emperor Constantius, and so easily was he offended by the slightest deviation from his imaginary standard of Christian truth, that he persecuted, with equal zeal, those who defended the *consubstantiality*, those who asserted the *similar substance*, and those who denied the *likeness*, of the Son of God. Three bishops, degraded and banished for those adverse opinions, might possibly meet in the same place of exile; and, according to the difference of their temper, might either pity or insult the blind enthusiasm of their antagonists, whose present sufferings would never be compensated by future happiness.

The disgrace and exile of the orthodox bishops of the West were designed as so many preparatory steps to the ruin of Athanasius himself.[133] Six-and-twenty months had elapsed, during which the Imperial court secretly laboured, by the most insidious arts, to remove him from Alexandria, and to withdraw the allowance which supplied his popular liberality. But when the primate of Egypt, deserted and proscribed by the Latin church, was left destitute of any foreign support, Constantius despatched two of his secretaries with a verbal commission to announce and execute the order of his banishment. As the justice of the sentence was publicly avowed by the whole party, the only motive which could restrain Constantius from giving his messengers the sanction of a written mandate must be imputed to his doubt of the event; and to a sense of the danger to which he might expose the second city and the most fertile province of the empire, if the people should persist in the resolution of defending, by force of arms, the innocence of their spiritual father. Such extreme caution afforded Athanasius a specious pretence respectfully to dispute the truth of an order which he could not reconcile either with the equity or with the former declarations of his gracious master. The civil powers of Egypt found themselves inadequate to the task of persuading or compelling the primate to abdicate his episcopal throne; and they were obliged to conclude a treaty with the popular leaders of Alexandria, by which it was stipulated that all proceedings and all hostilities should be suspended till the emperor's pleasure had been more distinctly ascertained. By this seeming moderation the catholics were deceived into a false and fatal security; while the legions of the Upper Egypt, and of Libya, advanced, by secret orders and hasty marches, to besiege, or rather to surprise, a capital habituated to sedition, and inflamed by religious zeal.[134] The position of Alexandria, between the sea and the lake Mareotis, facilitated the approach and landing of the troops, who were introduced into the heart of the city before any effectual measures could be taken, either to shut the gates, or to occupy the important posts of defence. At the hour of midnight, twenty-three days after the signature of the treaty, Syrianus, duke of Egypt, at the head of five thousand soldiers, armed and prepared for an assault, unexpectedly invested the church of St. Theonas, where the archbishop, with a part of his clergy and people, performed their nocturnal devotions. The doors of the sacred edifice yielded to the impetuosity of the attack, which was accompanied with every horrid circumstance of tumult and bloodshed; but, as the bodies of the slain, and the fragments of military weapons, remained the next day an unexceptionable evidence in the possession of the catholics, the enterprise of Syrianus may be considered as a successful irruption rather than as an absolute conquest. The other churches of the city were profaned by similar outrages; and, during at least four months, Alexandria was exposed to the insults of a licentious army, stimulated by the ecclesiastics of an hostile faction. Many of the faithful were killed, who may deserve the name of martyrs if their deaths were neither provoked nor revenged; bishops and presbyters were treated with cruel ignominy; consecrated virgins were stripped naked, scourged, and violated; the houses of wealthy citizens were plundered; and, under the mask of religious zeal, lust, avarice, and private resentment were gratified with impunity, and even with applause. The Pagans of Alexandria, who still formed a numerous and discontented party, were easily persuaded to desert a bishop whom they feared and esteemed. The hopes of some peculiar favours, and the apprehension of being involved in the general penalties of rebellion, engaged them to promise their support to the destined successor of Athanasius, the famous George of Cappadocia. The usurper, after receiving the consecration of an Arian synod, was placed on the episcopal throne by the arms of Sebastian, who had been appointed count of Egypt for the execution of that important design. In the use, as well as in the acquisition, of power, the tyrant George disregarded the laws of religion, of justice, and of humanity; and the same scenes of violence and scandal which had been exhibited in the capital were repeated in more than ninety episcopal cities of Egypt. Encouraged by success, Constantius ventured to approve the conduct of his ministers. By a public and passionate epistle, the emperor congratulates the deliverance of Alexandria from a popular tyrant, who deluded his blind votaries by the magic of his eloquence; expatiates on the virtues and piety of the most reverend George, the elected bishop; and aspires, as the patron and benefactor of the city, to surpass the fame of Alexander himself. But he solemnly declares his unalterable resolution to pursue with fire and sword the seditious adherents of the wicked Athanasius, who, by flying from justice, has confessed his guilt, and escaped the ignominious death which he had so often deserved.[135]

Athanasius had indeed escaped from the most imminent dangers; and the adventures of that extraordinary man deserve and fix our attention. On the memorable night when the church of St. Theonas was invested by the troops of Syrianus, the archbishop, seated on his throne, expected, with calm and intrepid dignity, the approach of death. While the public devotion was interrupted by shouts of rage and cries of terror, he animated his trembling congregation to express their religious confidence by chanting one of the psalms of David which celebrates the triumph of the God of Israel over the haughty and impious tyrant of

Egypt. The doors were at length burst open: a cloud of arrows was discharged among the people; the soldiers, with drawn swords, rushed forwards into the sanctuary; and the dreadful gleam of their armour was reflected by the holy luminaries which burnt round the altar.[136] Athanasius still rejected the pious importunity of the monks and presbyters who were attached to his person; and nobly refused to desert his episcopal station till he had dismissed in safety the last of the congregation. The darkness and tumult of the night favoured the retreat of the archbishop; and though he was oppressed by the waves of an agitated multitude, though he was thrown to the ground, and left without sense or motion, he still recovered his undaunted courage, and eluded the eager search of the soldiers, who were instructed by their Arian guides that the head of Athanasius would be the most acceptable present to the emperor. From that moment the primate of Egypt disappeared from the eyes of his enemies, and remained above six years concealed in impenetrable obscurity.[137]

The despotic power of his implacable enemy filled the whole extent of the Roman world; and the exasperated monarch had endeavoured, by a very pressing epistle to the Christian princes of Æthiopia, to exclude Athanasius from the most remote and sequestered regions of the earth. Counts, præfects, tribunes, whole armies, were successively employed to pursue a bishop and a fugitive; the vigilance of the civil and military powers was excited by the Imperial edicts; liberal rewards were promised to the man who should produce Athanasius, either alive or dead; and the most severe penalties were denounced against those who should dare to protect the public enemy.[138] But the deserts of Thebaïs were now peopled by a race of wild, yet submissive fanatics, who preferred the commands of their abbot to the laws of their sovereign. The numerous disciples of Antony and Pachomius received the fugitive primate as their father, admired the patience and humility with which he conformed to their strictest institutions, collected every word which dropped from his lips as the genuine effusions of inspired wisdom; and persuaded themselves that their prayers, their fasts, and their vigils, were less meritorious than the zeal which they expressed, and the dangers which they braved, in the defence of truth and innocence.[139] The monasteries of Egypt were seated in lonely and desolate places, on the summit of mountains, or in the islands of the Nile; and the sacred horn or trumpet of Tabenne was the well-known signal which assembled several thousand robust and determined monks, who, for the most part, had been the peasants of the adjacent country. When their dark retreats were invaded by a military force which it was impossible to resist, they silently stretched out their necks to the executioner; and supported their national character, that tortures could never wrest from an Egyptian the confession of a secret which he was resolved not to disclose.[140] The archbishop of Alexandria, for whose safety they eagerly devoted their lives, was lost among a uniform and well-disciplined multitude; and on the nearer approach of danger, he was swiftly removed, by their officious hands, from one place of concealment to another, till he reached the formidable deserts, which the gloomy and credulous temper of superstition had peopled with dæmons and savage monsters. The retirement of Athanasius, which ended only with the life of Constantius, was spent, for the most part, in the society of the monks, who faithfully served him as guards, as secretaries, and as messengers; but the importance of maintaining a more intimate connection with the catholic party tempted him, whenever the diligence of the pursuit was abated, to emerge from the desert, to introduce himself into Alexandria, and to trust his person to the discretion of his friends and adherents. His various adventures might have furnished the subject of a very entertaining romance. He was once secreted in a dry cistern, which he had scarcely left before he was betrayed by the treachery of a female slave;[141] and he was once concealed in a still more extraordinary asylum, the house of a virgin, only twenty years of age, and who was celebrated in the whole city for her exquisite beauty. At the hour of midnight, as she related her story many years afterwards, she was surprised by the appearance of the archbishop in a loose undress, who, advancing with hasty steps, conjured her to afford him the protection which he had been directed by a celestial vision to seek under her hospitable roof. The pious maid accepted and preserved the sacred pledge which was intrusted to her prudence and courage. Without imparting the secret to any one, she instantly conducted Athanasius into her most sacred chamber, and watched over his safety with the tenderness of a friend and the assiduity of a servant. As long as the danger continued, she regularly supplied him with books and provisions, washed his feet, managed his correspondence, and dexterously concealed from the eye of suspicion this familiar and solitary intercourse between a saint whose character required the most unblemished chastity, and a female whose charms might excite the most dangerous emotions.[142] During the six years of persecution and exile, Athanasius repeated his visits to his fair and faithful companion; and the formal declaration, that he *saw* the councils of Rimini and Seleucia,[143] forces us to believe that he was secretly present at the time and place of their convocation. The advantage of personally negotiating with his friends, and of observing and improving the divisions of his enemies, might justify, in a prudent statesman, so bold and dangerous an enterprise: and Alexandria was connected by trade and navigation with every seaport of the Mediterranean. From the depth of his inaccessible retreat the intrepid primate waged an incessant and offensive war against the protector of the Arians; and his seasonable writings, which were diligently circulated and eagerly perused, contributed to unite and animate the orthodox party. In his public apologies, which he addressed to the emperor himself, he sometimes affected the praise of moderation; whilst at the same time, in secret and vehement invectives, he exposed Constantius as a weak and wicked prince, the executioner of his family, the tyrant of the republic, and the Antichrist of the church. In the height of his prosperity, the victorious monarch, who had chastised the rashness of Gallus, and suppressed the revolt of Sylvanus, who had taken the diadem from the head of Vetranio, and vanquished in the field the legions of Magnentius, received from an invisible hand a wound which he could neither heal nor revenge; and the son of Constantine was the first of the Christian princes who experienced the strength of those principles which, in the cause of religion, could resist the most violent exertions of the civil power.[144]

The persecution of Athanasius and of so many respectable bishops, who suffered for the truth of their opinions, or at least for the integrity of their conscience, was a just subject of indignation and discontent to all Christians, except those who were blindly devoted to the Arian faction. The people regretted the loss of their faithful pastors, whose banishment was usually followed by the intrusion of a stranger[145] into the episcopal chair, and loudly complained that the right of election was violated, and that they were condemned to obey a mercenary usurper, whose person was unknown and whose principles were suspected. The catholics might prove to the world that they were not involved in the guilt and heresy of their ecclesiastical governor,

by publicly testifying their dissent, or by totally separating themselves from his communion. The first of these methods was invented at Antioch, and practised with such success that it was soon diffused over the Christian world. The doxology, or sacred hymn, which celebrates the *glory* of the Trinity, is susceptible of very nice, but material, inflections; and the substance of an orthodox or an heretical creed may be expressed by the difference of a disjunctive or a copulative particle. Alternate responses and a more regular psalmody[146] were introduced into the public service by Flavianus and Diodorus, two devout and active laymen, who were attached to the Nicene faith. Under their conduct a swarm of monks issued from the adjacent desert, bands of well-disciplined singers were stationed in the cathedral of Antioch, the Glory to the Father, AND the Son, AND the Holy Ghost[147] was triumphantly chanted by a full chorus of voices, and the catholics insulted, by the purity of their doctrine, the Arian prelate who had usurped the throne of the venerable Eustathius. The same zeal which inspired their songs prompted the more scrupulous members of the orthodox party to form separate assemblies, which were governed by the presbyters, till the death of their exiled bishop allowed the election and consecration of a new episcopal pastor.[148] The revolutions of the court multiplied the number of pretenders, and the same city was often disputed, under the reign of Constantius, by two, or three, or even four bishops, who exercised their spiritual jurisdiction over their respective followers, and alternately lost and regained temporal possessions of the church. The abuse of Christianity introduced into the Roman government new causes of tyranny and sedition; the bands of civil society were torn asunder by the fury of religious factions; and the obscure citizen, who might calmly have surveyed the elevation and fall of successive emperors, imagined and experienced that his own life and fortune were connected with the interests of a popular ecclesiastic. The example of the two capitals, Rome and Constantinople, may serve to represent the state of the empire and the temper of mankind under the reign of the sons of Constantine.

I. The Roman pontiff, as long as he maintained his station and his principles, was guarded by the warm attachment of a great people, and could reject with scorn the prayers, the menaces, and the oblations of an heretical prince. When the eunuchs had secretly pronounced the exile of Liberius, the well-grounded apprehension of a tumult engaged them to use the utmost precautions in the execution of the sentence. The capital was invested on every side, and the præfect was commanded to seize the person of the bishop, either by stratagem or by open force. The order was obeyed, and Liberius, with the greatest difficulty, at the hour of midnight, was swiftly conveyed beyond the reach of the Roman people before their consternation was turned into rage. As soon as they were informed of his banishment into Thrace, a general assembly was convened, and the clergy of Rome bound themselves, by a public and solemn oath, never to desert their bishop, never to acknowledge the usurper Felix, who, by the influence of the eunuchs, had been irregularly chosen and consecrated within the walls of a profane palace. At the end of two years their pious obstinacy subsisted entire and unshaken; and when Constantius visited Rome, he was assailed by the importunate solicitations of a people who had preserved, as the last remnant of their ancient freedom, the right of treating their sovereign with familiar insolence. The wives of many of the senators and most honourable citizens, after pressing their husbands to intercede in favour of Liberius, were advised to undertake a commission which in their hands would be less dangerous and might prove more successful. The emperor received with politeness these female deputies, whose wealth and dignity were displayed in the magnificence of their dress and ornaments; he admired their inflexible resolution of following their beloved pastor to the most distant regions of the earth, and consented that the two bishops, Liberius and Felix, should govern in peace their respective congregations. But the ideas of toleration were so repugnant to the practice, and even to the sentiments, of those times, that, when the answer of Constantius was publicly read in the Circus of Rome, so reasonable a project of accommodation was rejected with contempt and ridicule. The eager vehemence which animated the spectators on the decisive moment of a horse-race was now directed towards a different object, and the Circus resounded with the shout of thousands, who repeatedly exclaimed "One God, One Christ, One Bishop!" The zeal of the Roman people in the cause of Liberius was not confined to words alone, and the dangerous and bloody sedition which they excited soon after the departure of Constantius determined that prince to accept the submission of the exiled prelate, and to restore him to the undivided dominion of the capital. After some ineffectual resistance, his rival was expelled from the city by the permission of the emperor and the power of the opposite faction; the adherents of Felix were inhumanly murdered in the streets, in the public places, in the baths, and even in the churches; and the face of Rome, upon the return of a Christian bishop, renewed the horrid image of the massacres of Marius and the proscriptions of Sylla.[149]

II. Notwithstanding the rapid increase of Christians under the reign of the Flavian family, Rome, Alexandria, and the other great cities of the empire, still contained a strong and powerful faction of Infidels, who envied the prosperity, and who ridiculed, even in their theatres, the theological disputes of the church. Constantinople alone enjoyed the advantage of being born and educated in the bosom of the faith. The capital of the East had never been polluted by the worship of idols, and the whole body of the people had deeply imbibed the opinions, the virtues, and the passions which distinguished the Christians of that age from the rest of mankind. After the death of Alexander the episcopal throne was disputed by Paul and Macedonius. By their zeal and abilities they both deserved the eminent station to which they aspired; and if the moral character of Macedonius was less exceptionable, his competitor had the advantage of a prior election and a more orthodox doctrine. His firm attachment to the Nicene creed, which has given Paul a place in the calendar among saints and martyrs, exposed him to the resentment of the Arians. In the space of fourteen years he was five times driven from his throne, to which he was more frequently restored by the violence of the people than by the permission of the prince, and the power of Macedonius could be secured only by the death of his rival. The unfortunate Paul was dragged in chains from the sandy deserts of Mesopotamia to the most desolate places of Mount Taurus,[150] confined in a dark and narrow dungeon, left six days without food, and at length strangled, by the order of Philip, one of the principal ministers of the emperor Constantius.[151] The first blood which stained the new capital was spilt in this ecclesiastical contest, and many persons were slain on both sides in the furious and obstinate seditions of the people. The commission of enforcing a sentence of banishment against Paul had been intrusted to Hermogenes, the master-general of the cavalry, but the execution of it was fatal to himself. The catholics rose in the defence of their bishop; the palace of Hermogenes was consumed; the first military officer of the empire was dragged by the heels through the streets of Constantinople, and, after he expired, his lifeless corpse was exposed to their wanton insults.[152] The fate of Hermogenes instructed Philip, the Prætorian præfect, to act with more precaution on a similar occasion. In the most gentle and honourable terms he required the attendance of Paul in the baths of Zeuxippus, which had a private communication with the palace and the sea. A vessel, which lay ready at the garden stairs, immediately hoisted sail, and, while the people were still ignorant of the meditated sacrilege, their bishop was already embarked on his voyage to Thessalonica. They soon beheld, with surprise and indignation, the gates of the palace thrown open, and the usurper Macedonius seated by the side of the præfect on a lofty chariot, which was surrounded by troops of guards with drawn swords. The military procession advanced towards the cathedral; and the Arians and the catholics eagerly rushed to occupy that important post, and three thousand one hundred and fifty persons lost their lives in the confusion of the tumult. Macedonius, who was supported by a regular force, obtained a decisive victory, but his reign was disturbed by clamour and sedition, and the causes which appeared the least connected with the subject of dispute were sufficient to nourish and to kindle the flame of civil discord. As the chapel in which the body of the great Constantine had been deposited was in a ruinous condition, the bishop transported those venerable remains into the church of St. Acacius. This prudent and even pious measure was represented as a wicked profanation by the whole party which adhered to the Homoousian doctrine. The factions immediately flew to arms, the consecrated ground was used as their field of battle, and one of the ecclesiastical historians has observed, as a real fact, not as a figure of rhetoric, that the well before the church overflowed with a stream of blood which filled the porticoes and the adjacent courts. The writer who should impute these tumults solely to a religious principle would betray a very imperfect knowledge of human nature; yet it must be confessed that the motive which misled the sincerity of zeal, and the pretence which disguised the licentiousness of passion, suppressed the remorse which, in another cause, would have succeeded to the rage of the Christians of Constantinople.[153]

The cruel and arbitrary disposition of Constantius, which did not always require the provocations of guilt and resistance, was justly exasperated by the tumults of his capital and the criminal behaviour of a faction which opposed the authority and religion of their sovereign. The ordinary punishments of death, exile, and confiscation were inflicted with partial rigour, and the Greeks still revere the holy memory of two clerks, a reader and a subdeacon, who were accused of the murder of Hermogenes, and beheaded at the gates of Constantinople. By an edict of Constantius against the catholics, which has not been judged worthy of a place in the Theodosian code, those who refused to communicate with the Arian bishops, and particularly with Macedonius, were deprived of the immunities of ecclesiastics and of the rights of Christians; they were compelled to relinquish the possession of the churches, and were strictly prohibited from holding their assemblies within the walls of the city. The execution of this unjust law in the provinces of Thrace and Asia Minor was committed to the zeal of Macedonius; the civil and military powers were directed to obey his commands; and the cruelties exercised by this Semi-Arian tyrant in the support of the *Homoiousion* exceeded the commission and disgraced the reign of Constantius. The sacraments of the church were administered to the reluctant victims, who denied the vocation and abhorred the principles of Macedonius. The rites of baptism were conferred on women and children who, for that purpose, had been torn from the arms of their friends and parents; the mouths of the communicants were held open by a wooden engine while the consecrated bread was forced down their throat; the breasts of tender virgins were either burnt with red-hot eggshells, or inhumanly compressed between sharp and heavy boards.[154] The Novatians of Constantinople and the adjacent country, by their firm attachment to the Homoousian standard, deserved to be confounded with the catholics themselves. Macedonius was informed that a large district of Paphlagonia was almost entirely inhabited by those sectaries. He resolved either to convert or to extirpate them, and, as he distrusted on this occasion the efficacy of an ecclesiastical mission, he commanded a body of four thousand legionaries to march against the rebels, and to reduce the territory of Mantinium[155] under his spiritual dominion. The Novatian peasants, animated by despair and religious fury, boldly encountered the invaders of their country, and, though many of the Paphlagonians were slain, the Roman legions were vanquished by an irregular multitude, armed only with scythes and axes, and, except a few who escaped by an ignominious flight, four thousand soldiers were left dead on the field of battle. The successor of Constantius has expressed, in a concise but lively manner, some of the theological calamities which afflicted the empire, and more especially the East, in the reign of a prince who was the slave of his own passions and of those of his eunuchs. "Many were imprisoned, and persecuted, and driven into exile. Whole troops of those who are styled heretics were massacred, particularly at Cyzicus and at Samosata. In Paphlagonia, Bithynia, Galatia, and in many other provinces, towns and villages were laid waste and utterly destroyed."[156]

While the flames of the Arian controversy consumed the vitals of the empire, the African provinces were infested by their peculiar enemies, the savage fanatics, who, under the name of *Circumcellions*, formed the strength and scandal of the Donatist party.[157] The severe execution of the laws of Constantine had excited a spirit of discontent and resistance; the strenuous efforts of his son Constans to restore the unity of the church exasperated the sentiments of mutual hatred which had first occasioned the separation; and the methods of force and corruption employed by the two Imperial commissioners, Paul and Macarius, furnished the schismatics with a specious contrast between the maxims of the apostles and the conduct of their pretended successors.[158] The peasants who inhabited the villages of Numidia and Mauritania were a ferocious race, who had been imperfectly reduced under the authority of the Roman laws, who were imperfectly converted to the Christian faith, but who were actuated by a blind and furious enthusiasm in the cause of their Donatist teachers. They indignantly supported the exile of their bishops, the demolition of their churches, and the interruption of their secret assemblies. The violence of the officers of justice, who were usually sustained by a military guard, was sometimes repelled with equal violence, and the blood of some popular ecclesiastics, which had been shed in the quarrel, inflamed their rude followers with an eager desire of revenging the death of these holy martyrs. By their own cruelty and rashness the ministers of persecution sometimes provoked their fate, and the guilt of an accidental tumult precipitated the criminals into despair and rebellion. Driven from their native villages, the Donatist peasants assembled in formidable gangs on the edge of the Gætulian desert, and readily exchanged the habits of labour for a life of idleness and rapine, which was consecrated by the name of religion, and faintly condemned by the doc-

tors of the sect. The leaders of the Circumcellions assumed the title of captains of the saints; their principal weapon, as they were indifferently provided with swords and spears, was a huge and weighty club, which they termed an *Israelite*, and the well-known sound of "Praise be to God!" which they used as their cry of war, diffused consternation over the unarmed provinces of Africa. At first their depredations were coloured by the plea of necessity, but they soon exceeded the measure of subsistence, indulged without control their intemperance and avarice, burnt the villages which they had pillaged, and reigned the licentious tyrants of the open country. The occupations of husbandry and the administration of justice were interrupted; and, as the Circumcellions pretended to restore the primitive equality of mankind, and to reform the abuses of civil society, they opened a secure asylum for the slaves and debtors who flocked in crowds to their holy standard. When they were not resisted they usually contented themselves with plunder, but the slightest opposition provoked them to acts of violence and murder; and some catholic priests, who had imprudently signalised their zeal, were tortured by the fanatics with the most refined and wanton barbarity. The spirit of the Circumcellions was not always exerted against their defenceless enemies; they engaged, and sometimes defeated, the troops of the province, and in the bloody action of Bagai they attacked in the open field, but with unsuccessful valour, an advanced guard of the Imperial cavalry. The Donatists who were taken in arms received, and they soon deserved, the same treatment which might have been shown to the wild beasts of the desert. The captives died, without a murmur, either by the sword, the axe, or the fire; and the measures of retaliation were multiplied in a rapid proportion, which aggravated the horrors of rebellion and excluded the hope of mutual forgiveness. In the beginning of the present century the example of the Circumcellions has been renewed in the persecution, the boldness, the crimes, and the enthusiasm of the Camisards; and if the fanatics of Languedoc surpassed those of Numidia by their military achievements, the Africans maintained their fierce independence with more resolution and perseverance.[159]

Such disorders are the natural effects of religious tyranny; but the rage of the Donatists was inflamed by a frenzy of a very extraordinary kind; and which, if it really prevailed among them in so extravagant a degree, cannot surely be paralleled in any country or in any age.

Many of these fantatics were possessed with the horror of life, and the desire of martyrdom; and they deemed it of little moment by what means, or by what hands, they perished, if their conduct was sanctified by the intention of devoting themselves to the glory of the true faith, and the hope of eternal happiness.[160] Sometimes they rudely disturbed the festivals, and profaned the temples of Paganism, with the design of exciting the most zealous of the idolaters to revenge the insulted honour of their gods. They sometimes forced their way into the courts of justice, and compelled the affrighted judge to give orders for their immediate execution. They frequently stopped travellers on the public highways, and obliged them to inflict the stroke of martyrdom, by the promise of a reward if they consented, and by the threat of instant death if they refused to grant so very singular a favor. When they were disappointed of every other resource, they announced the day on which, in the presence of their friends and brethren, they should cast themselves headlong from some lofty rock; and many precipices were shown which had acquired fame by the number of religious suicides. In the actions of these desperate enthusiasts, who were admired by one party as the martyrs of God, and abhorred by the other as the victims of Satan, an impartial philosopher may discover the influence and the last abuse of that inflexible spirit which was originally derived from the character and principals of the Jewish nation.

The simple narrative of the intestine divisions which distracted the peace and dishonoured the triumph of the church, will confirm the remark of a Pagan historian, and justify the complaint of a venerable bishop. The experience of Ammianus had convinced him that the enmity of the Christians towards each other surpassed the fury of savage beasts against man;[161] and Gregory Nazianzen most pathetically laments that the kingdom of heaven was converted by discord into the image of chaos, of a nocturnal tempest, and of hell itself.[162] The fierce and partial writers of the times, ascribing *all* virtue to themselves, and imputing *all* guilt to their adversaries, have painted the battle of the angels and dæmons. Our calmer reason will reject such pure and perfect monsters of vice or sanctity, and will impute an equal, or at least an indiscriminate, measure of good and evil to the hostile sectaries, who assumed and bestowed the appellations of orthodox and heretics. They had been educated in the same religion and the same civil society. Their hopes and fears in the present, or in a future life, were balanced in the same proportion. On either side the error might be innocent, the faith sincere, the practice meritorious or corrupt. Their passions were excited by similar objects; and they might alternately abuse the favour of the court, or of the people. The metaphysical opinions of the Athanasians and the Arians could not influence their moral character; and they were alike actuated by the intolerant spirit which has been extracted from the pure and simple maxims of the Gospel.

A modern writer, who, with a just confidence, has prefixed to his own history the honourable epithets of political and philosophical,[163] accuses the timid prudence of Montesquieu, for neglecting to enumerate, among the causes of the decline of the empire, a law of Constantine, by which the exercise of the Pagan worship was absolutely suppressed, and a considerable part of his subjects was left destitute of priests, of temples, and of any public religion. The zeal of the philosophic historian for the rights of mankind has induced him to acquiesce in the ambiguous testimony of those ecclesiastics who have too lightly ascribed to their favourite hero the *merit* of a general persecution.[164] Instead of alleging this imaginary law, which would have blazed in the front of the Imperial codes, we may safely appeal to the original epistle which Constantine addressed to the followers of the ancient religion, at a time when he no longer disguised his conversion, nor dreaded the rivals of his throne. He invites and exhorts, in the most pressing terms, the subjects of the Roman empire to imitate the example of their master; but he declares that those who still refuse to open their eyes to the celestial light may freely enjoy their temples and their fancied gods. A report that the ceremonies of Paganism were suppressed is formally contradicted by the emperor himself, who wisely assigns, as the principle of his moderation, the invincible force of habit, of prejudice, and of superstition.[165] Without violating the sanctity of his promise, without alarming the fears of the Pagans, the artful monarch advanced, by slow and cautious steps, to undermine the irregular and decayed fabric of polytheism. The partial acts of severity which he occasionally exercised, though they were secretly prompted by a Christian zeal, were coloured by the fairest pretences of justice and the public good; and while Constantine designed to ruin the foundations, he seemed to reform the abuses, of the ancient religion. After the example of the wisest of his predecessors, he condemned, under the most rigorous penalties, the occult and impious arts of divination, which excited the vain hopes, and sometimes the criminal attempts, of those who were discontented with their present condition. An ignominious silence was imposed on the oracles, which had been publicly convicted of fraud and falsehood; the effeminate priests of the Nile were abolished; and Constantine discharged the duties of a Roman censor, when he gave orders for the demolition of several temples of Phœnicia, in which every mode of prostitution was devoutly practised in the face of day, and to the honour of Venus.[166] The Imperial city of Constantinople was, in some measure, raised at the expense, and was adorned with the spoils, of the opulent temples of Greece and Asia; the sacred property was confiscated; the statues of gods and heroes were transported, with rude familiarity, among a people who considered them as objects, not of adoration, but of curiosity; the gold and silver were restored to circulation; and the magistrates, the bishops, and the eunuchs, improved the fortunate occasion of gratifying, at once, their zeal, their avarice, and their resentment. But these depredations were confined to a small part of the Roman world; and the provinces had been long since accustomed to endure the same sacrilegious rapine, from the tyranny of princes and proconsuls who could not be suspected of any design to subvert the established religion.[167]

The sons of Constantine trod in the footsteps of their father with more zeal and with less discretion. The pretences of rapine and oppression were insensibly multiplied[168]; every indulgence was shown to the illegal behaviour of the Christians; every doubt was explained to the disadvantage of Paganism; and the demolition of the temples was celebrated as one of the auspicious events of the reign of Constans and Constantius.[169] The name of Constantius is prefixed to a concise law, which might have superseded the necessity of any future prohibitions. "It is our pleasure that in all places, and in all cities, the temples be immediately shut and carefully guarded, that none may have the power of offending. It is likewise our pleasure that all our subjects should abstain from sacrifices. If any one should be guilty of such an act, let him feel the sword of vengeance, and, after his execution, let his property be confiscated to the public use. We denounce the same penalties against the governors of the provinces, if they neglect to punish the criminals."[170] But there is the strongest reason to believe that this formidable edict was either composed without being published, or was published without being executed. The

evidence of facts, and the monuments which are still extant of brass and marble, continue to prove the public exercise of the Pagan worship during the whole reign of the sons of Constantine. In the East as well as in the West, in cities as well as in the country, a great number of temples were respected, or at least were spared; and the devout multitude still enjoyed the luxury of sacrifices, of festivals, and of processions, by the permission, or by the connivance, of the civil government. About four years after the supposed date of his bloody edict, Constantius visited the temples of Rome; and the decency of his behaviour is recommended by a Pagan orator as an example worthy of the imitation of succeeding princes. "That emperor," says Symmachus, "suffered the privileges of the vestal virgins to remain inviolate; he bestowed the sacerdotal dignities on the nobles of Rome, granted the customary allowance to defray the expenses of the public rites and sacrifices; and, though he had embraced a different religion, he never attempted to deprive the empire of the sacred worship of antiquity."[171] The senate still presumed to consecrate, by solemn decrees, the *divine* memory of their sovereigns; and Constantine himself was associated, after death, to those gods whom he had renounced and insulted during his life. The title, the ensigns, the prerogatives, of SOVEREIGN PONTIFF, which had been instituted by Numa, and assumed by Augustus, were accepted, without hesitation, by seven Christian emperors, who were invested with a more absolute authority over the religion which they had deserted than over that which they professed.[172]

The divisions of Christianity suspended the ruin of Paganism;[173] and the holy war against the infidels was less vigorously prosecuted by princes and bishops who were more immediately alarmed by the guilt and danger of domestic rebellion. The extirpation of idolatry[174] might have been justified by the established principles of intolerance: but the hostile sects, which alternately reigned in the Imperial court, were mutually apprehensive of alienating, and perhaps exasperating, the minds of a powerful, though declining faction. Every motive of authority and fashion, of interest and reason, now militated on the side of Christianity; but two or three generations elapsed before their victorious influence was universally felt. The religion which had so long and so lately been established in the Roman empire was still revered by a numerous people, less attached indeed to speculative opinion than to ancient custom. The honours of the state and army were indifferently bestowed on all the subjects of Constantine and Constantius; and a considerable portion of knowledge and wealth and valours was still engaged in the service of polytheism. The superstition of the senator and of the peasant, of the poet and the philosopher, was derived from very different causes, but they met with equal devotion in the temples of the gods. Their zeal was insensibly provoked by the insulting triumph of a proscribed sect; and their hopes were revived by the well-grounded confidence that the presumptive heir of the empire, a young and valiant hero, who had delivered Gaul from the arms of the barbarians, had secretly embraced the religion of his ancestors.

CHAPTER XXII

Julian is declared Emperor by the Legions of Gaul. His March and Success. The Death of Constantius. Civil Administration of Julian.

WHILE the Romans languished under the ignominious tyranny of eunuchs and bishops, the praises of Julian were repeated with transport in every part of the empire, except in the palace of Constantius. The barbarians of Germany had felt, and still dreaded, the arms of the young Cæsar; his soldiers were the companions of his victory; the grateful provincials enjoyed the blessings of his reign; but the favourites, who had opposed his elevation, were offended by his virtues; and they justly considered the friend of the people as the enemy of the court. As long as the fame of Julian was doubtful, the buffoons of the palace, who were skilled in the language of satire, tried the efficacy of those arts which they had so often practised with success. They easily discovered that his simplicity was not exempt from affectation: the ridiculous epithets of an hairy savage, of an ape invested with the purple, were applied to the dress and person of the philosophic warrior; and his modest despatches were stigmatised as the vain and elaborate fictions of a loquacious Greek, a speculative soldier, who had studied the art of war amidst the groves of the Academy.[1] The voice of malicious folly was at length silenced by the shouts of victory; the conqueror of the Franks and Alemanni could no longer be painted as an object of contempt; and the monarch himself was meanly ambitious of stealing from his lieutenant the honourable reward of his labours. In the letters crowned with laurel, which, according to ancient custom, were addressed to the provinces, the name of Julian was omitted. "Constantius had made his dispositions in person; *he* had signalised his valour in the foremost ranks; *his* military conduct had secured the victory; and the captive king of the barbarians was presented to *him* on the field of battle," from which he was at that time distant above forty days' journey.[2] So extravagant a fable was incapable, however, of deceiving the public credulity, or even of satisfying the pride of the emperor himself. Secretly conscious that the applause and favour of the Romans accompanied the rising fortunes of Julian, his discontented mind was prepared to receive the subtle poison of those artful sycophants who coloured their mischievous designs with the fairest appearances of truth and candour.[3] Instead of depreciating the merits of Julian, they acknowledged, and even exaggerated, his popular fame, superior talents, and important services. But they darkly insinuated that the virtues of the Cæsar might instantly be converted into the most dangerous crimes, if the inconstant multitude should prefer their inclinations to their duty; or if the general of a victorious army should be tempted from his allegiance by the hopes of revenge and independent greatness. The personal fears of Constantius were interpreted by his council as a laudable anxiety for the public safety; whilst in private, and perhaps in his own breast, he disguised, under the less odious appellation of fear, the sentiments of hatred and envy which he had secretly conceived for the inimitable virtues of Julian.

The apparent tranquility of Gaul, and the imminent danger of the eastern provinces, offered a specious pretence for the design which was artfully concerted by the Imperial ministers. They resolved to disarm the Cæsar; to recall those faithful troops who guarded his person and dignity; and to employ, in a distant war against the Persian monarch, the hardy veterans who had vanquished, on the banks of the Rhine, the fiercest nations of Germany. While Julian used the laborious hours of his winter quarters at Paris in the administration of power, which, in his hands, was the exercise of virtue, he was surprised by the hasty arrival of a tribune and a notary, with positive orders from the emperor, which *they* were directed to execute, and *he* was commanded not to oppose. Constantius signified his pleasure that four entire legions—the Celtæ and Petulants, the Heruli and the Batavians—should be separated from the standard of Julian, under which they had acquired their fame and discipline; that in each of the remaining bands three hundred of the bravest youths should be selected; and that this numerous detachment, the strength of the Gallic army, should instantly begin their march, and exert their utmost diligence to arrive, before the opening of the campaign, on the frontiers of Persia.[4] The Cæsar foresaw and lamented the consequences of this fatal mandate. Most of the auxiliaries, who engaged their voluntary service, had stipulated that they should never be obliged to pass the Alps. The public faith of Rome, and the personal honour of Julian, had been pledged for the observance of this condition. Such an act of treachery and oppression would destroy the confidence, and excite the resentment of the independent warriors of Germany, who considered truth as the noblest of their virtues, and freedom as the most valuable of their possessions. The legionaries, who enjoyed the title and privileges of Romans, were enlisted for the general defence of the republic; but those mercenary troops heard with cold indifference the antiquated names of the republic and of Rome. Attached, either from birth or long habit, to the climate and manners of Gaul, they loved and admired Julian; they despised, and perhaps hated, the emperor; they dreaded the laborious march, the Persian arrows, and the burning deserts of Asia. They claimed as their own the country which they had saved; and excused their want of spirit by pleading the sacred and more immediate duty of protecting their families and friends. The apprehensions of the Gauls were derived from the knowledge of the impending and inevitable danger. As soon as the provinces were exhausted of their military strength, the Germans would violate a treaty which had been imposed on their fears; and notwithstanding the abilities and valour of Julian, the general of a nominal army, to whom the public calamities would be imputed, must find himself, after a vain resistance, either a prisoner in the camp of the barbarians, or a criminal in the palace of Constantius. If Julian complied with the orders which he had received he subscribed his own destruction, and that of a people who deserved his affection. But a positive refusal was an act of rebellion and a declaration of war. The inexorable jealousy of the emperor, the peremptory, and perhaps insidious, nature of his commands, left not any room for a fair apology or candid interpretation; and the dependent station of the Cæsar scarcely allowed him to pause or to deliberate. Solitude increased the perplexity of Julian; he could no longer apply to the faithful counsels of Sallust, who had been removed from his office by the judicious malice of the eunuchs: he could not even enforce his representations by the concurrence of the ministers, who would have been afraid or ashamed to approve the ruin of Gaul. The moment had been chosen when Lupicinus,[5] the general of the cavalry, was despatched into Britain, to repulse the inroads of the Scots and Picts; and Florentius was occupied at Vienne by the assessment of the tribute. The latter, a crafty and corrupt statesman, declining to assume a responsible part on this dangerous occasion, eluded the pressing and repeated invitations of Julian, who represented to him that in every important measure the presence of the præfect was indispensable in the council of the prince. In the meanwhile the Cæsar was oppressed by the rude and importunate solicitations of the Imperial messengers, who presumed to suggest that, if he expected the return of his ministers, he could charge himself with the guilt of the delay, and reserve for them the merit of the execution. Unable to resist, unwilling to comply, Julian expressed in the most serious terms his wish, and even his intention, of resigning the purple, which he could not preserve with honour, but which he could not abdicate with safety.

After a painful conflict, Julian was compelled to acknowledge that obedience was the virtue of the most eminent subject, and that the sovereign alone was entitled to judge of the public welfare. He issued the necessary orders for carrying into execution the commands of Constantius; a part of the troops began their march for the Alps; and the detachments from the several garrisons moved towards their respective places of assembly. They advanced with difficulty through the trembling and affrighted crowds of provincials, who attempted to excite their pity by silent despair or loud lamentations; while the wives of the soldiers, holding their infants in their arms, accused the desertion of their husbands in the mixed language of grief, of tenderness, and of indignation. This scene of general distress afflicted the humanity of the Cæsar; he granted a sufficient number of post-waggons to transport the wives and families of the soldiers,[6] endeavoured to alleviate the hardships which he was constrained to inflict, and increased by the most laudable arts his own popularity and the discontent of the exiled troops. The grief of an armed multitude is soon converted into rage; their licentious murmurs, which every hour were communicated from tent to tent with more boldness and effect, prepared their minds for the most daring acts of sedition; and by the connivance of their tribunes a seasonable libel was secretly dispersed, which painted in lively colours the disgrace of the Cæsar, the oppression of the Gallic army, and the feeble vices of the tyrant of Asia. The servants of Constantius were astonished and alarmed by the progress of this dangerous spirit. They pressed the Cæsar to hasten the departure of the troops; but they imprudently rejected the honest and judicious advice of Julian, who proposed that they should not march through Paris, and suggested the danger and temptation of a last interview.

As soon as the approach of the troops was announced, the Cæsar went out to meet them, and ascended his tribunal, which had been erected in a plain before the gates of the city. After distinguishing the officers and soldiers who by their rank or merit deserved a peculiar attention, Julian addressed himself in a studied oration to the surrounding multitude: he celebrated their exploits with grateful applause; encouraged them to accept, with alacrity, the honour of serving under the eyes of a powerful and liberal monarch; and admonished them that the commands of Augustus required an instant and cheerful obedience. The soldiers, who were apprehensive of offending their general by an indecent clamour, or of belying their sentiments by false and venal acclamations, maintained an obstinate silence; and, after a short pause, were dismissed to their quarters. The principal officers were entertained by the Cæsar, who professed, in the warmest language of friendship, his desire and his inability to reward, according to their deserts, the brave companions of his victories. They retired from the feast full of grief and perplexity; and lamented the hardship of their fate, which tore them from their beloved general and their native country. The only expedient which could prevent their separation was boldly agitated and approved; the popular resentment was insensibly moulded into a regular conspiracy; their just reasons of complaint were heightened by passion, and their passions were inflamed by wine, as on the eve of their departure the troops were indulged in licentious festivity. At the hour of midnight the impetuous multitude, with swords, and bows, and torches in their hands, rushed into the suburbs; encompassed the palace;[7] and, careless of future dangers, pronounced the fatal and irrevocable words, JULIAN AUGUSTUS! The prince, whose anxious suspense was interrupted by their disorderly acclamations, secured the doors against their intrusion; and, as long as it was in his power, secluded his person and dignity from the accidents of a nocturnal tumult. At the dawn of day the soldiers, whose zeal was irritated by opposition, forcibly entered the palace, seized, with respectful violence, the object of their choice, guarded Julian with drawn swords through the streets of Paris, placed him on the tribunal, and with repeated shouts saluted him as their emperor. Prudence as well as loyalty inculcated the propriety of resisting their treasonable designs, and of preparing for his oppressed virtue the excuse of violence. Addressing himself by turns to the multitude and to individuals, he sometimes implored their mercy, and sometimes expressed his indignation; conjured them not to sully the fame of their immortal victories; ventured to promise that, if they would immediately return to their allegiance, he would undertake to obtain from the emperor not only a free and gracious pardon, but even the revocation of the orders which had excited their resentment. But the soldiers, who were conscious of their guilt, chose rather to depend on the gratitude of Julian than on the clemency of the emperor. Their zeal was insensibly turned into impatience, and their impatience into rage. The inflexible Cæsar sustained, till the third hour of the day, their prayers, their reproaches, and their menaces; nor did he yield till he had been repeatedly assured that, if he wished to live, he must consent to reign. He was exalted on a shield in the presence and amidst the unanimous acclamations of the troops; a rich military collar, which was offered by chance, supplied the want of a diadem;[8] the ceremony was concluded by the promise of a moderate donative;[9] and the new emperor, overwhelmed with real or affected grief, retired into the most secret recesses of his apartment.[10]

The grief of Julian could proceed only from his innocence; but his innocence must appear extremely doubtful[11] in the eyes of those who have learned to suspect the motives and the professions of princes. His lively and active mind was susceptible of the various impressions of hope and fear, of gratitude and revenge, of duty and of ambition, of the love of fame and of the fear of reproach. But it is impossible for us to calculate the respective weight and operation of these sentiments; or to ascertain the principles of action which might escape the observation, while they guided, or rather impelled, the steps of Julian himself. The discontent of the troops was produced by the malice of his enemies; their tumult was the natural effect of interest and of passion; and if Julian had tried to conceal a deep design under the appearances of chance, he must have employed the most consummate artifice without necessity, and probably without success. He solemnly declares, in the presence of Jupiter, of the Sun, of Mars, of Minerva, and of all the other deities, that till the close of the evening which preceded his elevation he was utterly ignorant of the designs of the soldiers;[12] and it may seem ungenerous to distrust the honour of a hero, and the truth of a philosopher. Yet the superstitious confidence that Constantius was the enemy, and that he himself was the favourite, of the gods, might prompt him to desire, to solicit, and even to hasten the auspicious moment of his reign, which was predestined to restore the ancient religion of mankind. When Julian had received the intelligence of the conspiracy, he resigned himself to a short slumber; and afterwards related to his friends that he had seen the Genius of the empire waiting with some impatience at his door, pressing for admittance, and reproaching his want of spirit and ambition.[13] Astonished and perplexed, he addressed his prayers to the great Jupiter, who immediately signified, by a clear and manifest omen, that he should submit to the will of heaven and of the army. The conduct which disclaims the ordinary maxims of reason excites our suspicion and eludes our inquiry. Whenever the spirit of fanaticism, at once so credulous and so crafty, has insinuated itself into a noble mind, it insensibly corrodes the vital principles of virtue and veracity.

To moderate the zeal of his party, to protect the persons of his enemies,[14] to defeat and to despise the secret enterprises which were formed against his life and dignity, were the cares which employed the first days of the reign of the new emperor. Although he was firmly resolved to maintain the station which he had assumed, he was still desirous of saving his country from the calamities of civil war, of declining a contest with the superior forces of Constantius, and of preserving his own character from the reproach of perfidy and ingratitude. Adorned with the designs of military and imperial pomp, Julian showed himself in the field of Mars to the soldiers, who glowed with ardent enthusiasm in the cause of their pupil, their leader, and their friend. He recapitulated their victories, lamented their sufferings, applauded their resolution, animated their hopes, and checked their impetuosity; nor did he dismiss the assembly till he had obtained a solemn promise from the troops that, if the emperor of the East would subscribe an equitable treaty, they would renounce any views of conquest, and satisfy themselves with the tranquil possession of the Gallic provinces. On this foundation he composed, in his own name, and in that of the army, a specious and moderate epistle,[15] which was delivered to Pentadius, his master of the offices, and to his chamberlain Eutherius; two ambassadors whom he appointed to receive the answer and observe the dispositions of Constantius. This epistle is inscribed with the modest appellation of Cæsar; but Julian solicits in a peremptory, though respectful manner, the confirmation of the title of Augustus. He acknowledges the irregularity of his own election, while he justifies in some measure, the resentment and violence of the troops which had extorted his reluctant consent. He allows the supremacy of his brother Constantius; and engages to send him an annual present of Spanish horses, to recruit his army with a select number of barbarian youths, and to accept from his choice a Prætorian præfect of approved discretion and fidelity. But he reserves for himself the nomination of his other civil and military officers, with the troops, the revenue, and the sovereignty of the provinces beyond the Alps. He admonishes the emperor to consult the dictates of justice; to distrust the arts of those venal flatterers who subsist only by the discord of princes; and to embrace the offer of a fair and honourable treaty, equally advantageous to the republic and to the house of Constantine. In this negotiation Julian claimed no more than he already possessed. The delegated authority which he had long exercised over the provinces of Gaul, Spain, and Britain, was still obeyed under a name more independent and august. The soldiers and the people rejoiced in revolution which was not stained even with the blood of the guilty. Florentius was a fugitive; Lupicinus a prisoner. The persons who were disaffected to the new government were disarmed and secured; and the vacant offices were distributed, according to the recommendation of merit, by a prince who despised the intrigues of the palace and the clamours of the soldiers.[16]

The negotiations of peace were accompanied and supported by the most vigorous preparations for war. The army, which Julian held in readiness for immediate action, was recruited and augmented by the disorders of the times. The cruel persecution of the faction of Magnentius had filled Gaul with numerous bands of outlaws and robbers. They cheerfully accepted the offer of a general pardon from a prince whom they could trust, submitted to the restraints of military discipline, and retained only their implacable hatred to the person and government of Constantius.[17] As soon as the season of the year permitted Julian to take the field, he appeared at the head of his legions; threw a bridge over the Rhine in the neighbourhood of Cleves; and prepared to chastise the perfidy of the Attuarii, a tribe of Franks, who presumed that they might ravage with impunity the frontiers of a divided empire. The difficulty, as well as glory, of this enterprise consisted in a laborious march; and Julian had conquered, as soon as he could penetrate into, a country which former princes had considered as inaccessible. After he had given peace to the barbarians, the emperor carefully visited the fortifications along the Rhine from Cleves to Basel; surveyed, with peculiar attention, the territories which he had recovered from the hands of the Alemanni; passed through Besançon,[18] which had severely suffered from their fury; and fixed his headquarters at Vienne for the ensuing winter. The barrier of Gaul was improved and strengthened with additional fortifications; and Julian entertained some hopes that the Germans, whom he had so often vanquished, might, in his absence, be restrained by the terror of his name. Vadomair[19] was the only prince of the Alemanni whom he esteemed or feared; and while the subtle barbarian affected to observe the faith of treaties, the progress of his arms threatened the state with an unseasonable and dangerous war. The policy of Julian condescended to surprise the prince of the Alemanni by his own arts: and Vadomair, who, in the character of a friend, had incautiously accepted an invitation from the Roman governors, was seized in the midst of the entertainment, and sent away prisoner into the heart of Spain. Before the barbarians were recovered from their amazement, the emperor appeared in arms on the banks of the Rhine, and, once more crossing the river, renewed the deep impressions of terror and respect which had been already made by four preceding expeditions.[20]

The ambassadors of Julian had been instruc-

ted to execute with the utmost diligence their important commission. But in their passage through Italy and Illyricum they were detained by the tedious and affected delays of the provincial governors; they were conducted by slow journeys from Constantinople to Cæsarea in Cappadocia; and when at length they were admitted to the presence of Constantius, they found that he had already conceived, from the despatches of his own officers, the most unfavourable opinion of the conduct of Julian and of the Gallic army. The letters were heard with impatience; the trembling messengers were dismissed with indignation and contempt; and the looks, the gestures, the furious language of the monarch, expressed the disorder of his soul. The domestic connection, which might have reconciled the brother and the husband of Helena, was recently dissolved by the death of that princess, whose pregnancy had been several times fruitless, and was at last fatal to herself.[21] The empress Eusebia had preserved, to the last moment of her life, the warm, and even jealous, affection which she had conceived for Julian; and her mild influence might have moderated the resentment of a prince who, since her death, was abandoned to his own passions, and to the arts of his eunuchs. But the terror of a foreign invasion obliged him to suspend the punishment of a private enemy; he continued his march towards the confines of Persia, and thought it sufficient to signify the conditions which might entitle Julian and his guilty followers to the clemency of their offended sovereign. He required that the presumptuous Cæsar should expressly renounce the appellation and rank of Augustus which he had accepted from the rebels; that he should descend to his former station of a limited and dependent minister; that he should vest the powers of the state and army in the hands of those officers who were appointed by the Imperial court; and that he should trust his safety to the assurances of pardon, which were announced by Epictetus, a Gallic bishop, and one of the Arian favourites of Constantius. Several months were ineffectually consumed in a treaty which was negotiated at the distance of three thousand miles between Paris and Antioch; and, as soon as Julian perceived that his moderate and respectful behaviour served only to irritate the pride of an implacable adversary, he boldly resolved to commit his life and fortune to the chance of a civil war. He gave a public and military audience to the questor Leonas: the haughty epistle of Constantius was read to the attentive multitude; and Julian protested, with the most flat-tering deference, that he was ready to resign the title of Augustus, if he could obtain the consent of those whom he acknowledged as the authors of his elevation. The faint proposal was impet-uously silenced; and the acclamations of "Jul-ian Augustus, continue to reign, by the author-ity of the army, of the people, of the republic which you have saved," thundered at once from every part of the field, and terrified the pale ambassador of Constantius. A part of the letter was afterwards read, in which the emperor ar-raigned the ingratitude of Julian, whom he had invested with the honours of the purple; whom he had educated with so much care and tender-ness; whom he had preserved in his infancy, when he was left a helpless orphan. "An or-phan!" interrupted Julian, who justified his cause by indulging his passions, "does the as-sassin of my family reproach me that I was left an orphan? He urges me to revenge those in-juries which I have long studied to forget." The assembly was dismissed; and Leonas, who with some difficulty had been protected from the popular fury, was sent back to his master with an epistle in which Julian expressed, in a strain of the most vehement eloquence, the sentiments of contempt, of hatred, and of resentment, which had been suppressed and embittered by the dis-simulation of twenty years. After this message, which might be considered as a signal of irrecon-cilable war, Julian, who some weeks before had celebrated the Christian festival of the Epiph-any,[22] made a public declaration that he com-mitted the care of his safety to the IMMORTAL GODS; and thus publicly renounced the religion as well as the friendship of Constantius.[23]

The situation of Julian required a vigorous and immediate resolution. He had discovered from intercepted letters that his adversary, sac-rificing the interest of the state to that of the monarch, had again excited the barbarians to invade the provinces of the West. The position of two magazines, one of them collected on the banks of the lake of Constance, the other formed at the foot of the Cottian Alps, seemed to indi-cate the march of two armies; and the size of those magazines, each of which consisted of six hundred thousand quarters of wheat, or rather flour,[24] was a threatening evidence of the strength and numbers of the enemy who prepared to sur-round him. But the Imperial legions were still in their distant quarters of Asia; the Danube was feebly guarded; and if Julian could occupy, by a sudden incursion, the important provinces of Illyricum, he might expect that a people of

soldiers would resort to his standard, and that the rich mines of gold and silver would contrib-ute to the expenses of the civil war. He pro-posed this bold enterprise to the assembly of the soldiers; inspired them with a just confidence in their general, and in themselves; and exhorted them to maintain their reputation of being ter-rible to the enemy, moderate to their fellow-citizens, and obedient to their officers. His spirited discourse was received with the loudest acclamations, and the same troops which had taken up arms against Constantius, when he summoned them to leave Gaul, now declared with alacrity that they would follow Julian to the farthest extremities of Europe or Asia. The oath of fidelity was administered; and the sol-diers, clashing their shields, and pointing their drawn swords to their throats, devoted them-selves, with horrid imprecations, to the service of a leader whom they celebrated as the deliv-erer of Gaul and the conqueror of the Germans.[25] This solemn engagement, which seemed to be dictated by affection rather than by duty, was singly opposed by Nebridius, who had been admitted to the office of Prætorian præfect. That faithful minister, alone and unassisted, as-serted the rights of Constantius in the midst of an armed and angry multitude, to whose fury he had almost fallen an honourable, but useless sacrifice. After losing one of his hands by the stroke of a sword, he embraced the knees of the prince whom he had offended. Julian covered the præfect with his Imperial mantle, and pro-tecting him from the zeal of his followers, dis-missed him to his own house, with less respect than was perhaps due to the virtue of an ene-my.[26] The high office of Nebridius was bestowed on Sallust; and the provinces of Gaul, which were now delivered from the intolerable op-pression of taxes, enjoyed the mild and equit-able administration of the friend of Julian, who was permitted to practise those virtues which he had instilled into the mind of his pupil.[27]

The hopes of Julian depended much less on the number of his troops than on the celerity of his motions. In the execution of a daring enter-prise he availed himself of every precaution, as far as prudence could suggest; and where pru-dence could no longer accompany his steps, he trusted the event to valour and to fortune. In the neighbourhood of Basel he assembled and divided his army.[28] One body, which consisted of ten thousand men, was directed, under the command of Nevitta, general of the cavalry, to advance through the midland parts of Rhætia and Noricum. A similar division of troops, un-

der the orders of Jovius and Jovinus, prepared
to follow the oblique course of the highways
through the Alps and the northern confines of
Italy. The instructions to the generals were conceived with energy and precision: to hasten
their march in close and compact columns, which,
according to the disposition of the ground,
might readily be changed into any order of battle; to secure themselves against the surprises of
the night by strong posts and vigilant guards;
to prevent resistance by their unexpected arrival; to elude examination by their sudden departure; to spread the opinion of their strength,
and the terror of his name; and to join their
sovereign under the walls of Sirmium. For himself Julian had reserved a more difficult and
extraordinary part. He selected three thousand
brave and active volunteers, resolved, like their
leader, to cast behind them every hope of a retreat; at the head of this faithful band he fear-
lessly plunged into the recesses of the Marcian,
or Black Forest, which conceals the sources of
the Danube;[29] and, for many days, the fate of
Julian was unknown to the world. The secrecy
of his march, his diligence, and vigour, surmounted every obstacle; he forced his way over
mountains and morasses, occupied the bridges
or swam the rivers, pursued his direct course[30]
without reflecting whether he traversed the territory of the Romans or of the barbarians, and
at length emerged, between Ratisbon and Vienna, at the place where he designed to embark
his troops on the Danube. By a well-concerted
stratagem he seized a fleet of light brigantines[31]
as it lay at anchor; secured a supply of coarse
provisions sufficient to satisfy the indelicate, but
voracious, appetite of a Gallic army; and boldly
committed himself to the stream of the Danube.
The labours of his mariners, who plied their
oars with incessant diligence, and the steady
continuance of a favourable wind, carried his
fleet above seven hundred miles in eleven days;[32]
and he had already disembarked his troops at
Bononia, only nineteen miles from Sirmium,
before his enemies could receive any certain intelligence that he had left the banks of the
Rhine. In the course of this long and rapid navigation, the mind of Julian was fixed on the object of his enterprise; and though he accepted
the deputation of some cities, which hastened to
claim the merit of an early submission, he passed
before the hostile stations, which were placed
along the river, without indulging the temptation of signalising a useless and ill-timed valour.
The banks of the Danube were crowded on
either side with spectators, who gazed on the

military pomp, anticipated the importance of
the event, and diffused through the adjacent
country the fame of a young hero, who advanced with more than mortal speed at the
head of the innumerable forces of the West.
Lucilian, who, with the rank of general of the
cavalry commanded the military powers of Illyricum, was alarmed and perplexed by the
doubtful reports, which he could neither reject
nor believe. He had taken some slow and irresolute measures for the purpose of collecting his
troops, when he was surprised by Dagalaiphus,
an active officer, whom Julian, as soon as he
landed at Bononia, had pushed forward with
some light infantry. The captive general, uncertain of his life or death, was hastily thrown
upon a horse, and conducted to the presence of
Julian, who kindly raised him from the ground,
and dispelled the terror and amazement which
seemed to stupefy his faculties. But Lucilian had
no sooner recovered his spirits than he betrayed
his want of discretion, by presuming to admonish his conqueror that he had rashly ventured,
with a handful of men, to expose his person in
the midst of his enemies. "Reserve for your master Constantius these timid remonstrances," replied Julian, with a smile of contempt; "when I
gave you my purple to kiss, I received you not
as a counsellor, but as a suppliant." Conscious
that success alone could justify his attempt, and
that boldness only could command success, he
instantly advanced, at the head of three thousand soldiers, to attack the strongest and most
populous city of the Illyrian provinces. As he
entered the long suburb of Sirmium, he was received by the joyful acclamations of the army
and people, who, crowned with flowers, and
holding lighted tapers in their hands, conducted
their acknowledged sovereign to the imperial
residence. Two days were devoted to the public
joy, which was celebrated by the games of the
Circus; but, early on the morning of the third
day, Julian marched to occupy the narrow pass
of Succi, in the defiles of Mount Hæmus;
which, almost in the midway between Sirmium
and Constantinople, separates the provinces of
Thrace and Dacia, by an abrupt descent towards the former, and a gentle declivity on the
side of the latter.[33] The defence of this important post was intrusted to the brave Nevitta,
who, as well as the generals of the Italian division, successfully executed the plan of the march
and junction which their master had so ably
conceived.[34]

The homage which Julian obtained from the
fears or the inclination of the people extended

far beyond the immediate effect of his arms.[35] The præfectures of Italy and Illyricum were administered by Taurus and Florentius, who united that important office with the vain honours of the consulship; and, as those magistrates had retired with precipitation to the court of Asia, Julian, who could not always restrain the levity of his temper, stigmatised their flight by adding, in all the Acts of the Year, the epithet of *fugitive* to the names of the two consuls. The provinces which had been deserted by their first magistrates acknowledged the authority of an emperor who, conciliating the qualities of a solider with those of a philosopher, was equally admired in the camps of the Danube and in the cities of Greece. From his palace, or, more properly, from his headquarters of Sirmium and Naissus, he distributed to the principal cities of the empire a laboured apology for his own conduct; published the secret despatches of Constantius; and solicited the judgment of mankind between two competitors, the one of whom had expelled, and the other had invited, the barbarians.[36] Julian, whose mind was deeply wounded by the reproach of ingratitude, aspired to maintain, by argument as well as by arms, the superior merits of his cause; and to excel not only in the arts of war, but in those of composition. His epistle to the senate and people of Athens[37] seems to have been dictated by an elegant enthusiasm, which prompted him to submit his actions and his motives to the degenerate Athenians of his own times, with the same humble deference as if he had been pleading in the days of Aristides before the tribunal of the Areopagus. His application to the senate of Rome, which was still permitted to bestow the titles of imperial power, was agreeable to the forms of the expiring republic. An assembly was summoned by Tertullus, præfect of the city; the epistle of Julian was read; and, as he appeared to be master of Italy, his claims were admitted without a dissenting voice. His oblique censure of the innovations of Constantine, and his passionate invective against the vices of Constantius, were heard with less satisfaction; and the senate, as if Julian had been present, unanimously exclaimed, "Respect, we beseech you, the author of your own fortune."[38] An artful expression, which, according to the chance of war, might be differently explained—as a manly reproof of the ingratitude of the usurper or as a flattering confession that a single act of such benefit to the state ought to atone for all the failings of Constantius.

The intelligence of the march and rapid progress of Julian was speedily transmitted to his rival, who, by the retreat of Sapor, had obtained some respite from the Persian war. Disguising the anguish of his soul under the semblance of contempt, Constantius professed his intention of returning into Europe, and of giving chase to Julian; for he never spoke of this military expedition in any other light than that of a hunting party.[39] In the camp of Hierapolis, in Syria, he communicated this design to his army; slightly mentioned the guilt and rashness of the Cæsar; and ventured to assure them that, if the mutineers of Gaul presumed to meet them in the field, they would be unable to sustain the fire of their eyes and the irresistible weight of their shout of onset. The speech of the emperor was received with military applause; and Theodotus, the president of the council of Hierapolis, requested, with tears of adulation, that *his* city might be adorned with the head of the vanquished rebel.[40] A chosen detachment was despatched away in post-waggons, to secure, if it were yet possible, the pass of Succi; the recruits, the horses, the arms, and the magazines, which had been prepared against Sapor, were appropriated to the service of the civil war; and the domestic victories of Constantius inspired his partisans with the most sanguine assurances of success. The notary Gaudentius had occupied in his name the provinces of Africa; the subsistence of Rome was intercepted; and the distress of Julian was increased by an unexpected event, which might have been productive of fatal consequences. Julian had received the submission of two legions and a cohort of archers who were stationed at Sirmium; but he suspected, with reason, the fidelity of those troops which had been distinguished by the emperor; and it was thought expedient, under the pretence of the exposed state of the Gallic frontier, to dismiss them from the most important scene of action. They advanced, with reluctance, as far as the confines of Italy; but, as they dreaded the length of the way and the savage fierceness of the Germans, they resolved, by the instigation of one of their tribunes, to halt at Aquileia, and to erect the banners of Constantius on the walls of that impregnable city. The vigilance of Julian perceived at once the extent of the mischief, and the necessity of applying an immediate remedy. By his order, Jovinus led back a part of the army into Italy; and the siege of Aquileia was formed with diligence and prosecuted with vigour. But the legionaries, who seemed to have rejected the yoke of discipline, conducted the defence of the place with skill and perseverance; invited the rest of Italy to imitate the example of their courage and loyalty; and threatened the retreat of Julian, if he should be forced to yield to the superior numbers of the armies of the East.[41]

But the humanity of Julian was preserved from the cruel alternative which he pathetically laments of destroying or of being himself destroyed: and the seasonable death of Constantius delivered the Roman empire from the calamities of civil war. The approach of winter could not detain the monarch at Antioch; and his favourites durst not oppose his impatient desire of revenge. A slight fever, which was perhaps occasioned by the agitation of his spirits, was increased by the fatigues of the journey, and Constantius was obliged to halt at the little town of Mopsucrene, twelve miles beyond Tarsus, where he expired, after a short illness, in the forty-fifth year of his age, and the twenty-fourth of his reign.[42] His genuine character, which was composed of pride and weakness, of superstition and cruelty, has been fully displayed in the preceding narrative of civil and ecclesiastical events. The long abuse of power rendered him a considerable object in the eyes of his contemporaries; but, as personal merit can alone deserve the notice of posterity, the last of the sons of Constantine may be dismissed from the world with the remark that he inherited the defects, without the abilities, of his father. Before Constantius expired, he is said to have named Julian for his successor; nor does it seem improbable that his anxious concern for the fate of a young and tender wife, whom he left with child, may have prevailed in his last moments over the harsher passions of hatred and revenge. Eusebius and his guilty associates made a faint attempt to prolong the reign of the eunuchs by the election of another emperor; but their intrigues were rejected with disdain by an army which now abhorred the thought of civil discord; and two officers of rank were instantly despatched to assure Julian that every sword in the empire would be drawn for his service. The military designs of that prince, who had formed three different attacks against Thrace, were prevented by this fortunate event. Without shedding the blood of his fellow-citizens, he escaped the dangers of a doubtful conflict, and acquired the advantages of a complete victory. Impatient to visit the place of his birth and the new capital of the empire, he advanced from Naissus through the mountains of Hæmus and the cities of Thrace. When he reached Heraclea, at the distance of sixty miles, all Constantinople was

poured forth to receive him; and he made his triumphal entry amidst the dutiful acclamations of the soldiers, the people, and the senate. An innumerable multitude pressed around him with eager respect, and were perhaps disappointed when they beheld the small stature and simple garb of a hero, whose inexperienced youth had vanquished the barbarians of Germany, and who had now traversed, in a successful career, the whole continent of Europe from the shores of the Atlantic to those of the Bosphorus.[43] A few days afterwards, when the remains of the deceased emperor were landed in the harbour, the subjects of Julian applauded the real or affected humanity of their sovereign. On foot, without his diadem, and clothed in a mourning habit, he accompanied the funeral as far as the church of the Holy Apostles, where the body was deposited: and if these marks of respect may be interpreted as a selfish tribute to the birth and dignity of his Imperial kinsman, the tears of Julian professed to the world that he had forgot the injuries, and remembered only the obligations, which he had received from Constantius.[44] As soon as the legions of Aquileia were assured of the death of the emperor, they opened the gates of the city, and, by the sacrifice of their guilty leaders, obtained an easy pardon from the prudence or lenity of Julian; who, in the thirty-second year of his age, acquired the undisputed possession of the Roman empire.[45]

Philosophy had instructed Julian to compare the advantages of action and retirement; but the elevation of his birth and the accidents of his life never allowed him the freedom of choice. He might perhaps sincerely have preferred the groves of the Academy and the society of Athens; but he was constrained, at first by the will, and afterwards by the injustice of Constantius, to expose his person and fame to the dangers of Imperial greatness; and to make himself accountable to the world and to posterity for the happiness of millions.[46] Julian recollected with terror the observation of his master Plato,[47] that the government of our flocks and herds is always committed to beings of a superior species; and that the conduct of nations requires and deserves the celestial powers of the Gods or of the Genii. From this principle he justly concluded that the man who presumes to reign should aspire to the perfection of the divine nature; that he should purify his soul from her mortal and terrestrial part; that he should extinguish his appetites, enlighten his understanding, regulate his passions, and subdue the wild beast which, according to the lively metaphor of Aristotle,[48] seldom fails to ascend the throne of a despot. The throne of Julian, which the death of Constantius fixed on an independent basis, was the seat of reason, of virtue, and perhaps of vanity. He despised the honours, renounced the pleasures, and discharged with incessant diligence the duties of his exalted station: and there were few among his subjects who would have consented to relieve him from the weight of the diadem, had they been obliged to submit their time and their actions to the rigorous laws which their philosophic emperor imposed on himself. One of his most intimate friends,[49] who had often shared the frugal simplicity of his table, has remarked that his light and sparing diet (which was usually of the vegetable kind) left his mind and body always free and active for the various and important business of an author, a pontiff, a magistrate, a general, and a prince. In one and the same day he gave audience to several ambassadors, and wrote or dictated a great number of letters to his generals, his civil magistrates, his private friends, and the different cities of his dominions. He listened to the memorials which had been received, considered the subject of the petitions, and signified his intentions more rapidly than they could be taken in shorthand by the diligence of his secretaries. He possessed such flexibility of thought, and such firmness of attention, that he could employ his hand to write, his ear to listen, and his voice to dictate; and pursue at once three several trains of ideas without hesitation, and without error. While his ministers reposed, the prince flew with agility from one labour to another; and, after a hasty dinner, retired into his library till the public business which he had appointed for the evening summoned him to interrupt the prosecution of his studies. The supper of the emperor was still less substantial than the former meal; his sleep was never clouded by the fumes of indigestion; and, except in the short interval of a marriage which was the effect of policy rather than love, the chaste Julian never shared his bed with a female companion.[50] He was soon awakened by the entrance of fresh secretaries, who had slept the preceding day; and his servants were obliged to wait alternately, while their indefatigable master allowed himself scarcely any other refreshment than the change of occupations. The predecessors of Julian, his uncle, his brother, and his cousin, indulged their puerile taste for the games of the Circus, under the specious pretence of complying with the inclinations of the

people; and they frequently remained the greatest part of the day as idle spectators, and as a part of the splendid spectacle, till the ordinary round of twenty-four races[51] was completely finished. On solemn festivals, Julian, who felt and professed an unfashionable dislike to these frivolous amusements, condescended to appear in the Circus; and, after bestowing a careless glance on five or six of the races, he hastily withdrew with the impatience of a philosopher, who considered every moment as lost that was not devoted to the advantage of the public or the improvement of his own mind.[52] By this avarice of time he seemed to protract the short duration of his reign; and, if the dates were less securely ascertained, we should refuse to believe that only sixteen months elapsed between the death of Constantius and the departure of his successor for the Persian war. The actions of Julian can only be preserved by the care of the historian; but the portion of his voluminous writings which is still extant remains as a monument of the application, as well as of the genius, of the emperor. The Misopogon, the Cæsars, several of his orations, and his elaborate work against the Christian religion, were composed in the long nights of the two winters, the former of which he passed at Constantinople, and the latter at Antioch.

The reformation of the Imperial court was one of the first and most necessary acts of the government of Julian.[53] Soon after his entrance into the palace of Constantinople he had occasion for the service of a barber. An officer, magnificently dressed, immediately presented himself. "It is a barber," exclaimed the prince, with affected surprise, "that I want, and not a receiver-general of the finances."[54] He questioned the man concerning the profits of his employment, and was informed that, besides a large salary and some valuable perquisites, he enjoyed a daily allowance for twenty servants and as many horses. A thousand barbers, a thousand cupbearers, a thousand cooks, were distributed in the several offices of luxury; and the number of eunuchs could be compared only with the insects of a summer's day.[55] The monarch who resigned to his subjects the superiority of merit and virtue was distinguished by the oppressive magnificence of his dress, his table, his buildings, and his train. The stately palaces erected by Constantine and his sons were decorated with many-coloured marbles and ornaments of massy gold. The most exquisite dainties were procured to gratify their pride rather than their taste; birds of the most distant climates, fish from the most remote seas, fruits out of their natural season, winter roses, and summer snows.[56] The domestic crowd of the palace surpassed the expense of the legions; yet the smallest part of this costly multitude was subservient to the use, or even to the splendour, of the throne. The monarch was disgraced, and the people was injured, by the creation and sale of an infinite number of obscure and even titular employments; and the most worthless of mankind might purchase the privilege of being maintained, without the necessity of labour, from the public revenue. The waste of an enormous household, the increase of fees and perquisites, which were soon claimed as a lawful debt, and the bribes which they extorted from those who feared their enmity or solicited their favour, suddenly enriched these haughty menials. They abused their fortune, without considering their past or their future condition; and their rapine and venality could be equalled only by the extravagance of their dissipations. Their silken robes were embroidered with gold, their tables were served with delicacy and profusion; the houses which they built for their own use would have covered the farm of an ancient consul; and the most honourable citizens were obliged to dismount from their horses and respectfully to salute an eunuch whom they met on the public highway. The luxury of the palace excited the contempt and indignation of Julian, who usually slept on the ground, who yielded with reluctance to the indispensable calls of nature, and who placed his vanity not in emulating, but in despising the pomp of royalty.

By the total extirpation of a mischief which was magnified even beyond its real extent, he was impatient to relieve the distress and to appease the murmurs of the people, who support with less uneasiness the weight of taxes if they are convinced that the fruits of their industry are appropriated to the service of the state. But in the execution of this salutary work Julian is accused of proceeding with too much haste and inconsiderate severity. By a single edict he reduced the palace of Constantinople to an immense desert, and dismissed with ignominy the whole train of slaves and dependents,[57] without providing any just, or at least benevolent, exceptions for the age, the services, or the poverty of the faithful domestics of the Imperial family. Such indeed was the temper of Julian, who seldom recollected the fundamental maxim of Aristotle, that true virtue is placed at an equal distance between the opposite vices. The splendid and effeminate dress of the Asiatics, the curls and paint, the collars and bracelets, which had appeared so ridiculous in the person of Constantine, were consistently rejected by his philosophic successor. But with the fopperies, Julian affected to renounce the decencies of dress; and seemed to value himself for his neglect of the laws of cleanliness. In a satirical performance, which was designed for the public eye, the emperor descants with pleasure, and even with pride, on the length of his nails and the inky blackness of his hands; protests that, although the greatest part of his body was covered with hair, the use of the razor was confined to his head alone; and celebrates with visible complacency the shaggy and *populous*[58] beard which he fondly cherished, after the example of the philosophers of Greece. Had Julian consulted the simple dictates of reason, the first magistrate of the Romans would have scorned the affectation of Diogenes, as well as that of Darius.

But the work of public reformation would have remained imperfect if Julian had only corrected the abuses, without punishing the crimes, of his predecessor's reign. "We are now delivered," says he, in a familiar letter to one of his intimate friends, "we are now surprisingly delivered from the voracious jaws of the Hydra.[59] I do not mean to apply that epithet to my brother Constantius. He is no more; may the earth lie light on his head! But his artful and cruel favourites studied to deceive and exasperate a prince whose natural mildness cannot be praised without some efforts of adulation. It is not, however, my intention that even those men should be oppressed: they are accused, and they shall enjoy the benefit of a fair and impartial trial." To conduct this inquiry, Julian named six judges of the highest rank in the state and army, and, as he wished to escape the reproach of condemning his personal enemies, he fixed this extraordinary tribunal at Chalcedon, on the Asiatic side of the Bosphorous, and transferred to the commissioners an absolute power to pronounce and execute their final sentence, without delay and without appeal. The office of president was exercised by the venerable præfect of the East, a *second* Sallust,[60] whose virtues conciliated the esteem of Greek sophists and of Christian bishops. He was assisted by the eloquent Mamertinus,[61] one of the consuls elect, whose merit is loudly celebrated by the doubtful evidence of his own applause. But the civil wisdom of two magistrates was overbalanced by the ferocious violence of four generals, Nevitta, Agilo, Jovinus, and Arbetio. Arbetio, whom the public would have seen with less surprise at the bar than on the bench, was supposed to possess the secret of the commission; the armed and angry leaders of the Jovian and Herculian bands encompassed the tribunal, and the judges were alternately swayed by the laws of justice and by the clamours of faction.[62]

The chamberlain Eusebius, who had so long abused the favour of Constantius, expiated, by an ignominious death, the insolence, the corruption, and cruelty of his servile reign. The executions of Paul and Apodemius (the former of whom was burnt alive) were accepted as an inadequate atonement by the widows and orphans of so many hundred Romans whom those legal tyrants had betrayed and murdered. But Justice herself (if we may use the pathetic expression of Ammianus[63]) appeared to weep over the fate of Ursulus, the treasurer of the empire, and his blood accused the ingratitude of Julian, whose distress had been seasonably relieved by the intrepid liberality of that honest minister. The rage of the soldiers, whom he had provoked by his indiscretion, was the cause and the excuse of his death; and the emperor, deeply wounded by his own reproaches and those of the public, offered some consolation to the family of Ursulus by the restitution of his confiscated fortunes. Before the end of the year in which they had been adorned with the ensigns of the prefecture and consulship,[64] Taurus and Florentius were reduced to implore the clemency of the inexorable tribunal of Chalcedon. The former was banished to Vercellæ in Italy, and a sentence of death was pronounced against the latter. A wise prince should have rewarded the crime of Taurus: the faithful minister, when he was no longer able to oppose the progress of a rebel, had taken refuge in the court of his benefactor and his lawful sovereign. But the guilt of Florentius justified the severity of the judges, and his escape served to display the magnanimity of Julian, who nobly checked the interested diligence of an informer, and refused to learn what place concealed the wretched fugitive from his just resentment.[65] Some months after the tribunal of Chalcedon had been dissolved, the prætorian vicegerent of Africa, the notary Gaudentius, and Artemius,[66] duke of Egypt, were executed at Antioch. Artemius had reigned the cruel and corrupt tyrant of a great province; Gaudentius had long practised the arts of calumny against the innocent, the virtuous, and even the person of Julian himself. Yet the circumstances of their trial and condemnation were so unskilfully managed that these wicked men obtained, in the public opinion, the glory of suffering for the obstinate loyalty with which they had supported the cause of Constantius. The rest of his servants were protected by a general act of oblivion, and they were left to enjoy with impunity the bribes which they had accepted either to defend the oppressed or to oppress the friendless. This measure, which, on the soundest principles of policy, may deserve our approbation, was executed in a manner which seemed to degrade the majesty of the throne. Julian was tormented by the importunities of a multitude, particularly of Egyptians, who loudly re-demanded the gifts which they had imprudently or illegally bestowed; he foresaw the endless prosecution of vexatious suits, and he engaged a promise, which ought always to have been sacred, that if they would repair to Chalcedon, he would meet them in person, to hear and determine their complaints. But as soon as they were landed, he issued an absolute order, which prohibited the watermen from transporting any Egyptian to Constantinople, and thus detained his disappointed clients on the Asiatic shore, till, their patience and money being utterly exhausted, they were obliged to return with indignant murmurs to their native country.[67]

The numerous army of spies, of agents, and informers, enlisted by Constantius to secure the repose of one man, and to interrupt that of millions, was immediately disbanded by his generous successor. Julian was slow in his suspicions, and gentle in his punishments, and his contempt of treason was the result of judgment, of vanity, and of courage. Conscious of superior merit, he was persuaded that few among his subjects would dare to meet him in the field, to attempt his life, or even to seat themselves on his vacant throne. The philosopher could excuse the hasty sallies of discontent, and the hero could despise the ambitious projects which surpassed the fortune or the abilities of the rash conspirators. A citizen of Ancyra had prepared for his own use a purple garment, and this indiscreet action, which, under the reign of Constantius, would have been considered as a capital offence,[68] was reported to Julian by the officious importunity of a private enemy. The monarch, after making some inquiry into the rank and character of his rival, despatched the informer with a present of a pair of purple slippers, to complete the magnificence of his Imperial habit. A more dangerous conspiracy was formed by ten of the domestic guards, who had resolved to assassinate Julian in the field of exercise near

Antioch. Their intemperance revealed their guilt, and they were conducted in chains to the presence of their injured sovereign, who, after a lively representation of the wickedness and folly of their enterprise, instead of a death of torture, which they deserved and expected, pronounced a sentence of exile against the two principal offenders. The only instance in which Julian seemed to depart from his accustomed clemency was the execution of a rash youth, who, with a feeble hand, had aspired to seize the reins of empire. But that youth was the son of Marcellus, the general of cavalry, who, in the first campaign of the Gallic war, had deserted the standard of the Cæsar and the republic. Without appearing to indulge his personal resentment, Julian might easily confound the crime of the son and of the father; but he was reconciled by the distress of Marcellus, and the liberality of the emperor endeavoured to heal the wound which had been inflicted by the hand of justice.[69]

Julian was not insensible of the advantages of freedom.[70] From his studies he had imbibed the spirit of ancient sages and heroes; his life and fortunes had depended on the caprice of a tyrant; and, when he ascended the throne, his pride was sometimes mortified by the reflection that the slaves who would not dare to censure his defects were not worthy to applaud his virtues.[71] He sincerely abhorred the system of oriental despotism which Diocletian, Constantine, and the patient habits of four score years, had established in the empire. A motive of superstition prevented the execution of the design which Julian had frequently meditated, of relieving his head from the weight of a costly diadem;[72] but he absolutely refused the title of *Dominus* or *Lord*,[73] a word which was grown so familiar to the ears of the Romans, that they no longer remembered its servile and humiliating origin. The office, or rather the name, of consul was cherished by a prince who contemplated with reverence the ruins of the republic; and the same behaviour which had been assumed by the prudence of Augustus was adopted by Julian from choice and inclination. On the calends of January, at break of day, the new consuls, Mamertinus and Nevitta, hastened to the palace to salute the emperor. As soon as he was informed of their approach, he leaped from his throne, eagerly advanced to meet them, and compelled the blushing magistrates to receive the demonstrations of his affected humility. From the palace they proceeded to the senate. The emperor, on foot, marched before their litters, and the gazing multitude admired the image of ancient times, or secretly blamed a conduct which, in their eyes, degraded the majesty of the purple.[74] But the behaviour of Julian was uniformly supported. During the games of the Circus, he had, imprudently or designedly, performed the manumission of a slave in the presence of the consul. The moment he was reminded that he had trespassed on the jurisdiction of *another* magistrate, he condemned himself to pay a fine of ten pounds of gold, and embraced this public occasion of declaring to the world that he was subject, like the rest of his fellow-citizens, to the laws,[75] and even to the forms, of the republic. The spirit of his administration, and his regard for the place of his nativity, induced Julian to confer on the senate of Constantinople the same honours, privileges, and authority which were still enjoyed by the senate of ancient Rome.[76] A legal fiction was introduced and gradually established, that one half of the national council had migrated into the East, and the despotic successors of Julian, accepting the title of Senators, acknowledged themselves the members of a respectable body which was permitted to represent the majesty of the Roman name. From Constantinople the attention of the monarch was extended to the municipal senates of the provinces. He abolished, by repeated edicts, the unjust and pernicious exemptions which had withdrawn so many idle citizens from the service of their country; and by imposing an equal distribution of public duties, he restored the strength, the splendour, or, according to the glowing expression of Libanius,[77] the soul of the expiring cities of his empire. The venerable age of Greece excited the most tender compassion in the mind of Julian, which kindled into rapture when he recollected the gods, the heroes, and the men superior to heroes and to gods, who had bequeathed to the latest posterity the monuments of their genius or the example of their virtues. He relieved the distress and restored the beauty of the cities of Epirus and Peloponnesus.[78] Athens acknowledged him for her benefactor, Argos for her deliverer. The pride of Corinth, again rising from her ruins with the honours of a Roman colony, exacted a tribute from the adjacent republics for the purpose of defraying the games of the Isthmus, which were celebrated in the amphitheatre with the hunting of bears and panthers. From this tribute the cities of Elis, of Delphi, and of Argos, which had inherited from their remote ancestors the sacred office of perpetuating the Olympic, the Pythian, and the Nemean games, claimed a just exemption. The immunity of Elis and Delphi was respected by the Corinthians, but the poverty of Argos tempted the insolence of oppression, and the feeble complaints of its deputies were silenced by the decree of a provincial magistrate, who seems to have consulted only the interest of the capital in which he resided. Seven years after this sentence Julian[79] allowed the cause to be referred to a superior tribunal, and his eloquence was interposed, most probably with success, in the defence of a city which had been the royal seat of Agamemnon,[80] and had given to Macedonia a race of kings and conquerors.[81]

The laborious administration of military and civil affairs, which were multiplied in proportion to the extent of the empire, exercised the abilities of Julian; but he frequently assumed the two characters of Orator[82] and of Judge,[83] which are almost unknown to the modern sovereigns of Europe. The arts of persuasion, so diligently cultivated by the first Cæsars, were neglected by the military ignorance and Asiatic pride of their successors, and, if they condescended to harangue the soldiers, whom they feared, they treated with silent disdain the senators, whom they despised. The assemblies of the senate, which Constantius had avoided, were considered by Julian as the place where he could exhibit with the most propriety the maxims of a republican and the talents of a rhetorician. He alternately practised, as in a school of declamation, the several modes of praise, of censure, of exhortation; and his friend Libanius has remarked that the study of Homer taught him to imitate the simple, concise style of Menelaus, the copiousness of Nestor, whose words descended like the flakes of a winter's snow, or the pathetic and forcible eloquence of Ulysses. The functions of a judge, which are sometimes incompatible with those of a prince, were exercised by Julian not only as a duty, but as an amusement; and although he might have trusted the integrity and discernment of his Prætorian præfects, he often placed himself by their side on the seat of judgment. The acute penetration of his mind was agreeably occupied in detecting and defeating the chicanery of the advocates, who laboured to disguise the truth of facts and to pervert the sense of the laws. He sometimes forgot the gravity of his station, asked indiscreet or unseasonable questions, and betrayed, by the loudness of his voice and the agitation of his body, the earnest vehemence with which he maintained his opinion against the judges, the advocates, and their clients. But his knowledge of his own temper prompted him to encourage, and even to solicit, the reproof of his friends and ministers: and whenever they ventured to oppose the irregular sallies of his passions, the spectators could observe the shame as well as the gratitude of their monarch. The decrees of Julian were almost always founded on the principles of justice, and he had the firmness to resist the two most dangerous temptations which assault the tribunal of a sovereign under the specious forms of compassion and equity. He decided the merits of the cause without weighing the circumstances of the parties; and the poor, whom he wished to relieve, were condemned to satisfy the just demands of a noble and wealthy adversary. He carefully distinguished the judge from the legislator;[84] and though he meditated a necessary reformation of the Roman jurisprudence, he pronounced sentence according to the strict and literal interpretation of those laws which the magistrates were bound to execute and the subjects to obey.

The generality of princes, if they were stripped of their purple and cast naked into the world, would immediately sink to the lowest rank of society, without a hope of emerging from their obscurity. But the personal merit of Julian was, in some measure, independent of his fortune. Whatever had been his choice of life, by the force of intrepid courage, lively wit, and intense application, he would have obtained, or at least he would have deserved, the highest honours of his profession, and Julian might have raised himself to the rank of minister or general of the state in which he was born a private citizen. If the jealous caprice of power had disappointed his expectations; if he had prudently declined the paths of greatness, the employment of the same talents in studious solitude would have placed beyond the reach of kings his present happiness and his immortal fame. When we inspect with minute, or perhaps malevolent, attention the portrait of Julian, something seems wanting to the grace and perfection of the whole figure. His genius was less powerful and sublime than that of Cæsar, nor did he possess the consummate prudence of Augustus. The virtues of Trajan appear more steady and natural, and the philosophy of Marcus is more simple and consistent. Yet Julian sustained adversity with firmness, and prosperity with moderation. After an interval of one hundred and twenty years from the death of Alexander Severus, the Romans beheld an emperor who made no distinction between his duties and his pleasures, who laboured to relieve the distress and to revive the spirit of his subjects, and who endeavoured always to connect authority with merit, and happiness with virtue. Even faction, and religious faction, was constrained to acknowledge the superiority of his genius in peace as well as in war, and to confess, with a sigh, that the apostate Julian was a lover of his country, and that he deserved the empire of the world.[85]

CHAPTER XXIII

The Religion of Julian. Universal Toleration. He attempts to restore and reform the Pagan Worship. To rebuild the Temple of Jerusalem. His Artful Persecution of the Christians. Mutual Zeal and Injustice.

THE character of Apostate has injured the reputation of Julian; and the enthusiasm which clouded his virtues has exaggerated the real and apparent magnitude of his faults. Our partial ignorance may represent him as a philosophic monarch, who studied to protect, with an equal hand, the religious factions of the empire, and to allay the theological fever which had inflamed the minds of the people from the edicts of Diocletian to the exile of Athanasius. A more accurate view of the character and conduct of Julian will remove this favourable prepossession for a prince who did not escape the general contagion of the times. We enjoy the singular advantage of comparing the pictures which have been delineated by his fondest admirers and his implacable enemies. The actions of Julian are faithfully related by a judicious and candid historian, the impartial spectator of his life and death. The unanimous evidence of his contemporaries is confirmed by the public and private declarations of the emperor himself; and his various writings express the uniform tenor of his religious sentiments, which policy would have prompted him to dissemble rather than to affect. A devout and sincere attachment for the gods of Athens and Rome constituted the ruling passion of Julian;[1] the powers of an enlightened understanding were betrayed and corrupted by the influence of superstitious prejudice; and the phantoms which existed only in the mind of the emperor had a real and pernicious effect on the government of the empire. The vehement zeal of the Christians, who despised the worship, and overturned the altars, of those fabulous deities, engaged their votary in a state of irreconcilable hostility with a very numerous party of his subjects; and he was sometimes tempted, by the desire of victory or the shame of a repulse, to violate the laws of prudence, and even of justice. The triumph of the party which he deserted and opposed has fixed a stain of infamy on the name of Julian; and the unsuccessful apostate has been overwhelmed with a torrent of pious invectives, of which the signal was given by the sonorous trumpet[2] of Gregory Nazianzen.[3] The interesting nature of the events which were crowded into the short reign of this active emperor deserves a just and circumstantial narrative. His motive, his counsels, and his actions, as far as they are connected with the history of religion, will be the subject of the present chapter.

The cause of his strange and fatal apostasy may be derived from the early period of his life when he was left an orphan in the hands of the murderers of his family. The names of Christ and of Constantius, the ideas of slavery and of religion, were soon associated in a youthful imagination, which was susceptible of the most lively impressions. The care of his infancy was intrusted to Eusebius, bishop of Nicomedia,[4] who was related to him on the side of his mother; and till Julian reached the twentieth year of his age, he received from his Christian preceptors the education not of a hero but of a saint. The emperor, less jealous of a heavenly than of an earthly crown, contented himself with the imperfect character of a catechumen, while he bestowed the advantages of baptism[5] on the nephews of Constantine.[6] They were even admitted to the inferior offices of the ecclesiastical order; and Julian publicly read the Holy Scriptures in the church of Nicomedia. The study of religion, which they assiduously cultivated, appeared to produce the fairest fruits of faith and devotion.[7] They prayed, they fasted, they distributed alms to the poor, gifts to the clergy, and oblations to the tombs of the martyrs; and the splendid monument of St. Mamas, at Cæsarea, was erected, or at least was undertaken, by the joint labour of Gallus and Julian.[8] They respectfully conversed with the bishops who were eminent for superior sanctity, and solicited the benediction of the monks and hermits who had introduced into Cappadocia the voluntary hardships of the ascetic life.[9] As the two princes advanced towards the years of manhood, they discovered, in their religious sentiments, the difference of their characters. The dull and obstinate understanding of Gallus embraced, with implicit zeal, the doctrines of Christianity, which never influenced his conduct, or moderated his passions. The mild disposition of the younger brother was less repugnant to the precepts of the Gospel; and his active curiosity might have been gratified by a theological system which explains the mysterious essence of the Deity, and opens the boundless prospect of invisible and future worlds. But the independent spirit of Julian refused to yield the passive and unresisting obedience which was required, in the name of religion, by the haughty ministers of the church. Their speculative opinions were imposed as positive laws, and guarded by the terrors of eternal punishments; but while they prescribed the rigid formulary of the thoughts, the words, and the actions of the young prince; whilst they silenced his objections, and severely checked the freedom of his inquiries, they secretly provoked his impatient genius to disclaim the authority of his ecclesiastical guides. He was educated in the lesser Asia, amidst the scandals of the Arian controversy.[10] The fierce contests of the Eastern bishops, the incessant alterations of their creeds, and the profane motives which appeared to actuate their conduct, insensibly strengthened the prejudice of Julian that they neither understood nor believed the religion for which they so fiercely contended. Instead of listening to the proofs of Christianity with that favourable attention which adds weight to the most respectable evidence, he heard with suspicion, and disputed with obstinacy and acuteness, the doctrines for which he already entertained an invincible aversion. Whenever the young princes were directed to compose declamations on the subject of the prevailing controversies, Julian always declared himself the advocate of Paganism, under the specious excuse that, in the defence of the weaker cause, his learning and ingenuity might be more advantageously exercised and displayed.

As soon as Gallus was invested with the honours of the purple, Julian was permitted to breathe the air of freedom, of literature, and of Paganism.[11] The crowd of sophists, who were attracted by the taste and liberality of their royal pupil, had formed a strict alliance between the learning and the religion of Greece;

and the poems of Homer, instead of being admired as the original productions of human genius, were seriously ascribed to the heavenly inspiration of Apollo and the muses. The deities of Olympus, as they are painted by the immortal bard, imprint themselves on the minds which are the least addicted to superstitious credulity. Our familiar knowledge of their names and characters, their forms and attributes, *seems* to bestow on those airy beings a real and substantial existence; and the pleasing enchantment produces an imperfect and momentary assent of the imagination to those fables which are the most repugnant to our reason and experience. In the age of Julian every circumstance contributed to prolong and fortify the illusion—the magnificent temples of Greece and Asia; the works of those artists who had expressed, in painting or in sculpture, the divine conceptions of the poet; the pomp of festivals and sacrifices; the successful arts of divination; the popular traditions of oracles and prodigies; and the ancient practice of two thousand years. The weakness of polytheism was, in some measure, excused by the moderation of its claims; and the devotion of the Pagans was not incompatible with the most licentious scepticism.[12] Instead of an indivisible and regular system, which occupies the whole extent of the believing mind, the mythology of the Greeks was composed of a thousand loose and flexible parts, and the servant of the gods was at liberty to define the degree and measure of his religious faith. The creed which Julian adopted for his own use was of the largest dimensions; and, by a strange contradiction, he disdained the salutary yoke of the Gospel, whilst he made a voluntary offering of his reason on the altars of Jupiter and Apollo. One of the orations of Julian is consecrated to the honour of Cybele, the mother of the gods, who required from her effeminate priests the bloody sacrifice so rashly performed by the madness of the Phrygian boy. The pious emperor condescends to relate, without a blush and without a smile, the voyage of the goddess from the shores of Pergamus to the mouth of the Tiber; and the stupendous miracle which convinced the senate and people of Rome that the lump of clay which their ambassadors had transported over the seas was endowed with life, and sentiment, and divine power.[13] For the truth of this prodigy he appeals to the public monuments of the city; and censures, with some acrimony, the sickly and affected taste of those men who impertinently derided the sacred traditions of their ancestors.[14]

But the devout philosopher, who sincerely embraced, and warmly encouraged, the superstition of the people, reserved for himself the privilege of a liberal interpretation, and silently withdrew from the foot of the altars into the sanctuary of the temple. The extravagance of the Grecian mythology proclaimed, with a clear and audible voice, that the pious inquirer, instead of being scandalised or satisfied with the literal sense, should diligently explore the occult wisdom, which had been disguised, by the prudence of antiquity, under the mask of folly and of fable.[15] The philosophers of the Platonic school,[16] Plotinus, Porphyry, and the divine Iamblichus, were admired as the most skilful masters of this allegorical science, which laboured to soften and harmonise the deformed features of Paganism. Julian himself, who was directed in the mysterious pursuit by Ædesius, the venerable successor of Iamblichus, aspired to the possession of a treasure which he esteemed, if we may credit his solemn asseverations, far above the empire of the world.[17] It was indeed a treasure which derived its value only from opinion; and every artist who flattered himself that he had extracted the precious ore from the surrounding dross claimed an equal right of stamping the name and figure the most agreeable to his peculiar fancy. The fable of Atys and Cybele had been already explained by Porphyry; but his labours served only to animate the pious industry of Julian, who invented and published his own allegory of that ancient and mystic tale. This freedom of interpretation, which might gratify the pride of the Platonists, exposed the vanity of their art. Without a tedious detail the modern reader could not form a just idea of the strange allusions, the forced etymologies, the solemn trifling, and the impenetrable obscurity of these sages, who professed to reveal the system of the universe. As the traditions of Pagan mythology were variously related, the sacred interpreters were at liberty to select the most convenient circumstances; and as they translated an arbitrary cipher, they could extract from *any* fable *any* sense which was adapted to their favourite system of religion and philosophy. The lascivious form of a naked Venus was tortured into the discovery of some moral precept, or some physical truth; and the castration of Atys explained the revolution of the sun between the tropics, or the separation of the human soul from vice and error.[18]

The theological system of Julian appears to have contained the sublime and important principles of natural religion. But as the faith which is not founded on revelation must remain destitute of any firm assurance, the disciple of Plato imprudently relapsed into the habits of vulgar superstition; and the popular and philosophic notion of the Deity seems to have been confounded in the practice, the writings, and even in the mind of Julian.[19] The pious emperor acknowledged and adored the Eternal Cause of the universe, to whom he ascribed all the perfections of an infinite nature, invisible to the eyes and inaccessible to the understanding of feeble mortals. The Supreme God had created, or rather, in the Platonic language, had generated, the gradual succession of dependent spirits, of gods, of dæmons, of heroes, and of men; and every being which derived its existence immediately from the First Cause received the inherent gift of immortailty. That so precious an advantage might not be lavished upon unworthy objects, the Creator had intrusted to the skill and power of the inferior gods the office of forming the human body, and of arranging the beautiful harmony of the animal, the vegetable, and the mineral kingdoms. To the conduct of these divine ministers he delegated the temporal government of this lower world; but their imperfect administration is not exempt from discord or error. The earth and its inhabitants are divided among them, and the characters of Mars or Minerva, of Mercury or Venus, may be distinctly traced in the laws and manners of their peculiar votaries. As long as our immortal souls are confined in a mortal prison, it is our interest, as well as our duty, to solicit the favour, and to deprecate the wrath, of the powers of heaven; whose pride is gratified by the devotion of mankind, and whose grosser parts may be supposed to derive some nourishment from the fumes of sacrifice.[20] The inferior gods might sometimes condescend to animate the statues, and to inhabit the temples, which were dedicated to their honour. They might occasionally visit the earth, but the heavens were the proper throne and symbol of their glory. The invariable order of the sun, moon, and stars was hastily admitted by Julian as a proof of their *eternal* duration; and their eternity was a sufficient evidence that they were the workmanship, not of an inferior deity, but of the Omnipotent King. In the system of the Platonists the visible was a type of the invisible world. The celestial bodies, as they were informed by a divine spirit, might be considered as the objects the most worthy of religious worship. The Sun, whose genial influence pervades and sustains the universe, justly claimed the adoration of mankind, as the bright representative of the Logos, the lively, the rational, the beneficent image of the intellectual Father.[21]

In every age the absence of genuine inspiration is supplied by the strong illusions of enthusiasm and the mimic arts of imposture. If, in the time of Julian, these arts had been practised only by the Pagan priests, for the support of an expiring cause, some indulgence might perhaps be allowed to the interest and habits of the sacerdotal character. But it may appear a subject of surprise and scandal that the philosophers themselves should have contributed to abuse the superstitious credulity of mankind,[22] and that the Grecian mysteries should have been supported by the magic or theurgy of the modern Platonists. They arrogantly pretended to control the order of nature, to explore the secrets of futurity, to command the service of the inferior dæmons, to enjoy the view and conversation of the superior gods, and, by disengaging the soul from her material bands, to re-unite that immortal particle with the Infinite and Divine Spirit.

The devout and fearless curiosity of Julian tempted the philosophers with the hopes of an easy conquest, which, from the situation of their young proselyte, might be productive of the most important consequences.[23] Julian imbibed the first rudiments of the Platonic doctrines from the mouth of Ædesius, who had fixed at Pergamus his wandering and persecuted school. But as the declining strength of that venerable sage was unequal to the ardour, the diligence, the rapid conception of his pupil, two of his most learned disciples, Chrysanthes and Eusebius, supplied, at his own desire, the place of their aged master. These philosophers seem to have prepared and distributed their respective parts; and they artfully contrived, by dark hints and affected disputes, to excite the impatient hopes of the *aspirant* till they delivered him into the hands of their associate, Maximus, the boldest and most skilful master of the Theurgic science. By his hands Julian was secretly initiated at Ephesus, in the twentieth year of his age. His residence at Athens confirmed this unnatural alliance of philosophy and superstition. He obtained the privilege of a solemn initiation into the mysteries of Eleusis, which, amidst the general decay of the Grecian worship, still retained some vestiges of their primæval sanctity; and such was the zeal of Julian that he afterwards invited the Eleusinian pontiff to the court of Gaul, for the sole purpose of consummating, by mystic rites and sacrifices, the great work of his sanctification. As these ceremonies were performed in the depth of caverns and in the silence of the night, and as the inviolable secret of the mysteries was preserved by the discretion of the initiated, I shall not presume to describe the horrid sounds and fiery apparitions which were presented to the senses or the imagination of the credulous aspirant,[24] till the visions of comfort and knowledge broke upon him in a blaze of celestial light.[25] In the caverns of Ephesus and Eleusis the mind of Julian was penetrated with sincere, deep, and unalterable enthusiasm; though he might sometimes exhibit the vicissitudes of pious fraud and hypocrisy which may be observed, or at least suspected, in the characters of the most conscientious fanatics. From that moment he consecrated his life to the service of the gods; and while the occupations of war, of government, and of study seemed to claim the whole measure of his time, a stated portion of the hours of the night was invariably reserved for the exercise of private devotion. The temperance which adorned the severe manners of the soldier and the philosopher was connected with some strict and frivolous rules of religious abstinence; and it was in honour of Pan or Mercury, of Hecate or Isis, that Julian, on particular days, denied himself the use of some particular food, which might have been offensive to his tutelar deities. By these voluntary fasts he prepared his senses and his understanding for the frequent and familiar visits with which he was honoured by the celestial powers. Notwithstanding the modest silence of Julian himself, we may learn from his faithful friend, the orator Libanius, that he lived in a perpetual intercourse with the gods and goddesses; that they descended upon earth to enjoy the conversation of their favourite hero; that they gently interrupted his slumbers by touching his hand or his hair; that they warned him of every impending danger, and conducted him, by their infallible wisdom, in every action of his life; and that he had acquired such an intimate knowledge of his heavenly guests, as readily to distinguish the voice of Jupiter from that of Minerva, and the form of Apollo from the figure of Hercules.[26] These sleeping or waking visions, the ordinary effects of abstinence and fanaticism, would almost degrade the emperor to the level of an Egyptian monk. But the useless lives of Antony or Pachomius were consumed in these vain occupations. Julian could break from the dream of superstition to arm himself for battle; and after vanquishing in the field the enemies of Rome, he calmly retired into his tent, to dictate the wise and salutary laws of an empire, or to indulge his genius in the elegant pursuits of literature and philosophy.

The important secret of the apostasy of Julian was intrusted to the fidelity of the *initiated*, with whom he was united by the sacred ties of friendship and religion.[27] The pleasing rumour was cautiously circulated among the adherents of the ancient worship; and his future greatness became the object of the hopes, the prayers, and the predictions of the Pagans in every province of the empire. From the zeal and virtues of their royal proselyte they fondly expected the cure of every evil and the restoration of every blessing; and instead of disapproving of the ardour of their pious wishes, Julian ingenuously confessed that he was ambitious to attain a situation in which he might be useful to his country and to his religion. But this religion was viewed with an hostile eye by the successor of Constantine, whose capricious passions alternately saved and threatened the life of Julian. The arts of magic and divination were strictly prohibited under a despotic government which condescended to fear them; and if the Pagans were reluctantly indulged in the exercise of their superstition, the rank of Julian would have excepted him from the general toleration. The apostate soon became the presumptive heir of the monarchy, and his death could alone have appeased the just apprehensions of the Christians.[28] But the young prince, who aspired to the glory of a hero rather than of a martyr, consulted his safety by dissembling his religion; and the easy temper of polytheism permitted him to join in the public worship of a sect which he inwardly despised. Libanius has considered the hypocrisy of his friend as a subject, not of censure, but of praise. "As the statues of the gods," says that orator, "which have been defiled with filth are again placed in a magnificent temple, so the beauty of truth was seated in the mind of Julian after it had been purified from the errors and follies of his education. His sentiments were changed; but as it would have been dangerous to have avowed his sentiments, his conduct still continued the same. Very different from the ass in Æsop, who disguised himself with a lion's hide, our lion was obliged to conceal himself under the skin of an ass; and, while he embraced the dictates of reason, to obey the laws of prudence and necessity."[29]

The dissimulation of Julian lasted above ten years, from his secret initiation at Ephesus to the beginning of the civil war; when he declared himself at once the implacable enemy of Christ and of Constantius. This state of constraint might contribute to strengthen his devotion; and as soon as he had satisfied the obligation of assisting, on solemn festivals, at the assemblies of the Christians, Julian returned, with the impatience of a lover, to burn his free and voluntary incense on the domestic chapels of Jupiter and Mercury. But as every act of dissimulation must be painful to an ingenuous spirit, the profession of Christianity increased the aversion of Julian for a religion which oppressed the freedom of his mind, and compelled him to hold a conduct repugnant to the noblest attributes of human nature—sincerity and courage.

The inclination of Julian might prefer the gods of Homer and of the Scipios to the new faith which his uncle had established in the Roman empire, and in which he himself had been sanctified by the sacrament of baptism. But, as a philosopher, it was incumbent on him to justify his dissent from Christianity, which was supported by the number of its converts, by the chain of prophecy, the splendour of miracles, and the weight of evidence. The elaborate work[30] which he composed amidst the preparations of the Persian war contained the substance of those arguments which he had long revolved in his mind. Some fragments have been transcribed and preserved by his adversary, the vehement Cyril of Alexandria;[31] and they exhibit a very singular mixture of wit and learning, of sophistry and fanaticism. The elegance of the style and the rank of the author recommended his writings to the public attention;[32] and in the impious list of the enemies of Christianity the celebrated name of Porphyry was effaced by the superior merit or reputation of Julian. The minds of the faithful were either seduced, or scandalised, or alarmed; and the Pagans, who sometimes presumed to engage in the unequal dispute, derived, from the popular work of their Imperial missionary, an inexhaustible supply of fallacious objections. But in the assiduous prosecution of these theological studies the emperor of the Romans imbibed the illiberal prejudices and passions of a polemic divine. He contracted an irrevocable obligation to maintain and propagate his religious opinions; and whilst he secretly applauded the strength and dexterity with which he wielded the weapons of controversy, he was tempted to distrust the sincerity, or to despise the understandings, of his antagonists, who could obstinately resist the force of reason and eloquence.

The Christians, who beheld with horror and indignation the apostasy of Julian, had much more to fear from his power than from his arguments. The Pagans, who were conscious of his fervent zeal, expected, perhaps with impatience, that the flames of persecution should be immediately kindled against the enemies of the gods; and that the ingenious malice of Julian would invent some cruel refinements of death and torture which had been unknown to the rude and inexperienced fury of his predecessors. But the hopes, as well as the fears, of the religious factions were apparently disappointed by the prudent humanity of a prince[33] who was careful of his own fame, of the public peace, and of the rights of mankind. Instructed by history and reflection, Julian was persuaded that, if the diseases of the body may sometimes be cured by salutary violence, neither steel nor fire can eradicate the erroneous opinions of the mind. The reluctant victim may be dragged to the foot of the altar; but the heart still abhors and disclaims the sacrilegious act of the hand. Religious obstinacy is hardened and exasperated by oppression; and, as soon as the persecution subsides, those who have yielded are restored as penitents, and those who have resisted are honoured as saints and martyrs. If Julian adopted the unsuccessful cruelty of Diocletian and his colleagues, he was sensible that he should stain his memory with the name of tyrant, and add new glories to the Catholic church, which had derived strength and increase from the severity of the Pagan magistrates. Actuated by these motives, and apprehensive of disturbing the repose of an unsettled reign, Julian surprised the world by an edict which was not unworthy of a statesman or a philosopher. He extended to all the inhabitants of the Roman world the benefits of a free and equal toleration; and the only hardship which he inflicted on the Christians was to deprive them of the power of tormenting their fellow-subjects, whom they stigmatised with the odious titles of idolaters and heretics. The Pagans received a gracious permission, or rather an express order, to open ALL their temples;[34] and they were at once delivered from the oppressive laws and arbitrary vexations which they had sustained under the reign of Constantine and of his sons. At the same time, the bishops and clergy who had been banished by the Arian monarch were recalled from exile, and restored to their respective churches; the Donatists, the Novatians, the Macedonians, the Eunomians, and those who, with a more prosperous fortune, adhered to the doctrine of the council of Nice. Julian, who understood and derided their theological disputes, invited to the palace the leaders of the hostile sects, that he might enjoy the agreeable spectacle of their furious encounters. The clamour of controversy sometimes provoked the emperor to exclaim, "Hear me! the Franks have heard me, and the Alemanni"; but he soon discovered that he was now engaged with more obstinate and implacable enemies; and though he exerted the powers of oratory to persuade them to live in concord, or at least in peace, he was perfectly satisfied, before he dismissed them from his presence, that he had nothing to dread from the union of the Christians. The impartial Ammianus has ascribed this affected clemency to the desire of fomenting the intestine divisions of the church; and the insidious design of undermining the foundations of Christianity was inseparably connected with the zeal which Julian professed to restore the ancient religion of the empire.[35]

As soon as he ascended the throne, he assumed, according to the custom of his predecessors, the character of supreme pontiff; not only as the most honourable title of Imperial greatness, but as a sacred and important office, the duties of which he was resolved to execute with pious diligence. As the business of the state prevented the emperor from joining every day in the public devotion of his subjects, he dedicated a domestic chapel to his tutelar deity the Sun; his gardens were filled with statues and altars of the gods; and each apartment of the palace displayed the appearance of a magnificent temple. Every morning he saluted the parent of light with a sacrifice; the blood of another victim was shed at the moment when the Sun sunk below the horizon; and the Moon, the Stars, and the Genii of the night received their respective and seasonable honours from the indefatigable devotion of Julian. On solemn festivals he regularly visited the temple of the god or goddess to whom the day was peculiarly consecrated, and endeavoured to excite the religion of the magistrates and people by the example of his own zeal. Instead of maintaining the lofty state of a monarch, distinguished by the splendour of his purple, and encompassed by the golden shields of his guards, Julian solicited, with respectful eagerness, the meanest offices which contributed to the worship of the gods. Amidst the sacred but licentious crowd of priests, of inferior ministers, and of female dancers, who were dedicated to the service of the temple, it was the business of the emperor to bring the wood, to blow the fire, to handle the knife, to slaughter the victim, and, thrusting his bloody hands into the bowels of the expiring animal, to draw forth the heart or liver, and to read, with the consummate skill of an haruspex, the imaginary signs of future events. The wisest of the Pagans censured this extravagant superstition, which affected to despise the restraints of prudence and decency. Under the reign of a prince who practised the rigid maxims of economy, the expense of religious worship consumed a very large portion of the revenue; a constant supply of the scarcest and most beautiful birds was transported from distant climates, to bleed on the altars of the gods; an hundred oxen were frequently sacrificed by Julian on one and the same day; and it soon became a popular jest, that, if he should return with conquest from the Persian war, the breed of horned cattle must infallibly be extinguished. Yet this expense may appear inconsiderable, when it is compared with the splendid presents which were offered, either by the hand or by the order of the emperor, to all the celebrated places of devotion in the Roman world; and with the sums allotted to repair and decorate the ancient temples, which had suffered the silent decay of time, or the recent injuries of Christian rapine. Encouraged by the example, the exhortations, the liberality of their pious sovereign, the cities and families resumed the practice of their neglected ceremonies. "Every part of the world," exclaims Libanius, with devout transport, "displayed the triumph of religion, and the grateful prospect of flaming altars, bleeding victims, the smoke of incense, and a solemn train of priests and prophets, without fear and without danger. The sound of prayer and of music was heard on the tops of the highest mountains; and the same ox afforded a sacrifice for the gods, and a supper for their joyous votaries."[36]

But the genius and power of Julian were unequal to the enterprise of restoring a religion which was destitute of theological principles, of moral precepts, and of ecclesiastical discipline; which rapidly hastened to decay and dissolution, and was not susceptible of any solid or consistent reformation. The jurisdiction of the supreme pontiff, more especially after that office had been united with the Imperial dignity, comprehended the whole extent of the Roman empire. Julian named for his vicars, in the several provinces, the priests and philosophers, whom he esteemed the best qualified to cooperate in the execution of his great design; and his pastoral letters,[37] if we may use that name, still represent a very curious sketch of his wishes and intentions. He directs that in every city the sacerdotal order should be composed, without any distinction of birth or fortune, of those persons who were the most conspicuous for their love of the gods and of men. "If they are guilty," continues he, "of any scandalous offence, they should be censured or degraded by the superior pontiff; but as long as they retain their rank, they are entitled to the respect of the magistrates and people. Their humility may be shown in the plainness of their domestic garb; their dignity, in the pomp of holy vestments. When they are summoned in their turn to officiate before the altar, they ought not, during the appointed number of days, to depart from the precincts of the temple; nor should a single day be suffered to elapse without the prayers and the sacrifice which they are obliged to offer for the prosperity of the state and of individuals. The exercise of their sacred functions requires an immaculate purity both of mind and body; and even when they are dismissed from the temple to the occupations of common life, it is incumbent on them to excel in decency and virtue the rest of their fellow-citizens. The priest of the gods should never be seen in theatres or taverns. His conversation should be chaste, his diet temperate, his friends of honourable reputation; and if he sometimes visits the Forum or the Palace, he should appear only as the advocate of those who have vainly solicited either justice or mercy. His studies should be suited to the sanctity of his profession. Licentious tales, or comedies, or satires, must be banished from his library, which ought solely to consist of historical and philosophical writings; of history, which is founded in truth, and of philosophy, which is connected with religion. The impious opinions of the Epicureans and sceptics deserve his abhorrence and contempt;[38] but he should diligently study the systems of Pythagoras, of Plato, and of the Stoics, which unanimously teach that there *are* gods; that the world is governed by their providence; that their goodness is the source of every temporal blessing; and that they have prepared for the human soul a future state of reward or punishment." The Imperial pontiff inculcates, in the most persuasive language, the duties of benevolence and hospitality; exhorts his inferior clergy to recommend the universal practice of those virtues; promises to assist their indigence from the public treasury; and declares his resolution of establishing hospitals in every city, where the poor should be received without any invidious distinction of country or of religion. Julian beheld with envy the wise and humane regulations of the church; and he very frankly confessed his intention to deprive the Christians of the applause, as well as advantage, which they had acquired by the exclusive practice of charity and beneficence.[39] The same spirit of imitation might dispose the emperor to adopt several ecclesiastical institutions, the use and importance of which were approved by the success of his enemies. But if these imaginary plans of reformation had been realised, the forced and imperfect copy would have been less beneficial to Paganism than honourable to Christianity.[40] The Gentiles, who peaceably followed the customs of their ancestors, were rather surprised than pleased with the introduction of foreign manners; and, in the short period of his reign, Julian had frequent occasions to complain of the want of fervour of his own party.[41]

The enthusiasm of Julian prompted him to embrace the friends of Jupiter as his personal friends and brethren; and though he partially overlooked the merit of Christian constancy, he admired and rewarded the noble perseverance of those Gentiles who had preferred the favour of the gods to that of the emperor.[42] If they cultivated the literature as well as the religion of the Greeks, they acquired an additional claim to the friendship of Julian, who ranked the Muses in the number of his tutelar deities. In the religion which he had adopted, piety and learning were almost synonymous;[43] and a crowd of poets, of rhetoricians, and of philosophers, hastened to the Imperial court to occupy the vacant places of the bishops who had seduced the credulity of Constantius. His successor esteemed the ties of common initiation as far more sacred than those of consanguinity; he chose his favourites among the sages who were deeply skilled in the occult sciences of magic and divination, and every impostor who pretended to reveal the secrets of futurity was assured of enjoying the present hour in honour and affluence.[44] Among the philosophers, Maximus obtained the most eminent rank in the friendship of his royal disciple, who communicated, with unreserved confidence, his actions, his sentiments, and his religious designs, during the anxious suspense of the civil war.[45] As soon as Julian had taken possession of the palace of Constantinople, he despatched an honourable and pressing invitation to Maximus, who then resided at Sardes in Lydia, with Chrysanthius, the associate of his art and studies. The prudent and superstitious Chrysanthius refused to undertake a journey which showed itself, according to the rules of divination, with the most threatening and malignant aspect; but his companion, whose fanat-

icism was of a bolder cast, persisted in his interrogations till he had extorted from the gods a seeming consent to his own wishes and those of the emperor. The journey of Maximus through the cities of Asia displayed the triumph of philosophic vanity, and the magistrates vied with each other in the honourable reception which they prepared for the friend of their sovereign. Julian was pronouncing an oration before the senate when he was informed of the arrival of Maximus. The emperor immediately interrupted his discourse, advanced to meet him, and, after a tender embrace, conducted him by the hand into the midst of the assembly, where he publicly acknowledged the benefits which he had derived from the instructions of the philosopher. Maximus,[46] who soon acquired the confidence, and influenced the councils, of Julian, was insensibly corrupted by the temptations of a court. His dress became more splendid, his demeanour more lofty, and he was exposed, under a succeeding reign, to a disgraceful inquiry into the means by which the disciple of Plato had accumulated, in the short duration of his favour, a very scandalous proportion of wealth. Of the other philosophers and sophists who were invited to the Imperial residence by the choice of Julian, or by the success of Maximus, few were able to preserve their innocence or their reputation.[47] The liberal gifts of money, lands, and houses were insufficient to satiate their rapacious avarice, and the indignation of the people was justly excited by the remembrance of their abject poverty and disinterested professions. The penetration of Julian could not always be deceived, but he was unwilling to despise the characters of those men whose talents deserved his esteem; he desired to escape the double reproach of imprudence and inconstancy, and he was apprehensive of degrading, in the eyes of the profane, the honour of letters and of religion.[48]

The favour of Julian was almost equally divided between the Pagans who had firmly adhered to the worship of their ancestors, and the Christians who prudently embraced the religion of their sovereign. The acquisition of new proselytes[49] gratified the ruling passions of his soul, superstition and vanity; and he was heard to declare, with the enthusiasm of a missionary, that if he could render each individual richer than Midas, and every city greater than Babylon, he should not esteem himself the benefactor of mankind unless, at the same time, he could reclaim his subjects from their impious revolt against the immortal gods.[50] A prince, who had studied human nature, and who possessed the treasures of the Roman empire, could adapt his arguments, his promises, and his rewards to every order of Christians;[51] and the merit of a seasonable conversion was allowed to supply the defects of a candidate, or even to expiate the guilt of a criminal. As the army is the most forcible engine of absolute power, Julian applied himself, with peculiar diligence, to corrupt the religion of his troops, without whose hearty concurrence every measure must be dangerous and unsuccessful, and the natural temper of soldiers made this conquest as easy as it was important. The legions of Gaul devoted themselves to the faith, as well as to the fortunes, of their victorious leader; and even before the death of Constantius, he had the satisfaction of announcing to his friends that they assisted, with fervent devotion and voracious appetite, at the sacrifices, which were repeatedly offered in his camp, of whole hecatombs of fat oxen.[52] The armies of the East, which had been trained under the standard of the cross and of Constantius, required a more artful and expensive mode of persuasion. On the days of solemn and public festivals the emperor received the homage, and rewarded the merit, of the troops. His throne of state was encircled with the military ensigns of Rome and the republic; the holy name of Christ was erased from the *Labarum*; and the symbols of war, of majesty, and of Pagan superstition were so dexterously blended that the faithful subject incurred the guilt of idolatry when he respectfully saluted the person or image of his sovereign. The soldiers passed successively in review, and each of them, before he received from the hand of Julian a liberal donative, proportioned to his rank and services, was required to cast a few grains of incense into the flame which burnt upon the altar. Some Christian confessors might resist, and others might repent; but the far greater number, allured by the prospect of gold and awed by the presence of the emperor, contracted the criminal engagement, and their future perseverance in the worship of the gods was enforced by every consideration of duty and of interest. By the frequent repetition of these arts, and at the expense of sums which would have purchased the service of half the nations of Scythia, Julian gradually acquired for his troops the imaginary protection of the gods, and for himself the firm and effectual support of the Roman legions.[53] It is indeed more than probable that the restoration and encouragement of Paganism revealed a multitude of pretended Christians, who, from motives of

temporal advantage, had acquiesced in the religion of the former reign, and who afterwards returned, with the same flexibility of conscience, to the faith which was professed by the successors of Julian.

While the devout monarch incessantly laboured to restore and propagate the religion of his ancestors, he embraced the extraordinary design of rebuilding the temple of Jerusalem. In a public epistle[54] to the nation or community of the Jews dispersed through the provinces, he pities their misfortunes, condemns their oppressors, praises their constancy, declares himself their gracious protector, and expresses a pious hope that, after his return from the Persian war, he may be permitted to pay his grateful vows to the Almighty in his holy city of Jerusalem. The blind superstition and abject slavery of those unfortunate exiles must excite the contempt of a philosophic emperor, but they deserved the friendship of Julian by their implacable hatred of the Christian name. The barren synagogue abhorred and envied the fecundity of the rebellious church; the power of the Jews was not equal to their malice, but their gravest rabbis approved the private murder of an apostate,[55] and their seditious clamours had often awakened the indolence of the Pagan magistrates. Under the reign of Constantine, the Jews became the subjects of their revolted children, nor was it long before they experienced the bitterness of domestic tyranny. The civil immunities which had been granted or confirmed by Severus were gradually repealed by the Christian princes; and a rash tumult, excited by the Jews of Palestine,[56] seemed to justify the lucrative modes of oppression which were invented by the bishops and eunuchs of the court of Constantius. The Jewish patriarch, who was still permitted to exercise a precarious jurisdiction, held his residence at Tiberias,[57] and the neighbouring cities of Palestine were filled with the remains of a people who fondly adhered to the promised land. But the edict of Hadrian was renewed and enforced, and they viewed from afar the walls of the holy city, which were profaned in their eyes by the triumph of the cross and the devotion of the Christians.[58]

In the midst of a rocky and barren country the walls of Jerusalem[59] enclosed the two mountains of Sion and Acra within an oval figure of about three English miles.[60] Towards the south, the upper town and the fortress of David were erected on the lofty ascent of Mount Sion; on the north side, the buildings of the lower town covered the spacious summit of Mount Acra;

and a part of the hill, distinguished by the name of Moriah, and levelled by human industry, was crowned with the stately temple of the Jewish nation. After the final destruction of the temple by the arms of Titus and Hadrian a ploughshare was drawn over the consecrated ground, as a sign of perpetual interdiction. Sion was deserted, and the vacant space of the lower city was filled with the public and private edifices of the Ælian colony, which spread themselves over the adjacent hill of Calvary. The holy places were polluted with monuments of idolatry, and, either from design or accident, a chapel was dedicated to Venus on the spot which had been sanctified by the death and resurrection of Christ.[61] Almost three hundred years after those stupendous events, the profane chapel of Venus was demolished by the order of Constantine, and the removal of the earth and stones revealed the holy sepulchre to the eyes of mankind. A magnificent church was erected on that mystic ground by the first Christian emperor, and the effects of his pious munificence were extended to every spot which had been consecrated by the footsteps of patriarchs, of prophets, and of the Son of God.[62]

The passionate desire of contemplating the original monuments of their redemption attracted to Jerusalem a successive crowd of pilgrims from the shores of the Atlantic Ocean and the most distant countries of the East:[63] and their piety was authorised by the example of the empress Helena, who appears to have united the credulity of age with the warm feelings of a recent conversion. Sages and heroes, who have visited the memorable scenes of ancient wisdom or glory, have confessed the inspiration of the genius of the place;[64] and the Christian who knelt before the holy sepulchre ascribed his lively faith and his fervent devotion to the more immediate influence of the Divine Spirit. The zeal, perhaps the avarice, of the clergy of Jerusalem cherished and multiplied these beneficial visits. They fixed, by unquestionable tradition, the scene of each memorable event. They exhibited the instruments which had been used in the passion of Christ; the nails and the lance that had pierced his hands, his feet, and his side; the crown of thorns that was planted on his head; the pillar at which he was scourged; and, above all, they showed the cross on which he suffered, and which was dug out of the earth in the reign of those princes who inserted the symbol of Christianity in the banners of the Roman legions.[65] Such miracles as seemed necessary to account for its extraordinary preservation and seasonable discovery were gradually propagated without opposition. The custody of the *true cross*, which on Easter Sunday was solemnly exposed to the people, was intrusted to the bishop of Jerusalem; and he alone might gratify the curious devotion of the pilgrims by the gift of small pieces, which they enchased in gold or gems, and carried away in triumph to their respective countries. But as this gainful branch of commerce must soon have been annihilated, it was found convenient to suppose that the marvellous wood possessed a secret power of vegetation, and that its substance, though continually diminished, still remained entire and unimpaired.[66] It might perhaps have been expected that the influence of the place and the belief of a perpetual miracle should have produced some salutary effects on the morals, as well as on the faith, of the people. Yet the most respectable of the ecclesiastical writers have been obliged to confess, not only that the streets of Jerusalem were filled with the incessant tumult of business and pleasure,[67] but that every species of vice—adultery, theft, idolatry, poisoning, murder—was familiar to the inhabitants of the holy city.[68] The wealth and pre-eminence of the church of Jerusalem excited the ambition of Arian as well as orthodox candidates; and the virtues of Cyril, who since his death has been honoured with the title of Saint, were displayed in the exercise, rather than in the acquisition, of his episcopal dignity.[69]

The vain and ambitious mind of Julian might aspire to restore the ancient glory of the temple of Jerusalem.[70] As the Christians were firmly persuaded that a sentence of everlasting destruction had been pronounced against the whole fabric of the Mosaic law, the Imperial sophist would have converted the success of his undertaking into a specious argument against the faith of prophecy and the truth of revelation.[71] He was displeased with the spiritual worship of the synagogue; but he approved the institutions of Moses, who had not disdained to adopt many of the rites and ceremonies of Egypt.[72] The local and national deity of the Jews was sincerely adored by a polytheist who desired only to multiply the number of the gods;[73] and such was the appetite of Julian for bloody sacrifice, that his emulation might be excited by the piety of Solomon, who had offered at the feast of the dedication twenty-two thousand oxen and one hundred and twenty thousand sheep.[74] These considerations might influence his designs; but the prospect of an immediate and important advantage would not suffer the impatient monarch to expect the remote and uncertain event of the Persian war. He resolved to erect, without delay, on the commanding eminence of Moriah, a stately temple, which might eclipse the splendour of the church of the Resurrection on the adjacent hill of Calvary; to establish an order of priests, whose interested zeal would detect the arts and resist the ambition of their Christian rivals; and to invite a numerous colony of Jews, whose stern fanaticism would be always prepared to second, and even to anticipate, the hostile measures of the Pagan government. Among the friends of the emperor (if the names of emperor and of friend are not incompatible) the first place was assigned, by Julian himself, to the virtuous and learned Alypius.[75] The humanity of Alypius was tempered by severe justice and manly fortitude; and while he exercised his abilities in the civil administration of Britain, he imitated, in his poetical compositions, the harmony and softness of the odes of Sappho. This minister, to whom Julian communicated, without reserve, his most careless levities and his most serious counsels, received an extraordinary commission to restore, in its pristine beauty, the temple of Jerusalem; and the diligence of Alypius required and obtained the strenuous support of the governor of Palestine. At the call of their great deliverer, the Jews from all the provinces of the empire assembled on the holy mountain of their fathers; and their insolent triumph alarmed and exasperated the Christian inhabitants of Jerusalem. The desire of rebuilding the temple has in every age been the ruling passion of the children of Israel. In this propitious moment the men forgot their avarice, and the women their delicacy; spades and pickaxes of silver were provided by the vanity of the rich, and the rubbish was transported in mantles of silk and purple. Every purse was opened in liberal contributions, every hand claimed a share in the pious labour; and the commands of a great monarch were executed by the enthusiasm of a whole people.[76]

Yet, on this occasion, the joint efforts of power and enthusiasm were unsuccessful; and the ground of the Jewish temple, which is now covered by a Mahometan mosque,[77] still continued to exhibit the same edifying spectacle of ruin and desolation. Perhaps the absence and death of the emperor, and the new maxims of a Christian reign, might explain the interruption of an arduous work, which was attempted only in the last six months of the life of Julian.[78] But the Christians entertained a natural and pious expectation that in this memorable contest the honour of religion would be vindicated by some signal miracle. An earthquake, a whirlwind, and a fiery eruption, which overturned and scattered the new foundations of the temple, are attested, with some variations, by contemporary and respectable evidence.[79] This public event is described by Ambrose,[80] bishop of Milan, in an epistle to the emperor Theodosius, which must provoke the severe animadversion of the Jews; by the eloquent Chrysostom,[81] who might appeal to the memory of the elder part of his congregation at Antioch; and by Gregory Nazianzen,[82] who published his account of the miracle before the expiration of the same year. The last of these writers has boldly declared that this preternatural event was not disputed by the infidels; and his assertion, strange as it may seem, is confirmed by the unexceptionable testimony of Ammianus Marcellinus.[83] The philosophic soldier, who loved the virtues without adopting the prejudices of his master, has recorded, in his judicious and candid history of his own times, the extraordinary obstacles which interrupted the restoration of the temple of Jerusalem. "Whilst Alypius, assisted by the governor of the province, urged with vigour and diligence the execution of the work, horrible balls of fire, breaking out near the foundations, with frequent and reiterated attacks, rendered the place, from time to time, inaccessible to the scorched and blasted workmen; and, the victorious element continuing in this manner obstinately and resolutely bent, as it were, to drive them to a distance, the undertaking was abandoned." Such authority should satisfy a believing, and must astonish an incredulous, mind. Yet a philosopher may still require the original evidence of impartial and intelligent spectators. At this important crisis any singular accident of nature would assume the appearance, and produce the effects, of a real prodigy. This glorious deliverance would be speedily improved and magnified by the pious art of the clergy of Jerusalem, and the active credulity of the Christian world; and, at the distance of twenty years, a Roman historian, careless of theological disputes, might adorn his work with the specious and splendid miracle.[84]

The restoration of the Jewish temple was secretly connected with the ruin of the Christian church. Julian still continued to maintain the freedom of religious worship, without distinguishing whether this universal toleration proceeded from his justice or his clemency. He affected to pity the unhappy Christians, who were mistaken in the most important object of their lives; but his pity was degraded by contempt, his contempt was embittered by hatred; and the sentiments of Julian were expressed in a style of sarcastic wit, which inflicts a deep and deadly wound whenever it issues from the mouth of a sovereign. As he was sensible that the Christians gloried in the name of their Redeemer, he countenanced, and perhaps enjoined, the use of the less honourable appellation of GALILÆANS.[85] He declared that, by the folly of the Galilæans, whom he describes as a sect of fanatics, contemptible to men and odious to the gods, the empire had been reduced to the brink of destruction; and he insinuates in a public edict that a frantic patient might sometimes be cured by salutary violence.[86] An ungenerous distinction was admitted into the mind and counsels of Julian, that, according to the difference of their religious sentiments, one part of his subjects deserved his favour and friendship, while the other was entitled only to the common benefits that his justice could not refuse to an obedient people.[87] According to a principle pregnant with mischief and oppression, the emperor transferred to the pontiffs of his own religion the management of the liberal allowances from the public revenue which had been granted to the church by the piety of Constantine and his sons. The proud system of clerical honours and immunities, which had been constructed with so much art and labour, was levelled to the ground; the hopes of testamentary donations were intercepted by the rigour of the laws; and the priests of the Christian sect were confounded with the last and most ignominious class of the people. Such of these regulations as appeared necessary to check the ambition and avarice of the ecclesiastics were soon afterwards imitated by the wisdom of an orthodox prince. The peculiar distinctions which policy has bestowed, or superstition has lavished, on the sacerdotal order, *must* be confined to those priests who profess the religion of the state. But the will of the legislator was not exempt from prejudice and passion; and it was the object of the insidious policy of Julian to deprive the Christians of all the temporal honours and advantages which rendered them respectable in the eyes of the world.[88]

A just and severe censure has been inflicted on the law which prohibited the Christians from teaching the arts of grammar and rhetoric.[89] The motives alleged by the emperor to justify this partial and oppressive measure might command, during his lifetime, the silence of slaves and the applause of flatterers. Julian abuses the ambiguous meaning of a word which might be indifferently applied to the language and the religion of the GREEKS: he contemptuously observes that the men who exalt the merit of implicit faith are unfit to claim or to enjoy the advantages of science; and he vainly contends that, if they refuse to adore the gods of Homer and Demosthenes, they ought to content themselves with expounding Luke and Matthew in the churches of the Galilæans.[90] In all the cities of the Roman world the education of the youth was intrusted to masters of grammar and rhetoric, who were elected by the magistrates, maintained at the public expense, and distinguished by many lucrative and honourable privileges. The edict of Julian appears to have included the physicians, and professors of all the liberal arts; and the emperor, who reserved to himself the approbation of the candidates, was authorised by the laws to corrupt, or to punish, the religious constancy of the most learned of the Christians.[91] As soon as the resignation of the more obstinate[92] teachers had established the unrivalled dominion of the Pagan sophists, Julian invited the rising generation to resort with freedom to the public schools, in a just confidence that their tender minds would receive the impressions of literature and idolatry. If the greatest part of the Christian youth should be deterred by their own scruples, or by those of their parents, from accepting this dangerous mode of instruction, they must, at the same time, relinquish the benefits of a liberal education. Julian had reason to expect that, in the space of a few years, the church would relapse into its primæval simplicity, and that the theologians, who possessed an adequate share of the learning and eloquence of the age, would be succeeded by a generation of blind and ignorant fanatics, incapable of defending the truth of their own principles, or of exposing the various follies of Polytheism.[93]

It was undoubtedly the wish and the design of Julian to deprive the Christians of the advantages of wealth, of knowledge, and of power; but the injustice of excluding them from all offices of trust and profit seems to have been the result of his general policy, rather than the immediate consequence of any positive law.[94] Superior merit might deserve and obtain some extraordinary exceptions; but the greater part of the Christian officers were gradually removed from their employments in the state, the army, and the provinces. The hopes of future candidates were extinguished by the declared partiality of a prince who maliciously reminded them that it was unlawful for a Christian to use the sword, either of justice or of war, and who studiously guarded the camp and the tribunals with the ensigns of idolatry. The powers of government were intrusted to the Pagans, who professed an ardent zeal for the religion of their ancestors; and as the choice of the emperor was often directed by the rules of divination, the favourites whom he preferred as the most agreeable to the gods did not always obtain the approbation of mankind.[95] Under the administration of their enemies, the Christians had much to suffer, and more to apprehend. The temper of Julian was averse to cruelty; and the care of his reputation, which was exposed to the eyes of the universe, restrained the philosophic monarch from violating the laws of justice and toleration which he himself had so recently established. But the provincial ministers of his authority were placed in a less conspicuous station. In the exercise of arbitrary power, they consulted the wishes, rather than the commands, of their sovereign; and ventured to exercise a secret and vexatious tyranny against the sectaries on whom they were not permitted to confer the honours of martyrdom. The emperor, who dissembled as long as possible his knowledge of the injustice that was exercised in his name, expressed his real sense of the conduct of his officers by gentle reproofs and substantial rewards.[96]

The most effectual instrument of oppression with which they were armed was the law that obliged the Christians to make full and ample satisfaction for the temples which they had destroyed under the preceding reign. The zeal of the triumphant church had not always expected the sanction of the public authority; and the bishops, who were secure of impunity, had often marched at the head of their congregations to attack and demolish the fortresses of the prince of darkness. The consecrated lands, which had increased the patrimony of the sovereign or of the clergy, were clearly defined, and easily restored. But on these lands, and on the ruins of Pagan superstition, the Christians had frequently erected their own religious edifices: and as it was necessary to remove the church before the temple could be rebuilt, the justice and piety of the emperor were applauded by one party, while the other deplored and execrated his sacrilegious violence.[97] After the ground was cleared, the restitution of those stately structures which had been levelled with the dust, and of the precious ornaments which had been converted to Christian uses, swelled into a very large account of damages and debt. The au-

thors of the injury had neither the ability nor the inclination to discharge this accumulated demand: and the impartial wisdom of a legislator would have been displayed in balancing the adverse claims and complaints by an equitable and temperate arbitration. But the whole empire, and particularly the East, was thrown into confusion by the rash edicts of Julian; and the Pagan magistrates, inflamed by zeal and revenge, abused the rigorous privilege of the Roman law, which substitutes, in the place of his inadequate property, the person of the insolvent debtor. Under the preceding reign, Mark, bishop of Arethusa,[98] had laboured in the conversion of his people with arms more effectual than those of persuasion.[99] The magistrates required the full value of a temple which had been destroyed by his intolerant zeal; but as they were satisfied of his poverty, they desired only to bend his inflexible spirit to the promise of the slightest compensation. They apprehended the aged prelate, they inhumanly scourged him, they tore his beard; and his naked body, anointed with honey, was suspended, in a net, between heaven and earth, and exposed to the stings of insects and the rays of a Syrian sun.[100] From this lofty station, Mark still persisted to glory in his crime, and to insult the impotent rage of his persecutors. He was at length rescued from their hands, and dismissed to enjoy the honour of his divine triumph. The Arians celebrated the virtue of their pious confessor; the Catholics ambitiously claimed his alliance;[101] and the Pagans, who might be susceptible of shame or remorse, were deterred from the repetition of such unavailing cruelty.[102] Julian spared his life: but if the bishop of Arethusa had saved the infancy of Julian,[103] posterity will condemn the ingratitude, instead of praising the clemency, of the emperor.

At the distance of five miles from Antioch, the Macedonian kings of Syria had consecrated to Apollo one of the most elegant places of devotion in the Pagan world.[104] A magnificent temple rose in honour of the god of light; and his colossal figure[105] almost filled the capacious sanctuary, which was enriched with gold and gems, and adorned by the skill of the Grecian artists. The deity was represented in a bending attitude, with a golden cup in his hand, pouring out a libation on the earth; as if he supplicated the venerable mother to give to his arms the cold and beauteous DAPHNE: for the spot was ennobled by fiction; and the fancy of the Syrian poets had transported the amorous tale from the banks of the Peneus to those of the Orontes. The ancient rites of Greece were imitated by the royal colony of Antioch. A stream of prophecy, which rivalled the truth and reputation of the Delphic oracle, flowed from the *Castalian* fountain of Daphne.[106] In the adjacent fields a stadium was built by a special privilege,[107] which had been purchased from Elis; the Olympic games were celebrated at the expense of the city; and a revenue of thirty thousand pounds sterling was annually applied to the public pleasures.[108] The perpetual resort of pilgrims and spectators insensibly formed, in the neighbourhood of the temple, the stately and populous village of Daphne, which emulated the splendour, without acquiring the title, of a provincial city. The temple and the village were deeply bosomed in a thick grove of laurels and cypresses, which reached as far as a circumference of ten miles, and formed in the most sultry summers a cool and impenetrable shade. A thousand streams of the purest water, issuing from every hill, preserved the verdure of the earth and the temperature of the air; the senses were gratified with harmonious sounds and aromatic odours; and the peaceful grove was consecrated to health and joy, to luxury and love. The vigorous youth pursued, like Apollo, the object of his desires; and the blushing maid was warned, by the fate of Daphne, to shun the folly of unseasonable coyness. The soldier and the philosopher wisely avoided the temptation of this sensual paradise;[109] where pleasure, assuming the character of religion, imperceptibly dissolved the firmness of manly virtue. But the groves of Daphne continued for many ages to enjoy the veneration of natives and strangers; the privileges of the holy ground were enlarged by the munificence of succeeding emperors; and every generation added new ornaments to the splendour of the temple.[110]

When Julian, on the day of the annual festival, hastened to adore the Apollo of Daphne, his devotion was raised to the highest pitch of eagerness and impatience. His lively imagination anticipated the grateful pomp of victims, of libations, and of incense; a long procession of youths and virgins, clothed in white robes, the symbol of their innocence; and the tumultuous concourse of an innumerable people. But the zeal of Antioch was diverted, since the reign of Christianity, into a different channel. Instead of hecatombs of fat oxen sacrificed by the tribes of a wealthy city to their tutelar deity, the emperor complains that he found only a single goose, provided at the expense of a priest, the pale and solitary inhabitant of this decayed temple.[111]

The altar was deserted, the oracle had been reduced to silence, and the holy ground was profaned by the introduction of Christian and funeral rites. After Babylas[112] (a bishop of Antioch, who died in prison in the persecution of Decius) had rested near a century in his grave, his body, by the order of the Cæsar Gallus, was transported into the midst of the grove of Daphne. A magnificent church was erected over his remains; a portion of the sacred lands was usurped for the maintenance of the clergy, and for the burial of the Christians of Antioch, who were ambitious of lying at the feet of their bishop; and the priests of Apollo retired, with their affrighted and indignant votaries. As soon as another revolution seemed to restore the fortune of Paganism, the church of St. Babylas was demolished, and new buildings were added to the mouldering edifice which had been raised by the piety of Syrian kings. But the first and most serious care of Julian was to deliver his oppressed deity from the odious presence of the dead and living Christians, who had so effectually suppressed the voice of fraud or enthusiasm.[113] The scene of infection was purified, according to the forms of ancient rituals; the bodies were decently removed; and the ministers of the church were permitted to convey the remains of St. Babylas to their former habitation within the walls of Antioch. The modest behaviour which might have assuaged the jealousy of an hostile government, was neglected on this occasion by the zeal of the Christians. The lofty car that transported the relics of Babylas was followed, and accompanied, and received, by an innumerable multitude, who chanted, with thundering acclamations, the Psalms of David the most expressive of their contempt for idols and idolaters. The return of the saint was a triumph; and the triumph was an insult on the religion of the emperor, who exerted his pride to dissemble his resentment. During the night which terminated this indiscreet procession the temple of Daphne was in flames; the statue of Apollo was consumed; and the walls of the edifice were left a naked and awful monument of ruin. The Christians of Antioch asserted, with religious confidence, that the powerful intercession of St. Babylas had pointed the lightnings of heaven against the devoted roof: but as Julian was reduced to the alternative of believing either a crime or a miracle, he chose, without hesitation, without evidence, but with some colour of probability, to impute the fire of Daphne to the revenge of the Galilæans.[114] Their offence, had it been sufficiently proved, might have justified the retaliation, which was immediately executed by the order of Julian, of shutting the doors, and confiscating the wealth, of the cathedral of Antioch. To discover the criminals who were guilty of the tumult, of the fire, or of secreting the riches of the church, several ecclesiastics were tortured;[115] and a presbyter, of the name of Theodoret, was beheaded by the sentence of the count of the East. But this hasty act was blamed by the emperor, who lamented, with real or affected concern, that the imprudent zeal of his ministers would tarnish his reign with the disgrace of persecution.[116]

The zeal of the ministers of Julian was instantly checked by the frown of their sovereign; but when the father of his country declares himself the leader of a faction, the licence of popular fury cannot easily be restrained, nor consistently punished. Julian, in a public composition, applauds the devotion and loyalty of the holy cities of Syria, whose pious inhabitants had destroyed, at the first signal, the sepulchres of the Galilæans; and faintly complains that they had revenged the injuries of the gods with less moderation than he should have recommended.[117] This imperfect and reluctant confession may appear to confirm the ecclesiastical narratives—that in the cities of Gaza, Ascalon, Cæsarea, Heliopolis, etc., the Pagans abused, without prudence or remorse, the moment of their prosperity; that the unhappy objects of their cruelty were released from torture only by death; that, as their mangled bodies were dragged through the streets, they were pierced (such was the universal rage) by the spits of cooks, and the distaffs of enraged women; and that the entrails of Christian priests and virgins, after they had been tasted by those bloody fanatics, were mixed with barley, and contemptuously thrown to the unclean animals of the city.[118] Such scenes of religious madness exhibit the most contemptible and odious picture of human nature; but the massacre of Alexandria attracts still more attention, from the certainty of the fact, the rank of the victims, and the splendour of the capital of Egypt.

George,[119] from his parents or his education, surnamed the Cappadocian, was born at Epiphania in Cilicia, in a fuller's shop. From this obscure and servile origin he raised himself by the talents of a parasite; and the patrons whom he assiduously flattered procured for their worthless dependent a lucrative commission, or contract, to supply the army with bacon. His employment was mean; he rendered it infamous. He accumulated wealth by the basest arts of fraud and corruption; but his malversations were so notorious, that George was compelled to escape from the pursuits of justice. After this disgrace, in which he appears to have saved his fortune at the expense of his honour, he embraced, with real or affected zeal, the profession of Arianism. From the love, or the ostentation, of learning, he collected a valuable library of history, rhetoric, philosophy, and theology;[120] and the choice of the prevailing faction promoted George of Cappadocia to the throne of Athanasius. The entrance of the new archbishop was that of a barbarian conqueror; and each moment of his reign was polluted by cruelty and avarice. The Catholics of Alexandria and Egypt were abandoned to a tyrant, qualified by nature and education to exercise the office of persecution; but he oppressed with an impartial hand the various inhabitants of his extensive diocese. The primate of Egypt assumed the pomp and insolence of his lofty station; but he still betrayed the vices of his base and servile extraction. The merchants of Alexandria were impoverished by the unjust and almost universal monopoly, which he acquired, of nitre, salt, paper, funerals, etc.: and the spiritual father of a great people condescended to practice the vile and pernicious arts of an informer. The Alexandrians could never forget, nor forgive, the tax which he suggested on all the houses of the city, under an obsolete claim that the royal founder had conveyed to his successors, the Ptolemies and the Cæsars, the perpetual property of the soil. The Pagans, who had been flattered with the hopes of freedom and toleration, excited his devout avarice; and the rich temples of Alexandria were either pillaged or insulted by the haughty prelate, who exclaimed in a loud and threatening tone, "How long will these sepulchres be permitted to stand?" Under the reign of Constantius he was expelled by the fury, or rather by the justice, of the people; and it was not without a violent struggle that the civil and military powers of the state could restore his authority, and gratify his revenge. The messenger who proclaimed at Alexandria the accession of Julian announced the downfall of the archbishop. George, with two of his obsequious ministers, count Diodorus, and Dracontius, master of the mint, were ignominiously dragged in chains to the public prison. At the end of twenty-four days the prison was forced open by the rage of a superstitious multitude, impatient of the tedious forms of judicial proceedings. The enemies of gods and men expired under their cruel insults; the lifeless bodies of the archbishop and his associates were carried in triumph through the streets on the back of a camel; and the inactivity of the Athanasian party[121] was esteemed a shining example of evangelical patience. The remains of these guilty wretches were thrown into the sea; and the popular leaders of the tumult declared their resolution to disappoint the devotion of the Christians, and to intercept the future honours of these *martyrs*, who had been punished, like their predecessors, by the enemies of their religion.[122] The fears of the Pagans were just, and their precautions ineffectual. The meritorious death of the archbishop obliterated the memory of his life. The rival of Athanasius was dear and sacred to the Arians, and the seeming conversion of those sectaries introduced his worship into the bosom of the Catholic church.[123] The odious stranger, disguising every circumstance of time and place, assumed the mask of a martyr, a saint, and a Christian hero;[124] and the infamous George of Cappadocia has been transformed[125] into the renowned St. George of England, the patron of arms, of chivalry, and of the garter.[126]

About the same time that Julian was informed of the tumult of Alexandria he received intelligence from Edessa that the proud and wealthy faction of the Arians had insulted the weakness of the Valentinians, and committed such disorders as ought not to be suffered with impunity in a well-regulated state. Without expecting the slow forms of justice, the exasperated prince directed his mandate to the magistrates of Edessa,[127] by which he confiscated the whole property of the church: the money was distributed among the soldiers; the lands were added to the domain; and this act of oppression was aggravated by the most ungenerous irony. "I show myself," says Julian, "the true friend of the Galilæans. Their *admirable* law has promised the kingdom of heaven to the poor; and they will advance with more diligence in the paths of virtue and salvation when they are relieved by my assistance from the load of temporal possessions. Take care," pursued the monarch, in a more serious tone, "take care how you provoke my patience and humanity. If these disorders continue, I will revenge on the magistrates the crimes of the people; and you will have reason to dread, not only confiscation and exile, but fire and the sword." The tumults of Alexandria were doubtless of a more bloody and dangerous nature: but a Christian bishop had fallen by the hands of the Pagans; and the public epistle of Julian affords a very lively proof of the partial spirit of his administration.

His reproaches to the citizens of Alexandria are mingled with expressions of esteem and tenderness; and he laments that, on this occasion, they should have departed from the gentle and generous manners which attested their Grecian extraction. He gravely censures the offence which they had committed against the laws of justice and humanity; but he recapitulates, with visible complacency, the intolerable provocations which they had so long endured from the impious tyranny of George of Cappadocia. Julian admits the principle that a wise and vigorous government should chastise the insolence of the people; yet, in consideration of their founder Alexander, and of Serapis their tutelar deity, he grants a free and gracious pardon to the guilty city, for which he again feels the affection of a brother.[128]

After the tumult of Alexandria had subsided, Athanasius, amidst the public acclamations, seated himself on the throne from whence his unworthy competitor had been precipitated: and as the zeal of the archbishop was tempered with discretion, the exercise of his authority tended not to inflame, but to reconcile, the minds of the people. His pastoral labours were not confined to the narrow limits of Egypt. The state of the Christian world was present to his active and capacious mind; and the age, the merit, the reputation of Athanasius, enabled him to assume, in a moment of danger, the office of Ecclesiastical Dictator.[129] Three years were not yet elapsed since the majority of the bishops of the West had, ignorantly or reluctantly, subscribed the Confession of Rimini. They repented, they believed, but they dreaded the unseasonable rigour of their orthodox brethren; and if their pride was stronger than their faith, they might throw themselves into the arms of the Arians, to escape the indignity of a public penance, which must degrade them to the condition of obscure laymen. At the same time the domestic differences concerning the union and distinction of the divine persons were agitated with some heat among the catholic doctors; and the progress of this metaphysical controversy seemed to threaten a public and lasting division of the Greek and Latin churches. By the wisdom of a select synod, to which the name and presence of Athanasius gave the authority of a general council, the bishops who had unwarily deviated into error were admitted to the communion of the church, on the easy condition of subscribing the Nicene Creed, without any formal acknowledgment of their past fault, or any minute definition of their scholastic opinions. The advice of the primate of Egypt had already prepared the clergy of Gaul and Spain, of Italy and Greece, for the reception of this salutary measure; and, notwithstanding the opposition of some ardent spirits,[130] the fear of the common enemy promoted the peace and harmony of the Christians.[131]

The skill and diligence of the primate of Egypt had improved the season of tranquillity before it was interrupted by the hostile edicts of the emperor.[132] Julian, who despised the Christians, honoured Athanasius with his sincere and peculiar hatred. For his sake alone he introduced an arbitrary distinction, repugnant at least to the spirit of his former declarations. He maintained that the Galilæans whom he had recalled from exile were not restored, by that general indulgence, to the possession of their respective churches; and he expressed his astonishment that a criminal, who had been repeatedly condemned by the judgment of the emperors, should dare to insult the majesty of the laws, and insolently usurp the archiepiscopal throne of Alexandria, without expecting the orders of his sovereign. As a punishment for the imaginary offence, he again banished Athanasius from the city; and he was pleased to suppose that this act of justice would be highly agreeable to his pious subjects. The pressing solicitations of the people soon convinced him that the majority of the Alexandrians were Christians; and that the greatest part of the Christians were firmly attached to the cause of their oppressed primate. But the knowledge of their sentiments, instead of persuading him to recall his decree, provoked him to extend to all Egypt the term of the exile of Athanasius. The zeal of the multitude rendered Julian still more inexorable: he was alarmed by the danger of leaving at the head of the tumultuous city a daring and popular leader; and the language of his resentment discovers the opinion which he entertained of the courage and abilities of Athanasius. The execution of the sentence was still delayed by the caution or negligence of Ecdicius, præfect of Egypt, who was at length awakened from his lethargy by a severe reprimand. "Though you neglect," says Julian, "to write to me on any other subject, at least it is your duty to inform me of your conduct towards Athanasius, the enemy of the gods. My intentions have been long since communicated to you. I swear by the great Serapis, that unless, on the calends of December, Athanasius has departed from Alexandria, nay, from Egypt, the officers of your government shall pay a fine of one hundred pounds of gold. You know my temper: I am slow to condemn, but I am still slower to forgive." This epistle was enforced by a short postscript written with the emperor's own hand. "The contempt that is shown for all the gods fills me with grief and indignation. There is nothing that I should see, nothing that I should hear, with more pleasure, than the expulsion of Athanasius from all Egypt. The abominable wretch! Under my reign, the baptism of several Grecian ladies of the highest rank has been the effect of his persecutions."[133] The death of Athanasius was not *expressly* commanded; but the præfect of Egypt understood that it was safer for him to exceed than to neglect the orders of an irritated master. The archbishop prudently retired to the monasteries of the Desert; eluded, with his usual dexterity, the snares of the enemy; and lived to triumph over the ashes of a prince who, in words of formidable import, had declared his wish that the whole venom of the Galilæan school were contained in the single person of Athanasius.[134]

I have endeavoured faithfully to represent the artful system by which Julian proposed to obtain the effects, without incurring the guilt of reproach, of persecution. But if the deadly spirit of fanaticism perverted the heart and understanding of a virtuous prince, it must, at the same time, be confessed, that the *real* sufferings of the Christians were inflamed and magnified by human passions and religious enthusiasm. The meekness and resignation which had distinguished the primitive disciples of the Gospel was the object of the applause, rather than of the imitation, of their successors. The Christians, who had now possessed above forty years the civil and ecclesiastical government of the empire, had contracted the insolent vices of prosperity,[135] and the habit of believing that the saints alone were entitled to reign over the earth. As soon as the enmity of Julian deprived the clergy of the privileges which had been conferred by the favour of Constantine, they complained of the most cruel oppression; and the free toleration of idolaters and heretics was a subject of grief and scandal to the orthodox party.[136] The acts of violence, which were no longer countenanced by the magistrates, were still committed by the zeal of the people. At Pessinus the altar of Cybele was overturned almost in the presence of the emperor; and in the city of Cæsarea, in Cappadocia, the temple of Fortune, the sole place of worship which had been left to the Pagans, was destroyed by the rage of a popular tumult. On these occasions, a prince who felt for the honour of the gods was not disposed to interrupt the course of justice; and his mind was still more deeply exasperated when he found that the fanatics, who had deserved and suffered the punishment of incendiaries, were rewarded with the honours of martyrdom.[137] The Christian subjects of Julian were assured of the hostile designs of their sovereign; and, to their jealous apprehension, every circumstance of his government might afford some grounds of discontent and suspicion. In the ordinary administration of the laws, the Christians, who formed so large a part of the people, must frequently be condemned; but their indulgent brethren, without examining the merits of the cause, presumed their innocence, allowed their claims, and imputed the severity of their judge to the partial malice of religious persecution.[138] These present hardships, intolerable as they might appear, were represented as a slight prelude of the impending calamities. The Christians considered Julian as a cruel and crafty tyrant, who suspended the execution of his revenge till he should return victorious from the Persian war. They expected that, as soon as he had triumphed over the foreign enemies of Rome, he would lay aside the irksome mask of dissimulation; that the amphitheatres would stream with the blood of hermits and bishops; and that the Christians who still persevered in the profession of the faith would be deprived of the common benefits of nature and society.[139] Every calumny[140] that could wound the reputation of the Apostate was credulously embraced by the fears and hatred of his adversaries; and their indiscreet clamours provoked the temper of a sovereign whom it was their duty to respect, and their interest to flatter. They still protested that prayers and tears were their only weapons against the impious tyrant, whose head they devoted to the justice of offended Heaven. But they insinuated, with sullen resolution, that their submission was no longer the effect of weakness; and that, in the imperfect state of human virtue, the patience which is founded on principle may be exhausted by persecution. It is impossible to determine how far the zeal of Julian would have prevailed over his good sense and humanity; but, if we seriously reflect on the strength and spirit of the church, we shall be convinced that, before the emperor could have extinguished the religion of Christ, he must have involved his country in the horrors of a civil war.[141]

CHAPTER XXIV

Residence of Julian at Antioch. His successful Expedition against the Persians. Passage of the Tigris. The Retreat and Death of Julian. Election of Jovian. He saves the Roman Army by a disgraceful Treaty.

THE philosophical fable which Julian composed under the name of the Cæsars[1] is one of the most agreeable and instructive productions of ancient wit.[2] During the freedom and equality of the days of the Saturnalia, Romulus prepared a feast for the deities of Olympus, who had adopted him as a worthy associate, and for the Roman princes, who had reigned over his martial people and the vanquished nations of the earth. The immortals were placed in just order on their thrones of state, and the table of the Cæsars was spread below the moon, in the upper region of the air. The tyrants, who would have disgraced the society of gods and men, were thrown headlong, by the inexorable Nemesis, into the Tartarean abyss. The rest of the Cæsars successively advanced to their seats; and as they passed, the vices, the defects, the blemishes of their respective characters, were maliciously noticed by old Silenus, a laughing moralist, who disguised the wisdom of a philosopher under the mask of a Bacchanal.[3] As soon as the feast was ended, the voice of Mercury proclaimed the will of Jupiter, that a celestial crown should be the reward of superior merit. Julius Cæsar, Augustus, Trajan, and Marcus Antoninus, were selected as the most illustrious candidates; the effeminate Constantine[4] was not excluded from this honourable competition; and the great Alexander was invited to dispute the prize of glory with the Roman heroes. Each of the candidates was allowed to display the merit of his own exploits; but, in the judgment of the gods, the modest silence of Marcus pleaded more powerfully than the elaborate orations of his haughty rivals. When the judges of this awful contest proceeded to examine the heart and to scrutinise the springs of action, the superiority of the Imperial Stoic appeared still more decisive and conspicuous.[5]

Alexander and Cæsar, Augustus, Trajan, and Constantine acknowledged, with a blush, that fame, or power, or pleasure, had been the important object of *their* labours; but the gods themselves beheld with reverence and love a virtuous mortal, who had practised on the throne the lessons of philosophy, and who, in a state of human imperfection, had aspired to imitate the moral attributes of the Deity. The value of this agreeable composition (the Cæsars of Julian) is enhanced by the rank of the author. A prince, who delineates with freedom the vices and virtues of his predecessors, subscribes, in every line, the censure or approbation of his own conduct.

In the cool moments of reflection, Julian preferred the useful and benevolent virtues of Antoninus; but his ambitious spirit was inflamed by the glory of Alexander, and he solicited, with equal ardor, the esteem of the wise and the applause of the multitude. In the season of life when the powers of the mind and body enjoy the most active vigour, the emperor, who was instructed by the experience and animated by the success of the German war, resolved to signalise his reign by some more splendid and memorable achievement. The ambassadors of the East, from the continent of India and the isle of Ceylon,[6] had respectfully saluted the Roman purple.[7] The nations of the West esteemed and dreaded the personal virtues of Julian both in peace and war. He despised the trophies of a Gothic victory,[8] and was satisfied that the rapacious barbarians of the Danube would be restrained from any future violation of the faith of treaties by the terror of his name and the additional fortifications with which he strengthened the Thracian and Illyrian frontiers. The successor of Cyrus and Artaxerxes was the only rival whom he deemed worthy of his arms, and he resolved, by the final conquest of Persia, to chastise the haughty nation which had so long resisted and insulted the majesty of Rome.[9] As soon as the Persian monarch was informed that the throne of Constantius was filled by a prince of a very different character, he condescended to make some artful or perhaps sincere overtures towards a negotiation of peace. But the pride of Sapor was astonished by the firmness of Julian, who sternly declared that he would never consent to hold a peaceful conference among the flames and ruins of the cities of Mesopotamia, and who added, with a smile of contempt, that it was needless to treat by ambassadors, as he himself had determined to visit speedily the court of Persia. The impatience of the emperor urged the diligence of the military preparations. The generals were named, a formidable army was destined for this important service, and Julian, marching from Constantinople through the provinces of Asia Minor, arrived at Antioch about eight months after the death of his predecessor. His ardent desire to march into the heart of Persia was checked by the indispensable duty of regulating the state of the empire, by his zeal to revive the worship of the gods, and by the advice of his wisest friends, who represented the necessity of allowing the salutary interval of winter quarters to restore the exhausted strength of the legions of Gaul and the discipline and spirit of the Eastern troops. Julian was persuaded to fix, till the ensuing spring, his residence at Antioch, among a people maliciously disposed to deride the haste and to censure the delays of their sovereign.[10]

If Julian had flattered himself that his personal connection with the capital of the East would be productive of mutual satisfaction to the prince and people, he made a very false estimate of his own character and of the manners of Antioch.[11] The warmth of the climate disposed the natives to the most intemperate enjoyment of tranquillity and opulence, and the lively licentiousness of the Greeks was blended with the hereditary softness of the Syrians. Fashion was the only law, pleasure the only pursuit, and the splendour of dress and furniture was the only distinction of the citizens of Antioch. The arts of luxury were honoured, the serious and manly virtues were the subject of ridicule, and the contempt for female modesty and reverent age announced the universal corruption of the capital of the East. The love of spectacles was the taste, or rather passion, of the Syrians; the most skilful artists were procured from the adjacent cities;[12] a considerable share of the revenue was devoted to the public amusements, and the magnificence of the games of the theatre and circus was considered as the happiness and as the glory of Antioch. The rustic manners of a prince who disdained such glory, and was insensible of such happiness, soon disgusted the delicacy of his subjects, and the effeminate Orientals could neither imitate nor admire the severe simplicity which Julian always maintained and sometimes affected. The days of festivity, consecrated by ancient custom to the honour of the gods, were the only occasions in which Julian relaxed his philosophic severity, and those festivals were the only days in which the Syrians of Antioch could reject the allurements of pleasure. The majority of the people supported the glory of the Christian name, which had been first invented by their ancestors:[13] they contented themselves with disobeying the moral precepts, but they were scrupulously attached to the speculative doctrines, of their religion. The church of Antioch was distracted by heresy and schism; but the Arians and the Athanasians, the followers of Meletius and those of Paulinus,[14] were actuated by the same pious hatred of their common adversary.

The strongest prejudice was entertained against the character of an apostate, the enemy and successor of a prince who had engaged the affections of a very numerous sect, and the removal of St. Babylas excited an implacable opposition to the person of Julian. His subjects complained with superstitious indignation, that famine had pursued the emperor's steps from Constantinople to Antioch, and the discontent of a hungry people was exasperated by the injudicious attempt to relieve their distress. The inclemency of the season had affected the harvests of Syria, and the price of bread[15] in the markets of Antioch had naturally risen in proportion to the scarcity of corn. But the fair and reasonable proportion was soon violated by the rapacious arts of monopoly. In this unequal contest, in which the produce of the land is claimed by one party as his exclusive property, is used by another as a lucrative object of trade, and is required by a third for the daily and necessary support of life, all the profits of the intermediate agents are accumulated on the head of the defenceless consumers. The hardships of their situation were exaggerated and increased by their own impatience and anxiety, and the apprehension of a scarcity gradually produced the appearances of a famine. When the luxurious citizens of Antioch complained of the high price of poultry and fish, Julian publicly delcared that a frugal city ought to be satisfied with a regular supply of wine, oil, and bread; but he acknowledged that it was the duty of a sovereign to provide for the subsistence of his people. With this salutary view the emperor ventured on a very dangerous and doubtful step, of fixing, by legal authority, the value of corn. He enacted that, in a time of scarcity, it should be sold at a price which had seldom been known in the most plentiful years; and that his own example might strengthen his laws, he sent into the market four hundred and twenty-two thousand *modii*, or measures, which were drawn by his order from the granaries of Hierapolis, of Chalcis, and even of Egypt. The consequences might have been foreseen, and were soon felt.

The Imperial wheat was purchased by the rich merchants; the proprietors of land or of corn withheld from the city the accustomed supply; and the small quantities that appeared in the market were secretly sold at an advanced and illegal price. Julian still continued to applaud his own policy, treated the complaints of the people as a vain and ungrateful murmur, and convinced Antioch that he had inherited the obstinacy, though not the cruelty, of his brother Gallus.[16] The remonstrances of the municipal senate served only to exasperate his inflexible mind. He was persuaded, perhaps with truth, that the senators of Antioch, who possessed lands or were concerned in trade, had themselves contributed to the calamities of their country; and he imputed the disrespectful boldness which they assumed to the sense, not of public duty, but of private interest. The whole body, consisting of two hundred of the most noble and wealthy citizens, were sent, under a guard, from the palace to the prison; and though they were permitted, before the close of evening, to return to their respective houses,[17] the emperor himself could not obtain the forgiveness which he had so easily granted. The same grievances were still the subject of the same complaints, which were industriously circulated by the wit and levity of the Syrian Greeks. During the licentious days of the Saturnalia, the streets of the city resounded with insolent songs, which derided the laws, the religion, the personal conduct, and even the *beard*, of the conqueror; and the spirit of Antioch was manifested by the connivance of the magistrates and the applause of the multitude.[18] The disciple of Socrates was too deeply affected by these popular insults; but the monarch, endowed with quick sensibility and possessed of absolute power, refused his passions the gratification of revenge. A tyrant might have proscribed, without distinction, the lives and fortunes of the citizens of Antioch; and the unwarlike Syrians must have patiently submitted to the lust, the rapaciousness, and the cruelty of the faithful legions of Gaul. A milder sentence might have deprived the capital of the East of its honours and privileges, and the courtiers, perhaps the subjects of Julian, would have applauded an act of justice which asserted the dignity of the supreme magistrate of the republic.[19] But instead of abusing or exerting the authority of the state to revenge his personal injuries, Julian contented himself with an inoffensive mode of retaliation, which it would be in the power of few princes to employ. He had been insulted by satires and libels; in his turn he composed, under the title of the *Enemy of the Beard*, an ironical confession of his own faults, and a severe satire of the licentious and effeminate manners of Antioch. This Imperial reply was publicly exposed before the gates of the palace; and the MISOPOGON[20] still remains a singular monument of the resentment, the wit, the humanity, and the indiscretion of Julian. Though he affected to laugh, he could not forgive.[21] His contempt was expressed, and his revenge might be gratified, by the nomination of a governor[22] worthy only of such subjects; and the emperor, for ever renouncing the ungrateful city, proclaimed his resolution to pass the ensuing winter at Tarsus in Cilicia.[23]

Yet Antioch possessed one citizen whose genius and virtues might atone, in the opinion of Julian, for the vice and folly of his country. The sophist Libanius was born in the capital of the East, he publicly professed the arts of rhetoric and declamation at Nice, Nicomedia, Constantinople, Athens, and, during the remainder of his life, at Antioch. His school was assiduously frequented by the Grecian youth; his disciples, who sometimes exceeded the number of eighty, celebrated their incomparable master; and the jealousy of his rivals, who persecuted him from one city to another, confirmed the favourable opinion which Libanius ostentatiously displayed of his superior merit. The preceptors of Julian had extorted a rash but solemn assurance that he would never attend the lectures of their adversary; the curiosity of the royal youth was checked and inflamed; he secretly procured the writings of this dangerous sophist, and gradually surpassed, in the perfect imitation of his style, the most laborious of his domestic pupils.[24] When Julian ascended the throne, he declared his impatience to embrace and reward the Syrian sophist, who had preserved in a degenerate age the Grecian purity of taste, of manners, and of religion. The emperor's prepossession was increased and justified by the discreet pride of his favourite. Instead of pressing, with the foremost of the crowd, into the palace of Constantinople, Libanius calmly expected his arrival at Antioch, withdrew from court on the first symptoms of coldness and indifference, required a formal invitation for each visit, and taught his sovereign an important lesson, that he might command the obedience of a subject, but that he must deserve the attachment of a friend. The sophists of every age, despising or affecting to despise the accidental distinctions of birth and fortune,[25] reserve their esteem for the superior qualities of the mind, with which they themselves are so plentifully endowed. Julian might disdain the acclamations of a venal court who adored the Imperial purple; but he was deeply flattered by the praise, the admonition, the freedom, and the envy of an independent philosopher, who refused his favours, loved his person, celebrated his fame, and protected his memory. The voluminous writings of Libanius still exist; for the most part they are the vain and idle compositions of an orator who cultivated the science of words—the productions of a recluse student, whose mind, regardless of his contemporaries, was incessantly fixed on the Trojan war and the Athenian commonwealth. Yet the sophist of Antioch sometimes descended from this imaginary elevation; he entertained a various and elaborate correspondence;[26] he praised the virtues of his own times; he boldly arraigned the abuses of public and private life; and he eloquently pleaded the cause of Antioch against the just resentment of Julian and Theodosius. It is the common calamity of old age[27] to lose whatever might have rendered it desirable; but Libanius experienced the peculiar misfortune of surviving the religion and the sciences to which he had consecrated his genius. The friend of Julian was an indignant spectator of the triumph of Christianity, and his bigotry, which darkened the prospect of the visible world, did not inspire Libanius with any lively hopes of celestial glory and happiness.[28]

The martial impatience of Julian urged him to take the field in the beginning of the spring, and he dismissed, with contempt and reproach, the senate of Antioch, who accompanied the emperor beyond the limits of their own territory, to which he was resolved never to return. After a laborious march of two days[29] he halted on the third at Berœa, or Aleppo, where he had the mortification of finding a senate almost entirely Christian, who received with cold and formal demonstrations of respect the eloquent sermon of the apostle of Paganism. The son of one of the most illustrious citizens of Berœa, who had embraced, either from interest or conscience, the religion of the emperor, was disinherited by his angry parent. The father and the son were invited to the Imperial table. Julian, placing himself between them, attempted without success to inculcate the lesson and example of toleration, supported, with affected calmness, the indiscreet zeal of the aged Christian, who seemed to forget the sentiments of nature and the duty of a subject, and at length, turning towards the afflicted youth, "Since you have lost a father," said he, "for my sake, it is incumbent on me to supply his place."[30] The emperor was received in a manner much more agreeable to his wishes at Batnæ, a small town pleasantly seated in a grove of cypresses, about twenty miles from the city of Hierapolis. The solemn rites of sacrifice were decently prepared by the inhabitants of Batnæ, who seemed attached to the worship of their tutelar deities, Apollo and Jupiter; but the serious piety of Julian was offended by the tumult of their applause, and he too clearly discerned that the smoke which arose from their altars was the incense of flattery rather than of devotion. The ancient and magnificent temple, which had sanctified for so many ages the city of Hierapolis,[31] no longer subsisted, and the consecrated wealth, which afforded a liberal maintenance to more than three hundred priests, might hasten its downfall. Yet Julian enjoyed the satisfaction of embracing a philosopher and a friend, whose religious firmness had withstood the pressing and repeated solicitations of Constantius and Gallus, as often as those princes lodged at his house in their passage through Hierapolis. In the hurry of military preparation, and the careless confidence of a familiar correspondence, the zeal of Julian appears to have been lively and uniform. He had now undertaken an important and difficult war, and the anxiety of the event rendered him still more attentive to observe and register the most trifling presages from which, according to the rules of divination, any knowledge of futurity could be derived.[32] He informed Libanius of his progress as far as Hierapolis by an elegant epistle,[33] which displays the facility of his genius and his tender friendship for the sophist of Antioch.

Hierapolis, situate almost on the banks of the Euphrates,[34] had been appointed for the general rendezvous of the Roman troops, who immediately passed the great river on the bridge of boats which was previously constructed.[35] If the inclinations of Julian had been similar to those of his predecessor, he might have wasted the active and important season of the year in the circus of Samosata or in the churches of Edessa. But as the warlike emperor, instead of Constantius, had chosen Alexander for his model, he advanced without delay to Carrhæ,[36] a very ancient city of Mesopotamia, at the distance of fourscore miles from Hierapolis. The temple of the Moon attracted the devotion of Julian, but the halt of a few days was principally employed in completing the immense preparations of the Persian war. The secret of the expedition had hitherto remained in his own breast; but as Carrhæ is the point of separation of the two great roads, he could no longer conceal whether it was his design to attack the dominions of Sapor on the side of the Tigris, or on that of the Euphrates. The emperor detached an army of thirty thousand men, under the command of his kinsman Procopius, and of Sebastian, who had been duke of Egypt. They were ordered to direct their march towards Nisibis, and to secure the frontier from the desultory incursions of the enemy, before they attempted the passage of the Tigris. Their subsequent operations were left to the discretion of the generals; but Julian expected that, after wasting with fire and sword the fertile districts of Media and Adiabene, they might arrive under the walls of Ctesiphon about the same time that he himself, advancing with equal steps along the banks of the Euphrates, should besiege the capital of the Persian monarchy. The success of this well-concerted plan depended, in a great measure, on the powerful and ready assistance of the king of Armenia, who, without exposing the safety of his own dominions, might detach an army of four thousand horse and twenty thousand foot to the assistance of the Romans.[37] But the feeble Arsaces Tiranus,[38] king of Armenia, had degenerated still more shamefully than his father Chosroes from the manly virtues of the great Tiridates; and as the pusillanimous monarch was averse to any enterprise of danger and glory, he could disguise his timid indolence by the more decent excuses of religion and gratitude. He expressed a pious attachment to the memory of Constantius, from whose hands he had received in marriage Olympias, the daughter of the præfect Ablavius; and the alliance of a female who had been educated as the destined wife of the emperor Constans exalted the dignity of a barbarian king.[39] Tiranus professed the Christian religion; he reigned over a nation of Christians; and he was restrained, by every principle of conscience and interest, from contributing to the victory which would consummate the ruin of the church. The alienated mind of Tiranus was exasperated by the indiscretion of Julian, who treated the king of Armenia as *his* slave, and as the enemy of the gods. The haughty and threatening style of the Imperial mandates[40] awakened the secret indignation of a prince who, in the humiliating state of dependence, was still conscious of his royal descent from the Arsacides, the lords of the East, and the rivals of the Roman power. The military dispositions of Julian were skilfully contrived to deceive the spies and to divert the attention of Sapor. The legions appeared to direct their march towards Nisibis and the Tigris. On a sudden they wheeled to the right, traversed the level and naked plain of Carrhæ, and reached, on the third day, the banks of the Euphrates, where the strong town of Nicephorium, or Callinicum, had been founded by the Macedonian kings. From thence the emperor pursued his march, above ninety miles, along the winding stream of the Euphrates, till at length, about one month after his departure from Antioch, he discovered the towers of Circesium, the extreme limit of the Roman dominions. The army of Julian, the most numerous that any of the Cæsars had ever led against Persia, consisted of sixty-five thousand effective and well-disciplined soldiers. The veteran bands of cavalry and infantry, of Romans and barbarians, had been selected from the different provinces, and a just pre-eminence of loyalty and valour was claimed by the hardy Gauls, who guarded the throne and person of their beloved prince. A formidable body of Scythian auxiliaries had been transported from another climate, and almost from another world, to invade a distant country of whose name and situation they were ignorant. The love of rapine and war allured to the Imperial standard several tribes of Saracens, or roving Arabs, whose service Julian had commanded, while he sternly refused the payment of the accustomed subsidies. The broad channel of the Euphrates[41] was crowded by a fleet of eleven hundred ships, destined to attend the motions and to satisfy the wants of the Roman army. The military strength of the fleet was composed of fifty armed galleys, and these were accompanied by an equal number of flat-bottomed boats, which might occasionally be connected into the form of temporary bridges. The rest of the ships, partly constructed of timber and partly covered with raw hides, were laden with an almost inexhaustible supply of arms and engines, of utensils and provisions. The vigilant humanity of Julian had embarked a very large magazine of vinegar and biscuit for the use of the soldiers, but he prohibited the indulgence of wine, and rigorously stopped a long string of superfluous camels that attempted to follow the rear of the army. The river Chaboras falls into the Euphrates at Circesium,[42] and, as soon as the trumpet gave the signal of march, the Romans passed the little stream which separated two mighty and hostile empires. The custom of ancient discipline required a military oration, and Julian embraced

every opportunity of displaying his eloquence. He animated the impatient and attentive legions by the example of the inflexible courage and glorious triumphs of their ancestors. He excited their resentment by a lively picture of the insolence of the Persians; and he exhorted them to imitate his firm resolution either to extirpate that perfidious nation, or to devote his life in the cause of the republic. The eloquence of Julian was enforced by a donative of one hundred and thirty pieces of silver to every soldier, and the bridge of the Chaboras was instantly cut away to convince the troops that they must place their hopes of safety in the success of their arms. Yet the prudence of the emperor induced him to secure a remote frontier, perpetually exposed to the inroads of the hostile Arabs. A detachment of four thousand men was left at Circesium, which completed, to the number of ten thousand, the regular garrison of that important fortress.[43]

From the moment that the Romans entered the enemy's country,[44] the country of an active and artful enemy, the order of march was disposed in three columns.[45] The strength of the infantry, and consequently of the whole army, was placed in the centre, under the peculiar command of their master-general Victor. On the right, the brave Nevitta led a column of several legions along the banks of the Euphrates, and almost always in sight of the fleet. The left flank of the army was protected by the column of cavalry. Hormisdas and Arinthæus were appointed generals of the horse, and the singular adventures of Hormisdas[46] are not undeserving of our notice. He was a Persian prince, of the royal race of the Sassanides, who, in the troubles of the minority of Sapor, had escaped from prison to the hospitable court of the great Constantine. Hormisdas at first excited the compassion, and at length acquired the esteem, of his new masters; his valour and fidelity raised him to the military honours of the Roman service; and, though a Christian, he might indulge the secret satisfaction of convincing his ungrateful country that an oppressed subject may prove the most dangerous enemy. Such was the disposition of the three principal columns. The front and flanks of the army were covered by Lucilianus with a flying detachment of fifteen hundred light-armed soldiers, whose active vigilance observed the most distant signs, and conveyed the earliest notice of any hostile approach. Dagalaiphus, and Secundinus duke of Osrhoene, conducted the troops of the rear-guard; the baggage securely proceeded in the intervals of the columns; and the ranks, from a motive either of use or ostentation, were formed in such open order that the whole line of march extended almost ten miles. The ordinary post of Julian was at the head of the centre column, but, as he preferred the duties of a general to the state of a monarch, he rapidly moved, with a small escort of light cavalry, to the front, the rear, the flanks, wherever his presence could animate or protect the march of the Roman army. The country which they traversed from the Chaboras to the cultivated lands of Assyria may be considered as a part of the desert of Arabia, a dry and barren waste, which could never be improved by the most powerful arts of human industry. Julian marched over the same ground which had been trod above seven hundred years before by the footsteps of the younger Cyrus, and which is described by one of the companions of his expedition, the sage and heroic Xenophon.[47] "The country was a plain throughout, as even as the sea, and full of wormwood; and if any other kind of shrubs or reeds grew there, they had all an aromatic smell, but no trees could be seen. Bustards and ostriches, antelopes and wild asses,[48] appeared to be the only inhabitants of the desert, and the fatigues of the march were alleviated by the amusements of the chase." The loose sand of the desert was frequently raised by the wind into clouds of dust, and a great number of the soldiers of Julian, with their tents, were suddenly thrown to the ground by the violence of an unexpected hurricane.

The sandy plains of Mesopotamia were abandoned to the antelopes and wild asses of the desert, but a variety of populous towns and villages were pleasantly situated on the banks of the Euphrates and in the islands which are occasionally formed by that river. The city of Anah, or Anatho,[49] the actual residence of an Arabian emir, is composed of two long streets, which enclose, within a natural fortification, a small island in the midst, and two fruitful spots on either side, of the Euphrates. The warlike inhabitants of Anatho showed a disposition to stop the march of a Roman emperor, till they were diverted from such fatal presumption by the mild exhortations of Prince Hormisdas, and the approaching terrors of the fleet and army. They implored and experienced the clemency of Julian, who transplanted the people to an advantageous settlement near Chalcis in Syria, and admitted Pusæus, the governor, to an honourable rank in his service and friendship. But the impregnable fortress of Thilutha could scorn the menace of a siege, and the emperor was obliged to content himself with an insulting promise that, when he had subdued the interior provinces of Persia, Thilutha would no longer refuse to grace the triumph of the conqueror. The inhabitants of the open towns, unable to resist and unwilling to yield, fled with precipitation, and their houses, filled with spoil and provisions, were occupied by the soldiers of Julian, who massacred, without remorse and without punishment, some defenceless women. During the march the Surenas, or Persian general, and Malek Rodosaces, the renowned emir of the tribe of Gassan,[50] incessantly hovered round the army; every straggler was intercepted, every detachment was attacked, and the valiant Hormisdas escaped with some difficulty from their hands. But the barbarians were finally repulsed, the country became every day less favourable to the operations of cavalry, and when the Romans arrived at Macepracta they perceived the ruins of the wall which had been constructed by the ancient kings of Assyria to secure their dominions from the incursions of the Medes. These preliminaries of the expedition of Julian appear to have employed about fifteen days, and we may compute near three hundred miles from the fortress of Circesium to the wall of Macepracta.[51]

The fertile province of Assyria,[52] which stretched beyond the Tigris, as far as the mountains of Media,[53] extended about four hundred miles from the ancient wall of Macepracta to the territory of Basra, where the united streams of the Euphrates and Tigris discharge themselves into the Persian Gulf.[54] The whole country might have claimed the peculiar name of Mesopotamia, as the two rivers, which are never more distant than fifty, approach, between Bagdad and Babylon, within twenty-five miles of each other. A multitude of artificial canals, dug without much labour in a soft and yielding soil, connected the rivers and intersected the plain of Assyria. The uses of these artificial canals were various and important. They served to discharge the superfluous waters from one river into the other at the season of their respective inundations. Subdividing themselves into smaller and smaller branches, they refreshed the dry lands and supplied the deficiency of rain. They facilitated the intercourse of peace and commerce, and, as the dams could be speedily broke down, they armed the despair of the Assyrians with the means of opposing a sudden deluge to the progress of an invading army. To the soil and climate of Assyria nature had denied some of her choicest gifts—the vine, the olive, and the fig-tree; but the food which supports the life of man, and particularly wheat and barley, were produced with inexhaustible fertility, and the husbandman, who committed his seed to the earth, was frequently rewarded with an increase of two or even of three hundred. The face of the country was interspersed with groves of innumerable palm-trees,[55] and the diligent natives celebrated, either in verse or prose, the three hundred and sixty uses to which the trunk, the branches, the leaves, the juice, and the fruit were skilfully applied. Several manufactures, especially those of leather and linen, employed the industry of a numerous people, and afforded valuable materials for foreign trade, which appears, however, to have been conducted by the hands of strangers. Babylon had been converted into a royal park, but near the ruins of the ancient capital new cities had successively arisen, and the populousness of the country was displayed in the multitudes of towns and villages, which were built of bricks dried in the sun and strongly cemented with bitumen, the natural and peculiar production of the Babylonian soil. While the successors of Cyrus reigned over Asia, the province of Assyria alone maintained, during a third part of the year, the luxurious plenty of the table and household of the Great King. Four considerable villages were assigned for the subsistence of his Indian dogs; eight hundred stallions and sixteen thousand mares were constantly kept, at the expense of the country, for the royal stables; and as the daily tribute which was paid to the satrap amounted to one English bushel of silver, we may compute the annual revenue of Assyria at more than twelve hundred thousand pounds sterling.[56]

The fields of Assyria were devoted by Julian to the calamities of war; and the philosopher retaliated on a guiltless people the acts of rapine and cruelty which had been committed by their haughty master in the Roman provinces. The trembling Assyrians summoned the rivers to their assistance; and completed with their own hands the ruin of their country. The roads were rendered impracticable; a flood of waters was poured into the camp; and, during several days, the troops of Julian were obliged to contend with the most discouraging hardships. But every obstacle was surmounted by the perseverance of the legionaries, who were inured to toil as well as to danger, and who felt themselves animated by the spirit of their leader. The damage was gradually repaired; the waters were restored to their proper channels; while groves of palm-

trees were cut down and placed along the broken parts of the road; and the army passed over the broad and deeper canals on bridges of floating rafts, which were supported by the help of bladders. Two cities of Assyria presumed to resist the arms of a Roman emperor; and they both paid the severe penalty of their rashness. At the distance of fifty miles from the royal residence of Ctesiphon, Perisabor, or Anbar, held the second rank in the province: a city, large, populous, and well fortified, surrounded with a double wall, almost encompassed by a branch of the Euphrates, and defended by the valour of a numerous garrison. The exhortations of Hormisdas were repulsed with contempt; and the ears of the Persian prince were wounded by a just reproach, that, unmindful of his royal birth, he conducted an army of strangers against his king and country. The Assyrians maintained their loyalty by a skilful as well as vigorous defence, till the lucky stroke of a battering-ram having opened a large breach by shattering one of the angles of the wall, they hastily retired into the fortifications of the interior citadel. The soldiers of Julian rushed impetuously into the town, and, after the full gratification of every military appetite, Perisabor was reduced to ashes; and the engines which assaulted the citadel were planted on the ruins of the smoking houses. The contest was continued by an incessant and mutual discharge of missile weapons; and the superiority which the Romans might derive from the mechanical powers of their balistæ and catapultæ was counterbalanced by the advantage of the ground on the side of the besieged. But as soon as an *Helepolis* had been constructed, which could engage on equal terms with the loftiest ramparts, the tremendous aspect of a moving turret, that would leave no hope of resistance or of mercy, terrified the defenders of the citadel into an humble submission; and the place was surrendered only two days after Julian first appeared under the walls of Perisabor. Two thousand five hundred persons of both sexes, the feeble remnant of a flourishing people, were permitted to retire: the plentiful magazines of corn, of arms, and of splendid furniture, were partly distributed among the troops and partly reserved for the public service; the useless stores were destroyed by fire or thrown into the stream of the Euphrates; and the fate of Amida was revenged by the total ruin of Perisabor.

The city, or rather fortress, of Maogamalcha, which was defended by sixteen large towers, a deep ditch, and two strong and solid walls of brick and bitumen, appears to have been constructed at the distance of eleven miles, as the safeguard of the capital of Persia. The emperor, apprehensive of leaving such an important fortress in his rear, immediately formed the siege of Maogamalcha; and the Roman army was distributed for that purpose into three divisions. Victor, at the head of the cavalry and of a detachment of heavy-armed foot, was ordered to clear the country as far as the banks of the Tigris and the suburbs of Ctesiphon. The conduct of the attack was assumed by Julian himself, who seemed to place his whole dependence in the military engines which he erected against the walls; while he secretly contrived a more efficacious method of introducing his troops into the heart of the city. Under the direction of Nevitta and Dagalaiphus, the trenches were opened at a considerable distance, and gradually prolonged as far as the edge of the ditch. The ditch was speedily filled with earth; and, by the incessant labour of the troops, a mine was carried under the foundations of the walls, and sustained at sufficient intervals by props of timber. Three chosen cohorts, advancing in a single file, silently explored the dark and dangerous passage; till their intrepid leader whispered back the intelligence that he was ready to issue from his confinement into the streets of the hostile city. Julian checked their ardour, that he might ensure their success; and immediately diverted the attention of the garrison by the tumult and clamour of a general assault. The Persians, who from their walls contemptuously beheld the progress of an impotent attack, celebrated with songs of triumph the glory of Sapor; and ventured to assure the emperor that he might ascend the starry mansion of Ormusd before he could hope to take the impregnable city of Maogamalcha. The city was already taken. History has recorded the name of a private soldier, the first who ascended from the mine into a deserted tower. The passage was widened by his companions, who pressed forwards with impatient valour. Fifteen hundred enemies were already in the midst of the city. The astonished garrison abandoned the walls, and their only hope of safety; the gates were instantly burst open; and the revenge of the soldier, unless it were suspended by lust or avarice, was satiated by an undistinguishing massacre. The governor, who had yielded on a promise of mercy, was burnt alive, a few days afterwards, on a charge of having uttered some disrespectful words against the honour of Prince Hormisdas. The fortifications were razed to the ground; and not a vestige was left that the city of Maogamalcha had ever existed. The neighbourhood of the capital of Persia was adorned with three stately palaces, laboriously enriched with every production that could gratify the luxury and pride of an Eastern monarch. The pleasant situation of the gardens along the banks of the Tigris was improved, according to the Persian taste, by the symmetry of flowers, fountains, and shady walks: and spacious parks were enclosed for the reception of the bears, lions, and wild boars, which were maintained at a considerable expense for the pleasure of the royal chase. The park-walls were broken down, the savage game was abandoned to the darts of the soldiers, and the palaces of Sapor were reduced to ashes, by the command of the Roman emperor. Julian, on this occasion, showed himself ignorant or careless of the laws of civility, which the prudence and refinement of polished ages have established between hostile princes. Yet these wanton ravages need not excite in our breasts any vehement emotions of pity or resentment. A simple, naked statue, finished by the hand of a Grecian artist, is of more genuine value than all these rude and costly monuments of barbaric labour; and, if we are more deeply affected by the ruin of a palace than by the conflagration of a cottage, our humanity must have formed a very erroneous estimate of the miseries of human life.[57]

Julian was an object of terror and hatred to the Persians; and the painters of that nation represented the invader of their country under the emblem of a furious lion, who vomited from his mouth a consuming fire.[58] To his friends and soldiers the philosophic hero appeared in a more amiable light; and his virtues were never more conspicuously displayed than in the last and most active period of his life. He practised, without effort, and almost without merit, the habitual qualities of temperance and sobriety. According to the dictates of that artificial wisdom which assumes an absolute dominion over the mind and body, he sternly refused himself the indulgence of the most natural appetites.[59] In the warm climate of Assyria, which solicited a luxurious people to the gratification of every sensual desire,[60] a youthful conqueror preserved his chastity pure and inviolate: nor was Julian ever tempted, even by a motive of curiosity, to visit his female captives of exquisite beauty,[61] who, instead of resisting his power, would have disputed with each other the honour of his embraces. With the same firmness that he resisted the allurements of love, he sustained the hardships of war. When the Romans marched through the flat and flooded country, their sovereign, on foot, at the head of his legions, shared their fatigues and animated their diligence. In every useful labour the hand of Julian was prompt and strenuous; and the Imperial purple was wet and dirty, as the coarse garment of the meanest soldier. The two sieges allowed him some remarkable opportunities of signalising his personal valour, which, in the improved state of the military art, can seldom be exerted by a prudent general. The emperor stood before the citadel of Perisabor, insensible of his extreme danger, and encouraged his troops to burst open the gates of iron, till he was almost overwhelmed under a cloud of missile weapons and huge stones that were directed against his person. As he examined the exterior fortifications of Maogamalcha, two Persians, devoting themselves for their country, suddenly rushed upon him with drawn scimitars: the emperor dexterously received their blows on his uplifted shield; and, with a steady and well-aimed thrust, laid one of his adversaries dead at his feet. The esteem of a prince who possesses the virtues which he approves is the noblest recompense of a deserving subject; and the authority which Julian derived from his personal merit enabled him to revive and enforce the rigour of ancient discipline. He punished with death, or ignominy, the misbehaviour of three troops of horse, who, in a skirmish with the Surenas, had lost their honour and one of their standards: and he distinguished with *obsidional*[62] crowns the valour of the foremost soldiers who had ascended into the city of Maogamalcha. After the siege of Perisabor the firmness of the emperor was exercised by the insolent avarice of the army, who loudly complained that their services were rewarded by a trifling donative of one hundred pieces of silver. His just indignation was expressed in the grave and manly language of a Roman. "Riches are the object of your desires; those riches are in the hands of the Persians; and the spoils of this fruitful country are proposed as the prize of your valour and discipline. Believe me," added Julian, "the Roman republic, which formerly possessed such immense treasures, is now reduced to want and wretchedness; since our princes have been persuaded, by weak and interested ministers, to purchase with gold the tranquillity of the barbarians. The revenue is exhausted; the cities are ruined; the provinces are dispeopled. For myself, the only inheritance that I have received from my royal ancestors is a soul incapable of fear; and as long

as I am convinced that every real advantage is seated in the mind, I shall not blush to acknowledge an honourable poverty, which in the days of ancient virtue was considered as the glory of Fabricius. That glory, and that virtue, may be your own, if you will listen to the voice of Heaven and of your leader. But if you will rashly persist, if you are determined to renew the shameful and mischievous examples of old seditions, proceed. As it becomes an emperor who has filled the first rank among men, I am prepared to die standing, and to despise a precarious life which every hour may depend on an accidental fever. If I have been found unworthy of the command, there are now among you (I speak it with pride and pleasure), there are many chiefs whose merit and experience are equal to the conduct of the most important war. Such has been the temper of my reign, that I can retire, without regret and without apprehension, to the obscurity of a private station."[63] The modest resolution of Julian was answered by the unanimous applause and cheerful obedience of the Romans, who declared their confidence of victory while they fought under the banners of their heroic prince. Their courage was kindled by his frequent and familiar asseverations (for such wishes were the oaths of Julian), "So may I reduce the Persians under the yoke!" "Thus may I restore the strength and splendour of the republic!" The love of fame was the ardent passion of his soul: but it was not before he trampled on the ruins of Maogamalcha that he allowed himself to say, "We have now provided some materials for the sophist of Antioch."[64]

The successful valour of Julian had triumphed over all the obstacles that opposed his march to the gates of Ctesiphon. But the reduction, or even the siege, of the capital of Persia was still at a distance: nor can the military conduct of the emperor be clearly apprehended without a knowledge of the country which was the theatre of his bold and skilful operations.[65] Twenty miles to the south of Bagdad, and on the eastern bank of the Tigris, the curiosity of travellers has observed some ruins of the palaces of Ctesiphon, which in the time of Julian was a great and populous city. The name and glory of the adjacent Seleucia were for ever extinguished; and the only remaining quarter of that Greek colony had resumed, with the Assyrian language and manners, the primitive appelation of Coche. Coche was situate on the western side of the Tigris; but it was naturally considered as a suburb of Ctesiphon, with which we may suppose it to have been connected by a permanent bridge of boats. The united parts contributed to form the common epithet of Al Modain, THE CITIES, which the Orientals have bestowed on the winter residence of the Sassanides; and the whole circumference of the Persian capital was strongly fortified by the waters of the river, by lofty walls, and by impracticable morasses. Near the ruins of Seleucia the camp of Julian was fixed, and secured by a ditch and rampart against the sallies of the numerous and enterprising garrison of Coche. In this fruitful and pleasant country the Romans were plentifully supplied with water and forage: and several forts, which might have embarrassed the motions of the army, submitted, after some resistance, to the efforts of their valour. The fleet passed from the Euphrates into an artificial deviation of that river, which pours a copious and navigable stream into the Tigris at a small distance *below* the great city. If they had followed this royal canal, which bore the name of Nahar-Malcha,[66] the intermediate situation of Coche would have separated the fleet and army of Julian; and the rash attempt of steering against the current of the Tigris, and forcing their way through the midst of a hostile capital, must have been attended with the total destruction of the Roman navy. The prudence of the emperor foresaw the danger, and provided the remedy. As he had minutely studied the operations of Trajan in the same country, he soon recollected that his warlike predecessor had dug a new and navigable canal, which, leaving Coche on the right hand, conveyed the waters of the Nahar-Malcha into the river Tigris at some distance *above* the cities. From the information of the peasants Julian ascertained the vestiges of this ancient work, which were almost obliterated by design or accident. By the indefatigable labour of the soldiers a broad and deep channel was speedily prepared for the reception of the Euphrates. A strong dyke was constructed to interrupt the ordinary current of the Nahar-Malcha: a flood of waters rushed impetuously into their new bed; and the Roman fleet, steering their triumphant course into the Tigris, derided the vain and ineffectual barriers which the Persians of Ctesiphon had erected to oppose their passage.

As it became necessary to transport the Roman army over the Tigris, another labour presented itself, of less toil, but of more danger, than the preceding expedition. The stream was broad and rapid, the ascent steep and difficult; and the entrenchments which had been formed on the ridge of the opposite bank were lined with a numerous army of heavy cuirassiers, dexterous archers, and huge elephants; who (according to the extravagant hyperbole of Libanius) could trample with the same ease a field of corn or a legion of Romans.[67] In the presence of such an enemy the construction of a bridge was impracticable; and the intrepid prince, who instantly seized the only possible expedient, concealed his design, till the moment of execution, from the knowledge of the barbarians, of his own troops, and even of his generals themselves. Under the specious pretence of examining the state of the magazines, fourscore vessels were gradually unladen; and a select detachment, apparently destined for some secret expedition, was ordered to stand to their arms on the first signal. Julian disguised the silent anxiety of his own mind with smiles of confidence and joy; and amused the hostile nations with the spectacle of military games, which he insultingly celebrated under the walls of Coche. The day was consecrated to pleasure; but, as soon as the hour of supper was past, the emperor summoned the generals to his tent, and acquainted them that he had fixed that night for the passage of the Tigris. They stood in silent and respectful astonishment; but when the venerable Sallust assumed the privilege of his age and experience, the rest of the chiefs supported with freedom the weight of his prudent remonstrances.[68] Julian contented himself with observing that conquest and safety depended on the attempt; that, instead of diminishing, the number of their enemies would be increased by successive reinforcements; and that a longer delay would neither contract the breadth of the stream nor level the height of the bank. The signal was instantly given, and obeyed: the most impatient of the legionaries leaped into five vessels that lay nearest to the bank; and, as they plied their oars with intrepid diligence, they were lost after a few moments in the darkness of the night. A flame arose on the opposite side; and Julian, who too clearly understood that his foremost vessels in attempting to land had been fired by the enemy, dexterously converted their extreme danger into a presage of victory. "Our fellow-soldiers," he eagerly exclaimed, "are already masters of the bank: see—they make the appointed signal; let us hasten to emulate and assist their courage." The united and rapid motion of a great fleet broke the violence of the current, and they reached the eastern shore of the Tigris with sufficient speed to extinguish the flames and rescue their adventurous companions. The difficulties of a steep and lofty ascent were increased by the weight of armour and the darkness of the night. A shower of stones, darts, and fire was incessantly discharged on the heads of the assailants; who, after an arduous struggle, climbed the bank and stood victorious upon the rampart. As soon as they possessed a more equal field, Julian, who with his light infantry had led the attack,[69] darted through the ranks a skilful and experienced eye; his bravest soldiers, according to the precepts of Homer,[70] were distributed in the front and rear; and all the trumpets of the Imperial army sounded to battle. The Romans, after sending up a military shout, advanced in measured steps to the animating notes of martial music; launched their formidable javelins, and rushed forwards with drawn swords to deprive the barbarians, by a closer onset, of the advantage of their missile weapons. The whole engagement lasted above twelve hours; till the gradual retreat of the Persians was changed into a disorderly flight, of which the shameful example was given by the principal leaders and the Surenas himself. They were pursued to the gates of Ctesiphon; and the conquerors might have entered the dismayed city,[71] if their general, Victor, who was dangerously wounded with an arrow, had not conjured them to desist from a rash attempt, which must be fatal if it were not successful. On *their* side the Romans acknowledged the loss of only seventy-five men; while they affirmed that the barbarians had left on the field of battle two thousand five hundred, or even six thousand, of their bravest soldiers. The spoil was such as might be expected from the riches and luxury of an Oriental camp; large quantities of silver and gold, splendid arms and trappings, and beds and tables of massive silver. The victorious emperor distributed, as the rewards of valour, some honourable gifts, civic, and mural, and naval crowns; which he, and perhaps he alone, esteemed more precious than the wealth of Asia. A solemn sacrifice was offered to the god of war, but the appearances of the victims threatened the most inauspicious events; and Julian soon discovered, by less ambiguous signs, that he had now reached the term of his prosperity.[72]

On the second day after the battle the domestic guards, the Jovians and Herculians, and the remaining troops, which composed near two-thirds of the whole army, were securely wafted over the Tigris.[73] While the Persians beheld from the walls of Ctesiphon the desolation of the adjacent country, Julian cast many an anxious look towards the North, in full expectation that, as he himself had victoriously penetrated to the

capital of Sapor, the march and junction of his lieutenants, Sebastian and Procopius, would be executed with the same courage and diligence. His expectations were disappointed by the treachery of the Armenian king, who permitted, and most probably directed, the desertion of his auxiliary troops from the camp of the Romans;[74] and by the dissensions of the two generals, who were incapable of forming or executing any plan for the public service. When the emperor had relinquished the hope of this important reinforcement, he condescended to hold a council of war, and approved, after a full debate, the sentiment of those generals who dissuaded the siege of Ctesiphon, as a fruitless and pernicious undertaking. It is not easy for us to conceive by what arts of fortification a city thrice besieged and taken by the predecessors of Julian could be rendered impregnable against an army of sixty thousand Romans, commanded by a brave and experienced general, and abundantly supplied with ships, provisions, battering engines, and military stores. But we may rest assured, from the love of glory, and contempt of danger, which formed the character of Julian, that he was not discouraged by any trivial or imaginary obstacles.[75] At the very time when he declined the siege of Ctesiphon, he rejected, with obstinacy and disdain, the most flattering offers of a negotiation of peace. Sapor, who had been so long accustomed to the tardy ostentation of Constantius, was surprised by the intrepid diligence of his successor. As far as the confines of India and Scythia, the satraps of the distant provinces were ordered to assemble their troops, and to march, without delay, to the assistance of their monarch. But their preparations were dilatory, their motions slow; and before Sapor could lead an army into the field, he received the melancholy intelligence of the devastation of Assyria, the ruin of his palaces, and the slaughter of his bravest troops, who defended the passage of the Tigris. The pride of royalty was humbled in the dust; he took his repasts on the ground; and the disorder of his hair expressed the grief and anxiety of his mind. Perhaps he would not have refused to purchase, with one half of his kingdom, the safety of the remainder; and he would have gladly subscribed himself, in a treaty of peace, the faithful and dependent ally of the Roman conqueror. Under the pretence of private business, a minister of rank and confidence was secretly despatched to embrace the knees of Hormisdas, and to request, in the language of a suppliant, that he might be introduced into the presence of the emperor. The Sassanian prince, whether he listened to the voice of pride or humanity, whether he consulted the sentiments of his birth or the duties of his situation, was equally inclined to promote a salutary measure which would terminate the calamities of Persia, and secure the triumph of Rome. He was astonished by the inflexible firmness of a hero who remembered, most unfortunately for himself and for his country, that Alexander had uniformly rejected the propositions of Darius. But as Julian was sensible that the hope of a safe and honourable peace might cool the ardour of his troops, he earnestly requested that Hormisdas would privately dismiss the minister of Sapor, and conceal this dangerous temptation from the knowledge of the camp.[76]

The honour, as well as interest, of Julian, forbade him to consume his time under the impregnable walls of Ctesiphon; and as often as he defied the barbarians, who defended the city, to meet him on the open plain, they prudently replied that, if he desired to exercise his valour, he might seek the army of the Great King. He felt the insult, and he accepted the advice. Instead of confining his servile march to the banks of the Euphrates and Tigris, he resolved to imitate the adventurous spirit of Alexander, and boldly to advance into the inland provinces, till he forced his rival to contend with him, perhaps in the plains of Arbela, for the empire of Asia. The magnanimity of Julian was applauded and betrayed by the arts of a noble Persian, who, in the cause of his country, had generously submitted to act a part full of danger, of falsehood, and of shame.[77] With a train of faithful followers he deserted to the Imperial camp; exposed, in a specious tale, the injuries which he had sustained; exaggerated the cruelty of Sapor, the discontent of the people, and the weakness of the monarchy; and confidently offered himself as the hostage and guide of the Roman march. The most rational grounds of suspicion were urged, without effect, by the wisdom and experience of Hormisdas; and the credulous Julian, receiving the traitor into his bosom, was persuaded to issue an hasty order, which, in the opinion of mankind, appeared to arraign his prudence and to endanger his safety. He destroyed in a single hour the whole navy, which had been transported above five hundred miles, at so great an expense of toil, of treasure, and of blood. Twelve, or, at the most, twenty-two, small vessels were saved, to accompany, on carriages, the march of the army, and to form occasional bridges for the passage of the rivers. A

supply of twenty days' provisions was reserved for the use of the soldiers; and the rest of the magazines, with a fleet of eleven hundred vessels, which rode at anchor in the Tigris, were abandoned to the flames by the absolute command of the emperor. The Christian bishops, Gregory and Augustin, insult the madness of the apostate, who executed, with his own hands, the sentence of divine justice. Their authority, of less weight, perhaps, in a military question, is confirmed by the cool judgment of an experienced soldier, who was himself spectator of the conflagration, and who could not disapprove the reluctant murmurs of the troops.[78] Yet there are not wanting some specious, and perhaps solid, reasons, which might justify the resolution of Julian. The navigation of the Euphrates never ascended above Babylon, nor that of the Tigris above Opis.[79] The distance of the last-mentioned city from the Roman camp was not very considerable; and Julian must soon have renounced the vain and impracticable attempt of forcing upwards a great fleet against the stream of a rapid river,[80] which in several places was embarrassed by natural or artificial cataracts.[81] The power of sails and oars was insufficient, it became necessary to tow the ships against the current of the river; the strength of twenty thousand soldiers was exhausted in this tedious and servile labour; and if the Romans continued to march along the banks of the Tigris, they could only expect to return home without achieving any enterprise worthy of the genius or fortune of their leader. If, on the contrary, it was advisable to advance into the inland country, the destruction of the fleet and magazines was the only measure which could save that valuable prize from the hands of the numerous and active troops which might suddenly be poured from the gates of Ctesiphon. Had the arms of Julian been victorious, we should now admire the conduct as well as the courage of a hero who, by depriving his soldiers of the hopes of a retreat, left them only the alternative of death or conquest.[82]

The cumbersome train of artillery and waggons, which retards the operations of a modern army, was in a great measure unknown in the camps of the Romans.[83] Yet, in every age, the subsistence of sixty thousand men must have been one of the most important cares of a prudent general; and that subsistence could only be drawn from his own or from the enemy's country. Had it been possible for Julian to maintain a bridge of communication on the Tigris, and to preserve the conquered places of

Assyria, a desolated province could not afford any large or regular supplies in a season of the year when the lands were covered by the inundation of the Euphrates,[84] and the unwholesome air was darkened with swarms of innumerable insects.[85] The appearance of the hostile country was far more inviting. The extensive region that lies between the river Tigris and the mountains of Media was filled with villages and towns; and the fertile soil, for the most part, was in a very improved state of cultivation. Julian might expect that a conqueror who possessed the two forcible instruments of persuasion, steel and gold, would easily procure a plentiful subsistence from the fears or avarice of the natives. But on the approach of the Romans this rich and smiling prospect was instantly blasted. Wherever they moved, the inhabitants deserted the open villages and took shelter in the fortified towns; the cattle was driven away; the grass and ripe corn were consumed with fire; and, as soon as the flames had subsided which interrupted the march of Julian, he beheld the melancholy face of a smoking and naked desert. This desperate but effectual method of defence can only be executed by the enthusiasm of a people who prefer their independence to their property; or by the rigour of an arbitrary government, which consults the public safety without submitting to their inclinations the liberty of choice. On the present occasion the zeal and obedience of the Persians seconded the commands of Sapor; and the emperor was soon reduced to the scanty stock of provisions which continually wasted in his hands. Before they were entirely consumed he might still have reached the wealthy and unwarlike cities of Ecbatana or Susa by the effort of a rapid and well-directed march;[86] but he was deprived of this last resource by his ignorance of the roads and by the perfidy of his guides. The Romans wandered several days in the country to the eastward of Bagdad; the Persian deserter, who had artfully led them into the snare, escaped from their resentment; and his followers, as soon as they were put to the torture, confessed the secret of the conspiracy. The visionary conquests of Hyrcania and India, which had so long amused, now tormented, the mind of Julian. Conscious that his own imprudence was the cause of the public distress, he anxiously balanced the hopes of safety or success without obtaining a satisfactory answer either from gods or men. At length, as the only practicable measure, he embraced the resolution of directing his steps towards the banks of the Tigris, with the design of saving the army by a hasty march to the confines of Corduene, a fertile and friendly province, which acknowledged the sovereignty of Rome. The desponding troops obeyed the signal of retreat, only seventy days after they had passed the Chaboras with the sanguine expectation of subverting the throne of Persia.[87]

As long as the Romans seemed to advance into the country, their march was observed and insulted from a distance by several bodies of Persian cavalry; who, showing themselves, sometimes in loose, and sometimes in closer order, faintly skirmished with the advanced guards. These detachments were, however, supported by a much greater force; and the heads of the columns were no sooner pointed towards the Tigris than a cloud of dust arose on the plain. The Romans, who now aspired only to the permission of a safe and speedy retreat, endeavoured to persuade themselves that this formidable appearance was occasioned by a troop of wild asses, or perhaps by the approach of some friendly Arabs. They halted, pitched their tents, fortified their camp, passed the whole night in continual alarms; and discovered at the dawn of day that they were surrounded by an army of Persians. This army, which might be considered only as the van of the barbarians, was soon followed by the main body of cuirassiers, archers, and elephants, commanded by Meranes, a general of rank and reputation. He was accompanied by two of the king's sons and many of the principal satraps; and fame and expectation exaggerated the strength of the remaining powers, which slowly advanced under the conduct of Sapor himself. As the Romans continued their march, their long array, which was forced to bend or divide, according to the varieties of the ground, afforded frequent and favourable opportunities to their vigilant enemies. The Persians repeatedly charged with fury; they were repeatedly repulsed with firmness; and the action at Maronga, which almost deserved the name of a battle, was marked by a considerable loss of satraps and elephants, perhaps of equal value in the eyes of their monarch. These splendid advantages were not obtained without an adequate slaughter on the side of the Romans: several officers of distinction were either killed or wounded; and the emperor himself, who, on all occasions of danger, inspired and guided the valour of his troops, was obliged to expose his person and exert his abilities. The weight of offensive and defensive arms, which still constituted the strength and safety of the Romans, disabled them from making any long or effectual pursuit; and as the horsemen of the East were trained to dart their javelins and shoot their arrows at full speed, and in every possible direction,[88] the cavalry of Persia was never more formidable than in the moment of a rapid and disorderly flight. But the most certain and irreparable loss of the Romans was that of time. The hardy veterans, accustomed to the cold climate of Gaul and Germany, fainted under the sultry heat of an Assyrian summer; their vigour was exhausted by the incessant repetition of march and combat; and the progress of the army was suspended by the precautions of a slow and dangerous retreat in the presence of an active enemy. Every day, every hour, as the supply diminished, the value and price of subsistence increased in the Roman camp.[89] Julian, who always contented himself with such food as a hungry soldier would have disdained, distributed, for the use of the troops, the provisions of the Imperial household, and whatever could be spared from the sumpter-horses of the tribunes and generals. But this feeble relief served only to aggravate the sense of the public distress; and the Romans began to entertain the most gloomy apprehensions that, before they could reach the frontiers of the empire, they should all perish, either by famine or by the sword of the barbarians.[90]

While Julian struggled with the almost insuperable difficulties of his situation, the silent hours of the night were still devoted to study and contemplation. Whenever he closed his eyes in short and interrupted slumbers, his mind was agitated with painful anxiety: nor can it be thought surprising that the Genius of the empire should once more appear before him, covering with a funeral veil his head and his horn of abundance, and slowly retiring from the Imperial tent. The monarch started from his couch, and, stepping forth to refresh his wearied spirits with the coolness of the midnight air, he beheld a fiery meteor, which shot athwart the sky, and suddenly vanished. Julian was convinced that he had seen the menacing countenance of the god of war;[91] the council which he summoned, of Tuscan Haruspices,[92] unanimously pronounced that he should abstain from action; but, on this occasion, necessity and reason were more prevalent than superstition; and the trumpets sounded at the break of day. The army marched through a hilly country; and the hills had been secretly occupied by the Persians. Julian led the van with the skill and attention of a consummate general; he was alarmed by the intelligence that his rear was

suddenly attacked. The heat of the weather had tempted him to lay aside his cuirass; but he snatched a shield from one of his attendants, and hastened, with a sufficient reinforcement, to the relief of the rear guard. A similar danger recalled the intrepid prince to the defence of the front; and, as he galloped between the columns, the centre of the left was attacked, and almost overpowered, by a furious charge of the Persian cavalry and elephants. This huge body was soon defeated by the well-timed evolution of the light infantry, who aimed their weapons, with dexterity and effect, against the backs of the horsemen, and the legs of the elephants. The barbarians fled: and Julian, who was foremost in every danger, animated the pursuit with his voice and gestures. His trembling guards, scattered and oppressed by the disorderly throng of friends and enemies, reminded their fearless sovereign that he was without armour; and conjured him to decline the fall of the impending ruin. As they exclaimed,[93] a cloud of darts and arrows was discharged from the flying squadrons; and a javelin, after razing the skin of his arm, transpierced the ribs, and fixed in the inferior part of the liver. Julian attempted to draw the deadly weapon from his side; but his fingers were cut by the sharpness of the steel, and he fell senseless from his horse. His guards flew to his relief; and the wounded emperor was gently raised from the ground, and conveyed out of the tumult of the battle into an adjacent tent. The report of the melancholy event passed from rank to rank; but the grief of the Romans inspired them with invincible valour, and the desire of revenge. The bloody and obstinate conflict was maintained by the two armies till they were separated by the total darkness of the night. The Persians derived some honour from the advantage which they obtained against the left wing, where Anatolius, master of the offices, was slain, and the præfect Sallust very narrowly escaped. But the event of the day was adverse to the barbarians. They abandoned the field; their two generals, Meranes and Nohordates,[94] fifty nobles or satraps, and a multitude of their bravest soldiers [were slain]: and the success of the Romans, if Julian had survived, might have been improved into a decisive and useful victory.

The first words that Julian uttered, after his recovery from the fainting fit into which he had been thrown by loss of blood, were expressive of his martial spirit. He called for his horse and arms, and was impatient to rush into the battle. His remaining strength was exhausted by the painful effort; and the surgeons, who examined his wound, discovered the symptoms of approaching death. He employed the awful moments with the firm temper of a hero and a sage; the philosophers who had accompanied him in this fatal expedition compared the tent of Julian with the prison of Socrates; and the spectators, whom duty, or friendship, or curiosity, had assembled round his couch, listened with respectful grief to the funeral oration of their dying emperor.[95] "Friends and fellow-soldiers, the seasonable period of my departure is now arrived, and I discharge, with the cheerfulness of a ready debtor, the demands of nature. I have learned from philosophy how much the soul is more excellent than the body; and that the separation of the nobler substance should be the subject of joy, rather than of affliction. I have learned from religion that an early death has often been the reward of piety;[96] and I accept, as a favour of the gods, the mortal stroke that secures me from the danger of disgracing a character which has hitherto been supported by virtue and fortitude. I die without remorse, as I have lived without guilt. I am pleased to reflect on the innocence of my private life; and I can affirm with confidence that the supreme authority, that emanation of the Divine Power, has been preserved in my hands pure and immaculate. Detesting the corrupt and destructive maxims of despotism, I have considered the happiness of the people as the end of government. Submitting my actions to the laws of prudence, of justice, and of moderation, I have trusted the event to the care of Providence. Peace was the object of my counsels, as long as peace was consistent with the public welfare; but when the imperious voice of my country summoned me to arms, I exposed my person to the dangers of war, with the clear foreknowledge (which I had acquired from the art of divination) that I was destined to fall by the sword. I now offer my tribute of gratitude to the Eternal Being, who has not suffered me to perish by the cruelty of a tyrant, by the secret dagger of conspiracy, or by the slow tortures of lingering disease. He has given me, in the midst of an honourable career, a splendid and glorious departure from this world; and I hold it equally absurd, equally base, to solicit, or to decline, the stroke of fate.—Thus much I have attempted to say; but my strength fails me, and I feel the approach of death.—I shall cautiously refrain from any word that may tend to influence your suffrages in the election of an emperor. My choice might be imprudent or injudicious; and if it should not be ratified by

the consent of the army, it might be fatal to the person whom I should recommend. I shall only, as a good citizen, express my hopes that the Romans may be blessed with the government of a virtuous sovereign." After this discourse, which Julian pronounced in a firm and gentle tone of voice, he distributed, by a military testament,[97] the remains of his private fortune; and making some inquiry why Anatolius was not present, he understood, from the answer of Sallust, that Anatolius was killed; and bewailed, with amiable inconsistency, the loss of his friend. At the same time he reproved the immoderate grief of the spectators; and conjured them not to disgrace, by unmanly tears, the fate of a prince who in a few moments would be united with heaven and with the stars.[98] The spectators were silent; and Julian entered into a metaphysical argument with the philosophers Priscus and Maximus on the nature of the soul. The efforts which he made, of mind as well as body, most probably hastened his death. His wound began to bleed with fresh violence: his respiration was embarrassed by the swelling of the veins: he called for a draught of cold water, and, as soon as he had drunk it, expired without pain, about the hour of midnight. Such was the end of that extraordinary man, in the thirty-second year of his age, after a reign of one year and about eight months from the death of Constantius. In his last moments he displayed, perhaps with some ostentation, the love of virtue and of fame, which had been the ruling passions of his life.[99]

The triumph of Christianity, and the calamities of the empire, may, in some measure, be ascribed to Julian himself, who had neglected to secure the future execution of his designs by the timely and judicious nomination of an associate and successor. But the royal race of Constantius Chlorus was reduced to his own person; and if he entertained any serious thoughts of investing with the purple the most worthy among the Romans, he was diverted from his resolution by the difficulty of the choice, the jealousy of power, the fear of ingratitude, and the natural presumption of health, of youth, and of prosperity. His unexpected death left the empire without a master, and without an heir, in a state of perplexity and danger which, in the space of fourscore years, had never been experienced, since the election of Diocletian. In a government which had almost forgotten the distinction of pure and noble blood, the superiority of birth was of little moment; the claims of official rank were accidental and precarious; and the candidates who might aspire to ascend the vacant throne could be supported only by the consciousness of personal merit, or by the hopes of popular favour. But the situation of a famished army, encompassed on all sides by an host of barbarians, shortened the moments of grief and deliberation. In this scene of terror and distress, the body of the deceased prince, according to his own directions, was decently embalmed; and, at the dawn of day, the generals convened a military senate, at which the commanders of the legions, and the officers both of cavalry and infantry, were invited to assist. Three or four hours of the night had not passed away without some secret cabals; and when the election of an emperor was proposed, the spirit of faction began to agitate the assembly. Victor and Arinthæus collected the remains of the court of Constantius; the friends of Julian attached themselves to the Gallic chiefs Dagalaiphus and Nevitta; and the most fatal consequences might be apprehended from the discord of two factions, so opposite in their character and interest, in their maxims of government, and perhaps in their religious principles. The superior virtues of Sallust could alone reconcile their divisions and unite their suffrages; and the venerable præfect would immediately have been declared the successor of Julian, if he himself, with sincere and modest firmness, had not alleged his age and infirmities, so unequal to the weight of the diadem. The generals, who were surprised and perplexed by his refusal, showed some disposition to adopt the salutary advice of an inferior officer,[100] that they should act as they would have acted in the absence of the emperor; that they should exert their abilities to extricate the army from the present distress; and, if they were fortunate enough to reach the confines of Mesopotamia, they should proceed with united and deliberate counsels in the election of a lawful sovereign. While they debated, a few voices saluted Jovian, who was no more than *first*[101] of the domestics, with the names of Emperor and Augustus. The tumultuary acclamation was instantly repeated by the guards who surrounded the tent, and passed, in a few minutes, to the extremities of the line. The new prince, astonished with his own fortune, was hastily invested with the Imperial ornaments, and received an oath of fidelity from the generals, whose favour and protection he so lately solicited. The strongest recommendation of Jovian was the merit of his father, Count Varronian, who enjoyed, in honourable retirement, the fruit of his long services. In the obscure freedom of a private station, the son indulged his taste for wine and women; yet he supported, with credit, the character of a Christian[102] and a soldier. Without being conspicuous for any of the ambitious qualifications which excite the admiration and envy of mankind, the comely person of Jovian, his cheerful temper, and familiar wit, had gained the affection of his fellow soldiers; and the generals of both parties acquiesced in a popular election which had not been conducted by the arts of their enemies. The pride of this unexpected elevation was moderated by the just apprehension that the same day might terminate the life and reign of the new emperor. The pressing voice of necessity was obeyed without delay; and the first orders issued by Jovian, a few hours after his predecessor had expired, were to prosecute a march which could alone extricate the Romans from their actual distress.[103]

The esteem of an enemy is more sincerely expressed by his fears; and the degree of fear may be accurately measured by the joy with which he celebrates his deliverance. The welcome news of the death of Julian, which a deserter revealed to the camp of Sapor, inspired the desponding monarch with a sudden confidence of victory. He immediately detached the royal cavalry, perhaps the ten thousand *Immortals*,[104] to second and support the pursuit; and discharged the whole weight of his united forces on the rear-guard of the Romans. The rear-guard was thrown into disorder; the renowned legions, which derived their title from Diocletian and his warlike colleague, were broke and trampled down by the elephants; and three tribunes lost their lives in attempting to stop the flight of their soldiers. The battle was at length restored by the persevering valour of the Romans; the Persians were repulsed with a great slaughter of men and elephants; and the army, after marching and fighting a long summer's day, arrived, in the evening, at Samara, on the banks of the Tigris, about one hundred miles above Ctesiphon.[105] On the ensuing day the barbarians, instead of harassing the march, attacked the camp of Jovian, which had been seated in a deep and sequestered valley. From the hills, the archers of Persia insulted and annoyed the wearied legionaries; and a body of cavalry, which had penetrated with desperate courage through the Prætorian gate, was cut in pieces, after a doubtful conflict, near the Imperial tent. In the succeeding night the camp of Carche was protected by the lofty dykes of the river; and the Roman army, though incessantly exposed to the vexatious pursuit of the Saracens, pitched their tents near the city of Dura[106] four days after the death of Julian. The Tigris was still on their left; their hopes and provisions were almost consumed; and the impatient soldiers, who had fondly persuaded themselves that the frontiers of the empire were not far distant, requested their new sovereign that they might be permitted to hazard the passage of the river. With the assistance of his wisest officers, Jovian endeavoured to check their rashness, by representing that, if they possessed sufficient skill and vigour to stem the torrent of a deep and rapid stream, they would only deliver themselves naked and defenceless to the barbarians, who had occupied the opposite banks. Yielding at length to their clamourous importunities, he consented, with reluctance, that five hundred Gauls and Germans, accustomed from their infancy to the waters of the Rhine and Danube, should attempt the bold adventure, which might serve either as an encouragement or as a warning for the rest of the army. In the silence of the night they swam the Tigris, surprised an unguarded post of the enemy, and displayed at the dawn of day the signal of their resolution and fortune. The success of this trial disposed the emperor to listen to the promises of his architects, who proposed to construct a floating bridge of the inflated skins of sheep, oxen, and goats, covered with a floor of earth and fascines.[107] Two important days were spent in the ineffectual labour; and the Romans, who already endured the miseries of famine, cast a look of despair on the Tigris, and upon the barbarians, whose numbers and obstinacy increased with the distress of the Imperial army.[108]

In this hopeless situation, the fainting spirits of the Romans were revived by the sound of peace. The transient presumption of Sapor had vanished: he observed, with serious concern, that, in the repetition of doubtful combats, he had lost his most faithful and intrepid nobles, his bravest troops, and the greatest part of his train of elephants: and the experienced monarch feared to provoke the resistance of despair, the vicissitudes of fortune, and the unexhausted powers of the Roman empire, which might soon advance to relieve, or to revenge, the successor of Julian. The Surenas himself, accompanied by another satrap, appeared in the camp of Jovian,[109] and declared that the clemency of his sovereign was not averse to signify the conditions on which he would consent to spare and to dismiss the Cæsar with the relics of his captive army. The hopes of safety subdued the firmness of the Romans; the emperor was compelled,

by the advice of his council and the cries of the soldiers, to embrace the offer of peace; and the præfect Sallust was immediately sent, with the general Arinthæus, to understand the pleasure of the Great King. The crafty Persian delayed, under various pretences, the conclusion of the agreement; started difficulties, required explanations, suggested expedients, receded from his concessions, increased his demands, and wasted four days in the arts of negotiation, till he had consumed the stock of provisions which yet remained in the camp of the Romans. Had Jovian been capable of executing a bold and prudent measure, he would have continued his march with unremitting diligence; the progress of the treaty would have suspended the attacks of the barbarians; and, before the expiration of the fourth day, he might have safely reached the fruitful province of Corduene, at the distance only of one hundred miles.[110] The irresolute emperor, instead of breaking through the toils of the enemy, expected his fate with patient resignation; and accepted the humiliating conditions of peace which it was no longer in his power to refuse. The five provinces beyond the Tigris, which had been ceded by the grandfather of Sapor, were restored to the Persian monarchy. He acquired, by a single article, the impregnable city of Nisibis, which had sustained, in three successive sieges, the effort of his arms. Singara and the castle of the Moors, one of the strongest places of Mesopotamia, were likewise dismembered from the empire. It was considered as an indulgence that the inhabitants of those fortresses were permitted to retire with their effects; but the conqueror rigorously insisted that the Romans should for ever abandon the king and kingdom of Armenia. A peace, or rather a long truce, of thirty years, was stipulated between the hostile nations; the faith of the treaty was ratified by solemn oaths and religious ceremonies; and hostages of distinguished rank were reciprocally delivered to secure the performance of the condition.[111]

The sophist of Antioch, who saw with indignation the sceptre of his hero in the feeble hand of a Christian successor, professes to admire the moderation of Sapor in contenting himself with so small a portion of the Roman empire. If he had stretched as far as the Euphrates the claims of his ambition, he might have been secure, says Libanius, of not meeting with a refusal. If he had fixed, as the boundary of Persia, the Orontes, the Cydnus, the Sangarius, or even the Thracian Bosphorus, flatterers would not have been wanting in the court of Jovian to convince the timid monarch that his remaining provinces would still afford the most ample gratifications of power and luxury.[112] Without adopting in its full force this malicious insinuation, we must acknowledge that the conclusion of so ignominious a treaty was facilitated by the private ambition of Jovian. The obscure domestic, exalted to the throne by fortune, rather than by merit, was impatient to escape from the hands of the Persians, that he might prevent the designs of Procopius, who commanded the army of Mesopotamia, and establish his doubtful reign over the legions and provinces which were still ignorant of the hasty and tumultuous choice of the camp beyond the Tigris.[113] In the neighbourhood of the same river, at no very considerable distance from the fatal station of Dura,[114] the ten thousand Greeks, without generals, or guides, or provisions, were abandoned, above twelve hundred miles from their native country, to the resentment of a victorious monarch. The difference of *their* conduct and success depended much more on their character than on their situation. Instead of tamely resigning themselves to the secret deliberations and private views of a single person, the united councils of the Greeks were inspired by the generous enthusiasm of a popular assembly, where the mind of each citizen is filled with the love of glory, the pride of freedom, and the contempt of death. Conscious of their superiority over the barbarians in arms and discipline, they disdained to yield, they refused to capitulate: every obstacle was surmounted by their patience, courage, and military skill; and the memorable retreat of the ten thousand exposed and insulted the weakness of the Persian monarchy.[115]

As the price of his disgraceful concessions, the emperor might perhaps have stipulated that the camp of the hungry Romans should be plentifully supplied,[116] and that they should be permitted to pass the Tigris on the bridge which was constructed by the hands of the Persians. But if Jovian presumed to solicit those equitable terms, they were sternly refused by the haughty tyrant of the East, whose clemency had pardoned the invaders of his country. The Saracens sometimes intercepted the stragglers on the march; but the generals and troops of Sapor respected the cessation of arms, and Jovian was suffered to explore the most convenient place for the passage of the river. The small vessels which had been saved from the conflagration of the fleet performed the most essential service. They first conveyed the emperor and his favourites, and afterwards transported, in many successive voyages, a great part of the army. But as every man was anxious for his personal safety and apprehensive of being left on the hostile shore, the soldiers, who were too impatient to wait the slow returns of the boats, boldly ventured themselves on light hurdles or inflated skins, and drawing after them their horses, attempted, with various success, to swim across the river. Many of these daring adventurers were swallowed by the waves; many others, who were carried along by the violence of the stream, fell an easy prey to the avarice or cruelty of the wild Arabs; and the loss which the army sustained in the passage of the Tigris was not inferior to the carnage of a day of battle. As soon as the Romans had landed on the western bank, they were delivered from the hostile pursuit of the barbarians; but in a laborious march of two hundred miles over the plains of Mesopotamia they endured the last extremities of thirst and hunger. They were obliged to traverse a sandy desert, which, in the extent of seventy miles, did not afford a single blade of sweet grass nor a single spring of fresh water, and the rest of the inhospitable waste was untrod by the footsteps either of friend or enemies. Whenever a small measure of flour could be discovered in the camp, twenty pounds weight were greedily purchased with ten pieces of gold,[117] the beasts of burden were slaughtered and devoured, and the desert was strewed with the arms and baggage of the Roman soldiers, whose tattered garments and meagre countenances displayed their past sufferings and actual misery. A small convoy of provisions advanced to meet the army as far as the castle of Ur; and the supply was the more grateful, since it declared the fidelity of Sebastian and Procopius. At Thilsaphata[118] the emperor most graciously received the generals of Mesopotamia, and the remains of a once flourishing army at length reposed themselves under the walls of Nisibis. The messengers of Jovian had already proclaimed, in the language of flattery, his election, his treaty, and his return, and the new prince had taken the most effectual measures to secure the allegiance of the armies and provinces of Europe by placing the military command in the hands of those officers who, from motives of interest or inclination, would firmly support the cause of their benefactor.[119]

The friends of Julian had confidently announced the success of his expedition. They entertained a fond persuasion that the temples of the gods would be enriched with the spoils of the East; that Persia would be reduced to the humble state of a tributary province, governed by the laws and magistrates of Rome; that the barbarians would adopt the dress, and manners, and language of their conquerors; and that the youth of Ecbatana and Susa would study the art of rhetoric under Grecian masters.[120] The progress of the arms of Julian interrupted his communication with the empire, and, from the moment that he passed the Tigris, his affectionate subjects were ignorant of the fate and fortunes of their prince. Their contemplation of fancied triumphs was disturbed by the melancholy rumour of his death, and they persisted to doubt, after they could no longer deny, the truth of that fatal event.[121] The messengers of Jovian promulgated the specious tale of a prudent and necessary peace; the voice of fame, louder and more sincere, revealed the disgrace of the emperor and the conditions of the ignominious treaty. The minds of the people were filled with astonishment and grief, with indignation and terror, when they were informed that the unworthy successor of Julian relinquished the five provinces which had been acquired by the victory of Galerius, and that he shamefully surrendered to the barbarians the important city of Nisibis, the firmest bulwark of the provinces of the East.[122] The deep and dangerous question, how far the public faith should be observed when it becomes incompatible with the public safety, was freely agitated in popular conversation, and some hopes were entertained that the emperor would redeem his pusillanimous behaviour by a splendid act of patriotic perfidy. The inflexible spirit of the Roman senate had always disclaimed the unequal conditions which were extorted from the distress of her captive armies; and, if it were necessary to satisfy the national honour by delivering the guilty general into the hands of the barbarians, the greatest part of the subjects of Jovian would have cheerfully acquiesced in the precedent of ancient times.[123]

But the emperor, whatever might be the limits of his constitutional authority, was the absolute master of the laws and arms of the state; and the same motives which had forced him to subscribe, now pressed him to execute the treaty of peace. He was impatient to secure an empire at the expense of a few provinces, and the respectable names of religion and honour concealed the personal fears and the ambition of Jovian. Notwithstanding the dutiful solicitations of the inhabitants, decency, as well as prudence, forbade the emperor to lodge in the palace of Nisibis; but the next morning after his arrival,

Bineses, the ambassador of Persia, entered the place, displayed from the citadel the standard of the Great King, and proclaimed, in his name, the cruel alternative of exile or servitude. The principal citizens of Nisibis, who till that fatal moment, had confided in the protection of their sovereign, threw themselves at his feet. They conjured him not to abandon, or at least not to deliver, a faithful colony to the rage of a barbarian tyrant, exasperated by the three successive defeats which he had experienced under the walls of Nisibis. They still possessed arms and courage to repel the invaders of their country; they requested only the permission of using them in their own defence, and, as soon as they had asserted their independence, they should implore the favour of being again admitted into the rank of his subjects. Their arguments, their eloquence, their tears, were ineffectual. Jovian alleged, with some confusion, the sanctity of oaths; and as the reluctance with which he accepted the present of a crown of gold convinced the citizens of their hopeless condition, the advocate Sylvanus was provoked to exclaim, "O emperor! may you thus be crowned by all the cities of your dominions!" Jovian, who in a few weeks had assumed the habits of a prince,[124] was displeased with freedom, and offended with truth; and as he reasonably supposed that the discontent of the people might incline them to submit to the Persian government, he published an edict, under pain of death, that they should leave the city within the term of three days. Ammianus has delineated in lively colours the scene of universal despair, which he seems to have viewed with an eye of compassion.[125] The martial youth deserted, with indignant grief, the walls which they had so gloriously defended; the disconsolate mourner dropped a last tear over the tomb of a son or husband, which must soon be profaned by the rude hand of a barbarian master; and the aged citizen kissed the threshold and clung to the doors of the house where he had passed the cheerful and careless hours of infancy. The highways were crowded with a trembling multitude; the distinctions of rank, and sex, and age, were lost in the general calamity. Every one strove to bear away some fragment from the wreck of his fortunes; and as they could not command the immediate service of an adequate number of horses or waggons, they were obliged to leave behind them the greatest part of their valuable effects. The savage insensibility of Jovian appears to have aggravated the hardships of these unhappy fugitives. They were seated, however, in a new-built quarter of Amida; and that rising city, with the reinforcement of a very considerable colony, soon recovered its former splendour and became the capital of Mesopotamia.[126] Similar orders were despatched by the emperor for the evacuation of Singara and the castle of the Moors, and for the restitution of the five provinces beyond the Tigris. Sapor enjoyed the glory and the fruits of his victory; and this ignominious peace has justly been considered as a memorable era in the decline and fall of the Roman empire. The predecessors of Jovian had sometimes relinquished the dominion of distant and unprofitable provinces; but, since the foundation of the city, the genius of Rome, the god Terminus, who guarded the boundaries of the republic, had never retired before the sword of a victorious enemy.[127]

After Jovian had performed those engagements which the voice of his people might have tempted him to violate, he hastened away from the scene of his disgrace, and proceeded with his whole court to enjoy the luxury of Antioch.[128] Without consulting the dictates of religious zeal, he was prompted, by humanity and gratitude, to bestow the last honours on the remains of his deceased sovereign;[129] and Procopius, who sincerely bewailed the loss of his kinsman, was removed from the command of the army, under the decent pretence of conducting the funeral. The corpse of Julian was transported from Nisibis to Tarsus, in a slow march of fifteen days, and, as it passed through the cities of the East, was saluted by the hostile factions with mournful lamentations and clamorous insults. The Pagans already placed their beloved hero in the rank of those gods whose worship he had restored, while the invectives of the Christians pursued the soul of the apostate to hell, and his body to the grave.[130] One party lamented the approaching ruin of their altars, the other celebrated the marvellous deliverance of the church. The Christians applauded, in lofty and ambiguous strains, the stroke of divine vengeance which had been so long suspended over the guilty head of Julian. They acknowledged that the death of the tyrant, at the instant he expired beyond the Tigris, was *revealed* to the saints of Egypt, Syria, and Cappadocia;[131] and instead of suffering him to fall by the Persian darts, their indiscretion ascribed the heroic deed to the obscure hand of some mortal or immortal champion of the

faith.[132] Such imprudent declarations were eagerly adopted by the malice or credulity of their adversaries,[133] who darkly insinuated or confidently asserted that the governors of the church had instigated and directed the fanaticism of a domestic assassin.[134] Above sixteen years after the death of Julian, the charge was solemnly and vehemently urged in a public oration addressed by Libanius to the emperor Theodosius. His suspicions are unsupported by fact or argument, and we can only esteem the generous zeal of the sophist of Antioch for the cold and neglected ashes of his friend.[135]

It was an ancient custom in the funerals, as well as in the triumphs of the Romans that the voice of praise should be corrected by that of satire and ridicule, and that, in the midst of the splendid pageants which displayed the glory of the living or of the dead, their imperfections should not be concealed from the eyes of the world.[136] This custom was practised in the funeral of Julian. The comedians, who resented his contempt and aversion for the theatre, exhibited, with the applause of a Christian audience, the lively and exaggerated representation of the faults and follies of the deceased emperor. His various character and singular manners afforded an ample scope for pleasantry and ridicule.[137] In the exercise of his uncommon talents he often descended below the majesty of his rank. Alexander was transformed into Diogenes —the philosopher was degraded into a priest. The purity of his virtue was sullied by excessive vanity; his superstition disturbed the peace and endangered the safety of a mighty empire; and his irregular sallies were the less entitled to indulgence, as they appeared to be the laborious efforts of art, or even of affectation. The remains of Julian were interred at Tarsus in Cilicia; but his stately tomb, which arose in that city on the banks of the cold and limpid Cydnus,[138] was displeasing to the faithful friends who loved and revered the memory of that extraordinary man. The philosopher expressed a very reasonable wish that the disciple of Plato might have reposed amidst the groves of the Academy,[139] while the soldier exclaimed, in bolder accents, that the ashes of Julian should have been mingled with those of Cæsar, in the field of Mars, and among the ancient monuments of Roman virtue.[140] The history of princes does not very frequently renew the example of a similar competition.

CHAPTER XXV

The Government and Death of Jovian. Election of Valentinian, who associates his Brother Valens, and makes the final Division of the Eastern and Western Empires. Revolt of Procopius. Civil and Ecclesiastical Administration. Germany. Britain. Africa. The East. The Danube. Death of Valentinian. His two Sons, Gratian and Valentinian II., succeed to the Western Empire.

THE death of Julian had left the public affairs of the empire in a very doubtful and dangerous situation. The Roman army was saved by an inglorious, perhaps a necessary, treaty;[1] and the first moments of peace were consecrated by the pious Jovian to restore the domestic tranquillity of the church and state. The indiscretion of his predecessor, instead of reconciling, had artfully fomented the religious war; and the balance which he affected to preserve between the hostile factions served only to perpetuate the contest by the vicissitudes of hope and fear, by the rival claims of ancient possession and actual favour. The Christians had forgotten the spirit of the Gospel, and the Pagans had imbibed the spirit of the church. In private families the sentiments of nature were extinguished by the blind fury of zeal and revenge; the majesty of the laws was violated or abused; the cities of the East were stained with blood; and the most implacable enemies of the Romans were in the bosom of their country. Jovian was educated in the profession of Christianity; and as he marched from Nisibis to Antioch, the banner of the Cross, the LABARUM of Constantine, which was again displayed at the head of the legions, announced to the people the faith of their new emperor. As soon as he ascended the throne he transmitted a circular epistle to all the governors of provinces, in which he confessed the divine truth and secured the legal establishment of the Christian religion. The insidious edicts of Julian were abolished, the ecclesiastical immunities were restored and enlarged, and Jovian condescended to lament that the distress of the times obliged him to diminish the measure of charitable distributions.[2] The Christians were unanimous in the loud and sincere applause which they bestowed on the pious successor of Julian; but they were still ignorant what creed or what synod he would choose for the standard of orthodoxy, and the peace of the church immediately revived those eager disputes which had been suspended during the season of persecution. The episcopal

leaders of the contending sects, convinced from experience how much their fate would depend on the earliest impressions that were made on the mind of an untutored soldier, hastened to the court of Edessa, or Antioch. The highways of the East were crowded with Homoousian, and Arian, and Semi-Arian, and Eunomian bishops, who struggled to outstrip each other in the holy race; the apartments of the palace resounded with their clamours, and the ears of the prince were assaulted, and perhaps astonished, by the singular mixture of metaphysical argument and passionate invective.[3] The moderation of Jovian, who recommended concord and charity, and referred the disputants to the sentence of a future council, was interpreted as a symptom of indifference; but his attachment to the Nicene Creed was at length discovered and declared by the reverence which he expressed for the *celestial*[4] virtues of the great Athanasius. The intrepid veteran of the faith, at the age of seventy, had issued from his retreat on the first intelligence of the tyrant's death. The acclamations of the people seated him once more on the archiepiscopal throne, and he wisely accepted or anticipated the invitation of Jovian. The venerable figure of Athanasius, his calm courage and insinuating eloquence, sustained the reputation which he had already acquired in the courts of four successive princes.[5] As soon as he had gained the confidence and secured the faith of the Christian emperor, he returned in triumph to his diocese, and continued, with mature counsels and undiminished vigour, to direct, ten years longer,[6] the ecclesiastical government of Alexandria, Egypt, and the Catholic church. Before his departure from Antioch, he assured Jovian that his orthodox devotion would be rewarded with a long and peaceful reign. Athanasius had reason to hope that he should be allowed either the merit of a successful prediction, or the excuse of a grateful though ineffectual prayer.[7]

The slightest force, when it is applied to assist and guide the natural descent of its object, operates with irresistible weight; and Jovian had the good fortune to embrace the religious opinions which were supported by the spirit of the times, and the zeal and numbers of the most powerful sect.[8] Under his reign Christianity obtained an easy and lasting victory; and as soon as the smile of royal patronage was withdrawn, the genius of Paganism, which had been fondly raised and cherished by the arts of Julian, sunk irrecoverably in the dust. In many cities the temples were shut or deserted; the philosophers, who had abused their transient favour, thought it prudent to shave their beards and disguise their profession; and the Christians rejoiced that they were now in a condition to forgive or to revenge the injuries which they had suffered under the preceding reign.[9] The consternation of the Pagan world was dispelled by a wise and gracious edict of toleration, in which Jovian explicitly declared that, although he should severely punish the sacrilegious rites of magic, his subjects might exercise, with freedom and safety, the ceremonies of the ancient worship. The memory of this law has been preserved by the orator Themistius, who was deputed by the senate of Constantinople to express their loyal devotion for the new emperor. Themistius expatiates on the clemency of the Divine Nature, the facility of human error, the rights of conscience, and the independence of the mind, and, with some eloquence, inculcates the principles of philosophical toleration, whose aid Superstition herself, in the hour of her distress, is not ashamed to implore. He justly observes that in the recent changes both religions had been alternately disgraced by the seeming acquisition of worthless proselytes, of those votaries of the reigning purple who could pass, without a reason and without a blush, from the church to the temple, and from the altars of Jupiter to the sacred table of the Christians.[10]

In the space of seven months the Roman troops, who were now returned to Antioch, had performed a march of fifteen hundred miles, in which they had endured all the hardships of war, of famine, and of climate. Notwithstanding their services, their fatigues, and the approach of winter, the timid and impatient Jovian allowed only to the men and horses a respite of six weeks. The emperor could not sustain the indiscreet and malicious raillery of the people of Antioch.[11] He was impatient to possess the palace of Constantinople, and to prevent the ambition of some competitor who might occupy the vacant allegiance of Europe; but he soon received the grateful intelligence that his author-

ity was acknowledged from the Thracian Bosphorus to the Atlantic ocean. By the first letters which he despatched from the camp of Mesopotamia, he had delegated the military command of Gaul and Illyricum to Malarich, a brave and faithful officer of the nation of the Franks, and to his father-in-law, Count Lucillian, who had formerly distinguished his courage and conduct in the defence of Nisibis. Malarich had declined an office to which he thought himself unequal, and Lucillian was massacred at Rheims, in an accidental mutiny of the Batavian cohorts.[12] But the moderation of Jovinus, master-general of the cavalry, who forgave the intention of his disgrace, soon appeased the tumult and confirmed the uncertain minds of the soldiers. The oath of fidelity was administered and taken with loyal acclamations, and the deputies of the Western armies[13] saluted their new sovereign as he descended from Mount Taurus to the city of Tyana, in Cappadocia. From Tyana he continued his hasty march to Ancyra, capital of the province of Galatia, where Jovian assumed, with his infant son, the name and ensigns of the consulship.[14] Dadastana,[15] an obscure town, almost at an equal distance between Ancyra and Nice, was marked for the fatal term of his journey and his life. After indulging himself with a plentiful, perhaps an intemperate supper, he retired to rest, and the next morning the emperor Jovian was found dead in his bed. The cause of this sudden death was variously understood. By some it was ascribed to the consequences of an indigestion, occasioned either by the quantity of the wine or the quality of the mushrooms which he had swallowed in the evening. According to others, he was suffocated in his sleep by the vapour of charcoal, which extracted from the walls of the apartment the unwholesome moisture of the fresh plaster.[16] But the want of a regular inquiry into the death of a prince whose reign and person were soon forgotten appears to have been the only circumstance which countenanced the malicious whispers of poison and domestic guilt.[17] The body of Jovian was sent to Constantinople to be interred with his predecessors, and the sad procession was met on the road by his wife Charito, the daughter of Count Lucillian, who still wept the recent death of her father, and was hastening to dry her tears in the embraces of an Imperial husband. Her disappointment and grief were embittered by the anxiety of maternal tenderness. Six weeks before the death of Jovian, his infant son had been placed in the curule chair, adorned with the title of *Nobilissimus* and the vain ensigns of the consulship. Unconscious of his fortune, the royal youth, who from his grandfather assumed the name of Varronian, was reminded only by the jealousy of the government that he was the son of an emperor. Sixteen years afterwards he was still alive; but he had already been deprived of an eye, and his afflicted mother expected, every hour, that the innocent victim would be torn from her arms, to appease with his blood the suspicions of the reigning prince.[18]

After the death of Jovian the throne of the Roman world remained ten days[19] without a master. The ministers and generals still continued to meet in council, to exercise their respective functions, to maintain the public order, and peaceably to conduct the army to the city of Nice in Bithynia, which was chosen for the place of the election.[20] In a solemn assembly of the civil and military powers of the empire, the diadem was again unanimously offered to the præfect Sallust. He enjoyed the glory of a second refusal; and, when the virtues of the father were alleged in favour of the son, the præfect, with the firmness of a disinterested patriot, declared to the electors that the feeble age of the one, and the inexperienced youth of the other, were equally incapable of the laborious duties of government. Several candidates were proposed, and, after weighing the objections of character or situation, they were successively rejected: but as soon as the name of Valentinian was pronounced, the merit of that officer united the suffrages of the whole assembly, and obtained the sincere approbation of Sallust himself. Valentinian[21] was the son of Count Gratian, a native of Cibalis, in Pannonia, who from an obscure condition had raised himself, by matchless strength and dexterity, to the military commands of Africa and Britain, from which he retired with an ample fortune and suspicious integrity. The rank and services of Gratian contributed, however, to smooth the first steps of the promotion of his son, and afforded him an early opportunity of displaying those solid and useful qualifications which raised his character above the ordinary level of his fellow-soldiers. The person of Valentinian was tall, graceful, and majestic. His manly countenance, deeply marked with the impression of sense and spirit, inspired his friends with awe, and his enemies with fear; and, to second the efforts of his undaunted courage, the son of Gratian had inherited the advantages of a strong and healthy constitution. By the habits of chastity and temperance, which restrain the appetites and in-

vigorate the faculties, Valentinian preserved his own and the public esteem. The avocations of a military life had diverted his youth from the elegant pursuits of literature; he was ignorant of the Greek language and the arts of rhetoric; but, as the mind of the orator was never disconcerted by timid perplexity, he was able, as often as the occasion prompted him, to deliver his decided sentiments with bold and ready elocution. The laws of martial discipline were the only laws that he had studied, and he was soon distinguished by the laborious diligence and inflexible severity with which he discharged and enforced the duties of the camp. In the time of Julian he provoked the danger of disgrace by the contempt which he publicly expressed for the reigning religion;[22] and it should seem, from his subsequent conduct, that the indiscreet and unseasonable freedom of Valentinian was the effect of military spirit rather than of Christian zeal. He was pardoned, however, and still employed by a prince who esteemed his merit,[23] and in the various events of the Persian war he improved the reputation which he had already acquired on the banks of the Rhine. The celerity and success with which he executed an important commission recommended him to the favour of Jovian, and to the honourable command of the second *school*, or company, of Targeteers of the domestic guards. In the march from Antioch he had reached his quarters at Ancyra, when he was unexpectedly summoned, without guilt and without intrigue, to assume, in the forty-third year of his age, the absolute government of the Roman empire.

The invitation of the ministers and generals at Nice was of little moment, unless it were confirmed by the voice of the army. The aged Sallust, who had long observed the irregular fluctuations of popular assemblies, proposed, under pain of death, that none of those persons whose rank in the service might excite a party in their favour, should appear in public on the day of the inauguration. Yet such was the prevalence of ancient superstition, that a whole day was voluntarily added to this dangerous interval because it happened to be the intercalation of the Bissextile.[24] At length, when the hour was supposed to be propitious, Valentinian showed himself from a lofty tribunal; the judicious choice was applauded, and the new prince was solemnly invested with the diadem and the purple, amidst the acclamations of the troops, who were disposed in martial order round the tribunal. But when he stretched forth his hand to address the armed multitude, a busy whisper was accidentally started in the ranks, and insensibly swelled into a loud and imperious clamour, that he should name, without delay, a colleague in the empire. The intrepid calmness of Valentinian obtained silence and commanded respect, and he thus addressed the assembly: "A few minutes since it was in *your* power, fellow-soldiers, to have left me in the obscurity of a private station. Judging from the testimony of my past life that I deserved to reign, you have placed me on the throne. It is now *my* duty to consult the safety and interest of the republic. The weight of the universe is undoubtedly too great for the hands of a feeble mortal. I am conscious of the limits of my abilities and the uncertainty of my life, and, far from declining, I am anxious to solicit, the assistance of a worthy colleague. But, where discord may be fatal, the choice of a faithful friend requires mature and serious deliberation. That deliberation shall be *my* care. Let *your* conduct be dutiful and consistent. Retire to your quarters; refresh your minds and bodies; and expect the accustomed donative on the accession of a new emperor."[25] The astonished troops, with a mixture of pride, of satisfaction, and of terror, confessed the voice of their master. Their angry clamours subsided into silent reverence, and Valentinian, encompassed with the eagles of the legions and the various banners of the cavalry and infantry, was conducted in warlike pomp to the palace of Nice. As he was sensible, however, of the importance of preventing some rash declaration of the soldiers, he consulted the assembly of the chiefs and their real sentiments were concisely expressed by the generous freedom of Dagalaiphus. "Most excellent prince," said that officer, "if you consider only your family, you have a brother; if you love the republic, look round for the most deserving of the Romans."[26] The emperor, who suppressed his displeasure without altering his intention, slowly proceeded from Nice to Nicomedia and Constantinople. In one of the suburbs of that capital,[27] thirty days after his own elevation, he bestowed the title of Augustus on his brother Valens: and as the boldest patriots were convinced that their opposition, without being serviceable to their country, would be fatal to themselves, the declaration of his absolute will was received with silent submission. Valens was now in the thirty-sixth year of his age, but his abilities had never been exercised in any employment, military or civil, and his character had not inspired the world with any sanguine expectations. He possessed, however, one quality which recommended him

to Valentinian, and preserved the domestic peace of the empire: a devout and grateful attachment to his benefactor, whose superiority of genius, as well as of authority, Valens humbly and cheerfully acknowledged in every action of his life.[28]

Before Valentinian divided the provinces, he reformed the administration of the empire. All ranks of subjects who had been injured or oppressed under the reign of Julian were invited to support their public accusations. The silence of mankind attested the spotless integrity of the præfect Sallust,[29] and his own pressing solicitations that he might be permitted to retire from the business of the state were rejected by Valentinian with the most honourable expressions of friendship and esteem. But among the favourites of the late emperor there were many who had abused his credulity or superstition, and who could no longer hope to be protected either by favour or justice.[30] The greater part of the ministers of the palace and the governors of the provinces were removed from their respective stations, yet the eminent merit of some officers was distinguished from the obnoxious crowd, and, notwithstanding the opposite clamours of zeal and resentment, the whole proceedings of this delicate inquiry appear to have been conducted with a reasonable share of wisdom and moderation.[31] The festivity of a new reign received a short and suspicious interruption from the sudden illness of the two princes, but as soon as their health was restored they left Constantinople in the beginning of the spring. In the castle or palace of Mediana, only three miles from Naissus, they executed the solemn and final division of the Roman empire.[32] Valentinian bestowed on his brother the rich præfecture of the *East*, from the Lower Danube to the confines of Persia; whilst he reserved for his immediate government the warlike præfectures of *Illyricum*, *Italy*, and *Gaul*, from the extremity of Greece to the Caledonian rampart and from the rampart of Caledonia to the foot of Mount Atlas. The provincial administration remained on its former basis, but a double supply of generals and magistrates was required for two councils and two courts; the division was made with a just regard to their peculiar merit and situation, and seven master-generals were soon created either of the cavalry or infantry. When this important business had been amicably transacted, Valentinian and Valens embraced for the last time. The emperor of the West established his temporary residence at Milan, and the emperor of the East returned to Constantinople to assume the dominion of fifty provinces, of whose language he was totally ignorant.[33]

The tranquillity of the East was soon disturbed by rebellion and the throne of Valens was threatened by the daring attempts of a rival whose affinity to the emperor Julian[34] was his sole merit, and had been his only crime. Procopius had been hastily promoted from the obscure station of a tribune and a notary to the joint command of the army of Mesopotamia; the public opinion already named him as the successor of a prince who was destitute of natural heirs; and a vain rumour was propagated by his friends or his enemies, that Julian, before the altar of the Moon at Carrhæ, had privately invested Procopius with the Imperial purple.[35] He endeavoured, by his dutiful and submissive behaviour, to disarm the jealousy of Jovian, resigned without a contest his military command, and retired, with his wife and family, to cultivate the ample patrimony which he possessed in the province of Cappadocia. These useful and innocent occupations were interrupted by the appearance of an officer with a band of soldiers, who, in the name of his new sovereigns, Valentinian and Valens, was despatched to conduct the unfortunate Procopius either to a perpetual prison or an ignominious death. His presence of mind procured him a longer respite and a more splendid fate. Without presuming to dispute the royal mandate, he requested the indulgence of a few moments to embrace his weeping family, and, while the vigilance of his guards was relaxed by a plentiful entertainment, he dexterously escaped to the sea-coast of the Euxine, from whence he passed over the country of Bosphorus. In that sequestered region he remained many months, exposed to the hardships of exile, of solitude, and of want; his melancholy temper brooding over his misfortunes, and his mind agitated by the just apprehension that, if any accident should discover his name, the faithless barbarians would violate, without much scruple, the laws of hospitality. In a moment of impatience and despair, Procopius embarked in a merchant-vessel which made sail for Constantinople, and boldly aspired to the rank of a sovereign because he was not allowed to enjoy the security of a subject. At first he lurked in the villages of Bithynia, continually changing his habitation and his disguise.[36] By degrees he ventured into the capital, trusted his life and fortune to the fidelity of two friends, a senator and an eunuch, and conceived some hopes of success from the intelligence which he obtained of the actual state of public affairs. The body of the people was infected with a spirit of discontent: they regretted the justice and the abilities of Sallust, who had been imprudently dismissed from the præfecture of the East. They despised the character of Valens, which was rude without vigour, and feeble without mildness. They dreaded the influence of his father-in-law, the patrician Petronius, a cruel and rapacious minister, who rigorously exacted all the arrears of tribute that might remain unpaid since the reign of the emperor Aurelian. The circumstances were propitious to the designs of an usurper. The hostile measures of the Persians required the presence of Valens in Syria; from the Danube to the Euphrates the troops were in motion, and the capital was occasionally filled with the soldiers who passed or repassed the Thracian Bosphorus. Two cohorts of Gauls were persuaded to listen to the secret proposals of the conspirators, which were recommended by the promise of a liberal donative; and as they still revered the memory of Julian, they easily consented to support the hereditary claim of his proscribed kinsman. At the dawn of day they were drawn up near the baths of Anastasia, and Procopius, clothed in a purple garment more suitable to a player than to a monarch, appeared, as if he rose from the dead, in the midst of Constantinople. The soldiers, who were prepared for his reception, saluted their trembling prince with shouts of joy and vows of fidelity. Their numbers were soon increased by a sturdy band of peasants collected from the adjacent country, and Procopius, shielded by the arms of his adherents, was successively conducted to the tribunal, the senate, and the palace. During the first moments of his tumultuous reign he was astonished and terrified by the gloomy silence of the people, who were either ignorant of the cause or apprehensive of the event. But his military strength was superior to any actual resistance; the malcontents flocked to the standard of rebellion; the poor were excited by the hopes, and the rich were intimidated by the fear, of a general pillage; and the obstinate credulity of the multitude was once more deceived by the promised advantages of a revolution. The magistrates were seized, the prisons and arsenals broke open, the gates and the entrance of the harbour were diligently occupied, and, in a few hours, Procopius became the absolute, though precarious, master of the Imperial city. The usurper improved this unexpected success with some degree of courage and dexterity. He artfully propagated the rumours and opinions the most favourable to his interest, while he deluded the populace by giving audience to the frequent but imaginary ambassadors of distant nations. The large bodies of troops stationed in the cities of Thrace and the fortresses of the Lower Danube were gradually involved in the guilt of rebellion, and the Gothic princes consented to supply the sovereign of Constantinople with the formidable strength of several thousand auxiliaries. His generals passed the Bosphorus, and subdued, without an effort, the unarmed but wealthy provinces of Bithynia and Asia. After an honourable defence the city and island of Cyzicus yielded to his power, the renowned legions of the Jovians and Herculians embraced the cause of the usurper whom they were ordered to crush, and, as the veterans were continually augmented with new levies, he soon appeared at the head of an army whose valour, as well as numbers, were not unequal to the greatness of the contest. The son of Hormisdas,[37] a youth of spirit and ability, condescended to draw his sword against the lawful emperor of the East, and the Persian prince was immediately invested with the ancient and extraordinary powers of a Roman proconsul. The alliance of Faustina, the widow of the emperor Constantius, who intrusted herself and her daughter to the hands of the usurper, added dignity and reputation to his cause. The princess Constantia, who was then about five years of age, accompanied, in a litter, the monarch of the army. She was shown to the multitude in the arms of her adopted father, and, as often as she passed through the ranks, the tenderness of the soldiers was inflamed into martial fury:[38] they recollected the glories of the house of Constantine, and they declared, with loyal acclamation, that they would shed the last drop of their blood in the defence of the royal infant.[39]

In the meanwhile Valentinian was alarmed and perplexed by the doubtful intelligence of the revolt of the East. The difficulties of a German war forced him to confine his immediate care to the safety of his own dominions; and, as every channel of communication was stopped or corrupted, he listened, with doubtful anxiety, to the rumours which were industriously spread that the defeat and death of Valens had left Procopius sole master of the Eastern provinces. Valens was not dead; but on the news of the rebellion, which he received at Cæsarea, he basely despaired of his life and fortune, proposed to negotiate with the usurper, and discovered his secret inclination to abdicate the Imperial purple. The timid monarch was saved from disgrace and ruin by the firmness of his

ministers, and their abilities soon decided in his favour the event of the civil war. In a season of tranquillity Sallust had resigned without a murmur, but, as soon as the public safety was attacked, he ambitiously solicited the pre-eminence of toil and danger, and the restoration of that virtuous minister to the præfecture of the East was the first step which indicated the repentance of Valens, and satisfied the minds of the people. The reign of Procopius was apparently supported by powerful armies and obedient provinces. But many of the principal officers, military as well as civil, had been urged, either by motives of duty or interest, to withdraw themselves from the guilty scene, or to watch the moment of betraying and deserting the cause of the usurper. Lupicinus advanced by hasty marches to bring the legions of Syria to the aid of Valens. Arintheus, who in strength, beauty, and valour excelled all the heroes of the age, attacked with a small troop a superior body of the rebels. When he beheld the faces of the soldiers who had served under his banner, he commanded them, with a loud voice, to seize and deliver up their pretended leader, and such was the ascendant of his genius that this extraordinary order was instantly obeyed.[40] Arbetio, a respectable veteran of the great Constantine, who had been distinguished by the honours of the consulship, was persuaded to leave his retirement, and once more to conduct an army into the field. In the heat of action, calmly taking off his helmet, he showed his grey hairs and venerable countenance, saluted the soldiers of Procopius by the endearing names of children and companions, and exhorted them no longer to support the desperate cause of a contemptible tyrant, but to follow their old commander, who had so often led them to honour and victory. In the two engagements of Thyatira[41] and Nacolia the unfortunate Procopius was deserted by his troops, who were seduced by the instructions and example of their perfidious officers. After wandering some time among the woods and mountains of Phrygia, he was betrayed by his desponding followers, conducted to the Imperial camp, and immediately beheaded. He suffered the ordinary fate of an unsuccessful usurper, but the acts of cruelty which were exercised by the conqueror, under the forms of legal justice, excited the pity and indignation of mankind.[42]

Such indeed are the common and natural fruits of despotism and rebellion. But the inquisition into the crime of magic, which, under the reign of the two brothers, was so rigorously prosecuted both at Rome and Antioch, was interpreted as the fatal symptom, either of the displeasure of Heaven or of the depravity of mankind.[43] Let us not hesitate to indulge a liberal pride that, in the present age, the enlightened part of Europe has abolished[44] a cruel and odious prejudice, which reigned in every climate of the globe and adhered to every system of religious opinions.[45] The nations and the sects of the Roman world admitted, with equal credulity and similar abhorrence, the reality of that infernal art[46] which was able to control the eternal order of the planets and the voluntary operations of the human mind. They dreaded the mysterious power of spells and incantations, of potent herbs and execrable rites, which could extinguish or recall life, inflame the passions of the soul, blast the works of creation, and extort from the reluctant dæmons the secrets of futurity. They believed, with the wildest inconsistency, that this preternatural dominion of the air, of earth, and of hell was exercised, from the vilest motives of malice or gain, by some wrinkled hags and itinerant sorcerers, who passed their obscure lives in penury and contempt.[47] The arts of magic were equally condemned by the public opinion and by the laws of Rome, but, as they tended to gratify the most imperious passions of the heart of man, they were continually proscribed and continually practised.[48] An imaginary cause is capable of producing the most serious and mischievous effects. The dark predictions of the death of an emperor or the success of a conspiracy were calculated only to stimulate the hopes of ambition and to dissolve the ties of fidelity, and the intentional guilt of magic was aggravated by the actual crimes of treason and sacrilege.[49] Such vain terrors disturbed the peace of society and the happiness of individuals, and the harmless flame which insensibly melted a waxen image might derive a powerful and pernicious energy from the affrighted fancy of the person whom it was maliciously designed to represent.[50] From the infusion of those herbs which were supposed to possess a supernatural influence it was an easy step to the use of more substantial poison, and the folly of mankind sometimes became the instrument and the mask of the most atrocious crimes. As soon as the zeal of informers was encouraged by the ministers of Valens and Valentinian, they could not refuse to listen to another charge too frequently mingled in the scenes of domestic guilt, a charge of a softer and less malignant nature, for which the pious though excessive rigour of Constantine had recently decreed the punishment of death.[51] This deadly and incoherent mixture of treason and magic, of poison and adultery, afforded infinite gradations of guilt and innocence, of excuse and aggravation, which in these proceedings appear to have been confounded by the angry or corrupt passions of the judges. They easily discovered that the degree of their industry and discernment was estimated by the Imperial court according to the number of executions that were furnished from their respective tribunals. It was not without extreme reluctance that they pronounced a sentence of acquittal, but they eagerly admitted such evidence as was stained with perjury or procured by torture to prove the most improbable charges against the most respectable characters. The progress of the inquiry continually opened new subjects of criminal prosecution; the audacious informer, whose falsehood was detected, retired with impunity; but the wretched victim who discovered his real or pretended accomplices was seldom permitted to receive the price of his infamy. From the extremity of Italy and Asia the young and the aged were dragged in chains to the tribunals of Rome and Antioch. Senators, matrons, and philosophers expired in ignominious and cruel tortures. The soldiers who were appointed to guard the prisons declared, with a murmur of pity and indignation, that their numbers were insufficient to oppose the flight or resistance of the multitude of captives. The wealthiest families were ruined by fines and confiscations; the most innocent citizens trembled for their safety; and we may form some notion of the magnitude of the evil from the extravagant assertion of an ancient writer, that in the obnoxious provinces the prisoners, the exiles, and the fugitives formed the greatest part of the inhabitants.[52]

When Tacitus describes the deaths of the innocent and illustrious Romans who were sacrificed to the cruelty of the first Cæsars, the art of the historian, or the merit of the sufferers, excites in our breasts the most lively sensations of terror, of admiration, and of pity. The coarse and undistinguishing pencil of Ammianus has delineated his bloody figures with tedious and disgusting accuracy. But as our attention is no longer engaged by the contrast of freedom and servitude, of recent greatness and of actual misery, we should turn with horror from the frequent executions which disgraced, both at Rome and Antioch, the reign of the two brothers.[53] Valens was of a timid,[54] and Valentinian of a choleric, disposition.[55] An anxious regard to his personal safety was the ruling principle of the administration of Valens. In the condition of a subject, he had kissed, with trembling awe, the hand of the oppressor; and when he ascended the throne, he reasonably expected that the same fears which had subdued his own mind would secure the patient submission of his people. The favourites of Valens obtained, by the privilege of rapine and confiscation, the wealth which his economy would have refused.[56] They urged, with persuasive eloquence, *that*, in all cases of treason, suspicion is equivalent to proof; *that* the power supposes the intention of mischief; *that* the intention is not less criminal than the act; and *that* a subject no longer deserves to live, if his life may threaten the safety, or disturb the repose, of his sovereign. The judgment of Valentinian was sometimes deceived, and his confidence abused; but he would have silenced the informers with a contemptuous smile, had they presumed to alarm his fortitude by the sound of danger. They praised his inflexible love of justice; and, in the pursuit of justice, the emperor was easily tempted to consider clemency as a weakness, and passion as a virtue. As long as he wrestled with his equals in the bold competition of an active and ambitious life, Valentinian was seldom injured, and never insulted, with impunity: if his prudence was arraigned, his spirit was applauded; and the proudest and most powerful generals were apprehensive of provoking the resentment of a fearless soldier. After he became master of the world, he unfortunately forgot that, where no resistance can be made, no courage can be exerted; and instead of consulting the dictates of reason and magnanimity, he indulged the furious emotions of his temper, at a time when they were disgraceful to himself, and fatal to the defenceless objects of his displeasure. In the government of his household, or of his empire, slight, or even imaginary offences—a hasty word, a casual omission, an involuntary delay—were chastised by a sentence of immediate death. The expressions which issued the most readily from the mouth of the emperor of the West were, "Strike off his head;"—"Burn him alive;"—"Let him be beaten with clubs till he expires;"[57] and his most favoured ministers soon understood that, by a rash attempt to dispute or suspend the execution of his sanguinary commands, they might involve themselves in the guilt and punishment of disobedience. The repeated gratification of this savage justice hardened the mind of Valentinian against pity and remorse; and the sallies of passion were confirmed by the habits of cruelty.[58] He could behold with calm satisfaction the convulsive agonies of torture and death: he reserved his friendship for those faithful servants whose temper was the most congenial to his own. The merit of Maximin, who had slaughtered the noblest families of Rome, was rewarded with the royal approbation, and the præfecture of Gaul. Two fierce and enormous bears, distinguished by the appellations of *Innocence* and *Mica Aurea*, could alone deserve to share the favour of Maximin. The cages of those trusty guards were always placed near the bedchamber of Valentinian, who frequently amused his eyes with the grateful spectacle of seeing them tear and devour the bleeding limbs of the malefactors who were abandoned to their rage. Their diet and exercises were carefully inspected by the Roman emperor; and when *Innocence* had earned her discharge, by a long course of meritorious service, the faithful animal was again restored to the freedom of her native woods.[59]

But in the calmer moments of reflection, when the mind of Valens was not agitated by fear, or that of Valentinian by rage, the tyrant resumed the sentiments, or at least the conduct, of the father of his country. The dispassionate judgment of the Western emperor could clearly perceive, and accurately pursue, his own and the public interest; and the sovereign of the East, who imitated with equal docility the various examples which he received from his elder brother, was sometimes guided by the wisdom and virtue of the præfect Sallust. Both princes invariably retained, in the purple, the chaste and temperate simplicity which had adorned their private life; and, under their reign, the pleasures of the court never cost the people a blush or a sigh. They gradually reformed many of the abuses of the times of Constantius; judiciously adopted and improved the designs of Julian and his successor; and displayed a style and spirit of legislation which might inspire posterity with the most favourable opinion of their character and government. It is not from the master of *Innocence* that we should expect the tender regard for the welfare of his subjects which prompted Valentinian to condemn the exposition of new-born infants,[60] and to establish fourteen skilful physicians, with stipends and privileges, in the fourteen quarters of Rome. The good sense of an illiterate soldier founded an useful and liberal institution for the education of youth, and the support of declining science.[61] It was his intention that the arts of rhetoric and grammar should be taught, in the

Greek and Latin languages, in the metropolis of every province; and as the size and dignity of the school was usually proportioned to the importance of the city, the academies of Rome and Constantinople claimed a just and singular pre-ëminence. The fragments of the literary edicts of Valentinian imperfectly represent the school of Constantinople, which was gradually improved by subsequent regulations. That school consisted of thirty-one professors in different branches of learning. One philosopher and two lawyers; five sophists and ten grammarians for the Greek, and three orators and ten grammarians for the Latin tongue; besides seven scribes, or, as they were then styled, antiquarians, whose laborious pens supplied the public library with fair and correct copies of the classic writers. The rule of conduct which was prescribed to the students is the more curious, as it affords the first outlines of the form and discipline of a modern university. It was required that they should bring proper certificates from the magistrates of their native province. Their names, professions, and places of abode, were regularly entered in a public register. The studious youth were severely prohibited from wasting their time in feasts or in the theatre; and the term of their education was limited to the age of twenty. The præfect of the city was empowered to chastise the idle and refractory by stripes or expulsion; and he was directed to make an annual report to the master of the offices, that the knowledge and abilities of the scholars might be usefully applied to the public service. The institutions of Valentinian contributed to secure the benefits of peace and plenty; and the cities were guarded by the establishment of the *Defensors*;[62] freely elected as the tribunes and advocates of the people, to support their rights, and to expose their grievances, before the tribunals of the civil magistrates, or even at the foot of the Imperial throne. The finances were diligently administered by two princes who had been so long accustomed to the rigid economy of a private fortune; but in the receipt and application of the revenue, a discerning eye might observe some difference between the government of the East and of the West. Valens was persuaded that royal liberality can be supplied only by public oppression, and his ambition never aspired to secure, by their actual distress, the future strength and prosperity of his people. Instead of increasing the weight of taxes, which in the space of forty years had been gradually doubled, he reduced, in the first years of his reign, one-fourth of the tribute of the East.[63] Valentinian appears to

have been less attentive and less anxious to relieve the burthens of his people. He might reform the abuses of the fiscal administration; but he exacted, without scruple, a very large share of the private property; as he was convinced that the revenues which supported the luxury of individuals would be much more advantageously employed for the defence and improvement of the state. The subjects of the East, who enjoyed the present benefit, applauded the indulgence of their prince. The solid, but less splendid merit of Valentinian was felt and acknowledged by the subsequent generation.[64]

But the most honourable circumstance of the character of Valentinian is the firm and temperate impartiality which he uniformly preserved in an age of religious contention. His strong sense, unenlightened, but uncorrupted, by study, declined, with respectful indifference, the subtle questions of theological debate. The government of the *Earth* claimed his vigilance, and satisfied his ambition; and while he remembered that he was the disciple of the church, he never forgot that he was the sovereign of the clergy. Under the reign of an apostate, he had signalised his zeal for the honour of Christianity: he allowed to his subjects the privilege which he had assumed for himself; and they might accept with gratitude and confidence the general toleration which was granted by a prince addicted to passion, but incapable of fear or of disguise.[65] The Pagans, the Jews, and all the various sects which acknowledged the divine authority of Christ, were protected by the laws from arbitrary power or popular insult; nor was any mode of worship prohibited by Valentinian, except those secret and criminal practices which abused the name of religion for the dark purposes of vice and disorder. The art of magic, as it was more cruelly punished, was more strictly proscribed: but the emperor admitted a formal distinction to protect the ancient methods of divination, which were approved by the senate and exercised by the Tuscan haruspices. He had condemned, with the consent of the most rational Pagans, the licence of nocturnal sacrifices; but he immediately admitted the petition of Prætextatus, proconsul of Achaia, who represented that the life of the Greeks would become dreary and comfortless if they were deprived of the invaluable blessing of the Eleusinian mysteries. Philosophy alone can boast (and perhaps it is no more than the boast of philosophy) that her gentle hand is able to eradicate from the human mind the latent and deadly principle of fanaticism. But this truce of twelve years, which was inforced by the wise and vigorous government of Valentinian, by suspending the repetition of mutual injuries, contributed to soften the manners, and abate the prejudices, of the religious factions.

The friend of toleration was unfortunately placed at a distance from the scene of the fiercest controversies. As soon as the Christians of the West had extricated themselves from the snares of the creed of Rimini, they happily relapsed into the slumber of orthodoxy; and the small remains of the Arian party, that still subsisted at Sirmium or Milan, might be considered rather as objects of contempt than of resentment. But in the provinces of the East, from the Euxine to the extremity of Thebais, the strength and numbers of the hostile factions were more equally balanced; and this equality, instead of recommending the counsels of peace, served only to perpetuate the horrors of religious war. The monks and bishops supported their arguments by invectives; and their invectives were sometimes followed by blows. Athanasius still reigned at Alexandria; the thrones of Constantinople and Antioch were occupied by Arian prelates; and every episcopal vacancy was the occasion of a popular tumult. The Homoousians were fortified by the reconciliation of fifty-nine Macedonian, or Semi-Arian, bishops; but their secret reluctance to embrace the divinity of the Holy Ghost clouded the splendour of the triumph; and the declaration of Valens, who, in the first years of his reign, had imitated the impartial conduct of his brother, was an important victory on the side of Arianism. The two brothers had passed their private life in the condition of catechumens; but the piety of Valens prompted him to solicit the sacraments of baptism before he exposed his person to the dangers of a Gothic war. He naturally addressed himself to Eudoxus,[66] bishop of the Imperial city; and if the ignorant monarch was instructed by that Arian pastor in the principles of heterodox theology, his misfortune, rather than his guilt, was the inevitable consequence of his erroneous choice. Whatever had been the determination of the emperor, he must have offended a numerous party of his Christian subjects; as the leaders both of the Homoousians and of the Arians believed that, if they were not suffered to reign, they were most cruelly injured and oppressed. After he had taken this decisive step, it was extremely difficult for him to preserve either the virtue, or the reputation, of impartiality. He never aspired, like Constantius, to the fame of a profound theologian; but, as he had received with simplicity and respect the tenets of Eudoxus, Valens resigned his conscience to the direction of his ecclesiastical guides, and promoted by the influence of his authority the re-union of the *Athanasian heretics* to the body of the Catholic church. At first he pitied their blindness; by degrees he was provoked at their obstinacy; and he insensibly hated those sectaries to whom he was an object of hatred. [67] The feeble mind of Valens was always swayed by the persons with whom he familiarly conversed; and the exile or imprisonment of a private citizen are the favours the most readily granted in a despotic court. Such punishments were frequently inflicted on the leaders of the Homoousian party; and the misfortune of fourscore ecclesiastics of Constantinople, who, perhaps accidentally, were burnt on shipboard, was imputed to the cruel and premeditated malice of the emperor and his Arian ministers. In every contest the catholics (if we may anticipate that name) were obliged to pay the penalty of their own faults, and of those of their adversaries. In every election the claims of the Arian candidate obtained the preference; and if they were opposed by the majority of the people, he was usually supported by the authority of the civil magistrate, or even by the terrors of a military force. The enemies of Athanasius attempted to disturb the last years of his venerable age; and his temporary retreat to his father's sepulchre has been celebrated as a fifth exile. But the zeal of a great people, who instantly flew to arms, intimidated the præfect: and the archbishop was permitted to end his life in peace and in glory, after a reign of forty-seven years. The death of Athanasius was the signal of the persecution of Egypt; and the Pagan minister of Valens, who forcibly seated the worthless Lucius on the archiepiscopal throne, purchased the favour of the reigning party by the blood and sufferings of their Christian brethren. The free toleration of the heathen and Jewish worship was bitterly lamented, as a circumstance which aggravated the misery of the catholics, and the guilt of the impious tyrant of the East.[68]

The triumph of the orthodox party has left a deep stain of persecution on the memory of Valens; and the character of a prince who derived his virtues, as well as his vices, from a feeble understanding and a pusillanimous temper, scarcely deserves the labour of an apology. Yet candour may discover some reasons to suspect that the ecclesiastical ministers of Valens often exceeded the orders, or even the intentions, of their master; and that the real measure of facts has been very liberally magnified by the vehement declamation and easy credulity of his antagonists.[69] 1. The silence of Valentinian may suggest a probable argument that the partial severities which were exercised in the name and provinces of his colleague amounted only to some obscure and inconsiderable deviations from the established system of religious toleration; and the judicious historian, who has praised the equal temper of the elder brother, has not thought himself obliged to contrast the tranquillity of the West with the cruel persecution of the East.[70] 2. Whatever credit may be allowed to vague and distant reports, the character, or at least the behaviour, of Valens may be most distinctly seen in his personal transactions with the eloquent Basil, archbishop of Cæsarea, who had succeeded Athanasius in the management of the Trinitarian cause.[71] The circumstantial narrative has been composed by the friends and admirers of Basil; and as soon as we have stripped away a thick coat of rhetoric and miracle, we shall be astonished by the unexpected mildness of the Arian tyrant, who admired the firmness of his character, or was apprehensive, if he employed violence, of a general revolt in the province of Cappadocia. The archbishop, who asserted, with inflexible pride,[72] the truth of his opinions and the dignity of his rank, was left in the free possession of his conscience and his throne. The emperor devoutly assisted at the solemn service of the cathedral; and, instead of a sentence of banishment, subscribed the donation of a valuable estate for the use of an hospital which Basil had lately founded in the neighbourhood of Cæsarea.[73] 3. I am not able to discover that any law (such as Theodosius afterwards enacted against the Arians) was published by Valens against the Athanasian sectaries; and the edict which excited the most violent clamours may not appear so extremely reprehensible. The emperor had observed that several of his subjects, gratifying their lazy disposition under the pretence of religion, had associated themselves with the monks of Egypt; and he directed the count of the East to drag them from their solitude, and to compel those deserters of society to accept the fair alternative of renouncing their temporal possessions, or of discharging the public duties of men and citizens.[74] The ministers of Valens seem to have extended the sense of this penal statute, since they claimed a right of enlisting the young and able-bodied monks in the Imperial armies. A detachment of cavalry and infantry, consisting of three thousand men, marched from Alexandria into the adjacent desert of Nitria,[75] which was peopled by five thousand monks. The soldiers were conducted by Arian priests; and it is reported that a considerable slaughter was made in the monasteries which disobeyed the commands of their sovereign.[76]

The strict regulations which have been framed by the wisdom of modern legislators to restrain the wealth and avarice of the clergy may be originally deduced from the example of the emperor Valentinian. His edict,[77] addressed to Damasus, bishop of Rome, was publicly read in the churches of the city. He admonished the ecclesiastics and monks not to frequent the houses of widows and virgins; and menaced their disobedience with the animadversion of the civil judge. The director was no longer permitted to receive any gift, or legacy, or inheritance, from the liberality of his spiritual daughter: every testament contrary to this edict was declared null and void: and the illegal donation was confiscated for the use of the treasury. By a subsequent regulation it should seem that the same provisions were extended to nuns and bishops; and that all persons of the ecclesiastical order were rendered incapable of receiving any testamentary gifts, and strictly confined to the natural and legal rights of inheritance. As the guardian of domestic happiness and virtue, Valentinian applied this severe remedy to the growing evil. In the capital of the empire the females of noble and opulent houses possessed a very ample share of independent property; and many of those devout females had embraced the doctrines of Christianity, not only with the cold assent of the understanding, but with the warmth of affection, and perhaps with the eagerness of fashion. They sacrificed the pleasures of dress and luxury; and renounced, for the praise of chastity, the soft endearments of conjugal society. Some ecclesiastic, of real or apparent sanctity, was chosen to direct their timorous conscience, and to amuse the vacant tenderness of their heart: and the unbounded confidence which they hastily bestowed was often abused by knaves and enthusiasts, who hastened from the extremities of the East, to enjoy, on a splendid theatre, the privileges of the monastic profession. By their contempt of the world, they insensibly acquired its most desirable advantages; the lively attachment, perhaps, of a young and beautiful woman, the delicate plenty of an opulent household, and the respectful homage of the slaves, the freedmen, and the clients of a senatorial family. The immense fortunes of the Roman ladies were gradually consumed in lavish alms and expensive pilgrimages; and the artful monk, who had assigned himself the first, or possibly the sole place, in the testament of his spiritual daughter, still presumed to declare, with the smooth face of hypocrisy, that *he* was only the instrument of charity, and the steward of the poor. The lucrative, but disgraceful, trade,[78] which was exercised by the clergy to defraud the expectations of the natural heirs, had provoked the indignation of a superstitious age: and two of the most respectable of the Latin fathers very honestly confess that the ignominious edict of Valentinian was just and necessary; and that the Christian priests had deserved to lose a privilege which was still enjoyed by comedians, charioteers, and the ministers of idols. But the wisdom and authority of the legislator are seldom victorious in a contest with the vigilant dexterity of private interest: and Jerom, or Ambrose, might patiently acquiesce in the justice of an ineffectual or salutary law. If the ecclesiastics were checked in the pursuit of personal emolument, they would exert a more laudable industry to increase the wealth of the church; and dignify their covetousness with the specious names of piety and patriotism.[79]

Damasus, bishop of Rome, who was constrained to stigmatise the avarice of his clergy by the publications of the law of Valentinian, had the good sense, or the good fortune, to engage in his service the zeal and abilities of the learned Jerom; and the grateful saint has celebrated the merit and purity of a very ambiguous character.[80] But the splendid vices of the church of Rome, under the reign of Valentinian and Damasus, have been curiously observed by the historian Ammianus, who delivers his impartial sense in these expressive words:—"The præfecture of Juventius was accompanied with peace and plenty, but the tranquillity of his government was soon disturbed by a bloody sedition of the distracted people. The ardour of Damasus and Ursinus to seize the episcopal seat surpassed the ordinary measure of human ambition. They contended with the rage of party; the quarrel was maintained by the wounds and death of their followers; and the præfect, unable to resist or to appease the tumult, was constrained by superior violence to retire into the suburbs. Damasus prevailed: the well-disputed victory remained on the side of his faction; one hundred and thirty-seven dead bodies[81] were found in the *Basilica* of Sicininus,[82] where the Christians hold their religious assemblies; and it was long before the angry minds of the peo-

ple resumed their accustomed tranquillity. When I consider the splendour of the capital, I am not astonished that so valuable a prize should inflame the desires of ambitious men, and produce the fiercest and most obstinate contests. The successful candidate is secure that he will be enriched by the offerings of matrons;[83] that, as soon as his dress is composed with becoming care and elegance, he may proceed in his chariot through the streets of Rome;[84] and that the sumptuousness of the Imperial table will not equal the profuse and delicate entertainments provided by the taste and at the expense of the Roman pontiffs. How much more rationally (continues the honest Pagan) would those pontiffs consult their true happiness, if, instead of alleging the greatness of the city as an excuse for their manners, they would imitate the exemplary life of some provincial bishops, whose temperance and sobriety, whose mean apparel and downcast looks, recommend their pure and modest virtue to the Deity and his true worshippers!"[85] The schism of Damasus and Ursinus was extinguished by the exile of the latter; and the wisdom of the præfect Prætextatus[86] restored the tranquillity of the city. Prætextatus was a philosophic Pagan, a man of learning, of taste, and politeness; who disguised a reproach in the form of a jest, when he assured Damasus that if he could obtain the bishopric of Rome, he himself would immediately embrace the Christian religion.[87] This lively picture of the wealth and luxury of the popes in the fourth century becomes the more curious as it represents the intermediate degree between the humble poverty of the apostolic fisherman and the royal state of a temporal prince whose dominions extend from the confines of Naples to the banks of the Po.

When the suffrage of the generals and of the army committed the sceptre of the Roman empire to the hands of Valentinian, his reputation in arms, his military skill and experience, and his rigid attachment to the forms as well as spirit of ancient discipline, were the principal motives of their judicious choice. The eagerness of the troops, who pressed him to nominate his colleague, was justified by the dangerous situation of public affairs; and Valentinian himself was conscious that the abilities of the most active mind were unequal to the defence of the distant frontiers of an invaded monarchy. As soon as the death of Julian had relieved the barbarians from the terror of his name, the most sanguine hopes of rapine and conquest excited the nations of the East, of the North, and of the

South. Their inroads were often vexatious, and sometimes formidable; but, during the twelve years of the reign of Valentinian, his firmness and vigilance protected his own dominions; and his powerful genius seemed to inspire and direct the feeble counsels of his brother. Perhaps the method of annals would more forcibly express the urgent and divided cares of the two emperors; but the attention of the reader, likewise, would be distracted by a tedious and desultory narrative. A separate view of the five great theatres of war—I. Germany; II. Britain; III. Africa; IV. The East; and V. The Danube—will impress a more distinct image of the military state of the empire under the reigns of Valentinian and Valens.

I. The ambassadors of the Alemanni had been offended by the harsh and haughty behaviour of Ursacius, master of the offices;[88] who, by an act of unseasonable parsimony, had diminished the value, as well as the quantity, of the presents to which they were entitled, either from custom or treaty, on the accession of a new emperor. They expressed, and they communicated to their countrymen, their strong sense of the national affront. The irascible minds of the chiefs were exasperated by the suspicion of contempt; and the martial youth crowded to their standard. Before Valentinian could pass the Alps, the villages of Gaul were in flames; before his general Dagalaiphus could encounter the Alemanni, they had secured the captives and the spoil in the forests of Germany. In the beginning of the ensuing year the military force of the whole nation, in deep and solid columns, broke through the barrier of the Rhine during the severity of a northern winter. Two Roman counts were defeated and mortally wounded; and the standard of the Heruli and Batavians fell into the hands of the conquerors, who displayed, with insulting shouts and menaces, the trophy of their victory.

The standard was recovered; but the Batavians had not redeemed the shame of their disgrace and flight in the eyes of their severe judge. It was the opinion of Valentinian that his soldiers must learn to fear their commander before they could cease to fear the enemy. The troops were solemnly assembled; and the trembling Batavians were enclosed within the circle of the Imperial army. Valentinian then ascended his tribunal; and, as if he disdained to punish cowardice with death, he inflicted a stain of indelible ignominy on the officers whose misconduct and pusillanimity were found to be the first occasion of the defeat. The Batavians were de-

graded from their rank, stripped of their arms, and condemned to be sold for slaves to the highest bidder. At this tremendous sentence the troops fell prostrate on the ground, deprecated the indignation of their sovereign, and protested that if he would indulge them in another trial, they would approve themselves not unworthy of the name of Romans, and of his soldiers. Valentinian, with affected reluctance, yielded to their entreaties: the Batavians resumed their arms; and, with their arms, the invincible resolution of wiping away their disgrace in the blood of the Alemanni.[89] The principal command was declined by Dagalaiphus; and that experienced general, who had represented, perhaps with too much prudence, the extreme difficulties of the undertaking, had the mortification, before the end of the campaign, of seeing his rival Jovinus convert those difficulties into a decisive advantage over the scattered forces of the barbarians. At the head of a well-disciplined army of cavalry, infantry, and light troops, Jovinus advanced, with cautious and rapid steps, to Scarponna,[90] in the territory of Metz, where he surprised a large division of the Alemanni before they had time to run to their arms; and flushed his soldiers with the confidence of an easy and bloodless victory. Another division, or rather army, of the enemy, after the cruel and wanton devastation of the adjacent country, reposed themselves on the shady banks of the Moselle. Jovinus, who had viewed the ground with the eye of a general, made his silent approach through a deep and woody vale, till he could distinctly perceive the indolent security of the Germans. Some were bathing their huge limbs in the river; others were combing their long and flaxen hair; others again were swallowing large draughts of rich and delicious wine. On a sudden they heard the sound of the Roman trumpet; they saw the enemy in their camp. Astonishment produced disorder; disorder was followed by flight and dismay; and the confused multitude of the bravest warriors was pierced by the swords and javelins of the legionaries and auxiliaries. The fugitives escaped to the third, and most considerable, camp in the Catalaunian plains, near Châlons in Champagne: the straggling detachments were hastily recalled to their standard; and the barbarian chiefs, alarmed and admonished by the fate of their companions, prepared to encounter in a decisive battle the victorious forces of the lieutenant of Valentinian. The bloody and obstinate conflict lasted a whole summer's day, with equal valour and with alternate success. The Romans at length prevailed, with the loss of about twelve hundred men. Six thousand of the Alemanni were slain, four thousand were wounded; and the brave Jovinus, after chasing the flying remnant of their host as far as the banks of the Rhine, returned to Paris, to receive the applause of his sovereign, and the ensigns of the consulship for the ensuing year.[91] The triumph of the Romans was indeed sullied by their treatment of the captive king, whom they hung on a gibbet, without the knowledge of their indignant general. This disgraceful act of cruelty, which might be imputed to the fury of the troops, was followed by the deliberate murder of Withicab, the son of Vadomair, a German prince, of a weak and sickly constitution, but of a daring and formidable spirit. The domestic assassin was instigated and protected by the Romans;[92] and the violation of the laws of humanity and justice betrayed their secret apprehension of the weakness of the declining empire. The use of the dagger is seldom adopted in public councils, as long as they retain any confidence in the power of the sword.

While the Alemanni appeared to be humbled by their recent calamities, the pride of Valentinian was mortified by the unexpected surprisal of Moguntiacum, or Mentz, the principal city of the Upper Germany. In the unsuspicious moment of a Christian festival, Rando, a bold and artful chieftain, who had long meditated his attempt, suddenly passed the Rhine, entered the defenceless town, and retired with a multitude of captives of either sex. Valentinian resolved to execute severe vengeance on the whole body of the nation. Count Sebastian, with the bands of Italy and Illyricum, was ordered to invade their country, most probably on the side of Rhætia. The emperor in person, accompanied by his son Gratian, passed the Rhine at the head of a formidable army, which was supported on both flanks by Jovinus and Severus, the two masters-general of the cavalry and infantry of the West. The Alemanni, unable to prevent the devastation of their villages, fixed their camp on a lofty and almost inaccessible mountain in the modern duchy of Wirtemberg, and resolutely expected the approach of the Romans. The life of Valentinian was exposed to imminent danger by the intrepid curiosity with which he persisted to explore some secret and unguarded path. A troop of barbarians suddenly rose from their ambuscade; and the emperor, who vigorously spurred his horse down a steep and slippery descent, was obliged to leave behind him his armour-bearer, and his helmet

magnificently enriched with gold and precious stones. At the signal of the general assault, the Roman troops encompassed and ascended the mountain of Solicinium on three different sides. Every step which they gained increased their ardour, and abated the resistance of the enemy: and after their united forces had occupied the summit of the hill, they impetuously urged the barbarians down the northern descent, where Count Sebastian was posted to intercept their retreat. After this signal victory Valentinian returned to his winter quarters at Trèves, where he indulged the public joy by the exhibition of splendid and triumphal games.[93] But the wise monarch, instead of aspiring to the conquest of Germany, confined his attention to the important and laborious defence of the Gallic frontier, against an enemy whose strength was renewed by a stream of daring volunteers, which incessantly flowed from the most distant tribes of the North.[94] The banks of the Rhine, from its source to the straits of the ocean, were closely planted with strong castles and convenient towers; new works and new arms were invented by the ingenuity of a prince who was skilled in the mechanical arts; and his numerous levies of Roman and barbarian youth were severely trained in all the exercises of war. The progress of the work, which was sometimes opposed by modest representations and sometimes by hostile attempts, secured the tranquillity of Gaul during the nine subsequent years of the administration of Valentinian.[95]

That prudent emperor, who diligently practised the wise maxims of Diocletian, was studious to foment and excite the intestine divisions of the tribes of Germany. About the middle of the fourth century, the countries, perhaps of Lusace and Thuringia, on either side of the Elbe, were occupied by the vague dominion of the BURGUNDIANS, a warlike and numerous people of the Vandal race,[96] whose obscure name insensibly swelled into a powerful kingdom, and has finally settled on a flourishing province. The most remarkable circumstance in the ancient manners of the Burgundians appears to have been the difference of their civil and ecclesiastical constitution. The appellation of *Hendinos* was given to the king or general, and the title of *Sinistus* to the high-priest of the nation. The person of the priest was sacred, and his dignity perpetual; but the temporal government was held by a very precarious tenure. If the events of war accused the courage or conduct of the king, he was immediately deposed; and the injustice of his subjects made him responsible for the fertility of the earth and the regularity of the seasons, which seemed to fall more properly within the sacerdotal department.[97] The disputed possession of some salt-pits[98] engaged the Alemanni and the Burgundians in frequent contests: the latter were easily tempted by the secret solicitations and liberal offers of the emperor; and their fabulous descent from the Roman soldiers who had formerly been left to garrison the fortresses of Drusus was admitted with mutual credulity, as it was conducive to mutual interest.[99] An army of fourscore thousand Burgundians soon appeared on the banks of the Rhine, and impatiently required the support and subsidies which Valentinian had promised; but they were amused with excuses and delays, till at length, after a fruitless expectation, they were compelled to retire. The arms and fortifications of the Gallic frontier checked the fury of their just resentment; and their massacre of the captives served to embitter the hereditary feud of the Burgundians and the Alemanni. The inconstancy of a wise prince may perhaps be explained by some alteration of circumstances; and perhaps it was the original design of Valentinian to intimidate rather than to destroy; as the balance of power would have been equally overturned by the extirpation of either of the German nations. Among the princes of the Alemanni, Macrianus, who, with a Roman name, had assumed the arts of a soldier and a statesman, deserved his hatred and esteem. The emperor himself, with a light and unincumbered band, condescended to pass the Rhine, marched fifty miles into the country, and would infallibly have seized the object of his pursuit, if his judicious measures had not been defeated by the impatience of the troops. Macrianus was afterwards admitted to the honour of a personal conference with the emperor; and the favours which he received fixed him, till the hour of his death, a steady and sincere friend of the republic.[100]

The land was covered by the fortifications of Valentinian; but the sea-coast of Gaul and Britain was exposed to the depredations of the Saxons. That celebrated name, in which we have a dear and domestic interest, escaped the notice of Tacitus; and in the maps of Ptolemy it faintly marks the narrow neck of the Cimbric peninsula, and three small islands towards the mouth of the Elbe.[101] This contracted territory, the present duchy of Schleswig, or perhaps of Holstein, was incapable of pouring forth the inexhaustible swarms of Saxons who reigned over the ocean, who filled the British island with their language, their laws, and their colonies,

and who so long defended the liberty of the North against the arms of Charlemagne.[102] The solution of this difficulty is easily derived from the similar manners and loose constitution of the tribes of Germany, which were blended with each other by the slightest accidents of war or friendship. The situation of the native Saxons disposed them to embrace the hazardous professions of fishermen and pirates; and the success of their first adventures would naturally excite the emulation of their bravest countrymen, who were impatient of the gloomy solitude of their woods and mountains. Every tide might float down the Elbe whole fleets of canoes, filled with hardy and intrepid associates, who aspired to behold the unbounded prospect of the ocean, and to taste the wealth and luxury of unknown worlds. It should seem probable, however, that the most numerous auxiliaries of the Saxons were furnished by the nations who dwelt along the shores of the Baltic. They possessed arms and ships, the art of navigation, and the habits of naval war; but the difficulty of issuing through the northern Columns of Hercules[103] (which during several months of the year are obstructed with ice) confined their skill and courage within the limits of a spacious lake. The rumour of the successful armaments which sailed from the mouth of the Elbe would soon provoke them to cross the narrow isthmus of Schleswig, and to launch their vessels on the great sea. The various troops of pirates and adventurers who fought under the same standard were insensibly united in a permanent society, at first of rapine, and afterwards of government. A military confederation was gradually moulded into a national body by the gentle operation of marriage and consanguinity; and the adjacent tribes, who solicited the alliance, accepted the name and laws of the Saxons. If the fact were not established by the most unquestionable evidence, we should appear to abuse the credulity of our readers by the description of the vessels in which the Saxon pirates ventured to sport in the waves of the German Ocean, the British Channel, and the Bay of Biscay. The keel of their large flat-bottomed boats was framed of light timber, but the sides and upper works consisted only of wicker, with a covering of strong hides.[104] In the course of their slow and distant navigations they must always have been exposed to the danger, and very frequently to the misfortune, of shipwreck; and the naval annals of the Saxons were undoubtedly filled with the accounts of the losses which they sustained on the coasts of Britain and Gaul. But the daring spirit of the pirates braved the perils both of the sea and of the shore: their skill was confirmed by the habits of enterprise; the meanest of their mariners was alike capable of handling an oar, of rearing a sail, or of conducting a vessel; and the Saxons rejoiced in the appearance of a tempest, which concealed their design, and dispersed the fleets of the enemy.[105] After they had acquired an accurate knowledge of the maritime provinces of the West they extended the scene of their depredations, and the most sequestered places had no reason to presume on their security. The Saxon boats drew so little water that they could easily proceed fourscore or an hundred miles up the great rivers; their weight was so inconsiderable that they were transported on waggons from one river to another; and the pirates who had entered the mouth of the Seine or of the Rhine might descend, with the rapid stream of the Rhone, into the Mediterranean. Under the reign of Valentinian the maritime provinces of Gaul were afflicted by the Saxons: a military count was stationed for the defence of the seacoast, or Armorican limit; and that officer, who found his strength or his abilities unequal to the task, implored the assistance of Severus, master-general of the infantry. The Saxons, surrounded and outnumbered, were forced to relinquish their spoil, and to yield a select band of their tall and robust youth to serve in the Imperial armies. They stipulated only a safe and honourable retreat; and the condition was readily granted by the Roman general, who meditated an act of perfidy,[106] imprudent as it was inhuman, while a Saxon remained alive and in arms to revenge the fate of his countrymen. The premature eagerness of the infantry, who were secretly posted in a deep valley, betrayed the ambuscade; and they would perhaps have fallen the victims of their own treachery, if a large body of cuirassiers, alarmed by the noise of the combat, had not hastily advanced to extricate their companions, and to overwhelm the undaunted valour of the Saxons. Some of the prisoners were saved from the edge of the sword to shed their blood in the amphitheatre; and the orator Symmachus complains that twenty-nine of those desperate savages, by strangling themselves with their own hands, had disappointed the amusement of the public. Yet the polite and philosophic citizens of Rome were impressed with the deepest horror when they were informed that the Saxons consecrated to the gods the tithe of their *human* spoil; and that they ascertained by lot the objects of the barbarous sacrifice.[107]

II. The fabulous colonies of Egyptians and Trojans, of Scandinavians and Spaniards, which flattered the pride and amused the credulity of our rude ancestors, have insensibly vanished in the light of science and philosophy.[108] The present age is satisfied with the simple and rational opinion that the islands of Great Britain and Ireland were gradually peopled from the adjacent continent of Gaul. From the coast of Kent, to the extremity of Caithness and Ulster, the memory of a Celtic origin was distinctly preserved in the perpetual resemblance of language, of religion, and of manners: and the peculiar characters of the British tribes might be naturally ascribed to the influence of accidental and local circumstances.[109] The Roman province was reduced to the state of civilised and peaceful servitude: the rights of savage freedom were contracted to the narrow limits of Caledonia. The inhabitants of that northern region were divided, as early as the reign of Constantine, between the two great tribes of the Scots and of the Picts[110] who have since experienced a very different fortune. The power, and almost the memory, of the Picts have been extinguished by their successful rivals; and the Scots, after maintaining for ages the dignity of an independent kingdom, have multiplied, by an equal and voluntary union, the honours of the English name. The hand of nature had contributed to mark the ancient distinction of the Scots and Picts. The former were the men of the hills, and the latter those of the plain. The eastern coast of Caledonia may be considered as a level and fertile country, which, even in a rude state of tillage, was capable of producing a considerable quantity of corn; and the epithet of *cruitnich*, or wheat-eaters, expressed the contempt or envy of the carnivorous highlander. The cultivation of the earth might introduce a more accurate separation of property, and the habits of a sedentary life; but the love of arms and rapine was still the ruling passion of the Picts; and their warriors, who stripped themselves for a day of battle, were distinguished, in the eyes of the Romans, by the strange fashion of painting their naked bodies with gaudy colours and fantastic figures. The western part of Caledonia irregularly rises into wild and barren hills, which scarcely repay the toil of the husbandman, and are most profitably used for the pasture of cattle. The highlanders were condemned to the occupations of shepherds and hunters; and as they seldom were fixed to any permanent habitation, they acquired the expressive name of Scots, which, in the Celtic tongue, is said to be equivalent to that of *wanderers*, or *vagrants*. The inhabitants of a barren land were urged to seek a fresh supply of food in the waters. The deep lakes and bays which intersect their country are plentifully stored with fish; and they gradually ventured to cast their nets in the waves of the ocean. The vicinity of the Hebrides, so profusely scattered along the western coast of Scotland, tempted their curiosity and improved their skill; and they acquired, by slow degrees, the art, or rather the habit, of managing their boats in a tempestuous sea, and of steering their nocturnal course by the light of the well-known stars. The two bold headlands of Caledonia almost touch the shores of a spacious island, which obtained, from its luxuriant vegetation, the epithet of *Green*; and has preserved, with a slight alteration, the name of Erin, or Ierne, or Ireland. It is *probable* that in some remote period of antiquity the fertile plains of Ulster received a colony of hungry Scots; and that the strangers of the North, who had dared to encounter the arms of the legions, spread their conquests over the savage and unwarlike natives of a solitary island. It is *certain* that, in the declining age of the Roman empire, Caledonia, Ireland, and the Isle of Man were inhabited by the Scots, and that the kindred tribes, who were often associated in military enterprise, were deeply affected by the various accidents of their mutual fortunes. They long cherished the lively tradition of their common name and origin: and the missionaries of the Isle of Saints, who diffused the light of Christianity over North Britain, established the vain opinion that their Irish countrymen were the natural, as well as spiritual, fathers of the Scottish race. The loose and obscure tradition has been preserved by the venerable Bede, who scattered some rays of light over the darkness of the eighth century. On this slight foundation a huge superstructure of fable was gradually reared by the bards and the monks; two orders of men who equally abused the privilege of fiction. The Scottish nation, with mistaken pride, adopted their Irish genealogy: and the annals of a long line of imaginary kings have been adorned by the fancy of Boethius and the classic elegance of Buchanan.[111]

Six years after the death of Constantine the destructive inroads of the Scots and Picts required the presence of his youngest son, who reigned in the Western empire. Constans visited his British dominions: but we may form some estimate of the importance of his achievements by the language of panegyric, which celebrates only his triumph over the elements, or, in other words, the good fortune of a safe and easy passage from the port of Boulogne to the harbour of Sandwich.[112] The calamities which the afflicted provincials continued to experience from foreign war and domestic tyranny were aggravated by the feeble and corrupt administration of the eunuchs of Constantius; and the transient relief which they might obtain from the virtues of Julian was soon lost by the absence and death of their benefactor. The sums of gold and silver which had been painfully collected, or liberally transmitted, for the payment of the troops, were intercepted by the avarice of the commanders; discharges, or, at least, exemptions, from the military service, were publicly sold; the distress of the soldiers, who were injuriously deprived of their legal and scanty subsistence, provoked them to frequent desertion; the nerves of discipline were relaxed, and the highways were infested with robbers.[113] The oppression of the good and the impunity of the wicked equally contributed to diffuse through the island a spirit of discontent and revolt; and every ambitious subject, every desperate exile, might entertain a reasonable hope of subverting the weak and distracted government of Britain. The hostile tribes of the North, who detested the pride and power of the King of the World, suspended their domestic feuds; and the barbarians of the land and sea, the Scots, the Picts, and the Saxons, spread themselves, with rapid and irresistible fury, from the wall of Antonius to the shores of Kent. Every production of art and nature, every object of convenience or luxury, which they were incapable of creating by labour or procuring by trade, was accumulated in the rich and fruitful province of Britain.[114] A philosopher may deplore the eternal discord of the human race, but he will confess that the desire of spoil is a more rational provocation than the vanity of conquest. From the age of Constantine to that of the Plantagenets this rapacious spirit continued to instigate the poor and hardy Caledonians: but the same people whose generous humanity seems to inspire the songs of Ossian was disgraced by a savage ignorance of the virtues of peace and of the laws of war. Their southern neighbours have felt, and perhaps exaggerated, the cruel depredations of the Scots and Picts;[115] and a valiant tribe of Caledonia, the Attacotti,[116] the enemies, and afterwards the soldiers, of Valentinian, are accused by an eyewitness of delighting in the taste of human flesh. When they hunted the woods for prey, it is said that they attacked the shepherd rather than his flock; and that they curiously selected the most delicate and brawny parts both of males and females, which they prepared for their horrid repasts.[117] If in the neighbourhood of the commercial and literary town of Glasgow a race of cannibals has really existed, we may contemplate in the period of the Scottish history the opposite extremes of savage and civilised life. Such reflections tend to enlarge the circle of our ideas, and to encourage the pleasing hope that New Zealand may produce in some future age the Hume of the Southern Hemisphere.

Every messenger who escaped across the British channel conveyed the most melancholy and alarming tidings to the ears of Valentinian, and the emperor was soon informed that the two military commanders of the province had been surprised and cut off by the barbarians. Severus, count of the domestics, was hastily despatched, and as suddenly recalled, by the court of Trèves. The representations of Jovinus served only to indicate the greatness of the evil, and, after a long and serious consultation, the defence, or rather the recovery, of Britain was intrusted to the abilities of the brave Theodosius. The exploits of that general, the father of a line of emperors, have been celebrated, with peculiar complacency, by the writers of the age; but his real merit deserved their applause, and his nomination was received, by the army and province, as a sure presage of approaching victory. He seized the favourable moment of navigation, and securely landed the numerous and veteran bands of the Heruli and Batavians, the Jovians and the Victors. In his march from Sandwich to London, Theodosius defeated several parties of the barbarians, released a multitude of captives, and, after distributing to his soldiers a small portion of the spoil, established the fame of disinterested justice by the restitution of the remainder to the rightful proprietors. The citizens of London, who had almost despaired of their safety, threw open their gates, and, as soon as Theodosius had obtained from the court of Trèves the important aid of a military lieutenant and a civil governor, he executed with wisdom and vigour the laborious task of the deliverance of Britain. The vagrant soldiers were recalled to their standard, an edict of amnesty dispelled the public apprehensions, and his cheerful example alleviated the rigour of martial discipline. The scattered and desultory warfare of the barbarians, who infested the land and sea, deprived him of the glory of a signal victory; but the prudent spirit and consummate art of the Roman general were displayed in the operations of two campaigns, which successively rescued every part of the province from the hands of a cruel and rapacious enemy. The splendour of the cities and the security of the fortifications were diligently restored by the paternal care of Theodosius, who with a strong hand confined the trembling Caledonians to the northern angle of the island, and perpetuated, by the name and settlement of the new province of *Valentia*, the glories of the reign of Valentinian.[118] The voice of poetry and panegyric may add, perhaps with some degree of truth, that the unknown regions of Thule were stained with the blood of the Picts, that the oars of Theodosius dashed the waves of the Hyperborean ocean, and that the distant Orkneys were the scene of his naval victory over the Saxon pirates.[119] He left the province with a fair as well as splendid reputation, and was immediately promoted to the rank of master-general of the cavalry by a prince who could applaud, without envy, the merit of his servants. In the important station of the Upper Danube, the conqueror of Britain checked and defeated the armies of the Alemanni, before he was chosen to suppress the revolt of Africa.

III. The prince who refuses to be the judge, instructs his people to consider him as the accomplice of his ministers. The military command of Africa had been long exercised by Count Romanus, and his abilities were not inadequate to his station; but as sordid interest was the sole motive of his conduct, he acted on most occasions as if he had been the enemy of the province, and the friend of the barbarians of the desert. The three flourishing cities of Oea, Leptis, and Sabrata, which, under the name of Tripoli, had long constituted a federal union,[120] were obliged, for the first time, to shut their gates against a hostile invasion; several of their most honourable citizens were surprised and massacred, the villages and even the suburbs were pillaged, and the vines and fruit-trees of that rich territory were extirpated by the malicious savages of Gætulia. The unhappy provincials implored the protection of Romanus; but they soon found that their military governor was not less cruel and rapacious than the barbarians. As they were incapable of furnishing the four thousand camels and the exorbitant present which he required before he would march to the assistance of Tripoli, his demand was equivalent to a refusal, and he might justly be accused as the author of the public calamity. In the annual assembly of the three cities, they nominated two deputies to lay at the feet of Valentinian the customary offering of a gold victory, and to accompany this tribute of duty, rather than of gratitude, with their humble complaint that they were ruined by the enemy and betrayed by their governor. If the severity of Valentinian had been rightly directed, it would have fallen on the guilty head of Romanus. But the count, long exercised in the arts of corruption, had despatched a swift and trusty messenger to secure the venal friendship of Remigius, master of the offices. The wisdom of the imperial council was deceived by artifice, and their honest indignation was cooled by delay. At length, when the repetition of complaint had been justified by the repetition of public misfortunes, the notary Palladius was sent from the court of Trèves to examine the state of Africa and the conduct of Romanus. The rigid impartiality of Palladius was easily disarmed; he was tempted to reserve for himself a part of the public treasure which he brought with him for the payment of the troops, and, from the moment that he was conscious of his own guilt, he could no longer refuse to attest the innocence and merit of the count. The charge of the Tripolitans was declared to be false and frivolous, and Palladius himself was sent back from Trèves to Africa with a special commission to discover and prosecute the authors of this impious conspiracy against the representatives of the sovereign. His inquiries were managed with so much dexterity and success, that he compelled the citizens of Leptis, who had sustained a recent siege of eight days, to contradict the truth of their own decrees and to censure the behaviour of their own deputies. A bloody sentence was pronounced, without hesitation, by the rash and headstrong cruelty of Valentinian. The president of Tripoli, who had presumed to pity the distress of the province, was publicly executed at Utica; four distinguished citizens were put to death as the accomplices of the imaginary fraud, and the tongues of two others were cut out by the express order of the emperor. Romanus, elated by impunity and irritated by resistance, was still continued in the military command, till the Africans were provoked, by his avarice, to join the rebellious standard of Firmus, the Moor.[121]

His father Nabal was one of the richest and most powerful of the Moorish princes who acknowledged the supremacy of Rome. But as he left, either by his wives or concubines, a very numerous posterity, the wealthy inheritance was eagerly disputed, and Zamma, one of his sons, was slain in a domestic quarrel by his brother Firmus. The implacable zeal with which Romanus prosecuted the legal revenge of this murder could be ascribed only to a motive of avarice or personal hatred; but on this occasion his claims were just, his influence was weighty, and Firmus clearly understood that he must either present his neck to the executioner, or appeal from the sentence of the Imperial consistory to his sword and to the people.[122] He was received as the deliverer of his country, and, as soon as it appeared that Romanus was formidable only to a submissive province, the tyrant of Africa became the object of universal contempt. The ruin of Cæsarea, which was plundered and burnt by the licentious barbarians, convinced the refractory cities of the danger of resistance; the power of Firmus was established, at least in the provinces of Mauritania and Numidia, and it seemed to be his only doubt whether he should assume the diadem of a Moorish king or the purple of a Roman emperor. But the imprudent and unhappy Africans soon discovered that, in this rash insurrection, they had not sufficiently consulted their own strength or the abilities of their leader. Before he could procure any certain intelligence that the emperor of the West had fixed the choice of a general, or that a fleet of transports was collected at the mouth of the Rhone, he was suddenly informed that the great Theodosius, with a small band of veterans, had landed near Igilgilis, or Gigeri, on the African coast, and the timid usurper sunk under the ascendant of virtue and military genius. Though Firmus possessed arms and treasures, his despair of victory immediately reduced him to the use of those arts which, in the same country and in a similar situation, had formerly been practised by the crafty Jugurtha. He attempted to deceive, by an apparent submission, the vigilance of the Roman general, to seduce the fidelity of his troops, and to protract the duration of the war by successively engaging the independent tribes of Africa to espouse his quarrel or to protect his flight. Theodosius imitated the example and obtained the success of his predecessor Metellus. When Firmus, in the character of a suppliant, accused his own rashness and humbly solicited the clemency of the emperor, the lieutenant of Valentinian received and dismissed him with a friendly embrace; but he diligently required the useful and substantial pledges of a sincere repentance, nor could he be persuaded, by the assurances of peace, to suspend for an instant the operations of an active war. A dark conspiracy was detected by the penetration of Theodosius, and he satisfied, without much reluctance, the public indignation which he had secretly excited. Several of the guilty accomplices of Firmus were abandoned, according to ancient custom, to the tumult of a military execution; many more, by the amputation of both their hands, continued to exhibit an instructive spectacle of horror; the hatred of the rebels was accompanied with fear, and the fear of the Roman soldiers was mingled with respectful admiration. Amidst the boundless plains of Gætulia and the innumerable valleys of Mount Atlas, it was impossible to prevent the escape of Firmus; and if the usurper could have tired the patience of his antagonist, he would have secured his person in the depth of some remote solitude, and expected the hopes of a future revolution. He was subdued by the perseverance of Theodosius, who had formed an inflexible determination that the war should end only by the death of the tyrant, and that every nation of Africa which presumed to support his cause should be involved in his ruin. At the head of a small body of troops, which seldom exceeded three thousand five hundred men, the Roman general advanced with a steady prudence, devoid of rashness or of fear, into the heart of a country where he was sometimes attacked by armies of twenty thousand Moors. The boldness of his charge dismayed the irregular barbarians; they were disconcerted by his seasonable and orderly retreats; they were continually baffled by the unknown resources of the military art; and they felt and confessed the just superiority which was assumed by the leader of a civilised nation. When Theodosius entered the extensive dominions of Igmazen, king of the Isaflenses, the haughty savage required, in words of defiance, his name and the object of his expedition. "I am," replied the stern and disdainful count, "I am the general of Valentinian, the lord of the world, who has sent me hither to pursue and punish a desperate robber. Deliver him instantly into my hands; and be assured, that, if thou dost not obey the commands of my invincible sovereign, thou and the people over whom thou reignest shall be utterly extirpated." As soon as Igmazen was satisfied that his enemy had strength and resolution to execute the fatal menace, he consented to purchase a necessary peace by the sacrifice of a guilty fugitive. The guards that were placed to secure the person of Firmus deprived him of the hopes of escape, and the Moorish tyrant, after wine had extinguished the sense of danger, disappointed the insulting triumph of the Romans by strangling himself in the night. His dead body, the only present which Igmazen could offer to

the conqueror, was carelessly thrown upon a camel; and Theodosius, leading back his victorious troops to Sitifi, was saluted by the warmest acclamations of joy and loyalty.[123]

Africa had been lost by the vices of Romanus; it was restored by the virtues of Theodosius; and our curiosity may be usefully directed to the inquiry of the respective treatment which the two generals received from the Imperial court. The authority of Count Romanus had been suspended by the master-general of the cavalry, and he was committed to safe and honourable custody till the end of the war. His crimes were proved by the most authentic evidence, and the public expected, with some impatience, the decree of severe justice. But the partial and powerful favour of Mellobaudes encouraged him to challenge his legal judges, to obtain repeated delays for the purpose of procuring a crowd of friendly witnesses, and, finally, to cover his guilty conduct by the additional guilt of fraud and forgery. About the same time the restorer of Britain and Africa, on a vague suspicion that his name and services were superior to the rank of a subject, was ignominiously beheaded at Carthage. Valentinian no longer reigned; and the death of Theodosius, as well as the impunity of Romanus, may justly be imputed to the arts of the ministers who abused the confidence and deceived the inexperienced youth of his sons.[124]

If the geographical accuracy of Ammianus had been fortunately bestowed on the British exploits of Theodosius, we should have traced, with eager curiosity, the distinct and domestic footsteps of his march. But the tedious enumeration of the unknown and uninteresting tribes of Africa may be reduced to the general remark, that they were all of the swarthy race of the Moors; that they inhabited the back settlements of the Mauritanian and Numidian provinces, the country, as they have since been termed by the Arabs, of dates and of locusts;[125] and that, as the Roman power declined in Africa, the boundary of civilised manners and cultivated land was insensibly contracted. Beyond the utmost limits of the Moors, the vast and inhospitable desert of the South extends above a thousand miles to the banks of the Niger. The ancients, who had a very faint and imperfect knowledge of the great peninsula of Africa, were sometimes tempted to believe that the torrid zone must ever remain destitute of inhabitants;[126] and they sometimes amused their fancy by filling the vacant space with headless men, or rather monsters,[127] with horned and cloven-footed satyrs,[128] with fabulous centaurs,[129] and with human pigmies, who waged a bold and doubtful warfare against the cranes.[130] Carthage would have trembled at the strange intelligence that the countries on either side of the equator were filled with innumerable nations who differed only in their colour from the ordinary appearance of the human species; and the subjects of the Roman empire might have anxiously expected that the swarms of barbarians which issued from the North would soon be encountered from the South by new swarms of barbarians, equally fierce and equally formidable. These gloomy terrors would indeed have been dispelled by a more intimate acquaintance with the character of their African enemies. The inaction of the negroes does not seem to be the effect either of their virtue or of their pusillanimity. They indulge, like the rest of mankind, their passions and appetites and the adjacent tribes are engaged in frequent acts of hostility.[131] But their rude ignorance has never invented any effectual weapons of defence or of destruction; they appear incapable of forming any extensive plans of government or conquest; and the obvious inferiority of their mental faculties has been discovered and abused by the nations of the temperate zone. Sixty thousand blacks are annually embarked from the coast of Guinea, never to return to their native country; but they are embarked in chains;[132] and this constant emigration which in the space of two centuries might have furnished armies to overrun the globe, accuses the guilt of Europe and the weakness of Africa.

IV. The ignominious treaty which saved the army of Jovian had been faithfully executed on the side of the Romans; and as they had solemnly renounced the sovereignty and alliance of Armenia and Iberia, those tributary Kingdoms were exposed, without protection, to the arms of the Persian monarch.[133] Sapor entered the Armenian territories at the head of a formidable host of cuirassiers, of archers, and of mercenary foot; but it was the invariable practice of Sapor to mix war and negotiation, and to consider falsehood and perjury as the most powerful instruments of regal policy. He affected to praise the prudent and moderate conduct of the king of Armenia; and the unsuspicious Tiranus was persuaded, by the repeated assurances of insidious friendship, to deliver his person into the hands of a faithless and cruel enemy. In the midst of a splendid entertainment, he was bound in chains of silver, as an honor due to the blood of the Arsacides; and, after a short con-

finement in the Tower of Oblivion at Ecbatana, he was released from the miseries of life, either by his own dagger or by that of an assassin. The kingdom of Armenia was reduced to the state of a Persian province; the administration was shared between a distinguished satrap and a favourite eunuch; and Sapor marched, without delay, to subdue the martial spirit of the Iberians. Sauromaces, who reigned in that country by the permission of the emperors, was expelled by a superior force, and, as an insult on the majesty of Rome, the king of kings placed a diadem on the head of his abject vassal Aspacuras. The city of Artogerassa[134] was the only place of Armenia which presumed to resist the effort of his arms. The treasure deposited in that strong fortress tempted the avarice of Sapor; but the danger of Olympias, the wife or widow of the Armenian king, excited the public compassion and animated the desperate valour of her subjects and soldiers. The Persians were surprised and repulsed under the walls of Artogerassa by a bold and well-concerted sally of the besieged. But the forces of Sapor were continually renewed and increased; the hopeless courage of the garrison was exhausted; the strength of the walls yielded to the assault; and the proud conqueror, after wasting the rebellious city with fire and sword, led away captive an unfortunate queen, who, in a more auspicious hour, had been the destined bride of the son of Constantine.[135] Yet if Sapor already triumphed in the easy conquest of two dependent kingdoms, he soon felt that a country is unsubdued as long as the minds of the people are actuated by an hostile and contumacious spirit. The satraps, whom he was obliged to trust, embraced the first opportunity of regaining the affection of their countrymen, and of signalising their immortal hatred to the Persian name. Since the conversion of the Armenians and Iberians, those nations considered the Christians as the favourites, and the Magians as the adversaries, of the Supreme Being; the influence of the clergy over a superstitious people was uniformly exerted in the cause of Rome; and as long as the successors of Constantine disputed with those of Artaxerxes the sovereignty of the intermediate provinces, the religious connection always threw a decisive advantage into the scale of the empire. A numerous and active party acknowledged Para, the son of Tiranus, as the lawful sovereign of Armenia, and his title to the throne was deeply rooted in the hereditary succession of five hundred years. By the unanimous consent of the Iberians, the country was equally divided between the rival princes; and Aspacuras, who owed his diadem to the choice of Sapor, was obliged to declare that his regard for his children, who were detained as hostages by the tyrant, was the only consideration which prevented him from openly renouncing the alliance of Persia. The emperor Valens, who respected the obligations of the treaty, and who was apprehensive of involving the East in a dangerous war, ventured with slow and cautious measures, to support the Roman party in the kingdoms of Iberia and Armenia. Twelve legions established the authority of Sauromaces on the banks of the Cyrus. The Euphrates was protected by the valour of Arintheus. A powerful army, under the command of Count Trajan, and of Vadomair king of the Alemanni, fixed their camp on the confines of Armenia. But they were strictly enjoined not to commit the first hostilities, which might be understood as a breach of the treaty; and such was the implicit obedience of the Roman general, that they retreated, with exemplary patience, under a shower of Persian arrows, till they had clearly acquired a just title to an honourable and legitimate victory. Yet these appearances of war insensibly subsided in a vain and tedious negotiation. The contending parties supported their claims by mutual reproaches of perfidy and ambition; and it should seem that the original treaty was expressed in very obscure terms, since they were reduced to the necessity of making their inconclusive appeal to the partial testimony of the generals of the two nations who had assisted at the negotiations.[136] The invasion of the Goths and Huns, which soon afterwards shook the foundations of the Roman empire, exposed the provinces of Asia to the arms of Sapor. But the declining age, and perhaps the infirmities of the monarch, suggested new maxims of tranquillity and moderation. His death, which happened in the full maturity of a reign of seventy years, changed in a moment the court and councils of Persia, and their attention was most probably engaged by domestic troubles and the distant efforts of a Carmanian war.[137] The remembrance of ancient injuries was lost in the enjoyment of peace. The kingdoms of Armenia and Iberia were permitted, by the mutual though tacit consent of both empires, to resume their doubtful neutrality. In the first years of the reign of Theodosius, a Persian embassy arrived at Constantinople to excuse the unjustifiable measures of the former reign, and to offer, as the tribute of friendship, or even of respect, a splendid present of gems, of silk, and of Indian elephants.[138]

In the general picture of the affairs of the East under the reign of Valens, the adventures of Para form one of the most striking and singular objects. The noble youth, by the persuasion of his mother Olympias, had escaped through the Persian host that besieged Artogerassa, and implored the protection of the emperor of the East. By his timid councils, Para was alternately supported, and recalled, and restored, and betrayed. The hopes of the Armenians were sometimes raised by the presence of their natural sovereign, and the ministers of Valens were satisfied that they preserved the integrity of the public faith, if their vassal was not suffered to assume the diadem and title of King. But they soon repented of their own rashness. They were confounded by the reproaches and threats of the Persian monarch. They found reason to distrust the cruel and inconstant temper of Para himself, who sacrificed, to the slightest suspicions, the lives of his most faithful servants, and held a secret and disgraceful correspondence with the assassin of his father and the enemy of his country. Under the specious pretence of consulting with the emperor on the subject of their common interest, Para was persuaded to descend from the mountains of Armenia, where his party was in arms, and to trust his independence and safety to the discretion of a perfidious court. The king of Armenia, for such he appeared in his own eyes and in those of his nation, was received with due honours by the governors of the provinces through which he passed but when he arrived at Tarsus in Cilicia, his progress was stopped under various pretences, his motions were watched with respectful vigilance, and he gradually discovered that he was a prisoner in the hands of the Romans. Para suppressed his indignation, dissembled his fears, and, after secretly preparing his escape, mounted on horseback with three hundred of his faithful followers. The officer stationed at the door of his apartment immediately communicated his flight to the consular of Cilicia, who overtook him in the suburbs, and endeavoured, without success, to dissuade him from prosecuting his rash and dangerous design. A legion was ordered to pursue the royal fugitive; but the pursuit of infantry could not be very alarming to a body of light cavalry; and upon the first cloud of arrows that was discharged into the air, they retreated with precipitation to the gates of Tarsus. After an incessant march of two days and two nights, Para and his Armenians reached the banks of the Euphrates; but the passage of the river, which they were obliged to swim, was attended with some delay and some loss. The country was alarmed, and the two roads, which were only separated by an interval of three miles, had been occupied by a thousand archers on horseback, under the command of a count and a tribune. Para must have yielded to superior force, if the accidental arrival of a friendly traveller had not revealed the danger and the means of escape. A dark and almost impervious path securely conveyed the Armenian troops through the thicket; and Para had left behind him the count and the tribune, while they patiently expected his approach along the public highways. They returned to the Imperial court to excuse their want of diligence or success; and seriously alleged that the king of Armenia, who was a skilful magician, had transformed himself and his followers, and passed before their eyes under a borrowed shape. After his return to his native kingdom, Para still continued to profess himself the friend and ally of the Romans: but the Romans had injured him too deeply ever to forgive, and the secret sentence of his death was signed in the council of Valens. The execution of the bloody deed was committed to the subtle prudence of Count Trajan, and he had the merit of insinuating himself into the confidence of the credulous prince, that he might find an opportunity of stabbing him to the heart. Para was invited to a Roman banquet, which had been prepared with all the pomp and sensuality of the East; the hall resounded with cheerful music, and the company was already heated with wine, when the count retired for an instant, drew his sword, and gave the signal of the murder. A robust and desperate barbarian instantly rushed on the king of Armenia, and though he bravely defended his life with the first weapon that chance offered to his hand, the table of the Imperial general was stained with the royal blood of a guest and an ally. Such were the weak and wicked maxims of the Roman administration, that, to attain a doubtful object of political interest, the laws of nations, and the sacred rights of hospitality, were inhumanly violated in the face of the world.[139]

V. During a peaceful interval of thirty years, the Romans secured their frontiers, and the Goths extended their dominions. The victories of the great Hermanric,[140] king of the Ostrogoths, and the most noble of the race of the Amali, have been compared, by the enthusiasm of his countrymen, to the exploits of Alexander: with this singular, and almost incredible, difference, that the martial spirit of the Gothic hero, instead of being supported by the vigour of youth, was displayed with glory and success in the extreme period of human life, between the age of fourscore and one hundred and ten years. The independent tribes were persuaded, or compelled, to acknowledge the king of the Ostrogoths as the sovereign of the Gothic nation: the chiefs of the Visigoths, or Thervingi, renounced the royal title, and assumed the more humble appellation of *Judges*; and, among those judges, Athanaric, Fritigern, and Alavivus were the most illustrious, by their personal merit, as well as by their vicinity to the Roman provinces. These domestic conquests, which increased the military power of Hermanric, enlarged his ambitious designs. He invaded the adjacent countries of the North, and twelve considerable nations, whose names and limits cannot be accurately defined, successively yielded to the superiority of the Gothic arms.[141] The Heruli, who inhabited the marshy lands near the lake Mæotis, were renowned for their strength and agility; and the assistance of their light infantry was eagerly solicited, and highly esteemed, in all the wars of the barbarians. But the active spirit of the Heruli was subdued by the slow and steady perseverance of the Goths; and, after a bloody action, in which the king was slain, the remains of that warlike tribe became an useful accession to the camp of Hermanric. He then marched against the Venedi; unskilled in the use of arms, and formidable only by their numbers, which filled the wide extent of the plains of modern Poland. The victorious Goths, who were not inferior in numbers, prevailed in the contest, by the decisive advantages of exercise and discipline. After the submission of the Venedi, the conqueror advanced, without resistance, as far as the confines of the Æstii,[142] an ancient people, whose name is still preserved in the province of Esthonia. Those distant inhabitants of the Baltic coast were supported by the labors of agriculture, enriched by the trade of amber, and consecrated by the peculiar worship of the Mother of the Gods. But the scarcity of iron obliged the Æstian warriors to content themselves with wooden clubs; and the reduction of that wealthy country is ascribed to the prudence, rather than to the arms, of Hermanric. His dominions, which extended from the Danube to the Baltic, included the native seats, and the recent acquisitions, of the Goths; and he reigned over the greatest part of Germany and Scythia with the authority of a conqueror, and sometimes with the cruelty of a tyrant. But he reigned over a part of the globe incapable of perpetuating and adorning the glory of its heroes. The name of Hermanric is almost buried in oblivion; his exploits are imperfectly known: and the Romans themselves appeared unconscious of the progress of an aspiring power which threatened the liberty of the North and the peace of the empire.[143]

The Goths had contracted an hereditary attachment for the Imperial house of Constantine, of whose power and liberality they had received so many signal proofs. They respected the public peace; and if an hostile band sometimes presumed to pass the Roman limit, their irregular conduct was candidly ascribed to the ungovernable spirit of the barbarian youth. Their contempt for two new and obscure princes, who had been raised to the throne by a popular election, inspired the Goths with bolder hopes; and, while they agitated some design of marching their confederate force under the national standard, [144] they were easily tempted to embrace the party of Procopius, and to foment, by their dangerous aid, the civil discord of the Romans. The public treaty might stipulate no more than ten thousand auxiliaries; but the design was so zealously adopted by the chiefs of the Visigoths, that the army which passed the Danube amounted to the number of thirty thousand men.[145] They marched with the proud confidence that their invincible valour would decide the fate of the Roman empire; and the provinces of Thrace groaned under the weight of the barbarians, who displayed the insolence of masters, and the licentiousness of enemies. But the intemperance which gratified their appetites retarded their progress; and before the Goths could receive any certain intelligence of the defeat and death of Procopius, they perceived, by the hostile state of the country, that the civil and military powers were resumed by his successful rival. A chain of posts and fortifications, skilfully disposed by Valens, or the generals of Valens, resisted their march, prevented their retreat, and intercepted their subsistence. The fierceness of the barbarians was tamed and suspended by hunger; they indignantly threw down their arms at the feet of the conqueror, who offered them food and chains: the numerous captives were distributed in all the cities of the East; and the provincials, who were soon familiarised with their savage appearance, ventured, by degrees, to measure their own strength with these formidable adversaries, whose name had so long been the object of their terror. The king of Scythia (and Hermanric alone could deserve so lofty a title) was

grieved and exasperated by this national calamity. His ambassadors loudly complained, at the court of Valens, of the infraction of the ancient and solemn alliance which had so long subsisted between the Romans and the Goths. They alleged that they had fulfilled the duty of allies, by assisting the kinsman and successor of the emperor Julian; they required the immediate restitution of the noble captives; and they urged a very singular claim, that the Gothic generals, marching in arms, and in hostile array, were entitled to the sacred character and privileges of ambassadors. The decent, but peremptory, refusal of these extravagant demands was signified to the barbarians by Victor, master-general of the cavalry, who expressed, with force and dignity, the just complaints of the emperor of the East.[146] The negotiation was interrupted, and the manly exhortations of Valentinian encouraged his timid brother to vindicate the insulted majesty of the empire.[147]

The splendour and magnitude of this Gothic war are celebrated by a contemporary historian:[148] but the events scarcely deserve the attention of posterity, except as the preliminary steps of the approaching decline and fall of the empire. Instead of leading the nations of Germany and Scythia to the banks of the Danube, or even to the gates of Constantinople, the aged monarch of the Goths resigned to the brave Athanaric the danger and glory of a defensive war, against an enemy who wielded with a feeble hand the powers of a mighty state. A bridge of boats was established upon the Danube, the presence of Valens animated his troops, and his ignorance of the art of war was compensated by personal bravery, and a wise deference to the advice of Victor and Arintheus, his masters-general of the cavalry and infantry. The operations of the campaign were conducted by their skill and experience; but they found it impossible to drive the Visigoths from their strong posts in the mountains, and the devastation of the plains obliged the Romans themselves to repass the Danube on the approach of winter. The incessant rains, which swelled the waters of the river, produced a tacit suspension of arms, and confined the emperor Valens, during the whole course of the ensuing summer, to his camp of Marcianopolis. The third year of the war was more favourable to the Romans, and more pernicious to the Goths. The interruption of trade deprived the barbarians of the objects of luxury, which they already confounded with the necessaries of life; and the desolation of a very extensive tract of country threatened them with the horrors of famine. Athanaric was provoked, or compelled, to risk a battle, which he lost, in the plains; and the pursuit was rendered more bloody by the cruel precaution of the victorious generals, who had promised a large reward for the head of every Goth that was brought into the Imperial camp. The submission of the barbarians appeased the resentment of Valens and his council: the emperor listened with satisfaction to the flattering and eloquent remonstrance of the senate of Constantinople, which assumed, for the first time, a share in the public deliberations; and the same generals, Victor and Arintheus, who had successfully directed the conduct of the war, were empowered to regulate the conditions of peace. The freedom of trade which the Goths had hitherto enjoyed was restricted to two cities on the Danube; the rashness of their leaders was severely punished by the suppression of their pensions and subsidies; and the exception, which was stipulated in favour of Athanaric alone, was more advantageous than honourable to the Judge of the Visigoths. Athanaric, who, on this occasion, appears to have consulted his private interest, without expecting the orders of his sovereign, supported his own dignity, and that of his tribe, in the personal interview which was proposed by the ministers of Valens. He persisted in his declaration that it was impossible for him, without incurring the guilt of perjury, ever to set his foot on the territory of the empire; and it is more than probable that his regard for the sanctity of an oath was confirmed by the recent and fatal examples of Roman treachery. The Danube, which separated the dominions of the two independent nations, was chosen for the scene of the conference. The emperor of the East, and the Judge of the Visigoths, accompanied by an equal number of armed followers, advanced in their respective barges to the middle of the stream. After the ratification of the treaty, and the delivery of hostages, Valens returned in triumph to Constantinople, and the Goths remained in a state of tranquillity about six years, till they were violently impelled against the Roman empire by an innumerable host of Scythians, who appeared to issue from the frozen regions of the North.[149]

The emperor of the West, who had resigned to his brother the command of the Lower Danube, reserved for his immediate care the defence of the Rhætian and Illyrian provinces, which spread so many hundred miles along the greatest of the European rivers. The active policy of Valentinian was continually employed in adding new fortifications to the security of the frontier; but the abuse of this policy provoked the just resentment of the barbarians. The Quadi complained that the ground for an intended fortress had been marked out on their territories, and their complaints were urged with so much reason and moderation, that Equitius, master-general of Illyricum, consented to suspend the prosecution of the work till he should be more clearly informed of the will of his sovereign. This fair occasion of injuring a rival, and of advancing the fortune of his son, was eagerly embraced by the inhuman Maximin, the præfect, or rather tyrant, of Gaul. The passions of Valentinian were impatient of control, and he credulously listened to the assurances of his favourite, that, if the government of Valeria, and the direction of the work, were intrusted to the zeal of his son Marcellinus, the emperor should no longer be importuned with the audacious remonstrances of the barbarians. The subjects of Rome, and the natives of Germany, were insulted by the arrogance of a young and worthless minister, who considered his rapid elevation as the proof and reward of his superior merit. He affected, however, to receive the modest application of Gabinius, king of the Quadi, with some attention and regard; but this artful civility concealed a dark and bloody design, and the credulous prince was persuaded to accept the pressing invitation of Marcellinus. I am at a loss how to vary the narrative of similar crimes; or how to relate that, in the course of the same year, but in remote parts of the empire, the inhospitable table of two Imperial generals was stained with the royal blood of two guests and allies, inhumanly murdered by their order, and in their presence. The fate of Gabinius, and of Para, was the same: but the cruel death of their sovereign was resented in a very different manner by the servile temper of the Armenians and the free and daring spirit of the Germans. The Quadi were much declined from that formidable power which, in the time of Marcus Antoninus, had spread terror to the gates of Rome. But they still possessed arms and courage; their courage was animated by despair, and they obtained the usual reinforcement of the cavalry of their Sarmatian allies. So improvident was the assassin Marcellinus, that he chose the moment when the bravest veterans had been drawn away to suppress the revolt of Firmus, and the whole province was exposed, with a very feeble defence, to the rage of the exasperated barbarians. They invaded Pannonia in the season of harvest, unmercifully destroyed every object of plunder which they could not easily transport, and either disregarded or demolished the empty fortifications. The princess Constantia, the daughter of the emperor Constantius, and the granddaughter of the great Constantine, very narrowly escaped. That royal maid, who had innocently supported the revolt of Procopius, was now the destined wife of the heir of the Western empire. She traversed the peaceful province with a splendid and unarmed train. Her person was saved from danger, and the republic from disgrace, by the active zeal of Messalla, governor of the provinces. As soon as he was informed that the village where she stopped only to dine was almost encompassed by the barbarians, he hastily placed her in his own chariot, and drove full speed till he reached the gates of Sirmium, which were at the distance of six-and-twenty miles. Even Sirmium might not have been secure if the Quadi and Sarmatians had diligently advanced during the general consternation of the magistrates and people. Their delay allowed Probus, the Prætorian præfect, sufficient time to recover his own spirits and to revive the courage of the citizens. He skilfully directed their strenuous efforts to repair and strengthen the decayed fortifications, and procured the seasonable and effectual assistance of a company of archers to protect the capital of the Illyrian provinces. Disappointed in their attempts against the walls of Sirmium, the indignant barbarians turned their arms against the master-general of the frontier, to whom they unjustly attributed the murder of their king. Equitius could bring into the field no more than two legions, but they contained the veteran strength of the Mæsian and Pannonian bands. The obstinacy with which they disputed the vain honours of rank and precedency was the cause of their destruction, and, while they acted with separate forces and divided councils, they were surprised and slaughtered by the active vigour of the Sarmatian horse. The success of this invasion provoked the emulation of the bordering tribes, and the province of Mæsia would infallibly have been lost if young Theodosius, the duke or military commander of the frontier, had not signalised, in the defeat of the public enemy, an intrepid genius worthy of his illustrious father and of his future greatness.[150]

The mind of Valentinian, who then resided at Trèves, was deeply affected by the calamities of Illyricum, but the lateness of the season suspended the execution of his designs till the ensuing spring. He marched in person, with a con-

siderable part of the forces of Gaul, from the banks of the Moselle; and to the suppliant ambassadors of the Sarmatians, who met him on the way, he returned a doubtful answer, that as soon as he reached the scene of action he should examine and pronounce. When he arrived at Sirmium he gave audience to the deputies of the Illyrian provinces, who loudly congratulated their own felicity under the auspicious government of Probus, his Prætorian præfect.[151] Valentinian, who was flattered by these demonstrations of their loyalty and gratitude, imprudently asked the deputy of Epirus, a Cynic philosopher of intrepid sincerity,[152] whether he was freely sent by the wishes of the province? "With tears and groans am I sent (replied Iphicles) by a reluctant people." The emperor paused, but the impunity of his ministers established the pernicious maxim that they might oppress his subjects without injuring his service. A strict inquiry into their conduct would have relieved the public discontent. The severe condemnation of the murder of Gabinius was the only measure which could restore the confidence of the Germans, and vindicate the honour of the Roman name. But the haughty monarch was incapable of the magnanimity which dares to acknowledge a fault. He forgot the provocation, remembered only the injury, and advanced into the country of the Quadi with an insatiate thirst of blood and revenge. The extreme devastation and promiscuous massacre of a savage war were justified in the eyes of the emperor, and perhaps in those of the world, by the cruel equity of retaliation;[153] and such was the discipline of the Romans, and the consternation of the enemy, that Valentinian repassed the Danube without the loss of a single man. As he had resolved to complete the destruction of the Quadi by a second campaign, he fixed his winter-quarters at Bregetio, on the Danube, near the Hungarian city of Presburg. While the operations of war were suspended by the severity of the weather, the Quadi made an humble attempt to deprecate the wrath of their conqueror, and, at the earnest persuasion of Equitius, their ambassadors were intoduced into the Imperial council. They approached the throne with bended bodies and dejected countenances, and, without daring to complain of the murder of their king, they affirmed, with solemn oaths, that the late invasion was the crime of some irregular robbers, which the public council of the nation condemned and abhorred. The answer of the emperor left them but little hope from his clemency or compassion. He reviled, in the most intemperate language, their baseness, their ingratitude, their insolence. His eyes, his voice, his colour, his gestures, expressed the violence of his ungoverned fury; and while his whole frame was agitated with convulsive passion a large blood-vessel suddenly burst in his body, and Valentinian fell speechless into the arms of his attendants. Their pious care immediately concealed his situation from the crowd, but in a few minutes the emperor of the West expired in an agony of pain, retaining his senses till the last, and struggling, without success, to declare his intentions to the generals and ministers who surrounded the royal couch. Valentinian was about fifty-four years of age, and he wanted only one hundred days to accomplish the twelve years of his reign.[154]

The polygamy of Valentinian is seriously attested by an ecclesiastical historian.[155] "The empress Severa (I relate the fable) admitted into her familiar society the lovely Justina, the daughter of an Italian governor; her admiration of those naked charms, which she had often seen in the bath, was expressed with such lavish and imprudent praise that the emperor was tempted to introduce a second wife into his bed; and his public edict extended to all the subjects of the empire the same domestic privilege which he had assumed for himself." But we may be assured, from the evidence of reason as well as history, that the two marriages of Valentinian with Severa and with Justina were *successively* contracted, and that he used the ancient permission of divorce, which was still allowed by the laws, though it was condemned by the church. Severa was the mother of Gratian, who seemed to unite every claim which could entitle him to the undoubted succession of the Western empire. He was the eldest son of a monarch whose glorious reign had confirmed the free and honourable choice of his fellow-soldiers. Before he had attained the ninth year of his age the royal youth received from the hands of his indulgent father the purple robe and diadem, with the title of Augustus; the election was solemnly ratified by the consent and applause of the armies of Gaul,[156] and the name of Gratian was added to the names of Valentinian and Valens in all the legal transactions of the Roman government. By his marriage with the granddaughter of Constantine, the son of Valentinian acquired all the hereditary rights of the Flavian family, which, in a series of three Imperial generations, were sanctified by time, religion, and the reverence of the people. At the death of his father the royal youth was in the seventeenth year of his age, and his virtues already justified the favourable opinion of the army and people. But Gratian resided, without apprehension, in the palace of Trèves, whilst at the distance of many hundred miles Valentinian suddenly expired in the camp of Bregetio. The passions which had been so long suppressed by the presence of a master immediately revived in the Imperial council, and the ambitious design of reigning in the name of an infant was artfully executed by Mellobaudes and Equitius, who commanded the attachment of the Illyrian and Italian bands. They contrived the most honourable pretences to remove the popular leaders and the troops of Gaul, who might have asserted the claims of the lawful successor; they suggested the necessity of extinguishing the hopes of foreign and domestic enemies by a bold and decisive measure. The empress Justina, who had been left in a palace about one hundred miles from Bregetio, was respectfully invited to appear in the camp with the son of the deceased emperor. On the sixth day after the death of Valentinian, the infant prince of the same name, who was only four years old, was shown, in the arms of his mother, to the legions, and solemnly invested, by military acclamation, with the titles and ensigns of supreme power. The impending dangers of a civil war were seasonably prevented by the wise and moderate conduct of the emperor Gratian. He cheerfully accepted the choice of the army, declared that he should always consider the son of Justina as a brother, not as a rival, and advised the empress, with her son Valentinian, to fix their residence at Milan, in the fair and peaceful province of Italy while he assumed the more arduous command of the countries beyond the Alps. Gratian dissembled his resentment till he could safely punish or disgrace the authors of the conspiracy; and though he uniformly behaved with tenderness and regard to his infant colleague, he gradually confounded, in the administration of the Western empire, the office of a guardian with the authority of a sovereign. The government of the Roman world was exercised in the united names of Valens and his two nephews; but the feeble emperor of the East, who succeeded to the rank of his elder brother, never obtained any weight or influence in the councils of the West.[157]

Manners of the Pastoral Nations. Progress of the Huns from China to Europe. Flight of the Goths. They pass the Danube. Gothic War. Defeat and Death of Valens. Gratian invests Theodosius with the Eastern Empire. His Character and Success. Peace and Settlement of the Goths.

IN the second year of the reign of Valentinian and Valens, on the morning of the twenty-first day of July, the greatest part of the Roman world was shaken by a violent and destructive earthquake. The impression was communicated to the waters; the shores of the Mediterranean were left dry by the sudden retreat of the sea; great quantities of fish were caught with the hand; large vessels were stranded on the mud; and a curious spectator[1] amused his eye, or rather his fancy, by contemplating the various appearance of valleys and mountains which had never, since the formation of the globe, been exposed to the sun. But the tide soon returned with the weight of an immense and irresistible deluge, which was severely felt on the coasts of Sicily, of Dalmatia, of Greece, and of Egypt; large boats were transported and lodged on the roofs of houses, or at the distance of two miles from the shore; the people, with their habitations, were swept away by the waters; and the city of Alexandria annually commemorated the fatal day on which fifty thousand persons had lost their lives in the inundation. This calamity, the report of which was magnified from one province to another, astonished and terrified the subjects of Rome, and their affrighted imagination enlarged the real extent of a momentary evil. They recollected the preceding earthquakes, which had subverted the cities of Palestine and Bithynia; they considered these alarming strokes as the prelude only of still more dreadful calamities; and their fearful vanity was disposed to confound the symptoms of a declining empire and a sinking world.[2] It was the fashion of the times to attribute every remarkable event to the particular will of the Deity; the alterations of nature were connected, by an invisible chain, with the moral and metaphysical opinions of the human mind; and the most sagacious divines could distinguish, according to the colour of their respective prejudices, that the establishment of heresy tended to produce an earthquake, or that a deluge was the inevitable consequence of the progress of sin and error. Without presuming to discuss the truth or propriety of these lofty speculations, the historian may content himself with an observation, which seems to be justified by experience, that man has much more to fear from the passions of his fellow-creatures than from the convulsions of the elements.[3] The mischievous effects of an earthquake or deluge, a hurricane or the eruption of a volcano, bear a very inconsiderable proportion to the ordinary calamities of war, as they are now moderated by the prudence or humanity of the princes of Europe, who amuse their own leisure and exercise the courage of their subjects in the practice of the military art. But the laws and manners of modern nations protect the safety and freedom of the vanquished soldier; and the peaceful citizen has seldom reason to complain that his life or even his fortune is exposed to the rage of war. In the disastrous period of the fall of the Roman empire, which may justly be dated from the reign of Valens, the happiness and security of each individual were personally attacked, and the arts and labours of ages were rudely defaced by the barbarians of Scythia and Germany. The invasion of the Huns precipitated on the provinces of the West the Gothic nation, which advanced, in less than forty years, from the Danube to the Atlantic, and opened a way, by the success of their arms, to the inroads of so many hostile tribes more savage than themselves. The original principle of motion was concealed in the remote countries of the North, and the curious observation of the pastoral life of the Scythians[4] or Tartars[5] will illustrate the latent cause of these destructive emigrations.

The different characters that mark the civilised nations of the globe may be ascribed to the use and the abuse of reason, which so variously shapes and so artificially composes the manners and opinions of an European or a Chinese. But the operation of instinct is more sure and simple than that of reason; it is much easier to ascertain the appetites of a quadruped than the speculations of a philosopher; and the savage tribes of mankind, as they approach nearer to the condition of animals, preserve a stronger resemblance to themselves and to each other. The uniform stability of their manners is the natural consequence of the imperfection of their faculties. Reduced to a similar situation, their wants, their desires, their enjoyments still continue the same; and the influence of food or climate, which, in a more improved state of society, is suspended or subdued by so many moral causes, most powerfully contributes to form and to maintain the national character of barbarians. In every age the immense plains of Scythia or Tartary have been inhabited by vagrant tribes of hunters and shepherds, whose indolence refuses to cultivate the earth, and whose restless spirit disdains the confinement of a sedentary life. In every age the Scythians and Tartars have been renowned for their invincible courage and rapid conquests. The thrones of Asia have been repeatedly overturned by the shepherds of the North, and their arms have spread terror and devastation over the most fertile and warlike countries of Europe.[6] On this occasion, as well as on many others, the sober historian is forcibly awakened from a pleasing vision, and is compelled, with some reluctance, to confess that the pastoral manners, which have been adorned with the fairest attributes of peace and innocence, are much better adapted to the fierce and cruel habits of a military life. To illustrate this observation, I shall now proceed to consider a nation of shepherds and of warriors in the three important articles of, I. Their diet; II. Their habitation; and III. Their exercises. The narratives of antiquity are justified by the experience of modern times;[7] and the banks of the Borysthenes, of the Volga, or of the Selinga will indifferently present the same uniform spectacle of similar and native manners.[8]

I. The corn, or even the rice, which constitutes the ordinary and wholesome food of a civilised people, can be obtained only by the patient toil of the husbandman. Some of the happy savages who dwell between the tropics are plentifully nourished by the liberality of nature, but in the climates of the North a nation of shepherds is reduced to their flocks and herds. The skilful practitioners of the medical art will determine (if they are able to determine) how far the temper of the human mind may be affected by the use of animal or of vegetable food; and whether the common association of carnivorous and cruel deserves to be considered in any other light than that of an innocent, perhaps a salutary, prejudice of humanity.[9] Yet, if it be true that the sentiment of compassion is imperceptibly weakened by the sight and practice of do-

mestic cruelty, we may observe that the horrid objects which are disguised by the arts of European refinement are exhibited in their naked and most disgusting simplicity in the tent of a Tartarian shepherd. The ox or the sheep are slaughtered by the same hand from which they were accustomed to receive their daily food; and the bleeding limbs are served, with very little preparation, on the table of their unfeeling murderer. In the military profession, and especially in the conduct of a numerous army, the exclusive use of animal food appears to be productive of the most solid advantages. Corn is a bulky and perishable commodity, and the large magazines, which are indispensably necessary for the subsistence of our troops, must be slowly transported by the labour of men or horses. But the flock and herds which accompany the march of the Tartars afford a sure and increasing supply of flesh and milk; in the far greater part of the uncultivated waste the vegetation of the grass is quick and luxuriant; and there are few places so extremely barren that the hardy cattle of the North cannot find some tolerable pasture. The supply is multiplied and prolonged by the undistinguishing appetite and patient abstinence of the Tartars. They indifferently feed on the flesh of those animals that have been killed for the table or have died of disease. Horseflesh, which in every age and country has been proscribed by the civilised nations of Europe and Asia, they devour with peculiar greediness, and this singular taste facilitates the success of their military operations. The active cavalry of Scythia is always followed, in their most distant and rapid incursions, by an adequate number of spare horses, who may be occasionally used either to redouble the speed or to satisfy the hunger of the barbarians. Many are the resources of courage and poverty. When the forage round a camp of Tartars is almost consumed, they slaughter the greatest part of their cattle, and preserve the flesh, either smoked or dried in the sun. On the sudden emergency of a hasty march, they provide themselves with a sufficient quantity of little balls of cheese, or rather of hard curd, which they occasionally dissolve in water, and this unsubstantial diet will support, for many days, the life, and even the spirits, of the patient warrior. But this extraordinary abstinence, which the Stoic would approve and the hermit might envy, is commonly succeeded by the most voracious indulgence of appetite. The wines of a happier climate are the most grateful present or the most valuable commodity that can be offered to the Tartars; and the only example of their industry seems to consist in the art of extracting from mare's milk a fermented liquor which possesses a very strong power of intoxication. Like the animals of prey, the savages, both of the old and new world, experience the alternate vicissitudes of famine and plenty, and their stomach is inured to sustain, without much inconvenience, the opposite extremes of hunger and of intemperance.

II. In the ages of rustic and martial simplicity, a people of soldiers and husbandmen are dispersed over the face of an extensive and cultivated country; and some time must elapse before the warlike youth of Greece or Italy could be assembled under the same standard, either to defend their own confines, or to invade the territories of the adjacent tribes. The progress of manufactures and commerce insensibly collects a large multitude within the walls of a city; but these citizens are no longer soldiers, and the arts which adorn and improve the state of civil society corrupt the habits of the military life. The pastoral manners of the Scythians seem to unite the different advantages of simplicity and refinement. The individuals of the same tribe are constantly assembled, but they are assembled in a camp, and the native spirit of these dauntless shepherds is animated by mutual support and emulation. The houses of the Tartars are no more than small tents, of an oval form, which afford a cold and dirty habitation for the promiscuous youth of both sexes. The palaces of the rich consist of wooden huts, of such a size that they may be conveniently fixed on large waggons, and drawn by a team perhaps of twenty or thirty oxen. The flocks and herds, after grazing all day in the adjacent pastures, retire, on the approach of night, within the protection of the camp. The necessity of preventing the most mischievous confusion in such a perpetual concourse of men and animals must gradually introduce, in the distribution, the order, and the guard of the encampment, the rudiments of the military art. As soon as the forage of a certain district is consumed, the tribe, or rather army, of shepherds makes a regular march to some fresh pastures, and thus acquires, in the ordinary occupations of the pastoral life, the practical knowledge of one of the most important and difficult operations of war. The choice of stations is regulated by the difference of the seasons; in the summer the Tartars advance towards the North, and pitch their tents on the banks of a river, or, at least, in the neighbourhood of a running stream. But in the winter they return to the South, and shelter their camp,

behind some convenient eminence, against the winds, which are chilled in their passage over the bleak and icy regions of Siberia. These manners are admirably adapted to diffuse among the wandering tribes the spirit of emigration and conquest. The connection between the people and their territory is of so frail a texture that it may be broken by the slightest accident. The camp, and not the soil, is the native country of the genuine Tartar. Within the precincts of that camp his family, his companions, his property, are always included, and in the most distant marches he is still surrounded by the objects which are dear or valuable or familiar in his eyes. The thirst of rapine, the fear or the resentment of injury, the impatience of servitude, have, in every age, been sufficient causes to urge the tribes of Scythia boldly to advance into some unknown countries, where they might hope to find a more plentiful subsistence or a less formidable enemy. The revolutions of the North have frequently determined the fate of the South; and in the conflict of hostile nations the victor and the vanquished have alternately drove, and been driven, from the confines of China to those of Germany.[10] These great emigrations, which have been sometimes executed with almost incredible diligence, were rendered more easy by the peculiar nature of the climate. It is well known that the cold of Tartary is much more severe than in the midst of the temperate zone might reasonably be expected; this uncommon rigour is attributed to the height of the plains, which rise, especially towards the east, more than half a mile above the level of the sea, and to the quantity of saltpetre with which the soil is deeply impregnated.[11] In the winter season, the broad and rapid rivers that discharge their waters into the Euxine, the Caspian, or the Icy Sea, are strongly frozen, the fields are covered with a bed of snow, and the fugitive or victorious tribes may securely traverse, with their families, their waggons, and their cattle, the smooth and hard surface of an immense plain.

III. The pastoral life, compared with the labours of agriculture and manufactures, is undoubtedly a life of idleness; and as the most honourable shepherds of the Tartar race devolve on their captives the domestic management of the cattle, their own leisure is seldom disturbed by any servile and assiduous cares. But this leisure, instead of being devoted to the soft enjoyments of love and harmony, is usefully spent in the violent and sanguinary exercise of the chase. The plains of Tartary are filled with a strong and serviceable breed of horses, which are easily trained for the purposes of war and hunting. The Scythians of every age have been celebrated as bold and skilful riders, and constant practice had seated them so firmly on horseback that they were supposed by strangers to perform the ordinary duties of civil life, to eat, to drink, and even to sleep, without dismounting from their steeds. They excel in the dexterous management of the lance; the long Tartar bow is drawn with a nervous arm, and the weighty arrow is directed to its object with unerring aim and irresistible force. These arrows are often pointed against the harmless animals of the desert, which increase and multiply in the absence of their most formidable enemy—the hare, the goat, the roebuck, the fallow-deer, the stag, the elk, and the antelope. The vigour and patience both of the men and horses are continually exercised by the fatigues of the chase, and the plentiful supply of game contributes to the subsistence and even luxury of a Tartar camp. But the exploits of the hunters of Scythia are not confined to the destruction of timid or innoxious beasts: they boldly encounter the angry wild boar when he turns against his pursuers, excite the sluggish courage of the bear, and provoke the fury of the tiger as he slumbers in the thicket. Where there is danger, there may be glory; and the mode of hunting which opens the fairest field to the exertions of valour may justly be considered as the image and as the school of war. The general hunting matches, the pride and delight of the Tartar princes, compose an instructive exercise for their numerous cavalry. A circle is drawn, of many miles in circumference, to encompass the game of an extensive district; and the troops that form the circle regularly advance towards a common centre, where the captive animals, surrounded on every side, are abandoned to the darts of the hunters. In this march, which frequently continues many days, the cavalry are obliged to climb the hills, to swim the rivers, and to wind through the valleys, without interrupting the prescribed order of their gradual progress. They acquire the habit of directing their eye and their steps to a remote object, of preserving their intervals, of suspending or accelerating their pace according to the motions of the troops on their right and left, and of watching and repeating the signals of their leaders. Their leaders study in this practical school the most important lesson of the military art, the prompt and accurate judgment of ground, of distance, and of time. To employ against a human enemy the same patience and valour, the same skill and discipline, is the only alteration which is required in real war, and the amusements of the chase serve as a prelude to the conquest of an empire.[12]

The political society of the ancient Germans has the appearance of a voluntary alliance of independent warriors. The tribes of Scythia, distinguished by the modern appellation of *Hords*, assume the form of a numerous and increasing family, which, in the course of successive generations, has been propagated from the same original stock. The meanest and most ignorant of the Tartars preserve with conscious pride the inestimable treasure of their genealogy, and, whatever distinctions of rank may have been introduced by the unequal distribution of pastoral wealth, they mutually respect themselves and each other as the descendants of the first founder of the tribe. The custom, which still prevails, of adopting the bravest and most faithful of the captives, may countenance the very probable suspicion that this extensive consanguinity is, in a great measure, legal and fictitious. But the useful prejudice which has obtained the sanction of time and opinion produces the effects of truth; the haughty barbarians yield a cheerful and voluntary obedience to the head of their blood, and their chief, or *mursa*, as the representative of their great father, exercises the authority of a judge in peace and of a leader in war. In the original state of the pastoral world, each of the *mursas* (if we may continue to use a modern appellation) acted as the independent chief of a large and separate family, and the limits of their peculiar territories were gradually fixed by superior force or mutual consent. But the constant operation of various and permanent causes contributed to unite the vagrant Hords into national communities, under the command of a supreme head. The weak were desirous of support, and the strong were ambitious of dominion; the power which is the result of union oppressed and collected the divided forces of the adjacent tribes; and, as the vanquished were freely admitted to share the advantages of victory, the most valiant chiefs hastened to range themselves and their followers under the formidable standard of a confederate nation. The most successful of the Tartar princes assumed the military command, to which he was entitled by the superiority either of merit or of power. He was raised to the throne by the acclamations of his equals, and the title of *Khan* expresses in the language of the North of Asia the full extent of the regal dignity. The right of hereditary succession was long confined to the blood of the founder of the monarchy; and at this moment all the Khans who reign from Crimea to the wall of China are the lineal descendants of the renowned Zingis.[13] But, as it is the indispensable duty of a Tartar sovereign to lead his warlike subjects into the field, the claims of an infant are often disregarded, and some royal kinsman, distinguished by his age and valour, is intrusted with the sword and sceptre of his predecessor. Two distinct and regular taxes are levied on the tribes to support the dignity of their national monarch and of their peculiar chief, and each of those contributions amounts to the tithe both of their property and of their spoil. A Tartar sovereign enjoys the tenth part of the wealth of his people; and as his own domestic riches of flocks and herds increase in a much larger proportion, he is able plentifully to maintain the rustic splendour of his court, to reward the most deserving or the most favoured of his followers, and to obtain from the gentle influence of corruption the obedience which might be sometimes refused to the stern mandates of authority. The manners of his subjects, accustomed, like himself, to blood and rapine, might excuse in their eyes such partial acts of tyranny as would excite the horror of a civilised people, but the power of a despot has never been acknowledged in the deserts of Scythia. The immediate jurisdiction of the Khan is confined within the limits of his own tribe, and the exercise of his royal prerogative has been moderated by the ancient institution of a national council. The Coroultai,[14] or Diet, of the Tartars was regularly held in the spring and autumn in the midst of a plain, where the princes of the reigning family and the mursas of the respective tribes may conveniently assemble on horseback with their martial and numerous trains, and the ambitious monarch who reviewed the strength, must consult the inclination, of an armed people. The rudiments of a feudal government may be discovered in the constitution of the Scythian or Tartar nations, but the perpetual conflict of those hostile nations has sometimes terminated in the establishment of a powerful and despotic empire. The victor, enriched by the tribute and fortified by the arms of dependent kings, has spread his conquests over Europe or Asia; the successful shepherds of the North have submitted to the confinement of arts, of laws, and of cities; and the introduction of luxury, after destroying the freedom of the people, has undermined the foundations of the throne.[15]

The memory of past events cannot long be preserved in the frequent and remote emigrations of illiterate barbarians. The modern Tartars are ignorant of the conquests of their ancestors;[16] and our knowledge of the history of the Scythians is derived from their intercourse with the learned and civilised nations of the South—the Greeks, the Persians, and the Chinese. The Greeks, who navigated the Euxine, and planted their colonies along the sea-coast, made the gradual and imperfect discovery of Scythia, from the Danube and the confines of Thrace, as far as the frozen Mæotis, the seat of eternal winter, and Mount Caucasus, which, in the language of poetry, was described as the utmost boundary of the earth. They celebrated, with simple credulity, the virtues of the pastoral life:[17] they entertained a more rational apprehension of the strength and numbers of the warlike barbarians,[18] who contemptuously baffled the immense armament of Darius, the son of Hystaspes.[19] The Persian monarchs had extended their western conquests to the banks of the Danube and the limits of European Scythia. The eastern provinces of their empire were exposed to the Scythians of Asia, the wild inhabitants of the plains beyond the Oxus and the Jaxartes, two mighty rivers, which direct their course towards the Caspian Sea. The long and memorable quarrel of Iran and Touran is still the theme of history or romance: the famous, perhaps the fabulous, valour of the Persian heroes, Rustan and Asfendiar, was signalised, in the defence of their country, against the Afrasiabs of the North;[20] and the invincible spirit of the same barbarians resisted, on the same ground, the victorious arms of Cyrus and Alexander.[21] In the eyes of the Greeks and Persians, the real geography of Scythia was bounded, on the east, by the mountains of Imaus or Caf; and their distant prospect of the extreme and inaccessible parts of Asia was clouded by ignorance, or perplexed by fiction. But those inaccessible regions are the ancient residence of a powerful and civilised nation,[22] which ascends, by a probable tradition, above forty centuries;[23] and which is able to verify a series of near two thousand years by the perpetual testimony of accurate and contemporary historians.[24] The annals of China[25] illustrate the state and revolutions of the pastoral tribes, which may still be distinguished by the vague appellation of Scythians or Tartars—the vassals, the enemies, and sometimes the conquerors of a great empire, whose policy has uniformly opposed the blind and impetuous valour of the barbarians of the North. From the mouth of the Danube to the sea of Japan, the whole longitude of Scythia is about one hundred and ten degrees, which, in that parallel, are equal to more than five thousand miles. The latitude of these extensive deserts cannot be so easily or so accurately measured; but, from the fortieth degree, which touches the wall of China, we may securely advance above a thousand miles to the northward, till our progress is stopped by the excessive cold of Siberia. In that dreary climate, instead of the animated picture of a Tartar camp, the smoke which issues from the earth, or rather from the snow, betrays the subterraneous dwellings of the Tongouses and the Samoiedes: the want of horses and oxen is imperfectly supplied by the use of reindeer and of large dogs; and the conquerors of the earth insensibly degenerate into a race of deformed and diminutive savages, who tremble at the sound of arms.[26]

The Huns, who under the reign of Valens threatened the empire of Rome, had been formidable, in a much earlier period, to the empire of China.[27] Their ancient, perhaps their original, seat was an extensive, though dry and barren, tract of country immediately on the north side of the great wall. Their place is at present occupied by the forty-nine Hordes or Banners of the Mongous, a pastoral nation, which consists of about two hundred thousand families.[28] But the valour of the Huns had extended the narrow limits of their dominions; and their rustic chiefs, who assumed the appellation of *Tanjou*, gradually became the conquerors and the sovereigns of a formidable empire. Towards the east their victorious arms were stopped only by the ocean; and the tribes, which are thinly scattered between the Amoor and the extreme peninsula of Corea, adhered with reluctance to the standard of the Huns. On the west, near the head of the Irtish, and in the valleys of Imaus, they found a more ample space, and more numerous enemies. One of the lieutenants of the Tanjou subdued, in a single expedition, twenty-six nations; the Igours,[29] distinguished above the Tartar race by the use of letters, were in the number of his vassals; and, by the strange connection of human events, the flight of one of those vagrant tribes recalled the victorious Parthians from the invasion of Syria.[30] On the side of the north, the ocean was assigned as the limit of the power of the Huns. Without enemies to resist their progress, or witnesses to contradict their vanity, they might securely achieve a real, or imaginary, conquest of the frozen regions of Siberia. The *Northern Sea* was fixed as the remote boundary of their empire. But the name of that sea, on whose shores the patriot Sovou embraced the life of a shepherd and an exile,[31] may be transferred, with much more probability, to the

Baikal, a capacious basin, above three hundred miles in length, which disdains the modest appellation of a lake,[32] and which actually communicates with the seas of the North, by the long course of the Angara, the Tonguska, and the Yenesei. The submission of so many distant nations might flatter the pride of the Tanjou; but the valour of the Huns could be rewarded only by the enjoyment of the wealth and luxury of the empire of the South. In the third century before the Christian era, a wall of fifteen hundred miles in length was constructed, to defend the frontiers of China against the inroads of the Huns;[33] but this stupendous work, which holds a conspicuous place in the map of the world, has never contributed to the safety of an unwarlike people. The cavalry of the Tanjou frequently consisted of two or three hundred thousand men, formidable by the matchless dexterity with which they managed their bows and their horses; by their hardy patience in supporting the inclemency of the weather; and by the incredible speed of their march, which was seldom checked by torrents or precipices, by the deepest rivers, or by the most lofty mountains.

They spread themselves at once over the face of the country; and their rapid impetuosity surprised, astonished, and disconcerted the grave and elaborate tactics of a Chinese army. The emperor Kaoti,[34] a soldier of fortune, whose personal merit had raised him to the throne, marched against the Huns with those veteran troops which had been trained in the civil wars of China. But he was soon surrounded by the barbarians; and, after a siege of seven days, the monarch, hopeless of relief, was reduced to purchase his deliverance by an ignominious capitulation. The successors of Kaoti, whose lives were dedicated to the arts of peace, or the luxury of the palace, submitted to a more permanent disgrace. They too hastily confessed the insufficiency of arms and fortifications. They were too easily convinced that, while the blazing signals announced on every side the approach of the Huns, the Chinese troops, who slept with the helmet on their head, and the cuirass on their back, were destroyed by the incessant labour of ineffectual marches.[35] A regular payment of money and silk was stipulated as the condition of a temporary and precarious peace; and the wretched expedient of disguising a real tribute under the names of a gift or subsidy was practised by the emperors of China as well as by those of Rome. But there still remained a more disgraceful article of tribute, which violated the sacred feelings of humanity and nature. The hardships of the savage life, which destroy in their infancy the children who are born with a less healthy and robust constitution, introduce a remarkable disproportion between the numbers of the two sexes. The Tartars are an ugly and even deformed race; and while they consider their own women as the instruments of domestic labour, their desires, or rather their appetites, are directed to the enjoyment of more elegant beauty. A select band of the fairest maidens of China was annually devoted to the rude embraces of the Huns;[36] and the alliance of the haughty Tanjous was secured by their marriage with the genuine, or adopted, daughters of the Imperial family, which vainly attempted to escape the sacrilegious pollution. The situation of these unhappy victims is described in the verses of a Chinese princess, who laments that she had been condemned by her parents to a distant exile, under a barbarian husband; who complains that sour milk was her only drink, raw flesh her only food, a tent her only palace; and who expresses, in a strain of pathetic simplicity, the natural wish that she were transformed into a bird, to fly back to her dear country, the object of her tender and perpetual regret.[37]

The conquest of China has been twice achieved by the pastoral tribes of the North: the forces of the Huns were not inferior to those of the Moguls, or of the Mantcheoux; and their ambition might entertain the most sanguine hopes of success. But their pride was humbled, and their progress was checked, by the arms and policy of Vouti,[38] the fifth emperor of the powerful dynasty of the Han. In his long reign of fifty-four years, the barbarians of the southern provinces submitted to the laws and manners of China; and the ancient limits of the monarchy were enlarged from the great river of Kiang to the port of Canton. Instead of confining himself to the timid operations of a defensive war, his lieutenants penetrated many hundred miles into the country of the Huns. In those boundless deserts, where it is impossible to form magazines, and difficult to transport a sufficient supply of provisions, the armies of Vouti were repeatedly exposed to intolerable hardships: and, of one hundred and forty thousand soldiers who marched against the barbarians, thirty thousand only returned in safety to the feet of their master. These losses, however, were compensated by splendid and decisive success. The Chinese generals improved the superiority which they derived from the temper of their arms, their chariots of war, and the service of their Tartar auxiliaries. The camp of the Tanjou was surprised in the midst of sleep and intemperance; and, though the monarch of the Huns bravely cut his way through the ranks of the enemy, he left above fifteen thousand of his subjects on the field of battle. Yet this signal victory, which was preceded and followed by many bloody engagements, contributed much less to the destruction of the power of the Huns, than the effectual policy which was employed to detach the tributary nations from their obedience. Intimidated by the arms, or allured by the promises, of Vouti and his successors, the most considerable tribes, both of the East and of the West, disclaimed the authority of the Tanjou. While some acknowledged themselves the allies or vassals of the empire, they all became the implacable enemies of the Huns: and the numbers of that haughty people, as soon as they were reduced to their native strength, might perhaps have been contained within the walls of one of the great and populous cities of China.[39] The desertion of his subjects, and the perplexity of a civil war, at length compelled the Tanjou himself to renounce the dignity of an independent sovereign, and the freedom of a warlike and high-spirited nation. He was received at Sigan, the capital of the monarchy, by the troops, the mandarins, and the emperor himself, with all the honours that could adorn and disguise the triumph of Chinese vanity.[40] A magnificent palace was prepared for his reception; his place was assigned above all the princes of the royal family; and the patience of the barbarian king was exhausted by the ceremonies of a banquet, which consisted of eight courses of meat, and of nine solemn pieces of music. But he performed, on his knees, the duty of a respectful homage to the emperor of China; pronounced, in his own name, and in the name of his successors, a perpetual oath of fidelity; and gratefully accepted a seal, which was bestowed as the emblem of his regal dependence. After this humiliating submission, the Tanjous sometimes departed from their allegiance, and seized the favourable moments of war and rapine; but the monarchy of the Huns gradually declined, till it was broken, by civil dissension, into two hostile and separate kingdoms. One of the princes of the nation was urged by fear and ambition to retire towards the south with eight hordes, which composed between forty and fifty thousand families. He obtained, with the title of Tanjou, a convenient territory on the verge of the Chinese provinces; and his constant attachment to the service of the empire was secured by weakness and the desire of revenge. From the time of this fatal schism, the Huns of the north continued to languish about fifty years, till they were oppressed on every side by their foreign and domestic enemies. The proud inscription[41] of a column, erected on a lofty mountain, announced to posterity that a Chinese army had marched seven hundred miles into the heart of their country. The Sienpi,[42] a tribe of Oriental Tartars, retaliated the injuries which they had formerly sustained; and the power of the Tanjous, after a reign of thirteen hundred years, was utterly destroyed before the end of the first century of the Christian era.[43]

The fate of the vanquished Huns was diversified by the various influence of character and situation.[44] Above one hundred thousand persons, the poorest, indeed, and the most pusillanimous of the people, were contented to remain in their native country, to renounce their peculiar name and origin, and to mingle with the victorious nation of the Sienpi. Fifty-eight hordes, about two hundred thousand men, ambitious of a more honourable servitude, retired towards the south, implored the protection of the emperors of China, and were permitted to inhabit and to guard the extreme frontiers of the province of Chansi and the territory of Ortous. But the most warlike and powerful tribes of the Huns maintained in their adverse fortune the undaunted spirit of their ancestors. The Western world was open to their valour, and they resolved, under the conduct of their hereditary chieftains, to discover and subdue some remote country which was still inaccessible to the arms of the Sienpi and to the laws of China.[45] The course of their emigration soon carried them beyond the mountains of Imaus and the limits of the Chinese geography; but *we* are able to distinguish the two great divisions of these formidable exiles, which directed their march towards the Oxus and towards the Volga. The first of these colonies established their dominion in the fruitful and extensive plains of the Sogdiana, on the eastern side of the Caspian, where they preserved the name of Huns, with the epithet of Euthalites or Nepthalites. Their manners were softened, and even their features were insensibly improved, by the mildness of the climate and their long residence in a flourishing province,[46] which might still retain a faint impression of the arts of Greece.[47] The *white* Huns, a name which they derived from the change of their complexions, soon abandoned the pastoral life of Scythia. Gorgo, which, under the appellation of Carizme, has since enjoyed a temporary splendour, was the residence of the king,

who exercised a legal authority over an obedient people. Their luxury was maintained by the labour of the Sogdians; and the only vestige of their ancient barbarism was the custom which obliged all the companions, perhaps to the number of twenty, who had shared the liberality of a wealthy lord, to be buried alive in the same grave.[48] The vicinity of the Huns to the provinces of Persia involved them in frequent and bloody contests with the power of that monarchy. But they respected, in peace, the faith of treaties; in war, the dictates of humanity; and their memorable victory over Peroses, or Firuz, displayed the moderation as well as the valour of the barbarians. The *second* division of their countrymen, the Huns who gradually advanced towards the north-west, were exercised by the hardships of a colder climate and a more laborious march. Necessity compelled them to exchange the silks of China for the furs of Siberia; the imperfect rudiments of civilised life were obliterated; and the native fierceness of the Huns was exasperated by their intercourse with the savage tribes, who were compared, with some propriety, to the wild beasts of the desert. Their independent spirit soon rejected the hereditary succession of the Tanjous; and each horde was governed by its peculiar mursa, their tumultuary council directed the public measures of the whole nation. As late as the thirteenth century their transient residence on the eastern banks of the Volga was attested by the name of Great Hungary.[49] In the winter they descended with their flocks and herds towards the mouth of that mighty river; and their summer excursions reached as high as the latitude of Saratoff, or perhaps the conflux of the Kama. Such at least were the recent limits of the black Calmucks,[50] who remained about a century under the protection of Russia, and who have since returned to their native seats on the frontiers of the Chinese empire. The march and the return of those wandering Tartars, whose united camp consists of fifty thousand tents or families, illustrate the distant emigrations of the ancient Huns.[51]

It is impossible to fill the dark interval of time which elapsed after the Huns of the Volga were lost in the eyes of the Chinese, and before they showed themselves to those of the Romans. There is some reason, however, to apprehend that the same force which had driven them from their native seats still continued to impel their march towards the frontiers of Europe. The power of the Sienpi, their implacable enemies, which extended above three thousand miles from east to west,[52] must have gradually oppressed them by the weight and terror of a formidable neighbourhood; and the flight of the tribes of Scythia would inevitably tend to increase the strength or to contract the territories of the Huns. The harsh and obscure appellations of those tribes would offend the ear, without informing the understanding, of the reader; but I cannot suppress the very natural suspicion *that* the Huns of the North derived a considerable reinforcement from the ruin of the dynasty of the South, which, in the course of the third century, submitted to the dominion of China; *that* the bravest warriors marched away in search of their free and adventurous countrymen; *and* that, as they had been divided by prosperity, they were easily reunited by the common hardships of their adverse fortune.[53] The Huns, with their flocks and herds, their wives and children, their dependents and allies, were transported to the west of the Volga, and they boldly advanced to invade the country of the Alani, a pastoral people, who occupied, or wasted, an extensive tract of the deserts of Scythia. The plains between the Volga and the Tanais were covered with the tents of the Alani, but their name and manners were diffused over the wide extent of their conquests; and the painted tribes of the Agathyrsi and Geloni were confounded among their vassals. Towards the north they penetrated into the frozen regions of Siberia, among the savages who were accustomed, in their rage or hunger, to the taste of human flesh; and their southern inroads were pushed as far as the confines of Persia and India. The mixture of Sarmatic and German blood had contributed to improve the features of the Alani, to whiten their swarthy complexions, and to tinge their hair with a yellowish cast, which is seldom found in the Tartar race. They were less deformed in their persons, less brutish in their manners, than the Huns; but they did not yield to those formidable barbarians in their martial and independent spirit; in the love of freedom, which rejected even the use of domestic slaves; and in the love of arms, which considered war and rapine as the pleasure and the glory of mankind. A naked scimitar, fixed in the ground, was the only object of their religious worship; the scalps of their enemies formed the costly trappings of their horses; and they viewed with pity and contempt the pusillanimous warriors who patiently expected the infirmities of age and the tortures of lingering disease.[54] On the banks of the Tanais the military power of the Huns and the Alani encountered each other with equal valour,

but with unequal success. The Huns prevailed in the bloody contest; the king of the Alani was slain; and the remains of the vanquished nation were dispersed by the ordinary alternative of flight or submission.[55] A colony of exiles found a secure refuge in the mountains of Caucasus, between the Euxine and the Caspian, where they still preserve their name and their independence. Another colony advanced, with more intrepid courage, towards the shores of the Baltic; associated themselves with the northern tribes of Germany; and shared the spoil of the Roman provinces of Gaul and Spain. But the greatest part of the nation of the Alani embraced the offers of an honourable and advantageous union; and the Huns, who esteemed the valour of their less fortunate enemies, proceeded, with an increase of numbers and confidence, to invade the limits of the Gothic empire.

The great Hermanric, whose dominions extended from the Baltic to the Euxine, enjoyed, in the full maturity of age and reputation, the fruit of his victories, when he was alarmed by the formidable approach of an host of unknown enemies,[56] on whom his barbarous subjects might, without injustice, bestow the epithet of barbarians. The numbers, the strength, the rapid motions, and the implacable cruelty of the Huns were felt, and dreaded, and magnified by the astonished Goths, who beheld their fields and villages consumed with flames and deluged with indiscriminate slaughter. To these real terrors they added the surprise and abhorrence which were excited by the shrill voice, the uncouth gestures, and the strange deformity of the Huns. These savages of Scythia were compared (and the picture had some resemblance) to the animals who walk very awkwardly on two legs, and to the misshapen figures, the *Termini*, which were often placed on the bridges of antiquity. They were distinguished from the rest of the human species by their broad shoulders, flat noses, and small black eyes, deeply buried in the head; and as they were almost destitute of beards, they never enjoyed either the manly graces of youth or the venerable aspect of age.[57] A fabulous origin was assigned worthy of their form and manners—that the witches of Scythia, who, for their foul and deadly practices, had been driven from society, had copulated in the desert with infernal spirits, and that the Huns were the offspring of this execrable conjunction.[58] The tale, so full of horror and absurdity, was greedily embraced by the credulous hatred of the Goths; but while it gratified their hatred it increased their fear, since the posterity of dæmons and witches might be supposed to inherit some share of the preternatural powers as well as of the malignant temper of their parents. Against these enemies, Hermanric prepared to exert the united forces of the Gothic state; but he soon discovered that his vassal tribes, provoked by oppression, were much more inclined to second than to repel the invasion of the Huns. One of the chiefs of the Roxolani[59] had formerly deserted the standard of Hermanric, and the cruel tyrant had condemned the innocent wife of the traitor to be torn asunder by wild horses. The brothers of that unfortunate woman seized the favourable moment of revenge. The aged king of the Goths languished some time after the dangerous wound which he received from their daggers; but the conduct of the war was retarded by his infirmities; and the public councils of the nation were distracted by a spirit of jealousy and discord. His death, which has been imputed to his own despair, left the reins of government in the hands of Withimer, who, with the doubtful aid of some Scythian mercenaries, maintained the unequal contest against the arms of the Huns and the Alani till he was defeated and slain in a decisive battle. The Ostrogoths submitted to their fate: and the royal race of the Amali will hereafter be found among the subjects of the haughty Attila. But the person of Witheric, the infant king, was saved by the diligence of Alatheus and Saphrax; two warriors of approved valour and fidelity, who, by cautious marches, conducted the independent remains of the nation of the Ostrogoths towards the Danastus, or Dniester, a considerable river, which now separates the Turkish dominions from the empire of Russia. On the banks of the Dniester the prudent Athanaric, more attentive to his own than to the general safety, had fixed the camp of the Visigoths; with the firm resolution of opposing the victorious barbarians, whom he thought it less advisable to provoke. The ordinary speed of the Huns was checked by the weight of baggage and the encumbrance of captives; but their military skill deceived and almost destroyed the army of Athanaric. While the Judge of the Visigoths defended the banks of the Dniester he was encompassed and attacked by a numerous detachment of cavalry, who, by the light of the moon, had passed the river in a fordable place; and it was not without the utmost efforts of courage and conduct that he was able to effect his retreat towards the hilly country. The undaunted general had already formed a new and judicious plan of defensive war; and the strong lines which he was preparing to construct between the mountains, the Pruth, and the Danube, would have secured the extensive and fertile territory that bears the modern name of Wallachia from the destructive inroads of the Huns.[60] But the hopes and measures of the Judge of the Visigoths were soon disappointed by the trembling impatience of his dismayed countrymen, who were persuaded by their fears that the interposition of the Danube was the only barrier that could save them from the rapid pursuit and invincible valour of the barbarians of Scythia. Under the command of Fritigern and Alavivus,[61] the body of the nation hastily advanced to the banks of the great river, and implored the protection of the Roman emperor of the East. Athanaric himself, still anxious to avoid the guilt of perjury, retired, with a band of faithful followers, into the mountainous country of Caucaland, which appears to have been guarded and almost concealed by the impenetrable forests of Transylvania.[62]

After Valens had terminated the Gothic war with some appearance of glory and success, he made a progress through his dominions of Asia, and at length fixed his residence in the capital of Syria. The five years[63] which he spent at Antioch were employed to watch, from a secure distance, the hostile designs of the Persian monarch; to check the depredations of the Saracens and Isaurians;[64] to enforce, by arguments more prevalent than those of reason and eloquence, the belief of the Arian theology; and to satisfy his anxious suspicions by the promiscuous execution of the innocent and the guilty. But the attention of the emperor was most seriously engaged by the important intelligence which he received from the civil and military officers who were intrusted with the defence of the Danube. He was informed that the North was agitated by a furious tempest; that the irruption of the Huns, an unknown and monstrous race of savages, had subverted the power of the Goths; and that the suppliant multitudes of that warlike nation, whose pride was now humbled in the dust, covered a space many miles along the banks of the river. With outstretched arms and pathetic lamentations they loudly deplored their past misfortunes and their present danger; acknowledged that their only hope of safety was in the clemency of the Roman government; and most solemnly protested that, if the gracious liberality of the emperor would permit them to cultivate the waste lands of Thrace, they should ever hold themselves bound, by the strongest obligations of duty and gratitude, to obey the laws and to guard the limits of the republic.

These assurances were confirmed by the ambassadors of the Goths, who impatiently expected from the mouth of Valens an answer that must finally determine the fate of their unhappy countrymen. The emperor of the East was no longer guided by the wisdom and authority of his elder brother, whose death happened towards the end of the preceding year; and as the distressful situation of the Goths required an instant and peremptory decision, he was deprived of the favourite resource of feeble and timid minds, who consider the use of the dilatory and ambiguous measures as the most admirable efforts of consummate prudence. As long as the same passions and interests subsist among mankind, the questions of war and peace, of justice and policy, which were debated in the councils of antiquity, will frequently present themselves as the subject of modern deliberation. But the most experienced statesman of Europe has never been summoned to consider the propriety or the danger of admitting or rejecting an innumerable multitude of barbarians, who are driven by despair and hunger to solicit a settlement on the territories of a civilised nation. When that important proposition, so essentially connected with the public safety, was referred to the ministers of Valens, they were perplexed and divided; but they soon acquiesced in the flattering sentiment which seemed the most favourable to the pride, the indolence, and the avarice of their sovereign. The slaves, who were decorated with the titles of præfects and generals, dissembled or disregarded the terrors of this national emigration—so extremely different from the partial and accidental colonies which had been received on the extreme limits of the empire. But they applauded the liberality of fortune which had conducted, from the most distant countries of the globe, a numerous and invincible army of strangers to defend the throne of Valens, who might now add to the royal treasures the immense sums of gold supplied by the provincials to compensate their annual proportion of recruits. The prayers of the Goths were granted, and their service was accepted by the Imperial court; and orders were immediately despatched by the civil and military governors of the Thracian diocese to make the necessary preparations for the passage and subsistence of a great people, till a proper and sufficient territory could be allotted for their future residence. The liberality of the emperor was accompanied, however, with two harsh and rigorous conditions, which prudence might justify on the side of the Romans, but which distress alone could extort

from the indignant Goths. Before they passed the Danube they were required to deliver their arms, and it was insisted that their children should be taken from them and dispersed through the provinces of Asia, where they might be civilised by the arts of education, and serve as hostages to secure the fidelity of their parents.

During this suspense of a doubtful and distant negotiation, the impatient Goths made some rash attempts to pass the Danube without the permission of the government whose protection they had implored. Their motions were strictly observed by the vigilance of the troops which were stationed along the river, and their foremost detachments were defeated with considerable slaughter; yet such were the timid councils of the reign of Valens, that the brave officers who had served their country in the execution of their duty were punished by the loss of their employments, and narrowly escaped the loss of their heads. The Imperial mandate was at length received for transporting over the Danube the whole body of the Gothic nation;[65] but the execution of this order was a task of labour and difficulty. The stream of the Danube, which in those parts is above a mile broad,[66] had been swelled by incessant rains, and in this tumultuous passage many were swept away and drowned by the rapid violence of the current. A large fleet of vessels, of boats, and of canoes, was provided; many days and nights they passed and repassed with indefatigable toil; and the most strenuous diligence was exerted by the officers of Valens that not a single barbarian, of those who were reserved to subvert the foundations of Rome, should be left on the opposite shore. It was thought expedient that an accurate account should be taken of their numbers; but the persons who were employed soon desisted, with amazement and dismay, from the prosecution of the endless and impracticable task;[67] and the principal historian of the age most seriously affirms that the prodigious armies of Darius and Xerxes, which had so long been considered as the fables of vain and credulous antiquity, were now justified, in the eyes of mankind, by the evidence of fact and experience. A probable testimony has fixed the number of the Gothic warriors at two hundred thousand men; and if we can venture to add the just proportion of women, of children, and of slaves, the whole mass of people which composed this formidable emigration must have amounted to near a million of persons, of both sexes and of all ages. The children of the Goths, those at least of a distinguished rank, were separated from the multitude. They were conducted without delay to the distant seats assigned for their residence and education; and as the numerous train of hostages or captives passed through the cities, their gay and splendid apparel, their robust and martial figure, excited the surprise and envy of the provincials. But the stipulation, the most offensive to the Goths and the most important to the Romans, was shamefully eluded. The barbarians, who considered their arms as the ensigns of honour and the pledges of safety, were disposed to offer a price which the lust or avarice of the Imperial officers was easily tempted to accept. To preserve their arms, the haughty warriors consented, with some reluctance, to prostitute their wives or their daughters; the charms of a beauteous maid, or a comely boy, secured the connivance of the inspectors, who sometimes cast an eye of covetousness on the fringed carpets and linen garments of their new allies,[68] or who sacrificed their duty to the mean consideration of filling their farms with cattle and their houses with slaves. The Goths, with arms in their hands, were permitted to enter the boats; and when their strength was collected on the other side of the river, the immense camp which was spread over the plains and the hills of the Lower Mæsia assumed a threatening and even hostile aspect. The leaders of the Ostrogoths, Alatheus and Saphrax, the guardians of their infant king, appeared soon afterwards on the northern banks of the Danube, and immediately despatched their ambassadors to the court of Antioch to solicit, with the same professions of allegiance and gratitude, the same favour which had been granted to the suppliant Visigoths. The absolute refusal of Valens suspended their progress, and discovered the repentance, the suspicions, and the fears of the Imperial council.

An undisciplined and unsettled nation of barbarians required the firmest temper and the most dexterous management. The daily subsistence of near a million of extraordinary subjects could be supplied only by constant and skilful diligence, and might continually be interrupted by mistake or accident. The insolence or the indignation of the Goths, if they conceived themselves to be the objects either of fear or of contempt, might urge them to the most desperate extremities, and the fortune of the state seemed to depend on the prudence, as well as the integrity, of the generals of Valens. At this important crisis the military government of Thrace was exercised by Lupicinus and Maximus, in whose venal minds the slightest hope of private emolument outweighed every consideration of public advantage, and whose guilt was only alleviated by their incapacity of discerning the pernicious effects of their rash and criminal administration. Instead of obeying the orders of their sovereign, and satisfying, with decent liberality, the demands of the Goths, they levied an ungenerous and oppressive tax on the wants of the hungry barbarians. The vilest food was sold at an extravagant price, and, in the room of wholesome and substantial provisions, the markets were filled with the flesh of dogs and of unclean animals who had died of disease. To obtain the valuable acquisition of a pound of bread, the Goths resigned the possession of an expensive though serviceable slave, and a small quantity of meat was greedily purchased with ten pounds of a precious but useless metal.[69] When their property was exhausted, they continued this necessary traffic by the sale of their sons and daughters; and notwithstanding the love of freedom which animated every Gothic breast, they submitted to the humiliating maxim that it was better for their children to be maintained in a servile condition than to perish in a state of wretched and helpless independence. The most lively resentment is excited by the tyranny of pretended benefactors, who sternly exact the debt of gratitude which they have cancelled by subsequent injuries; a spirit of discontent insensibly arose in the camp of the barbarians, who pleaded, without success, the merit of their patient and dutiful behaviour, and loudly complained of the inhospitable treatment which they had received from their new allies. They beheld around them the wealth and plenty of a fertile province, in the midst of which they suffered the intolerable hardships of artificial famine. But the means of relief, and even of revenge, were in their hands, since the rapaciousness of their tyrants had left to an injured people the possession and the use of arms. The clamours of a multitude, untaught to disguise their sentiments, announced the first symptoms of resistance, and alarmed the timid and guilty minds of Lupicinus and Maximus. Those crafty ministers, who substituted the cunning of temporary expedients to the wise and salutary counsels of general policy, attempted to remove the Goths from their dangerous station on the frontiers of the empire, and to disperse them, in separate quarters of cantonment, through the interior provinces. As they were conscious how ill they had deserved the respect or confidence of the barbarians, they diligently collected from every side a military force that might urge the tardy and reluctant march of a people who had not yet renounced the title or the duties of Roman subjects. But the generals of Valens, while their attention was solely directed to the discontented Visigoths, imprudently disarmed the ships and the fortifications which constituted the defence of the Danube. The fatal oversight was observed and improved by Alatheus and Saphrax, who anxiously watched the favourable moment of escaping from the pursuit of the Huns. By the help of such rafts and vessels as could be hastily procured, the leaders of the Ostrogoths transported, without opposition, their king and their army, and boldly fixed an hostile and independent camp on the territories of the empire.[70]

Under the name of Judges, Alavivus and Fritigern were the leaders of the Visigoths in peace and war; and the authority which they derived from their birth was ratified by the free consent of the nation. In a season of tranquillity their power might have been equal as well as their rank; but, as soon as their countrymen were exasperated by hunger and oppression, the superior abilities of Fritigern assumed the military command, which he was qualified to exercise for the public welfare. He restrained the impatient spirit of the Visigoths till the injuries and the insults of their tyrants should justify their resistance in the opinion of mankind: but he was not disposed to sacrifice any solid advantages for the empty praise of justice and moderation. Sensible of the benefits which would result from the union of the Gothic powers under the same standard, he secretly cultivated the friendship of the Ostrogoths; and while he professed an implicit obedience to the orders of the Roman generals, he proceeded by slow marches towards Marcianopolis, the capital of the Lower Mæsia, about seventy miles from the banks of the Danube. On that fatal spot the flames of discord and mutual hatred burst forth into a dreadful conflagration. Lupicinus had invited the Gothic chiefs to a splendid entertainment; and their martial train remained under arms at the entrance of the palace. But the gates of the city were strictly guarded, and the barbarians were sternly excluded from the use of a plentiful market, to which they asserted their equal claim of subjects and allies. Their humble prayers were rejected with insolence and derision; and as their patience was now exhausted, the townsmen, the soldiers, and the Goths were soon involved in a conflict of passionate altercation and angry reproaches. A blow was imprudently given; a sword was hastily drawn; and the first blood that was spilt in this accidental quarrel became the signal of a long and destructive war. In the midst of noise and brutal intemperance Lupicinus was informed by a secret messenger that many of his soldiers were slain and despoiled of their arms; and as he was already inflamed by wine and oppressed by sleep, he issued a rash command, that their death should be revenged by the massacre of the guards of Fritigern and Alavivus. The clamorous shouts and dying groans apprised Fritigern of his extreme danger; and, as he possessed the calm and intrepid spirit of a hero, he saw that he was lost if he allowed a moment of deliberation to the man who had so deeply injured him. "A trifling dispute," said the Gothic leader, with a firm but gentle tone of voice, "appears to have arisen between the two nations; but it may be productive of the most dangerous consequences, unless the tumult is immediately pacified by the assurance of our safety and the authority of our presence." At these words Fritigern and his companions drew their swords, opened their passage through the unresisting crowd, which filled the palace, the streets, and the gates of Marcianopolis, and, mounting their horses, hastily vanished from the eyes of the astonished Romans. The generals of the Goths were saluted by the fierce and joyful acclamations of the camp; war was instantly resolved, and the resolution was executed without delay: the banners of the nation were displayed according to the custom of their ancestors; and the air resounded with the harsh and mournful music of the barbarian trumpet.[71] The weak and guilty Lupicinus, who had dared to provoke, who had neglected to destroy, and who still presumed to despise his formidable enemy, marched against the Goths, at the head of such a military force as could be collected on this sudden emergency. The barbarians expected his approach about nine miles from Marcianopolis; and on this occasion the talents of the general were found to be of more prevailing efficacy than the weapons and discipline of the troops. The valour of the Goths was so ably directed by the genius of Fritigern, that they broke, by a close and vigorous attack, the ranks of the Roman legions. Lupicinus left his arms and standards, his tribunes and his bravest soldiers, on the field of battle; and their useless courage served only to protect the ignominious flight of their leader. "That successful day put an end to the distress of the barbarians and the security of the Romans: from that day the Goths, renouncing the precarious condition of strangers and exiles, assumed the character of citizens and masters, claimed an absolute dominion over the possessors of land, and held, in their own right, the northern provinces of the empire, which are bounded by the Danube." Such are the words of the Gothic historian,[72] who celebrates, with rude eloquence, the glory of his countrymen. But the dominion of the barbarians was exercised only for the purposes of rapine and destruction. As they had been deprived by the ministers of the emperor of the common benefits of nature and the fair intercourse of social life, they retaliated the injustice on the subjects of the empire; and the crimes of Lupicinus were expiated by the ruin of the peaceful husbandmen of Thrace, the conflagration of their villages, and the massacre or captivity of their innocent families. The report of the Gothic victory was soon diffused over the adjacent country; and while it filled the minds of the Romans with terror and dismay, their own hasty imprudence contributed to increase the forces of Fritigern and the calamities of the province. Some time before the great emigration a numerous body of Goths, under the command of Suerid and Colias, had been received into the protection and service of the empire.[73] They were encamped under the walls of Hadrianople: but the ministers of Valens were anxious to remove them beyond the Hellespont, at a distance from the dangerous temptation which might so easily be communicated by the neighbourhood and the success of their countrymen. The respectful submission with which they yielded to the order of their march might be considered as a proof of their fidelity; and their moderate request of a sufficient allowance of provisions and of a delay of only two days was expressed in the most dutiful terms. But the first magistrate of Hadrianople, incensed by some disorders which had been committed at his country-house, refused this indulgence; and arming against them the inhabitants and manufacturers of a populous city, he urged, with hostile threats, their instant departure. The barbarians stood silent and amazed, till they were exasperated by the insulting clamours and missile weapons of the populace: but when patience or contempt was fatigued, they crushed the undisciplined multitude, inflicted many a shameful wound on the backs of their flying enemies, and despoiled them of the splendid armour[74] which they were unworthy to bear. The resemblance of their sufferings and their actions soon united this victorious detachment to the nation of the Visigoths; the troops of Colias and Suerid expected the approach of the great Fritigern, ranged

themselves under his standard, and signalised their ardour in the siege of Hadrianople. But the resistance of the garrison informed the barbarians that in the attack of regular fortifications the efforts of unskilful courage are seldom effectual. Their general acknowledged his error, raised the siege, declared that "he was at peace with stone walls,"[75] and revenged his disappointment on the adjacent country. He accepted with pleasure the useful reinforcement of hardy workmen who laboured in the gold-mines of Thrace[76] for the emolument and under the lash of an unfeeling master:[77] and these new associates conducted the barbarians through the secret paths to the most sequestered places, which had been chosen to secure the inhabitants, the cattle, and the magazines of corn. With the assistance of such guides nothing could remain impervious or inaccessible: resistance was fatal; flight was impracticable; and the patient submission of helpless innocence seldom found mercy from the barbarian conqueror. In the course of these depredations a great number of the children of the Goths, who had been sold into captivity, were restored to the embraces of their afflicted parents; but these tender interviews, which might have revived and cherished in their minds some sentiments of humanity, tended only to stimulate their native fierceness by the desire of revenge. They listened with eager attention to the complaints of their captive children, who had suffered the most cruel indignities from the lustful or angry passions of their masters, and the same cruelties, the same indignities, were severely retaliated on the sons and daughters of the Romans.[78]

The imprudence of Valens and his ministers had introduced into the heart of the empire a nation of enemies; but the Visigoths might even yet have been reconciled by the manly confession of past errors and the sincere performance of former engagements. These healing and temperate measures seemed to concur with the timorous disposition of the sovereign of the East: but on this occasion alone Valens was brave; and his unseasonable bravery was fatal to himself and to his subjects. He declared his intention of marching from Antioch to Constantinople, to subdue this dangerous rebellion; and, as he was not ignorant of the difficulties of the enterprise, he solicited the assistance of his nephew, the emperor Gratian, who commanded all the forces of the West. The veteran troops were hastily recalled from the defence of Armenia; that important frontier was abandoned to the discretion of Sapor; and the immediate conduct of the Gothic war was intrusted, during the absence of Valens, to his lieutenants, Trajan and Profuturus, two generals who indulged themselves in a very false and favourable opinion of their own abilities. On their arrival in Thrace they were joined by Richomer, count of the domestics; and the auxiliaries of the West that marched under his banner were composed of the Gallic legions, reduced indeed by a spirit of desertion to the vain appearances of strength and numbers. In a council of war, which was influenced by pride rather than by reason, it was resolved to seek and to encounter the barbarians, who lay encamped in the spacious and fertile meadows near the most southern of the six mouths of the Danube.[79] Their camp was surrounded by the usual fortification of waggons;[80] and the barbarians, secure within the vast circle of the enclosure, enjoyed the fruits of their valour and the spoils of the province. In the midst of riotous intemperance, the watchful Fritigern observed the motions and penetrated the designs of the Romans. He perceived that the numbers of the enemy were continually increasing; and, as he understood their intention of attacking his rear as soon as the scarcity of forage should oblige him to remove his camp, he recalled to their standard his predatory detachments, which covered the adjacent country. As soon as they descried the flaming beacons[81] they obeyed with incredible speed the signal of their leader; the camp was filled with the martial crowd of barbarians; their impatient clamours demanded the battle, and their tumultuous zeal was approved and animated by the spirit of their chiefs. The evening was already far advanced; and the two armies prepared themselves for the approaching combat, which was deferred only till the dawn of day. While the trumpets sounded to arms, the undaunted courage of the Goths was confirmed by the mutual obligation of a solemn oath; and, as they advanced to meet the enemy, the rude songs which celebrated the glory of their forefathers were mingled with their fierce and dissonant outcries, and opposed to the artificial harmony of the Roman shout. Some military skill was displayed by Fritigern to gain the advantage of a commanding eminence; but the bloody conflict, which began and ended with the light, was maintained on either side by the personal and obstinate efforts of strength, valour, and agility. The legions of Armenia supported their fame in arms, but they were oppressed by the irresistible weight of the hostile multitude: the left wing of the Romans was thrown into disorder, and the

field was strewed with their mangled carcasses. This partial defeat was balanced, however, by partial success; and when the two armies, at a late hour of the evening, retreated to their respective camps, neither of them could claim the honours of the effects of a decisive victory. The real loss was more severely felt by the Romans, in proportion to the smallness of their numbers; but the Goths were so deeply confounded and dismayed by this vigorous, and perhaps unexpected, resistance, that they remained seven days within the circle of their fortifications. Such funeral rites as the circumstances of time and place would admit were piously discharged to some officers of distinguished rank; but the indiscriminate vulgar was left unburied on the plain. Their flesh was greedily devoured by the birds of prey, who in that age enjoyed very frequent and delicious feasts; and, several years afterwards, the white and naked bones which covered the wide extent of the fields presented to the eyes of Ammianus a dreadful monument of the battle of Salices.[82]

The progress of the Goths had been checked by the doubtful event of that bloody day; and the Imperial generals, whose army would have been consumed by the repetition of such a contest, embraced the more rational plan of destroying the barbarians by the wants and pressure of their own multitudes. They prepared to confine the Visigoths in the narrow angle of land between the Danube, the desert of Scythia, and the mountains of Hæmus, till their strength and spirit should be insensibly wasted by the inevitable operation of famine. The design was prosecuted with some conduct and success; the barbarians had almost exhausted their own magazines and the harvests of the country; and the diligence of Saturninus, the master-general of the cavalry, was employed to improve the strength and to contract the extent of the Roman fortifications. His labours were interrupted by the alarming intelligence that new swarms of barbarians had passed the unguarded Danube, either to support the cause or to imitate the example of Fritigern. The just apprehension that he himself might be surrounded and overwhelmed by the arms of hostile and unknown nations, compelled Saturninus to relinquish the siege of the Gothic camp; and the indignant Visigoths, breaking from their confinement, satiated their hunger and revenge by the repeated devastation of the fruitful country which extends above three hundred miles from the banks of the Danube to the straits of the Hellespont.[83] The sagacious Fritigern had successfully appealed to the passions as well as to the interest of his barbarian allies; and the love of rapine and the hatred of Rome seconded, or even prevented, the eloquence of his ambassadors. He cemented a strict and useful alliance with the great body of his countrymen who obeyed Alatheus and Saphrax as the guardians of their infant king: the long animosity of rival tribes was suspended by the sense of their common interest; the independent part of the nation was associated under one standard; and the chiefs of the Ostrogoths appear to have yielded to the superior genius of the general of the Visigoths. He obtained the formidable aid of the Taifalæ, whose military renown was disgraced and polluted by the public infamy of their domestic manners. Every youth, on his entrance into the world, was united by the ties of honourable friendship and brutal love to some warrior of the tribe; nor could he hope to be released from this unnatural connection till he had approved his manhood by slaying in single combat a huge bear or a wild boar of the forest.[84] But the most powerful auxiliaries of the Goths were drawn from the camp of those enemies who had expelled them from their native seats. The loose subordination and extensive possessions of the Huns and the Alani delayed the conquests and distracted the councils of that victorious people. Several of the hordes were allured by the liberal promises of Fritigern; and the rapid cavalry of Scythia added weight and energy to the steady and strenuous efforts of the Gothic infantry. The Sarmatians, who could never forgive the successor of Valentinian, enjoyed and increased the general confusion; and a seasonable irruption of the Alemanni into the provinces of Gaul engaged the attention and diverted the forces of the emperor of the West.[85]

One of the most dangerous inconveniences of the introduction of the barbarians into the army and the palace was sensibly felt in their correspondence with their hostile countrymen, to whom they imprudently or maliciously revealed the weakness of the Roman empire. A soldier of the life-guards of Gratian was of the nation of the Alemanni, and of the tribe of the Lentienses, who dwelt beyond the lake of Constance. Some domestic business obliged him to request a leave of absence. In a short visit to his family and friends he was exposed to their curious inquiries, and the vanity of the loquacious soldier tempted him to display his intimate acquaintance with the secrets of the state and the designs of his master. The intelligence that Gratian was preparing to lead the military force of Gaul and of the West to the assistance of his uncle Valens, pointed out to the restless spirit of the Alemanni the moment and the mode of a successful invasion. The enterprise of some light detachments, who in the month of February passed the Rhine upon the ice, was the prelude of a more important war. The boldest hopes of rapine, perhaps of conquest, outweighed the considerations of timid prudence or national faith. Every forest and every village poured forth a band of hardy adventurers; and the great army of the Alemanni, which on their approach was estimated at forty thousand men by the fears of the people, was afterwards magnified to the number of seventy thousand by the vain and credulous flattery of the Imperial court. The legions which had been ordered to march into Pannonia were immediately recalled or detained for the defence of Gaul; the military command was divided between Nanienus and Mellobaudes; and the youthful emperor, though he respected the long experience and sober wisdom of the former, was much more inclined to admire and to follow the martial ardour of his colleague, who was allowed to unite the incompatible characters of count of the domestics and of king of the Franks. His rival Priarius, king of the Alemanni, was guided, or rather impelled, by the same headstrong valour; and as their troops were animated by the spirit of their leaders, they met, they saw, they encountered each other near the town of Argentaria, or Colmar,[86] in the plains of Alsace. The glory of the day was justly ascribed to the missile weapons and well-practised evolutions of the Roman soldiers: the Alemanni, who long maintained their ground, were slaughtered with unrelenting fury: five thousand only of the barbarians escaped to the woods and mountains; and the glorious death of their king on the field of battle saved him from the reproaches of the people, who are always disposed to accuse the justice or policy of an unsuccessful war. After this signal victory, which secured the peace of Gaul and asserted the honour of the Roman arms, the emperor Gratian appeared to proceed without delay on his Eastern expedition; but, as he approached the confines of the Alemanni, he suddenly inclined to the left, surprised them by his unexpected passage of the Rhine, and boldly advanced into the heart of their country. The barbarians opposed to his progress the obstacles of nature and of courage; and still continued to retreat from one hill to another till they were satisfied, by repeated trials, of the power and perseverance of their enemies. Their submission was accepted as a proof, not indeed of their sincere repentance, but of their actual distress; and a select number of their brave and robust youth was exacted from the faithless nation, as the most substantial pledge of their future moderation. The subjects of the empire, who had so often experienced that the Alemanni could neither be subdued by arms nor restrained by treaties, might not promise themselves any solid or lasting tranquillity; but they discovered, in the virtues of their young sovereign, the prospect of a long and auspicious reign. When the legions climbed the mountains and scaled the fortifications of the barbarians, the valour of Gratian was distinguished in the foremost ranks: and the gilt and variegated armour of his guards was pierced and shattered by the blows which they had received in their constant attachment to the person of their sovereign. At the age of nineteen the son of Valentinian seemed to possess the talents of peace and war; and his personal success against the Alemanni was interpreted as a sure presage of his Gothic triumphs.[87]

While Gratian deserved and enjoyed the applause of his subjects, the emperor Valens, who at length had removed his court and army from Antioch, was received by the people of Constantinople as the author of the public calamity. Before he had reposed himself ten days in the capital he was urged by the licentious clamours of the Hippodrome to march against the barbarians whom he had invited into his dominions: and the citizens, who are always brave at a distance from any real danger, declared, with confidence, that if they were supplied with arms, *they* alone would undertake to deliver the province from the ravages of an insulting foe.[88] The vain reproaches of an ignorant multitude hastened the downfall of the Roman empire; they provoked the desperate rashness of Valens, who did not find, either in his reputation or in his mind, any motives to support with firmness the public contempt. He was soon persuaded by the successful achievements of his lieutenants to despise the power of the Goths, who, by the diligence of Fritigern, were now collected in the neighbourhood of Hadrianople. The march of the Taifalæ had been intercepted by the valiant Frigerid; the king of those licentious barbarians was slain in battle; and the suppliant captives were sent into distant exile to cultivate the lands of Italy, which were assigned for their settlement in the vacant territories of Modena and Parma.[89] The exploits of Sebastian,[90] who was recently engaged in the service of Valens,

and promoted to the rank of master-general of the infantry, were still more honourable to himself, and useful to the republic. He obtained the permission of selecting three hundred soldiers from each of the legions, and this separate detachment soon acquired the spirit of discipline and the exercise of arms, which were almost forgotten under the reign of Valens. By the vigour and conduct of Sebastian, a large body of the Goths was surprised in their camp; and the immense spoil which was recovered from their hands filled the city of Hadrianople and the adjacent plain. The splendid narratives which the general transmitted of his own exploits alarmed the Imperial court by the appearance of superior merit; and though he cautiously insisted on the difficulties of the Gothic war, his valour was praised, his advice was rejected; and Valens, who listened with pride and pleasure to the flattering suggestions of the eunuchs of the palace, was impatient to seize the glory of an easy and assured conquest. His army was strengthened by a numerous reinforcement of veterans; and his march from Constantinople to Hadrianople was conducted with so much military skill that he prevented the activity of the barbarians, who designed to occupy the intermediate defiles, and to intercept either the troops themselves or their convoys of provisions. The camp of Valens, which he pitched under the walls of Hadrianople, was fortified, according to the practice of the Romans, with a ditch and rampart; and a most important council was summoned to decide the fate of the emperor and of the empire. The party of reason and of delay was strenuously maintained by Victor, who had corrected, by the lessons of experience, the native fierceness of the Sarmatian character; while Sebastian with the flexible and obsequious eloquence of a courtier, represented every precaution and every measure that implied a doubt of immediate victory as unworthy of the courage and majesty of their invincible monarch. The ruin of Valens was precipitated by the deceitful arts of Fritigern and the prudent admonitions of the emperor of the West. The advantages of negotiating in the midst of war were perfectly understood by the general of the barbarians; and a Christian ecclesiastic was despatched, as the holy minister of peace, to penetrate and to perplex the councils of the enemy. The misfortunes, as well as the provocations, of the Gothic nation were forcibly and truly described by their ambassador, who protested, in the name of Fritigern, that he was still disposed to lay down his arms, or to employ them only in the defence of the empire, if he could secure for his wandering countrymen a tranquil settlement on the waste lands of Thrace, and a sufficient allowance of corn and cattle. But he added, in a whisper of confidential friendship, that the exasperated barbarians were averse to these reasonable conditions; and that Fritigern was doubtful whether he could accomplish the conclusion of the treaty unless he found himself supported by the presence and terrors of an Imperial army. About the same time, Count Richomer returned from the West to announce the defeat and submission of the Alemanni; to inform Valens that his nephew advanced by rapid marches at the head of the veteran and victorious legions of Gaul; and to request, in the name of Gratian and of the republic, that every dangerous and decisive measure might be suspended till the junction of the two emperors should ensure the success of the Gothic war. But the feeble sovereign of the East was actuated only by the fatal illusions of pride and jealousy. He disdained the importunate advice; he rejected the humiliating aid; he secretly compared the ignominious, at least the inglorious, period of his own reign with the fame of a beardless youth; and Valens rushed into the field to erect his imaginary trophy before the diligence of his colleague could usurp any share of the triumphs of the day.

On the 9th of August, a day which has deserved to be marked among the most inauspicious of the Roman calendar,[91] the emperor Valens, leaving, under a strong guard, his baggage and military treasure, marched from Hadrianople to attack the Goths, who were encamped about twelve miles from the city.[92] By some mistake of the orders, or some ignorance of the ground, the right wing or column of cavalry arrived in sight of the enemy whilst the left was still at a considerable distance; the soldiers were compelled, in the sultry heat of summer, to precipitate their pace; and the line of battle was formed with tedious confusion and irregular delay. The Gothic cavalry had been detached to forage in the adjacent country; and Fritigern still continued to practise his customary arts. He despatched messengers of peace, made proposals, required hostages, and wasted the hours, till the Romans, exposed without shelter to the burning rays of the sun, were exhausted by thirst, hunger, and intolerable fatigue. The emperor was persuaded to send an ambassador to the Gothic camp; the zeal of Richomer, who alone had courage to accept the dangerous commission, was applauded; and the

count of the domestics, adorned with the splendid ensigns of his dignity, had proceeded some way in the space between the two armies when he was suddenly recalled by the alarm of battle. The hasty and imprudent attack was made by Bacurius the Iberian, who commanded a body of archers and targeteers: and, as they advanced with rashness, they retreated with loss and disgrace. In the same moment the flying squadrons of Alatheus and Saphrax, whose return was anxiously expected by the general of the Goths, descended like a whirlwind from the hills, swept across the plain, and added new terrors to the tumultuous but irresistible charge of the barbarian host. The event of the battle of Hadrianople, so fatal to Valens and to the empire, may be described in a few words: the Roman cavalry fled; the infantry was abandoned, surrounded, and cut in pieces. The most skilful evolutions, the firmest courage, are scarcely sufficient to extricate a body of foot encompassed on an open plain by superior numbers of horse; but the troops of Valens, oppressed by the weight of the enemy and their own fears, were crowded into a narrow space, where it was impossible for them to extend their ranks, or even to use, with effect, their swords and javelins. In the midst of tumult, of slaughter, and of dismay, the emperor, deserted by his guards, and wounded, as it was supposed, with an arrow, sought protection among the Lancearii and the Mattiarii, who still maintained their ground with some appearance of order and firmness. His faithful generals, Trajan and Victor, who perceived his danger, loudly exclaimed that all was lost unless the person of the emperor could be saved. Some troops, animated by their exhortation, advanced to his relief: they found only a bloody spot, covered with a heap of broken arms and mangled bodies, without being able to discover their unfortunate prince either among the living or the dead. Their search could not indeed be successful, if there is any truth in the circumstances with which some historians have related the death of the emperor. By the care of his attendants, Valens was removed from the field of battle to a neighbouring cottage, where they attempted to dress his wound and to provide for his future safety. But this humble retreat was instantly surrounded by the enemy; they tried to force the door; they were provoked by a discharge of arrows from the roof; till at length, impatient of delay, they set fire to a pile of dry faggots, and consumed the cottage with the Roman emperor and his train. Valens perished in the flames; and a youth, who dropped from the window, alone escaped, to attest the melancholy tale and to inform the Goths of the inestimable prize which they had lost by their own rashness. A great number of brave and distinguished officers perished in the battle of Hadrianople, which equalled in the actual loss, and far surpassed in the fatal consequences, the misfortune which Rome had formerly sustained in the fields of Cannæ.[93] Two master-generals of the cavalry and infantry, two great officers of the palace, and thirty-five tribunes, were found among the slain; and the death of Sebastian might satisfy the world that he was the victim as well as the author of the public calamity. Above two-thirds of the Roman army were destroyed: and the darkness of the night was esteemed a very favourable circumstance, as it served to conceal the flight of the multitude, and to protect the more orderly retreat of Victor and Richomer, who alone, amidst the general consternation, maintained the advantage of calm courage and regular discipline.[94]

While the impressions of grief and terror were still recent in the minds of men, the most celebrated rhetorician of the age composed the funeral oration of a vanquished army and of an unpopular prince, whose throne was already occupied by a stranger. "There are not wanting," says the candid Libanius, "those who arraign the prudence of the emperor, or who impute the public misfortune to the want of courage and discipline in the troops. For my own part, I reverence the memory of their former exploits; I reverence the glorious death which they bravely received, standing and fighting in their ranks; I reverence the field of battle, stained with *their* blood and the blood of the barbarians. Those honourable marks have been already washed away by the rains; but the lofty monuments of their bones, the bones of generals of centurions, and of valiant warriors, claim a longer period of duration. The king himself fought and fell in the foremost ranks of the battle. His attendants presented him with the fleetest horses of the Imperial stable, that would soon have carried him beyond the pursuit of the enemy. They vainly pressed him to reserve his important life for the future service of the republic. He still declared that he was unworthy to survive so many of the bravest and most faithful of his subjects; and the monarch was nobly buried under a mountain of the slain. Let none, therefore, presume to ascribe the victory of the barbarians to fear, the weakness, or the imprudence of the Roman troops. The chiefs and the soldiers were animated by the virtue of their ancestors, whom they equalled in discipline and the arts of war. Their generous emulation was supported by the love of glory, which prompted them to contend at the same time with heat and thirst, with fire and the sword, and cheerfully to embrace an honourable death as their refuge against flight and infamy. The indignation of the gods has been the only cause of the success of our enemies." The truth of history may disclaim some parts of this panegyric, which cannot strictly be reconciled with the character of Valens or the circumstances of the battle; but the fairest commendation is due to the eloquence, and still more to the generosity, of the sophist of Antioch.[95]

The pride of the Goths was elated by this memorable victory; but their avarice was disappointed by the mortifying discovery that the richest part of the Imperial spoil had been within the walls of Hadrianople. They hastened to possess the reward of their valour; but they were encountered by the remains of a vanquished army with an intrepid resolution, which was the effect of their despair and the only hope of their safety. The walls of the city and the ramparts of the adjacent camp were lined with military engines that threw stones of an enormous weight, and astonished the ignorant barbarians by the noise and velocity, still more than by the real effects, of the discharge. The soldiers, the citizens, the provincials, the domestics of the palace, were united in the danger and in the defence; the furious assault of the Goths was repulsed; their secret arts of treachery and treason were discovered; and after an obstinate conflict of many hours they retired to their tents, convinced by experience that it would be far more advisable to observe the treaty which their sagacious leader had tacitly stipulated with the fortifications of great and populous cities. After the hasty and impolitic massacre of three hundred deserters, an act of justice extremely useful to the discipline of the Roman armies, the Goths indignantly raised the siege of Hadrianople. The scene of war and tumult was instantly converted into a silent solitude; the multitude suddenly disappeared; the secret paths of the woods and mountains were marked with the footsteps of the trembling fugitives, who sought a refuge in the distant cities of Illyricum and Macedonia; and the faithful officers of the household and the treasury cautiously proceeded in search of the emperor, of whose death they were still ignorant. The tide of the Gothic inundation rolled from the walls of Hadrianople to the suburbs of Constantinople. The barbarians were surprised with the splendid appearance of the capital of the East, the height and extent of the walls, the myriads of wealthy and affrighted citizens who crowded the ramparts, and the various prospect of the sea and land. While they gazed with hopeless desire on the inaccessible beauties of Constantinople, a sally was made from one of the gates by a party of Saracens,[96] who had been fortunately engaged in the service of Valens. The cavalry of Scythia was forced to yield to the admirable swiftness and spirit of the Arabian horses; their riders were skilled in the evolutions of irregular war; and the Northern barbarians were astonished and dismayed by the inhuman ferocity of the barbarians of the South. A Gothic soldier was slain by the dagger of an Arab, and the hairy, naked savage, applying his lips to the wound, expressed a horrid delight while he sucked the blood of his vanquished enemy.[97] The army of the Goths, laden with the spoils of the wealthy suburbs and the adjacent territory, slowly moved from the Bosphorus to the mountains which form the western boundary of Thrace. The important pass of Succi was betrayed by the fear or the misconduct of Maurus; and the barbarians, who no longer had any resistance to apprehend from the scattered and vanquished troops of the East, spread themselves over the face of a fertile and cultivated country, as far as the confines of Italy and the Hadriatic Sea.[98]

The Romans, who so coolly and so concisely mention the acts of *justice* which were exercised by the legions,[99] reserved their compassion and their eloquence for their own sufferings when the provinces were invaded and desolated by the arms of the successful barbarians. The simple circumstantial narrative (did such a narrative exist) of the ruin of a single town, of the misfortunes of a single family,[100] might exhibit an interesting and instructive picture of human manners; but the tedious repetition of vague and declamatory complaints would fatigue the attention of the most patient reader. The same censure may be applied, though not perhaps in an equal degree, to the profane and the ecclesiastical writers of this unhappy period; that their minds were inflamed by popular and religious animosity, and that the true size and colour of every object is falsified by the exaggerations of their corrupt eloquence. The vehement Jerom[101] might justly deplore the calamities inflicted by the Goths and their barbarous allies on his native country of Pannonia, and the wide extent

of the provinces from the walls of Constantinople, to the foot of the Julian Alps; the rapes, the massacres, the conflagrations, and, above all, the profanation of the churches that were turned into stables, and the contemptuous treatment of the relics of holy martyrs. But the saint is surely transported beyond the limits of nature and history when he affirms, "that in those desert countries nothing was left except the sky and the earth; that, after the destruction of the cities and the extirpation of the human race, the land was overgrown with thick forests and inextricable brambles; and that the universal desolation, announced by the prophet Zephaniah, was accomplished in the scarcity of the beasts, the birds, and even of the fish." These complaints were pronounced about twenty years after the death of Valens; and the Illyrian provinces, which were constantly exposed to the invasion and passage of the barbarians, still continued, after a calamitous period of ten centuries, to supply new materials for rapine and destruction. Could it even be supposed that a large tract of country had been left without cultivation and without inhabitants, the consequences might not have been so fatal to the inferior productions of animated nature. The useful and feeble animals, which are nourished by the hand of man, might suffer and perish if they were deprived of his protection; but the beasts of the forest, his enemies or his victims, would multiply in the free and undisturbed possession of their solitary domain. The various tribes that peopled the air or the waters are still less connected with the fate of the human species; and it is highly probable that the fish of the Danube would have felt more terror and distress from the approach of a voracious pike than from the hostile inroad of a Gothic army.

Whatever may have been the just measure of the calamities of Europe, there was reason to fear that the same calamities would soon extend to the peaceful countries of Asia. The sons of the Goths had been judiciously distributed through the cities of the East, and the arts of education were employed to polish and subdue the native fierceness of their temper. In the space of about twelve years their numbers had continually increased; and the children who in the first emigration were sent over the Hellespont had attained with rapid growth the strength and spirit of perfect manhood.[102] It was impossible to conceal from their knowledge the events of the Gothic war; and, as those daring youths had not studied the language of dissimulation, they betrayed their wish, their desire, perhaps their intention, to emulate the glorious example of their fathers. The danger of the times seemed to justify the jealous suspicions of the provincials; and these suspicions were admitted as unquestionable evidence that the Goths of Asia had formed a secret and dangerous conspiracy against the public safety. The death of Valens had left the East without a sovereign; and Julius, who filled the important station of master-general of the troops, with a high reputation of diligence and ability, thought it his duty to consult the senate of Constantinople, which he considered, during the vacancy of the throne, as the representative council of the nation. As soon as he had obtained the discretionary power of acting as he should judge most expedient for the good of the republic, he assembled the principal officers and privately concerted effectual measures for the execution of his bloody design. An order was immediately promulgated that, on a stated day, the Gothic youth should assemble in the capital cities of their respective provinces; and, as a report was industriously circulated that they were summoned to receive a liberal gift of lands and money, the pleasing hope allayed the fury of their resentment, and perhaps suspended the motions of the conspiracy. On the appointed day the unarmed crowd of the Gothic youth was carefully collected in the square or forum; the streets and avenues were occupied by the Roman troops, and the roofs of the houses were covered with archers and slingers. At the same hour, in all the cities of the East, the signal was given of indiscriminate slaughter; and the provinces of Asia were delivered, by the cruel prudence of Julius, from a domestic enemy, who in a few months might have carried fire and sword from the Hellespont to the Euphrates.[103] The urgent consideration of the public safety may undoubtedly authorise the violation of every positive law. How far that or any other consideration may operate to dissolve the natural obligations of humanity and justice, is a doctrine of which I still desire to remain ignorant.

The emperor Gratian was far advanced on his march towards the plains of Hadrianople when he was informed, at first by the confused voice of fame, and afterwards by the more accurate reports of Victor and Richomer, that his impatient colleague had been slain in battle, and that two-thirds of the Roman army were exterminated by the sword of the victorious Goths. Whatever resentment the rash and jealous vanity of his uncle might deserve, the resentment of a generous mind is easily subdued by the softer emotions of grief and compassion; and even the sense of pity was soon lost in the serious and alarming consideration of the state of the republic. Gratian was too late to assist, he was too weak to revenge, his unfortunate colleague; and the valiant and modest youth felt himself unequal to the support of a sinking world. A formidable tempest of the barbarians of Germany seemed ready to burst over the provinces of Gaul, and the mind of Gratian was oppressed and distracted by the administration of the Western empire. In this important crisis the government of the East and the conduct of the Gothic war required the undivided attention of a hero and a statesman. A subject invested with such ample command would not long have preserved his fidelity to a distant benefactor; and the Imperial council embraced the wise and manly resolution of conferring an obligation rather than of yielding to an insult. It was the wish of Gratian to bestow the purple as the reward of virtue; but at the age of nineteen it is not easy for a prince, educated in the supreme rank, to understand the true characters of his ministers and generals. He attempted to weigh, with an impartial hand, their various merits and defects; and whilst he checked the rash confidence of ambition, he distrusted the cautious wisdom which despaired of the republic. As each moment of delay diminished something of the power and resources of the future sovereign of the East, the situation of the times would not allow a tedious debate. The choice of Gratian was soon declared in favour of an exile, whose father, only three years before, had suffered, under the sanction of *his* authority, an unjust and ignominious death. The great Theodosius, a name celebrated in history and dear to the Catholic church,[104] was summoned to the Imperial court, which had gradually retreated from the confines of Thrace to the more secure station of Sirmium. Five months after the death of Valens the emperor Gratian produced before the assembled troops *his* colleague and *their* master, who, after a modest, perhaps a sincere resistance, was compelled to accept, amidst the general acclamations, the diadem, the purple, and the equal title of Augustus.[105] The provinces of Thrace, Asia, and Egypt, over which Valens had reigned, were resigned to the administration of the new emperor; but as he was specially intrusted with the conduct of the Gothic war, the Illyrian præfecture was dismembered, and the two great dioceses of Dacia and Macedonia were added to the dominions of the Eastern empire.[106]

The same province, and perhaps the same city,[107] which had given to the throne the virtues of Trajan and the talents of Hadrian, was the original seat of another family of Spaniards, who, in a less fortunate age, possessed, near fourscore years, the declining empire of Rome.[108] They emerged from the obscurity of municipal honours by the active spirit of the elder Theodosius, a general whose exploits in Britain and Africa have formed one of the most splendid parts of the annals of Valentinian. The son of that general, who likewise bore the name of Theodosius, was educated, by skilful preceptors, in the liberal studies of youth; but he was instructed in the art of war by the tender care and severe discipline of his father.[109] Under the standard of such a leader, young Theodosius sought glory and knowledge in the most distant scenes of military action; inured his constitution to the difference of seasons and climates; distinguished his valour by sea and land; and observed the various warfare of the Scots, the Saxons, and the Moors. His own merit, and the recommendation of the conqueror of Africa, soon raised him to a separate command; and, in the station of duke of Mæsia, he vanquished an army of Sarmatians; saved the province; deserved the love of the soldiers; and provoked the envy of the court.[110] His rising fortunes were soon blasted by the disgrace and execution of his illustrious father; and Theodosius obtained, as a favour, the permission of retiring to a private life in his native province of Spain. He displayed a firm and temperate character in the ease with which he adapted himself to this new situation. His time was almost equally divided between the town and country; the spirit which had animated his public conduct was shown in the active and affectionate performance of every social duty; and the diligence of the soldier was profitably converted to the improvement of his ample patrimony,[111] which lay between Valladolid and Segovia, in the midst of a fruitful district, still famous for a most exquisite breed of sheep.[112] From the innocent, but humble, labours of his farm, Theodosius was transported, in less than four months, to the throne of the Eastern empire: and the whole period of the history of the world will not perhaps afford a similar example of an elevation at the same time so pure and so honourable. The princes who peaceably inherit the sceptre of their fathers claim and enjoy a legal right, the more secure as it is absolutely distinct from the merits of their personal characters. The subjects who, in a monarchy or a popular state, acquire the possession of supreme power, may have raised themselves, by the superiority either of genius or virtue, above the heads of their equals: but their virtue is seldom exempt from ambition; and the cause of the successful candidate is frequently stained by the guilt of conspiracy or civil war. Even in those governments which allow the reigning monarch to declare a colleague or a successor, his partial choice, which may be influenced by the blindest passions, is often directed to an unworthy object. But the most suspicious malignity cannot ascribe to Theodosius, in his obscure solitude of Caucha, the arts, the desires, or even the hopes of an ambitious statesman; and the name of the Exile would long since have been forgotten, if his genuine and distinguished virtues had not left a deep impression in the Imperial court. During the season of prosperity he had been neglected; but, in the public distress, his superior merit was universally felt and acknowledged. What confidence must have been reposed in his integrity, since Gratian could trust that a pious son would forgive, for the sake of the republic, the murder of his father! What expectations must have been formed of his abilities, to encourage the hope that a single man could save, and restore, the empire of the East! Theodosius was invested with the purple in the thirty-third year of his age. The vulgar gazed with admiration on the manly beauty of his face and the graceful majesty of his person, which they were pleased to compare with the pictures and medals of the emperor Trajan; whilst intelligent observers discovered, in the qualities of his heart and understanding, a more important resemblance to the best and greatest of the Roman princes.

It is not without the most sincere regret that I must now take leave of an accurate and faithful guide, who has composed the history of his own times without indulging the prejudices and passions which usually affect the mind of a contemporary. Ammianus Marcellinus, who terminates his useful work with the defeat and death of Valens, recommends the more glorious subject of the ensuing reign to the youthful vigour and eloquence of the rising generation.[113] The rising generation was not disposed to accept his advice, or to imitate his example;[114] and, in the study of the reign of Theodosius, we are reduced to illustrate the partial narrative of Zosimus by the obscure hints of fragments and chronicles, by the figurative style of poetry or panegyric, and by the precarious assistance of the ecclesiastical writers, who, in the heat of religious faction, are apt to despise the profane virtues of sincerity and moderation. Conscious of these disadvantages, which will continue to involve a considerable portion of the decline and fall of the Roman empire, I shall proceed with doubtful and timorous steps. Yet I may boldly pronounce that the battle of Hadrianople was never revenged by any signal or decisive victory of Theodosius over the barbarians; and the expressive silence of his venal orators may be confirmed by the observation of the condition and circumstances of the times. The fabric of a mighty state, which has been reared by the labours of successive ages, could not be overturned by the misfortune of a single day, if the fatal power of the imagination did not exaggerate the real measure of the calamity. The loss of forty thousand Romans, who fell in the plains of Hadrianople, might have been soon recruited in the populous provinces of the East, which contained so many millions of inhabitants. The courage of a soldier is found to be the cheapest and most common quality of human nature; and sufficient skill to encounter an undisciplined foe might have been speedily taught by the care of the surviving centurions. If the barbarians were mounted on the horses, and equipped with the armour, of their vanquished enemies, the numerous studs of Cappadocia and Spain would have supplied new squadrons of cavalry; the thirty-four arsenals of the empire were plentifully stored with magazines of offensive and defensive arms; and the wealth of Asia might still have yielded an ample fund for the expenses of the war. But the effects which were produced by the battle of Hadrianople on the minds of the barbarians and of the Romans, extended the victory of the former, and the defeat of the latter, far beyond the limits of a single day. A Gothic chief was heard to declare, with insolent moderation, that, for his own part, he was fatigued with slaughter; but that he was astonished how a people who fled before him like a flock of sheep could still presume to dispute the possession of their treasures and provinces.[115] The same terrors which the name of the Huns had spread among the Gothic tribes were inspired, by the formidable name of the Goths, among the subjects and soldiers of the Roman empire.[116] If Theodosius, hastily collecting his scattered forces, had led them into the field to encounter a victorious enemy, his army would have been vanquished by their own fears; and his rashness could not have been excused by the chance of success. But the *great* Theodosius, an epithet which he honourably deserved on this momentous occasion, conducted himself as the firm and faithful guardian of the republic. He fixed his headquarters at Thessalonica, the capital of the Macedonian diocese;[117] from whence he could watch the irregular motions of the barbarians, and direct the operations of his lieutenants, from the gates of Constantinople to the shores of the Hadriatic. The fortifications and garrisons of the cities were strengthened; and the troops, among whom a sense of order and discipline was revived, were insensibly emboldened by the confidence of their own safety. From these secure stations they were encouraged to make frequent sallies on the barbarians, who infested the adjacent country; and, as they were seldom allowed to engage, without some decisive superiority, either of ground or of numbers, their enterprises were, for the most part, successful; and they were soon convinced, by their own experience, of the possibility of vanquishing their *invincible* enemies. The detachments of these separate garrisons were gradually united into small armies; the same cautious measures were pursued, according to an extensive and well-concerted plan of operations; the events of each day added strength and spirit to the Roman arms; and the artful diligence of the emperor, who circulated the most favourable reports of the success of the war, contributed to subdue the pride of the barbarians, and to animate the hopes and courage of his subjects. If, instead of this faint and imperfect outline, we could accurately represent the counsels and actions of Theodosius in four successive campaigns, there is reason to believe that his consummate skill would deserve the applause of every military reader. The republic had formerly been saved by the delays of Fabius; and, while the splendid trophies of Scipio, in the field of Zama, attract the eyes of posterity, the camps and marches of the dictator among the hills of Campania may claim a juster proportion of the solid and independent fame which the general is not compelled to share either with fortune or with his troops. Such was likewise the merit of Theodosius; and the infirmities of his body, which most unseasonably languished under a long and dangerous disease, could not oppress the vigour of his mind, or divert his attention from the public service.[118]

The deliverance and peace of the Roman provinces[119] was the work of prudence, rather than of valour: the prudence of Theodosius was seconded by fortune; and the emperor never failed to seize, and to improve, every favourable circumstance. As long as the superior genius of

Fritigern preserved the union and directed the motions of the barbarians, their power was not inadequate to the conquest of a great empire. The death of that hero, the predecessor and master of the renowned Alaric, relieved an impatient multitude from the intolerable yoke of discipline and discretion. The barbarians, who had been restrained by his authority, abandoned themselves to the dictates of their passions; and their passions were seldom uniform or consistent. An army of conquerors was broken into many disorderly bands of savage robbers; and their blind and irregular fury was not less pernicious to themselves than to their enemies. Their mischievous disposition was shown in the destruction of every object which they wanted strength to remove, or taste to enjoy; and they often consumed, with improvident rage, the harvests, or the granaries, which soon afterwards became necessary for their own subsistence. A spirit of discord arose among the independent tribes and nations, which had been united only by the bands of a loose and voluntary alliance. The troops of the Huns and the Alani would naturally upbraid the flight of the Goths, who were not disposed to use with moderation the advantages of their fortune: the ancient jealousy of the Ostrogoths and the Visigoths could not long be suspended; and the haughty chiefs still remembered the insults and injuries which they had reciprocally offered or sustained while the nation was seated in the countries beyond the Danube. The progress of domestic faction abated the more diffusive sentiment of national animosity; and the officers of Theodosius were instructed to purchase, with liberal gifts and promises, the retreat or service of the discontented party. The acquisition of Modar, a prince of the royal blood of the Amali, gave a bold and faithful champion to the cause of Rome. The illustrious deserter soon obtained the rank of master-general, with an important command; surprised an army of his countrymen, who were immersed in wine and sleep; and, after a cruel slaughter of the astonished Goths, returned with an immense spoil, and four thousand waggons, to the Imperial camp.[120] In the hands of a skilful politician the most different means may be successfully applied to the same ends; and the peace of the empire, which had been forwarded by the divisions, was accomplished by the re-union of the Gothic nation. Athanaric, who had been a patient spectator of these extraordinary events, was at length driven, by the chance of arms, from the dark recesses of the woods of Caucaland. He no

longer hesitated to pass the Danube; and a very considerable part of the subjects of Fritigern, who already felt the inconveniences of anarchy, were easily persuaded to acknowledge for their king a Gothic Judge, whose birth they respected, and whose abilities they had frequently experienced. But age had chilled the daring spirit of Athanaric; and instead of leading his people to the field of battle and victory, he wisely listened to the fair proposal of an honourable and advantageous treaty. Theodosius, who was acquainted with the merit and power of his new ally, condescended to meet him at the distance of several miles from Constantinople; and entertained him in the Imperial city, with the confidence of a friend, and the magnificence of a monarch. "The barbarian prince observed, with curious attention, the variety of objects which attracted his notice, and at last broke out into a sincere and passionate exclamation of wonder. I now behold (said he) what I never could believe, the glories of this stupendous capital! And as he cast his eyes around, he viewed and he admired the commanding situation of the city, the strength and beauty of the walls and public edifices, the capacious harbour crowded with innumerable vessels, the perpetual concourse of distant nations, and the arms and discipline of the troops. Indeed (continued Athanaric), the emperor of the Romans is a god upon earth; and the presumptuous man who dares to lift his hand against him is guilty of his own blood."[121] The Gothic king did not long enjoy this splendid and honourable reception; and, as temperance was not the virtue of his nation, it may justly be suspected that his mortal disease was contracted amidst the pleasures of the Imperial banquets. But the policy of Theodosius derived more solid benefit from the death than he could have expected from the most faithful services of his ally. The funeral of Athanaric was performed with solemn rites in the capital of the East; a stately monument was erected to his memory; and his whole army, won by the liberal courtesy and decent grief of Theodosius, enlisted under the standard of the Roman empire.[122] The submission of so great a body of the Visigoths was productive of the most salutary consequences; and the mixed influence of force, of reason, and of corruption, became every day more powerful and more extensive. Each independent chieftain hastened to obtain a separate treaty, from the apprehension that an obstinate delay might expose *him*, alone and unprotected, to the revenge or justice of the conqueror. The general, or rather the final, capitulation of the Goths, may be dated four years, one month, and twenty-five days, after the defeat and death of the emperor Valens.[123]

The provinces of the Danube had been already relieved from the oppressive weight of the Gruthungi, or Ostrogoths, by the voluntary retreat of Alatheus and Saphrax, whose restless spirit had prompted them to seek new scenes of rapine and glory. Their destructive course was pointed towards the West; but we must be satisfied with a very obscure and imperfect knowledge of their various adventures. The Ostrogoths impelled several of the German tribes on the provinces of Gaul; concluded, and soon violated, a treaty with the emperor Gratian; advanced into the unknown countries of the North; and, after an interval of more than four years, returned with accumulated force to the banks of the Lower Danube. Their troops were recruited with the fiercest warriors of Germany and Scythia; and the soldiers, or at least the historians, of the empire no longer recognised the name and countenances of their former enemies.[124] The general who commanded the military and naval powers of the Thracian frontier soon perceived that his superiority would be disadvantageous to the public service; and that the barbarians, awed by the presence of his fleet and legions, would probably defer the passage of the river till the approaching winter. The dexterity of the spies whom he sent into the Gothic camp allured the barbarians into a fatal snare. They were persuaded that, by a bold attempt, they might surprise, in the silence and darkness of the night, the sleeping army of the Romans; and the whole multitude was hastily embarked in a fleet of three thousand canoes.[125] The bravest of the Ostrogoths led the van; the main body consisted of the remainder of their subjects and soldiers; and the women and children securely followed in the rear. One of the nights without a moon had been selected for the execution of their design; and they had almost reached the southern bank of the Danube, in the firm confidence that they should find an easy landing and an unguarded camp. But the progress of the barbarians was suddenly stopped by an unexpected obstacle—a triple line of vessels, strongly connected with each other, and which formed an impenetrable chain of two miles and a half along the river. While they struggled to force their way in the unequal conflict, their right flank was overwhelmed by the irresistible attack of a fleet of galleys, which were urged down the stream by the united im-

pulse of oars and of the tide. The weight and velocity of those ships of war broke, and sunk, and dispersed the rude and feeble canoes of the barbarians: their valour was ineffectual; and Alatheus, the king or general of the Ostrogoths, perished, with his bravest troops, either by the sword of the Romans or in the waves of the Danube. The last division of this unfortunate fleet might regain the opposite shore; but the distress and disorder of the multitude rendered them alike incapable either of action or counsel; and they soon implored the clemency of the victorious enemy. On this occasion, as well as on many others, it is a difficult task to reconcile the passions and prejudices of the writers of the age of Theodosius. The partial and malignant historian, who misrepresents every action of his reign, affirms that the emperor did not appear in the field of battle till the barbarians had been vanquished by the valour and conduct of his lieutenant Promotus.[126] The flattering poet, who celebrated in the court of Honorius the glory of the father and of the son, ascribes the victory to the personal prowess of Theodosius; and almost insinuates that the king of the Ostrogoths was slain by the hand of the emperor.[127] The truth of history might perhaps be found in a just medium between these extreme and contradictory assertions.

The original treaty, which fixed the settlement of the Goths, ascertained their privileges, and stipulated their obligations, would illustrate the history of Theodosius and his successors. The series of their history has imperfectly preserved the spirit and substance of this singular agreement.[128] The ravages of war and tyranny had provided many large tracts of fertile but uncultivated land for the use of those barbarians who might not disdain the practice of agriculture. A numerous colony of the Visigoths was seated in Thrace; the remains of the Ostrogoths were planted in Phrygia and Lydia; their immediate wants were supplied by a distribution of corn and cattle; and their future industry was encouraged by an exemption from tribute during a certain term of years. The barbarians would have deserved to feel the cruel and perfidious policy of the Imperial court if they had suffered themselves to be dispersed through the provinces. They required and they obtained the sole possession of the villages and districts assigned for their residence; they still cherished and propagated their native manners and language; asserted, in the bosom of despotism, the freedom of their domestic government; and acknowledged the sovereignty of the em-

peror, without submitting to the inferior jurisdiction of the laws and magistrates of Rome.
The hereditary chiefs of the tribes and families
were still permitted to command their followers
in peace and war: but the royal dignity was
abolished; and the generals of the Goths were
appointed and removed at the pleasure of the
emperor. An army of forty thousand Goths was
maintained for the perpetual service of the empire of the East; and those haughty troops, who
assumed the title of *Foederati*, or allies, were distinguished by their gold collars, liberal pay, and
licentious privileges. Their native courage was
improved by the use of arms and the knowledge
of discipline; and, while the republic was
guarded or threatened by the doubtful sword of
the barbarians, the last sparks of the military
flame were finally extinguished in the minds of
the Romans.[129] Theodosius had the address to
persuade his allies that the conditions of peace,
which had been extorted from him by prudence
and necessity, were the voluntary expressions of
his sincere friendship for the Gothic nation.[130]
A different mode of vindication or apology was
opposed to the complaints of the people, who
loudly censured these shameful and dangerous
concessions.[131] The calamities of the War were
painted in the most lively colours; and the first
symptoms of the return of order, of plenty, and
security were diligently exaggerated. The advocates of Theodosius could affirm, with some appearance of truth and reason, that it was impossible to extirpate so many warlike tribes, who
were rendered desperate by the loss of their native country; and that the exhausted provinces
would be revived by a fresh supply of soldiers
and husbandmen. The barbarians still wore an
angry and hostile aspect; but the experience of
past times might encourage the hope that they
would acquire the habits of industry and obedience; that their manners would be polished by
time, education, and the influence of Christianity; and that their posterity would insensibly
blend with the great body of the Roman
people.[132]

Notwithstanding these specious arguments
and these sanguine expectations, it was apparent to every discerning eye that the Goths would
long remain the enemies, and might soon become the conquerors, of the Roman empire.
Their rude and insolent behaviour expressed
their contempt of the citizens and provincials,
whom they insulted with impunity.[133] To the
zeal and valour of the barbarians Theodosius
was indebted for the success of his arms: but
their assistance was precarious; and they were

sometimes seduced, by a treacherous and inconstant disposition, to abandon his standard at the
moment when their service was the most essential. During the civil war against Maximus a
great number of Gothic deserters retired into
the morasses of Macedonia, wasted the adjacent
provinces, and obliged the intrepid monarch to
expose his person and exert his power to suppress the rising flame of rebellion.[134] The public
apprehensions were fortified by the strong suspicion that these tumults were not the effect of
accidental passion, but the result of deep and
premeditated design. It was generally believed
that the Goths had signed the treaty of peace
with an hostile and insidious spirit; and that
their chiefs had previously bound themselves by
a solemn and secret oath never to keep faith
with the Romans, to maintain the fairest show
of loyalty and friendship, and to watch the favourable moment of rapine, of conquest, and of
revenge. But as the minds of the barbarians
were not insensible to the power of gratitude,
several of the Gothic leaders sincerely devoted
themselves to the service of the empire, or, at
least, of the emperor: the whole nation was insensibly divided into two opposite factions, and
much sophistry was employed in conversation
and dispute to compare the obligations of their
first and second engagements. The Goths who
considered themselves as the friends of peace, of
justice, and of Rome, were directed by the authority of Fravitta, a valiant and honourable
youth, distinguished above the rest of his countrymen by the politeness of his manners, the
liberality of his sentiments, and the mild virtues
of social life. But the more numerous faction adhered to the fierce and faithless Priulf, who inflamed the passions and asserted the independence of his warlike followers. On one of the
solemn festivals, when the chiefs of both parties
were invited to the Imperial table, they were insensibly heated by wine, till they forgot the
usual restraints of discretion and respect, and
betrayed in the presence of Theodosius the fatal
secret of their domestic disputes. The emperor,
who had been the reluctant witness of this extraordinary controversy, dissembled his fears
and resentment, and soon dismissed the tumultuous assembly. Fravitta, alarmed and exasperated by the insolence of his rival, whose departure from the palace might have been the signal
of a civil war, boldly followed him and, drawing
his sword, laid Priulf dead at his feet. Their
companions flew to arms; and the faithful
champion of Rome would have been oppressed
by superior numbers if he had not been pro-

tected by the seasonable interposition of the Imperial guards.[135] Such were the scenes of barbaric rage which disgraced the palace and table of the Roman emperor; and, as the impatient Goths could only be restrained by the firm and temperate character of Theodosius, the public safety seemed to depend on the life and abilities of a single man.[136]

CHAPTER XXVII

Death of Gratian. Ruin of Arianism. St. Ambrose. First Civil War, against Maximus. Character, Administration, and Penance, of Theodosius. Death of Valentinian II. Second Civil War, against Eugenius. Death of Theodosius.

THE fame of Gratian, before he had accomplished the twentieth year of his age, was equal to that of the most celebrated princes. His gentle and amiable disposition endeared him to his private friends, the graceful affability of his manners engaged the affection of the people; the men of letters, who enjoyed the liberality, acknowledged the taste and eloquence, of their sovereign; his valour and dexterity in arms were equally applauded by the soldiers; and the clergy considered the humble piety of Gratian as the first and most useful of his virtues. The victory of Colmar had delivered the West from a formidable invasion, and the grateful provinces of the East ascribed the merits of Theodosius to the author of *his* greatness and of the public safety. Gratian survived those memorable events only four or five years, but he survived his reputation, and, before he fell a victim to rebellion, he had lost, in a great measure, the respect and confidence of the Roman world.

The remarkable alteration of his character or conduct may not be imputed to the arts of flattery, which had besieged the son of Valentinian from his infancy, nor to the headstrong passion which that gentle youth appears to have escaped. A more attentive view of the life of Gratian may perhaps suggest the true cause of the disappointment of the public hopes. His apparent virtues, instead of being the hardy productions of experience and adversity, were the premature and artificial fruits of a royal education. The anxious tenderness of his father was continually employed to bestow on him those advantages which he might perhaps esteem the more highly as he himself had been deprived of them, and the most skilful masters of every science and of every art had laboured to form the mind and body of the young prince.[1] The knowledge which they painfully communicated was displayed with ostentation and celebrated with lavish praise. His soft and tractable disposition received the fair impression of their judicious precepts, and the absence of passion might easily be mistaken for the strength of reason. His preceptors gradually rose to the rank and consequence of ministers of state,[2] and, as they wisely dissembled their secret authority, he seemed to act with firmness, with propriety, and with judgment on the most important occasions of his life and reign. But the influence of this elaborate instruction did not penetrate beyond the surface, and the skilful preceptors, who so accurately guided the steps of their royal pupil, could not infuse into his feeble and indolent character the vigorous and independent principle of action which renders the laborious pursuit of glory essentially necessary to the happiness and almost to the existence of the hero. As soon as time and accident had removed those faithful counsellors from the throne, the emperor of the West insensibly descended to the level of his natural genius, abandoned the reins of government to the ambitious hands which were stretched forwards to grasp them, and amused his leisure with the most frivolous gratifications. A public sale of favour and injustice was instituted, both in the court and in the provinces, by the worthless delegates of his power, whose merit it was made *sacrilege* to question.[3] The conscience of the credulous prince was directed by saints and bishops,[4] who procured an Imperial edict to punish, as a capital offence, the violation, the neglect, or even the ignorance of the divine law.[5] Among the various arts which had exercised the youth of Gratian, he had applied himself, with singular inclination and success, to manage the horse, to draw the bow, and to dart the javelin; and these qualifications, which might be useful to a soldier, were prostituted to the viler purposes of hunting. Large parks were enclosed for the Imperial pleasures, and plentifully stocked with every species of wild beasts, and Gratian neglected the duties and even the dignity of his rank to consume whole days in the vain display of his dexterity and boldness in the chase. The pride and wish of the Roman emperor to excel in an art in which he might be surpassed by the meanest of his slaves reminded the numerous spectators of the examples of Nero and Commodus; but the chaste and temperate Gratian was a stranger to their monstrous vices, and his hands were stained only with the blood of animals.[6]

The behaviour of Gratian, which degraded his character in the eyes of mankind, could not have disturbed the security of his reign if the army had not been provoked to resent their peculiar injuries. As long as the young emperor was guided by the instructions of his masters, he professed himself the friend and pupil of the soldiers; many of his hours were spent in the familiar conversation of the camp, and the health, the comforts, the rewards, the honours of his faithful troops, appeared to be the object of his attentive concern. But, after Gratian more freely indulged his prevailing taste for hunting and shooting, he naturally connected himself with the most dexterous ministers of his favourite amusement. A body of the Alani was received into the military and domestic service of the palace, and the admirable skill which they were accustomed to display in the unbounded plains of Scythia was exercised on a more narrow theatre in the parks and enclosures of Gaul. Gratian admired the talents and customs of these favourite guards, to whom alone he intrusted the defence of his person; and, as if he meant to insult the public opinion, he frequently showed himself to the soldiers and people with the dress and arms, the long bow, the sounding quiver, and the fur garments of a Scythian warrior. The unworthy spectacle of a Roman prince who had renounced the dress and manners of his country filled the minds of the legions with grief and indignation.[7] Even the Germans, so strong and formidable in the armies of the empire, affected to disdain the strange and horrid appearance of the savages of the North, who, in the space of a few years, had wandered from the banks of the Volga to those of the Seine. A loud and licentious murmur was echoed through the camps and garrisons of the West; and as the mild indolence of Gratian neglected to extinguish the first symptoms of discontent, the want of love and respect was not supplied by the influence of fear. But the subversion of an established government is always a work of some real, and of much apparent difficulty; and the throne of Gratian was protected by the sanctions of custom, law, religion, and the nice balance of the civil and military powers which had been established by the policy of Constantine. It is not very important to inquire from what causes the revolt of Britain was produced. Accident is commonly the parent of disorder: the seeds of rebellion happened to fall on a soil which was supposed to be more fruitful than any other in tyrants and usurpers;[8] the legions of that sequestered island had been long famous for a spirit of presumption and arrogance;[9] and the name of Maximus was proclaimed by the tumultuary but unanimous voice both of the soldiers and of the provincials. The emperor, or the rebel, for his title was not yet ascertained by fortune, was a native of Spain, the countryman, the fellow-soldier, and the rival of Theodosius, whose elevation he had not seen without some emotions of envy and resentment; the events of his life had long since fixed him in Britain, and I should not be unwilling to find some evidence for the marriage which he is said to have contracted with the daughter of a wealthy lord of Caernarvonshire.[10] But this provincial rank might justly be considered as a state of exile and obscurity, and, if Maximus had obtained any civil or military office, he was not invested with the authority either of governor or general.[11] His abilities and even his integrity are acknowledged by the partial writers of the age, and the merit must indeed have been conspicuous that could extort such a confession in favour of the vanquished enemy of Theodosius. The discontent of Maximus might incline him to censure the conduct of his sovereign, and to encourage, perhaps without any views of ambition, the murmurs of the troops. But in the midst of the tumult he artfully or modestly refused to ascend the throne, and some credit appears to have been given to his own positive declaration that he was compelled to accept the dangerous present of the Imperial purple.[12]

But there was danger likewise in refusing the empire, and, from the moment that Maximus had violated his allegiance to his lawful sovereign, he could not hope to reign, or even to live, if he confined his moderate ambition within the narrow limits of Britain. He boldly and wisely resolved to prevent the designs of Gratian; the youth of the island crowded to his standard, and he invaded Gaul with a fleet and army which were long afterwards remembered as the emigration of a considerable part of the British nation.[13] The emperor, in his peaceful residence of Paris, was alarmed by their hostile approach, and the darts which he idly wasted on lions and bears might have been employed more honourably against the rebels. But his feeble efforts announced his degenerate spirit and desperate situation, and deprived him of the resources which he still might have found in the support of his subjects and allies. The armies of Gaul, instead of opposing the march of Maximus, received him with joyful and loyal acclamations, and the shame of the desertion was transferred from the people to the prince. The troops whose station more immediately attached them to the service of the palace abandoned the standard of Gratian the first time that it was displayed in the neighbourhood of Paris. The emperor of the West fled towards Lyons with a train of only three hundred horse, and in the cities along the road, where he hoped to find a refuge, or at least a passage, he was taught by cruel experience that every gate is shut against the unfortunate. Yet he might still have reached in safety the dominions of his brother, and soon have returned with the forces of Italy, and the East, if he had not suffered himself to be fatally deceived by the perfidious governor of the Lyonnese province. Gratian was amused by protestations of doubtful fidelity, and the hopes of a support which could not be effectual, till the arrival of Andragathius, the general of the cavalry of Maximus, put an end to his suspense. That resolute officer executed, without remorse, the orders or the intentions of the usurper. Gratian, as he rose from supper, was delivered into the hands of the assassin, and his body was denied to the pious and pressing entreaties of his brother Valentinian.[14] The death of the emperor was followed by that of his powerful general Mellobaudes, the king of the Franks, who maintained to the last moment of his life the ambiguous reputation which is the just recompense of obscure and subtle policy.[15] These executions might be necessary to the public safety, but the successful usurper, whose power was acknowledged by all the provinces of the West, had the merit and the satisfaction of boasting that, except those who had perished by the chance of war, his triumph was not stained by the blood of the Romans.[16]

The events of this revolution had passed in such rapid succession that it would have been impossible for Theodosius to march to the relief of his benefactor before he received the intelligence of his defeat and death. During the season of sincere grief or ostentatious mourning the Eastern emperor was interrupted by the arrival of the principal chamberlain of Maximus; and the choice of a venerable old man for an office which was usually exercised by eunuchs announced to the court of Constantinople the gravity and temperance of the British usurper. The ambassador condescended to justify or excuse the conduct of his master, and to protest, in specious language, that the murder of Gratian had been perpetrated, without his knowledge or consent, by the precipitate zeal of the soldiers. But he proceeded, in a firm and equal tone, to offer Theodosius the alternative of peace or war. The speech of the ambassador concluded with a spirited declaration that, although Maximus, as a Roman and as the father of his people, would choose rather to employ his forces in the common defence of the republic, he was armed and prepared, if his friendship should be rejected, to dispute in a field of battle the empire of the world. An immediate and peremptory answer was required, but it was extremely difficult for Theodosius to satisfy, on this important occasion, either the feelings of his own mind or the expectations of the public. The imperious voice of honour and gratitude called aloud for revenge. From the liberality of Gratian he had received the Imperial diadem; his patience would encourage the odious suspicion that he was more deeply sensible of former injuries than of recent obligations; and if he accepted the friendship, he must seem to share the guilt, of the assassin. Even the principles of justice and the interest of society would receive a fatal blow from the impunity of Maximus, and the example of successful usurpation would tend to dissolve the artificial fabric of government, and once more to replunge the empire in the crimes and calamities of the preceding age. But, as the sentiments of gratitude and honour should invariably regulate the conduct of an individual, they may be overbalanced in the mind of a sovereign by the sense of superior duties, and the maxims both of justice and humanity must permit the escape of an atrocious criminal if an innocent people would be involved in the consequences of his punishment. The assassin of Gratian had usurped, but he actually possessed, the most warlike provinces of the empire; the East was exhausted by the misfortunes, and even by the success, of the Gothic war; and it was seriously to be apprehended that, after the vital strength of the republic had been wasted in a doubtful and destructive contest, the feeble conqueror would remain an easy prey to the barbarians of the north. These weighty considerations engaged Theodosius to dissemble his resentment and to accept the alliance of the tyrant. But he stipulated that Maximus should content himself with the possession of the countries beyond the Alps. The brother of Gratian was confirmed and secured in the sovereignty of Italy, Africa, and the Western Illyricum, and some honourable conditions were inserted in the treaty to protect the memory and the laws of the deceased emperor.[17] According to the custom of the age, the images of the three Imperial colleagues were exhibited to the veneration of the people; nor should it be lightly supposed that, in the moment of a solemn reconciliation, Theodosius secretly cherished the intention of perfidy and revenge.[18]

The contempt of Gratian for the Roman soldiers had exposed him to the fatal effects of their resentment. His profound veneration for the Christian clergy was rewarded by the applause and gratitude of a powerful order, which has claimed in every age the privilege of dispensing honours, both on earth and in heaven.[19] The orthodox bishops bewailed his death, and their own irreparable loss; but they were soon comforted by the discovery that Gratian had committed the sceptre of the East to the hands of a prince whose humble faith and fervent zeal were supported by the spirit and abilities of a more vigorous character. Among the benefactors of the church, the fame of Constantine has been rivalled by the glory of Theodosius. If Constantine had the advantage of erecting the standard of the cross, the emulation of his successor assumed the merit of subduing the Arian heresy, and of abolishing the worship of idols in the Roman world. Theodosius was the first of the emperors baptised in the true faith of the Trinity. Although he was born of a Christian family, the maxims, or at least the practice, of the age encouraged him to delay the ceremony of his initiation till he was admonished of the danger of delay by the serious illness which threatened his life towards the end of the first year of his reign. Before he again took the field against the Goths, he received the sacrament of baptism[20] from Acholius, the orthodox bishop of Thessalonica:[21] and as the emperor ascended from the holy font, still glowing with the warm feelings of regeneration, he dictated a solemn edict, which proclaimed his own faith, and prescribed the religion of his subjects. "It is our pleasure (such is the Imperial style) that all the nations which are governed by our clemency and moderation should steadfastly adhere to the religion which was taught by St. Peter to the Romans, which faithful tradition has preserved, and which is now professed by the pontiff Damasus, and by Peter, bishop of Alexandria, a man of apostolic holiness. According to the discipline

of the apostles, and the doctrine of the Gospel, let us believe the sole deity of the Father, the Son, and the Holy Ghost, under an equal majesty and a pious Trinity. We authorise the followers of this doctrine to assume the title of Catholic Christians; and as we judge that all others are extravagant madmen, we brand them with the infamous name of Heretics, and declare that their conventicles shall no longer usurp the respectable appellation of churches. Besides the condemnation of Divine justice, they must expect to suffer the severe penalties, which our authority, guided by heavenly wisdom, shall think proper to inflict upon them."[22] The faith of a soldier is commonly the fruit of instruction, rather than of inquiry; but as the emperor always fixed his eyes on the visible landmarks of orthodoxy which he had so prudently constituted, his religious opinions were never affected by the specious texts, the subtle arguments, and the ambiguous creeds of the Arian doctors. Once indeed he expressed a faint inclination to converse with the eloquent and learned Eunomius, who lived in retirement at a small distance from Constantinople. But the dangerous interview was prevented by the prayers of the empress Flacilla, who trembled for the salvation of her husband; and the mind of Theodosius was confirmed by a theological argument adapted to the rudest capacity. He had lately bestowed on his eldest son Arcadius the name and honours of Augustus, and the two princes were seated on a stately throne to receive the homage of their subjects. A bishop, Amphilochius of Iconium, approached the throne, and, after saluting with due reverence the person of his sovereign, he accosted the royal youth with the same familiar tenderness which he might have used towards a plebeian child. Provoked by this insolent behaviour, the monarch gave orders that the rustic priest should be instantly driven from his presence. But while the guards were forcing him to the door, the dexterous polemic had time to execute his design, by exclaiming, with a loud voice, "Such is the treatment, O emperor! which the King of heaven has prepared for those impious men who affect to worship the Father, but refuse to acknowledge the equal majesty of his divine Son." Theodosius immediately embraced the bishop of Iconium, and never forgot the important lesson which he received from this dramatic parable.[23]

Constantinople was the principal seat and fortress of Arianism; and, in a long interval of forty years,[24] the faith of the princes and prelates who reigned in the capital of the East was rejected in the purer schools of Rome and Alexandria. The archiepiscopal throne of Macedonius, which had been polluted with so much Christian blood, was successively filled by Eudoxus and Damophilus. Their diocese enjoyed a free importation of vice and error from every province of the empire; the eager pursuit of religious controversy afforded a new occupation to the busy idleness of the metropolis: and we may credit the assertion of an intelligent observer, who describes, with some pleasantry, the effects of their loquacious zeal. "This city," says he, "is full of mechanics and slaves, who are all of them profound theologians, and preach in the shops and in the streets. If you desire a man to change a piece of silver, he informs you wherein the Son differs from the Father; if you ask the price of a loaf, you are told, by way of reply, that the Son is inferior to the Father; and if you inquire whether the bath is ready, the answer is, that the Son was made out of nothing."[25] The heretics, of various denominations, subsisted in peace under the protection of the Arians of Constantinople, who endeavoured to secure the attachment of those obscure sectaries, while they abused, with unrelenting severity, the victory which they had obtained over the followers of the council of Nice. During the partial reigns of Constantius and Valens, the feeble remnant of the Homoousians was deprived of the public and private exercise of their religion; and it has been observed, in pathetic language, that the scattered flock was left without a shepherd to wander on the mountains, or to be devoured by rapacious wolves.[26] But as their zeal, instead of being subdued, derived strength and vigour from oppression, they seized the first moments of imperfect freedom, which they acquired by the death of Valens, to form themselves into a regular congregation, under the conduct of an episcopal pastor. Two natives of Cappadocia, Basil and Gregory Nazianzen,[27] were distinguished above all their contemporaries[28] by the rare union of profane eloquence and of orthodox piety. These orators, who might sometimes be compared, by themselves and by the public, to the most celebrated of the ancient Greeks, were united by the ties of the strictest friendship. They had cultivated, with equal ardour, the same liberal studies in the schools of Athens; they had retired, with equal devotion, to the same solitude in the deserts of Pontus; and every spark of emulation or envy appeared to be totally extinguished in the holy and ingenuous breasts of Gregory and Basil. But the exaltation of Basil, from a private life to the archiepiscopal throne of Cæsarea, discovered to the world, and perhaps to himself, the pride of his character; and the first favour which he condescended to bestow on his friend was received, and perhaps was intended, as a cruel insult.[29] Instead of employing the superior talents of Gregory in some useful and conspicuous station, the haughty prelate selected, among the fifty bishoprics of his extensive province, the wretched village of Sasima,[30] without water, without verdure, without society, situate at the junction of three highways and frequented only by the incessant passage of rude and clamorous waggoners. Gregory submitted with reluctance to this humiliating exile: he was ordained bishop of Sasima; but he solemnly protests that he never consummated his spiritual marriage with this disgusting bride. He afterwards consented to undertake the government of his native church of Nazianzus,[31] of which his father had been bishop above five-and-forty years. But as he was still conscious that he deserved another audience and another theatre, he accepted, with no unworthy ambition, the honourable invitation which was addressed to him from the orthodox party of Constantinople. On his arrival in the capital, Gregory was entertained in the house of a pious and charitable kinsman; the most spacious room was consecrated to the uses of religious worship; and the name of *Anastasia* was chosen to express the resurrection of the Nicene faith. This private conventicle was afterwards converted into a magnificent church; and the credulity of the succeeding age was prepared to believe the miracles and visions which attested the presence, or at least the protection, of the Mother of God.[32] The pulpit of the Anastasia was the scene of the labours and triumphs of Gregory Nazianzen; and in the space of two years he experienced all the spiritual adventures which constitute the prosperous or adverse fortunes of a missionary.[33] The Arians, who were provoked by the boldness of his enterprise, represented his doctrine as if he had preached three distinct and equal Deities; and the devout populace was excited to suppress, by violence and tumult, the irregular assemblies of the Athanasian heretics. From the cathedral of St. Sophia there issued a motley crowd "of common beggars, who had forfeited their claim to pity; of monks, who had the appearance of goats or satyrs; and of women, more terrible than so many Jezebels." The doors of the Anastasia were broke open; much mischief was perpetrated, or attempted, with sticks, stones, and firebrands; and as a man lost his life in the affray, Gregory, who was summoned the next morning before the magistrate, had the satisfaction of supposing that he publicly confessed the name of Christ. After he was delivered from the fear and danger of a foreign enemy, his infant church was disgraced and distracted by intestine faction. A stranger, who assumed the name of Maximus[34] and the cloak of a Cynic philosopher, insinuated himself into the confidence of Gregory, deceived and abused his favourable opinion, and, forming a secret connection with some bishops of Egypt, attempted, by a clandestine ordination, to supplant his patron in the episcopal seat of Constantinople. These mortifications might sometimes tempt the Cappadocian missionary to regret his obscure solitude. But his fatigues were rewarded by the daily increase of his fame and his congregation; and he enjoyed the pleasure of observing that the greater part of his numerous audience retired from his sermons satisfied with the eloquence of the preacher,[35] or dissatisfied with the manifold imperfections of their faith and practice.[36]

The catholics of Constantinople were animated with joyful confidence by the baptism and edict of Theodosius; and they impatiently waited the effects of his gracious promise. Their hopes were speedily accomplished; and the emperor, as soon as he had finished the operations of the campaign, made his public entry into the capital at the head of a victorious army. The next day after his arrival he summoned Damophilus to his presence, and offered that Arian prelate the hard alternative of subscribing the Nicene creed, or of instantly resigning, to the orthodox believers, the use and possession of the episcopal palace, the cathedral of St. Sophia, and all the churches of Constantinople. The zeal of Damophilus, which in a catholic saint would have been justly applauded, embraced, without hesitation, a life of poverty and exile,[37] and his removal was immediately followed by the purification of the Imperial City. The Arians might complain, with some appearance of justice, that an inconsiderable congregation of sectaries should usurp the hundred churches which they were insufficient to fill, whilst the far greater part of the people was cruelly excluded from every place of religious worship. Theodosius was still inexorable; but as the angels who protected the catholic cause were only visible to the eyes of faith, he prudently reinforced those heavenly legions with the more effectual aid of temporal and carnal weapons, and the church of St. Sophia was occupied by a large body of the Imperial guards. If the mind of Gregory was susceptible of pride, he must have felt a very lively satisfaction when the emperor conducted him through the streets in solemn triumph, and, with his own hand, respectfully placed him on the archiepiscopal throne of Constantinople. But the saint (who had not subdued the imperfections of human virtue) was deeply affected by the mortifying consideration that his entrance into the fold was that of a wolf rather than of a shepherd; that the glittering arms which surrounded his person were necessary for his safety; and that he alone was the object of the imprecations of a great party, whom, as men and citizens, it was impossible for him to despise. He beheld the innumerable multitude, of either sex, and of every age, who crowded the streets, the windows, and the roofs of the houses; he heard the tumultuous voice of rage, grief, astonishment, and despair; and Gregory fairly confesses that on the memorable day of his installation the capital of the East wore the appearance of a city taken by storm, and in the hands of a barbarian conqueror.[38] About six weeks afterwards, Theodosius declared his resolution of expelling from all the churches of his dominions the bishops and their clergy who should obstinately refuse to believe, or at least to profess, the doctrine of the council of Nice. His lieutenant Sapor was armed with the ample powers of a general law, a special commission, and a military force;[39] and this ecclesiastical revolution was conducted with so much discretion and vigour, that the religion of the emperor was established, without tumult or bloodshed, in all the provinces of the East. The writings of the Arians, if they had been permitted to exist,[40] would perhaps contain the lamentable story of the persecution which afflicted the church under the reign of the impious Theodosius; and the sufferings of *their* holy confessors might claim the pity of the disinterested reader. Yet there is reason to imagine that the violence of zeal and revenge was in some measure eluded by the want of resistance; and that, in their adversity, the Arians displayed much less firmness than had been exerted by the orthodox party under the reigns of Constantius and Valens. The moral character and conduct of the hostile sects appear to have been governed by the same common principles of nature and religion: but a very material circumstance may be discovered, which tended to distinguish the degrees of their theological faith. Both parties in the schools, as well as in the temples, acknowledged and worshipped the divine majesty of Christ; and, as we are always prone to impute our own sentiments and passions to the Deity, it would be deemed more prudent and respectful to exaggerate than to circumscribe the adorable perfections of the Son of God. The disciple of Athanasius exulted in the proud confidence that he had entitled himself to the divine favour, while the follower of Arius must have been tormented by the secret apprehension that he was guilty perhaps of an unpardonable offence by the scanty praise and parsimonious honours which he bestowed on the Judge of the World. The opinions of Arianism might satisfy a cold and speculative mind; but the doctrine of the Nicene Creed, most powerfully recommended by the merits of faith and devotion, was much better adapted to become popular and successful in a believing age.

The hope that truth and wisdom would be found in the assemblies of the orthodox clergy induced the emperor to convene, at Constantinople, a synod of one hundred and fifty bishops, who proceeded, without much difficulty or delay, to complete the theological system which had been established in the council of Nice. The vehement disputes of the fourth century had been chiefly employed on the nature of the Son of God; and the various opinions which were embraced concerning the *Second*, were extended and transferred, by a natural analogy, to the *Third* person of the Trinity.[41] Yet it was found, or it was thought, necessary, by the victorious adversaries of Arianism, to explain the ambiguous language of some respectable doctors; to confirm the faith of the catholics; and to condemn an unpopular and inconsistent sect of Macedonians, who freely admitted that the Son was consubstantial to the Father, while they were fearful of seeming to acknowledge the existence of *Three* Gods. A final and unanimous sentence was pronounced to ratify the equal Deity of the Holy Ghost: the mysterious doctrine has been received by all the nations, and all the churches, of the Christian world; and their grateful reverence has assigned to the bishops of Theodosius the second rank among the general councils.[42] Their knowledge of religious truth may have been preserved by tradition, or it may have been communicated by inspiration; but the sober evidence of history will not allow much weight to the personal authority of the Fathers of Constantinople. In an age when the ecclesiastics had scandalously degenerated from the model of apostolical purity, the most worthless and corrupt were always the most eager to frequent and disturb the episcopal assemblies. The conflict and fermentation of so many opposite interests and tempers inflamed the passions of the bishops: and their ruling passions were, the love of gold and the love of dispute. Many of the same prelates who now applauded the orthodox piety of Theodosius had repeatedly changed, with prudent flexibility, their creeds and opinions; and in the various revolutions of the church and state, the religion of their sovereign was the rule of their obsequious faith. When the emperor suspended his prevailing influence, the turbulent synod was blindly impelled by the absurd or selfish motives of pride, hatred, and resentment. The death of Meletius, which happened at the council of Constantinople, presented the most favourable opportunity of terminating the schism of Antioch, by suffering his aged rival, Paulinus, peaceably to end his days in the episcopal chair. The faith and virtues of Paulinus were unblemished. But his cause was supported by the Western churches; and the bishops of the synod resolved to perpetuate the mischiefs of discord, by the hasty ordination of a perjured candidate,[43] rather than to betray the imagined dignity of the East, which had been illustrated by the birth and death of the Son of God. Such unjust and disorderly proceedings forced the gravest members of the assembly to dissent and to secede; and the clamorous majority, which remained masters of the field of battle, could be compared only to wasps or magpies, to a flight of cranes, or to a flock of geese.[44]

A suspicion may possibly arise that so unfavourable a picture of ecclesiastical synods has been drawn by the partial hand of some obstinate heretic or some malicious infidel. But the name of the sincere historian who has conveyed this instructive lesson to the knowledge of posterity must silence the impotent murmurs of superstition and bigotry. He was one of the most pious and eloquent bishops of the age; a saint, and a doctor of the church; the scourge of Arianism, and the pillar of the orthodox faith; a distinguished member of the council of Constantinople, in which, after the death of Meletius, he exercised the functions of president: in a word—Gregory Nazianzen himself. The harsh and ungenerous treatment which he experienced,[45] instead of derogating from the truth of his evidence, affords an additional proof of the spirit which actuated the deliberations of the synod. Their unanimous suffrage had confirmed the pretensions which the bishop of Constantinople derived from the choice of the people and the approbation of the emperor. But Gregory soon became the victim of malice and envy.

The bishops of the East, his strenuous adherents, provoked by his moderation in the affairs of Antioch, abandoned him, without support, to the adverse faction of the Egyptians, who disputed the validity of his election and rigorously asserted the obsolete canon that prohibited the licentious practice of episcopal translations. The pride, or the humility, of Gregory, prompted him to decline a contest which might have been imputed to ambition and avarice; and he publicly offered, not without some mixture of indignation, to renounce the government of a church which had been restored, and almost created, by his labours. His resignation was accepted by the synod, and by the emperor, with more readiness than he seems to have expected. At the time when he might have hoped to enjoy the fruits of his victory, his episcopal throne was filled by the senator Nectarius; and the new archbishop, accidentally recommended by his easy temper and venerable aspect, was obliged to delay the ceremony of his consecration till he had previously despatched the rites of his baptism.[46] After this remarkable experience of the ingratitude of princes and prelates, Gregory retired once more to his obscure solitude of Cappadocia, where he employed the remainder of his life, about eight years, in the exercises of poetry and devotion. The title of Saint has been added to his name; but the tenderness of his heart,[47] and the elegance of his genius, reflect a more pleasing lustre on the memory of Gregory Nazianzen.

It was not enough that Theodosius had suppressed the insolent reign of Arianism, or that he had abundantly revenged the injuries which the catholics sustained from the zeal of Constantius and Valens. The orthodox emperor considered every heretic as a rebel against the supreme powers of heaven and of earth; and each of these powers might exercise their peculiar jurisdiction over the soul and body of the guilty. The decrees of the council of Constantinople had ascertained the true standard of the faith; and the ecclesiastics who governed the conscience of Theodosius suggested the most effectual methods of persecution. In the space of fifteen years he promulgated at least fifteen severe edicts against the heretics,[48] more especially against those who rejected the doctrine of the Trinity; and to deprive them of every hope of escape, he sternly enacted that, if any laws or rescripts should be alleged in their favour, the judges should consider them as the illegal productions either of fraud or forgery. The penal statutes were directed against the ministers, the assemblies, and the persons of the heretics; and the passions of the legislator were expressed in the language of declamation and invective. I. The heretical teachers, who usurped the sacred titles of Bishops or Presbyters, were not only excluded from the privileges and emoluments so liberally granted to the orthodox clergy, but they were exposed to the heavy penalties of exile and confiscation, if they presumed to preach the doctrine, or to practise the rites, of their *accursed* sects. A fine of ten pounds of gold (above four hundred pounds sterling) was imposed on every person who should dare to confer, or receive, or promote, an heretical ordination: and it was reasonably expected that, if the race of pastors could be extinguished, their helpless flocks would be compelled, by ignorance and hunger, to return within the pale of the Catholic church. II. The rigorous prohibition of conventicles was carefully extended to every possible circumstance in which the heretics could assemble with the intention of worshipping God and Christ according to the dictates of their conscience. Their religious meetings, whether public or secret, by day or by night, in cities or in the country, were equally proscribed by the edicts of Theodosius; and the building, or ground, which had been used for that illegal purpose, was forfeited to the Imperial domain. III. It was supposed that the error of the heretics could proceed only from the obstinate temper of their minds; and that such a temper was a fit object of censure and punishment. The anathemas of the church were fortified by a sort of civil excommunication, which separated them from their fellow-citizens by a peculiar brand of infamy; and this declaration of the supreme magistrate tended to justify, or at least to excuse, the insults of a fanatic populace. The sectaries were gradually disqualified for the possession of honourable or lucrative employments; and Theodosius was satisfied with his own justice, when he decreed that, as the Eunomians distinguished the nature of the Son from that of the Father, they should be incapable of making their wills, or of receiving any advantage from testamentary donations. The guilt of the Manichæan heresy was esteemed of such magnitude that it could be expiated only by the death of the offender; and the same capital punishment was inflicted on the Audians, or *Quartodecimans*,[49] who should dare to perpetrate the atrocious crime of celebrating on an improper day the festival of Easter. Every Roman might exercise the right of public accusation; but the office of *Inquisitors* of the Faith, a name so deservedly abhorred, was first instituted under the reign of Theodosius. Yet we are assured that the execution of his penal edicts was seldom enforced; and that the pious emperor appeared less desirous to punish than to reclaim or terrify his refractory subjects.[50]

The theory of persecution was established by Theodosius, whose justice and piety have been applauded by the saints; but the practice of it, in the fullest extent, was reserved for his rival and colleague, Maximus, the first among the Christian princes who shed the blood of his Christian subjects on account of their religious opinions. The cause of the Priscillianists,[51] a recent sect of heretics who disturbed the provinces of Spain, was transferred, by appeal, from the synod of Bordeaux to the Imperial consistory of Trèves; and by the sentence of the Prætorian præfect, seven persons were tortured, condemned, and executed. The first of these was Priscillian[52] himself, bishop of Avila,[53] in Spain, who adorned the advantages of birth and fortune by the accomplishments of eloquence and learning. Two presbyters and two deacons accompanied their beloved master in his death, which they esteemed as a glorious martyrdom; and the number of religious victims was completed by the execution of Latronian, a poet, who rivalled the fame of the ancients; and of Euchrocia, a noble matron of Bordeaux, the widow of the orator Delphidius.[54] Two bishops, who had embraced the sentiments of Priscillian, were condemned to a distant and dreary exile;[55] and some indulgence was shown to the meaner criminals who assumed the merit of an early repentance. If any credit could be allowed to confessions extorted by fear or pain, and to vague reports, the offspring of malice and credulity, the heresy of the Priscillianists would be found to include the various abominations of magic, of impiety, and of lewdness.[56] Priscillian, who wandered about the world in the company of his spiritual sisters, was accused of praying stark-naked in the midst of the congregation; and it was confidently asserted, that the effects of his criminal intercourse with the daughter of Euchrocia had been suppressed by means still more odious and criminal. But an accurate, or rather a candid inquiry, will discover that, if the Priscillianists violated the laws of nature, it was not by the licentiousness, but by the austerity of their lives. They absolutely condemned the use of the marriage-bed; and the peace of families was often disturbed by indiscreet separations. They enjoined, or recommended, a total abstinence from all animal food; and their continual prayers, fasts, and vigils, inculcated a rule of strict and perfect devotion. The speculative tenets of the sect, concerning the person of Christ and the nature of the human soul, were derived from the Gnostic and Manichæan system; and this vain philosophy, which had been transported from Egypt to Spain, was ill adapted to the grosser spirits of the West. The obscure disciples of Priscillian suffered, languished, and gradually disappeared: his tenets were rejected by the clergy and people, but his death was the subject of a long and vehement controversy; while some arraigned, and others applauded, the justice of his sentence. It is with pleasure that we can observe the humane inconsistency of the most illustrious saints and bishops, Ambrose of Milan[57] and Martin of Tours,[58] who, on this occasion, asserted the cause of toleration. They pitied the unhappy men who had been executed at Trèves; they refused to hold communion with their episcopal murderers; and if Martin deviated from that generous resolution, his motives were laudable, and his repentance was exemplary. The bishops of Tours and Milan pronounced, without hesitation, the eternal damnation of heretics; but they were surprised and shocked by the bloody image of their temporal death, and the honest feelings of nature resisted the artificial prejudices of theology. The humanity of Ambrose and Martin was confirmed by the scandalous irregularity of the proceedings against Priscillian and his adherents. The civil and ecclesiastical ministers had transgressed the limits of their respective provinces. The secular judge had presumed to receive an appeal, and to pronounce a definitive sentence, in a matter of faith and episcopal jurisdiction. The bishops had disgraced themselves by exercising the functions of accusers in a criminal prosecution. The cruelty of Ithacius,[59] who beheld the tortures, and solicited the death of the heretics, provoked the just indignation of mankind; and the vices of that profligate bishop were admitted as a proof that his zeal was instigated by the sordid motives of interest. Since the death of Priscillian, the rude attempts of persecution have been refined and methodised in the holy office, which assigns their distinct parts to the ecclesiastical and secular powers. The devoted victim is regularly delivered by the priest to the magistrate, and by the magistrate to the executioner; and the inexorable sentence of the church, which declares the spiritual guilt of the offender, is expressed in the mild language of pity and intercession.

Among the ecclesiastics who illustrated the

reign of Theodosius, Gregory Nazianzen was distinguished by the talents of an eloquent preacher; the reputation of miraculous gifts added weight and dignity to the monastic virtues of Martin of Tours;[60] but the palm of episcopal vigour and ability was justly claimed by the intrepid Ambrose.[61] He was descended from a noble family of Romans; his father had exercised the important office of Prætorian præfect of Gaul; and the son, after passing through the studies of a liberal education, attained, in the regular gradation of civil honours, the station of consular of Liguria, a province which included the Imperial residence of Milan. At the age of thirty-four, and before he had received the sacrament of baptism, Ambrose, to his own surprise and to that of the world, was suddenly transformed from a governor to an archbishop. Without the least mixture, as it is said, of art or intrigue, the whole body of the people unanimously saluted him with the episcopal title; the concord and perseverance of their acclamations were ascribed to a preternatural impulse; and the reluctant magistrate was compelled to undertake a spiritual office for which he was not prepared by the habits and occupations of his former life. But the active force of his genius soon qualified him to exercise, with zeal and prudence, the duties of his ecclesiastical jurisdiction; and while he cheerfully renounced the vain and splendid trappings of temporal greatness, he condescended, for the good of the church, to direct the conscience of the emperors, and to control the administration of the empire. Gratian loved and revered him as a father; and the elaborate treatise on the faith of the Trinity was designed for the instruction of the young prince. After his tragic death, at a time when the empress Justina trembled for her own safety, and for that of her son Valentinian, the archbishop of Milan was despatched on two different embassies to the court of Trèves. He exercised, with equal firmness and dexterity, the powers of his spiritual and political characters; and perhaps contributed, by his authority and eloquence, to check the ambition of Maximus, and to protect the peace of Italy.[62] Ambrose had devoted his life and his abilities to the service of the church. Wealth was the object of his contempt; he had renounced his private patrimony; and he sold, without hesitation, the consecrated plate for the redemption of captives. The clergy and people of Milan were attached to their archbishop; and he deserved the esteem, without soliciting the favour, or apprehending the displeasure, of his feeble sovereigns.

The government of Italy, and of the young emperor, naturally devolved to his mother Justina, a woman of beauty and spirit, but who, in the midst of an orthodox people, had the misfortune of professing the Arian heresy, which she endeavoured to instil into the mind of her son. Justina was persuaded that a Roman emperor might claim, in his own dominions, the public exercise of his religion; and she proposed to the archbishop, as a moderate and reasonable concession, that he should resign the use of a single church, either in the city or suburbs of Milan. But the conduct of Ambrose was governed by very different principles.[63] The palaces of the earth might indeed belong to Cæsar, but the churches were houses of God; and, within the limits of his diocese, he himself, as the lawful successor of the apostles, was the only minister of God. The privileges of Christianity, temporal as well as spiritual, were confined to the true believers; and the mind of Ambrose was satisfied that his own theological opinions were the standard of truth and orthodoxy. The archbishop, who refused to hold any conference or negotiation with the instruments of Satan, declared, with modest firmness, his resolution to die a martyr rather than to yield to the impious sacrilege; and Justina, who resented the refusal as an act of insolence and rebellion, hastily determined to exert the Imperial prerogative of her son. As she desired to perform her public devotions on the approaching festival of Easter, Ambrose was ordered to appear before the council. He obeyed the summons with the respect of a faithful subject, but he was followed, without his consent, by an innumerable people: they pressed, with impetuous zeal, against the gates of the palace; and the affrighted ministers of Valentinian, instead of pronouncing a sentence of exile on the archbishop of Milan, humbly requested that he would interpose his authority to protect the person of the emperor, and to restore the tranquillity of the capital. But the promises which Ambrose received and communicated were soon violated by a perfidious court; and, during six of the most solemn days which Christian piety has set apart for the exercise of religion, the city was agitated by the irregular convulsions of tumult and fanaticism. The officers of the household were directed to prepare, first the Portian, and afterwards the new, *Basilica*, for the immediate reception of the emperor and his mother. The splendid canopy and hangings of the royal seat were arranged in the customary manner; but it was found necessary to defend them, by a strong guard, from the insults of the populace. The Arian ecclesiastics who ventured to show themselves in the streets were exposed to the most imminent danger of their lives; and Ambrose enjoyed the merit and reputation of rescuing his personal enemies from the hands of the enraged multitude.

But while he laboured to restrain the effects of their zeal, the pathetic vehemence of his sermons continually inflamed the angry and seditious temper of the people of Milan. The characters of Eve, of the wife of Job, of Jezebel, of Herodias, were indecently applied to the mother of the emperor; and her desire to obtain a church for the Arians was compared to the most cruel persecutions which Christianity had endured under the reign of Paganism. The measures of the court served only to expose the magnitude of the evil. A fine of two hundred pounds of gold was imposed on the corporate body of merchants and manufacturers: an order was signified, in the name of the emperor, to all the officers and inferior servants of the courts of justice, that, during the continuance of the public disorders, they should strictly confine themselves to their houses: and the ministers of Valentinian imprudently confessed that the most respectable part of the citizens of Milan was attached to the cause of their archbishop. He was again solicited to restore peace to his country, by a timely compliance with the will of his sovereign. The reply of Ambrose was couched in the most humble and respectful terms, which might, however, be interpreted as a serious declaration of civil war. "His life and fortune were in the hands of the emperor; but he would never betray the church of Christ, or degrade the dignity of the episcopal character. In such a cause he was prepared to suffer whatever the malice of the dæman could inflict; and he only wished to die in the presence of his faithful flock, and at the foot of the altar; *he* had not contributed to excite, but it was in the power of God alone to appease, the rage of the people: he deprecated the scenes of blood and confusion which were likely to ensue; and it was his fervent prayer that he might not survive to behold the ruin of a flourishing city, and perhaps the desolation of all Italy."[64] The obstinate bigotry of Justina would have endangered the empire of her son, if, in this contest with the church and people of Milan, she could have depended on the active obedience of the troops of the palace. A large body of Goths had marched to occupy the *Basilica*, which was the object of the dispute: and it might be expected from the Arian principles and barbarous manners of these foreign mercenaries, that they would not entertain any scruples in the execution of the most sanguinary orders. They were encountered on the sacred threshold by the archbishop, who, thundering against them a sentence of excommunication, asked them, in the tone of a father and a master, Whether it was to invade the house of God that they had implored the hospitable protection of the republic? The suspense of the barbarians allowed some hours for a more effectual negotiation; and the empress was persuaded by the advice of her wisest counsellors to leave the catholics in possession of all the churches of Milan; and to dissemble, till a more convenient season, her intentions of revenge. The mother of Valentinian could never forgive the triumph of Ambrose; and the royal youth uttered a passionate exclamation, that his own servants were ready to betray him into the hands of an insolent priest.

The laws of the empire, some of which were inscribed with the name of Valentinian, still condemned the Arian heresy, and seemed to excuse the resistance of the catholics. By the influence of Justina, an edict of toleration was promulgated in all the provinces which were subject to the court of Milan; the free exercise of their religion was granted to those who professed the faith of Rimini; and the emperor declared that all persons who should infringe this sacred and salutary constitution should be capitally punished, as the enemies of the public peace.[65] The character and language of the archbishop of Milan may justify the suspicion that his conduct soon afforded a reasonable ground, or at least a specious pretence, to the Arian ministers, who watched the opportunity of surprising him in some act of disobedience to a law which he strangely represents as a law of blood and tyranny. A sentence of easy and honourable banishment was pronounced, which enjoined Ambrose to depart from Milan without delay, whilst it permitted him to choose the place of his exile and the number of his companions. But the authority of the saints, who have preached and practised the maxims of passive loyalty, appeared to Ambrose of less moment than the extreme and pressing danger of the church. He boldly refused to obey; and his refusal was supported by the unanimous consent of his faithful people.[66] They guarded by turns the person of their archbishop; the gates of the cathedral and the episcopal palace were strongly secured; and the Imperial troops, who had formed the blockade, were unwilling to risk the attack of that impregnable fortress. The numerous poor, who had been relieved by the liberality of Ambrose, embraced the fair occasion of signalising their zeal and gratitude; and as the patience of the multitude might have been exhausted by the length and uniformity of nocturnal vigils, he prudently introduced into the church of Milan the useful institution of a loud and regular psalmody. While he maintained this arduous contest, he was instructed, by a dream, to open the earth in a place where the remains of two martyrs, Gervasius and Protasius,[67] had been deposited above three hundred years. Immediately under the pavement of the church two perfect skeletons were found,[68] with the heads separated from their bodies, and a plentiful effusion of blood. The holy relics were presented, in solemn pomp, to the veneration of the people; and every circumstance of this fortunate discovery was admirably adapted to promote the designs of Ambrose. The bones of the martyrs, their blood, their garments, were supposed to contain a healing power; and the preternatural influence was communicated to the most distant objects, without losing any part of its original virtue. The extraordinary cure of a blind man,[69] and the reluctant confessions of several dæmoniacs, appeared to justify the faith and sanctity of Ambrose; and the truth of those miracles is attested by Ambrose himself, by his secretary Paulinus, and by his proselyte, the celebrated Augustin, who, at that time, professed the art of rhetoric in Milan. The reason of the present age may possibly approve the incredulity of Justina and her Arian court, who derided the theatrical representations which were exhibited by the contrivance, and at the expense, of the archbishop.[70] Their effect, however, on the minds of the people, was rapid and irresistible; and the feeble sovereign of Italy found himself unable to contend with the favourite of Heaven. The powers likewise of the earth interposed in the defence of Ambrose: the disinterested advice of Theodosius was the genuine result of piety and friendship; and the mask of religious zeal concealed the hostile and ambitious designs of the tyrant of Gaul.[71]

The reign of Maximus might have ended in peace and prosperity, could he have contented himself with the possession of three ample countries, which now constitute the three most flourishing kingdoms of modern Europe. But the aspiring usurper, whose sordid ambition was not dignified by the love of glory and of arms, considered his actual forces as the instruments only of his future greatness, and his success was the immediate cause of his destruction. The wealth which he extorted[72] from the oppressed provinces of Gaul, Spain, and Britain, was employed in levying and maintaining a formidable army of barbarians, collected, for the most part, from the fiercest nations of Germany. The conquest of Italy was the object of his hopes and preparations; and he secretly meditated the ruin of an innocent youth, whose government was abhorred and despised by his catholic subjects. But as Maximus wished to occupy, without resistance, the passes of the Alps, he received, with perfidious smiles, Domninus of Syria, the ambassador of Valentinian, and pressed him to accept the aid of a considerable body of troops for the service of a Pannonian war. The penetration of Ambrose had discovered the snares of an enemy under the professions of friendship;[73] but the Syrian Domninus was corrupted or deceived by the liberal favour of the court of Trèves; and the council of Milan obstinately rejected the suspicion of danger with a blind confidence, which was the effect not of courage, but of fear. The march of the auxiliaries was guided by the ambassador; and they were admitted, without distrust, into the fortresses of the Alps. But the crafty tyrant followed, with hasty and silent footsteps, in the rear; and as he diligently intercepted all intelligence of his motions, the gleam of armour and the dust excited by the troops of cavalry first announced the hostile approach of a stranger to the gates of Milan. In this extremity, Justina and her son might accuse their own imprudence and the perfidious arts of Maximus; but they wanted time, and force, and resolution to stand against the Gauls and Germans, either in the field or within the walls of a large and disaffected city. Flight was their only hope; Aquileia their only refuge: and, as Maximus now displayed his genuine character, the brother of Gratian might expect the same fate from the hands of the same assassin. Maximus entered Milan in triumph; and if the wise archbishop refused a dangerous and criminal connection with the usurper, he might indirectly contribute to the success of his arms by inculcating from the pulpit the duty of resignation rather than that of resistance.[74] The unfortunate Justina reached Aquileia in safety; but she distrusted the strength of the fortifications; she dreaded the event of a siege; and she resolved to implore the protection of the great Theodosius, whose power and virtue were celebrated in all the countries of the West. A vessel was secretly provided to transport the Imperial family; they embarked with precipitation in one of the obscure harbours of Venetia, or Istria; traversed the whole extent of the Hadriatic and Ionian seas; turned the extreme promontory of Peloponnesus; and, after a long but successful navigation, reposed themselves in the port of Thessalonica. All the subjects of Valentinian deserted the cause of a prince who, by his abdication, had absolved them from the duty of allegiance; and if the little city of Æmona, on the verge of Italy, had not presumed to stop the career of his inglorious victory, Maximus would have obtained without a struggle the sole possession of the Western empire.

Instead of inviting his royal guests to the palace of Constantinople, Theodosius had some unknown reasons to fix their residence at Thessalonica; but these reasons did not proceed from contempt or indifference, as he speedily made a visit to that city, accompanied by the greatest part of his court and senate. After the first tender expressions of friendship and sympathy, the pious emperor of the East gently admonished Justina that the guilt of heresy was sometimes punished in this world as well as in the next; and that the public profession of the Nicene faith would be the most efficacious step to promote the restoration of her son, by the satisfaction which it must occasion both on earth and in heaven. The momentous question of peace or war was referred by Theodosius to the deliberation of his council; and the arguments which might be alleged on the side of honour and justice had acquired, since the death of Gratian, a considerable degree of additional weight. The persecution of the Imperial family, to which Theodosius himself had been indebted for his fortune, was now aggravated by recent and repeated injuries. Neither oaths nor treaties could restrain the boundless ambition of Maximus; and the delay of vigorous and decisive measures, instead of prolonging the blessings of peace, would expose the Eastern empire to the danger of an hostile invasion. The barbarians who had passed the Danube had lately assumed the character of soldiers and subjects, but their native fierceness was yet untamed; and the operations of a war, which would exercise their valour and diminish their numbers, might tend to relieve the provinces from an intolerable oppression. Notwithstanding these specious and solid reasons, which were approved by a majority of the council, Theodosius still hesitated whether he should draw the sword in a contest which could no longer admit any terms of reconciliation; and his magnanimous character was not disgraced by the apprehensions which he felt for the safety of his infant sons, and

the welfare of his exhausted people. In this moment of anxious doubt, while the fate of the Roman world depended on the resolution of a single man, the charms of the princess Galla most powerfully pleaded the cause of her brother Valentinian.[75] The heart of Theodosius was softened by the tears of beauty; his affections were insensibly engaged by the graces of youth and innocence; the art of Justina managed and directed the impulse of passion; and the celebration of the royal nuptials was the assurance and signal of the civil war. The unfeeling critics, who consider every amorous weakness as an indelible stain on the memory of a great and orthodox emperor, are inclined on this occasion to dispute the suspicious evidence of the historian Zosimus. For my own part, I shall frankly confess that I am willing to find, or even to seek, in the revolutions of the world some traces of the mild and tender sentiments of domestic life; and amidst the crowd of fierce and ambitious conquerors, I can distinguish, with peculiar complacency, a gentle hero who may be supposed to receive his armour from the hands of love. The alliance of the Persian king was secured by the faith of treaties; the martial barbarians were persuaded to follow the standard or to respect the frontiers of an active and liberal monarch; and the dominions of Theodosius, from the Euphrates to the Hadriatic, resounded with the preparations of war both by land and sea. The skilful disposition of the forces of the East seemed to multiply their numbers, and distracted the attention of Maximus. He had reason to fear that a chosen body of troops, under the command of the intrepid Arbogastes, would direct their march along the banks of the Danube, and boldly penetrate through the Rhætian provinces into the centre of Gaul. A powerful fleet was equipped in the harbours of Greece and Epirus, with an apparent design that, as soon as the passage had been opened by a naval victory, Valentinian and his mother should land in Italy, proceed without delay to Rome, and occupy the majestic seat of religion and empire. In the meanwhile Theodosius himself advanced, at the head of a brave and disciplined army, to encounter his unworthy rival, who, after the siege of Æmona, had fixed his camp in the neighbourhood of Siscia, a city of Pannonia, strongly fortified by the broad and rapid stream of the Save.

The veterans, who still remembered the long resistance, and successive resources, of the tyrant Magnentius, might prepare themselves for the labours of three bloody campaigns. But the contest with his successor, who, like him, had usurped the throne of the West, was easily decided in the term of two months,[76] and within the space of two hundred miles. The superior genius of the emperor of the East might prevail over the feeble Maximus, who in this important crisis showed himself destitute of military skill or personal courage; but the abilities of Theodosius were seconded by the advantage which he possessed of a numerous and active cavalry. The Huns, the Alani, and, after their example, the Goths themselves, were formed into squadrons of archers, who fought on horseback, and confounded the steady valour of the Gauls and Germans by the rapid motions of a Tartar war. After the fatigue of a long march in the heat of summer they spurred their foaming horses into the waters of the Save, swam the river in the presence of the enemy, and instantly charged and routed the troops who guarded the high ground on the opposite side. Marcellinus, the tyrant's brother, advanced to support them with the select cohorts, which were considered as the hope and strength of the army. The action, which had been interrupted by the approach of night, was renewed in the morning; and, after a sharp conflict, the surviving remnant of the bravest soldiers of Maximus threw down their arms at the feet of the conqueror. Without suspending his march, to receive the loyal acclamations of the citizens of Æmona, Theodosius pressed forwards to terminate the war by the death or captivity of his rival, who fled before him with the diligence of fear. From the summit of the Julian Alps he descended with such incredible speed into the plain of Italy that he reached Aquileia on the evening of the first day; and Maximus, who found himself encompassed on all sides, had scarcely time to shut the gates of the city. But the gates could not long resist the effort of a victorious enemy; and the despair, the disaffection, the indifference of the soldiers and people hastened the downfall of the wretched Maximus. He was dragged from his throne, rudely stripped of the Imperial ornaments, the robe, the diadem, and the purple slippers; and conducted, like a malefactor, to the camp and presence of Theodosius, at a place about three miles from Aquileia. The behaviour of the emperor was not intended to insult, and he showed some disposition to pity and forgive the tyrant of the West, who had never been his personal enemy, and was now become the object of his contempt. Our sympathy is the most forcibly excited by the misfortunes to which we are exposed; and the spectacle of a proud competitor now prostrate at his feet could not fail of producing very serious and solemn thoughts in the mind of the victorious emperor. But the feeble emotion of involuntary pity was checked by his regard for public justice and the memory of Gratian; and he abandoned the victim to the pious zeal of the soldiers, who drew him out of the Imperial presence and instantly separated his head from his body. The intelligence of his defeat and death was received with sincere or well-dissembled joy: his son Victor, on whom he had conferred the title of Augustus, died by the order, perhaps by the hand, of the bold Arbogastes; and all the military plans of Theodosius were successfully executed. When he had thus terminated the civil war, with less difficulty and bloodshed than he might naturally expect, he employed the winter months of his residence at Milan to restore the state of the afflicted provinces; and early in the spring he made, after the example of Constantine and Constantius, his triumphal entry into the ancient capital of the Roman empire.[77]

The orator, who may be silent without danger, may praise without difficulty and without reluctance;[78] and posterity will confess that the character of Theodosius[79] might furnish the subject of a sincere and ample panegyric. The wisdom of his laws and the success of his arms rendered his administration respectable in the eyes both of his subjects and of his enemies. He loved and practised the virtues of domestic life, which seldom hold their residence in the palaces of kings. Theodosius was chaste and temperate; he enjoyed, without excess, the sensual and social pleasures of the table, and the warmth of his amorous passions was never diverted from their lawful objects. The proud titles of Imperial greatness were adorned by the tender names of a faithful husband, an indulgent father; his uncle was raised, by his affectionate esteem, to the rank of a second parent; Theodosius embraced, as his own, the children of his brother and sister, and the expressions of his regard were extended to the most distant and obscure branches of his numerous kindred. His familiar friends were judiciously selected from among those persons who, in the equal intercourse of private life, had appeared before his eyes without a mask; the consciousness of personal and superior merit enabled him to despise the accidental distinction of the purple, and he proved by his conduct that he had forgotten all the injuries, while he most gratefully remembered all the favours and services which he had received before he ascended the throne of the Roman empire. The serious or lively tone of his conversation was adapted to the age, the rank, or the character of his subjects whom he admitted into his society; and the affability of his manners displayed the image of his mind. Theodosius respected the simplicity of the good and virtuous: every art, every talent, of an useful or even of an innocent nature, was rewarded by his judicious liberality; and, except the heretics, whom he persecuted with implacable hatred, the diffusive circle of his benevolence was circumscribed only by the limits of the human race. The government of a mighty empire may assuredly suffice to occupy the time and the abilities of a mortal; yet the diligent prince, without aspiring to the unsuitable reputation of profound learning, always reserved some moments of his leisure for the instructive amusement of reading. History, which enlarged his experience, was his favourite study. The annals of Rome, in the long period of eleven hundred years, presented him with a various and splendid picture of human life; and it has been particularly observed that, whenever he perused the cruel acts of Cinna, of Marius, or of Sylla, he warmly expressed his generous detestation of those enemies of humanity and freedom. His disinterested opinion of past events was usefully applied as the rule of his own actions, and Theodosius has deserved the singular commendation that his virtues always seemed to expand with his fortune; the season of his prosperity was that of his moderation, and his clemency appeared the most conspicuous after the danger and success of the civil war. The Moorish guards of the tyrant had been massacred in the first heat of the victory, and a small number of the most obnoxious criminals suffered the punishment of the law. But the emperor showed himself much more attentive to relieve the innocent than to chastise the guilty. The oppressed subjects of the West, who would have deemed themselves happy in the restoration of their lands, were astonished to receive a sum of money equivalent to their losses; and the liberality of the conqueror supported the aged mother and educated the orphan daughters of Maximus.[80] A character thus accomplished might almost excuse the extravagant supposition of the orator Pacatus that, if the elder Brutus could be permitted to revisit the earth, the stern republican would abjure, at the feet of Theodosius, his hatred of kings; and ingenuously confess that such a monarch was the most faithful guardian of the happiness and dignity of the Roman people.[81]

Yet the piercing eye of the founder of the republic must have discerned two essential imperfections, which might, perhaps, have abated his recent love of despotism. The virtuous mind of Theodosius was often relaxed by indolence,[82] and it was sometimes inflamed by passion.[83] In the pursuit of an important object his active courage was capable of the most vigorous exertions; but as soon as the design was accomplished, or the danger was surmounted, the hero sunk into inglorious repose, and, forgetful that the time of a prince is the property of his people, resigned himself to the enjoyment of the innocent but trifling pleasures of a luxurious court. The natural disposition of Theodosius was hasty and choleric; and, in a station where none could resist and few would dissuade the fatal consequence of his resentment, the humane monarch was justly alarmed by the consciousness of his infirmity and of his power. It was the constant study of his life to suppress or regulate the intemperate sallies of passion; and the success of his efforts enhanced the merit of his clemency. But the painful virtue which claims the merit of victory is exposed to the danger of defeat; and the reign of a wise and merciful prince was polluted by an act of cruelty which would stain the annals of Nero or Domitian. Within the space of three years the inconsistent historian of Theodosius must relate the generous pardon of the citizens of Antioch, and the inhuman massacre of the people of Thessalonica.

The lively impatience of the inhabitants of Antioch was never satisfied with their own situation, or with the character and conduct of their successive sovereigns. The Arian subjects of Theodosius deplored the loss of their churches; and, as three rival bishops disputed the throne of Antioch, the sentence which decided their pretensions excited the murmurs of the two unsuccessful congregations. The exigencies of the Gothic war, and the inevitable expense that accompanied the conclusion of the peace, had constrained the emperor to aggravate the weight of the public impositions; and the provinces of Asia, as they had not been involved in the distress, were the less inclined to contribute to the relief of Europe. The auspicious period now approached of the tenth year of his reign; a festival more grateful to the soldiers, who received a liberal donative, than to the subjects, whose voluntary offerings had been long since converted into an extraordinary and oppressive burden. The edicts of taxation interrupted the repose and pleasures of Antioch; and the tribunal of the magistrate was besieged by a suppliant crowd, who, in pathetic, but at first in respectful language, solicited the redress of their grievances. They were gradually incensed by the pride of their haughty rulers, who treated their complaints as a criminal resistance; their satirical wit degenerated into sharp and angry invectives; and, from the subordinate powers of government, the invectives of the people insensibly rose to attack the sacred character of the emperor himself. Their fury, provoked by a feeble opposition, discharged itself on the images of the Imperial family which were erected, as objects of public veneration, in the most conspicuous places of the city. The statues of Theodosius, of his father, of his wife Flaccilla, of his two sons Arcadius and Honorius, were insolently thrown down from their pedestals, broken in pieces, or dragged with contempt through the streets; and the indignities which were offered to the representations of Imperial majesty sufficiently declared the impious and treasonable wishes of the populace. The tumult was almost immediately suppressed by the arrival of a body of archers; and Antioch had leisure to reflect on the nature and consequences of her crime.[84] According to the duty of his office, the governor of the province despatched a faithful narrative of the whole transaction, while the trembling citizens intrusted the confession of their crime and the assurances of their repentance to the zeal of Flavian their bishop, and to the eloquence of the senator Hilarius, the friend, and most probably the disciple, of Libanius,[85] whose genius on this melancholy occasion was not useless to his country. But the two capitals, Antioch and Constantinople, were separated by the distance of eight hundred miles; and, notwithstanding the diligence of the Imperial posts, the guilty city was severely punished by a long and dreadful interval of suspense. Every rumour agitated the hopes and fears of the Antiochians, and they heard with terror that their sovereign, exasperated by the insult which had been offered to his own statues, and more especially to those of his beloved wife, had resolved to level with the ground the offending city, and to massacre, without distinction of age or sex, the criminal inhabitants,[86] many of whom were actually driven, by their apprehensions, to seek a refuge in the mountains of Syria and the adjacent desert. At length, twenty-four days after the sedition, the general Hellebicus, and Cæsarius, master of the offices, declared the will of the emperor and the sentence of Antioch. That proud capital was degraded from the rank of a city; and the metropolis of the East, stripped of its lands, its privileges, and its revenues, was subjected, under the humiliating denomination of a village, to the jurisdiction of Laodicea.[87] The baths, the circus, and the theatres were shut; and, that every source of plenty and pleasure might at the same time be intercepted, the distribution of corn was abolished by the severe instructions of Theodosius. His commissioners then proceeded to inquire into the guilt of individuals—of those who had perpetrated, and of those who had not prevented, the destruction of the sacred statues. The tribunal of Hellebicus and Cæsarius, encompassed with armed soldiers, was erected in the midst of the Forum. The noblest and most wealthy of the citizens of Antioch appeared before them in chains; the examination was assisted by the use of torture, and their sentence was pronounced or suspended, according to the judgment of these extraordinary magistrates. The houses of the criminals were exposed to sale, their wives and children were suddenly reduced from affluence and luxury to the most abject distress, and a bloody execution was expected to conclude the horrors of a day[88] which the preacher of Antioch, the eloquent Chrysostom, has represented as a lively image of the last and universal judgment of the world. But the ministers of Theodosius performed with reluctance the cruel task which had been assigned them; they dropped a gentle tear over the calamities of the people, and they listened with reverence to the pressing solicitations of the monks and hermits, who descended in swarms from the mountains.[89] Hellebicus and Cæsarius were persuaded to suspend the execution of their sentence; and it was agreed that the former should remain at Antioch, while the latter returned, with all possible speed, to Constantinople, and presumed once more to consult the will of his sovereign. The resentment of Theodosius had already subsided; the deputies of the people, both the bishop and the orator, had obtained a favourable audience; and the reproaches of the emperor were the complaints of injured friendship rather than the stern menaces of pride and power. A free and general pardon was granted to the city and citizens of Antioch; the prison-doors were thrown open; the senators, who despaired of their lives, recovered the possession of their houses and estates; and the capital of the East was restored to the enjoyment of her ancient dignity and splendour. Theodosius condescended to praise the senate of Constantinople, who had generously interceded for their distressed brethren; he rewarded the eloquence of Hilarius with the government of Palestine, and dismissed the bishop of Antioch with the warmest expressions of respect and gratitude. A thousand new statues arose to the clemency of Theodosius; the applause of his subjects was ratified by the approbation of his own heart; and the emperor confessed that, if the exercise of justice is the most important duty, the indulgence of mercy is the most exquisite pleasure of a sovereign.[90]

The sedition of Thessalonica is ascribed to a more shameful cause, and was productive of much more dreadful consequences. That great city, the metropolis of all the Illyrian provinces, had been protected from the dangers of the Gothic war by strong fortifications and a numerous garrison. Botheric, the general of those troops, and, as it should seem from his name, a barbarian, had among his slaves a beautiful boy, who excited the impure desires of one of the charioteers of the circus. The insolent and brutal lover was thrown into prison by the order of Botheric; and he sternly rejected the importunate clamours of the multitude, who, on the day of the public games, lamented the absence of their favourite, and considered the skill of a charioteer as an object of more importance than his virtue. The resentment of the people was embittered by some previous disputes; and, as the strength of the garrison had been drawn away for the service of the Italian war, the feeble remnant, whose numbers were reduced by desertion, could not save the unhappy general from their licentious fury. Botheric and several of his principal officers were inhumanly murdered; their mangled bodies were dragged about the streets; and the emperor, who then resided at Milan, was surprised by the intelligence of the audacious and wanton cruelty of the people of Thessalonica. The sentence of a dispassionate judge would have inflicted a severe punishment on the authors of the crime; and the merit of Botheric might contribute to exasperate the grief and indignation of his master. The fiery and choleric temper of Theodosius was impatient of the dilatory forms of a judicial inquiry; and he hastily resolved that the blood of his lieutenant should be expiated by the blood of the guilty people. Yet his mind still fluctuated between the counsels of clemency and of revenge; the zeal of the bishops had almost extorted from the reluctant emperor the promise of a general pardon; his passion was again inflamed by the flattering suggestions of his minister Rufinus; and, after Theodosius had despatched the messengers of death, he attempted, when it was too late, to prevent the execution of

his orders. The punishment of a Roman city was blindly committed to the undistinguishing sword of the barbarians; and the hostile preparations were concerted with the dark and perfidious artifice of an illegal conspiracy. The people of Thessalonica were treacherously invited, in the name of their sovereign, to the games of the circus; and such was their insatiate avidity for those amusements that every consideration of fear or suspicion was disregarded by the numerous spectators. As soon as the assembly was complete, the soldiers, who had secretly been posted round the circus, received the signal, not of the races, but of a general massacre. The promiscuous carnage continued three hours, without discrimination of strangers or natives, of age or sex, of innocence or guilt; the most moderate accounts state the number of the slain at seven thousand; and it is affirmed by some writers that more than fifteen thousand victims were sacrificed to the manes of Botheric. A foreign merchant, who had probably no concern in his murder, offered his own life and all his wealth to supply the place of *one* of his two sons; but while the father hesitated with equal tenderness, while he was doubtful to choose, and unwilling to condemn, the soldiers determined his suspense by plunging their daggers at the same moment into the breasts of the defenceless youths. The apology of the assassins, that they were obliged to produce the prescribed number of heads, serves only to increase, by an appearance of order and design, the horrors of the massacre, which was executed by the commands of Theodosius. The guilt of the emperor is aggravated by his long and frequent residence at Thessalonica. The situation of the unfortunate city, the aspect of the streets and buildings, the dress and faces of the inhabitants, were familiar, and even present, to his imagination; and Theodosius possessed a quick and lively sense of the existence of the people whom he destroyed.[91]

The respectful attachment of the emperor for the orthodox clergy had disposed him to love and admire the character of Ambrose, who united all the episcopal virtues in the most eminent degree. The friends and ministers of Theodosius imitated the example of their sovereign; and he observed, with more surprise than displeasure, that all his secret counsels were immediately communicated to the archbishop, who acted from the laudable persuasion that every measure of civil government may have some connection with the glory of God and the interest of the true religion. The monks and populace of

Callinicum, an obscure town on the frontier of Persia, excited by their own fanaticism, and by that of their bishop, had tumultuously burnt a conventicle of the Valentinians and a synagogue of the Jews. The seditious prelate was condemned by the magistrate of the provinces either to rebuild the synagogue or to repay the damage; and this moderate sentence was confirmed by the emperor. But it was not confirmed by the archbishop of Milan.[92] He dictated an epistle of censure and reproach, more suitable perhaps if the emperor had received the mark of circumcision and renounced the faith of his baptism. Ambrose considers the toleration of the Jewish as the persecution of the Christian religion; boldly declares that he himself and every true believer would eagerly dispute with the bishop of Callinicum the merit of the deed and the crown of martyrdom; and laments, in the most pathetic terms, that the execution of the sentence would be fatal to the fame and salvation of Theodosius. As this private admonition did not produce an immediate effect, the archbishop from his pulpit[93] publicly addressed the emperor on his throne;[94] nor would he consent to offer the oblation of the altar till he had obtained from Theodosius a solemn and positive declaration which secured the impunity of the bishop and monks of Callinicum. The recantation of Theodosius was sincere;[95] and, during the term of his residence at Milan, his affection for Ambrose was continually increased by the habits of pious and familiar conversation.

When Ambrose was informed of the massacre of Thessalonica, his mind was filled with horror and anguish. He retired into the country to indulge his grief and to avoid the presence of Theodosius. But as the archbishop was satisfied that a timid silence would render him the accomplice of his guilt, he represented in a private letter the enormity of the crime, which could only be effaced by the tears of penitence. The episcopal vigour of Ambrose was tempered by prudence; and he contented himself with signifying[96] an indirect sort of excommunication, by the assurance that he had been warned in a vision not to offer the oblation in the name or in the presence of Theodosius, and by the advice that he would confine himself to the use of prayer, without presuming to approach the altar of Christ, or to receive the holy eucharist with those hands that were still polluted with the blood of an innocent people. The emperor was deeply affected by his own reproaches and by those of his spiritual father; and after he had bewailed the mischievous and irreparable con-

sequences of his rash fury, he proceeded in the accustomed manner to perform his devotions in the great church of Milan. He was stopped in the porch by the archbishop, who, in the tone and language of an ambassador of Heaven, declared to his sovereign that private contrition was not sufficient to atone for a public fault or to appease the justice of the offended Deity. Theodosius humbly represented that, if he had contracted the guilt of homicide, David, the man after God's own heart, had been guilty not only of murder but of adultery. "You have imitated David in his crime, imitate then his repentance," was the reply of the undaunted Ambrose. The rigorous conditions of peace and pardon were accepted; and the public penance of the emperor Theodosius has been recorded as one of the most honourable events in the annals of the church. According to the mildest rules of ecclesiastical discipline which were established in the fourth century, the crime of homicide was expiated by the penitence of twenty years:[97] and as it was impossible in the period of human life to purge the accumulated guilt of the massacre of Thessalonica, the murderer should have been excluded from the holy communion till the hour of his death. But the archbishop, consulting the maxims of religious policy, granted some indulgence to the rank of his illustrious penitent, who humbled in the dust the pride of the diadem; and the public edification might be admitted as a weighty reason to abridge the duration of his punishment. It was sufficient that the emperor of the Romans, stripped of the ensigns of royalty, should appear in a mournful and suppliant posture; and that, in the midst of the church of Milan, he should humbly solicit, with sighs and tears, the pardon of his sins.[98] In this spiritual cure Ambrose employed the various methods of mildness and severity. After a delay of about eight months Theodosius was restored to the communion of the faithful; and the edict, which interposes a salutary interval of thirty days between the sentence and the execution, may be accepted as the worthy fruits of his repentance.[99] Posterity has applauded the virtuous firmness of the archbishop: and the example of Theodosius may prove the beneficial influence of those principles which could force a monarch, exalted above the apprehension of human punishment, to respect the laws and ministers of an invisible Judge. "The prince," says Montesquieu, "who is actuated by the hopes and fears of religion, may be compared to a lion, docile only to the voice, and tractable to the hand, of his keeper."[100] The motions of the royal animal will therefore depend on the inclination and interest of the man who has acquired such dangerous authority over him; and the priest who holds in his hand the conscience of a king may inflame or moderate his sanguinary passions. The cause of humanity and that of persecution have been asserted by the same Ambrose with equal energy and with equal success.

After the defeat and death of the tyrant of Gaul, the Roman world was in the possession of Theodosius. He derived from the choice of Gratian his honourable title to the provinces of the East; he had acquired the West by the right of conquest; and the three years which he spent in Italy were usefully employed to restore the authority of the laws and to correct the abuses which had prevailed with impunity under the usurpation of Maximus and the minority of Valentinian. The name of Valentinian was regularly inserted in the public acts, but the tender age and doubtful faith of the son of Justina appeared to require the prudent care of an orthodox guardian, and his specious ambition might have excluded the unfortunate youth, without a struggle and almost without a murmur, from the administration and even from the inheritance of the empire. If Theodosius had consulted the rigid maxims of interest and policy, his conduct would have been justified by his friends, but the generosity of his behaviour on this memorable occasion has extorted the applause of his most inveterate enemies. He seated Valentinian on the throne of Milan, and, without stipulating any present or future advantages, restored him to the absolute dominion of all the provinces from which he had been driven by the arms of Maximus. To the restitution of his ample patrimony Theodosius added the free and generous gift of the countries beyond the Alps which his successful valour had recovered from the assassin of Gratian.[101] Satisfied with the glory which he had acquired by revenging the death of his benefactor and delivering the West from the yoke of tyranny, the emperor returned from Milan to Constantinople, and, in the peaceful possession of the East, insensibly relapsed into his former habits of luxury and indolence. Theodosius discharged his obligation to the brother, he indulged his conjugal tenderness to the sister, of Valentinian; and posterity, which admires the pure and singular glory of his elevation, must applaud his unrivalled generosity in the use of victory.

The empress Justina did not long survive her return to Italy, and, though she beheld the triumph of Theodosius, she was not allowed to influence the government of her son.[102] The pernicious attachment to the Arian sect which Valentinian had imbibed from her example and instructions was soon erased by the lessons of a more orthodox education. His growing zeal for the faith of Nice, and his filial reverence for the character and authority of Ambrose, disposed the catholics to entertain the most favourable opinion of the virtues of the young emperor of the West.[103] They applauded his chastity and temperance, his contempt of pleasure, his application to business, and his tender affection for his two sisters, which would not, however, seduce his impartial equity to pronounce an unjust sentence against the meanest of his subjects. But this amiable youth, before he had accomplished the twentieth year of his age, was oppressed by domestic treason, and the empire was again involved in the horrors of a civil war. Arbogastes,[104] a gallant soldier of the nation of the Franks, held the second rank in the service of Gratian. On the death of his master he joined the standard of Theodosius, contributed, by his valour and military conduct, to the destruction of the tyrant, and was appointed, after the victory, master-general of the armies of Gaul. His real merit and apparent fidelity had gained the confidence both of the prince and people; his boundless liberality corrupted the allegiance of the troops; and, whilst he was universally esteemed as the pillar of the state, the bold and crafty barbarian was secretly determined either to rule or to ruin the empire of the West. The important commands of the army were distributed among the Franks; the creatures of Arbogastes were promoted to all the honours and offices of the civil government; the progress of the conspiracy removed every faithful servant from the presence of Valentinian; and the emperor, without power and without intelligence, insensibly sunk into the precarious and dependent condition of a captive.[105] The indignation which he expressed, though it might arise only from the rash and impatient temper of youth, may be candidly ascribed to the generous spirit of a prince who felt that he was not unworthy to reign. He secretly invited the archbishop of Milan to undertake the office of a mediator, as the pledge of his sincerity and the guardian of his safety. He contrived to apprise the emperor of the East of his helpless situation, and he declared that, unless Theodosius could speedily march to his assistance, he must attempt to escape from the palace, or rather prison, of Vienne, in Gaul, where he had imprudently fixed his residence in the midst of the hostile faction. But the hopes of relief were distant and doubtful; and, as every day furnished some new provocation, the emperor, without strength or counsel, too hastily resolved to risk an immediate contest with his powerful general. He received Arbogastes on the throne, and, as the count approached with some appearance of respect, delivered to him a paper which dismissed him from all his employments "My authority," replied Arbogastes, with insulting coolness, "does not depend on the smile or the frown of a monarch;" and he contemptuously threw the paper on the ground. The indignant monarch snatched at the sword of one of the guards, which he struggled to draw from its scabbard, and it was not without some degree of violence that he was prevented from using the deadly weapon against his enemy or against himself. A few days after this extraordinary quarrel, in which he had exposed his resentment and his weakness, the unfortunate Valentinian was found strangled in his apartment, and some pains were employed to disguise the manifest guilt of Arbogastes, and to persuade the world that the death of the young emperor had been the voluntary effect of his own despair.[106] His body was conducted with decent pomp to the sepulchre of Milan, and the archbishop pronounced a funeral oration to commemorate his virtue and his misfortunes.[107] On this occasion the humanity of Ambrose tempted him to make a singular breach in his theological system, and to comfort the weeping sisters of Valentinian by the firm assurance that their pious brother, though he had not received the sacrament of baptism, was introduced, without difficulty, into the mansions of eternal bliss.[108]

The prudence of Arbogastes had prepared the success of his ambitious designs, and the provincials, in whose breasts every sentiment of patriotism or loyalty was extinguished, expected, with tame resignation, the unknown master whom the choice of a Frank might place on the Imperial throne. But some remains of pride and prejudice still opposed the elevation of Arbogastes himself, and the judicious barbarians thought it more advisable to reign under the name of some dependent Roman. He bestowed the purple on the rhetorician Eugenius,[109] whom he had already raised from the place of his domestic secretary to the rank of master of the offices. In the course both of his private and public service the count had always approved the attachment and abilities of Eugenius; his learning and eloquence, supported by the gravity of his manners, recommended him to the esteem of the people, and the reluctance with which he seemed to ascend the throne may inspire a favourable prejudice of his virtue and moderation. The ambassadors of the new emperor were immediately despatched to the court of Theodosius, to communicate, with affected grief, the unfortunate accident of the death of Valentinian, and, without mentioning the name of Arbogastes, to request that the monarch of the East would embrace as his lawful colleague the respectable citizen who had obtained the unanimous suffrage of the armies and provinces of the West.[110] Theodosius was justly provoked that the perfidy of a barbarian should have destroyed in a moment the labours and the fruit of his former victory; and he was excited by the tears of his beloved wife[111] to revenge the fate of her unhappy brother, and once more to assert by arms the violated majesty of the throne. But as the second conquest of the West was a task of difficulty and danger, he dismissed, with splendid presents and an ambiguous answer, the ambassadors of Eugenius, and almost two years were consumed in the preparations of the civil war. Before he formed any decisive resolution, the pious emperor was anxious to discover the will of Heaven; and as the progress of Christianity had silenced the oracles of Delphi and Dodona, he consulted an Egyptian monk, who possessed, in the opinion of the age, the gift of miracles and the knowledge of futurity. Eutropius, one of the favourite eunuchs of the palace of Constantinople, embarked for Alexandria, from whence he sailed up the Nile as far as the city of Lycopolis, or of Wolves, in the remote province of Thebais.[112] In the neighbourhood of that city, and on the summit of a lofty mountain, the holy John[113] had constructed with his own hands an humble cell, in which he had dwelt above fifty years, without opening his door, without seeing the face of a woman, and without tasting any food that had been prepared by fire or any human art. Five days of the week he spent in prayer and meditation, but on Saturdays and Sundays he regularly opened a small window, and gave audience to the crowd of suppliants who successively flowed from every part of the Christian world. The eunuch of Theodosius approached the window with respectful steps, proposed his questions concerning the event of the civil war, and soon returned with a favourable oracle, which animated the courage of the emperor by the assurance of a bloody but infallible victory.[114] The accomplishment of the prediction was forwarded by all the means that human prudence could supply. The industry of the two master-generals, Stilicho and Timasius, was directed to recruit the numbers and to revive the discipline of the Roman legions. The formidable troops of barbarians marched under the ensigns of their national chieftains. The Iberian, the Arab, and the Goth, who gazed on each other with mutual astonishment, were enlisted in the service of the same prince; and the renowned Alaric acquired, in the school of Theodosius, the knowledge of the art of war which he afterwards so fatally exerted for the destruction of Rome.[115]

The emperor of the West, or, to speak more properly, his general Arbogastes, was instructed by the misconduct and misfortune of Maximus how dangerous it might prove to extend the line of defence against a skilful antagonist, who was free to press or to suspend, to contract or to multiply, his various methods of attack.[116] Arbogastes fixed his station on the confines of Italy; the troops of Theodosius were permitted to occupy, without resistance, the provinces of Pannonia, as far as the foot of the Julian Alps; and even the passes of the mountains were negligently, or perhaps artfully, abandoned to the bold invader. He descended from the hills, and beheld, with some astonishment, the formidable camp of the Gauls and Germans that covered with arms and tents the open country which extends to the walls of Aquileia and the banks of the Frigidus,[117] or Cold River.[118] This narrow theatre of the war circumscribed by the Alps and the Hadriatic, did not allow much room for the operations of military skill; the spirit of Arbogastes would have disdained a pardon; his guilt extinguished the hope of a negotiation; and Theodosius was impatient to satisfy his glory and revenge by the chastisement of the assassins of Valentinian. Without weighing the natural and artificial obstacles that opposed his efforts, the emperor of the East immediately attacked the fortifications of his rivals, assigned the post of honourable danger to the Goths, and cherished a secret wish that the bloody conflict might diminish the pride and numbers of the conquerors. Ten thousand of those auxiliaries, and Bacurius, general of the Iberians, died bravely on the field of battle. But the victory was not purchased by their blood; the Gauls maintained their advantage, and the approach of night protected the disorderly flight, or retreat, of the troops of Theodosius. The emperor retired to the adjacent hills, where he passed a disconsolate night, without sleep, without provisions, and without hopes,[119] except that strong assurance which, under the most desperate circumstances, the independent mind may derive from the contempt of fortune and of life. The triumph of Eugenius was celebrated by the insolent and dissolute joy of his camp, whilst the active and vigilant Arbogastes secretly detached a considerable body of troops to occupy the passes of the mountains and to encompass the rear of the Eastern army. The dawn of day discovered to the eyes of Theodosius the extent and the extremity of his danger, but his apprehensions were soon dispelled by a friendly message from the leaders of those troops, who expressed their inclination to desert the standard of the tyrant. The honourable and lucrative rewards which they stipulated as the price of their perfidy were granted without hesitation, and, as ink and paper could not easily be procured, the emperor subscribed on his own tablets the ratification of the treaty. The spirit of his soldiers was revived by this seasonable reinforcement, and they again marched with confidence to surprise the camp of a tyrant whose principal officers appeared to distrust either the justice or the success of his arms. In the heat of the battle a violent tempest,[120] such as is often felt among the Alps, suddenly arose from the East. The army of Theodosius was sheltered by their position from the impetuosity of the wind, which blew a cloud of dust in the faces of the enemy, disordered their ranks, wrested their weapons from their hands, and diverted or repelled their ineffectual javelins. This accidental advantage was skilfully improved: the violence of the storm was magnified by the superstitious terrors of the Gauls, and they yielded without shame to the invisible powers of heaven, who seemed to militate on the side of the pious emperor. His victory was decisive, and the deaths of his two rivals were distinguished only by the difference of their characters. The rhetorician Eugenius, who had almost acquired the dominion of the world, was reduced to implore the mercy of the conqueror, and the unrelenting soldiers separated his head from his body as he lay prostrate at the feet of Theodosius. Arbogastes, after the loss of a battle in which he had discharged the duties of a soldier and a general, wandered several days among the mountains. But when he was convinced that his cause was desperate, and his escape impracticable, the intrepid barbarian imitated the example of the ancient Romans, and turned his sword against his own breast. The fate of the empire was determined in a narrow corner of Italy; and the legitimate successor of the house of Valentinian embraced the archbishop of Milan, and graciously received the submission of the provinces of the West. Those provinces were involved in the guilt of rebellion; while the inflexible courage of Ambrose alone had resisted the claims of successful usurpation. With a manly freedom, which might have been fatal to any other subject, the archbishop rejected the gifts of Eugenius, declined his correspondence, and withdrew himself from Milan to avoid the odious presence of a tyrant whose downfall he predicted in discreet and ambiguous language. The merit of Ambrose was applauded by the conqueror, who secured the attachment of the people by his alliance with the church: and the clemency of Theodosius is ascribed to the humane intercession of the archbishop of Milan.[121]

After the defeat of Eugenius, the merit, as well as the authority, of Theodosius was cheerfully acknowledged by all the inhabitants of the Roman world. The experience of his past conduct encouraged the most pleasing expectations of his future reign; and the age of the emperor, which did not exceed fifty years, seemed to extend the prospect of the public felicity. His death, only four months after his victory, was considered by the people as an unforeseen and fatal event, which destroyed in a moment the hopes of the rising generation. But the indulgence of ease and luxury had secretly nourished the principles of disease.[122] The strength of Theodosius was unable to support the sudden and violent transition from the palace to the camp; and the increasing symptoms of a dropsy announced the speedy dissolution of the emperor. The opinion, and perhaps the interest, of the public had confirmed the division of the Eastern and Western empires; and the two royal youths, Arcadius and Honorius, who had already obtained, from the tenderness of their father, the title of Augustus, were destined to fill the thrones of Constantinople and of Rome. Those princes were not permitted to share the danger and glory of the civil war;[123] but as soon as Theodosius had triumphed over his unworthy rivals, he called his younger son, Honorius, to enjoy the fruits of the victory, and to receive the sceptre of the West from the hands of his dying father. The arrival of Honorius at Milan was welcomed by a splendid exhibition of the games of the circus; and the emperor, though he was oppressed by the weight of his disorder, contributed by his presence to the public joy. But the remains of his strength were exhausted by the painful effort which he made to assist at the spectacles of the morning. Honorius supplied, during the rest of the day, the place of his father; and the great Theodosius expired in the ensuing night. Notwithstanding the recent animosities of a civil war, his death was universally lamented. The barbarians, whom he had vanquished, and the churchmen, by whom he had been subdued, celebrated with loud and sincere applause the qualities of the deceased emperor which appeared the most valuable in their eyes. The Romans were terrified by the impending dangers of a feeble and divided administration; and every disgraceful moment of the unfortunate reigns of Arcadius and Honorius revived the memory of their irreparable loss.

In the faithful picture of the virtues of Theodosius, his imperfections have not been dissembled; the act of cruelty, and the habits of indolence, which tarnished the glory of one of the greatest of the Roman princes. An historian perpetually adverse to the fame of Theodosius has exaggerated his vices and their pernicious effects; he boldly asserts that every rank of subjects imitated the effeminate manners of their sovereign; that every species of corruption polluted the course of public and private life; and that the feeble restraints of order and decency were insufficient to resist the progress of that degenerate spirit which sacrifices, without a blush, the consideration of duty and interest to the base indulgence of sloth and appetite.[124] The complaints of contemporary writers, who deplore the increase of luxury and depravation of manners, are commonly expressive of their peculiar temper and situation. There are few observers who possess a clear and comprehensive view of the revolutions of society, and who are capable of discovering the nice and secret springs of action which impel, in the same uniform direction, the blind and capricious passions of a multitude of individuals. If it can be affirmed, with any degree of truth, that the luxury of the Romans was more shameless and dissolute in the reign of Theodosius than in the age of Constantine, perhaps, or of Augustus, the alteration cannot be ascribed to any beneficial improvements which had gradually increased the stock of national riches. A long period of calamity or decay must have checked the industry and diminished the wealth of the people; and their profuse luxury must have been the result of that indolent despair which enjoys the present hour and declines the thoughts of futurity. The uncertain condition of their property discouraged the subjects of Theodosius from engaging in those useful and laborious undertakings which require an immediate expense, and promise a slow and distant advantage. The frequent examples of ruin and desolation tempted them not to spare the remains of a patrimony which might, every hour, become the prey of the rapacious Goth. And the mad prodigality which prevails in the confusion of a shipwreck or a siege may serve to explain the progress of luxury amidst the misfortunes and terrors of a sinking nation.

The effeminate luxury, which infected the manners of courts and cities, had instilled a secret and destructive poison into the camps of the legions; and their degeneracy has been marked by the pen of a military writer, who had accurately studied the genuine and ancient principles of Roman discipline. It is the just and important observation of Vegetius, that the infantry was invariably covered with defensive armour from the foundation of the city to the reign of the emperor Gratian. The relaxation of discipline and the disuse of exercise rendered the soldiers less able and less willing to support the fatigues of the service; they complained of the weight of the armour, which they seldom wore; and they successively obtained the permission of laying aside both their cuirasses and their helmets. The heavy weapons of their ancestors, the short sword and the formidable *pilum*, which had subdued the world, insensibly dropped from their feeble hands. As the use of the shield is incompatible with that of the bow, they reluctantly marched into the field, condemned to suffer either the pain of wounds or the ignominy of flight, and always disposed to prefer the more shameful alternative. The cavalry of the Goths, the Huns, and the Alani, had felt the benefits and adopted the use of defensive armour; and, as they excelled in the management of missile weapons, they easily overwhelmed the naked and trembling legions, whose heads and breasts were exposed, without defence, to the arrows of the barbarians. The loss of armies, the destruction of cities, and the dishonour of the Roman name, ineffectually solicited the successors of Gratian to restore the helmets and cuirasses of the infantry. The enervated soldiers abandoned their own and the public defence; and their pusillanimous indolence may be considered as the immediate cause of the downfall of the empire.[125]

CHAPTER XXVIII

Final Destruction of Paganism. Introduction of the Worship of Saints and Relics among the Christians.

THE ruin of Paganism, in the age of Theodosius, is perhaps the only example of the total extirpation of any ancient and popular superstition, and may therefore deserve to be considered as a singular event in the history of the human mind. The Christians, more especially the clergy, had impatiently supported the prudent delays of Constantine and the equal toleration of the elder Valentinian; nor could they deem their conquest perfect or secure as long as their adversaries were permitted to exist. The influence which Ambrose and his brethren had acquired over the youth of Gratian and the piety of Theodosius was employed to infuse the maxims of persecution into the breasts of their Imperial proselytes. Two specious principles of religious jurisprudence were established, from whence they deduced a direct and rigorous conclusion against the subjects of the empire who still adhered to the ceremonies of their ancestors: *that* the magistrate is, in some measure, guilty of the crimes which he neglects to prohibit or to punish; and *that* the idolatrous worship of fabulous deities and real dæmons is the most abominable crime against the supreme majesty of the Creator. The laws of Moses and the examples of Jewish history[1] were hastily, perhaps erroneously, applied by the clergy to the mild and universal reign of Christianity.[2] The zeal of the emperors was excited to vindicate their own honour and that of the Deity; and the temples of the Roman world were subverted about sixty years after the conversion of Constantine.

From the age of Numa to the reign of Gratian, the Romans preserved the regular succession of the several colleges of the sacerdotal order.[3] Fifteen PONTIFFS exercised their supreme jurisdiction over all things and persons that were consecrated to the service of the gods; and the various questions which perpetually arose in a loose and traditionary system were submitted to the judgment of their holy tribunal. Fifteen grave and learned AUGURS observed the face of the heavens, and prescribed the actions of heroes according to the flight of birds. Fifteen keepers of the Sibylline books (their name of Quindecemvirs was derived from their number) occasionally consulted the history of future, and, as it should seem, of contingent events. Six Vestals devoted their virginity to the guard of the sacred fire and of the unknown pledges of the duration of Rome, which no mortal had been suffered to behold with impunity.[4] Seven Epulos prepared the table of the gods, conducted the solemn procession, and regulated the ceremonies of the annual festival. The three Flamens of Jupiter, of Mars, and of Quirinus, were considered as the peculiar ministers of the three most powerful deities, who watched over the fate of Rome and of the universe. The King of the Sacrifices represented the person of Numa and of his successors in the religious functions, which could be performed only by royal hands. The confraternities of the Salians, the Lupercals, etc., practised such rites as might extort a smile of contempt from every reasonable man, with a lively confidence of recommending themselves to the favour of the immortal gods. The authority which the Roman priests had formerly obtained in the counsels of the republic was gradually abolished by the establishment of monarchy and the removal of the seat of empire. But the dignity of their sacred character was still protected by the laws and manners of their country; and they still continued, more especially the college of pontiffs, to exercise in the capital, and sometimes in the provinces, the rights of their ecclesiastical and civil jurisdiction. Their robes of purple, chariots of state, and sumptuous entertainments attracted the admiration of the people; and they received, from the consecrated lands and the public revenue, an ample stipend, which liberally supported the splendour of the priesthood and all the expenses of the religious worship of the state. As the service of the altar was not incompatible with the command of armies, the Romans, after their consulships and triumphs, aspired to the place of pontiff or of augur; the seats of Cicero[5] and Pompey were filled, in the fourth century, by the most illustrious members of the senate; and the dignity of their birth reflected additional splendour on their sacerdotal character. The fifteen priests who composed the college of pontiffs enjoyed a more distinguished rank as the companions of their sovereign; and the Christian emperors condescended to accept the robe and ensigns which were appropriated to the office of supreme pontiff. But when Gratian ascended the throne, more scrupulous or more enlightened, he sternly rejected those profane symbols;[6] applied to the service of the state

or of the church the revenues of the priests and vestals; abolished their honours and immunities; and dissolved the ancient fabric of Roman superstition, which was supported by the opinions and habits of eleven hundred years. Paganism was still the constitutional religion of the senate. The hall or temple in which they assembled was adorned by the statue and altar of Victory;[7] a majestic female standing on a globe, with flowing garments, expanded wings, and a crown of laurel in her outstretched hand.[8] The senators were sworn on the altar of the goddess to observe the laws of the emperor and of the empire; and a solemn offering of wine and incense was the ordinary prelude of their public deliberations.[9] The removal of this ancient monument was the only injury which Constantius had offered to the superstition of the Romans. The altar of Victory was again restored by Julian, tolerated by Valentinian, and once more banished from the senate by the zeal of Gratian.[10] But the emperor yet spared the statues of the gods which were exposed to the public veneration: four hundred and twenty-four temples, or chapels, still remained to satisfy the devotion of the people, and in every quarter of Rome the delicacy of the Christians was offended by the fumes of idolatrous sacrifice.[11]

But the Christians formed the least numerous party in the senate of Rome;[12] and it was only by their absence that they could express their dissent from the legal, though profane, acts of a Pagan majority. In that assembly the dying embers of freedom were, for a moment, revived and inflamed by the breath of fanaticism. Four respectable deputations were successively voted to the Imperial court,[13] to represent the grievances of the priesthood and the senate, and to solicit the restoration of the altar of Victory. The conduct of this important business was intrusted to the eloquent Symmachus,[14] a wealthy and noble senator, who united the sacred characters of pontiff and augur with the civil dignities of proconsul of Africa and præfect of the city. The breast of Symmachus was animated by the warmest zeal for the cause of expiring Paganism; and his religious antagonists lamented the abuse of his genius and the inefficacy of his moral virtues.[15] The orator, whose petition is extant to the emperor Valentinian, was conscious of the difficulty and danger of the office which he had assumed. He cautiously avoids every topic which might appear to reflect on the religion of his sovereign; humbly declares that prayers and entreaties are his only arms; and artfully draws his arguments from the schools of rhetoric rather than from those of philosophy. Symmachus endeavours to seduce the imagination of a young prince, by displaying the attributes of the goddess of Victory; he insinuates that the confiscation of the revenues which were consecrated to the service of the gods was a measure unworthy of his liberal and disinterested character; and maintains that the Roman sacrifices would be deprived of their force and energy, if they were no longer celebrated at the expense as well as in the name of the republic. Even scepticism is made to supply an apology for superstition. The great and incomprehensible *secret* of the universe eludes the inquiry of man. Where reason cannot instruct, custom may be permitted to guide; and every nation seems to consult the dictates of prudence, by a faithful attachment to those rites and opinions which have received the sanction of ages. If those ages have been crowned with glory and prosperity—if the devout people has frequently obtained the blessings which they have solicited at the altars of the gods—it must appear still more advisable to persist in the same salutary practice, and not to risk the unknown perils that may attend any rash innovations. The test of antiquity and success was applied with singular advantage to the religion of Numa; and ROME herself, the celestial genius that presided over the fates of the city, is introduced by the orator to plead her own cause before the tribunal of the emperors. "Most excellent princes," says the venerable matron, "fathers of your country! pity and respect my age, which has hitherto flowed in an uninterrupted course of piety. Since I do not repent, permit me to continue in the practice of my ancient rites. Since I am born free, allow me to enjoy my domestic institutions. This religion has reduced the world under my laws. These rites have repelled Hannibal from the city, and the Gauls from the Capitol. Were my grey hairs reserved for such intolerable disgrace? I am ignorant of the new system that I am required to adopt; but I am well assured that the correction of old age is always an ungrateful and ignominious office."[16] The fears of the people supplied what the discretion of the orator had suppressed; and the calamities which afflicted or threatened the declining empire were unanimously imputed by the Pagans to the new religion of Christ and of Constantine.

But the hopes of Symmachus were repeatedly baffled by the firm and dexterous opposition of the archbishop of Milan, who fortified the emperors against the fallacious eloquence of the advocate of Rome. In this controversy Ambrose condescends to speak the language of a philosopher, and to ask, with some contempt, why it should be thought necessary to introduce an imaginary and invisible power as the cause of those victories, which were sufficiently explained by the valour and discipline of the legions. He justly derides the absurd reverence for antiquity, which could only tend to discourage the improvements of art and to replunge the human race into their original barbarism. From thence gradually rising to a more lofty and theological tone, he pronounces that Christianity alone is the doctrine of truth and salvation, and that every mode of Polytheism conducts its deluded votaries through the paths of error to the abyss of eternal perdition.[17] Arguments like these, when they were suggested by a favourite bishop, had power to prevent the restoration of the altar of Victory; but the same arguments fell with much more energy and effect from the mouth of a conqueror, and the gods of antiquity were dragged in triumph at the chariot-wheels of Theodosius.[18] In a full meeting of the senate the emperor proposed, according to the forms of the republic, the important question, whether the worship of Jupiter or that of Christ should be the religion of the Romans? The liberty of suffrages, which he affected to allow, was destroyed by the hopes and fears that his presence inspired; and the arbitrary exile of Symmachus was a recent admonition that it might be dangerous to oppose the wishes of the monarch. On a regular division of the senate, Jupiter was condemned and degraded by the sense of a very large majority; and it is rather surprising that any members should be found bold enough to declare, by their speeches and votes, that they were still attached to the interest of an abdicated deity.[19] The hasty conversion of the senate must be attributed either to supernatural or to sordid motives; and many of these reluctant proselytes betrayed, on every favourable occasion, their secret disposition to throw aside the mask of odious dissimulation. But they were gradually fixed in the new religion, as the cause of the ancient became more hopeless; they yielded to the authority of the emperor, to the fashion of the times, and to the entreaties of their wives and children,[20] who were instigated and governed by the clergy of Rome and the monks of the East. The edifying example of the Anician family was soon imitated by the rest of the nobility: the Bassi, the Paullini, the Gracchi, embraced the Christian religion; and "the luminaries of the world, the venerable assembly of Catos (such are the high-flown expressions of

Prudentius), were impatient to strip themselves of their pontifical garment—to cast the skin of the old serpent—to assume the snowy robes of baptismal innocence—and to humble the pride of the consular fasces before the tombs of the martyrs."[21] The citizens, who subsisted by their own industry, and the populace, who were supported by the public liberality, filled the churches of the Lateran and Vatican with an incessant throng of devout proselytes. The decrees of the senate, which proscribed the worship of idols, were ratified by the general consent of the Romans;[22] the splendour of the Capitol was defaced, and the solitary temples were abandoned to ruin and contempt.[23] Rome submitted to the yoke of the Gospel; and the vanquished provinces had not yet lost their reverence for the name and authority of Rome.

The filial piety of the emperors themselves engaged them to proceed with some caution and tenderness in the reformation of the eternal city. Those absolute monarchs acted with less regard to the prejudices of the provincials. The pious labour, which had been suspended near twenty years since the death of Constantius,[24] was vigorously resumed, and finally accomplished, by the zeal of Theodosius. Whilst that warlike prince yet struggled with the Goths, not for the glory, but for the safety of the republic, he ventured to offend a considerable party of his subjects, by some acts which might perhaps secure the protection of Heaven, but which must seem rash and unseasonable in the eye of human prudence. The success of his first experiments against the Pagans encouraged the pious emperor to reiterate and enforce his edicts of proscription: the same laws which had been originally published in the provinces of the East, were applied, after the defeat of Maximus, to the whole extent of the Western empire; and every victory of the orthodox Theodosius contributed to the triumph of the Christian and catholic faith.[25] He attacked superstition in her most vital part, by prohibiting the use of sacrifices, which he declared to be criminal as well as infamous; and if the terms of his edicts more strictly condemned the impious curiosity which examined the entrails of the victims,[26] every subsequent explanation tended to involve in the same guilt the general practice of *immolation*, which essentially constituted the religion of the Pagans. As the temples had been erected for the purpose of sacrifice, it was the duty of a benevolent prince to remove from his subjects the dangerous temptation of offending against the laws which he had enacted. A special commission was granted to Cynegius, the Prætorian præfect of the East, and afterwards to the counts Jovius and Gaudentius, two officers of distinguished rank in the West, by which they were directed to shut the temples, to seize or destroy the instruments of idolatry, to abolish the privileges of the priests, and to confiscate the consecrated property for the benefit of the emperor, of the church, or of the army.[27] Here the desolation might have stopped: and the naked edifices, which were no longer employed in the service of idolatry, might have been protected from the destructive rage of fanaticism. Many of those temples were the most splendid and beautiful monuments of Grecian architecture: and the emperor himself was interested not to deface the splendour of his own cities, or to diminish the value of his own possessions. Those stately edifices might be suffered to remain, as so many lasting trophies of the victory of Christ. In the decline of the arts, they might be usefully converted into magazines, manufactures, or places of public assembly: and perhaps, when the walls of the temple had been sufficiently purified by holy rites, the worship of the true Deity might be allowed to expiate the ancient guilt of idolatry. But as long as they subsisted, the Pagans fondly cherished the secret hope that an auspicious revolution, a second Julian, might again restore the altars of the gods: and the earnestness with which they addressed their unavailing prayers to the throne[28] increased the zeal of the Christian reformers to extirpate, without mercy, the root of superstition. The laws of the emperors exhibit some symptoms of a milder disposition:[29] but their cold and languid efforts were insufficient to stem the torrent of enthusiasm and rapine, which was conducted, or rather impelled, by the spiritual rulers of the church. In Gaul, the holy Martin, bishop of Tours,[30] marched at the head of his faithful monks to destroy the idols, the temples, and the consecrated trees of his extensive diocese; and, in the execution of this arduous task, the prudent reader will judge whether Martin was supported by the aid of miraculous powers or of carnal weapons. In Syria, the divine and excellent Marcellus,[31] as he is styled by Theodoret, a bishop animated with apostolic fervour, resolved to level with the ground the stately temples within the diocese of Apamea. His attack was resisted by the skill and solidity with which the temple of Jupiter had been constructed. The building was seated on an eminence: on each of the four sides the lofty roof was supported by fifteen massy columns, sixteen feet in circumference; and the large stones of which they were composed were firmly cemented with lead and iron. The force of the strongest and sharpest tools had been tried without effect. It was found necessary to undermine the foundations of the columns, which fell down as soon as the temporary wooden props had been consumed with fire; and the difficulties of the enterprise are described under the allegory of a black dæmon, who retarded, though he could not defeat, the operations of the Christian engineers. Elated with victory, Marcellus took the field in person against the powers of darkness; a numerous troop of soldiers and gladiators marched under the episcopal banner, and he successively attacked the villages and country temples of the diocese of Apamea. Whenever any resistance or danger was apprehended, the champion of the faith, whose lameness would not allow him either to fight or fly, placed himself at a convenient distance, beyond the reach of darts. But this prudence was the occasion of his death; he was surprised and slain by a body of exasperated rustics; and the synod of the province pronounced, without hesitation, that the holy Marcellus had sacrificed his life in the cause of God. In the support of this cause, the monks, who rushed with tumultuous fury from the desert, distinguished themselves by their zeal and diligence. They deserved the enmity of the Pagans; and some of them might deserve the reproaches of avarice and intemperance, which they indulged at the expense of the people, who foolishly admired their tattered garments, loud psalmody, and artificial paleness.[32] A small number of temples was protected by the fears, the venality, the taste, or the prudence of the civil and ecclesiastical governors. The temple of the Celestial Venus at Carthage, whose sacred precincts formed a circumference of two miles, was judiciously converted into a Christian church;[33] and a similar consecration had preserved inviolate the majestic dome of the Pantheon at Rome.[34] But in almost every province of the Roman world, an army of fanatics, without authority and without discipline, invaded the peaceful inhabitants; and the ruin of the fairest structures of antiquity still displays the ravages of *those* barbarians who alone had time and inclination to execute such laborious destruction.

In this wide and various prospect of devastation, the spectator may distinguish the ruins of the temple of Serapis, at Alexandria.[35] Serapis does not appear to have been one of the native gods, or monsters, who sprung from the fruitful soil of superstitious Egypt.[36] The first of the Ptolemies had been commanded, by a dream, to import the mysterious stranger from the coast of Pontus, where he had been long adored by the inhabitants of Sinope; but his attributes and his reign were so imperfectly understood, that it became a subject of dispute whether he represented the bright orb of day, or the gloomy monarch of the subterraneous regions.[37] The Egyptians, who were obstinately devoted to the religion of their fathers, refused to admit this foreign deity within the walls of their cities.[38] But the obsequious priests, who were seduced by the liberality of the Ptolemies, submitted, without resistance, to the power of the god of Pontus: an honourable and domestic genealogy was provided; and this fortunate usurper was introduced into the throne and bed of Osiris,[39] the husband of Isis, and the celestial monarch of Egypt. Alexandria, which claimed his peculiar protection, gloried in the name of the city of Serapis. His temple,[40] which rivalled the pride and magnificence of the Capitol, was erected on the spacious summit of an artificial mount, raised one hundred steps above the level of the adjacent parts of the city; and the interior cavity was strongly supported by arches, and distributed into vaults and subterraneous apartments. The consecrated buildings were surrounded by a quadrangular portico; the stately halls and exquisite statues displayed the triumph of the arts; and the treasures of ancient learning were preserved in the famous Alexandrian library, which had arisen with new splendour from its ashes.[41] After the edicts of Theodosius had severely prohibited the sacrifices of the Pagans, they were still tolerated in the city and temple of Serapis; and this singular indulgence was imprudently ascribed to the superstitious terrors of the Christians themselves: as if they had feared to abolish those ancient rites which could alone secure the inundations of the Nile, the harvests of Egypt, and the subsistence of Constantinople.[42]

At that time[43] the archiepiscopal throne of Alexandria was filled by Theophilus,[44] the perpetual enemy of peace and virtue; a bold, bad man, whose hands were alternately polluted with gold and with blood. His pious indignation was excited by the honours of Serapis; and the insults which he offered to an ancient chapel of Bacchus convinced the Pagans that he meditated a more important and dangerous enterprise. In the tumultuous capital of Egypt, the slightest provocation was sufficient to inflame a civil war. The votaries of Serapis, whose strength and numbers were much inferior to those of their antagonists, rose in arms at the instigation of the philosopher Olympius,[45] who exhorted them to die in the defence of the altars of the gods. These Pagan fanatics fortified themselves in the temple, or rather fortress, of Serapis; repelled the besiegers by daring sallies and a resolute defence; and, by the inhuman cruelties which they exercised on their Christian prisoners, obtained the last consolation of despair. The efforts of the prudent magistrate were usefully exerted for the establishment of a truce till the answer of Theodosius should determine the fate of Serapis. The two parties assembled without arms, in the principal square; and the Imperial rescript was publicly read. But when a sentence of destruction against the idols of Alexandria was pronounced, the Christians sent up a shout of joy and exultation, whilst the unfortunate Pagans, whose fury had given way to consternation, retired with hasty and silent steps, and eluded, by their flight or obscurity, the resentment of their enemies. Theophilus proceeded to demolish the temple of Serapis, without any other difficulties than those which he found in the weight and solidity of the materials; but these obstacles proved so insuperable that he was obliged to leave the foundations, and to content himself with reducing the edifice itself to a heap of rubbish, a part of which was soon afterwards cleared away, to make room for a church erected in honour of the Christian martyrs. The valuable library of Alexandria was pillaged or destroyed; and near twenty years afterwards, the appearance of the empty shelves excited the regret and indignation of every spectator whose mind was not totally darkened by religious prejudice.[46] The compositions of ancient genius, so many of which have irretrievably perished, might surely have been excepted from the wreck of idolatry, for the amusement and instruction of succeeding ages; and either the zeal or the avarice of the archbishop[47] might have been satiated with the rich spoils which were the reward of his victory. While the images and vases of gold and silver were carefully melted, and those of a less valuable metal were contemptuously broken and cast into the streets, Theophilus laboured to expose the frauds and vices of the ministers of the idols: their dexterity in the management of the loadstone; their secret methods of introducing an human actor into a hollow statue; and their scandalous abuse of the confidence of devout husbands and unsuspecting females.[48] Charges like these may seem to deserve some de-

gree of credit, as they are not repugnant to the crafty and interested spirit of superstition. But the same spirit is equally prone to the base practice of insulting and calumniating a fallen enemy; and our belief is naturally checked by the reflection that it is much less difficult to invent a fictitious story than to support a practical fraud. The colossal statue of Serapis[49] was involved in the ruin of his temple and religion. A great number of plates of different metals, artificially joined together, composed the majestic figure of the deity, who touched on either side the walls of the sanctuary. The aspect of Serapis, his sitting posture, and the sceptre which he bore in his left hand, were extremely similar to the ordinary representations of Jupiter. He was distinguished from Jupiter by the basket, or bushel, which was placed on his head; and by the emblematic monster which he held in his right hand; the head and body of a serpent branching into three tails, which were again terminated by the triple heads of a dog, a lion, and a wolf. It was confidently affirmed that, if any impious hand should dare to violate the majesty of the god, the heavens and the earth would instantly return to their original chaos. An intrepid soldier, animated by zeal, and armed with a weighty battle-axe, ascended the ladder; and even the Christian multitude expected with some anxiety the event of the combat.[50] He aimed a vigorous stroke against the cheek of Serapis; the cheek fell to the ground; the thunder was still silent, and both the heavens and the earth continued to preserve their accustomed order and tranquillity. The victorious soldier repeated his blows: the huge idol was overthrown and broken in pieces; and the limbs of Serapis were ignominiously dragged through the streets of Alexandria. His mangled carcase was burnt in the amphitheatre, amidst the shouts of the populace; and many persons attributed their conversion to this discovery of the impotence of their tutelar deity. The popular modes of religion, that propose any visible and material objects of worship, have the advantage of adapting and familiarising themselves to the senses of mankind; but this advantage is counterbalanced by the various and inevitable accidents to which the faith of the idolater is exposed. It is scarcely possible that, in every disposition of mind, he should preserve his implicit reverence for the idols, or the relics, which the naked eye and the profane hand are unable to distinguish from the most common productions of art or nature; and, if, in the hour of danger, their secret and miraculous virtue does not operate for their own preservation, he scorns the vain apologies of his priests, and justly derides the object and the folly of his superstitious attachment.[51] After the fall of Serapis, some hopes were still entertained by the Pagans that the Nile would refuse his annual supply to the impious masters of Egypt; and the extraordinary delay of the inundation seemed to announce the displeasure of the river-god. But this delay was soon compensated by the rapid swell of the waters. They suddenly rose to such an unusual height as to comfort the discontented party with the pleasing expectation of a deluge; till the peaceful river again subsided to the well-known and fertilising level of sixteen cubits, or about thirty English feet.[52]

The temples of the Roman empire were deserted or destroyed; but the ingenious superstition of the Pagans still attempted to elude the laws of Theodosius, by which all sacrifices had been severely prohibited. The inhabitants of the country, whose conduct was less exposed to the eye of malicious curiosity, disguised their *religious* under the appearance of *convivial* meetings. On the days of solemn festivals they assembled in great numbers under the spreading shade of some consecrated trees; sheep and oxen were slaughtered and roasted; and this rural entertainment was sanctified by the use of incense and by the hymns which were sung in honour of the gods. But it was alleged that, as no part of the animal was made a burnt-offering, as no altar was provided to receive the blood, and as the previous oblation of salt cakes and the concluding ceremony of libations were carefully omitted, these festal meetings did not involve the guests in the guilt or penalty of an illegal sacrifice.[53] Whatever might be the truth of the facts or the merit of the distinction,[54] these vain pretences were swept away by the last edict of Theodosius, which inflicted a deadly wound on the superstition of the Pagans.[55] This prohibitory law is expressed in the most absolute and comprehensive terms. "It is our will and pleasure," says the emperor, "that none of our subjects, whether magistrates or private citizens, however exalted or however humble may be their rank and condition, shall presume in any city or in any place to worship an inanimate idol by the sacrifice of a guiltless victim." The act of sacrificing and the practice of divination by the entrails of the victim are declared (without any regard to the object of the inquiry) a crime of high treason against the state, which can be expiated only by the death of the guilty. The rites of Pagan superstition which might

seem less bloody and atrocious are abolished as highly injurious to the truth and honour of religion; luminaries, garlands, frankincense, and libations of wine are specially enumerated and condemned; and the harmless claims of the domestic genius, of the household gods, are included in this rigorous proscription. The use of any of these profane and illegal ceremonies subjects the offender to the forfeiture of the house or estate where they have been performed; and if he has artfully chosen the property of another for the scene of his impiety, he is compelled to discharge, without delay, a heavy fine of twenty-five pounds of gold, or more than one thousand pounds sterling. A fine not less considerable is imposed on the connivance of the secret enemies of religion who shall neglect the duty of their respective stations, either to reveal or to punish the guilt of idolatry. Such was the persecuting spirit of the laws of Theodosius, which were repeatedly enforced by his sons and grandsons, with the loud and unanimous applause of the Christian world.[56]

In the cruel reigns of Decius and Diocletian Christianity had been proscribed, as a revolt from the ancient and hereditary religion of the empire; and the unjust suspicions which were entertained of a dark and dangerous faction were in some measure countenanced by the inseparable union and rapid conquests of the catholic church. But the same excuses of fear and ignorance cannot be applied to the Christian emperors, who violated the precepts of humanity and of the Gospel. The experience of ages had betrayed the weakness as well as folly of Paganism; the light of reason and of faith had already exposed to the greatest part of mankind the vanity of idols; and the declining sect, which still adhered to their worship, might have been permitted to enjoy in peace and obscurity the religious customs of their ancestors. Had the Pagans been animated by the undaunted zeal which possessed the minds of the primitive believers, the triumph of the church must have been stained with blood; and the martyrs of Jupiter and Apollo might have embraced the glorious opportunity of devoting their lives and fortunes at the foot of their altars. But such obstinate zeal was not congenial to the loose and careless temper of Polytheism. The violent and repeated strokes of the orthodox princes were broken by the soft and yielding substance against which they were directed; and the ready obedience of the Pagans protected them from the pains and penalties of the Theodosian Code.[57] Instead of asserting that the authority of the gods was superior to that of the emperor, they desisted, with a plaintive murmur, from the use of those sacred rites which their sovereign had condemned. If they were sometimes tempted by a sally of passion, or by the hopes of concealment, to indulge their favourite superstition, their humble repentance disarmed the severity of the Christian magistrate, and they seldom refused to atone for their rashness by submitting, with some secret reluctance, to the yoke of the Gospel. The churches were filled with the increasing multitude of these unworthy proselytes, who had conformed, from temporal motives, to the reigning religion; and whilst they devoutly imitated the postures and recited the prayers of the faithful, they satisfied their conscience by the silent and sincere invocation of the gods of antiquity.[58] If the Pagans wanted patience to suffer, they wanted spirit to resist; and the scattered myriads, who deplored the ruin of the temples, yielded, without a contest, to the fortune of their adversaries. The disorderly opposition[59] of the peasants of Syria and the populace of Alexandria to the rage of private fanaticism was silenced by the name and authority of the emperor. The Pagans of the West, without contributing to the elevation of Eugenius, disgraced by their partial attachment the cause and character of the usurper. The clergy vehemently exclaimed that he aggravated the crime of rebellion by the guilt of apostasy; that, by his permission, the altar of Victory was again restored; and that the idolatrous symbols of Jupiter and Hercules were displayed in the field against the invincible standard of the cross. But the vain hopes of the Pagans were soon annihilated by the defeat of Eugenius; and they were left exposed to the resentment of the conqueror, who laboured to deserve the favour of Heaven by the extirpation of idolatry.[60]

A nation of slaves is always prepared to applaud the clemency of their master who, in the abuse of absolute power, does not proceed to the last extremes of injustice and oppression. Theodosius might undoubtedly have proposed to his Pagan subjects the alternative of baptism or of death; and the eloquent Libanius has praised the moderation of a prince who never enacted, by any positive law, that all his subjects should immediately embrace and practise the religion of their sovereign.[61] The profession of Christianity was not made an essential qualification for the enjoyment of the civil rights of society, nor were any peculiar hardships imposed on the sectaries who credulously received the fables of Ovid and obstinately rejected the miracles of the Gospel. The palace, the schools, the army, and the senate were filled with declared and devout Pagans; they obtained, without distinction, the civil and military honours of the empire. Theodosius distinguished his liberal regard for virtue and genius by the consular dignity which he bestowed on Symmachus,[62] and by the personal friendship which he expressed to Libanius;[63] and the two eloquent apologists of Paganism were never required either to change or to dissemble their religious opinions. The Pagans were indulged in the most licentious freedom of speech and writing; the historical and philosophic remains of Eunapius, Zosimus,[64] and the fanatic teachers of the school of Plato, betray the most furious animosity, and contain the sharpest invectives, against the sentiments and conduct of their victorious adversaries. If these audacious libels were publicly known, we must applaud the good sense of the Christian princes, who viewed with a smile of contempt the last struggles of superstition and despair.[65] But the Imperial laws which prohibited the sacrifices and ceremonies of Paganism were rigidly executed; and every hour contributed to destroy the influence of a religion which was supported by custom rather than by argument. The devotion of the poet or the philosopher may be secretly nourished by prayer, meditation, and study; but the exercise of public worship appears to be the only solid foundation of the religious sentiments of the people, which derive their force from imitation and habit. The interruption of that public exercise may consummate, in the period of a few years, the important work of a national revolution. The memory of theological opinions cannot long be preserved without the artificial helps of priests, of temples, and of books.[66] The ignorant vulgar, whose minds are still agitated by the blind hopes and terrors of superstition, will be soon persuaded by their superiors to direct their vows to the reigning deities of the age; and will insensibly imbibe an ardent zeal for the support and propagation of the new doctrine, which spiritual hunger at first compelled them to accept. The generation that arose in the world after the promulgation of the Imperial laws was attracted within the pale of the Catholic church: and so rapid, yet so gentle, was the fall of Paganism, that only twenty-eight years after the death of Theodosius the faint and minute vestiges were no longer visible to the eye of the legislator.[67]

The ruin of the Pagan religion is described by the sophists as a dreadful and amazing prodigy, which covered the earth with darkness and restored the ancient dominion of chaos and of night. They relate in solemn and pathetic strains that the temples were converted into sepulchres, and that the holy places, which had been adorned by the statues of the gods, were basely polluted by the relics of Christian martyrs. "The monks" (a race of filthy animals, to whom Eunapius is tempted to refuse the name of men) "are the authors of the new worship, which, in the place of those deities who are conceived by the understanding, has substituted the meanest and most contemptible slaves. The heads, salted and pickled, of those infamous malefactors, who for the multitude of their crimes have suffered a just and ignominious death; their bodies, still marked by the impression of the lash and the scars of those tortures which were inflicted by the sentence of the magistrate; such" (continues Eunapius) "are the gods which the earth produces in our days; such are the martyrs, the supreme arbitrators of our prayers and petitions to the Deity, whose tombs are now consecrated as the objects of the veneration of the people."[68] Without approving the malice, it is natural enough to share the surprise of the sophist, the spectator of a revolution which raised those obscure victims of the laws of Rome to the rank of celestial and invisible protectors of the Roman empire. The grateful respect of the Christians for the martyrs of the faith was exalted, by time and victory, into religious adoration; and the most illustrious of the saints and prophets were deservedly associated to the honours of the martyrs. One hundred and fifty years after the glorious deaths of St. Peter and St. Paul, the Vatican and the Ostian road were distinguished by the tombs, or rather by the trophies, of those spiritual heroes.[69] In the age which followed the conversion of Constantine, the emperors, the consuls, and the generals of armies devoutly visited the sepulchres of a tentmaker and a fisherman;[70] and their venerable bones were deposited under the altars of Christ, on which the bishops of the royal city continually offered the unbloody sacrifice.[71] The new capital of the Eastern world, unable to produce any ancient and domestic trophies, was enriched by the spoils of dependent provinces. The bodies of St. Andrew, St. Luke, and St. Timothy had reposed near three hundred years in the obscure graves from whence they were transported, in solemn pomp, to the church of the apostles, which the magnificence of Constantine had founded on the banks of the Thracian Bosphorus.[72] About fifty years afterwards the same banks were honoured by the presence of Sam-

uel, the judge and prophet of the people of Israel. His ashes, deposited in a golden vase, and covered with a silken veil, were delivered by the bishops into each other's hands. The relics of Samuel were received by the people with the same joy and reverence which they would have shown to the living prophet; the highways, from Palestine to the gates of Constantinople, were filled with an uninterrupted procession; and the emperor Arcadius himself, at the head of the most illustrious members of the clergy and senate, advanced to meet his extraordinary guest, who had always deserved and claimed the homage of kings.[73] The example of Rome and Constantinople confirmed the faith and discipline of the catholic world. The honours of the saints and martyrs, after a feeble and ineffectual murmur of profane reason,[74] were universally established; and in the age of Ambrose and Jerom something was still deemed wanting to the sanctity of a Christian church, till it had been consecrated by some portion of holy relics, which fixed and inflamed the devotion of the faithful. In the long period of twelve hundred years, which elapsed between the reign of Constantine and the reformation of Luther, the worship of saints and relics corrupted the pure and perfect simplicity of the Christian model; and some symptoms of degeneracy may be observed even in the first generations which adopted and cherished this pernicious innovation.

I. The satisfactory experience that the relics of saints were more valuable than gold or precious stones[75] stimulated the clergy to multiply the treasures of the church. Without much regard for truth or probability, they invented names for skeletons, and actions for names. The fame of the apostles, and of the holy men who had imitated their virtues, was darkened by religious fiction. To the invincible band of genuine and primitive martyrs they added myriads of imaginary heroes, who had never existed, except in the fancy of crafty or credulous legendaries; and there is reason to suspect that Tours might not be the only diocese in which the bones of a malefactor were adored instead of those of a saint.[76] A superstitious practice, which tended to increase the temptations of fraud and credulity, insensibly extinguished the light of history and of reason in the Christian world.

II. But the progress of superstition would have been much less rapid and victorious if the faith of the people had not been assisted by the seasonable aid of visions and miracles to ascertain the authenticity and virtue of the most suspicious relics. In the reign of the younger Theodosius, Lucian,[77] a presbyter of Jerusalem, and the ecclesiastical minister of the village of Caphargamala, about twenty miles from the city, related a very singular dream, which, to remove his doubts, had been repeated on three successive Saturdays. A venerable figure stood before him, in the silence of the night, with a long beard, a white robe, and a gold rod; announced himself by the name of Gamaliel; and revealed to the astonished presbyter, that his own corpse, with the bodies of his son Abibas, his friend Nicodemus, and the illustrious Stephen, the first martyr of the Christian faith, were secretly buried in the adjacent field. He added, with some impatience, that it was time to release himself and his companions from their obscure prison; that their appearance would be salutary to a distressed world; and that they had made choice of Lucian to inform the bishop of Jerusalem of their situation and their wishes. The doubts and difficulties which still retarded this important discovery were successively removed by new visions; and the ground was opened by the bishop, in the presence of an innumerable multitude. The coffins of Gamaliel, of his son, and of his friend, were found in regular order; but when the fourth coffin, which contained the remains of Stephen, was shown to the light, the earth trembled, and an odour such as that of Paradise was smelt, which instantly cured the various diseases of seventy-three of the assistants. The companions of Stephen were left in their peaceful residence of Caphargamala; but the relics of the first martyr were transported, in solemn procession, to a church constructed in their honour on Mount Sion; and the minute particles of those relics, a drop of blood,[78] or the scrapings of a bone, were acknowledged, in almost every province of the Roman world, to possess a divine and miraculous virtue. The grave and learned Augustin,[79] whose understanding scarcely admits the excuse of credulity, has attested the innumerable prodigies which were performed in Africa by the relics of St. Stephen; and this marvellous narrative is inserted in the elaborate work of the City of God, which the bishop of Hippo designed as a solid and immortal proof of the truth of Christianity. Augustin solemnly declares that he has selected those miracles only which were publicly certified by the persons who were either the objects, or the spectators, of the power of the martyr. Many prodigies were omitted or forgotten; and Hippo had been less favourably treated than the other cities of the province. And yet the bishop enumerates above seventy miracles, of which three were resurrections from the dead, in the space of two years, and within the limits of his own diocese.[80] If we enlarge our view to all the diocese, and all the saints, of the Christian world, it will not be easy to calculate the fables, and the errors, which issued from this inexhaustible source. But we may surely be allowed to observe that a miracle, in that age of superstition and credulity, lost its name and its merit, since it could scarcely be considered as a deviation from the ordinary and established laws of nature.

III. The innumerable miracles, of which the tombs of the martyrs were the perpetual theatre, revealed to the pious believer the actual state and constitution of the invisible world; and his religious speculations appeared to be founded on the firm basis of fact and experience. Whatever might be the condition of vulgar souls in the long interval between the dissolution and the resurrection of their bodies, it was evident that the superior spirits of the saints and martyrs did not consume that portion of their existence in silent and inglorious sleep.[81] It was evident (without presuming to determine the place of their habitation, or the nature of their felicity) that they enjoyed the lively and active consciousness of their happiness, their virtue, and their powers; and that they had already secured the possession of their eternal reward. The enlargement of their intellectual faculties surpassed the measure of the human imagination; since it was proved by *experience* that they were capable of hearing and understanding the various petitions of their numerous votaries, who, in the same moment of time, but in the most distant parts of the world, invoked the name and assistance of Stephen or of Martin.[82] The confidence of their petitioners was founded on the persuasion that the saints, who reigned with Christ, cast an eye of pity upon earth; that they were warmly interested in the prosperity of the Catholic church; and that the individuals who imitated the example of their faith and piety were the peculiar and favourite objects of their most tender regard. Sometimes, indeed, their friendship might be influenced by considerations of a less exalted kind: they viewed with partial affection the places which had been consecrated by their birth, their residence, their death, their burial, or the possession of their relics. The meaner passions of pride, avarice, and revenge, may be deemed unworthy of a celestial breast; yet the saints themselves condescended to testify their grateful approbation of the liberality of their votaries; and the sharpest bolts of punishment were hurled against those impious wretches who violated their magnificent shrines, or disbelieved their supernatural power.[83] Atrocious, indeed, must have been the guilt, and strange would have been the scepticism, of those men, if they had obstinately resisted the proofs of a divine agency, which the elements, the whole range of the animal creation, and even the subtle and invisible operations of the human mind, were compelled to obey.[84] The immediate, and almost instantaneous, effects, that were supposed to follow the prayer, or the offence, satisfied the Christians of the ample measure of favour and authority which the saints enjoyed in the presence of the Supreme God; and it seemed almost superfluous to inquire whether they were continually obliged to intercede before the throne of grace, or whether they might not be permitted to exercise, according to the dictates of their benevolence and justice, the delegated powers of their subordinate ministry. The imagination, which had been raised by a painful effort to the contemplation and worship of the Universal Cause, eagerly embraced such inferior objects of adoration as were more proportioned to its gross conceptions and imperfect faculties. The sublime and simple theology of the primitive Christians was gradually corrupted: and the MONARCHY of heaven, already clouded by metaphysical subtleties, was degraded by the introduction of a popular mythology which tended to restore the reign of polytheism.[85]

IV. As the objects of religion were gradually reduced to the standard of the imagination, the rites and ceremonies were introduced that seemed most powerfully to affect the senses of the vulgar. If, in the beginning of the fifth century,[86] Tertullian, or Lactantius,[87] had been suddenly raised from the dead, to assist at the festival of some popular saint or martyr,[88] they would have gazed with astonishment and indignation on the profane spectacle which had succeeded to the pure and spiritual worship of a Christian congregation. As soon as the doors of the church were thrown open, they must have been offended by the smoke of incense, the perfume of flowers, and the glare of lamps and tapers, which diffused, at noon-day, a gaudy, superfluous, and, in their opinion, a sacrilegious light. If they approached the balustrade of the altar, they made their way through the prostrate crowd, consisting, for the most part, of strangers and pilgrims, who resorted to the city on the vigil of the feast; and who already felt the strong intoxication of fanaticism, and, perhaps, of wine. Their devout kisses were imprinted on the walls and pavement of the sacred edifice; and their fervent prayers were directed, whatever might be the language of their church, to the bones, the blood, or the ashes of the saint, which were usually concealed, by a linen or silken veil, from the eyes of the vulgar. The Christians frequented the tombs of the martyrs, in the hope of obtaining, from their powerful intercession, every sort of spiritual, but more especially of temporal, blessings. They implored the preservation of their health, or the cure of their infirmities; the fruitfulness of their barren wives, or the safety and happiness of their children. Whenever they undertook any distant or dangerous journey, they requested that the holy martyrs would be their guides and protectors on the road; and if they returned without having experienced any misfortune, they again hastened to the tombs of the martyrs, to celebrate, with grateful thanksgivings, their obligations to the memory and relics of those heavenly patrons. The walls were hung round with symbols of the favours which they had received; eyes, and hands, and feet, of gold and silver: and edifying pictures, which could not long escape the abuse of indiscreet or idolatrous devotion, represented the image, the attributes, and the miracles of the tutelar saint. The same uniform original spirit of superstition might suggest, in the most distant ages and countries, the same methods of deceiving the credulity, and of affecting the senses of mankind:[89] but it must ingenuously be confessed that the ministers of the catholic church imitated the profane model which they were impatient to destroy. The most respectable bishops had persuaded themselves that the ignorant rustics would more cheerfully renounce the superstitions of Paganism, if they found some resemblance, some compensation, in the bosom of Christianity. The religion of Constantine achieved, in less than a century, the final conquest of the Roman empire: but the victors themselves were insensibly subdued by the arts of their vanquished rivals.[90]

CHAPTER XXIX

Final Division of the Roman Empire between the Sons of Theodosius. Reign of Arcadius and Honorius. Administration of Rufinus and Stilicho. Revolt and Defeat of Gildo in Africa.

THE genius of Rome expired with Theodosius, the last of the successors of Augustus and Constantine who appeared in the field at the head of their armies, and whose authority was universally acknowledged throughout the whole extent of the empire. The memory of his virtues still continued, however, to protect the feeble and inexperienced youth of his two sons. After the death of their father, Arcadius and Honorius were saluted, by the unanimous consent of mankind, as the lawful emperors of the East and of the West; and the oath of fidelity was eagerly taken by every order of the state; the senates of old and new Rome, the clergy, the magistrates, the soldiers, and the people. Arcadius, who then was about eighteen years of age, was born in Spain in the humble habitation of a private family. But he received a princely education in the palace of Constantinople; and his inglorious life was spent in that peaceful and splendid seat of royalty, from whence he appeared to reign over the provinces of Thrace, Asia Minor, Syria, and Egypt, from the Lower Danube to the confines of Persia and Æthiopia. His younger brother, Honorius, assumed, in the eleventh year of his age, the nominal government of Italy, Africa, Gaul, Spain, and Britain; and the troops which guarded the frontiers of his kingdom were opposed, on one side, to the Caledonians, and on the other to the Moors. The great and martial præfecture of Illyricum was divided between the two princes: the defence and possession of the provinces of Noricum, Pannonia, and Dalmatia, still belonged to the Western empire; but the two large dioceses of Dacia and Macedonia, which Gratian had intrusted to the valour of Theodosius, were for ever united to the empire of the East. The boundary in Europe was not very different from the line which now separates the Germans and the Turks; and the respective advantages of territory, riches, populousness, and military strength, were fairly balanced and compensated in this final and permanent division of the Roman empire. The hereditary sceptre of the sons of Theodosius appeared to be the gift of nature and of their father; the

generals and ministers had been accustomed to adore the majesty of the royal infants; and the army and people were not admonished of their rights, and of their power, by the dangerous example of a recent election. The gradual discovery of the weakness of Arcadius and Honorius, and the repeated calamities of their reign, were not sufficient to obliterate the deep and early impressions of loyalty. The subjects of Rome, who still reverenced the persons, or rather the names, of their sovereigns, beheld with equal abhorrence the rebels who opposed, and the ministers who abused, the authority of the throne.

Theodosius had tarnished the glory of his reign by the elevation of Rufinus, an odious favourite, who in an age of civil and religious faction has deserved, from every party, the imputation of every crime. The strong impulse of ambition and avarice[1] had urged Rufinus to abandon his native country, an obscure corner of Gaul,[2] to advance his fortune in the capital of the East: the talent of bold and ready elocution[3] qualified him to succeed in the lucrative profession of the law; and his success in that profession was a regular step to the most honourable and important employments of the state. He was raised, by just degrees, to the station of master of the offices. In the exercise of his various functions, so essentially connected with the whole system of civil government, he acquired the confidence of a monarch who soon discovered his diligence and capacity in business, and who long remained ignorant of the pride, the malice, and the covetousness of his disposition. These vices were concealed beneath the mask of profound dissimulation;[4] his passions were subservient only to the passions of his master; yet, in the horrid massacre of Thessalonica, the cruel Rufinus inflamed the fury, without imitating the repentance, of Theodosius. The minister, who viewed with proud indifference the rest of mankind, never forgave the appearance of an injury; and his personal enemies had forfeited, in his opinion, the merit of all public services. Promotus, the master-general of the infantry, had saved the empire from the invasion of the Ostrogoths; but he indignantly supported the pre-eminence of a rival whose character and profession he despised; and, in the midst of a public council, the impatient soldier was provoked to chastise with a blow the indecent pride of the favourite. This act of violence was represented to the emperor as an insult which it was incumbent on *his* dignity to resent. The disgrace and exile of Promotus were signified by a peremptory order to repair without delay to a military station on the banks of the Danube; and the death of that general (though he was slain in a skirmish with the barbarians) was imputed to the perfidious arts of Rufinus.[5] The sacrifice of an hero gratified his revenge; the honours of the consulship elated his vanity; but his power was still imperfect and precarious as long as the important posts of præfect of the East, and of præfect of Constantinople, were filled by Tatian[6] and his son Proculus, whose united authority balanced for some time the ambition and favour of the master of the offices. The two præfects were accused of rapine and corruption in the administration of the laws and finances. For the trial of these illustrious offenders the emperor constituted a special commission: several judges were named to share the guilt and reproach of injustice; but the right of pronouncing sentence was reserved to the president alone, and that president was Rufinus himself. The father, stripped of the præfecture of the East, was thrown into a dungeon; but the son, conscious that few ministers can be found innocent where an enemy is their judge, had secretly escaped; and Rufinus must have been satisfied with the least obnoxious victim, if despotism had not condescended to employ the basest and most ungenerous artifice. The prosecution was conducted with an appearance of equity and moderation which flattered Tatian with the hope of a favourable event: his confidence was fortified by the solemn assurances and perfidious oaths of the president, who presumed to interpose the sacred name of Theodosius himself; and the unhappy father was at last persuaded to recall, by a private letter, the fugitive Proculus. He was instantly seized, examined, condemned, and beheaded in one of the suburbs of Constantinople, with a precipitation which disappointed the clemency of the emperor. Without respecting the misfortunes of a consular senator, the cruel judges of Tatian compelled him to behold the execution of his son: the fatal cord was fastened round his own neck; but in the moment when he expected, and perhaps desired, the relief of a speedy death, he was permitted to consume the miserable remnant of his old age in poverty and exile.[7] The punishment of the two præfects might perhaps be excused by the exceptionable parts of their own conduct; the enmity of Rufinus might be palliated by the jealous and unsociable nature of ambition. But he indulged a spirit of revenge, equally repugnant to prudence and to justice, when he degraded their native country of Lycia from the rank of Roman provinces, stigmatised a guiltless people with a mark of ignominy, and declared that the countrymen of Tatian and Proculus should for ever remain incapable of holding any employment of honour or advantage under the Imperial government.[8] The new præfect of the East (for Rufinus instantly succeeded to the vacant honours of his adversary) was not diverted, however, by the most criminal pursuits from the performance of the religious duties which in that age were considered as the most essential to salvation. In the suburb of Chalcedon, surnamed the *Oak*, he had built a magnificent villa, to which he devoutly added a stately church consecrated to the apostles St. Peter and St. Paul, and continually sanctified by the prayers and penance of a regular society of monks. A numerous and almost general synod of the bishops of the Eastern empire was summoned to celebrate at the same time the dedication of the church and the baptism of the founder. This double ceremony was performed with extraordinary pomp; and when Rufinus was purified in the holy font from all the sins that he had hitherto committed, a venerable hermit of Egypt rashly proposed himself as the sponsor of a proud and ambitious statesman.[9]

The character of Theodosius imposed on his minister the task of hypocrisy, which disguised, and sometimes restrained, the abuse of power; and Rufinus was apprehensive of disturbing the indolent slumber of a prince still capable of exerting the abilities and the virtue which had raised him to the throne.[10] But the absence, and soon afterwards the death, of the emperor confirmed the absolute authority of Rufinus over the person and dominions of Arcadius, a feeble youth, whom the imperious præfect considered as his pupil, rather than his sovereign. Regardless of the public opinion, he indulged his passions without remorse and without resistance; and his malignant and rapacious spirit rejected every passion that might have contributed to his own glory or the happiness of the people. His avarice,[11] which seems to have prevailed in his corrupt mind over every other sentiment, attracted the wealth of the East by the various arts of partial and general extortion—oppressive taxes, scandalous bribery, immoderate fines, unjust confiscations, forced or fictitious testaments, by which the tyrant despoiled of their lawful inheritance the children of strangers or enemies; and the public sale of justice, as well as of favour, which he instituted in the palace of Constantinople. The ambitious candidate eagerly solicited, at the expense of the fairest part of his patrimony, the honours and emoluments of some provincial government; the lives and fortunes of the unhappy people were abandoned to the most liberal purchaser; and the public discontent was sometimes appeased by the sacrifice of an unpopular criminal, whose punishment was profitable only to the præfect of the East, his accomplice and his judge. If avarice were not the blindest of the human passions, the motives of Rufinus might excite our curiosity, and we might be tempted to inquire with what view he violated every principle of humanity and justice to accumulate those immense treasures which he could not spend without folly nor possess without danger. Perhaps he vainly imagined that he laboured for the interest of an only daughter, on whom he intended to bestow his royal pupil and the august rank of empress of the East. Perhaps he deceived himself by the opinion that his avarice was the instrument of his ambition. He aspired to place his fortune on a secure and independent basis, which should no longer depend on the caprice of the young emperor; yet he neglected to conciliate the hearts of the soldiers and people by the liberal distribution of those riches which he had acquired with so much toil and with so much guilt. The extreme parsimony of Rufinus left him only the reproach and envy of ill-gotten wealth; his dependents served him without attachment; the universal hatred of mankind was repressed only by the influence of servile fear. The fate of Lucian proclaimed to the East that the præfect, whose industry was much abated in the despatch of ordinary business, was active and indefatigable in the pursuit of revenge. Lucian, the son of the præfect Florentius, the oppressor of Gaul and the enemy of Julian, had employed a considerable part of his inheritance, the fruit of rapine and corruption, to purchase the friendship of Rufinus and the high office of count of the East. But the new magistrate imprudently departed from the maxims of the court and of the times, disgraced his benefactor by the contrast of a virtuous and temperate administration, and presumed to refuse an act of injustice which might have tended to the profit of the emperor's uncle. Arcadius was easily persuaded to resent the supposed insult; and the præfect of the East resolved to execute in person the cruel vengeance which he meditated against this ungrateful delegate of his power. He performed with incessant speed the journey of seven or eight hundred miles from Constantinople to Antioch, entered the capital of Syria at the dead of night, and spread universal consternation among a people ignorant of his design, but not ignorant of his character. The count of the fifteen provinces of the East was dragged, like the vilest malefactor, before the arbitrary tribunal of Rufinus. Notwithstanding the clearest evidence of his integrity, which was not impeached even by the voice of an accuser, Lucian was condemned, almost without a trial, to suffer a cruel and ignominious punishment. The ministers of the tyrant, by the order and in the presence of their master, beat him on the neck with leather thongs armed at the extremities with lead; and when he fainted under the violence of the pain, he was removed in a close litter to conceal his dying agonies from the eyes of the indignant city. No sooner had Rufinus perpetrated this inhuman act, the sole object of his expedition, than he returned, amidst the deep and silent curses of a trembling people, from Antioch to Constantinople; and his diligence was accelerated by the hope of accomplishing, without delay, the nuptials of his daughter with the emperor of the East.[12]

But Rufinus soon experienced that a prudent minister should constantly secure his royal captive by the strong, though invisible, chain of habit; and that the merit, and much more easily the favour of the absent, are obliterated in a short time from the mind of a weak and capricious sovereign. While the præfect satiated his revenge at Antioch, a secret conspiracy of the favourite eunuchs, directed by the great chamberlain Eutropius, undermined his power in the palace of Constantinople. They discovered that Arcadius was not inclined to love the daughter of Rufinus, who had been chosen without his consent for his bride, and they contrived to substitute in her place the fair Eudoxia, the daughter of Bauto,[13] a general of the Franks in the service of Rome, and who was educated, since the death of her father, in the family of the sons of Promotus. The young emperor, whose chastity had been strictly guarded by the pious care of his tutor Arsenius,[14] eagerly listened to the artful and flattering descriptions of the charms of Eudoxia; he gazed with impatient ardour on her picture, and he understood the necessity of concealing his amorous designs from the knowledge of a minister who was so deeply interested to oppose the consummation of his happiness. Soon after the return of Rufinus, the approaching ceremony of the royal nuptials was announced to the people of Constantinople, who prepared to celebrate with false and hollow acclamations the fortune of his daughter. A splendid train of eunuchs and officers issued, in hymeneal pomp, from the gates of the palace, bearing aloft the diadem, the robes, and the inestimable ornaments of the future empress. The solemn procession passed through the streets of the city, which were adorned with garlands and filled with spectators; but when it reached the house of the sons of Promotus, the principal eunuch respectfully entered the mansion, invested the fair Eudoxia with the Imperial robes, and conducted her in triumph to the palace and bed of Arcadius.[15] The secrecy and success with which this conspiracy against Rufinus had been conducted imprinted a mark of indelible ridicule on the character of a minister who had suffered himself to be deceived, in a post where the arts of deceit and dissimulation constitute the most distinguished merit. He considered, with a mixture of indignation and fear, the victory of an aspiring eunuch who had secretly captivated the favour of his sovereign; and the disgrace of his daughter, whose interest was inseparably connected with his own, wounded the tenderness, or at least the pride, of Rufinus. At the moment when he flattered himself that he should become the father of a line of kings, a foreign maid, who had been educated in the house of his implacable enemies, was introduced into the Imperial bed; and Eudoxia soon displayed a superiority of sense and spirit to improve the ascendant which her beauty must acquire over the mind of a fond and youthful husband. The emperor would soon be instructed to hate, to fear, and to destroy the powerful subject whom he had injured; and the consciousness of guilt deprived Rufinus of every hope, either of safety or comfort, in the retirement of a private life. But he still possessed the most effectual means of defending his dignity, and perhaps of oppressing his enemies. The præfect still exercised an uncontrolled authority over the civil and military government of the East; and his treasures, if he could resolve to use them, might be employed to procure proper instruments for the execution of the blackest designs that pride, ambition, and revenge could suggest to a desperate statesman. The character of Rufinus seemed to justify the accusations that he conspired against the person of his sovereign to seat himself on the vacant throne; and that he had secretly invited the Huns and the Goths to invade the provinces of the empire and to increase the public confusion. The subtle præfect, whose life had been spent in the intrigues of the palace, opposed with equal arms the artful measures of the eunuch Eutropius; but the timid soul of Rufinus was astonished by the hostile approach of a more formidable rival, of the great Stilicho, the general, or rather the master, of the empire of the West.[16]

The celestial gift, which Achilles obtained, and Alexander envied, of a poet worthy to celebrate the actions of heroes, has been enjoyed by Stilicho, in a much higher degree than might have been expected from the declining state of genius and of art. The muse of Claudian,[17] devoted to his service, was always prepared to stigmatise his adversaries, Rufinus or Eutropius, with eternal infamy; or to paint, in the most splendid colours, the victories and virtues of a powerful benefactor. In the review of a period indifferently supplied with authentic materials, we cannot refuse to illustrate the annals of Honorius from the invectives, or the panegyrics, of a contemporary writer; but as Claudian appears to have indulged the most ample privilege of a poet and a courtier, some criticism will be requisite to translate the language of fiction or exaggeration into the truth and simplicity of historic prose. His silence concerning the family of Stilicho may be admitted as a proof that his patron was neither able nor desirous to boast of a long series of illustrious progenitors, and the slight mention of his father, an officer of barbarian cavalry in the service of Valens, seems to countenance the assertion that the general who so long commanded the armies of Rome was descended from the savage and perfidious race of the Vandals.[18] If Stilicho had not possessed the external advantages of strength and stature, the most flattering bard, in the presence of so many thousand spectators, would have hesitated to affirm that he surpassed the measure of the demi-gods of antiquity; and that, whenever he moved, with lofty steps, through the streets of the capital, the astonished crowd made room for the stranger, who displayed, in a private condition, the awful majesty of a hero. From his earliest youth he embraced the profession of arms; his prudence and valour were soon distinguished in the field; the horsemen and archers of the East admired his superior dexterity; and in each degree of his military promotions, the public judgment always pre-vented and approved the choice of the sover-eign. He was named by Theodosius to ratify a solemn treaty with the monarch of Persia: he supported, during that important embassy, the dignity of the Roman name; and after his re-turn to Constantinople his merit was rewarded by an intimate and honourable alliance with the Imperial family. Theodosius had been prompted, by a pious motive of fraternal affec-tion, to adopt, for his own, the daughter of his brother Honorius; the beauty and accomplish-ments of Serena[19] were universally admired by the obsequious court; and Stilicho obtained the preference over a crowd of rivals who ambi-tiously disputed the hand of the princess, and the favour of her adoptive father.[20] The assur-ance that the husband of Serena would be faith-ful to the throne which he was permitted to ap-proach engaged the emperor to exalt the for-tunes, and to employ the abilities, of the saga-cious and intrepid Stilicho. He rose through the successive steps of master of the horse, and count of the domestics, to the supreme rank of master-general of all the cavalry and infantry of the Roman, or at least of the Western, em-pire;[21] and his enemies confessed that he invari-ably disdained to barter for gold the rewards of merit, or to defraud the soldiers of the pay and gratifications which they deserved or claimed from the liberality of the state.[22] The valour and conduct which he afterwards displayed in the defence of Italy against the arms of Alaric and Radagaisus may justify the fame of his early achievements; and in an age less attentive to the laws of honour or of pride, the Roman gen-erals might yield the pre-eminence of rank to the ascendant of superior genius.[23] He lamented and revenged the murder of Promotus, his rival and his friend; and the massacre of many thousands of the flying Bastarnæ is represented by the poet as a bloody sacrifice which the Roman Achilles offered to the names of another Patroclus. The virtues and victories of Stilicho deserved the hatred of Rufinus: and the arts of calumny might have been successful, if the tender and vigilant Serena had not protected her husband against his domestic foes, whilst he vanquished in the field the enemies of the em-pire.[24] Theodosius continued to support an un-worthy minister, to whose diligence he dele-gated the government of the palace and of the East; but when he marched against the tyrant Eugenius, he associated his faithful general to the labours and glories of the civil war; and in the last moments of his life the dying monarch recommended to Stilicho the care of his sons and of the republic.[25] The ambition and the abilities of Stilicho were not unequal to the im-portant trust; and he claimed the guardianship of the two empires during the minority of Ar-cadius and Honorius.[26] The first measure of his administration, or rather of his reign, displayed to the nations the vigour and activity of a spirit worthy to command. He passed the Alps in the depth of winter; descended the stream of the Rhine, from the fortress of Basel to the marshes of Batavia; reviewed the state of the garrisons; repressed the enterprises of the Germans; and, after establishing along the banks a firm and honourable peace, returned with incredible speed to the palace of Milan.[27] The person and court of Honorius were subject to the master-general of the West; and the armies and prov-inces of Europe obeyed, without hesitation, a regular authority, which was exercised in the name of their young sovereign. Two rivals only remained to dispute the claims, and to provoke the vengeance, of Stilicho. Within the limits of Africa, Gildo, the Moor, maintained a proud and dangerous independence; and the minister of Constantinople asserted his equal reign over the emperor and the empire of the East.

The impartiality which Stilicho affected, as the common guardian of the royal brothers, en-gaged him to regulate the equal division of the arms, the jewels, and the magnificent wardrobe and furniture of the deceased emperor.[28] But the most important object of the inheritance consisted of the numerous legions, cohorts, and squadrons, of Romans or barbarians, whom the event of the civil war had united under the standard of Theodosius. The various multitudes of Europe and Asia, exasperated by recent ani-mosities, were overawed by the authority of a single man; and the rigid discipline of Stilicho protected the lands of the citizen from the ra-pine of the licentious soldier.[29] Anxious, how-ever, and impatient to relieve Italy from the presence of this formidable host, which could be useful only on the frontiers of the empire, he lis-tened to the just requisition of the minister of Arcadius, declared his intention of reconducting in person the troops of the East, and dexterously employed the rumour of a Gothic tumult to con-ceal his private designs of ambition and re-venge.[30] The guilty soul of Rufinus was alarmed by the approach of a warrior and a rival whose enmity he deserved; he computed, with in-creasing terror, the narrow space of his life and greatness; and, as the last hope of safety, he in-terposed the authority of the emperor Arcadius.

Stilicho, who appears to have directed his march along the sea-coast of the Hadriatic, was not far distant from the city of Thessalonica when he received a peremptory message to recall the troops of the East, and to declare that *his* nearer approach would be considered, by the Byzantine court, as an act of hostility. The prompt and unexpected obedience of the general of the West convinced the vulgar of his loyalty and moderation; and, as he had already engaged the affection of the Eastern troops, he recommended to their zeal the execution of his bloody design, which might be accomplished in his absence, with less danger perhaps, and with less reproach. Stilicho left the command of the troops of the East to Gainas, the Goth, on whose fidelity he firmly relied, with an assurance at least that the hardy barbarian would never be diverted from his purpose by any consideration of fear or remorse. The soldiers were easily persuaded to punish the enemy of Stilicho and of Rome; and such was the general hatred which Rufinus had excited, that the fatal secret, communicated to thousands, was faithfully preserved during the long march from Thessalonica to the gates of Constantinople. As soon as they had resolved his death, they condescended to flatter his pride; the ambitious præfect was seduced to believe that those powerful auxiliaries might be tempted to place the diadem on his head; and the treasures which he distributed with a tardy and reluctant hand were accepted by the indignant multitude as an insult rather than as a gift. At the distance of a mile from the capital, in the field of Mars, before the palace of Hebdomon, the troops halted; and the emperor, as well as his minister, advanced, according to ancient custom, respectfully to salute the power which supported their throne. As Rufinus passed along the ranks, and disguised, with studied courtesy, his innate haughtiness, the wings insensibly wheeled from the right and left, and enclosed the devoted victim within the circle of their arms. Before he could reflect on the danger of his situation, Gainas gave the signal of death; a daring and forward soldier plunged his sword into the breast of the guilty præfect, and Rufinus fell, groaned, and expired, at the feet of the affrighted emperor. If the agonies of a moment could expiate the crimes of a whole life, or if the outrages inflicted on a breathless corpse could be the object of pity, our humanity might perhaps be affected by the horrid circumstances which accompanied the murder of Rufinus. His mangled body was abandoned to the brutal fury of the populace of either sex, who hastened in crowds, from every quarter of the city, to trample on the remains of the haughty minister, at whose frown they had so lately trembled. His right hand was cut off, and carried through the streets of Constantinople, in cruel mockery, to extort contributions for the avaricious tyrant, whose head was publicly exposed, borne aloft on the point of a long lance.[31] According to the savage maxims of the Greek republics, his innocent family would have shared the punishment of his crimes. The wife and daughter of Rufinus were indebted for their safety to the influence of religion. *Her* sanctuary protected them from the raging madness of the people; and they were permitted to spend the remainder of their lives in the exercises of Christian devotion in the peaceful retirement of Jerusalem.[32]

The servile poet of Stilicho applauds with ferocious joy this horrid deed, which, in the execution, perhaps of justice, violated every law of nature and society, profaned the majesty of the prince, and renewed the dangerous examples of military licence. The contemplation of the universal order and harmony had satisfied Claudian of the existence of the Deity; but the prosperous impunity of vice appeared to contradict his moral attributes; and the fate of Rufinus was the only event which could dispel the religious doubts of the poet.[33] Such an act might vindicate the honour of Providence; but it did not much contribute to the happiness of the people. In less than three months they were informed of the maxims of the new administration, by a singular edict, which established the exclusive right of the treasury over the spoils of Rufinus; they silenced, under heavy penalties, the presumptuous claims of the subjects of the Eastern empire who had been injured by his rapacious tyranny.[34] Even Stilicho did not derive from the murder of his rival the fruit which he had proposed; and though he gratified his revenge, his ambition was disappointed. Under the name of a favourite, the weakness of Arcadius required a master, but he naturally preferred the obsequious arts of the eunuch Eutropius, who had obtained his domestic confidence; and the emperor contemplated with terror and aversion the stern genius of a foreign warrior. Till they were divided by the jealousy of power, the sword of Gainas, and the charms of Eudoxia, supported the favour of the great chamberlain of the palace: the perfidious Goth, who was appointed master-general of the East, betrayed, without scruple, the interest of his benefactor; and the same troops who had so lately massacred the enemy of Stilicho were engaged to support, against him, the independence of the throne of Constantinople. The favourites of Arcadius fomented a secret and irreconcilable war against a formidable hero, who aspired to govern and to defend the two empires of Rome and the two sons of Theodosius. They incessantly laboured, by dark and treacherous machinations, to deprive him of the esteem of the prince, the respect of the people, and the friendship of the barbarians. The life of Stilicho was repeatedly attempted by the dagger of hired assassins; and a decree was obtained from the senate of Constantinople, to declare him an enemy of the republic, and to confiscate his ample possessions in the provinces of the East. At a time when the only hope of delaying the ruin of the Roman name depended on the firm union and reciprocal aid of all the nations to whom it had been gradually communicated, the subjects of Arcadius and Honorius were instructed, by their respective masters, to view each other in a foreign and even hostile light; to rejoice in their mutual calamities; and to embrace, as their faithful allies, the barbarians whom they excited to invade the territories of their countrymen.[35] The natives of Italy affected to despise the servile and effeminate Greeks of Byzantium, who presumed to imitate the dress, and to usurp the dignity, of Roman senators;[36] and the Greeks had not yet forgot the sentiments of hatred and contempt which their polished ancestors had so long entertained for the rude inhabitants of the West. The distinction of two governments, which soon produced the separation of two nations, will justify my design of suspending the series of the Byzantine history, to prosecute, without interruption, the disgraceful but memorable reign of Honorius.

The prudent Stilicho, instead of persisting to force the inclinations of a prince and people who rejected his government, wisely abandoned Arcadius to his unworthy favourites; and his reluctance to involve the two empires in a civil war displayed the moderation of a minister who had so often signalised his military spirit and abilities. But if Stilicho had any longer endured the revolt of Africa, he would have betrayed the security of the capital, and the majesty of the Western emperor, to the capricious insolence of a Moorish rebel. Gildo,[37] the brother of the tyrant Firmus, had preserved and obtained, as the reward of his apparent fidelity, the immense patrimony which was forfeited by treason; long and meritorious service in the armies of Rome raised him to the dignity of a military count; the narrow policy of the court of Theodosius had adopted the mischievous expedient of supporting a legal government by the interest of a powerful family; and the brother of Firmus was invested with the command of Africa. His ambition soon usurped the administration of justice and of the finances, without account and without control; and he maintained, during a reign of twelve years, the possession of an office from which it was impossible to remove him without the danger of a civil war. During those twelve years the provinces of Africa groaned under the dominion of a tyrant who seemed to unite the unfeeling temper of a stranger with the partial resentments of domestic faction. The forms of law were often superseded by the use of poison; and if the trembling guests who were invited to the table of Gildo presumed to express their fears, the insolent suspicion served only to excite his fury, and he loudly summoned the ministers of death. Gildo alternately indulged the passions of avarice and lust; [38] and if his *days* were terrible to the rich, his *nights* were not less dreadful to husbands and parents. The fairest of their wives and daughters were prostituted to the embraces of the tyrant; and afterwards abandoned to a ferocious troop of barbarians and assassins, the black or swarthy natives of the desert, whom Gildo considered as the only guardians of his throne. In the civil war between Theodosius and Eugenius, the count, or rather the sovereign of Africa, maintained a haughty and suspicious neutrality; refused to assist either of the contending parties with troops or vessels, expected the declaration of fortune, and reserved for the conqueror the vain professions of his allegiance. Such professions would not have satisfied the master of the Roman world: but the death of Theodosius, and the weakness and discord of his sons, confirmed the power of the Moor, who condescended, as a proof of his moderation, to abstain from the use of the diadem and to supply Rome with the customary tribute, or rather subsidy, of corn. In every division of the empire, the five provinces of Africa were invariably assigned to the West; and Gildo had consented to govern that extensive country in the name of Honorius; but his knowledge of the character and designs of Stilicho soon engaged him to address his homage to a more distant and feeble sovereign. The ministers of Arcadius embraced the cause of a perfidious rebel; and the delusive hope of adding the numerous cities of Africa to the empire of the East tempted them to assert a claim which they were incapable of supporting either by reason or by arms.[39]

When Stilicho had given a firm and decisive answer to the pretensions of the Byzantine court, he solemnly accused the tyrant of Africa before the tribunal which had formerly judged the kings and nations of the earth; and the image of the republic was revived, after a long interval, under the reign of Honorius. The emperor transmitted an accurate and ample detail of the complaints of the provincials, and the crimes of Gildo, to the Roman senate; and the members of that venerable assembly were required to pronounce the condemnation of the rebel. Their unanimous suffrage declared him the enemy of the republic; and the decree of the senate added a sacred and legitimate sanction to the Roman arms.[40] A people who still remembered that their ancestors had been the masters of the world would have applauded, with conscious pride, the representation of ancient freedom, if they had not long since been accustomed to prefer the solid assurance of bread to the unsubstantial visions of liberty and greatness. The subsistence of Rome depended on the harvests of Africa; and it was evident that a declaration of war would be the signal of famine. The præfect Symmachus, who presided in the deliberations of the senate, admonished the minister of his just apprehension that, as soon as the revengeful Moor should prohibit the exportation of corn, the tranquillity, and perhaps the safety, of the capital would be threatened by the hungry rage of a turbulent multitude.[41] The prudence of Stilicho conceived, and executed without delay, the most effectual measure for the relief of the Roman people. A large and seasonable supply of corn, collected in the inland provinces of Gaul, was embarked on the rapid stream of the Rhone, and transported by an easy navigation from the Rhone to the Tiber. During the whole term of the African war, the granaries of Rome were continually filled, her dignity was vindicated from the humiliating dependence, and the minds of an immense people were quieted by the calm confidence of peace and plenty.[42]

The cause of Rome, and the conduct of the African war, were intrusted by Stilicho to a general active and ardent to avenge his private injuries on the head of the tyrant. The spirit of discord which prevailed in the house of Nabal had excited a deadly quarrel between two of his sons, Gildo and Mascezel.[43] The usurper pursued, with implacable rage, the life of his younger brother, whose courage and abilities he feared; and Mascezel, oppressed by superior power, took refuge in the court of Milan; where he soon received the cruel intelligence that his two innocent and helpless children had been murdered by their inhuman uncle. The affliction of the father was suspended only by the desire of revenge. The vigilant Stilicho already prepared to collect the naval and military forces of the Western empire; and he had resolved, if the tyrant should be able to wage an equal and doubtful war, to march against him in person. But as Italy required his presence, and as it might be dangerous to weaken the defence of the frontier, he judged it more advisable that Mascezel should attempt this arduous adventure at the head of a chosen body of Gallic veterans, who had lately served under the standard of Eugenius. These troops, who were exhorted to convince the world that they could subvert, as well as defend, the throne of an usurper, consisted of the *Jovian*, the *Herculian*, and the *Augustan* legions; of the *Nervian* auxiliaries; of the soldiers who displayed in their banners the symbol of a *lion*; and of the troops which were distinguished by the auspicious names of *Fortunate* and *Invincible*. Yet such was the smallness of their establishments, or the difficulty of recruiting, that these *seven* bands,[44] of high dignity and reputation in the service of Rome, amounted to no more than five thousand effective men.[45] The fleet of galleys and transports sailed in tempestuous weather from the port of Pisa, in Tuscany, and steered their course to the little island of Capraria, which had borrowed that name from the wild goats, its original inhabitants, whose place was now occupied by a new colony of a strange and savage appearance. "The whole island (says an ingenious traveller of those times) is filled, or rather defiled, by men who fly from the light. They call themselves *Monks* or solitaries, because they choose to live alone, without any witnesses of their actions. They fear the gifts of fortune, from the apprehension of losing them; and, lest they should be miserable, they embrace a life of voluntary wretchedness. How absurd is their choice! how perverse their understanding! to dread the evils, without being able to support the blessings, of the human condition. Either this melancholy madness is the effect of disease, or else the consciousness of guilt urges these unhappy men to exercise on their own bodies the tortures which are inflicted on fugitive slaves by the hand of justice."[46] Such was the contempt of a profane magistrate for the monks of Capraria, who were revered by the pious Mascezel as the chosen servants of God.[47] Some of them were persuaded, by his entreaties, to embark on board the fleet; and it is observed, to the praise of the Roman general, that his days and nights were employed in prayer, fasting, and the occupation of singing psalms. The devout leader, who with such a reinforcement appeared confident of victory, avoided the dangerous rocks of Corsica, coasted along the eastern side of Sardinia, and secured his ships against the violence of the south wind, by casting anchor in the safe and capacious harbour of Cagliari, at the distance of one hundred and forty miles from the African shores.[48]

Gildo was prepared to resist the invasion with all the forces of Africa. By the liberality of his gifts and promises, he endeavoured to secure the doubtful allegiance of the Roman soldiers, whilst he attracted to his standard the distant tribes of Gætulia and Æthiopia. He proudly reviewed an army of seventy thousand men, and boasted, with the rash presumption which is the forerunner of disgrace, that his numerous cavalry would trample under their horses' feet the troops of Mascezel, and involve, in a cloud of burning sand, the natives of the cold regions of Gaul and Germany.[49] But the Moor who commanded the legions of Honorius was too well acquainted with the manners of the countrymen to entertain any serious apprehension of a naked and disorderly host of barbarians, whose left arm, instead of a shield, was protected only by a mantle; who were totally disarmed as soon as they had darted their javelin from their right hand; and whose horses had never been taught to bear the control, or to obey the guidance, of the bridle. He fixed his camp of five thousand veterans in the face of a superior enemy, and, after the delay of three days, gave the signal of a general engagement.[50] As Mascezel advanced before the front with fair offers of peace and pardon, he encountered one of the foremost standard-bearers of the Africans, and, on his refusal to yield, struck him on the arm with his sword. The arm and the standard sunk under the weight of the blow, and the imaginary act of submission was hastily repeated by all the standards of the line. At this signal the disaffected cohorts proclaimed the name of their lawful sovereign; the barbarians, astonished by the defection of their Roman allies, dispersed, according to their custom, in tumultuary flight; and Mascezel obtained the honours of an easy and almost bloodless victory.[51] The tyrant escaped from the field of battle to the sea-shore, and threw himself into a small vessel, with the

hope of reaching in safety some friendly port of the empire of the East; but the obstinacy of the wind drove him back into the harbour of Tabraca,[52] which had acknowledged, with the rest of the province, the dominion of Honorius, and the authority of his lieutenant. The inhabitants, as a proof of their repentance and loyalty, seized and confined the person of Gildo in a dungeon; and his own despair saved him from the intolerable torture of supporting the presence of an injured and victorious brother.[53] The captives and the spoils of Africa were laid at the feet of the emperor; but Stilicho, whose moderation appeared more conspicuous and more sincere in the midst of prosperity, still affected to consult the laws of the republic, and referred to the senate and people of Rome the judgment of the most illustrious criminals.[54] Their trial was public and solemn; but the judges, in the exercise of this obsolete and precarious jurisdiction, were impatient to punish the African magistrates who had intercepted the subsistence of the Roman people. The rich and guilty province was oppressed by the Imperial ministers, who had a visible interest to multiply the number of the accomplices of Gildo; and if an edict of Honorius seems to check the malicious industry of informers, a subsequent edict, at the distance of ten years, continues and renews the prosecution of the offences which had been committed in the time of the general rebellion.[55] The adherents of the tyrant who escaped the first fury of the soldiers and the judges might derive some consolation from the tragic fate of his brother, who could never obtain his pardon for the extraordinary services which he had performed. After he had finished an important war in the space of a single winter, Mascezel was received at the court of Milan with loud applause, affected gratitude, and secret jealousy;[56] and his death, which perhaps was the effect of accident, has been considered as the crime of Stilicho. In the passage of a bridge, the Moorish prince, who accompanied the master-general of the West, was suddenly thrown from his horse into the river; the officious haste of the attendants was restrained by a cruel and perfidious smile which they observed on the countenance of Stilicho; and while they delayed the necessary assistance, the unfortunate Mascezel was irrecoverably drowned.[57]

The joy of the African triumph was happily connected with the nuptials of the emperor Honorius, and of his cousin Maria, the daughter of Stilicho; and this equal and honourable **alliance seemed to invest the powerful minister** with the authority of a parent over his submissive pupil. The muse of Claudian was not silent on this propitious day;[58] he sung, in various and lively strains, the happiness of the royal pair, and the glory of the hero who confirmed their union and supported their throne. The ancient fables of Greece, which had almost ceased to be the object of religious faith, were saved from oblivion by the genius of poetry. The picture of the Cyprian grove, the seat of harmony and love; the triumphant progress of Venus over her native seas, and the mild influence which her presence diffused in the palace of Milan, express to every age the natural sentiments of the heart in the just and pleasing language of allegorical fiction. But the amorous impatience which Claudian attributes to the young prince[59] must excite the smiles of the court; and his beauteous spouse (if she deserved the praise of beauty) had not much to fear or to hope from the passions of her lover. Honorius was only in the fourteenth year of his age; Serena, the mother of his bride, deferred, by art or persuasion, the consummation of the royal nuptials; Maria died a virgin, after she had been ten years a wife; and the chastity of the emperor was secured, or perhaps the debility, of his constitution.[60] His subjects, who attentively studied the character of their young sovereign, discovered that Honorius was without passions, and consequently without talents; and that his feeble and languid disposition was alike incapable of discharging the duties of his rank, or of enjoying the pleasures of his age. In his early youth he made some progress in the exercises of riding and drawing the bow; but he soon relinquished these fatiguing occupations, and the amusement of feeding poultry became the serious and daily care of the monarch of the West,[61] who resigned the reins of empire to the firm and skilful hand of his guardian Stilicho. The experience of history will countenance the suspicion that a prince who was born in the purple received a worse education than the meanest peasant of his dominions, and that the ambitious minister suffered him to attain the age of manhood without attempting to excite his courage or to enlighten his understanding.[62] The predecessors of Honorius were accustomed to animate by their example, or at least by their presence, the valour of the legions; and the dates of their laws attest the perpetual activity of their motions through the provinces of the Roman world. But the son of Theodosius passed the slumber of his life a captive in his palace, a stranger in his country, and the patient, almost the indifferent, spectator of the ruin of the Western empire, which was repeatedly attacked, and finally subverted, by the arms of the barbarians. In the eventful history of a reign of twenty-eight years, it will seldom be necessary to mention the name of the emperor Honorius.

CHAPTER XXX

Revolt of the Goths. They plunder Greece. Two great Invasions of Italy by Alaric and Radagaisus. They are repulsed by Stilicho. The Germans overrun Gaul. Usurpation of Constantine in the West. Disgrace and Death of Stilicho.

IF the subjects of Rome could be ignorant of their obligations to the great Theodosius, they were too soon convinced how painfully the spirit and abilities of their deceased emperor had supported the frail and mouldering edifice of the republic. He died in the month of January; and before the end of the winter of the same year, the Gothic nation was in arms.[1] The barbarian auxiliaries erected their independent standard, and boldly avowed the hostile designs which they had long cherished in their ferocious minds. Their countrymen, who had been condemned by the conditions of the last treaty to a life of tranquillity and labour, deserted their farms at the first sound of the trumpet, and eagerly resumed the weapons which they had reluctantly laid down. The barriers of the Danube were thrown open; the savage warriors of Scythia issued from their forests; and the uncommon severity of the winter allowed the poet to remark "that they rolled their ponderous waggons over the broad and icy back of the indignant river."[2] The unhappy natives of the provinces to the south of the Danube submitted to the calamities which, in the course of twenty years, were almost grown familiar to their imagination; and the various troops of barbarians who gloried in the Gothic name were irregularly spread from the woody shores of Dalmatia to the walls of Constantinople.[3] The interruption, or at least the diminution, of the subsidy which the Goths had received from the prudent liberality of Theodosius, was the specious pretence of their revolt: the affront was embittered by their contempt for the unwarlike sons of Theodosius; and their resentment was inflamed by the weakness or treachery of the minister of Arcadius. The frequent visits of Rufinus to the camp of the barbarians, whose arms and apparel he affected to imitate, were considered as a sufficient evidence of his guilty correspondence; and the public enemy, from a motive either of gratitude or of policy, was attentive, amidst the general devastation, to spare the private estates of the unpopular præfect. The Goths, instead of being impelled by the blind and headstrong passions of their chiefs, were now directed by the bold and artful genius of Alaric. That renowned leader was descended from the noble race of the Balti,[4] which yielded only to the royal dignity of the Amali: he had solicited the command of the Roman armies; and the Imperial court provoked him to demonstrate the folly of their refusal, and the importance of their loss. Whatever hopes might be entertained of the conquest of Constantinople, the judicious general soon abandoned an impracticable enterprise. In the midst of a divided court and a discontented people, the emperor Arcadius was terrified by the aspect of the Gothic arms: but the want of wisdom and valour was supplied by the strength of the city; and the fortifications, both of the sea and land, might securely brave the impotent and random darts of the barbarians. Alaric disdained to trample any longer on the prostrate and ruined countries of Thrace and Dacia, and he resolved to seek a plentiful harvest of fame and riches in a province which had hitherto escaped the ravages of war.[5]

The character of the civil and military officers on whom Rufinus had devolved the government of Greece confirmed the public suspicion that he had betrayed the ancient seat of freedom and learning to the Gothic invader. The proconsul Antiochus was the unworthy son of a respectable father; and Gerontius, who commanded the provincial troops, was much better qualified to execute the oppressive orders of a tyrant than to defend, with courage and ability, a country most remarkably fortified by the hand of nature. Alaric had traversed, without resistance, the plains of Macedonia and Thessaly, as far as the foot of Mount Oeta, a steep and woody range of hills, almost impervious to his cavalry. They stretched from east to west, to the edge of the sea-shore; and left, between the precipice and the Malian Gulf, an interval of three hundred feet, which in some places was contracted to a road capable of admitting only a single carriage.[6] In this narrow pass of Thermopylæ, where Leonidas and the three hundred Spartans had gloriously devoted their lives, the Goths might have been stopped, or destroyed, by a skilful general; and perhaps the view of that sacred spot might have kindled some sparks of military ardour in the breasts of the degenerate Greeks. The troops which had been posted to defend the straits of Thermopylæ retired, as they were directed, without attempting to disturb the secure and rapid passage of Alaric;[7] and the fertile fields of Phocis and Bœotia were instantly covered by a deluge of barbarians, who massacred the males of an age to bear arms, and drove away the beautiful females, with the spoil and cattle of the flaming villages. The travellers who visited Greece several years afterwards could easily discover the deep and bloody traces of the march of the Goths; and Thebes was less indebted for her preservation to the strength of her seven gates than to the eager haste of Alaric, who advanced to occupy the city of Athens and the important harbour of the Piræus. The same impatience urged him to prevent the delay and danger of a siege, by the offer of a capitulation; and as soon as the Athenians heard the voice of the Gothic herald, they were easily persuaded to deliver the greatest part of their wealth, as the ransom of the city of Minerva and its inhabitants. The treaty was ratified by solemn oaths, and observed with mutual fidelity. The Gothic prince, with a small and select train, was admitted within the walls; he indulged himself in the refreshment of the bath, accepted a splendid banquet which was provided by the magistrate, and affected to show that he was not ignorant of the manners of civilised nations.[8] But the whole territory of Attica, from the promontory of Sunium to the town of Megara, was blasted by his baleful presence; and, if we may use the comparison of a contemporary philosopher, Athens itself resembled the bleeding and empty skin of a slaughtered victim. The distance between Megara and Corinth could not much exceed thirty miles; but the *bad road*, an expressive name, which it still bears among the Greeks, was, or might easily have been made, impassable for the march of an enemy. The thick and gloomy woods of Mount Cithæron covered the inland country; the Scironian rocks approached the water's edge, and hung over the narrow and winding path, which was confined above six miles along the sea-shore.[9] The passage of those rocks, so infamous in every age, was terminated by the isthmus of Corinth; and a small body of firm and intrepid soldiers might have successfully defended a temporary entrenchment of five or six miles from the Ionian to the Ægean Sea. The confidence of the cities of Peloponnesus in their natural rampart had tempted them to neglect the care of their antique walls; and the avarice of the Roman governors had exhausted and betrayed the unhappy province.[10] Corinth, Argos, Sparta, yielded without resistance to the arms of the Goths; and the most fortunate of the inhabitants were saved by death from beholding the slavery of their families and the conflagration of their cities.[11] The vases and statues were distributed among the barbarians, with more regard to the value of the materials than to the elegance of the workmanship; the female captives submitted to the laws of war; the enjoyment of beauty was the reward of valour; and the Greeks could not reasonably complain of an abuse which was justified by the example of the heroic times.[12] The descendants of that extraordinary people, who had considered valour and discipline as the walls of Sparta, no longer remembered the generous reply of their ancestors to an invader more formidable than Alaric. "If thou art a god, thou wilt not hurt those who have never injured thee; if thou art a man, advance—and thou wilt find men equal to thyself."[13] From Thermopylæ to Sparta the leader of the Goths pursued his victorious march without encountering any mortal antagonists; but one of the advocates of expiring Paganism has confidently asserted that the walls of Athens were guarded by the goddess Minerva, with her formidable Ægis, and by the angry phantom of Achilles,[14] and that the conqueror was dismayed by the presence of the hostile deities of Greece. In an age of miracles it would perhaps be unjust to dispute the claim of the historian Zosimus to the common benefit, yet it cannot be dissembled that the mind of Alaric was ill prepared to receive, either in sleeping or waking visions, the impressions of Greek superstition. The songs of Homer and the fame of Achilles had probably never reached the ear of the illiterate *barbarian*; and the *Christian* faith, which he had devoutly embraced, taught him to despise the imaginary deities of Rome and Athens. The invasion of the Goths, instead of vindicating the honours, contributed, at least accidently, to extirpate the last remains of Paganism; and the mysteries of Ceres, which had subsisted eighteen hundred years, did not survive the destruction of Eleusis and the calamities of Greece.[15]

The last hope of a people who could no longer depend on their arms, their gods, or their sovereign, was placed in the powerful assistance of the general of the West; and Stilicho, who had not been permitted to repulse, advanced to chastise the invaders of Greece.[16] A numerous fleet was equipped in the ports of Italy; and the troops, after a short and prosperous navigation over the Ionian Sea, were safely disembarked on the isthmus, near the ruins of Corinth. The woody and mountainous country of Arcadia, the fabulous residence of Pan and the Dryads, became the scene of a long and doubtful conflict between two generals not unworthy of each other. The skill and perseverance of the Roman at length prevailed; and the Goths, after sustaining a considerable loss from disease and desertion, gradually retreated to the lofty mountain of Pholoe, near the sources of the Peneus, and on the frontiers of Elis—a sacred country, which had formerly been exempted from the calamities of war.[17] The camp of the barbarians was immediately besieged; the waters of the river[18] were diverted into another channel; and while they laboured under the intolerable pressure of thirst and hunger, a strong line of circumvallation was formed to prevent their escape. After these precautions Stilicho, too confident of victory, retired to enjoy his triumph in the theatrical games and lascivious dances of the Greeks; his soldiers, deserting their standards, spread themselves over the country of their allies, which they stripped of all that had been saved from the rapacious hands of the enemy. Alaric appears to have seized the favourable moment to execute one of those hardy enterprises in which the abilities of a general are displayed with more genuine lustre than in the tumult of a day of battle. To extricate himself from the prison of Peloponnesus it was necessary that he should pierce the entrenchments which surrounded his camp; that he should perform a difficult and dangerous march of thirty miles, as far as the Gulf of Corinth; and that he should transport his troops, his captives, and his spoil, over an arm of the sea, which, in the narrow interval between Rhium and the opposite shore, is at least half a mile in breadth.[19] The operations of Alaric must have been secret, prudent, and rapid, since the Roman general was confounded by the intelligence that the Goths, who had eluded his efforts, were in full possession of the important province of Epirus. This unfortunate delay allowed Alaric sufficient time to conclude the treaty which he secretly negotiated with the ministers of Constantinople. The apprehension of a civil war compelled Stilicho to retire, at the haughty mandate of his rivals, from the dominions of Arcadius; and he respected, in the enemy of Rome, the honourable character of the ally and servant of the emperor of the East.

A Grecian philosopher,[20] who visited Constantinople soon after the death of Theodosius, published his liberal opinions concerning the duties of kings and the state of the Roman republic. Synesius observes and deplores the fatal abuse which the imprudent bounty of the late emperor had introduced into the military service. The citizens and subjects had purchased an exemption from the indispensable duty of defending their country, which was supported by the arms of barbarian mercenaries. The fugitives of Scythia were permitted to disgrace the illustrious dignities of the empire; their ferocious youth, who disdained the salutary restraint of laws, were more anxious to acquire the riches than to imitate the arts of a people the object of their contempt and hatred; and the power of the Goths was the stone of Tantalus, perpetually suspended over the peace and safety of the devoted state. The measures which Synesius recommends are the dictates of a bold and generous patriot. He exhorts the emperor to revive the courage of his subjects by the example of manly virtue; to banish luxury from the court and from the camp; to substitute, in the place of the barbarian mercenaries, an army of men interested in the defence of their laws and of their property; to force, in such a moment of public danger, the mechanic from his shop and the philosopher from his school; to rouse the indolent citizen from his dream of pleasure; and to arm, for the protection of agriculture, the hands of the laborious husbandman. At the head of such troops, who might deserve the name and would display the spirit of Romans, he animates the son of Theodosius to encounter a race of barbarians who were destitute of any real courage; and never to lay down his arms till he had chased them far away into the solitudes of Scythia, or had reduced them to the state of ignominious servitude which the Lacedæmonians formerly imposed on the captive Helots.[21] The court of Arcadius indulged the zeal, applauded the eloquence, and neglected the advice of Synesius. Perhaps the philosopher, who addresses the emperor of the East in the language of reason and virtue which he might have used to a Spartan king, had not condescended to form a practicable scheme, consistent with the temper and circumstances of a degenerate age. Perhaps the pride of the ministers, whose business was

seldom interrupted by reflection, might reject, as wild and visionary, every proposal which exceeded the measure of their capacity, and deviated from the forms and precedents of office. While the oration of Synesius and the downfall of the barbarians were the topics of popular conversation, an edict was published at Constantinople which declared the promotion of Alaric to the rank of master-general of the Eastern Illyricum. The Roman provincials, and the allies who had respected the faith of treaties, were justly indignant that the ruin of Greece and Epirus should be so liberally rewarded. The Gothic conqueror was received as a lawful magistrate in the cities which he had so lately besieged. The fathers whose sons he had massacred, the husbands whose wives he had violated, were subject to his authority; and the success of his rebellion encouraged the ambition of every leader of the foreign mercenaries. The use to which Alaric applied his new command distinguishes the firm and judicious character of his policy. He issued his orders to the four magazines and manufactures of offensive and defensive arms, Margus, Ratiaria, Naissus, and Thessalonica, to provide his troops with an extraordinary supply of shields, helmets, swords, and spears; the unhappy provincials were compelled to forge the instruments of their own destruction; and the barbarians removed the only defect which had sometimes disappointed the efforts of their courage.[22] The birth of Alaric, the glory of his past exploits, and the confidence in his future designs, insensibly united the body of the nation under his victorious standards; and, with the unanimous consent of the barbarian chieftains, the master-general of Illyricum was elevated, according to ancient custom, on a shield, and solemnly proclaimed king of the Visigoths.[23] Armed with this double power, seated on the verge of the two empires, he alternately sold his deceitful promises to the courts of Arcadius and Honorius,[24] till he declared and executed his resolution of invading the dominions of the West. The provinces of Europe which belonged to the Eastern emperor were already exhausted, those of Asia were inaccessible, and the strength of Constantinople had resisted his attack. But he was tempted by the fame, the beauty, the wealth of Italy, which he had twice visited; and he secretly aspired to plant the Gothic standard on the walls of Rome, and to enrich his army with the accumulated spoils of three hundred triumphs.[25]

The scarcity of facts,[26] and the uncertainty of dates,[27] oppose our attempts to describe the circumstances of the first invasion of Italy by the arms of Alaric. His march, perhaps from Thessalonica, through the warlike and hostile country of Pannonia, as far as the foot of the Julian Alps; his passage of those mountains, which were strongly guarded by troops and entrenchments; the siege of Aquileia, and the conquest of the provinces of Istria and Venetia, appear to have employed a considerable time. Unless his operations were extremely cautious and slow, the length of the interval would suggest a probable suspicion that the Gothic king retreated towards the banks of the Danube, and reinforced his army with fresh swarms of barbarians, before he again attempted to penetrate into the heart of Italy. Since the public and important events escape the diligence of the historian, he may amuse himself with contemplating for a moment the influence of the arms of Alaric on the fortunes of two obscure individuals, a presbyter of Aquileia, and an husbandman of Verona. The learned Rufinus, who was summoned by his enemies to appear before a Roman synod,[28] wisely preferred the dangers of a besieged city; and the barbarians, who furiously shook the walls of Aquileia, might save him from the cruel sentence of another heretic, who, at the request of the same bishops, was severely whipped and condemned to perpetual exile on a desert island.[29] The *old man*[30] who had passed his simple and innocent life in the neighbourhood of Verona, was a stranger to the quarrels both of kings and of bishops; *his* pleasures, his desires, his knowledge, were confined within the little circle of his paternal farm; and a staff supported his aged steps on the same ground where he had sported in his infancy. Yet even this humble and rustic felicity (which Claudian describes with so much truth and feeling) was still exposed to the undistinguishing rage of war. His trees, his old *contemporary* trees,[31] must blaze in the conflagration of the whole country; a detachment of Gothic cavalry might sweep away his cottage and his family; and the power of Alaric could destroy this happiness, which he was not able either to taste or to bestow. "Fame," says the poet, "encircling with terror her gloomy wings, proclaimed the march of the barbarian army, and filled Italy with consternation:" the apprehensions of each individual were increased in just proportion to the measure of his fortune: and the most timid, who had already embarked their valuable effects, meditated their escape to the island of Sicily or the African coast. The public distress was aggravated by the fears and reproaches of superstition.[32] Every hour pro-

duced some horrid tale of strange and portentous accidents: the Pagans deplored the neglect of omens and the interruption of sacrifices; but the Christians still derived some comfort from the powerful intercession of the saints and martyrs.[33]

The emperor Honorius was distinguished, above his subjects, by the pre-eminence of fear as well as of rank. The pride and luxury in which he was educated had not allowed him to suspect that there existed on the earth any power presumptuous enough to invade the repose of the successor of Augustus. The arts of flattery concealed the impending danger till Alaric approached the palace of Milan. But when the sound of war had awakened the young emperor, instead of flying to arms with the spirit, or even the rashness, of his age, he eagerly listened to those timid counsellors who proposed to convey his sacred person and his faithful attendants to some secure and distant station in the provinces of Gaul. Stilicho alone[34] had courage and authority to resist this disgraceful measure, which would have abandoned Rome and Italy to the barbarians; but as the troops of the palace had been lately detached to the Rhætian frontier, and as the resource of new levies was slow and precarious, the general of the West could only promise that, if the court of Milan would maintain their ground during his absence, he would soon return with an army equal to the encounter of the Gothic king. Without losing a moment (while each moment was so important to the public safety), Stilicho hastily embarked on the Larian lake, ascended the mountains of ice and snow amidst the severity of an Alpine winter, and suddenly repressed, by his unexpected presence, the enemy, who had disturbed the tranquillity of Rhætia.[35] The barbarians, perhaps some tribes of the Alemanni, respected the firmness of a chief who still assumed the language of command; and the choice which he condescended to make of a select number of their bravest youth was considered as a mark of his esteem and favour. The cohorts, who were delivered from the neighbouring foe, diligently repaired to the Imperial standard; and Stilicho issued his orders to the most remote troops of the West, to advance, by rapid marches, to the defence of Honorius and of Italy. The fortresses of the Rhine were abandoned; and the safety of Gaul was protected only by the faith of the Germans, and the ancient terror of the Roman name. Even the legion which had been stationed to guard the wall of Britain against the Caledonians of the North was hastily recalled;[36]

and a numerous body of the cavalry of the Alani was persuaded to engage in the service of the emperor, who anxiously expected the return of his general. The prudence and vigour of Stilicho were conspicuous on this occasion, which revealed, at the same time, the weakness of the falling empire. The legions of Rome, which had long since languished in the gradual decay of discipline and courage, were exterminated by the Gothic and civil wars; and it was found impossible without exhausting and exposing the provinces, to assemble an army for the defence of Italy.

When Stilicho seemed to abandon his sovereign in the unguarded palace of Milan, he had probably calculated the term of his absence, the distance of the enemy, and the obstacles that might retard their march. He principally depended on the rivers of Italy, the Adige, the Mincius, the Oglio, and the Addua, which, in the winter or spring, by the fall of rains, or by the melting of the snows, are commonly swelled into broad and impetuous torrents.[37] But the season happened to be remarkably dry; and the Goths could traverse, without impediment, the wide and stony beds, whose centre was faintly marked by the course of a shallow stream. The bridge and passage of the Addua was secured by a strong detachment of the Gothic army; and as Alaric approached the walls, or rather the suburbs, of Milan, he enjoyed the proud satisfaction of seeing the emperor of the Romans fly before him. Honorius, accompanied by a feeble train of statesmen and eunuchs, hastily retreated towards the Alps, with a design of securing his person in the city of Arles, which had often been the royal residence of his predecessors. But Honorius[38] had scarcely passed the Po before he was overtaken by the speed of the Gothic cavalry;[39] since the urgency of the danger compelled him to seek a temporary shelter within the fortification of Asta, a town of Liguria or Piemont, situate on the banks of the Tanarus.[40] The siege of an obscure place, which contained so rich a prize, and seemed incapable of a long resistance, was instantly formed, and indefatigably pressed, by the king of the Goths; and the bold declaration, which the emperor might afterwards make, that his breast had never been susceptible of fear, did not probably obtain much credit even in his own court.[41] In the last and almost hopeless extremity, after the barbarians had already proposed the indignity of a capitulation, the Imperial captive was suddenly relieved by the fame, the approach, and at length the presence, of the hero whom he had

so long expected. At the head of a chosen and intrepid vanguard, Stilicho swam the stream of the Addua, to gain the time which he must have lost in the attack of the bridge; the passage of the Po was an enterprise of much less hazard and difficulty; and the successful action, in which he cut his way through the Gothic camp under the walls of Asta, revived the hopes and vindicated the honour of Rome. Instead of grasping the fruit of his victory, the barbarian was gradually invested, on every side, by the troops of the West, who successively issued through all the passes of the Alps; his quarters were straitened; his convoys were intercepted; and the vigilance of the Romans prepared to form a chain of fortifications, and to besiege the lines of the besiegers. A military council was assembled of the long-haired chiefs of the Gothic nation; of aged warriors, whose bodies were wrapped in furs, and whose stern countenances were marked with honourable wounds. They weighed the glory of persisting in their attempt against the advantage of securing their plunder; and they recommended the prudent measure of a seasonable retreat. In this important debate, Alaric displayed the spirit of the conqueror of Rome; and after he had reminded his countrymen of their achievements and of their designs, he concluded his animating speech by the solemn and positive assurance that he was resolved to find in Italy either a kingdom or a grave.[42]

The loose discipline of the barbarians always exposed them to the danger of a surprise; but, instead of choosing the dissolute hours of riot and intemperance, Stilicho resolved to attack the *Christian* Goths whilst they were devoutly employed in celebrating the festival of Easter.[43] The execution of the stratagem, or, as it was termed by the clergy, of the sacrilege, was intrusted to Saul, a barbarian and a Pagan, who had served, however, with distinguished reputation among the veteran generals of Theodosius. The camp of the Goths, which Alaric had pitched in the neighbourhood of Pollentia,[44] was thrown into confusion by the sudden and impetuous charge of the Imperial cavalry; but, in a few moments, the undaunted genius of their leader gave them an order and a field of battle; and, soon as they had recovered from their astonishment, the pious confidence that the God of the Christians would assert their cause added new strength to their native valour. In this engagement, which was long maintained with equal courage and success, the chief of the Alani, whose diminutive and savage form concealed a magnanimous soul, approved his suspected loyalty, by the zeal with which he fought and fell in the service of the republic; and the fame of this gallant barbarian has been imperfectly preserved in the verses of Claudian, since the poet, who celebrates his virtue, has omitted the mention of his name. His death was followed by the flight and dismay of the squadrons which he commanded; and the defeat of the wing of cavalry might have decided the victory of Alaric, if Stilicho had not immediately led the Roman and barbarian infantry to the attack. The skill of the general, and the bravery of the soldiers, surmounted every obstacle. In the evening of the bloody day, the Goths retreated from the field of battle; the entrenchments of their camp were forced, and the scene of rapine and slaughter made some atonement for the calamities which they had inflicted on the subjects of the empire.[45] The magnificent spoils of Corinth and Argos enriched the veterans of the West; the captive wife of Alaric, who had impatiently claimed his promise of Roman jewels and Patrician handmaids,[46] was reduced to implore the mercy of the insulting foe; and many thousand prisoners, released from the Gothic chains, dispersed through the provinces of Italy the praises of their heroic deliverer. The triumph of Stilicho[47] was compared by the poet, and perhaps by the public, to that of Marius; who, in the same part of Italy, had encountered and destroyed another army of Northern barbarians. The huge bones and the empty helmets of the Cimbri and of the Goths would easily be confounded by succeeding generations; and posterity might erect a common trophy to the memory of the two most illustrious generals, who had vanquished, on the same memorable ground, the two most formidable enemies of Rome.[48]

The eloquence of Claudian[49] has celebrated, with lavish applause, the victory of Pollentia, one of the most glorious days in the life of his patron; but his reluctant and partial muse bestows more genuine praise on the character of the Gothic king. His name is, indeed, branded with the reproachful epithets of pirate and robber, to which the conquerors of every age are so justly entitled; but the poet of Stilicho is compelled to acknowledge that Alaric possessed the invincible temper of mind which rises superior to every misfortune, and derives new resources from adversity. After the total defeat of his infantry, he escaped, or rather withdrew, from the field of battle, with the greatest part of his cavalry entire and unbroken. Without wasting a moment to lament the irreparable loss of so many brave companions, he left his victorious enemy to bind in chains the captive images of a Gothic king;[50] and boldly resolved to break through the unguarded passes of the Apennine, to spread desolation over the fruitful face of Tuscany, and to conquer or die before the gates of Rome. The capital was saved by the active and incessant diligence of Stilicho; but he respected the despair of his enemy; and, instead of committing the fate of the republic to the chance of another battle, he proposed to purchase the absence of the barbarians. The spirit of Alaric would have rejected such terms, the permission of a retreat, and the offer of a pension, with contempt and indignation; but he exercised a limited and precarious authority over the independent chieftains who had raised him, for *their* service, above the rank of his equals; they were still less disposed to follow an unsuccessful general, and many of them were tempted to consult their interest by a private negotiation with the minister of Honorius. The king submitted to the voice of his people, ratified the treaty with the empire of the West, and repassed the Po with the remains of the flourishing army which he had led into Italy. A considerable part of the Roman forces still continued to attend his motions: and Stilicho, who maintained a secret correspondence with some of the barbarian chiefs, was punctually appraised of the designs that were formed in the camp and council of Alaric. The king of the Goths, ambitious to signalise his retreat by some splendid achievement, had resolved to occupy the important city of Verona, which commands the principal passage of the Rhætian Alps; and, directing his march through the territories of those German tribes whose alliance would restore his exhausted strength, to invade, on the side of the Rhine, the wealthy and unsuspecting provinces of Gaul. Ignorant of the treason which had already betrayed his bold and judicious enterprise, he advanced towards the passes of the mountains, already possessed by the Imperial troops; where he was exposed, almost at the same instant, to a general attack in the front, on his flanks, and in the rear. In this bloody action, at a small distance from the walls of Verona, the loss of the Goths was not less heavy than that which they had sustained in the defeat of Pollentia; and their valiant king, who escaped by the swiftness of his horse, must either have been slain or made prisoner, if the hasty rashness of the Alani had not disappointed the measures of the Roman general. Alaric secured the remains of his army on the adjacent rocks; and prepared himself, with undaunted resolution, to maintain a siege against the superior numbers of the enemy, who invested him on all sides. But he could not oppose the destructive progress of hunger and disease; nor was it possible for him to check the continual desertion of his impatient and capricious barbarians. In this extremity he still found resources in his own courage, or in the moderation of his adversary; and the retreat of the Gothic king was considered as the deliverance of Italy.[51] Yet the people, and even the clergy, incapable of forming any rational judgment of the business of peace and war, presumed to arraign the policy of Stilicho, who so often vanquished, so often surrounded, and so often dismissed the implacable enemy of the republic. The first moment of the public safety is devoted to gratitude and joy; but the second is diligently occupied by envy and calumny.[52]

The citizens of Rome had been astonished by the approach of Alaric; and the diligence with which they laboured to restore the walls of the capital confessed their own fears, and the decline of the empire. After the retreat of the barbarians, Honorius was directed to accept the dutiful invitation of the senate, and to celebrate, in the Imperial city, the auspicious era of the Gothic victory, and of his sixth consulship.[53] The suburbs and the streets, from the Milvian bridge to the Palatine mount, were filled by the Roman people, who, in the space of an hundred years, had only thrice been honoured with the presence of their sovereigns. While their eyes were fixed on the chariot where Stilicho was deservedly seated by the side of his royal pupil, they applauded the pomp of a triumph which was not stained, like that of Constantine or of Theodosius, with civil blood. The procession passed under a lofty arch, which had been purposely erected: but in less than seven years, the Gothic conquerors of Rome might read, if they were able to read, the superb inscription of that monument, which attested the total defeat and destruction of their nation.[54] The emperor resided several months in the capital, and every part of his behaviour was regulated with care to conciliate the affection of the clergy, the senate, and the people of Rome. The clergy was edified by his frequent visits, and liberal gifts, to the shrines of the apostles. The senate, who, in the triumphal procession, had been excused from the humiliating ceremony of preceding on foot the Imperial chariot, was treated with the decent reverence which Stilicho always affected for that assembly. The people was repeatedly gratified by the attention and courtesy of Honorius in the public games, which were celebrated on that occasion with a magnificence not unworthy of the spectator. As soon as the appointed number of chariot-races was concluded, the decoration of the circus was suddenly changed; the hunting of wild beasts afforded a various and splendid entertainment; and the chase was succeeded by a military dance, which seems, in the lively description of Claudian, to present the image of a modern tournament.

In these games of Honorius, the inhuman combats of gladiators[55] polluted for the last time the amphitheatre of Rome. The first Christian emperor may claim the honour of the first edict which condemned the art and amusement of shedding human blood;[56] but this benevolent law expressed the wishes of the prince, without reforming an inveterate abuse which degraded a civilised nation below the condition of savage cannibals. Several hundred, perhaps several thousand, victims were annually slaughtered in the great cities of the empire; and the month of December, more peculiarly devoted to the combats of gladiators, still exhibited to the eyes of the Roman people a grateful spectacle of blood and cruelty. Amidst the general joy of the victory of Pollentia, a Christian poet exhorted the emperor to extirpate, by his authority, the horrid custom which had so long resisted the voice of humanity and religion.[57] The pathetic representations of Prudentius were less effectual than the generous boldness of Telemachus, an Asiatic monk, whose death was more useful to mankind than his life.[58] The Romans were provoked by the interruption of their pleasures; and the rash monk, who had descended into the arena, to separate the gladiators, was overwhelmed under a shower of stones. But the madness of the people soon subsided: they respected the memory of Telemachus, who had deserved the honours of martyrdom; and they submitted, without a murmur, to the laws of Honorius, which abolished for ever the human sacrifices of the amphitheatre. The citizens, who adhered to the manners of their ancestors, might perhaps insinuate that the last remains of a martial spirit were preserved in this school of fortitude, which accustomed the Romans to the sight of blood, and to the contempt of death: a vain and cruel prejudice, so nobly confuted by the valour of ancient Greece and of modern Europe![59]

The recent danger to which the person of the emperor had been exposed in the defenceless palace of Milan urged him to seek a retreat in some inaccessible fortress of Italy, where he might securely remain, while the open country was covered by a deluge of barbarians. On the coast of the Hadriatic, about ten or twelve miles from the most southern of the seven mouths of the Po, the Thessalians had founded the ancient colony of RAVENNA,[60] which they afterwards resigned to the natives of Umbria. Augustus, who had observed the opportunity of the place, prepared, at the distance of three miles from the old town, a capacious harbour for the reception of two hundred and fifty ships of war. This naval establishment, which included the arsenals and magazines, the barracks of the troops, and the houses of the artificers, derived its origin and name from the permanent station of the Roman fleet; the intermediate space was soon filled with buildings and inhabitants, and the three extensive and populous quarters of Ravenna gradually contributed to form one of the most important cities of Italy. The principal canal of Augustus poured a copious stream of the waters of the Po through the midst of the city, to the entrance of the harbour; the same waters were introduced into the profound ditches that encompassed the walls; they were distributed by a thousand subordinate canals into every part of the city, which they divided into a variety of small islands; the communication was maintained only by the use of boats and bridges; and the houses of Ravenna, whose appearance may be compared to that of Venice, were raised on the foundation of wooden piles. The adjacent country, to the distance of many miles, was a deep and impassable morass; and the artificial causeway which connected Ravenna with the continent might be easily guarded or destroyed on the approach of an hostile army. These morasses were interspersed, however, with vineyards; and though the soil was exhausted by four or five crops, the town enjoyed a more plentiful supply of wine than of fresh water.[61] The air, instead of receiving the sickly and almost pestilential exhalations of low and marshy grounds, was distinguished, like the neighbourhood of Alexandria, as uncommonly pure and salubrious; and this singular advantage was ascribed to the regular tides of the Hadriatic, which swept the canals, interrupted the unwholesome stagnation of the waters, and floated, every day, the vessels of the adjacent country into the heart of Ravenna. The gradual retreat of the sea has left the modern city at the distance of four miles from the Hadriatic, and as early as the fifth or sixth century of the Christian era the port of Augustus was converted into pleasant orchards, and a lonely grove of pines covered the ground where the Roman fleet once rode at anchor.[62] Even this alteration contrib-

uted to increase the natural strength of the place, and the shallowness of the water was a sufficient barrier against the large ships of the enemy. This advantageous situation was fortified by art and labour; and in the twentieth year of his age the emperor of the West, anxious only for his personal safety, retired to the perpetual confinement of the walls and morasses of Ravenna. The example of Honorius was imitated by his feeble successors, the Gothic kings, and afterwards the Exarchs, who occupied the throne and palace of the emperors; and till the middle of the eighth century Ravenna was considered as the seat of government and the capital of Italy.[63]

The fears of Honorius were not without foundation, nor were his precautions without effect. While Italy rejoiced in her deliverance from the Goths, a furious tempest was excited among the nations of Germany, who yielded to the irresistible impulse that appears to have been gradually communicated from the eastern extremity of the continent of Asia. The Chinese annals, as they have been interpreted by the learned industry of the present age, may be usefully applied to reveal the secret and remote causes of the fall of the Roman empire. The extensive territory to the north of the great wall was possessed after the flight of the Huns by the victorious Sienpi; who were sometimes broken into independent tribes, and sometimes re-united under a supreme chief; till at length, styling themselves *Topa*, or masters of the earth, they acquired a more solid consistence and a more formidable power. The Topa soon compelled the pastoral nations of the eastern desert to acknowledge the superiority of their arms; they invaded China in a period of weakness and intestine discord; and these fortunate Tartars, adopting the laws and manners of the vanquished people, founded an Imperial dynasty, which reigned near one hundred and sixty years over the northern provinces of the monarchy. Some generations before they ascended the throne of China, one of the Topa princes had enlisted in his cavalry a slave of the name of Moko, renowned for his valour, but who was tempted, by the fear of punishment, to desert his standard, and to range the desert at the head of an hundred followers. This gang of robbers and outlaws swelled into a camp, a tribe, a numerous people, distinguished by the appellation of *Geougen*; and their hereditary chieftains, the posterity of Moko the slave, assumed their rank among the Scythian monarchs. The youth of Toulun, the greatest of his descendants, was exercised by those misfortunes which are the school of heroes. He bravely struggled with adversity, broke the imperious yoke of the Topa, and became the legislator of his nation and the conqueror of Tartary. His troops were distributed into regular bands of an hundred and of a thousand men; cowards were stoned to death; the most splendid honours were proposed as the reward of valour; and Toulun, who had knowledge enough to despise the learning of China, adopted only such arts and institutions as were favourable to the military spirit of his government. His tents, which he removed in the winter season to a more southern latitude, were pitched during the summer on the fruitful banks of the Selinga. His conquests stretched from Corea far beyond the river Irtish. He vanquished, in the country to the north of the Caspian sea, the nation of the *Huns*; and the new title of *Khan*, or *Cagan*, expressed the fame and power which he derived from this memorable victory.[64]

The chain of events is interrupted, or rather is concealed, as it passes from the Volga to the Vistula, through the dark interval which separates the extreme limits of the Chinese and of the Roman geography. Yet the temper of the barbarians, and the experience of successive emigrations, sufficiently declare that the Huns, who were oppressed by the arms of the Geougen, soon withdrew from the presence of an insulting victor. The countries towards the Euxine were already occupied by their kindred tribes; and their hasty flight, which they soon converted into a bold attack, would more naturally be directed towards the rich and level plains through which the Vistula gently flows into the Baltic sea. The North must again have been alarmed and agitated by the invasion of the Huns; and the nations who retreated before them must have pressed with incumbent weight on the confines of Germany.[65] The inhabitants of those regions which the ancients have assigned to the Suevi, the Vandals, and the Burgundians, might embrace the resolution of abandoning to the fugitives of Sarmatia their woods and morasses, or at least discharging their superfluous numbers on the provinces of the Roman empire.[66] About four years after the victorious Toulun had assumed the title of Khan of the Geougen, another barbarian, the haughty Rhodogast, or Radagaisus,[67] marched from the northern extremities of Germany almost to the gates of Rome, and left the remains of his army to achieve the destruction of the West. The Vandals, the Suevi, and the Burgundians, formed the strength of this mighty host; but the

Alani, who had found an hospitable reception in their new seats, added their active cavalry to the heavy infantry of the Germans; and the Gothic adventurers crowded so eagerly to the standard of Radagaisus, that, by some historians, he has been styled the King of the Goths. Twelve thousand warriors, distinguished above the vulgar by their noble birth or their valiant deeds, glittered in the van;[68] and the whole multitude, which was not less than two hundred thousand fighting men, might be increased, by the accession of women, of children, and of slaves, to the amount of four hundred thousand persons. This formidable emigration issued from the same coast of the Baltic which had poured forth the myriads of the Cimbri and Teutones to assault Rome and Italy in the vigour of the republic. After the departure of those barbarians, their native country, which was marked by the vestiges of their greatness, long ramparts and gigantic moles,[69] remained, during some ages, a vast and dreary solitude; till the human species was renewed by the powers of generation, and the vacancy was filled by the influx of new inhabitants. The nations who now usurp an extent of land which they are unable to cultivate would soon be assisted by the industrious poverty of their neighbours, if the government of Europe did not protect the claims of dominion and property.

The correspondence of nations was in that age so imperfect and precarious, that the revolutions of the North might escape the knowledge of the court of Ravenna, till the dark cloud, which was collected along the coast of the Baltic, burst in thunder upon the banks of the Upper Danube. The emperor of the West, if his ministers disturbed his amusements by the news of the impending danger, was satisfied with being the occasion and the spectator of the war.[70] The safety of Rome was intrusted to the counsels and the sword of Stilicho; but such was the feeble and exhausted state of the empire, that it was impossible to restore the fortifications of the Danube, or to prevent by a vigorous effort the invasion of the Germans.[71] The hopes of the vigilant minister of Honorius were confined to the defence of Italy. He once more abandoned the provinces, recalled the troops, pressed the new levies, which were rigorously exacted and pusillanimously eluded; employed the most efficacious means to arrest or allure the deserters; and offered the gift of freedom and of two pieces of gold to all the slaves who would enlist.[72] By these efforts he painfully collected from the subjects of a great empire an army of thirty or forty thousand men, which in the days of Scipio or Camillus, would have been instantly furnished by the free citizens of the territory of Rome.[73] The thirty legions of Stilicho were reinforced by a large body of barbarian auxiliaries; the faithful Alani were personally attached to his service; and the troops of Huns and of Goths, who marched under the banners of their native princes Huldin and Sarus, were animated by interest and resentment to oppose the ambition of Radagaisus. The king of the confederate Germans passed without resistance the Alps, the Po, and the Apennine; leaving on one hand the inaccessible palace of Honorius securely buried among the marshes of Ravenna, and, on the other, the camp of Stilicho, who had fixed his head-quarters at Ticinum, or Pavia, but who seems to have avoided a decisive battle till he had assembled his distant forces. Many cities of Italy were pillaged or destroyed; and the siege of Florence[74] by Radagaisus is one of the earliest events in the history of that celebrated republic, whose firmness checked and delayed the unskilful fury of the barbarians. The senate and people trembled at their approach within an hundred and eighty miles of Rome, and anxiously compared the danger which they had escaped with the new perils to which they were exposed. Alaric was a Christian and a soldier, the leader of a disciplined army; who understood the laws of war, who respected the sanctity of treaties, and who had familiarly conversed with the subjects of the empire in the same camps and the same churches. The savage Radagaisus was a stranger to the manners, the religion, and even the language of the civilised nations of the South. The fierceness of his temper was exasperated by cruel superstition; and it was universally believed that he had bound himself by a solemn vow to reduce the city into a heap of stones and ashes, and to sacrifice the most illustrious of the Roman senators on the altars of those gods who were appeased by human blood. The public danger, which should have reconciled all domestic animosities, displayed the incurable madness of religious faction. The oppressed votaries of Jupiter and Mercury respected, in the implacable enemy of Rome, the character of a devout Pagan; loudly declared that they were more apprehensive of the sacrifices than of the arms of Radagaisus; and secretly rejoiced in the calamities of their country, which condemned the faith of their Christian adversaries.[75]

Florence was reduced to the last extremity; and the fainting courage of the citizens was sup-ported only by the authority of St. Ambrose, who had communicated in a dream the promise of a speedy deliverance.[76] On a sudden they beheld from their walls the banners of Stilicho, who advanced with his united force to the relief of the faithful city, and who soon marked that fatal spot for the grave of the barbarian host. The apparent contradictions of those writers who variously relate the defeat of Radagaisus, may be reconciled without offering much violence to their respective testimonies. Orosius and Augustin, who were intimately connected by friendship and religion, ascribe this miraculous victory to the providence of God rather than to the valour of man.[77] They strictly exclude every idea of chance, or even of bloodshed, and positively affirm that the Romans, whose camp was the scene of plenty and idleness, enjoyed the distress of the barbarians slowly expiring on the sharp and barren ridge of the hills of Fæsulæ, which rise above the city of Florence. Their extravagant assertion that not a single soldier of the Christian army was killed, or even wounded, may be dismissed with silent contempt; but the rest of the narrative of Augustin and Orosius is consistent with the state of the war and the character of Stilicho. Conscious that he commanded the *last* army of the republic, his prudence would not expose it in the open field to the headstrong fury of the Germans. The method of surrounding the enemy with strong lines of circumvallation, which he had twice employed against the Gothic king, was repeated on a larger scale and with more considerable effect. The examples of Cæsar must have been familiar to the most illiterate of the Roman warriors; and the fortifications of Dyrrachium, which connected twenty-four castles by a perpetual ditch and rampart of fifteen miles, afforded the model of an entrenchment which might confine and starve the most numerous host of barbarians.[78] The Roman troops had less degenerated from the industry than from the valour of their ancestors; and if the servile and laborious work offended the pride of the soldiers, Tuscany could supply many thousand peasants who would labour, though perhaps they would not fight, for the salvation of their native country. The imprisoned multitude of horses and men[79] was gradually destroyed by famine rather than by the sword; but the Romans were exposed during the progress of such an extensive work to the frequent attacks of an impatient enemy. The despair of the hungry barbarians would precipitate them against the fortifications of Stilicho; the general might

sometimes indulge the ardour of his brave auxiliaries, who eagerly pressed to assault the camp
of the Germans; and these various incidents
might produce the sharp and bloody conflicts
which dignify the narrative of Zosimus and the
Chronicles of Prosper and Marcellinus.[80] A
seasonable supply of men and provisions had
been introduced into the walls of Florence, and
the famished host of Radagaisus was in its turn
besieged. The proud monarch of so many warlike nations, after the loss of his bravest warriors, was reduced to confide either in the faith
of a capitulation, or in the clemency of Stilicho.[81] But the death of the royal captive, who
was ignominiously beheaded, disgraced the triumph of Rome and of Christianity; and the
short delay of his execution was sufficient to
brand the conqueror with the guilt of cool and
deliberate cruelty.[82] The famished Germans
who escaped the fury of the auxiliaries were sold
as slaves, at the contemptible price of as many
single pieces of gold; but the difference of food
and climate swept away great numbers of those
unhappy strangers; and it was observed that the
inhuman purchasers, instead of reaping the
fruits of their labour, were soon obliged to provide the expense of their interment. Stilicho informed the emperor and the senate of his success, and deserved a second time the glorious
title of Deliverer of Italy.[83]

The fame of the victory, and more especially
of the miracle, has encouraged a vain persuasion that the whole army, or rather nation, of
Germans who migrated from the shores of the
Baltic miserably perished under the walls of
Florence. Such indeed was the fate of Radagaisus himself, of his brave and faithful companions, and of more than one-third of the various
multitude of Sueves and Vandals, of Alani and
Burgundians, who adhered to the standard of
their general.[84] The union of such an army
might excite our surprise, but the causes of separation are obvious and forcible: the pride of
birth, the insolence of valour, the jealousy of
command, the impatience of subordination,
and the obstinate conflict of opinions, of interests, and of passions, among so many kings and
warriors, who were untaught to yield or to
obey. After the defeat of Radagaisus, two parts
of the German host, which must have exceeded
the number of one hundred thousand men, still
remained in arms between the Apennine and
the Alps, or between the Alps and the Danube.
It is uncertain whether they attempted to revenge the death of their general; but their irregular fury was soon diverted by the prudence

and firmness of Stilicho, who opposed their
march and facilitated their retreat, who considered the safety of Rome and Italy as the great
object of his care, and who sacrificed with too
much indifference the wealth and tranquillity
of the distant provinces.[85] The barbarians acquired, from the junction of some Pannonian
deserters, the knowledge of the country and of
the roads, and the invasion of Gaul, which
Alaric had designed, was executed by the remains of the great army of Radagaisus.[86]

Yet if they expected to derive any assistance
from the tribes of Germany who inhabited the
banks of the Rhine, their hopes were disappointed. The Alemanni preserved a state of inactive neutrality, and the Franks distinguished
their zeal and courage in the defence of the
empire. In the rapid progress down the Rhine
which was the first act of the administration of
Stilicho, he had applied himself with peculiar
attention to secure the alliance of the warlike
Franks, and to remove the irreconcilable enemies of peace and of the republic. Marcomir,
one of their kings, was publicly convicted before the tribunal of the Roman magistrate of
violating the faith of treaties. He was sentenced
to a mild but distant exile in the province of
Tuscany; and this degradation of the regal dignity was so far from exciting the resentment of
his subjects, that they punished with death the
turbulent Sunno, who attempted to revenge
his brother, and maintained a dutiful allegiance
to the princes who were established on the
throne by the choice of Stilicho.[87] When the
limits of Gaul and Germany were shaken by the
northern emigration, the Franks bravely encountered the single force of the Vandals, who,
regardless of the lessons of adversity, had again
separated their troops from the standard of their
barbarian allies. They paid the penalty of their
rashness; and twenty thousand Vandals, with
their king Godigisclus, were slain in the field of
battle. The whole people must have been extirpated if the squadrons of the Alani, advancing
to their relief, had not trampled down the infantry of the Franks, who, after an honourable
resistance, were compelled to relinquish the unequal contest. The victorious confederates pursued their march, and on the last day of the
year, in a season when the waters of the Rhine
were most probably frozen, they entered without opposition the defenceless provinces of Gaul.
This memorable passage of the Suevi, the Vandals, the Alani, and the Burgundians, who never afterwards retreated, may be considered as
the fall of the Roman empire in the countries

beyond the Alps; and the barriers, which had so long separated the savage and the civilised nations of the earth, were from that fatal moment levelled with the ground.[88]

While the peace of Germany was secured by the attachment of the Franks and the neutrality of the Alemanni, the subjects of Rome, unconscious of their approaching calamities, enjoyed the state of quiet and prosperity which had seldom blessed the frontiers of Gaul. Their flocks and herds were permitted to graze in the pastures of the barbarians; their huntsmen penetrated, without fear or danger, into the darkest recesses of the Hercynian wood.[89] The banks of the Rhine were crowned, like those of the Tiber, with elegant houses and well-cultivated farms; and if a poet descended the river, he might express his doubt on which side was situated the territory of the Romans.[90] This scene of peace and plenty was suddenly changed into a desert; and the prospect of the smoking ruins could alone distinguish the solitude of nature from the desolation of man. The flourishing city of Mentz was surprised and destroyed, and many thousand Christians were inhumanly massacred in the church. Worms perished after a long and obstinate siege; Strasburg, Spires, Rheims, Tournay, Arras, Amiens, experienced the cruel oppression of the German yoke; and the consuming flames of war spread from the banks of the Rhine over the greatest part of the seventeen provinces of Gaul. That rich and extensive country, as far as the ocean, the Alps, and the Pyrenees, was delivered to the barbarians, who drove before them in a promiscuous crowd the bishop, the senator, and the virgin, laden with the spoils of their houses and altars.[91] The ecclesiastics, to whom we are indebted for this vague description of the public calamities, embraced the opportunity of exhorting the Christians to repent of the sins which had provoked the Divine Justice, and to renounce the perishable goods of a wretched and deceitful world. But as the Pelagian controversy,[92] which attempts to sound the abyss of grace and predestination, soon became the serious employment of the Latin clergy, the Providence which had decreed, or foreseen, or permitted, such a train of moral and natural evils, was rashly weighed in the imperfect and fallacious balance of reason. The crimes and the misfortunes of the suffering people were presumptuously compared with those of their ancestors, and they arraigned the Divine Justice, which did not exempt from the common destruction, the feeble, the guiltless, the infant portion of the human species. These idle disputants overlooked the invariable laws of nature, which have connected peace with innocence, plenty with industry, and safety with valour. The timid and selfish policy of the court of Ravenna might recall the Palatine legions for the protection of Italy; the remains of the stationary troops might be unequal to the arduous task; and the barbarian auxiliaries might prefer the unbounded licence of spoil to the benefits of a moderate and regular stipend. But the provinces of Gaul were filled with a numerous race of hardy and robust youth, who, in the defence of their houses, their families, and their altars, if they had dared to die, would have deserved to vanquish. The knowledge of their native country would have enabled them to oppose continual and insuperable obstacles to the progress of an invader; and the deficiency of the barbarians in arms as well as in discipline removed the only pretence which excuses the submission of a populous country to the inferior numbers of a veteran army. When France was invaded by Charles the Fifth, he inquired of a prisoner how many *days* Paris might be distant from the frontier; "Perhaps *twelve*, but they will be days of battle:"[93] such was the gallant answer which checked the arrogance of that ambitious prince. The subjects of Honorius and those of Francis I. were animated by a very different spirit; and in less than two years the divided troops of the savages of the Baltic, whose numbers, were they fairly stated, would appear contemptible, advanced without a combat to the foot of the Pyrenæan mountains.

In the early part of the reign of Honorius, the vigilance of Stilicho had successfully guarded the remote island of Britain from her incessant enemies of the ocean, the mountains, and the Irish coast.[94] But those restless barbarians could not neglect the fair opportunity of the Gothic war, when the walls and stations of the province were stripped of the Roman troops. If any of the legionaries were permitted to return from the Italian expedition, their faithful report of the court and character of Honorius must have tended to dissolve the bounds of allegiance, and to exasperate the seditious temper of the British army. The spirit of revolt, which had formerly disturbed the age of Gallienus, was revived by the capricious violence of the soldiers; and the unfortunate, perhaps the ambitious, candidates, who were the objects of their choice, were the instruments, and at length the victims, of their passion.[95] Marcus was the first whom they placed on the throne, as the lawful emperor of Britain and of the West. They violated, by the hasty murder of Marcus, the oath of fidelity which they had imposed on themselves; and *their* disapprobation of his manners may seem to inscribe an honourable epitaph on his tomb. Gratian was the next whom they adorned with the diadem and the purple; and, at the end of four months, Gratian experienced the fate of his predecessor. The memory of the great Constantine, whom the British legions had given to the church and to the empire, suggested the singular motive of their third choice. They discovered in the ranks a private soldier of the name of Constantine, and their impetuous levity had already seated him on the throne, before they perceived his incapacity to sustain the weight of that glorious appellation.[96] Yet the authority of Constantine was less precarious, and his government was more successful, than the transient reigns of Marcus and of Gratian. The danger of leaving his inactive troops in those camps which had been twice polluted with blood and sedition urged him to attempt the reduction of the Western provinces. He landed at Boulogne with an inconsiderable force; and after he had reposed himself some days, he summoned the cities of Gaul, which had escaped the yoke of the barbarians, to acknowledge their lawful sovereign. They obeyed the summons without reluctance. The neglect of the court of Ravenna had absolved a deserted people from the duty of allegiance; their actual distress encouraged them to accept any circumstances of change, without apprehension, and, perhaps, with some degree of hope; and they might flatter themselves that the troops, the authority, and even the name of a Roman emperor, who fixed his residence in Gaul, would protect the unhappy country from the rage of the barbarians. The first successes of Constantine against the detached parties of the Germans were magnified by the voice of adulation into splendid and decisive victories, which the reunion and insolence of the enemy soon reduced to their just value. His negotiations procured a short and precarious truce; and if some tribes of the barbarians were engaged, by the liberality of his gifts and promises, to undertake the defence of the Rhine, these expensive and uncertain treaties, instead of restoring the pristine vigour of the Gallic frontier, served only to disgrace the majesty of the prince, and to exhaust what yet remained of the treasures of the republic. Elated however with this imaginary triumph, the vain deliverer of Gaul advanced into the provinces of the South, to encounter a more pressing and personal danger. Sarus the Goth was ordered to lay the head of the rebel at the feet of the emperor Honorius; and the forces of Britain and Italy were unworthily consumed in this domestic quarrel. After the loss of his two bravest generals, Justinian and Nevigastes, the former of whom was slain in the field of battle, the latter in a peaceful but treacherous interview, Constantine fortified himself within the walls of Vienna. The place was ineffectually attacked seven days; and the Imperial army supported, in a precipitate retreat, the ignominy of purchasing a secure passage from the freebooters and outlaws of the Alps.[97] Those mountains now separated the dominions of two rival monarchs: and the fortifications of the double frontier were guarded by the troops of the empire, whose arms would have been more usefully employed to maintain the Roman limits against the barbarians of Germany and Scythia.

On this side of the Pyrenees, the ambition of Constantine might be justified by the proximity of danger; but his throne was soon established by the conquest, or rather submission, of Spain, which yielded to the influence of regular and habitual subordination, and received the laws and magistrates of the Gallic præfecture. The only opposition which was made to the authority of Constantine proceeded not so much from the powers of government, or the spirit of the people, as from the private zeal and interest of the family of Theodosius. Four brothers[98] had obtained, by the favour of their kinsman, the deceased emperor, an honourable rank, and ample possessions, in their native country; and the grateful youths resolved to risk those advantages in the service of his son. After an unsuccessful effort to maintain their ground at the head of the stationary troops of Lusitania, they retired to their estates; where they armed and levied, at their own expense, a considerable body of slaves and dependents, and boldly marched to occupy the strong posts of the Pyrenæan mountains. This domestic insurrection alarmed and perplexed the sovereign of Gaul and Britain; and he was compelled to negotiate with some troops of barbarian auxiliaries, for the service of the Spanish war. They were distinguished by the title of *Honorarians*;[99] a name which might have reminded them of their fidelity to their lawful sovereign; and if it should candidly be allowed that the *Scots* were influenced by any partial affection for a British prince, the *Moors* and the *Marcomanni* could be tempted only by the profuse liberality of the usurper, who distributed among the barbarians the military, and even the civil, honours of

Spain. The nine bands of *Honorians*, which may be easily traced on the establishment of the Western empire, could not exceed the number of five thousand men; yet this inconsiderable force was sufficient to terminate a war which had threatened the power and safety of Constantine. The rustic army of the Theodosian family was surrounded and destroyed in the Pyrenees: two of the brothers had the good fortune to escape by sea to Italy or the East; the other two, after an interval of suspense, were executed at Arles; and if Honorius could remain insensible of the public disgrace, he might perhaps be affected by the personal misfortunes of his generous kinsmen. Such were the feeble arms which decided the possession of the Western provinces of Europe, from the wall of Antoninus to the Columns of Hercules. The events of peace and war have undoubtedly been diminished by the narrow and imperfect view of the historians of the times, who were equally ignorant of the causes and of the effects of the most important revolutions. But the total decay of the national strength had annihilated even the last resource of a despotic government; and the revenue of exhausted provinces could no longer purchase the military service of a discontented and pusillanimous people.

The poet, whose flattery has ascribed to the Roman eagle the victories of Pollentia and Verona, pursues the hasty retreat of Alaric from the confines of Italy, with a horrid train of imaginary spectres, such as might hover over an army of barbarians which was almost exterminated by war, famine, and disease.[100] In the course of this unfortunate expedition, the king of the Goths must indeed have sustained a considerable loss; and his harassed forces required an interval of repose to recruit their numbers and revive their confidence. Adversity had exercised and displayed the genius of Alaric; and the fame of his valour invited to the Gothic standard the bravest of the barbarian warriors, who, from the Euxine to the Rhine, were agitated by the desire of rapine and conquest. He had deserved the esteem, and he soon accepted the friendship, of Stilicho himself. Renouncing the service of the emperor of the East, Alaric concluded, with the court of Ravenna, a treaty of peace and alliance, by which he was declared master-general of the Roman armies throughout the præfecture of Illyricum; as it was claimed, according to the true and ancient limits, by the minister of Honorius.[101] The execution of the ambitious design, which was either stipulated or implied in the articles of the treaty, ap-

pears to have been suspended by the formidable irruption of Radagaisus; and the neutrality of the Gothic king may perhaps be compared to the indifference of Cæsar, who, in the conspiracy of Catiline, refused either to assist or to oppose the enemy of the republic. After the defeat of the Vandals, Stilicho resumed his pretensions to the provinces of the East; appointed civil magistrates for the administration of justice and of the finances; and declared his impatience to lead to the gates of Constantinople the united armies of the Romans and of the Goths. The prudence, however, of Stilicho, his aversion to civil war, and his perfect knowledge of the weakness of the state, may countenance the suspicion that domestic peace, rather than foreign conquest, was the object of his policy; and that his principal care was to employ the forces of Alaric at a distance from Italy. This design could not long escape the penetration of the Gothic king, who continued to hold a doubtful, and perhaps a treacherous, correspondence with the rival courts; who protracted, like a dissatisfied mercenary, his languid operations of Thessaly and Epirus; and who soon returned to claim the extravagant reward of his ineffectual services. From his camp near Æmona,[102] on the confines of Italy, he transmitted to the emperor of the West a long account of promises, of expenses, and of demands; called for immediate satisfaction, and clearly intimated the consequences of a refusal. Yet, if his conduct was hostile, his language was decent and dutiful. He humbly professed himself the friend of Stilicho, and the soldier of Honorius; offered his person and his troops to march, without delay, against the usurper of Gaul; and solicited, as a permanent retreat for the Gothic nation, the possession of some vacant province of the Western empire.

The political and secret transactions of two statesmen who laboured to deceive each other and the world must for ever have been concealed in the impenetrable darkness of the cabinet, if the debates of a popular assembly had not thrown some rays of light on the correspondence of Alaric and Stilicho. The necessity of finding some artificial support for a government which, from a principle, not of moderation, but of weakness, was reduced to negotiate with its own subjects, had insensibly revived the authority of the Roman senate: and the minister of Honorius respectfully consulted the legislative council of the republic. Stilicho assembled the senate in the palace of the Cæsars; represented, in a studied oration, the actual state of affairs;

proposed the demands of the Gothic king; and submitted to their consideration the choice of peace or war. The senators, as if they had been suddenly awakened from a dream of four hundred years, appeared on this important occasion to be inspired by the courage, rather than by the wisdom, of their predecessors. They loudly declared, in regular speeches or in tumultuary acclamations, that it was unworthy of the majesty of Rome to purchase a precarious and disgraceful truce from a barbarian king; and that, in the judgment of a magnanimous people, the chance of ruin was always preferable to the certainty of dishonour. The minister, whose pacific intentions were seconded only by the voices of a few servile and venal followers, attempted to allay the general ferment, by an apology for his own conduct, and even for the demands of the Gothic prince. "The payment of a subsidy, which had excited the indignation of the Romans, ought not (such was the language of Stilicho) to be considered in the odious light either of a tribute or of a ransom, extorted by the menaces of a barbarian enemy. Alaric had faithfully asserted the just pretensions of the republic to the provinces which were usurped by the Greeks of Constantinople: he modestly required the fair and stipulated recompense of his services; and if he had desisted from the prosecution of his enterprise, he had obeyed, in his retreat, the peremptory, though private, letters of the emperor himself. These contradictory orders (he would not dissemble the errors of his own family) had been procured by the intercession of Serena. The tender piety of his wife had been too deeply affected by the discord of the royal brothers, the sons of her adopted father; and the sentiments of nature had too easily prevailed over the stern dictates of the public welfare." These ostensible reasons, which faintly disguise the obscure intrigues of the palace of Ravenna, were supported by the authority of Stilicho; and obtained, after a warm debate, the reluctant approbation of the senate. The tumult of virtue and freedom subsided; and the sum of four thousand pounds of gold was granted, under the name of a subsidy, to secure the peace of Italy, and to conciliate the friendship of the king of the Goths. Lampadius alone, one of the most illustrious members of the assembly, still persisted in his dissent; exclaimed with a loud voice, "This is not a treaty of peace, but of servitude;"[103] and escaped the danger of such bold opposition by immediately retiring to the sanctuary of a Christian church.

But the reign of Stilicho drew towards its end; and the proud minister might perceive the symptoms of his approaching disgrace. The generous boldness of Lampadius had been applauded; and the senate, so patiently resigned to a long servitude, rejected with disdain the offer of invidious and imaginary freedom. The troops, who still assumed the name and prerogatives of the Roman legions, were exasperated by the partial affection of Stilicho for the barbarians: and the people imputed to the mischievous policy of the minister the public misfortunes, which were the natural consequence of their own degeneracy. Yet Stilicho might have continued to brave the clamours of the people, and even of the soldiers, if he could have maintained his dominion over the feeble mind of his pupil. But the respectful attachment of Honorius was converted into fear, suspicion, and hatred. The crafty Olympius,[104] who concealed his vices under the mask of Christian piety, had secretly undermined the benefactor by whose favour he was promoted to the honourable offices of the Imperial palace. Olympius revealed to the unsuspecting emperor, who had attained the twenty-fifth year of his age, that he was without weight or authority in his own government; and artfully alarmed his timid and indolent disposition by a lively picture of the designs of Stilicho, who already meditated the death of his sovereign, with the ambitious hope of placing the diadem on the head of his son Eucherius. The emperor was instigated by the new favourite to assume the tone of independent dignity; and the minister was astonished to find that secret resolutions were formed in the court and council, which were repugnant to his interest, or to his intentions. Instead of residing in the palace of Rome, Honorius declared that it was his pleasure to return to the secure fortress of Ravenna. On the first intelligence of the death of his brother Arcadius, he prepared to visit Constantinople, and to regulate, with the authority of a guardian, the provinces of the infant Theodosius.[105] The representation of the difficulty and expense of such a distant expedition checked this strange and sudden sally of active diligence; but the dangerous project of showing the emperor to the camp of Pavia, which was composed of the Roman troops, the enemies of Stilicho and his barbarian auxiliaries, remained fixed and unalterable. The minister was pressed, by the advice of his confidant, Justinian, a Roman advocate, of a lively and penetrating genius, to oppose a journey so prejudicial to his reputation and safety. His strenuous, but ineffectual, efforts confirmed the triumph of Olympius; and the prudent lawyer withdrew himself from the impending ruin of his patron.

In the passage of the emperor through Bologna a mutiny of the guards was excited and appeased by the secret policy of Stilicho, who announced his instructions to decimate the guilty, and ascribed to his own intercession the merit of their pardon. After this tumult, Honorius embraced, for the last time, the minister whom he now considered as a tyrant, and proceeded on his way to the camp of Pavia, where he was received by the loyal acclamations of the troops who were assembled for the service of the Gallic war. On the morning of the fourth day he pronounced, as he had been taught, a military oration in the presence of the soldiers, whom the charitable visits and artful discourses of Olympius had prepared to execute a dark and bloody conspiracy. At the first signal they massacred the friends of Stilicho, the most illustrious officers of the empire; two Prætorian præfects, of Gaul and of Italy; two masters-general of the cavalry and infantry; the master of the offices, the quæstor, the treasurer, and the count of the domestics. Many lives were lost, many houses were plundered; the furious sedition continued to rage till the close of the evening; and the trembling emperor, who was seen in the streets of Pavia without his robes or diadem, yielded to the persuasions of his favourite, condemned the memory of the slain, and solemnly approved the innocence and fidelity of their assassins. The intelligence of the massacre of Pavia filled the mind of Stilicho with just and gloomy apprehensions, and he instantly summoned, in the camp of Bologna, a council of the confederate leaders who were attached to his service, and would be involved in his ruin. The impetuous voice of the assembly called aloud for arms and for revenge; to march, without a moment's delay, under the banners of a hero whom they had so often followed to victory; to surprise, to oppress, to extirpate the guilty Olympius and his degenerate Romans, and perhaps to fix the diadem on the head of their injured general. Instead of executing a resolution which might have been justified by success, Stilicho hesitated till he was irrecoverably lost. He was still ignorant of the fate of the emperor; he distrusted the fidelity of his own party; and he viewed with horror the fatal consequences of arming a crowd of licentious barbarians against the soldiers and people of Italy. The confederates, impatient of his timorous and doubtful delay, hastily retired with fear and indignation. At the hour of mid-

night Sarus, a Gothic warrior, renowned among the barbarians themselves for his strength and valour, suddenly invaded the camp of his benefactor, plundered the baggage, cut in pieces the faithful Huns who guarded his person, and penetrated to the tent, where the minister, pensive and sleepless, meditated on the dangers of his situation. Stilicho escaped with difficulty from the sword of the Goth, and after issuing a last and generous admonition to the cities of Italy to shut their gates against the barbarians, his confidence or his despair urged him to throw himself into Ravenna, which was already in the absolute possession of his enemies. Olympius, who had assumed the dominion of Honorius, was speedily informed that his rival had embraced, as a suppliant, the altar of the Christian church. The base and cruel disposition of the hypocrite was incapable of pity or remorse; but he piously affected to elude, rather than to violate, the privilege of the sanctuary. Count Heraclian, with a troop of soldiers, appeared at the dawn of day before the gates of the church of Ravenna. The bishop was satisfied by a solemn oath that the Imperial mandate only directed them to secure the person of Stilicho: but as soon as the unfortunate minister had been tempted beyond the holy threshold, he produced the warrant for his instant execution. Stilicho supported with calm resignation the injurious names of traitor and parricide; repressed the unseasonable zeal of his followers, who were ready to attempt an ineffectual rescue; and, with a firmness not unworthy of the last of the Roman generals, submitted his neck to the sword of Heraclian.[106]

The servile crowd of the palace, who had so long adored the fortune of Stilicho, affected to insult his fall; and the most distant connection with the master-general of the West, which had so lately been a title to wealth and honours, was studiously denied, and rigorously punished. His family, united by a triple alliance with the family of Theodosius, might envy the condition of the meanest peasant. The flight of his son Eucherius was intercepted; and the death of that innocent youth soon followed the divorce of Thermantia, who filled the place of her sister Maria, and who, like Maria, had remained a virgin in the Imperial bed.[107] The friends of Stilicho who had escaped the massacre of Pavia were persecuted by the implacable revenge of Olympius, and the most exquisite cruelty was employed to extort the confession of a treasonable and sacrilegious conspiracy. They died in silence; their firmness justified the choice,[108] and perhaps absolved the innocence, of their patron; and the despotic power which could take his life without a trial, and stigmatise his memory without a proof, has no jurisdiction over the impartial suffrage of posterity.[109] The services of Stilicho are great and manifest; his crimes, as they are vaguely stated in the language of flattery and hatred, are obscure, at least, and improbable. About four months after his death an edict was published, in the name of Honorius, to restore the free communication of the two empires, which had been so long interrupted by the *public enemy*.[110] The minister, whose fame and fortune depended on the prosperity of the state, was accused of betraying Italy to the barbarians, whom he repeatedly vanquished at Pollentia, at Verona, and before the walls of Florence. His pretended design of placing the diadem on the head of his son Eucherius could not have been conducted without preparations or accomplices; and the ambitious father would not surely have left the future emperor, till the twentieth year of his age, in the humble station of tribune of the notaries. Even the religion of Stilicho was arraigned by the malice of his rival. The seasonable, and almost miraculous, deliverance was devoutly celebrated by the applause of the clergy, who asserted that the restoration of idols and the persecution of the church would have been the first measure of the reign of Eucherius. The son of Stilicho, however, was educated in the bosom of Christianity, which his father had uniformly professed and zealously supported.[111] Serena had borrowed her magnificent necklace from the statue of Vesta;[112] and the Pagans execrated the memory of the sacrilegious minister, by whose order the Sibylline books, the oracles of Rome, had been committed to the flames.[113] The pride and power of Stilicho constituted his real guilt. An honourable reluctance to shed the blood of his countrymen appears to have contributed to the success of his unworthy rival; and it is the last humiliation of the character of Honorius, that posterity has not condescended to reproach him with his base ingratitude to the guardian of his youth and the support of his empire.

Among the train of dependents whose wealth and dignity attracted the notice of their own times, *our* curiosity is excited by the celebrated name of the poet Claudian, who enjoyed the favour of Stilicho, and was overwhelmed in the ruin of his patron. The titular offices of tribune and notary fixed his rank in the Imperial court: he was indebted to the powerful intercession of Serena for his marriage with a rich heiress of the province of Africa;[114] and the statue of Claudian, erected in the forum of Trajan, was a monument of the taste and liberality of the Roman senate.[115] After the praises of Stilicho became offensive and criminal, Claudian was exposed to the enmity of a powerful and unforgiving courtier whom he had provoked by the insolence of wit. He had compared, in a lively epigram, the opposite characters of two Prætorian præfects of Italy; he contrasts the innocent repose of a philosopher, who sometimes resigned the hours of business to slumber, perhaps to study, with the interested diligence of a rapacious minister, indefatigable in the pursuit of unjust or sacrilegious gain. "How happy," continues Claudian, "how happy might it be for the people of Italy if Mallius could be constantly awake, and if Hadrian would always sleep!"[116] The repose of Mallius was not disturbed by this friendly and gentle admonition; but the cruel vigilance of Hadrian watched the opportunity of revenge, and easily obtained from the enemies of Stilicho the trifling sacrifice of an obnoxious poet. The poet concealed himself, however, during the tumult of the revolution, and consulting the dictates of prudence rather than of honour, he addressed, in the form of an epistle, a suppliant and humble recantation to the offended præfect. He deplores, in mournful strains, the fatal indiscretion into which he had been hurried by passion and folly; submits to the imitation of his adversary the generous examples of the clemency of gods, of heroes, and of lions; and expresses his hope that the magnanimity of Hadrian will not trample on a defenseless and contemptible foe, already humbled by disgrace and poverty, and deeply wounded by the exile, the tortures, and the death of his dearest friends.[117] Whatever might be the success of his prayer or the accidents of his future life, the period of a few years levelled in the grave the minister and the poet: but the name of Hadrian is almost sunk in oblivion, while Claudian is read with pleasure in every country which has retained or acquired the knowledge of the Latin language. If we fairly balance his merits and his defects, we shall acknowledge that Claudian does not either satisfy or silence our reason. It would not be easy to produce a passage that deserves the epithet of sublime or pathetic; to select a verse that melts the heart or enlarges the imagination. We should vainly seek in the poems of Claudian the happy invention and artificial conduct of an interesting fable, or the just and lively representation of the characters and situations of real life. For the service of his patron he published occasional panegyrics and invectives, and the design of these slavish compositions encouraged his propensity to exceed the limits of truth and nature. These imperfections, however, are compensated in some degree by the poetical virtues of Claudian. He was endowed with the rare and precious talent of raising the meanest, of adoring the most barren, and of diversifying the most similar topics; his colouring, more especially in descriptive poetry, is soft and splendid; and he seldom fails to display, and even to abuse, the advantages of a cultivated understanding, a copious fancy, an easy and sometimes forcible expression, and a perpetual flow of harmonious versification. To these commendations, independent of any accidents of time and place, we must add the peculiar merit which Claudian derived from the unfavourable circumstances of his birth. In the decline of arts and of empire, a native of Egypt,[118] who had received the education of a Greek, assumed in a mature age the familiar use and absolute command of the Latin language;[119] soared above the heads of his feeble contemporaries; and placed himself, after an interval of three hundred years, among the poets of ancient Rome.[120]

CHAPTER XXXI

Invasion of Italy by Alaric. Manners of the Roman Senate and People. Rome is thrice besieged, and at length pillaged, by the Goths. Death of Alaric. The Goths evacuate Italy. Fall of Constantine. Gaul and Spain are occupied by the Barbarians. Independence of Britain.

THE incapacity of a weak and distracted government may often assume the appearance and produce the effects of a treasonable correspondence with the public enemy. If Alaric himself had been introduced into the council of Ravenna, he would probably have advised the same measures which were actually pursued by the ministers of Honorius.[1] The king of the Goths would have conspired, perhaps with some reluctance, to destroy the formidable adversary by whose arms, in Italy as well as in Greece, he had been twice overthrown. *Their* active and interested hatred laboriously accomplished the disgrace and ruin of the great Stilicho. The valour of Sarus, his fame in arms, and his personal or hereditary influence over the confederate barbarians, could recommend him only to the friends of their country who despised or detested the worthless characters of Turpilio, Varanes, and Vigilantius. By the pressing instances of the new favourites, these generals, unworthy as they had shown themselves of the name of soldiers,[2] were promoted to the command of the cavalry, of the infantry, and of the domestic troops. The Gothic prince would have subscribed with pleasure the edict which the fanaticism of Olympius dictated to the simple and devout emperor. Honorius excluded all persons who were adverse to the catholic church from holding any office in the state; obstinately rejected the service of all those who dissented from his religion; and rashly disqualified many of his bravest and most skilful officers who adhered to the Pagan worship or who had imbibed the opinions of Arianism.[3] These measures, so advantageous to an enemy, Alaric would have approved, and might perhaps have suggested; but it may seem doubtful whether the barbarian would have promoted his interest at the expense of the inhuman and absurd cruelty which was perpetrated by the direction, or at least with the connivance, of the Imperial ministers. The foreign auxiliaries who had been attached to the person of Stilicho lamented his death; but the desire of revenge was checked by a natural apprehension for the safety of their wives and children, who were detained as hostages in the strong cities of Italy, where they had likewise deposited their most valuable effects. At the same hour, and as if by a common signal, the cities of Italy were polluted by the same horrid scenes of universal massacre and pillage, which involved in promiscuous destruction the families and fortunes of the barbarians. Exasperated by such an injury, which might have awakened the tamest and most servile spirit, they cast a look of indignation and hope towards the camp of Alaric, and unanimously swore to pursue with just and implacable war the perfidious nation that had so basely violated the laws of hospitality. By the imprudent conduct of the ministers of Honorius the republic lost the assistance, and deserved the enmity, of thirty thousand of her bravest soldiers; and the weight of that formidable army, which alone might have determined the event of the war, was transferred from the scale of the Romans into that of the Goths.

In the arts of negotiation, as well as in those of war, the Gothic king maintained his superior ascendant over an enemy whose seeming changes proceeded from the total want of counsel and design. From his camp, on the confines of Italy, Alaric attentively observed the revolutions of the palace, watched the progress of faction and discontent, disguised the hostile aspect of a barbarian invader, and assumed the more popular appearance of the friend and ally of the great Stilicho; to whose virtues, when they were no longer formidable, he could pay a just tribute of sincere praise and regret. The pressing invitation of the malcontents, who urged the king of the Goths to invade Italy, was enforced by a lively sense of his personal injuries; and he might speciously complain that the Imperial ministers still delayed and eluded the payment of the four thousand pounds of gold which had been granted by the Roman senate either to reward his services or to appease his fury. His decent firmness was supported by an artful moderation, which contributed to the success of his designs. He required a fair and reasonable satisfaction; but he gave the strongest assurances that, as soon as he had obtained it, he would immediately retire. He refused to trust the faith of the Romans, unless Aëtius and Jason, the sons of two great officers of state, were sent as hostages to his camp: but he offered to deliver in exchange several of the noblest youths of the Gothic nation. The modesty of Alaric was interpreted by the ministers of Ravenna as a sure evidence of his weakness and fear. They disdained either to negotiate a treaty or to assemble an army; and with a rash confidence, derived only from their ignorance of the extreme danger, irretrievably wasted the decisive moments of peace and war. While they expected, in sullen silence, that the barbarians should evacuate the confines of Italy, Alaric, with bold and rapid marches, passed the Alps and the Po; hastily pillaged the cities of Aquileia, Altinum, Concordia, and Cremona, which yielded to his arms; increased his forces by the accession of thirty thousand auxiliaries; and, without meeting a single enemy in the field, advanced as far as the edge of the morass which protected the impregnable residence of the emperor of the West. Instead of attempting the

hopeless siege of Ravenna, the prudent leader of the Goths proceeded to Rimini, stretched his ravages along the sea-coast of the Hadriatic, and meditated the conquest of the ancient mistress of the world. An Italian hermit, whose zeal and sanctity were respected by the barbarians themselves, encountered the victorious monarch, and boldly denounced the indignation of Heaven against the oppressors of the earth: but the saint himself was confounded by the solemn asseveration of Alaric that he felt a secret and præternatural impulse, which directed, and even compelled, his march to the gates of Rome. He felt that his genius and his fortune were equal to the most arduous enterprises; and the enthusiasm which he communicated to the Goths insensibly removed the popular and almost superstitious reverence of the nations for the majesty of the Roman name. His troops, animated by the hopes of spoil, followed the course of the Flaminian way, occupied the unguarded passes of the Apennine,[4] descended into the rich plains of Umbria; and, as they lay encamped on the banks of the Clitumnus, might wantonly slaughter and devour the milk-white oxen which had been so long reserved for the use of Roman triumphs.[5] A lofty situation and a seasonable tempest of thunder and lightning preserved the little city of Narni: but the king of the Goths, despising the ignoble prey, still advanced with unabated vigour; and after he had passed through the stately arches, adorned with the spoils of barbaric victories, he pitched his camp under the walls of Rome.[6]

During a period of six hundred and nineteen years the seat of empire had never been violated by the presence of a foreign enemy. The unsuccessful expedition of Hannibal[7] served only to display the character of the senate and people; of a senate degraded, rather than ennobled, by the comparison of an assembly of kings; and of a people to whom the ambassador of Pyrrhus ascribed the inexhaustible resources of the Hydra.[8] Each of the senators in the time of the Punic war had accomplished his term of military service, either in a subordinate or a superior station; and the decree which invested with temporary command all those who had been consuls, or censors, or dictators, gave the republic the immediate assistance of many brave and experienced generals. In the beginning of the war the Roman people consisted of two hundred and fifty thousand citizens of an age to bear arms.[9] Fifty thousand had already died in the defence of their country; and the twenty-three legions which were employed in the different camps of Italy, Greece, Sardinia, Sicily, and Spain, required about one hundred thousand men. But there still remained an equal number in Rome and the adjacent territory who were animated by the same intrepid courage; and every citizen was trained from his earliest youth in the discipline and exercises of a soldier. Hannibal was astonished by the constancy of the senate, who, without raising the siege of Capua or recalling their scattered forces, expected his approach. He encamped on the banks of the Anio, at the distance of three miles from the city: and he was soon informed that the ground on which he had pitched his tent was sold for an adequate price at a public auction; and that a body of troops was dismissed by an opposite road to reinforce the legions of Spain.[10] He led his Africans to the gates of Rome, where he found three armies in order of battle prepared to receive him; but Hannibal dreaded the event of a combat from which he could not hope to escape unless he destroyed the last of his enemies; and his speedy retreat confessed the invincible courage of the Romans.

From the time of the Punic war the uninterrupted succession of senators had preserved the name and image of the republic; and the degenerate subjects of Honorius ambitiously derived their descent from the heroes who had repulsed the arms of Hannibal and subdued the nations of the earth. The temporal honours which the devout Paula[11] inherited and despised are carefully recapitulated by Jerom, the guide of her conscience and the historian of her life. The genealogy of her father, Rogatus, which ascended as high as Agamemnon, might seem to betray a Grecian origin; but her mother, Blæsilla, numbered the Scipios, Æmilius Paulus, and the Gracchi in the list of her ancestors; and Toxotius, the husband of Paula, deduced his royal lineage from Æneas, the father of the Julian line. The vanity of the rich, who desired to be noble, was gratified by these lofty pretensions. Encouraged by the applause of their parasites, they easily imposed on the credulity of the vulgar; and were countenanced in some measure by the custom of adopting the name of their patron, which had always prevailed among the freedmen and clients of illustrious families. Most of those families, however, attacked by so many causes of external violence or internal decay, were gradually extirpated: and it would be more reasonable to seek for a lineal descent of twenty generations among the mountains of the Alps or in the peaceful solitude of Apulia, than on the theatre of Rome, the

seat of fortune, of danger, and of perpetual revolutions. Under each successive reign and from every province of the empire a crowd of hardy adventurers, rising to eminence by their talents or their vices, usurped the wealth, the honours, and the palaces of Rome; and oppressed or protected the poor and humble remains of consular families, who were ignorant, perhaps, of the glory of their ancestors.[12]

In the time of Jerom and Claudian the senators unanimously yielded the pre-eminence to the Anician line; and a slight view of *their* history will serve to appreciate the rank and antiquity of the noble families which contended only for the second place.[13]

During the five first ages of the city the name of the Anicians was unknown; they appear to have derived their origin from Præneste; and the ambition of those new citizens was long satisfied with the plebeian honours of tribunes of the people.[14] One hundred and sixty-eight years before the Christian era the family was ennobled by the prætorship of Anicius, who gloriously terminated the Illyrian war by the conquest of the nation and the captivity of their king.[15] From the triumph of that general three consulships in distant periods mark the succession of the Anician name.[16] From the reign of Diocletian to the final extinction of the Western empire that name shone with a lustre which was not eclipsed in the public estimation by the majesty of the Imperial purple.[17] The several branches to whom it was communicated united, by marriage or inheritance, the wealth and titles of the Annian, the Petronian, and the Olybrian houses; and in each generation the number of consulships was multiplied by an hereditary claim.[18] The Anician family excelled in faith and in riches: they were the first of the Roman senate who embraced Christianity; and it is probable that Anicius Julian, who was afterwards consul and præfect of the city, atoned for his attachment to the party of Maxentius by the readiness with which he accepted the religion of Constantine.[19] Their ample patrimony was increased by the industry of Probus, the chief of the Anician family, who shared with Gratian the honours of the consulship, and exercised four times the high office of Prætorian præfect.[20] His immense estates were scattered over the wide extent of the Roman world; and though the public might suspect or disapprove the methods by which they had been acquired, the generosity and magnificence of that fortunate statesman deserved the gratitude of his clients and the admiration of strangers.[21] Such was the respect entertained for his memory, that the two sons of Probus, in their earliest youth and at the request of the senate, were associated in the consular dignity: a memorable distinction, without example in the annals of Rome.[22]

"The marbles of the Anician palace," were used as a proverbial expression of opulence and splendour;[23] but the nobles and senators of Rome aspired in due gradation to imitate that illustrious family. The accurate description of the city, which was composed in the Theodosian age, enumerates one thousand seven hundred and eighty *houses*, the residence of wealthy and honourable citizens.[24] Many of these stately mansions might almost excuse the exaggeration of the poet—that Rome contained a multitude of palaces, and that each palace was equal to a city, since it included within its own precincts everything which could be subservient either to use or luxury: markets, hippodromes, temples, fountains, baths, porticos, shady groves, and artificial aviaries.[25] The historian Olympiodorus, who represents the state of Rome when it was besieged by the Goths,[26] continues to observe that several of the richest senators received from their estates an annual income of four thousand pounds of gold, above one hundred and sixty thousand pounds sterling; without computing the stated provision of corn and wine, which, had they been sold, might have equalled in value one-third of the money. Compared to this immoderate wealth, an ordinary revenue of a thousand or fifteen hundred pounds of gold might be considered as no more than adequate to the dignity of the senatorian rank, which required many expenses of a public and ostentatious kind. Several examples are recorded in the age of Honorius of vain and popular nobles who celebrated the year of their prætorship by a festival which lasted seven days and cost above one hundred thousand pounds sterling.[27] The estates of the Roman senators, which so far exceed the proportion of modern wealth, were not confined to the limits of Italy. Their possessions extended far beyond the Ionian and Ægean seas to the most distant provinces: the city of Nicopolis, which Augustus had founded as an eternal monument of the Actian victory, was the property of the devout Paula;[28] and it is observed by Seneca, that the rivers which had divided hostile nations now flowed through the lands of private citizens.[29] According to their temper and circumstances, the estates of the Romans were either cultivated by the labour of their slaves, or granted, for a certain and stipulated rent, to the industrious farmer. The economical

writers of antiquity strenuously recommend the former method wherever it may be practicable; but if the object should be removed by its distance or magnitude from the immediate eye of the master, they prefer the active care of an old hereditary tenant, attached to the soil and interested in the produce, to the mercenary administration of a negligent, perhaps an unfaithful, steward.[30]

The opulent nobles of an immense capital, who were never excited by the pursuit of military glory, and seldom engaged in the occupations of civil government, naturally resigned their leisure to the business and amusements of private life. At Rome commerce was always held in contempt; but the senators, from the first age of the republic, increased their patrimony and multiplied their clients by the lucrative practice of usury, and the obsolete laws were eluded or violated by the mutual inclinations and interest of both parties.[31] A considerable mass of treasure must always have existed at Rome, either in the current coin of the empire, or in the form of gold and silver plate; and there were many sideboards in the time of Pliny which contained more solid silver than had been transported by Scipio from vanquished Carthage.[32] The greater part of the nobles, who dissipated their fortunes in profuse luxury, found themselves poor in the midst of wealth, and idle in a constant round of dissipation. Their desires were continually gratified by the labour of a thousand hands; of the numerous train of their domestic slaves, who were actuated by the fear of punishment; and of the various professions of artificers and merchants, who were more powerfully impelled by the hopes of gain. The ancients were destitute of many of the conveniences of life which have been invented or improved by the progress of industry; and the plenty of glass and linen has diffused more real comforts among the modern nations of Europe than the senators of Rome could derive from all the refinements of pompous or sensual luxury.[33] Their luxury and their manners have been the subject of minute and laborious disquisition; but as such inquiries would divert me too long from the design of the present work, I shall produce an authentic state of Rome and its inhabitants which is more peculiarly applicable to the period of the Gothic invasion. Ammianus Marcellinus, who prudently chose the capital of the empire as the residence the best adapted to the historian of his own times, has mixed with the narrative of public events a lively representation of the scenes with which he was familiarly conversant. The judicious reader will not always approve the asperity of censure, the choice of circumstances, or the style of expression; he will perhaps detect the latent prejudices and personal resentments which soured the temper of Ammianus himself; but he will surely observe, with philosophic curiosity, the interesting and original picture of the manners of Rome.[34]

"The greatness of Rome (such is the language of the historian) was founded on the rare and almost incredible alliance of virtue and of fortune. The long period of her infancy was employed in a laborious struggle against the tribes of Italy, the neighbours and enemies of the rising city. In the strength and ardour of youth she sustained the storms of war, carried her victorious arms beyond the seas and the mountains, and brought home triumphal laurels from every country of the globe. At length, verging towards old age, and sometimes conquering by the terror only of her name, she sought the blessings of ease and tranquillity. The VENERABLE CITY, which had trampled on the necks of the fiercest nations, and established a system of laws, the perpetual guardians of justice and freedom, was content, like a wise and wealthy parent, to devolve on the Cæsars, her favourite sons, the care of governing her ample patrimony.[35] A secure and profound peace, such as had been once enjoyed in the reign of Numa, succeeded to the tumults of a republic; while Rome was still adored as the queen of the earth, and the subject nations still reverenced the name of the people and the majesty of the senate. But this native splendour (continues Ammianus) is degraded and sullied by the conduct of some nobles, who, unmindful of their own dignity and of that of their country, assume an unbounded licence of vice and folly. They contend with each other in the empty vanity of titles and surnames, and curiously select or invent the most lofty and sonorous appellations—Reburrus or Fabunius, Pagonius or Tarrasius[36]—which may impress the ears of the vulgar with astonishment and respect. From a vain ambition of perpetuating their memory, they affect to multiply their likeness in statues of bronze and marble; nor are they satisfied unless those statues are covered with plates of gold; an honourable distinction, first granted to Acilius the consul, after he had subdued by his arms and counsels the power of king Antiochus. The ostentation of displaying, of magnifying perhaps, the rent roll of the estates which they possess in all the provinces, from the rising to the setting sun, pro-

vokes the just resentment of every man who recollects that their poor and invincible ancestors were not distinguished from the meanest of the soldiers by the delicacy of their food or the splendour of their apparel. But the modern nobles measure their rank and consequence according to the loftiness of their chariots,[37] and the weighty magnificence of their dress. Their long robes of silk and purple float in the wind; and as they are agitated, by art or accident, they occasionally discover the under garments, the rich tunics, embroidered with the figures of various animals.[38] Followed by a train of fifty servants, and tearing up the pavement, they move along the streets with the same impetuous speed as if they travelled with post-horses; and the example of the senators is boldly imitated by the matrons and ladies, whose covered carriages are continually driving round the immense space of the city and suburbs. Whenever these persons of high distinction condescend to visit the public baths, they assume, on their entrance, a tone of loud and insolent command, and appropriate to their own use the conveniences which were designed for the Roman people. If, in these places of mixed and general resort, they meet any of the infamous ministers of their pleasures, they express their affection by a tender embrace, while they proudly decline the salutations of their fellow-citizens, who are not permitted to aspire above the honour of kissing their hands or their knees. As soon as they have indulged themselves in the refreshment of the bath, they resume their rings and the other ensigns of their dignity, select from their private wardrobe of the finest linen, such as might suffice for a dozen persons, the garments the most agreeable to their fancy, and maintain till their departure the same haughty demeanour, which perhaps might have been excused in the great Marcellus after the conquest of Syracuse. Sometimes indeed these heroes undertake more arduous achievements: they visit their estates in Italy, and procure themselves, by the toil of servile hands, the amusements of the chase.[39] If at any time, but more especially on a hot day, they have courage to sail in their painted galleys from the Lucrine lake[40] to their elegant villas on the sea-coast of Puteoli and Caieta,[41] they compare their own expeditions to the marches of Cæsar and Alexander. Yet should a fly presume to settle on the silken folds of their gilded umbrellas, should a sunbeam penetrate through some unguarded and imperceptible chink, they deplore their intolerable hardships, and lament in affected language that they were not born in the land of the Cimmerians,[42] the regions of eternal darkness. In these journeys into the country[43] the whole body of the household marches with their master. In the same manner as the cavalry and infantry, the heavy and the light armed troops, the advanced guard and the rear, are marshalled by the skill of their military leaders, so the domestic officers, who bear a rod as an ensign of authority, distribute and arrange the numerous train of slaves and attendants. The baggage and wardrobe move in the front, and are immediately followed by a multitude of cooks and inferior ministers employed in the service of the kitchens and of the table. The main body is composed of a promiscuous crowd of slaves, increased by the accidental concourse of idle or dependent plebeians. The rear is closed by the favourite band of eunuchs, distributed from age to youth, according to the order of seniority. Their numbers and their deformity excite the horror of the indignant spectators, who are ready to execrate the memory of Semiramis for the cruel art which she invented of frustrating the purposes of nature, and of blasting in the bud the hopes of future generations. In the exercise of domestic jurisdiction the nobles of Rome express an exquisite sensibility for any personal injury, and a contemptuous indifference for the rest of the human species. When they have called for warm water, if a slave has been tardy in his obedience, he is instantly chastised with three hundred lashes; but should the same slave commit a wilful murder, the master will mildly observe that he is a worthless fellow, but that if he repeats the offence he shall not escape punishment. Hospitality was formerly the virtue of the Romans; and every stranger who could plead either merit or misfortune was relieved or rewarded by their generosity. At present, if a foreigner, perhaps of no contemptible rank, is introduced to one of the proud and wealthy senators, he is welcomed indeed in the first audience with such warm professions and such kind inquiries, that he retires enchanted with the affability of his illustrious friend, and full of regret that he had so long delayed his journey to Rome, the native seat of manners as well as of empire. Secure of a favourable reception, he repeats his visit the ensuing day, and is mortified by the discovery that his person, his name, and his country are already forgotten. If he still has resolution to persevere, he is gradually numbered in the train of dependents, and obtains the permission to pay his assiduous and unprofitable court to a haughty patron, incapable of

gratitude or friendship, who scarcely deigns to remark his presence, his departure, or his return. Whenever the rich prepare a solemn and popular entertainment,[44] whenever they celebrate with profuse and pernicious luxury their private banquets, the choice of the guests is the subject of anxious deliberation. The modest, the sober, and the learned are seldom preferred; and the nomenclators, who are commonly swayed by interested motives, have the address to insert in the list of invitations the obscure names of the most worthless of mankind. But the frequent and familiar companions of the great are those parasites who practise the most useful of all arts, the art of flattery; who eagerly applaud each word and every action of their immortal patron; gaze with rapture on his marble columns and variegated pavements, and strenuously praise the pomp and elegance which he is taught to consider as a part of his personal merit. At the Roman tables the birds, the *squirrels*,[45] or the fish, which appear of an uncommon size, are contemplated with curious attention; a pair of scales is accurately applied to ascertain their real weight; and, while the more rational guests are disgusted by the vain and tedious repetition, notaries are summoned to attest by an authentic record the truth of such a marvellous event. Another method of introduction into the houses and society of the great is derived from the profession of gaming, or, as it is more politely styled, of play. The confederates are united by a strict and indissoluble bond of friendship, or rather of conspiracy; a superior degree of skill in the *Tesserarian* art (which may be interpreted the game of dice and tables[46]) is a sure road to wealth and reputation. A master of that sublime science, who in a supper or assembly is placed below a magistrate, displays in his countenance the surprise and indignation which Cato might be supposed to feel when he was refused the prætorship by the votes of a capricious people. The acquisition of knowledge seldom engages the curiosity of the nobles, who abhor the fatigue and disdain the advantages of study; and the only books which they peruse are the Satires of Juvenal, and the verbose and fabulous histories of Marius Maximus.[47] The libraries which they have inherited from their fathers are secluded, like dreary sepulchres, from the light of day.[48] But the costly instruments of the theatre, flutes, and enormous lyres, and hydraulic organs, are constructed for their use; and the harmony of vocal and instrumental music is incessantly repeated in the palaces of Rome. In those palaces sound is preferred to sense, and the care of the body to that of the mind. It is allowed as a salutary maxim, that the light and frivolous suspicion of a contagious malady is of sufficient weight to excuse the visits of the most intimate friends; and even the servants who are despatched to make the decent inquiries are not suffered to return home till they have undergone the ceremony of a previous ablution. Yet this selfish and unmanly delicacy occasionally yields to the more imperious passion of avarice. The prospect of gain will urge a rich and gouty senator as far as Spoleto; every sentiment of arrogance and dignity is subdued by the hopes of an inheritance, or even of a legacy; and a wealthy childless citizen is the most powerful of the Romans. The art of obtaining the signature of a favourable testament, and sometimes of hastening the moment of its execution, is perfectly understood; and it has happened that in the same house, though in different apartments, a husband and a wife, with the laudable design of over-reaching each other, have summoned their respective lawyers, to declare at the same time their mutual but contradictory intentions. The distress which follows and chastises extravagant luxury often reduces the great to the use of the most humiliating expedients. When they desire to borrow, they employ the base and supplicating style of the slave in the comedy; but when they are called upon to pay, they assume the royal and tragic declamation of the grandsons of Hercules. If the demand is repeated, they readily procure some trusty sycophant, instructed to maintain a charge of poison, or magic, against the insolent creditor, who is seldom released from prison till he has signed a discharge of the whole debt. These vices, which degrade the moral character of the Romans, are mixed with a puerile superstition that disgraces their understanding. They listen with confidence to the predictions of haruspices, who pretend to read in the entrails of victims the signs of future greatness and prosperity; and there are many who do not presume either to bathe or to dine, or to appear in public, till they have diligently consulted, according to the rules of astrology, the situation of Mercury and the aspect of the moon.[49] It is singular enough that this vain credulity may often be discovered among the profane sceptics who impiously doubt or deny the existence of a celestial power."

In populous cities, which are the seat of commerce and manufactures, the middle ranks of inhabitants, who derive their subsistence from the dexterity or labour of their hands, are commonly the most prolific, the most useful, and,

in that sense, the most respectable part of the community. But the plebeians of Rome, who disdained such sedentary and servile arts, had been oppressed from the earliest times by the weight of debt and usury, and the husbandman, during the term of his military service, was obliged to abandon the cultivation of his farm.[50] The lands of Italy, which had been originally divided among the families of free and indigent proprietors, were insensibly purchased or usurped by the avarice of the nobles; and in the age which preceded the fall of the republic, it was computed that only two thousand citizens were possessed of any independent substance.[51] Yet as long as the people bestowed by their suffrages the honours of the state, the command of the legions, and the administration of wealthy provinces, their conscious pride alleviated in some measure the hardships of poverty; and their wants were seasonably supplied by the ambitious liberality of the candidates, who aspired to secure a venal majority in the thirty-five tribes, or the hundred and ninety-three centuries, of Rome. But when the prodigal commons had imprudently alienated not only the *use*, but the *inheritance*, of power, they sunk, under the reign of the Cæsars, into a vile and wretched populace, which must, in a few generations, have been totally extinguished, if it had not been continually recruited by the manumission of slaves and the influx of strangers. As early as the time of Hadrian it was the just complaint of the ingenuous natives that the capital had attracted the vices of the universe and the manners of the most opposite nations. The intemperance of the Gauls, the cunning and levity of the Greeks, the savage obstinacy of the Egyptians and Jews, the servile temper of the Asiatics, and the dissolute, effeminate prostitution of the Syrians, were mingled in the various multitude, which, under the proud and false denomination of Romans, presumed to despise their fellow-subjects, and even their sovereigns, who dwelt beyond the precincts of the ETERNAL CITY.[52]

Yet the name of that city was still pronounced with respect: the frequent and capricious tumults of its inhabitants were indulged with impunity; and the successors of Constantine, instead of crushing the last remains of the democracy by the strong arm of military power, embraced the mild policy of Augustus, and studied to relieve the poverty and to amuse the idleness of an innumerable people.[53] I. For the convenience of the lazy plebeians, the monthly distributions of corn were converted into a daily allowance of bread; a great number of ovens were constructed and maintained at the public expense; and at the appointed hour, each citizen, who was furnished with a ticket, ascended the flight of steps which had been assigned to his peculiar quarter or division, and received, either as a gift or at a very low price, a loaf of bread of the weight of three pounds for the use of his family. II. The forests of Lucania, whose acorns fattened large droves of wild hogs,[54] afforded, as a species of tribute, a plentiful supply of cheap and wholesome meat. During five months of the year a regular allowance of bacon was distributed to the poorer citizens; and the annual consumption of the capital, at a time when it was much declined from its former lustre, was ascertained, by an edict of Valentinian the Third, at three millions six hundred and twenty-eight thousand pounds.[55] III. In the manners of antiquity the use of oil was indispensable for the lamp as well as for the bath, and the annual tax which was imposed on Africa for the benefit of Rome amounted to the weight of three millions of pounds, to the measure, perhaps, of three hundred thousand English gallons. IV. The anxiety of Augustus to provide the metropolis with sufficient plenty of corn was not extended beyond that necessary article of human subsistence; and when the popular clamour accused the dearness and scarcity of wine, a proclamation was issued by the grave reformer to remind his subjects that no man could reasonably complain of thirst, since the aqueducts of Agrippa had introduced into the city so many copious streams of pure and salubrious water.[56] This rigid sobriety was insensibly relaxed; and, although the generous design of Aurelian[57] does not appear to have been executed in its full extent, the use of wine was allowed on very easy and liberal terms. The administration of the public cellars was delegated to a magistrate of honourable rank; and a considerable part of the vintage of Campania was reserved for the fortunate inhabitants of Rome.

The stupendous aqueducts, so justly celebrated by the praises of Augustus himself, replenished the *Thermæ*, or baths, which had been constructed in every part of the city with Imperial magnificence. The baths of Antoninus Caracalla, which were open, at stated hours, for the indiscriminate service of the senators and the people, contained above sixteen hundred seats of marble; and more than three thousand were reckoned in the baths of Diocletian.[58] The walls of the lofty apartments were covered with curious mosaics, that imitated the art of the pencil in the elegance of design and the variety of colours. The Egyptian granite was beautifully encrusted with the precious green marble of Numidia; the perpetual stream of hot water was poured into the capacious basins through so many wide mouths of bright and massy silver; and the meanest Roman could purchase, with a small copper coin, the daily enjoyment of a scene of pomp and luxury which might excite the envy of the kings of Asia.[59] From these stately palaces issued a swarm of dirty and ragged plebeians, without shoes and without a mantle; who loitered away whole days in the street or Forum to hear news and to hold disputes; who dissipated in extravagant gaming the miserable pittance of their wives and children; and spent the hours of the night in obscure taverns and brothels in the indulgence of gross and vulgar sensuality.[60]

But the most lively and splendid amusement of the idle multitude depended on the frequent exhibition of public games and spectacles. The piety of Christian princes had suppressed the inhuman combats of gladiators; but the Roman people still considered the Circus as their home, their temple, and the seat of the republic. The impatient crowd rushed at the dawn of day to secure their places, and there were many who passed a sleepless and anxious night in the adjacent porticos. From the morning to the evening, careless of the sun or of the rain, the spectators, who sometimes amounted to the number of four hundred thousand, remained in eager attention; their eyes fixed on the horses and charioteers, their minds agitated with hope and fear for the success of the *colours* which they espoused; and the happiness of Rome appeared to hang on the event of a race.[61] The same immoderate ardour inspired their clamours and their applause as often as they were entertained with the hunting of wild beasts and the various modes of theatrical representation. These representations in modern capitals may deserve to be considered as a pure and elegant school of taste, and perhaps of virtue. But the Tragic and Comic Muse of the Romans, who seldom aspired beyond the imitation of Attic genius,[62] had been almost totally silent since the fall of the republic;[63] and their place was unworthily occupied by licentious farce, effeminate music, and splendid pageantry. The pantomimes,[64] who maintained their reputation from the age of Augustus to the sixth century, expressed, without the use of words, the various fables of the gods and heroes of antiquity; and the perfection of their art, which sometimes disarmed the gravity of the philosopher, always excited the applause and wonder of the people. The vast and magnificent theatres of Rome were filled by three thousand female dancers, and by three thousand singers, with the masters of the respective choruses. Such was the popular favour which they enjoyed, that, in a time of scarcity, when all strangers were banished from the city, the merit of contributing to the public pleasures exempted *them* from a law which was strictly executed against the professors of the liberal arts.[65]

It is said that the foolish curiosity of Elagabalus attempted to discover, from the quantity of spiders' webs, the number of the inhabitants of Rome. A more rational method of inquiry might not have been undeserving of the attention of the wisest princes, who could easily have resolved a question so important for the Roman government and so interesting to succeeding ages. The births and deaths of the citizens were duly registered; and if any writer of antiquity had condescended to mention the annual amount, or the common average, we might now produce some satisfactory calculation which would destroy the extravagant assertions of critics, and perhaps confirm the modest and probable conjectures of philosophers.[66] The most diligent researches have collected only the following circumstances, which, slight and imperfect as they are, may tend in some degree to illustrate the question of the populousness of ancient Rome. I. When the capital of the empire was besieged by the Goths, the circuit of the walls was accurately measured by Ammonius, the mathematician, who found it equal to twenty-one miles.[67] It should not be forgotten that the form of the city was almost that of a circle, the geometrical figure which is known to contain the largest space within any given circumference. II. The architect Vitruvius, who flourished in the Augustan age, and whose evidence, on this occasion, has peculiar weight and authority, observes that the innumerable habitations of the Roman people would have spread themselves far beyond the narrow limits of the city; and that the want of ground, which was probably contracted on every side by gardens and villas, suggested the common, though inconvenient, practice of raising the houses to a considerable height in the air.[68] But the loftiness of these buildings, which often consisted of hasty work and insufficient materials, was the cause of frequent and fatal accidents; and it was repeatedly enacted by Augustus, as well as by Nero, that the height of private edifices within the walls of Rome should not exceed the measure of seventy feet from the ground.[69] III. Juvenal[70] laments, as it should seem from his own experience, the hardships of the poorer citizens, to whom he addresses the salutary advice of emigrating, without delay, from the smoke of Rome, since they might purchase in the little towns of Italy a cheerful, commodious dwelling at the same price which they annually paid for a dark and miserable lodging. House-rent was therefore immoderately dear: the rich acquired, at an enormous expense, the ground, which they covered with palaces and gardens; but the body of the Roman people was crowded into a narrow space; and the different floors and apartments of the same house were divided, as it is still the custom of Paris and other cities, among several families of plebeians. IV. The total number of houses in the fourteen regions of the city is accurately stated in the description of Rome composed under the reign of Theodosius, and they amount to forty-eight thousand three hundred and eighty-two.[71] The two classes of *domus* and of *insulæ*, into which they are divided, include all the habitations of the capital, of every rank and condition, from the marble palace of the Anicii, with a numerous establishment of freedmen and slaves, to the lofty and narrow lodging-house where the poet Codrus and his wife were permitted to hire a wretched garret immediately under the tiles. If we adopt the same average which, under similar circumstances, has been found applicable to Paris,[72] and indifferently allow about twenty-five persons for each house, of every degree, we may fairly estimate the inhabitants of Rome at twelve hundred thousand: a number which cannot be thought excessive for the capital of a mighty empire, though it exceeds the populousness of the greatest cities of modern Europe.[73]

Such was the state of Rome under the reign of Honorius, at the time when the Gothic army formed the siege, or rather the blockade, of the city.[74] By a skilful disposition of his numerous forces, who impatiently watched the moment of an assault, Alaric encompassed the walls, commanded the twelve principal gates, intercepted all communication with the adjacent country, and vigilantly guarded the navigation of the Tiber, from which the Romans derived the surest and most plentiful supply of provisions. The first emotions of the nobles and of the people were those of surprise and indignation, that a vile barbarian should dare to insult the capital of the world; but their arrogance was

soon humbled by misfortune; and their unmanly rage, instead of being directed against
an enemy in arms, was meanly exercised on a
defenceless and innocent victim. Perhaps in the
person of Serena the Romans might have respected the niece of Theodosius, the aunt, nay
even the adoptive mother, of the reigning emperor; they abhorred the widow of Stilicho; and
they listened with credulous passion to the tale
of calumny which accused her of maintaining a
secret and criminal correspondence with the
Gothic invader. Actuated, or overawed, by the
same popular frenzy, the senate, without requiring any evidence of her guilt, pronounced the
sentence of her death. Serena was ignominiously strangled; and the infatuated multitude were
astonished to find that this cruel act of injustice
did not immediately produce the retreat of the
barbarians and the deliverance of the city. That
unfortunate city gradually experienced the distress of scarcity, and at length the horrid calamities of famine. The daily allowance of three
pounds of bread was reduced to one-half, to
one-third, to nothing; and the price of corn
still continued to rise in a rapid and extravagant proportion. The poorer citizens who were
unable to purchase the necessaries of life, solicited the precarious charity of the rich; and for
a while the public misery was alleviated by the
humanity of Læta, the widow of the emperor
Gratian, who had fixed her residence at Rome,
and consecrated, to the use of the indigent, the
princely revenue which she annually received
from the grateful successors of her husband.[75]
But these private and temporary donatives were
insufficient to appease the hunger of a numerous people; and the progress of famine invaded
the marble palaces of the senators themselves.
The persons of both sexes, who had been educated in the enjoyment of ease and luxury, discovered how little is requisite to supply the demands of nature; and lavished their unavailing
treasures of gold and silver to obtain the coarse
and scanty sustenance which they would formerly have rejected with disdain. The food the
most repugnant to sense or imagination, the ali-
ments the most unwholesome and pernicious to
the constitution, were eagerly devoured, and
fiercely disputed, by the rage of hunger. A dark
suspicion was entertained that some desperate
wretches fed on the bodies of their fellow-creatures whom they had secretly murdered; and
even mothers (such was the horrid conflict of
the two most powerful instincts implanted by
nature in the human breast), even mothers are
said to have tasted the flesh of their slaughtered

infants![76] Many thousands of the inhabitants of
Rome expired in their houses, or in the streets,
for want of sustenance; and as the public sepulchres without the walls were in the power of the
enemy, the stench which arose from so many
putrid and unburied carcasses infected the air;
and the miseries of famine were succeeded and
aggravated by the contagion of a pestilential
disease. The assurances of speedy and effectual
relief, which were repeatedly transmitted from
the court of Ravenna, supported, for some time,
the fainting resolution of the Romans, till at
length the despair of any human aid tempted
them to accept the offers of a preternatural deliverance. Pompeianus, præfect of the city, had
been persuaded, by the art or fanaticism of
some Tuscan diviners, that, by the mysterious
force of spells and sacrifices, they could extract
the lightning from the clouds, and point those
celestial fires against the camp of the barbarians.[77] The important secret was communicated
to Innocent, the bishop of Rome; and the successor of St. Peter is accused, perhaps without
foundation, of preferring the safety of the republic to the rigid severity of the Christian
worship. But when the question was agitated
in the senate; when it was proposed, as an essential condition, that those sacrifices should be
performed in the Capitol, by the authority and
in the presence of the magistrates; the majority
of that respectable assembly, apprehensive
either of the Divine or of the Imperial displeasure, refused to join in an act which appeared
almost equivalent to the public restoration of
Paganism.[78]

The last resource of the Romans was in the
clemency, or at least in the moderation, of the
king of the Goths. The senate, who in this emergency assumed the supreme powers of government, appointed two ambassadors to negotiate
with the enemy. This important trust was delegated to Basilius, a senator of Spanish extraction, and already conspicuous in the administration of provinces; and to John, the first
tribune of the notaries, who was peculiarly
qualified, by his dexterity in business, as well
as by his former intimacy with the Gothic
prince. When they were introduced into his
presence, they declared, perhaps in a more
lofty style than became their abject condition,
that the Romans were resolved to maintain
their dignity, either in peace or war; and that,
if Alaric refused them a fair and honourable
capitulation, he might sound his trumpets, and
prepare to give battle to an innumerable people, exercised in arms and animated by despair.

"The thicker the hay, the easier it is mowed," was the concise reply of the barbarian; and this rustic metaphor was accompanied by a loud and insulting laugh, expressive of his contempt for the menaces of an unwarlike populace, enervated by luxury before they were emaciated by famine. He then condescended to fix the ransom which he would accept as the price of his retreat from the walls of Rome: *all* the gold and silver in the city, whether it were the property of the state, or of individuals; *all* the rich and precious movables; and *all* the slaves who could prove their title to the name of *barbarians*. The ministers of the senate presumed to ask, in a modest and suppliant tone, "If such, O king! are your demands, what do you intend to leave us?" "YOUR LIVES," replied the haughty conqueror: they trembled and retired. Yet before they retired, a short suspension of arms was granted, which allowed some time for a more temperate negotiation. The stern features of Alaric were insensibly relaxed; he abated much of the rigour of his terms; and at length consented to raise the siege, on the immediate payment of five thousand pounds of gold, of thirty thousand pounds of silver, of four thousand robes of silk, of three thousand pieces of fine scarlet cloth, and of three thousand pounds weight of pepper.[79] But the public treasury was exhausted; the annual rents of the great estates in Italy and the provinces were intercepted by the calamities of war; the gold and gems had been exchanged, during the famine, for the vilest sustenance; the hoards of secret wealth were still concealed by the obstinacy of avarice; and some remains of consecrated spoils afforded the only resource that could avert the impending ruin of the city. As soon as the Romans had satisfied the rapacious demands of Alaric, they were restored, in some measure, to the enjoyment of peace and plenty. Several of the gates were cautiously opened; the importation of provisions from the river and the adjacent country was no longer obstructed by the Goths; the citizens resorted in crowds to the free market which was held during three days in the suburbs; and while the merchants who undertook this gainful trade made a considerable profit, the future subsistence of the city was secured by the ample magazines which were deposited in the public and private granaries. A more regular discipline than could have been expected was maintained in the camp of Alaric; and the wise barbarian justified his regard for the faith of treaties, by the just severity with which he chastised a party of licentious Goths who had insulted some Roman citizens on the road to Ostia. His army, enriched by the contributions of the capital, slowly advanced into the fair and fruitful province of Tuscany, where he proposed to establish his winter-quarters; and the Gothic standard became the refuge of forty thousand barbarian slaves, who had broke their chains, and aspired, under the command of their great deliverer, to revenge the injuries and the disgrace of their cruel servitude. About the same time he received a more honourable reinforcement of Goths and Huns, whom Adolphus,[80] the brother of his wife, had conducted, at his pressing invitation, from the banks of the Danube to those of the Tiber, and who had cut their way, with some difficulty and loss, through the superior numbers of the Imperial troops. A victorious leader, who united the daring spirit of a barbarian with the art and discipline of a Roman general, was at the head of an hundred thousand fighting men; and Italy pronounced with terror and respect the formidable name of Alaric.[81]

At the distance of fourteen centuries we may be satisfied with relating the military exploits of the conquerors of Rome, without presuming to investigate the motives of their political conduct. In the midst of his apparent prosperity, Alaric was conscious, perhaps, of some secret weakness, some internal defect; or perhaps the moderation which he displayed was intended only to deceive and disarm the easy credulity of the ministers of Honorius. The king of the Goths repeatedly declared that it was his desire to be considered as the friend of peace and of the Romans. Three senators, at his earnest request, were sent ambassadors to the court of Ravenna, to solicit the exchange of hostages and the conclusion of the treaty; and the proposals which he more clearly expressed during the course of the negotiations could only inspire a doubt of his sincerity, as they might seem inadequate to the state of his fortune. The barbarian still aspired to the rank of master-general of the armies of the West; he stipulated an annual subsidy of corn and money; and he chose the provinces of Dalmatia, Noricum, and Venetia for the seat of his new kingdom, which would have commanded the important communication between Italy and the Danube. If these modest terms should be rejected, Alaric showed a disposition to relinquish his pecuniary demands, and even to content himself with the possession of Noricum; an exhausted and impoverished country, perpetually exposed to the inroads of the barbarians of Germany.[82] But the hopes of peace were disappointed by the weak obstinacy, or interested views, of the minister Olympius. Without listening to the salutary remonstrances of the senate, he dismissed their ambassadors under the conduct of a military escort, too numerous for a retinue of honour, and too feeble for an army of defence. Six thousand Dalmatians, the flower of the Imperial legions, were ordered to march from Ravenna to Rome, through an open country which was occupied by the formidable myriads of the barbarians. These brave legionaries, encompassed and betrayed, fell a sacrifice to ministerial folly; their general, Valens, with an hundred soldiers, escaped from the field of battle; and one of the ambassadors, who could no longer claim the protection of the law of nations, was obliged to purchase his freedom with a ransom of thirty thousand pieces of gold. Yet Alaric, instead of resenting this act of impotent hostility, immediately renewed his proposals of peace, and the second embassy of the Roman senate, which derived weight and dignity from the presence of Innocent, bishop of the city, was guarded from the dangers of the road by a detachment of Gothic soldiers.[83]

Olympius[84] might have continued to insult the just resentment of a people who loudly accused him as the author of the public calamities, but his power was undermined by the secret intrigues of the palace. The favourite eunuchs transferred the government of Honorius and the empire to Jovius, the Prætorian præfect—an unworthy servant, who did not atone by the merit of personal attachment for the errors and misfortunes of his administration. The exile, or escape, of the guilty Olympius reserved him for more vicissitudes of fortune: he experienced the adventures of an obscure and wandering life; he again rose to power; he fell a second time into disgrace; his ears were cut off—he expired under the lash—and his ignominious death afforded a grateful spectacle to the friends of Stilicho. After the removal of Olympius, whose character was deeply tainted with religious fanaticism, the Pagans and heretics were delivered from the impolitic proscription which excluded them from the dignities of the state. The brave Gennerid,[85] a soldier of barbarian origin, who still adhered to the worship of his ancestors, had been obliged to lay aside the military belt; and though he was repeatedly assured by the emperor himself that laws were not made for persons of his rank or merit, he refused to accept any partial dispensation, and persevered in honourable disgrace till he had extorted a general act of justice from the distress of the Roman government. The conduct of Gennerid in the important station to which he was promoted or restored, of master-general of Dalmatia, Pannonia, Noricum, and Rhætia, seemed to revive the discipline and spirit of the republic. From a life of idleness and want his troops were soon habituated to severe exercise and plentiful subsistence, and his private generosity often supplied the rewards which were denied by the avarice or poverty of the court of Ravenna. The valour of Gennerid, formidable to the adjacent barbarians, was the firmest bulwark of the Illyrian frontier; and his vigilant care assisted the empire with a reinforcement of ten thousand Huns, who arrived on the confines of Italy, attended by such a convoy of provisions, and such a numerous train of sheep and oxen, as might have been sufficient not only for the march of an army but for the settlement of a colony. But the court and councils of Honorius still remained a scene of weakness and distraction, of corruption and anarchy. Instigated by the præfect Jovius, the guards rose in furious mutiny and demanded the heads of two generals and of the two principal eunuchs. The generals, under a perfidious promise of safety, were sent on ship-board and privately executed; while the favour of the eunuchs procured them a mild and secure exile at Milan and Constantinople. Eusebius the eunuch and the barbarian Allobich succeeded to the command of the bedchamber and of the guards; and the mutual jealousy of the subordinate ministers was the cause of their mutual destruction. By the insolent order of the count of the domestics, the great chamberlain was shamefully beaten to death with sticks before the eyes of the astonished emperor; and the subsequent assassination of Allobich, in the midst of a public procession, is the only circumstance of his life in which Honorius discovered the faintest symptom of courage or resentment. Yet before they fell, Eusebius and Allobich had contributed their part to the ruin of the empire by opposing the conclusion of a treaty which Jovius, from a selfish, and perhaps a criminal motive, had negotiated with Alaric, in a personal interview under the walls of Rimini. During the absence of Jovius the emperor was persuaded to assume a lofty tone of inflexible dignity, such as neither his situation nor his character could enable him to support; and a letter, signed with the name of Honorius, was immediately despatched to the Prætorian præfect, granting him a free permission to dispose of the public money, but sternly refusing to prostitute the military honours of Rome to the proud demands of a barbarian. This letter was imprudently communicated to Alaric himself; and the Goth, who in the whole transaction had behaved with temper and decency, expressed in the most outrageous language his lively sense of the insult so wantonly offered to his person and to his nation. The conference of Rimini was hastily interrupted; and the præfect Jovius, on his return to Ravenna, was compelled to adopt, and even to encourage, the fashionable opinions of the court. By his advice and example the principal officers of the state and army were obliged to swear that, without listening in *any* circumstances to *any* conditions of peace, they would still persevere in perpetual and implacable war against the enemy of the republic. This rash engagement opposed an insuperable bar to all future negotiation. The ministers of Honorius were heard to declare that, if they had only invoked the name of the Deity, they would consult the public safety, and trust their souls to the mercy of Heaven: but they had sworn by the sacred head of the emperor himself; they had touched in solemn ceremony that august seat of majesty and wisdom; and the violation of their oath would expose them to the temporal penalties of sacrilege and rebellion.[86]

While the emperor and his court enjoyed with sullen pride the security of the marshes and fortifications of Ravenna, they abandoned Rome, almost without defence, to the resentment of Alaric. Yet such was the moderation which he still preserved, or affected, that as he moved with his army along the Flaminian way he successively despatched the bishops of the towns of Italy to reiterate his offers of peace, and to conjure the emperor that he would save the city and its inhabitants from hostile fire and the sword of the barbarians.[87] These impending calamities were however averted, not indeed by the wisdom of Honorius, but by the prudence or humanity of the Gothic king, who employed a milder, though not less effectual, method of conquest. Instead of assaulting the capital he successfully directed his efforts against the *Port* of Ostia, one of the boldest and most stupendous works of Roman magnificence.[88] The accidents to which the precarious subsistence of the city was continually exposed in a winter navigation and an open road had suggested to the genius of the first Cæsar the useful design which was executed under the reign of Claudius. The artificial moles which formed the narrow entrance advanced far into the sea, and firmly repelled the fury of the waves, while the largest vessels securely rode at anchor within three deep and capacious basins which received the northern branch of the Tiber about two miles from the ancient colony of Ostia.[89] The Roman *Port* insensibly swelled to the size of an episcopal city,[90] where the corn of Africa was deposited in spacious granaries for the use of the capital. As soon as Alaric was in possession of that important place he summoned the city to surrender at discretion; and his demands were enforced by the positive declaration that a refusal, or even a delay, should be instantly followed by the destruction of the magazines on which the life of the Roman people depended. The clamours of that people and the terror of famine subdued the pride of the senate; they listened without reluctance to the proposal of placing a new emperor on the throne of the unworthy Honorius; and the suffrage of the Gothic conqueror bestowed the purple on Attalus, præfect of the city. The grateful monarch immediately acknowledged his protector as master-general of the armies of the West; Adolphus, with the rank of count of the domestics, obtained the custody of the person of Attalus; and the two hostile nations seemed to be united in the closest bands of friendship and alliance.[91]

The gates of the city were thrown open, and the new emperor of the Romans, encompassed on every side by the Gothic arms, was conducted in tumultuous procession to the palace of Augustus and Trajan. After he had distributed the civil and military dignities among his favourites and followers, Attalus convened an assembly of the senate, before whom, in a formal and florid speech, he asserted his resolution of restoring the majesty of the republic, and of uniting to the empire the provinces of Egypt and the East which had once acknowledged the sovereignty of Rome. Such extravagant promises inspired every reasonable citizen with a just contempt for the character of an unwarlike usurper, whose elevation was the deepest and most ignominious wound which the republic had yet sustained from the insolence of the barbarians. But the populace, with their usual levity, applauded the change of masters. The public discontent was favourable to the rival of Honorius; and the sectaries, oppressed by his persecuting edicts, expected some degree of countenance, or at least of toleration, from a prince who, in his native country of Ionia, had been educated in the Pagan superstition, and who had since received the sacrament of baptism from the hands of an Arian bishop.[92] The first days of the reign of Attalus were fair and prosperous. An officer of confidence was sent with an inconsiderable body of troops to secure the obedience of Africa; the greatest part of Italy submitted to the terror of the Gothic powers; and though the city of Bologna made a vigorous and effectual resistance, the people of Milan, dissatisfied perhaps with the absence of Honorius, accepted with loud acclamations the choice of the Roman senate. At the head of a formidable army, Alaric conducted his royal captive almost to the gates of Ravenna; and a solemn embassy of the principal ministers—of Jovius the Prætorian præfect, of Valens, master of the cavalry and infantry, of the quæstor Potamius, and of Julian, the first of the notaries—was introduced with martial pomp into the Gothic camp. In the name of their sovereign they consented to acknowledge the lawful election of his competitor, and to divide the provinces of Italy and the West between the two emperors. Their proposals were rejected with disdain; and the refusal was aggravated by the insulting clemency of Attalus, who condescended to promise that if Honorius would instantly resign the purple he should be permitted to pass the remainder of his life in the peaceful exile of some remote island.[93] So desperate indeed did the situation of the son of Theodosius appear to those who were the best acquainted with his strength and resources, that Jovius and Valens, his minister and his general, betrayed their trust, infamously deserted the sinking cause of their benefactor, and devoted their treacherous allegiance to the service of his more fortunate rival. Astonished by such examples of domestic treason, Honorius trembled at the approach of every servant, at the arrival of every messenger. He dreaded the secret enemies who might lurk in his capital, his palace, his bed-chamber; and some ships lay ready in the harbour of Ravenna to transport the abdicated monarch to the dominions of his infant nephew, the emperor of the East.

But there *is* a Providence (such at least was the opinion of the historian Procopius[94]) that watches over innocence and folly, and the pretensions of Honorius to its peculiar care cannot reasonably be disputed. At the moment when his despair, incapable of any wise or manly resolution, meditated a shameful flight, a seasonable reinforcement of four thousand veterans unexpectedly landed in the port of Ravenna. To these valiant strangers, whose fidelity had not been corrupted by the factions of the court, he committed the walls and gates of the city,

and the slumbers of the emperor were no longer disturbed by the apprehension of imminent and internal danger. The favourable intelligence which was received from Africa suddenly changed the opinions of men and the state of public affairs. The troops and officers whom Attalus had sent into that province were defeated and slain, and the active zeal of Heraclian maintained his own allegiance and that of his people. The faithful count of Africa transmitted a large sum of money, which fixed the attachment of the Imperial guards; and his vigilance in preventing the exportation of corn and oil introduced famine, tumult and discontent into the walls of Rome. The failure of the African expedition was the source of mutual complaint and recrimination in the party of Attalus, and the mind of his protector was insensibly alienated from the interest of a prince who wanted spirit to command or docility to obey. The most imprudent measures were adopted, without the knowledge or against the advice of Alaric, and the obstinate refusal of the senate to allow in the embarkation the mixture even of five hundred Goths, betrayed a suspicious and distrustful temper which in their situation was neither generous nor prudent. The resentment of the Gothic king was exasperated by the malicious arts of Jovius, who had been raised to the rank of patrician, and who afterwards excused his double perfidy by declaring without a blush that he had only *seemed* to abandon the service of Honorius more effectually to ruin the cause of the usurper. In a large plain near Rimini, and in the presence of an innumerable multitude of Romans and barbarians, the wretched Attalus was publicly despoiled of the diadem and purple; and those ensigns of royalty were sent by Alaric as the pledge of peace and friendship to the son of Theodosius.[95] The officers who returned to their duty were reinstated in their employments, and even the merit of a tardy repentance was graciously allowed; but the degraded emperor of the Romans, desirous of life and insensible of disgrace, implored the permission of following the Gothic camp in the train of a haughty and capricious barbarian.[96]

The degradation of Attalus removed the only real obstacle to the conclusion of the peace, and Alaric advanced within three miles of Ravenna to press the irresolution of the Imperial ministers, whose insolence soon returned with the return of fortune. His indignation was kindled by the report that a rival chieftain, that Sarus, the personal enemy of Adolphus, and the hereditary foe of the house of Balti, had been received into the palace. At the head of three hundred followers that fearless barbarian immediately sallied from the gates of Ravenna, surprised and cut in pieces a considerable body of Goths, re-entered the city in triumph, and was permitted to insult his adversary by the voice of a herald, who publicly declared that the guilt of Alaric had for ever excluded him from the friendship and alliance of the emperor.[97] The crime and folly of the court of Ravenna was expiated a third time by the calamities of Rome. The king of the Goths, who no longer dissembled his appetite for plunder and revenge, appeared in arms under the walls of the capital; and the trembling senate, without any hopes of relief, prepared by a desperate resistance to delay the ruin of their country. But they were unable to guard against the secret conspiracy of their slaves and domestics, who either from birth or interest were attached to the cause of the enemy. At the hour of midnight the Salarian gate was silently opened, and the inhabitants were awakened by the tremendous sound of the Gothic trumpet. Eleven hundred and sixty-three years after the foundation of Rome, the Imperial city, which had subdued and civilised so considerable a part of mankind, was delivered to the licentious fury of the tribes of Germany and Scythia.[98]

The proclamation of Alaric, when he forced his entrance into a vanquished city, discovered, however, some regard for the laws of humanity and religion. He encouraged his troops boldly to seize the rewards of valour, and to enrich themselves with the spoils of a wealthy and effeminate people; but he exhorted them at the same time to spare the lives of the unresisting citizens, and to respect the churches of the apostles St. Peter and St. Paul as holy and inviolable sanctuaries. Amidst the horrors of a nocturnal tumult several of the Christian Goths displayed the fervour of a recent conversion; and some instances of their uncommon piety and moderation are related, and perhaps adorned, by the zeal of ecclesiastical writers.[99] While the barbarians roamed through the city in quest of prey, the humble dwelling of an aged virgin, who had devoted her life to the service of the altar, was forced open by one of the powerful Goths. He immediately demanded, though in civil language, all the gold and silver in her possession, and was astonished at the readiness with which she conducted him to a splendid hoard of massy plate of the richest materials and the most curious workmanship.

The barbarian viewed with wonder and delight this valuable acquisition, till he was interrupted by a serious admonition, addressed to him in the following words: "These," said she, "are the consecrated vessels belonging to St. Peter: if you presume to touch them, the sacrilegious deed will remain on your conscience. For my part, I dare not keep what I am unable to defend." The Gothic captain, struck with reverential awe, despatched a messenger to inform the king of the treasure which he had discovered, and received a peremptory order from Alaric, that all the consecrated plate and ornaments should be transported, without damage or delay, to the church of the apostle. From the extremity, perhaps, of the Quirinal hill to the distant quarter of the Vatican, a numerous detachment of Goths, marching in order of battle through the principal streets, protected with glittering arms the long train of their devout companions who bore aloft on their heads the sacred vessels of gold and silver, and the martial shouts of the barbarians were mingled with the sound of religious psalmody. From all the adjacent houses a crowd of Christians hastened to join this edifying procession, and a multitude of fugitives, without distinction of age or rank, or even of sect, had the good fortune to escape to the secure and hospitable sanctuary of the Vatican. The learned work concerning the *City of God* was professedly composed by St. Augustin, to justify the ways of Providence in the destruction of the Roman greatness. He celebrates with peculiar satisfaction this memorable triumph of Christ, and insults his adversaries by challenging them to produce some similar example of a town taken by storm, in which the fabulous gods of antiquity had been able to protect either themselves or their deluded votaries.[100]

In the sack of Rome some rare and extraordinary examples of barbarian virtue have been deservedly applauded. But the holy precincts of the Vatican and the apostolic churches could receive a very small proportion of the Roman people: many thousand warriors, more especially of the Huns who served under the standard of Alaric, were strangers to the name, or at least to the faith, of Christ, and we may suspect, without any breach of charity or candour, that in the hour of savage licence, when every passion was inflamed and every restraint was removed, the precepts of the Gospel seldom influenced the behaviour of the Gothic Christians. The writers the best disposed to exaggerate their clemency have freely confessed that a cruel slaughter was made of the Romans,[101] and that the streets of the city were filled with dead bodies, which remained without burial during the general consternation. The despair of the citizens was sometimes converted into fury; and whenever the barbarians were provoked by opposition, they extended the promiscuous massacre to the feeble, the innocent, and the helpless. The private revenge of forty thousand slaves was exercised without pity or remorse; and the ignominious lashes which they had formerly received were washed away in the blood of the guilty or obnoxious families. The matrons and virgins of Rome were exposed to injuries more dreadful, in the apprehension of chastity, than death itself; and the ecclesiastical historian has selected an example of female virtue for the admiration of future ages.[102] A Roman lady, of singular beauty and orthodox faith, had excited the impatient desires of a young Goth, who, according to the sagacious remark of Sozomen, was attached to the Arian heresy. Exasperated by her obstinate resistance, he drew his sword, and, with the anger of a lover, slightly wounded her neck. The bleeding heroine still continued to brave his resentment and to repel his love, till the ravisher desisted from his unavailing efforts, respectfully conducted her to the sanctuary of the Vatican, and gave six pieces of gold to the guards of the church on condition that they should restore her inviolate to the arms of her husband. Such instances of courage and generosity were not extremely common. The brutal soldiers satisfied their sensual appetites without consulting either the inclination or the duties of their female captives; and a nice question of casuistry was seriously agitated, Whether those tender victims, who had inflexibly refused their consent to the violation which they sustained, had lost, by their misfortune, the glorious crown of virginity.[103] There were other losses indeed of a more substantial kind and more general concern. It cannot be presumed that all the barbarians were at all times capable of perpetrating such amorous outrages; and the want of youth, or beauty, or chastity, protected the greatest part of the Roman women from the danger of a rape. But avarice is an insatiate and universal passion; since the enjoyment of almost every object that can afford pleasure to the different tastes and tempers of mankind may be procured by the possession of wealth. In the pillage of Rome a just preference was given to gold and jewels, which contain the greatest value in the smallest compass and weight; but, after these portable riches had been removed by the more diligent robbers, the palaces of Rome were rudely stripped of their splendid and costly furniture. The sideboards of massy plate, and the variegated wardrobes of silk and purple, were irregularly piled in the waggons that always followed the march of a Gothic army. The most exquisite works of art were roughly handled or wantonly destroyed: many a statue was melted for the sake of the precious materials; and many a vase, in the division of the spoil, was shivered into fragments by the stroke of a battle-axe. The acquisition of riches served only to stimulate the avarice of the rapacious barbarians, who proceeded by threats, by blows, and by tortures, to force from their prisoners the confession of hidden treasure.[104] Visible splendour and expense were alleged as the proof of a plentiful fortune; the appearance of poverty was imputed to a parsimonious disposition; and the obstinacy of some misers, who endured the most cruel torments before they would discover the secret object of their affection, was fatal to many unhappy wretches, who expired under the lash for refusing to reveal their imaginary treasures. The edifices of Rome, though the damage has been much exaggerated, received some injury from the violence of the Goths. At their entrance through the Salarian gate they fired the adjacent houses to guide their march and to distract the attention of the citizens; the flames, which encountered no obstacle in the disorder of the night, consumed many private and public buildings, and the ruins of the palace of Sallust[105] remained in the age of Justinian a stately monument of the Gothic conflagration.[106] Yet a contemporary historian has observed that fire could scarcely consume the enormous beams of solid brass, and that the strength of man was insufficient to subvert the foundations of ancient structures. Some truth may possibly be concealed in his devout assertion, that the wrath of Heaven supplied the imperfections of hostile rage, and that the proud Forum of Rome, decorated with the statues of so many gods and heroes, was levelled in the dust by the stroke of lightning.[107]

Whatever might be the numbers of equestrian or plebeian rank who perished in the massacre of Rome, it is confidently affirmed that only one senator lost his life by the sword of the enemy.[108] But it was not easy to compute the multitudes who, from an honourable station and a prosperous fortune, were suddenly reduced to the miserable condition of captives and exiles. As the barbarians had more occasion for money than for slaves, they fixed at a moderate price the redemption of their indigent prisoners; and the ransom was often paid by the benevolence of their friends, or the charity of strangers.[109] The captives, who were regularly sold, either in open market or by private contract, would have legally regained their native freedom, which it was impossible for a citizen to lose or to alienate.[110] But as it was soon discovered that the vindication of their liberty would endanger their lives, and that the Goths, unless they were tempted to sell, might be provoked to murder their useless prisoners, the civil jurisprudence had been already qualified by a wise regulation, that they should be obliged to serve the moderate term of five years, till they had discharged by their labour the price of their redemption.[111] The nations who invaded the Roman empire had driven before them, into Italy, whole troops of hungry and affrighted provincials, less apprehensive of servitude than of famine. The calamities of Rome and Italy dispersed the inhabitants to the most lonely, the most secure, the most distant places of refuge. While the Gothic cavalry spread terror and desolation along the sea-coast of Campania and Tuscany, the little island of Igilium, separated by a narrow channel from the Argentarian promontory, repulsed, or eluded, their hostile attempts; and at so small a distance from Rome, great numbers of citizens were securely concealed in the thick woods of that sequestered spot.[112] The ample patrimonies which many senatorian families possessed in Africa invited them, if they had time and prudence to escape from the ruin of their country, to embrace the shelter of that hospitable province. The most illustrious of these fugitives was the noble and pious Proba,[113] the widow of the præfect Petronius. After the death of her husband, the most powerful subject of Rome, she had remained at the head of the Anician family, and successively supplied, from her private fortune, the expense of the consulships of her three sons. When the city was besieged and taken by the Goths, Proba supported with Christian resignation the loss of immense riches; embarked in a small vessel, from whence she beheld, at sea, the flames of her burning palace; and fled with her daughter Læta, and her grand-daughter, the celebrated virgin Demetrias, to the coast of Africa. The benevolent profusion with which the matron distributed the fruits or the price of her estates contributed to alleviate the misfortunes of exile and captivity. But even the family of Proba herself was not exempt from the rapacious oppression of Count Heraclian, who basely sold, in matrimonial prostitution, the noblest maidens of Rome to the lust or avarice of the Syrian merchants. The Italian fugitives were dispersed through the provinces, along the coast of Egypt and Asia, as far as Constantinople and Jerusalem; and the village of Bethlehem, the solitary residence of St. Jerom and his female converts, was crowned with illustrious beggars, of either sex and every age, who excited the public compassion by the remembrance of their past fortune.[114] This awful catastrophe of Rome filled the astonished empire with grief and terror. So interesting a contrast of greatness and ruin disposed the fond credulity of the people to deplore, and even to exaggerate, the afflictions of the queen of cities. The clergy, who applied to recent events the lofty metaphors of Oriental prophecy, were sometimes tempted to confound the destruction of the capital and the dissolution of the globe.

There exists in human nature a strong propensity to depreciate the advantages, and to magnify the evils, of the present times. Yet, when the first emotions had subsided, and a fair estimate was made of the real damage, the more learned and judicious contemporaries were forced to confess that infant Rome had formerly received more essential injury from the Gauls than she had now sustained from the Goths in her declining age.[115] The experience of eleven centuries has enabled posterity to produce a much more singular parallel; and to affirm with confidence, that the ravages of the barbarians whom Alaric had led from the banks of the Danube were less destructive than the hostilities exercised by the troops of Charles the Fifth, a catholic prince, who styled himself Emperor of the Romans.[116] The Goths evacuated the city at the end of six days, but Rome remained above nine months in the possession of the Imperialists; and every hour was stained by some atrocious act of cruelty, lust, and rapine. The authority of Alaric preserved some order and moderation among the ferocious multitude which acknowledged him for their leader and king; but the constable of Bourbon had gloriously fallen in the attack of the walls; and the death of the general removed every restraint of discipline from an army which consisted of three independent nations, the Italians, the Spaniards, and the Germans. In the beginning of the sixteenth century the manners of Italy exhibited a remarkable scene of the depravity of mankind. They united the sanguinary crimes that prevail in an unsettled state of society, with the polished vices which spring from the abuse of art and luxury; and the loose adventurers, who had violated every prejudice of patriotism and superstition to assault the palace of the Roman pontiff, must deserve to be considered as the most profligate of the *Italians*. At the same era the *Spaniards* were the terror both of the Old and New World; but their high-spirited valour was disgraced by gloomy pride, rapacious avarice, and unrelenting cruelty. Indefatigable in the pursuit of fame and riches, they had improved, by repeated practice, the most exquisite and effectual methods of torturing their prisoners: many of the Castilians who pillaged Rome were familiars of the holy inquisition; and some volunteers, perhaps, were lately returned from the conquest of Mexico. The *Germans* were less corrupt than the Italians, less cruel than the Spaniards; and the rustic, or even savage aspect of those Tramontane warriors often disguised a simple and merciful disposition. But they had imbibed, in the first fervour of the Reformation, the spirit, as well as the principles, of Luther. It was their favourite amusement to insult, or destroy, the consecrated objects of catholic superstition; they indulged, without pity or remorse, a devout hatred against the clergy of every denomination and degree who form so considerable a part of the inhabitants of modern Rome; and their fanatic zeal might aspire to subvert the throne of Antichrist, to purify, with blood and fire, the abominations of the spiritual Babylon.[117]

The retreat of the victorious Goths, who evacuated Rome on the sixth day,[118] might be the result of prudence, but it was not surely the effect of fear.[119] At the head of an army encumbered with rich and weighty spoils, their intrepid leader advanced along the Appian Way into the southern provinces of Italy, destroying whatever dared to oppose his passage, and contenting himself with the plunder of the unresisting country. The fate of Capua, the proud and luxurious metropolis of Campania, and which was respected, even in its decay, as the eighth city of the empire,[120] is buried in oblivion; whilst the adjacent town of Nola [121] has been illustrated, on this occasion, by the sanctity of Paulinus,[122] who was successively a consul, a monk, and a bishop. At the age of forty he renounced the enjoyment of wealth and honour, of society and literature, to embrace a life of solitude and penance; and the loud applause of the clergy encouraged him to despise the reproaches of his worldly friends, who ascribed this desperate act to some disorder of the mind or body.[123] An early and passionate attachment determined him to fix his humble dwelling in one of the suburbs of Nola, near the miraculous tomb of St. Felix, which the public devotion had already surrounded with five large and populous churches. The remains of his fortune, and of his understanding, were dedicated to the service of the glorious martyr; whose praise, on the day of his festival, Paulinus never failed to celebrate by a solemn hymn; and in whose name he erected a sixth church, of superior elegance and beauty, which was decorated with many curious pictures from the history of the Old and New Testament. Such assiduous zeal secured the favour of the saint,[124] or at least of the people; and, after fifteen years' retirement the Roman consul was compelled to accept the bishopric of Nola, a few months before the city was invested by the Goths. During the siege, some religious persons were satisfied that they had seen, either in dreams or visions, the divine form of their tutelar patron; yet it soon appeared by the event, that Felix wanted power, or inclination, to preserve the flock of which he had formerly been the shepherd. Nola was not saved from the general devastation;[125] and the captive bishop was protected only by the general opinion of his innocence and poverty. Above four years elapsed from the successful invasion of Italy by the arms of Alaric, to the voluntary retreat of the Goths under the conduct of his successor Adolphus; and, during the whole time, they reigned without control over a country which, in the opinion of the ancients, had united all the various excellences of nature and art. The prosperity, indeed, which Italy had attained in the auspicious age of the Antonines, had gradually declined with the decline of the empire. The fruits of a long peace perished under the rude grasp of the barbarians; and they themselves were incapable of tasting the more elegant refinements of luxury which had been prepared for the use of the soft and polished Italians. Each soldier, however, claimed an ample portion of the substantial plenty, the corn and cattle, oil and wine, that was daily collected and consumed, in the Gothic camp; and the principal warriors insulted the villas and gardens, once inhabited by Lucullus and Cicero, along the beauteous coast of Campania. Their trembling captives, the sons and daughters of Roman senators, presented, in goblets of gold and gems, large draughts of Falernian wine to the haughty victors, who stretched their huge limbs under the shade of plane-trees,[126] artificially disposed to exclude the scorching rays, and to admit the genial warmth, of the sun. These delights were enhanced by the memory of past hardships: the comparison of their native soil, the bleak and barren hills of Scythia, and the frozen banks of the Elbe and Danube, added new charms to the felicity of the Italian climate.[127]

Whether fame, or conquest, or riches were the object of Alaric, he pursued that object with an indefatigable ardour which could neither be quelled by adversity nor satiated by success. No sooner had he reached the extreme land of Italy than he was attracted by the neighbouring prospect of a fertile and peaceful island. Yet even the possession of Sicily he considered only an intermediate step to the important expedition which he already meditated against the continent of Africa. The straits of Rhegium and Messina[128] are twelve miles in length, and in the narrowest passage about one mile and a half broad; and the fabulous monsters of the deep, the rocks of Scylla and the whirlpool of Charybdis, could terrify none but the most timid and unskilled mariners. Yet as soon as the first division of the Goths had embarked, a sudden tempest arose, which sunk or scattered many of the transports; their courage was daunted by the terrors of a new element; and the whole design was defeated by the premature death of Alaric, which fixed, after a short illness, the fatal term of his conquests. The ferocious character of the barbarians was displayed in the funeral of a hero whose valour and fortune they celebrated with mournful applause. By the labour of a captive multitude they forcibly diverted the course of the Busentinus, a small river that washes the walls of Consentia. The royal sepulchre, adorned with the splendid spoils and trophies of Rome, was constructed in the vacant bed; the waters were then restored to their natural channel; and the secret spot where the remains of Alaric had been deposited was for ever concealed by the inhuman massacre of the prisoners who had been employed to execute the work.[129]

The personal animosities and hereditary feuds of the barbarians were suspended by the strong necessity of their affairs; and the brave Adolphus, the brother-in-law of the deceased monarch, was unanimously elected to succeed to his throne. The character and political system of the new king of the Goths may be best understood from his own conversation with an illustrious citizen of Narbonne, who afterwards, in a pilgrimage to the Holy Land, related it to St. Jerom, in the presence of the historian Orosius. "In the full confidence of valour and victory, I once aspired (said Adolphus) to change the face of the universe; to obliterate the name of Rome; to erect on its ruins the dominion of the Goths; and to acquire, like Augustus, the immortal fame of the founder of a new empire. By repeated experiments I was gradually convinced that laws are essentially necessary to maintain and regulate a well-constituted state; and that the fierce untractable humour of the Goths was incapable of bearing the salutary yoke of laws and civil government. From that moment I proposed to myself a different object of glory and ambition; and it is now my sincere wish that the gratitude of future ages should acknowledge the merit of a stranger, who employed the sword of the Goths. not to subvert, but to restore and maintain, the prosperity of the Roman empire."[130] With these pacific views the successor of Alaric suspended the operations of war, and seriously negotiated with the Imperial court a treaty of friendship and alliance. It was the interest of the ministers of Honorius, who were now released from the obligation of their extravagant oath, to deliver Italy from the intolerable weight of the Gothic powers; and they readily accepted their service against the tyrants and barbarians who infested the provinces beyond the Alps.[131] Adolphus, assuming the character of a Roman General, directed his march from the extremity of Campania to the southern provinces of Gaul. His troops, either by force or agreement, immediately occupied the cities of Narbonne, Toulouse, and Bordeaux; and though they were repulsed by Count Boniface from the walls of Marseilles, they soon extended their quarters from the Mediterranean to the ocean. The oppressed provincials might exclaim that the miserable remnant which the enemy had spared was cruelly ravished by their pretended allies; yet some specious colours were not wanting to palliate or justify the violence of the Goths. The cities of Gaul which they attacked might perhaps be considered as in a state of rebellion against the government of Honorius: the articles of the treaty or the secret instructions of the court might sometimes be alleged in favour of the seeming usurpations of Adolphus; and the guilt of any irregular unsuccessful act of hostility might always be imputed, with an appearance of truth, to the ungovernable spirit of a barbarian host impatient of peace or discipline. The luxury of Italy had been less effectual to soften the temper than to relax the courage of the Goths; and they had imbibed the vices, without imitating the arts and institutions, of civilised society.[132]

The professions of Adolphus were probably sincere, and his attachment to the cause of the republic was secured by the ascendant which a Roman princess had acquired over the heart and understanding of the barbarian king. Placidia,[133] the daughter of the great Theodosius, and of Galla, his second wife, had received a royal education in the palace of Constantinople; but the eventful story of her life is connected with the revolutions which agitated the Western empire under the reign of her brother Honorius. When Rome was first invested by the arms of Alaric, Placidia, who was then about twenty years of age, resided in the city; and her ready consent of the death of her cousin Serena has a cruel and ungrateful appearance, which, according to the circumstances of the action, may be aggravated or excused by the consideration of her tender age.[134] The victorious barbarians detained, either as a hostage or a captive,[135] the sister of Honorius; but while she was exposed to the disgrace of following round Italy the motions of a Gothic camp, she experienced, however, a decent and respectful treatment. The authority of Jornandes, who praises the beauty of Placidia, may perhaps be counterbalanced by the silence, the expressive silence, of her flatterers: yet the splendour of her birth, the bloom of youth, the elegance of manners, and the dexterous insinuations which she condescended to employ, made a deep impression on the mind of Adolphus; and the Gothic king aspired to call himself the brother of the emperor. The ministers of Honorius rejected with disdain the proposal of an alliance so injurious to every sentiment of Roman pride; and repeatedly urged the restitution of Placidia as an indispensable condition of the treaty of peace. But the daughter of Theodosius submitted without reluctance to the desires of the conqueror, a young and valiant prince, who yielded to Alaric in loftiness of stature, but who excelled in the more attractive qualities of grace and beauty. The marriage of Adolphus and Placidia[136] was consummated before the Goths retired from Italy; and the solemn, perhaps the anniversary, day of their nuptials was afterwards celebrated in the house of Ingenuus, one of the most illustrious citizens of Narbonne in Gaul. The bride, attired and adorned like a Roman empress, was placed on a throne of state; and the king of the Goths, who assumed on this occasion the Roman habit, contented himself with a less honourable seat by her side. The nuptial gift, which, according to the custom of his nation,[137] was offered to Placidia, consisted of the rare and magnificent spoils of her country. Fifty beautiful youths, in silken robes, carried a basin in each hand; and one of these basins was filled with pieces of gold, the other with precious stones of an inestimable value. Attalus, so long the sport of fortune and of the Goths, was appointed to lead the chorus of the Hymeneal song; and the degraded emperor might aspire to the praise of a skilful musician. The barbarians enjoyed the insolence of their triumph; and the provincials rejoiced in this alliance, which tempered, by the mild influence of love and reason, the fierce spirit of their Gothic lord.[138]

The hundred basins of gold and gems presented to Placidia at her nuptial feast formed an inconsiderable portion of the Gothic treasures; of which some extraordinary specimens may be selected from the history of the successors of Adolphus. Many curious and costly ornaments of pure gold, enriched with jewels, were found in their palace of Narbonne when it was pillaged in the sixth century by the Franks: sixty cups or chalices; fifteen *patens*, or plates, for the use of the communion; twenty boxes, or cases, to hold the books of the gospels: this consecrated wealth[139] was distributed by the son of Clovis among the churches of his dominions, and his pious liberality seems to upbraid some former sacrilege of the Goths. They possessed, with more security of conscience, the famous *missorium*, or great dish for the service of the table, of massy gold, of the weight of five hundred pounds, and of far superior value, from the precious stones, the exquisite workmanship, and the tradition that it had been presented by Aëtius, the patrician, to Torismond, king of the Goths. One of the successors of Torismond purchased the aid of the French monarch by the promise of this magnificent gift. When he was seated on the throne of Spain, he delivered it with reluctance to the ambassadors of Dagobert; despoiled them on the road; stipulated, after a long negotiation, the inadequate ransom of two hundred thousand pieces of gold; and preserved the *missorium* as the pride of the Gothic treasury.[140] When that treasury, after the conquest of Spain, was plundered by the Arabs, they admired and they have celebrated another object still more remarkable; a table of considerable size, of one single piece of solid emerald,[141] encircled with three rows of fine pearls, supported by three hundred and sixty-five feet of gems and massy gold, and estimated at the price of five hundred thousand pieces of gold.[142] Some portion of the Gothic treasures might be the gift of friendship or the tribute of obedience; but the far greater part had been the fruits of war and rapine, the spoils of the empire, and perhaps of Rome.

After the deliverance of Italy from the oppression of the Goths, some secret counsellor was permitted, amidst the factions of the palace, to heal the wounds of that afflicted country.[143] By a wise and humane regulation the eight provinces which had been the most deeply injured—Campania, Tuscany, Picenum, Samnium, Apulia, Calabria, Bruttium, and Lucania—obtained an indulgence of five years; the ordinary tribute was reduced to one-fifth, and even that fifth was destined to restore and support the useful institution of the public posts. By another law the lands which had been left without inhabitants or cultivation were granted, with some diminution of taxes, to the neighbours who should occupy or the strangers who should solicit them; and the new possessors were secured against the future claims of the fugitive proprietors. About the same time a general amnesty was published in the name of Honorius, to abolish the guilt and memory of all the *involuntary* offences which had been committed by his unhappy subjects during the term of the public disorder and calamity. A decent and respectful attention was paid to the restoration of the capital; the citizens were encouraged to rebuild the edifices which had been destroyed or damaged by hostile fire; and extraordinary supplies of corn were imported from the coast of Africa. The crowds that so lately fled before the sword of the barbarians were soon recalled by the hopes of plenty and pleasure; and Albinus, præfect of Rome, informed the court, with some anxiety and surprise, that in a single day he had taken an account of the arrival of fourteen thousand strangers.[144] In less than seven years the vestiges of the Gothic invasion were almost obliterated, and the city appeared to resume its former splendour and tranquillity. The venerable matron replaced her crown of laurel, which had been ruffled by the storms of war, and was still amused in the last moment of her decay with the prophecies of revenge, of victory, and of eternal dominion.[145]

This apparent tranquillity was soon disturbed by the approach of an hostile armament from the country which afforded the daily subsistence of the Roman people. Heraclian, count of Africa, who under the most difficult and distressful circumstances had supported with active loyalty the cause of Honorius, was tempted in the year of his consulship to assume the character of a rebel and the title of emperor. The

ports of Africa were immediately filled with the naval forces, at the head of which he prepared to invade Italy; and his fleet, when it cast anchor at the mouth of the Tiber, indeed surpassed the fleets of Xerxes and Alexander, if *all* the vessels, including the royal galley and the smallest boat, did actually amount to the incredible number of three thousand two hundred.[146] Yet with such an armament, which might have subverted or restored the greatest empires of the earth, the African usurper made a very faint and feeble impression on the provinces of his rival. As he marched from the port along the road which leads to the gates of Rome, he was encountered, terrified, and routed by one of the Imperial captains; and the lord of this mighty host, deserting his fortune and his friends, ignominiously fled with a single ship.[147] When Heraclian landed in the harbour of Carthage, he found that the whole province, disdaining such an unworthy ruler, had returned to their allegiance. The rebel was beheaded in the ancient temple of Memory, his consulship was abolished,[148] and the remains of his private fortune, not exceeding the moderate sum of four thousand pounds of gold, were granted to the brave Constantius, who had already defended the throne which he afterwards shared with his feeble sovereign. Honorius viewed with supine indifference the calamities of Rome and Italy,[149] but the rebellious attempts of Attalus and Heraclian against his personal safety awakened for a moment the torpid instinct of his nature. He was probably ignorant of the causes and events which preserved him from these impending dangers; and as Italy was no longer invaded by any foreign or domestic enemies, he peaceably existed in the palace of Ravenna, while the tyrants beyond the Alps were repeatedly vanquished in the name and by the lieutenants of the son of Theodosius.[150] In the course of a busy and interesting narrative I might possibly forget to mention the death of such a prince, and I shall therefore take the precaution of observing in this place that he survived the last siege of Rome about thirteen years.

The usurpation of Constantine, who received the purple from the legions of Britain, had been successful, and seemed to be secure. His title was acknowledged from the wall of Antoninus to the Columns of Hercules, and, in the midst of the public disorder, he shared the dominion and the plunder of Gaul and Spain with the tribes of barbarians whose destructive progress was no longer checked by the Rhine or Pyrenees. Stained with the blood of the kinsmen of

Honorius, he extorted from the court of Ravenna, with which he secretly corresponded, the ratification of his rebellious claims. Constantine engaged himself by a solemn promise to deliver Italy from the Goths, advanced as far as the banks of the Po, and, after alarming rather than assisting his pusillanimous ally, hastily returned to the palace of Arles, to celebrate with intemperate luxury his vain and ostentatious triumph. But this transient prosperity was soon interrupted and destroyed by the revolt of Count Gerontius, the bravest of his generals, who, during the absence of his son Constans, a prince already invested with the Imperial purple, had been left to command in the provinces of Spain. For some reason of which we are ignorant, Gerontius, instead of assuming the diadem, placed it on the head of his friend Maximus, who fixed his residence at Tarragona, while the active count pressed forwards through the Pyrenees to surprise the two emperors Constantine and Constans before they could prepare for their defence. The son was made prisoner at Vienne, and immediately put to death; and the unfortunate youth had scarcely leisure to deplore the elevation of his family, which had tempted or compelled him sacrilegiously to desert the peaceful obscurity of the monastic life. The father maintained a siege within the walls of Arles; but those walls must have yielded to the assailants had not the city been unexpectedly relieved by the approach of an Italian army. The name of Honorius, the proclamation of a lawful emperor, astonished the contending parties of the rebels. Gerontius, abandoned by his own troops, escaped to the confines of Spain, and rescued his name from oblivion by the Roman courage which appeared to animate the last moments of his life. In the middle of the night a great body of his perfidious soldiers surrounded and attacked his house, which he had strongly barricaded. His wife, a valiant friend of the nation of the Alani, and some faithful slaves, were still attached to his person; and he used with so much skill and resolution a large magazine of darts and arrows, that above three hundred of the assailants lost their lives in the attempt. His slaves, when all the missile weapons were spent, fled at the dawn of day; and Gerontius, if he had not been restrained by conjugal tenderness, might have imitated their example; till the soldiers, provoked by such obstinate resistance, applied fire on all sides to the house. In this fatal extremity he complied with the request of his barbarian friend and cut off his head. The wife of Gerontius, who conjured

him not to abandon her to a life of misery and disgrace, eagerly presented her neck to his sword: and the tragic scene was terminated by the death of the count himself, who after three ineffectual strokes, drew a short dagger and sheathed it in his heart.[151] The unprotected Maximus, whom he had invested with the purple, was indebted for his life to the contempt that was entertained of his power and abilities. The caprice of the barbarians, who ravaged Spain, once more seated this Imperial phantom on the throne: but they soon resigned him to the justice of Honorius; and the tyrant Maximus, after he had been shown to the people of Ravenna and Rome, was publicly executed.

The general, Constantius was his name, who raised by his approach the siege of Arles and dissipated the troops of Gerontius, was born a Roman; and this remarkable distinction is strongly expressive of the decay of military spirit among the subjects of the empire. The strength and majesty which were conspicuous in the person of that general[152] marked him in the popular opinion as a candidate worthy of the throne which he afterwards ascended. In the familiar intercourse of private life his manners were cheerful and engaging: nor would he sometimes disdain, in the license of convivial mirth, to vie with the pantomimes themselves in the exercises of their ridiculous profession. But when the trumpet summoned him to arms; when he mounted his horse, and, bending down (for such was his singular practice) almost upon the neck, fiercely rolled his large animated eyes round the field, Constantius then struck terror into his foes and inspired his soldiers with the assurance of victory. He had received from the court of Ravenna the important commission of extirpating rebellion in the provinces of the West; and the pretended emperor Constantine, after enjoying a short and anxious respite, was again besieged in his capital by the arms of a more formidable enemy. Yet this interval allowed time for a successful negotiation with the Franks and Alemanni; and his ambassador, Edobic, soon returned at the head of an army to disturb the operations of the siege of Arles. The Roman general, instead of expecting the attack in his lines, boldly, and perhaps wisely, resolved to pass the Rhone and to meet the barbarians. His measures were conducted with so much skill and secrecy, that, while they engaged the infantry of Constantius in the front, they were suddenly attacked, surrounded, and destroyed by the cavalry of his lieutenant Ulphilas, who had silently gained an advantageous post in their rear. The remains of the army of Edobic were preserved by flight or submission, and their leader escaped from the field of battle to the house of a faithless friend, who too clearly understood that the head of his obnoxious guest would be an acceptable and lucrative present for the Imperial general. On this occasion Constantius behaved with the magnanimity of a genuine Roman. Subduing or suppressing every sentiment of jealousy, he publicly acknowledged the merit and services of Ulphilas; but he turned with horror from the assassin of Edobic, and sternly intimated his commands that the camp should no longer be polluted by the presence of an ungrateful wretch who had violated the laws of friendship and hospitality. The usurper, who beheld from the walls of Arles the ruin of his last hopes, was tempted to place some confidence in so generous a conqueror. He required a solemn promise for his security; and after receiving, by the imposition of hands, the sacred character of a Christian presbyter, he ventured to open the gates of the city. But he soon experienced that the principles of honour and integrity, which might regulate the ordinary conduct of Constantius, were superseded by the loose doctrines of political morality. The Roman general indeed refused to sully his laurels with the blood of Constantine; but the abdicated emperor and his son Julian were sent, under a strong guard, into Italy; and before they reached the palace of Ravenna they met the ministers of death.

At a time when it was universally confessed that almost every man in the empire was superior in personal merit to the princes whom the accident of their birth had seated on the throne, a rapid succession of usurpers, regardless of the fate of their predecessors, still continued to arise. This mischief was peculiarly felt in the provinces of Spain and Gaul, where the principles of order and obedience had been extinguished by war and rebellion. Before Constantine resigned the purple, and in the fourth month of the siege of Arles, intelligence was received in the Imperial camp that Jovinus had assumed the diadem at Mentz, in the Upper Germany, at the instigation of Goar, king of the Alani, and of Guntiarius, king of the Burgundians; and that the candidate on whom with a formidable host of barbarians from the banks of the Rhine to those of the Rhone. Every circumstance is dark and extraordinary in the short history of the reign of Jovinus. It was natural to expect that a brave and skilful general, at the head of a victorius army, would have asserted, in a field of battle, the justice of the cause of Honorius. The hasty retreat of Constantius might be justified by weighty reasons; but he resigned without a struggle the possession of Gaul; and Dardanus, the Prætorian præfect, is recorded as the only magistrate who refused to yield obedience to the usurper.[153] When the Goths, two years after the siege of Rome, established their quarters in Gaul, it was natural to suppose that their inclinations could be divided only between the emperor Honorius, with whom they had formed a recent alliance, and the degraded Attalus, whom they reserved in their camp for the occasional purpose of acting the part of a musician or a monarch. Yet in a moment of disgust (for which it is not easy to assign a cause or a date) Adolphus connected himself with the usurper of Gaul; and imposed on Attalus the ignominious task of negotiating the treaty which ratified his own disgrace. We are again surprised to read, that, instead of considering the Gothic alliance as the firmest support of his throne, Jovinus upbraided, in dark and ambiguous language, the officious importunity of Attalus; that, scorning the advice of his great ally, he invested with the purple his brother Sebastian; and that he most imprudently accepted the service of Sarus, when that gallant chief, the soldier of Honorius, was provoked to desert the court of a prince who knew not how to reward or punish. Adolphus, educated among a race of warriors, who esteemed the duty of revenge as the most precious and sacred portion of their inheritance, advanced with a body of ten thousand Goths to encounter the hereditary enemy of the house of Balti. He attacked Sarus at an unguarded moment, when he was accompanied only by eighteen or twenty of his valiant followers. United by friendship, animated by despair, but at length oppressed by multitudes, this band of heroes deserved the esteem, without exciting the compassion, of their enemies; and the lion was no sooner taken in the toils[154] than he was instantly despatched. The death of Sarus dissolved the loose alliance which Adolphus still maintained with the usurpers of Gaul. He again listened to the dictates of love and prudence; and soon satisfied the brother of Placidia, by the assurance that he would immediately transmit to the palace of Ravenna the heads of the two tyrants, Jovinus and Sebastian. The king of the Goths executed his promise without difficulty or delay: the helpless brothers, unsupported by any personal merit, were abandoned by their barbarian auxiliaries;

and the short opposition of Valentia was expiated by the ruin of one of the oldest cities of Gaul. The emperor chosen by the Roman senate, who had been promoted, degraded, insulted, restored, again degraded, and again insulted, was finally abandoned to his fate; but when the Gothic king withdrew his protection, he was restrained, by pity or contempt, from offering any violence to the person of Attalus. The unfortunate Attalus, who was left without subjects or allies, embarked in one of the ports of Spain, in search of some secure and solitary retreat; but he was intercepted at sea, conducted to the presence of Honorius, led in triumph through the streets of Rome or Ravenna, and publicly exposed to the gazing multitude, on the second step of the throne of his *invincible* conqueror. The same measure of punishment with which, in the days of his prosperity, he was accused of menacing his rival, was inflicted on Attalus himself: he was condemned, after the amputation of two fingers, to a perpetual exile in the isle of Lipari, where he was supplied with the decent necessaries of life. The remainder of the reign Honorius was undisturbed by rebellion; and it may be observed that in the space of five years seven usurpers had yielded to the fortune of a prince who was himself incapable either of counsel or of action.

The situation of Spain, separated on all sides from the enemies of Rome, by the sea, by the mountains, and by intermediate provinces, had secured the long tranquillity of that remote and sequestered country; and we may observe, as a sure symptom of domestic happiness, that, in a period of four hundred years, Spain furnished very few materials to the history of the Roman empire. The footsteps of the barbarians, who, in the reign of Gallienus, had penetrated beyond the Pyrenees, were soon obliterated by the return of peace; and in the fourth century of the Christian era, the cities of Emerita or Merida, of Corduba, Seville, Bracara, and Tarragona, were numbered with the most illustrious of the Roman world. The various plenty of the animal, the vegetable, and the mineral kingdoms, was improved and manufactured by the skill of an industrious people; and the peculiar advantages of naval stores contributed to support an extensive and profitable trade.[155] The arts and sciences flourished under the protection of the emperors; and if the character of the Spaniards was enfeebled by peace and servitude, the hostile approach of the Germans, who had spread terror and desolation from the Rhine to the Pyrenees, seemed to rekindle some sparks of military ardour. As long as the defence of the mountains was intrusted to the hardy and faithful militia of the country, they successfully repelled the frequent attempts of the barbarians. But no sooner had the national troops been compelled to resign their post of the Honorian bands in the service of Constantine, than the gates of Spain were treacherously betrayed to the public enemy, about ten months before the sack of Rome by the Goths.[156] The consciousness of guilt, and the thirst of rapine, prompted the mercenary guards of the Pyrenees to desert their station; to invite the arms of the Suevi, the Vandals, and the Alani; and to swell the torrent which was poured with irresistible violence from the frontiers of Gaul to the sea of Africa. The misfortunes of Spain may be described in the language of its most eloquent historian, who has concisely expressed the passionate, and perhaps exaggerated, declamations of contemporary writers.[157] "The irruption of these nations was followed by the most dreadful calamities: as the barbarians exercised their indiscriminate cruelty on the fortunes of the Romans and the Spaniards, and ravaged with equal fury the cities and the open country. The progress of famine reduced the miserable inhabitants to feed on the flesh of their fellow-creatures; and even the wild beasts, who multiplied, without control, in the desert, were exasperated by the taste of blood and the impatience of hunger boldly to attack and devour their human prey. Pestilence soon appeared, the inseparable companion of famine; a large proportion of the people was swept away; and the groans of the dying excited only the envy of their surviving friends. At length the barbarians, satiated with carnage and rapine, and afflicted by the contagious evils which they themselves had introduced, fixed their permanent seats in the depopulated country. The ancient Gallicia, whose limits included the kingdom of Old Castille, was divided between the Suevi and the Vandals: the Alani were scattered over the provinces of Carthagena and Lusitania, from the Mediterranean to the Atlantic Ocean; and the fruitful territory of Bætica was allotted to the Silingi, another branch of the Vandalic nation. After regulating this partition, the conquerors contracted with their new subjects some reciprocal engagements of protection and obedience: the lands were again cultivated; and the towns and villages were again occupied by a captive people. The greatest part of the Spaniards was even disposed to prefer this new condition of poverty and barbarism to the severe oppressions of the Roman government; yet there were many who still asserted their native freedom, and who refused, more especially in the mountains of Gallicia, to submit to the barbarian yoke.[158]

The important present of the heads of Jovinus and Sebastian had approved the friendship of Adolphus, and restored Gaul to the obedience of his brother Honorius. Peace was incompatible with the situation and temper of the king of the Goths. He readily accepted the proposal of turning his victorious arms against the barbarians of Spain; the troops of Constantius intercepted his communication with the seaports of Gaul, and gently pressed his march towards the Pyrenees:[159] he passed the mountains, and surprised, in the name of the emperor, the city of Barcelona. The fondness of Adolphus for his Roman bride was not abated by time or possession; and the birth of a son, surnamed, from his illustrious grandsire, Theodosius, appeared to fix him for ever in the interest of the public. The loss of that infant, whose remains were deposited in a silver coffin in one of the churches near Barcelona, afflicted his parents; but the grief of the Gothic king was suspended by the labours of the field; and the course of his victories was soon interrupted by domestic treason. He had imprudently received into his service one of the followers of Sarus, a barbarian of a daring spirit, but of a diminutive stature, whose secret desire of revenging the death of his beloved patron was continually irritated by the sarcasms of his insolent master. Adolphus was assassinated in the palace of Barcelona; the laws of the succession were violated by a tumultuous faction;[160] and a stranger to the royal race, Singeric, the brother of Sarus himself, was seated on the Gothic throne. The first act of his reign was the inhuman murder of the six children of Adolphus, the issue of a former marriage, whom he tore, without pity, from the feeble arms of a venerable bishop.[161] The unfortunate Placidia, instead of the respectful compassion which she might have excited in the most savage breasts, was treated with cruel and wanton insult. The daughter of the emperor Theodosius, confounded among a crowd of vulgar captives, was compelled to march on foot above twelve miles, before the horse of a barbarian, the assassin of an husband whom Placidia loved and lamented.[162]

But Placidia soon obtained the pleasure of revenge; and the view of her ignominious sufferings might rouse an indignant people against the tyrant, who was assassinated on the seventh day of his usurpation. After the death of Sin-geric, the free choice of the nation bestowed the Gothic sceptre on Wallia, whose warlike and ambitious temper appeared, in the beginning of his reign, extremely hostile to the republic. He marched in arms from Barcelona to the shores of the Atlantic Ocean, which the ancients revered and dreaded as the boundary of the world. But when he reached the southern promontory of Spain,[163] and, from the rock now covered by the fortress of Gibralter, contemplated the neighbouring and fertile coast of Africa, Wallia resumed the designs of conquest which had been interrupted by the death of Alaric. The winds and waves again disappointed the enterprise of the Goths; and the minds of a superstitious people were deeply affected by the repeated disasters of storms and shipwrecks. In this disposition, the successor of Adolphus no longer refused to listen to a Roman ambassador, whose proposals were enforced by the real, or supposed, approach of a numerous army, under the conduct of the brave Constantius. A solemn treaty was stipulated and observed: Placidia was honourably restored to her brother; six hundred thousand measures of wheat were delivered to the hungry Goths;[164] and Wallia engaged to draw his sword in the service of the empire. A bloody war was instantly excited among the barbarians of Spain; and the contending princes are said to have addressed their letters, their ambassadors, and their hostages, to the throne of the Western emperor, exhorting him to remain a tranquil spectator of their contest, the events of which must be favourable to the Romans by the mutual slaughter of their common enemies.[165] The Spanish war was obstinately supported, during three campaigns, with desperate valour and various success; and the martial achievements of Wallia diffused through the empire the superior renown of the Gothic hero. He exterminated the Silingi, who had irretrievably ruined the elegant plenty of the province of Bætica. He slew, in battle, the king of the Alani; and the remains of those Scythian wanderers who escaped from the field, instead of choosing a new leader, humbly sought a refuge under the standard of the Vandals, with whom they were ever afterwards confounded. The Vandals themselves, and the Suevi, yielded to the efforts of the invincible Goths. The promiscuous multitude of barbarians, whose retreat had been intercepted, were driven into the mountains of Gallicia; where they still continued, in a narrow compass and on a barren soil, to exercise their domestic and implacable hostilities. In the pride of victory, Wallia was faithful to his engagements: he restored his Spanish conquests to the obedience of Honorius; and the tyranny of the Imperial officers soon reduced an oppressed people to regret the time of their barbarian servitude. While the event of the war was still doubtful, the first advantages obtained by the arms of Wallia had encouraged the court of Ravenna to decree the honours of a triumph to their feeble sovereign. He entered Rome like the ancient conquerors of nations; and if the monuments of servile corruption had not long since met with the fate which they deserved, we should probably find that a crowd of poets and orators, of magistrates and bishops, applauded the fortune, the wisdom, and the invincible courage of the emperor Honorius.[166]

Such a triumph might have been justly claimed by the ally of Rome, if Wallia, before he repassed the Pyrenees, had extirpated the seeds of the Spanish war. His victorious Goths, forty-three years after they had passed the Danube, were established, according to the faith of treaties, in the possession of the second Aquitain, a maritime province between the Garonne and the Loire, under the civil and ecclesiastical jurisdiction of Bourdeaux. That metropolis, advantageously situated for the trade of the ocean, was built in a regular and elegant form; and its numerous inhabitants were distinguished among the Gauls by their wealth, their learning, and the politeness of their manners. The adjacent province, which has been fondly compared to the garden of Eden, is blessed with a fruitful soil and a temperate climate; the face of the country displayed the arts and the rewards of industry; and the Goths, after their martial toils, luxuriously exhausted the rich vineyards of Aquitain.[167] The Gothic limits were enlarged by the additional gift of some neighbouring dioceses; and the successors of Alaric fixed their royal residence at Toulouse, which included five populous quarters, or cities, within the spacious circuit of its walls. About the same time, in the last years of the reign of Honorius, the GOTHS, the BURGUNDIANS, and the FRANKS, obtained a permanent seat and dominion in the provinces of Gaul. The liberal grant of the usurper Jovinus to his Burgundian allies was confirmed by the lawful emperor; the lands of the First, or Upper, Germany were ceded to those formidable barbarians; and they gradually occupied, either by conquest or treaty, the two provinces which still retain, with the titles of Duchy and of County, the national appellation of Burgundy.[168] The Franks, the valiant and faithful allies of the Roman republic, were soon tempted to imitate the invaders whom they had so bravely resisted. Trèves, the capital of Gaul, was pillaged by their lawless bands; and the humble colony which they so long maintained in the district of Toxandria, in Brabant, insensibly multiplied along the banks of the Meuse and Scheld, till their independent power filled the whole extent of the Second, or Lower, Germany. These facts may be sufficiently justified by historic evidence; but the foundation of the French monarchy by Pharamond, the conquests, the laws, and even the existence of that hero, have been justly arraigned by the impartial severity of modern criticism.[169]

The ruin of the opulent provinces of Gaul may be dated from the establishment of these barbarians, whose alliance was dangerous and oppressive, and who were capriciously impelled, by interest or passion, to violate the public peace. A heavy and partial ransom was imposed on the surviving provincials who had escaped the calamities of war; the fairest and most fertile lands were assigned to the rapacious strangers, for the use of their families, their slaves, and their cattle; and the trembling natives relinquished with a sigh the inheritance of their fathers. Yet these domestic misfortunes, which are seldom the lot of a vanquished people, had been felt and inflicted by the Romans themselves, not only in the insolence of foreign conquest, but in the madness of civil discord. The Triumvirs proscribed eighteen of the most flourishing colonies of Italy, and distributed their lands and houses to the veterans who revenged the death of Cæsar, and oppressed the liberty of their country. Two poets, of unequal fame, have deplored, in similar circumstances, the loss of their patrimony; but the legionaries of Augustus appear to have surpassed, in violence and injustice, the barbarians who invaded Gaul under the reign of Honorius. It was not without the utmost difficulty that Virgil escaped from the sword of the centurion who had usurped his farm in the neighbourhood of Mantua;[170] but Paulinus of Bourdeaux received a sum of money from his Gothic purchaser, which he accepted with pleasure and surprise; and, though it was much inferior to the real value of his estate, this act of rapine was disguised by some colours of moderation and equity.[171] The odious name of conquerors was softened into the mild and friendly appellation of the guests of the Romans; and the barbarians of Gaul, more especially the Goths, repeatedly declared that they were bound to the people by the ties of hospitality, and to the emperor by the duty of allegiance and military service. The title of Honorius and his successors, their laws and their civil magistrates, were still respected in the provinces of Gaul, of which they had resigned the possession to the barbarian allies; and the kings, who exercised a supreme and independent authority over their native subjects, ambitiously solicited the more honourable rank of master-generals of the Imperial armies.[172] Such was the involuntary reverence which the Roman name still impressed on the minds of those warriors who had borne away in triumph the spoils of the Capitol.

Whilst Italy was ravaged by the Goths, and a succession of feeble tyrants oppressed the provinces beyond the Alps, the British island separated itself from the body of the Roman empire. The regular forces which guarded that remote province had been gradually withdrawn; and Britain was abandoned without defence, to the Saxon pirates and the savages of Ireland and Caledonia. The Britons, reduced to this extremity, no longer relied on the tardy and doubtful aid of a declining monarchy. They assembled in arms, repelled the invaders, and rejoiced in the important discovery of their own strength.[173] Afflicted by similar calamities, and actuated by the same spirit, the Armorican provinces (a name which comprehended the maritime countries of Gaul between the Seine and the Loire)[174] resolved to imitate the example of the neighbouring island. They expelled the Roman magistrate, who acted under the authority of the usurper Constantine; and a free government was established among a people who had so long been subject to the arbitrary will of a master. The independence of Britain and Armorica was soon confirmed by Honorius himself, the lawful emperor of the West; and the letters by which he committed to the new states the care of their own safety might be interpreted as an absolute and perpetual abdication of the exercise and rights of sovereignty. This interpretation was, in some measure, justified by the event. After the usurpers of Gaul had successively fallen, the maritime provinces were restored to the empire. Yet their obedience was imperfect, and precarious: the vain, the inconstant, rebellious disposition of the people, was incompatible either with freedom or servitude;[175] and Armorica, though it could not long maintain the form of a republic,[176] was agitated by frequent and destructive revolts. Britain was irrecoverably lost.[177] But as the emperors wisely acquiesced in the independence of a remote province, the separation was not embittered by the reproach of tyranny or rebellion; and the claims of allegiance and protection were succeeded by the mutual and voluntary offices of national friendship.[178]

This revolution dissolved the artificial fabric of civil and military government; and the independent country, during a period of forty years, till the descent of the Saxons, was ruled by the authority of the clergy, the nobles, and the municipal towns.[179] I. Zosimus, who alone has preserved the memory of this singular transaction, very accurately observes that the letters of Honorius were addressed to the *cities* of Britain.[180] Under the protection of the Romans, ninety-two considerable towns had arisen in the several parts of that great province; and, among these, thirty-three cities were distinguished above the rest by their superior privileges and importance.[181] Each of these cities, as in all the other provinces of the empire, formed a legal corporation, for the purpose of regulating their domestic policy; and the powers of municipal government were distributed among annual magistrates, a select senate, and the assembly of the people, according to the original model of the Roman constitution.[182] The management of a common revenue, the exercise of civil and criminal jurisdiction, and the habits of public counsel and command, were inherent to these petty republics; and when they asserted their independence, the youth of the city, and of the adjacent districts, would naturally range themselves under the standard of the magistrate. But the desire of obtaining the advantages, and of escaping the burthens, of political society, is a perpetual and inexhaustible source of discord; nor can it reasonably be presumed that the restoration of British freedom was exempt from tumult and faction. The pre-eminence of birth and fortune must have been frequently violated by bold and popular citizens; and the haughty nobles, who complained that they were become the subjects of their own servants,[183] would sometimes regret the reign of an arbitrary monarch. II. The jurisdiction of each city over the adjacent country was supported by the patrimonial influence of the principal senators; and the smaller towns, the villages, and the proprietors of land, consulted their own safety by adhering to the shelter of these rising republics. The sphere of their attraction was proportioned to the respective degrees of their wealth and populousness; but the hereditary lords of ample possessions, who were not oppressed by the neighbourhood of any powerful city, aspired to the rank of independent princes, and boldly exercised the rights of peace and war. The gardens and villas, which exhibited some faint imitation of Italian elegance, would soon be converted into strong castles, the refuge, in time of danger, of the adjacent country:[184] the produce of the land was applied to purchase arms and horses; to maintain a military force of slaves, of peasants, and of licentious followers: and the chieftain might assume, within his own domain, the powers of a civil magistrate. Several of these British chiefs might be the genuine posterity of ancient kings; and many more would be tempted to adopt this honourable genealogy, and to vindicate there hereditary claims, which had been suspended by the usurpation of the Cæsars.[185] Their situation and their hopes would dispose them to affect the dress, the language, and the customs of their ancestors. If the *princes* of Britain relapsed into barbarism, while the *cities* studiously preserved the laws and manners of Rome, the whole island must have been gradually divided by the distinction of two national parties; again broken into a thousand subdivisions of war and faction by the various provocations of interest and resentment. The public strength, instead of being united against a foreign enemy, was consumed in obscure and intestine quarrels; and the personal merit which had placed a successful leader at the head of his equals might enable him to subdue the freedom of some neighbouring cities, and to claim a rank among the *tyrants*[186] who infested Britain after the dissolution of the Roman government. III. The British church might be composed of thirty or forty bishops,[187] with an adequate proportion of the inferior clergy; and the want of riches (for they seem to have been poor)[188] would compel them to deserve the public esteem by a decent and exemplary behaviour. The interest, as well as the temper, of the clergy, was favourable to the peace and union of their distracted country: those salutary lessons might be frequently inculcated in their popular discourses; and the episcopal synods were the only councils that could pretend to the weight and authority of a national assembly. In such councils, where the princes and magistrates sat promiscuously with the bishops, the important affairs of the state, as well as of the church, might be freely debated, differences reconciled, alliances formed, contributions imposed, wise resolutions often concerted, and sometimes executed; and there is reason to believe, that, in moments of extreme danger, a *Pendragon*, or Dictator, was elected by the general consent of the Britons. These pastoral cares, so worthy of the episcopal character,

were interrupted, however, by zeal and superstition; and the British clergy incessantly laboured to eradicate the Pelagian heresy, which they abhorred as the peculiar disgrace of their native country.[189]

It is somewhat remarkable, or rather it is extremely natural, that the revolt of Britain and Armorica should have introduced an appearance of liberty into the obedient provinces of Gaul. In a solemn edict,[190] filled with the strongest assurances of that paternal affection which princes so often express, and so seldom feel, the emperor Honorius promulgated his intention of convening an annual assembly of the *seven provinces*: a name peculiarly appropriated to Aquitain and the ancient Narbonnese, which had long since exchanged their Celtic rudeness for the useful and elegant arts of Italy.[191] Arles, the seat of government and commerce, was appointed for the place of the assembly, which regularly continued twenty-eight days, from the fifteenth of August to the thirteenth of September of every year. It consisted of the Prætorian præfect of the Gauls; of seven provincial governors, one consular, and six presidents; of the magistrates, and perhaps the bishops, of about sixty cities; and of a competent, though indefinite, number of the most honourable and opulent *possessors* of land, who might justly be considered as the representatives of their country. They were empowered to interpret and communicate the laws of their sovereign; to expose the grievances and wishes of their constituents; to moderate the excessive or unequal weight of taxes; and to deliberate on every subject of local or national importance that could tend to the restoration of the peace and prosperity of the seven provinces. If such an institution, which gave the people an interest in their own government, had been universally established by Trajan or the Antonines, the seeds of public wisdom and virtue might have been cherished and propagated in the empire of Rome. The privileges of the subject would have secured the throne of the monarch; the abuses of an arbitrary administration might have been prevented, in some degree, or corrected, by the interposition of these representative assemblies; and the country would have been defended against a foreign enemy by the arms of natives and freemen. Under the mild and generous influence of liberty, the Roman empire might have remained invincible and immortal; or if its excessive magnitude, and the instability of human affairs, had opposed such perpetual continuance, its vital and constituent members might have separately preserved their vigour and independence. But in the decline of the empire, when every principle of health and life had been exhausted, the tardy application of this partial remedy was incapable of producing any important or salutary effects. The emperor Honorius expresses his surprise that he must compel the reluctant provinces to accept a privilege which they should ardently have solicited. A fine of three, or even five, pounds of gold was imposed on the absent representatives, who seem to have declined this imaginary gift of a free constitution, as the last and most cruel insult of their oppressors.

CHAPTER XXXII

Arcadius Emperor of the East. Administration and Disgrace of Eutropius. Revolt of Gainas. Persecution of St. John Chrysostom. Theodosius II. Emperor of the East. His Sister Pulcheria. His Wife Eudocia. The Persian War, and Division of Armenia.

THE division of the Roman world between the sons of Theodosius marks the final establishment of the empire of the East, which, from the reign of Arcadius to the taking of Constantinople by the Turks, subsisted one thousand and fifty-eight years in a state of premature and perpetual decay. The sovereign of that empire assumed and obstinately retained the vain, and at length fictitious, title of Emperor of the ROMANS; and the hereditary appellations of CÆSAR and AUGUSTUS continued to declare that he was the legitimate successor of the first of men, who had reigned over the first of nations. The palace of Constantinople rivalled, and perhaps excelled, the magnificence of Persia; and the eloquent sermons of St. Chrysostom[1] celebrate, while they condemn, the pompous luxury of the reign of Arcadius. "The emperor," says he, "wears on his head either a diadem or a crown of gold, decorated with precious stones of inestimable value. These ornaments and his purple garments are reserved for his sacred person alone; and his robes of silk are embroidered with the figures of golden dragons. His throne is of massy gold. Whenever he appears in public he is surrounded by his courtiers, his guards, and his attendants. Their spears, their shields, their cuirasses, the bridles and trappings of their horses, have either the substance or the appearance of gold; and the large splendid boss in the midst of their shield is encircled with smaller bosses, which represent the shape of the human eye. The two mules that draw the chariot of the monarch are perfectly white, and shining all over with gold. The chariot itself, of pure and solid gold, attracts the admiration of the spectators, who contemplate the purple curtains, the snowy carpet, the size of the precious stones, and the resplendent plates of gold, that glitter as they are agitated by the motion of the carriage. The Imperial pictures are white, on a blue ground; the emperor appears seated on his throne, with his arms, his horses, and his guards beside him; and his vanquished enemies in chains at his feet." The successors of Constantine established their perpetual residence in the royal city which he had erected on the verge of Europe and Asia. Inaccessible to the menaces of their enemies, and perhaps to the complaints of their people, they received with each wind the tributary productions of every climate; while the impregnable strength of their capital continued for ages to defy the hostile attempts of the barbarians. Their dominions were bounded by the Hadriatic and the Tigris; and the whole interval of twenty-five days' navigation, which separated the extreme cold of Scythia from the torrid zone of Æthiopia,[2] was comprehended within the limits of the empire of the East. The populous countries of that empire were the seat of art and learning, of luxury and wealth; and the inhabitants, who had assumed the language and manners of Greeks, styled themselves, with some appearance of truth, the most enlightened and civilised portion of the human species. The form of government was a pure and simple monarchy; the name of the ROMAN REPUBLIC, which so long preserved a faint tradition of freedom, was confined to the Latin provinces; and the princes of Constantinople measured their greatness by the servile obedience of their people. They were ignorant how much this passive disposition enervates and degrades every faculty of the mind. The subjects who had resigned their will to the absolute commands of a master were equally incapable of guarding their lives and fortunes against the assaults of the barbarians or of defending their reason from the terrors of superstition.

The first events of the reign of Arcadius and Honorius are so intimately connected, that the rebellion of the Goths and the fall of Rufinus have already claimed a place in the history of the West. It has already been observed that Eutropius,[3] one of the principal eunuchs of the palace of Constantinople, succeeded the haughty minister whose ruin he had accomplished and whose vices he soon imitated. Every order of the state bowed to the new favourite; and their tame and obsequious submission encouraged him to insult the laws, and, what is still more difficult and dangerous, the manners of his country. Under the weakest of the predecessors of Arcadius the reign of the eunuchs had been secret and almost invisible. They insinuated themselves into the confidence of the prince; but their ostensible functions were confined to the menial service of the wardrobe and Imperial bedchamber. They might direct in a whisper the public counsels, and blast by their malicious suggestions the fame and fortunes of the most illustrious citizens; but they never presumed to stand forward in the front of empire,[4] or to profane the public honours of the state. Eutropius was the first of his artificial sex who dared to assume the character of a Roman magistrate and general.[5] Sometimes, in the presence of the blushing senate, he ascended the tribunal to pronounce judgment or to repeat elaborate harangues; and sometimes appeared on horseback, at the head of his troops, in the dress and armour of a hero. The disregard of custom and decency always betrays a weak and ill-regulated mind; nor does Eutropius seem to have compensated for the folly of the design by any superior merit or ability in the execution. His former habits of life had not introduced him to the study of the laws or the exercises of the field; his awkward and unsuccessful attempts provoked the secret contempt of the spectators; the Goths expressed their wish that *such* a general might always command the armies of Rome; and the name of the minister was branded with ridicule, more pernicious, perhaps, than hatred to a public character. The subjects of Arcadius were exasperated by the recollection that this deformed and decrepit eunuch,[6] who so perversely mimicked the actions of a man, was born in the most abject conditions of servitude; that before he entered the Imperial palace he had been successively sold and purchased by an hundred masters, who had exhausted his youthful strength in every mean and infamous office, and at length dismissed him in his old age to freedom and poverty.[7] While these disgraceful stories were circulated, and perhaps exaggerated, in private conversations, the vanity of the favourite was flattered with the most extraordinary honours. In the senate, in the capital, in the provinces, the statues of Eutropius were erected, in brass or marble, decorated with the symbols of his civil and military virtues, and inscribed with the pompous title of the third founder of Constantinople. He was promoted to the rank of *patrician*, which began to signify, in a popular and even legal acceptation, the father of the emperor: and the last year of the fourth century was polluted by the *consulship* of an eunuch and a slave. This strange and inexpiable prodigy[8] awakened, however, the prejudices of the Romans. The effeminate consul was rejected by the West as an indelible stain to the annals of the republic; and without invoking the shades of Brutus and Camillus, the colleague of Eutropius, a learned and respectable magistrate,[9] sufficiently represented the different maxims of the two administrations.

The bold and vigorous mind of Rufinus seems to have been actuated by a more sanguinary and revengeful spirit; but the avarice of the eunuch was not less insatiate than that of the præfect.[10] As long as he despoiled the oppressors who had enriched themselves with the plunder of the people, Eutropius might gratify his covetous disposition without much envy or injustice: but the progress of his rapine soon invaded the wealth which had been acquired by lawful inheritance or laudable industry. The usual methods of extortion were practised and improved; and Claudian has sketched a lively and original picture of the public auction of the state. "The impotence of the eunuch" (says that agreeable satirist) "has served only to stimulate his avarice: the same hand which, in his servile condition, was exercised in petty thefts to unlock the coffers of his master, now grasps the riches of the world; and this infamous broker of the empire appreciates and divides the Roman provinces from Mount Hæmus to the Tigris. One man, at the expense of his villa, is made proconsul of Asia; a second purchases Syria with his wife's jewels; and a third laments that he has exchanged his paternal estate for the government of Bithynia. In the antechamber of Eutropius a large tablet is exposed to public view, which marks the respective prices of the provinces. The different value of Pontus, of

Galatia, of Lydia is accurately distinguished. Lycia may be obtained for so many thousand pieces of gold; but the opulence of Phrygia will require a more considerable sum. The eunuch wishes to obliterate by the general disgrace his personal ignominy; and as he has been sold himself, he is desirous of selling the rest of mankind. In the eager contention, the balance, which contains the fate and fortunes of the province, often trembles on the beam; and till one of the scales is inclined by a superior weight, the mind of the impartial judge remains in anxious suspense.[11] Such" (continues the indignant poet) "are the fruits of Roman valour, of the defeat of Antiochus, and of the triumph of Pompey." This venal prostitution of public honours secured the impunity of *future* crimes; but the riches which Eutropius derived from confiscation were *already* stained with injustice; since it was decent to accuse and to condemn the proprietors of the wealth which he was impatient to confiscate. Some noble blood was shed by the hand of the executioner; and the most inhospitable extremities of the empire were filled with innocent and illustrious exiles. Among the generals and consuls of the East, Abundantius[12] had reason to dread the first effects of the resentment of Eutropius. He had been guilty of the unpardonable crime of introducing that abject slave to the palace of Constantinople; and some degree of praise must be allowed to a powerful and ungrateful favourite who was satisfied with the disgrace of his benefactor. Abundantius was stripped of his ample fortunes by an Imperial rescript, and banished to Pityus, on the Euxine, the last frontier of the Roman world; where he subsisted by the precarious mercy of the barbarians till he could obtain, after the fall of Eutropius, a milder exile at Sidon in Phœnicia. The destruction of Timasius[13] required a more serious and regular mode of attack. That great officer, the master-general of the armies of Theodosius, had signalised his valour by a decisive victory which he obtained over the Goths of Thessaly; but he was too prone, after the example of his sovereign, to enjoy the luxury of peace and to abandon his confidence to wicked and designing flatterers. Timasius had despised the public clamour by promoting an infamous dependent to the command of a cohort; and he deserved to feel the ingratitude of Bargus, who was secretly instigated by the favourite to accuse his patron of a treasonable conspiracy. The general was arraigned before the tribunal of Arcadius himself; and the principal eunuch stood by the side of the throne to suggest the questions and answers of his sovereign. But as this form of trial might be deemed partial and arbitrary, the further inquiry into the crimes of Timasius was delegated to Saturnius and Procopius; the former of consular rank, the latter still respected as the father-in-law of the emperor Valens. The appearances of a fair and legal proceeding were maintained by the blunt honesty of Procopius; and he yielded with reluctance to the obsequious dexterity of his colleague, who pronounced a sentence of condemnation against the unfortunate Timasius. His immense riches were confiscated in the name of the emperor and for the benefit of the favourite; and he was doomed to perpetual exile at Oasis, a solitary spot in the midst of the sandy deserts of Libya.[14] Secluded from all human converse, the master-general of the Roman armies was lost for ever to the world; but the circumstances of his fate have been related in a various and contradictory manner. It is insinuated that Eutropius despatched a private order for his secret execution.[15] It was reported that in attempting to escape from Oasis he perished in the desert of thirst and hunger, and that his dead body was found on the sands of Libya.[16] It has been asserted with more confidence that his son Syagrius, after successfully eluding the pursuit of the agents and emissaries of the court, collected a band of African robbers; that he rescued Timasius from the place of his exile; and that both the father and the son disappeared from the knowledge of mankind.[17] But the ungrateful Bargus, instead of being suffered to possess the reward of guilt, was soon afterwards circumvented and destroyed by the more powerful villainy of the minister himself, who retained sense and spirit enough to abhor the instrument of his own crimes.

The public hatred and the despair of individuals continually threatened, or seemed to threaten, the personal safety of Eutropius, as well as of the numerous adherents who were attached to his fortune and had been promoted by his venal favour. For their mutual defence he contrived the safeguard of a law which violated every principle of humanity and justice.[18] I. It is enacted, in the name and by the authority of Arcadius, that all those who shall conspire, either with subjects or with strangers, against the lives of any of the persons whom the emperor considers as the members of his own body, shall be punished with death and confiscation. This species of fictitious and metaphorical treason is extended to protect not only the *illustrious* officers of the state and army who are admitted into the sacred consistory, but likewise the principal domestics of the palace, the senators of Constantinople, the military commanders, and the civil magistrates of the provinces: a vague and indefinite list, which, under the successors of Constantine, included an obscure and numerous train of subordinate ministers. II. This extreme severity might perhaps be justified, had it been only directed to secure the representatives of the sovereign from any actual violence in the execution of their office. But the whole body of Imperial dependents claimed a privilege, or rather impunity, which screened them in the loosest moments of their lives from the hasty, perhaps the justifiable, resentment of their fellow-citizens: and, by a strange perversion of the laws, the same degree of guilt and punishment was applied to a private quarrel and to a deliberate conspiracy against the emperor and the empire. The edict of Arcadius most positively and most absurdly declares that in such cases of treason, *thoughts* and *actions* ought to be punished with equal severity; that the knowledge of a mischievous intention, unless it be instantly revealed, becomes equally criminal with the intention itself;[19] and that those rash men who shall presume to solicit the pardon of traitors shall themselves be branded with public and perpetual infamy. III. "With regard to the sons of traitors" (continues the emperor), "although they ought to share the punishment, since they will probably imitate the guilt of their parents, yet, by the special effect of our Imperial lenity, we grant them their lives; but, at the same time, we declare them incapable of inheriting, either on the father's or on the mother's side, or of receiving any gift or legacy from the testament either of kinsmen or of strangers. Stigmatised with hereditary infamy, excluded from the hopes of honours or fortune, let them endure the pangs of poverty and contempt till they shall consider life as a calamity and death as a comfort and relief." In such words, so well adapted to insult the feelings of mankind, did the emperor, or rather his favourite eunuch, applaud the moderation of a law which transferred the same unjust and inhuman penalties to the children of all those who had seconded or who had not disclosed these fictitious conspiracies. Some of the noblest regulations of Roman jurisprudence have been suffered to expire; but this edict, a convenient and forcible engine of ministerial tyranny, was carefully inserted in the codes of Theodosius and Justinian; and the same maxims have been revived in modern ages to protect the electors of Germany and the cardinals of the church of Rome.[20]

Yet these sanguinary laws, which spread terror among a disarmed and dispirited people, were of too weak a texture to restrain the bold enterprise of Tribigild[21] the Ostrogoth. The colony of that warlike nation, which had been planted by Theodosius in one of the most fertile districts of Phrygia,[22] impatiently compared the slow returns of laborious husbandry with the successful rapine and liberal rewards of Alaric; and their leader resented, as a personal affront, his own ungracious reception in the palace of Constantinople. A soft and wealthy province in the heart of the empire was astonished by the sound of war, and the faithful vassal who had been disregarded or oppressed was again respected as soon as he resumed the hostile character of a barbarian. The vineyards and fruitful fields between the rapid Marsyas and the winding Mæander[23] were consumed with fire; the decayed walls of the cities crumbled into dust at the first stroke of an enemy; the trembling inhabitants escaped from a bloody massacre to the shores of the Hellespont; and a considerable part of Asia Minor was desolated by the rebellion of Tribigild. His rapid progress was checked by the resistance of the peasants of Pamphylia; and the Ostrogoths, attacked in a narrow pass between the city of Selgæ[24] a deep morass, and the craggy cliffs of Mount Taurus, were defeated with the loss of their bravest troops. But the spirit of their chief was not daunted by misfortune, and his army was continually recruited by swarms of barbarians and outlaws who were desirous of exercising the profession of robbery under the more honourable names of war and conquest. The rumours of the success of Tribigild might for some time be suppressed by fear, or disguised by flattery; yet they gradually alarmed both the court and the capital. Every misfortune was exaggerated in dark and doubtful hints, and the future designs of the rebels became the subject of anxious conjecture. Whenever Tribigild advanced into the inland country, the Romans were inclined to suppose that he meditated the passage of Mount Taurus and the invasion of Syria. If he descended towards the sea, they imputed, and perhaps suggested, to the Gothic chief the more dangerous project of arming a fleet in the harbours of Ionia, and of extending his depredations along the maritime coast, from the mouth of the Nile to the port of Constantinople. The approach of danger and the obstinacy of Tribigild, who refused all terms of accommodation, compelled Eutropius to summon a council of war.[25] After claiming for himself the privilege of a veteran soldier, the eunuch intrusted the guard of Thrace and the Hellespont to Gainas the Goth, and the command of the Asiatic army to his favourite Leo; two generals who differently but effectually promoted the cause of the rebels. Leo,[26] who from the bulk of his body and the dulness of his mind was surnamed the Ajax of the East, had deserted his original trade of a woolcomber, to exercise with much less skill and success the military profession; and his uncertain operations were capriciously framed and executed with an ignorance of real difficulties and a timorous neglect of every favourable opportunity. The rashness of the Ostrogoths had drawn them into a disadvantageous position between the rivers Melas and Eurymedon, where they were almost besieged by the peasants of Pamphylia; but the arrival of an Imperial army, instead of completing their destruction, afforded the means of safety and victory. Tribigild surprised the unguarded camp of the Romans in the darkness of the night, seduced the faith of the greater part of the barbarian auxiliaries, and dissipated without much effort the troops which had been corrupted by the relaxation of discipline and the luxury of the capital. The discontent of Gainas, who had so boldly contrived and executed the death of Rufinus, was irritated by the fortune of his unworthy successor; he accused his own dishonourable patience under the servile reign of an eunuch; and the ambitious Goth was convicted, at least in the public opinion, of secretly fomenting the revolt of Tribigild, with whom he was connected by a domestic as well as by a national alliance.[27] When Gainas passed the Hellespont, to unite under his standard the remains of the Asiatic troops, he skilfully adapted his motions to the wishes of the Ostrogoths, abandoning by his retreat the country which they desired to invade, or facilitating by his approach the desertion of the barbarian auxiliaries. To the Imperial court he repeatedly magnified the valour, the genius, the inexhaustible resources of Tribigild, confessed his own inability to prosecute the war, and extorted the permission of negotiating with his invincible adversary. The conditions of peace were dictated by the haughty rebel; and the peremptory demand of the head of Eutropius revealed the author and the design of this hostile conspiracy.

The bold satirist, who has indulged his discontent by the partial and passionate censure of the Christian emperors, violates the dignity rather than the truth of history by comparing the son of Theodosius to one of those harmless and simple animals who scarcely feel that they are the property of their shepherd. Two passions, however—fear and conjugal affection—awakened the languid soul of Arcadius: he was terrified by the threats of a victorious barbarian, and he yielded to the tender eloquence of his wife Eudoxia, who, with a flood of artificial tears, presenting her infant children to their father, implored his justice for some real or imaginary insult which she imputed to the audacious eunuch.[28] The emperor's hand was directed to sign the condemnation of Eutropius; the magic spell, which during four years had bound the prince and the people, was instantly dissolved; and the acclamations that so lately hailed the merit and fortune of the favourite were converted into the clamours of the soldiers and people, who reproached his crimes and pressed his immediate execution. In this hour of distress and despair his only refuge was in the sanctuary of the church, whose privileges he had wisely, or profanely, attempted to circumscribe; and the most eloquent of the saints, John Chrysostom, enjoyed the triumph of protecting a prostrate minister, whose choice had raised him to the ecclesiastical throne of Constantinople. The archbishop, ascending the pulpit of the cathedral that he might be distinctly seen and heard by an innumerable crowd of either sex and of every age, pronounced a seasonable and pathetic discourse on the forgiveness of injuries and the instability of human greatness. The agonies of the pale and affrighted wretch, who lay grovelling under the table of the altar, exhibited a solemn and instructive spectacle; and the orator, who was afterwards accused of insulting the misfortunes of Eutropius, laboured to excite the contempt, that he might assuage the fury, of the people.[29] The powers of humanity, of superstition, and of eloquence prevailed. The empress Eudoxia was restrained, by her own prejudices or by those of her subjects, from violating the sanctuary of the church; and Eutropius was tempted to capitulate, by the milder arts of persuasion, and by an oath that his life should be spared.[30] Careless of the dignity of their sovereign, the new ministers of the palace immediately published an edict, to declare that his late favourite had disgraced the names of consul and patrician, to abolish his statues, to confiscate his wealth, and to inflict a perpetual exile in the island of Cyprus.[31] A despicable and decrepit eunuch could no longer alarm the fears of his enemies; nor was he capable of enjoying what yet remained—the comforts of peace, of solitude, and of a happy climate. But their implacable revenge still envied him the last moments of a miserable life, and Eutropius had no sooner touched the shores of Cyprus than he was hastily recalled. The vain hope of eluding, by a change of place, the obligation of an oath, engaged the empress to transfer the scene of his trial and execution from Constantinople to the adjacent suburb of Chalcedon. The consul Aurelian pronounced the sentence; and the motives of that sentence expose the jurisprudence of a despotic government. The crimes which Eutropius had committed against the people might have justified his death; but he was found guilty of harnessing to his chariot the *sacred* animals, who, from their breed or colour, were reserved for the use of the emperor alone.[32]

While this domestic revolution was transacted, Gainas[33] openly revolted from his allegiance, united his forces at Thyatira in Lydia with those of Tribigild, and still maintained his superior ascendant over the rebellious leader of the Ostrogoths. The confederate armies advanced without resistance to the straits of the Hellespont and the Bosphorus, and Arcadius was instructed to prevent the loss of his Asiatic dominions by resigning his authority and his person to the faith of the barbarians. The church of the holy martyr Euphemia, situate on a lofty eminence near Chalcedon,[34] was chosen for the place of the interview. Gainas bowed with reverence at the feet of the emperor, whilst he required the sacrifice of Aurelian and Saturninus, two ministers of consular rank; and their naked necks were exposed by the haughty rebel to the edge of the sword, till he condescended to grant them a precarious and disgraceful respite. The Goths, according to the terms of the agreement, were immediately transported from Asia into Europe; and the victorious chief, who accepted the title of master-general of the Roman armies, soon filled Constantinople with his troops, and distributed among his dependents the honours and rewards of the empire. In his early youth Gainas had passed the Danube as a suppliant and a fugitive: his elevation had been the work of valour and fortune, and his indiscreet or perfidious conduct was the cause of his rapid downfall. Notwithstanding the vigorous opposition of the archbishop, he importunately claimed for his Arian sectaries the possession of a peculiar church, and the pride of the catholics was offended by the public toleration of here-

sy.[35] Every quarter of Constantinople was filled with tumult and disorder; and the barbarians gazed with such ardour on the rich shops of the jewellers and the tables of the bankers which were covered with gold and silver, that it was judged prudent to remove those dangerous temptations from their sight. They resented the injurious precaution; and some alarming attempts were made during the night to attack and destroy with fire the Imperial palace.[36] In this state of mutual and suspicious hostility, the guards and the people of Constantinople shut the gates, and rose in arms to prevent or to punish the conspiracy of the Goths. During the absence of Gainas his troops were surprised and oppressed; seven thousand barbarians perished in this bloody massacre. In the fury of the pursuit the catholics uncovered the roof, and continued to throw down flaming logs of wood till they overwhelmed their adversaries, who had retreated to the church or conventicle of the Arians. Gainas was either innocent of the design or too confident of his success; he was astonished by the intelligence that the flower of his army had been ingloriously destroyed; that he himself was declared a public enemy; and that his countryman Fravitta, a brave and loyal confederate, had assumed the management of the war by sea and land. The enterprises of the rebel against the cities of Thrace were encountered by a firm and well-ordered defence: his hungry soldiers were soon reduced to the grass that grew on the margin of the fortifications; and Gainas, who vainly regretted the wealth and luxury of Asia, embraced a desperate resolution of forcing the passage of the Hellespont. He was destitute of vessels, but the woods of the Chersonesus afforded materials for rafts, and his intrepid barbarians did not refuse to trust themselves to the waves. But Fravitta attentively watched the progress of their undertaking. As soon as they had gained the middle of the stream, the Roman galleys,[37] impelled by the full force of oars, of the current, and of a favourable wind, rushed forwards in compact order and with irresistible weight, and the Hellespont was covered with the fragments of the Gothic shipwreck. After the destruction of his hopes and the loss of many thousands of his bravest soldiers, Gainas, who could no longer aspire to govern or to subdue the Romans, determined to resume the independence of a savage life. A light and active body of barbarian horse, disengaged from their infantry and baggage, might perform in eight or ten days a march of three hundred miles from the Hellespont to the Danube;[38] the garrisons of that important frontier had been gradually annihilated; the river in the month of December would be deeply frozen; and the unbounded prospect of Scythia was open to the ambition of Gainas. This design was secretly communicated to the national troops, who devoted themselves to the fortunes of their leader; and before the signal of departure was given, a great number of provincial auxiliaries, whom he suspected of an attachment to their native country, were perfidiously massacred. The Goths advanced by rapid marches through the plains of Thrace, and they were soon delivered from the fear of pursuit by the vanity of Fravitta, who, instead of extinguishing the war, hastened to enjoy the popular applause, and to assume the peaceful honours of the consulship. But a formidable ally appeared in arms to vindicate the majesty of the empire, and to guard the peace and liberty of Scythia.[39] The superior forces of Uldin, king of the Huns, opposed the progress of Gainas; an hostile and ruined country prohibited his retreat; he disdained to capitulate; and after repeatedly attempting to cut his way through the ranks of the enemy, he was slain, with his desperate followers, in the field of battle. Eleven days after the naval victory of the Hellespont, the head of Gainas, the inestimable gift of the conqueror, was received at Constantinople with the most liberal expressions of gratitude; and the public deliverance was celebrated by festivals and illuminations. The triumphs of Arcadius became the subject of epic poems;[40] and the monarch, no longer oppressed by any hostile terrors, resigned himself to the mild and absolute dominion of his wife, the fair and artful Eudoxia, who has sullied her fame by the persecution of St. John Chrysostom.

After the death of the indolent Nectarius, the successor of Gregory Nazianzen, the church of Constantinople was distracted by the ambition of rival candidates, who were not ashamed to solicit, with gold or flattery, the suffrage of the people or of the favourite. On this occasion Eutropius seems to have deviated from his ordinary maxims; and his uncorrupted judgment was determined only by the superior merit of a stranger. In a late journey into the East he had admired the sermons of John, a native and presbyter of Antioch, whose name has been distinguished by the epithet of Chrysostom, or the Golden Mouth.[41] A private order was despatched to the governor of Syria; and as the people might be unwilling to resign their favourite preacher, he was transported, with speed and secrecy, in a post-chariot, from Antioch to Constantinople. The unanimous and unsolicited consent of the court, the clergy, and the people ratified the choice of the minister; and, both as a saint and as an orator, the new archbishop surpassed the sanguine expectations of the public. Born of a noble and opulent family in the capital of Syria, Chrysostom had been educated, by the care of a tender mother, under the tuition of the most skilful masters. He studied the art of rhetoric in the school of Libanius; and that celebrated sophist, who soon discovered the talents of his disciple, ingenuously confessed that John would have deserved to succeed him had he not been stolen away by the Christians. His piety soon disposed him to receive the sacrament of baptism; to renounce the lucrative and honourable profession of the law; and to bury himself in the adjacent desert, where he subdued the lusts of the flesh by an austere penance of six years. His infirmities compelled him to return to the society of mankind; and the authority of Meletius devoted his talents to the service of the church: but in the midst of his family, and afterwards on the archiepiscopal throne, Chrysostom still persevered in the practice of the monastic virtues. The ample revenues, which his predecessors had consumed in pomp and luxury, he diligently applied to the establishment of hospitals; and the multitudes who were supported by his charity preferred the eloquent and edifying discourses of their archbishop to the amusements of the theatre or the circus. The monuments of that eloquence, which was admired near twenty years at Antioch and Constantinople, have been carefully preserved; and the possession of near one thousand sermons or homilies has authorised the critics[42] of succeeding times to appreciate the genuine merit of Chrysostom. They unanimously attribute to the Christian orator the free command of an elegant and copious language; the judgment to conceal the advantages which he derived from the knowledge of rhetoric and philosophy; an inexhaustible fund of metaphors and similitudes, of ideas and images, to vary and illustrate the most familiar topics; the happy art of engaging the passions in the service of virtue, and of exposing the folly as well as the turpitude of vice almost with the truth and spirit of a dramatic representation. The pastoral labours of the archbishop of Constantinople provoked and gradually united against him two sorts of enemies; the aspiring clergy, who envied his success, and the obstinate sinners, who were offended by his reproofs.

When Chrysostom thundered from the pulpit of St. Sophia against the degeneracy of the Christians, his shafts were spent among the crowd, without wounding or even marking the character of any individual. When he declaimed against the peculiar vices of the rich, poverty might obtain a transient consolation from his invectives: but the guilty were still sheltered by their numbers; and the reproach itself was dignified by some ideas of superiority and enjoyment. But as the pyramid rose towards the summit, it insensibly diminished to a point; and the magistrates, the ministers, the favourite eunuchs, the ladies of the court,[43] the empress Eudoxia herself, had a much larger share of guilt to divide among a smaller proportion of criminals. The personal applications of the audience were anticipated or confirmed by the testimony of their own conscience; and the intrepid preacher assumed the dangerous right of exposing both the offence and the offender to the public abhorrence. The secret resentment of the court encouraged the discontent of the clergy and monks of Constantinople, who were too hastily reformed by the fervent zeal of their archbishop. He had condemned from the pulpit the domestic females of the clergy of Constantinople, who, under the name of servants or sisters, afforded a perpetual occasion either of sin or of scandal. The silent and solitary ascetics, who had secluded themselves from the world, were entitled to the warmest approbation of Chrysostom; but he despised and stigmatised, as the disgrace of their holy profession, the crowd of degenerate monks, who, from some unworthy motives of pleasure or profit, so frequently infested the streets of the capital. To the voice of persuasion the archbishop was obliged to add the terrors of authority; and his ardour in the exercise of ecclesiastical jurisdiction was not always exempt from passion; nor was it always guided by prudence. Chrysostom was naturally of a choleric disposition.[44] Although he struggled, according to the precepts of the Gospel, to love his private enemies, he indulged himself in the privilege of hating the enemies of God and of the church; and his sentiments were sometimes delivered with too much energy of countenance and expression. He still maintained, from some considerations of health or abstinence, his former habits of taking his repasts alone; and this inhospitable custom,[45] which his enemies imputed to pride, contributed at least to nourish the infirmity of a morose and unsocial humour. Separated from that familiar intercourse which facilitates the

knowledge and the despatch of business, he reposed an unsuspecting confidence in his deacon Serapion; and seldom applied his speculative knowledge of human nature to the particular characters either of his dependents or of his equals. Conscious of the purity of his intentions, and perhaps of the superiority of his genius, the archbishop of Constantinople extended the jurisdiction of the Imperial city, that he might enlarge the sphere of his pastoral labours; and the conduct which the profane imputed to an ambitious motive, appeared to Chrysostom himself in the light of a sacred and indispensable duty. In his visitation through the Asiatic provinces he deposed thirteen bishops of Lydia and Phrygia; and indiscreetly declared that a deep corruption of simony and licentiousness had infected the whole episcopal order.[46] If those bishops were innocent, such a rash and unjust condemnation must excite a well-grounded discontent. If they were guilty, the numerous associates of their guilt would soon discover that their own safety depended on the ruin of the archbishop, whom they studied to represent as the tyrant of the Eastern church.

This ecclesiastical conspiracy was managed by Theophilus,[47] archbishop of Alexandria, an active and ambitious prelate, who displayed the fruits of rapine in monuments of ostentation. His national dislike to the rising greatness of a city which degraded him from the second to the third rank in the Christian world was exasperated by some personal disputes with Chrysostom himself.[48] By the private invitation of the empress, Theophilus landed at Constantinople, with a stout body of Egyptian mariners, to encounter the populace; and a train of dependent bishops, to secure by their voices the majority of a synod. The synod[49] was convened in the suburb of Chalcedon, surnamed the *Oak*, where Rufinus had erected a stately church and monastery; and their proceedings were continued during fourteen days or sessions. A bishop and a deacon accused the archbishop of Constantinople; but the frivolous or improbable nature of the forty-seven articles which they presented against him may justly be considered as a fair and unexceptionable panegyric. Four successive summons were signified to Chrysostom; but he still refused to trust either his person or his reputation in the hands of his implacable enemies, who, prudently declining the examination of any particular charges, condemned his contumacious disobedience, and hastily pronounced a sentence of deposition. The synod of the *Oak* immediately addressed the emperor to ratify and execute their judgment, and charitably insinuated that the penalties of treason might be inflicted on the audacious preacher, who had reviled, under the name of Jezebel, the empress Eudoxia herself. The archbishop was rudely arrested, and conducted through the city, by one of the Imperial messengers, who landed him, after a short navigation, near the entrance of the Euxine; from whence, before the expiration of two days, he was gloriously recalled.

The first astonishment of his faithful people had been mute and passive: they suddenly rose with unanimous and irresistible fury. Theophilus escaped, but the promiscuous crowd of monks and Egyptian mariners was slaughtered without pity in the streets of Constantinople.[50] A seasonable earthquake justified the interposition of Heaven; the torrent of sedition rolled forwards to the gates of the palace; and the empress, agitated by fear or remorse, threw herself at the feet of Arcadius, and confessed that the public safety could be purchased only by the restoration of Chrysostom. The Bosphorus was covered with innumerable vessels; the shores of Europe and Asia were profusely illuminated; and the acclamations of a victorious people accompanied, from the port to the cathedral, the triumph of the archbishop, who too easily consented to resume the exercise of his functions, before his sentence had been legally reversed by the authority of an ecclesiastical synod. Ignorant, or careless, of the impending danger, Chrysostom indulged his zeal, or perhaps his resentment; declaimed with peculiar asperity against *female* vices; and condemned the profane honours which were addressed, almost in the precincts of St. Sophia, to the statue of the empress. His imprudence tempted his enemies to inflame the haughty spirit of Eudoxia, by reporting, or perhaps inventing, the famous exordium of a sermon, "Herodias is again furious; Herodias again dances; she once more requires the head of John:" an insolent allusion, which, as a woman and a sovereign, it was impossible for her to forgive.[51] The short interval of a perfidious truce was employed to concert more effectual measures for the disgrace and ruin of the archbishop. A numerous council of the Eastern prelates, who were guided from a distance by the advice of Theophilus, confirmed the validity, without examining the justice, of the former sentence; and a detachment of barbarian troops was introduced into the city, to suppress the emotions of the people. On the vigil of

Easter the solemn administration of baptism was rudely interrupted by the soldiers, who alarmed the modesty of the naked catechumens, and violated, by their presence, the awful mysteries of the Christian worship. Arsacius occupied the church of St. Sophia and the archiepiscopal throne. The catholics retreated to the baths of Constantine, and afterwards to the fields, where they were still pursued and insulted by the guards, the bishops, and the magistrates. The fatal day of the second and final exile of Chrysostom was marked by the conflagration of the cathedral, of the senate-house, and of the adjacent buildings; and this calamity was imputed, without proof, but not without probability, to the despair of a persecuted faction.[52]

Cicero might claim some merit if his voluntary banishment preserved the peace of the republic;[53] but the submission of a Chrysostom was the indispensable duty of a Christian and a subject. Instead of listening to his humble prayer that he might be permitted to reside at Cyzicus or Nicomedia, the inflexible empress assigned for his exile the remote and desolate town of Cucusus, among the ridges of Mount Taurus, in the Lesser Armenia. A secret hope was entertained that the archbishop might perish in a difficult and dangerous march of seventy days in the heat of summer, through the provinces of Asia Minor, where he was continually threatened by the hostile attacks of the Isaurians, and the more implacable fury of the monks. Yet Chrysostom arrived in safety at the place of his confinement; and the three years which he spent at Cucusus, and the neighbouring town of Arabissus, were the last and most glorious of his life. His character was consecrated by absence and persecution; the faults of his administration were no longer remembered; but every tongue repeated the praises of his genius and virtue: and the respectful attention of the Christian world was fixed on a desert spot among the mountains of Taurus. From that solitude the archbishop, whose active mind was invigorated by misfortunes, maintained a strict and frequent correspondence[54] with the most distant provinces; exhorted the separate congregation of his faithful adherents to persevere in their allegiance; urged the destruction of the temples of Phœnicia, and the extirpation of heresy in the isle of Cyprus; extended his pastoral care to the missions of Persia and Scythia; negotiated, by his ambassadors, with the Roman pontiff and the emperor Honorius; and boldly appealed, from a partial synod, to the supreme tribunal of a free and general council. The mind of the illustrious exile was still independent; but his captive body was exposed to the revenge of the oppressors, who continued to abuse the name and authority of Arcadius.[55] An order was despatched for the instant removal of Chrysostom to the extreme desert of Pityus: and his guards so faithfully obeyed their cruel instructions, that, before he reached the sea-coast of the Euxine, he expired at Comana, in Pontus, in the sixtieth year of his age. The succeeding generation acknowledged his innocence and merit. The archbishops of the East, who might blush that their predecessors had been the enemies of Chrysostom, were gradually disposed, by the firmness of the Roman pontiff, to restore the honours of that venerable name.[56] At the pious solicitation of the clergy and people of Constantinople, his relics, thirty years after his death, were transported from their obscure sepulchre to the royal city.[57] The emperor Theodosius advanced to receive them as far as Chalcedon; and, falling prostrate on the coffin, implored, in the name of his guilty parents, Arcadius and Eudoxia, the forgiveness of the injured saint.[58]

Yet a reasonable doubt may be entertained whether any stain of hereditary guilt could be derived from Arcadius to his successor. Eudoxia was a young and beautiful woman, who indulged her passions and despised her husband: Count John enjoyed, at least, the familiar confidence of the empress; and the public named him as the real father of Theodosius the younger.[59] The birth of a son was accepted, however, by the pious husband as an event the most fortunate and honourable to himself, to his family, and to the Eastern world: and the royal infant, by an unprecedented favour, was invested with the titles of Cæsar and Augustus. In less than four years afterwards, Eudoxia, in the bloom of youth, was destroyed by the consequences of a miscarriage; and this untimely death confounded the prophecy of a holy bishop,[60] who, amidst the universal joy, had ventured to foretell that she should behold the long and auspicious reign of her glorious son. The catholics applauded the justice of Heaven, which avenged the persecution of St. Chrysostom; and perhaps the emperor was the only person who sincerely bewailed the loss of the haughty and rapacious Eudoxia. Such a domestic misfortune afflicted *him* more deeply than the public calamities of the East[61]—the licentious excursions, from Pontus to Palestine, of the Isaurian robbers, whose impunity accused the weakness of the government; and the earthquakes, the conflagrations,

the famine, and the flights of locusts,[62] which the popular discontent was equally disposed to attribute to the incapacity of the monarch. At length, in the thirty-first year of his age, after a reign (if we may abuse that word) of thirteen years, three months, and fifteen days, Arcadius expired in the palace of Constantinople. It is impossible to delineate his character; since, in a period very copiously furnished with historical materials, it has not been possible to remark one action that properly belongs to the son of the great Theodosius.

The historian Procopius[63] has indeed illuminated the mind of the dying emperor with a ray of human prudence, or celestial wisdom. Arcadius considered, with anxious foresight, the helpless condition of his son Theodosius, who was no more than seven years of age, the dangerous factions of a minority, and the aspiring spirit of Jezdegerd, the Persian monarch. Instead of tempting the allegiance of an ambitious subject by the participation of supeme power, he boldly appealed to the magnanimity of a king, and placed, by a solemn testament, the sceptre of the East in the hands of Jezdegerd himself. The royal guardian accepted and discharged this honourable trust with unexampled fidelity; and the infancy of Theodosius was protected by the arms and councils of Persia. Such is the singular narrative of Procopius; and his veracity is not disputed by Agathias,[64] while he presumes to dissent from his judgment, and to arraign the wisdom of a Christian emperor, who so rashly, though so fortunately, committed his son and his dominions to the unknown faith of a stranger, a rival, and a heathen. At the distance of one hundred and fifty years, this political question might be debated in the court of Justinian; but a prudent historian will refuse to examine the *propriety*, till he has ascertained the *truth*, of the testament of Arcadius. As it stands without a parallel in the history of the world, we may justly require that it should be attested by the positive and unanimous evidence of contemporaries. The strange novelty of the event, which excites our distrust, must have attracted their notice; and their universal silence annihilates the vain tradition of the succeeding age.

The maxims of Roman jurisprudence, if they could fairly be transferred from private property to public dominion, would have adjudged to the emperor Honorius the guardianship of his nephew, till he had attained, at least, the fourteenth year of his age. But the weakness of Honorius, and the calamities of his reign, disqualified him from prosecuting this natural claim; and such was the absolute separation of the two monarchies, both in interest and affection, that Constantinople would have obeyed with less reluctance the orders of the Persian, than those of the Italian court. Under a prince whose weakness is disguised by the external signs of manhood and discretion, the most worthless favourites may secretly dispute the empire of the palace, and dictate to submissive provinces the commands of a master whom they direct and despise. But the ministers of a child, who is incapable of arming them with the sanction of the royal name, must acquire and exercise an independent authority. The great officers of the state and army, who had been appointed before the death of Arcadius, formed an aristocracy which might have inspired them with the idea of a free republic; and the government of the Eastern empire was fortunately assumed by the præfect Anthemius,[65] who obtained, by his superior abilities, a lasting ascendant over the minds of his equals. The safety of the young emperor proved the merit and integrity of Anthemius; and his prudent firmness sustained the force and reputation of an infant reign. Uldin, with a formidable host of barbarians, was encamped in the heart of Thrace; he proudly rejected all terms of accommodation; and, pointing to the rising sun, declared to the Roman ambassadors that the course of that planet should alone terminate the conquests of the Huns. But the desertion of his confederates, who were privately convinced of the justice and liberality of the Imperial ministers, obliged Uldin to repass the Danube: the tribe of the Scyrri, which composed his rear-guard, was almost extirpated; and many thousand captives were dispersed, to cultivate, with servile labour, the fields of Asia.[66] In the midst of the public triumph, Constantinople was protected by a strong enclosure of new and more extensive walls; the same vigilant care was applied to restore the fortifications of the Illyrian cities; and a plan was judiciously conceived, which, in the space of seven years, would have secured the command of the Danube, by establishing on that river a perpetual fleet of two hundred and fifty armed vessels.[67]

But the Romans had so long been accustomed to the authority of a monarch, that the first, even among the females of the Imperial family, who displayed any courage or capacity, was permitted to ascend the vacant throne of Theodosius. His sister Pulcheria,[68] who was only two years older than himself, received at the age of sixteen the title of *Augusta*; and though her fa-

vour might be sometimes clouded by caprice or intrigue, she continued to govern the Eastern empire near forty years; during the long minority of her brother, and after his death in her own name, and in the name of Marcian, her nominal husband. From a motive either of prudence or religion, she embraced a life of celibacy; and notwithstanding some aspersions on the chastity of Pulcheria,[69] this resolution, which she communicated to her sisters Arcadia and Marina, was celebrated by the Christian world as the sublime effort of heroic piety. In the presence of the clergy and people the three daughters of Arcadius[70] dedicated their virginity to God; and the obligation of their solemn vow was inscribed on a tablet of gold and gems, which they publicly offered in the great church of Constantinople. Their palace was converted into a monastery, and all males—except the guides of their conscience, the saints who had forgotten the distinction of sexes—were scrupulously excluded from the holy threshold. Pulcheria, her two sisters, and a chosen train of favourite damsels, formed a religious community: they renounced the vanity of dress, interrupted by frequent fasts their simple and frugal diet, allotted a portion of their time to works of embroidery, and devoted several hours of the day and night to the exercises of prayer and psalmody. The piety of a Christian virgin was adorned by the zeal and liberality of an empress. Ecclesiastical history describes the splendid churches which were built at the expense of Pulcheria in all the provinces of the East, her charitable foundations for the benefit of strangers and the poor, the ample donations which she assigned for the perpetual maintenance of monastic societies, and the active severity with which she laboured to suppress the opposite heresies of Nestorius and Eutyches. Such virtues were supposed to deserve the peculiar favour of the Deity: and the relics of martyrs, as well as the knowledge of future events, were communicated in visions and revelations to the Imperial saint.[71] Yet the devotion of Pulcheria never diverted her indefatigable attention from temporal affairs; and she alone, among all the descendants of the great Theodosius, appears to have inherited any share of his manly spirit and abilities. The elegant and familiar use which she had acquired both of the Greek and Latin languages was readily applied to the various occasions of speaking or writing on public business: her deliberations were maturely weighed; her actions were prompt and decisive; and while she moved without noise or ostentation the wheel of government, she discreetly attributed to the genius of the emperor the long tranquillity of his reign. In the last years of his peaceful life Europe was indeed afflicted by the arms of Attila; but the more extensive provinces of Asia still continued to enjoy a profound and permanent repose. Theodosius the younger was never reduced to the disgraceful necessity of encountering and punishing a rebellious subject: and since we cannot applaud the vigour, some praise may be due to the mildness and prosperity, of the administration of Pulcheria.

The Roman world was deeply interested in the education of its master. A regular course of study and exercise was judiciously instituted; of the military exercises of riding, and shooting with the bow; of the liberal studies of grammar, rhetoric, and philosophy: the most skilful masters of the East ambitiously solicited the attention of their royal pupil, and several noble youths were introduced into the palace to animate his diligence by the emulation of friendship. Pulcheria alone discharged the important task of instructing her brother in the arts of government; but her precepts may countenance some suspicion of the extent of her capacity or of the purity of her intentions. She taught him to maintain a grave and majestic deportment; to walk, to hold his robes, to seat himself on his throne in a manner worthy of a great prince; to abstain from laughter, to listen with condescension, to return suitable answers; to assume by turns a serious or a placid countenance; in a word, to represent with grace and dignity the external figure of a Roman emperor. But Theodosius[72] was never excited to support the weight and glory of an illustrious name; and, instead of aspiring to imitate his ancestors, he degenerated (if we may presume to measure the degrees of incapacity) below the weakness of his father and his uncle. Arcadius and Honorius had been assisted by the guardian care of a parent, whose lessons were enforced by his authority and example. But the unfortunate prince who is born in the purple must remain a stranger to the voice of truth; and the son of Arcadius was condemned to pass his perpetual infancy encompassed only by a servile train of women and eunuchs. The ample leisure which he acquired by neglecting the essential duties of his high office was filled by idle amusements and unprofitable studies. Hunting was the only active pursuit that could tempt him beyond the limits of the palace; but he most assiduously laboured, sometimes by the light of a midnight lamp, in the mechanic occupations of painting and carv-

ing; and the elegance with which he transcribed religious books entitled the Roman emperor to the singular epithet of *Calligraphes*, or a fair writer. Separated from the world by an impenetrable veil, Theodosius trusted the persons whom he loved; he loved those who were accustomed to amuse and flatter his indolence; and as he never perused the papers that were presented for the royal signature, the acts of injustice the most repugnant to his character were frequently perpetrated in his name. The emperor himself was chaste, temperate, liberal, and merciful; but these qualities—which can only deserve the name of virtues when they are supported by courage and regulated by discretion—were seldom beneficial, and they sometimes proved mischievous, to mankind. His mind, enervated by a royal education, was oppressed and degraded by abject superstition: he fasted, he sung psalms, he blindly accepted the miracles and doctrines with which his faith was continually nourished. Theodosius devoutly worshipped the dead and living saints of the catholic church; and he once refused to eat till an insolent monk, who had cast an excommunication on his sovereign, condescended to heal the spiritual wound which he had inflicted.[73]

The story of a fair and virtuous maiden, exalted from a private condition to the Imperial throne, might be deemed an incredible romance, if such a romance had not been verified in the marriage of Theodosius. The celebrated Athenais[74] was educated by her father Leontius in the religion and sciences of the Greeks; and so advantageous was the opinion which the Athenian philosopher entertained of his contemporaries, that he divided his patrimony between his two sons, bequeathing to his daughter a small legacy of one hundred pieces of gold, in the lively confidence that her beauty and merit would be a sufficient portion. The jealousy and avarice of her brothers soon compelled Athenais to seek a refuge at Constantinople, and with some hopes, either of justice or favour, to throw herself at the feet of Pulcheria. That sagacious princess listened to her eloquent complaint, and secretly destined the daughter of the philosopher Leontius for the future wife of the emperor of the East, who had now attained the twentieth year of his age. She easily excited the curiosity of her brother by an interesting picture of the charms of Athenais: large eyes, a well-proportioned nose, a fair complexion, golden locks, a slender person, a graceful demeanour, an understanding improved by study, and a virtue tried by distress. Theodosius, concealed behind a curtain in the apartment of his sister, was permitted to behold the Athenian virgin: the modest youth immediately declared his pure and honourable love, and the royal nuptials were celebrated amidst the acclamations of the capital and the provinces. Athenais, who was easily persuaded to renounce the errors of Paganism, received at her baptism the Christian name of Eudocia: but the cautious Pulcheria withheld the title of Augusta till the wife of Theodosius had approved her fruitfulness by the birth of a daughter, who espoused fifteen years afterwards the emperor of the West. The brothers of Eudocia obeyed, with some anxiety, her Imperial summons; but as she could easily forgive their fortunate unkindness, she indulged the tenderness, or perhaps the vanity, of a sister, by promoting them to the rank of consuls and præfects. In the luxury of the palace she still cultivated those ingenuous arts which had contributed to her greatness, and wisely dedicated her talents to the honour of religion and of her husband. Eudocia composed a poetical paraphrase of the first eight books of the Old Testament and of the prophecies of Daniel and Zechariah; a cento of the verses of Homer, applied to the life and miracles of Christ, the legend of St. Cyprian, and a panegyric on the Persian victories of Theodosius; and her writings, which were applauded by a servile and superstitious age, have not been disdained by the candour of impartial criticism.[75] The fondness of the emperor was not abated by time and possession; and Eudocia, after the marriage of her daughter, was permitted to discharge her grateful vows by a solemn pilgrimage to Jerusalem. Her ostentatious progress through the East may seem inconsistent with the spirit of Christian humility: she pronounced from a throne of gold and gems an eloquent oration to the senate of Antioch, declared her royal intention of enlarging the walls of the city, bestowed a donative of two hundred pounds of gold to restore the public baths, and accepted the statues which were decreed by the gratitude of Antioch. In the Holy Land her alms and pious foundations exceeded the munificence of the great Helena; and though the public treasure might be impoverished by this excessive liberality, she enjoyed the conscious satisfaction of returning to Constantinople with the chains of St. Peter, the right arm of St. Stephen, and the undoubted picture of the Virgin, painted by St. Luke.[76] But this pilgrimage was the fatal term of the glories of Eudocia. Satiated with empty pomp, and unmindful perhaps of her obligations to Pulcheria, she ambitiously aspired to the government of the Eastern empire: the palace was distracted by female discord; but the victory was at last decided by the superior ascendant of the sister of Theodosius. The execution of Paulinus, master of the offices, and the disgrace of Cyrus, Prætorian præfect of the East, convinced the public that the favour of Eudocia was insufficient to protect her most faithful friends, and the uncommon beauty of Paulinus encouraged the secret rumour that his guilt was that of a successful lover.[77] As soon as the empress perceived that the affection of Theodosius was irretrievably lost, she requested the permission of retiring to the distant solitude of Jerusalem. She obtained her request, but the jealousy of Theodosius, or the vindictive spirit of Pulcheria, pursued her in her last retreat; and Saturninus, count of the domestics, was directed to punish with death two ecclesiastics, her most favoured servants. Eudocia instantly revenged them by the assassination of the count: the furious passions which she indulged on this suspicious occasion seemed to justify the severity of Theodosius; and the empress, ignominiously stripped of the honours of her rank,[78] was disgraced, perhaps unjustly, in the eyes of the world. The remainder of the life of Eudocia, about sixteen years, was spent in exile and devotion; and the approach of age, the death of Theodosius, the misfortunes of her only daughter, who was led a captive from Rome to Carthage, and the society of the Holy Monks of Palestine, insensibly confirmed the religious temper of her mind. After a full experience of the vicissitudes of human life, the daughter of the philosopher Leontius expired at Jerusalem, in the sixty-seventh year of her age; protesting with her dying breath that she had never transgressed the bounds of innocence and friendship.[79]

The gentle mind of Theodosius was never inflamed by the ambition of conquest or military renown; and the slight alarm of a Persian war scarcely interrupted the tranquillity of the East. The motives of this war were just and honourable. In the last year of the reign of Jezdegerd, the supposed guardian of Theodosius, a bishop, who aspired to the crown of martyrdom, destroyed one of the fire-temples of Susa.[80] His zeal and obstinacy were revenged on his brethren: the Magi excited a cruel persecution; and the intolerant zeal of Jezdegerd was imitated by his son Varanes, or Bahram, who soon afterwards ascended the throne. Some Christian fugitives, who escaped to the Roman frontier, were sternly demanded, and generously refused; and the refusal, aggravated by commercial disputes, soon kindled a war between the rival monarchies. The mountains of Armenia, and the plains of Mesopotamia, were filled with hostile armies; but the operations of two successive campaigns were not productive of any decisive or memorable events. Some engagements were fought, some towns were besieged, with various and doubtful success: and if the Romans failed in their attempt to recover the long-lost possession of Nisibis, the Persians were repulsed from the walls of a Mesopotamian city by the valour of a martial bishop, who pointed his thundering engine in the name of St. Thomas the Apostle. Yet the splendid victories which the incredible speed of the messenger Palladius repeatedly announced to the palace of Constantinople were celebrated with festivals and panegyrics. From these panegyrics the historians[81] of the age might borrow their extraordinary, and perhaps fabulous, tales; of the proud challenge of a Persian hero, who was entangled by the net, and despatched by the sword, of Areobindus the Goth; of the ten thousand *Immortals*, who were slain in the attack of the Roman camp; and of the hundred thousand Arabs, or Saracens, who were impelled by a panic terror to throw themselves headlong into the Euphrates. Such events may be disbelieved or disregarded; but the charity of a bishop, Acacius of Amida, whose name might have dignified the saintly calendar, shall not be lost in oblivion. Boldly declaring that vases of gold and silver are useless to a God who neither eats nor drinks, the generous prelate sold the plate of the church of Amida; employed the price in the redemption of seven thousand Persian captives; supplied their wants with affectionate liberality; and dismissed them to their native country, to inform their king of the true spirit of the religion which he persecuted. The practice of benevolence in the midst of war must always tend to assuage the animosity of contending nations; and I wish to persuade myself that Acacius contributed to the restoration of peace. In the conference which was held on the limits of the two empires, the Roman ambassadors degraded the personal character of their sovereign, by a vain attempt to magnify the extent of his power, when they seriously advised the Persians to prevent, by a timely accommodation, the wrath of a monarch who was yet ignorant of this distant war. A truce of one hundred years was solemnly ratified; and although the revolutions of Armenia might threaten the public tranquillity, the essential conditions of this treaty were respected near fourscore years by the successors of Constantine and Artaxerxes.

Since the Roman and Parthian standards first encountered on the banks of the Euphrates, the kingdom of Armenia[82] was alternately oppressed by its formidable protectors; and in the course of this History, several events, which inclined the balance of peace and war, have already related. A disgraceful treaty had resigned Armenia to the ambition of Sapor; and the scale of Persia appeared to preponderate. But the royal race of Arsaces impatiently submitted to the house of Sassan; the turbulent nobles asserted, or betrayed, their hereditary independence; and the nation was still attached to the *Christian* princes of Constantinople. In the beginning of the fifth century Armenia was divided by the progress of war and faction;[83] and the unnatural division precipitated the downfall of that ancient monarchy. Chosroes, the Persian vassal, reigned over the eastern and most extensive portion of the country; while the western province acknowledged the jurisdiction of Arsaces, and the supremacy of the emperor Arcadius. After the death of Arsaces, the Romans suppressed the regal government, and imposed on their allies the condition of subjects. The military command was delegated to the count of the Armenian frontier; the city of Theodosiopolis[84] was built and fortified in a strong situation, on a fertile and lofty ground, near the sources of the Euphrates; and the dependent territories were ruled by five satraps, whose dignity was marked by a peculiar habit of gold and purple. The less fortunate nobles, who lamented the loss of their king, and envied the honours of their equals, were provoked to negotiate their peace and pardon at the Persian court; and, returning with their followers to the palace of Artaxata, acknowledged Chosroes for their lawful sovereign. About thirty years afterwards, Artasires, the nephew and successor of Chosroes, fell under the displeasure of the haughty and capricious nobles of Armenia; and they unanimously desired a Persian governor in the room of an unworthy king. The answer of the archbishop Isaac, whose sanction they earnestly solicited, is expressive of the character of a superstitious people. He deplored the manifest and inexcusable vices of Artasires; and declared that he should not hesitate to accuse him before the tribunal of a Christian emperor, who would punish, without destroying, the sinner. "Our king," continued Isaac, "is too much addicted to licentious pleasures, but he has been purified in the holy water of baptism. He is a lover of women, but he does not adore the fire or the elements. He may deserve the reproach of lewdness, but he is an undoubted catholic; and his faith is pure, though his manners are flagitious. I will never consent to abandon my sheep to the rage of devouring wolves; and you would soon repent your rash exchange of the infirmities of a believer, for the specious virtues of an heathen."[85] Exasperated by the firmness of Isaac, the factious nobles accused both the king and the archbishop as the secret adherents of the emperor; and absurdly rejoiced in the sentence of condemnation, which, after a partial hearing, was solemnly pronounced by Bahram

himself. The descendants of Arsaces were degraded from the royal dignity,[86] which they had possessed above five hundred and sixty years;[87] and the dominions of the unfortunate Artasires, under the new and significant appellation of Persarmenia, were reduced into the form of a province. This usurpation excited the jealousy of the Roman government; but the rising disputes were soon terminated by an amicable, though unequal, partition of the ancient kingdom of Armenia; and a territorial acquisition, which Augustus might have despised, reflected some lustre on the declining empire of the younger Theodosius.

CHAPTER XXXIII

Death of Honorius. Valentinian III. Emperor of the West. Administration of his Mother Placidia. Aëtius and Boniface. Conquest of Africa by the Vandals.

DURING a long and disgraceful reign of twenty-eight years, Honorius, emperor of the West, was separated from the friendship of his brother, and afterwards of his nephew, who reigned over the East; and Constantinople beheld, with apparent indifference and secret joy, the calamities of Rome. The strange adventures of Placidia gradually renewed and cemented the alliance of the two empires. The daughter of the great Theodosius had been the captive and the queen of the Goths; she lost an affectionate husband; she was dragged in chains by his insulting assassin; she tasted the pleasure of revenge, and was exchanged, in the treaty of peace, for six hundred thousand measures of wheat. After her return from Spain to Italy, Placidia experienced a new persecution in the bosom of her family. She was averse to a marriage which had been stipulated without her consent; and the brave Constantius, as a noble reward for the tyrants whom he had vanquished, received, from the hand of Honorius himself, the struggling and reluctant hand of the widow of Adolphus. But her resistance ended with the ceremony of the nuptials; nor did Placidia refuse to become the mother of Honoria and Valentinian the Third, or to assume and exercise an absolute dominion over the mind of her grateful husband. The generous soldier, whose time had hitherto been divided between social pleasure and military service, was taught new lessons of avarice and ambition: he extorted the title of Augustus; and the servant of Honorius was associated to the

empire of the West. The death of Constantius, in the seventh month of his reign, instead of diminishing, seemed to increase, the power of Placidia; and the indecent familiarity[1] of her brother, which might be no more than the symptoms of a childish affection, were universally attributed to incestuous love. On a sudden, by some base intrigues of a steward and a nurse, this excessive fondness was converted into an irreconcilable quarrel: the debates of the emperor and his sister were not long confined within the walls of the palace; and as the Gothic soldiers adhered to their queen, the city of Ravenna was agitated with bloody and dangerous tumults, which could only be appeased by the forced or voluntary retreat of Placidia and her children. The royal exiles landed at Constantinople, soon after the marriage of Theodosius, during the festival of the Persian victories. They were treated with kindness and magnificence; but as the statues of the emperor Constantius had been rejected by the Eastern court, the title of Augusta could not decently be allowed to his widow. Within a few months after the arrival of Placidia a swift messenger announced the death of Honorius, the consequence of a dropsy; but the important secret was not divulged till the necessary orders had been despatched for the march of a large body of troops to the sea-coast of Dalmatia. The shops and the gates of Constantinople remained shut during seven days; and the loss of a foreign prince, who could neither be esteemed nor regretted, was celebrated with loud and affected demonstrations of the public grief.

While the ministers of Constantinople deliberated, the vacant throne of Honorius was usurped by the ambition of a stranger. The name of the rebel was John; he filled the confidential office of *Primicerius*, or principal secretary; and history has attributed to his character more virtues than can easily be reconciled with the violation of the most sacred duty. Elated by the submission of Italy, and the hope of an alliance with the Huns, John presumed to insult by an embassy, the majesty of the Eastern emperor; but when he understood that his agents had been banished, imprisoned, and at length chased away with deserved ignominy, John prepared to assert by arms the injustice of his claims. In such a cause the grandson of the great Theodosius should have marched in person; but the young emperor was easily diverted by his physicians from so rash and hazardous a design; and the conduct of the Italian expedition was prudently intrusted to Ardaburius and his son Aspar, who had already signalised their valour against the Persians. It was resolved that Ardaburius should embark with the infantry; whilst Aspar, at the head of the cavalry, conducted Placidia, and her son Valentinian, along the sea-coast of the Hadriatic. The march of the cavalry was performed with such active diligence, that they surprised, without resistance, the important city of Aquileia; when the hopes of Aspar were unexpectedly confounded by the intelligence that a storm had dispersed the Imperial fleet, and that his father, with only two galleys, was taken and carried a prisoner into the port of Ravenna. Yet this incident, unfortunate as it might seem, facilitated the conquest of Italy. Ardaburius employed, or abused, the courteous freedom which he was permitted to enjoy, to revive among the troops a sense of loyalty and gratitude; and, as soon as the conspiracy was ripe for execution, he invited, by private messages, and pressed the approach of Aspar. A shepherd, whom the popular credulity transformed into an angel, guided the Eastern cavalry, by a secret, and, it was thought, an impassable road, through the morasses of the Po: the gates of Ravenna, after a short struggle, were thrown open; and the defenceless tyrant was delivered to the mercy, or rather to the cruelty, of the conquerors. His right hand was first cut off, and after he had been exposed, mounted on an ass, to the public derision, John was beheaded in the circus of Aquileia. The emperor Theodosius, when he received the news of the victory, interrupted the horse-races; and singing, as he marched through the streets, a suitable psalm, conducted his people from the Hippodrome to the church, where he spent the remainder of the day in grateful devotion.[2]

In a monarchy which, according to various precedents, might be considered as elective, or hereditary, or patrimonial, it was impossible that the intricate claims of female and collateral succession should be clearly defined;[3] and Theodosius, by the right of consanguinity or conquest, might have reigned the sole legitimate emperor of the Romans. For a moment, perhaps, his eyes were dazzled by the prospect of unbounded sway; but his indolent temper gradually acquiesced in the dictates of sound policy. He contented himself with the possession of the East; and wisely relinquished the laborious task of waging a distant and doubtful war against the barbarians beyond the Alps, or of securing the obedience of the Italians and Africans, whose minds were alienated by the irreconcilable difference of language and interest. Instead of listening to the voice of ambition, Theodosius resolved to imitate the moderation of his grandfather, and to seat his cousin Valentinian on the throne of the West. The royal infant was distinguished at Constantinople by the title of *Nobilissimus:* he was promoted, before his departure from Thessalonica, to the rank and dignity of *Cæsar:* and, after the conquest of Italy, the patrician Helion, by the authority of Theodosius, and in the presence of the senate, saluted Valentinian the Third by the name of Augustus, and solemnly invested him with the diadem and the Imperial purple.[4] By the agreement of the three females who governed the Roman world, the son of Placidia was betrothed to Eudoxia, the daughter of Theodosius and Athenais; and, as soon as the lover and his bride had attained the age of puberty, this honourable alliance was faithfully accomplished. At the same time, as a compensation, perhaps, for the expenses of the war, the Western Illyricum was detached from the Italian dominions, and yielded to the throne of Constantinople.[5] The emperor of the East acquired the useful dominion of the rich and maritime province of Dalmatia, and the dangerous sovereignty of Pannonia and Noricum, which had been filled and ravaged above twenty years by a promiscuous crowd of Huns, Ostrogoths, Vandals, and *Bavarians*. Theodosius and Valentinian continued to respect the obligations of their public and domestic alliance; but the unity of the Roman government was finally dissolved. By a positive declaration, the validity of all future laws was limited to the dominions of their peculiar author; unless he should think proper to communicate them, subscribed with his own hand, for the approbation of his independent colleague.[6]

Valentinian, when he received the title of Augustus, was no more than six years of age; and his long minority was intrusted to the guardian care of a mother who might assert a female claim to the succession of the Western empire. Placidia envied, but she could not equal, the reputation and virtues of the wife and sister of Theodosius; the elegant genius of Eudocia, the wise and successful policy of Pulcheria. The mother of Valentinian was jealous of the power which she was incapable of exercising:[7] she reigned twenty-five years, in the name of her son; and the character of that unworthy emperor gradually countenanced the suspicion that Placidia had enervated his youth by a dissolute education, and studiously diverted his attention from every manly and honourable pursuit. Amidst the decay of military spirit, her armies were commanded by two generals, Aëtius[8] and Boniface,[9] who may be deservedly named as the last of the Romans. Their union might have supported a sinking empire; their discord was the fatal and immediate cause of the loss of Africa. The invasion and defeat of Attila has immortalised the fame of Aëtius; and though time has thrown a shade over the exploits of his rival, the defence of Marseilles, and the deliverance of Africa, attest the military talents of Count Boniface. In the field of battle, in partial encounters, in single combats, he was still the terror of the barbarians: the clergy, and particularly his friend Augustin, were edified by the Christian piety which had once tempted him to retire from the world; the people applauded his spotless integrity; the army dreaded his equal and inexorable justice, which may be displayed in a very singular example. A peasant, who complained of the criminal intimacy between his wife and a Gothic soldier, was directed to attend his tribunal the following day: in the evening the count, who had diligently informed himself of the time and place of the assignation, mounted his horse, rode ten miles into the country, surprised the guilty couple, punished the soldier with instant death, and silenced the complaints of the husband, by presenting him, the next morning, with the head of the adulterer. The abilities of Aëtius and Boniface might have been usefully employed against the public enemies in separate and important commands; but the experience of their past conduct should have decided the real favour and confidence of the empress Placidia. In the melancholy season of her exile and distress, Boniface alone had maintained her cause with unshaken fidelity; and the troops and treasures of Africa had essentially contributed to extinguish the rebellion. The same rebellion had been supported by the zeal and activity of Aëtius, who brought an army of sixty thousand Huns from the Danube to the confines of Italy, for the service of the usurper. The untimely death of John compelled him to accept an advantageous treaty; but he still continued, the subject and the soldier of Valentinian, to entertain a secret, perhaps a treasonable, correspondence with his barbarian allies, whose retreat had been purchased by liberal gifts and more liberal promises. But Aëtius possessed an advantage of singular moment in a female reign: he was present: he besieged with artful and assiduous flattery the palace of Ravenna; disguised his dark designs with the mask of loyalty and friendship; and at length deceived both his mistress and his absent rival, by a subtle conspiracy which a weak woman and a brave man could not easily suspect. He secretly persuaded [10] Placidia to recall Boniface from the government of Africa; he secretly advised Boniface to disobey the Imperial summons: to the one, he represented the order as a sentence of death; to the other, he stated the refusal as a signal of revolt; and when the credulous and unsuspectful count had armed the province in his defence, Aëtius applauded his sagacity in foreseeing the rebellion which his own perfidy had excited. A temperate inquiry into the real motives of Boniface would have restored a faithful servant to his duty and to the republic; but the arts of Aëtius still continued to betray and to inflame, and the count was urged by persecution to embrace the most desperate counsels. The success with which he eluded or repelled the first attacks could not inspire a vain confidence that, at the head of some loose disorderly Africans, he should be able to withstand the regular forces of the West, commanded by a rival whose military character it was impossible for him to despise. After some hesitation, the last struggles of prudence and loyalty, Boniface despatched a trusty friend to the court, or rather to the camp, of Gonderic, king of the Vandals, with the proposal of a strict alliance, and the offer of an advantageous and perpetual settlement.

After the retreat of the Goths the authority of

Honorius had obtained a precarious establishment in Spain, except only in the province of Gallicia, where the Suevi and the Vandals had fortified their camps in mutual discord and hostile independence. The Vandals prevailed, and their adversaries were besieged in the Nervasian hills, between Leon and Oviedo, till the approach of Count Asterius compelled, or rather provoked, the victorious barbarians to remove the scene of the war to the plains of Bætica. The rapid progress of the Vandals soon required a more effectual opposition, and the master-general Castinus marched against them with a numerous army of Romans and Goths. Vanquished in battle by an inferior enemy, Castinus fled with dishonour to Tarragona; and this memorable defeat, which has been represented as the punishment, was most probably the effect, of his rash presumption.[11] Seville and Carthagena became the reward, or rather the prey, of the ferocious conquerors; and the vessels which they found in the harbour of Carthagena might easily transport them to the isles of Majorca and Minorca, where the Spanish fugitives, as in a secure recess, had vainly concealed their families and their fortunes. The experience of navigation, and perhaps the prospect of Africa, encouraged the Vandals to accept the invitation which they received from Count Boniface, and the death of Gonderic served only to forward and animate the bold enterprise. In the room of a prince not conspicuous for any superior powers of the mind or body, they acquired his bastard brother, the terrible Genseric;[12] a name which in the destruction of the Roman empire has reserved an equal rank with the names of Alaric and Attila. The king of the Vandals is described to have been of a middle stature, with a lameness in one leg, which he had contracted by an accidental fall from his horse. His slow and cautious speech seldom declared the deep purposes of his soul: he disdained to imitate the luxury of the vanquished, but he indulged the sterner passions of anger and revenge. The ambition of Genseric was without bounds and without scruples, and the warrior could dexterously employ the dark engines of policy to solicit the allies who might be useful to his success, or to scatter among his enemies the seeds of hatred and contention. Almost in the moment of his departure he was informed that Hermanric, king of the Suevi, had presumed to ravage the Spanish territories which he was resolved to abandon. Impatient of the insult, Genseric pursued the hasty retreat of the Suevi as far as Merida, precipitated the king and his army into the river Anas, and calmly returned to the sea-shore to embark his victorious troops. The vessels which transported the Vandals over the modern Straits of Gibralter, a channel only twelve miles in breadth, were furnished by the Spaniards, who anxiously wished their departure, and by the African general, who had implored their formidable assistance.[13]

Our fancy, so long accustomed to exaggerate and multiply the martial swarms of barbarians that seemed to issue from the North, will perhaps be surprised by the account of the army which Genseric mustered on the coast of Mauritania. The Vandals, who in twenty years had penetrated from the Elbe to Mount Atlas, were united under the command of their warlike king; and he reigned with equal authority over the Alani, who had passed within the term of human life from the cold of Scythia to the excessive heat of an African climate. The hopes of the bold enterprise had excited many brave adventurers of the Gothic nation, and many desperate provincials were tempted to repair their fortunes by the same means which had occasioned their ruin. Yet this various multitude amounted only to fifty thousand effective men; and though Genseric artfully magnified his apparent strength by appointing eighty *chiliarchs*, or commanders of thousands, the fallacious increase of old men, of children, and of slaves, would scarcely have swelled his army to the number of fourscore thousand persons.[14] But his own dexterity and the discontents of Africa soon fortified the Vandal powers by the accession of numerous and active allies. The parts of Mauritania which border on the great desert and the Atlantic ocean were filled with a fierce and untractable race of men, whose savage temper had been exasperated rather than reclaimed by their dread of the Roman arms. The wandering Moors,[15] as they gradually ventured to approach the sea-shore and the camp of the Vandals, must have viewed with terror and astonishment the dress, the armour, the martial pride and discipline of the unknown strangers who had landed on their coast; and the fair complexions of the blue-eyed warriors of Germany formed a very singular contrast with the swarthy or olive hue which is derived from the neighbourhood of the torrid zone. After the first difficulties had in some measure been removed which arose from the mutual ignorance of their respective language, the Moors, regardless of any future consequence, embraced the alliance of the enemies of Rome, and a crowd of naked savages rushed from the woods and valleys of Mount Atlas, to satiate their revenge on the polished tyrants who had injuriously expelled them from the native sovereignty of the land.

The persecution of the Donatists[16] was an event not less favourable to the designs of Genseric. Seventeen years before he landed in Africa, a public conference was held at Carthage by the order of the magistrate. The catholics were satisfied that, after the invincible reasons which they had alleged, the obstinacy of the schismatics must be inexcusable and voluntary, and the emperor Honorius was persuaded to inflict the most rigorous penalties on a faction which had so long abused his patience and clemency. Three hundred bishops,[17] with many thousands of the inferior clergy, were torn from their churches, stripped of their ecclesiastical possessions, banished to the islands, and proscribed by the laws, if they presumed to conceal themselves in the provinces of Africa. Their numerous congregations, both in cities and in the country, were deprived of the rights of citizens and of the exercise of religious worship. A regular scale of fines, from ten to two hundred pounds of silver, was curiously ascertained, according to the distinctions of rank and fortune, to punish the crime of assisting at a schismatic conventicle; and if the fine had been levied five times without subduing the obstinacy of the offender, his future punishment was referred to the discretion of the Imperial court.[18] By these severities, which obtained the warmest approbation of St. Augustin,[19] great numbers of Donatists were reconciled to the Catholic church; but the fanatics who still persevered in their opposition were provoked to madness and despair; the distracted country was filled with tumult and bloodshed; the armed troops of Circumcellions alternately pointed their rage against themselves or against their adversaries; and the calendar of martyrs received on both sides a considerable augmentation.[20] Under these circumstances Genseric, a Christian, but an enemy of the orthodox communion, showed himself to the Donatists as a powerful deliverer, from whom they might reasonably expect the repeal of the odious and oppressive edicts of the Roman emperors.[21] The conquest of Africa was facilitated by the active zeal or the secret favour of a domestic faction; the wanton outrages against the churches and the clergy, of which the Vandals are accused, may be fairly imputed to the fanaticism of their allies; and the intolerant spirit which disgraced the triumph of Christianity contributed to the loss of the most important province of the West.[22]

The court and the people were astonished by the strange intelligence that a virtuous hero, after so many favours and so many services, had renounced his allegiance and invited the barbarians to destroy the province entrusted to his command. The friends of Boniface, who still believed that his criminal behaviour might be excused by some honourable motive, solicited, during the absence of Aëtius, a free conference with the Count of Africa; and Darius, an officer of high distinction, was named for the important embassy.[23] In their first interview at Carthage the imaginary provocations were mutually explained, the opposite letters of Aëtius were produced and compared, and the fraud was easily detected. Placidia and Boniface lamented their fatal error, and the count had sufficient magnanimity to confide in the forgiveness of his sovereign, or to expose his head to her future resentment. His repentance was fervent and sincere; but he soon discovered that it was no longer in his power to restore the edifice which he had shaken to its foundations. Carthage and the Roman garrisons returned with their general to the allegiance of Valentinian, but the rest of Africa was still distracted with war and faction; and the inexorable king of the Vandals, disdaining all terms of accommodation, sternly refused to relinquish the possession of his prey. The band of veterans who marched under the standard of Boniface, and his hasty levies of provincial troops, were defeated with considerable loss; the victorious barbarians insulted the open country; and Carthage, Cirta, and Hippo Regius, were the only cities that appeared to rise above the general inundation.

The long and narrow tract of the African coast was filled with frequent monuments of Roman art and magnificence; and the respective degrees of improvement might be accurately measured by the distance from Carthage and the Mediterranean. A simple reflection will impress every thinking mind with the clearest idea of fertility and cultivation: the country was extremely populous; the inhabitants reserved a liberal subsistence for their own use; and the annual exportation, particularly of wheat, was so regular and plentiful, that Africa deserved the name of the common granary of Rome and of mankind. On a sudden the seven fruitful provinces, from Tangier to Tripoli, were overwhelmed by the invasion of the Vandals, whose destructive rage has perhaps been exaggerated by popular animosity, religious zeal, and extravagant declamation. War in its fairest form implies a perpetual violation of humanity and justice; and the hostilities of barbarians are inflamed by the fierce and lawless spirit which incessantly disturbs their peaceful and domestic society. The Vandals, where they found resistance, seldom gave quarter; and the deaths of the valiant countrymen were expiated by the ruin of the cities under whose walls they had fallen. Careless of the distinction of age, or sex, or rank, they employed every species of indignity and torture to force from the captives a discovery of their hidden wealth. The stern policy of Genseric justified his frequent examples of military execution: he was not always the master of his own passions or of those of his followers; and the calamities of war were aggravated by the licentiousness of the Moors and the fanaticism of the Donatists. Yet I shall not easily be persuaded that it was the common practice of the Vandals to extirpate the olives and other fruit trees of a country where they intended to settle: nor can I believe that it was a usual stratagem to slaughter great numbers of their prisoners before the walls of a besieged city, for the sole purpose of infecting the air and producing a pestilence, of which they themselves must have been the first victims.[24]

The generous mind of Count Boniface was tortured by the exquisite distress of beholding the ruin which he had occasioned, and whose rapid progress he was unable to check. After the loss of a battle he retired to Hippo Regius, where he was immediately besieged by an enemy who considered him as the real bulwark of Africa. The maritime colony of *Hippo*,[25] about two hundred miles westward of Carthage, had formerly acquired the distinguishing epithet of *Regius* from the residence of Numidian kings; and some remains of trade and populousness still adhere to the modern city, which is known in Europe by the corrupted name of Bona. The military labours and anxious reflections of Count Boniface were alleviated by the edifying conversation of his friend St. Augustin;[26] till that bishop, the light and pillar of the Catholic church, was gently released, in the third month of the siege and in the seventy-sixth year of his age, from the actual and the impending calamities of his country. The youth of Augustin had been stained by the vices and errors which he so ingenuously confesses; but from the moment of his conversion to that of his death the manners of the bishop of Hippo were pure and austere, and the most

conspicuous of his virtues was an ardent zeal against heretics of every denomination—the Manichæans, the Donatists, and the Pelagians, against whom he waged a perpetual controversy. When the city, some months after his death, was burnt by the Vandals, the library was fortunately saved which contained his voluminous writings—two hundred and thirty-two separate books or treatises on theological subjects, besides a complete exposition of the psalter and the gospel, and a copious magazine of epistles and homilies.[27] According to the judgment of the most impartial critics, the superficial learning of Augustin was confined to the Latin language;[28] and his style, though sometimes animated by the eloquence of passion, is usually clouded by false and affected rhetoric. But he possessed a strong, capacious, argumentative mind; he boldly sounded the dark abyss of grace, predestination, free-will, and original sin; and the rigid system of Christianity which he framed or restored[29] has been entertained with public applause and secret reluctance by the Latin church.[30]

By the skill of Boniface, and perhaps by the ignorance of the Vandals, the siege of Hippo was protracted above fourteen months: the sea was continually open; and when the adjacent country had been exhausted by irregular rapine, the besiegers themselves were compelled by famine to relinquish their enterprise. The importance and danger of Africa were deeply felt by the regent of the West. Placidia implored the assistance of her Eastern ally; and the Italian fleet and army were reinforced by Aspar, who sailed from Constantinople with a powerful armament. As soon as the force of the two empires was united under the command of Boniface, he boldly marched against the Vandals; and the loss of a second battle irretrievably decided the fate of Africa. He embarked with the precipitation of despair, and the people of Hippo were permitted, with their families and effects, to occupy the vacant place of the soldiers, the greatest part of whom were either slain or made prisoners by the Vandals. The count, whose fatal credulity had wounded the vitals of the republic, might enter the palace of Ravenna with some anxiety, which was soon removed by the smiles of Placidia. Boniface accepted with gratitude the rank of patrician and the dignity of master-general of the Roman armies; but he must have blushed at the sight of those medals in which he was represented with the name and attributes of victory.[31] The discovery of his fraud, the displeasure of the empress, and the distinguished favour of his rival, exasperated the haughty and perfidious soul of Aëtius. He hastily returned from Gaul to Italy, with a retinue, or rather with an army, of barbarian followers; and such was the weakness of the government, that the two generals decided their private quarrel in a bloody battle. Boniface was successful; but he received in the conflict a mortal wound from the spear of his adversary, of which he expired within a few days, in such Christian and charitable sentiments that he exhorted his wife, a rich heiress of Spain, to accept Aëtius for her second husband. But Aëtius could not derive any immediate advantage from the generosity of his dying enemy: he was proclaimed a rebel by the justice of Placidia; and though he attempted to defend some strong fortresses, erected on his patrimonial estate, the Imperial power soon compelled him to retire into Pannonia, to the tents of his faithful Huns. The republic was deprived by their mutual discord of the service of her two most illustrious champions.[32]

It might naturally be expected, after the retreat of Boniface, that the Vandals would achieve without resistance or delay the conquest of Africa. Eight years however elapsed from the evacuation of Hippo to the reduction of Carthage. In the midst of that interval the ambitious Genseric, in the full tide of apparent prosperity, negotiated a treaty of peace, by which he gave his son Hunneric for an hostage, and consented to leave the Western emperor in the undisturbed possession of the three Mauritanias.[33] This moderation, which cannot be imputed to the justice, must be ascribed to the policy, of the conqueror. His throne was encompassed with domestic enemies, who accused the baseness of his birth, and asserted the legitimate claims of his nephews, the sons of Gonderic. Those nephews, indeed, he sacrificed to his safety, and their mother, the widow of the deceased king, was precipitated by his order into the river Ampsaga. But the public discontent burst forth in dangerous and frequent conspiracies; and the warlike tyrant is supposed to have shed more Vandal blood by the hand of the executioner than in the field of battle.[34] The convulsions of Africa, which had favoured his attack, opposed the firm establishment of his power; and the various seditions of the Moors and Germans, the Donatists and catholics, continually disturbed or threatened the unsettled reign of the conqueror. As he advanced towards Carthage he was forced to withdraw his troops from the Western provinces; the sea-coast was exposed to the naval enterprises of the Romans of Spain and Italy; and, in the heart of Numidia, the strong inland city of Cirta still persisted in obstinate independence.[35] These difficulties were gradually subdued by the spirit, the perserverance, and the cruelty of Genseric, who alternately applied the arts of peace and war to the establishment of his African kingdom. He subscribed a solemn treaty, with the hope of deriving some advantage from the term of its continuance and the moment of its violation. The vigilance of his enemies was relaxed by the protestations of friendship which concealed his hostile approach; and Carthage was at length surprised by the Vandals, five hundred and eighty-five years after the destruction of the city and republic by the younger Scipio.[36]

A new city had arisen from its ruins, with the title of a colony; and though Carthage might yield to the royal prerogatives of Constantinople, and perhaps to the trade of Alexandria, or the splendour of Antioch, she still maintained the second rank in the West; as the *Rome* (if we may use the style of contemporaries) of the African world. That wealthy and opulent metropolis[37] displayed, in a dependent condition, the image of a flourishing republic. Carthage contained the manufactures, the arms, and the treasures of the six provinces. A regular subordination of civil honours gradually ascended from the procurators of the streets and quarters of the city to the tribunal of the supreme magistrate, who, with the title of proconsul, represented the state and dignity of a consul of ancient Rome. Schools and *gymnasia* were instituted for the education of the African youth; and the liberal arts and manners, grammar, rhetoric, and philosophy, were publicly taught in the Greek and Latin languages. The buildings of Carthage were uniform and magnificent: a shady grove was planted in the midst of the capital; the *new* port, a secure and capacious harbour, was subservient to the commercial industry of citizens and strangers; and the splendid games of the circus and theatre were exhibited almost in the presence of the barbarians. The reputation of the Carthaginians was not equal to that of their country, and the reproach of Punic faith still adhered to their subtle and faithless character.[38] The habits of trade and the abuse of luxury had corrupted their manners; but their impious contempt of monks and the shameless practice of unnatural lusts are the two abominations which excite the pious vehemence of Salvian, the preacher of the age.[39] The king of the Vandals severely reformed the vices of a voluptuous people; and the ancient, noble, ingenuous freedom of Carthage (these expressions of Victor are not without energy) was reduced by Genseric into a state of ignominious servitude. After he had permitted his licentious troops to satiate their rage and avarice, he instituted a more regular system of rapine and oppression. An edict was promulgated, which enjoined all persons, without fraud or delay, to deliver their gold, silver, jewels, and valuable furniture or apparel to the royal officers; and the attempt to secrete any part of their patrimony was inexorably punished with death and torture as an act of treason against the state. The lands of the proconsular province, which formed the immediate district of Carthage, were accurately measured and divided among the barbarians; and the conqueror reserved for his peculiar domain the fertile territory of Byzacium and the adjacent parts of Numidia and Gætulia.[40]

It was natural enough that Genseric should hate those whom he had injured: the nobility and senators of Carthage, were exposed to his jealousy and resentment; and all those who refused the ignominious terms which their honour and religion forbade them to accept were compelled by the Arian tyrant to embrace the condition of perpetual banishment. Rome, Italy, and the provinces of the East, were filled with a crowd of exiles, of fugitives and of ingenuous captives, who solicited the public compassion: and the benevolent epistles of Theodoret still preserve the names and misfortunes of Cælestian and Maria.[41] The Syrian bishop deplores the misfortunes of Cælestian, who, from the state of a noble and opulent senator of Carthage, was reduced, with his wife, and family, and servants, to beg his bread in a foreign country; but he applauds the resignation of the Christian exile, and the philosophic temper which, under the pressure of such calamities, could enjoy more real happiness than was the ordinary lot of wealth and prosperity. The story of Maria, the daughter of the magnificent Eudæmon, is singular and interesting. In the sack of Carthage she was purchased from the Vandals by some merchants of Syria, who afterwards sold her as a slave in their native country. A female attendant, transported in the same ship, and sold in the same family, still continued to respect a mistress whom fortune had reduced to the common level of servitude; and the daughter of Eudæmon received from her grateful affection the domestic services which she had once required from her obedience. This remarkable behaviour divulged the real condition of Maria, who, in the absence of the bishop of Cyrrhus, was redeemed from slavery by the generosity of some soldiers of the garrison. The liberality of Theodoret provided for her decent maintenance; and she passed ten months among the deaconesses of the church, till she was unexpectedly informed that her father, who had escaped from the ruin of Carthage, exercised an honourable office in one of the Western provinces. Her filial impatience was seconded by the pious bishop: Theodoret, in a letter still extant, recommends Maria to the bishop of Ægæ, a maritime city of Cilicia, which was frequented, during the annual fair, by the vessels of the West; most earnestly requesting that his colleague would use the maiden with a tenderness suitable to her birth; and that he would intrust her to the care of such faithful merchants as would esteem it a sufficient gain if they restored a daughter, lost beyond all human hope, to the arms of her afflicted parent.

Among the insipid legends of ecclesiastical history, I am tempted to distinguish the memorable fable of the SEVEN SLEEPERS; [42] whose imaginary date corresponds with the reign of the younger Theodosius, and the conquest of Africa by the Vandals.[43] When the emperor Decius persecuted the Christians, seven noble youths of Ephesus concealed themselves in a spacious cavern in the side of an adjacent mountain where they were doomed to perish by the tyrant, who gave orders that the entrance should be firmly secured with a pile of huge stones. They immediately fell into a deep slumber, which was miraculously prolonged, without injuring the powers of life, during a period of one hundred and eighty-seven years. At the end of that time, the slaves of Adolius, to whom the inheritance of the mountain had descended, removed the stones, to supply materials for some rustic edifice: the light of the sun darted into the cavern, and the Seven Sleepers were permitted to awake. After a slumber, as they thought of a few hours, they were pressed by the calls of hunger; and resolved that Jamblichus, one of their number, should secretly return to the city to purchase bread for the use of his companions. The youth (if we may still employ that appellation) could no longer recognise the once familiar aspect of his native country; and his surprise was increased by the appearance of a large cross, triumphantly erected over the principal gate of Ephesus. His singular dress and obsolete language confounded the baker, to whom he offered an ancient medal of Decius as the current coin of the empire; and Jamblichus, on the suspicion of a secret treasure, was dragged before the judge. Their mutual inquiries produced the amazing discovery that two centuries were almost elapsed since Jamblichus and his friends had escaped from the rage of a Pagan tyrant. The bishop of Ephesus, the clergy, the magistrates, the people, and, as it is said, the emperor Theodosius himself, hastened to visit the cavern of the Seven Sleepers; who bestowed their benediction, related their story, and at the same instant peaceably expired. The origin of this marvellous fable cannot be ascribed to the pious fraud and credulity of the *modern* Greeks, since the authentic tradition may be traced within half a century of the supposed miracle. James of Sarug, a Syrian bishop, who was born only two years after the death of the younger Theodosius, has devoted one of his two hundred and thirty homilies to the praise of the young men of Ephesus.[44] Their legend, before the end of the sixth century, was translated from the Syriac into the Latin language, by the care of Gregory of Tours. The hostile communions of the East preserve their memory with equal reverence; and their names are honourably inscribed in the Roman, the Abyssinian, and the Russian calendar.[45] Nor has their reputation been confined to the Christian world. This popular tale, which Mahomet might learn when he drove his camels to the fairs of Syria, is introduced, as a divine revelation, into the Koran.[46] The story of the Seven Sleepers has been adopted and adorned by the nations, from Bengal to Africa, who profess the Mahometan religion;[47] and some vestiges of a similar tradition have been discovered in the remote extremities of Scandinavia.[48] This easy and universal belief, so expressive of the sense of mankind, may be ascribed to the genuine merit of the fable itself. We imperceptibly advance from youth to age without observing the gradual, but incessant, change of human affairs; and even in our larger experience of history, the imagination is accustomed, by a perpetual series of causes and effects, to unite the most distant revolutions. But if the interval between two memorable eras could be instantly annihilated; if it were possible, after a momentary slumber of two hundred years, to display the *new* world to the eyes of a spectator who still retained a lively and recent impression of the *old*, his surprise and his reflections would furnish the pleasing subject of a philosophical romance. The scene could not be more advantageously placed than in the two centuries which elapsed between the reigns of Decius and of Theodosius the Younger. During this period the seat of government had been transported from Rome to a new city on the banks of the Thracian Bosphorus and the abuse of military spirit had been suppressed by an artificial system of tame and ceremonious servitude. The throne of the persecuting Decius was filled by a succession of Christian and orthodox princes, who had extirpated the fabulous gods of antiquity: and the public devotion of the age was impatient to exalt the saints and martyrs of the Catholic church on the altars of Diana and Hercules. The union of the Roman empire was dissolved; its genius was humbled in the dust; and armies of unknown barbarians, issuing from the frozen regions of the North, had established their victorious reign over the fairest provinces of Europe and Africa.

CHAPTER XXXIV

The Character, Conquests, and Court of Attila, King of the Huns. Death of Theodosius the Younger. Elevation of Marcian to the Empire of the East.

THE WESTERN world was oppressed by the Goths and Vandals, who fled before the Huns; but the achievements of the Huns themselves were not adequate to their power and prosperity. Their victorious hordes had spread from the Volga to the Danube; but the public force was exhausted by the discord of independent chieftains; their valour was idly consumed in obscure and predatory excursions; and they often degraded their national dignity, by condescending, for the hopes of spoil, to enlist under the banners of their fugitive enemies. In the reign of ATTILA[1] the Huns again became the terrors of the world; and I shall now describe the character and actions of that formidable barbarian, who alternately insulted and invaded the East and the West and urged the rapid downfall of the Roman Empire.

In the tide of emigration which impetuously rolled from the confines of China to those of

Germany, the most powerful and populous tribes may commonly be found on the verge of the Roman provinces. The accumulated weight was sustained for a while by artificial barriers; and the easy condescension of the emperors invited, without satisfying, the insolent demands of the barbarians, who had acquired an eager appetite for the luxuries of civilised life. The Hungarians, who ambitiously insert the name of Attila among their native kings, may affirm with truth that the hordes which were subject to his uncle Roas, or Rugilas, had formed their encampments within the limits of modern Hungary,[2] in a fertile country which liberally supplied the wants of a nation of hunters and shepherds. In this advantageous situation, Rugilas, and his valiant brothers, who continually added to their power and reputation, commanded the alternative of peace or war with the two empires. His alliance with the Romans of the West was cemented by his personal friendship for the great Aëtius, who was always secure of finding in the barbarian camp an hospitable reception and a powerful support. At his solicitation, and in the name of John the usurper, sixty thousand Huns advanced to the confines of Italy; their march and their retreat were alike expensive to the state; and the grateful policy of Aëtius abandoned the possession of Pannonia to his faithful confederates. The Romans of the East were not less apprehensive of the arms of Rugilas, which threatened the provinces, or even the capital. Some ecclesiastical historians have destroyed the barbarians with lightning and pestilence;[3] but Theodosius was reduced to the more humble expedient of stipulating an annual payment of three hundred and fifty pounds of gold, and of disguising this dishonourable tribute by the title of general, which the king of the Huns condescended to accept. The public tranquillity was frequently interrupted by the fierce impatience of the barbarians and the perfidious intrigues of the Byzantine court. Four dependent nations, among whom we may distinguish the Bavarians, disclaimed the sovereignty of the Huns; and their revolt was encouraged and protected by a Roman alliance; till the just claims and formidable power of Rugilas were effectually urged by the voice of Eslaw, his ambassador. Peace was the unanimous wish of the senate: their decree was ratified by the emperor; and two ambassadors were named—Plinthas, a general of Scythian extraction, but of consular rank; and the quæstor Epigenes, a wise and experienced statesman, who was recommended to that office by his ambitious colleague.

The death of Rugilas suspended the progress of the treaty. His two nephews, Attila and Bleda, who succeeded to the throne of their uncle, consented to a personal interview with the ambassadors of Constantinople; but as they proudly refused to dismount, the business was transacted on horseback, in a spacious plain near the city of Margus, in the Upper Mæsia. The kings of the Huns assumed the solid benefits, as well as the vain honours, of the negotiation. They dictated the conditions of peace, and each condition was an insult on the majesty of the empire. Besides the freedom of a safe and plentiful market on the banks of the Danube, they required that the annual contribution should be augmented from three hundred and fifty to seven hundred pounds of gold; that a fine or ransom, of eight pieces of gold, should be paid for every Roman captive who had escaped from his barbarian master; that the emperor should renounce all treaties and engagements with the enemies of the Huns; and that all the fugitives who had taken refuge in the court or provinces of Theodosius should be delivered to the justice of their offended sovereign. This justice was rigorously inflicted on some unfortunate youths of a royal race. They were crucified on the territories of the empire, by the command of Attila: and, as soon as the king of the Huns had impressed the Romans with the terror of his name, he indulged them in a short and arbitrary respite, whilst he subdued the rebellious or independent nations of Scythia and Germany.[4]

Attila, the son of Mundzuk, deduced his noble, perhaps his regal, descent[5] from the ancient Huns, who had formerly contended with the monarchs of China. His features, according to the observation of a Gothic historian, bore the stamp of his national origin; and the portrait of Attila exhibits the genuine deformity of a modern Calmuck;[6] a large head, a swarthy complexion, small deep-seated eyes, a flat nose, a few hairs in the place of a beard, broad shoulders, and a short square body, of nervous strength, though of a disproportioned form. The haughty step and demeanor of the king of the Huns expressed the consciousness of his superiority above the rest of mankind; and he had a custom of fiercely rolling his eyes, as if he wished to enjoy the terror which he inspired. Yet this savage hero was not inaccessible to pity; his suppliant enemies might confide in the assurance of peace or pardon; and Attila was considered by his subjects as a just and indulgent master. He delighted in war; but, after he had ascended the throne in a mature age, his head, rather than his hand, achieved the conquest of the North; and the fame of an adventurous soldier was usefully exchanged for that of a prudent and successful general. The effects of personal valour are so inconsiderable, except in poetry or romance, that victory, even among barbarians, must depend on the degree of skill with which the passions of the multitude are combined and guided for the service of a single man. The Scythian conquerors, Attila and Zingis, surpassed their rude countrymen in art, rather than in courage; and it may be observed that the monarchies, both of the Huns and of the Moguls, were erected by their founders on the basis of popular superstition. The miraculous conception, which fraud and credulity ascribed to the virgin mother of Zingis, raised him above the level of human nature; and the naked prophet, who, in the name of the Deity, invested him with the empire of the earth, pointed the valour of the Moguls with irresistible enthusiasm.[7] The religious arts of Attila were not less skilfully adapted to the character of his age and country. It was natural enough that the Scythians should adore, with peculiar devotion, the god of war; but as they were incapable of forming either an abstract idea or a corporeal representation, they worshipped their tutelar deity under the symbol of an iron cimeter.[8] One of the shepherds of the Huns perceived that a heifer, who was grazing, had wounded herself in the foot, and curiously followed the track of the blood, till he discovered, among the long grass, the point of an ancient sword, which he dug out of the ground, and presented to Attila. That magnanimous, or rather that artful, prince accepted, with pious gratitude, this celestial favour; and, as the rightful possessor of the *sword of Mars*, asserted his divine and indefeasible claim to the dominion of the earth.[9] If the rites of Scythia were practised on this solemn occasion, a lofty altar, or rather pile of faggots, three hundred yards in length and in breadth, was raised in a spacious plain; and the sword of Mars was placed erect on the summit of this rustic altar, which was annually consecrated by the blood of sheep, horses, and of the hundredth captive.[10] Whether human sacrifices formed any part of the worship of Attila, or whether he propitiated the god of war with the victims which he continually offered in the field of battle, the favourite of Mars soon acquired a sacred character, which rendered his conquests more easy and more permanent; and the barbarian princes confessed, in the language of devotion or flattery, that they could not presume to gaze, with a steady eye, on the divine majesty of the king of the Huns.[11] His brother Bleda, who reigned over a considerable part of the nation, was compelled to resign his sceptre and his life. Yet even this cruel act was attributed to a supernatural impulse; and the vigour with which Attila wielded the sword of Mars convinced the world that it had been reserved alone for his invincible arm.[12] But the extent of his empire affords the only remaining evidence of the number and importance of his victories; and the Scythian monarch, however ignorant of the value of science and philosophy, might perhaps lament that his illiterate subjects were destitute of the art which could perpetuate the memory of his exploits.

If a line of separation were drawn between the civilised and the savage climates of the globe; between the inhabitants of cities, who cultivated the earth, and the hunters and shepherds, who dwelt in tents, Attila might aspire to the title of supreme and sole monarch of the barbarians.[13] He alone, among the conquerors of ancient and modern times, united the two mighty kingdoms of Germany and Scythia; and those vague appellations, when they are applied to his reign, may be understood with an ample latitude. Thuringia, which stretched beyond its actual limits as far as the Danube, was in the number of his provinces; he interposed, with the weight of a powerful neighbour, in the domestic affairs of the Franks; and one of his lieutenants chastised, and almost exterminated, the Burgundians of the Rhine. He subdued the islands of the ocean, the kingdoms of Scandinavia, encompassed and divided by the waters of the Baltic; and the Huns might derive a tribute of furs from that northern region, which has been protected from all other conquerors by the severity of the climate and the courage of the natives. Towards the East, it is difficult to circumscribe the dominion of Attila over the Scythian deserts; yet we may be assured that he reigned on the banks of the Volga; that the king of the Huns was dreaded, not only as a warrior, but as a magician;[14] that he insulted and vanquished the khan of the formidable Geougen; and that he sent ambassadors to negotiate an equal alliance with the empire of China. In the proud review of the nations who acknowledged the sovereignty of Attila, and who never entertained, during his lifetime, the thought of a revolt, the Gepidæ and the Ostrogoths were distinguished by their numbers, their bravery, and the personal merit of their chiefs. The renowned Ardaric, king of the Gepidæ, was the faithful and sagacious counsellor of the monarch, who esteemed his intrepid genius, whilst he loved the mild and discreet virtues of the noble Walamir, king of the Ostrogoths. The crowd of vulgar kings, the leaders of so many martial tribes, who served under the standard of Attila, were ranged in the submissive order of guards and domestics round the person of their master. They watched his nod; they trembled at his frown; and at the first signal of his will, they executed, without murmur or hesitation, his stern and absolute commands. In time of peace, the dependent princes, with their national troops, attended the royal camp in regular succession; but when Attila collected his military force he was able to bring into the field an army of five, or, according to another account, of seven hundred thousand barbarians.[15]

The ambassadors of the Huns might awaken the attention of Theodosius, by reminding him that they were his neighbours both in Europe and Asia; since they touched the Danube on one hand, and reached with the other as far as the Tanais. In the reign of his father Arcadius, a band of adventurous Huns had ravaged the provinces of the East, from whence they brought away rich spoils and innumerable captives. They advanced, by a secret path, along the shores of the Caspian Sea; traversed the snowy mountains of Armenia; passed the Tigris, the Euphrates, and the Halys; recruited their weary cavalry with the generous breed of Cappadocian horses; occupied the hilly country of Cilicia; and disturbed the festal songs and dances of the citizens of Antioch.[16] Egypt trembled at their approach; and the monks and pilgrims of the Holy Land prepared to escape their fury by a speedy embarkation. The memory of this invasion was still recent in the minds of the Orientals. The subjects of Attila might execute, with superior forces, the design which these adventurers had so boldly attempted; and it soon became the subject of anxious conjecture whether the tempest would fall on the dominions of Rome or of Persia. Some of the great vassals of the king of the Huns, who were themselves in the rank of powerful princes, had been sent to ratify an alliance and society of arms with the emperor, or rather with the general, of the West. They related, during their residence at Rome, the circumstances of an expedition which they had lately made into the East. After passing a desert and a morass supposed by the Ro-

mans to be the lake Mæotis, they penetrated through the mountains, and arrived, at the end of fifteen days' march, on the confines of Media, where they advanced as far as the unknown cities of Basic and Cursic.[17] They encountered the Persian army in the plains of Media; and the air, according to their own expression, was darkened by a cloud of arrows. But the Huns were obliged to retire before the numbers of the enemy. Their laborious retreat was affected by a different road; they lost the greatest part of their booty; and at length returned to the royal camp, with some knowledge of the country, and an impatient desire of revenge. In the free conversation of the Imperial ambassadors, who discussed, at the court of Attila, the character and designs of their formidable enemy, the ministers of Constantinople expressed their hope that his strength might be diverted and employed in a long and doubtful contest with the princes of the house of Sassan. The more sagacious Italians admonished their Eastern brethren of the folly and danger of such a hope; and convinced them, *that* the Medes and Persians were incapable of resisting the arms of the Huns; and *that* the easy and important acquisition would exalt the pride, as well as power, of the conqueror. Instead of contenting himself with a moderate contribution and a military title, which equalled him only to the generals of Theodosius, Attila would proceed to impose a disgraceful and intolerable yoke on the necks of the prostrate and captive Romans, who would then be encompassed on all sides by the empire of the Huns.[18]

While the powers of Europe and Asia were solicitous to avert the impending danger, the alliance of Attila maintained the Vandals in the possession of Africa. An enterprise had been concerted between the courts of Ravenna and Constantinople for the recovery of that valuable province; and the ports of Sicily were already filled with the military and naval forces of Theodosius. But the subtle Genseric, who spread his negotiations round the world, prevented their designs, by exciting the king of the Huns to invade the Eastern empire; and a trifling incident soon became the motive, or pretence, of a destructive war.[19] Under the faith of the treaty of Margus, a free market was held on the northern side of the Danube, which was protected by a Roman fortress surnamed Constantia. A troop of barbarians violated the commercial security; killed, or dispersed, the unsuspecting traders; and levelled the fortress with the ground. The Huns justified this outrage as an act of reprisal; alleged that the bishop of Margus had entered their territories, to discover and steal a secret treasure of their kings; and sternly demanded the guilty prelate, the sacrilegious spoil, and the fugitive subjects, who had escaped from the justice of Attila. The refusal of the Byzantine court was the signal of war; and the Mæsians at first applauded the generous firmness of their sovereign. But they were soon intimidated by the destruction of Viminiacum and the adjacent towns; and the people was persuaded to adopt the convenient maxim, that a private citizen, however innocent or respectable, may be justly sacrificed to the safety of his country. The bishop of Margus, who did not possess the spirit of a martyr, resolved to prevent the designs which he suspected. He boldly treated with the princes of the Huns; secured, by solemn oaths, his pardon and reward; posted a numerous detachment of barbarians, in silent ambush, on the banks of the Danube; and, at the appointed hour, opened, with his own hand, the gates of his episcopal city. This advantage, which had been obtained by treachery, served as a prelude to more honourable and decisive victories. The Illyrian frontier was covered by a line of castles and fortresses; and though the greatest part of them consisted only of a single tower, with a small garrison, they were commonly sufficient to repel, or to intercept, the inroads of an enemy who was ignorant of the art, and impatient of the delay, of a regular siege. But these slight obstacles were instantly swept away by the inundation of the Huns.[20] They destroyed, with fire and sword, the populous cities of Sirmium and Singidunum, of Ratiaria and Marcianopolis, of Naissus and Sardica; where every circumstance in the discipline of the people and the construction of the buildings had been gradually adapted to the sole purpose of defence. The whole breadth of Europe, as it extends above five hundred miles from the Euxine to the Hadriatic, was at once invaded, and occupied, and desolated, by the myriads of barbarians whom Attila led into the field. The public danger and distress could not, however, provoke Theodosius to interrupt his amusements and devotion, or to appear in person at the head of the Roman legions. But the troops which had been sent against Genseric were hastily recalled from Sicily; the garrisons, on the side of Persia, were exhausted; and a military force was collected in Europe, formidable by their arms and numbers, if the generals had understood the science of command, and their soldiers the duty of obedience. The armies of the Eastern empire were vanquished in three successive engagements; and the progress of Attila may be traced by the fields of battle. The two former, on the banks of the Utus, and under the walls of Marcianopolis, were fought in the extensive plains between the Danube and Mount Hæmus. As the Romans were pressed by a victorious enemy, they gradually, and unskilfully, retired towards the Chersonesus of Thrace; and that narrow peninsula, the last extremity of the land, was marked by their third and irreparable defeat. By the destruction of this army, Attila acquired the indisputable possession of the field. From the Hellespont to Thermopylæ and the suburbs of Constantinople he ravaged, without resistance and without mercy, the provinces of Thrace and Macedonia. Heraclea and Hadrianople might, perhaps, escape this dreadful irruption of the Huns; but the words the most expressive of total extirpation and erasure are applied to the calamities which they inflicted on seventy cities of the Eastern empire.[21] Theodosius, his court, and the unwarlike people, were protected by the walls of Constantinople; but those walls had been shaken by a recent earthquake, and the fall of fifty-eight towers had opened a large and tremendous breach. The damage indeed was speedily repaired; but this accident was aggravated by a superstitious fear that Heaven itself had delivered the Imperial city to the shepherds of Scythia, who were strangers to the laws, the language, and the religion of the Romans.[22]

In all their invasions of the civilised empires of the South, the Scythian shepherds have been uniformly actuated by a savage and destructive spirit. The laws of war, that restrain the exercise of national rapine and murder, are founded on two principles of substantial interest: the knowledge of the permanent benefits which may be obtained by a moderate use of conquest, and a just apprehension lest the desolation which we inflict on the enemy's country may be retaliated on our own. But these considerations of hope and fear are almost unknown in the pastoral state of nations. The Huns of Attila may without injustice be compared to the Moguls and Tartars before their primitive manners were changed by religion and luxury; and the evidence of Oriental history may reflect some light on the short and imperfect annals of Rome. After the Moguls had subdued the northern provinces of China, it was seriously proposed, not in the hour of victory and passion, but in calm deliberate council, to exterminate all the inhabitants of that populous country, that the vacant land might be converted to the pasture of cattle. The firmness of a Chinese mandarin,[23] who insinuated some principles of rational policy into the mind of Zingis, diverted him from the execution of this horrid design. But in the cities of Asia which yielded to the Moguls, the inhuman abuse of the rights of war was exercised with a regular form of discipline, which may, with equal reason though not with equal authority, be imputed to the victorious Huns. The inhabitants who had submitted to their discretion were ordered to evacuate their houses and to assemble in some plain adjacent to the city, where a division was made of the vanquished into three parts. The first class consisted of the soldiers of the garrison and the young men capable of bearing arms; and their fate was instantly decided: they were either enlisted among the Moguls, or they were massacred on the spot by the troops, who, with pointed spears and bended bows, had formed a circle round the captive multitude. The second class, composed of the young and beautiful women, of the artificers of every rank and profession, and of the more wealthy or honourable citizens, from whom a private ransom might be expected, was distributed in equal or proportionable lots. The remainder, whose life or death was alike useless to the conquerors, were permitted to return to the city, which in the meanwhile had been stripped of its valuable furniture; and a tax was imposed on those wretched inhabitants for the indulgence of breathing their native air. Such was the behaviour of the Moguls when they were not conscious of any extraordinary rigour.[24] But the most casual provocation, the slightest motive of caprice or convenience, often provoked them to involve a whole people in an indiscriminate massacre; and the ruin of some flourishing cities was executed with such unrelenting perseverance, that, according to their own expression, horses might run without stumbling over the ground where they had once stood. The three great capitals of Khorasan, Maru, Neisabour, and Herat, were destroyed by the armies of Zingis; and the exact account which was taken of the slain amounted to four millions three hundred and forty-seven thousand persons.[25] Timur, or Tamerlane, was educated in a less barbarous age and in the profession of the Mahometan religion; yet, if Attila equalled the hostile ravages of Tamerlane,[26] either the Tartar or the Hun might deserve the epithet of the Scourge of God.[27]

It may be affirmed with bolder assurance that the Huns depopulated the provinces of the empire by the number of Roman subjects whom they led away into captivity. In the hands of a wise legislator such an industrious colony might have contributed to diffuse through the deserts of Scythia the rudiments of the useful and ornamental arts; but these captives, who had been taken in war, were accidentally dispersed among the hordes that obeyed the empire of Attila. The estimate of their respective value was formed by the simple judgment of unenlightened and unprejudiced barbarians. Perhaps they might not understand the merit of a theologian profoundly skilled in the controversies of the Trinity and the Incarnation; yet they respected the ministers of every religion; and the active zeal of the Christian missionaries, without approaching the person or the palace of the monarch, successfully laboured in the propagation of the gospel.[28] The pastoral tribes, who were ignorant of the distinction of landed property, must have disregarded the use as well as the abuse of civil jurisprudence; and the skill of an eloquent lawyer could excite only their contempt or their abhorrence.[29] The perpetual intercourse of the Huns and the Goths had communicated the familiar knowledge of the two national dialects; and the barbarians were ambitious of conversing in Latin, the military idiom even of the Eastern empire.[30] But they disdained the language and the sciences of the Greeks; and the vain sophist or grave philosopher who had enjoyed the flattering applause of the schools, was mortified to find that his robust servant was a captive of more value and importance than himself. The mechanic arts were encouraged and esteemed, as they tended to satisfy the wants of the Huns. An architect in the service of Onegesius, one of the favourites of Attila, was employed to construct a bath: but this work was a rare example of private luxury; and the trades of the smith, the carpenter, the armourer, were much more adapted to supply a wandering people with the useful instruments of peace and war. But the merit of the physician was received with universal favour and respect: the barbarians, who despised death, might be apprehensive of disease; and the haughty conqueror trembled in the presence of a captive to whom he ascribed perhaps an imaginary power of prolonging or preserving his life.[31] The Huns might be provoked to insult the misery of their slaves, over whom they exercised a despotic command;[32] but their manners were not susceptible of a refined system of oppression, and the efforts of courage and diligence were often recompensed by the gift of freedom. The historian Priscus, whose embassy is a source of curious instruction, was accosted in the camp of Attila by a stranger, who saluted him in the Greek language, but whose dress and figure displayed the appearance of a wealthy Scythian. In the siege of Viminiacum he had lost, according to his own account, his fortune and liberty: he became the slave of Onegesius; but his faithful services against the Romans and the Acatzires had gradually raised him to the rank of the native Huns, to whom he was attached by the domestic pledges of a new wife and several children. The spoils of war had restored and improved his private property; he was admitted to the table of his former lord; and the apostate Greek blessed the hour of his captivity, since it had been the introduction to a happy and independent state, which he held by the honourable tenure of military service. This reflection naturally produced a dispute on the advantages and defects of the Roman government, which was severely arraigned by the apostate, and defended by Priscus in a prolix and feeble declamation. The freedman of Onegesius exposed, in true and lively colours, the vices of a declining empire of which he had so long been the victim; the cruel absurdity of the Roman princes, unable to protect their subjects against the public enemy, unwilling to trust them with arms for their own defence; the intolerable weight of taxes, rendered still more oppressive by the intricate or arbitrary modes of collection; the obscurity of numerous and contradictory laws; the tedious and expensive forms of judicial proceedings; the partial administration of justice; and the universal corruption which increased the influence of the rich and aggravated the misfortunes of the poor. A sentiment of patriotic sympathy was at length revived in the breast of the fortunate exile, and he lamented with a flood of tears the guilt or weakness of those magistrates who had perverted the wisest and most salutary institutions.[33]

The timid or selfish policy of the Western Romans had abandoned the Eastern empire to the Huns.[34] The loss of armies and the want of discipline or virtue were not supplied by the personal character of the monarch. Theodosius might still affect the style as well as the title of *Invincible Augustus*, but he was reduced to solicit the clemency of Attila who imperiously dictated these harsh and humiliating conditions of peace. I. The emperor of the East resigned, by an express or tacit convention, an extensive and important territory which stretched along the southern banks of the Danube, from Singidunum, or Belgrade, as far as Novæ, in the diocese of Thrace. The breadth was defined by the vague computation of fifteen days' journey; but, from the proposal of Attila to remove the situation of the national market, it soon appeared that he comprehended the ruined city of Naissus within the limits of his dominions. II. The king of the Huns required and obtained that his tribute or subsidy should be augmented from seven hundred pounds of gold to the annual sum of two thousand one hundred; and he stipulated the immediate payment of six thousand pounds of gold to defray the expenses, or to expiate the guilt, of the war. One might imagine that such a demand, which scarcely equalled the measure of private wealth, would have been readily discharged by the opulent empire of the East; and the public distress affords a remarkable proof of the impoverished, or at least of the disorderly, state of the finances. A large porportion of the taxes extorted from the people was detained and intercepted in their passage through the foulest channels to the treasury of Constantinople. The revenue was dissipated by Theodosius and his favourites in wasteful and profuse luxury, which was disguised by the names of imperial magnificence or Christian charity. The immediate supplies had been exhausted by the unforeseen necessity of military preparations. A personal contribution, rigorously but capriciously imposed on the members of the senatorian order, was the only expedient that could disarm without loss of time the impatient avarice of Attila: and the poverty of the nobles compelled them to adopt the scandalous resource of exposing to public auction the jewels of their wives and the hereditary ornaments of their palaces.[35] III. The king of the Huns appears to have established as a principle of national jurisprudence, that he could never lose the property which he had once acquired in the persons who had yielded either a voluntary or reluctant submission to his authority. From this principle he concluded, and the conclusions of Attila were irrevocable laws, that the Huns who had been taken prisoners in war should be released without delay and without ransom; that every Roman captive who had presumed to escape should purchase his right to freedom at the price of twelve pieces of gold; and that all the barbarians who had deserted the standard of Attila should be restored without any promise or stipulation of pardon. In the execution of this cruel and ignominious treaty the Imperial officers were forced to massacre several loyal and noble deserters who refused to devote themselves to certain death; and the Romans forfeited all reasonable claims to the friendship of any Scythian people by this public confession that they were destitute either of faith or power to protect the suppliant who had embraced the throne of Theodosius.[36]

The firmness of a single town, so obscure that except on this occasion it has never been mentioned by any historian or geographer, exposed the disgrace of the emperor and empire. Azimus, or Azimuntium, a small city of Thrace on the Illyrian borders,[37] had been distinguished by the martial spirit of its youth, the skill and reputation of the leaders whom they had chosen, and their daring exploits against the innumerable host of the barbarians. Instead of tamely expecting their approach, the Azimuntines attacked, in frequent and successful sallies, the troops of the Huns, who gradually declined the dangerous neighbourhood, rescued from their hands the spoil and the captives, and recruited their domestic force by the voluntary association of fugitives and deserters. After the conclusion of the treaty Attila still menaced the empire with implacable war, unless the Azimuntines were persuaded or compelled to comply with the conditions which their sovereign had accepted. The ministers of Theodosius confessed, with shame and with truth, that they no longer possessed any authority over a society of men who so bravely asserted their natural independence; and the king of the Huns condescended to negotiate an equal exchange with the citizens of Azimus. They demanded the restitution of some shepherds, who with their cattle had been accidentally surprised. A strict though fruitless inquiry was allowed; but the Huns were obliged to swear that they did not detain any prisoners belonging to the city before they could recover two surviving countrymen whom the Azimuntines had reserved as pledges for the safety of their lost companions. Attila, on his side, was satisfied and deceived by their solemn asseveration that the rest of the captives had been put to the sword; and that it was their constant practice immediately to dismiss the Romans and the deserters who had obtained the security of the public faith. This prudent and officious dissimulation may be condemned or excused by the casuists as they incline to the rigid decree of St. Augustin, or the milder sentiment of St. Jerom and St. Chrysostom: but every soldier, every statesman, must acknowledge that, if the race of the Azimuntines had been encouraged and multiplied, the barbarians would have ceased to trample on the majesty of the empire.[38]

It would have been strange, indeed, if Theodosius had purchased, by the loss of honour, a secure and solid tranquillity, or if his tameness had not invited the repetition of injuries. The Byzantine court was insulted by five or six successive embassies;[39] and the ministers of Attila were uniformly instructed to press the tardy or imperfect execution of the last treaty; to produce the names of fugitives and deserters who were still protected by the empire; and to declare, with seeming moderation, that, unless their sovereign obtained complete and immediate satisfaction, it would be impossible for him, were it even his wish, to check the resentment of his warlike tribes. Besides the motive of pride and interest which might prompt the king of the Huns to continue this train of negotiation, he was influenced by the less honourable view of enriching his favourites at the expense of his enemies. The Imperial treasury was exhausted to procure the friendly offices of the ambassadors and their principal attendants, whose favourable report might conduce to the maintenance of peace. The barbarian monarch was flattered by the liberal reception of his ministers; he computed with pleasure the value and splendour of their gifts, rigorously exacted the performance of every promise which would contribute to their private emolument, and treated as an important business of state the marriage of his secretary Constantius.[40] That Gallic adventurer, who was recommended by Aëtius to the king of the Huns, had engaged his service to the ministers of Constantinople for the stipulated reward of a wealthy and noble wife; and the daughter of Count Saturninus was chosen to discharge the obligations of her country. The reluctance of the victim, some domestic troubles, and the unjust confiscation of her fortune, cooled the ardour of her interested lover; but he still demanded, in the name of Attila, an equivalent alliance; and, after many ambiguous delays and excuses, the Byzantine court was compelled to sacrifice to this insolent stranger the widow of Armatius, whose birth, opulence, and beauty placed her in the most illustrious rank of the Roman matrons. For these importunate and oppressive embassies Attila claimed a suitable return; he weighed, with suspicious pride, the character and station of the Imperial envoys; but he condescended to promise that he would advance as far as Sardica to receive any minister who had been invested with the consular dignity. The council of Theodosius eluded this proposal by representing the desolate and ruined condition of Sardica; and even ventured to insinuate that every officer of the army or household was qualified to treat with the most powerful princes of Scythia. Maximin,[41] a respectable courtier, whose abilities had been long exercised in civil and military employments, accepted with reluctance the troublesome, and perhaps dangerous, commission of reconciling the angry spirit of the king of the Huns. His friend, the historian Priscus,[42] embraced the opportunity of observing the barbarian hero in the peaceful and domestic scenes of life: but the secret of the embassy, a fatal and guilty secret, was intrusted only to the interpreter Vigilius. The two last ambassadors of the Huns, Orestes, a noble subject of the Pannonian province, and Edecon, a valiant chieftain of the tribe of the Scyrri, returned at the same time from Constantinople to the royal camp. Their obscure names were afterwards illustrated by the extraordinary fortune and the contrast of their sons: the two servants of Attila became the fathers of the last Roman emperor of the West, and of the first barbarian king of Italy.

The ambassadors, who were followed by a numerous train of men and horses, made their first halt at Sardica, at the distance of three hundred and fifty miles, or thirteen days' journey, from Constantinople. As the remains of Sardica were still included within the limits of the empire, it was incumbent on the Romans to exercise the duties of hospitality. They provided, with the assistance of the provincials, a sufficient number of sheep and oxen, and invited the Huns to a splendid, or, at least, a plentiful supper. But the harmony of the entertainment was soon disturbed by mutual prejudice and indiscretion. The greatness of the emperor and the empire was warmly maintained by their ministers; the Huns, with equal ardour, asserted the superiority of their victorious monarch: the dispute was inflamed by the rash and unseasonable flattery of Vigilius, who passionately rejected the comparison of a mere mortal with the divine Theodosius; and it was with extreme difficulty that Maximin and Priscus were able to divert the conversation or to soothe the angry minds of the barbarians. When they rose from table the Imperial ambassador presented Edecon and Orestes with rich gifts of silk robes and Indian pearls, which they thankfully accepted. Yet Orestes could not

forbear insinuating that *he* had not always been treated with such respect and liberality: and the offensive distinction which was implied between his civil office and the hereditary rank of his colleague seems to have made Edecon a doubtful friend and Orestes an irreconcilable enemy. After this entertainment they travelled about one hundred miles from Sardica to Naissus. That flourishing city, which had given birth to the great Constantine, was levelled with the ground; the inhabitants were destroyed or dispersed; and the appearance of some sick persons, who were still permitted to exist among the ruins of the churches, served only to increase the horror of the prospect. The surface of the country was covered with the bones of the slain; and the ambassadors, who directed their course to the northwest, were obliged to pass the hills of modern Servia before they descended into the flat and marshy grounds which are terminated by the Danube. The Huns were masters of the great river: their navigation was performed in large canoes, hollowed out of the trunk of a single tree; the ministers of Theodosius were safely landed on the opposite bank; and their barbarian associates immediately hastened to the camp of Attila, which was equally prepared for the amusements of hunting or of war. No sooner had Maximin advanced about two miles from the Danube than he began to experience the fastidious insolence of the conqueror. He was sternly forbid to pitch his tents in a pleasant valley, lest he should infringe the distant awe that was due to the royal mansion. The ministers of Attila pressed him to communicate the business and the instructions which he reserved for the ear of their sovereign. When Maximin temperately urged the contrary practice of nations, he was still more confounded to find that the resolutions of the Sacred Consistory, those secrets (says Priscus) which should not be revealed to the gods themselves, had been treacherously disclosed to the public enemy. On his refusal to comply with such ignominious terms, the Imperial envoy was commanded instantly to depart; the order was recalled; it was again repeated; and the Huns renewed their ineffectual attempts to subdue the patient firmness of Maximin. At length, by the intercession of Scotta, the brother of Onegesius, whose friendship had been purchased by a liberal gift, he was admitted to the royal presence; but, instead of obtaining a decisive answer, he was compelled to undertake a remote journey towards the North, that Attila might enjoy the proud satisfaction of receiving in the same camp the ambassadors of the Eastern and Western empires. His journey was regulated by the guides, who obliged him to halt, to hasten his march, or to deviate from the common road, as it best suited the convenience of the king. The Romans who traversed the plains of Hungary suppose that they passed *several* navigable rivers, either in canoes or portable boats; but there is reason to suspect that the winding stream of the Theiss, or Tibiscus, might present itself in different places under different names. From the contiguous villages they received a plentiful and regular supply of provisions; mead instead of wine, millet in the place of bread, and a certain liquor named *camus*, which, according to the report of Priscus, was distilled from barley.[43] Such fare might appear coarse and indelicate to men who had tasted the luxury of Constantinople; but, in their accidental distress, they were relieved by the gentleness and hospitality of the same barbarians, so terrible and so merciless in war. The ambassadors had encamped on the edge of a large morass. A violent tempest of wind and rain, of thunder and lightning, overturned their tents, immersed their baggage and furniture in the water, and scattered their retinue, who wandered in the darkness of the night, uncertain of their road and apprehensive of some unknown danger, till they awakened by their cries the inhabitants of a neighbouring village, the property of the widow of Bleda. A bright illumination, and, in a few moments, a comfortable fire of reeds, was kindled by their officious benevolence: the wants, and even the desires, of the Romans were liberally satisfied; and they seem to have been embarrassed by the singular politeness of Bleda's widow, who added to her other favours the gift, or at least the loan, of a sufficient number of beautiful and obsequious damsels. The sunshine of the succeeding day was dedicated to repose, to collect and dry the baggage, and to the refreshment of the men and horses; but, in the evening, before they pursued their journey, the ambassadors expressed their gratitude to the bounteous lady of the village by a very acceptable present of silver cups, red fleeces, dried fruits, and Indian pepper. Soon after this adventure they rejoined the march of Attila, from whom they had been separated about six days; and slowly proceeded to the capital of an empire which did not contain, in the space of several thousand miles, a single city.

As far as we may ascertain the vague and obscure geography of Priscus, this capital appears to have been seated between the Danube, the Theiss, and the Carpathian hills, in the plains of Upper Hungary, and most probably in the neighbourhood of Jazberin, Agria, or Tokay.[44] In its origin it could be no more than an accidental camp, which, by the long and frequent residence of Attila, had insensibly swelled into a huge village, for the reception of his court, of the troops who followed his person, and of the various multitude of idle or industrious slaves and retainers.[45] The baths, constructed by Onegesius, were the only edifice of stone; the materials had been transported from Pannonia; and since the adjacent country was destitute even of large timber, it may be presumed that the meaner habitations of the royal village consisted of straw, of mud, or of canvas. The wooden houses of the more illustrious Huns were built and adorned with rude magnificence, according to the rank, the fortune, or the taste of the proprietors. They seem to have been distributed with some degree of order and symmetry; and each spot became more honourable as it approached the person of the sovereign. The palace of Attila, which surpassed all other houses in his dominions, was built entirely of wood, and covered an ample space of ground. The outward enclosure was a lofty wall, or palisade, of smooth square timber, intersected with high towers, but intended rather for ornament than defence. This wall, which seems to have encircled the declivity of a hill, comprehended a great variety of wooden edifices, adapted to the uses of royalty. A separate house was assigned to each of the numerous wives of Attila; and, instead of the rigid and illiberal confinement imposed by Asiatic jealousy, they politely admitted the Roman ambassadors to their presence, their table, and even to the freedom of an innocent embrace. When Maximin offered his presents to Cerca the principal queen, he admired the singular architecture of her mansion, the height of the round columns, the size and beauty of the wood, which was curiously shaped or turned, or polished or carved; and his attentive eye was able to discover some taste in the ornaments, and some regularity in the proportions. After passing through the guards who watched before the gate, the ambassadors were introduced into the private apartment of Cerca. The wife of Attila received their visit sitting, or rather lying, on a soft couch; the floor was covered with a carpet; the domestics formed a circle round the queen; and her damsels, seated on the ground, were employed in working the variegated embroidery which adorned the dress of the barbaric warriors. The Huns were ambitious of displaying those riches which were the fruit and evidence of their victories; the trappings of their horses, their swords, and even their shoes, were studded with gold and precious stones; and their tables were profusely spread with plates, and goblets, and vases of gold and silver, which had been fashioned by the labour of Grecian artists. The monarch alone assumed the superior pride of still adhering to the simplicity of his Scythian ancestors.[46] The dress of Attila, his arms, and the furniture of his horse, were plain, without ornament, and of a single colour. The royal table was served in wooden cups and platters; flesh was his only food; and the conqueror of the North never tasted the luxury of bread.

When Attila first gave audience to the Roman ambassadors on the banks of the Danube, his tent was encompassed with a formidable guard. The monarch himself was seated in a wooden chair. His stern countenance, angry gestures, and impatient tone astonished the firmness of Maximin; but Vigilius had more reason to tremble, since he distinctly understood the menace, that if Attila did not respect the law of nations, he would nail the deceitful interpreter to a cross, and leave his body to the vultures. The barbarians condescended, by producing an accurate list, to expose the bold falsehood of Vigilius, who had affirmed that no more than seventeen deserters could be found. But he arrogantly declared that he apprehended only the disgrace of contending with his fugitive slaves; since he despised their impotent efforts to defend the provinces which Theodosius had intrusted to their arms: "For what fortress" (added Attila), "what city, in the wide extent of the Roman empire, can hope to exist, secure and impregnable, if it is our pleasure that it should be erased from the earth?" He dismissed, however, the interpreter, who returned to Constantinople with his peremptory demand of more complete restitution, and a more splendid embassy. His anger gradually subsided, and his domestic satisfaction in a marriage which he celebrated on the road with the daughter of Eslam might perhaps contribute to mollify the native fierceness of his temper. The entrance of Attila into the royal village was marked by a very singular ceremony. A numerous troop of women came out to meet their hero and their king. They marched before him, distributed into long and regular files: the intervals between the files were filled by

white veils of thin linen, which the women on either side bore aloft in their hands, and which formed a canopy for a chorus of young virgins, who chanted hymns and songs in the Scythian language. The wife of his favourite Onegesius, with a train of female attendants, saluted Attila at the door of her own house, on his way to the palace; and offered, according to the custom of the country, her respectful homage, by entreating him to taste the wine and meat which she had prepared for his reception. As soon as the monarch had graciously accepted her hospitable gift, his domestics lifted a small silver table to a convenient height, as he sat on horseback; and Attila, when he had touched the goblet with his lips, again saluted the wife of Onegesius, and continued his march. During his residence at the seat of empire his hours were not wasted in the recluse idleness of a seraglio; and the king of the Huns could maintain his superior dignity without concealing his person from the public view. He frequently assembled his council, and gave audience to the ambassadors of the nations; and his people might appeal to the supreme tribunal, which he held at stated times, and, according to the Eastern custom, before the principal gate of his wooden palace. The Romans, both of the East and of the West, were twice invited to the banquet where Attila feasted with the princes and nobles of Scythia. Maximin and his colleagues were stopped on the threshold, till they had made a devout libation to the health and prosperity of the king of the Huns; and were conducted, after this ceremony, to their respective seats in a spacious hall. The royal table and couch, covered with carpets and fine linen, was raised by several steps in the midst of the hall; and a son, an uncle, or perhaps a favourite king, were admitted to share the simple and homely repast of Attila. Two lines of small tables, each of which contained three or four guests, were ranged in order on either hand; the right was esteemed the most honourable, but the Romans ingenuously confess that they were placed on the left; and that Beric, an unknown chieftain, most probably of the Gothic race, preceded the representatives of Theodosius and Valentinian. The barbarian monarch received from his cupbearer a goblet filled with wine, and courteously drank to the health of the most distinguished guest, who rose from his seat and expressed, in the same manner, his loyal and respectful vows. This ceremony was successively performed for all, or at least for the illustrious persons of the assembly; and a considerable time must have been consumed, since it was thrice repeated as each course or service was placed on the table. But the wine still remained after the meat had been removed; and the Huns continued to indulge their intemperance long after the sober and decent ambassadors of the two empires had withdrawn themselves from the nocturnal banquet. Yet before they retired they enjoyed a singular opportunity of observing the manners of the nation in their convivial amusements. Two Scythians stood before the couch of Attila, and recited the verses which they had composed to celebrate his valour and his victories. A profound silence prevailed in the hall; and the attention of the guests was captivated by the vocal harmony, which revived and perpetuated the memory of their own exploits: a martial ardour flashed from the eyes of the warriors, who were impatient for battle; and the tears of the old men expressed their generous despair that they could no longer partake the danger and glory of the field.[47] This entertainment, which might be considered as a school of military virtue, was succeeded by a farce that debased the dignity of human nature. A Moorish and a Scythian buffoon successively excited the mirth of the rude spectators, by their deformed figure, ridiculous dress, antic gestures, absurd speeches, and the strange unintelligible confusion of the Latin, the Gothic, and the Hunnic languages; and the hall resounded with loud and licentious peals of laughter. In the midst of this intemperate riot, Attila alone, without a change of countenance, maintained his steadfast and inflexible gravity, which was never relaxed, except on the entrance of Irnac, the youngest of his sons: he embraced the boy with a smile of paternal tenderness, gently pinched him by the cheek, and betrayed a partial affection, which was justified by the assurance of his prophets that Irnac would be the future support of his family and empire. Two days afterwards the ambassadors received a second invitation; and they had reason to praise the politeness, as well as the hospitality, of Attila. The king of the Huns held a long and familiar conversation with Maximin; but his civility was interrupted by rude expressions and haughty reproaches; and he was provoked, by a motive of interest, to support, with unbecoming zeal, the private claims of his secretary Constantius. "The emperor" (said Attila) "has long promised him a rich wife: Constantius must not be disappointed; nor should a Roman emperor deserve the name of liar." On the third day the ambassadors were dismissed; the freedom of several

captives was granted, for a moderate ransom, to their pressing entreaties; and, besides the royal presents, they were permitted to accept from each of the Scythian nobles the honourable and useful gift of a horse. Maximin returned, by the same road, to Constantinople; and though he was involved in an accidental dispute with Beric, the new ambassador of Attila, he flattered himself that he had contributed, by the laborious journey, to confirm the peace and alliance of the two nations.[48]

But the Roman ambassador was ignorant of the treacherous design which had been concealed under the mask of the public faith. The surprise and satisfaction of Edecon, when he contemplated the splendour of Constantinople, had encouraged the interpreter Vigilius to procure for him a secret interview with the eunuch Chrysaphius,[49] who governed the emperor and the empire. After some previous conversation, and a mutual oath of secrecy, the eunuch, who had not, from his own feelings or experience, imbibed any exalted notions of ministerial virtue, ventured to propose the death of Attila, as an important service, by which Edecon might deserve a liberal share of the wealth and luxury which he admired. The ambassador of the Huns listened to the tempting offer; and professed, with apparent zeal, his ability, as well as readiness, to execute the bloody deed: the design was communicated to the master of the offices, and the devout Theodosius consented to the assassination of his invincible enemy. But this perfidious conspiracy was defeated by the dissimulation, or the repentance, of Edecon; and though he might exaggerate his inward abhorrence for the treason which he seemed to approve, he dexterously assumed the merit of an early and voluntary confession. If we *now* review the embassy of Maximin and the behaviour of Attila, we must applaud the barbarian, who respected the laws of hospitality, and generously entertained and dismissed the minister of a prince who had conspired against his life. But the rashness of Vigilius will appear still more extraordinary, since he returned, conscious of his guilt and danger, to the royal camp accompanied by his son, and carrying with him a weighty purse of gold, which the favourite eunuch had furnished, to satisfy the demands of Edecon and to corrupt the fidelity of the guards. The interpreter was instantly seized and dragged before the tribunal of Attila, where he asserted his innocence with specious firmness, till the threat of inflicting instant death on his son extorted from him a sincere discovery of the criminal transaction. Under the name of ransom, or confiscation, the rapacious king of the Huns accepted two hundred pounds of gold for the life of a traitor whom he disdained to punish. He pointed his just indignation against a nobler object. His ambassadors, Eslaw and Orestes, were immediately despatched to Constantinople with a peremptory instruction, which it was much safer for them to execute than to disobey. They boldly entered the Imperial presence with the fatal purse hanging down from the neck of Orestes, who interrogated the eunuch Chrysaphius, as he stood beside the throne, whether he recognised the evidence of his guilt. But the office of reproof was reserved for the superior dignity of his colleague Eslaw, who gravely addressed the emperor of the East in the following words: "Theodosius is the son of an illustrious and respectable parent: Attila likewise is descended from a noble race; and *he* has supported, by his actions, the dignity which he inherited from his father Mundzuk. But Theodosius has forfeited his paternal honours, and, by consenting to pay tribute, has degraded himself to the condition of a slave. It is therefore just that he should reverence the man whom fortune and merit have placed above him, instead of attempting, like a wicked slave, clandestinely to conspire against his master." The son of Arcadius, who was accustomed only to the voice of flattery, heard with astonishment the severe language of truth: he blushed and trembled; nor did he presume directly to refuse the head of Chrysaphius, which Eslaw and Orestes were instructed to demand. A solemn embassy, armed with full powers and magnificent gifts, was hastily sent to deprecate the wrath of Attila; and his pride was gratified by the choice of Nomius and Anatolius, two ministers of consular or patrician rank, of whom the one was great treasurer, and the other was master-general of the armies of the East. He condescended to meet these ambassadors on the banks of the river Drenco; and though he at first affected a stern and haughty demeanour, his anger was insensibly mollified by their eloquence and liberality. He condescended to pardon the emperor, the eunuch, and the interpreter; bound himself by an oath to observe the conditions of peace; released a great number of captives; abandoned the fugitives and deserters to their fate; and resigned a large territory, to the south of the Danube, which he had already exhausted of its wealth and inhabitants. But this treaty was purchased at an expense which might have supported a vigorous and successful war; and the subjects of Theodosius were compelled to redeem the safety of a worthless favourite by oppressive taxes which they would more cheerfully have paid for his destruction.[50]

The emperor Theodosius did not long survive the most humiliating circumstance of an inglorious life. As he was riding or hunting in the neighbourhood of Constantinople, he was thrown from his horse into the river Lycus: the spine of his back was injured by the fall; and he expired some days afterwards, in the fiftieth year of his age, and the forty-third of his reign.[51] His sister Pulcheria, whose authority had been controlled both in civil and ecclesiastical affairs by the pernicious influence of the eunuchs, was unanimously proclaimed empress of the East; and the Romans, for the first time, submitted to a female reign. No sooner had Pulcheria ascended the throne than she indulged her own and the public resentment by an act of popular justice. Without any legal trial, the eunuch Chrysaphius was executed before the gates of the city; and the immense riches which had been accumulated by the rapacious favourite served only to hasten and to justify his punishment.[52] Amidst the general acclamations of the clergy and people, the empress did not forget the prejudice and disadvantage to which her sex was exposed; and she wisely resolved to prevent their murmurs by the choice of a colleague who would always respect the superior rank and virgin chastity of his wife. She gave her hand to Marcian, a senator, about sixty years of age, and the nominal husband of Pulcheria was solemnly invested with the Imperial purple. The zeal which he displayed for the orthodox creed, as it was established by the council of Chalcedon, would alone have inspired the grateful eloquence of the catholics. But the behaviour of Marcian in a private life, and afterwards on the throne, may support a more rational belief that he was qualified to restore and invigorate an empire which had been almost dissolved by the successive weakness of two hereditary monarchs. He was born in Thrace, and educated to the profession of arms; but Marcian's youth had been severely exercised by poverty and misfortune, since his only resource, when he first arrived at Constantinople, consisted in two hundred pieces of gold which he had borrowed of a friend. He passed nineteen years in the domestic and military service of Aspar and his son Ardaburius; followed those powerful generals to the Persian and African wars; and obtained, by their influence, the honourable rank of tribune and senator. His mild disposition and useful talents, without alarming the jealousy, recommended Marcian to the esteem and favour of his patrons; he had seen, perhaps he had felt, the abuses of a venal and oppressive administration; and his own example gave weight and energy to the laws which he promulgated for the reformation of manners.[53]

CHAPTER XXXV

Invasion of Gaul by Attila. He is repulsed by Aëtius and the Visigoths. Attila invades and evacuates Italy. The Deaths of Attila, Aëtius, and Valentinian the Third.

IT was the opinion of Marcian, that war should be avoided as long as it is possible to preserve a secure and honourable peace; but it was likewise his opinion that peace cannot be honourable or secure, if the sovereign betrays a pusillanimous aversion to war. This temperate courage dictated his reply to the demands of Attila, who insolently pressed the payment of the annual tribute. The emperor signified to the barbarians that they must no longer insult the majesty of Rome by the mention of a tribute; that he was disposed to reward, with becoming liberality, the faithful friendship of his allies; but that, if they presumed to violate the public peace, they should feel that he possessed troops, and arms, and resolution, to repel their attacks. The same language, even in the camp of the Huns, was used by his ambassador Apollonius, whose bold refusal to deliver the presents, till he had been admitted to a personal interview, displayed a sense of dignity, and a contempt of danger, which Attila was not prepared to expect from the degenerate Romans.[1] He threatened to chastise the rash successor of Theodosius; but he hesitated, whether he should first direct his invincible arms against the Eastern or the Western empire. While mankind awaited his decision with awful suspense, he sent an equal defiance to the courts of Ravenna and Constantinople; and his ministers saluted the two emperors with the same haughty declaration. "Attila, *my* lord, and *thy* lord, commands thee to provide a palace for his immediate reception."[2] But as the barbarian despised, or affected to despise, the Romans of the East, whom he had so often vanquished, he soon declared his resolution of suspending the easy conquest till he had achieved a more glorious and important enterprise. In the memorable invasions of Gaul and Italy, the Huns were naturally attracted by the wealth and fertility of those provinces; but the particular motives and provocations of Attila can only be explained by the state of the Western empire under the reign of Valentinian, or, to speak more correctly, under the administration of Aëtius.[3]

After the death of his rival Boniface, Aëtius had prudently retired to the tents of the Huns; and he was indebted to their alliance for his safety and his restoration. Instead of the suppliant language of a guilty exile, he solicited his pardon at the head of sixty thousand barbarians; and the empress Placidia confessed, by a feeble resistance, that the condescension which might have been ascribed to clemency was the effect of weakness or fear. She delivered herself, her son Valentinian, and the Western empire, into the hands of an insolent subject; nor could Placidia protect the son-in-law of Boniface, the virtuous and faithful Sebastian,[4] from the implacable persecution which urged him from one kingdom to another, till he miserably perished in the service of the Vandals. The fortunate Aëtius, who was immediately promoted to the rank of patrician, and thrice invested with the honours of the consulship, assumed, with the title of master of the cavalry and infantry, the whole military power of the state; and he is sometimes styled, by contemporary writers, the duke, or general, of the Romans of the West. His prudence, rather than his virtue, engaged him to leave the grandson of Theodosius in the possession of the purple; and Valentinian was permitted to enjoy the peace and luxury of Italy, while the patrician appeared in the glorious light of a hero and a patriot, who supported near twenty years the ruins of the Western empire. The Gothic historian ingenuously confesses that Aëtius was born for the salvation of the Roman republic;[5] and the following portrait, though it is drawn in the fairest colours, must be allowed to contain a much larger proportion of truth than of flattery. "His mother was a wealthy and noble Italian, and his father Gaudentius, who held a distinguished rank in the province of Scythia, gradually rose from the station of a military *domestic* to the dignity of master of the cavalry. Their son, who was enrolled almost in his infancy in the guards, was given as a hostage, first to Alaric, and afterwards to the Huns; and he successively obtained the civil and military honours of the palace, for which he was equally qualified by superior merit. The graceful figure of Aëtius was not above the middle stature; but his manly limbs were admirably formed for strength, beauty, and agility; and he excelled in the martial exercises of managing a horse, drawing a bow, and darting the javelin. He could patiently endure the want of food or of sleep; and his mind and body were alike capable of the most laborious efforts. He possessed the genuine courage that can despise not only dangers, but injuries: and it was impossible either to corrupt, or deceive, or intimidate the firm integrity of his soul."[6] The barbarians, who had seated themselves in the Western provinces, were insensibly taught to respect the faith and valour of the patrician Aëtius. He soothed their passions, consulted their prejudices, balanced their interest, and checked their ambition. A seasonable treaty which he concluded with Genseric protected Italy from the depredations of the Vandals; the independent Britons implored and acknowledged his salutary aid; the Imperial authority was restored and maintained in Gaul and Spain; and he compelled the Franks and the Suevi, whom he had vanquished in the field, to become the useful confederates of the republic.

From a principle of interest, as well as gratitude, Aëtius assiduously cultivated the alliance of the Huns. While he resided in their tents as an hostage or an exile, he had familiarly conversed with Attila himself, the nephew of his benefactor; and the two famous antagonists appear to have been connected by a personal and military friendship, which they afterwards confirmed by mutual gifts, frequent embassies, and the education of Carpilio, the son of Aëtius, in the camp of Attila. By the specious professions of gratitude and voluntary attachment, the patrician might disguise his apprehensions of the Scythian conqueror, who pressed the two empires with his innumerable armies. His demands were obeyed or eluded. When he claimed the spoils of a vanquished city, some vases of gold, which had been fraudulently embezzled, the civil and military governors of Noricum were immediately despatched to satisfy his complaints:[7] and it is evident, from their conversation with Maximin and Priscus in the royal village, that the valour and prudence of Aëtius had not saved the Western Romans from the common ignominy of tribute. Yet his dexterous policy prolonged the advantages of a salutary peace; and a numerous army of Huns and Alani, whom he had attached to his person, was employed in the defence of Gaul. Two colonies of these barbarians were judiciously fixed in the territories of Valence and Orleans;[8] and their active cavalry secured the important passages of the Rhône and of the Loire. These savage allies were not indeed less formidable to the subjects than to the enemies of Rome. Their original settlement was enforced with the licentious violence of conquest; and the province through which they marched was exposed to all the calamities of an hostile invasion.[9] Strangers to the emperor or the republic, the Alani of Gaul were devoted to the ambition of Aëtius; and though he might suspect that, in a contest with Attila himself, they would revolt to the standard of their national king, the patrician laboured to restrain, rather than to excite, their zeal and resentment against the Goths, the Burgundians, and the Franks.

The kingdom established by the Visigoths in the southern provinces of Gaul had gradually acquired strength and maturity; and the conduct of those ambitious barbarians, either in peace or war, engaged the perpetual vigilance of Aëtius. After the death of Wallia, the Gothic sceptre devolved to Theodoric, the son of the great Alaric;[10] and his prosperous reign of more than thirty years over a turbulent people may be allowed to prove that his prudence was supported by uncommon vigour, both of mind and body. Impatient of his narrow limits, Theodoric aspired to the possession of Arles, the wealthy seat of government and commerce; but the city was saved by the timely approach of Aëtius; and the Gothic king, who had raised the siege with some loss and disgrace, was persuaded, for an adequate subsidy, to divert the martial valour of his subjects in a Spanish war. Yet Theodoric still watched, and eagerly seized, the favourable moment of renewing his hostile attempts. The Goths besieged Narbonne, while the Belgic provinces were invaded by the Burgundians; and the public safety was threatened on every side by the apparent union of the enemies of Rome. On every side, the activity of Aëtius and his Scythian cavalry opposed a firm and successful resistance. Twenty thousand Burgundians were slain in battle; and the remains of the nation humbly accepted a dependent seat in the mountains of Savoy.[11] The walls of Narbonne had been shaken by the battering engines, and the inhabitants had endured the last extremities of famine, when Count Litorius, approaching in silence, and directing each horseman to carry behind him two sacks of flour, cut his way through the entrenchments of the besiegers. The siege was immediately raised; and the more decisive victory, which is ascribed to the personal conduct of Aëtius himself, was marked with the blood of eight thousand Goths. But in the absence of the patrician, who was hastily summoned to Italy by some public or private interest, Count Litorius succeeded to the command; and his presumption soon discovered that far different talents are required to lead a wing of cavalry, or to direct the operations of an important war. At the head of an army of Huns, he rashly advanced to the gates of Toulouse, full of careless contempt for an enemy whom his misfortunes had rendered prudent, and his situation made desperate. The predictions of the augurs had inspired Litorius with the profane confidence that he should enter the Gothic capital in triumph; and the trust which he reposed in his Pagan allies encouraged him to reject the fair conditions of peace which were repeatedly proposed by the bishops in the name of Theodoric. The king of the Goths exhibited in his distress the edifying contrast of Christian piety and moderation; nor did he lay aside his sackcloth and ashes till he was prepared to arm for the combat. His soldiers, animated with martial and religious enthusiasm, assaulted the camp of Litorius. The conflict was obstinate; the slaughter was mutual. The Roman general, after a total defeat, which could be imputed only to his unskilful rashness, was actually led through the streets of Toulouse, not in his own, but in an hostile triumph; and the misery which he experienced, in a long and ignominious captivity, excited the compassion of the barbarians themselves.[12] Such a loss, in a country whose spirit and finances were long since exhausted, could not easily be repaired; and the Goths, assuming, in their turn, the sentiments of ambition and revenge, would have planted their victorious standards on the banks of the Rhône, if the presence of Aëtius had not restored strength and discipline to the Romans.[13] The two armies expected the signal of a decisive action; but the generals, who were conscious of each other's force, and doubtful of their own superiority, prudently sheathed their swords in the field of battle; and their reconciliation was permanent and sincere. Theodoric, king of the Visigoths, appears to have deserved the love of his subjects, the confidence of his allies, and the esteem of mankind. His throne was surrounded by six valiant sons, who were educated with equal care in the exercises of the barbarian camp, and in those of the Gallic schools: from the study of the Roman jurisprudence they acquired the theory, at least, of law and justice; and the harmonious sense of Virgil contributed to soften the asperity of their native manners. [14] The two daughters of the Gothic king were given in marriage to the eldest sons of the kings of the Suevi and of the Vandals, who reigned in Spain and Africa; but these illustrious alliances were pregnant with guilt and discord. The queen of the Suevi bewailed the death of an husband, inhumanly massacred by her brother. The princess of the Vandals was the victim of a jealous tyrant, whom she called her father. The cruel Genseric suspected that his son's wife had conspired to poison him; the supposed crime was punished by the amputation of her nose and ears; and the unhappy daughter of Theodoric was ignominiously returned to the court of Toulouse in that deformed and mutilated condition. This horrid act, which must seem incredible to a civilised age, drew tears from every spectator; but Theodoric was urged, by the feelings of a parent and a king, to revenge such irreparable injuries. The Imperial ministers, who always cherished the discord of the barbarians, would have supplied the Goths with arms, and ships, and treasures, for the African war; and the cruelty of Genseric might have been fatal to himself, if the artful Vandal had not armed, in his cause, the formidable power of the Huns. His rich gifts and pressing solicitations inflamed the ambition of Attila; and the designs of Aëtius and Theodoric were prevented by the invasion of Gaul.[15]

The Franks, whose monarchy was still confined to the neighbourhood of the Lower Rhine, had wisely established the right of hereditary succession in the noble family of the Merovingians.[16] These princes were elevated on a buckler, the symbol of military command;[17] and the royal fashion of long hair was the ensign of their birth and dignity. Their flaxen locks, which they combed and dressed with singular care, hung down in flowing ringlets on their back and shoulders; while the rest of the nation were obliged, either by law or custom, to shave the hinder part of their head, to comb their hair over the forehead, and to content themselves with the ornament of two small whiskers.[18] The lofty stature of the Franks and their blue eyes denoted a Germanic origin; their close apparel accurately expressed the figure of their limbs; a weighty sword was suspended from a broad belt; their bodies were protected by a large shield: and these warlike barbarians were trained from their earliest youth to run, to leap, to swim; to dart the javelin or battle-axe with unerring aim; to advance without hesitation against a superior enemy; and to maintain, either in life or death, the invincible reputation of their ancestors.[19] Clodion, the first of their long-haired kings whose name and actions are mentioned in authentic history, held his residence at Dispargum,[20] a village or fortress, whose place may be assigned between Louvain and Brussels. From the report of his spies the king of the Franks was informed that the defenceless state of the second Belgic must yield, on the slightest attack, to the valour of his subjects. He boldly penetrated through the thickets and morasses of the Carbonarian forest;[21] occupied Tournay and Cambray, the only cities which existed in the fifth century; and extended his conquests as far as the river Somme, over a desolate country whose cultivation and populousness are the effects of more recent industry.[22] While Clodion lay encamped in the plains of Artois,[23] and celebrated with vain and ostentatious security the marriage perhaps of his son, the nuptial feast was interrupted by the unexpected and unwelcome presence of Aëtius, who had passed the Somme at the head of his light cavalry. The tables, which had been spread under the shelter of a hill along the banks of a pleasant stream, were rudely overturned; the Franks were oppressed before they could recover their arms or their ranks, and their unavailing valour was fatal only to themselves. The loaded waggons which had followed their march afforded a rich booty; and the virgin-bride with her female attendants submitted to the new lovers who were imposed on them by the chance of war. This advantage, which had been obtained by the skill and activity of Aëtius, might reflect some disgrace on the military prudence of Clodion; but the king of the Franks soon regained his strength and reputation, and still maintained the possession of his Gallic kingdom from the Rhine to the Somme.[24] Under his reign, and most probably from the enterprising spirit of his subjects, the three capitals, Mentz, Trèves, and Cologne, experienced the effects of hostile cruelty and avarice. The distress of Cologne was prolonged by the perpetual dominion of the same barbarians who evacuated the ruins of Trèves, and Trèves, which in the space of forty years had been four times besieged and pillaged, was disposed to lose the memory of her afflictions in the vain amusements of the circus.[25] The death of Clodion, after a reign of twenty years, exposed his kingdom to the discord and ambition of his two sons. Meroveus, the younger,[26] was persuaded to implore the protection of Rome; he was received at the Imperial court as the ally of Valentinian and the adopted son of the patrician Aëtius, and dismissed to his native country with splendid gifts and the strongest assurances of friendship and support. During his absence his elder brother had solicited with equal ardour the formidable aid of Attila; and the king of the Huns embraced an alliance which facilitated the passage of the Rhine, and justified by a specious and honourable pretence the invasion of Gaul.[27]

When Attila declared his resolution of supporting the cause of his allies the Vandals and the Franks, at the same time, and almost in the spirit of romantic chivalry, the savage monarch professed himself the lover and the champion of the princess Honoria. The sister of Valentinian was educated in the palace of Ravenna; and as her marriage might be productive of some danger to the state, she was raised, by the title of *Augusta*,[28] above the hopes of the most presumptuous subject. But the fair Honoria had no sooner attained the sixteenth year of her age than she detested the importunate greatness which must for ever exclude her from the comforts of honourable love: in the midst of vain and unsatisfactory pomp Honoria sighed, yielded to the impulse of nature, and threw herself into the arms of her chamberlain Eugenius. Her guilt and shame (such is the absurd language of imperious man) were soon betrayed by the appearances of pregnancy: but the disgrace of the royal family was published to the world by the imprudence of the empress Placidia, who dismissed her daughter, after a strict and shameful confinement, to a remote exile at Constantinople. The unhappy princess passed twelve or fourteen years in the irksome society of the sisters of Theodosius and their chosen virgins, to whose *crown* Honoria could no longer aspire, and whose monastic assiduity of prayer, fasting, and vigils she reluctantly imitated. Her impatience of long and hopeless celibacy urged her to embrace a strange and desperate resolution. The name of Attila was familiar and formidable at Constantinople, and his frequent embassies entertained a perpetual intercourse between his camp and the Imperial palace. In the pursuit of love, or rather of revenge, the daughter of Placidia sacrificed every duty and every prejudice, and offered to deliver her person into the arms of a barbarian of whose language she was ignorant, whose figure was scarcely human, and whose religion and manners she abhorred. By the ministry of a faithful eunuch she transmitted to Attila a ring, the pledge of her affection, and earnestly conjured him to claim her as a lawful spouse to whom he had been secretly betrothed. These indecent advances were received, however, with coldness and disdain; and the king of the Huns continued to multiply the number of his wives till his love was awakened by the more forcible passions of ambition and avarice. The invasion of Gaul was preceded and justified by a formal demand of the princess Honoria, with a just and equal share of the Imperial patrimony. His predecessors, the ancient Tanjous, had often addressed in the same hostile and peremptory manner the daughters of China; and the pretensions of Attila were not less offensive to the majesty of Rome. A firm but temperate refusal was communicated to his ambassadors. The right of female succession, though it might derive a specious argument from the recent examples of Placidia and Pulcheria, was strenuously denied, and the indissoluble engagements of Honoria were opposed to the claims of her Scythian lover.[29] On the discovery of her connection with the king of the Huns, the guilty princess had been sent away, as an object of horror, from Constantinople to Italy: her life was spared, but the ceremony of her marriage was performed with some obscure and nominal husband before she was immured in a perpetual prison, to bewail those crimes and misfortunes which Honoria might have escaped had she not been born the daughter of an emperor.[30]

A native of Gaul and a contemporary, the learned and eloquent Sidonius, who was afterwards bishop of Clermont, had made a promise to one of his friends that he would compose a regular history of the war of Attila. If the modesty of Sidonius had not discouraged him from the prosecution of this interesting work,[31] the historian would have related with the simplicity of truth those memorable events to which the poet, in vague and doubtful metaphors, has concisely alluded.[32] The kings and nations of Germany and Scythia, from the Volga perhaps to the Danube, obeyed the warlike summons of Attila. From the royal village in the plains of Hungary his standard moved towards the West, and after a march of seven or eight hundred miles he reached the conflux of the Rhine and the Neckar, where he was joined by the Franks who adhered to his ally, the elder of the sons of Clodion. A troop of light barbarians who roamed in quest of plunder might choose the winter for the convenience of passing the river on the ice, but the innumerable cavalry of the Huns required such plenty of forage and provisions as could be procured only in a milder season; the Hercynian forest supplied materials for a bridge of boats, and the hostile myriads were poured with resistless violence into the Belgic provinces.[33] The consternation of Gaul was universal, and the various fortunes of its cities have been adorned by tradition with martyrdoms and miracles.[34] Troyes was saved by the merits of St. Lupus; St. Servatius was removed from the world that he might not behold the ruin of Tongres; and the prayers of St. Genevieve diverted the march of Attila from the neighbourhood of Paris. But as the greatest part of the Gallic cities were alike destitute of saints and soldiers, they were besieged and stormed by the Huns, who practised, in the example of Metz,[35] their customary maxims of war. They involved in a promiscuous massacre the priests who served at the altar and the infants who, in the hour of danger, had been providently baptised by the bishop; the flourishing city was delivered to the flames, and a solitary chapel of St. Stephen marked the place where it formerly stood. From the Rhine and the Moselle, Attila advanced into the heart of Gaul, crossed the Seine at Auxerre, and after a long and laborious march fixed his camp under the walls of Orleans. He was desirous of securing his conquests by the possession of an advantageous post which commanded the passage of the Loire; and he depended on the secret invitation of Sangiban, king of the Alani, who had promised to betray the city and to revolt from the service of the empire. But this treacherous conspiracy was detected and disappointed: Orleans had been strengthened with recent fortifications, and the assaults of the Huns were vigorously repelled by the faithful valour of the soldiers or citizens who defended the place. The pastoral diligence of Anianus, a bishop of primitive sanctity and consummate prudence, exhausted every art of religious policy to support their courage till the arrival of the expected succours. After an obstinate siege the walls were shaken by the battering rams; the Huns had already occupied the suburbs, and the people who were incapable

of bearing arms lay prostrate in prayer. Anianus, who anxiously counted the days and
hours, despatched a trusty messenger to observe
from the rampart the face of the distant country. He returned twice without any intelligence
that could inspire hope or comfort; but in his
third report he mentioned a small cloud which
he had faintly descried at the extremity of the
horizon. "It is the aid of God!" exclaimed the
bishop in a tone of pious confidence; and the
whole multitude repeated after him "It is the
aid of God." The remote object, on which
every eye was fixed, became each moment
larger and more distinct; the Roman and Gothic banners were gradually perceived; and a
favourable wind, blowing aside the dust, discovered, in deep array, the impatient squadrons of Aëtius and Theodoric, who pressed forwards to the relief of Orleans.

The facility with which Attila had penetrated
into the heart of Gaul may be ascribed to his
insidious policy as well as to the terror of his
arms. His public declarations were skilfully
mitigated by his private assurances; he alternately soothed and threatened the Romans and
the Goths; and the courts of Ravenna and Toulouse, mutually suspicious of each other's intentions, beheld with supine indifference the
approach of their common enemy. Aëtius was
the sole guardian of the public safety; but his
wisest measures were embarrassed by a faction
which, since the death of Placidia, infested the
Imperial palace: the youth of Italy trembled at
the sound of the trumpet; and the barbarians,
who from fear or affection were inclined to the
cause of Attila, awaited with doubtful and venal
faith the event of the war. The patrician passed
the Alps at the head of some troops whose
strength and numbers scarcely deserved the
name of an army.[36] But on his arrival at Arles
or Lyons he was confounded by the intelligence
that the Visigoths, refusing to embrace the defence of Gaul, had determined to expect within
their own territories the formidable invader
whom they professed to despise. The senator
Avitus, who after the honourable exercise of the
Prætorian præfecture had retired to his estate
in Auvergne, was persuaded to accept the important embassy, which he executed with ability and success. He represented to Theodoric
that an ambitious conqueror who aspired to the
dominion of the earth could be resisted only by
the firm and unanimous alliance of the powers
whom he laboured to oppress. The lively eloquence of Avitus inflamed the Gothic warriors
by the description of the injuries which their

ancestors had suffered from the Huns, whose
implacable fury still pursued them from the
Danube to the foot of the Pyrenees. He strenuously urged that it was the duty of every Christian to save from sacrilegious violation the
churches of God and the relics of the saints;
that it was the interest of every barbarian who
had acquired a settlement in Gaul to defend the
fields and vineyards, which were cultivated
for his use, against the desolation of the Scythian shepherds. Theodoric yielded to the evidence of truth, adopted the measure at once the
most prudent and the most honourable, and
declared that as the faithful ally of Aëtius and
the Romans he was ready to expose his life and
kingdom for the common safety of Gaul.[37] The
Visigoths, who at that time were in the mature
vigour of their fame and power, obeyed with
alacrity the signal of war, prepared their arms
and horses, and assembled under the standard
of their aged king, who was resolved, with his
two eldest sons, Torismond and Theodoric, to
command in person his numerous and valiant
people. The example of the Goths determined
several tribes or nations that seemed to fluctuate between the Huns and the Romans. The
indefatigable diligence of the patrician gradually collected the troops of Gaul and Germany,
who had formerly acknowledged themselves the
subjects or soldiers of the republic, but who now
claimed the rewards of voluntary service and
the rank of independent allies; the Læti, the
Armoricans, the Breones, the Saxons, the Burgundians, the Sarmatians or Alani, the Ripuarians, and the Franks who followed Meroveus
as their lawful prince. Such was the various
army which, under the conduct of Aëtius and
Theodoric, advanced by rapid marches to relieve Orleans, and to give battle to the innumerable host of Attila.[38]

On their approach the king of the Huns immediately raised the siege, and sounded a
retreat to recall the foremost of his troops from
the pillage of a city which they had already
entered.[39] The valour of Attila was always
guided by his prudence; and as he foresaw the
fatal consequences of a defeat in the heart of
Gaul, he repassed the Seine, and expected the
enemy in the plains of Châlons, whose smooth
and level surface was adapted to the operations
of his Scythian cavalry. But in this tumultuary
retreat the vanguard of the Romans and their
allies continually pressed, and sometimes engaged, the troops whom Attila had posted in
the rear; the hostile columns, in the darkness of
the night and the perplexity of the roads, might

encounter each other without design; and the bloody conflict of the Franks and Gepidæ, in which fifteen thousand[40] barbarians were slain, was a prelude to a more general and decisive action. The Catalaunian fields[41] spread themselves round Châlons, and extend, according to the vague measurement of Jornandes, to the length of one hundred and fifty, and the breadth of one hundred miles, over the whole province, which is entitled to the appellation of a *champaign* country.[42] This spacious plain was distinguished, however, by some inequalities of ground; and the importance of an height which commanded the camp of Attila was understood and disputed by the two generals. The young and valiant Torismond first occupied the summit; the Goths rushed with irresistible weight on the Huns, who laboured to ascend from the opposite side: and the possession of this advantageous post inspired both the troops and their leaders with a fair assurance of victory. The anxiety of Attila prompted him to consult his priests and haruspices. It was reported that, after scrutinising the entrails of victims and scraping their bones, they revealed, in mysterious language, his own defeat, with the death of his principal adversary; and that the barbarian, by accepting the equivalent, expressed his involuntary esteem for the superior merit of Aëtius. But the unusual despondency which seemed to prevail among the Huns engaged Attila to use the expedient, so familiar to the generals of antiquity, of animating his troops by a military oration; and his language was that of a king who had often fought and conquered at their head.[43] He pressed them to consider their past glory, their actual danger, and their future hopes. The same fortune which opened the deserts and morasses of Scythia to their unarmed valour, which had laid so many warlike nations prostrate at their feet, had reserved the *joys* of this memorable field for the consummation of their victories. The cautious steps of their enemies, their strict alliance, and their advantageous posts, he artfully represented as the effects, not of prudence, but of fear. The Visigoths alone were the strength and nerves of the opposite army, and the Huns might securely trample on the degenerate Romans, whose close and compact order betrayed their apprehensions, and who were equally incapable of supporting the dangers or the fatigues of a day of battle. The doctrine of predestination, so favourable to martial virtue, was carefully inculcated by the king of the Huns; who assured his subjects that the warriors, protected by Heaven,

were safe and invulnerable amidst the darts of the enemy; but that the unerring Fates would strike their victims in the bosom of inglorious peace. "I myself," continued Attila, "will throw the first javelin, and the wretch who refuses to imitate the example of his sovereign is devoted to inevitable death." The spirit of the barbarians was rekindled by the presence, the voice, and the example of their intrepid leader; and Attila, yielding to their impatience, immediately formed his order of battle. At the head of his brave and faithful Huns, he occupied in person the centre of the line. The nations subject to his empire, the Rugians, the Heruli, the Thuringians, the Franks, the Burgundians, were extended, on either hand, over the ample space of the Catalaunian fields; the right wing was commanded by Ardaric, king of the Gepidæ; and the three valiant brothers who reigned over the Ostrogoths were posted on the left to oppose the kindred tribes of the Visigoths. The disposition of the allies was regulated by a different principle. Sangiban, the faithless king of the Alani, was placed in the centre: where his motions might be strictly watched, and his treachery might be instantly punished. Aëtius assumed the command of the left, and Theodoric of the right wing; while Torismond still continued to occupy the heights which appear to have stretched on the flank, and perhaps the rear, of the Scythian army. The nations from the Volga to the Atlantic were assembled on the plain of Châlons; but many of these nations had been divided by faction, or conquest, or emigration; and the appearance of similar arms and ensigns, which threatened each other, presented the image of a civil war.

The discipline and tactics of the Greeks and Romans form an interesting part of their national manners. The attentive study of the military operations of Xenophon, or Cæsar, or Frederic, when they are described by the same genius which conceived and executed them, may tend to improve (if such improvement can be wished) the art of destroying the human species. But the battle of Châlons can only excite our curiosity by the magnitude of the object; since it was decided by the blind impetuosity of barbarians, and has been related by partial writers, whose civil and ecclesiastical profession secluded them from the knowledge of military affairs. Cassiodorus, however, had familiarly conversed with many Gothic warriors who served in that memorable engagement; "a conflict," as they informed him, "fierce, various, obstinate, and bloody; such as could not be

paralleled either in the present or in past ages."
The number of the slain amounted to one hundred and sixty-two thousand, or, according to
another account, three hundred thousand persons;[44] and these incredible exaggerations suppose a real and effective loss, sufficient to justify
the historian's remark that whole generations
may be swept away by the madness of kings in
the space of a single hour. After the mutual and
repeated discharge of missile weapons, in which
the archers of Scythia might signalise their superior dexterity, the cavalry and infantry of the
two armies were furiously mingled in closer
combat. The Huns, who fought under the eyes
of their king, pierced through the feeble and
doubtful centre of the allies, separated their
wings from each other, and wheeling, with a
rapid effort, to the left, directed their whole
force against the Visigoths. As Theodoric rode
along the ranks to animate his troops, he received a mortal stroke from the javelin of An-
dages, a noble Ostrogoth, and immediately fell
from his horse. The wounded king was oppressed in the general disorder and trampled under
the feet of his own cavalry; and this important
death served to explain the ambiguous prophecy
of the haruspices. Attila already exulted in the
confidence of victory, when the valiant Torismond descended from the hills, and verified the
remainder of the prediction. The Visigoths, who
had been thrown into confusion by the flight,
or defection, of the Alani, gradually restored
their order of battle; and the Huns were undoubtedly vanquished, since Attila was compelled to retreat. He had exposed his person
with the rashness of a private soldier; but the
intrepid troops of the centre had pushed forwards beyond the rest of the line; their attack
was faintly supported; their flanks were unguarded; and the conquerors of Scythia and
Germany were saved by the approach of the
night from a total defeat. They retired within
the circle of waggons that fortified their camp;
and the dismounted squadrons prepared themselves for a defence to which neither their arms
nor their temper were adapted. The event was
doubtful: but Attila had secured a last and honourable resource. The saddles and rich furniture of the cavalry were collected by his order
into a funeral pile; and the magnanimous barbarian had resolved, if his entrenchments should
be forced, to rush headlong into the flames, and
to deprive his enemies of the glory which they
might have acquired by the death or captivity
of Attila.[45]

But his enemies had passed the night in equal
disorder and anxiety. The inconsiderate courage of Torismond was tempted to urge the pursuit, till he unexpectedly found himself, with a
few followers, in the midst of the Scythian waggons. In the confusion of a nocturnal combat he
was thrown from his horse; and the Gothic
prince must have perished like his father, if his
youthful strength and the intrepid zeal of his
companions had not rescued him from this dangerous situation. In the same manner, but on
the left of the line, Aëtius himself, separated
from his allies, ignorant of their victory, and
anxious for their fate, encountered and escaped
the hostile troops that were scattered over the
plains of Châlons; and at length reached the
camp of the Goths, which he could only fortify
with a slight rampart of shields till the dawn of
day. The Imperial general was soon satisfied
of the defeat of Attila, who still remained inactive within his entrenchments; and when he
contemplated the bloody scene, he observed,
with secret satisfaction, that the loss had principally fallen on the barbarians. The body of
Theodoric, pierced with honourable wounds,
was discovered under a heap of the slain: his
subjects bewailed the death of their king and
father; but their tears were mingled with songs
and acclamations, and his funeral rites were
performed in the face of a vanquished enemy.
The Goths, clashing their arms, elevated on a
buckler his eldest son Torismond, to whom they
justly ascribed the glory of their success; and
the new king accepted the obligation of revenge
as a sacred portion of his paternal inheritance.
Yet the Goths themselves were astonished by
the fierce and undaunted aspect of their formidable antagonist; and their historian has
compared Attila to a lion encompassed in his
den and threatening his hunters with redoubled
fury. The kings and nations who might have
deserted his standard in the hour of distress were
made sensible that the displeasure of their
monarch was the most imminent and inevitable
danger. All his instruments of martial music incessantly sounded a loud and animating strain
of defiance; and the foremost troops, who advanced to the assault, were checked or destroyed
by showers of arrows from every side of the entrenchments. It was determined in a general
council of war to besiege the king of the Huns in
his camp, to intercept his provisions, and to reduce him to the alternative of a disgraceful
treaty or an unequal combat. But the impatience of the barbarians soon disdained these
cautious and dilatory measures: and the mature
policy of Aëtius was apprehensive that, after the

extirpation of the Huns, the republic would be oppressed by the pride and power of the Gothic nation. The patrician exerted the superior ascendant of authority and reason to calm the passions which the son of Theodoric considered as a duty; represented, with seeming affection and real truth, the dangers of absence and delay; and persuaded Torismond to disappoint, by his speedy return, the ambitious designs of his brothers, who might occupy the throne and treasures of Toulouse.[46] After the departure of the Goths, and the separation of the allied army, Attila was surprised at the vast silence that reigned over the plains of Châlons: the suspicion of some hostile stratagem detained him several days within the circle of his waggons, and his retreat beyond the Rhine confessed the last victory which was achieved in the name of the Western empire. Meroveus and his Franks, observing a prudent distance, and magnifying the opinion of their strength by the numerous fires which they kindled every night, continued to follow the rear of the Huns till they reached the confines of Thuringia. The Thuringians served in the army of Attila: they traversed, both in their march and in their return, the territories of the Franks; and it was perhaps in this war that they exercised the cruelties which, about fourscore years afterwards, were revenged by the son of Clovis. They massacred their hostages, as well as their captives: two hundred young maidens were tortured with exquisite and unrelenting rage; their bodies were torn asunder by wild horses, or their bones were crushed under the weight of rolling waggons; and their unburied limbs were abandoned on the public roads as a prey to dogs and vultures. Such were those savage ancestors whose imaginary virtues have sometimes excited the praise and envy of civilised ages![47]

Neither the spirit, nor the forces, nor the reputation of Attila were impaired by the failure of the Gallic expedition. In the ensuing spring he repeated his demand of the princess Honoria and her patrimonial treasures. The demand was again rejected or eluded; and the indignant lover immediately took the field, passed the Alps, invaded Italy, and besieged Aquileia with an innumerable host of barbarians. Those barbarians were unskilled in the methods of conducting a regular siege, which, even among the ancients, required some knowledge, or at least some practice, of the mechanic arts. But the labour of many thousand provincials and captives, whose lives were sacrificed without pity, might execute the most painful and dangerous

work. The skill of the Roman artists might be corrupted to the destruction of their country. The walls of Aquileia were assaulted by a formidable train of battering rams, movable turrets, and engines that threw stones, darts, and fire;[48] and the monarch of the Huns employed the forcible impulse of hope, fear, emulation, and interest, to subvert the only barrier which delayed the conquest of Italy. Aquileia was at that period one of the richest, the most populous, and the strongest of the maritime cities of the Hadriatic coast. The Gothic auxiliaries, who appear to have served under their native princes, Alaric and Antala, communicated their intrepid spirit; and the citizens still remembered the glorious and successful resistance which their ancestors had opposed to a fierce, inexorable barbarian, who disgraced the majesty of the Roman purple. Three months were consumed without effect in the siege of Aquileia; till the want of provisions and the clamours of his army compelled Attila to relinquish the enterprise, and reluctantly to issue his orders that the troops should strike their tents the next morning, and begin their retreat. But as he rode round the walls, pensive, angry, and disappointed, he observed a stork preparing to leave her nest in one of the towers, and to fly with her infant family towards the country. He seized, with the ready penetration of a statesman, this trifling incident which chance had offered to superstition; and exclaimed, in a loud and cheerful tone, that such a domestic bird, so constantly attached to human society, would never have abandoned her ancient seats unless those towers had been devoted to impending ruin and solitude.[49] The favourable omen inspired an assurance of victory; the siege was renewed, and prosecuted with fresh vigour; a large breach was made in the part of the wall from whence the stork had taken her flight; the Huns mounted to the assault with irresistible fury; and the succeeding generation could scarcely discover the ruins of Aquileia.[50] After this dreadful chastisement, Attila pursued his march; and as he passed, the cities of Altinum, Concordia, and Padua were reduced into heaps of stones and ashes. The inland towns, Vicenza, Verona, and Bergamo, were exposed to the rapacious cruelty of the Huns. Milan and Pavia submitted, without resistance, to the loss of their wealth; and applauded the unusual clemency which preserved from the flames the public as well as private buildings, and spared the lives of the captive multitude. The popular traditions of Comum, Turin, or Modena may justly be suspected; yet they concur with more authentic evidence to prove that Attila spread his ravages over the rich plains of modern Lombardy, which are divided by the Po, and bounded by the Alps and Apennine.[51] When he took possession of the royal palace of Milan, he was surprised and offended at the sight of a picture which represented the Cæsars seated on their throne, and the princes of Scythia prostrate at their feet. The revenge which Attila inflicted on this monument of Roman vanity was harmless and ingenious. He commanded a painter to reverse the figures and the attitudes; and the emperors were delineated on the same canvas approaching in a suppliant posture to empty their bags of tributary gold before the throne of the Scythian monarch.[52] The spectators must have confessed the truth and propriety of the alteration; and were perhaps tempted to apply, on this singular occasion, the well-known fable of the dispute between the lion and the man.[53]

It is a saying worthy of the ferocious pride of Attila, that the grass never grew on the spot where his horse had trod. Yet the savage destroyer undesignedly laid the foundations of a republic which revived, in the feudal state of Europe, the art and spirit of a commercial industry. The celebrated name of Venice, or Venetia,[54] was formerly diffused over a large and fertile province of Italy, from the confines of Pannonia to the river Addua, and from the Po to the Rhætian and the Julian Alps. Before the irruption of the barbarians, fifty Venetian cities flourished in peace and prosperity: Aquileia was placed in the most conspicuous station: but the ancient dignity of Padua was supported by agriculture and manufactures; and the property of five hundred citizens, who were entitled to the equestrian rank, must have amounted, at the strictest computation, to one million seven hundred thousand pounds. Many families of Aquileia, Padua, and the adjacent towns, who fled from the sword of the Huns, found a safe, though obscure, refuge in the neighbouring islands.[55] At the extremity of the Gulf, where the Hadriatic feebly imitates the tides of the ocean, near an hundred small islands are separated by shallow water from the continent, and protected from the waves by several long slips of land, which admit the entrance of vessels through some secret and narrow channels.[56] Till the middle of the fifth century these remote and sequestered spots remained without cultivation, with few inhabitants, and almost without a name. But the manners of the Venetian fugitives, their arts and their government, were gradually formed by their new situation; and one of the epistles of Cassiodorus,[57] which describes their condition about seventy years afterwards, may be considered as the primitive monument of the republic. The minister of Theodoric compares them, in his quaint declamatory style, to waterfowl, who had fixed their nests on the bosom of the waves; and though he allows that the Venetian provinces had formerly contained many noble families, he insinuates that they were now reduced by misfortune to the same level of humble poverty. Fish was the common, and almost the universal, food of every rank: their only treasure consisted in the plenty of salt which they extracted from the sea: and the exchange of that commodity, so essential to human life, was substituted in the neighbouring markets to the currency of gold and silver. A people whose habitations might be doubtfully assigned to the earth or water soon became alike familiar with the two elements; and the demands of avarice succeeded to those of necessity. The islanders, who, from Grado to Chiozza, were intimately connected with each other, penetrated into the heart of Italy, by the secure, though laborious, navigation of the rivers and inland canals. Their vessels, which were continually increasing in size and number, visited all the harbours of the Gulf; and the marriage which Venice annually celebrates with the Hadriatic was contracted in her early infancy. The epistle of Cassiodorus, the Prætorian præfect, is addressed to the maritime tribunes; and he exhorts them, in a mild tone of authority, to animate the zeal of their countrymen for the public service, which required their assistance to transport the magazines of wine and oil from the province of Istria to the royal city of Ravenna. The ambiguous office of these magistrates is explained by the tradition, that, in the twelve principal islands, twelve tribunes, or judges, were created by an annual and popular election. The existence of the Venetian republic under the Gothic kingdom of Italy is attested by the same authentic record which annihilates their lofty claim of original and perpetual independence.[58]

The Italians, who had long since renounced the exercise of arms, were surprised, after forty years' peace, by the approach of a formidable barbarian, whom they abhorred as the enemy of their religion as well as of their republic. Amidst the general consternation, Aëtius alone was incapable of fear; but it was impossible that he should achieve alone and unassisted any military exploits worthy of his former renown.

The barbarians who had defended Gaul refused to march to the relief of Italy; and the succours promised by the Eastern emperor were distant and doubtful. Since Aëtius, at the head of his domestic troops, still maintained the field, and harassed or retarded the march of Attila, he never showed himself more truly great than at the time when his conduct was blamed by an ignorant and ungrateful people.[59] If the mind of Valentinian had been susceptible of any generous sentiments, he would have chosen such a general for his example and his guide. But the timid grandson of Theodosius, instead of sharing the dangers, escaped from the sound, of war; and his hasty retreat from Ravenna to Rome, from an impregnable fortress to an open capital, betrayed his secret intention of abandoning Italy as soon as the danger should approach his Imperial person. This shameful abdication was suspended, however, by the spirit of doubt and delay which commonly adheres to pusillanimous counsels, and sometimes corrects their pernicious tendency. The Western emperor, with the senate and people of Rome, embraced the more salutary resolution of deprecating, by a solemn and suppliant embassy, the wrath of Attila. This important commission was accepted by Avienus, who, from his birth and riches, his consular dignity, the numerous train of his clients, and his personal abilities, held the first rank in the Roman senate. The specious and artful character of Avienus[60] was admirably qualified to conduct a negotiation either of public or private interest: his colleague Trigetius had exercised the Prætorian præfecture of Italy; and Leo, bishop of Rome, consented to expose his life for the safety of his flock. The genius of Leo[61] was exercised and displayed in the public misfortunes; and he has deserved the appellation of *Great* by the successful zeal with which he laboured to establish his opinions and his authority, under the venerable names of orthodox faith and ecclesiastical discipline. The Roman ambassadors were introduced to the tent of Attila, as he lay encamped at the place where the slow-winding Mincius is lost in the foaming waves of the lake Benacus,[62] and trampled, with his Scythian cavalry, the farms of Catullus and Virgil.[63] The barbarian monarch listened with favourable, and even respectful, attention; and the deliverance of Italy was purchased by the immense ransom or dowry of the princess Honoria. The state of his army might facilitate the treaty and hasten his retreat. Their martial spirit was relaxed by the wealth and indolence of a warm climate. The shepherds of the North, whose ordinary food consisted of milk and raw flesh, indulged themselves too freely in the use of bread, of wine, and of meat prepared and seasoned by the arts of cookery; and the progress of disease revenged in some measure the injuries of the Italians.[64] When Attila declared his resolution of carrying his victorious arms to the gates of Rome, he was admonished by his friends, as well as by his enemies, that Alaric had not long survived the conquest of the eternal city. His mind, superior to real danger, was assaulted by imaginary terrors; nor could he escape the influence of superstition, which had so often been subservient to his designs.[65] The pressing eloquence of Leo, his majestic aspect and sacerdotal robes, excited the veneration of Attila for the spiritual father of the Christians. The apparition of the two apostles of St. Peter and St. Paul, who menaced the barbarian with instant death if he rejected the prayer of their successor, is one of the noblest legends of ecclesiastical tradition. The safety of Rome might deserve the interposition of celestial beings; and some indulgence is due to a fable which has been represented by the pencil of Raphael and the chisel of Algardi.[66]

Before the king of the Huns evacuated Italy, he threatened to return more dreadful, and more implacable, if his bride, the princess Honoria, were not delivered to his ambassadors within the term stipulated by the treaty. Yet, in the meanwhile, Attila relieved his tender anxiety, by adding a beautiful maid, whose name was Ildico, to the list of his innumerable wives.[67] Their marriage was celebrated with barbaric pomp and festivity, at his wooden palace beyond the Danube; and the monarch, oppressed with wine and sleep, retired at a late hour from the banquet to the nuptial bed. His attendants continued to respect his pleasures or his repose the greatest part of the ensuing day, till the unusual silence alarmed their fears and suspicions; and, after attempting to awaken Attila by loud and repeated cries, they at length broke into the royal apartment. They found the trembling bride sitting by the bedside, hiding her face with her veil, and lamenting her own danger, as well as the death of the king, who had expired during the night.[68] An artery had suddenly burst: and as Attila lay in a supine posture, he was suffocated by a torrent of blood, which, instead of finding a passage through the nostrils, regurgitated into the lungs and stomach. His body was solemnly exposed in the midst of the plain, under a silken pavilion; and the chosen squadrons of the Huns, wheeling round in measured evolutions, chanted a funeral song to the memory of a hero, glorious in his life, invincible in his death, the father of his people, the scourge of his enemies, and the terror of the world. According to their national custom, the barbarians cut off a part of their hair, gashed their faces with unseemly wounds, and bewailed their valiant leader as he deserved, not with the tears of women, but with the blood of warriors. The remains of Attila were enclosed within three coffins of gold, of silver, and of iron, and privately buried in the night: the spoils of nations were thrown into his grave; the captives who had opened the ground were inhumanly massacred; and the same Huns, who had indulged such excessive grief, feasted, with dissolute and intemperate mirth, about the recent sepulchre of their king. It was reported at Constantinople that, on the fortunate night in which he expired, Marcian beheld in a dream the bow of Attila broken asunder: and the report may be allowed to prove how seldom the image of that formidable barbarian was absent from the mind of a Roman emperor.[69]

The revolution which subverted the empire of the Huns established the fame of Attila, whose genius alone had sustained the huge and disjointed fabric. After his death the boldest chieftains aspired to the rank of kings; the most powerful kings refused to acknowledge a superior; and the numerous sons whom so many various mothers bore to the deceased monarch divided and disputed like a private inheritance the sovereign command of the nations of Germany and Scythia. The bold Ardaric felt and represented the disgrace of this servile partition; and his subjects, the warlike Gepidæ, with the Ostrogoths, under the conduct of three valiant brothers, encouraged their allies to vindicate the rights of freedom and royalty. In a bloody and decisive conflict on the banks of the river Netad in Pannonia, the lance of the Gepidæ, the sword of the Goths, the arrows of the Huns, the Suevic infantry, the light arms of the Heruli, and the heavy weapons of the Alani, encountered or supported each other; and the victory of Ardaric was accompanied with the slaughter of thirty thousand of his enemies. Ellac, the eldest son of Attila, lost his life and crown in the memorable battle of Netad; his early valour had raised him to the throne of the Acatzires, a Scythian people, whom he subdued; and his father, who loved the superior merit, would have envied the death, of Ellac.[70] His brother Dengisich, with an army of Huns still formidable in their flight and ruin, maintained his ground above

fifteen years on the banks of the Danube. The palace of Attila, with the old country of Dacia, from the Carpathian hills to the Euxine, became the seat of a new power which was erected by Ardaric, king of the Gepidæ. The Pannonian conquests, from Vienna to Sirmium, were occupied by the Ostrogoths; and the settlements of the tribes who had so bravely asserted their native freedom were irregularly distributed according to the measure of their respective strength. Surrounded and oppressed by the multitude of his father's slaves, the kingdom of Dengisich was confined to the circle of his waggons; his desperate courage urged him to invade the Eastern empire: he fell in battle, and his head, ignominiously exposed in the Hippodrome, exhibited a grateful spectacle to the people of Constantinople. Attila had fondly or superstitiously believed that Irnac, the youngest of his sons, was destined to perpetuate the glories of his race. The character of that prince, who attempted to moderate the rashness of his brother Dengisich, was more suitable to the declining condition of the Huns; and Irnac, with his subject hordes, retired into the heart of the Lesser Scythia. They were soon overwhelmed by a torrent of new barbarians, who followed the same road which their own ancestors had formerly discovered. The *Geougen*, or Avares, whose residence is assigned by the Greek writers to the shores of the ocean, impelled the adjacent tribes; till at length the Igours of the North, issuing from the cold Siberian regions which produce the most valuable furs, spread themselves over the desert as far as the Borysthenes and the Caspian gates, and finally extinguished the empire of the Huns.[71]

Such an event might contribute to the safety of the Eastern empire under the reign of a prince who conciliated the friendship, without forfeiting the esteem, of the barbarians. But the emperor of the West, the feeble and dissolute Valentinian, who had reached his thirty-fifth year without attaining the age of reason or courage, abused this apparent security to undermine the foundations of his own throne by the murder of the patrician Aëtius. From the instinct of a base and jealous mind, he hated the man who was universally celebrated as the terror of the barbarians and the support of the republic; and his new favourite, the eunuch Heraclius, awakened the emperor from the supine lethargy which might be disguised during the life of Placidia[72] by the excuse of filial piety. The fame of Aëtius, his wealth and dignity, the numerous and martial train of barbarian followers, his powerful dependents who filled the civil offices of the state, and the hopes of his son Gaudentius, who was already contracted to Eudoxia, the emperor's daughter, had raised him above the rank of a subject. The ambitious designs, of which he was secretly accused, excited the fears as well as the resentment of Valentinian. Aëtius himself, supported by the consciousness of his merit, his services, and perhaps his innocence, seems to have maintained a haughty and indiscreet behaviour. The patrician offended his sovereign by an hostile declaration; he aggravated the offence by compelling him to ratify with a solemn oath a treaty of reconciliation and alliance; he proclaimed his suspicions, he neglected his safety; and from a vain confidence that the enemy whom he despised was incapable even of a manly crime, he rashly ventured his person in the palace of Rome. Whilst he urged, perhaps with intemperate vehemence, the marriage of his son, Valentinian, drawing his sword—the first sword he had ever drawn—plunged it in the breast of a general who had saved his empire: his courtiers and eunuchs ambitiously struggled to imitate their master; and Aëtius, pierced with an hundred wounds, fell dead in the royal presence. Boethius, the Prætorian præfect, was killed at the same moment; and before the event could be divulged, the principal friends of the patrician were summoned to the palace and separately murdered. The horrid deed, palliated by the specious names of justice and necessity, was immediately communicated by the emperor to his soldiers, his subjects, and his allies. The nations who were strangers or enemies to Aëtius generously deplored the unworthy fate of a hero; the barbarians who had been attached to his service dissembled their grief and resentment; and the public contempt which had been so long entertained for Valentinian was at once converted into deep and universal abhorrence. Such sentiments seldom pervade the walls of a palace; yet the emperor was confounded by the honest reply of a Roman whose approbation he had not disdained to solicit. "I am ignorant, sir, of your motives or provocations; I only know that you have acted like a man who cuts off his right hand with his left."[73]

The luxury of Rome seems to have attracted the long and frequent visits of Valentinian, who was consequently more despised at Rome than in any other part of his dominions. A republican spirit was insensibly revived in the senate, as their authority, and even their supplies, became necessary for the support of his feeble government. The stately demeanour of an hereditary monarch offended their pride, and the pleasures of Valentinian were injurious to the peace and honour of noble families. The birth of the empress Eudoxia was equal to his own, and her charms and tender affection deserved those testimonies of love which her inconstant husband dissipated in vague and unlawful amours. Petronius Maximus, a wealthy senator of the Anician family, who had been twice consul, was possessed of a chaste and beautiful wife; her obstinate resistance served only to irritate the desires of Valentinian, and he resolved to accomplish them either by stratagem or force. Deep gaming was one of the vices of the court; the emperor, who, by chance or contrivance, had gained from Maximus a considerable sum, uncourteously exacted his ring as a security for the debt, and sent it by a trusty messenger to his wife, with an order in her husband's name that she should immediately attend the empress Eudoxia. The unsuspecting wife of Maximus was conveyed in her litter to the Imperial palace; the emissaries of her impatient lover conducted her to a remote and silent bed-chamber; and Valentinian violated, without remorse, the laws of hospitality. Her tears when she returned home, her deep affliction, and the bitter reproaches against a husband whom she considered as the accomplice of his own shame, excited Maximus to a just revenge; the desire of revenge was stimulated by ambition; and he might reasonably aspire, by the free suffrage of the Roman senate, to the throne of a detested and despicable rival. Valentinian, who supposed that every human breast was devoid like his own of friendship and gratitude, had imprudently admitted among his guards several domestics and followers of Aëtius. Two of these, of barbarian race, were persuaded to execute a sacred and honourable duty by punishing with death the assassin of their patron; and their intrepid courage did not long expect a favourable moment. Whilst Valentinian amused himself in the field of Mars with the spectacle of some military sports, they suddenly rushed upon him with drawn weapons, despatched the guilty Heraclius, and stabbed the emperor to the heart, without the least opposition from his numerous train, who seemed to rejoice in the tyrant's death. Such was the fate of Valentinian the Third,[74] the last Roman emperor of the family of Theodosius. He faithfully imitated the hereditary weakness of his cousin and his two uncles, without inheriting the gentleness, the purity, the innocence, which alleviate in their characters the want of spirit and ability. Valentinian was less excusable, since he had passions without virtues: even his religion was questionable; and though he never deviated into the paths of heresy, he scandalised the pious Christians by his attachment to the profane arts of magic and divination.

As early as the time of Cicero and Varro it was the opinion of the Roman augurs that the *twelve vultures* which Romulus had seen, represented the *twelve centuries* assigned for the fatal period of his city.[75] This prophecy, disregarded perhaps in the season of health and prosperity, inspired the people with gloomy apprehensions when the twelfth century, clouded with disgrace and misfortune, was almost elapsed;[76] and even posterity must acknowledge with some surprise that the arbitrary interpretation of an accidental or fabulous circumstance has been seriously verified in the downfall of the Western empire. But its fall was announced by a clearer omen than the flight of vultures: the Roman government appeared every day less formidable to its enemies, more odious and oppressive to its subjects.[77] The taxes were multiplied with the public distress; economy was neglected in proportion as it became necessary; and the injustice of the rich shifted the unequal burden from themselves to the people, whom they defrauded of the *indulgences* that might sometimes have alleviated their misery. The severe inquisition, which confiscated their goods and tortured their persons, compelled the subjects of Valentinian to prefer the more simple tyranny of the barbarians, to fly to the woods and mountains, or to embrace the vile and abject condition of mercenary servants. They abjured and abhorred the name of Roman citizens, which had formerly excited the ambition of mankind. The Armorican provinces of Gaul and the greatest part of Spain were thrown into a state of disorderly independence by the confederations of the Bagaudæ, and the Imperial ministers pursued with proscriptive laws and ineffectual arms the rebels whom they had made.[78] If all the barbarian conquerors had been annihilated in the same hour, their total destruction would not have restored the empire of the West: and if Rome still survived, she survived the loss of freedom, of virtue, and of honour.

CHAPTER XXXVI

Sack of Rome by Genseric, King of the Vandals. His Naval Depredations. Succession of the last Emperors of the West, Maximus, Avitus, Majorian, Severus, Anthemius, Olybrius, Glycerius, Nepos, Augustulus. Total Extinction of the Western Empire. Reign of Odoacer, the first Barbarian King of Italy.

THE loss or desolation of the provinces from the Ocean to the Alps impaired the glory and greatness of Rome: her internal prosperity was irretrievably destroyed by the separation of Africa. The rapacious Vandals confiscated the patrimonial estates of the senators, and intercepted the regular subsidies which relieved the poverty and encouraged the idleness of the plebeians. The distress of the Romans was soon aggravated by an unexpected attack; and the province, so long cultivated for their use by industrious and obedient subjects, was armed against them by an ambitious barbarian. The Vandals and Alani, who followed the successful standard of Genseric, had acquired a rich and fertile territory, which stretched along the coast above ninety days' journey from Tangier to Tripoli; but their narrow limits were pressed and confined, on either side, by the sandy desert and the Mediterranean. The discovery and conquest of the Black nations, that might dwell beneath the torrid zone, could not tempt the rational ambition of Genseric; but he cast his eyes towards the sea; he resolved to create a naval power, and his bold resolution was executed with steady and active perseverance. The woods of Mount Atlas afforded an inexhaustible nursery of timber; his new subjects were skilled in the arts of navigation and shipbuilding; he animated his daring Vandals to embrace a mode of warfare which would render every maritime country accessible to their arms; the Moors and Africans were allured by the hopes of plunder; and, after an interval of six centuries, the fleets that issued from the port of Carthage again claimed the empire of the Mediterranean. The success of the Vandals, the conquest of Sicily, the sack of Palermo, and the frequent descents on the coast of Lucania, awakened and alarmed the mother of Valentinian and the sister of Theodosius. Alliances were formed; and armaments, expensive and ineffectual, were prepared for the destruction of the common enemy, who reserved his courage to encounter those dangers which his policy could not prevent or elude. The designs of the Roman government were repeatedly baffled by his artful delays, ambiguous promises, and apparent concessions; and the interposition of his formidable confederate, the king of the Huns, recalled the emperors from the conquest of Africa to the care of their domestic safety. The revolutions of the palace, which left the Western empire without a defender and without a lawful prince, dispelled the apprehensions and stimulated the avarice of Genseric. He immediately equipped a numerous fleet of Vandals and Moors, and cast anchor at the mouth of the Tiber, about three months after the death of Valentinian and the elevation of Maximus to the Imperial throne.

The private life of the senator Petronius Maximus[1] was often alleged as a rare example of human felicity. His birth was noble and illustrious, since he descended from the Anician family; his dignity was supported by an adequate patrimony in land and money; and these advantages of fortune were accompanied with liberal arts and decent manners, which adorn or imitate the inestimable gifts of genius and virtue. The luxury of his palace and table was hospitable and elegant. Whenever Maximus appeared in public, he was surrounded by a train of grateful and obsequious clients;[2] and it is possible that among these clients he might deserve and possess some real friend. His merit was rewarded by the favour of the prince and senate; he thrice exercised the office of Prætorian præfect of Italy; he was twice invested with the consulship, and he obtained the rank of patrician. These civil honours were not incompatible with the enjoyment of leisure and tranquillity; his hours, according to the demands of pleasure or reason, were accurately distributed by a water-clock; and this avarice of time may be allowed to prove the sense which Maximus entertained of his own happiness. The injury which he received from the emperor Valentinian appears to excuse the most bloody revenge. Yet a philosopher might have reflected, that, if the resistance of his wife had been sincere, her chastity was still inviolate, and that it could never be restored if she had consented to the will of the adulterer. A patriot would have hesitated before he plunged himself and his country into those inevitable calamities which

must follow the extinction of the royal house of Theodosius.

The imprudent Maximus disregarded these salutary considerations: he gratified his resentment and ambition; he saw the bleeding corpse of Valentinian at his feet; and he heard himself saluted Emperor by the unanimous voice of the senate and people. But the day of his inauguration was the last day of his happiness. He was imprisoned (such is the lively expression of Sidonius) in the palace; and after passing a sleepless night, he sighed that he had attained the summit of his wishes, and aspired only to descend from the dangerous elevation. Oppressed by the weight of the diadem, he communicated his anxious thoughts to his friend and quæstor Fulgentius; and when he looked back with unavailing regret on the secure pleasures of his former life, the emperor exclaimed, "O fortunate Damocles, thy reign began and ended with the same dinner;" a well-known allusion, which Fulgentius afterwards repeated as an instructive lesson for princes and subjects.[3]

The reign of Maximus continued about three months. His hours, of which he had lost the command, were disturbed by remorse, or guilt, or terror; and his throne was shaken by the seditions of the soldiers, the people, and the confederate barbarians. The marriage of his son Palladius with the eldest daughter of the late emperor might tend to establish the hereditary succession of his family; but the violence which he offered to the empress Eudoxia could proceed only from the blind impulse of lust or revenge. His own wife, the cause of these tragic events, had been seasonably removed by death; and the widow of Valentinian was compelled to violate her decent mourning, perhaps her real grief, and to submit to the embraces of a presumptuous usurper, whom she suspected as the assassin of her deceased husband. These suspicions were soon justified by the indiscreet confession of Maximus himself; and he wantonly provoked the hatred of his reluctant bride, who was still conscious that she descended from a line of emperors. From the East, however, Eudoxia could not hope to obtain any effectual assistance: her father and her aunt Pulcheria were dead; her mother languished at Jerusalem in disgrace and exile; and the sceptre of Constantinople was in the hands of a stranger. She directed her eyes towards Carthage; secretly implored the aid of the king of the Vandals; and persuaded Genseric to improve the fair opportunity of disguising his rapacious designs by the specious names of honour, justice, and compassion.[4] Whatever abilities Maximus might have shown in a subordinate station, he was found incapable of administering an empire: and though he might easily have been informed of the naval preparations which were made on the opposite shores of Africa, he expected with supine indifference the approach of the enemy, without adopting any measures of defence, of negotiation, or of a timely retreat. When the Vandals disembarked at the mouth of the Tiber, the emperor was suddenly roused from his lethargy by the clamours of a trembling and exasperated multitude. The only hope which presented itself to his astonished mind was that of a precipitate flight, and he exhorted the senators to imitate the example of their prince. But no sooner did Maximus appear in the streets than he was assaulted by a shower of stones: a Roman or a Burgundian soldier claimed the honour of the first wound; his mangled body was ignominiously cast into the Tiber; the Roman people rejoiced in the punishment which they had inflicted on the author of the public calamities; and the domestics of Eudoxia signalised their zeal in the service of their mistress.[5]

On the third day after the tumult, Genseric boldly advanced from the port of Ostia to the gates of the defenceless city. Instead of a sally of the Roman youth, there issued from the gates an unarmed and venerable procession of the bishop at the head of his clergy.[6] The fearless spirit of Leo, his authority and eloquence, *again* mitigated the fierceness of a barbarian conqueror: the king of the Vandals promised to spare the unresisting multitude, to protect the buildings from fire, and to exempt the captives from torture; and although such orders were neither seriously given, nor strictly obeyed, the mediation of Leo was glorious to himself, and in some degree beneficial to his country. But Rome and its inhabitants were delivered to the licentiousness of the Vandals and Moors, whose blind passions revenged the injuries of Carthage. The pillage lasted fourteen days and nights; and all that yet remained of public or private wealth, of sacred or profane treasure, was diligently transported to the vessels of Genseric. Among the spoils, the splendid relics of two temples, or rather of two religions, exhibited a memorable example of the vicissitudes of human and divine things. Since the abolition of Paganism, the Capitol had been violated and abandoned; yet the statues of the gods and heroes were still respected, and the curious roof of gilt bronze was reserved for the rapacious hands of Genseric.[7] The holy instruments of the Jewish worship,[8] the gold table, and the gold candlestick with seven branches, originally framed according to the particular instructions of God himself, and which were placed in the sanctuary of his temple, had been ostentatiously displayed to the Roman people in the triumph of Titus. They were afterwards deposited in the temple of Peace; and at the end of four hundred years, the spoils of Jerusalem were transferred from Rome to Carthage, by a barbarian who derived his origin from the shores of the Baltic. These ancient monuments might attract the notice of curiosity as well as of avarice. But the Christian churches, enriched and adorned by the prevailing superstition of the times, afforded more plentiful materials for sacrilege; and the pious liberality of pope Leo, who melted six silver vases, the gift of Constantine, each of an hundred pounds weight, is an evidence of the damage which he attempted to repair. In the forty-five years that had elapsed since the Gothic invasion, the pomp and luxury of Rome were in some measure restored; and it was difficult either to escape, or to satisfy, the avarice of a conqueror who possessed leisure to collect, and ships to transport, the wealth of the capital. The Imperial ornaments of the palace, the magnificent furniture and wardrobe, the sideboards of massy plate, were accumulated with disorderly rapine: the gold and silver amounted to several thousand talents; yet even the brass and copper were laboriously removed. Eudoxia herself, who advanced to meet her friend and deliverer, soon bewailed the imprudence of her own conduct. She was rudely stripped of her jewels; and the unfortunate empress, with her two daughters, the only surviving remains of the great Theodosius, was compelled, as a captive, to follow the haughty Vandal, who immediately hoisted sail, and returned with a prosperous navigation to the port of Carthage.[9] Many thousand Romans of both sexes, chosen for some useful or agreeable qualifications, reluctantly embarked on board the fleet of Genseric; and their distress was aggravated by the unfeeling barbarians, who, in the division of the booty, separated the wives from their husbands, and the children from their parents. The charity of Deogratias, bishop of Carthage,[10] was their only consolation and support. He generously sold the gold and silver plate of the church to purchase the freedom of some, to alleviate the slavery of others, and to assist the wants and infirmities of a captive multitude, whose health was impaired by the hardships which they had suffered in the passage from Italy to Africa. By his order, two spacious churches were converted into hospitals: the sick were distributed in convenient beds, and liberally supplied with food and medicines; and the aged prelate repeated his visits both in the day and night, with an assiduity that surpassed his strength, and a tender sympathy which enhanced the value of his services. Compare this scene with the field of Cannæ; and judge between Hannibal and the successor of St. Cyprian.[11]

The deaths of Aëtius and Valentinian had relaxed the ties which held the barbarians of Gaul in peace and subordination. The sea-coast was infested by the Saxons; the Alemanni and the Franks advanced from the Rhine to the Seine; and the ambition of the Goths seemed to meditate more extensive and permanent conquests. The emperor Maximus relieved himself, by a judicious choice, from the weight of these distant cares; he silenced the solicitations of his friends, listened to the voice of fame, and promoted a stranger to the general command of the forces in Gaul. Avitus,[12] the stranger whose merit was so nobly rewarded, descended from a wealthy and honourable family in the diocese of Auvergne. The convulsions of the times urged him to embrace, with the same ardour, the civil and military professions; and the indefatigable youth blended the studies of literature and jurisprudence with the exercise of arms and hunting. Thirty years of his life were laudably spent in the public service; he alternately displayed his talents in war and negotiation; and the soldier of Aëtius, after executing the most important embassies, was raised to the station of Prætorian præfect of Gaul. Either the merit of Avitus excited envy, or his moderation was desirous of repose, since he calmly retired to an estate which he possessed in the neighbourhood of Clermont. A copious stream, issuing from the mountain, and falling headlong in many a loud and foaming cascade, discharged its waters into a lake about two miles in length, and the villa was pleasantly seated on the margin of the lake. The baths, the porticoes, the summer and winter apartments, were adapted to the purposes of luxury and use; and the adjacent country afforded the various prospects of woods, pastures, and meadows.[13] In this retreat, where Avitus amused his leisure with books, rural sports, the practice of husbandry, and the society of his friends,[14] he received the Imperial diploma, which constituted him master-general of the cavalry and infantry of Gaul. He assumed the military command; the barbarians suspended

their fury; and whatever means he might employ, whatever concessions he might be forced to make, the people enjoyed the benefits of actual tranquillity. But the fate of Gaul depended on the Visigoths; and the Roman general, less attentive to his dignity than to the public interest, did not disdain to visit Toulouse in the character of an ambassador. He was received with courteous hospitality by Theodoric, the king of the Goths; but while Avitus laid the foundations of a solid alliance with that powerful nation, he was astonished by the intelligence that the emperor Maximus was slain, and that Rome had been pillaged by the Vandals. A vacant throne, which he might ascend without guilt or danger, tempted his ambition:[15] and the Visigoths were easily persuaded to support his claim by their irresistible suffrage. They loved the person of Avitus; they respected his virtues; and they were not insensible of the advantage, as well as honour, of giving an emperor to the West. The season was now approaching in which the annual assembly of the seven provinces was held at Arles; their deliberations might perhaps be influenced by the presence of Theodoric and his martial brothers; but their choice would naturally incline to the most illustrious of their countrymen. Avitus, after a decent resistance, accepted the Imperial diadem from the representatives of Gaul; and his election was ratified by the acclamations of the barbarians and provincials. The formal consent of Marcian, emperor of the East, was solicited and obtained; but the senate, Rome, and Italy, though humbled by their recent calamities, submitted with a secret murmur to the presumption of the Gallic usurper.

Theodoric, to whom Avitis was indebted for the purple, had acquired the Gothic sceptre by the murder of his elder brother Torismond; and he justified this atrocious deed by the design which his predecessor had formed of violating his alliance with the empire.[16] Such a crime might not be incompatible with the virtues of a barbarian; but the manners of Theodoric were gentle and humane; and posterity may contemplate without terror the original picture of a Gothic king, whom Sidonius had intimately observed in the hours of peace and of social intercourse. In an epistle, dated from the court of Toulouse, the orator satisfies the curiosity of one of his friends, in the following description:[17] "By the majesty of his appearance, Theodoric would command the respect of those who are ignorant of his merit; and although he is born a prince, his merit would dignify a private station. He is of a middle stature, his body appears rather plump than fat, and in his well-proportioned limbs agility is united with muscular strength.[18] If you examine his countenance, you will distinguish a high forehead, large shaggy eyebrows, an aquiline nose, thin lips, a regular set of white teeth, and a fair complexion, that blushes more frequently from modesty than from anger. The ordinary distribution of his time, as far as it is exposed to the public view, may be concisely represented. Before daybreak he repairs, with a small train, to his domestic chapel, where the service is performed by the Arian clergy; but those who presume to interpret his secret sentiments consider this assiduous devotion as the effect of habit and policy. The rest of the morning is employed in the administration of his kingdom. His chair is surrounded by some military officers of decent aspect and behaviour: the noisy crowd of his barbarian guards occupies the hall of audience, but they are not permitted to stand within the veils or curtains that conceal the council-chamber from vulgar eyes. The ambassadors of the nations are successively introduced: Theodoric listens with attention, answers them with discreet brevity, and either announces or delays, according to the nature of their business, his final resolution. About eight (the second hour) he rises from his throne, and visits either his treasury or his stables. If he chooses to hunt, or at least to exercise himself on horseback, his bow is carried by a favourite youth; but when the game is marked, he bends it with his own hand, and seldom misses the object of his aim: as a king, he disdains to bear arms in such ignoble warfare; but as a soldier he would blush to accept any military service which he could perform himself. On common days his dinner is not different from the repast of a private citizen; but every Saturday many honourable guests are invited to the royal table, which, on these occasions, is served with the elegance of Greece, the plenty of Gaul, and the order and diligence of Italy.[19] The gold or silver plate is less remarkable for its weight than for the brightness and curious workmanship: the taste is gratified without the help of foreign and costly luxury; the size and number of the cups of wine are regulated with a strict regard to the laws of temperance; and the respectful silence that prevails is interrupted only by grave and instructive conversation. After dinner Theodoric sometimes indulges himself in a short slumber; and as soon as he wakes he calls for the dice and tables, encourages his friends to forget the royal majesty, and is delighted when

they freely express the passions which are excited by the incidents of play. At this game, which he loves as the image of war, he alternately displays his eagerness, his skill, his patience, and his cheeerful temper. If he loses, he laughs: he is modest and silent if he wins. Yet, notwithstanding this seeming indifference, his courtiers choose to solicit any favour in the moments of victory; and I myself, in my applications to the king, have derived some benefit from my losses.[20] About the ninth hour (three o'clock) the tide of business again returns, and flows incessantly till after sunset, when the signal of the royal supper dismisses the weary crowd of suppliants and pleaders. At the supper, a more familiar repast, buffoons and pantomimes are sometimes introduced, to divert, not to offend, the company by their ridiculous wit: but female singers, and the soft effeminate modes of music, are severely banished, and such martial tunes as animate the soul to deeds of valour are alone grateful to the ear of Theodoric. He retires from table; and the nocturnal guards are immediately posted at the entrance of the treasury, the palace, and the private apartments."

When the king of the Visigoths encouraged Avitus to assume the purple, he offered his person and his forces as a faithful soldier of the republic.[21] The exploits of Theodoric soon convinced the world that he had not degenerated from the warlike virtues of his ancestors. After the establishment of the Goths in Aquitain, and the passage of the Vandals into Africa, the Suevi, who had fixed their kingdom in Gallicia, aspired to the conquest of Spain, and threatened to extinguish the feeble remains of the Roman dominion. The provincials of Carthagena and Tarragona, afflicted by an hostile invasion, represented their injuries and their apprehensions. Count Fronto was despatched, in the name of the emperor Avitus, with advantageous offers of peace and alliance; and Theodoric interposed his weighty mediation to declare that, unless his brother-in-law, the king of the Suevi, immediately retired, he should be obliged to arm in the cause of justice and of Rome. "Tell him," replied the haughty Rechiarius, "that I despise his friendship and his arms; but that I shall soon try whether he will dare to expect my arrival under the walls of Toulouse." Such a challenge urged Theodoric to prevent the bold designs of his enemy: he passed the Pyrenees at the head of the Visigoths; the Franks and Burgundians served under his standard; and though he professed himself the dutiful servant of Avitus, he privately stipulated, for himself and his successors, the absolute possession of his Spanish conquests. The two armies, or rather the two nations, encountered each other on the banks of the river Urbicus, about twelve miles from Astorga; and the decisive victory of the Goths appeared for a while to have extirpated the name and kingdom of the Suevi. From the field of battle Theodoric advanced to Braga, their metropolis, which still retained the splendid vestiges of its ancient commerce and dignity.[22] His entrance was not polluted with blood; and the Goths respected the chastity of their female captives, more especially of the consecrated virgins: but the greatest part of the clergy and people were made slaves, and even the churches and altars were confounded in the universal pillage. The unfortunate king of the Suevi had escaped to one of the ports of the ocean; but the obstinacy of the winds opposed his flight: he was delivered to his implacable rival; and Rechiarius, who neither desired nor expected mercy, received, with manly constancy, the death which he would probably have inflicted. After this bloody sacrifice to policy or resentment, Theodoric carried his victorious arms as far as Merida, the principal town of Lusitania, without meeting any resistance, except from the miraculous powers of St. Eulalia; but he was stopped in the full career of success, and recalled from Spain before he could provide for the security of his conquests. In his retreat towards the Pyrenees he revenged his disappointment on the country through which he passed; and, in the sack of Polentia and Astorga he showed himself a faithless ally, as well as a cruel enemy. Whilst the king of the Visigoths fought and vanquished in the name of Avitus, the reign of Avitus had expired; and both the honour and interest of Theodoric were deeply wounded by the disgrace of a friend whom he had seated on the throne of the Western empire.[23]

The pressing solicitations of the senate and people persuaded the emperor Avitus to fix his residence at Rome, and to accept the consulship for the ensuing year. On the first day of January, his son-in-law, Sidonius Apollinaris, celebrated his praises in a panegyric of six hundred verses; but this composition, though it was rewarded with a brass statue,[24] seems to contain a very moderate proportion either of genius or of truth. The poet, if we may degrade that sacred name, exaggerates the merit of a sovereign and a father; and his prophecy of a long and glorious reign was soon contradicted by the

event. Avitus, at a time when the Imperial dignity was reduced to a pre-eminence of toil and danger, indulged himself in the pleasures of Italian luxury: age had not extinguished his amorous inclinations; and he is accused of insulting, with indiscreet and ungenerous raillery, the husbands whose wives he had seduced or violated.[25] But the Romans were not inclined either to excuse his faults or to acknowledge his virtues. The several parts of the empire became every day more alienated from each other; and the stranger of Gaul was the object of popular hatred and contempt. The senate asserted their legitimate claim in the election of an emperor; and their authority, which had been originally derived from the old constitution, was again fortified by the actual weakness of a declining monarchy. Yet even such a monarchy might have resisted the votes of an unarmed senate, if their discontent had not been supported, or perhaps inflamed, by Count Ricimer, one of the principal commanders of the barbarian troops who formed the military defence of Italy. The daughter of Wallia, king of the Visigoths, was the mother of Ricimer; but he was descended, on the father's side, from the nation of the Suevi:[26] his pride or patriotism might be exasperated by the misfortunes of his countrymen; and he obeyed with reluctance an emperor in whose elevation he had not been consulted. His faithful and important services against the common enemy rendered him still more formidable;[27] and, after destroying on the coast of Corsica a fleet of Vandals, which consisted of sixty galleys, Ricimer returned in triumph with the appellation of the Deliverer of Italy. He chose that moment to signify to Avitus that his reign was at an end; and the feeble emperor, at a distance from his Gothic allies, was compelled, after a short and unavailing struggle, to abdicate the purple. By the clemency, however, or the contempt of Ricimer,[28] he was permitted to descend from the throne to the more desirable station of bishop of Placentia: but the resentment of the senate was still unsatisfied; and their inflexible severity pronounced the sentence of his death. He fled towards the Alps, with the humble hope, not of arming the Visigoths in his cause, but of securing his person and treasures in the sanctuary of Julian, one of the tutelar saints of Auvergne.[29] Disease, or the hand of the executioner, arrested him on the road; yet his remains were decently transported to Brivas, or Brioude, in his native province, and he reposed at the feet of his holy patron.[30] Avitus left only one daughter, the wife of Sidonius Apollinaris, who inherited the patrimony of his father-in-law; lamenting, at the same time, the disappointment of his public and private expectations. His resentment prompted him to join, or at least to countenance, the measures of a rebellious faction in Gaul; and the poet had contracted some guilt, which it was incumbent on him to expiate by a new tribute of flattery to the succeeding emperor.[31]

The successor of Avitus presents the welcome discovery of a great and heroic character, such as sometimes arise, in a degenerate age, to vindicate the honour of the human species. The emperor Majorian has deserved the praises of his contemporaries and of posterity; and these praises may be strongly expressed in the words of a judicious and disinterested historian: "That he was gentle to his subjects; that he was terrible to his enemies; and that he excelled in *every* virtue *all* his predecessors who had reigned over the Romans."[32] Such a testimony may justify at least the panegyric of Sidonius; and we may acquiesce in the assurance that, although the obsequious orator would have flattered with equal zeal the most worthless of princes, the extraordinary merit of his object confined him, on this occasion, within the bounds of truth.[33] Majorian derived his name from his maternal grandfather, who, in the reign of the great Theodosius, had commanded the troops of the Illyrian frontier. He gave his daughter in marriage to the father of Majorian, a respectable officer, who administered the revenues of Gaul with skill and integrity; and generously preferred the friendship of Aëtius to the tempting offers of an insidious court. His son, the future emperor, who was educated in the profession of arms, displayed, from his early youth, intrepid courage, premature wisdom, and unbounded liberality in a scanty fortune. He followed the standard of Aëtius, contributed to his success, shared, and sometimes eclipsed, his glory, and at last excited the jealousy of the patrician, or rather of his wife, who forced him to retire from the service.[34] Majorian, after the death of Aëtius, was recalled and promoted: and his intimate connection with Count Ricimer was the immediate step by which he ascended the throne of the Western empire. During the vacancy that succeeded the abdication of Avitus, the ambitious barbarian, whose birth excluded him from the Imperial dignity, governed Italy, with the title of Patrician; resigned to his friend the conspicuous station of master-general of the cavalry and infantry, and, after an interval of some months, consented to the unanimous wish of the Romans, whose favour Majorian had solicited by a recent victory over the Alemanni.[35] He was invested with the purple at Ravenna: and the epistle which he addressed to the senate will best describe his situation and his sentiments. "Your election, Conscript Fathers! and the ordinance of the most valiant army, have made me your emperor.[36] May the propitious Deity direct and prosper the counsels and events of my administration to your advantage and to the public welfare! For my own part I did not aspire, I have submitted, to reign; nor should I have discharged the obligations of a citizen if I had refused, with base and selfish ingratitude, to support the weight of those labours which were imposed by the republic. Assist, therefore, the prince whom you have made; partake the duties which you have enjoined; and may our common endeavours promote the happiness of an empire which I have accepted from your hands. Be assured that, in our times, justice shall resume her ancient vigour, and that virtue shall become not only innocent but meritorious. Let none, except the authors themselves, be apprehensive of *delations*,[37] which, as a subject, I have always condemned, and, as a prince, will severely punish. Our own vigilance, and that of our father, the patrician Ricimer, shall regulate all military affairs and provide for the safety of the Roman world, which we have saved from foreign and domestic enemies.[38] You now understand the maxims of my government: you may confide in the faithful love and sincere assurances of a prince who has formerly been the companion of your life and dangers, who still glories in the name of senator, and who is anxious that you should never repent of the judgment which you have pronounced in his favour." The emperor, who, amidst the ruins of the Roman world, revived the ancient language of law and liberty, which Trajan would not have disclaimed, must have derived those generous sentiments from his own heart, since they were not suggested to his imitation by the customs of his age or the example of his predecessors.[39]

The private and public actions of Majorian are very imperfectly known: but his laws, remarkable for an original cast of thought and expression, faithfully represent the character of a sovereign who loved his people, who sympathised in their distress, who had studied the causes of the decline of the empire, and who was capable of applying (as far as such reformation was practicable) judicious and effectual remedies to the public disorders.[40] His regulations concerning the finances manifestly tended to remove, or at least to mitigate, the most intolerable grievances. I. From the first hour of his reign he was solicitous (I translate his own words) to relieve the *weary* fortunes of the provincials, oppressed by the accumulated weight of indictions and superindictions.[41] With this view, he granted an universal amnesty, a final and absolute discharge of all arrears of tribute, of all debts which, under any pretence, the fiscal officers might demand from the people. This wise dereliction of obsolete, vexatious, and unprofitable claims, improved and purified the sources of the public revenue; and the subject, who could now look back without despair, might labour with hope and gratitude for himself and for his country. II. In the assessment and collection of taxes Majorian restored the ordinary jurisdiction of the provincial magistrates, and suppressed the extraordinary commissions which had been introduced in the name of the emperor himself or of the Prætorian præfects. The favourite servants who obtained such irregular powers were insolent in their behaviour and arbitrary in their demands: they affected to despise the subordinate tribunals, and they were discontented if their fees and profits did not twice exceed the sum which they condescended to pay into the treasury. One instance of their extortion would appear incredible were it not authenticated by the legislator himself. They exacted the whole payment in gold: but they refused the current coin of the empire, and would accept only such ancient pieces as were stamped with the names of Faustina or the Antonines. The subject who was unprovided with these curious medals had recourse to the expedient of compounding with their rapacious demands; or, if he succeeded in the research, his imposition was doubled according to the weight and value of the money of former times.[42] III. "The municipal corporations (says the emperor), the lesser senates (so antiquity has justly styled them), deserve to be considered as the heart of the cities and the sinews of the republic. And yet so low are they now reduced, by the injustice of magistrates and the venality of collectors, that many of their members, renouncing their dignity and their country, have taken refuge in distant and obscure exile." He urges, and even compels, their return to their respective cities; but he removes the grievance which had forced them to desert the exercise of their municipal functions. They are directed, under the authority of the provincial magistrates, to resume their office of levying the tribute; but, instead of being made re-

sponsible for the whole sum assessed on their district, they are only required to produce a regular account of the payments which they have actually received, and of the defaulters who are still indebted to the public. IV. But Majorian was not ignorant that these corporate bodies were too much inclined to retaliate the injustice and oppression which they had suffered, and he therefore revives the useful office of the *defenders of cities*. He exhorts the people to elect, in a full and free assembly, some man of discretion and integrity who would dare to assert their privileges, to represent their grievances, to protect the poor from the tyranny of the rich, and to inform the emperor of the abuses that were committed under the sanction of his name and authority.

The spectator who casts a mournful view over the ruins of ancient Rome is tempted to accuse the memory of the Goths and Vandals for the mischief which they had neither leisure, nor power, nor perhaps inclination, to perpetrate. The tempest of war might strike some lofty turrets to the ground; but the destruction which undermined the foundations of those massy fabrics was prosecuted, slowly and silently, during a period of ten centuries; and the motives of interest, that afterwards operated without shame or control, were severely checked by the taste and spirit of the emperor Majorian. The decay of the city had gradually impaired the value of the public works. The circus and theatres might still excite, but they seldom gratified, the desires of the people: and the temples which had escaped the zeal of the Christians were no longer inhabited either by gods or men; the diminished crowds of the Romans were lost in the immense space of their baths and porticoes; and the stately libraries and halls of justice became useless to an indolent generation whose repose was seldom disturbed either by study or business. The monuments of consular or Imperial greatness were no longer revered as the immortal glory of the capital; they were only esteemed as an inexhaustible mine of materials, cheaper, and more convenient, than the distant quarry. Specious petitions were continually addressed to the easy magistrates of Rome which stated the want of stones or bricks for some necessary service: the fairest forms of architecture were rudely defaced for the sake of some paltry or pretended repairs; and the degenerate Romans, who converted the spoil to their own emolument, demolished, with sacrilegious hands, the labours of their ancestors. Majorian, who had often sighed over the desolation of the city, applied a severe remedy to the growing evil.[43] He reserved to the prince and senate the sole cognisance of the extreme cases which might justify the destruction of an ancient edifice; imposed a fine of fifty pounds of gold (two thousand pounds sterling) on every magistrate who should presume to grant such illegal and scandalous licence; and threatened to chastise the criminal obedience of their subordinate officers by a severe whipping and the amputation of both their hands. In the last instance the legislator might seem to forget the proportion of guilt and punishment; but his zeal arose from a generous principle, and Majorian was anxious to protect the monuments of those ages in which he would have desired and deserved to live. The emperor conceived that it was his interest to increase the number of his subjects; that it was his duty to guard the purity of the marriage-bed: but the means which he employed to accomplish these salutary purposes are of an ambiguous, and perhaps exceptionable, kind. The pious maids who consecrated their virginity to Christ were restrained from taking the veil till they had reached their fortieth year. Widows under that age were compelled to form a second alliance within the term of five years, by the forfeiture of half their wealth to their nearest relations or to the state. Unequal marriages were condemned or annulled. The punishment of confiscation and exile was deemed so inadequate to the guilt of adultery, that, if the criminal returned to Italy, he might, by the express declaration of Majorian, be slain with impunity.[44]

While the emperor Majorian assiduously laboured to restore the happiness and virtue of the Romans, he encountered the arms of Genseric, from his character and situation their most formidable enemy. A fleet of Vandals and Moors landed at the mouth of the Liris or Garigliano; but the Imperial troops surprised and attacked the disorderly barbarians, who were encumbered with the spoils of Campania; they were chased with slaughter to their ships, and their leader, the king's brother-in-law, was found in the number of the slain.[45] Such vigilance might announce the character of the new reign, but the strictest vigilance and the most numerous forces were insufficient to protect the long-extended coast of Italy from the depredations of a naval war. The public opinion had imposed a nobler and more arduous task on the genius of Majorian. Rome expected from him alone the restitution of Africa, and the design which he formed of attacking the Vandals in

their new settlements was the result of bold and judicious policy. If the intrepid emperor could have infused his own spirit into the youth of Italy; if he could have revived in the field of Mars the manly exercises in which he had always surpassed his equals; he might have marched against Genseric at the head of a *Roman* army. Such a reformation of national manners might be embraced by the rising generation; but it is the misfortune of those princes who laboriously sustain a declining monarchy, that, to obtain some immediate advantage, or to avert some impending danger, they are forced to countenance, and even to multiply, the most pernicious abuses. Majorian, like the weakest of his predecessors, was reduced to the disgraceful expedient of substituting barbarian auxiliaries in the place of his unwarlike subjects: and his superior abilities could only be displayed in the vigour and dexterity with which he wielded a dangerous instrument, so apt to recoil on the hand that used it. Besides the confederates who were already engaged in the service of the empire, the fame of his liberality and valour attracted the nations of the Danube, the Borysthenes, and perhaps of the Tanais. Many thousands of the bravest subjects of Attila, the Gepidæ, the Ostrogoths, the Rugians, the Burgundians, the Suevi, the Alani, assembled in the plains of Liguria, and their formidable strength was balanced by their mutual animosities.[46] They passed the Alps in a severe winter. The emperor led the way on foot and in complete armour, sounding with his long staff the depth of the ice or snow, and encouraging the Scythians, who complained of the extreme cold, by the cheerful assurance that they should be satisfied with the heat of Africa. The citizens of Lyons had presumed to shut their gates: they soon implored, and experienced, the clemency of Majorian. He vanquished Theodoric in the field, and admitted to his friendship and alliance a king whom he had found not unworthy of his arms. The beneficial though precarious reunion of the greatest part of Gaul and Spain was the effect of persuasion as well as of force;[47] and the independent Bagaudæ, who had escaped or resisted the oppression of former reigns, were disposed to confide in the virtues of Majorian. His camp was filled with barbarian allies; his throne was supported by the zeal of an affectionate people; but the emperor had foreseen that it was impossible without a maritime power to achieve the conquest of Africa. In the first Punic war the republic had exerted such incredible diligence that, within sixty days after the first stroke of the axe had been given in the forest, a fleet of one hundred and sixty galleys proudly rode at anchor in the sea.[48] Under circumstances much less favourable, Majorian equalled the spirit and perseverance of the ancient Romans. The woods of the Apennine were felled; the arsenals and manufactures of Ravenna and Misenum were restored; Italy and Gaul vied with each other in liberal contributions to the public service; and the Imperial navy of three hundred large galleys, with an adequate proportion of transports and smaller vessels, was collected in the secure and capacious harbour of Carthagena in Spain.[49] The intrepid countenance of Majorian animated his troops with a confidence of victory; and if we might credit the historian Procopius, his courage sometimes hurried him beyond the bounds of prudence. Anxious to explore with his own eyes the state of the Vandals, he ventured, after disguising the colour of his hair, to visit Carthage in the character of his own ambassador: and Genseric was afterwards mortified by the discovery that he had entertained and dismissed the emperor of the Romans. Such an anecdote may be rejected as an improbable fiction, but it is a fiction which would not have been imagined unless in the life of a hero.[50]

Without the help of a personal interview, Genseric was sufficiently acquainted with the genius and designs of his adversary. He practised his customary arts of fraud and delay, but he practised them without success. His applications for peace became each hour more submissive, and perhaps more sincere; but the inflexible Majorian had adopted the ancient maxim that Rome could not be safe as long as Carthage existed in a hostile state. The king of the Vandals distrusted the valour of his native subjects, who were enervated by the luxury of the South;[51] he suspected the fidelity of the vanquished people, who abhorred him as an Arian tyrant; and the desperate measure which he executed of reducing Mauritania into a desert[52] could not defeat the operations of the Roman emperor, who was at liberty to land his troops on any part of the African coast. But Genseric was saved from impending and inevitable ruin by the treachery of some powerful subjects, envious or apprehensive of their master's success. Guided by their secret intelligence, he surprised the unguarded fleet in the bay of Carthagena: many of the ships were sunk, or taken, or burnt; and the preparations of three years were destroyed in a single day.[53] After this event the behaviour of the two antagonists showed them superior

to their fortune. The Vandal, instead of being elated by this accidental victory, immediately renewed his solicitations for peace. The emperor of the West, who was capable of forming great designs and of supporting heavy disappointments, consented to a treaty, or rather to a suspension of arms, in the full assurance that before he could restore his navy he should be supplied with provocations to justify a second war. Majorian returned to Italy to prosecute his labours for the public happiness; and as he was conscious of his own integrity, he might long remain ignorant of the dark conspiracy which threatened his throne and his life. The recent misfortune of Carthagena sullied the glory which had dazzled the eyes of the multitude: almost every description of civil and military officers were exasperated against the Reformer, since they all derived some advantage from the abuses which he endeavoured to suppress; and the patrician Ricimer impelled the inconstant passions of the barbarians against a prince whom he esteemed and hated. The virtues of Majorian could not protect him from the impetuous sedition which broke out in the camp near Tortona at the foot of the Alps. He was compelled to abdicate the Imperial purple; five days after his abdication it was reported that he died of a dysentery,[54] and the humble tomb which covered his remains was consecrated by the respect and gratitude of succeeding generations.[55] The private character of Majorian inspired love and respect. Malicious calumny and satire excited his indignation, or if he himself were the object, his contempt; but he protected the freedom of wit, and in the hours which the emperor gave to the familiar society of his friends he could indulge his taste for pleasantry without degrading the majesty of his rank.[56]

It was not perhaps without some regret that Ricimer sacrificed his friend to the interest of his ambition: but he resolved in a second choice to avoid the imprudent preference of superior virtue and merit. At his command the obsequious senate of Rome bestowed the Imperial title on Libius Severus, who ascended the throne of the West without emerging from the obscurity of a private condition. History has scarcely deigned to notice his birth, his elevation, his character, or his death. Severus expired as soon as his life became inconvenient to his patron;[57] and it would be useless to discriminate his nominal reign in the vacant interval of six years between the death of Majorian and the elevation of Anthemius. During that period the government was in the hands of Ricimer alone; and although the modest barbarian disclaimed the name of king, he accumulated treasures, formed a separate army, negotiated private alliances, and ruled Italy with the same independent and despotic authority which was afterwards exercised by Odoacer and Theodoric. But his dominions were bounded by the Alps; and two Roman generals, Marcellinus and Ægidius, maintained their allegiance to the republic, by rejecting with disdain the phantom which he styled an emperor. Marcellinus still adhered to the old religion; and the devout Pagans, who secretly disobeyed the laws of the church and state, applauded his profound skill in the science of divination. But he possessed the more valuable qualifications of learning, virtue, and courage;[58] the study of the Latin literature had improved his taste, and his military talents had recommended him to the esteem and confidence of the great Aëtius, in whose ruin he was involved. By a timely flight Marcellinus escaped the rage of Valentinian, and boldly asserted his liberty amidst the convulsions of the Western empire. His voluntary or reluctant submission to the authority of Majorian was rewarded by the government of Sicily and the command of an army stationed in that island to oppose or to attack the Vandals; but his barbarian mercenaries, after the emperor's death, were tempted to revolt by the artful liberality of Ricimer. At the head of a band of faithful followers the intrepid Marcellinus occupied the province of Dalmatia, assumed the title of patrician of the West, secured the love of his subjects by a mild and equitable reign, built a fleet which claimed the dominion of the Hadriatic, and alternately alarmed the coasts of Italy and of Africa.[59] Ægidius, the master-general of Gaul, who equalled, or at least who imitated, the heroes of ancient Rome,[60] proclaimed his immortal resentment against the assassins of his beloved master. A brave and numerous army was attached to his standard: and though he was prevented by the arts of Ricimer and the arms of the Visigoths from marching to the gates of Rome, he maintained his independent sovereignty beyond the Alps and rendered the name of Ægidius respectable both in peace and war. The Franks, who had punished with exile the youthful follies of Childeric, elected the Roman general for their king; his vanity rather than his ambition was gratified by that singular honour; and when the nation at the end of four years repented of the injury which they had offered to the Merovingian family, he patiently acquiesced in the restoration of the lawful prince. The authority of Ægidius ended only with his life, and the suspicions of poison and secret violence, which derived some countenance from the character of Ricimer, were eagerly entertained by the passionate credulity of the Gauls.[61]

The kingdom of Italy, a name to which the Western empire was gradually reduced, was afflicted under the reign of Ricimer, by the incessant depredations of the Vandal pirates.[62] In the spring of each year they equipped a formidable navy in the port of Carthage, and Genseric himself, though in a very advanced age, still commanded in person the most important expeditions. His designs were concealed with impenetrable secrecy till the moment that he hoisted sail. When he was asked by his pilot what course he should steer, "Leave the determination to the winds (replied the barbarian, with pious arrogance): *they* will transport us to the guilty coast whose inhabitants have provoked the divine justice"; but if Genseric himself deigned to issue more precise orders, he judged the most wealthy to be the most criminal. The Vandals repeatedly visited the coasts of Spain, Liguria, Tuscany, Campania, Lucania, Bruttium, Apulia, Calabria, Venetia, Dalmatia, Epirus, Greece, and Sicily: they were tempted to subdue the island of Sardinia, so advantageously placed in the centre of the Mediterranean; and their arms spread desolation or terror from the Columns of Hercules to the mouth of the Nile. As they were more ambitious of spoil than of glory, they seldom attacked any fortified cities, or engaged any regular troops in the open field. But the celerity of their motions enabled them almost at the same time to threaten and to attack the most distant objects which attracted their desires; and as they always embarked a sufficient number of horses, they had no sooner landed than they swept the dismayed country with a body of light cavalry. Yet, notwithstanding the example of their king, the native Vandals and Alani insensibly declined this toilsome and perilous warfare; the hardy generation of the first conquerors was almost extinguished, and their sons, who were born in Africa, enjoyed the delicious baths and gardens which had been acquired by the valour of their fathers. Their place was readily supplied by a various multitude of Moors and Romans, of captives and outlaws; and those desperate wretches, who had already violated the laws of their country, were the most eager to promote the atrocious acts which disgraced the victories of Genseric. In the treatment of his unhappy prisoners he sometimes consulted his avarice, and sometimes indulged his cruelty; and the massacre of five hundred noble citizens of Zante or Zacynthus, whose mangled bodies he cast into the Ionian Sea, was imputed by the public indignation to his latest posterity.

Such crimes could not be excused by any provocations, but the war which the king of the Vandals prosecuted against the Roman empire was justified by a specious and reasonable motive. The widow of Valentinian, Eudoxia, whom he had led captive from Rome to Carthage, was the sole heiress of the Theodosian house; her eldest daughter, Eudocia, became the reluctant wife of Hunneric, his eldest son; and the stern father, asserting a legal claim which could not easily be refuted or satisfied, demanded a just proportion of the Imperial patrimony. An adequate, or at least a valuable, compensation was offered by the Eastern emperor to purchase a necessary peace. Eudoxia and her younger daughter Placidia were honourably restored, and the fury of the Vandals was confined to the limits of the Western empire. The Italians, destitute of a naval force, which alone was capable of protecting their coasts, implored the aid of the more fortunate nations of the East, who had formerly acknowledged in peace and war the supremacy of Rome. But the perpetual division of the two empires had alienated their interest and their inclinations; the faith of a recent treaty was alleged; and the Western Romans, instead of arms and ships, could only obtain the assistance of a cold and ineffectual mediation. The haughty Ricimer, who had long struggled with the difficulties of his situation, was at length reduced to address the throne of Constantinople in the humble language of a subject; and Italy submitted, as the price and security of the alliance, to accept a master from the choice of the emperor of the East.[63] It is not the purpose of the present chapter, or even of the present volume, to continue the distinct series of the Byzantine history; but a concise view of the reign and character of the emperor Leo may explain the last efforts that were attempted to save the falling empire of the West.[64]

Since the death of the younger Theodosius, the domestic repose of Constantinople had never been interrupted by war or faction. Pulcheria had bestowed her hand, and the sceptre of the East, on the modest virtue of Marcian: he gratefully reverenced her august rank and virgin chastity; and, after her death, he gave his people the example of the religious worship that was due to the memory of the Imperial saint.[65] Attentive to the prosperity of his own dominions, Marcian seemed to behold with indifference the misfortunes of Rome; and the obstinate refusal of a brave and active prince to draw his sword against the Vandals was ascribed to a secret promise which had formerly been exacted from him when he was a captive in the power of Genseric.[66] The death of Marcian, after a reign of seven years, would have exposed the East to the danger of a popular election, if the superior weight of a single family had not been able to incline the balance in favour of the candidate whose interest they supported. The patrician Aspar might have placed the diadem on his own head, if he would have subscribed the Nicene creed.[67] During three generations the armies of the East were successively commanded by his father, by himself, and by his son Ardaburius; his barbarian guards formed a military force that overawed the palace and the capital; and the liberal distribution of his immense treasures rendered Aspar as popular as he was powerful. He recommended the obscure name of Leo of Thrace, a military tribune, and the principal steward of his household. His nomination was unanimously ratified by the senate; and the servant of Aspar received the Imperial crown from the hands of the patriarch or bishop, who was permitted to express, by this unusual ceremony, the suffrage of the Deity.[68] This emperor, the first of the name of Leo, has been distinguished by the title of the *Great*, from a succession of princes who gradually fixed in the opinion of the Greeks a very humble standard of heroic, or at least of royal, perfection. Yet the temperate firmness with which Leo resisted the oppression of his benefactor showed that he was conscious of his duty and of his prerogative. Aspar was astonished to find that his influence could no longer appoint a præfect of Constantinople: he presumed to reproach his sovereign with a breach of promise, and, insolently shaking his purple, "It is not proper (said he) that the man who is invested with this garment should be guilty of lying." "Nor is it proper (replied Leo) that a prince should be compelled to resign his own judgment, and the public interest, to the will of a subject."[69] After this extraordinary scene, it was impossible that the reconciliation of the emperor and the patrician could be sincere; or, at least, that it could be solid and permanent. An army of Isaurians[70] was secretly levied and introduced into Constantinople; and while Leo undermined the authority, and prepared the disgrace, of the family of Aspar, his mild and cautious behaviour restrained them from any rash and desperate attempts, which might have been fatal to themselves or their enemies. The measures of peace and war were affected by this internal revolution. As long as Aspar degraded the majesty of the throne, the secret correspondence of religion and interest engaged him to favour the cause of Genseric. When Leo had delivered himself from the ignominious servitude, he listened to the complaints of the Italians; resolved to extirpate the tyranny of the Vandals; and declared his alliance with his colleague Anthemius, whom he solemnly invested with the diadem and purple of the West.

The virtues of Anthemius have perhaps been magnified, since the Imperial descent, which he could only deduce from the usurper Procopius, has been swelled into a line of emperors.[71] But the merit of his immediate parents, their honours, and their riches, rendered Anthemius one of the most illustrious subjects of the East, His father, Procopius, obtained, after his Persian embassy, the rank of general and patrician; and the name of Anthemius was derived from his maternal grandfather, the celebrated præfect, who protected, with so much ability and success, the infant reign of Theodosius. The grandson of the præfect was raised above the condition of a private subject by his marriage with Euphemia, the daughter of the emperor Marcian. This splendid alliance, which might supersede the necessity of merit, hastened the promotion of Anthemius to the successive dignities of count, of master-general, of consul, and of patrician; and his merit or fortune claimed the honours of a victory which was obtained on the banks of the Danube over the Huns. Without indulging an extravagant ambition, the son-in-law of Marcian might hope to be his successor; but Anthemius supported the disappointment with courage and patience; and his subsequent elevation was universally approved by the public, who esteemed him worthy to reign till he ascended the throne.[72] The emperor of the West marched from Constantinople, attended by several counts of high distinction, and a body of guards almost equal to the strength and numbers of a regular army: he entered Rome in triumph, and the choice of Leo was confirmed by the senate, the people, and the barbarian confederates of Italy.[73] The solemn inauguration of Anthemius was followed by the nuptials of his daughter and the patrician Ricimer; a fortunate event, which was considered as the firmest security of the union and happiness of the state. The wealth of two empires was ostentatiously displayed; and many senators completed their ruin, by an expensive effort to disguise their poverty. All serious business was suspended during this festival; the courts of justice were shut; the streets of Rome, the theatres, the places of public and private resort, resounded with hymenæal song and dances: and the royal bride, clothed in silken robes, with a crown on her head, was conducted to the palace of Ricimer, who had changed his military dress for the habit of a consul and a senator. On this memorable occasion, Sidonius, whose early ambition had been so fatally blasted, appeared as the orator of Auvergne, among the provincial deputies who addressed the throne with congratulations or complaints.[74] The calends of January were now approaching, and the venal poet, who had loved Avitus and esteemed Majorian, was persuaded by his friends to celebrate, in heroic verse, the merit, the felicity, the second consulship, and the future triumphs of the emperor Anthemius. Sidonius pronounced, with assurance and success, a panegyric which is still extant; and whatever might be the imperfections, either of the subject or of the composition, the welcome flatterer was immediately rewarded with the præfecture of Rome; a dignity which placed him among the illustrious personages of the empire, till he wisely preferred the more respectable character of a bishop, and a saint.[75]

The Greeks ambitiously commend the piety and catholic faith of the emperor whom they gave to the West; nor do they forget to observe that, when he left Constantinople, he converted his palace into the pious foundation of a public bath, a church, and an hospital for old men.[76] Yet some suspicious appearances are found to sully the theological fame of Anthemius. From the conversation of Philotheus, a Macedonian sectary, he had imbibed the spirit of religious toleration; and the heretics of Rome would have assembled with impunity, if the bold and vehement censure which pope Hilary pronounced in the church of St. Peter had not obliged him to abjure the unpopular indulgence.[77] Even the Pagans, a feeble and obscure remnant, conceived some vain hopes, from the indifference, or partiality, of Anthemius; and his singular friendship for the philosopher Severus, whom he promoted to the consulship, was ascribed to a secret project of reviving the ancient worship of the gods.[78] These idols were crumbled into dust: and the mythology which had once been the creed of nations was so universally disbelieved, that it might be employed without scandal, or at least without suspicion, by Christian poets.[79] Yet the vestiges of superstition were not absolutely obliterated, and the festival of the Lupercalia, whose origin had preceded the foundation of Rome, was still celebrated under the reign of Anthemius. The savage and simple rites were expressive of an early state of society before the invention of arts and agriculture. The rustic deities who presided over the toils and pleasures of the pastoral life, Pan, Faunus, and their train of satyrs, were such as the fancy of shepherds might create, sportive, petulant, and lascivious; whose power was limited, and whose malice was inoffensive. A goat was the offering the best adapted to their character and attributes; the flesh of the victim was roasted on willow spits; and the riotous youths, who crowded to the feast, ran naked about the fields, with leather thongs in their hands, communicating, as it was supposed, the blessing of fecundity to the women whom they touched.[80] The altar of Pan was erected, perhaps by Evander the Arcadian, in a dark recess in the side of the Palatine hill, watered by a perpetual fountain, and shaded by a hanging grove. A tradition that, in the same place, Romulus and Remus were suckled by the wolf, rendered it still more sacred and venerable in the eyes of the Romans; and this sylvan spot was gradually surrounded by the stately edifices of the Forum.[81] After the conversion of the Imperial city, the Christians still continued, in the month of February, the annual celebration of the Lupercalia; to which they ascribed a secret and mysterious influence on the genial powers of the animal and vegetable world. The bishops of Rome were solicitous to abolish a profane custom so repugnant to the spirit of Christianity; but their zeal was not supported by the authority of the civil magistrate: the inveterate abuse subsisted till the end of the fifth century, and pope Gelasius, who purified the capital from the last stain of idolatry, appeased, by a formal apology, the murmurs of the senate and people.[82]

In all his public declarations the emperor Leo assumes the authority, and professes the affection of a father for his son Anthemius, with whom he had divided the administration of the universe.[83] The situation, and perhaps the character, of Leo dissuaded him from exposing his person to the toils and dangers of an African war. But the powers of the Eastern empire were strenuously exerted to deliver Italy and the Mediterranean from the Vandals; and Genseric, who had so long oppressed both the land and sea, was threatened from every side with a formidable invasion. The campaign was opened by a bold and successful enterprise of the præ-

fect Heraclius.[84] The troops of Egypt, Thebais, and Libya were embarked under this command: and the Arabs, with a train of horses and camels, opened the roads of the desert. Heraclius landed on the coast of Tripoli, surprised and subdued the cities of that province, and prepared, by a laborious march, which Cato had formerly executed,[85] to join the Imperial army under the walls of Carthage. The intelligence of this loss extorted from Genseric some insidious and ineffectual propositions of peace: but he was still more seriously alarmed by the reconciliation of Marcellinus with the two empires. The independent patrician had been persuaded to acknowledge the legitimate title of Anthemius, whom he accompanied in his journey to Rome; the Dalmatian fleet was received into the harbours of Italy; the active valour of Marcellinus expelled the Vandals from the island of Sardinia; and the languid efforts of the West added some weight to the immense preparations of the Eastern Romans. The expense of the naval armament, which Leo sent against the Vandals has been distinctly ascertained; and the curious and instructive account displays the wealth of the declining empire. The Royal demesnes, or private patrimony of the prince, supplied seventeen thousand pounds of gold; forty-seven thousand pounds of gold, and seven hundred thousand of silver, were levied and paid into the treasury by the Prætorian præfects. But the cities were reduced to extreme poverty; and the diligent calculation of fines and forfeitures, as a valuable object of the revenue, does not suggest the idea of a just, or merciful, administration. The whole expense, by whatsoever means it was defrayed, of the African campaign, amounted to the sum of one hundred and thirty thousand pounds of gold, about five millions two hundred thousand pounds sterling, at a time when the value of money appears, from the comparative price of corn, to have been somewhat higher than in the present age.[86] The fleet that sailed from Constantinople to Carthage consisted of eleven hundred and thirteen ships, and the number of soldiers and mariners exceeded one hundred thousand men. Basiliscus, the brother of the empress Verina, was intrusted with this important command. His sister, the wife of Leo, had exaggerated the merit of his former exploits against the Scythians. But the discovery of his guilt, or incapacity, was reserved for the African war; and his friends could only save his military reputation by asserting that he had conspired with Aspar to spare Genseric, and to betray the last hope of the Western empire.

Experience has shown that the success of an invader most commonly depends on the vigour and celerity of his operations. The strength and sharpness of the first impression are blunted by delay; the health and spirit of the troops insensibly languish in a distant climate; the naval and military force, a mighty effort which perhaps can never be repeated, is silently consumed; and every hour that is wasted in negotiation accustoms the enemy to contemplate and examine those hostile terrors which, on their first appearance, he deemed irresistible. The formidable navy of Basiliscus pursued its prosperous navigation from the Thracian Bosphorus to the coast of Africa. He landed his troops at Cape Bona, or the promontory of Mercury, about forty miles from Carthage.[87] The army of Heraclius, and the fleet of Marcellinus, either joined or seconded the Imperial lieutenant; and the Vandals who opposed his progress by sea or land were successively vanquished.[88] If Basiliscus had seized the moment of consternation, and boldly advanced to the capital, Carthage must have surrendered, and the kingdom of the Vandals was extinguished. Genseric beheld the danger with firmness, and eluded it with his veteran dexterity. He protested, in the most respectful language, that he was ready to submit his person and his dominions to the will of the emperor; but he requested a truce of five days to regulate the terms of his submission; and it was universally believed that his secret liberality contributed to the success of this public negotiation. Instead of obstinately refusing whatever indulgence his enemy so earnestly solicited, the guilty, or the credulous, Basiliscus consented to the fatal truce; and his imprudent security seemed to proclaim that he already considered himself as the conqueror of Africa. During this short interval the wind became favourable to the designs of Genseric. He manned his largest ships of war with the bravest of the Moors and Vandals; and they towed after them many large barks filled with combustible materials. In the obscurity of the night, these destructive vessels were impelled against the unguarded and unsuspecting fleet of the Romans, who were awakened by the sense of their instant danger. Their close and crowded order assisted the progress of the fire, which was communicated with rapid and irresistible violence; and the noise of the wind, the crackling of the flames, the dissonant cries of the soldiers and mariners, who could neither command nor obey, increased the horror of the nocturnal tumult. Whilst they laboured to extricate themselves from the fire-ships, and to save at least a part of the navy, the galleys of Genseric assaulted them with temperate and disciplined valour; and many of the Romans, who escaped the fury of the flames, were destroyed or taken by the victorious Vandals. Among the events of that disastrous night, the heroic, or rather desperate, courage of John, one of the principal officers of Basiliscus, has rescued his name from oblivion. When the ship which he had bravely defended was almost consumed, he threw himself in his armour into the sea, disdainfully rejected the esteem and pity of Genso, the son of Genseric, who pressed him to accept honourable quarter, and sunk under the waves; exclaiming, with his last breath, that he would never fall alive into the hands of those impious dogs. Actuated by a far different spirit, Basiliscus, whose station was the most remote from danger, disgracefully fled in the beginning of the engagement, returned to Constantinople with the loss of more than half of his fleet and army, and sheltered his guilty head in the sanctuary of St. Sophia, till his sister, by her tears and entreaties, could obtain his pardon from the indignant emperor. Heraclius effected his retreat through the desert; Marcellinus retired to Sicily, where he was assassinated, perhaps at the instigation of Ricimer, by one of his own captains; and the king of the Vandals expressed his surprise and satisfaction that the Romans themselves should remove from the world his most formidable antagonists.[89] After the failure of this great expedition, Genseric again became the tyrant of the sea: the coasts of Italy, Greece, and Asia, were again exposed to his revenge and avarice; Tripoli and Sardinia returned to his obedience; he added Sicily to the number of his provinces; and, before he died, in the fulness of years and of glory, he beheld the final extinction of the empire of the West.[90]

During his long and active reign the African monarch had studiously cultivated the friendship of the barbarians of Europe, whose arms he might employ in a seasonable and effectual diversion against the two empires. After the death of Attila he renewed his alliance with the Visigoths of Gaul; and the sons of the elder Theodoric, who successively reigned over that warlike nation, were easily persuaded, by the sense of interest, to forget the cruel affront which Genseric had inflicted on their sister.[91] The death of the emperor Majorian delivered Theodoric the Second from the restraint of fear, and perhaps of honour; he violated his recent treaty with the Romans; and the ample territory of

Narbonne, which he firmly united to his dominions, became the immediate reward of his
perfidy. The selfish policy of Ricimer encouraged him to invade the provinces which were in
the possession of Ægidius, his rival; but the
active count, by the defence of Arles and the
victory of Orleans, saved Gaul, and checked
during his lifetime the progress of the Visigoths.
Their ambition was soon rekindled; and the design of extinguishing the Roman empire in
Spain and Gaul was conceived and almost completed in the reign of Euric, who assassinated
his brother Theodoric, and displayed, with a
more savage temper, superior abilities both in
peace and war. He passed the Pyrenees at the
head of a numerous army, subdued the cities
of Saragossa and Pampeluna, vanquished in
battle the martial nobles of the Tarragonese
province, carried his victorious arms into the
heart of Lusitania, and permitted the Suevi to
hold the kingdom of Gallicia under the Gothic
monarchy of Spain.[92] The efforts of Euric were
not less vigorous or less successful in Gaul; and
throughout the country that extends from the
Pyrenees to the Rhône and the Loire, Berry and
Auvergne were the only cities or dioceses which
refused to acknowledge him as their master.[93]
In the defence of Clermont, their principal
town, the inhabitants of Auvergne sustained
with inflexible resolution the miseries of war,
pestilence, and famine; and the Visigoths, relinquishing the fruitless siege, suspended the hopes
of that important conquest. The youth of the
province were animated by the heroic and almost incredible valour of Ecdicius, the son of
the emperor Avitus,[94] who made a desperate
sally with only eighteen horsemen, boldly attacked the Gothic army, and, after maintaining
a flying skirmish, retired safe and victorious
within the walls of Clermont. His charity was
equal to his courage: in a time of extreme scarcity four thousand poor were fed at his expense;
and his private influence levied an army of Burgundians for the deliverance of Auvergne. From
his virtues alone the faithful citizens of Gaul derived any hopes of safety or freedom; and even
such virtues were insufficient to avert the impending ruin of their country, since they were
anxious to learn, from his authority and example, whether they should prefer the alternative
of exile or servitude.[95] The public confidence
was lost; the resources of the state were exhausted; and the Gauls had too much reason to
believe that Anthemius, who reigned in Italy,
was incapable of protecting his distressed subjects beyond the Alps. The feeble emperor could

only procure for their defence the service of
twelve thousand British auxiliaries. Riothamus,
one of the independent kings or chieftains of the
island, was persuaded to transport his troops to
the continent of Gaul: he sailed up the Loire,
and established his quarters in Berry, where the
people complained of these oppressive allies, till
they were destroyed or dispersed by the arms of
the Visigoths.[96]

One of the last acts of jurisdiction which the
Roman senate exercised over their subjects of
Gaul was the trial and condemnation of Arvandus, the Prætorian præfect. Sidonius, who re-
joices that he lived under a reign in which he
might pity and assist a state-criminal, has expressed, with tenderness and freedom, the faults
of his indiscreet and unfortunate friend.[97] From
the perils which he had escaped, Arvandus imbibed confidence rather than wisdom; and such
was the various, though uniform, imprudence
of his behaviour, that his prosperity must appear much more surprising than his downfall.
The second præfecture, which he obtained
within the term of five years, abolished the
merit and popularity of his preceding administration. His easy temper was corrupted by
flattery and exasperated by opposition; he was
forced to satisfy his importunate creditors with
the spoils of the province; his capricious insolence offended the nobles of Gaul; and he sunk
under the weight of the public hatred. The
mandate of his disgrace summoned him to justify his conduct before the senate; and he passed
the sea of Tuscany with a favourable wind, the
presage, as he vainly imagined, of his future fortunes. A decent respect was still observed for the
Præfectorian rank; and on his arrival at Rome
Arvandus was committed to the hospitality,
rather than to the custody, of Flavius Asellus,
the count of the sacred largesses, who resided in
the Capitol.[98] He was eagerly pursued by his
accusers, the four deputies of Gaul, who were
all distinguished by their birth, their dignities,
or their eloquence. In the name of a great province, and according to the forms of Roman
jurisprudence, they instituted a civil and criminal action, requiring such restitution as might
compensate the losses of individuals, and such
punishment as might satisfy the justice of the
state. Their charges of corrupt oppression were
numerous and weighty; but they placed their
secret dependence on a letter which they had
intercepted, and which they could prove, by the
evidence of his secretary, to have been dictated
by Arvandus himself. The author of this letter
seemed to dissuade the king of the Goths from

a peace with the *Greek* emperor: he suggested the attack of the Britons on the Loire; and he recommended a division of Gaul, according to the law of nations, between the Visigoths and the Burgundians.[99] These pernicious schemes, which a friend could only palliate by the reproaches of vanity and indiscretion, were susceptible of a treasonable interpretation; and the deputies had artfully resolved not to produce their most formidable weapons till the decisive moment of the contest. But their intentions were discovered by the zeal of Sidonius. He immediately apprised the unsuspecting criminal of his danger; and sincerely lamented, without any mixture of anger, the haughty presumption of Arvandus, who rejected, and even resented, the salutary advice of his friends. Ignorant of his real situation, Arvandus showed himself in the Capitol in the white robe of a candidate, accepted indiscriminate salutations and offers of service, examined the shops of the merchants, the silks, and gems, sometimes with the indifference of a spectator and sometimes with the attention of a purchaser; and complained of the times, of the senate, of the prince, and of the delays of justice. His complaints were soon removed. An early day was fixed for his trial; and Arvandus appeared, with his accusers, before a numerous assembly of the Roman senate. The mournful garb which they affected excited the compassion of the judges, who were scandalised by the gay and splendid dress of their adversary: and when the præfect Arvandus, with the first of the Gallic deputies, were directed to take their places on the senatorial benches, the same contrast of pride and modesty was observed in their behaviour. In this memorable judgment, which presented a lively image of the old republic, the Gauls exposed, with force and freedom, the grievances of the province; and as soon as the minds of the audience were sufficiently inflamed, they recited the fatal epistle. The obstinacy of Arvandus was founded on the strange supposition that a subject could not be convicted of treason, unless he had actually conspired to assume the purple. As the paper was read, he repeatedly, and with a loud voice, acknowledged it for his genuine composition; and his astonishment was equal to his dismay when the unanimous voice of the senate declared him guilty of a capital offence. By their decree he was degraded from the rank of a præfect to the obscure condition of a plebeian, and ignominiously dragged by servile hands to the public prison. After a fortnight's adjournment the senate was again convened to pronounce the sentence of his death: but while he expected, in the island of Æsculapius, the expiration of the thirty days allowed by an ancient law to the vilest malefactors,[100] his friends interposed, the emperor Anthemius relented, and the præfect of Gaul obtained the milder punishment of exile and confiscation. The faults of Arvandus might deserve compassion; but the impunity of Seronatus accused the justice of the republic, till he was condemned and executed on the complaint of the people of Auvergne. That flagitious minister, the Catiline of his age and country, held a secret correspondence with the Visigoths to betray the province which he oppressed: his industry was continually exercised in the discovery of new taxes and obsolete offences; and his extravagant vices would have inspired contempt if they had not excited fear and abhorrence.[101]

Such criminals were not beyond the reach of justice; but whatever might be the guilt of Ricimer, that powerful barbarian was able to contend or to negotiate with the prince whose alliance he had condescended to accept. The peaceful and prosperous reign which Anthemius had promised to the West was soon clouded by misfortune and discord. Ricimer, apprehensive or impatient of a superior, retired from Rome and fixed his residence at Milan; an advantageous situation, either to invite or to repel the warlike tribes that were seated between the Alps and the Danube.[102] Italy was gradually divided into two independent and hostile kingdoms; and the nobles of Liguria, who trembled at the near approach of a civil war, fell prostrate at the feet of the patrician, and conjured him to spare their unhappy country. "For my own part," replied Ricimer, in a tone of insolent moderation, "I am still inclined to embrace the friendship of the Galatian;[103] but who will undertake to appease his anger, or to mitigate the pride which always rises in proportion to our submission?" They informed him that Epiphanius, bishop of Pavia,[104] united the wisdom of the serpent with the innocence of the dove; and appeared confident that the eloquence of such an ambassador must prevail against the strongest opposition, either of interest or passion. Their recommendation was approved; and Epiphanius, assuming the benevolent office of mediation, proceeded without delay to Rome where he was received with the honours due to his merit and reputation. The oration of a bishop in favour of peace may be easily supposed: he argued that, in all possible circumstances, the forgiveness of injuries must be an act of mercy, or magnanimity, or prudence; and he seriously admonished the emperor to avoid a contest with a fierce barbarian, which might be fatal to himself, and must be ruinous to his dominions. Anthemius acknowledged the truth of his maxims; but he deeply felt, with grief and indignation, the behaviour of Ricimer; and his passion gave eloquence and energy to his discourse. "What favours," he warmly exclaimed, "have we refused to this ungrateful man? What provocations have we not endured? Regardless of the majesty of the purple, I gave my daughter to a Goth; I sacrificed my own blood to the safety of the republic. The liberality which ought to have secured the eternal attachment of Ricimer has exasperated him against his benefactor. What wars has he not excited against the empire? How often has he instigated and assisted the fury of hostile nations? Shall I now accept his perfidious friendship? Can I hope that he will respect the engagements of a treaty, who has already violated the duties of a son?" But the anger of Anthemius evaporated in these passionate exclamations: he insensibly yielded to the proposals of Epiphanius; and the bishop returned to his diocese with the satisfaction of restoring the peace of Italy by a reconciliation,[105] of which the sincerity and continuance might be reasonably suspected. The clemency of the emperor was extorted from his weakness; and Ricimer suspended his ambitious designs till he had secretly prepared the engines with which he resolved to subvert the throne of Anthemius. The mask of peace and moderation was then thrown aside. The army of Ricimer was fortified by a numerous reinforcement of Burgundians and Oriental Suevi: he disclaimed all allegiance to the Greek emperor, marched from Milan to the gates of Rome, and, fixing his camp on the banks of the Anio, impatiently expected the arrival of Olybrius, his Imperial candidate.

The senator Olybrius, of the Anician family, might esteem himself the lawful heir of the Western empire. He had married Placidia, the younger daughter of Valentinian, after she was restored by Genseric, who still detained her sister Eudoxia, as the wife, or rather as the captive, of his son. The king of the Vandals supported, by threats and solicitations, the fair pretensions of his Roman ally; and assigned, as one of the motives of the war, the refusal of the senate and people to acknowledge their lawful prince, and the unworthy preference which they had given to a stranger.[106] The friendship of the public enemy might render Olybrius still more unpopular to the Italians; but when Ricimer meditated the ruin of the emperor Anthemius, he tempted, with the offer of a diadem, the candidate who could justify his rebellion by an illustrious name and a royal alliance. The husband of Placidia, who, like most of his ancestors, had been invested with the consular dignity, might have continued to enjoy a secure and splendid fortune in the peaceful residence of Constantinople; nor does he appear to have been tormented by such a genius as cannot be amused or occupied unless by the administration of an empire. Yet Olybrius yielded to the importunities of his friends, perhaps of his wife; rashly plunged into the dangers and calamities of a civil war; and, with the secret connivance of the emperor Leo, accepted the Italian purple, which was bestowed, and resumed, at the capricious will of a barbarian. He landed without obstacle (for Genseric was master of the sea) either at Ravenna or the port of Ostia, and immediately proceeded to the camp of Ricimer, where he was received as the sovereign of the Western world.[107]

The patrician, who had extended his posts from the Anio to the Milvian bridge, already possessed two quarters of Rome, the Vatican and the Janiculum, which are separated by the Tiber from the rest of the city;[108] and it may be conjectured that an assembly of seceding senators imitated, in the choice of Olybrius, the forms of a legal election. But the body of the senate and people firmly adhered to the cause of Anthemius; and the more effectual support of a Gothic army enabled him to prolong his reign, and the public distress, by a resistance of three months, which produced the concomitant evils of famine and pestilence. At length Ricimer made a furious assault on the bridge of Hadrian, or St. Angelo; and the narrow pass was defended with equal valour by the Goths till the death of Gilimer, their leader. The victorious troops, breaking down every barrier, rushed with irresistible violence into the heart of the city, and Rome (if we may use the language of a contemporary pope) was subverted by the civil fury of Anthemius and Ricimer.[109] The unfortunate Anthemius was dragged from his concealment and inhumanly massacred by the command of his son-in-law, who thus added a third, or perhaps a fourth, emperor to the number of his victims. The soldiers, who united the rage of factious citizens with the savage manners of barbarians, were indulged without control in the licence of rapine and murder: the crowd of slaves and plebeians, who were unconcerned in the event, could only gain by the indiscriminate pillage; and the face of the city exhibited the strange contrast of stern cruelty and dissolute intemperance.[110] Forty days after this calamitous event, the subject, not of glory, but of guilt, Italy was delivered, by a painful disease, from the tyrant Ricimer, who bequeathed the command of his army to his nephew Gundobald, one of the princes of the Burgundians. In the same year all the principal actors in this great revolution were removed from the stage; and the whole reign of Olybrius, whose death does not betray any symptoms of violence, is included within the term of seven months. He left one daughter, the offspring of his marriage with Placidia; and the family of the great Theodosius, transplanted from Spain to Constantinople, was propagated in the female line as far as the eighth generation.[111]

Whilst the vacant throne of Italy was abandoned to lawless barbarians,[112] the election of a new colleague was seriously agitated in the council of Leo. The empress Verina, studious to promote the greatness of her own family, had married one of her nieces to Julius Nepos, who succeeded his uncle Marcellinus in the sovereignty of Dalmatia, a more solid possession than the title which he was persuaded to accept of Emperor of the West. But the measures of the Byzantine court were so languid and irresolute, that many months elapsed after the death of Anthemius, and even of Olybrius, before their destined successor could show himself, with a respectable force, to his Italian subjects. During that interval, Glycerius, an obscure soldier, was invested with the purple by his patron Gundobald; but the Burgundian prince was unable or unwilling to support his nomination by a civil war: the pursuits of domestic ambition recalled him beyond the Alps,[113] and his client was permitted to exchange the Roman sceptre for the bishopric of Salona. After extinguishing such a competitor, the emperor Nepos was acknowledged by the senate, by the Italians, and by the provincials of Gaul; his moral virtues and military talents were loudly celebrated; and those who derived any private benefit from his government announced in prophetic strains the restoration of the public felicity.[114] Their hopes (if such hopes had been entertained) were confounded within the term of a single year; and the treaty of peace, which ceded Auvergne to the Visigoths, is the only event of his short and inglorious reign. The most faithful subjects of Gaul were sacrificed by the Italian emperor to the hope of domestic security;[115] but his repose

was soon invaded by a furious sedition of the barbarian confederates, who, under the command of Orestes, their general, were in full march from Rome to Ravenna. Nepos trembled at their approach; and, instead of placing a just confidence in the strength of Ravenna, he hastily escaped to his ships, and retired to his Dalmatian principality, on the opposite coast of the Hadriatic. By this shameful abdication he protracted his life about five years, in a very ambiguous state between an emperor and an exile, till he was assassinated at Salona by the ungrateful Glycerius, who was translated, perhaps as the reward of his crime, to the archbishopric of Milan.[116]

The nations who had asserted their independence after the death of Attila were established, by the right of possession or conquest, in the boundless countries to the north of the Danube; or in the Roman provinces between the river and the Alps. But the bravest of their youth enlisted in the army of confederates, who formed the defence and the terror of Italy;[117] and in this promiscuous multitude, the names of the Heruli, the Sciri, the Alani, the Turcilingi, and the Rugians, appear to have predominated. The example of these warriors was imitated by Orestes,[118] the son of Tatullus, and the father of the last Roman emperor of the West. Orestes, who has been already mentioned in this history, had never deserted his country. His birth and fortunes rendered him one of the most illustrious subjects of Pannonia. When that province was ceded to the Huns, he entered into the service of Attila, his lawful sovereign, obtained the office of his secretary, and was repeatedly sent ambassador to Constantinople, to represent the person and signify the commands of the imperious monarch. The death of that conqueror restored him to his freedom; and Orestes might honourably refuse either to follow the sons of Attila into the Scythian desert, or to obey the Ostrogoths, who had usurped the dominion of Pannonia. He preferred the service of the Italian princes, the successors of Valentinian; and, as he possessed the qualifications of courage, industry, and experience, he advanced with rapid steps in the military profession, till he was elevated, by the favour of Nepos himself, to the dignities of patrician and master general of the troops. These troops had been long accustomed to reverence the character and authority of Orestes, who affected their manners, conversed with them in their own language, and was intimately connected with their national chieftains by long habits of familiarity and friendship. At his solicitation they rose in arms against the obscure Greek who presumed to claim their obedience; and when Orestes, from some secret motive, declined the purple, they consented, with the same facility, to acknowledge his son Augustulus as the emperor of the West. By the abdication of Nepos, Orestes had now attained the summit of his ambitious hopes; but he soon discovered, before the end of the first year, that the lessons of perjury and ingratitude which a rebel must inculcate will be retorted against himself, and that the precarious sovereign of Italy was only permitted to choose whether he would be the slave or the victim of his barbarian mercenaries. The dangerous alliance of these strangers had oppressed and insulted the last remains of Roman freedom and dignity. At each revolution their pay and privileges were augmented; but their insolence increased in a still more extravagant degree; they envied the fortune of their brethren in Gaul, Spain, and Africa, whose victorious arms had acquired an independent and perpetual inheritance; and they insisted on their peremptory demand that a *third* part of the lands of Italy should be immediately divided among them. Orestes, with a spirit which, in another situation, might be entitled to our esteem, chose rather to encounter the rage of an armed multitude than to subscribe the ruin of an innocent people. He rejected the audacious demand; and his refusal was favourable to the ambition of Odoacer, a bold barbarian, who assured his fellow-soldiers that, if they dared to associate under his command, they might soon extort the justice which had been denied to their dutiful petitions. From all the camps and garrisons of Italy the confederates, actuated by the same resentment and the same hopes, impatiently flocked to the standard of this popular leader; and the unfortunate patrician, overwhelmed by the torrent, hastily retreated to the strong city of Pavia, the episcopal seat of the holy Epiphanites. Pavia was immediately besieged, the fortifications were stormed, the town was pillaged; and although the bishop might labour, with much zeal and some success, to save the property of the church and the chastity of female captives, the tumult could only be appeased by the execution of Orestes.[119] His brother Paul was slain in an action near Ravenna; and the helpless Augustulus, who could no longer command the respect, was reduced to implore the clemency, of Odoacer.

That successful barbarian was the son of Edecon; who, in some remarkable transactions, particularly described in a preceding chapter had been the colleague of Orestes himself. The honour of an ambassador should be exempt from suspicion; and Edecon had listened to a conspiracy against the life of his sovereign. But this apparent guilt was expiated by his merit or repentance: his rank was eminent and conspicuous; he enjoyed the favour of Attila; and the troops under his command, who guarded in their turn the royal village, consisted of a tribe of Sciri, his immediate and hereditary subjects. In the revolt of the nations they still adhered to the Huns; and, more than twelve years afterwards, the name of Edecon is honourably mentioned in their unequal contest with the Ostrogoths; which was terminated, after two bloody battles, by the defeat and dispersion of the Sciri.[120] Their gallant leader, who did not survive this national calamity, left two sons, Onulf and Odoacer, to struggle with adversity, and to maintain as they might, by rapine or service, the faithful followers of their exile. Onulf directed his steps towards Constantinople, where he sullied, by the assassination of a generous benefactor, the fame which he had acquired in arms. His brother Odoacer led a wandering life among the barbarians of Noricum, with a mind and a fortune suited to the most desperate adventures; and when he had fixed his choice, he piously visited the cell of Severinus, the popular saint of the country, to solicit his approbation and blessing. The lowness of the door would not admit the lofty stature of Odoacer: he was obliged to stoop; but in that humble attitude the saint could discern the symptoms of his future greatness; and addressing him in a prophetic tone, "Pursue (said he) your design; proceed to Italy, you will soon cast away this coarse garment of skins; and your wealth will be adequate to the liberality of your mind."[121] The barbarian, whose daring spirit accepted and ratified the prediction, was admitted into the service of the Western empire, and soon obtained an honourable rank in the guards. His manners were gradually polished, his military skill was improved, and the confederates of Italy would not have elected him for their general unless the exploits of Odoacer had established a high opinion of his courage and capacity.[122] Their military acclamations saluted him with the title of king; but he abstained during his whole reign from the use of the purple and diadem,[123] lest he should offend those princes whose subjects, by their accidental mixture, had formed the victorious army which time and policy might insensibly unite into a great nation.

Royalty was familiar to the barbarians, and the submissive people of Italy was prepared to obey, without a murmur, the authority which he should condescend to exercise as the vice-gerent of the emperor of the West. But Odoacer had resolved to abolish that useless and expensive office; and such is the weight of antique prejudice, that it required some boldness and penetration to discover the extreme facility of the enterprise. The unfortunate Augustulus was made the instrument of his own disgrace; he signified his resignation to the senate; and that assembly, in their last act of obedience to a Roman prince, still affected the spirit of freedom and the forms of the constitution. An epistle was addressed, by their unanimous decree, to the emperor Zeno, the son-in-law and successor of Leo, who had lately been restored, after a short rebellion, to the Byzantine throne. They solemnly "disclaim the necessity, or even the wish, of continuing any longer the Imperial succession in Italy; since, in their opinion, the majesty of a sole monarch is sufficient to pervade and protect, at the same time, both the East and the West. In their own name, and in the name of the people, they consent that the seat of universal empire shall be transferred from Rome to Constantinople; and they basely renounce the right of choosing their master, the only vestige that yet remained of the authority which had given laws to the world. The republic (they repeat that name without a blush) might safely confide in the civil and military virtues of Odoacer; and they humbly request that the emperor would invest him with the title of Patrician, and the administration of the *diocese* of Italy." The deputies of the senate were received at Constantinople with some mark of displeasure and indignation: and when they were admitted to the audience of Zeno, he sternly reproached them with their treatment of the two emperors, Anthemius and Nepos, whom the East had successively granted to the prayers of Italy. "The first (continued he) you have murdered; the second you have expelled: but the second is still alive, and whilst he lives he is your lawful sovereign." But the prudent Zeno soon deserted the hopeless cause of his abdicated colleague. His vanity was gratified by the title of sole emperor, and by the statues erected to his honour in the several quarters of Rome; he entertained a friendly, though ambiguous, correspondence with the *patrician* Odoacer; and he gratefully accepted the Imperial ensigns, the sacred ornaments of the throne and palace, which the barbarian was not unwilling to remove from the sight of the people.[124]

In the space of twenty years since the death of Valentinian, nine emperors had successively disappeared; and the son of Orestes, a youth recommended only by his beauty, would be the least entitled to the notice of posterity, if his reign, which was marked by the extinction of the Roman empire in the West, did not leave a memorable era in the history of mankind.[125] The patrician Orestes had married the daughter of Count *Romulus*, of Petovio in Noricum; the name of *Augustus*, notwithstanding the jealousy of power, was known at Aquileia as a familiar surname; and the appellations of the two great founders, of the city and of the monarchy, were thus strangely united in the last of their successors.[126] The son or Orestes assumed and disgraced the names of Romulus Augustus: but the first was corrupted into Momyllus by the Greeks, and the second has been changed by the Latins into the contemptible diminutive Augustulus. The life of this inoffensive youth was spared by the generous clemency of Odoacer; who dismissed him, with his whole family, from the Imperial palace, fixed his annual allowance at six thousand pieces of gold, and assigned the castle of Lucullus, in Campania, for the place of his exile or retirement.[127] As soon as the Romans breathed from the toils of the Punic war, they were attracted by the beauties and the pleasures of Campania; and the country-house of the elder Scipio at Liternum exhibited a lasting model of their rustic simplicity.[128] The delicious shores of the bay of Naples were crowded with villas; and Sylla applauded the masterly skill of his rival, who had seated himself on the lofy promontory of Misenum, that commands, on every side, the sea and land, as far as the boundaries of the horizon.[129] The villa of Marius was purchased within a few years, by Lucullus, and the price had increased from two thousand five hundred, to more than fourscore thousand, pounds sterling.[130] It was adorned by the new proprietor with Grecian arts and Asiatic treasures; and the houses and gardens of Lucullus obtained a distinguished rank in the list of Imperial palaces.[131] When the Vandals became formidable to the sea-coast, the Lucullan villa, on the promontory of Misenum, gradually assumed the strength and appellation of a strong castle, the obscure retreat of the last emperor of the West. About twenty years after that great revolution it was converted into a church and monastery, to receive the bones of St. Severinus. They securely reposed, amidst the broken trophies of Cimbric and Armenian victories, till the beginning of the tenth century; when the fortifications, which might afford a dangerous shelter to the Saracens, were demolished by the people of Naples.[132]

Odoacer was the first barbarian who reigned in Italy, over a people who had once asserted their just superiority above the rest of mankind. The disgrace of the Romans still excites our respectful compassion, and we fondly sympathise with the imaginary grief and indignation of their degenerate posterity. But the calamities of Italy had gradually subdued the proud consciousness of freedom and glory. In the age of Roman virtue the provinces were subject to the arms, and the citizens to the laws, of the republic, till those laws were subverted by civil discord, and both the city and the provinces became the servile property of a tyrant. The forms of the constitution, which alleviated or disguised their abject slavery, were abolished by time and violence; the Italians alternately lamented the presence or the absence of the sovereigns whom they detested or despised; and the succession of five centuries inflicted the various evils of military licence, capricious despotism, and elaborate oppression. During the same period, the barbarians had emerged from obscurity and contempt, and the warriors of Germany and Scythia were introduced into the provinces, as the servants, the allies, and at length the masters, of the Romans, whom they insulted or protected. The hatred of the people was suppressed by fear; they respected the spirit and splendour of the martial chiefs who were invested with the honours of the empire; and the fate of Rome had long depended on the sword of those formidable strangers. The stern Ricimer, who trampled on the ruins of Italy, had exercised the power, without assuming the title, of a king; and the patient Romans were insensibly prepared to acknowledge the royalty of Odoacer and his barbaric successors.

The king of Italy was not unworthy of the high station to which his valour and fortune had exalted him: his savage manners were polished by the habits of conversation; and he respected, though a conqueror and a barbarian, the institutions, and even the prejudices, of his subjects. After an interval of seven years, Odoacer restored the consulship of the West. For himself he modestly, or proudly, declined an honour which was still accepted by the emperors of the East; but the curule chair was successively filled by eleven of the most illustrious senators;[133] and the list is adorned by the respectable name of Bas-

ilius, whose virtues claimed the friendship and grateful applause of Sidonius, his client.[134] The laws of the emperors were strictly enforced, and the civil administration of Italy was still exercised by the Prætorian præfect and his subordinate officers. Odoacer devolved on the Roman magistrates the odious and oppressive task of collecting the public revenue; but he reserved for himself the merit of seasonable and popular indulgence.[135] Like the rest of the barbarians, he had been instructed in the Arian heresy; but he revered the monastic and episcopal characters; and the silence of the catholics attests the toleration which they enjoyed. The peace of the city required the interposition of his præfect Basilius in the choice of a Roman pontiff: the decree which restrained the clergy from alienating their lands was ultimately designed for the benefit of the people, whose devotion would have been taxed to repair the dilapidations of the church.[136] Italy was protected by the arms of its conqueror; and its frontiers were respected by the barbarians of Gaul and Germany, who had so long insulted the feeble race of Theodosius. Odoacer passed the Hadriatic, to chastise the assassins of the emperor Nepos, and to acquire the maritime province of Dalmatia. He passed the Alps, to rescue the remains of Noricum from Fava, or Feletheus, king of the Rugians, who held his residence beyond the Danube. The king was vanquished in battle, and led away prisoner; a numerous colony of captives and subjects was transplanted into Italy; and Rome, after a long period of defeat and disgrace, might claim the triumph of her barbarian master.[137]

Notwithstanding the prudence and success of Odoacer, his kingdom exhibited the sad prospect of misery and desolation. Since the age of Tiberius, the decay of agriculture had been felt in Italy; and it was a just subject of complaint that the life of the Roman people depended on the accidents of the winds and waves.[138] In the division and the decline of the empire, the tributary harvests of Egypt and Africa were withdrawn; the numbers of the inhabitants continually diminished with the means of subsistence; and the country was exhausted by the irretrievable losses of war, famine,[139] and pestilence. St. Ambrose has deplored the ruin of a populous district, which had been once adorned with the flourishing cities of Bologna, Modena, Rhegium, and Placentia.[140] Pope Gelasius was a subject of Odoacer; and he affirms, with strong exaggeration, that in Æmilia, Tuscany, and the adjacent provinces. the human species was almost extirpated.[141] The plebians of Rome, who were fed by the hand of their master, perished or disappeared as soon as his liberality was suppressed; the decline of the arts reduced the industrious mechanic to idleness and want; and the senators, who might support with patience the ruin of their country, bewailed their private loss of wealth and luxury. One third of those ample estates, to which the ruin of Italy is originally imputed,[142] was extorted for the use of the conquerors. Injuries were aggravated by insults; the sense of actual sufferings was embittered by the fear of more dreadful evils; and as new lands were allotted to new swarms of barbarians, each senator was apprehensive lest the arbitrary surveyors should approach his favourite villa, or his most profitable farm. The least unfortunate were those who submitted without a murmur to the power which it was impossible to resist. Since they desired to live, they owed some gratitude to the tyrant who had spared their lives; and since he was the absolute master of their fortunes, the portion which he left must be accepted as his pure and voluntary gift.[143] The distress of Italy was mitigated by the prudence and humanity of Odoacer, who had bound himself, as the price of his elevation, to satisfy the demands of a licentious and turbulent multitude. The kings of the barbarians were frequently resisted, deposed, or murdered, by their *native* subjects; and the various bands of Italian mercenaries, who associated under the standard of an elective general, claimed a larger privilege of freedom and rapine. A monarchy destitute of national union and hereditary right hastened to its dissolution. After a reign of fourteen years Odoacer was oppressed by the superior genius of Theodoric, king of the Ostrogoths; a hero alike excellent in the arts of war and of government, who restored an age of peace and prosperity, and whose name still excites and deserves the attention of mankind.

CHAPTER XXXVII

Origin, Progress, and Effects of the Monastic Life. Conversion of the Barbarians to Christianity and Arianism. Persecution of the Vandals in Africa. Extinction of Arianism among the Barbarians.

THE indissoluble connection of civil and ecclesiastical affairs has compelled and encouraged me to relate the progress, the persecutions, the establishment, the divisions, the final triumph, and the gradual corruption of Christianity. I have purposely delayed the consideration of two religious events interesting in the study of human nature, and important in the decline and fall of the Roman empire. I. The institution of the monastic life;[1] and II. The conversion of the northern barbarians.

I. Prosperity and peace introduced the distinction of the *vulgar* and the *Ascetic Christians*.[2] The loose and imperfect practice of religion satisfied the conscience of the multitude. The prince or magistrate, the soldier or merchant, reconciled their fervent zeal and implicit faith with the exercise of their profession, the pursuit of their interest, and the indulgence of their passions: but the Ascetics, who obeyed and abused the rigid precepts of the Gospel, were inspired by the savage enthusiasm which represents man as a criminal, and God as a tyrant. They seriously renounced the business and the pleasures of the age; abjured the use of wine, of flesh, and of marriage; chastised their body, mortified their affections, and embraced a life of misery, as the price of eternal happiness. In the reign of Constantine the Ascetics fled from a profane and degenerate world to perpetual solitude or religious society. Like the first Christians of Jerusalem,[3] they resigned the use or the property of their temporal possessions; established regular communities of the same sex and a similar disposition; and assumed the names of *Hermits*, *Monks*, and *Anachorets*, expressive of their lonely retreat in a natural or artificial desert. They soon acquired the respect of the world, which they despised; and the loudest applause was bestowed on this DIVINE PHILOSOPHY,[4] which surpassed, without the aid of science or reason, the laborious virtues of the Grecian schools. The monks might indeed contend with the Stoics in the contempt of fortune, of pain, and of death: the Pythagorean silence and submission were revived in their servile discipline; and they disdained as firmly as the Cynics themselves all the forms and decencies of civil society. But the votaries of this Divine Philosophy aspired to imitate a purer and more perfect model. They trod in the footsteps of the prophets, who had retired to the desert;[5] and they restored the devout and contemplative life, which had been instituted by the Essenians in Palestine and Egypt. The philosophic eye of Pliny had surveyed with astonishment a solitary people, who dwelt among the palm-trees near the Dead Sea; who subsisted without money; who were propagated without women; and who derived from the disgust and repentance of mankind a perpetual supply of voluntary associates.[6]

Egypt, the fruitful parent of superstition, afforded the first example of the monastic life. Antony,[7] an illiterate[8] youth of the lower parts of Thebais, distributed his patrimony,[9] deserted his family and native home, and executed his *monastic* penance with original and intrepid fanaticism. After a long and painful novitiate among the tombs and in a ruined tower, he boldly advanced into the desert three days' journey to the eastward of the Nile; discovered a lonely spot, which possessed the advantages of shade and water; and fixed his last residence on Mount Colzim, near the Red Sea, where an ancient monastery still preserves the name and memory of the saint.[10] The curious devotion of the Christians pursued him to the desert; and when he was obliged to appear at Alexandria, in the face of mankind, he supported his fame with discretion and dignity. He enjoyed the friendship of Athanasius, whose doctrine he approved; and the Egyptian peasant respectfully declined a respectful invitation from the emperor Constantine. The venerable patriarch (for Antony attained the age of one hundred and five years) beheld the numerous progeny which had been formed by his example and his lessons. The prolific colonies of monks multiplied with rapid increase on the sands of Libya, upon the rocks of Thebais, and in the cities of the Nile. To the south of Alexandria, the mountain, and adjacent desert, of Nitria was peopled by five thousand anachorets; and the traveller may still investigate the ruins of fifty monasteries, which were planted in that barren soil by the disciples of Antony.[11] In the Upper Thebais, the vacant island of Tabenne,[12] was occupied by Pachomius and fourteen hundred of his brethren. That holy abbot successively founded nine monasteries of men, and one of women; and the festival of Easter sometimes collected fifty thousand religious persons, who followed his *angelic* rule of discipline.[13] The stately and populous city of Oxyrinchus, the seat of Christian orthodoxy, had devoted the temples, the public edifices, and even the ramparts, to pious and charitable uses; and the bishop, who might preach in twelve churches, computed ten thousand females, and twenty thousand males, of the monastic profession.[14] The Egyptians, who gloried in this marvellous revolution, were disposed to hope, and to believe, that the number of the monks was equal to the remainder of the people;[15] and posterity might repeat the saying which had formerly been applied to the sacred animals of the same country, that in Egypt it was less difficult to find a god than a man.

Athanasius introduced into Rome the knowledge and practice of the monastic life; and a school of this new philosophy was opened by the disciples of Antony, who accompanied their primate to the holy threshold of the Vatican. The strange and savage appearance of these Egyptians excited, at first, horror and contempt, and, at length, applause and zealous imitation. The senators, and more especially the matrons, transformed their palaces and villas into religious houses; and the narrow institution of *six* Vestals was eclipsed by the frequent monasteries, which were seated on the ruins of ancient temples and in the midst of the Roman Forum.[16] Inflamed by the example of Antony, a Syrian youth, whose name was Hilarion,[17] fixed his dreary abode on a sandy beach between the sea and a morass about seven miles from Gaza. The austere penance, in which he persisted forty-eight years, diffused a similar enthusiasm; and the holy man was followed by a train of two or three thousand anachorets, whenever he visited the innumerable monasteries of Palestine. The fame of Basil[18] is immortal in the monastic history of the East. With a mind that had tasted the learning and eloquence of Athens; with an ambition scarcely to be satisfied by the archbishopric of Cæsarea, Basil retired to a savage solitude in Pontus; and deigned, for a while, to give laws to the spiritual colonies which he profusely scattered along the coast of the Black Sea. In the West, Martin of Tours,[19] a soldier, a hermit, a bishop, and a saint, established the monasteries of Gaul; two thousand of his disciples followed him to the grave; and his eloquent historian challenges the deserts of Thebais to produce, in a more favourable climate, a champion of equal virtue. The progress of the monks was not less rapid or universal than that of Christianity itself. Every province, and, at last, every city, of the empire was filled with their increasing multitudes; and the bleak and barren isles, from Lerins to Lipari, that arise out of the Tuscan Sea, were chosen by the anachorets for the place of their voluntary exile. An easy and perpetual intercourse by sea and land connected the provinces of the Roman world; and the life of Hilarion displays the facility with which an indigent hermit of Palestine might traverse Egypt, embark for Sicily, escape to Epirus, and finally settle in the island of Cyprus.[20] The Latin Christians embraced the religious institutions of Rome. The pilgrims who visited Jerusalem eagerly copied, in the most distant climates of the earth, the faithful model of the monastic life. The disciples of Antony spread themselves beyond the tropic, over the Christian empire of Æthiopia.[21] The monastery of Banchor,[22] in Flintshire, which contained above two thousand brethren, dispersed a numerous colony among the barbarians of Ireland;[23] and Iona, one of the Hebrides, which was planted by the Irish monks, diffused over the northern regions a doubtful ray of science and superstition.[24]

These unhappy exiles from social life were impelled by the dark and implacable genius of superstition. Their mutual resolution was supported by the example of millions, of either sex, of every age, and of every rank; and each proselyte who entered the gates of a monastery was persuaded that he trod the steep and thorny path of eternal happiness.[25] But the operation of these religious motives was variously determined by the temper and situation of mankind. Reason might subdue, or passion might suspend, their influence; but they acted most forcibly on the infirm minds of children and females; they were strengthened by secret remorse or accidental misfortune; and they might derive some aid from the temporal considerations of vanity or interest. It was naturally supposed that the pious and humble monks, who had renounced the world to accomplish the work of their salvation, were the best qualified for the spiritual government of the Christians. The reluctant hermit was torn from his cell, and seated amidst the acclamations of the people, on the episcopal throne: the monasteries of Egypt, of Gaul, and of the East, supplied a regular succession of saints and bishops; and ambition soon discovered the secret road which led to the possession of wealth and honours.[26] The popular monks, whose reputation was connected with the fame and success of the order, assiduously laboured to multiply the number of their fellow-captives. They insinuated themselves into noble and opulent families; and the specious arts of flattery and seduction were employed to secure those proselytes who might bestow wealth or dignity on the monastic profession. The indignant father bewailed the loss, perhaps, of an only son;[27] the credulous maid was betrayed by

vanity to violate the laws of nature; and the matron aspired to imaginary perfection by renouncing the virtues of domestic life. Paula yielded to the persuasive eloquence of Jerom;[28] and the profane title of mother-in-law of God[29] tempted that illustrious widow to consecrate the virginity of her daughter Eustochium. By the advice, and in the company, of her spiritual guide, Paula abandoned Rome and her infant son; retired to the holy village of Bethlem; founded an hospital and four monasteries; and acquired, by her alms and penance, an eminent and conspicuous station in the Catholic church. Such rare and illustrious penitents were celebrated as the glory and example of their age; but the monasteries were filled by a crowd of obscure and abject plebeians,[30] who gained in the cloister much more than they had sacrificed in the world. Peasants, slaves, and mechanics might escape from poverty and contempt to a safe and honourable profession, whose apparent hardships were mitigated by custom, by popular applause, and by the secret relaxation of discipline.[31] The subjects of Rome, whose persons and fortunes were made responsible for unequal and exorbitant tributes, retired from the oppression of the Imperial government; and the pusillanimous youth preferred the penance of a monastic, to the dangers of a military, life. The affrighted provincials of every rank, who fled before the barbarians, found shelter and subsistence; whole legions were buried in these religious sanctuaries; and the same cause which relieved the distress of individuals impaired the strength and fortitude of the empire.[32]

The monastic profession of the ancients[33] was an act of voluntary devotion. The inconstant fanatic was threatened with the eternal vengeance of the God whom he deserted; but the doors of the monastery were still open for repentance. Those monks whose conscience was fortified by reason or passion were at liberty to resume the character of men and citizens; and even the spouses of Christ might accept the legal embraces of an earthly lover.[34] The examples of scandal, and the progress of superstition, suggested the propriety of more forcible restraints. After a sufficient trial, the fidelity of the novice was secured by a solemn and perpetual vow; and his irrevocable engagement was ratified by the laws of the church and state. A guilty fugitive was pursued, arrested, and restored to his perpetual prison; and the interposition of the magistrate oppressed the freedom and merit which had alleviated, in some degree, the abject slavery of the monastic discipline.[35] The actions of a monk, his words, and even his thoughts, were determined by an inflexible rule[36] or a capricious superior: the slightest offences were corrected by disgrace or confinement, extraordinary fasts, or bloody flagellation; and disobedience, murmur, or delay were ranked in the catalogue of the most heinous sins.[37] A blind submission to the commands of the abbot, however absurd, or even criminal, they might seem, was the ruling principle, the first virtue of the Egyptian monks; and their patience was frequently exercised by the most extravagant trials. They were directed to remove an enormous rock; assiduously to water a barren staff that was planted in the ground, till, at the end of three years, it should vegetate and blossom like a tree; to walk into a fiery furnace; or to cast their infant into a deep pond: and several saints, or madmen, have been immortalised in monastic story by their thoughtless and fearless obedience.[38] The freedom of the mind, the source of every generous and rational sentiment, was destroyed by the habits of credulity and submission; and the monk, contracting the vices of a slave, devoutly followed the faith and passions of his ecclesiastical tyrant. The peace of the Eastern church was invaded by a swarm of fanatics, incapable of fear, or reason, or humanity; and the Imperial troops acknowledged, without shame, that they were much less apprehensive of an encounter with the fiercest barbarians.[39]

Superstition has often framed and consecrated the fantastic garments of the monks:[40] but their apparent singularity sometimes proceeds from their uniform attachment to a simple and primitive model, which the revolutions of fashion have made ridiculous in the eyes of mankind. The father of the Benedictines expressly disclaims all idea of choice or merit; and soberly exhorts his disciples to adopt the coarse and convenient dress of the countries which they may inhabit.[41] The monastic habits of the ancients varied with the climate and their mode of life; and they assumed, with the same indifference, the sheepskin of the Egyptian peasants or the cloak of the Grecian philosophers. They allowed themselves the use of linen in Egypt, where it was a cheap and domestic manufacture; but in the West they rejected such an expensive article of foreign luxury.[42] It was the practice of the monks either to cut or shave their hair; they wrapped their heads in a cowl, to escape the sight of profane objects; their legs and feet were naked, except in the extreme cold of winter; and their slow and feeble steps were supported by a long staff. The aspect of a genuine anachoret was horrid and disgusting: every sensation that is offensive to man was thought acceptable to God; and the angelic rule of Tabenne condemned the salutary custom of bathing the limbs in water and of anointing them with oil.[43] The austere monks slept on the ground, on a hard mat or a rough blanket; and the same bundle of palm-leaves served them as a seat in the day and a pillow in the night. Their original cells were low narrow huts, built of the slightest materials; which formed, by the regular distribution of the streets, a large and populous village, enclosing, within the common wall, a church, a hospital, perhaps a library, some necessary offices, a garden, and a fountain or reservoir of fresh water. Thirty or forty brethren composed a family of separate discipline and diet; and the great monasteries of Egypt consisted of thirty or forty families.

Pleasure and guilt are synonymous terms in the language of the monks, and they had discovered, by experience, that rigid fasts and abstemious diet are the most effectual preservatives against the impure desires of the flesh.[44] The rules of abstinence which they imposed, or practised, were not uniform or perpetual: the cheerful festival of the Pentecost was balanced by the extraordinary mortification of Lent; the fervour of new monasteries was insensibly relaxed; and the voracious appetite of the Gauls could not imitate the patient and temperate virtue of the Egyptians.[45] The disciples of Antony and Pachomius were satisfied with their daily pittance[46] of twelve ounces of bread, or rather biscuit,[47] which they divided into two frugal repasts, of the afternoon and of the evening. It was esteemed a merit, and almost a duty, to abstain from the boiled vegetables which were provided for the refectory; but the extraordinary bounty of the abbot sometimes indulged them with the luxury of cheese, fruit, salad, and the small dried fish of the Nile.[48] A more ample latitude of sea and river fish was gradually allowed or assumed; but the use of flesh was long confined to the sick or travellers: and when it gradually prevailed in the less rigid monasteries of Europe, a singular distinction was introduced; as if birds, whether wild or domestic, had been less profane than the grosser animals of the field. Water was the pure and innocent beverage of the primitive monks; and the founder of the Benedictines regrets the daily portion of half a pint of wine which had been extorted from him by the intemperance of the age.[49] Such an allowance might be easily supplied by the vineyards of Italy; and his victorious disciples, who passed the Alps, the Rhine, and the Baltic, required, in the place of wine, an adequate compensation of strong beer or cider.

The candidate who aspired to the virtue of evangelical poverty, abjured, at his first entrance into a regular community, the idea, and even the name, of all separate or exclusive possession.[50] The brethren were supported by their manual labour; and the duty of labour was strenuously recommended as a penance, as an exercise, and as the most laudable means of securing their daily subsistence.[51] The garden and fields, which the industry of the monks had often rescued from the forest or the morass, were diligently cultivated by their hands. They performed, without reluctance, the menial offices of slaves and domestics; and the several trades that were necessary to provide their habits, their utensils, and their lodging, were exercised within the precincts of the great monasteries. The monastic studies have tended, for the most part, to darken, rather than to dispel, the cloud of superstition. Yet the curiosity or zeal of some learned solitaries has cultivated the ecclesiastical and even the profane sciences: and posterity must gratefully acknowledge that the monuments of Greek and Roman literature have been preserved and multiplied by their indefatigable pens.[52] But the more humble industry of the monks, especially in Egypt, was contented with the silent, sedentary occupation of making wooden sandals, or of twisting the leaves of the palm-tree into mats and baskets. The superfluous stock, which was not consumed in domestic use, supplied, by trade, the wants of the community: the boats of Tabenne, and the other monasteries of Thebais, descended the Nile as far as Alexandria; and, in a Christian market, the sanctity of the workmen might enhance the intrinsic value of the work.

But the necessity of manual labour was insensibly superseded. The novice was tempted to bestow his fortune on the saints in whose society he was resolved to spend the remainder of his life; and the pernicious indulgence of the laws permitted him to receive, for their use, any future accessions of legacy or inheritance.[53] Melania contributed her plate, three hundred pounds' weight of silver, and Paula contracted an immense debt for the relief of their favourite monks, who kindly imparted the merits of their prayers and penance to a rich and liberal sinner.[54] Time continually increased, and accidents could seldom diminish, the estates of the popular monasteries, which spread over the adjacent country and cities: and, in the first century of their institution, the infidel Zosimus has maliciously observed, that, for the benefit of the poor, the Christian monks had reduced a great part of mankind to a state of beggary.[55] As long as they maintained their original fervour, they approved themselves, however, the faithful and benevolent stewards of the charity which was intrusted to their care. But their discipline was corrupted by prosperity: they gradually assumed the pride of wealth, and at last indulged the luxury of expense. Their public luxury might be excused by the magnificence of religious worship, and the decent motive of erecting durable habitations for an immortal society. But every age of the church has accused the licentiousness of the degenerate monks; who no longer remembered the object of their institution, embraced the vain and sensual pleasures of the world which they had renounced,[56] and scandalously abused the riches which had been acquired by the austere virtues of their founders.[57] Their natural descent, from such painful and dangerous virtue, to the common vices of humanity, will not, perhaps, excite much grief or indignation in the mind of a philosopher.

The lives of the primitive monks were consumed in penance and solitude, undisturbed by the various occupations which fill the time, and exercise the faculties, of reasonable, active, and social beings. Whenever they were permitted to step beyond the precincts of the monastery, two jealous companions were the mutual guards and spies of each other's actions; and, after their return, they were condemned to forget, or, at least, to suppress, whatever they had seen or heard in the world. Strangers, who professed the orthodox faith, were hospitably entertained in a separate apartment; but their dangerous conversation was restricted to some chosen elders of approved discretion and fidelity. Except in their presence, the monastic slave might not receive the visits of his friends or kindred; and it was deemed highly meritorious, if he afflicted a tender sister, or an aged parent, by the obstinate refusal of a word or look.[58] The monks themselves passed their lives, without personal attachments, among a crowd which had been formed by accident, and was detained, in the same prison, by force or prejudice. Recluse fanatics have few ideas or sentiments to communicate: a special licence of the abbot regulated the time and duration of their familiar visits; and, at their silent meals, they were enveloped in their cowls, inaccessible, and almost invisible, to each other.[59] Study is the resource of solitude; but education had not prepared and qualified for any liberal studies the mechanics and peasants who filled the monastic communities. They might work; but the vanity of spiritual perfection was tempted to disdain the exercise of manual labour; and the industry must be faint and languid which is not excited by the sense of personal interest.

According to their faith and zeal, they might employ the day, which they passed in their cells, either in vocal or mental prayer: they assembled in the evening, and they were awakened in the night, for the public worship of the monastery. The precise moment was determined by the stars, which are seldom clouded in the serene sky of Egypt; and a rustic horn, or trumpet, the signal of devotion, twice interrupted the vast silence of the desert.[60] Even sleep, the last refuge of the unhappy, was rigorously measured: the vacant hours of the monk heavily rolled along, without business or pleasure; and, before the close of each day, he had repeatedly accused the tedious progress of the sun.[61] In this comfortless state, superstition still pursued and tormented her wretched votaries.[62] The repose which they had sought in the cloister was disturbed by tardy repentance, profane doubts, and guilty desires; and, while they considered each natural impulse as an unpardonable sin, they perpetually trembled on the edge of a flaming and bottomless abyss. From the painful struggles of disease and despair, these unhappy victims were sometimes relieved by madness or death; and, in the sixth century, a hospital was founded at Jerusalem for a small portion of the austere penitents who were deprived of their senses.[63] Their visions, before they attained this extreme and acknowledged term of frenzy, have afforded ample materials of supernatural history. It was their firm persuasion that the air which they breathed was peopled with invisible enemies; with innumerable demons, who watched every occasion, and assumed every form, to terrify, and above all to tempt, their unguarded virtue. The imagination, and even the senses, were deceived by the illusions of distempered fanaticism; and the hermit, whose midnight prayer was oppressed by involuntary slumber, might easily confound the phantoms of horror or delight which had occupied his sleeping and his waking dreams.[64]

The monks were divided into two classes: the *Coenobites*, who lived under a common and regular discipline; and the *Anachorets*, who indulged their unsocial, independent fanaticism.[65] The most devout, or the most ambitious, of the spiritual brethren renounced the convent, as they had renounced the world. The fervent monasteries of Egypt, Palestine, and Syria were surrounded by a *Laura*,[66] a distant circle of solitary cells; and the extravagant penance of the Hermits was stimulated by applause and emulation.[67] They sunk under the painful weight of crosses and chains; and their emaciated limbs were confined by collars, bracelets, gauntlets, and greaves of massy and rigid iron. All superfluous incumbrance of dress they contemptuously cast away; and some savage saints of both sexes have been admired, whose naked bodies were only covered by their long hair. They aspired to reduce themselves to the rude and miserable state in which the human brute is scarcely distinguished above his kindred animals; and the numerous sect of Anachorets derived their name from their humble practice of grazing in the fields of Mesopotamia with the common herd.[68] They often usurped the den of some wild beast whom they affected to resemble; they buried themselves in some gloomy cavern, which art or nature had scooped out of the rock; and the marble quarries of Thebais are still inscribed with the monuments of their penance.[69] The most perfect Hermits are supposed to have passed many days without food, many nights without sleep, and many years without speaking; and glorious was the *man* (I abuse that name) who contrived any cell, or seat, of a peculiar construction, which might expose him, in the most inconvenient posture, to the inclemency of the seasons.

Among these heroes of the monastic life, the name and genius of Simeon Stylites[70] have been immortalised by the singular invention of an aërial penance. At the age of thirteen the young Syrian deserted the profession of a shepherd, and threw himself into an austere monastery. After a long and painful novitiate, in which Simeon was repeatedly saved from pious suicide, he established his residence on a mountain, about thirty or forty miles to the east of Antioch. Within the space of a *mandra*, or circle of stones, to which he had attached himself by a ponderous chain, he ascended a column, which was successively raised from the height of nine, to that of sixty, feet from the ground.[71] In this last and lofty station, the Syrian Anachoret resisted the heat of thirty summers, and the cold of as many winters. Habit and exercise instructed him to maintain his dangerous situation without fear or giddiness, and successively to assume the different postures of devotion. He sometimes prayed in an erect attitude, with his outstretched arms in the figure of a cross; but his most familiar practice was that of bending his meagre skeleton from the forehead to the feet; and a curious spectator, after numbering twelve hundred and forty-four repetitions, at length desisted from the endless account. The progress of an ulcer in his thigh[72] might shorten, but it could not disturb, this *celestial* life; and the patient Hermit expired without descending from his column. A prince, who should capriciously inflict such tortures, would be deemed a tyrant; but it would surpass the power of a tyrant to impose a long and miserable existence on the reluctant victims of his cruelty. This voluntary martyrdom must have gradually destroyed the sensibility both of the mind and body; nor can it be presumed that the fanatics who torment themselves are susceptible of any lively affection for the rest of mankind. A cruel, unfeeling temper has distinguished the monks of every age and country: their stern indifference, which is seldom mollified by personal friendship, is inflamed by religious hatred; and their merciless zeal has strenuously administered the holy office of the Inquisition.

The monastic saints, who excite only the contempt and pity of a philosopher, were respected and almost adored by the prince and people. Successive crowds of pilgrims from Gaul and India saluted the divine pillar of Simeon; the tribes of Saracens disputed in arms the honour of his benediction; the queens of Arabia and Persia gratefully confessed his supernatural virtue; and the angelic Hermit was consulted by the younger Theodosius in the most important concerns of the church and state. His remains were transported from the mountain of Telenissa, by a solemn procession of the patriarch, the master-general of the East, six bishops, twenty-one counts or tribunes, and six thousand soldiers; and Antioch revered his bones as her glorious ornament and impregnable defence. The fame of the apostles and martyrs was gradually eclipsed by these recent and popular Anachorets; the Christian world fell prostrate before their shrines; and the miracles ascribed to their relics exceeded, at least in number and duration, the spiritual exploits of their lives. But the golden legend of their lives[73] was embellished by the artful credulity of their interested brethren; and a believing age was easily persuaded that the slightest caprice of an Egyptian or a Syrian monk had been sufficient to interrupt the eternal laws of the universe. The favourites of Heaven were accustomed to cure inveterate diseases with a touch, a word, or a distant message; and to expel the most obstinate demons from the souls or bodies which they possessed. They familiarly accosted, or imperiously commanded, the lions and serpents of the desert; infused vegetation into a sapless trunk; suspended iron on the surface of the water; passed the Nile on the back of a crocodile; and refreshed themselves in a fiery furnace. These extravagant tales, which display the fiction, without the genius, of poetry, have seriously affected the reason, the faith, and the morals of the Christians. Their credulity debased and vitiated the faculties of the mind: they corrupted the evidence of history; and superstition gradually extinguished the hostile light of philosophy and science. Every mode of religious worship which had been practised by the saints, every mysterious doctrine which they believed, was fortified by the sanction of divine revelation, and all the manly virtues were oppressed by the servile and pusillanimous reign of the monks. If it be possible to measure the interval between the philosophic writings of Cicero and the sacred legend of Theodoret, between the character of Cato and that of Simeon, we may appreciate the memorable revolution which was accomplished in the Roman empire within a period of five hundred years.

II. The progress of Christianity has been marked by two glorious and decisive victories: over the learned and luxurious citizens of the Roman empire; and over the warlike barbarians of Scythia and Germany, who subverted the empire and embraced the religion of the Romans. The Goths were the foremost of these savage proselytes; and the nation was indebted for its conversion to a countryman, or at least to a subject, worthy to be ranked among the inventors of useful arts who have deserved the remembrance and gratitude of posterity. A great number of Roman provincials had been led away into captivity by the Gothic bands who ravaged Asia in the time of Gallienus; and of these captives many were Christians, and several belonged to the ecclesiastical order. Those involuntary missionaries, dispersed as slaves in the villages of Dacia, successively laboured for the salvation of their masters. The seeds which they planted of the evangelic doctrine were gradually propagated; and before the end of a century the pious work was achieved by the labours of Ulphilas, whose ancestors had been transported beyond the Danube from a small town of Cappadocia.

Ulphilas, the bishop and apostle of the

Goths,[74] acquired their love and reverence by his blameless life and indefatigable zeal, and they received with implicit confidence the doctrines of truth and virtue which he preached and practised. He executed the arduous task of translating the Scriptures into their native tongue, a dialect of the German or Teutonic language; but he prudently suppressed the four books of Kings, as they might tend to irritate the fierce and sanguinary spirit of the barbarians. The rude, imperfect idiom of soldiers and shepherds, so ill qualified to communicate any spiritual ideas, was improved and modulated by his genius; and Ulphilas, before he could frame his version, was obliged to compose a new alphabet of twenty-four letters; four of which he invented to express the peculiar sounds that were unknown to the Greek and Latin pronunciation.[75] But the prosperous state of the Gothic church was soon afflicted by war and intestine discord, and the chieftains were divided by religion as well as by interest. Fritigern, the friend of the Romans, became the proselyte of Ulphilas; while the haughty soul of Athanaric disdained the yoke of the empire and of the Gospel. The faith of the new converts was tried by the persecution which he excited. A waggon, bearing aloft the shapeless image of Thor, perhaps, or of Woden, was conducted in solemn procession through the streets of the camp, and the rebels who refused to worship the god of their fathers were immediately burnt with their tents and families. The character of Ulphilas recommended him to the esteem of the Eastern court, where he twice appeared as the minister of peace; he pleaded the cause of the distressed Goths, who implored the protection of Valens; and the name of *Moses* was applied to this spiritual guide, who conducted his people through the deep waters of the Danube to the Land of Promise.[76] The devout shepherds, who were attached to his person and tractable to his voice, acquiesced in their settlement at the foot of the Mæsian mountains, in a country of woodlands and pastures, which supported their flocks and herds, and enabled them to purchase the corn and wine of the more plentiful provinces. These harmless barbarians multiplied in obscure peace and the profession of Christianity.[77]

Their fiercer brethren, the formidable Visigoths, universally adopted the religion of the Romans, with whom they maintained a perpetual intercourse of war, of friendship, or of conquest. In their long and victorious march from the Danube to the Atlantic Ocean they converted their allies; they educated the rising generation; and the devotion which reigned in the camp of Alaric, or the court of Toulouse, might edify or disgrace the palaces of Rome and Constantinople.[78] During the same period Christianity was embraced by almost all the barbarians who established their kingdoms on the ruins of the Western empire; the Burgundians in Gaul, the Suevi in Spain, the Vandals in Africa, the Ostrogoths in Pannonia, and the various bands of mercenaries that raised Odoacer to the throne of Italy. The Franks and the Saxons still persevered in the errors of Paganism; but the Franks obtained the monarchy of Gaul by their submission to the example of Clovis; and the Saxon conquerors of Britain were reclaimed from their savage superstition by the missionaries of Rome. These barbarian proselytes displayed an ardent and successful zeal in the propagation of the faith. The Merovingian kings and their successors, Charlemagne and the Othos, extended by their laws and victories the dominion of the cross. England produced the apostle of Germany; and the evangelic light was gradually diffused from the neighbourhood of the Rhine to the nations of the Elbe, the Vistula, and the Baltic.[79]

The different motives which influenced the reason or the passions of the barbarian converts cannot easily be ascertained. They were often capricious and accidental; a dream, an omen, the report of a miracle, the example of some priest or hero, the charms of a believing wife, and, above all, the fortunate event of a prayer or vow which, in a moment of danger, they had addressed to the God of the Christians.[80] The early prejudices of education were insensibly erased by the habits of frequent and familiar society; the moral precepts of the Gospel were protected by the extravagant virtues of the monks; and a spiritual theology was supported by the visible power of relics, and the pomp of religious worship. But the rational and ingenious mode of persuasion which a Saxon bishop[81] suggested to a popular saint might sometimes be employed by the missionaries who laboured for the conversion of infidels. "Admit," says the sagacious disputant, "whatever they are pleased to assert of the fabulous and carnal genealogy of their gods and goddesses, who are propagated from each other. From this principle deduce their imperfect nature and human infirmities, the assurance they were *born*, and the probability that they will *die*. At what time, by what means, from what cause, were the eldest of the gods or goddesses produced? Do they still continue, or have they ceased, to propagate? If they have ceased, summon your antagonist to declare the reason of this strange alteration. If they still continue, the number of the gods must become infinite; and shall we not risk, by the indiscreet worship of some impotent deity, to excite the resentment of his jealous superior? The visible heavens and earth, the whole system of the universe, which may be conceived by the mind, is it created or eternal? If created, how or where could the gods themselves exist before the creation? If eternal, how could they assume the empire of an independent and pre-existing world? Urge these arguments with temper and moderation; insinuate, at seasonable intervals, the truth and beauty of the Christian revelation; and endeavour to make the unbelievers ashamed without making them angry." This metaphysical reasoning, too refined perhaps for the barbarians of Germany, was fortified by the grosser weight of authority and popular consent. The advantage of temporal prosperity had deserted the Pagan cause and passed over to the service of Christianity. The Romans themselves, the most powerful and enlightened nation of the globe, had renounced their ancient superstition; and if the ruin of their empire seemed to accuse the efficacy of the new faith, the disgrace was already retrieved by the conversion of the victorious Goths. The valiant and fortunate barbarians who subdued the provinces of the West successively received and reflected the same edifying example. Before the age of Charlemagne, the Christian nations of Europe might exult in the exclusive possession of the temperate climates, of the fertile lands which produced corn, wine, and oil; while the savage idolaters and their helpless idols were confined to the extremities of the earth, the dark and frozen regions of the North.[82]

Christianity, which opened the gates of Heaven to the barbarians, introduced an important change in their moral and political condition. They received, at the same time, the use of letters, so essential to a religion whose doctrines are contained in a sacred book; and while they studied the divine truth, their minds were insensibly enlarged by the distant view of history, of nature, of the arts, and of society. The version of the Sciptures into their native tongue, which had facilitated their conversion, must excite, among their clergy, some curiosity to read the original text, to understand the sacred liturgy of the church, and to examine, in the writings of the fathers, the chain of ecclesiastical tradition. These spiritual gifts were preserved in the Greek and Latin languages, which conceal-ed the inestimable monuments of ancient learning. The immortal productions of Virgil, Cicero, and Livy, which were accessible to the Christian barbarians, maintained a silent intercourse between the reign of Augustus and the times of Clovis and Charlemagne. The emulation of mankind was encouraged by the remembrance of a more perfect state; and the flame of science was secretly kept alive, to warm and enlighten the mature age of the Western world. In the most corrupt state of Christianity the barbarians might learn justice from the *law*, and mercy from the *gospel*; and if the knowledge of their duty was insufficient to guide their actions or to regulate their passions, they were sometimes restrained by conscience, and frequently punished by remorse. But the direct authority of religion was less effectual than the holy communion, which united them with their Christian brethren in spiritual friendship. The influence of these sentiments contributed to secure their fidelity in the service or the alliance of the Romans, to alleviate the horrors of war, to moderate the insolence of conquest, and to preserve, in the downfall of the empire, a permanent respect for the name and institutions of Rome. In the days of Paganism the priests of Gaul and Germany reigned over the people, and controlled the jurisdiction of the magistrates; and the zealous proselytes transferred an equal, or more ample, measure of devout obedience to the pontiffs of the Christian faith. The sacred character of the bishops was supported by their temporal possessions; they obtained an honourable seat in the legislative assemblies of soldiers and freemen; and it was their interest, as well as their duty, to mollify by peaceful counsels the fierce spirit of the barbarians. The perpetual correspondence of the Latin clergy, the frequent pilgrimages to Rome and Jerusalem, and the growing authority of the popes, cemented the union of the Christian republic, and gradually produced the similar manners and common jurisprudence which have distinguished from the rest of mankind the independent, and even hostile, nations of modern Europe.

But the operation of these causes was checked and retarded by the unfortunate accident which infused a deadly poison into the cup of salvation. Whatever might be the early sentiments of Ulphilas, his connections with the empire and the church were formed during the reign of Arianism. The apostle of the Goths subscribed the creed of Rimini; professed with freedom, and perhaps with sincerity, that the Son was not equal or consubstantial to the FATHER;[83] communicated these errors to the clergy and people; and infected the barbaric world with an heresy[84] which the great Theodosius proscribed and extinguished among the Romans. The temper and understanding of the new proselytes were not adapted to metaphysical subtleties; but they strenuously maintained what they had piously received as the pure and genuine doctrines of Christianity. The advantage of preaching and expounding the Scriptures in the Teutonic language promoted the apostolic labours of Ulphilas and his successors; and they ordained a competent number of bishops and presbyters for the instruction of the kindred tribes. The Ostrogoths, the Burgundians, the Suevi, and the Vandals, who had listened to the eloquence of the Latin clergy,[85] preferred the more intelligible lessons of their domestic teachers; and Arianism was adopted as the national faith of the warlike converts who were seated on the ruins of the Western empire. This irreconcilable difference of religion was a perpetual source of jealousy and hatred; and the reproach of *Barbarian* was embittered by the more odious epithet of *Heretic.* The heroes of the North, who had submitted with some reluctance to believe that all their ancestors were in hell,[86] were astonished and exasperated to learn that they themselves had only changed the mode of their eternal condemnation. Instead of the smooth applause which Christian kings are accustomed to expect from their loyal prelates, the orthodox bishops and their clergy were in a state of opposition to the Arian courts; and their indiscreet opposition frequently became criminal, and might sometimes be dangerous.[87] The pulpit, that safe and sacred organ of sedition, resounded with the names of Pharaoh and Holofernes;[88] the public discontent was inflamed by the hope or promise of a glorious deliverance; and the seditious saints were tempted to promote the accomplishment of their own predictions. Notwithstanding these provocations, the catholics of Gaul, Spain, and Italy enjoyed, under the reign of the Arians, the free and peaceful exercise of their religion. Their haughty masters respected the zeal of a numerous people, resolved to die at the foot of their altars, and the example of their devout constancy was admired and imitated by the barbarians themselves. The conquerors evaded, however, the disgraceful reproach, or confession, of fear, by attributing their toleration to the liberal motives of reason and humanity; and while they affected the language, they imperceptibly imbibed the spirit, of genuine Christianity.

The peace of the church was sometimes interrupted. The catholics were indiscreet, the barbarians were impatient; and the partial acts of severity or injustice, which had been recommended by the Arian clergy, were exaggerated by the orthodox writers. The guilt of persecution may be imputed to Euric, king of the Visigoths who suspended the exercise of ecclesiastical, or, at least, of episcopal functions, and punished the popular bishops of Aquitain with imprisonment, exile, and confiscation.[89] But the cruel and absurd enterprise of subduing the minds of a whole people was undertaken by the Vandals alone. Genseric himself, in his early youth, had renounced the orthodox communion; and the apostate could neither grant nor expect a sincere forgiveness. He was exasperated to find that the Africans, who had fled before him in the field, still presumed to dispute his will in synods and churches; and his ferocious mind was incapable of fear or of compassion. His catholic subjects were oppressed by intolerant laws and arbitrary punishments. The language of Genseric was furious and formidable; the knowledge of his intentions might justify the most unfavourable interpretation of his actions; and the Arians were reproached with the frequent executions which stained the palace and the dominions of the tyrant. Arms and ambition were, however, the ruling passions of the monarch of the sea. But Hunneric, his inglorious son, who seemed to inherit only his vices, tormented the catholics with the same unrelenting fury which had been fatal to his brother, his nephews, and the friends and favourites of his father; and even to the Arian patriarch, who was inhumanly burnt alive in the midst of Carthage. The religious war was preceded and prepared by an insidious truce; persecution was made the serious and important business of the Vandal court; and the loathsome disease which hastened the death of Hunneric revenged the injuries, without contributing to the deliverance, of the church. The throne of Africa was successively filled by the two nephews of Hunneric; by Gundamund, who reigned about twelve, and by Thrasimund, who governed the nation above twenty-seven, years. Their administration was hostile and oppressive to the orthodox party. Gundamund appeared to emulate, or even to surpass, the cruelty of his uncle; and if at length he relented, if he recalled the bishops, and restored the freedom of Athanasian worship, a premature death intercepted the benefits of his tardy clemency. His brother, Thrasimund, was the greatest and most accomplished of the Vandal kings, whom he excelled in beauty, prudence, and magnanimity of soul. But this magnanimous character was degraded by his intolerant zeal and deceitful clemency. Instead of threats and tortures, he employed the gentle, but efficacious, powers of seduction. Wealth, dignity, and the royal favour were the liberal rewards of apostacy; the catholics who had violated the laws might purchase their pardon by the renunciation of their faith; and whenever Thrasimund mediated any rigorous measure, he patiently waited till the indiscretion of his adversaries furnished him with a specious opportunity. Bigotry was his last sentiment in the hour of death; and he exacted from his successor a solemn oath that he would never tolerate the sectaries of Athanasius. But his successor, Hilderic, the gentle son of the savage Hunneric, preferred the duties of humanity and justice to the vain obligation of an impious oath; and his accession was gloriously marked by the restoration of peace and universal freedom. The throne of that virtuous, though feeble, monarch was usurped by his cousin Gelimer, a zealous Arian: but the Vandal kingdom, before he could enjoy or abuse his power, was subverted by the arms of Belisarius; and the orthodox party retaliated the injuries which they had endured.[90]

The passionate declamations of the catholics, the sole historians of this persecution, cannot afford any distinct series of causes and events, any impartial view of characters or counsels; but the most remarkable circumstances that deserve either credit or notice may be referred to the following heads: I. In the original law, which is still extant,[91] Hunneric expressly declares, and the declaration appears to be correct, that he had faithfully transcribed the regulations and penalties of the Imperial edicts against the heretical congregations, the clergy, and the people, who dissented from the established religion. If the rights of conscience had been understood, the catholics must have condemned their past conduct, or acquiesced in their actual sufferings. But they still persisted to refuse the indulgence which they claimed. While they trembled under the lash of persecution, they praised the *laudable* severity of Hunneric himself, who burnt or banished great numbers of Manichæans;[92] and they rejected with horror the ignominious compromise that the disciples of Arius and of Athanasius should enjoy a reciprocal and similar toleration in the territories of the Romans and in those of the Vandals.[93] II. The practice of a conference,

which the catholics had so frequently used to insult and punish their obstinate antagonists, was retorted against themselves.[94] At the command of Hunneric, four hundred and sixty-six orthodox bishops assembled at Carthage; but when they were admitted into the hall of audience, they had the mortification of beholding the Arian Cyrila, exalted on the patriarchal throne. The disputants were separated, after the mutual and ordinary reproaches of noise and silence, of delay and precipitation, of military force and of popular clamour. One martyr and one confessor were selected among the catholic bishops; twenty-eight escaped by flight, and eighty-eight by conformity; forty-six were sent into Corsica to cut timber for the royal navy; and three hundred and two were banished to the different parts of Africa, exposed to the insults of their enemies, and carefully deprived of all the temporal and spiritual comforts of life.[95] The hardships of ten years' exile must have reduced their numbers; and if they had complied with the law of Thrasimund, which prohibited any episcopal consecrations, the orthodox church of Africa must have expired with the lives of its actual members. They disobeyed; and their disobedience was punished by a second exile of two hundred and twenty bishops into Sardinia, where they languished fifteen years, till the accession of the gracious Hilderic.[96] The two islands were judiciously chosen by the malice of their Arian tyrants. Seneca, from his own experience, has deplored and exaggerated the miserable state of Corsica,[97] and the plenty of Sardinia was overbalanced by the unwholesome quality of the air.[98] III. The zeal of Genseric and his successors for the conversion of the catholics must have rendered them still more jealous to guard the purity of the Vandal faith. Before the churches were finally shut, it was a crime to appear in a barbarian dress; and those who presumed to neglect the royal mandate were rudely dragged backwards by their long hair.[99] The palatine officers, who refused to profess the religion of their prince, were ignominiously stripped of their honours and employments; banished to Sardinia and Sicily; or condemned to the servile labours of slaves and peasants in the fields of Utica. In the districts which had been peculiarly allotted to the Vandals, the exercise of the catholic worship was more strictly prohibited; and severe penalties were denounced against the guilt both of the missionary and the proselyte. By these arts the faith of the barbarians was preserved, and their zeal was inflamed;

they discharged with devout fury the office of spies, informers, or executioners; and whenever their cavalry took the field, it was the favourite amusement of the march to defile the churches and to insult the clergy of the adverse faction.[100] IV. The citizens who had been educated in the luxury of the Roman province were delivered, with exquisite cruelty, to the Moors of the desert. A venerable train of bishops, presbyters, and deacons, with a faithful crowd of four thousand and ninety-six persons, whose guilt is not precisely ascertained, were torn from their native homes by the command of Hunneric. During the night they were confined, like a herd of cattle, amidst their own ordure: during the day they pursued their march over the burning sands; and if they fainted under the heat and fatigue, they were goaded or dragged along till they expired in the hands of their tormentors.[101] These unhappy exiles, when they reached the Moorish huts, might excite the compassion of a people whose native humanity was neither improved by reason nor corrupted by fanaticism: but if they escaped the dangers, they were condemned to share the distress, of a savage life. V. It is incumbent on the authors of persecution previously to reflect whether they are determined to support it in the last extreme. They excite the flame which they strive to extinguish; and it soon becomes necessary to chastise the contumacy, as well as the crime, of the offender. The fine, which he is unable or unwilling to discharge, exposes his person to the severity of the law; and his contempt of lighter penalties suggests the use and propriety of capital punishment. Through the veil of fiction and declamation we may clearly perceive that the catholics, more especially under the reign of Hunneric, endured the most cruel and ignominious treatment.[102] Respectable citizens, noble matrons, and consecrated virgins were stripped naked and raised in the air by pulleys, with a weight suspended at their feet. In this painful attitude their naked bodies were torn with scourges, or burnt in the most tender parts with red-hot plates of iron. The amputation of the ears, the nose, the tongue, and the right hand was inflicted by the Arians; and although the precise number cannot be defined, it is evident that many persons, among whom a bishop,[103] and a proconsul,[104] may be named, were entitled to the crown of martyrdom. The same honour has been ascribed to the memory of Count Sebastian, who professed the Nicene creed with unshaken constancy; and Genseric might detest as an heretic the brave and ambi-

tious fugitive whom he dreaded as a rival.[105] VI. A new mode of conversion, which might subdue the feeble and alarm the timorous, was employed by the Arian ministers. They imposed, by fraud or violence, the rites of baptism; and punished the apostacy of the catholics, if they disclaimed this odious and profane ceremony, which scandalously violated the freedom of the will and the unity of the sacrament.[106] The hostile sects had formerly allowed the validity of each other's baptism; and the innovation, so fiercely maintained by the Vandals, can be imputed only to the example and advice of the Donatists. VII. The Arian clergy surpassed in religious cruelty the king and his Vandals; but they were incapable of cultivating the spiritual vineyard which they were so desirous to possess. A patriarch[107] might seat himself on the throne of Carthage; some bishops, in the principal cities, might usurp the place of their rivals; but the smallness of their numbers, and their ignorance of the Latin language,[108] disqualified the barbarians for the ecclesiastical ministry of a great church; and the Africans, after the loss of their orthodox pastors, were deprived of the public exercise of Christianity. VIII. The emperors were the natural protectors of the Homoousian doctrine; and the faithful people of Africa, both as Romans, and as catholics, preferred their lawful sovereignty to the usurpation of the barbarous heretics. During an interval of peace and friendship Hunneric restored the cathedral of Carthage, at the intercession of Zeno, who reigned in the East, and of Placidia, the daughter and relict of emperors and the sister of the queen of the Vandals.[109] But this decent regard was of short duration; and the haughty tyrant displayed his contempt for the religion of the empire by studiously arranging the bloody images of persecution in all the principal streets through which the Roman ambassador must pass in his way to the palace.[110] An oath was required from the bishops who were assembled at Carthage, that they would support the succession of his son Hilderic, and that they would renounce all foreign or *transmarine* correspondence. This engagement, consistent, as it should seem, with their moral and religious duties, was refused by the more sagacious members[111] of the assembly. Their refusal, faintly coloured by the pretence that it is unlawful for a Christian to swear, must provoke the suspicions of a jealous tyrant.

The catholics, oppressed by royal and military force, were far superior to their adversaries in numbers and learning. With the same weapons which the Greek[112] and Latin fathers had already provided for the Arian controversy, they repeatedly silenced or vanquished the fierce and illiterate successors of Ulphilas. The consciousness of their own superiority might have raised them above the arts and passions of religious warfare. Yet, instead of assuming such honourable pride, the orthodox theologians were tempted, by the assurance of impunity, to compose fictions which must be stigmatised with the epithets of fraud and forgery. They ascribed their own polemical works to the most venerable names of Christian antiquity; the characters of Athanasius and Augustin were awkwardly personated by Vigilius and his disciples;[113] and the famous creed, which so clearly expounds the mysteries of the Trinity and the Incarnation, is deduced, with strong probability, from this African school.[114] Even the Scriptures themselves were profaned by their rash and sacrilegious hands. The memorable text which asserts the unity of the THREE who bear witness in heaven[115] is condemned by the universal silence of the orthodox fathers, ancient versions, and authentic manuscripts.[116] It was first alleged by the catholic bishops whom Hunneric summoned to the conference of Carthage.[117] An allegorical interpretation, in the form perhaps of a marginal note, invaded the text of the Latin Bibles which were renewed and corrected in a dark period of ten centuries.[118] After the invention of printing,[119] the editors of the Greek Testament yielded to their own prejudices, or those of the times;[120] and the pious fraud, which was embraced with equal zeal at Rome and at Geneva, has been infinitely multiplied in every country and every language of modern Europe.

The example of fraud must excite suspicion: and the specious miracles by which the African catholics have defended the truth and justice of their cause may be ascribed, with more reason, to their own industry than to the visible protection of Heaven. Yet the historian who views this religious conflict with an impartial eye may condescend to mention *one* preternatural event, which will edify the devout and surprise the incredulous. Tipasa,[121] a maritime colony of Mauritania, sixteen miles to the east of Cæsarea, had been distinguished in every age by the orthodox zeal of its inhabitants. They had braved the fury of the Donatists;[122] they resisted or eluded the tyranny of the Arians. The town was deserted on the approach of an heretical bishop: most of the inhabitants who could procure ships passed over to the coast of Spain; and

the unhappy remnant, refusing all communion with the usurper, still presumed to hold their pious, but illegal, assemblies. Their disobedience exasperated the cruelty of Hunneric. A military count was despatched from Carthage to Tipasa: he collected the catholics in the Forum, and, in the presence of the whole province, deprived the guilty of their right hands and their tongues. But the holy confessors continued to speak without tongues; and this miracle is attested by Victor, an African bishop, who published an history of the persecution within two years after the event.[123] "If any one," says Victor, "should doubt of the truth, let him repair to Constantinople, and listen to the clear and perfect language of Restitutus, the subdeacon, one of these glorious sufferers, who is now lodged in the palace of the emperor Zeno, and is respected by the devout empress." At Constantinople we are astonished to find a cool, a learned, and unexceptionable witness, without interest, and without passion. Æneas of Gaza, a Platonic philosopher, has accurately described his own observations on these African sufferers. "I saw them myself: I heard them speak: I diligently inquired by what means such an articulate voice could be formed without any organ of speech: I used my eyes to examine the report of my ears: I opened their mouth, and saw that the whole tongue had been completely torn away by the roots; an operation which the physicians generally suppose to be mortal."[124] The testimony of Æneas of Gaza might be confirmed by the superfluous evidence of the emperor Justinian, in a perpetual edict; of Count Marcellinus, in his Chronicle of the times; and of pope Gregory the First, who had resided at Constantinople as the minister of the Roman pontiff.[125] They all lived within the compass of a century; and they all appeal to their personal knowledge or the public notoriety for the truth of a miracle which was repeated in several instances, displayed on the greatest theatre of the world, and submitted during a series of years to the calm examination of the senses. This supernatural gift of the African confessors, who spoke without tongues, will command the assent of those, and of those only, who already believe that their language was pure and orthodox. But the stubborn mind of an infidel is guarded by secret, incurable suspicion; and the Arian, or Socinian, who has seriously rejected the doctrine of the Trinity, will not be shaken by the most plausible evidence of an Athanasian miracle.

The Vandals and the Ostrogoths persevered

in the profession of Arianism till the final ruin of the kingdoms which they had founded in Africa and Italy. The barbarians of Gaul submitted to the orthodox dominion of the Franks; and Spain was restored to the catholic church by the voluntary conversion of the Visigoths.

This salutary revolution[126] was hastened by the example of a royal martyr, whom our calmer reason may style an ungrateful rebel. Leovigild, the Gothic monarch of Spain, deserved the respect of his enemies and the love of his subjects: the catholics enjoyed a free toleration, and his Arian synods attempted, without much success, to reconcile their scruples by abolishing the unpopular rite of a *second* baptism. His eldest son Hermenegild, who was invested by his father with the royal diadem and the fair principality of Bætica, contracted an honourable and orthodox alliance with a Merovingian princess, the daughter of Sigebert, king of Austrasia, and of the famous Brunechild. The beauteous Ingundis, who was no more than thirteen years of age, was received, beloved, and persecuted in the Arian court of Toledo; and her religious constancy was alternately assaulted with blandishments and violence by Goisvintha, the Gothic queen, who abused the double claim of maternal authority.[127] Incensed by her resistance, Goisvintha seized the catholic princess by her long hair, inhumanly dashed her against the ground, kicked her till she was covered with blood, and at last gave orders that she should be stripped and thrown into a basin or fishpond.[128] Love and honour might excite Hermenegild to resent this injurious treatment of his bride; and he was gradually persuaded that Ingundis suffered for the cause of divine truth. Her tender complaints, and the weighty arguments of Leander, archbishop of Seville, accomplished his conversion; and the heir of the Gothic monarchy was initiated in the Nicene faith by the solemn rites of confirmation.[129] The rash youth, inflamed by zeal, and perhaps by ambition, was tempted to violate the duties of a son and a subject; and the catholics of Spain, although they could not complain of persecution, applauded his pious rebellion against an heretical father. The civil war was protracted by the long and obstinate sieges of Merida, Cordova, and Seville, which had strenuously espoused the party of Hermenegild. He invited the orthodox barbarians, the Suevi, and the Franks, to the destruction of his native land: he solicited the dangerous aid of the Romans, who possessed Africa and a part of the Spanish coast; and his holy ambassador, the archbishop Leander, effectually negotiated in person with the Byzantine court. But the hopes of the catholics were crushed by the active diligence of a monarch who commanded the troops and treasures of Spain; and the guilty Hermenegild, after his vain attempts to resist or to escape, was compelled to surrender himself into the hands of an incensed father. Leovigild was still mindful of that sacred character; and the rebel, despoiled of the regal ornaments, was still permitted, in a decent exile, to profess the catholic religion. His repeated and unsuccessful treasons at length provoked the indignation of the Gothic king; and the sentence of death, which he pronounced with apparent reluctance, was privately executed in the tower of Seville. The inflexible constancy with which he refused to accept the Arian communion, as the price of his safety, may excuse the honours that have been paid to the memory of St. Hermenegild. His wife and infant son were detained by the Romans in ignominious captivity; and this domestic misfortune tarnished the glories of Leovigild, and embittered the last moments of his life.

His son and successor, Recared, the first catholic king of Spain, had imbibed the faith of his unfortunate brother, which he supported with more prudence and success. Instead of revolting against his father, Recared patiently expected the hour of his death. Instead of condemning his memory, he piously supposed that the dying monarch had abjured the errors of Arianism, and recommended to his son the conversion of the Gothic nation. To accomplish that salutary end, Recared convened an assembly of the Arian clergy and nobles, declared himself a catholic, and exhorted them to imitate the example of their prince. The laborious interpretation of doubtful texts, or the curious pursuit of metaphysical arguments, would have excited an endless controversy; and the monarch discreetly proposed to his illiterate audience two substantial and visible arguments—the testimony of Earth and of Heaven. The *Earth* had submitted to the Nicene synod: the Romans, the barbarians, and the inhabitants of Spain unanimously professed the same orthodox creed; and the Visigoths resisted, almost alone, the consent of the Christian world. A superstitious age was prepared to reverence, as the testimony of Heaven, the preternatural cures which were performed by the skill or virtue of the catholic clergy; the baptismal fonts of Osset in Bætica,[130] which were spontaneously replenished each year on the vigil of Easter;[131] and the miraculous shrine of St. Martin of

Tours, which had already converted the Suevic prince and people of Gallicia.[132] The catholic king encountered some difficulties on this important change of the national religion. A conspiracy, secretly fomented by the queen-dowager, was formed against his life; and two counts excited a dangerous revolt in the Narbonnese Gaul. But Recared disarmed the conspirators, defeated the rebels, and executed severe justice, which the Arians, in their turn, might brand with the reproach of persecution. Eight bishops, whose names betray their barbaric origin, abjured their errors; and all the books of Arian theology were reduced to ashes, with the house in which they had been purposely collected. The whole body of the Visigoths and Suevi were allured or driven into the pale of the catholic communion; the faith, at least of the rising generation, was fervent and sincere; and the devout liberality of the barbarians enriched the churches and monasteries of Spain. Seventy bishops, assembled in the council of Toledo, received the submission of their conquerors; and the zeal of the Spaniards improved the Nicene creed, by declaring the procession of the Holy Ghost from the Son, as well as from the Father; a weighty point of doctrine, which produced, long afterwards, the schism of the Greek and Latin churches.[133] The royal proselyte immediately saluted and consulted pope Gregory, surnamed the Great, a learned and holy prelate whose reign was distinguished by the conversion of heretics and infidels. The ambassadors of Recared respectfully offered on the threshold of the Vatican his rich presents of gold and gems; they accepted, as a lucrative exchange, the hairs of St. John the Baptist; a cross which enclosed a small piece of the true wood; and a key that contained some particles of iron which had been scraped from the chains of St. Peter.[134]

The same Gregory, the spiritual conqueror of Britain, encouraged the pious Theodelinda, queen of the Lombards, to propagate the Nicene faith among the victorious savages, whose recent Christianity was polluted by the Arian heresy. Her devout labours still left room for the industry and success of future missionaries, and many cities of Italy were still disputed by hostile bishops. But the cause of Arianism was gradually suppressed by the weight of truth, of interest, and of example; and the controversy, which Egypt had derived from the Platonic school, was terminated, after a war of three hundred years, by the final conversion of the Lombards of Italy.[135]

The first missionaries who preached the Gospel to the barbarians appealed to the evidence of reason, and claimed the benefit of toleration.[136] But no sooner had they established their spiritual dominion than they exhorted the Christian kings to extirpate, without mercy, the remains of Roman or barbaric superstition. The successors of Clovis inflicted one hundred lashes on the peasants who refused to destroy their idols; the crime of sacrificing to the demons was punished by the Anglo-Saxon laws with the heavier penalties of imprisonment and confiscation; and even the wise Alfred adopted, as an indispensable duty, the extreme rigour of the Mosaic institutions.[137] But the punishment and the crime were gradually abolished among a Christian people; the theological disputes of the schools were suspended by propitious ignorance; and the intolerant spirit which could find neither idolaters nor heretics, was reduced to the persecution of the Jews. That exiled nation had founded some synagogues in the cities of Gaul; but Spain, since the time of Hadrian, was filled with their numerous colonies.[138] The wealth which they accumulated by trade and the management of the finances invited the pious avarice of their masters; and they might be oppressed without danger, as they had lost the use, and even the remembrance, of arms. Sisebut, a Gothic king who reigned in the beginning of the seventh century, proceeded at once to the last extremes of persecution.[139] Ninety thousand Jews were compelled to receive the sacrament of baptism; the fortunes of the obstinate infidels were confiscated, their bodies were tortured, and it seems doubtful whether they were permitted to abandon their native country. The excessive zeal of the catholic king was moderated even by the clergy of Spain, who solemnly pronounced an inconsistent sentence: *that* the sacraments should not be forcibly imposed; but *that* the Jews who had been baptised should be constrained, for the honour of the church, to persevere in the external practice of a religion which they disbelieved and detested. Their frequent relapses provoked one of the successors of Sisebut to banish the whole nation from his dominions; and a council of Toledo published a decree that every Gothic king should swear to maintain this salutary edict. But the tyrants were unwilling to dismiss the victims whom they delighted to torture, or to deprive themselves of the industrious slaves over whom they might exercise a lucrative oppression. The Jews still continued in Spain, under the weight of the civil and ecclesiastical laws, which in the same country have been faithfully transcribed in the

Code of the Inquisition. The Gothic kings and bishops at length discovered that injuries will produce hatred, and that hatred will find the opportunity of revenge. A nation, the secret or professed enemies of Christianity, still multiplied in servitude and distress; and the intrigues of the Jews promoted the rapid success of the Arabian conquerors.[140]

As soon as the barbarians withdrew their powerful support, the unpopular heresy of Arius sunk into contempt and oblivion. But the Greeks still retained their subtle and loquacious disposition: the establishment of an obscure doctrine suggested new questions and new disputes; and it was always in the power of an ambitious prelate or a fanatic monk to violate the peace of the church, and perhaps of the empire. The historian of the empire may overlook those disputes which were confined to the obscurity of schools and synods. The Manichæans, who laboured to reconcile the religions of Christ and of Zoroaster, had secretly introduced themselves into the provinces: but these foreign sectaries were involved in the common disgrace of the Gnostics, and the Imperial laws were executed by the public hatred. The rational opinions of the Pelagians were propagated from Britain to Rome, Africa, and Palestine, and silently expired in a superstitious age. But the East was distracted by the Nestorian and Eutychian controversies, which attempted to explain the mystery of the incarnation, and hastened the ruin of Christianity in her native land. These controversies were first agitated under the reign of the younger Theodosius: but their important consequences extend far beyond the limits of the present volume. The metaphysical chain of argument, the contests of ecclesiastical ambition, and their political influence on the decline of the Byzantine empire, may afford an interesting and instructive series of history, from the general councils of Ephesus and Chalcedon to the conquest of the East by the successors of Mahomet.

CHAPTER XXXVIII

Reign and Conversion of Clovis. His Victories over the Alemanni, Burgundians, and Visigoths. Establishment of the French Monarchy in Gaul. Laws of the Barbarians. State of the Romans. The Visigoths of Spain. Conquest of Britain by the Saxons.

THE Gauls,[1] who impatiently supported the Roman yoke, received a memorable lesson from one of the lieutenants of Vespasian, whose weighty sense has been refined and expressed by the genius of Tacitus.[2] "The protection of the republic has delivered Gaul from internal discord and foreign invasions. By the loss of national independence you have acquired the name and privileges of Roman citizens. You enjoy, in common with ourselves, the permanent benefits of civil government; and your remote situation is less exposed to the accidental mischiefs of tyranny. Instead of exercising the rights of conquest, we have been contented to impose such tributes as are requisite for your own preservation. Peace cannot be secured without armies, and armies must be supported at the expense of the people. It is for your sake, not for our own, that we guard the barrier of the Rhine against the ferocious Germans, who have so often attempted, and who will always desire, to exchange the solitude of their woods and morasses for the wealth and fertility of Gaul. The fall of Rome would be fatal to the provinces, and you would be buried in the ruins of that mighty fabric which has been raised by the valour and wisdom of eight hundred years. Your imaginary freedom would be insulted and oppressed by a savage master, and the expulsion of the Romans would be succeeded by the eternal hostilities of the barbarian conquerors."[3] This salutary advice was accepted, and this strange prediction was accomplished. In the space of four hundred years the hardy Gauls, who had encountered the arms of Cæsar, were imperceptibly melted into the general mass of citizens and subjects: the Western empire was dissolved; and the Germans who had passed the Rhine fiercely contended for the possession of Gaul, and excited the contempt or abhorrence of its peaceful and polished inhabitants. With that conscious pride which the preeminence of knowledge and luxury seldom fails to inspire, they derided the hairy and gigantic savages of the North; their rustic manners, dissonant joy, voracious appetite, and their horrid appearance, equally disgusting to the sight and to the smell. The liberal studies were still cultivated in the schools of Autun and Bordeaux, and the language of Cicero and Virgil was familiar to the Gallic youth. Their ears were astonished by the harsh and unknown sounds of the Germanic dialect, and they ingeniously lamented that the trembling muses fled from the harmony of a Burgundian lyre. The Gauls were endowed with all the advantages of art and nature, but, as they wanted courage to defend them, they were justly condemned to obey, and even to flatter, the victorious barbarians by whose clemency they held their precarious fortunes and their lives.[4]

As soon as Odoacer had extinguished the Western empire, he sought the friendship of the most powerful of the barbarians. The new sovereign of Italy resigned to Euric, king of the Visigoths, all the Roman conquests beyond the Alps, as far as the Rhine and the Ocean;[5] and the senate might confirm this liberal gift with some ostentation of power, and without any real loss of revenue or dominion. The lawful pretensions of Euric were justified by ambition and success, and the Gothic nation might aspire under his command to the monarchy of Spain and Gaul. Arles and Marseilles surrendered to his arms: he oppressed the freedom of Auvergne, and the bishop condescended to purchase his recall from exile by a tribute of just but reluctant praise. Sidonius waited before the gates of the palace among a crowd of ambassadors and suppliants, and their various business at the court of Bordeaux attested the power and the renown of the king of the Visigoths. The Heruli of the distant ocean, who painted their naked bodies with its cærulean colour, implored his protection; and the Saxons respected the maritime provinces of a prince who was destitute of any naval force. The tall Burgundians submitted to his authority; nor did he restore the captive Franks till he had imposed on that fierce nation the terms of an unequal peace. The Vandals of Africa cultivated his useful friendship, and the Ostrogoths of Pannonia were supported by his powerful aid against the oppression of the neighbouring Huns. The North (such are the lofty strains of the poet) was agitated or appeased by the nod of Euric, the great king of Persia consulted the oracle of the West, and the aged god of the Tiber was protected by the swelling genius of the Garonne.[6] The fortune of nations has often depended on accidents; and France may ascribe her greatness to the premature death of the Gothic king at a time when his son Alaric

was a helpless infant, and his adversary Clovis[7] an ambitious and valiant youth.

While Childeric, the father of Clovis, lived an exile in Germany, he was hospitably entertained by the queen as well as by the king of the Thuringians. After his restoration Bafina escaped from her husband's bed to the arms of her lover, freely declaring that, if she had known a man wiser, stronger, or more beautiful than Childeric, that man should have been the object of her preference.[8] Clovis was the offspring of this voluntary union, and when he was no more than fifteen years of age he succeeded, by his father's death, to the command of the Salian tribe. The narrow limits of his kingdom[9] were confined to the island of the Batavians, with the ancient dioceses of Tournay and Arras;[10] and at the baptism of Clovis the number of his warriors could not exceed five thousand. The kindred tribes of the Franks who had seated themselves along the Belgic rivers, the Scheldt, the Meuse, the Moselle, and the Rhine, were governed by their independent kings of the Merovingian race—the equals, the allies, and sometimes the enemies, of the Salic prince. But the Germans, who obeyed in peace the hereditary jurisdiction of their chiefs, were free to follow the standard of a popular and victorious general; and the superior merit of Clovis attracted the respect and allegiance of the national confederacy. When he first took the field, he had neither gold and silver in his coffers, nor wine and corn in his magazines;[11] but he imitated the example of Cæsar, who in the same country had acquired wealth by the sword, and purchased soldiers with the fruits of conquest. After each successful battle or expedition the spoils were accumulated in one common mass; every warrior received his proportionable share, and the royal prerogative submitted to the equal regulations of military law. The untamed spirit of the barbarians was taught to acknowledge the advantages of regular discipline.[12] At the annual review of the month of March their arms were diligently inspected, and when they traversed a peaceful territory they were prohibited from touching a blade of grass. The justice of Clovis was inexorable, and his careless or disobedient soldiers were punished with instant death. It would be superfluous to praise the valour of a Frank, but the valour of Clovis was directed by cool and consummate prudence.[13] In all his transactions with mankind he calculated the weight of interest, of passion, and of opinion; and his measures were sometimes adapted to the sanguinary manners of the Germans, and sometimes moderated by the milder genius of Rome and Christianity. He was intercepted in the career of victory, since he died in the forty-fifth year of his age: but he had already accomplished, in a reign of thirty years, the establishment of the French monarchy in Gaul.

The first exploit of Clovis was the defeat of Syagrius, the son of Ægidius, and the public quarrel might on this occasion be inflamed by private resentment. The glory of the father still insulted the Merovingian race; the power of the son might excite the jealous ambition of the king of the Franks. Syagrius inherited, as a patrimonial estate, the city and diocese of Soissons: the desolate remnant of the second Belgic, Rheims and Troyes, Beauvais and Amiens, would naturally submit to the count or patrician;[14] and after the dissolution of the Western empire he might reign with the title, or at least with the authority, of king of the Romans.[15] As a Roman, he had been educated in the liberal studies of rhetoric and jurisprudence; but he was engaged by accident and policy in the familiar use of the Germanic idiom. The independent barbarians resorted to the tribunal of a stranger who possessed the singular talent of explaining, in their native tongue, the dictates of reason and equity. The diligence and affability of their judge rendered him popular, the impartial wisdom of his decrees obtained their voluntary obedience, and the reign of Syagrius over the Franks and Burgundians seemed to revive the original institution of civil society.[16] In the midst of these peaceful occupations Syagrius received, and boldly accepted, the hostile defiance of Clovis, who challenged his rival in the spirit, and almost in the language of chivalry, to appoint the day and the field[17] of battle. In the time of Cæsar, Soissons would have poured forth a body of fifty thousand horse; and such an army might have been plentifully supplied with shields, cuirasses, and military engines from the three arsenals or manufactures of the city.[18] But the courage and numbers of the Gallic youth were long since exhausted, and the loose bands of volunteers or mercenaries who marched under the standard of Syagrius were incapable of contending with the national valour of the Franks. It would be ungenerous, without some more accurate knowledge of his strength and resources, to condemn the rapid flight of Syagrius, who escaped after the loss of a battle to the distant court of Toulouse. The feeble minority of Alaric could not assist or protect an unfortunate fugitive; the pusillanimous[19] Goths were intimidated by the menaces of Clo-

vis: and the Roman *king*, after a short confinement, was delivered into the hands of the executioner. The Belgic cities surrendered to the king of the Franks, and his dominions were enlarged towards the east by the ample diocese of Tongres,[20] which Clovis subdued in the tenth year of his reign.

The name of the Alemanni has been absurdly derived from their imaginary settlement on the banks of the *Leman* lake.[21] That fortunate district, from the lake to Avenche and Mount Jura, was occupied by the Burgundians.[22] The northern parts of Helvetia had indeed been subdued by the ferocious Alemanni, who destroyed with their own hands the fruits of their conquest. A province, improved and adorned by the arts of Rome, was again reduced to a savage wilderness, and some vestige of the stately Vindonissa may still be discovered in the fertile and populous valley of the Aar.[23] From the source of the Rhine to its conflux with the Main and the Moselle, the formidable swarms of the Alemanni commanded either side of the river by the right of ancient possession or recent victory. They had spread themselves into Gaul over the modern provinces of Alsace and Lorraine; and their bold invasion of the kingdom of Cologne summoned the Salic prince to the defence of his Ripuarian allies. Clovis encountered the invaders of Gaul in the plain of Tolbiac, about twenty-four miles from Cologne, and the two fiercest nations of Germany were mutually animated by the memory of past exploits and the prospect of future greatness. The Franks after an obstinate struggle gave way, and the Alemanni, raising a shout of victory, impetuously pressed their retreat. But the battle was restored by the valour, the conduct, and perhaps by the piety, of Clovis; and the event of the bloody day decided for ever the alternative of empire or servitude. The last king of the Alemanni was slain in the field, and his people were slaughtered and pursued till they threw down their arms and yielded to the mercy of the conqueror. Without discipline it was impossible for them to rally: they had contemptuously demolished the walls and fortifications which might have protected their distress; and they were followed into the heart of their forests by an enemy not less active or intrepid than themselves. The great Theodoric congratulated the victory of Clovis, whose sister Albofleda the king of Italy had lately married; but he mildly interceded with his brother in favour of the suppliants and fugitives who had implored his protection. The Gallic territories which were possessed by the Alemanni became the prize of their conqueror; and the haughty nation, invincible or rebellious to the arms of Rome, acknowledged the sovereignty of the Merovingian kings, who graciously permitted them to enjoy their peculiar manners and institutions under the government of official, and, at length, of hereditary dukes. After the conquest of the Western provinces, the Franks alone maintained their ancient habitations beyond the Rhine. They gradually subdued and civilised the exhausted countries as far as the Elbe and the mountains of Bohemia, and the peace of Europe was secured by the obedience of Germany.[24]

Till the thirtieth year of his age Clovis continued to worship the gods of his ancestors.[25] His disbelief, or rather disregard of Christianity, might encourage him to pillage with less remorse the churches of an hostile territory: but his subjects of Gaul enjoyed the free exercise of religious worship, and the bishops entertained a more favourable hope of the idolater than of the heretics. The Merovingian prince had contracted a fortunate alliance with the fair Clotilda, the niece of the king of Burgundy, who in the midst of an Arian court was educated in the profession of the catholic faith. It was her interest as well as her duty to achieve the conversion[26] of a Pagan husband; and Clovis insensibly listened to the voice of love and religion. He consented (perhaps such terms had been previously stipulated) to the baptism of his eldest son; and though the sudden death of the infant excited some superstitious fears, he was persuaded a second time to repeat the dangerous experiment. In the distress of the battle of Tolbiac, Clovis loudly invoked the God of Clotilda and the Christians; and victory disposed him to hear with respectful gratitude the eloquent[27] Remigius,[28] bishop of Rheims, who forcibly displayed the temporal and spiritual advantages of his conversion. The king declared himself satisfied of the truth of the catholic faith; and the political reasons which might have suspended his public profession were removed by the devout or loyal acclamations of the Franks, who showed themselves alike prepared to follow their heroic leader to the field of battle or to the baptismal font. The important ceremony was performed in the cathedral of Rheims with every circumstance of magnificence and solemnity that could impress an awful sense of religion on the minds of its rude proselytes.[29] The new Constantine was immediately baptised with three thousand of his warlike subjects, and their example was imitated by the remainder of the

gentle barbarians, who, in obedience to the victorious prelate, adored the cross which they had burnt, and burnt the idols which they had formerly adored.[30] The mind of Clovis was susceptible of transient fervour: he was exasperated by the pathetic tale of the passion and death of Christ; and instead of weighing the salutary consequences of that mysterious sacrifice, he exclaimed with indiscreet fury, "Had I been present at the head of my valiant Franks, I would have revenged his injuries."[31] But the savage conqueror of Gaul was incapable of examining the proofs of a religion which depends on the laborious investigation of historic evidence and speculative theology. He was still more incapable of feeling the mild influence of the Gospel, which persuades and purifies the heart of a genuine convert. His ambitious reign was a perpetual violation of moral and Christian duties: his hands were stained with blood in peace as well as in war; and, as soon as Clovis had dismissed a synod of the Gallician church, he calmly assassinated *all* the princes of the Merovingian race.[32] Yet the king of the Franks might sincerely worship the Christian God as a Being more excellent and powerful than his national deities; and the signal deliverance and victory of Tolbiac encouraged Clovis to confide in the future protection of the Lord of Hosts. Martin, the most popular of the saints, had filled the Western world with the fame of those miracles which were incessantly performed at his holy sepulchre of Tours. His visible or invisible aid promoted the cause of a liberal and orthodox prince; and the profane remark of Clovis himself, that St. Martin was an expensive friend,[33] need not be interpreted as the symptom of any permanent or rational scepticism. But earth as well as heaven rejoiced in the conversion of the Franks. On the memorable day when Clovis ascended from the baptismal font, he alone in the Christian world deserved the name and prerogatives of a catholic king. The emperor Anastasius entertained some dangerous errors concerning the nature of the divine incarnation; and the barbarians of Italy, Africa, Spain, and Gaul were involved in the Arian heresy. The eldest, or rather the only son of the church, was acknowledged by the clergy as their lawful sovereign or glorious deliverer; and the arms of Clovis were strenuously supported by the zeal and favour of the catholic faction.[34]

Under the Roman empire the wealth and jurisdiction of the bishops, their sacred character and perpetual office, their numerous dependents, popular eloquence, and provincial assemblies had rendered them always respectable, and sometimes dangerous. Their influence was augmented with the progress of superstition; and the establishment of the French monarchy may, in some degree, be ascribed to the firm alliance of an hundred prelates, who reigned in the discontented or independent cities of Gaul. The slight foundations of the *Armorican* republic had been repeatedly shaken or overthrown; but the same people still guarded their domestic freedom; asserted the dignity of the Roman name; and bravely resisted the predatory inroads and regular attacks of Clovis, who laboured to extend his conquests from the Seine to the Loire. Their successful opposition introduced an equal and honourable union. The Franks esteemed the valour of the Armoricans;[35] and the Armoricans were reconciled by the religion of the Franks. The military force which had been stationed for the defence of Gaul consisted of one hundred different bands of cavalry or infantry; and these troops, while they assumed the title and privileges of Roman soldiers, were renewed by an incessant supply of the barbarian youth. The extreme fortifications and scattered fragments of the empire were still defended by their hopeless courage. But their retreat was intercepted, and their communication was impracticable: they were abandoned by the Greek princes of Constantinople, and they piously disclaimed all connection with the Arian usurpers of Gaul. They accepted, without shame or reluctance, the generous capitulation which was proposed by a catholic hero; and the spurious or legitimate progeny of the Roman legions was distinguished in the succeeding age by their arms, their ensigns, and their peculiar dress and institutions. But the national strength was increased by these powerful and voluntary accessions; and the neighbouring kingdoms dreaded the numbers as well as the spirit of the Franks. The reduction of the northern provinces of Gaul, instead of being decided by the chance of a single battle, appears to have been slowly effected by the gradual operation of war and treaty; and Clovis acquired each object of his ambition by such efforts or such concessions as were adequate to its real value. *His* savage character and the virtues of Henry IV. suggest the most opposite ideas of human nature; yet some resemblance may be found in the situation of two princes who conquered France by their valour, their policy, and the merits of a seasonable conversion.[36]

The kingdom of the Burgundians, which was defined by the course of two Gallic rivers, the Saone and the Rhône, extended from the forest of Vosges to the Alps and the sea of Marseilles.[37] The sceptre was in the hands of Gundobald. That valiant and ambitious prince had reduced the number of royal candidates by the death of two brothers, one of whom was the father of Clotilda;[38] but his imperfect prudence still permitted Godegesil, the youngest of his brothers, to possess the dependent principality of Geneva. The Arian monarch was justly alarmed by the satisfaction and the hopes which seemed to animate his clergy and people after the conversion of Clovis; and Gundobald convened at Lyons an assembly of his bishops, to reconcile, if it were possible, their religious and political discontents. A vain conference was agitated between the two factions. The Arians upbraided the catholics with the worship of three Gods: the catholics defended their cause by theological distinctions; and the usual arguments, objections, and replies were reverberated with obstinate clamour, till the king revealed his secret apprehensions by an abrupt but decisive question, which he addressed to the orthodox bishops: "If you truly profess the Christian religion, why do you not restrain the king of the Franks? He has declared war against me, and forms alliances with my enemies for my destruction. A sanguinary and covetous mind is not the symptom of a sincere conversion: let him show his faith by his works." The answer of Avitus, bishop of Vienne, who spoke in the name of his brethren, was delivered with the voice and countenance of an angel. "We are ignorant of the motives and intentions of the king of the Franks: but we are taught by Scripture that the kingdoms which abandon the divine laws are frequently subverted; and that enemies will arise on every side against those who have made God their enemy. Return, with thy people, to the law of God, and he will give peace and security to thy dominions." The king of Burgundy, who was not prepared to accept the condition which the catholics considered as essential to the treaty, delayed and dismissed the ecclesiastical conference, after reproaching his bishops, that Clovis, their friend and proselyte, had privately tempted the allegiance of his brother.[39]

The allegiance of his brother was already seduced; and the obedience of Godegesil, who joined the royal standard with the troops of Geneva, more effectually promoted the success of the conspiracy. While the Franks and Burgundians contended with equal valour, his seasonable desertion decided the event of the battle;

and as Gundobald was faintly supported by the disaffected Gauls, he yielded to the arms of Clovis, and hastily retreated from the field, which appears to have been situate between Langres and Dijon. He distrusted the strength of Dijon, a quadrangular fortress, encompassed by two rivers and by a wall thirty feet high and fifteen thick, with four gates and thirty-three towers:[40] he abandoned to the pursuit of Clovis the important cities of Lyons and Vienne; and Gundobald still fled with precipitation till he had reached Avignon, at the distance of two hundred and fifty miles from the field of battle. A long siege and an artful negotiation admonished the king of the Franks of the danger and difficulty of his enterprise. He imposed a tribute on the Burgundian prince, compelled him to pardon and reward his brother's treachery, and proudly returned to his own dominions with the spoils and captives of the southern provinces. This splendid triumph was soon clouded by the intelligence that Gundobald had violated his recent obligations, and that the unfortunate Godegesil, who was left at Vienne with a garrison of five thousand Franks,[41] had been besieged, surprised, and massacred by his inhuman brother. Such an outrage might have exasperated the patience of the most peaceful sovereign; yet the conqueror of Gaul dissembled the injury, released the tribute, and accepted the alliance and military service of the king of Burgundy. Clovis no longer possessed those advantages which had assured the success of the preceding war; and his rival, instructed by adversity, had found new resources in the affections of his people. The Gauls or Romans applauded the mild and impartial laws of Gundobald, which almost raised them to the same level with their conquerors. The bishops were reconciled and flattered by the hopes which he artfully suggested of his approaching conversion; and though he eluded their accomplishment to the last moment of his life, his moderation secured the peace and suspended the ruin of the kingdom of Burgundy.[42]

I am impatient to pursue the final ruin of that kingdom, which was accomplished under the reign of Sigismond, the son of Gundobald. The catholic Sigismond has acquired the honours of a saint and martyr;[43] but the hands of the royal saint were stained with the blood of his innocent son, whom he inhumanly sacrificed to the pride and resentment of a stepmother. He soon discovered his error, and bewailed the irreparable loss. While Sigismond embraced the corpse of the unfortunate youth, he received a severe admonition from one of his attendants: "It is not his situation, O king! it is thine which deserves pity and lamentation." The reproaches of a guilty conscience were alleviated, however, by his liberal donations to the monastery of Agaunum, or St. Maurice, in Vallais; which he himself had founded in honour of the imaginary martyrs of the Thebæan legion.[44] A full chorus of perpetual psalmody was instituted by the pious king; he assiduously practised the austere devotion of the monks; and it was his humble prayer that Heaven would inflict in this world the punishment of his sins. His prayer was heard: the avengers were at hand; and the provinces of Burgundy were overwhelmed by an army of victorious Franks. After the event of an unsuccessful battle, Sigismond, who wished to protract his life that he might prolong his penance, concealed himself in the desert in a religious habit till he was discovered and betrayed by his subjects, who solicited the favour of their new masters. The captive monarch, with his wife and two children, was transported to Orleans, and buried alive in a deep well by the stern command of the sons of Clovis, whose cruelty might derive some excuse from the maxims and examples of their barbarous age. Their ambition, which urged them to achieve the conquest of Burgundy, was inflamed or disguised by filial piety: and Clotilda, whose sanctity did not consist in the forgiveness of injuries, pressed them to revenge her father's death on the family of his assassin. The rebellious Burgundians, for they attempted to break their chains, were still permitted to enjoy their national laws under the obligation of tribute and military service; and the Merovingian princes peaceably reigned over a kingdom whose glory and greatness had been first overthrown by the arms of Clovis.[45]

The first victory of Clovis had insulted the honour of the Goths. They viewed his rapid progress with jealousy and terror; and the youthful fame of Alaric was oppressed by the more potent genius of his rival. Some disputes inevitably arose on the edge of their contiguous dominions; and after the delays of fruitless negotiation a personal interview of the two kings was proposed and accepted. This conference of Clovis and Alaric was held in a small island of the Loire, near Amboise. They embraced, familiarly conversed, and feasted together; and separated with the warmest professions of peace and brotherly love. But their apparent confidence concealed a dark suspicion of hostile and treacherous designs; and their mutual complaints solicited, eluded, and disclaimed a final arbitration. At Paris, which he already considered as his royal seat, Clovis declared to an assembly of the princes and warriors the pretence and the motive of a Gothic war. "It grieves me to see that the Arians still possess the fairest portion of Gaul. Let us march against them with the aid of God; and, having vanquished the heretics, we will possess and divide their fertile provinces."[46] The Franks, who were inspired by hereditary valour and recent zeal, applauded the generous design of their monarch; expressed their resolution to conquer or die, since death and conquest would be equally profitable; and solemnly protested that they would never shave their beards till victory should absolve them from that inconvenient vow. The enterprise was promoted by the public or private exhortations of Clotilda. She reminded her husband how effectually some pious foundation would propitiate the Deity and his servants: and the Christian hero, darting his battle-axe with a skilful and nervous hand, "There (said he), on that spot where my *Francisca*[47] shall fall, will I erect a church in honour of the holy apostles." This ostentatious piety confirmed and justified the attachment of the catholics, with whom he secretly corresponded; and their devout wishes were gradually ripened into a formidable conspiracy. The people of Aquitain was alarmed by the indiscreet reproaches of their Gothic tyrants, who justly accused them of preferring the dominion of the Franks; and their zealous adherent Quintianus, bishop of Rodez,[48] preached more forcibly in his exile than in his diocese. To resist these foreign and domestic enemies, who were fortified by the alliance of the Burgundians, Alaric collected his troops, far more numerous than the military powers of Clovis. The Visigoths resumed the exercise of arms, which they had neglected in a long and luxurious peace;[49] a select band of valiant and robust slaves attended their masters to the field;[50] and the cities of Gaul were compelled to furnish their doubtful and reluctant aid. Theodoric, king of the Ostrogoths, who reigned in Italy, had laboured to maintain the tranquillity of Gaul; and he assumed, or affected, for that purpose the impartial character of a mediator. But the sagacious monarch dreaded the rising empire of Clovis, and he was firmly engaged to support the national and religious cause of the Goths.

The accidental or artificial prodigies which adorned the expedition of Clovis were accepted, by a superstitious age, as the manifest declaration of the Divine favour. He marched from Paris; and as he proceeded with decent reverence through the holy diocese of Tours, his anxiety tempted him to consult the shrine of St. Martin, the sanctuary, and the oracle of Gaul. His messengers were instructed to remark the words of the Psalm which should happen to be chanted at the precise moment when they entered the church. Those words most fortunately expressed the valour and victory of the champions of Heaven, and the application was easily transferred to the new Joshua, the new Gideon, who went forth to battle against the enemies of the Lord.[51] Orleans secured to the Franks a bridge on the Loire; but, at the distance of forty miles from Poitiers, their progress was intercepted by an extraordinary swell of the river Vigenna or Vienne; and the opposite banks were covered by the encampment of the Visigoths. Delay must be always dangerous to barbarians, who consume the country through which they march; and had Clovis possessed leisure and materials, it might have been impracticable to construct a bridge, or to force a passage, in the face of a superior enemy. But the affectionate peasants, who were impatient to welcome their deliverer, could easily betray some unknown or unguarded ford: the merit of the discovery was enhanced by the useful interposition of fraud or fiction; and a white hart, of singular size and beauty, appeared to guide and animate the march of the catholic army. The counsels of the Visigoths were irresolute and distracted. A crowd of impatient warriors, presumptuous in their strength, and disdaining to fly before the robbers of Germany, excited Alaric to assert in arms the name and blood of the conqueror of Rome. The advice of the graver chieftains pressed him to elude the first ardour of the Franks; and to expect, in the southern provinces of Gaul, the veteran and victorious Ostrogoths, whom the king of Italy had already sent to his assistance. The decisive moments were wasted in idle deliberation; the Goths too hastily abandoned, perhaps, an advantageous post; and the opportunity of a secure retreat was lost by their slow and disorderly motions. After Clovis had passed the ford, as it is still named, of the *Hart*, he advanced with bold and hasty steps to prevent the escape of the enemy. His nocturnal march was directed by a flaming meteor suspended in the air above the cathedral of Poitiers; and this signal, which might be previously concerted with the orthodox successor of St. Hilary, was compared to the column of fire that guided the Israelites in the desert. At the third hour of the day, about ten miles beyond

Poitiers, Clovis overtook, and instantly attacked, the Gothic army, whose defeat was already prepared by terror and confusion. Yet they rallied in their extreme distress, and the martial youths, who had clamorously demanded the battle, refused to survive the ignominy of flight. The two kings encountered each other in single combat. Alaric fell by the hand of his rival; and the victorious Frank was saved, by the goodness of his cuirass and the vigour of his horse, from the spears of two desperate Goths, who furiously rode against him to revenge the death of their sovereign. The vague expression of a mountain of the slain serves to indicate a cruel, though indefinite, slaughter; but Gregory has carefully observed that his valiant countryman Apollinaris, the son of Sidonius, lost his life at the head of the nobles of Auvergne. Perhaps these suspected catholics had been maliciously exposed to the blind assault of the enemy; and perhaps the influence of religion was superseded by personal attachment or military honour.[52]

Such is the empire of Fortune (if we may still disguise our ignorance under that popular name), that it is almost equally difficult to foresee the events of war, or to explain their various consequences. A bloody and complete victory has sometimes yielded no more than the possession of the field; and the loss of ten thousand men has sometimes been sufficient to destroy, in a single day, the work of ages. The decisive battle of Poitiers was followed by the conquest of Aquitain. Alaric had left behind him an infant son, a bastard competitor, factious nobles, and a disloyal people; and the remaining forces of the Goths were oppressed by the general consternation, or opposed to each other in civil discord. The victorious king of the Franks proceeded without delay to the siege of Angoulême. At the sound of his trumpets the walls of the city imitated the example of Jericho, and instantly fell to the ground; a splendid miracle, which may be reduced to the supposition that some clerical engineers had secretly undermined the foundations of the rampart.[53] At Bordeaux, which had submitted without resistance, Clovis established his winter quarters; and his prudent economy transported from Toulouse the royal treasures, which were deposited in the capital of the monarchy. The conqueror penetrated as far as the confines of Spain;[54] restored the honours of the catholic church; fixed in Aquitain a colony of Franks;[55] and delegated to his lieutenants the easy task of subduing or extirpating the nation of the Visigoths. But the Visigoths were protected by the wise and powerful monarch of Italy. While the balance was still equal, Theodoric had perhaps delayed the march of the Ostrogoths; but their strenuous efforts successfully resisted the ambition of Clovis; and the army of the Franks, and their Burgundian allies, was compelled to raise the siege of Arles, with the loss, as it is said, of thirty thousand men. These vicissitudes inclined the fierce spirit of Clovis to acquiesce in an advantageous treaty of peace. The Visigoths were suffered to retain the possession of Septimania, a narrow tract of sea-coast, from the Rhône to the Pyrenees; but the ample province of Aquitain, from those mountains to the Loire, was indissolubly united to the kingdom of France.[56]

After the success of the Gothic war, Clovis accepted the honours of the Roman consulship. The emperor Anastasius ambitiously bestowed on the most powerful rival of Theodoric the title and ensigns of that eminent dignity; yet, from some unknown cause, the name of Clovis has not been inscribed in the *Fasti* either of the East or West.[57] On the solemn day, the monarch of Gaul, placing a diadem on his head, was invested, in the church of St. Martin, with a purple tunic and mantle. From thence he proceeded on horseback to the cathedral of Tours; and, as he passed through the streets, profusely scattered, with his own hand, a donative of gold and silver to the joyful multitude, who incessantly repeated their acclamations of *Consul* and *Augustus*. The actual or legal authority of Clovis could not receive any new accessions from the consular dignity. It was a name, a shadow, an empty pageant; and if the conqueror had been instructed to claim the ancient prerogatives of that high office, they must have expired with the period of its annual duration. But the Romans were disposed to revere, in the person of their master, that antique title which the emperors condescended to assume: the barbarian himself seemed to contract a sacred obligation to respect the majesty of the republic; and the successors of Theodosius, by soliciting his friendship, tacitly forgave, and almost ratified, the usurpation of Gaul.

Twenty-five years after the death of Clovis this important concession was more formally declared in a treaty between his sons and the emperor Justinian. The Ostrogoths of Italy, unable to defend their distant acquisitions, had resigned to the Franks the cities of Arles and Marseilles: of Arles, still adorned with the seat of a Prætorian præfect, and of Marseilles, enriched by the advantages of trade and navigation.[58] This transaction was confirmed by the

Imperial authority; and Justinian, generously yielding to the Franks the sovereignty of the countries beyond the Alps, which they already possessed, absolved the provincials from their allegiance; and established on a more lawful, though not more solid, foundation, the throne of the Merovingians.[59] From that era they enjoyed the right of celebrating at Arles the games of the circus; and by a singular privilege, which was denied even to the Persian monarch, the *gold* coin, impressed with their name and image, obtained a legal currency in the empire.[60] A Greek historian of that age has praised the private and public virtues of the Franks, with a partial enthusiasm which cannot be sufficiently justified by their domestic annals.[61] He celebrates their politeness and urbanity, their regular government, and orthodox religion; and boldly asserts that these barbarians could be distinguished only by their dress and language from the subjects of Rome. Perhaps the Franks already displayed the social disposition, and lively graces, which, in every age, have disguised their vices, and sometimes concealed their intrinsic merit. Perhaps Agathias, and the Greeks, were dazzled by the rapid progress of their arms, and the splendour of their empire. Since the conquest of Burgundy, Gaul, except the Gothic province of Septimania, was subject, in its whole extent, to the sons of Clovis. They had extinguished the German kingdom of Thuringia, and their vague dominion penetrated beyond the Rhine, into the heart of their native forests. The Alemanni and Bavarians, who had occupied the Roman provinces of Rhætia and Noricum, to the south of the Danube, confessed themselves the humble vassals of the Franks; and the feeble barrier of the Alps was incapable of resisting their ambition. When the last survivor of the sons of Clovis united the inheritance and conquests of the Merovingians, his kingdom extended far beyond the limits of modern France. Yet modern France, such has been the progress of arts and policy, far surpasses, in wealth, populousness, and power, the spacious but savage realms of Clotaire or Dagobert.[62]

The Franks, or French, are the only people of Europe who can deduce a perpetual succession from the conquerors of the Western empire. But their conquest of Gaul was followed by ten centuries of anarchy and ignorance. On the revival of learning, the students who had been formed in the schools of Athens and Rome disdained their barbarian ancestors; and a long period elapsed before patient labour could provide the requisite materials to satisfy, or rather to excite, the curiosity of more enlightened times.[63] At length the eye of criticism and philosophy was directed to the antiquities of France; but even philosophers have been tainted by the contagion of prejudice and passion. The most extreme and exclusive systems, of the personal servitude of the Gauls, or of their voluntary and equal alliance with the Franks, have been rashly conceived, and obstinately defended; and the intemperate disputants have accused each other of conspiring against the prerogative of the crown, the dignity of the nobles, or the freedom of the people. Yet the sharp conflict has usefully exercised the adverse powers of learning and genius; and each antagonist, alternately vanquished and victorious, has extirpated some ancient errors, and established some interesting truths. An impartial stranger, instructed by their discoveries, their disputes, and even their faults, may describe, from the same original materials, the state of the Roman provincials, after Gaul had submitted to the arms and laws of the Merovingian kings.[64]

The rudest, or the most servile, condition of human society, is regulated however by some fixed and general rules. When Tacitus surveyed the primitive simplicity of the Germans, he discovered some permanent maxims, or customs, of public and private life, which were preserved by faithful tradition till the introduction of the art of writing, and of the Latin tongue.[65] Before the election of the Merovingian kings, the most powerful tribe, or nation, of the Franks, appointed four venerable chieftains to compose the *Salic* laws;[66] and their labours were examined and approved in three successive assemblies of the people. After the baptism of Clovis, he reformed several articles that appeared incompatible with Christianity: the Salic law was again amended by his sons; and at length, under the reign of Dagobert, the code was revised and promulgated in its actual form, one hundred years after the establishment of the French monarchy. Within the same period, the customs of the *Ripuarians* were transcribed and published; and Charlemagne himself, the legislator of his age and country, had accurately studied the *two* national laws which still prevailed among the Franks.[67] The same care was extended to their vassals; and the rude institutions of the *Alemanni* and *Bavarians* were diligently compiled and ratified by the supreme authority of the Merovingian kings. The *Visigoths* and *Burgundians*, whose conquests in Gaul preceded those of the Franks, showed less impatience to attain one of the principal benefits of civilised society. Euric was the first of the Gothic princes who expressed in writing the manners and customs of his people; and the composition of the Burgundian laws was a measure of policy rather than of justice, to alleviate the yoke and regain the affections of their Gallic subjects.[68] Thus, by a singular coincidence, the Germans framed their artless institutions at a time when the elaborate system of Roman jurisprudence was finally consummated. In the Salic laws, and the Pandects of Justinian, we may compare the first rudiments, and the full maturity, of civil wisdom; and whatever prejudices may be suggested in favour of barbarism, our calmer reflections will ascribe to the Romans the superior advantages, not only of science and reason, but of humanity and justice. Yet the laws of the barbarians were adapted to their wants and desires, their occupations and their capacity; and they all contributed to preserve the peace, and promote the improvements, of the society for whose use they were originally established. The Merovingians, instead of imposing a uniform rule of conduct on their various subjects, permitted each people, and each family, of their empire freely to enjoy their domestic institutions;[69] nor were the Romans excluded from the common benefits of this legal toleration.[70] The children embraced the *law* of their parents, the wife that of her husband, the freedman that of his patron; and in all causes where the parties were of different nations, the plaintiff or accuser was obliged to follow the tribunal of the defendant, who may always plead a judicial presumption of right or innocence. A more ample latitude was allowed, if every citizen, in the presence of the judge, might declare the law under which he desired to live, and the national society to which he chose to belong. Such an indulgence would abolish the partial distinctions of victory: and the Roman provincials might patiently acquiesce in the hardships of their condition, since it depended on themselves to assume the privilege, if they dared to assert the character, of free and warlike barbarians.[71]

When justice inexorably requires the death of a murderer, each private citizen is fortified by the assurance that the laws, the magistrate, and the whole community, are the guardians of his personal safety. But in the loose society of the Germans, revenge was always honourable, and often meritorious: the independent warrior chastised, or vindicated, with his own hand, the injuries which he had offered or received; and he had only to dread the resentment of the sons and kinsmen of the enemy whom he had sacrificed to his selfish or angry passions. The magistrate, conscious of his weakness, interposed, not to punish, but to reconcile; and he was satisfied if he could persuade or compel the contending parties to pay and to accept the moderate fine which had been ascertained as the price of blood.[72] The fierce spirit of the Franks would have opposed a more rigorous sentence; the same fierceness despised these ineffectual restraints; and, when their simple manners had been corrupted by the wealth of Gaul, the public peace was continually violated by acts of hasty or deliberate guilt. In every just government the same penalty is inflicted, or at least is imposed, for the murder of a peasant or a prince. But the national inequality established by the Franks in their criminal proceedings was the last insult and abuse of conquest.[73] In the calm moments of legislation they solemnly pronounced that the life of a Roman was of smaller value than that of a barbarian. The *Antrustion*,[74] a name expressive of the most illustrious birth or dignity among the Franks, was appreciated at the sum of six hundred pieces of gold; while the noble provincial, who was admitted to the king's table, might be legally murdered at the expense of three hundred pieces. Two hundred were deemed sufficient for a Frank of ordinary condition; but the meaner Romans were exposed to disgrace and danger by a trifling compensation of one hundred, or even fifty, pieces of gold. Had these laws been regulated by any principle of equity or reason, the public protection should have supplied, in just proportion, the want of personal strength. But the legislator had weighed in the scale, not of justice, but of policy, the loss of a soldier against that of a slave: the head of an insolent and rapacious barbarian was guarded by a heavy fine; and the slightest aid was afforded to the most defenceless subjects. Time insensibly abated the pride of the conquerors, and the patience of the vanquished; and the boldest citizen was taught by experience that he might suffer more injuries than he could inflict. As the manners of the Franks became less ferocious, their laws were rendered more severe; and the Merovingian kings attempted to imitate the impartial rigour of the Visigoths and Burgundians.[75] Under the empire of Charlemagne murder was universally punished with death; and the use of capital punishments has been liberally multiplied in the jurisprudence of modern Europe.[76]

The civil and military professions, which had been separated by Constantine, were again united by the barbarians. The harsh sound of the Teutonic appellations was mollified into the Latin titles of Duke, of Count, or of Præfect; and the same officer assumed, within his district, the command of the troops and the administration of justice.[77] But the fierce and illiterate chieftain was seldom qualified to discharge the duties of a judge, which require all of the faculties of a philosophic mind, laboriously cultivated by experience and study; and his rude ignorance was compelled to embrace some simple and visible methods of ascertaining the cause of justice. In every religion the Deity has been invoked to confirm the truth, or to punish the falsehood, of human testimony; but this powerful instrument was misapplied and abused by the simplicity of the German legislators. The party accused might justify his innocence, by producing before their tribunal a number of friendly witnesses, who solemnly declared their belief or assurance that he was not guilty. According to the weight of the charge this legal number of *compurgators* was multiplied: seventy-two voices were required to absolve an incendiary or assassin; and when the chastity of a queen of France was suspected, three hundred gallant nobles swore, without hesitation, that the infant prince had been actually begotten by her deceased husband.[78] The sin and scandal of manifest and frequent perjuries engaged the magistrates to remove these dangerous temptations, and to supply the defects of human testimony by the famous experiments of fire and water. These extraordinary trials were so capriciously contrived, that in some cases guilt, and innocence in others, could not be proved without the interposition of a miracle. Such miracles were readily provided by fraud and credulity; the most intricate causes were determined by this easy and infallible method; and the turbulent barbarians, who might have disdained the sentence of the magistrate, submissively acquiesced in the judgment of God.[79]

But the trials by single combat gradually obtained superior credit and authority among a warlike people, who could not believe that a brave man deserved to suffer, or that a coward deserved to live.[80] Both in civil and criminal proceedings, the plaintiff, or accuser, the defendant, or even the witness, were exposed to mortal challenge from the antagonist who was destitute of legal proofs; and it was incumbent on them either to desert their cause or publicly to maintain their honour in the lists of battle. They fought either on foot or on horseback, according to the custom of their nation;[81] and the decision of the sword or lance was ratified by the sanction of Heaven, of the judge, and of the people. This sanguinary law was introduced into Gaul by the Burgundians; and their legislator Gundobald[82] condescended to answer the complaints and objections of his subject Avitus. "Is it not true," said the king of Burgundy to the bishop, "that the event of national wars and private combats is directed by the judgment of God; and that his providence awards the victory to the juster cause?" By such prevailing arguments, the absurd and cruel practice of judicial duels, which had been peculiar to some tribes of Germany, was propagated and established in all the monarchies of Europe, from Sicily to the Baltic. At the end of ten centuries the reign of legal violence was not totally extinguished; and the ineffectual censures of saints, of popes, and of synods, may seem to prove that the influence of superstition is weakened by its unnatural alliance with reason and humanity. The tribunals were stained with the blood, perhaps, of innocent and respectable citizens; the law, which now favours the rich, then yielded to the strong; and the old, the feeble, and the infirm, were condemned either to renounce their fairest claims and possessions, to sustain the dangers of an unequal conflict,[83] or to trust the doubtful aid of a mercenary champion. This oppressive jurisprudence was imposed on the provincials of Gaul who complained of any injuries in their persons and property. Whatever might be the strength or courage of individuals, the victorious barbarians excelled in the love and exercise of arms; and the vanquished Roman was unjustly summoned to repeat, in his own person, the bloody contest which had been already decided against his country.[84]

A devouring host of one hundred and twenty thousand Germans had formerly passed the Rhine under the command of Ariovistus. One-third part of the fertile lands of the Sequani was appropriated to their use; and the conqueror soon repeated his oppressive demand of another third, for the accommodation of a new colony of twenty-four thousand barbarians whom he had invited to share the rich harvest of Gaul.[85] At the distance of five hundred years the Visigoths and Burgundians, who revenged the defeat of Ariovistus, usurped the same unequal proportion of *two-thirds* of the subject lands. But this distribution, instead of spreading over the province, may be reasonably confined to the peculiar districts where the victorious people had been planted by their own choice or by the policy of their leader. In these districts each barbarian was connected by the ties of hospitality with some Roman provincial. To this unwelcome guest the proprietor was compelled to abandon two-thirds of his patrimony: but the German, a shepherd and a hunter, might sometimes content himself with a spacious range of wood and pasture, and resign the smallest, though most valuable, portion to the toil of the industrious husbandman.[86] The silence of ancient and authentic testimony has encouraged an opinion that the rapine of the *Franks* was not moderated or disguised by the forms of a legal division; that they dispersed themselves over the provinces of Gaul without order or control; and that each victorious robber, according to his wants, his avarice, and his strength, measured with his sword the extent of his new inheritance. At a distance from their sovereign the barbarians might indeed be tempted to exercise such arbitrary depredation; but the firm and artful policy of Clovis must curb a licentious spirit which would aggravate the misery of the vanquished whilst it corrupted the union and discipline of the conquerors. The memorable vase of Soissons is a monument and a pledge of the regular distribution of the Gallic spoils. It was the duty and the interest of Clovis to provide rewards for a successful army, and settlements for a numerous people, without inflicting any wanton or superfluous injuries on the loyal catholics of Gaul. The ample fund which he might lawfully acquire of the Imperial patrimony, vacant lands, and Gothic usurpations, would diminish the cruel necessity of seizure and confiscation, and the humble provincials would more patiently acquiesce in the equal and regular distribution of their loss.[87]

The wealth of the Merovingian princes consisted in their extensive domain. After the conquest of Gaul they still delighted in the rustic simplicity of their ancestors; the cities were abandoned to solitude and decay; and their coins, their charters, and their synods, are still inscribed with the names of the villas or rural palaces in which they successively resided. One hundred and sixty of these *palaces*, a title which need not excite any unseasonable ideas of art or luxury, were scattered through the provinces of their kingdom; and if some might claim the honours of a fortress, the far greater part could be esteemed only in the light of profitable farms. The mansion of the long-haired kings was surrounded with convenient yards and stables for the cattle and the poultry; the garden was planted with useful vegetables; the various trades, the labours of agriculture, and even the arts of hunting and fishing, were exercised by servile hands for the emolument of the sovereign; his magazines were filled with corn and wine, either for sale or consumption; and the whole administration was conducted by the strictest maxims of private economy.[88] This ample patrimony was appropriated to supply the hospitable plenty of Clovis and his successors, and to reward the fidelity of their brave companions, who, both in peace and war, were devoted to their personal service. Instead of a horse or a suit of armour, each companion, according to his rank, or merit, or favour, was invested with a *benefice*, the primitive name and most simple form of the feudal possessions. These gifts might be resumed at the pleasure of the sovereign; and his feeble prerogative derived some support from the influence of his liberality. But this dependent tenure was gradually abolished[89] by the independent and rapacious nobles of France, who established the perpetual property and hereditary succession of their benefices; a revolution salutary to the earth, which had been injured or neglected by its precarious masters.[90] Besides these royal and beneficiary estates, a large proportion had been assigned, in the division of Gaul, of *allodial* and *Salic* lands: they were exempt from tribute, and the Salic lands were equally shared among the male descendants of the Franks.[91]

In the bloody discord and silent decay of the Merovingian line a new order of tyrants arose in the provinces, who, under the appellation of *Seniors* or Lords, usurped a right to govern and a licence to oppress the subjects of their peculiar territory. Their ambition might be checked by the hostile resistance of an equal: but the laws were extinguished; and the sacrilegious barbarians, who dared to provoke the vengeance of a saint or bishop,[92] would seldom respect the landmarks of a profane and defenceless neighbour. The common or public rights of nature, such as they had always been deemed by the Roman jurisprudence,[93] were severely restrained by the German conquerors, whose amusement, or rather passion, was the exercise of hunting. The vague dominion which MAN has assumed over the wild inhabitants of the earth, the air, and the waters, was confined to some fortunate individuals of the human species. Gaul was again overspread with woods; and the animals, who were reserved for the use or pleasure of the lord, might ravage with impunity the fields of his industrious vassals. The chase was the sacred privilege of the nobles and their domestic servants. Plebeian transgressors were legally chastised with stripes and imprisonment;[94] but in an age which admitted a slight composition for the life of a citizen, it was a capital crime to destroy a stag or a wild bull within the precincts of the royal forests.[95]

According to the maxims of ancient war, the conqueror became the lawful master of the enemy whom he had subdued and spared:[96] and the fruitful cause of personal slavery, which had been almost suppressed by the peaceful sovereignty of Rome, was again revived and multiplied by the perpetual hostilities of the independent barbarians. The Goth, the Burgundian, or the Frank, who returned from a successful expedition, dragged after him a long train of sheep, of oxen, and of human captives, whom he treated with the same brutal contempt. The youths of an elegant form and ingenuous aspect were set apart for the domestic service; a doubtful situation, which alternately exposed them to the favourable or cruel impulse of passion. The useful mechanics and servants (smiths, carpenters, tailors, shoemakers, cooks, gardeners, dyers, and workmen in gold and silver, etc.) employed their skill for the use or profit of their master. But the Roman captives who were destitute of art, but capable of labour, were condemned, without regard to their former rank, to tend the cattle and cultivate the lands of the barbarians. The number of the hereditary bondsmen who were attached to the Gallic estates was continually increased by new supplies; and the servile people, according to the situation and temper of their lords, was sometimes raised by precarious indulgence, and more frequently depressed by capricious despotism.[97] An absolute power of life and death was exercised by these lords; and when they married their daughters, a train of useful servants, chained on the waggons to prevent their escape, was sent as a nuptial present into a distant country.[98] The majesty of the Roman laws protected the liberty of each citizen against the rash effects of his own distress or despair. But the subjects of the Merovingian kings might alienate their personal freedom; and this act of legal suicide, which was familiarly practised, is expressed in terms most disgraceful and afflicting to the dignity of human nature.[99] The example of the poor, who purchased life by the sacrifice of all that can render life desirable, was gradually imitated by the feeble and the devout, who, in times of public disorder, pusillanimously crowded to shelter themselves under the battlements of a powerful chief and around the shrine of a popular saint. Their submission was accepted by these temporal or spiritual patrons; and the hasty transaction irrecoverably fixed their own condition and that of their latest posterity. From the reign of Clovis, during five successive centuries, the laws and manners of Gaul uniformly tended to promote the increase, and to confirm the duration, of personal servitude. Time and violence almost obliterated the intermediate ranks of society, and left an obscure and narrow interval between the noble and the slave. This arbitrary and recent division has been transformed by pride and prejudice into a *national* distinction, universally established by the arms and the laws of the Merovingians. The nobles, who claimed their genuine or fabulous descent from the independent and victorious Franks, have asserted and abused the indefeasible right of conquest over a prostrate crowd of slaves and plebeians, to whom they imputed the imaginary disgrace of a Gallic or Roman extraction.

The general state and revolutions of *France*, a name which was imposed by the conquerors, may be illustrated by the particular example of a province, a diocese, or a senatorial family. Auvergne had formerly maintained a just preeminence among the independent states and cities of Gaul. The brave and numerous inhabitants displayed a singular trophy—the sword of Cæsar himself, which he had lost when he was repulsed before the walls of Gergovia.[100] As the common offspring of Troy, they claimed a fraternal alliance with the Romans;[101] and if each province had imitated the courage and loyalty of Auvergne, the fall of the Western empire might have been prevented or delayed. They firmly maintained the fidelity which they had reluctantly sworn to the Visigoths; but when their bravest nobles had fallen in the battle of Poitiers, they accepted without resistance a victorious and catholic sovereign. This easy and valuable conquest was achieved and possessed by Theodoric, the eldest son of Clovis: but the remote province was separated from his Austrasian dominions by the intermediate kingdoms of Soissons, Paris, and Orleans, which formed, after their father's death, the inheritance of his three brothers. The king of Paris, Childebert, was tempted by the neighbourhood and beauty of Auvergne.[102] The upper country, which rises towards the south into the mountains of the Cevennes, presented a rich and various prospect of woods and pastures; the sides of the hills were clothed with vines; and each eminence was crowned with a villa or castle. In the Lower Auvergne, the river Allier flows through the fair and spacious plain of Limagne; and the inexhaustible fertility of the soil supplied, and still supplies, without any interval of repose, the constant repetition of the same harvests.[103] On the false report that their lawful sovereign had been slain in Germany, the city and diocese of Auvergne were betrayed by the grandson of Sidonius Apollinaris. Childebert enjoyed this clandestine victory; and the free subjects of Theodoric threatened to desert his standard if he indulged his private resentment while the nation was engaged in the Burgundian war. But the Franks of Austrasia soon yielded to the persuasive eloquence of their king. "Follow me," said Theodoric, "into Auvergne; I will lead you into a province where you may acquire gold, silver, slaves, cattle, and precious apparel, to the full extent of your wishes. I repeat my promise; I give you the people and their wealth as your prey; and you may transport them at pleasure into your own country." By the execution of this promise Theodoric justly forfeited the allegiance of a people whom he devoted to destruction. His troops, reinforced by the fiercest barbarians of Germany,[104] spread desolation over the fruitful face of Auvergne; and two places only, a strong castle and a holy shrine, were saved or redeemed from their licentious fury. The castle of Meroliac[105] was seated on a lofty rock, which rose an hundred feet above the surface of the plain; and a large reservoir of fresh water was enclosed with some arable lands within the circle of its fortifications. The Franks beheld with envy and despair this impregnable fortress: but they surprised a party of fifty stragglers; and, as they were oppressed by the number of their captives, they fixed at a trifling ransom the alternative of life or death for these wretched victims, whom the cruel barbarians were prepared to massacre on the refusal of the garrison. Another detachment penetrated as far as Brivas, or Brioude, where the inhabitants, with their valuable effects, had taken refuge in the sanctuary of St. Julian. The doors of the church resisted the assault, but a daring soldier entered through a window of the choir and opened a passage to his companions. The clergy and people, the sacred and the profane spoils, were rudely torn from the altar; and the sacrilegious division was made at a small distance from the town of Brioude. But this act of impiety was severely chastised by the devout son of Clovis. He punished with death the most atrocious offenders; left their secret accomplices to the vengeance of St. Julian; released the captives; restored the plunder; and extended the rights of sanctuary five miles round the sepulchre of the holy martyr.[106]

Before the Austrasian army retreated from Auvergne, Theodoric exacted some pledges of the future loyalty of a people whose just hatred could be restrained only by their fear. A select band of noble youths, the sons of the principal senators, was delivered to the conqueror as the hostages of the faith of Childebert and of their countrymen. On the first rumour of war or conspiracy these guiltless youths were reduced to a state of servitude; and one of them, Attalus,[107] whose adventures are more particularly related, kept his master's horses in the diocese of Trèves. After a painful search he was discovered in this unworthy occupation, by the emissaries of his grandfather, Gregory bishop of Langres; but his offers of ransom were sternly rejected by the avarice of the barbarian, who required an exorbitant sum of ten pounds of gold for the freedom of his noble captive. His deliverance was effected by the hardy stratagem of Leo, a slave belonging to the kitchens of the bishop of Langres.[108] An unknown agent easily introduced him into the same family. The barbarian purchased Leo for the price of twelve pieces of gold; and was pleased to learn that he was deeply skilled in the luxury of an episcopal table: "Next Sunday," said the Frank, "I shall invite my neighbours and kinsmen. Exert thy art, and force them to confess that they have never seen or tasted such an entertainment, even in the king's house." Leo assured him that, if he would provide a sufficient quantity of poultry, his wishes should be satisfied. The master, who already aspired to the merit of elegant hospitality, assumed as his own the praise which the voracious guests unanimously bestowed on his cook; and the dexterous Leo insensibly acquired the trust and management of his household. After the patient expectation of a whole year, he cautiously whispered his design to Attalus, and exhorted him to prepare for flight in the ensuing night. At the hour of midnight the intemperate guests retired from table, and the Frank's son-in-law, whom Leo attended to his apartment with a nocturnal potation, condescended to jest on the facility with which he might betray his trust. The intrepid slave, after sustaining this dangerous raillery, entered his master's bed-chamber; removed his spear and shield; silently drew the fleetest horses from the stable; unbarred the ponderous gates; and excited Attalus to save his life and liberty by incessant diligence. Their apprehensions urged them to leave their horses on the banks of the Meuse;[109]

they swam the river, wandered three days in the adjacent forest, and subsisted only by the accidental discovery of a wild plum-tree. As they lay concealed in a dark thicket, they heard the noise of horses; they were terrified by the angry countenance of their master, and they anxiously listened to his declaration that, if he could seize the guilty fugitives, one of them he would cut in pieces with his sword, and would expose the other on a gibbet. At length Attalus and his faithful Leo reached the friendly habitation of a presbyter of Rheims, who recruited their fainting strength with bread and wine, concealed them from the search of their enemy, and safely conducted them beyond the limits of the Austrasian kingdom to the episcopal palace of Langres. Gregory embraced his grandson with tears of joy, gratefully delivered Leo with his whole family from the yoke of servitude, and bestowed on him the property of a farm, where he might end his days in happiness and freedom. Perhaps this singular adventure, which is marked with so many circumstances of truth and nature, was related by Attalus himself to his cousin or nephew, the first historian of the Franks. Gregory of Tours[110] was born about sixty years after the death of Sidonius Apollinaris; and their situation was almost similar, since each of them was a native of Auvergne, a senator, and a bishop. The difference of their style and sentiments may, therefore, express the decay of Gaul; and clearly ascertain how much, in so short a space, the human mind had lost of its energy and refinement.[111]

We are now qualified to despise the opposite, and perhaps artful, misrepresentations which have softened or exaggerated the oppression of the Romans of Gaul under the reign of the Merovingians. The conquerors never promulgated any *universal* edict of servitude or confiscation: but a degenerate people, who excused their weakness by the specious names of politeness and peace, was exposed to the arms and laws of the ferocious barbarians, who contemptuously insulted their possessions, their freedom, and their safety. Their personal injuries were partial and irregular; but the great body of the Romans survived the revolution, and still preserved the property and privileges of citizens. A large portion of their lands was exacted for the use of the Franks: but they enjoyed the remainder exempt from tribute;[112] and the same irresistible violence which swept away the arts and manufactures of Gaul destroyed the elaborate and expensive system of Imperial despotism. The provincials must frequently deplore the savage

jurisprudence of the Salic or Ripuarian laws; but their private life, in the important concerns of marriage, testaments, or inheritance, was still regulated by the Theodosian Code; and a discontented Roman might freely aspire or descend to the title and character of a barbarian. The honours of the state were accessible to his ambition: the education and temper of the Romans more peculiarly qualified them for the offices of civil government; and as soon as emulation had rekindled their military ardour, they were permitted to march in the ranks, or even at the head, of the victorious Germans. I shall not attempt to enumerate the generals and magistrates whose names[113] attest the liberal policy of the Merovingians. The supreme command of Burgundy, with the title of Patrician, was successively intrusted to three Romans; and the last and most powerful, Mummolus,[114] who alternately saved and disturbed the monarchy, had supplanted his father in the station of count of Autun, and left a treasure of thirty talents of gold and two hundred and fifty talents of silver. The fierce and illiterate barbarians were excluded, during several generations, from the dignities, and even from the orders, of the church.[115] The clergy of Gaul consisted almost entirely of native provincials; the haughty Franks fell prostrate at the feet of their subjects who were dignified with the episcopal character; and the power and riches which had been lost in war were insensibly recovered by superstition.[116] In all temporal affairs the Theodosian Code was the universal law of the clergy; but the barbaric jurisprudence had liberally provided for their personal safety: a subdeacon was equivalent to two Franks; the *antrustion* and priest were held in similar estimation; and the life of a bishop was appreciated far above the common standard, at the price of nine hundred pieces of gold.[117] The Romans communicated to their conquerors the use of the Christian religion and Latin language;[118] but their language and their religion had alike degenerated from the simple purity of the Augustan and Apostolic age. The progress of superstition and barbarism was rapid and universal: the worship of the saints concealed from vulgar eyes the God of the Christians, and the rustic dialect of peasants and soldiers was corrupted by a Teutonic idiom and pronunciation. Yet such intercourse of sacred and social communion eradicated the distinctions of birth and victory; and the nations of Gaul were gradually confounded under the name and government of the Franks.

The Franks, after they mingled with their

Gallic subjects, might have imparted the most valuable of human gifts, a spirit and system of constitutional liberty. Under a king, hereditary but limited, the chiefs and counsellors might have debated at Paris in the palace of the Cæsars: the adjacent field, where the emperors reviewed their mercenary legions, would have admitted the legislative assembly of freemen and warriors; and the rude model which had been sketched in the woods of Germany[119] might have been polished and improved by the civil wisdom of the Romans. But the careless barbarians, secure of their personal independence, disdained the labour of government: the annual assemblies of the month of March were silently abolished, and the nation was separated and almost dissolved by the conquest of Gaul.[120] The monarchy was left without any regular establishment of justice, of arms, or of revenue. The successors of Clovis wanted resolution to assume, or strength to exercise, the legislative and executive powers which the people had abdicated: the royal prerogative was distinguished only by a more ample privilege of rapine and murder; and the love of freedom, so often invigorated and disgraced by private ambition, was reduced among the licentious Franks to the contempt of order and the desire of impunity. Seventy-five years after the death of Clovis, his grandson Gontran, king of Burgundy, sent an army to invade the Gothic possessions of Septimania, or Languedoc. The troops of Burgundy, Berry, Auvergne, and the adjacent territories were excited by the hopes of spoil. They marched without discipline under the banners of German or Gallic counts: their attack was feeble and unsuccessful, but the friendly and hostile provinces were desolated with indiscriminate rage. The cornfields, the villages, the churches themselves, were consumed by fire; the inhabitants were massacred or dragged into captivity; and, in the disorderly retreat, five thousand of these inhuman savages were destroyed by hunger or intestine discord. When the pious Gontran reproached the guilt or neglect of their leaders, and threatened to inflict, not a legal sentence, but instant and arbitrary execution, they accused the universal and incurable corruption of the people. "No one," they said, "any longer fears or respects his king, his duke, or his count. Each man loves to do evil, and freely indulges his criminal inclinations. The most gentle correction provokes an immediate tumult, and the rash magistrate who presumes to censure or restrain his seditious subjects seldom escapes alive from their revenge."[121] It has been reserved for the same nation to expose, by their intemperate vices, the most odious abuse of freedom, and to supply its loss by the spirit of honour and humanity which now alleviates and dignifies their obedience to an absolute sovereign.

The Visigoths had resigned to Clovis the greatest part of their Gallic possessions; but their loss was amply compensated by the easy conquest and secure enjoyment of the provinces of Spain. From the monarchy of the Goths, which soon involved the Suevic kingdom of Gallicia, the modern Spaniards still derive some national vanity, but the historian of the Roman empire is neither invited nor compelled to pursue the obscure and barren series of their annals.[122] The Goths of Spain were separated from the rest of mankind by the lofty ridge of the Pyrenæan mountains: their manners and institutions, as far as they were common to the Germanic tribes, have been already explained. I have anticipated in the preceding chapter the most important of their ecclesiastical events—the fall of Arianism and the persecution of the Jews: and it only remains to observe some interesting circumstances which relate to the civil and ecclesiastical constitution of the Spanish kingdom.

After their conversion from idolatry or heresy, the Franks and the Visigoths were disposed to embrace, with equal submission, the inherent evils and the accidental benefits of superstition. But the prelates of France, long before the extinction of the Merovingian race, had degenerated into fighting and hunting barbarians. They disdained the use of synods, forgot the laws of temperance and chastity, and preferred the indulgence of private ambition and luxury to the general interest of the sacerdotal profession.[123] The bishops of Spain respected themselves, and were respected by the public: their indissoluble union disguised their vices, and confirmed their authority; and the regular discipline of the church introduced peace, order, and stability into the government of the state. From the reign of Recared, the first catholic king, to that of Witiza, the immediate predecessor of the unfortunate Roderic, sixteen national councils were successively convened. The six metropolitans, Toledo, Seville, Merida, Braga, Tarragona, and Narbonne, presided according to their respective seniority; the assembly was composed of their suffragan bishops, who appeared in person or by their proxies, and a place was assigned to the most holy or opulent of the Spanish abbots. During the first three days of the convocation, as long as they agitated the ecclesiastical questions of doctrine and discipline, the profane laity was excluded from their debates, which were conducted, however, with decent solemnity. But on the morning of the fourth day the doors were thrown open for the entrance of the great officers of the palace, the dukes and counts of the provinces, the judges of the cities, and the Gothic nobles; and the decrees of Heaven were ratified by the consent of the people. The same rules were observed in the provincial assemblies, the annual synods, which were empowered to hear complaints and to redress grievances; and a legal government was supported by the prevailing influence of the Spanish clergy. The bishops, who in each revolution were prepared to flatter the victorious and to insult the prostrate, laboured with diligence and success to kindle the flames of persecution, and to exalt the mitre above the crown. Yet the national councils of Toledo, in which the free spirit of the barbarians was tempered and guided by episcopal policy, have established some prudent laws for the common benefit of the king and people. The vacancy of the throne was supplied by the choice of the bishops and palatines; and after the failure of the line of Alaric, the regal dignity was still limited to the pure and noble blood of the Goths. The clergy, who anointed their lawful prince, always recommended, and sometimes practised, the duty of allegiance: and the spiritual censures were denounced on the heads of the impious subjects who should resist his authority, conspire against his life, or violate by an indecent union the chastity even of his widow. But the monarch himself, when he ascended the throne, was bound by a reciprocal oath to God and his people that he would faithfully execute his important trust. The real or imaginary faults of his administration were subject to the control of a powerful aristocracy; and the bishops and palatines were guarded by a fundamental privilege that they should not be degraded, imprisoned, tortured, nor punished with death, exile, or confiscation, unless by the free and public judgment of their peers.[124]

One of these legislative councils of Toledo examined and ratified the code of laws which had been compiled by a succession of Gothic kings, from the fierce Euric to the devout Egica. As long as the Visigoths themselves were satisfied with the rude customs of their ancestors, they indulged their subjects of Aquitain and Spain in the enjoyment of the Roman law. Their gradual improvement in arts, in policy, and at length in religion, encouraged them to imitate and to supersede these foreign institutions, and

to compose a code of civil and criminal jurisprudence for the use of a great and united people. The same obligations and the same privileges were communicated to the nations of the Spanish monarchy; and the conquerors, insensibly renouncing the Teutonic idiom, submitted to the restraints of equity, and exalted the Romans to the participation of freedom. The merit of this impartial policy was enhanced by the situation of Spain under the reign of the Visigoths. The provincials were long separated from their Arian masters by the irreconcilable difference of religion. After the conversion of Recared had removed the prejudices of the catholics, the coasts both of the Ocean and Mediterranean were still possessed by the Eastern emperors, who secretly excited a discontented people to reject the yoke of the barbarians, and to assert the name and dignity of Roman citizens. The allegiance of doubtful subjects is indeed most effectually secured by their own persuasion that they hazard more in a revolt than they can hope to obtain by a revolution; but it has appeared so natural to oppress those whom we hate and fear, that the contrary system well deserves the praise of wisdom and moderation.[125]

While the kingdoms of the Franks and Visigoths were established in Gaul and Spain, the Saxons achieved the conquest of Britain, the third great diocese of the præfecture of the West. Since Britain was already separated from the Roman empire, I might without reproach decline a story familiar to the most illiterate, and obscure to the most learned, of my readers. The Saxons, who excelled in the use of the oar or the battle-axe, were ignorant of the art which could alone perpetuate the fame of their exploits; the provincials, relapsing into barbarism, neglected to describe the ruin of their country; and the doubtful tradition was almost extinguished before the missionaries of Rome restored the light of science and Christianity. The declamations of Gildas, the fragments or fables of Nennius, the obscure hints of the Saxon laws and chronicles, and the ecclesiastical tales of the venerable Bede,[126] have been illustrated by the diligence, and sometimes embellished by the fancy, of succeeding writers, whose works I am not ambitious either to censure or to transcribe.[127] Yet the historian of the empire may be tempted to pursue the revolutions of a Roman province till it vanishes from his sight; and an Englishman may curiously trace the establishment of the barbarians from whom he derives his name, his laws, and perhaps his origin.

About forty years after the dissolution of the

Roman government Vortigern appears to have obtained the supreme, though precarious, command of the princes and cities of Britain. That unfortunate monarch has been almost unanimously condemned for the weak and mischievous policy of inviting[128] a formidable stranger to repel the vexatious inroads of a domestic foe. His ambassadors are despatched by the gravest historians to the coast of Germany: they address a pathetic oration to the general assembly of the Saxons, and those warlike barbarians resolve to assist with a fleet and army the suppliants of a distant and unknown island. If Britain had indeed been unknown to the Saxons, the measure of its calamities would have been less complete. But the strength of the Roman government could not always guard the maritime province against the pirates of Germany: the independent and divided states were exposed to their attacks, and the Saxons might sometimes join the Scots and the Picts in a tacit or express confederacy of rapine and destruction. Vortigern could only balance the various perils which assaulted on every side his throne and his people; and his policy may deserve either praise or excuse if he preferred the alliance of *those* barbarians whose naval power rendered them the most dangerous enemies, and the most serviceable allies. Hengist and Horsa, as they ranged along the eastern coast with three ships, were engaged by the promise of an ample stipend to embrace the defence of Britain, and their intrepid valour soon delivered the country from the Caledonian invaders. The Isle of Thanet, a secure and fertile district, was alloted for the residence of these German auxiliaries, and they were supplied according to the treaty with a plentiful allowance of clothing and provisions. This favourable reception encouraged five thousand warriors to embark with their families in seventeen vessels, and the infant power of Hengist was fortified by this strong and seasonable reinforcement. The crafty barbarian suggested to Vortigern the obvious advantage of fixing, in the neighbourhood of the Picts, a colony of faithful allies: a third fleet, of forty ships, under the command of his son and nephew, sailed from Germany, ravaged the Orkneys, and disembarked a new army on the coast of Northumberland or Lothian, at the opposite extremity of the devoted land. It was easy to foresee, but it was impossible to prevent, the impending evils. The two nations were soon divided and exasperated by mutual jealousies. The Saxons magnified all that they had done and suffered in the cause of an ungrateful people; while the Britons regretted the liberal rewards which could not satisfy the avarice of those haughty mercenaries. The causes of fear and hatred were inflamed into an irreconcilable quarrel. The Saxons flew to arms; and if they perpetrated a treacherous massacre during the security of a feast, they destroyed the reciprocal confidence which sustains the intercourse of peace and war.[129]

Hengist, who boldly aspired to the conquest of Britain, exhorted his countrymen to embrace the glorious opportunity: he painted in lively colours the fertility of the soil, the wealth of the cities, the pusillanimous temper of the natives, and the convenient situation of a spacious solitary island, accessible on all sides to the Saxon fleets. The successive colonies which issued in the period of a century from the mouths of the Elbe, the Weser, and the Rhine, were principally composed of three valiant tribes or nations of Germany; the *Jutes*, the *old Saxons*, and the *Angles*. The Jutes, who fought under the peculiar banner of Hengist, assumed the merit of leading their countrymen in the paths of glory, and of erecting in Kent the first independent kingdom. The fame of the enterprise was attributed to the primitive Saxons, and the common laws and language of the conquerors are described by the national appellation of a people which, at the end of four hundred years, produced the first monarchs of South Britain. The Angles were distinguished by their numbers and their success; and they claimed the honour of fixing a perpetual name on the country of which they occupied the most ample portion. The barbarians, who followed the hopes of rapine either on the land or sea, were insensibly blended with this triple confederacy; the *Frisians*, who had been tempted by their vicinity to the British shores, might balance during a short space the strength and reputation of the native Saxons; the *Danes*, the *Prussians*, the *Rugians*, are faintly described; and some adventurous *Huns*, who had wandered as far as the Baltic, might embark on board the German vessels for the conquest of a new world.[130] But this arduous achievement was not prepared or executed by the union of national powers. Each intrepid chieftain, according to the measure of his fame and fortunes, assembled his followers; equipped a fleet of three, or perhaps of sixty, vessels; chose the place of the attack, and conducted his subsequent operations according to the events of the war and the dictates of his private interest. In the invasion of Britain many heroes vanquished and fell; but only seven victorious leaders assumed, or at least maintained, the title of kings.

Seven independent thrones, the Saxon Heptarchy, were founded by the conquerors; and seven families, one of which has been continued, by female succession, to our present sovereign, derived their equal and sacred lineage from Woden, the god of war. It has been pretended that this republic of kings was moderated by a general council and a supreme magistrate. But such an artificial scheme of policy is repugnant to the rude and turbulent spirit of the Saxons: their laws are silent, and their imperfect annals afford only a dark and bloody prospect of intestine discord.[131]

A monk, who in the profound ignorance of human life has presumed to exercise the office of historian, strangely disfigures the state of Britain at the time of its separation from the Western empire. Gildas[132] describes in florid language the improvements of agriculture, the foreign trade which flowed with every tide into the Thames and the Severn, the solid and lofty construction of public and private edifices: he accuses the sinful luxury of the British people; of a people, according to the same writer, ignorant of the most simple arts, and incapable, without the aid of the Romans, of providing walls of stone or weapons of iron for the defence of their native land.[133] Under the long dominion of the emperors, Britain had been insensibly moulded into the elegant and servile form of a Roman province, whose safety was intrusted to a foreign power. The subjects of Honorius contemplated their new freedom with surprise and terror; they were left destitute of any civil or military constitution; and their uncertain rulers wanted either skill, or courage, or authority to direct the public force against the common enemy. The introduction of the Saxons betrayed their internal weakness, and degraded the character both of the prince and people. Their consternation magnified the danger, the want of union diminished their resources, and the madness of civil factions was more solicitous to accuse than to remedy the evils which they imputed to the misconduct of their adversaries. Yet the Britons were not ignorant, they could not be ignorant, of the manufacture or the use of arms: the successive and disorderly attacks of the Saxons allowed them to recover from their amazement, and the prosperous or adverse events of the war added discipline and experience to their native valour.

While the continent of Europe and Africa yielded, without resistance, to the barbarians, the British island, alone and unaided, maintained a long, vigorous, though an unsuccessful, struggle, against the formidable pirates who, almost at the same instant, assaulted the northern, the eastern, and the southern coasts. The cities, which had been fortified with skill, were defended with resolution; the advantages of ground, hills, forests, and morasses, were diligently improved by the inhabitants; the conquest of each district was purchased with blood; and the defeats of the Saxons are strongly attested by the discreet silence of their annalist. Hengist might hope to achieve the conquest of Britain; but his ambition, in an active reign of thirty-five years, was confined to the possession of Kent; and the numerous colony which he had planted in the North was extirpated by the sword of the Britons. The monarchy of the West Saxons was laboriously founded by the persevering efforts of three martial generations. The life of Cerdic, one of the bravest of the children of Woden, was consumed in the conquest of Hampshire and the Isle of Wight; and the loss which he sustained in the battle of Mount Badon reduced him to a state of inglorious repose. Kenric, his valiant son, advanced into Wiltshire; besieged Salisbury, at that time seated on a commanding eminence; and vanquished an army which advanced to the relief of the city. In the subsequent battle of Marlborough,[134] his British enemies displayed their military science. Their troops were formed in three lines; each line consisted of three distinct bodies; and the cavalry, the archers, and the pikemen were distributed according to the principles of Roman tactics. The Saxons charged in one weighty column, boldly encountered with their short swords the long lances of the Britons, and maintained an equal conflict till the approach of night. Two decisive victories, the death of three British kings, and the reduction of Cirencester, Bath, and Gloucester, established the fame and power of Ceaulin, the grandson of Cerdic, who carried his victorious arms to the banks of the Severn.

After a war of an hundred years the independent Britons still occupied the whole extent of the western coast, from the wall of Antoninus to the extreme promontory of Cornwall; and the principal cities of the inland country still opposed the arms of the barbarians. Resistance became more languid, as the number and boldness of the assailants continually increased. Winning their way by slow and painful efforts, the Saxons, the Angles, and their various confederates, advanced from the North, from the East, and from the South, till their victorious banners were united in the centre of the island. Beyond the Severn the Britons still asserted their national freedom, which survived the heptarchy, and even the monarchy of the Saxons. The bravest warriors, who preferred exile to slavery, found a secure refuge in the mountains of Wales: the reluctant submission of Cornwall was delayed for some ages;[135] and a band of fugitives acquired a settlement in Gaul, by their own valour, or the liberality of the Merovingian kings.[136] The western angle of Armorica acquired the new appellations of *Cornwall* and the *Lesser Britain*; and the vacant lands of the Osismii were filled by a strange people, who, under the authority of their counts and bishops, preserved the laws and language of their ancestors. To the feeble descendants of Clovis and Charlemagne, the Britons of Armorica refused the customary tribute, subdued the neighbouring dioceses of Vannes, Rennes, and Nantes, and formed a powerful, though vassal, state, which has been united to the crown of France.[137]

In a century of perpetual, or at least implacable, war, much courage, and some skill, must have been exerted for the defence of Britain. Yet if the memory of its champions is almost buried in oblivion, we need not repine; since every age, however destitute of science or virtue, sufficiently abounds with acts of blood and military renown. The tomb of Vortimer, the son of Vortigern, was erected on the margin of the sea-shore, as a landmark formidable to the Saxons, whom he had thrice vanquished in the fields of Kent. Ambrosius Aurelian was descended from a noble family of Romans;[138] his modesty was equal to his valour, and his valour, till the last fatal action,[139] was crowned with splendid success. But every British name is effaced by the illustrious name of ARTHUR,[140] the hereditary prince of the Silures, in South Wales, and the elective king or general of the nation. According to the most rational account, he defeated, in twelve successive battles, the Angles of the North and the Saxons of the West; but the declining age of the hero was embittered by popular ingratitude and domestic misfortunes. The events of his life are less interesting than the singular revolutions of his fame. During a period of five hundred years the tradition of his exploits was preserved, and rudely embellished, by the obscure bards of Wales and Armorica, who were odious to the Saxons, and unknown to the rest of mankind. The pride and curiosity of the Norman conquerors prompted them to inquire into the ancient history of Britain; they listened with fond credulity to the tale of Arthur, and eagerly applauded the merit of a prince who had triumphed over the Saxons, their common enemies. His romance, transcribed in the Latin of Jeffrey of Monmouth, and afterwards translated into the fashionable idiom of the times, was enriched with the various, though incoherent, ornaments which were familiar to the experience, the learning, or the fancy of the twelfth century. The progress of a Phrygian colony, from the Tiber to the Thames, was easily engrafted on the fable of the Æneid; and the royal ancestors of Arthur derived their origin from Troy, and claimed their alliance with the Cæsars. His trophies were decorated with captive provinces and Imperial titles; and his Danish victories avenged the recent injuries of his country. The gallantry and superstition of the British hero, his feasts and tournaments, and the memorable institution of his Knights of the *Round Table*, were faithfully copied from the reigning manners of chivalry; and the fabulous exploits of Uther's son appear less incredible than the adventures which were achieved by the enterprising valour of the Normans. Pilgrimage, and the holy wars, introduced into Europe the specious miracles of Arabian magic. Fairies and giants, flying dragons and enchanted palaces, were blended with the more simple fictions of the West; and the fate of Britain depended on the art, or the predictions, of Merlin. Every nation embraced and adorned the popular romance of Arthur and the Knights of the Round Table: their names were celebrated in Greece and Italy; and the voluminous tales of Sir Lancelot and Sir Tristram were devoutly studied by the princes and nobles who disregarded the genuine heroes and historians of antiquity. At length the light of science and reason was rekindled; the talisman was broken; the visionary fabric melted into air; and by a natural, though unjust, reverse of the public opinion, the severity of the present age is inclined to question the *existence* of Arthur.[141]

Resistance, if it cannot avert, must increase the miseries of conquest; and conquest has never appeared more dreadful and destructive than in the hands of the Saxons, who hated the valour of their enemies, disdained the faith of treaties, and violated, without remorse, the most sacred objects of the Christian worship. The fields of battle might be traced, almost in every district, by monuments of bones; the fragments of falling towers were stained with blood; the last of the Britons, without distinction of age or sex, was massacred,[142] in the ruins of Anderida;[143] and the repetition of such calamities was frequent and familiar under the Saxon heptarchy. The arts and religion, the laws and language, which the Romans had so carefully planted in Britain, were extirpated by their barbarous successors. After the destruction of the principal churches, the bishops who had declined the crown of martyrdom retired with the holy relics into Wales and Armorica; the remains of their flocks were left destitute of any spiritual food; the practice, and even the remembrance, of Christianity were abolished; and the British clergy might obtain some comfort from the damnation of the idolatrous strangers. The kings of France maintained the privileges of their Roman subjects; but the ferocious Saxons trampled on the laws of Rome and of the emperors. The proceedings of civil and criminal jurisdiction, the titles of honour, the forms of office, the ranks of society, and even the domestic rights of marriage, testament, and inheritance, were finally suppressed; and the indiscriminate crowd of noble and plebeian slaves was governed by the traditionary customs which had been coarsely framed for the shepherds and pirates of Germany. The language of science, of business, and of conversation, which had been introduced by the Romans, was lost in the general desolation. A sufficient number of Latin or Celtic words might be assumed by the Germans to express their new wants and ideas;[144] but those *illiterate* Pagans preserved and established the use of their national dialect.[145] Almost every name, conspicuous either in the church or state, reveals its Teutonic origin;[146] and the geography of *England* was universally inscribed with foreign characters and appellations. The example of a revolution so rapid and so complete may not easily be found; but it will excite a probable suspicion that the arts of Rome were less deeply rooted in Britain than in Gaul or Spain; and that the native rudeness of the country and its inhabitants was covered by a thin varnish of Italian manners.

This strange alteration has persuaded historians, and even philosophers, that the provincials of Britain were totally exterminated; and that the vacant land was again peopled by the perpetual influx and rapid increase of the German colonies. Three hundred thousand Saxons are *said* to have obeyed the summons of Hengist;[147] the entire emigration of the Angles was attested, in the age of Bede, by the solitude of their native country;[148] and our experience has shown the free propagation of the human race, if they are cast on a fruitful wilderness, where their steps are unconfined, and their subsistence is plentiful. The Saxon kingdoms displayed the face of recent discovery and cultivation: the towns were small, the villages were distant; the husbandry was languid and unskilful; four sheep were equivalent to an acre of the best land;[149] an ample space of wood and morass was resigned to the vague dominion of nature; and the modern bishopric of Durham, the whole territory from the Tyne to the Tees, had returned to its primitive state of a savage and solitary forest.[150] Such imperfect population might have been supplied, in some generations, by the English colonies; but neither reason nor facts can justify the unnatural supposition that the Saxons of Britain remained alone in the desert which they had subdued. After the sanguinary barbarians had secured their dominion and gratified their revenge, it was their interest to preserve the peasants, as well as the cattle, of the unresisting country. In each successive revolution the patient herd becomes the property of its new masters; and the salutary compact of food and labour is silently ratified by their mutual necessities. Wilfrid, the apostle of Sussex,[151] accepted from his royal convert the gift of the peninsula of Selsey, near Chichester, with the persons and property of its inhabitants, who then amounted to eighty-seven families. He released them at once from spiritual and temporal bondage; and two hundred and fifty slaves of both sexes were baptised by their indulgent master. The kingdom of Sussex, which spread from the sea to the Thames, contained seven thousand families: twelve hundred were ascribed to the Isle of Wight; and, if we multiply this vague computation, it may seem probable that England was cultivated by a million of servants, or *villains*, who were attached to the estates of their arbitrary landlords. The indigent barbarians were often tempted to sell their children or themselves into perpetual, and even foreign, bondage;[152] yet the special exemptions which were granted to *national* slaves[153] sufficiently declare that they were much less numerous than the strangers and captives who had lost their liberty, or changed their masters, by the accidents of war. When time and religion had mitigated the fierce spirit of the Anglo-Saxons, the laws encouraged the frequent practice of manumission; and their subjects, of Welsh or Cambrian extraction, assumed the respectable station of inferior freemen, possessed of lands, and entitled to the rights of civil society.[154] Such gentle treatment might secure the allegiance of a fierce people, who had been recently subdued on the confines of Wales and Cornwall. The sage Ina, the legislator of Wessex, united the two nations in the bands of domestic alliance; and four British lords of Somersetshire may be honourably distinguished in the court of a Saxon monarch.[155]

The independent Britons appear to have relapsed into the state of original barbarism from whence they had been imperfectly reclaimed. Separated by their enemies from the rest of mankind, they soon became an object of scandal and abhorrence to the catholic world.[156] Christianity was still professed in the mountains of Wales; but the rude schismatics, in the *form* of the clerical tonsure, and in the *day* of the celebration of Easter, obstinately resisted the imperious mandates of the Roman pontiffs. The use of the Latin language was insensibly abolished, and the Britons were deprived of the arts and learning which Italy communicated to her Saxon proselytes. In Wales and Armorica, the Celtic tongue, the native idiom of the West, was preserved and propagated; and the *Bards*, who had been the companions of the Druids, were still protected, in the sixteenth century, by the laws of Elizabeth. Their chief, a respectable officer of the courts of Pengwern, or Aberfraw, or Caermarthen, accompanied the king's servants to war: the monarchy of the Britons, which he sung in the front of battle, excited their courage, and justified their depredations; and the songster claimed for his legitimate prize the fairest heifer of the spoil. His subordinate ministers, the masters and disciples of vocal and instrumental music, visited, in their respective circuits, the royal, the noble, and the plebeian houses; and the public poverty, almost exhausted by the clergy, was oppressed by the importunate demands of the bards. Their rank and merit were ascertained by solemn trials, and the strong belief of supernatural inspiration exalted the fancy of the poet and of his audience.[157] The last retreats of Celtic freedom, the extreme territories of Gaul and Britain, were less adapted to agriculture than to pasturage: the wealth of the Britons consisted in their flocks and herds; milk and flesh were their ordinary food; and bread was sometimes esteemed, or rejected, as a foreign luxury. Liberty had peopled the mountains of Wales and the morasses of Armorica: but their populousness has been maliciously ascribed to the loose practice of polygamy; and the houses of these licentious barbarians have been supposed to contain ten wives, and perhaps fifty children.[158] Their disposition was rash and choleric: they were bold in action and in speech;[159] and as they were ignorant of the arts of peace, they alternately indulged their passions in foreign and domestic war. The cavalry of Armorica, the spearmen of Gwent, and the archers of Merioneth, were equally formidable; but their poverty could seldom procure either shields or helmets; and the inconvenient weight would have retarded the speed and agility of their desultory operations. One of the greatest of the English monarchs was requested to satisfy the curiosity of a Greek emperor concerning the state of Britain; and Henry II. could assert, from his personal experience, that Wales was inhabited by a race of naked warriors, who encountered, without fear, the defensive armour of their enemies.[160]

By the revolution of Britain the limits of science as well as of empire were contracted. The dark cloud which had been cleared by the Phœnician discoveries, and finally dispelled by the arms of Cæsar, again settled on the shores of the Atlantic, and a Roman province was again lost among the fabulous Islands of the Ocean. One hundred and fifty years after the reign of Honorius the gravest historian of the times[161] describes the wonders of a remote isle, whose eastern and western parts are divided by an antique wall, the boundary of life and death, or, more properly, of truth and fiction. The east is a fair country, inhabited by a civilised people: the air is healthy, the waters are pure and plentiful, and the earth yields her regular and fruitful increase. In the west, beyond the wall, the air is infectious and mortal; the ground is covered with serpents; and this dreary solitude is the region of departed spirits, who are transported from the opposite shores in substantial boats and by living rowers. Some families of fishermen, the subjects of the Franks, are excused from tribute, in consideration of the mysterious office which is performed by these Charons of the ocean. Each in his turn is summoned, at the hour of midnight, to hear the voices, and even the names, of the ghosts: he is sensible of their weight, and he feels himself impelled by an unknown, but irresistible, power. After this dream of fancy, we read with astonishment that the name of this island is *Brittia*; that it lies in the ocean, against the mouth of the Rhine, and less than thirty miles from the continent; that it is possessed by three nations, the Frisians, the Angles, and the Britons; and that some Angles had appeared at Constantinople in the train of the French ambassadors. From these ambassadors Procopius might be informed of a singular, though not improbable, adventure, which announces the spirit, rather than the delicacy, of an English heroine. She had been betrothed to Radiger, king of the Varni, a tribe of Germans who touched the ocean and the Rhine; but the perfidious lover was tempted, by motives of policy, to prefer his father's widow, the sister of Theodebert, king of the Franks.[162] The forsaken princess of the Angles, instead of bewailing, revenged her disgrace. Her warlike subjects are *said* to have been ignorant of the use, and even of the form, of a horse; but she boldly sailed from Britain to the mouth of the Rhine, with a fleet of four hundred ships and an army of one hundred thousand men. After the loss of a battle, the captive Radiger implored the mercy of his victorious bride, who generously pardoned his offence, dismissed her rival, and compelled the king of the Varni to discharge with honour and fidelity the duties of a husband.[163] This gallant exploit appears to be the last naval enterprise of the Anglo-Saxons. The arts of navigation, by which they had acquired the empire of Britain and of the sea, were soon neglected by the indolent barbarians, who supinely renounced all the commercial advantages of their insular situation. Seven independent kingdoms were agitated by perpetual discord; and the *British world* was seldom connected, either in peace or war, with the nations of the continent.[164]

I have now accomplished the laborious narrative of the decline and fall of the Roman empire, from the fortunate age of Trajan and the Antonines to its total extinction in the West, about five centuries after the Christian era. At that unhappy period the Saxons fiercely struggled with the natives for the possession of Britain: Gaul and Spain were divided between the powerful monarchies of the Franks and Visigoths and the dependent kingdoms of the Suevi and Burgundians: Africa was exposed to the cruel persecution of the Vandals and the savage insults of the Moors: Rome and Italy, as far as the banks of the Danube, were afflicted by an army of barbarian mercenaries, whose lawless tyranny was succeeded by the reign of Theodoric the Ostrogoth. All the subjects of the empire, who, by the use of the Latin language, more particularly deserved the name and privileges of Romans, were oppressed by the disgrace and calamities of foreign conquest; and the victorious nations of Germany established a new system of manners and government in the western countries of Europe. The majesty of Rome was faintly represented by the princes of Constantinople, the feeble and imaginary successors of Augustus. Yet they continued to reign over the East, from the Danube to the Nile and Tigris; the Gothic and Vandal kingdoms of Italy and Africa were subverted by the arms of Justinian; and the history of the *Greek* emperors may still afford a long series of instructive lessons and interesting revolutions.

GENERAL OBSERVATIONS ON THE FALL OF THE ROMAN EMPIRE IN THE WEST

THE Greeks, after their country had been reduced into a province, imputed the triumphs of Rome, not to the merit, but to the FORTUNE, of the republic. The inconstant goddess who so blindly distributes and resumes her favours, had *now* consented (such was the language of envious flattery) to resign her wings, to descend from her globe, and to fix her firm and immutable throne on the banks of the Tiber.[1] A wiser Greek, who has composed, with a philosophic spirit, the memorable history of his own times, deprived his countrymen of this vain and delusive comfort, by opening to their view the deep foundations of the greatness of Rome.[2] The fidelity of the citizens to each other and to the state was confirmed by the habits of education and the prejudices of religion. Honour, as well as virtue, was the principle of the republic; the ambitious citizens laboured to deserve the solemn glories of a triumph; and the ardour of the Roman youth was kindled into active emulation as often as they beheld the domestic images of their ancestors.[3] The temperate struggles of the patricians and plebeians had finally established the firm and equal balance of the constitution, which united the freedom of popular assemblies with the authority and wisdom of a senate and the executive powers of a regal magistrate. When the consul displayed the standard of the republic, each citizen bound himself, by the obligation of an oath, to draw his sword in the cause of his country till he had discharged the sacred duty by a military service of ten years. This wise institution continually poured into the field the rising generations of freemen and soldiers; and their numbers were reinforced by the warlike and populous states of Italy, who, after a brave resistance, had yielded to the valour and embraced the alliance of the Romans. The sage historian, who excited the virtue of the younger Scipio and beheld the ruin of Carthage,[4] has accurately described their military system;

their levies, arms, exercises, subordination, marches, encampments; and the invincible legion, superior in active strength to the Macedonian phalanx of Philip and Alexander. From these institutions of peace and war Polybius has deduced the spirit and success of a people incapable of fear and impatient of repose. The ambitious design of conquest, which might have been defeated by the seasonable conspiracy of mankind, was attempted and achieved; and the perpetual violation of justice was maintained by the political virtues of prudence and courage. The arms of the republic, sometimes vanquished in battle, always victorious in war, advanced with rapid steps to the Euphrates, the Danube, the Rhine, and the Ocean; and the images of gold, or silver, or brass, that might serve to represent the nations and their kings, were successively broken by the *iron* monarchy of Rome.[5]

The rise of a city, which swelled into an empire, may deserve, as a singular prodigy, the reflection of a philosophic mind. But the decline of Rome was the natural and inevitable effect of immoderate greatness. Prosperity ripened the principle of decay; the causes of destruction multiplied with the extent of conquest; and as soon as time or accident had removed the artificial supports, the stupendous fabric yielded to the pressure of its own weight. The story of its ruin is simple and obvious; and instead of inquiring *why* the Roman empire was destroyed, we should rather be surprised that it had subsisted so long. The victorious legions, who, in distant wars, acquired the vices of strangers and mercenaries, first oppressed the freedom of the republic, and afterwards violated the majesty of the purple. The emperors, anxious for their personal safety and the public peace, were reduced to the base expedient of corrupting the discipline which rendered them alike formidable to their sovereign and to the enemy; the vigour of the military government was relaxed and finally dissolved by the partial institutions of Constantine; and the Roman world was overwhelmed by a deluge of barbarians.

The decay of Rome has been frequently ascribed to the translation of the seat of empire; but this history has already shown that the powers of Government were *divided* rather than *removed*. The throne of Constantinople was erected in the East; while the West was still possessed by a series of emperors who held their residence in Italy, and claimed their equal inheritance of the legions and provinces. This dangerous novelty impaired the strength and fomented the vices of a double reign: the instruments of an oppressive and arbitrary system were multiplied; and a vain emulation of luxury, not of merit, was introduced and supported between the degenerate successors of Theodosius. Extreme distress, which unites the virtue of a free people, embitters the factions of a declining monarchy. The hostile favourites of Arcadius and Honorius betrayed the republic to its common enemies; and the Byzantine court beheld with indifference, perhaps with pleasure, the disgrace of Rome, the misfortunes of Italy, and the loss of the West. Under the succeeding reigns the alliance of the two empires was restored; but the aid of the Oriental Romans was tardy, doubtful, and ineffectual; and the national schism of the Greeks and Latins was enlarged by the perpetual difference of language and manners, of interests, and even of religion. Yet the salutary event approved in some measure the judgment of Constantine. During a long period of decay his impregnable city repelled the victorious armies of barbarians, protected the wealth of Asia, and commanded, both in peace and war, the important straits which connect the Euxine and Mediterranean seas. The foundation of Constantinople more essentially contributed to the preservation of the East than to the ruin of the West.

As the happiness of a *future* life is the great object of religion, we may hear without surprise or scandal that the introduction, or at least the abuse of Christianity, had some influence on the decline and fall of the Roman empire. The clergy successfully preached the doctrines of patience and pusillanimity; the active virtues of society were discouraged; and the last remains of military spirit were buried in the cloister: a large portion of public and private wealth was consecrated to the specious demands of charity and devotion; and the soldiers' pay was lavished on the useless multitudes of both sexes who could only plead the merits of abstinence and chastity. Faith, zeal, curiosity, and more earthly passions of malice and ambition, kindled the flame of theological discord; the church, and even the state, were distracted by religious factions, whose conflicts were sometimes bloody and always implacable; the attention of the emperors was diverted from camps to synods; the Roman world was oppressed by a new species of tyranny; and the persecuted sects became the secret enemies of their country. Yet party-spirit, however pernicious or absurd, is a principle of union as well as of dissension. The bishops, from eighteen hundred pulpits, inculcated the duty of passive obedience to a lawful and orthodox sovereign; their frequent assemblies and perpetual correspondence maintained the communion of distant churches; and the benevolent temper of the Gospel was strengthened, though confirmed, by the spiritual alliance of the catholics. The sacred indolence of the monks was devoutly embraced by a servile and effeminate age; but if superstition had not afforded a decent retreat, the same vices would have tempted the unworthy Romans to desert, from baser motives, the standard of the republic. Religious precepts are easily obeyed which indulge and sanctify the natural inclinations of their votaries; but the pure and genuine influence of Christianity may be traced in its beneficial, though imperfect, effects on the barbarian proselytes of the North. If the decline of the Roman empire was hastened by the conversion of Constantine, his victorious religion broke the violence of the fall, and mollified the ferocious temper of the conquerors.

This awful revolution may be usefully applied to the instruction of the present age. It is the duty of a patriot to prefer and promote the exclusive interest and glory of his native country: but a philosopher may be permitted to enlarge his views, and to consider Europe as one great republic, whose various inhabitants have attained almost the same level of politeness and cultivation. The balance of power will continue to fluctuate, and the prosperity of our own or the neighbouring kingdoms may be alternately exalted or depressed; but these partial events cannot essentially injure our general state of happiness, the system of arts, and laws, and manners, which so advantageously distinguish, above the rest of mankind, the Europeans and their colonies. The savage nations of the globe are the common enemies of civilised society; and we may inquire, with anxious curiosity, whether Europe is still threatened with a repetition of those calamities which formerly oppressed the arms and institutions of Rome. Perhaps the same reflections will illustrate the fall of that mighty empire, and explain the probable causes of our actual security.

I. The Romans were ignorant of the extent of their dangers and the number of their enemies. Beyond the Rhine and Danube the northern countries of Europe and Asia were filled with innumerable tribes of hunters and shepherds, poor, voracious, and turbulent; bold in arms, and impatient to ravish the fruits of industry. The barbarian world was agitated by the rapid impulse of war; and the peace of Gaul or Italy was shaken by the distant revolutions of China.

The Huns, who fled before a victorious enemy, directed their march towards the West; and the torrent was swelled by the gradual accession of captives and allies. The flying tribes who yielded to the Huns assumed in *their* turn the spirit of conquest; the endless column of barbarians pressed on the Roman empire with accumulated weight; and, if the foremost were destroyed, the vacant space was instantly replenished by new assailants. Such formidable emigrations no longer issue from the North; and the long repose, which has been imputed to the decrease of population, is the happy consequence of the progress of arts and agriculture. Instead of some rude villages thinly scattered among its woods and morasses, Germany now produces a list of two thousand three hundred walled towns: the Christian kingdoms of Denmark, Sweden, and Poland have been successively established; and the Hanse merchants, with the Teutonic knights, have extended their colonies along the coast of the Baltic as far as the Gulf of Finland. From the Gulf of Finland to the Eastern Ocean, Russia now assumes the form of a powerful and civilised empire. The plough, the loom, and the forge are introduced on the banks of the Volga, the Oby, and the Lena; and the fiercest of the Tartar hordes have been taught to tremble and obey. The reign of independent barbarism is now contracted to a narrow span; and the remnant of Calmucks or Uzbecks, whose forces may be almost numbered, cannot seriously excite the apprehensions of the great republic of Europe.[6] Yet this apparent security should not tempt us to forget that new enemies and unknown dangers may *possibly* arise from some obscure people, scarcely visible in the map of the world. The Arabs or Saracens, who spread their conquests from India to Spain, had languished in poverty and contempt till Mahomet breathed into those savage bodies the soul of enthusiasm.

II. The empire of Rome was firmly established by the singular and perfect coalition of its members. The subject nations, resigning the hope and even the wish of independence, embraced the character of Roman citizens; and the provinces of the West were reluctantly torn by the barbarians from the bosom of their mother country.[7] But this union was purchased by the loss of national freedom and military spirit; and the servile provinces, destitute of life and motion, expected their safety from the mercenary troops and governors who were directed by the orders of a distant court. The happiness of an hundred millions depended on the personal merit of one or two men, perhaps children, whose minds were corrupted by education, luxury, and despotic power. The deepest wounds were inflicted on the empire during the minorities of the sons and grandsons of Theodosius; and, after those incapable princes seemed to attain the age of manhood, they abandoned the church to the bishops, the state to the eunuchs, and the provinces to the barbarians. Europe is now divided into twelve powerful, though unequal kingdoms, three respectable commonwealths, and a variety of smaller, though independent states: the chances of royal and ministerial talent are multiplied, at least, with the number of its rulers; and a Julian, or Semiramis, may reign in the North, while Arcadius and Honorius again slumber on the thrones of the South. The abuses of tyranny are restrained by the mutual influence of fear and shame; republics have acquired order and stability; monarchies have imbibed the principles of freedom, or, at least, of moderation; and some sense of honour and justice is introduced into the most defective constitutions by the general manners of the times. In peace, the progress of knowledge and industry is accelerated by the emulation of so many active rivals: in war, the European forces are exercised by temperate and undecisive contests. If a savage conqueror should issue from the deserts of Tartary, he must repeatedly vanquish the robust peasants of Russia, the numerous armies of Germany, the gallant nobles of France, and the intrepid freemen of Britain; who, perhaps, might confederate for their common defence. Should the victorious barbarians carry slavery and desolation as far as the Atlantic Ocean, ten thousand vessels would transport beyond their pursuit the remains of civilised society; and Europe would revive and flourish in the American world, which is already filled with her colonies and institutions.[8]

III. Cold, poverty, and a life of danger and fatigue fortify the strength and courage of barbarians. In every age they have oppressed the polite and peaceful nations of China, India, and Persia, who neglected, and still neglect, to counterbalance these natural powers by the resources of military art. The warlike states of antiquity, Greece, Macedonia, and Rome, educated a race of soldiers; exercised their bodies, disciplined their courage, multiplied their forces by regular evolutions, and converted the iron which they possessed into strong and serviceable weapons. But this superiority insensibly declined with their laws and manners: and the feeble policy of Constantine and his successors armed and instructed, for the ruin of the empire, the rude valour of the barbarian mercenaries. The military art has been changed by the invention of gunpowder; which enables man to command the two most powerful agents of nature, air and fire. Mathematics, chemistry, mechanics, architecture, have been applied to the service of war; and the adverse parties oppose to each other the most elaborate modes of attack and of defence. Historians may indignantly observe that the preparations of a siege would found and maintain a flourishing colony;[9] yet we cannot be displeased that the subversion of a city should be a work of cost and difficulty; or that an industrious people should be protected by those arts which survive and supply the decay of military virtue. Cannon and fortifications now form an impregnable barrier against the Tartar horse; and Europe is secure from any future irruption of barbarians; since, before they can conquer, they must cease to be barbarous. Their gradual advances in the science of war would always be accompanied, as we may learn from the example of Russia, with a proportionable improvement in the arts of peace and civil policy; and they themselves must deserve a place among the polished nations whom they subdue.

Should these speculations be found doubtful or fallacious, there still remains a more humble source of comfort and hope. The discoveries of ancient and modern navigators, and the domestic history or tradition of the most enlightened nations, represent the *human savage* naked both in mind and body, and destitute of laws, of arts, of ideas, and almost of language.[10] From this abject condition, perhaps the primitive and universal state of man, he has gradually arisen to command the animals, to fertilise the earth, to traverse the ocean, and to measure the heavens. His progress in the improvement and exercise of his mental and corporeal faculties[11] has been irregular and various; infinitely slow in the beginning, and increasing by degrees with redoubled velocity: ages of laborious ascent have been followed by a moment of rapid downfall; and the several climates of the globe have felt the vicissitudes of light and darkness. Yet the experience of four thousand years should enlarge our hopes and diminish our apprehensions: we cannot determine to what height the human species may aspire in their advance towards perfection; but it may safely be presumed that no people, unless the face of nature is changed, will relapse into their original barbarism. The improvements of society may be viewed under a threefold aspect. 1. The poet or philosopher illustrates his age and country by the efforts of a *single* mind; but these superior powers of reason or fancy are rare and spontaneous productions; and the genius of Homer, or Cicero, or Newton, would excite less admiration if they could be created by the will of a prince or the lessons of a preceptor. 2. The benefits of law and policy, of trade and manufactures, of arts and sciences, are more solid and permanent; and *many* individuals may be qualified, by education and discipline, to promote, in their respective stations, the interest of the community. But this general order is the effect of skill and labour; and the complex machinery may be decayed by time, or injured by violence. 3. Fortunately for mankind, the more useful, or, at least, more necessary arts, can be performed without superior talents or national subordination; without powers of *one*, or the union of *many*. Each village, each family, each individual, must always possess both ability and inclination to perpetuate the use of fire[12] and of metals; the propagation and service of domestic animals; the methods of hunting and fishing; the rudiments of navigation; the imper-

fect cultivation of corn or other nutritive grain; and the simple practice of the mechanic trades. Private genius and public industry may be extirpated, but these hardy plants survive the tempest, and strike an everlasting root into the most unfavourable soil. The splendid days of Augustus and Trajan were eclipsed by a cloud of ignorance; and the barbarians subverted the laws and palaces of Rome. But the scythe, the invention or emblem of Saturn,[13] still continued annually to mow the harvests of Italy; and the human feasts of the Læstrigons[14] have never been renewed on the coast of Campania.

Since the first discovery of the arts, war, commerce, and religious zeal have diffused among the savages of the Old and New World these inestimable gifts: they have been successively propagated; they can never be lost. We may therefore acquiesce in the pleasing conclusion that every age of the world has increased and still increases the real wealth, the happiness, the knowledge, and perhaps the virtue, of the human race.[15]

CHAPTER XXXIX

Zeno and Anastasius, Emperors of the East. Birth, Education, and First Exploits of Theodoric the Ostrogoth. His Invasion and Conquest of Italy. The Gothic Kingdom of Italy. State of the West. Military and Civil Government. The Senator Boethius. Last Acts and Death of Theodoric.

AFTER the fall of the Roman empire in the West, an interval of fifty years, till the memorable reign of Justinian, is faintly marked by the obscure names and imperfect annals of Zeno, Anastasius, and Justin, who successively ascended the throne of Constantinople. During the same period, Italy revived and flourished under the government of a Gothic king who might have deserved a statue among the best and bravest of the ancient Romans.

Theodoric the Ostrogoth, the fourteenth in lineal descent of the royal line of the Amali,[1] was born in the neighbourhood of Vienna[2] two years after the death of Attila. A recent victory had restored the independence of the Ostrogoths; and the three brothers, Walamir, Theodemir, and Widimir, who ruled that warlike nation with united counsels, had separately pitched their habitations in the fertile, though desolate, province of Pannonia. The Huns still threatened their revolted subjects, but their hasty attack was repelled by the single forces of

Walamir, and the news of his victory reached the distant camp of his brother in the same auspicious moment that the favourite concubine of Theodemir was delivered of a son and heir. In the eighth year of his age, Theodoric was reluctantly yielded by his father to the public interest, as the pledge of an alliance which Leo, emperor of the East, had consented to purchase by an annual subsidy of three hundred pounds of gold. The royal hostage was educated at Constantinople with care and tenderness. His body was formed to all the exercises of war, his mind was expanded by the habits of liberal conversation; he frequented the schools of the most skilful masters, but he disdained or neglected the arts of Greece; and so ignorant did he always remain of the first elements of science, that a rude mark was contrived to represent the signature of the illiterate king of Italy.[3] As soon as he had attained the age of eighteen he was restored to the wishes of the Ostrogoths, whom the emperor aspired to gain by liberality and confidence. Walamir had fallen in battle; the youngest of the brothers, Widimir, had led away into Italy and Gaul an army of barbarians; and the whole nation acknowledged for their king the father of Theodoric. His ferocious subjects admired the strength and stature of their young prince,[4] and he soon convinced them that he had not degenerated from the valour of his ancestors. At the head of six thousand volunteers he secretly left the camp in quest of adventures, descended the Danube as far as Singidunum or Belgrade, and soon returned to his father with the spoils of a Sarmatian king whom he had vanquished and slain. Such triumphs, however, were productive only of fame, and the invincible Ostrogoths were reduced to extreme distress by the want of clothing and food. They unanimously resolved to desert their Pannonian encampments, and boldly to advance into the warm and wealthy neighbourhood of the Byzantine court, which already maintained in pride and luxury so many bands of confederate Goths. After proving, by some acts of hostility, that they could be dangerous, or at least troublesome, enemies, the Ostrogoths sold at a high price their reconciliation and fidelity, accepted a donative of lands and money, and were intrusted with the defence of the lower Danube under the command of Theodoric, who succeeded after his father's death to the hereditary throne of the Amali.[5]

An hero, descended from a race of kings, must have despised the base Isaurian who was invested with the Roman purple, without any endowments of mind or body, without any advantages of royal birth or superior qualifications. After the failure of the Theodosian line, the choice of Pulcheria and of the senate might be justified in some measure by the characters of Marcian and Leo; but the latter of these princes confirmed and dishonoured his reign by the perfidious murder of Aspar and his sons, who too rigorously exacted the debt of gratitude and obedience. The inheritance of Leo and of the East was peaceably devolved on his infant grandson, the son of his daughter Ariadne; and her Isaurian husband, the fortunate Trascalisseus, exchanged that barbarous sound for the Grecian appellation of Zeno. After the decease of the elder Leo, he approached with unnatural respect the throne of his son, humbly received as a gift the second rank in the empire, and soon excited the public suspicion on the sudden and premature death of his young colleague, whose life could no longer promote the success of his ambition. But the palace of Constantinople was ruled by female influence, and agitated by female passions; and Verina, the widow of Leo, claiming his empire as her own, pronounced a sentence of deposition against the worthless and ungrateful servant on whom she alone had bestowed the sceptre of the East.[6] As soon as she sounded a revolt in the ears of Zeno, he fled with precipitation into the mountains of Isauria; and her brother Basiliscus, already infamous by his African expedition,[7] was unanimously proclaimed by the servile senate. But the reign of the usurper was short and turbulent. Basiliscus presumed to assassinate the lover of his sister; he dared to offend the lover of his wife, the vain and insolent Harmatius, who, in the midst of Asiatic luxury, affected the dress, the demeanour, and the surname of Achilles.[8] By the conspiracy of the malcontents, Zeno was recalled from exile; the armies, the capital, the person of Basiliscus, were betrayed; and his whole family was condemned to the long agony of cold and hunger by the inhuman conqueror, who wanted courage to encounter or to forgive his enemies. The haughty spirit of Verina was still incapable of submission or repose. She provoked the enmity of a favourite general, embraced his cause as soon as he was disgraced, created a new emperor in Syria and Egypt, raised an army of seventy thousand men, and persisted to the last moment of her life in a fruitless rebellion, which, according to the fashion of the age, had been predicted by Christian hermits and Pagan magicians. While the East was afflicted by the passions of Verina, her daughter Ariadne was distinguished by the female virtues of mildness and fidelity; she followed her husband in his exile, and after his restoration she implored his clemency in favour of her mother. On the decease of Zeno, Ariadne, the daughter, the mother, and the widow of an emperor, gave her hand and the Imperial title to Anastasius, an aged domestic of the palace, who survived his elevation above twenty-seven years, and whose character is attested by the acclamation of the people, "Reign as you have lived!"[9]

Whatever fear or affection could bestow was profusely lavished by Zeno on the king of the Ostrogoths; the rank of patrician and consul, the command of the Palatine troops, an equestrian statue, a treasure in gold and silver of many thousand pounds, the name of son, and the promise of a rich and honourable wife. As long as Theodoric condescended to serve, he supported with courage and fidelity the cause of his benefactor; his rapid march contributed to the restoration of Zeno; and in the second revolt, the *Walamirs*, as they were called, pursued and pressed the Asiatic rebels, till they left an easy victory to the Imperial troops.[10] But the faithful servant was suddenly converted into a formidable enemy, who spread the flames of war from Constantinople to the Hadriatic; many flourishing cities were reduced to ashes, and the agriculture of Thrace was almost extirpated by the wanton cruelty of the Goths, who deprived their captive peasants of the right hand that guided the plough.[11] On such occasions Theodoric sustained the loud and specious reproach of disloyalty, of ingratitude, and of insatiate avarice, which could be only excused by the hard necessity of his situation. He reigned, not as the monarch, but as the minister of a ferocious people, whose spirit was unbroken by slavery, and impatient of real or imaginary insults. Their poverty was incurable, since the most liberal donatives were soon dissipated in wasteful luxury, and the most fertile estates became barren in their hands; they despised, but they envied, the laborious provincials; and when their subsistence had failed, the Ostrogoths embraced the familiar resources of war and rapine. It had been the wish of Theodoric (such, at least, was his declaration) to lead a peaceful, obscure, obedient life, on the confines of Scythia, till the Byzantine court, by splendid and fallacious promises, seduced him to attack a confederate tribe of Goths, who had been engaged in the party of Basiliscus. He marched from his station in Mæsia, on the solemn assurance that before he reached Adrianople he should meet a plentiful convoy of provisions, and a reinforcement of eight thousand horse and thirty thousand foot, while the legions of Asia were encamped at Heraclea to second his operations. These measures were disappointed by mutual jealousy. As he advanced into Thrace, the son of Theodemir found an inhospitable solitude, and his Gothic followers, with an heavy train of horses, of mules, and of waggons, were betrayed by their guides among the rocks and precipices of Mount Sondis, where he was assaulted by the arms and invectives of Theodoric, the son of Triarius. From a neighbouring height his artful rival harangued the camp of the *Walamirs*, and branded their leader with the opprobrious names of child, of madman, of perjured traitor, the enemy of his blood and nation. "Are you ignorant," exclaimed the son of Triarius, "that it is the constant policy of the Romans to destroy the Goths by each other's swords? Are you insensible that the victor in this unnatural contest will be exposed, and justly exposed, to their implacable revenge? Where are those warriors, my kinsmen and thy own, whose widows now lament that their lives were sacrificed to thy rash ambition? Where is the wealth which thy soldiers possessed when they were first allured from their native homes to enlist under thy standard? Each of them was then master of three or four horses; they now follow thee on foot like slaves, through the deserts of Thrace; those men who were tempted by the hope of measuring gold with a bushel, those brave men who are as free and as noble as thyself." A language so well suited to the temper of the Goths excited clamour and discontent; and the son of Theodemir, apprehensive of being left alone, was compelled to embrace his brethren, and to imitate the example of Roman perfidy.[12]

In every state of his fortune the prudence and firmness of Theodoric were equally conspicuous: whether he threatened Constantinople at the head of the confederate Goths, or retreated with a faithful band to the mountains and sea-coast of Epirus. At length the accidental death of the son of Triarius[13] destroyed the balance which the Romans had been so anxious to preserve, the whole nation acknowledged the supremacy of the Amali, and the Byzantine court subscribed an ignominious and oppressive treaty.[14] The senate had already declared that it was necessary to choose a party among the Goths, since the public was unequal to the support of their united forces. A subsidy of two thousand pounds of gold, with the ample pay of thirteen thousand men, were required for the least considerable of their armies;[15] and the Isaurians, who guarded not the empire but the emperor, enjoyed, besides the privilege of rapine, an annual pension of five thousand pounds. The sagacious mind of Theodoric soon perceived that he was odious to the Romans, and suspected by the barbarians; he understood the popular murmur, that his subjects were exposed in their frozen huts to intolerable hardships, while their king was dissolved in the luxury of Greece; and he prevented the painful alternative of encountering the Goths as the champion, or of leading them to the field as the enemy, of Zeno. Embracing an enterprise worthy of his courage and ambition, Theodoric addressed the emperor in the following words:—"Although your servant is maintained in affluence by your liberality, graciously listen to the wishes of my heart! Italy, the inheritance of your predecessors, and Rome itself, the head and mistress of the world, now fluctuate under the violence and oppression of Odoacer the mercenary. Direct me, with my national troops, to march against the tyrant. If I fall, you will be relieved from an expensive and troublesome friend: if, with the Divine permission, I succeed, I shall govern in your name, and to your glory, the Roman senate, and the part of the republic delivered from slavery by my victorious arms." The proposal of Theodoric was accepted, and perhaps had been suggested, by the Byzantine court. But the forms of the commission or grant appear to have been expressed with a prudent ambiguity, which might be explained by the event; and it was left doubtful whether the conqueror of Italy should reign as the lieutenant, the vassal, or the ally, of the emperor of the East.[16]

The reputation both of the leader and of the war diffused a universal ardour; the *Walamirs* were multiplied by the Gothic swarms already engaged in the service, or seated in the provinces, of the empire; and each bold barbarian who had heard of the wealth and beauty of Italy was impatient to seek, through the most perilous adventures, the possession of such enchanting objects. The march of Theodoric must be considered as the emigration of an entire people; the wives and children of the Goths, their aged parents, and most precious effects were carefully transported; and some idea may be formed of the heavy baggage that now followed the camp by the loss of two thousand waggons which had been sustained in a single action in the war of Epirus. For their subsistence, the Goths depended on the magazines of corn, which was ground in portable mills by the hands of their women, on the milk and flesh of their flocks and herds, on the casual produce of the chase, and upon the contributions which they might impose on all who should presume to dispute the passage or to refuse their friendly assistance. Notwithstanding these precautions, they were exposed to the danger, and almost to the distress, of famine, in a march of seven hundred miles, which had been undertaken in the depth of a rigorous winter. Since the fall of the Roman power, Dacia and Pannonia no longer exhibited the rich prospect of populous cities, well-cultivated fields, and convenient highways: the reign of barbarism and desolation was restored; and the tribes of Bulgarians, Gepidæ, and Sarmatians, who had occupied the vacant province, were prompted by their native fierceness, or the solicitations of Odoacer, to resist the progress of his enemy. In many obscure though bloody battles, Theodoric fought and vanquished: till at length, surmounting every obstacle by skilful conduct and persevering courage, he descended from the Julian Alps, and displayed his invincible banners on the confines of Italy.[17]

Odoacer, a rival not unworthy of his arms, had already occupied the advantageous and well-known post of the river Sontius, near the ruins of Aquileia, at the head of a powerful host, whose independent *kings*[18] or leaders disdained the duties of subordination, and the prudence of delays. No sooner had Theodoric granted a short repose and refreshment to his wearied cavalry, than he boldly attacked the fortifications of the enemy; the Ostrogoths showed more ardour to acquire, than the mercenaries to defend, the lands of Italy, and the reward of the first victory was the possession of the Venetian province as far as the walls of Verona. In the neighbourhood of that city, on the steep banks of the rapid Adige, he was opposed by a new army, reinforced in its numbers, and not impaired in its courage: the contest was more obstinate, but the event was still more decisive; Odoacer fled to Ravenna, Theodoric advanced to Milan, and the vanquished troops saluted their conqueror with loud acclamations of respect and fidelity. But their want either of constancy or of faith soon exposed him to the most imminent danger; his vanguard, with several Gothic counts, which had been rashly intrusted to a deserter, was betrayed and destroyed near Faenza by his double treachery; Odoacer again appeared master of the field, and the invader, strongly entrenched in his camp of Pavia, was reduced to solicit the aid of a kindred nation, the Visigoths of Gaul. In the course of this history the most voracious appetite for war will be abundantly satiated; nor can I much lament that our dark and imperfect materials do not afford a more ample narrative of the distress of Italy, and of the fierce conflict which was finally decided by the abilities, experience, and valour of the Gothic king. Immediately before the battle of Verona he visited the tent of his mother[19] and sister, and requested that on a day, the most illustrious festival of his life, they would adorn him with the rich garments which they had worked with their own hands. "Our glory," said he, "is mutual and inseparable. You are known to the world as the mother of Theodoric, and it becomes me to prove that I am the genuine offspring of those heroes from whom I claim my descent." The wife or concubine of Theodemir was inspired with the spirit of the German matrons, who esteemed their sons' honour far above their safety; and it is reported that in a desperate action, when Theodoric himself was hurried along by the torrent of a flying crowd, she boldly met them at the entrance of the camp, and, by her generous reproaches, drove them back on the swords of the enemy.[20]

From the Alps to the extremity of Calabria, Theodoric reigned by the right of conquest: the Vandal ambassadors surrendered the island of Sicily as a lawful appendage of his kingdom, and he was accepted as the deliverer of Rome by the senate and people, who had shut their gates against the flying usurper.[21] Ravenna alone, secure in the fortifications of art and nature, still sustained a siege of almost three years, and the daring sallies of Odoacer carried slaughter and dismay into the Gothic camp. At length, destitute of provisions and hopeless of relief, that unfortunate monarch yielded to the groans of his subjects and the clamours of his soldiers. A treaty of peace was negotiated by the bishop of Ravenna; the Ostrogoths were admitted into the city; and the hostile kings consented, under the sanction of an oath, to rule with equal and undivided authority the provinces of Italy. The event of such an agreement may be easily foreseen. After some days had been devoted to the semblance of joy and friendship, Odoacer, in the midst of a solemn banquet, was stabbed by the hand, or at least by the command, of his rival. Secret and effectual orders had been previously despatched; the faithless and rapacious mercenaries at the same moment, and without resistance, were universally massacred; and the royalty of Theodoric was proclaimed by the Goths, with the tardy, reluctant, ambiguous consent of the emperor of the East. The design of a conspiracy was imputed, according to the usual forms, to the prostrate tyrant, but his innocence and the guilt of his conqueror[22] are sufficiently proved by the advantageous treaty which *force* would not sincerely have granted, nor *weakness* have rashly infringed. The jealousy of power, and the mischiefs of discord, may suggest a more decent apology, and a sentence less rigorous may be pronounced against a crime which was necessary to introduce into Italy a generation of public felicity. The living author of this felicity was audaciously praised in his own presence by sacred and profane orators;[23] but history (in his time she was mute and inglorious) has not left any just representation of the events which displayed, or of the defects which clouded, the virtues of Theodoric.[24] One record of his fame, the volume of public epistles composed by Cassiodorus in the royal name, is still extant, and has obtained more implicit credit than it seems to deserve.[25] They exhibit the forms, rather than the substance, of his government; and we should vainly search for the pure and spontaneous sentiments of the barbarian amidst the declamation and learning of a sophist, the wishes of a Roman senator, the precedents of office, and the vague professions which, in every court, and on every occasion, compose the language of discreet ministers. The reputation of Theodoric may repose with more confidence on the visible peace and prosperity of a reign of thirty-three years, the unanimous esteem of his own times, and the memory of his wisdom and courage, his justice and humanity, which was deeply impressed on the minds of the Goths and Italians.

The partition of the lands of Italy, of which Theodoric assigned the third part to his soldiers, is *honourably* arraigned as the sole injustice of his life. And even this act may be fairly justified by the example of Odoacer, the rights of conquest, the true interest of the Italians, and the sacred duty of subsisting a whole people, who, on the faith of his promises, had transported themselves into a distant land.[26] Under the reign of Theodoric, and in the happy climate of Italy, the Goths soon multiplied to a formidable host of two hundred thousand men,[27] and the whole amount of their families may be computed by the ordinary addition of women and children. Their invasion of property, a part of which must have been already vacant, was disguised by the generous but improper name of *hospitality*; these unwelcome guests were irregularly dispersed over the face of Italy, and the lot of each barbarian was adequate to his birth and office, the number of his followers, and the rustic wealth which he possessed in slaves and cattle. The distinctions of noble and plebeian were acknowledged,[28] but the lands of every freeman were exempt from taxes, and he enjoyed the inestimable privilege of being subject only to the laws of his country.[29] Fashion, and even convenience, soon persuaded the conquerors to assume the more elegant dress of the natives, but they still persisted in the use of their mother tongue; and their contempt for the Latin schools was applauded by Theodoric himself, who gratified their prejudices, or his own, by declaring that the child who had trembled at a rod would never dare to look upon a sword.[30] Distress might sometimes provoke the indigent Roman to assume the ferocious manners which were insensibly relinquished by the rich and luxurious barbarian;[31] but these mutual conversions were not encouraged by the policy of a monarch who perpetuated the separation of the Italians and Goths, reserving the former for the arts of peace, and the latter for the service of war. To accomplish this design, he studied to protect his industrious subjects, and to moderate the violence, without enervating the valour, of his soldiers, who were maintained for the public defence. They held their lands and benefices as a military stipend: at the sound of the trumpet they were prepared to march under the conduct of their provincial officers, and the whole extent of Italy was distributed into the several quarters of a well-regulated camp. The service of the palace and of the frontiers was performed by choice or by rotation, and each extraordinary fatigue was recompensed by an increase of pay and occasional donatives. Theodoric had convinced his brave companions that empire must be acquired and defended by the same arts. After his example, they strove to excel in the use not only of the lance and sword, the instruments of their victories, but of the missile weapons, which they were too much inclined to neglect: and the lively image of war was displayed in the daily exercise and annual reviews of the Gothic cavalry. A firm though gentle discipline imposed the habits of modesty, obedience, and temperance; and the Goths were instructed to spare the people, to reverence the laws, to understand the duties of civil society, and to disclaim the barbarous licence of judicial combat and private revenge.[32]

Among the barbarians of the West the victory of Theodoric had spread a general alarm. But as soon as it appeared that he was satisfied with conquest and desirous of peace, terror was changed into respect, and they submitted to a powerful mediation, which was uniformly employed for the best purposes of reconciling their quarrels and civilising their manners.[33] The ambassadors who resorted to Ravenna from the most distant countries of Europe admired his wisdom, magnificence,[34] and courtesy; and, if he sometimes accepted either slaves or arms, white horses or strange animals, the gift of a sun-dial, a water-clock, or a musician, admonished even the princes of Gaul of the superior art and industry of his Italian subjects. His domestic alliances,[35] a wife, two daughters, a sister, and a niece, united the family of Theodoric with the kings of the Franks, the Burgundians, the Visigoths, the Vandals, and the Thuringians, and contributed to maintain the harmony, or at least the balance, of the great republic of the West.[36] It is difficult in the dark forests of Germany and Poland to pursue the emigrations of the Heruli, a fierce people who disdained the use of armour, and who condemned their widows and aged parents not to survive the loss of their husbands or the decay of their strength.[37] The king of these savage warriors solicited the friendship of Theodoric, and was elevated to the rank of his son, according to the barbaric rites of a military adoption.[38] From the shores of the Baltic the Æstians or Livonians laid their offerings of native amber[39] at the feet of a prince whose fame had excited them to undertake an unknown and dangerous journey of fifteen hundred miles. With the country[40] from whence the Gothic nation derived their origin he maintained a frequent and friendly correspondence: the Italians were clothed in the rich sables[41] of Sweden; and one of its sovereigns, after a voluntary or reluctant abdication, found an hospitable retreat in the palace of Ravenna. He had reigned over one of the thirteen populous tribes who cultivated a small portion of the great island or peninsula of Scandinavia, to which the vague appellation of Thule has been sometimes applied. That northern region was peopled, or had been explored, as high as the sixty-eighth degree of latitude, where the natives of the polar circle enjoy and lose the presence of the sun at each summer and winter solstice during an equal period of forty days.[42] The long night of his absence or death was the mournful season of distress and anxiety, till the messengers, who had been sent to the mountain tops, descried the first rays of returning light, and proclaimed to the plain below the festival of his resurrection.[43]

The life of Theodoric represents the rare and meritorious example of a barbarian who sheathed his sword in the pride of victory and the vigour of his age. A reign of three and thirty years was consecrated to the duties of civil government, and the hostilities, in which he was sometimes involved, were speedily terminated by the conduct of his lieutenants, the discipline of his troops, the arms of his allies, and even by the terror of his name. He reduced, under a strong and regular government, the unprofitable countries of Rhætia, Noricum, Dalmatia, and Pannonia, from the source of the Danube and the territory of the Bavarians[44] to the petty kingdom erected by the Gepidæ on the ruins of Sirmium. His prudence could not safely intrust the bulwark of Italy to such feeble and turbulent neighbours; and his justice might claim the lands which they oppressed, either as a part of his kingdom, or as the inheritance of his father. The greatness of a servant, who was named perfidious because he was successful, awakened the jealousy of the emperor Anastasius; and a war was kindled on the Dacian frontier, by the protection which the Gothic king, in the vicissitude of human affairs, had granted to one of the descendants of Attila. Sabinian, a general illustrious by his own and father's merit, advanced at the head of ten thousand Romans; and the provisions and arms, which filled a long train of waggons, were distributed to the fiercest of the Bulgarian tribes. But in the fields of Margus the Eastern powers were defeated by the inferior forces of the Goths and Huns; the flower and even the hope of the Roman armies was irretrievably destroyed; and such was the temperance with which Theodoric had inspired his victorious troops, that, as their leader had not given the signal of pillage, the rich spoils of the enemy lay untouched at their feet.[45] Exasperated by this disgrace, the Byzantine court despatched two hundred ships and eight thousand men to plunder the sea-coast of Calabria and Apulia: they assaulted the ancient city of Tarentum, interrupted the trade and agriculture of a happy country, and sailed back to the Hellespont, proud of their piratical victory over a people whom they still presumed to consider as their *Roman* brethren.[46] Their retreat was possibly hastened by the activity of Theodoric; Italy was covered by a fleet of a thousand light vessels,[47] which he constructed with incredible despatch; and his firm moderation was soon rewarded by a solid and honourable peace. He maintained with a powerful hand the balance of the West, till it was at length overthrown by the ambition of Clovis; and although unable to assist his rash and unfortunate kinsman the king of the Visigoths, he saved the remains of his family and people, and checked the Franks in the midst of their victorious career. I am not desirous to prolong or repeat[48] this narrative of military events, the least interesting of the reign of Theodoric; and shall be content to add that the Alemanni were protected,[49] that an inroad of the Burgundians was severely chastised, and that the conquest of Arles and Marseilles opened a free communication with the Visigoths, who revered him both as their national protector, and as the guardian of his grandchild, the infant son of Alaric. Under this respectable character, the king of Italy restored the Prætorian præfecture of the Gauls, reformed some abuses in the civil government of Spain, and accepted the annual tribute and apparent submission of its military governor, who wisely refused to trust his person in the palace of Ravenna.[50] The Gothic sovereignty was established from Sicily to the Danube, from Sirmium or Belgrade to the Atlantic Ocean; and the Greeks themselves have acknowledged that Theodoric reigned over the fairest portion of the Western empire.[51]

The union of the Goths and Romans might have fixed for ages the transient happiness of Italy; and the first of nations, a new people of free subjects and enlightened soldiers, might have gradually arisen from the mutual emulation of their respective virtues. But the sublime merit of guiding or seconding such a revolution was not reserved for the reign of Theodoric: he wanted either the genius or the opportunities of a legislator;[52] and while he indulged the Goths in the enjoyment of rude liberty, he servilely copied the institutions, and even the abuses, of the political system which had been framed by Constantine and his successors. From a tender regard to the expiring prejudices of Rome, the barbarian declined the name, the purple, and the diadem of the emperors; but he assumed, under the hereditary title of king, the whole substance and plenitude of Imperial prerogative.[53] His addresses to the Eastern throne were respectful and ambiguous: he celebrated in pompous style the harmony of the two republics, applauded his own government as the perfect similitude of a sole and undivided empire, and claimed above the kings of the earth the same pre-eminence which he modestly allowed to the person or rank of Anastasius. The alliance of the East and West was annually declared by the unanimous choice of two consuls; but it should seem that the Italian candidate, who was named by Theodoric, accepted a formal confirmation from the sovereign of Constantinople.[54] The Gothic palace of Ravenna reflected the image of the court of Theodosius or Valentinian. The Prætorian præfect, the præfect of Rome, the quæstor, the master of the offices, with the public and patrimonial treasurers, whose functions are painted in gaudy colours by the rhetoric of Cassiodorus, still continued to act as the ministers of state. And the subordinate care of justice and the revenue was delegated to seven consulars, three correctors, and five presidents, who governed the fifteen *regions* of Italy according to the principles, and even the forms, of Roman jurisprudence.[55] The violence of the conquerors was abated or eluded by the slow artifice of judicial proceedings; the civil administration, with its honours and emoluments, was confined to the Italians; and the people still preserved their dress and language, their laws and customs, their personal freedom, and two-thirds of their landed property. It had been the object of Augustus to conceal the introduction of monarchy; it was the policy of Theodoric to disguise the reign of a barbarian.[56]

If his subjects were sometimes awakened from this pleasing vision of a Roman government, they derived more substantial comfort from the character of a Gothic prince who had penetration to discern, and firmness to pursue, his own and the public interest. Theodoric loved the virtues which he possessed, and the talents of which he was destitute. Liberius was promoted to the office of Prætorian præfect for his unshaken fidelity to the unfortunate cause of Odoacer. The ministers of Theodoric, Cassiodorus,[57] and Boethius, have reflected on his reign the lustre of their genius and learning. More prudent or more fortunate than his colleague, Cassiodorus preserved his own esteem without forfeiting the royal favour; and after passing thirty years in the honours of the world, he was blessed with an equal term of repose in the devout and studious solitude of Squillace.

As the patron of the republic, it was the interest and duty of the Gothic king to cultivate the affections of the senate[58] and people. The nobles of Rome were flattered by sonorous epithets and formal professions of respect, which had been more justly applied to the merit and authority of their ancestors. The people enjoyed, without fear or danger, the three blessings of a capital, order, plenty, and public amusements. A visible diminution of their numbers may be found even in the measure of liberality;[59] yet Apulia, Calabria, and Sicily poured their tribute of corn into the granaries of Rome; an allowance of bread and meat was distributed to the indigent citizens; and every office was deemed honourable which was consecrated to the care of their health and happiness. The public games, such as a Greek ambassador might politely applaud, exhibited a faint and feeble copy of the magnificence of the Cæsars; yet the musical, the gymnastic, and the pantomime arts, had not totally sunk in oblivion; the wild beasts of Africa still exercised in the amphitheatre the courage and dexterity of the hunters; and the indulgent Goth either patiently tolerated or gently restrained the blue and green factions, whose contests so often filled the circus with clamour, and even with blood.[60] In the seventh year of his peaceful reign, Theodoric visited the old capital of the world; the senate and people advanced in solemn procession to salute a second Trajan, a new Valentinian; and he nobly supported that character, by the assurance of a just and legal government,[61] in a discourse which he was not afraid to pronounce in public and to inscribe on a tablet of brass. Rome, in this august ceremony, shot a last ray of declining glory;

and a saint, the spectator of this pompous scene, could only hope, in his pious fancy, that it was excelled by the celestial splendour of the New Jerusalem.[62] During a residence of six months, the fame, the person, and the courteous demeanour of the Gothic king excited the admiration of the Romans, and he contemplated, with equal curiosity and surprise, the monuments that remained of their ancient greatness. He imprinted the footsteps of a conqueror on the Capitoline hill, and frankly confessed that each day he viewed with fresh wonder the Forum of Trajan and his lofty column. The theatre of Pompey appeared, even in its decay, as a huge mountain, artificially hollowed and polished, and adorned by human industry; and he vaguely computed that a river of gold must have been drained to erect the colossal amphitheatre of Titus.[63] From the mouths of fourteen aqueducts a pure and copious stream was diffused into every part of the city; among these the Claudian water, which arose at the distance of thirty-eight miles in the Sabine mountains, was conveyed along a gentle though constant declivity of solid arches, till it descended on the summit of the Aventine hill. The long and spacious vaults which had been constructed for the purpose of common sewers subsisted after twelve centuries in their pristine strength; and these subterraneous channels have been preferred to all the visible wonders of Rome.[64] The Gothic kings, so injuriously accused of the ruin of antiquity, were anxious to preserve the monuments of the nation whom they had subdued.[65] The royal edicts were framed to prevent the abuses, the neglect, or the depredations of the citizens themselves; and a professed architect, the annual sum of two hundred pounds of gold, twenty-five thousand tiles, and the receipt of customs from the Lucrine port, were assigned for the ordinary repairs of the walls and public edifices. A similar care was extended to the statues of metal or marble of men or animals. The spirit of the horses which have given a modern name to the Quirinal was applauded by the barbarians;[66] the brazen elephants of the *Via sacra* were diligently restored;[67] the famous heifer of Myron deceived the cattle, as they were driven through the forum of peace;[68] and an officer was created to protect those works of art, which Theodoric considered as the noblest ornament of his kingdom.

After the example of the last emperors, Theodoric preferred the residence of Ravenna, where he cultivated an orchard with his own hands.[69] As often as the peace of his kingdom was threatened (for it was never invaded) by the barbarians, he removed his court to Verona[70] on the northern frontier, and the image of his palace, still extant on a coin, represents the oldest and most authentic model of Gothic architecture. These two capitals, as well as Pavia, Spoleto, Naples, and the rest of the Italian cities, acquired under his reign the useful or splendid decorations of churches, aqueducts, baths, porticoes, and palaces.[71] But the happiness of the subject was more truly conspicuous in the busy scene of labour and luxury, in the rapid increase and bold enjoyment of national wealth. From the shades of Tibur and Præneste, the Roman senators still retired in the winter season to the warm sun and salubrious springs of Baiæ; and their villas, which advanced on solid moles into the bay of Naples, commanded the various prospect of the sky, the earth, and the water. On the eastern side of the Hadriatic a new Campania was formed in the fair and fruitful province of Istria, which communicated with the palace of Ravenna by an easy navigation of one hundred miles. The rich productions of Lucania and the adjacent provinces were exchanged at the Marcilian fountain, in a populous fair annually dedicated to trade, intemperance, and superstition. In the solitude of Comum, which had once been animated by the mild genius of Pliny, a transparent basin above sixty miles in length still reflected the rural seats which encompassed the margin of the Larian lake; and the gradual ascent of the hills was covered by a triple plantation of olives, of vines, and of chestnut-trees.[72] Agriculture revived under the shadow of peace, and the number of husbandmen was multiplied by the redemption of captives.[73] The iron-mines of Dalmatia, a gold-mine in Bruttium, were carefully explored, and the Pomptine marshes, as well as those of Spoleto, were drained and cultivated by private undertakers, whose distant reward must depend on the continuance of the public prosperity.[74] Whenever the seasons were less propitious, the doubtful precautions of forming magazines of corn, fixing the price, and prohibiting the exportation, attested at least the benevolence of the state; but such was the extraordinary plenty which an industrious people produced from a grateful soil, that a gallon of wine was sometimes sold in Italy for less than three farthings, and a quarter of wheat at about five shillings and sixpence.[75] A country possessed of so many valuable objects of exchange soon attracted the merchants of the world, whose beneficial traffic was encouraged and protected by the liberal

spirit of Theodoric. The free intercourse of the provinces by land and water was restored and extended; the city gates were never shut either by day or by night; and the common saying, that a purse of gold might be safely left in the fields, was expressive of the conscious security of the inhabitants.

A difference of religion is always pernicious and often fatal to the harmony of the prince and people: the Gothic conqueror had been educated in the profession of Arianism, and Italy was devoutly attached to the Nicene faith. But the persuasion of Theodoric was not infected by zeal: and he piously adhered to the heresy of his fathers, without condescending to balance the subtile arguments of theological metaphysics. Satisfied with the private toleration of his Arian sectaries, he justly conceived himself to be the guardian of the public worship, and his external reverence for a superstition which he despised may have nourished in his mind the salutary indifference of a statesman or philosopher. The catholics of his dominions acknowledged, perhaps with reluctance, the peace of the church; their clergy, according to the degrees of rank or merit, were honourably entertained in the palace of Theodoric; he esteemed the living sanctity of Cæsarius[76] and Epiphanius,[77] the orthodox bishops of Arles and Pavia; and presented a decent offering on the tomb of St. Peter, without any scrupulous inquiry into the creed of the apostle.[78] His favourite Goths, and even his mother, were permitted to retain or embrace the Athanasian faith, and his long reign could not afford the example of an Italian catholic who, either from choice or compulsion, had deviated into the religion of the conqueror.[79] The people, and the barbarians themselves, were edified by the pomp and order of religious worship; the magistrates were instructed to defend the just immunities of ecclesiastical persons and possessions; the bishops held their synods, the metropolitans exercised their jurisdiction, and the privileges of sanctuary were maintained or moderated according to the spirit of the Roman jurisprudence.[80] With the protection, Theodoric assumed the legal supremacy, of the church; and his firm administration restored or extended some useful prerogatives which had been neglected by the feeble emperors of the West. He was not ignorant of the dignity and importance of the Roman pontiff, to whom the venerable name of POPE was now appropriated. The peace or the revolt of Italy might depend on the character of a wealthy and popular bishop, who claimed such ample dominion both in heaven and earth; who had been declared in a numerous synod to be pure from all sin, and exempt from all judgment.[81] When the chair of St. Peter was disputed by Symmachus, and Laurence, they appeared at his summons before the tribunal of an Arian monarch, and he confirmed the election of the most worthy or the more obsequious candidate. At the end of his life, in a moment of jealousy and resentment, he prevented the choice of the Romans, by nominating a pope in the palace of Ravenna. The danger and furious contests of a schism were mildly restrained, and the last decree of the senate was enacted to extinguish, if it were possible, the scandalous venality of the papal elections.[82]

I have descanted with pleasure on the fortunate condition of Italy, but our fancy must not hastily conceive that the golden age of the poets, a race of men without vice or misery, was realised under the Gothic conquest. The fair prospect was sometimes overcast with clouds; the wisdom of Theodoric might be deceived, his power might be resisted, and the declining age of the monarch was sullied with popular hatred and patrician blood. In the first insolence of victory he had been tempted to deprive the whole party of Odoacer of the civil and even the natural rights of society;[83] a tax, unseasonably imposed after the calamities of war, would have crushed the rising agriculture of Liguria; a rigid pre-emption of corn, which was intended for the public relief, must have aggravated the distress of Campania. These dangerous projects were defeated by the virtue and eloquence of Epiphanius and Boethius, who, in the presence of Theodoric himself, successfully pleaded the cause of the people:[84] but, if the royal ear was open to the voice of truth, a saint and a philosopher are not always to be found at the ear of kings. The privileges of rank, or office, or favour were too frequently abused by Italian fraud and Gothic violence, and the avarice of the king's nephew was publicly exposed, at first by the usurpation, and afterwards by the restitution, of the estates which he had unjustly extorted from his Tuscan neighbours. Two hundred thousand barbarians, formidable even to their master, were seated in the heart of Italy; they indignantly supported the restraints of peace and discipline; the disorders of their march were always felt and sometimes compensated; and where it was dangerous to punish, it might be prudent to dissemble, the sallies of their native fierceness. When the indulgence of Theodoric had remitted two-thirds of the Ligurian tribute, he condescended to explain the

difficulties of his situation, and to lament the heavy though inevitable burdens which he imposed on his subjects for their own defence.[85] These ungrateful subjects could never be cordially reconciled to the origin, the religion, or even the virtues of the Gothic conqueror; past calamities were forgotten, and the sense of suspicion of injuries was rendered still more exquisite by the present felicity of the times.

Even the religious toleration which Theodoric had the glory of introducing into the Christian world was painful and offensive to the orthodox zeal of the Italians. They respected the armed heresy of the Goths; but their pious rage was safely pointed against the rich and defenceless Jews, who had formed their establishments at Naples, Rome, Ravenna, Milan, and Genoa, for the benefit of trade and under the sanction of the laws.[86] Their persons were insulted, their effects were pillaged, and their synagogues were burnt by the mad populace of Ravenna and Rome, inflamed, as it should seem, by the most frivolous or extravagant pretences. The government which could neglect, would have deserved such an outrage. A legal inquiry was instantly directed; and, as the authors of the tumult had escaped in the crowd, the whole community was condemned to repair the damage, and the obstinate bigots, who refused their contributions, were whipped through the streets by the hand of the executioner. This simple act of justice exasperated the discontent of the catholics, who applauded the merit and patience of these holy confessors. Three hundred pulpits deplored the persecution of the church; and if the chapel of St. Stephen at Verona was demolished by the command of Theodoric, it is probable that some miracle hostile to his name and dignity had been performed on that sacred theatre. At the close of a glorious life, the king of Italy discovered that he had excited the hatred of a people whose happiness he had so assiduously laboured to promote; and his mind was soured by indignation, jealousy, and the bitterness of unrequited love. The Gothic conqueror condescended to disarm the unwarlike natives of Italy, interdicting all weapons of offence, and excepting only a small knife for domestic use. The deliverer of Rome was accused of conspiring with the vilest informers against the lives of senators whom he suspected of a secret and treasonable correspondence with the Byzantine court.[87] After the death of Anastasius, the diadem had been placed on the head of a feeble old man, but the powers of government were assumed by his nephew Justinian, who already meditated the extirpation of heresy and the conquest of Italy and Africa. A rigorous law, which was published at Constantinople, to reduce the Arians, by the dread of punishment, within the pale of the church, awakened the just resentment of Theodoric, who claimed for his distressed brethren of the East the same indulgence which he had so long granted to the catholics of his dominions. At his stern command the Roman pontiff, with four *illustrious* senators, embarked on an embassy of which he must have alike dreaded the failure or the success. The singular veneration shown to the first pope who had visited Constantinople was punished as a crime by this jealous monarch; the artful or peremptory refusal of the Byzantine court might excuse an equal, and would provoke a larger, measure of retaliation; and a mandate was prepared in Italy to prohibit, after a stated day, the exercise of the catholic worship. By the bigotry of his subjects and enemies the most tolerant of princes was driven to the brink of persecution, and the life of Theodoric was too long, since he lived to condemn the virtue of Boethius and Symmachus.[88]

The senator Boethius[89] is the last of the Romans whom Cato or Tully could have acknowledged for their countrymen. As a wealthy orphan, he inherited the patrimony and honours of the Anician family, a name ambitiously assumed by the kings and emperors of the age, and the appellation of Manlius asserted his genuine or fabulous descent from a race of consuls and dictators who had repulsed the Gauls from the Capitol, and sacrificed their sons to the discipline of the republic. In the youth of a Boethius the studies of Rome were not totally abandoned; a Virgil[90] is now extant corrected by the hand of a consul; and the professors of grammar, rhetoric, and jurisprudence were maintained in their privileges and pensions by the liberality of the Goths. But the erudition of the Latin language was insufficient to satiate his ardent curiosity; and Boethius is said to have employed eighteen laborious years in the schools of Athens,[91] which were supported by the zeal, the learning, and the diligence of Proclus and his disciples. The reason and piety of their Roman pupil were fortunately saved from the contagion of mystery and magic which polluted the groves of the Academy; but he imbibed the spirit, and imitated the method, of his dead and living masters, who attempted to reconcile the strong and subtle sense of Aristotle with the devout contemplation and sublime fancy of Plato. After his return to Rome, and his marriage with the daughter of his friend the patrician Symmachus, Boethius still continued, in a palace of ivory and marble, to prosecute the same studies.[92] The church was edified by his profound defence of the orthodox creed against the Arian, the Eutychian, and the Nestorian heresies; and the catholic unity was explained or exposed in a formal treatise by the *indifference* of three distinct though consubstantial persons. For the benefit of his Latin readers, his genius submitted to teach the first elements of the arts and sciences of Greece. The geometry of Euclid, the music of Pythagoras, the arithmetic of Nicomachus, the mechanics of Archimedes, the astronomy of Ptolemy, the theology of Plato, and the logic of Aristotle, with the commentary of Porphyry, were translated and illustrated by the indefatigable pen of the Roman senator. And he alone was esteemed capable of describing the wonders of art, a sun-dial, a water-clock, or a sphere which represented the motions of the planets. From these abstruse speculations Boethius stooped—or, to speak more truly, he rose—to the social duties of public and private life; the indigent were relieved by his liberality, and his eloquence, which flattery might compare to the voice of Demosthenes or Cicero, was uniformly exerted in the cause of innocence and humanity. Such conspicuous merit was felt and rewarded by a discerning prince: the dignity of Boethius was adorned with the titles of consul and patrician, and his talents were usefully employed in the important station of master of the offices. Notwithstanding the equal claims of the East and West, his two sons were created, in their tender youth, the consuls of the same year.[93] On the memorable day of their inauguration they proceeded in solemn pomp from their palace to the Forum amidst the applause of the senate and people; and their joyful father, the true consul of Rome, after pronouncing an oration in the praise of his royal benefactor, distributed a triumphal largess in the games of the circus. Prosperous in his fame and fortunes, in his public honours and private alliances, in the cultivation of science and consciousness of virtue, Boethius might have been styled happy, if that precarious epithet could be safely applied before the last term of the life of man.

A philosopher, liberal of his wealth and parsimonious of his time, might be insensible to the common allurements of ambition, the thirst of gold and employment. And some credit may be due to the asseveration of Boethius, that he had reluctantly obeyed the divine Plato, who enjoins every virtuous citizen to rescue the state from the usurpation of vice and ignorance. For the integrity of his public conduct he appeals to the memory of his country. His authority has restrained the pride and oppression of the royal officers, and his eloquence had delivered Paulianus from the dogs of the palace. He had always pitied, and often relieved, the distress of the provincials, whose fortunes were exhausted by public and private rapine; and Boethius alone had courage to oppose the tyranny of the barbarians, elated by conquest, excited by avarice, and, as he complains, encouraged by impunity. In these honourable contests his spirit soared above the consideration of danger, and perhaps of prudence; and we may learn from the example of Cato that a character of pure and inflexible virtue is the most apt to be misled by prejudice, to be heated by enthusiasm, and to confound private enmities with public justice. The disciple of Plato might exaggerate the infirmities of nature and the imperfections of society; and the mildest form of a Gothic kingdom, even the weight of allegiance and gratitude, must be insupportable to the free spirit of a Roman patriot. But the favour and fidelity of Boethius declined in just proportion with the public happiness, and an unworthy colleague was imposed to divide and control the power of the master of the offices. In the last gloomy season of Theodoric he indignantly felt that he was a slave; but as his master had only power over his life, he stood, without arms and without fear, against the face of an angry barbarian, who had been provoked to believe that the safety of the senate was incompatible with his own. The senator Albinus was accused and already convicted on the presumption of *hoping*, as it was said, the liberty of Rome. "If Albinus be criminal," exclaimed the orator, "the senate and myself are all guilty of the same crime. If we are innocent, Albinus is equally entitled to the protection of the laws." These laws might not have punished the simple and barren wish of an unattainable blessing; but they would have shown less indulgence to the rash confession of Boethius, that, had he known of a conspiracy, the tyrant never should.[94] The advocate of Albinus was soon involved in the danger and perhaps the guilt of his client; their signature (which they denied as a forgery) was affixed to the original address inviting the emperor to deliver Italy from the Goths; and three witnesses of honourable rank, perhaps of infamous reputation, attested the treasonable designs of the Roman patrician.[95] Yet his innocence must be presumed, since he was deprived by Theo-

doric of the means of justification, and rigorously confined in the tower of Pavia, while the senate, at the distance of five hundred miles, pronounced a sentence of confiscation and death against the most illustrious of its members. At the command of the barbarians, the occult science of a philosopher was stigmatised with the names of sacrilege and magic.[96] A devout and dutiful attachment to the senate was condemned as criminal by the trembling voices of the senators themselves; and their ingratitude deserved the wish or prediction of Boethius, that, after him, none should be found guilty of the same offence.[97]

While Boethius, oppressed with fetters, expected each moment the sentence or the stroke of death, he composed in the tower of Pavia the *Consolation of Philosophy*; a golden volume not unworthy of the leisure of Plato or Tully, but which claims incomparable merit from the barbarism of the times and the situation of the author. The celestial guide whom he had so long invoked at Rome and Athens now condescended to illumine his dungeon, to revive his courage, and to pour into his wounds her salutary balm. She taught him to compare his long prosperity and his recent distress, and to conceive new hopes from the inconstancy of fortune. Reason had informed him of the precarious condition of her gifts; experience had satisfied him of their real value; he had enjoyed them without guilt, he might resign them without a sigh, and calmly disdain the impotent malice of his enemies, who had left him happiness, since they had left him virtue. From the earth Boethius ascended to heaven in search of the SUPREME GOOD; explored the metaphysical labyrinth of chance and destiny, of prescience and free-will, of time and eternity; and generously attempted to reconcile the perfect attributes of the Diety with the apparent disorders of his moral and physical government. Such topics of consolation, so obvious, so vague, or so abstruse, are ineffectual to subdue the feelings of human nature. Yet the sense of misfortune may be diverted by the labour of thought; and the sage who could artfully combine in the same work the various riches of philosophy, poetry, and eloquence, must already have possessed the intrepid calmness which he affected to seek. Suspense, the worst of evils, was at length determined by the ministers of death, who executed, and perhaps exceeded, the inhuman mandate of Theodoric. A strong cord was fastened round the head of Boethius, and forcibly tightened till his eyes almost started from their sockets; and some mercy may be discovered in the milder torture of beating him with clubs till he expired.[98] But his genius survived to diffuse a ray of knowledge over the darkest ages of the Latin world; the writings of the philosopher were translated by the most glorious of the English kings,[99] and the third emperor of the name of Otho removed to a more honourable tomb the bones of a catholic saint who, from his Arian persecutors, had acquired the honours of martyrdom and the fame of miracles.[100] In the last hours of Boethius he derived some comfort from the safety of his two sons, of his wife, and of his father-in-law, the venerable Symmachus. But the grief of Symmachus was indiscreet, and perhaps disrespectful: he had presumed to lament, he might dare to revenge, the death of an injured friend. He was dragged in chains from Rome to the palace of Ravenna, and the suspicions of Theodoric could only be appeased by the blood of an innocent and aged senator.[101]

Humanity will be disposed to encourage any report which testifies the jurisdiction of conscience and the remorse of kings; and philosophy is not ignorant that the most horrid spectres are sometimes created by the powers of a disordered fancy, and the weakness of a distempered body. After a life of virtue and glory, Theodoric was now descending with shame and guilt into the grave: his mind was humbled by the contrast of the past, and justly alarmed by the invisible terrors of futurity. One evening, as it is related, when the head of a large fish was served on the royal table,[102] he suddenly exclaimed that he beheld the angry countenance of Symmachus, his eyes glaring fury and revenge, and his mouth armed with long sharp teeth, which threatened to devour him. The monarch instantly retired to his chamber, and, as he lay trembling with aguish cold under a weight of bed-clothes, he expressed in broken murmurs to his physician Elpidius his deep re-

pentance for the murders of Boethius and Symmachus.[103] His malady increased, and, after a dysentery which continued three days, he expired in the palace of Ravenna, in the thirty-third, or, if we compute from the invasion of Italy, in the thirty-seventh year of his reign. Conscious of his approaching end, he divided his treasures and provinces between his two grandsons, and fixed the Rhône as their common boundary.[104] Amalaric was restored to the throne of Spain. Italy, with all the conquests of the Ostrogoths, was bequeathed to Athalaric, whose age did not exceed ten years, but who was cherished as the last male offspring of the line of Amali, by the short-lived marriage of his mother Amalasuntha with a royal fugitive of the same blood.[105] In the presence of the dying monarch the Gothic chiefs and Italian magistrates mutually engaged their faith and loyalty to the young prince and to his guardian mother; and received, in the same awful moment, his last salutary advice to maintain the laws, to love the senate and people of Rome, and to cultivate with decent reverence the friendship of the emperor.[106] The monument of Theodoric was erected by his daughter Amalasuntha in a conspicuous situation, which commanded the city of Ravenna, the harbour, and the adjacent coast. A chapel of a circular form, thirty feet in diameter, is crowned by a dome of one entire piece of granite: from the centre of the dome four columns arose, which supported in a vase of porphyry the remains of the Gothic king, surrounded by the brazen statues of the twelve apostles.[107] His spirit, after some previous expiation, might have been permitted to mingle with the benefactors of mankind, if an Italian hermit had not been witness in a vision to the damnation of Theodoric,[108] whose soul was plunged by the ministers of divine vengeance into the volcano of Lipari, one of the flaming mouths of the infernal world.[109]

CHAPTER XL

Elevation of Justin the Elder. Reign of Justinian. I. The Empress Theodora. II. Factions of the Circus, and Sedition of Constantinople. III. Trade and Manufacture of Silk. IV. Finances and Taxes. V. Edifices of Justinian. Church of St. Sophia. Fortifications and Frontiers of the Eastern Empire. VI. Abolition of the Schools of Athens and the Consulship of Rome.

THE emperor Justinian was born[1] near the ruins of Sardica (the modern Sophia), of an obscure race[2] of barbarians,[3] the inhabitants of a wild and desolate country, to which the names of Dardania, of Dacia, and of Bulgaria have been successively applied. His elevation was prepared by the adventurous spirit of his uncle Justin, who, with two other peasants of the same village, deserted for the profession of arms the more useful employment of husbandmen or shepherds.[4] On foot, with a scanty provision of biscuit in their knapsacks, the three youths followed the high road of Constantinople, and were soon enrolled, for their strength and stature, among the guards of the emperor Leo. Under the two succeeding reigns, the fortunate peasant emerged to wealth and honours; and his escape from some dangers which threatened his life was afterwards ascribed to the guardian angel who watches over the fate of kings. His long and laudable service in the Isaurian and Persian wars would not have preserved from oblivion the name of Justin; yet they might warrant the military promotion which, in the course of fifty years, he gradually obtained—the rank of tribune, of count, and of general, the dignity of senator, and the command of the guards, who obeyed him as their chief at the important crisis when the emperor Anastasius was removed from the world. The powerful kinsmen whom he had raised and enriched were excluded from the throne; and the eunuch Amantius, who reigned in the palace, had secretly resolved to fix the diadem on the head of the most obsequious of his creatures. A liberal donative, to conciliate the suffrage of the guards, was intrusted for that purpose in the hands of their commander. But these weighty arguments were treacherously employed by Justin in his own favour; and as no competitor presumed to appear, the Dacian peasant was invested with the purple by the unanimous consent of the soldiers, who knew him to be brave and gentle; of the clergy and people, who believed him to be orthodox; and of the provincials, who yielded a blind and implicit submission to the will of the capital. The elder Justin, as he is distinguished from another emperor of the same family and name, ascended the Byzantine throne at the age of sixty-eight years; and, had he been left to his own guidance, every moment of a nine-years' reign must have exposed to his subjects the impropriety of their choice. His ignorance was similar to that of Theodoric; and it is remarkable that, in an age not destitute of learning, two contemporary monarchs had never been instructed in the knowledge of the alphabet. But the genius of Justin was far inferior to that of the Gothic king: the experience of a soldier had not qualified him for the government of an empire; and, though personally brave, the consciousness of his own weakness was naturally attended with doubt, distrust, and political apprehension. But the official business of the state was diligently and faithfully transacted by the quæstor Proclus;[5] and the aged emperor adopted the talents and ambition of his nephew Justinian, an aspiring youth, whom his uncle had drawn from the rustic solitude of Dacia, and educated at Constantinople as the heir of his private fortune, and at length of the Eastern empire.

Since the eunuch Amantius had been defrauded of his money, it became necessary to deprive him of his life. The task was easily accomplished by the charge of a real or fictitious conspiracy; and the judges were informed, as an accumulation of guilt, that he was secretly addicted to the Manichæan heresy.[6] Amantius lost his head; three of his companions, the first domestics of the palace, were punished either with death or exile; and their unfortunate candidate for the purple was cast into a deep dungeon, overwhelmed with stones, and ignominiously thrown without burial into the sea. The ruin of Vitalian was a work of more difficulty and danger. That Gothic chief had rendered himself popular by the civil war which he boldly waged against Anastasius for the defence of the orthodox faith; and after the conclusion of an advantageous treaty, he still remained in the neighbourhood of Constantinople at the head of a formidable and victorious army of barbarians. By the frail security of oaths he was tempted to relinquish this advantageous situation, and to trust his person within the walls of a city whose inhabitants, particularly the *blue* faction, were artfully incensed against him by the remembrance even of his pious hostilities. The emperor and his nephew embraced him as the faithful and worthy champion of the church and state, and gratefully adorned their favourite with the titles of consul and general; but in the seventh month of his consulship Vitalian was stabbed with seventeen wounds at the royal banquet,[7] and Justinian, who inherited the spoil, was accused as the assassin of a spiritual brother, to whom he had recently pledged his faith in the participation of the Christian mysteries.[8] After the fall of his rival, he was promoted, without any claim of military service, to the office of master-general of the Eastern armies, whom it was his duty to lead into the field against the public enemy. But, in the pursuit of fame, Justinian might have lost his present dominion over the age and weakness of his uncle; and instead of acquiring by Scythian or Persian trophies the applause of his countrymen,[9] the prudent warrior solicited their favour in the churches, the circus, and the senate of Constantinople. The catholics were attached to the nephew of Justin, who, between the Nestorian and Eutychian heresies, trod the narrow path of inflexible and intolerant orthodoxy.[10] In the first days of the new reign he prompted and gratified the popular enthusiasm against the memory of the deceased emperor. After a schism of thirty-four years, he reconciled the proud and angry spirit of the Roman pontiff, and spread among the Latins a favourable report of his pious respect for the apostolic see. The thrones of the East were filled with catholic bishops devoted to his interest, the clergy and the monks were gained by his liberality, and the people were taught to pray for their future sovereign, the hope and pillar of the true religion. The magnificence of Justinian was displayed in the superior pomp of his public spectacles, an object not less sacred and important in the eyes of the multitude than the creed of Nice of Chalcedon; the expense of his consulship was esteemed at two hundred and eighty-eight thousand pieces of gold; twenty lions and thirty leopards were produced at the same time in the amphitheatre; and a numerous train of horses, with their rich trappings, was bestowed as an extraordinary gift on the victorious charioteers of the circus. While he indulged the people of Constantinople, and received the addresses of foreign kings, the nephew of Justin assiduously cultivated the friendship of the senate. That venerable name seemed to qualify its members to declare the sense of the nation, and to regulate the succession of the Imperial throne. The feeble Anastasius had permitted the vigour of government to degenerate into the form or substance of an aristocracy, and the military officers who had obtained the senatorial rank were followed by their domestic guards, a band of veterans whose arms or acclamations might fix in a tumultuous moment the diadem of the East. The treasures of the state were lavished to procure the voices of the senators, and their unanimous wish that he would be pleased to adopt Justinian for his colleague was communicated to the emperor. But this request, which too clearly admonished him of his approaching end, was unwelcome to the jealous temper of an aged monarch desirous to retain the power which he was incapable of exercising; and Justin, holding his purple with both his hands, advised them to prefer, since an election was so profitable, some older candidate. Notwithstanding this reproach, the senate proceeded to decorate Justinian with the royal epithet of *nobilissimus;* and their decree was ratified by the affection or the fears of his uncle. After some time the languor of mind and body to which he was reduced by an incurable wound in his thigh indispensably required the aid of a guardian. He summoned the patriarch and senators, and in their presence solemnly placed the diadem on the head of his nephew, who was conducted from the palace to the circus, and saluted by the loud and joyful applause of the people. The life of Justin was prolonged about four months; but from the instant of this ceremony he was considered as dead to the empire, which acknowledged Justinian in the forty-fifth year of his age, for the lawful sovereign of the East.[11]

From his elevation to his death, Justinian governed the Roman empire thirty-eight years, seven months, and thirteen days. The events of his reign, which excite our curious attention by their number, variety, and importance, are diligently related by the secretary of Belisarius, a rhetorician, whom eloquence had promoted to the rank of senator and præfect of Constantinople. According to the vicissitudes of courage or servitude, of favour or disgrace, Procopius[12] successively composed the *history,* the *panegyric,* and the *satire* of his own times. The eight books of the Persian, Vandalic, and Gothic wars,[13] which are continued in the five books of Agathias, deserve our esteem as a laborious and successful imitation of the Attic, or at least of the Asiatic, writers of ancient Greece. His facts are collected from the personal experience and free conversation of a soldier, a statesman, and a traveller; his style continually aspires, and often attains, to the merit of strength and elegance; his reflections, more especially in the speeches, which he too frequently inserts, contain a rich fund of political knowledge; and the historian, excited by the generous ambition of pleasing and instructing posterity, appears to disdain the prejudices of the people and the flattery of courts. The writings of Procopius[14] were read and applauded by his contemporaries:[15] but, although he respectfully laid them at the foot of the throne, the pride of Justinian must have been wounded by the praise of a hero who perpetually eclipses the glory of his inactive sovereign. The conscious dignity of independence was subdued by the hopes and fears of a slave; and the secretary of Belisarius laboured for pardon and reward in the six books of the Imperial *edifices*. He had dexterously chosen a subject of apparent splendour, in which he could loudly celebrate the genius, the magnificence, and the piety of a prince who, both as a conqueror and legislator, had surpassed the puerile virtues of Themistocles and Cyrus.[16] Disappointment might urge the flatterer to secret revenge; and the first glance of favour might again tempt him to suspend and suppress a libel[17] in which the Roman Cyrus is degraded into an odious and contemptible tyrant, in which both the emperor and his consort Theodora are seriously represented as two dæmons who had assumed a human form for the destruction of mankind.[18] Such base inconsistency must doubtless sully the reputation, and detract from the credit, of Procopius: yet, after the venom of his malignity has been suffered to exhale, the residue of the *anecdotes*, even the most disgraceful facts, some of which had been tenderly hinted in his public history, are established by their internal evidence, or the authentic monuments of the times.[19] From these various materials I shall now proceed to describe the reign of Justinian, which will deserve and occupy an ample space. The present chapter will explain the elevation and character of Theodora, the factions of the circus, and the peaceful administration of the sovereign of the East. In the three succeeding chapters I shall

relate the wars of Justinian, which achieved the conquest of Africa and Italy; and I shall follow the victories of Belisarius and Narses, without disguising the vanity of their triumphs, or the hostile virtue of the Persian and Gothic heroes. The series of this volume will embrace the jurisprudence and theology of the emperor; the controversies and sects which still divide the Oriental church; the reformation of the Roman law which is obeyed or respected by the nations of modern Europe.

I. In the exercise of supreme power, the first act of Justinian was to divide it with the woman whom he loved, the famous Theodora,[20] whose strange elevation cannot be applauded as the triumph of female virtue. Under the reign of Anastasius, the care of the wild beasts maintained by the green faction at Constantinople was intrusted to Acacius, a native of the isle of Cyprus, who, from his employment, was surnamed the master of the bears. This honourable office was given after his death to another candidate, notwithstanding the diligence of his widow, who had already provided a husband and a successor. Acacius had left three daughters, Comito,[21] Theodora, and Anastasia, the eldest of whom did not then exceed the age of seven years. On a solemn festival, these helpless orphans were sent by their distressed and indignant mother, in the garb of suppliants, into the midst of the theatre: the green faction received them with contempt, the blues with compassion; and this difference, which sunk deep into the mind of Theodora, was felt long afterwards in the administration of the empire. As they improved in age and beauty, the three sisters were successively devoted to the public and private pleasures of the Byzantine people; and Theodora, after following Comito on the stage, in the dress of a slave, with a stool on her head, was at length permitted to exercise her independent talents. She neither danced, nor sung, nor played on the flute; her skill was confined to the pantomime art; she excelled in buffoon characters; and as often as the comedian swelled her cheeks, and complained with a ridiculous tone and gesture of the blows that were inflicted, the whole theatre of Constantinople resounded with laughter and applause. The beauty of Theodora[22] was the subject of more flattering praise, and the source of more exquisite delight. Her features were delicate and regular; her complexion, though somewhat pale, was tinged with a natural colour; every sensation was instantly expressed by the vivacity of her eyes; her easy motions displayed the graces of a small but elegant figure; and either love or adulation might proclaim that painting and poetry were incapable of delineating the matchless excellence of her form. But this form was degraded by the facility with which it was exposed to the public eye, and prostituted to licentious desire. Her venal charms were abandoned to a promiscuous crowd of citizens and strangers, of every rank and of every profession: the fortunate lover who had been promised a night of enjoyment was often driven from her bed by a stronger or more wealthy favourite; and when she passed through the streets, her presence was avoided by all who wished to escape either the scandal or the temptation. The satirical historian has not blushed[23] to describe the naked scenes which Theodora was not ashamed to exhibit in the theatre.[24] After exhausting the arts of sensual pleasure,[25] she most ungratefully murmured against the parsimony of Nature;[26] but her murmurs, her pleasures, and her arts, must be veiled in the obscurity of a learned language. After reigning for some time the delight and contempt of the capital, she condescended to accompany Ecebolus, a native of Tyre, who had obtained the government of the African Pentapolis. But this union was frail and transient; Ecebolus soon rejected an expensive or faithless concubine; she was reduced at Alexandria to extreme distress; and in her laborious return to Constantinople, every city of the East admired and enjoyed the fair Cyprian, whose merit appeared to justify her descent from the peculiar island of Venus. The vague commerce of Theodora, and the most detestable precautions, preserved her from the danger which she feared; yet once, and once only, she became a mother. The infant was saved and educated in Arabia by his father, who imparted to him on his death-bed that he was the son of an empress. Filled with ambitious hopes, the unsuspecting youth immediately hastened to the palace of Constantinople, and was admitted to the presence of his mother. As he was never more seen, even after the decease of Theodora, she deserves the foul imputation of extinguishing with his life a secret so offensive to her imperial virtue.

In the most abject state of her fortune and reputation, some vision, either of sleep or of fancy, had whispered to Theodora the pleasing assurance that she was destined to become the spouse of a potent monarch. Conscious of her approaching greatness, she returned from Paphlagonia to Constantinople; assumed, like a skilful actress, a more decent character; relieved her poverty by the laudable industry of spinning wool; and affected a life of chastity and solitude in a small house, which she afterwards changed into a magnificent temple.[27] Her beauty, assisted by art or accident, soon attracted, captivated, and fixed, the patrician Justinian, who already reigned with absolute sway under the name of his uncle. Perhaps she contrived to enhance the value of a gift which she had so often lavished on the meanest of mankind; perhaps she inflamed, at first by modest delays, and at last by sensual allurements, the desires of a lover who, from nature or devotion, was addicted to long vigils and abstemious diet. When his first transports had subsided, she still maintained the same ascendant over his mind by the more solid merit of temper and understanding. Justinian delighted to ennoble and enrich the object of his affection: the treasures of the East were poured at her feet, and the nephew of Justin was determined, perhaps by religious scruples, to bestow on his concubine the sacred and legal character of a wife. But the laws of Rome expressly prohibited the marriage of a senator with any female who had been dishonoured by a servile origin or theatrical profession: the empress Lupicina or Euphemia, a barbarian of rustic manners, but of irreproachable virtue, refused to accept a prostitute for her niece; and even Vigilantia, the superstitious mother of Justinian, though she acknowledged the wit and beauty of Theodora, was seriously apprehensive lest the levity and arrogance of that artful paramour might corrupt the piety and happiness of her son. These obstacles were removed by the inflexible constancy of Justinian. He patiently expected the death of the empress; he despised the tears of his mother, who soon sunk under the weight of her affliction; and a law was promulgated, in the name of the emperor Justin, which abolished the rigid jurisprudence of antiquity. A glorious repentance (the words of the edict) was left open for the unhappy females who had prostituted their persons on the theatre, and they were permitted to contract a legal union with the most illustrious of the Romans.[28] This indulgence was speedily followed by the solemn nuptials of Justinian and Theodora; her dignity was gradually exalted with that of her lover; and, as soon as Justin had invested his nephew with the purple, the patriarch of Constantinople placed the diadem on the heads of the emperor and empress of the East. But the usual honours which the severity of Roman manners had allowed to the wives of princes could not satisfy either the ambition of

Theodora or the fondness of Justinian. He seated her on the throne as an equal and independent colleague in the sovereignty of the empire, and an oath of allegiance was imposed on the governors of the provinces in the joint names of Justinian and Theodora.[29] The Eastern world fell prostrate before the genius and fortune of the daughter of Acacius. The prostitute who, in the presence of innumerable spectators, had polluted the theatre of Constantinople, was adored as a queen in the same city, by grave magistrates, orthodox bishops, victorious generals, and captive monarchs.[30]

Those who believe that the female mind is totally depraved by the loss of chastity will eagerly listen to all the invectives of private envy or popular resentment, which have dissembled the virtues of Theodora, exaggerated her vices, and condemned with rigour the venal or voluntary sins of the youthful harlot. From a motive of shame or contempt, she often declined the servile homage of the multitude, escaped from the odious light of the capital, and passed the greatest part of the year in the palaces and gardens which were pleasantly seated on the sea-coast of the Propontis and the Bosphorus. Her private hours were devoted to the prudent as well as grateful care of her beauty, the luxury of the bath and table, and the long slumber of the evening and the morning. Her secret apartments were occupied by the favourite women and eunuchs, whose interests and passions she indulged at the expense of justice: the most illustrious personages of the state were crowded into a dark and sultry antechamber; and when at last, after tedious attendance, they were admitted to kiss the feet of Theodora, they experienced, as her humour might suggest, the silent arrogance of an empress or the capricious levity of a comedian. Her rapacious avarice to accumulate an immense treasure may be excused by the apprehension of her husband's death, which could leave no alternative between ruin and the throne; and fear as well as ambition might exasperate Theodora against two generals who, during a malady of the emperor, had rashly declared that they were not disposed to acquiesce in the choice of the capital. But the reproach of cruelty, so repugnant even to her softer vices, has left an indelible stain on the memory of Theodora. Her numerous spies observed and zealously reported every action, or word, or look, injurious to their royal mistress. Whomsoever they accused were cast into her peculiar prisons,[31] inaccessible to the inquiries of justice; and it was rumoured that the torture of the rack or scourge had been inflicted in the presence of a female tyrant, insensible to the voice of prayer or of pity.[32] Some of these unhappy victims perished in deep unwholesome dungeons, while others were permitted, after the loss of their limbs, their reason, or their fortune, to appear in the world, the living monuments of her vengeance, which was commonly extended to the children of those whom she had suspected or injured. The senator or bishop whose death or exile Theodora had pronounced, was delivered to a trusty messenger, and his diligence was quickened by a menace from her own mouth. "If you fail in the execution of my commands, I swear by him who liveth for ever that your skin shall be flayed from your body."[33]

If the creed of Theodora had not been tainted with heresy, her exemplary devotion might have atoned, in the opinion of her contemporaries, for pride, avarice, and cruelty; but if she employed her influence to assuage the intolerant fury of the emperor, the present age will allow some merit to her religion, and much indulgence to her speculative errors.[34] The name of Theodora was introduced, with equal honour, in all the pious and charitable foundations of Justinian; and the most benevolent institution of his reign may be ascribed to the sympathy of the empress for her less fortunate sisters, who had been seduced or compelled to embrace the trade of prostitution. A palace, on the Asiatic side of the Bosphorus, was converted into a stately and spacious monastery, and a liberal maintenance was assigned to five hundred women who had been collected from the streets and brothels of Constantinople. In this safe and holy retreat they were devoted to perpetual confinement; and the despair of some, who threw themselves headlong into the sea, was lost in the gratitude of the penitents who had been delivered from sin and misery by their generous benefactress.[35] The prudence of Theodora is celebrated by Justinian himself; and his laws are attributed to the sage counsels of his most reverend wife, whom he had received as the gift of the Deity.[36] Her courage was displayed amidst the tumult of the people and the terrors of the court. Her chastity, from the moment of her union with Justinian, is founded on the silence of her implacable enemies; and although the daughter of Acacius might be satiated with love, yet some applause is due to the firmness of a mind which could sacrifice pleasure and habit to the stronger sense either of duty or interest. The wishes and prayers of Theodora could never obtain the blessing of a lawful son, and she buried an infant daughter, the sole offspring of her marriage.[37] Notwithstanding this disappointment, her dominion was permanent and absolute; she preserved, by art or merit, the affections of Justinian; and their seeming dissensions were always fatal to the courtiers who believed them to be sincere. Perhaps her health had been impaired by the licentiousness of her youth; but it was always delicate, and she was directed by her physicians to use the Pythian warm-baths. In this journey the empress was followed by the Prætorian præfect, the great treasurer, several counts and patricians, and a splendid train of four thousand attendants: the highways were repaired at her approach; a palace was erected for her reception; and as she passed through Bithynia she distributed liberal alms to the churches, the monasteries, and the hospitals, that they might implore Heaven for the restoration of her health.[38] At length, in the twenty-fourth year of her marriage, and the twenty-second of her reign, she was consumed by a cancer;[39] and the irreparable loss was deplored by her husband, who, in the room of a theatrical prostitute, might have selected the purest and most noble virgin of the East.[40]

II. A material difference may be observed in the games of antiquity: the most eminent of the Greeks were actors, the Romans were merely spectators. The Olympic stadium was open to wealth, merit, and ambition; and if the candidates could depend on their personal skill and activity, they might pursue the footsteps of Diomede and Menelaus, and conduct their own horses in the rapid career.[41] Ten, twenty, forty chariots, were allowed to start at the same instant; a crown of leaves was the reward of the victor, and his fame, with that of his family and country, was chanted in lyric strains more durable than monuments of brass and marble. But a senator, or even a citizen, conscious of his dignity, would have blushed to expose his person or his horses in the circus of Rome. The games were exhibited at the expense of the republic, the magistrates, or the emperors; but the reins were abandoned to servile hands; and if the profits of a favourite charioteer sometimes exceeded those of an advocate, they must be considered as the effects of popular extravagance, and the high wages of a disgraceful profession. The race, in its first institution, was a simple contest of two chariots, whose drivers were distinguished by *white* and *red* liveries: two additional colours, a light *green* and a cærulean *blue*, were afterwards introduced; and, as the races were repeated twenty-five times, one hundred chariots contributed in the same day to the pomp of the circus. The four *factions* soon acquired a legal establishment and a mysterious origin, and their fanciful colours were derived from the various appearances of nature in the four seasons of the year; the red dog-star of summer, the snows of winter, the deep shades of autumn, and the cheerful verdure of the spring.[42] Another interpretation preferred the elements to the seasons, and the struggle of the green and blue was supposed to represent the conflict of the earth and sea. Their respective victories announced either a plentiful harvest or a prosperous navigation, and the hostility of the husbandmen and mariners was somewhat less absurd than the blind ardour of the Roman people, who devoted their lives and fortunes to the colour which they had espoused. Such folly was disdained and indulged by the wisest princes; but the names of Caligula, Nero, Vitellius, Verus, Commodus, Caracalla, and Elagabalus, were enrolled in the blue or green factions of the circus: they frequented their stables, applauded their favourites, chastised their antagonists, and deserved the esteem of the populace by the natural or affected imitation of their manners. The bloody and tumultuous contest continued to disturb the public festivity till the last age of the spectacles of Rome; and Theodoric, from a motive of justice or affection, interposed his authority to protect the greens against the violence of a consul and a patrician who were passionately addicted to the blue faction of the circus.[43]

Constantinople adopted the follies, though not the virtues, of ancient Rome; and the same factions which had agitated the circus raged with redoubled fury in the hippodrome. Under the reign of Anastasius, this popular frenzy was inflamed by religious zeal; and the greens, who had treacherously concealed stones and daggers under baskets of fruit, massacred at a solemn festival three thousand of their blue adversaries.[44] From the capital this pestilence was diffused into the provinces and cities of the East, and the sportive distinction of two colours produced two strong and irreconcilable factions, which shook the foundations of a feeble government.[45] The popular dissensions, founded on the most serious interest or holy pretence, have scarcely equalled the obstinacy of this wanton discord, which invaded the peace of families, divided friends and brothers, and tempted the female sex, though seldom seen in the circus, to espouse the inclinations of their lovers, or to contradict the wishes of their husbands. Every law, either human or divine, was trampled under foot; and as long as the party was successful, its deluded followers appeared careless of private distress or public calamity. The licence, without the freedom, of democracy, was revived at Antioch and Constantinople, and the support of a faction became necessary to every candidate for civil or ecclesiastical honours. A secret attachment to the family or sect of Anastasius was imputed to the greens; the blues were zealously devoted to the cause of orthodoxy and Justinian,[46] and their grateful patron protected, about five years, the disorders of a faction whose seasonable tumults overawed the palace, the senate, and the capitals of the East. Insolent with royal favour, the blues affected to strike terror by a peculiar and barbaric dress—the long hair of the Huns, their close sleeves and ample garments, a lofty step, and a sonorous voice. In the day they concealed their two-edged poniards, but in the night they boldly assembled in arms and in numerous bands, prepared for every act of violence and rapine. Their adversaries of the green faction, or even inoffensive citizens, were stripped and often murdered by these nocturnal robbers, and it became dangerous to wear any gold buttons or girdles, or to appear at a late hour in the streets of a peaceful capital. A daring spirit, rising with impunity, proceeded to violate the safeguard of private houses; and fire was employed to facilitate the attack, or to conceal the crimes, of these factious rioters. No place was safe or sacred from their depredations; to gratify either avarice or revenge they profusely spilt the blood of the innocent; churches and altars were polluted by atrocious murders, and it was the boast of the assassins that their dexterity could always inflict a mortal wound with a single stroke of their dagger. The dissolute youth of Constantinople adopted the blue livery of disorder; the laws were silent, and the bonds of society were relaxed; creditors were compelled to resign their obligations; judges to reverse their sentence; masters to enfranchise their slaves; fathers to supply the extravagance of their children; noble matrons were prostituted to the lust of their servants; beautiful boys were torn from the arms of their parents; and wives, unless they preferred a voluntary death, were ravished in the presence of their husbands.[47] The despair of the greens, who were persecuted by their enemies and deserted by the magistrate, assumed the privilege of defence, perhaps of retaliation; but those who

survived the combat were dragged to execution, and the unhappy fugitives, escaping to woods and caverns, preyed without mercy on the society from whence they were expelled. Those ministers of justice who had courage to punish the crimes and to brave the resentment of the blues became the victims of their indiscreet zeal: a præfect of Constantinople fled for refuge to the holy sepulchre, a count of the East was ignominiously whipped, and a governor of Cilicia was hanged, by the order of Theodora, on the tomb of two assassins whom he had condemned for the murder of his groom, and a daring attack upon his own life.[48] An aspiring candidate may be tempted to build his greatness on the public confusion, but it is the interest as well as duty of a sovereign to maintain the authority of the laws. The first edict of Justinian, which was often repeated and sometimes executed, announced his firm resolution to support the innocent, and to chastise the guilty, of every denomination and *colour*. Yet the balance of justice was still inclined in favour of the blue faction, by the secret affection, the habits, and the fears of the emperor; his equity, after an apparent struggle, submitted without reluctance to the implacable passions of Theodora, and the empress never forgot or forgave the injuries of the comedian. At the accession of the younger Justin, the proclamation of equal and rigorous justice indirectly condemned the partiality of the former reign. "Ye blues, Justinian is no more! ye greens, he is still alive!"[49]

A sedition, which almost laid Constantinople in ashes, was excited by the mutual hatred and momentary reconciliation of the two factions. In the fifth year of his reign Justinian celebrated the festival of the ides of January: the games were incessantly disturbed by the clamorous discontent of the greens; till the twenty-second race the emperor maintained his silent gravity; at length, yielding to his impatience, he condescended to hold, in abrupt sentences, and by the voice of a crier, the most singular dialogue[50] that ever passed between a prince and his subjects. Their first complaints were respectful and modest; they accused the subordinate ministers of oppression, and proclaimed their wishes for the long life and victory of the emperor. "Be patient and attentive, ye insolent railers!" exclaimed Justinian; "be mute, ye Jews, Samaritans, and Manichæans!" The greens still attempted to awaken his compassion. "We are poor, we are innocent, we are injured, we dare not pass through the streets: a general persecution is exercised against our name and colour.

Let us die, O emperor! but let us die by your command, and for your service!" But the repetition of partial and passionate invectives degraded, in their eyes, the majesty of the purple; they renounced allegiance to the prince who refused justice to his people, lamented that the father of Justinian had been born, and branded his son with the opprobrious names of a homicide, an ass, and a perjured tyrant. "Do you despise your lives?" cried the indignant monarch. The blues rose with fury from their seats, their hostile clamours thundered in the hippodrome, and their adversaries, deserting the unequal contest, spread terror and despair through the streets of Constantinople. At this dangerous moment, seven notorious assassins of both factions, who had been condemned by the præfect, were carried round the city, and afterwards transported to the place of execution in the suburb of Pera. Four were immediately beheaded; a fifth was hanged; but, when the same punishment was inflicted on the remaining two, the rope broke, they fell alive to the ground, the populace applauded their escape, and the monks of St. Conon, issuing from the neighbouring convent, conveyed them in a boat to the sanctuary of the church.[51] As one of these criminals was of the blue, and the other of the green, livery, the two factions were equally provoked by the cruelty of their oppressor or the ingratitude of their patron, and a short truce was concluded till they had delivered their prisoners and satisfied their revenge. The palace of the præfect, who withstood the seditious torrent, was instantly burnt, his officers and guards were massacred, the prisons were forced open, and freedom was restored to those who could only use it for the public destruction. A military force which had been despatched to the aid of the civil magistrate was fiercely encountered by an armed multitude, whose numbers and boldness continually increased: and the Heruli, the wildest barbarians in the service of the empire, overturned the priests and their relics, which, from a pious motive, had been rashly interposed to separate the bloody conflict. The tumult was exasperated by this sacrilege; the people fought with enthusiasm in the cause of God; the women, from the roofs and windows, showered stones on the heads of the soldiers, who darted firebrands against the houses; and the various flames, which had been kindled by the hands of citizens and strangers, spread without control over the face of the city. The conflagration involved the cathedral of St. Sophia, the baths of Zeuxippus, a part of the palace from the first

entrance to the altar of Mars, and the long portico from the palace to the forum of Constantine: a large hospital, with the sick patients, was consumed; many churches and stately edifices were destroyed; and an immense treasure of gold and silver was either melted or lost. From such scenes of horror and distress the wise and wealthy citizens escaped over the Bosphorus to the Asiatic side, and during five days Constantinople was abandoned to the factions, whose watchword, NIKA, *vanquish!* has given a name to this memorable sedition.[52]

As long as the factions were divided, the triumphant blues and desponding greens appeared to behold with the same indifference the disorders of the state. They agreed to censure the corrupt management of justice and the finance; and the two responsible ministers, the artful Tribonian and the rapacious John of Cappadocia, were loudly arraigned as the authors of the public misery. The peaceful murmurs of the people would have been disregarded: they were heard with respect when the city was in flames; the quæstor and the præfect were instantly removed, and their offices were filled by two senators of blameless integrity. After this popular concession Justinian proceeded to the hippodrome to confess his own errors, and to accept the repentance of his grateful subjects; but they distrusted his assurances, though solemnly pronounced in the presence of the holy gospels; and the emperor, alarmed by their distrust, retreated with precipitation to the strong fortress of the palace. The obstinacy of the tumult was now imputed to a secret and ambitious conspiracy, and a suspicion was entertained that the insurgents, more especially the green faction, had been supplied with arms and money by Hypatius and Pompey, two patricians who could neither forget with honour, nor remember with safety, that they were the nephews of the emperor Anastasius. Capriciously trusted, disgraced, and pardoned by the jealous levity of the monarch, they had appeared as loyal servants before the throne, and, during five days of the tumult, they were detained as important hostages; till at length, the fears of Justinian prevailing over his prudence, he viewed the two brothers in the light of spies, perhaps of assassins, and sternly commanded them to depart from the palace. After a fruitless representation that obedience might lead to involuntary treason, they retired to their houses, and in the morning of the sixth day Hypatius was surrounded and seized by the people, who, regardless of his virtuous resistance and the tears of his wife, transported their favourite to the Forum of Constantine, and, instead of a diadem, placed a rich collar on his head. If the usurper, who afterwards pleaded the merit of his delay, had complied with the advice of his senate, and urged the fury of the multitude, their first irresistible effort might have oppressed or expelled his trembling competitor. The Byzantine palace enjoyed a free communication with the sea, vessels lay ready at the garden-stairs, and a secret resolution was already formed to convey the emperor with his family and treasures to a safe retreat at some distance from the capital.

Justinian was lost, if the prostitute whom he raised from the theatre had not renounced the timidity as well as the virtues of her sex. In the midst of a council where Belisarius was present, Theodora alone displayed the spirit of a hero, and she alone, without apprehending his future hatred, could save the emperor from the imminent danger and his unworthy fears. "If flight," said the consort of Justinian, "were the only means of safety, yet I should disdain to fly. Death is the condition of our birth, but they who have reigned should never survive the loss of dignity and dominion. I implore Heaven that I may never be seen, not a day, without my diadem and purple; that I may no longer behold the light when I cease to be saluted with the name of queen. If you resolve, O Cæsar! to fly, you have treasures; behold the sea, you have ships; but tremble lest the desire of life should expose you to wretched exile and ignominious death. For my own part, I adhere to the maxim of antiquity, that the throne is a glorious sepulchre." The firmness of a woman restored the courage to deliberate and act, and courage soon discovers the resources of the most desperate situation. It was an easy and a decisive measure to revive the animosity of the factions; the blues were astonished at their own guilt and folly, that a trifling injury should provoke them to conspire with their implacable enemies against a gracious and liberal benefactor; they again proclaimed the majesty of Justinian; and the greens, with their upstart emperor, were left alone in the hippodrome. The fidelity of the guards was doubtful; but the military force of Justinian consisted in three thousand veterans, who had been trained to valour and discipline in the Persian and Illyrian wars. Under the command of Belisarius and Mundus, they silently marched in two divisions from the palace, forced their obscure way through narrow passages, expiring flames, and

falling edifices, and burst open at the same moment the two opposite gates of the hippodrome. In this narrow space the disorderly and affrighted crowd was incapable of resisting on either side a firm and regular attack; the blues signalised the fury of their repentance, and it is computed that above thirty thousand persons were slain in the merciless and promiscuous carnage of the day. Hypatius was dragged from his throne, and conducted with his brother Pompey to the feet of the emperor; they implored his clemency, but their crime was manifest, their innocence uncertain, and Justinian had been too much terrified to forgive. The next morning the two nephews of Anastasius, with eighteen *illustrious* accomplices, of patrician or consular rank, were privately executed by the soldiers, their bodies were thrown into the sea, their palaces razed, and their fortunes confiscated. The hippodrome itself was condemned, during several years, to a mournful silence; with the restoration of the games the same disorders revived, and the blue and green factions continued to afflict the reign of Justinian, and to disturb the tranquillity of the Eastern empire.[53]

III. That empire, after Rome was barbarous, still embraced the nations whom she had conquered beyond the Hadriatic, and as far as the frontiers of Æthiopia and Persia. Justinian reigned over sixty-four provinces and nine hundred and thirty-five cities;[54] his dominions were blessed by nature with the advantages of soil, situation, and climate, and the improvements of human art had been perpetually diffused along the coast of the Mediterranean and the banks of the Nile from ancient Troy to the Egyptian Thebes. Abraham[55] had been relieved by the well-known plenty of Egypt; the same country, a small and populous tract, was still capable of exporting each year two hundred and sixty thousand quarters of wheat for the use of Constantinople;[56] and the capital of Justinian was supplied with the manufactures of Sidon fifteen centuries after they had been celebrated in the poems of Homer.[57] The annual powers of vegetation, instead of being exhausted by two thousand harvests, were renewed and invigorated by skilful husbandry, rich manure, and seasonable repose. The breed of domestic animals was infinitely multiplied. Plantations, buildings, and the instruments of labour and luxury, which are more durable than the term of human life, were accumulated by the care of successive generations. Tradition preserved, and experience simplified, the humble practice of the arts; society was enriched by the division of labour and the facility of exchange; and every Roman was lodged, clothed, and subsisted by the industry of a thousand hands. The invention of the loom and distaff has been piously ascribed to the gods. In every age a variety of animal and vegetable productions, hair, skins, wool, flax, cotton, and at length *silk*, have been skilfully manufactured to hide or adorn the human body; they were stained with' an infusion of permanent colours, and the pencil was successfully employed to improve the labours of the loom. In the choice of those colours[58] which imitate the beauties of nature, the freedom of taste and fashion was indulged; but the deep purple[59] which the Phœnicians extracted from a shell-fish was restrained to the sacred person and palace of the emperor, and the penalties of treason were denounced against the ambitious subjects who dared to usurp the prerogative of the throne.[60]

I need not explain that *silk*[61] is originally spun from the bowels of a caterpillar, and that it composes the golden tomb from whence a worm emerges in the form of a butterfly. Till the reign of Justinian, the silkworms who feed on the leaves of the white mulberry-tree were confined to China; those of the pine, the oak, and the ash were common in the forests both of Asia and Europe; but as their education is more difficult, and their produce more uncertain, they were generally neglected, except in the little island of Ceos, near the coast of Attica. A thin gauze was procured from their webs, and this Cean manufacture, the invention of a woman, for female use, was long admired both in the East and at Rome. Whatever suspicions may be raised by the garments of the Medes and Assyrians, Virgil is the most ancient writer who expressly mentions the soft wool which was combed from the trees of the Seres or Chinese;[62] and this natural error, less marvellous than the truth, was slowly corrected by the knowledge of a valuable insect, the first artificer of the luxury of nations. That rare and elegant luxury was censured, in the reign of Tiberius, by the gravest of the Romans; and Pliny, in affected though forcible language, has condemned the thirst of gain, which explored the last confines of the earth for the pernicious purpose of exposing to the public eye naked draperies and transparent matrons.[63] A dress which showed the turn of the limbs and colour of the skin might gratify vanity or provoke desire; the silks which had been closely woven in China were sometimes unravelled by the Phœnician women, and the

precious materials were multiplied by a looser texture, and the intermixture of linen threads.[64] Two hundred years after the age of Pliny the use of pure or even of mixed silks was confined to the female sex, till the opulent citizens of Rome and the provinces were insensibly familiarised with the example of Elagabalus, the first who, by this effeminate habit, had sullied the dignity of an emperor and a man. Aurelian complained that a pound of silk was sold at Rome for twelve ounces of gold; but the supply increased with the demand, and the price diminished with the supply. If accident or monopoly sometimes raised the value even above the standard of Aurelian, the manufacturers of Tyre and Berytus were sometimes compelled, by the operation of the same causes, to content themselves with a ninth part of that extravagant rate.[65] A law was thought necessary to discriminate the dress of comedians from that of senators, and of the silk exported from its native country the far greater part was consumed by the subjects of Justinian. They were still more intimately acquainted with a shell-fish of the Mediterranean, surnamed the silk-worm of the sea: the fine wool or hair by which the mother-of-pearl affixes itself to the rock is now manufactured for curiosity rather than use; and a robe obtained from the same singular materials was the gift of the Roman emperor to the satraps of Armenia.[66]

A valuable merchandise of small bulk is capable of defraying the expense of land-carriage, and the caravans traversed the whole latitude of Asia in two hundred and forty-three days from the Chinese ocean to the sea-coast of Syria. Silk was immediately delivered to the Romans by the Persian merchants,[67] who frequented the fairs of Armenia and Nisibis; but this trade, which in the intervals of truce was oppressed by avarice and jealousy, was totally interrupted by the long wars of the rival monarchies. The Great King might proudly number Sogdiana, and even *Serica*, among the provinces of his empire, but his real dominion was bounded by the Oxus, and his useful intercourse with the Sogdoites, beyond the river, depended on the pleasure of their conquerors, the white Huns and the Turks, who successively reigned over that industrious people. Yet the most savage dominion has not extirpated the seeds of agriculture and commerce in a region which is celebrated as one of the four gardens of Asia; the cities of Samarcand and Bochara are advantageously seated for the exchange of its various productions, and their merchants purchased from the Chinese[68] the raw or manufactured silk which they transported into Persia for the use of the Roman empire. In the vain capital of China the Sogdian caravans were entertained as the suppliant embassies of tributary kingdoms, and, if they returned in safety, the bold adventure was rewarded with exorbitant gain. But the difficult and perilous march from Samarcand to the first town of Shensi could not be performed in less than sixty, eighty, or one hundred days; as soon as they had passed the Jaxartes they entered the desert, and the wandering hordes, unless they are restrained by armies and garrisons, have always considered the citizen and the traveller as the objects of lawful rapine. To escape the Tartar robbers and the tyrants of Persia, the silk-caravans explored a more southern road: they traversed the mountains of Thibet, descended the streams of the Ganges or the Indus, and patiently expected, in the ports of Guzerat and Malabar, the annual fleets of the West.[69] But the dangers of the desert were found less intolerable than toil, hunger, and the loss of time; the attempt was seldom renewed, and the only European who has passed that unfrequented way applauds his own diligence that, in nine months after his departure from Pekin, he reached the mouth of the Indus. The ocean, however, was open to the free communication of mankind. From the great river to the tropic of Cancer the provinces of China were subdued and civilised by the emperors of the North; they were filled about the time of the Christian era with cities and men, mulberry-trees and their precious inhabitants; and if the Chinese, with the knowledge of the compass, had possessed the genius of the Greeks or Phœnicians, they might have spread their discoveries over the southern hemisphere. I am not qualified to examine, and I am not disposed to believe, their distant voyages to the Persian Gulf or the Cape of Good Hope; but their ancestors might equal the labours and success of the present race, and the sphere of their navigation might extend from the isles of Japan to the straits of Malacca, the Pillars, if we may apply that name, of an Oriental Hercules.[70] Without losing sight of land, they might sail along the coast to the extreme promontory of Achin, which is annually visited by ten or twelve ships laden with the productions, the manufactures, and even the artificers of China; the island of Sumatra and the opposite peninsula are faintly delineated[71] as the regions of gold and silver, and the trading cities named in the geography of Ptolemy may indicate that this wealth was not solely derived from the mines. The direct interval between Sumatra and Ceylon is about three hundred leagues; the Chinese and Indian navigators were conducted by the flight of birds and periodical winds, and the ocean might be securely traversed in square-built ships, which, instead of iron, were sewed together with the strong thread of the cocoanut. Ceylon, Serendib, or Taprobana was divided between two hostile princes, one of whom possessed the mountains, the elephants, and the luminous carbuncle, and the other enjoyed the more solid riches of domestic industry, foreign trade, and the capacious harbour of Trinquemale, which received and dismissed the fleets of the East and West. In this hospitable isle, at an equal distance (as it was computed) from their respective countries, the silk-merchants of China, who had collected in their voyages aloes, cloves, nutmeg, and sandal-wood, maintained a free and beneficial commerce with the inhabitants of the Persian Gulf. The subjects of the Great King exalted, without a rival, his power and magnificence; and the Roman, who confounded their vanity by comparing his paltry coin with a gold medal of the emperor Anastasius, had sailed to Ceylon, in an Æthiopian ship, as a simple passenger.[72]

As silk became of indispensable use, the emperor Justinian saw with concern that the Persians had occupied by land and sea the monopoly of this important supply, and that the wealth of his subjects was continually drained by a nation of enemies and idolators. An active government would have restored the trade of Egypt and the navigation of the Red Sea, which had decayed with the prosperity of the empire; and the Roman vessels might have sailed for the purchase of silk to the ports of Ceylon, of Malacca, or even of China. Justinian embraced a more humble expedient, and solicited the aid of his Christian allies, the Æthiopians of Abyssinia, who had recently acquired the arts of navigation, the spirit of trade, and the seaport of Adulis,[73] still decorated with the trophies of a Grecian conqueror. Along the African coast they penetrated to the equator in search of gold, emeralds, and aromatics; but they wisely declined an unequal competition, in which they must be always prevented by the vicinity of the Persians to the markets of India: and the emperor submitted to the disappointment till his wishes were gratified by an unexpected event. The Gospel had been preached to the Indians: a bishop already governed the

Christians of St. Thomas on the pepper-coast of Malabar; a church was planted in Ceylon, and the missionaries pursued the footsteps of commerce to the extremities of Asia.[74] Two Persian monks had long resided in China, perhaps in the royal city of Nankin, the seat of a monarch addicted to foreign superstitions, and who actually received an embassy from the isle of Ceylon. Amidst their pious occupations they viewed with a curious eye the common dress of the Chinese, the manufactures of silk, and the myriads of silkworms, whose education (either on trees or in houses) had once been considered as the labour of queens.[75] They soon discovered that it was impracticable to transport the short-lived insect, but that in the eggs a numerous progeny might be preserved and multiplied in a distant climate. Religion or interest had more power over the Persian monks than the love of their country: after a long journey they arrived at Constantinople, imparted their project to the emperor, and were liberally encouraged by the gifts and promises of Justinian. To the historians of that prince a campaign at the foot of Mount Caucasus has seemed more deserving of a minute relation than the labours of these missionaries of commerce, who again entered China, deceived a jealous people by concealing the eggs of the silkworm in a hollow cane, and returned in triumph with the spoils of the East. Under their direction the eggs were hatched at the proper season by the artificial heat of dung; the worms were fed with mulberry-leaves; they lived and laboured in a foreign climate; a sufficient number of butterflies was saved to propagate the race, and trees were planted to supply the nourishment of the rising generations. Experience and reflection corrected the errors of a new attempt, and the Sogdoite ambassadors acknowledged in the succeeding reign that the Romans were not inferior to the natives of China in the education of the insects and the manufactures of silk,[76] in which both China and Constantinople have been surpassed by the industry of modern Europe. I am not insensible of the benefits of elegant luxury; yet I reflect with some pain that if the importers of silk had introduced the art of printing, already practised by the Chinese, the comedies of Menander and the entire decads of Livy would have been perpetuated in the editions of the sixth century. A larger view of the globe might at least have promoted the improvement of speculative science; but the Christian geography was forcibly extracted from texts of Scripture, and the study of nature was the surest symptom of an unbelieving mind. The orthodox faith confined the habitable world to *one* temperate zone, and represented the earth as an oblong surface, four hundred days' journey in length, two hundred in breadth, encompassed by the ocean and covered by the solid crystal of the firmament.[77]

IV. The subjects of Justinian were dissatisfied with the times and with the government. Europe was overrun by the barbarians and Asia by the monks: the poverty of the West discouraged the trade and manufactures of the East: the produce of labour was consumed by the unprofitable servants of the church, the state, and the army; and a rapid decrease was felt in the fixed and circulating capitals which constitute the national wealth. The public distress had been alleviated by the economy of Anastasius, and that prudent emperor accumulated an immense treasure while he delivered his people from the most odious or oppressive taxes. Their gratitude universally applauded the abolition of the *gold of affliction*, a personal tribute on the industry of the poor,[78] but more intolerable, as it should seem, in the form than in the substance, since the flourishing city of Edessa paid only one hundred and forty pounds of gold, which was collected in four years from ten thousand artificers.[79] Yet such was the parsimony which supported this liberal disposition, that, in a reign of twenty-seven years, Anastasius saved from his annual revenue the enormous sum of thirteen millions sterling, or three hundred and twenty thousand pounds of gold.[80] His example was neglected, and his treasure was abused, by the nephew of Justin. The riches of Justinian were speedily exhausted by alms and buildings, by ambitious wars and ignominious treaties. His revenues were found inadequate to his expenses. Every art was tried to extort from the people the gold and silver which he scattered with a lavish hand from Persia to France:[81] his reign was marked by the vicissitudes, or rather by the combat, of rapaciousness and avarice, of splendour and poverty; he lived with the reputation of hidden treasures,[82] and bequeathed to his successor the payment of his debts.[83] Such a character has been justly accused by the voice of the people and of posterity: but public discontent is credulous; private malice is bold; and a lover of truth will peruse with a suspicious eye the instructive anecdotes of Procopius. The secret historian represents only the vices of Justinian, and those vices are darkened by his malevolent pencil. Ambiguous actions are imputed to the worst motives: error is confounded with guilt, accident with design, and laws with abuses; the partial injustice of a moment is dexterously applied as the general maxim of a reign of thirty-two years: the emperor alone is made responsible for the faults of his officers, the disorders of the times, and the corruption of his subjects; and even the calamities of nature, plagues, earthquakes, and inundations, are imputed to the prince of the dæmons, who had mischieviously assumed the form of Justinian.[84]

After this precaution I shall briefly relate the anecdotes of avarice and rapine under the following heads: I. Justinian was so profuse that he could not be liberal. The civil and military officers, when they were admitted into the service of the palace, obtained a humble rank and a moderate stipend; they ascended by seniority to a station of affluence and repose; the annual pensions, of which the most honourable class was abolished by Justinian, amounted to four hundred thousand pounds; and this domestic economy was deplored by the venal or indigent courtiers as the last outrage on the majesty of the empire. The posts, the salaries of physicians, and the nocturnal illuminations were objects of more general concern; and the cities might justly complain that he usurped the municipal revenues which had been appropriated to these useful institutions. Even the soldiers were injured; and such was the decay of military spirit, that they were injured with impunity. The emperor refused at the return of each fifth year the customary donative of five pieces of gold, reduced his veterans to beg their bread, and suffered unpaid armies to melt away in the wars of Italy and Persia. II. The humanity of his predecessors had always remitted, in some auspicious circumstance of their reign, the arrears of the public tribute, and they dexterously assumed the merit of resigning those claims which it was impracticable to enforce. "Justinian, in the space of thirty-two years, has never granted a similar indulgence; and many of his subjects have renounced the possession of those lands whose value is insufficient to satisfy the demands of the treasury. To the cities which had suffered by hostile inroads Anastasius promised a general exemption of seven years: the provinces of Justinian have been ravaged by the Persians and Arabs, the Huns and Sclavonians; but his vain and ridiculous dispensation of a single year has been confined to those places which were actually taken by the enemy." Such is the language of the secret historian, who expressly denies that *any* indulgence was granted to Palestine after the revolt of the Samaritans;

a false and odious charge, confuted by the authentic record which attests a relief of thirteen centenaries of gold (fifty-two thousand pounds) obtained for that desolate province by the intercession of St. Sabas.[85] III. Procopius has not condescended to explain the system of taxation, which fell like a hailstorm upon the land, like a devouring pestilence on its inhabitants: but we should become the accomplices of his malignity if we imputed to Justinian alone the ancient, though rigorous principle, that a whole district should be condemned to sustain the partial loss of the persons or property of individuals. The *Annona*, or supply of corn for the use of the army and capital, was a grievous and arbitrary exaction, which exceeded, perhaps in a tenfold proportion, the ability of the farmer; and his distress was aggravated by the partial injustice of weights and measures, and the expense and labour of distant carriage. In a time of scarcity an extraordinary requisition was made to the adjacent provinces of Thrace, Bithynia, and Phrygia: but the proprietors, after a wearisome journey and a perilous navigation, received so inadequate a compensation, that they would have chosen the alternative of delivering both the corn and price at the doors of their granaries. These precautions might indicate a tender solicitude for the welfare of the capital; yet Constantinople did not escape the rapacious despotism of Justinian. Till his reign the straits of the Bosphorus and Hellespont were open to the freedom of trade, and nothing was prohibited except the exportation of arms for the service of the barbarians. At each of these gates of the city a prætor was stationed, the minister of Imperial avarice; heavy customs were imposed on the vessels and their merchandise; the oppression was retaliated on the helpless consumer; the poor were afflicted by the artificial scarcity and exorbitant price of the market; and a people accustomed to depend on the liberality of their prince might sometimes complain of the deficiency of water and bread.[86] The *aërial* tribute, without a name, a law, or a definite object, was an annual gift of one hundred and twenty thousand pounds, which the emperor accepted from his Prætorian præfect; and the means of payment were abandoned to the discretion of that powerful magistrate. IV. Even such a tax was less intolerable than the privilege of monopolies, which checked the fair competition of industry, and, for the sake of a small and dishonest gain, imposed an arbitrary burden on the wants and luxury of the subject. "As soon (I transcribe the Anecdotes) as the exclusive sale of silk was usurped by the Imperial treasurer, a whole people, the manufacturers of Tyre and Berytus, was reduced to extreme misery, and either perished with hunger or fled to the hostile dominions of Persia." A province might suffer by the decay of its manufactures, but in this example of silk Procopius has partially overlooked the inestimable and lasting benefit which the empire received from the curiosity of Justinian. His addition of one-seventh to the ordinary price of copper-money may be interpreted with the same candour; and the alteration, which might be wise, appears to have been innocent; since he neither alloyed the purity nor enhanced the value of the gold coin,[87] the legal measure of public and private payments. V. The ample jurisdiction required by the farmers of the revenue to accomplish their engagements might be placed in an odious light, as if they had purchased from the emperor the lives and fortunes of their fellow-citizens. And a more direct sale of honours and offices was transacted in the palace, with the permission, or at least with the connivance, of Justinian and Theodora. The claims of merit, even those of favour, were disregarded, and it was almost reasonable to expect that the bold adventurer who had undertaken the trade of a magistrate should find a rich compensation for infamy, labour, danger, the debts which he had contracted, and the heavy interest which he paid. A sense of the disgrace and mischief of this venal practice at length awakened the slumbering virtue of Justinian; and he attempted, by the sanction of oaths[88] and penalties, to guard the integrity of his government: but at the end of a year of perjury his rigorous edict was suspended, and corruption licentiously abused her triumph over the impotence of the laws. VI. The testament of Eulalius, count of the domestics, declared the emperor his sole heir, on condition, however, that he should discharge his debts and legacies, allow to his three daughters a decent maintenance, and bestow each of them in marriage, with a portion of ten pounds of gold. But the splendid fortune of Eulalius had been consumed by fire, and the inventory of his goods did not exceed the trifling sum of five hundred and sixty-four pieces of gold. A similar instance in Grecian history admonished the emperor of the honourable part prescribed for his imitation. He checked the selfish murmurs of the treasury, applauded the confidence of his friend, discharged the legacies and debts, educated the three virgins under the eye of the empress Theodora, and doubled the marriage-portion which had satisfied the tenderness of their father.[89] The humanity of a prince (for princes cannot be generous) is entitled to some praise; yet even in this act of virtue we may discover the inveterate custom of supplanting the legal or natural heirs which Procopius imputes to the reign of Justinian. His charge is supported by eminent names and scandalous examples; neither widows nor orphans were spared; and the art of soliciting, or extorting, or supposing testaments, was beneficially practised by the agents of the palace. This base and mischievous tyranny invades the security of private life; and the monarch who has indulged an appetite for gain will soon be tempted to anticipate the moment of succession, to interpret wealth as an evidence of guilt, and to proceed, from the claim of inheritance, to the power of confiscation. VII. Among the forms of rapine a philosopher may be permitted to name the conversion of Pagan or heretical riches to the use of the faithful; but in the time of Justinian this holy plunder was condemned by the sectaries alone, who became the victims of his orthodox avarice.[90]

Dishonour might be ultimately reflected on the character of Justinian; but much of the guilt, and still more of the profit, was intercepted by the ministers, who were seldom promoted for their virtues, and not always selected for their talents.[91] The merits of Tribonian the quæstor will hereafter be weighed in the reformation of the Roman law; but the economy of the East was subordinate to the Prætorian præfect; and Procopius has justified his anecdotes by the portrait which he exposes, in his public history, of the notorious vices of John of Cappadocia.[92] His knowledge was not borrowed from the schools,[93] and his style was scarcely legible; but he excelled in the powers of native genius, to suggest the wisest counsels, and to find expedients in the most desperate situations. The corruption of his heart was equal to the vigour of his understanding. Although he was suspected of magic and Pagan superstition, he appeared insensible to the fear of God or the reproaches of man; and his aspiring fortune was raised on the death of thousands, the poverty of millions, the ruin of cities, and the desolation of provinces. From the dawn of light to the moment of dinner, he assiduously laboured to enrich his master and himself at the expense of the Roman world; the remainder of the day was spent in sensual and obscene pleasures, and the silent hours of the night were interrupted by the perpetual dread of the justice of an assassin. His abilities, perhaps his vices, recommended him to the lasting friendship of Justinian: the emperor yielded with reluctance to the fury of the people; his victory was displayed by the immediate restoration of their enemy; and they felt above ten years, under his oppressive administration, that he was stimulated by revenge rather than instructed by misfortune. Their murmurs served only to fortify the resolution of Justinian; but the præfect, in the insolence of favour, provoked the resentment of Theodora, disdained a power before which every knee was bent, and attempted to sow the seeds of discord between the emperor and his beloved consort. Even Theodora herself was constrained to dissemble, to wait a favourable moment, and, by an artful conspiracy, to render John of Cappadocia the accomplice of his own destruction. At a time when Belisarius, unless he had been a hero, must have shown himself a rebel, his wife Antonina, who enjoyed the secret confidence of the empress, communicated his feigned discontent to Euphemia, the daughter of the præfect; the credulous virgin imparted to her father the dangerous project; and John, who might have known the value of oaths and promises, was tempted to accept a nocturnal, and almost treasonable, interview with the wife of Belisarius. An ambuscade of guards and eunuchs had been posted by the command of Theodora; they rushed with drawn swords to seize or to punish the guilty minister: he was saved by the fidelity of his attendants; but, instead of appealing to a gracious sovereign who had privately warned him of his danger, he pusillanimously fled to the sanctuary of the church. The favourite of Justinian was sacrificed to conjugal tenderness or domestic tranquillity; the conversion of a præfect into a priest extinguished his ambitious hopes; but the friendship of the emperor alleviated his disgrace, and he retained in the mild exile of Cyzicus an ample portion of his riches. Such imperfect revenge could not satisfy the unrelenting hatred of Theodora; the murder of his old enemy, the bishop of Cyzicus, afforded a decent pretence; and John of Cappadocia, whose actions had deserved a thousand deaths, was at last condemned for a crime of which he was innocent. A great minister, who had been invested with the honours of consul and patrician, was ignominiously scourged like the vilest of malefactors; a tattered cloak was the sole remnant of his fortunes; he was transported in a bark to the place of his banishment at Antinopolis in Upper Egypt, and the præfect of the East begged his bread through the cities which had trembled at his name. During an exile of seven years, his life was protracted and threatened by the ingenious cruelty of Theodora; and when her death permitted the emperor to recall a servant whom he had abandoned with regret, the ambition of John of Cappadocia was reduced to the humble duties of the sacerdotal profession. His successors convinced the subjects of Justinian that the arts of oppression might still be improved by experience and industry; the frauds of a Syrian banker were introduced into the administration of the finances; and the example of the præfect was diligently copied by the quæstor, the public and private treasurer, the governors of provinces, and the principal magistrates of the Eastern empire.[94]

V. The *edifices* of Justinian were cemented with the blood and treasure of his people; but those stately structures appeared to announce the prosperity of the empire, and actually displayed the skill of their architects. Both the theory and practice of the arts which depend on mathematical science and mechanical power were cultivated under the patronage of the emperors; the fame of Archimedes was rivalled by Proclus and Anthemius; and if their *miracles* had been related by intelligent spectators, they might now enlarge the speculations, instead of exciting the distrust, of philosophers. A tradition has prevailed that the Roman fleet was reduced to ashes in the port of Syracuse by the burning-glasses of Archimedes;[95] and it is asserted that a similar expedient was employed by Proclus to destroy the Gothic vessels in the harbour of Constantinople, and to protect his benefactor Anastasius against the bold enterprise of Vitalian.[96] A machine was fixed on the walls of the city, consisting of a hexagon mirror of polished brass, with many smaller and movable polygons to receive and reflect the rays of the meridian sun; and a consuming flame was darted to the distance, perhaps, of two hundred feet.[97] The truth of these two extraordinary facts is invalidated by the silence of the most authentic historians; and the use of burning-glasses was never adopted in the attack or defence of places.[98] Yet the admirable experiments of a French philosopher[99] have demonstrated the possibility of such a mirror; and, since it is possible, I am more disposed to attribute the art to the greatest mathematicians of antiquity, than to give the merit of the fiction to the idle fancy of a monk or a sophist. According to another story, Proclus applied sulphur to the destruction of the Gothic fleet;[100] in a modern imagination, the name of sulphur is instantly connected with the suspicion of gunpowder, and that suspicion is propagated by the secret arts of his disciple Anthemius.[101] A citizen of Tralles in Asia had five sons, who were all distinguished in their respective professions by merit and success. Olympius excelled in the knowledge and practice of the Roman jurisprudence. Dioscorus and Alexander became learned physicians; but the skill of the former was exercised for the benefit of his fellow-citizens, while his more ambitious brother acquired wealth and reputation at Rome. The fame of Metrodorus the grammarian, and of Anthemius the mathematician and architect, reached the ears of the emperor Justinian, who invited them to Constantinople; and while the one instructed the rising generation in the schools of eloquence, the other filled the capital and provinces with more lasting monuments of his art. In a trifling dispute relative to the walls or windows of their contiguous houses, he had been vanquished by the eloquence of his neighbour Zeno; but the orator was defeated in his turn by the master of mechanics, whose malicious, though harmless, stratagems are darkly represented by the ignorance of Agathias. In a lower room, Anthemius arranged several vessels or caldrons of water, each of them covered by the wide bottom of a leathern tube, which rose to a narrow top, and was artificially conveyed among the joists and rafters of the adjacent building. A fire was kindled beneath the caldron; the steam of the boiling water ascended through the tubes; the house was shaken by the efforts of imprisoned air, and its trembling inhabitants might wonder that the city was unconscious of the earthquake which they had felt. At another time, the friends of Zeno, as they sat at table, were dazzled by the intolerable light which flashed in their eyes from the reflecting mirrors of Anthemius; they were astonished by the noise which he produced from the collision of certain minute and sonorous particles; and the orator declared in tragic style to the senate, that a mere mortal must yield to the power of an antagonist who shook the earth with the trident of Neptune, and imitated the thunder and lightning of Jove himself. The genius of Anthemius, and his colleague Isidore the Milesian, was excited and employed by a prince whose taste for architecture had degenerated into a mischievous and costly passion. His favourite architects submitted their designs and difficulties to Justinian, and discreetly confessed how much their laborious meditations were surpassed by the intuitive knowledge or celestial inspiration of an emperor whose views were always directed to the benefit of his people, the glory of his reign, and the salvation of his soul.[102]

The principal church, which was dedicated by the founder of Constantinople to Saint Sophia, or the eternal wisdom, had been twice destroyed by fire; after the exile of John Chrysostom and during the *Nika* of the blue and green factions. No sooner did the tumult subside than the Christian populace deplored their sacrilegious rashness; but they might have rejoiced in the calamity, had they foreseen the glory of the new temple, which at the end of forty days was strenuously undertaken by the piety of Justinian.[103] The ruins were cleared away, a more spacious plan was described, and, as it required the consent of some proprietors of ground, they obtained the most exorbitant terms from the eager desires and timorous conscience of the monarch. Anthemius formed the design, and his genius directed the hands of ten thousand workmen, whose payment in pieces of fine silver was never delayed beyond the evening. The emperor himself, clad in a linen tunic, surveyed each day their rapid progress, and encouraged their diligence by his familiarity, his zeal, and his rewards. The new cathedral of St. Sophia was consecrated by the patriarch, five years, eleven months, and ten days from the first foundation; and in the midst of the solemn festival Justinian exclaimed with devout vanity, "Glory be to God, who hath thought me worthy to accomplish so great a work; I have vanquished thee, O Solomon!"[104] But the pride of the Roman Solomon, before twenty years had elapsed, was humbled by an earthquake, which overthrew the eastern part of the dome. Its splendour was again restored by the perseverance of the same prince; and in the thirty-sixth year of his reign Justinian celebrated the second dedication of a temple which remains, after twelve centuries, a stately monument of his fame. The architecture of St. Sophia, which is now converted into the principal mosque, has been imitated by the Turkish sultans, and that venerable pile continues to excite the fond admiration of the Greeks, and the more rational curiosity of European travellers. The eye of the spectator is disappointed by an irregular prospect of half-domes and shelving roofs: the western front, the principal approach, is destitute of simplicity and magnificence; and the scale of dimensions has been much surpassed by several of the Latin cathedrals. But the architect who first erected an *aërial* cupola is entitled to the praise of bold design and skilful execution. The dome of St. Sophia, illuminated by four-and-twenty windows, is formed with so small a curve, that the depth is equal only to one-sixth of its diameter; the measure of that diameter is one hundred and fifteen feet, and the lofty centre, where a crescent has supplanted the cross, rises to the perpendicular height of one hundred and eighty feet above the pavement. The circle which encompasses the dome lightly reposes on four strong arches, and their weight is firmly supported by four massy piles, whose strength is assisted on the northern and southern sides by four columns of Egyptian granite. A Greek cross, inscribed in a quadrangle, represents the form of the edifice; the exact breadth is two hundred and forty-three feet, and two hundred and sixty-nine may be assigned for the extreme length, from the sanctuary in the east to the nine western doors which open into the vestibule, and from thence into the *narthex* or exterior portico. That portico was the humble station of the penitents. The nave or body of the church was filled by the congregation of the faithful; but the two sexes were prudently distinguished, and the upper and lower galleries were allotted for the more private devotion of the women. Beyond the northern and southern piles, a balustrade, terminated on either side by the thrones of the emperor and the patriarch, divided the nave from the choir; and the space, as far as the steps of the altar, was occupied by the clergy and singers. The altar itself, a name which insensibly became familiar to Christian ears, was placed in the eastern recess, artificially built in the form of a demicylinder; and this sanctuary communicated by several doors with the sacristy, the vestry, the baptistery, and the contiguous buildings, subservient either to the pomp of worship, or the private use of the ecclesiastical ministers. The memory of past calamities inspired Justinian with a wise resolution that no wood, except for the doors, should be admitted into the new edifice; and the choice of the materials was applied to the strength, the lightness, or the splendour of the respective parts. The solid piles which sustained the cupola were composed of huge blocks of freestone, hewn into squares and triangles, fortified by circles of iron, and firmly cemented by the infusion of lead and quicklime; but the weight of the cupola was diminished by the levity of its substance, which consists either of pumice-stone that floats in the water, or of bricks, from the isle of Rhodes, five times less ponderous than the ordinary sort. The whole frame of the edifice was constructed of brick; but those base materials were concealed by a crust of marble; and the inside of St. Sophia, the cupola, the two larger and the six smaller semidomes, the walls, the hundred columns, and the pavement, delight even the eyes of barbarians with a rich and variegated picture.

A poet,[105] who beheld the primitive lustre of St. Sophia, enumerates the colours, the shades, and the spots of ten or twelve marbles, jaspers, and porphyries, which nature had profusely diversified, and which were blended and contrasted as it were by a skilful painter. The triumph of Christ was adorned with the last spoils of Paganism, but the greater part of these costly stones was extracted from the quarries of Asia Minor, the isles and continent of Greece, Egypt, Africa, and Gaul. Eight columns of porphyry, which Aurelian had placed in the Temple of the Sun, were offered by the piety of a Roman matron; eight others of green marble were presented by the ambitious zeal of the magistrates of Ephesus: both are admirable by their size and beauty, but every order of architecture disclaims their fantastic capitals. A variety of ornaments and figures was curiously expressed in mosaic; and the images of Christ, of the Virgin, of saints, and of angels, which have been defaced by Turkish fanaticism, were dangerously exposed to the superstition of the Greeks. According to the sanctity of each object, the precious metals were distributed in thin leaves or in solid masses. The balustrade of the choir, the capitals of the pillars, the ornaments of the doors and galleries, were of gilt bronze. The spectator was dazzled by the glittering aspect of the cupola. The sanctuary contained forty thousand pound weight of silver, and the holy vases and vestments of the altar were of the purest gold, enriched with inestimable gems. Before the structure of the church had arisen two cubits above the ground, forty-five thousand two hundred pounds were already consumed, and the whole expense amounted to three hundred and twenty thousand. Each reader, according to the measure of his belief, may estimate their value either in gold or silver; but the sum of one million sterling is the result of the lowest computation. A magnificent temple is a laudable monument of national taste and religion, and the enthusiast who entered the dome of St. Sophia might be tempted to suppose that it was the residence, or even the workmanship, of the Deity. Yet how dull is the artifice, how insignificant is the labour, if it be compared with the formation of the vilest insect that crawls upon the surface of the temple!

So minute a description of an edifice which time has respected may attest the truth and excuse the relation of the innumerable works, both in the capital and provinces, which Justinian constructed on a smaller scale and less durable foundations.[106] In Constantinople alone, and the adjacent suburbs, he dedicated twenty-five churches to the honour of Christ, the Virgin, and the saints. Most of these churches were decorated with marble and gold; and their various situation was skilfully chosen in a populous square or a pleasant grove, on the margin of the sea-shore or on some lofty eminence which overlooked the continents of Europe and Asia. The church of the Holy Apostles at Constantinople, and that of St. John at Ephesus, appear to have been framed on the same model: their domes aspired to imitate the cupolas of St. Sophia, but the altar was more judiciously placed under the centre of the dome, at the junction of four stately porticoes, which more accurately expressed the figure of the Greek cross. The Virgin of Jerusalem might exult in the temple erected by her imperial votary on a most ungrateful spot, which afforded neither ground nor materials to the architect. A level was formed by raising part of a deep valley to the height of the mountain. The stones of a neighbouring quarry were hewn into regular forms; each block was fixed on a peculiar carriage drawn by forty of the strongest oxen, and the roads were widened for the passage of such enormous weights. Lebanon furnished her loftiest cedars for the timbers of the church; and the seasonable discovery of a vein of red marble supplied its beautiful columns, two of which, the supporters of the exterior portico, were esteemed the largest in the world. The pious munificence of the emperor was diffused over the Holy Land; and if reason should condemn the monasteries of both sexes which were built or restored by Justinian, yet charity must applaud the wells which he sunk, and the hospitals which he founded, for the relief of the weary pilgrims. The schismatical temper of Egypt was ill entitled to the royal bounty; but in Syria and Africa some remedies were applied to the disasters of wars and earthquakes, and both Carthage and Antioch, emerging from their ruins, might revere the name of their gracious benefactor.[107] Almost every saint in the calendar acquired the honours of a temple—almost every city of the empire obtained the solid advantages of bridges, hospitals, and aque-ducts; but the severe liberality of the monarch disdained to indulge his subjects in the popular luxury of baths and theatres. While Justinian laboured for the public service, he was not unmindful of his own dignity and ease. The Byzantine palace, which had been damaged by the conflagration, was restored with new magnificence; and some notion may be conceived of the whole edifice by the vestibule or hall, which, from the doors perhaps, or the roof, was surnamed *chalce*, or the brazen. The dome of a spacious quadrangle was supported by massy pillars; the pavement and walls were incrusted with many-coloured marbles—the emerald green of Laconia, the fiery red, and the white Phrygian stone, intersected with veins of a sea-green hue. The mosaic paintings of the dome and sides represented the glories of the African and Italian triumphs. On the Asiatic shore of the Propontis, at a small distance to the east of Chalcedon, the costly palace and gardens of Heræum,[108] were prepared for the summer residence of Justinian, and more especially of Theodora. The poets of the age have celebrated the rare alliance of nature and art, the harmony of the nymphs of the groves, the fountains and the waves; yet the crowd of attendants who followed the court complained of their inconvenient lodgings,[109] and the nymphs were too often alarmed by the famous Porphyrio, a whale of ten cubits in breadth and thirty in length, who was stranded at the mouth of the river Sangaris after he had infested more than half a century the seas of Constantinople.[110]

The fortifications of Europe and Asia were multiplied by Justinian; but the repetition of those timid and fruitless precautions exposes, to a philosophic eye, the debility of the empire.[111] From Belgrade to the Euxine, from the conflux of the Save to the mouth of the Danube, a chain of above fourscore fortified places was extended along the banks of the great river. Single watchtowers were changed into spacious citadels; vacant walls, which the engineers contracted or enlarged according to the nature of the ground, were filled with colonies or garrisons; a strong fortress defended the ruins of Trajan's bridge;[112] and several military stations affected to spread beyond the Danube the pride of the Roman name. But that name was divested of its terrors; the barbarians, in their annual inroads, passed and contemptuously repassed before these useless bulwarks; and the inhabitants of the frontier, instead of reposing under the shadow of the general defence, were compelled to guard with incessant vigilance their separate habitations.

The solitude of ancient cities was replenished; the new foundations of Justinian acquired, perhaps too hastily, the epithets of impregnable and populous; and the auspicious place of his own nativity attracted the grateful reverence of the vainest of princes. Under the name of *Justiniana prima*, the obscure village of Tauresium became the seat of an archbishop and a præfect, whose jurisdiction extended over seven warlike provinces of Illyricum;[113] and the corrupt appellation of *Giustendil* still indicates, about twenty miles to the south of Sophia, the residence of a Turkish sanjak.[114] For the use of the emperor's countrymen, a cathedral, a palace, and an aqueduct were speedily constructed; the public and private edifices were adapted to the greatness of a royal city; and the strength of the walls resisted, during the lifetime of Justinian, the unskilful assaults of the Huns and Sclavonians. Their progress was sometimes retarded, and their hopes of rapine were disappointed, by the innumerable castles which, in the provinces of Dacia, Epirus, Thessaly, Macedonia, and Thrace, appeared to cover the whole face of the country. Six hundred of these forts were built or repaired by the emperor; but it seems reasonable to believe that the far greater part consisted only of a stone or brick tower in the midst of a square or circular area, which was surrounded by a wall and ditch, and afforded in a moment of danger some protection to the peasants and cattle of the neighbouring villages.[115] Yet these military works, which exhausted the public treasure, could not remove the just apprehensions of Justinian and his European subjects. The warm-baths of Anchialus, in Thrace, were rendered as safe as they were salutary; but the rich pastures of Thessalonica were foraged by the Scythian cavalry; the delicious vale of Tempe, three hundred miles from the Danube, was continually alarmed by the sound of war;[116] and no unfortified spot, however distant or solitary, could securely enjoy the blessings of peace. The straits of Thermopylæ, which seemed to protect, but which had so often betrayed, the safety of Greece, were diligently strengthened by the labours of Justinian. From the edge of the sea-shore, through the forests and valleys, and as far as the summit of the Thessalian mountains, a strong wall was continued which occupied every practicable entrance. Instead of a hasty crowd of peasants, a garrison of two thousand soldiers was stationed along the rampart, granaries of corn and reservoirs of water were provided for their use, and, by a precaution that inspired the cowardice which it foresaw, convenient fortresses were erected for their retreat. The walls of Corinth, overthrown by an earthquake, and the mouldering bulwarks of Athens and Platæa, were carefully restored; the barbarians were discouraged by the prospect of successive and painful sieges, and the naked cities of Peloponnesus were covered by the fortifications of the isthmus of Corinth. At the extremity of Europe, another peninsula, the Thracian Chersonesus, runs three days' journey into the sea, to form, with the adjacent shores of Asia, the straits of the Hellespont. The intervals between eleven populous towns were filled by lofty woods, fair pastures, and arable lands; and the isthmus, of thirty-seven stadia or furlongs, had been fortified by a Spartan general nine hundred years before the reign of Justinian.[117] In an age of freedom and valour the slightest rampart may prevent a surprise; and Procopius appears insensible of the superiority of ancient times, while he praises the solid construction and double parapet of a wall whose long arms stretched on either side into the sea, but whose strength was deemed insufficient to guard the Chersonesus, if each city, and particularly Gallipoli and Sestus, had not been secured by their peculiar fortifications. The *long* wall, as it was emphatically styled, was a work as disgraceful in the object as it was respectable in the execution. The riches of a capital diffuse themselves over the neighbouring country, and the territory of Constantinople, a paradise of nature, was adorned with the luxurious gardens and villas of the senators and opulent citizens. But their wealth served only to attract the bold and rapacious barbarians; the noblest of the Romans, in the bosom of peaceful indolence, were led away into Scythian captivity; and their sovereign might view from his palace the hostile flames which were insolently spread to the gates of the Imperial city. At the distance only of forty miles, Anastasius was constrained to establish a last frontier; his long wall of sixty miles, from the Propontis to the Euxine, proclaimed the impotence of his arms; and as the danger became more imminent, new fortifications were added by the indefatigable prudence of Justinian.[118]

Asia Minor, after the submission of the Isaurians,[119] remained without enemies and without fortifications. Those bold savages, who had disdained to be the subjects of Gallienus, persisted two hundred and thirty years in a life of independence and rapine. The most successful princes respected the strength of the mountains and the despair of the natives: their fierce spirit was sometimes soothed with gifts, and sometimes restrained by terror; and a military count, with three legions, fixed his permanent and ignominious station in the heart of the Roman provinces.[120] But no sooner was the vigilance of power relaxed or diverted, than the light-armed squadrons descended from the hills, and invaded the peaceful plenty of Asia. Although the Isaurians were not remarkable for stature or bravery, want rendered them bold, and experience made them skilful in the exercise of predatory war. They advanced with secrecy and speed to the attack of villages and defenceless towns; their flying parties have sometimes touched the Hellespont, the Euxine, and the gates of Tarsus, Antioch, or Damascus;[121] and the spoil was lodged in their inaccessible mountains, before the Roman troops had received their orders, or the distant province had computed its loss. The guilt of rebellion and robbery excluded them from the rights of national enemies; and the magistrates were instructed by an edict, that the trial or punishment of an Isaurian, even on the festival of Easter, was a meritorious act of justice and piety.[122] If the captives were condemned to domestic slavery, they maintained, with their sword or dagger, the private quarrel of their masters; and it was found expedient for the public tranquillity to prohibit the service of such dangerous retainers. When their countryman Tarcalissæus or Zeno ascended the throne, he invited a faithful and formidable band of Isaurians, who insulted the court and city, and were rewarded by an annual tribute of five thousand pounds of gold. But the hopes of fortune depopulated the mountains, luxury enervated the hardiness of their minds and bodies, and, in proportion as they mixed with mankind, they became less qualified for the enjoyment of poor and solitary freedom. After the death of Zeno, his successor Anastasius suppressed their pensions, exposed their persons to the revenge of the people, banished them from Constantinople, and prepared to sustain a war which left only the alternative of victory or servitude. A brother of the last emperor usurped the title of Augustus; his cause was powerfully supported by the arms, the treasures, and the magazines collected by Zeno; and the native Isaurians must have formed the smallest portion of the hundred and fifty thousand barbarians under his standard, which was sanctified for the first time by the presence of a fighting bishop. Their disorderly numbers were vanquished in the plains of Phrygia by the valour and discipline of the Goths, but a war of six years almost exhausted the courage of the emperor.[123] The Isaurians retired to their mountains, their fortresses were successively besieged and ruined, their communication with the sea was intercepted, the bravest of their leaders died in arms, the surviving chiefs before their execution were dragged in chains through the hippodrome, a colony of their youth was transplanted into Thrace, and the remnant of the people submitted to the Roman government. Yet some generations elapsed before their minds were reduced to the level of slavery. The populous villages of Mount Taurus were filled with horsemen and archers; they resisted the imposition of tributes, but they recruited the armies of Justinian; and his civil magistrates, the proconsul of Cappadocia, the count of Isauria, and the prætors of Lycaonia and Pisidia, were invested with military power to restrain the licentious practice of rapes and assassinations.[124]

If we extend our view from the tropic to the mouth of the Tanais, we may observe, on one hand, the precautions of Justinian to curb the savages of Æthiopia,[125] and, on the other, the long walls which he constructed in Crimæa for the protection of his friendly Goths, a colony of three thousand shepherds and warriors.[126] From that peninsula to Trebizond the eastern curve of the Euxine was secured by forts, by alliance, or by religion; and the possession of *Lazica*, the Colchos of ancient, the Mingrelia of modern, geography, soon became the object of an important war. Trebizond, in after times the seat of a romantic empire, was indebted to the liberality of Justinian for a church, an aqueduct, and a castle, whose ditches are hewn in the solid rock. From that maritime city a frontier line of five hundred miles may be drawn to the fortress of Circesium, the last Roman station on the Euphrates.[127] Above Trebizond immediately, and five days' journey to the south, the country rises into dark forests and craggy mountains, as savage though not so lofty as the Alps and the Pyrenees. In this rigorous climate,[128] where the snows seldom melt, the fruits are tardy and tasteless; even honey is poisonous: the most industrious tillage would be confined to some pleasant valleys, and the pastoral tribes obtained a scanty sustenance from the flesh and milk of their cattle. The *Chalybians*[129] derived their name and temper from the iron quality of the soil; and, since the days of Cyrus, they might produce, under the various appellations of Chaldæans and Zanians, an uninterrupted prescription of war and rapine. Under the reign of Justinian they acknowledged the god and the emperor of the Romans, and seven fortresses were built in the most accessible passes to exclude the ambition of the Persian monarch.[130] The principal source of the Euphrates descends from the Chalybian mountains, and seems to flow towards the west and the Euxine: bending to the south-west, the river passes under the walls of Satala and Melitene (which were restored by Justinian as the bulwarks of the lesser Armenia), and gradually approaches the Mediterranean Sea, till at length, repelled by Mount Taurus,[131] the Euphrates inclines his long and flexible course to the south-east and the Gulf of Persia. Among the Roman cities beyond the Euphrates we distinguish two recent foundations, which were named from Theodosius and the relics of the martyrs, and two capitals, Amida and Edessa, which are celebrated in the history of every age. Their strength was proportioned by Justinian to the danger of their situation. A ditch and palisade might be sufficient to resist the artless force of the cavalry of Scythia, but more elaborate works were required to sustain a regular siege against the arms and treasures of the Great King. His skilful engineers understood the methods of conducting deep mines, and of raising platforms to the level of the rampart. He shook the strongest battlements with his military engines, and sometimes advanced to the assault with a line of movable turrets on the backs of elephants. In the great cities of the East the disadvantage of space, perhaps of position, was compensated by the zeal of the people, who seconded the garrison in the defence of their country and religion; and the fabulous promise of the Son of God, that Edessa should never be taken, filled the citizens with valiant confidence and chilled the besiegers with doubt and dismay.[132] The subordinate towns of Armenia and Mesopotamia were diligently strengthened, and the posts which appeared to have any command of ground or water were occupied by numerous forts substantially built of stone, or more hastily erected with the obvious materials of earth and brick. The eye of Justinian investigated every spot, and his cruel precautions might attract the war into some lonely vale, whose peaceful natives, connected by trade and marriage, were ignorant of national discord and the quarrels of princes. Westward of the Euphrates a sandy desert extends above six hundred miles to the Red Sea. Nature had interposed a vacant solitude between the ambition of two rival empires; the Arabians, till Mahomet arose, were formidable only as robbers; and in the proud security of peace the fortifications of Syria were neglected on the most vulnerable side.

But the national enmity, at least the effects of that enmity, had been suspended by a truce which continued above fourscore years. An ambassador from the emperor Zeno accompanied the rash and unfortunate Perozes in his expedition against the Nephthalites, or White Huns, whose conquests had been stretched from the Caspian to the heart of India, whose throne was enriched with emeralds,[133] and whose cavalry was supported by a line of two thousand elephants.[134] The Persians were twice circumvented, in a situation which made valour useless and flight impossible, and the double victory of the Huns was achieved by military stratagem. They dismissed their royal captive after he had submitted to adore the majesty of a barbarian, and the humiliation was poorly evaded by the casuistical subtlety of the Magi, who instructed Perozes to direct his attention to the rising sun. The indignant successor of Cyrus forgot his danger and his gratitude; he renewed the attack with headstrong fury, and lost both his army and his life.[135] The death of Perozes abandoned Persia to her foreign and domestic enemies, and twelve years of confusion elapsed before his son Cabades or Kobad could embrace any designs of ambition or revenge. The unkind parsimony of Anastasius was the motive or pretence of a Roman war;[136] the Huns and Arabs marched under the Persian standard, and the fortifications of Armenia and Mesopotamia were at that time in a ruinous or imperfect condition. The emperor returned his thanks to the governor and people of Martyropolis for the prompt surrender of a city which could not be successfully defended, and the conflagration of Theodosiopolis might justify the conduct of their prudent neighbours. Amida sustained a long and destructive siege: at the end of three months the loss of fifty thousand of the soldiers of Cabades was not balanced by any prospect of success, and it was in vain that the Magi deduced a flattering prediction from the indecency of the women on the ramparts, who had revealed their most secret charms to the eyes of the assailants. At length, in a silent night, they ascended the most accessible tower, which was guarded only by some monks, oppressed, after the duties of a festival, with sleep and wine. Scaling-ladders were applied at the dawn of day; the presence of Cabades, his stern command, and his drawn sword, compelled the Persians to vanquish, and, before it was sheathed, fourscore thousand of the inhabitants had expiated the blood of their companions. After the siege of Amida the war continued three years, and the unhappy frontier tasted the full measure of its calamities. The gold of Anastasius was offered too late, the number of his troops was defeated by the number of their generals, the country was stripped of its inhabitants, and both the living and the dead were abandoned to the wild beasts of the desert. The resistance of Edessa and the deficiency of spoil inclined the mind of Cabades to peace; he sold his conquests for an exorbitant price; and the same line, though marked with slaughter and devastation, still separated the two empires. To avert the repetition of the same evils, Anastasius resolved to found a new colony, so strong that it should defy the power of the Persian, so far advanced towards Assyria that its stationary troops might defend the province by the menace or operation of offensive war. For this purpose the town of Dara,[137] fourteen miles from Nisibis, and four days' journey from the Tigris, was peopled and adorned: the hasty works of Anastasius were improved by the perseverance of Justinian, and, without insisting on places less important, the fortifications of Dara may represent the military architecture of the age. The city was surrounded with two walls, and the interval between them, of fifty paces, afforded a retreat to the cattle of the besieged. The inner wall was a monument of strength and beauty: it measured sixty feet from the ground, and the height of the towers was one hundred feet; the loopholes, from whence an enemy might be annoyed with missile weapons, were small, but numerous; the soldiers were planted along the rampart, under the shelter of double galleries; and a third platform, spacious and secure, was raised on the summit of the towers. The exterior wall appears to have been less lofty, but more solid, and each tower was protected by a quadrangular bulwark. A hard rocky soil resisted the tools of the miners, and on the south-east, where the ground was more tractable, their approach was retarded by a new work, which advanced in the shape of a half-moon. The double and treble ditches were filled with a stream of water, and in the management of the river the most skilful labour was employed to supply the inhabitants, to distress the besiegers, and to prevent the mischiefs of a natural or artificial inundation. Dara continued more than sixty years to fulfil the wishes of its founders and to provoke the jealousy of the Persians, who incessantly complained that this impregnable fortress had been constructed in manifest violation of the treaty of peace between the two empires.

Between the Euxine and the Caspian the countries of Colchos, Iberia, and Albania are intersected in every direction by the branches of Mount Caucasus, and the two principal *gates*, or passes, from north to south, have been frequently confounded in the geography both of the ancients and moderns. The name of *Caspian* or *Albanian* gates is properly applied to Derbend,[138] which occupies a short declivity between the mountains and the sea; the city, if we give credit to local tradition, had been founded by the Greeks, and this dangerous entrance was fortified by the kings of Persia with a mole, double walls, and doors of iron. The *Iberian* gates[139] are formed by a narrow passage of six miles in Mount Caucasus, which opens from the northern side of Iberia or Georgia into the plain that reaches to the Tanais and the Volga. A fortress, designed by Alexander perhaps, or one of his successors, to command that important pass, had descended by right of conquest or inheritance to a prince of the Huns, who offered it for a moderate price to the emperor; but while Anastasius paused, while he timorously computed the cost and the distance, a more vigilant rival interposed, and Cabades forcibly occupied the straits of Caucasus. The Albanian and Iberian gates excluded the horsemen of Scythia from the shortest and most practicable roads, and the whole front of the mountains was covered by the rampart of Gog and Magog, the long wall which has excited the curiosity of an Arabian caliph[140] and a Russian conqueror.[141] According to a recent description, huge stones, seven feet thick, twenty-one feet in length or height, are artifically joined, without iron or cement, to compose a wall which runs above three hundred miles from the shores of Derbend, over the hills and through the valleys of Daghestan and Georgia. Without a vision such a work might be undertaken by the policy of Cabades; without a miracle it might be accomplished by his son, so formidable to the Romans under the name of Chosroes, so dear to the Orientals under the appellation of Nushirwan. The Persian monarch held in his hand the keys both of peace and war; but he stipulated in every treaty that Justinian should contribute to the expense of a common barrier which equally protected the two empires from the inroads of the Scythians.[142]

VI. Justinian suppressed the schools of Athens and the consulship of Rome, which had given so many sages and heroes to mankind. Both these institutions had long since degenerated from their primitive glory, yet some reproach may be justly inflicted on the avarice and jealousy of a prince by whose hand such venerable ruins were destroyed.

Athens, after her Persian triumphs, adopted the philosophy of Ionia and the rhetoric of Sicily; and these studies became the patrimony of a city whose inhabitants, about thirty thousand males, condensed, within the period of a single life, the genius of ages and millions. Our sense of the dignity of human nature is exalted by the simple recollection that Isocrates[143] was the companion of Plato and Xenophon; that he assisted, perhaps with the historian Thucydides, at the first representations of the Œdipus of Sophocles and the Iphigenia of Euripides; and that his pupils Æschines and Demosthenes contended for the crown of patriotism in the presence of Aristotle, the master of Theophrastus, who taught at Athens with the founders of the Stoic and Epicurean sects.[144] The ingenious youth of Attica enjoyed the benefits of their domestic education, which was communicated without envy to the rival cities. Two thousand disciples heard the lessons of Theophrastus;[145] the schools of rhetoric must have been still more populous than those of philosophy; and a rapid succession of students diffused the fame of their teachers as far as the utmost limits of the Grecian language and name. Those limits were enlarged by the victories of Alexander; the arts of Athens survived her freedom and dominion; and the Greek colonies which the Macedonians planted in Egypt, and scattered over Asia, undertook long and frequent pilgrimages to worship the Muses in their favourite temple on the banks of the Ilissus. The Latin conquerors respectfully listened to the instructions of their subjects and captives; the names of Cicero and Horace were enrolled in the schools of Athens; and after the perfect settlement of the Roman empire, the natives of Italy, of Africa, and of Britain, conversed in the groves of the Academy with their fellow-students of the East. The studies of philosophy and eloquence are congenial to a popular state, which encourages the freedom of inquiry, and submits only to the force of persuasion. In the republics of Greece and Rome the art of speaking was the powerful engine of patriotism or ambition; and the schools of rhetoric poured forth a colony of statesmen and legislators. When the liberty of public debate was suppressed, the orator, in the honourable profession of an advocate, might plead the cause of innocence and justice; he might abuse his talents in the more profitable trade of panegyric; and the same precepts continued to dictate the fanciful declamations of the sophist, and the chaster beauties of historical composition. The systems which professed to unfold the nature of God, of man, and of the universe, entertained the curiosity of the philosophic student; and according to the temper of his mind, he might doubt with the Sceptics, or decide with the Stoics, sublimely speculate with Plato, or severely argue with Aristotle. The pride of the adverse sects had fixed an unattainable term of moral happiness and perfection: but the race was glorious and salutary; the disciples of Zeno, and even those of Epicurus, were taught both to act and to suffer; and the death of Petronius was not less effectual than that of Seneca to humble a tyrant by the discovery of his impotence. The light of science could not indeed be confined within the walls of Athens. Her incomparable writers address themselves to the human race; the living masters emigrated to Italy and Asia; Berytus, in later times, was devoted to the study of the law; astonomy and physic were cultivated in the museum of Alexandria; but the Attic schools of rhetoric and philosophy maintained their superior reputation from the Peloponnesian war to the reign of Justinian. Athens, though situate in a barren soil, possessed a pure air, a free navigation, and the monuments of ancient art. That sacred retirement was seldom disturbed by the business of trade or government; and the last of the Athenians were distinguished by their lively wit, the purity of their taste and language, their social manners, and some traces, at least in discourse, of the magnanimity of their fathers. In the suburbs of the city, the *Academy* of the Platonists, the *Lyceum* of the Peripatetics, the *Portico* of the Stoics, and the *Garden* of the Epicureans, were planted with trees and decorated with statues; and the philosophers, instead of being immured in a cloister, delivered their instructions in spacious and pleasant walks, which at different hours were consecrated to the exercises of the mind and body. The genius of the founders still lived in those venerable seats; the ambition of succeeding to the masters of human reason excited a generous emulation; and the merit of the candidates was determined, on each vacancy, by the free voices of an enlightened people. The Athenian professors were paid by their disciples: according to their mutual wants and abilities, the price appears to have varied from a mina to a talent; and Isocrates himself, who derides the avarice of the sophists, required, in his school of rhetoric, about thirty pounds from each of his hundred pupils. The wages of industry are just and honourable, yet the same Isocrates shed tears at the first receipt of a stipend: the Stoic might blush when he was hired to preach the contempt of money; and I should be sorry to discover that Aristotle or Plato so far degenerated from the example of Socrates as to exchange knowledge for gold. But some property of lands and houses was settled, by the permission of the laws, and the legacies of deceased friends, on the philosophic chairs of Athens. Epicurus bequeathed to his disciples the gardens which he had purchased for eighty minæ or two hundred and fifty pounds, with a fund sufficient for their frugal subsistence and monthly festivals;[146] and the patrimony of Plato afforded an annual rent, which, in eight centuries, was gradually increased from three to one thousand pieces of gold.[147] The schools of Athens were protected by the wisest and most virtuous of the Roman princes. The library, which Hadrian founded, was placed in a portico adorned with pictures, statues, and a roof of alabaster, and supported by one hundred columns of Phrygian marble. The public salaries were assigned by the generous spirit of the Antonines; and each professor, of politics, of rhetoric, of the Platonic, the Peripatetic, the Stoic, and the Epicurean philosophy, received an annual stipend of ten thousand drachmæ, or more than three hundred pounds sterling.[148] After the death of Marcus, these liberal donations, and the privileges attached to the *thrones* of science, were abolished and revived, diminished and enlarged; but some vestige of royal bounty may be found under the successors of Constantine; and their arbitrary choice of an unworthy candidate might tempt the philosophers of Athens to regret the days of independence and poverty.[149] It is remarkable that the impartial favour of the Antonines was bestowed on the four adverse sects of philosophy, which they considered as equally useful, or at least as equally innocent. Socrates had formerly been the glory and the reproach of his country; and the first lessons of Epicurus so strangely scandalised the pious ears of the Athenians, that by his exile, and that of his antagonists, they silenced all vain disputes concerning the nature of the gods. But in the ensuing year they recalled the hasty decree, restored the liberty of the schools, and were convinced by the experience of ages that the moral character of philosophers is not affected by the diversity of their theological speculations.[150]

The Gothic arms were less fatal to the schools of Athens than the establishment of a new religion, whose ministers superseded the exercise of reason, resolved every question by an article of faith, and condemned the infidel or sceptic to eternal flame. In many a volume of laborious controversy they exposed the weakness of the understanding and the corruption of the heart, insulted human nature in the sages of antiquity, and proscribed the spirit of philosophical inquiry, so repugnant to the doctrine, or at least to the temper, of a humble believer. The surviving sect of the Platonists, whom Plato would have blushed to acknowledge, extravagantly mingled a sublime theory with the practice of superstition and magic; and as they remained alone in the midst of a Christian world, they indulged a secret rancour against the government of the church and state, whose severity was still suspended over their heads. About a century after the reign of Julian,[151] Proclus[152] was permitted to teach in the philosophic chair of the Academy; and such was his industry, that he frequently, in the same day, pronounced five lessons, and composed seven hundred lines. His sagacious mind explored the deepest questions of morals and metaphysics, and he ventured to urge eighteen arguments against the Christian doctrine of the creation of the world. But in the intervals of study he *personally* conversed with Pan, Æsculapius, and Minerva, in whose mysteries he was secretly initiated, and whose prostrate statues he adored; in the devout persuasion that the philosopher, who is a citizen of the universe, should be the priest of its various deities. An eclipse of the sun announced his approaching end; and his Life, with that of his scholar Isidore,[153] compiled by two of their most learned disciples, exhibits a deplorable picture of the second childhood of human reason. Yet the golden chain, as it was fondly styled, of the Platonic succession, continued forty-four years from the death of Proclus to the edict of Justinian,[154] which imposed a perpetual silence on the schools of Athens, and excited the grief and indignation of the few remaining votaries of Grecian science and superstition. Seven friends and philosophers, Diogenes, and Hermias, Eulalius and Priscian, Damascius, Isidore, and Simplicius, who dissented from the religion of their sovereign, embraced the resolution of seeking in a foreign land the freedom which was denied in their native country. They had heard, and they credulously believed, that the republic of Plato was realised in the despotic government of Persia, and that a patriot king reigned over the happiest and most virtuous of nations. They were soon astonished by the natural discovery that Persia resembled the other countries of the globe; that Chosroes, who affected the name of a philosopher, was vain, cruel, and ambitious; that bigotry, and a spirit of intolerance, prevailed among the Magi; that the nobles were haughty, the courtiers servile, and the magistrates unjust; that the guilty sometimes escaped, and that the innocent were often oppressed. The disappointment of the philosophers provoked them to overlook the real virtues of the Persians; and they were scandalised, more deeply perhaps than became their profession, with the plurality of wives and concubines, the incestuous marriages, and the custom of exposing dead bodies to the dogs and vultures, instead of hiding them in the earth, or consuming them with fire. Their repentance was expressed by a precipitate return, and they loudly declared that they had rather die on the borders of the empire than enjoy the wealth and favour of the barbarian. From this journey, however, they derived a benefit which reflects the purest lustre on the character of Chosroes. He required that the seven sages who had visited the court of Persia should be exempted from the penal laws which Justinian enacted against his Pagan subjects; and this privilege, expressly stipulated in a treaty of peace, was guarded by the vigilance of a powerful mediator.[155] Simplicius and his companions ended their lives in peace and obscurity; and as they left no disciples, they terminate the long list of Grecian philosophers, who may be justly praised, notwithstanding their defects, as the wisest and most virtuous of their contemporaries. The writings of Simplicius are now extant. His physical and metaphysical commentaries on Aristotle have passed away with the fashion of the times; but his moral interpretation of Epictetus is preserved in the library of nations, as a classic book, most excellently adapted to direct the will, to purify the heart, and to confirm the understanding, by a just confidence in the nature both of God and man.

About the same time that Pythagoras first invented the appellation of philosopher, liberty and the consulship were founded at Rome by the elder Brutus. The revolutions of the consular office, which may be viewed in the successive lights of a substance, a shadow, and a name, have been occasionally mentioned in the present history. The first magistrates of the republic had been chosen by the people, to exercise, in the senate and in the camp, the powers of peace and war, which were afterwards translated to the emperors. But the tradition of ancient dignity was long revered by the Romans and barbarians. A Gothic historian applauds the consulship of Theodoric as the height of all temporal glory and greatness;[156] the king of Italy himself congratulates those annual favourites of fortune who, without the cares, enjoyed the splendour of the throne; and at the end of a thousand years two consuls were created by the sovereigns of Rome and Constantinople for the sole purpose of giving a date to the year and a festival to the people. But the expenses of this festival, in which the wealthy and the vain aspired to surpass their predecessors, insensibly arose to the enormous sum of fourscore thousand pounds; the wisest senators declined a useless honour which involved the certain ruin of their families, and to this reluctance I should impute the frequent chasms in the last age of the consular *Fasti*. The predecessors of Justinian had assisted from the public treasures the dignity of the less opulent candidates; the avarice of that prince preferred the cheaper and more convenient method of advice and regulation.[157] Seven *processions* or spectacles were the number to which his edict confined the horse and chariot races, the athletic sports, the music and pantomimes of the theatre, and the hunting of wild beasts; and small pieces of silver were discreetly substituted to the gold medals, which had always excited tumult and drunkenness when they were scattered with a profuse hand among the populace. Notwithstanding these precautions and his own example, the succession of consuls finally ceased in the thirteenth year of Justinian, whose despotic temper might be gratified by the silent extinction of a title which admonished the Romans of their ancient freedom.[158] Yet the annual consulship still lived in the minds of the people; they fondly expected its speedy restoration; they applauded the gracious condescension of successive princes, by whom it was assumed in the first year of their reign; and three centuries elapsed, after the death of Justinian, before that obsolete dignity, which had been suppressed by custom, could be abolished by law.[159] The imperfect mode of distinguishing each year by the name of a magistrate was usefully supplied by the date of a permanent era: the creation of the world, according to the Septuagint version, was adopted by the Greeks;[160] and the Latins, since the age of Charlemagne, have computed their time from the birth of Christ.[161]

NOTES

CHAPTERS I—XL

Chapter I

1. Dion Cassius (l. liv. p. 736), with the annotations of Reimar, who has collected all that Roman vanity has left upon the subject. The marble of Ancyra, on which Augustus recorded his own exploits, asserts that *he compelled* the Parthians to restore the ensigns of Crassus.

2. Strabo (l. xvi. p. 780), Pliny the elder (Hist. Natur. l. vi. c. 28, 29), and Dion Cassius (l. liii. p. 723 and l. liv. p. 734), have left us very curious details concerning these wars. The Romans made themselves masters of Mariaba, a city of Arabia Felix, well known to the Orientals (see Abulfeda and the Nubian geography, p. 5). They were arrived within three days' journey of the Spice country, the rich object of their invasion.

3. By the slaughter of Varus and his three legions. First book of the Annals of Tacitus. Sueton, in August, c. 23 and Velleius Paterculus, l. ii. c. 117, etc. Augustus did not receive the melancholy news with all the temper and firmness that might have been expected from his character.

4. Tacit. Annal. l. ii., Dion Cassius, l. lvi. p. 833, and the speech of Augustus himself, in Julian's Cæsars. It receives great light from the learned notes of his French translator M. Spanheim.

5. Germanicus, Suetonius Paulinus, and Agricola, were checked and recalled in the course of their victories. Corbulo was put to death. Military merit, as it is admirably expressed by Tacitus, was, in the strictest sense of the word, *imperatoria virtus*.

6. Cæsar himself conceals that ignoble motive; but it is mentioned by Suetonius, c. 47. The British pearls proved, however, of little value, on account of their dark and livid colour. Tacitus observes, with reason (in Agricola, c. 12), that it was an inherent defect. "Ego facilius crediderim, naturam margaritis deesse quam nobis avaritiam."

7. Claudius, Nero, and Domitian. A hope is expressed by Pomponius Mela, l. iii. c. 6. (He wrote under Claudius) that, by the success of the Roman arms, the island and its savage inhabitants would soon be better known.

8. The admirable abridgment given by Tacitus, in the Life of Agricola, and copiously, though perhaps not completely, illustrated by our own antiquarians, Camden and Horsley.

9. The Irish writers, jealous of their national honour, are extremely provoked on this occasion, both with Tacitus and with Agricola.

10. Horsley's Britannia Romana, l. i. c. 10.

11. The poet Buchanan celebrates, with elegance and spirit (see his Sylvæ v.), the unviolated independence of his native country. But, if the single testimony of Richard of Cirencester was sufficient to create a Roman province of Vespasiano to the north of the wall, that independence would be reduced within very narrow limits.

12. Appian (in Procem.) and the uniform imagery of Ossian's Poems, which, according to every hypothesis, were composed by a native Caledonian. [Gibbon believed that *Ossian* was translated from the Gaelic. Many now believe the poems to have been fabricated by Macpherson.]

13. Pliny's Panegyric, which seems founded on facts.

14. Dion Cassius, l. lxvii.

15. Herodotus, l. iv. c. 94. Julian in the Cæsars, with Spanheim's observations.

16. Plin. Epist. viii. 9.

17. Dion Cassius, l. lxviii. p. 1123, 1131. Julian in Cæsaribus, Eutropius, viii. 2, 6. Aurelius Victor in Epitome.

18. Memoir of M. d'Anville, on the Province of Dacia, in the Academie des Inscriptions, tom. xxviii. p. 444-468.

19. Trajan's sentiments are represented in a very just and lively manner in the Cæsars of Julian.

20. Eutropius and Sextus Rufus have endeavoured to perpetuate the illusion. See a very sensible dissertation of M. Freret in the Academie des Inscriptions, tom. xxi. p. 55

21. Dion Cassius, l. lxviii.

22. Ovid, Fast. l. ii. ver. 667. Livy, under the reign of Tarquin.

23. St. Augustin is highly delighted with the proof of the weakness of Terminus, and the vanity of the Augurs. The City of God, iv. 29.

24. Augustan History, p. 5. Jerome's Chronicle, and all the Epitomisers. It is somewhat surprising that this memorable event should be omitted by Dion, or rather by Xiphilin.

25. Dion, l. lxix. p. 1158. Hist. August. p. 5, 8. If all our historians were lost, medals, inscriptions, and other monuments, would be sufficient to record the travels of Hadrian.

26. Augustan History.

27. We must, however, remember, that, in the time of Hadrian, a rebellion of the Jews raged with religious fury, though only in a single province: Pausanias (l. viii. c. 43) mentions two necessary and successful wars, conducted by the generals of Pius. 1st, Against, the wandering Moors, who were driven into the solitudes of Atlas. 2nd, Against the Brigantes of Britain, who had invaded the Roman province. Both these wars (with several other hostilities) are mentioned in the Augustan History, p. 19.

28. Appian of Alexandria, in the preface to his History of the Roman Wars.

29. Dion, l. lxxi. Hist. August. in Marco, b. iv. 9–22. The Parthian victories gave birth to a crowd of contemptible historians, whose memory has been rescued from oblivion, and exposed to ridicule, in a very lively piece of criticism of Lucian.

30. The poorest rank of soldiers possessed above forty pounds sterling (Dionys, Halicarn, iv. 17), a very high qualification, at a time when money was so scarce, that an ounce of silver was equivalent to seventy pound weight of brass. The populace, excluded by the ancient constitution, were indiscriminately admitted by Marius. Sallust. de Bell. Jugurth. c. 91.

31. Cæsar formed his legion Alauda, of Gauls and strangers: but it was during the licence of civil war; and after the victory, he gave them the freedom of the city for their reward.

32. Vegetius de Re Militari, l. i. c. 2–7.

33. The oath of service and fidelity to the emperor was annually renewed by the troops, on the first of January.

34. Tacitus calls the Roman eagles, Bellorum Deos. They were placed in a chapel in the camp, and with the other deities received the religious worship of the troops.

35. Gronovius de Pecunia vetere, l. iii. p. 120, etc. The emperor Domitian raised the annual stipend of the legionaries to twelve pieces of gold, which, in his time, was equivalent to about ten of our guineas. This pay, somewhat higher than our own, had been, and was afterwards, gradually increased, according to the progress of wealth and military government. After twenty years' service, the veteran received three thousand denarii (about one hundred pounds sterling), or a proportionable allowance of land. The pay and advantages of the guards were, in general, about double those of the legions.

36. Exercitus ab exercitando, Varro de Linguâ Latinâ, l. iv. Cicero in Tusculan. l. ii. 37. There is room for a very interesting work, which should lay open the connection between the languages and manners of nations.

37. Vegetius, l. ii. and the rest of his first book.

38. The Pyrrhic dance is extremely well illustrated by M. le Beau, in the Academie des Inscriptions, tom. xxxv. p. 262, etc. That learned academician, in a series of memoirs, has collected all the passages of the ancients that relate to the Roman legion.

39. Joseph. de Bell. Judaico, l. iii. c. 5. We are indebted to this Jew for some very curious details of Roman discipline.

40. Plin. Panegyr. c. 13. Life of Hadrian, in the Augustan History, 1–14.

41. See an admirable digression on the Roman discipline, in the sixth book of his history.

42. Vegetius de Re Militari, l. ii. c. 4, etc. Considerable part of his very perplexed abridgment was taken from the regulations of Trajan and Hadrian; and the legion, as he describes it, cannot suit any other age of the Roman empire.

43. Vegetius de Re Militari, l. ii. c. 1. In the purer age of Cæsar and Cicero, the word miles was almost confined to the infantry. Under the lower empire, and in the times of chivalry, it was appropriated almost as exclusively to the men at arms, who fought on horseback.

44. In the time of Polybius and Dionysius of Halicarnassus (l. v. c. 45), the steel point of the pilum seems to have been much longer. In the time of Vegetius, it was reduced to a foot, or even nine inches. I have chosen a medium.

45. For the legionary arms, see Lipsius de Militiâ Romanâ, l. iii. c. 2–7.

46. See the beautiful comparison of Virgil, Georgic. ii. v. 279.

47. M. Guichard, Memoires Militaires, tom. i. c. 4 and Nouveaux Memoires, tom, i. p. 293–311 has treated the subject like a scholar and an officer.

48. Arrian's Tactics. With the true partiality of a Greek, Arrian rather chose to describe the phalanx, of which he had read, than the legions which he had commanded.

49. Polyb. l. xvii.

50. Veget. de Re Militari, l. ii. c. 6. His positive testimony, which might be supported by circumstantial evidence, ought surely to silence those critics who refuse the Imperial legion its proper body of cavalry.

51. Livy almost throughout, particularly xlii. 61.

52. Plin. Hist. Natur. xxxiii. 2. The true sense of that very curious passage was first discovered and illustrated by M. de Beaufort, Republique Romaine, l. ii. c. 2.

53. As in the instance of Horace and Agricola. This appears to have been a defect in the Roman discipline; which Hadrian endeavoured to remedy, by ascertaining the legal age of a tribune.

54. Arrian's Tactics, 4.

55. Such, in particular, was the state of the Batavians. Tacit. Germania, c 29.

56. Marcus Antoninus obliged the vanquished Quadi and Marcomanni to supply him with a large body of troops, which he immediately sent into Britain. Dion Cassius, l. lxxi.

57. Tacit. Annal. iv. 5. Those who fix a regular proportion of as many foot, and twice as many

horse, confound the auxiliaries of the emperors, with the Italian allies of the republic.

58. Vegetius, ii. 2. Arrian, in his order of march and battle against the Alani.

59. The subject of the ancient machines is treated with great knowledge and ingenuity by the Chevalier Folard (Polybe, tom. ii. p. 233–290). He prefers them in many respects to our modern cannon and mortars. We may observe, that the use of them in the field gradually became more prevalent, in proportion as personal valour and military skill declined with the Roman empire. When men were no longer found, their place was supplied by machines. See Vegetius, ii. 25. Arrian.

60. Vegetius finishes his second book, and the description of the legion, with the following emphatic words: "Universa quæ in quoque belli genere necessaria esse creduntur, secum legio debet ubique portare, ut in quovis loco fixerit castra, armatam facial civitatem."

61. For the Roman Castrametation, Polybius, l. vi. with Lipsius de Militiâ Romanâ, Joseph. de Bell. Jud. l. iii. c. 5. Vegetius, i. 21–25, iii. 9 and Memoires de Guichard, tom. i. c. 1

62. Cicero in Tusculan. ii. 37. Joseph. de Bell. Jud. l. iii. 5. Frontinus, iv. 1

63. Vegetius, i. 9. Memoires de l'Academie des Inscriptions, tom. xxv. p. 187.

64. Those evolutions are admirably well explained by M. Guichard, Nouveaux Memoires, tom. i. p. 141–234.

65. Tacitus (Annal iv. 5) has given us a state of the legions under Tiberius: and Dion Cassius (l. lv. p. 794) under Alexander Severus. I have endeavoured to fix on the proper medium between these two periods. See likewise Lipsius de Magnitudine Romanâ, l. i. c. 4, 5.

66. The Romans tried to disguise, by the pretence of religious awe, their ignorance and terror. Tacit. Germania, c. 34.

67. Plutarch, in Marc. Anton. And yet, if we may credit Orosius, these monstrous castles were no more than ten feet above the water, vi. 19.

68. Lipsius, de Magnitud. Rom. l. i. c. 5. The sixteen last chapters of Vegetius relate to naval affairs.

69. Voltaire, Siècle de Louis XIV. c. 29. It must, however, be remembered, that France still feels that extraordinary effort.

70. Strabo, l. ii. It is natural enough to suppose, that Arragon is derived from Tarraconensis, and several moderns who have written in Latin, use those words as synonymous. It is however certain, that the Arragon, a little stream which falls from the Pyrenees into the Ebro, first gave its name to a country, and gradually to a kingdom. D'Anville, Geographie du Moyen Age, p. 181.

71. One hundred and fifteen *cities* appear in the Notitia of Gaul; and it is well known that this appellation was applied not only to the capital town, but to the whole territory of each state. But Plutarch and Appian increase the number of tribes to three or four hundred.

72. D'Anville. Notice de l'Ancienne Gaule.

73. Whitaker's History of Manchester, vol. i. c. 3.

74. The Italian Veneti, though often confounded with the Gauls, were more probably of Illyrian origin. M. Freret, Memoires de l'Academie des Inscriptions, tom. xviii.

75. Maffei Verona illustrata, l. 1.

76. The first contrast was observed by the ancients. Florus, i. 11. The second must strike every modern traveller.

77. Pliny (Hist. Natur. l. iii) [6] follows the division of Italy by Augustus.

78. Tournefort, Voyages en Grèce et Asie Mineure, lettre xviii.

79. The name of Illyricum originally belonged to the sea-coast of the Adriatic, and was gradually extended by the Romans from the Alps to the Euxine Sea. Severini Pannonia, i. l. c. 3.

80. A Venetian traveller, the Abbate Fortis, has lately given us some account of those very obscure countries. But the geography and antiquities of the western Illyricum can be expected only from the munificence of the emperor, its sovereign.

81. The Save rises near the confines of *Istria*, and was considered by the more early Greeks as the principal stream of the Danube.

82. Periplus of Arrian. He examined the coasts of the Euxine, when he was governor of Cappadocia.

83. The progress of religion is well known. The use of letters was introduced among the savages of Europe about fifteen hundred years before Christ; and the Europeans carried them to America, about fifteen centuries after the Christian era. But in a period of three thousand years, the Phœnician alphabet received considerable alterations, as it passed through the hands of the Greeks and Romans.

84. Dion Cassius, lib. lxviii. p. 1131 [c. 14].

85. Ptolemy and Strabo, with the modern geographers, fix the Isthmus of Suez as the boundary of Asia and Africa. Dionysius, Mela, Pliny, Sallust, Hirtius, and Solinus, have preferred for that purpose the western branch of the Nile, or even the great Catabathmus, or descent, which last would assign to Asia, not only Egypt, but part of Libya.

86. The long range, moderate height, and gentle declivity of mount Atlas are very unlike a solitary mountain which rears its head into the clouds, and seems to support the heavens. The peak of Teneriffe, on the contrary, rises a league and a half above the surface of the sea, and as it was frequently visited by the Phœnicians, might engage the notice of the Greek poets. Buffon, Histoire Naturelle, tom. i. p. 312. Histoire des Voyages, tom. ii.

87. M. de Voltaire, tom. xiv. p. 297, unsupported by either fact or probability, has generously bestowed the Canary Islands on the Roman empire.

88. Bergier, Hist. des Grands Chemins, l. iii. c. 1, 2, 3, 4, a very useful collection.

89. Templeman's Survey of the Globe: but I distrust both the doctor's learning and his maps.

Chapter II

1. They were erected about midway between Lahor and Delhi. The conquests of Alexander in Hindostan were confined to the Punjab, a country watered by the five great streams of the Indus.

2. M. de Guignes, Histoire des Huns, l. xv. xvi. and xvii.

3. There is not any writer who describes in so lively a manner as Herodotus, the true genius of Polytheism. The best commentary may be found in Mr. Hume's Natural History of Religion; and the best contrast in Bossuet's Universal History. Some obscure traces of an intolerant spirit appear in the conduct of the Egyptians (Juvenal, Sat. xv.); and the Christians as well as Jews, who lived under the Roman empire, formed a very important exception: so important, indeed, that the discussion will require a distinct chapter of this work.

4. The rights, powers, and pretensions of the sovereign of Olympus, are very clearly described in the xvth book of the Iliad: in the Greek original, I mean; for Mr. Pope, without perceiving it, has improved the theology of Homer.

5. Cæsar de Bell. Gall. vi. 17. Within a century or two the Gauls themselves applied to their gods the names of Mercury, Mars, Apollo, etc.

6. The admirable work of Cicero, de Naturâ Deorum, is the best clue we have to guide us through the dark and profound abyss. He represents with candour, and confutes with subtlety, the opinions of the philosophers.

7. I do not pretend to assert that, in this irreligious age, the natural terrors of superstition, dreams, omens, apparitions, etc., had lost their efficacy.

8. Socrates, Epicurus, Cicero, and Plutarch, always inculcated decent reverence for the religion of their own country, and of mankind. The devotion of Epicurus was assiduous and exemplary. Diogen. Laert. x. 10.

9. Polybius, l. vi. c. 53, 54 [cap. 56]. Juvenal, Sat. xiii. laments, that in his time this apprehension had lost much of its effect.

10. See the fate of Syracuse, Tarentum, Ambracia, Corinth, etc., the conduct of Verres, in Cicero (Actio ii. Orat. 4), and the usual practice of governors, in the viiith Satire of Juvenal.

11. Sueton. in Claud.—Plin. Hist. Nat. xxx. i.

12. Pelloutier Histoire des Celtes, tom. vi. p. 230–252.

13. Seneca Consolat. ad Helviam, p. 74. Edit. Lips.

14. Dionysius Halicarn. Antiquitat. Roman. l. ii.

15. In the year of Rome 701, the temple of Isis

and Serapis was demolished by the order of the Senate (Dion Cassius, l. xl. p. 252), and even by the hands of the consul (Valerius Maximus, 1, 3). After the death of Cæsar, it was restored at the public expense (Dion, l. xlvii. p. 501). When Augustus was in Egypt, he revered the majesty of Serapis (Dion, l. ii. p. 647;) but in the Pomærium of Rome, and a mile round it, he prohibited the worship of the Egyptian gods (Dion. l. liii. p. 679, l. liv. p. 735). They remained, however, very fashionable under his reign (Ovid. de Art. Amand. l. i.) and that of his successor, till the justice of Tiberius was provoked to some acts of severity. (Tacit. Annal. ii. 85. Joseph. Antiquit. l. xviii. c. 3.)

16. Tertullian in Apologetic, c. 6, p. 74. Edit. Havercamp. I am inclined to attribute their establishment to the devotion of the Flavian family.

17. See Livy, l. xi. and xxix.

18. Macrob. Saturnalia, l. iii. c. 9. He gives us a form of evocation.

19. Minutius Felix in Octavio, p. 54. Arnobius, l. vi. p. 115.

20. Tacit. Annal. xi. 24. The Orbis Romanus of the learned Spanheim is a complete history of the progressive admission of Latium, Italy, and the provinces, to the freedom of Rome.

21. Herodotus, v. 97. It should seem, however, that he followed a large and popular estimation.

22. Athenæus Deipnosophist, l. vi. p. 272. Edit. Casaubon. Meursius de Fortunâ Atticâ, c. 4.

23. See a very accurate collection of the numbers of each Lustrum in M. de Beaufort, Republique Romaine, l. iv. c. 4.

24. Appian. de Bell. civil. l. i. Velleius Paterculus, l. ii. c. 15, 16, 17.

25. Mæcenas had advised him to declare by one edict, all his subjects, citizens. But we may justly suspect that the historian Dion was the author of a counsel, so much adapted to the practice of his own age, and so little to that of Augustus.

26. The senators were obliged to have one-third of their own landed property in Italy. Plin. l. vi. ep. 19. The qualification was reduced by Marcus to one-fourth. Since the reign of Trajan, Italy had sunk nearer to the level of the provinces.

27. The first part of the Verona Illustrata of the Marquis Maffei, gives the clearest and most comprehensive view of the state of Italy under the Cæsars.

28. Pausanias, l. vii. [c]. The Romans condescended to restore the names of those assemblies, when they could no longer be dangerous.

29. They are frequently mentioned by Cæsar. The Abbé Dubos attempts, with very little success,

to prove that the assemblies of Gaul were continued under the emperors. Histoire de l'Etablissement de la Monarchie Francoise, l. i. c. 4.

30. Seneca in Consolat. ad Helviam, c. 6.

31. Memnon apud Photium, c. 33 [p. 231 edit. Bekker]. Valer. Maxim. ix. 2. Plutarch [Sulla cap. 24] and Dion Cassius swell the massacre to 150,000 citizens; but I should esteem the smaller number to be more than sufficient.

32. Twenty-five colonies were settled in Spain (Plin. Hist. Natur. iii. 3, 4, iv. 35): and nine in Britain, of which London, Colchester, Lincoln, Chester, Gloucester, and Bath, still remain considerable cities (Richard of Cirencester, p. 36, and Whitaker's History of Manchester, l. i. c. 3).

33. Aul. Gell. Noctes Atticæ, xvi. 13. The emperor Hadrian expressed his surprise, that the cities of Utica, Gades, and Itatica, which already enjoyed the rights of *Municipia*, should solicit the title of *colonies*. Their example, however, became fashionable, and the empire was filled with honorary colonies. Spanheim, de Usu Numismatum, Dissertat. xiii.

34. Spanheim, Orbis Roman, c. 8. p. 62.

35. Aristid. in Romæ Encomio, tom. i. p. 218. Edit. Jebb.

36. Tacit. Annal. xi. 23, 24. Hist. iv. 74.

37. Plin. Hist. Natur. iii. 5. Augustine, The City of God, xix. 7. Lipsius de pronunciatione Linguæ Latinæ, c. 3.

38. Apuleius and Augustin will answer for Africa; Strabo for Spain and Gaul; Tacitus, in the Life of Agricola, for Britain; and Velleius Paterculus for Pannonia. To them we may add the language of the Inscriptions.

39. The Celtic was preserved in the mountains of Wales, Cornwall, and Armorica. We may observe that Apuleius reproaches an African youth, who lived among the populace, with the use of the Punic; whilst he had almost forgot Greek, and neither could nor would speak Latin (Apolog. p. 596). The greater part of St. Austin's congregations were strangers to the Punic.

40. Spain alone produced Columella, the Senecas, Lucan, Martial, and Quintilian.

41. There is not, I believe, from Dionysius to Libanus, a single Greek critic who mentions Virgil or Horace. They seem ignorant that the Romans had any good writers.

42. The curious reader may see in Dupin (Bibliotheque Ecclesiastique, tom. xix. p. 1, c. 8), how much the use of the Syriac and Egyptian languages was still preserved.

43. Juvenal, Sat. iii. and xv. Ammian. Marcellin. xxii. 16.

44. Dion Cassius, l. lxxvii. [5] p. 1275. The first instance happened under the reign of Septimius Severus.

45. Valerius Maximus, l. ii. c. 2, n. 2. The emperor Claudius disfranchised an eminent Grecian for not understanding Latin. He was probably in some public office. Suetonius in Claud. c. 16.

46. In the camp of Lucullus, an ox sold for a drachma, and a slave for four drachmæ, or about three shillings. Plutarch. in Lucullus.

47. Diodorus Siculus in Eclog. Hist. l. xxxiv. and xxxvi. Florus, iii. 19, 20.

48. See a remarkable instance of severity in Cicero in Verrem, v. 3.

49. See in Gruter, and the other collectors, a great number of inscriptions addressed by slaves to their wives, children, fellow-servants, masters, etc. They are all most probably of the Imperial age.

50. Augustan History [Spartian Hadr. 18] and Dissertation of M. de Burigny, in the xxxvth volume of the Academy of Inscriptions, upon the Roman slaves.

51. Dissertation of M. de Burigny in the xxxviith volume, on the Roman freedmen.

52. Spanheim, Orbis Roman, l. i. c. 16, p. 124, etc.

53. Seneca de Clementiâ, l. i. c. 24. The original is much stronger, "Quantum periculum immineret si servi nostri numerare nos cœpissent."

54. Pliny (Hist. Natur. l. xxxiii.) and Athenæus (Deipnosophist. l. vi. p. 272). The latter boldly asserts, that he knew very many (παμπολλοι) Romans who possessed, not for use, but ostentation, ten and even twenty thousand slaves.

55. In Paris there are not more than 43,700 domestics of every sort, and not a twelfth part of the inhabitants. Messange Recherches sur la Population, p. 186.

56. A learned slave sold for many hundred pounds sterling: Atticus always bred and taught them himself. Cornel. Nepos in Vit. c. 13.

57. Many of the Roman physicians were slaves. Middleton's Dissertation and Defence.

58. Their ranks and offices are very copiously enumerated by Pignorius de Servis.

59. Tacit. Annal. xiv. 43. They were all executed for not preventing their master's murder.

60. Apuleius in Apolog. p. 548, edit. Delphin.

61. Plin. Hist. Natur. l. xxxiii. 47.

62. Compute twenty millions in France, twenty-two in Germany, four in Hungary, ten in Italy with its islands, eight in Great Britain and Ireland, eight in Spain and Portugal, ten or twelve in the European Russia, six in Poland, six in Greece and Turkey, four in Sweden, three in Denmark and Norway, four in the Low Countries. The whole would amount to one hundred and five or one hundred and seven millions. Voltaire, de Histoire Generale.

63. Joseph. de Bell. Judaico. l. ii. c. 16. The oration of Agrippa, or rather of the historian, is a fine picture of the Roman empire.

64. Sueton. in August. c. 28. Augustus built in Rome the temple and forum of Mars the Avenger; the temple of Jupiter Tonans in the Capitol; that of Apollo Palatine, with public libraries; the portico and basilica of Caius and Lucius, the porticos of Livia and Octavia, and the theatre of Marcel-

lus. The example of the sovereign was imitated by his ministers and generals; and his friend Agrippa left behind him the immortal monument of the Pantheon.

65. Maffei, Verona illustrata, l. iv. p. 68.

66. Xth book of Pliny's Epistles. He mentions the following works, carried on at the expense of the cities. At Nicomedia, a new forum, an aqueduct, and a canal, left unfinished by a king; at Nice, a gymnasium, and a theatre which had already cost near ninety thousand pounds; baths at Prusa and Claudiopolis; and an aqueduct of sixteen miles in length for the use of Sinope.

67. Hadrian afterwards made a very equitable regulation, which divided all treasure-trove between the right of property and that of discovery. Hist. August. p. 9 [Spartian Hadr. c. 18].

68. Philostrat. in Vit. Sophist. l. ii. p. 548.

69. Aulus Gellius, in Noct. Attic. i. 2, ix. 2, xviii. 10, xix. 12, Philostrat. p. 564.

70. Philostrat. l. ii. p. 548, 560. Pausanias, l. i. and vii. 10. The Life of Herodes, in the xxxth volume of the Memoirs of the Academy of Inscriptions.

71. It is particularly remarked of Athens by Dicæarchus, de Statu Græciæ, p. 8, inter Geographos Minores, edit. Hudson.

72. Donatus de Roma Vetere, l. iii. c. 4, 5, 6. Nardini Roma Antica, l. iii. 11, 12, 13, and a MS. description of ancient Rome, by Bernardus Oricellarius, or Rucellai, of which I obtained a copy from the library of the Canon Ricardi at Florence. Two celebrated pictures of Timanthes and of Protogenes are mentioned by Pliny, as in the Temple of Peace: and the Laocoon was found in the baths of Titus.

73. Montfaucon l'Antiquité Expliquée, tom. iv. p. 2, l. i. c. 9. Fabretti has composed a very learned treatise on the aqueducts of Rome.

74. Ælian. Hist. Var. l. ix. c. 16. He lived in the time of Alexander Severus. See Fabricius, Biblioth. Græca, l. iv. c. 21.

75. Joseph. de Bell. Jud. ii. 16. The number, however, is mentioned, and should be received with a degree of latitude.

76. Plin. Hist. Natur. iii. 5.

77. Plin. Hist. Natur. iii. 3, 4, iv. 35. The list seems authentic and accurate: the division of the provinces, and the different condition of the cities, are minutely distinguished.

78. Strabon. Geograph. l. xvii. p. 1189.

79. Joseph. de Bell. Jud. ii. 16. Philostrat. in Vit. Sophist. l. ii. p. 548, edit. Olear.

80. Tacit. Annal. iv. 55. I have taken some pains in consulting and comparing modern travellers, with regard to the fate of those eleven cities of Asia: seven or eight are totally destroyed, Hypæpe, Tralles, Laodicea, Ilium, Halicarnassus, Miletus, Ephesus, and we may add Sardis. Of the remaining three, Pergamus is a straggling village of two or three thousand inhabitants; Magnesia, under the name of Guzel-hissar, a town of some con-

sequence, and Smyrna, a great city, peopled by an hundred thousand souls. But even at Smyrna, while the Franks have maintained commerce, the Turks have ruined the arts.

81. See a very exact and pleasing description of the ruins of Laodicea, in Chandler's Travels through Asia Minor, p. 225, etc.

82. Strabo, l. xii. p. 866. He had studied at Tralles.

83. Dissertation of M. de Boze, Mem. de l'Academie, tom. xviii. Aristides pronounced an oration which is still extant, to recommend concord to the rival cities.

84. The inhabitants of Egypt, exclusive of Alexandria, amounted to seven millions and a half (Joseph. de Bell. Jud. ii. 16). Under the military government of the Mamalukes, Syria was supposed to contain sixty thousand villages (Histoire de Timur Bec, l. v. c. 20).

85. The following Itinerary may serve to convey some idea of the direction of the road, and of the distance between the principal towns. I. From the wall of Antoninus to York, 222 Roman miles. II. London 227. III. Rhutupiæ or Sandwich 67. IV. The navigation to Boulogne 45. V. Rheims 174. VI. Lyons 330. VII. Milan 324. VIII. Rome 426. IX. Brundusium 360. X. The navigation to Dyrrachium 40. XI. Byzantium 711. XII. Ancyra 283. XIII. Tarsus 301. XIV. Antioch 141. XV. Tyre 252. XVI. Jerusalem 168. In all 4080 Roman, or 3740 English miles. See the Itineraries published by Wesseling, his annotations; Gale and Stukeley for Britain, and M. d'Anville for Gaul and Italy.

86. Montfaucon, l'Antiquité Expliquée (tom. iv. p. 2, l. i. c. 5), has described the bridges of Narni, Alcantara, Nismes, etc.

87. Bergier Histoire des grands Chemins de l'Empire Romain, l. ii. c. 1–28.

88. Procopius in Hist. Arcanâ, c. 30. Bergier Hist. des grands Chemins, l. iv. Codex Theodosian. l. viii. tit. v. vol. ii. p. 506–563, with Godefroy's learned commentary.

89. In the time of Theodosius, Cæsarius, a magistrate of high rank, went post from Antioch to Constantinople. He began his journey at night, was in Cappadocia (165 miles from Antioch) the ensuing evening, and arrived at Constantinople the sixth day about noon. The whole distance was 725 Roman, or 665 English miles. See Libanius Orat. xxii. and the Itineraria, p. 572–581.

90. Pliny, though a favourite and a minister, made an apology for granting post-horses to his wife on the most urgent business. Epist. x. 121, 122.

91. Bergier Hist. des grands Chemins, l. iv. c. 49.

92. Plin. Hist. Natur. xix. 1.

93. It is not improbable that the Greeks and Phœnicians introduced some new arts and productions into the neighborhood of Marseilles and Gades.

94. Homer, Odyss. l. ix. v. 358.

95. Plin. Hist. Natur. l. xiv.

96. Strab. Geograph. l. iv. p. 223. The intense cold of a Gallic winter was almost proverbial among the ancients.

97. In the beginning of the fourth century, the orator Eumenius (Panegyric. Veter. viii. 6, edit. Delphin.) speaks of the vines in the territory of Autun, which were decayed through age, and the first plantation of which was totally unknown. The Pagus Arebrignus is supposed by M. d'Anville to be the district of Beaune, celebrated, even at present, for one of the first growths of Burgundy.

98. Plin. Hist. Natur. l. xv.

99. Plin. Hist. Natur. l. xix.

100. Harte's Essays on Agriculture, in which he has collected all that the ancients and moderns have said of Lucerne.

101. Tacit. Germania, c. 45. Plin. Hist. Nat. xxxviii. 11.The latter observed, with some humour, that even fashion had not yet found out the use of amber. Nero sent a Roman knight to purchase great quantities on the spot where it was produced, the coast of modern Prussia.

102. Called Taprobana by the Romans, and Serendib by the Arabs. It was discovered under the reign of Claudius, and gradually became the principal mart of the East.

103. Plin. Hist. Natur. l. vi. Strabo, l. xvii.

104. Hist. August. p. 224. A silk garment was considered as an ornament to a woman, but as a disgrace to a man.

105. The two great pearl fisheries were the same as at present, Ormuz and Cape Comorin. As well as we can compare ancient with modern geography, Rome was supplied with diamonds from the mine of Jumelpur, in Bengal, which is described in the Voyages de Tavernier, tom. ii. p. 281.

106. Tacit. Annal. iii. 52 (in a speech of Tiberius).

107. Plin. Hist. Natur. xii. 18. In another place he computes half that sum; Quingenties H. S. for India exclusive of Arabia.

108. The proportion which was 1 to 10, and 12½, rose to 14 2-5ths, the legal regulation of Constantine. See Arbuthnot's Tables of ancient Coins, c. v.

109. Among many other passages, see Pliny (Hist. Natur. iii. 5), Aristides (de Urbe Româ), and Tertullian (de Animâ, c. 30).

110. Herodes Atticus gave the sophist Polemo above eight thousand pounds for three declamations. Philostrat. l. i. p. 558 [vita Herodes, cap. 7]. The Antonines founded a school at Athens, in which professors of grammar, rhetoric, politics, and the four great sects of philosophy, were maintained at the public expense for the instruction of youth. The salary of a philosopher was ten thousand drachmæ, between three and four hundred pounds a year. Similar establishments were formed in the other great cities of the empire. Lucian in Eunuch. tom. ii. p. 353 edit. Reitz. Philostrat. l. ii. p. 566. Hist. August. p. 21. Dion Cassius, l. lxxi. p. 1195. Juvenal himself, in a morose satire, which in every line betrays his own disappointment and envy, is obliged, however, to say—

——O Juvenes, circumspicit et agitat vos.
Materiamque sibi Ducis indulgentia quærit.
                                              —Satir. vii. 20.

111. Longin, de Sublim. c. 43, p. 229, edit. Toll. Here too we may say of Longinus, "his own example strengthens all his laws." Instead of proposing his sentiments with a manly boldness, he insinuates them with the most guarded caution, puts them into the mouth of a friend; and, as far as we can collect from a corrupted text, makes a show of refuting them himself.

.   .   .

Chapter III

1. Orosius, vi. 18.

2. Julius Cæsar introduced soldiers, strangers, and half-barbarians, into the senate (Sueton. in Cæsar, c. 77, 80). The abuse became still more scandalous after his death.

3. Dion Cassius, l. iii. [c. 42], p. 693. Suetonius in August. c. 55.

4. Dion (l. iii. p. 698) gives us a prolix and bombast speech on this great occasion. I have borrowed from Suetonius and Tacitus the general language of Augustus.

5. *Imperator* (from which we have derived Emperor) signified under the republic no more than *general*, and was emphatically bestowed by the soldiers, when on the field of battle they proclaimed their victorious leader worthy of that title. When the Roman *emperors* assumed it in that sense, they

placed it after their name, and marked how often they had taken it.

6. Dion. l. liii. p. 703, etc.

7. Livy Epitom. l. xiv. Valer. Maxim. vi. 3.

8. See in the viiith book of Livy, the conduct of Manlius Torquatus and Papirius Cursor. They violated the laws of nature and humanity, but they asserted those of military discipline; and the people, who abhorred the action, was obliged to respect the principle.

9. By the lavish but unconstrained suffrages of the people, Pompey had obtained a military command scarcely inferior to that of Augustus. Among the extraordinary acts of power executed by the former, we may remark the foundation of twentynine cities, and the distribution of three or four millions sterling to his troops. The ratification

of his acts met with some opposition and delays in the senate. See Plutarch, Appian, Dion Cassius, and the first book of the epistles to Atticus.

10. Under the commonwealth, a triumph could only be claimed by the general, who was authorised to take the Auspices in the name of the people. By an exact consequence drawn from this principle of policy and religion, the triumph was reserved to the emperor; and his most successful lieutenants were satisfied with some marks of distinction, which, under the name of triumphal honours, were invented in their favour.

11. Cicero (de Legibus, iii. 3) gives the consular office the name of *Regia potestas;* and Polybius (l. vi. c. 3) observes three powers in the Roman constitution. The monarchical was represented and exercised by the consuls.

12. As the tribunitian power (distinct from the annual office) was first invented for the Dictator Cæsar (Dion, l. xliv. p. 384), we may easily conceive that it was given as a reward for having so nobly asserted, by arms, the sacred rights of the tribunes and people. Commentaries, De Bell. Civil. l. i.

13. Augustus exercised nine annual consulships without interruption. He then most artfully refused that magistracy, as well as the dictatorship, absented himself from Rome and waited till the fatal effects of tumult and faction forced the senate to invest him with a perpetual consulship. Augustus, as well as his successors, affected, however, to conceal so invidious a title.

14. See a fragment of a Decree of the Senate, conferring on the emperor Vespasian all the powers granted to his predecessors, Augustus, Tiberius, and Claudius. This curious and important monument is published in Gruter's Inscriptions, No. ccxlii.

15. Two consuls were created on the Calends of January; but in the course of the year others were substituted in their places, till the annual number seems to have amounted to no less than twelve. The prætors were usually sixteen or eighteen (Lipsius in Excurs. D. ad Tacit. Annal. l. i.). I have not mentioned the Ædiles or Quæstors. Officers of the police or revenue easily adapt themselves to any form of government. In the time of Nero, the tribunes legally possessed the right of *intercession*, though it might be dangerous to exercise it (Tacit. Annal. xvi. 26). In the time of Trajan, it was doubtful whether the tribuneship was an office or a name (Plin. Epist. i. 23).

16. The tyrants themselves were ambitious of the consulship. The virtuous princes were moderate in the pursuit, and exact in the discharge of it. Trajan revived the ancient oath, and swore before the consul's tribunal that he would observe the laws (Plin. Panegyric. c. 64).

17. Quoties Magistratuum Comitiis interesset. Tribus cum candidatis suis circuibat: supplicabatque more solemni. Ferebat et ipse suffragium in tribubus, ut unus e populo. Suetonius in August.

c. 56.

18. Tum primum Comitia e campo ad patres translata sunt. Tacit. Annal. i. 15. The word *primum* seems to allude to some faint and unsuccessful efforts, which were made towards restoring them to the people.

19. Dion Cassius (l. liii. p. 703-714) has given a very loose and partial sketch of the Imperial system. To illustrate and often to correct him, I have meditated Tacitus, examined Suetonius, and consulted the following moderns: the Abbé de la Bleterie, in the Memoires de l'Academie des Inscriptions, tom. xix. xxi. xxiv. xxv. xxvii. Beaufort, Republique Romaine, tom. i. p. 255-275. The Dissertations of Noodt and Gronovius, *de lege Regia;* printed at Leyden, in the year 1731. Gravina de Imperio Romano, p. 479-544 of his Opuscula. Maffei Verona Illustrata, t. i. p. 245, etc.

20. A weak prince will always be governed by his domestics. The power of slaves aggravated the shame of the Romans; and the senate paid court to a Pallas or a Narcissus. There is a chance that a modern favourite may be a gentleman.

21. Treatise of Vandale de Consecratione Principum. It would be easier for me to copy than it has been to verify the quotations of that learned Dutchman.

22. Dissertation of the Abbé Mongault in the first volume of the Academy of Inscriptions.

23. Jurandasque tuum per nomen ponimus *aras,* says Horace to the emperor himself, and Horace was well acquainted with the court of Augustus.

24. See Cicero in Philippic. i. 6. Julian in Cæsaribus. Inque Deûm templis jurabit Roma per umbras, is the indignant expression of Lucan, but it is a patriotic, rather than a devout indignation.

25. Dion Cassius, l. liii. p. 710, with the curious Annotations of Reimar.

26. As Octavianus advanced to the banquet of the Cæsars, his colour changed like that of the Camelion; pale at first, then red, afterwards black, he at last assumed the mild livery of Venus and the graces (Cæsars, p. 309). This image employed by Julian, in his ingenious fiction, is just and elegant; but when he considers this change of character as real, and ascribes it to the power of philosophy, he does too much honour to philosophy, and to Octavianus.

27. Two centuries after the establishment of monarchy, the emperor Marcus Antoninus recommends the character of Brutus as a perfect model of Roman virtue.

28. It is much to be regretted that we have lost the part of Tacitus which treated of that transaction. We are forced to content ourselves with the popular rumours of Josephus, and the imperfect hints of Dion and Suetonius.

29. Augustus restored the ancient severity of discipline. After the civil wars, he dropped the endearing name of Fellow-Soldiers, and called them only Soldiers (Sueton. in August. c. 25). See the

use Tiberius made of the senate in the mutiny of the Pannonian legions (Tacit. Annals, i. [25]).

30. These words seem to have been the constitutional language. See Tacit. Annal. xiii. 4.

31. The first was Camillus Scribonianus, who took up arms in Dalmatia against Claudius, and was deserted by his own troops in five days. The second, L. Antonius, in Germany, who rebelled against Domitian; and the third, Avidius Cassius, in the reign of M. Antoninus. The two last reigned but a few months, and were cut off by their own adherents. We may observe, that both Camillus and Cassius coloured their ambition with the design of restoring the republic: a task, said Cassius, peculiarly reserved for his name and family.

32. Velleius Paterculus, l. ii. c. 121. Sueton. in Tiber. c. 20.

33. Sueton. in Tit. c. 6. Plin. in Præfat. Hist. Natur.

34. This idea is frequently and strongly inculcated by Tacitus. Hist. i. 5, 16; ii. 76.

35. The emperor Vespasian, with his usual good sense, laughed at the genealogists, who deduced his family from Flavius, the founder of Reate (his native country), and one of the companions of Hercules. Suet. in Vespasian. c. 12.

36. Dion. l. lxviii. p. 1121. Plin. Secund. in Panegyric.

37. Felicior Augusto, MELIOR TRAJANO. Eutrop. viii. 5.

38. Dion (l. lxix. p. 1249) affirms the whole to have been a fiction, on the authority of his father, who being governor of the province where Trajan died, had very good opportunities of sifting this mysterious transaction. Yet Dodwell (Prælect. Camden. xvii.) has maintained that Hadrian was called to the certain hope of the empire during the lifetime of Trajan.

39. Dion (lxx. p. 1171). Aurel. Victor.

40. The deification of Antinous, his medals, statues, temples, city, oracles, and constellation, are well known, and still dishonour the memory of Hadrian. Yet we may remark, that of the first fifteen emperors, Claudius was the only one whose taste in love was entirely correct. For the honours of Antinous, see Spanheim, Commentaire sur les Cæsars de Julien, p. 80.

41. Hist. August. p. 13. Aurelius Victor in Epitom.

42. Without the help of medals and inscriptions we should be ignorant of this fact, so honourable to the memory of Pius.

43. During the twenty-three years of Pius's reign, Marcus was only two nights absent from the palace, and even those were at different times. Hist. August. p. 25.

44. He was fond of the theatre, and not insensible to the charms of the fair sex. Marcus Antoninus, i. 16. Hist. August. p. 20, 21. Julian in Cæsar.

45. The enemies of Marcus charged him with hypocrisy, and with a want of that simplicity which distinguished Pius and even Verus (Hist. August. 6, 34). This suspicion, unjust as it was, may serve to account for the superior applause bestowed upon personal qualifications, in preference to the social virtues. Even Marcus Antoninus has been called a hypocrite; but the wildest scepticism never insinuated that Cæsar might possibly be a coward, or Tully a fool. Wit and valour are qualifications more easily ascertained, than humanity or the love of justice.

46. Tacitus has characterised, in a few words, the principles of the portico: Doctores sapientiæ secutus est, qui sola bona quæ honesta, mala tantum quæ turpia; potentiam, nobilitatem, cæteraque extra animum, neque bonis neque malis adnumerant. Tacit. Hist. iv. 5.

47. Before he went on the second expedition against the Germans, he read lectures of philosophy to the Roman people, during three days. He had already done the same in the cities of Greece and Asia. Hist. August. in Cassio, c. 3.

48. Dion, l. lxxi. [c. 23] p. 1190. Hist. August. in Avid. Cassio [c. 8].

49. Hist. August. in Marc. Antonin. c. 18.

50. Vitellius consumed in mere eating, at least six millions of our money in about seven months. It is not easy to express his vices with dignity, or even decency. Tacitus fairly calls him a hog; but it is by substituting to a coarse word a very fine image. "At Vitellius, umbraculis hortorum abditus, ut *ignava animalia*, quibus si cibum suggeras jacent torpentque, præterita, instantia, futura, pari oblivione dimiserat. Atque illum nemore Arcino desidem et marcentem, etc." Tacit. Hist. iii. 36, ii. 95. Sueton. in Vitell. c. 13. Dion Cassius, l. lxv. p. 1062.

51. The execution of Helvidius Priscus, and of the virtuous Eponina, disgraced the reign of Vespasian.

52. Voyage de Chardin en Perse, vol. iii. p. 293.

53. The practice of raising slaves to the great offices of state is still more common among the Turks than among the Persians. The miserable countries of Georgia and Circassia supply rulers to the greatest part of the East.

54. Chardin says, that European travellers have diffused among the Persians some ideas of the freedom and mildness of our governments. They have done them a very ill office.

55. They alleged the example of Scipio and Cato (Tacit. Annal. iii. 66). Marcellus Epirus and Crispus Vibius had acquired two millions and a half under Nero. Their wealth, which aggravated their crimes, protected them under Vespasian. Tacit. Hist. iv. 43. Dialog. de Orator. c. 8. For one accusation, Regulus, the just object of Pliny's satire, received from the senate the consular ornaments, and a present of sixty thousand pounds.

56. The crime of *majesty* was formerly a treasonable offence against the Roman people. As tribunes of the people, Augustus and Tiberius applied it to their own persons, and extended it to an

infinite latitude.

57. After the virtuous and unfortunate widow of Germanicus had been put to death, Tiberius received the thanks of the senate for his clemency. She had not been publicly strangled; nor was the body drawn with a hook to the Gemoniæ, where those of common malefactors were exposed. Tacit. Annal. vi. 25. Sueton. in Tiberio, c. 53.

58. Seriphus was a small rocky island in the Ægean Sea, the inhabitants of which were despised for their ignorance and obscurity. The place

of Ovid's exile is well known, by his just, but unmanly lamentations. It should seem, that he only received an order to leave Rome in so many days, and to transport himself to Tomi. Guards and gaolers were unnecessary.

59. Under Tiberius, a Roman knight attempted to fly to the Parthians. He was stopt in the Straits of Sicily; but so little danger did there appear in the example, that the most jealous of tyrants disdained to punish it. Tacit. Annal. vi. 14.

60. Cicero ad Familiares, iv. 7.

Chapter IV

1. See the complaints of Avidius Cassius, Hist. August. p. 45. These are, it is true, the complaints of faction; but even faction exaggerates, rather than invents.

2. Hist. August. p. 34.

3. Dion Cassius, l. lxxi. p. 1195. Hist. August. p. 33. Commentaire de Spanheim sur les Cesars de Julien, p. 289. The deification of Faustina is the only defect which Julian's criticism is able to discover in the all-accomplished character of Marcus.

4. Commodus was the first *Porphyrogenetus* (born since his father's accession to the throne). By a new strain of flattery, the Egyptian medals date by the years of his life; as if they were synonymous to those of his reign. Tillemont, Hist. des Empereurs, tom. ii. p. 752.

5. Hist. August. p. 46.

6. Dion Cassius, l. lxxii. p. 1203.

7. According to Tertullian (Apolog. c. 25), he died at Sirmium. But the situation of Vindobona, or Vienna, where both the Victors place his death, is better adapted to the operations of the war against the Marcomanni and Quadi.

8. Herodian, l. i. p. 12.

9. Herodian, l. i. p. 16.

10. This universal joy is well described (from the medals as well as historians) by Mr. Wotton, Hist. of Rome, p. 192, 193.

11. Manilius, the confidential secretary of Avidius Cassius, was discovered after he had lain concealed several years. The emperor nobly relieved the public anxiety by refusing to see him and burning his papers without opening them. Dion Cassius, l. lxxii. p. 1200.

12. Maffei degli Amphitheatri, p. 126.

13. Dion, l. lxxii. p. 1205. Herodian, l. i. p. 16. Hist. August. p. 46.

14. In a note upon the Augustan History, p. 96, Casaubon has collected a number of particulars concerning these celebrated brothers.

15. Dion, l. xxii. p. 1210. Herodian, l. i. p. 22. Hist. August. p. 48. Dion gives a much less odious character of Perennis than the other historians. His moderation is almost a pledge of his veracity.

16. During the second Punic war, the Romans imported from Asia the worship of the mother of the gods. Her festival, the *Megalesia*, began on the

fourth of April, and lasted six days. The streets were crowded with mad processions, the theatres with spectators, and the public tables with unbidden guests. Order and police were suspended, and pleasure was the only serious business of the city. See Ovid. de Fastis, l. iv. 189, etc.

17. Herodian, l. i. p. 23, 28.

18. Cicero pro Flacco, c. 27.

19. One of these dear-bought promotions occasioned a current bon mot, that Julius Solon was *banished* into the senate.

20. Dion (l. lxxii. p. 12, 13) observes, that no freedman had possessed riches equal to those of Cleander. The fortune of Pallas amounted, however, to upwards of five and twenty hundred thousand pounds; *Ter millies*.

21. Dion, l. lxxii. p. 12, 13. Herodian, l. i. p. 29. Hist. August. p. 52. These baths were situated near the *Porta Capena*. Nardini Roma Antica, p. 79.

22. Hist. August. p. 48.

23. Herodian, l. i. p. 28. Dion, l. lxxii. p. 1215. The latter says, that two thousand persons died every day at Rome, during a considerable length of time.

24. Tuncque primum tres præfecti prætorio fuere: inter quos libertinus. From some remains of modesty, Cleander declined the title, whilst he assumed the powers, of Prætorian præfect. As the other freedmen were styled, from their several departments, a rationibus, ab epistolis; Cleander called himself a pugione, as intrusted with the defence of his master's person. Salmasius and Casaubon seem to have talked very idly upon this passage.

25. Ὁι τῆς πόλεως πέζοι στρατιῶται. Herodian, l. i. p. 31. It is doubtful whether he means the Prætorian infantry, or the cohortes urbanæ, a body of six thousand men, but whose rank and discipline were not equal to their numbers. Neither Tillemont nor Wotton choose to decide this question.

26. Dion Cassius, l. lxxii. p. 1215. Herodian, l. i. p. 32. Hist. August. p. 48.

27. The African lions, when pressed by hunger, infested the open villages and cultivated country, and they infested them with impunity. The royal

beast was reserved for the pleasures of the emperor and the capital; and the unfortunate peasant, who killed one of them, though in his own defence, incurred a very heavy penalty. This extraordinary *game-law* was mitigated by Honorius, and finally repealed by Justinian. Codex Theodos. tom. v. p. 92, et Comment Gothofred.

28. Spanheim de Numismat. Dissertat. xii. tom. ii. p. 493.

29. Dion, l. lxxii. p. 1216. Hist. August. p. 49.

30. The ostrich's neck is three feet long, and composed of seventeen vertebræ. Buffon, Hist. Naturelle.

31. Commodus killed a camelopardalis or giraffe (Dion, l. lxxii. p. 1211), the tallest, the most gentle, and the most useless of the large quadrupeds. This singular animal, a native only of the interior parts of Africa, has not been seen in Europe since the revival of letters, and though M. de Buffon (Hist. Naturelle, tom. xiii.) has endeavoured to describe, he has not ventured to delineate, the giraffe.

32. Herodian, l. i. p. 37. Hist. August. p. 50.

33. The virtuous and even the wise princes forbade the senators and knights to embrace this scandalous profession, under pain of infamy, or, what was more dreaded by those profligate wretches, of exile. The tyrants allured them to dishonour by threats and rewards. Nero once produced, in the arena, forty senators and sixty knights. Lipsius, Saturnalia, l. ii. c. 2. He has happily corrected a passage of Suetonius, in Nerone, c. 12.

34. Lipsius, l. ii. c. 7, 8. Juvenal, in the eighth satire, gives a picturesque description of this combat.

35. Hist. August. p. 50. Dion, l. lxxii. p. 1220. He received for each time, *decies* about £8000 sterling.

36. Victor tells us, that Commodus only allowed his antagonists a leaden weapon, dreading most probably the consequences of their despair.

37. They were obliged to repeat six hundred and twenty-six times, *Paulus first of the Secutors*, etc.

38. Dion, l. lxxii. p. 1221. He speaks of his own baseness and danger.

39. He mixed, however, some prudence with his courage, and passed the greatest part of his time in a country retirement; alleging his advanced age, and the weakness of his eyes. "I never saw him in the senate," says Dion, "except during the short reign of Pertinax." All his infirmities had suddenly left him, and they returned as suddenly upon the murder of that excellent prince. Dion, l. lxxii. p. 1227.

40. The præfects were changed almost hourly or daily; and the caprice of Commodus was often fatal to his most favourite chamberlains. Hist. August. p. 46, 51.

41. Dion, l. lxxii. p. 1222. Herodian, l. i. p. 43. Hist. August. p. 52.

42. Pertinax was a native of Alba Pompeia, in Piedmont, and son of a timber-merchant. The order

of his employments (it is marked by Capitolinus) well deserves to be set down, as expressive of the form of government and manners of the age. 1. He was a centurion. 2. Præfect of a cohort in Syria, in the Parthian war, and in Britain. 3. He obtained an *Ala*, or squadron of horse, in Mæsia. 4. He was commissary of provisions on the Æmilian way. 5. He commanded the fleet upon the Rhine. 6. He was procurator of Dacia, with a salary of about £1600 a year. 7. He commanded the Veterans of a legion. 8. He obtained the rank of senator. 9. Of prætor. 10. With the command of the first legion in Rhætia and Noricum. 11. He was consul about the year 175. 12. He attended Marcus into the east. 13. He commanded an army on the Danube. 14. He was consular legate of Mæsia. 15. Of Dacia. 16. Of Syria. 17. Of Britain. 18. He had the care of the public provisions at Rome. 19. He was proconsul of Africa. 20. Præfect of the city. Herodian (l. i. p. 48) does justice to his disinterested spirit; but Capitolinus, who collected every popular rumour, charges him with a great fortune acquired by bribery and corruption.

43. Julian in the Cæsars taxes him with being accessory to the death of Commodus.

44. Capitolinus gives us the particulars of these tumultuary votes, which were moved by one senator, and repeated, or rather chanted, by the whole body. Hist. August. p. 52.

45. The senate condemned Nero to be put to death *more majorum*. Sueton. c. 49.

46. Dion (l. lxxiii. p. 1223) speaks of these entertainments, as a senator who had supped with the emperor; Capitolinus (Hist. August. p. 58), like a slave, who had received his intelligence from one of the scullions.

47. *Decies.* The blameless economy of Pius left his successors a treasure of *vicies septies millies*, above two and twenty millions sterling. Dion, l. lxxiii. p. 1231.

48. Besides the design of converting these useless ornaments into money, Dion (l. lxxiii. p. 1229) assigns two secret motives of Pertinax. He wished to expose the vices of Commodus and to discover by the purchasers those who most resembled him.

49. Though Capitolinus has picked up many idle tales of the private life of Pertinax, he joins with Dion and Herodian in admiring his public conduct.

50. Leges, rem surdam, inexorabilem esse. T. Liv. ii. 3.

51. If we credit Capitolinus (which is rather difficult), Falco behaved with the most petulant indecency to Pertinax, on the day of his accession. The wise emperor only admonished him of his youth and inexperience. Hist. August. p. 55.

52. The modern bishopric of Liege. This soldier probably belonged to the Batavian horseguards, who were mostly raised in the duchy of Gueldres and the neighbourhood, and were distinguished by their valour, and by the boldness with which they

swam their horses across the broadest and most rapid rivers. Tacit. Hist. iv. 12. Dion, l. lv. p. 797. Lipsius de magnitudine Româ, l. i. c. 4.

53. Dion, l. lxxiii. p. 1232. Herodian, l. ii. p. 60. Hist. August. p. 58. Victor in Epitom. and in Cæsarib. Eutropius, viii. 16.

Chapter V

1. They were originally nine or ten thousand men (for Tacitus and Dion are not agreed upon the subject), divided into as many cohorts. Vitellius increased them to sixteen thousand, and as far as we can learn from inscriptions, they never afterwards sunk much below that number. Lipsius de magnitudine Româ, i. 4.

2. Sueton. in August. c. 49.

3. Tacit. Annal. iv. 2. Sueton. in Tiber. c. 37. Dion Cassius, l. lvii. p. 867.

4. In the civil war between Vitellius and Vespasian, the Prætorian camp was attacked and defended with all the machines used in the siege of the best fortified cities. Tacit. Hist. iii. 84.

5. Close to the walls of the city, on the broad summit of the Quirinal and Viminal hills. Nardini Roma Antica, p. 174. Donatus de Roma Antiqua, p. 46.

6. Claudius, raised by the soldiers to the empire, was the first who gave a donative. He gave quina dena, £120 (Sueton. in Claud. c. 10): when Marcus, with his colleague Lucius Verus, took quiet possession of the throne, he gave vicena, £160 to each of the guards. Hist. August. p. 25. (Dion, l. lxxiii. p. 1231.) We may form some idea of the amount of these sums, by Hadrian's complaint, that the promotion of a Cæsar had cost him ter millies, two millions and a half sterling.

7. Cicero de Legibus, iii. 3. The first book of Livy, and the second of Dionysius of Halicarnassus, show the authority of the people, even in the election of the kings.

8. They were originally recruited in Latium, Etruria, and the old colonies (Tacit. Annal. iv. 5). The emperor Otho compliments their vanity, with the flattering titles of Italiæ Alumni Romana vere juventus. Tacit. Hist. i. 84.

9. In the siege of Rome by the Gauls. See Livy, v. 48. Plutarch, in Camillus.

10. Dion, l. lxxiii. p. 1234. Herodian, l. ii. p. 63. Hist. August. p. 60. Though the three historians agree that it was in fact an auction, Herodian alone affirms that it was proclaimed as such by the soldiers.

11. Spartianus softens the most odius parts of the character and elevation of Julian.

12. Dion Cassius, at that time prætor, had been a personal enemy to Julian, l. lxxiii. p. 1235.

13. Hist. August. p. 61. We learn from thence one curious circumstance, that the new emperor, whatever had been his birth, was immediately aggregated to the number of Patrician families.

14. Dion, l. lxxiii. p. 1235. Hist. August. p. 61. I have endeavoured to blend into one consistent story the seeming contradictions of the two writers.

15. Dion, l. lxxiii. p. 1235.

16. The Postumian and the Cejonian; the former of whom was raised to the consulship in the fifth year after its institution.

17. Spartianus, in his undigested collections, mixes up all the virtues and all the vices that enter into the human composition, and bestows them on the same object. Such, indeed, are many of the characters in the Augustan History.

18. Hist. August. p. 80, 84.

19. Pertinax, who governed Britain a few years before, had been left for dead, in a mutiny of the soldiers. Hist. August. p. 54. Yet they loved and regretted him; admirantibus eam virtutem cui irascebantur.

20. Suetonius in. Galba, c. 10.

21. Hist. August. p. 76.

22. Herod. l. ii. p. 68. The chronicle of John Malala, of Antioch, shows the zealous attachment of his countrymen to these festivals, which at once gratified their superstition and their love of pleasure.

23. A king of Thebes, in Egypt, is mentioned in the Augustan History, as an ally, and, indeed, as a personal friend of Niger. If Spartianus is not, as I strongly suspect, mistaken, he has brought to light a dynasty of tributary princes totally unknown to history.

24. Dion, l. lxxiii. p. 1238. Herod. l. ii. p. 67. A verse in every one's mouth at that time seems to express the general opinion of the three rivals; Optimus est Niger, bonus Afer, pessimus Albus. Hist. August. p. 75.

25. Herodian, l. ii. p. 71.

26. See an account of that memorable war in Velleius Paterculus, ii. 110, etc., who served in the army of Tiberius.

27. Such is the reflection of Herodian, l. ii. p. 74. Will the modern Austrians allow the influence?

28. In the letter to Albinus, already mentioned, Commodus accuses Severus, as one of the ambitious generals who censured his conduct, and wished to occupy his place. Hist. August. p. 80.

29. Pannonia was too poor to supply such a sum. It was probably promised in the camp, and paid at Rome, after the victory. In fixing the sum, I have adopted the conjecture of Casaubon. Hist. August. p. 66. Comment. p. 115.

30. Herodian, l. ii. p. 78. Severus was declared emperor on the banks of the Danube, either at Carnuntum, according to Spartianus (Hist. August. p. 65), or else at Sabaria, according to

Victor. Mr. Hume, in supposing that the birth and dignity of Severus were too much inferior to the Imperial crown, and that he marched in Italy as general only, has not considered this transaction with his usual accuracy (Essay on the original contract).

31. Velleius Paterculus, l. ii. c. 3. We must reckon the march from the nearest verge of Pannonia, and extend the sight of the city as far as two hundred miles.

32. This is not a puerile figure of rhetoric, but an allusion to a real fact recorded by Dion, l. lxxi. p. 1181. It probably happened more than once.

33. Dion, l. lxxiii. p. 1233. Herodian, l. ii. p. 81. There is no surer proof of the military skill of the Romans, than their first surmounting the idle terror, and afterwards disdaining the dangerous use, of elephants in war.

34. Hist. August. p. 62, 63.

35. Victor and Eutropius, viii. 17, mention a combat near the Milvian bridge, the Ponte Molle, unknown to the better and more ancient writers.

36. Dion, l. lxxiii. p. 1240. Herodian, l. ii. p. 83. Hist. August. p. 63.

37. From these sixty-six days, we must first deduct sixteen, as Pertinax was murdered on the 28th of March, and Severus most probably elected on the 13th of April (see Hist. August. p. 65, and Tillemont, Hist. des Empereurs, tom. iii. p. 393, Note 7). We cannot allow less than ten days after his election, to put a numerous army in motion. Forty days remain for this rapid march, and as we may compute about eight hundred miles from Rome to the neighbourhood of Vienna, the army of Severus marched twenty miles every day, without halt or intermission.

38. Dion, l. lxxiv. p. 1241. Herodian, l. ii. p. 84.

39. Dion (l. lxxiv. p. 1244), who assisted at the ceremony as a senator, gives a most pompous description of it.

40. Herodian, l. iii. [c. 7] p. 112.

41. Though it is not, most assuredly, the intention of Lucan, to exalt the character of Cæsar, yet the idea he gives of that hero, in the tenth book of the Pharsalia, where he describes him, at the same time, making love to Cleopatra, sustaining a siege against the power of Egypt, and conversing with the sages of the country, is, in reality, the noblest panegyric.

42. Reckoning from his election, April 13, 193, to the death of Albinus, February 19, 197. Tillemont's Chronology.

43. Herodian, l. ii. [c. 13] p. 85.

44. Whilst Severus was very dangerously ill, it was industriously given out that he intended to appoint Niger and Albinus his successors. As he could not be sincere with respect to both, he might not be so with regard to either. Yet Severus carried his hypocrisy so far as to profess that intention in the memoirs of his own life.

45. Hist. August, p. 65.

46. This practice, invented by Commodus,

proved very useful to Severus. He found, at Rome, the children of many of the principal adherents of his rivals; and he employed them more than once to intimidate, or seduce, the parents.

47. Herodian, l. iii. p. 96. Hist. August. p. 67, 68.

48. Hist. August. p. 84. Spartianus has inserted this curious letter at full length.

49. Consult the third book of Herodian, and the seventy-fourth book of Dion Cassius.

50. Dion, l. lxxv. p. 1260.

51. Dion, l. lxxv. [c. 6] p. 1261. Herodian, l. iii. p. 110. Hist. August. p. 68. The battle was fought in the plain of Trevoux, three or four leagues from Lyons. Tillemont, tom. iii. p. 406, Note 18.

52. Montesquieu, Considerations sur la Grandeur et la Decadence des Romains, c. xii.

53. Most of these, as may be supposed, were small open vessels; some, however, were galleys of two, and a few of three ranks of oars.

54. The engineer's name was Priscus. His skill saved his life, and he was taken into the service of the conqueror. For the particular facts of the siege consult Dion Cassius (l. lxxv. [c. 10] p. 1251), and Herodian (l. iii. [c. 6] p. 95): for the theory of it, the fanciful chevalier de Folard may be looked into. Polybe, tom. i. p. 76.

55. Notwithstanding the authority of Spartianus and some modern Greeks, we may be assured from Dion and Herodian, that Byzantium, many years after the death of Severus, lay in ruins.

56. Dion, l. lxxiv. p. 1250.

57. Dion (l. lxxv. p. 1264); only 29 senators are mentioned by him, but 41 are named in the Augustan History, p. 69, among whom were six of the name of Pescennius. Herodian (l. iii. p. 115) speaks in general of the cruelties of Severus.

58. Aurelius Victor.

59. Dion, l. lxxvi. p. 1272. Hist. August. p. 67 [Spartian. Severus, c. 8]. Severus celebrated the secular games with extraordinary magnificence, and he left in the public granaries a provision of corn for seven years, at the rate of 75,000 modii, or about 2500 quarters per day. I am persuaded, that the granaries of Severus were supplied for a long term; but I am not less persuaded, that policy on one hand, and admiration on the other, magnified the hoard far beyond its true contents. [Hist. Aug. p. 73. Spar. Sev. c. 23.]

60. See Spanheim's treatise of ancient medals, the inscriptions, and our learned travellers, Spon and Wheeler, Shaw, Pocock, etc., who, in Africa, Greece, and Asia, have found more monuments of Severus than of any other Roman emperor whatsoever.

61. He carried his victorious arms to Seleucia and Ctesiphon, the capitals of the Parthian monarchy. I shall have occasion to mention this war in its proper place.

62. Etiam in Britannis was his own just and emphatic expression. Hist. August. 72 [Spart. Sev. c. 23].

63. Herodian, l. iii. p. 115. Hist. August. p. 68.

64. Upon the insolence and privileges of the soldiers, the 16th Satire, falsely ascribed to Juvenal, may be consulted; the style and circumstances of it would induce me to believe that it was composed under the reign of Severus, or that of his son.

65. Hist. August. p. 75.

66. Herodian, l. iii. p. 131.

67. Dion, l. lxxiv. p. 1243.

68. One of his most daring and wanton acts of power, was the castration of an hundred free Romans, some of them married men, and even fathers of families; merely that his daughter, on her marriage with the young emperor, might be attended by a train of eunuchs worthy of an eastern queen. Dion, lxxvi. p. 1271.

69. Dion, l. lxxvi. p. 1274. Herodian, l. iii. p. 122, 129. The grammarian of Alexandria seems, as it is not unusual, much better acquainted with this mysterious transaction, and more assured of the guilt of Plautianus, than the Roman senator ventures to be.

70. Appian in Proem [cap. 6].

71. Dion Cassius seems to have written with no other view, than to form these opinions into an historical system. The Pandects will show how assiduously the lawyers, on their side, laboured in the cause of prerogative.

Chapter VI

1. Hist. August. p. 71 [Spart. Sever. c. 18]. "Omnia fui et nihil expedit."

2. Dion Cassius, l. lxxvi. [c. 16] p. 1284.

3. About the year 186 M. de Tillemont is miserably embarrassed with a passage of Dion, in which the empress Faustina, who died in the year 175, is introduced as having contributed to the marriage of Severus and Julia (l. lxxiv. p. 1243). The learned compiler forgot, that Dion is relating, not a real fact, but a dream of Severus; and dreams are circumscribed to no limits of time or space. Hist. des Empereurs, tom. iii. p. 389, Note 6.

4. Hist. August. p. 65 [Spart. Sev. c. 3].

5. Hist. August. [Spart. Carac. c. 10] p. 85.

6. Dion Cassius, l. lxxvii. [c. 18] p. 1304, 1314.

7. See a Dissertation of Menage, at the end of his edition of Diogenes Laertius, de Fœminis Philosophis.

8. Dion, l. lxxvi. [c. 16] p. 1285. Aurelius Victor [De Cæs. xx. 23].

9. Bassianus was his first name, as it had been that of his maternal grandfather. During his reign he assumed the appellation of Antoninus, which is employed by lawyers and ancient historians. After his death, the public indignation loaded him with the nick-names of Tarantus and Caracalla. The first was borrowed from a celebrated gladiator, the second from a long Gallic gown which he distributed to the people of Rome.

10. The elevation of Caracalla is fixed by the accurate M. de Tillemont to the year 198: the association of Geta to the year 208.

11. Herodian, l. iii. p. 130. The Lives of Caracalla and Geta in the Augustan History.

12. Dion, l. lxxvi. p. 1280, etc. Herodian, l. iii. p. 132, etc.

13. Ossian's Poems, vol. i. p. 175.

14. That the Caracul of Ossian is the Caracalla of the Roman History is, perhaps, the only point of British antiquity in which Mr. Macpherson and Mr. Whitaker are of the same opinion, and yet the opinion is not without difficulty. In the Caledonian war, the son of Severus was known only by the appellation of Antoninus; and it may seem strange that the Highland bard should describe him by a nick-name, invented four years afterwards, scarcely used by the Romans till after the death of that emperor, and seldom employed by the most ancient historians. Dion, l. lxxvii. p. 1317. Hist. August. p. 89. Aurel. Victor. Euseb. in Chron. ad ann. 214.

15. Dion, l. lxxvi. p. 1282. Hist. August. p. 71. Aurel. Victor.

16. Dion, l. lxxvi. p. 1283. Hist. August. p. 89.

17. Dion, l. lxxvi. p. 1284. Herodian, l. iii. p. 135.

18. Mr. Hume is justly surprised at a passage in Herodian (l. iv. p. 139), who, on this occasion, represents the Imperial palace as equal in extent to the rest of Rome. The whole region of the Palatine Mount on which it was built, occupied, at most, a circumference of eleven or twelve thousand feet (Notitia and Victor, in Nardini's Roma Antica). But we should recollect that the opulent senators had almost surrounded the city with their extensive gardens and suburban palaces, the greatest part of which had been gradually confiscated by the emperors. If Geta resided in the gardens that bore his name in the Janiculum; and if Caracalla inhabited the gardens of Mæcenas on the Esquiline, the rival brothers were separated from each other by the distance of several miles; and yet the intermediate space was filled by the imperial gardens of Sallust, of Lucullus, of Agrippa, of Domitian, of Caius, etc., all skirting round the city, and all connected with each other, and with the palace, by bridges thrown over the Tiber and the streets. But this explanation of Herodian would require, though it ill deserves, a particular dissertation, illustrated by a map of ancient Rome.

19. Herodian, l. iv. p. 139.

20. Herodian, l. iv. p. 144.

21. Caracalla consecrated, in the temple of Serapis, the sword with which, as he boasted, he had slain his brother Geta. Dion, l. lxxvii. p. 1307.

22. Herodian, l. iv. p. 147. In every Roman camp there was a small chapel near the head quarters, in which the statues of the tutelar deities were preserved and adored; and we may remark, that the eagles, and other military ensigns, were in the first rank of these deities: an excellent institution, which confirmed discipline by the sanction of religion. Lipsius de Militia Romanâ, iv. 5, v. 2.

23. Herodian, l. iv. p. 148. Dion, l. lxxvii. p. 1289.

24. Geta was placed among the gods. Sit *divus*, dum non sit *vivus*, said his brother. Hist. August. p. 91. Some marks of Geta's consecration are still found upon medals.

25. Dion, l. lxxvii. p. 1301.

26. Dion, l. lxxvii. p. 1290. Herodian, l. iv. p. 150. Dion (p. 1298) says, that the comic poets no longer durst employ the name of Geta in their plays, and that the estates of those who mentioned it in their testaments, were confiscated.

27. Caracalla had assumed the names of several conquered nations; Pertinax observed that the name of *Geticus* (he had obtained some advantage of the Goths or Getæ) would be a proper addition to Parthicus, Alemannicus, etc. Hist. August. p. 89.

28. Dion, l. lxxvii. p. 1291. He was probably descended from Helvidius Priscus and Thrasea Pætus, those patriots whose firm, but useless and unseasonable, virtue has been immortalised by Tacitus.

29. It is said that Papinian was himself a relation of the empress Julia.

30. Tacit. Annal. xiv. ii.

31. Hist. August. p. 88.

32. With regard to Papinian, see Heineccius's Historia Juris Romani, l. 330, etc.

33. Tiberius and Domitian never moved from the neighbourhood of Rome. Nero made a short journey into Greece. "Et laudatorum Principum usus ex æquo quamvis procul agentibus. Sævi proximis ingruunt." Tacit. Hist. iv. 75.

34. Dion, l. lxxvii. p. 1294.

35. Dion, l. lxxvii. p. 1307. Herodian, l. iv. p. 158. The former represents it as a cruel massacre, the latter as a perfidious one too. It seems probable, that the Alexandrians had irritated the tyrant by their railleries, and perhaps by their tumults.

36. Dion, l. lxxvii. p. 1296.

37. Dion, l. lxxvi. p. 1284. Mr. Wotton (Hist. of Rome, p. 330) suspects that this maxim was invented by Caracalla himself, and attributed to his father.

38. Dion (l. lxxviii. p. 1343) informs us, that the extraordinary gifts of Caracalla to the army amounted annually to seventy millions of drachmæ (about two millions three hundred and fifty thousand pounds). There is another passage in Dion, concerning the military pay, infinitely curious; were it not obscure, imperfect, and probably corrupt The best sense seems to be, that the Præ-

torian guards received twelve hundred and fifty drachmæ (forty pounds) a year (Dion, l. lxxvii. p. 1307). Under the reign of Augustus, they were paid at the rate of two drachmæ, or denarii, per day, 720 a year (Tacit. Annal. i. 17). Domitian, who increased the soldiers' pay one fourth, must have raised the Prætorians to 960 drachmæ (Gronovius de Pecunia Veteri, l. iii. c. 2). These successive augmentations ruined the empire, for, with the soldiers' pay, their numbers too were increased. We have seen the Prætorians alone increased from 10,000 to 50,000 men.

39. Dion, l. lxxviii. p. 1312. Herodian, l. iv. p. 168.

40. The fondness of Caracalla for the name and ensigns of Alexander, is still preserved on the medals of that emperor. Spanheim, de Usu Numismatum, Dissertat. xii. Herodian (l. iv. p. 154) had seen very ridiculous pictures, in which a figure was drawn, with one side of the face like Alexander, and the other like Caracalla.

41. Herodian, l. iv. p. 619. Hist. August. p. 94.

42. Dion, l. lxxviii. p. 1350. Elagabalus reproached his predecessor, with daring to seat himself on the throne; though, as Prætorian præfect, he could not have been admitted into the senate after the voice of the crier had cleared the house. The personal favour of Plautianus and Sejanus had broke through the established rule. They rose indeed from the equestrian order; but they preserved the præfecture with the rank of senator, and even with the consulship.

43. He was a native of Cæsarea, in Numidia, and began his fortune by serving in the household of Plautian, from whose ruin he narrowly escaped. His enemies asserted that he was born a slave, and had exercised, among other infamous professions, that of gladiator. The fashion of aspersing the birth and condition of an adversary, seems to have lasted from the time of the Greek orators to the learned grammarians of the last age.

44. Both Dion and Herodian speak of the virtues and vices of Macrinus, with candour and impartiality; but the author of his Life, in the Augustan History, seems to have implicitly copied some of the venal writers, employed by Elagabalus, to blacken the memory of his predecessor.

45. Dion, l. lxxxiii. p. 1336. The sense of the author is as clear as the intention of the emperor; but M. Wotton has mistaken both, by understanding the distinction, not of veterans and recruits, but of old and new legions. History of Rome, p. 347.

46. Dion, l. lxxviii. p. 1330. The abridgment of Xiphilin, though less particular, is in this place clearer than the original.

47. According to Lampridius (Hist. August. p. 135), Alexander Severus lived twenty-nine years, three months, and seven days. As he was killed March 19, 235, he was born December 12, 205, and was consequently about this time thirteen years old, as his elder cousin might be about sev-

enteen. This computation suits much better the history of the young princes, than that of Herodian (l. v. p. 181), who represents them as three years younger; whilst, by an opposite error of chronology, he lengthens the reign of Elagabalus two years beyond its real duration. For the particulars of the conspiracy, see Dion, l. lxxviii. p. 1339. Herodian, l. v. p. 184.

48. By a most dangerous proclamation of the pretended Antoninus, every soldier who brought in his officer's head, became entitled to his private estate, as well as to his military commission.

49. Dion, l. lxxviii. p. 1345. Herodian, l. v. p. 186. The battle was fought near the village of Immæ, about two and twenty miles from Antioch.

50. Dion, l. lxxix. [c. 4] p. 1353.

51. Dion, l. lxxix. [c. 14] p. 1363. Herodian, l. v. [c. 5] p. 189.

52. This name is derived by the learned from two Syriac words, *Ela* a God, and *Gabal*, to form, the forming or plastic God, a proper, and even happy epithet for the Sun. Wotton's History of Rome, p. 378.

53. Herodian, l. v. [c. 5] p. 190.

54. He broke into the sanctuary of Vesta, and carried away a statue, which he supposed to be the Palladium; but the vestals boasted, that, by a pious fraud, they had imposed a counterfeit image on the profane intruder. Hist. August. p. 103.

55. Dion, l. lxxix. [c. 12] p. 1360. Herodian, l. v. [c. 6] p. 193. The subjects of the empire were obliged to make liberal presents to the new-married couple; and whatever they had promised during the life of Elagabalus, was carefully exacted under the administration of Mamæa.

56. The invention of a new sauce was liberally rewarded; but, if it was not relished, the inventor was confined to eat of nothing else, till he had discovered another more agreeable to the Imperial palate. Hist. August. [Lamprid. Heliog. c. 29], p. 111.

57. He never would eat sea-fish except at a great distance from the sea; he then would distribute vast quantities of the rarest sorts, brought at an immense expense, to the peasants of the inland country. Hist. Aug. [Lamprid. Heliog. c. 23], p. 109.

58. Dion, l. lxxix. p. 1358. Herodian, l. v. p. 192.

59. Hierocles enjoyed that honour. Dion, l. lxxix. p. 1363, 1364. A dancer was made præfect of the city, a charioteer præfect of the watch, a barber præfect of the provisions. Hist. August. p. 105.

60. Even the credulous compiler of his Life, in the Augustan History (p. 111), is inclined to suspect that his vices may have been exaggerated.

61. Dion, l. lxxix. p. 1365. Herodian, l. v. p. 195–201. Hist. August. p. 105. The last of the three historians seems to have followed the best authors in his account of the revolution.

62. The era of the death of Elagabalus, and of the accession of Alexander, has employed the learning and ingenuity of Pagi, Tillemont, Valsecchi, Vignoli, and Torre bishop of Adria. The question is most assuredly intricate; but I still adhere to the authority of Dion; the truth of whose calculations is undeniable, and the purity of whose text is justified by the agreement of Xiphilin, Zonaras, and Cedrenus. Elagabalus reigned three years, nine months, and four days, from his victory over Macrinus, and was killed March 10, 222. But what shall we reply to the medals, undoubtedly genuine, which reckon the fifth year of his tribunitian power? We shall reply, with the learned Valsecchi, that the usurpation of Macrinus was annihilated, and that the son of Caracalla dated his reign from his father's death. After resolving this great difficulty, the smaller knots of this question may be easily untied, or cut asunder.

63. Hist. August. p. 114. By this unusual precipitation, the senate meant to confound the hopes of pretenders, and prevent the factions of the armies.

64. Metellus Numidicus, the censor, acknowledged to the Roman people in a public oration that had kind Nature allowed us to exist without the help of women, we should be delivered from a very troublesome companion; and he could recommend matrimony, only as the sacrifice of private pleasure to public duty. Aulus Gellius, i. 6.

65. Tacit. Annal. xiii. 5.

66. Hist. August. p. 102, 107 [Lamprid. Heliog. c. 4 and 18].

67. Dion, l. lxxx. [c. 2] p. 1369. Herodian, l. vi. [c. 1] p. 206. Hist. August. [Lamprid. Alexander Sev. c. 49] p. 131. Herodian represents the Patrician as innocent. The Augustan History, on the authority of Dexippus, condemns him, as guilty of a conspiracy against the life of Alexander. It is impossible to pronounce between them: but Dion is an irreproachable witness of the jealousy and cruelty of Mamæa toward the young empress, whose hard fate Alexander lamented, but durst not oppose.

68. Herodian, l. vi. p. 203. Hist. August. p. 119. The latter insinuates, that when any law was to be passed, the council was assisted by a number of able lawyers and experienced senators, whose opinions were separately given and taken down in writing.

69. See his Life in the Augustan History. The undistinguishing compiler has buried these interesting anecdotes under a load of trivial and unmeaning circumstances.

70. See the 13th Satire of Juvenal.

71. Hist. August. p. 119.

72. See in the Hist. August. p. 116, 117, the whole contest between Alexander and the senate, extracted from the journals of that assembly. It happened on the sixth of March, probably of the year 223, when the Romans had enjoyed, almost a twelvemonth, the blessings of his reign. Before the appellation of Antoninus was offered him as a

title of honour, the senate waited to see whether Alexander would not assume it, as a family name.

73. It was a favourite saying of the emperor's, *Se milites magis servare quam seipsum; quod salus publica in his esset.* Hist. August. p. 130.

74. Though the author of the Life of Alexander (Hist. August. p. 132) mentions the sedition raised against Ulpian by the soldiers, he conceals the catastrophe, as it might discover a weakness in the administration of his hero. From this designed omission, we may judge of the weight and candour of that author.

75. For an account of Ulpian's fate and his own danger, see the mutilated conclusion of Dion's History, l. lxxx, p. 1371.

76. Annot. Reimar. ad Dion Cassius, l. lxxx. p. 1369.

77. Julius Cæsar had appeased a sedition with the same word *Quirites;* which thus opposed to *Soldiers,* was used in a sense of contempt, and reduced the offenders to the less honourable condition of mere citizens. Tacit. Annal. i. 42.

78. Hist. August. p. 132.

79. From the Metelli. Hist. August. [Lamprid. Alexander Sev. c. 44] p. 119. The choice was judicious. In one short period of twelve years, the Metelli could reckon seven consulships and five triumphs. Velleius Paterculus, ii. 11, and the Fasti.

80. The Life of Alexander, in the Augustan History, is the mere idea of a perfect prince, an awkward imitation of the Cyropædia. The account of his reign, as given by Herodian, is rational and moderate, consistent with the general history of the age; and, in some of the most invidious particulars, confirmed by the decisive fragments of Dion. Yet from a very paltry prejudice, the greater number of our modern writers abuse Herodian, and copy the Augustan History. Mess. de Tillemont and Wotton. From the opposite prejudice, the emperor Julian (in Cæsarib. p. 315) dwells with a visible satisfaction on the effeminate weakness of the *Syrian,* and the ridiculous avarice of his mother.

81. According to the more accurate Dionysius, the city itself was only an hundred stadia, or twelve miles and a half, from Rome; though some outposts might be advanced farther on the side of Etruria. Nardini, in a professed treatise, has combated the popular opinion and the authority of two popes, and has removed Veii from Civita Castellana, to a little spot called Isola, in the midway between Rome and the lake Bracciano.

82. Cf. Livy, b. iv. c. 59 and b. v. c. 7. In the Roman Census, property, power, and taxation, were commensurate with each other.

83. Plin. Hist. Natur. l. xxxiii. c. 3. Cicero de Offic. ii. 22. Plutarch in Æmilius Paulus.

84. See a fine description of this accumulated wealth of ages, in Lucan's Phars. l. iii. v. 155.

85. Tacit. in Annal. i. 11. It seems to have existed in the time of Appian.

86. Plutarch. in Pompey.

87. Strabo, l. xvii. p. 798.

88. Velleius Paterculus, l. ii. c. 39. He seems to give the preference to the revenue of Gaul.

89. The Euboic, the Phœnician, and the Alexandrian talents were double in weight to the Attic. Hooper on ancient weights and measures, p. iv. c. 5. It is very probable, that the same talent was carried from Tyre to Carthage.

90. Polyb. l. xv. c. 2.

91. Diodorus Siculus, l. v. Cadiz was built by the Phœnicians a little more than a thousand years before Christ. Vell. Paterc. i. 2.

92. Appian in Punicis, p. 84.

93. Strabo, l. iii. p. 148.

94. Plin. Hist. Natur. l. xxxiii. c. 3. He mentions likewise a silver mine in Dalmatia, that yielded every day fifty pounds to the state.

95. Strabo, l. x. p. 485. Tacit. Annal. iii. 69 and iv. 30. Tournefort (Voyages au Levant, Lettre viii.) gives a very lively picture of the actual misery of Gyarus.

96. Lipsius de magnitudine Romanâ (l. ii. c. 3) computes the revenue at one hundred and fifty millions of gold crowns; but his whole book, though learned and ingenious, betrays a very heated imagination.

97. Tacit. Annal. xiii. 31.

98. Pliny (Hist. Natur. l. vi. c. 28 [s. 32]; l. xii. c. 18). His observation, that the Indian commodities were sold at Rome at a hundred times their original price, may give us some notion of the produce of the customs, since that original price amounted to more than eight hundred thousand pounds.

99. The ancients were unacquainted with the art of cutting diamonds.

100. M. Bouchaud, in his treatise de l'Impot chez les Romains, has transcribed this catalogue from the Digest, and attempts to illustrate it by a very prolix commentary.

101. Tacit. Annal. i. 78. Two years afterwards, the reduction of the poor kingdom of Cappadocia gave Tiberius a pretence for diminishing the excise to one half; but the relief was of very short duration.

102. Dion Cassius, l. lv. p. 794, l. lvi. p. 825.

103. The sum is only fixed by conjecture.

104. As the Roman law subsisted for many ages, the *Cognati,* or relations on the mother's side, were not called to the succession. This harsh institution was gradually undermined by humanity, and finally abolished by Justinian.

105. Plin. Panegyric. c. 37.

106. Heineccius in the Antiquit. Juris Romani, l. ii.

107. Horat. l. ii. Sat. v. Petron. c. 116, etc. Plin. l. ii. Epist. 20.

108. Cicero in Philipp. ii. c. 16.

109. See his Epistles. Every such will gave him an occasion of displaying his reverence to the dead, and his justice to the living. He reconciled both in

his behaviour to a son who had been disinherited by his mother (v. 1).

110. Tacit. Annal. xiii. 50. The Spirit of Laws, xiii. 19.

111. Pliny's Panegyric, the Augustan History, and Burman de Vectigal, passim.

112. The tributes (properly so called) were not farmed; since the good princes often remitted many millions of arrears.

113. The situation of the new citizens is minutely described by Pliny (Panegyric, c. 37, 38, 39).

Trajan published a law very much in their favour.

114. Dion, l. lxxvii. p. 1295.

115. He who paid ten *aurei*, the usual tribute, was charged with no more than the third part of an aureus, and proportional pieces of gold were coined by Alexander's order. Hist. August. p. 127, with the commentary of Salmasius.

116. See the Lives of Agricola, Vespasian, Trajan, Severus, and his three competitors; and indeed of all the eminent men of those times.

Chapter VII

1. There had been no example of three successive generations on the throne; only three instances of sons who succeeded their fathers. The marriages of the Cæsars (notwithstanding the permission, and the frequent practice, of divorces) were generally unfruitful.

2. Hist. August. p. 138 [Capitol. Max. c. 1 *seqq.*].

3. Hist. August. p. 140. Herodian, l. vi. p. 223. Aurelius Victor. By comparing these authors, it should seem, that Maximin had the particular command of the Triballian horse, with the general commission of disciplining the recruits of the whole army. His biographer ought to have marked, with more care, his exploits, and the successive steps of his military promotions.

4. Original letter of Alexander Severus, Hist. August. p. 149.

5. Hist. August. p. 135. I have softened some of the most improbable circumstances of this wretched biographer. From this ill-worded narration, it should seem, that the prince's buffoon having accidentally entered the tent, and awakened the slumbering monarch, the fear of punishment urged him to persuade the disaffected soldiers to commit the murder.

6. Herodian, l. vi. p. 223–227.

7. Caligula, the eldest of the four, was only twenty-five years of age when he ascended the throne; Caracalla was twenty-three, Commodus nineteen, and Nero no more than seventeen.

8. It appears that he was totally ignorant of the Greek language: which, from its universal use in conversation and letters, was an essential part of every liberal education.

9. Hist. August. p. 141. Herodian, l. vii. p. 237. The latter of these historians has been most unjustly censured for sparing the vices of Maximin.

10. The wife of Maximin, by insinuating wise counsels with female gentleness, sometimes brought back the tyrant to the way of truth and humanity. See Ammianus Marcellinus, l. xiv. c. 1, where he alludes to the fact which he had more fully related under the reign of the Gordians. We may collect from the medals, that Paullina was the name of this benevolent empress: and from the title of *Diva*,

that she died before Maximin. (Valesius ad loc. cit. Ammian.) Spanheim de U. et P. N. tom. ii. p. 300.

11. He was compared to Spartacus and Athenio. Hist. August. p. 141.

12. Herodian, l. vii. [c. 3 and 4] p. 238. Zosim. l. i. [c. 13 and 18] p. 15.

13. In the fertile territory of Byzacium, one hundred and fifty miles to the south of Carthage. This city was decorated, probably by the Gordians, with the title of colony, and with a fine amphitheatre, which is still in a very perfect state. See Itinerar. Wesseling, p. 59, and Shaw's Travels, p. 117.

14. Herodian, l. vii. [c. 4 and 5] p. 239. Hist. August. p. 153 [Capitol. Gordiani, c. 7 *seq.*].

15. Hist. August. p. 152. The celebrated house of Pompey *in carinis*, was usurped by Marc Antony, and consequently became, after the Triumvir's death, a part of the Imperial domain. The emperor Trajan allowed and even encouraged the rich senators to purchase those magnificent and useless places (Plin. Panegyric. c. 50): and it may seem probable that, on this occasion, Pompey's house came into the possession of Gordian's great-grandfather.

16. The Claudian, the Numidian, the Carystian, and the Synnadian. The colours of Roman marbles have been faintly described and imperfectly distinguished. It appears, however, that the Carystian was a sea-green, and that the marble of Synnada was white mixed with oval spots of purple. Salmasius ad Hist. August. p. 164.

17. Hist. August. p. 151, 152. He sometimes gave five hundred pair of gladiators, never less than one hundred and fifty. He once gave for the use of the circus one hundred Sicilian, and as many Cappadocian horses. The animals designed for hunting were chiefly bears, boars, bulls, stags, elks, wild asses, etc. Elephants and lions seem to have been appropriated to Imperial magnificence.

18. See the original letter, in the Augustan History, p. 152, which at once shows Alexander's respect for the authority of the senate, and his esteem for the proconsul appointed by that assembly.

19. By each of his concubines, the younger Gordian left three or four children. His literary productions were by no means contemptible.

20. Herodian, l. vii. p. 243. Hist. August. p. 144.

21. Quod tamen patres dum periculosum existimant inermes armato resistere, approbaverunt. *Aurelius Victor.*

22. Even the servants of the house, the scribes, etc., were excluded, and their office was filled by the senators themselves. We are obliged to the Augustan History, p. 159, for preserving this curious example of the old discipline of the commonwealth.

23. This spirited speech, translated from the Augustan historian, p. 156, seems transcribed by him from the original registers of the senate.

24. Herodian, l. vii. p. 224.

25. Herodian, l. vii. p. 247, l. viii. p. 277. Hist. August. p. 156-158.

26. Herodian, l. vii. p. 254. Hist. August. p. 150-160. We may observe, that one month and six days, for the reign of Gordian, is a just correction of Casaubon and Panvinius, instead of the absurd reading of one year and six months. Commentar. p. 193. Zosimus relates, l. i. p. 17, that the two Gordians perished by a tempest in the midst of their navigation. A strange ignorance of history, or a strange abuse of metaphors!

27. Augustan History, p. 166, from the registers of the senate; the date is confessedly faulty, but the coincidence of the Apollinarian games enables us to correct it.

28. He was descended from Cornelius Balbus, a noble Spaniard, and the adopted son of Theophanes the Greek historian. Balbus obtained the freedom of Rome by the favour of Pompey, and preserved it by the eloquence of Cicero (see Orat. pro Cornel. Balbo). The friendship of Cæsar (to whom he rendered the most important secret services in the civil war) raised him to the consulship and the pontificate, honours never yet possessed by a stranger. The nephew of this Balbus triumphed over the Garamantes. See Dictionnaire de Bayle, au mot *Balbus,* where he distinguishes the several persons of that name, and rectifies, with his usual accuracy, the mistakes of former writers concerning them.

29. Zonaras, l. xii. p. 622. But little dependence is to be had on the authority of a moderate Greek, so grossly ignorant of the history of the third century, that he creates several imaginary emperors, and confounds those who really existed.

30. Herodian, l. vii. p. 256, supposes that the senate was at first convoked in the Capitol, and is very eloquent on the occasion. The Augustan History, p. 116, seems much more authentic.

31. In Herodian, l. vii. p. 249, and in the Augustan History, we have three several orations of Maximin to his army, on the rebellion of Africa and Rome: M. de Tillemont has very justly observed, that they neither agree with each other, nor with truth. Histoire des Empereurs, tom. iii. p. 799.

32. The carelessness of the writers of that age leaves us in a singular perplexity. 1. We know that Maximus and Balbinus were killed during the Capitoline games. Herodian, l. viii. p. 285. The authority of Censorinus (de Die Natali, c. 18) enables us to fix those games with certainty to the year 238, but leaves us in ignorance of the month or day. 2. The election of Gordian by the senate is fixed, with equal certainty, to the 27th of May; but we are at a loss to discover whether it was in the same or the preceding year. Tillemont and Muratori, who maintain the two opposite opinions, bring into the field a desultory troop of authorities, conjectures, and probabilities. The one seems to draw out, the other to contract, the series of events between those periods, more than can be well reconciled to reason and history. Yet it is necessary to choose between them.

33. Velleius Paterculus, l. ii. c. 24. The president de Montesquieu (in his dialogue between Sulla and Eucrates) expresses the sentiments of the dictator, in a spirited and even a sublime manner.

34. Muratori (Annali d'Italia, tom. ii. p. 294) thinks the melting of the snows suits better with the months of June or July, than with that of February. The opinion of a man who passed his life between the Alps and the Apennines, is undoubtedly of great weight; yet I observe, 1. That the long winter, of which Muratori takes advantage, is to be found only in the Latin version, and not in the Greek text of Herodian. 2. That the vicissitude of suns and rains, to which the soldiers of Maximin were exposed (Herodian, l. viii. p. 277) denotes the spring rather than the summer. We may observe likewise, that these several streams, as they melted into one, composed the Timavus, so poetically (in every sense of the word) described by Virgil. They are about twelve miles to the east of Aquileia. See Cluver. Italia Antiqua, tom. i. p. 189, etc.

35. Herodian, l. viii. p. 272. The Celtic deity was supposed to be Apollo, and received under that name the thanks of the senate. A temple was likewise built to Venus the bald, in honour of the women of Aquileia, who had given up their hair to make ropes for the military engines.

36. Herodian, l. viii. p. 279. Hist. August. p. 146. The duration of Maximin's reign has not been defined with much accuracy, except by Eutropius, who allows him three years and a few days (l. ix. 1); we may depend on the integrity of the text, as the Latin original is checked by the Greek version of Pæanius.

37. Eight Roman feet and one third, which are equal to above eight English feet, as the two measures are to each other in the proportion of 967 to 1000. See Graves's discourse on the Roman foot. We are told that Maximin could drink in a day an amphora (or about seven gallons of wine), and eat thirty or forty pounds of meat. He could move a loaded waggon, break a horse's leg with his fist,

crumble stones in his hand, and tear up small trees by the roots. See his Life in the Augustan History.

38. See the congratulatory letter of Claudius Julianus the consul, to the two emperors, in the Augustan History.

39. Hist. August. p. 171 [Capitol. c. 15].

40. Herodian, l. viii. [c. 12] p. 258.

41. Herodian, l. viii. [c. 7] p. 213.

42. The observation had been made imprudently enough in the acclamations of the senate, and with regard to the soldiers it carried the appearance of a wanton insult. Hist. August. p. 170.

43. Discordiæ tacitæ, et quæ intelligerentur potius quam viderentur. Hist. August. p. 170. This well-chosen expression is probably stolen from some better writer.

44. Herodian, l. viii. p. 287, 288.

45. Quia non alius erat in præsenti, is the expression of the Augustan History.

46. Quintus Curtius (l. x. c. 9) pays an elegant compliment to the emperor of the day, for having, by his happy accession, extinguished so many firebrands, sheathed so many swords, and put an end to the evils of a divided government. After weighing with attention every word of the passage, I am of opinion that it suits better with the elevation of Gordian, than with any other period of the Roman history. In that case, it may serve to decide the age of Quintus Curtius. Those who place him under the first Cæsars, argue from the purity of his style, but are embarrassed by the silence of Quintilian, in his accurate list of Roman historians.

47. Hist. August. p. 161. From some hints in the two letters, I should expect that the eunuchs were not expelled the palace without some degree of gentle violence, and that young Gordian rather approved of, than consented to, their disgrace.

48. Duxit uxorem filiam Misithei, quem causâ eloquentiæ dignum parentela suâ putavit; et præfectum statim fecit; post quod, non puerile jam et contemptibile videbatur imperium.

49. Hist. August. p. 162. Aurelius Victor. Porphyrius in Vit. Plotin. ap. Fabricium Biblioth. Græc. l. iv. c. 36. The philosopher Plotinus accompanied the army, prompted by the love of knowledge, and by the hope of penetrating as far as India.

50. About twenty miles from the little town of Circesium, on the frontier of the two empires.

51. The inscription (which contained a very singular pun) was erased by the order of Licinius,

who claimed some degree of relationship to Philip (Hist. August. p. 165); but the *tumulus* or mound of earth which formed the sepulchre, still subsisted in the time of Julian. Ammian. Marcellin. xxiii. 5.

52. Aurelius Victor. Eutrop. ix. 2. Orosius, vii. 20. Ammianus Marcellinus, xxiii. 5. Zosimus, l. i. p. 19. Philip, who was a native of Bostra, was about forty years of age.

53. Can the epithet of *Aristocracy* be applied with any propriety, to the government of Algiers? Every military government floats between the extremes of absolute monarchy and wild democracy.

54. The military republic of the Mamalukes in Egypt, would have afforded M. de Montesquieu (Considerations sur la Grandeur et la Decadence des Romains, c. 16) a juster and more noble parallel.

55. The Augustan History (p. 163, 164) cannot, in this instance, be reconciled with itself or with probability. How could Philip condemn his predecessor, and yet consecrate his memory? How could he order his public execution, and yet, in his letters to the senate, exculpate himself from the guilt of his death? Philip, though an ambitious usurper, was by no means a mad tyrant. Some chronological difficulties have likewise been discovered by the nice eyes of Tillemont and Muratori, in this supposed association of Philip to the empire.

56. The account of the last supposed celebration, though in an enlightened period of history, was so very doubtful and obscure, that the alternative seems not doubtful. When the popish jubilees, the copy of the secular games, were invented by Boniface VIII., the crafty pope pretended that he only revived an ancient institution. M. de Chais Lettres sur les Jubilès.

57. Either of a hundred, or a hundred and ten years. Varro and Livy adopted the former opinion, but the infallible authority of the Sibyl consecrated the latter (Censorinus de Die Natal. c. 17). The emperors Claudius and Philip, however, did not treat the oracle with implicit respect.

58. The idea of the secular games is best understood from the poem of Horace, and the description of Zosimus, l. ii. p. 167, etc.

59. The received calculation of Varro assigns to the foundation of Rome an era that corresponds with the 754th year before Christ. But so little is the chronology of Rome to be depended on, in the more early ages, that Sir Isaac Newton has brought the same event as low as the year 627.

Chapter VIII

1. An ancient chronologist quoted by Velleius Paterculus (l. i. c. 6) observes, that the Assyrians, the Medes, the Persians, and the Macedonians, reigned over Asia one thousand nine hundred and ninety-five years, from the accession of Ninus to the defeat of Antiochus by the Romans. As the lat-

ter of these great events happened 289 years before Christ, the former may be placed 2184 years before the same era. The Astronomical Observations, found at Babylon by Alexander, went fifty years higher.

2. In the five hundred and thirty-eighth year of

the era of Seleucus. Agathias, l. ii. p. 63. This great event (such is the carelessness of the Orientals) is placed by Eutychius as high as the tenth year of Commodus, and by Moses of Chorene as low as the reign of Philip. Ammianus Marcellinus has so servilely copied (xxiii. 6) his ancient materials, which are indeed very good, that he describes the family of the Arsacides as still seated on the Persian throne in the middle of the fourth century.

3. The tanner's name was Babec; the soldier's, Sassan: from the former Artaxerxes obtained the surname of Babegan: from the latter all his descendants have been styled *Sassanides*.

4. D'Herbelot. Bibliotheque Orientale. Ardshir.

5. Dion Cassius, l. lxxx. Herodian, l. vi. p. 207. Abulpharagius Dynast. p. 80.

6. Moses Chorenensis, l. ii. c. 65-71.

7. Hyde and Prideaux, working up the Persian legends and their own conjectures into a very agreeable story, represent Zoroaster as a contemporary of Darius Hystaspes. But it is sufficient to observe, that the Greek writers, who lived almost in the age of Darius, agree in placing the era of Zoroaster many hundred, or even thousand, years before their own time. The judicious criticism of Mr. Moyle perceived, and maintained against his uncle Dr. Prideaux, the antiquity of the Persian prophet. See his work, vol. ii.

8. That ancient idiom was called the *Zend*. The language of the commentary, the Pehlvi, though much more modern, has ceased many ages ago to be a living tongue. This fact alone (if it is allowed as authentic) sufficiently warrants the antiquity of those writings, which M. d'Anquetil has brought into Europe, and translated into French.

9. Hyde de Religione veterum Pers. c. 21.

10. I have principally drawn this account from the Zendavesta of M. d'Anquetil, and the Sadder, subjoined to Dr. Hyde's treatise. It must, however, be confessed, that the studied obscurity of a prophet, the figurative style of the East, and the deceitful medium of a French or Latin version, may have betrayed us into error and heresy in this abridgment of Persian theology.

11. The modern Parsees (and in some degree the Sadder) exalt Ormusd into the first and omnipotent cause, whilst they degrade Ahriman into an inferior but rebellious spirit. Their desire of pleasing the Mahometans may have contributed to refine their theological system.

12. Herodotus, l. i. c. 131. But Dr. Prideaux thinks, with reason, that the use of temples was afterwards permitted in the Magian religion.

13. Hyde de Relig. Pers. c. 8. Notwithstanding all their distinctions and protestations, which seem sincere enough, their tyrants, the Mahometans, have constantly stigmatised them as idolatrous worshippers of the Fire.

14. See the Sadder, the smallest part of which consists of moral precepts. The ceremonies enjoined are infinite and trifling. Fifteen genuflexions, prayers, etc., were required whenever the devout Persian cut his nails or made water; or as often as he put on the sacred girdle. Sadder, Art. 14, 50, 60.

15. Zendavesta, tom. i. p. 224, and Precis du Systeme de Zoroastre, tom. iii.

16. Hyde de Religione Persarum, c. 19.

17. Hyde de Religione Persarum, c. 28. Both Hyde and Prideaux affect to apply to the Magian the terms consecrated to the Christian hierarchy.

18. Ammian. Marcellin. xxiii. 6. He informs us (as far as we may credit him) of two curious particulars; 1, that the Magi derived some of their most secret doctrines from the Indian Brachmans; and 2, that they were a tribe or family, as well as order.

19. The divine institution of tithes exhibits a singular instance of conformity between the law of Zoroaster and that of Moses. Those who cannot otherwise account for it, may suppose, if they please, that the Magi of the latter times inserted so useful an interpolation into the writings of their prophet.

20. Sadder, Art. 8.

21. Plato in Alcibiad.

22. Pliny (Hist. Natur. l. xxx. c. 1) observes, that magic held mankind by the triple chain of religion, of physic, and of astronomy.

23. Agathias, l. iv. p. 134.

24. Mr. Hume, in the Natural History of Religion, remarks that the most refined and philosophic sects are the most intolerant.

25. Cicero de Legibus, ii. 10. Xerxes, by the advice of the Magi, destroyed the temples of Greece.

26. Hyde de Rel. Persar. c. 23, 24. D'Herbelot Bibliothèque Orientale *Zordusht*. Life of Zoroaster in tom. ii. of the Zendavesta.

27. Compare Moses of Chorene, l. ii. c. 74 with Ammian. Marcellin. xxiii. 6. Hereafter I shall make use of these passages.

28. Rabbi Abraham in the Tarikh Schickard, p. 108, 109.

29. Basnage, Histoire des Juifs, l. viii. c. 3. Sozomen, l. ii. c. 1. Manes, who suffered an ignominious death, may be deemed a Magian as well as a Christian heretic.

30. Hyde de Religione Persar. c. 21.

31. These colonies were extremely numerous. Seleucus Nicator founded thirty-nine cities, all named from himself, or some of his relations (Appian in Syriac. p. 124). The æra of Seleucus (still in use among the Eastern Christians) appears as late as the year 508, of Christ 196, on the medals of the Greek cities within the Parthian empire. Moyle, vol. i. p. 273, etc., and M. Freret, Mem. de l'Academie, tom. xix.

32. The modern Persians distinguish that period as the dynasty of the kings of the nations. Plin. Hist. Nat. vi. 25.

33. Eutychius (tom. i. p. 367, 371, 375) relates the siege of the island of Mesene in the Tigris, with some circumstances not unlike the story of Nisus and Scylla.

34. Agathias, ii. 164. The princes of Segestan defended their independence during many years. As romances generally transport to an ancient period the events of their own time, it is not impossible that the fabulous exploits of Rustan prince of Segestan may have been grafted on this real history.

35. We can scarcely attribute to the Persian monarchy the sea-coast of Gedrosia or Macran, which extends along the Indian Ocean from Cape Jast (the promontory of Capella) to Cape Goadel. In the time of Alexander, and probably many ages afterwards, it was thinly inhabited by a savage people of Icthyophagi, or Fishermen, who knew no arts, who acknowledged no master, and who were divided by inhospitable deserts from the rest of the world. (Arrian de Reb. Indicis.) In the twelfth century, the little town of Taiz (supposed by M. d'Anville to be the Tesa of Ptolemy) was peopled and enriched by the resort of the Arabian merchants. (Geographie Nubiens, p. 58; d'Anville Geographie Ancienne, tom. ii. p. 283.) In the last age the whole country was divided between three princes, one Mahometan and two Idolaters, who maintained their independence against the successors of Shaw Abbas. (Voyages de Tavernier, part. i. l. v. p. 635.)

36. Chardin, tom. iii. c. 1, 2, 3.

37. Dion, l. xxviii. p. 1335.

38. For the precise situation of Babylon, Seleucia, Ctesiphon, Modain, and Bagdad, cities often confounded with each other, see an excellent Geographical Tract of M. d'Anville, in Mem. de l'Academie, tom. xxx.

39. Tacit. Annal. xi. 42. Plin. Hist. Nat. vi. 26.

40. This may be inferred from Strabo, l. xvi. p. 743.

41. That most curious traveller Bernier, who followed the camp of Aurengzebe from Delhi to Cashmir, describes with great accuracy the immense moving city. The guard of cavalry consisted of 35,000 men, that of infantry of 10,000. It was computed that the camp contained 150,000 horses, mules, and elephants; 50,000 camels, 50,000 oxen, and between 300,000 and 400,000 persons. Almost all Delhi followed the court, whose magnificence supported its industry.

42. Dion, l. lxxi. [c. 2] p. 1178. Hist. August. [Capit. Verro], p. 38. Eutrop. viii. 10. Euseb. in Chronic. Quadratus (quoted in the Augustan History) attempted to vindicate the Romans, by alleging that the citizens of Seleucia had first violated their faith.

43. Dion, l. lxxv. p. 1263. Herodian, l. iii. p. 120. Hist. August. [Spart. Sever. c. 16], p. 70.

44. The polished citizens of Antioch called those of Edessa mixed barbarians. It was, however, some praise, that of the three dialects of the Syriac, the purest and most elegant (the Aramæan) was spoken at Edessa. This remark of M. Bayer (Hist. Edess. p. 5) has borrowed from George of Malatia, a Syrian writer.

45. Dion, l. lxxv. p. 1248, 1249, 1250. M. Bayer has neglected to use this most important passage.

46. This kingdom, from Osrhoes, who gave a new name to the country, to the last Abgarus, had lasted 353 years. See the learned work of M. Bayer, Historia Osrhoena et Edessena.

47. Xenophon, in the preface of the Cyropædia, gives a clear and magnificent idea of the extent of the empire of Cyrus. Herodotus (l. iii. c. 7-9, etc.) enters into a curious and particular description of the twenty great Satrapies into which the Persian empire was divided by Darius Hystaspes.

48. Herodian, vi. 209, 212.

49. There were two hundred scythed chariots at the battle of Arbela, in the host of Darius. In the vast army of Tigranes, which was vanquished by Lucullus, seventeen thousand horse only were completely armed. Antiochus brought fifty-four elephants into the field against the Romans: by his frequent wars and negotiations with the princes of India, he had once collected an hundred and fifty of those great animals; but it may be questioned whether the most powerful monarch of Hindostan ever formed a line of battle of seven hundred elephants. Instead of three or four thousand elephants, which the Great Mogul was supposed to possess, Tavernier (Voyages, part ii. l. i. p. 198) discovered, by a more accurate inquiry, that he had only five hundred for his baggage, and eighty or ninety for the service of war. The Greeks have varied with regard to the number which Porus brought into the field: but Quintus Curtius (viii. 13), in this instance judicious and moderate, is contented with eighty-five elephants, distinguished by their size and strength. In Siam, where these animals are the most numerous and the most esteemed, eighteen elephants are allowed as a sufficient proportion for each of the nine brigades into which a just army is divided. The whole number, of one hundred and sixty-two elephants of war, may sometimes be doubled. Hist. des Voyages, tom. ix. p. 260.

50. Hist. August. p. 133.

51. M. de Tillemont has already observed, that Herodian's geography is somewhat confused.

52. Moses of Chorene (Hist. Armen. l. ii. c. 71) illustrates this invasion of Media, by asserting that Chosroes, king of Armenia, defeated Artaxerxes and pursued him to the confines of India. The exploits of Chosroes have been magnified; and he acted as a dependent ally to the Romans.

53. For the account of this war, see Herodian, l. vi. [cap. 5], p. 209, 212. The old abbreviators and modern compilers have blindly followed the Augustan History.

54. Eutychius, tom. ii. p. 180, vers. Pocock. The great Chosroes Noushirwan sent the Code of Artaxerxes to all his satraps, as the invariable rule of their conduct.

55. D'Herbelot Bibliothèque Orientale, au mot Ardshir. We may observe, that after an ancient period of fables, and a long interval of darkness,

the modern histories of Persia begin to assume an air of truth with the dynasty of the Sassanides.

56. Herodian, l. vi. p. 214. Ammianus Marcellinus, l. xxiii. c. 6. Some differences may be observed between the two historians, the natural effects of the changes produced by a century and a half.

57. The Persians are still the most skilful horsemen, and their horses the finest, in the East.

58. From Herodotus, Xenophon, Herodian, Ammianus, Chardin, etc., I have extracted such *probable* accounts of the Persian nobility, as seem either common to every age, or particular to that of the Sassanides.

Chapter IX

1. The modern philosophers of Sweden seem agreed that the waters of the Baltic gradually sink in a regular proportion, which they have ventured to estimate at half an inch every year. Twenty centuries ago, the flat country of Scandinavia must have been covered by the sea; while the high lands rose above the waters, as so many islands of various forms and dimensions. Such indeed is the notion given us by Mela, Pliny, and Tacitus, of the vast countries round the Baltic. See in the Bibliothèque Raisonnée, tom. xl. and xlv. a large abstract of Dalin's History of Sweden, composed in the Swedish language.

2. In particular, Hume, the Abbé du Bos, and M. Pelloutier, Hist. des Celtes, tom. i.

3. Diodorus Siculus, l. v. p. 340, Edit. Wessel. Herodian, l. vi. p. 221. Jornandes, c. 55. On the banks of the Danube, the wine, when brought to table, was frequently frozen into great lumps, *frusta vini.* Ovid. Epist. ex Ponto, l. iv. 7, 9, 10. Virgil. Georgic. l. iii. 355. The fact is confirmed by a soldier and a philosopher, who had experienced the intense cold of Thrace. Xenophon, Anabasis, l. vii. p. 560. Edit. Hutchinson.

4. Buffon Histoire Naturelle, tom. xii. p. 79, 116.

5. Cæsar de Bell. Gallic. vi. 23, etc. The most inquisitive of the Germans were ignorant of its utmost limits, although some of them had travelled in it more than sixty days' journey.

6. Cluverius (Germania Antiqua, l. iii. c. 47) investigates the small and scattered remains of the Hercynian wood.

7. Charlevoix Histoire du Canada.

8. Olaus Rudbeck asserts that the Swedish women often bear ten or twelve children, and not uncommonly twenty or thirty; but the authority of Rudbeck is much to be suspected.

9. In hos artus, in hæc corpora, quæ miramur, excrescunt. Tacit. Germania, 3, 20. Cluver. l. i. c. 15.

10. Plutarch. in Caius Marius. The Cimbri, by way of amusement, often slid down mountains of snow on their broad shields.

11. The Romans made war in all climates, and by their excellent discipline were in a great measure preserved in health and vigour. It may be remarked, that man is the only animal which can live and multiply in every country from the equator to the poles. The hog seems to approach the nearest to our species in that privilege.

12. Tacit. German. c. 3. The emigration of the Gauls followed the course of the Danube, and discharged itself on Greece and Asia. Tacitus could discover only one inconsiderable tribe that retained any traces of a Gallic origin.

13. His work, entitled Atlantica, is uncommonly scarce. Bayle has given two most curious extracts from it. Republique des Lettres Janvier et Fevrier, 1685.

14. Tacit. Germ. ii. 19. Literarum secreta viri pariter ac fœminæ ignorant. We may rest contented with this decisive authority, without entering into the obscure disputes concerning the antiquity of the Runic characters. The learned Celsius, a Swede, a scholar, and a philosopher, was of opinion, that they were nothing more than the Roman letters, with the curves changed into straight lines for the ease of engraving. See Pelloutier, Histoire des Celtes, l. ii. c. 11. Dictionnaire Diplomatique, tom. i. p. 223. We may add, that the oldest Runic inscriptions are supposed to be of the third century, and the most ancient writer who mentions the Runic characters is Venantius Fortunatus (Carm. vii. 18), who lived towards the end of the sixth century—

Barbara fraxineis pingatur RUNA tabellis.

15. Recherches Philosophiques sur les Americains, tom. iii. p. 228. The author of that very curious work is, if I am not misinformed, a German by birth.

16. The Alexandrian Geographer is often criticised by the accurate Cluverius.

17. See Cæsar, and Whitaker's History of Manchester, vol. i.

18. Tacit. Germ. 15.

19. When the Germans commanded the Ubii of Cologne to cast off the Roman yoke, and with their new freedom to resume their ancient manners, they insisted on the immediate demolition of the walls of the colony. "Postulamus a vobis, muros coloniæ, munimenta servitii detrahatis; etiam fera animalia, si clausa teneas, virtutis obliviscuntur." Tacit. Hist. iv. 64.

20. The straggling villages of Silesia are several miles in length. Cluver. l. i. c. 13.

21. One hundred and forty years after Tacitus, a few more regular structures were erected near the Rhine and Danube. Herodian, l. vii. p. 234.

22. Tacit. Germ. 17.

23. Tacit. Germ. 5.

24. Cæsar de Bell. Gall. vi. 21.

25. Tacit. Germ. 26. Cæsar, vi. 22.

26. Tacit. Germ. 6.

27. It is said that the Mexicans and Peruvians, without the use of either money or iron, had made a very great progress in the arts. Those arts, and the monuments they produced, have been strangely magnified. Recherches sur les Americains, tom. ii. p. 153, etc.

28. Tacit. Germ. 15.

29. Tacit. Germ. 22, 23.

30. Tacit. Germ. 24. The Germans might borrow the *arts* of play from the Romans, but the *passion* is wonderfully inherent in the human species.

31. Tacit. Germ. 14.

32. Plutarch. in Camillus. T. Liv. v. 33.

33. Dubos. Hist. de la Monar. Franç., i. p. 193.

34. The Helvetian nation, which issued from the country called Switzerland, contained, of every age and sex 368,000 persons (Cæsar de Bell. Gall. i. 29). At present, the number of people in the Pays de Vaud (a small district on the banks of the Leman Lake, much more distinguished for politeness than for industry) amounts to 112,591. See an excellent tract of M. Muret, in the Memoires de la Societé de Bern.

35. Paul Diaconus, c. 1, 2, 3. Machiavel, Davila, and the rest of Paul's followers, represent these emigrations too much as regular and concerted measures.

36. Sir William Temple and Montesquieu have indulged, on this subject, the usual liveliness of their fancy.

37. Machiavel Hist. di Firenze, l. i. Mariana Hist. Hispan. l. v. c. 1.

38. Robertson's Charles V. Hume's Political Essays.

39. Tacit. German. 44, 45. Frenshemius (who dedicated his supplement to Livy to Christina of Sweden) thinks proper to be very angry with the Roman who expressed so very little reverence for Northern queens.

40. May we not suspect that superstition was the parent of despotism? The descendants of Odin (whose race was not extinct till the year 1060) are said to have reigned in Sweden above a thousand years. The temple of Upsal was the ancient seat of religion and empire. In the year 1153 I find a singular law, prohibiting the use and profession of arms to any except the king's guards. Is it not probable that it was coloured by the pretence of reviving an old institution? Dalling's History of Sweden in the Bibliothèque Raisonnée, xl. xlv.

41. Tacit. Germ. c. 43.

42. Tacit. Germ. c. 11, 12, 13, etc.

43. Grotius changes an expression of Tacitus, *pertractantur* into *prætractantur*. The correction is equally just and ingenious.

44. Even in *our* ancient parliament, the barons often carried a question, not so much by the number of votes, as by that of their armed followers.

45. Cæsar de Bell. Gall. vi. 23.

46. Minuunt controversias is a very happy expression of Cæsar's.

47. Reges ex nobilitate, duces ex virtute sumunt. Tacit. Germ. 7.

48. Cluver. Germ. Ant. l. i. c. 38.

49. Cæsar, vi. 22. Tacit. Germ. 26.

50. Tacit. Germ. 7.

51. Tacit. Germ. 13, 14.

52. The Spirit of Laws, xxx. 3. The brilliant imagination of Montesquieu is corrected, however, by the dry cold reason of the Abbé de Mably. Observations sur l'Histoire de France, tom. i. p. 356.

53. Gaudent muneribus, sed nec data imputant, nec acceptis obligantur. Tacit. Germ. c. 21.

54. The adulteress was whipped through the village. Neither wealth nor beauty could inspire compassion, or procure her a second husband. Germ. c. 18, 19.

55. Ovid considers the theatre as the best adapted to collect the beauties of Rome, and to melt them into tenderness and sensuality.

56. Tacit. Hist. iv. 61, 65.

57. The marriage present was yoke of oxen, horses, and arms. Germ. c. 18. Tacitus is somewhat too florid on the subject.

58. The change of *exigere* into *exugere* is a most excellent correction.

59. Tacit. Germ. c. 7. Plutarch in Caius Marius. Before the wives of the Teutones destroyed themselves and their children they had offered to surrender on condition that they should be received as the slaves of the vestal virgins.

60. Tacitus has employed a few lines, and Cluverius one hundred and twenty-four pages, on this obscure subject. The former discovers in Germany the gods of Greece and Rome. The latter is positive, that under the emblems of the sun, the moon, and the fire, his pious ancestors worshipped the Trinity in unity.

61. The sacred wood, described with such sublime horror by Lucan, was in the neighborhood of Marseilles; but there were many of the same kind in Germany.

62. Tacit. Germania, c. 7.

63. Tacit. Germania, c. 40.

64. Robertson's Hist. of Charles V. vol. i. note 10.

65. Tacit. Germ. c. 7. These standards were only the heads of wild beasts.

66. Tacit. Annal. xiii. 57.

67. Cæsar, Diodorus, and Lucan seem to ascribe this doctrine to the Gauls, but M. Pelloutier (Histoire des Celtes, l. iii. c. 18) labours to reduce their expressions to a more orthodox sense.

68. Concerning this gross but alluring doctrine of the Edda, see Fable xx. in the curious version of that book, published by M. Mallet, in his Introduction to the History of Denmark.

69. Tacit. Germ. c. 3. Diodor. Sicul. l. v. Strabo, l. iv. p. 197. The classical reader may remember the rank of Demodocus in the Phæacian court, and the ardour infused by Tyrtæus into the fainting

Spartans. Yet there is little probability that the Greeks and the Germans were the same people. Much learned trifling might be spared if our antiquarians would condescend to reflect, that similar manners will naturally be produced by similar situations.

70. Missilia spargunt, Tacit. Germ. c. 6. Either that historian used a vague expression, or he meant that they were thrown at random.

71. It was their principal distinction from the Sarmatians, who generally fought on horseback.

72. The relation of this enterprise occupies a great part of the fourth and fifth books of the History of Tacitus, and is more remarkable for its eloquence than perspicuity. Sir Henry Saville has observed several inaccuracies.

73. Tacit. Hist. iv. 13: like them he had lost an eye.

74. It was contained between the two branches of the old Rhine, as they subsisted before the face of the country was changed by art and nature. Cluver. Germ. Antiq. l. iii. c. 30, 37.

75. Cæsar de Bell. Gall. l. vi. 23.

76. They are mentioned however in the fourth and fifth centuries by Nazarius, Ammianus, Claudian, etc., as a tribe of Franks. Cluver. Germ. Antiq. l. iii. c. xiii.

77. *Urgentibus* is the common reading, but good sense, Lipsius, and some MSS. declare for *Vergentibus*.

78. Tacit. Germania, c. 33. The pious Abbé de la Bleterie is very angry with Tacitus, talks of the devil who was a murderer from the beginning, etc., etc.

79. Many traces of this policy may be discovered in Tacitus and Dion: and many more may be inferred from the principles of human nature.

80. Hist. August. p. 31. Ammian. Marcellin. l. xxxi. c. 5. Aurel. Victor. The emperor Marcus was reduced to sell the rich furniture of the palace, and to enlist slaves and robbers.

81. The Marcomanni, a colony, who, from the banks of the Rhine, occupied Bohemia and Moravia, had once erected a great and formidable monarchy under their king Maroboduus. Strabo, l. vii. Vell. Pat. ii. 105. Tacit. Annal. ii. 63.

82. Wotton (Hist. of Rome, p. 166) increases the prohibition to ten times the distance. His reasoning is specious, but not inclusive. Five miles were sufficient for a fortified barrier.

83. Dion, l. lxxi. and lxxii.

84. See an excellent dissertation on the origin and migrations of nations, in the Mem. de l'Acad. des Inscript. tom. xviii. p. 48-71. It is seldom that the antiquarian and the philosopher are so happily blended.

85. Should we suspect that Athens contained only 21,000 citizens, and Sparta no more than 39,000? See Hume and Wallace on the number of mankind in ancient and modern times.

Chapter X

1. The expression used by Zosimus and Zonaras may signify that Marinus commanded a centenary, a cohort, or a legion.

2. His birth at Bubalia, a little village in Pannonia (Eutrop. ix. Victor in Cæsarib. et epitom.) seems to contradict, unless it was merely accidental, his supposed descent from the Decii. Six hundred years had bestowed nobility on the Decii; but at the commencement of that period they were only Plebeians of merit, and among the first who shared the consulship with the haughty Patricians. Plebeiæ Deciorum animæ, etc. Juvenal, Sat. viii. 254. See the spirited speech of Decius, in Livy, x. 9, 10.

3. Zosimus, l. i. [c. 22] p. 20. Zonaras, l. xii. p. 624.

4. Prefaces of Cassiodorus and Jornandes: it is surprising that the latter should be omitted in the excellent edition published by Grotius, of the Gothic writers.

5. On the authority of Ablavius, Jornandes quotes some old Gothic chronicles in verse. De Reb. Geticis, c. 4.

6. Jornandes c. 3.

7. The Prolegomena of Grotius has some large extracts from Adam of Bremen and Saxo Grammaticus. The former wrote in the year 1077, the latter flourished about the year 1200.

8. Voltaire, Hist. de Charles XII. l. iii. When the Austrians desired the aid of the court of Rome against Gustavus Adolphus, they always represented that conqueror as the lineal successor of Alaric. Harte's Hist. of Gustavus, vol. ii. p. 123.

9. Adam of Bremen in Grotii Prolegomenis, p. 104. The temple of Upsal was destroyed by Ingo king of Sweden, who began his reign in the year 1075, and about fourscore years afterwards a Christian cathedral was erected on its ruins. Dalin's Hist. of Sweden, in Bibliothèque Raisonnée.

10. Mallet, Introd. à l'Hist. du Dannemarc.

11. Mallet. c. iv. p. 55 has collected from Strabo, Pliny, Ptolemy, and Stephanus Byzantinus, the vestiges of such a city and people.

12. This wonderful expedition of Odin, which, by deducing the enmity of the Goths and Romans from so memorable a cause, might supply the noble groundwork of an epic poem, cannot safely be received as authentic history. According to the obvious sense of the Edda, and the interpretation of the most skilful critics, As-gard, instead of denoting a real city of the Asiatic Sarmatia, is the fictitious appellation of the mystic abode of the gods, the Olympus of Scandinavia: from whence the prophet was supposed to descend when he announced his new religion to the Gothic nations,

who were already seated in the southern parts of Sweden.

13. Tacit. Germ. c. 44.

14. Tacit. Annal. ii. 62. If we could yield a firm assent to the navigations of Pytheas of Marseilles, we must allow that the Goths had passed the Baltic at least three hundred years before Christ.

15. Ptolemy, l. ii.

16. By the German colonies who followed the arms of the Teutonic knights. The conquest and conversion of Prussia were completed by those adventurers in the thirteenth century.

17. Pliny (Hist. Natur. iv. 14) and Procopius (in Bell. Vandal. l. i. c. 1) agree in this opinion. They lived in distant ages, and possessed different means of investigating the truth.

18. The *Ostro* and *Visi*, the eastern and western Goths, obtained those denominations from their original seats in Scandinavia. In all their future marches and settlements they preserved, with their names, the same relative situation. When they first departed from Sweden, the infant colony was contained in three vessels. The third being a heavy sailer lagged behind, and the crew, which afterwards swelled into a nation, received from that circumstance the appellation of Gepidæ or Loiterers. Jornandes, c. 17.

19. Fragment of Peter Patricius in the Excerpta Legationum; and with regard to its probable date, Tillemont, Hist. des Empereurs, tom. iii. p. 346.

20. Omnium harum gentium insigne, rotunda scuta, breves gladii, et erga reges obsequium. Tacit. Germania, c. 43. The Goths probably acquired their iron by the commerce of amber.

21. Jornandes, c. 13, 14.

22. The Heruli, and the Uregundi or Burgundi, are particularly mentioned. Mascou's History of the Germans, l. v. A passage in the Augustan History, p. 28, seems to allude to this great emigration. The Marcomannic war was partly occasioned by the pressure of barbarous tribes, who fled before the arms of more northern barbarians.

23. D'Anville, Geographie Ancienne, and the third part of his incomparable map of Europe.

24. Tacit. Germ. c. 46.

25. Cluver. Germ. Antiq. l. iii. c. 43.

26. The Venedi, the *Slavi*, and the Antes, were the three great tribes of the same people. Jornandes, c. 24.

27. Tacitus most assuredly deserves that title, and even his cautious suspense is a proof of his diligent inquiries.

28. Genealogical History of the Tartars, p. 593. Bell (vol. ii. p. 379) traversed the Ukraine in his journey from Petersburgh to Constantinople. The modern face of the country is a just representation of the ancient, since, in the hands of the Cossacks, it still remains in a state of nature.

29. In the sixteenth chapter of Jornandes, instead of *secundo* Mæsiam, we may venture to substitute *secundam*, the second Mæsia, of which Marcianopolis was certainly the capital (Hierocles

de Provinciis, and Wesseling ad locum, p. 636 Itinerar.). It is surprising how this palpable error of the scribe could escape the judicious correction of Grotius.

30. The place is still called Nicop. The little stream, on whose banks it stood, falls into the Danube. D'Anville, Geographie Ancienne, tom. i. p. 307.

31. Stephan. Byzant. de Urbibus, p. 740. Wesseling Itinerar. p. 136. Zonaras, by an odd mistake, ascribes the foundation of Philippopolis to the immediate predecessor of Decius.

32. Ammian. xxxi. 5.

33. Aurel. Victor [de Cæsar], c. 29.

34. *Victoriæ Carpicæ*, on some medals of Decius, insinuate these advantages.

35. Claudius (who afterwards reigned with so much glory) was posted in the pass of Thermopylæ with 200 Dardanians, 100 heavy and 160 light horse, 60 Cretan archers, and 1000 well armed recruits. See an original letter from the emperor to his officer, in the Augustan History, p. 200. [Trebell. Pollio in Claud. c. 16.]

36. Jornandes, c. 16-18. Zosimus, l. i. [c. 22] p. 22. In the general account of this war, it is easy to discover the opposite prejudices of the Gothic and the Grecian writers. In carelessness alone they are alike.

37. Montesquieu, Grandeur et Decadence des Romains, c. viii. He illustrates the nature and use of the censorship with his usual ingenuity, and with uncommon precision.

38. Vespasian and Titus were the last censors (Pliny, Hist. Natur. vii. 49. Censorinus de Die Natali). The modesty of Trajan refused an honour which he deserved, and his example became a law to the Antonines. Pliny's Panegyric, c. 45 and 60.

39. Yet in spite of this exemption Pompey appeared before that tribunal during his consulship. The occasion indeed was equally singular and honourable. Plutarch in Pompey.

40. Original speech, in the Augustan Hist. p. 173, 174 [Treb. Poll. c. 2].

41. This transaction might deceive Zonaras, who supposes that Valerian was actually declared the colleague of Decius, l. xii. p. 625.

42. Hist. August. p. 174 [Treb. Poll. l. c.] The emperor's reply is omitted.

43. Such as the attempts of Augustus towards a reformation of manners. Tacit. Annal. iii. 24.

44. Tillemont, Histoire des Empereurs, tom. iii. p. 598. As Zosimus and some of his followers mistake the Danube for the Tanais, they place the field of battle in the plains of Scythia.

45. Aurelius Victor allows two distinct actions for the deaths of the two Decii; but I have preferred the account of Jornandes.

46. I have ventured to copy from Tacitus (Annal. i. 64) the picture of a similar engagement between a Roman army and a German tribe.

47. Jornandes, c. 18. Zosimus, l. i. [c. 23] p. 22.

Zonaras, l. xii. [c. 20] p. 627. Aurelius Victor. [Epitome c. 29].

48. The Decii were killed before the end of the year two hundred and fifty-one, since the new princes took possession of the consulship on the ensuing calends of January.

49. Hist. August. p. 223 [Vopesc. Aur. c. 42] gives them a very honourable place among the small number of good emperors who reigned between Augustus and Diocletian.

50. Hæc ubi Patres comperere . . . decernunt. Victor in Cæsaribus [c. 30].

51. Zonaras, l. xii. [c. 21] p. 628.

52. A *Sella*, a *Toga*, and a golden *Patera* of five pounds weight, were accepted with joy and gratitude by the wealthy king of Egypt (Livy, xxvii. 4). *Quina Millia Æris*, a weight of copper in value about eighteen pounds sterling, was the usual present made to foreign ambassadors (Livy, xxxi. 9).

53. See the firmness of a Roman general so late as the time of Alexander Severus, in the Excerpta Legationum, p. 25, edit. Louvre.

54. Jornandes, c. 19, and Victor in Cæsaribus.

55. These improbable accusations are alleged by Zosimus, l. i. p. 23, 24.

56. Jornandes, c. 19. The Gothic writer at least observed the peace which his victorious countrymen had sworn to Gallus.

57. Zosimus, l. i. p. 25, 26.

58. Victor in Cæsaribus, [c. 30].

59. Zonaras, l. xii. p. 628.

60. Banduri Numismata, p. 94.

61. Eutropius, l. ix. c. 6 says tertio mense. Eusebius omits this emperor.

62. Zosimus, l. i. p. 28. Eutropius and Victor station Valerian's army in Rhætia.

63. He was about seventy at the time of his accession, or, as it is more probable, of his death. Hist. August. p. 173. Tillemont, Hist. des Empereurs, tom. iii. p. 893, note 1.

64. Inimicus Tyrannorum. Hist. August. p. 173. In the glorious struggle of the senate against Maximin, Valerian acted a very spirited part. Hist. August. p. 156.

65. According to the distinction of Victor, he seems to have received the title of *Imperator* from the army, and that of Augustus from the senate.

66. From Victor and from the medals, Tillemont (tom. iii. p. 710) very justly infers that Gallienus was associated to the empire about the month of August of the year 253.

67. Various systems have been formed to explain a difficult passage in Gregory of Tours, l. i. c. 9.

68. The Geographer of Ravenna, i. 11, by mentioning *Mauringania* on the confines of Denmark, as the ancient seat of the Franks, gave birth to an ingenious system of Leibnitz.

69. Cluver. Germania Antiqua, l. iii. c. 20. M. Freret, in the Memoires des l'Academie des Inscriptions, tom. xviii.

70. Most probably under the reign of Gordian,

from an accidental circumstance fully canvassed by Tillemont, tom. iii. p. 710, 1181.

71. Plin. Hist. Natur. xvi. 1. The panegyrists frequently allude to the morasses of the Franks.

72. Tacit. Germania, c. 30, 37.

73. In a subsequent period, most of those old names are occasionally mentioned. See some vestiges of them in Cluver. Germ. Antiq. l. iii.

74. Simler de Republica Helvet. cum notis Fuselin.

75. Zosimus, l. i. p. 27.

76. M. de Brequigny (Mem. de l'Acad. tom. xxx.) has given us a very curious life of Posthumus. A series of the Augustan History from Medals and Inscriptions has been more than once planned, and is still much wanted.

77. Aurel. Victor, c. 33. Instead of *Pæne direpto*, both the sense and the expression require *deleto;* though, indeed, for different reasons, it is alike difficult to correct the text of the best, and the worst, writers.

78. In the time of Ausonius (the end of the fourth century) Herda or Lerida was in a very ruinous state, which probably was the consequence of this invasion. Aus. ep. 25, 8.

79. Valesius is therefore mistaken in supposing that the Franks had invaded Spain by the sea.

80. Aurel. Victor. Eutrop. ix. 6.

81. Tacit. Germania, 38.

82. Cluver. Germ. Antiq. iii. 25.

83. Sic Suevi a cateri Germanus, sic suevorum ingenui, a Servis separantur—A proud separation.

84. Cæsar in Bello Gallico, iv. 7.

85. Victor in Caracal. [c. 21]. Dion. Cassius, lxvii. [c. 13] p. 1350.

86. This etymology (far different from those which amuse the fancy of the learned) is preserved by Asinius Quadratus, an original historian, quoted by Agathias, i. c. 5.

87. The Suevi engaged Cæsar in this manner, and the manœuvre deserved the approbation of the conqueror (Bell. Gall. i. 48.)

88. Hist. August. p. 215, 216. [Vopis. Aurel. c. 18, 21]. Dexippus in the Excerpta Legationum, p. 8. Hieronym. Chron. Orosius, vii. 22.

89. Zosimus, l. i. p. 34.

90. Aurel. Victor, in Gallieno et Probo. His complaints breathe an uncommon spirit of freedom.

91. Zonaras, l. xii. p. 631.

92. One of the Victors calls him King of the Marcomanni; the other, of the Germans.

93. Tillemont, Hist. des Empereurs, tom. iii. p. 398, etc.

94. See Lives of Claudius, Aurelian, and Probus, in the Augustan History.

95. It is about half a league in breadth. Genealogical History of the Tartars, p. 598.

96. M. de Peyssonel, who had been French consul at Caffa, in his Observations sur les Peuples Barbares, qui ont habité les bords du Danube.

97. Euripides in Iphigenia Among the Tauri.

98. Strabo, l. vii. p. 309. The first kings of Bosphorus were the allies of Athens.

99. Appian in Mithridat.

100. It was reduced by the arms of Agrippa. Orosius, vi. 21. Eutropius, vii. 9. The Romans once advanced within three days' march of the Tanais. Tacit. Annal. xii. 17.

101. See the Toxaris of Lucian, if we credit the sincerity and the virtues of the Scythian, who relates a great war of his nation against the kings of Bosphorus.

102. Zosimus, l. i. p. 28.

103. Strabo, l. xi. Tacit. Hist. iii. 47.—They were called *Camaræ*.

104. See a very natural picture of the Euxine navigation, in the sixteenth letter of Tournefort.

105. Arrian places the frontier garrison at Dioscurias, or Sebastopolis, forty-four miles to the east of Pityus. The garrison of Phasis consisted in his time of only four hundred foot. Periplus of the Euxine.

106. Zosimus, l. i. p. 30.

107. Arrian (in Periplo Maris Euxin. p. 130) calls the distance 2610 stadia.

108. Xenophon. Anabasis, l. iv. [c. 8, 22] p. 348.

109. Arrian, p. 129. The general observation is Tournefort's.

110. Epistle of Gregory Thaumaturgus, bishop of Neo-Cæsarea, quoted by Mascon, v. 37.

111. Zosimus, l. i. [c. 33] p. 32, 33.

112. Itiner. Hierosolym. p. 572. Wesseling.

113. Zosimus, l. i. [c. 35] p. 32, 33.

114. He besieged the place with 400 galleys, 150,000 foot, and a numerous cavalry. Plutarch in Lucul. [c. 9]. Appian in Mithridat. Cicero pro Lege Maniliâ, c. 8.

115. Strabo, l. xii. p. 573.

116. Pocock's Description of the East, l. ii. c. 23, 24.

117. Zosimus, l. i. [c. 35] p. 33.

118. Syncellus tells an unintelligible story of Prince *Odenathus*, who defeated the Goths, and who was killed by Prince *Odenathus* [p. 382, ed. Paris].

119. Voyages de Chardin, tom. i. p. 45. He sailed with the Turks from Constantinople to Caffa.

120. Syncellus (p. 382) speaks of this expedition as undertaken by the Heruli.

121. Strabo, l. xi. p. 495.

122. Plin. Hist. Natur. iii. 7.

123. Hist. August. p. 181. Victor, c. 33. Orosius, vii. 42. Zosimus, l. i. [c. 39] p. 35. Zonaras, l. xii. [c. 26] 635. Syncellus, p. 382 [vol. i. p. 717, ed. Bonn]. It is not without some attention, that we can explain and conciliate their imperfect hints. We can still discover some traces of the partiality of Dexippus, in the relation of his own and his countrymen's exploits.

124. Syncellus, p. 382. This body of Heruli was for a long time faithful and famous.

125. Claudius, who commanded on the Danube, thought with propriety and acted with spirit.

His colleague was jealous of his fame. Hist. August. p. 181.

126. Jornandes, c. 20.

127. Zosimus and the Greeks (as the author of the Philopatris) give the name of Scythians to those whom Jornandes, and the Latin writers, constantly represent as Goths.

128. Hist. August. p. 178. Jornandes, c. 20.

129. Strabo, l. xiv. p. 640. Vitruvius, l. i. c. 1, præfat. l. vii. Tacit. Annal. iii. 61. Plin. Hist. Nat. xxxvi. 14.

130. The length of St. Peter's is 840 Roman palms; each palm is very little short of nine English inches. Greaves's Miscellanies, vol. i. p. 233; On the Roman foot.

131. The policy, however, of the Romans induced them to abridge the extent of the sanctuary or asylum, which by successive privileges had spread itself two stadia round the temple. Strabo, l. xiv. p. 641. Tacit. Annal. iii. 60, etc.

132. They offered no sacrifices to the Grecian gods. Epistol. Gregor. Thaumat.

133. Zonaras, l. xii. p. 635. Such an anecdote was perfectly suited to the taste of Montaigne. He makes use of it in his agreeable Essay on Pedantry, l. i. c. 24.

134. Moses Chorenensis, l. ii. c. 71, 73, 74. Zonaras, l. xii. p. 628. The authentic relation of the Armenian historian serves to rectify the confused account of the Greek. The latter talks of the children of Tiridates, who at that time was himself an infant.

135. Hist. August. p. 191. As Macrinus was an enemy to the Christians, they charged him with being a magician.

136. Zosimus, l. i. p. 33. Hist. August. p. 174.

137. Victor. in Cæsar. Eutropius, ix. 7.

138. Zosimus, l. i. p. 33. Zonaras, l. xii. p. 630. Peter Patricius in the Excerpta Legat. p. 20.

139. Hist. August. p. 185. The reign of Cyriades appears in that collection prior to the death of Valerian; but I have preferred a probable series of events to the doubtful chronology of a most inaccurate writer.

140. The sack of Antioch, anticipated by some historians, is assigned, by the decisive testimony of Ammianus Marcellinus, to the reign of Gallienus, xxiii. 5.

141. Zosimus, l. i. [c. 36] p. 35.

142. John Malala, tom. i. p. 391 [ed. Oxon.; p. 127, ed. Ven.; p. 296, ed. Bonn]. He corrupts this probable event by some fabulous circumstances.

143. Zonaras, l. xii. p. 630. Deep valleys were filled up with the slain. Crowds of prisoners were driven to water like beasts, and many perished for want of food.

144. Zosimus, l. i. p. 25, asserts that Sapor, had he not preferred spoil to conquest, might have remained master of Asia.

145. Peter Patricius in Excerpt. Leg. p. 29.

146. Syrorum agrestium manû. Sextus Rufus, c. 23. Rufus Victor, the Augustan History (p.

192), and several inscriptions agree in making Odenathus a citizen of Palmyra.

147. He possessed so powerful an interest among the wandering tribes, that Procopius (Bellersic, l. ii. c. 5) and John Malala (tom. i. p. 391) style him prince of the Saracens.

148. Peter Patricius, p. 25.

149. The pagan writers lament, the Christian insult, the misfortunes of Valerian. Their various testimonies are accurately collected by Tillemont, tom. iii. p. 739, etc. So little has been preserved of eastern history before Mahomet, that the modern Persians are totally ignorant of the victory of Sapor, an event so glorious to their nation. Bibliothèque Orientale.

150. One of these epistles is from Artavasdes, king of Armenia: since Armenia was then a province in Persia, the king, the kingdom, and the epistle, must be fictitious.

151. See his Life in the Augustan History.

152. There is still extant a very pretty Epithalamium, composed by Gallienus for the nuptials of his nephews:—

Ite ait, O Juvenes, pariter surdate medullis

Omnibus, inter vos; non murmura vestra columbæ,

Brachia non hederæ, non vincant oscula conchæ.

153. He was on the point of giving Plotinus a ruined city of Campania, to try the experiment of realising Plato's Republic. Life of Plotinus, by Porphyry, in Fabricius's Biblioth. Græc. l. iv.

154. A medal which bears the head of Gallienus has perplexed the antiquarians by its legend and reverse; the former *Gallienæ Augustæ*, the latter *Ubique Pax*. M. Spanheim supposes that the coin was struck by some of the enemies of Gallienus, and was designed as a severe satire on that effeminate prince. But as the use of irony may seem unworthy of the gravity of the Roman mint, M. de Vallemont has deduced from a passage of Trebellius Pollio (Hist. August. p. 198) an ingenious and natural solution. *Galliena* was first cousin to the emperor. By delivering Africa from the usurper Celsus, she deserved the title of Augusta. On a medal in the French king's collection, we read a similar inscription of *Faustina Augusta* round the head of Marcus Aurelius. With regard to the *Ubique Pax*, it is easily explained by the vanity of Gallienus, who seized, perhaps, the occasion of some momentary calm. Nouvelles de la Republique des Lettres, Janvier 1700, p. 21-34.

155. This singular character has, I believe, been fairly transmitted to us. The reign of his immediate successor was short and busy; and the historians who wrote before the elevation of the family of Constantine could not have the most remote interest to misrepresent the character of Gallienus.

156. Pollio expresses the most minute anxiety to complete the number.

157. The place of his reign is somewhat doubtful: but there *was* a tyrant in Pontus, and we are acquainted with the seat of all the others.

158. Tillemont, tom. iii. p. 1163, reckons them somewhat differently.

159. Speech of Marius, in the Augustan History, p. 197. [Pollio. xxx. Tyranni de Mario.] The accidental identity of names was the only circumstance that could tempt Pollio to imitate Sallust.

160. Vos, O Pompilius sanguis; is Horace's address to the Pisos. Art. Poet. v. 292, with Dacier's and Sanadon's notes.

161. Tacit. Annal. xv. 48. Hist. i. 15. In the former of these passages we may venture to change *paterna* into *materna*. In every generation from Augustus to Alexander Severus, one or more Pisos appear as consuls. A Piso was deemed worthy of the throne by Augustus (Tacit. Annal. i. 13). A second headed a formidable conspiracy against Nero; and a third was adopted, and declared Cæsar by Galba.

162. Hist. August. p. 195. The senate, in a moment of enthusiasm, seems to have presumed on the approbation of Gallienus.

163. Hist. August. p. 196.

164. The association of the brave Palmyrenian was the most popular act of the whole reign of Gallienus. Hist. August. p. 180.

165. Gallienus had given the titles of Cæsar and Augustus to his son Saloninus, slain at Cologne by the usurper Posthumus. A second son of Gallienus succeeded to the name and rank of his elder brother. Valerian, the brother of Gallienus, was also associated to the empire: several other brothers, sisters, nephews, and nieces of the emperor, formed a very numerous royal family. Tillemont, tom. iii. and M. de Brequigny in the Memoires de l'Academie, tom. xxxii. p. 262.

166. Hist. August. p. 188.

167. Regillianus had some bands of Roxolani in his service. Posthumus a body of Franks. It was perhaps in the character of auxiliaries that the latter introduced themselves into Spain.

168. The Augustan History, p. 177, calls it *servile bellum*. Diodor. Sicul. l. xxxiv.

169. Plin. Hist. Natur. v. 10.

170. Diodor. Sicul. l. xvii. [c. 52] p. 590. Edit. Wesseling.

171. See a very curious letter of Hadrian in Aug. Hist. [Vopis. Sat. c. 8] p. 245.

172. Such as the sacrilegious murder of a divine cat. Diodor Sicul. l. i. [c. 83].

173. Hist. August. p. 195. This long and terrible sedition was first occasioned by a dispute between a soldier and a townsman about a pair of shoes.

174. Dionysius apud Euseb. Hist. Eccl. v. vii. p. 21. Ammian. xxii. 16.

175. Scaliger, Animadver. ad Euseb. Chron. p. 258. Three dissertations of M. Bonamy in the Mem. de l'Academie, tom. ix.

176. Strabo. l. xii. p. 569.

177. Hist. August. p. 197 [xxiv. 25].

178. See Cellarius, Georg. Antiq. tom. ii. p. 137, upon the limits of Isauria.

179. Hist. August. p. 177 [xxiii. 5].

180. Hist. August. p. 177. Zosimus, l. i. p. 24, 26. Zonaras, l. xii. p. 623. Euseb. Chronicon. Victor in Epitom. Victor in Cæsar [c. 33]. Eutropius, ix. 5. Orosius, vii. 21.

181. Euseb. Hist. Eccles. vii. 21. The fact is taken from the Letters of Dionysius, who, in the time of those troubles, was bishop of Alexandria.

182. In a great number of parishes 11,000 persons were found between fourteen and eighty: 5305 between forty and seventy. See Buffon, Histoire Naturelle, tom. ii. p. 500.

Chapter XI

1. *Pons Aureoli*, thirteen miles from Bergamo, and thirty-two from Milan. See Cluver. Italia Antiq. tom. i. p. 245. Near this place, in the year 1703, the obstinate battle of Cassano was fought between the French and Austrians. The excellent relation of the Chevalier de Folard, who was present, gives a very distinct idea of the ground. See Polybe de Folard, tom. iii. p. 223-248.

2. On the death of Gallienus, see Trebellius Pollio in Hist. August. p. 181. [Gallieni II., c. 14.] Zosimus, l. i. [c. 40] p. 37. Zonaras, l. xii. [c. 25] p. 634. [ed. Paris; p. 602, ed. Bonn]. Eutrop. ix. 8. Aurelius Victor in Epitom. [c. 33.] Victor in Cæsar. [c. 33.] I have compared and blended them all, but have chiefly followed Aurelius Victor, who seems to have had the best memoirs.

3. Some supposed him, oddly enough, to be a bastard of the younger Gordian. Others took advantage of the province of Dardania to deduce his origin from Dardanus and the ancient kings of Troy.

4. *Notoria*, a periodical and official despatch which the emperors received from the *frumentarii*, or agents dispersed through the provinces. Of these we may speak hereafter.

5. Hist. August. p. 208. [Pollio, Claud. c. 17.] Gallienus describes the plate, vestments, etc., like a man who loved and understood those splendid trifles.

6. Julian (Orat. i. p. 6) affirms that Claudius acquired the empire in a just and even holy manner. But we may distrust the partiality of a kinsman.

7. Hist. August. p. 203. [Pollio, Claud. c. 5.] There are some trifling differences concerning the circumstances of the last defeat and death of Aureolus.

8. Aurelius Victor in Gallien. [De Cæsar. c. 33.] The people loudly prayed for the damnation of Gallienus. The senate decreed that his relations and servants should be thrown down headlong from the Gemonian stairs. An obnoxious officer of the revenue had his eyes torn out whilst under examination.

9. Zonaras, l. xii. [c. 26] p. 635 [ed. Paris; p. 604, ed. Bonn].

10. Zonaras on this occasion mentions Posthumus; but the registers of the senate (Hist. August. p. 203. [Pollio. Claud. c. 4]) prove that Tetricus was already emperor of the western provinces.

11. The Augustan History mentions the smaller, Zonaras the larger, number; the lively fancy of Montesquieu induced him to prefer the latter.

12. Trebell. Pollio in Hist. August. p. 204 [Claud. c. 7].

13. Hist. August. in Claud. Aurelian. et Prob. Zosimus, l. i. [c. 42-46] p. 38-42. Zonaras, l. xii. [c. 26], p. 636 [ed. Paris; p. 605, ed. Bonn]. Aurel. Victor in Epitom. Victor Junior in Cæsar. Eutrop. ix. 8. Euseb. in Chron. [An. CCLXXI.]

14. According to Zonaras (l. xii. [c. 26] p. 636 [ed. Par.; p. 605, ed. Bonn]) Claudius, before his death, invested him with the purple; but this singular fact is rather contradicted than confirmed by other writers.

15. See the Life of Claudius by Pollio, and the Orations of Mamertinus, Eumenius, and Julian. See likewise the Cæsars of Julian, p. 313. In Julian it was not adulation, but superstition and vanity.

16. Zosimus, l. i. [c. 47] p. 42. Pollio (Hist. August. p. 206 [Claud. c. 12]) allows him virtues, and says, that, like Pertinax, he was killed by the licentious soldiers. According to Dexippus, he died of a disease.

17. Theoclius (as quoted in the Augustan History, p. 211 [Vopisc. Aurel. c. 6]) affirms that in one day he killed with his own hand forty-eight Sarmatians, and in several subsequent engagements nine hundred and fifty. This heroic valour was admired by the soldiers, and celebrated in their rude songs, the burden of which was *mille, mille, mille, occidit.*

18. Acholius (ap. Hist. August. p. 213 [Vopisc. Aurel. c. 13]) describes the ceremony of the adoption, as it was performed at Byzantium, in the presence of the emperor and his great officers.

19. Hist. August. p. 211 [Vopisc. Aurel. c. 7]. This laconic epistle is truly the work of a soldier; it abounds with military phrases and words, some of which cannot be understood without difficulty. *Ferramenta samiata* is well explained by Salmasius. The former of the words means all weapons of offence, and is contrasted with *Arma*, defensive armour. The latter signifies keen and well sharpened.

20. Zosimus, l. i. [c. 48, p. 43] p. 45.

21. Dexippus (ap. Excerpta Legat. p. 12 [ed. Paris; p. 8, ed. Ven.; p. 19, ed. Bonn]) relates the whole transaction under the name of Vandals. Aurelian married one of the Gothic ladies to his general Bonosus, who was able to drink with the Goths and discover their secrets. Hist. August. p. 247. [Vopisc. Bonosus, c. 15.]

22. Hist. August. p. 222. [Vopisc. Aurel. c. 39.] Eutrop. ix. 15 [c. 9]. Sextus Rufus, c. 8. Lactantius de Mortibus Persecutorum, c. 9.

23. The Wallachians still preserve many traces of the Latin language, and have boasted, in every age, of their Roman descent. They are surrounded by, but not mixed with, the barbarians. See a Memoir of M. d'Anville on ancient Dacia, in the Academy of Inscriptions, tom. xxx.

24. See the first chapter of Jornandes. The Vandals, however (c. 22), maintained a short independence between the rivers Marisia and Grissia (Maros and Keres), which fell into the Theiss.

25. Dexippus, p. 7-12 [ed. Paris; p. 5, *sqq.* ed. Ven.; p. 11, *sqq.* ed. Bonn]. Zosimus, l. i. [c. 49] p. 43. Vopiscus in Aurelian. in Hist. August. However these historians differ in names (Alemanni, Juthungi, and Marcomanni), it is evident that they mean the same people and the same war; but it requires some care to conciliate and explain them.

26. Cantoclarus, with his usual accuracy, chooses to translate three hundred thousand; his version is equally repugnant to sense and to grammar.

27. We may remark, as an instance of bad taste, that Dexippus applies to the light infantry of the Alemanni the technical terms proper only to the Grecian phalanx.

28. In Dexippus we at present read Rhodanus: M. de Valois very judiciously alters the word to Eridanus.

29. The emperor Claudius was certainly of the number; but we are ignorant how far this mark of respect was extended; if to Cæsar and Augustus, it must have produced a very awful spectacle; a long line of the masters of the world.

30. Vopiscus in Hist. August. p. 210. [Aurel. c. 6.]

31. Dexippus gives them a subtle and prolix oration, worthy of a Grecian sophist.

32. Hist. August. p. 215. [Vopisc. Aurel. c. 18.]

33. Dexippus, p. 12 [ed. Paris; p. 8, ed. Ven.; p. 21, ed. Bonn].

34. Victor Junior in Aurelian [Epit. 35, 2].

35. Vopiscus in Hist. August. p. 216. [Aurel. c. 21.]

36. The little river, or rather torrent, of Metaurus, near Fano, has been immortalised by finding such an historian as Livy, and such a poet as Horace.

37. It is recorded by an inscription found at Pesaro. See Gruter, cclxxvi. 3.

38. One should imagine, he said, that you were assembled in a Christian church, not in the temple of all the gods.

39. Vopiscus, in Hist. August. p. 215, 216 [Aurel. c. 18, *sqq.*], gives a long account of these ceremonies from the registers of the senate.

40. Plin. Hist. Natur. iii. 5 [§ 9]. To confirm our idea, we may observe that for a long time Mount Cælius was a grove of oaks, and Mount Viminal was overrun with osiers; that in the fourth century the Aventine was a vacant and solitary retirement;

that till the time of Augustus the Esquiline was an unwholesome burying-ground; and that the numerous inequalities remarked by the ancients in the Quirinal sufficiently prove that it was not covered with buildings. Of the seven hills, the Capitoline and Palatine only, with the adjacent valleys, were the primitive habitation of the Roman people. But this subject would require a dissertation.

41. Exspatiantia tecta multas addidere urbes, is the expression of Pliny.

42. Hist. August. p. 222. [Vopisc. Aurel. c. 39.] Both Lipsius and Isaac Vossius have eagerly embraced this measure.

43. See Nardini, Roma Antica, l. i. c. 8.

44. Tacit. Hist. iv. 23.

45. For Aurelian's walls, see Vopiscus in Hist. August. p. 216, 222. [Aurel. c. 21 and 39.] Zosimus, l. i. [c. 49] p. 43. Eutropius, ix. 15 [9]. Aurel. Victor in Aurelian. Victor Junior in Aurelian. Euseb. Hieronym. et Idatius in Chronic.

46. His competitor was Lollianus, or Ælianus, if, indeed, these names mean the same person. See Tillemont, tom. iii. p. 1177.

47. The character of this prince by Julius Aterianus (ap. Hist. August. p. 187 [Pollio, xxx. Tyranni, c. 5]) is worth transcribing, as it seems fair and impartial. Victorino, qui post Junium Posthumum Gallias rexit, neminem existimo præferendum; non in virtute Trajanum; non Antoninum in clementia: non in gravitate Nervam: non in gubernando ærario Vespasianum; non in censura totius vitæ ac severitate militari Pertinacem vel Severum. Sed omnia hæc libido et cupiditas voluptatis mulierariæ sic perdidit, ut nemo audeat virtutes ejus in literas mittere quem constat omnium judicio meruisse puniri.

48. He ravished the wife of Attitianus, an *actuary*, or army agent. Hist. August. p. 186. [Pollio, l. c.] Aurel. Victor in Aurelian.

49. Pollio assigns her an article among the thirty tyrants. Hist. August. p. 200. [xxx. Tyranni, c. 30.]

50. Pollio in Hist. August. p. 196. [xxx. Tyranni, c. 23.] Vopiscus in Hist. August. p. 220. [Aurel. c. 32.] The two Victors, in the lives of Gallienus and Aurelian. Eutrop. ix. 13 [c. 9]. Euseb. in Chron. Of all these writers, only the two last (but with strong probability) place the fall of Tetricus before that of Zenobia. M. de Boze (in the Academy of Inscriptions, tom. xxx.) does not wish, and Tillemont (tom. iii. p. 1189) does not dare, to follow them. I have been fairer than the one, and bolder than the other.

51. Victor Junior in Aurelian. Eumenius mentions *Batavicæ;* some critics, without any reason, would fain alter the word to *Bagaudicæ.*

52. Eumen. in Vet. Panegyr. iv. 8.

53. Vopiscus in Hist. August. p. 246 [in Proculo, c. 13]. Autun was not restored till the reign of Diocletian. See Eumenius de restaurandis scholis.

54. Almost everything that is said of the manners of Odenathus and Zenobia is taken from their

Lives in the Augustan History, by Trebellius Pollio: see p. 192, 198 [xxx. Tyranni, c. 14 and 29].

55. She never admitted her husband's embraces but for the sake of posterity. If her hopes were baffled, in the ensuing *month* she reiterated the experiment.

56. Hist. August. p. 192, 193. [Pollio, xxx. Tyranni, c. 14.] Zosimus, l. i. [c. 39] p. 36. Zonaras, l. xii. [c. 24] p. 633 [ed. Paris; p. 600, ed. Bonn]. The last is clear and probable, the others confused and inconsistent. The text of Syncellus, if not corrupt, is absolute nonsense.

57. Odenathus and Zenobia often sent him, from the spoils of the enemy, presents of gems and toys, which he received with infinite delight.

58. Some very unjust suspicions have been cast on Zenobia, as if she was accessory to her husband's death.

59. Hist. August. p. 180, 181. [Pollio, Gallieni II. c. 13.]

60. See in Hist. August. p. 198 [Pollio, xxx. Tyranni, c. 29], Aurelian's testimony to her merit; and for the conquest of Egypt, Zosimus, l. i. [c. 44] p. 39, 40.

61. Timolaus, Herennianus, and Vabalathus. It is supposed that the two former were already dead before the war. On the last, Aurelian bestowed a small province of Armenia, with the title of King; several of his medals are still extant. See Tillemont, tom. iii. p. 1190.

62. Zosimus, l. i. [c. 50] p. 44.

63. Vopiscus (in Hist. August. p. 217 [Aurel. c. 23, *seq.*]) gives us an authentic letter, and a doubtful vision, of Aurelian. Apollonius of Tyana was born about the same time as Jesus Christ. His life (that of the former) is related in so fabulous a manner by his disciples, that we are at a loss to discover whether he was a sage, an impostor, or a fanatic.

64. Zosimus, l. i. [c. 54] p. 46.

65. At a place called Immæ. Eutropius, Sextus Rufus, and Jerome mention only this first battle.

66. Vopiscus, in Hist. August. p. 217 [Aurel. c. 25], mentions only the second.

67. Zosimus, l. i. [c. 50, *sqq.*] p. 44–48. His account of the two battles is clear and circumstantial.

68. It was five hundred and thirty-seven miles from Seleucia, and two hundred and three from the nearest coast of Syria, according to the reckoning of Pliny, who, in a few words (Hist. Natur. v. 25), gives an excellent description of Palmyra.

69. Some English travellers from Aleppo *discovered* the ruins of Palmyra about the end of the last century. Our curiosity has since been gratified in a more splendid manner by Messieurs Wood and Dawkins. For the history of Palmyra we may consult the masterly dissertation of Dr. Halley in the Philosophical Transactions: Lowthorp's Abridgment, vol. iii. p. 518.

70. Vopiscus in Hist. August. p. 218. [Aurel. c. 26.]

71. From a very doubtful chronology I have endeavoured to extract the most probable date.

72. Hist. August. p. 218. [Vopisc. Aurel. c. 28.] Zosimus, l. i. [c. 55] p. 50. Though the camel is a heavy beast of burden, the dromedary, which is either of the same or of a kindred species, is used by the natives of Asia and Africa on all occasions which require celerity. The Arabs affirm that he will run over as much ground in one day as their fleetest horses can perform in eight or ten. See Buffon, Hist. Naturelle, tom. xi. p. 222; and Shaw's Travels, p. 167.

73. Pollio in Hist. August. p. 199. [xxx. Tyranni, de Zenobia, c. 29.]

74. Vopiscus in Hist. August. p. 219. [Aurel. c. 30.] Zosimus, l. i. [c. 56, p. 49] p. 51.

75. Hist. August. p. 219. [Vopisc. Aurel. c. 31.]

76. See Vopiscus in Hist. August. p. 220, 242. [Aurel. c. 32; Firmus, c. 2.] As an instance of luxury, it is observed that he had glass windows. He was remarkable for his strength and appetite, his courage and dexterity. From the letter of Aurelian we may justly infer that Firmus was the last of the rebels, and consequently that Tetricus was already suppressed.

77. See the triumph of Aurelian, described by Vopiscus. He relates the particulars with his usual minuteness; and on this occasion they *happen* to be interesting. Hist. August. p. 220. [Vopisc. Aurel. c. 33, *seq.*]

78. Among barbarous nations women have often combated by the side of their husbands. But it is *almost* impossible that a society of Amazons should ever have existed either in the old or new world.

79. The use of *braccæ*, breeches, or trousers, was still considered in Italy as a Gallic and barbarian fashion. The Romans, however, had made great advances towards it. To encircle the legs and thighs with *fasciæ*, or bands, was understood, in the time of Pompey and Horace, to be a proof of ill health or effeminacy. In the age of Trajan the custom was confined to the rich and luxurious. It gradually was adopted by the meanest of the people. See a very curious note of Casaubon, ad. Sueton. in August. c. 82.

80. Most probably the former; the latter, seen on the medals of Aurelian, only denote (according to the learned Cardinal Noris) an oriental victory.

81. The expression of Calpurnius (Eclog. i. 50), Nullos ducet *captiva* triumphos, as applied to Rome, contains a very manifest allusion and censure.

82. Vopiscus in Hist. August. p. 199. [xxx. Tyranni, Zenobia, c. 29.] Hieronym. in Chron. Prosper in Chron. Baronius supposes that Zenobius, bishop of Florence in the time of St. Ambrose, was of her family.

83. Vopisc. in Hist. August. p. 222. [Aurel. c. 39.] Eutropius, ix. 13 [9]. Victor Junior. But Pollio, in Hist. August. p. 196 [xxx. Tyranni, de Tetrico, sen. c. 23], says that Tetricus was made corrector of all Italy.

84. Hist. August. p. 197. [Vopisc. xxx. Tyranni, de Tetrico jun. c. 24.]

85. Vopiscus in Hist. August. 222. [Aurel. c. 39.] Zosimus, l. i. [c. 61, p. 53] p. 56. He placed it in the images of Belus and of the Sun, which he has brought from Palmyra. It was dedicated in the fourth year of his reign (Euseb. in Chron. [an. CCLXXV.]), but was most assuredly begun immediately on his accession.

86. See in the Augustan History, p. 210 [Vopisc. Aurel. c. 5], the omens of his fortune. His devotion to the sun appears in his letters, on his medals, and is mentioned in the Cæsars of Julian. Commentaire de Spanheim, p. 109.

87. Vopiscus in Hist. August. p. 221 [Aurel. c. 37.]

88. Hist. August. p. 222. [Vopisc. Aurel. c. 38.] Aurelian calls these soldiers *Hiberi*, *Riparienses*, *Castriani*, and *Dacisci*.

89. Zosimus, l. i. [c. 61, p. 53] p. 56. Eutropius, ix. 14 [9]. Aurel. Victor. [de Cæsar. 35.]

90. Hist. August. p. 222. [Vopisc. Aurel. c. 39.] Aurel. Victor. [de Cæsar. 35.]

91. It already raged before Aurelian's return from Egypt. See Vopiscus, who quotes an original letter. Hist. August. p. 244. [Vopisc. Firmus, c. 5.]

92. Vopiscus in Hist. August. p. 222. [Aurel. c. 39.] The two Victors. Eutropius, ix. 14 [9]. Zosimus (l. i. p. 43) mentions only three senators, and places their death before the eastern war.

93. Nulla catenati feralis pompa senatûs
    Carnificum lassabit opus; nec carcere pleno
    Infelix raros numerabit curia Patres.
                Calpurn. Eclog. i. 60.

94. According to the younger Victor [Epitome, c. 35], he sometimes wore the diadem. *Deus* and *Dominus* appear on his medals.

95. It was the observation of Diocletian. See Vopiscus in Hist. August. p. 224. [Aurel. c. 44.]

96. Vopiscus in Hist. August. p. 221. [Aurel. c. 35, *seq*.] Zosimus, l. i. [c. 62] p. 57. Eutrop. ix. 15 [9]. The two Victors.

Chapter XII

1. Vopiscus in Hist. August. p. 222. [Aurel. c. 41.] Aurelius Victor mentions a formal deputation from the troops to the senate.

2. Vopiscus, our principal authority, wrote at Rome sixteen years only after the death of Aurelian; and, besides the recent notoriety of the facts, constantly draws his materials from the Journals of the Senate and the original papers of the Ulpian library. Zosimus and Zonaras appear as ignorant of this transaction as they were in general of the Roman constitution.

3. Liv. i. 17. Dionys. Halicarn, l. ii. [c. 57] p. 115. Plutarch in Numa Pompilius. The first of these writers relates the story like an orator, the second like a lawyer, and the third like a moralist, and none of them probably without some intermixture of fable.

4. Vopiscus (in Hist. August. p. 227 [Tacit. c. 4]) calls him "primæ sententiæ consularis;" and soon afterwards *Princeps senatûs*. It is natural to suppose that the monarchs of Rome, disdaining that humble title, resigned it to the most ancient of the senators.

5. The only objection to this genealogy is, that the historian was named Cornelius, the emperor Claudius. But under the Lower Empire surnames were extremely various and uncertain.

6. Zonaras, l. xii. [c. 28] p. 637 [ed. Paris; p. 608, ed. Bonn]. The Alexandrian Chronicle, by an obvious mistake, transfers that age to Aurelian.

7. In the year 273 he was ordinary consul. But he must have been Suffectus many years before, and most probably under Valerian.

8. *Bis millies octingenties*. Vopiscus in Hist. August. p. 229. [Tacit. c. 10.] This sum, according to the old standard, was equivalent to eight hundred and forty thousand Roman pounds of silver, each of the value of three pounds sterling. But in the age of Tacitus the coin had lost much of its weight and purity.

9. After his accession he gave orders that ten copies of the historian should be annually transcribed and placed in the public libraries. The Roman libraries have long since perished, and the most valuable part of Tacitus was preserved in a single MS., and discovered in a monastery of Westphalia. See Bayle, Dictionnaire, Art. *Tacite*, and Lipsius ad Annal. ii. 9.

10. Vopiscus in Hist. August. p. 227. [Tacit. c. 4.]

11. Hist. August. p. 228 [*ib*. c. 7]. Tacitus addressed the Prætorians by the appellation of *sanctissimi milites*, and the people by that of *sacratissimi Quirites*.

12. In his manumissions he never exceeded the number of an hundred, as limited by the Caninian law, which was enacted under Augustus, and at length repealed by Justinian. See Casaubon ad locum Vopisci.

13. See the Lives of Tacitus, Florianus, and Probus, in the Augustan History; we may be well assured that whatever the soldier gave the senator had already given.

14. Vopiscus in Hist. August. p. 216. [Aurel. c. 20.] The passage is perfectly clear, yet both Casaubon and Salmasius wish to correct it.

15. Vopiscus in Hist. August. p. 230, 232, 233. [Florian. c. 5 and 6.] The senators celebrated the happy restoration with hecatombs and public rejoicings.

16. Hist. August. p. 228. [Vopisc. Tacit. c. 8.]

17. Vopiscus in Hist. August. p. 230. [Tacit. c.

13.] Zosimus, l. i. [c. 63] p. 57. Zonaras, l. xii. [c. 28] p. 637 [ed. Paris; p. 608, ed. Bonn]. Two passages in the Life of Probus (p. 236, 238 [Vopisc. Probus, c. 8 and 12]) convince me that these Scythian invaders of Pontus were Alani. If we may believe Zosimus (l. i. [c. 64] p. 58), Florianus pursued them as far as the Cimmerian Bosphorus. But he had scarcely time for so long and difficult an expedition.

18. Eutropius [9, c. 10] and Aurelius Victor [c. 36] only say that he died; Victor Junior adds, that it was of a fever. Zosimus [i. 63, p. 55] and Zonaras [xii. c. 28] affirm that he was killed by the soldiers. Vopiscus [Tacit. c. 13] mentions both accounts, and seems to hesitate. Yet surely these jarring opinions are easily reconciled.

19. According to the two Victors, he reigned exactly two hundred days.

20. Hist. August. p. 231. [Vopiscus, Florian. c. 1.] Zosimus, l. i. [c. 64, p. 56] p. 58, 59. Zonaras, l. xii. [c. 29, p. 609] p. 637. Aurelius Victor [de Cæsar. c. 37] says that Probus assumed the empire in Illyricum; an opinion which (though adopted by a very learned man) would throw that period of history into inextricable confusion.

21. Hist. August. p. 229. [Vopisc. Tacit. c. 10.]

22. He was to send judges to the Parthians, Persians, and Sarmatians, a president to Taprobana, and a proconsul to the Roman island (supposed by Casaubon and Salmasius to mean Britain). Such a history as mine (says Vopiscus with proper modesty) will not subsist a thousand years to expose or justify the prediction.

23. For the private life of Probus, see Vopiscus in Hist. August. p. 234-237. [Probus, c. 3, *sqq.*]

24. According to the Alexandrian chronicle, he was fifty at the time of his death.

25. The letter was addressed to the Prætorian præfect, whom (on condition of his good behaviour) he promised to continue in his great office. See Hist. August. p. 237. [Vopisc. Probus, c. 10.]

26. Vopiscus in Hist. August. p. 237 [in Probo, c. 11]. The date of the letter is assuredly faulty. Instead of *Non. Februar.* we may read *Non. August.*

27. Hist. August. p. 238. [Vopisc. *ib.* c. 12.] It is odd that the senate should treat Probus less favourably than Marcus Antoninus. That prince had received, even before the death of Pius, *Jus quintæ relationis.* See Capitolin. in Hist. August. p. 24 [in M. Anton. c. 6].

28. See the dutiful letter of Probus to the senate after his German victories. Hist. August. p. 239. [Vopisc. Prob. c. 15.]

29. The date and duration of the reign of Probus are very correctly ascertained by Cardinal Noris in his learned work, De Epochis Syro-Macedonum, p. 96-105. A passage of Eusebius connects the second year of Probus with the eras of several of the Syrian cities.

30. Vopiscus in Hist. August. p. 239. [Prob. c. 16.]

31. Zosimus (l. i. [c. 69, *sqq.*] p. 62-65) tells us a very long and trifling story of Lydius the Isaurian robber.

32. Zosim. l. i. [c. 7] p. 65. Vopiscus in Hist. August. p. 239, 240. [Prob. c. 17.] But it seems incredible that the defeat of the savages of Æthiopia could affect the Persian monarch.

33. Besides these well-known chiefs, several others are named by Vopiscus (Hist. August. p. 241 [Prob. c. 22]), whose actions have not reached our knowledge.

34. See the Cæsars of Julian [p. 314], and Hist. August. p. 238, 240, 241. Vopisc. Prob. c. 13, c. 18, *sqq.*

35. Zosimus, l. i. [c. 68] p. 62. Hist. August. p. 238. [Vopisc. Probus, c. 13, 14.] But the latter supposes the punishment inflicted with the consent of their kings: if so, it was partial, like the offence.

36. See Cluver, Germania Antiqua, l. iii. Ptolemy places in their country the city of Calisia, probably Calish in Silesia.

37. *Feralis umbra* is the expression of Tacitus: it is surely a very bold one.

38. Tacit. Germania (c. 43).

39. Vopiscus in Hist. August. p. 238 [Prob. c. 14.]

40. Hist. August. p. 238, 239. [Vopisc. Probus, c. 14, *sqq.*] Vopiscus quotes a letter [c. 15] from the emperor to the senate, in which he mentions his design of reducing Germany into a province.

41. Strabo, l. vii. [p. 290]. According to Velleius Paterculus (ii. 108, 109), Maroboduus led his Marcomanni into Bohemia: Cluverius (German. Antiq. iii. 8) proves that it was from Swabia.

42. These settlers, from the payment of tithes, were denominated *Decumates.* Tacit. Germania, c. 29.

43. See notes de l'Abbé de la Bléterie à la Germanie de Tacite, p. 183. His account of the wall is chiefly borrowed (as he says himself) from the *Alsatia Illustrata* of Schœpflin.

44. See Recherches sur les Chinois et les Egyptiens, tom. ii. p. 81-102. The anonymous author is well acquainted with the globe in general, and with Germany in particular: with regard to the latter, he quotes a work of M. Hanselman; but he seems to confound the wall of Probus, designed against the Alemanni, with the fortification of the Mattiaci, constructed in the neighbourhood of Frankfort against the Catti.

45. He distributed about fifty or sixty barbarians to a *Numerus,* as it was then called, a corps with whose established number we are not exactly acquainted.

46. Camden's Britannia, Introduction, p. 136; but he speaks from a very doubtful conjecture.

47. Zosimus, l. i. [c. 68] p. 62. According to Vopiscus, another body of Vandals was less faithful.

48. Hist. August. p. 240. [Vopisc. Probus, c. 18.] They were probably expelled by the Goths. Zosim. l. i. [c. 71] p. 66.

49. Hist. August. p. 240. [Vopisc. l. c.]

50. Panegyr. Vet. v. 18. Zosimus, l. i. [c. 71] p. 66.

51. Vopiscus in Hist. August. p. 245, 246 [in Saturnino, c. 10]. The unfortunate orator had studied rhetoric at Carthage; and was therefore more probably a Moor (Zosim. l. i. [c. 66] p. 60) than a Gaul, as Vopiscus calls him.

52. Zonaras, l. xii. [c. 29] p. 638 [ed. Par.; p. 609, ed. Bonn.]

53. A very surprising instance is recorded of the prowess of Proculus. He had taken one hundred Sarmatian virgins. The rest of the story he must relate in his own language: Ex his unâ nocte decem inivi; omnes tamen, quod in me erat, mulieres intra dies quindecim reddidi. Vopiscus in Hist. August. p. 246 [in Proculo, 12].

54. Proculus, who was a native of Albengue on the Genoese coast, armed two thousand of his own slaves. His riches were great, but they were acquired by robbery. It was afterwards a saying of his family, sibi non placere esse vel principes vel latrones. Vopiscus in Hist. August. p. 247 [in Proculo, 13].

55. Hist. August. p. 240. [Vopisc. in Probo, c. 19.]

56. Zosim. l. i. [c. 71] p. 66.

57. Hist. August. p. 236. [Vopisc. in Probo, c. 9.]

58. Aurel. Victor. in Prob. [De Cæsar, c. 37.] But the policy of Hannibal, unnoticed by any more ancient writer, is irreconcilable with the history of his life. He left Africa when he was nine years old, returned to it when he was forty-five, and immediately lost his army in the decisive battle of Zama. Livius, xxx. 35.

59. Hist. August. p. 240. [Vopisc. Probus, c. 18.] Eutrop. ix. 17 [7]. Aurel. Victor. in Prob. Victor Junior. He revoked the prohibition of Domitian, and granted a general permission of planting vines to the Gauls, the Britons, and the Pannonians.

60. Julian [Cæsares, p. 314] bestows a severe, and indeed excessive, censure on the rigour of Probus, who, as he thinks, almost deserved his fate.

61. Vopiscus in Hist. August. p. 241 [in Probo, c. 20]. He lavishes on this idle hope a large stock of very foolish eloquence.

62. Turris ferrata. It seems to have been a movable tower, and cased with iron.

63. [Hic] Probus, et vere probus situs est; Victor omnium gentium Barbararum: victor etiam tyrannorum. [Vopisc. Prob. c. 21]

64. Yet all this may be conciliated. He was born at Narbonne in Illyricum, confounded by Eutropius with the more famous city of that name in Gaul. His father might be an African, and his mother a noble Roman. Carus himself was educated in the capital. See Scaliger, Animadversion, ad Euseb. Chron. p. 241.

65. Probus had requested of the senate an equestrian statue and a marble palace, at the public expense, as a just recompense of the singular merit of Carus. Vopiscus in Hist. August. p. 249 [in Caro, c. 6].

66. Vopiscus in Hist. August. p. 242, 249 [in Probo, c. 24; in Caro, c. 3]. Julian excludes the emperor Carus and both his sons from the banquet of the Cæsars.

67. John Malala, tom. i. p. 401 [ed. Oxon.; p. 129, ed. Ven.; p. 303, ed. Bonn]. But the authority of that ignorant Greek is very slight. He ridiculously derives from Carus the city of Carrhæ and the province of Caria, the latter of which is mentioned by Homer.

68. Hist. August. p. 249. [Vopisc. Carus, c. 5.] Carus congratulated the senate that one of their own order was made emperor.

69. Hist. August. p. 242. [Vopisc. Probus, c. 24.]

70. See the first eclogue of Calphurnius. The design of it is preferred by Fontenelle to that of Virgil's Pollio. See tom. iii. p. 148.

71. Hist. August. p. 250. [Vopisc. Carus, c. 7.] Eutropius, ix. 18 [12]. Pagi, Annal.

72. Agathias, l. iv. p. 135 [ed. Paris; p. 94, ed. Ven.; c. 24, p. 261, ed. Bonn]. We find one of his sayings in the Bibliothèque Orientale of M. d'Herbelot. "The definition of humanity includes all other virtues." [Bahram did not succeed Artaxerxes. Three monarchs intervened.]

73. Synesius tells this story of Carinus; and it is much more natural to understand it of Carus than (as Petavius and Tillemont choose to do) of Probus.

74. Vopiscus in Hist. August. p. 250. [Vopisc. Carus, c. 8.] Eutropius, ix. 18 [12]. The two Victors.

75. To the Persian victory of Carus, I refer the dialogue of the *Philopatris*, which has so long been an object of dispute among the learned. But to explain and justify my opinion would require a dissertation.

76. Hist. August. p. 250. [Vopisc. Carus, c. 8.] Yet Eutropius, Festus Rufus, the two Victors, Jerome, Sidonius, Apollinaris, Syncellus, and Zonaras, all ascribe the death of Carus to lightning.

77. See Nemesian. Cynegeticon, v. 71, etc.

78. See Festus and his commentators, on the word *Scribonianum*. *Places* struck by lightning were surrounded with a wall; *things* were buried with mysterious ceremony.

79. Vopiscus in Hist. August. p. 250. [Carus, c. 9] Aurelius Victor seems to believe the prediction, and to approve the retreat.

80. Nemesian. Cynegeticon, v. 69. He was a contemporary, but a poet.

81. *Cancellarius*. This word, so humble in its origin, has by a singular fortune risen into the title of the first great office of state in the monarchies of Europe. See Casaubon and Salmasius, ad Hist. August. p. 253. [Vopisc. Carinus, c. 15.]

82. Vopiscus in Hist. August. p. 253, 254 [id. ib. c. 15, 16]. Eutropius, ix. 19 [13]. Victor Junior. The reign of Diocletian indeed was so long and prosperous, that it must have been very unfavourable to the reputation of Carinus.

83. Vopiscus in Hist. August. p. 255 [in Carino, 19]. He calls him Carus, but the sense is sufficiently obvious, and the words were often confounded.

84. See Calphurnius, Eclog. vii. 43. We may ob-

serve that the spectacles of Probus were still recent, and that the poet is seconded by the historian.

85. The philosopher Montaigne (Essays, iii. 6) gives a very just and lively view of Roman magnificence in these spectacles.

86. Vopiscus in Hist. August. p. 240. [Probus, c. 19.]

87. They are called *Onagri;* but the number is too inconsiderable for mere wild asses. Cuper (de Elephantis Exercitat. ii. 7) has proved from Oppian, Dion, and an anonymous Greek, that zebras had been seen at Rome. They were brought from some island of the ocean, perhaps Madagascar.

88. Carinus gave an hippopotamus (see Calphurn. Eclog. vii. 66). In the latter spectacles I do not recollect any crocodiles, of which Augustus once exhibited thirty-six. Dion Cassius, l. lv. [c. 10] p. 781.

89. Capitolin. in Hist. August. p. 164, 165. [Gordian. III. c. 33.] We are not acquainted with the animals which he calls *archeleontes;* some read *argoleontes,* others *agrioleontes:* both corrections are very nugatory.

90. Plin. Hist. Natur. viii. 6, from the annals of Piso.

91. See Maffei, Verona Illustrata, p. iv. l. i. c. 2.

92. Maffei, l. ii. c. 2. The height was very much exaggerated by the ancients. It reached almost to the heavens, according to Calphurnius (Eclog. vii. 23); and surpassed the ken of human sight, according to Ammianus Marcellinus (xvi. 10). Yet how trifling to the great pyramid of Egypt, which rises 500 feet perpendicular! [The height was 157 feet.]

93. According to different copies of Victor, we read 77,000 or 87,000 spectators; but Maffei (l. ii. c. 12) finds room on the open seats for no more than 34,000. The remainder were contained in the upper covered galleries.

94. See Maffei, l. ii. c. 5–12. He treats the very difficult subject with all possible clearness, and like an architect as well as an antiquarian.

95. Calphurn. Eclog. vii. 64–73. These lines are curious, and the whole eclogue has been of infinite use to Maffei. Calphurnius, as well as Martial (see his first book), was a poet; but when they described the amphitheatre, they both wrote from their own senses, and to those of the Romans.

96. Consult Plin. Hist. Natur. xxxiii. 16, xxxvii. 11.

97. Balteus en gemmis, en inlita porticus auro Certatim radiant, etc. Calphurn. vii. [v. 47.]

98. Et Martis vultus et Apollinis esse putavi, says Calphurnius [Ecl. vii. 83]; but John Malala, who had perhaps seen pictures of Carinus, describes him as thick, short, and white, tom. i. p. 403.

99. With regard to the time when these Roman games were celebrated, Scaliger, Salmasius, and Cuper have given themselves a great deal of trouble to perplex a very clear subject.

100. Nemesianus (in the Cynegeticon [v. 80, sqq.]) seems to anticipate in his fancy that auspicious day.

101. He won all the crowns from Nemesianus, with whom he vied in didactic poetry. The senate erected a statue to the son of Carus, with a very ambiguous inscription, "To the most powerful of orators." See Vopiscus in Hist. August. p. 251 [Numerian. c. 11.]

102. A more natural cause, at least, than that assigned by Vopiscus (Hist. August. p. 251 [Numerian, c. 12]), incessantly weeping for his father's death.

103. In the Persian war Aper was suspected of a design to betray Carus. Hist. August. p. 250. [Vopiscus, Carus, c. 8.]

104. We are obliged to the Alexandrian Chronicle, p. 274, for the knowledge of the time and place where Diocletian was elected emperor.

105. Hist. August. p. 251. [Vopisc. Numer. c. 12.] Eutrop. ix. 88 [c. 12]. Hieronym. in Chron. According to these *judicious* writers, the death of Numerian was discovered by the stench of his dead body. Could no aromatics be found in the Imperial household?

106. Aurel. Victor. [De Cæsar. c. 39.] Eutropius, ix. 20 [c. 13]. Hieronym. in Chron.

107. Vopiscus in Hist. August. p. 252. [Numer. c. 13.] The reason why Diocletian killed *Aper* (a wild boar) was founded on a prophecy and a pun, as foolish as they are well known. [Vopisc. l. c.]

108. Eutropius [lib. ix. c. 13] marks its situation very accurately; it was between the Mons Aureus and Viminiacum. M. d'Anville (Géographie Ancienne, tom. i. p. 304) places Margus at Kastolatz in Servia, a little below Belgrade and Semendria.

109. Hist. August. p. 254. [Vopisc. Carin. c. 17.] Eutropius, ix. 20 [13]. Aurelius Victor. Victor in Epitome.

Chapter XIII

1. Eutrop. ix. 19 [13]. Victor in Epitome [c. 39]. The town seems to have been properly called Doclia, from a small tribe of Illyrians (see Cellarius, Geograph. Antiqua, tom. i. p. 393); and the original name of the fortunate slave was probably Docles; he first lengthened it to the Grecian harmony of Diocles, and at length to the Roman maj-

esty of Diocletianus. He likewise assumed the Patrician name of Valerius, and it is usually given him by Aurelius Victor.

2. See Dacier on the sixth satire of the second book of Horace. Cornel. Nepos, in Vit. Eumen. c. 1.

3. Lactantius (or whoever was the author of the

little treatise De Mortibus Persecutorum) accuses Diocletian of *timidity* in two places, c. 7, 8. In chap. 9 he says of him, "erat in omni tumultu meticulosus et animi disjectus."

4. In this enconium Aurelius Victor seems to convey a just, though indirect, censure of the cruelty of Constantius. It appears from the Fasti that Aristobolus remained præfect of the city, and that he ended with Diocletian the consulship which he had commenced with Carinus.

5. Aurelius Victor styles Diocletian "Parentem potius quam Dominum." [De Cæsar. 39.] See Hist. August. p. 30. [Capitol. M. Anton. Phil. c. 19.]

6. The question of the time when Maximian received the honours of Cæsar and Augustus has divided modern critics and given occasion to a great deal of learned wrangling. I have followed M. de Tillemont (Histoire des Empereurs, tom. iv. p. 500–505), who has weighed the several reasons and difficulties with his scrupulous accuracy.

7. In an oration delivered before him (Panegyr. Vet. i. 8) Mamertinus expresses a doubt whether his hero, in imitating the conduct of Hannibal and Scipio, had ever heard of their names. From thence we may fairly infer that Maximian was more desirous of being considered as a soldier than as a man of letters: and it is in this manner that we can often translate the language of flattery into that of truth.

8. Lactantius de M. P. c. 8. Aurelius Victor [de Cæsar. c. 39]. As among the Panegyrics we find orations pronounced in praise of Maximian, and others which flatter his adversaries at his expense, we derive some knowledge from the contrast.

9. See the second and third Panegyrics, particularly iii. [ii.] 3, 10, 14; but it would be tedious to copy the diffuse and affected expressions of their false eloquence. With regard to the titles, consult Aurel. Victor, Lactantius de M. P. c. 52. Spanheim de Usu Numismatum, etc. Dissertat. xii. 8.

10. Aurelius Victor. Victor in Epitome. Eutrop. ix. 22 [14]. Lactant. de M. P. c. 7. Hieronym. in Chron.

11. It is only among the modern Greeks that Tillemont can discover his appellation of Chlorus. Any remarkable degree of paleness seems inconsistent with the *rubor* mentioned in Panegyric v. 19.

12. Julian, the grandson of Constantius, boasts that his family was derived from the warlike Mæsians. Misopogon, p. 348. The Dardanians dwelt on the edge of Mæsia.

13. Galerius married Valeria, the daughter of Diocletian; if we speak with strictness, Theodora, the wife of Constantius, was daughter only to the wife of Maximian. Spanheim, Dissertat. xi. 2.

14. This division agrees with that of the four præfectures; yet there is some reason to doubt whether Spain was not a province of Maximian. See Tillemont, tom. iv. p. 517.

15. Julian in Cæsarib. p. 315. Spanheim's notes to the French translation, p. 122.

16. The general name of *Bagaudæ* (in the signification of Rebels) continued till the fifth century in Gaul. Some critics derive it from a Celtic word, *Bagad*, a tumultuous assembly. Scaliger ad Euseb. Du Cange Glossar.

17. Chronique de Froissart, vol. i. c. 182, ii. 73, 79. The *naïveté* of his story is lost in our best modern writers.

18. Cæsar de Bell. Gallic. vi. 13. Orgetorix, the Helvetian, could arm for his defence a body of ten thousand slaves.

19. Their oppression and misery are acknowledged by Eumenius (Panegyr. vi. 8), Gallias efferatas injuriis.

20. Panegyr. Vet. ii. 4. Aurelius Victor [de Cæsar. c. 39].

21. Ælianus and Amandus. We have medals coined by them. Goltzius in Thes. R. A. p. 117, 121.

22. Levibus prœliis domuit. Eutrop. ix. 20 [13].

23. The fact rests indeed on very slight authority, a Life of St. Babolinus, which is probably of the seventh century. See Duchesne Scriptores Rer. Francicar. tom. i. p. 662.

24. Aurelius Victor [de Cæsar. c. 39] calls them Germans. Eutropius (ix. 21 [13]) gives them the name of Saxons. But Eutropius lived in the ensuing century, and seems to use the language of his own times.

25. The three expressions of Eutropius [ix. 13], Aurelius Victor [de Cæsar. 39], and Eumenius, "vilissime natus," "Bataviæ alumnus," and "Menapiæ civis," gives us a very doubtful account of the birth of Carausius. Dr. Stukely however (Hist. of Carausius, p. 62), chooses to make him a native of St. David's and a prince of the blood royal of Britain. The former idea he had found in Richard of Cirencester, p. 44.

26. Panegyr. v. 12. Britain at this time was secure, and slightly guarded.

27. Panegyr. Vet. v. 11, vii. 9. The orator Eumenius wished to exalt the glory of the hero (Constantius) with the importance of the conquest. Notwithstanding our laudable partiality for our native country, it is difficult to conceive that, in the beginning of the fourth century, England deserved *all* these commendations. A century and a half before it hardly paid its own establishment. See Appian in Procem.

28. As a great number of medals of Carausius are still preserved, he is become a very favourite object of antiquarian curiosity, and every circumstance of his life and actions has been investigated with sagacious accuracy. Dr. Stukely in particular has devoted a large volume to the British emperor. I have used his materials, and rejected most of his fanciful conjectures.

29. When Mamertinus pronounced his first panegyric the naval preparations of Maximian were completed; and the orator presaged an assured victory. His silence in the second panegyric might alone inform us that the expedition had not succeeded.

30. Aurelius Victor, Eutropius, and the medals (Pax Augg.), inform us of this temporary reconciliation; though I will not presume (as Dr. Stukely has done, Medallic History of Carausius, p. 86, etc.) to insert the identical articles of the treaty.

31. With regard to the recovery of Britain, we obtain a few hints from Aurelius Victor and Eutropius.

32. John Malala, in Chron. Antiochen. tom. i. p. 408, 409 [ed. Oxon.; p. 132, ed. Ven.; p. 308, ed. Bonn].

33. Zosim. l. i. p. 3 [l. ii. c. 34]. That partial historian seems to celebrate the vigilance of Diocletian, with a design of exposing the negligence of Constantine; we may, however, listen to an orator: "Nam quid ego alarum et cohortium castra percenseam, toto Rheni et Istri et Euphratis limite restituta." Panegyr. Vet. iv. 18.

34. Ruunt omnes in sanguinem suum populi, quibus non contigit esse Romanis, obstinatæque feritatis pœnas nunc sponte persolvunt. Panegyr. Vet. iii. 16. Mamertinus illustrates the fact by the example of almost all the nations of the world.

35. He complained, though not with the strictest truth, "Jam fluxisse annos quindecim in quibus, in Illyrico, ad ripam Danubii relegatus cum gentibus barbaris luctaret." Lactant. de M. P. c. 18.

36. In the Greek text of Eusebius we read six thousand, a number which I have preferred to the sixty thousand of Jerome, Orosius, Eutropius, and his Greek translator Pæanius.

37. Panegyr. Vet. vii. 21.

38. There was a settlement of the Sarmatians in the neighbourhood of Treves, which seems to have been deserted by those lazy barbarians; Ausonius speaks of them in his Mosella [v. 5, sqq.]:—

Unde iter ingrediens nemorosa per avia
    solum,
Et nulla humani spectans vestigia cultus;

   .   .   .   .   .

Arvaque Sauromatum nuper metata colonis.
There was a town of the Carpi in the Lower Mæsia.

39. See the rhetorical exultation of Eumenius. Panegyr. vii. 9.

40. Scaliger (Animadvers. ad Euseb. p. 243) decides, in his usual manner, that the Quinquegentiani, or five African nations, were the five great cities, the Pentapolis of the inoffensive province of Cyrene.

41. After his defeat Julian stabbed himself with a dagger, and immediately leaped into the flames. Victor in Epitome [c. 39].

42. Tu ferocissimos Mauritaniæ populos inaccessis montium jugis et naturali munitione fidentes, expugnasti, recepisti, transtulisti. Panegyr. Vet. vi. 8.

43. See the description of Alexandria in Hirtius de Bell. Alexandrin, c. 5.

44. Eutrop. ix. 24 [15]. Orosius, vii. 25. John Malala in Chron. Antioch. p. 409, 410 [ed. Oxon.; p. 132, ed. Ven.; p. 309, ed. Bonn]. Yet Eumenius

assures us that Egypt was pacified by the clemency of Diocletian.

45. Eusebius (in Chron. [An. CCXCIII.]) places their destruction several years sooner, and at a time when Egypt itself was in a state of rebellion against the Romans.

46. Strabo, l. xvii. p. 819. Pomponius Mela, l. i. c. 4. His words are curious: "Intra, si credere libet, vix homines magisque semiferi; Ægipanes, et Blemmyes, et 'Satyri.'"

47. Ausus sese inserere fortunæ et provocare arna Romana.

48. See Procopius de Bell. Persic. l. i. c. 19.

49. He fixed the public allowance of corn for the people of Alexandria at two millions of medimni; about four hundred thousand quarters. Chron. Paschal. p. 276. Procop. Hist. Arcan. c. 26.

50. John Antioch. in Excerp. Valesian, p. 834. Suidas in Diocletian.

51. See a short history and confutation of Alchymy, in the works of that philosophical compiler, La Mothe le Vayer, tom. i. p. 327–353.

52. See the education and strength of Tiridates in the Armenian history of Moses of Chorene, l. ii. c. 76. He could seize two wild bulls by the horns and break them off with his hands.

53. If we give credit to the younger Victor [Epit. 41], who supposes that in the year 323 Licinius was only sixty years of age, he could scarcely be the same person as the patron of Tiridates; but we know from much better authority (Euseb. Hist. Ecclesiast. l. x. c. 8) that Licinius was at that time in the last period of old age: sixteen years before, he is represented with grey hairs and as the contemporary of Galerius. See Lactant. c. 32. Lucinius was probably born about the year 250.

54. See the sixty-second and sixty-third books of Dion Cassius [l. lxiii. c. 5].

55. Moses of Chorene, Hist. Armen. l. ii. c. 74. The statues had been erected by Valarsaces, who reigned in Armenia about 130 years before Christ, and was the first king of the family of Arsaces (see Moses, Hist. Armen. l. ii. 2, 3). The deification of the Arsacides is mentioned by Justin (xli. 5) and by Ammianus Marcellinus (xxiii. 6).

56. The Armenian nobility was numerous and powerful. Moses mentions many families which were distinguished under the reign of Valarsaces (l. ii. 7), and which still subsisted in his own time, about the middle of the fifth century. See the preface of his editors.

57. She was named Chosroiduchta, and had not the os patulum like other women. (Hist. Armen. l. ii. c. 79.) I do not understand the expression.

58. In the Armenian History (l. ii. 78), as well as in the Geography (p. 367), China is called Zenia, or Zenastan. It is characterised by the production of silk, by the opulence of the natives, and by their love of peace, above all the other nations of the earth.

59. Vou-ti, the first emperor of the seventh dynasty, who then reigned in China, had political

transactions with Fergana, a province of Sogdiana, and is said to have received a Roman embassy (Histoire des Huns, tom. i. p. 38). In those ages the Chinese kept a garrison at Kashgar, and one of their generals, about the time of Trajan, marched as far as the Caspian Sea. With regard to the intercourse between China and the western countries, a curious memoir of M. de Guignes may be consulted, in the Académie des Inscriptions, tom. xxii. p. 355.

60. See Hist. Armen. l. ii. c. 81.

61. Ipsos Persas ipsumque Regem ascitis Sacis, et Rufiis, et Gellis, petit frater Ormies. Panegyric. Vet. iii. [ii.] 17. The Sacæ were a nation of wandering Scythians, who encamped towards the sources of the Oxus and the Jaxartes. The Gelli were the inhabitants of Ghilan, along the Caspian Sea, and who so long, under the name of Dilemites, infested the Persian monarchy. See D'Herbelot, Bibliothèque Orientale.

62. Moses of Chorene takes no notice of this second revolution, which I have been obliged to collect from a passage of Ammianus Marcellinus (l. xxiii. c. 5). Lactantius speaks of the ambition of Narses: "Concitatus domesticis exemplis avi sui Saporis ad occupandum orientem magnis copiis inhiabat." De Mort. Persecut. c. 9.

63. We may readily believe that Lactantius ascribes to cowardice the conduct of Diocletian. Julian, in his oration, says that he remained with all the forces of the empire; a very hyperbolical expression.

64. Our five abbreviators, Eutropius, Festus, the two Victors, and Orosius, all relate the last and great battle; but Orosius is the only one who speaks of the two former.

65. The nature of the country is finely described by Plutarch, in the Life of Crassus; and by Xenophon, in the first book of the Anabasis.

66. See Foster's Dissertation in the second volume of the translation of the Anabasis by Spelman; which I will venture to recommend as one of the best versions extant.

67. Hist. Armen. l. ii. c. 76. I have transferred this exploit of Tiridates from an imaginary defeat to the real one of Galerius.

68. Ammian. Marcellin. l. xiv. [c. 11.] The mile, in the hands of Eutropius (ix. 24 [15]), of Festus (c. 25), and of Orosius (vii. 25), easily increased to several miles.

69. Aurelius Victor. Jornandes de Rebus Geticis, c. 21.

70. Aurelius Victor [de Cæsar. c. 39] says, "Per Armenian in hostes contendit, quæ ferme sola, seu facilior vincendi via est." He followed the conduct of Trajan and the idea of Julius Cæsar.

71. Xenophon's Anabasis, l. iii. [c. 4, § 35.] For that reason the Persian cavalry encamped sixty stadia from the enemy.

72. The story is told by Ammianus, l. xxii. Instead of saccum some read scutum.

73. The Persians confessed the Roman superiority in morals as well as in arms. Eutrop. ix. 24. But this respect and gratitude of enemies is very seldom to be found in their own accounts.

74. The account of the negotiation is taken from the fragments of Peter the Patrician, in the Excerpta Legationum published in the Byzantine Collection. Peter lived under Justinian; but it is very evident, by the nature of his materials, that they are drawn from the most authentic and respectable writers.

75. Adeo Victor (says Aurelius [de Cæsar. c. 39]) ut ni Valerius, cujus nutu omnia gerebantur, abnuisset, Romani fasces in provinciam novam ferrentur. Verum pars terrarum tamen nobis utilior quæsita.

76. He had been governor of Sumium (Pet. Patricius in Excerpt. Legat. p. 30) [ed. Paris; p. 21, ed. Ven.; p. 135, ed. Bonn]. This province seems to be mentioned by Moses of Chorene (Geograph. p. 360), and lay to the east of Mount Ararat.

77. By an error of the geographer Ptolemy, the position of Singara is removed from the Aboras to the Tigris, which may have produced the mistake of Peter in assigning the latter river for the boundary instead of the former. The line of the Roman frontier traversed, but never followed, the course of the Tigris.

78. Procopius de Ædificiis, l. ii. c. 6.

79. Three of the provinces, Zabdicene, Arzanene, and Carduene, are allowed on all sides. But instead of the other two, Peter (in Excerpt Leg. p. 30) inserts Rehimene and Sophene. I have preferred Ammianus (l. xxv. 7), because it might be proved that Sophene was never in the hands of the Persians, either before the reign of Diocletian or after that of Jovian. For want of correct maps, like those of M. d'Anville, almost all the moderns, with Tillemont and Valesius at their head, have imagined that it was in respect to Persia, and not to Rome, that the five provinces were situate beyond the Tigris.

80. Xenophon's Anabasis, l. iv. [c. 3 init.] Their bows were three cubits in length, their arrows two; they rolled down stones that were each a waggonload. The Greeks found a great many villages in that rude country.

81. According to Eutropius (vi. 9, as the text is represented by the best MSS.), the city of Tigranocerta was in Arzanene. The names and situation of the other three may be faintly traced.

82. Compare Herodotus, l. i. c. 98, with Moses Chorenens. Hist. Armen. l. ii. c. 84, and the map of Armenia given by his editors.

83. Hiberi, locorum potentes, Caspiâ viâ Sarmatam in Armenios raptim effundunt. Tacit. Annal. vi. 33. See Strabon. Geograph. l. xi. p. 500.

84. Peter Patricius (in Excerpt. Leg. p. 30 [ed. Paris; p. 21, ed. Ven; p. 135, ed. Bonn]) is the only writer who mentions the Iberian article of the treaty.

85. Euseb. in Chron. Pagi ad annum. Till the

discovery of the treatise De Mortibus Persecutorum, it was not certain that the triumph and the Vicennalia were celebrated at the same time.

86. At the time of the Vicennalia, Galerius seems to have kept his station on the Danube. See Lactant. de M. P. c. 38.

87. Eutropius (ix. 27 [16]) mentions them as a part of the triumph. As the *persons* had been restored to Narses, nothing more than their *images* could be exhibited.

88. Livy gives us a speech of Camillus on that subject (v. 51-54), full of eloquence and sensibility, in opposition to a design of removing the seat of government from Rome to the neighbouring city of Veii.

89. Julius Cæsar was reproached with the intention of removing the empire to Ilium or Alexandria. See Sueton. in Cæsar. c. 79. According to the ingenious conjecture of Le Fèvre and Dacier, the third ode of the third book of Horace was intended to divert Augustus from the execution of a similar design.

90. See Aurelius Victor [de Cæsar. c. 39], who likewise mentions the buildings erected by Maximian at Carthage, probably during the Moorish war. We shall insert some verses of Ausonius de Clar. Urb. v.:—

Et Mediolani mira omnia: copia rerum;
Innumeræ cultæque domus; facunda virorum
Ingenia, et mores læti: tum duplice muro
Amplificata loci species; populique voluptas
Circus; et inclusi moles cuneata Theatri;
Templa, Palatinæque arces, opulensque Moneta,
Et regio *Herculei* celebris sub honore lavacri.
Conctaque marmoreis ornata Peristyla signis;
Mœniaque in valli formam circumdata labro,
Omnia quæ magnis operum velut æmula formis
Excellunt: nec juncta premit vicinia Romæ.

91. Lactant. de M. P. c. 17. Libanius, Orat. vi. p. 203 [ed. Morell. Paris, 1627].

92. Lactant. de M. P. c. 17. On a similar occasion, Ammianus mentions the *dicacitas plebis* as not very agreeable to an Imperial ear. (See l. xvi. c. 10.) [Ammianus just says the opposite: "dicacitate plebis oblectabatur" (about Constantius)].

93. Lactantius accuses Maximian of destroying fictis criminationibus lumina senatûs (de M. P. c. 8). Aurelius Victor speaks very doubtfully of the faith of Diocletian towards his friends.

94. Truncatæ vires urbis, imminuto prætoriarum cohortium atque in armis vulgi numero. Aurelius Victor [de Cæsar. c. 39]. Lactantius attributes to Galerius the prosecution of the same plan (c. 26).

95. They were old corps stationed in Illyricum; and, according to the ancient establishment, they each consisted of six thousand men. They had acquired much reputation by the use of the *plumbatæ*, or darts loaded with lead. Each soldier carried five of these, which he darted from a considerable distance with great strength and dexterity. See Vegetius, i. 17.

96. See the Theodosian Code, l. vi. tit. ii. with Godefroy's commentary.

97. See the 12th dissertation in Spanheim's excellent work de Usu Numismatum. From medals, inscriptions, and historians, he examines every title separately, and traces it from Augustus to the moment of its disappearing.

98. Pliny (in Panegyr. c. 3, 55, etc.) speaks of *Dominus* with execration, as synonymous to Tyrant, and opposite to Prince. And the same Pliny regularly gives that title (in the tenth book of the epistles) to his friend rather than master, the virtuous Trajan. This strange contradiction puzzles the commentators who think, and the translators who can write.

99. Synesius de Regno, edit. Petav. p. 15. I am indebted for this quotation to the Abbé de la Bléterie.

100. See Van Dale de Consecratione, p. 354, etc. It was customary for the emperors to mention (in the preamble of laws) their *numen, sacred majesty, divine oracles, etc.* According to Tillemont, Gregory Nazianzen complains most bitterly of the profanation, especially when it was practised by an Arian emperor.

101. See Spanheim de Usu Numismat. Dissert. xii.

102. Aurelius Victor. Eutropius, ix. 26 [16]. It appears by the Panegyrists that the Romans were soon reconciled to the name and ceremony of adoration.

103. The innovations introduced by Diocletian are chiefly deduced, 1st, from some very strong passages in Lactantius; and, secondly, from the new and various offices which, in the Theodosian code, appear *already* established in the beginning of the reign of Constantine.

104. Lactant. de M. P. c. 7.

105. Indicta lex nova quæ sane illorum temporum modestiâ tolerabilis, in perniciem processit. Aurel. Victor [de Cæsar. c. 39]; who has treated the character of Diocletian with good sense, though in bad Latin.

106. Solus omnium, post conditum Romanum Imperium, qui ex tanto fastigio sponte ad privatæ vitæ statum civilitatemque remearet. Eutrop. ix. 28 [16].

107. The particulars of the journey and illness are taken from Lactantius (c. 17), who may *sometimes* be admitted as an evidence of public facts, though very seldom of private anecdotes.

108. Aurelius Victor [de Cæsar. c. 39] ascribes the abdication, which had been so variously accounted for, to two causes; first, Diocletian's contempt of ambition; and secondly, his apprehension of impending troubles. One of the panegyrists (vi. [v.] 9) mentions the age and infirmities of Diocletian as a very natural reason for his retirement.

109. The difficulties as well as mistakes attending the dates both of the year and of the day of Diocletian's abdication are perfectly cleared up by

Tillemont, Hist. des Empereurs, tom. iv. p. 525, note 19, and by Pagi ad annum.

110. See Panegyr. Veter. vi. [v.] 9. The oration was pronounced after Maximian had reassumed the purple.

111. Eumenius pays him a very fine compliment: "At enim divinum illum virum, qui primus imperium et participavit et posuit, consilii et facti sui non pœnitet; nec amisisse se putat quod sponte transcripsit. Felix beatusque vere quem vestra, tantorum principum, colunt obsequia privatum." Panegyr. Vet. vii. [vi.] 15.

112. We are obliged to the younger Victor [Epit. c. 39] for this celebrated bon mot. Eutropius [l. ix. c. 16] mentions the thing in a more general manner.

113. Hist. August. p. 223, 224. [Vopisc. Aurel. c. 43.] Vopiscus had learned this conversation from his father.

114. The younger Victor [Epit. c. 39] slightly mentions the report. But as Diocletian had disobliged a powerful and successful party, his memory has been loaded with every crime and misfortune. It has been affirmed that he died raving mad, that he was condemned as a criminal by the Roman senate, etc.

115. See the Itiner. p. 269, 272, edit. Wessel.

116. The Abate Fortis, in his Viaggio in Delmazia, p. 43 (printed at Venice in the year 1774, in two small volumes in quarto), quotes a MS. account of the antiquities of Salona, composed by Giambattista Giustiniani about the middle of the sixteenth century.

117. Adam's Antiquities of Diocletian's Palace at Spalatro, p. 6. We may add a circumstance or two from the Abate Fortis: the little stream of the Hyader, mentioned by Lucan, produces most exquisite trout, which a sagacious writer, perhaps a monk, supposes to have been one of the principal reasons that determined Diocletian in the choice of his retirement. Fortis, p. 45. The same author (p. 38) observes that a taste for agriculture is reviving

at Spalatro; and that an experimental farm has lately been established near the city by a society of gentlemen.

118. Constantin. Orat. ad Cœtum Sanct. c. 25. In this sermon, the emperor, or the bishop who composed it for him, affects to relate the miserable end of all the persecutors of the church.

119. Constantin. Porphyr. de Statu Imper. p. 86 [ed. Paris; vol. iii. p. 125, ed. Bonn].

120. D'Anville, Géographie Ancienne, tom. i. p. 162.

121. Messieurs Adam and Clerisseau, attended by two draughtsmen, visited Spalatro in the month of July, 1757. The magnificent work which their journey produced was published in London seven years afterwards.

122. I shall quote the words of the Abate Fortis. "E'bastevolmente nota agli amatori dell' Architettura, e dell' Antichità, l'opera del Signor ADAMS, che a donato molto a que' superbi vestigi coll' abituale eleganza del suo toccalapis e del bulino. In generale la rozzezza del scalpello, e'l cattivo gusto del secolo vi gareggiano colla magnificenza del fabricato." See Viaggio in Dalmazia, p. 40.

123. The orator Eumenius was secretary to the emperors Maximian and Constantius, and Professor of Rhetoric in the college of Autun. His salary was six hundred thousand sesterces, which, according to the lowest computation of that age, must have exceeded three thousand pounds a year. He generously requested the permission of employing it in rebuilding the college. See his Oration De Restaurandis Scholis [c. 11]; which, though not exempt from vanity, may atone for his panegyrics.

124. Porphyry died about the time of Diocletian's abdication. The life of his master Plotinus, which he composed, will give us the most complete idea of the genius of the sect and the manners of its professors. This very curious piece is inserted in Fabricius, Bibliotheca Græca, tom. iv. p. 88-148.

Chapter XIV

1. M. de Montesquieu (Considérations sur la Grandeur et la Décadence des Romains, c. 17) supposes, on the authority of Orosius and Eusebius, that, on this occasion, the empire, for the first time, was *really* divided into two parts. It is difficult, however, to discover in what respect the plan of Galerius differed from that of Diocletian.

2. Hic non modo amabilis, sed etiam venerabilis Gallis fuit; præcipue quod Diocletiani suspectam prudentiam, et Maximiani sanguinariam violentiam imperio ejus evaserant. Eutrop. Breviar. x. i.

3. Divitiis Provincialium (mel. *provinciarum*) ac privatorum studens, fisci commoda non admodum affectans; ducensque melius publicas opes a privatis haberi, quam intra unum claustrum reservari. Id. ibid. He carried this maxim so far, that, when-

ever he gave an entertainment, he was obliged to borrow a service of plate.

4. Lactantius de Mort. Persecutor. c. 18. Were the particulars of this conference more consistent with truth and decency, we might still ask how they came to the knowledge of an obscure rhetorician? But there are many historians who put us in mind of the admirable saying of the great Condé to Cardinal de Retz: "Ces coquins nous font parler et agir comme ils auroient fait eux-mêmes à norte place."

5. Sublatus nuper a pecoribus et silvis (says Lactantius de M. P. c. 19) statim Scutarius, continuo Protector, mox Tribunus, postridie Cæsar, accepit Orientem. Aurelius Victor is too liberal in giving him the whole portion of Diocletian.

6. His diligence and fidelity are acknowledged even by Lactantius, de M. P. c. 18.

7. These schemes, however, rest only on the very doubtful authority of Lactantius de M. P. c. 20.

8. This tradition, unknown to the contemporaries of Constantine, was invented in the darkness of monasteries, was embellished by Jeffrey of Monmouth and the writers of the twelfth century, has been defended by our antiquarians of the last age, and is seriously related in the ponderous History of England compiled by Mr. Carte (vol. i. p. 147). He transports, however, the kingdom of Coil, the imaginary father of Helena, from Essex to the wall of Antoninus.

9. Eutropius (x. 2) expresses, in a few words, the real truth, and the occasion of the error, "*ex obscuriori matrimonio* ejus filius." Zosmius (l. ii. [c. 8] p. 78) eagerly seized the most unfavourable report, and is followed by Orosius (vii. 25), whose authority is oddly enough overlooked by the indefatigable but partial Tillemont. By insisting on the divorce of Helena, Diocletian acknowledged her marriage.

10. There are three opinions with regard to the place of Constantine's birth. 1. Our English antiquarians were used to dwell with rapture on the words of his panegyrist, "Britannias illic oriendo nobiles fecisti." But this celebrated passage may be referred with as much propriety to the accession as to the nativity of Constantine. 2. Some of the modern Greeks have ascribed the honour of his birth to Drepanum, a town on the gulf of Nicomedia (Cellarius, tom. ii. p. 174), which Constantine dignified with the name of Helenopolis, and Justianian adorned with many splendid buildings (Procop. de Edificiis, v. 2). It is indeed probable enough that Helena's father kept an inn at Drepanum, and that Constantinus might lodge there when he returned from a Persian embassy in the reign of Aurelian. But in the wandering life of a soldier, the place of his marriage, and the places where his children are born, have very little connection with each other. 3. The claim of Naissus is supported by the anonymous writer, published at the end of Ammianus, p. 710 [vol. ii. p. 295, ed. Bip.], and who in general copied very good materials: and it is confirmed by Julius Firmicus (de Astrologia, l. i. c. 4), who flourished under the reign of Constantine himself. Some objections have been raised against the integrity of the text, and the application of the passage, of Firmicus; but the former is established by the best MSS., and the latter is very ably defended by Lipsius de Magnitudine Romana, l. iv. c. 11, et Supplement.

11. Literis minus instructus. Anonym. ad Ammian. p. 710.

12. Galerius, or perhaps his own courage, exposed him to single combat with a Sarmatian (Anonym. p. 710), and with a monstrous lion. See Praxagoras apud Photium, p. 63. Praxagoras, an Athenian philosopher, had written a life of Constantine in two books, which are now lost. He was a contemporary.

13. Zosimus, l. ii. [c. 8] p. 78, 79. Lactantius de M. P. c. 24. The former tells a very foolish story, that Constantine caused all the post-horses which he had used to be hamstrung. Such a bloody execution, without preventing a pursuit, would have scattered suspicions, and might have stopped his journey.

14. Anonym. p. 710. Panegyr. Veter. vii. 7. But Zosimus, l. ii. [c. 9] p. 79, Eusebius de Vit. Constant. l. i. c. 21, and Lactantius de M. P. c. 24, suppose, with less accuracy, that he found his father on his death-bed.

15. Cunctis qui aderant annitentibus, sed præcipue Croco (*alii Eroco*) [Erich?] Alemannorum Rege, auxilii gratiâ Constantium comitato, imperium capit. Victor Junior, c. 41. This is perhaps the first instance of a barbarian king who assisted the Roman arms with an independent body of his own subjects. The practice grew familiar, and at last became fatal.

16. His panegyrist Eumenius (vii. 8) ventures to affirm, in the presence of Constantine, that he put spurs to his horse, and tried, but in vain, to escape from the hands of his soldiers.

17. Lactantius de M. P. c. 25. Eumenius (vii. 8) gives a rhetorical turn to the whole transaction.

18. The choice of Constantine by his dying father, which is warranted by reason, and insinuated by Eumenius, seems to be confirmed by the most unexceptionable authority, the concurring evidence of Lactantius (de M. P. c. 24) and of Libanius (Oratio i.), of Eusebius (in Vit. Constantin. l. i. c. 21) and of Julian (Oratio i. [p. 7]).

19. Of the three sisters of Constantine, Constantia married the emperor Licinius, Anastasia the Cæsar Bassianus, and Eutropia the consul Nepotianus. The three brothers were, Dalmatius, Julius Constantius, and Annibalianus, of whom we shall have occasion to speak hereafter.

20. See Gruter Inscrip. p. 178. The six princes are all mentioned, Diocletian and Maximian as the senior Augusti, and fathers of the emperors. They jointly dedicate, for the use of *their own* Romans, this magnificent edifice. The architects have delineated the ruins of these *Thermæ;* and the antiquarians, particularly Donatus and Nardini, have ascertained the ground which they covered. One of the great rooms is now the Carthusian church; and even one of the porter's lodges is sufficient to form another church, which belongs to the Feuillans.

21. See Lactantius de M. P. c. 26, 31.

22. The sixth Panegyric represents the conduct of Maximian in the most favourable light; and the ambiguous expression of Aurelius Victor [de Cæsar. c. 40], "retractante diu," may signify either that he contrived, or that he opposed, the conspiracy. See Zosimus, l. ii. [c. 9] p. 79, and Lactantius de M. P. c. 26.

23. The circumstances of this war, and the death of Severus, are very doubtfully and variously told in our ancient fragments (see Tillemont, Hist.

des Empereurs, tom. iv. part. i. p. 555). I have endeavoured to extract from them a consistent and probable narration.

24. The sixth Panegyric was pronounced to celebrate the elevation of Constantine; but the prudent orator avoids the mention either of Galerius or of Maxentius. He introduces only one slight allusion to the actual troubles, and to the majesty of Rome.

25. With regard to this negotiation, see the fragments of an anonymous historian, published by Valesius at the end of his edition of Ammianus Marcellinus, p. 711. These fragments have furnished us with several curious, and, as it should seem, authentic anecdotes.

26. Lactantius de M. P. c. 27. The former of these reasons is probably taken from Virgil's Shepherd: "Illam . . . ego huic nostræ similem, Melibœe, putavi, etc." Lactantius delights in these poetical allusions.

27. Castra super Tusci si ponere Tybridis undas
   (jubeas)
   Hesperios audax veniam metator in agros.
   Tu quoscunque voles in planum effundere muros,
   His aries actus disperget saxa lacertis;
   Illa licet penitus tolli quam jusseris urbem
   Roma sit.   Lucan. Pharsal. i. 381.

28. Lactantius de M. P. c. 27. Zosim. l. ii. [c. 10] p. 82. The latter insinuates that Constantine, in his interview with Maximian, had promised to declare war against Galerius.

29. M. de Tillemont (Hist. des Empereurs, tom. iv. part. i. p. 559) has proved that Licinius, without passing through the intermediate rank of Cæsar, was declared Augustus, the 11th of November, A.D. 307, after the return of Galerius from Italy.

30. Lactantius de M. P. c. 32. When Galerius declared Licinius Augustus with himself, he tried to satisfy his younger associates, by inventing for Constantine and Maximin (not Maxentius, see Baluze, p. 81) the new title of sons of the Augusti. But when Maximin acquainted him that he had been saluted Augustus by the army, Galerius was obliged to acknowledge him, as well as Constantine, as equal associates in the Imperial dignity.

31. See Panegyr. Vet. vi. [v.] 9. Audi doloris nostri liberam vocem, etc. The whole passage is imagined with artful flattery, and expressed with an easy flow of eloquence.

32. Lactantius de M. P. c. 28. Zosim. l. ii. [c. 11] p. 82. A report was spread that Maxentius was the son of some obscure Syrian, and had been substituted by the wife of Maximian as her own child. See Aurelius Victor [Epit. 40], Anonym. Valesian. [§12], and Panegyr. Vet. ix. 3, 4.

33. Ab urbe pulsum, ab Italia fugatum, ab Illyrico repudiatum, tuis provinciis, tuis copiis, tuo palatio recepisti. Eumen. in Panegyr. Vet. vii. [vi.] 14.

34. Lactantius de M. P. c. 29. Yet after the resignation of the purple, Constantine still continued to Maximian the pomp and honours of the Imperial dignity; and on all public occasions gave the right-hand place to his father-in-law. Panegyr. Vet. viii. 15.

35. Zosim. l. ii. [c. 11] p. 82. Eumenius in Panegyr. Vet. vii. 16-21. The latter of these has undoubtedly represented the whole affair in the most favourable light for his sovereign. Yet even from this partial narrative we may conclude that the repeated clemency of Constantine, and the reiterated treasons of Maximian, as they are described by Lactantius (de M. P. c. 29, 30), and copied by the moderns, are destitute of any historical foundation.

36. Aurelius Victor, c. 40. But that lake was situated on the upper Pannonia, near the borders of Noricum; and the province of Valeria (a name which the wife of Galerius gave to the drained country) undoubtedly lay between the Drave and the Danube (Sextus Rufus, c. 8). I should therefore suspect that Victor has confounded the lake Pelso with the Volocean marshes, or, as they are now called, the lake Sabaton. It is placed in the heart of Valeria, and its present extent is not less than twelve Hungarian miles (about seventy English) in length, and two in breadth. See Severini Pannonia, l. i. c. 9.

37. Lactantius (de M. P. c. 33) and Eusebius (l. viii. c. 16) describe the symptoms and progress of his disorder with singular accuracy and apparent pleasure.

38. If any (like the late Dr. Jortin, Remarks on Ecclesiastical History, vol. ii. p. 307-356) still delight in recording the wonderful deaths of the persecutors, I would recommend to their perusal an admirable passage of Grotius (Hist. l. vii. p. 332) concerning the last illness of Philip II. of Spain.

39. See Eusebius, l. ix. 6, 10. Lactantius de M. P. c. 36. Zosimus is less exact, and evidently confounds Maximian with Maximin.

40. See the eighth Panegyr. in which Eumenius displays, in the presence of Constantine, the misery and the gratitude of the city of Autun.

41. Eutropius, x. 2. Panegyr. Veter. vii. 10, 11, 12. A great number of the French youth were likewise exposed to the same cruel and ignominious death.

42. Julian excludes Maxentius from the banquet of the Cæsars with abhorrence and contempt; and Zosimus (l. ii. [c. 14] p. 85) accuses him of every kind of cruelty and profligacy.

43. Zosimus, l. ii. [c. 14] p. 83-85. Aurelius Victor. [Cæsar. 40.]

44. The passage of Aurelius Victor (l. c.] should be read in the following manner: Primus instituto pessimo, munerum specie, Patres Oratoresque pecuniam conferre prodigenti sibi cogeret.

45. Panegyr. Vet. ix. 3. Euseb. Hist. Eccles. viii. 14, et in Vit. Constant. i. 33, 34. Rufinus, c. 17. The virtuous matron, who stabbed herself to escape the violence of Maxentius, was a Christian, wife to the præfect of the city, and her name was

Sophronia. It still remains a question among the casuists, Whether, on such occasions, suicide is justifiable?

46. Prætorianis cædem vulgi quondam annuerit, is the vague expression of Aurelius Victor. [Cæsar. 40]. See more particular, though somewhat different, accounts of a tumult and massacre which happened at Rome, in Eusebius (l. viii. c. 14), and in Zosimus (l. ii. [c. 13] p. 84).

47. See in the Panegyrics (ix. 14) a lively description of the indolence and vain pride of Maxentius. In another place [ib. c. 3] the orator observes that the riches which Rome had accumulated in a period of 1060 years were lavished by the tyrant on his mercenary bands; redemptis ad civile latrocinium manibus ingesserat.

48. After the victory of Constantine it was universally allowed that the motive of delivering the republic from a detested tyrant would, at any time, have justified his expedition into Italy. Euseb. in Vit. Constantin. l. i. c. 26. Panegyr. Vet. ix. 2.

49. Zosimus, l. ii. [c. 14] p. 84, 85. Nazarius in Panegyr. x. 7-13.

50. See Panegyr. Vet. ix. [viii.] 2. Omnibus fere tuis Comitibus et Ducibus non solum tacite mussantibus, sed etiam aperte timentibus; contra consilia hominum, contra Haruspicum monita, ipse per temet liberandæ urbis tempus venisse sentires. The embassy of the Romans is mentioned only by Zonaras (l. xiii. [c. 1.]), and by Cedrenus (in Compend. Hist. p. 270 [ed. Paris; vol. i. p. 474, ed. Bonn]); but those modern Greeks had the opportunity of consulting many writers which have since been lost, among which we may reckon the Life of Constantine by Praxagoras. Photius (p. 63) has made a short extract from that historical work.

51. Zosimus (l. ii. [c. 15] p. 86) has given us this curious account of the forces on both sides. He makes no mention of any naval armaments, though we are assured (Panegyr. Vet. ix. 25) that the war was carried on by sea as well as by land; and that the fleet of Constantine took possession of Sardinia, Corsica, and the ports of Italy.

52. Panegyr. Vet. ix. 3. It is not surprising that the orator should diminish the numbers with which his sovereign achieved the conquest of Italy; but it appears somewhat singular that he should esteem the tyrant's army at no more than 100,000 men.

53. The three principal passages of the Alps between Gaul and Italy are those of Mount St. Bernard, Mount Cenis, and Mount Genevre. Tradition, and a resemblance of names (Alpes Penninæ), had assigned the first of these for the march of Hannibal (see Simler de Alpibus). The Chevalier de Folard (Polyb. tom. iv.) and M. d'Anville have led him over Mount Genevre. But notwithstanding the authority of an experienced officer and a learned geographer, the pretensions of Mount Cenis are supported in a specious, not to say a con-

vincing manner, by M. Grosley, Observations sur l'Italie, tom. i. p. 40, etc.

54. La Brunette near Suse, Demont, Exiles, Fenestrelles, Coni, etc.

55. See Ammian. Marcellin. xv. 10. His description of the roads over the Alps is clear, lively, and accurate.

56. Zosimus as well as Eusebius hasten from the passage of the Alps to the decisive action near Rome. We must apply to the two Panegyrics for the intermediate actions of Constantine.

57. The Marquis Maffei has examined the siege and battle of Verona with that degree of attention and accuracy which was due to a memorable action that happened in his native country. The fortifications of that city, constructed by Gallienus, were less extensive than the modern walls, and the amphitheatre was not included within their circumference. See Verona Illustrata, part. i. p. 142, 150.

58. They wanted chains for so great a multitude of captives; and the whole council was at a loss; but the sagacious conqueror imagined the happy expedient of converting into fetters the swords of the vanquished. Panegyr. Vet. ix. 9.

59. Panegyr. Vet. ix. 10.

60. Literas calamitatum suarum indices supprimebat. Panegyr. Vet. ix. 15.

61. Remedia malorum potius quam mala differebat, is the fine censure which Tacitus passes on the supine indolence of Vitellius.

62. The Marquis Maffei has made it extremely probable that Constantine was still at Verona, the 1st of September, A.D. 312, and that the memorable era of the Indictions was dated from his conquest of the Cisalpine Gaul.

63. See Panegyr. Vet. xi. 16 [ix. 14?]. Lactantius de M. P. c. 44.

64. Illo die hostem Romanorum esse periturum. [Lact. l. c.] The vanquished prince became of course the enemy of Rome.

65. See Panegyr. Vet. ix. 16, x. 27. The former of these orators magnifies the hoards of corn which Maxentius had collected from Africa and the islands. And yet, if there is any truth in the scarcity mentioned by Eusebius (in Vit. Constantin. l. i. c. 36), the Imperial granaries must have been open only to the soldiers.

66. Maxentius . . . tandem urbe in Saxa Rubra, millia ferme novem ægerrime progressus. Aurelius Victor. [de Cæsar. 40]. See Cellarius Geograph. Antiq. tom. i. p. 463. Saxa Rubra was in the neighborhood of the Cremera, a trifling rivulet, illustrated by the valour and glorious death of the three hundred Fabii.

67. The post which Maxentius had taken, with the Tiber in his rear, is very clearly described by the two Panegyrists, ix. 16, x. 28.

68. Exceptis latrocinii illius primis auctoribus, qui desperatâ veniâ, locum quem pugnæ sumpserant texere corporibus. Panegyr. Vet. ix. 17.

69. A very idle rumour soon prevailed, that

Maxentius, who had not taken any precaution for his own retreat, had contrived a very artful snare to destroy the army of the pursuers; but that the wooden bridge, which was to have been loosened on the approach of Constantine, unluckily broke down under the weight of the flying Italians. M. de Tillemont (Hist. des Empereurs, tom. iv. part i. p. 576) very seriously examines whether, in contradiction to common sense, the testimony of Eusebius and Zosimus ought to prevail over the silence of Lactantius, Nazarius, and the anonymous but contemporary orator who composed the ninth Panegyric.

70. Zosimus, l. ii. [c. 15, sq.] p. 86-88, and the two Panegyrics, the former of which was pronounced a few months afterwards, afford the clearest notion of this great battle. Lactantius, Eusebius, and even the Epitomes, supply several useful hints.

71. Zosimus, the enemy of Constantine, allows (l. ii. [c. 17] p. 88) that only a few of the friends of Maxentius were put to death; but we may remark the expressive passage of Nazarius (Panegyr. Vet. x. 6): Omnibus qui labefactari statum ejus poterant cum stirpe deletis. The other orator (Panegyr. Vet. ix. 20, 21) contents himself with observing that Constantine, when he entered Rome, did not imitate the cruel massacres of Cinna, of Marius, or of Sylla.

72. See the two Panegyrics, and the laws of this and the ensuing year, in the Theodosian Code.

73. Panegyr. Vet. ix. 20. Lactantius de M. P. c. 44. Maximin, who had confessedly the eldest Cæsar, claimed, with some show of reason, the first rank among the Augusti.

74. Adhuc cuncta opera quæ magnifice construxerat, urbis fanum, atque basilicam, Flavii meritis patres sacravere. Aurelius Victor. [de Cæsar. 40.] With regard to the theft of Trajan's trophies, consult Flaminius Vacca, apud Montfaucon, Diarium Italicum, p. 250, and l'Antiquité Expliquée of the latter, tom. iv. p. 171.

75. Prætoriæ legiones ac subsidia factionibus aptiora quam urbi Romæ, sublata penitus; simul arma atque usus indumenti militaris. Aurelius Victor. [l. c.] Zosimus (l. ii. [c. 17] p. 89) mentions this fact as an historian, and it is very pompously celebrated in the ninth Panegyric.

76. Ex omnibus provinciis optimates viros Curiæ tuæ pigneraveris; ut Senatûs dignitas . . . ex totius Orbis flore consisterat. Nazarius in Panegyr. Vet. x. [ix.] 35. The word pigneraveris might almost seem maliciously chosen. Concerning the senatorial tax, see Zosimus, l. ii. [c. 38] p. 115; the second title of the sixth book of the Theodosian Code, with Godefroy's Commentary; and Mémoires de l'Académie des Inscriptions, tom. xxviii. p. 726.

77. From the Theodosian Code we may now begin to trace the motions of the emperors; but the dates both of time and place have frequently been altered by the carelessness of transcribers.

78. Zosimus (l. ii. [c. 17] p. 89) observes, that

before the war the sister of Constantine had been betrothed to Licinius. According to the younger Victor [Epit. c. 39], Diocletian was invited to the nuptials; but having ventured to plead his age and infirmities, he received a second letter filled with reproaches for his supposed partiality to the cause of Maxentius and Maximin.

79. Zosimus mentions the defeat and death of Maximin as ordinary events; but Lactantius expatiates on them (de M. P. c. 45-50), ascribing them to the miraculous interposition of Heaven. Licinius at that time was one of the protectors of the church.

80. Lactantius de M. P. c. 50. Aurelius Victor touches on the different conduct of Licinius, and of Constantine, in the use of victory.

81. The sensual appetites of Maximin were gratified at the expense of his subjects. His eunuchs, who forced away wives and virgins, examined their naked charms with anxious curiosity, lest any part of their body should be found unworthy of the royal embraces. Coyness and disdain were considered as treason, and the obstinate fair one was condemned to be drowned. A custom was gradually introduced that no person should marry a wife without the permission of the emperor, "ut ipse in omnibus nuptiis prægustator esset". Lactantius de M. P. c. 38.

82. Lactantius de M. P. c. 39.

83. Diocletian at last sent cognatum suum, quendam militarem ac potentem virum, to intercede in favour of his daughter (Lactantius de M. P. c. 41). We are not sufficiently acquainted with the history of these times to point out the person who was employed.

84. Valeria quoque per varias provincias quindecim mensibus plebeio cultû pervagata. Lactantius de M. P. c. 51. There is some doubt whether we should compute the fifteen months from the moment of her exile, or from that of her escape. The expression of pervagata seems to denote the latter; but in that case we must suppose that the treatise of Lactantius was written after the first civil war between Licinius and Constantine. See Cuper, p. 254.

85. Ita illis pudicitia et conditio exitio fuit. Lactantius de M. P. c. 51. He relates the misfortunes of the innocent wife and daughter of Diocletian with a very natural mixture of pity and exultation.

86. The curious reader who consults the Valesian Fragment, p. 713, will probably accuse me of giving a bold and licentious paraphrase; but if he considers it with attention, he will acknowledge that my interpretation is probable and consistent.

87. The situation of Æmona, or, as it is now called, Laybach, in Carniola (d'Anville, Géographie Ancienne, tom. i. p. 187), may suggest a conjecture. As it lay to the north-east of the Julian Alps, that important territory became a natural object of dispute between the sovereigns of Italy and of Illyricum.

88. Cibalis or Cibalæ (whose name is still pre-

served in the obscure ruins of Swilei) was situated
about fifty miles from Sirmium, the capital of
Illyricum, and about one hundred from Tauru-
num, or Belgrade, and the conflux of the Danube
and the Save. The Roman garrisons and cities on
those rivers are finely illustrated by M. d'Anville,
in a memoir inserted in l'Académie des Inscriptions, tom. xxviii.

89. Zosimus (l. ii. [c. 18] p. 90, 91) gives a very
particular account of this battle; but the descriptions of Zosimus are rhetorical rather than military.

90. Zosimus, l. ii. [c. 19] p. 92, 93. Anonym.
Valesian. p. 713. The Epitomes furnish some circumstances; but they frequently confound the two
wars between Licinius and Constantine.

91. Petrus Patricius in Excerpt. Legat. p. 27
[ed. Paris; p. 19, ed. Ven.; p. 129, ed. Bonn]. If it
should be thought that γάμβρος signifies more
properly a son-in-law, we might conjecture that
Constantine, assuming the name as well as the
duties of a father, had adopted his younger brothers and sisters, the children of Theodora. But in
the best authors γάμβρος sometimes signifies a husband, sometimes a father-in-law, and sometimes a
kinsman in general. See Spanheim Observat. ad
Julian. Orat. i. p. 72.

92. Zosimus, l. ii. [c. 20] p. 93. Anonym. Valesian, p. 713. Eutropius, x. 4. Aurelius Victor,
Euseb. in Chron. [An. CCCXVIII.] Sozomen, l. i.
c. 2. Four of these writers affirm that the promotion
of the Cæsars was an article of the treaty. It is however certain that the younger Constantine and
Licinius were not yet born; and it is highly probable that the promotion was made the 1st of
March, A.D. 317. The treaty had probably stipulated that the two Cæsars might be created by the
western, and one only by the eastern emperor; but
each of them reserved to himself the choice of the
persons.

93. Codex Theodosian, l. xi. tit. 27, tom. iv. p.
188, with Godefroy's observations. See likewise, l.
v. tit. 7, 8.

94. Omnia foris placida domi prospera, annonæ
ubertate, fructuum copiâ, etc. Panegyr. Vet. x. 38.
This oration of Nazarius was pronounced on the
day of the Quinquennalia of the Cæsars, the 1st of
March, A.D. 321,

95. See the edict of Constantine, addressed to
the Roman people, in the Theodosian Code, l. ix.
tit. 24, tom. iii. p. 189.

96. His son very fairly assigns the true reason of
the repeal. "Ne sub specie atrocioris judicii aliqua
in ulciscendo crimine dilatio nasceretur." Cod.
Theod. tom. iii. p. 193.

97. Eusebius (in Vitâ Constant. l. iii. c. 1)
chooses to affirm that in the reign of this hero the
sword of justice hung idle in the hands of the magistrates. Eusebius himself (l. iv. c. 29, 54) and the
Theodosian Code will inform us that this excessive
lenity was not owing to the want either of atrocious
criminals or of penal laws.

98. Nazarius in Panegyr. Vet. x. [36]. The victory of Crispus over the Alemanni is expressed on
some medals.

99. See Zosimus, l. ii. [c. 21] p. 93, 94; though
the narrative of that historian is neither clear nor
consistent. The Panegyric of Optatianus (c. 32)
mentions the alliance of the Sarmatians with the
Carpi and Getæ, and points out the several fields of
battle. It is supposed that the Sarmatian games,
celebrated in the month of November, derived
their origin from the success of this war.

100. In the Cæsars of Julian (p. 329. Commentaire de Spanheim, p. 252). Constantine boasts
that he had recovered the province (Dacia) which
Trajan had subdued. But it is insinuated by
Silenus that the conquests of Constantine were like
the gardens of Adonis, which fade and wither almost the moment they appear.

101. Jornandes de Rebus Geticis, c. 21. I know
not whether we may entirely depend on his authority. Such an alliance has a very recent air, and
scarcely is suited to the maxims of the beginning
of the fourth century.

102. Eusebius in Vit. Constantin. l. i. c. 8. This
passage, however, is taken from a general declamation on the greatness of Constantine, and not
from any particular account of the Gothic war.

103. Constantinus tamen, vir ingens, et omnia
efficere nitens quæ animo præparasset, simul principatum totius orbis affectans, Licinio bellum in-
tulit. Eutropius, x. 5 [4]. Zosimus, l. ii. [c. 18] p.
89. The reasons which they have assigned for the
first civil war may, with more propriety, be applied to the second.

104. Zosimus, l. ii. [c. 22] p. 94, 95.

105. Constantine was very attentive to the privileges and comforts of his fellow-veterans (Convet-
erani), as he now began to style them. See the
Theodosian Code, l. vii. tit. 10, tom. ii. p. 419, 429.

106. Whilst the Athenians maintained the empire of the sea, their fleet consisted of three, and
afterwards of four, hundred galleys of three ranks
of oars, all completely equipped and ready for
immediate service. The arsenal in the port of
Piræus had cost the republic a thousand talents,
about two hundred and sixteen thousand pounds.
See Thucydides de Bel. Pelopon. l. ii. c. 13; and
Meursius de Fortuna Attica, c. 19.

107. Zosimus, l. ii. [c. 22] p. 95, 96. This great
battle is described in the Valesian fragment (p.
714) [ad fin. Amm. Marcell. vol. ii. p. 300, ed.
Bip.] in a clear though concise manner. "Licinius
vero circum Hadrianopolin maximo exercitu late-
ra ardui montis impleverat; illuc toto agmine Constantinus inflexit. Cum bellum terrâ marique tra-
heretur, quamvis per arduum suis nitentibus, atta-
men disciplinâ militari et felicitate, Constantinus
Licinii confusum et sine ordine agentem vicit exercitum; leviter femore sauciatus."

108. Zosimus, l. ii. [c. 24] p. 97, 98. The current
always sets out of the Hellespont; and when it is
assisted by a north wind, no vessel can attempt the

passage. A south wind renders the force of the current almost imperceptible. See Tournefort's Voyage au Levant. Let. xi.

109. Aurelius Victor. [de Cæsar. c. 41.] Zosimus, l. ii. [c. 25] p. 93. According to the latter, Martinianus was Magister Officiorum (he uses the Latin appellation in Greek). Some medals seem to intimate that during his short reign he received the title of Augustus.

110. Eusebius (in Vitâ Constantin. l. ii. c. 16, 17) ascribes this decisive victory to the pious prayers of the emperor. The Valesian fragment (p. 714) [Amm. Marcell. vol. ii. p. 301, ed. Bip.] mentions a body of Gothic auxiliaries, under their chief Aliquaca, who adhered to the party of Licinius.

111. Zosimus, l. ii. [c. 28] p. 102. Victor Junior in Epitome. [c. 41.] Anonym. Valesian, p. 714.

112. Contra religionem sacramenti Thessalonicæ privatus occisus est. Eutropius, x. 6 [4]; and his evidence is confirmed by Jerome (in Chronic.), as well as by Zosimus, l. ii. [c. 28] p. 102. The Valesian writer is the only one who mentions the soldiers, and it is Zonaras alone who calls in the assistance of the senate. Eusebius prudently slides over this delicate transaction. But Sozomen, a century afterwards, ventures to assert the treasonable practices of Licinius.

113. See the Theodosian Code, l. xv. tit. 15, tom. v. p. 404, 405. These edicts of Constantine betray a degree of passion and precipitancy very unbecoming the character of a lawgiver.

Chapter XV

1. Dum Assyrios penes, Medosque, et Persas Oriens fuit, despectissima pars servientium. Tacit. Hist. v. 8. Herodotus, who visited Asia whilst it obeyed the last of those empires, slightly mentions the Syrians of Palestine, who, according to their own confession, had received from Egypt the rite of circumcision. See l. ii. c. 104.

2. Diodorus Siculus, l. xl. [Eclog. 1, vol. ii. p. 542, ed. Wesseling.] Dion Cassius, l. xxxvii. [c. 16] p. 121. Tacit. Hist. v. 1-9. Justin, xxxvi, 2, 3.

3. Tradidit arcano quæcunque volumine Moses:
   Non monstrare vias eadem nisi sacra colenti,
   Quæsitum ad fontem solos deducere verpos.
   [Juvenal, Sat. xiv. 102.]
The letter of this law is not to be found in the present volume of Moses. But the wise, the humane Maimonides openly teaches that, if an idolater fall into the water, a Jew ought not to save him from instant death. See Basnage, Histoire des Juifs, l. vi. c. 28 [l. v. c. 24].

4. A Jewish sect, which indulged themselves in a sort of occasional conformity, derived from Herod, by whose example and authority they had been seduced, the name of Herodians. But their numbers were so inconsiderable, and their duration so short, that Josephus has not thought them worthy of his notice. See Prideaux's Connection, vol. ii. p. 285.

5. Cicero pro Flacco, c. 28.

6. Philo de Legatione. Augustus left a foundation for a perpetual sacrifice. Yet he approved of the neglect which his grandson Caius expressed towards the temple of Jerusalem. See Sueton. in August. c 93, and Casaubon's notes on that passage.

7. See in particular, Joseph. Antiquit. xvii. 6, xviii. 3; and De Bell. Judaic. i. 33, and ii. 9, edit. Havercamp.

8. Jussi a Caio Cesare, effigiem ejus in templo locare, arma potius sumpsere. Tacit. Hist. v. 9. Philo and Josephus give a very circumstantial, but

a very rhetorical, account of this transaction, which exceedingly perplexed the governor of Syria. At the first mention of this idolatrous proposal king Agrippa fainted away, and did not recover his senses until the third day.

9. For the enumeration of the Syrian and Arabian deities, it may be observed that Milton has comprised in one hundred and thirty very beautiful lines the two large and learned syntagmas which Selden had composed on that abstruse subject.

10. "How long will this people provoke me? and how long will it be ere they *believe* me, for all the *signs* which I have shown among them?" (Numbers xiv. 11.) It would be easy, but it would be unbecoming, to justify the complaint of the Deity from the whole tenor of the Mosaic history.

11. All that relates to the Jewish proselytes has been very ably treated by Basnage, Hist. des Juifs, l. v. c. 6, 7.

12. See Exod. xxxiv, 23, Deut. xvi. 16, the commentators, and a very sensible note in the Universal History, vol. i. p. 603, edit. fol.

13. When Pompey, using or abusing the right of conquest, entered into the Holy of Holies, it was observed with amazement, "Nullâ intus Deûm effigie, vacuam sedem et inania arcana." Tacit. Hist. v. 9. It was a popular saying, with regard to the Jews,

Nil præter nubes et cœli numen adorant.

14. A second kind of circumcision was inflicted on a Samaritan or Egyptian proselyte. The sullen indifference of the Talmudists, with respect to the conversion of strangers, may be seen in Basnage, Histoire des Juifes, l. v. c. 6.

15. These arguments were urged with great ingenuity by the Jew Orobio, and refuted with equal ingenuity and candour by the Christian Limborch. See the Amica Collatio (it well deserves that name), or account of the dispute between them.

16. Jesus . . . circumcisus erat; cibis utebatur

Judaicis; vestitû simili; purgatos scabie mittebat ad sacerdotes; Paschata et alios dies festos religiosè observabat: si quos sanavit sabbatho, ostendit non tantum ex lege, sed et ex receptis sententis, talia opera sabbatho non interdicta. Grotius de Veritate Religionis Christianæ, l. v. c. 7. A little afterwards (c. 12) he expatiates on the condescension of the apostles.

17. Pæne omnes Christum Deum sub legis observatione credebant. Sulpicius Severus, ii. 31. See Eusebius, Hist. Ecclesiast, l. iv. c. 5.

18. Mosheim de Rebus Christianis ante Constantinum Magnum, p. 153. In this masterly performance, which I shall often have occasion to quote, he enters much more fully into the state of the primitive church than he has an opportunity of doing in his General History.

19. Eusebius, l. iii. c. 5. Le Clerc, Hist. Ecclesiast. p. 605. During this occasional absence, the bishop and church of Pella still retained the title of Jerusalem. In the same manner, the Roman pontiffs resided seventy years at Avignon; and the patriarchs of Alexandria have long since transferred their episcopal seat to Cairo.

20. Dion Cassius, l. lxix. [c. 12]. The exile of the Jewish nation from Jerusalem is attested by Aristo of Pella (apud Euseb. l. iv. c. 6), and is mentioned by several ecclesiastical writers; though some of them too hastily extend this interdiction to the whole country of Palestine.

21. Eusebius, l. iv. c. 6. Sulpicius Severus, ii. 31. By comparing their unsatisfactory accounts, Mosheim (p. 327, etc.) has drawn out a very distinct representation of the circumstances and motives of this revolution.

22. Le Clerc (Hist. Ecclesiast. p. 477, 535) seems to have collected from Eusebius, Jerome, Epiphanius, and other writers, all the principal circumstances that relate to the Nazarenes or Ebionites. The nature of their opinions soon divided them into a stricter and a milder sect; and there is some reason to conjecture that the family of Jesus Christ remained members, at least, of the latter and more moderate party.

23. Some writers have been pleased to create an Ebion, the imaginary author of their sect and name. But we can more safely rely on the learned Eusebius than on the vehement Tertullian, or the credulous Epiphanius. According to Le Clerc, the Hebrew word *Ebjonim* may be translated into Latin by that of *Pauperes*. See Hist. Ecclesiast. p. 477.

24. See the very curious Dialogue of Justin Martyr with the Jew Tryphon. The conference between them was held at Ephesus, in the reign of Antoninus Pius, and about twenty years after the return of the church of Pella to Jerusalem. For this date consult the accurate note of Tillemont, Mémoires Ecclésiastiques, tom. ii. p. 511.

25. Of all the systems of Christianity, that of Abyssinia is the only one which still adheres to the Mosaic rites (Geddes's Church History of Æthio-

pia, and Dissertations de La Grand sur la Relation du P. Lobo). The eunuch of the queen Candace might suggest some suspicions; but as we are assured (Socrates, i. 19; Sozomen, ii. 24; Ludolphus, p. 281) that the Æthiopians were not converted till the fourth century, it is more reasonable to believe that they respected the sabbath, and distinguished the forbidden meats, in imitation of the Jews, who, in a very early period, were seated on both sides of the Red Sea. Circumcision had been practised by the most ancient Æthiopians, from motives of health and cleanliness, which seem to be explained in the Recherches Philosophiques sur les Américains, tom. ii. p. 117.

26. Beausobre, Histoire du Manichéisme, l. i. c. 3, has stated their objections, particularly those of Faustus, the adversary of Augustin, with the most learned impartiality.

27. Apud ipsos fides obstinata, misericordia in promptû: adversus omnes alios hostile odium. Tacit. Hist. v. 5. Surely Tacitus had seen the Jews with too favourable an eye. The perusal of Josephus must have destroyed the antithesis.

28. Dr. Burnet (Archæologia, l. ii. c. 7) has discussed the first chapters of Genesis with too much wit and freedom.

29. The milder Gnostics considered Jehovah, the Creator, as a Being of a mixed nature between God and the Dæmon. Others confounded him with the evil principle. Consult the second century of the general history of Mosheim, which gives a very distinct, though concise, account of their strange opinions on this subject.

30. See Beausobre, Hist. du Manichéisme, l. i. c. 4. Origen and St. Augustin were among the allegorists.

31. Hegesippus, ap. Euseb. l. iii. 32; iv. 22. Clemens Alexandrin. Stromat. vii. 17.

32. In the account of the Gnostics of the second and third centuries, Mosheim is ingenious and candid; Le Clerc dull, but exact; Beausobre almost always an apologist; and it is much to be feared that the primitive fathers are very frequently calumniators.

33. See the catalogues of Irenæus and Epiphanius. It must indeed be allowed that those writers were inclined to multiply the number of sects which opposed the *unity* of the church.

34. Eusebius, l. iv. c. 15. Sozomen, l. ii. c. 32. See in Bayle, in the article of *Marcion*, a curious detail of a dispute on that subject. It should seem that some of the Gnostics (the Basilidians) declined, and even refused, the honour of martyrdom. Their reasons were singular and abstruse. See Mosheim, p. 539.

35. See a very remarkable passage of Origen (Proem. ad Lucam.). That indefatigable writer, who had consumed his life in the study of the Scriptures, relies for their authenticity on the inspired authority of the church. It was impossible that the Gnostics could receive our present Gospels, many parts of which (particularly in the

resurrection of Christ) are directly, and as it might seem designedly, pointed against their favourite tenets. It is therefore somewhat singular that Ignatius (Epist. ad Smyrn. Patr. Apostol. tom. ii. p. 34) should choose to employ a vague and doubtful tradition, instead of quoting the certain testimony of the evangelists.

36. Faciunt favos et vespæ; faciunt ecclesias et Marcionitæ, is the strong expression of Tertullian, which I am obliged to quote from memory. [Adv. Marcion, iv. 5] In the time of Epiphanius (advers. Hæreses, p. 302 [ed. Paris, 1622]) the Marcionites were very numerous in Italy, Syria, Egypt, Arabia, and Persia.

37. Augustin is a memorable instance of this gradual progress from reason to faith. He was, during several years, engaged in the Manichæan sect.

38. The unanimous sentiment of the primitive church is very clearly explained by Justin Martyr, Apolog. Major [c. 25, p. 59, ed. Bened.]; by Athenagoras, Legat. c. 22, etc.; and by Lactantius, Institut. Divin. ii. 14-19.

39. Tertullian (Apolog. c. 23) alleges the confession of the dæmons themselves as often as they were tormented by the Christian exorcists.

40. Tertullian has written a most severe treatise against idolatry, to caution his brethren against the hourly danger of incurring that guilt. Recogita silvam, et quantæ latitant spinæ. De Coronâ Militis. c. 10.

41. The Roman senate was always held in a temple or consecrated place (Aulus Gellius, xiv. 7). Before they entered on business, every senator dropped some wine and frankincense on the altar. Sueton. in August. c. 35.

42. See Tertullian, De Spectaculis. This severe reformer shows no more indulgence to a tragedy of Euripides than to a combat of gladiators. The dress of the actors particularly offends him. By the use of the lofty buskin they impiously strive to add a cubit to their stature: c. 23.

43. The ancient practice of concluding the entertainment with libations may be found in every classic. Socrates and Seneca, in their last moments, made a noble application of this custom. Postremo stagnum calidæ aquæ introiit, respergens proximos servorum, additâ voce, libare se liquorem illum Jovi Liberatori. Tacit. Annal. xv. 64.

44. See the elegant but idolatrous hymn of Catullus on the nuptials of Manlius and Julia. O Hymen, Hymenæe Iö! Quis huic Deo compararier ausit?

45. The ancient funerals (in those of Misenus and Pallas) are no less accurately described by Virgil than they are illustrated by his commentator Servius. The pile itself was an altar, the flames were fed with the blood of victims, and all the assistants were sprinkled with lustral water.

46. Tertullian de Idololatria, c. 11.

47. See every part of Montfaucon's Antiquities. Even the reverses of the Greek and Roman coins were frequently of an idolatrous nature. Here, indeed, the scruples of the Christian were suspended by a stronger passion.

48. Tertullian de Idololatria, c. 20, 21, 22. If a Pagan friend (on the occasion perhaps of sneezing) used the familiar expression of "Jupiter bless you," the Christian was obliged to protest against the divinity of Jupiter.

49. Consult the most laboured work of Ovid, his imperfect Fasti. He finished no more than the first six months of the year. The compilation of Macrobius is called the Saturnalia, but it is only a small part of the first book that bears any relation to the title.

50. Tertullian has composed a defence, or rather panegyric, of the rash action of a Christian soldier, who, by throwing away his crown of laurel, had exposed himself and his brethren to the most imminent danger. By the mention of the emperors (Severus and Caracalla) it is evident, notwithstanding the wishes of M. de Tillemont, that Tertullian composed his treatise De Coronâ long before he was engaged in the errors of the Montanists. See Mémoires Ecclésiastiques, tom. iii. p. 384.

51. In particular, the first book of the Tusculan Questions, and the treatise De Senectute, and the Somnium Scipionis, contain, in the most beautiful language, everything that Grecian philosophy or Roman good sense could possibly suggest on this dark but important object.

52. The pre-existence of human souls, so far at least as that doctrine is compatible with religion, was adopted by many of the Greek and Latin fathers. See Beausobre, Hist. du Manichéisme, l. vi. c. 4.

53. See Cicero pro Cluent. c. 61. Cæsar ap. Sallust. de Bell. Catilin. c. 51. Juvenal. Satir. ii. 149.

Esse aliquid manes, et subterranea regna,

. . . . . .

Nec pueri credunt, nisi qui nondum ære lavantur.

54. The eleventh book of the Odyssey gives a very dreary and incoherent account of the infernal shades. Pindar and Virgil have embellished the picture; but even those poets, though more correct than their great model, are guilty of very strange inconsistencies. See Bayle, Responses aux Questions d'un Provincial, part iii. c. 22.

55. See the sixteenth epistle of the first book of Horace, the thirteenth Satire of Juvenal, and the second Satire of Persius: these popular discourses express the sentiment and language of the multitude.

56. If we confine ourselves to the Gauls, we may observe that they intrusted not only their lives, but even their money, to the security of another world. Vetus ille mos Gallorum occurrit (says Valerius Maximus, l. ii. c. 6, § 10) quos, memoria proditum est, pecunias mutuas, quæ his apud inferos redderentur, dare solitos. The same custom is more darkly insinuated by Mela, l. iii. c. 2. It is almost needless to add that the profits of trade hold a just

proportion to the credit of the merchant, and that the Druids derived from their holy profession a character of responsibility which could scarcely be claimed by any other order of men.

57. The right reverend author of the Divine Legation of Moses assigns a very curious reason for the omission, and most ingeniously retorts it on the unbelievers.

58. See Le Clerc (Prolegomena ad Hist. Ecclesiast. sect. 1, c. 8). His authority seems to carry the greater weight, as he has written a learned and judicious commentary on the books of the Old Testament.

59. Joseph. Antiquitat. l. xiii. c. 10 [§ 5, *sq.*]; De Bell. Jud. ii. 8 [§ 2]. According to the most natural interpretation of his words, the Sadducees admitted only the Pentateuch; but it has pleased some modern critics to add the Prophets to their creed, and to suppose that they contented themselves with rejecting the traditions of the Pharisees. Dr. Jortin has argued that point in his Remarks on Ecclesiastical History, vol. ii. p. 103.

60. This expectation was countenanced by the twenty-fourth chapter of St. Matthew, and by the first epistle of St. Paul to the Thessalonians. Erasmus removes the difficulty by the help of allegory and metaphor; and the learned Grotius ventures to insinuate, that, for wise purposes, the pious deception was permitted to take place.

61. See Burnet's Sacred Theory, part iii. c. 5. This tradition may be traced as high as the author of the Epistle of Barnabas, who wrote in the first century, and who seems to have been half a Jew.

62. The primitive church of Antioch computed almost 6000 years from the creation of the world to the birth of Christ. Africanus, Lactantius, and the Greek church have reduced that number to 5500, and Eusebius has contented himself with 5200 years. These calculations were formed on the Septuagint, which was universally received during the six first centuries. The authority of the Vulgate and of the Hebrew text has determined the moderns, Protestants as well as Catholics, to prefer a period of about 4000 years; though, in the study of profane antiquity, they often find themselves straitened by those narrow limits.

63. Most of these pictures were borrowed from a misrepresentation of Isaiah, Daniel, and the Apocalypse. One of the grossest images may be found in Irenæus (l. v. [c. 23] p. 455 [ed. Oxon. 1702]), the disciple of Papias, who had seen the apostle St. John.

64. See the second dialogue of Justin with Tryphon, and the seventh book of Lactantius. It is unnecessary to allege all the intermediate fathers, as the fact is not disputed. Yet the curious reader may consult Daillè de Usu Patrum, l. ii. c. 4.

65. The testimony of Justin of his own faith and that of his orthodox brethren, in the doctrine of a Millennium, is delivered in the clearest and most solemn manner (Dialog. cum Tryphonte Jud. p. 177, 178, edit. Benedictin.). If in the beginning of this important passage there is anything like an inconsistency, we may impute it, as we think proper, either to the author or to his transcribers.

66. Dupin, Bibliothèque Ecclésiastique, tom. i. p. 223, tom. ii. p. 366, and Mosheim, p. 720; though the latter of these learned divines is not altogether candid on this occasion.

67. In the council of Laodicea (about the year 360) the Apocalypse was tacitly excluded from the sacred canon by the same churches of Asia to which it is addressed; and we may learn from the complaint of Sulpicius Severus that their sentence had been ratified by the greater number of Christians of his time. From what causes then is the Apocalypse at present so generally received by the Greek, the Roman, and the Protestant churches? The following ones may be assigned:—1. The Greeks were subdued by the authority of an impostor, who, in the sixth century, assumed the character of Dionysius the Areopagite. 2. A just apprehension that the grammarians might become more important than the theologians engaged the council of Trent to fix the seal of their infallibility on all the books of Scripture contained in the Latin Vulgate, in the number of which the Apocalypse was fortunately included (Fr. Paolo, Istoria del Concilio Tridentino, l. ii.). 3. The advantage of turning those mysterious prophecies against the See of Rome inspired the Protestants with uncommon veneration for so useful an ally. See the ingenious and elegant discourses of the present bishop of Lichfield on that unpromising subject.

68. Lactantius (Institut. Divin. vii. 15, etc.) relates the dismal tale of futurity with great spirit and eloquence.

69. On this subject every reader of taste will be entertained with the third part of Burnet's Sacred Theory. He blends philosophy, Scripture, and tradition, into one magnificent system; in the description of which he displays a strength of fancy not inferior to that of Milton himself.

70. And yet, whatever may be the language of individuals, it is still the public doctrine of all the Christian churches; nor can even our own refuse to admit the conclusions which must be drawn from the eighth and the eighteenth of her Articles. The Jansenists, who have so diligently studied the works of the fathers, maintain this sentiment with distinguished zeal; and the learned M. de Tillemont never dismisses a virtuous emperor without pronouncing his damnation. Zuinglius is perhaps the only leader of a party who has ever adopted the milder sentiment, and he gave no less offence to the Lutherans than to the Catholics. See Bossuet, Histoire des Variations des Eglises Protestantes, l. ii. c. 19–22.

71. Justin and Clemens of Alexandria allow that some of the philosophers were instructed by the Logos; confounding its double signification of the human reason and of the Divine Word.

72. Tertullian, de Spectaculis, c. 30. In order to ascertain the degree of authority which the zealous

African had acquired, it may be sufficient to allege the testimony of Cyprian, the doctor and guide of all the western churches (see Prudent. Hym. xiii. 100). As often as he applied himself to his daily study of the writings of Tertullian, he was accustomed to say "*Da mihi magistrum;* Give me my master." (Hieronym. de Viris Illustribus, tom. i. p. 284 [c. 53, tom. ii. p. 878, ed. Vallars.]).

73. Notwithstanding the evasions of Dr. Middleton, it is impossible to overlook the clear traces of visions and inspiration which may be found in the apostolic fathers.

74. Irenæus adv. Hæres. Proem. p. 3. Dr. Middleton (Free Inquiry, p. 96, etc.) observes that, as this pretension of all others was the most difficult to support by art, it was the soonest given up. The observation suits his hypothesis.

75. Athenagoras in Legatione. Justin Martyr, Cohort. ad Gentes. Tertullian advers. Marcionem, l. iv. These descriptions are not very unlike the prophetic fury for which Cicero (de Divinat. ii. 54) expresses so little reverence.

76. Tertullian (Apolog. c. 23) throws out a bold defiance to the Pagan magistrates. Of the primitive miracles, the power of exorcising is the only one which has been assumed by Protestants.

77. Irenæus adv. Hæreses, l. ii. c. 56, 57, l. v. c. 6. Mr. Dodwell (Dissertat. ad Irenæum, ii. 42) concludes that the second century was still more fertile in miracles than the first.

78. Theophilus ad Autolycum, l. i. p. 345, edit. Benedictin. Paris, 1742 [p. 35, ed. Oxon. 1684].

79. Dr. Middleton sent out his Introduction in the year 1747, published his Free Inquiry in 1749, and before his death, which happened in 1750, he had prepared a vindication of it against his numerous adversaries.

80. The university of Oxford conferred degrees on his opponents. From the indignation of Mosheim (p. 221) we may discover the sentiments of the Lutheran divines.

81. It may seem somewhat remarkable that Bernard of Clairvaux, who records so many miracles of his friend St. Malachi, never takes any notice of his own, which, in their turn, however, are carefully related by his companions and disciples. In the long series of ecclesiastical history, does there exist a single instance of a saint asserting that he himself possessed the gift of miracles?

82. The conversion of Constantine is the era which is most usually fixed by Protestants. The more rational divines are unwilling to admit the miracles of the fourth, whilst the more credulous are unwilling to reject those of the fifth century.

83. The imputations of Celsus and Julian, with the defence of the fathers, are very fairly stated by Spanheim, Commentaire sur les Césars de Julian, p. 468.

84. Plin. Epist. x. 97.

85. Tertullian, Apolog. c. 44. He adds, however, with some degree of hesitation, "Aut si [et] aliud, jam non Christianus."

86. The philosopher Peregrinus (of whose life and death Lucian has left us so entertaining an account) imposed, for a long time, on the credulous simplicity of the Christians of Asia.

87. See a very judicious treatise of Barbeyrac sur la Morale des Pères.

88. Lactant. Institut. Divin. l. vi. c. 20, 21, 22.

89. Consult a work of Clemens of Alexandria, entitled The Pædagogue, which contains the rudiments of ethics, as they were taught in the most celebrated of the Christian schools.

90. Tertullian, de Spectaculis, c. 23. Clemens Alexandrin, Pædagog. l. iii. c. 8.

91. Beausobre, Hist. Critique du Manichéisme, l. vii. c. 3. Justin, Gregory of Nyssa, Augustin, etc., strongly inclined to this opinion.

92. Some of the Gnostic heretics were more consistent; they rejected the use of marriage.

93. See a chain of tradition, from Justin Martyr to Jerome, in the Morale des Pères, c. iv. 6–26.

94. See a very curious Dissertation on the Vestals, in the Mémoires de l'Académie des Inscriptions, tom. iv. p. 161–227. Notwithstanding the honours and rewards which were bestowed on those virgins, it was difficult to procure a sufficient number; nor could the dread of the most horrible death always restrain their incontinence.

95. Cupiditatem procreandi aut unam scimus aut nullam. Minucius Felix, c. 31. Justin. Apolog. Major. Anthenagoras in Legat. c. 28. Tertullian de Cultu Femin. l. ii.

96. Eusebius, l. vi. 8. Before the fame of Origen had excited envy and persecution, this extraordinary action was rather admired than censured. As it was his general practice to allegorise Scripture, it seems unfortunate that, in this instance only, he should have adopted the literal sense.

97. Cyprian. Epist. 4, and Dodwell, Dissertat. Cyprianic. iii. Something like this rash attempt was long afterwards imputed to the founder of the order of Fontevrault. Bayle has amused himself and his readers on that very delicate subject.

98. Dupin (Bibliothèque Ecclésiastique, tom. i. p. 195) gives a particular account of the dialogue of the ten virgins, as it was composed by Methodius, bishop of Tyre. The praises of virginity are excessive.

99. The Ascetics (as early as the second century) made a public profession of mortifying their bodies, and of abstaining from the use of flesh and wine. Mosheim, p. 310.

100. See the Morale des Pères. The same patient principles have been revived since the Reformation by the Socinians, the modern Anabaptists, and the Quakers. Barclay, the Apologist of the Quakers, has protected his brethren by the authority of the primitive Christians; p. 542–549.

101. Tertullian, Apolog. c. 21; De Idololatriâ, c. 17, 18. Origen contra Celsum, l. v. p. 253 [c. 33, tom. i. p. 602, ed. Bened.], l. vii. p. 349 [c. 26, p. 712], l. viii. p. 423–428 [c. 68 *sq.* p. 793 *sq.*].

102. Tertullian (de Coronâ Militis, c. 11) sug-

gested to them the expedient of deserting; a counsel which, if it had been generally known, was not very proper to conciliate the favour of the emperors towards the Christian sect.

103. As well as we can judge from the mutilated representation of Origen (l. viii. p. 423 [c. 73, tom. i. p. 796, ed. Bened.]), his adversary, Celsus, had urged his objection with great force and candour.

104. The aristocratical party in France, as well as in England, has strenuously maintained the divine origin of bishops. But the Calvinistical presbyters were impatient of a superior; and the Roman Pontiff refused to acknowledge an equal. See Fra Paolo.

105. In the history of the Christian hierarchy, I have, for the most part, followed the learned and candid Mosheim.

106. For the prophets of the primitive church, see Mosheim, Dissertationes ad Hist. Eccles. pertinentes, tom. ii. p. 132–208.

107. See the epistles of St. Paul, and of Clemens, to the Corinthians.

108. Hooker's Ecclesiastical Polity, l. vii.

109. See Jerome ad Titum, c. i. and Epistol. 85 (in the Benedictine edition, 101) [Ep. 146, ed. Vallars. tom. i. p. 1074], and the elaborate apology of Blondel, pro sententiâ Hieronymi. The ancient state, as it is described by Jerome, of the bishop and presbyters of Alexandria, receives a remarkable confirmation from the patriarch Eutychius (Annal. tom. i. p. 330, Vers. Pocock); whose testimony I know not how to reject, in spite of all the objections of the learned Pearson in his Vindiciæ Ignatianæ, part i. c. 11.

110. See the introduction to the Apocalypse. Bishops, under the name of angels, were already instituted in the seven cities of Asia. And yet the epistle of Clemens (which is probably of as ancient a date) does not lead us to discover any traces of episcopacy either at Corinth or Rome.

111. Nulla Ecclesia sine Episcopo, has been a fact as well as a maxim since the time of Tertullian and Irenæus.

112. After we have passed the difficulties of the first century, we find the episcopal government universally established, till it was interrupted by the republican genius of the Swiss and German reformers.

113. See Mosheim in the first and second centuries. Ignatius (ad Smyrnæos, c. 8, etc.) is fond of exalting the episcopal dignity. Le Clerc (Hist. Eccles. p. 569) very bluntly censures his conduct. Mosheim, with a more critical judgment (p. 161), suspects the purity even of the smaller epistles.

114. Nonne et Laici sacerdotes sumus? Tertullian, Exhort. ad Castitat. c. 7. As the human heart is still the same, several of the observations which Mr. Hume has made on Enthusiasm (Essays, vol. i. p. 76, quarto edit.) may be applied even to real inspiration.

115. Acta Concil. Carthag. apud and Cyprian. edit. Fell, p. 158. This council was composed of eighty-seven bishops from the provinces of Mauritania, Numidia, and Africa; some presbyters and deacons assisted at the assembly; præsente plebis maximâ parte.

116. Aguntur præterea per Græcias illas, certis in locis concilia, etc. Tertullian de Jejuniis, c. 13. The African mentions it as a recent and foreign institution. The coalition of the Christian churches is very ably explained by Mosheim, p. 164–170.

117. Cyprian, in his admired treatise De Unitate Ecclesiæ, p. 75–86 [p. 108, ed. Oxon.].

118. We may appeal to the whole tenor of Cyprian's conduct, of his doctrine, and of his epistles. Le Clerc, in a short Life of Cyprian (Bibliothèque Universelle, tom. xii. p. 207–378), has laid him open with great freedom and accuracy.

119. If Novatus, Felicissimus, etc., whom the bishop of Carthage expelled from his church, and from Africa, were not the most detestable monsters of wickedness, the zeal of Cyprian must occasionally have prevailed over his veracity. For a very just account of these obscure quarrels, see Mosheim, p. 497–512.

120. Mosheim, p. 269, 574. Dupin, Antiquæ Eccles. Disciplin. p. 19, 20.

121. Tertullian, in a distinct treatise, has pleaded against the heretics the right of prescription, as it was held by the apostolic churches.

122. The journey of St. Peter to Rome is mentioned by most of the ancients (see Eusebius, ii 25), maintained by all the Catholics, allowed by some Protestants (see Pearson and Dodwell de Success. Episcop. Roman.), but has been vigorously attacked by Spanheim (Miscellanea Sacra, iii. 3). According to father Hardouin, the monks of the thirteenth century, who composed the Æneid, represented St. Peter under the allegorical character of the Trojan hero.

123. It is in French only that the famous allusion to St. Peter's name is exact. Tu es Pierre, et sur cette pierre.—The same is imperfect in Greek, Latin, Italian, etc., and totally unintelligible in our Teutonic languages.

124. Irenæus adv. Hæreses, iii. 3; Tertullian de Præscription, c. 36; and Cyprian Epistol. 27, 55, 71, 75. Le Clerc (Hist. Eccles. p. 764) and Mosheim (p. 258, 578) labour in the interpretation of these passages. But the loose and rhetorical style of the fathers often appears favourable to the pretensions of Rome.

125. See the sharp epistle from Firmilianus, bishop of Cæsarea, to Stephen, bishop of Rome, ap. Cyprian. Epistol. 75.

126. Concerning this dispute of the re-baptism of heretics, see the epistles of Cyprian, and the seventh book of Eusebius.

127. For the origin of these words, see Mosheim, p. 141. Spanheim, Hist. Ecclesiast. p. 633. The distinction of Clerus and Laicus was established before the time of Tertullian.

128. The community instituted by Plato is more perfect than that which Sir Thomas More had

imagined for his Utopia. The community of women, and that of temporal goods, may be considered as inseparable parts of the same system.

129. Joseph Antiquitat. xviii. 2 [c. 1, § 5, ed. Oxon. 1720]. Philo, de Vit. Contemplativ.

130. See the Acts of the Apostles, c. 2, 4, 5, with Grotius's Commentary. Mosheim, in a particular dissertation, attacks the common opinion with very inconclusive arguments.

131. Justin Martyr, Apolog. Major, c. 89. Tertullian, Apolog. c. 39.

132. Irenæus ad Hæres. l. iv. c. 26, 34. Origen in Num. Hom. 11. Cyprian de Unitat. Eccles. Constitut. Apostol. l. ii. c. 34, 35, with the notes of Cotelerius. The Constitutions introduce this divine precept by declaring that priests are as much above kings as the soul is above the body. Among the tithable articles, they enumerate corn, wine, oil, and wool. On this interesting subject, consult Prideaux's History of Tithes, and Fra Paolo delle Materie Beneficiarie; two writers of a very different character.

133. The same opinion, which prevailed about the year one thousand, was productive of the same effects. Most of the donations express their motive, "appropinquante mundi fine." See Mosheim's General History of the Church, vol. i. p. 457.

134. Tum summa cura est fratribus
  (Ut sermo testatur loquax)
  Offerre fundis venditis,
  Sestertiorum millia,
  Addicta avorum prædia
  Fœdis sub auctionibus,
  Successor exheres gemit,
  Sanctis egens parentibus.
  Hæc occuluntur abditis
  Ecclesiarum in angulis.
  Et summa pietas creditur
  Nudare dulces liberos.
   Prudent. περὶ στεφάνων. Hymn 2
      [v. 73, sqq.].

The subsequent conduct of the deacon Laurence only proves how proper a use was made of the wealth of the Roman church; it was undoubtedly very considerable; but Fra Paolo (c. 3) appears to exaggerate when he supposes that the successors of Commodus were urged to persecute the Christians by their own avarice, or that of their Prætorian præfects.

135. Cyprian, Epistol. 62.

136. Tertullian de Præscriptione, c. 30.

137. Diocletian gave a rescript, which is only a declaration of the old law:—"Collegium, si nullo speciali privilegio subnixum sit, hæreditatem capere non posse, dubium non est." Fra Paolo (c. 4) thinks that these regulations had been much neglected since the reign of Valerian.

138. Hist. August. p. 131. [Lampr. Alex. Sever. c. 49.] The ground had been public; and was now disputed between the society of Christians and that of butchers.

139. Constitut. Apostol. ii. 35.

140. Cyprian de Lapsis, p. 89 [p. 126, ed. Oxon.]. Epistol. 65. The charge is confirmed by the 19th and 20th canon of the council of Illiberis.

141. See the apologies of Justin, Tertullian, etc.

142. The wealth and liberality of the Romans to their most distant brethren is gratefully celebrated by Dionysius of Corinth, ap. Euseb. l. iv. c. 23.

143. See Lucian in Peregrin. [c. 13.] Julian (Epist. 49) seems mortified that the Christian charity maintains not only their own, but likewise the heathen poor.

144. Such, at least, has been the laudable conduct of more modern missionaries, under the same circumstances. Above three thousand new-born infants are annually exposed in the streets of Pekin. See Le Comte, Mémoires sur la Chine, and the Recherches sur les Chinois et les Egyptiens, tom. i. p. 61.

145. The Montanists and the Novatians, who adhered to this opinion with the greatest rigour and obstinacy, found *themselves* at last in the number of excommunicated heretics. See the learned and copious Mosheim, Secul. ii. and iii.

146. Dionysius ap. Euseb. iv. 23. Cyprian, de Lapsis.

147. Cave's Primitive Christianity, part iii. c. 5. The admirers of antiquity regret the loss of this public penance.

148. See in Dupin, Bibliothèque Ecclésiastique, tom. ii. p. 304–313, a short but rational exposition of the canons of those councils which were assembled in the first moments of tranquillity after the persecution of Diocletian. This persecution had been much less severely felt in Spain than in Galatia; a difference which may, in some measure, account for the contrast of their regulations.

149. Cyprian Epist. 69 [59].

150. The arts, the manners, and the vices of the priests of the Syrian goddess are very humorously described by Apuleius, in the eighth book of his Metamorphoses.

151. The office of Asiarch was of this nature, and it is frequently mentioned in Aristides, the Inscriptions, etc. It was annual and elective. None but the vainest citizens could desire the honour; none but the most wealthy could support the expense. See in the Patres Apostol. tom. ii. p. 200 [Epist. Eccl. Smyrn. de Martyrio Polycarpi, c. 12], with how much indifference Philip the Asiarch conducted himself in the martyrdom of Polycarp. There were likewise Bithyniarchs, Lyciarchs, etc.

152. The modern critics are not disposed to believe what the fathers almost unanimously assert, that St. Matthew composed a Hebrew gospel, of which only the Greek translation is extant. It seems, however, dangerous to reject their testimony.

153. Under the reigns of Nero and Domitian, and in the cities of Alexandria, Antioch, Rome, and Ephesus. See Mill, Prolegomena ad. Nov. Testament, and Dr. Lardner's fair and extensive collection, vol. xv.

154. The Alogians (Epiphanius de Hæres. 51

[p. 455. ed. Paris, 1622]) disputed the genuineness of the Apocalypse, because the church of Thyatira was not yet founded. Epiphanius, who allows the fact, extricates himself from the difficulty by ingeniously supposing that St. John wrote in the spirit of prophecy. See Abauzit, Discours sur l'Apocalypse.

155. The epistles of Ignatius and Dionysius (ap. Euseb. iv. 23) point out many churches in Asia and Greece. That of Athens seems to have been one of the least flourishing.

156. Lucian in Alexandro, c. 25. Christianity, however, must have been very unequally diffused over Pontus; since, in the middle of the third century, there were no more than seventeen believers in the extensive diocese of Neo-Cæsarea. See M. de Tillemont, Mémoires Ecclésiast. tom. iv. p. 675, from Basil and Gregory of Nyssa, who were themselves natives of Cappadocia.

157. According to the ancients, Jesus Christ suffered under the consulship of the two Gemini, in the year 29 of our present era. Pliny was sent into Bithynia (according to Pagi) in the year 110.

158. Plin. Epist. x. 97.

159. Chrysostom. Opera, tom. vii. p. 658, 810 [edit. Savil. ii. 422, 529].

160. John Malala, tom. ii. p. 144 [ed. Oxon.; p. 420, ed. Bonn]. He draws the same conclusion with regard to the populousness of Antioch.

161. Chrysostom, tom. i. p. 592. I am indebted for these passages, though not for my inference, to the learned Dr. Lardner. Credibility of the Gospel History, vol. xii. p. 370.

162. Basnage, Histoire des Juifs, l. ii. c. 20, 21, 22, 23, has examined with the most critical accuracy the curious treatise of Philo which describes the Therapeutæ. By proving that it was composed as early as the time of Augustus, Basnage has demonstrated, in spite of Eusebius (l. ii. c. 17), and a crowd of modern Catholics, that the Therapeutæ were neither Christians nor monks. It still remains probable that they changed their name, preserved their manners, adopted some new articles of faith, and gradually became the fathers of the Egyptian Ascetics.

163. See a letter of Hadrian in the Augustan History, p. 245. [Vopisc. Saturn. c. 1.]

164. For the succession of Alexandrian bishops, consult Renaudot's History, p. 24, etc. This curious fact is preserved by the patriarch Eutychius (Annal. tom. i. p. 332, Vers. Pocock), and its internal evidence would alone be a sufficient answer to all the objections which Bishop Pearson has urged in the Vindiciæ Ignatianæ.

165. Ammian. Marcellin. xxii. 16.

166. Origen contra Celsum, l. i. p. 40 [c. 52, tom. i. p. 368, ed. Bened.]

167. Ingens multitudo is the expression of Tacitus, xv. 44.

168. T. Liv. xxxix. 13, 15, 16, 17. Nothing could exceed the horror and consternation of the senate on the discovery of the Bacchanalians, whose depravity is described, and perhaps exaggerated, by Livy.

169. Eusebius, l. vi. c. 43. The Latin translator (M. de Valois) has thought proper to reduce the number of presbyters to forty-four.

170. This proportion of the presbyters and of the poor to the rest of the people was originally fixed by Burnet (Travels into Italy, p. 168), and is approved by Moyle (vol. ii. p. 151). They were both unacquainted with the passage of Chrysostom, which converts their conjecture almost into a fact.

171. Serius trans Alpes, religione Dei susceptâ. Sulpicius Severus, l. ii. [p. 383, ed. Lugd. Bat. 1647]. With regard to Africa, see Tertullian ad Scapulam, c. 3. It is imagined that the Scyllitan martyrs were the first (Acta Sincera Ruinart. p. 34). One of the adversaries of Apuleius seems to have been a Christian. Apolog. p. 499, 497, edit. Delphin.

172. Tum primum intra Gallias martyria visa. Sulp. Severus, l. ii. [l. c.] These were the celebrated martyrs of Lyons. See Eusebius, v. i. Tillemont, Mém. Ecclésiast. tom. ii. p. 316. According to the Donatists, whose assertion is confirmed by the tacit acknowledgment of Augustin, Africa was the last of the provinces which received the Gospel. Tillemont, Mém. Ecclésiast. tom. i. p. 754.

173. Raræ in aliquibus civitatibus ecclesiæ, paucorum Christianorum devotione, resurgerent. Acta Sincera, p. 130. Gregory of Tours, l. i. c. 28. Mosheim, p. 207, 449. There is some reason to believe that, in the beginning of the fourth century, the extensive dioceses of Liege, of Treves, and of Cologne, composed a single bishopric, which had been very recently founded. See Mémoires de Tillemont, tom. vi. part i. p. 43, 411.

174. The date of Tertullian's Apology is fixed, in a dissertation of Mosheim, to the year 198.

175. In the fifteenth century there were a few who had either inclination or courage to question whether Joseph of Arimathea founded the monastery of Glastonbury, and whether Dionysius the Areopagite preferred the residence of Paris to that of Athens.

176. The stupendous metamorphosis was performed in the ninth century. See Mariana (Hist. Hispan. l. vii. c. 13, tom. i. p. 285, edit. Hag. Com. 1733), who, in every sense, imitates Livy; and the honest detection of the legend of St. James by Dr. Geddes, Miscellanies, vol. ii. p. 221.

177. Justin Martyr, Dialog. cum Tryphon, p. 341 [c. 117, p. 211, ed. Bened.]. Irenæus adv. Hæres. l. i. c. 10. Tertullian adv. Jud. c. 7. See Mosheim, p. 203.

178. See the fourth century of Mosheim's History of the Church. Many, though very confused circumstances, that relate to the conversion of Iberia and Armenia, may be found in Moses of Chorene, l. ii. c. 78-89.

179. According to Tertullian, the Christian faith had penetrated into parts of Britain inaccessible to the Roman arms. About a century afterwards, Os-

sian, the son of Fingal, is *said* to have disputed, in his extreme old age, with one of the foreign missionaries, and the dispute is still extant in verse, and in the Erse language. See Mr. Macpherson's Dissertation on the Antiquity of Ossian's Poems, p. 10.

180. The Goths, who ravaged Asia in the reign of Gallineus, carried away great numbers of captives; some of whom were Christians, and became missionaries. See Tillemont, Mémoires Ecclésiast. tom. iv. p. 44.

181. The legend of Abgarus, fabulous as it is, affords a decisive proof that many years before Eusebius wrote his history the greatest part of the inhabitants of Edessa had embraced Christianity. Their rivals, the citizens of Carrhæ, adhered, on the contrary, to the cause of Paganism, as late as the sixth century.

182. According to Bardesanes (ap. Euseb. Præpar. Evangel.), there were some Christians in Persia before the end of the second century. In the time of Constantine (see his epistle to Sapor [Euseb.], Vit. l. iv. c. 13) they composed a flourishing church. Consult Beausobre, Hist. Critique du Manichéisme, tom. i. p. 180, and the Bibliotheca Orientalis of Assemani.

183. Origen contra Celsum, l. viii. p. 424 [c. 69, tom. i. p. 794, ed. Bened.].

184. Minucius Felix, p. 8 [ed. Lugd. B. 1652], with Wowerus's notes. Celsus ap. Origen, l. iii. p. 138, 142 [c. 49, tom. i. p. 479, ed Bened.]. Julian ap. Cyril. l. vi. p. 206, edit. Spanheim.

185. Euseb. Hist. Eccles. iv. 3. Hieronym. Epist. 83. [Ep. 70, tom. i. p. 424, ed. Vallars.]

186. The story is prettily told in Justin's Dialogues. Tillemont (Mém. Ecclésiast. tom. ii. p. 384), who relates it after him, is sure that the old man was a disguised angel.

187. Eusebius, v. 28. It may be hoped that none, except the heretics, gave occasion to the complaint of Celsus (ap. Origen, l. ii. p. 77 [c. 27, tom. i. p. 411, ed. Bened.]), that the Christians were perpetually correcting and altering their Gospels.

188. Plin. Epist. x. 97. Fuerunt alii similis amentiæ, cives Romani. . . . Multi enim omnis ætatis, *omnis ordinis*, utriusquæ sexûs, et jam vocantur in periculum et vocabuntur.

189. Tertullian ad Scapulam. Yet even his rhetoric rises no higher than to claim a tenth part of Carthage.

190. Cyprian. Epist. 79 [80].

191. Dr. Lardner, in his first and second volumes of Jewish and Christian testimonies, collects and illustrates those of Pliny the younger, of Tacitus, of Galen, of Marcus Antoninus, and perhaps of Epictetus (for it is doubtful whether that philosopher means to speak of the Christians). The new sect is totally unnoticed by Seneca, the elder Pliny, and Plutarch.

192. If the famous prophecy of the Seventy Weeks had been alleged to a Roman philosopher, would he not have replied in the words of Cicero, "Quæ tandem ista auguratio est, annorum potius quam aut mensium aut dierum?" De Divinatione, ii. 30. Observe with what irreverence Lucian (in Alexandro, c. 13), and his friend Celsus, ap. Origen (l. vii. [c. 14] p. 327), express themselves concerning the Hebrew prophets.

193. The philosophers, who derided the more ancient predictions of the Sibyls, would easily have detected the Jewish and Christian forgeries, which have been so triumphantly quoted by the fathers, from Justin Martyr to Lactantius. When the Sibylline verses had performed their appointed task, they, like the system of the millennium, were quietly laid aside. The Christian Sibyl had unluckily fixed the ruin of Rome for the year 195, A. U. C. 948.

194. The fathers, as they are drawn out in battle array by Dom Calmet (Dissertations sur la Bible, tom. iii. p. 295–308), seem to cover the whole earth with darkness, in which they are followed by most of the moderns.

195. Origen ad Matth. c. 27, and a few modern critics, Beza, Le Clerc, Lardner, etc., are desirous of confining it to the land of Judea.

196. The celebrated passage of Phlegon is now wisely abandoned. When Tertullian assures the Pagans that the mention of the prodigy is found in Arcanis (not Archivis) vestris (see his Apology, c. 21), he probably appeals to the Sibylline verses, which relate it exactly in the words of the Gospel.

197. Seneca Quæst. Natur. l. i. 15, vi. 1, vii. 17. Plin. Hist. Natur. l. ii.

198. Plin. Hist. Natur. ii. 30.

199. Virgil. Georgic. i. 466. Tibullus, ii. 5, 75. Ovid. Metamorph. xv. 782. Lucan. Pharsal. i. 535. The last of these poets places this prodigy before the civil war.

200. See a public epistle of M. Antony in Joseph. Antiquit. xiv. 12 [§ 3]. Plutarch in Cæsar. [c. 69] p. 471. Appian. Bell. Civil. l. iv. Dion Cassius, l. xlv. [c. 17] p. 431. Julius Obsequens, c. 128. His little treatise is an abstract of Livy's prodigies.

Chapter XVI

1. In Cyrene they massacred 220,000 Greeks; in Cyprus, 240,000; in Egypt a very great multitude. Many of these unhappy victims were sawn asunder, according to a precedent to which David had given the sanction of his example. The victorious Jews devoured the flesh, licked up the blood, and twisted the entrails like a girdle round their bodies. See Dion Cassius, l. lxviii. [c. 32] p. 1145.

2. Without repeating the well-known narratives of Josephus, we may learn from Dion (l. lxix. [c. 14] p. 1162), that in Hadrian's war 580,000 Jews were cut off by the sword, besides an infinite number which perished by famine, by disease, and by fire.

3. For the sect of the Zealots, see Basnage, Histoire des Juifs, l. i. c. 17; for the characters of the Messiah, according to the Rabbis, l. v. c. 11, 12, 13; for the actions of Barchochebas, l. vii. c. 12. [Hist. of Jews, iii. 115.]

4. It is to Modestinus, a Roman lawyer (l. vi. regular.), that we are indebted for a distinct knowledge of the edict of Antoninus. See Casaubon ad Hist. August. p. 27.

5. See Basnage, Histoire des Juifs, l. iii. c. 2, 3. The office of Patriarch was suppressed by Theodosius the younger.

6. We need only mention the Purim, or deliverance of the Jews from the rage of Haman, which, till the reign of Theodosius, was celebrated with insolent triumph and riotous intemperance. Basnage, Hist. des Juifs, l. vi. c. 17, l. viii. c. 6.

7. According to the false Josephus, Tsepho, the grandson of Esau, conducted into Italy the army of Æneas, king of Carthage. Another colony of Idumæans, flying from the wrath of David, took refuge in the dominions of Romulus. For these, or for other reasons of equal weight, the name of Edom was applied by the Jews to the Roman empire.

8. From the arguments of Celsus, as they are represented and refuted by Origen (l. v. [c. 59] p. 247–259), we may clearly discover the distinction that was made between the Jewish *people* and the Christian *sect*. See in the Dialogue of Minucius Felix (p. 5, 6) a fair and not inelegant description of the popular sentiments with regard to the desertion of the established worship.

9. Cur nullas aras habent? templa nulla? nulla nota simulacra? . . . Unde autem, vel quis ille, aut ubi, Deus unicus, solitarius, destitutus? Minucius Felix, p. 10. The Pagan interlocutor goes on to make a distinction in favour of the Jews, who had once a temple, altars, victims, etc.

10. It is difficult (says Plato) to attain, and dangerous to publish, the knowledge of the true God. See the Théologie des Philosophes, in the Abbé d'Olivet's French translation of Tully de Naturâ Deorum, tom. i. p. 275.

11. The author of the Philopatris perpetually treats the Christians as a company of dreaming enthusiasts, δαιμόνιοι αἰθέριοι, αἰθεροβατοῦντες, ἀεροβατοῦντες, etc.; and in one place manifestly alludes to the vision in which St. Paul was transported to the third heaven. In another place, Triephon, who personates a Christian, after deriding the gods of Paganism, proposes a mysterious oath:—

Ὑψιμέδοντα θεὸν, μέγαν, ἄμβροτον, οὐρανίωνα,
Υἱὸν πατρὸς, πνεῦμα ἐκ πατρὸς ἐκπορευόμενον,
Ἕν ἐκ τριῶν, καὶ ἐξ ἑνὸς τρία.

Ἀριθμέειν με διδάσκεις, (is the profane answer of Critias), καὶ ὅρκος ἡ ἀριθμητική οὐκ οἶδα γάρ τι λέγεις ἐν τρία, τρία ἕν!

12. According to Justin Martyr (Apolog. Major, c. 70–85), the dæmon, who had gained some imperfect knowledge of the prophecies, purposely contrived this resemblance, which might deter, though by different means, both the people and the philosophers from embracing the faith of Christ.

13. In the first and second books of Origen, Celsus treats the birth and character of our Saviour with the most impious contempt. The orator Libanius praises Porphyry and Julian for confuting the folly of a sect which style a dead man of Palestine, God, and the Son of God. Socrates, Hist. Ecclesiast. iii. 23.

14. The emperor Trajan refused to incorporate a company of 150 firemen for the use of the city of Nicomedia. He disliked all associations. See Plin. Epist. x. 42, 43.

15. The proconsul Pliny had published a general edict against unlawful meetings. The prudence of the Christians suspended their Agapæ; but it was impossible for them to omit the exercise of public worship.

16. As the prophecies of the Antichrist, approaching conflagration, etc., provoked those Pagans whom they did not convert, they were mentioned with caution and reserve; and the Montanists were censured for disclosing too freely the dangerous secret. See Mosheim, p. 413.

17. Neque enim dubitabam, qualecunque esset quod faterentur (such are the words of Pliny) pervicaciam certe et inflexibilem obstinationem debere puniri. [Epist. x. 97.]

18. See Mosheim's Ecclesiastical History, vol. i. p. 101, and Spanheim, Remarques sur les Césars de Julien, p. 468, etc.

19. See Justin Martyr, Apolog. i. 35 [c. 27? ed. Ben.], ii. 14 [c. 12, p. 97, ed. Ben.]. Athenagoras, in Legation, c. 27. Tertullian, Apolog. c. 7, 8, 9. Minucius Felix, p. 9, 10, 30, 31. The last of these writers relates the accusation in the most elegant and circumstantial manner. The answer of Tertullian is the boldest and most vigorous.

20. In the persecution of Lyons, some Gentile slaves were compelled, by the fear of tortures, to

accuse their Christian master. The church of Lyons, writing to their brethren of Asia, treat the horrid charge with proper indignation and contempt. Euseb. Hist. Eccles. v. i.

21. See Justin Martyr, Apolog. i. 35 [c. 27? ed. Ben.]. Irenæus adv. Hæres. i. 24. Clemens Alexandrin. Stromat. l. iii. p. 438 [c. 2, p. 514, ed. Oxon. 1715]. Euseb. iv. 8. It would be tedious and disgusting to relate all that the succeeding writers have imagined, all that Epiphanius has received, and all that Tillemont has copied. M. de Beausobre (Hist. du Manichéisme, l. ix. c. 8, 9) has exposed, with great spirit, the disingenuous arts of Augustin and Pope Leo I.

22. When Tertullian became a Montanist, he aspersed the morals of the church which he had so resolutely defended. "Sed majoris est Agape, quia per hanc adolescentes tui cum sororibus dormiunt. Appendices scilicet gulæ lascivia et luxuria." De Jejuniis, c. 17. The 35th canon of the council of Illiberis provides against the scandals which too often polluted the vigils of the church, and disgraced the Christian name in the eyes of unbelievers.

23. Tertullian (Apolog. c. 2) expatiates on the fair and honourable testimony of Pliny, with much reason, and some declamation.

24. In the various compilation of the Augustan History (a part of which was composed under the reign of Constantine) there are not six lines which relate to the Christians; nor has the diligence of Xiphilin discovered their name in the large history of Dion Cassius.

25. An obscure passage of Suetonius (in Claud. c. 25) may seem to offer a proof how strangely the Jews and Christians of Rome were confounded with each other.

26. See, in the eighteenth and twenty-fifth chapters of the Acts of the Apostles, the behaviour of Gallio, proconsul of Achaia, and of Festus, procurator of Judæa.

27. In the time of Tertullian and Clemens of Alexandria the glory of martyrdom was confined to St. Peter, St. Paul, and St. James. It was gradually bestowed on the rest of the apostles by the more recent Greeks, who prudently selected for the theatre of their preaching and sufferings some remote country beyond the limits of the Roman empire. See Mosheim, p. 81; and Tillemont, Mémoires Ecclésiastiques, tom. i. part. iii.

28. Tacit. Annal. xv. 38–44. Sueton. in Neron. c. 38. Dion Cassius, l. lxii. [c. 16] p. 1014. Orosius, vii. 7.

29. The price of wheat (probably of the *modius*) was reduced as low as *terni Nummi;* which would be equivalent to about fifteen shillings the English quarter.

30. We may observe that the rumour is mentioned by Tacitus with a very becoming distrust and hesitation, whilst it is greedily transcribed by Suetonius, and solemnly confirmed by Dion.

31. This testimony is alone sufficient to expose the anachronism of the Jews, who place the birth of Christ near a century sooner. (Basnage, Histoire des Juifs, l. v. c. 14, 15.) We may learn from Josephus (Antiquitat. xviii. 3 [c. 2, § 2, ed. Oxon. 1720]) that the procuratorship of Pilate corresponded with the last ten years of Tiberius, A.D. 27–37. As to the particular time of the death of Christ, a very early tradition fixed it to the 25th of March, A.D. 29, under the consulship of the two Gemini (Tertullian adv. Judæos, c. 8). This date, which is adopted by Pagi, Cardinal Norris, and Le Clerc, seems at least as probable as the vulgar era, which is placed (I know not from what conjectures) four years later.

32. *Odio humani generis convicti*. These words may either signify the hatred of mankind towards the Christians, or the hatred of the Christians towards mankind. I have preferred the latter sense, as the most agreeable to the style of Tacitus, and to the popular error, of which a precept of the Gospel (see Luke xiv. 26) had been, perhaps, the innocent occasion. My interpretation is justified by the authority of Lipsius; of the Italian, the French, and the English translators of Tacitus; of Mosheim (p. 102), of Le Clerc (Historia Ecclesiast. p. 427), of Dr. Lardner (Testimonies, vol. i. p. 345), and of the Bishop of Gloucester (Divine Legation, vol. iii, p. 38). But as the word *convicti* does not unite very happily with the rest of the sentence, James Gronovius has preferred the reading of *conjuncti*, which is authorised by the valuable MS. of Florence.

33. Tacit. Annal. xv. 44.

34. Nardini Roma Antica, p. 487. Donatus de Româ Antiquâ, l. iii. p. 449.

35. Sueton. in Nerone, c. 16. The epithet of *malefica*, which some sagacious commentators have translated *magical*, is considered by the more rational Mosheim as only synonymous to the *exitiabilis* of Tacitus.

36. The passage concerning Jesus Christ which was inserted into the text of Josephus between the time of Origen and that of Eusebius, may furnish an example of no vulgar forgery. The accomplishment of the prophecies, the virtues, miracles, and resurrection of Jesus, are distinctly related. Josephus acknowledges that he was the Messiah, and hesitates whether he should call him a man. If any doubt can still remain concerning this celebrated passage, the reader may examine the pointed objections of Le Fevre (Havercamp. Joseph. tom. ii. p. 267–273), the laboured answers of Daubuz (p. 187–232), and the masterly reply (Bibliothèque Ancienne et Moderne, tom. vii. p. 237–288) of an anonymous critic, whom I believe to have been the learned Abbé de Longuerue.

37. See the lives of Tacitus by Lipsius and the Abbé de la Bleterie, Dictionnaire de Bayle à l'article TACITE, and Fabricius, Biblioth, Latin. tom. ii. p. 386, edit. Ernest.

38. Principatum Divi Nervæ, et imperium Trajani, uberiorem securioremque materiam, senectuti se posui. Tacit. Hist. i. l.

39. See Tacit. Annal. ii. 61, iv. 4.

40. The player's name was Aliturus. Through the same channel, Josephus (de Vitâ suâ, c. 3), about two years before, had obtained the pardon and release of some Jewish priests who were prisoners at Rome.

41. The learned Dr. Lardner (Jewish and Heathen Testimonies, vol. ii. p. 102, 103) has proved that the name of Galilæans was a very ancient, and perhaps the primitive, appellation of the Christians.

42. Joseph Antiquitat. xviii. 1, 2. Tillemont, Ruine des Juifs, p. 742. The sons of Judas were crucified in the time of Claudius. His grandson Eleazar, after Jerusalem was taken, defended a strong fortress with 960 of his most desperate followers. When the battering-ram had made a breach, they turned their swords against their wives, their children, and at length against their own breasts. They died to the last man.

43. See Dodwell. Paucitat. Mart. l. xiii. The Spanish Inscription in Gruter, p. 238, No. 9, is a manifest and acknowledged forgery, contrived by that noted impostor Cyriacus of Ancona to flatter the pride and prejudices of the Spaniards. See Ferreras, Histoire d'Espagne, tom. i. p. 192.

44. The Capitol was burnt during the civil war between Vitellius and Vespasian, the 19th of December, A.D. 69. On the 10th of August, A.D. 70, the Temple of Jerusalem was destroyed by the hands of the Jews themselves, rather than by those of the Romans.

45. The new Capitol was dedicated by Domitian. Sueton. in Domitian. c. 5. Plutarch in Poplicola [c. 15], tom. i. p. 230, edit. Bryant. The gilding alone cost 12,000 talents (above two millions and a half). It was the opinion of Martial (l. ix. Epigram 4), that, if the emperor had called in his debts, Jupiter himself, even though he had made a general auction of Olympus would have been unable to pay two shillings in the pound.

46. With regard to the tribute, see Dion Cassius, l. lxvi. [c. 7] p. 1082, with Reimarus's notes; Spanheim, de Usu Numismatum, tom. ii. p. 571; and Basnage, Histoire des Juifs, l. vii. c. 2.

47. Suetonius (in Domitian. c. 12) had seen an old man of ninety publicly examined before the procurator's tribunal. This is what Martial calls Mentula tributis damnata.

48. This appellation was at first understood in the most obvious sense, and it was supposed that the brothers of Jesus were the lawful issue of Joseph and Mary. A devout respect for the virginity of the mother of God suggested to the Gnostics, and afterwards to the orthodox Greeks, the expedient of bestowing a second wife on Joseph. The Latins (from the time of Jerome) improved on that hint, asserted the perpetual celibacy of Joseph, and justified by many similar examples the new interpretation that Jude, as well as Simon and James, who are styled the brothers of Jesus Christ, were only his first-cousins. See Tillemont, Mém. Ecclé-

siast. tom. i. part iii.; and Beausobre, Hist. Critique du Manichéisme, l. ii. c. 2.

49. Thirty-nine πλέθρα, squares of an hundred feet each, which, if strictly computed, would scarcely amount to nine acres. But the probability of circumstances, the practice of other Greek writers, and the authority M. de Valois, incline me to believe that the πλέθρον is used to express the Roman jugerum.

50. Eusebius, iii. 20. The story is taken from Hegesippus.

51. See the death and character of Sabinus in Tacitus (Hist. iii. 74, 75). Sabinus was the elder brother, and, till the accession of Vespasian, had been considered as the principal support of the Flavian family.

52. Flavium Clementem patruelem suum contemptissimæ inertiæ . . . ex tenuissimâ suspicione interemit. Sueton. in Domitian. c. 15.

53. The isle of Pandataria, according to Dion. Bruttius Præsens (apud Euseb. iii. 18) banishes her to that of Pontia, which was not far distant from the other. That difference, and a mistake, either of Eusebius or of his transcribers, have given occasion to suppose two Domitillas, the wife and the niece of Clemens. See Tillemont, Mémoires Ecclésiastiques, tom. ii. p. 224.

54. Dion, l. lxvii. [c. 14] p. 1112. If the Bruttius Præsens, from whom it is probable that he collected this account, was the correspondent of Pliny (Epistol. vii. 3), we may consider him as a contemporary writer.

55. Suet. in Domit. c. 17. Philostratus in Vit. Apollon. l. viii.

56. Dion, l. lxviii. [c. 1] p. 1118. Plin. Epistol. iv. 22.

57. Plin. Epistol. x. 97. The learned Mosheim expresses himself (p. 147, 232) with the highest approbation of Pliny's moderate and candid temper. Notwithstanding Dr. Lardner's suspicions (see Jewish and Heathen Testimonies, vol. ii. p. 46), I am unable to discover any bigotry in his language or proceedings.

58. Plin. Epist. v. 8. He pleaded his first cause A.D. 81; the year after the famous eruptions of Mount Vesuvius, in which his uncle lost his life.

59. Plin. Epist. x. 98. Tertullian (Apolog. c. 5) considers this rescript as a relaxation of the ancient penal laws, "quas Trajanus ex parte frustratus est:" and yet Tertullian, in another part of his Apology, exposes the inconsistency of prohibiting inquiries and enjoining punishments.

60. Eusebius (Hist. Ecclesiast. l. iv. c. 9) has preserved the edict of Hadrian. He has likewise (c. 13) given us one still more favourable under the name of Antoninus, the authenticity of which is not so universally allowed. The second Apology of Justin contains some curious particulars relative to the accusations of Christians.

61. See Tertullian (Apolog. c. 40). The Acts of the Martyrdom of Polycarp exhibit a lively picture

of these tumults, which were usually fomented by the malice of the Jews.

62. These regulations are inserted in the above-mentioned edicts of Hadrian and Pius. See the Apology of Melito (apud Euseb. l. iv. c. 26).

63. See the rescript of Trajan, and the conduct of Pliny. The most authentic Acts of the Martyrs abound in these exhortations.

64. In particular, see Tertullian (Apolog. c. 2, 3) and Lactantius (Institut. Divin. v. 9). Their reasonings are almost the same; but we may discover that one of these apologists had been a lawyer, and the other a rhetorician.

65. See two instances of this kind of torture in the Acta Sincera Martyrum, published by Ruinart, p. 160, 399. Jerome, in his Legend of Paul the Hermit, tells a strange story of a young man who was chained naked on a bed of flowers, and assaulted by a beautiful and wanton courtesan. He quelled the rising temptation by biting off his tongue.

66. The conversion of his wife provoked Claudius Herminianus, governor of Cappadocia, to treat the Christians with uncommon severity. Tertullian ad Scapulam, c. 3.

67. Tertullian, in his epistle to the governor of Africa, mentions several remarkable instances of lenity and forbearance which had happened within his knowledge.

68. Neque enim in universum aliquid quod quasi certam formam habeat, constitui potest: an expression of Trajan, which gave a very great latitude to the governors of provinces.

69. In metalla damnamur, in insulas relegamur. Tertullian, Apolog. c. 12. The mines of Numidia contained nine bishops, with a proportionable number of their clergy and people, to whom Cyprian addressed a pious epistle of praise and comfort. See Cyprian. Epistol. 76, 77.

70. Though we cannot receive with entire confidence either the epistles or the acts of Ignatius (they may be found in the second volume of the Apostolic Fathers), yet we may quote that bishop of Antioch as one of these *exemplary* martyrs. He was sent in chains to Rome as a public spectacle; and when he arrived at Troas he received the pleasing intelligence that the persecution of Antioch was already at an end.

71. Among the martyrs of Lyons (Euseb. l. v. c. 1) the slave Blandina was distinguished by more exquisite tortures. Of the five martyrs so much celebrated in the Acts of Felicitas and Perpetua, two were of a servile, and two others of a very mean, condition.

72. Origen. advers. Celsum. l. iii. p. 116 [c. 8, tom. i. p. 452, ed. Bened.]. His words deserve to be transcribed:—" Ὀλίγοι κατὰ καιροὺς, καὶ σφόδρα εὐαρίθμητοι ὑπὲρ τῆς Χριστιανῶν θεοσεβείας τεθνήκασι."

73. If we recollect that all the Plebeians of Rome were not Christians, and that all the Christians were not saints and martyrs, we may judge with how much safety religious honours can be ascribed to bones or urns indiscriminately taken from the public burial-place. After ten centuries of a very free and open trade some suspicions have arisen among the more learned Catholics. They now require, as a proof of sanctity and martyrdom, the letters B. M., a vial full of red liquor supposed to be blood, or the figure of a palm-tree. But the two former signs are of little weight, and with regard to the last, it is observed by the critics—1. That the figure, as it is called, of a palm, is perhaps a cypress, and perhaps only a stop, the flourish of a comma used in the monumental inscriptions. 2. That the palm was the symbol of victory among the Pagans. 3. That among the Christians it served as the emblem, not only of martyrdom, but in general of a joyful resurrection. See the epistle of P. Mabillon on the worship of unknown saints, and Muratori sopra le Antichità Italiane, Dissertat. lviii.

74. As a specimen of these legends, we may be satisfied with 10,000 Christian soldiers crucified in one day, either by Trajan or Hadrian, on Mount Ararat. See Baronius ad Martyrologium Romanum; Tillemont, Mém. Ecclésiast. tom. ii. part ii. p. 438; and Geddes's Miscellanies, vol. ii. p. 203. The abbreviation of MIL., which may signify either *soldiers* or *thousands*, is said to have occasioned some extraordinary mistakes.

75. Dionysius ap. Euseb. l. vi. c. 41. One of the seventeen was likewise accused of robbery.

76. The letters of Cyprian exhibit a very curious and original picture both of the *man* and of the *times*. See likewise the two Lives of Cyprian, composed with equal accuracy, though with very different views; the one by Le Clerc (Bibliothèque Universelle, tom. xii. p. 208-378), the other by Tillemont, Mémoires Ecclésiastiques, tom. iv. part i. p. 76-459.

77. See the polite but severe epistle of the clergy of Rome to the bishop of Carthage (Cyprian. Epist. 8, 9). Pontius labours with the greatest care and diligence to justify his master against the general censure.

78. In particular those of Dionysius of Alexandria, and Gregory Thaumaturgus of Neo-Cæsarea. See Euseb. Hist. Ecclesiast. l. vi. c. 40; and Mémoires de Tillemont, tom. iv. part. ii. p. 685.

79. See Cyprian. Epist. 16, and his Life by Pontius.

80. We have an original Life of Cyprian by the deacon Pontius, the companion of his exile and the spectator of his death; and we likewise possess the ancient proconsular Acts of his martyrdom. These two relations are consistent with each other, and with probability; and what is somewhat remarkable, they are both unsullied by any miraculous circumstances.

81. It should seem that these were circular orders, sent at the same time to all the governors. Dionysius (ap. Euseb. l. vii. c. 11) relates the history of his own banishment from Alexandria almost in the same manner. But as he escaped and

survived the persecution, we must account him either more or less fortunate than Cyprian.

82. See Plin. Hist. Natur. v. 3; Cellarius, Geograph. Antiq. part iii. p. 96; Shaw's Travels, p. 90; and for the adjacent country (which is terminated by Cape Bona, or the promontory of Mercury) l'Afrique de Marmol. tom. ii. p. 494. There are the remains of an aqueduct near Curubis, or Curbis, at present altered into Gurbes; and Dr. Shaw read an inscription which styles that city *Colonia Fulvia*. The deacon Pontius (in Vit. Cyprian. c. 12) calls it "Apricum et competentem locum, hospitium pro voluntate secretum, et quicquid apponi eis ante promissum est, qui regnum et justitiam Dei quærunt."

83. See Cyprian. Epistol. 77, edit. Fell.

84. Upon his conversion he had sold those gardens for the benefit of the poor. The indulgence of God (most probably the liberality of some Christian friend) restored them to Cyprian. See Pontius, c. 15.

85. When Cyprian, a twelvemonth before, was sent into exile, he dreamt that he should be put to death the next day. The event made it necessary to explain that word as signifying a year. Pontius, c. 12.

86. Pontius (c. 15) acknowledges that Cyprian, with whom he supped, passed the night custodiâ delicatâ. The bishop exercised a last and very proper act of jurisdiction, by directing that the younger females, who watched in the street, should be removed from the dangers and temptations of a nocturnal crowd. Act. Proconsularia, c. 2.

87. See the original sentence in the Acts, c. 4; and in Pontius, c. 17. The latter expresses it in a more rhetorical manner.

88. Pontius, c. 19. M. de Tillemont (Mémoires, tom. iv. part i. p. 450, note 50) is not pleased with so positive an exclusion of any former martyrs of the episcopal rank.

89. Whatever opinion we may entertain of the character or principles of Thomas Becket, we must acknowledge that he suffered death with a constancy not unworthy of the primitive martyrs. See Lord Lyttelton's History of Henry II., vol. ii. p. 592, etc.

90. See in particular the treatise of Cyprian de Lapsis, p. 87-98, edit. Fell. [p. 121.] The learning of Dodwell (Dissertat. Cyprianic. xii. xiii.), and the ingenuity of Middleton (Free Inquiry, p. 162, etc.), have left scarcely anything to add concerning the merit, the honours, and the motives of the martyrs.

91. Cyprian. Epistol. 5, 6, 7, 22, 24; and de Unitat. Ecclesiæ. The number of pretended martyrs has been very much multiplied by the custom which was introduced of bestowing that honourable name on confessors.

92. Certatim gloriosa in certamina ruebatur; multoque avidius tum martyria gloriosis mortibus quærebantur, quam nunc Episcopatus pravis ambitionibus appetuntur. Sulpicius Severus, l. ii. [p.

385, ed. Lugd. Bat. 1647.] He might have omitted the word *nunc*.

93. See Epist. ad Roman. c. 4, 5, ap. Patres Apostol. tom. ii. p. 27. It suited the purpose of Bishop Pearson (see Vindiciæ Ignatianæ, part ii. c. 9) to justify, by a profusion of examples and authorities, the sentiments of Ignatius.

94. The story of Polyeuctes, on which Corneille has founded a very beautiful tragedy, is one of the most celebrated, though not perhaps the most authentic, instances of this excessive zeal. We should observe that the 60th canon of the council of Illiberis refuses the title of martyrs to those who exposed themselves to death by publicly destroying the idols.

95. See Epictetus, Discourses, iv. 7 (though there is some doubt whether he alludes to the Christians); Marcus Aurelius, Meditations, xi. 3; Lucian in Peregrin.

96. Tertullian ad Scapul. c. 5. The learned are divided between three persons of the same name, who were all proconsuls of Asia. I am inclined to ascribe this story to Antoninus Pius, who was afterwards emperor; and who may have governed Asia under the reign of Trajan.

97. Mosheim, de Rebus Christ. ante Constantin. p. 235.

98. See the Epistle of the Church of Smyrna, ap. Euseb. Hist. Eccles. l. iv. c. 15.

99. In the second Apology of Justin there is a particular and very curious instance of this legal delay. The same indulgence was granted to accused Christians in the persecution of Decius: and Cyprian (de Lapsis) expressly mentions the "Dies negantibus præstitutus."

100. Tertullian considers flight from persecution as an imperfect, but very criminal, apostasy, as an impious attempt to elude the will of God, etc. He has written a treatise on this subject (see p. 536-544, edit. Rigalt.), which is filled with the wildest fanaticism and the most incoherent declamation. It is, however, somewhat remarkable that Tertullian did not suffer martyrdom himself.

101. The *Libellatici*, who are chiefly known by the writings of Cyprian, are described with the utmost precision in the copious commentary of Mosheim, p. 483-489.

102. Plin. Epistol. x. 97. Dionysius Alexandrin. ap. Euseb. l. vi. c. 41. Ad prima statim verba minantis inimici maximus fratrum numerus fidem suam prodidit: nec prostratus est persecutionis impetu, sed voluntario lapsu seipsum prostravit. Cyprian. Opera, p. 89. Among these deserters were many priests and even bishops.

103. It was on this occasion that Cyprian wrote his treatise De Lapsis, and many of his epistles. The controversy concerning the treatment of penitent apostates does not occur among the Christians of the preceding century. Shall we ascribe this to the superiority of their faith and courage, or to our less intimate knowledge of their history?

104. See Mosheim, p. 97. Sulpicius Severus was the first author of this computation; though he seemed desirous of reserving the tenth and greatest persecution for the coming of the Antichrist.

105. The testimony given by Pontius Pilate is first mentioned by Justin. The successive improvements which the story acquired (as it has passed through the hands of Tertullian, Eusebius, Epiphanius, Chrysostom, Orosius, Gregory of Tours, and the authors of the several editions of the Acts of Pilate), are very fairly stated by Dom Calmet, Dissertat. sur l'Ecriture, tom. iii. p. 651, etc.

106. On this miracle, as it is commonly called, of the Thundering Legion, see the admirable criticism of Mr. Moyle, in his Works, vol. ii. p. 81-390.

107. Dion Cassius, or rather his abbreviator Xiphilin, l. lxxii. [c. 4] p. 1206. Mr. Moyle (p. 266) has explained the condition of the church under the reign of Commodus.

108. Compare the Life of Caracalla, in the Augustan History, with the epistle of Tertullian to Scapula. Dr. Jortin (Remarks on Ecclesiastical History, vol. ii. p. 5, etc.) considers the cure of Severus, by the means of holy oil, with a strong desire to convert it into a miracle.

109. Tertullian de Fugâ, c. 13. The present was made during the feast of the Saturnalia; and it is a matter of serious concern to Tertullian that the faithful should be confounded with the most infamous professions which purchased the connivance of the government.

110. Euseb. l. v. c. 23, 24. Mosheim, p. 435-447.

111. Judæos fieri sub gravi pœnâ vetuit. Idem etiam de Christianis sanxit. Hist. August. p. 70. [Spart. Sever. c. 17.]

112. Sulpicius Severus, l. ii. p. 384 [ed. Lugd. Bat. 1647]. This computation (allowing for a single exception) is confirmed by the History of Eusebius and by the writings of Cyprian.

113. The antiquity of Christian churches is discussed by Tillemont (Mémoires Ecclésiastiques, tom. iii. part ii. p. 68-72) and by Mr. Moyle (vol. i. p. 378-398). The former refers the first construction of them to the peace of Alexander Severus; the latter, to the peace of Gallienus.

114. See the Augustan History, p. 130. [Lamprid. Alex. Sever. c. 45.] The emperor Alexander adopted their method of publicly proposing the names of those persons who were candidates for ordination. It is true that the honour of this practice is likewise attributed to the Jews.

115. Euseb. Hist. Ecclesiast. l. vi. c. 21. Hieronym. de Script. Eccles. c. 54 [vol. ii. p. 879, ed. Vallars.]. Mamæa was styled a holy and pious woman, both by the Christians and the Pagans. From the former, therefore, it was impossible that she should deserve that honourable epithet.

116. See the Augustan History, p. 123. [Lampr. Alex. Sever. c. 29.] Mosheim (p. 465) seems to refine too much on the domestic religion of Alexander. His design of building a public temple to Christ (Hist. August. p. 129 [Lampr. Alex. Sever. c. 43]), and the objection which was suggested either to him, or in similar circumstances to Hadrian, appear to have no other foundation than an improbable report, invented by the Christians, and credulously adopted by an historian of the age of Constantine.

117. Euseb. l. vi. c. 28. It may be presumed that the success of the Christians had exasperated the increasing bigotry of the Pagans. Dion Cassius, who composed his history under the former reign, had most probably intended for the use of his master those counsels of persecution which he ascribes to a better age, and to the favourite of Augustus. Concerning this oration of Mæcenas, or rather of Dion, I may refer to my own unbiased opinion (vol. i. p. 55, note 25), and to the Abbé de la Bléterie (Mémoires de l'Académie, tom xxiv. p. 303; tom. xxv. p. 432).

118. Orosius, l. vii. c. 19, mentions Origen as the object of Maximin's resentment; and Firmilianus, a Cappadocian bishop of that age, gives a just and confined idea of this persecution (apud Cyprian. Epist. 75).

119. The mention of those princes who were publicly supposed to be Christians, as we find it in an epistle of Dionysius of Alexandria (ap. Euseb. l. vii. c. 10), evidently alludes to Philip and his family; and forms a contemporary evidence that such a report had prevailed; but the Egyptian bishop, who lived at an humble distance from the court of Rome, expresses himself with a becoming diffidence concerning the truth of the fact. The epistles of Origen (which were extant in the time of Eusebius, see l. vi. c. 36) would most probably decide this curious, rather than important, question.

120. Euseb. l. vi. c. 34. The story, as is usual, has been embellished by succeeding writers, and is confuted, with much superfluous learning, by Frederick Spanheim (Opera Varia, tom. ii. p. 400, etc.).

121. Lactantius, de Mortibus Persecutorum, c. 3, 4. After celebrating the felicity and increase of the church under a long succession of good princes, he adds, "Extitit post annos plurimos, execrabile animal, Decius, qui vexaret Ecclesiam."

122. Euseb. l. vi. c. 39. Cyprian. Epistol. 55. The see of Rome remained vacant from the martyrdom of Fabianus, the 20th of January, A.D. 250, till the election of Cornelius, the 4th of June, A.D. 251. Decius had probably left Rome, since he was killed before the end of that year.

123. Euseb. l. vii. c. 10. Mosheim (p. 548) has very clearly shown that the præfect Macrianus, and the Egyptian Magus, are one and the same person.

124. Eusebius (l. vii. c. 13) gives us a Greek version of this Latin edict, which seems to have been very concise. By another edict he directed that the Cæmeteria should be restored to the Christians.

125. Euseb. l. vii. c. 30. Lactantius de M. P. c.

6. Hieronym. in Chron. p. 177 [Anno ab. Abr. 2290, tom, viii. p. 757, ed. Vallars.]. Orosius, l. vii. c. 23. Their language is in general so ambiguous and incorrect, that we are at a loss to determine how far Aurelian had carried his intentions before he was assassinated. Most of the moderns (except Dodwell, Dissertat. Cyprian. xi. 64) have seized the occasion of gaining a few extraordinary martyrs.

126. Paul was better pleased with the title of *Ducenarius* than with that of bishop. The *Ducenarius* was an imperial procurator, so called from his salary of two hundred *sestertia*, or £1600 a year. (See Salmasius ad Hist. August. p. 124.) Some critics suppose that the bishop of Antioch had actually obtained such an office from Zenobia, while others consider it only as a figurative expression of his pomp and insolence.

127. Simony was not unknown in those times; and the clergy sometimes bought what they intended to sell. It appears that the bishopric of Carthage was purchased by a wealthy matron, named Lucilla, for her servant Majorinus. The price was 400 *Folles*. (Monument. Antiq. ad calcem Optati, p. 263.) Every *Follis* contained 125 pieces of silver, and the whole sum may be computed at about £2400.

128. If we are desirous of extenuating the vices of Paul, we must suspect the assembled bishops of the East of publishing the most malicious calumnies in circular epistles addressed to all the churches of the empire (ap. Euseb. l. vii. c. 30).

129. His heresy (like those of Noetus and Sabellius, in the same century) tended to confound the mysterious distinction of the divine persons. See Mosheim, p. 702, etc.

130. Euseb. Hist. Ecclesiast. l. vii. c. 30. We are entirely indebted to him for the curious story of Paul of Samosata.

131. The era of martyrs, which is still in use among the Copts and the Abyssinians, must be reckoned from the 29th of August, A.D. 284; as the beginning of the Egyptian year was nineteen days earlier than the real accession of Diocletian. See Dissertation Préliminaire à l'Art de vérifier les Dates.

132. The expression of Lactantius (de M. P. c. 15), "sacrificio pollui coegit," implies their antecedent conversion to the faith; but does not seem to justify the assertion of Mosheim (p. 912), that they had been privately baptised.

133. M. de Tillemont (Mémoires Ecclésiastiques, tom. v. part. i. p. 11, 12) has quoted from the Spicilegium of Dom Luc d'Archeri a very curious instruction which bishop Theonas composed for the use of Lucian.

134. Lactantius de M. P. c. 10.

135. Eusebius, Hist. Ecclesiast. l. viii. c. 1. The reader who consults the original will not accuse me of heightening the picture. Eusebius was about sixteen years of age at the accession of the emperor Diocletian.

136. We might quote, among a great number of instances, the mysterious worship of Mithras and the Taurobolia; the latter of which became fashionable in the time of the Antonines (see a Dissertation of M. de Boze, in the Mémoires de l'Académie des Inscriptions, tom. ii. p. 443). The romance of Apuleius is as full of devotion as of satire.

137. The impostor Alexander very strongly recommended the oracle of Trophonius at Mallos, and those of Apollo at Claros and Miletus (Lucian, tom. ii. p. 236, edit. Reitz [Alexand. c. 29]). The last of these, whose singular history would furnish a very curious episode, was consulted by Diocletian before he published his edicts of persecution (Lactantius de M. P. c. 11).

138. Besides the ancient stories of Pythagoras and Aristeas, the cures performed at the shrine of Æsculapius, and the fables related of Apollonius of Tyana, were frequently opposed to the miracles of Christ; though I agree with Dr. Lardner (see Testimonies, vol. iii. p. 253, 352), that, when Philostratus composed the Life of Apollonius, he had no such intention.

139. It is seriously to be lamented that the Christian fathers, by acknowledging the supernatural, or, as they deem it, the infernal part of Paganism, destroy with their own hands the great advantage which we might otherwise derive from the liberal concessions of our adversaries.

140. Julian ([tom. i.] p. 301, edit. Spanheim) expresses a pious joy that the providence of the gods had extinguished the impious sects, and for the most part destroyed the books of the Pyrrhonians and Epicureans, which had been very numerous, since Epicurus himself composed no less than 300 volumes. See Diogenes Laertius, l. x. c. 26.

141. Cumque alios audiam mussitare indignanter, et dicere opportere statui per Senatum, abolleantur ut hæc scripta, quibus Christiana Religio comprobetur, et vetustatis opprimatur auctoritas. Arnobius adversus Gentes, l. iii. p. 103, 104, [p. 98, 99, ed. Ant. 1604]. He adds very properly, Erroris convincite Ciceronem . . . nam intercipere scripta, et publicatam velle submergere lectionem, non est Deum [Deos] defendere sed veritatis testificationem timere.

142. Lactantius (Divin. Institut. l. v. c. 2, 3) gives a very clear and spirited account of two of these philosophic adversaries of the faith. The large treatise of Porphyry against the Christians consisted of thirty books, and was composed in Sicily about the year 270.

143. See Socrates, Hist. Ecclesiast. l. i. c. 9, and Codex Justinian. l. i. tit. i. l. 3.

144. Eusebius l. viii. c. 4, c. 17. He limits the number of military martyrs, by a remarkable expression (σπανίως τούτων εἶς που καὶ δεύτερος), of which neither his Latin nor French translator have rendered the energy. Notwithstanding the authority of Eusebius, and the silence of Lactantius, Ambrose, Sulpicius, Orosius, etc., it has been long

believed that the Thebæan legion, consisting of 6000 Christians, suffered martyrdom by the order of Maximian, in the valley of the Pennine Alps. The story was first published about the middle of the fifth century, by Eucherius bishop of Lyons, who received it from certain persons, who received it from Isaac bishop of Geneva, who is said to have received it from Theodore bishop of Octodurum. The abbey of St. Maurice still subsists, a rich monument of the credulity of Sigismund, king of Burgundy. See an excellent Dissertation in the thirty-sixth volume of the Bibliothèque Raisonnée, p. 427-454.

145. See the Acta Sincera, p. 299. The accounts of his martyrdom, and of that of Marcellus, bear every mark of truth and authenticity.

146. Acta Sincera, p. 302.

147. De M. P. c. 11. Lactantius (or whoever was the author of this little treatise) was, at that time, an inhabitant of Nicomedia; but it seems difficult to conceive how he could acquire so accurate a knowledge of what passed in the Imperial cabinet.

148. The only circumstance which we can discover is the devotion and jealousy of the mother of Galerius. She is described by Lactantius as Deorum montium cultrix; mulier admodum superstitiosa. She had a great influence over her son, and was offended by the disregard of some of her Christian servants.

149. The worship and festival of the god Terminus are elegantly illustrated by M. de Boze, Mém. de l'Académie des Inscriptions, tom. i. p. 50.

150. In our only MS. of Lactantius we read *profectus;* but reason, and the authority of all the critics, allow us, instead of that word, which destroys the sense of the passage, to substitute *præfectus.*

151. Lactantius, de M. P. c. 12, gives a very lively picture of the destruction of the church.

152. Mosheim (p. 922-926), from many scattered passages of Lactantius and Eusebius, has collected a very just and accurate notion of this edict; though he sometimes deviates into conjecture and refinement.

153. Many ages afterwards Edward I. practised, with great success, the same mode of persecution against the clergy of England. See Hume's History of England, vol. ii. p. 300, last 4to edition.

154. Lactantius only calls him quidam, etsi non recte, magno tamen animo, etc., M. P. c. 13. Eusebius (l. viii. c. 5) adorns him with secular honours. Neither have condescended to mention his name; but the Greeks celebrate his memory under that of John. See Tillemont, Mémoires Ecclésiastiques, tom. v. part ii. p. 320.

155. Lactantius de M. P. c. 13, 14 [14, 15]. Potentissimi quondam Eunuchi necati, per quos Palatium et ipse constabat. Eusebius (l. viii. c. 6) mentions the cruel executions of the eunuchs Gorgonius and Dorotheus, and of Anthimus bishop of Nicomedia; and both those writers describe, in a vague but tragical manner, the horrid scenes which were acted even in the Imperial presence.

156. See Lactantius, Eusebius, and Constantine, ad Cœtum Sanctorum, c. xxv. Eusebius confesses his ignorance of the cause of this fire.

157. Tillemont, Mémoires Ecclésiast. tom. v. part. i. p. 43.

158. See the Acta Sincera of Ruinart, p. 353; those of Felix of Thibara, or Tibiur, appear much less corrupted than in the other editions, which afford a lively specimen of legendary licence.

159. See the first book of Optatus of Milevis against the Donatists. Paris, 1700, edit. Dupin. He lived under the reign of Valens.

160. The ancient monuments, published at the end of Optatus, p. 261, etc., describe, in a very circumstantial manner, the proceedings of the governors in the destruction of churches. They made a minute inventory of the plate, etc., which they found in them. That of the church of Cirta, in Numidia, is still extant. It consisted of two chalices of gold and six of silver; six urns, one kettle, seven lamps, all likewise of silver; besides a large quantity of brass utensils and wearing apparel.

161. Lactantius (Institut. Divin. v. 11) confines the calamity to the *conventiculum,* with its congregation. Eusebius (viii. 11) extends it to a whole city, and introduces something very like a regular siege. His ancient Latin translator, Rufinus, adds the important circumstance of the permission given to the inhabitants of retiring from thence. As Phrygia reached to the confines of Isauria, it is possible that the restless temper of those independent barbarians may have contributed to this misfortune.

162. Eusebius, l. viii. c. 6. M. de Valois (with some probability) thinks that he has discovered the Syrian rebellion in an oration of Libanius; and that it was a rash attempt of the tribune Eugenius, who with only five hundred men seized Antioch and might perhaps allure the Christians by the promise of religious toleration. From Eusebius (l. ix. c. 8), as well as from Moses of Chorene (Hist. Armen. l. ii. 77, etc.), it may be inferred that Christianity was already introduced into Armenia.

163. See Mosheim, p. 938; the text of Eusebius very plainly shows that the governors, whose powers were enlarged, not restrained, by the new laws, could punish with death the most obstinate Christians as an example to their brethren.

164. Athanasius, p. 833, ap. Tillemont, Mém. Ecclésiast. tom. v. part i. p. 90.

165. Eusebius, l. viii. c. 13. Lactantius de M. P. c. 15. Dodwell (Dissertat. Cyprian. xi. 75) represents them as inconsistent with each other. But the former evidently speaks of Constantius in the station of Cæsar, and the latter of the same prince in the rank of Augustus.

166. Datianus is mentioned in Gruter's Inscriptions as having determined the limits between the territories of Pax Julia and those of Ebora, both cities in the southern part of Lusitania. If we recollect the neighbourhood of those places to Cape St.

Vincent, we may suspect that the celebrated deacon and martyr of that name has been inaccurately assigned by Prudentius, etc., to Saragossa or Valentia. See the pompous history of his sufferings, in the Mémoires de Tillemont, tom. v. part ii. p. 58-85. Some critics are of opinion that the department of Constantius, as Cæsar, did not include Spain, which still continued under the immediate jurisdiction of Maximian.

167. Eusebius, l. viii. c. 11. Gruter, Inscrip. p. 1171, No. 18. Rufinus has mistaken the office of Adauctus, as well as the place of his martyrdom.

168. Eusebius, l. viii. c. 14. But as Maxentius was vanquished by Constantine, it suited the purpose of Lactantius to place his death among those of the persecutors.

169. The epitaph of Marcellus is to be found in Gruter, Inscrip. p. 1172, No. 3, and it contains all that we know of his history. Marcellinus and Marcellus, whose names follow in the list of popes, are supposed by many critics to be different persons; but the learned Abbé de Longuerue was convinced that they were one and the same.

Veridicus rector lapsis quia crimina flere
Prædixit miseris, fuit omnibus hostis amarus.
Hinc furor, hinc odium; sequitur discordia, lites,
Seditio, cædes; solvuntur fœdera pacis.
Crimen ob alterius, Christum qui in pace negavit
Finibus expulsus patriæ est feritate Tyranni.
Hæc breviter Damasus voluit comperta referre:
Marcelli populus meritum cognoscere posset.

We may observe that Damasus was made bishop of Rome, A.D. 366.

170. Optatus contr. Donatist. l. i. c. 17, 18.

171. The Acts of the Passion of St. Boniface, which abound in miracles and declamation, are published by Ruinart (p. 283-291), both in Greek and Latin, from the authority of very ancient manuscripts.

172. During the four first centuries there exist few traces of either bishops or bishoprics in the western Illyricum. It has been thought probable that the primate of Milan extended his jurisdiction over Sirmium, the capital of that great province. See the Geographia Sacra of Charles de St. Paul, p. 68-76, with the observations of Lucas Holstenius.

173. The eighth book of Eusebius, as well as the supplement concerning the martyrs of Palestine, principally relate to the persecution of Galerius and Maximin. The general lamentations with which Lactantius opens the fifth book of his Divine Institutions allude to their cruelty.

174. Eusebius (l. viii. c. 17) has given us a Greek version, and Lactanius (de M. P. c. 34) the Latin original, of this memorable edict. Neither of these writers seems to recollect how directly it contradicts whatever they have just affirmed of the remorse and repentance of Galerius.

175. Eusebius, l. ix. c. 1. He inserts the epistle of the præfect.

176. See Eusebius, l. viii. c. 14, l. ix. c. 2-8. Lac-

tantius de M. P. c. 36. These writers agree in representing the arts of Maximin: but the former relates the execution of several martyrs, while the latter expressly affirms, occidi servos Dei vetuit.

177. A few days before his death he published a very ample edict of toleration, in which he imputes all the severities which the Christians suffered to the judges and governors, who had misunderstood his intentions. See the edict in Eusebius, l. ix. c. 10.

178. Such is the *fair* deduction from two remarkable passages in Eusebius, l. viii. c. 2, and de Martyr. Palestin. c. 12. The prudence of the historian has exposed his own character to censure and suspicion. It was well known that he himself had been thrown into prison; and it was suggested that he had purchased his deliverance by some dishonourable compliance. The reproach was urged in his lifetime, and even in his presence, at the council of Tyre. See Tillemont, Mémoires Ecclésiastiques, tom. viii. part i. p. 67.

179. The ancient, and perhaps authentic, account of the sufferings of Tarachus and his companions (Acta Sincera Ruinart, p. 419-448) is filled with strong expressions of resentment and contempt, which could not fail of irritating the magistrate. The behaviour of Ædesius to Hierocles, præfect of Egypt, was still more extraordinary. λόγοις τε καὶ ἔργοις τὸν δικαστὴν ... περιβαλὼν. Euseb. de Martyr. Palestin. c. 5.

180. Euseb. de Martyr. Palestin. c. 13.

181. Augustin. Collat. Carthagin. Dei. iii. c. 13, ap. Tillemont, Mémoires Ecclésiastiques, tom. v. part i. p. 46. The controversy with the Donatists has reflected some, though perhaps a partial, light on the history of the African church.

182. Eusebius de Martyr. Palestin. c. 13. He closes his narration by assuring us that these were the martyrdoms inflicted in Palestine during the *whole* course of the persecution. The ninth chapter of his eighth book, which relates to the province of Thebais in Egypt, may seem to contradict our moderate computation; but it will only lead us to admire the artful management of the historian. Choosing for the scene of the most exquisite cruelty the most remote and sequestered country of the Roman empire, he relates that in Thebais from ten to one hundred persons had frequently suffered martyrdom in the same day. But when he proceeds to mention his own journey into Egypt, his language insensibly becomes more cautious and moderate. Instead of a large but definite number, he speaks of many Christians (πλείους), and most artfully selects two ambiguous words (ἱστορήσαμεν and ὑπομείναντας) which may signify either what he had seen or what he had heard; either the expectation or the execution of the punishment. Having thus provided a secure evasion, he commits the equivocal passage to his readers and translators; justly conceiving that their piety would induce them to prefer the most favourable sense. There was perhaps some malice in the remark of Theodorus Metochita, that all who, like

Eusebius, had been conversant with the Egyptians, delighted in an obscure and intricate style. (See Valesius ad loc.)

183. When Palestine was divided into three, the præfecture of the East contained forty-eight provinces. As the ancient distinctions of nations were long since abolished, the Romans distributed the provinces according to a general proportion of their extent and opulence.

184. Ut gloriari possint nullum se innocentium peremisse, nam et ipse audivi aliquos gloriantes,

quia administratio sua, in hâc parte, fuerit incruenta. Lactant. Institut. Divin. v. 11.

185. Grot. Annal. de Rebus Belgicis, l. i. p. 12, edit. fol.

186. Fra Paolo (Istoria del Concilio Tridentino, l. iii.) reduces the number of the Belgic martyrs to 50,000. In learning and moderation Fra Paolo was not inferior to Grotius. The priority of time gives some advantage to the evidence of the former, which he loses on the other hand by the distance of Venice from the Netherlands.

Chapter XVII

1. Polybius, l. iv. [c. 45] p. 423, edit. Casaubon. He observes that the peace of the Byzantines was frequently disturbed, and the extent of their territory contracted, by the inroads of the wild Thracians.

2. The navigator Byzas, who was styled the son of Neptune, founded the city 656 years before the Christian era. His followers were drawn from Argos and Megara. Byzantium was afterwards rebuilt and fortified by the Spartan general Pausanias. See Scaliger, Animadvers. ad Euseb. p. 81. Ducange, Constantinopolis, l. i. part i. cap. 15, 16. With regard to the wars of the Byzantines against Philip, the Gauls, and the kings of Bithynia, we should trust none but the ancient writers who lived before the greatness of the Imperial city had excited a spirit of flattery and fiction.

3. The Bosphorus has been very minutely described by Dionysius of Byzantium, who lived in the time of Domitian (Hudson, Geograph. Minor. tom. iii.), and by Gilles or Gyllius, a French traveller of the sixteenth century. Tournefort (Lettre XV.) seems to have used his own eyes, and the learning of Gyllius.

4. There are very few conjectures so happy as that of Le Clerc (Bibliothèque Universelle, tom. i. p. 148), who supposes that the harpies were only locusts. The Syriac or Phœnician name of those insects, their noisy flight, the stench and devastation which they occasion, and the north wind which drives them into the sea, all contribute to form the striking resemblance.

5. The residence of Amycus was in Asia, between the old and the new castles, at a place called Laurus Insana. That of Phineus was in Europe, near the village of Mauromole and the Black Sea. See Gyllius de Bosph. l. ii. c. 23. Tournefort, Lettre XV.

6. The deception was occasioned by several pointed rocks, alternately covered and abandoned by the waves. At present there are two small islands, one towards either shore: that of Europe is distinguished by the column of Pompey.

7. The ancients computed one hundred and twenty stadia, or fifteen Roman miles. They measured only from the new castles, but they

carried the straits as far as the town of Chalcedon.

8. Ducas. Hist. c. 34 [p. 136, ed. Paris; p. 108, ed. Ven.; p. 242, ed. Bonn]. Leunclavius Hist. Turcica Mussulmanica, l. xv. p. 577. Under the Greek empire these castles were used as state prisons, under the tremendous name of Lethe, or towers of oblivion.

9. Darius engraved in Greek and Assyrian letters, on two marble columns, the names of his subject nations, and the amazing numbers of his land and sea forces. The Byzantines afterwards transported these columns into the city, and used them for the altars of their tutelar deities. Herodotus, l. iv. c. 87.

10. Namque artissimo inter Europam Asiamque divortio Byzantium in extremâ Europâ posuere Græci, quibus, Pythium Apollinem consulentibus ubi conderent urbem, redditum oraculum est, quærerent sedem cæcorum terris adversam. Eâ ambage Chalcedonii monstrabantur, quod priores illuc advecti, prævisâ locorum utilitate pejora legissent. Tacit. Annal. xii. 63.

11. Strabo, l. vii. p. 492 [320, ed. Casaubon]. Most of the antlers are now broken off; or, to speak less figuratively, most of the recesses of the harbour are filled up. See Gyllius de Bosphoro Thracio, l. i. c. 5.

12. Procopius de Ædificiis, l. i. c. 5. His description is confirmed by modern travellers. See Thevenot. part. i. l. i. c. 15. Tournefort, Lettre XII. Niebuhr, Voyage d'Arabie, p. 22.

13. See Ducange, C. P. l. i. part i. c. 16, and his Observations sur Villehardouin, p. 289. The chain was drawn from the Acropolis near the modern Kiosk to the tower of Galata, and was supported at convenient distances by large wooden piles.

14. Thevenot (Voyages au Levant, part i. l. i. c. 14) contracts the measure to 125 small Greek miles. Belon (Observations, l. ii. c. 1) gives a good description of the Propontis, but contents himself with the vague expression of one day and one night's sail. When Sandys (Travels. p. 21) talks of 150 furlongs in length as well as breadth, we can only suppose some mistake of the press in the text of that judicious traveller.

15. See an admirable dissertation of M. d'An-

ville upon the Hellespont or Dardanelles, in the Mémoires de l'Académie des Inscriptions, tom. xxviii. p. 318-346. Yet even that ingenious geographer is too fond of supposing new, and perhaps imaginary *measures*, for the purpose of rendering ancient writers as accurate as himself. The stadia employed by Herodotus in the description of the Euxine, the Bosphorus, etc. (l. iv. c. 85), must undoubtedly be all of the same species; but it seems impossible to reconcile them either with truth or with each other.

16. The oblique distance between Sestus and Abydus was thirty stadia. The improbable tale of Hero and Leander is exposed by M. Mahudel, but is defended on the authority of poets and medals by M. de la Nauze. See the Académie des Inscriptions, tom. vii. Hist. p. 74, Mem. p. 240.

17. See the seventh book of Herodotus, who has erected an elegant trophy to his own fame and to that of his country. The review appears to have been made with tolerable accuracy; but the vanity, first of the Persians, and afterwards of the Greeks, was interested to magnify the armament and the victory. I should much doubt whether the *invaders* have ever outnumbered the *men* of any country which they attacked.

18. See Wood's Observations on Homer, p. 320. I have, with pleasure, selected this remark from an author who in general seems to have disappointed the expectation of the public as a critic, and still more as a traveller. He had visited the banks of the Hellespont; he had read Strabo; he ought to have consulted the Roman itineraries. How was it possible for him to confound Ilium and Alexandria Troas (Observations, p. 340, 341), two cities which were sixteen miles distant from each other?

19. Demetrius of Scepsis wrote sixty books on thirty lines of Homer's catalogue. The thirteenth Book of Strabo is sufficient for *our* curiosity.

20. Strabo, l. xiii. p. 595. The disposition of the ships, which were drawn up on dry land, and the posts of Ajax and Achilles, are very clearly described by Homer. See Iliad, viii. 220.

21. Zosim. l. ii. [c. 30] p. 105. Sozomen, l. ii. c. 3. Theophanes, p. 18 [p. 14, ed. Ven.; vol. i. p. 34, ed. Bonn]. Nicephorus Callistus, l. vii. p. 48. Zonaras tom. ii. l. xiii. [c. 3] p. 6. Zosimus places the new city between Ilium and Alexandria, but this apparent difference may be reconciled by the large extent of its circumference. Before the foundation of Constantinople, Thessalonica is mentioned by Cedrenus (p. 283) [vol. i. p. 496, ed. Bonn], and Sardica by Zonaras, as the intended capital. They both suppose, with very little probability, that the emperor, if he had not been prevented by a prodigy, would have repeated the mistake of the *blind* Chalcedonians.

22. Pocock's Description of the East, vol. ii. part ii. p. 127. His plan of the seven hills is clear and accurate. That traveller is seldom so satisfactory.

23. See Belon, Observations, c. 72-76. Among a variety of different species, the Pelamides, a sort of Thunnies, were the most celebrated. We may learn from Polybius, Strabo, and Tacitus, that the profits of the fishery constituted the principal revenue of Byzantium.

24. See the eloquent description of Busbequius, epistol. i. p. 64. Est in Europa; habet in conspectu Asiam, Egyptum, Africamque à dextrâ: quæ tametsi contiguæ non sunt, maris tamen navigandique commoditate veluti junguntur. A sinistrâ vero Pontus est Euxinus, etc.

25. Datur hæc venia antiquitati, ut miscendo humana divinis, primordia urbium augustiora faciat. T. Liv. in procem.

26. He says, in one of his laws, pro commoditate Urbis quam æterno nomine, jubente Deo, donavimus. Cod. Theodos. l. xiii. tit. v. leg. 7.

27. The Greeks, Theophanes, Cedrenus, and the author of the Alexandrian Chronicle, confine themselves to vague and general expressions. For a more particular account of the vision we are obliged to have recourse to such Latin writers as William of Malmesbury. See Ducange, C. P. l. i. p. 24, 25.

28. See Plutarch in Romulus. Among other ceremonies, a large hole, which had been dug for that purpose, was filled up with handfuls of earth, which each of the settlers brought from the place of his birth, and thus adopted his new country.

29. Philostorgius, l. ii. c. 9. This incident, though borrowed from a suspected writer, is characteristic and probable.

30. See in the Mémoires de l'Académie, tom. xxxv. p. 747-758, a dissertation of M. d'Anville on the extent of Constantinople. He takes the plan inserted in the Imperium Orientale of Banduri as the most complete; but by a series of very nice observations he reduces the extravagant proportion of the scale, and, instead of 9500, determines the circumference of the city as consisting of about 7800 French *toises*.

31. Codinus, Antiquitat. Const. p. 12 [p. 25, ed. Bonn]. He assigns the church of St. Anthony as the boundary on the side of the harbour. It is mentioned in Ducange, l. iv. c. 6; but I have tried, without success, to discover the exact place where it was situated.

32. The new wall of Theodosius was constructed in the year 413. In 447 it was thrown down by an earthquake, and rebuilt in three months by the diligence of the præfect Cyrus. The suburb of the Blachernæ was first taken into the city in the reign of Heraclius. Ducange, Const. l. i. c. 10, 11.

33. The measurement is expressed in the Notitia by 14,075 feet. It is reasonable to suppose that these were Greek feet; the proportion of which has been ingeniously determined by M. d'Anville. He compares the 180 feet with 78 Hashemite cubits, which in different writers are assigned for the heights of St. Sophia. Each of these cubits was equal to 27 French inches.

34. The accurate Thevenot (l. i. c. 15) walked in one hour and three-quarters round two of the sides of the triangle, from the Kiosk of the Seraglio to the seven towers. D'Anville examines with care, and receives with confidence, this decisive testimony, which gives a circumference of ten or twelve miles. The extravagant computation of Tournefort (Lettre XI.) of thirty-four or thirty miles, without including Scutari, is a strange departure from his usual character.

35. The sycæ, or fig-trees, formed the thirteenth region, and were very much embellished by Justinian. It has since borne the names of Pera and Galata. The etymology of the former is obvious; that of the latter is unknown. See Ducange, Const. l. i. 22, and Gyllius de Byzant. l. iv. c. 10.

36. One hundred and eleven stadia, which may be translated into modern Greek miles each of seven stadia, or 660, sometimes only 600, French toises. See D'Anville, Mesures Itinéraires, p. 53.

37. When the ancient texts, which describe the size of Babylon and Thebes, are settled, the exaggerations reduced, and the measures ascertained, we find that those famous cities filled the great but not incredible circumference of about twenty-five or thirty miles. Compare D'Anville, Mém. de l'Académie, tom. xxviii. p. 235, with his Description de l'Egypte, p. 201, 202.

38. If we divide Constantinople and Paris into equal squares of 50 French toises, the former contains 850, and the latter 1160, those divisions.

39. Six hundred centenaries, or sixty thousand pounds' weight of gold. This sum is taken from Codinus, Antiquit. Const. p. 11 [p. 23, ed. Bonn]; but unless that contemptible author had derived his information from some purer sources, he would probably have been unacquainted with so obsolete a mode of reckoning.

40. For the forests of the Black Sea, consult Tournefort, Lettre XVI.; for the marble quarries of Proconnesus, see Strabo, l. xiii. p. 588. The latter had already furnished the materials of the stately buildings of Cyzicus.

41. See the Codex Theodos. l. xiii. tit. iv. leg. 1. This law is dated in the year 334, and was addressed to the præfect of Italy, whose jurisdiction extended over Africa. The commentary of Godefroy on the whole title well deserves to be consulted.

42. Constantinopolis dedicatur pœne omnium urbium nuditate. Hieronym. Chron. p. 181. See Codinus, p. 8, 9 [p. 16 sq. ed. Bonn]. The author of the Antiquitat. Const. l. iii. (apud Banduri Imp. Orient. tom. i. p. 41) enumerates Rome, Sicily, Antioch, Athens, and a long list of other cities. The provinces of Greece and Asia Minor may be supposed to have yielded the richest booty.

43. Hist. Compend. p. 369 [vol. i. p. 648, ed. Bonn]. He describes the statue, or rather bust, of Homer with a degree of taste which plainly indicates that Cedrenus copied the style of a more fortunate age.

44. Zosim. l. ii. [c. 30] p. 106. Chron. Alexandrin. vel Paschal. p. 284. Ducange, Const. l. i. c. 24. Even the last of those writers seems to confound the Forum of Constantine with the Augusteum, or court of the palace. I am not satisfied whether I have properly distinguished what belongs to the one and the other.

45. The most tolerable account of this column is given by Pocock, Description of the East, vol. ii. part ii. p. 131. But it is still in many instances perplexed and unsatisfactory.

46. Ducange, Const. l. i. c. 24, p. 76, and his notes ad Alexiad. p. 382. The statue of Constantine or Apollo was thrown down under the reign of Alexius Comnenus.

47. Tournefort (Lettre XII.) computes the Atmeidan at four hundred paces. If he means geometrical paces of five feet each, it was three hundred *toises* in length, about forty more than the great circus of Rome. See d'Anville, Mesures Itinéraires, p. 73.

48. The guardians of the most holy relics would rejoice if they were able to produce such a chain of evidence as may be alleged on this occasion. See Banduri ad Antiquitat. Const. p. 668. Gyllius de Byzant. l. ii. c. 13. 1. The original consecration of the tripod and pillar in the temple of Delphi may be proved from Herodotus and Pausanias. 2. The Pagan Zosimus agrees with the three ecclesiastical historians, Eusebius, Socrates, and Sozomen, that the sacred ornaments of the temple of Delphi were removed to Constantinople by the order of Constantine; and among these the serpentine pillar of the Hippodrome is particularly mentioned. 3. All the European travellers who have visited Constantinople, from Buondelmonte to Pocock, describe it in the same place, and almost in the same manner; the differences between them are occasioned only by the injuries which it has sustained from the Turks. Mahomet the Second broke the under jaw of one of the serpents with a stroke of his battle-axe. Thevenot, l. i. c. 17.

49. The Latin name *Cochlea* was adopted by the Greeks, and very frequently occurs in the Byzantine history. Ducange, Const. l. ii. c. 1, p. 104.

50. There are three topographical points which indicate the situation of the palace. 1. The staircase which connected it with the Hippodrome or Atmeidan. 2. A small artificial port on the Propontis, from whence there was an easy ascent, by a flight of marble steps, to the gardens of the palace. 3. The Augusteum was a spacious court, one side of which was occupied by the front of the palace, and another by the church of St. Sophia.

51. Zeuxippus was an epithet of Jupiter, and the baths were a part of old Byzantium. The difficulty of assigning their true situation has not been felt by Ducange. History seems to connect them with St. Sophia and the palace; but the original plan inserted in Banduri places them on the other side of the city, near the harbour. For their beauties see Chron. Paschal, p. 285, and Gyllius de Byzant.

l. ii. c. 7. Christodorus (see Antiquitat. Const. l. vii.) composed inscriptions in verse for each of the statues. He was a Theban poet in genius as well as in birth:—

Bœotum in crasso jurares aëre natum.

52. See the Notitia. Rome only reckoned 1780 large houses, *domus;* but the word must have had a more dignified signification. No *insulæ* are mentioned at Constantinople. The old capital consisted of 424 streets, the new of 322.

53. Liutprand Legatio ad Imp. Nicephorum, p. 153. The modern Greeks have strangely disfigured the antiquities of Constantinople. We might excuse the errors of the Turkish or Arabian writers; but it is somewhat astonishing that the Greeks, who had access to the authentic materials preserved in their own language, should prefer fiction to truth, and loose tradition to genuine history. In a single page of Codinus we may detect twelve unpardonable mistakes: the reconciliation of Severus and Niger, the marriage of their son and daughter, the siege of Byzantium by the Macedonians, the invasion of the Gauls which recalled Severus to Rome, the *sixty* years which elapsed from his death to the foundation of Constantinople, etc.

54. Montesquieu, Grandeur et Décadence des Romains, c. 17.

55. Themist. Orat. iii. p. 48, edit. Hardouin. Sozomen, l. ii. c. 3. Zosim. l. ii. [c. 31] p. 107. Anonym. Valesian. p. 175. If we could credit Codinus (p. 10) [p. 20, *sq.*, ed. Bonn], Constantine built houses for the senators on the exact model of their Roman palaces, and gratified them, as well as himself, with the pleasure of an agreeable surprise; but the whole story is full of fictions and inconsistencies.

56. The law by which the younger Theodosius, in the year 438, abolished this tenure, may be found among the Novellæ of that emperor at the end of the Theodosian Code, tom. vi. nov. 12. M. de Tillemont (Hist. des Empereurs, tom. iv. p. 371) has evidently mistaken the nature of these estates. With a grant from the Imperial demesnes, the same condition was accepted as a favour, which would justly have been deemed a hardship if it had been imposed upon private property.

57. The passages of Zosimus, of Eunapius, of Sozomen, and of Agathias, which relate to the increase of buildings and inhabitants at Constantinople, are collected and connected by Gyllius de Byzant, l. i. c. 3. Sidonius Apollinaris (in Panegyr. Anthem. 56, p. 279, edit. Sirmond) describes the moles that were pushed forwards into the sea; they consisted of the famous Puzzolan sand, which hardens in the water.

58. Sozomen, l. ii. c. 3. Philostorg. l. ii. c. 9. Codin. Antiquitat. Const. p. 8 [p. 16, ed. Bonn]. It appears by Socrates, l. ii. c. 13, that the daily allowance of the city consisted of eight myriads of σίτου, which we may either translate, with Valesius, by the words modii of corn, or consider as expressive of the number of loaves of bread.

59. See Cod. Theodos. l. xiii. and xiv. and Cod. Justinian. Edict. xii. tom. ii. p. 648, edit. Genev. See the beautiful complaint of Rome in the poem of Claudian de Bell. Gildonico, ver. 60-62:—

Cum subiit par Roma mihi, divisaque sumsit
Æquales Aurora togas; Ægyptia rura
In partem cessere novam.

60. The regions of Constantinople are mentioned in the Code of Justinian, and particularly described in the Notitia of the younger Theodosius; but as the four last of them are not included within the wall of Constantine, it may be doubted whether this division of the city should be referred to the founder.

61. Senatum constituit secundiordinis; *Claros* vocavit. Anonym. Valesian. p. 715. The senators of old Rome were styled *Clarissimi.* See a curious note of Valesius ad Ammian. Marcellin. xxii. 9. From the eleventh epistle of Julian it should seem that the place of senator was considered as a burthen rather than as an honour; but the Abbé de la Blèterie (Vie de Jovien, tom. ii. p. 371) has shown that this epistle could not relate to Constantinople. Might we not read, instead of the celebrated name of Βυζαντίοις, the obscure but more probable word Βισανθηνοις? Bisanthe or Rhœdestus, now Rhodosto, was a small maritime city of Thrace. See Stephan. Byz. de Urbibus, p. 225 [ed. Lugd. B. 1694], and Cellar. Geograph. tom. i. p. 849.

62. Cod. Theodos. l. xiv. 13. [Add Cod. Just. xi. 20.—S.] The commentary of Godefroy (tom. v. p. 220) is long, but perplexed; nor indeed is it easy to ascertain in what the Jus Italicum could consist after the freedom of the city had been communicated to the whole empire.

63. Julian (Orat. i. p. 8) celebrates Constantinople as not less superior to all other cities than she was inferior to Rome itself. His learned commentator (Spanheim, p. 75, 76) justifies this language by several parallel and contemporary instances. Zosimus, as well as Socrates and Sozomen, flourished after the division of the empire between the two sons of Theodosius, which established a perfect *equality* between the old and the new capital.

64. Codinus (Antiquitat. p. 8 [p. 17, ed. Bonn.]) affirms that the foundations of Constantinople were laid in the year of the world 5837 (A.D. 329), on the 26th of September, and that the city was dedicated the 11th of May, 5838 (A.D. 330). He connects these dates with several characteristic epochs, but they contradict each other; the authority of Codinus is of little weight, and the space which he assigns must appear insufficient. The term of ten years is given us by Julian (Orat. i. p. 8); and Spanheim labours to establish the truth of it (p. 69-75), by the help of two passages from Themistius (Orat. iv. p. 58) and of Philostorgius (l. ii. c. 9), which form a period from the year 324 to the year 334. Modern critics are divided con-

cerning this point of chronology, and their different sentiments are very accurately described by Tillemont, Hist. des Empereurs, tom. iv. p. 619-625.

65. Themistius, Orat. iii. p. 47. Zosim. l. ii. [c. 32]p. 108. Constantine himself, in one of his laws (Cod. Theod. l. xv. tit. i. [leg. 23?]), betrays his impatience.

66. Cedrenus and Zonaras, faithful to the mode of superstition which prevailed in their own times, assure us that Constantinople was consecrated to the virgin Mother of God.

67. The earliest and most complete account of this extraordinary ceremony may be found in the Alexandrian Chronicle, p. 285. Tillemont, and the other friends of Constantine, who are offended with the air of Paganism which seems unworthy of a Christian prince, had a right to consider it as doubtful, but they were not authorised to omit the mention of it.

68. Sozomen, l. ii. c. 3. Ducange, C. P. l. i. c. 6. Velut ipsius Romæ filiam, is the expression of Augustine, The City of God, l. v. c. 25.

69. Eutropius, l. x. c. 8. Julian. Orat. i. p. 8. Ducange, C. P. l. i. c. 5. The name of Constantinople is extant on the metals of Constantine.

70. The lively Fontenelle (Dialogues des Morts, xii.) affects to deride the vanity of human ambition, and seems to triumph in the disappointment of Constantine, whose immortal name is now lost in the vulgar appellation of Istambol, a Turkish corruption of εἰς τὴν πόλιν. Yet the original name is still preserved, 1. By the nations of Europe. 2. By the modern Greeks. 3. By the Arabs, whose writings are diffused over the wide extent of their conquests in Asia and Africa. See d'Herbelot, Bibliothèque Orientale, p. 275. 4. By the more learned Turks, and by the emperor himself in his public mandates. Cantemir's History of the Othman Empire, p. 51.

71. The Theodosian code was promulgated A.D. 438. See the Prolegomena of Godefroy, c. i. p. 185.

72. Pancirolus, in his elaborate Commentary, assigns to the Notitia a date almost similar to that of the Theodosian Code; but his proofs, or rather conjectures, are extremely feeble. I should be rather inclined to place this useful work between the final division of the empire (A.D. 395) and the successful invasion of Gaul by the barbarians (A.D. 407). See Histoire des Anciens Peuples de l'Europe, tom. vii. p. 40.

73. Scilicet externæ superbiæ sueto, non inerat notitia nostri (perhaps nostræ); apud quos vis Imperii valet, inania transmittuntur. Tacit. Annal. xv. 31. The gradation from the style of freedom and simplicity to that of form and servitude may be traced in the Epistles of Cicero, of Pliny, and of Symmachus.

74. The emperor Gratian, after confirming a law of precedency published by Valentinian, the father of his Divinity, thus continues: Siquis igitur indebitum sibi locum usurpaverit, nullâ se ignora-

tione defendat; sitque plane sacrilegii reus, qui divina præcepta neglexerit. Cod. Theod. l. vi. tit. v. leg. 2.

75. Consult the Notitia Dignitatum at the end of the Theodosian Code, tom. vi. p. 316.

76. Pancirolus ad Notitiam utriusque Imperii, p. 39. But his explanations are obscure, and he does not sufficiently distinguish the painted emblems from the effective ensigns of office.

77. In the Pandects, which may be referred to the reigns of the Antonines, Clarissimus is the ordinary and legal title of a senator.

78. Pancirol. p. 12-17. I have not taken any notice of the two inferior ranks, Perfectissimus and Egregius, which were given to many persons who were not raised to the senatorial dignity.

79. Cod. Theodos. l. vi. tit. vi. The rules of precedency are ascertained with the most minute accuracy by the emperors, and illustrated with equal prolixity by their learned interpreter.

80. Cod. Theodos. l. vi. tit. xxii.

81. Ausonius (in Gratiarum Actione) basely expatiates on this unworthy topic, which is managed by Mamertinus (Panegyr. Vet. xi. [x.] 16, 19) with somewhat more freedom and ingenuity.

82. Cum de Consulibus in annum creandis, solus mecum volutarem . . . te Consulem et designavi, et declaravi, et priorem nuncupavi; are some of the expressions employed by the emperor Gratian to his preceptor the poet Ausonius.

83. Immanesque . . . dentes
   Qui secti ferro in tabulas auroque micantes,
   Inscripti rutilum cælato Consule nomen
   Per proceres et vulgus eant.
      Claud. de Cons. Stilichon. iii. 346.
Montfaucon has represented some of these tablets or dypticks [diptychs]; see Supplément à l'Antiquité, tom. iii. p. 220.

84. Consule lætatur post plurima sæcula viso
   Pallanteus apex: agnoscunt rostra curules
   Auditas quondam proavis: desuetaque cingit
   Regius auratis fora fascibus Ulpia lictor.
      Claud. in vi. Cons. Honorii, 643.
From the reign of Carus to the sixth consulship of Honorius there was an interval of one hundred and twenty years, during which the emperors were always absent from Rome on the first day of January. See the Chronologie de Tillemont, tom. iii., iv. and v.

85. See Claudian in Cons. Prob. et Olybrii, 178, etc.; and in iv. Cons. Honorii, 585, etc.; though in the latter it is not easy to separate the ornaments of the emperor from those of the consul. Ausonius received from the liberality of Gratian a vestis palmata, or robe of state, in which the figure of the emperor Constantius was embroidered.

86. Cernis ut armorum proceres legumque potentes
   Patricios sumunt habitus, et more Gabino
   Discolor incedit legio, positisque parumper
   Bellorum signis, sequitur vexilla Quirini?
   Lictori cedunt aquilæ, ridetque togatus

> Miles, et in mediis effulget curia castris?
> > Claud. in iv. Cons. Honorii, 5.
> ——*strictasque* procul radiare *secures*.
> > In Cons. Prob. 231.

87. See Valesius ad Ammian. Marcellin. l. xxii. c. 7.

88.
> Auspice mox lætum sonuit clamore tribunal,
> Te fastos ineunte quater; solemnia ludit
> Omina Libertas: deductum Vindice morem
> Lex servat, famulusque jugo laxatus herili
> Ducitur, et grato remeat securior ictu.
> > Claud. in iv. Cons. Honorii, 611.

89. Celebrant quidem solemnes istos dies omnes ubique urbes quæ sub legibus agunt; et Roma de more, et Constantinopolis de imitatione, et Antiochia pro luxu, et discincta Carthago, et domus fluminis Alexandria, sed Treviri Principis beneficio. Ausonius in Grat. Actione [p. 715, ed. Amst. 1671].

90. Claudian (in Cons. Mall. Theodori, 279-331) describes, in a lively and fanciful manner, the various games of the circus, the theatre, and the amphitheatre, exhibited by the new consul. The sanguinary combats of gladiators had already been prohibited. Twenty centenaria equal 2000 pounds in gold. Procopius says 20 centenaria equaled 144,000 solidi, and there were 72 solidi to the pound. With the solidus worth 10s, the sum would be £72,000.]

91. Procopius in Hist. Arcana, c. 26.

92. In Consulatu honos sine labore suscipitur. (Mamertin. in Panegyr. Vet. xi. [x.] 2). This exalted idea of the consulship is borrowed from an Oration (iii. p. 107) pronounced by Julian in the servile court of Constantius. See the Abbé de la Bléterie (Mémoires de l'Académie, tom. xxiv. p. 289), who delights to pursue the vestiges of the old constitution, and who sometimes finds them in his copious fancy.

93. Intermarriages between the Patricians and Plebeians were prohibited by the laws of the XII Tables; and the uniform operations of human nature may attest that the custom survived the law. See in Livy (iv. 1-6) the pride of family urged by the consul, and the rights of mankind asserted by the tribune Canuleius.

94. See the animated picture drawn by Sallust, in the Jugurthine war, of the pride of the nobles, and even of the virtuous Metellus, who was unable to brook the idea that the honour of the consulship should be bestowed on the obscure merit of his lieutenant Marius (c. 64). Two hundred years before, the race of the Metelli themselves were confounded among the Plebeians of Rome; and from the etymology of their name of *Cæcilius*, there is reason to believe that those haughty nobles derived their origin from a sutler.

95. In the year of Rome 800 very few remained, not only of the old Patrician families, but even of those which had been created by Cæsar and Augustus. (Tacit. Annal. xi. 25.) The family of Scaurus (a branch of the Patrician Æmilii) was degraded so low that his father, who exercised the trade of a charcoal merchant, left him only ten slaves and somewhat less than three hundred pounds sterling. (Valerius Maximus, l. iv. c. 4, n. 11. Aurel. Victor in Scauro. [De Viris Ill. 72]). The family was saved from oblivion by the merit of the son.

96. Tacit. Annal. xi. 25. Dion Cassius, l. lii. [c. 42] p. 693. The virtues of Agricola, who was created a Patrician by the emperor Vespasian, reflected honour on that ancient order; but his ancestors had not any claim beyond an Equestrian nobility.

97. This failure would have been almost impossible if it were true, as Casaubon compels Aurelius Victor to affirm (ad Sueton. in Cæsar. c. 42; see Hist. August. p. 203 [Trebell. Poll. Claud. c. 3], and Casaubon Comment. p. 220), that Vespasian created at once a thousand Patrician families. But this extravagant number is too much even for the whole Senatorial order, unless we should include all the Roman knights who were distinguished by the permission of wearing the laticlave.

98. Zosimus, l. ii. [c. 40] p. 118; and Godefroy ad Cod. Theodos. l. vi. tit. vi.

99. Zosimus, l. ii. [c. 33] p. 109, 110. If we had not fortunately possessed this satisfactory account of the division of the power and provinces of the Prætorian præfects, we should frequently have been perplexed amidst the copious details of the Code, and the circumstantial minuteness of the Notitia.

100. See a law of Constantine himself. A præfectis autem prætorio provocare, non sinimus. Cod. Justinian. l. vii. tit. lxii. leg. 19. Charisius, a lawyer of the time of Constantine (Heinec. Hist. Juris Romani, p. 349), who admits this law as a fundamental principle of jurisprudence, compares the Prætorian præfects to the masters of the horse of the ancient dictators. Pandect. l. i. tit. xi.

101. When Justinian, in the exhausted condition of the empire, instituted a Prætorian præfect for Africa, he allowed him a salary of one hundred pounds of gold. Cod. Justinian. l. i. tit. xxvii. leg. i.

102. For this, and the other dignities of the empire, it may be sufficient to refer to the ample commentaries of Pancirolus and Godefroy, who have diligently collected and accurately digested in their proper order all the legal and historical materials. From those authors Dr. Howell (History of the World, vol. ii. p. 24-77) has deduced a very distinct abridgment of the state of the Roman empire.

103. Tacit. Annal. vi. 11. Euseb. in Chron. p. 155. Dion Cassius, in the oration of Mæcenas (l. lii. [c. 21] p. 675), describes the prerogatives of the præfect of the city as they were established in his own time.

104. The fame of Messalla has been scarcely equal to his merit. In the earliest youth he was recommended by Cicero to the friendship of Brutus. He followed the standard of the republic till

it was broken in the fields of Philippi: he then accepted and deserved the favour of the most moderate of the conquerors; and uniformly asserted his freedom and dignity in the court of Augustus. The triumph of Messalla was justified by the conquest of Aquitain. As an orator he disputed the palm of eloquence with Cicero himself. Messalla cultivated every muse, and was the patron of every man of genius. He spent his evenings in philosophic conversation with Horace; assumed his place at table between Delia and Tibullus; and amused his leisure by encouraging the poetical talents of young Ovid.

105. Incivilem esse potestatem contestans, says the translator of Eusebius. Tacitus expresses the same idea in other words: quasi nescius exercendi.

106. See Lipsius, Excursus D. ad 1 lib. Tacit. Annal.

107. Heineccii Element. Juris Civilis secund. ordinem Pandect. tom. i. p. 70. See likewise Spanheim de Usu Numismatum, tom. ii. dissertat. x. p. 119. In the year 450 Marcian published a law that *three* citizens should be annually created prætors of Constantinople by the choice of the senate, but with their own consent. Cod. Justinian. l. i. tit. xxxix. leg. 2.

108. Quidquid igitur intra urbem admittitur, ad. P. U. videtur pertinere; sed et siquid intra centesimum milliarium. Ulpian in Pandect. l. i. tit. xii. n. 1. He proceeds to enumerate the various offices of the præfect, who, in the code of Justinian (l. i. tit. xxxix. leg. 3), is declared to precede and command all city magistrates sine injuriâ ac detrimento honoris alieni.

109. Besides our usual guides, we may observe that Felix Cantelorius has written a separate treatise, De Præfecto Urbis; and that many curious details concerning the police of Rome and Constantinople are contained in the fourteenth book of the Theodosian Code.

110. Eunapius affirms that the proconsul of Asia was independent of the præfect; which must, however, be understood with some allowance: the jurisdiction of the vice-præfect he most assuredly disclaimed. Pancirolus, p. 161.

111. The proconsul of Africa had four hundred apparitors; and they all received large salaries, either from the treasury or the province. See Pancirol. p. 26, and Cod. Justinian, l. xii. tit. lvi. ilvi.

112. In Italy there was likewise the *Vicar of Rome*. It has been much disputed whether his jurisdiction measured one hundred miles from the city, or whether it stretched over the ten southern provinces of Italy.

113. The Table taken from Marquardt (Becker's Handbuch der Römischen Alterthümer, vol. iii. part i. p. 240), shows the division of the empire under the four Prætorian præfects.

114. Among the works of the celebrated Ulpian there was one, in ten books, concerning the office of a proconsul, whose duties in the most essential articles were the same as those of an ordinary governor of a province.

115. The presidents, or consulars, could impose only two ounces; the vice-præfects, three; the proconsuls, count of the East, and præfect of Egypt, six. See Heineccii Jur. Civil. tom. i. p. 75. Pandect l. xlviii. tit. xix. n. 8. Cod. Justinian. l. i. tit. liv. leg. 4, 6.

116. Ut nulli patriæ suæ administratio sine speciali principis permissu permittatur. Cod. Justinian. l. i. tit. xli. This law was first enacted by the emperor Marcus, after the rebellion of Cassius (Dion, l. lxxi. [c. 31, p. 1195]). The same regulation is observed in China, with equal strictness, and with equal effect.

117. Pandect. l. xxiii. tit. ii. n. 38, 57, 63.

118. In jure continetur, ne quis in administratione constitutus aliquid compararet. Cod. Theod. l. viii. tit. xv. leg. 1. This maxim of common law was enforced by a series of edicts (see the remainder of the title) from Constantine to Justin. From this prohibition, which is extended to the meanest officers of the governor, they except only clothes and provisions. The purchase within five years may be recovered; after which, on information, it devolves to the treasury.

119. Cessent rapaces jam nunc officialium manus; cessent, inquam; nam si moniti non cessaverint, gladiis præcidentur, etc. Cod. Theod. l. i. tit. vii. leg. 1. Zeno enacted that all governors should remain in the province, to answer any accusations, fifty days after the expiration of their power. Cod. Justinian, l. i. tit. xlix. leg. 1.

120. Summâ igitur ope et alacri studio has leges nostras accipite; et vosmetipsos sic eruditos ostendite, ut spes vos pulcherrima foveat; toto legitimo opere perfecto, posse etiam nostram rempublicam in partibus ejus vobis credendis gubernari. Justinian. in procem. Institutionum.

121. The splendour of the school of Berytus, which preserved in the East the language and jurisprudence of the Romans, may be computed to have lasted from the third to the middle of the sixth century. Heinecc. Jur. Rom. Hist. p. 351–356.

122. As in a former period I have traced the civil and military promotion of Pertinax, I shall here insert the civil honours of Mallius Theodorus. 1. He was distinguished by his eloquence while he pleaded as an advocate in the court of the Prætorian præfect. 2. He governed one of the provinces of Africa, either as president or consular, and deserved, by his administration, the honour of a brass statue. 3. He was appointed vicar, or vice-præfect of Macedonia. 4. Quæstor. 5. Count of the sacred largesses. 6. Prætorian præfect of the Gauls; whilst he might yet be represented as a young man. 7. After a retreat, perhaps a disgrace, of many years, which Mallius (confounded by some critics with the poet Manilius, see Fabricius Bibliothec. Latin edit. Ernest. tom. i. c. 18, p. 501)

employed in the study of the Grecian philosophy, he was named Prætorian præfect of Italy, in the year 397. 8. While he still exercised that great office, he was created, in the year 399, consul for the West; and his name, on account of the infamy of his colleague, the eunuch Eutropius, often stands alone in the Fasti. 9. In the year 408 Mallius was appointed a second time Prætorian præfect of Italy. Even in the venal panegyric of Claudian we may discover the merit of Mallius Theodorus, who, by a rare felicity, was the intimate friend both of Symmachus and of St. Augustin. See Tillemont, Hist. des Emp. tom. v. p. 1110–1114.

123. Mamertinus in Panegyr. Vet. xi. [x.] 20. Asterius apud Photium, p. 1500.

124. The curious passage of Ammianus (l. xxx. c. 4), in which he paints the manners of contemporary lawyers, affords a strange mixture of sound sense, false rhetoric, and extravagant satire. Godefroy (Prolegom. ad Cod. Theod. c. i. p. 185) supports the historian by similar complaints and authentic facts. In the fourth century many camels might have been laden with law-books. Eunapius in Vit. Ædesii, p. 72.

125. See a very splendid example in the Life of Agricola, particularly c. 20, 21. The lieutenant of Britain was intrusted with the same powers which Cicero, proconsul of Cilicia, had exercised in the name of the senate and people.

126. The Abbé Dubos, who has examined with accuracy (see Hist. de la Monarchie Françoise tom. i. p. 41–100, edit. 1742) the institutions of Augustus and of Constantine, observes that, if Otho had been put to death the day before he executed his conspiracy, Otho would now appear in history as innocent as Corbulo.

127. Zosimus, l. ii. [c. 33] p. 110. Before the end of the reign of Constantius the *magistri militum* were already increased to four. See Valesius ad Ammian. l. xvi. c. 7.

128. Though the military counts and dukes are frequently mentioned, both in history and the codes, we must have recourse to the Notitia for the exact knowledge of their number and stations. For the institution, rank, privileges, etc., of the counts in general, see Cod. Theod. l. vi. tit. xii.–xx. with the commentary of Godefroy.

129. Zosimus, l. ii. [c. 34] p. 111. The distinction between the two classes of Roman troops is very darkly expressed in the historians, the laws, and the Notitia. Consult, however, the copious *paratitlon* or abstract, which Godefroy has drawn up, of the seventh book, de Re Militari, of the Theodosian Code, l. vii. tit. i. leg. 18; l. viii. tit. i. leg. 10.

130. Ferox erat in suos miles et rapax, ignavus vero in hostes et fractus. Ammian. l. xxii. c. 4. He observes that they loved downy beds and houses of marble, and that their cups were heavier than their swords.

131. Cod. Theod. l. vii. tit. i. leg. 1; tit. xii. leg. 1. See Howell's Hist. of the World, vol. ii. p. 19.

That learned historian, who is not sufficiently known, labours to justify the character and policy of Constantine.

132. Ammian, l. xix. c. 2. He observes (c. 5) that the desperate sallies of two Gallic legions were like a handful of water thrown on a great conflagration.

133. Pancirolus ad Notitiam, p. 96. Mémoires de l'Académie des Inscriptions, tom. xxv. p. 491.

134. Romana acies unius prope formæ erat et hominum et armorum genere. —Regia acies varia magis multis gentibus dissimilitudine armorum auxiliorumque erat. T. Liv. l. xxxvii. c. 39, 40. Flaminius [Flamininus], even before the event, had compared the army of Antiochus to a supper in which the flesh of one vile animal was diversified by the skill of the cooks. See the Life of Flaminius [Flamininus] in Plutarch.

135. Agathias, l. v. p. 157, edit. Louvre [c. 13, p. 305, ed. Bonn].

136. Valentinian (Cod. Theodos. l. vii. tit. xiii. leg. 3) fixes the standard at five feet seven inches, about five feet four inches and a half English measure. It had formerly been five feet ten inches, and in the best corps six Roman feet. Sed tunc erat amplior multitudo, et plures militiam sequebantur armatam. Vegetius de Re Militari, l. i. c. 5.

137. See the two titles, De Veteranis and De Filiis Veteranorum [tit. xx. xxii.], in the seventh book of the Theodosian Code. The age at which their military service was required varied from twenty-five to sixteen. If the sons of the veterans appeared with a horse, they had a right to serve in the cavalry; two horses gave them some valuable privileges.

138. Cod. Theod. l. vii. tit. xiii. leg. 7. According to the historian Socrates (see Godefroy ad loc.), the same emperor Valens sometimes required eighty pieces of gold for a recruit. In the following law it is faintly expressed that slaves shall not be admitted inter optimas lectissimorum militum turmas.

139. The person and property of a Roman knight, who had mutilated his two sons, were sold at public auction by order of Augustus. (Sueton, in August. c. 24.) The moderation of that artful usurper proves that this example of severity was justified by the spirit of the times. Ammianus makes a distinction between the effeminate Italians and the hardy Gauls (l. xv. c. 12). Yet only fifteen years afterwards, Valentinian, in a law addressed to the præfect of Gaul, is obliged to enact that these cowardly deserters shall be burnt alive. (Cod. Theod. l. vii. tit. xiii. leg. 5.) Their numbers in Illyricum were so considerable that the province complained of a scarcity of recruits. (Id. leg. 10.)

140. They were called *Murci. Murcidus* is found in Plautus and Festus to denote a lazy and cowardly person, who, according to Arnobius and Augustin, was under the immediate protection of the goddess *Murcia.* From this particular instance of cowardice *murcare* is used as synonymous to *muti-*

lare by the writers of the middle Latinity. See Lindenbrogius and Valesius ad Ammian. Marcellin. l. xv. c. 12.

141. Malarichus—adhibitis Francis quorum ea tempestate in palatio multitudo florebat, erectius jam loquebatur tumultuabaturque. Ammian. l. xv. c. 5.

142. Barbaros omnium primus, ad usque fasces auxerat et trabeas consulares. Ammian. l. xxi. c. 10. Eusebius (in Vit. Constantin. l. iv. c. 7) and Aurelius Victor seem to confirm the truth of this assertion; yet in the thirty-two consular Fasti of the reign of Constantine I cannot discover the name of a single barbarian. I should therefore interpret the liberality of that prince as relative to the ornaments, rather than to the office, of the consulship.

143. Cod. Theod. l. vi. tit. 8.

144. By a very singular metaphor, borrowed from the military character of the first emperors, the steward of their household was styled the count of their camp (comes castrensis). Cassiodorus very seriously represents to him that his own fame, and that of the empire, must depend on the opinion which foreign ambassadors may conceive of the plenty and magnificence of the royal table. (Variar. l. vi. epistol. 9.)

145. Gutherius (de Officiis Dumûs Augustæ, l. ii. c. 20, l. iii.) has very accurately explained the functions of the master of the offices, and the constitution of the subordinate *scrinia*. But he vainly attempts, on the most doubtful authority, to deduce from the time of the Antonines, or even of Nero, the origin of a magistrate who cannot be found in history before the reign of Constantine.

146. Tacitus (Annal. xi. 22) says that the first quæstors were elected by the people sixty-four years after the foundation of the republic; but he is of opinion that they had, long before that period, been annually appointed by the consuls, and even by the kings. But this obscure point of antiquity is contested by other writers.

147. Tacitus (Annal. xi. 22) seems to consider twenty as the highest number of quæstors; and Dion (l. xliii. [c. 47] p. 374) insinuates that, if the dictator Cæsar once created forty, it was only to facilitate the payment of an immense debt of gratitude. Yet the augmentation which he made of prætors subsisted under the succeeding reigns.

148. Sueton. in August. c. 65, and Torrent. ad loc. Dion Cas. p. 755.

149. The youth and inexperience of the quæstors, who entered on that important office in their twenty-fifth year (Lips. Excurs. ad Tacit. l. iii. D.), engaged Augustus to remove them from the management of the treasury; and though they were restored by Claudius, they seem to have been finally dismissed by Nero. (Tacit. Annal. xiii. 29. Sueton. in Aug. c. 36, in Claud. c. 24. Dion, p. 696 [l. liii. c. 2], 961 [l. lx. c. 24], etc. Plin. Epistol. x. 20, et alibi.) In the provinces of the Imperial division, the place of the quæstors was more ably supplied by the *procurators* (Dion Cas. p. 707 [l. liii. c. 15]; Tacit. in Vit. Agricol. c. 15); or, as they were afterwards called, *rationales*. (Hist. August. p. 130 [Lamprid. Alex. Sever. cc. 45, 46]). But in the provinces of the senate we may still discover a series of quæstors till the reign of Marcus Antoninus. (See the Inscriptions of Gruter, the Epistles of Pliny, and a decisive fact in the Augustan History, p. 64 [Spartian. Sever. c. 2].) From Ulpian we may learn (Pandect. l. i. tit. 13) that, under the government of the House of Severus, their provincial administration was abolished; and in the subsequent troubles the annual or triennial elections of quæstors must have naturally ceased.

150. Cum patris nomine et epistolas ipse dictaret, et edicta conscriberet, orationesque in senatu recitaret, etiam quæstoris vice. Sueton. in Tit. c. 6. The office must have acquired new dignity, which was occasionally executed by the heir apparent of the empire. Trajan intrusted the same care to Hadrian, his quæstor and cousin. See Dodwell, Prælection. Cambden. x. xi. p. 362–394.

151. ————Terris edicta daturus,
    Supplicibus responsa, venis. Oracula
      regis
    Eloquio crevere tuo; nec dignius unquam
    Majestas meminit sese Romana locutam.
Claudian in Consulat. Mall. Theodor. 33. See likewise Symmachus (Epistol. i. 17) and Cassiodorus (Variar. vi. 5).

152. Cod. Theod. l. vi. tit. 30. Cod. Justinian. l. xii. tit. 24.

153. In the departments of the two counts of the treasury the eastern part of the *Notitia* happens to be very defective. It may be observed that we had a treasury chest in London, and a gyneceum or manufacture at Winchester. But Britain was not thought worthy either of a mint or of an arsenal. Gaul alone possessed three of the former and eight of the latter.

154. Cod. Theod. l. vi. tit. xxx. leg. 2; and Godefroy ad loc.

155. Strabon. Geograph. l. xii. p. 809 [p. 535, edit. Casaub]. The other temple of Comana, in Pontus, was a colony from that of Cappadocia, l. xii. p. 835 [p. 557, ed. Casaub.]. The president Des Brosses (see his Saluste, tom. ii. p. 21) conjectures that the deity adored in both Comanas was Beltis, the Venus of the East, the goddess of generation; a very different being indeed from the goddess of war.

156. Cod. Theod. l. x. tit. vi. de Grege Dominico. Godefroy has collected every circumstance of antiquity relative to the Cappadocian horses. One of the finest breeds, the Palmatian, was the forfeiture of a rebel, whose estate lay about sixteen miles from Tyana, near the great road between Constantinople and Antioch.

157. Justinian (Novell. 30) subjected the province of the count of Cappadocia to the immediate authority of the favourite eunuch, who presided over the sacred bedchamber.

158. Cod. Theod. l. vi. tit. xxx, leg. 4, etc.

159. Pancirolus, p. 102, 136. The appearance of these military domestics is described in the Latin poem of Corippus, De Laudibus Justin. l. iii. 157-179, p. 419, 420 of the Appendix Hist. Byzantin. Rom. 1777.

160. Ammianus Marcellinus, who served so many years, obtained only the rank of a protector. The first ten among these honourable soldiers were *Clarissimi*.

161. Xenophon, Cyropæd. l. viii. [c. 2, §§ 10, 11.] Brisson, de Regno Persico, l. i. No. 190, p. 264. The emperors adopted with pleasure this Persian metaphor.

162. For the *Agentes in Rebus*, see Ammian. l. xv. c. 3, l. xvi. c. 5, l. xxii. c. 7, with the curious annotations of Valesius. Cod. Theod. l. vi. tit. xxvii. xxviii. xxix. Among the passages collected in the Commentary of Godefroy, the most remarkable is one from Libanius, in his discourse concerning the death of Julian.

163. The Pandects (l. xlviii. tit. xviii.) contains the sentiments of the most celebrated civilians on the subject of torture. They strictly confine it to slaves; and Ulpian himself is ready to acknowledge that Res est fragilis, et periculosa, et quæ veritatem fallat. [§ 23.]

164. In the conspiracy of Piso against Nero, Epicharis (libertina mulier) was the only person tortured; the rest were *intacti tormentis*. It would be superfluous to add a weaker, and it would be difficult to find a stronger, example. Tacit. Annal. xv. 57.

165. Dicendum . . . de institutis Atheniensium, Rhodiorum, doctissimorum hominum, apud quos etiam (id quod acerbissimum est) liberi, civesque torquentur. Cicero, Partit. Orat. c. 34. We may learn from the trial of Philotas the practice of the Macedonians. (Diodor. Sicul. l. xvii. [c. 80] p. 604. Q. Curt. l. vi. c. 11.)

166. Heineccius (Element. Jur. Civil. part vii. p. 81) has collected these exemptions into one view.

167. This definition of the sage Ulpian (Pandect. l. xlviii. tit. iv.) seems to have been adapted to the court of Caracalla, rather than to that of Alexander Severus. See the Codes of Theodosius and Justinian ad leg. Juliam majestatis.

168. Arcadius Charisius is the oldest lawyer quoted in the Pandects to justify the universal practice of torture in all cases of treason; but this maxim of tyranny, which is admitted by Ammianus (l. xix. c. 12) with the most respectful terror, is enforced by several laws of the successors of Constantine. See Cod. Theod. l. ix. tit. xxxv. In majestatis crimine omnibus æqua est conditio. [leg. 1.]

169. Montesquieu, The Spirit of Laws, xiii. 12.

170. Mr. Hume (Essays, vol. i. p. 389) has seen this important truth with some degree of perplexity.

171. The cycle of indictions, which may be traced as high as the reign of Constantius, or perhaps of his father Constantine, is still employed by the Papal court: but the commencement of the year has been very reasonably altered to the first of January. See l'Art de vérifier les Dates, p. xi.; and Dictionnaire Raison. de la Diplomatique, tom. ii. p. 25; two accurate treatises, which come from the workshop of the Benedictines.

172. The first twenty-eight titles of the eleventh book of the Theodosian Code are filled with the circumstantial regulations on the important subject of tributes; but they suppose a clearer knowledge of fundamental principles than it is at present in our power to attain.

173. The title concerning the Decurions (l. xii. tit. i.) is the most ample in the whole Theodosian Code; since it contains not less than one hundred and ninety-two distinct laws to ascertain the duties and privileges of that useful order of citizens.

174. Habemus enim et hominum numerum qui delati sunt, et agrorum modum. Eumenius in Panegyr. Vet. viii. [vii.] 6. See Cod. Theod. l. xiii. tit. x. xi. with Godefroy's Commentary.

175. Siquis sacrilegâ vitem falce succiderit; aut feracium ramorum fœtus hebetaverit, quo declinet fidem Censuum, et mentiatur callide paupertatis ingenium, mox detectus capitale subibit exitium, et bona ejus in Fisci jura migrabunt. Cod. Theod. l. xiii. tit. xi. leg. 1. Although this law is not without its studied obscurity, it is, however, clear enough to prove the minuteness of the inquisition, and the disproportion of the penalty.

176. The astonishment of Pliny would have ceased. Equidem miror P. R. victis gentibus [in tributo] semper argentum imperitasse, non aurum. Hist. Natur. xxxiii. 15.

177. Some precautions were taken (see Cod. Theod. l. xi. tit. ii. and Cod. Justinian. l. x. tit. xxvii. leg. 1, 2, 3) to restrain the magistrates from the abuse of their authority, either in the exaction or in the purchase of corn: but those who had learning enough to read the orations of Cicero against Verres (iii. de Frumento) might instruct themselves in all the various arts of oppression, with regard to the weight, the price, the quality, and the carriage. The avarice of an unlettered governor would supply the ignorance of precept or precedent.

178. Cod. Theod. l. xi. tit. xxviii. leg. 2, published the 24th of March, A.D. 395, by the emperor Honorius, only two months after the death of his father Theodosius. He speaks of 528,042 Roman jugera, which I have reduced to the English measure. The jugerum contained 28,800 square Roman feet.

179. Godefroy (Cod. Theod. tom. v. p. 116 [l. xiv. tit. x. leg. 2]) argues with weight and learning on the subject of the capitation; but while he explains the *caput* as a share or measure of property, he too absolutely excludes the idea of a personal assessment.

180. Quid profuerit (*Julianus*) anhelantibus extremâ penuriâ Gallis, hinc maxime claret, quod primitus partes eas ingressus, pro *capitibus* singulis tributi nomine vicenos quinos aureos reperit flagi-

tari; discedens vero septenos tantum, munera universa complentes. Ammian. l. xvi. c. 5.

181. In the calculation of any sum of money under Constantine and his successors, we need only refer to the excellent discourse of Mr. Greaves on the Denarius for the proof of the following principles: 1. That the ancient and modern Roman pound, containing 5256 grains of Troy weight, is about one-twelfth lighter than the English pound, which is composed of 5760 of the same grains. 2. That the pound of gold, which had once been divided into forty-eight *aurei*, was at this time coined into seventy-two smaller pieces of the same denomination. 3. That five of these aurei were the legal tender for a pound of silver, and that consequently the pound of gold was exchanged for fourteen pounds eight ounces of silver, according to the Roman, or about thirteen pounds according to the English weight. 4. That the English pound of silver is coined into sixty-two shillings. From these elements we may compute the Roman pound of gold, the usual method of reckoning large sums, at forty pounds sterling, and we may fix the currency of the *aureus* at somewhat more than eleven shillings.

182.   Geryones nos esse puta, monstrumque
          tributum,
       Hic *capita* ut vivam, tu mihi tolle *tria*.
              Sidon. Apollinar. Carm. xiii.
                         [v. 19.]
The reputation of Father Sirmond led me to expect more satisfaction than I have found in his note (p. 144) on this remarkable passage. The words, suo *vel suorum* nomine, betray the perplexity of the commentator.

183. This assertion, however formidable it may seem, is founded on the original registers of births, deaths, and marriages, collected by public authority, and now deposited in the *Contrôle Général* at Paris. The annual average of births throughout the whole kingdom, taken in five years (from 1770 to 1774, both inclusive), is 479,649 boys and 449,269 girls, in all 928,918 children. The province of French Hainault alone furnishes 9906 births; and we are assured, by an actual enumeration of the people, annually repeated from the year 1773 to the year 1776, that, upon an average, Hainault contains 257,097 inhabitants. By the rules of fair analogy, we might infer that the ordinary proportion of annual births to the whole people is about 1 to 26; and that the kingdom of France contains 24,151,868 persons of both sexes and of every age. If we content ourselves with the more moderate proportion of 1 to 25, the whole population will amount to 23,222,950. From the diligent researches of the French government (which are not unworthy of our own imitation) we may hope to obtain a still greater degree of certainty on this important subject.

184. Cod. Theod. l. v. tit. ix. x. xi. Cod. Justinian. l. xi. tit. lxiii. Coloni appellantur qui condi-

tionem debent genitali solo, propter agriculturam sub dominio possessorum. Augustine, The City of God, l. x. c. i.

185. The ancient jurisdiction of (*Augustodunum*) Autun in Burgundy, the capital of the Ædui, comprehended the adjacent territory of (*Noviodunum*) Nevers. See d'Anville, Notice de l'Ancienne Gaule, p. 491. The two dioceses of Autun and Nevers are now composed, the former of 610, and the latter of 160 parishes. The registers of births, taken during eleven years, in 476 parishes of the same province of Burgundy, and multiplied by the moderate proportion of 25 (see Messance, Recherches sur la Population, p. 142), may authorise us to assign an average number of 656 persons for each parish, which, being again multiplied by the 770 parishes of the dioceses of Nevers and Autun, will produce the sum of 505,120 persons for the extent of country which was once possessed by the Ædui.

186. We might derive an additional supply of 301,750 inhabitants from the dioceses of Châlons (*Cabillonum*) and of Maçon (*Matisco*); since they contain, the one 200, and the other 260 parishes. This accession of territory might be justified by very specious reasons. 1. Châlons and Maçon were undoubtedly within the original jurisdiction of the Ædui. (See d'Anville, Notice, p. 187, 443.) 2. In the Notitia of Gaul they are enumerated not as *Civitates*, but merely as *Castra*. 3. They do not appear to have been episcopal seats before the fifth and sixth centuries. Yet there is a passage in Eumenius (Panegyr. Vet. viii. [vii.] 7) which very forcibly deters me from extending the territory of the Ædui, in the reign of Constantine, along the beautiful banks of the navigable Saône.

187. Eumenius in Panegyr. Vet. viii. [vii.] 11.

188. L'Abbé du Bos. Hist. Critique de la M. F. tom. i. p. 121.

189. See Cod. Theod. l. xiii. tit. i. and iv.

190. Zosimus, l. ii. [c. 38] p. 115. There is probably as much passion and prejudice in the attack of Zosimus as in the elaborate defence of the memory of Constantine by the zealous Dr. Howell. Hist. of the World, vol. ii. p. 20.

191. Cod. Theod. l. xi. tit. vii. leg. 3.

192. See Lipsius de Magnitud. Romanâ, l. ii. c. 9. The Tarragonese Spain presented the emperor Claudius with a crown of gold of seven, and Gaul with another of nine, *hundred* pounds weight. I have followed the rational emendation of Lipsius.

193. Cod. Theod. l. xii. tit. xiii. The senators were supposed to be exempt from the *Aurum Coronarium;* but the *Auri Oblatio*, which was required at their hands, was precisely of the same nature.

194. The great Theodosius, in his judicious advice to his son (Claudian, in iv. Consulat. Honorii, 214, etc.), distinguishes the station of a Roman prince from that of a Parthian monarch. Virtue was necessary for the one; birth might suffice for the other.

Chapter XVIII

1. On ne se trompera point sur Constantin en croyant tout le mal qu'en dit Eusèbe, et tout le bien qu'en dit Zosime. Fleury, Hist. Ecclésiastique, tom. iii. p. 233. Eusebius and Zosimus form indeed the two extremes of flattery and invective. The intermediate shades are expressed by those writers whose character or situation variously tempered the influence of their religious zeal.

2. The virtues of Constantine are collected for the most part from Eutropius and the younger Victor, two sincere pagans, who wrote after the extinction of his family. Even Zosimus and the *Emperor* Julian acknowledged his personal courage and military achievements.

3. See Eutropius, x. 6 [4]. In primo Imperii tempore optimis principibus, ultimo mediis comparandus. From the ancient Greek version of Pœanius (edit. Havercamp. p. 697), I am inclined to suspect that Eutropius had originally written *vix* mediis; and that the offensive monosyllable was dropped by the wilful inadvertency of transcribers. Aurelius Victor expresses the general opinion by a vulgar and indeed obscure proverb. *Trachala* decem annis præstantissimus; duodecim sequentibus *latro;* decem novissimis *pupillus* ob immodicas profusiones. [Epit. c. 41.]

4. Julian, Orat. i. p. 8, in a flattering discourse pronounced before the son of Constantine; and Cæsares, p. 335. Zosimus [l. ii. c. 38], p. 114, 115. The stately buildings of Constantinople, etc., may be quoted as a lasting and unexceptionable proof of the profuseness of their founder.

5. The impartial Ammianus deserves all our confidence. Proximorum fauces aperuit primus omnium Constantinus. l. xvi. c. 8. Eusebius himself confesses the abuse (Vit. Constantin. l. iv. c. 29, 54); and some of the Imperial laws feebly point out the remedy. See p. 337.

6. Julian, in the Cæsars, attempts to ridicule his uncle. His suspicious testimony is confirmed, however, by the learned Spanheim, with the authority of medals (see Commentaire, p. 156, 299, 397, 459). Eusebius (Orat. c. 5) alleges that Constantine dressed for the public, not for himself. Were this admitted, the vainest coxcomb could never want an excuse.

7. Zosimus [l. ii. c. 20] and Zonaras agree in representing Minervina as the concubine of Constantine; but Ducange has very gallantly rescued her character, by producing a decisive passage from one of the panegyrics: "Ab ipso fine pueritiæte te matrimonii legibus dedisti."

8. Ducange (Familiæ Byzantinæ, p. 44) bestows on him, after Zonaras, the name of Constantine; a name somewhat unlikely, as it was already occupied by the elder brother. That of Hannibalianus is mentioned in the Paschal Chronicle, and is approved by Tillemont, Hist. des Empereurs, tom. iv. p. 527.

9. Jerom. in Chron. The poverty of Lactantius may be applied either to the praise of the disinterested philosopher, or to the shame of the unfeeling patron. See Tillemont, Mém. Ecclésiast. tom. vi. part i. p. 345. Dupin, Bibliothèque Ecclésiast. tom. i. p. 205. Lardner's Credibility of the Gospel History, part ii. vol. vii. p. 66.

10. Euseb. Hist. Ecclesiast. l. x. c. 9. Eutropius (x. 4) styles him "egregium virum;" and Julian (Orat. i.) very plainly alludes to the exploits of Crispus in the civil war. See Spanheim, Comment. p. 92.

11. Compare Idatius and the Paschal Chronicle with Ammianus (l. xiv. c. 5). The *year* in which Constantius was created Cæsar seems to be more accurately fixed by the two chronologists; but the historian who lived in his court could not be ignorant of the *day* of the anniversary. For the appointment of the new Cæsar to the provinces of Gaul, see Julian, Orat. i. p. 12; Godefroy, Chronol. Legum, p. 26; and Blondel, de la Primauté de l'Eglise, p. 1183.

12. Cod. Theod. l. ix. tit. iv. [tit. 1, leg. 4.] Godefroy suspected the secret motives of this law. Comment. tom. iii. p. 9.

13. Ducange, Fam. Byzant. p. 28. Tillemont, tom. iv. p. 610.

14. His name was Porphyrius Optatianus. The date of his panegyric, written according to the taste of the age in vile acrostics, is settled by Scaliger ad Euseb. p. 250; Tillemont, tom. iv. p. 607; and Fabricius, Biblioth. Latin. l. iv. c. 1.

15. Zosim. l. ii. [c. 29] p. 103. Godefroy, Chronol. Legum. p. 28.

16. Ἀκρίτως *without a trial*, is the strong and most probably the just expression of Suidas. The elder Victor, who wrote under the next reign, speaks with becoming caution. "Natû grandior, incertum quâ causâ, patris judicio occidisset." [De Cæsar. c. 41.] If we consult the succeeding writers, Eutropius, the younger Victor, Orosius, Jerom, Zosimus, Philostorgius, and Gregory of Tours, their knowledge will appear gradually to increase as their means of information must have diminished, a circumstance which frequently occurs in historical disquisition.

17. Ammianus (l. xiv. c. 11) uses the general expression of *peremptum*. Codinus (p. 34) [p. 63, ed. Bonn] beheads the young prince; but Sidonius Apollinaris (Epistol. v. 8), for the sake perhaps of an antithesis to Fausta's *warm* bath, chooses to administer a draught of *cold* poison.

18. Sorosis filium, commodæ indolis juvenem. Eutropius, x. 6 [4]. May I not be permitted to conjecture that Crispus had married Helena, the daughter of the emperor Licinius, and that on the

748

happy delivery of the princess, in the year 322, a general pardon was granted by Constantine? See Ducange, Fam. Byzant. p. 47, and the law (l. ix. tit. xxxvii.) of the Theodosian code, which has so much embarrassed the interpreters. Godefroy, tom. iii. p. 267.

19. See the Life of Constantine, particularly [Euseb.] l. ii. c. 19, 20. Two hundred and fifty years afterwards Evagrius (l. iii. c. 41) deduced from the silence of Eusebius a vain argument against the reality of the fact.

20. Histoire de Pierre le Grand, par Voltaire, part ii. c. 10.

21. In order to prove that the statue was erected by Constantine, and afterwards concealed by the malice of the Arians, Codinus very readily creates (p. 34 [p. 63, ed. Bonn]) two witnesses, Hippolytus and the younger Herodotus, to whose imaginary histories he appeals with unblushing confidence.

22. Zosimus (l. ii. [c. 29] p. 103) may be considered as our original. The ingenuity of the moderns, assisted by a few hints from the ancients, has illustrated and improved his obscure and imperfect narrative.

23. Philostorgius, l. ii. c. 4. Zosimus (l. ii. p. 104 [c. 29], 116 [c. 39]) imputes to Constantine the death of two wives, of the innocent Fausta, and of an adulteress who was the mother of his three successors. According to Jerom, three or four years elapsed between the death of Crispus and that of Fausta. The elder Victor is prudently silent.

24. If Fausta was put to death, it is reasonable to believe that the private apartments of the palace were the scene of her execution. The orator Chrysostom indulges his fancy by exposing the naked empress on a desert mountain to be devoured by wild beasts.

25. Julian. Orat. i. [p. 9]. He seems to call her the mother of Crispus. She might assume that title by adoption. At least, she was not considered as his mortal enemy. Julian compares the fortune of Fausta with that of Parysatis, the Persian queen. A Roman would have more naturally recollected the second Agrippina:—

Et moi, qui sur le trône ai suivi mes ancêtres:
Moi, fille, femme, sœur, et mère de vos maîtres.

26. Monod. in Constantin. Jun. c. 4, ad Calcem Eutrop. edit. Havercamp. The orator styles her the most divine and pious of queens.

27. Interfecit numerosos amicos. Eutrop. x. 6 [4].

28. Saturni aurea sæcula quis requirat?
Sunt hæc gemmea, sed Neroniana.
Sidon. Apollinar. v. 8.

It is somewhat singular that these satirical lines should be attributed, not to an obscure libeller or a disappointed patriot, but to Ablavius, prime minister and favourite of the emperor. We may now perceive that the imprecations of the Roman people were dictated by humanity as well as by superstition. Zosim. l. ii. [c. 30] p. 105.

29. Euseb. Orat. in Constantin. c. 3. These dates are sufficiently correct to justify the orator.

30. Zosim. l. ii. [c. 39] p. 117. Under the predecessors of Constantine, *Nobilissimus* was a vague epithet rather than a legal and determined title.

31. Adstruunt nummi veteres ac singulares. Spanheim de Usu Numismat. Dissertat. xii. vol. ii. p. 357. Ammianus speaks of this Roman king (l. xiv. c. 1, and Valesius ad loc.). The Valesian fragment styles him King of kings; and the Paschal Chronicle (p. 286 [p. 228, ed. Ven.; vol. i. p. 532, ed. Bonn]), by employing the word Pῆγα, acquires the weight of Latin evidence.

32. His dexterity in martial exercises is celebrated by Julian (Orat. i. p. 11, Orat. ii. p. 53) and allowed by Ammianus (l. xxi. c. 16).

33. Euseb. in Vit. Constantin. l. iv. c. 51. Julian, Orat. i. p. 11–16, with Spanheim's elaborate Commentary. Libanius, Orat. iii. p. 109 [ed. Paris, 1627]. Constantius studied with laudable diligence; but the dulness of his fancy prevented him from succeeding in the art of poetry, or even of rhetoric.

34. Eusebius (l. iv. c. 51, 52), with a design of exalting the authority and glory of Constantine, affirms that he divided the Roman empire as a private citizen might have divided his patrimony. His distribution of the provinces may be collected from Eutropius, the two Victors, and the Valesian fragment.

35. Calocerus, the obscure leader of this rebellion, or rather tumult, was apprehended and burnt alive in the market-place of Tarsus, by the vigilance of Dalmatius. See the elder Victor, the Chronicle of Jerom, and the doubtful traditions of Theophanes and Cedrenus.

36. Cellarius has collected the opinions of the ancients concerning the European and Asiatic Sarmatia; and M. d'Anville has applied them to modern geography with the skill and accuracy which always distinguish that excellent writer.

37. Ammian. l. xvii. c. 12. The Sarmatian horses were castrated to prevent the mischievous accidents which might happen from the noisy and ungovernable passions of the males.

38. Pausanias, l. i. [c. 21, § 5] p. 50, edit. Kuhn. That inquisitive traveller had carefully examined a Sarmatian cuirass which was preserved in the temple of Æsculapius at Athens.

39. Aspicis et mitti sub adunco toxica ferro
Et telum causas mortis habere duas.
Ovid, ex Ponto, l. iv. ep. 7, ver. 11.

See in the Recherches sur les Américains, tom. ii. p. 236–271, a very curious dissertation on poisoned darts. The venom was commonly extracted from the vegetable reign; but that employed by the Scythians appears to have been drawn from the viper and a mixture of human blood. The use of poisoned arms, which has been spread over both worlds, never preserved a savage tribe from the arms of a disciplined enemy.

40. The nine books of Poetical Epistles which

Ovid composed during the seven first years of his melancholy exile, possess, besides the merit of elegance, a double value. They exhibit a picture of the human mind under very singular circumstances; and they contain many curious observations, which no Roman, except Ovid, could have an opportunity of making. Every circumstance which tends to illustrate the history of the barbarians has been drawn together by the very accurate Count de Buat, Hist. Ancienne des Peuples de l'Europe, tom. iv. c. xvi. p. 286–317.

41. The Sarmatian Jazygæ were settled on the banks of the Pathissus or Tibiscus, when Pliny, in the year 79, published his Natural History. See l. iv. c. 25. In the time of Strabo and Ovid, sixty or seventy years before, they appear to have inhabited beyond the Getæ, along the coast of the Euxine.

42. Principes Sarmatarum Jazygum penes quos civitatis regimen . . . plebem quoque et vim equitum, quâ solâ valent, offerebant. Tacit. Hist. iii. 5. This offer was made in the civil war between Vitellius and Vespasian.

43. This hypothesis of a Vandal king reigning over Sarmatian subjects seems necessary to reconcile the Goth Jornandes with the Greek and Latin historians of Constantine. It may be observed that Isidore, who lived in Spain under the dominion of the Goths, gives them for enemies, not the Vandals, but the Sarmatians. See his Chronicle in Grotius, p. 709.

44. [No other author mentions Constantine's defeat by the Goths.]

45. I may stand in need of some apology for having used, without scruple, the authority of Constantine Porphyrogenitus, in all that relates to the wars and negotiations of the Chersonites. I am aware that he was a Greek of the tenth century, and that his accounts of ancient history are frequently confused and fabulous. But on this occasion his narrative is, for the most part, consistent and probable; nor is there much difficulty in conceiving that an emperor might have access to some secret archives which had escaped the diligence of meaner historians. For the situation and history of Chersone, see Peyssonel, des Peuples barbares qui ont habité les Bords du Danube, c. xvi. 84–90. [Gibbon has confused the inhabitants of the city of Cherson, the ancient Chersonesus, with the people of the Chersonesus Taurica.]

46. The Gothic and Sarmatian wars are related in so broken and imperfect a manner, that I have been obliged to compare the following writers, who mutually supply, correct, and illustrate each other. Those who will take the same trouble may acquire a right of criticising my narrative. Ammianus, l. xvii. c. 12. Anonym. Valesian. p. 715. Eutropius, x. 7 [4]. Sextus Rufus de Provinciis, c. 26. Julian, Orat. i. p. 9, and Spanheim, Comment. p. 94. Hieronym. in Chron. Euseb. in Vit. Constantin. l. iv. c. 6. Socrates, l. i. c. 18. Sozomen, l. i. c. 8. Zosimus, l. ii. [c. 21] p. 108. Jornandes de Reb. Geticis, c. 22. Isidorus in Chron. p. 709; in Hist.

Gothorum Grotii. Constantin. Porphyrogenitus de Administrat. Imperii, c. 53, p. 208, edit. Meursii [p. 144 *sqq.* ed. Paris; vol. iii. p. 244 *sqq.* ed. Bonn].

47. Eusebius (in Vit. Const. l. iv. c. 50) remarks three circumstances relative to these Indians. 1. They came from the shores of the eastern ocean; a description which might be applied to the coast of China or Coromandel. 2. They presented shining gems and unknown animals. 3. They protested their kings had erected statues to represent the supreme majesty of Constantine.

48. Funus relatum in urbem sui nominis, quod sane P. R. ægerrime tulit. Aurelius Victor [de Cæsar. c. 41]. Constantine prepared for himself a stately tomb in the church of the Holy Apostles. Euseb. l. iv. c. 60. The best, and indeed almost the only account of the sickness, death, and funeral of Constantine, is contained in the fourth book of his Life by Eusebius.

49. Eusebius (l. iv. c. 68) terminates his narrative by this loyal declaration of the troops, and avoids all the invidious circumstances of the subsequent massacre.

50. The character of Dalmatius is advantageously, though concisely, drawn by Eutropius (x. 9 [5]). Dalmatius Cæsar prosperrimâ indole, neque patruo absimilis, *haud multo* post oppressus est factione militari. As both Jerom and the Alexandrian Chronicle mention the third year of the Cæsar, which did not commence till the 18th or 24th of September, A.D. 337, it is certain that these military factions continued above four months.

51. I have related this singular anecdote on the authority of Philostorgius, l. ii. c. 16. But if such a pretext was ever used by Constantius and his adherents, it was laid aside with contempt as soon as it served their immediate purpose. Athanasius (tom. i. p. 856) mentions the oath which Constantius had taken for the security of his kinsmen.

52. Conjuga sobrinarum diu ignorata, tempore addito percrebuisse. Tacit. Annal. xii. 6, and Lipsius ad loc. The repeal of the ancient law, and the practice of five hundred years, were insufficient to eradicate the prejudices of the Romans, who still considered the marriages of cousins-german as a species of imperfect incest (Augustine, The City of God, xv. 16); and Julian, whose mind was biassed by superstition and resentment, stigmatises these unnatural alliances between his own cousins with the opprobrious epithet of γαμῶν τε οὐ γαμῶν (Orat. vii. p. 228). The jurisprudence of the canons has since revived and enforced this prohibition, without being able to introduce it either into the civil or the common law of Europe. See, on the subject of these marriages, Taylor's Civil Law, p. 331; Brouer, de Jure Connub. l. ii. c. 12; Hericourt, des Loix Ecclésiastiques, part iii. c. 5; Fleury, Institutions du Droit Canonique, tom. i. p. 331, Paris, 1767; and Fra Paolo, Istoria del Concilio Trident. l. viii.

53. Julian (ad S. P. Q. Athen. p. 270) charges his cousin Constantius with the whole guilt of a

massacre from which he himself so narrowly escaped. His assertion is confirmed by Athanasius, who, for reasons of a very different nature, was not less an enemy of Constantius (tom. i. p. 856). Zosimus [ii. 40] joins in the same accusation. But the three abbreviators, Eutropius and the Victors, use very qualifying expressions:—"sinente poitus quam jubente;" "incertum quo suasore;" "vi militum."

54. Euseb. in Vit. Constantin. l. iv. c. 69. Zosimus, l. ii. [c. 39] p. 117. Idat. in Chron. See two notes of Tillemont, Hist. des Empereurs, tom. iv. p. 1086-1091. The reign of the eldest brother at Constantinople is noticed only in the Alexandrian Chronicle.

55. Agathias, who lived in the sixth century, is the author of this story (l. iv. p. 135, edit. Louvre [c. 25, p. 262, ed. Bonn]). He derived his information from some extracts of the Persian Chronicles, obtained and translated by the interpreter Sergius during his embassy at that court. The coronation of the mother of Sapor is likewise mentioned by Schikard (Tarikh, p. 116) and d'Herbelot (Bibliothèque Orientale, p. 763).

56. D'Herbelot, Bibliothèque Orientale, p. 764.

57. Sextus Rufus (c. 26), who on this occasion is no contemptible authority, affirms that the Persians sued in vain for peace, and that Constantine was preparing to march against them: yet the superior weight of the testimony of Eusebius obliges us to admit the preliminaries, if not the ratification, of the treaty. See Tillemont, Hist. des Empereurs, tom. iv. p. 420.

58. Julian. Orat. i. p. 20.

59. Julian. Orat. i. p. 20, 21. Moses of Chorene, l. ii. c. 89, l. iii. c. 1-9, p. 226-240. The perfect agreement between the vague hints of the contemporary orator and the circumstantial narrative of the national historian, gives light to the former and weight to the latter. For the credit of Moses it may be likewise observed that the name of Antiochus is found a few years before in a civil office of inferior dignity. See Godefroy, Cod. Theod. tom. vi. p. 350.

60. Ammianus (xiv. 4) gives a lively description of the wandering and predatory life of the Saracens, who stretched from the confines of Assyria to the cataracts of the Nile. It appears from the adventures of Malchus, which Jerom has related in so entertaining a manner, that the high road between Beræa and Edessa was infested by these robbers. See Hieronym. tom. i. p. 256.

61. We shall take from Eutropius the general idea of the war (x. 10 [6]). A Persis enim multa et gravia perpessus, sæpe captis oppidis, obsessis urbibus, cæsis exercitibus, nullumque ei contra Saporem prosperum prœlium fuit, nisi quod apud Singaram, etc. This honest account is confirmed by the hints of Ammianus, Rufus, and Jerom. The two first orations of Julian, and the third oration of Libanius, exhibit a more flattering picture; but the recantation of both those orators after the death of Constantius, while it restores us to the possession

of the truth, degrades their own character and that of the emperor. The commentary of Spanheim on the first oration of Julian is profusely learned. See likewise the judicious observations of Tillemont, Hist. des Empereurs, tom. iv. p. 656.

62. Acerrimâ nocturnâ concertatione pugnatum est, nostrorum copiis ingenti strage confossis. Ammian. xviii. 5. See likewise Eutropius, x. 10 [6], and S Rufus, c. 27.

63. Libanius, Orat. iii. p. 133, with Julian. Orat. i. p. 24, and Spanheim's Commentary, p. 179.

64. See Julian. Orat. i. p. 27; Orat. ii. p. 62, etc.; with the Commentary of Spanheim (p. 188-202), who illustrates the circumstances, and ascertains the time of the three sieges of Nisibis. Their dates are likewise examined by Tillemont (Hist. des Empereurs, tom. iv. p. 668, 671, 674). Something is added from Zosimus, l. iii. [c. 8] p. 151 and the Alexandrian Chronicle, p. 290.

65. Sallust. Fragment. lxxxiv. edit. Brosses, and Plutarch in Lucullus. Nisibis is now reduced to one hundred and fifty houses; the marshy lands produce rice, and the fertile meadows, as far as Mosul and the Tigris, are covered with the ruins of towns and villages. See Niebuhr, Voyages, tom. ii. p. 300-309.

66. The miracles which Theodoret (l. ii. c. 30) ascribes to St. James, bishop of Edessa, were at least performed in a worthy cause, the defence of his country. He appeared on the walls under the figure of the Roman emperor, and sent an army of gnats to sting the trunks of the elephants, and to discomfit the host of the new Senacherib.

67. Julian. Orat. i. p. 27. Though Niebuhr (tom. ii. p. 307) allows a very considerable swell to the Mygdonius, over which he saw a bridge of twelve arches; it is difficult, however, to understand this parallel of a trifling rivulet with a mighty river. There are many circumstances obscure, and almost unintelligible, in the description of these stupendous waterworks.

68. We are obliged to Zonaras (tom. ii. l. xiii. [c. 7] p. 11 [15]) for this invasion of the Massagetæ, which is perfectly consistent with the general series of events to which we are darkly led by the broken history of Ammianus.

69. The causes and the events of this civil war are related with much perplexity and contradiction. I have chiefly followed Zonaras and the younger Victor. The monody (ad calcem Eutrop. edit. Havercamp.) pronounced on the death of Constantine might have been very instructive; but prudence and false taste engaged the orator to involve himself in vague declamation.

70. Quarum (gentium) obsides pretio quæsitos pueros venustiores, quod cultius habuerat, libidine hujusmodi arsisse pro certo habetur. [De Cæs. 41] Had not the depraved taste of Constans been publicly avowed, the elder Victor, who held a considerable office in his brother's reign, would not have asserted it in such positive terms.

71. Julian. Orat. i. and ii. Zosim. l. ii. [c. 42] p.

134. Victor in Epitome [c. 41]. There is reason to believe that Magnentius was born in one of those barbarian colonies which Constantius Chlorus had established in Gaul (see this History, p. 313). His behaviour may remind us of the patriot earl of Leicester, the famous Simon de Montfort, who could persuade the good people of England that he, a Frenchman by birth, had taken arms to deliver them from foreign favourites.

72. This ancient city had once flourished under the name of Illiberis (Pomponius Mela, ii. 5). The munificence of Constantine gave it new splendour, and his mother's name. Helena (it is still called Elne) became the seat of a bishop, who long afterwards transferred his residence to Perpignan, the capital of modern Rousillon. See d'Anville, Notice de l'Ancienne Gaule, p. 380; Longuerue, Description de la France, p. 223; and the Marca Hispanica, l. i. c. 2.

73. Zosimus, l. ii. [c. 42] p. 119, 120; Zonaras, tom. ii. l. xiii. [c. 6] p. 13; and the Abbreviators.

74. Eutropius (x. 10 [6]) describes Vetranio with more temper, and probably with more truth, than either of the two Victors. Vetranio was born of obscure parents in the wildest parts of Mæsia; and so much had his education been neglected, that, after his elevation, he studied the alphabet.

75. The doubtful, fluctuating conduct of Vetranio is described by Julian in his first oration [p. 30, sqq.], and accurately explained by Spanheim, who discusses the situation and behaviour of Constantina.

76. See Peter the Patrician, in the Excerpta Legationum, p. 28 [ed. Paris.; cap. 14, p. 130, ed. Bonn].

77. Zonaras, tom. ii. l. xiii. [c. 7] p. 15. The position of Sardica, near the modern city of Sophia, appears better suited to this interview than the situation of either Naissus or Sirmium, where it is placed by Jerom, Socrates, and Sozomen.

78. See the two first orations of Julian, particularly p. 31; and Zosimus, l. ii. [c. 44] p. 122. The distinct narrative of the historian serves to illustrate the diffuse but vague descriptions of the orator.

79. The younger Victor assigns to his exile the emphatical appellation of "voluptarium otium." [Epit. c. 41.] Socrates (l. ii. c. 28) is the voucher for the correspondence with the emperor, which would seem to prove that Vetranio was, indeed, prope ad stultitiam simplicissimus.

80. Eum Constantius . . . facundiæ vi dejectum Imperio in privatum otium removit. Quæ gloria post natum Imperium soli processit eloquio clementiâque, etc. Aurelius Victor [de Cæsar. c. 42]. Julian and Themistius (Orat. iii. and iv.) adorn this exploit with all the artificial and gaudy colouring of their rhetoric.

81. Busbequius (p. 112) traversed the Lower Hungary and Sclavonia at a time when they were reduced almost to a desert, by the reciprocal hostilities of the Turks and Christians. Yet he mentions with admiration the unconquerable fertility of the soil; and observes that the height of the grass was sufficient to conceal a loaded waggon from his sight. See likewise Browne's Travels, in Harris's Collection, vol. ii. p. 762, etc.

82. Zosimus gives a very large account of the war and the negotiation (l. ii. [c. 45-54] p. 123-130). But as he neither shows himself a soldier nor a politician, his narrative must be weighed with attention, and received with caution.

83. This remarkable bridge, which is flanked with towers and supported on large wooden piles, was constructed, A.D. 1566, by Sultan Soliman, to facilitate the march of his armies into Hungary. See Browne's Travels, and Busching's System of Geography, vol. ii. p. 90.

84. This position, and the subsequent evolutions, are clearly, though concisely, described by Julian, Orat. i. p. 36.

85. Sulpicius Severus, l. ii. p. 405 [ed. Lugd. Bat. 1647]. The emperor passed the day in prayer with Valens, the Arian bishop of Mursa, who gained his confidence by announcing the success of the battle. M. de Tillemont (Hist. des Empereurs, tom. iv. p. 1110) very properly remarks the silence of Julian with regard to the personal prowess of Constantius in the battle of Mursa. The silence of flattery is sometimes equal to the most positive and authentic evidence.

86. Julian. Orat i. p. 36, 37; and Orat. ii. p. 59, 60. Zonaras, tom. ii. l. xliii. [c. 8] p. 17. Zosimus, l. ii. [c. 49-52] p. 130-133. The last of these celebrates the dexterity of the archer Menelaus, who could discharge three arrows at the same time; an advantage which, according to his apprehension of military affairs, materially contributed to the victory of Constantius.

87. According to Zonaras [l. c.], Constantius, out of 80,000 men, lost 30,000; and Magnentius lost 24,000 out of 36,000. The other articles of this account seem probable and authentic, but the numbers of the tyrants' army must have been mistaken, either by the author or his transcribers. Magnentius had collected the whole force of the West, Romans and barbarians, into one formidable body, which cannot fairly be estimated at less than 100,000 men. Julian. Orat. i. p. 34, 35.

88. Ingentes R. I. vires eâ dimicatione consumptæ sunt, ad quælibet bella externa idoneæ, quæ multum triumphorum possent securitatisque conferre. Eutropius, x. 13 [6]. The younger Victor expresses himself to the same effect.

89. On this occasion we must prefer the unsuspected testimony of Zosimus and Zonaras to the flattering assertions of Julian. The younger Victor paints the character of Magnentius in a singular light: "Sermonis acer, animi turmidi, et immodice timidus; artifex tamen ad occultandam audaciæ specie formidenem." [Epit. c. 43.] Is it most likely that in the battle of Mursa his behaviour was governed by nature or by art? I should incline for the latter.

90. Julian. Orat. i. p. 38, 39. In that place, however, as well as in Oration ii. p. 97, he insinuates the general disposition of the senate, the people, and the soldiers of Italy, towards the party of the emperor.

91. The elder Victor describes in a pathetic manner the miserable condition of Rome: "Cujus stolidum ingenium adeo P. R. patribusque exitio fuit, uti passim domus, fora, viæ, templaque, cruore, cadaveribusque opplerentur, bustorum modo." [De Cæsar. c. 42.] Athanasius (tom. i. p. 677) deplores the fate of several illustrious victims, and Julian (Orat. ii. p. 58) execrates the cruelty of Marcellinus, the implacable enemy of the house of Constantine.

92. Zosim. l. ii. [c. 53] p. 133. Victor in Epitome [c. 42]. The panegyrists of Constantius, with their usual candour, forget to mention this accidental defeat.

93. Zonaras, tom. ii. l. xiii. [c. 8] p. 17. Julian, in several places of the two orations, expatiates on the clemency of Constantius to the rebels.

94. Zosim. l. ii. [c. 53] p. 133. Julian. Orat. i. p. 40, ii. p. 74.

95. Ammian. xv. 6. Zosim. l. ii. [c. 53] p. 133. Julian, who (Orat. i. p. 40) inveighs against the cruel effects of the tyrant's despair, mentions (Orat. i. p. 34) the oppressive edicts which were dictated by his necessities, or by his avarice. His subjects were compelled to purchase the Imperial demesnes; a doubtful and dangerous species of property, which, in case of a revolution, might be imputed to them as a treasonable usurpation.

96. The medals of Magnentius celebrate the victories of the *two* Augusti, and of the Cæsar. The Cæsar was another brother named Desiderius. See Tillemont, Hist. des Empereurs, tom. iv. p. 757.

97. Julian. Orat. i. p. 40. ii. p. 74; with Spanheim, p. 263. His Commentary illustrates the transactions of this civil war. Mons Seleuci was a small place in the Cottian Alps, a few miles distant from Vapincum, or Gap, an episcopal city of Dauphiné. See d'Anville, Notice de la Gaule, p. 464; and Longuerue, Description de la France, p. 327.

98. Zosimus, l. ii. [c. 53] p. 134. Liban. Orat. x. p. 268, 269. The latter most vehemently arraigns this cruel and selfish policy of Constantius.

99. Julian, Orat. i. p. 40. Zosimus, l. ii. [c. 53] p. 134. Socrates, l. ii. c. 32. Sozomen, l. iv. c. 7. The younger Victor describes his death with some horrid circumstances: Transfosso latere, ut erat vasti corporis, vulnere naribusque et ore cruorem effundens, exspiravit. [Epit. c. 42.] If we can give credit to Zonaras, the tyrant, before he expired, had the pleasure of murdering with his own hands his mother and his brother Desiderius.

100. Julian (Orat. ii. p. 58, 59) seems at a loss to determine whether he inflicted on himself the punishment of his crimes, whether he was drowned in the Drave, or whether he was carried by the avenging dæmons from the field of battle to his destined place of eternal tortures.

101. Ammian. xiv. 5, xxi. 16.

Chapter XIX

1. Ammianus (l. xiv. c. 6) imputes the first practice of castration to the cruel ingenuity of Semiramis, who is supposed to have reigned above nineteen hundred years before Christ. The use of eunuchs is of high antiquity, both in Asia and Egypt. They are mentioned in the law of Moses, Deuteron. xxiii. 1. See Goguet, Origines des Loix, etc., Part i. l. i. c. 3.

2. Eunuchum dixti velle te;
Quia solæ utuntur his reginæ—
Terent. Eunuch. act. i. scene 2.
This play is translated from Menander, and the original must have appeared soon after the eastern conquests of Alexander.

3. Miles . . . spadonibus
Servire rugosis potest.
Horat. Carm. v. 9 [Epod. ix. 13], and
Dacier ad loc.
By the word *spado* the Romans very forcibly expressed their abhorrence of this mutilated condition. The Greek appellation of eunuchs, which insensibly prevailed, had a milder sound and a more ambiguous sense.

4. We need only mention Posides, a freedman and eunuch of Claudius, in whose favour the emperor prostituted some of the most honourable rewards of military valour. See Sueton. in Claudio, c. 28. Posides employed a great part of his wealth in building.

Ut *spado* vincebat Capitolia nostra Posides.
Juvenal. Sat. xiv. [91.]

5. Castrari mares vetuit. Sueton. in Domitian. c. 7. See Dion Cassius, l. lxvii. [c. 2] p. 1101; l. lxviii. [c. 2] p. 1119.

6. There is a passage in the Augustan History, p. 137, in which Lampridius, whilst he praises Alexander Severus and Constantine for restraining the tyranny of the eunuchs, deplores the mischiefs which they occasioned in other reigns. Huc accedit, quod eunuchos nec in consiliis nec in ministeriis habuit; qui soli principes perdunt, dum eos more gentium aut regum Persarum volunt vivere; qui a populo etiam amicissimum semovent; qui internuntii sunt, aliud quàm respondetur [sæpe], referentes; claudentes principem suum, et agentes ante omnia ne quid sciat. [Lampr. Alex. Sev. c. 66.]

7. Xenophon (Cyropædia, l. vii. [5 § 60] p. 540) has stated the specious reasons which engaged Cyrus to intrust his person to the guard of eunuchs. He had observed in animals, that, although

the practice of castration might tame their ungovernable fierceness, it did not diminish their strength or spirit; and he persuaded himself that those who were separated from the rest of human kind would be more firmly attached to the person of their benefactor. But a long experience has contradicted the judgment of Cyrus. Some particular instances may occur of eunuchs distinguished by their fidelity, their valour, and their abilities; but if we examine the general history of Persia, India, and China, we shall find that the power of the eunuchs has uniformly marked the decline and fall of every dynasty.

8. See Ammianus Marcellinus, l. xxi. c. 16; l. xxii. c. 4. The whole tenor of his impartial history serves to justify the invectives of Mamertinus, of Libanius, and of Julian himself, who have insulted the vices of the court of Constantius.

9. Aurelius Victor censures the negligence of his sovereign in choosing the governors of the provinces and the generals of the army, and concludes his history with a very bold observation, as it is much more dangerous under a feeble reign to attack the ministers than the master himself. "Uti verum absolvam brevi, ut Imperatore ipso clarius, ita apparitorum plerisque magis atrox nihil." [De Cæsar. c. 42.]

10. Apud quem (si vere dici debeat) multum Constantius potuit. Ammian. l. xviii. c. 4.

11. Gregory Nazianzen (Orat. iii. p. 90) reproaches the apostate with his ingratitude towards Mark, bishop of Arethusa, who had contributed to save his life; and we learn, though from a less respectable authority (Tillemont, Hist. des Empereurs, tom. iv. p. 916), that Julian was concealed in the sanctuary of a church.

12. The most authentic account of the education and adventures of Julian is contained in the epistle or manifesto which he himself addressed to the senate and people of Athens. Libanius (Orat. Parentalis), on the side of the Pagans, and Socrates (l. iii. c. 1), on that of the Christians, have preserved several interesting circumstances.

13. For the promotion of Gallus see Idatius, Zosimus, and the two Victors. According to Philostorgius (l. iv. c. 1), Theophilus, an Arian bishop, was the witness, and, as it were, the guarantee of this solemn engagement. He supported that character with generous firmness; but M. de Tillemont (Hist. des Empereurs, tom. iv. p. 1120) thinks it very improbable that a heretic should have possessed such virtue.

14. Julian was at first permitted to pursue his studies at Constantinople, but the reputation which he acquired soon excited the jealousy of Constantius; and the young prince was advised to withdraw himself to the less conspicuous scenes of Bithynia and Ionia.

15. See Julian ad S. P. Q. A. p. 271. Jerom. in Chron. Aurelius Victor. Eutropius, x. 14 [7]. I shall copy the words of Eutropius, who wrote his abridgment about fifteen years after the death of Gallus, when there was no longer any motive either to flatter or to depreciate his character. "Multis incivilibus gestis Gallus Cæsar . . . vir naturâ ferus et ad tyrannidem pronior, si suo jure imperare licuisset."

16. Megæra quædam mortalis, inflammatrix sævientis assidua, humani cruoris avida, etc. Ammian. Marcellin. l. xiv. c. 1. The sincerity of Ammianus would not suffer him to misrepresent facts or characters, but his love of *ambitious* ornaments frequently betrayed him into an unnatural vehemence of expression.

17. His name was Clematius of Alexandria, and his only crime was a refusal to gratify the desires of his mother-in-law; who solicited his death, because she had been disappointed of his love. Ammian. l. xiv. c. 1.

18. See in Ammianus (l. xiv. c. 1, 7) a very ample detail of the cruelties of Gallus. His brother Julian (p. 272) insinuates that a secret conspiracy had been formed against him; and Zosimus names (l. ii. [c. 55] p. 135) the persons engaged in it; a minister of considerable rank, and two obscure agents, who were resolved to make their fortune.

19. Zonaras, l. xiii. [c. 8] tom. ii. p. 17, 18. The assassins had seduced a great number of legionaries; but their designs were discovered and revealed by an old woman in whose cottage they lodged.

20. In the present text of Ammianus [xiv. 7] we read *Asper*, quidem, sed ad *lenitatem* propensior; which forms a sentence of contradictory nonsense. With the aid of an old manuscript, Valesius has rectified the first of these corruptions, and we perceive a ray of light in the substitution of the word *vafer*. If we venture to change *lenitatem* into *levitatem*, this alteration of a single letter will render the whole passage clear and consistent.

21. Instead of being obliged to collect scattered and imperfect hints from various sources, we now enter into the full stream of the history of Ammianus, and need only refer to the seventh and ninth chapters of his fourteenth book. Philostorgius, however (l. iii. c. 28), though partial to Gallus, should not be entirely overlooked.

22. She had preceded her husband, but died of a fever on the road, at a little place in Bithynia called Cœnum Gallicanum.

23. The Thebæan legions, which were then quartered at Hadrianople, sent a deputation to Gallus, with a tender of their services. Ammian. l. xiv. c. 11. The Notitia (s. 6, 20, 38, edit. Labb.) mentions three several legions which bore the name of Thebæan. The zeal of M. de Voltaire to destroy a despicable though celebrated legend has tempted him on the slightest grounds to deny the existence of a Thebæan legion in the Roman armies. See Œuvres de Voltaire, tom. xv. p. 414, quarto edition.

24. See the complete narrative of the journey and death of Gallus in Ammianus, l. xiv. c. 11. Julian complains that his brother was put to death

without a trial; attempts to justify, or at least to excuse, the cruel revenge which he had inflicted on his enemies; but seems at last to acknowledge that he might justly have been deprived of the purple.

25. Philostorgius, l. iv. c. 1. Zonaras, l. xiii. [c. 9] tom. ii. p. 19. But the former was partial towards an Arian monarch, and the latter transcribed, without choice or criticism, whatever he found in the writings of the ancients.

26. See Ammianus Marcellin. l. xv. c. 1, 3, 8. Julian himself, in his epistle to the Athenians, draws a very lively and just picture of his own danger and of his sentiments. He shows, however, a tendency to exaggerate his sufferings, by insinuating, though in obscure terms, that they lasted above a year; a period which cannot be reconciled with the truth of chronology.

27. Julian has worked the crimes and misfortunes of the family of Constantine into an allegorical fable, which is happily conceived and agreeably related. It forms the conclusion of the seventh Oration, from whence it has been detached and translated by the Abbé de la Bléterie, Vie de Jovien, tom. ii. p. 385-408.

28. She was a native of Thessalonica in Macedonia, of a noble family, and the daughter as well as sister of consuls. Her marriage with the emperor may be placed in the year 352. In a divided age the historians of all parties agree in her praises. See their testimonies collected by Tillemont, Hist. des Empereurs, tom. iv. p. 750-754.

29. Libanius and Gregory Nazianzen have exhausted the arts as well as the powers of their eloquence to represent Julian as the first of heroes, or the worst of tyrants. Gregory was his fellow-student at Athens; and the symptoms, which he so tragically describes, of the future wickedness of the apostate, amount only to some bodily imperfections, and to some peculiarities in his speech and manner. He protests, however, that he *then* foresaw and foretold the calamities of the church and state (Greg. Nazianzen, Orat. iv. p. 121, 122).

30. Succumbere tot necessitatibus tamque crebris unum se, quod nunquam fecerat, aperte demonstrans. Ammian. l. xv. c. 8. He then expresses, in their own words, the flattering assurances of the courtiers.

31. Tantum a temperatis moribus Juliani differens fratris quantum inter Vespasiani filios fuit, Domitianum et Titum. Ammian. l. xiv. c. 11. The circumstances and education of the two brothers were so nearly the same as to afford a strong example of the innate difference of characters.

32. Ammianus, l. xv. c. 8. Zosimus, l. iii. [c. 2] p. 137, 138.

33. Julian, ad S. P. Q. A. p. 275, 276. Libanius, Orat. x. p. 268. Julian did not yield till the gods had signified their will by repeated visions and omens. His piety then forbade him to resist.

34. Julian himself relates (p. 274), with some humour, the circumstances of his own metamor-

phosis, his downcast looks, and his perplexity at being thus suddenly transported into a new world, where every object appeared strange and hostile.

35. See Ammian. Marcellin. l. xv. c. 8. Zosimus, l. iii. [c. 2] p. 139. Aurelius Victor. Victor Junior in Epitom. [c. 42] Eutrop. x. 14 [7].

36. Militares omnes horrendo fragore scuta genibus illidentes; quod est prosperitatis indicium plenum; nam contra cum hastis clypei feriuntur, iræ documentum est et doloris . . . Ammianus adds, with a nice distinction, Eumque ut potiori reverentia servaretur, nec supra modum laudabant nec infra quam decebat [xv. 8].

37. Ἔλλαβε πορφύρεος θάνατος, καὶ μοιρα κραταιή. The word *purple*, which Homer had used as a vague but common epithet for death, was applied by Julian to express very aptly, the nature and object of his own apprehensions.

38. He represents, in the most pathetic terms (p. 277), the distress of his new situation. The provision for his table was however so elegant and sumptuous, that the young philosopher rejected it with disdain. Quum legeret libellum assidue, quem Constantius ut privignum ad studia mittens manú suâ conscripserat, prælicenter disponens quid in convivio Cæsaris impendi deberet, Phasianum, et vulvam et sumen exigi petuit et inferri. Ammian. Marcellin. l. xvi. c. 5.

39. If we recollect that Constantine, the father of Helena, died above eighteen years before in a mature old age, it will appear probable that the daughter, though a virgin, could not be very young at the time of her marriage. She was soon afterwards delivered of a son, who died immediately, quòd obstetrix corrupta mercede, mox natum præsecto plusquam convenerat umbilico necavit. She accompanied the emperor and empress in their journey to Rome, and the latter, quæsitum venenum bibere per fraudem illexit, ut quotiescunque concepisset, immaturum abjiceret partum. Ammian. l. xvi. c. 10. Our physicians will determine whether there exists such a poison. For my own part, I am inclined to hope that the public malignity imputed the effects of accident as the guilt of Eusebia.

40. Ammianus (xv. 5) was perfectly well informed of the conduct and fate of Sylvanus. He himself was one of the few followers who attended Ursicinus in his dangerous enterprise.

41. For the particulars of the visit of Constantius to Rome, see Ammianus, l. xvi. c. 10. We have only to add that Themistius was appointed deputy from Constantinople, and that he composed his fourth oration for this ceremony.

42. Hormisdas, a fugitive prince of Persia, observed to the emperor, that, if he made such a horse, he must think of preparing a similar stable (the Forum of Trajan). Another saying of Hormisdas is recorded, "that one thing only had *displeased* him, to find that men died at Rome as well as elsewhere." If we adopt this reading of the text of Ammianus (*displicuisse* instead of *placuisse*), we

may consider it as a reproof of Roman vanity. The contrary sense would be that of a misanthrope.

43. When Germanicus visited the ancient monuments of Thebes, the eldest of the priests explained to him the meaning of these hieroglyphics. Tacit, Annal ii. c. 60. But it seems probable that before the useful invention of an alphabet these natural or arbitrary signs were the common characters of the Egyptian nation. See Warburton's Divine Legation of Moses, vol. iii. p. 69-243.

44. See Plin. Hist. Natur. l. xxxvi. c. 14, 15.

45. Ammian. Marcellin. l. xvii. c. 4. He gives us a Greek interpretation of the hieroglyphics, and his commentator Lindenbrogius adds a Latin inscription, which, in twenty verses of the age of Constantius, contain a short history of the obelisk.

46. See Donat. Roma Antiqua, l. iii. c. 14, l. iv. c. 12; and the learned, though confused, Dissertation of Bargæus on Obelisks, inserted in the fourth volume of Grævius's Roman Antiquities, p. 1897-1936. This dissertation is dedicated to Pope Sixtus V., who erected the obelisk of Constantius in the square before the patriarchal church of St. John Lateran.

47. The events of this Quadian and Sarmation war are related by Ammianus, xvi. 10, xvii. 12, 13, xix. 11.

48. Genti Sarmatarum, magno decore considens apud eos, regem dedit. Aurelius Victor [Cæsar. 42]. In a pompous oration pronounced by Constantius himself, he expatiates on his own exploits with much vanity and some truth.

49. Ammian. xvi. 9.

50. Ammianus (xvii. 5) transcribes the haughty letter. Themistius (Orat. iv. p. 57, edit. Petav.) takes notice of the silk covering. Idatius and Zonaras mention the journey of the ambassador; and Peter the Patrician (in Excerpt. Legat. p. 28 [ed. Paris; c. 15, p. 131, ed. Bonn]) has informed us of his conciliating behaviour.

51. Ammianus, xvii. 5, and Valesius ad loc. The sophist, or philosopher (in that age these words were almost synonymous), was Eustathius the Cappadocian, the disciple of Jamblichus, and the friend of St. Basil. Eunapius (in vit. Ædesii, p. 44-47) fondly attributes to this philosophic ambassador the glory of enchanting the barbarian king by the persuasive charms of reason and eloquence. See Tillemont, Hist. de Empereurs, tom. iv. p. 828, 1132.

52. Ammian. xviii. 5, 6, 8. The decent and respectful behaviour of Antoninus towards the Roman general sets him in a very interesting light; and Ammianus himself speaks of the traitor with some compassion and esteem.

53. This circumstance, as it is noticed by Ammianus, serves to prove the veracity of Herodotus (l. i. c. 133), and the permanency of the Persian manners. In every age the Persians have been addicted to intemperance, and the wines of Shiraz have triumphed over the law of Mahomet. Bris-

son de Regno Pers. l. ii. p. 462-472, and Chardin Voyages en Perse, tom. iii. p. 90.

54. Ammian. l. xviii. 6, 7, 8, 10.

55. For the description of Amida, see d'Herbelot, Bibliothèque Orientale, p. 108; Histoire de Timur Bec, par Cherefeddin Ali, l. iii. c. 41. Ahmed Arabsiades, tom. i. p. 331, c. 43; Voyages de Tavernier, tom. i. p. 301; Voyages d'Otter, tom. ii. p. 273; and Voyages de Niebuhr, tom. ii. p. 324-328. The last of these travellers, a learned and accurate Dane, has given a plan of Amida, which illustrates the operations of the siege.

56. Diarbekir, which is styled Amid, or Kara-Amid, in the public writings of the Turks, contains above 16,000 houses, and is the residence of a pasha with three tails. The epithet of *Kara* is derived from the *blackness* of the stone which composes the strong and ancient wall of Amida.

57. The operations of the siege of Amida are very minutely described by Ammianus (xix. 1-9), who acted an honourable part in the defence, and escaped with difficulty when the city was stormed by the Persians.

58. Of these four nations the Albanians are too well known to require any description. The Segestans [*Sacastenè, St. Martin*] inhabited a large and level country, which still preserves their name, to the south of Khorasan and the west of Hindostan. (See Geographia Nubiensis, p. 133; and d'Herbelot, Bibliothèque Orientale, p. 797.) Notwithstanding the boasted victory of Bahram (page 294), the Segestans, above fourscore years afterwards, appear as an independent nation, the ally of Persia. We are ignorant of the situation of the Vertæ and Chionites, but I am inclined to place them (at least the latter) towards the confines of India and Scythia. See Ammian. xvi. 9.

59. Ammianus has marked the chronology of this year by three signs, which do not perfectly coincide with each other, or with the series of the history. 1. The corn was ripe when Sapor invaded Mesopotamia: "Cum jam stipulâ flavente turgerent;" a circumstance which, in the latitude of Aleppo, would naturally refer us to the month of April or May. See Harmer's Observations on Scripture, vol. i. p. 41. Shaw's Travels, p. 335, edit. 4to. 2. The progress of Sapor was checked by the overflowing of the Euphrates, which generally happens in July and August. Plin. Hist. Nat. v. 21. Viaggi di Pietro della Valle, tom. i. p. 696. 3. When Sapor had taken Amida, after a siege of seventy-three days, the autumn was far advanced: "Autumno præcipiti hædorumque improbo sidere exorto." To reconcile these apparent contradictions, we must allow for some delay in the Persian king, some inaccuracy in the historian, and some disorder in the seasons.

60. The account of these sieges is given by Ammianus, xx. 6, 7.

61. For the identity of Virtha and Tecrit, see d'Anville, Géographie Ancienne, tom. ii. p. 201. For the siege of that castle by Timur Bec, or Tam-

erlane, see Cherefeddin, l. iii. c. 33. The Persian biographer exaggerates the merit and difficulty of this exploit, which delivered the caravans of Bagdad from a formidable gang of robbers.

62. Ammianus (xviii. 5, 6, xix. 3, xx. 2) represents the merit and disgrace of Ursicinus with that faithful attention which a soldier owed to his general. Some partiality may be suspected, yet the whole account is consistent and probable.

63. Ammian. xx. 11. Omisso vano incepto, hiematurus Antiochiæ redit in Syriam ærumnosam, perpessus et ulcerum sed et atrocia, diuque defienda. It is *thus* that James Gronovius has restored an obscure passage; and he thinks that this correction alone would have deserved a new edition of his author; whose sense may now be darkly perceived. I expected some additional light from the recent labours of the learned Ernestus. (Lipsiæ, 1773.)

64. The ravages of the Germans, and the distress of Gaul, may be collected from Julian himself. Orat. ad S. P. Q. Athen. p. 277. Ammian. xv. 11 [8?] Libanius, Orat. x. Zosimus, l. iii. [c. 3] p. 140. Sozomen, l. iii. c. 1. [Mamertin. Grat. Act. c. iv.]

65. Ammianus (xvii. 8). This name seems to be derived from the Toxandri of Pliny, and very frequently occurs in the histories of the middle age. Toxandria was a country of woods and morasses, which extended from the neighbourhood of Tongres to the conflux of the Vahal and the Rhine. See Valesius, Notit. Galliar. p. 558.

66. The paradox of P. Daniel, that the Franks never obtained any permanent settlement on this side of the Rhine before the time of Clovis, is refuted with much learning and good sense by Mr. Biet, who has proved, by a chain of evidence, their uninterrupted possession of Toxandria one hundred and thirty years before the accession of Clovis. The Dissertation of M. Biet was crowned by the Academy of Soissons in the year 1736, and seems to have been justly preferred to the discourse of his more celebrated competitor, the Abbé le Bœuf, an antiquarian whose name was happily expressive of his talents.

67. The private life of Julian in Gaul, and the severe discipline which he embraced, are displayed by Ammianus (xvi. 5), who professes to praise, and by Julian himself, who affects to ridicule (Misopogon, p. 340) a conduct which, in a prince of the house of Constantine, might justly excite the surprise of mankind.

68. Aderat Latine quoque disserendi sufficiens sermo. Ammianus, xvi. 5. But Julian, educated in the schools of Greece, always considered the language of the Romans as a foreign and popular dialect, which he might use on necessary occasions.

69. We are ignorant of the actual office of this excellent minister, whom Julian afterwards created præfect of Gaul. Sallust was speedily recalled by the jealousy of the emperor; and we may still read a sensible but pedantic discourse (p. 240-252), in which Julian deplores the loss of so valuable a

friend, to whom he acknowledges himself indebted for his reputation. See La Bléterie, Préface à la Vie de Jovien, p. 20.

70. Ammianus (xvi. 2, 3) appears much better satisfied with the success of this first campaign than Julian himself; who very fairly owns that he did nothing of consequence, and that he fled before the enemy.

71. Ammian. xvi. 7. Libanius speaks rather more advantageously of the military talents of Marcellus, Orat. x. p. 272. And Julian insinuates that he would not have been so easily recalled, unless he had given other reasons of offence to the court, p. 278.

72. Severus, non discors, non arrogans, sed lon ga militiæ frugalitate compertus; et eum recta præeuntem securturus, ut ductorem morigerus miles. Ammian. xvi. 11. Zosimus, l. iii. [c. 2] p. 140.

73. On the design and failure of the co-operation between Julian and Barbatio, see Ammianus (xvi. 11), and Libanius, Orat. x. p. 273.

74. Ammianus (xvi. 12) describes with his inflated eloquence the figure and character of Chnodomar. Audax et fidens ingenti robore lacertorum, ubi ardor prœlii sperabatur immanis, equo spumante, sublimior, erectus in jaculum formidandæ vastitatis, armorumque nitore conspicuus: antea strenuus et miles, et utilis præter cæteros ductor . . . Decentium Cæsarem superavit æquo Marte congressus.

75. After the battle Julian ventured to revive the rigour of ancient discipline by exposing these fugitives in female apparel to the derision of the whole camp. In the next campaign these troops nobly retrieved their honour. Zosimus, l. iii. [c. 3] p. 142.

76. Julian himself (ad S. P. Q. Athen. p. 279) speaks of the battle of Strasburg with the modesty of conscious merit; ἐμαχεσάμην οὐκ ἀκλεως, ἴσως καὶ εἰς ὑμας ἀφίκετο ἡ τοιαύτη μάχη. Zosimus compares it with the victory of Alexander over Darius; and yet we are at a loss to discover any of those strokes of military genius which fix the attention of ages on the conduct and success of a single day.

77. Ammianus, xvi. 12. Libanius adds 2000 more to the number of the slain (Orat. x. p. 274). But these trifling differences disappear before the 60,000 barbarians whom Zosimus has sacrificed to the glory of his hero (l. iii. [c. 3] p. 141). We might attribute this extravagant number to the carelessness of transcribers, if this credulous or partial historian had not swelled the army of 35,000 Alemanni to an innumerable multitude of barbarians, πληθος ἄπειρον βαρβάρων. It is our own fault if this detection does not inspire us with proper distrust on similar occasions.

78. Ammian. xvi. 12. Libanius. Orat. x. p. 276.

79. Libanius (Orat. iii. p. 137) draws a very lively picture of the manners of the Franks.

80. Ammianus, xvii. 2. Libanius, Orat. x. p. 278. The Greek orator, by misapprehending a passage of Julian, has been induced to represent the

Franks as consisting of a thousand men; and, as his head was always full of the Peloponnesian war, he compares them to the Lacedæmonians, who were besieged and taken in the island of Sphacteria.

81. Julian. ad S. P. Q. Athen. p. 280. Libanius, Orat. x. p. 278. According to the expression of Libanius, the emperor δωρα ὠνόμαζε, which La Blé-terie understands (Vie de Julien, p. 118) as an honest confession, and Valesius (ad Ammian. xvii. 2) as a mean evasion, of the truth. Dom Bouquet (Historiens de France, tom. i. p. 733), by substituting another word, ἐνόμισε, would suppress both the difficulty and the spirit of this passage.

82. Ammian. xvii. 8; Zosimus, l. iii. [c. 4, sq.] p. 146-150 (his narrative is darkened by a mixture of fable); and Julian. ad S.P.Q. Athen. p. 280. His expression, ὑπεδεξάμην μὲν μοῖραν τοῦ Σαλίων ἔθνους, Χαμάβους δὲ ἐξήλασα. This difference of treatment confirms the opinion that the Salian Franks were permitted to retain the settlements in Toxandria.

83. This interesting story, which Zosimus has abridged, is related by Eunapius (in Excerpt. Legationum, p. 15, 16, 17 [ed. Paris; p. 11 sq. ed. Ven.; cap. i. p. 41 sqq. ed. Bonn]), with all the amplifications of Grecian rhetoric: but the silence of Libanius, of Ammianus, and of Julian himself, renders the truth of it extremely suspicious.

84. Libanius, the friend of Julian, clearly insinuates (Orat. iv. p. 178) that his hero had composed the history of his Gallic campaigns. But Zosimus (l. iii. [c. 2] p. 140) seems to have derived his information only from the Orations (λόγοι) and the Epistles of Julian. The discourse which is addressed to the Athenians contains an accurate, though general, account of the war against the Germans.

85. See Ammian. xvii. 1, 10, xviii. 2; and Zosim. l. iii. p. 144. Julian. ad S. P. Q. Athen. p. 280.

86. Ammian. xviii. 2. Libanius, Orat. x. p. 279, 280. Of these seven posts, four are at present towns of some consequence—Bingen, Andernach, Bonn, and Nuyss. The other three, Tricesimæ, Quadriburgium, and Castra Herculis, or Heraclea, no longer subsist; but there is room to believe that, on the ground of Quadriburgium, the Dutch have constructed the fort of Schenk, a name so offensive to the fastidious delicacy of Boileau. See D'Anville, Notice de l'Ancienne Gaule, p. 183; Boileau, Epitre iv. and the notes.

87. We may credit Julian himself, Orat. ad S. P.Q. Atheniensem, p. 279, sq., who gives a very particular account of the transaction. Zosimus adds two hundred vessels more, l. iii. [c. 5] p. 145. If we computed the 600 corn ships of Julian at only seventy tons each, they were capable of exporting 120,000 quarters (see Arbuthnot's Weights and Measures, p. 237), and the country which could bear so large an exportation must already have attained an improved state of agriculture.

88. The troops once broke out into a mutiny, immediately before the second passage of the Rhine. Ammian. xvii. 9.

89. Ammian. xvi. 5, xviii. 1. Mamertinus in Panegyr. Vet. xi. 4.

90. Ammian. xvii. 3. Julian. Epistol. xvii. edit. Spanheim. Such a conduct almost justifies the encomium of Mamertinus. Ita illi anni spatia divisa sunt, ut aut Barbaros domitet, aut civibus jura restituat; perpetuum professus, aut contra hostem, aut contra vitia, certamen.

91. Libanius, Orat. Parental. in Imp. Julian. c. 38, in Fabricius Bibliothec. Græc. tom. vii. p. 263, 264.

92. See Julian. in Misopogon, p. 340, 341. The primitive state of Paris is illustrated by Henry Valesius (ad Ammian. xx. 4), his brother Hadrian Valesius, or de Valois, and M. d'Anville (in their respective Notitias of ancient Gaul), the Abbé de Longuerue (Description de la France, tom. i. p. 12, 13), and M. Bonamy (in the Mém. de l'Académie des Inscriptions, tom. xv. p. 656-691).

93. Τὴν φίλην Λευκετίαν. Julian. in Misopogon, p. 340. Leucetia, or Lutetia, was the ancient name of the city which, according to the fashion of the fourth century, assumed the territorial appellation of Parisii.

94. Julian. in Misopogon. p. 359, 360.

Chapter XX

1. The date of the Divine Institutions of Lactantius has been accurately discussed, difficulties have been started, solutions proposed, and an expedient imagined of two *original* editions—the former published during the persecutions of Diocletian, the latter under that of Licinius. See Dufresnoy, Præfat. p. v. Tillemont, Mém. Ecclésiast. tom. vi. p. 465-470. Lardner's Credibility, part ii. vol. vii. p. 78-86. For my own part, I am *almost* convinced that Lactantius dedicated his Institutions to the sovereign of Gaul, at a time when Galerius, Maximin, and even Licinius, persecuted the Christians; that is, between the years 306 and 311.

2. Lactant. Divin. Institut. i. 1, vii. 26. The first and most important of these passages is indeed wanting in twenty-eight manuscripts, but it is found in nineteen. If we weigh the comparative value of those manuscripts, one of 900 years old, in the king of France's library, may be alleged in its favour; but the passage is omitted in the correct manuscript of Bologna, which the P. de Montfaucon ascribes to the sixth or seventh century (Diarium Italic. p. 409). The taste of most of the editors (except Isæus, see Lactant. edit. Dufresnoy, tom. i. p. 596) has felt the genuine style of Lactantius.

3. Euseb. in Vit. Constant. l. i. c. 27-32.

4. Zosimus, l. ii. [c. 29] p. 104.

5. That rite was *always* used in making a cate-chumen (see Bingham's Antiquities, l. x. c. i. p. 419; Dom Chardon, Hist. des Sacremens, tom. i. p. 62), and Constantine received it for the *first* time (Euseb. in Vit. Constant. l. iv. c. 61) immediately before his baptism and death. From the connection of these two facts, Valesius (ad loc. Euseb.) has drawn the conclusion which is reluctantly admitted by Tillemont (Hist. des Empereurs, tom. iv. p. 628), and opposed with feeble arguments by Mosheim (p. 968).

6. Euseb. in Vit Constant. l. iv. c. 61, 62, 63. The legend of Constantine's baptism at Rome, thirteen years before his death, was invented in the eighth century, as a proper motive for his *donation*. Such has been the gradual progress of knowledge, that a story, of which Cardinal Baronius (Annal. Ecclesiast. A.D. 324, No. 43-49) declared himself the unblushing advocate, is now feebly supported, even within the verge of the Vatican. See the Antiquitates Christianæ, tom. ii. p. 232— a work published with six approbations at Rome, in the year 1751, by Father Mamachi, a learned Dominican.

7. The quæstor, or secretary, who composed the law of the Theodosian Code, makes his master say with indifference, "hominibus supra dictæ religionis" (l. xvi. tit. ii. leg. 1). The minister of ecclesiastical affairs was allowed a more devout and respectful style, τῆς ἐνθέσμου καὶ ἁγιωτάτης καθολικῆς θρησκείας; the legal, most holy, and catholic worship. See Euseb. Hist. Eccles. l. x. c. 6.

8. Cod. Theodos. l. ii. tit. viii. leg. 1. Cod. Justinian. l. iii. tit. xii. leg. 3. Constantine styles the Lord's day *dies solis*, a name which could not offend the ears of his Pagan subjects.

9. Cod. Theodos. l. xvi. tit. x. leg. 1. Godefroy, in the character of a commentator, endeavours (tom. vi. p. 257) to excuse Constantine; but the more zealous Baronius (Annal. Eccles. A.D. 321, No. 18) censures his profane conduct with truth and asperity.

10. Theodoret (l. i. c. 18) seems to insinuate that Helena gave her son a Christian education; but we may be assured, from the superior authority of Eusebius (in Vit. Constant. l. iii. c. 47), that she herself was indebted to Constantine for the knowledge of Christianity.

11. See the medals of Constantine in Ducange and Banduri. As few cities had retained the privilege of coining, almost all the medals of that age issued from the mint under the sanction of the Imperial authority.

12. The panegyric of Eumenius (vii. [vi.] inter Panegyr. Vet.), which was pronounced a few months before the Italian war, abounds with the most unexceptionable evidence of the Pagan superstition of Constantine, and of his particular veneration for Apollo, or the Sun; to which Julian alludes (Orat. vii. p. 228, ἀπολείπων σέ). See Commentaire de Spanheim sur les Césars, p. 317.

13. Constantin. Orat. ad Sanctos, c. 25. But it might easily be shown that the Greek translator has improved the sense of the Latin original; and the aged emperor might recollect the persecution of Diocletian with a more lively abhorrence than he had actually felt in the days of his youth and Paganism.

14. See Euseb. Hist. Eccles. l. viii. 13, l. ix. 9; and in Vit. Const. l. i. c. 16, 17. Lactant. Divin. Institut. i. 1. Cæcilius de Mort. Persecut. c. 25.

15. Cæcilius (de Mort. Persecut. c. 48) has preserved the Latin original; and Eusebius (Hist. Eccles. l. x. c. 5) has given a Greek translation of this perpetual edict, which refers to some provisional regulations.

16. A panegyric of Constantine, pronounced seven or eight months after the edict of Milan (see Gothofred. Chronolog. Legum, p. 7; and Tillemont, Hist. des Empereurs, tom. iv. p. 246), uses the following remarkable expression:—"Summe rerum sator, cujus tot nomina sunt, quot linguas gentium esse voluisti, quem enim te ipse dici velis scire non possumus." (Panegyr. Vet. ix. [viii.] 26.) In explaining Constantine's progress in the faith, Mosheim (p. 971, etc.) is ingenious, subtle, prolix.

17. See the elegant description of Lactantius (Divin. Institut. v. 8), who is much more perspicuous and positive than becomes a discreet prophet.

18. The political system of the Christians is explained by Grotius, de Jure Belli et Pacis, l. i. c. 3, 4. Grotius was a republican and an exile, but the mildness of his temper inclined him to support the established powers.

19. Tertullian, Apolog. c. 32, 34, 35, 36. Tamen nunquam Albiniani, nec Nigriani vel Cassiani inveniri potuerunt Christiani. Ad Scapulam, c. 2. If this assertion be strictly true, it excludes the Christians of that age from all civil and military employments, which would have compelled them to take an active part in the service of their respective governors. See Moyle's Works, vol. ii. p. 349.

20. See the artful Bossuet (Hist. des Variations des Eglises Protestantes, tom. iii. p. 210-258), and the malicious Bayle (tom. ii. p. 620). I *name* Bayle, for he was certainly the author of the Avis aux Réfugiés; consult the Dictionnaire Critique de Chauffepié tom. i. part. ii. p. 145.

21. Buchanan is the earliest, or at least the most celebrated, of the reformers, who has justified the theory of resistance. See his Dialogue de Jure Regni apud Scotos, tom. ii. p. 28, 30, edit. fol. Ruddiman.

22. Lactant. Divin. Institut. i. 1. Eusebius, in the course of his History, his Life, and his Oration, repeatedly inculcates the divine right of Constantine to the empire.

23. Our imperfect knowledge of the persecution of Licinius is derived from Eusebius (Hist. Eccles. l. x. c. 8; Vit. Constantin. l. i. c. 49-56, l. ii. c. 1, 2). Aurelius Victor mentions his cruelty in general terms.

24. Euseb. in Vit. Constant. l. ii. c. 24-42, 48-60.

25. In the beginning of the last century the papists of England were only a *thirtieth*, and the protestants of France only a *fifteenth*, part of the respective nations to whom their spirit and power were a constant object of apprehension. See the relations which Bentivoglio (who was then nuncio at Brussels, and afterwards cardinal) transmitted to the court of Rome (Relazione, tom. ii. p. 211, 241). Bentivoglio was curious, well-informed, but somewhat partial.

26. This careless temper of the Germans appears almost uniformly in the history of the conversion of each of the tribes. The legions of Constantine were recruited with Germans (Zosimus, l. ii. [c. 15] p. 86); and the court even of his father had been filled with Christians. See the first book of the Life of Constantine, by Eusebius.

27. De his qui arma projiciunt in *pace*, placuit eos abstinere a communione. Concil. Arelat. Canon iii. The best critics apply these words to the *peace of the church*.

28. Eusebius always considers the second civil war against Licinius as a sort of religious crusade. At the invitation of the tyrant, some Christian officers had resumed their *zones;* or, in other words, had returned to the military service. Their conduct was afterwards censured by the twelfth canon of the Council of Nice; if this particular application may be received, instead of the loose and general sense of the Greek interpreters, Balsamon, Zonaras, and Alexis Aristenus. See Beveridge, Pandect. Eccles, Græc, tom. i. p. 72, tom. ii. p. 78. Annotation.

29. Nomen ipsum *crucis* absit non modo a corpore civium Romanorum, sed etiam a cogitatione, oculis, auribus. Cicero pro Rabirio, c. 5. The Christian writers, Justin, Minucius Felix, Tertullian, Jerom, and Maximus of Turin, have investigated with tolerable success the figure or likeness of a cross in almost every object of nature or art; in the intersection of the meridian and equator, the human face, a bird flying, a man swimming, a mast and yard, a plough, a *standard*, etc., etc., etc. See Lipsius de Cruce, l. i. c. 9.

30. See Aurelius Victor [de Cæsar. c. 41], who considers this law as one of the examples of Constantine's piety. An edict so honourable to Christianity deserved a place in the Theodosian Code, instead of the indirect mention of it which seems to result from the comparison of the fifth and eighteenth titles of the ninth book.

31. Eusebius, in Vit. Constantin. l. i. c. 40. This statue, or at least the cross and inscription, may be ascribed with more probability to the second, or even the third, visit of Constantine to Rome. Immediately after the defeat of Maxentius, the minds of the senate and people were scarcely ripe for this public monument.

32. Agnoscas, regina, libens mea signa necesse
est;

In quibus effigies *crucis* aut gemmata
refulget
Aut longis solido ex auro præfertur in
hastis.
Hoc signo invictus, transmissis Alpibus
ultor
Servitium solvit miserabile Constantinus.
.   .   .   .
Christus *purpureum* gemmanti textus in auro
Signabat *Labarum*, clipeorum insignia
Christus
Scripserat; ardebat summis *crux* addita
cristis.
                Prudent. in Symmachum, l. i.
                        464, 486.

33. The derivation and meaning of the word *Labarum* or *Laborum*, which is employed by Gregory Nazianzen, Ambrose, Prudentius, etc., still remain totally unknown, in spite of the efforts of the critics, who have ineffectually tortured the Latin, Greek, Spanish, Celtic, Teutonic, Illyric, Armenian, etc., in search of an etymology. See Ducange, in Gloss. Med. and infim. Latinitat. sub voce *Labarum*, and Godefroy, ad Cod. Theodos. tom. ii. p. 143.

34. Euseb. in Vit. Constantin. l. i. c. 30, 31. Baronius (Annal. Eccles. A.D. 312, No. 26) has engraved a representation of the Labarum.

35. Transversâ X literâ, summo capite circumflexo, Christum in scutis notat. Cæcilius de M. P. c. 44. Cuper (ad M. P. in edit. Lactant. tom. ii. p. 500) and Baronius (A.D. 312, No. 25) have engraved from ancient monuments several specimens —as thus, ☦ or ☧—of these monograms, which became extremely fashionable in the Christian world.

36. Euseb. in Vit. Constantin. l. ii. c. 7, 8, 9. He introduces the Labarum before the Italian expedition; but his narrative seems to indicate that it was never shown at the head of an army, till Constantine, above ten years afterwards, declared himself the enemy of Licinius and the deliverer of the church.

37. See Cod. Theod. l. vi. tit. xxv. Sozomen, l. i. c. 2 [c. 4]. Theophan. Chronograph. p. 11. Theophanes lived towards the end of the eighth century, almost five hundred years after Constantine. The modern Greeks were not inclined to display in the field the standard of the empire and of Christianity; and though they depended on every superstitious hope of *defence*, the promise of *victory* would have appeared too bold a fiction.

38. The Abbé du Voisin, p. 103, etc., alleges several of these medals, and quotes a particular dissertation of a Jesuit, the Père de Grainville, on this subject.

39. Tertullian, de Coronâ, c. 3. Athanasius, tom. i. p. 101 [p. 89, ed. Bened. 1698; de Incarn. Verbi Dei, c. 48]. The learned Jesuit Petavius (Dogmata Theolog. l. xv. c. 9, 10) has collected many similar passages on the virtues of the cross, which in the last age embarrassed our protestant disputants.

40. Cæcilius, de M. P. c. 44. It is certain that this historical declamation was composed and published while Licinius, sovereign of the East, still preserved the friendship of Constantine and of the Christians. Every reader of taste must perceive that the style is of a very different and inferior character to that of Lactantius; and such indeed is the judgment of Le Clerc and Lardner (Bibliothèque Ancienne et Moderne, tom. iii. p. 438; Credibility of the Gospel, etc., part ii. vol. vii. p. 94). Three arguments from the title of the book, and from the names of Donatus and Cæcilius, are produced by the advocates for Lactantius (see the P. Lestocq, tom. ii. p. 46–60). Each of these proofs is singly weak and defective; but their concurrence has great weight. I have often fluctuated, and shall *tamely* follow the Colbert MS. in calling the author (whoever he was) Cæcilius.

41. Cæcilius, de M. P. c. 46. There seems to be some reason in the observation of M. de Voltaire (Œuvres, tom. xiv. p. 307), who ascribes to the success of Constantine the superior fame of his Labarum above the angel of Licinius. Yet even this angel is favourably entertained by Pagi, Tillemont, Fleury, etc., who are fond of increasing their stock of miracles.

42. Besides these well-known examples, Tollius (Preface to Boileau's translation of Longinus) has discovered a vision of Antigonus, who assured his troops that he had seen a pentagon (the symbol of safety) with these words, "In this conquer." But Tollius has most inexcusably omitted to produce his authority; and his own character, literary as well as moral, is not free from reproach (see Chauffepié, Dictionnaire Critique, tom. iv. p. 460). Without insisting on the silence of Diodorus, Plutarch, Justin, etc., it may be observed that Polyænus, who in a separate chapter (l. iv. c. 6) has collected nineteen military stratagems of Antigonus, is totally ignorant of this remarkable vision.

43. Instinctu Divinitatis, mentis magnitudine. The inscription on the triumphal arch of Constantine, which has been copied by Baronius, Gruter, etc., may still be perused by every curious traveller.

44. Habes profecto aliquid cum illâ mente Divinâ secretum; quæ delegatâ nostrâ Diis Minoribus curâ uni se tibi dignatur ostendere. Panegyr. Vet. ix. [viii.] 2.

45. M. Freret (Mémoires de l'Académie des Inscriptions, tom. iv. p. 411–437) explains, by physical causes, many of the prodigies of antiquity; and Fabricius, who is abused by both parties, vainly tries to introduce the celestial cross of Constantine among the solar halos. Bibliothec. Græc. tom. vi. p. 8–29.

46. Nazarius inter Panegyr. Vet. x. [ix.] 14, 15. It is unnecessary to name the moderns, whose undistinguishing and ravenous appetite has swallowed even the Pagan bait of Nazarius.

47. The apparitions of Castor and Pollux, particularly to announce the Macedonian victory, are attested by historians and public monuments. See Cicero de Naturâ Deorum, ii. 2, iii. 5, 6. Florus, ii. 12. Valerius Maximus, l. i. c. 8, No. 1. Yet the most recent of these miracles is omitted, and indirectly denied, by Livy (xlv. 1).

48. Eusebius [Vit. Constant.], l. i. c. 28, 29, 30. The silence of the same Eusebius, in his Ecclesiastical History, is deeply felt by those advocates for the miracle who are not absolutely callous.

49. The narrative of Constantine seems to indicate that he saw the cross in the sky before he passed the Alps against Maxentius. The scene has been fixed by provincial vanity at Treves, Besançon, etc. See Tillemont, Hist. des Empereurs, tom. iv. p. 573.

50. The pious Tillemont (Mém. Ecclés. tom. vii. p. 1317) rejects with a sigh the useful Acts of Artemius, a veteran and a martyr, who attests as an eye-witness the vision of Constantine.

51. Gelasius Cyzic. in Act. Concil. Nicen. l. i. c. 4.

52. The advocates for the vision are unable to produce a single testimony from the Fathers of the fourth and fifth centuries, who in their voluminous writings repeatedly celebrate the triumph of the church and of Constantine. As these venerable men had not any dislike to a miracle, we may suspect (and the suspicion is confirmed by the ignorance of Jerom) that they were all unacquainted with the Life of Constantine by Eusebius. This tract was recovered by the diligence of those who translated or continued his Ecclesiastical History, and who have represented in various colours the vision of the cross.

53. Godefroy was the first who, in the year 1643 (Not. ad Philostorgium, l. i. c. 6, p. 16), expressed any doubt of a miracle which had been supported with equal zeal by Cardinal Baronius and the Centuriators of Magdeburg. Since that time many of the protestant critics have inclined towards doubt and disbelief. The objections are urged with great force by M. Chauffepié (Dictionnaire Critique, tom. iv. p. 6–11); and in the year 1774 a doctor of Sorbonne, the Abbé du Voisin, published an apology, which deserves the praise of learning and moderation.

54.   Lors Constantin dit ces propres paroles:
      J'ai renversé le culte des idoles:
      Sur les débris de leurs temples fumants
      Au Dieu du Ciel j'ai prodigué l'encens.
      Mais tous mes soins pour sa grandeur
         suprême
      N'eurent jamais d'autre objet que moi-
         même;
      Les saints autels n'étoient à mes regards
      Qu'un marchepié du trone des Césars.
      L'ambition, la fureur, les délices
      Etoient mes dieux, avoient mes sacrifices.
      L'or des Chrétiens, leurs intrigues, leur
         sang
      Ont cimenté ma fortune et mon rang.

The poem which contains these lines may be read with pleasure, but cannot be named with decency.

55. This favourite was probably the great Osius, bishop of Cordova, who preferred the pastoral care of the whole church to the government of a particular diocese. His character is magnificently though concisely expressed by Athanasius (tom. i. p. 703 [tom. ii. p. 535, ed. Bened. 1777]). See Tillemont. Mém. Ecclés. tom. vii. p. 524–561. Osius was accused, perhaps unjustly, of retiring from court with a very ample fortune.

56. See Eusebius (in Vit. Constant. passim), and Zosimus, l. ii. [c. 19] p. 104.

57. The Christianity of Lactantius was of a moral rather than of a mysterious cast. "Erat pæne rudis (says the orthodox Bull) disciplinæ Christianæ, et in rhetoricâ melius quam in theologiâ versatus." Defensio Fidei Nicenæ, sect. ii. c. 14.

58. Fabricius, with his usual diligence, has collected a list of between three and four hundred authors quoted in the Evangelical Preparation of Eusebius. See Bibl. Græc. l. v. c. 4, tom. vi. p. 37–56.

59. See Constantin. Orat ad Sanctos, c. 19, 20. He chiefly depends on a mysterious acrostic, composed in the sixth age after the Deluge by the Erythræan Sibyl, and translated by Cicero into Latin. The initial letters of the thirty-four Greek verses form this prophetic sentence:—JESUS CHRIST, SON OF GOD, SAVIOUR OF THE WORLD.

60. In his paraphrase of Virgil the emperor has frequently assisted and improved the literal sense of the Latin text. See Blondel, des Sibylles, l. i. c. 14, 15, 16.

61. The different claims of an elder and younger son of Pollio, of Julia, of Drusus, of Marcellus, are found to be incompatible with chronology, history, and the good sense of Virgil.

62. See Lowth, de Sacrâ Poesi Hebræorum Prælect. xxi. p. 289–293. In the examination of the fourth eclogue, the respectable bishop of London has displayed learning, taste, ingenuity, and a temperate enthusiasm, which exalts his fancy without degrading his judgment.

63. The distinction between the public and the secret parts of divine service, the *missa catechumenorum* and the *missa fidelium*, and the mysterious veil which piety or policy had cast over the latter, are very judiciously explained by Thiers, Exposition du Saint Sacrement, l. i. c. 8–12, p. 59–91; but as on this subject the papists may reasonably be suspected, a Protestant reader will depend with more confidence on the learned Bingham, Antiquities, l. x. c. 5.

64. See Eusebius in Vit. Const. l. iv. c. 15–32, and the whole tenor of Constantine's sermon. The faith and devotion of the emperor has furnished Baronius with a specious argument in favour of his early baptism.

65. Zosimus, l. ii. [c. 29] p. 105.

66. Eusebius in Vit. Constant. l. iv. c. 15, 16.

67. The theory and practice of antiquity, with regard to the sacrament of baptism, have been copiously explained by Dom Chardon, Hist. des Sacremens, tom. p. i. 3–405; Dom Martenne, de Ritibus Ecclesiæ Antiquis, tom. i.; and by Bingham, in the tenth and eleventh books of his Christian Antiquities. One circumstance may be observed in which the modern churches have materially departed from the ancient custom. The sacrament of baptism (even when it was administered to infants) was immediately followed by confirmation and the holy communion.

68. The Fathers, who censured this criminal delay, could not deny the certain and victorious efficacy even of a death-bed baptism. The ingenious rhetoric of the Chrysostom could find only three arguments against these prudent Christians. 1. That we should love and pursue virtue for her own sake, and not merely for the reward. 2. That we may be surprised by death without an opportunity of baptism. 3. That, although we shall be placed in heaven, we shall only twinkle like little stars, when compared to the suns of righteousness who have run their appointed course with labour, with success, and with glory. Chrysostom, in Epist. ad Hebræos, Homil. xiii. apud. Chardon, Hist. des Sacremens, tom. i. p. 49. I believe that this delay of baptism, though attended with the most pernicious consequences, was never condemned by any general or provincial council, or by any public act or declaration of the church. The zeal of the bishops was easily kindled on much slighter occasions.

69. Zosimus, l. ii. [c. 29] p. 104. For this disingenuous falsehood he has deserved and experienced the harshest treatment from all the ecclesiastical writers, except Cardinal Baronius (A.D. 324, No. 15–28,) who had occasion to employ the infidel on a particular service against the Arian Eusebius.

70. Eusebius [Vit. Constant.], l. iv. c. 61, 62, 63. The bishop of Cæsarea supposes the salvation of Constantine with the most perfect confidence.

71. See Tillemont, Hist. des Empereurs, tom. iv. p. 429. The Greeks, the Russians, and, in the darker ages, the Latins themselves, have been desirous of placing Constantine in the catalogue of saints.

72. See the third and fourth books of his Life. He was accustomed to say that, whether Christ was preached in pretence or in truth, he should still rejoice (l. iii. c. 58).

73. M. de Tillemont (Hist. des Empereurs, tom. iv. p. 374, 616) has defended with strength and spirit the virgin purity of Constantinople against some malevolent insinuations of the Pagan Zosimus.

74. The author of the Histoire Politique et Philosophique des deux Indes (tom. i. p. 9) condemns a law of Constantine which gave freedom to all the slaves who should embrace Christianity. The emperor did indeed publish a law which restrained the Jews from circumcising, perhaps from keeping, any Christian slaves (see Euseb. in Vit. Constant. l. iv. c. 27, and Cod. Theod. l. xvi. tit. ix., with Godefroy's Commentary, tom. vi. p. 247). But

this imperfect exception related only to the Jews; and the great body of slaves, who were the property of Christian or Pagan masters, could not improve their temporal condition by changing their religion. I am ignorant by what guides the Abbé Raynal was deceived, as the total absence of quotations is the unpardonable blemish of his entertaining history.

75. See Acta Sti. Silvestri, and Hist. Eccles. Nicephor. Callist. l. vii. c. 34, ap. Baronium Annal. Eccles. A.D. 324, No. 67, 74. Such evidence is contemptible enough; but these circumstances are in themselves so probable, that the learned Dr. Howell (History of the World, vol. iii. p. 14) has not scrupled to adopt them.

76. The conversion of the barbarians under the reign of Constantine is celebrated by the ecclesiastical historians (see Sozomen, l. ii. c. 6, and Theodoret, l. i. c. 23, 24). But Rufinus, the Latin translator of Eusebius, deserves to be considered as an original authority. His information was curiously collected from one of the companions of the Apostle of Æthiopia, and from Bacurius, an Iberian prince, who was count of the domestics. Father Mamachi has given an ample compilation on the progress of Christianity, in the first and second volumes of his great but imperfect work.

77. See in Eusebius (in Vit. Constant. l. iv. c. 9, sqq.) the pressing and pathetic epistle of Constantine in favour of his Christian brethren of Persia.

78. See Basnage, Hist. des Juifs, tom. vii. p. 182, tom. viii. p. 333, tom. ix. p. 810. The curious diligence of this writer pursues the Jewish exiles to the extremities of the globe.

79. Theophilus had been given in his infancy as a hostage by his countrymen of the isle of Diva, and was educated by the Romans in learning and piety. The Maldives, of which Male, or Diva, may be the capital, are a cluster of 1900 or 2000 minute islands in the Indian Ocean. The ancients were imperfectly acquainted with the Maldives, but they are described in the two Mahometan travellers of the ninth century, published by Renaudot. Geograph. Nubiensis, p. 30, 31. D'Herbelot, Bibliothèque Orientale, p. 704. Hist. Générale des Voyages, tom. viii.

80. Philostorgius, l. iii. c. 4, 5, 6, with Godefroy's learned observations. The historical narrative is soon lost in an inquiry concerning the seat of Paradise, strange monsters, etc.

81. See the epistle of Osius, ap. Athanasium, vol. i. p. 840. The public remonstrance which Osius was forced to address to the son contained the same principles of ecclesiastical and civil government which he had secretly instilled into the mind of the father.

82. M. de la Bastie (Mémoires de l'Académie des Inscriptions, tom. xv. p. 38–61) has evidently proved that Augustus and his successors exercised in person all the sacred functions of pontifex maximus, or high priest, of the Roman empire.

83. Something of a contrary practice had insensibly prevailed in the church of Constantinople; but the rigid Ambrose commanded Theodosius to retire below the rails, and taught him to know the difference between a king and a priest. See Theodoret, l. v. c. 18.

84. At the table of the emperor Maximus, Martin, bishop of Tours, received the cup from an attendant, and gave it to the presbyter his companion, before he allowed the emperor to drink; the empress waited on Martin at table. Sulpicius Severus, in Vit. Sti. Martin, c. 23, and Dialogue ii. 7. Yet it may be doubted whether these extraordinary compliments were paid to the bishop or the saint. The honours usually granted to the former character may be seen in Bingham's Antiquities, l. ii. c. 9, and Vales. ad Theodoret, l. iv. c. 6. See the haughty ceremonial which Leontius, bishop of Tripoli, imposed on the empress. Tillemont, Hist. des Empereurs, tom. iv. p. 754. (Patres Apostol. tom. ii. p. 179.)

85. Plutarch, in his treatise of Isis and Osiris, informs us that the kings of Egypt, who were not already priests, were initiated, after their election, into the sacerdotal order.

86. The numbers are not ascertained by any ancient writer or original catalogue; for the partial lists of the eastern churches are comparatively modern. The patient diligence of Charles a Sto. Paolo, of Luke Holstenius, and of Bingham, has laboriously investigated all the episcopal sees of the Catholic church, which was almost commensurate with the Roman empire. The ninth book of the Christian Antiquities is a very accurate map of ecclesiastical geography.

87. On the subject of the rural bishops, or Chorepiscopi, who voted in synods, and conferred the minor orders, see Thomassin, Discipline de l'Eglise, tom. i. p. 447, etc. and Chardon, Hist. des Sacramens, tom. v. p. 395, etc. They do not appear till the fourth century; and this equivocal character, which had excited the jealousy of the prelates, was abolished before the end of the tenth, both in the East and the West.

88. Thomassin (Discipline de l'Eglise, tom. ii. l. ii. c. 1–8, p. 673–721) has copiously treated of the election of bishops during the five first centuries, both in the East and in the West; but he shows a very partial bias in favour of the episcopal aristocracy. Bingham (l. iv. c. 2) is moderate; and Chardon (Hist. des Sacramens, tom. v. p. 106–128) is very clear and concise.

89. Incredibilis multitudo, non solum ex eo oppido (Tours), sed etiam ex vicinis urbibus ad suffragia ferenda convenerat, etc. Sulpicius Severus, in Vit. Martin. c. 7. The council of Laodicea (canon xiii.) prohibits mobs and tumults; and Justinian confines the right of election to the nobility. Novell. cxxiii. 1.

90. The epistles of Sidonius Apollinaris (iv. 25, vii. 5, 9) exhibit some of the scandals of the Gallican church; and Gaul was less polished and less corrupt than the East.

91. A compromise was sometimes introduced by law or by consent; either the bishops or the people chose one of the three candidates who had been named by the other party.

92. All the examples quoted by Thomassin (Discipline de l'Eglise, tom. ii. l. ii. c. vi. p. 704–714) appear to be extraordinary acts of power, and even of oppression. The confirmatie of the bishop of Alexandria is mentioned by Philostorgius as a more regular proceeding (Hist. Eccles. l. ii. 11).

93. The celibacy of the clergy during the first five or six centuries is a subject of discipline, and indeed of controversy, which has been very diligently examined. See in particular Thomassin Discipline de l'Eglise, tom. i. l. ii. c. lx. lxi. p. 886–902; and Bingham's Antiquities, l. iv. c. 5. By each of these learned but partial critics one half of the truth is produced, and the other is concealed.

94. Diodorus Siculus attests and approves the hereditary succession of the priesthood among the Egyptians, the Chaldeans, and the Indians (l. i. [c. 73] p. 84, l. ii. [c. 29 and 40] p. 142, 153, edit. Wesseling). The Magi are described by Ammianus as a very numerous family: "Per sæcula multa ad præsens unâ eâdemque prosapiâ multitudo creata, Deorum cultibus dedicatur" (xxiii. 6). Ausonius celebrates the *Stirps Druidarum* (De Professorib. Burdigal. iv. [7]); but we may infer from the remark of Cæsar (Bell. Gall. vi. 13), that in the Celtic hierarchy some room was left for choice and emulation.

95. The subject of the vocation, ordination, obedience, etc., of the clergy, is laboriously discussed by Thomassin (Discipline de l'Eglise, tom. ii. p. 1–83) and Bingham (in the 4th book of his Antiquities, more especially the 4th, 6th, and 7th chapters). When the brother of St. Jerom was ordained in Cyprus, the deacons forcibly stopped his mouth, lest he should make a solemn protestation which might invalidate the holy rites.

96. The charter of immunities, which the clergy obtained from the Christian emperors, is obtained in the 16th book of the Theodosian code; and is illustrated with tolerable candour by the learned Godefroy, whose mind was balanced by the opposite prejudices of a civilian and a Protestant.

97. Justinian. Novell. ciii. Sixty presbyters or priests, one hundred deacons, forty deaconesses, ninety sub-deacons, one hundred and ten readers, twenty-five chanters, and one hundred doorkeepers; in all, five hundred and twenty-five. This moderate number was fixed by the emperor to relieve the distress of the church, which had been involved in debt and usury by the expense of a much higher establishment.

98. Universus clerus ecclesiæ Carthaginiensis . . . fere *quingenti* vel amplius; inter quos quamplurimi erant lectores infantuli. Victor Vitensis, de Persecut. Vandal. v. 9, p. 78, edit. Ruinart. This remnant of a more prosperous state still subsisted under the oppression of the Vandals.

99. The number of *seven* orders has been fixed in the Latin church, exclusive of the episcopal character. But the four inferior ranks, the minor orders, are now reduced to empty and useless tithes.

100. See Cod. Theodos. l. xvi. tit. ii. leg. 42, 43. Godefroy's Commentary, and the Ecclesiastical History of Alexandria, show the danger of these pious institutions, which often disturbed the peace of that turbulent capital.

101. The edict of Milan (de M. P. c. 48) acknowledges, by reciting, that there existed a species of landed property, ad jus corporis eorum, id est, ecclesiarum non hominum singulorum pertinentia. Such a solemn declaration of the supreme magistrate must have been received in all the tribunals as a maxim of civil law.

102. Habeat unusquisque licentiam sanctissimo Catholicæ (*ecclesiæ*) venerabilique concilio, decedens bonorum quod optavit relinquere. Cod. Theodos. l. xvi. tit. ii. leg. 4. This law was published at Rome, A.D. 321, at a time when Constantine might foresee the probability of a rupture with the emperor of the East.

103. Eusebius, Hist. Eccles. l. x. 6, in Vit. Constantin. l. iv. c. 28. He repeatedly expatiates on the liberality of the Christian hero, which the bishop himself had an opportunity of knowing, and even of tasting.

104. Eusebius, Hist. Eccles. l. x. c. 2, 3, 4. The bishop of Cæsarea, who studied and gratified the taste of his master, pronounced in public an elaborate description of the church of Jerusalem (in Vit. Const. l. iv. c. 46). It no longer exists, but he has inserted in the Life of Constantine (l. iii. c. 36) a short account of the architecture and ornaments. He likewise mentions the church of the Holy Apostles at Constantinople (l. iv. c. 58).

105. See Justinian, Novell. cxxiii. 3. The revenue of the patriarchs, and the most wealthy bishops, is not expressed: the highest annual valuation of a bishopric is stated at *thirty*, and the lowest at *two*, pounds of gold; the medium might be taken at *sixteen*, but these valuations are much below the real value.

106. See Baronius (Annal. Eccles. A.D. 324, No. 58, 65, 70, 71). Every record which comes from the Vatican is justly suspected; yet these rent-rolls have an ancient and authentic colour; and it is at least evident that, if forged, they were forged in a period when *farms*, not *kingdoms*, were the objects of papal avarice.

107. See Thomassin, Discipline de l'Eglise, tom. iii. l. ii. c. 13, 14, 15, p. 689–706. The legal division of the ecclesiastical revenue does not appear to have been established in the time of Ambrose and Chrysostom. Simplicius and Gelasius, who were bishops of Rome in the latter part of the fifth century, mention it in their pastoral letters as a general law, which was already confirmed by the custom of Italy.

108. Ambrose, the most strenuous asserter of ecclesiastical privileges, submits without a murmur to the payment of the land-tax. "Si tributum petit

Imperator, non negamus; agri ecclesiæ solvunt tributum; solvimus quæ sunt Cæsaris Cæsari, and quæ sunt Dei Deo; tributum Cæsaris est; non negatur." Baronius labours to interpret this tribute as an act of charity rather than of duty (Annal. Eccles. A.D. 387); but the words, if not the intentions of Ambrose, are more candidly explained by Thomassin, Discipline de l'Eglise, tom. iii. l. i. c. 34, p. 268.

109. In Ariminensi synodo super ecclesiarum et clericorum privilegiis tractatû habito, usque eo dispositio progressa est, ut juga quæ viderentur ad ecclesiam pertinere, a publicâ functione cessarent inquietudine desistente; quod nostra videtur dudum sanctio repulsisse. Cod. Theod. l. xvi. tit. ii. leg. 15. Had the synod of Rimini carried this point, such practical merit might have atoned for some speculative heresies.

110. From Eusebius (in Vit. Constant. l. iv. c. 27) and Sozomen (l. i. c. 9) we are assured that the episcopal jurisdiction was extended and confirmed by Constantine; but the forgery of a famous edict, which was never fairly inserted in the Theodosian Code (see at the end, tom. vi. p. 303), is demonstrated by Godefroy in the most satisfactory manner. It is strange that M. de Montesquieu, who was a lawyer as well as a philosopher, should allege this edict of Constantine (The Spirit of Laws, xxiii. 21) without intimating any suspicion.

111. The subject of ecclesiastical jurisdiction has been involved in a mist of passion, of prejudice, and of interest. Two of the fairest books which have fallen into my hands are the Institutes of Canon Law, by the Abbé de Fleury, and the Civil History of Naples, by Giannone. Their moderation was the effect of situation as well as of temper. Fleury was a French ecclesiastic, who respected the authority of the parliaments; Giannone was an Italian lawyer, who dreaded the power of the church. And here let me observe that, as the general propositions which I advance are the result of *many* particular and imperfect facts, I must either refer the reader to those modern authors who have expressly treated the subject, or swell these notes to a disagreeable and disproportionate size.

112. Tillemont has collected from Rufinus, Theodoret, etc. the sentiments and language of Constantine. Mém. Ecclés. tom. iii. p. 749, 750.

113. See Cod. Theod. l. ix. tit. xlv. leg. 4. In the works of Fra Paolo (tom. iv. p. 192, etc.) there is an excellent discourse on the origin, claims, abuses, and limits of sanctuaries. He justly observes that ancient Greece might perhaps contain fifteen or twenty *asyla* or sanctuaries; a number which at present may be found in Italy within the walls of a single city.

114. The penitential jurisprudence was continually improved by the canons of the councils. But as many cases were still left to the discretion of the bishops, they occasionally published, after the example of the Roman prætor, the rules of discipline which they proposed to observe. Among the ca-

nonical epistles of the fourth century, those of Basil the Great were the most celebrated. They are inserted in the Pandects of Beveridge (tom. ii. p. 47–151), and are translated by Chardon, Hist. des Sacremens, tom. iv. p. 219–277.

115. Basil. Epistol. xlvii. in Baronius (Annal. Eccles. A.D. 370, No. 91), who declares that he purposely relates it to convince governors that they were not exempt from a sentence of excommunication. In his opinion, even a royal head is not safe from the thunders of the Vatican; and the cardinal shows himself much more consistent than the lawyers and theologians of the Gallican church.

116. The long series of his ancestors, as high as Eurysthenes, the first Doric king of Sparta, and the fifth in lineal descent from Hercules, was inscribed in the public registers of Cyrene, a Lacedæmonian colony. (synes. Epist. lvii. p. 197, edit. Petav.) Such a pure and illustrious pedigree of seventeen hundred years, without adding the royal ancestors of Hercules, cannot be equalled in the history of mankind.

117. Synesius (de Regno, p. 2 [ed. Par. 1612]) pathetically deplores the fallen and ruined state of Cyrene, πόλις Ἑλληνὶς, παλαιὸν ὄνομα καὶ σεμνὸν, καὶ ἐν ᾠδῇ μυρίᾳ τῶν πάλαι σοφῶν, νῦν πένης καὶ κατηφὴς, καὶ μέγα ἐρείπιον. Ptolemais, a new city, 82 miles to the westward of Cyrene, assumed the metropolitan honours of the Pentapolis, or Upper Libya, which were afterwards transferred to Sozusa. See Wesseling, Itinerar. p. 67, 68, 732. Cellarius Geograph. tom. ii. part ii. p. 72, 74. Carolus a Sto. Paulo, Geograph. Sacra, p. 273. D'Anville, Géographie Ancienne, tom. iii. p. 43, 44. Mémoires de l'Acad. des Inscriptions, tom. xxxvii. p. 363–391.

118. Synesius had previously represented his own disqualifications (Epist. cv. p. 246–250). He loved profane studies and profane sports; he was incapable of supporting a life of celibacy; he disbelieved the resurrection; and he refused to preach *fables* to the people, unless he might be permitted to *philosophise* at home. Theophilus, primate of Egypt, who knew his merit, accepted this extraordinary compromise. See the Life of Synesius in Tillemont, Mém. Ecclés. tom. xii. p. 499–554.

119. See the invective of Synesius, Epist. lvii. p. 191–201. The promotion of Andronicus was illegal, since he was a native of Berenice, in the same province. The instruments of tortures are curiously specified—the πιεστήριον, or press, the δακτυλήθρα, the ποδοστράβη, the ῥινολάβις, the φτάγρα, and the χειλοστρόφιον, that variously pressed or distended the fingers, the feet, the nose, the ears, and the lips of the victims.

120. The sentence of excommunication is expressed in a rhetorical style. (Synesius, Epist. lviii. p. 201–203.) The method of involving whole families, though somewhat unjust, was improved into national interdicts.

121. See Synesius, Epist. xlvii. p. 186, 187; Epist. lxxii. p. 218, 219; Epist. lxxxix, p. 230, 231.

122. See Thomassin (Discipline de l'Eglise, tom.

ii. l. iii. c. 83, p. 1761–1770) and Bingham (Antiquities, vol. i. l. xiv. c. 4, p. 688–717). Preaching was considered as the most important office of the bishop; but this function was sometimes intrusted to such presbyters as Chrysostom and Augustin.

123. Queen Elizabeth used this expression and practised this art whenever she wished to prepossess the minds of her people in favour of any extraordinary measure of government. The hostile effects of this *music* were apprehended by her successor, and severely felt by his son. "When pulpits drum ecclesiastic," etc. See Haylin's Life of Archbishop Laud, p. 153.

124. Those modest orators acknowledged that, as they were destitute of the gift of miracles, they endeavoured to acquire the arts of eloquence.

125. The council of Nice, in the fourth, fifth, sixth, and seventh canons, has made some fundamental regulations concerning synods, metropolitans, and primates. The Nicene canons have been variously tortured, abused, interpolated, or forged, according to the interest of the clergy. The *Suburbicarian* churches, assigned (by Rufinus) to the bishop of Rome, have been made the subject of vehement controversy. (See Sirmond, Opera, tom. iv. p. 1–238.)

126. We have only thirty-three or forty-seven episcopal subscriptions; but Ado, a writer indeed of small account, reckons six hundred bishops in the council of Arles. Tillemont, Mém. Ecclés. tom. vi. p. 422.

127. See Tillemont, tom. vi. p. 915, and Beausobre, Hist. du Manichéisme, tom. i. p. 529. The name of *bishop*, which is given by Eutychius to the 2048 ecclesiastics (Annal. tom. i. p. 440, vers. Pocock), must be extended far beyond the limits of an orthodox or even episcopal ordination.

128. See Euseb. in Vit. Constantin. l. iii. c. 6–21. Tillemont. Mém. Ecclésiastiques, tom. vi. p. 669–759.

129. Sancimus igitur vicem legum obtinere, quæ a quatuor Sanctis Conciliis . . . expositæ sunt aut firmatæ. Prædictarum enim quatuor synodorum dogmata sicut sanctas Scripturas et regulas sicut leges observamus. Justinian, Novell. cxxxi. Beveridge (ad Pandect. proleg. p. 2) remarks that the emperors never made new laws in ecclesiastical matters; and Giannone observes, in a very different spirit, that they gave a legal sanction to the canons of councils. Istoria Civile di Napoli, tom. i. p. 136.

130. See the article CONCILE in the Encyclopédie, tom. iii. p. 668–679, édition de Lucques. The author, M. le docteur Bouchaud, has discussed, according to the principles of the Gallican church, the principal questions which relate to the form and constitution of general, national, and provincial councils. The editors (see Preface, p. xvi.) have reason to be proud of *this* article. Those who consult their immense compilation seldom depart so well satisfied.

Chapter XXI

1. Eusebius in Vit. Constantin. l. iii. c. 63, 64, 65, 66.

2. After some examination of the various opinions of Tillemont, Beausobre, Lardner, etc., I am convinced that Manes did not propagate his sect, even in Persia, before the year 270. It is strange that a philosophic and foreign heresy should have penetrated so rapidly into the African provinces; yet I cannot easily reject the edict of Diocletian against the Manichæans, which may be found in Baronius. (Annal. Eccl. A.D. 287.)

3. Constantinus enim, cum limatius superstitionum quæerret sectas, Mannichæorum et similium, etc., Ammian. xv. 13. Strategius, who from this commission obtained the surname of *Musonianus*, was a Christian of the Arian sect. He acted as one of the counts at the council of Sardica. Libanius praises his mildness and prudence. Vales. ad locum Ammian.

4. Cod. Theod. l. xvi. tit. v. leg. 2. As the general law is not inserted in the Theodosian Code, it is probable that, in the year 438, the sects which it had condemned were already extinct.

5. Sozomen, l. i. c. 22. Socrates, l. i. c. 10. These historians have been suspected, but I think without reason, of an attachment to the Novatian doctrine. The emperor said to the bishop, "Acesius, take a ladder, and get up to heaven by yourself." Most of the Christian sects have, by turns, borrowed the ladder of Acesius.

6. The best materials for this part of ecclesiastical history may be found in the edition of Optatus Milevitanus, published (Paris, 1700) by M. Dupin, who has enriched it with critical notes, geographical discussions, original records, and an accurate abridgment of the whole controversy. M. de Tillemont has bestowed on the Donatists the greatest part of a volume (tom. vi. part i.): and I am indebted to him for an ample collection of all the passages of his favourite St. Augustin which relate to those heretics.

7. Schisma igitur illo tempore confusæ mulieris iracundia peperit; ambitus nutrivit; avaritia roboravit. Optatus, l. i. c. 19. The language of Purpurius is that of a furious madman. Dicitur te necasse filios sororis tuæ duos. Purpurius respondit: Putas me terreri à te . . . occidi; et occido eos qui contra me faciunt. Acta Concil. Cirtensis, ad calc. Optat. p. 274. When Cæcilian was invited to an assembly of bishops, Purpurius said to his brethren, or rather to his accomplices, "Let him come hither to receive our imposition of hands, and we will

break his head by way of penance." Optat. l. i. c. 19.

8. The councils of Arles, of Nice, and of Trent, confirmed the wise and moderate practice of the church of Rome. The Donatists, however, had the advantage of maintaining the sentiment of Cyprian, and of a considerable part of the primitive church. Vincentius Lirinensis (p. 332, ap. Tillemont, Mém. Ecclés. tom. vi. p. 138) has explained why the Donatists are eternally burning with the Devil, while St. Cyprian reigns in heaven with Jesus Christ.

9. See the sixth book of Optatus Milevitanus, p. 91–100.

10. Tillemont, Mém. Ecclésiastiques, tom. vi. part i. p. 253. He laughs at their partial credulity. He revered Augustin, the great doctor of the system of predestination.

11. Plato Ægyptum peregravit ut a sacerdotibus barbaris numeros et cælestia acciperet. Cicero de Finibus, v. 29. The Egyptians might still preserve the traditional creed of the patriarchs. Josephus has persuaded many of the Christian fathers that Plato derived a part of his knowledge from the Jews; but this vain opinion cannot be reconciled with the obscure state and unsocial manners of the Jewish people, whose scriptures were not accessible to Greek curiosity till more than one hundred years after the death of Plato. See Marsham, Canon. Chron. p. 144. Le Clerc, Epistol. Critic. vii. p. 177–194.

12. The modern guides who lead me to the knowledge of the Platonic system are Cudworth (Intellectual System, p. 568–620), Basnage (Hist. des Juifs, l. iv. c. 4, p. 53–86), Le Clerc (Epist. Crit. vii. p. 194–209), and Brucker (Hist. Philosoph. tom. i. p. 675–706). As the learning of these writers was equal, and their intention different, an inquisitive observer may derive instruction from their disputes, and certainty from their agreement.

13. Brucker, Hist. Philosoph. tom. i. p. 1349–1357. The Alexandrian school is celebrated by Strabo (l. xvii. [p. 794, ed. Casaub.]) and Ammianus (xxii. 16).

14. Joseph Antiquitat. l. xii. c. 1, 3. Basnage, Hist. des Juits, l. vii. c. 7.

15. For the origin of the Jewish philosophy, see Eusebius, Præparat. Evangel. viii. 9, 10. According to Philo, the Therapeutæ studied philosophy; and Brucker has proved (Hist. Philosoph. tom. ii. p. 787) that they gave the preference to that of Plato.

16. See Calmet, Dissertations sur la Bible, tom. ii. p. 277. The book of the Wisdom of Solomon was received by many of the fathers as the work of that monarch; and although rejected by the Protestants for want of a Hebrew original, it has obtained, with the rest of the Vulgate, the sanction of the council of Trent.

17. The Platonism of Philo, which was famous to a proverb, is proved beyond a doubt by Le Clerc (Epist. Crit. viii. p. 211–228). Basnage (Hist. des Juifs, l. iv. c. 5) has clearly ascertained that the theological works of Philo were composed before the death, and most probably before the birth, of Christ. In such a time of darkness the knowledge of Philo is more astonishing than his errors. Bull, Defens. Fid. Nicen. s. i. c. i. p. 12.

18. Mens agitat molem, et magno se corpore miscet.

Besides this material soul, Cudworth has discovered (p. 562) in Amelius, Porphyry, Plotinus, and, as he thinks, in Plato himself, a superior spiritual hypercosmian soul of the universe. But this double soul is exploded by Brucker, Basnage, and Le Clerc, as an idle fancy of the latter Platonists.

19. Petav. Dogmata Theologica, tom. ii. l. viii. c. 2. 791. Bull, Defens. Fid. Nicen. s. i. c. 1, p. 8, 13. This notion, till it was abused by the Arians, was freely adopted in the Christian theology. Tertullian (adv. Praxeam, c. 16) has a remarkable and dangerous passage. After contrasting, with indiscreet wit, the nature of God and the actions of Jehovah, he concludes: Scilicet ut hæc de filio Dei non credenda fuisse, si non scripta essent; fortasse non credenda de Patre licet scripta.

20. The Platonists admired the beginning of the Gospel of St. John, as containing an exact transcript of their own principles. Augustine, The City of God, x. 29. Amelius apud Cyril. advers Julian l. viii. p. 283. But in the third and fourth centuries the Platonists of Alexandria might improve their Trinity by the secret study of the Christian theology.

21. See Beausobre, Hist. Critique du Manichéisme, tom. i. p. 377. The Gospel according to St. John is supposed to have been published about seventy years after the death of Christ.

22. The sentiments of the Ebionites are fairly stated by Mosheim (p. 331) and Le Clerc (Hist. Ecclés. p. 535). The Clementines, published among the apostolical Fathers, are attributed by the critics to one of these sectaries.

23. Staunch polemics, like Bull (Judicium Ecclés. Cathol. c. 2), insist on the orthodoxy of the Nazarenes; which appears less pure and certain in the eyes of Mosheim (p. 330).

24. The humble condition and sufferings of Jesus have always been a stumbling-block to the Jews. "Deus . . . contrariis coloribus Messiam depinxerat; futurus erat Rex, Judex, Pastor," etc. See Limborch et Orobio Amica Collat. p. 8, 19, 53–76, 192–234. But this objection has obliged the believing Christians to lift up their eyes to a spiritual and everlasting kingdom.

25. Justin Martyr. Dialog. cum Tryphonte, p. 143, 144. See Le Clerc, Hist. Ecclés. p. 615. Bull, and his editor Grabe (Judicium Eccles. Cathol. c. 7, and Appendix), attempt to distort either the sentiments or the words of Justin; but their violent correction of the text is rejected even by the Benedictine editors.

26. The Arians reproached the orthodox party with borrowing their Trinity from the Valentin-

ians and Marcionites. See Beausobre, Hist. du Manichéisme, l. iii. c. 5, 7.

27. Non dignum est ex utero credere Deum, et Deum Christum . . . non dignum est ut tanta majestas per sordes et squalores mulieris transire credatur. The Gnostics asserted the impurity of matter and of marriage; and they were scandalised by the gross interpretations of the fathers, and even of Augustin himself. See Beausobre, tom. ii. p. 523.

28. Apostolis adhuc in sæculo superstitibus apud Judæam Christi sanguine recente, et phantasma corpus Domini asserebatur. Cotelerius thinks (Patres Apostol. tom. ii. p. 24) that those who will not allow the Docetes to have arisen in the time of the Apostles may with equal reason deny that the sun shines at noonday. These Docetes, who formed the most considerable party among the Gnostics, were so called, because they granted only a seeming body to Christ.

29. Some proofs of the respect which the Christians entertained for the person and doctrine of Plato may be found in De la Mothe le Vayer, tom. v. p. 135, etc., edit. 1757; and Basnage, Hist. des Juifs, tom. iv. p. 29, 79, etc.

30. Doleo bona fide, Platonem omnium hæreticorum condimentarium factum. Tertullian. de Anima, c. 23. Petavius (Dogm. Theolog. tom. iii. proleg. 2) shows that this was a general complaint. Beausobre (tom. i. l. iii. c. 9, 10) has deduced the Gnostic errors from Platonic principles; and as, in the school of Alexandria, those principles were blended with the Oriental philosophy (Brucker, tom. i. p. 1356), the sentiment of Beausobre may be reconciled with the opinion of Mosheim (General History of the Church, vol. i. p. 37).

31. If Theophilus, bishop of Antioch (see Dupin, Bibliothèque Ecclésiastique, tom. i. p. 66), was the first who employed the word Triad, Trinity, that abstract term, which was already familiar to the schools of philosophy, must have been introduced into the theology of the Christians after the middle of the second century.

32. Athanasius, tom. i. p. 808. His expressions have an uncommon energy; and as he was writing to monks, there could not be any occasion for him to affect a rational language.

33. In a treatise which professed to explain the opinions of the ancient philosophers concerning the nature of the gods, we might expect to discover the theological Trinity of Plato. But Cicero very honestly confessed that, though he had translated the Timæus, he could never understand that mysterious dialogue. See Hieronym. præf. ad l. xii. in Isaiam, tom. v. p. 154 [tom. iv. p. 494, ed. Vallars.].

34. Tertullian. in Apolog. c. 46. See Bayle, Dictionnaire, au mot Simonide. His remarks on the presumption of Tertullian are profound and interesting.

35. Lactantius, iv. 8. Yet the Probole, or Prolatio, which the most orthodox divines borrowed without scruple from the Valentinians, and illustrated by the comparisons of a fountain and stream, the sun and its rays, etc., either meant nothing, or

favoured a material idea of the divine generation. See Beausobre, tom. i. l. iii. c. 7, p. 548.

36. Many of the primitive writers have frankly confessed that the Son owed his being to the will of the Father. See Clarke's Scripture Trinity, p. 280–287. On the other hand, Athanasius and his followers seem unwilling to grant what they are afraid to deny. The schoolmen extricate themselves from this difficulty by the distinction of a preceding and a concomitant will. Petav. Dogm. Theolog. tom. ii. l. vi. c. 8, p. 587–603.

37. See Petav. Dogm. Theolog. tom. ii. l. ii. c. 10, p. 159.

38. Carmenque Christo quasi Deo dicere secum invicem. Plin. Epist. x. 97. The sense of Deus, θεός Elohim, in the ancient languages, is critically examined by Le Clerc (Ars Critica, p. 150–156), and the propriety of worshipping a very excellent creature is ably defended by the Socinian Emlyn (Tracts, p. 29–36, 51–145).

39. See Daillé, de Usu Patrum, and Le Clerc, Bibliothèque Universelle, tom. x. p. 409. To arraign the faith of the Ante-Nicene fathers was the object, or at least has been the effect, of the stupendous work of Petavius on the Trinity (Dogm. Theolog. tom. ii.); nor has the deep impression been erased by the learned defence of Bishop Bull.

40. The most ancient creeds were drawn up with the greatest latitude. See Bull (Judicium Eccles. Cathol.), who tries to prevent Episcopius from deriving any advantage from this observation.

41. The heresies of Praxeas, Sabellius, etc., are accurately explained by Mosheim (p. 425, 680–714). Praxeas, who came to Rome about the end of the second century, deceived, for some time, the simplicity of the bishop, and was confuted by the pen of the angry Tertullian.

42. Socrates acknowledges that the heresy of Arius proceeded from his strong desire to embrace an opinion the most diametrically opposite to that of Sabellius.

43. The figure and manners of Arius, the character and numbers of his first proselytes, are painted in very lively colours by Epiphanius (tom. i. Hæres. lxix. 3, p. 729 [ed. Paris, 1622]), and we cannot but regret that he should soon forget the historian, to assume the task of controversy.

44. See Philostorgius (l. i. c. 3) ,and Godefroy's ample Commentary. Yet the credibility of Philostorgius is lessened, in the eyes of the orthodox, by his Arianism; and in those of rational critics, by his passion, his prejudice, and his ignorance.

45. Sozomen (l. i. c. 15) represents Alexander as indifferent, and even ignorant, in the beginning of the controversy; while Socrates (l. i. c. 5) ascribes the origin of the dispute to the vain curiosity of his theological speculations. Dr. Jortin (Remarks on Ecclesiastical History, vol. ii. p. 178) has censured, with his usual freedom, the conduct of Alexander; πρὸς ὀργὴν ἐξαπτέται . . . ὁμοίως φρόνειν ἐκέλευσε.

46. The flames of Arianism might burn for some time in secret; but there is reason to believe that

they burst out with violence as early as the year 319. Tillemont, Mém. Ecclés. tom. vi. p. 774–780.

47. Quid credidit? Certe, *aut* tria nomina audiens tres Deos esse credidit, et idololatra effectus est; *aut* in tribus vocabulis trinominem credens Deum, in Sabellii hæresim incurrit; *aut* edoctus ab Arianis unum esse verum Deum Patrem, filium et spiritum sanctum credidit creaturas. Aut extra hæc quid credere portuerit nescio. Hieronym. adv. Luciferianos [tom. ii. p. 184, ed. Vallars.]. Jerom reserves for the last the orthodox system, which is more complicated and difficult.

48. As the doctrine of absolute creation from nothing was gradually introduced among the Christians (Beausobre, tom. ii. p. 165–215), the dignity of the *workman* very naturally rose with that of the *work*.

49. The metaphysics of Dr. Clarke (Scripture Trinity, p. 276–280) could digest an eternal generation from an infinite cause.

50. This profane and absurd simile is employed by several of the primitive fathers, particularly by Athenagoras, in his Apology to the emperor Marcus and his son; and it is alleged, without censure, by Bull himself. See Defens. Fid. Nicen. sect. iii. c. 5, No. 4.

51. See Cudworth's Intellectual System, p. 559, 579. This dangerous hypothesis was countenanced by the two Gregories, of Nyssa and Nazianzen, by Cyril of Alexandria, John of Damascus, etc. See Cudworth, p. 603. Le Clerc, Bibliothèque Universelle, tom. xviii. p. 97–105.

52. Augustin seems to envy the freedom of the philosophers. Liberis verbis loquuntur philosophi . . . Nos autem non dicimus duo vel tria principia, duos vel tres Deos. The City of God, x. 23-24.

53. Boethius, who was deeply versed in the philosophy of Plato and Aristotle, explains the unity of the Trinity by the *indifference* of the three persons. See the judicious remarks of Le Clerc, Bibliothèque Choisie, tom. xvi. p. 225, etc.

54. If the Sabellians were startled at this conclusion, they were driven down another precipice into the confession that the Father was born of a virgin, that *he* had suffered on the cross; and this deserved the odious epithet of *Patripassians*, with which they were branded by their adversaries. See the invectives of Tertullian against Praxeas, and the temperate reflections of Mosheim (p. 423, 681); and Beausobre, tom. i. l. iii. c. 6, p. 533.

55. The transactions of the council of Nice are related by the ancients, not only in a partial, but in a very imperfect manner. Such a picture as Fra Paolo would have drawn can never be recovered; but such rude sketches as have been traced by the pencil of bigotry, and that of reason, may be seen in Tillemont (Mém. Ecclés. tom. vi. p. 669–759), and in Le Clerc (Bibliothèque Universelle, tom. x. p. 435–454).

56. We are indebted to Ambrose (De Fide, l. iii. cap. ult.) for the knowledge of this curious anecdote. Hoc verbum posuerunt Patres, quod viderunt adversariis esse formidini; ut tanquam evaginato ab ipsis gladio, ipsum nefandæ caput hæreseos amputarent.

57. See Bull. Defens. Fid. Nicen. sect. ii. c. i. p. 25–36. He thinks it his duty to reconcile two orthodox synods.

58. According to Aristotle, the stars were homoousian to each other. "That *Homoousius* means of one substance in *kind*, hath been shown by Petavius, Curcellæus, Cudworth, Le Clerc, etc., and to prove it would be *actum agere*." This is the just remark of Dr. Jortin (vol. ii. p. 212), who examines the Arian controversy with learning, candour, and ingenuity.

59. See Petavius (Dogm. Theolog. tom. ii. l. iv. c. 16, p. 453, etc.), Cudworth (p. 559), Bull (sect. iv. p. 285–290, edit. Grab.). The περιχώρησις, or *circumincessio*, is perhaps the deepest and darkest corner of the whole theological abyss.

60. The third section of Bull's Defence of the Nicene Faith, which some of his antagonists have called nonsense, and others heresy, is consecrated to the supremacy of the Father.

61. The ordinary appellation with which Athanasius and his followers chose to compliment the Arians was that of *Ariomanites*.

62. Epiphanius, tom. i. Hæres. lxxii. 4, p. 837. See the adventures of Marcellus, in Tillemont (Mém. Ecclés. tom. vii. p. 880–899). His work, in *one* book, of the Unity of God, was answered in the *three* books, which are still extant, of Eusebius. After a long and careful examination, Petavius (tom. ii. l. i. c. 14, p. 78) has reluctantly pronounced the condemnation of Marcellus.

63. Athanasius, in his epistle concerning the synods of Seleucia and Rimini (tom. i. p. 886–905 [p. 735 *seqq.*, ed. Bened.]), has given an ample list of Arian creeds, which has been enlarged and improved by the labours of the indefatigable Tillemont. (Mém. Ecclés. tom. vi. p. 477).

64. Erasmus, with admirable sense and freedom, has delineated the just character of Hilary. To revise his text, to compose the annals of his life, and to justify his sentiments and conduct, is the province of the Benedictine editors.

65. Absque episcopo Eleusio et paucis cum eo, ex majore parte Asianæ decem provinciæ, inter quas consisto, vere Deum nesciunt. Atque utinam penitus nescirent! cum procliviore enim veniâ ignorarent quam obtrectarent. Hilar. de Synodis, sive de Fide Orientalium, c. 63, p. 1186, edit. Benedict. In the celebrated parallel between atheism and superstition, the bishop of Poitiers would have been surprised in the philosophic society of Bayle and Plutarch.

66. Hilarius ad Constantium, l. i. c. 4, 5, p. 1227, 1228. This remarkable passage deserved the attention of Mr. Locke, who has transcribed it (vol. iii. p. 470) into the model of his new commonplace book.

67. In Philostorgius (l. iii. c. 15) the character and adventures of Aëtius appear singular enough,

though they are carefully softened by the hand of a friend. The editor Godefroy (p. 153), who was more attached to his principles than to his author, has collected the odious circumstances which his various adversaries have preserved or invented.

68. According to the judgment of a man who respected both those sectaries, Aëtius had been endowed with a stronger understanding, and Eunomius had acquired more art and learning (Philostorgius, l. viii. c. 18). The confession and apology of Eunomius (Fabricius, Bibliot. Græc. tom. viii. p. 258–305) is one of the few heretical pieces which have escaped.

69. Yet, according to the opinion of Estius and Bull (p. 297), there is one power, that of creation, which God *cannot* communicate to a creature. Estius, who so accurately defined the limits of Omnipotence, was a Dutchman by birth, and by trade a scholastic divine. Dupin, Bibliot. Ecclés. tom. xvii. p. 45.

70. Sabinus (ap. Socrat. l. ii. c. 39) had copied the acts; Athanasius and Hilary have explained the divisions of this Arian synod; the other circumstances which are relative to it are carefully collected by Baronius and Tillemont.

71. Fideli et piâ intelligentiâ . . . De Synod. c. 77, p. 1193. In his short apological notes (first published by the Benedictines from a MS. of Chartres) he observes that he used this cautious expression, quia intelligerem et impiam, p. 1206. See p. 1146. Philostorgius, who saw those objects through a different medium, is inclined to forget the difference of the important diphthong. See in particular viii. 17, and Godefroy, p. 352.

72. Testor Deum cœli atque terræ me cum neutrum audissem, semper tamen utrumque sensisse. . . . Regeneratus pridem et in episcopatu aliquantisper manens fidem Nicenam nunquam nisi exsulaturus audivi. Hilar. de Synodis, c. xci. p. 1205. The Benedictines are persuaded that he governed the diocese of Poitiers several years before his exile.

73. Seneca (Epist. lviii.) complains that even the τὸ ὄν of the Platonists (the *ens* of the bolder schoolmen) could not be expressed by a Latin noun.

74. The preference which the fourth council of the Lateran at length gave to a *numerical* rather than a *generical* unity (see Petav. tom. ii. l. iv. c. 13, p. 424) was favoured by the Latin language: τρίας seems to excite the idea of substance, *trinitas* of qualities.

75. Ingemuit totus orbis, et Arianum se esse miratus est. Hieronym, adv. Lucifer, tom. i. p. 145. [Tom. ii. p. 191, ed. Vallars.]

76. The story of the council of Rimini is very elegantly told by Sulpicius Severus (Hist. Sacra. l. ii. p. 419–430. edit. Lugd. Bat. 1647), and by Jerom, in his dialogue against the Luciferians. The design of the latter is to apologise for the conduct of the Latin bishops, who were deceived, and who repented.

77. Eusebius, in Vit. Constant. l. ii. c. 64–72.

The principles of toleration and religious indifference contained in this epistle have given great offence to Baronius, Tillemont, etc., who suppose that the emperor had some evil counsellor, either Satan or Eusebius, at his elbow. See Jortin's Remarks, tom. ii. p. 183.

78. Eusebius in Vit. Constantin. l. iii. c. 13.

79. Theodoret has preserved (l. i. c. 20) an epistle from Constantine to the people of Nicomedia, in which the monarch declares himself the public accuser of one of his subjects; he styles Eusebius ὁ τὴν τυραννικῆς ὠμότητος συμμύστης; and complains of his hostile behavior during the civil war.

80. See in Socrates (l. i. c. 8), or rather in Theodoret (l. i. c. 12), an original letter of Eusebius of Cæsarea, in which he attempts to justify his subscribing the Homoousion. The character of Eusebius has always been a problem; but those who have read the second critical epistle of Le Clerc (Ars Critica, tom. iii. p. 30–69) must entertain a very unfavourable opinion of the orthodoxy and sincerity of the bishop of Cæsarea.

81. Athanasius, tom. i. p. 727 [tom. i. p. 247, ed. Bened.); Philostorgius, l. i. c. 10; and Godefroy's Commentary, p. 41.

82. Socrates, l. i. c. 9. In his circular letters, which were addressed to the several cities, Constantine employed against the heretics the arms of ridicule and *comic* raillery.

83. We derive the original story from Athanasius (tom. i. p. 670), who expresses some reluctance to stigmatise the memory of the dead. He might exaggerate; but the perpetual commerce of Alexandria and Constantinople would have rendered it dangerous to invent. Those who press the literal narrative of the death of Arius (his bowels suddenly burst out in a privy) must make their option between *poison* and *miracle*.

84. The change in the sentiments, or at least in the conduct of Constantine, may be traced in Eusebius (in Vit. Constant. l. iii. c. 23, l. iv. c. 41), Socrates (l. i. c. 23–39), Sozomen (l.ii. c. 16–34), Theodoret (l. i. c. 14–34), and Philostorgius (l.ii. c. 1–17). But the first of these writers was too near the scene of action, and the others were too remote from it. It is singular enough that the important task of continuing the history of the church should have been left for two laymen and a heretic.

85. Quia etiam tum catechumenus sacramentum fidei merito videretur potuisse nescire. Sulp. Sever. Hist. Sacra, l. ii. p. 410.

86. Socrates, l. ii. c. 2. Sozomen, l. iii. c. 18. Athanas. tom. i. p. 813, 834 [tom. i. p. 289, ed. Bened. Patav. 1777]. He observes that the eunuchs are the natural enemies of the *Son*. Compare Dr. Jortin's Remarks on Ecclesiastical History, vol. iv. p. 3, with a certain genealogy in *Candide* (ch. iv.), which ends with one of the first companions of Christopher Columbus.

87. Sulpicius Severus in Hist. Sacra. l. ii. p. 405, 406.

88. Cyril (apud Baron. A.D. 353, No. 26) ex-

pressly observes that in the reign of Constantine the cross had been found in the bowels of the earth; but that it had appeared, in the reign of Constantius, in the midst of the heavens. This opposition evidently proves that Cyril was ignorant of the stupendous miracle to which the conversion of Constantine is attributed; and this ignorance is the more surprising, since it was no more than twelve years after his death that Cyril was consecrated bishop of Jerusalem by the immediate successor of Eusebius of Cæsarea. See Tillemont, Mém. Ecclés. tom. viii. p. 715.

89. It is not easy to determine how far the ingenuity of Cyril might be assisted by some natural appearances of a solar halo.

90. Philostorgius, l. iii. c. 26. He is followed by the author of the Alexandrian Chronicle, by Cedrenus, and by Nicephorus (see Gothofred. Dissert. p. 188). They could not refuse a miracle, even from the hand of an enemy.

91. So curious a passage well deserves to be transcribed. Christianam religionem absolutam et simplicem, anili superstitione confundens; in quâ scrutandâ perplexius, quam componendâ gravius excitaret discidia plurima; quæ progressa fusius aluit concertatione verborum, ut catervis antistitum jumentis publicis ultro citroque discurrentibus, per synodos (quas appellant) dum ritum omnem ad suum trahere conantur (Valesius reads conatur) rei vehiculariæ concideret nervos. Ammianus, xxi. 16.

92. Athanas, tom. i. p. 870.

93. Socrates, l. ii. c. 35–47. Sozomen, l. iv. c. 12–30. Theodoret, l. ii. c. 18–32. Philostorg. l. iv. c. 4–12, l. v. c. 1–4, l. vi. c. 1–5.

94. Sozomen, l. iv. c. 23. Athanas. tom. i. p. 831 [tom. i. p. 281, ed. Ben.]. Tillemont (Mém. Ecclés. tom. vii. p. 947) has collected several instances of the haughty fanaticism of Constantius from the detached treatises of Lucifer of Cagliari. The very titles of these treatises inspire zeal and terror:— "Moriendum pro Dei Filio." "De Regibus Apostaticis." "De non conveniendo cum Hæretico." "De non parcendo in Deum delinquentibus."

95. Sulp. Sever. Hist. Sacra. l. ii. p. 418–430. The Greek historians were very ignorant of the affairs of the West.

96. We may regret that Gregory Nazianzen composed a panegyric instead of a life of Athanasius, but we should enjoy and improve the advantage of drawing our most authentic materials from the rich fund of his own epistles and apologies (tom. i. p. 670–951). I shall not imitate the example of Socrates (l. ii. c. 1), who published the first edition of his history without giving himself the trouble to consult the writings of Athanasius. Yet even Socrates, the more curious Sozomen, and the learned Theodoret, connect the life of Athanasius with the series of ecclesiastical history. The diligence of Tillemont (tom. viii.) and of the Benedictine editors has collected every fact and examined every difficulty.

97. Sulpicius Severus (Hist. Sacra. l. ii. p. 396) calls him a lawyer, a jurisconsult. This character cannot now be discovered either in the life or writings of Athanasius.

98. Dicebatur enim fatidicarum sortium fidem, quæve augurales portenderent alites scientissime callens aliquoties præedixisse futura. Ammianus, xv. 7. A prophecy, or rather a joke, is related by Sozomen (l. iv. c. 10), which evidently proves (if the crows speak Latin) that Athanasius understood the language of the crows.

99. The irregular ordination of Athanasius was slightly mentioned in the councils which were held against him (see Philostorg. l. ii. c. 11, and Godefroy, p. 71); but it can scarcely be supposed that the assembly of the bishops of Egypt would solemnly attest a *public* falsehood. Athanas. tom. i. p. 726.

100. See the History of the Fathers of the Desert, published by Rosweide; and Tillemont, Mém. Ecclés. tom. vii., in the Lives of Antony Pachomius, etc. Athanasius himself, who did not disdain to compose the life of his friend Antony, has carefully observed how often the holy monk deplored and prophesied the mischiefs of the Arian heresy. Athanas. tom. ii. p. 492, 498, etc. [tom. i. p. 677, ed. Bened.]

101. At first Constantine threatened in *speaking*, but requested in *writing*, καὶ ἀγράφως μὲν ἠπείλει, γράφων δὲ ἠξίου. His letters gradually assumed a menacing tone; but while he required that the entrance of the church should be open to *all*, he avoided the odious name of Arius. Athanasius, like a skilful politician, has accurately marked these distinctions (tom. i. p. 788 [tom. i. p. 140, ed. Bened.]), which allowed him some scope for excuse and delay.

102. The Meletians in Egypt, like the Donatists in Africa, were produced by an episcopal quarrel which arose from the persecution. I have not leisure to pursue the obscure controversy, which seems to have been misrepresented by the partiality of Athanasius and the ignorance of Epiphanius. See Mosheim's General History of the Church, vol. i. p. 201.

103. The treatment of the six bishops is specified by Sozomen (l. ii. c. 25); but Athanasius himself, so copious on the subject of Arsenius and the chalice, leaves this grave accusation without a reply.

104. Athanas. tom. i. p. 788 [tom. i. p. 147, ed. Bened.]. Socrates, l. i. c. 28. Sozomen, l. ii. c. 25. The emperor, in his Epistle of Convocation (Euseb. in Vit. Constant. l. iv. c. 42), seems to prejudge some members of the clergy, and it was more than probable that the synod would apply those reproaches to Athanasius.

105. See, in particular, the second Apology of Athanasius (tom. i. p. 763–808), and his Epistles to the Monks (p. 808–866) [tom. i. p. 271 *sqq.* ed. Bened.]. They are justified by original and authentic documents; but they would inspire more confidence if he appeared less innocent, and his enemies less absurd.

106. Eusebius in Vit. Constantin. l. iv. c. 41-47.

107. Athanas. tom. i. p. 804 [tom. i. p. 159, ed. Bened. 1777]. In a church dedicated to St. Athanasius, this situation would afford a better subject for a picture than most of the stories of miracles and martyrdoms.

108. Athanas. tom. i. p. 729 [tom. i. p. 104, ed. Bened.]. Eunapius has related (in Vit. Sophist. p. 36, 37 [in Ædesio], edit. Commelin) a strange example of the cruelty and credulity of Constantine on a similar occasion. The eloquent Sopater, a Syrian philosopher, enjoyed his friendship, and provoked the resentment of Ablavius, his Prætorian præfect. The corn-fleet was detained for want of a south wind; the people of Constantinople were discontented; and Sopater was beheaded, on a charge that he had *bound* the winds by the power of magic. Suidas adds, that Constantine wished to prove, by this execution, that he had absolutely renounced the superstition of the Gentiles.

109. In his return he saw Constantius twice—at Viminiacum, and at Cæsarea in Cappadocia (Athanas. tom. i. p. 676 [tom. i. p. 236, ed. Bened.]). Tillemont supposes that Constantine introduced him to the meeting of the three royal brothers in Pannonia. (Mémoires Ecclés. tom. viii. p. 69.)

110. See Beveridge, Pandect. tom. i. p. 429-452, and tom. ii. Annotation. p. 182; Tillemont, Mém. Ecclés. tom. vi. p. 310-324. St. Hilary of Poitiers has mentioned this synod of Antioch with too much favour and respect. He reckons ninety-seven bishops.

111. This magistrate, so odious to Athanasius, is praised by Gregory Nazianzen, tom. i. Orat. xxi. p. 390, 391 [ed. Par. 1630].

Sæpe premente Deo fert Deus alter opem.

For the credit of human nature, I am always pleased to discover some good qualities in those men whom party has represented as tyrants and monsters.

112. The chronological difficulties which perplex the residence of Athanasius at Rome are strenuously agitated by Valesius (Observat. ad Calcem, tom. ii.; Hist. Eccles. l. i. c. 1-5) and Tillemont (Mém. Ecclés. tom. viii. p. 674, etc.). I have followed the simple hypothesis of Valesius, who allows only one journey after the intrusion of Gregory.

113. I cannot forbear transcribing a judicious observation of Wetstein (Prolegomen. N. T. p. 19): —Si tamen Historiam Ecclesiasticam velimus consulere, patebit jam inde a seculo quarto, cum, ortis controversiis, ecclesiæ Græciæ doctores in duas partes scinderentur, ingenio, eloquentiâ, numero, tantum non æquales, eam partem quæ vincere cupiebat Romam confugisse, majestatemque pontificis comiter coluisse, eoque pacto oppressis per pontificem et episcopos Latinos adversariis prævaluisse, atque orthodoxiam in conciliis stabilivisse. Eam ob causam Athanasius, non sine comitatu Romam petiit, pluresque annos ibi hæsit.

114. Philostorgius, l. iii. c. 12. If any corruption was used to promote the interest of religion, an advocate of Athanasius might justify or excuse this questionable conduct by the example of Cato and Sidney, the former of whom is *said* to have given, and the latter to have received, a bribe in the cause of liberty.

115. The canon which allows appeals to the Roman pontiffs has almost raised the council of Sardica to the dignity of a general council, and its acts have been ignorantly or artfully confounded with those of the Nicene synod. See Tillemont, tom. viii. p. 689; and Geddes's Tracts, vol. ii. p. 419-460.

116. As Athanasius dispersed secret invectives against Constantius (see the Epistle to the Monks) at the same time that he assured him of his profound respect, we might distrust the professions of the archbishop. Tom. i. p. 677.

117. Notwithstanding the discreet silence of Athanasius and the manifest forgery of a letter inserted by Socrates, these menaces are proved by the unquestionable evidence of Lucifer of Cagliari, and even of Constantius himself. See Tillemont, tom. viii. p. 693.

118. I have always entertained some doubts concerning the retractation of Ursacius and Valens (Athanas. tom. i. p. 776 [tom. i. p. 139, ed, Bened. 1777]). Their epistles to Julius bishop of Rome, and to Athanasius himself, are of so different a cast from each other, that they cannot both be genuine: the one speaks the language of criminals who confess their guilt and infamy, the other of enemies, who solicit on equal terms an honourable reconciliation.

119. The circumstances of his second return may be collected from Athanasius himself, tom. i. p. 769, and 822, 843 [tom. i. p. 283, ed. Bened.]. Socrates, l. ii. c. 15. Sozomen, l. iii. c. 19. Theodoret, l. ii. c. 11, 12. Philostorgius, l. iii. c. 12.

120. Athanasius (tom. i. p. 677, 678 [tom. i. p. 239, ed. Bened.]) defends his innocence by pathetic complaints, solemn assertions, and specious arguments. He admits that letters had been forged in his name, but he requests that his own secretaries and those of the tyrant may be examined, whether those letters had been written by the former or received by the latter.

121. Athanas. tom. i. p. 825-844.

122. Athanas. tom. i. p. 861. Theodoret, l. ii. c. 16. The emperor declared that he was more desirous to subdue Athanasius than he had been to vanquish Magnentius or Sylvanus.

123. The affairs of the council of Milan are so imperfectly and erroneously related by the Greek writers, that we must rejoice in the supply of some letters of Eusebius, extracted by Baronius from the archives of the church of Vercellæ, and of an old Life of Dionysius of Milan, published by Bollandus. See Baronius, A.D. 355, and Tillemont, tom. vii. p. 1415.

124. The honours, presents, feasts, which seduced so many bishops, are mentioned with indignation by those who were too pure or too proud to accept

them. "We combat" (says Hilary of Poitiers) "against Constantius the Antichrist, who strokes the belly instead of scourging the back;" qui non dorsa cædit, sed ventrem palpat. Hilarius contra Constant. c. 5, p. 1240.

125. Something of this opposition is mentioned by Ammianus (xv. 7), who had a very dark and superficial knowledge of ecclesiastical history. Liberius . . . perseveranter renitebatur, nec visum hominem, nec auditum damnare, nefas ultimum sæpe exclamans; aperte scilicet recalcitrans Imperatoris arbitrio. Id enim ille Athanasio semper infestus, etc.

126. More properly by the orthodox part of the council of Sardica. If the bishops of both parties had fairly voted, the division would have been 94 to 76. M. de Tillemont (see tom. viii. p. 1147–1158) is justly surprised that so small a majority should have proceeded so vigorously against their adversaries, the principal of whom they immediately deposed.

127. Sulp. Severus, in Hist. Sacra, l. ii. p. 412.

128. The exile of Liberius is mentioned by Ammianus, xv. 7. See Theodoret, l. ii. c. 16. Athanas. tom. i. p. 834–837 [tom. i. p. 161, ed. Bened.]. Hilar. Fragment. i.

129. The life of Osius is collected by Tillemont (tom. vii. p. 524–561), who, in the most extravagant terms, first admires and then reprobates the bishop of Cordova. In the midst of their lamentations on his fall, the prudence of Athanasius may be distinguished from the blind and intemperate zeal of Hilary.

130. The confessors of the West were successively banished to the deserts of Arabia or Thebaïs, the lonely places of Mount Taurus, the wildest parts of Phrygia, which were in the possession of the impious Montanists, etc. When the heretic Aëtius was too favorably entertained at Mopsuestia in Cilicia, the place of his exile was changed, by the advice of Acacius, to Amblada, a district inhabited by savages, and infested by war and pestilence. Philostorg. l. v. c. 2.

131. See the cruel treatment and strange obstinacy of Eusebius, in his own letters, published by Baronius, A.D. 356, No. 92–102.

132. Cæterum exules satis constat, totius orbis studiis celebratos, pecuniasque eis in sumptum affatim congestas, legationibus quoque eos plebis catholicæ ex omnibus fere provinciis frequentatos. Sulp. Sever. Hist. Sacra. p. 414. Athanas. tom. i. p. 836, 840.

133. Ample materials for the history of this third persecution of Athanasius may be found in his own works. See particularly his very able Apology to Constantius (tom. i. p. 673 [tom. i. p. 233 sqq. ed. Bened.]), his first Apology for his flight (p. 701 [tom. i. p. 253 sqq. ed. Bened.]), his prolix Epistle to the Solitaries (p. 808), and the original Protest of the People of Alexandria against the violences committed by Syrianus (p. 866 [p. 311, ed. Bened.]). Sozomen (l. iv. c. 9) has thrown into the narrative two or three luminous and important circumstances.

134. Athanasius had lately sent for Antony and some of his chosen monks. They descended from their mountain, announced to the Alexandrians the sanctity of Athanasius, and were honourably conducted by the archbishop as far as the gates of the city. Athanas. tom. ii. p. 491, 492 [tom. i. p. 677 sq. ed. Bened. 1777]. See likewise Rufinus, iii. 164, in Vit. Patr. p. 524.

135. Athanas. tom. i p. 694 [tom. i. p. 249, ed. Bened.]. The emperor, or his Arian secretaries, while they express their resentment, betray their fears and esteem of Athanasius.

136. These minute circumstances are curious, as they are literally transcribed from the protest which was publicly presented three days afterwards by the catholics of Alexandria. See Athanas. tom. i. p. 867 [tom. i. p. 311, ed. Bened. 1777].

137. The Jansenists have often compared Athanasius and Arnauld, and have expatiated with pleasure on the faith and zeal, the merit and exile, of those celebrated doctors. This concealed parallel is very dexterously managed by the Abbé de la Bléterie, Vie de Jovien, tom. i. p. 130.

138. Hinc jam toto orbe profugus [agitur] Athanasius, nec ullus ei tutus ad latendum supererat locus. Tribuni, Præfecti, Comites, exercitus quoque, ad pervestigandum eum moventur edictis Imperialibus; præmia delatoribus proponuntur, si quis eum vivum, si id minus, caput certe Athanasii detulisset. Rufin. l. i. c. 18.

139. Gregor. Nazianzen. tom. i. Orat. xxi. p. 384, 385. See Tillemont, Mém. Ecclés. tom. vii. p. 176–410, 820–880.

140. Et nulla tormentorum vis inveniri adhuc potuit, quæ obdurato illius tractûs latroni invito elicere potuit, ut nomen proprium dicat. Ammian. xxii. 16, and Valesius ad locum.

141. Rufin. l. i. c. 18. Sozomen, l. iv. c. 10. This and the following story will be rendered impossible if we suppose that Athanasius always inhabited the asylum which he accidentally or occasionally had used.

142. Palladius (Hist. Lausiac. c. 136 in Vit. Patrum, p. 776 [p. 230, ed. Paris, Pallad. 1555]), the original author of this anecdote, had conversed with the damsel, who in her old age still remembered so pious and honourable a connection. I cannot indulge the delicacy of Baronius, Valesius, Tillemont, etc., who almost reject a story so unworthy, as they deem it, of the gravity of ecclesiastical history.

143. Athanas. tom. i. p. 869 [tom. i. p. 572, ed. Bened. 1777]. I agree with Tillemont (tom. viii. p. 1197), that his expressions imply a personal, though perhaps secret, visit to the synods.

144. The epistle of Athanasius to the monks is filled with reproaches, which the public must feel to be true (vol. i. p. 834, 856 [tom. i. p. 304, ed. Bened.]); and, in compliment to his readers, he has introduced the comparisons of Pharaoh, Ahab,

Belshazzar, etc. The boldness of Hilary was attended with less danger, if he published his invective in Gaul after the revolt of Julian; but Lucifer sent his libels to Constantius, and almost challenged the reward of martyrdom. See Tillemont, tom. vii. p. 905.

145. Athanasius (tom. i. p. 811) complains in general of this practice, which he afterwards exemplifies (p. 861 [tom. i. p. 307, ed. Bened.]) in the pretended election of Felix. Three eunuchs represented the Roman people, and three prelates, who followed the court, assumed the functions of the bishops of the Suburbicarian provinces.

146. Thomassin (Discipline de l'Eglise, tom. i. l. ii. c. 72, 73, p. 966–984) has collected many curious facts concerning the origin and progress of church-singing, both in the East and West.

147. Philostorgius, l. iii. c. 13. Godefroy has examined this subject with singular accuracy (p. 147, etc.). There were three heterodox forms: "To the Father *by* the Son, *and* in the Holy Ghost;" "To the Father *and* the Son, *in* the Holy Ghost;" and "To the Father *in* the Son *and* the Holy Ghost."

148. After the exile of Eustathius, under the reign of Constantine, the rigid party of the orthodox formed a separation which afterwards degenerated into a schism, and lasted above fourscore years. See Tillemont, Mém. Ecclés. tom. vii. p. 35–54, 1137–1158, tom, viii. p. 573–632, 1314–1332. In many churches the Arians and Homoousians, who had renounced each other's *communion*, continued for some time to join in prayer. Philostorgius, l. iii. c. 14.

149. See, on this ecclesiastical revolution of Rome, Ammianus, xv. 7. Athanas. tom. i. p. 834, 861 [tom. i. p. 307, ed. Bened.]. Sozomen, l. iv. c. 15. Theodoret, l. ii. c. 17. Sulp. Sever. Hist. Sacra, l. ii. p. 413. Hieronym. Chron. Marcellin. et Faustin. Libell. p. 3, 4. Tillemont, Mém. Ecclés. tom. vi. p. 336.

150. Cucusus was the last stage of his life and sufferings. The situation of that lonely town, on the confines of Cappadocia, Cilicia, and the Lesser Armenia, has occasioned some geographical perplexity; but we are directed to the true spot by the course of the Roman road from Cæsarea to Anazarbus. See Cellarii Geograph. tom. ii. p. 213; Wesseling, ad Itinerar. p. 179, 703.

151. Athanasius (tom. i. p. 703, 813, 814 [tom. i. p. 275, ed. Bened.]) affirms, in the most positive terms, that Paul was murdered; and appeals, not only to common fame, but even to the unsuspicious testimony of Philagrius, one of the Arian persecutors. Yet he acknowledges that the heretics attributed to disease the death of the bishop of Constantinople. Athanasius is servilely copied by Socrates (l. ii. c. 26); but Sozomen, who discovers a more liberal temper, presumes (l. iv. c. 2) to insinuate a prudent doubt.

152. Ammianus (xiv. 10) refers to his own account of this tragic event. But we no longer possess that part of his history.

153. See Socrates, l. ii. c. 6, 7, 12, 13, 15, 16, 26, 27, 38; and Sozomen, l. iii. 3, 4, 7, 9, l. iv. c. 2, 21. The acts of St. Paul of Constantinople, of which Photius has made an abstract (Phot. Biblioth. p. 1419–1430), are an indifferent copy of these historians; but a modern Greek, who could write the Life of a saint without adding fables and miracles, is entitled to some commendation.

154. Socrates, l. ii. c. 27, 38. Sozomen, l. iv. c. 21. The principal assistants of Macedonius, in the work of persecution, were the two bishops of Nicomedia and Cyzicus, who were esteemed for their virtues, and especially for their charity. I cannot forbear reminding the reader that the difference between the *Homoousion* and *Homoiousion* is almost invisible to the nicest theological eye.

155. We are ignorant of the precise situation of Mantinium. In speaking of these *four* bands of legionaries, Socrates, Sozomen, and the author of the Acts of St. Paul, use the indefinite terms of ἀριθμοί, φάλαγγες, τάγματα, which Nicephorus very properly translates *thousands*. Vales. ad. Socrat. l. ii. c. 38.

156. Julian. Epistol. lii. p. 436, edit. Spanheim.

157. See Optatus Milevitanus (particularly iii. 4), with the Donatist history by M. Dupin, and the original pieces at the end of his edition. The numerous circumstances which Augustin has mentioned, of the fury of the Circumcellions against others and against themselves, have been laboriously collected by Tillemont, Mém. Ecclés. tom. vi. p. 147–165; and he has often though without design, exposed the injuries which had provoked those fanatics.

158. It is amusing enough to observe the language of opposite parties when they speak of the same men and things. Gratus, bishop of Carthage, begins the acclamations of an orthodox synod, "Gratias Deo omnipotenti et Christo Jesu . . . qui imperavit religiosissimo Constanti Imperatori, ut votum gereret unitatis, et mitteret ministros sancti operis *famulos Dei* Paulum et Macarium." Monument. Vet. ad Calcem Optati, p. 313. "Ecce subito," (says the Donatist author of the Passion of Marculus) "de Constantis regis tyrannicâ domo . . . pollutum Macarianæ persecutionis murmur increpuit, et *duabus bestiis* ad Africam missis, eodem scilicet Macario et Paulo, execrandum prorsus ac dirum ecclesiæ certamen indictum est; ut populus Christianus ad unionem cum traditoribus faciendam, nudatis militum gladiis et draconum præsentibus signis, et tubarum vocibus cogeretur." Monument. p. 304.

159. The Histoire des Camisards, in 3 vols. 12mo., Villefranche, 1760, may be recommended as accurate and impartial. It requires some attention to discover the religion of the author.

160. The Donatist suicides alleged in their justification the example of Razias, which is related in the 14th chapter of the second book of the Maccabees.

161. Nullas infestas hominibus bestias, ut sunt sibi ferales plerique Christianorum, expertus. Ammian. xxii. 5.

162. Gregor. Nazianzen, Orat. i. p. 33. See Tillemont, tom. vi. p. 501, quarto edit.

163. Histoire Politique et Philosophique des Etablissemens des Européens dans les deux Indes, tom. i. p. 9.

164. According to Eusebius (in Vit. Constantin. l. ii. c. 45) the emperor prohibited, both in cities and in the country, τὰ μυσαρὰ . . . τῆς εἰδωλολατρείας; the abominable acts or parts of idolatry. Socrates (l. i. c. 18) and Sozomen (l. ii. c. 4, 5) have represented the conduct of Constantine with a just regard to truth and history, which has been neglected by Theodoret (l. v. c. 21) and Orosius (vii. 28). Tum deinde (says the latter) primus Constantinus *justo* ordine et *pio* vicem vertit edicto; siquidem statuit citra ullam hominum cædem, paganorum templa claudi.

165. See Eusebius in Vit. Constantin. l. ii. c. 56, 60. In the sermon to the assembly of saints which the emperor pronounced when he was mature in years and piety, he declares to the idolaters (c. xi.) that they are permitted to offer sacrifices and to exercise every part of their religious worship.

166. See Eusebius, in Vit. Constantin. l. iii. c. 54–58, and l. iv. c. 23, 25. These acts of authority may be compared with the suppression of the Bacchanals, and the demolition of the temple of Isis, by the magistrates of Pagan Rome.

167. Eusebius (in Vit. Constant. l. iii. c. 54) and Libanius (Orat. pro Templis, p. 9, 10, edit. Gothofred.) both mention the pious sacrilege of Constantine, which they viewed in very different lights. The latter expressly declares that "he made use of the sacred money, but made no alteration in the legal worship; the temples indeed were impoverished, but the sacred rites were performed there." Lardner's Jewish and Heathen Testimonies, vol. iv. p. 140.

168. Ammianus (xxii. 4) speaks of some court eunuchs who were spoliis templorum pasti. Libanius says (Orat. pro Templ. p. 23) that the emperor often gave away a temple, like a dog, or a horse, or a slave, or a gold cup: but the devout philosopher takes care to observe that these sacrilegious favourites very seldom prospered.

169. See Gothofred. Cod. Theodos. tom. vi. p. 262. Liban. Orat. Parental. c. x. in Fabric. Bibl. Græc. tom. vii. p. 235 [ed. Hamb. 1715].

170. Placuit omnibus locis atque urbibus universis claudi protinus templa, et accessu vetitis omnibus licentiam delinquendi perditis abnegari. Volumus etiam cunctos a sacrificiis abstinere. Quod siquis aliquid forte hujusmodi perpetraverit, gladio [ultore] sternatur: facultates etiam perempti fisco decernimus vindicari: et similiter adfligi rectores provinciarum si facinora vindicare neglexerint. Cod. Theodos. l. xvi. tit. x. leg. 4. Chronology has discovered some contradiction in the date of this extravagant law; the only one, perhaps, by which the negligence of magistrates is punished by death and confiscation. M. de la Bastie (Mém. de l'Acédémie, tom. xv. p. 98) con-

jectures, with a show of reason, that this was no more than the minutes of a law, the heads of an intended bill, which were found in Scriniis Memoriæ, among the papers of Constantius, and afterwards inserted, as a worthy model, in the Theodosian Code.

171. Symmach. Epistol. x. 54 [p. 289, ed. Paris, 1604].

172. The fourth Dissertation of M. de la Bastie, sur le Souverain Pontificat des Empereurs Romains (in the Mém. de l'Acad. tom. xv. 75–144), is a very learned and judicious performance, which explains the state, and proves the toleration, of Paganism from Constantine to Gratian. The assertion of Zosimus [iv. 36], that Gratian was the first who refused the pontifical robe, is confirmed beyond a doubt; and the murmurs of bigotry on that subject are almost silenced.

173. As I have freely anticipated the use of *pagans* and paganism, I shall now trace the singular revolutions of those celebrated words. 1. Πάγη, in the Doric dialect, so familiar to the Italians, signifies a fountain; and the rural neighbourhood which frequented the same fountain derived the common appellation of *pagus* and *pagans* (Festus sub voce, and Servius ad Virgil. Georgic. ii. 382). 2. By an easy extension of the word, *pagan* and rural became almost synonymous (Plin. Hist. Natur. xxviii. 5); and the meaner rustics acquired that name, which has been corrupted into *peasants* in the modern languages of Europe. 3. The amazing increase of the military order introduced the necessity of a correlative term (Hume's Essays, vol. i. p. 555); and all the *people* who were not enlisted in the service of the prince were branded with the contemptuous epithet of pagans (Tacit. Hist. iii. 24, 43, 77. Juvenal. Satir. 16 [v. 32]. Tertullian de Pallio, c. 4). 4. The Christians were the soldiers of Christ; their adversaries who refused his *sacrament*, or military oath of baptism, might deserve the metaphorical name of pagans; and this popular reproach was introduced as early as the reign of Valentinian (A.D. 365) into Imperial laws (Cod. Theodos. l. xvi. tit. ii. leg. 18) and theological writings. 5. Christianity gradually filled the cities of the empire: the old religion, in the time of Prudentius (advers. Symmachum, l. i. [v. 575 *sqq.*] ad fin.) and Orosius (in Præfat. Hist.), retired and languished in obscure villages; and the word *pagans*, with its new signification, reverted to its primitive origin. 6. Since the worship of Jupiter and his family has expired, the vacant title of Pagans has been successively applied to all the idolaters and polytheists of the old and new world. 7. The Latin Christians bestowed it, without scruple, on their mortal enemies the Mahometans; and the purest *Unitarians* were branded with the unjust reproach of idolatry and paganism. See Gerard Vossius, Etymologicon Linguæ Latinæ, in his works, tom. i. p. 420; Godefroy's Commentary on the Theodosian Code, tom. vi. p. 250; and Ducange mediæ et infimæ Latinitat. Glossar.

174. In the pure language of Ionia and Athens, Εἴδωλον and Λατρεία were ancient and familiar words. The former expressed a likeness, an apparition (Homer. Odys. xi. 602), a representation, an *image*, created either by fancy or art. The latter denoted any sort of *service* or slavery. The Jews of Egypt, who translated the Hebrew Scriptures, restrained the use of these words (Exod. xx. 4, 5) to the religious worship of an image. The peculiar idiom of the Hellenists, or Grecian Jews, has been adopted by the sacred and ecclesiastical writers; and the reproach of *idolatry* (Εἰδωλολατρεία) has stigmatised that visible and abject mode of superstition which some sects of Christianity should not hastily impute to the polytheists of Greece and Rome.

Chapter XXII

1. Omnes qui plus poterant in palatio, adulandi professores jam docti, recte consulta, prospereque completa vertebant in deridiculum: talia sine modo strepentes insulse; in odium venit cum victoriis suis; capella, non homo; ut hirsutum Julianum carpentes, appellantesque loquacem talpam, et purpuratam simiam, et litterionem Græcum: et his congruentia plurima atque vernacula principi resonantes, audire hæc taliaque gestienti, virtutes ejus obruere verbis impudentibus conabantur, ut segnem incessentes et timidum et umbratilem, gestaque secus verbis comptioribus exornantem. Ammianus, xvii. 11.

2. Ammian. xvi. 12 [*fin.*]. The orator Themistius (iv. p. 56, 57) believed whatever was contained in the Imperial letters, which were addressed to the senate of Constantinople. Aurelius Victor, who published his Abridgment in the last year of Constantius, ascribes the German victories to the *wisdom* of the emperor and the *fortune* of the Cæsar. Yet the historian, soon afterwards, was indebted to the favour or esteem of Julian for the honour of a brass statue, and the important offices of consular of the second Pannonia and præfect of the city. Ammian. xxi. 10.

3. Callido nocendi artificio, accusatoriam diritatem laudum titulis peragebant. . . . Hæ voces fuerunt ad inflammanda odia probris omnibus potentiores. See Mamertin. in Actione Gratiarum in Vet. Panegyr. xi. 4, 5.

4. The minute interval which may be interposed between the *hieme adultâ* and the *primo vere* of Ammianus (xx. 1, 4), instead of allowing a sufficient space for a march of three thousand miles, would render the orders of Constantius as extravagant as they were unjust. The troops of Gaul could not have reached Syria till the end of autumn. The memory of Ammianus must have been inaccurate, and his language incorrect.

5. Ammianus, xx. 1. The valour of Lupicinus and his military skill are acknowledged by the historian, who, in his affected language, accuses the general of exalting the horns of his pride, bellowing in a tragic tone, and exciting a doubt whether he was more cruel or avaricious. The danger from the Scots and Picts was so serious, that Julian himself had some thoughts of passing over into the island.

6. He granted them the permission of the *cursus clavularis*, or *clabularis*. These post-waggons are often mentioned in the Code, and were supposed to carry fifteen hundred pounds weight. See Vales. ad Ammian. xx. 4.

7. Most probably the palace of the baths (*Thermarum*), of which a solid and lofty hall still subsists in the *Rue de la Harpe*. The buildings covered a considerable space of the modern quarter of the university; and the gardens, under the Merovingian kings, communicated with the abbey of St. Germain des Prez. By the injuries of time and the Normans this ancient palace was reduced in the twelfth century to a maze of ruins, whose dark recesses were the scene of licentious love.

> Explicat aula sinus montemque amplecti-
> tur alis;
> Multiplici latebrâ scelerum tersura rubo-
> rem. . . . . . . pereuntis sæpe pudoris
> Celatura nefas, Venerisque accommoda
> furtis.

(These lines are quoted from the Architrenius, l. iv. c. 8, a poetical work of John de Hauteville, or Hanville, a monk of St. Alban's, about the year 1190. See Warton's History of English Poetry, vol. i. dissert. ii.) Yet such *thefts* might be less pernicious to mankind than the theological disputes of the Sorbonne, which have been since agitated on the same ground. Bonamy, Mém. de l'Académie, tom. xv. p. 678–682.

8. Even in this tumultuous moment Julian attended to the forms of superstitious ceremony, and obstinately refused the inauspicious use of a female necklace, or a horse-collar, which the impatient soldiers would have employed in the room of a diadem.

9. An equal proportion of gold and silver, five pieces of the former, one pound of the latter; the whole amounting to about five pounds ten shillings of our money.

10. For the whole narrative of this revolt we may appeal to authentic and original materials; Julian himself (ad S. P. Q. Atheniensem, p. 282, 283, 284), Libanius (Orat. Parental. c. 44–48, in Fabricius Biblioth. Græc. tom, vii. p. 269–273), Ammianus (xx. 4), and Zosimus (l. iii. [c. 9], p. 151, 152, 153), who, in the reign of Julian, appears to follow the more respectable authority of Eunapius. With such guides we *might* neglect the abbreviators and ecclesiastical historians.

11. Eutropius, a respectable witness, uses a doubtful expression, "consensu militum" (x. 15 [7]). Gregory Nazianzen, whose ignorance might excuse his fanaticism, directly charges the apostate with presumption, madness, and impious rebellion, αὐθάδεια, ἀπόνοια; ἀσέβεια. Orat. iii. p. 67.

12. Julian. ad S. P. Q. Athen. p. 284. The *devout* Abbé de la Bléterie (Vie de Julien, p. 159) is almost inclined to respect the *devout* protestations of a Pagan.

13. Ammian. xx. 5, with the note of Lindenbrogius on the Genius of the empire. Julian himself, in a confidential letter to his friend and physician Oribasius (Epist. xvii. p. 384), mentions another dream, to which, before the event, he gave credit; of a stately tree thrown to the ground, of a small plant striking a deep root into the earth. Even in his sleep the mind of the Cæsar must have been agitated by the hopes and fears of his fortune. Zosimus (l. iii. [c. 9] p. 155) relates a subsequent dream.

14. The difficult situation of the prince of a rebellious army is finely described by Tacitus (Hist. i. 80-85). But Otho had much more guilt and much less abilities than Julian.

15. To this ostensible epistle he added, says Ammianus, private letters, objurgatorias et mordaces, which the historian had not seen, and would not have published. Perhaps they never existed.

16. See the first transactions of his reign, in Julian ad S. P. Q. Athen. p. 285, 286. Ammianus, xx. 5, 8. Liban. Orat. Parent. c. 49, 50, p. 273-275.

17. Liban. Orat. Parent. c. 50, p. 275, 276. A strange disorder, since it continued above seven years. In the factions of the Greek republics the exiles amounted to 20,000 persons; and Isocrates assures Philip that it would be easier to raise an army from the vagabonds than from the cities. See Hume's Essays, tom. i. p. 426, 427.

18. Julian (Epist. xxxviii. p. 414) gives a short description of Vesontio, or Besançon; a rocky peninsula almost encircled by the river Doubs; once a magnificent city, filled with temples, etc., now reduced to a small town, emerging however from its ruins.

19. Vadomair entered into the Roman service, and was promoted from a barbarian kingdom to the military rank of duke of Phœnicia. He still retained the same artful character (Ammian. xxi. 3); but, under the reign of Valens, he signalised his valour in the Armenian war (xxix. 1).

20. Ammian. xx. 10, xxi. 3, 4. Zosimus, l. iii. [c. 10] p. 155.

21. Her remains were sent to Rome, and interred near those of her sister Constantina, in the suburb of the *Via Nomentana*. Ammian. xxi. 1. Libanius has composed a very weak apology, to justify his hero from a very absurd charge of poisoning his wife, and rewarding her physician with his mother's jewels. (See the seventh of seventeen new orations, published at Venice 1754, from a MS. in St. Mark's library, p. 117-127.) Elpidius, the Præ-

torian præfect of the East, to whose evidence the accuser of Julian appeals, is arraigned by Libanius as *effeminate* and ungrateful; yet the religion of Elpidius is praised by Jerom (tom. i. p. 243), and his humanity by Ammianus (xxi. 6).

22. Feriarum die, quem celebrantes mense Januario, Christiani *Epiphania* dictitant, progressus, in eorum ecclesiam, solemniter numine orato discessit. Ammian. xxi. 2. Zonaras observes that it was on Christmas Day, and his assertion is not inconsistent; since the churches of Egypt, Asia, and perhaps Gaul, celebrated on the same day (the 6th of January) the nativity and the baptism of their Saviour. The Romans, as ignorant as their brethren of the real date of his birth, fixed the solemn festival to the 25th of December, the *Brumalia*, or winter solstice, when the Pagans annually celebrated the birth of the sun. See Bingham's Antiquities of the Christian Church, l. xx. c. 4; and Beausobre, Hist. Critique du Manichéisme, tom. ii. p. 690-700.

23. The public and secret negotiations between Constantius and Julian must be extracted, with some caution, from Julian himself (Orat. ad S. P. Q. Athen. p. 286), Libanius (Orat. Parent. c. 51, p. 276), Ammianus (xx. 9), Zosimus (l. iii. [c. 9] p. 154), and even Zonaras (tom. ii. l. xiii. [c. 10] p. 20, 21, 22), who, on this occasion, appears to have possessed and used some valuable materials.

24. Three hundred myriads, or three millions, of *medimni*, a corn-measure familiar to the Athenians, and which contained six Roman *modii*. Julian explains, like a soldier and a statesman, the danger of his situation, and the necessity and advantages of an offensive war (ad S. P. Q. Athen. p. 286, 287).

25. See his oration, and the behaviour of the troops, in Ammian. xxi. 5.

26. He sternly refused his hand to the suppliant præfect, whom he sent into Tuscany (Ammian. xxi. 5). Libanius, with savage fury, insults Nebridius, applauds the soldiers, and almost censures the humanity of Julian (Orat. Parent. c. 53, p. 278).

27. Ammian. xxi. 8. In this promotion Julian obeyed the law which he publicly imposed on himself. Neque civilis quisquam judex nec militaris [militiæ] rector, alio quodam præter merita suffragante, ad potiorem veniat gradum. (Ammian. xx. 5.) Absence did not weaken his regard for Sallust, with whose name (A.D. 363) he honoured the consulship.

28. Ammianus (xxi. 8) ascribes the same practice and the same motive to Alexander the Great and other skilful generals.

29. This wood was a part of the great Hercynian forest, which, in the time of Cæsar, stretched away from the country of the Rauraci (Basel) into the boundless regions of the North. See Culver. Germania Antiqua, l. iii. c. 47.

30. Compare Libanius, Orat. Parent. c. 53, p. 278, 279, with Gregory Nazianzen, Orat. iii. p. 68.

Even the saint admires the speed and secrecy of this march. A modern divine might apply to the progress of Julian the lines which were originally designed for another apostate:—

> ———So eagerly the fiend,
> O'er bog, or steep, through strait, rough, dense, or rare,
> With head, hands, wings, or feet, pursues his way,
> And swims, or sinks, or wades, or creeps, or flies.

31. In that interval the *Notitia* places two or three fleets, the Lauriacensis (at Lauriacum, or Lorch), the Arlapensis, the Maginensis; and mentions five legions, or cohorts, of Liburnarii, who should be a sort of marines. Sect. lviii. edit. Labb.

32. Zosimus alone (l. iii. [c. 10] p. 156) has specified this interesting circumstance. Mamertinus (in Panegyr. Vet. xi. [x.] 6, 7, 8), who accompanied Julian, as count of the sacred largesses, describes this voyage in a florid and picturesque manner, challenges Triptolemus and the Argonauts of Greece, etc.

33. The description of Ammianus, which might be supported by collateral evidence, ascertains the precise situation of the *Augustiæ Succorum*, or passes of *Succi*. M. d'Anville, from the trifling resemblance of names, has placed them between Sardica and Naissus. For my own justification, I am obliged to mention the *only* error which I have discovered in the maps or writings of that admirable geographer.

34. Whatever circumstances we may borrow elsewhere, Ammianus (xxi. 8, 9, 10) still supplies the series of the narrative.

35. Ammian. xxi. 9, 10. Libanius, Orat. Parent. c. 54, p. 279, 280. Zosimus, l. iii. [c. 10] p. 156, 157.

36. Julian (ad S. P. Q. Athen. p. 286) positively asserts that he intercepted the letters of Constantius to the barbarians; and Libanius as positively affirms that he read them on his march to the troops and the cities. Yet Ammianus (xxi. 3) expresses himself with cool and candid hesitation, si *famæ solius* admittenda est fides. He specifies, however, an intercepted letter from Vadomair to Constantius, which supposes an intimate correspondence between them: "Cæsar tuus disciplinam non habet."

37. Zosimus mentions his epistles to the Athenians, the Corinthians, and the Lacedæmonians. The substance was probably the same, though the address was properly varied. The epistle to the Athenians is still extant (p. 268–287), and has afforded much valuable information. It deserves the praises of the Abbé de la Blétterie (Préf. à l'Histoire de Jovien, p. 24, 25), and is one of the best manifestoes to be found in any language.

38. *Auctori tuo reverentium rogamus.* Ammian. xxi. It is amusing enough to observe the secret conflicts of the senate between flattery and fear. See Tacit. Hist. i. 85.

39. Tanquam venaticiam prædam caperet: hoc enim ad leniendum suorum metum subinde prædicabat. Ammian. xxi. 7.

40. See the speech and preparations in Ammianus, xxi. 13. The vile Theodotus afterwards implored and obtained his pardon from the merciful conqueror, who signified his wish of diminishing his enemies and increasing the number of his friends (xxii. 14).

41. Ammian. xxi. 7, 11, 12. He seems to describe, with superfluous labour, the operations of the siege of Aquileia, which on this occasion maintained its impregnable fame. Gregory Nazianzen (Orat. iii. p. 68) ascribes this accidental revolt to the wisdom of Constantius, whose assured victory he announces with some appearance of truth. Constantio, quem credebat proculdubio fore victorem: nemo enim omnium tunc ab hac constanti sententia discrepabat. Ammian. xxi. 7.

42. His death and character are faithfully delineated by Ammianus (xxi. 14, 15, 16); and we are authorised to despise and detest the foolish calumny of Gregory (Orat. iii. p. 68), who accuses Julian of contriving the death of his benefactor. The private repentance of the emperor, that he had spared and promoted Julian (p. 69, and Orat. xxi. p. 389), is not improbable in itself, nor incompatible with the public verbal testament which prudential considerations might dictate in the last moments of his life.

43. In describing the triumph of Julian, Ammianus (xxii. 1, 2) assumes the lofty tone of an orator or poet; while Libanius (Orat. Parent. c. 56, p. 281) sinks to the grave simplicity of an historian.

44. The funeral of Constantius is described by Ammianus (xxi. 16), Gregory Nazianzen (Orat. iv. p. 119), Mamertinus (in Panegyr. Vet. xi. 27), Libanius (Orat. Parent. c. lvii. p. 283), and Philostorgius (l. vi. c. 6, with Godefroy's Dissertations, p. 265). These writers, and their followers, Pagans, Catholics, Arians, beheld with very different eyes both the dead and the living emperor.

45. The day and year of the birth of Julian are not perfectly ascertained. The day is probably the sixth of November, and the year must be either 331 or 332. Tillemont, Hist. des Empereurs, tom. iv. p. 693. Ducange, Fam. Byzantin. p. 50. I have preferred the earlier date.

46. Julian himself (p. 253–267) has expressed these philosophical ideas with much eloquence and some affectation, in a very elaborate epistle to Themistius. The Abbé de la Blétterie (tom. ii. p. 146–193), who has given an elegant translation, is inclined to believe that it was the celebrated Themistius, whose orations are still extant.

47. Julian ad Themist. p. 258. Petavius (not. p. 95) observes that this passage is taken from the fourth book of De Legibus; but either Julian quoted from memory, or his MSS. were different from ours. Xenophon opens the Cyropædia with a similar reflection.

48. Ὁ δὲ ἄνθρωπον κελεύων ἄρχειν, προστίθησι καὶ θήριον. Aristot. ap. Julian. [in Epist. ad Themis-

tium] p. 261. The MS. of Vossius, unsatisfied with the single beast, affords the stronger reading of θήρια, which the experience of despotism may warrant.

49. Libanius (Orat. Parentalis, c. lxxxiv. lxxxv. p. 310, 311, 312) has given this interesting detail of the private life of Julian. He himself (in Misopogon, p. 350) mentions his vegetable diet, and upbraids the gross and sensual appetite of the people of Antioch.

50. Lectulus . . . Vestalium toris purior, is the praise which Mamertinus (Panegyr. Vet. xi. [x.] 13) addresses to Julian himself. Libanius affirms, in sober peremptory language, that Julian never knew a woman before his marriage, or after the death of his wife (Orat. Parent. c. lxxxviii. p. 313). The chastity of Julian is confirmed by the impartial testimony of Ammianus (xxv. 4), and the partial silence of the Christians. Yet Julian ironically urges the reproach of the people of Antioch, that he *almost always* (ὡς ἔπιπαν, in Misopogon, p. 345) lay alone. This suspicious expression is explained by the Abbé de la Bléterie (Hist. de Jovien, tom. ii. p. 103. 109) with candour and ingenuity.

51. See Salmasius ad Sueton. in Claud. c. xxi. A twenty-fifth race, or *missus*, was added, to complete the number of one hundred chariots, four of which, the four colours, started each heat.

Centum quadrijugos agitabo ad flumina currus.

It appears that they ran five or seven times round the *Meta* (Sueton, in Domitian. c. 4); and (from the measure of the Circus Maximus at Rome, the Hippodrome at Constantinople, etc.) it might be about a four-mile course.

52. Julian, in Misopogon, p. 340. Julius Cæsar had offended the Roman people by reading his despatches during the actual race. Augustus indulged their taste, or his own, by his constant attention to the important business of the Circus, for which he professed the warmest inclination. Sueton. in August. c. xlv.

53. The reformation of the palace is described by Ammianus (xxii. 4), Libanius (Orat. Parent. c. lxii. p. 288, etc.), Mamertinus (in Panegyr. Vet. xi. [x.] 11), Socrates (l. iii. c. 1), and Zonaras (tom. ii. l. xiii. [c. 12] p. 24).

54. Ego non *rationalem* jussi sed tonsorem acciri. Zonaras uses the less natural image of a *senator*. Yet an officer of the finances, who was satiated with wealth, might desire and obtain the honours of the senate.

55. Μαγείρους μὲν χιλίους, κουρέας δὲ οὐκ ἐλάττους, οἰνοχόους δὲ πλείους, σμήνη τραπεζοπιῶν, εὐνούχους ὑπὲρ τὰς μυίας παρὰ τοῖς ποιμέσιν ἐν ἦρι, are the original words of Libanius, which I have faithfully quoted, lest I should be suspected of magnifying the abuses of the royal household.

56. The expressions of Mamertinus [l. c.] are lively and forcible. Quin etiam prandiorum et cœnarum elaboratas magnitudines Respublica sentiebat; cum quæsitissimæ dapes non gustu, sed difficultatibus æstimarentur; miracula avium, longinqui maris pisces, alieni temporis poma, æstivæ nives, hibernæ rosæ.

57. Yet Julian himself was accused of bestowing whole towns on the eunuchs (Orat. vii. against Polyclet. p. 117-127). Libanius contents himself with a cold but positive denial of the fact, which seems indeed to belong more properly to Constantius. This charge, however, may allude to some unknown circumstance.

58. In the Misopogon (p. 338, 339) he draws a very singular picture of himself, and the following words are strangely characteristic: αὐτὸς προσέθεικα τὸν βαθὺν τουτονὶ πώγωνα. . . ταῦτά τοι διαθέοντων ἀνέχομαι τῶν φθειρῶν ὥσπερ ἐν λοχμῇ τῶν θηρίων. The friends of the Abbé de la Bléterie adjured him, in the name of the French nation, not to translate this passage, so offensive to their delicacy (Hist. de Jovien, tom. ii. p. 94). Like him, I have contented myself with a transient allusion; but the little animal which Julian *names*, is a beast familiar to man, and signifies love.

59. Julian, Epist. xxiii. p. 389. He uses the words πολυκέφαλον ὕδραν, in writing to his friend Hermogenes, who, like himself, was conversant with the Greek poets.

60. The two Sallusts, the præfect of Gaul and the præfect of the East, must be carefully distinguished (Hist. des Empereurs, tom. iv. p. 696). I have used the surname of *Secundus* as a convenient epithet. The second Sallust extorted the esteem of the Christians themselves; and Gregory Nazianzen, who condemned his religion, has celebrated his virtues (Orat. iii. p. 90). See a curious note of the Abbé de la Bléterie, Vie de Julien, p. 363.

61. Mamertinus praises the emperor (xi. [x.] 1) for bestowing the offices of treasurer and præfect on a man of wisdom, firmness, integrity, etc., like himself. Yet Ammianus ranks him (xxi. 1) among the ministers of Julian, quorum merita nôrat et fidem.

62. The proceedings of this chamber of justice are related by Ammianus (xxii. 3) and praised by Libanius (Orat. Parent. c. 74, p. 299, 300).

63. Ursuli vero necem ipsa mihi videtur flêsse Justitia [Amm. l. c.]. Libanius, who imputes his death to the soldiers, attempts to criminate the count of the largesses.

64. Such respect was still entertained for the venerable names of the commonwealth, that the public was surprised and scandalised to hear Taurus summoned as a criminal under the consulship of Taurus. The summons of his colleague Florentius was probably delayed till the commencement of the ensuing year.

65. Ammian. xxii. 7.

66. For the guilt and punishment of Artemius, see Julian (Epist. x. p. 379) and Ammianus (xxii. 11, and Vales, ad loc.). The merit of Artemius, who demolished temples, and was put to death by an apostate, has tempted the Greek and Latin churches to honour him as a martyr. But as eccle-

siastical history attests that he was not only a tyrant, but an Arian, it is not altogether easy to
justify this indiscreet promotion. Tillemont, Mém.
Ecclés. tom. vii. p. 1319.

67. See Ammian. xxii. 6, and Vales. ad locum;
and the Codex Theodosianus, l. ii. tit. xxix. leg. i.;
and Godefroy's Commentary, tom. i. p. 218, ad;
locum.

68. The president Montesquieu (Considérations
sur la Grandeur, etc., des Romains, c. xiv. in his
works, tom. iii. p. 448, 449) excuses this minute and
absurd tyranny, by supposing that actions the
most indifferent in our eyes might excite, in a Roman mind, the idea of guilt and danger. This
strange apology is supported by a strange misapprehension of the English laws, "chez une nation
. . . où il est défendu de boire á la santé d'une cer-
taine personne."

69. The clemency of Julian, and the conspiracy
which was formed against his life at Antioch, are
described by Ammianus (xxii. 9, 10, and Vales. ad
loc.) and Libanius (Orat. Parent. c. 99, p. 323).

70. According to some, says Aristotle (as he is
quoted by Julian ad Themist. p. 261), the form of
absolute government, the παμβασίλεια, is contrary
to nature. Both the prince and the philosopher
choose, however, to involve this eternal truth in
artful and laboured obscurity.

71. That sentiment is expressed almost in the
words of Julian himself. Ammian. xxii. 10.

72. Libanius (Orat. Parent. c. 95, p. 330), who
mentions the wish and design of Julian, insinuates
in mysterious language (θεῶν οὕτω γνόντων . . . ἀλλ'
ἦν ἀμείνων ὁ κωλύων) that the emperor was restrained by some particular revelation.

73. Julian in Misopogon, p. 343. As he never
abolished, by any public law, the proud appellations of Despot, or Dominus, they are still extant on
his medals (Ducange, Fam. Byzantin. p. 38, 39);
and the private displeasure which he affected to
express only gave a different tone to the servility of
the court. The Abbé de la Blétérie (Hist. de Jovien, tom. ii. p. 99–102) has curiously traced the
origin and progress of the word Dominus under the
Imperial government.

74. Ammian. xxii. 7. The consul Mamertinus
(in Panegyr. Vet. xi. [x.] 28, 29, 30) celebrates the
auspicious day, like an eloquent slave, astonished
and intoxicated by the condescension of his
master.

75. Personal satire was condemned by the laws
of the twelve tables:—

> Si mala condiderit in quem quis carmina,
> jus est,
> Judiciumque ———
>
> Horat. Sat. ii. 1, 82.

Julian (in Misopogon, p. 337) owns himself subject to the law; and the Abbé de la Blétérie (Hist.
de Jovien, tom. ii. p. 92) has eagerly embraced a
declaration so agreeable to his own system, and
indeed to the true spirit of the Imperial constitution.

76. Zosimus, l. iii. [c. 11] p. 158.

77. Ἡ τῆς βούλης ἰσχὺς ψύχη πόλεως ἔστιν. See
Libanius (Orat. Parent. c. 71. p. 296), Ammianus
(xxii. 9), and the Theodosian Code (l. xii. tit. i.
leg. 50–55) with Godefroy's Commentary (tom. iv.
p. 390–402). Yet the whole subject of the Curia,
notwithstanding very ample materials, still remains the most obscure in the legal history of the
empire.

78. Quæ paulo ante arida et siti anhelantia vise-
bantur, ea nunc perlui, mundari, madere; Fora,
Deambulacra, Gymnasia, lætis et gaudentibus
populis frequentari; dies festos, et celebrari veteres,
et novos in honorem principis consecrari (Mamertin. xi. [x.] 9). He particularly restored the city of
Nicopolis, and the Actiac games, which had been
instituted by Augustus.

79. Julian, Epist. xxxv. p. 407–411. This epistle,
which illustrates the declining age of Greece, is
omitted by the Abbé de la Blétérie; and strangely
disfigured by the Latin translator, who, by rendering ἀτέλεια, tributum, and ἰδιῶται, populus, directly
contradicts the sense of the original.

80. He reigned in Mycenæ, at the distance of
fifty stadia, or six miles, from Argos: but those
cities, which alternately flourished, are confounded
by the Greek poets. Strabo, l. viii. p. 579, edit.
Amstel. 1707 [p. 377, edit. Casaub.].

81. Marsham, Canon. Chron. p. 421. This pedigree from Temenus and Hercules may be suspicious; yet it was allowed, after a strict inquiry by
the judges of the Olympic games (Herodot. l. v. c.
22), at a time when the Macedonian kings were
obscure and unpopular in Greece. When the
Achæan league declared against Philip, it was
thought decent that the deputies of Argos should
retire (T. Liv. xxxii. 22).

82. His eloquence is celebrated by Libanius
(Orat. Parent. c. 75, 76, p. 300, 301), who distinctly mentions the orators of Homer. Socrates
(l. iii. c. 1.) has rashly asserted that Julian was the
only prince since Julius Cæsar who harangued the
senate. All the predecessors of Nero (Tacit. Annal.
xiii. 3.), and many of his successors, possessed the
faculty of speaking in public; and it might be
proved by various examples that they frequently
exercised it in the senate.

83. Ammianus (xxii. 10) has impartially stated
the merits and defects of his judicial proceedings.
Libanius (Orat. Parent. c. 90, 91, p. 315, etc.) has
seen only the fair side; and his picture, if it flatters
the person, expresses at least the duties of the
judge. Gregory Nazianzen (Orat. iv. p. 120), who
suppresses the virtues and exaggerates even the
venial faults of the Apostate, triumphantly asks,
Whether such a judge was fit to be seated between
Minos and Rhadamanthus in the Elysian fields?

84. Of the laws which Julian enacted in a reign
of sixteen months, fifty-four have been admitted
into the codes of Theodosius and Justinian. (Gothofred. Chron. Legum. p. 64–67.) The Abbé de la
Blétérie (tom. ii. p. 329–336) has chosen one of
these laws to give an idea of Julian's Latin style,

which is forcible and elaborate, but less pure than his Greek.

85. . . . . Ductor fortissimus armis,
  Conditor et legum celeberrimus, ore ma-
    nuque
  Consultor patriæ, sed non consultor ha-
    bendæ

Religionis, amans tercentûm millia Divûm.
Perfidus ille Deo, quamvis non prefidus
  orbi.
      Prudent. Apotheosis, 450, etc.
The consciousness of a generous sentiment seems to have raised the Christian poet above his usual mediocrity.

Chapter XXIII

1. I shall transcribe some of his own expressions from a short religious discourse which the Imperial pontiff composed to censure the bold impiety of a Cynic. Ἀλλ' ὅμως οὕτω δή τι τοὺς θεοὺς πέφρικα, καὶ φιλῶ, καὶ σέβω, καὶ ἄζομαι, καὶ πάνθ' ἁπλῶς τὰ τοιαῦτα πρὸς αὐτοὺς πάσχω, ὅσαπερ ἄν τις καὶ οἷα πρὸς ἀγαθοὺς δεσπότας, πρὸς διδασκάλους, πρὸς πατέρας, πρὸς κηδεμόνας. Orat. vii. p. 212. The variety and copiousness of the Greek tongue seems inadequate to the fervour of his devotion.

2. The orator, with some eloquence, much enthusiasm, and more vanity, addresses his discourse to heaven and earth, to men and angels, to the living and the dead; and above all, to the great Constantius (εἴ τις αἴσθησις, an odd Pagan expression). He concludes with a bold assurance that he has erected a monument not less durable, and much more portable, than the Columns of Hercules. See Greg. Nazianzen, Orat. iii. p. 50, iv. p. 134.

3. See this long invective, which has been injudiciously divided into two orations in Gregory's Works, tom. i. p. 49–134, Paris, 1630. It was published by Gregory and his friend Basil (iv. p. 133), about six months after the death of Julian, when his remains had been carried to Tarsus (iv. p. 120), but while Jovian was still on the throne (iii. p. 54, iv. p. 117). I have derived much assistance from a French version and remarks, printed at Lyons 1735.

4. Nicomediæ ab Eusebio educatus Episcopo, quem genere longius contingebat (Ammian. xxii. 9). Julian never expresses any gratitude towards that Arian prelate; but he celebrates his preceptor the eunuch Mardonius, and describes his mode of education, which inspired his pupil with a passionate admiration for the genius, and perhaps the religion, of Homer. Misopogon, p. 351, 352.

5. Greg. Naz. iii. p. 70. He laboured to efface that holy mark in the blood, perhaps, of a Taurobolium. Baron. Annal. Eccles. A.D. 361, No. 3, 4.

6. Julian himself (Epist. li. p. 434) assures the Alexandrians that he had been a Christian (he must mean a sincere one) till the twentieth year of his age.

7. See his Christian, and even ecclesiastical education, in Gregory (iii. p. 58), Socrates (l. iii. c. 1), and Sozomen (l. v. c. 2). He escaped very narrowly from being a bishop, and perhaps a saint.

8. The share of the work which had been allotted to Gallus was prosecuted with vigour and success;

but the earth obstinately rejected and subverted the structures which were imposed by the sacrilegious hand of Julian. Greg. iii. p. 59, 60, 61. Such a partial earthquake, attested by many living spectators, would form one of the clearest miracles in ecclesiastical story.

9. The *philosopher* (Fragment, p. 288) ridicules the iron chains, etc., of these solitary fanatics (see Tillemont, Mém. Ecclés. tom. ix. p. 661, 662), who had forgot that man is by nature a gentle and social animal, ἀνθρώπου φύσει πολιτικοῦ ζώου καὶ ἡμέρου. The *Pagan* supposes that because they had renounced the gods, they were possessed and tormented by evil dæmons.

10. See Julian apud Cyril. l. vi. p. 206, l. viii. p. 253, 262. "You persecute," says he, "those heretics who do not mourn the dead man precisely in the way which you approve." He shows himself a tolerable theologian; but he maintains that the Christian Trinity is not derived from the doctrine of Paul, of Jesus, or of Moses.

11. Libanius, Orat. Parentalis, c. 9, 10, p. 232, etc. Greg. Nazianzen, Orat. iii. p. 61. Eunap. Vit. Sophist. in Maximo, p. 88 *seq.*, edit. Commelin. [1596].

12. A modern philosopher has ingeniously compared the different operation of theism and polytheism, with regard to the doubt or conviction which they produce in the human mind. See Hume's Essays, vol. ii. p. 444–457, in 8vo. edit. 1777.

13. The Idæan mother landed in Italy about the end of the second Punic war. The miracle of Claudia, either virgin or matron, who cleared her fame by disgracing the graver modesty of the Roman ladies, is attested by a cloud of witnesses. Their evidence is collected by Drakenborch (ad Silium Italicum, xvii. 33); but we may observe that Livy (xxix. 14) slides over the transaction with discreet ambiguity.

14. I cannot refrain from transcribing the emphatical words of Julian: ἐμοὶ δὲ δοκεῖ ταῖς πόλεσι πιστεύειν μᾶλλον τὰ τοιαῦτα, ἢ τουτοισὶ τοῖς κομψοῖς, ὧν τὸ ψυχάριον δριμὺ μὲν, ὑγιὲς δὲ οὐδὲ ἐν βλέπει. Orat. v. p. 161. Julian likewise declares his firm belief in the *ancilia*, the holy shields, which dropped from heaven on the Quirinal hill; and pities the strange blindness of the Christians, who preferred the *cross* to these celestial trophies. Apud Cyril. l. vi. p. 194.

15. See the principles of allegory, in Julian (Orat. vii. p. 216, 222). His reasoning is less absurd than that of some modern theologians, who assert that an extravagant or contradictory doctrine *must* be divine, since no man alive could have thought of inventing it.

16. Eunapius has made these sophists the subject of a partial and fanatical history; and the learned Brucker (Hist. Philosoph. tom. ii. p. 217–303) has employed much labour to illustrate their obscure lives and incomprehensible doctrines.

17. Julian, Orat. vii. p. 222. He swears with the most fervent and enthusiastic devotion; and trembles lest he should betray too much of these holy mysteries, which the profane might deride with an impious Sardonic laugh.

18. See the fifth oration of Julian. But all the allegories which ever issued from the Platonic school are not worth the short poem of Catullus on the same extraordinary subject. The transition of Atys from the wildest enthusiasm to sober pathetic complaint for his irretrievable loss, must inspire a man with pity, an eunuch with despair.

19. The true religion of Julian may be deduced from the Cæsars, p. 308, with Spanheim's notes and illustrations; from the fragments in Cyril, l. ii. p. 57, 58; and especially from the theological oration in Solem Regem, p. 130–158, addressed, in the confidence of friendship, to the præfect Sallust.

20. Julian adopts this gross conception by ascribing it to his favourite Marcus Antoninus (Cæsares, p. 333). The Stoics and Platonists hesitated between the analogy of bodies and the purity of spirits; yet the gravest philosophers inclined to the whimsical fancy of Aristophanes and Lucian, that an unbelieving age might starve the immortal gods. See Observations de Spanheim, p. 284, 444, etc.

21. Ἥλιον λέγω, τὸ ζῶν ἄγαλμα καὶ ἔμψυχον, καὶ ἔννουν, καὶ ἀγαθοεργὸν τοῦ νοητοῦ πατρὸς. Julian, Epist. li. [p. 434]. In another place (apud Cyril. l. ii. p. 69) he calls the sun God, and the throne of God. Julian believed the Platonician Trinity; and only blames the Christians for preferring a mortal to an immortal *Logos*.

22. The sophists of Eunapius perform as many miracles as the saints of the desert; and the only circumstance in their favour is, that they are of a less gloomy complexion. Instead of devils with horns and tails, Iamblichus evoked the genii of love, Eros and Anteros, from two adjacent fountains. Two beautiful boys issued from the water, fondly embraced him as their father, and retired at his command. P. 26, 27.

23. The dexterous management of these sophists, who played their credulous pupil into each other's hands, is fairly told by Eunapius [in Maximo, p. 85 *seqq.*, ed. Commel.] with unsuspecting simplicity. The Abbé de la Bléterie understands, and neatly describes, the whole comedy. (Vie de Julian, p. 61–67.)

24. When Julian, in a momentary panic, made the sign of the cross, the demons instantly disappeared (Greg. Naz. Orat. iii. p. 71). Gregory supposes that they were frightened, but the priests declared that they were indignant. The reader, according to the measure of his faith, will determine this profound question.

25. A dark and distant view of the terrors and joys of initiation is shown by Dion Chrysostom, Themistius, Proclus, and Stobæus. The learned author of the Divine Legation has exhibited their words (vol. i. p. 239, 247, 248, 280, edit. 1765), which he dexterously or forcibly applies to his own hypothesis.

26. Julian's modesty confined him to obscure and occasional hints: but Libanius expatiates with pleasure on the fasts and visions of the religious hero. (Legat. ad. Julian. p. 157, and Orat. Parental. c. lxxxiii. p. 309, 310.)

27. Libanius, Orat. Parent. c. x. p. 233, 234. Gallus had some reason to suspect the secret apostasy of his brother; and in a letter, which may be received as geniune, he exhorts Julian to adhere to the religion of their *ancestors;* an argument which, as it should seem, was not yet perfectly ripe. See Julian. Op. p. 454 [ed. Spanheim, Lips. 1696], and Hist. de Jovien, tom. ii. p. 141.

28. Gregory (iii. p. 50), with inhuman zeal, censures Constantius for sparing the infant apostate (κάκως σώθεντα). His French translator (p. 265) cautiously observes that such expressions must not be prises à la lettre.

29. Libanius, Orat. Parental. c. ix. p. 233.

30. Fabricius (Biblioth. Græc. l. v. c. viii. p. 88–90) and Lardner (Heathen Testimonies, vol. iv. p. 44–47) have accurately compiled all that can now be discovered of Julian's work against the Christians.

31. About seventy years after the death of Julian he executed a task which had been feebly attempted by Philip of Side, a prolix and contemptible writer. Even the work of Cyril has not entirely satisfied the most favourable judges: and the Abbé de la Bléterie (Préface à l'Hist. de Jovien, p. 30, 32) wishes that some *théologien philosophe* (a strange centaur) would undertake the refutation of Julian.

32. Libanius (Orat. Parental. c. lxxxvii. p. 313), who has been suspected of assisting his friend, prefers this divine vindication (Orat. ix. in necem Julian. p. 257, edit. Morel.) to the writings of Porphyry. His judgment may be arraigned (Socrates, l. iii. c. 23), but Libanius cannot be accused of flattery to a dead prince.

33. Libanius (Orat. Parent. c. lviii. p. 283, 284) has eloquently explained the tolerating principles and conduct of his Imperial friend. In a very remarkable epistle to the people of Bostra, Julian himself (Epist. lii. [p. 436]) professes his moderation, and betrays his zeal, which is acknowledged by Ammianus and exposed by Gregory. (Orat. iii. p. 72.)

34. In Greece the temples of Minerva were opened by his express command, before the death

of Constantius (Liban. Orat. Parent. c. 55, p. 280); and Julian declares himself a Pagan in his public manifesto to the Athenians. This unquestionable evidence may correct the hasty assertion of Ammianus, who seems to suppose Constantinople to be the place where he discovered his attachment to the gods.

35. Ammianus, xxii. 5. Sozomen, l. v. c. 5. Bestia moritur, tranquillitas redit . . . omnes episcopi qui de propriis sedibus fuerant exterminati per indulgentiam novi principis ad ecclesias redeunt. Jerom. adversus Luciferianos, tom. ii. p. 143 [tom. ii. p. 191, ed. Vallars.]. Optatus accuses the Donatists for owing their safety to an apostate (l. ii. c. 16, p. 36, 37, edit. Dupin).

36. The restoration of the Pagan worship is described by Julian (Misopogon, p. 346), Libanius (Orat. Parent. c. 60, p. 286, 287, and Orat. Consular. ad Julian. p. 245, 246, edit. Morel.), Ammianus (xxii. 12), and Gregory Nazianzen (Orat. iv. p. 121). These writers agree in the essential, and even minute, facts; but the different lights in which they view the extreme devotion of Julian are expressive of the gradations of self-applause, passionate admiration, mild reproof, and partial invective.

37. See Julian. Epistol. xlix. lxii. lxiii., and a long and curious fragment, without beginning or end (p. 288-305). The supreme pontiff derides the Mosaic history and the Christian discipline, prefers the Greek poets to the Hebrew prophets, and palliates, with the skill of a Jesuit, the *relative* worship of images.

38. The exultation of Julian (p. 301) that these impious sects, and even their writings, are extinguished, may be consistent enough with the sacerdotal character; but it is unworthy of a philosopher to wish that any opinions and arguments the most repugnant to his own should be concealed from the knowledge of mankind.

39. Yet he insinuates that the Christians, under the pretence of charity, inveigled children from their religion and parents, conveyed them on shipboard, and devoted those victims to a life of poverty or servitude in a remote country (p. 305). Had the charge been proved, it was his duty not to complain but to punish.

40. Gregory Nazianzen is facetious, ingenious, and argumentative (Orat. iii. p. 101, 102, etc.). He ridicules the folly of such vain imitation; and amuses himself with inquiring what lessons, moral or theological, could be extracted from the Grecian fables.

41. He accuses one of his pontiffs of a secret confederacy with the Christian bishops and presbyters (Epist. lxii.). Ὁρῶν οὖν πολλὴν μὲν ὀλιγωρίαν οὖσαν ἡμῖν πρὸς τοὺς θεούς; and again, ἡμᾶς δὲ οὕτω ῥαθύμως, etc. Epist. lxiii.

42. He praises the fidelity of Callixene, priestess of Ceres, who had been twice as constant as Penelope, and rewards her with the priesthood of the Phrygian goddess at Pessinus (Julian. Epist. xxi.

[p. 389]). He applauds the firmness of Sopater of Hierapolis, who had been repeatedly pressed by Constantius and Gallus to *apostatise* (Epist. xxvii. p. 401).

43. Ὁ δὲ νομίζων ἀδελφὰ λόγους τε καὶ θεων ἱερά. Orat. Parent. c. 77, p. 302. The same sentiment is frequently inculcated by Julian, Libanius, and the rest of their party.

44. The curiosity and credulity of the emperor, who tried every mode of divination, are fairly exposed by Ammianus, xxii. 12.

45. Julian. Epist. xxxviii. Three other epistles (xv. xvi. xxxix.), in the same style of friendship and confidence, are addressed to the philosopher Maximus.

46. Eunapius (in Maximo, p. 77, 78, 79, and in Chrysanthio, p. 147, 148 [p. 94 *sqq.* and 191 *sqq.*, ed. Comm.]) has minutely related these anecdotes, which he conceives to be the most important events of the age. Yet he fairly confesses the frailty of Maximus. His reception at Constantinople is described by Libanius (Orat. Parent. c. 76, p. 301) and Ammianus (xxii. 7).

47. Chrysanthius, who had refused to quit Lydia, was created high-priest of the province. His cautious and temperate use of power secured him after the revolution: and he lived in peace; while Maximus, Priscus, etc., were persecuted by the Christian ministers. See the adventures of those fanatic sophists, collected by Brucker, tom. ii. p. 281-293.

48. See Libanius (Orat. Parent. c. 100, 101, p. 324, 325, 326) and Eunapius (Vit. Sophist. in Proæresio, p. 126 [p. 160, ed. Comm.]). Some students, whose expectations perhaps were groundless or extravagant, retired in disgust (Greg. Naz. Orat. iv. p. 120). It is strange that we should not be able to contradict the title of one of Tillemont's chapters (Hist. des Empereurs, tom. iv. p. 960), "La Cour de Julien est pleine de philosophes et de gens perdus."

49. Under the reign of Louis XIV. his subjects of every rank aspired to the glorious title of *Convertisseur*, expressive of their zeal and success in making proselytes. The word and the idea are growing obsolete in France; may they never be introduced into England!

50. See the strong expressions of Libanius, which were probably those of Julian himself (Orat. Parent. c. 59, p. 285).

51. When Gregory Nazianzen (Orat. x. p. 167) is desirous to magnify the Christian firmness of his brother Cæsarius, physician to the Imperial court, he owns that Cæsarius disputed with a formidable adversary, πόλυν ἐν ὁπλοῖς, καὶ μέγαν ἐν λόγων δεινότητι. In his invectives he scarcely allows any share of wit or courage to the apostate.

52. Julian. Epist. xxxviii. [p. 415]. Ammianus, xxii. 12. Adeo ut in dies pæne singulos milites carnis distentione saginâ victitantes incultus, potusque aviditate correpti, humeris impositi transeuntium per plateas, ex publicis ædibus . . . ad sua di-

versoria portarentur. The devout prince and the indignant historian describe the same scene; and in Illyricum or Antioch similar causes must have produced similar effects.

53. Gregory (Orat. iii. p. 74, 75, 83–86) and Libanius (Orat. Parent. c. lxxxi. lxxxii. p. 307, 308), περὶ ταύτην τὴν σπουδήν, οὐκ ἀρνοῦμαι πλοῦτον ἀνηλῶσθαι μέγαν. The sophist owns and justifies the expense of these military conversions.

54. Julian's epistle (xxv.) is addressed to the community of the Jews. Aldus (Venet. 1499) has branded it with an εἰ γνήσιος; but this stigma is justly removed by the subsequent editors, Petavius and Spanheim. The epistle is mentioned by Sozomen (l. v. c. 22), and the purport of it is confirmed by Gregory (Orat. iv. p. 111), and by Julian himself (Fragment. p. 295).

55. The Misnah denounced death against those who abandoned the foundation. The judgment of zeal is explained by Marsham (Canon. Chron. p. 161, 162, edit. fol. London, 1672) and Basnage (Hist. des Juifs, tom. viii. p. 120). Constantine made a law to protect Christian converts from Judaism. Cod. Theod. l. xvi. tit. viii. leg. 1. Godefroy, tom. vi. p. 215.

56. Et interea (during the civil war of Magnentius) Judæorum seditio, qui Patricium nefarie in regni speciem sustulerunt, oppressa. Aurelius Victor, in Constantio, c. xlii. See Tillemont. Hist. des Empereurs, tom. iv. p. 379, in 4to.

57. The city and synagogue of Tiberias are curiously described by Reland, Palestin. tom. ii. p. 1036–1042.

58. Basnage has fully illustrated the state of the Jews under Constantine and his successors (tom. viii. c. iv. p. 111–153).

59. Reland (Palestin. l. i. p. 309, 390, l. iii. p. 838) describes, with learning and perspicuity, Jerusalem and the face of the adjacent country.

60. I have consulted a rare and curious treatise of M. d'Anville (sur l'Ancienne Jérusalem, Paris, 1747, p. 75). The circumference of the ancient city (Euseb. Preparat. Evangel. l. ix. c. 36) was 27 stadia, or 2550 toises. A plan taken on the spot assigns no more than 1980 for the modern town. The circuit is defined by natural landmarks, which cannot be mistaken or removed.

61. See two curious passages in Jerom (tom. i. p. 102, tom. vi. p. 315), and the ample details of Tillemont (Hist. des Empereurs, tom. i. p. 569, tom. ii. p. 289, 294, 4to. edition).

62. Eusebius in Vit. Constantin. l. iii. c. 25–47, 51–53. The emperor likewise built churches at Bethlehem, the Mount of Olives, and the oak of Mambre. The holy sepulchre is described by Sandys (Travels, p. 125–133), and curiously delineated by Le Bruyn (Voyage au Levant, p. 288–296).

63. The Itinerary from Bordeaux to Jerusalem was composed in the year 333, for the use of pilgrims; among whom Jerom (tom. i. p. 126) mentions the Britons and the Indians. The causes of this superstitious fashion are discussed in the learned and judicious preface of Wesseling (Itinerar. p. 537–545).

64. Cicero (de Finibus. v. 1) has beautifully expressed the common sense of mankind.

65. Baronius (Annal. Eccles. A.D. 326, No. 42–50) and Tillemont (Mém. Ecclés. tom. vii. p. 8–16) are the historians and champions of the miraculous invention of the cross, under the reign of Constantine. Their oldest witnesses are Paulinus, Sulpicius Severus, Rufinus, Ambrose, and perhaps Cyril of Jerusalem. The silence of Eusebius and the Bordeaux pilgrim, which satisfies those who think, perplexes those who believe. See Jortin's sensible remarks, vol. ii. p. 238–248.

66. This multiplication is asserted by Paulinus (Epist. xxxvi.; see Dupin. Bibliot. Ecclés. tom. iii. p. 149), who seems to have improved a rhetorical flourish of Cyril into a real fact. The same supernatural privilege must have been communicated to the Virgin's milk (Erasmi Opera, tom. i. p. 778, Lugd. Batav. 1703, in Colloq. de Peregrinat. Riligionis ergo), saints' heads, etc., and other relics, which are repeated in so many different churches.

67. Jerom (tom. i. p. 103), who resided in the neighbouring village of Bethlehem, describes the vices of Jerusalem from his personal experience.

68. Gregor. Nyssen. apud Wesseling, p. 539. The whole epistle, which condemns either the use or the abuse of religious pilgrimage, is painful to the catholic divines, while it is dear and familiar to our protestant polemics.

69. He renounced his orthodox ordination, officiated as a deacon, and was re-ordained by the hands of the Arians. But Cyril afterwards changed with the times, and prudently conformed to the Nicene faith. Tillemont (Mém. Ecclés. tom. viii.), who treats his memory with tenderness and respect, has thrown his virtues into the text, and his faults into the notes, in decent obscurity, at the end of the volume.

70. Imperii sui memoriam magnitudine operum gestiens propagare. Ammian. xxiii. 1. The temple of Jerusalem had been famous even among the Gentiles. They had many temples in each city (at Sichem five, at Gaza eight, at Rome four hundred and twenty-four); but the wealth and religion of the Jewish nation was centred in one spot.

71. The secret intentions of Julian are revealed by the late bishop of Gloucester, the learned and dogmatic Warburton; who, with the authority of a theologian, prescribes the motives and conduct of the Supreme Being. The discourse entitled Julian (2nd edition, London, 1751) is strongly marked with all the peculiarities which are imputed to the Warburtonian school.

72. I shelter myself behind Maimonides, Marsham, Spencer, Le Clerc, Warburton, etc., who have fairly derided the fears, the folly, and the falsehood of some superstitious divines. See Divine Legation, vol. iv. p. 25, etc.

73. Julian (Fragment. p. 295) respectfully styles him μέγας θεός, and mentions him elsewhere (Epist.

lxiii.) with still higher reverence. He doubly condemns the Christians, for believing and for renouncing the religion of the Jews. Their Deity was a *true*, but not the *only*, God. Apud Cyril. l. ix. p. 305, 306.

74. 1 Kings viii. 63. 2 Chronicles vii. 5. Joseph. Antiquitat. Judaic. l. viii. c. 4 [§5], p. 431, edit. Havercamp. As the blood and smoke of so many hecatombs might be inconvenient, Lightfoot, the Christian Rabbi, removes them by a miracle. Le Clerc (ad loca) is bold enough to suspect the fidelity of the numbers.

75. Julian, Epist. xxix. xxx. [p. 402, *sqq.*] La Bléterie has neglected to translate the second of these epistles.

76. See the zeal and impatience of the Jews in Gregory Nazianzen (Orat. iv. p. 111) and Theodoret (l. iii. c. 20).

77. Built by Omar, the second khalif, who died A.D. 644. This great mosque covers the whole consecrated ground of the Jewish temple, and constitutes almost a square of 760 *toises*, or one Roman mile, in circumference. See d'Anville, Jerusalem, p. 45.

78. Ammianus records the consuls of the year 363, before he proceeds to mention the *thoughts* of Julian. Templum . . . instaurare sumptibus *cogitabat* immodicis. Warburton has a secret wish to anticipate the design; but he must have understood, from former examples, that the execution of such a work would have demanded many years.

79. The subsequent witnesses, Socrates, Sozomen, Theodoret, Philostorgius, etc., add contradictions rather than authority. Compare the objections of Basnage (Hist. des Juifs, tom. viii. p. 157–168) with Warburton's answers (Julian, p. 174–258). The bishop has ingeniously explained the miraculous crosses which appeared on the garments of the spectators by a similar instance and the natural effects of lightning.

80. Ambros. tom. ii. Epist. xl. p. 946, edit. Benedictin. He composed this fanatic epistle (A.D. 388) to justify a bishop who had been condemned by the civil magistrate for burning a synagogue.

81. Chrysostom, tom. i. p. 580, advers. Judæos et Gentes [c. 16], tom. ii. p. 574, de Sto. Babylâ [c. 22], edit. Montfaucon. I have followed the common and natural supposition; but the learned Benedictine, who dates the composition of these sermons in the year 383, is confident they were never pronounced from the pulpit.

82. Greg. Nazianzen, Orat. iv. p. 110–113. Τὸ δὲ οὖν περιβόητον πᾶσι θαῦμα καὶ οὐδὲ τοῖς ἀθέοις αὐτοῖς ἀπιστούμενον, λέξων ἐρχόμαι.

83. Ammian. xxiii. 1. Cum itaque rei fortiter instaret Alypius, juvaretque provinciæ rector, metuendi globi flammarum prope fundamenta crebris assultibus erumpentes fecere locum exustis aliquoties operantibus inaccessum; hocque modo elemento destinatius repellente, cessavit inceptum. Warburton labours (p. 60–90) to extort a confession of the miracle from the mouths of Julian and

Libanius, and to employ the evidence of a rabbi who lived in the fifteenth century. Such witnesses can only be received by a very favourable judge.

84. Dr. Lardner, perhaps alone of the Christian critics, presumes to doubt the truth of this famous miracle (Jewish and Heathen Testimonies, vol. iv. p. 47–71). The silence of Jerom would lead to a suspicion that the same story which was celebrated at a distance might be despised on the spot.

85. Greg. Naz. Orat. iii. p. 81. And this law was confirmed by the invariable practice of Julian himself. Warburton has justly observed (p. 35) that the Platonists believed in the mysterious virtue of words; and Julian's dislike for the name of Christ might proceed from superstition as well as from contempt.

86. Fragment. Julian. p. 288. He derides the μωρία Γαλιλαίων (Epist. vii.) and so far loses sight of the principles of toleration as to wish (Epist. xlii. [p. 424]) ἄκοντας ἰᾶσθαι.

87. Οὐ γάρ μοι θέμις ἐστὶ κομιζέμεν ἢ ἐλεαίρειν
     Ανερας, οἵ κε θεοῖσιν ἀπέχθωντ' ἀθανάτοισιν.

These two lines, which Julian has changed and perverted in the true spirit of a bigot (Epist. xlix. [p. 432]), are taken from the speech of Æolus, when he refuses to grant Ulysses a fresh supply of winds (Odyss. x. 73). Libanius (Orat. Parent. c. lix. p. 286) attempts to justify this partial behaviour by an apology, in which persecution peeps through the mask of candour.

88. These laws, which affected the clergy, may be found in the slight hints of Julian himself (Epist. lii. [p. 433, *sqq.*]), in the vague declamations of Gregory (Orat. iii. p. 86, 87), and in the positive assertions of Sozomen (l. v. c. 5).

89. Inclemens . . . perenni obruendum silentio. Ammian. xxii. 10, xxv. 5.

90. The edict itself, which is still extant among the epistles of Julian (xlii. [p. 422]), may be compared with the loose invectives of Gregory (Orat. iii. p. 96). Tillemont (Mém. Ecclés. tom. vii. p. 1291–1294) has collected the seeming differences of ancients and moderns. They may be easily reconciled. The Christians were *directly* forbid to teach, they were *indirectly* forbid to learn; since they would not frequent the schools of the Pagans.

91. Codex Theodos. l. xiii. tit. iii. de medicis et professoribus, leg. 5 (published the 17th of June, received, at Spoleto in Italy, the 29th of July, A.D. 363) with Godefroy's Illustrations, tom. v. p. 31.

92. Orosius celebrates their disinterested resolution: Sicut a majoribus nostris compertum habemus, omnes ubique propemodum . . . officium quam fidem deserere maluerunt, vii. 30. Proæresius, a Christian sophist, refused to accept the partial favour of the emperor. Hieronym. in Chron. p. 185, edit. Scaliger [tom. viii. p. 805, ed. Vallars.]. Eunapius in Proæresio, p. 126 [p. 160, ed. Comm.].

93. They had recourse to the expedient of composing books for their own schools. Within a few months Apollinaris produced his Christian imita-

tions of Homer (a sacred history in xxiv. books), Pindar, Euripides, and Menander; and Sozomen is satisfied that they equalled, or excelled, the originals.

94. It was the instruction of Julian to his magistrates (Epist. vii.) προτιμᾶσθαι μέντοι τοὺς θεοσεβεῖς καὶ πάνυ φημὶ δεῖν. Sozomen (l. v. c. 18) and Socrates (l. iii. c. 13) must be reduced to the standard of Gregory (Orat. iii. p. 95), not less prone to exaggeration, but more restrained by the actual knowledge of his contemporary readers.

95. Ψηφῷ θεῶν καὶ διδόυς καὶ μὴ διδόυς. Libanius, Orat. Parent. c. 88, p. 314.

96. Greg. Naz. Orat. iii. p. 74, 91, 92. Socrates, l. iii. c. 14. Theodoret, l. iii. c. 6. Some drawback may however be allowed for the violence of *their* zeal, not less partial than the zeal of Julian.

97. If we compare the gentle language of Libanius (Orat. Parent. c. 60, p. 286) with the passionate exclamations of Gregory (Orat. iii. p. 86, 87), we may find it difficult to persuade ourselves that the two orators are really describing the same events.

98. Restan, or Arethusa, at the equal distance of sixteen miles between Emesa (*Hems*) and Epiphania (*Hamath*), was founded, or at least named, by Seleucus Nicator. Its peculiar era dates from the year of Rome 685, according to the medals of the city. In the decline of the Seleucides, Emesa and Arethusa were usurped by the Arab Sampsiceramus, whose posterity, the vassals of Rome, were not extinguished in the reign of Vespasian. See d'Anville's Maps and Géographie Ancienne, tom. ii. p. 134; Wesseling, Itineraria, p. 188; and Noris. Epoch. Syro-Macedon., p. 80, 481, 482.

99. Sozomen, l. v. c. 10. It is surprising that Gregory and Theodoret should suppress a circumstance which, in their eyes, must have enhanced the religious merit of the confessor.

100. The sufferings and constancy of Mark, which Gregory has so tragically painted (Orat. iii. p. 88–91), are confirmed by the unexceptionable and reluctant evidence of Libanius. Μάρκος ἐκεῖνος κρεμάμενος, καὶ μαστιγούμενος, καὶ τοῦ πώγωνος αὐτῷ τιλλομένου, πάντα ἐνεγκὼν ἀνδρείως, νῦν ἰσόθεός ἐστι ταῖς τιμαῖς, κἂν φανῇ που, περιμάχητος εὐθύς. Epist. 730, p. 350, 351. Edit. Wolf. Amstel. 1738.

101. Περιμάχητος, certatim eum sibi (Christiani) vindicant. It is thus that La Croze and Wolfius (ad loc.) have explained a Greek word whose true signification had been mistaken by former interpreters, and even by Le Clerc (Bibliothèque Ancienne et Moderne, tom. iii. p. 371). Yet Tillemont is strangely puzzled to understand (Mém. Ecclés. tom. vii. p. 1309) *how* Gregory and Theodoret could mistake a Semi-Arian bishop for a saint.

102. See the probable advice of Sallust (Greg. Nazianzen, Orat. iii. 90, 91). Libanius intercedes for a similar offender, lest they should find many *Marks;* yet he allows that, if Orion had secreted the consecrated wealth, he deserved to suffer the punishment of Marsyas—to be flayed alive (Epist. 730, p. 349–351).

103. Gregory (Orat. iii. p. 90) is satisfied that, by saving the apostate, Mark had deserved still more than he had suffered.

104. The grove and temple of Daphne are described by Strabo (l. xvi. p. 1089, 1090, edit. Amstel. 1707 [p. 750, ed. Casaub.]), Libanius (Nænia, p. 185–188; Antiochic. Orat. xi. p. 380, 381 [ed. Morell. 1627]), and Sozomen (l. v. c. 19). Wesseling (Itinerar. p. 581) and Casaubon (ad Hist. August p. 64) illustrate this curious subject.

105. Simulacrum in eo Olympiaci Jovis imitamenti æquiparans magnitudinem. Ammian. xxii. 13. The Olympic Jupiter was sixty feet high, and his bulk was consequently equal to that of a thousand men. See a curious *Mémoire* of the Abbé Gedoyn (Académie des Inscriptions, tom. ix. p. 198.)

106. Hadrian read the history of his future fortunes on a leaf dipped in the Castalian stream; a trick which, according to the physician Vandale (de Oraculis, p. 281, 282), might be easily performed by chemical preparations. The emperor stopped the source of such dangerous knowledge, which was again opened by the devout curiosity of Julian.

107. It was purchased, A.D. 44, in the year 92 of the era of Antioch (Noris. Epoch. Syro-Maced. p. 139–174) for the term of ninety Olympiads. But the Olympic games of Antioch were not regularly celebrated till the reign of Commodus. See the curious details in the Chronicle of John Malala (tom. i. p. 291, 320, 372–381 [ed. Oxon.; p. 225, 248, and 283 *sqq.*, ed. Bonn.]), a writer whose merit and authority are confined within the limits of his native city.

108. Fifteen talents of gold, bequeathed by Sosibius, who died in the reign of Augustus. The theatrical merits of the Syrian cities, in the age of Constantine, are compared in the Expositio totius Mundi, p. 6 (Hudson, Geograph. Minor. tom. iii.).

109. Avidio Cassio Syriacas legiones dedi luxuriâ diffluentes et *Daphnicis* moribus. These are the words of the emperor Marcus Antoninus, in an original letter preserved by his biographer in Hist. August. p. 41 [Vulcat. Gallic. in Vitâ Avid. Cass. c. 6]. Cassius dismissed or punished every soldier who was seen at Daphne.

110. Aliquantum agrorum Daphnensibus dedit (*Pompey*), quo lucus ibi spatiosior fieret; delectatus amœnitate loci et aquarum abundantiâ. Eutropius, vi. 14 [11]. Sextus Rufus, de Provinciis, c. 16.

111. Julian (Misopogon, p. 361, 362) discovers his own character with that naïveté, that unconscious simplicity, which always constitutes genuine humour.

112. Babylas is named by Eusebius in the succession of the bishops of Antioch (Hist. Eccles. l. vi. c. 29, 39). His triumph over two emperors (the first fabulous, the second historical) is diffusely celebrated by Chrysostom (tom. ii. p. 536–577, edit. Montfaucon). Tillemont (Mém. Ecclés. tom.

iii. part ii. p. 287–302, 459–465) becomes almost a sceptic.

113. Ecclesiastical critics, particularly those who love relics, exult in the confession of Julian (Misopogon, p. 361) and Libanius (Nænia, p. 185) that Apollo was disturbed by the vicinity of *one* dead man. Yet Ammianus (xxii. 12) clears and purifies the whole ground, according to the rites which the Athenians formerly practised in the isle of Delos.

114. Julian (in Misopogon, p. 361) rather insinuates than affirms their guilt. Ammianus (xxii. 13) treats the imputation as *levissimus rumor,* and relates the story with extraordinary candour.

115. Quo tam atroci casû repente consumpto, ad id usque imperatoris ira provexit, ut quæstiones agitari juberet solito acriores (yet Julian blames the lenity of the magistrates of Antioch), et majorem ecclesiam Antiochiæ claudi. [Amm. l. c.] This interdiction was performed with some circumstances of indignity and profanation: and the seasonable death of the principal actor, Julian's uncle, is related with much superstitious complacency by the Abbé de la Blèterie, Vie de Julien, p. 362–369.

116. Besides the ecclesiastical historians, who are more or less to be suspected, we may allege the passion of St. Theodore, in the Acta Sincera of Ruinart, p. 591. The complaint of Julian gives it an original and authentic air.

117. Julian. Misopogon, p. 361.

118. See Gregory Nazianzen (Orat. iii. p. 87). Sozomen (l. v. c. 9) may be considered as an original, though not impartial, witness. He was a native of Gaza, and had conversed with the confessor Zeno, who, as bishop of Maiuma, lived to the age of an hundred (l. vii. c. 28). Philostorgius (l. vii. c. 4, with Godefroy's Dissertations, p. 284) adds some tragic circumstances of Christians who were *literally* sacrificed at the altars of the gods, etc.

119. The life and death of George of Cappadocia are described by Ammianus (xxii. 11), Gregory Nazianzen (Orat. xxi. p. 382, 385, 389, 390), and Epiphanius (Hæres. lxxvi. [p. 912, ed. Paris, 1622]). The invectives of the two saints might not deserve much credit, unless they were confirmed by the testimony of the cool and impartial infidel.

120. After the massacre of George, the emperor Julian repeatedly sent orders to preserve the library for his own use, and to torture the slaves who might be suspected of secreting any books. He praises the merit of the collection, from whence he had borrowed and transcribed several manuscripts while he pursued his studies in Cappadocia. He could wish indeed that the works of the Galilæans might perish; but he requires an exact account even of those theological volumes, lest other treatises more valuable should be confounded in their loss. Julian. Epist. ix. xxxvi. [p. 377, 411].

121. Philostorgius, with cautious malice, insinuates their guilt, καὶ τὴν Ἀθανασίου γνώμην στρατηγῆσαι τῆς πράξεως, l. vii. c. 2. Godefroy, p. 267.

122. Cineres projecit in mare, id metuens ut clamabat, ne, collectis supremis, ædes illis exstruerentur ut reliquis, qui deviare a religione compulsi, pertulere cruciabiles pœnas, adusque gloriosam mortem intemeratâ fide progressi, et nunc Martyres appellantur. Ammian. xxii. 11. Epiphanius proves to the Arians that George was not a martyr.

123. Some Donatists (Optatus Milev. p. 60, 303, edit. Dupin; and Tillemont, Mém. Ecclés. tom. vi. p. 713, in 4to.) and Priscillianists (Tillemont, Mém. Ecclés. tom. viii. p. 517, in 4to.) have in like manner usurped the honours of catholic saints and martyrs.

124. The saints of Cappadocia, Basil and the Gregories, were ignorant of their holy companion. Pope Gelasius (A.D. 494), the first catholic who acknowledges St. George, places him among the martyrs "qui Deo magis quam hominibus noti sunt." He rejects his Acts as the composition of heretics. Some, perhaps not the oldest, of the spurious Acts are still extant; and, through a cloud of fiction, we may yet distinguish the combat which St. George of Cappadocia sustained, in the presence of Queen *Alexandra,* against the *magician Athanasius.*

125. This transformation is not given as absolutely certain, but as *extremely* probable. See the Longueruana, tom. i. p. 194.

126. A curious history of the worship of St. George, from the sixth century (when he was already revered in Palestine, in Armenia, at Rome, and at Treves in Gaul), might be extracted from Dr. Heylin (History of St. George, and edition, London, 1633, in 4to. p. 429) and the Bollandists (Act SS. Mens. April. tom. iii. p. 100–163). His fame and popularity in Europe, and especially in England, proceeded from the Crusades.

127. Julian. Epist. xliii. [p. 424.]

128. Julian. Epist. x. [p. 378.] He allowed his friends to assuage his anger. Ammian. xxii. 11.

129. See Athanas. ad Rufin. tom. ii. p. 40, 41; and Greg. Nazianzen, Orat. xxi. p. 395, 396; who justly states the temperate zeal of the primate as much more meritorious than his prayers, his fasts, his persecutions, etc.

130. I have not leisure to follow the blind obstinacy of Lucifer of Cagliari. See his adventures in Tillemont (Mém. Ecclés. tom. vii. p. 900–926); and observe how the colour of the narrative insensibly changes, as the confessor becomes a schismatic.

131. Assensus est huic sententiæ Occidens, et, per tam necessarium concilium, Satanæ faucibus mundus ereptus. The lively and artful dialogue of Jerom against the Luciferians (tom. ii. p. 135–155 [tom. ii. p. 193, ed. Vallars.]) exhibits an original picture of the ecclesiastical policy of the times.

132. Tillemont, who supposes that George was massacred in August, crowds the actions of Athanasius into a narrow space (Mém. Ecclés. tom. viii. p. 360). An original fragment, published by the Marquis Maffei, from the old Chapter Library

of Verona (Osservazioni Letterarie, tom. iii. p. 60–92), affords many important dates, which are authenticated by the computation of Egyptian months.

133. Τὸν μιαρὸν, ὃς ἐτόλμησεν Ἑλληνίδας, ἐπ᾽ ἐμοῦ, γυναῖκας τῶν ἐπισήμων βαπτίσαι, διώκεσθαι. [Julian. Ep. vi. p. 376.] I have preserved the ambiguous sense of the last word, the ambiguity of a tyrant who wished to find or to create guilt.

134. The three epistles of Julian which explain his intentions and conduct with regard to Athanasius should be disposed in the following chronological order, xxvi. x. vi. See likewise Greg. Nazianzen, xxi. p. 393; Sozomen, l. v. c. 15; Socrates, l. iii. c. 14; Theodoret, l. iii. c. 9; and Tillemont, Mém. Ecclés. tom. viii. p. 361–368, who has used some materials prepared by the Bollandists.

135. See the fair confession of Gregory (Orat. iii. p. 61, 62).

136. Hear the furious and absurd complaint of Optatus (de Schismat. Donatist, l. ii. c. 16, 17).

137. Greg. Nazianzen, Orat. iii. p. 91, iv. p. 133. He praises the rioters of Cæsarea, τούτων δὲ τῶν μεγαλοφνῶν καὶ θερμῶν εἰς εὐσεβείαν. See Sozomen, l. v. 4, 11. Tillemont (Mém. Ecclés. tom. vii. p. 649, 650) owns that their behaviour was not dans l'ordre commun; but he is perfectly satisfied, as the great St. Basil always celebrated the festival of these blessed martyrs.

138. Julian determined a lawsuit against the new Christian city at Maiuma, the port of Gaza; and his sentence, though it might be imputed to bigotry, was never reversed by his successors. Sozomen, l. v. c. 3. Reland, Palestin. tom. ii. p. 791.

139. Gregory (Orat. iii. p. 93, 94, 95; Orat. iv. p. 114) pretends to speak from the information of Julian's confidants, whom Orosius (vii. 30) could not have seen.

140. Gregory (Orat. iii. p. 91) charges the Apostate with secret sacrifices of boys and girls; and positively affirms that the dead bodies were thrown into the Orontes. See Theodoret, l. iii. c. 26, 27; and the equivocal candour of the Abbé de la Bléterie, Vie de Julien, p. 351, 352. Yet *contemporary* malice could not impute to Julian the troops of martyrs, more especially in the West, which Baronius so greedily swallows, and Tillemont so faintly rejects (Mém. Ecclés. tom. vii. p. 1295–1315).

141. The resignation of Gregory is truly edifying (Orat. iv. p. 123, 124). Yet, when an officer of Julian attempted to seize the church of Nazianzus, he would have lost his life if he had not yielded to the zeal of the bishop and people (Orat. xix. p. 308). See the reflections of Chrysostom, as they are alleged by Tillemont (Mém. Ecclés. tom. vii. p. 575).

Chapter XXIV

1. See this fable or satire, p. 306–336 of the Leipzig edition of Julian's works. The French version of the learned Ezekiel Spanheim (Paris, 1683) is coarse, languid, and correct; and his notes, proofs, illustrations, etc., are piled on each other till they form a mass of 557 close-printed quarto pages. The Abbé de la Bléterie (Vie de Jovien, tom. i. p. 241–393) has more happily expressed the spirit, as well as the sense, of the original, which he illustrates with some concise and curious notes.

2. Spanheim (in his preface) has most learnedly discussed the etymology, origin, resemblance, and disagreement of the Greek *satyrs*, a dramatic piece, which was acted after the tragedy; and the Latin *satires* (from *Satura*), a *miscellaneous* composition, either in prose or verse. But the Cæsars of Julian are of such an original cast, that the critic is perplexed to which class he should ascribe them.

3. This mixed character of Silenus is finely painted in the sixth eclogue of Virgil.

4. Every impartial reader must perceive and condemn the partiality of Julian against his uncle Constantine and the Christian religion. On this occasion the interpreters are compelled, by a more sacred interest, to renounce their allegiance, and to desert the cause of their author.

5. Julian was secretly inclined to prefer a Greek to a Roman. But when he seriously compared a

hero with a philosopher, he was sensible that mankind had much greater obligations to Socrates than to Alexander (Orat. ad Themistium, p. 264).

6. Inde nationibus Indicis certatim cum donis optimates mittentibus . . . ab usque Divis et *Serendivis*. Ammian. xxii. 7. This island, to which the names of Taprobana, Serendib, and Ceylon, have been successively applied, manifests how imperfectly the seas and lands to the east of Cape Comorin were known to the Romans. 1. Under the reign of Claudius, a freedman, who farmed the customs of the Red Sea, was accidentally driven by the winds upon this strange and undiscovered coast: he conversed six months with the natives: and the king of Ceylon, who heard for the first time of the power and justice of Rome, was persuaded to send an embassy to the emperor (Plin. Hist. Nat. vi. 24). 2. The geographers (and even Ptolemy) have magnified above fifteen times the real size of this new world, which they extended as far as the equator, and the neighbourhood of China.

7. These embassies had been sent to Constantius. Ammianus, who unwarily deviates into gross flattery, must have forgotten the length of the way, and the short duration of the reign of Julian.

8. Gothos sæpe fallaces et perfidos; hostes quærere se meliores aiebat: illis enim sufficere merca-

tores Galatas per quos ubique sine conditionis discrimine venumdantur. [Ammian. xxii. 7.] Within less than fifteen years these Gothic slaves threatened and subdued their masters.

9. Alexander reminds his rival Cæsar, who depreciated the fame and merit of an Asiatic victory, that Crassus and Antony had felt the Persian arrows; and that the Romans, in a war of three hundred years, had not yet subdued the single province of Mesopotamia or Assyria (Cæsares, p. 324).

10. The design of the Persian war is declared by Ammianus (xxii. 7, 12), Libanius (Orat. Parent. c. 79, 80, p. 305, 306 [Fabric. Bibl. Græc. ed. Hamb. 1715]), Zosimus (l. iii. [c. 11] p. 158), and Socrates (l. iii. c. 19).

11. The Satire of Julian and the Homilies of St. Chrysostom exhibit the same picture of Antioch. The miniature which the Abbé de la Bléterie has copied from thence (Vie de Julian, p. 332) is elegant and correct.

12. Laodicea furnished charioteers; Tyre and Berytus, comedians; Cæsarea, pantomimes; Heliopolis, singers; Gaza, gladiators; Ascalon, wrestlers; and Castabala, rope-dancers. See the Expositio totius Mundi, p. 6, in the third tome of Hudson's Minor Geographers.

13. Χριστόν δὲ ἀγαπῶντες ἔχετε πολιοῦχον ἀντὶ τοῦ Διός. The people of Antioch ingeniously professed their attachment to the *Chi* (Christ), and the *Kappa* (Constantius). Julian in Misopogon, p. 357.

14. The schism of Antioch, which lasted eighty-five years (A.D. 330–415), was inflamed, while Julian resided in that city, by the indiscreet ordination of Paulinus. See Tillemont. Mém. Ecclés. tom. vii. p. 803 of the quarto edition (Paris, 1701,etc.), which henceforward I shall quote.

15. Julian states three different proportions, of five, ten, or fifteen *modii* of wheat, for one piece of gold, according to the degrees of plenty and scarcity (in Misopogon, p. 369). From this fact, and from some collateral examples, I conclude that, under the successors of Constantine, the moderate price of wheat was about thirty-two shillings the English quarter, which is equal to the average price of the sixty-four first years of the present century. See Arbuthnot's Tables of Coins, Weights, and Measures, p. 88, 89. Plin. Hist. Natur. xviii. 12. Mém. de l'Académie des Inscriptions, tom. xxviii. p. 718–721. Smith's Inquiry into the Nature and Causes of the Wealth of Nations, Bk. I, ch. 11. This last I am proud to quote, as the work of a sage and a friend.

16. Nunquam a proposito declinabat, Galli similis fratris, licet incruentus. Ammian. xxii. 14. The ignorance of the most enlightened princes may claim some excuse; but we cannot be satisfied with Julian's own defence (in Misopogon, p. 368, 369), or the elaborate apology of Libanius (Orat. Parental. c. xcvii. p. 321).

17. Their short and easy confinement is gently touched by Libanius (Orat. Parental. c. xcviii. p. 322, 323).

18. Libanius (ad Antiochenos de Imperatoris ira, c. 17, 18, 19, in Fabricius, Biblioth. Græc. tom. vii. p. 221–223), like a skilful advocate, severely censures the folly of the people, who suffered for the crime of a few obscure and drunken wretches.

19. Libanius (ad Antiochen. c. vii. p. 213) reminds Antioch of the recent chastisement of Cæsarea; and even Julian (in Misopogon, p. 355) insinuates how severely Tarentum had expiated the insult to the Roman ambassadors.

20. On the subject of the Misopogon, see Ammianus (xxii. 14), Libanius (Orat. Parentalis, c. xcix. p. 323), Gregory Nazianzen (Orat. iv. p. 133 [ed. Paris, 1609]), and the Chronicle of Antioch, by John Malala (tom. ii. p. 15, 16 [ed. Ox.; p. 328, ed. Bonn]). I have essential obligations to the translation and notes of the Abbé de la Bléterie (Vie de Jovien, tom. ii. p. 1:138).

21. Ammianus [l. c.] very justly remarks, Coactus dissimulare pro tempore irâ sufflabatur internâ. The elaborate irony of Julian at length bursts forth into serious and direct invective.

22. Ipse autem Antiochiam egressurus, Heliopoliten quendam Alexandrum Syracæ jurisdictioni præfecit, turbulentum et sævum; dicebatque non illum meruisse, sed Antiochensibus avaris et contumeliosis hujusmodi judicem convenire. Ammian. xxiii. 2. Libanius (Epist. 722, p. 346, 347 [ed. Wolf. Amst. 1738]), who confesses to Julian himself that he had shared the general discontent, pretends that Alexander was an useful, though harsh, reformer of the manners and religion of Antioch.

23. Julian, in Misopogon, p. 364. Ammian. xxiii. 2, and Valesius ad loc. Libanius, in a professed oration, invites him to return to his loyal and penitent city of Antioch.

24. Libanius, Orat. Parent. c. vii. p. 230, 231.

25. Eunapius reports that Libanius refused the honorary rank of Prætorian præfect, as less illustrious than the title of Sophist (in Vit. Sophist. p. 135 [p. 175, ed. Comm.]). The critics have observed a similar sentiment in one of the epistles (xviii. [p. 7] ed. Wolf.) of Libanius himself.

26. Near two thousand of his letters—a mode of composition in which Libanius was thought to excel—are still extant, and already published. The critics may praise their subtle and elegant brevity; yet Dr. Bentley (Dissertation upon Phalaris, p. 487) might justly though quaintly observe that "you feel, by the emptiness and deadness of them, that you converse with some dreaming pedant, with his elbow on his desk."

27. His birth is assigned to the year 314. He mentions [Ep. 866] the seventy-sixth year of his age (A.D. 390), and seems to allude to some events of a still later date.

28. Libanius has composed the vain, prolix, but curious narrative of his own life (tom. ii. p. 1–84, edit. Morell.), of which Eunapius (p. 130–135) has left a concise and unfavourable account. Among the moderns, Tillemont (Hist. des Empereurs, tom. iv. p. 571–576), Fabricius (Biblioth. Græc.

tom. vii. p. 376–414), and Lardner (Heathen Testimonies, tom. iv. p. 127–163) have illustrated the character and writings of this famous sophist.

29. From Antioch to Litarbe, on the territory of Chalcis, the road, over hills and through morasses, was extremely bad; and the loose stones were cemented only with sand (Julian. Epist. xxvii.). It is singular enough that the Romans should have neglected the great communication between Antioch and the Euphrates. See Wesseling, Itinerar. p. 190. Bergier, Hist. des Grands Chemins, tom. ii. p. 100.

30. Julian alludes to this incident (Epist. xxvii.), which is more distinctly related by Theodoret (l. iii. c. 22). The intolerant spirit of the father is applauded by Tillemont (Hist. des Empereurs, tom. iv. p. 534), and even by la Bléterie (Vie de Julien, p. 413).

31. See the curious treatise de Deâ Syriâ, inserted among the works of Lucian (tom. iii. p. 451–490, edit. Reitz.). The singular appellation of *Ninus veius* (Ammian. xiv. 8) might induce a suspicion that Hierapolis had been the royal seat of the Assyrians.

32. Julian (Epist. xxviii. [xxvii.]) kept a regular account of all the fortunate omens; but he suppresses the inauspicious signs, which Ammianus (xxiii. 2) has carefully recorded.

33. Julian, Epist. xxvii. p. 399–402.

34. I take the earliest opportunity of acknowledging my obligations to M. d'Anville for his recent geography of the Euphrates and Tigris (Paris, 1780, in 4to.), which particularly illustrates the expedition of Julian. [Hierapolis was about twenty-two miles from the Euphrates.]

35. There are three passages within a few miles of each other: 1. Zeugma, celebrated by the ancients; 2. Bir, frequented by the moderns; and, 3. The bridge of Menbigz [Manbedj] or Hierapolis, at the distance of four parasangs from the city.

36. Haran, or Carrhæ, was the ancient residence of the Sabæans and of Abraham. See the Index Geographicus of Schultens (ad calcem Vit. Saladin.), a work from which I have obtained much *Oriental* knowledge concerning the ancient and modern geography of Syria and the adjacent countries.

37. See Xenophon, Cyropæd, l. iii. [c. 1, § 34] p. 189, edit. Hutchinson. Artavasdes might have supplied Marc Antony with 16,000 horse, armed and disciplined after the Parthian manner (Plutarch, in M. Antonio [c. 50], tom. v. p. 117).

38. Moses of Chorene (Hist. Armeniac. l. iii. c. 11, p. 241 [ed. Whiston, Lond. 1736]) fixes his accession (A.D. 354) to the 17th year of Constantius.

39. Ammian. xx. 11. Athanasius (tom. i. p. 856) says, in general terms, that Constantius gave his brother's widow τοῖς βαρβάροις, an expression more suitable to a Roman than a Christian.

40. Ammianus (xxiii. 2) uses a word much too soft for the occasion, *monuerat.* Muratori (Fabricius, Bibliothec. Græc. tom. vii. p. 86) has published an epistle from Julian to the satrap Arsaces; fierce, vulgar, and (though it might deceive Sozomen, l. vi. c. 5 [c. 1]), most probably spurious. La Bléterie (Hist. de Jovien, tom. ii. p. 339) translates and rejects it.

41. Latissimum flumen Euphraten artabat. Ammian. xxiii. 3. Somewhat higher, at the fords of Thapsacus, the river is four stadia, or 800 yards, almost half an English mile, broad (Xenophon, Anabasis, l. i. [c. 4, § 11] p. 41, edit. Hutchinson, with Foster's Observations, p. 29, etc., in the second volume of Spelman's translation). If the breadth of the Euphrates at Bir and Zeugma is no more than 130 yards (Voyages de Niebuhr, tom. ii. p. 335), the enormous difference must chiefly arise from the depth of the channel.

42. Munimentum tutissimum et fabrè politum, cujus mœnia Abora (the Orientals aspirate Chaboras or Chabour) et Euphrates ambiunt flumina, velut spatium insulare fingentes. Ammian. xxiii. 5.

43. The enterprise and armament of Julian are described by himself (Epist. xxvii.), Ammianus Marcellinus (xxiii. 3, 4, 5), Libanius (Orat. Parent. c. 108, 109, p. 332, 333), Zosimus (l. iii. [c. 11] p. 160, 161, 162), Sozomen (l. vi. c. 1), and John Malala (tom. ii. p. 17 [ed. Ox.; p. 328, ed. Bonn]).

44. Before he enters Persia, Ammianus copiously describes (xxiii. 6, p. 396–419, edit. Gronov. in 4to) the eighteen great satrapies or provinces (as far as the Seric or Chinese frontiers) which were subject to the Sassanides.

45. Ammianus (xxiv. 1) and Zosimus (l. iii. [c. 14] p. 162, 163) have accurately expressed the order of march.

46. The adventures of Hormisdas are related with some mixture of fable (Zosimus, l. ii. [c. 27] p. 100–102; Tillemont, Hist. des Empereurs, tom. iv. p. 198). It is almost impossible that he should be the brother (frater germanus) of an *eldest* and *posthumous* child; nor do I recollect that Ammianus ever gives him that title.

47. See the first book of the Anabasis [c. 5], p. 45, 46. This pleasing work is original and authentic. Yet Xenophon's memory, perhaps many years after the expedition, has sometimes betrayed him; and the distances which he marks are often larger than either a soldier or a geographer will allow.

48. Mr. Spelman, the English translator of the Anabasis (vol. i. p. 51), confounds the antelope with the roebuck, and the wild ass with the zebra.

49. See Voyages de Tavernier, part. i. l. iii. p. 316, and more especially Viaggi di Pietro della Valle, tom. i. lett. xvii. p. 671, etc. He was ignorant of the old name and condition of Anah. Our blind travellers *seldom* possess any previous knowledge of the countries which they visit. Shaw and Tournefort deserve an honourable exception.

50. Famosi nominis latro, says Ammianus—a high encomium for an Arab. The tribe of Gassan had settled on the edge of Syria, and reigned some time in Damascus, under a dynasty of thirty-one kings or emirs, from the time of Pompey to that of

the Khalif Omar. D'Herbelot, Bibliothèque Orientale, p. 360. Pococke, Specimen Hist. Arabicæ, p. 75–78. The name of Rodosaces does not appear in the list.

51. See Ammianus (xxiv. 1, 2), Libanius (Orat. Parental. c. 110, 111, p. 334), Zosimus (l. iii. [c. 15] p. 164–168).

52. The description of Assyria is furnished by Herodotus (l. i. c. 192, etc.), who sometimes writes for children, and sometimes for philosophers; by Strabo (l. xvi. p. 1070–1082 [p. 736–746, ed. Casaub.]); and by Ammianus (l. xxiii. c. 6). The most useful of the modern travellers are Tavernier (part. i. l. ii. p. 226–258), Otter (tom. ii. p. 35–69, and 189–224), and Niebuhr (tom. ii. p. 172–288). Yet I much regret that the *Irak Arabi* of Abulfeda has not been translated.

53. Ammianus remarks that the primitive Assyria, which comprehended Ninus (Nineveh) and Arbela, had assumed the more recent and peculiar appellation of Adiabene; and he seems to fix Teredon, Vologesia, and Apollonia, as the *extreme* cities of the actual province of Assyria.

54. The two great rivers unite at Apamea, or Corna (one hundred miles from the Persian Gulf), into the broad stream of the Pasitigris, or Shat-ul-Arab. The Euphrates formerly reached the sea by a separate channel, which was obstructed and diverted by the citizens of Orchoe, about twenty miles to the south-east of modern Basra (D'Anville, in the Mémoires de l'Acad. des Inscriptions, tom. xxx. p. 170–191).

55. The learned Kæmpfer, as a botanist, an antiquary, and a traveller, has exhausted (Amœnitat. Exoticæ, Fascicul. iv. p. 660–764) the whole subject of palm-trees.

56. Assyria yielded to the Persian satrap an *artaba* of silver each day. The well-known proportion of weights and measures (see Bishop Hooper's elaborate Inquiry), the specific gravity of water and silver, and the value of that metal, will afford, after a short process, the annual revenue which I have stated. Yet the Great King received no more than 1000 Euboic, or Tyrian, talents (£252,000) from Assyria. The comparison of two passages in Herodotus (l. i. c. 192, l. iii. c. 89–96) reveals an important difference between the *gross* and the *net* revenue of Persia; the sums paid by the province, and the gold or silver deposited in the royal treasure. The monarch might annually save three millions six hundred thousand pounds, of the seventeen or eighteen millions raised upon the people.

57. The operations of the Assyrian war are circumstantially related by Ammianus (xxiv. 2, 3, 4, 5), Libanius (Orat. Parent. c. 112–123, p. 335–347), Zosimus (l. iii. [c. 18] p. 168–180), and Gregory Nazianzen (Orat. iv. p. 113, 144). The *military* criticisms of the saint are devoutly copied by Tillemont, his faithful slave.

58. Libanius de ulciscendâ Juliani nece, c. 13, p. 162 [in Fabric. Bibl. Græc. vol. vii.]

59. The famous examples of Cyrus, Alexander,

and Scipio, were acts of justice. Julian's chastity was voluntary, and, in his opinion, meritorious.

60. Sallust (ap. Vet. Scholiast. Juvenal. Satir. i. 104) observes, that nihil corruptius moribus. The matrons and virgins of Babylon freely mingled with the men in licentious banquets: and as they felt the intoxication of wine and love, they gradually, and almost completely, threw aside the incumbrance of dress; ad ultimum ima corporum velamenta projiciunt. Q. Curtius. v. 1.

61. Ex virginibus autem, quæ speciosæ sunt captæ, ut in Perside, ubi feminarum pulchritudo excellit, nec contrectare aliquam voluit nec videre. Ammian. xxiv. 4. The native race of Persians is small and ugly; but it has been improved by the perpetual mixture of Circassian blood (Herodot. l. iii. c. 97. Buffon, Hist. Naturelle, tom. iii. p. 420).

62. Obsidionalibus coronis donati. Ammian. xxiv. 4. Either Julian or his historian were unskilful antiquaries. He should have given *mural* crowns. The *obsidional* were the reward of a general who had delivered a besieged city (Aulus Gellius, Noct. Attic. v. 6).

63. I give this speech as original and genuine. Ammianus might hear, could transcribe, and was incapable of inventing, it. I have used some slight freedoms, and conclude with the most forcible sentence.

64. Ammian. xxiv. 3. Libanius, Orat. Parent. c. 122, p. 346.

65. M. d'Anville (Mém. de l'Académie des Inscriptions, tom. xxviii. p. 246–259) has ascertained the true position and distance of Babylon, Seleucia, Ctesiphon, Bagdad, etc. The Roman traveller, Pietro della Valle (tom. i. lett. xvii. p. 650–780), seems to be the most intelligent spectator of that famous province. He is a gentleman and a scholar, but intolerably vain and prolix.

66. The Royal Canal (*Nahar-Malcha*) might be successively restored, altered, divided, etc. (Cellarius, Geograph. Antiq. tom. ii. p. 453): and these changes may serve to explain the seeming contradictions of antiquity. In the time of Julian it must have fallen into the Euphrates *below* Ctesiphon.

67 Καὶ μεγέθεσιν ἐλεφάντων, οἷς ἴσον ἔργον διὰ σταχύων ἐλθεῖν καὶ φάλαγγος. [Or. Parent. c. 125.] Rien n'est beau que le vrai; a maxim which should be inscribed on the desk of every rhetorician.

68. Libanius alludes to the most powerful of the generals. I have ventured to name *Sallust*. Ammianus [xxiv. 6] says, of all the leaders, quòd acri metú territi duces concordi precatú fieri prohibere tentarent.

69. Hinc Imperator . . . (says Ammianus) ipse cum levis armaturæ auxiliis per prima postremaque discurrens, etc. Yet Zosimus, his friend, does not allow him to pass the river till two days after the battle.

70. Secundum Homericam dispositionem. A similar disposition is ascribed to the wise Nestor, in the fourth book of the Iliad; and Homer was never absent from the mind of Julian.

71. Persas terrore subito miscuerunt, versisque agminibus totius gentis, apertas Ctesiphontis portas victor miles intrâsset, ni major prædaram occasio fuisset, quam cura victoriæ (Sextus Rufus de Provinciis, c. 28). Their avarice might dispose them to hear the advice of Victor.

72. The labour of the canal, the passage of the Tigris, and the victory, are described by Ammianus (xxiv. 5, 6), Libanius (Orat. Parent. c. 124-128, p. 347-353), Greg. Nazianzen (Orat. iv. p. 115), Zosimus (l. iii. [c. 24, p. 159 *sqq.*] p. 181-183), and Sextus Rufus (de Provinciis, c. 28).

73. The fleet and army were formed in three divisions, of which the first only had passed during the night (Ammian. xxiv. 6). The πᾶσα δορυφορία, whom Zosimus transports on the third day (l. iii. [c. 26] p. 183), might consist of the protectors, among whom the historian Ammianus, and the future emperor Jovian, actually served; some *schools* of the *domestics;* and perhaps the Jovians and Herculians, who often did duty as guards.

74. Moses of Chorene (Hist. Armen. l. iii. c. 15, p. 246) supplies us with a national tradition and a spurious letter. I have borrowed only the leading circumstance, which is consistent with truth, probability, and Libanius (Orat. Parent. c. 131, p. 355).

75. Civitas inexpugnabilis, facinus audax et importunum. Ammianus, xxiv. 7. His fellow-soldier, Eutropius, turns aside from the difficulty: Assyriamque populatus, castra apud Ctesiphontem stativa aliquandiu habuit: remeansque victor, etc., x. 16 [8]. Zosimus is artful or ignorant, and Socrates inaccurate.

76. Libanius, Orat. Parent. c. 130, p. 354, c. 139, p. 361. Socrates, l. iii. c. 21. The ecclesiastical historian imputes the refusal of peace to the advice of Maximus. Such advice was unworthy of a philosopher; but the philosopher was likewise a magician, who flattered the hopes and passions of his master.

77. The arts of this new Zopyrus (Greg. Nazianzen, Orat. iv. p. 115, 116 [ed. Par. 1609]) may derive some credit from the testimony of two abbreviators (Sextus Rufus and Victor), and the casual hints of Libanius (Orat. Parent. c. 134, p. 357) and Ammianus (xxiv. 7). The course of genuine history is interrupted by a most unseasonable chasm in the text of Ammianus.

78. See Ammianus (xxiv. 7), Libanius, (Orat. Parentalis, c. 132, 133, p. 356, 357), Zosimus (l. iii. [c. 26] p. 183), Zonaras (tom. ii. l. xiii. [c. 13] p. 26), Gregory (Orat. iv. p. 116), and Augustine (The City of God, l. iv. c. 29, l. v. c. 21). Of these Libanius alone attempts a faint apology for his hero; who, according to Ammianus, pronounced his own condemnation by a tardy and ineffectual attempt to extinguish the flames.

79. Consult Herodotus (l. i. c. 194), Strabo (l. xvi. p. 1074 [p. 739, ed. Casaub.]), and Tavernier (part i. l. ii. p. 152).

80. A celeritate Tigris incipit vocari, ita appellant Medi sagittam. Plin. Hist. Natur. vi. 31.

81. One of these dykes, which produces an artificial cascade or cataract, is described by Tavernier (part i. l. ii. p. 226) and Thevenot (part ii. l. i. p. 193). The Persians, or Assyrians, laboured to interrupt the navigation of the river (Strabo, l. xvi. p. 1075 [p. 740]. D'Anville, l'Euphrate et le Tigre, p. 98, 99).

82. Recollect the successful and applauded rashness of Agathocles and Cortez, who burnt their ships on the coast of Africa and Mexico.

83. See the judicious reflections of the author of the Essai sur la Tactique, tom. ii. p. 287-353, and the learned remarks of M. Guichardt, Nouveaux Mémoires Militaires, tom. i. p. 351-382, on the baggage and subsistence of the Roman armies.

84. The Tigris rises to the south, the Euphrates to the north, of the Armenian mountains. The former overflows in March, the latter in July. These circumstances are well explained in the Geographical Dissertation of Foster, inserted in Spelman's Expedition of Cyrus, vol. ii. p. 26.

85. Ammianus (xxiv. 8) describes, as he had felt, the inconveniency of the flood, the heat, and the insects. The lands of Assyria, oppressed by the Turks, and ravaged by the Curds or Arabs, yield an increase of ten, fifteen, and twenty fold, for the seed which is cast into the ground by the wretched and unskilful husbandmen. Voyages de Niebuhr, tom. ii. p. 279, 285.

86. Isidore of Charax (Mansion, Parthic. p. 5, 6, in Hudson, Geograph. Minor. tom. ii.) reckons 129 schœni from Seleucia, and Thevenot (part i. l. i. ii. p. 209-245) 128 hours of march from Bagdad to Ecbatana, or Hamadan. These measures cannot exceed an ordinary parasang, or three Roman miles.

87. The march of Julian from Ctesiphon is circumstantially, but not clearly, described by Ammianus (xxiv. 7, 8), Libanius (Orat. Parent. c. 134, p. 357), and Zosimus (l. iii. [c. 26] p. 183). The two last seem ignorant that their conqueror was retreating; and Libanius absurdly confines him to the banks of the Tigris.

88. Chardin, the most judicious of modern travellers, describes (tom. iii. p. 57, 58, etc., edit. in 4to.) the education and dexterity of the Persian horsemen. Brissonius (de Regno Persico, p. 650, 661, etc.) has collected the testimonies of antiquity.

89. In Mark Antony's retreat, an attic chœnix sold for fifty drachmæ, or, in other words, a pound of flour for twelve or fourteen shillings; barley bread was sold for its weight in silver. It is impossible to peruse the interesting narrative of Plutarch (Life of Antony) without perceiving that Mark Antony and Julian were pursued by the same enemies and involved in the same distress.

90. Ammian. xxiv. 8, xxv. 1. Zosimus, l. iii. [c. 27, *seq.*] p. 184, 185, 186. Libanius, Orat. Parent. c. 134, 135, p. 357, 358, 359. The sophist of Antioch appears ignorant that the troops were hungry.

91. Ammian. xxv. 2. Julian had sworn in a passion, numquam se Marti sacra facturum (xxiv. 6). Such whimsical quarrels were not uncommon be-

tween the gods and their insolent votaries; and even the prudent Augustus, after his fleet had been twice shipwrecked, excluded Neptune from the honours of public processions. See Hume's Philosophical Reflections. Essays, vol. ii. p. 418.

92. They still retained the monopoly of the vain but lucrative science, which had been invented in Etruria; and professed to derive their knowledge of signs and omens from the ancient books of Tarquitius, a Tuscan sage.

93. Clamabant hinc inde *candidati* (see the note of Valesius) quos disjecerat terror, ut fugientium molem tanquam ruinam male compositi culminis declinaret. Ammian. xxv. 3.

94. Sapor himself declared to the Romans that it was his practice to comfort the families of his deceased satraps by sending them, as a present, the heads of the guards and officers who had not fallen by their master's side. Libanius, de nece Julian. ulcis. c. xiii. p. 163.

95. The character and situation of Julian might countenance the suspicion that he had previously composed the elaborate oration, which Ammianus heard, and has transcribed. The version of the Abbé de la Bléterie is faithful and elegant. I have followed him in expressing the Platonic idea of emanations, which is darkly insinuated in the original.

96. Herodotus (l. i. c. 31) has displayed that doctrine in an agreeable tale. Yet the Jupiter (in the 16th book of the Iliad), who laments with tears of blood the death of Sarpedon his son, had a very imperfect notion of happiness, or glory beyond the grave.

97. The soldiers who made their verbal or nuncupatory testaments upon actual service (in procinctû) were exempted from the formalities of the Roman law. See Heineccius (Antiquit. Jur. Roman. tom. i. p. 504) and Montesquieu (Esprit des Loix, l. xxvii.).

98. This union of the human soul with the divine etherial substance of the universe is the ancient doctrine of Pythagoras and Plato, but it seems to exclude any personal or conscious immortality. See Warburton's learned and rational observations. Divine Legation, vol. ii. p. 199–216.

99. The whole relation of the death of Julian is given by Ammianus (xxv. 3), an intelligent spectator. Libanius, who turns with horror from the scene, has supplied some circumstances (Orat. Parental. c. 136–140, p. 359–362). The calumnies of Gregory, and the legends of more recent saints, may now be *silently* despised.

100. Honoratior aliquis miles; perhaps Ammianus himself. The modest and judicious historian describes the scene of the election, at which he was undoubtedly present (xxv. 5).

101. The *primus* or *primicerius* enjoyed the dignity of a senator; and, though only a tribune, he ranked with the military dukes. Cod. Theodosian. l. vi. tit. xxiv. [leg. 11]. These privileges are perhaps more recent than the time of Jovian.

102. The ecclesiastical historians, Socrates (l. iii.

c. 22), Sozomen (l. vi. c. 3), and Theodoret (l. iv. c. 1), ascribe to Jovian the merit of a confessor under the preceding reign, and piously suppose that he refused the purple till the whole army unanimously exclaimed that they were Christians. Ammianus, calmly pursuing his narrative, overthrows the legend by a single sentence. Hostiis pro Joviano extisque inspectis, pronuntiatum est, etc. (xxv. 6).

103. Ammianus (xxv. 10) has drawn from the life an impartial portrait of Jovian, to which the younger Victor has added some remarkable strokes. The Abbé de la Bléterie (Histoire de Jovien, tom. i. p. 1–238) has composed an elaborate history of his short reign—a work remarkably distinguished by elegance of style, critical disquisition, and religious prejudice.

104. Regius equitatus. It appears from Procopius that the Immortals, so famous under Cyrus and his successors, were revived, if we may use that improper word, by the Sassanides. Brisson. de Regno Persico, p. 268, etc.

105. The obscure villages of the inland country are irrecoverably lost; nor can we name the field of battle where Julian fell: but M. d'Anville has demonstrated the precise situation of Sumere, Carche, and Dura, along the banks of the Tigris (Géographie Ancienne, tom. ii. p. 248; l'Euphrate et le Tigre, p. 95, 97). In the ninth century, Sumere, or Samara, became, with a slight change of name, the royal residence of the khalifs of the house of Abbas.

106. Dura was a fortified place in the wars of Antiochus against the rebels of Media and Persia (Polybius, l. v. c. 48, 52, p. 548, 552, edit. Casaubon, in 8vo.)

107. A similar expedient was proposed to the leaders of the ten thousand, and wisely rejected. Xenophon, Anabasis, l. iii. [c. v. §§ 9–11] p. 255, 256, 257. It appears from our modern travellers that rafts floating on bladders perform the trade and navigation of the Tigris.

108. The first military acts of the reign of Jovian are related by Ammianus (xxv. 6), Libanius (Orat. Parent. c. 143, p. 364), and Zosimus (l. iii. [c. 30] p. 189, 190, 191). Though we may distrust the fairness of Libanius, the ocular testimony of Eutropius (uno a Persis atque altero prœlio victus, x. 17 [9]) must incline us to suspect that Ammianus has been too jealous of the honour of the Roman arms.

109. Sextus Rufus (de Provinciis, c. 29) embraces a poor subterfuge of national vanity. Tanta reverentia nominis Romani fuit, ut a Persis primus de pace sermo haberetur.

110. It is presumptuous to controvert the opinion of Ammianus, a soldier and a spectator. Yet it is difficult to understand *how* the mountains of Corduene could extend over the plain of Assyria as low as the conflux of the Tigris and the Great Zab, or *how* an army of sixty thousand men could march one hundred miles in four days.

111. The treaty of Dura is recorded with grief or indignation by Ammianus (xxv. 7), Libanius

(Orat. Parent. c. 142, p. 364), Zosimus (l. iii. [c. 31] p. 190, 191), Gregory Nazianzen (Orat. iv. p. 117, 118, who imputes the distress to Julian, the deliverance to Jovian), and Eutropius (x. 17 [9]). The last-mentioned writer, who was present in a military station, styles this peace necessariam quidem sed ignobilem.

112. Libanius, Orat. Parent. c. 143, p. 364, 365.

113. Conditionibus . . . dispendiosis Romanæ reipublicæ impositis . . . quibus cupidior regni quam gloriæ Jovianus, imperio rudis, adquievit. Sextus Rufus de Provinciis, c. 29. La Bléterie has expressed, in a long, direct oration, these specious considerations of public and private interest (Hist. de Jovien, tom. i. p. 39, etc.).

114. The generals were murdered on the banks of the Zabatus (Anabasis, l. ii. [c. v. § 1] p. 156, l. iii. [c. iii. § 6] p. 226), or Great Zab, a river of Assyria, 400 feet broad, which falls into the Tigris fourteen hours below Mosul. The error of the Greeks bestowed on the Great and Lesser Zab the names of the *Wolf* (Lycus) and the *Goat* (Capros). They created these animals to attend the *Tiger* of the East.

115. The *Cyropædia* is vague and languid; the *Anabasis* circumstantial and animated. Such is the eternal difference between fiction and truth.

116. According to Rufinus, an immediate supply of provisions was stipulated by the treaty, and Theodoret affirms that the obligation was faithfully discharged by the Persians. Such a fact is probable, but undoubtedly false. See Tillemont, Hist. des. Empereurs, tom. iv. p. 702.

117. We may recollect some lines of Lucan (Pharsal. iv. 95), who describes a similar distress of Cæsar's army in Spain:—

Sæva fames aderat ————
Miles eget: toto censû non prodigus emit
Exiguam Cererem. Proh lucri pallida tabes!
Non deest prolato jejunus venditor auro.

See Guichardt (Nouveaux Mémoires Militaries, tom. i. p. 379-382). His analysis of the two campaigns in Spain and Africa is the noblest monument that has ever been raised to the fame of Cæsar.

118. M. d'Anville (see his Maps, and l'Euphrate et le Tigre, p. 92, 93) traces their march, and assigns the true position of Hatra, Ur, and Thilsaphata, which Ammianus has mentioned. He does not complain of the Samiel, the deadly hot wind, which Thevenot (Voyages, part ii. l. i. p. 192) so much dreaded.

119. The retreat of Jovian is described by Ammianus (xxv. 9), Libanius (Orat. Parent c. 143, p. 365), and Zosimus (l. iii. [c. 33] p. 194).

120. Libanius (Orat. Parent. c. 145, p. 366). Such were the natural hopes and wishes of a rhetorician.

121. The people of Carrhæ, a city devoted to Paganism, buried the inauspicious messenger under a pile of stones (Zosimus, l. iii. [c. 34] p. 196). Libanius, when he received the fatal intelligence, cast his eye on his sword; but he recollected that Plato had condemned suicide, and that he must live to compose the Panegyric of Julian (Libanius de Vitâ suâ, tom. ii. p. 45, 46 [ed. Morell. Paris. 1627]).

122. Ammianus and Eutropius may be admitted as fair and credible witnesses of the public language and opinions. The people of Antioch reviled an ignominious peace which exposed them to the Persians on a naked and defenceless frontier (Excerpt. Valesiana, p. 845, ex Johanne Antiocheno.).

123. The Abbé de la Bléterie (Hist. de Jovien, tom. i. p. 212-227), though a severe casuist, has pronounced that Jovian was not bound to execute his promise: since he *could not* dismember the empire, nor alienate, without their consent, the allegiance of his people. I have never found much delight or instruction in such political metaphysics.

124. At Nisibis he performed a *royal* act. A brave officer, his namesake, who had been thought worthy of the purple, was dragged from supper, thrown into a well, and stoned to death without any form of trial or evidence of guilt. Ammian. xxv. 8.

125. See xxv. 9, and Zosimus, l. iii. [c. 33] p. 194. 195.

126. Chron. Paschal. p. 300 [tom. i. p. 554, ed Bonn]. The ecclesiastical Notitiæ may be consulted.

127. Zosimus, l. iii. [c. 32] p. 192, 193. Sextus Rufus de Provinciis, c. 29. Augustine, The City of God, l. iv. c. 29. This general position must be applied and interpreted with some caution.

128. Ammianus, xxv. 10. Zosimus, l. iii. [c. 34] p. 196. He might be edax, et vino Venerique indulgens. But I agree with La Bléterie (tom. i. p. 148-154) in rejecting the foolish report of a Bacchanalian riot (ap. Suidam) celebrated at Antioch by the emperor, his *wife*, and a troop of concubines.

129. The Abbé de la Bléterie (tom. i. p. 156, 209) handsomely exposes the brutal bigotry of Baronius, who would have thrown Julian to the dogs, ne cespititiâ quidem sepulturâ dignus.

130. Compare the sophist and the saint (Libanius, Monod. tom. ii. p. 251, and Orat. Parent. c. 145, p. 367, c. 156, p. 377, with Gregory Nazianzen, Orat. iv. p. 125-132). The Christian orator faintly mutters some exhortations to modesty and forgiveness: but he is well satisfied that the real sufferings of Julian will far exceed the fabulous torments of Ixion or Tantalus.

131. Tillemont (Hist. des Empereurs, tom. iv. p. 549) has collected these visions. Some saint or angel was observed to be absent in the night on a secret expedition, etc.

132. Sozomen (l. vi. 2) applauds the Greek doctrine of *tyrannicide:* but the whole passage, which a Jesuit might have translated, is prudently suppressed by the president Cousin.

133. Immediately after the death of Julian an uncertain rumour was scattered, telo cecidisse Romano. It was carried by some deserters to the Persian camp; and the Romans were reproached as the assassins of the emperor by Sapor and his sub-

jects (Ammian. xxv. 6; Libanius de ulciscendâ Juliani nece, c. xiii. p. 162, 163). It was urged, as a decisive proof, that no Persian had appeared to claim the promised reward (Liban. Orat. Parent. c. 141, p. 363). But the flying horseman who darted the fatal javelin might be ignorant of its effect, or he might be slain in the same action. Ammianus neither feels nor inspires a suspicion.

134. Οστις ἐντολὴν πληρῶν τῷ σφῶν αὐτῶν ἄρχοντι. This dark and ambiguous expression may point to Athanasius, the first without a rival of the Christian clergy (Libanius de ulcis. Jul. nece, c. 5, p. 149. La Bléterie, Hist. de Jovien, tom. i. p. 179).

135. The orator (Fabricius, Biblioth. Græc. tom. vii. p. 145–179) scatters suspicions, demands an inquiry, and insinuates that proofs might still be obtained. He ascribes the success of the Huns to the criminal neglect of revenging Julian's death.

136. At the funeral of Vespasian, the comedian who personated that frugal emperor anxiously inquired how much it cost?—Fourscore thousand pounds (centies).—Give me the tenth part of the sum, and throw my body into the Tiber. Sueton.

in Vespasian, c. 19, with the notes of Casaubon and Gronovius.

137. Gregory (Orat. iv. p. 119, 120 [ed. Paris, 1609; Orat. v. c. 16, 18, p. 157, seqq. ed. Bened. 1778]) compares this supposed ignominy and ridicule to the funeral honours of Constantius, whose body was chaunted over Mount Taurus by a choir of angels.

138. Quintus Curtius, l. iii. c. 4. The luxuriancy of his descriptions has been often censured. Yet it was almost the duty of the historian to describe a river whose waters had nearly proved fatal to Alexander.

139. Libanius, Orat. Parent. c. 156, p. 377. Yet he acknowledges with gratitude the liberality of the two royal brothers in decorating the tomb of Julian (de ulcis. Jul. nece, c. 7, p. 152).

140. Cujus suprema et cineres, si qui tunc justè consuleret, non Cydnus videre deberet, quamvis gratissimus amnis et liquidus: sed ad perpetuandam gloriam recte factorum præterlambere Tiberis, intersecans urbem æternam, divorumque veterum monumenta præstringens. Ammian. xxv. 10.

Chapter XXV

1. The medals of Jovian adorn him with victories, laurel crowns, and prostrate captives. Ducange, Famil. Byzantin. p. 52. Flattery is a foolish suicide; she destroys herself with her own hands.

2. Jovian restored to the church τὸν ἀρχαῖον κόσμον; a forcible and comprehensive expression (Philostorgius, l. viii. c. 5, with Godefroy's Dissertations, p. 329. Sozomen, l. vi. c. 3). The new law which condemned the rape or marriage of nuns (Cod. Theod. l. ix. tit. xxv. leg. 2) is exaggerated by Sozomen, who supposes that an amorous glance, the adultery of the heart, was punished with death by the evangelic legislator.

3. Compare Socrates, l. iii. c. 25, and Philostorgius, l. viii. c. 6, with Godefroy's Dissertations, p. 330.

4. The word celestial faintly expresses the impious and extravagant flattery of the emperor to the archbishop, τῆς πρὸς τὸν θεὸν τῶν ὅλων ὁμοιώσεως (See the original epistle in Athanasius, tom. ii. p. 33.) Gregory Nazianzen (Orat. xxi. p. 392) celebrates the friendship of Jovian and Athanasius. The primate's journey was advised by the Egyptian monks (Tillemont, Mém. Ecclés. tom. viii. p. 221).

5. Athanasius, at the court of Antioch, is agreeably represented by La Bléterie (Hist. de Jovien, tom. i. p. 121–148): he translates the singular and original conferences of the emperor, the primate of Egypt, and the Arian deputies. The Abbé is not satisfied with the coarse pleasantry of Jovian; but his partiality for Athanasius assumes, in his eyes, the character of justice.

6. The true era of his death is perplexed with

some difficulties (Tillemont, Mém. Ecclés. tom viii. p. 719–723). But the date (A.D. 373, May 2) which seems the most consistent with history and reason is ratified by his authentic Life (Maffei, Osservazioni Letterarie, tom. iii. p. 81).

7. See the observations of Valesius and Jortin (Remarks on Ecclesiastical History, vol. iv. p. 38) on the original letter of Athanasius, which is preserved by Theodoret (l. iv. c. 3). In some MSS. this indiscreet promise is omitted; perhaps by the Catholics, jealous of the prophetic fame of their leader.

8. Athanasius (apud Theodoret, l. iv. c. 3) magnifies the number of the orthodox, who composed the whole world, πάρεξ ὀλίγων τῶν τὰ Ἀρείου φρονούντων. This assertion was verified in the space of thirty or forty years.

9. Socrates, l. iii. c. 24. Gregory Nazianzen (Orat. iv. p. 131) and Libanius (Orat. Parentalis, c. 148, p. 369) express the living sentiments of their respective factions.

10. Themistius, Orat. v. p. 63–71, edit. Harduin, Paris, 1684. The Abbé de la Bléterie judiciously remarks (Hist. de Jovien, tom. i. p. 199) that Sozomen has forgot the general toleration; and Themistius the establishment of the Catholic religion. Each of them turned away from the object which he disliked, and wished to suppress the part of the edict the least honourable, in his opinion, to the emperor Jovian.

11. Οἱ δὲ Ἀντιοχεῖς οὐχ ἡδέως διέκειντο πρὸς αὐτὸν· ἀλλ᾽ ἐπέσκωπτον αὐτὸν ᾠδαῖς καὶ παρῳδίαις καὶ τοῖς καλουμένοις φαμώσσοις (famosis libellis). Johan. Antiochen. in Excerpt. Valesian. p. 845. The libels of

Antioch may be admitted on very slight evidence.

12. Compare Ammianus (xxv. 10), who omits the name of the Batavians, with Zosimus (l. iii. [c. 35] p. 197), who removes the scene of action from Rheims to Sirmium.

13. Quos capita scholarum ordo castrensis appellat. Ammian. xxv. 10, and Vales. ad locum.

14. Cujus vagitus, pertinaciter reluctantis, ne in curuli sellâ veheretur ex more, id quod mox accidit portendebat. [Amm. l. c.] Augustus and his successors respectfully solicited a dispensation of age for the sons or nephews whom they raised to the consulship. But the curule chair of the first Brutus had never been dishonoured by an infant.

15. The Itinerary of Antoninus fixes Dadastana 125 Roman miles from Nice, 117 from Ancyra (Wesseling, Itinerar. p. 142). The pilgrim of Bordeaux, by omitting some stages, reduces the whole space from 242 to 181 miles. Wesseling, p. 574.

16. See Ammianus (xxv. 10), Eutropius (x. 18 [9]), who might likewise be present; Jerom (tom. i. p. 26 [tom. i. p. 341 ed. Vallars.] ad Heliodorum), Orosius (vii. 31), Sozomen (l. vi. c. 6), Zosimus (l. iii. [c. 35] p. 197, 198), and Zonaras (tom. ii. l. xiii. [c. 14] p. 28, 29). We cannot expect a perfect agreement, and we shall not discuss minute differences.

17. Ammianus, unmindful of his usual candour and good sense, compares the death of the harmless Jovian to that of the second Africanus, who had excited the fears and resentment of the popular faction.

18. Chrysostom, tom. i. p. 336–349, edit. Montfaucon. The Christian orator attempts to comfort a widow by the examples of illustrious misfortunes; and observes, that, of nine emperors (including the Cæsar Gallus) who had reigned in his time, only two (Constantine and Constantius) died a natural death. Such vague consolations have never wiped away a single tear.

19. Ten days appear scarcely sufficient for the march and election. But it may be observed—1. That the generals might command the expeditious use of the public posts for themselves, their attendants, and messengers. 2. That the troops, for the ease of the cities, marched in many divisions; and that the head of the column might arrive at Nice when the rear halted at Ancyra.

20. Ammianus, xxvi. 1; Zosimus, l. iii. [c. 36] p. 198; Philostorgius, l. viii. c. 8; and Godefroy, Dissertat. p. 334. Philostorgius, who appears to have obtained some curious and authentic intelligence, ascribes the choice of Valentinian to the præfect Sallust, the master-general Arintheus, Dagalaiphus count of the domestics, and the patrician Datianus, whose pressing recommendations from Ancyra had a weighty influence in the election.

21. Ammianus (xxx. 7, 9) and the younger Victor [Epit. c. 45] have furnished the portrait of Valentinian, which naturally precedes and illustrates the history of his reign.

22. At Antioch, where he was obliged to attend the emperor to the temple, he struck a priest who had presumed to purify him with lustral water (Sozomen, l. vi. c. 6. Theodoret, l. iii. c. 16). Such public defiance might become Valentinian; but it could leave no room for the unworthy delation of the philosopher Maximus, which supposes some more private offence (Zosimus, l. iv. [c. 2] p. 200, 201.)

23. Socrates, l. iv. A previous exile to Melitene, or Thebais (the first might be possible), is interposed by Sozomen (l. vi. c. 6) and Philostorgius (l. vii. c. 7, with Godefroy's Dissertations, p. 293).

24. Ammianus, in a long, because unseasonable, digression (xxvi. 1, and Valesius ad locum), rashly supposes that he understands an astronomical question, of which his readers are ignorant. It is treated with more judgment and propriety by Censorinus (de Die Natali, c. 20), and Macrobius (Saturnal. l. i. c. 12–16). The appellation of Bissextile, which marks the inauspicious year (Augustin. ad Januarium, Epist. 119), is derived from the repetition of the sixth days of the calends of March.

25. Valentinian's first speech is full in Ammianus (xxvi. 2); concise and sententious in Philostorgius (l. viii. c. 8).

26. Si tuos amas, Imperator optime, habes fratrem; si Rempublicam, quære quem vestias. Ammian. xxvi. 4. In the division of the empire, Valentinian retained that sincere counsellor for himself (c. 6).

27. In suburbano, Ammian. xxvi. 4. The famous Hebdomon, or field of Mars, was distant from Constantinople either seven stadia or seven miles. See Valesius and his brother, ad loc.; and Ducange, Const. l. ii. p. 140, 141, 172, 173.

28. Participem quidem legitimum potestatis; sed in modum apparitoris morigerum, ut progrediens aperiet textus. Ammian. xxvi. 4.

29. Notwithstanding the evidence of Zonaras, Suidas, and the Paschal Chronicle, M. de Tillemont (Hist. des Empereurs, tom. v. p. 671) wishes to disbelieve these stories si advantageuses à un payen.

30. Eunapius celebrates and exaggerates the sufferings of Maximus (p. 82, 83 [p. 102, ed. Comm.]); yet he allows that this sophist or magician, the guilty favourite of Julian, and the personal enemy of Valentinian, was dismissed on the payment of a small fine.

31. The loose assertions of a general disgrace (Zosimus, l. iv. [c. 2] p. 201) are detected and refuted by Tillemont (tom. v. p. 21).

32. Ammianus, xxvi. 5.

33. Ammianus says, in general terms, subagrestis ingenii, nec bellicis nec liberalibus studiis eruditus. Ammian. xxxi. 14. The orator Themistius, with the genuine impertinence of a Greek, wished for the first time to speak the Latin language, the dialect of his sovereign, τὴν διάλεκτον κρατοῦσαν Orat. vi. p. 71.

34. The uncertain degree of alliance or consanguinity, is expressed by the words ἀνέψιος, cognatus, consobrinus (see Valesius ad Ammian. xxiii.

3). The mother of Procopius might be a sister of Basilina and Count Julian, the mother and uncle of the Apostate. Ducange, Fam. Byzantin. p. 49.

35. Ammian. xxiii. 3, xxvi. 6. He mentions the report with much hesitation: susurravit obscurior fama; nemo enim dicti auctor exstitit verus. It serves, however, to mark that Procopius was a Pagan. Yet his religion does not appear to have promoted, or obstructed, his pretensions.

36. One of his retreats was a country-house of Eunomius, the heretic. The master was absent, innocent, ignorant; yet he narrowly escaped a sentence of death, and was banished into the remote parts of Mauritania (Philostorg. l. ix. c. 5, 8, and Godefroy's Dissert. p. 369–378).

37. Hormisdæ maturo juveni Hormisdæ regalis illius filio, potestatem Proconsulis detulit; et civilia, more veterum, et bella, recturo. Ammian. xxvi. 8. The Persian prince escaped with honour and safety, and was afterwards (A.D. 380) restored to the same extraordinary office of proconsul of Bithynia (Tillemont, Hist. des Empereurs, tom. v. p. 204). I am ignorant whether the race of Sassan was propagated. I find (A.D. 514) a pope Hormisdas; but he was a native of Frusino, in Italy (Pagi. Brev. Pontific. tom. i. p. 247).

38. The infant rebel was afterwards the wife of the emperor Gratian, but she died young and childless. See Ducange, Fam. Byzantin. p. 48, 59.

39. Sequimini culminis summi prosapiam, was the language of Procopius, who affected to despise the obscure birth and fortuitous election of the upstart Pannonian. Ammian. xxvi. 7.

40. Et dedignatus hominem superare certamine despicabilem, auctoritatis et celsi fiduciâ corporis, ipsis hostibus jussit, suum vincire rectorem: atque ita turmarum antesignanus umbratilis comprensus suorum manibus. The strength and beauty of Arintheus, the new Hercules, are celebrated by St. Basil, who supposes that God had created him as an inimitable model of the human species. The painters and sculptors could not express his figure: the historians appeared fabulous when they related his exploits (Ammian. xxvi. [c. 8] and Vales. ad loc.).

41. The same field of battle is placed by Ammianus in Lycia, and by Zosimus at Thyatira, which are at the distance of 150 miles from each other. But Thyatira alluitur Lyco (Plin. Hist. Natur. v. 31; Cellarius, Geograph. Antiq. tom. ii. p. 79): and the transcribers might easily convert an obscure river into a well-known province.

42. The adventures, usurpation, and fall of Procopius, are related, in a regular series, by Ammianus (xxvi. 6, 7, 8, 9, 10) and Zosimus (l. iv. [c. 4 seq.] p. 203–210). They often illustrate, and seldom contradict, each other. Themistius (Orat. vii. p. 91, 92) adds some base panegyric; and Eunapius (p. 83, 84 [p. 104, ed. Comm.]) some malicious satire.

43. Libanius de ulciscend. Julian. nece, c. ix. [x.] p. 158, 159. The sophist deplores the public frenzy, but he does not (after their deaths) impeach the justice of the emperors.

44. The French and English lawyers of the present age allow the *theory*, and deny the *practice*, of witchcraft (Denisart, Recueil de Décisions de Jurisprudence, au mot *Sorciers*, tom. iv. p. 553. Blackstone's Commentaries, vol. iv. p. 60). As private reason always prevents, or outstrips, public wisdom, the president Montesquieu (The Spirit of Laws, l. xii. c. 5, 6) rejects the *existence* of magic.

45. See Œuvres de Bayle, tom. iii. p. 567–589. The sceptic of Rotterdam exhibits, according to his custom, a strange medley of loose knowledge and lively wit.

46. The Pagans distinguished between good and bad magic, the Theurgic and the Goetic (Hist. de l'Académie, etc., tom. vii. p. 25). But they could not have defended this obscure distinction against the acute logic of Bayle. In the Jewish and Christian system, *all* demons are infernal spirits; and *all* commerce with them is idolatry, apostasy, etc., which deserves death and damnation.

47. The Canidia of Horace (Carm. l. v. Od. 5 [Epod. 5], with Dacier's and Sanadon's illustrations) is a vulgar witch. The Erichtho of Lucan (Pharsal. vi. 430–827) is tedious, disgusting, but sometimes sublime. She chides the delay of the Furies; and threatens, with tremendous obscurity, to pronounce their real names; to reveal the true infernal countenance of Hecate; to invoke the secret powers that lie *below* hell, etc.

48. Genus hominum potentibus infidum, sperantibus fallax, quod in civitate nostrâ et vetabitur semper et retinebitur. Tacit. Hist. i. 22. See Augustine, The City of God, l. viii. c. 19, and the Theodosian Code, l. ix. tit. xvi. with Godefroy's Commentary.

49. The persecution of Antioch was occasioned by a criminal consultation. The twenty-four letters of the alphabet were arranged round a magic tripod: and a dancing ring, which had been placed in the centre, pointed to the four first letters in the name of the future emperor, Θ. ε. ο. Δ. Theodorus (perhaps with many others, who owned the fatal syllables) was executed. Theodosius succeeded. Lardner (Heathen Testimonie, vol. iv. p. 353–372) has copiously and fairly examined this dark transaction of the reign of Valens.

50. Limus ut hic durescit, et hæc ut cera liquescit
Uno eodemque igni ————
Virgil. Bucolic. viii. 80.
Devovet absentes, simulacraque cerea figit.
Ovid. in Epist. Hypsil. ad Jason. 91 [Ep. vi.]. Such vain incantations could affect the mind, and increase the disease, of Germanicus. Tacit. Annal. ii. 69.

51. See Heineccius Antiquitat. Juris Roman. tom. ii. p. 353, etc. Cod. Theodosian. l. ix. tit. 7, with Godefroy's Commentary.

52. The cruel persecution of Rome and Antioch is described, and most probably exaggerated, by Ammianus (xxviii. 1, xxix. 1, 2) and Zosimus (l. iv. [c. 13] p. 216–218). The philosopher Maximus,

with some justice, was involved in the charge of magic (Eunapius in Vit. Sophist. p. 88, 89, [p. 110, ed. Comm.]); and young Chrysostom, who had accidentally found one of the proscribed books, gave himself for lost. (Tillemont, Hist. des Empereurs, tom. v. p. 340).

53. Consult the six last books of Ammianus, and more particularly the portraits of the two royal brothers (xxx. 8, 9, xxxi. 14). Tillemont has collected (tom. v. p. 12–18, p. 127–133) from all antiquity their virtues and vices.

54. The younger Victor asserts that he was valde timidus [Epit. c. 46]; yet he behaved, as almost every man would do, with decent resolution at the *head* of an army. The same historian attempts to prove that his anger was harmless. Ammianus observes, with more candour and judgment, incidentia crimina ad contemptam vel læsam principis amplitudinem trahens, in sanguinem sæviebat [xxxi. 14].

55. Cum esset in acerbitatem naturæ calore propensior . . . pœnas per ignes augebat et gladios. Ammian. xxx. 8. See xxvii. 7.

56. I have transferred the reproach of avarice from Valens to his servants. Avarice more properly belongs to ministers than to kings, in whom that passion is commonly extinguished by absolute possession.

57. He sometimes expressed a sentence of death with a tone of pleasantry: "Abi, Comes, et muta ei caput, qui sibi mutari provinciam cupit." A boy, who had slipped too hastily a Spartan hound; an armourer, who had made a polished cuirass that wanted some grains of the legitimate weight, etc., were the victims of his fury.

58. The innocents of Milan were an agent and three apparitors, whom Valentinian condemned for signifying a legal summons. Ammianus (xxvii. 7) strangely supposes that all who had been unjustly executed were worshipped as martyrs by the Christians. His impartial silence does not allow us to believe that the great chamberlain Rhodanus was burnt alive for an act of oppression (Chron. Paschal. p. 302 [tom. i. p. 558, ed. Bonn]).

59. Ut bene meritam in silvas jussit abire *Innoxiam*. Ammian. xxix. 3, and Valesius ad locum.

60. See the Code of Justinian, l. viii. tit. lii. leg. 2. Unusquisque sobolem suam nutriat. Quod si exponendam putaverit animadversioni quæ constituta est subjacebit. For the present I shall not interfere in the dispute between Noodt and Binkershoek, how far or how long this unnatural practice had been condemned or abolished by law, philosophy, and the more civilised state of society.

61. These salutary institutions are explained in the Theodosian Code, l. xiii. tit. iii. *De Professoribus et Medicis;* and l. xiv. tit. ix. *De Studiis liberalibus Urbis Romæ.* Besides our usual guide (Godefroy), we may consult Giannone (Istoria di Napoli, tom. i. p. 105–111), who has treated the interesting subject with the zeal and curiosity of a man of letters who studies his domestic history.

62. Cod. Theodos. l. i. tit. xi. with Godefroy's *Paratitlon,* which diligently gleans from the rest of the code.

63. Three lines of Ammianus (xxxi. 14) countenance a whole oration of Themistius (viii. p. 101–120), full of adulation, pedantry, and commonplace morality. The eloquent M. Thomas (tom. i. p. 366–396) has amused himself with celebrating the virtues and genius of Themistius, who was not unworthy of the age in which he lived.

64. Zosimus, l. iv. [c. 3] p. 202. Ammian. xxx. 9. His reformation of costly abuses might entitle him to the praise of, in provinciales admodum parcus, tributorum ubique molliens sarcinas. By some his frugality was styled avarice (Jerom. Chron. p. 186 [tom. viii. p. 809, ed. Vallars.]).

65. Testes sunt leges a me in exordio Imperii mei datæ; quibus unicuique quod animo imbibisset colendi libera facultas tributa est. Cod. Theodos. l. ix. tit. xvi. leg. 9. To this declaration of Valentinian we may add the various testimonies of Ammianus (xxx. 9), Zosimus (l. iv. [c. 3] p. 204), and Sozomen (l. vi. c. 7, 21). Baronius would naturally blame such rational toleration (Annal. Eccles. A.D. 370, No. 129–132, A.D. 376, No. 3, 4).

66. Eudoxus was of a mild and timid disposition. When he baptised Valens (A.D. 367) he must have been extremely old, since he had studied theology fifty-five years before, under Lucian, a learned and pious martyr. Philostorg. l. ii. c. 14–16, l. iv. c. 4 with Godefroy, p. 82, 206, and Tillemont, Mém Ecclés. tom. v. p. 474–480, etc.

67. Gregory Nazianzen (Orat. xxv. p. 432) insults the persecuting spirit of the Arians, as an infallible symptom of error and heresy.

68. This sketch of the ecclesiastical government of Valens is drawn from Socrates (l. iv.), Sozomen (l. vi.), Theodoret (l. iv.), and the immense compilations of Tillemont (particularly tom. vi. viii. and ix.).

69. Dr. Jortin (Remarks on Ecclesiastical History, vol. iv. p. 78) has already conceived and intimated the same suspicion.

70. This reflection is so obvious and forcible, that Orosius (l. vii. c. 32, 33) delays the persecution till after the death of Valentinian. Socrates, on the other hand, supposes (l. iii. [iv.] c. 32) that it was appeased by a philosophical oration which Themistius pronounced in the year 374 (Orat. xii. p. 154, in Latin only). Such contradictions diminish the evidence and reduce the term of the persecution of Valens.

71. Tillemont, whom I follow and abridge, has extracted (Mém. Ecclés. tom. viii. p. 153–167) the most authentic circumstances from the Panegyrics of the two Gregories; the brother and the friend of Basil. The letters of Basil himself (Dupin, Bibliothéque Ecclésiastique, tom. ii. p. 155–180) do not present the image of a very lively persecution.

72. Basilius Cæsariensis episcopus Cappadociæ clarus habetur . . . qui multa continentiæ et ingenii bona uno superbiæ malo perdidit [Chron

Ann. 2392, tom. viii. p. 816, ed. Vallars.]. This irreverent passage is perfectly in the style and character of St. Jerom. It does not appear in Scaliger's edition of his Chronicle; but Isaac Vossius found it in some old MSS. which had not been reformed by the monks.

73. This noble and charitable foundation (almost a new city) surpassed in merit, if not in greatness, the pyramids, or the walls of Babylon. It was principally intended for the reception of lepers (Greg. Nazianzen. Orat. xx. p. 439).

74. Cod. Theodos. l. xii. tit. i. leg. 63. Godefroy (tom. iv. p. 409–413) performs the duty of a commentator and advocate. Tillemont (Mém. Ecclés. tom. viii. p. 808) *supposes* a second law to excuse his orthodox friends, who had misrepresented the edict of Valens, and suppressed the liberty of choice.

75. See D'Anville, Description de l'Egypte, p. 74. Hereafter I shall consider the monastic institutions.

76. Socrates, l. iv. c. 24, 25. Orosius, l. vii. c. 33. Jerom. in Chron. p. 189 [tom. viii. p. 816, ed. Vallars.], and tom. ii. p. 212. The monks of Egypt performed many miracles, which prove the truth of their faith. Right, says Jortin (Remarks, vol. iv. p. 79), but what proves the truth of those miracles?

77. Cod. Theodos. l. xvi. tit. ii. leg. 20. Godefroy (tom. vi. p. 49), after the example of Baronius, impartially collects all that the fathers have said on the subject of this important law; whose spirit was long afterwards revived by the emperor Frederic II., Edward I. of England, and other Christian princes who reigned after the twelfth century.

78. The expressions which I have used are temperate and feeble, if compared with the vehement invectives of Jerom (tom. i. p. 13, 45, 144, etc. [tom. i. p. 259, etc., ed. Vallars.]). In *his* turn he was reproached with the guilt which he imputed to his brother monks: and the *Sceleratus*, the *Versipellis*, was publicly accused as the lover of the widow Paula (tom. ii. p. 363). He undoubtedly possessed the affections both of the mother and the daughter; but he declares that he never abused his influence to any selfish or sensual purpose.

79. Pudet dicere, sacerdotes idolorum, mimi et aurigæ, et scorta, hæreditates capiunt: solis *clericis* ac *monachis* hâc [hoc] lege prohibetur. Et non prohibetur a persecutoribus, sed a principibus Christianis. Nec de lege queror; sed doleo cur *meruerimus* hanc legem. Jerom (tom. i. p. 13 [tom. i. p. 258, ed. Vallars.]) discreetly insinuates the secret policy of his patron Damasus.

80. Three words of Jerom, *sanctæ memoriæ Damasus* (tom. ii. p. 109 [Ep. ad Pammachium. tom. i. p. 228, ed. Vallars.]), wash away all his stains, and blind the devout eyes of Tillemont (Mém. Ecclés. tom. viii. p. 386–424).

81. Jerom himself is forced to allow, crudelissimæ interfectiones diversi sexús perpetratæ (in Chron. p. 186 [tom. viii. p. 809, ed. Vallars.]). But an original *libel* or petition of two presbyters of the adverse party has unaccountably escaped. They affirm that the doors of the basilica were burnt, and that the roof was untiled; that Damasus marched at the head of his own clergy, gravediggers, charioteers, and hired gladiators; that none of *his* party were killed, but that one hundred and sixty dead bodies were found. This petition is published by the P. Sirmond, in the first volume of his works.

82. The *Basilica* of Sicininus, or Liberius, is probably the church of Sancta Maria Maggiore, on the Esquiline hill. Baronius, A.D. 367, No. 3; and Donatus, Roma Antiqua et Nova, l. iv. c. 3, p. 462.

83. The enemies of Damasus styled him *Auriscalpius Matronarum*, the ladies' ear-scratcher.

84. Gregory Nazianzen (Orat. xxxii. p. 526) describes the pride and luxury of the prelates who reigned in the Imperial cities; their gilt car, fiery steeds, numerous train, etc. The crowd gave way as to a wild beast.

85. Ammian. xxvii. 3. Perpetuo Numini, *verisque* ejus cultoribus. The incomparable pliancy of a polytheist!

86. Ammianus, who makes a fair report of his præfecture (xxvii. 9), styles him *præclaræ indolis, gravitatisque*, senator (xxii. 7, and Vales. ad loc.). A curious inscription (Gruter MCII. No. 2) records, in two columns, his religious and civil honours. In one line he was Pontiff of the Sun and of Vesta, Augur, Quindecemvir, Hierophant, etc., etc. In the other, 1. Quæstor candidatus, more probably titular. 2. Prætor. 3. Corrector of Tuscany and Umbria. 4. Consular of Lusitania. 5. Proconsul of Achaia. 6. Præfect of Rome. 7. Prætorian præfect of Italy. 8. Of Illyricum. 9. Consul, elect; but he died before the beginning of the year 385. See Tillemont, Hist. des Empereurs, tom. v. p. 241, 736.

87. Facite me Romanæ urbis episcopum, et ero protinus Christianus (Jerom, tom. ii. p. 165 [contra Joann. Ierosol. tom. ii. p. 415, ed. Vallars.]). It is more than probable that Damasus would not have purchased his conversion at such a price.

88. Ammian. xxvi. 5. Valesius adds a long and good note on the master of the offices.

89. Ammian. xxvii. 1. Zosimus, l. iv. [c. 9] p. 208. The disgrace of the Batavians is suppressed by the contemporary soldier, from a regard for military honour, which could not affect a Greek rhetorician of the succeeding age.

90. See D'Anville, Notice de l'Ancienne Gaule, p. 587. The name of the Moselle, which is not specified by Ammianus, is clearly understood by Mascou (Hist. of the Ancient Germans, vii. 2).

91. The battles are described by Ammianus (xxvii. 2) and by Zosimus (l. iv. [c. 9] p. 209), who supposes Valentinian to have been present.

92. Studio solicitante nostrorum, occubuit. Ammian. xxvii. 10.

93. The expedition of Valentinian is related by Ammianus (xxvii. 10); and celebrated by Auson-

ius (Mosell. 421, etc.), who foolishly supposes that the Romans were ignorant of the sources of the Danube.

94. Immanis enim natio, jam inde ab incunabulis primis varietate casuum imminuta; ita sæpius adolescit, ut fuisse longis sæculis æstimetur intacta. Ammian. xxviii. 5. The Count de Buat (Hist. des Peuples de l'Europe, tom. vi. p. 370), ascribes the fecundity of the Alemanni to their easy adoption of strangers.

95. Ammian. xxviii. 2. Zosimus, l. iv. [c. 16] p. 214. The younger Victor mentions the mechanical genius of Valentinian: nova arma meditari; fingere terrâ seu limo simulacra. [Epit. c. 45.]

96. Bellicosos et pubis immensæ viribus affluentes; et ideo metuendos finitimis universis. Ammian. xxviii. 5.

97. I am always apt to suspect historians and travellers of improving extraordinary facts into general laws. Ammianus ascribes a similar custom to Egypt; and the Chinese have imputed it to the Ta-tsin, or Roman empire (De Guignes, Hist. des Huns, tom. ii. part i. p. 79).

98. Salinarum finiumque causâ Alemannis sæpe jurgabant. Ammian. xxviii. 5. Possibly they disputed the possession of the *Sala*, a river which produced salt, and which had been the object of ancient contention. Tacit. Annal. xiii. 57, and Lipsius ad loc.

99. Jam inde temporibus priscis sobolem se esse Romanam Burgundii sciunt: and the vague tradition gradually assumed a more regular form (Oros. l. vii. c. 32). It is annihilated by the decisive authority of Pliny, who composed the History of Drusus, and served in Germany (Plin. Secund. Epist. iii. 5), within sixty years after the death of that hero. *Germanorum genera* quinque; Vindili, quorum pars *Burgundiones*, etc. (Hist. Natur. iv. 28).

100. The wars and negotiations relative to the Burgundians and Alemanni are distinctly related by Ammianus Marcellinus (xxviii. 5, xxix. 4, xxx. 3). Orosius (l. vii. c. 32), and the Chronicles of Jerom and Cassiodorus, fix some dates and add some circumstances.

101. Ἐπὶ τόν αὐχένα τῆς Κιμβρικῆς Χερσονήσου, Σάξονες. At the northern extremity of the peninsula (the Cimbric promontory of Pliny, iv. 27) Ptolemy fixes the remnant of the *Cimbri*. He fills the interval between the *Saxons* and the Cimbri with six obscure tribes, who were united, as early as the sixth century, under the national appellation of *Danes*. See Cluver German. Antiq. l. iii. c. 21, 22, 23.

102. M. d'Anville (Etablissement des Etats de l'Europe, etc., p. 19–26) has marked the extensive limits of the Saxony of Charlemagne.

103. The fleet of Drusus had failed in their attempt to pass, or even to approach, the *Sound* (styled, from an obvious resemblance, the Columns of Hercules), and the naval enterprise was never resumed (Tacit. de Moribus German, c. 34). The knowledge which the Romans acquired of the naval powers of the Baltic (c. 44, 45) was obtained by their land journeys in search of amber.

104.   Quin et Aremoricus piratem *Saxona* tractus
            Sperabat; cui pelle salum sulcare Britannum
            Ludus; et assuto glaucum mare findere lembo.
                          Sidon. in Panegyr. Avit. 369.

The genius of Cæsar imitated, for a particular service, these rude, but light vessels, which were likewise used by the natives of Britain (Comment. de Bell. Civil. i. 54, and Guichardt, Nouveaux Mémoires Militaires, tom. ii. p. 41, 42). The British vessels would now astonish the genius of Cæsar.

105. The best original account of the Saxon pirates may be found in Sidonius Apollinaris (l. viii. Epist. 6, p. 223, edit. Sirmond), and the best commentary in the Abbé du Bos (Hist. Critique de la Monarchie Françoise, etc., tom. i. l. i. c. 16, p. 148–155. See likewise p. 77, 78).

106. Ammian. (xxviii. 5) justifies this breach of faith to pirates and robbers; and Orosius (l. vii. c. 32) more clearly expresses their real guilt; virtute atque agilitate terribiles.

107. Symmachus (l. ii. Epist. 46) still presumes to mention the sacred names of Socrates and philosophy. Sidonius, bishop of Clermont, might condemn (l. viii. Epist. 6), with *less* inconsistency, the human sacrifices of the Saxons.

108. In the beginning of the last century the learned Camden was obliged to undermine with respectful scepticism, the romance of *Brutus* the Trojan, who is now buried in silent oblivion, with *Scota*, the daughter of Pharaoh, and her numerous progeny. Yet I am informed that some champions of the *Milesian colony* may still be found among the original natives of Ireland. A people dissatisfied with their present condition grasp at any visions of their past or future glory.

109. Tacitus, or rather his father-in-law Agricola, might remark the German or Spanish complexion of some British tribes. But it was their sober, deliberate opinion: "In universum tamen æstimanti Gallos vicinum solum occupâsse credibile est Eorum sacra deprehendas . . . sermo haud multum diversus" (in Vit. Agricol. c. xi.). Cæsar had observed their common religion (Comment. de Bello Gallico, vi. 13); and in his time the emigration from the Belgic Gaul was a recent, or at least an historical event (v. 12). Camden, the British Strabo, has modestly ascertained our genuine antiquities (Britannia, vol. i. Introduction, p. ii.–xxxi.).

110. In the dark and doubtful paths of Caledonian antiquity, I have chosen for my guides two learned and ingenious Highlanders, whom their birth and education had peculiarly qualified for that office. See Critical Dissertations on the Origin, Antiquities, etc., of the Caledonians, by Dr. John Macpherson, London, 1768, in 4to.; and Introduction to the History of Great Britain and

Ireland, by James Macpherson, Esq., London, 1773, in 4to. third edit. Dr. Macpherson was a minister in the Isle of Skye: and it is a circumstance honourable for the present age, that a work replete with erudition and criticism should have been composed in the most remote of the Hebrides.

111. The Irish descent of the Scots has been revived, in the last moments of its decay, and strenuously supported, by the Rev. Mr. Whitaker (Hist. of Manchester, vol. i. p. 430, 431; and Genuine History of the Britons asserted, etc., p. 154–293). Yet he acknowledges, 1. *That* the Scots of Ammianus Marcellinus (A.D. 340) were already settled in Caledonia, and that the Roman authors do not afford any hints of their emigration from another country. 2. *That all* the accounts of such emigrations, which have been asserted or received, by Irish bards, Scotch historians, or English antiquaries (Buchanan, Camden, Usher, Stillingfleet, etc.), are totally fabulous. 3. *That* three of the Irish tribes, which are mentioned by Ptolemy (A.D. 150), were of Caledonian extraction. 4. *That* a younger branch of Caledonian princes, of the house of Fingal, acquired and possessed the monarchy of Ireland. After these concessions, the remaining difference between Mr. Whitaker and his adversaries is minute and obscure. The *genuine history*, which he produces, of a Fergus, the cousin of Ossian, who was transplanted (A.D. 324) from Ireland to Caledonia, is built on a conjectural supplement to the Erse poetry, and the feeble evidence of Richard of Cirencester, a monk of the fourteenth century. The lively spirit of the learned and ingenious antiquarian has tempted him to forget the nature of a question which he so *vehemently* debates, and so *absolutely* decides.

112. Hieme tumentes ac sævientes undas calcâstis Oceani sub remis vestris; ... insperatum imperatoris faciem Britannus expavit. Julius Firmicus Maternus de Errore Profan. Relig. p. 464 [p. 59, ed. Lugd. B. 1672] edit. Gronov. ad calcem Minuc. Fel. See Tillemont (Hist. des Empereurs, tom. iv. p. 336).

113. Libanius, Orat. Parent. c. xxxix. p. 264. This curious passage has escaped the diligence of our British antiquaries.

114. The Caledonians praised and coveted the gold, the steeds, the lights, etc., of the *stranger*. See Dr. Blair's Dissertation on Ossian, vol. ii. p. 343; and Mr. Macpherson's Introduction, p. 242–286.

115. Lord Lyttelton has circumstantially related (History of Henry II. vol. i. p. 182), and Sir David Dalrymple has slightly mentioned (Annals of Scotland, vol. i. p. 69), a barbarous inroad of the Scots, at a time (A.D. 1137) when law, religion, and society must have softened their primitive manners.

116. Attacotti bellicosa hominum natio. Ammian. xxvii. 8. Camden (Introduct. p. clii.) has restored their true name in the text of Jerom. The bands of Attacotti which Jerom had seen in Gaul were afterwards stationed in Italy and Illyricum (Notitia, S. viii. xxxix. xl.).

117. Cum ipse adolescentulus in Galliâ viderim Attacottos (or Scotos) gentem Brittannicam humanis vesci carnibus; et cum per silvas porcorum greges, et armentorum pecudumque reperiant, pastorum *nates* et feminarum *papillas* solere ab scindere; et has solas ciborum delicias arbitrari. Such is the evidence of Jerom (tom. ii. p. 75 [adv. Jovinianum, l. ii. tom. ii. p. 335, ed. Vallars.]), whose veracity I find no reason to question.

118. Ammianus has concisely represented (xx. 1, xxvi. 4, xxvii. 8, xxviii. 3) the whole series of the British war.

119.   Horrescit...ratibus...impervia Thule.
Ille ... nec falso nomine Pictos
Edomuit. Scotumque vago mucrone secutus
Fregit Hyperboreas remis audacibus undas.

   Claudian, in iii. Cons. Honorii,
ver. 53, etc.

————Maduerunt Saxone fuso
Orcades: incaluit Pictorum sanguine Thule.
Scotorum cumulos flevit glacialis Ierne.
   In iv. Cons. Hon. ver. 31, etc.

See likewise Pacatus (in Panegyr. Vet. xii. 5). But it is not easy to appreciate the intrinsic value of flattery and metaphor. Compare the *British* victories of Bolanus (Statius, Silv. v. 2) with his real character (Tacit. in Vit. Agricol. c. 16).

120. Ammianus frequently mentions their concilium annuum, legitimum, etc. Leptis and Sabrata are long since ruined; but the city of Oea, the native country of Apuleius, still flourishes under the provincial denomination of *Tripoli*. See Cellarius (Geograph. Antiqua, tom. ii. part ii. p. 81), D'Anville (Géographie Ancienne, tom. iii. p. 71, 72), and Marmol (Afrique, tom. ii. p. 562).

121. Ammian. xxviii. 6. Tillemont (Hist. des Empereurs, tom. v. p. 25, 676) has discussed the chronological difficulties of the history of Count Romanus.

122. The chronology of Ammianus is loose and obscure; and Orosius (l. vii. c. 33, p. 551, edit. Havercamp.) seems to place the revolt of Firmus after the deaths of Valentinian and Valens. Tillemont (Hist. des Emp. tom. v. p. 691) endeavours to pick his way. The patient and sure-footed mule of the Alps may be trusted in the most slippery paths.

123. Ammian. xxix. 5. The text of this long chapter (fifteen quarto pages) is broken and corrupted; and the narrative is perplexed by the want of chronological and geographical landmarks.

124. Ammian. xxviii. 4. Orosius, l. vii. c. 33, p. 551, 552. Jerom. in Chron. p. 187.

125. Leo Africanus (in the Viaggi di Ramusio, tom. i. fol. 78–83) has traced a curious picture of the people and the country, which are more

minutely described in the Afrique de Marmol, tom. iii. p. 1–54.

126. This uninhabitable zone was gradually reduced, by the improvements of ancient geography, from forty-five to twenty-four, or even sixteen degrees of latitude. See a learned and judicious note of Dr. Robertson, Hist. of America, vol. i. p. 426.

127. Intra, si credere libet, vix jam homines et magis semiferi . . . Blemmyes, Satyri, etc. Pomponius Mela, i. 4, p. 26, edit. Voss. in 8vo. Pliny *philosophically* explains (vi. 35) the irregularities of nature, which he had *credulously* admitted (v. 8).

128. If the satyr was the orang-outang, the great human ape (Buffon, Hist. Nat. tom. xiv. p. 43, etc.), one of that species might actually be shown alive at Alexandria in the reign of Constantine. Yet some difficulty will still remain about the conversation which St. Anthony held with one of these pious savages in the desert of Thebais (Jerom. in Vit. Paul. Eremit. tom. i. p. 238).

129. St. Anthony likewise met one of *these* monsters, whose existence was seriously asserted by the emperor Claudius. The public laughed; but his præfect of Egypt had the address to send an artful preparation, the embalmed corpse of an *Hippocentaur*, which was preserved almost a century afterwards in the Imperial palace. See Pliny (Hist. Natur. vii. 3), and the judicious observations of Fréret (Mémoires de l'Acad. tom. vii. p. 321, etc.).

130. The fable of the pigmies is as old as Homer (Iliad, iii. 6). The pigmies of India and Æthiopia were (trispithami) twenty-seven inches high. Every spring their cavalry (mounted on rams and goats) marched in battle array to destroy the cranes' eggs, aliter (says Pliny) futuris gregibus non resisti. Their houses were built of mud, feathers, and egg-shells. See Pliny (vi. 35, vii. 2) and Strabo (l. ii. p. 121 [p. 70, ed. Casaub.]).

131. The third and fourth volumes of the valuable Histoire des Voyages describe the present state of the negroes. The nations of the sea-coast have been polished by European commerce, and those of the inland country have been improved by Moorish colonies.

132. Histoire Philosophique et Politique, etc., tom. iv. p. 192.

133. The evidence of Ammianus is original and decisive (xxvii. 12). Moses of Chorene (l. iii. c. 17, p. 249, and c. 34, p. 269) and Procopius (de Bell. Persico, l. i. c. 5, p. 17, edit. Louvre [tom. i. p. 29, ed. Bonn]) have been consulted; but those historians, who confound distinct facts, repeat the same events, and introduce strange stories, must be used with diffidence and caution.

134. Perhaps Artagera, or Ardis, under whose walls Caius, the grandson of Augustus, was wounded. This fortress was situate above Amida, near one of the sources of the Tigris. See D'Anville, Géographie Ancienne, tom. ii. p. 106.

135. Tillemont (Hist. des Empereurs, tom. v. p. 701) proves from chronology that Olympias must have been the mother of Para.

136. Ammianus (xxvii. 12, xxix. 1, xxx. 1, 2) has described the events, without the dates, of the Persian war. Moses of Chorene (Hist. Armen. l. iii. c. 28, p. 261, c. 31, p. 266, c. 35, p. 271) affords some additional facts; but it is extremely difficult to separate truth from fable.

137. Artaxerxes was the successor and brother (*the cousin-german*) of the great Sapor, and the guardian of his son Sapor III. (Agathias, l. iv. [c. 26] p. 136, edit. Louvre [p. 263, ed. Bonn.]). See the Universal History, vol. xi. p. 86, 161. The authors of that unequal work have compiled the Sassanian dynasty with erudition and diligence; but it is a preposterous arrangement to divide the Roman and Oriental accounts into two distinct histories.

138. Pacatus in Panegyr. Vet. xii. 22; and Orosius, l. vii. c. 34. Ictumque tum fœdus est, quo universus Oriens usque ad nunc (A.D. 416) tranquilissime fruitur.

139. See in Ammianus (xxx. 1) the adventures of Para. Moses of Chorene calls him Tiridates; and tells a long and not improbable story of his son Gnelus, who afterwards made himself popular in Armenia, and provoked the jealousy of the reigning king (l. iii. c. 21, etc., p. 253, etc.). [Para is not the same as Tiridates, who was the father of Gnel, first husband of Pharandsem, the future wife of Arsaces, and the mother of Para.]

140. The concise account of the reign and conquests of Hermanric seems to be one of the valuable fragments which Jornandes (c. 23) borrowed from the Gothic histories of Ablavius, or Cassiodorus.

141. M. de Buat (Hist. des Peuples de l'Europe, tom. vi. p. 311–329) investigates, with more industry than success, the nations subdued by the arms of Hermanric. He denies the existence of the *Vasinobroncæ*, on account of the immoderate length of their name. Yet the French envoy to Ratisbon, or Dresden, must have traversed the country of the *Mediomatrici*.

142. The edition of Grotius (Jornandes, p. 642) exhibits the name of *Æstri*. But reason and the Ambrosian MS. have restored the *Æstii*, whose manners and situation are expressed by the pencil of Tacitus (Germania, c. 45).

143. Ammianus (xxxi. 3) observes, in general terms, Ermenrichi . . . bellicosissimi Regis, et per multa variaque fortiter facta, vicinis gentibus formidati, etc.

144. Valens . . . docetur relationibus Ducum, gentem Gothorum, eâ tempestate intactam ideoque sævissimam, conspirantem in unum, ad pervadenda parari collimitia Thraciarum. Ammian. xxvi. 6.

145. M. de Buat (Hist. des Peuples de l'Europe, tom. vi. p. 332) has curiously ascertained the real number of these auxiliaries. The 3000 of Ammianus, and the 10,000 of Zosimus, were only the first divisions of the Gothic army.

146. The march and subsequent negotiation are

described in the Fragments of Eunapius (Excerpt. Legat. p. 18, edit. Louvre [p. 47, ed. Bonn]). The provincials, who afterwards became familiar with the barbarians, found that their strength was more apparent than real. They were tall of stature, but their legs were clumsy and their shoulders were narrow.

147. Valens enim, ut consulto placuerat fratri, cujus regebatur arbitrio, arma concussit in Gothos ratione justâ permotus. Ammianus (xxvii. 4) then proceeds to describe, not the country of the Goths, but the peaceful and obedient province of Thrace, which was not affected by the war.

148. Eunapius, in Excerpt. Legat. p. 18, 19 [p. 47, 48, ed. Bonn]. The Greek sophist must have considered as *one* and the *same* war, the whole series of Gothic history till the victories and peace of Theodosius.

149. The Gothic war is described by Ammianus (xxvii. 5), Zosimus (l. iv. [c. 10] p. 211–214), and Themistius (Orat. x. p. 129–141). The orator Themistius was sent from the senate of Constantinople to congratulate the victorious emperor; and his servile eloquence compares Valens *on* the Danube to Achilles *in* the Scamander. Jornandes forgets a war peculiar to the *Visi*-Goths, and inglorious to the Gothic name (Mascou's Hist. of the Germans, vii. 3).

150. Ammianus (xxix. 6) and Zosimus (l. iv. [c. 16] p. 219, 220) carefully mark the origin and progress of the Quadic and Sarmatian war.

151. Ammianus (xxx. 5), who acknowledges the merit, has censured, with becoming asperity, the oppressive administration of Petronius Probus. When Jerom translated and continued the Chronicle of Eusebius (A.D. 380; see Tillemont, Mém. Eclés. tom. xii. p. 53, 626), he expressed the truth, or at least the public opinion of his country, in the following words: "Probus P. P. Illyrici iniquissimis tributorum exactionibus, ante provincias quas regebat, quam a Barbaris vastarentur, *erasit*." (Chron. edit. Scaliger, p. 187; Animadvers. p. 259.) The saint afterwards formed an intimate and tender friendship with the widow of Probus; and the name of Count Equitius, with less propriety, but without much injustice, has been substituted in the text.

152. Julian (Orat. vi. p. 198) represents his friend Iphicles as a man of virtue and merit, who had made himself ridiculous and unhappy by adopting the extravagant dress and manners of the Cynics.

153. Ammian. xxx. 5. Jerom, who exaggerates the misfortune of Valentinian, refuses him even this last consolation of revenge. Vastato genitali solo, et *inultam* patriam derelinquens (tom. i. p. 26 [Ep. ad Heliodor. tom. i. p. 341, ed. Vallars.]).

154. See, on the death of Valentinian, Ammianus (xxx. 6), Zosimus (l. vi. [c. 17] p. 221), Victor (in Epitom. [c. 45]), Socrates (l. iv. c. 31), and Jerom (in Chron. p. 187 [tom. viii. p. 815, ed. Vallars.], and tom. i. p. 26, ad Heliodor. [tom. i. p. 341, ed. Vallars.]). There is much variety of circumstances among them; and Ammianus is so eloquent that he writes nonsense.

155. Socrates (l. iv. c. 31) is the only original witness of this foolish story, so repugnant to the laws and manners of the Romans, that it scarcely deserved the formal and elaborate dissertation of M. Bonamy (Mém. de l'Académie, tom. xxx. p. 394–405). Yet I would preserve the natural circumstance of the bath, instead of following Zosimus, who represents Justina as an old woman, the widow of Magnentius.

156. Ammianus (xxvii. 6) describes the form of this military election, and *august* investiture. Valentinian does not appear to have consulted, or even informed, the senate of Rome.

157. Ammianus, xxx. 10. Zosimus, l. iv. [c. 19] p. 222, 223. Tillemont has proved (Hist. des Empereurs, tom. v. p. 707–709) that Gratian *reigned* in Italy, Africa, and Illyricum. I have endeavoured to express his authority over his brother's dominions, as he used it, in an ambiguous style.

Chapter XXVI

1. Such is the bad taste of Ammianus (xxvi. 10), that it is not easy to distinguish his facts from his metaphors. Yet he positively affirms that he saw the rotten carcase of a ship, ad *secundum lapidem*, at Methone, or Modon, in Peloponnesus.

2. The earthquakes and inundations are variously described by Libanius (Orat. de ulciscendâ Juliani nece, c. x. in Fabricius, Bibl. Græc. tom. vii. p. 158, with a learned note of Olearius), Zosimus (l. iv. [c. 18] p. 221), Sozomen (l. vi. c. 2), Cedrenus (p. 310, 314 [tom. i. p. 543, 550, ed. Bonn]), and Jerom (in Chron. p. 186 [tom. viii. p. 809, ed. Vallars.], and tom. i. p. 250, in Vit. Hilarion [tom. ii. p. 36 ed. Vallars.]). Epidaurus must have been overwhelmed, had not the prudent citizens placed St. Hilarion, an Egyptian monk, on the beach. He made the sign of the cross; the mountain-wave stopped, bowed, and returned.

3. Dicæarchus the Peripatetic composed a formal treatise to prove this obvious truth, which is not the most honourable to the human species (Cicero, de Officiis, ii. 5).

4. The original Scythians of Herodotus (l. iv. c. 47–57, 99–101) were confined by the Danube and the Palus Mæotis within a square of 4000 stadia (400 Roman miles). See D'Anville (Mém. de l'Académie, tom. xxxv. p. 573–591). Diodorus Siculus (tom. i. l. ii. [c. 43] p. 155, edit. Wesseling) has marked the gradual progress of the *name* and nation.

5. The *Tatars* or Tartars were a primitive tribe, the rivals, and at length the subjects, of the Moguls. In the victorious armies of Zingis Khan and his successors, the Tartars formed the vanguard; and the name which first reached the ears of foreigners was applied to the whole nation (Fréret, in the Hist. de l'Académie, tom. xviii. p. 60). In speaking of all or any of the northern shepherds of Europe or Asia, I indifferently use the appellations of *Scythians* or *Tartars*.

6. Imperium Asiæ *ter* quæsivere: ipsi perpetuo ab alieno imperio, aut intacti, aut invicti, mansere. Since the time of Justin (ii. 3) they have multiplied this account. Voltaire, in a few words (tom. x. p. 64, Hist. Générale, c. 156), has abridged the Tartar conquests.

Oft o'er the trembling nations from afar

Has Scythia breath'd the living cloud of war.

7. The fourth book of Herodotus affords a curious though imperfect portrait of the Scythians. Among the moderns, who describe the uniform scene, the Khan of Khowaresm, Abulghazi Bahadur, expresses his native feelings; and his Genealogical History of the *Tatars* has been copiously illustrated by the French and English editors. Carpin, Ascelin, and Rubruquis (in the Hist. des Voyages, tom. vii.), represent the Moguls of the fourteenth century. To these guides I have added Gerbillon and the other Jesuits (Description de la Chine, par Du Halde, tom. iv.), who accurately surveyed the Chinese Tartary, and that honest and intelligent traveller, Bell of Antermony (two volumes in 4to, Glasgow, 1763).

8. The Uzbeks are the most altered from their primitive manners; 1, by the profession of the Mahometan religion; and 2, by the possession of the cities and harvests of the Great Bucharia.

9. Il est certain que les grands mangeurs de viande sont en général cruels et féroces plus que les autres hommes. Cette observation est de tous les lieux, et de tous les tems: la barbarie Angloise est connue, etc. Emile de Rousseau, tom. i. p. 274. Whatever we may think of the general observation, *we* shall not easily allow the truth of his example. The good-natured complaints of Plutarch, and the pathetic lamentations of Ovid, seduce our reason by exciting our sensibility.

10. These Tartar emigrations have been discovered by M. de Guignes (Histoire des Huns, tom. i. ii.), a skilful and laborious interpreter of the Chinese language, who has thus laid open new and important scenes in the history of mankind.

11. A plain in the Chinese Tartary, only eighty leagues from the great wall, was found by the missionaries to be three thousand geometrical paces above the level of the sea. Montesquieu, who has used and abused the relations of travellers, deduces the revolutions of Asia from this important circumstance, that heat and cold, weakness and strength, touch each other without any temperate zone (The Spirit of Laws, l. xvii. c. 3).

12. Petit de la Croix (Vie de Gengiscan, l. iii. c.

7) represents the full glory and extent of the Mogul chase. The Jesuits Gerbillon and Verbiest followed the emperor Kamhi when he hunted in Tartary (Du Halde, Description de la Chine, tom. iv. p. 81, 290, etc., folio edit.). His grandson, Kien-long, who unites the Tartar discipline with the laws and learning of China, describes (Eloge de Moukden, p. 273–285), as a poet, the pleasures which he had often enjoyed as a sportsman.

13. See the second volume of the Genealogical History of the Tartars, and the lists of the Khans at the end of the life of Gengis, or Zingis. Under the reign of Timur, or Tamerlane, one of his subjects, a descendant of Zingis, still bore the regal appellation of Khan; and the conqueror of Asia contented himself with the title of Emir or Sultan. Abulghazi, part v. c. 4. D'Herbelot, Bibliothèque Orientale, p. 878.

14. See the Diets of the ancient Huns (De Guignes, tom. ii. p. 26), and a curious description of those of Zingis (Vie de Gengiscan, l. i. c. 6, l. iv. c. 11). Such assemblies are frequently mentioned in the Persian history of Timur, though they served only to countenance the resolutions of their master.

15. Montesquieu labours to explain a difference, which has not existed, between the liberty of the Arabs and the *perpetual* slavery of the Tartars (The Spirit of Laws, l. xvii. c. 5, l. xviii. c. 19. etc.).

16. Abulghazi Khan, in the two first parts of his Genealogical History, relates the miserable fables and traditions of the Uzbek Tartars concerning the times which preceded the reign of Zingis.

17. In the thirteenth book of the Iliad, Jupiter turns away his eyes from the bloody fields of Troy to the plains of Thrace and Scythia. We would not, by changing the prospect, behold a more peaceful or innocent scene.

18. Thucydides, l. ii. c. 97.

19. See the fourth book of Herodotus. When Darius advanced into the Moldavian desert, between the Danube and the Dniester, the king of the Scythians sent him a mouse, a frog, a bird, and five arrows; a tremendous allegory!

20. These wars and heroes may be found under their respective *titles*, in the Bibliothèque Orientale of D'Herbelot. They have been celebrated in an epic poem of sixty thousand rhymed couplets, by Ferdusi, the Homer of Persia. See the history of Nadir Shah, p. 145, 165. The public must lament that Mr. Jones has suspended the pursuit of Oriental learning.

21. The Caspian Sea, with its rivers and adjacent tribes, are laboriously illustrated in the Examen Critique des Historiens d'Alexandre, which compares the true geography and the errors produced by the vanity or ignorance of the Greeks.

22. The original seat of the nation appears to have been in the north-west of China, in the provinces of Chensi and Chansi. Under the two first dynasties the principal town was still a movable camp; the villages were thinly scattered; more land was employed in pasture than in tillage; the exer-

cise of hunting was ordained to clear the country from wild beasts; Petcheli (where Pekin stands) was a desert; and the southern provinces were peopled with Indian savages. The dynasty of the *Han* (before Christ 206) gave the empire its actual form and extent.

23. The era of the Chinese monarchy has been variously fixed from 2952 to 2132 years before Christ; and the year 2637 has been chosen for the lawful epoch by the authority of the present emperor. The difference arises from the uncertain duration of the two first dynasties; and the vacant space that lies beyond them, as far as the real, or fabulous, times of Fohi or Hoangti. Sematsien dates his authentic chronology from the year 841: the thirty-six eclipses of Confucius (thirty-one of which have been verified) were observed between the years 722 and 480 before Christ. The *historical period* of China does not ascend above the Greek Olympiads.

24. After several ages of anarchy and despotism, the dynasty of the Han (before Christ 206) was the era of the revival of learning. The fragments of ancient literature were restored; the characters were improved and fixed; and the future preservation of books was secured by the useful inventions of ink, paper, and the art of printing. Ninety-seven years before Christ, Sematsien published the first history of China. His labours were illustrated and continued by a series of one hundred and eighty historians. The substance of their works is still extant; and the most considerable of them are now deposited in the king of France's library.

25. China has been illustrated by the labours of the French; of the missionaries at Pekin, and Messrs. Fréret and De Guignes at Paris. The substance of the three preceding notes is extracted from the *Chou-king*, with the preface and notes of M. de Guignes, Paris, 1770; The *Tong-Kien-Kang-Mou*, translated by the P. de Mailla, under the name of Hist. Générale de la Chine, tom. i. p. xlix.–cc.; the Mémoires sur la Chine, Paris, 1776, etc., tom. i. p. 1–323, tom. ii. p. 5–364; the Histoire des Huns, tom. i. p. 1–131, tom. v. p. 345–362; and the Mémoires de l'Académie des Inscriptions, tom. x. p. 377–402, tom. xv. p. 495–564, tom. xviii. p. 178–295, tom. xxxvi. p. 164–238.

26. See the Histoire Générale des Voyages, tom. xviii.; and the Genealogical History, vol. ii. p. 620–664.

27. M. de Guignes (tom. ii. p. 1–124) has given the original history of the ancient Hiong-nou, or Huns. The Chinese geography of their country (tom. i. part ii. p. lv.–lxiii.) seems to comprise a part of their conquests.

28. See in Du Halde (tom. iv. p. 18–65) a circumstantial description, with a correct map, of the country of the Mongous.

29. The Igours, or Vigours, were divided into three branches—hunters, shepherds, and husbandmen; and the last class was despised by the two former. See Abulghazi, part ii. c. 7.

30. Mémoires de l'Académie des Inscriptions, tom. xxv. p. 17–33. The comprehensive view of M. de Guignes has compared these distant events.

31. The fame of Sovou, or So-ou, his merit, and his singular adventures, are still celebrated in China. See the Eloge de Moukden, p. 20, and notes, p. 241–247; and Mémoires sur la Chine, tom. iii. p. 317–360.

32. See Isbrand Ives in Harris's Collection, vol. ii. p. 931; Bell's Travels, vol. i. p. 247–254; and Gmelin. in the Hist. Générale des Voyages, tom. xviii. p. 283–329. They all remark the vulgar opinion, that the *holy sea* grows angry and tempestuous if any one presumes to call it a *lake*. This grammatical nicety often excites a dispute between the absurd superstition of the mariners and the absurd obstinacy of travellers.

33. The construction of the wall of China is mentioned by Du Halde (tom. ii. p. 45) and De Guignes (tom. ii. p. 59).

34. See the life of Lieoupang, or Kaoti, in the Hist. de la Chine, published at Paris, 1777, etc., tom. i. p. 442–522. This voluminous work is the translation (by the P. de Mailla) of the *Tong-Kien-Kang-Mou*, the celebrated abridgment of the great History of Semakouang (A.D. 1084) and his continuators.

35. See a free and ample memorial, presented by a Mandarin to the emperor Venti (before Christ 180–157), in Du Halde (tom. ii. p. 412–426), from a collection of State papers, marked with the red pencil by Kamhi himself (p. 384–612). Another memorial from the minister of war (Kang-Mou, tom. ii. p. 555) supplies some curious circumstances of the manners of the Huns.

36. A supply of women is mentioned as a customary article of treaty and tribute (Hist. de la Conquête de la Chine par les Tartares Mantcheoux, tom. i. p. 186, 187, with the note of the editor).

37. De Guignes, Hist. des Huns, tom. ii. p. 62.

38. See the reign of the emperor Vouti, in the Kang-Mou, tom. iii. p. 1–98. His various and inconsistent character seems to be impartially drawn.

39. This expression is used in the memorial to the emperor Venti (Du Halde, tom. ii. p. 417). Without adopting the exaggerations of Marco Polo and Isaac Vossius, we may rationally allow for Pekin two millions of inhabitants. The cities of the south, which contain the manufactures of China, are still more populous.

40. See the Kang-Mou, tom. iii. p. 150, and the subsequent events under the proper years. This memorable festival is celebrated in the Eloge de Moukden, and explained in a note by the P. Gaubil, p. 89, 90.

41. This inscription was composed on the spot by Pankou, President of the Tribunal of History (Kang-Mou, tom. iii. p. 392). Similar monuments have been discovered in many parts of Tartary (Histoires des Huns, tom. ii. p. 122).

42. M. de Guignes (tom. i. p. 189) has inserted a short account of the Sienpi.

43. The era of the Huns is placed by the Chinese 1210 years before Christ. But the series of their kings does not commence till the year 230 (Hist. des Huns, tom. ii. p. 21, 123).

44. The various accidents of the downfall and flight of the Huns are related in the Kang-Mou, tom. iii. p. 88, 91, 95, 139, etc. The small numbers of each horde may be ascribed to their losses and divisions.

45. M. de Guignes has skilfully traced the foot-steps of the Huns through the vast deserts of Tar-tary (tom. ii. p. 123, 277, etc. 325, etc.).

46. Mohammed, sultan of Carizme, reigned in Sogdiana when it was invaded (A.D. 1218) by Zingis and his Moguls. The Oriental historians (see D'Herbelot, Petit de la Croix, etc.) celebrate the populous cities which he ruined, and the fruit-ful country which he desolated. In the next cen-tury the same provinces of Chorasmia and Mawa-ralnahr were described by Abulfeda (Hudson, Geograph. Minor. tom. iii.). Their actual misery may be seen in the Genealogical History of the Tartars, p. 423–469.

47. Justin (xli. 6) has left a short abridgment of the Greek kings of Bactriana. To their industry I should ascribe the new and extraordinary trade which transported the merchandises of India into Europe by the Oxus, the Caspian, the Cyrus, the Phasis, and the Euxine. The other ways, both of the land and sea, were possessed by the Seleu-cides and the Ptolemies. (See l'Esprit des Loix, l. xxi.)

48. Procopius de Bell. Persico, l. i. c. 3, p. 9 [tom. i. p. 16, ed. Bonn.].

49. In the thirteenth century, the monk Rubru-quis (who traversed the immense plain of Kipzak in his journey to the court of the Great Khan) ob-served the remarkable name of *Hungary*, with the traces of a common language and origin (Hist. des Voyages, tom. vii. p. 269).

50. Bell (vol. i. p. 29–34) and the editors of the Genealogical History (p. 539) have described the Calmucks of the Volga in the beginning of the present century.

51. This great transmigration of 300,000 Cal-mucks, or Torgouts, happened in the year 1771. The original narrative of Kien-long, the reigning emperor of China, which was intended for the in-scription of a column, has been translated by the missionaries of Pekin (Mémoires sur la Chine, tom. i. p. 401–418). The emperor affects the smooth and specious language of the Son of Hea-ven, and the Father of his People.

52. The Kang-Mou (tom. iii. p. 447) ascribes to their conquests a space of 14,000 *lis*. According to the present standard, 200 *lis* (or more accurate-ly 193) are equal to one degree of latitude; and one English mile consequently exceeds three miles of China. But there are strong reasons to believe that the ancient *li* scarcely equalled one-half of the

modern. See the elaborate researches of M. d'An-ville, a geographer who is not a stranger in any age or climate of the globe. (Mémoires de l'Acad. tom. ii. p. 125–502. Mesures Itinéraires, p. 154–167.)

53. See the Histoire des Huns, tom. ii. p. 125–144. The subsequent history (p. 145–277) of three or four Hunnic dynasties evidently proves that their martial spirit was not impaired by a long residence in China.

54. Utque hominibus quietis et placidis otium est voluptabile, ita illos pericula juvant et bella. Judicatur ibi beatus qui in prœlio profuderit ani-mam: senescentes etiam et fortuitis mortibus mun-do digressos, ut degeneres et ignavos, conviciis atrocibus insectantur. [Ammian. xxxi. 2.] We must think highly of the conquerors of *such* men.

55. On the subject of the Alani, see Ammianus (xxxi. 2), Jornandes (de Rebus Geticis, c. 24), M. de Guignes (Hist. des Huns, tom. ii. p. 279), and the Genealogical History of the Tartars (tom. ii. p. 617).

56. As we are possessed of the authentic history of the Huns, it would be impertinent to repeat or to refute the fables which misrepresent their origin and progress, their passage of the mud or water of the Mæotis in pursuit of an ox or stag, les Indes qu'ils avoient découvertes, etc. (Zosimus l. iv. [c. 20] p. 224. Sozomen, l. vi. c. 37. Procopius, Hist. Miscell. c. 5. Jornandes, c. 24. Grandeur et Déca-dence, etc., des Romains, c. 17.)

57. Prodigiosæ formæ, et pandi; ut bipedes ex-istimes bestias; vel quales in commarginandis pon-tibus, effigiati stipites dolantur incompti. Ammian. xxxi. 2. Jornandes (c. 24) draws a strong carica-ture of a Calmuck face. Species pavendâ nigredine . . . quædam deformis offa, non facies; habensque magis puncta quam lumina. See Buffon, Hist. Naturelle, tom. iii. p. 380.

58. This execrable origin, which Jornandes (c. 24) describes with the rancour of a Goth, might be originally derived from a more pleasing fable of the Greeks (Herodot. l. iv. c. 9, etc.).

59. The Roxolani may be the fathers of the 'Pῶς, the *Russians* (D'Anville, Empire de Russie, p. 1–10), whose residence (A.D. 862) about Novogrod Veliki cannot be very remote from that which the Geographer of Ravenna (i. 12, iv. 4, 46, v. 28, 30) assigns to the Roxolani (A.D. 886).

60. The text of Ammianus seems to be imperfect or corrupt; but the nature of the ground explains, and almost defines, the Gothic rampart. Mémoires de l'Académie, etc. tom. xxviii. p. 444–462.

61. M. de Buat (Hist. des Peuples de l'Europe, tom. vi. p. 407) has conceived a strange idea, that Alavivus was the same person as Ulphilas the Gothic bishop; and that Ulphilas, the grandson of a Cappadocian captive, became a temporal prince of the Goths.

62. Ammianus (xxxi. 3) and Jornandes (de Re-bus Geticis, c. 24) describe the subversion of the Gothic empire by the Huns.

63. The chronology of Ammianus is obscure

and imperfect. Tillemont has laboured to clear and settle the annals of Valens.

64. Zosimus, l. iv. [c. 20] p. 223. Sozomen, l. vi. c. 38. The Isaurians, each winter, infested the roads of Asia Minor, as far as the neighbourhood of Constantinople. Basil, Epist. ccl. apud Tillemont, Hist. des Empereurs, tom. v. p. 106.

65. The passage of the Danube is exposed by Ammianus (xxxi. 3, 4), Zosimus (l. iv. [c. 20] p. 223, 224), Eunapius in Excerpt. Legat. (p. 19, 20 [p. 49, 50, ed. Bonn]), and Jornandes (c. 25, 26). Ammianus declares (c. 5) that he means only ipsas rerum digerere *summitates*. But he often takes a false measure of their importance, and his superfluous prolixity is disagreeably balanced by his unseasonable brevity.

66. Chishull, a curious traveller, has remarked the breadth of the Danube, which he passed to the south of Bucharest, near the conflux of the Argish (p. 77). He admires the beauty and spontaneous plenty of Mæsia, or Bulgaria.

67. Quem qui scire velit, Libyci velit æquoris idem

Discere quam multæ Zephyro turbentur arenæ.

Ammianus has inserted in his prose these lines of Virgil (Georgic. l. ii. 105), originally designed by the poet to express the impossibility of numbering the different sorts of vines. See Plin. Hist. Natur. l. xiv.

68. Eunapius and Zosimus curiously specify these articles of Gothic wealth and luxury. Yet it must be presumed that they were the manufactures of the provinces, which the barbarians had acquired as the spoils of war, or as the gifts or merchandise of peace.

69. *Decem libras;* the word *silver* must be understood. Jornandes betrays the passions and prejudices of a Goth. The servile Greeks, Eunapius and Zosimus, disguise the Roman oppression, and execrate the perfidy of the barbarians. Ammianus, a patriot historian, slightly and reluctantly touches on the odious subject. Jerom, who wrote almost on the spot, is fair, though concise. Per avaritiam Maximi ducis, ad rebellionem fame *coacti* sunt (in Chron. [tom. viii. p. 817, ed. Vallars.]).

70. Ammianus, xxxi. 4, 5.

71. Vexillis de *more* sublatis, auditisque *triste sonantibus classicis*. Ammian. xxxi. 5. These are the *rauca cornua* of Claudian (in Rufin. ii. 57), the large horns of the *Uri*, or wild bull—such as have been more recently used by the Swiss cantons of Uri and Unterwald (Simler de Republicâ Helvet. l. ii. p. 201, edit. Fuselin. Tigur. 1734). Their military horn is finely, though perhaps casually, introduced in an original narrative of the battle of Nancy (A.D. 1477). "Attendant le combat le dit cor fut corné par trois fois, tant que le vent du souffleur pouvoit durer: ce qui esbahit fort Monsieur de Bourgoigne; *car dêja à Morat l'avoit ouy.*" (See the Pièces Justificatives in the 4to edition of Philippe de Comines, tom. iii. p. 493.)

72. Jornandes de Rebus Geticis, c. 26, p. 648, edit. Grot. These *splendidi panni* (they are comparatively such) are undoubtedly transcribed from the larger histories of Priscus, Ablavius, or Cassiodorus.

73. Cum populis suis longe ante suscepti. We are ignorant of the precise date and circumstances of their transmigration.

74. An imperial manufacture of shields, etc., was established at Hadrianople; and the populace were headed by the *Fabricenses*, or workmen (Vales. ad Ammian. xxxi. 6).

75. Pacem sibi esse cum parietibus memorans. Ammian. xxxi. 6.

76. These mines were in the country of the Bessi, in the ridge of mountains, the Rhodope, that runs between Philippi and Philippopolis, two Macedonian cities, which derived their name and origin from the father of Alexander. From the mines of Thrace he annually received the value, not the weight, of a thousand talents (£200,000)—a revenue which paid the phalanx and corrupted the orators of Greece. See Diodor. Siculus, tom. ii. l. xvi. [c. 8] p. 88, edit. Wesseling. Godefroy's Commentary on the Theodosian Code, tom. iii. p. 496. Cellarius, Geograph. Antiq. tom. i. p. 676, 857. D'Anville, Géographie Ancienne, tom. i. p. 336.

77. As those unhappy workmen often ran away, Valens had enacted severe laws to drag them from their hiding-places. Cod. Theodosian, l. x. tit. xix. leg. 5, 7.

78. See Ammianus xxxi. 5, 6. The historian of the Gothic war loses time and space by an unseasonable recapitulation of the ancient inroads of the barbarians.

79. The Itinerary of Antoninus (p. 226, 227, edit. Wesseling) marks the situation of this place about sixty miles north of Tomi, Ovid's exile; and the name of *Salices* (the willows) expresses the nature of the soil.

80. This circle of waggons, the *Carrago*, was the usual fortification of the barbarians (Vegetius de Re Militari, l. iii. c. 10. Valesius ad Ammian. xxxi. 7). The practice and the name were preserved by their descendants as late as the fifteenth century. The *Charroy*, which surrounded the *Ost*, is a word familiar to the readers of Froissart, or Comines.

81. Statim ut accensi malleoli [Amm. xxxi. 7]. I have used the literal sense of real torches or beacons; but I almost suspect that it is only one of those turgid metaphors, those false ornaments, that perpetually disfigure the style of Ammianus.

82. Indicant nunc usque albentes ossibus campi. Ammian. xxxi. 7. The historian might have viewed these plains, either as a soldier or as a traveller. But his modesty has suppressed the adventures of his own life subsequent to the Persian wars of Constantius and Julian. We are ignorant of the time when he quitted the service and retired to Rome, where he appears to have composed his History of his Own Times.

83. Ammian. xxxi. 8.

84. Hanc Taifalorum gentem turpem, et ob-
scenæ vitæ flagitiis ita accipimus mersam, ut apud
eos nefandi concubitús fœdere copulentur maribus
puberes, ætatis viriditatem in eorum pollutis usi-
bus consumpturi. Porro, si qui jam adultus aprum
exceperit solus, vel interemerit ursum immanem,
colluvione liberatur incesti. Ammian. xxxi. 9.
Among the Greeks likewise, more especially among
the Cretans, the holy bands of friendship were confirmed and sullied by unnatural love.

85. Ammian. xxxi. 8, 9. Jerom (tom. i. p. 26
[tom. i. p. 342, ed. Vallars.]) enumerates the nations, and marks a calamitous period of twenty
years. This epistle to Heliodorus was composed in
the year 397 (Tillemont, Mém. Ecclés. tom. xii.
p. 645).

86. The field of battle, *Argentaria* or *Argentovaria*,
is accurately fixed by M. d'Anville (Notice de
l'Ancienne Gaule, p. 96–99) at twenty-three Gallic
leagues, or thirty-four and a half Roman miles, to
the south of Strasburg. From its ruins the adjacent
town of *Colmar* has arisen.

87. The full and impartial narrative of Ammianus (xxxi. 10) may derive some additional light
from the Epitome of Victor, the Chronicle of Jerom, and the History of Orosius (l. vii. c. 33, p.
552, edit. Havercamp).

88. Moratus paucissimos dies, seditione popu-
larium levium pulsus. Ammian. xxxi. 11. Socrates,
(l. iv. c. 38) supplies the dates and some circumstances.

89. Vivosque omnes circa Mutinam, Regium-
que, et Parmam, Italica oppida, rura culturos ex-
terminavit. Ammianus, xxxi. 9. Those cities and
districts, about ten years after the colony of the
Taifalæ, appear in a very desolate state. See Muratori, Dissertazioni sopra le Antichità Italiane, tom.
i. Dissertat. xxi. p. 354.

90. Ammian. xxxi. 11. Zosimus, l. iv. [c. 23] p.
228–230. The latter expatiates on the desultory exploits of Sebastian, and despatches in a few lines
the important battle of Hadrianople. According
to the ecclesiastical critics, who hate Sebastian, the
praise of Zosimus is disgrace (Tillemont, Hist. des
Empereurs, tom. v. p. 121). His prejudice and ignorance undoubtedly render him a very questionable judge of merit.

91. Ammianus (xxxi. 12, 13) almost alone describes the councils and actions which were terminated by the fatal battle of Hadrianople. We
might censure the vices of his style, the disorder
and perplexity of his narrative; but we must now
take leave of this impartial historian; and reproach
is silenced by our regret for such an irreparable
loss.

92. The difference of the eight miles of Ammianus, and the twelve of Idatius, can only embarrass those critics (Valesius ad loc.) who suppose a
great army to be a mathematical point, without
space or dimensions.

93. Nec ulla, annalibus, præter Cannensem pug-

nam, ita ad internecionem res legitur gesta. Ammian. xxxi. 13. According to the grave Polybius,
no more than 370 horse and 3000 foot escaped
from the field of Cannæ; 10,000 were made prisoners; and the number of the slain amounted to
5630 horse and 70,000 foot (Polyb. l. iii. [c. 117] p.
371, edit. Casaubon, in 8vo.). Livy (xxii. 49) is
somewhat less bloody; he slaughters only 2700
horse and 40,000 foot. The Roman army was supposed to consist of 87,200 effective men (xxii. 36).

94. We have gained some faint light from Jerom
(tom. i. p. 26 [tom. i. p. 342, ed. Vallars.], and in
Chron. p. 188 [tom. viii. p. 817, ed. Vallars.]),
Victor (in Epitome), Orosius (l. vii. c. 33, p. 554),
Jornandes (c. 27), Zosimus (l. iv. [c. 24] p. 230),
Socrates (l. iv. c. 38), Sozomen (l. vi. c. 40), Idatius (in Chron.). But their united evidence, if
weighed against Ammianus alone, is light and unsubstantial.

95. Libanius de ulciscend. Julian. Nece, c. 3, in
Fabricius, Bibliot. Græc. tom. vii. p. 146–148.

96. Valens had gained, or rather purchased, the
friendship of the Saracens, whose vexatious inroads
were felt on the borders of Phœnicia, Palestine,
and Egypt. The Christian faith had been lately introduced among a people reserved in a future age
to propagate another religion (Tillemont, Hist.
des Empereurs, tom. v. p. 104, 106, 141; Mém.
Ecclés. tom. vii. p. 593).

97. Crinitus quidam, nudus omnia præter pu-
bem, subraucum et lugubre strepens. Ammian.
xxxi. 16, and Vales. ad loc. The Arabs often fought
naked—a custom which may be ascribed to their
sultry climate and ostentatious bravery. The description of this unknown savage is the lively portrait of Derar, a name so dreadful to the Christians
of Syria. See Ockley's Hist. of the Saracens, vol. i.
p. 72, 84, 87.

98. The series of events may still be traced in the
last pages of Ammianus (xxxi. 15, 16). Zosimus (l.
iv. [c. 22] p. 227, 231), whom we are now reduced
to cherish, misplaces the sally of the Arabs before
the death of Valens. Eunapius (in Excerpt. Legat.
p. 20 [p. 51, ed. Bonn]) praises the fertility of
Thrace, Macedonia, etc.

99. Observe with how much indifference Cæsar
relates, in the Commentaries of the Gallic war,
that he put to death the whole senate of the Veneti,
who had yielded to his mercy (iii. 16); *that* he laboured to extirpate the whole nation of the Eburones (vi. 43); *that* forty thousand persons were
massacred at Bourges by the just revenge of his
soldiers, who spared neither age nor sex (vii. 27),
etc.

100. Such are the accounts of the sack of Mad-
geburg, by the ecclesiastic and the fisherman,
which Mr. Harte has transcribed (Hist. of Gustavus Adolphus, vol. i. p. 313–320), with some apprehension of violating the *dignity* of history.

101. Et vastatis urbibus, hominibusque inter-
fectis, solitudinem et *raritatem bestiarum* quoque
fieri, *et volatilium, pisciumque:* testis Illyricum est,

testis Thracia, testis in quo ortus sum solum (Pannonia); ubi præter cœlum et terram, et crescentes vepres, et condensa silvarum *cuncta perierunt.* Tom. vii. p. 250, ad 1. Cap. Sophonias; and tom. i. p. 26 [tom. i. p. 342, ed. Vallars.].

102. Eunapius (in Excerpt. Legat. p. 20 [p. 50, ed. Bonn]) foolishly supposes a preternatural growth of the young Goths, that he may introduce Cadmus's armed men, who sprung from the dragon's teeth, etc. Such was the Greek eloquence of the times.

103. Ammianus evidently approves this execution, efficacia velox et salutaris, which concludes his work (xxxi. 16). Zosimus, who is curious and copious (l. iv. [c. 26] p. 233–236), mistakes the date, and labours to find the reason why Julius did not consult the emperor Theodosius, who had not yet ascended the throne of the East.

104. A life of Theodosius the Great was composed in the last century (Paris, 1679, in 4to; 1680, in 12mo), to inflame the mind of the young dauphin with Catholic zeal. The author, Fléchier, afterwards bishop of Nismes, was a celebrated preacher; and his history is adorned or tainted with pulpit eloquence; but he takes his learning from Baronius, and his principles from St. Ambrose and St. Augustin.

105. The birth, character, and elevation of Theodosius, are marked in Pacatus (in Panegyr. Vet. xii. 10, 11, 12), Themistius (Orat. xiv. p. 182), Zosimus (l. iv. [c. 24] p. 231), Augustine (The City of God, v. 26), Orosius (l. vii. c. 34), Sozomen (l. vii. c. 2), Socrates (l. v. c. 2), Theodoret (l. v. c. 5), Philostorgius (l. ix. c. 17, with Godefroy, p. 393), the Epitome of Victor, and the Chronicles of Prosper, Idatius, and Marcellinus, in the Thesaurus Temporum of Scaliger.

106. Tillemont, Hist. des Empereurs, tom. v. p. 716, etc.

107. *Italica,* founded by Scipio Africanus for his wounded veterans of *Italy.* The ruins still appear, about a league above Seville, but on the opposite bank of the river. See the Hispania Illustrata of Nonius—a short though valuable treatise—c. xvii. p. 64–67.

108. I agree with Tillemont (Hist. des Empereurs, tom. v. p. 726), in suspecting the royal pedigree, which remained a secret till the promotion of Theodosius. Even after that event, the silence of Pacatus outweighs the venal evidence of Themistius, Victor, and Claudian, who connect the family of Theodosius with the blood of Trajan and Hadrian.

109. Pacatus compares, and consequently prefers, the youth of Theodosius, to the military education of Alexander, Hannibal, and the second Africanus, who, like him, had served under their fathers (xii. 8).

110. Ammianus (xxix. 6) mentions this victory of Theodosius Junior Dux Mæsiæ, primâ etiam tum lanugine juvenis, princeps postea perspectissimus. The same fact is attested by Themistius and

Zosimus; but Theodoret (l. v. c. 5), who adds some curious circumstances, strangely applies it to the time of the interregnum.

111. Pacatus (in Panegyr. Vet. xii. 9) prefers the rustic life of Theodosius to that of Cincinnatus; the one was the effect of choice, the other of poverty.

112. M. d'Anville (Géographie Ancienne, tom. i. p. 25) has fixed the situation of Caucha, or Coca, in the old province of Gallicia, where Zosimus and Idatius have placed the birth or patrimony of Theodosius.

113. Let us hear Ammianus himself. Hæc, ut miles quondam at Græcus, a principatu Cæsaris Nervæ exorsus, adusque Valentis interitum, pro virium explicavi mensurâ: opus veritatem professum nunquam, ut arbitror, sciens, silentio ausus corrumpere vel mendacio. Scribant reliqua potiores ætate, doctrinisque florentes. Quos id, si libuerit, aggressuros, procudere linguas ad majores moneo stilos. Ammian. xxxi. 16. The first thirteen books, a superficial epitome of two hundred and fifty-seven years, are now lost; the last eighteen, which contain no more than twenty-five years, still preserve the copious and authentic history of his own times.

114. Ammianus was the last subject of Rome who composed a profane history in the Latin language. The East, in the next century, produced some rhetorical historians, Zosimus, Olympiodorus, Malchus, Candidus, etc. See Vossius de Historicis Græcis, l. ii. c. 18; de Historicis Latinis, l. ii. c. 10, etc.

115. Chrysostom, tom. i. p. 344, edit. Montfaucon. I have verified and examined this passage; but I should never, without the aid of Tillemont (Hist. des Emp. tom. v. p. 152), have detected an historical anecdote in a strange medley of moral and mystic exhortations, addressed, by the preacher of Antioch, to a young widow.

116. Eunapius, in Excerpt. Legation. p. 21 [p. 52, ed. Bonn].

117. See Godefroy's Chronology of the Laws. Codex Theodos. tom. i. Prolegomen. p. xcix.–civ.

118. Most writers insist on the illness and long repose of Theodosius at Thessalonica: Zosimus, to diminish his glory; Jornandes, to favour the Goths; and the ecclesiastical writers, to introduce his baptism.

119. Compare Themistius (Orat. xiv. p. 181) with Zosimus (l. iv. [c. 25] p. 232), Jornandes (c. xxvii. p. 649), and the prolix Commentary of M. de Buat (Hist. des Peuples, etc., tom. vi. p. 477–552). The Chronicles of Idatius and Marcellinus allude, in general terms, to magna certamina, *magna multaque prælia.* The two epithets are not easily reconciled.

120. Zosimus (l. iv. [c. 25] p. 232) styles him a Scythian, a name which the more recent Greeks seem to have appropriated to the Goths.

121. The reader will not be displeased to see the original words of Jornandes, or the author whom

he transcribed. Regiam urbem ingressus est, miransque, En, inquit, cerno quod sæpe incredulus audiebam, famam videlicet tantæ urbis. Et huc illuc oculos volvens, nunc situm urbis, commeatumque navium, nunc mœnia clara prospectans, miratur; populosque diversarum gentium, quasi fonte in uno e diversis partibus scaturiente undâ, sic quoque militem ordinatum aspiciens; Deus, inquit, sine dubio est terrenus Imperator, et quisquis adversus eum manum moverit, ipse sui sanguinis reus existit. Jornandes (c. xxviii. p. 650) proceeds to mention his death and funeral.

122. Jornandes, c. xxviii. p. 650. Even Zosimus (l. iv. [c. 34] p. 246) is compelled to approve the generosity of Theodosius, so honourable to himself and so beneficial to the public.

123. The short, but authentic, hints in the *Fasti* of Idatius (Chron. Scaliger. p. 52) are stained with contemporary passion. The fourteenth oration of Themistius is a compliment to Peace and the consul Saturninus (A.D. 383).

124. Ἔθνος τι Σπύθικον πᾶσιν ἄγνωστον. Zosimus, l. iv. [c. 38] p. 252.

125. I am justified, by reason and example, in applying this Indian name to the μονόξυλα of the barbarians, the single trees hollowed into the shape of a boat, πληθεῖ μονοξύλων ἐμβιβάσαντες. Zosimus, l. iv. [c. 38] p. 253.

> Ausi Danubium quondam tranare Gruthungi
> In lintres fregere nemus: ter mille ruebant
> Per fluvium plenæ cuneis immanibus alni.
>   Claudian, in iv. Cons. Hon. 623.

126. Zosimus, l. iv. [c. 38] p. 252–255. He too frequently betrays his poverty of judgment by disgracing the most serious narratives with trifling and incredible circumstances.

127.   ———Odothæi Regis *opima*

> Retulit   Ver. 632.

The *opima* were the spoils which a Roman general could only win from the king, or general, of the enemy, whom he had slain with his own hands: and no more than three such examples are celebrated in the victorious ages of Rome.

128. See Themistius, Orat. xvi. p. 211. Claudian (in Eutrop. l. ii. 152) mentions the Phrygian colony:—

> ———Ostrogothis colitur mistisque Gruthungis
> Phryx ager———

and then proceeds to name the rivers of Lydia, the Pactolus, and Hermus.

129. Compare Jornandes (c. 21, 28), who marks the condition and number of the Gothic *Fœderati*, with Zosimus (l. iv. p. 258), who mentions their golden collars; and Pacatus (in Panegyr. Vet. xii. 37), who applauds, with false or foolish joy, their bravery and discipline.

130. Amator pacis generisque Gothorum, is the praise bestowed by the Gothic historian (c. xxix.), who represents his nation as innocent, peaceable men, slow to anger and patient of injuries. According to Livy, the Romans conquered the world in their own defence.

131. Besides the partial invectives of Zosimus (always discontented with the Christian reigns), see the grave representations which Synesius addresses to the emperor Arcadius (de Regno, p. 25, 26, edit. Petav. [Paris, 1612]). The philosophic bishop of Cyrene was near enough to judge; and he was sufficiently removed from the temptation of fear or flattery.

132. Themistius (Orat. xvi. p. 211, 212) composes an elaborate and rational apology, which is not, however, exempt from the puerilities of Greek rhetoric. Orpheus could *only* charm the wild beasts of Thrace; but Theodosius enchanted the men and women whose predecessors in the same country had torn Orpheus in pieces, etc.

133. Constantinople was deprived, half a day, of the public allowance of bread, to expiate the murder of a Gothic soldier: κινοῦντες τὸ Σκυθικόν was the guilt of the people. Libanius, Orat. xii. p. 394, edit. Morel.

134. Zosimus, l. iv. [c. 48] p. 267–271. He tells a long and ridiculous story of the adventurous prince, who roved the country with only five horsemen, of a spy whom they detected, whipped, and killed in an old woman's cottage, etc.

135. Compare Eunapius (in Excerpt. Legat. p. 21, 22 [p. 53, 54, ed. Bonn.] with Zosimus (l. iv. [c. 56] p. 279). The difference of circumstances and names must undoubtedly be applied to the same story. Fravitta, or Travitta, was afterwards consul (A.D. 401), and still continued his faithful service to the eldest son of Theodosius (Tillemont, Hist. des Empereurs, tom. v. p. 467).

136. Les Goths ravagèrent tout depuis le Danube jusqu'au Bosphore; exterminèrent Valens et son armée; et ne repassèrent le Danube que pour abandonner l'affreuse solitude qu'ils avoient faite (Œuvres de Montesquieu, tom. iii. p. 479; Considérations sur les *Causes* de la Grandeur et de la Décadence des Romains, c. xvii.). The president Montesquieu seems ignorant that the Goths, after the defeat of Valens, never abandoned the Roman territory. It is now thirty years, says Claudian (de Bello Getico, 166, etc., A.D. 404),

> Ex quo jam patrios gens hæc oblita Triones,
> Atque Istrum transvecta semel, vestigiâ fixit
> Threicio funesta solo———

The error is inexcusable; since it disguises the principal and immediate cause of the fall of the Western empire of Rome.

1. Valentinian was less attentive to the religion of his son; since he intrusted the education of Gratian to Ausonius, a professed Pagan. (Mém. de l'Académie des Inscriptions, tom. xv. p. 125–138). The poetical fame of Ausonius condemns the taste of his age.

2. Ausonius was successively promoted to the Prætorian præfecture of Italy (A.D. 377) and of Gaul (A.D. 378); and was at length invested with the consulship (A.D. 379). He expressed his gratitude in a servile and insipid piece of flattery (Actio Gratiarum, p. 699–736 [ed. Toll. Amst. 1671]), which has survived more worthy productions.

3. Disputare de principali judicio non oportet. Sacrilegii enim instar est dubitare, an is dignus sit, quem elegerit imperator. Codex Justinian. l. ix. tit. xxix. leg. 2. This convenient law was revived and promulgated, after the death of Gratian, by the feeble court of Milan.

4. Ambrose composed, for his instruction, a theological treatise on the faith of the Trinity: and Tillemont (Hist. des Empereurs, tom. v. p. 158, 169) ascribes to the archbishop the merit of Gratian's intolerant laws.

5. Qui divinæ legis sanctitatem [aut] nesciendo omittunt, aut negligendo violant, et offendunt, sacrilegium committunt. Codex Justinian. l. ix. tit. xxix. leg. 1. Theodosius indeed may claim his share in the merit of this comprehensive law.

6. Ammianus (xxxi. 10) and the younger Victor [Epit. c. 47] acknowledge the virtues of Gratian; and accuse, or rather lament, his degenerate taste. The odious parallel of Commodus is saved by "licet incruentus;" and perhaps Philostorgius (l. x. c. 10 [5], and Godefroy, p. 412) had guarded, with some similar reserve, the comparison of Nero.

7. Zosimus (l. iv. [c. 35] p. 247) and the younger Victor ascribe the revolution to the favour of the Alani and the discontent of the Roman troops. Dum exercitum negligeret, et paucos ex Alanis, quos ingenti auro ad se transtulerat, anteferret veteri ac Romano militi [Epit. c. 47].

8. Britannia fertilis provincia tyrannorum, is a memorable expression used by Jerom in the Pelagian controversy, and variously tortured in the disputes of our national antiquaries. The revolutions of the last age appeared to justify the image of the sublime Bossuet, "cette ile, plus orageuse que les mers qui l'environment."

9. Zosimus says of the British soldiers, τῶν ἄλλων ἁπάντων πλέον αὐθαδείᾳ καὶ θυμῷ νικωμένους [l. c.].

10. Helena the daughter of Eudda. Her chapel may still be seen at Caersegont, now Caer-narvon. (Carte's Hist. of Englsnd, vol. i. p. 168, from Rowland's Mona Antiqua.) The prudent reader may not perhaps be satisfied with such Welch evidence.

11. Camden (vol. i. introduct. p. ci.) appoints him governor of Britain; and the father of our antiquities is followed, as usual, by his blind progeny. Pacatus and Zosimus had taken some pains to prevent this error or fable; and I shall protect myself by their decisive testimonies. Regali habitú exulem suum, illi exules orbis induerunt (in Panegyr. Vet. xii. 23), and the Greek historian still less equivocally, αὐτὸς (Maximus) δὲ οὐδὲ εἰς ἀρχὴν ἔντιμον ἔτυχε προελθών (l. iv. [c. 35] p. 248).

12. Sulpicius Severus, Dialog. ii. 7. Orosius, l. vii. c. 34, p. 556. They both acknowledge (Sulpicius had been his subject) his innocence and merit. It is singular enough that Maximus should be less favourably treated by Zosimus, the partial adversary of his rival.

13. Archbishop Usher (Antiquitat. Britan. Eccles. p. 107, 108) has diligently collected the legends of the island and the continent. The whole emigration consisted of 30,000 soldiers and 100,000 plebeians, who settled in Bretagne. Their destined brides, St. Ursula with 11,000 noble and 60,000 plebeian virgins, mistook their way, landed at Cologne, and were all most cruelly murdered by the Huns. But the plebeian sisters have been defrauded of their equal honours; and, what is still harder, John Trithemius presumes to mention the children of these British virgins.

14. Zosimus (l. iv. [c. 35] p. 248, 249) has transported the death of Gratian from Lugdunum in Gaul (Lyons) to Singidunum in Mæsia. Some hints may be extracted from the Chronicles; some lies may be detected in Sozomen (l. vii. c. 13) and Socrates (l. v. c. 11). Ambrose is our most authentic evidence (tom. i. Enarrat. in Psalm lxi. p. 961, tom. ii. Epist. xxiv. p. 888, etc., and de Obitú Valentinian. Consolat. No. 28, p. 1182).

15. Pacatus (xii. 28) celebrates his fidelity; while his treachery is marked in Prosper's Chronicle as the cause of the ruin of Gratian. Ambrose, who has occasion to exculpate himself, only condemns the death of Vallio, a faithful servant of Gratian (tom. ii. Epist. xxiv. p. 891, edit. Benedict.).

16. He protested, nullum ex adversariis nisi in acie occubuisse. Sulp. Severus in Vit. B. Martin c. 23. The orator of Theodosius bestow's reluctant, and therefore weighty, praise on his clemency. Si cui ille, pro ceteris, sceleribus, suit, minus crudelis fuisse videtur (Panegyr. Vet. xii. 28).

17. Ambrose mentions the laws of Gratian, quas non abrogavit hostis (tom. ii. Epist. xvii. p. 827).

18. Zosimus, l. iv. [c. 37] p. 251, 252. We may disclaim his odious suspicions, but we cannot reject the treaty of peace which the friends of Theodosius have absolutely forgotten, or slightly mentioned.

19. Their oracle, the archbishop of Milan, assigns to his pupil Gratian an high and respectable

place in heaven (tom. ii. de Obit. Val. Consol. p. 1193).

20. For the baptism of Theodosius, see Sozomen (l. vii. c. 4), Socrates (l. v. c. 6), and Tillemont (Hist. des Empereurs, tom. v. p. 728).

21. Ascolius, or Acholius, was honoured by the friendship and the praises of Ambrose, who styles him, murus fidei atque sanctitatis (tom. ii. Epist. xv. p. 820); and afterwards celebrates his speed and diligence in running to Constantinople, Italy, etc. (Epist. xvi. p. 822)—a virtue which does not appertain either to a *wall* or a *bishop*.

22. Codex Theodos. l. xvi. tit. i. leg. 2, with Godefroy's Commentary, tom. vi. p. 5–9. Such an edict deserved the warmest praises of Baronius, auream sanctionem, edictum pium et salutare.— sic itur ad astra.

23. Sozomen, l. vii. c. 6. Theodoret, l. v. c. 16. Tillemont is displeased (Mém. Ecclés. tom. vi. p. 627, 628) with the terms of "rustic bishop," "obscure city." Yet I must take leave to think that both Amphilochius and Iconium were objects of inconsiderable magnitude in the Roman empire.

24. Sozomen, l. vii. c. 5. Socrates, l. v. c. 7. Marcellin. in Chron. The account of forty years must be dated from the election or intrusion of Eusebius, who wisely exchanged the bishopric of Nicomedia for the throne of Constantinople.

25. See Jortin's Remarks on Ecclesiastical History, vol. iv. p. 71. The thirty-third Oration of Gregory Nazianzen affords indeed some similar ideas, even some still more ridiculous; but I have not yet found the *words* of this remarkable passage, which I allege on the faith of a correct and liberal scholar.

26. See the thirty-second Oration of Gregory Nazianzen, and the account of his own life, which he has composed in 1800 iambics. Yet every physician is prone to exaggerate the inveterate nature of the disease which he has cured.

27. I confess myself deeply indebted to the *two* Lives of Gregory Nazianzen, composed, with very different views, by Tillemont (Mém. Ecclés. tom. ix. p. 305–560, 692–731), and Le Clerc (Bibliothèque Universelle, tom. xviii. p. 1–128).

28. Unless Gregory Nazianzen mistook thirty years in his own age, he was born, as well as his friend Basil, about the year 329. The preposterous chronology of Suidas has been graciously received, because it removes the scandal of Gregory's father, a saint likewise, begetting children after he became a bishop (Tillemont, Mém. Ecclés. tom. ix. p. 693–697).

29. Gregory's Poem on his own Life contains some beautiful lines (tom. ii. p. 8 [ed. Paris, 1609]), which burst from the heart, and speak the pangs of injured and lost friendship:—

......πόνοι κοινοὶ λόγων,

Ὁμόστεγός τε καὶ συνέστιος βίος,

Νοῦς εἶς ἐν ἀμφοῖν . . . .

Διεσκέδασται πάντα, κάρριπται χαμαί.

Αὖραι φέρουσι τὰς παλαιὰς ἐλπίδας.

In the Midsummer Night's Dream, Helena addresses the same pathetic complaint to her friend Hermia:—

Is all the counsel that we two have shared,
The sisters' vows, etc.

Shakspeare had never read the poems of Gregory Nazianzen; he was ignorant of the Greek language; but his mother-tongue, the language of Nature, is the same in Cappadocia and in Britain.

30. This unfavourable portrait of Sasima is drawn by Gregory Nazianzen (tom. ii. de Vita suâ, p. 7, 8). Its precise situation, forty-nine miles from Archelais, and thirty-two from Tyana, is fixed in the Itinerary of Antoninus (p. 144, edit. Wesseling).

31. The name of Nazianzus has been immortalised by Gregory; but his native town, under the Greek or Roman title of Diocæsarea (Tillemont, Mém. Ecclés. tom. ix. p. 692), is mentioned by Pliny (vi. 3), Ptolemy, and Hierocles (Itinerar. Wesseling, p. 709). It appears to have been situate on the edge of Isauria.

32. See Ducange, Constant. Christiana, l. iv. p. 141, 142. The θεία δύναμις of Sozomen (l. vii. c. 5) is interpreted to mean the Virgin Mary.

33. Tillemont (Mém. Ecclés. tom. ix. p. 432, etc.) diligently collects, enlarges, and explains, the oratorical and poetical hints of Gregory himself.

34. He pronounced an oration (tom. i. Orat. xxiii. p. 409) in his praise; but after their quarrel the name of Maximus was changed into that of Heron (see Jerom, tom. i. in Catalog. Script. Eccles. p. 301 [tom. ii. p. 930, ed. Vallars.]). I touch slightly on these obscure and personal squabbles.

35. Under the modest emblem of a dream, Gregory (tom. ii. Carmen ix. p. 78) describes his own success with some human complacency. Yet it should seem, from his familiar conversation with his auditor St. Jerom (tom. i. Epist. ad Nepotian. p. 14 [tom. i. p. 261, ed. Vallars.]), that the preacher understood the true value of popular applause.

36. Lacrimæ auditorum laudes tuæ sint, is the lively and judicious advice of St. Jerom [loc. cit.].

37. Socrates (l. v. c. 7) and Sozomen (l. vii. c. 5) relate the evangelical words and actions of Damophilus without a word of approbation. He considered, says Socrates, that it is difficult to *resist* the powerful; but it was easy, and would have been profitable, to *submit*.

38. See Gregory Nazianzen, tom. ii. de Vitâ suâ, p. 21, 22. For the sake of posterity, the bishop of Constantinople records a stupendous prodigy. In the month of November, it was a cloudy morning, but the sun broke forth when the procession entered the church.

39. Of the three ecclesiastical historians, Theodoret alone (l. v. c. 2) has mentioned this important commission of Sapor, which Tillemont (Hist. des Empereurs, tom. v. p. 728), judiciously removes from the reign of Gratian to that of Theodosius.

40. I do not reckon Philostorgius, though he mentions (l. ix. c. 19) the expulsion of Damophilus. The Eunomian historian has been carefully strained through an orthodox sieve.

41. Le Clerc has given a curious extract (Bibliothèque Universelle, tom. xviii. p. 91–105) of the theological sermons which Gregory Nazianzen pronounced at Constantinople against the Arians, Eunomians, Macedonians, etc. He tells the Macedonians, who deified the Father and the Son, without the Holy Ghost, that they might as well be styled *Tritheists as Ditheists*. Gregory himself was almost a Tritheist, and his monarchy of heaven resembles a well-regulated aristocracy.

42. The first general council of Constantinople now triumphs in the Vatican; but the popes had long hesitated, and their hesitation perplexes and almost staggers the humble Tillemont (Mém. Ecclés. tom. ix. p. 499, 500).

43. Before the death of Meletius, six or eight of his most popular ecclesiastics, among whom was Flavian, had *abjured*, for the sake of peace, the bishopric of Antioch (Sozomen, l. vii. c. 3, 11; Socrates, l. v. c. 5). Tillemont thinks it his duty to disbelieve the story; but he owns that there are many circumstances in the life of Flavian that *seem* inconsistent with the praises of Chrysostom and the character of a saint (Mém. Ecclés. tom. x. p. 541).

44. Consult Gregory Nazianzen, de vitâ suâ, tom. ii. p. 25–28. His general and particular opinion of the clergy and their assemblies may be seen in verse and prose (tom. i. Orat. i. p. 33; Epist. lv. p. 814, tom. ii.; Carmen x. p. 81). Such passages are faintly marked by Tillemont, and fairly produced by Le Clerc.

45. See Gregory, tom. ii. de Vitâ suâ, p. 28–31. The fourteenth, twenty-seventh, and thirty-second Orations were pronounced in the several stages of this business. The peroration of the last (tom. i. p. 528), in which he takes a solemn leave of men and angels, the city and the emperor, the East and the West, etc., is pathetic, and almost sublime.

46. The whimsical ordination of Nectarius is attested by Sozomen (l. vii. c. 8); but Tillemont observes (Mém. Ecclés. tom. ix. p. 719), Après tout, ce narré de Sozomène est si honteux pour tous ceux qu'il y mêle, et surtout pour Théodose, qu'il vaut mieux travailler â le détruire qu'á le soutenir: an admirable canon of criticism!

47. I can only be understood to mean that such was his natural temper when it was not hardened or inflamed by religious zeal. From his retirement he exhorts Nectarius to prosecute the heretics of Constantinople.

48. See the Theodosian Code, l. xvi. tit. v. leg. 6–23, with Godefroy's commentary on each law, and his general summary, or *Paratitlon*, tom. vi. p. 104–110.

49. They always kept their Easter, like the Jewish Passover, on the fourteenth day of the first moon after the vernal equinox; and thus pertinaciously opposed the Roman church and Nicene synod, which had *fixed* Easter to a Sunday. Bingham's Antiquities, l. xx. c. 5, vol. ii. p. 309, fol. edit.

50. Sozomen, l. vii. c. 12.

51. See the Sacred History of Sulpicius Severus (l. ii. p. 437–452, edit. Lugd. Bat. 1647), a correct and original writer. Dr. Lardner (Credibility, etc., part ii. vol. ix. p. 256–350) has laboured this article with pure learning, good sense, and moderation. Tillemont (Mém. Ecclés. tom. viii. p. 491–527) has raked together all the dirt of the fathers—an useful scavenger!

52. Sulpicius Severus mentions the arch-heretic with esteem and pity. Felix profecto, si non pravo studio corrupisset optimum ingenium; prorsus multa in eo animi et corporis bona cerneres. (Hist. Sacra, l. ii. p. 439.) Even Jerom (tom. i. in Script. Eccles. p. 302 [tom. ii. p. 934, ed. Vallars.]) speaks with temper of Priscillian and Latronian.

53. The bishopric (in Old Castile) is now worth 20,000 ducats a-year (Busching's Geography, vol. ii. p. 308), and is therefore much less likely to produce the author of a new heresy.

54. Exprobrabatur mulieri viduæ nimia religio, et diligentius culta divinitas (Pacat. in Panegyr. Vet. xii. 29). Such was the idea of a humane though ignorant polytheist.

55. One of them was sent in Syllinam insulam quæ ultra Britanniam est. What must have been the ancient condition of the rocks of Scilly (Camden's Britannia, vol. ii. p. 1519)?

56. The scandalous calumnies of Augustin, pope Leo, etc., which Tillemont swallows like a child, and Lardner refutes like a man, may suggest some candid suspicions in favour of the older Gnostics.

57. Ambrose. tom. ii. Epist. xxiv. p. 891.

58. In the Sacred History, and the Life of St. Martin, Sulpicius Severus uses some caution; but he declares himself more freely in the Dialogues (iii. 15). Martin was reproved, however, by his own conscience and by an angel; nor could he afterwards perform miracles with so much ease.

59. The catholic presbyter (Sulp. Sever. l. ii. p. 448), and the Pagan orator (Pacat. in Panegyr. Vet. xxi. 29), reprobate with equal indignation the character and conduct of Ithacius.

60. The Life of St. Martin, and the Dialogues concerning his miracles, contain facts adapted to the grossest barbarism, in a style not unworthy of the Augustin age. So natural is the alliance between good taste and good sense, that I am always astonished by this contrast.

61. The short and superficial Life of St. Ambrose, by his deacon Paulinus (Appendix ad edit. Benedict. p. i.–xv.), has the merit of original evidence. Tillemont (Mém. Ecclés. tom. x. p. 78–306) and the Benedictine editors (p. xxxi.–lxiii.) have laboured with their usual diligence.

62. Ambrose himself (tom. ii. Epist. xxiv. p. 888–891) gives the emperor a very spirited account of his own embassy.

63. His own representation of his principles and conduct (tom. ii. Epist. xx. xxi. xxii. p. 852–880) is one of the curious monuments of ecclesiastical antiquity. It contains two letters to his sister Marcellina, with a petition to Valentinian, and the sermon *de Basilicis non tradendis*.

64. Retz had a similar message from the queen to request that he would appease the tumult of Paris. It was no longer in his power, etc. A quoi j'ajoutai tout ce que vous pouvez vous imaginer de respect, de douleur, de regret, et de soumission, etc. (Mémoires, tom. i. p. 140). Certainly I do not compare either the causes or the men; yet the coadjutor himself had some idea (p. 84) of imitating St. Ambrose.

65. Sozomen alone (l. vii. c. 13) throws this luminous fact into a dark and perplexed narrative.

66. Excubabat pia plebs in ecclesiâ mori parata cum episcopo suo . . . Nos adhuc frigidi excitabamur tamen civitate attonitâ atque turbatâ. Augustine, Confessions, ix. 15.

67. Tillemont, Mém. Ecclés. tom. ii. p. 78, 498. Many churches in Italy, Gaul, etc., were dedicated to these unknown martyrs, of whom St. Gervase seems to have been more fortunate than his companion.

68. Invenimus miræ magnitudinis viros duos, ut prisca ætas ferebat, tom. ii. Epist. xxii. p. 875. The size of these skeletons was fortunately, or skilfully, suited to the popular prejudice of the gradual decrease of the human stature, which has prevailed in every age since the time of Homer.

Grandiaque effossis mirabitur ossa sepulchris.

69. Ambros. tom. ii. Epist. xxii. p. 875. Augusine, Confessions, ix. 16, The City of God, l. xxii. c. 8. Paulin. in Vitâ St. Ambros. c. 14, in Append. Benedict. p. 4. The blind man's name was Severus; he touched the holy garment, recovered his sight, and devoted the rest of his life (at least twenty-five years) to the service of the church. I should recommend this miracle to our divines, if it did not prove the worship of relics as well as the Nicene creed.

70. Paulin. in Vit. St. Ambros. c. 5 [15], in Append. Benedict. p. 5.

71. Tillemont, Mém. Ecclés. tom. x. p. 190, 750. He partially allows the mediation of Theodosius, and capriciously rejects that of Maximus, though it is attested by Prosper, Sozomen, and Theodoret.

72. The modest censure of Sulpicius (Dialog. iii. 15 [p. 576]) inflicts a much deeper wound than the feeble declamation of Pacatus (xii. 25, 26).

73. Esto tutior adversus hominem, pacis involucro [bellum] tegentem, was the wise caution of Ambrose (tom. ii. p. 891) after his return from his second embassy.

74. Baronius (A.D. 387, No. 63) applies to this season of public distress some of the penitential sermons of the archbishop.

75. The flight of Valentinian and the love of Theodosius for his sister are related by Zosimus (l. iv. [c. 43] p. 263, 264). Tillemont produces some

weak and ambiguous evidence to antedate the second marriage of Theodosius (Hist. des Empereurs, tom. v. p. 740), and consequently to refute ces contes de Zosime qui seroient trop contraires à la piété de Théodose.

76. See Godefroy's Chronology of the Laws, Cod. Theodos. tom. i. p. cxix.

77. Besides the hints which may be gathered from chronicles and ecclesiastical history, Zosimus (l. iv. [c. 40, *seq.*] p. 259–267), Orosius (l. vii. c. 35), and Pacatus (in Panegyr. Vet. xii. 30–47), supply the loose and scanty materials of this civil war. Ambrose (tom. ii. Epist. xl. p. 952, 953) darkly alludes to the well-known events of a magazine surprised, an action at Petovio, a Sicilian, perhaps a naval, victory, etc. Ausonius (p. 236, edit. Toll.) applauds the peculiar merit and good fortune of Aquileia.

78. Quam promptum laudare principem, tam tutum siluisse de principe (Pacat. in Panegyr. Vet. xii. 2). Latinus Pacatus Drepanius, a native of Gaul, pronounced this oration at Rome (A.D. 388). He was afterwards proconsul of Africa; and his friend Ausonius praises him as a poet second only to Virgil. See Tillemont, Hist. des Empereurs, tom. v. p. 303.

79. See the fair portrait of Theodosius by the younger Victor; the strokes are distinct and the colours are mixed. The praise of Pacatus is too vague; and Claudian always seems afraid of exalting the father above the son.

80. Ambros. tom. ii. Epist. xl. p. 955. Pacatus, from the want of skill or of courage, omits this glorious circumstance.

81. Pacat. in Panegyr. Vet. xii. 20.

82. Zosimus, l. iv. [c. 50] p. 271, 272. His partial evidence is marked by an air of candour and truth. He observes these vicissitudes of sloth and activity, not as a vice but as a singularity in the character of Theodosius.

83. This choleric temper is acknowledged and excused by Victor [Epit. c. 48]. Sed habes (says Ambrose in decent and manly language to his sovereign) naturæ impetum, quem si quis lenire velit, cito vertes ad misericordiam: si quis stimulet, in magis exsuscitas, ut eum revocare vix possis (tom. ii. Epist. li. p. 998). Theodosius (Claud. in iv. Cons. Hon. 266, etc.) exhorts his son to moderate his anger.

84. The Christians and Pagans agreed in believing that the sedition of Antioch was excited by the dæmons. A gigantic woman (says Sozomen, l. vii. c. 23) paraded the streets with a scourge in her hand. An old man, says Libanius (Orat. xii. p. 396), transformed himself into a youth, then a boy, etc.

85. Zosimus, in his short and disingenuous account (l. iv. [c. 41] p. 258, 259), is certainly mistaken in sending Libanius himself to Constantinople. His own orations fix him at Antioch.

86. Libanius (Orat. i. p. 6, edit. Venet.) declares, that under such a reign the fear of a massa-

cre was groundless and absurd, especially in the emperor's absence; for his presence, according to the eloquent slave, might have given a sanction to the most bloody acts.

87. Laodicea, on the sea-coast, sixty-five miles from Antioch (see Noris, Epoch. Syro-Maced. Dissert. iii. p. 230). The Antiochians were offended that the dependent city of Seleucia should presume to intercede for them.

88. As the days of the tumult depend on the *movable* festival of Easter, they can only be determined by the previous determination of the year. The year 387 has been preferred, after a laborious inquiry, by Tillemont (Hist. des Emp. tom. v. p. 741–744) and Montfaucon (Chrysostom, tom. xiii. p. 105–110).

89. Chrysostom opposes *their* courage, which was not attended with much risk, to the cowardly flight of the Cynics.

90. The sedition of Antioch is represented in a lively and almost dramatic manner by two orators who had their respective shares of interest and merit. See Libanius (Orat. xiv. xv. [xii. xiii.] p. 389–420, edit. Morel.; Orat. i. p. 1–14, Venet. 1754) and the twenty orations of St. John Chrysostom, *de Statuis* (tom. ii. p. 1–225, edit. Montfaucon). I do not pretend to *much* personal acquaintance with Chrysostom; but Tillemont (Hist. des Empereurs, tom. v. p. 263–283) and Hermant (Vie de St. Chrysostome, tom. i. p. 137–224) had read him with pious curiosity and diligence.

91. The original evidence of Ambrose (tom. ii. Epist. li. p. 998), Augustine (The City of God, v. 26), and Paulinus (in Vit. Ambros. c. 24), is delivered in vague expressions of horror and pity. It is illustrated by the subsequent and unequal testimonies of Sozomen (l. vii. c. 25), Theodoret (l. v. c. 17), Theophanes (Chronograph. p. 62 [tom. i. p. 113, ed. Bonn.]), Cedrenus (p. 317 [tom. i. p. 556, ed. Bonn.]), and Zonaras (tom. ii. l. xiii. [c. 18] p. 34). Zosimus *alone*, the partial enemy of Theodosius, most unaccountably passes over in silence the worst of his actions.

92. See the whole transaction in Ambrose (tom. ii. Epist. xl. xli. p. 946–956), and his biographer Paulinus (c. 23). Bayle and Barbeyrac (Morales des Pères, c. xvii. p. 325, etc.) have justly condemned the archbishop.

93. His sermon is a strange allegory of Jeremiah's rod, of an almond-tree, of the woman who washed and anointed the feet of Christ. But the peroration is direct and personal.

94. Hodie, Episcope, de me proposuisti. Ambrose modestly confessed it; but he sternly reprimanded Timesius, general of the horse and foot, who had presumed to say that the monks of Callinicum deserved punishment.

95. Yet, five years afterwards, when Theodosius was absent from his spiritual guide, he tolerated the Jews, and condemned the destruction of their synagogues. Cod. Theodos. l. xvi. tit. viii. leg. 9, with Godefroy's Commentary, tom. vi. p. 225.

96. Ambros. tom. ii. Epist. li. p. 997–1001. His epistle is a miserable rhapsody on a noble subject. Ambrose could act better than he could write. His compositions are destitute of taste or genius; without the spirit of Tertullian, the copious elegance of Lactantius, the lively wit of Jerom, or the grave energy of Augustin.

97. According to the discipline of St. Basil (Canon lvi.), the voluntary homicide was *four* years a mourner; *five* an hearer; *seven* in a prostrate state; and *four* in a standing posture. I have the original (Beveridge, Pandect. tom. ii. p. 47–151) and a translation (Chardon, Hist. des Sacremens, tom. iv. p. 219–277) of the Canonical Epistles of St. Basil.

98. The penance of Theodosius is authenticated by Ambrose (tom. ii. de Obit. Theodos. c. 34, p. 1207), Augustine (The City of God, v. 26), and Paulinus (in Vit. Ambros. c. 24). Socrates is ignorant; Sozomen (l. vii. c. 25) concise; and the copious narrative of Theodoret (l. v. c. 18) must be used with precaution.

99. Codex Theodos. l. ix. tit. xl. leg. 13. The date and circumstances of this law are perplexed with difficulties; but I feel myself inclined to favour the honest efforts of Tillemont (Hist. des Emp. tom. v. p. 721) and Pagi (Critica, tom. i. p. 578).

100. Un prince qui aime la religion, et qui la craint, est un lion qui cède à la main qui le flatte, ou à la voix qui l'appaise. The Spirit of Laws, l. xxiv. c. 2.

101. Τοῦτο περὶ τοὺς εὐεργέτας καθῆκον ἔδοξεν εἶναι, is the niggard praise of Zosimus himself (l. iv. [c. 48] p. 267). Augustin says, with some happiness of expression, Valentinianum . . . misericordissimâ veneratione restituit.

102. Sozomen, l. vii. c. 14. His chronology is very irregular.

103. See Ambrose (tom. ii. de Obit. Valentinian. c. 15, etc., p. 1178, c. 36, etc., p. 1184). When the young emperor gave an entertainment, he fasted himself; he refused to see an handsome actress, etc. Since he ordered his wild beasts to be killed, it is ungenerous in Philostorgius (l. xi. c. 1) to reproach him with the love of that amusement.

104. Zosimus (l. iv. [c. 53] p. 275) praises the enemy of Theodosius. But he is detested by Socrates (l. v. c. 25) and Orosius (l. vii. c. 35).

105. Gregory of Tours (l. ii. c. 9, p. 165, in the second volume of the Historians of France) has preserved a curious fragment of Sulpicius Alexander, an historian far more valuable than himself.

106. Godefroy (Dissertat. ad Philostorg. p. 429–434) has diligently collected all the circumstances of the death of Valentinian II. The variations and the ignorance of contemporary writers prove that it was secret.

107. De Obitû Valentinian. tom. ii. p. 1173–1196. He is forced to speak a discreet and obscure language: yet he is much bolder than any layman, or perhaps any other ecclesiastic, would have dared to be.

108. See c. 51, p. 1188; c. 75, p. 1193. Dom Chardon (Hist. des Sacremens, tom. i. p. 86), who owns that St. Ambrose most strenuously maintains the *indispensable* necessity of baptism, labours to reconcile the contradiction.

109.   Quem sibi Germanus famulum delegerat exul,

is the contemptuous expression of Claudian (iv. Cons. Hon. 74). Eugenius professed Christianity; but his secret attachment to Paganism (Sozomen, l. vii. c. 22; Philostorg. l. xi. c. 2) is probable in a grammarian, and would secure the friendship of Zosimus (l. iv. [c. 54] p. 276, 277).

110. Zosimus (l. iv. [c. 55] p. 278) mentions this embassy; but he is diverted by another story from relating the event.

111. Συνετάραξεν ἡ τούτου γαμετὴ Γάλλα τὰ βασίλεια, τὸν ἀδελφὸν ὀλοφυρομένη. Zosim. l. iv. [c. 55] p. 277. He afterwards says ([c. 57] p. 280) that Galla died in childbed; and intimates that the affliction of her husband was extreme but short.

112. Lycopolis is the modern Siut, or Osiot, a town of Said, about the size of St. Denys, which drives a profitable trade with the kingdom of Sennaar, and has a very convenient fountain, "cujus potú signa virginitatis eripiuntur." See D'Anville, Description de l'Egypte, p. 181. Abulfeda, Descript. Egypt. p. 14; and the curious Annotations, p. 25, 92, of his editor Michaelis.

113. The Life of John of Lycopolis is described by his two friends, Rufinus (l. ii. c. i. p. 449) and Palladius (Hist. Lausiac. c. 43, p. 738), in Rosweyde's great Collection of the Vitæ Patrum. Tillemont (Mém. Ecclés. tom. x. p. 718, 720) has settled the chronology.

114. Sozomen, l. vii. c. 22. Claudian (in Eutrop. l. i. 312) mentions the eunuch's journey: but he most contemptuously derives the Egyptian dreams and the oracles of the Nile.

115. Zosimus, l. iv. [c. 57] p. 280; Socrates, l. vii. 10. Alaric himself (de Bell. Getico, 524) dwells with more complacency on his early exploits against the Romans.

      . . . Tot Augustos Hebro qui teste fugavi.

Yet his vanity could scarcely have proved this *plurality* of flying emperors.

116. Claudian (in iv. Cons. Honor. 77, etc.) contrasts the military plans of the two usurpers:—

      . . . Novitas audere priori

Suadebat; cautumque dabant exempla sequentem.

His nova moliri præceps: his quærere tuta Providus. Hic fusis, collectis viribus ille;

Hic vagus excurrens; hic intra claustra reductus;

Dissimiles, sed morte pares . . .

117. The Frigidus, a small though memorable stream in the country of Goretz, now called the Vipao, falls into the Sontius, or Lisonzo, above Aquileia, some miles from the Hadriatic. See D'Anville's ancient and modern maps, and the Italia Antiqua of Cluverius (tom. i. p. 188).

118. Claudian's wit is intolerable: the snow was dyed red; the cold river smoked; and the channel must have been choked with carcasses if the current had not been swelled with blood.

119. Theodoret affirms that St. John and St. Philip appeared to the waking or sleeping emperor, on horseback, etc. This is the first instance of apostolic chivalry, which afterwards became so popular in Spain and in the Crusades.

120.   Te propter, gelidis Aquilo de monte procellis

Obruit adversas acies; revolutaque tela

Vertit in auctores, et turbine reppulit hastas.

O nimium dilecte Deo, cui fundit ab antris

Æolus armatas hiemes; cui militat Æther, Et conjurati veniunt ad classica venti.

These famous lines of Claudian (in iii. Cons. Honor. 93, A.D. 396) are alleged by his contemporaries, Augustin and Orosius, who suppress the Pagan deity of Æolus, and add some circumstances from the information of eye-witnesses. Within four months after the victory, it was compared by Ambrose to the miraculous victories of Moses and Joshua.

121. The events of this civil war are gathered from Ambrose (tom. ii. Epist. lxii. p. 1022), Paulinus (in Vit. Ambros. c. 26–34), Augustine (The City of God, v. 26), Orosius (l. vii. c. 35), Sozomen (l. vii. c. 24), Theodoret (l. v. c. 24), Zosimus (l. iv. [c. 58] p. 281, 282), Claudian (in. iii. Cons. Hon. 63–105; in iv. Cons. Hon. 70–117), and the Chronicles published by Scaliger.

122. This disease, ascribed by Socrates (l. v. c. 26) to the fatigues of war, is represented by Philostorgius (l. xi. c. 2) as the effect of sloth and intemperance; for which Photius calls him an impudent liar (Godefroy, Dissert. p. 438).

123. Zosimus supposes that the boy Honorius accompanied his father (l. iv. [c. 58] p. 280). Yet the quanto flagrabant pectora voto is all that flattery would allow to a contemporary poet, who clearly describes the emperor's refusal, and the journey of Honorius, *after* the victory (Claudian in iii. Cons. 78–125).

124. Zosimus, l. iv. [c. 33] p. 244.

125. Vegetius, de Re Militari, l. i. c. 20. The series of calamities, which he marks, compel us to believe that the *Hero* to whom he dedicates his book is the last and most inglorious of the Valentinians.

Chapter XXVIII

1. St. Ambrose (tom. ii. de Obit. Theodos. p. 1208 [ed. Bened.]) expressly praises and recommends the zeal of Josiah in the destruction of idolatry. The language of Julius Firmicus Maternus on the same subject (de Errore Profan. Relig. p. 467, edit. Gronov. [Rotterod. 1743]) is piously inhuman. Nec filio jubet (the Mosaic Law) parci, nec fratri, et per amatam conjugem gladium vindicem ducit, etc.

2. Bayle (tom. ii. p. 406, in his Commentaire Philosophique) justifies and limits these intolerant laws by the temporal reign of Jehovah over the Jews. The attempt is laudable.

3. See the outlines of the Roman hierarchy in Cicero (de Legibus, ii. 7, 8), Livy (i. 20), Dionysius Halicarnassensis (l. ii. [c. 63, *sqq.*] p. 119-129, edit. Hudson), Beaufort (République Romaine, tom. i. p. 1-90), and Moyle (vol. i. p. 10-55). The last is the work of an English whig, as well as of a Roman antiquary.

4. These mystic, and perhaps imaginary, symbols have given birth to various fables and conjectures. It seems probable that the Palladium was a small statue (three cubits and a half high) of Minerva, with a lance and distaff; that it was usually inclosed in a *seria*, or barrel; and that a similar barrel was placed by its side to disconcert curiosity or sacrilege. See Mezeriac (Comment. sur les Epitres d'Ovide, tom. i. p. 60-66) and Lipsius (tom. iii. p. 610, de Vestâ, etc., c. 10).

5. Cicero frankly (ad Atticum, l. ii. Epist. 5) or indirectly (ad Familiar. l. xv. Epist 4) confesses that the *Augurate* is the supreme object of his wishes. Pliny is proud to tread in the footsteps of Cicero (l. iv. Epist. 8), and the chain of tradition might be continued from history and marbles.

6. Zosimus, l. iv. [c. 36] p. 249, 250. I have suppressed the foolish pun about *Pontifex* and *Maximus*.

7. This statue was transported from Tarentum to Rome, placed in the *Curia Julia* by Cæsar, and decorated by Augustus with the spoils of Egypt.

8. Prudentius (l. ii. [in Symm.] in initio) has drawn a very awkward portrait of Victory; but the curious reader will obtain more satisfaction from Montfaucon's Antiquities (tom. i. p. 341).

9. See Suetonius (in August. c. 35) and the Exordium of Pliny's Panegyric.

10. These facts are mutually allowed by the two advocates Symmachus and Ambrose.

11. The *Notitia Urbis*, more recent than Constantine, does not find one Christian church worthy to be named among the edifices of the city. Ambrose (tom. ii. Epist. xvii. p. 825) deplores the public scandals of Rome, which continually offended the eyes, the ears, and the nostrils of the faithful.

12. Ambrose repeatedly affirms, in contradiction to common sense (Moyle's Works, vol. ii. p.

147), that the Christians had a majority in the senate.

13. The *first* (A.D. 382) to Gratian, who refused them audience. The *second* (A.D. 384) to Valentinian, when the field was disputed by Symmachus and Ambrose. The *third* (A.D. 388) to Theodosius; and the *fourth* (A.D. 392) to Valentinian. Lardner (Heathen Testimonies, vol. iv. p. 372-399) fairly represents the whole transaction.

14. Symmachus, who was invested with all the civil and sacerdotal honours, represented the emperor under the two characters of *Pontifex Maximus* and *Princeps Senatus*. See the proud inscription at the head of his works.

15. As if any one, says Prudentius (in Symmach. i. 639), should dig in the mud with an instrument of gold and ivory. Even saints, and polemic saints, treat this adversary with respect and civility.

16. See the fifty-fourth Epistle of the tenth book of Symmachus [p. 289, ed. Paris, 1604]. In the form and disposition of his ten books of Epistles, he imitated the younger Pliny, whose rich and florid style he was supposed by his friends to equal or excel (Macrob. Saturnal, l. v. c. i.). But the luxuriancy of Symmachus consists of barren leaves, without fruits, and even without flowers. Few facts and few sentiments can be extracted from his verbose correspondence.

17. See Ambrose (tom. ii. Epist. xvii. xviii. p. 825-833). The former of these epistles is a short caution; the latter is a formal reply to the petition or *libel* of Symmachus. The same ideas are more copiously expressed in the poetry, if it may deserve that name, of Prudentius, who composed his two books against Symmachus (A.D. 404) while that senator was still alive. It is whimsical enough that Montesquieu (Considérations, etc., c. xix. tom. iii. p. 487) should overlook the two professed antagonists of Symmachus, and amuse himself with descanting on the more remote and indirect confutations of Orosius, St. Augustin, and Salvian.

18. See Prudentius (in Symmach. l. i. 545, etc.). The Christian agrees with the Pagan Zosimus (l. iv. [c. 59] p. 283) in placing this visit of Theodosius after the *second* civil war, gemini bis victor cæde Tyranni (l. i. 410). But the time and circumstances are better suited to his first triumph.

19. Prudentius, after proving that the sense of the senate is declared by a legal majority, proceeds to say (609, etc.),

> Adspice quam pleno subsellia nostra Senatú
> Decernant infame Jovis pulvinar, et omne
> Idolum longe purgatâ ex urbe fugandum.
> Qua vocat egregii sententia Principis, illuc
> Libera, tum pedibus, tum corde, frequentia
>   transit.

Zosimus ascribes to the conscript fathers an heathenish courage which few of them are found to possess.

20. Jerom specifies the pontiff Albinus, who was surrounded with such a believing family of children and grandchildren as would have been sufficient to convert even Jupiter himself—an extraordinary proselyte! (tom. i. ad Lætam, p. 54 [Ep. cvii. tom. i. p. 671, ed. Vallars.]).

21. Exsultare Patres videas, pulcherrima mundi
  Lumina; Conciliumque senúm gestire Catonum
  Candidiore togâ niveum pietatis amictum
  Sumere; et exuvias deponere pontificales.
The fancy of Prudentius is warmed and elevated by victory.

22. Prudentius, after he has described the conversion of the senate and people, asks, with some truth and confidence,

  Et dubitamus adhuc Romam, tibi, Christe, dicatam
  In leges transîsse tuas?

23. Jerom exults in the desolation of the Capitol and the other temples of Rome (tom. i. p. 54, tom. ii. p. 95).

24. Libanius (Orat. pro Templis, p. 10, Genev. 1634, published by James Godefroy, and now extremely scarce) accuses Valentinian and Valens of prohibiting sacrifices. Some partial order may have been issued by the Eastern emperor; but the idea of any general law is contradicted by the silence of the Code and the evidence of ecclesiastical history.

25. See his laws in the Theodosian Code, l. xvi. tit. x. leg. 7–11.

26. Homer's sacrifices are not accompanied with any inquisition of entrails (see Feithius, Antiquitat. Homer. l. i. c. 10, 16. The Tuscans, who produced the first *Haruspices*, subdued both the Greeks and the Romans (Cicero de Divinatione, ii. 23).

27. Zosimus, l. iv. [c. 37] p. 245, 249. Theodoret, l. v. c. 21. Idatius in Chron. Prosper. Aquitan. l. iii. c. 38 apud Baronium, Annal. Eccles. A.D. 389, No. 52. Libanius (pro Templis, p. 10) labours to prove that the commands of Theodosius were not direct and positive.

28. Cod. Theodos. l. xvi. tit. x. leg. 8, 18. There is room to believe that this temple of Edessa, which Theodosius wished to save for civil uses, was soon afterwards a heap of ruins (Libanius pro Templis. p. 26, 27, and Godefroy's notes, p. 59).

29. See this curious oration of Libanius pro Templis, pronounced, or rather composed, about the year 390. I have consulted with advantage Dr. Lardner's version and remarks (Heathen Testimonies, vol. iv. p. 135–163).

30. See the Life of Martin by Sulpicius Severus, c. 9–14. The saint once mistook (as Don Quixote might have done) an harmless funeral for an idolatrous procession, and imprudently committed a miracle.

31. Compare Sozomen (l. vii. c. 15) with The-

odoret (l. v. c. 21). Between them they relate the crusade and death of Marcellus.

32. Libanius pro Templis, p. 10–13. He rails at these black-garbed men, the Christian monks, who eat more than elephants. Poor elephants! *they* are temperate animals.

33. Prosper. Aquitan. l. iii. c. 38, apud Baronium; Annal. Eccles. A.D. 389, No. 58, etc. The temple had been shut some time, and the access to it was overgrown with brambles.

34. Donatus, Roma Antiqua et Nova, l. iv. c. 4, p. 468. This consecration was performed by Pope Boniface IV. I am ignorant of the favourable circumstances which had preserved the Pantheon above two hundred years after the reign of Theodosius.

35. Sophronius composed a recent and separate history (Jerom. in Script. Eccles. tom. i. p. 303), which has furnished materials to Socrates (l. v. c. 16), Theodoret (l. v. c. 22), and Rufinus (l. ii. c. 22). Yet the last, who had been at Alexandria before and after the event, may deserve the credit of an original witness.

36. Gerard Vossius (Opera, tom. v. p. 80, and de Idololatriâ, l. i. c. 29) strives to support the strange notion of the Fathers, that the patriarch Joseph was adored in Egypt as the bull Apis and the god Serapis.

37. Origo dei nondum nostris celebrata, Ægyptiorum antistites *sic* memorant, etc. Tacit. Hist. iv. 83. The Greeks who had travelled into Egypt were alike ignorant of this new deity.

38. Macrobius, Saturnal. l. i. c. 7. Such a living fact decisively proves his foreign extraction.

39. At Rome, Isis and Serapis were united in the same temple. The precedency which the queen assumed may seem to betray her unequal alliance with the stranger of Pontus. But the superiority of the female sex was established in Egypt as a civil and religious institution (Diodor. Sicul. tom. i. l. i. [c. 27] p. 31, edit. Wesseling), and the same order is observed in Plutarch's Treatise of Isis and *Osiris;* whom he identifies with Serapis.

40. Ammianus (xxii. 16). The Exposito totius Mundi (p. 8, in Hudson's Geograph. Minor. tom. iii.), and Rufinus (l. ii. c. 22), celebrate the *Serapeum* as one of the wonders of the world.

41. See Mémoires de l'Acad. des Inscriptions, tom. ix. p. 397–416. The *old* library of the Ptolemies was *totally* consumed in Cæsar's Alexandrian war. Marc Antony gave the whole collection of Pergamus (200,000 volumes) to Cleopatra, as the foundation of the *new* library of Alexandria.

42. Libanius (pro Templis, p. 21) indiscreetly provokes his Christian masters by this insulting remark.

43. We may choose between the date of Marcellinus (A.D. 389) or that of Prosper (A.D. 391). Tillemont (Hist. des. Emp. tom. v. p. 310, 756) prefers the former, and Pagi the latter.

44. Tillemont, Mém. Ecclés. tom. xi. p. 441–500. The ambiguous situation of Theophilus—a

saint, as the friend of Jerom; a *devil*, as the enemy of Chrysostom—produces a sort of impartiality; yet, upon the whole, the balance is justly inclined against him.

45. Lardner (Heathen Testimonies, vol. iv. p. 411) has alleged a beautiful passage from Suidas, or rather from Damascius, which shows the devout and virtuous Olympius, not in the light of a warrior, but of a prophet.

46. Nos vidimus armaria librorum, quibus direptis, exinanita ea a nostris hominibus, nostris temporibus memorent. Orosius, l. vi. c. 15, p. 421, edit. Havercamp. Though a bigot and a controversial writer, Orosius seems to blush.

47. Eunapius, in the Lives of Antoninus and Ædesius, execrates the sacrilegious rapine of Theophilus. Tillemont (Mém. Ecclés. tom. xiii. p. 453) quotes an epistle of Isidore of Pelusium, which reproaches the primate with the *idolatrous* worship of gold, the auri *sacra* fames.

48. Rufinius names the priest of Saturn who, in the character of the god, familiarly conversed with many pious ladies of quality; till he betrayed himself, in a moment of transport, when he could not disguise the tone of his voice. The authentic and impartial narrative of Æschines (see Bayle, Dictionnaire Critique, Scamandre), and the adventure of Mundus (Joseph. Antiquitat. Judaic. l. xviii. c. 3 [§ 4], p. 877, edit. Havercamp), may prove that such amorous frauds have been practised with success.

49. See the images of Serapis, in Montfaucon (tom. ii. p. 297): but the description of Macrobius (Saturnal. l. i. c. 20) is much more picturesque and satisfactory.

50. Sed fortes tremuere manus, motique verendâ
    Majestate loci, si robora sacra ferirent
    In sua credebant redituras membra secures.

(Lucan. iii. 419). "Is it true" (said Augustus to a veteran of Italy, at whose house he supped) "that the man who gave the first blow to the golden statue of Anaitis was instantly deprived of his eyes and of his life?"—"*I* was that man" (replied the clear-sighted veteran), "and you now sup on one of the legs of the goddess." (Plin. Hist. Natur. xxxiii. 24).

51. The History of the Reformation affords frequent examples of the sudden change from superstition to contempt.

52. Sozomen, l. vii. c. 20. I have supplied the measure. The same standard of the inundation, and consequently of the cubit, has uniformly subsisted since the time of Herodotus. See Fréret, in the Mém. de l'Académie des Inscriptions, tom. xvi. p. 344–353. Greaves's Miscellaneous Works, vol. i. p. 233. The Egyptian cubit is about twenty-two inches of the English measure.

53. Libanius (pro Templis, p. 15, 16, 17) pleads their cause with gentle and insinuating rhetoric. From the earliest age such feasts had enlivened the country: and those of Bacchus (Georgic. ii. 380) had produced the theatre of Athens. See Godefroy, ad loc., Liban., and Codex Theodos. tom. vi. p. 284 [ed. Lugd. 1665].

54. Honorius tolerated these rustic festivals (A.D. 399). "Absque ullo sacrificio, atque ullâ superstitione damnabili." But nine years afterwards he found it necessary to reiterate and enforce the same proviso (Codex Theodos. l. xvi. tit. x. leg. 17, 19).

55. Cod. Theodos. l. xvi. tit. x. leg. 12. Jortin (Remarks on Eccles. History, vol. iv. p. 134) censures, with becoming asperity, the style and sentiment of this intolerant law.

56. Such a charge should not be lightly made; but it may surely be justified by the authority of St. Augustin, who thus addresses the Donatists: "Quis nostrûm, quis vestrûm non laudat leges ab Imperatoribus datas adversus sacrificia Paganorum? Et certe longe ibi pœna severior constituta est; illius quippe impietatis capitale supplicium est." Epist. xciii. No. 10 [tom. ii. p. 308, ed. Bened. 1797], quoted by Le Clerc (Bibliothèque Choisie, tom. viii. p. 277), who adds some judicious reflections on the intolerance of the victorious Christians.

57. Orosius, l. vii. c. 28, p. 537. Augustin (Enarrat. in Psalm cxl. apud Lardner, Heathen Testimonies, vol. iv. p. 458) insults their cowardice. "Quis eorum comprehensus est in sacrificio (cum his legibus ista prohiberentur) et non negavit?"

58. Libanius (pro Templis, p. 17, 18) mentions, without censure, the occasional conformity, and as it were theatrical play, of these hypocrites.

59. Libanius concludes his apology (p. 32) by declaring to the emperor that, unless he expressly warrants the destruction of the temples, ἴσθι τοὺς τῶν ἀγρῶν δεσπότας, καὶ αὐτοῖς, καὶ τῷ νόμῳ βοηθήσοντας, the proprietors will defend themselves and the laws.

60. Paulinus, in Vit. Ambros. c. 26. Augustine, The City of God, l. v. c. 26. Theodoret, l. v. c. 24.

61. Libanius suggests the form of a persecuting edict which Theodosius might enact (pro Templis, p. 31): a rash joke and a dangerous experiment. Some princes would have taken his advice.

62. Denique pro meritis terrestribus æqua rependens
    Munera, sacricolis summos impertit honores,
    Dux bonus, et certare sinit cum laude suorum:
    Nec pago implicitos per debita culmina mundi
    Ire viros prohibet.
    Ipse magistratum tibi consulis, ipse tribunal
    Contulit.
        Prudent. in Symmach. i. 617, etc.

63. Libanius (pro Templis, p. 32) is proud that Theodosius should thus distinguish a man who even in his *presence* would swear by Jupiter. Yet this presence seems to be no more than a figure of rhetoric.

64. Zosimus, who styles himself Count and Ex-advocate of the Treasury, reviles, with partial and indecent bigotry, the Christian princes, and even the father of his sovereign. His work must have been privately circulated, since it escaped the invectives of the ecclesiastical historians prior to Evagrius (l. iii. c. 40–41), who lived towards the end of the sixth century.

65. Yet the Pagans of Africa complained that the times would not allow them to answer with freedom the City of God; nor does St. Augustin (v. 26) deny the charge.

66. The Moors of Spain, who secretly preserved the Mahometan religion above a century, under the tyranny of the Inquisition, possessed the Koran, with the peculiar use of the Arabic tongue. See the curious and honest story of their expulsion in Geddes (Miscellanies, vol. i. p. 1–198).

67. Paganos qui supersunt, quanquam jam nullos esse credamus, etc. Cod. Theodos. l. xvi. tit. x. leg. 22, A.D. 423. The younger Theodosius was afterwards satisfied that his judgment had been somewhat premature.

68. See Eunapius, in the Life of the sophist Ædesius; in that of Eustathius he foretells the ruin of Paganism, καί τι μυθῶδες, καὶ ἀειδὲς, σκότος τυραννήσει τὰ ἐπὶ γῆς κάλλιστα.

69. Caius (apud Euseb. Hist. Eccles. l. ii. c. 25), a Roman presbyter, who lived in the time of Zephyrinus (A.D. 202–219), is an early witness of this superstitious practice.

70. Chrysostom. Quod Christus sit Deus. Tom. s. nov. edit. No. 9. I am indebted for this quotation to Benedict the XIVth's pastoral letter on the Jubilee of the year 1750. See the curious and entertaining letters of M. Chais, tom. iii.

71. Male facit ergo Romanus episcopus? qui, super mortuorum hominum, Petri and Pauli, secundum nos, ossa veneranda . . . offert Domino sacrificia, et tumulos eorum, Christi arbitratur altaria. Jerom. tom. ii. advers. Vigilant. p. 153. [Tom. ii. p. 395, ed. Vallars.]

72. Jerom (tom. ii. p. 122 [contra Vigilant. c. 5, tom. ii. p. 391, ed. Vallars.]) bears witness to these translations, which are neglected by the ecclesiastical historians. The passion of St. Andrew at Patræ is described in an epistle from the clergy of Achaia, which Baronius (Annal. Eccles. A.D. 60, No. 34) wishes to believe, and Tillemont is forced to reject. St. Andrew was adopted as the spiritual founder of Constantinople (Mém. Ecclés. tom. i. p. 317–323, 588–594).

73. Jerom (tom. ii. p. 122 [l. c. ed. Vallars.]) pompously describes the translation of Samuel, which is noticed in all the chronicles of the times.

74. The Presbyter Vigilantius, the protestant of his age, firmly, though ineffectually, withstood the superstition of monks, relics, saints, fasts, etc., for which Jerom compares him to the Hydra, Cerberus, the Centaurs, etc., and considers him only as the organ of the Dæmon (tom. ii. p. 120–126 [tom. ii. p. 387–402, ed. Vallars.]). Whoever will

peruse the controversy of St. Jerom and Vigilantius, and St. Augustin's account of the miracles of St. Stephen, may speedily gain some idea of the spirit of the Fathers.

75. M. de Beausobre (Hist. du Manichéisme, tom. ii. p. 648) has applied a worldly sense to the pious observation of the clergy of Smyrna, who carefully preserved the relics of St. Polycarp the martyr.

76. Martin of Tours (see his Life, c. 8, by Sulpicius Severus) extorted this confession from the mouth of the dead man. The error is allowed to be natural; the discovery is supposed to be miraculous. Which of the two was likely to happen most frequently?

77. Lucian composed in Greek his original narrative, which has been translated by Avitus, and published by Baronius (Annal. Eccles. A.D. 415, No. 7–16). The Benedictine editors of St. Augustin have given (at the end of the work De Civitate Dei) two several copies, with many various readings. It is the character of falsehood to be loose and inconsistent. The most incredible parts of the legend are smoothed and softened by Tillemont (Mém. Ecclés. tom. ii. p. 9, etc.).

78. A phial of St. Stephen's blood was annually liquefied at Naples till he was superseded by St. Januarius (Ruinart. Hist. Persecut. Vandal. p. 529).

79. Augustin composed the two-and-twenty books de Civitate Dei in the space of thirteen years, A.D. 413–426. (Tillemont, Mém. Ecclés. tom. xiv. p. 608, etc.) His learning is too often borrowed, and his arguments are too often his own; but the whole work claims the merit of a magnificent design, vigorously, and not unskilfully, executed.

80. See Augustine, The City of God, xxii. 8, and the Appendix, which contains two books of St. Stephen's miracles, by Evodius, bishop of Uzalis. Freculphus (apud Basnage, Hist. des Juifs, tom. viii. p. 249) has preserved a Gallic or Spanish proverb, "Whoever pretends to have read all the miracles of St. Stephen, he lies."

81. Burnet (de Statú Mortuorum, p. 56–84) collects the opinions of the Fathers, as far as they assert the sleep or repose of human souls till the day of judgment. He afterwards exposes (p. 91, etc.) the inconveniences which must arise if they possessed a more active and sensible existence.

82. Vigilantius placed the souls of the prophets and martyrs, either in the bosom of Abraham (in loco refrigerii), or else under the altar of God. Nec posse [de] suis tumulis et ubi voluerint adesse præsentes. But Jerom (tom. ii. p. 122 [tom. ii. 392, ed. Vallars.]) sternly refutes this blasphemy. Tu Deo leges pones? Tu apostolis vincula injicies, ut usque ad diem judicii teneantur custodiâ, nec sint cum Domino suo; de quibus scriptum est, Sequuntur Agnum quocunque vadit. Si Agnus ubique, ergo, et hi, qui cum Agno sunt, ubique esse credendi sunt. Et cum diabolus et dæmones toto vagentur in orbe, etc.

83. Fleury, Discours sur l'Hist. Ecclésiastique, iii. p. 80.

84. At Minorca, the relics of St. Stephen converted in eight days 540 Jews; with the help, indeed, of some unwholesome severities, such as burning the synagogue, driving the obstinate infidels to starve among the rocks, etc. See the original letter of Severus bishop of Minorca (ad calcem St. Augustin. de Civ. Dei), and the judicious remarks of Basnage (tom. viii. p. 245–251).

85. Mr. Hume (Essays, vol. ii. p. 434) observes, like a philosopher, the natural flux and reflux of polytheism and theism.

86. D'Aubigné (see his own Mémoires, p. 156–160) frankly offered, with the consent of the Huguenot ministers, to allow the first 400 years as the rule of faith. The Cardinal du Perron haggled for forty years more, which were indiscreetly given. Yet neither party would have found their account in this foolish bargain.

87. The worship practised and inculcated by Tertullian, Lactantius, Arnobius, etc., is so *extremely* pure and spiritual, that their declamations against the Pagan sometimes glance against the Jewish ceremonies.

88. Faustus the Manichæan accuses the Catholics of idolatry. Vertitis idola in martyres . . . quos votis similibus colitis. M. de Beausobre (Hist. Critique du Manichéisme, tom. ii. p. 629–700), a protestant, but a philosopher, has represented, with candour and learning, the introduction of *Christian idolatry* in the fourth and fifth centuries.

89. The resemblance of superstition, which could not be imitated, might be traced from Japan to Mexico. Warburton has seized this idea, which he distorts by rendering it too general and absolute (Divine Legation, vol. iv. p. 126, etc.).

90. The imitation of Paganism is the subject of Dr. Middleton's agreeable letter from Rome. Warburton's animadversions obliged him to connect (vol. iii. p. 120–132) the history of the two religions, and to prove the antiquity of the Christian copy.

Chapter XXIX

1. Alecto, envious of the public felicity, convenes an infernal synod; Megæra recommends her pupil Rufinus, and excites him to deeds of mischief, etc. But there is as much difference between Claudian's fury and that of Virgil, as between the characters of Turnus and Rufinus.

2. It is evident (Tillemont, Hist. des Emp. tom. v. p. 770), though De Marca is ashamed of his countryman, that Rufinus was born at Elusa, the metropolis of Novempopulania, now a small village of Gascony (D'Anville, Notice de l'Ancienne Gaule, p. 289).

3. Philosotorgius, l. xi. c. 3, with Godefroy's Dissert. p. 440.

4. A passage of Suidas is expressive of his profound dissimulation; βαθυγνώμων ἄνθρωπος καὶ κρυψίνους.

5. Zosimus, l. iv. [c. 51] p. 272, 273.

6. Zosimus, who describes the fall of Tatian and his son (l. iv. [c. 52] p. 273, 274), asserts their innocence; and even *his* testimony may outweigh the charges of their enemies (Cod. Theod. tom iv. p. 489), who accuse them of oppressing the *Curiæ.* The connection of Tatian with the Arians, while he was præfect of Egypt (A.D. 373), inclines Tillemont to believe that he was guilty of every crime (Hist. des Emp. tom. v. p. 360; Mém. Ecclés. tom. vi. p. 589).

7. ————Juvenum rorantia colla
Ante patrum vultus strictâ cecidere securi.
Ibat grandævus nato moriente superstes
Post trabeas exsul.   In Rufin. i. 248.
The *facts* of Zosimus explain the *allusions* of Claudian; but his classic interpreters were ignorant of the fourth century. The *fatal cord* I found, with the help of Tillemont, in a sermon of St. Asterius of Amasea.

8. This odious law is recited and repealed by Arcadius (A.D. 396), in the Theodosian Code, l. ix. tit. xxxviii. leg. 9. The sense, as it is explained by Claudian (in Rufin. i. 232) and Godefroy (tom. iii. p. 279), is perfectly clear.

————Exscindere cives
Funditus, et nomen gentis delere laborat.
The scruples of Pagi and Tillemont can arise only from their zeal for the glory of Theodosius.

9. Ammonius . . . Rufinum propriis manibus suscepit sacro fonte mundatum. See Rosweyde's Vitæ Patrum, p. 947. [Heraclidis Paradisus in Append. ad Vit. Patr. p. 941 *b.*] Sozomen (l. viii. c. 17) mentions the church and monastery: and Tillemont (Mém. Ecclés. tom. ix. p. 593) records this synod, in which St. Gregory of Nyssa performed a conspicuous part.

10. Montesquieu (The Spirit of Laws, l. xii. c. 12) praises one of the laws of Theodosius, addressed to the præfect Rufinus (l. ix. tit. iv. leg. unic.), to discourage the prosecution of treasonable or sacrilegious words. A tyrannical statute always proves the existence of tyranny; but a laudable edict may only contain the specious professions or ineffectual wishes of the prince or his ministers. This, I am afraid, is a just though mortifying canon of criticism.

11 ————————fluctibus auri
Expleri calor ille nequit————————.

Congestæ cumulantur opes; orbisque rapinas
Accipit una domus.
This character (Claudian, in Rufin. i. 184–220) is

confirmed by Jerom, a disinterested witness (de-
decus insatiabilis avaritiæ, tom. i. ad Heliodor. p.
26 [Epist. lx. tom. i. p. 342, ed. Vallars.]), by Zosimus (l. v. [c. 1] p. 286), and by Suidas, who copied
the history of Eunapius.

12. —————— Cætera segnis;
Ad facinus velox; penitus regione remotas
Impiger ire vias.

This allusion of Claudian (in Rufin. i. 241) is again
explained by the circumstantial narrative of Zosimus (l. v. [c. 2] p. 288, 289).

13. Zosimus (l. iv. [c. 33] p. 243) praises the
valour, prudence, and integrity of Bauto the
Frank. See Tillemont, Hist. des Empereurs, tom.
v. p. 771.

14. Arsenius escaped from the palace of Constantinople, and passed fifty-five years in rigid penance in the monasteries of Egypt. See Tillemont,
Mém. Ecclés. tom. xiv. p. 676–702; and Fleury,
Hist. Eccles. tom. v. p. 1, etc.; but the latter, for
want of authentic materials, has given too much
credit to the legend of Metaphrastes.

15. This story (Zosimus, l. v. [c. 3] p. 290)
proves that the hymeneal rites of antiquity were
still practised, without idolatry, by the Christians
of the East; and the bride was *forcibly* conducted
from the house of her parents to that of her husband. Our form of marriage requires, with less
delicacy, the express and public consent of a
virgin.

16. Zosimus (l. v. [c. 4] p. 290), Orosius (l. vii. c.
37), and the Chronicle of Marcellinus. Claudian
(in Rufin. ii. 7–100) paints, in lively colours, the
distress and guilt of the præfect.

17. Stilicho, directly or indirectly, is the perpetual theme of Claudian. The youth and private
life of the hero are vaguely expressed in the poem
on his first consulship, 35–140.

18. Vandalorum imbellis, avaræ, perfidæ, et
dolosæ gentis genere editus. Orosius, l. vii. c. 38.
Jerom (tom. i. ad Gerontiam, p. 93) calls him a
semi-barbarian.

19. Claudian, in an imperfect poem, has drawn
a fair, perhaps a flattering, portrait of Serena. That
favourite niece of Theodosius was born, as well as
her sister Thermantia, in Spain; from whence, in
their earliest youth, they were honourably conducted to the palace of Constantinople.

20. Some doubt may be entertained whether
this adoption was legal, or only metaphorical (see
Ducange, Fam. Byzant. p. 75). An old inscription
gives Stilicho the singular title of *Pro-gener Divi
Theodosii*.

21. Claudian (Laus Serenæ, 190, 193) expresses,
in poetic language, the "dilectus equorum," and
the "gemino mox idem culmine duxit agmina."
The inscription adds, "count of the domestics,"
an important command, which Stilicho, in the
height of his grandeur, might prudently retain.

22. The beautiful lines of Claudian (in i. Cons.
Stilich. ii. 113) display *his* genius: but the integrity
of Stilicho (in the military administration) is much
more firmly established by the unwilling evidence
of Zosimus (l. v. [c. 34] p. 345).

23. —————— Si bellica nubes
Ingrueret, quamvis annis et jure minori,
Cedere grandævos equitum peditumque
magistros
Adspiceres.
Claudian, Laus Seren. v. 196, etc.

A modern general would deem their submission
either heroic patriotism or abject servility.

24. Compare the poem on the first consulship
(i. 95–115) with the *Laus Serenæ* (227–237, where
it unfortunately breaks off). We may perceive the
deep, inveterate malice of Rufinus.

25. —————— Quem *fratribus* ipse
Discedens, clipeum defensoremque dedisti. (iv. Cons. Hon. 432.)

Yet the nomination was private (iii. Cons. Hon.
142) cunctos discedere . . . jubet—and may therefore be suspected. Zosimus and Suidas apply to
Stilicho and Rufinus the same equal title of 'Επίτ
ροποι, guardians or procurators.

26. The Roman law distinguishes two sorts of
minority, which expired at the age of fourteen and
of twenty-five. The one was subject to the *tutor*,
or guardian, of the person; the other, to the *curator*,
or trustee, of the estate (Heineccius, Antiquitat.
Rom. ad Jurisprudent. pertinent. l. i. tit. xxii.
xxiii. p. 218–232). But these legal ideas were never
accurately transferred into the constitution of an
elective monarchy.

27. See Claudian (i. Cons. Stilich. i. 188–242);
but he must allow more than fifteen days for the
journey and return between Milan and Leyden.

28. I. Cons. Stilich. ii. 88–94. Not only the robes
and diadems of the deceased emperor, but even
the helmets, sword-hilts, belts, cuirasses, etc., were
enriched with pearls, emeralds, and diamonds.

29. —————— Tantoque remoto
Principe, mutatas orbis non sensit habenas.

This high commendation (i. Cons. Stil. i. 149) may
be justified by the fears of the dying emperor (de
Bell. Gildon. 292–301), and the peace and good
order which were enjoyed after his death (i. Cons.
Stil. i. 150–168).

30. Stilicho's march and the death of Rufinus
are described by Claudian (in Rufin. l. ii. 101–
453), Zosimus (l. v. [c. 7] p. 296, 297), Sozomen
(l. viii. c. 1), Socrates (l. vi. c. 1), Philostorgius (l.
xi. c. 3, with Godefroy, p. 441), and the Chronicle
of Marcellinus.

31. The *dissection* of Rufinus, which Claudian
performs with the savage coolness of an anatomist
(in Rufin. ii. 405–415), is likewise specified by Zosimus [v. c. 7] and Jerom (tom. i. p. 26 [Epist. lx.
tom. i. p. 342, ed. Vallars.]).

32. The Pagan Zosimus mentions their sanctuary and pilgrimage. The sister of Rufinus, Sylvania,
who passed her life at Jerusalem, is famous in monastic history. 1. The studious virgin had diligently, and even repeatedly, perused the commentators on the Bible, Origen, Gregory, Basil,

etc., to the amount of five millions of lines. 2. At the age of threescore she could boast that she had never washed her hands, face, or any part of her whole body, except the tips of her fingers, to receive the communion. See the Vitæ Patrum, p. 779, 977.

33. See the beautiful exordium of his invective against Rufinus, which is curiously discussed by the sceptic Bayle, Dictionnaire Critique, RUFIN. Not. E.

34. See the Theodosian Code, l. ix. tit. xlii. leg. 14, 15. The new ministers attempted, with inconsistent avarice, to seize the spoils of their predecessor and to provide for their own future security.

35. See Claudian (i. Cons. Stilich. l. i. 275, 292, 296, l. ii. 83), and Zosimus, l. v. [c. 11] p. 302.

36. Claudian turns the consulship of the eunuch Eutropius into a national reflection (l. ii. 135):

————————Plaudentem cerne senatum,
Et Byzantinos proceres, Graiosque Quirites:
O patribus plebes, O digni consule patres.

It is curious to observe the first symptoms of jealousy and schism between old and new Rome, between the Greeks and Latins.

37. Claudian may have exaggerated the vices of Gildo; but his Moorish extraction, his notorious actions, and the complaints of St. Augustin, may justify the poet's invectives. Baronius (Annal. Eccles. A.D. 398, No. 35–56) has treated the African rebellion with skill and learning.

38.   Instat terribilis vivis, morientibus hæres,
    Virginibus raptor, thalamis obscenus
        adulter.
    Nulla quies: oritur prædâ cessante libido,
    Divitibusque dies, et nox metuenda ma-
        ritis.
————————Mauris clarissima quæque
Fastidita datur.
        De Bello Gildonico, 165, 189.

Baronius condemns, still more severely, the licentiousness of Gildo; as his wife, his daughter, and his sister, were examples of perfect chastity. The adulteries of the African soldiers are checked by one of the Imperial laws.

39.   Inque tuam sortem numerosas transtulit
        urbes.

Claudian (de Bell. Gildonico, 230–324) has touched, with political delicacy, the intrigues of the Byzantine court, which are likewise mentioned by Zosimus (i. v. [c. 11] p. 302).

40. Symmachus (l. iv. epist. 4) expresses the judicial forms of the senate; and Claudian (i. Cons. Stilich. l. i. 325, etc.) seems to feel the spirit of a Roman.

41. Claudian finely displays these complaints of Symmachus, in a speech of the goddess of Rome before the throne of Jupiter (de Bell. Gildon. 28–128).

42. See Claudian (in Eutrop. l. i. 401, etc.; i. Cons. Stil. l. i. 306, etc.; ii. Cons. Stilich. 91, etc.).

43. He was of a mature age, since he had formerly (A.D. 373) served against his brother Firmus (Ammian. xxix. 5). Claudian, who understood the court of Milan, dwells on the injuries, rather than

the merits, of Mascezel (de Bell. Gild. 389–414). The Moorish war was not worthy of Honorius or Stilicho, etc.

44. Claudian, Bell. Gild. 415–423. The change of discipline allowed him to use indifferently the names of Legio, Cohors, Manipulus. See the Notitia Imperii, S. 38, 40.

45. Orosius (l. vii. c. 36, p. 565) qualifies this account with an expression of doubt (ut aiunt); and it scarcely coincides with the δυνάμεις ἀδρὰς of Zosimus (l. v. [c. 11] p. 303). Yet Claudian, after some declamation about Cadmus's soldiers, frankly owns that Stilicho sent a small army, lest the rebel should fly, ne timeare times (i. Cons. Stilich. l. i. 314, etc.).

46. Claud. Rutil. Numatian. Itinerar. lib. i. 439–448. He afterwards (ib. 515–526) mentions a religious madman on the isle of Gorgona. For such profane remarks, Rutilius and his accomplices are styled, by his commentator Barthius, rabiosi canes diaboli. Tillemont (Mém. Ecclés. tom. xii. p. 471) more calmly observes that the unbelieving poet praises where he means to censure.

47. Orosius, l. vii. c. 36, p. 564. Augustin commends two of these savage saints of the Isle of Goats (Epist. lxxxi. apud Tillemont, Mém. Ecclés. tom. xiii. p. 317, and Baronius, Annal. Eccles. A.D. 398, No. 51).

48. Here the first book of the Gildonic war is terminated. The rest of Claudian's poem has been lost; and we are ignorant how or where the army made good their landing in Africa.

49. Orosius must be responsible for the account. The presumption of Gildo and his various train of barbarians is celebrated by Claudian (i. Cons. Stil. l. i. 345–355).

50. St. Ambrose, who had been dead about a year, revealed in a vision the time and place of the victory. Mascezel afterwards related his dream to Paulinus, the original biographer of the saint, from whom it might easily pass to Orosius.

51. Zosimus (l. v. [c. 11] p. 303) supposes an obstinate combat; but the narrative of Orosius appears to conceal a real fact under the disguise of a miracle.

52. Tabraca lay between the two Hippos (Cellarius, tom. ii. p. 112; D'Anville, tom. iii. p. 84). Orosius has distinctly named the field of battle, but our ignorance cannot define the precise situation.

53. The death of Gildo is expressed by Claudian (i. Cons. Stil. l. 357) and his best interpreters, Zosimus and Orosius.

54. Claudian (iii. Cons. Stilich. 99–119) describes their trial (tremuit quos Africa nuper, cernunt rostra reos), and applauds the restoration of the ancient constitution. It is here that he introduces the famous sentence so familiar to the friends of despotism:

————————Nunquam libertas gratior exstat
Quam sub rege pio.

But the freedom which depends on royal piety scarcely deserves that appellation.

55. See the Theodosian Code, l. ix. tit. xxxix. leg. 3, tit. xl. leg. 19.

56. Stilicho, who claimed an equal share in all the victories of Theodosius and his son, particularly asserts that Africa was recovered by the wisdom of *his* counsels (see an inscription produced by Baronius).

57. I have softened the narrative of Zosimus, which, in its crude simplicity, is almost incredible (l. v. [c. 11] p. 303). Orosius damns the victorious general (p. 538 [lib. vii. c. 36]) for violating the right of sanctuary.

58. Claudian, as the poet laureat, composed a serious and elaborate epithalamium of 340 lines; besides some gay Fescennines, which were sung in a more licentious tone on the wedding night.

59.   —————Calet obvius ire
    Jam princeps, tardumque cupit discedere
    solem.

Nobilis haud aliter *sonipes*—
(de Nuptiis Honor. et Mariæ, 287) and more freely in the Fescennines 112–126 [iv. 14].
  Dices, *O quoties*, hoc mihi dulcius
  Quam flavos *decies* vincere Sarmatas.
.   .   .   .
  Tum victor mandido prosilias toro
  Nocturni referens vulnera prœlii.

60. See Zosimus, l. v. [c. 28] p. 333.

61. Procopius de Bell. Vandal. l. i. c. 2 [tom. i. p. 316, ed. Bonn.]. I have borrowed the general practice of Honorius, without adopting the singular, and, indeed, improbable tale, which is related by the Greek historian.

62. The lessons of Theodosius, or rather Claudian (iv. Cons. Honor. 214–418) might compose a fine institution for the future prince of a great and free nation. It was far above Honorius and his degenerate subjects.

Chapter XXX

1. The revolt of the Goths and the blockade of Constantinople are distinctly mentioned by Claudian (in Rufin. l. ii. 7–100), Zosimus (l. v. [c. 5] p. 292), and Jornandes (de Rebus Geticis, c. 29).

2.   —————Alii per terga ferocis
  Danubi solidata ruunt; expertaque remos
  Frangunt stagna rotis.
            [Claud. ib. v. 24.]
Claudian and Ovid often amuse their fancy by interchanging the metaphors and properties of *liquid* water and *solid* ice. Much false wit has been expended in this easy exercise.

3. Jerom. tom. i. p. 26 [Epist. lx. tom. i. p. 342, ed. Vallars.]. He endeavours to comfort his friend Heliodorus, bishop of Altinum, for the loss of his nephew Nepotian, by a curious recapitulation of all the public and private misfortunes of the times. See Tillemont, Mém. Ecclés. tom. xii. p. 200, etc.

4. *Baltha*, or *bold:* origo mirifica, says Jornandes (c. 29). This illustrious race long continued to flourish in France, in the Gothic province of Septimania, or Languedoc, under the corrupted appellation of *Baux:* and a branch of that family afterwards settled in the kingdom of Naples (Grotius in Prolegom. ad Hist. Gothic. p. 53). The lords of Baux, near Arles, and of seventy-nine subordinate places, were independent of the counts of Provence (Longuerue, Description de la France, tom. i. p. 357).

5. Zosimus (l. v. [c. 5] p. 293–295) is our best guide for the conquest of Greece: but the hints and allusion of Claudian are so many rays of historic light.

6. Compare Herodotus (l. vii. c. 176) and Livy (xxxvi. 15). The narrow entrance of Greece was probably enlarged by each successive ravisher.

7. He passed, says Eunapius (in Vit. Philosoph.

p. 93, edit. Commelin, 1596), through the straits, διὰ τῶν τυλῶν (of Thermopylæ) παρῆλθεν, σῶπερ διὰ σταδίου καὶ ἱπποκρότου πεδίου τρέχων.

8. In obedience to Jerom and Claudian (in Rufin. l. ii. 191), I have mixed some darker colours in the mild representation of Zosimus, who wished to soften the calamities of Athens.
  Nec fera Cecropias traxissent vincula matres.
Synesius (Epist. cxxxv. p. 272, edit. Petav.) observes that Athens, whose sufferings he imputes to the proconsul's avarice, was at that time less famous for her schools of philosophy than for her trade of honey.

9.   —————Vallata mari Scironia rupes,
  Et duo continuo connectens æquora muro
  Isthmos.
        Claudian de Bell. Getico, 188.
The Scironian rocks are described by Pausanias (l. i. c. 44, p. 107, edit. Kuhn) and our modern travellers Wheeler (p. 436) and Chandler (p. 298). Hadrian made the road passable for two carriages [Pausan. i. c. 44, § 6, ed. Bekker].

10. Claudian (in Rufin. l. ii. 186, and de Bello Getico, 611, etc.) vaguely, though forcibly, delineates the scene of rapine and destruction.

11. Τρὶς μάκαρες Δαναοὶ καὶ τετράκις, etc. These generous lines of Homer (Odyss. l. v. 306) were transcribed by one of the captive youths of Corinth: and the tears of Mummius may prove that the rude conqueror, though he was ignorant of the value of an original picture, possessed the purest source of good taste, a benevolent heart (Plutarch, Symposiac. l. ix. tom. ii. p. 737, edit. Wechel. [tom. viii. p. 939, ed. Reiske]).

12. Homer perpetually describes the exemplary patience of these female captives, who gave their charms, and even their hearts, to the murderers of their fathers, brothers, etc. Such a passion (of

Eriphile for Achilles) is touched with admirable delicacy by Racine.

13. Plutarch (in Pyrrhus) gives the genuine answer in the Laconic dialect. Pyrrhus attacked Sparta with 25,000 foot, 2000 horse, and 24 elephants: and the defence of that open town is a fine comment on the laws of Lycurgus, even in the last stage of decay.

14. Such, perhaps, as Homer (Iliad, xx. 164) has so nobly painted him.

15. Eunapius (in Vit. Philosoph. p. 90–93) intimates that a troop of monks betrayed Greece and followed the Gothic camp.

16. For Stilicho's Greek war compare the honest narrative of Zosimus (l. v. [c. 7] p. 295, 296) with the curious circumstantial flattery of Claudian (i. Cons. Stilich. l. i. 172–186; iv. Cons. Hon. 459–487). As the event was not glorious, it is artfully thrown into the shade.

17. The troops who marched through Elis delivered up their arms. This security enriched the Eleans, who were lovers of a rural life. Riches begat pride: they disdained their privilege, and they suffered. Polybius advises them to retire once more within their magic circle. See a learned and judicious discourse on the Olympic games, which Mr. West has prefixed to his translation of Pindar.

18. Claudian (in iv. Cons. Hon. 480) alludes to the fact without naming the river; perhaps the Alpheus (i. Cons. Stil. l. i. 185).

——————Et Alpheus Geticis angustus acervis
Tardior ad Siculos etiamnum pergit amores.

Yet I should prefer the Peneus, a shallow stream in a wide and deep bed which runs through Elis and falls into the sea below Cyllene. It had been joined with the Alpheus to cleanse the Augean stable. (Cellarius, tom. i. p. 760. Chandler's Travels, p. 286.)

19. Strabo, l. viii. p. 517 [p. 335, ed. Casaub.]. Plin. Hist. Natur. iv. 3. Wheeler, p. 308. Chandler, p. 275. They measured from different points the distance between the two lands.

20. Synesius passed three years (A.D. 397–400) at Constantinople as deputy from Cyrene to the emperor Arcadius. He presented him with a crown of gold, and pronounced before him the instructive oration de Regno (p. 1–32, edit. Petav. Paris, 1612). The philosopher was made bishop of Ptolemais, A.D. 410, and died about 430. See Tillemont, Mém. Ecclés. tom. xii. p. 499, 554, 683–685.

21. Synesius de Regno, p. 21–26.

22. ——————qui fœdera rumpit
Ditatur: qui servat, eget: vastator Achivæ
Gentis, et Epirum nuper populatus in-
ultam
Præsidet Illyrico: jam, quos obsedit,
amicos
Ingreditur muros; illis responsa daturus
Quorum conjugibus potitur, natosque pe-
remit.

Claudian in Eutrop. l. ii. 212. Alaric applauds his own policy (de Bell. Getic. 533–543) in the use

which he had made of this Illyrian jurisdiction.

23. Jornandes, c. 29, p. 651 [ed. Grot. 1655; p. 81, ed. Lugd. B. 1597]. The Gothic historian adds, with unusual spirit, Cum suis deliberans suasit suo labore quærere regna, quam alienis per otium subjacere.

24. ——————Discors odiisque anceps civilibus orbis
Non sua vis tutata diu, dum fœdera fallax
Ludit, et alternæ perjuria venditat aluæ.
Claudian de Bell. Get. 565.

25. Alpibus Italiæ ruptis penetrabis ad Urbem. This authentic prediction was announced by Alaric, or at least by Claudian (de Bell. Getico, 547), seven years before the event. But as it was not accomplished within the term which had been rashly fixed, the interpreters escaped through an ambiguous meaning.

26. Our best materials are 970 verses of Claudian, in the poem on the Getic war, and the beginning of that which celebrates the sixth consulship of Honorius. Zosimus is totally silent; and we are reduced to such scraps, or rather crumbs, as we can pick from Orosius and the Chronicles.

27. Notwithstanding the gross errors of Jornandes, who confounds the Italian wars of Alaric (c. 29), his date of the consulship of Stilicho and Aurelian (A.D. 400) is firm and respectable. It is certain from Claudian (Tillemont, Hist. des Emp. tom. v. p. 804), that the battle of Pollentia was fought A.D. 403; but we cannot easily fill the interval.

28. Tantum Romanæ urbis judicium fugis, ut magis obsidionem barbaricam, quam pacatæ urbis judicium velis sustinere. Jerom, tom. ii. p. 239. Rufinus understood his own danger; the peaceful city was inflamed by the beldam Marcella and the rest of Jerom's faction.

29. Jovinian, the enemy of fasts and of celibacy, who was persecuted and insulted by the furious Jerom (Jortin's Remarks, vol. iv. p. 104, etc.). See the original edict of banishment in the Theodosian Code, l. xvi. tit. v. leg. 53.

30. This epigram (de Sene Veronensi qui surburbium nusquam egressus est) is one of the earliest and most pleasing compositions of Claudian. Cowley's imitation (Hurd's edition, vol. ii. p. 241) has some natural and happy strokes: but it is much inferior to the original portrait, which is evidently drawn from the life.

31. Ingentem meminit parvo qui germine
quercum
Æquævumque videt consenuisse nemus.
A neighbouring wood born with himself
he sees,
And loves his old contemporary trees.

In this passage Cowley is perhaps superior to his original; and the English poet, who was a good botanist, has concealed the oaks under a more general expression.

32. Claudian de Bell. Get. 199–266. He may seem prolix: but fear and superstition occupied as large a space in the minds of the Italians.

33. From the passages of Paulinus which Baronius has produced (Annal. Eccles. A.D. 403, No. 51) it is manifest that the general alarm had pervaded all Italy, as far as Nola in Campania, where that famous penitent had fixed his abode.

34. Solus erat Stilicho, etc., is the exclusive commendation which Claudian bestows (de Bell. Get. 267), without condescending to except the emperor. How insignificant must Honorius have appeared in his own court!

35. The face of the country and the hardiness of Stilicho are finely described (de Bell. Get. 340–363).

36. Venit et extremis legio prætenta Britannis
   Quæ Scoto dat frena truci.
   De Bell. Get. 416.
Yet the most rapid march from Edinburgh, or Newcastle, to Milan, must have required a longer space of time than Claudian seems willing to allow for the duration of the Gothic war.

37. Every traveller must recollect the face of Lombardy (see Fontenelle, tom. v. p. 279), which is often tormented by the capricious and irregular abundance of waters. The Austrians before Genoa were encamped in the dry bed of the Polcevera. "Ne sarebbe" (says Muratori) "mai passato per mente a que' buoni Alemanni, che quel picciolo torrente potesse, per cosi dire, in un instante cangiarsi in un terribil gigante." (Annal. d'Italia, tom. xvi. p. 443, Milan, 1753, 8vo. edit.)

38. Claudian does not clearly answer our question, Where was Honorius himself? Yet the flight is marked by the pursuit; and my idea of the Gothic war is justified by the Italian critics, Sigonius (tom. i. p. ii. p. 369, de Imp. Occident. l. x.) and Muratori (Annali d'Italia, tom. iv. p. 45).

39. One of the roads may be traced in the Itineraries (p. 98, 288, 294, with Wesseling's Notes). Asta lay some miles on the right hand.

40. Asta, or Asti, a Roman colony, is now the capital of a pleasant county, which, in the sixteenth century, devolved to the dukes of Savoy (Leandro Alberti, Descrizzione d'Italia, p. 382).

41. Nec me timor impulit ullus. He might hold this proud language the next year at Rome, five hundred miles from the scene of danger (vi. Cons. Hon. 449).

42. Hanc ego vel victor regno, vel morte tenebo
   Victus, humum.
The speeches (de Bell. Get. 479–549) of the Gothic Nestor and Achilles are strong, characteristic, adapted to the circumstances, and possibly not less genuine than those of Livy.

43. Orosius (l. vii. c. 37) is shocked at the impiety of the Romans, who attacked on Easter Sunday such pious Christians. Yet, at the same time, public prayers were offered at the shrine of St. Thomas of Edessa for the destruction of the Arian robber. See Tillemont (Hist. des. Emp. tom. v. p. 529), who quotes a homily which has been erroneously ascribed to St. Chrysostom.

44. The vestiges of Pollentia are twenty-five miles to the south-east of Turin. *Urbs,* in the same neighbourhood, was a royal chase of the kings of Lombardy, and a small river, which excused the prediction, "penetrabis ad urbem." (Cluver. Ital. Antiq. tom. i. p. 83–85.)

45. Orosius wishes, in doubtful words, to insinuate the defeat of the Romans. "Pugnantes vicimus, victores victi sumus." Prosper (in Chron.) makes it an equal and bloody battle; but the Gothic writers, Cassiodorus (in Chron.) and Jornandes (de Reb. Get. c. 30), claim a decisive victory.

46. Demens Ausonidum gemmata monilia matrum,
   Romanasque altâ famulas cervice petebat.
   De Bell. Get. 627.

47. Claudian (de Bell. Get. 580–647) and Prudentius (in Symmach. l. ii. 694–719) celebrate, without ambiguity, the Roman victory of Pollentia. They are poetical and party writers; yet some credit is due to the most suspicious witnesses who are checked by the recent notoriety of facts.

48. Claudian's peroration is strong and elegant; but the identity of the Cimbric and Gothic fields must be understood (like Virgil's Philippi, Georgic i. 490) according to the loose geography of a poet. Vercellæ and Pollentia are sixty miles from each other; and the latitude is still greater if the Cimbri were defeated in the wide and barren plain of Verona (Maffei, Verona Illustrata, p. i. p. 54–62).

49. Claudian and Prudentius must be strictly examined, to reduce the figures and extort the historic sense of those poets.

50. Et gravant en airain ses frêles avantages
   De mes états conquis enchainer les images.
The practice of exposing in triumph the images of kings and provinces was familiar to the Romans. The bust of Mithridates himself was twelve feet high, of massy gold (Freinshem. Supplement. Livian. ciii. 47).

51. The Getic war and the sixth consulship of Honorius obscurely connect the events of Alaric's retreat and losses.

52. Taceo de Alarico . . . sæpe victo, sæpe concluso, semperque dimisso. Orosius, l. vii. c. 37, p. 567. Claudian (vi. Cons. Hon. 320) drops the curtain with a fine image.

53. The remainder of Claudian's poem on the sixth consulship of Honorius describes the journey, the triumph, and the games (330–660).

54. See the inscription in Mascou's History of the Ancient Germans, viii. 12. The words are positive and indiscreet: Getarum nationem in omne, ævum domitam, etc.

55. On the curious though horrid subject of the gladiators, consult the two books of the Saturnalia Lipsius, who, as an *antiquarian,* is inclined to excuse the practice of *antiquity* (tom. iii. p. 483–545).

56. Cod. Theodos. l. xv. tit. xii. leg. 1. The Commentary of Godefroy affords large materials (tom. v. p. 396) for the history of gladiators.

57. See the peroration of Prudentius (in Symmach. l. ii. 1121–1131), who had doubtless read

the eloquent invective of Lactantius (Divin. Institut. l. vi. c. 20). The Christian apologists have not spared these bloody games, which were introduced in the religious festivals of Paganism.

58. Theodoret, l. v. c. 26. I wish to believe the story of St. Telemachus. Yet no church has been dedicated, no altar has been erected, to the only monk who died a martyr in the cause of humanity.

59. Crudele gladiatorum spectaculum et inhumanum *nonnullis* videri solet; et *haud scio* an ita sit, ut nunc fit. Cicero Tusculan. ii. 17. He faintly censures the *abuse*, and warmly defends the *use*, of these sports; oculis nulla poterat esse fortior contra dolorem et mortem disciplina. Seneca (Epist. v. i.) shows the feelings of a man.

60. This account of Ravenna is drawn from Strabo (l. v. p. 327 [p. 213, ed. Casaub.]), Pliny (iii. 20), Stephen of Byzantium (sub voce 'Ράβεννα, p. 651, edit. Berkel.), Claudian (in vi. Cons. Honor. 494, etc)., Sidonius Apollinaris (l. i. Epist. 5, 8), Jornandes (de Reb. Get. c. 29), Procopius (de Bell. Gothic. l. i. c. i. p. 309, edit. Louvre [tom. ii. p. 8, ed. Bonn]), and Cluverius (Ital. Antiq. tom. i. p. 301-307). Yet I still want a local antiquarian, and a good topographical map.

61. Martial (Epigram iii. 56, 57) plays on the trick of the knave who had sold him wine instead of water; but he seriously declares that a cistern at Ravenna is more valuable than a vineyard. Sidonius complains that the town is destitute of fountains and aqueducts, and ranks the want of fresh water among the local evils, such as the croaking of frogs, the stinging of gnats, etc.

62. The fable of Theodore and Honoria, which Dryden has so admirably transplanted from Boccaccio (Giornata iii. novell. viii.) was acted in the wood of *Chiassi*, a corrupt word from *Classis*, the naval station, which, with the intermediate road or suburb, the *Via Cæsaris*, constituted the *triple* city of Ravenna.

63. From the year 404 the dates of the Theodosian Code became sedentary at Constantinople and Ravenna. See Godefroy's Chronology of the Laws, tom. i. p. cxlviii., etc.

64. See M. de Guignes, Hist. des Huns, tom. i. p. 179-189, tom. ii. p. 295, 334-338.

65. Procopius (de Bell. Vandal. l. i. c. iii. p. 182 [ed. Paris; tom. i. p. 319, ed. Bonn]) has observed an emigration from the Palus Mæotis to the north of Germany, which he ascribes to famine. But his views of ancient history are strangely darkened by ignorance and error.

66. Zosimus (l. v. [c. 26] p. 331) uses the general description of the nations beyond the Danube and the Rhine. Their situation, and consequently their names, are manifestly shown, even in the various epithets which each ancient writer may have casually added.

67. The name of Rhadagast was that of a local deity of the Obotrites (in Mecklenburg). A hero might naturally assume the appellation of his tutelar god; but it is not probable that the barbar-

ians should worship an unsuccessful hero. See Mascou, Hist. of the Germans, viii. 14.

68. Olympiodorus (apud Photium, p. 180 [p. 57, ed. Bekker]) uses the Latin word 'Οπτιμάτοι, which does not convey any precise idea. I suspect that they were the princes and nobles with their faithful companions—the knights with their squires, as they would have been styled some centuries afterwards.

69. Tacit. de Moribus Germanorum, c. 37.

70. ———Cujus agendi

Spectator vel causa fui,

Claudian, vi. Cons. Hon. 439,

is the modest language of Honorius, in speaking of the Gothic war, which he had seen somewhat nearer.

71. Zosimus (l. v. [c. 26] p. 331) transports the war and the victory of Stilicho beyond the Danube. A strange error, which is awkwardly and imperfectly cured by reading "Αρνον for "Ιστρον (Tillemont, Hist. des Emp. tom. v. p. 807). In good policy, we must use the service of Zosimus, without esteeming or trusting him.

72. Codex Theodos. l. vii. tit. xiii. leg. 16. The date of this law (A.D. 406, May 18) satisfies me, as it had done Godefroy (tom. ii. p. 387), of the true year of the invasion of Radagaisus. Tillemont, Pagi, and Muratori prefer the preceding year; but they are bound, by certain obligations of civility and respect, to St. Paulinus of Nola.

73. Soon after Rome had been taken by the Gauls, the senate, on a sudden emergency, armed ten legions, 3000 horse and 42,000 foot—a force which the city could not have sent forth under Augustus (Livy, vii. 25). This declaration may puzzle an antiquary, but it is clearly explained by Montesquieu.

74. Machiavel has explained, at least as a philosopher, the origin of Florence, which insensibly descended, for the benefit of trade, from the rock of Fæsulæ to the banks of the Arno (Istoria Florentina, tom. i. l. ii. p. 36; Londra, 1747). The triumvirs sent a colony to Florence, which, under Tiberius (Tacit. Annal. i. 79), deserved the reputation and name of a *flourishing* city. See Culver. Ital. Antiq. tom. i. p. 507, etc.

75. Yet the Jupiter of Radagaisus, who worshipped Thor and Woden, was very different from the Olympic or Capitoline Jove. The accommodating temper of polytheism might unite those various and remote deities; but the genuine Romans abhorred the human sacrifices of Gaul and Germany.

76. Paulinus (in Vit. Ambros. c. 50) relates this story, which he received from the mouth of Pansophia herself, a religious matron of Florence. Yet the archbishop soon ceased to take an active part in the business of the world, and never became a popular saint.

77. Augustine, The City of God, v. 23. Orosius, l. vii. c. 37, p. 567-571. The two friends wrote in Africa ten or twelve years after the victory, and

their authority is implicitly followed by Isidore of Seville (in Chron. p. 713, edit. Grot.). How many interesting facts might Orosius have inserted in the vacant space which is devoted to pious nonsense!

78. Franguntur montes, planumque per ardua Cæsar

 Ducit opus: pandit fossas, turritaque summis

 Disponit castella jugis, magnoque recessû

 Amplexusfines,saltus,nemorosaquetesqua

 Et silvas, vastâque feras indagine claudit.

Yet the simplicity of truth (Cæsar, de Bell. Civ. iii. 44) is far greater than the amplifications of Lucan (Pharsal. l. vi. 29–63).

79. The rhetorical expressions of Orosius, "in arido et aspero montis jugo," "in unum ac parvum verticem," are not very suitable to the encampment of a great army. But Fæsulæ, only three miles from Florence, might afford space for the head-quarters of Radagaisus, and would be comprehended within the circuit of the Roman lines.

80. See Zosimus, l. v. [c. 26] p. 331, and the Chronicles of Prosper and Marcellinus.

81. Olympiodorus (apud Photium, p. 180 [p. 57, ed. Bekk.]), uses an expression (προσηταιρίσατο) which would denote a strict and friendly alliance, and render Stilicho still more criminal. The paulisper retentus, deinde interfectus, of Orosius [p. 570], is sufficiently odious.

82. Orosius, piously inhuman, sacrifices the king and people—Agag and the Amalekites—without a symptom of compassion. The bloody actor is less detestable than the cool, unfeeling historian.

83. And Claudian's muse, was she asleep? had she been ill-paid? Methinks the seventh consulship of Honorius (A.D. 407) would have furnished the subject of a noble poem. Before it was discovered that the state could no longer be saved, Stilicho (after Romulus, Camillus, and Marius) might have been worthily surnamed the fourth founder of Rome.

84. A luminous passage of Prosper's Chronicle, "*In tres partes, per diversos principes, divisus exercitus,*" reduces the miracle of Florence, and connects the history of Italy, Gaul, and Germany.

85. Orosius and Jerom positively charge him with instigating the invasion. "Excitatæ a Stilichone gentes," etc. They must mean *indirectly.* He saved Italy at the expense of Gaul.

86. The Count de Buat is satisfied that the Germans who invaded Gaul were the *two-thirds* that yet remained of the army of Radagaisus. See the Histoire Ancienne des Peuples de l'Europe (tom. vii. p. 87, 121, Paris, 1772), an elaborate work, which I had not the advantage of perusing till the year 1777. As early as 1771, I find the same idea expressed in a rough draught of the present History. I have since observed a similar intimation in Mascou (viii. 15). Such agreement, without mutual communication, may add some weight to our common sentiment.

87. ____Provincia missos

Expellet citius fasces, quam Francia reges Quos dederis.

Claudian (i. Cons. Stil. l. i. 235, etc.) is clear and satisfactory. These kings of France are unknown to Gregory of Tours; but the author of the Gesta Francorum mentions both Sunno and Marcomir, and names the latter as the father of Pharamond (in tom. ii. p. 543). He seems to write from good materials, which he did not understand.

88. See Zosimus (l. vi. [c. 3] p. 373), Orosius (l. vii. c. 40, p. 576), and the Chronicles. Gregory of Tours (l. ii. c. 9, p. 165, in the second volume of the Historians of France) has preserved a valuable fragment of Renatus Profuturus Frigeridus, whose three names denote a Christian, a Roman subject, and a semi-barbarian.

89. Claudian (i. Cons. Stil. l. i. 221, etc.; l. ii. 186) describes the peace and prosperity of the Gallic frontier. The Abbé Dubos (Hist. Critique, etc., tom. i. p. 174) would read *Alba* (a nameless rivulet of the Ardennes) instead of *Albis;* and expatiates on the danger of the Gallic cattle grazing beyond the *Elbe.* Foolish enough! In poetical geography, the Elbe and the Hercynian signify any river or any wood in Germany. Claudian is not prepared for the strict examination of our antiquaries.

90. ——Geminasque viator

 Cum videat ripas, quæ sit Romana requirat.

91. Jerom, tom. i. p. 93 [Epist. cxxiii. c. 16, tom. i. p. 908, ed. Vallars.]. See, in the first volume of the Historians of France, p. 777, 782, the proper extracts from the Carmen de Providentiâ Divinâ, and Salvian. The anonymous poet was himself a captive, with his bishop and fellow-citizens.

92. The Pelagian doctrine, which was first agitated A.D. 405, was condemned, in the space of ten years, at Rome and Carthage. St. Augustin fought and conquered; but the Greek church was favourable to his adversaries; and (what is singular enough) the people did not take any part in a dispute which they could not understand.

93. See the Mémoires de Guillaume du Bellay, l. vi. In French, the original reproof is less obvious and more pointed, from the double sense of the word *journée,* which alike signifies a day's travel or a battle.

94. Claudian (i. Cons. Stil. l. ii. 250). It is supposed that the Scots of Ireland invaded by sea the whole western coast of Britain; and some slight credit may be given even to Nennius and the Irish traditions (Carte's Hist. of England, vol. i. p. 169). Whitaker's Genuine History of the Britons, p. 199. The sixty-six Lives of St. Patrick, which were extant in the ninth century, must have contained as many thousand lies; yet we may believe that, in one of these Irish inroads, the future apostle was led away captive (Usher, Antiquit. Eccles. Britann. p. 431; and Tillemont, Mém. Ecclés. tom. xvi. p. 456, 782, etc.).

95. The British usurpers are taken from Zosimus

(l. vi. [c. 2] p. 371–375), Orosius (l. vii. v. 40, p. 576, 577), Olympiodorus (apud Photium, p. 180, 181 [p. 57, ed. Bekker]), the ecclesiastical historians, and the Chronicles. The Latins are ignorant of Marcus.

96. Cum in Constantino *inconstantiam* . . . execrarentur (Sidonius Apollinaris, l. v. Epist. 9, p. 139, edit. secund. Sirmond.). Yet Sidonius might be tempted, by so fair a pun, to stigmatise a prince who had disgraced his grandfather.

97. *Bagaudæ* is the name which Zosimus applies to them; perhaps they deserved a less odious character (see Dubos, Hist. Critique, tom. i. p. 203). We shall hear of them again.

98. Verinianus, Didymus, Theodosius, and Lagodius, who in modern courts would be styled princes of the blood, were not distinguished by any rank or privileges above the rest of their fellow-subjects.

99. These *Honoriani* or *Honoriaci* consisted of two bands of Scots or Attacotti, two of Moors, two of Marcomanni, the Victores, the Ascarii, and the Gallicani (Notitia Imperii, sect. xxxviii. edit. Lab.). They were part of the sixty-five *Auxilia Palatina*, and are properly styled ἐν τῇ αὐλῇ τάξεις by Zosimus (l. vi. [c. 4] p. 374).

100. ———Comitantur euntem
Pallor, et atra Fames; et saucia lividus ora
Luctus; et inferno stridentes agmine Morbi.
Claudian in vi. Cons. Hon. 321, etc.

101. These dark transactions are investigated by the Count de Buat (Hist. des Peuples de l'Europe, tom. vii. c. iii.-viii. p. 69–206), whose laborious accuracy may sometimes fatigue a superficial reader.

102. See Zosimus, l. v. [c. 29] p. 334, 335. He interrupts his scanty narrative to relate the fable of Æmona, and of the ship Argo, which was drawn overland from that place to the Hadriatic. Sozomen (l. viii. c. 25; l. ix. c. 4) and Socrates (l. vii. c. 10) cast a pale and doubtful light, and Orosius (l. vii. c. 38, p. 571) is abominably partial.

103. Zosimus, l. v. [c. 29] p. 338, 339. He repeats the words of Lampadius as they were spoken in Latin, "Non est ista pax, sed pactio servitutis," and then translates them into Greek for the benefit of his readers.

104. He came from the coast of the Euxine, and exercised a splendid office, λαμπρᾶς δὲ στρατείας ἐν τοῖς βασιλείοις ἠξιωμένος. His actions justify his character, which Zosimus (l. v. [c. 32] p. 340) exposes with visible satisfaction. Augustin revered the piety of Olympius, whom he styles a true son of the church (Baronius, Annal. Eccles. A.D. 408, No. 19, etc.; Tillemont, Mém. Ecclés. tom. xiii. p. 467, 468). But these praises, which the African saint so unworthily bestows, might proceed as well from ignorance as from adulation.

105. Zosimus, l. v. [c. 31] p. 338, 339. Sozomen,

l. ix. c. 4. Stilicho offered to undertake the journey to Constantinople, that he might divert Honorius from the vain attempt. The Eastern empire would not have obeyed, and could not have been conquered.

106. Zosimus (l. v. [c. 30, *sqq.*] p. 336–345) has copiously, though not clearly, related the disgrace and death of Stilicho. Olympiodorus (apud Phot. p. 177 [p. 56, ed. Bekker]), Orosius (l. vii. c. 38, p. 571, 572), Sozomen (l. ix. c. 4), and Philostorgius (l. xi. c. 3, l. xii. c. 2), afford supplemental hints.

107. Zosimus, l. v. [c. 28] p. 333. The marriage of a Christian with two sisters scandalises Tillemont (Hist. des Empereurs, tom. v. p. 557), who expects, in vain, that Pope Innocent I. should have done something in the way either of censure or of dispensation.

108. Two of his friends are honourably mentioned (Zosimus, l. v. [c. 35] p. 346)—Peter, chief of the school of notaries, and the great chamberlain Deuterius. Stilicho had secured the bedchamber; and it is surprising that, under a feeble prince, the bedchamber was not able to secure him.

109. Orosius (l. vii. c. 38, p. 571, 572) seems to copy the false and furious manifestos which were dispersed through the provinces by the new administration.

110. See the Theodosian Code, l. vii. tit. xvi. leg. 1; l. ix. tit. xlii. leg. 22. Stilicho is branded with the name of *prædo publicus*, who employed his wealth *ad omnem ditandam, inquietandamque Barbariem.*

111. Augustin himself is satisfied with the effectual laws which Stilicho had enacted against heretics and idolaters, and which are still extant in the Code. He only applies to Olympius for their confirmation (Baronius, Annal. Eccles. A.D. 408, No. 19).

112. Zosimus, l. v. [c. 38] p. 351. We may observe the bad taste of the age, in dressing their statues with such awkward finery.

113. See Rutilius Numatianus (Itinerar. l. ii. 41–60), to whom religious enthusiasm has dictated some elegant and forcible lines. Stilicho likewise stripped the gold plates from the doors of the Capitol, and read a prophetic sentence which was engraven under them (Zosimus, l. v. [c. 38] p. 352). These are foolish stories; yet the charge of *impiety* adds weight and credit to the praise, which Zosimus reluctantly bestows, of his virtues.

114. At the nuptials of Orpheus (a modest comparison!) all the parts of animated nature contributed their various gifts, and the gods themselves enriched their favourite. Claudian had neither flocks, nor herds, nor vines, nor olives. His wealthy bride was heiress to them all. But he carried to Africa a recommendatory letter from Serena, his Juno, and was made happy (Epist. ii. ad Serenam).

115. Claudian feels the honour like a man who deserved it (in præfat. Bell. Get.). The original inscription, on marble, was found at Rome, in the

fifteenth century, in the house of Pomponius Lætus. The statue of a poet, far superior to Claudian,
should have been erected, during his lifetime, by
the men of letters, his countrymen and contemporaries. It was a noble design.

116. See Epigram xxx.:—

> Mallius indulget somno noctesque di-
>   esque:
> Insomnis *Pharius* sacra, profana, rapit.
> Omnibus, hoc, Italæ gentes, exposcite
>   votis,
> Mallius ut vigilet, dormiat ut Pharius.

Hadrian was a Pharian (of Alexandria). See his
public life in Godefroy, Cod. Theodos. tom. vi. p.
364. Mallius did not always sleep. He composed
some elegant dialogues on the Greek systems of
natural philosophy (Claud. in Mall. Theodor.
Cons. 61–112).

117. See Claudian's first Epistle. Yet in some
places an air of irony and indignation betrays his
secret reluctance.

118. National vanity has made him a Floren-
tine, or a Spaniard. But the first Epistle of Claudian proves him a native of Alexandria (Fabricius,
Biblioth. Latin. tom. iii. p. 191–202, edit. Ernest.).

119. His first Latin verses were composed during
the consulship of Probinus, A.D. 395:—

> Romanos bibimus primum, te consule,
>   fontes,
> Et Latiæ cessit Graia Thalia togæ.

Besides some Greek epigrams, which are still extant, the Latin poet had composed, in Greek, the
Antiquities of Tarsus, Anazarbus, Berytus, Nice,
etc. It is more easy to supply the loss of good poetry
than of authentic history.

120. Strada (Prolusion v. vi.) allows him to
contend with the five heroic poets, Lucretius, Virgil, Ovid, Lucan, and Statius. His patron is the
accomplished courtier Balthazar Castiglione. His
admirers are numerous and passionate. Yet the
rigid critics reproach the exotic weeds or flowers
which spring too luxuriantly in his Latian soil.

Chapter XXXI

1. The series of events, from the death of Stilicho
to the arrival of Alaric before Rome, can only be
found in Zosimus, l. v. [c. 35–37] p. 347–350.

2. The expression of Zosimus is strong and
lively, καταφρόνησιν ἐμποιῆσαι τοῖς πολεμίοις ἀρκοῦν-
τας, sufficient to excite the contempt of the enemy.

3. Eos qui catholicæ sectæ sunt inimici, intra
palatium militare prohibemus. Nullus nobis sit
aliquâ ratione conjunctus, qui a nobis fide et religione discordat. Cod. Theodos, l. xvi. tit. v. leg.
42, and Godefroy's Commentary, tom. vi. p. 164.
This law was applied in the utmost latitude and
rigorously executed. Zosimus, l. v. [c. 46] p. 364.

4. Addison (see his Works, vol. ii. p. 54, edit.
Baskerville) has given a very picturesque description of the road through the Apennine. The Goths
were not at leisure to observe the beauties of the
prospect; but they were pleased to find that the
Saxa Intercisa, a narrow passage which Vespasian
had cut through the rock (Cluver. Italia Antiq.
tom. i. p. 618), was totally neglected.

5.   Hinc albi, Clitumne, Greges, et maxima
          taurus
      Victima sæpe, tuo perfusi flumine sacro,
      Romanos ad templa Deum duxere tri-
          umphos.   Georg. ii. 147.

Besides Virgil, most of the Latin poets, Propertius,
Lucan, Silius Italicus, Claudian, etc., whose passages may be found in Cluverius and Addison,
have celebrated the triumphal victims of Clitumnus.

6. Some ideas of the march of Alaric are borrowed from the journey of Honorius over the same
ground (see Claudian in vi. Cons. Hon. 494–522).
The measured distance between Ravenna and
Rome was 254 Roman miles. Itinerar. Wesseling,
p. 126.

7. The march and retreat of Hannibal are described by Livy, l. xxvi. c. 7, 8, 9, 10, 11; and the
reader is made a spectator of the interesting scene.

8. These comparisons were used by Cineas, the
counsellor of Pyrrhus, after his return from his embassy, in which he had diligently studied the discipline and manners of Rome. See Plutarch in
Pyrrhus.

9. In the three *census* which were made of the
Roman people about the time of the second Punic
war, the numbers stand as follows (see Livy, Epitom. l. xx. Hist. l. xxvii. 36, xxix .37), 270, 213, 137,
108, 214,000. The fall of the second and the rise of
the third appears so enormous, that several critics,
notwithstanding the unanimity of the MSS., have
suspected some corruption of the text of Livy.
(See Drakenbroch ad xxvii. 36, and Beaufort, République Romaine, tom. i. p. 325). They did not
consider that the second *census* was taken only at
Rome, and that the numbers were diminished, not
only by the death, but likewise by the *absence*, of
many soldiers. In the third *census*, Livy expressly
affirms that the legions were mustered by the care
of particular commissaries. From the numbers on
the list we must always deduct one-twelfth above
threescore and incapable of bearing arms. See
Population de la France, p. 72.

10. Livy considers these two incidents as the
effects only of chance and courage. I suspect that
they were both managed by the admirable policy
of the senate.

11. See Jerom, tom. i. p. 169, 170, ad Eustochium [Epist. cviii. tom. i. p. 684, ed. Vallars.]; he
bestows on Paula the splendid titles of Gracchorum
stirps, soboles Scipionum, Pauli hæres, cujus vo-
cabulum trahit, Martiæ Papyriæ Matris Africani

vera et germana propago. This particular description supposes a more solid title than the surname of Julius, which Toxotius shared with a thousand families of the western provinces. See the Index of Tacitus, of Gruter's Inscriptions, etc.

12. Tacitus (Annal. iii. 55) affirms that, between the battle of Actium and the reign of Vespasian, the senate was gradually filled with *new* families from the Municipia and colonies of Italy.

13.   Nec quisquam Procerum tentet (licet ære vetusto
    Floreat, et claro cingatur Roma senatû)
    Se jactare parem; sed primâ sede relictâ
    Aucheniis, de jure licet certare secundo.
        Claud. in Prob. et Olybrii Coss. 18.

Such a compliment paid to the obscure name of the Auchenii has amazed the critics; but they all agree that, whatever may be the true reading, the sense of Claudian can be applied only to the Anician family.

14. The earliest date on the annals of Pighius is that of M. Anicius Gallus, Trib. Pl. A.U.C. 506. Another Tribune, Q. Anicius, A.U.C. 508, is distinguished by the epithet of Prænestinus. Livy (xlv. 43) places the Anicii below the great families of Rome.

15. Livy, xliv. 30, 31, xlv. 3, 26, 43. He fairly appreciates the merit of Anicius, and justly observes that his fame was clouded by the superior lustre of the Macedonian, which preceded the Illyrian, triumph.

16. The dates of the three consulships are A.U.C. 593, 818, 967: the two last under the reigns of Nero and Caracalla. The second of these consuls distinguished himself only by his infamous flattery (Tacit. Annal. xv. 74); but even the evidence of crimes, if they bear the stamp of greatness and antiquity, is admitted, without reluctance, to prove the genealogy of a noble house.

17. In the sixth century the nobility of the Anician name is mentioned (Cassiodor. Variar. l. x. Ep. 11, 12) with singular respect by the minister of a Gothic king of Italy.

18.   ———Fixus in omnes
    Cognatos procedit honos; quemcumque requiras
    Hâc de stirpe virum, certum est de Consule nasci.
    Per fasces numerantur avi, semperque renatâ
    Nobilitate virent, et prolem fata sequuntur.

(Claudian in Prob. et Olyb. Consulat. 12, etc.) The Annii, whose name seems to have merged in the Anician, mark the Fasti with many consulships from the time of Vespasian to the fourth century.

19. The title of first Christian senator may be justified by the authority of Prudentius (in Symmach. i. 553) and the dislike of the Pagans to the Anician family. See Tillemont, Hist. des Empereurs, tom. iv. p. 183, v. p. 44. Baron. Annal. A.D. 312, No. 78; A.D. 322, No. 2.

20. Probus . . . claritudine generis et potentiâ et opûm amplitudine cognitus Orbi Romano, per quem universum pœne patrimonia sparsa possedit, juste an secus non judicioli est nostri. Ammian. Marcellin. xxvii. 11. His children and widow erected for him a magnificent tomb in the Vatican, which was demolished in the time of pope Nicholas V. to make room for the new church of St. Peter. Baronius, who laments the ruin of this Christian monument, has diligently preserved the inscriptions and basso-relievos. See Annal. Eccles. A.D. 395, No. 5–17.

21. Two Persian satraps travelled to Milan and Rome to hear St. Ambrose and to see Probus. (Paulin. in Vit. Ambros.) Claudian (in Cons. Probin. et. Olybr. 30–60) seems at a loss how to express the glory of Probus.

22. See the poem which Claudian addressed to the two noble youths.

23. Secundinus, the Manichæan, ap. Baron. Annal. Eccles. A.D. 390, No. 34.

24. See Nardini, Roma Antica, p. 89, 498, 500.

25.   Quid loquar inclusas inter laquearia silvas?
    Vernula quâ vario carmine ludit avis?
        Claud. Rutil. Numatian. Itinerar.
            ver. 111.

The poet lived at the time of the Gothic invasion. A moderate palace would have covered Cincinnatus's farm of four acres (Val. Max. iv. 4, 7). In laxitatem ruris excurrunt, says Seneca, Epist. 114. See a judicious note of Mr. Hume, Essays, vol. i. p. 562, last 8vo edition.

26. This curious account of Rome in the reign of Honorius is found in a fragment of the historian Olympiodorus, ap. Photium, p. 197 [p. 63, ed. Bekker].

27. The sons of Alypius [Olympius in Bekker's ed.], of Symmachus, and of Maximus, spent, during their respective prætorships, twelve, or twenty, or forty, *centenaries* (or hundredweight of gold). See Olympiodor. ap. Phot. p. 197 [p. 63, ed. Bekker]. This popular estimation allows some latitude; but it is difficult to explain a law in the Theodosian Code (l. vi. tit. iv. leg. 5) which fixes the expense of the first prætor at 25,000, of the second at 20,000, and of the third at 15,000 *folles*. The name of *follis* (see Mém. de l'Académie des Inscriptions, tom. xxviii. p. 727) was equally applied to a purse of 125 pieces of silver, and to a small copper coin of the value of $\frac{1}{2825}$ part of that purse. In the former sense, the 25,000 *folles* would be equal to £150,000; in the latter to five or six pounds sterling. The one appears extravagant, the other is ridiculous. There must have existed some third and middle value, which is here understood; but ambiguity is an inexcusable fault in the language of laws.

28. Nicopolis . . . in Actiaco littore sita possessionis vestræ nunc pars vel maxima est. Jerom. in præfat. Comment. ad Epistol. ad Titum, tom. ix. p. 243. M. de Tillemont supposes, strangely

enough, that it was part of Agamemnon's inheritance. Mém. Ecclés. tom. xii. p. 85.

29. Seneca, Epist. lxxxix. His language is of the declamatory kind: but declamation could scarcely exaggerate the avarice and luxury of the Romans. The philosopher himself deserved some share of the reproach, if it be true that his rigorous exaction of *Quadringenties*, above three hundred thousand pounds, which he had lent at high interest, provoked a rebellion in Britain. (Dion Cassius, l. lxii. [c. 2] p. 1003.) According to the conjecture of Gale (Antoninus's Itinerary in Britain, p. 92), the same Faustinus possessed an estate near Bury, in Suffolk, and another in the kingdom of Naples.

30. Volusius, a wealthy senator (Tacit. Annal. iii. 30), always preferred tenants born on the estate. Columella, who received this maxim from him, argues very judiciously on the subject. De Re Rustica, l. i. c. 7, p. 408, edit. Gesner. Leipzig, 1735.

31. Valesius (ad Ammian. xiv. 6) has proved, from Chrysostom and Augustin, that the senators were not allowed to lend money at usury. Yet it appears from the Theodosian Code (see Godefroy ad l. ii. tit. xxxiii. tom. i. p. 230–239) that they were permitted to take six per cent, or one-half of the legal interest; and, what is more singular, this permission was granted to the *young* senators.

32. Plin. Hist. Natur. xxxiii. 50. He states the silver at only 4380 pounds, which is increased by Livy (xxx. 45) to 100,023; the former seems too little for an opulent city, the latter too much for any private sideboard.

33. The learned Arbuthnot (Tables of Ancient Coins, etc., p. 153) has observed with humour, and I believe with truth, that Augustus had neither glass to his windows nor a shirt to his back. Under the lower empire the use of linen and glass became somewhat more common.

[Glass was in general use during the reign of Augustus, and linen in that of Tiberius.]

34. It is incumbent on me to explain the liberties which I have taken with the text of Ammianus. 1. I have melted down into one piece the sixth chapter of the fourteenth and the fourth of the twenty-eighth book. 2. I have given order and connection to the confused mass of materials. 3. I have softened *some* extravagant hyperboles and pared away some superfluities of the original. 4. I have developed some observations which were insinuated rather than expressed. With these allowances my version will be found, not literal indeed, but faithful and exact.

35. Claudian, who seems to have read the history of Ammianus, speaks of this great revolution in a much less courtly style:

> Postquam jura ferox in se communia Cæsar
> Transtulit; et lapsi mores; desuetaque priscis
> Artibus, in gremium pacis servile recessi.
> De Bell. Gildonico, v. 49.

36. The minute diligence of antiquarians has not been able to verify these extraordinary names. I am of opinion that they were invented by the historian himself, who was afraid of any personal satire or application. It is certain, however, that the simple denominations of the Romans were gradually lengthened to the number of four, five, or even seven, pompous surnames; as, for instance, Marcus Mæcius Mæmmius Furius Balburius Cæcilianus Placidus. See Norris, Cenotaph. Pisan. Dissert. iv. p. 438.

37. The *carrucæ*, or coaches of the Romans, were often of solid silver curiously carved and engraved; and the trappings of the mules or horses were embossed with gold. This magnificence continued from the reign of Nero to that of Honorius; and the Appian way was covered with the splendid equipages of the nobles, who came out to meet St. Melania when she returned to Rome six years before the Gothic siege (Seneca, Epist. lxxxvii.; Plin. Hist. Natur. xxxiii. 49; Paulin. Nolan. apud Baron. Annal. Eccles. A.D. 397, No. 5). Yet pomp is well exchanged for convenience; and a plain modern coach that is hung upon springs is much preferable to the silver or gold *carts* of antiquity, which rolled on the axletree, and were exposed, for the most part, to the inclemency of the weather.

38. In a homily of Asterius, bishop of Amasia, M. de Valois has discovered (ad Ammian. xiv. 6) that this was a new fashion; that bears, wolves, lions, and tigers, woods, hunting-matches, etc., were represented in embroidery; and that the more pious coxcombs substituted the figure or legend of some favourite saint.

39. See Pliny's Epistles, i. 6. Three large wild boars were allured and taken in the toils without interrupting the studies of the philosophic sportsman.

40. The change from the inauspicious word *Avernus*, which stands in the text, is immaterial. The two lakes, Avernus and Lucrinus, communicated with each other, and were fashioned by the stupendous moles of Agrippa into the Julian port, which opened through a narrow entrance into the gulf of Puteoli. Virgil, who resided on the spot, has described (Georgic ii. 161) this work at the moment of its execution: and his commentators, especially Catrou, have derived much light from Strabo, Suetonius, and Dion. Earthquakes and volcanoes have changed the face of the country, and turned the Lucrine lake, since the year 1538, into the Monte Nuovo. See Camillo Pellegrino Discorsi della Campania Felice, p. 239, 244, etc. Antonii Sanfelicii Campania, p. 13, 88.

41. The regna Cumana et Puteolana; loca cætero quivalde expetenda, interpellantium autem multitudine pæne fugienda. Cicero ad Attic. xiv. 16.

42. The proverbial expression of *Cimmerian darkness* was originally borrowed from the description of Homer (in the eleventh book of the Odyssey) which he applies to a remote and fabulous country

on the shores of the ocean. See Erasmi Adagia, in his Works, tom. ii. p. 593, the Leyden edition.

43. We may learn from Seneca Epist. cxxiii., three curious circumstances relative to the journeys of the Romans. 1. They were preceded by a troop of Numidian light-horse, who announced by a cloud of dust the approach of a great man. 2. Their baggage-mules transported not only the precious vases but even the fragile vessels of crystal and *murra*, which last is almost proved, by the learned French translator of Seneca (tom. iii. p. 402–422), to mean the porcelain of China and Japan. 3. The beautiful faces of the young slaves were covered with a medicated crust, or ointment, which secured them against the effects of the sun and frost.

44. Distributio solemnium sportularum. The *sportulæ*, or *sportellæ*, were small baskets supposed to contain a quantity of hot provisions of the value of 100 quadrantes, or twelvepence halfpenny, which were ranged in order in the hall, and ostentatiously distributed to the hungry or servile crowd who waited at the door. This indelicate custom is very frequently mentioned in the epigrams of Martial and the satires of Juvenal. See likewise Suetonius, in Claud. c. 21; in Neron. c. 16; in Domitian. c. 4, 7. These baskets of provisions were afterwards converted into large pieces of gold and silver coin, or plate, which were mutually given and accepted even by the persons of the highest rank (see Symmach. Epist. iv. 55, ix. 124, and Miscell. p. 256 [ed. Paris, 1604]), on solemn occasions, of consulships, marriages, etc.

45. The want of an English name obliges me to refer to the common genus of squirrels, the Latin *glis*, the French *loir;* a little animal who inhabits the woods and remains torpid in cold weather (see Plin. Hist. Natur. viii. 82; Buffon, Hist. Naturelle, tom. viii. 158; Pennant's Synopsis of Quadrupeds, p. 289). The art of rearing and fattening great numbers of *gliers* was practised in Roman villas as a profitable article of rural economy (Varro, de Re Rusticâ, iii. 15). The excessive demand of them for luxurious tables was increased by the foolish prohibitions of the censors; and it is reported that they are still esteemed in modern Rome, and are frequently sent as presents by the Colonna princes (see Brotier, the last editor of Pliny, tom. ii. p. 458, apud Barbou, 1779).

46. This game, which might be translated by the more familiar names of *trictrac*, or *backgammon;* was a favourite amusement of the gravest Romans; and old Mucius Scævola, the lawyer, had the reputation of a very skilful player. It was called *ludus duodecim scriptorum*, from the twelve *scripta* or lines which equally divided the *alveolus* or table. On these the two armies, the white and the black, each consisting of fifteen men, or *calculi*, were regularly placed and alternately moved according to the laws of the game and the chances of the *tesseræ* or dice. Dr. Hyde, who diligently traces the history and varieties of the *nerdiludium* (a name of Persic

etymology) from Ireland to Japan, pours forth on this trifling subject a copious torrent of classic and Oriental learning. See Syntagma Dissertat. tom. ii. p. 217–405.

47. Marius Maximus, homo omnium verbosissimus, qui et mythistoricis se voluminibus implicavit. Vopiscus in Hist. August. p. 242 [Vopisc. Firm. c. 1.] He wrote the Lives of the Emperors from Trajan to Alexander Severus. See Gerard Vossius de Historicis Latin. l. ii. c. 3, in his Works, vol. iv. p. 57.

48. This satire is probably exaggerated. The Saturnalia of Macrobius, and the Epistles of Jerom, afford satisfactory proofs that Christian theology and classic literature were studiously cultivated by several Romans of both sexes and of the highest rank.

49. Macrobius, the friend of these Roman nobles, considered the stars as the cause, or at least the signs, of future events (de Somn. Scipion. l. i. c. 19, p. 68).

50. The histories of Livy (see particularly vi. 36) are full of the extortions of the rich and the sufferings of the poor debtors. The melancholy story of a brave old soldier (Dionys. Hal. l. vi. c. 26, p. 347, edit. Hudson, and Livy, ii. 23) must have been frequently repeated in those primitive times, which have been so undeservedly praised.

51. Non esse in civitate duo millia hominum qui rem haberent. Cicero, Offic. ii. 21, and Comment. Paul. Manut. in edit. Græv. This vague computation was made A.U.C. 649, in a speech of the tribune Philippus, and it was his object, as well as that of the Gracchi (see Plutarch), to deplore, and perhaps to exaggerate, the misery of the common people.

52. See the third Satire (60–125) of Juvenal, who indignantly complains,

   ——Quamvis quota portio fæcia Achæi!
   Jampridem Syrus in Tiberim defluxit
      Orontes;
   Et linguam et mores, etc.

Seneca, when he proposes to comfort his mother (Consolat. ad Helv. c. 6) by the reflection that a great part of mankind were in a state of exile, reminds her how few of the inhabitants of Rome were born in the city.

53. Almost all that is said of the bread, bacon, oil, wine, etc., may be found in the fourteenth book of the Theodosian Code, which expressly treats of the *police* of the great cities. See particularly the titles iii. iv. xv. xvi. xvii. xxiv. The collateral testimonies are produced in Godefroy's Commentary, and it is needless to transcribe them. According to a law of Theodosius, which appreciates in money the military allowance, a piece of gold (eleven shillings) was equivalent to eighty pounds of bacon, or to eighty pounds of oil, or to twelve modii (or pecks) of salt (Cod. Theod. l. viii. tit. iv. leg. 17). This equation, compared with another seventy pounds of bacon for an *amphora* (Cod.

Theod. l. xiv. tit. iv. leg. 4), fixes the price of wine at about sixteenpence the gallon.

54. The anonymous author of the Description of the World (p. 14, in tom. iii. Geograph. Minor. Husdon) observes of Lucania, in his barbarous Latin, Regio obtima, et ipsa omnibus habundans, et lardum multum foras emittit: propter quod est in montibus, cujus æscam animalium variam.

55. See Novell. ad calcem Cod. Theod. D. Valent. l. i. tit. xv. [tom. vi. App. p. 28, ed. Gothofr.]. This law was published at Rome, June 29th, A.D. 452.

56. Sueton. in August. c. 42. The utmost debauch of the emperor himself, in his favourite wine of Rhætia, never exceeded a *sextarius* (an English pint). Id. c. 77. Torrentius ad loc. and Arbuthnot's Tables, p. 86.

57. His design was to plant vineyards along the sea-coast of Etruria (Vopiscus, in Hist. August. p. 225 [in Aurel. c. 48]), the dreary, unwholesome, uncultivated *Maremme* of modern Tuscany.

58. Olympiodor, apud Phot. p. 197 [p. 63, ed. Bekker].

59. Seneca (Epistol. lxxxvi.) compares the baths of Scipio Africanus, at his villa of Liternum, with the magnificence (which was continually increasing) of the public baths of Rome, long before the stately Thermæ of Antoninus and Diocletian were erected. The *quadrans* paid for admission was the quarter of the *as*, about one-eighth of an English penny.

60. Ammianus (l. xiv. c. 6, and l. xxviii. c. 4), after describing the luxury and pride of the nobles of Rome, exposes, with equal indignation, the vices and follies of the common people.

61. Juvenal, Satir. xi. 191, etc. The expressions of the historian Ammianus are not less strong and animated than those of the satirist; and both the one and the other painted from the life. The numbers which the great Circus was capable of receiving are taken from the *original Notitiæ* of the city. The differences between them prove that they did not transcribe each other; but the sum may appear incredible, though the country on these occasions flocked to the city.

62. Sometimes, indeed, they composed original pieces.

————Vestigia Græca

Ausi deserere et celebrare domestica facta. Horat. Epistol. ad Pisones, 285, and the learned though perplexed note of Dacier, who might have allowed the name of tragedies to the *Brutus* and the *Decius* of Pacuvius, or to the *Cato* of Maternus. The *Octavia*, ascribed to one of the Senecas, still remains a very unfavourable specimen of Roman tragedy.

63. In the time of Quintillian and Pliny a tragic poet was reduced to the imperfect method of hiring a great room, and reading his play to the company, whom he invited for that purpose. (See Dialog. de Oratoribus, c. 9, 10, and Plin. Epistol. vii. 17.)

64. See the dialogue of Lucian, entitled de Saltatione, tom. ii. p. 265–317, edit. Reitz. The pantomimes obtained the honourable name of χειροσό-φοι; and it was required that they should be conversant with almost every art and science. Burette (in the Mémoires de l'Académie des Inscriptions, tom. i. p. 127, etc.) has given a short history of the art of pantomimes.

65. Ammianus, l. xiv. c. 6. He complains, with decent indignation, that the streets of Rome were filled with crowds of females, who might have given children to the state, but whose only occupation was to curl and dress their hair, and jactari volubilibus gyris, dum exprimunt innumera simulacra, quæ finxere fabulæ theatrales.

66. Lipsius (tom. iii. p. 423, de Magnitud. Romana, l. iii. c. 3) and Isaac Vossius (Observat. Var. p. 26–34) have indulged strange dreams, of four, or eight, or fourteen millions in Rome. Mr. Hume (Essays, vol. i. p. 450–457), with admirable good sense and scepticism, betrays some secret disposition to extenuate the populousness of ancient times.

67. Olympiodor. ap. Phot. p. 197 [p. 63, ed. Bekker]. See Fabricius, Biblioth. Græc. tom. ix. p. 400.

68. In eâ autem majestate urbis, et vicium infinitâ frequentiâ innumerabiles habitationes opus fuit explicare. Ergo cum recipere non posset area plana tantam multitudinem [ad habitandum] in urbe, ad auxilium altitudinis ædificiorum res ipsa coëgit devenire. Vitruv. ii. 8. This passage, which I owe to Vossius, is clear, strong, and comprehensive.

69. The successive testimonies of Pliny, Aristides, Claudian, Rutilius, etc., prove the insufficiency of these restrictive edicts. See Lipsius, de Magnitud. Romana, l. iii. c. 4.

————Tabulata tibi jam tertia fumant;

Tu nescis; nam si gradibus trepidatur ab imis

Ultimus ardebit, quem tegula sola tuetur
A pluviâ.   Juvenal, Satir. iii. 199.

70. Read the whole third Satire, but particularly 166, 223, etc. The description of a crowded *insula*, or lodging-house, in Petronius (c. 95, 97), perfectly tallies with the complaints of Juvenal; and we learn from legal authority that, in the time of Augustus (Heineccius, Hist. Juris Roman. c. iv. p. 181), the ordinary rent of the several *cænacula*, or apartments of an *insula*, annually produced forty thousand sesterces, between three and four hundred pounds sterling (Pandect. l. xix. tit. ii. No. 30), a sum which proves at once the large extent and high value of those common buildings.

71. This sum total is composed of 1780 *domus*, or great houses, of 46,602 *insulæ*, or plebeian habitations (see Nardini, Roma Antica, l. iii. p. 88); and these numbers are ascertained by the agreement of the texts of the different *Notitiæ*. Nardini, l. viii. p. 498, 500.

72. See that accurate writer M. de Messance, Recherches sur la Population, p. 175–187. From probable or certain grounds he assigns to Paris 23,565 houses, 71,114 families, and 576,630 inhabitants.

73. This computation is not very different from that which M. Brotier, the last editor of Tacitus (tom. ii. p. 380), has assumed from similar principles; though he seems to aim at a degree of precision which it is neither possible nor important to obtain.

74. For the events of the first siege of Rome, which are often confounded with those of the second and third, see Zosimus, l. v. [c. 38–42] p. 350–354; Sozomen, l. ix. c. 6; Olympiodorus, ap. Phot. p. 180 [p. 57, ed. Bekk.]; Philostorgius, l. xii. c. 3; and Godefroy, Dissertat. p. 467–475.

75. The mother of Læta was named Pissumena. Her father, family, and country are unknown. Ducange, Fam. Byzantin. p. 59.

76. Ad nefandos cibos erupit esurientium rabies, et sua invicem membra aniarunt, dum mater non parcit lactenti infantiæ; et recipit utero, quem paullò ante effuderat. Jerom. ad. Principiam, tom. i. p. 121 [Ep. cxxvii. tom. i. p. 953, ed. Vallars.]. The same horrid circumstance is likewise told of the sieges of Jerusalem and Paris. For the latter, compare the tenth book of the Henriade, and the Journal de Henri IV. tom. i. p. 47–83; and observe that a plain narrative of facts is much more pathetic than the most laboured descriptions of epic poetry.

77. Zosimus (l. v. [c. 41] p. 355, 356) speaks of these ceremonies like a Greek unacquainted with the national superstition of Rome and Tuscany. I suspect that they consisted of two parts, the secret and the public; the former were probably an imitation of the arts and spells by which Numa had drawn down Jupiter and his thunder on Mount Aventine.

> ——Quid agant laqueis, quæ carmina dicant,
> Quâque trahant superis sedibus arte Jovem,
> Scire nefas homini.

The ancilia or shields of Mars, the pignora Imperii, which were carried in solemn procession on the calends of March, derived their origin from this mysterious event (Ovid. Fast. iii. 259–398). It was probably designed to revive this ancient festival, which had been suppressed by Theodosius. In that case we recover a chronological date (March the 1st, A.D. 409) which has not hitherto been observed.

78. Sozomen (l. ix. c. 6) insinuates that the experiment was actually though unsuccessfully made, but he does not mention the name of Innocent; and Tillemont (Mém. Ecclés. tom. x. p. 645) is determined not to believe that a pope could be guilty of such impious condescension.

79. Pepper was a favourite ingredient of the most expensive Roman cookery, and the best sort commonly sold for fifteen denarii, or ten shillings, the pound. See Pliny, Hist. Natur. xii. 14. It was brought from India; and the same country, the coast of Malabar, still affords the greatest plenty; but the improvement of trade and navigation has multiplied the quantity and reduced the price. See Histoire Politique et Philosophique, etc., tom. i. p. 457.

80. This Gothic chieftain is called, by Jornandes and Isidore, Athaulphus; by Zosimus and Orosius, Ataulphus; and by Olympiodorus, Adaoulphus. I have used the celebrated name of Adolphus, which seems to be authorised by the practice of the Swedes, the sons or brothers of the ancient Goths.

81. The treaty between Alaric and the Romans, etc., is taken from Zosimus, l. v. [c. 41, sqq.] p. 354, 355, 358, 359, 362, 363. The additional circumstances are too few and trifling to require any other quotation.

82. Zosimus, l. v. [c. 48] p. 367, 368, 369.

83. Zosimus, l. v. [c. 45] p. 360, 361, 362. The bishop, by remaining at Ravenna, escaped the impending calamities of the city. Orosius, l. vii. c. 39, p. 573.

84. For the adventures of Olympius and his successors in the ministry, see Zosimus, l. v. [c. 46] p. 363, 365, 366; and Olympiodor. ap. Phot. p. 180, 181 [p. 57, ed. Bekk.].

85. Zosimus (l. v. [c. 46] p. 364) relates this circumstance with visible complacency, and celebrates the character of Gennerid as the last glory of expiring Paganism. Very different were the sentiments of the council of Carthage, who deputed four bishops to the court of Ravenna, to complain of the law which had been just enacted, that all conversions to Christianity should be free and voluntary. See Baronius, Annal. Eccles. A.D. 409, No. 12; A.D. 410, No. 47, 48.

86. Zosimus, l. v. [c. 47–49] p. 367, 368, 369. This custom of swearing by the head, or life, or safety, or genius, of the sovereign, was of the highest antiquity, both in Egypt (Genesis xlii. 15) and Scythia. It was soon transferred, by flattery, to the Cæsars; and Tertullian complains that it was the only oath which the Romans of his time affected to reverence. See an elegant Dissertation of the Abbé Massieu on the Oaths of the Ancients, in the Mém. de l'Académie des Inscriptions, tom. i. p. 208, 209.

87. Zosimus, l. v. [c. 50] p. 368, 369. I have softened the expressions of Alaric, who expatiates in too florid a manner on the history of Rome.

88. See Sueton. in Claud. c. 20; Dion Cassius, l. lx. [c. 11] p. 949, edit. Reimar; and the lively description of Juvenal, Satir. xii. 75, etc. In the sixteenth century, when the remains of this Augustan port were still visible, the antiquarians sketched the plan (see D'Anville, Mém. de l'Académie des Inscriptions, tom. xxx. p. 198), and declared with enthusiasm that all the monarchs of Europe would be unable to execute so great a work (Bergier, Hist. des Grands Chemins des Romains, tom. ii. p. 356).

89. The *Ostia Tiberina* (see Cluver. Italia Antiq. l. iii. p. 870–879), in the plural number, the two mouths of the Tiber, were separated by the Holy Island, an equilateral triangle, whose sides were each of them computed at about two miles. The colony of Ostia was founded immediately beyond the left, or southern, and the *Port* immediately beyond the right, or northern, branch of the river; and the distance between their remains measures something more than two miles on Cingolani's map. In the time of Strabo the sand and mud deposited by the Tiber had choked the harbour of Ostia; the progress of the same cause has added much to the size of the Holy Island, and gradually left both Ostia and the Port at a considerable distance from the shore. The dry channels (fiumi morti) and the large estuaries (stagno di Ponente, di Levante) mark the changes of the river and the efforts of the sea. Consult, for the present state of this dreary and desolate tract, the excellent map of the ecclesiastical state by the mathematicians of Benedict XIV.; an actual survey of the *Agro Romano*, in six sheets, by Cingolani, which contains 113,819 *rubbia* (about 570,000 acres); and the large topographical map of Ameti, in eight sheets.

90. As early as the third (Lardner's Credibility of the Gospel, part ii. vol. iii. p. 89–92), or at least the fourth century (Carol. a Sancto Paulo, Notit. Eccles. p. 47), the Port of Rome was an episcopal city, which was demolished, as it should seem, in the ninth century, by pope Gregory IV., during the incursions of the Arabs. It is now reduced to an inn, a church, and the house or palace of the bishop, who ranks as one of six cardinal bishops of the Roman church. See Eschinard, Descrizione di Roma et dell' Agro Romano, p. 328.

91. For the elevation of Attalus, consult Zosimus, l. vi. [c. 6, 7] p. 377–380; Sozomen, l. ix. c. 8, 9; Olympiodor. ap. Phot. p. 180, 181 [p. 57, ed. Bekk.]; Philostorg. l. xii. c. 3, and Godefroy, Dissertat. p. 470.

92. We may admit the evidence of Sozomen for the Arian baptism, and that of Philostorgius for the Pagan education, of Attalus. The visible joy of Zosimus, and the discontent which he imputes to the Anician family, are very unfavourable to the Christianity of the new emperor.

93. He carried his insolence so far as to declare that he should mutilate Honorius before he sent him into exile. But this assertion of Zosimus [l. vi. c. 8] is destroyed by the more impartial testimony of Olympiodorus, who attributes the ungenerous proposal (which was absolutely rejected by Attalus) to the baseness and perhaps the treachery of Jovius.

94. Procop. de Bell. Vandal. l. i. c. 2 [tom. i. p. 318, ed. Bonn].

95. See the cause and circumstances of the fall of Attalus in Zosimus, l. vi. [c. 9–12], p. 380–383. Sozomen, l. ix. c. 8. Philostorg. l. xii. c. 3. The two acts of indemnity in the Theodosian Code, l. ix. tit. xxxviii. leg. 11, 12, which were published the 12th of February and the 8th of August, A.D. 410, evidently relate to this usurper.

96. In hoc, Alaricus, imperatore, facto, infecto, refecto, ac defecto . . . mimum risit, et ludum spectavit imperii. Orosius, l. vii. c. 42, p. 582.

97. Zosimus, l. vi. [c. 13] p. 384. Sozomen, l. ix. c. 9. Philostorgius. l. xii. c. 3. In this place the text of Zosimus is mutilated, and we have lost the remainder of his sixth and last book, which ended with the sack of Rome. Credulous and partial as he is, we must take our leave of that historian with some regret.

98. Adest Alaricus, trepidam Romam obsidet, turbat, irrumpit. Orosius, l. vii. c. 39, p. 573. He despatches this great event in seven words; but he employs whole pages in celebrating the devotion of the Goths. I have extracted from an improbable story of Procopius the circumstances which had an air of probability. Procop. de Bell. Vandal. l. i. c. 2 [tom. i. p. 315, ed. Bonn]. He supposes that the city was surprised while the senators slept in the afternoon; but Jerom, with more authority and more reason, affirms that it was in the night, nocte Moab capta est; nocte cecidit murus ejus, tom. i. p. 121, ad Principiam [Epist. cxxvii. c. 12, tom. i. p. 953, ed. Vallars.].

99. Orosius (l. vii. c. 39, p. 573–576) applauds the piety of the Christian Goths without seeming to perceive that the greatest part of them were Arian heretics. Jornandes (c. 30, p. 653 [p. 86, ed. Lugd. B. 1597]) and Isidore of Seville (Chron. p. 714, edit. Grot.), who were both attached to the Gothic cause, have repeated and embellished these edifying tales. According to Isidore, Alaric himself was heard to say that he waged war with the Romans, and not with the Apostles. Such was the style of the seventh century; two hundred years before, the fame and merit had been ascribed, not to the Apostles, but to Christ.

100. See Augustine, The City of God, l. i. c. 1–6. He particularly appeals to the examples of Troy, Syracuse, and Tarentum.

101. Jerom (tom. i. p. 121, ad Principiam [Ep. cxxvii. tom. i. p. 953, ed. Vallars.]) has applied to the sack of Rome all the strong expressions of Virgil:—

> Quis cladem illius noctis, quis funera
> fando,
>
> Explicet, etc.

Procopius (l. i. c. 2 [tom. i. p. 316, ed. Bonn]) positively affirms that great numbers were slain by the Goths. Augustine (The City of God, l. i. c. 12, 13) offers Christian comfort for the death of those whose bodies (*multa corpora*) had remained (*in tantâ strage*) unburied. Baronius, from the different writings of the Fathers, has thrown some light on the sack of Rome. Annal. Eccles. A.D. 410, No. 16–44.

102. Sozomen, l. ix. c. 10. Augustine (The City of God, l. i. c. 17) intimates that some virgins or matrons actually killed themselves to escape violation; and though he admires their spirit, he is

obliged, by his theology, to condemn their rash presumption. Perhaps the good bishop of Hippo was too easy in the belief, as well as too rigid in the censure, of this act of female heroism. The twenty maidens (if they ever existed) who threw themselves into the Elbe when Magdeburg was taken by storm, have been multiplied to the number of twelve hundred. See Harte's History of Gustavus Adolphus, vol. i. p. 308.

103. See Augustine, The City of God, l. i. c. 16–18. He treats the subject with remarkable accuracy: and after admitting that there cannot be any crime where there is no consent, he adds, Sed quia non solum quod ad dolorem, verum etiam quod ad libidinem, pertinet, in corpore alieno perpetrari potest; quicquid tale factum fuerit, etsi retentam constantissimo animo pudicitiam non excutit, pudorem tamen incutit, ne credatur factum cum mentis etiam voluntate, quod fieri fortasse sine carnis aliquâ voluptate non potuit. In c. 18 he makes some curious distinctions between moral and physical virginity.

104. Marcella, a Roman lady, equally respectable for her rank, her age, and her piety, was thrown on the ground and cruelly beaten and whipped, cæsam fustibus flagellisque, etc. Jerom, tom. i. p. 121, ad Principiam [Ep. cxxvii. c. 13, tom. i. p. 953, ed. Vallars]. See Augustine, The City of God, l. i. c. 10. The modern Sacco di Roma, p. 108, gives an idea of the various methods of torturing prisoners for gold.

105. The historian Sallust, who usefully practised the vices which he has so eloquently censured, employed the plunder of Numidia to adorn his palace and gardens on the Quirinal hill. The spot where the house stood is now marked by the church of St. Susanna, separated only by a street from the baths of Diocletian, and not far distant from the Salarian gate. See Nardini, Roma Antica, p. 192, 193, and the great Plan of Modern Rome, by Nolli.

106. The expressions of Procopius are distinct and moderate (de Bell. Vandal. l. i. c. 2 [tom. i. p. 316, ed. Bonn]). The chronicle of Marcellinus speaks too strongly, partem urbis Romæ cremavit; and the words of Philostorgius ἐν ἐρειπίοις δὲ τῆς πόλεως κειμένης, (l. xii. c. 3) convey a false and exaggerated idea. Bargæus has composed a particular dissertation (see tom. iv. Antiquit. Rom. Græv.) to prove that the edifices of Rome were not subverted by the Goths and Vandals.

107. Orosius, l. ii. c. 19, p. 143. He speaks as if he disapproved all statues; vel Deum vel hominem mentiuntur. They consisted of the kings of Alba and Rome from Æneas, the Romans illustrious either in arms or arts, and the deified Cæsars. The expression which he uses of Forum is somewhat ambiguous, since there existed five principal Fora; but as they were all contiguous and adjacent, in the plain which is surrounded by the Capitoline, the Quirinal, the Esquiline, and the Palatine hills, they might fairly be considered as one. See the

Roma Antiqua of Donatus, p. 162–201, and the Roma Antica of Nardini, p. 212–273. The former is more useful for the ancient descriptions, the latter for the actual topography.

108. Orosius (l. ii. c. 19, p. 142) compares the cruelty of the Gauls and the clemency of the Goths. Ibi vix quemquam inventum senatorem, qui vel absens evaserit; hic vix quemquam requiri, qui forte ut latens perierit. But there is an air of rhetoric, and perhaps of falsehood, in this antithesis; and Socrates (l. vii. c. 10) affirms, perhaps by an opposite exaggeration, that many senators were put to death with various and exquisite tortures.

109. Multi . . . Christiani captivi ducti sunt. Augustine, The City of God, l. i. c. 14; and the Christians experienced no peculiar hardships.

110. See Heineccius, Antiquitat. Juris Roman. tom. i. p. 96.

111. Appendix Cod. Theodos. xvi. in Sirmond. Opera, tom. i. p. 735. This edict was published on the 11th of December, A.D. 408, and is more reasonable than properly belonged to the ministers of Honorius.

112. Eminus Igilii sylvosa cacumina miror;
    Quem fraudare nefas laudis honore suæ.
Hæc proprios nuper tutata est insula saltus;
    Sive loci ingenio, seu domini genio.
Gurgite cum modico victricibus obstitit armis,
    Tanquam longinquo dissociata mari.
Hæc multos lacerâ suscepit ab urbe fugatos,
    Hîc fessis posito certa timore salus.
Plurima terreno populaverat æquora bello,
    Contra naturam classe timendus eques:
Unum, mira fides, vario discrimine portum!
    Tam prope Romanis, tam procul esse Getis.
           Rutilius, in Itinerar. l. i. 325.
The island is now called Giglio. See Cluver. Ital. Antiq. l. ii. p. 502.

113. As the adventures of Proba and her family are connected with the life of St. Augustin, they are diligently illustrated by Tillemont, Mém. Eclés. tom. xiii. p. 620–635. Some time after their arrival in Africa, Demetrias took the veil and made a vow of virginity; an event which was considered as of the highest importance to Rome and to the world. All the Saints wrote congratulatory letters to her; that of Jerom is still extant (tom. i. p. 62–73, ad Demetriad. de servandâ Virginitat. [Epist. cxxx. tom. i. p. 969, ed. Vallars.]), and contains a mixture of absurd reasoning, spirited declamation, and curious facts, some of which relate to the siege and sack of Rome.

114. See the pathetic complaint of Jerom (tom. v. p. 400) in his preface to the second book of his Commentaries on the Prophet Ezekiel.

115. Orosius, though with some theological partiality, states this comparison, l. ii. c. 19, p. 142, l. vii. c. 39, p. 575. But, in the history of the taking of Rome by the Gauls, everything is uncertain, and perhaps fabulous. See Beaufort sur l'Incertitude, etc., de l'Histoire Romaine, p. 356; and Melot, in the Mém. de l'Académie des Inscript. tom. xv. p. 1–21.

116. The reader who wishes to inform himself of the circumstances of this famous event may peruse an admirable narrative in Dr. Robertson's History of Charles V. vol. ii. p. 283; or consult the Annali d'Italia of the learned Muratori, tom. xiv. p. 230–244, octavo edition. If he is desirous of examining the originals, he may have recourse to the eighteenth book of the great, but unfinished, history of Guicciardini. But the account which most truly deserves the name of authentic and original is a little book, entitled *Il Sacco di Roma*, composed, within less than a month after the assault of the city, by the *brother* of the historian Guicciardini, who appears to have been an able magistrate and a dispassionate writer.

117. The furious spirit of Luther, the effect of temper and enthusiasm, has been forcibly attacked (Bossuet, Hist. des Variations des Eglises Protestantes, livre i. p. 20–36) and feebly defended (Seckendorf, Comment. de Lutheranismo, especially l. i. No. 78, p. 120, and l. iii. No. 122, p. 556).

118. Marcellinus, in Chron. Orosius (l. vii. c. 39, p. 575), asserts that he left Rome on the *third* day; but this difference is easily reconciled by the successive motions of great bodies of troops.

119. Socrates (l. vii. c. 10) pretends, without any colour of truth or reason, that Alaric fled on the report that the armies of the Eastern empire were in full march to attack him.

120. Ausonius de Claris Urbibus, p. 233, edit. Toll. The luxury of Capua had formerly surpassed that of Sybaris itself. See Athenæus Deipnosophist. l. xii. [c. 36] p. 528, edit. Casaubon.

121. Forty-eight years before the foundation of Rome (about 800 before the Christian era) the Tuscans built Capua and Nola, at the distance of twenty-three miles from each other: but the latter of the two cities never emerged from a state of mediocrity.

122. Tillemont (Mém. Ecclés. tom. xiv. p. 1–146) has compiled, with his usual diligence, all that relates to the life and writings of Paulinus, whose retreat is celebrated by his own pen and by the praises of St. Ambrose, St. Jerom, St. Augustin, Sulpicius Severus, etc., his Christian friends and contemporaries.

123. See the affectionate letters of Ausonius (Epist. xix.–xxv. p. 650–698, edit. Toll.) to his colleague, his friend, and his disciple, Paulinus. The religion of Ausonius is still a problem (see Mém. de l'Académie des Inscriptions, tom. xv. p. 123–138). I believe that it was such in his own time, and consequently that in his heart he was a Pagan.

124. The humble Paulinus once presumed to say that he believed St. Felix *did* love him; at least, as a master loves his little dog.

125. See Jornandes, de Reb. Get. c. 30, p. 653. Philostorgius, l. xii. c. 3. Augustine, The City of God, l. i. c. 10. Baronius, Annal. Eccles. A.D. 410, No. 45, 46.

126. The *platanus*, or plane-tree, was a favourite of the ancients, by whom it was propagated, for the sake of shade, from the East to Gaul. Pliny, Hist. Natur. xii. 3, 4, 5. He mentions several of an enormous size; one in the Imperial villa at Velitræ, which Caligula called his nest, as the branches were capable of holding a large table, the proper attendants, and the emperor himself, whom Pliny quaintly styles *pars umbræ*; an expression which might, with equal reason, be applied to Alaric.

127. The prostrate South to the destroyer yields
Her boasted titles and her golden fields;
With grim delight the brood of winter view
A brighter day, and skies of azure hue;
Scent the new fragrance of the opening rose,
And quaff the pendent vintage as it grows.

See Gray's Poems, published by Mr. Mason, p. 197. Instead of compiling tables of chronology and natural history, why did not Mr. Gray apply the powers of his genius to finish the philosophic poem of which he has left such an exquisite specimen?

128. For the perfect description of the Straits of Messina, Scylla, Charybdis, etc., see Cluverius (Ital. Antiq. l. iv. p. 1293, and Silicia Antiq. l. i. p. 60–76), who had diligently studied the ancients and surveyed with a curious eye the actual face of the country.

129. Jornandes, de Reb. Get. c. 30, p. 654 [p. 87, ed. Lugd. B. 1597].

130. Orosius, l. vii. c. 43, p. 584, 585. He was sent by St. Augustin, in the year 415, from Africa to Palestine, to visit St. Jerom and to consult with him on the subject of Pelagian controversy.

131. Jornandes supposes, without much probability, that Adolphus visited and plundered Rome a second time (more locustarum erasit). Yet he agrees with Orosius in supposing that a treaty of peace was concluded between the Gothic prince and Honorius. See Oros. l. vii. c. 43, p. 584, 585. Jornandes, de Reb. Geticis, c. 31, p. 654, 655 [p. 88, ed. Lugd. B.].

132. The retreat of the Goths from Italy and their first transactions in Gaul are dark and doubtful. I have derived much assistance from Mascou (Hist. of the Ancient Germans, l. viii. c. 29, 35, 36, 37), who has illustrated and connected the broken chronicles and fragments of the times.

133. See an account of Placidia in Ducange, Fam. Byzant. p. 72; and Tillemont, Hist. des Empereurs, tom. v. p. 260, 386, etc., tom. vi. p. 240.

134. Zosim. l. v. [c. 38] p. 350.

135. Zosim. l. vi. [c. 12] p. 383. Orosius (l vii.

c. 40, p. 567) and the Chronicles of Marcellinus and Idatius seem to suppose that the Goths did not carry away Placidia till after the last siege of Rome.

136. See the pictures of Adolphus and Placidia, and the account of their marriage, in Jornandes, de Reb. Geticis, c. 31, p. 654, 655 [p. 88, ed. Lugd. B.] With regard to the place where the nuptials were stipulated, or consummated, or celebrated, the MSS. of Jornandes vary between two neighbouring cities, Forli and Imola (Forum Livii and Forum Cornelii). It is fair and easy to reconcile the Gothic historian with Olympiodorus (see Mascou, l. viii. c. 36): but Tillemont grows peevish, and swears that it is not worth while to try to conciliate Jornandes with any good authors.

137. The Visigoths (the subjects of Adolphus) restrained, by subsequent laws, the prodigality of conjugal love. It was illegal for a husband to make any gift or settlement for the benefit of his wife during the first year of their marriage; and his liberality could not at any time exceed the tenth part of his property. The Lombards were somewhat more indulgent: they allowed the *morgingcap* immediately after the wedding night; and this famous gift, the reward of virginity, might equal the fourth part of the husband's substance. Some cautious maidens, indeed, were wise enough to stipulate beforehand a present which they were too sure of not deserving. See Montesquieu, The Spirit of Laws, l. xix. c. 25. Muratori, delle Antichità Italiane, tom. i. Dissertazione xx. p. 243.

138. We owe the curious detail of this nuptial feast to the historian Olympiodorus, ap. Photium, p. 185, 188 [p. 59, ed. Bekk.].

139. See in the great collection of the Historians of France by Dom Bouquet, tom. ii. Greg. Turonens. l. iii. c. 10, p. 191. Gesta Regum Francorum, c. 23, p. 557. The anonymous writer, with an ignorance worthy of his times, supposes that these instruments of Christian worship had belonged to the temple of Solomon. If he has any meaning, it must be that they were found in the sack of Rome.

140. Consult the following original testimonies in the Historians of France, tom. ii. Fredegarii Scholastici Chron. c. 73, p. 441. Fredegar. Fragment. iii. p. 463. Gesta Regis Dagobert. c. 29, p. 587. The accession of Sisenand to the throne of Spain happened A.D. 631. The 200,000 pieces of gold were appropriated by Dagobert to the foundation of the church of St. Denys.

141. The president Goguet (Oirgine des Loix, etc., tom. ii. p. 239) is of opinion that the stupendous pieces of emerald, the statues and columns which antiquity has placed in Egypt, at Gades, at Constantinople, were in reality artificial compositions of coloured glass. The famous emerald dish which is shown at Genoa is supposed to countenance the suspicion.

142. Elmacin. Hist. Saracenica, l. i. p. 85; Roderic. Tolet. Hist. Arab. c. 9. Cardonne, Hist. de l'Afrique et de l'Espagne sous les Arabes, tom. i. p. 83. It was called the Table of Solomon, according to the custom of the Orientals, who ascribe to that prince every ancient work of knowledge or magnificence.

143. His three laws are inserted in the Theodosian Code, l. xi. tit. xxviii. leg. 7; l. xiii. tit. xi. leg. 12; l. xv. tit. xiv. leg. 14. The expressions of the last are very remarkable, since they contain not only a pardon, but an apology.

144. Olympiodorus ap. Phot. p. 188 [p. 59, ed. Bekk.]. Philostorgius (l. xii. c. 5) observes, that when Honorius made his triumphal entry he encouraged the Romans, with his hand and voice (χειρὶ καὶ γλώττη), to rebuild their city; and the Chronicle of Prosper commends Heraclian, qui in Romanæ urbis reparationem strenuum exhibuerat ministerium.

145. The date of the voyage of Claudius Rutilius Numatianus is clogged with some difficulties; but Scaliger has deduced from astronomical characters that he left Rome the 14th of September, and embarked at Porto the 9th of October, A.D. 416. See Tillemont, Hist. des Empereurs, tom. v. p. 820. In this poetical Itinerary, Rutilius (l. i. 115, etc.) addresses Rome in a high strain of congratulation:

Erige crinales lauros, seniumque sacrati
Verticis in virides, Roma, recinge comas, etc.

146. Orosius composed his history in Africa only two years after the event; yet his authority seems to be overbalanced by the improbability of the fact. The Chronicle of Marcellinus gives Heraclian 700 ships and 3000 men: the latter of these numbers is ridiculously corrupt; but the former would please me very much.

147. The Chronicle of Idatius affirms, without the least appearance of truth, that he advanced as far as Otriculum, in Umbria, where he was overthrown in a great battle, with the loss of fifty thousand men.

148. See Cod. Theod. l. xv. tit. xiv. leg. 13. The legal acts performed in his name, even the manumission of slaves, were declared invalid till they had been formally repeated.

149. I have disdained to mention a very foolish, and probably a false, report (Procop. de Bell. Vandal. l. i. c. 2 [tom. i. p. 316, ed. Bonn]), that Honorius was alarmed by the *loss* of Rome till he understood that it was not a favourite chicken of that name, but *only* the capital of the world, which had been lost. Yet even this story is some evidence of the public opinion.

150. The materials for the lives of all these tyrants are taken from six contemporary historians, two Latins and four Greeks: Orosius, l. vii. c. 42, p. 581, 582, 583; Renatus Profuturus Frigeridus, apud Gregor. Turon. l. ii. c. 9, in the Historians of France, tom. ii. p. 165, 166; Zosimus, l. vi. [c. 2] p. 370, 371; Olympiodorus, apud Phot. p. 180, 181, 184, 185 [p. 57 *sqq.*, ed. Bekk.]; Sozomen, l. ix. c. 12, 13, 14, 15; and Philostorgius, l. xii. c. 5, 6, with Godefroy's Dissertations, p. 477-481; besides the four Chronicles of Prosper Tyro, Prosper of Aquitain, Idatius, and Marcellinus.

151. The praises which Sozomen has bestowed on this act of despair appear strange and scandalous in the mouth of an ecclesiastical historian. He observes (p. 379 [ed. Cantab. 1720]) that the wife of Gerontius was a *Christian;* and that her death was worthy of her religion, and of immortal fame.

152. Εἶδος ἄξιον τυραννίδος, is the expression of Olympiodorus, which he seems to have borrowed from *Æolus,* a tragedy of Euripides, of which some fragments only are now extant (Euripid. Barnes, tom. ii. p. 443, ver. 38). This allusion may prove that the ancient tragic poets were still familiar to the Greeks of the fifth century.

153. Sidonius Apollinaris (l. v. Epist. 9, p. 139, and Not. Sirmond. p. 58), after stigmatising the *inconstancy* of Constantine, the *facility* of Jovinus, the *perfidy* of Gerontius, continues to observe that *all* the vices of these tyrants were united in the person of Dardanus. Yet the præfect supported a respectable character in the world, and even in the church; held a devout correspondence with St. Augustin and St. Jerom; and was complimented by the latter (tom. iii. p. 66) with the epithets of Christianorum Nobilissime and Nobilium Christianissime.

154. The expression may be understood almost literally: Olympiodorus says, μόλις σάκκοις ἐζώγρησαν. Σάκκος (or σάκος) may signify a sack or a loose garment; and this method of entangling and catching an enemy, laciniis contortis, was much practised by the Huns (Ammian. xxxi. 2). Il fut pris vif avec des filets, is the translation of Tillemont, Hist. des Empereurs, tom. v. p. 608.

155. Without recurring to the more ancient writers, I shall quote three respectable testimonies which belong to the fourth and seventh centuries: the Expositio totius Mundi (p. 16, in the third volume of Hudson's Minor Geographers), Ausonius (de Claris Urbibus, p. 242, edit. Toll.), and Isidore of Seville (Præfat. ad Chron. ap Grotium, Hist. Goth. p. 707). Many particulars relative to the fertility and trade of Spain may be found in Nonnius, Hispania, Illustrata; and in Huet, Hist. du Commerce des Anciens, c. 40, p. 228–234.

156. The date is accurately fixed in the Fasti and the Chronicle of Idatius. Orosius (l. vii. c. 40, p. 578) imputes the loss of Spain to the treachery of the Honorians; while Sozomen (l. ix. c. 12) accuses only their negligence.

157. Idatius wishes to apply the prophecies of Daniel to these national calamities, and is therefore obliged to accommodate the circumstances of the event to the terms of the prediction.

158. Mariana de Rebus Hispanicis, l. v. c. 1, tom. i. p. 148. Hag. Comit. 1733. He had read in Orosius (l. vii. c. 41, p. 579) that the barbarians had turned their swords into ploughshares; and that many of the provincials preferred inter Barbaros pauperem libertatem, quam inter Romanos tributariam solicitudinem, sustinere.

159. This mixture of force and persuasion may be fairly inferred from comparing Orosius and Jornandes, the Roman and the Gothic historian.

160. According to the system of Jornandes (c. 33, p. 659 [ed. Grot.]), the true hereditary right to the Gothic sceptre was vested in the *Amali;* but those princes, who were the vassals of the Huns, commanded the tribes of the Ostrogoths in some distant parts of Germany or Scythia.

161. The murder is related by Olympiodorus; but the number of the children is taken from an epitaph of suspected authority.

162. The death of Adolphus was celebrated at Constantinople with illuminations and Circensian games. (See Chron. Alexandrin.) It may seem doubtful whether the Greeks were actuated on this occasion by their hatred of the barbarians or of the Latins.

163. Quòd *Tartessiacis* avus hujus Vallia terris

　Vandalicas turmas, et juncti Martis Alanos

　Stravit, et occiduam texêre cadavera *Calpen.*

　　　Sidon. Appollinar. in Panegyr.
　　　　　Anthem. 363, p. 300,
　　　　　　edit. Sirmond.

164. This supply was very acceptable: the Goths were insulted by the Vandals of Spain with the epithet of *Truli,* because in their extreme distress they had given a piece of gold for a *trula,* or about half a pound of flour. Olympiod. apud Phot. p. 189 [p. 60, ed. Bekk.].

165. Orosius inserts a copy of these pretended letters. Tu cum omnibus pacem habe, omniumque obsides accipe; nos nobis confligimus, nobis perimus, tibi vincimus; immortalis vero quæstus erit Reipublicæ tuæ, si utrique pereamus [p. 586]. The idea is just; but I cannot persuade myself that it was entertained or expressed by the barbarians.

166. Romam triumphans ingreditur is the formal expression of Prosper's Chronicle. The facts which relate to the death of Adolphus and the exploits of Wallia are related from Olympiodorus (ap Phot. p. 188 [p. 59, 60, ed. Bekk.]), Orosius (l. vii. c. 43, p. 584–587), Jornandes (de Rebus Geticis, c. 31, 32), and the Chronicles of Idatius and Isidore.

167. Ausonius (de Claris Urbibus, p. 257–262 [No. 14]) celebrates Bourdeaux with the partial affection of a native. See in Salvian (de Gubern. Dei, p. 228, Paris, 1608) a florid description of the provinces of Aquitain and Novempopulania.

168. Orosius (l. vii. c. 32, p. 550) commends the mildness and modesty of these Burgundians, who treated their subjects of Gaul as their Christian brethren. Mascou has illustrated the origin of their kingdom in the four first annotations at the end of his laborious History of the Ancient Germans, vol. ii. p. 555–572 of the English translation.

169. See Mascou, l. viii. c. 43, 44, 45. Except in a short and suspicious line of the Chronicle of Prosper (in tom. i. p. 638), the name of Pharamond is never mentioned before the seventh century.

The author of the Gesta Francorum (in tom. ii. p. 543) suggests, probably enough, that the choice of Pharamond, or at least of a king, was recommended to the Franks by his father Marcomir, who was an exile in Tuscany.

170. O Lycida, vivi pervenimus: advena nostri
  (Quod nunquam veriti sumus) ut possessor agelli
  Diceret: Hæc mea sunt; veteres migrate coloni.
  Nunc victi tristes, etc.

See the whole of the ninth eclogue, with the useful Commentary of Servius. Fifteen miles of the Mantuan territory were assigned to the veterans, with a reservation in favour of the inhabitants of three miles round the city. Even in this favour they were cheated by Alfenus Varus, a famous lawyer and one of the commissioners, who measured eight hundred paces of water and morass.

171. See the remarkable passage of the Eucharisticon of Paulinus, 575, apud Mascou, l. viii. c. 42.

172. This important truth is established by the accuracy of Tillemont (Hist. des Emp. tom. v. p. 641) and by the ingenuity of the Abbé Dubos (Hist. de l'Etablissement de la Monarchie Françoise dans les Gaules, tom. i. p. 259).

173. Zosimus (l. vi. [c. 5] 376 [c. 10], 383) relates in a few words the revolt of Britain and Armorica. Our antiquarians, even the great Camden himself, have been betrayed into many gross errors by their imperfect knowledge of the history of the continent.

174. The limits of Armorica are defined by two national geographers, Messieurs de Valois and d'Anville, in their Notitias of Ancient Gaul. The word had been used in a more extensive, and was afterwards contracted to a much narrower, signification.

175. Gens inter geminos notissima clauditur amnes,
  Armoricana prius veteri cognomine dicta.
  Torva, ferox, ventosa, procax, incauta, rebellis;
  Inconstans, disparque sibi novitatis amore;
  Prodiga verborum, sed non et prodiga facti.

Erricus, Monach. in Vit. St. Germani, l. v. apud Vales. Notit. Galliarum, p. 43. Valesius alleges several testimonies to confirm this character; to which I shall add the evidence of the presbyter Constantine (A.D. 488), who, in the Life of St. Germain, calls the Armorican rebels mobilem et indisciplinatum populum. See the Historians of France, tom. i. p. 643.

176. I thought it necessary to enter my protest against this part of the system of the Abbé Dubos, which Montesquieu has so vigorously opposed. See The Spirit of Laws, l. xxx. c. 24.

177. Βρεταννίαν μέντοι 'Ρωμαῖοι ἀνασώσασθαι οὐκέτι ἔσχον, are the words of Procopius (de Bell. Vandal. l. i. c. 2, p. 181, Louvre edition [tom. i. p. 318, ed. Bonn]), in a very important passage which has been too much neglected. Even Bede (Hist. Gent. Anglican. l. i. c. 12, p' 50, edit. Smith) acknowledges that the Romans finally left Britain in the reign of Honorius. Yet our modern historians and antiquarians extend the term of their dominion; and there are some who allow only the interval of a few months between their departure and the arrival of the Saxons.

178. Bede has not forgot the occasional aid of the legions against the Scots and Picts; and more authentic proof will hereafter be produced that the independent Britons raised 12,000 men for the service of the emperor Anthemius in Gaul.

179. I owe it to myself and to historic truth to declare that some *circumstances* in this paragraph are founded only on conjecture and analogy. The stubbornness of our language has sometimes forced me to deviate from the *conditional* into the *indicative* mood.

180. Πρὸς τὰς ἐν Βρεταννίᾳ πόλεις. Zosimus, l. vi. [c. 10] p. 383.

181. Two cities of Britain were *municipia*, nine *colonies*, ten *Latii jure donatæ*, twelve *stipendiariæ* of eminent note. This detail is taken from Richard of Cirencester, de Sitû Britanniæ, p. 36; and though it may not seem probable that he wrote from the MSS. of a Roman general, he shows a genuine knowledge of antiquity, very extraordinary for a monk of the fourteenth century.

182. See Maffei, Verona Illustrata, part. i. l. v. p. 83–106.

183. Leges restituit, libertatemque reducit,
  Et servos famulis non sinit esse suis.
    Itinerar. Rutil. l. i. 215.

184. An inscription (apud Sirmond, Not. ad Sidon. Appollinar. p. 59) describes a castle, cum muris et portis, tuitioni omnium, erected by Dardanus on his own estate near Sisteron in the second Narbonnese, and named by him Theopolis.

185. The establishment of their power would have been easy indeed if we could adopt the impracticable scheme of a lively and learned antiquarian, who supposes that the British monarchs of the several tribes continued to reign, though with subordinate jurisdiction, from the time of Claudius to that of Honorius. See Whitaker's History of Manchester, vol. i. p. 247–257.

186. 'Αλλ' οὖσα ὑπὸ τυράννοις ἀπ' αὐτοῦ ἔμενε. Procopius, de Bell. Vandal. l. i. c. 2, p. 181 [ed. Paris; tom. i. p. 318, ed. Bonn]. Britannia fertilis provincia tyrannorum, was the expression of Jerom in the year 415 (tom. ii. p. 255, ad Ctesiphont. [Epist. cxxxiii. c. 9, tom. i. p. 1032, ed. Vallars.]). By the pilgrims who resorted every year to the Holy Land, the monk of Bethlem received the earliest and most accurate intelligence.

187. See Bingham's Eccles. Antiquities, vol. i. l. ix. c. 6, p. 394.

188. It is reported of *three* British bishops who assisted at the council of Rimini, A.D. 359, tam

pauperes fuisse ut nihil [proprium] haberent. Sulpicius Severus, Hist. Sacra, l. ii. p. 420. Some of their brethren, however, were in better circumstances.

189. Consult Usher, de Antiq. Eccles. Britannicar. c. 8–12.

190. See the correct text of this edict, as published by Sirmond (Not. ad Sidon. Apollin. p. 147). Hincmar of Rheims, who assigns a place to the *bishops*, had probably seen (in the ninth century) a more perfect copy. Dubos, Hist. Critique de la Monarchie Françoise, tom. i. p. 241–255.

191. It is evident from the *Notitia* that the seven provinces were the Viennensis, the maritime Alps, the first and second Narbonnese, Novempopulania, and the first and second Aquitain. In the room of the first Aquitain, the Abbé Dubos, on the authority of Hincmar, desires to introduce the first Lugdunensis or Lyonnese.

Chapter XXXII

1. Father Montfaucon, who, by the command of his Benedictine superiors, was compelled (see Longueruana, tom. i. p. 205) to execute the laborious edition of St. Chrysostom, in thirteen volumes in folio (Paris, 1738), amused himself with extracting from that immense collection of morals some curious *antiquities*, which illustrate the manners of the Theodosian age (see Chrysostom, Opera, tom. xiii. p. 192–196), and his French Dissertation, in the Mémoires de l'Acad. des Inscriptions, tom. xiii. p. 474–490.

2. According to the loose reckoning, that a ship could sail with a fair wind 1000 stadia, or 125 miles, in the revolution of a day and night, Diodorus Siculus computes ten days from the Palus Mæotis to Rhodes, and four days from Rhodes to Alexandria. The navigation of the Nile, from Alexandria to Syene, under the tropic of Cancer, required, as it was against the stream, ten days more. Diodor. Sicul. tom. i. l. iii. [c. 33] p. 200, edit. Wesseling. He might, without much impropriety, measure the extreme heat from the verge of the torrid zone; but he speaks of the Mæotis, in the 47th degree of northern latitude, as if it lay within the polar circle.

3. Barthius, who adored his author with the blind superstition of a commentator, gives the preference to the two books which Claudian composed against Eutropius, above all his other productions (Baillet, Jugemens des Savans, tom. iv. p. 227). They are indeed a very elegant and spirited satire, and would be more valuable in an historical light, if the invective were less vague and more temperate.

4. After lamenting the progress of the eunuchs in the Roman palace, and defining their proper functions, Claudian adds,

————A fronte recedant
    Imperii.

                                        In Eutrop. i. 422.
Yet it does not appear that the eunuch had assumed any of the efficient offices of the empire, and he is styled only Præpositus sacri cubiculi in the edict of his banishment. See Cod. Theod. l. ix. tit. xl. leg. 17.

5. Jamque oblita sui, nec sobria divitiis mens
    In miseras leges hominumque negoti a ludit:

Judicat eunuchus . . .
    Arma etiam violare parat. . . .
Claudian (in Eutrop. i. 229–270), with that mixture of indignation and humour which always pleases in a satiric poet, describes the insolent folly of the eunuch, the disgrace of the empire, and the joy of the Goths.

———— Gaudet, cum viderit, hostis,
    Et sentit jam deesse viros.

6. The poet's lively description of his deformity (i. 110–125) is confirmed by the authentic testimony of Chrysostom (tom. iii. [in Eutrop. i. c. 3] p. 384, edit. Montfaucon), who observes that, when the paint was washed away, the face of Eutropius appeared more ugly and wrinkled than that of an old woman. Claudian remarks (i. 469), and the remark must have been founded on experience, that there was scarcely any interval between the youth and the decrepit age of a eunuch.

7. Eutropius appears to have been a native of Armenia or Assyria. His three services, which Claudian more particularly describes, were these: —1. He spent many years as the catamite of Ptolemy, a groom or soldier of the Imperial stables. 2. Ptolemy gave him to the old general Arintheus, for whom he very skilfully exercised the profession of a pimp. 3. He was given, on her marriage, to the daughter of Arintheus; and the future consul was employed to comb her hair, to present the silver ewer, to wash and to fan his mistress in hot weather. See l. i. 31–137.

8. Claudian (l. i. in Eutrop. 1–22), after enumerating the various prodigies of monstrous births, speaking animals, showers of blood or stones, double suns, etc., adds, with some exaggeration,

Omnia cesserunt eunucho consule monstra.
The first book concludes with a noble speech of the goddess of Rome to her favourite Honorius, deprecating the *new* ignominy to which she was exposed.

9. Fl. Mallius Theodorus, whose civil honours and philosophical works have been celebrated by Claudian in a very elegant panegyric.

10. Μεθύων δὲ ἤδη τῷ πλούτῳ, drunk with riches, is the forcible expression of Zosimus (l. v. [c. 10] p. 301); and the avarice of Eutropius is equally execrated in the Lexicon of Suidas and the Chronicle

of Marcellinus. Chrysostom had often admonished the favourite of the vanity and danger of immoderate wealth, tom. iii. p. 381 [in Eutrop. i. c. 1].

11.   ——certantum sæpe duorum

      Diversum suspendit onus: cum pondere judex

      Vergit, et in geminas nutat provincia lances.

Claudian (i. 192–209) so curiously distinguishes the circumstances of the sale that they all seem to allude to particular anecdotes.

12. Claudian (in Eutrop. i. 154–170) mentions the *guilt* and exile of Abundantius; nor could he fail to quote the example of the artist who made the first trial of the brazen bull which he presented to Phalaris. See Zosimus, l. v. [c. 10] p. 302; Jerom, tom. i. p. 26 [Ep. lx. c. 16, tom. i. p. 342, ed. Vallars.]. The difference of place is easily reconciled; but the decisive authority of Asterius of Amasia (Orat. iv. p. 76, apud Tillemont, Hist. des Empereurs, tom. v. p. 435) must turn the scale in favour of Pityus.

13. Suidas (most probably from the history of Eunapius) has given a very unfavourable picture of Timasius. The account of his accuser, the judges, trial, etc., is perfectly agreeable to the practice of ancient and modern courts. (See Zosimus, l. v. [c. 9] p. 298, 299, 300.) I am almost tempted to quote the romance of a great master (Fielding's Works, vol. iv. p. 49, etc., 8vo. edit.), which may be considered as the history of human nature.

14. The great Oasis was one of the spots in the sands of Libya, watered with springs, and capable of producing wheat, barley, and palm-trees. It was about three days' journey from north to south, about half a day in breadth, and at the distance of about five days' march to the west of Abydus, on the Nile. See D'Anville, Description de l'Egypte, p. 186, 187, 188. The barren desert which encompasses Oasis (Zosimus l. v. [c. 9] p. 300) has suggested the idea of comparative fertility, and even the epithet of the *happy island* (Herodot. iii. 26).

15. The line of Claudian, in Eutrop. l. i. 180,

      Marmaricus claris violatur cædibus Hammon,

evidently alludes to *his* persuasion of the death of Timasius.

16. Sozomen, l. viii. c. 7. He speaks from report, ὡς τινος ἐπυθόμην.

17. Zosimus, l. v. [c. 9] p. 300. Yet he seems to suspect that this rumour was spread by the friends of Eutropius.

18. See the Theodosian Code, l. ix. tit. 14, ad legem Corneliam de Sicariis, leg. 3, and the Code of Justinian, l. ix. tit. viii. ad legem Juliam de Majestate, leg. 5. The alteration of the *title*, from murder to treason, was an improvement of the subtle Tribonian. Godefroy, in a formal dissertation, which he has inserted in his Commentary, illustrates this law of Arcadius, and explains all the difficult passages which had been perverted by the

juriconsults of the darker ages. See tom. iii. p. 88–111.

19. Bartolus understands a simple and naked consciousness, without any sign of approbation or concurrence. For this opinion, says Baldus, he is now roasting in hell. For my own part, continues the discreet Heineccius (Element. Jur. Civil. l. iv. p. 411), I must approve the theory of Bartolus; but in practise I should incline to the sentiment of Baldus. Yet Bartolus was gravely quoted by the lawyers of Cardinal Richelieu; and Eutropius was indirectly guilty of the murder of the virtuous De Thou.

20. Godefroy, tom. iii. p. 89. It is, however, suspected that this law, so repugnant to the maxims of Germanic freedom, has been surreptitiously added to the golden bull.

21. A copious and circumstantial narrative (which he might have reserved for more important events) is bestowed by Zosimus (l. v. [c. 10, *sqq.*] p. 304–312) on the revolt of Tribigild and Gainas. See likewise Socrates, l. vi. c. 6, and Sozomen, l. viii. c. 4. The second book of Claudian against Eutropius is a fine though imperfect piece of history.

22. Claudian (in Eutrop. l. ii. 237–250) very accurately observes that the ancient name and nation of the Phrygians extended very far on every side, till their limits were contracted by the colonies of the Bithynians of Thrace, of the Greeks, and at last of the Gauls. His description (ii. 257–272) of the fertility of Phrygia, and of the four rivers that produced gold, is just and picturesque.

23. Xenophon, Anabasis, l. i. [c. 2, § 8] p. 11, 12, edit. Hutchinson; Strabo, l. xii. p. 865, edit. Amstel. [p. 577, ed. Casaub.]; Q. Curt. l. iii. c. 1. Claudian compares the junction of the Marsyas and Mæander to that of the Saone and the Rhône, with this difference, however, that the smaller of the Phrygian rivers is not accelerated but retarded by the larger.

24. Selgæ, a colony of the Lacedæmonians, had formerly numbered twenty thousand citizens; but in the age of Zosimus it was reduced to a πολίχνη or small town. See Cellarius, Geograph. Antiq. tom. ii. p. 117.

25. The council of Eutropius, in Claudian, may be compared to that of Domitian in the fourth Satire of Juvenal. The principal members of the former were, juvenes protervi lascivique senes; one of them had been a cook, a second a woolcomber. The language of their original profession exposes their assumed dignity; and their trifling conversation about tragedies, dancers, etc., is made still more ridiculous by the importance of the debate.

26. Claudian (l. ii. 376–461) has branded him with infamy; and Zosimus, in more temperate language, confirms his reproaches. L. v. [c. 14] p. 305.

27. The *conspiracy* of Gainas and Tribigild, which is attested by the Greek historian, had not reached the ears of Claudian, who attributes the revolt of the Ostrogoth to his own *martial spirit* and the advice of his wife.

28. This anecdote, which Philostorgius alone has preserved (l. xi. c. 6, and Gothofred, Dissertat. p. 451-456), is curious and important, since it connects the revolt of the Goths with the secret intrigues of the palace.

29. See the Homily [i. in Eutrop.] of Chrysostom, tom. iii. p. 381-386, of which the exordium is particularly beautiful; Socrates, l. vi. c. 5; Sozomen, l. viii. c. 7. Montfaucon (in his Life of Chrysostom, tom. xiii. p. 135) too hastily supposes that Tribigild was *actually* in Constantinople, and that he commanded the soldiers who were ordered to seize Eutropius. Even Claudian, a Pagan poet (Præfat. ad. l. ii. in Eutrop. 27), has mentioned the flight of the eunuch to the sanctuary.

Suppliciterque pias humilis prostratus ad aras
Mitigat iratas voce tremente nurus.

30. Chrysostom, in another homily [in Eutr. ii. c. 1] (tom. iii. p. 386), affects to declare that Eutropius would not have been taken, had he not deserted the church. Zosimus (l. v. [c. 18] p. 313), on the contrary, pretends that his enemies forced him (ἐξαρπάσαντες αὐτὸν) from the sanctuary. Yet the promise is an evidence of some treaty; and the strong assurance of Claudian (Præfat. ad. l. ii. 46),

Sed tamen exemplo non feriere tuo,

may be considered as an evidence of some promise.

31. Cod. Theod. l. ix. tit. xl. leg. 14 [leg. 17]. The date of that law (Jan. 17, A.D. 399) is erroneous and corrupt, since the fall of Eutropius could not happen till the autumn of the same year. See Tillemont, Hist. des Empereurs, tom. v. p. 780.

32. Zosimus, l. v. [c. 18] p. 313. Philostorgius, l. xi. c. 6.

33. Zosimus (l. v. [c. 18-22] p. 313-323), Socrates (l. vi. c. 4 [6]), Sozomen (l. viii. c. 4), and Theodoret (l. v. c. 32, 33), represent, though with some various circumstances, the conspiracy, defeat, and death of Gainas.

34. Ὁσίας Εὐφημίας μαρτύριον is the expression of Zosimus himself (l. v. [c. 18] p. 314), who inadvertently uses the fashionable language of the Christians. Evagrius describes (l. ii. c. 3) the situation, architecture, relics, and miracles of that celebrated church, in which the general council of Chalcedon was afterwards held.

35. The pious remonstrances of Chrysostom, which do not appear in his own writings, are strongly urged by Theodoret; but his insinuation that they were successful is disproved by facts. Tillemont (Hist. des. Empereurs, tom. v. p. 383) has discovered that the emperor, to satisfy the rapacious demands of Gainas, was obliged to melt the plate of the church of the Apostles.

36. The ecclesiastical historians, who sometimes guide and sometimes follow the public opinion, most confidently assert that the palace of Constantinople was guarded by legions of angels.

37. Zosimus (l. v. [c. 20] p. 319) mentions these galleys by the name of *Liburnians*, and observes that they were as swift (without explaining the difference between them) as the vessels with fifty oars; but that they were far inferior in speed to the *triremes*, which had been long disused. Yet he reasonably concludes, from the testimony of Polybius, that galleys of a still larger size had been constructed in the Punic wars. Since the establishment of the Roman empire over the Mediterranean, the useless art of building large ships of war had probably been neglected, and at length forgotten.

38. Chishull (Travels, p. 61-63, 72-76) proceeded from Gallipoli, through Hadrianople, to the Danube, in about fifteen days. He was in the train of an English ambassador, whose baggage consisted of seventy-one waggons. That learned traveller has the merit of tracing a curious and unfrequented route.

39. The narrative of Zosimus, who actually leads Gainas beyond the Danube, must be corrected by the testimony of Socrates [l. vi. c. 6] and Sozomen [l. viii. c. 4], that he was killed in *Thrace*, and by the precise and authentic dates of the Alexandrian or Paschal Chronicle, p. 307 [ed. Paris; tom. i. p. 567, ed. Bonn]. The naval victory of the Hellespont is fixed to the month Apellæus, the tenth of the calends of January (December 23); the head of Gainas was brought to Constantinople the third of the nones of January (January 3), in the month Audynæus.

40. Eusebius Scholasticus acquired much fame by his poem on the Gothic war, in which he had served. Near forty years afterwards, Ammonius recited another poem on the same subject, in the presence of the emperor Theodosius. See Socrates, l. vi. c. 6.

41. The sixth book of Socrates, the eighth of Sozomen, and the fifth of Theodoret, afford curious and authentic materials for the Life of John Chrysostom. Besides those general historians, I have taken for my guides the four principal biographers of the saint:—1. The author of a partial and passionate Vindication of the Archbishop of Constantinople, composed in the form of a dialogue, and under the name of his zealous partisan, Palladius, bishop of Helenopolis (Tillemont, Mém. Ecclés. tom. xi. p. 500-533). It is inserted among the works of Chrysostom, tom. xiii. p. 1-90, edit. Montfaucon. 2. The moderate Erasmus (tom. iii. Epist. MCL. p. 1331-1347, edit. Lugd. Bat.). His vivacity and good sense were his own; his errors, in the uncultivated state of ecclesiastical antiquity, were almost inevitable. 3. The learned Tillemont (Mém. Ecclésiastiques, tom. xi. p. 1-405, 547-626, etc. etc.), who compiles the Lives of the saints with incredible patience and religious accuracy. He has minutely searched the voluminous works of Chrysostom himself. 4. Father Montfaucon, who has perused those works with the curious diligence of an editor, discovered several new homilies, and again reviewed and composed the Life of Chrysostom (Opera Chrysostom. tom. xiii. p. 91-177).

42. As I am *almost* a stranger to the voluminous sermons of Chrysostom, I have given my confi-

dence to the two most judicious and moderate of the ecclesiastical critics, Erasmus (tom. iii. p. 1344) and Dupin (Bibliothèque Ecclésiastique, tom. iii. p. 38); yet the good taste of the former is sometimes vitiated by an excessive love of antiquity, and the good sense of the latter is always restrained by prudential considerations.

43. The females of Constantinople distinguished themselves by their enmity or their attachment to Chrysostom. Three noble and opulent widows—Marsa, Castricia, and Eugraphia—were the leaders of the persecution (Pallad. Dialog. tom. xiii. p. 14 [c. 4, p. 35, ed. Paris, 1680]). It was impossible that they should forgive a preacher who reproached their affectation to conceal, by the ornaments of dress, their age and ugliness (Pallad. p. 27). Olympias, by equal zeal, displayed in a more pious cause, has obtained the title of saint. See Tillemont, Mém. Ecclés. tom. xi. p. 416–440.

44. Sozomen, and more especially Socrates, have defined the real character of Chrysostom with a temperate and impartial freedom very offensive to his blind admirers. Those historians lived in the next generation, when party violence was abated, and had conversed with many persons intimately acquainted with the virtues and imperfections of the saint.

45. Palladius (tom˙ xiii. p. 40, etc. [c. xii. p. 102, ed. Paris, 1680]) very seriously defends the archbishop. 1. He never tasted wine. 2. The weakness of his stomach required a peculiar diet. 3. Business, or study, or devotion, often kept him fasting till sunset. 4. He detested the noise and levity of great dinners. 5. He saved the expense for the use of the poor. 6. He was apprehensive, in a capital like Constantinople, of the envy and reproach of partial invitations.

46. Chrysostom declares his free opinion (tom. ix. hom. iii. in Act. Apostol. p. 29) that the number of bishops who might be saved bore a very small proportion to those who would be damned.

47. See Tillemont, Mém. Ecclés. tom. xi. p. 441–500.

48. I have purposely omitted the controversy which arose among the monks of Egypt concerning Origenism and Anthropomorphism, the dissimulation and violence of Theophilus, his artful management of the simplicity of Epiphanius, the persecution and flight of the long or tall brothers, the ambiguous support which they received at Constantinople from Chrysostom, etc. etc.

49. Photius (p. 53–60 [p. 17, sqq. ed. Bekk.]) has preserved the original acts of the synod of the Oak, which destroy the false assertion that Chrysostom was condemned by no more than thirty-six bishops, of whom twenty-nine were Egyptians. Forty-five bishops subscribed his sentence. See Tillemont, Mém. Ecclés. tom. xi. p. 595.

50. Palladius owns (p. 30 [c. 8, p. 75]) that if the people of Constantinople had found Theophilus, they would certainly have thrown him into the sea. Socrates mentions (l. vi. c. 17) a battle between the mob and the sailors of Alexandria, in which many wounds were given, and some lives were lost. The massacre of the monks is observed only by the Pagan Zosimus (l. v. [c. 23] p. 324), who acknowledges that Chrysostom had a singular talent to lead the illiterate multitude, ἦν γὰρ ὁ ἄνθρωπος ἄλογον ὄχλον ὑπαγαγέσθαι δεινός.

51. See Socrates, l. vi. c. 18. Sozomen, l. viii. c. 20. Zosimus (l. v. [c. 24] p. 324, 327) mentions, in general terms, his invectives against Eudoxia. The homily which begins with those famous words is rejected as spurious. Montfaucon, tom. xiii. p. 151. Tillemont, Mém. Ecclés. tom. xi. p. 603.

52. We might naturally expect such a charge from Zosimus (l. v. [c. 24] p. 327; but it is remarkable enough that it should be confirmed by Socrates, l. vi.c. 18, and the Paschal Chronicle, p. 307 [ed. Paris; tom. i. p. 568, ed. Bonn].

53. He displays those specious motives (Post Reditum, c. 13, 14) in the language of an orator and a politician.

54. Two hundred and forty-two of the epistles of Chrysostom are still extant (Opera, tom. iii. p. 528–736 [ed. Bened.]). They are addressed to a great variety of persons, and show a firmness of mind much superior to that of Cicero in his exile. The fourteenth epistle contains a curious narrative of the dangers of his journey.

55. After the exile of Chrysostom, Theophilus published an *enormous* and *horrible* volume against him, in which he perpetually repeats the polite expressions of hostem humanitatis, sacrilegorum principem, immundum dæmonem; he affirms that John Chrysostom had delivered his soul to be adulterated by the devil; and wishes that some farther punishment, adequate (if possible) to the magnitude of his crimes, may be inflicted on him. St. Jerom, at the request of his friend Theophilus, translated this edifying performance from Greek into Latin. See Facundus Hermian. Defens. pro iii. Capitul. l. vi. c. 5 [p. 260, ed. Paris, 1629], published by Sirmond, Opera, tom. ii. p. 595, 596, 597.

56. His name was inserted by his successor Atticus in the dyptics of the church of Constantinople, A.D. 418. Ten years afterwards he was revered as a saint. Cyril, who inherited the place and the passions of his uncle Theophilus, yielded with much reluctance. See Facund. Hermian. l. vi. c. 1 [p. 142, ed. Par. 1629]; Tillemont, Mém. Ecclés. tom. xiv. p. 277–283.

57. Socrates, l. vii. c. 45; Theodoret, l. v. c. 36. This event reconciled the Joanites, who had hitherto refused to acknowledge his successors. During his lifetime the Joanites were respected by the catholics as the true and orthodox communion of Constantinople. Their obstinacy gradually drove them to the brink of schism.

58. According to some accounts (Baronius, Annal. Eccles. A.D. 438, No. 9, 10), the emperor was forced to send a letter of invitation and excuses before the body of the ceremonious saint could be moved from Comana.

59. Zosimus, l. v. [c. 18] p. 315. The chastity of an empress should not be impeached without producing a witness; but it is astonishing that the witness should write and live under a prince whose legitimacy he dared to attack. We must suppose that this history was a party libel, privately read and circulated by the Pagans. Tillemont (Hist. des Empereurs, tom. v. p. 782) is not averse to brand the reputation of Eudoxia.

60. Porphyry of Gaza. His zeal was transported by the order which he had obtained for the destruction of eight Pagan temples of that city. See the curious details of his life (Baronius, A.D. 401, No. 17–51), originally written in Greek, or perhaps in Syriac, by a monk, one of his favourite deacons.

61. Philostorg. l. xi. c. 8, and Godefroy, Dissertat. p. 457.

62. Jerom (tom. vi. p. 73, 76) describes in lively colours the regular and destructive march of the locusts, which spread a dark cloud between heaven and earth over the land of Palestine. Seasonable winds scattered them, partly into the Dead Sea and partly into the Mediterranean.

63. Procopius, de Bell. Persic. l. i. c. 2, p. 8, edit. Louvre [tom. i. p. 14, ed. Bonn].

64. Agathias, l. vi. [c. 26] p. 136, 137 [p. 264, ed. Bonn]. Although he confesses the prevalence of the tradition, he asserts that Procopius was the first who had committed it to writing. Tillemont (Hist. des Empereurs, tom. vi. p. 597) argues very sensibly on the merits of this fable. His criticism was not warped by any ecclesiastical authority: both Procopius and Agathias are half Pagans.

65. Socrates, l. vii. c. 1. Anthemius was the grandson of Philip, one of the ministers of Constantius, and the grandfather of the emperor Anthemius. After his return from the Persian embassy, he was appointed consul and Prætorian præfect of the East, in the year 405; and held the præfecture about ten years. See his honours and praises in Godefroy, Cod. Theod. tom. vi. p. 350; Tillemont, Hist. des Emp. tom. vi. p. 1, etc.

66. Sozomen, l. ix. c. 5. He saw some Scyrri at work near Mount Olympus, in Bithynia, and cherished the vain hope that those captives were the last of the nation.

67. Cod. Theod. l. vii. tit. xvii.; l. xv. tit. i. leg. 49.

68. Sozomen has filled three chapters with a magnificent panegyric of Pulcheria (l. ix. c. 1, 2, 3); and Tillemont (Mémoires Ecclés. tom. xv. p. 171–184) has dedicated a separate article to the honour of St. Pulcheria, virgin and empress.

69. Suidas (Excerpta, p. 68, in Script. Byzant.) pretends, on the credit of the Nestorians, that Pulcheria was exasperated against their founder, because he censured her connection with the beautiful Paulinus, and her incest with her brother Theodosius.

70. See Ducange, Famil. Byzantin. p. 70. Flaccilla, the eldest daughter, either died before Arcadius, or, if *she* lived till the year 431 (Marcellin.

Chron.), some defect of mind or body must have excluded her from the honours of her rank.

71. She was admonished, by repeated dreams, of the place where the relics of the forty martyrs had been buried. The ground had successively belonged to the house and garden of a woman of Constantinople, to a monastery of Macedonian monks, and to a church of St. Thrysus, erected by Cæsarius, who was consul A.D. 397; and the memory of the relics was almost obliterated. Notwithstanding the charitable wishes of Dr. Jortin (Remarks, tom. iv. p. 234), it is not easy to acquit Pulcheria of some share in the pious fraud, which must have been transacted when she was more than five-and-thirty years of age.

72. There is a remarkable difference between the two ecclesiastical historians who in general bear so close a resemblance. Sozomen (l. ix. c. 1) ascribes to Pulcheria the government of the empire and the education of her brother, whom he scarcely condescends to praise. Socrates, though he affectedly disclaims all hopes of favour or fame, composes an elaborate panegyric on the emperor, and cautiously suppresses the merits of his sister (l. vii. c. 22, 42). Philostorgius (l. xii. c. 7) expresses the influence of Pulcheria in gentle and courtly language, τάς βασιλικάς σημειώσεις ὑπηρετουμένη καὶ διευθύνουσα. Suidas (Excerpt. p. 53) gives a true character of Theodosius; and I have followed the example of Tillemont (tom. vi. p. 25) in borrowing some strokes from the modern Greeks.

73. Theodoret, l. v. c. 37. The bishop of Cyrrhus, one of the first men of his age for his learning and piety, applauds the obedience of Theodosius to the divine laws.

74. Socrates (l. vii. c. 21) mentions her name (Athenais, the daughter of Leontius, an Athenian sophist), her baptism, marriage, and poetical genius. The most ancient account of her history is in John Malala (part ii. p. 20, 21, edit. Venet. 1733 [p. 354, 355, ed. Bonn]) and in the Paschal Chronicle (p. 311, 312 [ed. Paris; tom. i. p. 576, 577, ed. Bonn]). Those authors had probably seen original pictures of the empress Eudocia. The modern Greeks, Zonaras, Cedrenus, etc., have displayed the love, rather than the talent, of fiction. From Nicephorus, indeed, I have ventured to assume her age. The writer of a romance would not have *imagined* that Athenais was near twenty-eight years old when she inflamed the heart of a young emperor.

75. Socrates, l. vii. c. 21. Photius, p. 413–420 [p. 128, 129, ed. Bekk.]. The Homeric cento is still extant, and has been repeatedly printed; but the claim of Eudocia to that insipid performance is disputed by the critics. See Fabricius, Biblioth. Græc. tom. i. p. 357. The *Ionia*, a miscellaneous dictionary of history and fable, was compiled by another empress of the name of Eudocia who lived in the eleventh century; and the work is still extant in manuscript.

76. Baronius (Annal. Eccles. A.D. 438, 439) is

copious and florid; but he is accused of placing the lies of different ages on the same level of authenticity.

77. In this short view of the disgrace of Eudocia I have imitated the caution of Evagrius (l. i. c. 21) and Count Marcellinus (in Chron. A.D. 440 and 444 [p. 26]). The two authentic dates assigned by the latter overturn a great part of the Greek fictions; and the celebrated story of the *apple*, etc., is fit only for the Arabian Nights, where something not very unlike it may be found.

78. Priscus (in Excerpt. Legat. p. 69 [ed. Paris; p. 208, ed. Bonn]), a contemporary and a courtier, drily mentions her Pagan and Christian names without adding any title of honour or respect.

79. For the *two* pilgrimages of Eudocia, and her long residence at Jerusalem, her devotion, alms, etc., see Socrates (l. vii. c. 47) and Evagrius (l. i. c. 20, 21, 22). The Paschal Chronicle may sometimes deserve regard; and, in the domestic history of Antioch, John Malala becomes a writer of good authority. The Abbé Guenée, in a memoir on the fertility of Palestine, of which I have only seen an extract, calculates the gifts of Eudocia at 20,488 pounds of gold, above 800,000 pounds sterling.

80. Theodoret, l. v. c. 39. Tillemont, Mém. Ecclés. tom. xii. p. 356–364. Assemanni, Bibliot. Oriental. tom. iii. p. 396, tom. iv. p. 61. Theodoret blames the rashness of Abdas, but extols the constancy of his martyrdom. Yet I do not clearly understand the casuistry which prohibits our repairing the damage which we have unlawfully committed.

81. Socrates (l. vii. c. 18, 19, 20, 21) is the best author for the Persian war. We may likewise consult the three Chronicles, the Paschal, and those of Marcellinus and Malala.

82. This account of the ruin and division of the kingdom of Armenia is taken from the third book of the Armenian history of Moses of Chorene. Deficient as he is in every qualification of a good historian, his local information, his passions, and his prejudices are strongly expressive of a native and contemporary. Procopius (de Ædificiis, l. iii. c.

1–5) relates the same facts in a very different manner; but I have extracted the circumstances, the most probable in themselves and the least inconsistent with Moses of Chorene.

83. The western Armenians used the Greek language and characters in their religious offices; but the use of that hostile tongue was prohibited by the Persians in the eastern provinces, which were obliged to use the Syriac, till the invention of the Armenian letters by Mesrobes in the beginning of the fifth century, and the subsequent version of the Bible into the Armenian language; an event which relaxed the connection of the church and nation with Constantinople.

84. Moses Choren. l. iii. c. 59, p. 309 and p. 358 [ed. Whiston, Lond. 1736]. Procopius, de Ædeficiis, l. iii. c. 5. Theodosiopolis stands, or rather stood, about thirty-five miles to the east of Arzeroum, the modern capital of Turkish Armenia. See D'Anville, Géographie Ancienne, tom. ii. p. 99, 100.

85. Moses Choren. l. iii. c. 63, p. 316. According to the institution of St. Gregory, the Apostle of Armenia, the archbishop was always of the royal family; a circumstance which, in some degree, corrected the influence of the sacerdotal character, and united the mitre with the crown.

86. A branch of the royal house of Arsaces still subsisted with the rank and possessions (as it should seem) of Armenian satraps. See Moses Choren. l. iii. c. 65, p. 321.

87. Valarsaces was appointed king of Armenia by his brother the Parthian monarch, immediately after the defeat of Antiochus Sidetes (Moses Choren. l. ii. c. 2, p. 85), one hundred and thirty years before Christ. Without depending on the various and contradictory periods of the reigns of the last kings, we may be assured that the ruin of the Armenian kingdom happened after the council of Chalcedon, A.D. 431 (l. iii. c. 61, p. 312); and under Varanes, or Bahram, king of Persia (l. iii. c. 64, p. 317), who reigned from A.D. 420 to 440. See Assemanni, Bibliot. Oriental. tom. iii. p. 396.

Chapter XXXIII

1. Τὰ συνεχῆ κατὰ στόμα φιλήματα, is the expression of Olympiodorus (apud Photium, p. 196 [p. 62 b, ed. Bekk.]); who means, perhaps, to describe the same caresses which Mahomet bestowed on his *daughter* Phatemah. Quando (says the prophet himself), quando subit mihi desiderium Paradisi, osculor eam, et ingero linguam meam in os ejus. But this sensual indulgence was justified by miracle and mystery; and the anecdote has been communicated to the public by the Reverend Father Maracci, in his Version and Confutation of the Koran, tom. i. p. 32.

2. For these revolutions of the Western empire

consult Olympiodor. apud Phot. p. 192, 193, 196, 197, 200 [p. 61–63, ed. Bekk.]; Sozomen, l. ix. c. 16; Socrates, l. vii. 23, 24; Philostorgius, l. xii. c. 10, 11 [12–14], and Godefroy, Dissertat. p. 486; Procopius, de Bell. Vandal. l. i. c. 3, p. 182, 183 [ed. Paris; tom. i. p. 319 seqq. ed. Bonn]; Theophanes, in Chronograph, p. 72, 73 [ed. Par.; tom. i. p. 129–131, ed. Bonn]; and the Chronicles.

3. See Grotius de Jure Belli et Pacis, l. ii. c. 7. He has laboriously, but vainly, attempted to form a reasonable system of jurisprudence from the various and discordant modes of royal succession.

which have been introduced by fraud or force, by time or accident.

4. The original writers are not agreed (see Muratori, Annali d'Italia, tom. iv. p. 139) whether Valentinian received the Imperial diadem at Rome or Ravenna. In this uncertainty, I am willing to believe that some respect was shown to the senate.

5. The Count de Buat (Hist. des Peuples de l'Europe, tom. vii. p. 292–300) has established the reality, explained the motives, and traced the consequences, of this remarkable cession.

6. See the first *Novel* of Theodosius, by which he ratifies and communicates (A.D. 438) the Theodosian Code. About 40 years before that time the unity of legislation had been proved by an exception. The Jews, who were numerous in the cities of Apulia and Calabria, produced a law of the East to justify their exemption from municipal offices (Cod. Theod. l. xvi. tit. viii. leg. 13); and the Western emperor was obliged to invalidate, by a special edict, the law, quam constat meis partibus esse damnosam. Cod. Theod. l. xi. [xii.] tit. i. leg. 158.

7. Cassiodorus (Variar. l. xi. Epist. i. p. 238 [p. 161, ed. Venet.]) has compared the regencies of Placidia and Amalasuntha. He arraigns the weakness of the mother of Valentinian, and praises the virtues of his royal mistress. On this occasion flattery seems to have spoken the language of truth.

8. Philostorgius, l. xii. c. 12 [14], and Godefroy's Dissertat. p. 493, etc.; and Renatus Frigeridus, apud Gregor. Turon. l. ii. c. 8, in tom. ii. p. 163. The father of Aëtius was Gaudentius, an illustrious citizen of the province of Scythia and master-general of the cavalry; his mother was a rich and noble Italian. From his earliest youth, Aëtius, as a soldier and a hostage, had conversed with the barbarians.

9. For the character of Boniface see Olympiodorus, apud Phot. p. 196 [p. 62 b, ed. Bekk.]; and St. Augustin, apud Tillemont, Mémoires Ecclés. tom. xiii. p. 712–715, 886. The bishop of Hippo at length deplored the fall of his friend, who, after a solemn vow of chastity, had married a second wife of the Arian sect, and who was suspected of keeping several concubines in his house.

10. Procopius (de Bell. Vandal. l. i. c. 3, 4, p. 182–186 [tom. i. p. 319–328, ed. Bonn]) relates the fraud of Aëtius, the revolt of Boniface, and the loss of Africa. This anecdote, which is supported by some collateral testimony (see Ruinart, Hist. Persecut. Vandal. p. 420, 421) seems agreeable to the practice of ancient and modern courts, and would be naturally revealed by the repentance of Boniface.

11. See the Chronicles of Prosper and Idatius [Sirmond, Op. tom. ii. p. 298]. Salvian (de Gubernat. Dei, l. vii. p. 246, Paris, 1608) ascribes the victory of the Vandals to their superior piety. They fasted, they prayed, they carried a Bible in the front of the Host, with the design, perhaps, of reproaching the perfidy and sacrilege of their enemies.

12. Gizericus (his name is variously expressed) staturâ mediocris et equi casû claudicans, animo profundus, sermone rarus, luxuriæ contemptor, irâ turbidus, habendi cupidus, ad solicitandas gentes providentissimus, semina contentionum jacere, odia miscere paratus. Jornandes, de Rebus Geticis, c. 33, p. 675. This portrait, which is drawn with some skill and a strong likeness, must have been copied from the Gothic history of Cassiodorus.

13. See the Chronicle of Idatius. That bishop, a Spaniard and a contemporary, places the passage of the Vandals in the month of May, of the year of Abraham (which commences in October) 2444. This date, which coincides with A.D. 429, is confirmed by Isidore, another Spanish bishop, and is justly preferred to the opinion of those writers who have marked for that event one of the two preceding years. See Pagi Critica, tom. ii. p. 205, etc.

14. Compare Procopius (de Bell. Vandal. l. i. c. 5, p. 190 [tom. i. p. 334, ed. Bonn]) and Victor Vitensis (de Persecutione Vandal. l. i. c. 1, p. 3, edit. Ruinart). We are assured by Idatius that Genseric evacuated Spain, cum Vandalis *omnibus* eorumque familiis [Sirm. Op. tom. ii. p. 299]; and Possidius (in Vit. Augustin. c. 28, apud Ruinart, p. 427) describes his army as manus ingens immanium gentium Vandalorum et Alanorum, commixtam secum habens Gothorum gentem, aliarumque diversarum personas.

15. For the manners of the Moors see Procopius (de Bell. Vandal. l. ii. c. 6, p. 249 [tom. i. p. 434, ed. Bonn]); for their figure and complexion, M. de Buffon (Histoire Naturelle, tom. iii. p. 430). Procopius says in general that the Moors had joined the Vandals before the death of Valentinian (de Bell. Vandal. l. i. c. 5, p. 190 [tom. i. p. 334, ed. Bonn]); and it is probable that the independent tribes did not embrace any uniform system of policy.

16. See Tillemont, Mémoires Ecclés. tom. xiii. p. 516–558; and the whole series of the persecution, in the original monuments, published by Dupin at the end of Optatus, p. 323–515.

17. The Donatist bishops, at the conference of Carthage, amounted to 279; and they asserted that their whole number was not less than 400. The Catholics had 286 present, 120 absent, besides sixty-four vacant bishoprics.

18. The fifth title of the sixteenth book of the Theodosian Code exhibits a series of the Imperial laws against the Donatists, from the year 400 to the year 428. Of these the 54th law, promulgated by Honorius, A.D. 414, is the most severe and effectual.

19. St. Augustin altered his opinion with regard to the proper treatment of heretics. His pathetic declaration of pity and indulgence for the Manichæans has been inserted by Mr. Locke (vol. iii. p. 469) among the choice specimens of his commonplace book. Another philosopher, the celebrated Bayle (tom. ii. p. 445–496), has refuted, with superfluous diligence and ingenuity, the arguments

by which the bishop of Hippo justified, in his old age, the persecution of the Donatists.

20. See Tillemont, Mém. Ecclés. tom. xiii. p. 586–592, 806. The Donatists boasted of *thousands* of these voluntary martyrs. Augustin asserts, and probably with truth, that these numbers were much exaggerated; but he sternly maintains that it was better that *some* should burn themselves in this world than that *all* should burn in hell flames.

21. According to St. Augustin and Theodoret, the Donatists were inclined to the principles, or at least to the party, of the Arians, which Genseric supported. Tillemont, Mém. Ecclés. tom. vi. p. 68.

22. See Baronius, Annal. Eccles. A.D. 428, No. 7, A.D. 439, No. 35. The cardinal, though more inclined to seek the cause of great events in heaven than on the earth, has observed the apparent connection of the Vandals and the Donatists. Under the reign of the barbarians, the schismatics of Africa enjoyed an obscure peace of one hundred years; at the end of which we may again trace them by the light of the Imperial persecutions. See Tillemont, Mém. Ecclés. tom. vi. p. 192, etc.

23. In a confidential letter to Count Boniface, St. Augustin, without examining the grounds of the quarrel, piously exhorts him to discharge the duties of a Christian and a subject; to extricate himself without delay from his dangerous and guilty situation; and even, if he could obtain the consent of his wife, to embrace a life of celibacy and penance (Tillemont, Mém. Ecclés. tom. xiii. p. 890). The bishop was intimately connected with Darius, the minister of peace (id. tom. xiii. p. 928).

24. The original complaints of the desolation of Africa are contained—1. In a letter from Capreolus, bishop of Carthage, to excuse his absence from the council of Ephesus (ap. Ruinart, p. 428). 2. In the Life of St. Augustin by his friend and colleague Possidius (ap. Ruinart, p. 427). 3. In the History of the Vandalic Persecution, by Victor Vitensis (l. i. c. 1, 2, 3, edit. Ruinart). The last picture, which was drawn sixty years after the event, is more expressive of the author's passions than of the truth of facts.

25. See Cellarius, Geograph. Antiq. tom. ii. part ii. p. 112. Leo African. in Ramusio, tom. i. fol. 70. L'Afrique de Marmol, tom. ii. p. 434, 437. Shaw's Travels, p. 46, 47. The old Hippo Regius was finally destroyed by the Arabs in the seventh century; but a new town, at the distance of two miles, was built with the materials; and it contained in the sixteenth century about three hundred families of industrious, but turbulent, manufacturers. The adjacent territory is renowned for a pure air, a fertile soil, and plenty of exquisite fruits.

26. The Life of St. Augustin, by Tillemont, fills a quarto volume (Mém. Ecclés. tom. xiii.) of more than one thousand pages; and the diligence of that learned Jansenist was excited, on this occasion, by factious and devout zeal for the founder of his sect.

27. Such at least is the account of Victor Vitensis (de Persecut. Vandal. l. i. c. 3); though

Gennadius seems to doubt whether any person had read, or even collected, *all* the works of St. Augustin (see Hieronym. Opera, tom. i. p. 319, in Catalog. Scriptor. Eccles.). They have been repeatedly printed; and Dupin (Bibliothèque Ecclés. tom. iii. p. 158–257) has given a large and satisfactory abstract of them as they stand in the last edition of the Benedictines. My personal acquaintance with the bishop of Hippo does not extend beyond the *Confessions* and the *City of God*.

28. In his early youth (Confess. i. 23) St. Augustin disliked and neglected the study of Greek; and he frankly owns that he read the Platonists in a Latin version (Confess. vii. 13). Some modern critics have thought that his ignorance of Greek disqualified him from expounding the Scriptures; and Cicero or Quintilian would have required the knowledge of that language in a professor of rhetoric.

29. These questions were seldom agitated from the time of St. Paul to that of St. Augustin. I am informed that the Greek fathers maintain the natural sentiments of the Semi-Pelagians; and that the orthodoxy of St. Augustin was derived from the Manichæan school.

30. The church of Rome has canonised Augustin and reprobated Calvin. Yet, as the *real* difference between them is invisible even to a theological microscope, the Molinists are oppressed by the authority of the saint, and the Jansenists are disgraced by their resemblance to the heretic. In the meanwhile the Protestant Arminians stand aloof and deride the mutual perplexity of the disputants (see a curious Review of the Controversy by Le Clerc, Bibliothèque Universelle, tom. xiv. p. 144–398). Perhaps a reasoner still more independent may smile in *his* turn when he peruses an Arminian Commentary on the Epistle to the Romans.

31. Ducange, Fam. Byzant. p. 67. On one side, the head of Valentinian; on the reverse, Boniface with a scourge in one hand and a palm in the other, standing in a triumphal car, which is drawn by four horses, or, in another medal, by four stags; an unlucky emblem! I should doubt whether another example can be found of the head of a subject on the reverse of an Imperial medal. See Science des Médailles, by the Père Jobert, tom. i. p. 132–150, edit. of 1739, by the Baron de la Bastie.

32. Procopius (de Bell. Vandal. l. i. c. 3, p. 185 [tom. i. p. 325, ed. Bonn]) continues the history of Boniface no farther than his return to Italy. His death is mentioned by Prosper [Ann. 432] and Marcellinus; the expression of the latter, that Aëtius the day before had provided himself with a *longer* spear, implies something like a regular duel.

33. See Procopius, de Bell. Vandal. l. i. c. 4, p. 186 [tom. i. p. 327, ed. Bonn]. Valentinian published several humane laws to relieve the distress of his Numidian and Mauritanian subjects; he discharged them in a great measure from the payment of their debts, reduced their tribute to one-eighth, and gave them a right of appeal from their

provincial magistrates to the præfect of Rome. Cod. Theod. tom. vi. Novell. p. 11, 12.

34. Victor Vitensis, de Persecut. Vandal. l. ii. c. 5, p. 26. The cruelties of Genseric towards his subjects are strongly expressed in Prosper's Chronicle, A.D. 442.

35. Possidius, in Vit. Augustin. c. 28, apud Ruinart, p. 428.

36. See the Chronicles of Idatius, Isidore, Prosper, and Marcellinus. They mark the same year, but different days, for the surprisal of Carthage.

37. The picture of Carthage, as it flourished in the fourth and fifth centuries, is taken from the Expositio totius Mundi, p. 17, 18, in the third volume of Hudson's Minor Geographers; from Ausonius de Claris Urbibus, p. 228, 229; and principally from Salvian, de Gubernatione Dei, l. vii. p. 257, 258. I am surprised that the *Notitia* should not place either a mint or an arsenal at Carthage, but only a gynecæum, or female manufacture.

38. The anonymous author of the Expositio totius Mundi compares, in his barbarous Latin, the country and the inhabitants; and, after stigmatising their want of faith, he coolly concludes, Difficile autem inter eos inventitur bonus, tamen in multis pauci boni esse possunt. P. 18.

39. He declares that the peculiar vices of each country were collected in the sink of Carthage (l. vii. p. 257). In the indulgence of vice the Africans applauded their manly virtue. Et illi se magis virilis fortitudinis esse crederent, qui maxime viros feminei usûs probrositate fregissent (p. 268). The streets of Carthage were polluted by effeminate wretches, who publicly assumed the countenance, the dress, and the character, of women (p. 264). If a monk appeared in the city, the holy man was pursued with impious scorn and ridicule; detestantibus ridentium cachinnis (p. 289).

40. Compare Procopius, de Bell. Vandal. l. i. c. 5, p. 189, 190 [tom. i. p. 332 *sqq.*, ed. Bonn]; and Victor Vitensis, de Persecut. Vandal. l. i. c. 4.

41. Ruinart (p. 444-457) has collected from Theodoret and other authors the misfortunes, real and fabulous, of the inhabitants of Carthage.

42. The choice of fabulous circumstances is of small importance; yet I have confined myself to the narrative which was translated from the Syriac by the care of Gregory of Tours (de Gloriâ Martyrûm, l. i. c. 95, in Max. Bibliothecâ Patrum, tom. xi. p. 856), to the Greek acts of their martyrdom (apud Photium, p. 1400, 1401 [p. 467, ed. Bekk.]), and to the Annals of the Patriarch Eutychius (tom. i. p. 391, 531, 532, 535, vers. Pocock [Oxon. 1658]).

43. Two Syriac writers, as they are quoted by Assemanni (Bibliot. Oriental. tom. i. p. 336, 338), place the resurrection of the Seven Sleepers in the year 736 (A.D. 425) or 748 (A.D. 437) of the era of the Seleucides. Their Greek acts, which Photius had read, assign the date of the thirty-eighth year of the reign of Theodosius, which may coincide either with A.D. 439 or 446. The period which had elapsed since the persecution of Decius is easily ascertained; and nothing less than the ignorance of Mahomet or the legendaries could suppose an interval of three or four hundred years.

44. James, one of the orthodox fathers of the Syrian church, was born A.D. 452; he began to compose his sermons A.D. 474; he was made bishop of Batnæ, in the district of Sarug and province of Mesopotamia, A.D. 519, and died A.D. 521. (Assemanni, tom. i. p. 288, 289.) For the homily *de Pueris Ephesinis*, see p. 335-339: though I could wish that Assemanni had translated the text of James of Sarug instead of answering the objections of Baronius.

45. See the *Acta Sanctorum* of the Bollandists (Mensis Julii, tom. vi. p. 375-397). This immense calendar of Saints, in one hundred and twenty-six years (1644-1770), and in fifty volumes in folio, has advanced no farther than the 7th day of October. The suppression of the Jesuits has most probably checked an undertaking which, through the medium of fable and superstition, communicates much historical and philosophical instruction.

46. See Maracci Alcoran. Sura xviii. tom. ii. p. 420-427, and tom. i. part iv. p. 103. With such an ample privilege Mahomet has not shown much taste or ingenuity. He has invented the dog (Al Rakim) of the Seven Sleepers; the respect of the sun, who altered his course twice a day that he might not shine into the cavern; and the care of God himself, who preserved their bodies from putrefaction by turning them to the right and left.

47. See D'Herbelot, Bibliothèque Orientale, p. 139; and Renaudot, Hist. Patriarch. Alexandrin, p. 39, 40.

48. Paul, the deacon of Aquileia (de Gestis Langobardorum, l. i. c. 4, p. 745, 746, edit. Grot.), who lived towards the end of the eighth century, has placed in a cavern under a rock on the shore of the ocean the Seven Sleepers of the North, whose long repose was respected by the barbarians. Their dress declared them to be Romans; and the deacon conjectures that they were reserved by Providence as the future apostles of those unbelieving countries.

Chapter XXXIV

1. The authentic materials for the history of Attila may be found in Jornandes (de Rebus Geticis, c. 34–50, p. 660–688, edit. Grot.) and Priscus (Excerpta de Legationibus, p. 33–76, Paris, 1648 [p. 140–220, ed. Bonn]). I have not seen the Lives of Attila, composed by Juvencus Cælius Calanus Dalmatinus, in the twelfth century, or by Nicolas Olahus, archbishop of Gran, in the sixteenth. See Mascou's History of the Germans, ix. 23, and Maffei Osservazioni Litterarie, tom. i. p. 88, 89. Whatever the modern Hungarians have added must be fabulous; and they do not seem to have excelled in the art of fiction. They suppose that when Attila invaded Gaul and Italy, married innumerable wives, etc., he was one hundred and twenty years of age. Thevrocz Chron. p. i. c. 22, in Script. Hungar. tom. i. p. 76.

2. Hungary has been successively occupied by three Scythian colonies:—1. The Huns of Attila; 2. The Abares, in the sixth century; and, 3. The Turks or Magyars, A.D. 889, the immediate and genuine ancestors of the modern Hungarians, whose connection with the two former is extremely faint and remote. The *Prodromus* and *Notitia* of Matthew Belius appear to contain a rich fund of information concerning ancient and modern Hungary. I have seen the extracts in Bibliothèque Ancienne et Moderne, tom. xxii. p. 1–51, and Bibliothèque Raisonée, tom. xvi. p. 127–175.

3. Socrates, l. vii. c. 43; Theodoret, l. v. c. 37. Tillemont, who always depends on the faith of his ecclesiastical authors, strenuously contends (Hist. des Emp. tom. vi. p. 136, 607) that the wars and personages were not the same.

4. See Priscus, p. 47, 48 [ed. Par.; pp. 166–170, ed. Bonn], and Hist. des Peuples de l'Europe, tom. vii. c. xii. xiii. xiv. xv.

5. Priscus, p. 39 [p. 150, ed. Bonn]. The modern Hungarians have deduced his genealogy, which ascends, in the thirty-fifth degree, to Ham the son of Noah; yet they are ignorant of his father's real name. (De Guignes, Hist. des Huns, tom. ii. p. 297.)

6. Compare Jornandes (c. 35, p. 661) with Buffon, Hist. Naturelle, tom. iii. p. 380. The former had a right to observe, originis suæ signa restituens. The character and portrait of Attila are probably transcribed from Cassiodorus.

7. Abulpharag. Dynast. vers. Pocock, p. 281 [ed. Oxon. 1663]; Genealogical History of the Tartars, by Abulghazi Bahader Khan, part iii. c. 15, part iv. c. 3; Vie de Gengiscan, par Petit de la Croix, l. i. c. 1, 6. The relations of the missionaries who visited Tartary in the thirteenth century (see the seventh volume of the Histoire des Voyages) express the popular language and opinions; Zingis is styled the son of God, etc., etc.

8. Nec templum apud eos visitur, aut delubrum, ne tugurium quidem culmo tectum cerni usquam potest; sed *gladius* barbarico ritû humi figitur nudus, eumque ut Martem regionum quas circumcircant præsulem verecundius colunt. Ammian. Marcellin. xxxi. 2, and the learned Notes of Lindenbrogius and Valesius.

9. Priscus relates this remarkable story, both in his own text (p. 65 [p. 201, ed. Bonn]) and in the quotation made by Jornandes (c. 35, p. 662). He might have explained the tradition or fable, which characterised this famous sword, and the name as well as attributes of the Scythian deity whom he has translated into the Mars of the Greeks and Romans.

10. Herodot. l. iv. c. 62. For the sake of economy, I have calculated by the smallest stadium. In the human sacrifices, they cut off the shoulder and arm of the victim, which they threw up into the air, and drew omens and presages from the manner of their falling on the pile.

11. Priscus, p. 55 [p. 182, ed. Bonn]. A more civilised hero, Augustus himself, was pleased if the person on whom he fixed his eyes seemed unable to support their divine lustre. Sueton. in August. c. 79.

12. The Count de Buat (Hist. des Peuples de l'Europe, tom. vii. p. 428, 429) attempts to clear Attila from the murder of his brother, and is almost inclined to reject the concurrent testimony of Jornandes and the contemporary Chronicles.

13. Fortissimarum gentium dominus, qui inauditâ ante se potentiâ, solus Scythica et Germanica regna possedit. Jornandes, c. 49, p. 684; Priscus, p. 64, 65 [p. 199–201, ed. Bonn]. M. de Guignes, by his knowledge of the Chinese, has acquired (tom. ii. p. 295–301) an adequate idea of the empire of Attila.

14. See Hist. des Huns, tom. ii. p. 296. The Geougen believed that the Huns could excite at pleasure storms of wind and rain. This phenomenon was produced by the stone *Gezi*, to whose magic power the loss of a battle was ascribed by the Mahometan Tartars of the fourteenth century. See Cherefeddin Ali, Hist. de Timur Bec, tom. i. p. 82, 83.

15. Jornandes, c. 35, p. 661; c. 37, p. 667. See Tillemont, Hist. des Empereurs, tom. vi. p. 129, 138. Corneille has represented the pride of Attila to his subject kings, and his tragedy opens with these two ridiculous lines:—

Ils ne sont pas venus, nos deux rois! qu'on leur die

Qu'ils se font trop attendre, et qu'Attila s'ennuie.

The two kings of the Gepidæ and the Ostrogoths are profound politicians and sentimental lovers; and the whole piece exhibits the defects, without the genius, of the poet.

16. ———alii per Caspia clustara
Armeniasque nives, inopino tramite ducti
Invadunt Orientis opes: jam pascua fu-
    mant
Cappadocum, volucrumque parens Ar-
    gæus equorum.
Jam rubet altus Halys, nec se defendit
    iniquo
Monte Cilix; Syriæ tractus vastantur
    amœni;
Assuetumque choris, et lætâ plebe ca-
    norum,
Proterit imbellem sonipes hostilis Oron-
    tem.
                Claudian, in Rufin. l. ii. 28–35.
See likewise, in Eutrop. l. i. 243–251, and the
strong description of Jerom, who wrote from his
feelings, tom. i. p. 26, ad Heliodor. p. 200, ad
Ocean. [p. 342 and 460 ed. Vallars.]. Philostor-
gius (l. ix. c. 8 [17]) mentions this irruption.

17. [Basic and Cursic are not cities, but the
names of the two commanders of the bands of
Huns who invaded Persia.]

18. See the original conversation in Priscus, p.
64, 65 [ed. Par.; p. 198–201, ed. Bonn].

19. Priscus, p. 331. His history contained a
copious and elegant account of the war (Evagrius,
l. i. c. 17); but the extracts which relate to the embassies are the only parts that have reached our
times. The original work was accessible, however,
to the writers from whom we borrow our imperfect knowledge, Jornandes, Theophanes, Count
Marcellinus, Prosper-Tyro, and the author of the
Alexandrian, or Paschal, Chronicle. M. de Buat
(Hist. des Peuples de l'Europe, tom. vii. c. xv.) has
examined the cause, the circumstances, and the
duration of this war; and will not allow it to extend
beyond the year four hundred and forty-four.

20. Procopius, de Ædificiis, l. iv. c. 5 [tom. iii.
p. 286, ed. Bonn]. These fortresses were afterwards
restored, strengthened, and enlarged by the emperor Justinian; but they were soon destroyed by
the Abares, who succeeded to the power and possessions of the Huns.

21. Septuaginta civitates (says Prosper-Tyro) de-
prædatione vastatæ. The language of Count Marcellinus is still more forcible. Pene totam Europam,
invasis excisisque civitatibus atque castellis, conrasit.

22. Tillemont (Hist. des Empereurs, tom. vi. p.
106, 107) has paid great attention to this memorable earthquake, which was felt as far from Constantinople as Antioch and Alexandria, and is
celebrated by all the ecclesiastical writers. In the
hands of a popular preacher, an earthquake is an
engine of admirable effect.

23. He represented to the emperor of the Moguls that the four provinces (Petcheli, Chantong,
Chansi, and Leaotong) which he already possessed
might annually produce, under a mild administration, 500,000 ounces of silver, 400,000 measures of
rice, and 800,000 pieces of silk. Gaubil, Hist. de la
Dynastie des Mongous, p. 58, 59. Yelutchousay

(such was the name of the mandarin) was a wise
and virtuous minister, who saved his country and
civilised the conquerors. See p. 102, 103.

24. Particular instances would be endless; but
the curious reader may consult the Life of Gengiscan, by Petit de la Croix, the Histoire des Mongous,
and the fifteenth book of the History of the Huns.

25. At Maru, 1,300,000; at Herat, 1,600,000; at
Neisabour, 1,747,000. D'Herbelot, Bibliothèque
Orientale, p. 380, 381. I use the orthography of
D'Anville's maps. It must, however, be allowed,
that the Persians were disposed to exaggerate their
losses, and the Moguls to magnify their exploits.

26. Cherefeddin Ali, his servile panegyrist, would
afford us many horrid examples. In his camp before Delhi, Timur massacred 100,000 Indian prisoners, who had smiled when the army of their
countrymen appeared in sight (Hist. de Timur
Bec, tom. iii. p. 90). The people of Ispahan supplied 70,000 human skulls for the structure of several lofty towers (id. tom. i. p. 434). A similar tax
was levied on the revolt of Bagdad (tom. iii. p.
370); and the exact account, which Cherefeddin
was not able to procure from the proper officers, is
stated by another historian (Ahmed Arabsiada,
tom. ii. p. 175, vers. Manger) at 90,000 heads.

27. The ancients, Jornandes, Priscus, etc., are
ignorant of this epithet. The modern Hungarians
have imagined that it was applied, by a hermit of
Gaul, to Attila, who was pleased to insert it among
the titles of his royal dignity. Mascou, ix. 23, and
Tillemont, Hist. des Empereurs, tom. vi. p. 143.

28. The missionaries of St. Chrysostom had converted great numbers of the Scythians, who dwelt
beyond the Danube in tents and waggons. Theodoret, l. v. c. 31; Photius, p. 1517 [p. 508 b, ed.
Bekk.]. The Mahometans, the Nestorians, and the
Latin Christians, thought themselves secure of
gaining the sons and grandsons of Zingis, who
treated the rival missionaries with impartial favour.

29. The Germans, who exterminated Varus and
his legions, had been particularly offended with
the Roman laws and lawyers. One of the barbarians, after the effectual precautions of cutting
out the tongue of an advocate, and sewing up his
mouth, observed with much satisfaction that the
viper could no longer hiss. Florus, iv. 12.

30. Priscus, p. 59 [p. 190, ed. Bonn]. It should
seem that the Huns preferred the Gothic and
Latin languages to their own, which was probably
a harsh and barren idiom.

31. Philip de Comines, in his admirable picture
of the last moments of Lewis XI. (Mémoires, l. vi.
c. 12), represents the insolence of his physician,
who, in five months, extorted 54,000 crowns and a
rich bishopric from the stern avaricious tyrant.

32. Priscus (p. 61 [p. 194, ed. Bonn]) extols the
equity of the Roman laws, which protected the
life of a slave. Occidere solent (says Tacitus of the
Germans) non disciplinâ et servitate, sed impetu
et irâ, ut inimicum, nisi quòd impune. De Moribus
Germ. c. 25. The Heruli, who were the subjects of

Attila, claimed and exercised the power of life and death over their slaves. See a remarkable instance in the second book of Agathias.

33. See the whole conversation in Priscus, p. 59–62 [p. 189–197, ed. Bonn].

34. Nova iterum Orienti assurgit ruina . . . quum nulla ab Occidentalibus ferrentur auxilia. Prosper-Tyro composed his Chronicle in the West; and his observation implies a censure.

35. According to the description, or rather invective, of Chrysostom, an auction of Byzantine luxury must have been very productive. Every wealthy house possessed a semicircular table of massy silver, such as two men could scarcely lift; a vase of solid gold of the weight of forty pounds; cups, dishes, of the same metal, etc.

36. The articles of the treaty, expressed without much order or precision, may be found in Priscus (p. 34, 35, 36, 37, 53, etc. [ed. Par.; p. 142–148, 178, etc., ed. Bonn]). Count Marcellinus dispenses some comfort by observing—1. That Attila himself solicited the peace and presents which he had formerly refused; and, 2. That, about the same time, the ambassadors of India presented a fine large tame tiger to the emperor Theodosius.

37. Priscus, p. 35, 36 [p. 143, 144, ed. Bonn]. Among the hundred and eighty-two forts or castles of Thrace enumerated by Procopius (de Ædificiis, l. iv. c. xi. tom. ii. p. 92, edit. Paris [tom. iii. p. 306, ed. Bonn]), there is one of the name of Esimontou, whose position is doubtfully marked, in the neighbourhood of Anchialus and the Euxine Sea. The name and walls of Azimuntium might subsist till the reign of Justinian; but the race of its brave defenders had been carefully extirpated by the jealousy of the Roman princes.

38. The peevish dispute of St. Jerom and St. Augustin, who laboured by different expedients to reconcile the *seeming* quarrel of the two apostles, St. Peter and St. Paul, depends on the solution of an important question (Middleton's Works, vol. ii. p. 5–10), which has been frequently agitated by catholic and protestant divines, and even by lawyers and philosophers of every age.

39. Montesquieu (Considérations sur la Grandeur, etc., c. xix.) has delineated, with a bold and easy pencil, some of the most striking circumstances of the pride of Attila and the disgrace of the Romans. He deserves the praise of having read the Fragments of Priscus, which have been too much disregarded.

40. See Priscus, p. 69, 71, 72, etc. [p. 208, 213, ed. Bonn]. I would fain believe that this adventurer was afterwards crucified by the order of Attila, on a suspicion of treasonable practices; but Priscus (p. 57 [p. 185, 186, ed. Bonn]) has too plainly distinguished *two* persons of the name of Constantius, who, from the similar events of their lives, might have been easily confounded.

41. In the Persian treaty, concluded in the year 422, the wise and eloquent Maximin had been the assessor of Ardaburius (Socrates, l. vii. c. 20).

When Marcian ascended the throne, the office of Great Chamberlain was bestowed on Maximin, who is ranked in a public edict among the four principal ministers of state (Novell. ad Calc. Cod. Theod. p. 31 [tit. ii.]). He executed a civil and military commission in the eastern provinces; and his death was lamented by the savages of Æthiopia, whose incursions he had repressed. See Priscus, p. 40, 41 [p. 153, 154, ed. Bonn].

42. Priscus was a native of Panium in Thrace, and deserved by his eloquence an honourable place among the sophists of the age. His Byzantine history, which related to his own times, was comprised in seven books. See Fabricius Biblioth. Græc. tom. vi. p. 235, 236. Notwithstanding the charitable judgment of the critics, I suspect that Priscus was a Pagan.

43. The Huns themselves still continued to despise the labours of agriculture: they abused the privilege of a victorious nation; and the Goths, their industrious subjects, who cultivated the earth dreaded their neighbourhood, like that of so many ravenous wolves (Priscus, p. 45 [p. 163, ed. Bonn]). In the same manner the Sarts and Tadgics provide for their own subsistence, and for that of the Usbec Tartars, their lazy and rapacious sovereigns. See Genealogical History of the Tartars, p. 423, 455, etc.

44. It is evident that Priscus passed the Danube and the Theiss, and that he did not reach the foot of the Carpathian hills. Agria, Tokay, and Jazberin are situate in the plains circumscribed by this definition. M. de Buat (Histoire des Peuples, etc., tom. vii. p. 461) has chosen Tokay; Otrokosci (p. 180, apud Mascou, ix. 23), a learned Hungarian, has preferred Jazberin, a place about thirty-six miles westward of Buda and the Danube.

45. The royal village of Attila may be compared to the city of Karacorum, the residence of the successors of Zingis, which, though it appears to have been a more stable habitation, did not equal the size or splendour of the town and abbey of St. Denys in the 13th century (see Rubruquis, in the Histoire Générale des Voyages, tom. vii. p. 286). The camp of Aurengzebe, as it is so agreeably described by Bernier (tom. ii. p. 217–235), blended the manners of Scythia with the magnificence and luxury of Hindostan.

46. When the Moguls displayed the spoils of Asia in the diet of Toncal, the throne of Zingis was still covered with the original black felt carpet on which he had been seated when he was raised to the command of his warlike countrymen. See Vie de Gengiscan, l. iv. c. 9.

47. If we may believe Plutarch (in Demetrius, tom. v. p. 24), it was the custom of the Scythians, when they indulged in the pleasures of the table, to awaken their languid courage by the martial harmony of twanging their bow-strings.

48. The curious narrative of this embassy, which required few observations, and was not susceptible

of any collateral evidence, may be found in Priscus, p. 49–70 [ed. Par.; p. 170–209, ed. Bonn]. But I have not confined myself to the same order; and I had previously extracted the historical circumstances, which were less intimately connected with the journey and business of the Roman ambassadors.

49. M. de Tillemont has very properly given the succession of chamberlains who reigned in the name of Theodosius. Chrysaphius was the last, and, according to the unanimous evidence of history, the worst of these favourites (see Hist. des Empereurs, tom. vi. p. 117–119; Mém. Ecclés. tom. xv. p. 438). His partiality for his godfather, the heresiarch Eutyches, engaged him to persecute the orthodox party.

50. This secret conspiracy, and its important consequences, may be traced in the fragments of Priscus, p. 37, 38, 39, 54, 70, 71, 72 [p. 146–150, 180, 210–214, ed. Bonn]. The chronology of that historian is not fixed by any precise date; but the series of negotiations between Attila and the East-ern empire must be included within the three or four years which are terminated, A.D. 450, by the death of Theodosius.

51. Theodorus the Reader (see Vales. Hist. Eccles. tom. iii. p. 563) and the Paschal Chronicle mention the fall without specifying the injury; but the consequence was so likely to happen, and so unlikely to be invented, that we may safely give credit to Nicephorus Callistus, a Greek of the fourteenth century.

52. Pulcheriæ nutû (says Count Marcellinus) suâ cum avaritiâ interemptus est. She abandoned the eunuch to the pious revenge of a son whose father had suffered at his instigation.

53. Procopius, de Bell. Vandal. l. i. c. 4 [tom. i. p. 325, *sqq.* ed. Bonn]; Evagrius, l. ii. c. 1; Theophanes, p. 90, 91 [ed. Par.; tom. i. p. 161–164, ed. Bonn]; Noveil, ad Calcem Cod. Theod. tom. vi. p. 30. The praises which St. Leo and the catholics have bestowed on Marcian are diligently transcribed by Baronius, as an encouragement for future princes.

Chapter XXXV

1. See Priscus, p. 39, 72 [p. 213, 214, ed. Bonn].

2. The Alexandrian or Paschal Chronicle, which introduces this haughty message during the lifetime of Theodosius, may have anticipated the date; but the dull annalist was incapable of inventing the original and genuine style of Attila.

3. The second book of the Histoire Critique de l'Etablissement de la Monarchie Françoise, tom. i. p. 189–424, throws great light on the state of Gaul when it was invaded by Attila; but the ingenious author, the Abbé Dubos, too often bewilders himself in system and conjecture.

4. Victor Vitensis (de Persecut. Vandal. l. i. c. 6, p. 8, edit. Ruinart) calls him, acer consilio et strenuus in bello: but his courage, when he became unfortunate, was censured as desperate rashness; and Sebastian deserved, or obtained, the epithet of *præceps* (Sidon. Apollinar. Carmen ix. 281). His adventures at Constantinople, in Sicily, Gaul, Spain, and Africa, are faintly marked in the Chronicles of Marcellinus and Idatius. In his distress he was always followed by a numerous train; since he could ravage the Hellespont and Propontis and seize the city of Barcelona.

5. Reipublicæ Romanæ singulariter natus, qui superbiam Suevorum, Francorumque barbariem immensis cœdibus servire Imperio Romano coegisset. Jornandes de Rebus Geticis, c. 34, p. 660.

6. This portrait is drawn by Renatus Profuturus Frigeridus, a contemporary historian, known only by some extracts which are preserved by Gregory of Tours (l. ii. c. 8, in tom. ii. p. 163). It was probably the duty, or at least the interest, of Renatus, to magnify the virtues of Aëtius; but he would have shown more dexterity if he had not insisted on his patient *forgiving* disposition.

7. The embassy consisted of Count Romulus; of Promotus, president of Noricum; and of Romanus, the military duke. They were accompanied by Tatullus, an illustrious citizen of Petovio, in the same province, and father of Orestes, who had married the daughter of Count Romulus. See Priscus, p. 57, 65 [p. 185, 198, ed. Bonn]. Cassiodorus (Variar. i. 4) mentions another embassy which was executed by his father and Carpilio, the son of Aëtius; and, as Attila was no more, he could safely boast of their manly, intrepid behaviour in his presence.

8. Deserta Valentinæ urbis rura Alanis partienda traduntur. Prosper. Tyronis Chron. in Historiens de France, tom. i. p. 639. A few lines afterwards, Prosper observes that lands in the *ulterior* Gaul were assigned to the Alani. Without admitting the correction of Dubos (tom. i. p. 300), the reasonable supposition of *two* colonies or garrisons of Alani will confirm his arguments and remove his objections.

9. See Prosper, Tyro, p. 639. Sidonius (Panegyr. Avit. 246) complains, in the name of Auvergne, his native country—

Litorius Scythicos equites tunc forte, subacto
Celsus Aremorico, Geticum rapiebat in agmen
Per terras, Arverne, tuas: qui proxima quæque
Discursu, flammis, ferro, feritate, rapinis,
Delebant; pacis fallentes nomen inane.

Another poet, Paulinus of Perigord, confirms the complaint:

Nam socium vix ferre queas, qui durior hoste.

See Dubos, tom. i. p. 330.

10. Theodoric II., the son of Theodoric I., declares to Avitus his resolution of repairing, or expiating, the fault which his *grandfather* had committed.

> Quæ *noster*, peccavit *avus*, quem fuscat id unum,
> Quod te, Roma, capit.
>
> Sidon. Panegyric. Avit. 505.

This character, applicable only to the great Alaric, establishes the genealogy of the Gothic kings, which has hitherto been unnoticed.

11. The name of *Sapaudia*, the origin of *Savoy*, is first mentioned by Ammianus Marcellinus [l. xv. c. 11]; and two military posts are ascertained by the Notitia within the limits of that province; a cohort was stationed at Grenoble in Dauphiné; and Ebredunum, or Iverdun, sheltered a fleet of small vessels which commanded the lake of Neufchâtel. See Valesius, Notit. Galliarum, p. 503. D'Anville, Notice de l'Ancienne Gaule, p. 284, 579.

12. Salvian has attempted to explain the moral government of the Deity; a task which may be readily performed by supposing that the calamities of the wicked are *judgments*, and those of the righteous, *trials*.

13. ——Capto terrarum damna patebant
> Litorio: in Rhodanum proprios producere fines,
> Theudoridæ fixum; nec erat pugnare necesse,
> Sed migrare Getis. Rabidam trux asperat iram
> Victor; quôd sensit Scythicum sub mœnibus hostem
> Imputat, et nihil est gravius, si forsitan unquam
> Vincere contingat, trepido.
>
> Panegyr. Avit. 300, etc.

Sidonius then proceeds, according to the duty of a panegyrist, to transfer the whole merit from Aëtius to his minister Avitus.

14. Theodoric II. revered, in the person of Avitus, the character of his preceptor.

> ——Mihi Romula dudum
> Per te jura placent; parvumque ediscere jussit
> Ad tua verba pater, docili quo prisca *Maronis*
> Carmine molliret Scythicos mihi pagina mores.
>
> Sidon. Panegyric. Avit. 495, etc.

15. Our authorities for the reign of Theodoric I. are, Jornandes de Rebus Geticis, c. 34, 36, and the Chronicles of Idatius and the two Prospers, inserted in the Historians of France, tom. i. p. 612–640. To these we may add Salvian de Gubernatione Dei, l. vii. p. 243, 244, 245, and the Panegyric of Avitus by Sidonius.

16. Reges *Crinitos* [super] se creavisse de primâ, et ut ita dicam, nobiliori suorum familiâ (Greg. Turon. l. ii. c. 9, p. 166, of the second volume of the Historians of France). Gregory himself does not mention the *Merovingian* name, which may be

traced, however, to the beginning of the seventh century, as the distinctive appellation of the royal family, and even of the French monarchy. An ingenious critic has deduced the Merovingians from the great Maroboduus; and he has clearly proved that the prince who gave his name to the first race was more ancient than the father of Childeric. See Mémoires de l'Académie des Inscriptions, tom. xx. p. 52–90, from tom. xxx. p. 557–587.

17. This German custom, which may be traced from Tacitus to Gregory of Tours, was at length adopted by the emperors of Constantinople. From a MS. of the tenth century, Montfaucon has delineated the representation of a similar ceremony, which the ignorance of the age had applied to king David. See Monumens de la Monarchie Françoise, tom. i. Discours Préliminaire.

18. Cæsaries prolixa ... crinium flagellis per terga dismissis, etc. See the Preface to the third volume of the Historians of France and the Abbé Le Bœuf (Dissertat. tom. iii. p. 47–79). This peculiar fashion of the Merovingians has been remarked by natives and strangers; by Priscus (tom. i. p. 608 [p. 152, ed. Bonn]), by Agathias (tom. ii. p. 49 [l. i. c. 3, p. 19, ed. Bonn]), and by Gregory of Tours (l. iii. 18, vi. 24, viii. 10, tom. ii. p. 196, 278, 316).

19. See an original picture of the figure, dress, arms, and temper of the ancient Franks, in Sidonius Apollinaris (Panegyr., Majorian. 238–254); and such pictures, though coarsely drawn, have a real and intrinsic value. Father Daniel (Hist. de la Milice Françoise, tom. i. p. 2–7) has illustrated the description.

20. Dubos, Hist. Critique, etc., tom. i. p. 271, 272. Some geographers have placed Dispargum on the German side of the Rhine. See a note of the Benedictine Editors to the Historians of France, tom. ii. p. 166.

21. The Carbonarian wood was that part of the great forest of the Ardennes which lay between the Escaut, or Scheldt, and the Meuse. Vales. Notit. Gall. p. 126.

22. Gregor. Turon, l. ii. c. 9, in tom. ii. p. 166, 167; Fredegar. Epitom. c. 9, p. 395; Gesta Reg. Francor. c. 5, in tom. ii. p. 544; Vit. St. Remig. ab Hincmar, in tom. iii. p. 373.

23. —— Francus quâ Cloio patentes
> Atrebatum terras pervaserat.
>
> Panegyr. Majorian. 212.

The precise spot was a town or village called Vicus *Helena;* and both the name and the place are discovered by modern geographers at Lens. See Vales. Notit. Gall. p. 246. Longuerue, Description de la France, tom. ii. p. 88.

24. See a vague account of the action in Sidonius, Panegyr. Majorian. 212–230. The French critics, impatient to establish their monarchy in Gaul, have drawn a strong argument from the silence of Sidonius, who dares not insinuate that the vanquished Franks were compelled to repass the Rhine. Dubos, tom. i. p. 322.

25. Salvian (de Gubernat. Dei. l. vi.) has expressed, in vague and declamatory language, the misfortunes of these three cities, which are distinctly ascertained by the learned Mascou, Hist. of the Ancient Germans, ix. 21.

26. Priscus in relating the contest does not name the two brothers; the second of whom he had seen at Rome, a beardless youth, with long flowing hair (Historians of France, tom. i. p. 607, 608 [p. 152, ed. Bonn]). The Benedictine Editors are inclined to believe that they were the sons of some unknown king of the Franks who reigned on the banks of the Neckar; but the arguments of M. de Foncemagne (Mém. de l'Académie, tom. viii. p. 464) seem to prove that the succession of Clodion was disputed by his two sons, and that the younger was Meroveus, the father of Childeric.

27. Under the Merovingian race the throne was hereditary; but all the sons of the deceased monarch were equally entitled to their share of his treasures and territories. See the Dissertations of M. de Foncemagne, in the sixth and eighth volumes of the Mémoires de l'Académie.

28. A medal is still extant which exhibits the pleasing countenance of Honoria, with the title of Augusta; and on the reverse, the improper legend of *Salus Reipublicæ* round the monogram of Christ. See Ducange, Famil. Byzantin. p. 67, 73.

29. See Priscus, p. 39, 40 [p. 151, 152, ed. Bonn]. It might be fairly alleged that, if females could succeed to the throne, Valentinian himself, who had married the daughter and heiress of the younger Theodosius, would have asserted her right to the Eastern empire.

30. The adventures of Honoria are imperfectly related by Jornandes, de Successione Regn. c. 97, and de Reb. Get. c. 42, p. 674; and in the Chronicles of Prosper and Marcellinus; but they cannot be made consistent or probable, unless we separate, by an interval of time and place, her intrigue with Eugenius and her invitation of Attila.

31. Exegeras mihi, ut promitterem tibi Attilæ bellum stylo me posteris intimaturum . . . cœperam scribere, sed operis arrepti fasce perspecto, tæduit inchoasse. Sidon. Apoll. l. viii. Epist. 15, p. 246.

32. ———Subito cum rupta tumultu
    Barbaries totas in te transfuderat Arctos,
    Gallia. Pugnacem Rugum comitante Gelono,
    Gepida trux sequitur; Scyrum Burgundio cogit:
    Chunus, Bellonotus, Neurus, Basterna, *Toringus,*
    Bructerus, ulvosâ vel quem Nicer abluit undâ
    Prorumpit Francus. Cecidit cito secta bipenni
    Hercynia in lintres, et Rhenum texuit alno.
    Et jam terrificis diffuderat Attila turmis
    In campos, se, Belga, tuos.
                  Panegyr. Avit. 319, etc.

33. The most authentic and circumstantial account of this war is contained in Jornandes (de Reb. Geticis, c. 36–41, p. 662–672), who has sometimes abridged, and sometimes transcribed, the larger history of Cassiodorus. Jornandes, a quotation which it would be superfluous to repeat, may be corrected and illustrated by Gregory of Tours, l. ii. c. 5, 6, 7, and the Chronicles of Idatius, Isidore, and the two Prospers. All the ancient testimonies are collected and inserted in the Historians of France; but the reader should be cautioned against a supposed extract from the Chronicle of Idatius (among the fragments of Fredegarius, tom. ii. p. 462), which often contradicts the genuine text of the Gallician bishop.

34. The *ancient* legendaries deserve some regard, as they are obliged to connect their fables with the real history of their own times. See the Lives of St. Lupus, St. Anianus, the bishops of Metz, Ste. Genevieve, etc., in the Historians of France, tom. i. p. 644, 645, 649, tom. iii. p. 369.

35. The scepticism of the Count de Buat (Hist. des Peuples, tom. vii. p. 539, 540) cannot be reconciled with any principles of reason or criticism. Is not Gregory of Tours precise and positive in his account of the destruction of Metz? At the distance of no more than an hundred years could he be ignorant, could the people be ignorant, of the fate of a city, the actual residence of his sovereigns, the kings of Austrasia? The learned Count, who seems to have undertaken the apology of Attila and the barbarians, appeals to the false Idatius, *parcens* civitatibus Germaniæ et Galliæ, and forgets that the true Idatius had explicitly affirmed, plurimæ civitates *effractæ*, among which he enumerates Metz.

36.   ———Vix liquerat Alpes
    Aëtius, tenue, et rarum sine milite ducens
    Robur, in auxiliis Geticum male credulus agmen
    Incassum propriis præsumens adfore castris.
                Panegyr. Avit. 328, etc.

37. The policy of Attila, of Aëtius, and of the Visigoths, is imperfectly described in the Panegyric of Avitus and the thirty-sixth chapter of Jornandes. The poet and the historian were both biased by personal or national prejudices. The former exalts the merit and importance of Avitus; orbis, Avite, salus, etc.! The latter is anxious to show the Goths in the most favourable light. Yet their agreement, when they are fairly interpreted, is a proof of their veracity.

38. The review of the army of Aëtius is made by Jornandes, c. 36, p. 664, edit. Grot. tom. ii. p. 23, of the Historians of France, with the notes of the Benedictine editor. The *Læti* were a promiscuous race of barbarians, born or naturalised in Gaul; and the Riparii, or *Ripuarii*, derived their name from their posts on the three rivers, the Rhine, the Meuse, and the Moselle; the *Armoricans* possessed the independent cities between the Seine and the

Loire. A colony of *Saxons* had been planted in the diocese of Bayeux; the *Burgundians* were settled in Savoy; and the *Breones* were a warlike tribe of Rhætians, to the east of the lake of Constance.

39. Aurelianensis urbis obsidio, oppugnatio, irruptio, nec direptio. Sidon. Apollin. l. viii. Epist. 15, p. 246. The preservation of Orleans might easily be turned into a miracle, obtained and foretold by the holy bishop.

40. The common editions read xcm; but there is some authority of manuscripts (and almost any authority is sufficient) for the more reasonable number of xvm.

41. Châlons, or Duro-Catalaunum, afterwards *Catalauni*, had formerly made a part of the territory of Rheims, from whence it is distant only twenty-seven miles. See Vales. Notit. Gall. p. 136; D'Anville, Notice de l'Ancienne Gaule, p. 212, 279.

42. The name of Campania, or Champagne, is frequently mentioned by Gregory of Tours; and that great province, of which Rheims was the capital, obeyed the command of a duke. Vales. Notit. p. 120–123.

43. I am sensible that these military orations are usually composed by the historian; yet the old Ostrogoths, who had served under Attila, might repeat his discourse to Cassiodorus; the ideas, and even the expressions, have an original Scythian cast; and I doubt whether an Italian of the sixth century would have thought of the hujus certaminis *gaudia*.

44. The expressions of Jornandes, or rather of Cassiodorus, are extremely strong. Bellum atrox, multiplex, immane, pertinax, cui simile nulle usquam narrat antiquitas: ubi talia gesta referuntur, ut nihil esset quod in vitâ suâ conspicere potuisset egregius, qui hujus miraculi privaretur aspectú [c. 40, p. 668]. Dubos (Hist. Critique, tom. i. p. 392, 393) attempts to reconcile the 162,000 of Jornandes with the 300,000 of Idatius and Isidore, by supposing that the larger number included the total destruction of the war, the effects of disease, the slaughter of the unarmed people, etc.

45. The Count de Buat (Hist. des Peuples, etc., tom. vii. p. 554–573), still depending on the *false*, and again rejecting the *true*, Idatius, has divided the defeat of Attila into two great battles; the former near Orleans, the latter in Champagne: in the one, Theodoric was slain; in the other, he was revenged.

46. Jornandes de Rebus Geticis, c. 41, p. 671. The policy of Aëtius and the behaviour of Torismond are extremely natural; and the patrician, according to Gregory of Tours (l. ii. c. 7, p. 163), dismissed the prince of the Franks by suggesting to him a similar apprehension. The false Idatius ridiculously pretends that Aëtius paid a clandestine nocturnal visit to the kings of the Huns and of the Visigoths; from each of whom he obtained a bribe of ten thousand pieces of gold as the price of an undisturbed retreat.

47. These cruelties, which are passionately deplored by Theodoric, the son of Clovis (Gregory of Tours, l. iii. c. 10, p. 190), suit the time and circumstances of the invasion of Attila. His residence in Thuringia was long attested by popular tradition; and he is supposed to have assembled a *couroultai*, or diet, in the territory of Eisenach. See Mascou, ix. 30, who settles with nice accuracy the extent of ancient Thuringia, and derives its name from the Gothic tribe of the Thervingi.

48. Machinis constructis, omnibusque tormentorum generibus adhibitis. Jornandes, c. 42, p. 673. In the thirteenth century the Moguls battered the cities of China with large engines constructed by the Mahometans or Christians in their service, which threw stones from 150 to 300 pounds weight. In the defence of their country the Chinese used gunpowder, and even bombs, above an hundred years before they were known in Europe; yet even those celestial, or infernal, arms were insufficient to protect a pusillanimous nation. See Gaubil, Hist. des Mongous, p. 70, 71, 155, 157, etc.

49. The same story is told by Jornandes and by Procopius (de Bell. Vandal. l. i. c. 4, p. 187, 188 [tom. i. p. 330, ed. Bonn]): nor is it easy to decide which is the original. But the Greek historian is guilty of an inexcusable mistake in placing the siege of Aquileia *after* the death of Aëtius.

50. Jornandes, about an hundred years afterwards, affirms that Aquileia was so completely ruined, ita ut vix ejus vestigia, ut appareant, reliquerint. See Jornandes de Reb. Geticis, c. 42, p. 673. Paul. Diacon. l. ii. c. 14, p. 785 [Grot. Hist. Goth.]. Liutprand, Hist. l. iii. c. 2. The name of Aquileia was sometimes applied to Forum Julii (Civildad del Friuli), the more recent capital of the Venetian province.

51. In describing this war of Attila, a war so famous but so imperfectly known, I have taken for my guides two learned Italians who considered the subject with some peculiar advantages: Sigonius, de Imperio Occidentali, l. xiii. in his Works, tom. i. p. 495–502; and Muratori, Annali d'Italia, tom. iv. p. 229–236, 8vo edition.

52. This anecdote may be found under two different articles (μεδιόλανον and κόρυκοs) of the miscellaneous compilation of Suidas.

53.   Leo respondit, humanâ hoc pictum manû:
      Videres hominem dejectum, si pingere
      Leones scirent.
         Appendix ad Phædrum, Fab. xxv.
The lion in Phædrus very foolishly appeals from pictures to the amphitheatre; and I am glad to observe that the native taste of La Fontaine (l. iii. fable x.) has omitted this most lame and impotent conclusion.

54. Paul the Deacon (de Gestis Langobard, l. ii. c. 14 [seqq.], p. 784) describes the provinces of Italy about the end of the eighth century. *Venetia* non solum in paucis insulis quas nunc Venetias dicimus, constat; sed ejus terminus a Pannoniæ finibus usque Adduam fluvium protelatur. The his-

tory of that province till the age of Charlemagne forms the first and most interesting part of the Verona Illustrata (p. 1–388), in which the Marquis Scipio Maffei has shown himself equally capable of enlarged views and minute disquisitions.

55. This emigration is not attested by any contemporary evidence; but the fact is proved by the event, and the circumstances might be preserved by tradition. The citizens of Aquileia retired to the Isle of Gradus, those of Padua to Rivus Altus, or Rialto, where the city of Venice was afterwards built, etc.

56. The topography and antiquities of the Venetian islands, from Gradus to Clodia, or Chioggia, are accurately stated in the Dissertatio Chorographica de Italiâ Medii Ævi, p. 151–155.

57. Cassiodor. Variar. l. xii. Epist. 24. Maffei (Verona Illustrata, part i. p. 240–254) has translated and explained this curious letter, in the spirit of a learned antiquarian and a faithful subject, who considered Venice as the only legitimate offspring of the Roman republic. He fixes the date of the epistle, and consequently the præfecture, of Cassiodorus, A.D. 523; and the Marquis's authority has the more weight as he had prepared an edition of his works and actually published a dissertation on the true orthography of his name. See Osservazioni Letterarie, tom. ii. p. 290–339.

58. See, in the second volume of Amelot de la Houssaie, Histoire du Gouvernement de Venise, a translation of the famous *Squittenio*. This book, which has been exalted far above its merits, is stained in every line with the disingenuous malevolence of party: but the principal evidence, genuine and apocryphal, is brought together, and the reader will easily choose the fair medium.

59. Sirmond (Not. ad Sidon, Apollin. p. 19) has published a curious passage from the Chronicle of Prosper. Attila, redintegratis viribus, quas in Gallia amiserat, Italiam ingredi per Pannonias intendit; nihil duce nostro Aëtio secundum prioris belli opera prospiciente, etc. He reproaches Aëtius with neglecting to guard the Alps and with a design to abandon Italy; but this rash censure may at least be counterbalanced by the favourable testimonies of Idatius and Isidore.

60. See the original portraits of Avienus and his rival Basilius delineated and contrasted in the epistles (i. 9, p. 22) of Sidonius. He had studied the characters of the two chiefs of the senate; but he attached himself to Basilius as the more solid and disinterested friend.

61. The character and principles of Leo may be traced in one hundred and forty-one original epistles, which illustrate the ecclesiastical history of his long and busy pontificate, from A.D. 440 to 461. See Dupin, Bibliothèque Ecclésiastique, tom. iii. part ii. p. 120–165.

62. ——tardis ingens ubi flexibus errat
Mincius, et tenerâ prætexit arundine ripas
. . . .
Anne lacus tantos, te Lari maxime, teque

Fluctibus, et fremitu assurgens *Benace* marino.

63. The Marquis Maffei (Verona Illustrata, part i. p. 95, 129, 221, part ii. p. 2, 6) has illustrated with taste and learning this interesting topography. He places the interview of Attila and St. Leo near Ariolica, or Ardelica, now Peschiera, at the conflux of the lake and river; ascertains the villa of Catullus, in the delightful peninsula of Sirmio, and discovers the Andes of Virgil in the village of Bandes, precisely situate, quâ se subducere colles incipiunt, where the Veronese hills imperceptibly slope down into the plain of Mantua.

64. Si statim infesto agmine urbem petiissent, prande discrimen esset: sed in Venetiâ quo fere tractu Italia mollissima est, ipsâ soli cœlique clementiâ robur elanguit. Ad hoc panis usû carnisque coctæ, et dulcedine vini mitigatos, etc. This passage of Florus (iii. 3) is still more applicable to the Huns than to the Cimbri, and it may serve as a commentary on the *celestial* plague with which Idatius and Isidore have afflicted the troops of Attila.

65. The historian Priscus had positively mentioned the effect which this example produced on the mind of Attila. Jornandes, c. 42, p. 673.

66. The picture of Raphael is in the Vatican; the basso (or perhaps the alto) relievo of Algardi on one of the altars of St. Peter's (see Dubos, Réflexions sur la Poésie et sur la Peinture, tom. i. p. 519, 520). Baronius (Annal. Eccles. A.D. 452, No. 57, 58) bravely sustains the truth of the apparition; which is rejected, however, by the most learned and pious Catholics.

67. Attila, ut Priscus historicus refert, extinctionis suæ tempore, puellam Ildico nomine, decoram valde, sibi [in] matrimonium post innumerabiles uxores . . . socians. Jornandes, c. 49, p. 683, 684. He afterwards adds (c. 50, p. 686) Filii Attilæ, quorum per licentiam libidinis pœne populus fuit. Polygamy has been established among the Tartars of every age. The rank of plebeian wives is regulated only by their personal charms: and the faded matron prepares, without a murmur, the bed which is destined for her blooming rival. But in royal families the daughters of Khans communicate to their sons a prior right of inheritance. See Genealogical History, p. 406, 407, 408.

68. The report of her *guilt* reached Constantinople, where it obtained a very different name; and Marcellinus observes, that the tyrant of Europe was slain in the night by the hand and the knife of a woman. Corneille, who has adapted the genuine account to his tragedy, describes the irruption of blood in forty bombast lines, and Attila exclaims, with ridiculous fury,
——S'il ne veut s'arrêter (*his blood*),
(Dit-il) on me payera ce qui m'en va coûter.

69. The curious circumstances of the death and funeral of Attila are related by Jornandes (c. 49, p. 683, 684, 685), and were probably transcribed from Priscus.

70. See Jornandes, de Rebus Geticis, c. 50, p. 685, 686, 687, 688. His distinction of the national arms is curious and important. Nam ibi admirandum reor fuisse spectaculum, ubi cernere erat cunctis, pugnantem Gothum ense furentem, Gepidam in vulnere suorum cuncta tela frangentem, Suevum pede, Hunnum sagittâ præsumere, Alanum gravi, Herulum, levi, armaturâ, aciem instruere. I am not precisely informed of the situation of the river Netad.

71. Two modern historians have thrown much new light on the ruin and division of the empire of Attila—M. de Buat, by his laborious and minute diligence (tom. viii. p. 3–31, 68–94); and M. de Guignes, by his extraordinary knowledge of the Chinese language and writers. See Hist. des Huns, tom. ii. p. 315–319.

72. Placidia died at Rome, November 27, A.D. 450. She was buried at Ravenna, where her sepulchre, and even her corpse, seated in a chair of cypress-wood, were preserved for ages. The empress received many compliments from the orthodox clergy; and St. Peter Chrysologus assured her that her zeal for the Trinity had been recompensed by an august trinity of children. See Tillemont, Hist. des Emp. tom. vi. p. 240.

73. Aëtium Placidus mactavit semivir amens, is the expression of Sidonius (Panegyr. Avit. 359). The poet knew the world, and was not inclined to flatter a minister who had injured or disgraced Avitus and Majorian, the successive heroes of his song.

74. With regard to the cause and circumstances of the deaths of Aëtius and Valentinian, our information is dark and imperfect. Procopius (de Bell. Vandal. l. i. c. 4, p. 186, 187, 188 [tom. i. p. 327–331, ed. Bonn]) is a fabulous writer for the events which precede his own memory. His narrative must therefore be supplied and corrected by five or six Chronicles, none of which were composed in Rome or Italy, and which can only express, in broken sentences, the popular rumours as they were conveyed to Gaul, Spain, Africa, Constantinople, or Alexandria.

75. This interpretation of Vettius, a celebrated augur, was quoted by Varro in the xviiith book of his Antiquities. Censorinus, de Die Natali, c. 17, p. 90, 91, edit. Havercamp.

76. According to Varro, the twelfth century would expire A.D. 447; but the uncertainty of the true era of Rome might allow some latitude of anticipation or delay. The poets of the age, Claudian (de Bell. Getico, 265) and Sidonius (in Panegyr. Avit. 357), may be admitted as fair witnesses of the popular opinion.

> Dunc reputant annos, interceptoque volatû
> Vulturis, incidunt properatis sæcula metis.
>
> .   .   .   .   .   .
>
> Jam prope fata tui bissenas Vulturis alas
> Implebant; scis namque tuos, scis, Roma,
> labores.

See Dubos, Hist. Critique, tom. i. p. 340–346.

77. The fifth book of Salvian is filled with pathetic lamentations and vehement invectives. His immoderate freedom serves to prove the weakness, as well as the corruption, of the Roman government. His book was published after the loss of Africa (A.D. 439), and before Attila's war (A.D. 451).

78. The Bagaudæ of Spain, who fought pitched battles with the Roman troops, are repeatedly mentioned in the Chronicle of Idatius. Salvian has described their distress and rebellion in very forcible language. Itaque nomen civium Romanorum . . . nunc ultro repudiatur ac fugitur, nec vile tamen [tantum] sed etiam abominabile pœne habetur . . . Et hinc est ut etiam hi qui ad barbaros non confugiunt, barbari tamen esse coguntur, scilicet ut est pars magna Hispanorum, et non minima Gallorum . . . De Bagaudis nunc mihi sermo est, qui per malos judices et cruentos spoliati, afflicti, necati postquam jus Romanæ libertatis amiserant, etiam honorem Romani nominis perdiderunt . . . Vocamus rebelles, vocamus perditos quos compulimus criminosos. De Gubernat. Dei, l. v. p. 158, 159.

Chapter XXXVI

1. Sidonius Apollinaris composed the thirteenth epistle of the second book to refute the paradox of his friend Serranus, who entertained a singular though generous enthusiasm for the deceased emperor. This epistle, with some indulgence, may claim the praise of an elegant composition; and it throws much light on the character of Maximus.

2. Clientum prævia, pedisequa, circumfusa, populositas, is the train which Sidonius himself (l. i. Epist. 9) assigns to another senator of consular rank.

3.   Districtus ensis cui super impiâ
     Cervice pendet, non Siculæ dapes
     Dulcem elaborabunt saporem:

> Non avium citharæque cantus
> Somnum reducent.
>
> Horat. Carm. iii. 1.

Sidonius concludes his letter with the story of Damocles, which Cicero (Tusculan. v. 20, 21) had so inimitably told.

4. Notwithstanding the evidence of Procopius, Evagrius, Idatius, Marcellinus, etc., the learned Muratori (Annali d'Italia, tom. vi. p. 249) doubts the reality of this invitation, and observes, with great truth, "Non si può dii quanto sia facile il popolo a sognare e spacciar voci false." But his argument, from the interval of time and place, is extremely feeble. The figs which grew near Car-

thage were produced to the senate of Rome on the third day.

5. . . . Infidoque tibi Burgundio ductu
	Extorquet trepidas mactandi principis iras.
		Sidon. in Panegyr. Avit. 442.

A remarkable line, which insinuates that Rome and Maximus were betrayed by their Burgundian mercenaries.

6. The apparent success of pope Leo may be justified by Prosper, and the *Historia Miscellan.*; but the improbable notion of Baronius (A.D. 455, No. 13) that Genseric spared the three apostolical churches is not countenanced even by the doubtful testimony of the *Liber Pontificalis*.

7. The profusion of Catulus, the first who gilt the roof of the Capitol, was not universally approved (Plin. Hist. Natur. xxxiii. 18); but it was far exceeded by the emperor's, and the external gilding of the temple cost Domitian 12,000 talents (£2,400,000). The expressions of Claudian and Rutilius (*luce metalli æmula . . . fastigia astris*, and *confunduntque vagos delubra micantia visus*) manifestly prove that this splendid covering was not removed either by the Christians or the Goths (see Donatus, Roma Antiqua, l. ii. c. 6, p. 125). It should seem that the roof of the Capitol was decorated with gilt statues, and chariots drawn by four horses.

8. The curious reader may consult the learned and accurate treatise of Hadrian Reland, de Spoliis Templi Hierosolymitani in Arcú Titiano Romæ conspicuis, in 12mo. Trajecti ad Rhenum, 1716.

9. The vessel which transported the relics of the Capitol was the only one of the whole fleet that suffered shipwreck. If a bigoted sophist, a Pagan bigot, had mentioned the accident, he might have rejoiced that this cargo of sacrilege was lost in the sea.

10. See Victor Vitensis, de Persecut. Vandal. l. i. c. 8, p. 11, 12, edit. Ruinart. Deogratias governed the church of Carthage only three years. If he had not been privately buried, his corpse would have been torn piecemeal by the mad devotion of the people.

11. The general evidence for the death of Maximus, and the sack of Rome by the Vandals, is comprised in Sidonius (Panegyr. Avit. 441–450), Procopius (de Bell. Vandal. l. i. c. 4, 5, p. 188, 189 [tom. i. p. 332, ed. Bonn.], and l. ii. c. 9, p. 255 [tom. i. p. 445, *sq.*, ed. Bonn]), Evagrius (l. ii. c. 7), Jornandes (de Reb. Geticis, c. 45, p. 677), and the Chronicles of Idatius, Prosper, Marcellinus, and Theophanes, under the proper year.

12. The private life and elevation of Avitus must be deduced, with becoming suspicion, from the panegyric pronounced by Sidonius Apollinaris, his subject, and his son-in-law.

13. After the example of the younger Pliny, Sidonius (l. ii. Epist. 2) has laboured the florid, prolix, and obscure description of his villa, which bore the name (*Avitacum*), and had been the property,

of Avitus. The precise situation is not ascertained. Consult, however, the notes of Savaron and Sirmond.

14. Sidonius (l. ii. Epist. 9) has described the country life of the Gallic nobles, in a visit which he made to his friends, whose estates were in the neighbourhood of Nismes. The morning hours were spent in the *sphæristerium* or tennis-court, or in the library, which was furnished with *Latin* authors, profane and religious—the former for the men, the latter for the ladies. The table was twice served, at dinner and supper, with hot meat (boiled and roast) and wine. During the intermediate time, the company slept, took the air on horseback, and used the warm bath.

15. Seventy lines of panegyric (505–575) which describe the importunity of Theodoric and of Gaul, struggling to overcome the modest reluctance of Avitus, are blown away by three words of an honest historian. Romanum *ambisset* Imperium (Greg. Turon. l. ii. c. 11, in tom. ii. p. 168).

16. Isidore, archbishop of Seville, who was himself of the blood-royal of the Goths, acknowledges and almost justifies (Hist. Goth. p. 718) the crime which their slave Jornandes had basely dissembled (c. 43, p. 675).

17. This elaborate description (l. i. Ep. ii. p. 2–7) was dictated by some political motive. It was designed for the public eye, and had been shown by the friends of Sidonius before it was inserted in the collection of his epistles. The first book was published separately. See Tillemont, Mémoires Ecclés. tom. xvi. p. 264.

18. I have suppressed, in this portrait of Theodoric, several minute circumstances and technical phrases, which could be tolerable, or indeed intelligible, to those only who, like the contemporaries of Sidonius, had frequented the markets where naked slaves were exposed to sale (Dubos, Hist. Critique, tom. i. p. 404).

19. Videas ibi elegantiam Græcam, abundantiam Gallicanam; celeritatem Italam; publicam pompam, privatam diligentiam, regiam disciplinam.

20. Tunc etiam ego aliquid obsecraturus feliciter vincor, et mihi tabula perit ut causa salvetur [p. 6]. Sidonius of Auvergne was not a subject of Theodoric; but he might be compelled to solicit either justice or favour at the court of Toulouse.

21. Theodoric himself had given a solemn and voluntary promise of fidelity, which was understood both in Gaul and Spain:—
——Romæ sum, te duce, Amicus,
	Principe te, MILES.
					Sidon. Panegyr. Avit. 511.

22.	Quæque sinú pelagi jactat se Bracara
		dives.
			Auson. de Claris Urbibus, p. 245
						[Emerita, ix.].

From the design of the king of the Suevi, it is evident that the navigation from the ports of Gallicia to the Mediterranean was known and practised.

The ships of Bracara, or Braga, cautiously steered along the coast, without daring to lose themselves in the Atlantic.

23. This Suevic war is the most authentic part of the Chronicle of Idatius, who, as bishop of Iria Flavia, was himself a spectator and a sufferer. Jornandes (c. 44, p. 675, 676, 677) has expatiated with pleasure on the Gothic victory.

24. In one of the porticoes or galleries belonging to Trajan's library, among the statues of famous writers and orators. Sidon. Apoll. l. ix. Epist. 16, p. 284; Carm. viii. p. 350.

25. Luxuriose agere volens a senatoribus projectus est, is the concise expression of Gregory of Tours (l. ii. c. xi. in tom. ii. p. 168). An old Chronicle (in tom. ii. p. 649) mentions an indecent jest of Avitus, which seems more applicable to Rome than to Trèves.

26. Sidonius (Panegyr. Anthem. 302 [360], etc.) praises the royal birth of Ricimer, the lawful heir, as he chooses to insinuate, both of the Gothic and Suevic kingdoms.

27. See the Chronicle of Idatius. Jornandes (c. xliv. p. 676 [c. 45, p. 678]) styles him, with some truth, virum egregium, et pene tunc in Italiâ ad exercitum singularem.

28. Parcens innocentiæ Aviti, is the compassionate but contemptuous language of Victor Tunnunensis (in Chron. apud Scaliger Euseb.). In another place he calls him vir totius simplicitatis. This commendation is more humble, but it is more solid and sincere, than the praises of Sidonius.

29. He suffered, as it is supposed, in the persecution of Diocletian (Tillemont, Mém. Ecclés. tom. v. p. 279, 696). Gregory of Tours, his peculiar votary, has dedicated to the glory of Julian the Martyr an entire book (de Gloriâ Martyrum, l. ii. in Max. Bibliot. Patrum, tom. xi. p. 861–871), in which he relates about fifty foolish miracles performed by his relics.

30. Gregory of Tours (l. ii. c. xi. p. 168) is concise, but correct, in the reign of his countryman. The words of Idatius, "caret imperio, caret et vitâ" [Hist. de France, i. p. 621], seem to imply that the death of Avitus was violent; but it must have been secret, since Evagrius (l. ii. c. 7) could suppose that he died of the plague.

31. After a modest appeal to the examples of his brethren, Virgil and Horace, Sidonius honestly confesses the debt, and promises payment:—

Sic mihi diverso nuper sub Marte cadenti
Jussisti placido victor ut essem animo.
Serviat ergo tibi servati lingua poetæ,
Atque meæ vitæ laus tua sit pretium.
Sidon. Apoll. Carm. iv. p. 308.

See Dubos, Hist. Critique, tom. i. p. 448, etc.

32. The words of Procopius deserve to be transcribed: αὖτος γὰρ ὁ Μαιορῖνος ξύμπαντας τοὺς πώποτε ᾽Ρωμαίων βεβασιλευκότας ὑπεραίρων ἀρετῇ πάσῃ; and afterwards, ἀνὴρ τὰ μὲν εἰς τοὺς ὑπηκόους μέτριος γεγονώς, φοβερὸς δὲ τὰ ἐς τοὺς παλεμίους (de Bell. Vandal. l. i. c. 7, p. 194 [tom. i. p. 340 and 342, ed.

Bonn])—a concise but comprehensive definition of royal virtue.

33. The Panegyric was pronounced at Lyons before the end of the year 458, while the emperor was still consul. It has more art than genius, and more labour than art. The ornaments are false or trivial; the expression is feeble and prolix; and Sidonius wants the skill to exhibit the principal figure in a strong and distinct light. The private life of Majorian occupies about two hundred lines, 107–305.

34. She pressed his immediate death, and was scarcely satisfied with his disgrace. It should seem that Aëtius, like Belisarius and Marlborough, was governed by his wife, whose fervent piety, though it might work miracles (Gregor. Turon. l. ii. c. 7, p. 162), was not incompatible with base and sanguinary counsels.

35. The Alemanni had passed the Rhætian Alps, and were defeated in the Campi Canini, or Valley of Bellinzone, through which the Ticino flows, in its descent from Mount Adula, to the Lago Maggiore (Cluver. Italia Antiq. tom. i. p. 100, 101). This boasted victory over nine hundred barbarians (Panegyr. Majorian. 373, etc.) betrays the extreme weakness of Italy.

36. Imperatorem me factum, P. C. electionis vestræ arbitrio, et fortissimi exercitús ordinatione agnoscite (Novell. Majorian. tit. iii. p. 34, ad Calcem Cod. Theodos.). Sidonius proclaims the unanimous voice of the empire:—

——Postquam ordine vobis
Ordo omnis regnum dederat; plebs, curia, miles,
Et collega simul. [Carm. v.] 386.

This language is ancient and constitutional; and we may observe that the clergy were not yet considered as a distinct order of the state.

37. Either dilationes, or delationes, would afford a tolerable reading; but there is much more sense and spirit in the latter, to which I have therefore given the preference.

38. Ab externo hoste et a domesticâ clade liberavimus: by the latter, Majorian must understand the tyranny of Avitus, whose death he consequently avowed as a meritorious act. On this occasion Sidonius is fearful and obscure; he describes the twelve Cæsars, the nations of Africa, etc., that he may escape the dangerous name of Avitus (305–369).

39. See the whole edict or epistle of Majorian to the senate (Novell. tit. iv. p. 34.) Yet the expression regnum nostrum bears some taint of the age, and does not mix kindly with the word respublica, which he frequently repeats.

40. See the laws of Majorian (they are only nine in number, but very long and various), at the end of the Theodosian Code, Novell. l. iv. p. 32–37. Godefroy has not given any commentary on these additional pieces.

41. Fessas provincialium variâ atque multiplici tributorum exactione fortunas, et extraordinariis

fiscalium solutionum oneribus attritas, etc. Novell. Majorian. tit. iv. p. 34.

42. The learned Greaves (vol. i. p. 329, 330, 331) has found, by a diligent inquiry, that *aurei* of the Antonines weighed one hundred and eighteen, and those of the fifth century only sixty-eight English grains. Majorian gives currency to all gold coin, excepting only the *Gallic solidus*, from its deficiency, not in the weight, but in the standard.

43. The whole edict (Novell. Majorian. tit. vi. p. 35) is curious. "Antiquarum ædium dissipatur speciosa constructio; et ut [earum] aliquid reparetur, magna diruuntur. Hinc jam occasio nascitur, ut etiam unusquisque privatum ædificium construens, per gratiam judicum . . . præsumere de publicis locis necessaria, et transferre non dubitet," etc. With equal zeal, but with less power, Petrarch, in the fourteenth century, repeated the same complaints (Vie de Petrarque, tom. i. p. 326, 327). If I prosecute this History, I shall not be unmindful of the decline and fall of the *city* of Rome —an interesting object, to which my plan was originally confined.

44. The emperor chides the lenity of Rogatian, consular of Tuscany, in a style of acrimonius reproof, which sounds almost like personal resentment (Novell. tit. ix. p. 37). The law of Majorian which punished obstinate widows was soon afterwards repealed by his successor Severus (Novell. Sever. tit. i. p. 37).

45. Sidon. Panegyr. Majorian. 385–440.

46. The review of the army, and passage of the Alps, contain the most tolerable passages of the Panegyric (470–552). M. de Buat (Hist. des Peuples, etc., tom. viii. p. 49–55) is a more satisfactory commentator than either Savaron or Sirmond.

47. Τὰ μὲν ὅπλοις, τα δὲ λόγοις, is the just and forcible distinction of Priscus (Excerpt. Legat. p. 42 [p. 156, ed. Bonn]), in a short fragment which throws much light on the history of Majorian. Jornandes has suppressed the defeat and alliance of the Visigoths, which were solemnly proclaimed in Gallicia, and are marked in the Chronicle of Idatius.

48. Florus, l. ii. c. 2. He amuses himself with the poetical fancy that the trees had been transformed into ships; and, indeed, the whole transaction, as it is related in the first book of Polybius, deviates too much from the probable course of human events.

49.　Interea duplici texis dum littore classem
　Inferno superoque mari, cadit omnis in
　　æquor
　Silva tibi, etc.
　　　　Sidon. Panegyr. Majorian.
　　　　　　　　441–461.
The number of ships, which Priscus fixes at 300, is magnified, by an indefinite comparison with the fleets of Agamemnon, Xerxes, and Augustus.

50. Procopius de Bell. Vandal. l. i. c. 7, p. 194 [tom. i. p. 341, ed. Bonn]. When Genseric conducted his unknown guest into the arsenal of Carthage, the arms clashed of their own accord. Ma-

jorian had tinged his yellow locks with a black colour.

51. Spoliisque potitus
　Immensis, robur luxú jam perdidit omne,
　Quo valuit dum pauper erat.
　　　　　Panegyr. Majorian. 330.
He afterwards applies to Genseric, unjustly as it should seem, the vices of his subjects.

52. He burnt the villages and poisoned the springs (Priscus, p. 42 [p. 156, ed. Bonn]). Dubos (Hist. Critique, tom. i. p. 475) observes that the magazines which the Moors buried in the earth might escape his destructive search. Two or three hundred pits are sometimes dug in the same place, and each pit contains at least four hundred bushels of corn. Shaw's Travels, p. 139.

53. Idatius, who was safe in Gallicia from the power of Ricimer, boldly and honestly declares, Vandali per proditores admoniti, etc.: he dissembles, however, the name of the traitor.

54. Procop. de Bell. Vandal. l. i. c. 7, p. 194 [tom. i. p. 342, ed. Bonn]. The testimony of Idatius is fair and impartial: "Majorianum de Galliis Romam redeuntem, et Romano imperio vel nomini res necessarias ordinantem, Richimer livore percitus, et *invidorum* consilio fultus, fraude interficit circumventum" [Sirmondi Op. tom. ii. p. 311]. Some read *Suevorum*, and I am unwilling to efface either of the words, as they express the different accomplices who united in the conspiracy against Majorian.

55. See the Epigrams of Ennodius, No. cxxxv. inter Sirmond. Opera, tom. i. p. 1903. It is flat and obscure; but Ennodius was made bishop of Pavia fifty years after the death of Majorian, and his praise deserves credit and regard.

56. Sidonius gives a tedious account (l. i. Epist. xi. p. 25–31) of a supper at Arles, to which he was invited by Majorian a short time before his death. He had no intention of praising a deceased emperor; but a casual disinterested remark, "Subrisit Augustus; ut erat, auctoritate servatâ, cum se communioni dedisset, joci plenus," outweighs the six hundred lines of his venal panegyric.

57. Sidonius (Panegyr. Anthem. 317) dismisses him to heaven:—

　Auxerat Augustus naturæ lege Severus
　Divorum numerum.
And an old list of the emperors, composed about the time of Justinian, praises his piety, and fixes his residence at Rome (Sirmond. Not. ad Sidon, p. 111, 112).

58. Tillemont, who is always scandalised by the virtues of infidels, attributes this advantageous portrait of Marcellinus (which Suidas has preserved) to the partial zeal of some Pagan historian (Hist. des Empereurs. tom. vi. p. 330).

59. Procopius de Bell. Vandal. l. i. c. 6, p. 191 [tom. i. p. 336, ed. Bonn]. In various circumstances of the life of Marcellinus, it is not easy to reconcile the Greek historian with the Latin Chronicles of the times.

60. I must apply to Ægidius the praises which Sidonius (Panegyr. Majorian. 553) bestows on a nameless master-general, who commanded the rear-guard of Majorian. Idatius, from public report, commends his Christian piety; and Priscus mentions (p. 42 [p. 156, 157, ed. Bonn]) his military virtues.

61. Greg. Turon. l. ii. c. 12, in tom. ii. p. 168. The Père Daniel, whose ideas were superficial and modern, has started some objections against the story of Childeric (Hist. de France, tom. i. Préface Historique, p. lxxviii. etc.); but they have been fairly satisfied by Dubos (Hist. Critique, tom. i. p. 460–510), and by two authors who disputed the prize of the Academy of Soissons (p. 131–177, 310–339). With regard to the term of Childeric's exile, it is necessary either to prolong the life of Ægidius beyond the date assigned by the Chronicle of Idatius, or to correct the text of Gregory, by reading *quarto* anno, instead of *octavo*.

62. The naval war of Genseric is described by Priscus (Excerpta Legation. p. 42 [p. 157, ed. Bonn]), Procopius (de Bell. Vandal. l. i. c. 5, p. 189, 190, and c. 22, p. 228 [tom. i. p. 332, *sqq*., and p. 399, ed. Bonn]), Victor Vitensis (de Persecut. Vandal. l. i. c. 17, and Ruinart, p. 467–481), and in the three panegyrics of Sidonius, whose chronological order is absurdly transposed in the editions both of Savaron and Sirmond. (Avit. Carm. vii. 441–451. Majorian. Carm. v. 327–350, 385–440. Anthem. Carm. ii. 348–386.) In one passage the poet seems inspired by his subject, and expresses a strong idea by a lively image:—

——Hinc Vandalus hostis
Urget; et in nostrum numerosâ classe quotannis
Militat excidium; conversoque ordine fati
Torrida Caucaseos infert mihi Byrsa furores.
[Carm. ii. 347.]

63. The poet himself is compelled to acknowledge the distress of Ricimer:—

Præterea invictus Ricimer, quem publica fata
Respiciunt, *proprio* solus vix *Marte* repellit
Piratam per rura vabum.
[Carm. ii. 352.]

Italy addresses her complaint to the Tiber; and Rome, at the solicitation of the river-god, transports herself to Constantinople, renounces her ancient claims, and implores the friendship of Aurora, the goddess of the East. This fabulous machinery, which the genius of Claudian had used and abused, is the constant and miserable resource of the muse of Sidonius.

64. The original authors of the reigns of Marcian, Leo, and Zeno, are reduced to some imperfect fragments, whose deficiencies must be supplied from the more recent compilations of Theophanes, Zonaras, and Cedrenus.

65. St. Pulcheria died A.D. 453, four years before her nominal husband; and her festival is celebrated on the 10th of September by the modern Greeks: she bequeathed an immense patrimony to pious, or at least to ecclesiastical uses. See Tillemont. Mémoires Ecclés. tom. xv. p. 181–184.

66. See Procopius de Bell. Vandal. l. i. c. 4, p. 185 [tom. i. p. 325, ed. Bonn].

67. From this disability of Aspar to ascend the throne, it may be inferred that the stain of *Heresy* was perpetual and indelible, while that of *Barbarism* disappeared in the second generation.

68. Theophanes, p. 95 [ed. Par.; tom. i. p. 170, ed. Bonn]. This appears to be the first origin of a ceremony which all the Christian princes of the world have since adopted; and from which the clergy have deduced the most formidable consequences.

69. Cedrenus (p. 346 [ed. Par.; tom. i. p. 607, ed. Bonn]), who was conversant with the writers of better days, has preserved the remarkable words of Aspar, Βασιλεῦ, τὸν ταύτην τὴν ἀλουργίδα περιβεβλημένον οὐ Χρῆ διαψεύδεσθαι.

70. The power of the Isaurians agitated the Eastern empire in the two succeeding reigns of Zeno and Anastasius; but it ended in the destruction of those barbarians, who maintained their fierce independence about two hundred and thirty years.

71. ——Tali tu civis ab urbe
Procopio genitore micas; cui prisca propago
Augustis venit a *proavis.*

The poet (Sidon. Panegyr. Anthem. 67–306) then proceeds to relate the private life and fortunes of the future emperor, with which he must have been very imperfectly acquainted.

72. Sidonius discovers, with tolerable ingenuity, that this disappointment added new lustre to the virtues of Anthemius (210, etc.), who declined one sceptre, and reluctantly accepted another (22, etc.).

73. The poet again celebrates the unanimity of all orders of the state (15–22); and the Chronicle of Idatius mentions the forces which attended his march.

74. Interveni etenim nuptiis Patricii Ricimeris, cui filia perennis Augusti in spem publicæ securitatis copulabatur. The journey of Sidonius from Lyons, and the festival of Rome, are described with some spirit. L. i. Epist. 5, p. 9–13; Epist. 9. p. 21.

75. Sidonius (l. i. Epist. 9, p. 23, 24) very fairly states his motive, his labour, and his reward. "Hic ipse Panegyricus, si non judicium, certe eventum, boni operis, accepit." He was made bishop of Clermont A.D. 471. Tillemont, Mém. Ecclés. tom. xvi. p. 750.

76. The palace of Anthemius stood on the banks of the Propontis. In the ninth century, Alexius, the son-in-law of the emperor Theophilus, obtained permission to purchase the ground, and ended his days in a monastery which he founded on that delightful spot. Ducange, Constantinopolis Christiana, p. 117, 152.

77. Papa Hilarius ... apud beatum Petrum Apostolum, palam ne id fieret, clarâ voce con-

strinxit, in tantum ut non ea facienda cum interpositione juramenti idem promitteret Imperator. Gelasius Epistol. ad Andronicum, apud Baron. A.D. 467, No. 3. The cardinal observes, with some complacency, that it was much easier to plant heresies at Constantinople than at Rome.

78. Damascius, in the Life of the philosopher Isidore, apud Photium, p. 1040 [p. 340a, ed. Bekk.]. Damascius, who lived under Justinian, composed another work, consisting of 570 præternatural stories of souls, dæmons, apparitions, the dotage of Platonic Paganism.

79. In the poetical works of Sidonius, which he afterwards condemned (l. ix. Epist. 16, p. 285), the fabulous deities are the principal actors. If Jerom was scourged by the angels for only reading Virgil, the bishop of Clermont, for such a vile imitation, deserved an additional whipping from the Muses.

80. Ovid (Fast. l. ii. 267-452) has given an amusing description of the follies of antiquity, which still inspired so much respect, that a grave magistrate, running naked through the streets, was not an object of astonishment or laughter.

81. See Dionys. Halicarn. l. i. [c. 79] p. 25, 65, edit. Hudson. The Roman antiquaries, Donatus (l. ii. c. 18, p. 173, 174) and Nardini (p. 386, 387), have laboured to ascertain the true situation of the Lupercal.

82. Baronius published, from the MSS. of the Vatican, this epistle of Pope Gelasius (A.D. 496, No. 28-45), which is entitled Adversus Andromachum Senatorem, cæterosque Romanos, qui Lupercalia secundum morem pristinum colenda constituebant. Gelasius always supposes that his adversaries are nominal Christians, and, that he may not yield to them in absurd prejudice, he imputes to this harmless festival all the calamities of the age.

83. Itaque nos quibus totius mundi regimen commisit superna provisio.... Pius et triumphator semper Augustus filius noster Anthemius, licet Divina Majestas et nostra creatio pietati ejus plenam Imperii commiserit, potestatem, etc. ... Such is the dignified style of Leo, whom Anthemius respectfully names Dominus et Pater meus Princeps sacratissimus Leo. See Novell, Anthem. tit. ii. iii. p. 38, ad calcem Cod. Theod.

84. The expedition of Heraclius is clouded with difficulties (Tillemont, Hist. des Empereurs, tom. vi. p. 640), and it requires some dexterity to use the circumstances afforded by Theophanes, without injury to the more respectable evidence of Procopius.

85. The march of Cato from Berenice, in the province of Cyrene, was much longer than that of Heraclius from Tripoli. He passed the deep sandy desert in thirty days, and it was found necessary to provide, besides the ordinary supplies, a great number of skins filled with water, and several *Psylli*, who were supposed to possess the art of sucking the wounds which had been made by the serpents of their native country. See Plutarch in Caton. Uticens. [c. 56] tom. iv. p. 275; Strabon. Geograph. l. xvii. p. 1193 [p. 836, ed. Casaub.].

86. The principal sum is clearly expressed by Procopius (de Bell. Vandal. l. i. c. 6, p. 191 [tom. i. p. 335, ed. Bonn]); the smaller constituent parts, which Tillemont (Hist. des Empereurs, tom. vi. p. 396) has laboriously collected from the Byzantine writers, are less certain and less important. The historian Malchus laments the public misery (Excerpt. ex Suida in Corp. Hist. Byzant. p. 58); but he is surely unjust when he charges Leo with hoarding the treasures which he extorted from the people [p. 270, ed. Bonn].

87. This promontory is forty miles from Carthage (Procop. l. i. c. 6, p. 192 [De Bell. Vandal. tom. i. p. 377, ed. Bonn]), and twenty leagues from Sicily (Shaw's Travels, p. 89). Scipio landed farther in the bay, at the fair promontory; see the animated description of Livy, xxix. 26, 27.

88. Theophanes (p. 100 [tom. i. p. 179, ed. Bonn]) affirms that many ships of the Vandals were sunk. The assertion of Jornandes (de Successione Regn.), that Basiliscus attacked Carthage, must be understood in a very qualified sense.

89. Damascius in Vit. Isidor. apud Phot. p. 1048 [p. 342, ed. Bekk.]. It will appear, by comparing the three short chronicles of the times, that Marcellinus had fought near Carthage, and was killed in Sicily.

90. For the African war see Procopius (de Bell. Vandal. l. i. c. 6, p. 191, 192, 193 [tom. i. p. 335, sqq., ed bonn]), Theophanes (p. 99, 100, 101, [ed. Par.; tom. i. p. 179 sqq., ed. Bonn]), Cedrenus (p. 349, 350 [tom. i. p. 613, ed. Bonn]), and Zonaras (tom. ii. l. xiv. p. 50, 51). Montesquieu (Considérations sur la Grandeur, etc., c. xx. tom. iii. p. 497) has made a judicious observation on the failure of these great naval armaments.

91. Jornandes is our best guide through the reigns of Theodoric II. and Euric (de Rebus Geticis, c. 44, 45, 46, 47, p. 675-681). Idatius ends too soon, and Isidore is too sparing of the information which he might have given on the affairs of Spain. The events that relate to Gaul are laboriously illustrated in the third book of the Abbé Dubos, Hist. Critique, tom. i. p. 424-620.

92. See Mariana, Hist. Hispan. tom. i. l. v. c. 5, p. 162.

93. An imperfect, but original, picture of Gaul, more especially of Auvergne, is shown by Sidonius; who, as a senator and afterwards as a bishop, was deeply interested in the fate of his country. See l. v. [vii.] Epist. 1, 5, 9, etc.

94. Sidonius, l. iii. Epist. 3, p. 65-68; Greg. Turon. l. ii. c. 24, in tom. ii. p. 174; Jornandes, c. 45, p. 679. Perhaps Ecdicius was only the son-in-law of Avitus, his wife's son by another husband.

95. Si nullæ a republicâ vires, nulla præsidia, si nullæ, quantum rumor est, Anthemii principis opes, statuit, et auctore, nobilitas, seu patriam dimitere seu capillos (Sidon. l. ii. Epist. 1, p. 33).

The last words (Sirmond, Not. p. 25) may likewise denote the clerical tonsure, which was indeed the choice of Sidonius himself.

96. The history of these Britons may be traced in Jornandes (c. 45, p. 678), Sidonius (l. iii. Epistol. 9, p. 73, 74), and Gregory of Tours (l. ii. c. 18, in tom. ii. p. 170). Sidonius (who styles these mercenary troops argutos, armatos, tumultuosos, virtute, numero, contubernio, contumaces) addresses their general in a tone of friendship and familiarity.

97. See Sidonius, l. i. Epist. 7, p. 15–20, with Sirmond's notes. This letter does honour to his heart as well as to his understanding. The prose of Sidonius, however vitiated by a false and affected taste, is much superior to his insipid verses.

98. When the Capitol ceased to be a temple, it was appropriated to the use of the civil magistrate; and it is still the residence of the Roman senator. The jewellers, etc., might be allowed to expose their precious wares in the porticoes.

99. Hæc ad regem Gothorum, charta videbatur emitti pacem cum Græco Imperatore dissuadens, Britannos super Ligerim sitos impugnari oportere demonstrans, cum Burgundionibus jure gentium Gallias dividi debere confirmans.

100. Senatûsconsultum Tiberianum (Sirmond, Not. p. 17); but that law allowed only ten days between the sentence and execution; the remaining twenty were added in the reign of Theodosius.

101. Catilina seculi nostri. Sidonius, l. ii. Epist. 1, p. 33; l. v. Epist. 13, p. 143; l. vii. Epist. 7, p. 185. He execrates the crimes and applauds the punishment of Seronatus, perhaps with the indignation of a virtuous citizen, perhaps with the resentment of a personal enemy.

102. Ricimer, under the reign of Anthemius, defeated and slew in battle Beorgor, king of the Alani (Jornandes, c. 45, p. 678). His sister had married the king of the Burgundians, and he maintained an intimate connection with the Suevic colony established in Pannonia and Noricum.

103. Galatam concitatum. Sirmond (in his notes to Ennodius [tom. i. p. 659]) applies this appellation to Anthemius himself. The emperor was probably born in the province of Galatia, whose inhabitants, the Gallo-Grecians, were supposed to unite the vices of a savage and a corrupted people.

104. Epiphanius was thirty years bishop of Pavia (A.D. 467–497; see Tillemont, Mém. Ecclés. tom. xvi. p. 788.) His name and actions would have been unknown to posterity if Ennodius, one of his successors, had not written his Life (Sirmond, Opera, tom. i. p. 1647–1692); in which he represents him as one of the greatest characters of the age.

105. Ennodius (p. 1659–1664) has related this embassy of Epiphanius; and his narrative, verbose and turgid as it must appear, illustrates some curious passages in the fall of the Western empire.

106. Priscus Excerpt. Legation. p. 74 [p. 219, ed. Bonn]. Procopius de Bell. Vandal. l. i. c. 6, p. 191 [tom. i. p. 336, ed. Bonn]. Eudoxia and her daughter were restored after the death of Majorian. Perhaps the consulship of Olybrius (A.D. 464) was bestowed as a nuptial present.

107. The hostile appearance of Olybrius is fixed (notwithstanding the opinion of Pagi) by the duration of his reign. The secret connivance of Leo is acknowledged by Theophanes and the Paschal Chronicle. We are ignorant of his motives; but in this obscure period our ignorance extends to the most public and important facts.

108. Of the fourteen regions, or quarters, into which Rome was divided by Augustus, only one, the Janiculum, lay on the Tuscan side of the Tiber. But, in the fifth century, the Vatican suburb formed a considerable city; and in the ecclesiastical distribution, which had been recently made by Simplicius, the reigning pope, two of the seven regions or parishes of Rome depended on the church of St. Peter. See Nardini Roma Antica, p. 67. It would require a tedious dissertation to mark the circumstances in which I am inclined to depart from the topography of that learned Roman.

109. Nuper Anthemii et Ricimeris civili furore subversa est. Gelasius (in Epist. ad Andromach. apud Baron. A.D. 496, No. 42), Sigonius (tom. i. l. xiv. de Occidentali Imperio, p. 542, 543), and Muratori (Annali d'Italia tom. iv. p. 308, 309), with the aid of a less imperfect MS. of the Historia Miscella, have illustrated this dark and bloody transaction.

110. Such had been the sæva ac deformis urbe totâ facies, when Rome was assaulted and stormed by the troops of Vespasian (see Tacit. Hist. iii. 82, 83); and every cause of mischief had since acquired much additional energy. The revolution of ages may bring round the same calamities; but ages may revolve without producing a Tacitus to describe them.

111. See Ducange, Familiæ Byzantin. p. 74, 75. Areobindus, who appears to have married the niece of the emperor Justinian, was the eighth descendant of the elder Theodosius.

112. The last revolutions of the Western empire are faintly marked in Theophanes (p. 102 [tom. i. p. 184, ed. Bonn]), Jornandes (c. 45, p. 679), the Chronicle of Marcellinus, and the Fragments of an anonymous writer, published by Valesius at the end of Ammianus (p. 716, 717 [tom. ii. p. 303 sq., ed. Bipon.] If Photius had not been so wretchedly concise, we should derive much information from the contemporary histories of Malchus and Candidus. See his Extracts, p. 172–179 [p. 54–56, ed. Bekk.].

113. See Greg. Turon. l. ii. c. 28, in tom. ii. p. 175. Dubos, Hist. Critique, tom. i. p. 613. By the murder or death of his two brothers, Gundobald acquired the sole possession of the kingdom of Burgundy, whose ruin was hastened by their discord.

114. Julius Nepos armis pariter summus Augustus ac moribus. Sidonius, l. v. Ep. 16, p. 146. Nepos had given to Ecdicius the title of Patrician.

which Anthemius had promised, decessoris Anthemii fidem absolvit. See l. viii. Ep. 7, p. 224 [l. v. Ep. 16, p. 146].

115. Epiphanius was sent ambassador from Nepos to the Visigoths for the purpose of ascertaining the *fines Imperii Italici* (Ennodius in Sirmond, tom. i. p. 1665–1669). His pathetic discourse concealed the disgraceful secret which soon excited the just and bitter complaints of the bishop of Clermont.

116. Malchus, apud Phot. p. 172 [p. 54 b. ed. Bekk.]. Ennod. Epigram, lxxxii. in Sirmond Oper. tom. i. p. 1879. Some doubt may however be raised on the identity of the emperor and the archbishop.

117. Our knowledge of these mercenaries who subverted the Western empire is derived from Procopius (de Bell. Gothico. l. i. c. i. p. 308 [tom. ii. p. 6, ed. Bonn]). The popular opinion and the recent historians represent Odoacer in the false light of a *stranger* and a *king*, who invaded Italy with an army of foreigners, his native subjects.

118. Orestes, qui eo tempore quando Attila ad Italiam venit, se illi junxit, et ejus notarius factus fuerat. Anonym. Vales. p. 716 [Amm. Marc. tom. ii. p. 303, ed. Bipon.] He is mistaken in the date; but we may credit his assertion that the secretary of Attila was the father of Augustulus.

119. See Ennodius (in Vit. Epiphan. Sirmond, tom. i. p. 1669, 1670). He adds weight to the narrative of Procopius, though we may doubt whether the devil actually contrived the siege of Pavia to distress the bishop and his flock.

120. Jornandes, c. 53, 54, p. 692–695. M. de Buat (Hist. des Peuples de l'Europe, tom. viii. p. 221–228) has clearly explained the origin and adventures of Odoacer. I am almost inclined to believe that he was the same who pillaged Angers, and commanded a fleet of Saxon pirates on the ocean. Greg. Turon. l. ii. c. 18, in tom. ii. p. 170.

121. Vade ad Italiam, vade vilissimis nunc pellibus coopertus: sed multis cito plurima largiturus. Anonym. Vales. p. 717 [Amm. Marc. ii. p. 305, ed. Bipon.]. He quotes the Life of St. Severinus, which is extant, and contains much unknown and valuable history; it was composed by his disciple Eugippius (A.D. 511), thirty years after his death. See Tillemont, Mém. Ecclés. tom. xvi. p. 168–181.

122. Theophanes, who calls him a Goth, affirms that he was educated, nursed (τράφευτος), in Italy (p. 102 [tom. i. p. 184, ed. Bonn]); and as this strong expression will not bear a literal interpretation, it must be explained by long service in the Imperial guards.

123. Nomen regis Odoacer assumpsit, cum tamen neque purpurâ nec regalibus uteretur insignibus. Cassiodor. in Chron. A.D. 476. He seems to have assumed the abstract title of a king without applying it to any particular nation or country.

124. Malchus, whose loss excites our regret, has preserved (in Excerpt. Legat. p. 93 [ed. Par.; p. 235, ed. Bonn]) this extraordinary embassy from the senate to Zeno. The anonymous fragment (p. 717) and the extract from Candidus (apud Phot. p. 176 [p. 55, ed. Bekk.]) are likewise of some use.

125. The precise year in which the Western empire was extinguished is not positively ascertained. The vulgar era of A.D. 476 *appears* to have the sanction of authentic chronicles. But the two dates assigned by Jornandes (c. 46, p. 680) would delay that great event to the year 479; and though M. de Buat has overlooked *his* evidence, he produces (tom. viii. p. 261–288) many collateral circumstances in support of the same opinion.

126. See his medals in Ducange (Fam. Byzantin. p. 81), Priscus (Excerpt. Legat. p. 57 [p. 185, ed. Bonn]). Maffei (Osservazioni Letterarie, tom. ii. p. 314). We may allege a famous and similar case. The meanest subjects of the Roman empire assumed the *illustrious* name of *Patricius*, which, by the conversion of Ireland, has been communicated to a whole nation.

127. Ingrediens autem Ravennam deposuit Augustulum de regno, cujus infantiam misertus concessit ei sanguinem; et quia pulcher erat, tamen donavit ei reditum sex millia solidos, et misit eum intra Campaniam cum parentibus suis libere vivere. Anonym. Vales. p. 716 [Amm. Marc. tom. ii. p. 303, ed. Bipon.]. Jornandes says (c. 46, p. 680), in Lucullano Campaniæ castello exsilii pœna damnavit.

128. See the eloquent Declamation of Seneca (Epist. lxxxvi.). The philosopher might have recollected that all luxury is relative; and that the elder Scipio, whose manners were polished by study and conversation, was himself accused of that vice by his ruder contemporaries (Livy, xxix. 19).

129. Sylla, in the language of a soldier, praised his *peritia castrametandi* (Plin. Hist. Natur. xviii. 7). Phædrus, who makes its shady walks (*læta viridia*) the scene of an insipid fable (ii. 5), has thus described the situation:—

Cæsar Tiberius quum petens Neapolim,
In Misenensem villam venisset suam;
Quæ monte summo posita Luculli manu
Prospectat Siculum et despicit Tuscum mare.

130. From seven myriads and a half to two hundred and fifty myriads of drachmæ. Yet even in the possession of Marius it was a luxurious retirement. The Romans derided his indolence; they soon bewailed his activity. See Plutarch in Caius Marius.

131. Lucullus had other villas of equal, though various, magnificence at Baiæ, Naples, Tusculum, etc. He boasted that he changed his climate with the storks and cranes. Plutarch, in the life of Lucullus.

132. Severinus died in Noricum, A.D. 482. Six years afterwards his body, which scattered miracles as it passed, was transported by his disciples into Italy. The devotion of a Neapolitan lady invited the saint to the Lucullan villa, in the place of Augustulus, who was probably no more. See Ba-

ronius (Annal. Eccles. A.D. 496, No. 50, 51) and Tillemont (Mém. Ecclés. tom. xvi. p. 178–181), from the original Life by Eugippius. The narrative of the last migration of Severinus to Naples is likewise an authentic piece.

133. The consular Fasti may be found in Pagi or Muratori. The consuls named by Odoacer, or perhaps by the Roman senate, appear to have been acknowledged in the Eastern empire.

134. Sidonius Apollinaris (l. i. Epist. 9, p. 22, edit. Sirmond) has compared the two leading senators of his time (A.D. 468), Gennadius Avienus and Cæcina Basilius. To the former he assigns the specious, to the latter the solid, virtues of public and private life. A Basilius junior, possibly his son, was consul in the year 480.

135. Epiphanius interceded for the people of Pavia; and the king first granted an indulgence of five years, and afterwards relieved them from the oppression of Pelagius, the Prætorian præfect (Ennodius, in Vit. St. Epiphan, in Sirmond. Oper. tom. i. p. 1670–1672).

136. See Baronius, Annal. Eccles. A.D. 483, No. 10–15. Sixteen years afterwards the irregular proceedings of Basilius were condemned by pope Symmachus in a Roman synod.

137. The wars of Odoacer are concisely mentioned by Paul the Deacon (de Gest. Langobard. l.i.c. 19, p. 757, edit. Grot.) and in the two Chronicles of Cassiodorus and Cuspinian. The Life of St. Severinus, by Eugippius, which the Count de Buat (Hist. des Peuples, etc., tom. viii. c. 1, 4, 8, 9) has diligently studied, illustrates the ruin of Noricum and the Bavarian antiquities.

138. Tacit. Annal. iii. 54. The Recherches sur l'Administration des Terres chez les Romains (p. 351–361) clearly state the progress of internal decay.

139. A famine, which afflicted Italy at the time of the irruption of Odoacer, king of the Heruli, is eloquently described in prose and verse by a French poet (Les Mois, tom. ii. p. 174, 206, edit. in 12mo.). I am ignorant from whence he derives his information; but I am well assured that he relates some facts incompatible with the truth of history.

140. See the xxxixth epistle of St. Ambrose [tom. ii. p. 944, ed. Bened.] as it is quoted by Muratori, sopra le Antichità Italiane, tom. i. Dissert. xxi. p. 354.

141. Æmilia, Tuscia, ceteræque provinciæ in quibus hominum prope nullus exsistit. Gelasius, Epist. ad Andromachum, ap. Baronium Annal. Eccles. A.D. 496, No. 36.

142. Verumque confitentibus, latifundia perdidere Italiam. Plin. Hist. Natur. xviii. 7 [§ 3].

143. Such are the topics of consolation, or rather of patience, which Cicero (ad Familiares, lib. ix. Epist. 17) suggests to his friend Papirius Pætus, under the military despotism of Cæsar. The argument, however, of "vivere pulcherrimum duxi," is more forcibly addressed to a Roman philosopher, who possessed the free alternative of life or death.

Chapter XXXVII

1. The origin of the monastic institution has been laboriously discussed by Thomassin (Discipline de l'Eglise, tom. i. p. 1419–1426) and Helyot (Hist. des Ordres Monastiques, tom. i. p. 1–66). These authors are very learned and tolerably honest, and their difference of opinion shows the subject in its full extent. Yet the cautious Protestant, who distrusts *any* Popish guides, may consult the seventh book of Bingham's Christian Antiquities.

2. See Euseb. Demonstrat. Evangel. (l. i. p. 20, 21, edit. Græc. Rob. Stephani, Paris, 1545). In his Ecclesiastical History, published twelve years after the Demonstration, Eusebius (l. ii. c. 17) asserts the Christianity of the Therapeutæ; but he appears ignorant that a similar institution was actually revived in Egypt.

3. Cassian (Collat. xviii. 5 [Max. Bibl. Patr. t. vii. p. 208]) claims this origin for the institution of the *Cænobites*, which gradually decayed till it was restored by Antony and his disciples.

4. Ὠφελιμώτατον γάρ τι χρῆμα εἰς ἀνθρώπους ἐλθοῦσα παρὰ Θεοῦ ἡ τοιαύτη φιλοσοφία. These are the expressive words of Sozomen, who copiously and agreeably describes (l. i. c. 12, 13, 14) the origin and progress of this monkish philosophy (see Suicer. Thesaur. Eccles. tom. ii. p. 1441). Some modern writers, Lipsius (tom. iv. p. 448; Manuduct. ad Philosoph. Stoic. iii. 13) and La Mothe de Vayer (tom. ix. de la Vertu des Payens, p. 228–262), have compared the Carmelites to the Pythagoreans, and the Cynics to the Capucins.

5. The Carmelites derive their pedigree in regular succession from the prophet Elijah (see the Theses of Beziers, A.D. 1682, in Bayle's Nouvelles de la République des Lettres, Œuvres, tom. i. p. 82, etc.; and the prolix irony of the Ordres Monastiques, an anonymous work, tom. i. p. 1–433; Berlin, 1751). Rome and the inquisition of Spain silenced the profane criticism of the Jesuits of Flanders (Helyot, Hist. des Ordres Monastiques, tom. i. p. 282–300), and the statue of Elijah the Carmelite has been erected in the church of St. Peter (Voyages du P. Labat, tom. iii. p. 87).

6. Plin. Hist. Natur. v. 15. Gens sola, et in toto orbe præter ceteras mira, sine ullâ feminâ, omni venere abdicatâ, sine pecuniâ, socia palmarum. Ita per seculorum millia (incredibile dictu) gens æterna est in quâ nemo nascitur. Tam fecunda illis aliorum vitæ pœnitentia est. He places them just beyond the noxious influence of the lake, and names Engaddi and Masada as the nearest towns.

The Laura and monastery of St. Sabas could not be far distant from this place. See Reland, Palestin. tom. i. p. 295; tom. ii. p. 763, 874, 880, 890.

7. See Athanas. Op. tom. ii. p. 450–505 [tom. i. p. 793–866, ed. Bened. 1698], and the Vit. Patrum, p. 26–74, with Rosweyde's Annotations. The former is the Greek original; the latter, a very ancient Latin version by Evagrius, the friend of St. Jerom.

8. Τράμματα μὲν μάθειν οὐκ ἠνέσχετο. Athanas. tom. ii. in Vit. St. Anton. p. 452 [p. 795, ed. Bened. 1698; cf. c. 72, p. 849], and the assertion of his total ignorance has been received by many of the ancients and moderns. But Tillemont (Mém. Ecclés. tom. vii. p. 666) shows, by some probable arguments, that Antony could read and write in the Coptic, his native tongue; and that he was only a stranger to the *Greek letters*. The philosopher Synesius (p. 51 [ed. Par. 1612]) acknowledges that the natural genius of Antony did not require the aid of learning.

9. *Aruræ* autem erant ei trecentæ uberes, et valde optimæ (Vit. Patr. l. v. [l. i.] p. 36). If the *Arura* be a square measure of an hundred Egyptian cubits (Rosweyde, Onomasticon ad Vit. Patrum, p. 1014, 1015 [p. 1009]), and the Egyptian cubit of all ages be equal to twenty-two English inches (Greaves, vol. i. p. 233), the arura will consist of about three-quarters of an English acre.

10. The description of the monastery is given by Jerom (tom. i. p. 248, 249, in Vit. Hilarion [tom. ii. p. 31, ed. Vallars.]), and the P. Sicard (Missions du Levant, tom. v. p. 122–200). Their accounts cannot always be reconciled: the father painted from his fancy, and the Jesuit from his experience.

11. Jerom, tom. i. p. 146, ad Eustochium [Ep. 22, p. 119, ed. Vall.]; Hist. Lausiac. c. 7, in Vit. Patrum, p. 712 [p. 982]. The P. Sicard (Missions du Levant, tom. ii. p. 29–79) visited and has described this desert, which now contains four monasteries, and twenty or thirty monks. See D'Anville, Description de l'Egypte, p. 74.

12. Tabenne is a small island in the Nile, in the diocese of Tentyra or Dendera, between the modern town of Girge and the ruins of ancient Thebes (D'Anville, p. 194). M. de Tillemont doubts whether it was an isle; but I may conclude, from his own facts, that the primitive name was afterwards transferred to the great monastery of Bau or Pabau (Mém. Ecclés. tom. vii. p. 678, 688).

13. See in the Codex Regularum (published by Lucas Holstenius, Rome, 1661) a preface of St. Jerom to his Latin version of the Rule of Pachomius, tom. i. p. 61 [tom. i. p. 25, ed. Augsb. 1759].

14. Rufin. c. 5, in Vit. Patrum, p. 459. He calls it civitas ampla valde et populosa, and reckons twelve churches. Strabo (l. xvii. p. 1166 [p. 812, ed. Casaub.]) and Ammianus (xxii. 16) have made honourable mention of Oxyrinchus, whose inhabitants adored a small fish in a magnificent temple.

15. Quanti populi habentur in urbibus, tantæ pene habentur in desertis multitudines monachorum. Rufin. c. 7, in Vit. Patrum, p. 461. He congratulates the fortunate change.

16. The introduction of the monastic life into Rome and Italy is occasionally mentioned by Jerom, tom. i. p. 119, 120, 199.

17. See the Life of Hilarion, by St. Jerom (tom. i. p. 241, 252 [tom. ii. p. 15, 24, ed. Vall.]). The stories of Paul, Hilarion, and Malchus, by the same author, are admirably told; and the only defect of these pleasing compositions is the want of truth and common sense.

18. His original retreat was in a small village on the banks of the Iris, not far from Neo-Cæsarea. The ten or twelve years of his monastic life were disturbed by long and frequent avocations. Some critics have disputed the authenticity of his ascetic rules; but the external evidence is weighty, and they can only prove that it is the work of a real or affected enthusiast. See Tillemont, Mém. Ecclés. tom. ix. p. 636–644; Helyot, Hist. des Ordres Monastiques, tom. i. p. 175–181.

19. See his Life, and the three Dialogues by Sulpicius Severus, who asserts (Dialog. i. 16) that the booksellers of Rome were delighted with the quick and ready sale of his popular work.

20. When Hilarion sailed from Parætonium to Cape Pachynus, he offered to pay his passage with a book of the Gospels. Posthumian, a Gallic monk, who had visited Egypt, found a merchant-ship bound from Alexandria to Marseilles, and performed the voyage in thirty days (Sulp. Sever. Dialog. i. 1). Athanasius, who addressed his Life of St. Anthony to the foreign monks, was obliged to hasten the composition, that it might be ready for the sailing of the fleets (tom. ii. p. 451 [tom. i. p. 794, ed. Bened. 1698]).

21. See Jerom (tom. i. p. 126), Assemanni, Bibliot. Orient. tom. iv. p. 92, p. 857–919, and Geddes, Church History of Æthiopia, p. 29, 30, 31. The Abyssinian monks adhere very strictly to the primitive institution.

22. Camden's Britannia, vol. i. p. 666, 667.

23. All that learning can extract from the rubbish of the dark ages is copiously stated by Archbishop Usher in his Britannicarum Ecclesiarum Antiquitates, cap. xvi. p. 425–503.

24. This small though not barren spot, Iona, Hy, or Columbkill, only two miles in length and one mile in breadth, has been distinguished—1. By the monastery of St. Columba, founded A.D. 566, whose abbot exercised an extraordinary jurisdiction over the bishops of Caledonia; 2. By a *classic* library, which afforded some hopes of an entire Livy; and, 3. By the tombs of sixty kings, Scots, Irish, and Norwegians, who reposed in holy ground. See Usher (p. 311, 360–370) and Buchanan (Rer. Scot. l. ii. p. 15, edit. Ruddiman).

25. Chrysostom (in the first tome of the Benedictine edition) has consecrated three books to the praise and defence of the monastic life. He is encouraged, by the example of the ark, to presume

that none but the elect (the monks) can possibly be saved (l. i. p. 55, 56). Elsewhere, indeed, he becomes more merciful (l. iii. p. 83, 84), and allows different degrees of glory, like the sun, moon, and stars. In his lively comparison of a king and a monk (l. iii. p. 116–121), he supposes (what is hardly fair) that the king will be more sparingly rewarded, and more rigorously punished.

26. Thomassin (Discipline de l'Eglise, tom. i. p. 1426–1469) and Mabillon (Œuvres Posthumes, tom. ii. p. 115–158). The monks were gradually adopted as a part of the ecclesiastical hierarchy.

27. Dr. Middleton (vol. i. p. 110) liberally censures the conduct and writings of Chrysostom, one of the most eloquent and successful advocates for the monastic life.

28. Jerom's devout ladies form a very considerable portion of his works: the particular treatise, which he styles the Epitaph of Paula (tom. i. p. 169–192 [Ep. 108, tom. i. p. 684, ed. Vallars.]), is an elaborate and extravagant panegyric. The exordium is ridiculously turgid:—"If all the members of my body were changed into tongues, and if all my limbs resounded with a human voice, yet should I be incapable," etc.

29. Socrus Dei esse cœpisti (Jerom. tom. i. p. 140, ad Eustochium), Rufinus (in Hieronym. Op. tom. iv. p. 223), who was justly scandalised, asks his adversary, From what Pagan poet he had stolen an expression so impious and absurd?

30. Nunc autem veniunt *plerumque* ad hanc professionem servitutis Dei, et ex conditione servili, vel etiam liberati, vel propter hoc a Dominis liberati sive liberandi; et ex vitâ rusticanâ, et ex opificum exercitatione, et plebeio labore. Augustin. de Oper. Monach. c. 22, ap. Thomassin, Discipline de l'Eglise, tom. iii. p. 1094. The Egyptian, who blamed Arsenius, owned that he led a more comfortable life as a monk than as a shepherd. See Tillemont, Mém. Ecclés. tom. xiv. p. 679.

31. A Dominican friar (Voyages du P. Labat, tom. i. p. 10), who lodged at Cadiz in a convent of his brethren, soon understood that their repose was never interrupted by nocturnal devotion; "quoiqu'on ne laisse pas de sonner pour l'édification du peuple."

32. See a very sensible preface of Lucas Holstenius to the Codex Regularum. The emperors attempted to support the obligation of public and private duties; but the feeble dykes were swept away by the torrent of superstition; and Justinian surpassed the most sanguine wishes of the monks (Thomassin, tom. i. p. 1782–1799, and Bingham, l. vii. c. 3, p. 253).

33. The monastic institutions, particularly those of Egypt, about the year 400, are described by four curious and devout travellers—Rufinus (Vit. Patrum, l. ii. iii. p. 424–536), Posthumian (Sulp. Sever. Dialog. i.), Palladius (Hist. Lausiac. in Vit. Patrum, p. 709–863 [783]), and Cassian (see in tom. vii. Bibliothec. Max. Patrum, his four first

books of Institutes, and the twenty-four Collations or Conferences).

34. The example of Malchus (Jerom. tom. i. p. 256 [tom. ii. p. 44, ed. Vallars.]), and the design of Cassian and his friend (Collation xxiv. 1), are incontestable proofs of their freedom, which is elegantly described by Erasmus in his Life of St. Jerom. See Chardon, Hist. des Sacremens, tom. vi. p. 279–300.

35. See the Laws of Justinian (Novell. cxxiii. No. 42 [Auth. Coll. ix. tit. vii.]), and of Lewis the Pious (in the Historians of France, tom. vi. p. 427), and the actual jurisprudence of France, in Denissart (Decisions, etc., tom. iv. p. 855, etc.).

36. The ancient Codex Regularum, collected by Benedict Anianinus, the reformer of the monks in the beginning of the ninth century, and published in the seventeenth by Lucas Holstenius, contains thirty different rules for men and women. Of these seven were composed in Egypt, one in the East one in Cappadocia, one in Italy, one in Africa, four in Spain, eight in Gaul or France, and one in England.

37. The rule of Columbanus, so prevalent in the West inflicts one hundred lashes for very slight offences (Cod. Reg. part ii. p. 174 [tom. i. p. 178, ed. 1759]). Before the time of Charlemagne the abbots indulged themselves in mutilating their monks, or putting out their eyes—a punishment much less cruel than the tremendous *vade* in *pace* (the subterraneous dungeon, or sepulchre), which was afterwards invented. See an admirable discourse of the learned Mabillon (Œuvres Posthumes, tom. ii. p. 321–336), who, on this occasion, seems to be inspired by the genius of humanity. For such an effort, I can forgive his defence of the holy tear of Vendome (p. 361–399).

38. Sulp. Sever. Dialog. i. 12, 13, p. 532, etc. [ed. Lugd. B. 1647]; Cassian. Institut. l. iv. c. 26, 27. "Præcipua ibi virtus et prima est obedientia." Among the Verba seniorum (in Vit. Patrum, l. v. p. 617), the fourteenth libel or discourse is on the subject of obedience; and the Jesuit Rosweyde, who published that huge volume for the use of convents, has collected all the scattered passages in his two copious indexes.

39. Dr. Jortin (Remarks on Ecclesiastical History, vol. iv. p. 161) has observed the scandalous valour of the Cappadocian monks, which was exemplified in the banishment of Chrysostom.

40. Cassian has simply, though copiously, described the monastic habit of Egypt (Institut. l. i.), to which Sozomen (l. iii. c. 14) attributes such allegorical meaning and virtue.

41. Regul. Benedict. cap. 55, in Cod. Regul. part ii. p. 51 [tom. i. p. 130, ed. Augsb. 1759].

42. See the Rule of Ferreolus, bishop of Usez (cap. 31, in Cod. Regul. part ii. p. 136 [tom. i. p. 162]), and of Isidore, bishop of Seville (cap. 13, in Cod. Regul. part ii. p. 214 [tom. i. p. 193]).

43. Some partial indulgences were granted for the hands and feet. "Totum autem corpus nemo

unguet nisi causâ infirmitatis, nec lavabitur aquâ nudo corpore, nisi languor perspicuus sit." (Regul. Pachom. xcii. part. i. p. 78 [tom. i. p. 31].)

44. St. Jerom, in strong but indiscreet language, expresses the most important use of fasting and abstinence: "Non quod Deus universitatis Creator et Dominus, intestinorum nostrorum rugitû, et inanitate ventris, pulmonisque ardore delectetur, sed quod aliter pudicitia tuta esse non possit." (Op. tom. i. p. 137, ad Eustochium [Ep. 22, tom. i. p. 94, ed. Vallars.].) See the twelfth and twenty-second Collations of Cassian, de Castitate and de Illusionibus Nocturnis.

45. Edacitas in Græcas gula est, in Gallis natura (Dialog. i. c. 4, p. 521). Cassian fairly owns that the perfect model of abstinence cannot be imitated in Gaul, on account of the aërum temperies, and the qualitas nostræ fragilitatis (Institut. iv. 11). Among the Western rules, that of Columbanus is the most austere: he had been educated amidst the poverty of Ireland, as rigid, perhaps, and inflexible as the abstemious virtue of Egypt. The rule of Isidore of Seville is the mildest: on holidays he allows the use of flesh.

46. "Those who drink only water, and have no nutritious liquor, ought at least to have a pound and a half (twenty-four ounces) of bread every day." State of Prisons, p. 40, by Mr. Howard.

47. See Cassian. Collat. ii. 19, 20, 21. The small loaves or biscuit of six ounces each had obtained the name of Paximacia (Rosweyde, Onomasticon, p. 1045 [1033]). Pachomius, however, allowed his monks some latitude in the quantity of their food; but he made them work in proportion as they ate (Pallad. in Hist. Lausiac. c. 38, 39, in Vit. Patrum, l. viii. p. 736, 737).

48. See the banquet to which Cassian (Collation viii. 1) was invited by Serenus, an Egyptian abbot.

49. See the Rule of St. Benedict, cap. 39, 40 (in Cod. Reg. part ii. p. 41, 42 [tom. i. p. 129, ed. 1759]). Licet legamus vinum omnino monachorum non esse, sed quia nostris temporibus id monachis persuaderi non potest; he allows them a Roman hemina, a measure which may be ascertained from Arbuthnot's Tables.

50. Such expressions as my book, my cloak, my shoes (Cassian. Institut. l. iv. c. 13) were not less severely prohibited among the Western monks (Cod. Regul. part ii. p. 174 [tom. i. p. 178], 235, 288); and the Rule of Columbanus punished them with six lashes. The ironical author of the Ordres Monastiques, who laughs at the foolish nicety of modern convents, seems ignorant that the ancients were equally absurd.

51. Two great masters of ecclesiastical science, the P. Thomassin (Discipline de l'Eglise, tom. iii. p. 1090-1139) and the P. Mabillon (Etudes Monastiques, tom. i. p. 116-155), have seriously examined the manual labour of the monks, which the former considers as a merit, and the latter as a duty.

52. Mabillon (Etudes Monastiques, tom. i. p. 47-55) has collected many curious facts to justify the literary labours of his predecessors both in the East and West. Books were copied in the ancient monasteries of Egypt (Cassian. Institut. l. iv. c. 12), and by the disciples of St. Martin (Sulp. Sever. in Vit. Martin. c. 7, p. 473). Cassiodorus has allowed an ample scope for the studies of the monks; and we shall not be scandalised if their pen sometimes wandered from Chrysostom and Augustin to Homer and Virgil.

53. Thomassin (Discipline de l'Eglise, tom. iii. p. 118, 145, 146, 171-179) has examined the revolution of the civil, canon, and common law. Modern France confirms the death which monks have inflicted on themselves, and justly deprives them of all right of inheritance.

54. See Jerom (tom. i. p. 176, 183). The monk Pambo made a sublime answer to Melania, who wished to specify the value of her gift:—"Do you offer it to me, or to God? If to God, HE who suspends the mountains in a balance need not be informed of the weight of your plate." (Pallad. Hist. Lausiac. c. 10, in the Vit. Patrum, l. viii. p. 715.)

55. Τὸ πολὺ μέρος τῆς γῆς ᾠκειώσαντο, προφάσει τοῦ μεταδιδόναι πάντων πτωχοῖς, πάντας (ὡς εἰπεῖν) πτωχοὺς καταστήσαντες. Zosim. l. v. [c. 23] p. 325. Yet the wealth of the Eastern monks was far surpassed by the princely greatness of the Benedictines.

56. The sixth general council (the Quinisext in Trullo, Canon xlvii. in Beveridge, tom. i. p. 213) restrains women from passing the night in a male, or men in a female, monastery. The seventh general council (the second Nicene, Canon xx. in Beveridge, tom. i. p. 325) prohibits the erection of double or promiscuous monasteries of both sexes; but it appears from Balsamon that the prohibition was not effectual. On the irregular pleasures and expenses of the clergy and monks, see Thomassin, tom. iii. p. 1334-1368.

57. I have somewhere heard or read the frank confession of a Benedictine abbot: "My vow of poverty has given me an hundred thousand crowns a year; my vow of obedience has raised me to the rank of a sovereign prince." I forget the consequences of his vow of chastity.

58. Pior, an Egyptian monk, allowed his sister to see him; but he shut his eyes during the whole visit. See Vit. Patrum, l. iii. p. 504. Many such examples might be added.

59. The 7th, 8th, 29th, 30th, 31st, 34th, 57th, 60th, 86th, and 95th articles of the Rule of Pachomius, impose most intolerable laws of silence and mortification.

60. The diurnal and nocturnal prayers of the monks are copiously discussed by Cassian, in the third and fourth books of his Institutions; and he constantly prefers the liturgy which an angel had dictated to the monasteries of Tabennœ.

61. Cassian, from his own experience, describes the acedia, or listlessness of mind and body, to which a monk was exposed when he sighed to find

himself alone. Sæpiusque egreditur et ingreditur cellam, et Solem velut ad occasum tardius properantem crebrius intuetur (Institut. x. 2).

62. The temptations and sufferings of Stagirius were communicated by that unfortunate youth to his friend St. Chrysostom. See Middleton's Works, vol. i. p. 107-110. Something similar introduces the life of every saint; and the famous Inigo, or Ignatius, the founder of the Jesuits (Vida d'Inigo de Guiposcoa, tom. i. p. 29-38) may serve as a memorable example.

63. Fleury, Hist. Ecclésiastique, tom. vii. p. 46. I have read somewhere in the Vitæ Patrum, but I cannot recover the place, that *several*, I believe *many*, of the monks, who did not reveal their temptations to the abbot, became guilty of suicide.

64. See the seventh and eighth Collations of Cassian, who gravely examines why the dæmons were grown less active and numerous since the time of St. Antony. Rosweyde's copious index to the Vitæ Patrum will point out a variety of infernal scenes. The devils were most formidable in a female shape.

65. For the distinction of the *Cœnobites* and the *Hermits*, especially in Egypt, see Jerom (tom. i. p. 45, ad Rusticum [Ep. 125, tom. i. p. 932, ed. Vallars.]), the first Dialogue of Sulpicius Severus, Rufinus (c. 22, in Vit. Patrum, l. ii. p. 478), Palladius (c. 7, 69, in Vit. Patrum, l. viii. p. 712, 758), and, above all, the eighteenth and nineteenth Collations of Cassian. These writers, who compare the common and solitary life, reveal the abuse and danger of the latter.

66. Suicer. Thesaur. Ecclesiast. tom. ii. p. 205, 218. Thomassin (Discipline de l'Eglise, tom. i. p. 1501, 1502) gives a good account of these cells. When Gerasimus founded his monastery, in the wilderness of Jordan, it was accompanied by a Laura of seventy cells.

67. Theodoret, in a large volume (the Philotheus in Vit. Patrum, l. ix. p. 793-863) has collected the lives and miracles of thirty Anachorets. Evagrius (l. i. c. 21) more briefly celebrates the monks and hermits of Palestine.

68. Sozomen, l. vi. c. 33. The great St. Ephrem composed a panegyric on these βόσκοι, or grazing monks (Tillemont, Mém. Ecclés. tom. viii. p. 292).

69. The P. Sicard (Missions du Levant, tom. ii. p. 217-233) examined the caverns of the Lower Thebais with wonder and devotion. The inscriptions are in the old Syriac character, which was used by the Christians of Abyssinia.

70. See Theodoret (in Vit. Patrum, l. ix. p. 848-854), Antony (in Vit. Patrum, l. i. p. 170-177), Cosmas (in Asseman. Bibliot. Oriental. tom. i. p. 239-253), Evagrius (l. i. c. 13, 14), and Tillemont (Mém. Ecclés. tom. xv. p. 347-392).

71. The narrow circumference of two cubits, or three feet, which Evagrius assigns for the summit of the column, is inconsistent with reason, with facts, and with the rules of architecture. The people who saw it from below might be easily deceived.

72. I must not conceal a piece of ancient scandal concerning the origin of this ulcer. It has been reported that the Devil, assuming an angelic form, invited him to ascend, like Elijah, into a fiery chariot. The saint too hastily raised his foot, and Satan seized the moment of inflicting this chastisement on his vanity.

73. I know not how to select or specify the miracles contained in the *Vitæ Patrum* of Rosweyde, as the number very much exceeds the thousand pages of that voluminous work. An elegant specimen may be found in the Dialogues of Sulpicius Severus and his Life of St. Martin. He reveres the monks of Egypt; yet he insults them with the remark that *they* never raised the dead; whereas the bishop of Tours had restored *three* dead men to life.

74. On the subject of Ulphilas and the conversion of the Goths, see Sozomen, l. vi. c. 37; Socrates, l. iv. c. 33; Theodoret, l. iv. c. 37; Philostorg. l. ii. c. 5. The heresy of Philostorgius appears to have given him superior means of information.

75. A mutilated copy of the four Gospels in the Gothic version was published A.D. 1665, and is esteemed the most ancient monument of the Teutonic language, though Wetstein attempts, by some frivolous conjectures, to deprive Ulphilas of the honour of the work. Two of the four additional letters express the *W* and our own *Th*. See Simon, Hist. Critique du Nouveau Testament, tom. ii. p. 219-223. Mill. Prolegom. p. 151, edit. Kuster. Wetstein, Prolegom. tom. i. p. 114.

76. Philostorgius erroneously places this passage under the reign of Constantine; but I am much inclined to believe that it preceded the great emigration.

77. We are obliged to Jornandes (de Reb. Get. c. 51, p. 688) for a short and lively picture of these lesser Goths. Gothi minores, populus immensus, cum suo Pontifice ipsoque primate Wulfila. The last words, if they are not mere tautology, imply some temporal jurisdiction.

78. At non ita Gothi non ita Vandali; malis licet doctoribus instituti, meliores tamen etiam in hâc parte quam nostri. Salvian de Gubern. Dei, l. vii. p. 243 [ed. Par. 1608].

79. Mosheim has slightly sketched the progress of Christianity in the North, from the fourth to the fourteenth century. The subject would afford materials for an ecclesiastical and even philosophical history.

80. To such a cause has Socrates (l. vii. c. 30) ascribed the conversion of the Burgundians, whose Christian piety is celebrated by Orosius (l. vii. c. 19 [32]).

81. See an original and curious epistle from Daniel, the first bishop of Winchester (Beda, Hist. Eccles. Anglorum, l. v. c. 18, p. 203, edit. Smith), to St. Boniface, who preached the Gospel among the savages of Hesse and Thuringia. Epistol. Bonifacii, lxvii. in the Maxima Bibliotheca Patrum, tom. xiii. p. 93.

82. The sword of Charlemagne added weight to

the argument; but when Daniel wrote this epistle (A.D. 723), the Mahometans, who reigned from India to Spain, might have retorted it against the Christians.

83. The opinions of Ulphilas and the Goths inclined to semi-Arianism, since they would not say that the Son was a *creature*, though they held communion with those who maintained that heresy. Their apostle represented the whole controversy as a question of trifling moment which had been raised by the passions of the clergy. Theodoret, l. iv. c. 37.

84. The Arianism of the Goths has been imputed to the emperor Valens: "Itaque justo Dei judicio ipsi eum vivum incenderunt, qui propter eum etiam mortui, vitio erroris arsuri sunt." Orosius, l. vii. c. 33, p. 554. This cruel sentence is confirmed by Tillemont (Mém. Ecclés. tom. vi. p. 604–610), who coolly observes, "un seul homme entraîna dans l'enfer un nombre infini de Septentrionaux," etc. Salvian (de Gubern. Dei, l. v. p. 150, 151) pities and excuses their involuntary error.

85. Orosius affirms, in the year 416 (l. vii. c. 41, p. 580), that the churches of Christ (of the catholics) were filled with Huns, Suevi, Vandals, Burgundians.

86. Radbod, king of the Frisons, was so much scandalised by this rash declaration of a missionary, that he drew back his foot after he had entered the baptismal font. See Fleury, Hist. Ecclés. tom. ix. p. 167.

87. The epistles of Sidonius, bishop of Clermont under the Visigoths, and of Avitus, bishop of Vienne under the Burgundians, explain, sometimes in dark hints, the general dispositions of the catholics. The history of Clovis and Theodoric will suggest some particular facts.

88. Genseric confessed the resemblance by the severity with which he punished such indiscreet allusions. Victor Vitensis, i. 7, p. 10.

89. Such are the contemporary complaints of Sidonius, bishop of Clermont (l. vii. c. 6, p. 182, etc., edit. Sirmond). Gregory of Tours, who quotes this Epistle (l. ii. c. 25, in tom. ii. p. 174), extorts an unwarrantable assertion, that, of the nine vacancies in Aquitain, some had been produced by episcopal *martyrdoms*.

90. The original monuments of the Vandal persecution are preserved in the five books of the history of Victor Vitensis (de Persecutione Vandalicâ), a bishop who was exiled by Hunneric; in the Life of St. Fulgentius, who was distinguished in the persecution of Thrasimund (in Biblioth. Max. Patrum, tom. ix. p. 4–16); and in the first book of the Vandalic War, by the impartial Procopius (c. 7, 8, p. 196, 197, 198, 199 [ed. Paris; tom. i. p. 344 *sqq*., ed. Bonn]). Dom. Ruinart, the last editor of Victor, has illustrated the whole subject with a copious and learned apparatus of notes and supplement. (Paris, 1694.)

91. Victor, iv. 2, p. 65. Hunneric refuses the name of Catholics to the *Homoousians*. He describes,

as the veri Divinæ Majestatis cultores, his own party, who professed the faith, confirmed by more than a thousand bishops, in the synods of Rimini and Seleucia.

92. Victor, ii. 1, p. 21, 22, *Laudabilior . . .* videbatur. In the MSS. which omit this word, the passage is unintelligible. See Ruinart, Not. p. 164.

93. Victor, ii. 2, p. 22, 23 [21, 22]. The clergy of Carthage called these conditions *periculosæ*; and they seem, indeed, to have been proposed as a snare to entrap the catholic bishops.

94. See the narrative of this conference and the treatment of the bishops in Victor, ii. 13–18, p. 35–42, and the whole fourth book, p. 63–71. The third book, p. 42–62, is entirely filled by their apology or confession of faith.

95. See the list of the African bishops, in Victor, p. 117–140, and Ruinart's notes, p. 215–397. The schismatic name of *Donatus* frequently occurs, and they appear to have adopted (like our fanatics of the last age) the pious appellations of *Deodatus, Deogratias, Quidvultdeus, Habetdeum*, etc.

96. Fulgent. Vit. c. 16–29. Thrasimund affected the praise of moderation and learning; and Fulgentius addressed three books of controversy to the Arian tyrant, whom he styles *piissime Rex*. Biblioth. Maxim. Patrum, tom. ix. p. 41. Only sixty bishops are mentioned as exiles in the Life of Fulgentius; they are increased to one hundred and twenty by Victor Tunnunensis and Isidore; but the number of two hundred and twenty is specified in the *Historia Miscella* and a short authentic chronicle of the times. See Ruinart, p. 570, 571.

97. See the base and insipid epigrams of the Stoic, who could not support exile with more fortitude than Ovid. Corsica might not produce corn, wine, or oil; but it could not be destitute of grass, water, and even fire.

98. Si ob gravitatem cœli interissent, *vile* damnum. Tacit. Annal. ii. 85. In this application Thrasimund would have adopted the reading of some critics, *utile* damnum.

99. See these preludes of a *general* persecution, in Victor, ii. c. 3, 4, 7, and the two edicts of Hunneric, l. ii. p. 35, l. iv. p. 64.

100. See Procopius de Bell. Vandal. l. i. c. 7 [c. 8], p. 197, 198 [tom. i. p. 344 *sqq*., ed. Bonn]. A Moorish prince endeavoured to propitiate the God of the Christians by his diligence to erase the marks of the Vandal sacrilege.

101. See this story in Victor, ii. 8–12, p. 30–34. Victor describes the distress of these confessors as an eye-witness.

102. See the fifth book of Victor. His passionate complaints are confirmed by the sober testimony of Procopius and the public declaration of the emperor Justinian. Cod. l. i. tit. xxvii.

103. Victor, ii. 18, p. 41.

104. Victor, v. 4, p. 74, 75. His name was Victorianus, and he was a wealthy citizen of Adrumetum, who enjoyed the confidence of the king,

by whose favour he had obtained the office, or at least the title, of proconsul of Africa.

105. Victor, i. 6, p. 8, 9. After relating the firm resistance and dexterous reply of Count Sebastian, he adds, quare alio [aliius] generis argumento postea bellicosum virum occidit.

106. Victor, v. 12, 13. Tillemont, Mém. Ecclés. tom. vi. p. 609.

107. *Primate* was more properly the title of the bishop of Carthage; but the name of *patriarch* was given by the sects and nations to their principal ecclesiastic. See Thomassin, Discipline de l'Elgise, tom. i. p. 155, 158.

108. The patriarch Cyrila himself publicly declared that he did not understand Latin (Victor, ii. 18, p. 42): Nescio Latine; and he might converse with tolerable ease, without being capable of disputing or preaching in that language. His Vandal clergy were still more ignorant; and small confidence could be placed in the Africans who had conformed.

109. Victor, ii. 1, 2, p. 22.

110. Victor, v. 7, p. 77. He appeals to the ambassador himself, whose name was Uranius.

111. *Astutiores,* Victor, iv. 4, p. 70. He plainly intimates that their quotation of the Gospel, "Non jurabitis in toto," was only meant to elude the obligation of an inconvenient oath. The forty-six bishops who refused were banished to Corsica; the three hundred and two who swore were distributed through the provinces of Africa.

112. Fulgentius, bishop of Ruspæ, in the Byzacene province, was of a senatorial family and had received a liberal education. He could repeat all Homer and Menander before he was allowed to study Latin, his native tongue (Vit. Fulgent. c. 1). Many African bishops might understand Greek, and many Greek theologians were translated into Latin.

113. Compare the two prefaces to the Dialogue of Vigilius of Thapsus (p. 118, 119, edit. Chiflet). He might amuse his learned reader with an innocent fiction; but the subject was too grave, and the Africans were too ignorant.

114. The P. Quesnel started this opinion, which has been favourably received. But the three following truths, however surprising they may seem, are *now* universally acknowledged (Gerard Vossius, tom. vi. p. 516–522; Tillemont, Mém. Ecclés. tom. viii. p. 667–671). 1. St. Athanasius is not the author of the creed which is so frequently read in our churches. 2. It does not appear to have existed within a century after his death. 3. It was originally composed in the Latin tongue, and, consequently, in the Western provinces. Gennadius, a patriarch of Constantinople, was so much amazed by this extraordinary composition, that he frankly pronounced it to be the work of a drunken man. Petav. Dogmat. Theologica, tom. ii. l. vii. c. 8, p. 687.

115. 1 John v. 7. See Simon, Hist. Critique du Nouveau Testament, part i. c. xviii. p. 203–218;

and part ii. c. ix. p. 99–121; and the elaborate Prolegomena and Annotations of Dr. Mill and Wetstein to their editions of the Greek Testament. In 1689, the papist Simon strove to be free; in 1707, the Protestant Mill wished to be a slave; in 1751, the Arminian Wetstein used the liberty of his times and of his sect.

116. Of *all* the MSS. now extant, above fourscore in number, some of which are more than 1200 years old (Wetstein ad loc.). The *orthodox* copies of the Vatican, of the Complutensian editors, of Robert Stephens, are become invisible; and the *two* MSS. of Dublin and Berlin are unworthy to form an exception. See Emlyn's Works, vol. ii. p. 227–255, 269–299; and M. de Missy's four ingenious letters, in tom. viii. and ix. of the Journal Britannique.

117. Or, more properly, by the *four* bishops who composed and published the profession of faith in the name of their brethren. They styled this text luce clarius (Victor Vitensis de Persecut. Vandal. l. iii. c. 11, p. 54). It is quoted soon afterwards by the African polemics Vigilius and Fulgentius.

118. In the eleventh and twelfth centuries the Bibles were corrected by Lanfranc, archbishop of Canterbury, and by Nicolas, cardinal and librarian of the Roman church, secundum orthodoxam fidem (Wetstein, Prolegom. p. 84, 85). Notwithstanding these corrections, the passage is still wanting in twenty-five Latin MSS. (Wetstein ad loc.), the oldest and the fairest; two qualities seldom united, except in manuscripts.

119. The art which the Germans had invented was applied in Italy to the profane writers of Rome and Greece. The original Greek of the New Testament was published about the same time (A.D. 1514, 1516, 1520) by the industry of Erasmus and the munificence of Cardinal Ximenes. The Complutensian Polyglot cost the cardinal 50,000 ducats. See Mattaire, Annal. Typograph. tom. ii. p. 2–8, 125–133; and Wetstein, Prolegomena, p. 116–127.

120. The three witnesses have been established in our Greek Testaments by the prudence of Erasmus; the honest bigotry of the Complutensian editors; the typographical fraud or error of Robert Stephens in the placing a crotchet; and the deliberate falsehood or strange misapprehension of Theodore Beza.

121. Plin. Hist. Natural. v. 1; Itinerar. Wesseling, p. 15; Cellarius, Geograph. Antiq. tom. ii. part ii. p. 127. This Tipasa (which must not be confounded with another in Numidia) was a town of some note, since Vespasian endowed it with the right of Latium.

122. Optatus Milevitanus de Schism. Donatist. l. ii. p. 38.

123. Victor Vitensis, v. 6. p. 76. Ruinart, p. 483–487.

124. Æneas Gazæus in Theophrasto, in Biblioth. Patrum, tom. viii. p. 664, 665. He was a Christian, and composed this Dialogue (the Theophrastus) on the immortality of the soul and the

resurrection of the body; besides twenty-five Epistles, still extant. See Cave (Hist. Litteraria, p. 297) and Fabricius (Biblioth. Græc. tom. i. p. 422).

125. Justinian. Codex, l. i. tit. xxvii. [leg. 1]; Marcellin. in Chron. p. 45, in Thesaur. Temporum Scaliger; Procopius, de Bell. Vandal. l. i. c. 8, p. 196 [ed. Par.; tom. i. p. 345, ed. Bonn]; Gregor. Magnus, Dialog. iii. 32. None of these witnesses have specified the number of the confessors, which is fixed at sixty in an old menology (apud Ruinart, p. 486). Two of them lost their speech by fornication; but the miracle is enhanced by the singular instance of a boy who had *never* spoken before his tongue was cut out.

126. See the two general historians of Spain, Mariana (Hist. de Rebus Hispaniæ, tom. i. l. v. c. 12–15, p. 182–194) and Ferreras (French translation tom. ii. p. 206–247). Mariana almost forgets that he is a Jesuit, to assume the style and spirit of a Roman classic. Ferreras, an industrious compiler, reviews his facts and rectifies his chronology.

127. Goisvintha successively married two kings of the Visigoths: Athanigild, to whom she bore Brunechild, the mother of Ingundis; and Leovigild, whose two sons, Hermenegild and Recared, were the issue of a former marriage.

128. Iracundiæ furore succensa, adprehensam per comam capitis puellam in terram conlidit, et diu calcibus verberatam, ac sanguine cruentatam, jussit exspoliari, et piscinæ immergi. Greg. Turon. l. v. c. 39, in tom. ii. p. 255. Gregory is one of our best originals for this portion of history.

129. The catholics, who admitted the baptism of heretics, repeated the rite, or, as it was afterwards styled, the sacrament, of confirmation, to which they ascribed many mystic and marvellous prerogatives, both visible and invisible. See Chardon, Hist. des Sacremens, tom. i. p. 405–552.

130. Osset, or Julia Constantia, was opposite to Seville, on the northern side of the Bætis (Plin. Hist. Natur. iii. 3): and the authentic reference of Gregory of Tours (Hist. Francor. l. vi. c. 43, p. 288) deserves more credit than the name of Lusitania (de Gloriâ Martyr. c. 24), which has been eagerly embraced by the vain and superstitious Portuguese (Ferreras, Hist. d'Espagne, tom. ii. p. 166.)

131. This miracle was skilfully performed. An Arian king sealed the doors and dug a deep trench round the church without being able to intercept the Easter supply of baptismal water.

132. Ferreras (tom. ii. p. 168–175, A.D. 550) has illustrated the difficulties which regard the time and circumstances of the conversion of the Suevi. They had been recently united by Leovigild to the Gothic monarchy of Spain.

133. This addition to the Nicene, or rather the Constantinopolitan creed, was first made in the eighth council of Toledo, A.D. 653; but it was expressive of the popular doctrine (Gerard Vossius, tom. vi. p. 527, de tribus Symbolis).

134. See Gregor. Magn. l. vii. Epist. 126, apud Baronium, Annal. Eccles. A.D. 599, No. 25, 26 [l. ix. Ep. 122, tom. ii. p. 1031, ed. Bened.].

135. Paul Warnefrid (de Gestis Langobard. l. iv. c. 44, p. 853, edit. Grot.) allows that Arianism still prevailed under the reign of Rotharis (A.D. 636–652). The pious *deacon* does not attempt to mark the precise era of the national conversion, which was accomplished, however, before the end of the seventh century.

136. Quorum fidei et conversioni ita congratulatus esse rex perhibetur, ut nullum tamen cogeret ad Christianismum. . . . Didicerat enim a doctoribus auctoribusque suæ salutis, servitium Christi voluntarium non coactitium esse debere. Bedæ Hist. Ecclesiastic. l. i. c. 26, p. 62, edit. Smith.

137. See the Historians of France, tom. iv. p. 114; and Wilkins, Leges Anglo-Saxonicæ, p. 11, 31. Siquis sacrificium immolaverit præter Deo soli morte moriatur.

138. The Jews pretend that they were introduced into Spain by the fleets of Solomon and the arms of Nebuchadnezzar; that Hadrian transported forty thousand families of the tribe of Judah, and ten thousand of the tribe of Benjamin, etc. Basnage, Hist. des Juifs, tom. vii. c. 9, p. 240–256.

139. Isidore, at that time archbishop of Seville, mentions, disapproves, and congratulates, the zeal of Sisebut (Chron. Goth. p. 728 [ed. Grot.]). Baronius (A.D. 614, No. 41) assigns the number on the evidence of Aimoin (l. iv. c. 22): but the evidence is weak, and I have not been able to verify the quotation (Historians of France, tom. iii. p. 127).

140. Basnage (tom. viii. c. 13, p. 388–400) faithfully represents the state of the Jews: but he might have added, from the canons of the Spanish councils and the laws of the Visigoths, many curious circumstances essential to his subject, though they are foreign to mine.

Chapter XXXVIII

1. In this chapter I shall draw my quotations from the Recueil des Historiens des Gaules et de la France, Paris, 1738–1767, in eleven volumes in folio. By the labour of Dom Bouquet and the other Benedictines, all the original testimonies, as far as A.D. 1060, are disposed in chronological order, and illustrated with learned notes. Such a national work, which will be continued to the year 1500, might provoke our emulation.

2. Tacitus, The Histories, iv. 73, 74. To abridge Tacitus would indeed be presumptuous; but I may select the general ideas which he applies

to the present state and future revolutions of Gaul.

3. Eadem semper causa Germanis transcendendi in Gallias, libido atque avaritia, et mutandæ sedis amor; ut relictis paludibus et solitudinibus suis, fecundissimum hoc solum vosque ipsos possiderent. . . . Nam pulsis Romanis quid aliud quam bella omnium inter se gentium exsistent?

4. Sidonius Apollinaris ridicules, with affected wit and pleasantry, the hardships of his situation (Carm. xii. in tom. i. p. 811).

5. See Procopius de Bell. Gothico, l. i. c. 12, in tom. ii. p. 31 [tom. ii. p. 64, ed. Bonn]. The character of Grotius inclines me to believe that he has not substituted the *Rhine* for the *Rhône* (Hist. Gothorum, p. 175) without the authority of some MS.

6. Sidonius, l. viii. Epist. 3, 9, in tom. i. p. 800. Jornandes de Rebus Geticis (c. 47, p. 680) justifies in some measure this portrait of the Gothic hero.

7. I use the familiar appellation of *Clovis*, from the Latin *Chlodovechus* or *Chlodovæus*. But the *Ch* expresses only the German aspiration; and the true name is not different from *Luduin* or *Lewis* (Mém. de l'Académie des Inscriptions, tom. xx. p. 68).

8. Greg. Turon. l. ii. c. 12, in tom. ii. p. 168. Bafina speaks the language of nature: the Franks, who had seen her in their youth, might converse with Gregory in their old age; and the bishop of Tours could not wish to defame the mother of the first Christian king.

9. The Abbé Dubos (Hist. Critique de l'Etablissement de la Monarchie Françoise dans les Gaules, tom. i. p. 630-650) has the merit of defining the primitive kingdom of Clovis, and of ascertaining the genuine number of his subjects.

10. Ecclesiam incultam ac negligentiâ civium Paganorum prætermissam, veprium densitate oppletam, etc. Vit. St. Vedasti, in tom. iii. p. 372. This description supposes that Arras was possessed by the Pagans many years before the baptism of Clovis.

11. Gregory of Tours (l. v. c. i. tom. ii. p. 232) contrasts the poverty of Clovis with the wealth of his grandsons. Yet Remigius (in tom. iv. p. 52) mentions his *paternas opes*, as sufficient for the redemption of captives.

12. See Gregory (l. ii. c. 27, 37, in tom. iii. p. 175, 181, 182). The famous story of the vase of Soissons explains both the power and character of Clovis. As a point of controversy, it has been strangely tortured by Boulainvilliers, Dubos, and the other political antiquarians.

13. The Duke of Nivernois, a noble statesman, who has managed weighty and delicate negotiations, ingeniously illustrates (Mém. de l'Acad. des Inscriptions, tom. xx. p. 147-184) the political system of Clovis.

14. M. Biet (in a Dissertation which deserved the prize of the Academy of Soissons, p. 178-226) has accurately defined the nature and extent of the kingdom of Syagrius, and his father; but he too readily allows the slight evidence of Dubos

(tom. ii. p. 54-57) to deprive him of Beauvais and Amiens.

15. I may observe that Fredegarius, in his epitome of Gregory of Tours (tom. ii. p. 398 [c. 15]), has prudently substituted the name of *Patricius* for the incredible title of *Rex Romanorum*.

16. Sidonius (l. v. Epist. 5, in tom. i. p. 794), who styles him the Solon, the Amphion, of the barbarians, addresses this imaginary king in the tone of friendship and equality. From such offices of arbitration, the crafty Deioces had raised himself to the throne of the Medes (Herodot. l. i. c. 96-100).

17. Campum sibi præparari jussit. M. Biet (p. 226-251) has diligently ascertained this field of battle at Nogent, a Benedictine abbey, about ten miles to the north of Soissons. The ground was marked by a circle of Pagan sepulchres; and Clovis bestowed the adjacent lands of Leuilly and Coucy on the church of Rheims.

18. See Cæsar. Comment. de Bell. Gallic. ii. 4, in tom. i. p. 220, and the Notitiæ, tom. i. p. 126. The three *Fabricæ* of Soissons were, *Scutaria, Balistaria*, and *Clinabaria*. The last supplied the complete armour of the heavy cuirassiers.

19. The epithet must be confined to the circumstances; and history cannot justify the French prejudice of Gregory (l. ii. c. 27, in tom. ii. p. 175), ut Gothorum pavere *mos* est.

20. Dubos has satisfied me (tom. i. p. 277-286) that Gregory of Tours, his transcribers or his readers, have repeatedly confounded the German kingdom of *Thuringia*, beyond the Rhine, and the Gallic *city* of *Tongria*, on the Meuse, which was more anciently the country of the Eburones, and more recently the diocese of Liege.

21. Populi habitantes juxta *Lemannum* lacum, *Alemanni* dicuntur. Servius, ad Virgil. Georgic. iv. 278. Dom Bouquet (tom. i. p. 817) has only alleged the more recent and corrupt text of Isidore of Seville.

22. Gregory of Tours sends St. Lupicinus inter illa Jurensis deserti secreta, quæ, inter Burgundiam Alamanniamque sita, Aventicæ adjacent civitati, in tom. i. p. 648. M. de Watteville (Hist. de la Confédération Helvétique, tom. i. p. 9, 10) has accurately defined the Helvetian limits of the duchy of Alemannia, and the Transjurane Burgundy. They were commensurate with the dioceses of Constance and Avenche, or Lausanne, and are still discriminated in modern Switzerland by the use of the German or French language.

23. See Guilliman de Rebus Helveticis, l. i. c. 3, p. 11, 12. Within the ancient walls of Vindonissa, the castle of Hapsburg, the abbey of Königsfeld, and the town of Bruck, have successively arisen. The philosophic traveller may compare the monuments of Roman conquest, of feudal or Austrian tyranny, of monkish superstition, and of industrious freedom. If he be truly a philosopher, he will applaud the merit and happiness of his own times.

24. Gregory of Tours (l. ii. 30, 37, in tom. ii. p.

176, 177, 182), the Gesta Francorum (in tom. ii. p. 551), and the epistle of Theodoric (Cassiodor. Variar. l. ii. Ep. 41, in tom. iv. p. 4) represent the defeat of the Alemanni. Some of their tribes settled in Rhætia, under the protection of Theodoric, whose successors ceded the colony and their country to the grandson of Clovis. The state of the Alemanni under the Merovingian kings may be seen in Mascou (Hist. of the Ancient Germans, xi. 8, etc.; Annotation xxxvi.) and Guilliman (de Reb. Helvet. l. ii. c. 10–12, p. 72–80).

25. Clotilda, or rather Gregory, supposes that Clovis worshipped the gods of Greece and Rome. The fact is incredible, and the mistake only shows how completely, in less than a century, the national religion of the Franks had been abolished, and even forgotten.

26. Gregory of Tours relates the marriage and conversion of Clovis (l. ii. c. 28–31, in tom. ii. p. 175–178). Even Fredegarius, or the nameless Epitomiser (in tom. ii. p. 398–400), the author of the Gesta Francorum (in tom. ii. p. 548–552), and Aimoin himself (l. i. c. 13–16, in tom. iii. p. 37–40), may be heard without disdain. Tradition might long preserve some curious circumstances of these important transactions.

27. A traveller, who returned from Rheims to Auvergne, had stolen a copy of his Declamations from the secretary or bookseller of the modest archbishop (Sidonius, Apollinar. l. ix. Epist. 7). Four epistles of Remigius, which are still extant (in tom. iv. p. 51, 52, 53), do not correspond with the splendid praise of Sidonius.

28. Hincmar, one of the successors of Remigius (A.D. 845–882), has composed his Life (in tom. iii. p. 373–380). The authority of ancient MSS. of the church of Rheims might inspire some confidence, which is destroyed, however, by the selfish and audacious fictions of Hincmar. It is remarkable enough that Remigius, who was consecrated at the age of twenty-two (A.D. 457), filled the episcopal chair seventy-four years (Pagi Critica, in Baron. tom. ii. p. 384, 572).

29. A vial (the *Sainte Ampoulle*) of holy or rather celestial oil was brought down by a white dove, for the baptism of Clovis; and it is still used and renewed in the coronation of the kings of France. Hincmar (he aspired to the primacy of Gaul) is the first author of this fable (in tom. iii. p. 377), whose slight foundations the Abbé de Vertot (Mémoires de l'Académie des Inscriptions, tom. ii. p. 619–633) has undermined with profound respect and consummate dexterity.

30. Mitis depone colla, Sicamber: adora quod incendisti, incende quod adorasti. Greg. Turon. l. ii. c. 31, in tom. ii. p. 177.

31. Si ego ibidem cum Francis meis fuissem, injurias ejus vindicassem. This rash expression, which Gregory has prudently concealed, is celebrated by Fredegarius (Epitom. c. 21, in tom. ii. p. 400), Aimoin (l. i. c. 16, in tom. iii. p. 40), and the Chroniques de St. Denys (l. i. c. 20, in tom. iii.

p. 171), as an admirable effusion of Christian zeal.

32. Gregory (l. ii. c. 40–43, in tom. ii. p. 183–185), after coolly relating the repeated crimes and affected remorse of Clovis, concludes, perhaps undesignedly, with a lesson which ambition will never hear—"His ita transactis . . . obiit."

33. After the Gothic victory, Clovis made rich offerings to St. Martin of Tours. He wished to redeem his war-horse by the gift of one hundred pieces of gold, but the enchanted steed could not move from the stable till the price of his redemption had been doubled. This *miracle* provoked the king to exclaim, Vere B. Martinus est bonus in auxilio, sed carus in negotio. (Gesta Francorum, in tom. ii. p. 554, 555.)

34. See the epistle from Pope Anastasius to the royal convert (in tom. iv. p. 50, 51). Avitus, bishop of Vienne, addressed Clovis on the same subject (p. 49); and many of the Latin bishops would assure him of their joy and attachment.

35. Instead of the Ἀρβόρυχοι, an unknown people, who now appear in the text of Procopius [Bell. Goth. l. i. c. 12], Hadrian de Valois has restored the proper name of the Ἀρμόρυχοι; and this easy correction has been almost universally approved. Yet an unprejudiced reader would naturally suppose that Procopius means to describe a tribe of Germans in the alliance of Rome, and not a confederacy of Gallic cities which had revolted from the empire.

36. This important digression of Procopius (de Bell. Gothic. l. i. c. 12, in tom. ii. p. 29–36 [tom. ii. p. 62, *sqq.*, ed. Bonn]) illustrates the origin of the French monarchy. Yet I must observe, 1. That the Greek historian betrays an inexcusable ignorance of the geography of the West; 2. That these treaties and privileges, which should leave some lasting traces, are totally invisible in Gregory of Tours, the Salic laws, etc.

37. Regnum circa Rhodanum aut Ararium cum provinciâ Massiliensi retinebant. Greg. Turon. l. ii. c. 32, in tom. ii. p. 178. The province of Marseilles, as far as the Durance, was afterwards ceded to the Ostrogoths; and the signatures of twenty-five bishops are supposed to represent the kingdom of Burgundy, A.D. 519. (Concil. Epaon. in tom. iv. p. 104, 105.) Yet I would except Vindonissa. The bishop, who lived under the Pagan Alemanni, would naturally resort to the synods of the next Christian kingdom. Mascou (in his four first annotations) has explained many circumstances relative to the Burgundian monarchy.

38. Mascou (Hist. of the Germans, xi. 10), who very reasonably distrusts the testimony of Gregory of Tours, has produced a passage from Avitus (Epist. v.) to prove that Gundobald affected to deplore the tragic event which his subjects affected to applaud.

39. See the original conference (in tom. iv. p. 99–102). Avitus, the principal actor, and probably the secretary of the meeting, was bishop of Vienne. A short account of his person and works may be

found in Dupin (Bibliothèque Ecclésiastique, tom. v. p. 5–10).

40. Gregory of Tours (l. iii. c. 19, in tom. ii. p. 197) indulges his genius, or rather transcribes some more eloquent writer, in the description of Dijon —a castle, which already deserved the title of a city. It depended on the bishops of Langres till the twelfth century, and afterwards became the capital of the dukes of Burgundy. Longuerue, Description de la France, part i. p. 280.

41. The Epitomiser of Gregory of Tours (in tom. ii. p. 401) has supplied this number of Franks, but he rashly supposes that they were cut in pieces by Gundobald. The prudent Burgundian spared the soldiers of Clovis, and sent these captives to the king of the Visigoths, who settled them in the territory of Toulouse.

42. In this Burgundian war I have followed Gregory of Tours (l. ii. c. 32, 33, in tom. ii. p. 178, 179), whose narrative *appears* so incompatible with that of Procopius (de Bell. Goth. l. i. c. 12, in tom. ii. p. 31, 32 [tom. ii. p. 63, *sqq.*, ed. Bonn]), that some critics have supposed *two* different wars. The Abbé Dubos (Hist. Critique, etc., tom. ii. p. 126–162) has distinctly represented the causes and the events.

43. See his Life or legend (in tom. iii. p. 402). A martyr! how strangely has that word been distorted from its original sense of a common witness! St. Sigismond was remarkable for the cure of fevers.

44. Before the end of the fifth century, the church of St. Maurice, and his Thebæan legion, had rendered Agaunum a place of devout pilgrimage. A promiscuous community of both sexes had introduced some deeds of darkness, which were abolished (A.D. 515) by the regular monastery of Sigismond. Within fifty years, his *angels of light* made a nocturnal sally to murder their bishop and his clergy. See, in the Bibliothèque Raisonnée (tom. xxxvi. p. 435–438), the curious remarks of a learned librarian of Geneva.

45. Marius, bishop of Avenche (Chron. in tom. ii. p. 15), has marked the authentic dates, and Gregory of Tours (l. iii. c. 5, 6, in tom. ii. p. 188, 189) has expressed the principal facts, of the life of Sigismond and the conquest of Burgundy. Procopius (in tom. ii. p. 34 [tom. ii. p. 65, ed. Bonn]) and Agathias (in tom. ii. p. 49) show their remote and imperfect knowledge.

46. Gregory of Tours (l. ii. c. 37, in tom. ii. p. 181) inserts the short but persuasive speech of Clovis. Valde moleste fero, quod hi Ariani partem teneant Galliarum (the author of the Gesta Francorum, in tom. ii. p. 553, adds the precious epithet of *optimam*), eamus cum Dei adjutorio, et, superatis eis, redigamus terram in ditionem nostram.

47. Tunc rex projecit a se in directum Bipennem suam quod est *Francisca*, etc. (Gesta Franc. in tom. ii. p. 554.) The form and use of this weapon are clearly described by Procopius (in tom. ii. p. 37 [Bell. Goth. l. ii. c. 25, tom. ii. p. 247, 248, ed. Bonn]). Examples of its *national* appellation in Latin and French may be found in the Glossary of Ducange and the large Dictionnaire de Trevoux.

48. It is singular enough that some important and authentic facts should be found in a Life of Quintianus, composed in rhyme in the old *patois* of Rouergue (Dubos, Hist. Critique, etc., tom. ii. p. 179).

49. Quamvis fortitudini vestræ confidentiam tribuat parentum vestrorum innumerabilis multitudo; quamvis Attilam potentem reminiscamini Visigotharum viribus inclinatum; tamen quia populorum ferocia corda longa pace mollescunt, cavete subito in aleam mittere, quos constat tantis temporibus exercitia non habere. Such was the salutary but fruitless advice of peace, of reason, and of Theodoric (Cassiodor. l. iii. Ep. 2 [ed. Rotom. 1679]).

50. Montesquieu (The Spirit of Laws, l. xv. c. 13) mentions and approves the law of the Visigoths (l. ix. tit. 2, in tom. iv. p. 425), which obliged all masters to arm and send or lead into the field a tenth of their slaves.

51. This mode of divination, by accepting as an omen the first sacred words which in particular circumstances should be presented to the eye or ear, was derived from the Pagans; and the Psalter or Bible was substituted to the poems of Homer and Virgil. From the fourth to the fourteenth century, these *sortes sanctorum*, as they are styled, were repeatedly condemned by the decrees of councils, and repeatedly practised by kings, bishops, and saints. See a curious dissertation of the Abbé du Resnel, in the Mémoires de l'Académie, tom. xix. p. 287–310.

52. After correcting the text or excusing the mistake of Procopius, who places the defeat of Alaric near Carcassonne, we may conclude, from the evidence of Gregory, Fortunatus, and the author of the Gesta Francorum, that the battle was fought *in campo Vocladensi*, on the banks of the Clain, about ten miles to the south of Poitiers. Clovis overtook and attacked the Visigoths near Vivonne, and the victory was decided near a village still named Champagné St. Hilaire. See the Dissertations of the Abbé le Bœuf, tom. i. p. 304–331.

53. Angoulême is in the road from Poitiers to Bordeaux, and, although Gregory delays the siege, I can more readily believe that he confounded the order of history than that Clovis neglected the rules of war.

54. Pyrenæos montes usque Perpinianum subjecit, is the expression of Rorico, which betrays his recent date, since Perpignan did not exist before the tenth century (Marca Hispanica, p. 458). This florid and fabulous writer (perhaps a monk of Amiens—see the Abbé le Bœuf, Mém. de l'Académie, tom. xvii. p. 228–245) relates, in the *allegorical* character of a shepherd, the general history of his countrymen the Franks; but his narrative ends with the death of Clovis.

55. The author of the Gesta Francorum positively affirms that Clovis fixed a body of Franks in

the Saintonge and Bourdelois; and he is not injudiciously followed by Rorico, electos milites, atque fortissimos, cum parvulis, atque mulieribus. Yet it should seem that they soon mingled with the Romans of Aquitain, till Charlemagne introduced a more numerous and powerful colony (Dubos, Hist. Critique, tom. ii. p. 215).

56. In the composition of the Gothic war I have used the following materials, with due regard to their unequal value:—Four epistles from Theodoric, king of Italy (Cassiodor. l. iii. Epist. 1–4, in tom. iv. p. 3–5), Procopius (de Bell. Goth. l. i. c. 12, in tom. ii. p. 32, 33), Gregory of Tours (l. ii. c. 35, 36, 37, in tom. ii. p. 181–183), Jornandes (de Reb. Geticis, c. 58, in tom. ii. p. 28), Fortunatus (in Vit. St. Hilarii, in tom. iii. p. 380), Isidore (in Chron. Goth. in tom. ii. p. 702), the Epitome of Gregory of Tours (in tom. ii. p. 401), the author of the Gesta Francorum (in tom. ii. p. 553–555), the Fragments of Fredegarius (in tom. ii. p. 463), Aimoin (l. i. c. 20, in tom. iii. p. 41, 42), and Rorico (l. iv. in tom. iii. p. 14–19).

57. The *Fasti* of Italy would naturally reject a consul, the enemy of their sovereign; but any ingenious hypothesis that might explain the silence of Constantinople and Egypt (the Chronicle of Marcellinus, and the Paschal) is overturned by the similar silence of Marius, bishop of Avenche, who composed his *Fasti* in the kingdom of Burgundy. If the evidence of Gregory of Tours were less weighty and positive (l. ii. c. 38, in tom. ii. p. 183), I could believe that Clovis, like Odoacer, received the lasting title and honours of *Patrician* (Pagi Critica, tom. ii. p. 474, 492).

58. Under the Merovingian kings, Marseilles still imported from the East, paper, wine, oil, linen, silk, precious stones, spices, etc. The Gauls or Franks traded to Syria, and the Syrians were established in Gaul. See M. de Guignes, Mém. de l'Académie, tom. xxxvii. p. 471–475.

59. Οὐ γάρ ποτε ᾤοντο Γαλλίας ξὺν τῷ ἀσφαλεῖ κεκτῆσθαι Φράγγοι, μὴ τοῦ αὐτοκράτορος τὸ ἔργον ἐπισφραγίσαντος τοῦτό] γε. This strong declaration of Procopius (de Bell. Gothic. l. iii. cap. 33, in tom. ii. p. 41 [tom. ii. p. 417, ed. Bonn]) would almost suffice to justify the Abbé Dubos.

60. The Franks, who probably used the mints of Trèves, Lyons, and Arles, imitated the coinage of the Roman emperors, of seventy-two *solidi*, or pieces, to the pound of gold. But as the Franks established only a decuple proportion of gold and silver, ten shillings will be a sufficient valuation of their solidus of gold. It was the common standard of the barbaric fines, and contained forty *denarii*, or silver threepences. Twelve of these denarii made a *solidus*, or *shilling*, the twentieth part of the ponderal and numeral *livre*, or pound of silver, which has been so strangely reduced in modern France. See Le Blanc, Traité Historique des Monnoyes de France, p. 37–43, etc.

61. Agathias, in tom. ii. p. 47 [p. 17, ed. Bonn]. Gregory of Tours exhibits a very different picture.

Perhaps it would not be easy, within the same historical space, to find more vice and less virtue. We are continually shocked by the union of savage and corrupt manners.

62. M. de Foncemagne has traced, in a correct and elegant dissertation (Mém. de l'Académie, tom. viii. p. 505–528), the extent and limits of the French monarchy.

63. The Abbé Dubos (Histoire Critique, tom. i. p. 29–36) has truly and agreeably represented the slow progress of these studies; and he observes that Gregory of Tours was only once printed before the year 1560. According to the complaint of Heineccius (Opera, tom. iii. Sylloge iii. p. 248, etc.), Germany received with indifference and contempt the codes of barbaric laws which were published by Heroldus, Lindebrogius, etc. At present those laws (as far as they relate to Gaul), the history of Gregory of Tours, and all the monuments of the Merovingian race, appear in a pure and perfect state, in the first four volumes of the Historians of France.

64. In the space of [*about*] thirty years (1728–1765) this interesting subject has been agitated by the free spirit of the Count de Boulainvilliers (Mémoires Historiques sur l'Etat de la France, particularly tom. i. p. 15–49), the learned ingenuity of the Abbé Dubos (Histoire Critique de l'Etablissement de la Monarchie Françoise dans les Gaules, 2 vols. in 4to.), the comprehensive genius of the President de Montesquieu (The Spirit of Laws, particularly l. xxviii. xxx. xxxi.), and the good sense and diligence of the Abbé de Mably (Observations sur l'Histoire de France, 2 vols. 12mo.).

65. I have derived much instruction from two learned works of Heineccius—the *History* and the *Elements* of the Germanic law. In a judicious preface to the Elements, he considers, and tries to excuse, the defects of that barbarous jurisprudence.

66. Latin appears to have been the original language of the Salic law. It was probably composed in the beginning of the fifth century, before the era (A.D. 421) of the real or fabulous Pharamond. The preface mentions the four cantons which produced the four legislators; and many provinces—Franconia, Saxony, Hanover, Brabant, etc.—have claimed them as their own. See an excellent Dissertation of Heineccius, de Lege Salicâ, tom. iii. Sylloge iii. p. 247–267.

67. Eginhard, in Vit. Caroli Magni, c. 29, in tom. v. p. 100. By these two laws most critics understand the Salic and the Ripuarian. The former extended from the Carbonarian forest to the Loire (tom. iv. p. 151 [Lex Sal. tit. L.]), and the latter might be obeyed from the same forest to the Rhine (tom. iv. p. 232).

68. Consult the ancient and modern prefaces of the several codes, in the fourth volume of the Historians of France. The original prologue to the Salic law expresses (though in a foreign dialect) the genuine spirit of the Franks more forcibly than the ten books of Gregory of Tours.

69. The Ripuarian law declares and defines this indulgence in favour of the plaintiff (tit. xxxi. in tom. iv. p. 240); and the same toleration is understood or expressed in all the codes except that of the Visigoths of Spain. Tanta diversitas legum (says Agobard in the ninth century) quanta non solum in [singulis] regionibus, aut civitatibus, sed etiam in multis domibus habetur. Nam plerumque contingit ut simul eant aut sedeant quinque homines, et nullus eorum communem legem cum altero habeat (in tom. vi. p. 356). He foolishly proposes to introduce an uniformity of law as well as of faith.

70. Inter Romanos negotia causarum Romanis legibus præcipimus terminari. Such are the words of a general constitution promulgated by Clotaire, the son of Clovis, and sole monarch of the Franks (in tom. iv. p. 116), about the year 560.

71. This liberty of choice has been aptly deduced (The Spirit of Laws, l. xxviii. 2) from a constitution of Lothaire I. (Leg. Langobard. l. ii. tit. lvii. in Codex Lindebrog. p. 664), though the example is too recent and partial. From a various reading in the Salic law (tit. xliv. not. xlv.), the Abbé de Mably (tom. i. p. 290–293) has conjectured that at first a *barbarian* only, and afterwards any *man* (consequently a Roman), might live according to the law of the Franks. I am sorry to offend this ingenious conjecture by observing that the stricter sense (*barbarum*) is expressed in the reformed copy of Charlemagne, which is confirmed by the Royal and Wolfenbüttel MSS. The looser interpretation (*hominem*) is authorised only by the MS. of Fulda, from whence Heroldus published his edition. See the four original texts of the Salic law, in tom. iv. p. 147, 173, 196, 220.

72. In the heroic times of Greece, the guilt of murder was expiated by a pecuniary satisfaction to the family of the deceased (Feithius Antiquitat. Homer. l. ii. c. 8). Heineccius, in his preface to the Elements of Germanic Law, favourably suggests that at Rome and Athens homicide was only punished with exile. It is true; but exile was a *capital* punishment for a citizen of Rome or Athens.

73. This proportion is fixed by the Salic (tit. xliv. in tom. iv. p. 147) and the Ripuarian (tit. vii. xi. xxxvi. in tom. iv. p. 237, 241) laws; but the latter does not distinguish any difference of Romans. Yet the orders of the clergy are placed above the Franks themselves, and the Burgundians and Alemanni between the Franks and the Romans.

74. The *Antrustiones, qui in truste Dominicâ sunt, leudi, fideles*, undoubtedly represent the first order of Franks; but it is a question whether their rank was personal or hereditary. The Abbé de Mably (tom. i. p. 334–347) is not displeased to mortify the pride of birth (The Spirit of Laws, l. xxx. c. 25) by dating the *origin* of French nobility from the reign of Clotaire II. (A.D. 615).

75. See the Burgundian laws (tit. ii. in tom. iv. p. 257), the code of the Visigoths (l. vi. tit. v. in tom. iv. p. 383), and the constitution of *Childebert*, not of Paris, but most evidently of Austrasia (in

tom. iv. p. 112). Their premature severity was sometimes rash and excessive. Childebert condemned not only murderers but robbers; quomodo sine lege involavit, sine lege moriatur; and even the negligent judge was involved in the same sentence. The Visigoths abandoned an unsuccessful surgeon to the family of his deceased patient, ut quod de eo facere voluerint habeant potestatem (l. xi. tit. i. in tom. iv. p. 435).

76. See in the sixth volume of the works of Heineccius, the Elementa Juris Germanici, l. ii. p. ii. No. 261, 262, 280–283. Yet some vestiges of these pecuniary compositions for murder have been traced in Germany as late as the sixteenth century.

77. The whole subject of the Germanic judges, and their jurisdiction, is copiously treated by Heineccius (Element. Jur. Germ. l. iii. No. 1–72). I cannot find any proof that, under the Merovingian race, the *scabini*, or assessors, were chosen by the people.

78. Gregor. Turon. l. viii. c. 9, in tom. ii. p. 316. Montesquieu observes (Esprit des Loix, l. xxviii. c. 13) that the Salic law did not admit these *negative proofs* so universally established in the barbaric codes. Yet this obscure concubine (Fredegundis), who became the wife of the grandson of Clovis, must have followed the Salic law.

79. Muratori, in the Antiquities of Italy, has given two Dissertations (xxxviii. xxxix.) on the *judgments of God*. It was expected that *fire* would not burn the innocent, and that the pure element of *water* would not allow the guilty to sink into its bosom.

80. Montesquieu (The Spirit of Laws, l. xxviii. c. 17) has condescended to explain and excuse "la manière de penser de nos pères" on the subject of judicial combats. He follows this strange institution from the age of Gundobald to that of St. Lewis; and the philosopher is sometimes lost in the legal antiquarian.

81. In a memorable duel at Aix-la-Chapelle (A.D. 820), before the emperor Lewis the Pious, his biographer observes, secundum legem propriam, utpote quia uterque Gothus erat, equestri pugnâ [prœlio] congressus est (Vit. Lud. Pii. c. 33, in tom. vi. p. 103). Ermoldus Nigellus (l. iii. 543–628, in tom. vi. p. 48–50), who describes the duel, admires the *ars nova* of fighting on horseback, which was unknown to the Franks.

82. In his original edict published at Lyons (A.D. 501), Gundobald establishes and justifies the use of judicial combat. (Leg. Burgund. tit. xlv. in tom. iii. p. 267, 268.) Three hundred years afterwards, Agobard, bishop of Lyons, solicited Lewis the Pious to abolish the law of an Arian tyrant (in tom. vi. p. 356–358). He relates the conversation of Gundobald and Avitus.

83. "Accidit (says Agobard), ut non solum valentes viribus, sed etiam infirmi et senes lacessantur ad [certamen et] pugnam, etiam pro vilissimis rebus. Quibus feralibus certaminibus contingunt

homicidia injusta, et crudeles ac perversi eventus judiciorum" [tom. vi. p. 357]. Like a prudent rhetorician, he suppresses the legal privilege of hiring champions.

84. Montesquieu (The Spirit of Laws, xxviii. c. 14), who understands *why* the judicial combat was admitted by the Burgundians, Ripuarians, Alemanni, Bavarians, Lombards, Thuringians, Frisons, and Saxons, is satisfied (and Agobard seems to countenance the assertion) that it was not allowed by the Salic law. Yet the same custom, at least in cases of treason, is mentioned by Ermoldus Nigellus (l. iii. 543, in tom. vi. p. 48) and the anonymous biographer of Lewis the Pious (c. 46, in tom. vi. p. 112), as the "mos antiquus Francorum, more Francis solito," etc., expressions too general to exclude the noblest of their tribes.

85. Cæsar de Bell. Gall. l. i. c. 31, in tom. i. p. 213.

86. The obscure hints of a division of lands occasionally scattered in the laws of the Burgundians (tit. liv. No. 1, 2, in tom. iv. p. 271, 272) and Visigoths (l. x. tit. i. No. 8, 9, 16, in tom. iv. p. 428, 429, 430) are skilfully explained by the President Montesquieu (The Spirit of Laws, l. xxx. c. 7, 8, 9). I shall only add that, among the Goths, the division seems to have been ascertained by the judgment of the neighbourhood; that the barbarians frequently usurped the remaining *third*; and that the Romans might recover their right, unless they were barred by a prescription of fifty years.

87. It is singular enough that the President de Montesquieu (The Spirit of Laws, l. xxx. c. 7) and the Abbé de Mably (Observations, tom. i. p. 21, 22) agree in this strange supposition of arbitrary and private rapine. The Count de Boulainvilliers (Etat de la France, tom. i. p. 22, 23) shows a strong understanding through a cloud of ignorance and prejudice.

88. See the rustic edict, or rather code, of Charlemagne, which contains seventy distinct and minute regulations of that great monarch (in tom. v. p. 652–657). He requires an account of the horns and skins of the goats, allows his fish to be sold, and carefully directs that the larger villas (*Capitaneæ*) shall maintain one hundred and thirty geese, and the smaller (*Mansionales*) fifty hens and twelve geese. Mabillon (de Re Diplomaticâ) has investigated the names, the number, and the situation of the Merovingian villas.

89. From a passage of the Burgundian law (tit. i. No. 4 [3] in tom. iv. p. 257) it is evident that a deserving son might expect to hold the lands which his father had received from the royal bounty of Gundobald. The Burgundians would firmly maintain their privilege, and their example might encourage the beneficiaries of France.

90. The revolutions of the benefices and fiefs are clearly fixed by the Abbé de Mably. His accurate distinction of *times* gives him a merit to which even Montesquieu is a stranger.

91. See the Salic law (tit. lxii. in tom. iv. p. 156).

The origin and nature of these Salic lands, which in times of ignorance were perfectly understood, now perplex our most learned and sagacious critics.

92. Many of the two hundred and six miracles of St. Martin (Greg. Turon. in Maximâ Bibliothecâ Patrum, tom. xi. p. 896–932) were repeatedly performed to punish sacrilege. Audite hæc omnes (exclaims the bishop of Tours) potestatem habentes, after relating how some horses ran mad that had been turned into a sacred meadow.

93. Heinec. Element. Jur. German. l. ii. p. 1, No. 8.

94. Jonas, bishop of Orleans (A.D. 821–826; Cave, Hist. Litteraria, p. 443), censures the *legal* tyranny of the nobles. Pro feris, quas cura hominum non aluit, sed Deus in commune mortalibus ad utendum concessit, pauperes a potentioribus spoliantur, flagellantur, ergastulis detruduntur, et multa alia patiuntur. Hoc enim qui faciunt, *lege mundi* se facere juste posse contendunt. De Institutione Laicorum, l. ii. c. 23, apud Thomassin, Discipline de l'Eglise, tom. iii. p. 1348.

95. On a mere suspicion, Chundo, a chamberlain of Gontram, king of Burgundy, was stoned to death (Greg. Turon. l. x. c. 10, in tom. ii. p. 369). John of Salisbury (Policrat. l. i. c. 4) asserts the rights of nature, and exposes the cruel practice of the twelfth century. See Heineccius, Elem. Jur. Germ. l. ii. p. 1, No. 51–57.

96. The custom of enslaving prisoners of war was totally extinguished in the thirteenth century by the prevailing influence of Christianity; but it might be proved, from frequent passages of Gregory of Tours, etc., that it was practised without censure under the Merovingian race; and even Grotius himself (de Jure Belli et Pacis, l. iii. c. 7), as well as his commentator Barbeyrac, have laboured to reconcile it with the laws of nature and reason.

97. The state, professions, etc., of the German, Italian, and Gallic slaves, during the middle ages, are explained by Heineccius (Element. Jur. Germ. l. i. No. 28–47), Muratori (Dissertat. xiv. xv.), Ducange (Gloss. sub voce *Servi*), and the Abbé de Mably (Observations, tom. ii. p. 3, etc., p. 237, etc.).

98. Gregory of Tours (l. vi. c. 45, in tom. ii. p 289) relates a memorable example, in which Chilperic only abused the private rights of a master. Many families, which belonged to his *domus fiscales* in the neighbourhood of Paris, were forcibly sent away into Spain.

99. Licentiam habeatis mihi qualemcunque volueritis disciplinam ponere; vel venumdare, aut quod vobis placuerit de me facere. Marculf. Formul. l. ii. 28, in tom. iv. p. 497. The *Formula* of Lindenbrogius (p. 559), and that of Anjou (p. 565), are to the same effect. Gregory of Tours (l. vii. c. 45, in tom. ii. p. 311) speaks of many persons who sold themselves for bread in a great famine.

100. When Cæsar saw it, he laughed (Plutarch.

in Cæsar [The Lives of the Noble Grecians and Romans]); yet he relates his unsuccessful siege of Gergovia with less frankness than we might expect from a great man to whom victory was familiar. He acknowledges, however, that in one attack he lost forty-six centurions and seven hundred men (de Bell. Gallico, l. vi. [vii.] c. 44–53, in tom. i. p. 270–272).

101. Audebant se quondam fratres Latio dicere, et sanguine ab Iliaco populos computare (Sidon. Apollinar. l. vii. Epist. 7, in tom. i. p. 799). I am not informed of the degrees and circumstances of this fabulous pedigree.

102. Either the first or second partition among the sons of Clovis had given Berry to Childebert (Greg. Turon. l. iii. c. 12, in tom. ii. p. 192). Velim (said he), Arvernam *Lemanem*, quæ tantæ jocunditatis gratiâ refulgere dicitur, oculis cernere (l. iii. c. 9, p. 191). The face of the country was concealed by a thick fog when the king of Paris made his entry into Clermont.

103. For the description of Auvergne, see Sidonius (l. iv. Epist. 21, in tom. i. p. 793), with the notes of Savaron and Sirmond (p. 279 and 51 of their respective editions). Boulainvilliers (Etat de la France, tom. ii. p. 242–268), and the Abbé de la Longuerue (Description de la France, part i. p. 132–139).

104. Furorem gentium, quæ de ulteriore Rheni amnis parte venerant, superare non poterat (Greg. Turon. l. iv. c. 50, in tom. ii. 229), was the excuse of another king of Austrasia (A.D. 574) for the ravages which his troops committed in the neighbourhood of Paris.

105. From the name and situation, the Benedictine editors of Gregory of Tours (in tom. ii. p. 192) have fixed this fortress at a place named *Chastel Merliac*, two miles from Mauriac, in the Upper Auvergne. In this description I translate *infra* as if I read *intra;* the two prepositions are perpetually confounded by Gregory or his transcribers, and the sense must always decide.

106. See these revolutions and wars of Auvergne in Gregory of Tours (l. ii. c. 37, in tom. ii. p. 183, and l. iii. c. 9, 12, 13, p. 191, 192, de Miraculis St. Julian. c. 13, in tom. ii. p. 466). He frequently betrays his extraordinary attention to his native country.

107. The story of Attalus is related by Gregory of Tours (l. iii. c. 15, in tom. ii. p. 193–195). His editor, the P. Ruinart, confounds this Attalus, who was a youth (*puer*) in the year 532, with a friend of Sidonius of the same name, who was count of Autun fifty or sixty years before. Such an error, which cannot be imputed to ignorance, is excused in some degree by its own magnitude.

108. This Gregory, the great-grandfather of Gregory of Tours (in tom. ii. p. 197, 490), lived ninety-two years, of which he passed forty as count of Autun, and thirty-two as bishop of Langres. According to the poet Fortunatus, he displayed equal merit in these different stations:—

Nobilis antiquâ decurrens prole parentum,
Nobilior gestis, nunc super astra manet.
Arbiter ante ferox, dein pius ipse sacerdos,
Quos domuit judex, fovit amore patris.

109. As M. de Valois and the P. Ruinart are determined to change the *Mosella* of the text into *Mosa*, it becomes me to acquiesce in the alteration. Yet, after some examination of the topography, I could defend the common reading.

110. The parents of Gregory (Gregorius Florentius Georgius) were of noble extraction (*natalibus . . . illustres*), and they possessed large estates (*latifundia*) both in Auvergne and Burgundy. He was born in the year 539, was consecrated bishop of Tours in 573, and died in 593 or 595, soon after he had terminated his history. See his Life by Odo, abbot of Clugny (in tom. ii. p. 129–135), and a new Life in the Mémoires de l'Académie, etc., tom. xxvi. p. 598–637.

111. Decedente atque immo potius pereunte ab urbibus Gallicanis liberalium culturâ literarum, etc. (in præfat. in tom. ii. p. 137), is the complaint of Gregory himself, which he fully verifies by his own work. His style is equally devoid of elegance and simplicity. In a conspicuous station he still remained a stranger to his own age and country; and in a prolix work (the five last books contain ten years) he has omitted almost everything that posterity desires to learn. I have tediously acquired, by a painful perusal, the right of pronouncing this unfavourable sentence.

112. The Abbé de Mably (tom. i. p. 247–267) has diligently confirmed this opinion of the President de Montesquieu (The Spirit of Laws, l. xxx. c. 13).

113. See Dubos, Hist. Critique de la Monarchie Françoise, tom. ii. l. vi. c. 9, 10. The French antiquarians establish as a *principle* that the Romans and barbarians may be distinguished by their names. Their names undoubtedly form a reasonable *presumption;* yet, in reading Gregory of Tours, I have observed Gondulphus, of Senatorian or Roman extraction (l. vi. c. 11, in tom. ii. p. 273), and Claudius, a barbarian (l. vii. c. 29, p. 303).

114. Eunius Mummolus is repeatedly mentioned by Gregory of Tours, from the fourth (c. 42, p. 224) to the seventh (c. 40, p. 310) book. The computation by talents is singular enough; but if Gregory attached any meaning to that obsolete word, the treasures of Mummolus must have exceeded £100,000 sterling.

115. See Fleury, Discours iii. sur l'Histoire Ecclésiastique.

116. The bishop of Tours himself has recorded the complaint of Chilperic, the grandson of Clovis. Ecce pauper remansit fiscus noster; ecce divitiæ nostræ ad ecclesias sunt translatæ: nulli penitus nisi soli Episcopi regnant (l. vi. c. 46, in tom. ii. p. 291).

117. See the Ripuarian Code (tit. xxxvi. in tom. iv. p. 241). The Salic law does not provide for the safety of the clergy; and we might suppose, on the

behalf of the more civilised tribe, that they had
not foreseen such an impious act as the murder of
a priest. Yet Prætextatus, archbishop of Rouen,
was assassinated by the order of queen Fredegundis
before the altar (Greg. Turon. l. viii. c. 31, in tom.
ii. p. 326).

118. M. Bonamy (Mém. de l'Académie des Inscriptions, tom. xxiv. p. 582–670) has ascertained
the *Lingua Romana Rustica*, which, through the
medium of the *Romance*, has gradually been polished
into the actual form of the French language. Under
the Carlovingian race the kings and nobles of
France still understood the dialect of their German
ancestors.

119. Ce beau système a été trouvé dans les bois.
Montesquieu, The Spirit of Laws, l. xi. c. 6.

120. See the Abbé de Mably, Observations, etc.,
tom. i. p. 34–56. It should seem that the institution
of national assemblies, which are coeval with the
French nation, has never been congenial to its
temper.

121. Gregory of Tours (l. viii. c. 30, in tom. ii. p.
325–326) relates, with much indifference, the
crimes, the reproof, and the apology. Nullus Regem metuit, nullus Ducem, nullus Comitem reve-
retur; et si fortassis alicui ista displicent, et ea, pro
longævitate vitæ vestræ, emendare conatur, statim
seditio in populo, statim tumultus exoritur, et in
tantum unusquisque contra seniorem, sævâ inten-
tione grassatur, ut vix se credat evadere, si tandem
silere nequiverit.

122. Spain in these dark ages has been peculiar-
ly unfortunate. The Franks had a Gregory of
Tours; the Saxons, or Angles, a Bede; the Lom-
bards, a Paul Warnefrid, etc. But the history of the
Visigoths is contained in the short and imperfect
Chronicles of Isidore of Seville and John of Biclar.

123. Such are the complaints of St. Boniface,
the apostle of Germany and the reformer of Gaul
(in tom. iv. p. 94). The fourscore years which he
deplores of licence and corruption would seem to
insinuate that the barbarians were admitted into
the clergy about the year 660.

124. The acts of the councils of Toledo are still
the most authentic records of the church and constitution of Spain. The following passages are particularly important:—iii. 17, 18; iv. 75; v. 2, 3, 4,
5, 8; vi. 11, 12, 13, 14, 17, 18; vii. 1; xiii. 2, 3, 6. I
have found Mascou (Hist. of the Ancient Germans, xv. 29, and Annotations, xxvi. and xxxiii.)
and Ferreras (Hist. Générale de l'Espagne, tom.
ii.) very useful and accurate guides.

125. The Code of the Visigoths, regularly divided into twelve books, has been correctly published by Dom Bouquet (in tom. iv. p. 283–460).
It has been treated by the President De Montesquieu (The Spirit of Laws, l. xxviii. c. 1) with excessive severity. I dislike the style; I detest the
superstition; but I shall presume to think that the
civil jurisprudence displays a more civilised and
enlightened state of society than that of the Burgundians or even of the Lombards.

126. See Gildas de Excidio Britanniæ, c. 11–25,
p. 4–9, edit. Gale; Nennius, Hist. Britonum, c. 28,
35–65, p. 105–115, edit. Gale; Bede, Hist. Ecclesiast. Gentis Anglorum, l. i. c. 12–16, p. 49–53,
c. 22, p. 58, edit. Smith; Chron. Saxonicum,
p. 11–23, etc., edit. Gibson. The Anglo-Saxon
laws were published by Wilkins, London, 1731, in
folio; and the Leges Wallicæ, by Wotton and
Clarke, London, 1730, in folio.

127. The laborious Mr. Carte and the ingenious Mr. Whitaker are the two modern writers to
whom I am principally indebted. The particular
historian of Manchester embraces, under that obscure title, a subject almost as extensive as the general history of England.

128. This *invitation*, which may derive some
countenance from the loose expressions of Gildas
and Bede, is framed into a regular story by Witi-
kind, a Saxon monk of the tenth century (see
Cousin, Hist. de l'Empire d'Occident, tom. ii. p.
356). Rapin, and even Hume, have too freely used
this suspicious evidence without regarding the precise and probable testimony of Nennius: Interea
venerunt tres Chiulæ à Germaniâ *in exilio pulsæ*,
in quibus erant Hors et Hengist [c. 28].

129. Nennius imputes to the Saxons the murder
of three hundred British chiefs; a crime not unsuitable to their savage manners. But we are not
obliged to believe (see Jeffrey of Monmouth, l.
viii. c. 9–12) that Stonehenge is their monument,
which the giants had formerly transported from
Africa to Ireland, and which was removed to
Britain by the order of Ambrosius and the art of
Merlin.

130. All these tribes are expressly enumerated
by Bede (l. i. c. 15, p. 52, l. v. c. 9, p. 190); and
though I have considered Mr. Whitaker's remarks
(Hist. of Manchester, vol. ii. p. 538–543), I do not
perceive the absurdity of supposing that the Frisians, etc., were mingled with the Anglo-Saxons.

131. Bede has enumerated seven kings—two
Saxons, a Jute, and four Angles—who successively
acquired in the heptarchy an indefinite supremacy
of power and renown. But their reign was the
effect, not of law, but of conquest; and he observes,
in similar terms, that one of them subdued the
Isles of Man and Anglesey; and that another imposed a tribute on the Scots and Picts (Hist. Eccles. l. ii. c. 5, p. 83).

132. See Gildas de Excidio Britanniæ, c. i. p. 1,
edit. Gale.

133. Mr. Whitaker (History of Manchester, vol.
ii. p. 503, 516) has smartly exposed this glaring
absurdity, which had passed unnoticed by the
general historians, as they were hastening to more
interesting and important events.

134. At Beran-birig, or Barbury-castle, near
Marlborough. The Saxon Chronicle assigns the
name and date. Camden (Britannia, vol. i. p. 128)
ascertains the place; and Henry of Huntingdon
(Scriptores post Bedam, p. 314) relates the circumstances of this battle. They are probable and char-

acteristic; and the historians of the twelfth century might consult some materials that no longer exist.

135. Cornwall was finally subdued by Athelstan (A.D. 927–941), who planted an English colony at Exeter, and confined the Britons beyond the river Tamar. See William of Malmesbury, l. ii. in the Scriptores post Bedam, p. 50. The spirit of the Cornish knights was degraded by servitude: and it should seem, from the romance of Sir Tristram, that their cowardice was almost proverbial.

136. The establishment of the Britons in Gaul is proved in the sixth century by Procopius [Bell. Goth. iv. 20], Gregory of Tours, the second council of Tours (A.D. 567), and the least suspicious of their chronicles and lives of saints. The subscription of a bishop of the Britons to the first council of Tours (A.D. 461, or rather 481), the army of Riothamus, and the loose declamation of Gildas (alii transmarinas petebant regiones, c. 25, p. 8), may countenance an emigration as early as the middle of the fifth century. Beyond that era the Britons of Armorica can be found only in romance; and I am surprised that Mr. Whitaker (Genuine History of the Britons, p. 214–221) should so faithfully transcribe the gross ignorance of Carte, whose venial errors he has so rigorously chastised.

137. The antiquities of *Bretagne*, which have been the subject even of political controversy, are illustrated by Hadrian Valesius (Notitia Galliarum, sub voce *Britannia Cismarina*, p. 98–100), M. d'Anville (Notice de l'Ancienne Gaule, *Corisopiti, Curiosolites, Osismii, Vorganium*, p. 248, 258, 508, 720, and Etats de l'Europe, p. 76–80), Longuerue (Description de la France, tom. i. p. 84–94), and the Abbé de Vertot (Hist. Critique de l'Etablissement des Bretons dans les Gaules, 2 vols. in 12mo. Paris 1720). I may assume the merit of examining the original evidence which they have produced.

138. Bede, who in his chronicle (p. 28) places Ambrosius under the reign of Zeno (A.D. 474–491), observes that his parents had been "purpurâ induti;" which he explains, in his ecclesiastical history, by "regium nomen et insigne ferentibus" (l. i. c. 16, p. 53). The expression of Nennius (c. 44, p. 110, edit. Gale) is still more singular, "Unus de *consulibus* gentis Romanicæ est pater meus."

139. By the unanimous, though doubtful, conjecture of our antiquarians, Ambrosius is confounded with Natanleod, who (A.D. 508) lost his own life and five thousand of his subjects in a battle against Cerdic, the West Saxon (Chron. Saxon. p. 17, 18).

140. As I am a stranger to the Welsh bards, Myrdhin, Llomarch, and Taliessin, my faith in the existence and exploits of Arthur principally rests on the simple and circumstantial testimony of Nennius (Hist. Brit. c. 62, 63, p. 114). Mr. Whitaker (Hist. of Manchester, vol. ii. p. 31–71) has framed an interesting, and even probable, narrative of the wars of Arthur: though it is impossible to allow the reality of the round table.

141. The progress of romance and the state of learning in the middle ages are illustrated by Mr. Thomas Warton, with the taste of a poet and the minute diligence of an antiquarian. I have derived much instruction from the two learned dissertations prefixed to the first volume of his History of English Poetry.

142. Hoc anno (490) Ælla et Cissa obsederunt Andredes-Ceaster; et interfecerunt omnes qui id incolerent; adeo ut ne unus Brito ibi superstes fuerit (Chron. Saxon. p. 15); an expression more dreadful in its simplicity than all the vague and tedious lamentations of the British Jeremiah.

143. Andredes-Ceaster, or Anderida, is placed by Camden (Britannia, vol. i. p. 258) at Newenden, in the marshy grounds of Kent, which might be formerly covered by the sea, and on the edge of the great forest (Anderida) which overspread so large a portion of Hampshire and Sussex.

144. Dr. Johnson affirms that *few* English words are of British extraction. Mr. Whitaker, who understands the British language, has discovered more than *three thousand*, and actually produces a long and various catalogue (vol. ii. p. 235–329). It is possible, indeed, that many of these words may have been imported from the Latin or Saxon into the native idiom of Britain.

145. In the beginning of the seventh century the Franks and the Anglo-Saxons mutually understood each other's language, which was derived from the same Teutonic root (Bede. l. i. c. 25, p. 60).

146. After the first generation of Italian or Scottish missionaries, the dignities of the church were filled with Saxon proselytes.

147. Carte's History of England, vol. i. p. 195. He quotes the British historians; but I much fear that Jeffrey of Monmouth (l. vi. c. 15) is his only witness.

148. Bede, Hist. Ecclesiast. l. i. c. 15, p. 52. The fact is probable and well attested: yet such was the loose intermixture of the German tribes, that we find, in a subsequent period, the law of the Angli and Warini of Germany (Lindenbrog. Codex, p. 479–486).

149. See Dr. Henry's useful and laborious History of Great Britain, vol. ii. p. 388.

150. Quicquid (says John of Tinemouth) inter Tynam et Tesam fluvios extitit, sola eremi vastitudo tunc temporis fuit, et idcirco nullius ditioni servivit, eo quod sola indomitorum et silvestrium animalium spelunca et habitatio fuit (apud Carte, vol. i. p. 195). From Bishop Nicholson (English Historical Library, p. 65, 98) I understand that fair copies of John of Tinemouth's ample collections are preserved in the libraries of Oxford, Lambeth, etc.

151. See the mission of Wilfrid, etc., in Bede, Hist. Eccles. l. iv. c. 13, 16, p. 155, 156, 159.

152. From the concurrent testimony of Bede (l. ii. c. 1, p. 78) and William of Malmesbury (l. iii. p. 102), it appears that the Anglo-Saxons, from

the first to the last age, persisted in this unnatural practice. Their youths were publicly sold in the market of Rome.

153. According to the laws of Ina they could not be lawfully sold beyond the seas.

154. The life of a *Wallus*, or *Cambricus*, *homo*, who possessed a hyde of land, is fixed at 120 shillings, by the same laws (of Ina, tit. xxxii. in Leg. Anglo-Saxon. p. 20) which allowed 200 shillings for a free Saxon, and 1200 for a Thane (see likewise Leg. Anglo-Saxon, p. 71). We may observe that these legislators, the West-Saxons and Mercians, continued their British conquests after they became Christians. The laws of the four kings of Kent do not condescend to notice the existence of any subject Britons.

155. See Carte's Hist. of England, vol. i. p. 278.

156. At the conclusion of his history (A.D. 731), Bede describes the ecclesiastical state of the island, and censures the implacable, though impotent, hatred of the Britons against the English nation and the catholic church (l. v. c. 23, p. 219).

157. Mr. Pennant's Tour in Wales (p. 426–449) has furnished me with a curious and interesting account of the Welsh bards. In the year 1568 a session was held at Caerwys by the special command of queen Elizabeth, and regular degrees in vocal and instrumental music were conferred on fifty-five minstrels. The prize (a silver harp) was adjudged by the Mostyn family.

158. Regio longe lateque diffusa, milite, magis quam credibile sit, referta. Partibus equidem in illis miles unus quinquaginta generat, sortitus more barbaro denas aut amplius uxores. This reproach of William of Poitiers (in the Historians of France, tom. xi. p. 88) is disclaimed by the Benedictine editors.

159. Giraldus Cambrensis confines this gift of bold and ready eloquence to the Romans, the French and the Britons. The malicious Welshman insinuates that the English taciturnity might pos-sibly be the effect of their servitude under the Normans.

160. The picture of Welsh and Armorican manners is drawn from Giraldus (Descript. Cambriæ, c. 6–15, inter Script. Camden. p. 886–891) and the authors quoted by the Abbé de Vertot (Hist. Critique, tom. ii. p. 259–266).

161. See Procopius de Bell. Gothic. l. iv. c. 20, p. 620–625 [ed. Paris; tom. ii. p. 559 *sqq.*, ed. Bonn]. The Greek historian is himself so confounded by the wonders which he relates, that he weakly attempts to distinguish the islands of *Brittia* and *Britain*, which he has identified by so many inseparable circumstances.

162. Theodebert, grandson of Clovis and king of Austrasia, was the most powerful and warlike prince of the age; and this remarkable adventure may be placed between the years 534 and 547, the extreme terms of his reign. His sister Theudechildis retired to Sens, where she founded monasteries and distributed alms (see the notes of the Benedictine editors, in tom. ii. p. 216). If we may credit the praises of Fortunatus (l. vi. carm. 5, in tom. ii. p. 507), Radiger was deprived of a most valuable wife.

163. Perhaps she was the sister of one of the princes or chiefs of the Angles who landed, in 527 and the following years, between the Humber and the Thames, and gradually founded the kingdoms of East Anglia and Mercia. The English writers are ignorant of her name and existence; but Procopius may have suggested to Mr. Rowe the character and situation of Rodogune in the tragedy of the Royal Convert.

164. In the copious history of Gregory of Tours we cannot find any traces of hostile or friendly intercourse between France and England, except in the marriage of the daughter of Caribert, king of Paris, quam in Cantia regis *cujusdam* filius matrimonio copulavit (l. ix. c. 26, in tom. ii. p. 348). The bishop of Tours ended his history and his life almost immediately before the conversion of Kent.

General Observations

1. Such are the figurative expressions of Plutarch (Opera, tom. ii. p. 318, edit. Wechel [Frankf. 1620]), to whom, on the faith of his son Lamprias (Fabricius, Bibliot. Græc. tom. iii. p. 341), I shall boldly impute the malicious declamation, περὶ τῆς Ῥωμαίων τυχης. The same opinions had prevailed among the Greeks two hundred and fifty years before Plutarch; and to confute them is the professed intention of Polybius (Hist. l. i. [c. 63] p. 90, edit. Gronov. Amstel. 1670).

2. See the inestimable remains of the sixth book of Polybius, and many other parts of his general history, particularly a digression in the seventeenth book [l. xviii. c. 12–15], in which he compares the phalanx and the legion.

3. Sallust, de Bell. Jugurthin. c. 4. Such were the generous professions of P. Scipio and Q. Maximus. The Latin historian had read, and most probably transcribes, Polybius, their contemporary and friend.

4. While Carthage was in flames Scipio repeated two lines of the Iliad, which express the destruction of Troy, acknowledging to Polybius, his friend and preceptor (Polyb. [Fragm. l. xxxix *sub fin.*] in Excerpt. de Virtut. et Vit. tom. ii. p. 1455–1465), that while he recollected the vicissitudes of human affairs he inwardly applied them to the future calamities of Rome (Appian. in Libycis [l. viii. c. 132], p. 136, edit. Toll.).

5. See Daniel ii. 31–40. "And the fourth king-

dom shall be strong as *iron*; forasmuch as iron breaketh in pieces and subdueth all things." The remainder of the prophecy (the mixture of iron and *clay*) was accomplished, according to St. Jerom, in his own time. Sicut enim in principio nihil Romano Imperio fortius et durius, ita in fine rerum nihil imbecillius: quum et in bellis civilibus et adversus diversas nationes, aliarum gentium barbararum auxilio indigemus (Opera, tom. v. p. 572).

6. The French and English editors of the Genealogical History of the Tartars have subjoined a curious, though imperfect, description of their present state. We might question the independence of the Calmucks, or Eluths, since they have been recently vanquished by the Chinese, who, in the year 1759, subdued the lesser Bucharia, and advanced into the country of Badakshan, near the sources of the Oxus (Mémoires sur les Chinois, tom. i. p. 325–400). But these conquests are precarious, nor will I venture to ensure the safety of the Chinese empire.

7. The prudent reader will determine how far this general proposition is weakened by the revolt of the Isaurians, the independence of Britain and Armorica, the Moorish tribes, or the Bagaudæ of Gaul and Spain (vol. i. p. 414, vol. iv. pp. 130, 178, 252).

8. America now contains about six millions of European blood and descent; and their numbers, at least in the North, are continually increasing. Whatever may be the changes of their political situation, they must preserve the manners of Europe; and we may reflect with some pleasure that the English language will probably be diffused over an immense and populous continent.

9. On avoit fait venir (for the siege of Turin) 140 pièces de canon; et il est à remarquer que chaque gros canon monté revient à environ 2000 écus: il y avoit 100,000 boulets; 106,000 cartouches d'une façon, et 300,000 d'une autre; 21,000 bombes; 27,700 grenades, 15,000 sacs à terre, 30,000 instruments pour la pionnage; 1,200,000 livres de poudre. Ajoutez à ces munitions le plomb, le fer, et le fer-blanc, les cordages, tout ce qui sert aux mineurs, le souphre, le salpêtre, les outils de toute espèce. Il est certain que les frais de tous ces préparatifs de destruction suffiroient pour fonder et pour faire fleurir la plus nombreuse colonie. Voltaire, Siècle de Louis XIV. c. xx. in his Works, tom. xi. p. 391.

10. It would be an easy, though tedious, task to produce the authorities of poets, philosophers, and historians. I shall therefore content myself with appealing to the decisive and authentic testimony of Diodorus Siculus (tom. i. l. i. p. 11, 12, l. iii. [c. 14 *sqq.*] p. 184, etc., edit. Wesseling). The Ichthyophagi, who in his time wandered along the shores of the Red Sea, can only be compared to the natives of New Holland (Dampier's Voyages, vol. i. p. 464–469). Fancy, or perhaps reason, may still suppose an extreme and absolute state of nature far below the level of these savages, who had acquired some arts and instruments.

11. See the learned and rational work of the President Goguet, de l'Origine des Loix, des Arts, et des Sciences. He traces from facts or conjectures (tom. i. p. 147–337, edit. 12mo.) the first and most difficult steps of human invention.

12. It is certain, however strange, that many nations have been ignorant of the use of fire. Even the ingenious natives of Otaheite, who are destitute of metals, have not invented any earthen vessels capable of sustaining the action of fire and of communicating the heat to the liquids which they contain.

13. Plutarch. Quæst. Rom. in tom. ii. p. 275 [tom. vii. p. 112, ed. Reiske]. Macrob. Saturnal. l. i. c. 7, p. 152, edit. London. The arrival of Saturn (of his religious worship) in a ship may indicate that the savage coast of Latium was first discovered and civilised by the Phœnicians.

14. In the ninth and tenth books of the Odyssey, Homer has embellished the tales of fearful and credulous sailors who transformed the cannibals of Italy and Sicily into monstrous giants.

15. The merit of discovery has too often been stained with avarice, cruelty, and fanaticism; and the intercourse of nations has produced the communication of disease and prejudice. A singular exception is due to the virtue of our own times and country. The five great voyages, successively undertaken by the command of his present Majesty, were inspired by the pure and generous love of science and mankind. The same prince, adapting his benefactions to the different stages of society, has founded a school of painting in his capital, and has introduced into the islands of the South Sea the vegetables and animals most useful to human life.

Chapter XXXIX

·1: **Jornandes** (de Rebus Geticis, c. 13, 14, p. 629, 630, edit. Grot.) has drawn the pedigree of Theodoric from Gapt, one of the *Anses* or Demigods, who lived about the time of Domitian. Cassiodorus, the first who celebrates the royal race of the Amali (Variar. viii. 5, ix. 25, x. 2, xi. 1), reckons the grandson of Theodoric as the xviith in descent. Peringsciold (the Swedish commentator of Cochlœus, Vit. Theodoric. p. 271, etc., Stockholm, 1699) labours to connect this genealogy with the legends or traditions of his native country.

2. More correctly on the banks of the lake Pelso (Nieusiedler-see) near Carnuntum, almost on the same spot where Marcus Antoninus composed his

Meditations (Jornandes, c. 52, p. 689. Severin. Pannonia Illustrata, p. 22. Cellarius, Geograph. Antiq. tom. i. p. 350).

3. The four first letters of his name (ΘΕΟΔ) were inscribed on a gold plate, and when it was fixed on the paper the king drew his pen through the intervals (Anonym. Valesian. ad calcem Amm. Marcellin. p. 722 [tom. ii. p. 313, ed. Bipon.]). This authentic fact, with the testimony of Procopius, or at least of the contemporary Goths (Gothic. l. i. c. 2, p. 312 [ed. Paris; tom. ii. p. 14, ed. Bonn]), far outweighs the vague praises of Ennodius (Sirmond. Opera, tom. i. p. 1596) and Theophanes (Chronograph. p. 112 [ed. Par.; p. 202, 203, ed. Bonn]).

4. Statura est quæ resignet proceritate regnantem (Ennodius, p. 1614). The bishop of Pavia (I mean the ecclesiastic who wished to be a bishop) then proceeds to celebrate the complexion, eyes, hands, etc., of his sovereign.

5. The state of the Ostrogoths and the first years of Theodoric are found in Jornandes (c. 52–56, p. 689–696) and Malchus (Excerpt. Legat. p. 78–80 [ed. Par.; p. 244–248, ed. Bonn]), who erroneously styles him the son of Walamir.

6. Theophanes (p. 111 [p. 200, ed. Bonn]) inserts a copy of her *sacred* letters to the provinces; ἴστε ὅτι τὸ βασίλειον ἡμέτερόν ἐστι . . . καὶ ὅτι προχειρησάμεθα βασιλέα Τρασκαλλισαῖον, etc. Such female pretensions would have astonished the slaves of the *first* Cæsars.

7. Vol. iv. p. 284, *seq*

8. Suidas, tom. i. p. 332, 333, edit. Kuster.

9. The contemporary histories of Malchus and Candidus are lost; but some extracts or fragments have been saved by Photius (lxxviii. lxxix. p. 100–102 [p. 54–56, ed. Bekk.]), Constantine Porphyrogenitus (Excerpt. Leg. p. 78–97), and in various articles of the Lexicon of Suidas. The Chronicles of Marcellinus (Imago Historiæ) are originals for the reigns of Zeno and Anastasius; and I must acknowledge, almost for the last time, my obligations to the large and accurate collections of Tillemont (Hist. des Emp. tom. vi. p. 472–652).

10. In ipsis congressionis tuæ foribus cessit invasor, cum *profugo* per te sceptra redderentur de salute dubitanti. Ennodius then proceeds (p. 1596, 1597, tom. i. Sirmond) to transport his hero (on a flying dragon?) into Æthiopia, beyond the tropic of Cancer. The evidence of the Valesian Fragment (p. 717), Liberatus (Brev. Eutych. c. 25, p. 118), and Theophanes (p. 112 [p. 203, ed. Bonn]), is more sober and rational.

11. This cruel practice is specially imputed to the *Triarian* Goths, less barbarous, as it should seem, than the *Walamirs*; but the son of Theodemir is charged with the ruin of many Roman cities (Malchus, Excerpt. Leg. p. 95 [ed. Par.; p. 238, ed. Bonn]).

12. Jornandes (c. 56, 57, p. 696) displays the services of Theodoric, confesses his rewards, but dissembles his revolt, of which such curious details

have been preserved by Malchus (Excerpt. Legat. p. 78–97 [p. 244 *sqq.*, ed. Bonn]). Marcellinus, a domestic of Justinian, under whose ivth consulship (A.D. 534) he composed his Chronicle (Scaliger, Thesaurus Temporum, P. ii. p. 34–57), betrays his prejudice and passion; in [apud] Græciam debacchantem . . . Zenonis munificentiâ pene pacatus . . . beneficiis nunquam satiatus, etc. [p. 368, 369, and 370, ed. Sirmond].

13. As he was riding in his own camp an unruly horse threw him against the point of a spear which hung before a tent, or was fixed on a waggon (Marcellin. in Chron. Evagrius, l. iii. c. 25).

14. See Malchus (p. 91 [ed. Par.; p. 268, ed. Bonn]) and Evagrius (l. iii. c. 35).

15. Malchus, p. 85 [p. 256, ed. Bonn]. In a single action, which was decided by the skill and discipline of Sabinian, Theodoric could lose 5000 men.

16. Jornandes (c. 57, p. 696, 697) has abridged the great history of Cassiodorus. See, compare, and reconcile, Procopius (Gothic. l. i. c. i.), the Valesian Fragment (p. 718 [ad Calcem Amm. Marc. tom. ii. p. 306, ed. Bip.]), Theophanes (p. 113 [p. 203, ed. Bonn]), and Marcellinus (in Chron.).

17. Theodoric's march is supplied and illustrated by Ennodius (p. 1598–1602), when the bombast of the oration is translated into the language of common sense.

18. Tot reges, etc. (Ennodius, p. 1602). We must recollect how much the royal title was multiplied and degraded, and that the mercenaries of Italy were the fragments of many tribes and nations.

19. See Ennodius, p. 1603, 1604. Since the orator, in the king's presence, could mention and praise his mother, we may conclude that the magnanimity of Theodoric was not hurt by the vulgar reproaches of concubine and bastard.

20. This anecdote is related on the modern but respectable authority of Sigonius (Op. tom. i. p. 580; De Occident. Imp. l. xv.); his words are curious:—"Would you return?" etc. She presented and almost displayed the original recess.

21. Hist. Miscell. l. xv., a Roman history from Janus to the ninth century, an Epitome of Eutropius, Paulus Diaconus, and Theophanes, which Muratori has published from a MS. in the Ambrosian library (Script. Rerum Italicarum, tom. i. p. 100).

22. Procopius (Gothic. l. i. c. i.) approves himself an impartial sceptic; φασὶ . . . δολερῷ τρόπῳ ἔκτεινε [tom. ii. p. 10, ed. Bonn]. Cassiodorus (in Chron.) and Ennodius (p. 1605) are loyal and credulous, and the testimony of the Valesian Fragment (p. 718 [Amm. tom. ii. p. 307, ed. Bip.]) may justify their belief. Marcellinus spits the venom of a Greek subject—perjuriis illectus, interfectusque est (in Chron. [anno 489]).

23. The sonorous and servile oration of Ennodius was pronounced at Milan or Ravenna in the

years 507 or 508 (Sirmond, tom. i. p. 1615). Two or three years afterwards the orator was rewarded with the bishopric of Pavia, which he held till his death in the year 521. (Dupin, Bibliot. Eccles. tom. v. p. 11-14. See Saxii Onomasticon, tom. ii. p. 12.)

24. Our best materials are occasional hints from Procopius and the Valesian Fragment, which was discovered by Sirmond and is published at the end of Ammianus Marcellinus. The author's name is unknown, and his style is barbarous; but in his various facts he exhibits the knowledge, without the passions, of a contemporary. The President Montesquieu had formed the plan of a history of Theodoric, which at a distance might appear a rich and interesting subject.

25. The best edition of the *Variarum Libri* xii. is that of Joh. Garretius (Rotomagi, 1679, in Opp. Cassiodor. 2 vols. in fol.); but they deserved and required such an editor as the Marquis Scipio Maffei, who thought of publishing them at Verona. The *Barbara Eleganza* (as it is ingeniously named by Tiraboschi) is never simple, and seldom perspicuous.

26. Procopius, Gothic. l. i. c. i.; Variarum, ii. Maffei (Verona Illustrata, P. i. p. 228) exaggerates the injustice of the Goths, whom he hated as an Italian noble. The plebeian Muratori crouches under their oppression.

27. Procopius, Goth. l. iii. c. 4 and 21 [tom. ii. p. 295 and 366, ed. Bonn]. Ennodius describes (p. 1612, 1613) the military arts and increasing numbers of the Goths.

28. When Theodoric gave his sister to the king of the Vandals, she sailed for Africa with a guard of 1000 noble Goths, each of whom was attended by five armed followers (Procop. Vandal. l. i. c. 8 [tom. i. p. 346, ed. Bonn]). The Gothic nobility must have been as numerous as brave.

29. See the acknowledgment of Gothic liberty (Var. v. 30).

30. Procopius, Goth. l. i. c. 2 [tom. ii. p. 14, ed. Bonn]. The Roman boys learnt the language (Var. viii. 21) of the Goths. Their general ignorance is not destroyed by the exceptions of Amalasuntha, a female, who might study without shame, or of Theodatus, whose learning provoked the indignation and contempt of his countrymen.

31. A saying of Theodoric was founded on experience: "Romanus miser imitatur Gothum; et utilis (*dives*) Gothus imitatur Romanum." See the Fragment and Notes of Valesius, p. 719 [Amm. ii. p. 308, ed. Bip.]).

32. The view of the military establishment of the Goths in Italy is collected from the Epistles of Cassiodorus (Var. i. 24, 40; iii. 3, 24, 48; iv. 13, 14; v. 26, 27; viii. 3, 4, 25). They are illustrated by the learned Mascou (Hist. of the Germans, l. xi. 40-44; Annotation xiv.).

33. See the clearness and vigour of his negotiations in Ennodius (p. 1607) and Cassiodorus (Var. iii. 1, 2, 3, 4; iv. 13; v. 43, 44), who gives the different styles of friendship, counsel, expostulation, etc.

34. Even of his table (Var. vi. 9) and palace (vii. 5). The admiration of strangers is represented as the most rational motive to justify these vain expenses, and to stimulate the diligence of the officers to whom these provinces were intrusted.

35. See the public and private alliances of the Gothic monarch, with the Burgundians (Var. i. 45, 46), with the Franks (ii. 40), with the Thuringians (iv. 1), and with the Vandals (v. 1); each of these epistles affords some curious knowledge of the policy and manners of the barbarians.

36. His political system may be observed in Cassiodorus (Var. iv. 1, ix. 1), Jornandes (c. 58, p. 698, 699), and the Valesian Fragment (p. 720, 721 [Amm. tom. ii. p. 311, ed. Bip.]). Peace, honourable peace, was the constant aim of Theodoric.

37. The curious reader may contemplate the Heruli of Procopius (Goth. l. ii. c. 14), and the patient reader may plunge into the dark and minute researches of M. de Buat (Hist. des Peuples Anciens, tom. ix. p. 348-396).

38. Variarum, iv. 2. The spirit and forms of this martial institution are noticed by Cassiodorus; but he seems to have only translated the sentiments of the Gothic king into the language of Roman eloquence.

39. Cassiodorus, who quotes Tacitus to the Æstians, the unlettered savages of the Baltic (Var. v. 2), describes the amber for which their shores have ever been famous as the gum of a tree hardened by the sun and purified and wafted by the waves. When that singular substance is analysed by the chemists, it yields a vegetable oil and a mineral acid.

40. Scanzia, or Thule, is described by Jornandes (c. 3, p. 610-613) and Procopius (Goth. l. ii. c. 15). Neither the Goth nor the Greek had visited the country: both had conversed with the natives in their exile at Ravenna or Constantinople.

41. *Saphirinas pelles.* In the time of Jornandes they inhabited *Suethans*, the proper Sweden; but that beautiful race of animals has gradually been driven into the eastern parts of Siberia. See Buffon (Hist. Nat. tom. xiii. p. 309-313, quarto edition); Pennant (System of Quadrupeds, vol. i. p. 322-328); Gmelin (Hist. Gén. des Voyages, tom. xviii. p. 257, 258); and Levesque (Hist. de Russie, tom. v. p. 165, 166, 514, 515).

42. In the system or romance of M. Bailly (Lettres sur les Sciences et sur l'Atlantide, tom. i. p. 249-256, tom. ii. p. 114-139), the phœnix of the Edda, and the annual death and revival of Adonis and Osiris, are the allegorical symbols of the absence and return of the sun in the Arctic regions. This ingenious writer is a worthy disciple of the great Buffon; nor is it easy for the coldest reason to withstand the magic of their philosophy.

43. Αὕτη τε Θουλίταις ἡ μεγίστη τῶν ἑορτων ἔστι, says Procopius [tom. ii. p. 207, ed. Bonn]. At present a rude Manicheism (generous enough) prevails

among the Samoyedes in Greenland and in Lapland (Hist. des Voyages, tom. xviii. p. 508, 509, tom. xix. p. 105, 106, 527, 528); yet, according to Grotius, Samojutæ cœlum atque astra adorant, numina haud aliis iniquiora (de Rebus Belgicis, l. iv. p. 338, folio edition); a sentence which Tacitus would not have disowned.

44. See the Hist. des Peuples Anciens, etc., tom. ix. p. 255-273, 396-501. The Count de Buat was French minister at the court of Bavaria: a liberal curiosity prompted his inquiries into the antiquities of the country, and that curiosity was the *germ* of twelve respectable volumes.

45. See the Gothic transactions on the Danube and in Illyricum, in Jornandes (c. 58, p. 699), Ennodius (p. 1607-1610), Marcellinus (in Chron. p. 44, 47, 48), and Cassiodorus (in Chron. and Var. iii. 23, 50; iv. 13; vii. 4, 24; viii. 9, 10, 11, 21; ix. 8, 9).

46. I cannot forbear transcribing the liberal and classic style of Count Marcellinus: Romanus comes domesticorum, et Rusticus comes scholariorum cum centum armatis navibus, totidemque dromonibus, octo millia militum armatorum secum ferentibus, ad devastanda Italiæ littora processerunt, et usque ad Tarentum antiquissimam civitatem aggressi sunt; remensoque mari inhonestam victoriam quam piratico ausu Romani ex Romanis rapuerunt, Anastasio Cæsari reportarunt (in Chron. p. 48 [anno 508]). See Variar. i. 16, ii. 38.

47. See the royal orders and instructions (Var. iv. 15; v. 16-20). These armed boats should be still smaller than the thousand vessels of Agamemnon at the siege of Troy [Manso, p. 121].

48. Vol. iv. p. 357, *seq.*

49. Ennodius (p. 1610) and Cassiodorus, in the royal name (Var. ii. 41), record his salutary protection of the Alemanni.

50. The Gothic transactions in Gaul and Spain are represented with some perplexity in Cassiodorus (Var. iii. 32, 38, 41, 43, 44; v. 39), Jornandes (c. 58, p. 698, 699), and Procopius (Goth. l. i. c. 12). I will neither hear nor reconcile the long and contradictory arguments of the Abbé Dubos and the Count de Buat, about the wars of Burgundy.

51. Theophanes, p. 113 [p. 203, ed. Bonn].

52. Procopius affirms that no laws whatsoever were promulgated by Theodoric and the succeeding kings of Italy (Goth. l. ii. c. 6 [tom. ii. p. 170, ed. Bonn]). He must mean in the Gothic language. A Latin edict of Theodoric is still extant, in one hundred and fifty-four articles.

53. The image of Theodoric is engraved on his coins; his modest successors were satisfied with adding their own name to the head of the reigning emperor (Muratori, Antiquitat. Italiæ Medii Ævi, tom. ii. dissert. xxvii. p. 577-579. Giannone, Istoria Civile di Napoli, tom. i. p. 166).

54. The alliance of the emperor and the king of Italy are represented by Cassiodorus (Var. i. 1; ii. 1, 2, 3; vi 1) and Procopius (Goth. l. ii. c. 6; l. iii.

c. 21 [tom. ii. p. 369, ed. Bonn]), who celebrate the friendship of Anastasius and Theodoric: but the figurative style of compliment was interpreted in a very different sense at Constantinople and Ravenna.

55. To the seventeen provinces of the Notitia, Paul Warnefrid the deacon (De Reb. Longobard. l. ii. c. 14-22) has subjoined an eighteenth, the Apennine (Muratori, Script. Rerum Italicarum, tom. i. p. 431-433). But of these, Sardinia and Corsica were possessed by the Vandals, and the two Rhætias, as well as the Cottian Alps, seem to have been abandoned to a military government. The state of the four provinces that now form the kingdom of Naples is laboured by Giannone (tom. i. p. 172, 178) with patriotic diligence.

56. See the Gothic history of Procopius (l. i. c. 1, l. ii. c. 6), the Epistles of Cassiodorus (passim, but especially the fifth and sixth books [vi. and vii.], which contain the *formulæ*, or patents of offices), and the Civil History of Giannone (tom. i. l. ii. iii.). The Gothic counts, which he places in every Italian city, are annihilated, however, by Maffei (Verona Illustrata, P. i. l. viii. p. 227); for those of Syracuse and Naples (Var. vi. 22, 23) were special and temporary commissions.

57. Two Italians of the name of Cassiodorus, the father (Var. i. 24 [4], 40) and the son (ix. 24, 25), were successively employed in the administration of Theodoric. The son was born in the year 479: his various epistles as quæstor, master of the offices, and Prætorian præfect, extend from 509 to 539, and he lived as a monk about thirty years. (Tiraboschi, Storia della Letteratura Italiana, tom. iii. p. 7-24. Fabricius, Biblioth. Lat. Med. Ævi. tom. i. p. 357, 358, edit. Mansi.)

58. See his regard for the senate in Cochlœus (Vit. Theod. viii. p. 72-80).

59. No more than 120,000 *modii*, or four thousand quarters (Anonym. Valesian, p. 721 [Amm. ii. p. 310, ed. Bip.], and Var. i. 35, vi. 18, xi. 5, 39).

60. See his regard and indulgence for the spectacles of the circus, the amphitheatre, and the theatre, in the Chronicle and Epistles of Cassiodorus (Var. i. 20, 27, 30, 31, 32, iii. 51, iv. 51, illustrated by the fourteenth Annotation of Mascou's History), who has contrived to sprinkle the subject with ostentatious, though agreeable, learning.

61. Anonym. Vales. p. 721 [l. c. ed. Bip.]. Marius Aventicensis in Chron. In the scale of public and personal merit, the Gothic conqueror is at least as much *above* Valentinian as he may seem *inferior* to Trajan.

62. Vit. Fulgentii in Baron. Annal. Eccles. A.D. 500, No. 10.

63. Cassiodorus describes in his pompous style the Forum of Trajan (Var. vii. 6), the theatre of Marcellus (iv. 51), and the amphitheatre of Titus (v. 42); and his descriptions are not unworthy of the reader's perusal. According to the modern prices, the Abbé Barthelemy computes that the brickwork and masonry of the Coliseum would

now cost twenty millions of French livres (Mém. de l'Académie des Inscriptions, tom. xxviii. p. 585, 586). How small a part of that stupendous fabric!

64. For the aqueducts and cloacæ see Strabo (l. v. p. 360 [p. 235, ed. Casaub.]), Pliny (Hist. Nat. xxxvi. 24 [§ 3]), Cassiodorus (Var. iii. 30, 31, vi. 6), Procopius (Goth. l. i. c. 19), and Nardini (Roma Antica, p. 514–522). How such works could be executed by a king of Rome is yet a problem.

65. For the Gothic care of the buildings and statues, see Cassiodorus (Var. i. 21, 25, ii. 34, iv. 30, vii. 6, 13, 15), and the Valesian Fragment (p. 721 [Amm. tom. ii. p. 310, ed. Bip.]).

66. Var. vii. 15. These horses of Monte Cavallo had been transported from Alexandria to the baths of Constantine (Nardini, p. 188). Their sculpture is disdained by the Abbé Dubos (Réflexions sur la Poésie et sur la Peinture, tom. i. section 39), and admired by Winckelman (Hist. de l'Art, tom. ii. p. 159).

67. Var. x. 30. They were probably a fragment of some triumphal car (Cuper de Elephantis, ii. 10).

68. Procopius (Goth. l. iv. c. 21 [tom. ii. p. 571, ed. Bonn]) relates a foolish story of Myron's cow, which is celebrated by the false wit of thirty-six Greek epigrams (Antholog. l. iv. p. 302–306, edit. Hen. Steph.; Auson. Epigram. lviii.–lxviii.).

69. See an epigram of Ennodius (ii. 3, p. 1893, 1894) on this garden and the royal gardener.

70. His affection for that city is proved by the epithet of "Verona tua," and the legend of the hero; under the barbarous name of Dietrich of Bern (Peringsciold ad Cochlœum, p. 240), Maffei traces him with knowledge and pleasure in his native country (l. ix. p. 230–236).

71. See Maffei (Verona Illustrata, Part. i. p. 231, 232, 308, etc.). He imputes Gothic architecture, like the corruption of language, writing, etc., not to the barbarians, but to the Italians themselves. Compare his sentiments with those of Tiraboschi (tom. iii. p. 61).

72. The villas, climate, and landscape of Baiæ (Var. ix. 6; see Cluver. Italia Antiq. l. iv. c. 2, p. 1119, etc.), Istria (Var. xii. 22, 26), and Comum (Var. xi. 14, compare with Pliny's two villas, ix. 7), are agreeably painted in the epistles of Cassiodorus.

73. In Liguria numerosa agricolarum progenies (Ennodius, p. 1678, 1679, 1680). St. Epiphanius of Pavia redeemed by prayer or ransom 6000 captives from the Burgundians of Lyons and Savoy. Such deeds are the best of miracles.

74. The political economy of Theodoric (see Anonym. Vales. p. 721 [Amm. tom. ii. p. 311, ed. Bip.] and Cassiodorus, in Chron.) may be distinctly traced under the following heads: iron-mine (Var. iii. 25); gold-mine (ix. 3); Pomptine marshes (ii. 32, 33); Spoleto (ii. 21); corn (i. 34, x. 27, 28, xi. 11, 12); trade (vi. 7, vii. 9, 23); fair of Leucothoe or St. Cyprian in Lucania (viii. 33); plenty (xii. 4); the cursus, or public post (i. 29, ii.

31, iv. 47, v. 5, vi. 6, vii. 33); the Flaminian way (xii. 18).

75. LX modii tritici in solidum ipsius tempore fuerunt, et vinum xxx amphoras in solidum (Fragment. Vales. [p. 311, ed. Bip.]). Corn was distributed from the granaries at xv or xxv modii for a piece of gold, and the price was still moderate.

76. See the Life of St. Cæsarius in Baronius (A.D. 508, No. 12, 13, 14). The king presented him with 300 gold solidi, and a discus of silver of the weight of sixty pounds.

77. Ennodius in Vit. St. Epiphanii, in Sirmond Op. tom. i. p. 1672–1690. Theodoric bestowed some important favours on this bishop, whom he used as a counsellor in peace and war.

78. Devotissimus ac si catholicus (Anonym. Vales. p. 720 [p. 310, ed. Bip.]); yet his offering was no more than two silver candlesticks (cerostrata) of the weight of seventy pounds, far inferior to the gold and gems of Constantinople and France (Anastasius in Vit. Pont. in Hormisda, p. 34, edit. Paris [tom. i. p. 93, ed. Rom. 1718]).

79. The tolerating system of his reign (Ennodius, p. 1612, Anonym. Vales. p. 719 [p. 308, ed. Bip.], Procop. Goth. l. i. c. 1, l. ii. c. 6) may be studied in the Epistles of Cassiodorus, under the following heads: bishops (Var. i. 9, viii. 15, 24, xi. 23); immunities (i. 26, ii. 29, 30); church lands (iv. 17, 20); sanctuaries (ii. 11, iii. 47); church plate (xii. 20); discipline (iv. 44); which prove at the same time that he was the head of the church as well as of the state.

80. We may reject a foolish tale of his beheading a catholic deacon who turned Arian (Theodor. Lector. No. 17). Why is Theodoric surnamed Afer? From Vafer? (Vales. ad loc.) A light conjecture.

81. Ennodius, p. 1621, 1622, 1636, 1638. His libel was approved and registered (synodaliter) by a Roman council (Baronius, A.D. 503, No. 6. Franciscus Pagi in Breviar. Pont. Rom. tom. i. p. 242).

82. See Cassiodorus (Var. viii. 15, ix. 15, 16), Anastasius (in Symmacho, p. 31 [p. 84, ed. Rom.]), and the seventeenth Annotation of Mascou. Baronius, Pagi, and most of the catholic doctors, confess, with an angry growl, this Gothic usurpation.

83. He disabled them—a licentia testandi; and all Italy mourned—lamentabili justitio. I wish to believe that these penalties were enacted against the rebels who had violated their oath of allegiance; but the testimony of Ennodius (p. 1675–1678) is the more weighty, as he lived and died under the reign of Theodoric.

84. Ennodius, in Vit. Epiphan. p. 1689, 1690. Boethius de Consolatione Philosophiæ, l. i. pros. iv. p. 45, 46, 47 [ed. Callyus, Par. 1680]. Respect, but weigh, the passions of the saint and the senator; and fortify or alleviate their complaints by the various hints of Cassiodorus (ii. 8, iv. 36, viii. 5).

85. Immanium expensarum pondus ... pro ipsorum salute, etc.; yet these are no more than words.

86. The Jews were settled at Naples (Procopius, Goth. l. i. c. 8 [tom. ii. p. 44, ed. Bonn]), at Genoa (Var. ii. 27, iv. 33), Milan (v. 37), Rome (iv. 43). See likewise Basnage, Hist. des Juifs, tom. viii. c. 7, p. 254.

87. Rex avidus communis exitii, etc. (Boethius, l. i. p. 55): rex dolum Romanis tendebat (Anonym. Vales. p. 723). These are hard words: they speak the passions of the Italians, and those (I fear) of Theodoric himself.

88. I have laboured to extract a rational narrative from the dark, concise, and various hints of the Valesian Fragment (p. 722, 723, 724 [p. 313, sqq. ed. Bip.]), Theophanes (p. 145 [tom. i. p. 261, ed. Bonn]), Anastasius (in Johanne, p. 35 [p. 94, ed. Rom.]), and the Hist. Miscella (p. 103, edit. Muratori [Milan, 1723]). A gentle pressure and paraphrase of their words is no violence. Consult likewise Muratori (Annali d'Italia, tom. iv. p. 471–478), with the Annals and Breviary (tom. i. p. 259–263) of the two Pagis, the uncle and the nephew.

89. Le Clerc has composed a critical and philosophical Life of Anicius Manlius Severinus Boethius (Bibliot. Choisie, tom. xvi. p. 168–275); and both Tiraboschi (tom. iii.) and Fabricius (Bibliot. Latin.) may be usefully consulted. The date of his birth may be placed about the year 470, and his death in 524, in a premature old age (Consol. Phil. Metrica, i. p. 5).

90. For the age and value of this MS., now in the Medicean library at Florence, see the Cenotaphia Pisana (p. 430–447) of Cardinal Noris.

91. The Athenian studies of Boethius are doubtful (Baronius, A.D. 510, No. 3, from a spurious tract, De Disciplina Scholarum), and the term of eighteen years is doubtless too long: but the simple fact of a visit to Athens is justified by much internal evidence (Brucker, Hist. Crit. Philosoph. tom. iii. p. 524–527), and by an expression (though vague and ambiguous) of his friend Cassiodorus (Var. i. 45), "longè positas Athenas introisti."

92. Bibliothecæ comptos ebore ac vitro parietes, etc. (Consol. Phil. l. i. pros. v. p. 74). The Epistles of Ennodius (vi. 6, vii. 13, viii. 1, 31, 37, 40) and Cassiodorus (Var. i. 39, iv. 6, ix. 21) afford many proofs of the high reputation which he enjoyed in his own times. It is true that the bishop of Pavia wanted to purchase of him an old house at Milan, and praise might be tendered and accepted in part of payment.

93. Pagi, Muratori, etc., are agreed that Boethius himself was consul in the year 510, his two sons in 522, and in 487, perhaps, his father. A desire of ascribing the last of these consulships to the philosopher had perplexed the chronology of his life. In his honours, alliances, children, he celebrates his own felicity—his past felicity (p. 109, 110).

94. Si ego scissem tu nescisses. Boethius adopts this answer (l. i. pros. 4, p. 53) of Julius Canus, whose philosophic death is described by Seneca (De Tranquillitate Animi, c. 14).

95. The characters of his two delators, Basilius (Var. ii. 10, 11, iv. 22) and Opilio (v. 41, viii. 16), are illustrated, not much to their honour, in the Epistles of Cassiodorus, which likewise mention Decoratus (v. 31), the worthless colleague of Boethius (l. iii. pros. 4, p. 193).

96. A severe inquiry was instituted into the crime of magic (Var. iv. 22, 23, ix. 18); and it was believed that many necromancers had escaped by making their gaolers mad: for *mad*, I should read *drunk*.

97. Boethius had composed his own Apology (p. 53), perhaps more interesting than his Consolation. We must be content with the general view of his honours, principles, persecution, etc. (l. i. pros. 4, p. 42–62), which may be compared with the short and weighty words of the Valesian Fragment (p. 723 [Amm. tom. ii. p. 314, ed. Bip.]). An anonymous writer [Sinner, Catalog. MSS. Bibliot. Bern. tom. i. p. 287) charges him home with honourable and patriotic treason.

98. He was executed in Agro Calventiano (Calvenzano, between Marignano and Pavia), Anonym. Vales. p. 723 [p. 315, ed. Bip.], by order of Eusebius, count of Ticinum or Pavia. The place of his confinement is styled the *baptistery*, an edifice and name peculiar to cathedrals. It is claimed by the perpetual tradition of the church of Pavia. The tower of Boethius subsisted till the year 1584, and the draught is yet preserved (Tiraboschi, tom. iii. p. 47, 48).

99. See the Biographia Britannica, ALFRED, tom. i. p. 80, 2nd edition. The work is still more honourable if performed under the learned eye of Alfred by his foreign and domestic doctors. For the reputation of Boethius in the middle ages consult Brucker (Hist. Crit. Philosoph. tom. iii. p. 565, 566).

100. The inscription on his new tomb was composed by the preceptor of Otho the Third, the learned pope Silvester II., who, like Boethius himself, was styled a magician by the ignorance of the times. The catholic martyr had carried his head in his hands a considerable way (Baronius, A.D. 526, No. 17, 18); yet on a similar tale, a lady of my acquaintance once observed, "La distance n'y fait rien; il n'y a que le premier pas qui coûte."

101. Boethius applauds the virtues of his father-in-law (l. i. pros. 4, p. 59, l. ii. pros. 4, p. 118). Procopius (Goth. l. i. c. i. [tom. ii. p. 11, ed. Bonn]), the Valesian Fragment (p. 724 [p. 316, ed. Bip.]), and the Historia Miscella (l. xv. p. 105 [103?]), agree in praising the superior innocence or sanctity of Symmachus; and in the estimation of the legend, the guilt of his murder is equal to the imprisonment of a pope.

102. In the fanciful eloquence of Cassiodorus, the variety of sea and river fish are an evidence of extensive dominion; and those of the Rhine, of Sicily, and of the Danube, were served on the

table of Theodoric (Var. xii. 44). The monstrous turbot of Domitian (Juvenal, Satir. iv. 39) had been caught on the shores of the Hadriatic.

103. Procopius, Goth. l. i. c. 1 [tom. ii. p. 11, ed. Bonn]. But he might have informed us whether he had received this curious anecdote from common report, or from the mouth of the royal physician.

104. Procopius, Goth. l. i. c. 1, 2, 12, 13. This partition had been directed by Theodoric, though it was not executed till after his death. Rengi hereditatem superstes reliquit (Isidor. Chron. p. 721, edit. Grot.).

105. Berimund, the third in descent from Hermanric, king of the Ostrogoths, had retired into Spain, where he lived and died in obscurity (Jornandes, c. 33, p. 202, edit. Muratori). See the discovery, nuptials, and death of his grandson Eutharic (c. 58, p. 220). His Roman games might render him popular (Cassiodor. in Chron.), but Eutharic was asper in religione (Anonym. Vales. p. 722, 723 [p. 313, ed. Bip.]).

106. See the counsels of Theodoric, and the professions of his successor, in Procopius (Goth. l. i. c. 1, 2), Jornandes (c. 59 [p. 700, 701, ed. Grot.]), and Cassiodorus (Var. viii. 1–7). These epistles are the triumph of his ministerial eloquence.

107. Anonym. Vales. p. 724 [p. 316, ed. Bip.]. Agnellus de Vitis Pont. Raven. in Muratori Script. Rerum Ital. tom. ii. P. i. p. 67. Alberti Descrizione d'Italia, p. 311.

108. This legend is related by Gregory I. (Dialog. iv. 30 [tom. ii. p. 420, ed. Bened.]), and approved by Baronius (A.D. 526, No. 28); and both the pope and cardinal are grave doctors, sufficient to establish a *probable* opinion.

109. Theodoric himself, or rather Cassiodorus, had described in tragic strains the volcanos of Lipari (Cluver. Sicilia, p. 406–410), and Vesuvius ([Var.] iv. 50).

Chapter XL

1. There is some difficulty in the date of his birth (Ludewig in Vit. Justiniani, p. 125); none in the place—the district Bederiana—the village Tauresium, which he afterwards decorated with his name and splendour (D'Anville, Hist. de l'Acad. etc., tom. xxxi. p. 287–292).

2. The names of these Dardanian peasants are Gothic, and almost English: *Justinian* is a translation of *uprauda* (*upright*); his father *Sabatius* (in Græco-barbarous language *stipes*) was styled in his village *Istock* (*Stock*); his mother Bigleniza was softened into Vigilantia.

3. Ludewig (p. 127–135) attempts to justify the Anician name of Justinian and Theodora, and to connect them with a family from which the house of Austria has been derived.

4. See the Anecdotes of Procopius (c. 6) with the notes of N. Alemannus. The satirist would not have sunk, in the vague and decent appellation of γεωργος, the βουκολος and συφορβος of Zonaras. Yet why are those names disgraceful?—and what German baron would not be proud to descend from the Eumæus of the Odyssey?

5. His virtues are praised by Procopius (Persic. l. i. c. 11 [tom. i. p. 52, ed. Bonn]). The quæstor Proclus was the friend of Justinian and the enemy of every other adoption.

6. Manichæan signifies Eutychian. Hear the furious acclamations of Constantinople and Tyre, the former no more than six days after the decease of Anastasius. *They* produced, the latter applauded, the eunuch's death (Baronius, A.D. 518, P. ii. No. 15; Fleury, Hist. Ecclés. tom. vii. p. 200, 205, from the Councils, tom. v. p. 182, 207).

7. His power, character, and intentions are perfectly explained by the Count de Buat (tom. ix. p. 54–81). He was great-grandson of Aspar, heredi-tary prince in the Lesser Scythia, and count of the Gothic *fœderati* of Thrace. The Bessi, whom he could influence, are the minor Goths of Jornandes (c. 51).

8. Justiniani patricii factione dicitur interfectus fuisse (Victor Tununensis Chron. in Thesaur. Temp. Scaliger, P. ii. p. 7). Procopius (Anecdot. c. 7 [c. 6, tom. iii. p. 46, ed. Bonn]) styles him a tyrant, but acknowledges the αδελφοπιστια, which is well explained by Alemannus.

9. In his earliest youth (plane adolescens) he had passed some time as a hostage with Theodoric. For this curious fact Alemannus (ad Procop. Anecdot. c. 9, p. 34 [tom. iii. p. 383, ed. Bonn] of the first edition) quotes a MS. history of Justinian, by his preceptor Theophilus. Ludewig (p. 143) wishes to make him a soldier.

10. The ecclesiastical history of Justinian will be shown hereafter. See Baronius, A.D. 518–521, and the copious article *Justinianus* in the index to the seventh volume of his Annals.

11. The reign of the elder Justin may be found in the three Chronicles of Marcellinus, Victor, and John Malala (tom. ii. p. 130–150 [ed. Oxon.; l. xvii. p. 410–424, ed. Bonn]), the last of whom (in spite of Hody, Prolegom. No. 14, 39, edit. Oxon.) lived soon after Justinian (Jortin's Remarks, etc., vol. iv. p. 383); in the Ecclesiastical History of Evagrius (l. iv. c. 1, 2, 3, 9), and the Excerpta of Theodorus Lector (No. 37 [l. ii.]), and in Cedrenus (p. 363–366 [ed. Par.; tom. i. p. 636–642, ed. Bonn]) and Zonaras (l. xiv. p. 58–60), who may pass for an original.

12. See the characters of Procopius and Agathias in La Mothe le Vayer (tom. viii. p. 144–174), Vossius (de Historicis Græcis, l. ii. c. 22), and Fabricius (Bibliot. Græc. l. v. c. 5, tom. vi. p. 248–

278). Their religion, an honourable problem, betrays occasional conformity, with a secret attachment to Paganism and Philosophy.

13. In the seven first books, two Persic, two Vandalic, and three Gothic, Procopius has borrowed from Appian the division of provinces and wars: the eighth book, though it bears the name of Gothic, is a miscellaneous and general supplement down to the spring of the year 553, from whence it is continued by Agathias till 559 (Pagi, Critica, A.D. 579, No. 5).

14. The literary fate of Procopius has been somewhat unlucky. 1. His books de Bello Gothico were stolen by Leonard Aretin, and published (Fulginii, 1470; Venet. 1471, apud Janson. Mattaire, Annal. Typograph. tom. i. edit. posterior, p. 290, 304, 279, 299) in his own name (see Vossius de Hist. Lat. l. iii. c. 5, and the feeble defence of the Venice Giornale de' Letterati, tom. xix. p. 207). 2. His works were mutilated by the first Latin translators, Christopher Persona (Giornale, tom. xix. p. 340–348) and Raphael de Volaterra (Huet. de Claris Interpretibus, p. 166), who did not even consult the MS. of the Vatican library, of which they were præfects (Aleman. in Præfat. Anecdot.). 3. The Greek text was not printed till 1607, by Hoeschelius of Augsburg (Dictionnaire de Bayle, tom. ii. p. 782). 4. The Paris edition was imperfectly executed by Claude Maltret, a Jesuit of Toulouse (in 1663), far distant from the Louvre press and the Vatican MS., from which, however, he obtained some supplements. His promised commentaries, etc., have never appeared. The Agathias of Leyden (1594) has been wisely reprinted by the Paris editor, with the Latin version of Bonaventura Vulcanius, a learned interpreter (Huet., p. 176).

15. Agathias in Præfat. p. 7, 8, l. iv. p. 136 [ed. Par.; p. 11, 264, ed. Bonn]; Evagrius, l. iv. c. 12. See likewise Photius, cod. lxiii. p. 65 [p. 21, ed. Bekk.].

16. Κύρου παιδεία (says he, Præfat. ad l. de Ædificiis περὶ κτισμάτων) is no more than Κύρου παιδία —a pun! In these five books Procopius affects a Christian as well as a courtly style.

17. Procopius discloses himself (Præfat. ad Anecdot. c. 1, 2, 5), and the anecdotes are reckoned as the ninth book by Suidas (tom. iii. p. 186, ed. Kuster). The silence of Evagrius is a poor objection. Baronius (A.D. 548, No. 24) regrets the loss of this secret history: it was then in the Vatican library, in his own custody, and was first published sixteen years after his death, with the learned but partial notes of Nicholas Alemannus (Lugd. 1623).

18. Justinian an ass—the perfect likeness of Domitian—Anecdot. c. 8—Theodora's lovers driven from her bed by rival dæmons—her marriage foretold with a great dæmon—a monk saw the prince of the dæmons, instead of Justinian, on the throne —the servants who watched beheld a face without features, a body walking without a head, etc., etc.

Procopius declares his own and his friends' belief in these diabolical stories (c. 12).

19. Montesquieu (Considérations sur la Grandeur et la Décadence des Romains, c. xx.) gives credit to these anecdotes, as connected, 1, with the weakness of the empire, and, 2, with the instability of Justinian's laws.

20. For the life and manners of the empress Theodora see the Anecdotes; more especially c. 1–5, 9, 10–15, 16, 17, with the learned notes of Alemannus—a reference which is always implied.

21. Comito was afterwards married to Sittas duke of Armenia, the father, perhaps, at least she might be the mother, of the empress Sophia. Two nephews of Theodora may be the sons of Anastasia (Aleman. p. 30, 31).

22. Her statue was raised at Constantinople on a porphyry column. See Procopius (de Ædif. l. i. c. 11), who gives her portrait in the Anecdotes (c. 10 [tom. iii. p. 69, ed. Bonn]). Aleman. (p. 47) produces one from a mosaic at Ravenna, loaded with pearls and jewels, and yet handsome.

23. A fragment of the Anecdotes (c. 9), somewhat too naked, was suppressed by Alemannus, though extant in the Vatican MS.; nor has the defect been supplied in the Paris or Venice editions. La Mothe le Vayer (tom. viii. p. 155) gave the first hint of this curious and genuine passage (Jortin's Remarks, vol. iv. p. 366), which he had received from Rome, and it has been since published in the Menagiana (tom. iii. p. 254–259), with a Latin version.

24. After the mention of a narrow girdle (as none could appear stark naked in the theatre), Procopius thus proceeds: ἀναπεπτωκυῖα τε ἐν τῷ ἐδάφει ὑπτία ἔκειτο. Θῆτες δέ τινες . . . κριθὰς αὐτῇ ὑπερθεν τῶν αἰδοίων ἐρρίπτουν, ἃς δὴ οἱ χῆνες, οἳ ἐς τοῦτο παρεσκευασμένοι ἐτύγχανον, τοῖς στόμασιν ἐνθένδε κατὰ μίαν ἀνελόμενοι ἤσθιον. I have heard that a learned prelate, now deceased, was fond of quoting this passage in conversation.

25. Theodora surpassed the Crispa of Ausonius (Epigram lxxi.), who imitated the capitalis luxus of the females of Nola. See Quintilian Institut. viii. 6, and Torrentius ad Horat. Sermon. l. i. sat. 2, v. 101. At a memorable supper thirty slaves waited round the table; ten young men feasted with Theodora. Her charity was universal.

Et lassata viris, necdum satiata, recessit.

26. Ἡ δὲ κἀκ τῶν τριῶν τρυπημάτων ἐργαζομένη ἐνεκάλει τῇ φύσει, δυσφορουμένη ὅτι δὴ μὴ καὶ τοὺς τιτθοὺς αὐτῇ εὐρύτερον ἢ νῦν εἶσι τρυπῴη, ὅπως δυνατὴ εἴη καὶ ἐκείνῃ ἐργάζεσθαι. She wished for a fourth altar on which she might pour libations to the god of love.

27. Anonym. de Antiquitat. C. P. l. iii. 132, in Banduri Imperium Orient. tom. i. p. 47. Ludewig (p. 154) argues sensibly that Theodora would not have immortalised a brothel: but I apply this fact to her second and chaster residence at Constantinople.

28. See the old law in Justinian's Code (l. v. tit.

v. leg. 7, tit. xxvii. leg. 1) under the years 336 and 454. The new edict (about the year 521 or 522, Aleman. p. 38, 96) very awkwardly repeals no more than the clause of mulieres *scenicæ*, libertinæ, tabernariæ. See the novels 89 and 117, and a Greek rescript from Justinian to the bishops (Aleman. p. 41).

29. I swear by the Father, etc., by the Virgin Mary, by the four Gospels, quæ in manibus teneo, and by the Holy Archangels Michael and Gabriel, puram conscientiam germanumque servitium me servaturum, sacratissimis DDNN. Justiniano et Theodoræ conjugi ejus (Novell. viii. tit. 3). Would the oath have been binding in favour of the widow? Communes tituli et triumphi, etc. (Aleman. p. 47, 48).

30. "Let greatness own her, and she's mean no more," etc.
Without Warburton's critical telescope, I should never have seen, in this general picture of triumphant vice, any personal allusion to Theodora.

31. Her prisons, a labyrinth, a Tartarus (Anecdot. c. 4), were under the palace. Darkness is propitious to cruelty, but it is likewise favourable to calumny and fiction.

32. A more jocular whipping was inflicted on Saturninus, for presuming to say that his wife, a favourite of the empress, had not been found ἄτρητος (Anecdot. c. 17 [tom. iii. p. 104, ed. Bonn]).

33. Per viventem in sæcula excoriari te faciam. Anastasius de Vitis Pont. Roman. in Vigilio, p. 40.

34. Ludewig. p. 161–166. I give him credit for the charitable attempt, although *he* hath not much charity in his temper.

35. Compare the Anecdotes (c. 17) with the Edifices (l. i. c. 9). How differently may the same fact be stated! John Malala (tom. ii. p. 174, 175 [p. 440, 441, ed. Bonn]) observes, that on this, or a similar occasion, she released and clothed the girls whom she had purchased from the stews at five aurei apiece.

36. Novel. viii. 1. An allusion to Theodora. Her enemies read the name Dæmonodora (Aleman. p. 66 [Procop. tom. iii. p. 415, ed. Bonn]).

37. St. Sabas refused to pray for a son of Theodora, lest he should prove a heretic worse than Anastasius himself (Cyril in Vit. St. Sabæ, apud Aleman. p. 70, 109 [Procop. tom. iii. p. 421, 462, ed. Bonn]).

38. See John Malala, tom. ii. p. 174 [p. 441, ed. Bonn]. Theophanes, p. 158 [tom. i. p. 286, ed. Bonn]. Procopius de Ædific. l. v. c. 3.

39. Theodora Chalcedonensis synodi inimica canceris plagâ toto corpore perfusa vitam prodigiose finivit (Victor Tununensis in Chron.). On such occasions an orthodox mind is steeled against pity. Alemannus (p. 12, 13) understands the εὐσεβῶς ἐκοιμήθη of Theophanes as civil language, which does not imply either piety or repentance; yet two years after her death St. Theodora is celebrated by Paul Silentiarius (in Proem. ver. 58–62).

40. As she persecuted the popes, and rejected a council, Baronius exhausts the names of Eve, Dalila, Herodias, etc.; after which he has recourse to his infernal dictionary: civis inferni—alumna dæmonum—satanico agitata spiritû—œstro percita diabolico, etc. etc. (A.D. 548, No. 24).

41. Read and feel the twenty-third book of the Iliad, a living picture of manners, passions, and the whole form and spirit of the chariot-race. West's Dissertation on the Olympic Games (sect. xii.–xvii.) affords much curious and authentic information.

42. The four colours, *albati, russati, prasini, veneti*, represent the four seasons, according to Cassiodorus (Var. iii. 51), who lavishes much wit and eloquence on this theatrical mystery. Of these colours, the three first may be fairly translated, *white, red,* and *green*. *Venetus* is explained by *cæruleus*, a word various and vague: it is properly the sky reflected in the sea; but custom and convenience may allow *blue* as an equivalent. (Robert. Stephan. sub voce. Spence's Polymetis, p. 228.)

43. See Onuphrius Panvinius de Ludis Circensibus, l. i. c. 10, 11; the seventeenth Annotation on Mascou's History of the Germans; and Aleman. ad c. vii.

44. Marcellin. in Chron. p. 47 [anno 501]. Instead of the vulgar word *veneta*, he uses the more exquisite terms of *cærulea* and *cærealis*. Baronius (A.D. 501, No. 4, 5, 6) is satisfied that the blues were orthodox; but Tillemont is angry at the supposition, and will not allow any martyrs in a playhouse (Hist. des Emp. tom. vi. p. 554).

45. See Procopius (Persic. l. i. c. 24). In describing the vices of the factions and of the government, the *public* is not more favourable than the *secret* historian. Aleman. (p. 26 [tom. iii. p. 373, ed. Bonn]) has quoted a fine passage from Gregory Nazianzen, which proves the inveteracy of the evil.

46. The partiality of Justinian for the blues (Anecdot. c. 7 [tom. iii. p. 53, ed. Bonn]) is attested by Evagrius (Hist. Eccles. l. iv. c. 32), John Malala (tom. ii. p. 138, 139 [p. 152, ed. Oxon.; lib. xviii. p. 425, ed. Bonn]), especially for Antioch, and Theophanes (p. 142 [p. 256, ed. Bonn]).

47. A wife (says Procopius) who was seized and almost ravished by a blue-coat, threw herself into the Bosphorus. The bishops of the second Syria (Aleman. p. 26 [tom. iii. p. 374, ed. Bonn]) deplore a similar suicide, the guilt or glory of female chastity, and name the heroine.

48. The doubtful credit of Procopius (Anecdot. c. 17) is supported by the less partial Evagrius, who confirms the fact, and specifies the names. The tragic fate of the præfect of Constantinople is related by John Malala (tom. ii. p. 139 [p. 416, ed. Bonn]).

49. See John Malala (tom. ii. p. 147 [p. 422, ed. Bonn]); yet he owns that Justinian was attached to the blues. The seeming discord of the emperor and Theodora is perhaps viewed with too much jealousy and refinement by Procopius (Anecdot.

c. 10 [t. iii. p. 70, ed. Bonn]). See Aleman. Præfat. p. 6.

50. This dialogue, which Theophanes has preserved, exhibits the popular language, as well as the manners, of Constantinople in the sixth century. Their Greek is mingled with many strange and barbarous words, for which Ducange cannot always find a meaning or etymology.

51. See this church and monastery in Ducange, C. P. Christiana, l. iv. p. 182.

52. The history of the *Nika* sedition is extracted from Marcellinus (in Chron. [an. 532]), Procopius (Persic. l. i. c. 26 [c. 24, tom. i. p. 119, ed. Bonn]), John Malala (tom. ii. p. 213–218 [ed. Ox.; p. 473–477, ed. Bonn]), Chron. Paschal. (p. 336–340, tom. i. p. 620 *sqq.* [ed. Bonn]), Theophanes (Chronograph. p. 154–158 [ed. Par. tom. i. p. 278–286, ed. Bonn]), and Zonaras (l. xiv. p. 61–63).

53. Marcellinus says, in general terms, innumeris populis in circo trucidatis. Procopius numbers 30,000 victims [tom. i. p. 129, ed. Bonn]; and the 35,000 of Theophanes are swelled to 40,000 by the more recent Zonaras [tom. ii. p. 63]. Such is the usual progress of exaggeration.

54. Hierocles, a contemporary of Justinian, composed his Συνέκδημος (Itineraria, p. 631), or review of the eastern provinces and cities, before the year 535 (Wesseling, in Præfat. and Not. ad p. 623, etc.).

55. See the Book of Genesis (xii. 10), and the administration of Joseph. The annals of the Greeks and Hebrews agree in the early arts and plenty of Egypt: but this antiquity supposes a long series of improvement; and Warburton, who is almost stifled by the Hebrew, calls aloud for the Samaritan, chronology (Divine Legation, vol. iii. p. 29, etc.).

56. Eight millions of Roman modii, besides a contribution of 80,000 aurei for the expenses of water-carriage, from which the subject was graciously excused. See the thirteenth Edict of Justinian [c. viii.]; the numbers are checked and verified by the agreement of the Greek and Latin texts.

57. Homer's Iliad, vi. 289. These veils, πέπλοι παμποίκιλοι, were the work of the Sidonian women. But this passage is more honourable to the manufactures than to the navigation of Phœnicia, from whence they had been imported to Troy in Phrygian bottoms.

58. See in Ovid (de Arte Amandi, iii. 269, etc.) a poetical list of twelve colours borrowed from flowers, the elements, etc. But it is almost impossible to discriminate by words all the nice and various shades both of art and nature.

59. By the discovery of cochineal, etc., we far surpass the colours of antiquity. Their royal purple had a strong smell, and a dark cast as deep as bull's blood—obscuritas rubens (says Cassiodorus, Var. l. 1, c. 2) nigredo sanguinea. The President Goguet (Origine des Loix et des Arts, part ii. l. ii. c. 2, p. 184–215) will amuse and satisfy the reader.

I doubt whether his book, especially in England, is as well known as it deserves to be.

60. Historical proofs of this jealousy have been occasionally introduced, and many more might have been added; but the arbitrary acts of despotism were justified by the sober and general declarations of law (Codex Theodosian. l. x. tit. 21, leg. 3; Codex Justinian. l. xi. tit. 8, leg. 5). An inglorious permission, and necessary restriction, was applied to the *mimæ*, the female dancers (Cod. Theodos. l. xv. tit. 7, leg. 11).

61. In the history of insects (far more wonderful than Ovid's Metamorphoses) the silkworm holds a conspicuous place. The bombyx of the isle of Ceos, as described by Pliny (Hist. Natur. xi. 26, 27, with the notes of the two learned Jesuits, Hardouin and Brotier), may be illustrated by a similar species in China (Mémoires sur les Chinois, tom. ii. p. 575–598); but our silkworm, as well as the white mulberry-tree, were unknown to Theophrastus and Pliny.

62. Georgic. ii. 121. Serica quando venerint in usum planissime non scio: suspicor tamen in Julii Cæsaris ævo, nam ante non invenio, says Justus Lipsius (Excursus i. ad Tacit. Annal. ii. 32). See Dion Cassius (l. xliii. [c. 24] p. 358, edit. Reimar), and Pausanias (l. vi. [c. 26, § 6–9] p. 519), the first who describes, however strangely, the Seric insect.

63. Tam longinquo orbe petitur, ut in publico matrona transluceat . . . ut denudet fœminas vestis (Plin. vi. 20, xi. 26). Varro and Publius Syrus had already played on the Toga vitrea, ventus textilis, and nebula linea (Horat. Sermon. i. 2, 101, with the notes of Torrentius and Dacier).

64. On the texture, colours, names, and use of the silk, half-silk, and linen garments of antiquity, see the profound, diffuse, and obscure researches of the great Salmasius (in Hist. August. p. 127, 309, 310, 339, 341, 342, 344, 388–391, 395, 513), who was ignorant of the most common trades of Dijon or Leyden.

65. Flavius Vopiscus in Aurelian. c. 45, in Hist. August. p. 224. See Salmasius ad Hist. Aug. p. 392, and Plinian. Excercitat. in Solinum, p. 694, 695. The Anecdotes of Procopius (c. 25) state a partial and imperfect rate of the price of silk in the time of Justinian.

66. Procopius de Ædif. l. iii. c. 1. These *pinnes de mer* are found near Smyrna, Sicily, Corsica, and Minorca; and a pair of gloves of their silk was presented to Pope Benedict XIV.

67. Procopius, Persic. l. i. c. 20; l. ii. c. 25; Gothic. l. iv. c. 17. Menander in Excerpt. Legat. p. 107 [ed. Par.; p. 296, ed. Bonn]. Of the Parthian or Persian empire, Isidore of Charax (in Stathmis Parthicis, p. 7, 8, in Hudson, Geograph, Minor. tom. ii.) has marked the roads, and Ammianus Marcellinus (l. xxiii. c. 6, p. 400) has enumerated the provinces.

68. The blind admiration of the Jesuits confounds the different periods of the Chinese history. They are more critically distinguished by M. de

Guignes (Hist. des Huns, tom. i. part i. in the Tables, part ii. in the Geography. Mémoires de l'Académie des Inscriptions, tom. xxxii. xxxvi. xlii. xliii.), who discovers the gradual progress of the truth of the annals and the extent of the monarchy, till the Christian era. He has searched with a curious eye the connections of the Chinese with the nations of the West; but these connections are slight, casual, and obscure; nor did the Romans entertain a suspicion that the Seres or Sinæ possessed an empire not inferior to their own.

69. The roads from China to Persia and Hindostan may be investigated in the relations of Hackluyt and Thevenot (the ambassadors of Sharokh, Anthony Jenkinson, the Père Greuber, etc. See likewise Hanway's Travels, vol. i. p. 345-357). A communication through Thibet has been lately explored by the English sovereigns of Bengal.

70. For the Chinese navigation to Malacca and Achin, perhaps to Ceylon, see Renaudot (on the two Mahometan Travellers, p. 8-11, 13-17, 141-157), Dampier (vol. ii. p. 136), the Hist. Philosophique des deux Indes (tom. i. p. 98), and the Hist. Générale des Voyages (tom. vi. p. 201).

71. The knowledge, or rather ignorance, of Strabo, Pliny, Ptolemy, Arrian, Marcian, etc., of the countries eastward of Cape Comorin, is finely illustrated by D'Anville (Antiquité Géographique de l'Inde, especially p. 161-198). Our geography of India is improved by commerce and conquest; and has been illustrated by the excellent maps and memoirs of Major Rennell. If he extends the sphere of his inquiries with the same critical knowledge and sagacity, he will succeed, and may surpass, the first of modern geographers.

72. The Taprobane of Pliny (vi. 24), Solinus (c. 56), and Salmas. Plinianæ Exercitat. (p. 781, 782), and most of the ancients, who often confound the islands of Ceylon and Sumatra, is more clearly described by Cosmas Indicopleustes; yet even the Christian topographer has exaggerated its dimensions. His information on the Indian and Chinese trade is rare and curious (l. ii. p. 138, l. xi. p. 337, 338, edit. Montfaucon [Coll. Nova Patrum, tom. ii. Paris, 1706]).

73. See Procopius, Persic. (l. ii. c. 20 [l. i. c. 19]). Cosmas affords some interesting knowledge of the port and inscription of Adulis (Topograph. Christ. l. ii. p. 139, 140-143), and of the trade of the Axumites along the African coast of Barbaria or Zingi (p. 138, 139), and as far as Taprobane (l. xi. p. 339).

74. See the Christian missions in India, in Cosmas (l. iii. p. 178, 179, l. xi. p. 337), and consult Asseman. Bibliot. Orient. (tom. iv. p. 413-548).

75. The invention, manufacture, and general use of silk in China, may be seen in Duhalde (Description Générale de la Chine, tom. ii. p. 165, 205-223). The province of Chekian is the most renowned both for quantity and quality.

76. Procopius, Bell. Gothic. iv. c. 17. Theophanes, Byzant. apud Phot. Cod. lxxxiv. [lxiv.] p. 38 [ed. Hoeschel.; p. 26 a, ed. Bekk.]. Zonaras, tom. ii. l. xiv. p. 69). Pagi (tom. ii. p. 602) assigns to the year 552 this memorable importation. Menander (in Excerpt. Legat. p. 107 [p. 295, 296, ed. Bonn]) mentions the admiration of the Sogdoites; and Theophylact Simocatta (l. vii. c. 9) darkly represents the two rival kingdoms in (China) the country of silk.

77. Cosmas, surnamed Indicopleustes, or the Indian navigator, performed his voyage about the year 522, and composed at Alexandria, between 535 and 547, Christian Topography (Montfaucon, Præfat. c. i.), in which he refutes the impious opinion that the earth is a globe; and Photius had read this work (Cod. xxxvi. p. 9, 10 [p. 7, ed. Bekk.]), which displays the prejudices of a monk, with the knowledge of a merchant: the most valuable part has been given in French and in Greek by Melchisedec Thevenot (Relations Curieuses, part i.), and the whole is since published in a splendid edition by Père Montfaucon (Collectio Nova Patrum, Paris, 1706, 2 vols. in fol. tom. ii. p. 113-346). But the editor, a theologian, might blush at not discovering the Nestorian heresy of Cosmas, which has been detected by La Croze (Christianisme des Indes, tom. i. p. 40-56).

78. Evagrius (l. iii. c. 39, 40) is minute and grateful, but angry with Zosimus for calumniating the great Constantine. In collecting all the bonds and records of the tax, the humanity of Anastasius was diligent and artful: fathers were sometimes compelled to prostitute their daughters (Zosim. Hist. l. ii. c. 38, p. 165, 166, Lipsiæ, 1784 [p. 104, ed. Bonn]. Timotheus of Gaza chose such an event for the subject of a tragedy (Suidas, tom. iii. p. 475), which contributed to the abolition of the tax (Cedrenus, p. 357 [ed. Par.; tom. i. p. 627, ed. Bonn])—an happy instance (if it be true) of the use of the theatre.

79. See Josua Stylites, in the Bibliotheca Orientalis of Asseman (tom. i. p. 268). This capitation-tax is slightly mentioned in the Chronicle of Edessa.

80. Procopius (Anecdot. c. 19 [tom. iii. p. 113, ed. Bonn]) fixes this sum from the report of the treasurers themselves. Tiberius had *vicies ter millies;* but far different was his empire from that of Anastasius.

81. Evagrius (l. iv. c. 30), in the next generation, was moderate and well informed; and Zonaras (l. xiv. c. 61), in the twelfth century, had read with care, and thought without prejudice: yet their colours are almost as black as those of the Anecdotes.

82. Procopius (Anecdot. c. 30) relates the idle conjectures of the times. The death of Justinian, says the secret historian, will expose his wealth or poverty.

83. See Corippus de Laudibus Justini Aug. l. ii. v. 260, etc., 389, etc.

"Plurima sunt vivo nimium neglecta parente,
Unde tot exhaustus contraxit debita fiscus."

Centenaries of gold were brought by strong arms into the Hippodrome:

"Debita persolvit genitoris, cauta recepit."

84. The Anecdotes (c. 11–14, 18, 20–30) supply many facts and more complaints.

85. One to Scythopolis, capital of the second Palestine, and twelve for the rest of the province. Aleman. (p. 59 [Procop. tom. iii. p. 407, 408, ed. Bonn]) honestly produces this fact from a MS. Life of St. Sabas, by his disciple Cyril, in the Vatican library, and since published by Cotelerius.

86. John Malala (tom. ii. p. 232 [p. 488, ed. Bonn]) mentions the want of bread, and Zonaras (l. xiv. p. 63) the leaden pipes, which Justinian, or his servants, stole from the aqueducts.

87. For an aureus, one-sixth of an ounce of gold, instead of 210, he gave no more than 180 folles or ounces of copper. A disproportion of the mint, below the market price, must have soon produced a scarcity of small money. In England, *twelve* pence in copper would sell for no more than *seven* pence (Smith's Inquiry into the Wealth of Nations, Bk. i. ch. 4). For Justinian's gold coin, see Evagrius (l. iv. c. 30).

88. The oath is conceived in the most formidable words (Novell. viii. tit. 3). The defaulters imprecate on themselves, quicquid habent telorum armamentaria cœli; the part of Judas, the leprosy of Giezi, the tremor of Cain, etc., besides all temporal pains.

89. A similar or more generous act of friendship is related by Lucian of Eudamidas of Corinth (in Toxare, c. 22, 23, tom. ii. p. 530), and the story has produced an ingenious, though feeble, comedy of Fontenelle.

90. John Malala, tom. ii. p. 101, 102, 103 [p. 171–173, ed. Oxon.; 439, 440, ed. Bonn].

91. One of these, Anatolius, perished in an earthquake—doubtless a judgment! The complaints and clamours of the people in Agathias (l. v. p. 146, 147 [ed. Par.; p. 284 *sq.*, ed. Bonn]) are almost an echo of the anecdote. The aliena pecunia reddenda of Corippus (l. ii. 381, etc. [Laud. Just. Min.]) is not very honourable to Justinian's memory.

92. See the history and character of John of Cappadocia in Procopius (Persic. l. i. c. 24, 25, l. ii. c. 30. Vandal. l. i. c. 13. Anecdot. c. 2, 17, 22). The agreement of the history and anecdotes is a mortal wound to the reputation of the præfect.

93. Οὐ γὰρ ἄλλο οὐδὲν ἐς γραμματιστοῦ φοιτῶν ἔμαθεν, ὅτι μὴ γράμματα, καὶ ταῦτα κακὰ κακῶς γράψαι —a forcible expression [Pers. i. c. 24].

94. The chronology of Procopius is loose and obscure; but with the aid of Pagi I can discern that John was appointed Prætorian præfect of the East in the year 530; that he was removed in January, 532—restored before June, 533—banished in 541 —and recalled between June, 548, and April 1, 549. Aleman. (p. 96, 97 [Procop. tom. iii. p. 449, 450, ed. Bonn]) gives the list of his ten successors— a rapid series in a part of a single reign.

95. This conflagration is hinted by Lucian (in Hippia, c. 2) and Galen (l. iii. de Temperamentis, tom. i. p. 81, edit. Basil) in the second century. A thousand years afterwards it is positively affirmed by Zonaras (l. ix. p. 424) on the faith of Dion Cassius, by Tzetzes (Chiliad ii. 119, etc.), Eustathius (ad Iliad, E. p. 338), and the scholiast of Lucian. See Fabricius (Biblioth. Græc. l. iii. c. 22, tom. ii. p. 551, 552 [ed, Hamb. 1716]), to whom I am more or less indebted for several of these quotations.

96. Zonaras (l. xiv. p. 55) affirms the fact, without quoting any evidence.

97. Tzetzes describes the artifice of these burning-glasses, which he had read, perhaps with no learned eyes, in a mathematical treatise of Anthemius. That treatise, περὶ παραδόξων μηχανημάτων, has been lately published, translated, and illustrated by M. Dupuys, a scholar and a mathematician (Mémoires de l'Académie des Inscriptions, tom. xlii. p. 392–451).

98. In the siege of Syracuse, by the silence of Polybius, Plutarch, Livy; in the siege of Constantinople, by that of Marcellinus and all the contemporaries of the sixth century.

99. Without any previous knowledge of Tzetzes or Anthemius, the immortal Buffon imagined and executed a set of burning-glasses, with which he could inflame planks at the distance of 200 feet (Supplément à l'Hist. Naturelle, tom. i. p. 399– 483, quarto edition). What miracles would not his genius have performed for the public service, with royal expense, and in the strong sun of Constantinople or Syracuse!

100. John Malala (tom. ii. p. 120–124 [p. 403– 406, ed. Bonn]) relates the fact; but he seems to confound the names or persons of Proclus and Marinus.

101. Agathias, l. v. p. 149–152 [ed. Par.; p. 289–294, ed. Bonn]. The merit of Anthemius as an architect is loudly praised by Procopius (de Ædif. l. i. c. 1 [tom. iii. p. 174, ed. Bonn]) and Paulus Silentiarius (part i. 134, etc. [p. 15, ed. Bonn]).

102. See Procopius (de Ædificiis, l. i. c. 1, l. ii. c. 3). He relates a coincidence of dreams which supposes some fraud in Justinian or his architect. They both saw, in a vision, the same plan for stopping an inundation at Dara. A stone-quarry near Jerusalem was revealed to the emperor (l. v. c. 6 [tom. iii. p. 323, ed. Bonn]): an angel was tricked into the perpetual custody of St. Sophia (Anonym. de Antiq. C. P. l. iv. p. 70).

103. Among the crowd of ancients and moderns who have celebrated the edifice of St. Sophia, I shall distinguish and follow, 1. Four original spectators and historians: Procopius (de Ædific. l. i. c. 1), Agathias (l. v. p. 152, 153 [p. 296, 297, ed. Bonn]), Paul Silentiarius (in a poem of 1026 hexameters, ad calcem Annæ Comnen. Alexiad.), and Evagrius (l. iv. c. 31). 2. Two legendary Greeks of a later period: George Codinus (de Origin. C. P. p. 64–74 [ed. Par.; p. 130–148, ed.

Bonn]), and the anonymous writer of Banduri (Imp. Orient. tom. i. l. iv. p. 65–80). 3. The great Byzantine antiquarian, Ducange (Comment. ad Paul Silentiar. p. 525–598, and C. P. Christ. l. iii. p. 5–78). 4. Two French travellers—the one, Peter Gyllius (de Topograph. C. P. l. ii. c. 3, 4) in the sixteenth; the other, Grelot (Voyage de C. P. p. 95–164, Paris, 1680, in 4to): he has given plans, prospects, and inside views of St. Sophia; and his plans, though on a smaller scale, appear more correct than those of Ducange. I have adopted and reduced the measures of Grelot: but as no Christian can now ascend the dome, the height is borrowed from Evagrius, compared with Gyllius, Greaves, and the Oriental Geographer.

104. Solomon's temple was surrounded with courts, porticoes, etc.; but the proper structure of the house of God was no more (if we take the Egyptian or Hebrew cubit at 22 inches) than 55 feet in height, 36⅔ in breadth, and 110 in length —a small parish church, says Prideaux (Connection, vol. i. p. 144, folio); but few sanctuaries could be valued at four or five millions sterling!

105. Paul Silentiarius, in dark and poetic language, describes the various stones and marbles that were employed in the edifice of St. Sophia (P. ii. ver. 129, 133, etc. etc. [p. 27 sqq., ed. Bonn]): 1. The *Carystian*—pale, with iron veins. 2. The *Phrygian*—of two sorts, both of a rosy hue; the one with a white shade, the other purple, with silver flowers. 3. The *Porphyry of Egypt*—with small stars. 4. The *green marble of Laconia.* 5. The *Carian*—from Mount Iassis, with oblique veins, white and red. 6. The *Lydian*—pale, with a red flower. 7. The *African*, or *Mauritanian*—of a gold or saffron hue. 8. The *Celtic*—black, with white veins. 9. The *Bosphoric*—white, with black edges. Besides the *Proconnesian*, which formed the pavement; the *Thessalian, Molossian*, etc., which are less distinctly painted.

106. The six books of the Edifices of Procopius are thus distributed: the *first* is confined to Constantinople; the *second* includes Mesopotamia and Syria; the *third*, Armenia and the Euxine; the *fourth*, Europe; the *fifth*, Asia Minor and Palestine; the *sixth*, Egypt and Africa. Italy is forgot by the emperor or the historian, who published this work of adulation before the date (A.D. 555) of its final conquest.

107. Justinian once gave forty-five centenaries of gold (£180,000) for the repairs of Antioch after the earthquake (John Malala, tom. ii. p. 146–149 [p. 422–424, ed. Bonn]).

108. For the Heræum, the palace of Theodora, see Gyllius (de Bosphoro Thracio, l. iii. c. xi.), Aleman. (Not. ad Anec. p. 80, 81 [Procop. tom. iii. p. 431, 432, ed. Bonn], who quotes several epigrams of the Anthology) and Ducange (C. P. Christ. l. iv. c. 13, p. 175, 176).

109. Compare, in the Edifices (l. i. c. 11) and in the Anecdotes (c. 8, 15), the different styles of adulation and malevolence: stripped of the paint, or cleansed from the dirt, the object appears to be the same.

110. Procopius, Goth. iii. 29; most probably a stranger and wanderer, as the Mediterranean does not breed whales. Balænæ quoque in nostra maria penetrant (Plin. Hist. Natur. ix. 2 [5]). Between the polar circle and the tropic, the cetaceous animals of the ocean grow to the length of 50, 80, or 100 feet. (Hist. des Voyages, tom. xv. p. 289. Pennant's British Zoology, vol. iii. p. 35.)

111. Montesquieu observes (tom. iii. p. 503, Considérations sur la Grandeur et la Décadence des Romains, c. xx.) that Justinian's empire was like France in the time of the Norman inroads— never so weak as when every village was fortified.

112. Procopius affirms (l. iv. c. 6 [tom. iii. p. 289, ed. Bonn]) that the Danube was stopped by the ruins of the bridge. Had Apollodorus, the architect, left a description of his own work, the fabulous wonders of Dion Cassius (l. lxviii. [c. 13] p. 1129) would have been corrected by the genuine picture. Trajan's bridge consisted of twenty or twenty-two stone piles with wooden arches; the river is shallow, the current gentle, and the whole interval no more than 443 (Reimar ad Dion, from Marsigli) or 515 *toises* (D'Anville, Géographie Ancienne, tom. i. p. 305).

113. Of the two Dacias, *Mediterranea* and *Ripensis*, Dardania, Prævalitana, the second Mæsia, and the second Macedonia. See Justinian (Novell. xi. [Præf.]), who speaks of his castles beyond the Danube, and of homines semper bellicis sudoribus inhærentes.

114. See D'Anville (Mémoires de l'Académie, etc. tom. xxxi. p. 289, 290). Rycaut (Present State of the Turkish Empire, p. 97, 316), Marsigli (Stato Militare del Imperio Ottomano, p. 130). The sanjak of Guistendil is one of the twenty under the beglerbeg of Rumelia, and his district maintains 48 *zaims* and 588 *timariots*.

115. These fortifications may be compared to the castles in Mingrelia (Chardin, Voyages en Perse, tom. i. p. 60, 131)—a natural picture.

116. The valley of Tempe is situate along the river Peneus, between the hills of Ossa and Olympus: it is only five miles long, and in some places no more than 120 feet in breadth. Its verdant beauties are elegantly described by Pliny (Hist. Natur. l. iv. 15), and more diffusely by Ælian (Hist. Var. l. iii. c. i.).

117. Xenophon Hellenic. l. iii. c. 2. After a long and tedious conversation with the Byzantine declaimers, how refreshing is the truth, the simplicity, the elegance of an Attic writer!

118. See the long wall in Evagrius (l. iv. [iii.] c. 38). This whole article is drawn from the fourth book of the Edifices, except Anchialus (l. iii. c. 7).

119. Turn back to p. 113 above. In the course of this history I have sometimes mentioned, and much oftener slighted, the hasty inroads of the Isaurians, which were not attended with any consequences.

120. Trebellius Pollio in Hist. August. p. 197 [Triginta Tyr. 25], who lived under Diocletian, or Constantine. See likewise Pancirolus ad Notit. Imp. Orient. c. 115, 141. See Cod. Theodos. l. ix. tit. 35, leg. 37 [7], with a copious collective Annotation of Godefroy, tom. iii. p. 256, 257.

121. See the full and wide extent of their inroads in Philostorgius (Hist. Eccles. l. xi. c. 8), with Godefroy's learned Dissertations.

122. Cod. Justinian. l. ix. tit. 12, leg. 10. The punishments are severe—a fine of an hundred pounds of gold, degradation, and even death. The public peace might afford a pretence, but Zeno was desirous of monopolising the valour and service of the Isaurians.

123. The Isaurian war and the triumph of Anastasius are briefly and darkly represented by John Malala (tom. ii. p. 106, 107 [p. 393, 394, ed. Bonn], Evagrius (l. iii. c. 35), Theophanes (p. 118-120 [ed. Par.; tom. i. p. 212-215, ed. Bonn]), and the Chronicle of Marcellinus.

124. Fortes ea regio (says Justinian) viros habet, nec in ullo differt ab Isauriâ, though Procopius (Persic. l. i. c. 18 [tom. i. p. 96, ed. Bonn]) marks an essential difference between their military character; yet in former times the Lycaonians and Pisidians had defended their liberty against the Great King (Xenophon. Anabasis, l. iii. c. 2). Justinian introduces some false and ridiculous erudition of the ancient empire of the Pisidians, and of Lycaon, who, after visiting Rome (long before Æneas), gave a name and people to Lycaonia (Novell. 24, 25, 27, 30).

125. See Procopius, Persic. l. i. c. 19. The altar of national concord, of annual sacrifice and oaths, which Diocletian had erected in the Isle of Elephantine, was demolished by Justinian with less policy than zeal.

126. Procopius de Ædificiis, l. iii. c. 7 [p. 262, ed. Bonn]; Bell. Goth. iv. c. 3, 4 [p. 469, seq., ed. Bonn]. These unambitious Goths had refused to follow the standard of Theodoric. As late as the fifteenth and sixteenth century the name and nation might be discovered between Caffa and the Straits of Azoph (D'Anville, Mémoires de l'Académie, tom. xxx. p. 240). They well deserved the curiosity of Busbequius (p. 321-326); but seem to have vanished in the more recent account of the Missions du Levant (tom. i.), Tott, Peysonnel, etc.

127. For the geography and architecture of this Armenian border see the Persian Wars and Edifices (l. ii. c. 4-7; l. iii. c. 2-7) of Procopius.

128. The country is described by Tournefort (Voyage au Levant, tom. iii. lettre xvii. xviii.). That skilful botanist soon discovered the plant that infects the honey (Plin. xxi. 44, 45): he observes that the soldiers of Lucullus might indeed be astonished at the cold, since, even in the plain of Erzerum, snow sometimes falls in June, and the harvest is seldom finished before September. The hills of Armenia are below the fortieth degree of latitude; but in the mountainous country which I

inhabit it is well known that an ascent of some hours carries the traveller from the climate of Languedoc to that of Norway; and a general theory has been introduced that, under the line, an elevation of 2400 toises is equivalent to the cold of the polar circle (Remond, Observations sur les Voyages de Coxe dans la Suisse, tom. ii. p. 104).

129. The identity or proximity of the Chalybians, or Chaldæans, may be investigated in Strabo (l. xii. p. 825, 826 [p. 548, 549, ed. Casaub.]), Cellarius (Geograph. Antiq. tom. ii. p. 202-204), and Fréret (Mém. de l'Académie, tom. iv. p. 594). Xenophon supposes, in his romance (Cyropæd. l. iii. [c. 2]), the same barbarians against whom he had fought in his retreat (Anabasis, l. iv. [c. 3]).

130. Procopius, Persic. l. i. c. 15; De Ædific. l. iii. c. 6.

131. Ni Tauros obstet in nostra maria venturus (Pomponius Mela, iii. 8). Pliny, a poet as well as a naturalist (v. 20), personifies the river and mountain and describes their combat. See the course of the Tigris and Euphrates in the excellent treatise of D'Anville.

132. Procopius (Persic. l. ii. c. 12 [tom. i. p. 208, ed. Bonn]) tells the story with the tone, half sceptical, half superstitious, of Herodotus. The promise was not in the primitive lie of Eusebius, but dates at least from the year 400; and a third lie, the Veronica, was soon raised on the two former (Evagrius, l. iv. c. 27). As Edessa has been taken, Tillemont must disclaim the promise (Mém. Ecclés. tom. i. p. 362, 383, 617).

133. They were purchased from the merchants of Adulis who traded to India (Cosmas, Topograph. Christ. l. xi. p. 339); yet, in the estimate of precious stones, the Scythian emerald was the first, the Bactrian the second, the Æthiopian only the third (Hill's Theophrastus, p. 61, etc., 92). The production, mines, etc., of emeralds, are involved in darkness; and it is doubtful whether we possess any of the twelve sorts known to the ancients (Goguet, Origine des Loix, etc., part ii. l. ii. c. 2, art. 3). In this war the Huns got, or at least Perozes lost, the finest pearl in the world, of which Procopius relates a ridiculous fable.

134. The Indo-Scythæ continued to reign from the time of Augustus (Dionys. Perieget. 1088, with the Commentary of Eustathius, in Hudson, Geograph. Minor. tom. iv.) to that of the elder Justin (Cosmas, Topograph. Christ. l. xi. p. 338, 339). On their origin and conquests see D'Anville (sur l'Inde, p. 18, 45, etc., 69, 85, 89). In the second century they were masters of Larice or Guzerat.

135. See the fate of Phirouz or Perozes and its consequences, in Procopius (Persic. l. i. c. 3-6), who may be compared with the fragments of Oriental history (D'Herbelot, Bibliot. Orient. p. 351, and Texeira, History of Persia, translated or abridged by Stephens, l. i. c. 32, p. 132-138). The chronology is ably ascertained by Assemani (Bibliot. Orient. tom. iii. p. 396-427).

136. The Persian war, under the reigns of Anas-

tasius and Justin, may be collected from Procopius (Persic. l. i. c. 7, 8, 9), Theophanes (in Chronograph. p. 124-127 [ed. Par.; tom. i. p. 222-229, ed. Bonn]), Evagrius (l. iii. c. 37), Marcellinus (in Chron. p. 47 [p. 372, sq., ed. Sirmond.]), and Josua Stylites (apud Asseman. tom. i. p. 272-281).

137. The description of Dara is amply and correctly given by Procopius (Persic. l. i. c. 10, l. ii. c. 13; De Ædific. l. ii. c. 1, 2, 3; l. iii. c. 5). See the situation in D'Anville (l'Euphrate et le Tigre, p. 53, 54, 55), though he seems to double the interval between Dara and Nisibis.

138. For the city and pass of Derbend see D'Herbelot (Bibliot. Orient. p. 157, 291, 807), Petit de la Croix (Hist. de Gengiscan, l. iv. c. 9), Histoire Généalogique des Tartars (tom. i. p. 120), Olearius (Voyage en Perse, p. 1039-1041), and Corneille le Bruyn (Voyages, tom. i. p. 146, 147): his view may be compared with the plan of Olearius, who judges the wall to be of shells and gravel hardened by time.

139. Procopius, though with some confusion, always denominates them Caspian (Persic. l. i. c. 10). The pass is now styled Tatar-topa, the Tartar-gates (D'Anville, Géographie Ancienne, tom. ii. p. 119, 120).

140. The imaginary rampart of Gog and Magog, which was seriously explored and believed by a caliph of the ninth century, appears to be derived from the gates of Mount Caucasus, and a vague report of the wall of China (Geograph. Nubiensis, p. 267-270; Mémoires de l'Académie, tom. xxxi. p. 210-219).

141. See a learned dissertation of Baier, de muro Caucaseo, in Comment. Acad. Petropol. ann. 1726, tom. i. p. 425-463; but it is destitute of a map or plan. When the Czar Peter I. became master of Derbend in the year 1722, the measure of the wall was found to be 3285 Russian orgygiæ, or fathom, each of seven feet English; in the whole somewhat more than four miles in length.

142. See the fortifications and treaties of Chosroes or Nushirwan, in Procopius (Persic. l. i. c. 16, 22, l. ii.) and D'Herbelot (p. 682).

143. The life of Isocrates extends from Olymp. lxxxvi. 1, to cx. 3 (ante Christ. 436-338). See Dionys. Halicarn. tom. ii. p. 149, 150, edit. Hudson. Plutarch (sive anonymus), in Vit. X. Oratorum, p. 1538-1543, edit. H. Steph. Phot. cod. cclix. p. 1453 [p. 486 b, ed. Bekk.].

144. The schools of Athens are copiously though concisely represented in the Fortuna Attica of Meursius (c. viii. p. 59-73, in tom. i. Opp.). For the state and arts of the city, see the first book of Pausanias, and a small tract of Dicæarchus (in the second volume of Hudson's Geographers), who wrote about Olymp. cxvii. (Dodwell's Dissertat. sect. 4).

145. Diogen. Laert. de Vit. Philosoph. l. v. [c. 2] segm. 37, p. 289.

146. See the Testament of Epicurus in Diogen.

Laert. l. x. [c. 1] segm. 16-20, p. 611, 612. A single epistle (ad Familiares, xiii. 1) displays the injustice of the Areopagus, the fidelity of the Epicureans, the dexterous politeness of Cicero, and the mixture of contempt and esteem with which the Roman senators considered the philosophy and philosophers of Greece.

147. Damascius, in Vit. Isidor. apud Photium, cod. ccxlii. p. 1057 [p. 346 a, ed. Bekk.].

148. See Lucian (in Eunuch. tom. ii. [c. 3, sqq.] p. 350-359, edit Reitz), Philostratus (in Vit. Sophist. l. ii. c. 2), and Dion Cassius, or Xiphilin (l. lxxi. [c. 31] p. 1195), with their editors Du Soul, Olearius, and Reimar, and, above all, Salmasius (ad Hist. August. p. 72). A judicious philosopher (Smith's Wealth of Nations, vol. ii. p. 340-374) prefers the free contributions of the students to a fixed stipend for the professor.

149. Brucker, Hist. Crit. Philosoph. tom. ii. p. 310, etc.

150. The birth of Epicurus is fixed to the year 342 before Christ (Bayle), Olympiad cix. 3; and he opened his school at Athens, Olymp. cxviii. 3, 306 years before the same era. This intolerant law (Athenæus, l. xiii. p. 610; Diogen. Laertius, l. v. [c. 2] s. 38, p. 290; Julius Pollux, ix. 5) was enacted in the same or the succeeding year (Sigonius, Opp. tom. v. p. 62; Menagius, ad Diogen. Laert. p. 204; Corsini, Fasti Attici, tom. iv. p. 67, 68). Theophrastus, chief of the Peripatetics, and disciple of Aristotle, was involved in the same exile.

151. This is no fanciful era: the Pagans reckoned their calamities from the reign of their hero. Proclus, whose nativity is marked by his horoscope (A.D. 412, February 8, at C. P.), died 124 years ἀπὸ Ἰουλιανοῦ βασιλέως, A.D. 485 (Marin. in Vitâ Procli, c. 36).

152. The Life of Proclus, by Marinus, was published by Fabricius (Hamburg, 1700, et ad Calcem Biblioth. Latin. Lond. 1703). See Suidas (tom. iii. p. 185, 186), Fabricius (Biblioth. Græc. l. v. c. 26, p. 449-552), and Brucker (Hist. Crit. Philosoph. tom. ii. p. 319-326).

153. The Life of Isidore was composed by Damascius (apud Photium, cod. ccxlii. p. 1028-1076 [p. 335-353, ed. Bekk.]). See the last age of the Pagan philosophers in Brucker (tom. ii. p. 341-351).

154. The suppression of the schools of Athens is recorded by John Malala (tom. ii. p. 187 [p. 451, ed. Bonn], sub Decio Cos. Sol.), and an anonymous Chronicle in the Vatican library (apud Aleman. p. 106 [Procop. tom. iii. p. 459, ed. Bonn]).

155. Agathias (l. ii. p. 69, 70, 71 [ed. Par.; p. 130-136, ed. Bonn]) relates this curious story. Chosroes ascended the throne in the year 531, and made his first peace with the Romans in the beginning of 533, a date most compatible with his young fame and the old age of Isidore (Asseman. Biblioth. Orient. tom. iii. p. 404; Pagi, tom. ii. p. 543, 550).

156. Cassiodor. Variarum Epist. vi. 1. Jornan-

des, c. 57, p. 696, edit. Grot. Quod summum bonum primumque in mundo decus edicitur.

157. See the regulations of Justinian (Novell. cv.), dated at Constantinople, July 5, and addressed to Strategius, treasurer of the empire.

158. Procopius, in Anecdot. c. 26 [tom. iii. p. 144, ed. Bonn]. Aleman. p. 106 [p. 459, ed. Bonn]. In the eighteenth year after the consulship of Basilius, according to the reckoning of Marcellinus, Victor, Marius, etc., the secret history was composed, and, in the eyes of Procopius, the consulship was finally abolished.

159. By Leo, the philosopher (Novell. xciv. A.D. 886–911). See Pagi (Dissertat. Hypatica, p. 325–362) and Ducange (Gloss. Græc. p. 1635, 1636.) Even the title was vilified: consulatus codicilli . . . vilescunt, says the emperor himself.

160. According to Julius Africanus, etc., the world was created the first of September, 5508 years, three months, and twenty-five days before the birth of Christ (see Pezron, Antiquité des Tems défendue, p. 20–28); and this era has been used by the Greeks, the Oriental Christians, and even by the Russians, till the reign of Peter I. The period,

however, arbitrary, is clear and convenient. Of the 7296 years which are supposed to elapse since the creation, we shall find 3000 of ignorance and darkness; 2000 either fabulous or doubtful; 1000 of ancient history, commencing with the Persian empire and the republics of Rome and Athens; 1000 from the fall of the Roman empire in the West to the discovery of America; and the remaining 296 will almost complete three centuries of the modern state of Europe and mankind. I regret this chronology, so far preferable to our double and perplexed method of counting backwards and forwards the years before and after the Christian era.

161. The era of the world has prevailed in the East since the sixth general council (A.D. 681). In the West the Christian era was first invented in the sixth century: it was propagated in the eighth by the authority and writings of venerable Bede; but it was not till the tenth that the use became legal and popular. See l'Art de vérifier les Dates, Dissert. Préliminaire, p. iii. xii.; Dictionnaire Diplomatique, tom. i. p. 329–337: the works of a laborious society of Benedictine monks.

MAPS: VOLUME I

I. THE EXTENT OF THE ROMAN EMPIRE

VENEDAE

BUDINI

HUNS

Dak (Ural) R.

SARMATIA

Rha (Volga) R.

Aorsi

CASPIAN SEA

Borysthenes (Dnieper) R.

SCYTHIANS

BASTARNAE

Roxolani

Tanais

ALANS

Udii

Legae

Tyras (Dniester) R.

Costoboci

Tanais (Don) R.

CARPATHIAN MTS.

Olbia

Lake Maeotis
Sea of Azov

Phanagoria

CAUCASIAN MTS.

Tyra

Tauric
Chersonese

Theodosia

Pityus

COLCHIS

IBERIA

ALBANIA

Harmozica

Cyrus R.

Caspii

Napoca

Patavissa

Apulum

DACIA

Sarmizegethusa

Troesmis

Heraclea

Dioscurias

Phasis

Araxes R.

Isis R.

EUXINE (BLACK) SEA

MEDIA

Ister (Danube) R.

UPPER MOESIA

LOWER MOESIA

Callatis

Sinope

Amisus

Trapezus

GREATER ARMENIA

Cotyora

Naissus

Mesembria

Odessus

Amastris

PAPHLAGONIA

Neocaesarea

Euphrates R.

DARDANIA

Sardica

Hebrus R.

Apollonia

Heraclea

PONTUS

Nicopolis

LESSER ARMENIA

Arsanias R.

Scodra

Scupi

Philippopolis

Hadrianopolis

Byzantium

Chalcedon

BITHYNIA

Amasia

Melitene

Amida

ASSYRIA

Lissus

Lychnidus

Abdera

Lysimachia

Nicomedia

Nicopolis

Tavium

Nisibis

Singara

Nineveh

MACEDONIA

Dyrrhachium

Edessa

Thessalonica

Nicaea

Prusa

Cyzicus

GALATIA

Ancyra

CAPPADOCIA

Caesarea

Samosata

MESOPOTAMIA

Edessa

Hatra

Apollonia

Beroea

Larissa

MYSIA

Cotyaeum

Pessinus

Archelais

Carrhae

Nicephorium

EPIRUS

Ambracia

Pergamum

Sardis

LYCAONIA

Iconium

Tyrrhus

Hierapolis

Euphrates R.

Ctesiphon

Nicopolis

Delphi

Chalcis

Athens

Ephesus

Meander R.

PISIDIA

CILICIA

Tarsus

Alexandria

Antioch

Apamea

Palmyra

Babylon

Seleucia

ACHAIA

Patrae

Elis

Lesbos

Magnesia

Miletus

CARIA

Halicarnassus

Cnidus

LYDIA

PAMPHYLIA

Attalia

LYCIA

Myra

Celenderis

Seleucia

Laodicea

Epiphania

Emesa

SYRIA

SYRIAN DESERT

Sparta

Salamis

Soli

Tripolis

Byblus

Damascus

RHODES

Paphos

CYPRUS

Sidon

Tyre

Phoenicia

CRETE

AEGEAN SEA

Cnossus

Ptolemais

Caesarea

Joppe

Palestine

Pella

Philadelphia

Jerusalem

Bostra

Gaza

Petra

ARABIA
PETRAEA

Ptolemais

Apollonia

Darnis

Cyrene

Chersonesus

Pelusium

Aelana

Arsinoe

Barca

Paraetonium

Derris

Alexandria

Sais

Arsinoe

Berenice

MAJOR

CYRENAICA

LIBYA

Memphis

ARABIA DESERTA

Ammonium

EGYPT

Oxyrynchus

Antinopolis

Philotera

Hermopolis

Myoshormus

Panopolis

Albus Portus

RED

Ptolemais

Coptus

SEA

Tentyra

Thebae

Diospolis

Berenice

Ombos

Syene

V·R·

AT THE DEATH OF TRAJAN

II. ITALY

III. ROME UNDER THE EMPERORS

IV. BYZANTINE CONSTANTINOPLE

(BLACK) SEA

COLCHIS IBERIA

Harmene
Sinope
Sebastopolis (Phasis)
Harmozica

Amnias R.
Halys R.
Amisus
Themiscyra
Cotyora
Tripolis
Trapezus (Trebizond)
Athena
Rhizus
Acampsis R.
Cyrus R.

NIA
PONTUS
PARYADRES MTS.
Pharnacia (Cerasus)
Zigana
LYCHNITIS L.

Amasia
Comana
Neocaesarea (Cabira)
Domana
Araxes R.
Armavira
Artaxata

Zela
Gaziura
Lycus R.
Theodosiopolis (Carana)
Phasis R.

Nicopolis
Satala
MT. ABUS

Sebastia
ARMENIA MINOR
Euphrates R.
ARMENIA
Melazgird
L. ARSISSA

Halys R.
Arsanias (Eastern Euphrates) R.
L. THOSPITIS
Van

Caesarea (Mazaca)
Arsamosata
ANTITAURUS MTS.

MT. ARGAEUS
Melitene
SOPHENE
Tigranocerta
GORDYENE

CAPPADOCIA
CATAONIA
Comana
Amida
Tigris R.

TAURUS MTS.
MASIUS MTS.

Sarus
Augusta
COMMAGENE
Samosata
Tela
Dara
Nisibis
Sapphe (Bezabde)
Greater Zab R.

Cilician
Gates
Pyramus R.
AMANUS MTS.
Zeugma
Apamea (Europus)
Edessa
Carrhae
Resaina
MYGDONIA
Ninus
(Nineveh)
Gaugamela
Arbela

CIA
Tarsus
Adana
Mopsuestia
Issus
Cyrrhus
Carchemish
OSRHOENE
Batnae
Singara
Larissa
ASSYRIA

Aegeae
Cilician &
Syrian Gates
Hierapolis
MESOPOTAMIA
Hatra
Caenae

Seleucia
ANTIOCH
Chalybon
(Beroea)
Nicephorium
Thapsacus
Sura
Zenobia

Laodicea
Apamea
Orontes R.
SYRIA
Chaboras R.

Epiphania
Circesium
Phaliga
Dura

Aradus
Antaradus
Homs
PALMYRENE
Doura
Opis

Tripolis
Laodicea
Palmyra (Tadmor)
Corsote
Anah

Byblus
COELE
SYRIA
Thilabus
Diacira
Sittace

Berytus
Chalcis
SYRIAN DESERT
Sippara
Cunaxa

Sidon
Sarepta
Heliopolis
Damascus

Tyre
Caesarea Philippi
BABYLONIA
Seleucia Ctesiphon

Ptolemais
(Ake)
PALESTINE
PHOENICIA
LEBANON MTS.
Tiberias
Bostra
BABYLON
Borsippa
Vologesia

Caesarea

V. R.

50 100 150 200 MILES

V. ASIA MINOR

VI. THE EMPIRE OF ATTILA

CALEDONIA

PICTS

WALL OF ANTONINUS

Clyde R.

Tweed R.

Trimontium

CHEVIOT HILLS

Brémenium
Habitancum

Blatobulgium

HADRIAN'S WALL

Corstopitum

Luguvallium

Uxellodunum
Voreda
Brocavum

CUMBRIAN MTS.

Vinovia

Lavatrae

Galava

Clanoventa

BRIGANTES

Cataractonium

MONAPIA
(I. of Man)

Isurium

Ilkley

Eburacum (York)

PARISI

Bremetennacum

Cambodunum
Legiolium

Coccium

Anavio

Aquae

Lindum (Lincoln)

IRISH SEA

Causennae

ICENI

Branodunum

SIMONA

Canovium

Deva (Chester)

LEAD

LEAD

Segontium

ORDOVICES

CORNOVII

CORITANI

Venta Icenorum

Gariannonum

Viroconium

Letocetum

Ratae

LEAD

Durobrivae

Bravonium

Venonae

Camboritum?

NORTH SEA

CAMBRIAN MTS.

Magnae

Bannaventa

TRINOVANTES

DEMETAE

GOLD

SILURES

Gobannium

Lactodorum

Camulodunum

Maridunum

Glevum (Gloucester)

Durocobrivae

Isca Silurum

Venta Silurum

Corinium

Verulamium

IRON
DOBUNI

Aquae Sulis (Bath)

Cunetio

R. LONDINIUM (London)

Regulbium

LEAD

BELGAE

Calleva Atrebatum

Durobrivae

Durovernum
(Canterbury)

Rutupiae

DUROTRIGES

Venta Belgarum
(Winchester)

Portus Lemanis

Dubrae

CANTII

IRON

Anderida

DUMNONII

Isca
Dumnoniorum
(Exeter)

Moridunum

Clausentum
(Bittern)

Regnum
(Chichester)

STR. OF DOVER

TIN

Durnovaria

Gesoriacum
(Boulogne)

VECTIS
(I. of Wight)

ENGLISH CHANNEL

·V·R·

VII. ROMAN BRITAIN

PRINTED IN THE U.S.A.

THE GREAT IDEAS, *Volumes 2 and 3*

••••••••••••••••••••••••••••••	FAMILY
ANGEL	FATE
ANIMAL	FORM
ARISTOCRACY	GOD
ART	GOOD AND EVIL
ASTRONOMY	GOVERNMENT
BEAUTY	HABIT
BEING	HAPPINESS
CAUSE	HISTORY
CHANCE	HONOR
CHANGE	HYPOTHESIS
CITIZEN	IDEA
CONSTITUTION	IMMORTALITY
COURAGE	INDUCTION
CUSTOM AND	INFINITY
CONVENTION	JUDGMENT
DEFINITION	JUSTICE
DEMOCRACY	KNOWLEDGE
DESIRE	LABOR
DIALECTIC	LANGUAGE
DUTY	LAW
EDUCATION	LIBERTY
ELEMENT	LIFE AND DEATH
EMOTION	LOGIC
ETERNITY	LOVE
EVOLUTION	MAN
EXPERIENCE	MATHEMATICS